April 18–23, 2015
Seoul, Republic of Korea

Association for
Computing Machinery

Advancing Computing as a Science & Profession

SIGCHI

I0888103

CHI 2015
CROSSINGS

CHI 2015

Proceedings of the

33rd Annual CHI Conference on Human Factors in Computing Systems

Sponsored by:

ACM SIGCHI

Supported by:

Samsung, Golfzon, Google, Microsoft, NAVER, SK Planet, AutoDesk, Daumkakao, Disney Research, FuturePlay, Hyundai Motor Group, Language Grid, LG, NSF, Adobe Systems, H9Works, Yonsei University, KIPFA, and Samsung Art & Design Institute

Association for
Computing Machinery

Advancing Computing as a Science & Profession

The Association for Computing Machinery
2 Penn Plaza, Suite 701
New York, New York 10121-0701

Notice to Past Authors of ACM-Published Articles
ACM intends to create a complete electronic archive of all articles and/or other material previously published by ACM. If you have written a work that has been previously published by ACM in any journal or conference proceedings prior to 1978, or any SIG Newsletter at any time, and you do NOT want this work to appear in the ACM Digital Library, please inform permissions@acm.org, stating the title of the work, the author(s), and where and when published.

ISBN: 978-1-4503-3145-6 (Digital)

ISBN: 978-1-4503-3777-9 (Print)

Additional copies may be ordered prepaid from:

ACM Order Department
PO Box 30777
New York, NY 10087-0777, USA

Phone: 1-800-342-6626 (USA and Canada)
+1-212-626-0500 (Global)
Fax: +1-212-944-1318
E-mail: acmhelp@acm.org
Hours of Operation: 8:30 am – 4:30 pm ET

Printed in the USA

From the General and Technical Program Chairs

Welcome to CHI 2015, the premier international forum for human-computer interaction (HCI). In its early days, HCI focused on optimizing interactions between a user and a computer. Today, computers pervade our world, impacting our lives in varied and subtle ways. By never focusing solely on technology itself but always on innovations and their effects throughout human lives, HCI has increasingly come to mean *human-centered innovation*.

The theme for the conference this year is *CROSSINGS* which represents our excitement about crossing into Asia and also reflects CHI's core principle of crossing disciplines, crossing people and technology, crossing research and business, crossing physical and digital, … crossing you and me.

This year's conference brings CHI to Asia for the first time in its 33-year history, continuing the SIGCHI commitment to making CHI a truly international community. The city of Seoul represents one of many innovation centers in Asia and provides a fantastic opportunity to showcase groundbreaking content from across the region. In addition to an exciting technical program, we are holding four special symposia devoted to breakthrough insights and innovations from the Chinese, Japanese and ASEAN research communities.

The exciting keynote program features speakers who will bring fresh perspectives to CHI including Dean ***Lou Yongqi*** of Tongji University, China, a prominent global thinker on social and sustainable design; Executive VP ***Donghoon Chang***, MFA, head of Samsung Electronic's design strategy; Senior Research Fellow ***David Min***, PhD, head of the Software Center at LG Electronics; and ***PSY***, the media record breaker and innovator discussing creative methods and the impact of social media on to cross cultural boundaries.

CHI is honored this year to be the forum chosen by the recipient of one of ACM's top awards, the Athena Lecturer Award, ***Susan T. Dumais*** who developed novel algorithms and interfaces for interactive retrieval that have made it easier for people to find, use and make sense of information. She will present insights from her experiences at a special keynote session at the conference.

CHI 2015 includes two days of focused workshops and four days of technical content, including CHI's prestigious technical program, with 16 parallel sessions of rigorously reviewed research Papers, engaging Panels, Case Studies and Special Interest Groups (SIGs), an extensive Course program and invited talks from SIGCHI's award winners: Leysia Palen, Jean Scholtz, Michel Beaudouin-Lafon, Jim Hollan, Susan Dray and the new inductees to the CHI Academy.

We also host student research, design, and game competitions, and last-minute SIGs for discussing current topics. The popular alt.chi forum entered its tenth year of provocation to the HCI community. Interactivity's hands-on demonstrations showcase the best of interactive technology and innovation. The program also highlights more than 200 Work-In-Progress posters. Evening events include the CHI 2015 conference reception, Sponsors and University events, local performances and the Job Fair. Across all tracks, CHI received over 2800 submissions and accepted nearly 1000 that will appear in the ACM Digital Library.

We are deeply indebted to an enormous number of volunteers, without whom CHI 2015 would not be possible, including over 3800 reviewers, over 200 senior members of the program committee, nearly 100 members of the CHI 2015 conference organization committee and, of course, the more than 180 student volunteers. We are also deeply grateful to the ongoing support of the Korean HCI society who demonstrated incredible hospitality by moving their own conference's time and location to make room for

CHI in Seoul and who provided tremendous resources from their membership to support CHI logistically and in attracting novel content from around Asia.

We hope you will see fresh insights, strengthen connections and find new collaborators in Asia. *Above all, we hope you enjoy this unique experience of CHI 2015!*

General Conference Chairs

Bo Begole
Huawei, USA

Jinwoo Kim
Yonsei University, Korea

Technical Program Chairs

Kori Inkpen
Microsoft Research, USA

Woontack Woo
KAIST, Korea

From ACM SIGCHI's President and Vice President for Conferences

SIGCHI is proud to sponsor the premier annual conference in the field of human-computer interaction. We are extremely grateful to the CHI 2015 Conference Chairs Jinwoo Kim and Bo Begole, to Technical Program Chairs Woontack Woo and Kori Inkpen, and to their wonderful crew, who succeeded to build an impressive program and experience.

CHI 2015 is in Seoul, Korea, the first CHI ever in Asia. CHI started in Gaithersburg, MD, USA, in March 1982. That first conference in Gaithersburg drew over 900 attendees, and since then CHI, with the official name: "ACM Conference on Human Factors in Computing Systems" moved to annual, originally moving between the USA and Canada. Starting with 1993 CHI traveled between locations in Europe and North America. This year is another big step forward, made possible thanks to the Korean HCI Society that helped understand and navigate the local context, that moved its annual conference 3 months earlier to December 2014, and at the same time supported CHI's Technical Program meeting.

CHI has continued to grow and broaden its range of topics and contributing disciplines: the founding psychologists and software engineers began to meet new visions from ethnography, sociology, communication sciences and arts, among others. Relevant industries, as well as research institutes and academia, showed an increasing — and often long-lasting — interest and involvement (through volunteers and through sponsorship for conference expenses). This year's Conference Committee truly succeeded in crossing borders of all kind, providing new and unique opportunities for all participants to meet something entirely different.

CHI is an ideal forum for people to meet formally as well as informally, to exchange knowledge and views, to share experiences, and to learn. The CHI conference brings together professionals from research and practice; people from industry, academia, and from government; long-term veterans of HCI, young professionals and students; all in an environment designed to encourage interaction. We invite you to actively participate in that interaction: introduce yourself to people, interact with presenters and speakers, renew old friendships and make new ones

CHI is organized on behalf of ACM's Special Interest Group on Computer-Human Interaction (SIGCHI), an international community of professionals who share an interest in the many diverse facets of HCI. SIGCHI is committed both to advancing the field of HCI, to facilitate exchange of information within the SIGCHI community, and to support students to enter the domain.

The CHI conference is arguably the single most visible activity of SIGCHI, but we also sponsor and support a wide range of specialized conferences and workshops in areas ranging from interactive systems design to user interface technology to computer-supported cooperative work to "intelligent" user interfaces. Visit the SIGCHI website at **http://www.sigchi.org** to find our conference schedule, listing upcoming as well as past conferences.

SIGCHI and ACM produce some of the most respected publications in the field. All members receive interactions, a highly-acclaimed magazine covering the broad field of HCI and user interface design. ACM Transactions on Computer-Human Interactions (ToCHI), now in its 21st year, is our flagship journal – a quarterly publication with the top-quality archival research aimed at researchers and those translating research into practice.

SIGCHI is truly an international organization, with around 40 local chapters and 3 student chapters in 25 countries on 6 continents. We encourage all SIGCHI members to join their local chapter — or if there isn't one in your area, we would love to help you create one. And don't forget virtual communities! SIGCHI hosts dozens of electronic mailing lists on topics ranging from HCI and the Web, to HCI educations, to public policy and beyond. Those lists range from dozens of subscribers to thousands, and are an excellent way to keep up with the field and with friends and colleagues.

Finally, on behalf of ACM SGICHI, we again want to thank the conference committee and all of the hundreds of volunteers who make this conference possible. Their work makes this a rewarding experience for all of us.

Gerrit C. van der Veer
SIGCHI President

John "Scooter" Morris
SIGCHI Vice-President for Conferences

About SIGCHI

CHI 2015 is sponsored by ACM's Special Interest Group on Computer-Human Interaction (ACM SIGCHI). ACM, the Association for Computing Machinery, is an educational and scientific society uniting the world's computing educators, researchers, and professionals to inspire dialogue, share resources, and address the field's challenges. ACM strengthens the profession's collective voice through strong leadership, promotion of the highest standards, and recognition of technical excellence. ACM supports the professional growth of its members by providing opportunities for life-long learning, career development, and professional networking. ACM offers its more than 100,000 worldwide members cutting edge technical information through world class journals and magazines, dynamic special interest groups, and globally recognized conferences.

Visit www.acm.org for more information about the ACM.

SIGCHI is the premier international society for professionals, academics, and students who are interested in human-computer interaction (HCI). We provide a forum for the discussion of all aspects of HCI through our conferences, including our flagship CHI conference, publications, web sites, email discussion groups, and other services. We advance education in HCI through courses, workshops, and outreach, and we promote informal access to a wide range of individuals and organizations involved in HCI. Members can be involved in HCI-related activities with others in their region through local SIGCHI chapters. Come to the SIGCHI Town Hall meeting on Wednesday, April 22, at 12:50 to 14:30 in Room 308 or visit www.sigchi.org to learn more about SIGCHI.

Membership Information

Please contact ACM's Member Services Dept.
Online: www.acm.org
Tel: +1-800-342-6626 (USA/Canada)
+1-212-626-0500 (International)
Fax: +1-212-944-1318
Email: acmhelp@acm.org

Write:

Association for Computing Machinery, Inc.
General Post Office
P.O. Box 30777
New York, NY 10087-0777, USA

CHI 2015 Papers and Notes Chairs' Welcome

The CHI Papers and Notes programme is continuing to grow and this year! We are pleased that CHI continues to be the leading conference for research in human-computer interaction.

This year we considered more than 2120 submissions, ~600 of which were notes. This represents a continuation of ~4% annual growth in submissions. We accepted 486 submissions (~23%): 379 papers and 107 notes.

The CHI review process demands a tremendous amount of work from all areas of the human-computer interaction community. As co-chairs of the process, we are amazed at the ability of the community to organize itself to accomplish this task. We would like to thank the 2809 individual reviewers for their careful consideration of these papers. Every submission received at least three external reviews.

We also deeply appreciate the huge amount of time donated to this process by the 225-member program committee, who paid their own way to attend the face-to-face program committee meeting, an event larger than most ACM conferences.

We are proud of the work of the CHI 2015 program committee and hope that you enjoy these papers and notes, which represent the best research in human-computer interaction.

CHI 2015 Paper and Notes Chairs

Andy Cockburn
University of Canterbury

Janna McGrenere
University of British Columbia

Table of Contents

Visualizing Data

Session Chair: Christophe Hurter, *IRIT, France*

Interaction in 3D Space

Session Chair: Kening Zhu, *City University of Hong Kong, China*

Understanding & Evaluating Performance

Session Chair: Richard Davis, *Singapore Management University, Singapore*

Music & Art

Session Chair: Jonathan Hook, *University of York, UK*

Supporting Change in Developing Countries

Session Chair: Anirudha Joshi, *Indian Institute of Technology, Bombay, India*

Privacy, Security & Interruptions

Session Chair: Emilee Rader, *Michigan State University, USA*

Making & Sharing Assistive Technologies

Session Chair: Suranga Nanayakkara, *Singapore University of Technology and Design, Singapore*

Matching & Facilitating Social Interactions

Session Chair: Jofish Kaye, *Yahoo!, USA*

Reflecting Upon Design Reflection

Session Chair: Ron Wakkary, *Simon Fraser University, Canada*

Makers & Hackers

Session Chair: Ellen Yi-Luen Do, *Georgia Institute of Technology, USA*

How Fast Can You Type on Your Phone?

Session Chair: Michael Rohs, *University of Hannover, Germany*

Understand & Enhancing Learning

Session Chair: Chris Quintana, *University of Michigan, USA*

Family Communication

Crowdsourcing Fans & Friends

Managing Personal Privacy

Health Sensors & Monitoring

Collaborative Tables, Walls & Rooms

Session Chair: Harald Reiterer, *University of Konstanz, Germany*

The Value of Things

Session Chair: Mark Blythe, *Northumbria University, UK*

Phones for more than Just Talking & Text

Session Chair: Naomi Yamashita, *NTT Communication Science Laboratories, Japan*

Search & Recommendations

Session Chair: Susan Dumais, *Microsoft Research, USA*

Kids Haptic, Wearable, Tangible Learning

Motivation & Participation

Sustainability & Recycling

Tangible Interactions

New Evaluation Approaches

Evaluating Crowdsourcing

Smart Smartphone Authentication

Interactive Video & Collaborative Annotations

Session Chair: Amy Ogan, *Carnegie Mellon University, USA*

HCI for the Elderly

Session Chair: Maria Wolters, *University of Edinburgh, UK*

The Impact of Crowd Work on Workers

Session Chair: Jaime Teevan, *Microsoft Research, USA*

Social Media and Mobile Camera Privacy

Session Chair: Pam Briggs, *Northumbria University, UK*

DIY Healthcare: Apps & Wearables

Session Chair: David Coyle, *University College Dublin*

Social Embodied Interaction

Session Chair: Gina Venolia, *Microsoft Research, USA*

Innovation in Theories & Products

Session Chair: Volker Wulf, *University of Siegen, Germany*

Design and 3D Object Fabrication

Session Chair: David Kim, *Microsoft Research, UK*

Understanding & Extending Touch Interfaces

Session Chair: Theophanis Tsandilas, *INRIA, France*

Sharing & Collaboration @ Work

Session Chair: Steven Drucker, *Microsoft Research, USA*

Families and Their Use of Technology

Session Chair: Jennifer Marlow, *Carnegie Mellon University, USA*

Understanding Crowdwork in Many Domains

Session Chair: Uichin Lee, *Korea Advanced Institute of Science and Technology, South Korea*

Eco-Green: Encouraging Energy Conservation

Session Chair: Germaine Irwin, *University of Maryland Baltimore County, USA*

Sports Tracking & Training

Session Chair: Hao-Hua Chu, *National Taiwan University, Taiwan*

Feeling & Communicating Emotions

Session Chair: Rongrong Wang, *Samsung Research America, USA*

Critical Design

Session Chair: Giulio Jacucci, *University of Helsinki, Finland*

HMDs in Augmented & Virtual Reality

Session Chair: Shahram Izadi, *Microsoft Research, UK*

Tangible Interaction with Phones

Session Chair: Shengdong Zhao, *National University of Singapore, Singapore*

UI Impact on Performance & Decisions

Session Chair: Tom Gross, *University of Bamberg, Germany*

Player Performance & Experience in Games

Session Chair: Jan Smeddinck, *University of Bremen, Germany*

Neighborhoods & Disadvantaged Communities

Session Chair: Katharina Reinecke, *University of Michigan, USA*

Enhanced Security with Passwords & CAPTCHAs

Session Chair: Serge Egelman, *University of California, Berkeley, USA*

Accessibility at Home & on The Go

Session Chair: Hironobu Takagi, *IBM Research, Japan*

Visualizing Statistics & Graphs

Session Chair: Benjamin Bach, *INRIA, France*

2683 (s|qu)eries: Visual Regular Expressions for Querying and Exploring Event Sequences
Emanuel Zgraggen, *Microsoft Research & Brown University*
Steven M. Drucker, Danyel Fisher, Robert DeLine, *Microsoft Research*

2693 Statsplorer: Guiding Novices in Statistical Analysis
Chat Wacharamanotham, Krishna Subramanian, Sarah Theres Völkel, Jan Borchers, *RWTH Aachen University*

2703 Investigating the Direct Manipulation of Ranking Tables for Time Navigation
Romain Vuillemot, *Harvard University*
Charles Perin, *INRIA, Univ Paris-Sud, & CNRS-LIMSI*

2707 Dynamic Opacity Optimization for Scatter Plots
Justin Matejka, Fraser Anderson, George Fitzmaurice, *Autodesk Research*

2711 Evaluating How Level of Detail of Visual History Affects Process Memory
Eric D. Ragan, John R. Goodall, *Oak Ridge National Laboratory*
Albert Tung, *Rio Hondo College*

Understanding Everyday Use of Mobile Phones

Session Chair: Matt Jones, *Swansea University, UK*

2729 Demand in My Pocket: Mobile Devices and the Data Connectivity Marshalled in Support of Everyday Practice
Carolynne Lord, Mike Hazas, Adrian K. Clear, Oliver Bates, Rosalind Whittam, Janine Morley, Adrian Friday, *Lancaster University*

2739 An In-Situ Study of Mobile App & Mobile Search Interactions
Juan Pablo Carrascal, *Pompeu Fabra University*
Karen Church, *Yahoo Labs*

2749 The Composition and Use of Modern Mobile Phonebooks
Frank Bentley, Ying-Yu Chen, *Yahoo Labs*

GUI Size, Resolution & Layout

Session Chair: Enrico Rukzio, *Institute of Media Informatics, Germany*

2759 Effects of Display Size and Resolution on User Behavior and Insight Acquisition in Visual Exploration
Khairi Reda, *Argonne National Laboratory & University of Hawai'i at Mānoa*
Andrew E. Johnson, *University of Illinois at Chicago*
Michael E. Papka, *Argonne National Laboratory & Northern Illinois University*
Jason Leigh, *University of Hawai'i at Mānoa*

2769 Subjective and Objective Effects of Tablet's Pixel Density
Lars Lischke, Sven Mayer, Katrin Wolf, Alireza Sahami Shirazi, Niels Henze, *University of Stuttgart*

2773 Push-Edge and Slide-Edge: Scrolling by Pushing Against the Viewport Edge
Sylvain Malacria, *University College London & INRIA Lille*
Jonathan Aceituno, *Inria Lille & University of Lille*
Philip Quinn, *University of Canterbury*
Géry Casiez, *Inria Lille & University of Lille*
Andy Cockburn, *University of Canterbury*
Nicolas Roussel, *Inria Lille*

2777 Investigating Visual Feedforward for Target Expansion Techniques
Maxime Guillon, *University Grenoble Alpes & Aesculap SAS*
François Leitner, *Aesculap SAS*
Laurence Nigay, *University Grenoble Alpes*

2787 GACA: Group-Aware Command-based Arrangement of Graphic Elements
Pengfei Xu, *HKUST*
Hongbo Fu, *City University of Hong Kong*
Chiew-Lan Tai, *HKUST*
Takeo Igarashi, *The University of Tokyo*

Kids Social, Emotional & Special Needs

Session Chair: Konstantinos Kazakos, *Newcastle University, UK*

2797 Designing Social and Emotional Skills Training: The Challenges and Opportunities for Technology Support
Petr Slovák, *Microsoft Research & Vienna University of Technology*
Ran Gilad-Bachrach, *Microsoft Research*
Geraldine Fitzpatrick, *Vienna University of Technology*

2801 Designing Autism Research for Maximum Impact
Elizabeth J. Carter, Jennifer Hyde, *Carnegie Mellon University*

2805 Networked Empowerment on Facebook among Parents of Children with Special Needs
Tawfiq Ammari, Sarita Schoenebeck, *University of Michigan*

HCI for Civic Engagement

Session Chair: John Vines, *Newcastle University, UK*

Security Feedback & Warnings

Session Chair: Alexander De Luca, *University of Munich, Germany*

Wellness & Wearables

Session Chair: Marianna Obrist, *University of Sussex, UK*

Task Interruption & Resumption

Session Chair: Martin Halvey, *University of Strathclyde, UK*

Using Random Body Parts for Input

Session Chair: Patrick Baudisch, *Hasso Plattner Institute, Germany*

Brain & Physiological Data use for HCI

Session Chair: Jacob Robert, *Tufts University, USA*

Software Engineering Tools

Session Chair: Feng Tian, *Chinese Academy of Sciences, China*

HCI at Home

Session Chair: David Geerts, *Social Spaces, Belgium*

Voting & Volunteerism

Session Chair: Andres Monroy-Hernandez, *Microsoft Research, USA*

Socio-Political Interactions

Session Chair: Liang Gou, *Almaden, USA*

Understanding Health through Online Behavior

Session Chair: Mary Czerwinski, *Microsoft Research, USA*

Natural User Interfaces for InfoVis

Session Chair: Bongshin Lee, *Microsoft Research, USA*

UX Methods 4

Session Chair: Benjamin Hanrahan, *Xerox Research Center Europe, France*

Augmented & Virtual Reality in the Real World

Session Chair: Morten Fjeld, *Chalmers University of Technology, Sweden*

Gesture Elicitation & Recognition

Session Chair: Niels Henze, *University of Stuttgart, Germany*

Programming Environments

Session Chair: Joonhwan Lee, *Seoul National University, Republic of Korea*

Understanding Gamers

Session Chair: Toni-Jan Keith Monserrat, *National University of Singapore, Singapore*

Bridging Communities

Session Chair: Edward Cutrell, *Microsoft Research India, India*

Gender & Technology

Session Chair: Antonella De Angeli, *University of Trento, Italy*

CHI 2015 Organization

General Conference Chairs
Jinwoo Kim, *Yonsei University, Korea*
Bo Begole, *Huawei, USA*

Technical Program

Technical Program Chairs
Woontack Woo, *KAIST, Korea*
Kori Inkpen, *Microsoft Research, USA*

Papers
Andy Cockburn, *University of Canterbury, New Zealand*
Joanna McGrenere, *University of British Columbia, Canada*
Jun Rekimoto, *University of Toyko, Japan*

Case Studies
Danielle Cooley, *DGCooley Consulting, USA*
Joonhwan Lee, *Seoul National University, Korea*

Courses
Regina Bernhaupt, *ICS-IRIT, France*
Matt Jones, *Swansea University, UK*

Interactivity
Julie Rico Williamson, *University of Glasgow, UK*
Juhyun Eune, *Seoul National University, Korea*

Video Showcase
Jinwook Seo, *Seoul National University, Korea*
Rodrigo de Oliveira, *Google, USA*

SIGs
Enrico Rukzio, *Ulm University, Germany*
Simone Barbosa, *PUC-Rio, Brazil*

Doctoral Consortium
Si-Jung "Jun" Kim, *University of Central Florida, USA*
Jaime Teevan, *Microsoft Research, USA*
Sue Fussell, *Cornell University, USA*

Workshops
Juergen Steimle, *Max Planck Institute for Informatics, Germany*
Bongshin Lee, *Microsoft Research, USA*

Works in Progress
Shamsi Iqbal, *Microsoft Research, USA*
Shaun Lawson, *University of Lincoln, UK*
Shendong Zhao, *National University of Singapore, Singapore*

Student Research Competition
Seungyon "Claire" Lee, *Google, USA*
Geehyuk Lee, *KAIST, Korea*

Student Design Competition
Youn-Kyung Lim, *KAIST, Korea*
Anirudha Joshi, *ITT Bombay, India*

Student Game Competition
Floyd Muller, *RMIT University, Australia*
Alessandro Canossa, *Northeastern University, USA*
Soojin Jun, *Yonsei University, Korea*

alt.chi
Silvia Lindtner, *University of California, Irvine, USA*
Morgan Ames, *Intel, USA*
Henry Duh, *University of Tasmania, Australia*

TOCHI Papers
Jeffrey Nichols, *IBM Research, USA*

Best of CHI Awards
Mark Billinghurst, *University of Canterbury, New Zealand*

Panels
Khai Truong, *University of North Carolina, Charlotte, USA*
Elaine M. Huang, *University of Zurich, Switzerland*

Conference Theme Chair
Kyle Hyunsuk Kim, *Hongik University, Korea*

Industry Liaison
Garett Dworman, *TecEd, USA*

Operations

Chair's Assistant
Yoojin Lee, *Yonsei University, Korea*

Chair's Assistant
Nik Martelaro, *Stanford University, USA*

Student Volunteer
Jon Haber, *University of Calgary, Canada*
Siroberto Scerbo, *Virginia Tech, USA*
Jieun Wee, *Seoul National University, Korea*

Technology Liaisons
Sara Drenner, *University of Minnesota-Twin Cities, USA*
Scooter Morris, *University of California, San Francisco, USA*

Webmaster
Juho Kim, *MIT, USA*
TJ Monserrat, *National University of Singapore, Singapore*

Social Media
Max Wilson, *Nottingham University, UK*
Kwangsu Cho, *Sungkyunkwan University, Korea*

Data Managerment
Max Van Kleek, *University of Southampton, UK*
BoYu Gao, *Konkuk University, Korea*

Proceedings
Deana Brown, *Georgia Tech, USA*
Jaejeung Kim, *KAIST, Korea*

Infrastructure Accessibility Chair
Jongbae Kim, *Yonsei University, Korea*

Digital Accessibility Chair
Jeff Bigham, *University of Rochester, USA*

Scheduling
Christophe Hurter, *ENAC, France*
Juho Kim, *MIT, USA*

Mobile Apps
Stephen Oney, *Carnegie Mellon University, USA*
Eiji Hayashi, *Carnegie Mellon University, USA*
Jason Wiese, *Carnegie Mellon University, USA*
Célia Martinie, *Université Paul Sabatier, France*

Video Previews
Fanny Chevalier, *INRIA, France*
Stéphane Huo, *Université Paris-Sud, France*

Posters
Hyun Joo Song, *Seoul National University, Korea*

Translations
Sue Fussell, *Cornell University, USA*
Naomi Yamashita, *NTT, Japan*

Local Hospitality
Junho Choi, *Yonsei University, Korea*

Sponsors, Exhibits & Recruitment
Carol Klyver, *Foundations of Excellence, USA*

Registration
Yvonne Lopez, *Executive Events, Inc. USA*
Brooke Daley, *Executive Events, Inc. USA*

PCS Liaisons
Max van Kleek, *University of Southampton, UK*
Carol Klyver, *Foundations of Excellence, USA*
Scooter Morris, *University of California, San Francisco, USA*

Substitutional Reality: Using the Physical Environment to Design Virtual Reality Experiences

Adalberto L. Simeone[†*] adalberto.simeone@port.ac.uk
Eduardo Velloso[*] e.velloso@lancaster.ac.uk
Hans Gellersen[*] h.gellersen@lancaster.ac.uk

[†]University of Portsmouth
Portsmouth, United Kingdom
[*]Lancaster University
Lancaster, United Kingdom

Figure 1. Two Virtual Environments based on the layout of a real room (middle): a medieval courtyard (left) and the bridge of a spaceship (right). In these *Substitutional Environments*, every physical object is paired, with some degree of discrepancy, to a contextually appropriate virtual object.

ABSTRACT

Experiencing Virtual Reality in domestic and other uncontrolled settings is challenging due to the presence of physical objects and furniture that are not usually defined in the Virtual Environment. To address this challenge, we explore the concept of Substitutional Reality in the context of Virtual Reality: a class of Virtual Environments where every physical object surrounding a user is paired, with some degree of discrepancy, to a virtual counterpart. We present a model of potential substitutions and validate it in two user studies. In the first study we investigated factors that affect participants' suspension of disbelief and ease of use. We systematically altered the virtual representation of a physical object and recorded responses from 20 participants. The second study investigated users' levels of engagement as the physical proxy for a virtual object varied. From the results, we derive a set of guidelines for the design of future Substitutional Reality experiences.

Author Keywords

Virtual Reality, Substitutional Reality, Passive Haptics

ACM Classification Keywords

H.5.1 Information Interfaces and Presentation: Artificial, augmented and virtual realities

INTRODUCTION

Virtual Reality (VR) has been applied in many contexts, including: archaeology, industrial design, training, therapy, and gaming. Despite a renewed commercial interest [14], its adoption in the home environment has been slow to take off. In contrast to VR laboratories, domestic spaces are filled with furniture and objects that may not be present in a simulation. As a consequence, home VR is constrained to the user's immediate surroundings. We envision a VR experience that incorporates physical objects into the virtual world by using them to represent objects relevant to the virtual context. We call this type of experience *Substitutional Reality* (SR) [24].

In an SR environment, every physical object and architectural feature is replaced in the Virtual Environment (VE) by a counterpart. This leverages the physicality of the real world to provide tangibility to virtual objects and contributes to a higher sense of presence [7]. For example, a living room can be substituted with a courtyard or the bridge of a spaceship (see Figure 1) and a suitable physical object (e.g., a torch or umbrella) can be replaced by a sword or a lightsaber.

Previous research has focused on scenarios where the virtual object is modelled on the physical proxy. However, to give content authors creative freedom and flexibility in the design of virtual worlds, SR experiences should be designed around the idea that a mismatch between virtual elements and their physical proxy is to be expected. In this work, we explore the question of how far designers can push this mismatch before breaking the VR illusion. Our approach builds on the concept of *passive haptics* [7], i.e. receiving feedback from touching a physical object that is registered to a virtual object.

We propose a multi-layer model of substitution which illustrates increasing levels of mismatch between the virtual counterpart and the physical object. At the bottom level, the substituted object is simply a replica of the original one. At the top level, the appearance of a substituted object has few, if any, connections to the appearance and function of the phys-

CHI 2015, April 18-23 2015, Seoul, Republic of Korea
Copyright is held by the owner/author(s). Publication rights licensed to ACM.
ACM 978-1-4503-3145-6/15/04...$15.00
http://dx.doi.org/10.1145/2702123.2702389

ical one. We investigate the impact of this mismatch on the user experience in the VE through two studies.

In the first, we focused on a single baseline object, a real mug, and systematically presented participants with virtual objects representing the different types of substitution defined in the model. Our goal was to explore which factors have the greatest impact on the believability of the experience. In the second, we took the inverse route. We asked participants to hit a moving target with a virtual Lightsaber. However, the physical objects they held changed between a 1:1 Lightsaber replica, an umbrella, and a torch. We investigated those scenarios in which the user is required to interact with objects that might be common in the context of the SR experience (e.g., historical or imaginary objects) but are rarely found in homes. Our goal was to evaluate whether different objects (that can be manipulated similarly to the virtual one) can provide comparable levels of engagement to actual replicas.

Results from our studies show that, in the absence of exact replicas, those objects that present similar affordances [5] in the parts most likely to be interacted with, are the best candidates for substitution. For example, a torch for a Lightsaber or a pen for a magic wand. We found that the believability of the pairing is affected by the material used by the virtual counterpart. Those with variations in their tactile feedback, temperature, or weight had the most impact. However, participants found moderate mismatches (an oil lamp for a real mug) to be believable and with little impact on the experience. Pairings having extreme mismatches (a box for a real mug) were found to negatively affect the illusion.

RELATED WORK

The concept of *Substitutional Reality* implies the modification of the normally perceived reality through artificial means. Suzuki et al. [24], defined a *Substitutional Reality System* that, through a headset, was capable of manipulating users' perception of reality. It alternated a live video feed with previously recorded scenes so that users did not perceive any discontinuity. A related concept, *Virtualized Reality* [10] focused on the process of reconstructing virtual versions of real scenes. This way, users could experience real events from potentially unlimited viewpoints without any degradation in terms of visual and auditive realism during the reconstruction process. In the next section we define our vision of Substitutional Reality in the context of Virtual Reality. In the remainder of this section, we describe other research that shares common themes to those we investigated.

Passive Haptics — Previous work has shown that passive haptics can enhance the sense of presence. In a study by Hoffman [7], participants were immersed in a virtual kitchen environment and divided into two groups. In one, the interactive objects in the environment were purely virtual. In the other, the virtual objects were mapped to physical counterparts. Results showed that participants in the physical objects group guessed the object properties more accurately than those in the group subjected to the purely virtual condition. In a study by Insko et al. [8], participants had to place a book on a chair at the opposite end of a pit room by navigating on a ledge that separated them from the fall below. In one condition this ledge was substituted with a real wooden plank whereas in the other, the ledge was only virtual. Results showed that behavioural presence, heart rate, and skin conductivity changes had significant differences in the passive haptics condition. Indeed, participants could feel a height difference between the ledge they stood on and the floor below, enhancing the illusion of standing on the edge of a pit.

Passive haptics have also been used in studies using VR for medical purposes. In a study by Carlin et al. [2], a patient gradually interacted with a virtual spider to counteract her fear. A physical spider toy replica was mapped into the environment so that when the patient's virtual hand reached to touch the virtual spider, she could sense the furry texture of the toy. A Virtual Human paired to a mannequin was used by a system enabling inter-personal touch between a trainee physician and the agent posing as a breast-exam patient [13]. The results show that the use of passive haptics in the form of the mannequin and a physical breast simulator engaged participants to behave similar to human-human interaction.

Desktop VR — Nowadays, end-users can experience VR through headsets and conventional input devices. Past research on semi-immersive setups based on desktop displays has shown advantages in terms of better performance in a visual search task [21] in those scenarios not necessitating full immersion (e.g., browsing a scientific dataset). A drawback of this class of systems is the inability of using locomotion interfaces to move in the VE, which is considered to be beneficial to the sense of presence [26]. However, desktop SR could represent a first stepping stone as there are many scenarios in which substituting the user's immediate surroundings would suffice (e.g., racing or flight simulators). Augmented Reality (AR) [19] instead studies the real-time integration of virtual objects into the physical environment. Conversely, SR focuses on the integration of physical elements into a VE.

Visuo-Haptic Feedback — The biggest drawback of passive haptics is that any virtual alteration must also be reflected on the physical proxy, if visual fidelity is to be maintained. This can prove to be impractical. Haptic devices on the other hand, provide a more dynamic tactile experience. Works in the domain of Visuo-Haptic feedback have explored the use of these devices in conjunction with AR systems [3, 11]. In these works, users interact with a Phantom haptic device which is subsequently removed from the augmented video feed and substituted with a virtual object. For example in Knoerlein et al. [11], users play an AR version of ping-pong through the haptic device while seeing a virtual racket. Similarly, in Cosco et al. [3] users perform various tool-based tasks while interacting with a Phantom haptic device, replaced with a virtual tool. The benefits in terms of the haptic sensations come with the drawback of tying the user to the device. This negates the benefits of walking locomotion interfaces (unless the device can move with the user) and could be difficult to implement in domestic environments.

Robotic Manipulation — McNeely presented a robot that, when the user is about to touch a virtual object, places a physical object in their reach [17]. Tachi et al. [25], presented a *Shape Approximation Device*, a robot whose effector is capable of simulating contact with a variety of surfaces such as those having vertices, edges, and concave or convex parts.

Space Warping — The mapping between real and virtual objects has traditionally focused on a 1:1 match. In a study by Kohli et al. [12], the authors build on the concept that the sense of vision can take precedence over other senses in case of a conflict. They developed a technique called *Redirected Touching* which alters the way the user's virtual hand moves in the VE compared to its real movement.

Sensory Mismatch — Hinckley et al. [6] pioneered in a 1994 paper the use of a real object associated to a similar but not identical virtual object where a doll head model was used to control a brain visualization. The mismatch between visual feedback and other senses has also been investigated in studies on neurology and perception [1, 16]. In the context of AR, Kwon et al. [15] studied the extent to which mismatches in terms of shape and size affect user performance. They found better results when size and shape matched but no significant differences when size alone was altered. Steinicke et al. [23] presented a taxonomy of redirected walking techniques supporting ubiquitous passive haptic feedback. In the VR literature on locomotion interfaces, *redirected walking* refers to a range of techniques that are used to allow walking in VEs larger than the physical environment where the simulation is taking place. In the context of their work, redirected walking techniques are used to bring the user to a proxy object when they reach a similar object in the VE.

These works approach the problem of providing tactile feedback in a VE by building a physical environment that matches it as closely as possible or vice versa, the VE is designed as a copy of the physical environment. We approach the problem from a different angle. We focus on domestic environments where it is impractical to radically rearrange furniture or build matching props. Thus, instead of studying 1:1 physical/virtual pairings, our research assumes the existence of a mismatch and studies the extent to which it can be pushed.

SUBSTITUTIONAL REALITY

The Virtual Reality continuum introduced by Milgram [18] defines a range of possible "realities" altering our senses in different ways. At one end is the *Real Environment*, i.e. our normal experience of the world in which we live. At the other end is *Virtual Reality* where, in theory, every sense can be artificially stimulated. In between is the notion of Mixed Reality (MR), encompassing Augmented Reality and Augmented Virtuality [19]. These types of systems are usually characterised by adding or subtracting elements of either side of the continuum to the user experience.

Milgram defined a class of MR environments where *"real physical objects in the user's environment play a role in (or interfere with) the computer generated scene"* [18]. This class was named "Hybrid Reality". Since then, this term has been used in different contexts from location-based games [4] to large-scale data visualization [20].

VR systems and devices are now able to create highly visually and aurally convincing experiences. Current technology however, is still not able to stimulate our other senses with the same resolution. In particular, even though some technologies provide the experience of tactile feedback (e.g., haptic devices) and locomotion (e.g., omni-directional treadmills), these devices still are not able to mimic how we experience the real world. For example, haptic devices only stimulate the parts of the body where they touch, and are therefore unable to affect the body as a whole. Similarly, while treadmills allow users to navigate endlessly large spaces, they are unable to render physical obstacles or other terrain properties, such as ridges and uneven elevations.

To address the difficulty in rendering convincing physical and haptic experiences in VEs, we explore the concept of *Substitutional Reality* in the context of VR. That is, a class of MR environments in which a substitution process adapts a VE to the physical world. By substituting each physical element with a virtual counterpart, a VE is able to leverage physical properties to create convincing bodily experiences. We define the VE in which a substitution process has matched each virtual element with a physical element with varying degrees of mismatch, a *Substitutional Environment* (SE). If taken to extreme this would entail VEs that replicate the physical world. If any creative freedom is to be allowed, an SR system must be able to alter the elements in the virtual world to match the desired theme and feel of the SR experience.

To assist the design of how these elements can be altered, we provide a layered model of modification in which at each level the virtual element gets further away from its physical counterpart. Although we use the term *object*, this model applies to both small manipulable objects and large architectural features (e.g., walls, floors). To illustrate its structure, we use the example of a mug that exists in the real world, but is substituted in the VE with increasing levels of mismatch.

Replica — The basis of our model is constituted by substituted objects that are 1:1 replicas of their physical proxy. In a VE, the object will appear as a 3D model of the real one. It will present the same affordances and allow exactly the same interaction as its physical counterpart. In our example, the mug would be rendered as-is in the VE, matching every single one of its characteristics, from the material to little imperfections on its surface. Substitution at this level is the most realistic, but higher-fidelity systems would require either real-time reconstruction or pre-built models of existing objects.

Aesthetic — At this level, virtual and physical objects begin to differ, albeit from an aesthetic perspective. Physical properties regarding the appearance of a virtual object are altered without affecting the way the object is perceived. For example, in the VE the *material* of the mug might appear to be made out of glass or wood. This in turn affects the way an object can be perceived in terms of *temperature* and *weight*. If the mug is rendered as one carved out of ice, users might expect it to be colder to the touch and weigh differently.

Addition/Subtraction — Here, elements of either reality do not have counterparts in the other. Addition happens when parts of an object are rendered where there is no physical counterpart and subtraction happens when parts of a physical object do not have a virtual representation. Physical properties can be altered to varying degrees. For example, the *size* of the mug can be altered to portray a bigger or smaller version, or the mug might appear to lack a handle or have two on either side where the physical proxy only has one. Whereas this allows the design of richer environments (e.g., a room can be rendered as the captain's cabin in a pirate ship), this creates the risk of accidentally bumping into physical objects (e.g., in the said ship, going for a swim in the sea visible from the windows would result in bumping your head on the wall) and attempting to grasp non-existent parts of objects (reaching for the handle of a virtual glass, whose physical proxy lacks one).

Function — The alteration reaches the functional level when there is a mismatch between the affordances of physical and virtual elements. The concept of "affordance" introduced by Gibson [5] refers to the interaction possibilities perceived by the observer of an object. For instance, a mug *affords* drinking and pouring. In SR there could be a mismatch between the affordances portrayed by a substitutive object and those related to the physical proxy. However, users will interact with an object based on the affordances perceived by its virtual appearance. When some of these affordances are not shared, a functional mismatch appears. For example, the mug might be rendered as an oil lamp as they share some affordances (we can pour liquids in both) but are intended for two different functions (drinking or lighting). A mug and a similarly sized virtual box would have a greater functional mismatch: we can no longer pour liquids in both while the virtual box might have a lid. Affordances suggested by the virtual object but not present in the real object have a greater potential of negatively affecting the suspension of disbelief.

Category — Here, the substitution reaches the highest extreme. The virtual appearance of the object no longer has any connection to its physical counterpart. For example, if its *shape* is altered, a mug might be substituted by a box or a spherical ball. If we imagine these two objects to be sized within the bounding box of the original mug, parts of the space it occupies will appear to be empty (sphere) or filled (box). In addition, they no longer will share common affordances. As the virtual object distances itself from its proxy, the set of possible objects it can be substituted with increases and so does the likelihood of running into issues concerning the believability of the substitution and its ease of interaction. It is worth noting that the alteration does not have to be gradual, as the modification of specific physical properties can be enough to sever any recognizable connection the virtual object had with the original proxy.

We designed two studies that investigated the impact of the alterations defined in this model from two opposing perspectives. In the first study, we hypothesised that each substitution type would affect the believability of the experience to different degrees. To test this assumption and evaluate the extent of their effect, we presented participants with a physical object, a mug. However, in each trial of the study, the mug was matched to a different virtual object that exemplified a substitution type from the model. In the second study, we assumed that SR systems would frequently involve users in scenarios in which they need to interact with objects they might not possess (such as dangerous or imaginary objects, with the exception of props). Thus, we evaluated participants' engagement while wielding a Lightsaber replica and while wielding two substitutive objects: a torch and an umbrella. However, in the SE they were all perceived as the same Lightsaber.

APPARATUS

Here, we describe the physical room in which the two studies took place, the corresponding virtual room experienced by participants while immersed, and the equipment they used.

The Physical Room — Participants of our studies were tracked through a combination of 9 OptiTrack Flex 3 cameras. All cameras were placed at a height of 2.5 m. Four of these were placed at the corners. A fifth one was placed in the middle of the wall facing the entrance. The remaining four cameras were placed in the middle of the side walls, each oriented towards one half of the room's volume. Participants interacted with the environment in areas with optimal tracking coverage. In the first study they were sitting on a (real) sofa / (virtual) bench and did not incur tracking issues. In the second study, participants were instructed about the extents of the zone in which they could move while still being tracked, an area of 3 $m \times 2.75$ m. We furnished our study room with furniture commonly found in a living room (see Figure 1): a desk with chair, a sofa, a cabinet, and a television plus stand. We measured the room's extents (5.9 $m \times 3$ m) and each object's bounding box. These measures were used to model the virtual objects substituting their real counterparts.

The Virtual Room — We designed two VEs using the Unity 4.5 engine. We built custom scripts in order to use VRPN data streamed by Motive, the software controlling the OptiTrack cameras. The data packets contained information on the absolute position and orientation of all tracked objects.

The User — Participants wore an *Oculus Rift* Development Kit 1 headset, working wirelessly through an HDMI receiver and an external battery inside a backpack. Absolute positioning and orientation data was provided by an optical marker attached to the Oculus Rift through a custom 3D printed mount. We mapped tracking data received from this marker to a stereoscopic camera representing the user's head in the VE. Participants also wore two fingerless gloves with optical markers attached on top. The markers were mapped to the position and orientation of two virtual forearm plus hand models that the user saw in the VE. We told participants that the movements of their fingers would not affect the pose of their virtual representation.

FIRST USER STUDY

In the first study, participants were immersed in an SE where our mock living room had been substituted by a medieval courtyard. Our goal for this study was to investigate the impact on the suspension of disbelief and ease of interaction that artificially increasing the mismatch between the virtual object and its physical counterpart could have. A baseline object, a replica of the real mug was recreated in the VE with the exact same size, shape, and visual appearance. The real mug measured 7 $m \times 10$ $m \times 8$ cm and weighed 290 g. We considered various substituted objects, each altering a physical property exemplifying one of the substitution levels we previously described (see Figure 2). The substituted objects were:

Aesthetic — We altered the *material* of the mug, resulting in one appearing to be made out of *glass* and another appearing to be made out of *wood*; in addition, we also wanted to test the effect of materials suggesting explicit differences in terms of temperature, thus we designed a *hot* mug that appeared to be on fire and an *icy* one that appeared to be carved out of ice with a particle effect showing the ice sublimating.

Addition/Subtraction — We altered the *size* of the baseline mug with a *smaller* one (50% of the size) and a *bigger* one (150% of the size).

Function — We tested a *combination* of factors, i.e. different material, size, and addition and removal of features. The two resulting objects were a wooden basket of similar shape and size to the mug, save for the absence of the handles on the side and a lighted oil lamp in which one handle was approximated by the real handle of the mug (while the second was absent from the physical proxy).

Category — We wanted to test the effect a severely different *shape* had, thus we considered two substitutive objects: a box having the same bounding box of the mug and a sphere inscribed in said bounding box.

Figure 2. In the picture each pair of objects exemplifying a different substitution type is shown. The *replica* mug used as baseline *(a)* then each pair of substitutive objects: *(Aesthetic)* glass *(b)* and wooden mug *(c)*; hot *(d)* and icy mug *(e)*; *(Addition/Subtraction)* big *(f)* and small mug *(g)*; *(Function)* basket *(h)* and lamp *(i)*; *(Category)* box *(j)* and sphere *(k)*.

Since the impact of this mismatch was not known beforehand, we designed the virtual objects substituting furniture and other decorative elements that were not part of the main focus of the study by following a principle of plausibility. We chose the substitutive objects among those we believed participants would find plausible to find in such an outdoor environment. As it can be observed from Figure 1, wooden fences delimited the room on its two sides, while a stone arch with metal gate was placed in lieu of the real door leading into the room; the entrance to another house delimited the other end. The real-world desk from which the investigator controlled the experiment was substituted with a set of crates arranged in the same L-shape and size of its physical counterpart. The TV stand was substituted by a wooden beam to which a set of swords were attached (whose bounding box corresponded to the TV screen). Participants were sitting on a wooden bench that was modelled to the exact same size and shape of the real-world sofa, save for the absence of cushions which were replaced by a thicker wooden frame. Ambient sounds of birds and the wind played in the background.

Since we required a surface for the purpose of this study, we moved the cabinet in front of the sofa so that the objects of study could be placed on top. In the SE, the cabinet was replaced by a barrel having the same bounding box. Two objects were placed on top: a wine bottle (identical to the one in the real world) and a mug (the physical proxy we successively altered in the study). The real objects are shown in Figure 3. We augmented both objects with optical trackers (placed on top). The appearance of the wine bottle did not change during the course of the study. Its purpose was to support more complex interactions (such as pouring wine into the mug).

Task

Before beginning the first study, the investigator explained to the participants the concept of SR and the main implications it had on their surroundings: every virtual object they saw would be paired by a physical proxy. We informed participants that once immersed within the VE they would be presented with a number of different objects they had to interact with. We explained that the virtual appearance of the mug would change in each session. We asked participants to grab and feel the object, attempt to manipulate and use it in conjunction with the wine bottle.

Participants

Twenty participants (11 male, 9 female) aged 20-43 ($M = 27.35, SD = 5.12$) took part in the first study. One additional participant left the study midway due to nausea and was thus excluded from the analysis. We asked them to rate their experience with computer games and VR, on a scale of 1 (rarely play games/use VR technologies) to 7 (very frequently play games/use VR technologies). Our sample constituted of average gamers ($M = 4.64, SD = 1.35$) with low experience with VR technologies ($M = 2.50, SD = 1.50$). Each participant received £8.

Procedure

Before starting they completed a demographics questionnaire. They then put on the Oculus Rift and the two tracked gloves. The investigator placed the two real objects on the cabinet/barrel. Participants were not aware of what the real object looked like before the study began. At the end of each session, it was moved and then placed back for the successive session. Each participant was allowed to freely manipulate the virtual object for one minute, after which, we asked the participant to answer a set of questions on the experience of interacting with the object. Five of these questions required participants to rate on a 7-point scale how similar the virtual object felt to the real one in terms of *physical* properties such as *size*, *shape* (regardless of the apparent size), *temperature*, *material*, and *weight*. A value of 1 meant that the virtual object was completely different from the physical one; a value of 7 meant that they were exactly the same.

Two additional questions asked participants to rate on a 7-point scale the *perceived* properties of the object. The first, asked them to rate the *ease* of grabbing and manipulating the object, where 1 meant that the interaction was *very hard* and 7 meant that it was *very easy*. The second question asked how likely they were to believe that they were actually manipulating the virtual object, considering the overall mismatch between the two objects. A value of 1 meant that they were *completely distracted* from the idea of actually manipulating the virtual object, while a value of 7 meant that they were *completely absorbed* in the idea of actually manipulating it.

The investigator posed these questions while the participants were still wearing the Oculus Rift but after they had placed the object back on the barrel. The objects were presented in a balanced order. After completing each session, we asked participants to fill an SUS questionnaire on the sense of presence in the VE [22].

Results

We collected for each participant 77 responses ($7\ questions \times 11\ objects$), for a total of 1540. We compared the mean scores for each object in each category using a repeated-measures one-way ANOVA (Greenhouse-Geisser corrected when necessary) and post-hoc pairwise comparisons (Bonferroni corrected). The questionnaire results are summarised in Table 1.

		Material (Physical)	Temp. (Physical)	Size (Physical)	Shape (Physical)	Weight (Physical)	Ease (Perceived)	Suspension of Disbelief (Perceived)
Replica	Mean	4.95	5.74	6.05	6.35	4.78	6.25	5.85
Mug	SD	2.01	1.69	1.05	0.88	1.22	0.91	1.18
Aesthetic	Glass	0.55	0.26	0.20	0.10	0.85	0.00	0.20
(Material)	Wood	*†-2.01*	-1.57	-0.29	-0.13	-0.83	-0.36	-1.57
Aesthetic	Hot	**-2.70*	**-4.34*	-0.05	0.05	0.00	-0.55	**-2.55*
(Temp.)	Icy	**-2.20*	**-3.58*	0.10	0.05	-0.20	-0.20	*†-1.85*
Addition	Big *(Size)*	0.05	-0.29	**-4.60*	-0.65	**-3.00*	-0.78	-1.06
Subtraction	Small *(Size)*	0.15	-0.54	**-3.15*	-0.75	0.17	**-2.14*	**-2.90*
Function	Lamp	-1.70	**-2.84*	*†-1.30*	**-4.00*	-0.17	-1.20	-1.38
(Combined)	Basket	**-2.45*	**-2.14*	-0.25	**-2.45*	-0.61	-0.70	-1.27
Categorical	Sphere	-1.19	-1.33	**-1.81*	**-4.53*	-1.31	**-1.66*	**-3.38*
(Shape)	Box	-0.89	-0.99	-0.52	**-4.82*	-1.48	-1.07	**-2.79*

Table 1. The first two rows report the replica mug's mean and standard deviation for each property, respectively. The remaining rows report the differences in the mean score of the object to the baseline, with statistically significant differences marked with † ($p < 0.05$) and * ($p < 0.01$).

The inflexibility of passive haptics showed in the participants' scores regarding their perception of the objects' *materials*. We found significant differences for the *Basket* ($M = 2.5$, $SD = 1.73$), the *Wooden* ($M = 2.94$, $SD = 1.95$), *Icy* ($M = 2.75$, $SD = 1.65$), and *Hot* mugs ($M = 2.25$, $SD = 1.65$). As expected, we found significant differences in terms of *temperature* for the *Icy* ($M = 2.16$, $SD = 1.12$) and *Hot* mugs ($M = 1.4$, $SD = 1.1$). Interestingly, participants expected the two objects that appeared to be made out of wood to be warmer: the *Wooden* ($M = 4.16$, $SD = 1.72$) mug and the *Basket* ($M = 3.6$, $SD = 1.6$). *Weight* was not a property we could alter in the substitutive objects. We did ask participants how much they thought the virtual representation should weigh compared to the one they were holding. We found a significant difference for the *Small* mug ($M = 1.78$, $SD = 1.06$). The *Box* trended towards significance ($M = 3.29$, $SD = 1.36$, $p = 0.57$). Indeed, we found that unambiguously communicating the correct material was not trivial. Some participants thought that the box was made out of paper, others of a concrete-like material.

Regarding differences between the visual appearance of the substitutive object and the physical proxy in terms of *size*, participants found the *Big* ($M = 2.9$, $SD = 1.83$) and *Small* mugs ($M = 1.45$, $SD = 0.6$), the *Sphere* ($M = 4.24$, $SD = 1.52$), and the *Lamp* ($M = 4.75$, $SD = 1.62$) to significantly vary. On the perception of the object's *shape*, we found significant differences regarding the *Sphere* ($M = 1.82$, $SD = 1.38$), the *Box* ($M = 1.53$, $SD = 0.8$), the *Lamp* ($M = 2.35$, $SD = 1.23$) and the *Basket* ($M = 3.9$, $SD = 1.58$).

Overall, we found that the objects that participants thought detracted from their suspension of disbelief were those that had a different shape or temperature. We found significant differences for the box ($M = 2.91$, $SD = 2.19$), the sphere ($M = 2.5$, $SD = 1.24$), the *Hot* mug ($M = 3.81$, $SD = 2.32$), and the *Icy* mug ($M = 4.21$, $SD = 2.04$). The *Small* mug ($M = 2.86$, $SD = 1.75$) was found to be less believable, while the bigger one was not. No significant differences from the believability of the baseline object were found for both the *Basket* ($M = 4.69$, $SD = 1.49$) and the *Lamp* ($M = 4.5$, $SD = 1.51$). Concerning the *ease* of interaction, only the *Small* mug ($M = 4.43$, $SD = 1.79$) and the *Sphere* ($M = 4.75$, $SD = 1.14$) were found to affect participants during manipulation, highlighting the issue *addition/subtraction* substitutions were likely to lead to. Finally, the mean SUS score, the sum of 6 or 7 ratings for each participant, was 2.5 ($SD = 1.79$).

Figure 3. From left to right, top to bottom: the real mug and wine bottle used as physical props in the first study; the torch, umbrella, and Force FX replica of Darth Vader's Lightsaber used in the second study.

SECOND USER STUDY

In the second user study, participants were immersed in an SE where our mock living room had been turned into the bridge of a futuristic spaceship. Furniture was replaced by futuristic equivalents. An ambient sound of the engine humming played in the background. Our goal for this study was to investigate whether objects whose function differs from the one portrayed in the VE can be used to provide similar levels of engagement and support the suspension of disbelief as well as exact replicas. Often games present players with scenarios where they need to interact with various objects, such as guns, wizards' staves, swords, etc. In the context of SR it will be necessary to design experiences around the fact that these objects (especially the imaginary ones) are very unlikely to be found in users' living rooms. Thus, in most cases, the need to find a substitutive object becomes a necessity.

We designed a scenario in which participants needed to hit a moving target with a virtual Lightsaber matched to a physical proxy. We chose a replica as a baseline and two objects representative of substitution at the functional level. We did not consider categorical substitution as in the first study we found it to impact negatively the suspension of disbelief. Likewise, in a real world scenario we could not assume that users would possess examples of addition/subtraction or aesthetic substitution, e.g., Lightsabers of different sizes/colours. Our baseline object was a Force FX 1:1 replica of Darth Vader's Lightsaber from Star Wars ®. It consisted of a metal hilt and light tube, measuring 114 $cm \times 10\ cm \times 8\ cm$ and weighing 725 g. The other two objects were common household items: an umbrella (measuring 94 $cm \times 4\ cm \times 4\ cm$, weighing 520 g) and a torch (measuring 26 $cm \times 5\ cm \times 5\ cm$, weighing 214 g). These objects, shown in Figure 3, were chosen because they can be manipulated similar to the Lightsaber. However, they differ in shape, size, and perceived function.

Task

We asked participants to hit a moving blue sphere with their virtual Lightsaber. Each physical proxy had an optical tracker attached to it so that the movements and orientation of the virtual Lightsaber corresponded to those of the physical objects. We instructed them to stand in a specific spot in the room and explained that they could move, however the target was always in reach of the Lightsaber. The target moved across a pattern consisting of 9 positions arranged in a 3×3 grid centred at a distance of 1 m in front of the participant's starting position. The sphere stayed in a position for two seconds before moving to another randomly chosen grid-position (excluding the current one); the movement took one second. Once hit, the sphere turned green and a Lightsaber sound was played; it stayed green for one second before turning back blue. We instructed participants that hits performed while the sphere was green did not count. After hitting the sphere a total of nine times, the trial stopped.

Participants and Procedure

The same 20 participants who took part to the first study also took part to the second one. Each trial started after a countdown of three seconds. Participants repeated each session four times, the first of which was considered as training and was thus excluded from the analysis. They completed 3 *objects* × 3 *repetitions* for a total of 9 trials. Participants did not see any of the objects before the completion of the study. One of the investigators handed participants the objects when they were already wearing the headset. After completing each object's three trials, we asked participants to rate from 1 to 7 the following questions: how much they felt *engaged* or distracted in the idea of being a Jedi on a spaceship; their degree of *preference* for each object; how physically and mentally *exerted* they felt. In addition, we asked participants to guess which object they were really holding. Finally, we asked them to fill an SUS questionnaire.

Results

Results from the second study are summarised in Table 2. We measured average completion times: the *torch* was the fastest, followed by the *Lightsaber* and the umbrella; however, we did not find any significant differences. In terms of *engagement*, we found a significant effect for the object being used ($F_{2,57} = 294.83$, $p < 0.01$). When asked which object participants considered more supportive to the idea of actually wielding a Lightsaber, they gave the torch the highest rating, followed by the replica and then the umbrella. Pairwise comparison found a significant difference between the torch and the umbrella ($p < 0.01$).

We found a significant difference in terms of *preference* ($F_{2,57} = 287.68$, $p < 0.01$), with the torch being preferred to the umbrella ($p < 0.01$). When we asked to clarify the motivations for their preference, all participants stated that the weight was the main reason. Indeed we found a significant difference in terms of *physical exertion* ($F_{2,57} = 106.11$, $p < 0.02$), with the torch being reported as less tiring than both the replica and the umbrella ($p < 0.01$). This was further highlighted by their mean scores. No differences were found in terms of mental exertion. We asked participants to guess which object they were holding: out of 60 possible answers, 17 guessed correctly (28.33%). The mean SUS score, the sum of 6 or 7 ratings for each participant, was 2.5 ($SD = 1.91$).

Object	Time (s)	Engagement	Preference	Physical Ex.	Mental Ex.
Lightsaber	25.72 *(7.83)*	5.40 *(1.75)*	5.15 *(1.31)*	4.00 *(1.41)*	3.30 *(1.87)*
Umbrella	24.07 *(5.19)*	4.50 *(1.43)*	4.65 *(1.63)*	3.95 *(1.79)*	3.45 *(1.79)*
Torch	22.66 *(4.13)*	5.95 *(1.00)*	6.00 *(1.08)*	2.55 *(1.96)*	3.45 *(1.99)*
	Quantitative	*Qualitative*			

Table 2. Mean quantitative and qualitative results; in parentheses, the standard deviation.

DISCUSSION

We categorised our findings from the two studies in four main areas: design implications, content authoring, a discussion of open challenges, and of other application areas.

Design Implications

SR systems should prefer functional substitution for manipulable objects.

Overall, our results show that the choice of which substitutive object to assign to a real one is largely affected by the shape. However, if the extent of the substitution is maintained at the **functional** level, we found that there is a large leeway in terms of how much this can be altered. For instance, participants commented that the lamp object was regarded as being believable, however what broke the illusion was the missing handle (on one side, the mug handle approximated the lamp's). In the second study, more participants preferred the torch rather than the actual replica. The torch approximated only the hilt of the Lightsaber. Although it is unknown whether in reality the energy blade would have a significant weight, we believe the torch's lesser weight made it easier to manipulate than the replica (whose hilt was made out of metal) and the umbrella (also heavier).

Minimise mismatch with the manipulable parts of an object.

In order to minimise the impact that any mismatch has on the suspension of disbelief, we believe designers of SR systems should place greater emphasis in making substitutive objects closer to the proxy's physical appearance in the parts users are most likely to contact. For example, a pen would thus be a good candidate for a magic wand. The way a user would hold it is similar and the virtual magic wand can have a different shape at the opposite end from the hilt, as the user will be less likely to interact with it from that side.

Maintain correct proprioceptive feedback even if it conflicts with the real pose.
Regarding the **addition** or **subtraction** of features, smaller objects had a significant negative impact on the believability of the objects. This is largely due to the higher difficulty experienced by users in finding the physical object. Participants commented that it was harder to guess where the physical object was. They unexpectedly hit the real object while they saw their hand still distant from the virtual object. Objects that appeared bigger than they really were, did not cause a significant impact on the believability of the interaction. However, they reported some issues when their own hands could go through the bigger object's mesh. As we previously stated, we attached a single marker to the user's palm. With more sophisticated tracking systems it could be possible to track all fingers and use inverse kinematics to alter the pose of the fingers. For example, have the fingers appear to correctly grab a bigger looking object even though in reality, the fingers would be inside the object's mesh.

Out-of-reach objects allow for greater categorical mismatch.
We believe **categorical** substitution to be more suited for those objects that are least likely to be interacted with by the user, e.g., decorative or out-of-reach objects. If, however, there are no more suitable substitution options, we found that even though the extents of the mismatch broke the believability of the illusion, participants had few issues in actually being able to manipulate the objects.

Materials can affect users' expectation on the physical properties of the object.
Graphical realism, or substitution of **aesthetic** features is another key aspect that designers should keep in mind while creating SR experiences. We observed that participants experienced difficulties in understanding what objects were made of. This, in turn, caused users to perceive objects differently and thus generate assumptions based on the idea they had of the material. For example, 4 participants had conflicting opinions about the *box* object. For some, it appeared to be made out of paper, others of stone or concrete. One participant commented that *"The environment influenced my perception of the materials; as this looks like a medieval courtyard, I would not expect to find plastic here"*. As highlighted by our results, the ambient temperature of a material also needs to be taken into consideration as it was shown to have a significant impact on the believability of the illusion. In this regard, one participant commented while interacting with the hot mug, that *"if I had been wearing gloves, I would have believed it"*, similar to how oven mittens shield us from high temperatures.

The relation between an object's visual appearance and the physical properties it suggests can be manipulated by designers. They can alter the visual appearance of a material to influence users' expectations. For example, if a user is holding a virtual box, it could appear to be made out of iron if heavy or tin if light. In this way the user's suspension of disbelief will be improved by not perceiving a mismatch in terms of weight, even though there might be mismatches on other physical properties, e.g., the physical object might be made of a different material, such as plastic or have a different shape.

Substitutive objects can engage users as much as replicas.
Another observation we made, based on the results and the interviews with our participants, is that using objects that approximate the portrayed virtual object might be a better strategy than pursuing realistic physical-virtual object pairings. Even assuming that it could be practical to build high-fidelity replicas of objects needed in an SR system, even for dangerous or imaginary objects, using them might not be *fun*. Indeed, one of the main comments made by participants was that the Lightsaber replica and the umbrella were too heavy. This was also highlighted by the participants finding the torch to require less physical exertion. A convincing illusion of holding a machine gun or a longsword might constitute the goal of an "ultimate display". However, the real objects have considerable weights and require training to be used effectively. Thus, we believe this finding to generalise to other scenarios, that is: exact replicas are not necessary to maintain the suspension of disbelief; a substitutive object can be chosen among those able to provide a similar interactive experience to the one they portray; however it should not have undesirable qualities (e.g., being too heavy or fragile) even at the cost of increasing the mismatch with the actual object.

Reality-based VEs might have stricter presence requirements.
Although we did not find any significant differences in terms of the sense of presence in the two SEs, we collected some observations that highlight subjective differences between the two. One participant commented that *"I have really been in an environment similar to the [courtyard in the first study] so I know what to expect; I have never been on a spaceship and it seemed less real because I don't know what to compare it to"*. Another commented: *"Oh we are in Italy, aren't we?"*. We believe these and similar other comments to be an indicator of the first VE being more believable than the second as it was similar to places participants had really been to. This could implicate that it will be harder to maintain the suspension of disbelief while visiting VEs that look like common or really existing places. Users will form expectations based on their real experience of similar places that the VE needs to maintain in order to be perceived as believable. Conversely, designers will have more creative freedom when involving users in imaginary environments, as users will have less preconceived expectations.

Content Authoring

In our two studies we authored the SE manually. That is, we created a VE based on actual measurements. However, SR designers will have to design experiences that have to adapt to a wide variety of room environments. One key requirement is that future SR systems will need to have knowledge of the surrounding environment. This information ranges from data about the size and layout of the real environment in which a system is deployed (e.g., the user's house) to knowledge of the available objects' physical properties. The system will then enforce pairings between virtual objects and their physical counterparts, according to the requirements of the particular experience.

We envision two main avenues to recreate the user's own environment. On one end, an SR system could give users the means to create the basic layout of the environment, similar to *The Sims*' build mode. On the other end, it could be completely automatic. There are various mounts available to attach a depth camera to an Oculus Rift and it is conceivable that future headsets might have these sensors already built-in. Reconstruction systems such as the Kinect Fusion [9] allow users to capture the point cloud of any room. The advantage of SR is that it does not need a perfect approximation of the environment as its fundamental concept rests on non-perfect virtual-real pairings. Thus, we believe the tolerance of an environment resulting from a Kinect-Fusion capture would be acceptable for the purpose of extracting its basic layout features. Concerning the actual positional tracking of the user, the Oculus DK2 shipped with an add-on that is able to detect the user's head movements and orientation within 2.5 *m*. It is conceivable that off-the shelf tracking systems having greater range will become available in the near future.

Object recognition from 3D point-cloud datasets would then be the ideal method to detect which objects are available in a room and which substitutive objects would be the ideal candidates. However, manual labelling of objects the user wishes to be interactive in the SE would be the most cost-effective solution in the medium term. The SR system would then have to match the available objects with the substitutive objects needed in the game. This could be achieved by a rule-based system that privileged pairings that minimised the negative effects on the suspension of disbelief and ease of interaction. When no objects satisfying a rule are available, those having greater mismatch would be chosen. For example if an actual tablet cannot be found to substitute a futuristic one, then a book could be a good match as it could have similar size and affordances. The guidelines we presented in the previous section illustrate how such a system could favour these pairings.

Open Challenges

We believe that a similar investigation to the one we presented can be conducted to understand how the mismatch between larger physical objects and their virtual portrayal can impact real-walking locomotion interfaces.

In our studies, participants were not familiar with the objects used. In the first study, we observed that participants identified the object as a mug after manipulating it. In the second, the majority of users (71.67%) were not able to identify the object they held. Future research on SR systems deployed in real homes could investigate whether the user experience is affected by interacting with familiar objects.

Another challenge is represented by the disparity between the size of the VE and the space available in the real environment in which an SR experience takes place. A VR game can require very large spaces. For example, consider Carla: she is playing an SR experience at home. The SR system is able to adapt the locations in the VE to the rooms available in her own home. When the experience requires her to transition to another area, it would then be necessary to implement such a mechanism while avoiding her to wander outside the real boundaries (e.g., if her front door is also mapped to a virtual door). A naive implementation could require her to turn 180° when she reaches the door leading to the outside, as in the work of Williams et al. [27]. Upon completing the turn, she would find herself in a new environment, where the layout of her home continues to delimit the space she is allowed to explore. For example, if she is outside in a modern city environment, the real walls could be substituted by cars parked on one side of the street and a building façade on the other. In other outdoor environments, trees or fences could delimit the space available as we have done in the first study.

The existence of disparities between the user and their virtual avatar constitutes another challenge. In a VR game, the user is the real protagonist. In traditional computer games, the user impersonates a different character. Frequently, the abilities and skills of the game character differ from the user's real ones. In VR, this is no longer possible and our virtual avatar would be limited to our abilities. However it might still be desirable to provide "superhuman" capabilities. If our character possesses extraordinary strength, then designers can use the expectations we form based on an object's material to corroborate the illusion. For example, a cushion could be substituted by a heavy boulder that children playing the role of a superhero could throw on enemies.

Other Application Scenarios

The concept we have presented is not restricted to the domain of games. We envision that it can also have applications in educational contexts. For example, a museum could allocate a room for an SE that portrayed how everyday life was back in a different historical period. In this scenario, visitors could be immersed in an SR system that substituted the real environment with a Roman villa. Physical props could be used to provide a more engaging hands-on experience. For example, learning how the Romans prepared food by interacting with virtual utensils matched to physical proxies. Other areas of interest include training and simulation: fire-fighters or paramedics can simulate rescue operations taking place in virtual replicas of physical environments that are altered to look like an emergency is taking place. Sports represent another scenario: rock-climbers could substitute artificial walls with a mountain-side; hikers could experience remote environments while actually walking inside their own homes.

CONCLUSION

In this paper we investigated the concept of Substitutional Reality — Virtual Environments where the physical world is substituted with virtual counterparts. In particular, we studied how the mismatch between the virtual and the physical objects affects the user experience. A greater mismatch can increase the range of environments that can substitute the physical environment, but can also become an obstacle to the interaction and to the believability of the experience. We investigated the factors affecting this mismatch in two user studies.

Participants found the more believable substitutive objects to be those that do not have significant variations in the part most likely to be interacted with (a handle). They reported the mismatch to become significant when the virtual appearance suggested variations in terms of tactile feedback, temperature, and weight not portrayed by the physical proxy. However, we showed that designers can use these notions to simulate superhuman abilities (by matching heavy-looking materials with light objects) and increase the extent of the mismatch in the parts of objects least likely to be interacted with (a sword blade). In those cases where the exact object required by the experience might not be available (imaginary ones, for example), participants found interacting with a similar object as engaging as interacting with an actual replica. We envision that users will be able to participate in Virtual Reality experiences that can adapt to any uncontrolled environment. To this end, we believe our research will support future designers of Substitutional Reality systems and experiences.

ACKNOWLEDGEMENTS

The first author was supported by a Marie Curie Intra European Fellowship *(3STARS)* within the 7th European Community Framework Programme. We thank Dr Wendy Powell, Dr John Hardy, Kiel Long, and Tim Dykes for their feedback.

REFERENCES

1. Barbagli, F., Salisbury, K., Ho, C., Spence, C., and Tan, H. Z. Haptic discrimination of force direction and the influence of visual information. *ACM TAP 3*, 2 (Apr. 2006), 125–135.
2. Carlin, A. S., Hoffman, H. G., and Weghorst, S. Virtual reality and tactile augmentation in the treatment of spider phobia: a case report. *Behav. Res. Ther. 35*, 2 (1997), 153–158.
3. Cosco, F., Garre, C., Bruno, F., Muzzupappa, M., and Otaduy, M. A. Visuo-haptic mixed reality with unobstructed tool-hand integration. *IEEE TVCG 19*, 1 (2013), 159–172.
4. e Silva, A. d. S., and Delacruz, G. C. Hybrid reality games reframed potential uses in educational contexts. *SAGE GAC 1*, 3 (2006), 231–251.
5. Gibson, J. J. The theory of affordances. *Perceiving, Acting and Knowing* (1977).
6. Hinckley, K., Pausch, R., Goble, J. C., and Kassell, N. F. Passive real-world interface props for neurosurgical visualization. In *Proc. CHI '94*, 452–458.
7. Hoffmann, H. Physically touching virtual objects using tactile augmentation enhances the realism of virtual environments. In *Proc. VR '98*, 59–63.
8. Insko, B. E. *Passive haptics significantly enhances virtual environments*. PhD thesis, UNC, 2001.
9. Izadi, S., Kim, D., Hilliges, O., Molyneaux, D., Newcombe, R., Kohli, P., Shotton, J., Hodges, S., Freeman, D., Davison, A., et al. Kinectfusion: real-time 3d reconstruction and interaction using a moving depth camera. In *Proc. UIST '11*, 559–568.
10. Kanade, T., Rander, P., and Narayanan, P. Virtualized reality: Constructing virtual worlds from real scenes. *IEEE Multimedia 4*, 1 (1997), 34–47.
11. Knoerlein, B., Székely, G., and Harders, M. Visuo-haptic collaborative augmented reality ping-pong. In *Proc. ACE '07*, 91–94.
12. Kohli, L., Whitton, M. C., and Brooks, F. Redirected touching: The effect of warping space on task performance. In *Proc. 3DUI '12*, 105–112.
13. Kotranza, A., and Lok, B. Virtual human+ tangible interface= mixed reality human an initial exploration with a virtual breast exam patient. In *Proc. VR '08*, 99–106.
14. Kushner, D. Virtual reality's moment. *IEEE Spectrum 51*, 1 (Jan. 2014), 34–37.
15. Kwon, E., Kim, G. J., and Lee, S. Effects of sizes and shapes of props in tangible augmented reality. In *Proc. ISMAR '09*, 201–202.
16. Matsuoka, Y., Allin, S. J., and Klatzky, R. L. The tolerance for visual feedback distortions in a virtual environment. *Physiol. Behav. 77*, 4 (2002), 651–655.
17. McNeely, W. A. Robotic graphics: a new approach to force feedback for virtual reality. In *Proc. VR '93*, 336–341.
18. Milgram, P., and Kishino, F. A taxonomy of mixed reality visual displays. *IEICE Trans. Inf.& Syst. 77*, 12 (1994), 1321–1329.
19. Milgram, P., Takemura, H., Utsumi, A., and Kishino, F. Augmented reality: A class of displays on the reality-virtuality continuum. In *Proc. SPIE 2351* (1995), 282–292.
20. Reda, K., Febretti, A., Knoll, A., Aurisano, J., Leigh, J., Johnson, A. E., Papka, M. E., and Hereld, M. Visualizing large, heterogeneous data in hybrid-reality environments. *IEEE CGA 33*, 4 (2013), 38–48.
21. Robertson, G., Czerwinski, M., and Van Dantzich, M. Immersion in desktop virtual reality. In *Proc. UIST '97*, 11–19.
22. Slater, M., Usoh, M., and Steed, A. Taking steps: The influence of a walking technique on presence in virtual reality. *ACM TOCHI 2*, 3 (Sept. 1995), 201–219.
23. Steinicke, F., Bruder, G., Kohli, L., Jerald, J., and Hinrichs, K. Taxonomy and implementation of redirection techniques for ubiquitous passive haptic feedback. In *Cyberworlds '08*, 217–223.
24. Suzuki, K., Wakisaka, S., and Fujii, N. Substitutional reality system: a novel experimental platform for experiencing alternative reality. *Sci. Rep. 2* (2012).
25. Tachi, S., Maeda, T., Hirata, R., and Hoshino, H. A construction method of virtual haptic space. In *Proc. ICAT '94*, 131–138.
26. Usoh, M., Arthur, K., Whitton, M. C., Bastos, R., Steed, A., Slater, M., and Brooks Jr, F. P. Walking > walking-in-place > flying, in virtual environments. In *Proc. SIGGRAPH '99*, 359–364.
27. Williams, B., Narasimham, G., Rump, B., McNamara, T. P., Carr, T. H., Rieser, J., and Bodenheimer, B. Exploring large virtual environments with an hmd when physical space is limited. In *Proc. APGV '07*, 41–48.

The Semantic Paintbrush: Interactive 3D Mapping and Recognition in Large Outdoor Spaces

Ondrej Miksik[1†⋆] Vibhav Vineet[2◇⋆] Morten Lidegaard[1†] Ram Prasaath[◇] Matthias Nießner[2]
Stuart Golodetz[1†] Stephen L. Hicks[1‡] Patrick Pérez[3] Shahram Izadi[4] Philip H. S. Torr[1†]
[1]University of Oxford [2]Stanford University [3]Technicolor R&I [4]Microsoft Research

(a) (b) (c) (d) (e)

Figure 1: (a) Our system comprises of an off-the-shelf pair of optical see-through glasses, with additional stereo RGB-Infrared cameras, and an additional handheld infrared/visible light laser. (b) The passive stereo cameras are used for extended range and outdoor depth estimation. (c) The user can see these reconstructions immediately using the heads-up display, and can use a laser pointer to draw onto the 3D world to semantically segment objects (once segmented these labels will propagate to new parts of the scene). (d) The laser pointer can also be triangulated precisely in the stereo infrared images allowing for interactive 'cleaning up' of the model during capture. (e) Final output, the semantic map of the scene.

ABSTRACT

We present an augmented reality system for large scale 3D reconstruction and recognition in outdoor scenes. Unlike existing prior work, which tries to reconstruct scenes using *active* depth cameras, we use a purely passive stereo setup, allowing for outdoor use and extended sensing range. Our system not only produces a map of the 3D environment in real-time, it also allows the user to draw (or 'paint') with a laser pointer directly onto the reconstruction to *segment* the model into objects. Given these examples our system then learns to segment other parts of the 3D map during online acquisition. Unlike typical object recognition systems, ours therefore very much places the user 'in the loop' to segment particular objects of interest, rather than learning from predefined databases. The laser pointer additionally helps to 'clean up' the stereo reconstruction and final 3D map, *interactively*. Using our system, within minutes, a user can capture a full 3D map, segment it into objects of interest, and refine parts of the model during capture. We provide full technical details of our system to aid replication, as well as quantitative evaluation of system components. We demonstrate the possibility of using our system for helping the visually impaired navigate through spaces. Beyond this use, our system can be used for playing large-scale augmented reality games, shared online to augment streetview data, and used for more detailed car and person navigation.

Author Keywords

3D reconstruction, laser pointer interaction, semantic segmentation, stereo, augmented reality, visually impaired

⋆ O. Miksik and V. Vineet assert joint first authorship.

† Department of Engineering Science
‡ Nuffield Department of Clinical Neurosciences
◇ Work was done at the University of Oxford.
ondra.miksik@gmail.com, vibhav.vineet@gmail.com | http://www.miksik.co.uk

CHI '15, Apr 18 – 23 2015, Seoul, Korea
Copyright 2015 ACM 978-1-4503-3145-6/15/04$15.00.
http://dx.doi.org/10.1145/2702123.2702222

INTRODUCTION

Maps help us to navigate and discover the world. In recent times, companies such as Google and Microsoft have applied reconstruction techniques to aerial and/or street-level imagery to produce virtual 3D maps on a *global scale*. These digital 3D maps form the basis of many of the navigation systems we use in our cars and mobile devices today.

Whilst much progress has been made in 3D mapping, particularly with the advent of real-time depth cameras, most of these virtual maps are still at a *geometric* level, representing the 3D structure of the scene, as opposed to understanding or *recognizing* the higher level objects or scene structure. Furthermore, these maps are captured ahead of time, and often at a coarse level, instead of being captured *live* and reflecting the detailed nature of the scene. Finally, these maps are often general-purpose and not *personalized* to specific objects or areas of interest for specific users.

In this paper, we present a new mapping system that is capable of creating large-scale semantic maps of outdoor scenes *interactively*. The word 'interactive' is of particular importance, as this not only implies live capture of the map, but also a system that keeps the user 'in the loop' to guide the mapping towards objects and elements of the map that are of particular interest.

More specifically, we present a novel augmented reality (AR) system for large scale 3D reconstruction and recognition in outdoor scenes. Unlike prior work, which tries to reconstruct scenes using *active* depth cameras, we use a purely passive stereo setup, allowing for outdoor use and extended range sensing. This allows us to reconstruct large and/or distant structures, such as building facades, roads and cars.

Our system not only produces a map of the 3D environment in real-time, it also allows the user to draw (or 'paint') with a laser pointer directly onto the reconstruction. The user simply points at an object with the laser pointer, performs a brush-like stroke, and then issues a voice command to interactively segment and label the 3D scene into different object classes. Unlike typical object recognition systems, which work in a 'closed-world' scenario, with a fixed, pre-trained set of object classifiers, our system is fully interactive, allowing the user to add new classes on the fly, and even correct object labels.

The laser pointer is additionally triangulated by the stereo camera rig during capture, which provides a strong 3D prior to help *interactively* 'clean up' the stereo reconstruction and final 3D map. Stereo algorithms typically break in textureless regions, causing major errors. Here, these errors can be quickly and interactively cleaned up by the user, in an online manner. To our knowledge, this is the first such system that allows the user to see the results of object and stereo estimation in real time and interactively correct them.

With our system, within minutes, a user can capture a full 3D map, segment it into objects of interest and refine parts of the model during capture, all by simply exploring the space and moving a handheld laser pointer device, metaphorically 'painting' or 'brushing' onto the world. We provide full technical details of our system to aid replication, as well as quantitative evaluation of system components.

We are particularly interested in application scenarios that can exploit these large-scale semantic 3D maps. We demonstrate the possibility of using our system for helping the visually impaired navigate through spaces. Here, the semantic segmentation allows us to highlight objects of interest using the AR glasses. The metric and precise reconstruction can be used for navigation, and the laser pointer can be used to pinpoint objects within proximity. Beyond this use, these semantic maps can used for playing large-scale AR games, shared online to augment streetview data, and used for more detailed car and person navigation.

Our contributions can therefore be summarized as follows:

- A novel augmented reality hardware system comprising of transparent LED glasses, attached RGB-Infrared stereo cameras, and a one-button laser pointer.
- A large-scale dense mapping system that can operate in outdoor scenes, in real-time. This provides the ability to reconstruct objects at greater distances and in direct sunlight, beyond the capabilities of active depth cameras such as the Kinect.
- Extensions to KinectFusion [22] to support visual odometry for pose estimation alongside stereo data input.
- The ability for users to semantically segment captured 3D maps into object regions using a simple laser pointer and 'brushing' metaphor.
- A machine learning pipeline for learning from these object examples to automatically segment the captured 3D models, in real-time, at scale, and with noisier data than previous systems *e.g.* [32].
- Integration of accurate yet sparse measurements from a laser pointer to interactively improve the quality of the stereo depth estimation and reconstruction.
- A first prototype of our semantic mapping system for the visually impaired.

RELATED WORK

In the past years, there have been rapid developments in algorithms and systems for indoor and outdoor mapping, at varying scales. Offline structure from motion (SfM) and multi-view stereo (MVS) techniques work directly on photos taken of the same scene from different viewpoints (potentially from online repositories and heterogeneous sets of cameras). These systems typically utilize computationally expensive feature matching and bundle adjustment techniques and require minutes, hours or even days to create 3D models. The output can be sparse [31] or dense point clouds [1], or even detailed and connected surface models [9].

Algorithms based on Simultaneous Localization and Mapping (SLAM) [18, 4] instead perform real-time mapping using a single monocular cameras. Early on, they represented the world by a small number of reconstructed 3D points. With the advent of *dense* real-time methods such as DTAM [23], they have moved to reconstructing detailed surfaces. However, they can still only reconstruct very small environments.

Recently LSD-SLAM [5] demonstrated large-scale semi-dense point cloud reconstruction using only a monocular mobile phone camera. The method is based on a variant of semi-dense whole image alignment for camera tracking [6]. Other notable systems focusing on city-scale reconstructions use passive cameras (*e.g.* Taneja *et al.* [30]). Chen *et al.* [2] localizes landmarks at city-scale on mobile devices. Geiger *et al.* [10] use stereo camera input to build a dense 3D reconstruction of scene in real-time.

Another approach is to replace the challenges of depth estimation using passive cameras with the use of active depth sensors, such as structured light or time-of-flight systems. The ability to compute (noisy) real-time depth maps cheaply has led to a resurgence of dense 3D reconstruction algorithms, demonstrating real-time performance [22] even at large scales [25], [34]. However, these systems rely on active sensors, which limits their use outdoors (*i.e.* in direct sunlight or at extended sensing ranges). The ability of such systems to reconstruct objects such as buildings at long-range is thus limited.

Whilst these systems have demonstrated impressive 3D mapping results, they stop purely at geometry reconstruction. Instead another important area is the recognition of scene objects. A great deal of work has focused on developing efficient and accurate algorithms predicting object labels at the pixel level. Examples include the models of Ladicky *et al.* [19] or Munoz *et al.* [21]. Recently many others have focused on labeling *voxels* or other 3D representations. Some of them focus on indoor scenes [33], and others on outdoor scenes [29], [36]. Some other recent works have also tried to jointly optimize for both the tasks of reconstruction and recognition, and so incorporate the synergy effects between these two high level vision tasks [12].

However, these methods are far from real-time and require offline processing. A more recent trend has explored real-time or online object recognition directly during 3D mapping [28], in particular to help compress 3D models further and aid in relocalization. SemanticPaint [32] takes this concept further by allowing users to label the scene during capture by *touching* surfaces and providing an online learning framework to infer class labels for unseen parts of the world. We build on that framework in this paper, but change the algorithm to handle large scale outdoor mapping using far nosier stereo data. Furthermore, we fundamentally change the input modality. Using a laser pointer allows for the correction of failures in the estimated stereo depth, which are endemic when moving to outdoor scenes. This ability to create semantic segmentations of the map and correct both the geometry and labels is a critical part of our system.

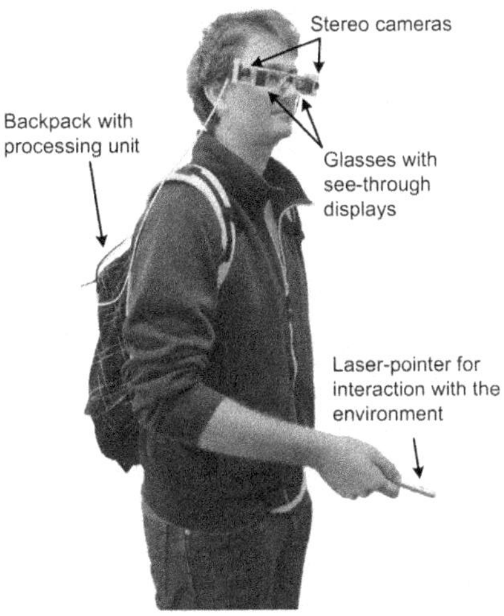

Figure 2: The main hardware components of our system.

Laser pointers have been used extensively for HCI scenarios, especially for interacting with large displays in intuitive ways [35, 26, 17]. Our approach uses the laser pointer as a means for interactively segmenting the scene into objects of interest. However, as a by-product the laser pointer can be precisely triangulated through the stereo pair. This allows us to also refine the 3D model, based on accurate 3D measurements taken from the laser pointer. This is in the spirit of systems such as [11] and other scanning laser depth sensors. However, our method puts the user 'in the loop' allowing the laser to refine parts that the user cares about or observes as noisy. In contrast to [24], our method allows to label any unknown (indoor/outdoor) environment into objects and semantic parts.

We demonstrate our real-time large scale-semantic mapping system in the context of helping visually impaired users to navigate through outdoor spaces. Here, laser pointing devices have a long history as digital aids for the partially sighted (see [16] for a review). We however take further inspiration from a relatively new trend of helping the visually impaired through augmented vision [14, 8]. The basic principle is based on capturing images using a regular camera or depth sensor, and enhancing features of the image such as edges [8] or objects of interest [14]. These enhanced images are then displayed to the user on head-mounted AR-glasses, hence stimulating the residual vision of the user.

SYSTEM OVERVIEW

In this section, we describe our system from a hardware, user interaction, and software perspective.

Hardware

The hardware for our system is shown in Fig. 2 and Fig. 3. It is composed of optical see-through AR glasses (EPSON MOVERIO BT-200) with a resolution of 960×540 and field of view of approx. 23° corresponding to a 40" virtual screen at 2.5 metres. Attached to these glasses are a pair of Omnivision RGB-Infrared (RGB-I) cameras (OV4682 RGB IR) with a resolution of 2688x1520 pixels. These cameras are capable of imaging both visible and infrared (IR) spectra. The cameras are set apart with a baseline of 22cm, calibrated, and using a stereo algorithm (described in the next section), natural features in the RGB image of the left camera are *matched* with those in the right, to estimate the disparity of the scene. This allows a *dense* depth map to be computed per frame. Additionally, we use a standard red laser operating at visible and IR spectra between 680-730nm, with output far less than 5mW making its usage eye safe. This laser emits both red light for the user to see, but also IR light which can be sensed by the IR sensitive pixels of the stereo cameras. This laser point can be triangulated and used to help localize the pointer with respect to the 3D reconstruction.

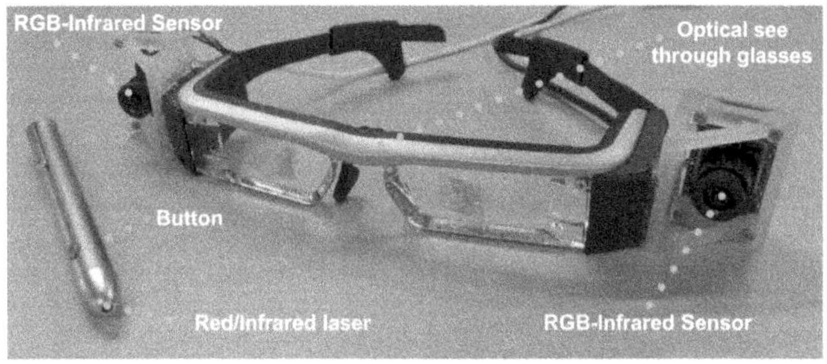

Figure 3: The main hardware components of our augmented reality glasses. See text for details.

User Interface and Interaction

As the user wears the AR glasses, they are provided with immediate feedback, as the reconstruction is captured live. The reconstruction is based on a scalable variant of the KinectFusion system [25]. Our system not only produces a map of the 3D environment in real-time, it also allows the user to draw (or 'paint') with a laser pointer directly onto the reconstruction.

In Fig. 9 and the accompanying supplementary video, we show how the laser pointer is used for interaction. In a basic scenario, a user wears the AR glasses and carries the laser pointer and backpack with processing unit (see Fig. 2). The user simply points at an object with the laser, performs a stroke, and then issues a voice command to interactively segment and label the 3D scene into different object classes. Unlike typical object recognition systems, our system therefore very much places the user 'in the loop' to segment particular objects of interest, rather than learning from predefined databases. The laser pointer is additionally triangulated by the stereo camera rig during capture, which provides a strong 3D prior to help 'clean up' the stereo reconstruction and final 3D map, *interactively*. Stereo algorithms typically break in textureless regions, causing major errors and outliers. Here, these errors can be quickly and interactively cleaned up by the user, in an online manner. The immediate feedback is visualized on the AR glasses. Our system also supports multi-user interactions, this scenario is thoroughly discussed in the Applications section.

SOFTWARE PIPELINE

The entire pipeline consists of several steps (*cf.* Fig. 4). First, we capture a pair of frames from the RGB-I cameras, which we separate into a pair of color and IR images. Next, we estimate the depth and camera pose from the color images, and detect and track the laser dot in the IR images. Then, the system fuses the input data to the current 3D model and performs 3D inference to propagate the semantic information and improves the reconstruction by high quality depth from triangulated laser dots. The user interacts with the system at all stages, by moving with the wearable AR device and by laser pointer to label the objects and improve the depth. The output of the system is continuously visualized with the optical see-through glasses.

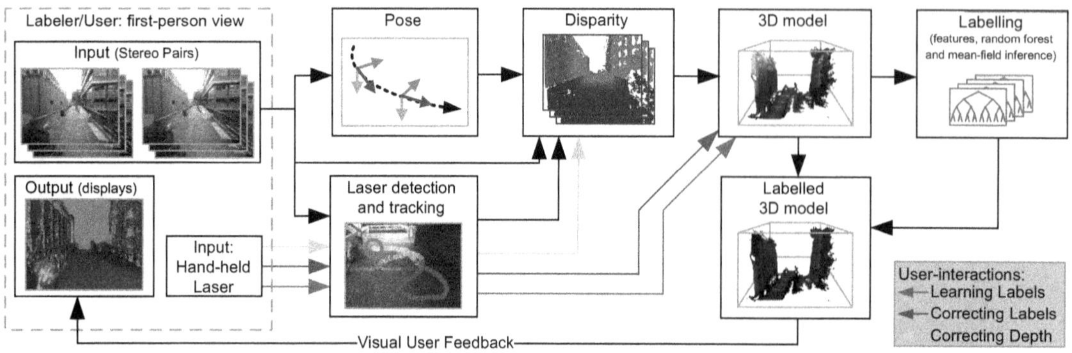

Figure 4: Overview of the system.

We first describe the more standard or known components of our system to aid replication, before moving onto the more novel and interactive aspects.

Surface Reconstruction The depth data generated using the stereo pairs are generally noisy. In order to generate high-quality surfaces, we follow the scalable hash-based fusion approach of Nießner *et al.* [25]. The key property of this approach is that it is able to generate high-quality surfaces of large-scale indoor scenes by fusing noisy depth data measured over time. However, there are two main drawbacks of this system: 1) the system is fully dependent on Kinect data, hence it fails to work in an outdoor environment and 2) the method depends on the ICP approach for camera pose estimation. Their pose estimation system generally fails with noisy depth from stereo. In our work, the first key contribution is to adapt this scalable hashing to work with outdoor scenes given stereo pairs and also to solve the issues associated with camera tracking.

Given the noisy depth data generated using stereo image pairs and pose estimate obtained by the visual odometry (described later), we incrementally fuse them into a single 3D volume using a truncated signed distance function (TSDF) [3] within a volumetric data structure. Each voxel is represented by a color, the TSDF encoding the distance of the voxel to the closest surface interface, and a weight that measures the confidence of that voxel belonging to the surface.

Camera calibration

First an offline calibration process is performed on the two RGB-I cameras. This comprises of: 1) *intrinsic calibration* to compute the geometric parameters of each IR camera lens (focal length, principal point, radial and tangential distortion); 2) *stereo calibration* to compute the geometric relationship between the two cameras, expressed as a rotation matrix and translation vector; 3) *stereo rectification* to correct the camera image planes to ensure they are scanline-aligned to simplify disparity computation. For more details please see [13].

Depth Estimation

Given a stereo image pair, we compute the depth as $z_i = bf/d_i$ where z_i is the depth for a corresponding disparity value d_i of ith pixel, b is the stereo camera baseline and f is the camera focal length. For disparity estimation, we use an approach of Geiger *et al.* [10] which forms a triangulation on a set of support points that can be robustly matched. This reduces the matching ambiguities and allows efficient exploitation of the disparity search space without any global optimization. Hence, the method can be easily parallelized.

Visual Odometry

For camera pose estimation, we use the FOVIS feature-based visual odometry method [15]. First, we preprocess an input pair of images by spatially smoothing them with a Gaussian filter and building a three-level image pyramid, in which each pyramid level corresponds to one octave in scale space. Then, we extract a set of sparse local features representing corner-like structures. For this, we use a FAST detector [27] with an adaptively-chosen threshold to detect a sufficient number of features. The feature extraction step is "biased" by bucketing to ensure features are uniformly distributed across space and scale.

To constrain the matching stage into a local search windows, an initial rotation of the image plane dealing with small motions in 3D is estimated. Feature matching stage associates the extracted features with descriptors, usually local binary patterns of normalized intensity values and features are matched using a mutual-consistency check. A robust estimate is performed by RANSAC [7] and the final transformation is estimated on the inliers. Robustness is further increased by "keyframes" that reduce drift when the camera viewpoint does not change significantly.

THE LASER PAINTBRUSH

Fig. 5 outlines the main process of laser pointer tracking. Since we use cameras with IR sensitive pixels, and emit IR from the laser, we can readily localize the laser pointer in the IR input images. In most cases, the IR images will contain high-intensity pixels associated with the laser dot and some spurious noise. Due to the presence of noise, we cannot simply extract pixels with the highest intensity. Hence we "track" a local window around the laser dot.

A user first initializes the tracker by pointing the laser into a predefined rectangle in the center of the image. To avoid the spurious noise (often with higher-intensity values than the laser dot), we need to keep the tracked window as local as possible. However, we also need to handle even rapid motion of the camera or the laser pointer itself (or both) resulting in a very large displacement in the image plane. To this end, the laser pointer tracker uses a Kalman filter, which predicts a pose of a local window in frame $t + 1$. In this frame, we move the local window into the predicted position, and threshold the patch. The tracker automatically switches into the "re-detection" mode if the mean intensity of a patch is higher than some fraction α of the highest intensity, the thresholded pixels are not connected, or the number of thresholded pixels is much higher than the expected size of the laser dot at a given distance.

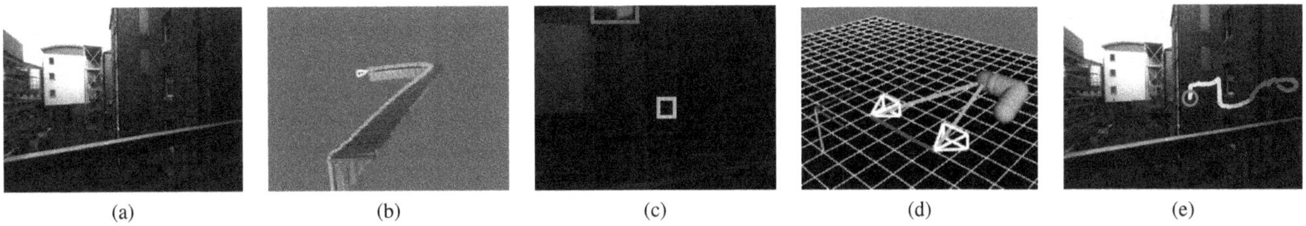

Figure 5: Laser pointer tracker: a) color images (left camera), b) part of visual odometry c) filtered images with local window (green) which is necessary since the image often contains brighter areas (blue), d) triangulation, e) tracked and triangulated (mapped) points projected onto the RGB frame.

Next, the measured pose is used to "correct" the Kalman filter prediction. If the laser tracker is in the "re-detection mode", it attempts to re-initialize in a small area close to the last known position – this is important since the laser dot intensity is often decreased to the level of noise (or can even completely disappear) due to diffraction and other optical effects. Further robustness is ensured by epipolar constraints; we run two laser trackers (left and right camera) in parallel and if the predictions do not satisfy the epipolar constraint, the tracker switches to the re-detection mode.

The final step is a 3D triangulation of the tracked 2D points observed in left and right images. To this end we implement simple and efficient linear triangulation as described in [13]. We then use the 6DoF pose estimated from the visual odometry as a means to back-project this 3D point into world space (from camera space). This adds a desirable temporal consistency of the 3D points, allowing 3D point tracks to be built up over time to detect 'brush' strokes and other gestures.

Interactive Improvement of Disparity

Whilst the laser pointer provides the main method for user input, it also carries another important benefit: The triangulated 3D point is very robustly matched and consequently a high-quality depth/disparity estimate is provided at a single sparse point. In general, dense depth/disparity estimation in large outdoor areas using passive stereo is a difficult problem. Although there has been a tremendous progress over the past decade, the typical output of a real-world sequence suffers from several issues – disparity estimates in homogeneous and/or over-exposed (saturated) areas are usually incorrect or completely missing. Moreover, most algorithms evaluate disparity independently per stereo-pair, *i.e.* disparity evaluated on a video sequence typically exhibits a "flickering" effect.

Our applications allows to, at least partially, recover incorrect and/or missing disparity values by laser interactions. A user labels the scene surface by laser pointer. The laser tracker is able to find such dots, which are triangulated and used to obtain high-quality depth estimates. These can be used as prior in disparity estimation algorithm. To this end, we modified approach of Geiger *et al.* [10]. A desirable side-effect is, that the tracked points are stable over time, hence also the prior is stabilized and the estimated disparity within regions corrected by interactions is more temporarily consistent.

Fig. 6 shows the steps used in disparity correction using the sparse 3D laser point. The method of Geiger *et al.* [10] robustly matches a set of sparse corner-like features (called support points) first and forms a Delaunay triangulation which serves as prior (a piece-wise linear function) in a generative model for stereo matching. This reduces the disparity search space to plausible regions and tends to disambiguate dense matching even without any global optimization method.

In order to improve disparity by interactivity, we inject the tracked laser points into a set of the support points before it computes triangulation. Feature matches in homogeneous areas are often incorrect, hence we form a convex hull around tracked points and remove all support points from its interior. We prefer this conservative strategy since we can always add missing matches by laser interactions; however, we need to make sure there are no incorrect matches (support points for prior). We consider three situations for each triangle: 1) if all three vertices of a triangle are laser points, we decrease the weight of feature matching term in the final energy function by β_{decr} (*cf.* [10], Eq. 8) and rely much more on the prior since we are very certain about the correct disparity value from the laser points. 2) if at least one vertex is a laser point, we decrease the weight of the feature matching term only by some fraction of β_{decr}. Finally, if no vertex of a triangle is obtained by laser pointer, we maintain the current state.

Unfortunately, all real-world measurements contain some level of noise, which includes our laser tracker, triangulation, and pose estimation (projection of 3D point to a current frame). In order to handle noisy input data and make disparity estimates more robust in the case of planar surfaces, we find connected components of triangles, fit a plane (using RANSAC with least squares refinement on inliers) into all support points obtained by the laser tracker, and share the estimated plane as a more robust prior (this can be viewed as a regularization) by all triangles within a connected component. In the case of unreliable surface measurements, a user can easily add more support points in these regions in order to clean them up during refinement.

Interactive Learning of Semantic Labels

In addition to map refinement, the laser is used to mark objects of interest through simple gestures such as strokes. Our system is then able to learn a classifier for labeled parts of a scene, where the semantic labels l_s are provided through speech recognition. Note that the user need not precisely label every voxel belonging to the object and can instead roughly mark a small set of voxel and the algorithm will automatically propagate labels to the other voxels belonging to the same part of a scene. Laser interaction is more convenient in this outdoor scenario than touch gestures, which are used in the SemanticPaint system [32]. The laser allows interaction at a distance and does not corrupt the 3D reconstruction; moving hands in front of a camera causes serious issues if corresponding depth values are not segmented and masked out properly.

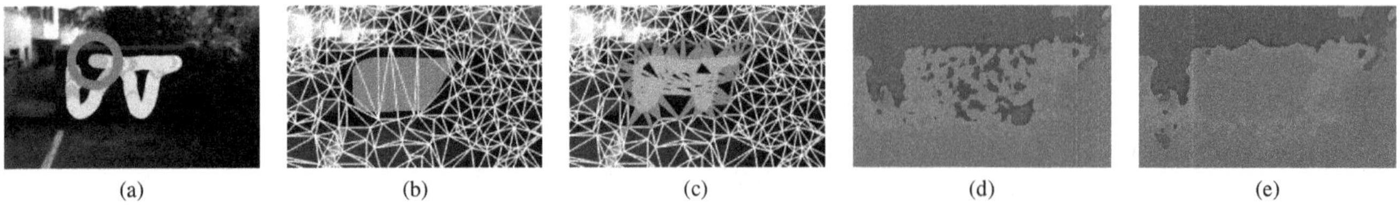

Figure 6: Disparity correction: a) tracked laser point, b) removed support points c) support points provided by interaction, d) disparity without interactivity, e) improved disparity

At the heart of our system is a densely-connected pairwise dynamic Conditional Random Field (CRF) defined on voxels. In such a model, each voxel i in the 3D reconstruction volume $\mathcal{V}$ of the scene is represented by a discrete random variable x_i that represents the semantic class $l \in \mathcal{L}$ (*e.g.* road, sidewalk, wall, ...) that the voxel belongs to. The unary potentials are evaluated by streaming decision forests that are extremely fast both to test and train online on voxel oriented patches (VOP) features. For the pairwise potentials, we employ the standard Potts model that enforces smoothness but preserves edges (we use RGB, surface normal vector and 3D world coordinate as features). These potentials take form of mixture of Gaussian kernels that allow efficient, filter based inference which is a message passing algorithm. Although the CRF is defined on continuously changing data, its energy landscape changes only gradually from one frame to the next. This allow us to amortize the optimization cost over multiple frames and a GPU implementation allows super real-time speeds (one update of the messages requires 6 ms).

AUGMENTED VISUALIZATION

The last step of our pipeline involves rendering our synthetic scene on the (full-color) displays of the glasses. These displays are transparent, allowing our raycasted 3D model to be superimposed over the user's view of their physical environment. For interactive segmentation of the scene, superimposing the two in this way provides a natural way of interacting with the 3D model, providing users with a way to verify the accuracy of the interactive labeling of the scene in real time. Our rendering through the glasses shows various semantic classes using a number of easily-distinguished colors. Fig. 8 shows some visualization examples.

Interactive Reduction of Visual Clutter

In addition to its uses for semantic labeling and improving disparity, the laser pointer can also be used to select individual semantic classes for visualization. That is, the user points at a part of the scene that is labeled with a particular class and the system then highlights all parts of the scene that belong to that class, whilst graying out those parts that belong to other classes. This provides a useful way of reducing the visual clutter in a scene, *e.g.* it might be useful for a visually-impaired person trying to follow a footpath to be able to prominently highlight the footpath and grey out classes such as the road and the surrounding buildings. The user can either select a class that should be highlighted until the system is informed otherwise (which is useful for tasks such as following a footpath), or switch into interactive highlighting mode, in which case the class being highlighted changes in real time as the user moves the laser pointer around. This could also be augmented with audio feedback for visually impaired users to determine the type of objects in view.

Map Sharing

In order to allow optional multi-user interactions, we need to share information between users. For ease of exposition, we discuss a two user scenario. We assume that users A and B are close to each other so they observe almost the same part of the scene. In our scenario, only user A builds a single common map and provides raycasted visualizations to user B. At the beginning, we estimate a relative pose between the users and run visual odometry for each of them. Then, the user B sends only a 6DoF pose and receives a raycasted visualization from her own perspective so both users can interact. Though this approach adds computational load on the A, this is not an issue in practice, since raycasting takes only 5 ms. Though our map sharing method is simple and efficient, the quality depends on precision of visual odometry. In order to prevent drifting, we re-estimate a relative pose between the users every 500 frames.

EXPERIMENTAL RESULTS

Qualitative Results

Propagation of User Labels The user indicates the surface of objects in the physical world using the laser pointer. Our system interprets such indications as a paint stroke, and voice input is used to associate an object class label to the corresponding voxels. Then, our mean-field inference engine (see our related paper [32]) propagates these labels through the reconstructed scene very efficiently. Thanks to the pairwise potentials we use, the result is a spatially smooth segmentation that adheres to object boundaries. Examples of label propagation are shown in Fig. 7 and supplementary material.

Semantic Labelling Our system learns a streaming decision forest classifier in a background CPU thread given the labels provided by the user. At some point, the user selects 'test mode', and the forest starts classifying all voxels. In Fig. 8 and supplementary material shows the final smooth results obtained by running our mean-field inference procedure on our decision forest predictions. We show results on four new challenging sequences captured using a head-mounted display (the last two columns belong to the same sequence). The images clearly indicate the sharp boundaries that we manage to achieve between different conflicting semantic classes. For example, observe the extremely accurate boundary between the pavement and the road in the sequence in the third column.

Quantitative Results

We evaluate the accuracy of our mean-field filtering of the forest predictions, based on a variety of test sequences captured from outdoor scenes. For each sequence, a series of keyframes were hand-labeled with object segmentations. Keyframes were selected to ensure full coverage of the scene. These ground-truth images are then projected and aggregated onto the underlying TSDF, and then back-projected to all the views of each sequence. We use the results to calculate global accuracies for each of our semantic classes (see Table 1).

Figure 7: Label propagation. Our efficient inference engine smoothly propagates class labels from the voxels indicated by the user to the rest of the volume. Here we show examples from four sequences. The first row shows the raw sequences; the second row shows the labelling after a couple of propagation steps; the third and fourth rows shows the labelling at later stages of the propagation. The pairwise terms in our energy encourage a smooth segmentation that respects object boundaries.

Class	Bgd.	Bld.	Road	Pavement	Tree	Bin
2D Labelling	87.6	85.4	86.2	86.9	82.3	80.5
3D Labelling	88.5	89.3	88.9	89.2	89.3	84.0

Table 1: Global accuracies (true positives / total numbers) for each class we use. The first column shows results for labelling in the image domain; the second column shows results for labelling in 3D and then projecting those labels to 2D.

Computational Efficiency

The inherently volumetric nature of our approach parallelizes well on modern GPU architectures. For our experiments we employed laptops with an Nvidia GeForce GTX 880M with 8 GB of GPU RAM, and quadcore Intel i7 processor with 24 GB of CPU RAM. We provide approximate system timings in Table 2. Although the timings change as a function of the number of visible voxels and resolution, in all tests we observed interactive frame rates. Numbers are provided for $4 \times 4 \times 4$ cm^3 voxel resolution, 1024×768 pixels and we do not fuse voxels beyond 20 m. The semantic segmentation pipeline runs on a GPU while the disparity estimation, laser tracker, disparity correction, visual odometry and forest learning run on the CPU. Note that the forest learning runs asynchronously in a background thread so it does not influence reconstruction and labeling. This thread continuously samples new labeled training data from the current view frustum and updates itself. This ensures an up-to-date forest is available for classification whenever the user requests it. As shown in Table 2, the most time consuming step is disparity estimation, but this can be implemented on GPU as well. Note, the reconstruction and labeling are independent of forest update step.

For a two-user scenario, we established a peer-to-peer wireless network. Since we transfer only 6DoF pose and raycasted visualizations, the data transfer is fast enough. Latency is not a huge issue, since we accumulate all the interactions over multiple frames and transfer the data when user is satisfied.

Finally, the size of the environment that our system is able to map is limited by 1) drift of the visual odometry, 2) battery life of a laptop under heavy load (1 hour) and 3) GPU and CPU RAM. Considering these limits, we were able to run our system in environments of up to 100-500 meters. A standard scene can be reconstructed and labeled at human walking speeds and we use no post-processing.

APPLICATIONS

So far we have described and evaluated our novel mapping system, and uncovered its low-level interactive capabilities. Whilst the focus of our work is technical, we believe the system as a whole could have dramatic impact for HCI applications. We demonstrate one potential application area in the next section, and discuss others afterwards.

Semantic Maps for the Visually Impaired

There are more than 285 million people in the world living with sight loss which has a significant impact on their daily lives. Over 85% of these individuals have some remaining vision [20]. Recently, there has been an interest in developing smart glasses [14, 8], which seek to provide these people with additional information from the nearby environment through stimulation of the residual vision. The aim is to increase the information level regarding the close environment using depth and/or image edges. This rather simplistic, though effective,

Figure 8: Final mean-field inference results for four sequences (the last two columns belong to the same sequence). Our streaming decision forest is able to learn to make per-voxel predictions about the object classes present in the scene. Each pixel is classified independently, and so the forest predictions can be somewhat noisy. The mean-field inference effectively smooths these predictions to produce a final labelling output to display to the user.

Disparity Estimation	Laser Tracker	Disparity Correction	VO	Fusion	Forest Update	Forest Evaluation	Mean-field	Wifi latency
80 ms	2 ms	3 ms	20 ms	15 ms	170 ms	5 ms	2-10 ms	5-10 ms

Table 2: Approximate system timing per frame. Despite small fluctuations we observed consistently good, interactive frame rates. Note, the reconstruction and labeling are independent of forest update step.

method for information extracting, enables the user to more independently traverse and navigate areas by providing the user with richer information than residual vision could provide.

We believe our live semantic maps can be directly used to highlight user-specific objects learned through online teaching with a carer/helper/trainer. This will present the visually impaired user with even more information regarding the nearby environment to understand the surrounding environment more clearly. Examples of these user-specific objects or regions could be stairs, road-crossings, bus-stops, entry or exit doors, sidewalk, restrooms, ticket machines or booths.

The basic scenario is that a visually impaired and a helper, both wearing smart-glasses displaying individual views of a shared 3D reconstructed environment, label the user-specific objects or regions of interest through usage of a laser pointer handled by the helper. The user can learn to use the system within familiar environments highlighting only regions that the user finds useful with help from the carer. The objects are labeled and learned by the system online, hence immediate response can be provided to both users. Fig. 9 shows a demonstration of this scenario.

At a later stage, once the objects are labeled, the visually impaired user can return to the same scene, and view the semantic map using the heads-up display. The transparency of the displays is advantageous for a visually-impaired person using the glasses to navigate around a pre-labeled scene, since it allows them to enhance, rather than replace, their remaining vision with the spatial information provided by the 3D mapping. Furthermore, transparent displays allow other people to see the wearer's eyes, which is helpful for social interaction.

Once a scene has been labeled by a sighted user, it can easily be converted into a form that is suitable for assisting a visually-impaired person to understand the nature of their environment, and navigate safely around it. Existing techniques such as those of Hicks *et al.* [14] have shown the usefulness of whole-image techniques, such as depth-to-brightness mapping, for helping visually-impaired individuals to avoid obstacles. The inclusion of semantic labeling has the potential to add an additional dimension to this kind of system by providing the wearer with more information about the objects around them and the boundaries between surfaces in their local environment (*e.g.* between a footpath and a road).

Other Applications for Semantic Maps

Personalized semantic maps with known object segmentations could also be used for a variety of other way-finding and navigation applications, either for robots or end users. For example, imagine self driving cars or quadcopters being able to follow particular paths and avoid obstacles. Additionally, users could interact with these robots, asking them to find particular instances of objects by semantically breaking down the world and using the laser pointer (*e.g.* 'please go to *that* building'). Furthermore, if such a model was maintained and updated over time, finding points of interest could be as simple as uttering a few words (*e.g.* 'where is the nearest bus stop').

These personalized maps could also be interactively captured, shared online and played back. For example, a user could give fine details for navigation to a friend, by actually capturing their path through the city, and then sharing it online, allowing for a detailed retracing of the steps, potentially with audio feedback. Another aspect is the ability for users to add semantic information to online maps. Here, by crowd-sourcing multiple personalized maps, a larger corpus of semantic maps could be generated. Users could use these semantic labels for searching, *e.g.* 'find the nearest bus stop to my map location', or 'please find the entrance to the building'. This latter point is also very important, as it allows a level of detail not yet available in regular maps, allowing for a more fine-grained level of way finding and navigation. Finally, augmented reality mobile gaming could be a rich source of application. Imagine quickly scanning in and labeling an outdoor space, and then associating object classes with aspects of the game. For example, game characters could hid behind particular objects, or follow particular paths or enter buildings. Such augmented reality scenarios could be expanded for planning the renovation of buildings and cities, automating inventory, and town planning.

Figure 9: A potential application area for semantic 3D maps for aiding visually impaired people to navigate outdoor spaces. The basic scenario is that a visually impaired and a helper, both wearing smart-glasses displaying individual views of a shared 3D reconstructed environment, label the user-specific objects or regions of interest through usage of a laser pointer handled by the helper. As shown in (a and b) the helper is indicating the object 'tree' using the laser pointer. Our system then starts to learn this 'tree' model. We first track and detect the laser dots in the IR images (c). These points are detected and tracked over a sequence of frames (d). After interaction, the label propagates to segment the tree (e and f), and other instances are detected in the scene (g).

User Experience The proposed system has been used by 15 users. All users felt comfortable with it. In particular, they liked the system performing a 3D reconstruction and labeling at interactive framerates and the laser pointer providing a natural means of interacting at a distance in outdoors environment as opposed to touching. The users also liked the see-through glasses allowing to see the real world with overlayed outputs providing an extra information about the environment.

Though the users provided a positive feedback in general, they also suggested a few modifications to make the system more comfortable, mostly on the hardware side. They suggested in particular to balance the center of gravity of the AR glasses better to prevent sliding off from the user's nose. Another recommendation was to change the position of wires in order to less resctrict the motion of user's head. On software side, the users mostly complained about drift of the visual odometry.

LIMITATIONS Despite very encouraging results, our system is not without limitations. As with all recognition algorithms, the segmentation results are not always voxel-perfect, as shown in the results and accompanying video. One possibility, however, is to allow the user to interactively make corrections to help reduce such errors. We believe additional modes of interaction such as voice priors (*e.g.* 'walls are vertical'), as well as more intelligently sampling the training examples could further improve results. From a computational standpoint, our system is fairly GPU heavy, which limits us to laptop only uses currently. With the advent of mobile GPGPU there are likely ways of addressing this in future work.

Further, our system is currently state based; *i.e.*, it requires the use of voice commands to switch between annotation, training, and test modes. We are planning an extension where both the learning and forest predictions are always turned on. This will require considerable care to avoid 'drift' in the learned category models: the feedback loop would mean that small errors could quickly get amplified. Finally, algorithmic parameters such as the pairwise weights are currently set at compile time (these are cross-validated and common across datasets shown). Given a small training set (perhaps boot-strapping), more reliable settings could be automatically selected online.

Since our system uses an IR laser pointer with output far less than 5mW, the pointer will not work in direct sunlight, but the IR laser can be replaced *e.g.* by LIDAR-based pointer. In general, the system works well in an urban environment, but fails in areas where the visual odometry and/or disparity estimation fail (*e.g.* those containing highly reflective or specular surfaces, or textureless regions).

CONCLUSIONS

In this paper, we have presented an interactive 3D mapping system that can semantically label large unknown outdoor scenes. The system can take advantage of interactive input from the user in order to guide the mapping towards objects and elements of interest in the scene. Rather than using active depth cameras, we capture our input using a passive stereo approach, making it possible to reconstruct large or distant structures outdoors.

Our system comprises a pair of see-through glasses, two RGB-Infrared stereo cameras, and a one-button laser pointer. The laser pointer helps the user highlight objects of interest and, in combination with voice commands, can provide semantic labels for objects (even distant objects) in an online fashion. The laser pointer can also be used to provide accurate, sparse measurements to the system in order to improve the estimated stereo depth, and thereby improve the final reconstruction.

We believe our mapping system could be of particular use for the visually-impaired, who in many cases can benefit from a more accurate understanding of the nature of objects in their environment. Whilst we have focused our work on the technical details, we feel this could be a high impact area for future work. For example, our system's ability to differentiate footpaths from roads has the potential to be extremely helpful in providing visually-impaired people with a safer way to navigate independently outdoors.

REFERENCES

1. Agarwal, S., Furukawa, Y., Snavely, N., Simon, I., Curless, B., Seitz, S. M., and Szeliski, R. Building Rome in a Day. *CACM* (2011).
2. Chen, D. M., Baatz, G., Köser, K., Tsai, S. S., Vedantham, R., Pylvänäinen, T., Roimela, K., Chen, X., Bach, J., Pollefeys, M., Girod, B., and Grzeszczuk, R. City-scale landmark identification on mobile devices. In *CVPR* (2011), 737–744.
3. Curless, B., and Levoy, M. A volumetric method for building complex models from range images. In *SIGGRAPH* (1996), 303–312.
4. Davison, A. J., Reid, I. D., Molton, N. D., and Stasse, O. MonoSLAM: Real-Time Single Camera SLAM. *PAMI 29*, 6 (2007).
5. Engel, J., Schöps, T., and Cremers, D. LSD-SLAM: Large-Scale Direct Monocular SLAM. In *ECCV* (2014).
6. Engel, J., Sturm, J., and Cremers, D. Semi-Dense Visual Odometry for a Monocular Camera. In *ICCV* (2013).
7. Fischler, M. A., and Bolles, R. C. Random Sample Consensus: A Paradigm for Model Fitting with Applications to Image Analysis and Automated Cartography. *CACM 24*, 6 (1981).
8. Froissard, B., Konik, H., Trmeau, A., and Dinet, . Contribution of augmented reality solutions to assist visually impaired people in their mobility. In *Universal Access in Human-Computer Interaction. Design for All and Accessibility Practice*. Springer, 2014, 182–191.
9. Furukawa, Y., Curless, B., Seitz, S. M., and Szeliski, R. Reconstructing Building Interiors from Images. In *ICCV* (2009).
10. Geiger, A., Ziegler, J., and Stiller, C. StereoScan: Dense 3d Reconstruction in Real-time. In *IVS* (2011).
11. Habbecke, M., and Kobbelt, L. LaserBrush: A Flexible Device for 3D Reconstruction of Indoor Scenes. In *SPM* (2008).
12. Hane, C., Zach, C., Cohen, A., Angst, R., and Pollefeys, M. Joint 3d scene reconstruction and class segmentation. In *CVPR* (2013), 97–104.
13. Hartley, R., and Zisserman, A. *Multiple view geometry in computer vision*. Cambridge university press, 2003.
14. Hicks, S. L., Wilson, I., van Rheede, J. J., MacLaren, R. E., Downes, S. M., and Kennard, C. Improved mobility with depth-based residual vision glasses. *Investigative Ophthalmology & Visual Science 55*, 5 (2014).
15. Huang, A. S., Bachrach, A., Henry, P., Krainin, M., Maturana, D., Fox, D., and Roy, N. Visual Odometry and Mapping for Autonomous Flight Using an RGB-D Camera. In *ISRR* (2011).

This research was supported by Technicolor, EPSRC, the Leverhulme Trust, the ERC grant ERC-2012-AdG 321162-HELIOS, the NIHR i4i grant II-LB-1111-20005 and a Royal Society Brian Mercer Award for Innovation.

16. Iannacci, F., Turnquist, E., Avrahami, D., and Patel, S. N. The Haptic Laser: Multi-Sensation Tactile Feedback for At-a-Distance Physical Space Perception and Interaction. In *CHI* (2011).
17. Jr., D. R. O., and Nielsen, T. Laser Pointer Interaction. In *CHI* (2001).
18. Klein, G., and Murray, D. W. Parallel tracking and mapping for small ar workspaces. In *ISMAR* (2007).
19. Ladický, L., Russell, C., Kohli, P., and Torr, P. H. S. Associative Hierarchical CRFs for Object Class Image Segmentation. In *ICCV* (2009).
20. Mariotti, S. P. Global Data on Visual Impairments 2010. Tech. rep., World Health Organization, 2010.
21. Munoz, D., Bagnell, J. A., and Hebert, M. Stacked Hierarchical Labeling. In *ECCV* (2010).
22. Newcombe, R. A., Izadi, S., Hilliges, O., Molyneaux, D., Kim, D., Davison, A. J., Kohli, P., Shotton, J., Hodges, S., and Fitzgibbon, A. KinectFusion: Real-Time Dense Surface Mapping and Tracking. In *ISMAR* (2011).
23. Newcombe, R. A., Lovegrove, S. J., and Davison, A. J. DTAM: Dense Tracking and Mapping in Real-Time. In *ICCV* (2011).
24. Nguyen, T., Grasset, R., Schmalstieg, D., and Reitmayr, G. Interactive syntactic modeling with a single-point laser range finder and camera. In *ISMAR* (2013).
25. Nießner, M., Zollhöfer, M., Izadi, S., and Stamminger, M. Real-time 3d reconstruction at scale using voxel hashing. *TOG 32*, 6 (2013), 169.
26. Qin, Y., Shi, Y., Jiang, H., and Yu, C. Structured Laser Pointer: Enabling Wrist-Rolling Movements as a New Interactive Dimension. In *AVI* (2010).
27. Rosten, E., and Drummond, T. Machine learning for high-speed corner detection. In *ECCV* (2006).
28. Salas-Moreno, R. F., Newcombe, R. A., Strasdat, H., Kelly, P. H. J., and Davison, A. J. SLAM++: SLAM at the Level of Objects. In *CVPR* (2013).
29. Sengupta, S., Greveson, E., Shahrokni, A., and Torr, P. H. S. Urban 3d semantic modelling using stereo vision. In *ICRA* (2013), 580–585.
30. Taneja, A., Ballan, L., and Pollefeys, M. City-scale change detection in cadastral 3d models using images. In *CVPR* (2013), 113–120.
31. Triggs, B., McLauchlan, P. F., Hartley, R. I., and Fitzgibbon, A. W. Bundle adjustment - a modern synthesis. In *Workshop on Vision Algorithms* (1999).
32. Valentin, J., Vineet, V., Cheng, M.-M., Kim, D., Shotton, J., Kohli, P., Niessner, M., Criminisi, A., Izadi, S., and Torr, P. H. S. SemanticPaint: Interactive 3D Labeling and Learning at your Fingertips. *ACM TOG* (2015).
33. Valentin, J. P. C., Sengupta, S., Warrell, J., Shahrokni, A., and Torr, P. H. S. Mesh based semantic modelling for indoor and outdoor scenes. In *CVPR* (2013), 2067–2074.
34. Whelan, T., Johannsson, H., Kaess, M., Leonard, J. J., and Mcdonald, J. Robust real-time visual odometry for dense rgb-d mapping. In *ICRA* (2013).
35. Wienss, C., Nikitin, I., Goebbels, G., Troche, K., Göbel, M., Nikitina, L., and Müller, S. Sceptre – An Infrared Laser Tracking System for Virtual Environments. In *VRST* (2006).
36. Xiong, X., Munoz, D., Bagnell, J. A., and Hebert, M. 3-D Scene Analysis via Sequenced Predictions over Points and Regions. In *ICRA* (2011).

User-Defined Game Input for Smart Glasses in Public Space

Ying-Chao Tung, Chun-Yen Hsu, Han-Yu Wang, Silvia Chyou, Jhe-Wei Lin, Pei-Jung Wu, Andries Valstar, Mike Y. Chen
Mobile and HCI Research Lab, National Taiwan University
{tony61507,hcythomas0125,huw12313212,silvia.chyou,evin92,eziay77,sanderwebs}@gmail.com, mikechen@csie.ntu.edu.tw

ABSTRACT
Smart glasses, such as Google Glass, provide always-available displays not offered by console and mobile gaming devices, and could potentially offer a pervasive gaming experience. However, research on input for games on smart glasses has been constrained by the available sensors to date. To help inform design directions, this paper explores user-defined game input for smart glasses beyond the capabilities of current sensors, and focuses on the interaction in public settings. We conducted a user-defined input study with 24 participants, each performing 17 common game control tasks using 3 classes of interaction and 2 form factors of smart glasses, for a total of 2448 trials. Results show that users significantly preferred non-touch and non-handheld interaction over using handheld input devices, such as in-air gestures. Also, for touch input without handheld devices, users preferred interacting with their palms over wearable devices (51% vs 20%). In addition, users preferred interactions that are less noticeable due to concerns with social acceptance, and preferred in-air gestures in front of the torso rather than in front of the face (63% vs 37%).

Author Keywords
Game; input; Control; Smart glasses; Guessability; User-defined; Public space; Pervasive gaming; Wearable.

ACM Classification Keywords
K.8.0. General: Games; H.5.2.Information Interfaces

INTRODUCTION
Smart glasses provide always-available displays and offer the opportunity for instantly available information and pervasive gaming experiences. Compared to game consoles and mobile gaming devices, smart glasses do not have touchscreens and currently do not support handheld controllers specifically designed for gaming. Current smart glasses, such as Google Glass and the Epson Moverio, support input via voice, touchpads, cameras, gyroscopes, accelerometers, and GPS. Games

CHI 2015, April 18–23, 2015, Seoul, Republic of Korea.

http://dx.doi.org/10.1145/2702123.2702214

Figure 1. A study participant performing an in-air gesture to drag an object seen through the immersive smart glasses in a public coffee shop.

designed specifically for Google Glass [27] utilize these sensors as game control. For example, "Clay Shooter" utilizes the user's voice to trigger a shotgun, and "Shape Splitter" detects in-air gestures via the built-in cameras. For the Epson Moverio glasses, wired trackpads are used as handheld inputs.

To better inform the interaction design of games for smart glasses, we aimed to explore the design space without being constrained by the capabilities of current sensors. We used the guessability study methodology [42], and presented the *effects* of game controls to the participants in a real-world, public environment. We then elicited what the participants felt was the most appropriate *causes* to invoke the corresponding effects.

For input tasks, we analyzed 90 popular games to identify the game controls used by more than one game, which resulted in a set of 17 tasks. We also explored the form factors of smart glasses displays, and included both types in the study: 1) *immersive*, with display content spanning the user's field

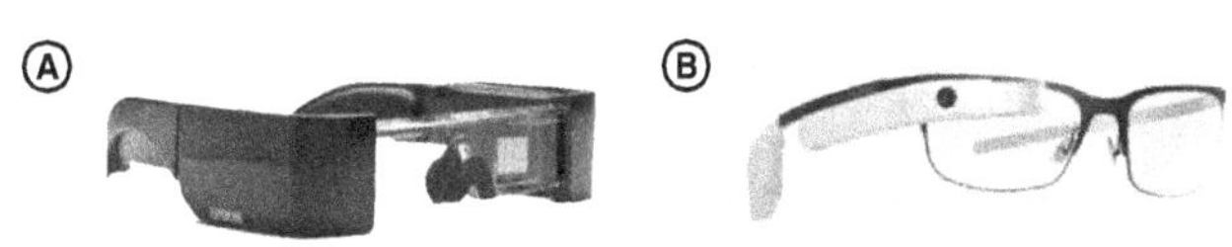

Figure 2. (A) Epson Moverio, (B) Google Glass.

of view (e.g. Epson and Sony's smart glasses), and 2) *off-to-the-side*, with display content in the corners of the user's field of view (e.g. Google Glass).

In order to compare different types of interaction while keeping the experiment tractable, we grouped the different types of input into the following 3 classes:

- *handheld*: input types that make use of handheld controllers, such as smartphones and the wired trackpads used by Sony's SmartEyeglass and Epson's Moverio glasses.
- *touch*: non-handheld touch input, such as gesturing and tapping on body surfaces, and touch-sensing wearable devices (e.g. smart rings, watches, and glasses). These provide tactile feedback.
- *non-touch*: non-handheld, non-touch input, such as in-air gestures, head/body movement, and voice recognition. These do not have tactile feedback.

We recruited 24 participants and asked them to wear the two form factors of smart glasses in a coffee shop. On-screen instructions prompted participants to perform each of the 17 common game control tasks using the 3 classes of input types. For each game control task, form factor, and input type, participants first explored all possible interactions they could think of, then reported the one they most preferred. After completing the 3 types of interactions for that task and form factor, they then rated their preferences for 3 interactions. Overall, each participant reported 102 interactions, for a total of 2448.

We collected quantitative and qualitative data through video analysis, preference ratings, and interviews. Our key observations are as follows:

- Participants significantly preferred non-handheld, non-touch interactions over handheld interactions (3.81 vs 3.68 on a 5-point Likert scale, $p<0.01$).
- For touch input without using handheld devices, users preferred interacting with their body surface over wearable devices (80% vs 20%), and the most frequently used body surface was the palm (51%).
- Participants preferred interactions that are more subtle due to concerns with social acceptance. Also, participants preferred using in-air gestures in front of the torso than in front of the face (63% vs 37%), even though those gestures were reported to be less intuitive and less precise.
- There is a significant mismatch between participants' preferred input methods and those supported by the current smart glasses. For example, less than 2% of the participants used voice and less than 2% of the participants used touch input on the smart glasses – which are Google Glass' two primary input methods. In addition, current cameras can only detect in-air gestures in front of users' faces, missing most 63% of the gestures performed.

The contribution of this paper are as follows: (1) the first quantitative and qualitative characterization of user-defined input for games on smart glasses, including a taxonomy, (2) set of user-defined input for common game tasks, which is reflective of user behavior. (3) insight into users' mental models when playing smart glasses games in a public space, and an understanding of implications for mobile input technology and user interface design. Our results will help designers create better smart glasses experience informed by user behavior.

RELATED WORK

Game Input

There are many previous works exploring new kinds of game controls and pushing the limit of game design. Vickers et al.[40] showed the possibility to use eye gestures as game inputs; Christian et al.[8] provided novel techniques for users to interact with games by head-gesture; Harada et al.[18] and Sporka et al.[36] both indicated that the voice input greatly expanded the scope of games that could be played hands-free and just counted on voice input; Baba et al.[4] presented a game prototype which treated skin contact as controller input; Nacke et al.[30] even considered using biofeedback (including EMG, EDA, EKG, RESP, TEMP) as game input methods; Hsu et al.[21] compared different game inputs, including head gestures, voice control, handheld controller, joysticks, eye winking and glass touchpad, for First-Person Shooter(FPS) games on smart glasses.

Mobile Input Technology

Some works related to mobile systems had defined designer-made input methods. These systems could be divided into two main categories, *touch* and *non-touch* inputs.

Harrison et al.[19] created *OmniTouch*, a wearable depth-sensing and projected system that enables interactive multi-touch applications on any surface of the user's body. Moreover, *Skinput*[20], a technology that appropriates the human body for acoustic transmission, and allows the skin to be used as an input surface. Chan et al. presented FingerPad[7], a nail-mounted device that turns the tip of the index finger into a touchpad, allowing private and subtle interaction while on the move. Baudisch et al.[17] illustrated a concept of imaginary interface with sensing several gestures on the user's palms. Recently, Serrano et al.[35] explored the use of *Hand-to-Face* input to interact with head-worn displays(HWD) and provided a set of guidelines for developing effective Hand-to-Face interactions based on two main factors they found, social acceptability and cultural effect.

Kim et al.[25] developed a wrist-worn architecture, which supports discrete gesture recognition with reconstructing a 3D hand model in the air. Similarly, Jing et al.[22] implemented *Magic Ring*, a finger ring shaped input device using inertial sensors to detect subtle finger gestures; Colaço et al.[9] built a head-mounted display, *Mime*, sensing 3D gestures in front of the user's eyes.

Gestures in HCI

Gesture-based interfaces are already common in a variety of application domains such as gaming, virtual or augmented reality and mobile devices[24]. Aigner et al.[1] conducted a study of human preferences in usage of gesture types for HCI and indicated that, depending on the meaning of the gesture, there is preference in the usage of gesture types; Nielsen et al.[31] pointed out some important issues in choosing the set of gestures for the interface from a user-centred view such as the learning rate, ergonomics, and intuition; Grijincu et al.[16] presented a video-based gesture dataset and a methodology for annotating video-based gesture datasets; Recently, Piumsomboon et al.[32] have developed a user-defined gesture set for augmented reality applications. In our work, we focus on exploring relevant input gestures for gaming on smart glasses in public space.

User Elicitation Studies

User-elicitation studies are a specific type of participatory design methodology that involves end-users in the design of control-sets[29]. These studies had been used to design user interfaces of various types including multi-touch gestures on small and large surfaces[2, 43] and multi-modal interactions [29, 26]. There is also some evidence that user-defined control sets are more complete than those sets defined solely by experts[33, 43].

In a user-elicitation study, users were shown referents (an action's effects) and were asked to demonstrate the interactions that resulted in a given referent[43]. In this work, we draw upon the user-elicitation methodology to identify user expectations and suggestions for smart glass gaming.

DEVELOPING A USER-DEFINED GAME INPUT SET

Overview

We developed a user-defined game input set by having 24 participants perform game tasks with smart glasses. To avoid bias from visual hints[11], no elements specific to PCs, consoles and mobile games were shown. Similarly, no specific game title was assumed. Instead, participants acted in a simple blocks world of geometry shapes or in the shape of a basic human avatar. Each participant saw the effect of a game input (e.g. an object moving left and right) and was asked to perform the game input action he or she thought would use to cause that effect (e.g. performing an in-air gesture to drag the object left and right, see Figure 1).

Seventeen game tasks were presented, and game inputs were elicited for three different interaction methods (*handheld*, *touch*, *non-touch*) with 2 smart glasses (Google Glass, Epson Moverio). The system did not attempt to sense the user's input action, but we used a camera to record the whole process. Participants used the think-aloud protocol and were interviewed about the input details. They also provided subjective preference ratings.

The final user-defined game input set was developed in light of the *agreement* found in the participants' preferred input action for each game task. The more participants that used the same action for a given task, the more likely that input action would be assigned to the task. In the end, our user-defined game input set emerged as a surprisingly consistent collection founded on actual user behavior.

Interaction Methods

In our study, we asked users to define three input manners to satisfy three interaction requirements individually in each task. These three interaction types, classified according to familiar interactions explored by previous works, were *handheld*, *touch*, and *non-touch*. *handheld*, one of these types, required users to create a game input by interacting with common portable handheld devices, mobile phones. Another method was *touch*, which asked users to design an input action by touching any skin, clothes or accessories on their own bodies. The last method, *non-touch*, was that users were asked to define an input method without touching any tangible object, such as, moving eyeballs, rotating their heads, voice control or in-air gestures.

#	Task	Used in Famous Game
1	Select single from many	Clash of Clans, Plague Inc.
2	Vertical menu	Puzzle&Dragon, PeggleHD
3	Horizontal menu	Clash of Clans, PeggleHD
4	Move left and right	Temple Run, Super Mario
5	Move in 4 directions	1943, RaidenX
6	Switch 2 objects	Candy Crush, Bejeweled
7	Move object to position	World of Goo, The Sim
8	Draw a path	Draw Something, P&D
9	Throw an object (in-2D)	Angry Birds, PeggleHD
10	Follow the beats	RockSmith, Guitar Hero
11	Rotate an object (Z-axis)	Zuma, PeggleHD
12	Rotate an object (Y-axis)	Spore, The Sim
13	Avatar jump	Temple Run, Super Mario
14	Avatar 3D move	Spore, Tintin
15	Avatar attack	Minecraft, Terraria
16	Avatar squat	Temple Run, Minecraft
17	Control 3D viewport	The Sim, Spore

Table 1. Summary of our general casual game task set. We named several famous games which use these tasks.

Game Tasks

Casual game is one of the game categories with the most players[13], and it is shown high potential in public gaming[34, 5]. We chose top 90 casual games[38] from existing platforms, including PCs, consoles and mobile games (30 games for each) by crawling and analyzing the sale and download count data from famous gaming websites[3, 39, 37, 14]. We invited 3 experienced game developers to review these top 90 casual games. In these games, they found 26 game tasks in total, and removed 9 tasks which were only used once in specific games. Finally, we got a set of general casual game task (shown in Table 1) with 17 tasks, which can completely support 90% of our top casual games.

Form Factor of Glasses

We explored the form factors of smart glasses displays, and included both types in the study: 1) *immersive*, with display content spanning users' field of view (e.g. Epson Moverio), and 2) *off-to-the-side*, with display content in the corners of users' field of view (e.g. Google Glass). The display of the Epson Moverio is located in front of the user's eyes with 960×540 resolution[12]. And Google Glass locates its display above the user's right eye with 640×360 resolution[15] (see Figure 2).

Method	Mean	Std.	L.Bound	U.Bound
handheld	3.68	0.79	3.63	3.74
touch	3.77	0.81	3.72	3.83
non-touch	3.81	0.90	3.75	3.87

Table 2. Summary of user preference of 3 different interaction methods, it provides mean value, standard deviation, and 95% confidence interval for mean (Lower Bound and Upper Bound).

Participants

We recruited twenty-four participants with an equal male-female ratio for our study. Their average age was 23.2 (*sd* = 2.72). All participants are right-handed and none of them had past experience with smart glasses usage. About their gaming experience, according to our investigation, 14 users were daily game players, 9 were weekly players and 1 was a monthly player. Participants spent 1.36 hours (*sd* = 0.89) on average to play games one time. Moreover, 58% of them indicated that their main gaming platforms were mobile phones, 38% were on PCs, and only 4% were on consoles. Another important factor of the gaming experience is the user's familiarity with game controllers. The results showed that average familiarity scores were 2.50 for gamepad (*sd* = 1.24), 3.96 for touchscreen (*sd* = 0.62) and 4.22 for keyboard and mouse (*sd* = 0.74) on a 5-point Likert Scale for degree of familiarity (1 means very unfamiliar, 5 means very familiar).

Environment

According to the previous works[41, 28], the social acceptability of mobile-input was influenced by whether participants believed a bystander could interpret the intention of the input action. Therefore, to provide a game input set suited for a real-world environment, we chose a Starbucks cafe near our college. The visitor flow of the cafe, on average, was 72.5 persons per hour. In our investigation, participants indicated that the cafe was comparatively a public space with average 4.17 points (*sd*=0.65) on a 5-point Likert Scale for degree of field publicity (1 means very private, 5 means very public).

Procedure

Participants wore two different glasses (Google Glass and Epson Moverio) and our software randomly presented 17 game tasks (Table 1) to participants. For each game task, participants performed an input action in 3 different interaction methods (*handheld*, *touch* and *non-touch* interaction). The study was conducted using a counterbalanced measures design, alternating the glass's form and the interaction method. After each game input, participants were shown a 5-point Likert scale concerning subjective preference and conducted a short interview about input detail. With 24 participants, 17 game tasks, 2 glass forms and 3 interaction methods, a total of $24 \times 17 \times 2 \times 3 = 2448$ game input actions were made.

RESULTS

Our results include game input taxonomies, a user-defined game input set, user ratings, subjective responses, and qualitative observations for each interaction method.

Preference Between Interaction Methods

Table 2 shows the average rating of 3 interaction methods. Three interaction types had a significant rating difference ($F_{0.05}(2, 2445)=4.61$, $p = .01$). We found that the user rating preference for *non-touch* was significantly higher than for *handheld* ($p = .009$). And we didn't find a significant difference between *touch* and *non-touch* ($p = .688$).

In the interview conducted after the rating, we asked why users gave *handheld* a lower preference score. The general reason was that users had to take their controller, e.g. phone, out of their pocket first. Users thought the handheld controller was not always-available and was not hands-free compared to the other interaction methods in this study. After analysing the video recording, we found that most participants simply used the handheld device as a trackpad. In addition, the user behavior and mental model were similar to the previous work by Liang et al.[26]. Considering the users' preferences and the reasons mentioned above, our report will focus on the results of *touch* and *non-touch* interaction.

Behavior with Different Form Factor of Glasses

In our study, for each of the two glasses, there are 1224 game input pairs with the user, task and interaction method. We found 119 pairs of game input (9.72% of all) were designed differently with distinct smart glasses forms. The influence of game input in each interaction method was 1.22% for *handheld*, 7.35% for *touch* and 20.59% for *non-touch*.

While using *non-touch* as interaction method, users who designed distinctive game input action mentioned that they were eager to use direct control and perfom a in-air gesture in front of the screen with the Epson Moverio. However, it is difficult to perform the same input with Google Glass because of the small screen size. On the other hand, users' reasons to define different input with different glasses for *touch* and *handheld* interaction methods seem to be random as users were unable to motivate their choice to define a different input.

Although the form factor of smart glasses influenced the design of game inputs, there was almost no difference in the user preference ratings for user-defined game inputs between the 2 different glasses: ($F_{0.05}(1, 2446)=.36$, $p=.549$).

Classification of Game Inputs

Taxonomy of Game Input

As the authors, we manually classified the input actions along four dimensions: *form*, *binding*, *nature*, and *flow*. Within each dimension, there are multiple categories as shown in Table 4. To verify the objectivity (or inter-rater reliability), we invited an independent rater who performed the same categorization using 170 trials (10 trials were randomly selected for each task). The inter-rater reliability is shown in Table 3. The lowest Kappa value, .688, is greater than .6, which is rated as *substantial* and thus is sufficient to establish the validity of the categorization. In addition, the average Kappa value is .897. A Kappa value of .8 and higher is considered *almost perfect*[23].

The scope of the *Form* dimension is applied separately to different interaction methods. There are 11 *Form* categories with *touch* input. 4 of them (*palm*, *back of hand*, *forearm*, *wrist*) are performed with both hands. 2 of them (*leg*, *face*) use a

#	Task	Kappa Value
1	Select single from many	0.863
2	Vertical menu	1.000
3	Horizontal menu	0.688
4	Move left and right	0.825
5	Move in 4 directions	1.000
6	Switch 2 objects	0.804
7	Move object to position	1.000
8	Draw a path	1.000
9	Throw an object (in-2D)	1.000
10	Follow the beats	0.697
11	Rotate an object (Z-axis)	0.867
12	Rotate an object (Y-axis)	1.000
13	Avatar jump	0.867
14	Avatar 3D move	0.880
15	Avatar attack	1.000
16	Avatar squat	0.878
17	Control 3D viewport	0.878
	Average	**0.897**

Table 3. Inter-rater reliability for each task.

Taxonomy of Game Inputs		
Form ***(touch)***	*palm*	I.b. finger and palm.
	fingers	I.b. fingers.
	leg	I.b. finger and leg.
	back of hand	I.b. finger and back of hand.
	forearm	I.b. finger and forearm.
	face	I.b. finger and face.
	wrist	I.b. finger and wrist.
	ring	I.b. finger and ring.
	watch	I.b. finger and watch.
	glasses	I.b. finger and glasses.
	necklace	I.b. finger and necklace.
Form ***(non-touch)***	*finger*	Using finger to perform in-air gesture.
	hand	Using hand to perform in-air gesture.
	head	Using head to perform input.
	voice	Using voice control.
Binding	*direct*	Directly control in front of screen.
	surface	Absolute mapping screen to surface.
	independent	No binding b. screen and input.
Nature	*symbolic*	Input visually depicts a symbol.
	physical	Input acts physically on objects.
	metaphorical	Input indicates a metaphor.
	abstract	Input mapping is arbitrary.
Flow	*discrete*	Response occurs *after the user acts.*
	continuous	Response occurs *before the user acts.*

Table 4. Taxonomy of game inputs based on 2448 input actions. The abbreviation "I.b." means "Interaction between". The abbreviation "b." means "between".

single hand to interact with other body parts. *fingers* is a single hand input and it is merely an interaction between fingers, e.g. a pinch. And rest of them (*ring*, *watch*, *glasses*, *necklace*) are interactions with accessories. There are 4 form categories with the *non-touch* interaction method. *Finger* is a special case of *hand*, but it is worth distinguishing because of its similarity to mouse actions and direct-touch.

In the *Nature* dimension, *symbolic* inputs are visual depiction. For example, a user poses the v-sign in the air in order to select menu option 2, or forms his hand as a gun to throw an object. *physical* inputs with the virtual object should be similar to the real world interaction with the physical object. *metaphorical* inputs occur when an input acts on, with, or like something else. For instance, users trace a finger in a circle to simulate the "object rotation", or view the palm as a trackpad to perform gestures. As it should be, the input itself is usually not enough to reveal its metaphorical nature; the answer lies in the user's mental model which could be understood by the interview afterwards. Finally, *abstract* inputs have no *symbolic*, *physical*, or *metaphorical* connection to their game tasks. The mapping is arbitrary, which does not necessarily mean it is poor. Pinch-touching thumb and index finger to perform "avatar jump", for example, would be an abstract input.

The *Binding* dimension is defined as the relationship between the input area and the smart glass's screen. *direct* binding means the user performs the inputs in the screen region directly, such as using an in-air gesture right in front of the screen to drag or touch virtual objects. A game input binding is called a *surface* binding if the user absolutely maps the screen onto another surface and performs the game inputs on it. Dragging a finger on the palm to move the object on the screen, for example, is a *surface* binding input. For inputs categorized as *independent* inputs it means that there is no binding between the screen and the input area. Thus the input can be performed in any position, like the "pinch to jump".

A game input's *Flow* is *discrete* if the input is performed, delimited, recognized, and responded to as an event. An example is punching in the air to perform "avatar attack". *Flow* is *continuous* if ongoing recognition is required, such as during most of our participants' "Control 3D viewport" rotating the imaginary camera by hands.

Taxonometric Breakdown of Input Actions in our Data

We found that our taxonomy adequately describes even widely differing input actions made by our users. Figure 3 and 4 show for each dimension the percentage distribution between the categories. The *Form* dimension for *touch* input and the the *Form* dimension for *non-touch* input are both dominated with hand related input. And *Form* dimension for *touch* input is consisted of *On-Body*(80.3%) and *Wearable*(19.7%) interaction. We found that the forms of *touch* inputs are more complicated than those of *non-touch*. Nonetheless, the binding of *touch* is more consistent. About 75% of the inputs are independent of the screen. In addition, we were surprised that no user designed a *direct* binding or *physical* nature input with *touch* input. And we found that for the *Flow* dimension, the percentage distribution is similar to *touch* and *non-touch* interaction.

User-Defined Game Input Set

The goal of this work is to present a user-defined game input set for smart glasses used in a public environment. This section gives the process by which the set was created and properties of the set. Unlike the input sets for existing games

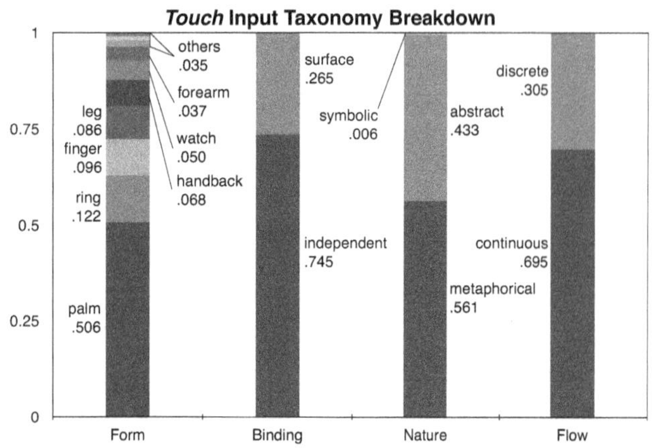

Figure 3. Percentage of game inputs in each taxonomy dimension with *touch* interaction. The "others" on the form dimension is consisted of glasses (0.0164), necklace (0.0088), face (0.0075) and wrist (0.0025).

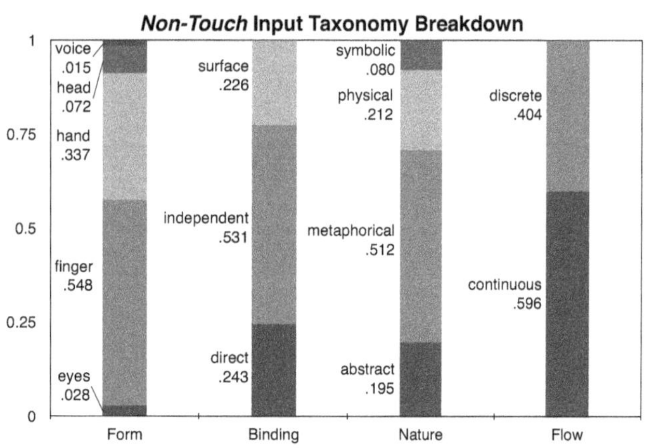

Figure 4. Percentage of game inputs in each taxonomy dimension with *non-touch* interaction.

on smart glasses, the set we have found is based on observed user behavior.

Agreement

All 24 participants have provided game input for each and every game task, smart glasses form and interaction method. For each game task, we made groups of identical actions used by participants. Group size was then used to compute an *Agreement Score* that reflects the consensus among participants regarding the action used for a certain game task. A task with a .31 agreement score means that, two randomly picked participants will have a 31% chance to perform an identical input action for this task. The definition and formula of the agreement score can be found in previous work. [42].

$$A = \frac{\sum_{t \epsilon T} \sum_{P_i \subseteq P_t} \left(\frac{|P_i|}{|P_t|} \right)^2}{|T|} \quad (1)$$

In eq. 1, t is a task in the set of all tasks T, P_t is the set of proposed input actions for task t, and P_i is a subset of identical input actions from P_t. The range for A is $\left[|P_t|^{-1}, 1\right]$.

As an example, consider the agreement for *draw a path* with *touch* input, it had four groups of identical input actions with group sizes 34, 4, 5 and 5. we compute

$$A_{touch-path} = \left(\frac{34}{48}\right)^2 + \left(\frac{4}{48}\right)^2 + \left(\frac{5}{48}\right)^2 + \left(\frac{5}{48}\right)^2 = 0.53 \quad (2)$$

The participant agreement for our study is pictured in Figure 5. The overall agreement for *touch* and *non-touch* inputs were A_{touch}=0.25 and $A_{non-touch}$=0.27, respectively. When comparing the agreement of *touch* and *non-touch* inputs, we clearly see that their patterns are extremely similar. The average difference of agreement between these two interaction methods was .056. This implies that the agreement score was influenced more by the game tasks than by the interaction methods.

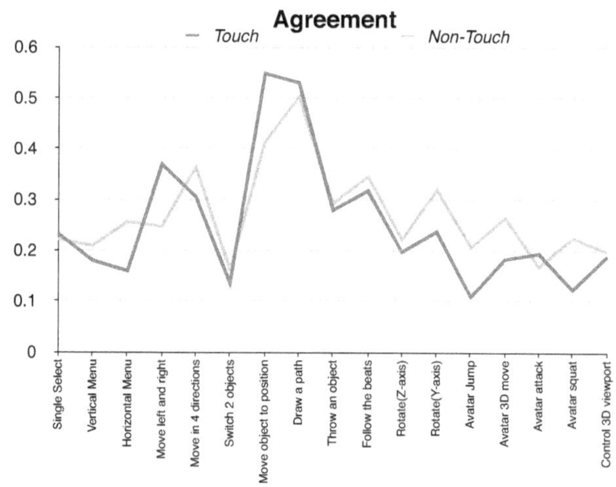

Figure 5. Agreement for each game task. The tasks are listed in the same order as they appear in Table 1.

Properties of the User-defined Game Input Set

The user-defined game input set was developed by taking the largest groups with identical input actions for each game task and assigning those actions to the game tasks. The resulting user-defined game input set covers 41.32% and 40.07% of all game inputs proposed for both the *touch* and the *non-touch* interaction class respectively. Our user defined set is useful, therefore, not just for what it contains, but also for what it omits.

All the inputs in our final *touch* input set are finger based (see Figure 7). Most of them use a single finger tip to perform gestures on different surfaces. The most preferable surface for *touch* input is the hand palm. This way, the hand palm acts as a trackpad or a proxy touch-screen. The other touch inputs are finger interactions with single hand. More specifically, participants used their thumb to interact with their index finger or the ring on the finger.

For *non-touch* input set (see Figure 8), even though we informed users beforehand that they were not limited to using their hands when providing game input, the results show that users still preferred to use hand input over voice control, eye gestures and head tilting. Additionally, users would make use of direct-control if they had to perform precise tasks, such as selecting an object from many or moving an object to a specific position. On the other hand, for tasks with lower precision requirements, such as selecting a single option from 4 or making an avatar jump, users would prefer using an indirect-control. For examples: the user taps 4 different areas in front of their chest or the user raises his hands slightly.

Taxonometric Breakdown of User-Defined Game Inputs
As expected, the taxonometric breakdown of the final user-defined game input set (Figure 7 and 8) is similar to the proportions of all control actions proposed (Figure 3 and 4). Across all taxonomy categories, the average difference between these two sets was only 5.61%, (*touch* input 6.31% and *non-touch* input 4.91%, respectively).

Mental Model Observations

Social Acceptance and Input Area
To our surprise, approximately 63% of the in-air gestures were not performed in front of the face (See Figure 9.2). This behavior conflicts with the current "Google Glass" design. There were 7 participants who performed most gestures in front of their face. They indicated that input in front of the face was more precise and intuitive. At the same time, the other 17 participants preferred to perform in-air gestures in front of or below their chest. Among them, there were 3 participants who didn't perform a single in-air gesture in front of their face. These users indicated that moving a finger in front of their face was weird and not socially acceptable. They also noted that there was a hand fatigue problem if they had to lift their hand in front of their face all the time, so they thought that it was not suitable for gaming.

Bias by Existing Game Input
Although we were careful not to show elements from traditional game platforms like PCs, consoles and mobile games, participants still often reasoned based on their previous gaming experience. For example, some input actions were performed as if using a touch-screen in front of their face (see Figure 8{A,F,G}). Some actions were like using an imaginary trackpad on an in-air surface or on the hand palm(see Figure 7{B,D,E,H,I,K,N,Q} and Figure 8{H,I}). Even with simple shapes and basic characters, it was clear how deeply rooted the previous gaming experience is. Some quotes reveal this: "So I just click a button like on a game controller", "Can I just imagine there is a trackpad on my palm?" and "It's an imaginary touch-screen."

Identical Gestures on Different Surfaces
In our study, we found several identical gestures performed by our users on different surfaces. Take the task "Move in 4 directions" for example, although 57% of the gestures were performed by moving a finger on the palm with *touch* inputs(Figure 7.E). The rest of the gestures were mostly using identical gestures (moving a finger), but then on the different surfaces such as the back of the hand, the leg, the forearm and on the even face. The same phenomenon could also be observed when comparing the game input of the user-defined input set with *touch* and *non-touch* inputs for the

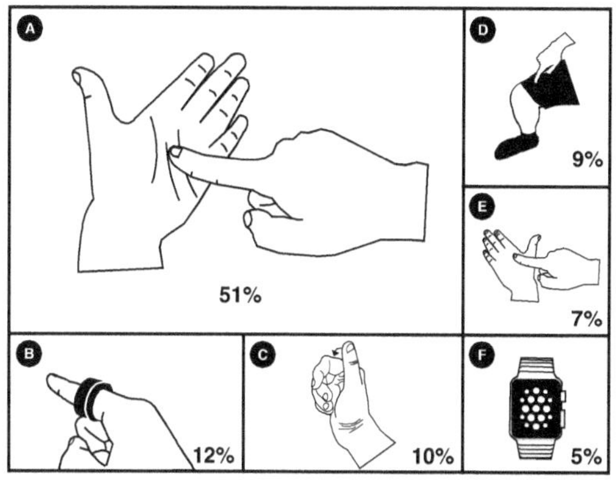

Figure 6. The top 6 *touch* input forms. Percentage indicates the portion of *touch* input actions. (A)Interaction between finger and palm. (B)Interaction between finger and ring. (C)Interaction between fingers. (D)Interaction between finger and leg. (E)Interaction between finger and back of hand. (F)Interaction between finger and watch.

tasks "Move left and right", "Move in 4 directions", "Draw a Path", "Throw an Object". Participants used the hand palm or an imaginary in-air surface. (See Figure 7 and Figure 8 {D,E,H,I}).

In these cases, the surface did not influence the meaning of the gestures. We have asked users why they chose the palm as their input area. The general response was that it required the least physical movement, such as "I chose the left palm to perform a gesture on because it is near to my right hand".

DISCUSSION

Implications for Touch Input Technology
Our results showed that the hand palm was the most favorite area for users to perform *touch* inputs on. Half of the game inputs with *touch* input used a finger to perform a gesture on the palm (See Figure 6). According to the mental model mentioned above, users utilized the metaphor of a trackpad and a touch-screen on the palm in several cases. Since this metaphor leads to the same input actions as on trackpads and touch-screens, current gesture interpreting algorithms like Dollar N[10] could be employed here.

Implications for Non-Touch Interaction Technology
For *non-touch* interaction methods, our taxonomy shows that performing in-air gestures with fingers and hands are still the dominant forms for smart glass gaming (Figure 9.1{A,B}). There was only a small number of participants that used head-gestures, eye-gestures or voice controls, 7%, 3% and 1% respectively. Before our study, both Google Glass and Mime[15, 9] supplied their own in-air gesture sets to increase the diversity of their input. However, our results show that 63% of the in-air gestures are not performed in front of the user's face in the public space due to the social acceptance issues and physical tiring problems mentioned before (see Figure 9.2). Therefore, if the developers of head-worn devices want to implement in-air gestures for input, they will need to have the capability to sense gestures in a wide range of areas near the user other than only right in front of the face. Take

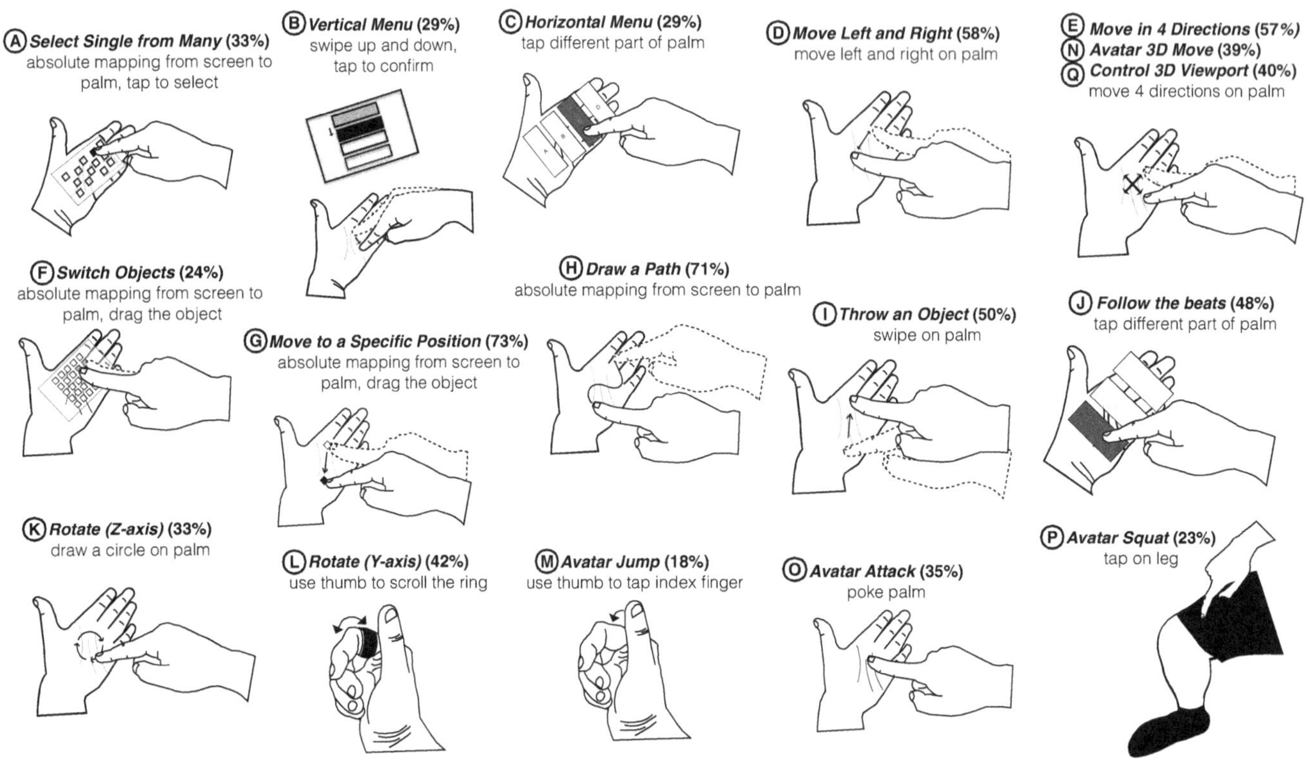

Figure 7. The user-defined game input set with *touch* inputs. The percentages indicate the portion of users who performed the pictured input action for the game task. Note that, there are 3 tasks ("Move in 4 directions", "Avatar 3D Move", and "Control 3D viewport") have been assigned with an identical input action.

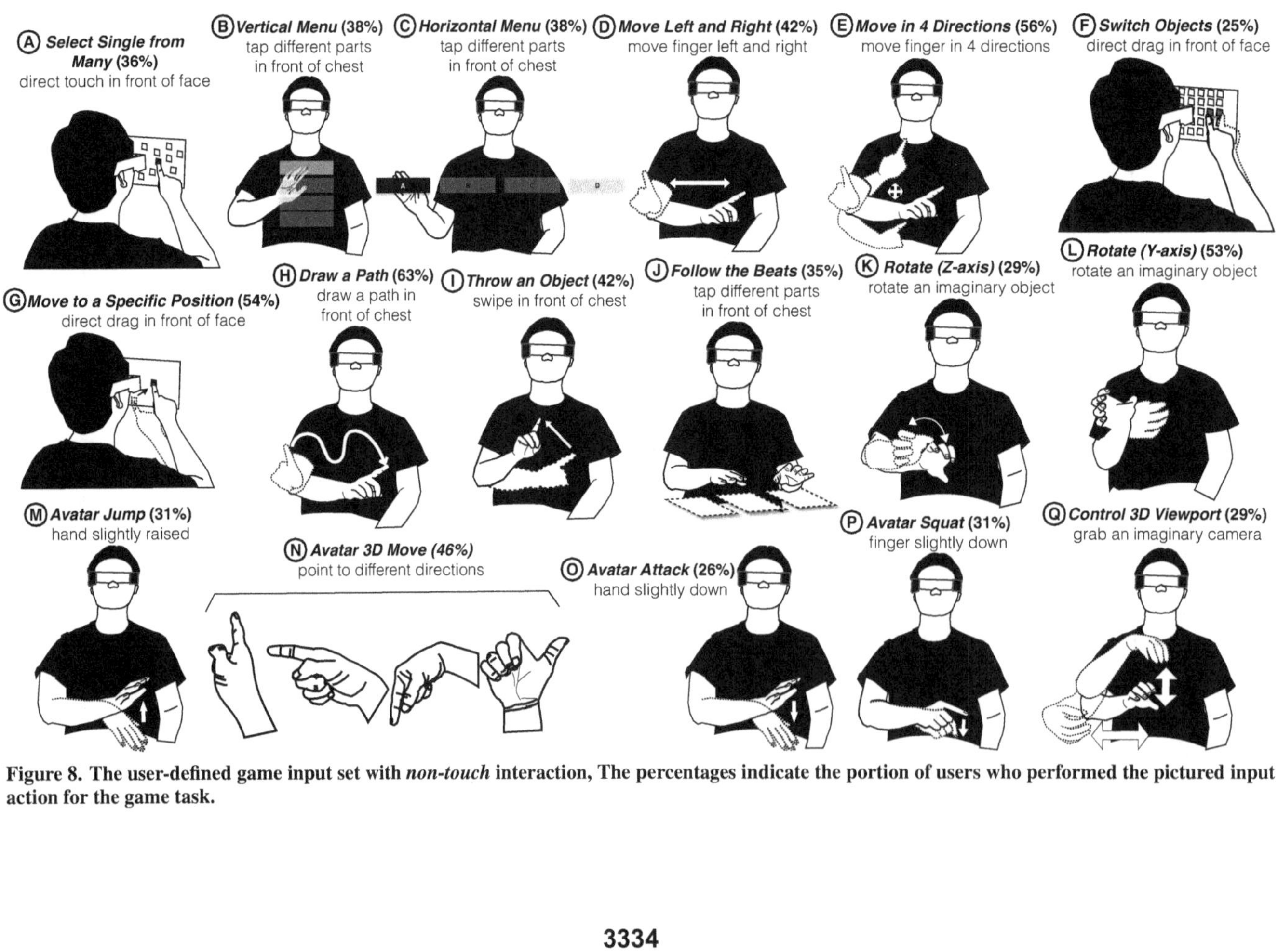

Figure 8. The user-defined game input set with *non-touch* interaction, The percentages indicate the portion of users who performed the pictured input action for the game task.

CV-based sensing technologies for example, instead of a regular lens, we could use a wide-angle lens or fish-eye lens to implement a system to cater to the user's preference [6].

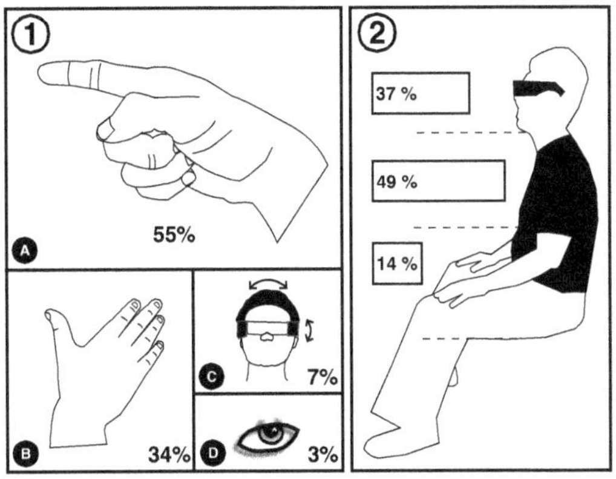

Figure 9. 1.The top 4 *non-touch* interaction forms. Percentages indicate the portion of *non-touch* game inputs that consisted of the pictured input. (A)Using a finger to perform an in-air gesture. (B)Using the full hand to perform an in-air gesture. (C)Using head-tilting to perform game input. (D)Using eye-gestures to perform game input. 2.The distribution of the in-air gesture input area. Half of the in-air gestures (49%) were performed in front of the chest, 14% in front of or below the belly, and only 37% of the gestures were performed in front of the face.

Implications for Game Design

According to the agreement scores we found that, no matter if using *touch* interaction or *non-touch* input, the average agreement between users was only .26, and the highest agreement was just about .55 (see Figure 5). In this case, guessing the game inputs would become a frustrating experience for players. It indicated that game developers should design the visual guide carefully to lead users performing the input action, or show an instruction to explain the input methods.

Contribution to non-gaming scenarios

When we first set out to explore interaction design for smart glasses, we focused on a specific domain in order to gain deeper insight and to keep the study tractable. Looking back at the results, some the study findings do apply to non-gaming scenarios. For example, many of our tasks are also used in non-gaming applications, such as "Select single from many", "Vertical menu", "Horizontal menu", "Move left and right", "Move in 4 directions", "Move object to position", "Draw a path" and "Rotate an object". Also, study results showed several facts that are useful for general cases: (1) Social acceptance of input is a significant concern in public space; (2) Performing in-air gestures in front of the face is weird and not socially acceptable; (3) If the input surface does not have an influence on the meaning of the gestures, users prefer to perform the gestures on a surface reached with least movement.

Limitation and Next Steps

As we know, there are many different places known as public space, and users may behave differently in each specific place. Furthermore, in our study, we did not ask users to define any input actions to interact with tangible objects in public space, such as, tables or chairs in the cafe shop. We only made participants experience two types of smart glasses. Therefore, our user-defined game input set might not be suitable to be applied to games on other types of head-worn devices. Moreover, our participants were all literate Taiwanese adults; undoubtedly, children, elders, participants from other cultures, or uneducated participants would behave differently. That is to say, these issues are worthy of investigation, but exceed the range of our current work.

An important next step is to validate our user-defined game input set with a wearable system, which can sense all *touch* and *non-touch* input actions listed in our set.

CONCLUSION

This paper explored user-defined game input for smart glasses beyond the capabilities of current sensors, and focused on gaming interaction in a public setting. We conducted a user-defined input study with 24 participants, each performing 17 common game control tasks using *handheld*, *touch* and *non-touch* interaction methods with two form factors of smart glasses in a public cafe, which lead to a total of 2448 game inputs. Our results indicate that participants significantly preferred *non-touch* interactions over *handheld* interactions (3.81 vs 3.68, $p < 0.01$). And the most frequently used body surface was the palm (51%). Also, participants preferred using in-air gestures in front of the torso over gestures in front of the face(63% vs 37%) due to concerns with social acceptance and the hand fatigue. Furthermore, we indicated the mismatch between participants' preferred input methods and those supported by current smart glasses. Finally, we presented insight into users' mental models, and an understanding of implications for input technology and interface design. This work represents a necessary step in bringing glasses gaming closer to the hands and minds of smart glasses users.

REFERENCES

1. Aigner, R., Wigdor, D., Benko, H., Haller, M., Lindbauer, D., Ion, A., Zhao, S., and Koh, J. Understanding mid-air hand gestures: A study of human preferences in usage of gesture types for hci. *Microsoft Research TechReport MSR-TR-2012-111* (2012).
2. Anthony, L., Brown, Q., Nias, J., Tate, B., and Mohan, S. Interaction and recognition challenges in interpreting children's touch and gesture input on mobile devices. ITS'12, 225–234.
3. App Annie. `http://www.appannie.com`.
4. Baba, T., Ushiama, T., Tsuruno, R., and Tomimatsu, K. Video game that uses skin contact as controller input. SIGGRAPH'07,
5. Biskupski, A., Fender, A. R., Feuchtner, T. M., Karsten, M., and Willaredt, J. D. Drunken ed: A balance game for public large screen displays. CHI EA'14, 289–292.
6. Chan, L., Hsieh, C.-H., Chen, Y.-L., Yang, S., Huang, D.-Y., Liang, R.-H., and Chen, B.-Y. Cyclops: Wearable and single-piece full-body gesture input device. CHI'15,
7. Chan, L., Liang, R.-H., Tsai, M.-C., Cheng, K.-Y., Su, C.-H., Chen, M. Y., Cheng, W.-H., and Chen, B.-Y. Fingerpad: Private and subtle interaction using fingertips. UIST'13,

8. Christian, S., Alves, J., Ferreira, A., Jesus, D., Freitas, R., and Vieira, N. Volcano salvation: Interaction through gesture and head tracking. CHI EA'14, 297–300.

9. Colaço, A., Kirmani, A., Yang, H. S., Gong, N.-W., Schmandt, C., and Goyal, V. K. Mime: Compact, low power 3d gesture sensing for interaction with head mounted displays. UIST'13, 227–236.

10. Dollar N Multistroke Recognizer. `http://depts.washington.edu/aimgroup/proj/dollar/ndollar.html`.

11. Epps, J., Lichman, S., and Wu, M. A study of hand shape use in tabletop gesture interaction. 748–753.

12. Epson BT-100 Specs. `http://www.epson.com.au/products/ProjectorAccessories/Moverio_BT-100_specs.asp`.

13. Essential Facts About The Computer And Video Game Industry. `http://www.theesa.com/facts/pdfs/esa_ef_2014.pdf`.

14. GameStop. `http://www.gamestop.com`.

15. Google Glass wiki. `http://en.wikipedia.org/wiki/Google_Glass#Features`.

16. Grijincu, D., Nacenta, M. A., and Kristensson, P. O. User-defined interface gestures: Dataset and analysis. ITS'14, 25–34.

17. Gustafson, S., Holz, C., and Baudisch, P. Imaginary phone: Learning imaginary interfaces by transferring spatial memory from a familiar device. UIST'11, 283–292.

18. Harada, S., Wobbrock, J. O., and Landay, J. A. Voice games: Investigation into the use of non-speech voice input for making computer games more accessible. INTERACT'11, 11–29.

19. Harrison, C., Benko, H., and Wilson, A. D. Omnitouch: Wearable multitouch interaction everywhere. UIST'11, 441–450.

20. Harrison, C., Tan, D., and Morris, D. Skinput: Appropriating the body as an input surface. CHI'10, 453–462.

21. Hsu, C.-Y., Tung, Y.-C., Wang, H.-Y., Chyou, S., Lin, J.-W., and Chen, M. Y. Glass shooter: Exploring first-person shooter game control with google glass. ICMI'14, 70–71.

22. Jing, L., Cheng, Z., Zhou, Y., Wang, J., and Huang, T. Magic ring: A self-contained gesture input device on finger. MUM'13, 39:1–39:4.

23. Cohen's kappa - Wikipedia, the free encyclopedia. `http://en.wikipedia.org/wiki/Cohen's_kappa`.

24. Karam, M., et al. A taxonomy of gestures in human computer interactions.

25. Kim, D., Hilliges, O., Izadi, S., Butler, A. D., Chen, J., Oikonomidis, I., and Olivier, P. Digits: Freehand 3d interactions anywhere using a wrist-worn gloveless sensor. UIST'12, 167–176.

26. Liang, H.-N., Williams, C., Semegen, M., Stuerzlinger, W., and Irani, P. User-defined surface+motion gestures for 3d manipulation of objects at a distance through a mobile device. APCHI'12, 299–308.

27. Google Glass Mini Games. `https://developers.google.com/glass/samples/mini-games`.

28. Montero, C. S., Alexander, J., Marshall, M. T., and Subramanian, S. Would you do that?: Understanding social acceptance of gestural interfaces. MobileHCI'10, 275–278.

29. Morris, M. R. Web on the wall: Insights from a multimodal interaction elicitation study. ITS'12, 95–104.

30. Nacke, L. E., Kalyn, M., Lough, C., and Mandryk, R. L. Biofeedback game design: Using direct and indirect physiological control to enhance game interaction. CHI'11, 103–112.

31. Nielsen, M., Störring, M., Moeslund, T. B., and Granum, E. A procedure for developing intuitive and ergonomic gesture interfaces for hci. In *Gesture-Based Communication in Human-Computer Interaction*. Springer, 2004, 409–420.

32. Piumsomboon, T., Clark, A., Billinghurst, M., and Cockburn, A. User-defined gestures for augmented reality. CHI'13, 955–960.

33. Pyryeskin, D., Hancock, M., and Hoey, J. Comparing elicited gestures to designer-created gestures for selection above a multitouch surface. ITS'12, 1–10.

34. Reis, S. Expanding the magic circle in pervasive casual play. ICEC'12, 486–489.

35. Serrano, M., Ens, B. M., and Irani, P. P. Exploring the use of hand-to-face input for interacting with head-worn displays. CHI'14, 3181–3190.

36. Sporka, A. J., Kurniawan, S. H., Mahmud, M., and Slavík, P. Non-speech input and speech recognition for real-time control of computer games. Assets'06, 213–220.

37. Steam. `http://store.steampowered.com`.

38. Top 90 Casual Games List. `http://ppt.cc/hO2j`, Analyzed at 2014-08-14.

39. VGChartz. `http://www.vgchartz.com`.

40. Vickers, S., Istance, H., and Hyrskykari, A. Performing locomotion tasks in immersive computer games with an adapted eye-tracking interface. *ACM Trans. Access. Comput. 5*, 1 (Sept. 2013), 2:1–2:33.

41. Williamson, J. R., Brewster, S., and Vennelakanti, R. Mo!games: Evaluating mobile gestures in the wild. ICMI'13, 173–180.

42. Wobbrock, J. O., Aung, H. H., Rothrock, B., and Myers, B. A. Maximizing the guessability of symbolic input. CHI EA'05, 1869–1872.

43. Wobbrock, J. O., Morris, M. R., and Wilson, A. D. User-defined gestures for surface computing. CHI'09, 1083–1092.

Retargeting Technical Documentation to Augmented Reality

Peter Mohr, Bernhard Kerbl, Michael Donoser, Dieter Schmalstieg, and Denis Kalkofen
Graz University of Technology
{ mohr | kerbl | donoser | schmalstieg | kalkofen }@icg.tugraz.at

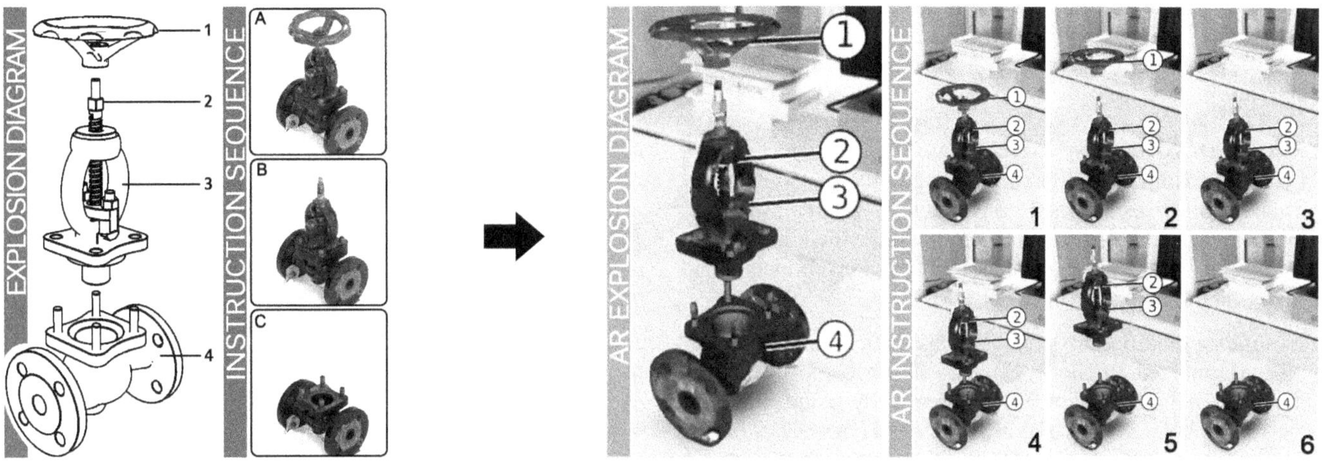

(a) (c) (d)

Figure 1. Retargeted 2D documentation. (a) The input documentation consists of an annotated explosion diagram and a sequence of images presenting disassembly instructions. (b) From analyzing the 2D explosion diagram, our system is able to generate a 3D explosion diagram presented in AR. Moreover, our system generates 3D annotations in AR based on the input 2D documentation. (c) In addition, our system is able to analyze image sequences in order to create 3D animations from it. This allows to present animated 3D documentations in AR. Here we show six key-frames from the resulting AR animation.

ABSTRACT

We present a system which automatically transfers printed technical documentation, such as handbooks, to three-dimensional Augmented Reality. Our system identifies the most frequent forms of instructions found in printed documentation, such as image sequences, explosion diagrams, textual annotations and arrows indicating motion. The analysis of the printed documentation works automatically, with minimal user input. The system only requires the documentation itself and a CAD model or 3D scan of the object described in the documentation. The output is a fully interactive Augmented Reality application, presenting the information from the printed documentation in 3D, registered to the real object.

Author Keywords

Augmented reality; virtual reality; retargeting

ACM Classification Keywords

H.5.1 Information Interfaces and Presentation: Multimedia Information Systems-Artificial, augmented and virtual realities

CHI 2015, April 18 - 23, 2015, Seoul, Republic of Korea

ACM 978-1-4503-3145-6/15/04$15.00
http://dx.doi.org/10.1145/2702123.2702490

INTRODUCTION

Printed technical documentation is an essential requirement for understanding and using technical products and many other artifacts found in our daily life. We use handbooks to understand how things work and manuals to learn how to assemble or maintain them. Most documentation still exists on paper and relies on graphical illustrations and accompanying textual explanations to convey the relevant information to the reader. However, the use of printed manuals arguably introduces a cognitive seam, since users have to match the images in the manual with the physical object. In addition, inferring actions from a sequence of 2D images can be a mentally demanding task.

Augmented Reality (AR) overcomes this seam by presenting the documentation directly registered to the object in the 3D space surrounding the user. It has been shown that this can actually reduce the cognitive load when using technical documentation [8]. However, authoring AR documentation is a complex and time-consuming process. It requires skills with 3D modeling and animation tools and additional expertise with AR requirements such as registration and tracking. Meanwhile, a large amount of traditional documentation exists on paper (or in two-dimensional digital form), but remains unused for AR applications. To close this gap, we propose a system capable of automatically transferring traditional printed documentation to AR. We demonstrate our approach on several graphical elements commonly found in traditional documentations. Specifically, we present the transfer of annotations labeling parts of the object, arrows indicating motions, explosion diagrams revealing an object's internal structure, and structural diagrams conveying the assembly or disassembly, translation and rotation of parts. Together, these illustrative elements cover the most frequent documentation styles.

We demonstrate that the conventions kept by illustrators allow to automatically interpret the images with only minimal help from the user. Thus, it becomes feasible to produce AR experiences from existing documentation at only a fraction of the effort it would take with conventional 3D modeling and animation software.

RELATED WORK

Documentations exhibit a variety of graphical elements, but usually follow established conventions. We identified the most frequent elements – in the following called diagrams – from books [18], online databases of popular products[1 2] and scientific publications [1, 7, 12].

A number of different strategies has been proposed to author Augmented Reality manuals. The two most common methods define behavior either directly by using commercially available modeling tools, such as Maya or 3DS MAX, or by scripting all actions and transitions between actions using specialized script languages [11, 3]. In both approaches, the user must define the manual from scratch. However, this requires excessive knowledge of both the modeling tool or the scripting language and the functionality of the object for which the manual was generated. In addition, manual authoring, either by programming or by using animation tools, is usually a very time consuming task.

An alternative approach is to build AR manuals from recorded videos [20]. This allows to author complicated manuals without additional knowledge about any programming language or animation tool. However, if the video is viewed from a different point of view than the one it was recorded from, it has to be warped to the new point of view, which is prone to rendering artifacts.

Zauner et al. [27] as well as Gupta et al. [6] proposed to generate instructions from 3D recordings of actions. However, both 2D and 3D recordings require the user to record all steps of an instruction, ignoring any existing documentation material. In contrast, our approach makes use of existing documentation material without any adjustment required. We achieve this by computing animations from 2D documentation material.

Our approach is inspired by the work of Li et al. [13], who generate an animated 2D explosion diagram from a single image. Their system requires the user to manually define all parts and all animations in the diagram. This is not practical for complex structures or multiple images in a sequence.

Recently, Shao et al. [24] presented a system which derives simple animations from interpreting 2D sketches. This reduces the effort required to generate animations between two images. However, this approach only works for simple structures. Since the user has to generate proxy geometry for every single part of the object, this system can handle only objects which consist of a small number of parts. Furthermore, the user has to re-create the 3D model for every image. Therefore, this approach does not scale easily to image sequences and large product databases.

Bergig et al. [2] present a system which is able to automatically generate 3D reconstructions of simple 2D sketches. Even though this system does not require any interaction to derive 3D geometry, it is limited by the capabilities of the sketch reconstruction approach. Their approach can handle only a few simple shapes. In contrast, we aim at the transfer of 2D documentations of complex structures, which may even be presented in multiple different configurations.

[1]http://service.lego.com/en-us/buildinginstructions
[2]http://www.ikea.com/ms/en_US/customer_service/assembly_instructions.html

OVERVIEW

Our system generates interactive AR presentations from 2D documentation, given as a collection of images, and a 3D CAD model of the target object. The CAD model must be structured such that individually movable parts of the target object can be distinguished. If no CAD model exists, we use an RGB-D sensor (Microsoft Kinect) to obtain a 3D scan which can only be used for annotation transfer. However, oftentimes a 3D CAD model will already be available from the manufacturer of the target object, and the RGB-D sensor is only required for registering the CAD model with the real-world target object.

In the following, we outline our approach to analyze every major type of diagram. The result of our analysis is a 3D scene description including 3D animations representing instructions. Our results can be presented on a desktop PC using a Virtual Reality (VR) viewer or in the user's real world environment through an Augmented Reality display. The modules required to implement our approach are illustrated in Figure 3.

Annotated diagrams

A typical illustration is an annotated diagram, which allows to identify parts of an object by external labels, connected with leader lines to the referred parts (Figure 2(a)). The labels are often cross-referenced with more extensive textual descriptions.

The first step for interpreting annotations (and any other diagram considered in this paper) is to determine camera parameters that were used to create the image, with respect to the coordinate systems used in the corresponding CAD model. Rendering the CAD model with the obtained parameters allows us to determine which part of the target object is covered by a given pixel in the image. Around the target object, we detect leader lines, identify the part of the target object from which the leader line originates and decode the text labels attached to the leader line.

Action diagrams

Action diagrams use auxiliary diagrammatic elements to present instructions within a single image. A common form uses arrows to encode the transformations which have to be applied to a part to perform the presented action (Figure 2(b)).

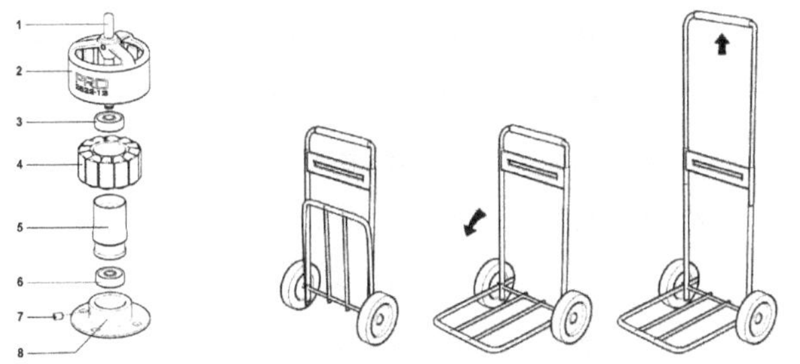

(a) (b)

Figure 2. Diagrams used in traditional 2D documentations. (a) Explosion diagrams are commonly used to present the structure of an object. In addition, annotations identify parts. (b) Sequences of images are often used to represent an action. The images show the object in key poses. Occasionally, arrows are presented to demonstrate the necessary transformations of parts to perform the action. Images adapted from [18].

Like annotations, arrows are complementary graphical elements that cannot be derived from a CAD model. However, their special shape allows detecting them in the image and interpreting the intended motion and direction. The intention of the arrow can be interpreted by comparing its pointing direction to valid displacement directions of parts nearby.

Explosion diagrams

Another popular form of technical reference is the explosion diagram, which reveals the internal structure of an object in a single image. Explosions reposition each part of the object along one or more explosion axes. The position of parts is determined based on the structure of the assembly, i. e., parts are arranged on each explosion axis according to the order in which they can be removed (Figure 2(a)). The resulting diagram avoids occlusions and simultaneously encodes blocking relationships between the individual parts.

Detecting which parts are shown in which displaced position is an essential problem considered in this paper. To retarget explosion diagrams, we use disassembly planning [26] to determine the order in which parts may be removed and generate valid displacements for candidate parts. The candidate parts are then rendered with these displacements, and the resulting image is compared to the input image using robust image matching techniques.

Structural diagrams

Complex instructions are most commonly represented by image sequences, where each image represents one step of the procedure [7]. The most basic form is the structural diagram, where each consecutive image adds, removes or reconfigures one or multiple parts. Since each image portrays the object at a single point in time only, the procedure has to be interpreted by comparing one image to the next and identifying their differences. Note that structural diagrams change the structure of the object from one image to next, while explosion diagrams offset parts to present the structure of an object.

To retarget structural diagrams, we must thus determine which parts are added, removed, translated or rotated in each consecutive image. By using motion planning, we obtain a set of candidate configurations of the CAD model, which we can

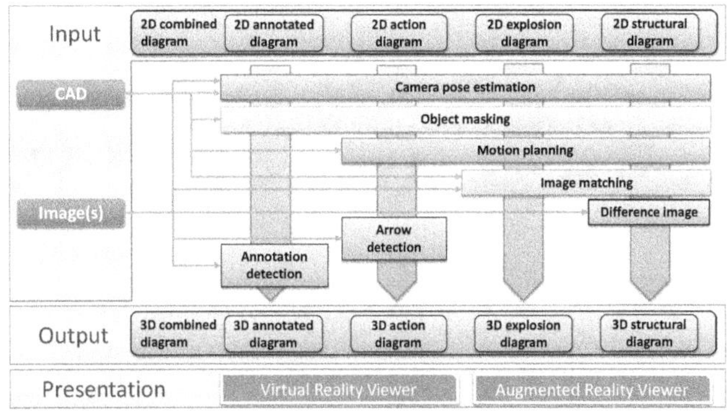

Figure 3. System Overview. Given an input image of a 2D diagram and a 3D CAD model of the object of interest, our system is able to generate interactive 3D diagrams, which it can display in an Augmented Reality environment. Our system consists of several modules. This overview shows which of these modules are used to retarget a specific type of input diagram. Once a 3D diagram is created, we present it either in Virtual Reality or within the user's real world environment by using an AR display.

use to search for the one depicted in the diagram. To reduce the search space, we can use robust image differencing to determine the area of change. For each image pair, we use the area of change to discard motions occurring outside of these regions.

Combined Diagrams

Documentation often combines multiple types of diagrams. For example, labels may be used in an image sequence to name the relevant parts of the presented instruction (Figure 2(a)). Also, partially exploded objects or sequences of action diagrams (Figure 2(b)) are commonly used in image sequences to present both an action and the object configuration after applying it to the object. Our system is able to analyze and retarget all these combinations.

Augmented Reality interface

The analyzed diagrams are transformed into 3D overlays and presented in AR, registered to the physical object. The user can interactively step through the instruction sequence and explore the individual elements of the documentation.

ANNOTATED DIAGRAMS

We transfer 2D image data to 3D space by projecting a 3D model of the object of interest to 2D image space. If this rendering of the object fits to its input image, we can relate image elements to 3D structure. We segment all labels and their corresponding leader lines in image space. Subsequently, we generate 3D annotations relative to the 3D model by using the relations we found between image elements and 3D structures. This process is illustrated in Figure 4.

Estimating camera parameters

The 3D model needs to be rendered using the same camera parameters as the input image. Since the original camera is unknown, we need to approximate the intrinsic and extrinsic parameters. In principle, these parameters can be found automatically [28]. In practice, automatic extraction of reliable 2D-to-3D point correspondences from a single, highly stylized image is not robust in many cases. Thus, we opted for a

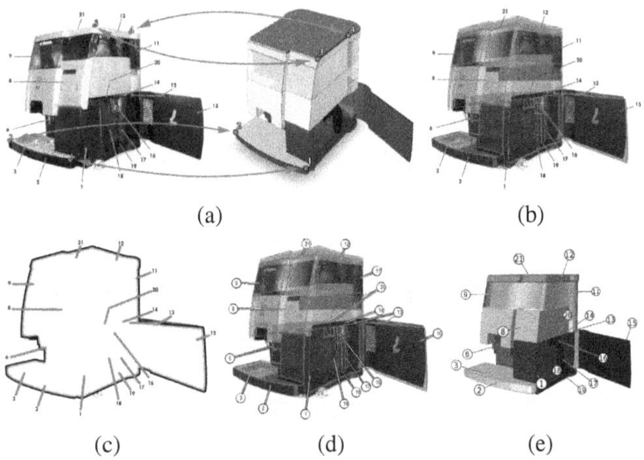

Figure 4. Retargeting annotations. (a) To estimate the camera pose, the user interactively defines corresponding points between the 3D model and the input image. (b) With the estimated camera pose, the rendering of the 3D model fits the 2D input image. This is illustrated by adding the rendering as semi-transparent blue layer on top of the input image. (c) Searching for MSER with an eccentricity close to 1 allows to identify leader lines. The mask defined by the rendering enables to detect their starting and ending points. (d) Running an OCR tool around the end point decodes text labels (e), which allows to add 3D annotations to the 3D model.

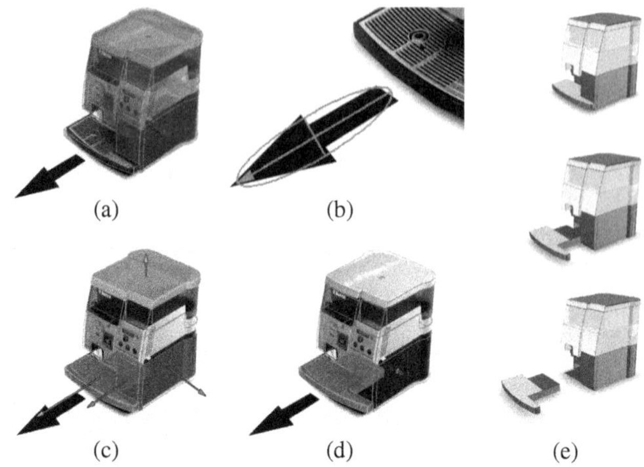

Figure 5. Retargeting action diagrams. (a) The input image with a semi-transparent overlay of the 3D CAD model. (b) We detect the arrow and its direction in 2D image space. (c) We analyze the 3D CAD model to find all removable parts and their directions. (d) By comparing the assembly directions to the direction of the arrow, we reduce the set of possible part motions. The part which is closest to the shaft of the arrow is selected. (e) The animation is defined by the path which was derived during motion planing.

manual definition of point correspondences and field of view by providing a basic user interface (UI). The UI is a side-by-side arrangement of a 2D image viewer and a 3D viewer, wherein the user selects four or more points both in the input image and on the freely rotatable 3D model (Figure 4a). The camera pose is then determined using POSIT [5]. This procedure needs to be done only once for a set of instruction images that use the same camera parameters, which covers the majority of examples we have analyzed.

Annotation detection

By computing maximally stable extremal regions (MSER) [17], we search the 2D documentation for leader lines and labels. MSER provides an efficient means for segmenting connected components in an image. For every connected component, we calculate its eccentricity. If the eccentricity value is close to 1, we assume that the region contains a leader line. We then determine the end points of the line by fitting an ellipse to the region. Rendering the CAD model using the camera parameters estimated in the previous step yields a mask for looking up whether a pixel is occupied by the model. The pixel coincident with the end point inside the mask is used to look up the annotated part and defines the 3D anchor point, where the leader line is attached to the 3D object. The region around the other end point is automatically scanned with a standard optical character recognition (OCR) tool to decode a text label.

ACTION DIAGRAMS

Action diagrams encode instructions within a single image, mostly by using arrows. Therefore, to retarget action diagrams, we need to identify and interpret arrows and the parts of the target object they are referring to. We start by detecting and analyzing each arrow in 2D space (Figure 5(b)). Subsequently, we use motion planning to identify the set of geometrically feasible motions of each part (Figure 5(c)). We then identify a set of parts the arrow might refer to by selecting those which can be moved similarly to the motion encoded in the arrow. To present the action in 3D, we animate the selected part using the corresponding movement, as suggested by the motion planner (Figure 5(e)).

Motion planning

We assume that input images show only geometrically feasible configurations, which have been generated by moving parts without penetrating other parts of the object. To find such valid motions for each part in the CAD model, we need to test whether or not a motion causes collisions. Using Minkowski differences of polyhedra [16], we detect for a given direction of motion how far each part can be displaced. By default, we test for the principal axes in local and global coordinates of the part.

Arrow interpretation

In order to identify an arrow, we begin by computing MSER regions outside the target object. Among all candidates with connected components, we select the ones with exactly two concavities along the boundary, and we determine the main axis by ellipse fitting (Figure 5(b)). The tip of the arrow is the extremal point on this axis closer to the concavities. To identify candidate actions, we search for parts which could be removed in the direction indicated by the arrow. Therefore, we project the motion vectors that have been computed during motion planning to image space using the camera parameters we have estimated before (Figure 5(c)). We compare the projected directions to the direction of the arrow. We select part motions as candidates if the angle between their projected motion vector and the arrow vector is below a given threshold. If there is more than one candidate, the part which is closest to the shaft of the arrow is chosen (Figure 5(d)).

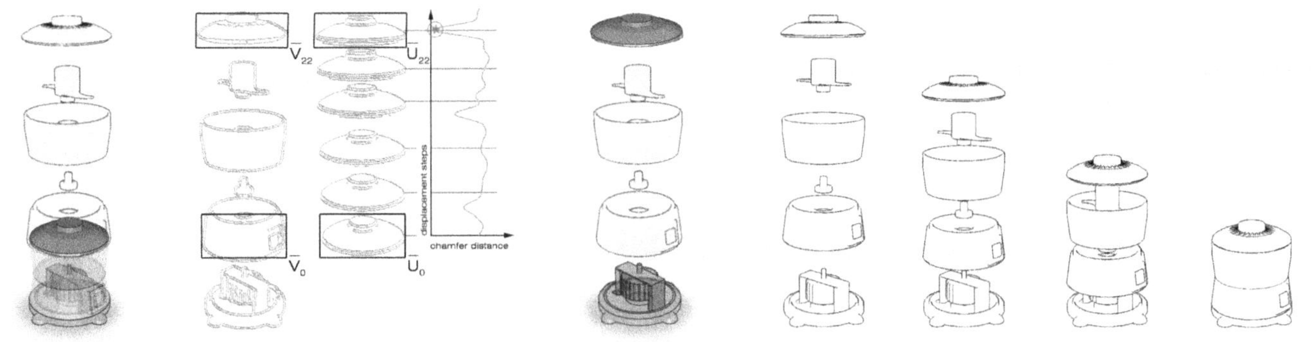

(a) (b) (c) (d)

Figure 6. Retargeting explosion diagrams. (a) The 2D input image and the object rendered semi-transparently using the estimated camera parameters. The motion planner generates candidate places for the lid (red part) first. (b) Our matching compares renderings of the lid within its bounding rectangle $\bar{U}$ at geometrically possible locations $\bar{V}$. The orientation of the local gradient, as used during image matching, has been color coded from red (horizontal) to green (vertical). The chamfer distance between $\bar{V}_i$ and $\bar{U}_i$ has been plotted in the line chart. The red star in the line chart highlights the minimal chamfer distance $\bar{U}_{22} \rightarrow \bar{V}_{22}$. (c) The lid is placed corresponding to the analysis. (d) To replicate the entire 2D explosion diagram, we search for the optimal placement of each part. We generate animations by consecutively applying the motions that were identified by our candidate evaluation algorithm. This example shows output key frames of a generated 2D animation for collapsing the input explosion diagram. Note that occlusions are correctly resolved with the 3D model.

EXPLOSION DIAGRAMS

In order to retarget explosion diagrams, we need to find a sequence of unblocked motions of parts such that the resulting 3D scene setup visually matches the input 2D explosion diagram. The problem of detecting such sequences has been considered in assembly planning [1, 26, 21]. Thus, we incorporate our motion planning system into a sequencing approach similar to Srinivasan et al. [25]. This generates a set of feasible candidate explosions in 3D space. We find the candidate that matches the input image best by comparing the it with rendered images of each candidate setup (Figure 6).

By using only motions which we identified as geometrically feasible, we generate candidate displacements of each part in discrete locations. The CAD model is rendered to a texture with its parts displaced according to feasible motions. The resulting image U is compared to the input image V using a variation of directional chamfer matching (DCM), as given in Equation 1 [15]. To emphasize relevant edge features of the CAD model for DCM, we assign a random color to each part and add contour lines to the scene before rendering. We then apply a Canny edge detector [4] and store the normalized vector of the locally detected 2D gradient in $\hat{U}(\mathbf{u})$ and $\hat{V}(\mathbf{v})$, respectively. Our notation employs the zero norm $||\cdot||_0$ to count the non-zero pixel values in an image. With a small constant ϵ, we obtain a continuous distance function d_{DCM} for comparing images U and V:

$$d_{DCM}(U,V) = \frac{1}{||\hat{U}||_0} \sum_{\mathbf{u_i} \in U} \min_{\mathbf{v_j} \in V} \frac{|\mathbf{v_j} - \mathbf{u_i}|}{|(\hat{U}(\mathbf{u_i}) \cdot \hat{V}(\mathbf{v_j}))| + \epsilon} \tag{1}$$

Reducing the size of the test area

Calculating the DCM over the entire image for each candidate explosion is computationally demanding. However, if a part is visible in the explosion diagram, we search specifically for this part at valid candidate locations. We generate a new image template $\bar{U} \subset U$ for each candidate motion by projecting the displaced 3D part into 2D image space and calculating its bounding rectangle. The search space in V is restricted to the matching bounding coordinates $\bar{V} \subset V$. We refer to the procedure of finding the place of the template $\bar{U}$ in V as local template fitting (see Figure 6(b)).

Reducing number of tests

While restricting the image matching to the bounding rectangles of displaced parts helps to increase system performance, the amount of possible combinations of part displacement easily becomes very large. Even with the restriction to geometrically feasible motions, the search space grows quickly with the number of parts and candidate displacements. Thus, we accelerate the system with a greedy search approach. Instead of generating all possible configurations in advance, we combine candidate generation and evaluation to progressively find the best fit for a given input image. In each iteration, each movable part is offset according to its geometrically feasible candidate motions without modifying the others. The displacement that produced the smallest local distance value according to $d_{DCM}(\bar{U}, \bar{V})$ is applied to the corresponding part. The search continues as long as at least one tested part displacement yields a distance that is significantly smaller than the currently stored minimum. If multiple choices are available, the motion that introduces the largest improvement is chosen and applied. If no such motion exists, the algorithm terminates. Note that exploding a part may unblock others, which results in additional feasible motions of the formerly blocked parts. Thus, blocking information of the remaining parts needs to be continuously updated.

STRUCTURAL DIAGRAMS

Structural diagrams appear in 2D documentations as sequences of at least two images. Every two consecutive input images differ with regard to changes in configuration that are applied to one or multiple parts. Given a pair of input images, we can restrict candidate motions to those which fall in the image region where visual changes are observed. This allows us to reject candidate motion based on where parts have been moved, rather than on their matching score with the target image. Early rejection of candidate motion based on the region of change is essential to increase system performance. Therefore, we must ensure reliable identification of these regions.

Difference images

In order to evaluate the relevance of a candidate motion with regard to the visible region of change, we need to compute the difference image $\texttt{diff}(U_1, U_2)$ of the rendering of the object before and after applying the candidate motion, and the difference between the two consecutive input images, $\texttt{diff}(V_1, V_2)$. Computing the percentage of overlap of the two regions (Equation 2) allows us to discard motions that are not related to the observed differences in the input images, i.e., where the coverage falls below a given threshold.

$$coverage = \frac{||\texttt{diff}(V_1, V_2) \cap \texttt{diff}(U_1, U_2)||_0}{||\texttt{diff}(V_1, V_2)||_0} \quad (2)$$

We generate $\texttt{diff}(U_1, U_2)$ by rendering all parts in the object except for the current candidate to the depth buffer in the first pass. In a second pass, we enable the color buffer and render the part before and after applying candidate motion. The resulting pixels in the color buffer correspond to the region of change $\texttt{diff}(U_1, U_2)$ (Figure 7(b)). The method used for obtaining $\texttt{diff}(V_1, V_2)$ differs based on the type of input images. Difference images from input with clear distinct colors, such as LEGO assembly manuals, can be directly computed by subtraction and thresholding. However, a reasonable amount of assembly instructions are simple black-and-white closed-line drawings, as known from do-it-yourself furniture [3]. For such line drawings, we apply a silhouette check to identify the background area in both images and reject motions that exhibit a low foreground coverage. A flood-fill from the four image corners (which are assumed to be empty) creates enhanced versions of the input images, where background and foreground pixels have a unique color. By conjoining the foreground regions of V_1 and V_2, we receive a generous enclosure for the area of visible change. Change detection in photographic material is most challenging. Simple image differencing is defeated by lighting, reflection, shadows and surface texture. For robust determination of the region of change, we employ SIFT flow [14], which densely relates pixels from the source image to the most similar pixel in the destination image.

Global bi-directional chamfer distance matching

Local template fitting works well for detecting detached and isolated parts, as they appear in explosion diagrams. However, this approach performs poorly when trying to verify subtle structural changes, which include reconfiguring, removing or attaching parts. The possibility to compare between images in a sequence obviates the necessity to depict each action individually. Involved parts may be partially obscured or simply disappear from one image to the next, thus making local fitting inapplicable. Consequently, a more thorough

[3]www.ikea.com

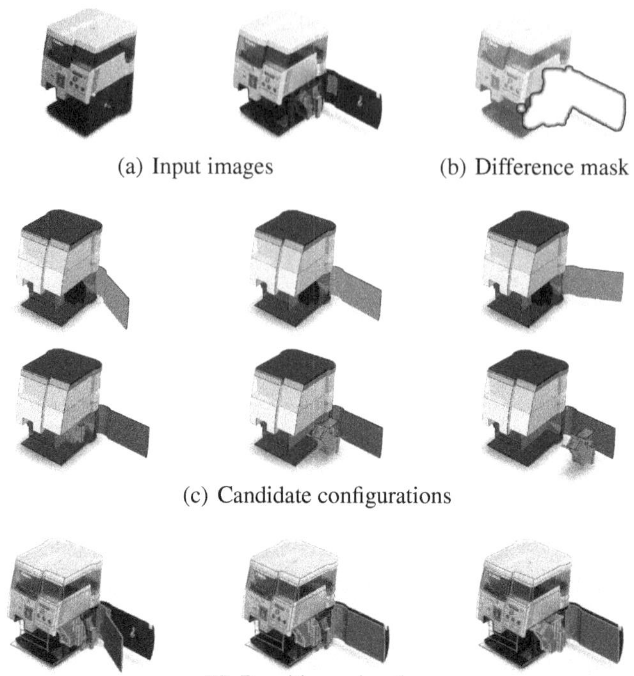

(a) Input images (b) Difference mask

(c) Candidate configurations

(d) Resulting animation

Figure 7. Retargeting structural diagrams. (a) Input images. (b) We generate a difference image, which reveals changes between the images. Our system creates a set candidate configurations by moving and rotating all parts of the machine which are identified by the difference image. (d) From all candidate configurations, the one which fits the target image best is selected. The motion which had to be applied to transform the object in the selected configuration is used to create the 3D animation. In this case, a rotation is generated to open the service door, and the brewing unit is removed.

analysis of the entire image domain is required. For a full analysis and comparison of two images U and V, we compute the DCM over the entire image area in both direction $U \rightarrow V$ and $V \rightarrow U$. We refer to this global image matching of U and V as the bi-directional chamfer distance (BCM):

$$d_{BCM}(U, V) = d_{DCM}(U, V) + d_{DCM}(V, U) \quad (3)$$

Finding a candidate rendering U that minimizes $d_{BCM}(U, V)$ ensures a strong visual similarity between U and target image V. For a scene with n parts and up to c feasible configurations per part, evaluating all possible setups requires $\mathcal{O}(c^n)$ comparisons. Since this quickly becomes infeasible even for moderately complex objects, we use the greedy algorithm mentioned before to progressively select the best structural improvement based on individual part motions. However, greedy global matching may at early stages favor part configurations that approximately resemble multiple unmatched parts in the target image. To suppress this effect, we put an additional emphasis on local consistency to penalize discrepancies in the subimage regions $\bar{U}$ and $\bar{V}$ enclosing the projection of the currently tested part. Thus, the distance function uses a weighted bidirectional chamfer matching (WBC):

$$d_{WBC}(U, V) = \underbrace{d_{BCM}(U, V)}_{\text{global matching}} + \underbrace{\lambda\, d_{DCM}(\bar{U}, \bar{V})}_{\text{local fitting}} \quad (4)$$

The additional weighting of local consistency for $\bar{U}$ and $\bar{V}$ is controlled by the parameter λ. In practice, we found that choosing $\lambda \approx 0.25$ yields satisfactory results for all examined sequences.

Candidate generation

Similar to explosion diagrams, we generate candidate configurations by iteratively moving and testing parts based on geometrically feasible motions. In addition, we allow to move parts outside the visible area in order to handle instructions which require to append or to remove parts. The instructions shown in Figure 7(a) present multiple consecutive actions. To access the brewing unit from the coffee machine, the hatch has to be opened before the unit can be removed. Since we iteratively change candidate configurations, our system succeeds in correctly recreating the depicted motions. This example demonstrates that our algorithm is robust to hidden or incomplete input data. Although the brewing unit is completely obscured by the closed hatch, its removal was successfully detected by our system (Figure 7(d)).

Since structural diagrams may also encode actions requiring to rotate a part, we additionally generate candidates that involve part rotations. Candidate rotation axes are generated by combining principal axes with the origin of either the local coordinate system or the center of gravity of a part. The testing of rotations starts with the part in default configuration, and proceeds by increasing the angle of rotation in discreet steps. Testing rotations around an axis terminates after reaching 360° or if a collision with another part occurs. For example, to analyze the input images in Figure 7, our system generates and evaluates candidate configurations by rotating the service door of the coffee machine around its hinge.

COMBINED DIAGRAMS

Traditional 2D documentation often consists of diagrams which combine aspects of annotated, structural, explosion and action diagrams. A typical example is to use annotations in any of the other diagrams (Figure 2(a)). Another very common combination is to show one or multiple parts in displaced positions (explosion diagram), before showing their final position on the object in the next image of a sequence (structural diagram). Displaced parts may further be highlighted with diagrammatic elements such as arrows or leader lines. Consider the example in Figure 8(a), which shows two images in a sequence of a LEGO assembly manual. Instructions to add bricks are given by showing the brick and leader line connecting the brick to the intended location on the object (as used in action diagrams). In addition, some bricks just appear in the second image.

The system we present is able to handle all kinds of combinations. Interpreting the mixed sequence displayed in Figure 8(a) can be achieved by employing the approach that is used for analyzing structural diagrams. Since WBC considers both global and local features, it is applicable to partial explosions as well. The additional visual information that is conveyed by arrows in sequences can be processed by the established methods for arrow diagrams and may be used to complement candidate selection. However, we found that for

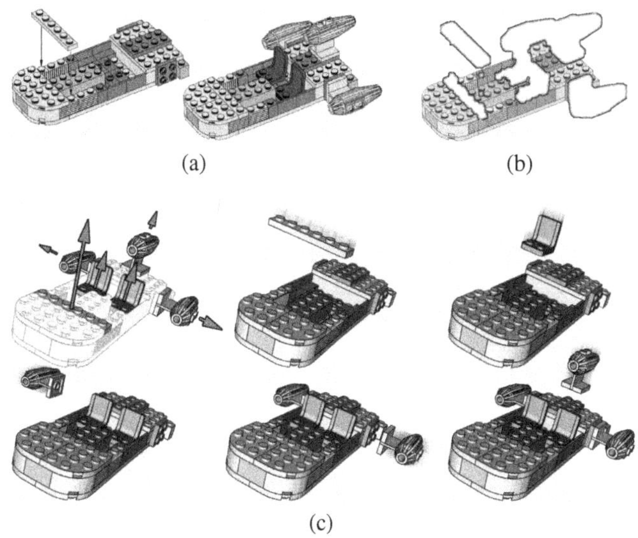

Figure 8. Retargeting combined diagrams. (a) Two input images illustrate multiple assembly steps. (b) We derive a difference image from the inputs, which indicates where changes occurred. (c) Our analysis yields a set of motions and corresponding parts, in this example indicated by red arrows. The key frames show the animation generated from the computed motions. ©2014 The LEGO Group, used with permission.

all assessed sequences, our algorithm for retargeting structural diagrams was able to reproduce the portrayed instructions without interpreting the arrows. Moreover, since we approximate any displayed object configurations by accumulating several part motions, our system is able to retarget image pairs which convey multiple instructions at once. This includes manipulations of multiple parts between two images as well as multiple consecutive actions. For example, Figure 8(a) shows two images taken from a LEGO instruction which adds six bricks from one image to the next. Since our system correctly identifies the configurations in both images it is able to generate the correct motion to animation.

Our approach to generate 3D annotations is independent of other elements present in the diagram. Therefore, we can handle annotations, which appear in any of the other diagrams. Only the current configuration of the parts depicted in the image is required to render a mask which matches the input image. Since DCM is robust against image noise and smaller artifacts, additional graphical elements do not influence the candidate matching. Figure 1 shows an example of an annotated explosion diagram, which we successfully analyzed before retargeting to AR.

AUGMENTED REALITY INTERFACE

Our analysis of 2D documentations reveals any combination of an annotated 3D model and a set of consecutive 3D motions. Our final goal is to easily relate the information to real world objects using an AR interface. Therefore, we register the 3D model to its real world counterpart and track the user's display to make the augmentation visible. Since we present the documentation in a dynamic and often visually complex environment, we also provide interactive visualization tools as part of the AR interface.

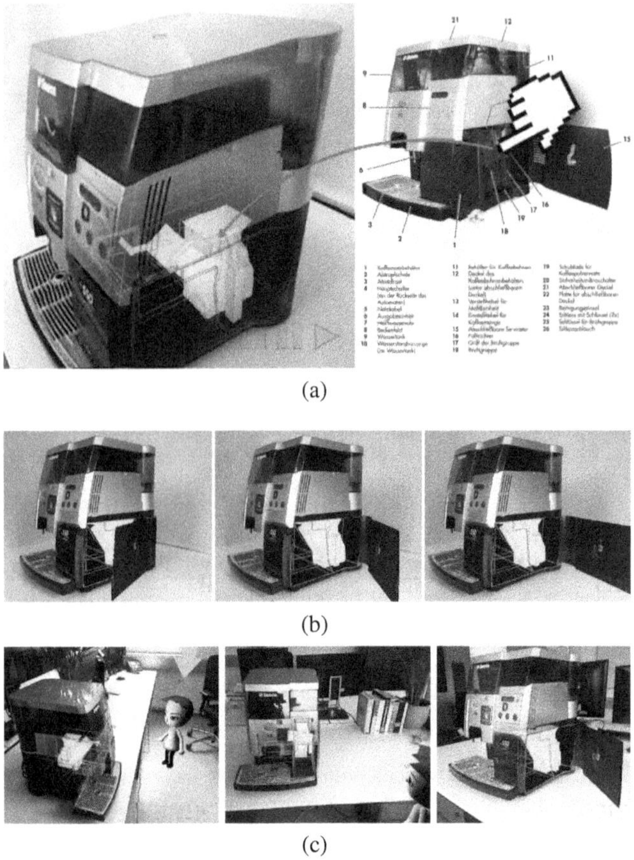

Figure 9. Interaction. (a) The relation between 2D image elements and 3D structure allows us to manipulate the 3D visualization with 2D interactions. Selection of the brewing unit triggers highlighting of the corresponding 3D object. If the selected object in the real world is occluded, we provide the user with a ghosted view x-ray visualization. (b) We allow to replicate an optimized object overview configuration in a 2D image by computing the steps for transforming the real world object into the one depicted in the 2D documentation (e.g., opening the service door). (c) The optimized object configuration is most effective from the point of view used in the 2D documentation. We extract the point of view from which the 2D image was generated and present it to the user by showing an avatar. This example shows the user navigating to the extracted point of view.

Registration and tracking

The registration of the 3D model to its physical counterpart uses an RGB-D sensor and PCL-Kinfu, which is an implementation of KinectFusion [19] using the Point Cloud Library (PCL) [23]. Our system registers the 3D model automatically to the point cloud received from the RGB-D sensor using an implementation of Sample Consensus Initial Alignment (SAC-IA) [22]. Camera tracking is realized using PCL-Kinfu and initialized with SAC-IA.

Visualization

The registered 3D model allows to present the 2D documentation within the real world environment of the user. However, in AR, we usually have to cope with a visually complex background and dynamic camera motion. Therefore, AR documentations demand special techniques to provide effective visualizations. To reduce the visual complexity of our AR visualizations, we allow animations to be presented as video phantoms [9]. This resembles a real-time photomontage (Figure 1, Figure 9(b)) and thus reduces the visual complexity by decreasing the amount of virtual objects in AR.

Interaction

Traditional diagrams have been optimized to present their information from a carefully chosen vantage point. However, interactive diagrams can become confusing, if many parts are animated, or the user chooses a poor point of view. Thus, we let the user interactively control the progress of an animation by influencing the displacement of all or individual parts at runtime. Furthermore, the relation between 2D image data and 3D objects allows us to connect interactions in image space to 3D visualizations in AR. For example, we allow to quickly find 3D parts in AR by interactively selecting 2D elements in image space. Consider the example in Figure 9(a). The 2D illustration is taken from a traditional handbook. It is showing the object of interest in a configuration, which was optimized for visibility. Note the open door, which reveals the parts inside the machine. While optimized 2D graphics support selection tasks, our system adds support to identify the selected elements within the real world environment. Thus, selecting an element in image space activates highlighting of the related 3D structure in AR. If the selected element is hidden in the real world, we provide the user with ghosted view visualization [10] (Figure 9(a)). Notice the transparency modulation, which creates the impression of seeing through the closed real world door.

While ghosted views enable effective exploration of hidden objects, they fail to create effective visualizations for visually complex structures. However, since our 2D input graphics provide optimized visualization, we furthermore provide the user with a replicate of the 2D configuration in 3D AR. We implement this by computing the object configuration shown in the optimized 2D image. To provide a smooth animation from the object configuration in reality to the one depicted in 2D, we furthermore derive the configuration of the real world object in front of the user. Therefore, we run our diagram analysis using a screenshot of the live video and the optimized 2D graphics. Figure 9(b) shows the resulting animation from using the images seen in Figure 9(a) as input. The selected brewing unit is clearly shown after replicating the object configuration used in the traditional documentation material.

Replicating the object configuration from an optimized 2D illustration works best from a point of view which is close to the one used in 2D. During camera estimation, we derive this point in space, and, thus, we can guide the user to these optimized points of view. As demonstrated in Figure 9(c) we provide this information to the user by adding an avatar looking at the object to the scene. The avatar indicates the point of view the image was taken from, and thus for which the configuration of the object is optimized.

PERFORMANCE

To evaluate the performance of our system, we choose a set of objects, which have been illustrated in different styles. The results are listed in Table 1. The table shows the number of parts the object consist of (#Parts), the number of images in the sequence (#Images) and the time used to retarget the input

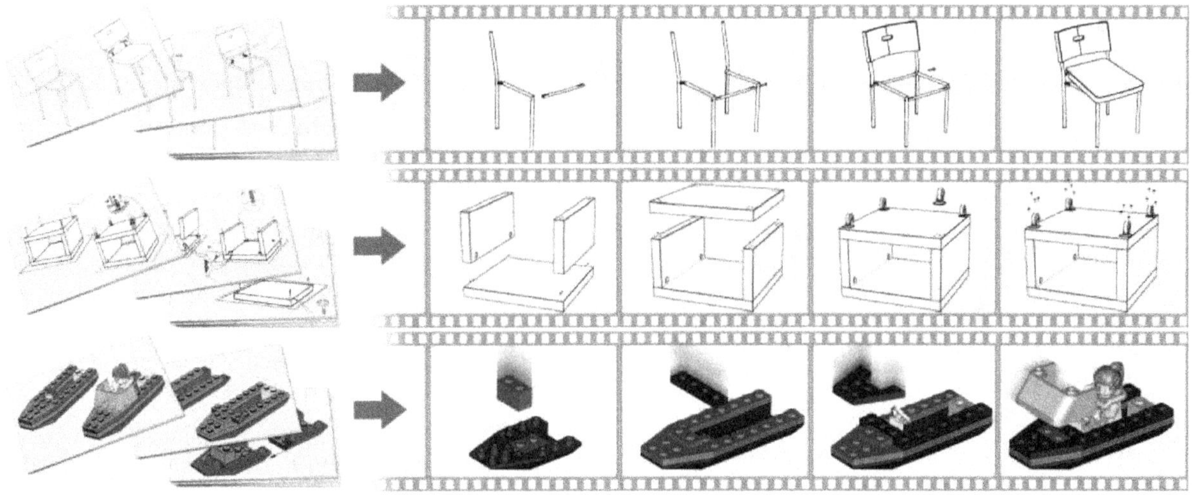

Figure 10. Various examples. ©IKEA Chair Herman and Table Lack, used with permission. LEGO Boat, ©2014 The LEGO Group, used with permission.

Table 1. Assessed test cases. We list the number of parts involved, as well as the length of the input documentation material and runtimes for retargeting.

Testcase	#Parts	#Images	Runtime
Valve (Fig. 1)	4	3	8s
Coffee Machine (Fig. 4)	6	4	9s
Mixer (Fig. 6)	6	*1	45s
LEGO Boat (Fig. 10)	18	8	1m 27s
LEGO Landspeeder (Fig. 8)	39	14	4m 10s
IKEA Chair Herman (Fig. 10)	10	8	5m 58s
IKEA Table Lack (Fig. 10)	42	5	16m 29s
LEGO Tower	42	7	2m 21s
LEGO House	88	13	10m 25s

* Explosion diagram, single image only

data to a 3D diagram (Runtime). The runtimes were recorded on a personal computer with an i7-4771 CPU @ 3.50 Ghz, 16 GB RAM and an NVidia GeForce GTX 780 Ti with 3 GB graphics memory. Input diagrams and resulting animations for test cases that are not shown elsewhere are depicted in Figure 10 and in the supplementary video. Although the LEGO Landspeeder and the IKEA Table Lack have a similar part count, the manual of the latter takes significantly longer to retarget. This results from the different illustration styles used and the number of parts involved in each step of the manuals. Photos and renderings allow us to apply image differencing to obtain tight areas of change for early rejection of unrelated candidate motions. However, this is not possible for line drawings. Furthermore, the manual of the IKEA Table depicts a larger number of instructions in each individual diagram. This is possible, because many parts of the object have no sequential dependency (e.g., wheels and screws can be added in parallel). Consequently, a high number of movable parts has to be considered at each point in time. The performance of our approach thus depends strongly on the employed illustrating style and the overall structure of the examined object.

LIMITATIONS

Our current implementation has several limitations. The pose estimation is the basis for the data extraction in our approach. Therefore, an erroneous estimation will propagate through the entire pipeline. If the error is exceeds a certain threshold, the system will fail to associate image regions with 3D objects. In addition, invisible elements in an image cannot be extracted with our current implementation. For example, if several screws have to be removed from an assembly within a single step often only a few representatives are shown in an image, while others remain occluded. Since our system can only detect visible elements it will fail to retarget such cases. A similar problem occurs when parts are small and those barely visible in the image. We provide visual examples for the described limitations in the accompanying video material.

CONCLUSIONS AND FUTURE WORK

We presented a system to generate interactive 3D documentations from 2D image data. The resulting 3D scene can be presented on a regular desktop or tablet computer, or can be displayed directly within the user's real world environment. Thus, our system enables to reuse existing 2D documentation material to create 3D documentations. Therefore, we believe that our approach will become a key enabling technology to move from traditional 2D to modern interactive 3D documentation.

The central idea for transfer of 2D documentation to 3D is to replicate the 2D image by rendering a 3D model of the object of interest. This relates 2D image elements to 3D objects. We have demonstrated how this relation can be used to interact in 2D image space in order to control the corresponding 3D visualization. Thus, we believe that applications of our system will not substitute 2D documentations entirely. Instead, they will combine 2D and 3D data to provide the user with best of both presentation and interaction spaces.

While our system is able to handle images present in existing 2D documentation, it is not limited to documentation material. Our system can generate 3D animations from any image or photo sequence which shows an object in different configurations. Therefore, our system furthermore provides a new tool to control 3D animations by images.

Several direction for future work exist. For example, some documentations present instructions by visualizing both the cause and the effect of an action within a single image. This is usually done by adding commonly known glyphs to abstract the depicted effect. To retarget cause and effect visualizations, we need to extend our system to be able to identify such glyphs and to subsequently derive the class of possible motion from it. Another direction of future work is concerned with retargeting documentations which depict interactions with soft tissue or deformable objects. Generating candidate configurations of 3D deformable objects presents additional challenges such as a large amount of candidate configurations and complex models describing the deformations.

ACKNOWLEDGMENTS

This work was funded by a grant from the Competence Centers for Excellent Technologies (COMET) 843272 with support from AVL List GmbH and the Austrian Science Fund (FWF) under contract P-24021.

REFERENCES

1. Agrawala, M., Phan, D., Heiser, J., Haymaker, J., Klingner, J., Hanrahan, P., and Tversky, B. Designing effective step-by-step assembly instructions. ACM Trans. Graph. 22, 3 (2003), 828–837.
2. Bergig, O., Hagbi, N., El-Sana, J., and Billinghurst, M. In-place 3d sketching for authoring and augmenting mechanical systems. In Proc. of ISMAR (2009), 87–94.
3. Butz, A. Betty: Planning and generating animations for the visualization of movements and spatial relations. In Proc. of Advanced Visual Interfaces (1994), 53–58.
4. Canny, J. A computational approach to edge detection. IEEE Trans. Pattern Anal. Mach. Intell. 8, 6 (June 1986), 679–698.
5. Dementhon, D. F., and Davis, L. S. Model-based object pose in 25 lines of code. Int. J. Comput. Vision 15, 1-2 (June 1995), 123–141.
6. Gupta, A., Fox, D., Curless, B., and Cohen, M. F. Duplotrack a real-time system for authoring and guiding duplo block assembly. In UIST (2012), 389–402.
7. Heiser, J., Phan, D., Agrawala, M., Tversky, B., and Hanrahan, P. Identification and validation of cognitive design principles for automated generation of assembly instructions. In Proc. of AVI (2004), 311–319.
8. Henderson, S., and Feiner, S. Exploring the benefits of augmented reality documentation for maintenance and repair. IEEE TVCG 17, 10 (2011), 1355–1368.
9. Kalkofen, D., Tatzgern, M., and Schmalstieg, D. Explosion diagrams in augmented reality. In Proc of IEEE VR (2009), 71–78.
10. Kalkofen, D., Veas, E. E., Zollmann, S., Steinberger, M., and Schmalstieg, D. Adaptive ghosted views for augmented reality. In IEEE ISMAR (2013), 1–9.
11. Ledermann, F., and Schmalstieg, D. April: A high-level framework for creating augmented reality presentations. In Proc. of IEEE VR (2005), 187–194.
12. Li, W., Agrawala, M., Curless, B., and Salesin, D. Automated generation of interactive 3d exploded view diagrams. ACM Trans. Graph. 27, 3 (2008).
13. Li, W., Agrawala, M., and Salesin, D. Interactive image-based exploded view diagrams. In Prof of Graphics Interface (2004), 203–212.
14. Liu, C., Yuen, J., Torralba, A., Sivic, J., and Freeman, W. T. Sift flow: Dense correspondence across different scenes. In Proc. of ECCV (2008), 28–42.
15. Liu, M.-Y., Tuzel, O., Veeraraghavan, A., and Chellappa, R. Fast directional chamfer matching. In Proc. of CVPR (2010), 1696–1703.
16. Lozano-Perez, T. Spatial planning: A configuration space approach. IEEE Trans. Comput. 32, 2 (1983), 108–120.
17. Matas, J., Chum, O., Urban, M., and Pajdla, T. Robust wide baseline stereo from maximally stable extremal regions. In Proc. of BMVC (2002).
18. Mijksenaar, P., and Westendorp, P. Open Here: The Art of Instructional Design. Thames & Hudson, 1999.
19. Newcombe, R. A., Izadi, S., Hilliges, O., Molyneaux, D., Kim, D., Davison, A. J., Kohli, P., Shotton, J., Hodges, S., and Fitzgibbon, A. W. Kinectfusion: Real-time dense surface mapping and tracking. In ISMAR, IEEE (2011), 127–136.
20. Petersen, N., and Stricker, D. Learning task structure from video examples for workflow tracking and authoring. In Proc of ISMAR (2012), 237–246.
21. Romney, B., Godard, C., Goldwasser, M., and Ramkumar, G. An efficient system for geometric assembly sequence generation and evaluation. In Proc. of Computers in Engineering (1995), 699–712.
22. Rusu, R. B., Blodow, N., and Beetz, M. Fast point feature histograms (fpfh) for 3d registration. In ICRA, IEEE (2009), 3212–3217.
23. Rusu, R. B., and Cousins, S. 3D is here: Point Cloud Library (PCL). Proc. of ICRA (2011).
24. Shao, T., Li, W., Zhou, K., Xu, W., Guo, B., and Mitra, N. J. Interpreting concept sketches. TOG 32, 4 (2013).
25. Srinivasan, H., and Gadh, R. Efficient geometric disassembly of multiple components from an assembly using wave propagation. Mech. Design 122 (2000), 179.
26. Wilson, R. H., and Latombe, J.-C. Geometric reasoning about mechanical assembly. In Proc. Algorithmic Foundations of Robotics (1995), 203–220.
27. Zauner, J., Haller, M., Brandl, A., and Hartmann, W. Authoring of a mixed reality assembly instructor for hierarchical structures. In ISMAR (2003), 237–246.
28. Zheng, Y., Kuang, Y., Sugimoto, S., strm, K., and Okutomi, M. Revisiting the pnp problem: A fast, general and optimal solution. In ICCV (2013), 2344–2351.

Soft-Constraints to Reduce Legacy and Performance Bias to Elicit Whole-body Gestures with Low Arm Fatigue

Jaime Ruiz
Computer Science Department
Colorado State University, USA
jgruiz@cs.colostate.edu

Daniel Vogel
Cheriton School of Computer Science
University of Waterloo, CANADA
dvogel@uwaterloo.ca

ABSTRACT

Participant biases can influence proposed gestures in elicitation studies. There is a *legacy bias* from previous experience with, or even knowledge of, existing input devices, interfaces, and technologies. There is also a *performance bias*, where the artificial study setting does not encourage consideration of long-term aspects such as fatigue. These biases make it especially difficult to uncover gestures appropriate for whole-body gestural input. We propose using soft constraints to correct for legacy and performance biases by penalizing physical movements. We use wrist weights as a soft constraint to elicit whole-body gestures with low arm fatigue. We show soft constraints encourage a wider range of gestures using subtler arm movements or alternate body parts and lower consumed endurance for arm movements.

Author Keywords

Elicitation studies, whole-body gestures

ACM Classification Keywords

H.5.m. Info. interfaces and presentation (e.g., HCI): Misc.

INTRODUCTION

Gesture elicitation studies have become a widely used tool to inform the design of gesture sets. In a gestural elicitation study, participants are shown a system action (the "referent") and asked to propose a gesture to trigger it (the "symbol"). If suitable agreement is found among participants, a consensus gesture set may be defined [8]. In practice few gestures may have high agreement, but elicited gestures are useful to inform design [6,8]. An advantage of these studies is they should not be confined to current technologies. The focus is on user desires, not limitations of recognition technology or previous design decisions [4]. Researchers have shown that user-proposed gestures are easier to perform [5], easier to learn and recall [7], and more suitable than designer-created gestures [5]. These advantages have led to elicitation studies for technologies including touchscreens [8], mobile devices [6], and multimodal systems [3].

CHI 2015, April 18 - 23 2015, Seoul, Republic of Korea
Copyright 2015 ACM 978-1-4503-3145-6/15/04...$15.00
http://dx.doi.org/10.1145/2702123.2702583

Despite the benefits of elicitation studies, Morris et al. [4] argue *legacy bias* is a potential problem with elicitation studies. This is when prior experience with interfaces and technologies make it hard to uncover new gestures for an emerging medium. In previous work, participants have proposed touch gestures resembling legacy mouse input [8]. For whole-body gestures (performed by moving any part of the body without a device), we extend the definition of legacy bias beyond direct experience. We include secondhand knowledge of current body tracking capabilities and gestures portrayed in popular culture such as gaming system advertisements or science fiction films.

With this extended definition of legacy bias, we argue elicited whole-body gestures may have more to do with what is easy to track with current sensing technologies or more expressive for the sake of cinematic performance. For example, we found that for map panning, participants often mimic a gesture popularized by the Microsoft Kinect and the film *Minority Report*: they raise their arm to chest level and move it left and right (e.g. Figure 2a). Frequent use of large arm gestures like this can cause "gorilla arm" fatigue [2]. Alternative gestures using other body parts or more subtle arm movements may be more appropriate.

We believe legacy bias is compounded by what we call *performance bias*. This is when the artificial, time-limited study setting biases participants against considering long-term performance. It is difficult to get participants to consider aspects such as fatigue when their primary goal is to complete the study quickly and receive remuneration.

Morris et al. [4] proposed three techniques to overcome legacy bias: producing multiple gestures per action; priming to think about system capabilities; and running group studies. In a mid-air gesture elicitation pilot, they found that producing multiple gestures and priming resulted in a wider variety of gestures that took advantage of depth sensor capabilities. However, producing multiple gestures takes time, group studies are difficult to coordinate, and in pilot studies, we found priming with information to encourage consideration of long-term fatigue was unsuccessful.

We propose imposing *soft constraints* to reduce legacy and performance biases in gesture elicitation studies. We define a soft constraint as something that physically penalizes or encourages certain types of movement (in contrast to a *hard constraint* to prevent movement, such as wearing a straight jacket). In our study, we use wrist weights to penalize large arm movements and our results demonstrate that this soft constraint can counteract legacy and performance bias to elicit more alternative gestures with lower arm fatigue.

STUDY

Our study uses a typical elicitation study protocol [6,8] where each participant is asked to propose gestures for common interaction tasks. The difference is that each participant proposes gestures under two conditions: a *control* condition with no constraints and a *constraint* condition in which weights were fastened around the wrists. We chose wrist weights as a soft constraint for two reasons: first, current whole-body gestures tend to use tiring large arm movements; second, the *Consumed Endurance (CE)* metric enables us to quantify a reduction in arm fatigue [2]. To provide participants time to adjust to the soft constraint, we repeat elicitation with the *constraint* condition twice.

We had three primary hypotheses:

H1. The wrist weight soft constraint will decrease the likelihood of participants proposing legacy gestures used in commercial systems (e.g. Microsoft Xbox).

H2. The wrist weight soft constraint will encourage gestures with lower *Consumed Endurance (CE)* [2].

H3. The second time gestures are elicited with the wrist weight soft constraint, they will have lower CE and fewer legacy gestures.

Participants

Fourteen volunteers (7 female) were recruited between the ages of 21-34 ($\mu = 25$, $\sigma = 3.3$). All received $10 remuneration. Note that we did not control recruitment for people with and without gestural system experience since our definition of legacy bias includes indirect exposure.

Apparatus

Images portraying action referents were ordered and displayed with custom C# software and projected on a wall. Participants stood approximately 3m from the wall and their movements were logged as time-stamped skeleton segment positions using the Microsoft Kinect SDK and depth camera (v1). Audio and video was recorded for all sessions.

Task

For each action referent, participants were asked to propose a whole-body gesture that matched well and was "easy to perform" (fatigue is a key part of the latter). Participants were told to choose any stationary body movement that could be recognized by a person 3m away. We explicitly said the system was not an eye tracker. The 18 action referents are listed in Table 1 classified by interaction category (navigation-based actions and command actions) and usage context (a map application and interacting with tiled widgets). All actions were shown as simulated screen captures (a map or a grid of pictures) with overlaid arrows or words to convey the action. A description of each action was read aloud by the experimenter and participants were asked to design a gesture while "thinking aloud" so their thought process could be recorded. Once a gesture was chosen, they performed it 4 times while body movement was recorded.

Category	Context	Action Referent
Navigation	Map Application	Move Cursor
		Pan Left/Right
		Pan Up/Down
		Zoom In
		Zoom out
	Tiled Widgets	Cursor Left/Right
		Cursor Up/Down
Command	Map Application	Cancel
		Confirm
		Help
		Select
	Tiled Widgets	Delete
		Drag Left/Right
		Drag Up/Down
		Release Object
		Select
		Undo
		View Details

Table 1. Referent system actions used to elicit gestures (grouped by interaction category and application context).

Design and Procedure

Participants proposed gestures in 3 blocks, where all 18 action referents where seen in each block. The order of usage context (map and tiled widgets) in each block was counterbalanced across participants. Block 1 was the CONTROL condition without any wrist weights. In blocks 2 and 3 the wrist weights were worn. This deterministic condition ordering is used because soft constraints produce a strong carryover effect for subsequent non-constrained conditions. The second constraint block allowed participants to refine or change their gesture given the longer exposure to the weights. These two condition-block combinations are referred to as CONSTRAINT and CONSTRAIN-FINAL. When weights were added in block 2, we found some additional explanation was necessary so participants did not think it was as an endurance test. We simply asked them to "not muscle through" since the weights are heavy. With 14 participants each performing 3 condition blocks of 18 action referents, we collected 756 gestures (with each gesture performed 4 times). Each study session lasted about one hour.

Data Analysis and Coding

Two people coded gestures independently using synchronized audio, video, and Kinect skeleton data. This classified body part(s) used and their motion characteristics (e.g. whole arm, head nod, foot tap, etc.). Given the objective data and the think-aloud description audio, coding disagreements did not exist. Coded gestures were further examined for *legacy gestures*. A legacy gesture was designed as gestures resembling touch pinch-to-zoom, touch tapping, or a gesture used in the Microsoft Xbox with Kinect user guide. To quantify arm fatigue, we calculated Consumed Endurance *(CE)* [2] for both arms for each gesture performance using the CE Workbench [1] and our skeleton logs.

RESULTS

Whole Arm and Legacy Gestures

Out of 252 proposed gestures in the CONTROL condition, 196 (78%) used whole arm movements and 156 (62%) were identified as legacy gestures. As expected, the CONTROL condition exhibits a strong legacy bias. Further examination found that 108 of the 156 legacy gestures were proposed for the navigation action referents. This is not surprising given navigation actions are common on commercial gestural interfaces (e.g. Xbox). Out of 252 proposed gestures in the CONSTRAINT condition, 147 (58%) used whole arm gestures and 111 legacy gestures (44%). Observations for the 252 proposed gestures in the CONSTRAINT-FINAL were similar; there were 145 whole arm gestures (57%) and 109 legacy gestures (43%). There was a significant effect for condition on the frequency of arm and non-arm gestures (χ^2=21.91, p < .001). Pair-wise comparisons shows the CONTROL condition to have significantly higher arm gestures than the CONSTRAINT and CONSTRAINT-FINAL conditions (χ^2=18.68, p < .001 and χ^2=17.17, p < .001 respectively). We also observed a significant effect of condition on the frequency of legacy gestures (χ^2=21.91, p < .001). Again, pairwise comparisons show the CONTROL condition to have a higher frequency of legacy gestures than the CONSTRAINT (χ^2=15.71, p < .001) and CONSTRAINT-FINAL (χ^2=17.15, p < .001) conditions. There were no observed differences in the frequency of arm movements or legacy gestures between the CONSTRAINT and CONSTRAINT-FINAL conditions (p >.9 in all cases). The observed differences in the frequency of arm and legacy gestures between the CONTROL and CONSTRAINT conditions supports H1.

Consumed Endurance (CE) of Arms

Analysis of variance (ANOVA) showed a significant effect of action referent ($F_{17, 221}$ = 5.59, p < .001) and condition ($F_{2, 26}$ = 20.7, p < .001) on mean CE of proposed gestures. Post hoc tests using Bonferroni correction showed the CONTROL condition had higher CE than CONSTRAINT and CONSTRAINT-FINAL conditions (all p < .001), but no difference was found between CONSTRAINT and CONSTRAINT-FINAL. Figure 1 illustrates CE by action referent and condition for map and tile contexts. Given the high percentage of whole arm gestures in the navigation category, we examined the effect of task category on CE. ANOVA showed navigation actions have higher CE than command actions ($F_{1,13}$ = 7.02, p < .05). It also showed a category × condition interaction ($F_{34,26}$ = 14.0, p < .001). Post-hoc analysis found navigation and command categories to be significantly different for the CONTROL condition (all p < .01), but no significant differences were found between navigation and command categories for CONSTRAINT or CONSTRAINT-FINAL conditions. The reduction in CE when constraints were applied supports H2, but no statistical evidence supports H3.

DISCUSSION

Our results show that by adding wrist weights as soft constraints, participants propose alternate gestures. This includes gestures other than those used in legacy systems (H1

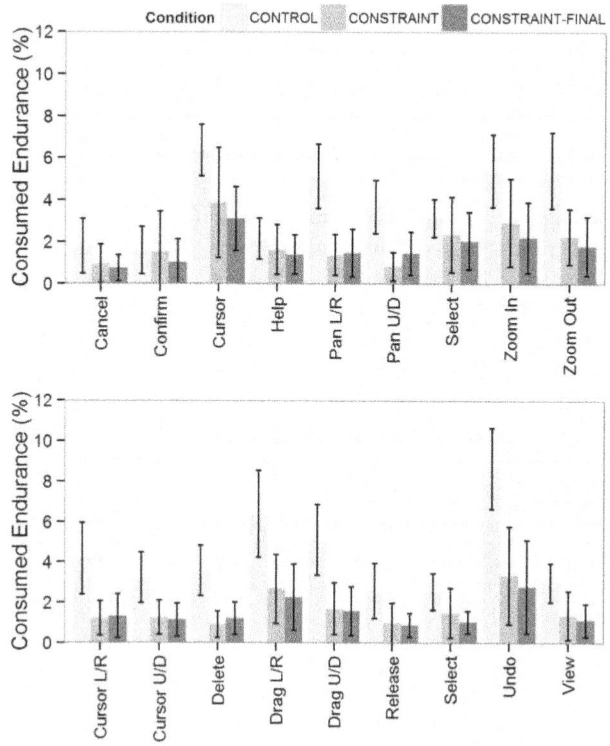

Figure 1 Consumed Endurance for each action referent: (top) map context; (bottom) tiled widget context. SEM error bars.

supported) and gestures with lower arm fatigue (H2 supported). We expected the need for additional time to adjust to the wrist weights, but we did not find evidence for this (H3 not supported).

Limitations

A possible limitation of soft constraints like wrist weights is that they could create a new bias favouring uncommon, less natural gestures. Like all elicitation studies, participants were instructed to propose gestures to match the task and were easy to perform. These instructions favour natural gestures, but if the only natural choice uses large arm movements, then the wrist weight soft constraints discourage it. This why we chose wrist weights and not a straightjacket – the hope is that if a large arm gesture was so compelling to use, the participant would propose it regardless of the increased wrist weight. This is why we suggest soft constraints, not hard constraints.

Perhaps due to the compelling nature of using arm gestures for some referents, participants sometimes proposed legacy gestures with higher arm fatigue even with wrist weights. This may be the soft constraints working as they should, allowing participants to selectively ignore their effect. Or, it may be that soft constraints reduce legacy and performance biases, but not completely. As future work, we plan on exploring how soft constraints can be combined with other bias reducing techniques, such as those from Morris et al. [4]

The current CE metric only applies to arms, so our study only quantifies arm fatigue. When subtler arm gestures are proposed, whole body fatigue is likely decreased. However, if proposed gestures use alternate body parts, such as using the head or foot while arms remain at the sides, whole body fatigue may decrease or increase. Future work is required to derive CE equations for these alternate body movements.

Elicited Gesture Characteristics and Agreement

Agreement scores, a metric for gesture consensus among participants, can generate gesture sets [6,8]. However, abstract referents and novel device form factors lead to low scores [6]. This was the case here. Scores were low and decreased further when constraints were added. Of course, our intention is not to generate a user-defined gesture set but to test if constraints can lower arm fatigue. As discussed above, a side effect of soft constraints is a more diverse collection of gestures, which would certainly be useful to inform design. We illustrate elicited gestures for six representative referents in Figure 2. With a soft-constraint, participants minimized the use of whole arm movements, making more subtle arm motions or abandoning arm and hands and used head or foot gestures instead. Foot gestures were only suggested in the constraint conditions.

Other Soft Constraints

Many other soft constraints are possible. For whole body fatigue, a body suit with elasticized tethers could dampen all movement. For low mobility gesture elicitation, participants could wear "age suits" like those worn by auto designers. Constraints could also be used to elicit context specific gestures such as walking on a treadmill to elicit walking gestures or blindfolds for eyes-free gestures.

CONCLUSION

We introduce the use of physical soft constraints in gesture elicitation studies. An elicitation study for whole-body gestures comparing proposed gestures with and without a wrist weight constraint and found that soft constraints reduced arm fatigue by generating more diverse, non-legacy gestures using different body parts and more subtle movements. We attribute this to soft constraints counteracting our expanded definition of legacy bias and our identification of a performance bias in elicitation studies.

REFERENCES

1. Hincapié-Ramos, J.D., et al. The Consumed Endurance Workbench: A Tool to Assess Arm Fatigue During Mid-air Interactions. Proc of DIS 2014, (2014), 109–112.
2. Hincapié-Ramos, J.D., et al. Consumed Endurance: A Metric to Quantify Arm Fatigue of Mid-air Interactions. Proc of CHI '14, ACM (2014), 1063–1072.
3. Morris, M.R. Web on the Wall: Insights from a Multimodal Interaction Elicitation Study. Proc of ITS '12, ACM (2012), 95–104.
4. Morris, M.R., Danielescu, A., Drucker, S., et al. Reducing Legacy Bias in Gesture Elicitation Studies. Interactions 21, 3 (2014), 40–45.
5. Morris, M.R., Wobbrock, J.O., and Wilson, A.D. Understanding users' preferences for surface gestures. Proc of GI 2010, (2010), 261–268.
6. Ruiz, J., Li, Y., and Lank, E. User-defined motion gestures for mobile interaction. Proc of CHI '11, ACM (2011), 197–206.
7. Wobbrock, J.O., Aung, H.H., Rothrock, B., and Myers, B.A. Maximizing the guessability of symbolic input. Ext. abstracts of CHI '05, (2005), 1869.
8. Wobbrock, J.O., Morris, M.R., and Wilson, A.D. User-defined gestures for surface computing. Proc of CHI '09, (2009), 1083.

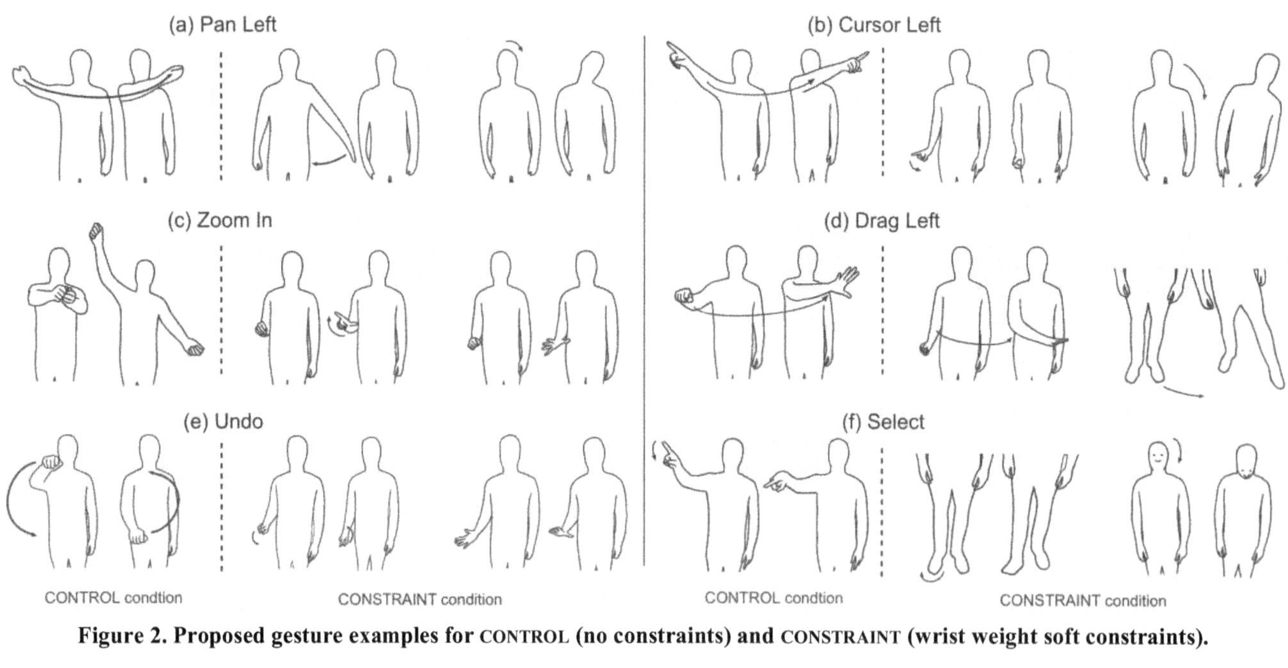

Figure 2. Proposed gesture examples for CONTROL (no constraints) and CONSTRAINT (wrist weight soft constraints).

Unistroke Gesture Recognition Through Polyline Approximation and Alignment

Vittorio Fuccella
Department of Informatics, University of Salerno
Via Giovanni Paolo II, 80084 Fisciano (SA)
vfuccella@unisa.it

Gennaro Costagliola
Department of Informatics, University of Salerno
Via Giovanni Paolo II, 80084 Fisciano (SA)
gencos@unisa.it

ABSTRACT
We present a novel gesture recognizer suitable for fast prototyping of gesture-based applications. The recognizer uses a nearest neighbor approach, and requires a small number of samples for each class. The similarity between two gestures is calculated through a three steps procedure: firstly, each gesture is approximated to a polyline, in order to extract its main movements; then, the two polylines are aligned to obtain an equal number of segments from both of them; lastly, the distance is found by summing the contribution of each pair of segments. We tested the recognizer on two different datasets and found that it performs more accurately than a state-of-art method.

Author Keywords
Gesture-based interaction; gesture recognition; unistroke gestures; PolyRec;

ACM Classification Keywords
H.5.2. Information Interfaces and Presentation: User Interfaces; I.5.2. Pattern Recognition: Design methodology Classifier design and evaluation

INTRODUCTION
Most of the applications for the latest mobile devices support a gesture-based interaction. Some of these, as in the case of text entry [1, 5, 4], exploit unistroke gestures, for their usability and for the ease with which they can be interpreted by the computer. Lately, the HCI scientific community has produced interesting solutions to the problem of gesture recognition, with the proposal of unistroke recognizers as *$1* [9] and *Protractor* [6].

We present a new gesture recognizer that, like its two aforementioned predecessors, is scale and (optionally) rotation invariant. Furthermore, its use is suitable for fast prototyping due to the following desirable features: it can run in real time on any recent device; it needs a few prototypes for each class and does not need to be tuned to a specific dataset; it can be used through a small number of method calls and does not need to link additional libraries.

http://dx.doi.org/10.1145/2702123.2702505

Differently from its predecessors, our recognizer does not sample gestures through a predetermined number of points at a fixed distance. Instead, only a small number of dominant points are extracted from gestures during preprocessing. Each gesture is then represented through a *polyline* whose segments identify the main movements in the gesture.

Every time two gestures are compared the best point-to-point correspondence is found. In order to enable a comparison, the two polylines are reduced to an equal number of segments. To this aim, their initial sampling is adjusted *on-the-fly*, possibly adding new sampled points to one or both of them. This method solves the problems reported (see [5] and [9]) with uniform sampling: "misalignment" in one-to-one correspondence and "unwanted flexibility" in *elastic matching*.

To find the distance between two gestures, the segments of each polyline are treated as vectors, characterized by magnitude and direction, and compared in pairs with those of the other polyline. The distance is obtained by summing the contribution of each pair of segments. Golden search (see [9]) is used to find the distance at the best angle.

We tested the recognizer on two different datasets with a number of different classes sufficient to prove its effectiveness for common gesture-based applications. The method that we use as a benchmark is *Protractor* [6], which was shown to be more powerful than previous approaches.

THE RECOGNIZER
Our recognizer uses a nearest neighbor approach. The distance between two gestures is calculated through the following three steps:

1. **Preprocessing**: each gesture is approximated to a polyline, in order to extract its dominant points;
2. **Alignment**: the two polylines are aligned to obtain an equal number of segments from both of them;
3. **Calculation**: the distance is found by summing the contribution of each pair of corresponding segments.

Step 1 - Preprocessing
Prior to any processing, an input gesture contains the points sampled from the device, which are variable in number and are usually obtained by capturing the position of the pointer (finger or pen) at regular time intervals. The points sampled in our preprocessing are the so-called *dominant* points, namely those where the gesture shows a greater curvature. The result is a broken line, which we call a *polyline*.

We relied on the Douglas-Peucker reducer [3] (DP, in the following), which works as follows: initially, the endpoints of the curve are selected, i.e., the *polyline* is formed by the segment connecting the endpoints; then the algorithm breaks the curve in the point which is the furthest from the line segment, adds it to the polyline, and calls itself recursively on the two parts of the curve. The curve is broken only if the selected point is at a distance greater than a *tolerance* threshold. The result of the execution of DP on an arrow sample gesture is shown in Figure 1(a).

In order to obtain a smoother polyline, an iterative *LineFusion* procedure (see [2]) is executed. At each iteration, the point between the segments having the smallest direction change is removed. The process ends when the smallest direction change exceeds a minimum threshold θ. Figure 1(b) shows the result of this step: in two consecutive iterations, two sampled points are removed from the shaft of the arrow.

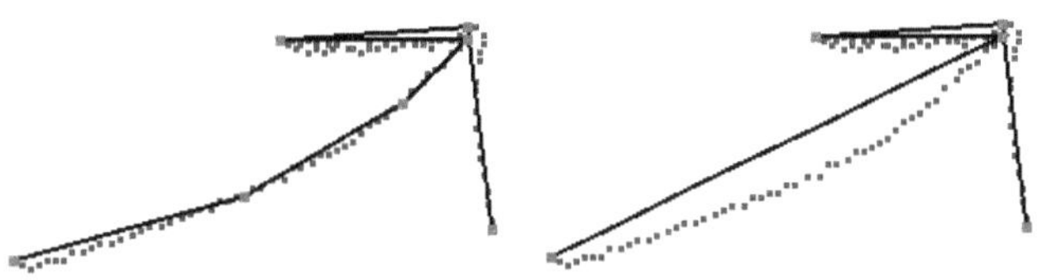

(a) Douglas-Peucker (b) LineFusion

Figure 1: Points (highlighted in red) sampled on an arrow sample gesture.

It is worth noting that the worst-case complexity of DP is $O(N^2)$, with N being the number of points in the input gesture. However, the preprocessing step can be executed only once on each template, so as not to overly burden the recognition procedure.

Step 2 - Alignment

The alignment is used to have the same number of segments in the two polylines, in order to enable a comparison between them. After preprocessing, a polyline is composed of a variable number of segments connecting the dominant points of the gesture. In step 2, we establish a mapping between the sampled points of the two gestures. The mapping is based on the similarity between the vertices of their respective polylines. The similarity is determined using two features:

- $pos(p)$: the position of the point within the gesture, calculated as the ratio between the length up to p and the total length;
- $angle(p)$: the difference of direction between the two segments of the polyline that meet at vertex p.

It is possible that one or more vertices of a polyline do not have a mapping on the other polyline and vice versa. For each unmapped vertex in a polyline, an additional vertex will be inserted in the other polyline. To perform the alignment we use a modified version of Needleman-Wunsch [7] (NW, in the sequel), an algorithm used, mainly in applications in bioinformatics, for the alignment of strings. NW calculates an optimal alignment between two strings based on a scoring scheme. The possible alignments are evaluated through a similarity function and the most similar is chosen. The final alignment is composed of two strings of equal length where two corresponding letters are the same (*match*) or are different (*mismatch*). In the latter case, a letter is aligned to a gap in the other string.

Here we use the same idea to align gestures' points. In particular, the effect is to associate two vertices of the polylines only when they are quite similar (*match*), while a new point is sampled on one of them in the opposite case (*mismatch*). In particular, given two polylines P with vertices $p_1, ..., p_n$ and Q with vertices $q_1, ..., q_m$, we define the similarity function F recursively as follows:

- Basis:
  $F_{i,0} = i \times g$ for $i = 0, ..., n$
  $F_{0,j} = j \times g$ for $j = 0, ..., m$.
- Step:

$$F_{i,j} = max \begin{cases} F_{i-1,j-1} + s(p_i, q_j), & Match(p_i, q_j) \\ F_{i,j-1} + g, & Insert(P, q_j) \\ F_{i-1,j} + g, & Insert(Q, p_i) \end{cases} \quad (1)$$

  for $i = 1, ..., n; j = 1, ..., m$.

where $s(p_i, q_j)$ is the similarity score between p_i and q_j; g is a *gap penalty*, i.e. a constant cost added in case of insertion in P or Q. The similarity score is calculated as follows:

$$s(p_i, q_j) = 1-[b \times pDiff(i,j)+(1-b) \times aDiff(i,j)] \quad (2)$$

Where:

- $pDiff(i,j) = |pos(p_i) - pos(q_j)|$;
- $aDiff(i,j) = |angle(p_i) - angle(q_j)|/2\pi$;
- b is a constant which determines a balancing of the weight of the two features.

The alignment, composed of pairs of mapped vertices, is determined by finding the *maximum-match pathway* in the matrix built from F (see [7] for a more detailed description): starting from the bottom right cell and going down to its upper left cell, we determine the option chosen in Equation (1) used to calculate the value in each cell in the *pathway*. In particular,

- $Match(p_i, q_j)$: vertices p_i from P and q_j from Q are matched, i.e. the pair (p_i, q_j) is added to the alignment;
- $Insert(P, q_j)$: a new vertex mapped to q_j is added in P, i.e., the pair $(-, q_j)$ is added to the alignment;
- $Insert(Q, p_i)$: a new vertex mapped to p_i is added in Q, i.e.,the pair $(p_i, -)$ is added to the alignment.

The insertion of a vertex in a polyline occurs between the closest vertices having a correspondence in the other polyline. For instance, from the alignment $\ldots(p_{m'}, q_{m'})(-, q_j)(p_{m''}, q_{m''})\ldots$, we determine that a new vertex p mapped to q_j must be added in P between $p_{m'}$

and $p_{m''}$. The ideal position of the new sampled vertex p in the subgesture delimited by $p_{m'}$ and $p_{m''}$ is established proportionally to the position of q_j in the subgesture delimited by $q_{m'}$ and $q_{m''}$. In practice, the raw point closest to that position is sampled.

$$pos(p) = pos(p_{m'}) + \frac{length(q_{m'},q_j) \times length(p_{m'},p_{m''})}{length(q_{m'},q_{m''})}$$

An example of polyline alignment is shown in Figure 2. The figure shows the result of the application of alignment on two gestures reduced to two polylines P and Q. Before alignment (see Figure 2a), P and Q contain 8 and 9 vertices, respectively. The alignment returned by NW is the following: (p_1, q_1) $(p_2, -)$ (p_3, q_2) $(-, q_3)$ (p_4, q_4) (p_5, q_5) (p_6, q_6) $(-, q_7)$ (p_7, q_8) (p_8, q_9). As a result, two vertices corresponding to q_3 and q_7 are inserted in P and one corresponding to p_2 in Q (see Figure 2b).

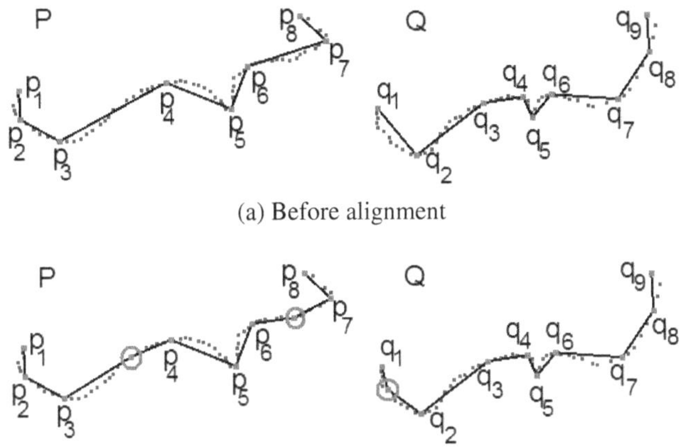

(a) Before alignment

(b) After alignment

Figure 2: Alignment of two polylines. After alignment, 2 new vertices (marked through a circle) are sampled from P and one from Q.

Step 3 - Distance

To calculate the distance between two gestures, we derive a sequence of vectors for each of the polylines representing them: each segment of the polyline is transformed into a vector whose magnitude is equal to the relative length of the segment and whose direction is represented by the slope of the segment, i.e. the angle between the segment and the horizontal axis. Here, we also consider as a part of the polyline the segment connecting its endpoints. Formally, the magnitude of the i-th vector corresponding to the i-th segment of a polyline P is calculated as: $|\vec{P_i}| = length(P_i)/length(P)$. At this step, the two gestures are approximated through polylines having the same number of segments. The distance between them is calculated by summing the magnitude of the vectors obtained from the difference of each pair of vectors in the corresponding sequences of vectors. Let us consider two polylines P and Q, both composed of n segments, their distance will be:

$$D(P,Q) = penalty \times \sum_{i=1}^{n} |\vec{P_i} - \vec{Q_i}|,$$

Param	Explanation	Value
t	tolerance in Douglas-Peucker	gesture diagonal / 26
θ	threshold for LineFusion	22 degrees
g	gap penalty in Equation (1)	0.4
b	balancing in Equation (2)	0.6

Table 1: Parameter settings for the recognizer, obtained in a tuning phase.

where *penalty* is a factor calculated on the basis of the number of *matches* and *mismatches* in the alignment step: $penalty = 1 + (mismatches/(matches + mismatches))$. The rationale for its use is that it increases the distance D proportionally to the number of *mismatches*, which itself expresses a distance between two gestures. The use of relative length to establish the magnitude of the vectors makes our recognizer scale invariant.

Rotation

Before calculating the distance, our recognizer rotates the gestures in order to reduce noise in gesture orientation: it determines the gesture's *indicative angle*, defined as the direction from the centroid to the first point of the gesture. Our recognizer can be used both in a rotation sensitive and in a rotation invariant context. In the former case, the gesture is rotated at 0. In the latter case, we adopt the strategy used in [6], i.e., the indicative angle of a gesture is aligned with the closest direction of the eight major orientations. Then, the *Golden Section Search* (GSS) is used to determine the distance at the best angle.

Setting Parameters

To establish default values for the parameters (reported in Table 1) we performed a tuning on a dataset composed of 400 curves [10], previously used in literature to test algorithms for finding corners in digital curves. To this aim, we measured the values of an objective function in correspondence of all the possible combinations of parameter values (discretized at regular steps and varied within plausible ranges). To avoid a combinatorial explosion, we separately tuned the parameters for preprocessing and those for the NW procedure.

For preprocessing, the objective function (to be minimized) was chosen as the absolute difference between the ideal number of sampled points (e.g., for a polyline representing a triangle, the ideal number of sampled points is 4: the two endpoints and two internal corners) and the number of points sampled through our preprocessing. We chose the values of t and θ which minimized the above difference (averaged on all the curves). To establish the value of the parameters used in the NW procedure, we simply ran our recognizer on the whole dataset and chose the values for g and b which maximized the recognition accuracy.

EVALUATION

We evaluated our recognizer in a rotation invariant context by testing it on two different unistroke datasets. The performance was compared to that of Protractor [6]. The main features of the datasets are summarized in Table 2. The first

Dataset	Classes	Symbols	Writers	Source
$1	16	4800	10	[9]
ILGDB	21	1923	11	[8]

Table 2: Features of the two datasets used in our evaluation.

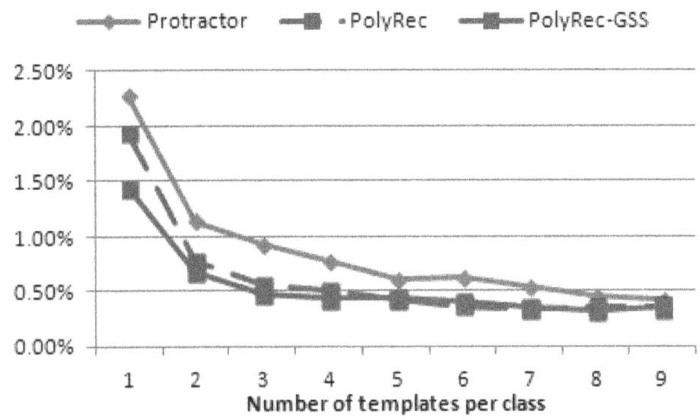

Figure 3: Error rate by the number of templates for each class on dataset *$1*.

dataset is the one introduced to evaluate the $1 recognizer [9]. The second dataset is the one presented in [8].

Methods

We performed a writer-dependent test for both our recognizer and Protractor [6]. The procedure we followed for testing with *$1* dataset is the same used in [9]: for each user, speed and gesture class, we randomly chose the templates and performed 100 trials for each number of training examples. For *ILGDB* we followed a slightly different procedure as data are already split in training set and test set. The difference is that we chose template and unknown gestures from training set and test set, respectively. The experiment was conducted on a Dell Precision T5400 workstation equipped with an Intel Xeon CPU at 2.50 GHz running Microsoft Windows XP operating system and the Java Run-Time Environment 6.

Results

The results of the recognition tests are shown in Figures 3 and 4, for the two datasets $1 and ILGDB, respectively. To

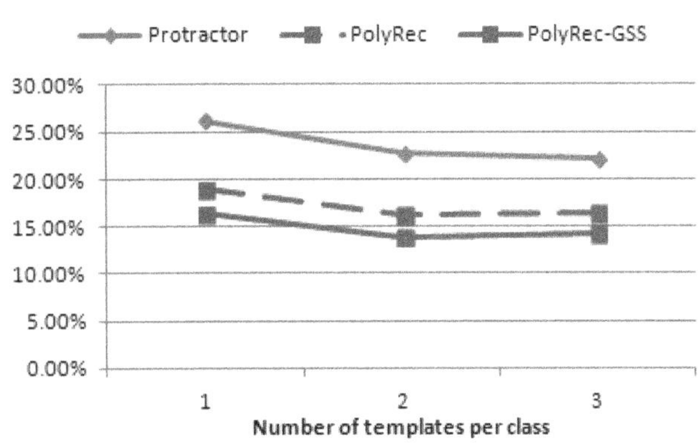

Figure 4: Error rate by the number of templates for each class on dataset *ILGDB*.

evaluate the improvement due to the use of the GSS rotation schema, we report the performance of our recognizer with and without it, represented through continuous and dashed lines, respectively. Both charts show a clear advantage in terms of recognition accuracy for our (*PolyRec*) recognizer. This advantage (both with and without GSS) with respect to Protractor was sought to be highly significant on both datasets ($p < .001$) through a Poisson regression model.

DISCUSSION AND CONCLUSION

We presented a unistroke gesture recognizer which offers significant advantages in terms of accuracy with respect to its predecessors. Our recognizer samples the dominant points of the trajectory of a gesture, enabling a better interpretation of the basic movements composing the gesture. The recognizer is suitable for fast prototyping as it does not need parameter tuning on specific datasets, since the use of the default values reported in Table 1 has proven effective in our tests. Our Java implementation can be freely downloaded at `http://sourceforge.net/p/polyrec`.

REFERENCES

1. Blickenstorfer, C. H. Graffiti: Wow!!!! *Pen Computing Magazine* (1995), 30–31.
2. Costagliola, G., Fuccella, V., and Di Capua, M. Interpretation of strokes in radial menus: The case of the keyscretch text entry method. *JVLC 24*, 4 (2013), 234 – 247.
3. Douglas, D., and Peucker, T. Algorithms for the reduction of the number of points required to represent a digitized line or its caricature. *The Canadian Cartographer 10*, 2 (1973), 112–122.
4. Fuccella, V., De Rosa, M., and Costagliola, G. Novice and expert performance of keyscretch: A gesture-based text entry method for touch-screens. *IEEE THMS 44*, 4 (2014), 511–523.
5. Kristensson, P.-O., and Zhai, S. Shark2: a large vocabulary shorthand writing system for pen-based computers. In *Proc. of UIST '04*, ACM (2004), 43–52.
6. Li, Y. Protractor: A fast and accurate gesture recognizer. In *Proc. of CHI '10*, ACM (2010), 2169–2172.
7. Needleman, S. B., and Wunsch, C. D. A general method applicable to the search for similarities in the amino acid sequence of two proteins. *Journal of Molecular Biology 48*, 3 (1970), 443–453.
8. Renau-Ferrer, N., Li, P., Delaye, A., and Anquetil, E. The ilgdb database of realistic pen-based gestural commands. In *Proc. of ICPR'12* (2012), 3741–3744.
9. Wobbrock, J. O., Wilson, A. D., and Li, Y. Gestures without libraries, toolkits or training: A $1 recognizer for user interface prototypes. In *Proc. of UIST '07*, ACM (2007), 159–168.
10. Xiong, Y., and LaViola, J. J. J. A shortstraw-based algorithm for corner finding in sketch-based interfaces. *Computers & Graphics 34*, 5 (2010), 513 – 527.

Gesture On: Enabling Always-On Touch Gestures for Fast Mobile Access from the Device Standby Mode

Hao Lü and Yang Li
Google Inc.
1600 Amphitheatre Parkway
Mountain View, CA 94043
hlv@google.com, yangli@acm.org

ABSTRACT
A significant percentage of mobile interaction involves short-period usages that originate from the standby mode—users wake up a device by pressing the power button, unlock the device by authenticating themselves, and then search for a target app or functionality on the device. These additional steps preceding a target task imposes significant overhead on users for each mobile device access. To address the issue, we developed *Gesture On*, a system that enables gesture shortcuts in the standby mode by which a user can draw a gesture on the touchscreen before the screen is turned on. Based on the gesture, our system directly brings up a target item onto the screen that bypasses all these additional steps in a mobile access. This paper examines several challenges in realizing Gesture On, including robustly rejecting accidental touches when the device is in standby, battery consumption incurred for continuous sensing and gesture-based user authentication methods for automatically device unlocking. Our analyses based on a set of user data indicated that Gesture On demonstrates a feasible approach for leveraging the standby mode for fast access to mobile content.

Author Keywords
Gesture-based interaction; gesture recognition; mobile computing; power efficiency; standby mode.

ACM Classification Keywords
H.5.2. [User Interfaces]: Input devices and strategies, Prototyping. I.5.2. [Pattern Recognition]: Classifier design and evaluation.

INTRODUCTION
A large number of mobile accesses have a rather short time span (e.g., a previous study reports 49.8% of the logged app usage is shorter than 5 seconds [3]) and originate from the standby mode of a mobile device [3,5], i.e., when the screen is off. To access a mobile functionality such as making a phone call, users will need to first press the power button to wake up the screen, unlock the phone by authenticating themselves, and then locate the target application before they can perform the desired action (see Figure 1a). These steps preceding a target action are always needed for many common mobile accesses, such as sending a text message, checking email, jotting down a note, or searching for a restaurant. They impose significant overhead for each mobile access from the standby mode.

Due to the frequent occurrences of these standby-originated accesses, reducing the overhead in these tasks can significantly improve the efficiency of mobile interaction. Existing commercial products and prior research literatures have investigated this issue in several aspects. Gesture Search alleviates the effort by allowing users to quickly access mobile content using mnemonic gesture shortcuts [10]. However, it still requires the user to activate the device and locate and invoke Gesture Search in the first place. The always-on speech feature has recently been enabled in Motorola's Moto X smartphone[1]. It allows the user to wake up the phone from standby to a speech input interface that is readying for a set of voice commands by speaking the phrase "Okay, Google Now". The person can

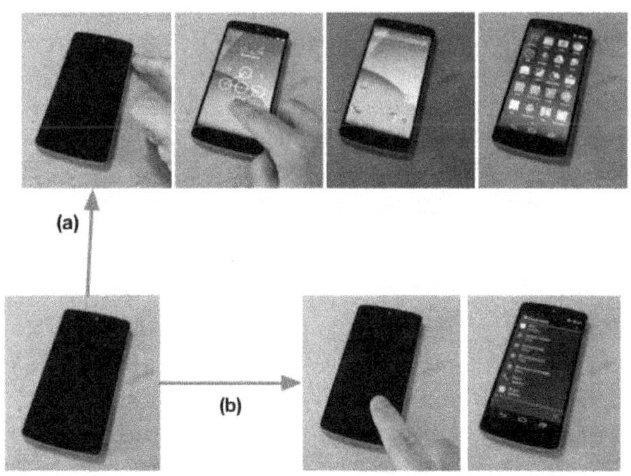

Figure 1. (a) Existing mobile systems require additional steps before the user can perform a target action, including pressing the power button, unlocking the device, and locating the target application. (b) Gesture On eliminates all these steps by directly accessing a target item from the device's standby mode by drawing a gesture on the touchscreen before it is turned on.

CHI 2015, Apr 18-23, 2015, Seoul, Republic of Korea
ACM 978-1-4503-3145-6/15/04.
http://dx.doi.org/10.1145/2702123.2702610

then speak out a command to quickly perform a common action, such as sending a text message, making a phone call, and navigating to a place. This always-on speech feature eliminates the extra interaction steps from waking up the device to getting to the target application. However, the method suffers several drawbacks. It requires the user to utter a special phrase before speaking a target command. In addition, speech input is not always appropriate or feasible (e.g., in a shared office, on a bus or in a noisy restaurant). Finally, further authentication is still needed if the desired action is considered privacy sensitive.

To address these issues, we developed *Gesture On*, a system that enables touchscreen gestures when a device is in the standby mode. With Gesture On, a user can draw a symbolic gesture on the touchscreen before the screen is even turned on; based on the recognition of the gesture, it directly brings up a target item onto the screen. Because symbolic gestures can often be drawn without visual feedback (such as trajectories), they can be articulated when the screen is off [7]. Gesture On overrides the default kernel behavior of mobile platforms by constantly monitoring and analyzing touchscreen input when the device is in standby. When a symbolic gesture is detected on the device touchscreen, Gesture On wakes up the device, authenticates the user based on the gesture, and performs the corresponding action, e.g., drawing a triangle to launch the Camera app or a circle to invoke the Alarm Clock.

In this paper, we examine several technical challenges in realizing Gesture On. First, Gesture On needs to differentiate the desired gesture input from accidental touches. There are many accidental touches registered on the touchscreen throughout the day when a device is in standby, e.g., when a user grab their device or when the device rests in a pocket. To avoid wasting computational power or triggering unwanted actions, Gesture On needs to identify and discard accidental touches as fast as possible. We also investigated the potential impact on battery consumption due to the continuous sensing as required by Gesture On. Second, to avoid a dedicated step for user authentication, we intend to authenticate the user based on the biometric information as demonstrated by a touch gesture itself.

The paper makes the following contributions:

- A gesture shortcut system that is embedded at the core of a mobile platform, which enables touchscreen gesture shortcuts when the device is in the standby mode;
- A set of methods for differentiating symbolic (particularly alphanumeric) gestures from accidental touches in the standby mode, and a thorough analysis over the characteristics of these touch behaviors;
- An examination of the impact on mobile battery consumption with the continuous sensing of Gesture On and the architectural design for addressing it;
- A preliminary investigation of methods for authenticating users based on their touchscreen gestures, and how gesture-based authentication can be integrated into an interaction flow.

In the rest of the paper, we first provide an overview of the related work. Next, we discuss our methods of learning and validating a gesture recognizer for differentiating desired gestures from accident touches, including our data collection procedure and an analysis over the collected data. Then, we investigate implicit user authentication methods, by creating and validating a classifier for authenticating users based on their touchscreen gestures. Finally we discuss our implementation and limitations and then conclude the paper.

RELATED WORK

To ease the effort for searching and activating a target functionality or command, previous work has investigated a variety of gesture shortcut systems [2,10,16]. However, these systems only address part of the problem in that they themselves need to be invoked before a user can benefit from these approaches. The benefit of reducing the interaction overhead from the very beginning of the interaction process—the standby mode—has attracted significant effort from both research and commercial products. A large body of work exploits various input capabilities of mobile devices to allow waking up a device and launching an application faster.

Motion gestures utilizing on-device accelerometers and gyroscopes can wake up the device from standby and launch a specific action. For example, many smart watches can be turned on when a user twist the wrist[2]. Google Glass[3] can wake up when a user looks up beyond a certain angle. A flipping gesture [18] is used by Moto X to allow a user to launch the camera for taking photos.

Touchscreen have also been used to wake up devices and perform predefined actions. For example, Nexus 9 tablet[4] allows a user to double tap the touchscreen to wake up the device. Previous methods have also demonstrated using a directional swipe to wake up the phone and execute an action that corresponds to the direction of the swipe[5]. Compared to these methods, Gesture On allows a richer set of gesture input by enabling alphanumeric gestures. It is the first work that examines accidental touches and the user authentication challenges using these gestures.

Other on-device sensors including proximity sensor, light sensor, IR sensors have also been used to wake up a device. For example, Moto X smartphones employ all these sensor data to infer when a user is intending to check the phone and automatically wakes up the phone to show useful information such as time and notifications.

[2] Android Wear. https://www.android.com/wear/
[3] Google Glass. https://www.google.com/glass
[4] Nexus 9. www.google.com/nexus/9/
[5] Android lock screen. http://www.android.com

Lastly, speech input through microphones is an expressive modality for waking up the device and performing actions. Again with Moto X, a user can speak the specific phrase, i.e., "Okay, Google Now", to wake up the phone to a voice listening interface[6] that is readying for a rich set of voice commands. In contrast, Gesture On does not require a separate activation step and allows users to directly articulate their target gestures for both activating the device and bringing up the target action.

Prior work has extensively studied methods for recognizing touchscreen gestures, e.g., [2,9,11,22]. Most of the prior recognition systems focused on gestures with well-defined touch characteristics, such as the trajectory of a rectangle shape [9,22]. These systems do not attempt to reject out-of-vocabulary gestures, and for any unknown input, they always output the best matched gesture class from a given gesture set. In contrast, accidental touches studied in this paper often do not have well-defined trajectories. Wed need to efficiently rule them out for further processing.

Little work has been devoted to discerning intended gestures from accidental touches. Recently, Schwarz et al. [19] used a set of spatiotemporal touch features (e.g., touch area, trajectory size, trajectory smoothness) to differentiate and filter out touch events from the hand palm. The accidental touches as concerned by us include palm touches, e.g., when the user fetches a phone. Thus, we borrowed several features of [19] to differentiate trajectory-based gestures from accidental touches.

Another related area is user authentication on mobile devices, which has been a longstanding problem. Much work has focused on replacing user passcodes with other forms of authentication methods that are more user friendly. For example, fingerprint readers[7] allow users to press or swipe their fingers to authenticate themselves. Trusted physical tokens [8] are another genre of technologies that authenticates the user by touching a trusted token on the device via NFC[8] or by simply connecting a trusted token via Bluetooth[9]. Face recognition has also been used in commercial mobile platforms such as Android devices , which unlocks the device by simply asking the user to face the device camera.

Previous work has also looked at touchscreen gestures for user authentication. Feng et al. [4] investigated methods for identifying users by observing a series of simple touchscreen gestures (e.g., swipe up, swipe down), but in a post-login setting. GEAT [20] authenticates users by how they perform (about 3) touch gestures from a set of 10 simple gestures. Because these systems need multiple gesture observations, they are not ideal for the authentication scenario we want to address here that only observes a single unknown alphanumerical gesture.

[6] Google Now. https://www.google.com/landing/now/

[7] iPhone 6. http://www.apple.com/iphone-6/

[8] Motorola Skip uses NFC to unlock smartphones.

[9] Android 5 supports adding any Bluetooth device as trusted token.

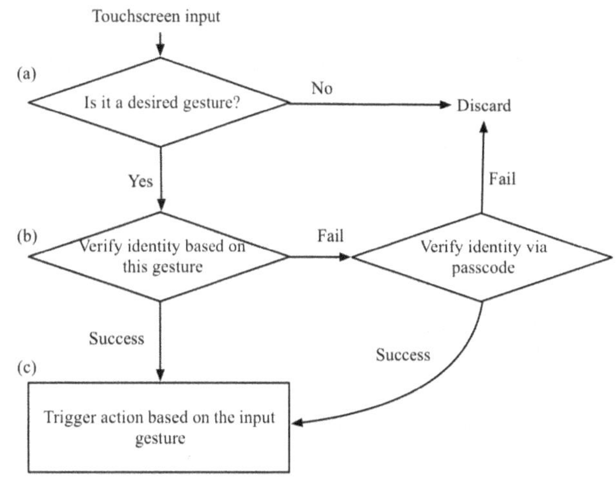

Figure 2. The processing flow of Gesture On: The two main components are (a) filtering out accidental touch input, and (b) verifying user identity based on this gesture. The gesture action component (c) is pluggable and we use Gesture Search in our first prototype to trigger search activity.

Handwritten signatures have been extensively investigated for user authentication or identification [17]. Sherman et al. [21] studies the security and memorability of using user-defined free-form multi-touch gestures for authentication. These forms of data have rich biometric characteristics of the user.

Gesture On investigates authenticating users only based on their touch gestures for launching actions, which avoids the need of additional hardware or extra user action. In contrast to the existing touch-based authentication, Gesture On does not authenticate against a user-defined signature, but a set of simple gestures that contain much less biometric characteristics.

Contextual information has also been used for user authentication. For example, a user can set home location to be trusted in Android and the device will automatically authenticate the user at home. CASA [6] provides a probabilistic framework for choosing an appropriate form of authentication according to the available contextual information. It balances between security and usability. We also took into account such a tradeoff in Gesture On that can benefit from these authentication frameworks.

THE DESIGN OF THE GESTURE-ON SYSTEM

In this section, we discuss the design of Gesture On. Assume Alice wants to make a phone call to her friend Bob. Typically, she would take out the phone, press the power button, unlock the phone with a passcode, locate and tap on the contacts app, and then search for Bob.

With Gesture On, after taking out the phone, Alice only needs to draw a letter "B" on the blank screen. Gesture On will wake up the phone, authenticate the user, and search the device with the gesture using Gesture Search [10]. Based on a list of presented search results, Alice can tap on

Bob's name from the search results to immediately make a phone call.

The detailed processing flow is illustrated in Figure 2. When a sequence of touch events occurs, Gesture On first determines whether the touch events are gesture input intended by the user. If not, it ignores the touch events, otherwise Gesture On wakes up the device and continues to process the gesture. If the user originally has set passcode protection, Gesture On will first verify if the input gesture is from the same user—authentication. If the gesture does not authenticate the user, the passcode guard will be shown and a correct passcode needs to be provided before the Gesture On can proceed. After authentication, Gesture On will launch Gesture Search with the input gesture as a search query.

Gesture On processes multi-touch input to filter out accidental touches, and authenticates the user. The handling of a detected gesture to fire desired actions can be delegated to a gesture shortcut system. For example, our current implementation sends the detected gesture as a query to Gesture Search [10] that allows random access to mobile content using alphanumerical gestures. Alternatively, we can connect Gesture On with other gesture shortcut systems, e.g., drawing a rectangle to invoke the camera functionality and a circle to bring up the Clock app.

In addition to flexibility, an important reason to separate the detection of target gestures (from accidental touches) from the recognition of them for invoking actions is to reduce unnecessary computation thus battery consumption caused by the accidental touches. As discussed later in the paper, detecting gestures from accident touches needs to run continuously but the recognition only needs to be performed when a gesture is detected. By separating the two and making detection an independent and compact component, we can run the detection on a low-power DSP to filter out the accidental touches while the CPU is in the sleep mode. Later, we will discuss our experimentation with such an architecture by evaluating of our gesture detection component on an ARM Cortex-M3 DSP[10], which shows that the separation allows a minimal impact on the power consumption.

The rest of paper focuses on the two key components to Gesture On are (1) algorithms for filtering out accidental touches, and (2) methods for authenticating users based on their input gestures.

DETECTING GESTURES FROM ACCIDENTAL TOUCHES

When a mobile device is in the standby mode, many screen contacts could register touch events. These touch events are accidental and not meant for initiating interaction. For example, when a person takes out a phone from the pocket or simply grabs the phone in their hand, their fingers could easily contact the screen and register touch events. Even when a phone rests in the pocket, depending on the fabrics of the cloth, screen contacts with the body over the cloth could also register touch events. Discerning intended gestures from accidental touches is crucial so as to avoid battery drain that is caused by unnecessary processing of the touch events and false activation of unwanted actions. In this section we discuss our methods for filtering out these accidental touches.

Most touchscreens nowadays detect multi-touch input. Although Gesture On focuses on enabling single-touch gestures for mobile access, both the accidental and the intended gesture input may contain touch input from multiple body parts simultaneously. For instance, when a user grabs a phone, multiple fingers could contact the screen, which generate accidental touches. Accidental touches can also co-occur with intended gestures. For example, while gesturing with one finger, a user may have touched the bezel of the phone unconsciously with the holding hand, which has become frequently occurred as many smartphones or tablets today are becoming frameless. It is even difficult for the user to realize accidental touches in the standby mode because there is no visual feedback in this mode while the screen is in sleep. Consequently, although the target gestures we aim to support are single-stroke, we need to handle multi-touch input that consists of one or multiple parallel touch trajectories (or touch strokes).

In our method, we classify each touch stroke as either accidental or intended given its context in a multi-touch input—the stroke being evaluated in relation to other co-occurring strokes as well as other sensor data such as acceleration. The classification only takes place at the end of each stroke, i.e., when a touched finger lifts up.

Data Collection

To understand how intended touch gestures are different from accidental touches, we collected touch data about these behaviors from users that consists of two consecutive stages: one for collecting accidental touch events and one for collecting intended gestures.

In the first stage of the experiment, a participant was given a customized Nexus 5 smartphone and was asked to use it as their primary phone (replacing their own phone) for a minimum of three consecutive days. The customized Nexus 5 contained a modified Linux kernel that we instrumented to enable logging touch events when the phone is in the standby mode and an Android app that we developed to log other types of sensor data. Because replacing the kernel on the phone can cause factory reset, we could not use participants' own devices for this study.

The second stage involved a laboratory study session in which we asked each participant of the first stage to perform a set of gesture tasks on the same device. Each participant needed to draw a set of symbolic gestures in five conditions involving both sitting and walking situations.

[10] http://www.arm.com/products/processors/cortex-m/cortex-m3.php

The sitting situation includes: 1) the user gestures on the phone that is resting on a table, 2) the user gestures with one hand and holds the phone with the other hand—the two-handed situation, and 3) the user gestures with the thumb of the hand that is holding the phone—the single-handed situation. The walking situation includes 4) the two-handed and 5) the single-handed situation while the user is walking.

For each of the 5 conditions, our data collection tool instructed the user to draw 3 samples for each alphanumeric symbol (i.e., the 26 English letters and 10 digits). When the instruction for drawing a specific gesture symbol shows at the top of the screen (see Figure 3), the participant is supposed to draw the gesture on the blank canvas and no visual feedback is provided while the participant performs the gesture. The order for which symbol to draw is randomized. This procedure resulted in a total of 540 gestures per participant.

We collected the same types of sensor data when touch events occur in both stages of the data collection study. The first set of data comes from the touchscreen sensor. For each touch event, we collect:

- The number of touches (each with an ID);
- The action of the touch event (i.e., move, release);
- The on-screen location of the touch event;
- The size (in pixels) of the touch area;
- The pressure associated with the touch event.

The second set of sensor data comes from other sensors. We recorded the readings from the proximity sensor, light sensor, accelerometer, magnetometer, and gyroscope. While these sensor data are not directly related to touch events, prior work has shown the strong correlation between these sensor dimensions and the screen touches [14]. We sampled these sensor readings within a 2-second

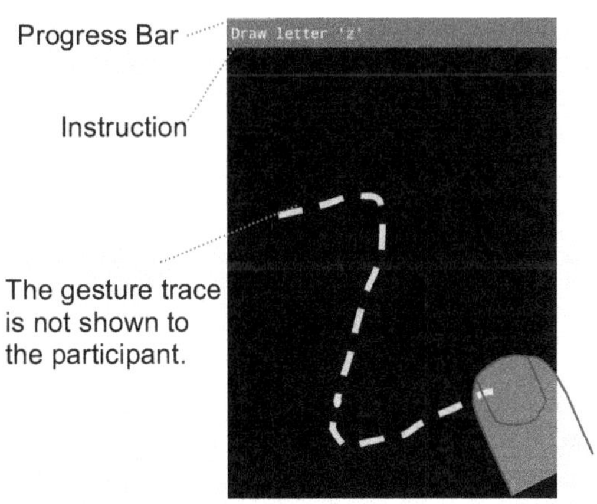

Figure 3. The interface for collecting gestures in the laboratory study. To simulate our target situation where no visual feedback is provided on the screen in the standby mode, the interface does not render the trajectory of the gesture while the participant performs it. The task automatically progresses when each gesture is finished.

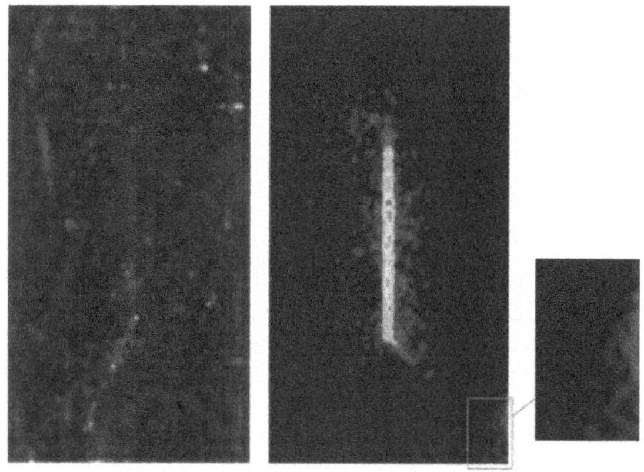

(a) (b)

Figure 4. The heatmap of stroke locations as measured from the farthest point of a stroke to the bezel for (a) accidental touches, and (b) desired gesture inputs.

window before, during and after each touch event.

Collected Data and Features

We recruited 14 participants (8 female, 6 males, aged from 20-30). All were Nexus 5 users and right-handed. The total time span of the first stage of data collection was 1,359 hours, about 4 days per participant on average. During this period of time, a total of 3,834 screen-turned-on events were observed, about 68 screen-turned-on events per day per participant on average.

For the accidental touch data, we collected a total of 642,670 touch strokes. Notice that we treated all the touches occurred when the screen is off as accidental because no touch interaction is supported in the standby mode during the data collection. For intended gestures, we acquired a total of 9,995 touch strokes from the laboratory session. Based on this dataset, we analyzed different characteristics these two types of behaviors demonstrate, by which we extract useful features for automatically classifying them for our gesture detection purpose.

On-Screen Locations

We found accidental touches and intend gestures have distinct location distributions. A touch stroke consists of a sequence of touch points and we use the point that is the farthest to the bezel as the stroke's location. Our data indicated that strokes of accidental touch were scattered across the screen and many were near the bezels (see Figure 4a). In contrast, strokes of intended gestures were mostly cluttered at the center of the screen (see Figure 4b). However, we observed a noticeable amount of touch strokes of intended gestures occurred at the lower right corner of the screen (see Figure 4b). By looking into the data, we found all these near-corner touches co-occurred with other finger touches for articulating gestures, during the single-handed condition. Because all of our participants were right-handed, we infer that these touch events were actually resulted from the participants' accidental palm contact with the touchscreen.

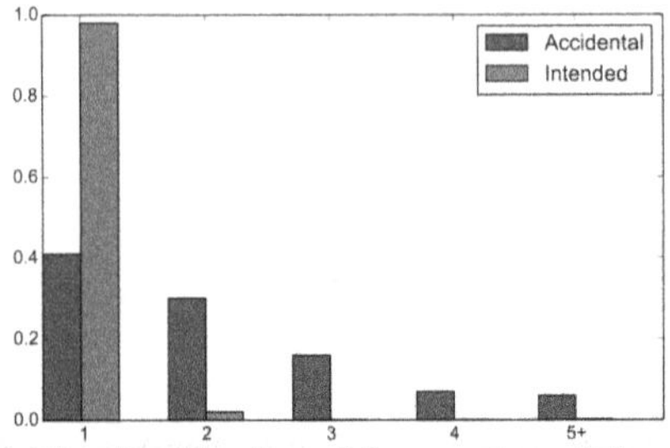

Figure 5. The distribution of the number of simultaneous touches from accidental touches and desired gestures. 60% of accidental touches involved more than 2 fingers or body parts, while the majority of intended gestures involved a single touch finger.

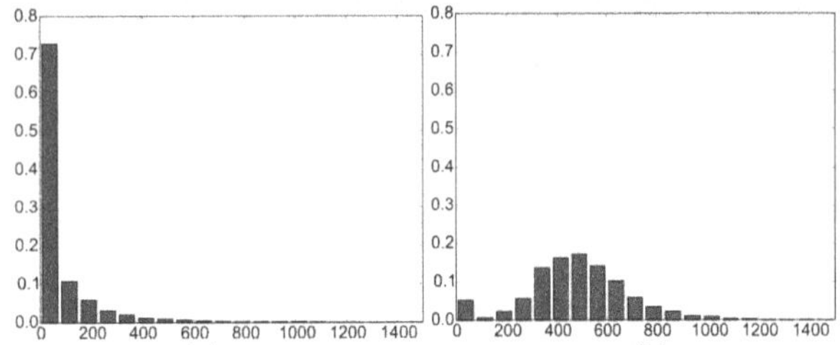

(a) (b)

Figure 6. The distribution of the larger dimension of the bounding box of each touch stroke. The majority of accidental touches had small bounding boxes (a). In contrast, the bounding size of the intended gestures were widely spread (b). The touch strokes that had small bounding boxes in (b) were mostly resulted from part of a multi-stroke gesture such as the dots in letter "i" or "j".

Number of Simultaneous Touches

Another important aspect that we examined was simultaneous touches from multiple fingers. Single-stroke gestures, i.e., our target gesture type, should ideally only involve a single finger touching at a time. However, as discussed previously, accidental contacts with touchscreens can result in simultaneous touches while performing a gesture, although such situations are extremely rare compared to accidental touches that often involved more than one finger registered (see Figure 5).

Touch Movement

The movement range of a touch stroke can be a great indicator to whether the stroke is intended or accidental, because many intended gestures have a trajectory with a significant length while accidental touches involve relatively less movement. Our data confirmed our intuition that the touch strokes of intended gestures often had much larger bounding boxes than accidental touches (see Figure 6).

Time Duration

We hypothesize that touch strokes in intended gestures would have relatively more concentrated time durations, while accidental touches are more random and could have very brief or extended time duration, e.g., when grabbing the phone in hand. This hypothesis was confirmed by our data (see Figure 7). The majority of accident touches have a very short duration while some lasted for an extended time period (>1400 milliseconds).

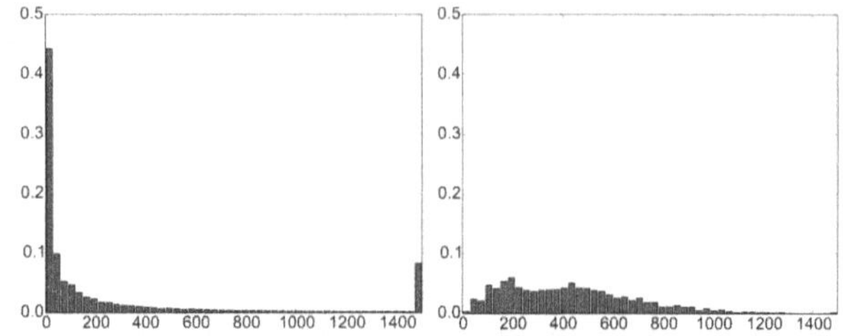

(a) (b)

Figure 7. The distribution of time duration (ms) of a touch stroke: (a) the strokes from accidental touches mostly had a very brief duration with a long tail spread for an extended time period, and (b) the strokes from intended gestures had a relatively more concentrated duration.

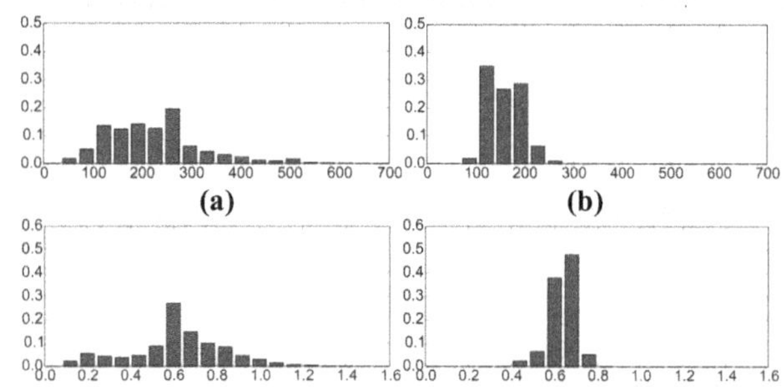

Figure 8. The distribution of touch width and pressure: (a) the widths from accidental touches, (b) the widths from intended gestures, (c) the pressure from accidental touches and (d) the pressure from desired gestures. In both metrics, accidental touches resulted in larger variations.

Touch Size and Pressure

A user typically performs an intended gesture by drawing with the fingertip as in our laboratory study that leads to a relatively consistent contact area size and pressure value. In contrast, accidental touches could be much more varying in these measures. For example, when a phone rests in the back pocket of a jean, the entire screen could be pushed against the body and the touch area from such a contact can be large so is the sensed pressure. Because the Nexus 5 phone, i.e., our experimental device, is only able to detect the major width of a touch area (a hardware limitation), we use the touch width instead of the actual size to characterize touch area differences between these two types of touch behaviors (see Figure 8).

Proximity

A proximity sensor is able to detect nearby objects and their distance from the sensor. However, Nexus 5 phones only report two values, 0 for "near" and 5 for "far", to indicate whether there is an object within a given range (i.e., 5cm). For smartphones, the proximity sensor is typically located on the top near the headset for detecting if the person is holding the phone against their ear during a phone call, to disable the screen to avoid accidental touches.

Because the proximity sensor is located at the top bezel, it is difficult to trigger the "near" signal while the user is gesturing on the touchscreen (see Figure 4). However, because accidental touches are more scattered around, the proximity sensors can be more easily triggered to send a "near" signal. The statistics about proximity sensor readings based on our data has also confirmed this (see Figure 9). Because the proximity reading may change in the course of a gesture articulation, i.e., switching between 1 and 5, we used the average proximity for each sample that resulted numerical values between 1 and 5 as shown in Figure 9. Overall, more than half of the accidental touches took place when the "near" signal was triggered. In contrast, few intended gestures were associated with the "near" proximity value.

Motion Sensors

Prior work has shown that motion signals can be useful to assist touch screen interaction and to enable finger tapping beyond the touchscreen [13,14]. We noticed that accidental touches and intended gestures generated different distributions for the standard deviation of the acceleration magnitudes during a touch stroke (see Figure 10). Intuitively, when performing a gesture on a touchscreen, users try to keep the phone stable, which might not be the case for accidental touches.

Features for Learning

Based on the above observation from our dataset, we choose the measures listed in Table 1 as our features in training a classifier for detecting intended gesture input from accidental touches.

Training and Validation

We chose to use a decision tree model for our gesture detector because our features are good indicators themselves. We also experimented with other classification models that achieved similar precision and recall, but a

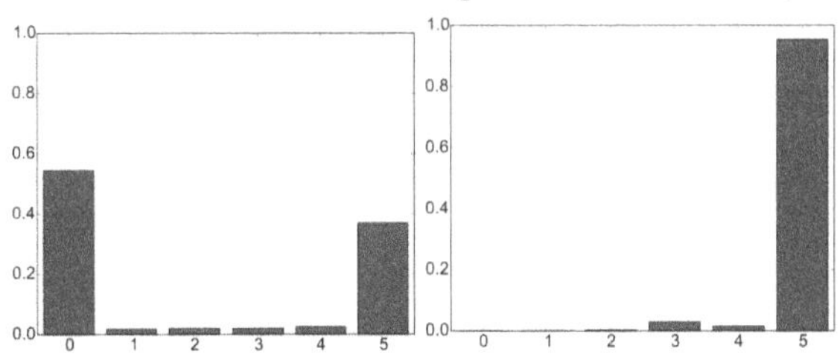

(a) (b)

Figure 9. The distribution of the average proximity during a touch stroke: (a) the proximity during accident touches. Many touches that were recorded as "near" might have taken place when the phone was a pocket, and (b) the proximity of intended gestures is rarely detected as "near".

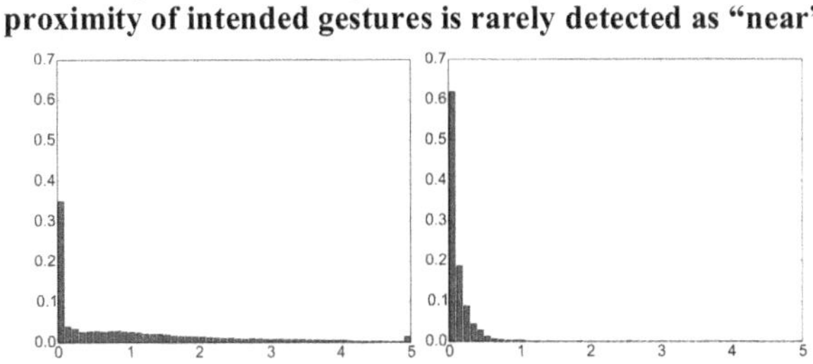

(a) (b)

Figure 10. The distribution of the standard deviation of the acceleration magnitudes during a touch stroke: (a) the distribution of accidental touches, and (b) that of intended gestures. The acceleration from accidental touches tends to have a larger deviation and thus is less stable.

1	Maximum distance of the stroke to device bezels
2	Larger dimension of the bounding box of the stroke
3	Time duration of the touch stroke
4	Maximum number of simultaneous touches when the stroke is generated
5	Maximum width of a touch area associated with the stroke
6	Maximum pressure of a touch area associated with the stroke
7	Average proximity while the stroke is generated
8	Deviation of acceleration magnitudes in the course of a stroke

Table 1. The features used for detecting intended gestures from accidental touches.

decision tree has relatively lower computational cost and is easier for us to port the detector onto low-power DSP chips for continuous sensing as discussed in the following sections.

For evaluation, we used a cross-user validation strategy. Each user's data was classified using a model that was learned from all other users' data. This simulates the user-independent setting where learning from specific users is not required after the system is deployed. Based on our dataset, we acquired 98.2% precision and 97.6% recall on detecting gestures from accidental touches. For accidental touches, this translates to 0.028% of them being misclassified as intended gestures, which is about 3 false activations per user per day.

USER AUTHENTICATION BASED ON A GESTURE

After a touch stroke is detected as an intended gesture, Gesture On checks if the device is locked with a passcode. If it is not locked, the gesture is directly sent to the connected gesture shortcut system for triggering the target action. If it is locked, Gesture On will try to authenticate the user based on the gesture, to avoid the overhead of requiring an additional authentication step. If the authentication fails, Gesture On will fall back to the default system authentication interface, e.g., via a passcode. Unlike prior work for user authentication using handwritten signatures, a gesture here often has much simpler trajectories, such as a circle for letter 'o'. These gestures have much less biometric information than a signature does. In this section, we discuss an initial investigation into this problem.

Authenticating a user through a simple gesture reduces interaction overhead but can sacrifice security due to false accepted gestures. The more accurate Gesture On can authenticate a user, the higher efficiency and better security it can achieve. To authenticate a user based on a single symbolic gesture, the system would need to first collect a sample of gesture data from the user before the user can use it, similar to collecting fingerprint data before using the fingerprint reader to authenticate. Since the biometric information might vary when a person draws different symbols, we require a user to draw at least one sample for each gesture symbol. The more gesture samples there are, the better the system can model the user's biometric profile.

To formalize our problem, verifying a person here is to calculate the probability that a person is as claimed given the gesture, i.e., $P(u(g) = u^*|g, G^*)$, where $u(g)$ is the person who perform the gesture g, u^* is the claimed user—the person who owns the device, and G^* is the pre-collected gesture sample set of u^*. Because the biometric information can vary from symbol to symbol, we introduce a hidden variable s for the gesture symbol that the person intends to perform by which gives the following equation:

$$P(u(g) = u^*|g, G^*) = \sum_{s \in S} P(u(g) = u^*|g, s, G^*)P(s|g)$$

where S is the target symbol set, G^* is the set of gesture samples for S collected from the owner u^*. $P(s|g)$ can be computed using a user-independent gesture recognizer such as a handwriting recognizer. We can calculate $P(u(g) = u^*|g, s, G^*)$ as the following:

$$max_{g_i \in G_s^*} P(u(g) = u(g_i)|s)$$

$P(u(g) = u(g_i)|s)$ is the probability of whether two gesture samples are authored by the same user given that these gestures are intended for a specific symbol. In the following section, we discuss our initial exploration in estimating this probability by learning a binary classifier for each gesture symbol.

Data Collection

Although the gesture data we collected in our laboratory study can still be used here, it is limited in the sample size (only 14 participants), which is insufficient for training and validating our classification method. Thus, we used another dataset that was collected from 94 participants on their own touchscreen mobile devices, via a crowdsourcing platform [1]. Participants finished the data collection tasks remotely on their own rather than in a controlled laboratory environment, which resembles a realistic situation.

Each participant contributed 5 samples for each English letter. This amounts to 470 samples per letter symbol. Since the classification involves a pair of gestures, there are C_{470}^2 =110,215 training pairs for each letter symbol.

Feature Extraction & Classification

Each gesture sample pair consists of five groups of features. First, in the preprocessing step, each gesture in the pair is resampled to 129 equidistant points and is aligned with each other using Protractor [9]. These points split the gesture into 128 path segments, and we then partition these segments to form 8 segment groups with each group containing 16 consecutive segments (thus 17 points). Based on these segment groups, we compute the following features for each pair of gesture samples.

- $d_i, 1 \le i \le 8$. d_i is the cosine distance between the i-th group's point coordinate sequence of the two gesture samples in the pair;
- $c_i, 1 \le i \le 8$. c_i is the cosine distance between i-th group's point curvature sequence of the two gestures;
- $s_i, 1 \le i \le 8$. s_i is the ratio between the i-th group's displacement of the two gestures. The displacement is the Euclidean distance between the beginning and end points of a group;
- $v_i, 1 \le i \le 8$. v_i is the ratio between the i-th group's velocity of the two gestures. The velocity is the displacement divided by the duration of a group;
- $a_i, 1 \le i \le 8$. a_i is the ratio between the i-th group's acceleration of the two gestures. The acceleration is the velocity divided by the duration.

On top of the above features, we used the ratio between the bounding circle's diameters of the two gestures. The displacement, velocity and acceleration have been used previously for signature-based verification [17]. In contrast to prior work, based on these features, we used a data-driven approach and trained an SVM classifier with radial basis kernels for each letter symbol.

Validation and Results

Similar to evaluating our gesture detector, we split our dataset for training and testing across users. For each letter symbol, we randomly pick 5 participants (a total of 25 gestures) to create a test dataset of 300 sample pairs. We use the rest participants' data to form the training sample pairs. We chose 5 participants for testing because it simulates a scenario of 4 attackers who try to pass the authentication test—a reasonable amount of attacks.

For each letter, we repeat the above process for 5 times and report the average false positive rate (or false acceptance rate, FAR) and false negative rate (or false rejection rate, FRR) (see Figure 11). FAR reflects how easily a person can break in the device (the vulnerability). FRR indicates how likely the system will reject an authentic user's gesture. Because Gesture On falls back to the default passcode interface when authentication fails, higher FRR means the reduction to the interaction efficiency. The average false positive rate was 25.8% and the average false negative rate was 25.5% across gesture symbols.

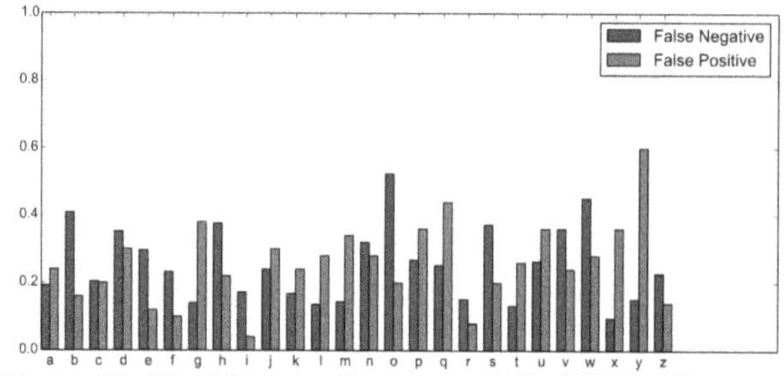

Figure 11. The false negative rate and the false positive rate for each letter symbol. Gestures for some symbols are more discriminative for differentiating users than others.

There are two extremes along the spectrum of interaction efficiency and security. Gesture On always fires an action without the authentication process (FAR=100%). This maximally reduces the authentication overhead, but at the expense of security. In the other extreme, Gesture On always asks the person to go through the passcode interface (FRR=100%), which does not reduce authentication overhead, nor sacrifice security.

It is worth mentioning that we can thus adjust the decision boundary of the binary classification to trade efficiency for security, or vice versa. We can expose this decision to users and let them finely-tune such a balance. For example, we offer three levels of authentication in a setting UI: a default level using a .5 decision threshold that yields the above FAR and FRR, a high-security level using a higher threshold for a low FAR, a low-security level using a lower threshold for a low FRR.

Before implementing our own solution, we experimented with a state-of-the-art solution from signature verification research [17]. With this previous method, we were only able to achieve 35%-40% FRR and FAR on single symbol verification. The fact that this previous method was able to achieve less than 2% FRR and FAR [17] for signature-based authentication indicated that a single-letter symbol often contain significantly less biometrics than handwritten signatures.

IMPLEMENTATION

Gesture On consists of two components. First, we implemented a virtual driver (for Nexus 5) in the Linux kernel that listens to and processes touchscreen events when the device is in the standby mode. The driver writes all the touch events to on-device storage files in our data collection study. To enable touch sensing in the standby mode, we modified the kernel to keep the touch sensor and its microcontroller active, and held a wake lock on CPU.

Second, we implemented an Android service that listens to all other sensor events and the touch events from our driver. This part can be alternatively implemented in the driver as well but it is much easier to implement using Android platform for our fast prototyping purpose. The communication between the service and the driver is through *sysfs* [15]. We used Weka [12] to train and validate our decision tree and SVM models.

POWER EFFICIENCY

The implementation of Gesture On that we discussed serves the purposes for data collection and prototyping and it works around the existing architecture of Nexus 5. However, while utilizing the sensors is relatively cheap, such an implementation requires Gesture On to hold a wake lock on CPU that consumes precious battery power.

A more power efficient solution is to move the gesture detection component that requires continuous sensing to a separate, low-power DSP (i.e., a sensor hub). The DSP only wakes up the CPU when a gesture input is detected, for more expensive computation such as gesture recognition and user authentication.

In fact, many today's mobile devices have already been utilizing such an architecture with a low-power DSP solution (MPU) for continuous sensing. For example, Apple iPhone 5s uses a M8 for processing sensor data in the background; Motorola Moto X uses a TI C55x DSP[11] for always-on voice command. This architectural design has a much less impact on the battery life.

Due to the limited access allowed to the current platform cores, we are yet able to harness these on-device DSP for our prototype. Instead, to examine the power efficiency Gesture On in such an architecture, we used a standalone low-power DSP through a development board. We chose NXP ARM Cortex-M3 as our DSP that has been used in iPhone 5s, and LPCXpresso1549 as the development board that offers good development support.

We ported our gesture detection component onto the DSP and used a Monsoon power monitor to measure the energy consumption of the entire development board. The development board uses a constant voltage of 5.04V during the experiment. We let the DSP perform 50,000 detection tasks, each consisting of featurizing and classifying a touch stroke with 30 touch events and 120 acceleration readings. We subtracted the energy consumption when the DSP is idle from that of the detection tasks. The mean energy consumption of each detection task is 0.02μAh, which is negligible compared to the entire battery capacity of Nexus 5 (2300mAh). Because there were about 811 accidental touch strokes per day per user based on our data, the average battery consumption for ruling out accidental touches is about 16μAh.

DISCUSSION

There are several ways to improve our authentication accuracy. We can utilize other sensor data such as the accelerometer in addition to the trajectories. The acceleration associated with touch events has been shown effective on user authentication [20]. Another direction is to allow a user to perform more than one gesture although this approach requires an additional authentication gesture that hampers the interaction efficiency. Alternatively, we can allow the user to use a pre-determined secretive gesture prefix or postfix for the desired gesture, e.g., a pigtail postfix. A prefix or postfix still allows the user to both authenticate and issue a target gesture in a single step. This approach can improve the authentication accuracy with introducing minimal extra effort for gesturing.

Our user authentication method requires a user to provide at least one example for each gesture in the target set. This requirement might be acceptable for 36 alphanumeric symbols. However, it is not feasible to a language with a large number of characters, e.g., Chinese characters. Future

[11] http://www.ti.com/lsds/ti/dsp/c5000_dsp/overview.page

work can explore the approach of clustering characters with a similar biometric profile such that such a requirement can be relaxed.

Our learned model for detecting gestures from accidental touches may not apply to another device with a different form factor. We conducted our feature analyses based on the data collected from Nexus 5 smartphones and some features are dependent of the specific form factor of the device (e.g., the bezel distance would be different on a larger device). This limitation would require device manufacturers to train a model for each device form factor.

Lastly, while our evaluation validates the accuracy performance and feasibility with Gesture On in an offline fashion, a user study with the deployed system is necessary to understand how such a system impacts the user's mobile experience. In the future, we want to deploy the system to users and iterate on the design of the interaction flow and UI to balance the efficiency and security.

CONCLUSION

We present Gesture On, a system that enables touchscreen gesture shortcuts from the standby mode. We discussed the design and implementation of two key components: gesture detection from accidental touches and user authentication based on a single gesture. Our experiments indicated that Gesture On demonstrated a useful approach for fast mobile access.

REFERENCES

1. Amini, S. and Li, Y. CrowdLearner: rapidly creating mobile recognizers using crowdsourcing. *Proc. UIST 2013*, ACM Press (2013), 163–172.
2. Appert, C. and Zhai, S. Using strokes as command shortcuts. *Proc. CHI 2009*, 2289–2298.
3. Böhmer, M., Hecht, B., Schöning, J., Krüger, A., and Bauer, G. Falling asleep with Angry Birds, Facebook and Kindle: a large scale study on mobile application usage. *Proc. MobileHCI 2011*, 47–56.
4. Feng, T., Liu, Z., Kwon, K.-A., Shi, W., Carbunar, B., Jiang, Y., and Nguyen, N. Continuous mobile authentication using touchscreen gestures. *2012 IEEE Conference on Technologies for Homeland Security (HST)*, IEEE (2012), 451–456.
5. Ferreira, D., Goncalves, J., Kostakos, V., Barkhuus, L., and Dey, A.K. Contextual experience sampling of mobile application micro-usage. *Proc. MobileHCI 2014*, ACM Press (2014), 91–100.
6. Hayashi, E., Das, S., Amini, S., Hong, J., and Oakley, I. CASA: context-aware scalable authentication. *Proceedings of the Ninth Symposium on Usable Privacy and Security - SOUPS '13*, Article No. 3.
7. Kane, S.K., Wobbrock, J.O., and Ladner, R.E. Usable gestures for blind people : understanding preference and performance. *Proc. CHI 2011*, 413–422.
8. Kennedy, P.R., Hall, T.G., and Hardy, D.A. Security token and method for wireless applications. Patent US6084968, 2000.
9. Li, Y. Protractor : a fast and accurate gesture recognizer. *Proc. CHI 2010*, ACM Press (2010), 2169–2172.
10. Li, Y. Gesture search: a tool for fast mobile data access. *Proc. UIST 2010*, ACM Press (2010), 87–96.
11. Lü, H., Fogarty, J., and Li, Y. Gesture Script: recognizing gestures and their structure using rendering scripts and interactively trained parts. *Proc. CHI 2014*, ACM Press (2014), 1685–1694.
12. Mark Hall, Eibe Frank, Geoffrey Holmes, Bernhard Pfahringer, Peter Reutemann, I.H.W. The WEKA Data Mining Software: An Update. *SIGKDD Explorations 11*, 1 (2009).
13. Mcgrath, W. and Li, Y. Detecting Tapping Motion on the Side of Mobile Devices By Probabilistically Combining Hand Postures. *Proc. UIST 2014*, 215–219.
14. Miluzzo, E., Varshavsky, A., Balakrishnan, S., and Choudhury, R.R. Tapprints: your finger taps have fingerprints. *Proc. MobiSys 2012*, 323–336.
15. Mochel, P. The sysfs filesystem. *Linux Symposium*, (2005), 313–326.
16. Ouyang, T. and Li, Y. Bootstrapping personal gesture shortcuts with the wisdom of the crowd and handwriting recognition. *Proc. CHI 2012*, 2895–2904.
17. Pirlo, G., Cuccovillo, V., Impedovo, D., and Mignone, P. On-line Signature Verification by Multi-Domain Classification. *Proceedings of International Conference on Frontiers in Handwriting Recognition (ICFHR 2014)*, IEEE (2014), 67–72.
18. Ruiz, J. and Li, Y. DoubleFlip: : a motion gesture delimiter for mobile interaction. *Proc. CHI 2011*, 2717–2720.
19. Schwarz, J., Xiao, R., Mankoff, J., Hudson, S.E., and Harrison, C. Probabilistic palm rejection using spatiotemporal touch features and iterative classification. *Proc. CHI 2014*, 2009–2012.
20. Shahzad, M., Liu, A.X., and Samuel, A. Secure unlocking of mobile touch screen devices by simple gestures. *Proc. MobiCom 2013*, 39–50.
21. Sherman, M., Clark, G., Yang, Y., Sugrim, S., Modig, A., Lindqvist, J., Oulasvirta, A., and Roos, T. User-generated free-form gestures for authentication. *Proc. MobiSys 2014*, 176–189.
22. Wobbrock, J.O., Wilson, A.D., and Li, Y. Gestures without libraries, toolkits or training: a $1 recognizer for user interface prototypes. *Proc. UIST 2007*, 159–168.

Optimizing Touchscreen Keyboards for Gesture Typing

Brian A. Smith[1,2*] **Xiaojun Bi**[2] **Shumin Zhai**[2]

[1]Columbia University
New York, NY, USA
brian@cs.columbia.edu

[2]Google Inc.
Mountain View, CA, USA
{xiaojunbi, zhai}@acm.org

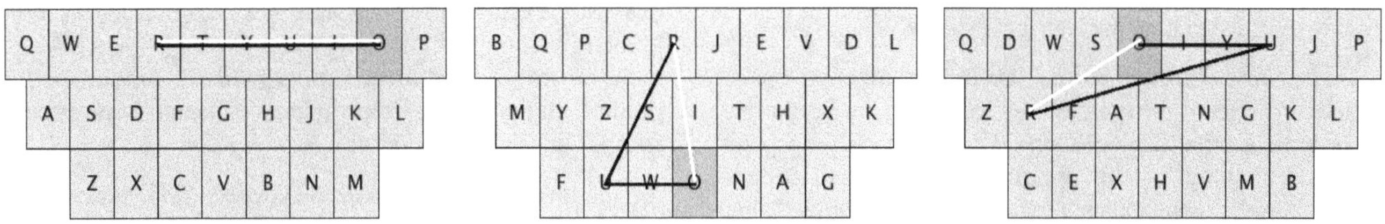

(a) Qwerty (b) GK-D (c) GK-T

Figure 1. Keyboards optimized for gesture typing. The 'o' key is shaded to mark the beginning of the word gestures for "or" (white) and "our" (black). (a) The Qwerty keyboard suffers from the problem of gesture ambiguity. Many pairs of words (such as "or" and "our" shown here) share the same gesture on Qwerty. (b) The GK-D keyboard ("Gesture Keyboard—Double optimized") is the best compromise for gesture clarity and gesture speed. Here, the gestures for "or" and "our" are noticeably different. (c) The GK-T keyboard ("Gesture Keyboard—Triple optimized") is the best compromise for gesture clarity, gesture speed, and Qwerty similarity. Again, the two gestures are noticeably different.

ABSTRACT
Despite its growing popularity, gesture typing suffers from a major problem not present in touch typing: gesture ambiguity on the Qwerty keyboard. By applying rigorous mathematical optimization methods, this paper systematically investigates the optimization space related to the accuracy, speed, and Qwerty similarity of a gesture typing keyboard. Our investigation shows that optimizing the layout for gesture clarity (a metric measuring how unique word gestures are on a keyboard) drastically improves the accuracy of gesture typing. Moreover, if we also accommodate gesture speed, or both gesture speed and Qwerty similarity, we can still reduce error rates by 52% and 37% over Qwerty, respectively. In addition to investigating the optimization space, this work contributes a set of optimized layouts such as GK-D and GK-T that can immediately benefit mobile device users.

Author Keywords
Gesture typing; touchscreen keyboard optimization; text entry; word-gesture keyboard; shape writing

ACM Classification Keywords
H.5.2. [Information interfaces and presentation]: User Interfaces—Input devices and strategies.

INTRODUCTION
Gesture typing has gained large-scale adoption on mobile devices since its conception in the early 2000's [24]. Today, gesture typing can be found on all major mobile computing platforms in products such as ShapeWriter, Swype, SwiftKey, SlideIT, TouchPal, and Google Keyboard. Compared to touch typing (tapping), gesture typing offers several advantages. It supports a gradual and seamless transition from visually guided tracing to recall-based gesturing, allows users to approximate words with gestures rather than tapping each key exactly, and mitigates one major problem plaguing regular touchscreen typing: the lack of tactile feedback.

Despite these benefits, gesture typing suffers from an inherent problem: highly ambiguous word gestures. Bi, Azenkot, Partridge, and Zhai [2] showed that the error rate for gesture typing is approximately 5–10% higher than for touch typing. This problem occurs because when gesture typing, the input finger must inevitably cross unintended letters before reaching the intended one. The Qwerty layout itself further exacerbates this problem. Because common vowels such as 'u,' 'i,' and 'o' are arranged together on Qwerty, many pairs of words (such as "or" and "our") have identical gestures, and many others (such as "but" and "bit") have very similar gestures. Figure 1(a) shows the gestures for "or" and "our"—their superstrings "for" and "four" also have identical gestures. In fact, our analysis over a 40,000-word lexicon showed that 6.4% of words have another word with an identical gesture on Qwerty.

Given Qwerty's obvious problems, rearranging the keys to make word gestures more distinct should reduce the error

CHI 2015, April 18–23, 2015, Seoul, Republic of Korea.
ACM 978-1-4503-3145-6/15/04.
http://dx.doi.org/10.1145/2702123.2702357

* This work was done while Brian Smith was an intern at Google Inc.

rate when gesture typing. However, a layout optimized for gesture clarity (distinctness) might increase the length of each gesture (reducing typing speed) or may be difficult for users to learn. Many questions arise when deciding whether or not to introduce a new layout for gesture typing. For example, if the layout is exclusively optimized for clarity, to what degree will it improve in accuracy over Qwerty? What is the relationship between gesture clarity and gesture typing speed? Can we design an optimized layout similar to Qwerty in order to ease the learning process?

In this paper, we explore the layout optimization space related to gesture typing by applying a rigorous mathematical optimization. Our research not only deepens the understanding of the optimization space of gesture typing, but also contributes a set of optimized layouts that significantly outperform Qwerty (in terms of both gesture clarity and speed) and can immediately benefit mobile device users.

RELATED WORK

Stroke-Based Virtual Keyboards

Cirrin [14] and Quikwriting [17] are the first virtual keyboards designed specifically for word-level unistroke text entry. In both of those keyboards, users trace gestures that alternate from the center of a radial layout to one or more zones around the center (representing characters), with one articulation per character. However, since these gestures are completely determined by character layout without statistical pattern recognition, the letter layout has to be one-dimensional and most word-gestures defined on these layouts are very complex.

SHARK [24] and SHARK^2 [11] introduced gesture typing (also known as shape writing and the word-gesture keyboard paradigm) as we know it today. In these systems, users gesture words by swiping from letter to letter on a virtual Qwerty keyboard. The word gestures are much simpler than they are on Cirrin and Quikwriting, but since SHARK and SHARK^2 have no central "dead zone" for strokes to cross from character to character (and users must stroke over other characters instead), they suffer from an inherent ambiguity between word gestures (see Figure 1(a)). Even with sophisticated models for predicting users' intended words, Bi et al. [2] found that the error rate from gesture typing is 5–10% higher than that from touch typing.

Keyboard Layout Optimization

As has been widely published [18, 19, 21], Qwerty was designed to reduce jamming in mechanical typewriters by placing common digraphs (consecutive letter pairs) on opposite sides of the keyboard. Though this works well for two-handed or two-finger typing, researchers have long acknowledged that this is unsuitable for one-finger typing [9, 12]. There have been many proposed optimized keyboard layouts over the years for both bimanual [15] and unimanual typing [5, 6, 8, 13, 18, 20, 21]. Most of these layouts were optimized for touch typing, but the Square OSK layout [18] was optimized for stroking.

We should emphasize, however, that existing optimized layouts are predominantly optimized for typing speed (essentially minimizing finger travel distance), and that optimizing for word gesture clarity (as we optimize for along with gesture typing speed and Qwerty similarity) is an entirely different, and often conflicting, problem. As an example, the Dvorak layout arranges common letters in the home row to make bimanual typing faster [19], but this also makes word gestures more similar (and less unique, hurting gesture clarity) since many paths between keys become straight lines on the home row.

As another example, the ATOMIK [21] and Square ATOMIK [23] keyboards were optimized for speed with a bias for having keys appear in alphabetical order. Although these keyboards were tuned so that the gestures for 17 common words were short and memorable, they were not specifically optimized for gesture clarity. In fact, these keyboards predate gesture typing altogether. Other examples include Quasi-Qwerty [6], which was optimized for speed and familiarity, and the Sath keyboards [8], which were optimized for those metrics plus tap interpretation clarity for improved spell checking.

Few optimized layouts have gained widespread adoption. This is likely due to both learnability and the complexity of tapping input: users may type with one, two, or even ten fingers, and a good layout must accommodate each. However, the increasing popularity of gesture typing may offer a better chance at introducing new layouts since most users gesture words with one finger and our optimized layouts significantly improve both accuracy and speed over Qwerty.

OPTIMIZATION METRICS

Gesture Clarity

The gesture clarity metric is the most important metric in our optimization. The purpose of this metric is to measure how unique the word gestures on a keyboard layout are. We based the metric on the location channel in SHARK^2 [11] and represent each word's gesture as its *ideal trace,* the polyline connecting the key centers of the word's letters. We define the *nearest neighbor* of a word w to be the word whose ideal trace is closest to w's ideal trace. This is the word that is most likely to be confused with w when gesture typing, independent from the language model. The closer a word is to its nearest neighbor, the more likely its gesture will be misrecognized. The gesture clarity metric score for a given keyboard layout is simply the average distance (weighted by words' frequencies) between each word and its nearest neighbor on that keyboard layout:

$$\text{Clarity} = \sum_{w \in L} f_w \, d_w, \tag{1}$$

$$\text{where } d_w = \min_{x \in L - \{w\}} d(w, x) \text{ and } \sum_{w \in L} f_w = 1.$$

L is a 40,000-word lexicon, f_w is the frequency of w, and d_w is the distance between w and its nearest neighbor. We compute the distance between two ideal traces w and x via *proportional shape matching*. Each gesture is sampled into N equidistant points, and the distance is simply the average of the distance between corresponding points:

$$d(w, x) = \frac{1}{N} \sum_{i=1}^{N} \|w_i - x_i\|_2 \qquad (2)$$

Time Complexity Refinements

Since the gesture clarity metric compares the gestures of every pair of words to find each word's nearest neighbor, its time complexity is $\Theta(N \cdot |L|^2)$. Here, L is the number of words in the lexicon and N is the number of sample points in each word gesture. Its quadratic time complexity with respect to L stands in stark contrast to the time complexities of earlier optimization metrics (which are exclusively linear with respect to L), making optimization using it intractable. For our 40,000-word lexicon, there are nearly 800 million pairs of word gestures to compare for each keyboard layout that we examine during the optimization process.

To make the metric more tractable, we made two key algorithmic refinements. First, when searching for the nearest neighbor for each word, we only considered prospective neighbors that started and ended with characters that were located within one key diagonal of the word's starting and ending character, respectively. This is similar to the initial template-pruning step employed in SHARK[2] [11], where the distance threshold in this case is the diagonal length of a key. Second, we used a small number of gesture sample points N to represent each word's gesture. If N were too large, the computation would be very expensive. If N were too small, word gestures (especially longer ones) might not be represented properly, leading to incorrectly chosen nearest neighbors.

In order to see how small we could make N without affecting the integrity of our results, we performed a small experiment. First, we found each word's nearest neighbor on Qwerty using very fine sampling (N = 100). Then, we repeated this step for smaller values of N down to N = 20 and counted the number of nearest neighbors that were identical to the N = 100 case. Figure 2 shows the results. When the number of sample points is reduced to 40, 96.9% of the nearest neighbors are the same as they were before. We used this value for N in our algorithm.

Gesture Speed

The gesture speed metric estimates how quickly users can gesture type on a keyboard layout. We based this metric on the CLC model by Cao and Zhai [7]. The model (which stands for "curves, line segments, and corners") stems from

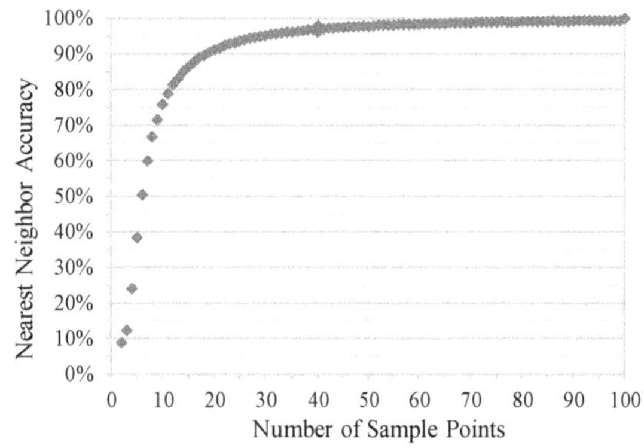

Figure 2. Word gesture neighbor sensitivity. The nearest neighbor that we find for a word depends on how finely the word gestures are sampled. Here, we show the percentage of nearest neighbors that are the same as when 100 sample points are used. The red dot signifies 40 points, the amount we used.

human motor control theory, and was designed to predict the amount of time it takes for a person to make an arbitrary pen stroke gesture. To do this, the model partitions the gesture into segments, where each segment is a curve (with a constant radius of curvature), a straight line, or a corner (whose interior angle does not need to be 90°). The time that it takes for a person to gesture each type of segment is modeled with a different function. For line segments, the time is modeled with a power function that echoes how people tend to gesture faster with longer lines:

$$T(\overline{AB}) = m \cdot (\|\overline{AB}\|_2)^n. \qquad (3)$$

Here, $\overline{AB}$ is a line segment, the output T is in milliseconds, $\|\overline{AB}\|_2$ is the length of $\overline{AB}$ in millimeters, and both m and n are constants (found to be 68.8 and 0.469 respectively in Cao and Zhai's original formulation).

A polyline gesture is simply a collection of individual line segments. The time to complete this type of gesture is modeled as simply the sum of the individual line segments' functions:

$$T(P) = \sum_{\overline{AB} \in P} T(\overline{AB}), \qquad (4)$$

where P is the polyline and $\overline{AB}$ is a segment in the polyline. Although Cao and Zhai found that the angles between polyline segments (that is, of a polyline's corners) have an effect on gesture entry time, the magnitude of the effect was small: less than 40 ms per corner compared to 200–700 ms per segment. Hence, the model uses corners to delineate segments but omits their 40 ms contribution.

As with the gesture clarity metric, each word in the lexicon is represented as its ideal trace. To help compute the metric, we store a table of the weighted number of occurrences of each bigram in our lexicon. The weighted number of occurrences $o(i—j)$ of a bigram $i—j$ (for letters i and j) is calculated as follows:

$$o(i\text{—}j) = \sum_{w \in L} f_w \cdot (\#\text{ occurrences of } i\text{—}j \text{ in } w) \quad (5)$$

Here, L is the lexicon, w is a word in the lexicon, and f_w is the frequency of word w in L. Each bigram is represented by a different line segment in the CLC model. Hence, to estimate G, the average time it takes to complete a word gesture, we calculate the following:

$$G = \sum_{i,j \in \alpha} o(i\text{—}j) \cdot T(\overline{K_i K_j}) \quad (6)$$

Here, i and j are both letters in alphabet α, the set of lowercase letters from 'a' to 'z.' K_i and K_j are the key centers of the i and j keys, respectively, $\overline{K_i K_j}$ is the line segment connecting the key centers, and the function T is defined in Equation 3. Hence, G is measured in milliseconds.

The last step is to convert the gesture duration G into words per minute (WPM), a measure of typing speed. Doing so gives us our gesture speed metric score:

$$\text{Speed} = \frac{60{,}000}{G} \quad (7)$$

60,000 represents the number of milliseconds in one minute. When calculating the gesture typing speed of a keyboard layout, we do not consider the effects of the space bar or capitalization (and the Shift key). One of the key contributions of gesture typing is the fact that spaces are automatically added between word gestures, eliminating the need for 1 in approximately every 5.7 characters typed [24]. Moreover, most of today's gesture-typing systems apply capitalization and diacritics automatically.

We should also note that, because the CLC model omits the cost of gesturing corners and the cost of traveling from the end of one gesture to the beginning of the next, the calculated speeds generally overestimate the speeds at which users would actually type. Rick [18] proposed an alternative to the CLC model that is also based on Fitts's law, and although we ultimately chose to use the CLC model for our metric, we implemented Rick's model (without key taps for single-character words) to compare the models' behaviors. We found that Rick's model consistently output lower speed estimates than the CLC model, but that they both followed the same overall trend. More specifically, the mean (std. dev.) ratio between Rick's model's predicted speeds and the CLC model's predicted speeds for our final set of optimized layouts is 0.310 (0.004). After normalizing the metrics as described on the next page, the mean (std. dev.) ratio becomes 0.995 (0.016).

Qwerty Similarity

As has been thoroughly studied [18, 19, 21], the key obstacle to the widespread adoption of optimized layouts is the arduous process of learning the new layouts. The Qwerty similarity metric measures how similar a given keyboard layout is to Qwerty. By making a new layout more similar to Qwerty (and hence less alien to longtime users of Qwerty), we hope to bridge the gap between the short-term frustration of learning the new layout and the long-term benefits that the layout provides.

The metric is based on the constraint that Bi, Smith, and Zhai [6] used when creating the Quasi-Qwerty layout. In that optimization (which was for typing speed only), keys were not allowed to move more than one slot away from their Qwerty locations. Dunlop and Levine [8] later relaxed this constraint in their multi-objective keyboard optimization by using the total squared Euclidean distance between keys' positions and their Qwerty locations instead. Since a keyboard layout is essentially a grid of keys, we use the total Manhattan distance between keys' positions and their Qwerty locations to measure Qwerty similarity. Like Dunlop and Levine's metric, this allows more freedom than the hard constraint used by Quasi-Qwerty. However, unlike Dunlop and Levine's metric, individual keys are not punished so severely if they move far from their Qwerty locations. This allows us to consider layouts in which a few keys move very far from their Qwerty locations.

The Qwerty similarity metric for a given keyboard layout is computed as follows:

$$\text{Similarity} = \sum_{i \in \alpha} \left(\left| k_{i_x} - q_{i_x} \right| + \left| k_{i_y} - q_{i_y} \right| \right) \quad (8)$$

where i is a letter in alphabet α, the set of lowercase letters from 'a' to 'z,' and k_{i_x} and q_{i_x} are the x-indices of the i key on the given keyboard layout and Qwerty, respectively. Unlike K_i and K_j in Equation 6, which are points with units of millimeters, k_i and q_i are unit-less ordered pairs of integers that represent the 2D index of key i's slot in the keyboard grid. In most of today's touchscreen keyboard layouts, the second and third rows are offset from the first row by half of a key width. Hence, in order to properly calculate the Manhattan distance for this metric, we treat the second and third rows as if they are shifted to the left by another half of a key width so that the second row is left-aligned with the first row. The resulting representation of keyboard layouts is actually identical to the one used for creating Quasi-Qwerty [6]. The Qwerty similarity metric is the only one that uses this modified keyboard representation.

OPTIMIZATION PROCEDURE

We frame the problem of designing a touchscreen keyboard for gesture typing as a multi-objective optimization, where the three objectives are improving (1) gesture clarity, (2) gesture speed, and (3) Qwerty similarity. There are multiple ways of judging how well a layout meets these objectives. One way is to create a simple objective function that somehow combines the objectives' associated metric scores (for example, by summing the scores in a linear combination). However, such an approach would force us to decide how much each metric should count for in deriving a single optimal layout, when in fact we are more interested in understanding the behavior of each of the metrics and the inherent tradeoffs between them.

As a result, although we still employ a simple objective function as part of our optimization's second phase, we use another approach called Pareto optimization for the optimization at large. Pareto optimization has recently been used to optimize both keyboard layouts [5] and keyboard algorithms [4]. In this approach, we calculate an optimal set of layouts called a *Pareto optimal set* or a *Pareto front*. Each layout in the set is *Pareto optimal*, which means that none of its metric scores can be improved without hurting the other scores. If a layout is not Pareto optimal, then it is *dominated*, which means that there exists a Pareto optimal layout that is better than it with respect to at least one metric and no worse than it with respect to the others. By calculating the Pareto optimal set of keyboard layouts rather than a single keyboard layout, we can analyze the tradeoffs inherent in choosing a keyboard layout and give researchers the freedom to choose one that best meets their constraints.

Our optimization procedure is composed of three phases, described in detail in the subsections below.

Phase 1: Metric Normalization

In the first phase, we perform a series of optimizations for each metric individually to estimate the minimum and maximum possible raw values for each metric. We then normalize each of the metric's scores in a linear fashion so that the worst possible score is mapped to 0.0 and the best possible score is mapped to 1.0. Normalizing the scores allows us to weight the metrics appropriately in Phase 2.

We use local neighborhood search to perform the optimizations. In order to more reliably find the global extrema instead of local extrema, we incorporate a simulated annealing process similar to the Metropolis random walk algorithm [10, 20]). Each optimization starts with a random keyboard layout using the same footprint as Qwerty and runs for 2,000 iterations. At each iteration, we swap the locations of two randomly chosen keys in the current layout to create a new candidate layout. If the new layout is better than the current layout, we keep the new layout with 100% probability. Otherwise, we only keep the new layout with a probability specified by a user-controlled "temperature." Higher temperatures increase this probability, and allow us to escape from local extrema.

In total, we performed 10–30 optimizations for each metric. We found that the range for the raw gesture typing clarity metric scores was [0.256 key widths, 0.533 key widths], that the range for the raw gesture typing speed metric scores was [50.601 WPM, 77.929 WPM], and that the range for the raw Qwerty similarity metric scores was [0, 148]. Qwerty's raw scores for the three metrics are 2.390 mm, 62.652 WPM, and 0, respectively.

Phase 2: Pareto Front Initialization

In this phase, we generate an initial Pareto front of keyboard layouts by performing even more local neighborhood searches. The searches are identical to the ones we perform in Phase 1, except this time we seek to maximize the score from linear combinations of all three metric scores. We use 22 different weightings for the linear combinations and perform roughly 15 full 2000-iteration local neighborhood searches for each weighting. The purpose is to ensure that the Pareto front includes a broad range of Pareto optimal keyboard layouts.

The Pareto front starts out empty at the very beginning of this phase, but we update it with each new candidate keyboard layout that we encounter during the searches (at each iteration of each search). To update the front, we compare the candidate layout with the layouts already on the front. Then, we add the candidate layout to the front if it is Pareto optimal (possibly displacing layouts already on the front that are now dominated by the candidate layout). The candidate layout is added whether it is ultimately kept in the particular local neighborhood search or not. This approach is similar to the one that Bi et al. [4] used to optimize keyboard correction and completion algorithms.

Phase 3: Pareto Front Expansion

In the last phase, we perform roughly 200 passes over the Pareto front to help "fill out" the front by finding Pareto optimal layouts that are similar to those already on the front. In each pass, we swap two keys in each layout on the front to generate a set of candidate layouts, then update the front with any candidate layouts that are Pareto optimal. This phase is similar to the optimization used by Dunlop and Levine [8]. However, by including Phase 2, we can ensure that all possible solutions are reachable without the need to swap more than two keys at a time.

Optimization Parameters

We based our optimization's keyboard representation on dimensions of the Nexus 5 [16] Android keyboard. Since most of today's touchscreen keyboards have very similar profiles, our results should be applicable to any touchscreen keyboard. Each key is represented by its entire touch-sensitive area (with boundaries placed between the center points of neighboring keys) and is 109 × 165 px (6.22 × 9.42 mm) in size.

Our lexicon consists of 40,000 words. Before starting the optimization, we converted words with diacritics to their Anglicized forms ("naïve" to "naive," for example), removed all punctuation marks from words (such as "can't"), and made all words completely lowercase. Since gesture typing systems automatically handle diacritics, capitalization, and punctuation marks within words, this should not hurt the integrity of our optimization.

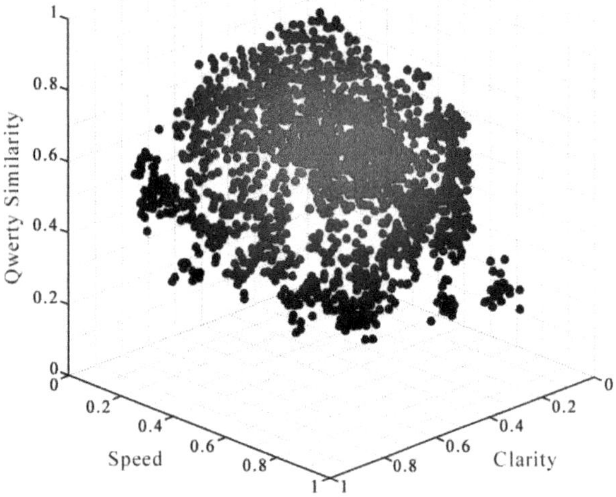

Figure 3. 3D Pareto front. The keyboard layouts with lighter colors are farther from the origin.

Optimization Runtime

Due to the complexity and scope of our work, it took four machines (with 32 threads apiece) running continuously over the course of nearly three weeks to obtain the results presented below.

OPTIMIZED KEYBOARD LAYOUTS

Figure 3 shows the final Pareto front of keyboard layouts optimized for gesture typing. Overall, the front is composed of 1,725 keyboard layouts chosen from the 900,000+ candidate layouts that we examined in all. No single layout on the front is better than all of the others—each layout is better than the others in some way, and the tradeoffs that are inherent in choosing a suitable layout from the front are reflected in the front's convex shape.

More specifically, the front can be viewed as a three-dimensional design space of performance goals that one can choose from for different usage scenarios. Layouts with high gesture clarity scores, gesture speed scores, and Qwerty similarity scores are more apt to exhibit lower error rates, expert-level gesture entry times, and initial gesture entry times (respectively) than those with low scores. However, since each layout on the front represents a compromise between these three goals, the choice of layout for a particular user or usage scenario depends on the relative importance of each goal. For example, a fast but less accurate user may prefer a layout biased towards clarity, while a user who gesture types very accurately may prefer a layout biased toward speed. Nevertheless, if we know nothing about users' preferences or wish to choose a layout that can best accommodate a wide variety of preferences, it is reasonable to use one that is in the middle of the convex surface (serving each goal on a roughly equal basis) as Dunlop and Levine did [8].

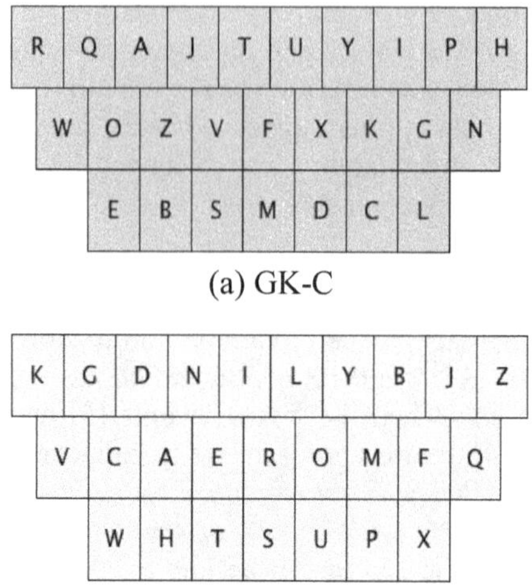

(b) GK-S

Figure 4. Single-optimized keyboard layouts. (a) Our GK-C keyboard ("Gesture Keyboard—Clarity") is optimized for gesture typing clarity only. (b) Our GK-S keyboard ("Gesture Keyboard—Speed") is optimized for gesture typing speed only.

We will now highlight layouts optimized for each of the three metrics as well as layouts that serve roughly equal combinations of metrics. These layouts may serve as useful references to researchers and designers, and will later (in the user study) help us test the effectiveness of our optimization and its associated metrics.

Single-Optimized Keyboard Layouts

Figure 4(a) shows GK-C ("Gesture Keyboard—Clarity"), the layout optimized exclusively for gesture typing clarity. Figure 4(b) shows GK-S, which was optimized exclusively for speed. The layout optimized for Qwerty similarity is simply Qwerty itself, and is shown in Figure 1(a).

Double-Optimized Keyboard Layout

Figure 1(b) shows GK-D (where the 'D' stands for "double-optimized"). This keyboard offers a roughly equal compromise between gesture typing clarity and gesture typing speed without regard to learnability (Qwerty similarity). To find this layout, we projected the three-dimensional Pareto front onto the clarity–speed plane to derive a 2D Pareto front between clarity and speed, then chose the layout on the 2D front that was closest to the 45° line. Figure 5 shows the 2D Pareto front and GK-D.

Triple-Optimized Keyboard Layout

Figure 1(c) shows GK-T, where the 'T' stands for "triple optimized." This keyboard offers a roughly equal compromise between all three metrics: gesture typing clarity, gesture typing speed, and Qwerty similarity. It is the one on the three-dimensional Pareto front that is closest to the 45° line through the space. As Figure 5 illustrates, it is possible to accommodate the extra dimension of Qwerty similarity without a big sacrifice to clarity and speed.

Layout	Gesture Typing Clarity		Gesture Typing Speed		Qwerty Similarity	
	Normalized	Raw (key widths)	Normalized	Raw (WPM)	Normalized	Raw (key slots)
Qwerty	0.489	0.391	0.441	62.653	1.000	0
Sath Trapezoidal [8]	0.568	0.413	0.704	69.843	0.730	40
GK-C	1.038	0.543	0.317	59.256	0.554	66
GK-S	0.283	0.334	1.000	77.940	0.311	102
GK-D	0.743	0.462	0.739	70.793	0.324	100
GK-T	0.709	0.452	0.704	69.830	0.716	42
Square ATOMIK [21]	0.362	0.356	0.878	74.591	N/A	N/A
Square OSK [18]	0.381	0.361	0.979	77.358	N/A	N/A

Table 1. Keyboard metric score comparison. Shaded rows signify previous layouts.

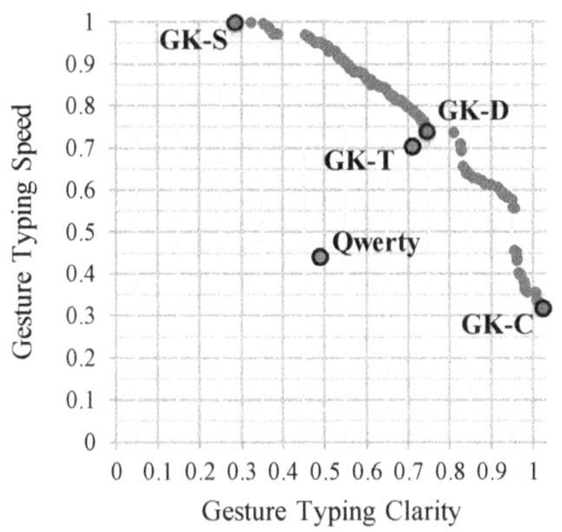

Figure 5. 2D Pareto front for gesture typing clarity and gesture typing speed. GK-D, our double-optimized layout, is the point on the front nearest the 45° line. Note that Qwerty is far worse in both dimensions than GK-D, and that GK-T (which accommodates yet another dimension) is only slightly worse on these two dimensions than GK-D.

Discussion
Table 1 shows the metric scores for our optimized layouts as well as previous optimized layouts. Together, these optimized layouts give us a good understanding of what is possible in the optimization space for gesture typing.

First, we can improve gesture clarity by 38.8% by optimizing for clarity alone: GK-C's raw metric score is 0.543 key widths while Qwerty's is 0.391 key widths. Likewise, we also see that we can improve gesture speed by 24.4% by optimizing for speed alone (resulting in GK-S).

Second, the 2D Pareto front for gesture clarity and gesture speed (Figure 5) shows that these two metrics conflict with each other. It forms a roughly -45° line, indicating that optimizing for one leads to the decrease in the other. As GK-C and GK-S illustrate, the clarity metric tends to arrange common letters far apart in a radial fashion while the speed metric clusters common letters close together.

However, despite the conflict, it is possible to arrange common letters close together while keeping word gestures relatively distinct, achieving large improvements in both clarity and speed. In GK-D (our double-optimized keyboard), letters in common n-grams such as "*the*," "*and*," and "*ing*" are arranged together while the n-grams themselves are spaced apart. This arrangement offers a 17.9% improvement in gesture clarity and a 13.0% improvement in gesture speed over Qwerty.

Third, accommodating Qwerty similarity (as GK-T does) does little harm to gesture clarity or gesture speed. GK-T's gesture clarity is only 0.01 key widths lower than GK-D's, and GK-T's predicted speed is only 1 WPM lower than GK-D's. Meanwhile, GK-T's Manhattan distance from Qwerty is just 42 key slots, while GK-D's is 102 key slots.

Comparison with Previous Optimized Layouts
The key difference between our proposed keyboard layouts and previous optimized layouts is that our layouts are optimized for multiple gesture typing factors while previous layouts are predominantly optimized for tapping speed. As Table 1 shows, previous layouts such as Sath Trapezoidal [8], Square ATOMIK [23], and Square OSK [18] have high gesture speed scores but low gesture clarity scores.

USER STUDY
Since the main focus of this work is to computationally discover the optimization space for gesture typing, the conclusions that we have made so far are based on theoretical metrics. Of the three metrics that we established, only one (gesture speed) is based on a model that directly predicts its respective performance goal (in this case, words per minute). The others, gesture clarity and Qwerty similarity, do not directly measure their performance goals (error rate and learnability, respectively). Hence, we performed an empirical study to give us a sense of how the metric scores correspond to real performance and whether the optimization itself is effective.

Experimental Setup
In the study, participants gesture typed a set of 22 words with each keyboard layout using a Nexus 5 [16] smartphone in portrait mode. As in Bi et al. [5], participants had to gesture each word seven times in succession. We instructed

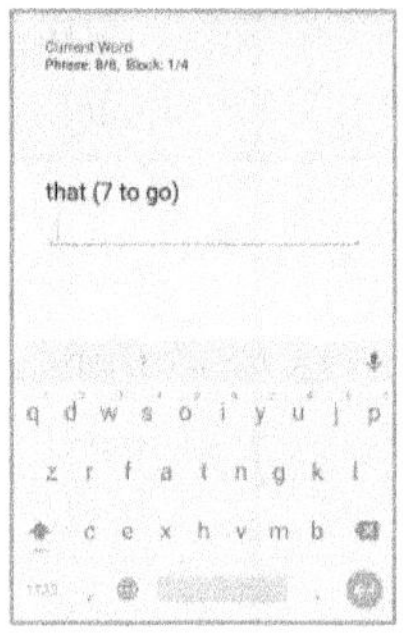

Figure 6. User study application. The layout shown is GK-T.

the participants to gesture as quickly as possible and ignore any errors, which, for us, achieved two goals. First, it allowed us to stress test the keyboard's gesture decoder by providing it very sloppy gestures (the resulting data is also more differentiable in evaluating accuracy). Second, it simulated a type of expert input behavior: entering words first and coming back to fix mistakes later.

Our study was a within-subject design that tested three keyboard layouts: Qwerty (our baseline), GK-D (the roughly equal compromise for clarity and speed only), and GK-T (the roughly equal compromise for clarity, speed, and Qwerty similarity). To conduct the experiment, we created Android implementations of GK-D and GK-T based on the Android [1] keyboard, and developed an Android application (Figure 6) to collect users' gesture typing data.

All participants started with Qwerty but used the other two layouts in alternating order. The first three words served as a warm-up phase to familiarize participants with the task (we did not collect their data), and the other 19 words are from the list proposed by Zhai and Kristensson [22]: "*the and you that is in of know not they get have were are bit quick fox jumps lazy*." These words cover all letters of the English alphabet and approximate both letter frequencies and digraph frequencies in English. They were divided into groups of four or five with short breaks in between.

To measure gesture typing accuracy, we compare each committed word with the respective requested word using a strict binary string equality comparison. The committed word is the word that appears after the participant lifts his or her finger from the screen and the keyboard algorithm applies any word corrections that it sees fit. To measure gesture entry times, we recorded either (1) the length of time from when a word was presented on the screen to when the word was committed (for the first repetition of a word), or (2) the length of time between when the last word was committed to when the current word is committed (for subsequent repetitions of a word).

The entry times for the first repetitions of words offer a rough (but by no means perfect) perspective of our keyboards' learnability, while the entry times for latter repetitions of the word are a rough estimate of expert-level entry times. The rationale for the latter is that by repeating the same word in a row, users will reach a stage where the

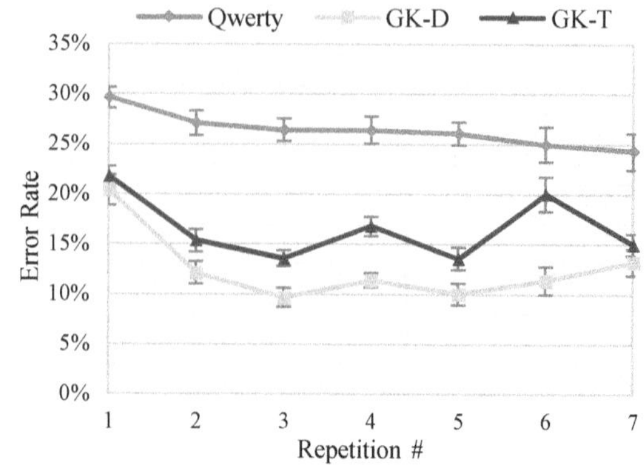

Figure 7. Error rates across 14 participants for Qwerty, GK-D, and GK-T. GK-D's and GK-T's average error rate is 52% and 31% less than Qwerty's, respectively. Error bars indicate standard errors.

input behavior is mostly governed by motor control ability, which reflects expert input behavior. However, this is only a limited proxy for the study of the complex learning process and expert-level typing performance at scale, which may require a longitudinal logging study of real keyboard use, notwithstanding privacy and other challenges associated with such methods.

A total of 14 volunteers (9 female, 5 male) participated in the experiment. 3 were age 18–25, 9 were 26–35, and 2 were 36–45. 8 of them primarily use Android smartphones and the rest iPhones. 13 were at least somewhat familiar with gesture typing, and 5 were at least somewhat familiar with alternative keyboard layouts. All of them were right-handed. Each experiment lasted less than an hour.

Experimental Results

Error Rate

Figure 7 shows participants' overall error rates with each layout and how those error rates changed as participants made successive repetitions of each word. The mean (std. dev.) error rate for Qwerty, GK-D, and GK-T were 26.4% (7.2%), 12.6% (6.6%), and 16.6% (6.2%), respectively. This means that the error rates for GK-D and GK-T were 52% and 37% less than Qwerty, respectively. The keyboard layout has a significant main effect on the overall error rate ($F_{2,26} = 35.46$, $p < 0.001$). Pairwise mean comparison over all repetitions showed that the differences were significant ($p < 0.01$) for every pair of keyboards except GK-D vs. GK-T. For Repetitions 2–6, however, the difference is significant ($p < 0.01$) for every pair of keyboards.

Initial Gesture Entry Time

Figure 8 shows how long, on average, it took participants to gesture words per repetition × layout. We noticed that participants often planned out their gestures in the first repetition, but resorted to motor memory in later repetitions. The mean (std. dev.) initial entry time was 2,655 ms (502 ms), 5,870 ms (1,190 ms), and 5,468 ms (1,140 ms) for Qwerty, GK-D, and GK-T, respectively. The keyboard

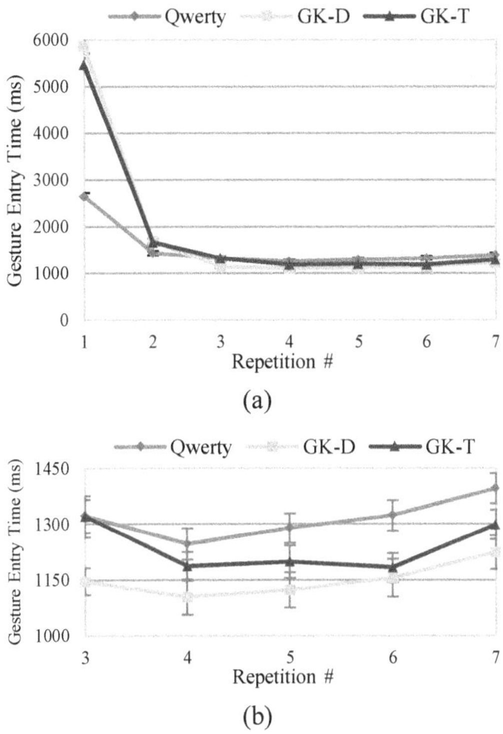

Figure 8. Gesture entry times across 14 participants for Qwerty, GK-D, and GK-T. Error bars indicate standard errors. (a) The initial entry time (Repetition 1) using GK-D and GK-T is over twice as long as it is using Qwerty. (b) For Repetitions 3–7 (approximating expert usage), the average entry time for GK-D and GK-T are 12.5% and 6.0% faster (respectively) than they are for Qwerty.

layout has a significant main effect on the initial entry time ($F_{2,26}$ = 75.26, $p < 0.001$). Pairwise mean comparison showed that the differences were significant ($p < 0.01$) for each pair of keyboards except GK-D vs. GK-T.

Expert-Level Gesture Entry Time

Figure 8(b) shows the expert-level entry time (Repetitions 3–7) in detail. The mean (std. dev.) entry time in this case is 1,315 ms (300 ms) for Qwerty, 1,150 ms (333 ms) for GK-D, and 1,237 ms (310 ms) for GK-T. The keyboard layout has a significant main effect on the expert-level entry time ($F_{2,26}$ = 12.46, $p < 0.001$). The expert-level entry time for GK-D and GK-T is 12.5% and 6.0% faster than that for Qwerty. Pairwise mean comparison showed the differences were significant ($p < 0.01$) for each pair of keyboards except GK-D vs. GK-T.

Discussion

The results from the user study lead to several findings, although we stress (as described earlier) that they are limited by the fact that our experiment was conducted in a single session. First, keyboards optimized for gesture clarity are more accurate than those without. The error rates for GK-D and GK-T are 52% and 37% less than Qwerty, respectively. Second, including both gesture typing clarity and gesture typing speed in the optimization process results in layouts that outperform Qwerty in terms of both accuracy and expert typing speed. Both GK-D and GK-T significantly outperform Qwerty in both of these metrics. Third, considering the Qwerty similarity metric has only minor effects on accuracy and speed. The differences we observed between the expert-level entry times for GK-D and GK-T were not statistically significant. Finally, the Qwerty similarity metric is not very effective in improving learnability. Though the mean initial entry time for GK-T was lower than that of GK-D, we did not observe a statistically significant difference between the two. This is likely due to the relative leniency of the Qwerty similarity metric compared to Quasi-Qwerty's hard constraint [6] and Dunlop and Levine's squared distance metric [8].

The findings also give us a better sense of how a layout's gesture clarity and Qwerty similarity scores correspond to real performance (recall that the gesture speed scores are based on an empirically derived model). For example, the gesture clarity score increase from 0.489 in Qwerty to 0.743 in GK-D (an increase by 0.254—see Table 1) corresponds to a decrease in the mean error rate from 26.4% to 12.6%. Yet, the Qwerty similarity score increase from 0.324 to 0.716 does not improve learnability as we have defined it, while the increase from 0.716 to 1.000 drastically does.

Still, we do not know the exact relationship between these two metrics' scores and the corresponding real-world performance measures. Conversely, the problem of finding metrics that empirically model gesture typing error rate and keyboard learnability remains to be solved. In the case of learnability, Quasi-Qwerty's constraint improves it [6] but cannot be used as a continuous model, and squared distance has not yet been shown to model it in its various degrees. Determining those relationships requires empirically testing many more layouts (using a variety of values for each metric score), and remains promising future work.

CONCLUSION

The present work, for the first time, defines a multidimensional optimization space for gesture typing (comprising gesture clarity, gesture speed, and Qwerty similarity) and systematically explores that space. In the process, we contribute a set of optimized layouts such as GK-D (optimized for both gesture clarity and gesture speed) and GK-T (optimized for gesture clarity, gesture speed, and Qwerty similarity) that can immediately benefit users. Though limited, our empirical study of these layouts led to the following findings.

First, optimizing the layouts for gesture clarity drastically improves gesture typing accuracy. By incorporating gesture clarity as an optimization dimension, GK-D and GK-T reduced error rates by 52% and 37% over Qwerty, respectively. Second, gesture clarity and gesture speed conflict with each other, but despite the conflict, incorporating both in the optimization process leads to superior performance over Qwerty with respect to both metrics. GK-D and GK-T, for example, improved expert-level entry times by 12.5% and 6.0% over Qwerty, respectively. Third, Qwerty similarity as we have defined it has only a minor conflict with gesture clarity and gesture speed, but is not effective in improving learnability.

FUTURE WORK

Although the nature, size, and complexity of this work have surpassed its precedents in the literature [6, 8, 12, 18], many questions beyond the scope of this work require further research. These include further, larger, and longitudinal empirical studies of the multiple optimality dimensions. Further empirical investigation may redefine some or all of the optimality dimensions identified in this work in order to advance the gesture typing paradigm toward new shorthand writing systems that tolerate user errors, require minimal visual attention and motor effort, and remain easy to learn.

ACKNOWLEDGEMENTS

We would like to thank Kurt Partridge, other colleagues at Google, and the CHI reviewers for their valuable insights and contributions to this work.

REFERENCES

1. Android Developers. https://source.android.com.
2. Bi, X., Azenkot, S., Partridge, K., and Zhai, S. Octopus: evaluating touchscreen keyboard correction and recognition algorithms via "remulation." In *Proc. CHI 2013*, ACM Press (2013), 543–552.
3. Bi, X., Chelba, C., Ouyang, T., Partridge, K., and Zhai, S. Bimanual gesture keyboard. In *Proc. UIST 2012*, ACM Press (2012), 137–146.
4. Bi, X., Ouyang, T., and Zhai, S. Both complete and correct? Multiobjective optimization of a touchscreen keyboard. In *Proc. CHI 2014*, ACM Press (2014), 2297–2306.
5. Bi, X., Smith, B.A., and Zhai, S. Multilingual touchscreen keyboard design and optimization. *Human–Computer Interaction 27*, 4 (2012), 352–382.
6. Bi, X., Smith, B.A., and Zhai, S. Quasi-Qwerty soft keyboard optimization. In *Proc. CHI 2010*, ACM Press (2010), 283–286.
7. Cao, X. and Zhai, S. Modeling human performance of pen stroke gestures. In *Proc. CHI 2007*, ACM Press (2007), 1495–1504.
8. Dunlop, M.D. and Levine, J. Multidimensional Pareto optimization of touchscreen keyboards for speed, familiarity, and improved spell checking. In *Proc. CHI 2012*, ACM Press (2012), 2669–2678.
9. Getschow, C.O., Rosen, M.J., and Goodenough-Trepagnier, C. A systematic approach to design a minimum distance alphabetical keyboard. In *Proc. RESNA 1986*, RESNA (1986), 396–398.
10. Hastings, W.K. Monte Carlo sampling methods using Markov chains and their applications. In *Biometrika 57*, 1 (1970), 97–109.
11. Kristensson, P.O. and Zhai, S. SHARK^2: a large vocabulary shorthand writing system for pen-based computers. In *Proc. UIST 2004*, ACM Press (2004), 43–52.
12. Lewis, J.R., Kennedy, P.J., and LaLomia, M.J. Development of a digram-based typing key layout for single finger/stylus input. In *Proc. Hum. Fact. Ergon. Soc. 1999*, Sage Publications (1999), 415–419.
13. MacKensie, I.S. and Zhang, S. The design and evaluation of a high-performance soft keyboard. In *Proc. CHI 1999*, ACM Press (1999), 25–31.
14. Mankoff, J. and Abowd, G.D. Cirrin: a word-level unistroke keyboard for pen input. In *Proc. UIST 1998*, ACM Press (1998), 213–214.
15. Oulasvirta, A., Reichel, A., Li, W., Zhang, Y., Bachnynskyi, M., Vertanen, K., and Kristensson, P.O. Improving two-thumb text entry on touchscreen devices. In *Proc. CHI 2013*, ACM Press (2013), 2765–2774.
16. Nexus 5 – Google. http://www.google.com/nexus/5/
17. Perlin, K. Quikwriting: continuous stylus-based text entry. In *Proc. UIST 1998*, ACM Press (1998), 215–216.
18. Rick, J. Performance optimizations of virtual keyboards for stroke-based text entry on a touch-based tabletop. In *Proc. UIST 2010*, ACM Press (2010), 77–86.
19. Yamada, H. A historical study of typewriters and typing methods: from the position of planning Japanese parallels. *Information Processing 2*, 4 (1980), 175–202.
20. Zhai, S., Hunter, M., and Smith, B.A. The Metropolis keyboard—an exploration of quantitative techniques for virtual keyboard design. In *Proc. UIST 2000*, ACM Press (2000), 119–128.
21. Zhai, S., Hunter, M., and Smith, B.A. Performance optimization of virtual keyboards. *Human–Computer Interaction 17*, 2 (2002), 229–269.
22. Zhai, S. and Kristensson, P.O. Interlaced QWERTY – accommodating ease of visual search and input flexibility in shape writing. In *Proc. CHI 2008*, ACM Press (2008), 593–596.
23. Zhai, S. and Kristensson, P.O. Introduction to shape writing. *Text Entry Systems: Mobility, Accessibility, Universality*. Morgan Kaufmann, 2010. 139–158.
24. Zhai, S. and Kristensson, P.O. Shorthand writing on stylus keyboard. In *Proc. CHI 2003*, ACM Press (2003), 97–104.
25. Zhai, S. and Kristensson, P.O. The word-gesture keyboard: reimagining keyboard interaction. *Communications of the ACM 55*, 9 (2012), 91–101.

Design and Evaluation of a Self-Correcting Gesture Interface based on Error Potentials from EEG

Felix Putze
Karlsruhe Institute of Technology
Karlsruhe, Germany
felix.putze@kit.edu

Christoph Amma
Karlsruhe Institute of Technology
Karlsruhe, Germany
christoph.amma@kit.edu

Tanja Schultz
Karlsruhe Institute of Technology
Karlsruhe, Germany
tanja.schultz@kit.edu

ABSTRACT
Any user interface which automatically interprets the user's input using natural modalities like gestures makes mistakes. System behavior depending on such mistakes will confuse the user and lead to an erroneous interaction flow. The automatic detection of error potentials in electroencephalographic data recorded from a user allows the system to detect such states of confusion and automatically bring the interaction back on track. In this work, we describe the design of such a self-correcting gesture interface, implement different strategies to deal with detected errors, use a simulation approach to analyze performance and costs of those strategies and execute a user study to evaluate user satisfaction. We show that self-correction significantly improves gesture recognition accuracy at lower costs and with higher acceptance than manual correction.

Author Keywords
Error-Potentials; Self-Correction; Adaptive Interface; Gesture Recognition; Simulation; User Study

ACM Classification Keywords
H.5.m. Information Interfaces and Presentation (e.g. HCI): Miscellaneous

INTRODUCTION
Intuitive human-computer interaction (HCI) has been a highly active field of research in the last decade. Natural input modalities like speech or gestures have become broadly available. However, while those input techniques are an important step towards intuitive and efficient HCI, there are some important aspects which are still lacking. One major challenge when using machine learning and pattern recognition techniques to interpret user input is the introduction of a substantial error chance compared to traditional input devices like keyboards. Reasons are on the one hand limitations of generalizing from a finite set of training samples for data of high intrinsic variability and on the other hand ambiguities of complex, natural input patterns. Recognition errors often lead to an inefficient and unsatisfying interaction.

CHI 2015, April 18–23 2015, Seoul, Republic of Korea

ACM 978-1-4503-3145-6/15/04$15.00.
http://dx.doi.org/10.1145/2702123.2702184

In this paper, we propose the design of an error-aware gesture interface which is able to pro-actively detect erroneous system behavior in reaction to the input of a user. To detect errors, we exploit the fact that a discrepancy between the expected and the observed system behavior results in characteristic patterns of brain activity. Such a pattern is called Error Potential (ErrP) and can be measured using Electroencephalography (EEG) almost immediately after erroneous system feedback is presented following a user action. Therefore, identifying ErrPs allows the design of systems that proactively recover from errors.

While the general feasibility of ErrP detection from EEG has been established at least in the context of Brain-Computer-Interfaces (BCIs, see next section), there is a lack of investigations concentrating on the design of the actual error recovery behavior and the related usability implications. In this paper, we describe the design of an error-aware gesture recognizer. This recognizer uses ErrP detection and implements different strategies for error correction. Our main focus is to provide a thorough evaluation of the proposed error-aware recognizer, looking at both objective and subjective metrics. For this purpose, we use a comprehensive simulation employing data from multiple user studies.

RELATED WORK
In this section, we give an overview of related work on error recovery. Recovery from error states is a feature which is required for any type of interaction in which the interpretation of user input is error-prone, for example from speech or handwriting recognition. Most mature in that regard are probably spoken dialog systems which often need elaborate recovery strategies. For example, Bohus and Rudnicky [1] described ten distinct strategies to recover from non-understanding situations and empirically evaluated the performance impact of the different strategies. Most of their presented strategies involved one of several alternatives of "reprompting" the user after a non-understanding. Another approach is to identify erroneous sections of a speech recognition result and propose other likely alternatives [16].

Most of those systems make use of confidence scores to estimate the presence of recognition errors [5, 16]. However, when statistical models are unreliable and generate incorrect results, it is unreasonable to expect a very reliable confidence estimate. For example, Vu et al. [18] showed that confidence scores in ASR correlated well to recognition performance for well-trained models but confidence reliability deteriorated for models which were trained on small data corpora or data which did not match the testing data. This indicates that in order to provide self-correcting behavior for a user interface, we need additional information sources on the presence of an error besides confidence scores. One promising candidate in this regard is the detection of ErrPs.

Unsurprisingly, the idea to use ErrP detection for improving interaction has been first introduced in the context of BCIs, for which the necessary equipment for EEG recordings is already in place. BCIs as input or control device suffer from far-from-perfect recognition rates. A standard technique to remedy this is to always repeat each input several times. This increases robustness but leads to a low transfer rate [8]. The detection of ErrPs allows increasing accuracy and therefore the potential transfer rate. Combaz et al. [2] showed how they can detect ErrPs during operation of a P300 speller BCI. They suggest using the second best recognition result of the BCI in case of a detected ErrP and showed in simulations how this would improve performance. Spüler et al. [15] pursued a different approach and deleted the previously given input in case an ErrP was detected. They then prompted the user to repeat the input command. The authors showed how they can use an online ErrP classifier to significantly increase transfer rate. A similar approach was chosen by Schmidt et al. [13], who showed that they were able to reliably detect ErrPs online and demonstrated a significant increase in communication speed for their gaze-independent "Center Speller" BCI. The work by Margaux et al. [11] is one of the few examples of studies which do not only regard objective criteria but also investigate subjective evaluation of error-aware interfaces. For a P300 speller with second-best correction, the authors showed that a majority of participants "reported a preference in favor of a spelling including automatic correction". However, the authors also noted large individual differences regarding the subjective evaluation of their error-aware BCI. Llera et al. [9] used detected ErrPs to adapt the weight parameters of a logistic regression model for BCI operation to better represent the (assumingly) misclassified trial. They used simulation and offline analysis of data from eight participants to show that this process improved classification accuracy.

The number of studies which transfer ErrP detection to other input modalities – like gestures – is limited. Förster et al. [4] used classification of ErrPs during operation of a gesture recognition system to improve its performance by adaptation of the gesture recognizer. However, their system did not immediately react to the detected ErrPs by error correction. Instead, it focused on improving gesture recognition accuracy by selective online adaptation: Gesture trials which were classified correctly (i.e., did not result in an ErrP) were added to the training data to train a personalized gesture recognizer. This addressed the challenge of unsupervised adaptation that the addition of misclassified trials can result in performance degradation instead of improvement. Vi and Subramanian [17] proposed an ErrP recognition system based on a consumer-level EEG device. They performed person-dependent ErrP classification, using a test set of 80 trials of Flanker Task execution and achieved a classification accuracy of about 0.7. Using a simulation of ErrP classification with different error rates, they also showed that a non-perfect ErrP detection rate between 0.65 and 0.8 was beneficial for the enhancement of interactive systems for detecting user errors in spatial selection with the Flick technique on a touch surface. The authors analyzed accuracy improvements of allowing manual corrections when an ErrP is detected, but did not analyze costs or other usability aspects.

Corpus	Modalities	Size	Used for ...
BCI-ErrP	EEG	20	training of ErrP classifier (already existed)
Gesture-ErrP	EEG+IMU	11	evaluating ErrP classifier on gesture task
Gesture-Sim	IMU	20	evaluating accuracy & cost of recovery strategies
Recovery-Study	IMU	10	evaluating user satisfaction

Table 1. Overview over the different data corpora used in the paper. Size is given in number of sessions.

While there exists a large corpus of usability investigations on gesture-based interaction systems, we are not aware of many studies on the impact and handling of recognition errors. The cited related work on results from error-aware BCIs cannot be directly transferred to other HCI applications (e.g., gesture-based interfaces) for a number of reasons: 1) Errors of a gesture-based interface might generate different or no ErrPs compared to BCI input. 2) The feasibility of error recovery behavior depends on attributes of the input modality (number of classes, input recognition accuracy, error distribution, etc.), which differ between gesture and BCI input. 3) The acceptance of error recovery behavior is specific to the modality, as expectations on system performance, judgment of own performance, frequency of user errors vs. system errors, the costs of recovery behavior and many other factors differ between gesture-based interfaces and BCIs. 4) Some approaches for error recovery are modality specific (e.g., approaches using spatial re-arrangement for gesture interfaces). For those reasons, it is necessary to study the development and evaluation of error-recovery strategies which can make use of ErrP detection outside of a BCI application. We do this for the example of a gesture recognizer. Our main focus is on a thorough (objective and subjective) evaluation of different error recovery behaviors. For this purpose, we use a comprehensive simulation employing data from multiple user studies.

STRUCTURE OF THE PAPER

In this section, we describe how we design and systematically evaluate the necessary components for an EEG-based self-correcting gesture interface. This also defines the structure of our paper. First, we briefly introduce an existing ErrP classifier which is trained on the so-called *BCI-ErrP* corpus of participants operating a simple BCI task simulating feedback errors. Second, we introduce the experimantal setup, consisting of the gesture task, the employed gesture recognizer and the self-correcting interface. For the latter, we define several recovery strategies which are employed to respond to detected gesture recognition errors. Third, we evaluate the ErrP classifier by transferring its trained models to data of participants perceiving correct and erroneous feedback in the actual gesture task. We call this data of simultaneous gesture and EEG recordings the *Gesture-ErrP* corpus. We then use an additional larger corpus – called *Gesture-Sim* – of 20 participants performing the gesture task without parallel EEG recordings to evaluate the performance and associated costs of a large number of recovery strategy variants in a comprehensive simulation. We finally perform a user study with 10 participants – generating the *Recovery-Study* corpus – using three selected recovery strategies together with simulated ErrP classification to compare user satisfaction between different automatic and manual strategies. Table 1 gives an overview of the different employed corpora.

Most of the presented results use evaluation methods which employ partial simulation of system components. Note that while this is an established method to evaluate error-aware interfaces (see for example [17]), simulation is no complete substitution for the evaluation of a complete end-to-end system. This should be considered when interpreting the results of the paper. On the upside, simulation allows us to generate results which are more general than results for few concrete end-to-end systems.

EEG-BASED ERROR RECOGNITION

In this section, we briefly review the employed methods for ErrP classification. A typical ErrP can be measured at fronto-central electrode positions and occurs in a window of about 150ms to 600ms after a stimulus (i.e., the feedback), with its most pronounced components being a negative peak around 250ms and a positive peak around 350ms [3]. The exact contour and latency of an ErrP varies with tasks and individuals [6]. Figure 1, which is taken from [12] shows a Grand Average of an ErrP pattern as difference between brain activity following error-free and erroneous feedback.

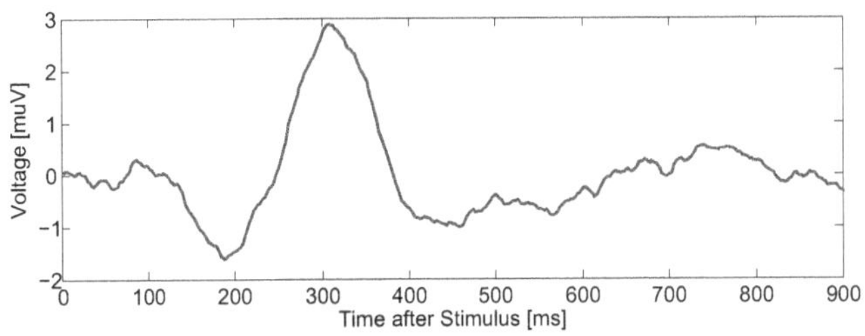

Figure 1. Grand Average of an ErrP (difference of correct and erroneous feedback) after a feedback stimulus in reaction to user input.

For the present investigation, we leveraged an existing ErrP classification system which is described and evaluated in [12]. In summary, this system extracts EEG data from a window of 1s duration after the presentation of a feedback. It preprocesses the data by re-referencing data to a common average and by removing ocular artifacts using Independent Component Analysis (ICA). The signal is then downsampled and the signals from two electrodes (Fz and Cz) used as features for a Support Vector Machine with a radial basis function kernel[1]. For each participant, the system is trained on available training data from other persons as well as a number of available calibration trials recorded from the current test person. This calibration data is also used to select only those training sessions which are closest to the data from the present test person. Additional details on the design of the ErrP classifier can be found in [12].

To validate this classification setup, we tested it on a corpus (originally described in [12]) using a highly controllable and easily executable task for elicitation of ErrPs. The employed paradigm to evoke ErrPs was operation of a mockup-BCI (selecting one of two presented options with mental commands) that simulated an error rate of 30%. For this task, EEG data was recorded at 500Hz using a BrainVision actiCHamp system with 32 active electrodes, of which 23 where used for ICA calculation and feature extraction[2]: Fz, F3, F7, FC5, FC1, C3, T7, CP5, CP1, P3, P7, O1, O2, P4, CP6, CP2, Cz, C4, T8, FC6, FC2, F4, F8. Impedance was kept below $16k\Omega$ for all electrodes. Pz was used as reference electrode and an additional light sensor attached to the stimulus presentation screen was used for synchronization. Using this setup, the *BCI-ErrP* corpus was recorded with data from 20 participants. On this data, the authors of [12] achieved an F-score of 0.86, corresponding to an accuracy of 0.92, using leave-one-person-out cross-validation with 125 calibration trials.

When applying the existing ErrP classifier to a gesture recognition context (see next section), we will use the BCI-ErrP corpus as training data. We use calibration data from the users of the gesture recognizer as calibration data. The rest of the classification setup remains unchanged.

EXPERIMENTAL SETUP

In this section, we describe the main parts of the experimental setup besides the ErrP recognition: The gesture task, the gesture recognition component and the self-correcting interface. To evaluate the potential for an ErrP classifier and corresponding error recovery strategies in a realistic, non-BCI related interaction task, we designed an experiment using a simple gesture recognizer for pointing gestures. This experiment consists of a pointing gesture task, a gesture recognizer and the self-correcting interface.

Gesture Task

In the employed task, participants selected and dragged images presented on a large projected display to a certain spot of a 2x3 matrix, depending on the content of the image (Step 1 and 2 in Figure 2 show the interface of the task). We used data from a wireless sensor wristband equipped with an inertial-measurement-unit (IMU) placed on the participant's right hand to classify the six possible pointing gestures. Figure 3 shows a participant performing the gesture task.

Before execution of the actual experiment, each participant trained a predefined movement sequence: From a resting position, the participant moved the arm to point at the bottom left corner, paused for about a second, moved the arm to the target cell of the matrix in a smooth motion, paused for about a second and returned to the resting position. This schema ensured consistent execution quality across all participants. The

[1]Note that the recording of additional channels is still necessary to perform ICA.

[2]Different subsets of electrodes were used in different setups and therefore not all were available for all sessions.

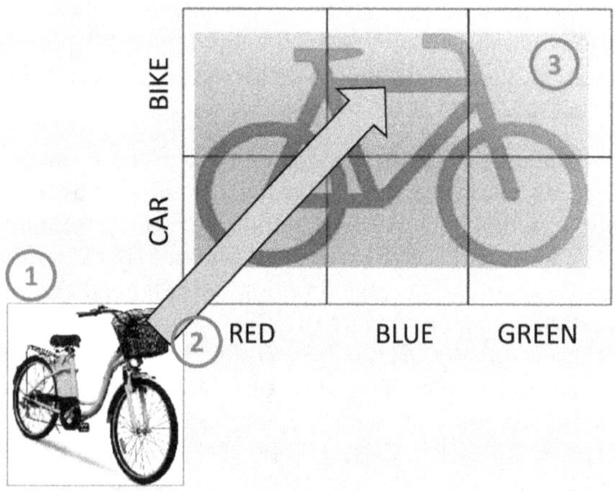

Figure 2. The gesture task: Image is shown (step 1) and moved by pointing gesture (step 2). Then, feedback on the recogized category is shown (step 3).

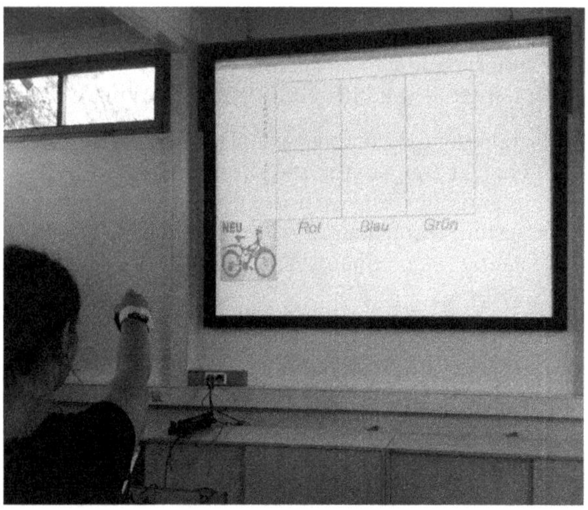

Figure 3. Execution of the gesture task.

task supported the participant in the correct execution by giving acoustic feedback in the form of a beep when a pausing position could be left. When the gesture was completed, the recognition result was displayed as a large overlay showing an abstract pictogram representing the selected category (Step 3 in Figure 2). At this point, an ErrP classifier can evaluate the subsequently recorded EEG to recognize whether an error has occurred. As recognition of ErrPs, and triggered effects in EEG in general, depend on temporal patterns in the range of milliseconds, it is important to provide such a stimulus-locking. Note that the selected window for ErrP classification does not contain systematic movement or system stimuli besides the presented feedback.

Gesture Recognition

We designed a simple person-independent gesture recognition system for recognizing the pointing gestures. The recognizer was designed to discriminate six different classes, corresponding to the six matrix cells of the gesture task. Arm motion was sensed with a sensor equipped wristband. We used a jNode sensor [14], an open research sensor platform which contains a 9 degrees-of-freedom inertial measurement unit (IMU). Sensor data was sampled at 50 Hz and sent wirelessly to a computer. We applied a standard processing chain consisting of segmentation, feature extraction and classification stages. It should be noted that the gesture recognizer was deliberately not optimized towards high accuracy. An almost perfect recognizer would not be of use in our scenario, since we are investigating recovery strategies from errors. We targeted an accuracy of 75%.

We employed a two-stage segmentation process, which first identifies segments of motion and then separates the actual pointing gesture from other hand movements. In the first stage, the motion data is segmented into parts containing motion and parts that are considered to contain no motion (idle). A motion segment is detected whenever the angular rate exceeds a given empirically determined threshold. The motion segment ends if the angular rate is below the threshold and stays below it for at least 200 ms.

In the second stage of the segmentation process, we model the movement sequence with a finite state automaton. Since the movement sequence follows a strict schema, this is a feasible approach for the case of this study. The finite state automaton has four states called `UNDEFINED`, `POINTSTART`, `GESTURE`, and `POINTEND` (see Figure 4). Whenever the segmentation stage detects a motion/idle change, we check for a state transition. The start state is `UNDEFINED`, which captures all motion that occurs between two gestural interactions. The `POINTSTART` state corresponds to the initial pointing on the picture at the bottom left corner of the display. The transition into the state `POINTSTART` is performed if the acceleration in the axis perpendicular to the back of the hand is within a range of 0.98 m/s^2 of an experimentally determined reference value. This means, the orientation of the hand in 3d space is compared to a reference orientation based on the measured earth acceleration. The reference orientation depends on the height and distance of the projected image relative to the user and is therefore dependent on the local environment. The next motion segment triggers transition into the state `GESTURE`, which indicates the execution of the actual gesture. The next idle segment consequently triggers transition into the state `POINTEND`, indicating the pause at the target position. The next motion segment leads to the transition back into `UNDEFINED`. The motion segment corresponding to the state `GESTURE` is used for the actual classification of the gesture.

For the classification stage, we used a Gaussian mixture model (GMM) with five Gaussians per class for maximum likelihood classification. Features were computed on the complete gesture segment associated with the `GESTURE` state in the finite state automaton. Preprocessing consists of a mean subtraction to compensate constant offsets introduced by gravity (mean calculated on previous trials) and signal smoothing with a running average filter of order five. Due to the drift and noise present in inertial sensor readings, there is no established technique to reconstruct the actual trajectory performed in 3d space. As a result, we could not simply compute the direction and length of the performed gesture re-

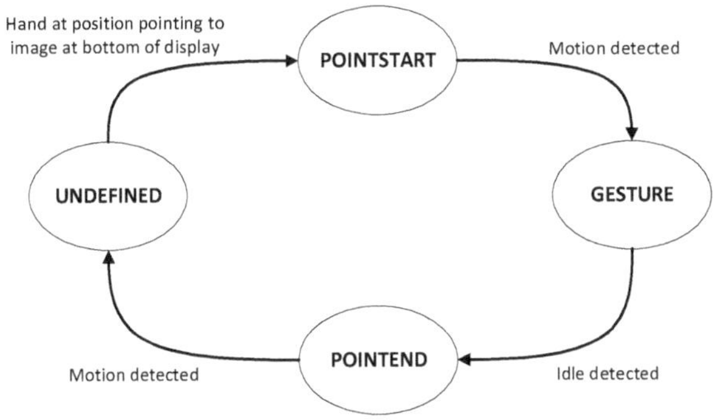

Figure 4. Finite state automaton that controls the second state of the gesture segmentation process.

liably. Instead, we computed the angle of motion in each of the three axes, the L_2-norm of these three angles and the duration of the gesture segment. The angles were computed by integrating the angular rate measurements from the gyroscope over the whole gesture segment. The resulting feature space therefore had five dimensions. The classifier was evaluated in crossvalidation, yielding a person-independent recognition accuracy of 77% (on the *Gesture-Sim* corpus) and therefore the gesture recognizer is suitable for our experiments. We also computed a confidence estimate for the gesture classification: Scores of the GMMs for each feature vector were normalized to a probability distribution across classes. The distance between the normalized score of the highest and second-highest scoring class was used as a confidence estimate of the classification result.

Self-Correcting Interface

For the described scenario, the self-correcting interface is designed as follows: The gesture classifier receives input from the IMU and outputs a probability distribution for six classes corresponding to the six possible matrix cells. The most likely class is used to present feedback on the recognized class to the user. The EEG data following this feedback is analyzed; in case the ErrP detector triggers, a recovery behavior is started to correct the error. The exact nature of this recovery behavior depends on the implementation of the recovery strategy. Different strategies can have different characteristics in terms of recovery accuracy, recovery costs and other factors.

In the evaluation section, we will show how the existing ErrP classifier performs on erroneous feedback during the gesture task. In the experiments comparing different recovery strategies, however, the ErrP component was replaced with a simulated ErrP classifier that receives the ground truth gesture class and the output of the gesture classifier to detect ErrPs with a recall and precision of both 0.8. The results from the isolated analysis of the ErrP classifier justify this simplification of the experimental setup as they show that we are able to achieve this performance from real EEG data. Simulating the ErrP classification allowed us a better control over the distribution of errors and therefore a better comparability between sessions. Furthermore, it reduced the setup time, and thereby allowed us to record data from a larger number of participants. It should be noted that the existing ErrP classifier we describe in the previous section can also be operated in online mode, therefore the results from the experiment can be generalized to an end-to-end system with EEG-based classifier.

Next, we defined the notion for the different recovery strategies we analyzed. The most basic strategy is the `REPROMPT` strategy. `REPROMPT` reacts to a detected error by prompting the user to repeat the input. The initial gesture data is discarded and the second gesture is used as the final classification result. We did not repeat the correction procedure after the first repetition as frequent handling of the same error might lead to unexpected EEG signal patterns. The `2ND-BEST` strategy is a modification of `REPROMPT` in that it does not always reprompt if an error is detected. Instead, it inspects the probability distribution of the remaining classes without the allegedly rejected one and picks the now highest scoring class (i.e., the originally second best). However, this estimate might be unreliable as it is based on a probability distribution that has just been indicated as erroneous by the ErrP classifier. Therefore, we only used the second best class if its re-normalized confidence (i.e., probability mass of the first best class distributed equally across all remaining classes) is above a certain threshold T (which is varied during evaluation). Otherwise, the user was asked to repeat the input. Figure 5 shows the control flow of both correction strategies (`REPROMPT` is a special case of `2ND-BEST` with threshold $T = \infty$).

As we also want to compare the automatic correction strategies with user-triggered correction, we define the `MANUAL` strategy that requires the user to actively report a system error. This could for example be executed with a "manual override" command or a correction gesture. In our experiments, we used a two-handed keyboard command issued by the user as trigger. When triggered, the system performed a reprompt of the last trial. This strategy has the advantage of near-perfect recognition of error events but does impose additional overhead for the user. Note that the `MANUAL` strategy still allows only one correction attempt per trial and can therefore still result in recognition errors. This restriction keeps `MANUAL` comparable to the other strategies that also allow at most one correction attempt. We finally call the recovery strategy that does not provide any mechanism to recover from detected error situations `NONE`.

EVALUATION

In this section, we systematically evaluate several aspects of the proposed approach: First, we show that ErrP classification is feasible in the proposed gesture task. Second, we introduce our simulation approach to evaluate different correction strategies. Third, we present the simulation results on correction accuracy and correction costs. Fourth, we show how the simulation results can be generalized to systems at different performance levels. Fifth, we show results of a user study comparing correction strategies.

ErrP Classification on Gesture Task

To understand how the existing ErrP classifier generalizes for more realistic HCI applications, we investigated how the

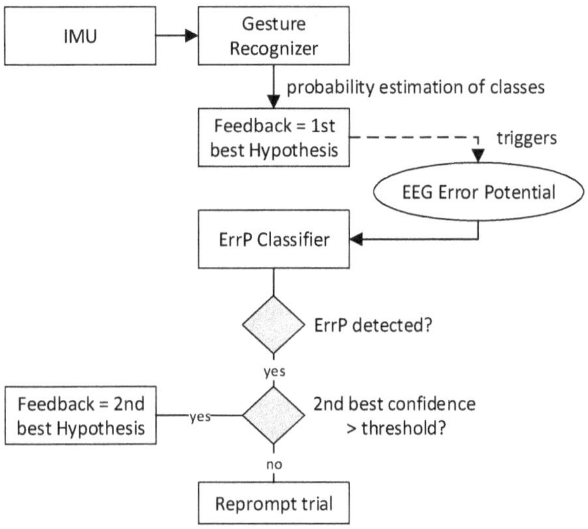

Figure 5. Flowchart of the 2ND-BEST strategy.

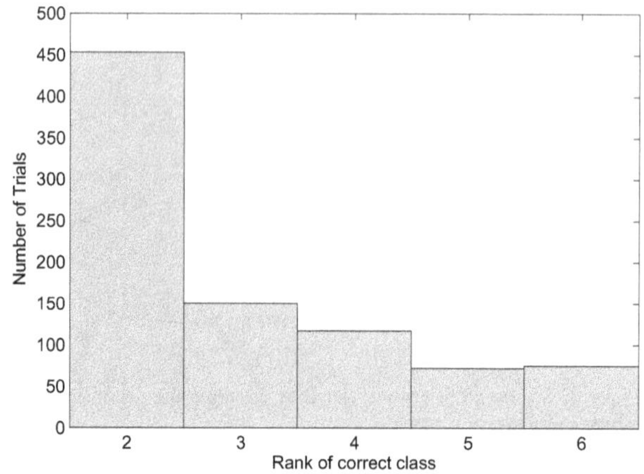

Figure 6. Histogram of ranks of the correct gesture class within the recognition results. Ranks are ordered by assigned probability (only for originally misclassified trials).

trained model transferred to data from the actual gesture scenario. As Iturrate et al. [6] showed, transfer between different tasks may result in performance degradation as characteristics of the ErrP patterns, for example onset latency, change. Therefore, we recorded the *Gesture-ErrP* corpus, which contains data from 11 participants performing the gesture task while wearing the EEG headset. Feedback was presented in the form of a pictogram symbolizing the selected class. It was presented on a fixed position (to avoid systematic eye movement artifacts) as a large, high-contrast overlay and participants were instructed to pay attention to the feedback to improve the recognition accuracy. This procedure was chosen to increase the likelihood and timing precision of the generated ErrP, as participants will not miss feedback or perceive it with a delay. We then evaluated the system trained on the *BCI-ErrP* corpus on the new data set. Using 60 calibration trials, we achieved an accuracy of 78.3%, corresponding to an F-score of 0.69, a precision of 0.72 and a recall of 0.67. This result shows that recognition of ErrPs in the presented real-life gesture scenario is feasible with limited calibration time. While those values are a bit lower than the values assumed for the self-correcting interface, it is known from Putze et al. [12] that accuracy can be improved by adding additional calibration trials.

Simulation-based Evaluation of Recovery Strategies

Using the described setup for the gesture task, we recorded IMU data of a total of 20 sessions from 20 participants. All participants were university students or employees. During the experiments, participants first performed a number of training trials and then three blocks with 35 trials each. Between two blocks was a pause of several minutes for the participant to rest. This is the *Gesture-Sim* corpus which we use to evaluate the baseline gesture classifier and to simulate the effects of different recovery strategies.

First, we describe the gesture classification performance in more detail. Inspecting the average confidence values yielded by the gesture classifier, we see a difference of 0.84 vs. 0.64 for the correct and the incorrect results, respectively. The confidence values are indistinguishable for practical purposes with an average p of 0.158 (two-sided t-test on each fold). This result indicates that the confidence value alone is not reliable enough to detect errors on its own. An additional knowledge source, like the proposed EEG-based ErrP detection, is necessary to reliably identify errors. For all misclassified trials, Figure 6 shows a histogram of the position of the correct label within the recognition results for the corresponding trial sorted by probability. We see that of all wrong classification results, in 52.2% of the cases, the second best estimate is the correct one. This indicates that we can successfully pursue a 2ND-BEST strategy.

In the following, we evaluate the different recovery strategies for their impact on recognition accuracy of the gesture recognizer and the associated costs in the form of additional gestures. We do this in simulation, where we use the actual results from the gesture recognizer for each trial but simulate the ErrP classification and recovery strategy, including any additional gesture classifications during recovery. This method gives us the opportunity to evaluate a large number of recovery strategies with different parameters to study and compare their effects.

To quantify the effect of the different recovery strategies, we define the *corrected recognition accuracy* to be the fraction of correctly identified gestures after applying the effects of any recovery behavior of the system. Corrected recognition accuracy takes into account the error of the gesture recognizer as well as both types of errors of the ErrP classifier (false positives and false negatives). See the appendix for the equation used to calculate corrected recognition accuracy.

We also assess the costs of each correction strategy to measure system efficiency. As a metric, we calculate the costs of a correction as the average number of additional user inputs (gestures or key presses) necessary to perform the correction. As performing a gesture and receiving the corresponding feedback is the most complex operation in our scenario, this cost measure is highly correlated to task execution time. For REPROMPT, this amounts to one gesture for each detected error, including false alarms. Those costs are reduced

Metric	Definition
Corrected accuracy	Gesture accuracy after application of correction behavior.
Correction costs	Number of additional gestures for application of correction behavior.
Cost benefit ratio	Ratio of difference between corrected accuracy and accuracy and correction costs.

Table 2. Overview of employed evaluation metrics.

for 2ND-BEST which in favorable cases corrects errors without any additional costs for the user. For MANUAL, we have no false alarms but additional costs for triggering the correction. We favorably assume that the signal to trigger manual correction is always issued correctly by the user. Correction costs can be estimated in cross-validation by counting the number of (automatically or manually triggered) reprompts.

Simulation Results

To assess the performance of the different strategies using the above metrics, we performed a block-wise leave-one-out crossvalidation of the gesture recognition system and calculated a number of statistics on errors and confidence values. The crossvalidation simulates online recognition, i.e., normalization parameters for each trial are only calculated from the data previous to this trial in chronological order. For each fold, we evaluate the gesture classifier on the testing block and estimate corrected recognition accuracy for the different correction strategies. Table 3 summarizes the results, averaged across all folds. We see that for all correction strategies, the corrected accuracy exceeds the baseline accuracy (i.e., NONE) and therefore improves the overall performance of the gesture classifier. As expected, MANUAL yields the highest improvement, followed by REPROMPT. Still, 2ND-BEST ranks only 3.1 to 9.9% worse than REPROMPT (depending on the selected threshold, see below) and provides a statistically significant improvement over NONE (block-wise one-sided paired t-test, $t = 4.38$, $p = 0.002$). A caveat is that while 2ND-BEST fixes a number of erroneously classified gestures, it also reacts to a number of false positives with no chance of recovery (in contrast to REPROMPT which can still generate a valid final result in case of a false positive). To some degree, this is mitigated by the confidence threshold t applied to the second best result: With $T = 0$, the corrected accuracy of 2ND-BEST is 71%, i.e., below the raw accuracy of NONE. Using a confidence threshold of 0.7, the strategy suggested the second best result for 53% of all error trials. This yields a tuning parameter with which the designer can select between different trade-offs between accuracy and correction costs: Table 3 lists results for three different parameter settings to demonstrate this.

Strategy	Corr. Accuracy	Corr. Costs
NONE	77.0%	0
MANUAL	93.0%	0.46
REPROMPT	86.8%	0.34
ROW-COL-REPROMPT	76.4%	0.34
SELECTIVE-REPROMPT	88.1%	0.34
2ND-BEST (T=0.5)	78.2%	0.14
2ND-BEST (T=0.7)	81.4%	0.19
2ND-BEST (T=0.9)	84.1%	0.27

Table 3. Performance measures of different error correction strategies.

It is surprisingly difficult to beat the simple 2ND-BEST strategy (and its special case REPROMPT) in terms of corrected accuracy. We explored a number of other strategies that use elaborate mechanisms to improve the recovery process. For example, the ROW-COL-REPROMPT strategy tries to estimate the correct row or column (by identifying the row or column with the highest cumulative confidence after removing the first best result) from the initial gesture and only reprompts this reduced set. Indeed, corrected accuracy of the gesture recognizer rises to 88% when only the one missing dimension (i.e., row or column) has to be estimated from the reprompt. However, errors in the automatic selection of the correct row or column, which inevitably prevent a successful correction, lead to a non-competitive corrected accuracy of 76.4%, which is worse than NONE. An alternative which performs better is SELECTIVE-REPROMPT. It also limits the number of reprompted items, but selects the three best classes from the initial gesture input, including the one marked as incorrect by the ErrP detector. This leads to a corrected accuracy of 88.1%, reducing the number of errors by 9.8% relative to REPROMPT. However, we achieve this error reduction only by re-arranging those items into one row[3]. Thus, we pay for this benefit by the fact that we are required to re-arrange the matrix for the reprompt (e.g., moving the three candidates to a joint row) to actually benefit from a simplified pointing and classification task. Informal user tests showed that this is highly confusing to users.

Generalizing Simulation Results

Up to this point, we analyzed the benefit of error recovery using the empirically determined gesture recognition accuracy of 77.0% (on average) yielded by the employed gesture recognizer. Similarly, we used performance values for the ErrP classifier which were plausible for the system described in [12]. However, the benefit of error recovery depends on the performance of both components, gesture recognition and ErrP detection: A very high gesture recognition accuracy demands a high ErrP classification accuracy. Otherwise, nearly all detected errors will be false alarms. In case of rather low gesture recognition accuracy, even an ErrP detector with comparably low accuracy can lead to substantial benefits. For this reason, we analyze the system for different performance levels of gesture recognizer and ErrP classifier in Figure 7. For every configuration, we calculate the *benefit cost ratio*, which is the ratio of absolute improvement of correction accuracy to the corresponding correction costs. See the appendix for how to calculate benefit cost ratio.

We can make a number of noteworthy observations: Unsurprisingly, the benefit-cost ratio increased with performance of the ErrP classifier for a fixed accuracy of the gesture recognizer. In contrast, benefit-cost ratio did not develop monotonously for a fixed ErrP classification accuracy. This is because for very low gesture recognition accuracy, the costs of frequent reprompts are high, regardless of ErrP classification performance; for very high gesture recognition accuracy, the ErrP classifier has to be very precise to actually detect

[3]other options like simply discarding the other items or training new models with a-priori probabilities from the original trial lead to worse recognition accuracy.

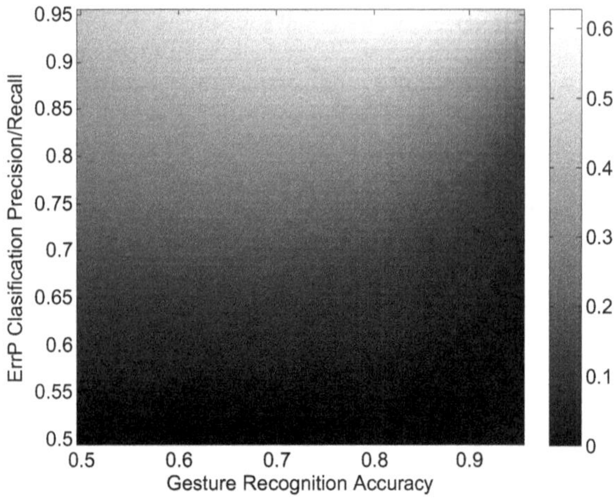

Figure 7. Benefit-cost ratio of REPROMPT over NONE for different performance levels of gesture recognizer and ErrP classifier.

the few misclassified gestures. Highest benefit-cost ratio can be achieved for gesture recognizers in the accuracy range of 70% to 85%. This is an encouraging result as this is a plausible range for many real-world gesture recognition tasks. Figure 7 can be used to decide whether the application of a self-correcting interface is beneficial for a concrete gesture recognizer and a concrete available ErrP classification accuracy.

In the previous analysis, we treated precision and recall identically. Relaxing this constraint enables the trade-off between precision and recall as an additional design parameter: As false positives and missed errors are not symmetrical in their influence on the performance of a recovery strategy, we now look at the impact of different precision/recall values of the ErrP classifier. For example, it may be favorable to tune the classifier towards a higher precision at the cost of reduced recall, to avoid false alarms which might invalidate correct gesture inputs. In [12], Putze et al. showed that it was possible to achieve a precision of 0.96 by modifying the class balance of training data. Simultaneously, this step reduced recall to 0.76. While this resulted in a slightly lower F-Score of 0.84 compared to the optimal system, it is the number of false positives (which depends on the precision of the classifier) that causes the most trouble for automatic recovery; this is especially true for 2ND-BEST, which cannot recover successfully in case of a false positive. To investigate the impact of the trade-off between both performance metrics, we adjusted precision and recall of the ErrP detector by $+0.1$ and -0.1, respectively. As a consequence, relative corrected recognition accuracy improved by 3.5% for REPROMPT and 6.3% for 2ND-BEST. The overall ranking of recovery strategies stayed the same, although the gap to the MANUAL strategy was reduced, as it did not benefit from the adjustment.

User Satisfaction of Recovery Strategies

The results up to this point indicate that is is possible to develop a self-correcting interface that significantly improves the accuracy of the employed gesture recognizer. However, usability of such a system does not only depend on efficiency and effectiveness and we still have to investigate whether users will accept the different correction strategies. In [7] Jameson systematically analyzed a number of undesired side-effects of introducing such an adaptive interface. He discussed the cause and the effects and ways to remedy them. For application, the most relevant side-effects are "Inadequate Control over Interaction Style" and "Inadequate Predictability and Comprehensibility", as the user has no control over when a correction is triggered and has no way to predict when an error is detected. Another important aspect is "Imperfect System Performance" (of the ErrP classifier), which may lead to negative user experience when a correct interpretation is discarded. To investigate whether those challenges affect user satisfaction, we recorded the *Recovery-Study* corpus, a user study in which we compared REPROMPT and 2ND-BEST (with $T = 0.7$) to the MANUAL correction strategy. This strategy selection allowed a comparison of recovery strategies with different levels of autonomy. After a training phase with the gesture recognizer, each participant performed 35 trials for each of the three strategies in random order and filled out a usability questionnaire. Averaged across all participants, raw recognition accuracy was 76.2%. Table 4 describes the actual performance of the different correction strategies. Compared to the simulation results, we can conclude that in simulation we made satisfactory predictions on accuracy and correction costs. Table 5 summarizes the items of the questionnaire and the results. Items were presented with a 5-point Likert-scale, with 1 indicating no agreement and 5 indicating the highest possible agreement. In the following, we analyze the corresponding questionnaire responses. Given the limited sample size, not all results are significant, but the tendencies give a good impression on the perception of the different strategies.

Strategy	Corr. Accuracy	Corr. Costs
MANUAL	91.7%	0.52
REPROMPT	84.0%	0.37
2ND-BEST (T=0.7)	79.7%	0.18

Table 4. Performance measures of the different error correction strategies for the *Recovery-Study* corpus.

Questionnaire Item	REPROMPT	2ND-BEST	MANUAL
felt supported	3.6	3	3.1
system reacts proactively	4.4*	3.5*	2.1
errors corrected reliably	3.1	3.2	2.6
system strenuous	2.9	2.4	2.8
correction tedious	3.0	2.4*	3.5
system predictable	3.4	3.1	2.5
system impedes user	2.5	2.4	2.9
system confusing	2.2*	2.9	3.0
system intuitive	4.6*	4.3	4.1
user has control	4.0*	3.4	3.3
felt observed	1.3	1.8	1.8
pleasant experience	3.3	3.7	3.0

Table 5. Subjective evaluation of correction strategies. 1 = strong rejection, 5 = strong agreement. An asterisk denotes a significant difference (two-sided, paired t-test, $\alpha = 0.05$) between MANUAL and the respective automatic strategy.

We see that users are not daunted by the self-correcting interfaces. By tendency, the self-correcting systems are evaluated more positively compared to the system with manual correction regarding all presented questionnaire items. However, there was a difference between REPROMPT and 2ND-BEST in which items they more distinctively differed from MANUAL. Due to the reduced number of manual interventions necessary, automatic correction by the 2ND-BEST strategy was perceived as less strenuous, less tedious and more pleasant than manual correction. Comparing both automatic strategies regarding ease-of-use, users preferred the REPROMPT strategy. REPROMPT was evaluated as the least confusing, most predictable, most intuitive strategy. For REPROMPT, there also was a stronger perception of pro-active behavior compared to both other strategies. The reason we see for this difference between both self-correction strategies is that 2ND-BEST provided the more complex behavior as it adds new elements to the interaction flow, while REPROMPT only repeats elements which are already familiar to the user. Both behaviors also differ in their handling of false positives. While reprompting a user after presented feedback can be interpreted as a confirmation of an unreliable classification, the 2ND-BEST behavior explicitly discards the initial classification result and gives the user no opportunity to counter this behavior.

Interestingly, REPROMPT and 2ND-BEST were both perceived as (slightly) more reliable in terms of error correction than MANUAL (3.1 and 3.2 vs. 2.6). This result is in contrast to the higher corrected accuracy of MANUAL. Based on post-hoc interviews with the participants, we postulate that this is because participants did not attribute the high corrected accuracy of MANUAL to the system, but to their own additional effort to report errors.

CONCLUSION

In this paper, we showed that it is possible to improve accuracy of a gesture recognizer using ErrP classification to enable pro-active recovery from recognition errors. We discussed all components necessary for an end-to-end error-aware interface and evaluated different recovery strategies, looking at both objective and subjective evaluation metrics. We showed that an error-aware interface can achieve corrected recognition accuracy close to manual correction, while maintaining much lower correction costs. We compared different recovery strategies, showing a trade-off between achieved corrected accuracy and recovery costs as well as differences in subjective assessment between strategies.

In this paper, we did not only report results for one specific self-correcting gesture recognizer but for a whole family of recognizers with different (gesture and ErrP) accuracy levels and correction strategies. In the discussion of related work we argued that the concrete design of error recovery strategies depends on the employed modalities and recognizers. The methods that we employed in this paper enable us to assess the benefit of different strategies in different situations: The simulation-based evaluation of recovery strategies can be easily extended to other strategies and recognizers. In addition to the simulation, the user study in the *Recovery-Study* showed a number of general criteria (e.g., intuitiveness, perceived performance, control) by which different recovery strategies can be evaluated for user satisfaction. When transferring the results of this paper to another modality or domain, one may have to adjust the recovery strategies and consequently the evaluation of Equation 1. Another aspect that needs to be adapted to new application areas is the employed cost model. It may require adjustments as requesting additional user input may be more or less costly (e.g., finger flicks vs. full-arm movements) or measured on a completely different scale (e.g., time, as some gestures take longer to perform than others) than in this paper. This may also change the user preference for different recovery strategies.

One limitation of the described approach is that it relies on time-locked evaluation of EEG data relative to feedback presentation. This works well for situations were the system can give instantaneous feedback in an unambiguous way, for example global feedback on a graphical user interface. Detection of error states becomes more challenging when feedback is given more locally, is not obviously erroneous or is spreading across longer periods of time. In such cases, the ErrP classification has to rely on additional information sources (e.g., eye tracking to estimate when a presented feedback was perceived) or become less reliant on temporal alignment (e.g., by using methods by Marathe et al. [10]). Another limitation is induced by the fundamental challenges of BCIs: Long setup time, low signal-to-noise ratio, requirement for additional equipment. Those challenges may restrict the applicability to scenarios in which such characteristics are acceptable and are outweighed by the benefits of the error correction. Finally, the work needs to be extended to a full end-to-end system. Such a system would feature additional interactions between the different components, for example potential changes in ErrP patterns in reaction to system error recovery.

APPENDIX

This appendix gives the equations for the calculation of corrected accuracy and benefit cost ratio when employing different correction strategies. The *corrected accuracy* can be calculated as follows:

$$\begin{aligned}\hat{a} =& a \cdot (1 - p_{cor}) + a \cdot p_{cor} \cdot a_{FP} \\ &+ (1 - a) \cdot p_{incor} \cdot a_{TP}\end{aligned} \quad (1)$$

In Equation 1, p_{cor} is the probability of detecting an ErrP if the gesture input was classified correctly (i.e., the false positive rate of the ErrP classifier) and p_{incorr} is the probability of detecting an ErrP if the gesture input was classified incorrectly (i.e., the precision of the ErrP classifier). a is the raw accuracy of the gesture recognizer and can be estimated during crossvalidation. a_{TP} and a_{FP} are the probabilities of a successful recovery when an ErrP was identified correctly (i.e., true positive) or incorrectly (i.e., false positive) for the initial gesture input. For REPROMPT, we simply have $a = a_{TP} = a_{FP}$, as every detected ErrP leads to an additional unmodified gesture trial. For a pure 2ND-BEST strategy (i.e., $T = 0$), we have $a_{TP} = p_{2ND}$ and $a_{FP} = 0$, where p_{2ND} is the probability that the second best estimate is correct, given the first one was already excluded. p_{2ND} can be estimated from the histogram in Figure 6 as the fraction of second best results of all wrongly classified gesture trials (52.2% in our case). For `2ND-BEST` with $T > 0$, we have:

$$a_{TP} = P(c_{2ND} \leq T) \cdot a + P(c_{2ND} > T) \cdot p_{2ND}$$
$$a_{FP} = P(c_{2ND} \leq T) \cdot a \quad (2)$$

In Equation 2, c_{2ND} is the re-normalized confidence of the second best recognition result (i.e., the probability mass of the first best recognition result is distributed proportionally across the other results). Again, the necessary probabilities can be estimated from the histogram in Figure 6 by counting only the trials with high confidence.

To quantify the efficiency of a correction strategy, we define the *benefit cost ratio* b as the ratio between absolute improvement in accuracy $\hat{a} - a$ and the correction costs c. b can be interpreted as the expected improvement in gesture recognition accuracy per necessary additional gesture. To simplify the analysis, we set $q = p_{cor} = 1 - p_{incorr}$, i.e., we used identical values for precision and recall of the ErrP classifier. Using the definition of b, c and q in Equation 1, we can calculate the benefit-cost ratio as follows:

$$b = \frac{\hat{a} - a}{c} = \frac{(2q-1)(a-a^2)}{a(1-q) + (1-a)q} \quad (3)$$

REFERENCES

1. Bohus, D., and Rudnicky, A. I. Sorry, i didn't catch that! In *Recent Trends in Discourse and Dialogue*, no. 39 in Text, Speech and Language Technology. Springer Netherlands, 2008, 123–154.
2. Combaz, A., Chumerin, N., Manyakov, N. V., Robben, A., Suykens, J. A. K., and Van Hulle, M. M. Towards the detection of error-related potentials and its integration in the context of a p300 speller brain–computer interface. *Neurocomputing 80* (2012), 73–82.
3. Ferrez, P. W., and José del R. Millan. Error-related EEG potentials generated during simulated brain computer interaction. *IEEE Transactions on Biomedical Engineering 55*, 3 (2008), 923–929.
4. Förster, K., Biasiucci, A., Chavarriaga, R., Millan, J. d. R., Roggen, D., and Tröster, G. On the use of brain decoded signals for online user adaptive gesture recognition systems. In *Pervasive Computing*, no. 6030 in Lecture Notes in Computer Science. Springer Berlin Heidelberg, 2010, 427–444.
5. Große, P. W., Holzapfel, H., and Waibel, A. Confidence based multimodal fusion for person identification. In *Proceedings of the 16th International Conference on Multimedia* (New York, USA, 2008).
6. Iturrate, I., Chavarriaga, R., Montesano, L., Minguez, J., and Millan, J. d. R. Latency correction of error potentials between different experiments reduces calibration time for single-trial classification. *Proceedings of Annual International Conference of the Engineering in Medicine and Biology Society. 2012* (2012), 3288–3291.
7. Jameson, A. D. Understanding and dealing with usability side effects of intelligent processing. *AI Magazine 30*, 4 (2009), 23–40.
8. Krusienski, D. J., Sellers, E. W., McFarland, D. J., Vaughan, T. M., and Wolpaw, J. R. Toward enhanced p300 speller performance. *Journal of Neuroscience Methods 167*, 1 (2008), 15–21.
9. Llera, A., van Gerven, M. A. J., Gómez, V. M., Jensen, O. K., and Kappen, H. J. On the use of interaction error potentials for adaptive brain computer interfaces. *Neural Networks 24*, 10 (2011), 1120–1127.
10. Marathe, A. R., Ries, A. J., and McDowell, K. A novel method for single-trial classification in the face of temporal variability. In *Foundations of Augmented Cognition*, no. 8027 in Lecture Notes in Computer Science. Springer Berlin Heidelberg, 2013, 345–352.
11. Margaux, P., Emmanuel, M., Sébastien, D., Olivier, B., and Jérémie, M. Objective and subjective evaluation of online error correction during p300-based spelling. *Adv. in Hum.-Comp. Int. 2012* (2012).
12. Putze, F., Heger, D., and Schultz, T. Reliable subject-adapted recognition of EEG error potentials using limited calibration data. In *6th International Conference on Neural Engineering* (San Diego, USA, 2013).
13. Schmidt, N. M., Blankertz, B., and Treder, M. S. Online detection of error-related potentials boosts the performance of mental typewriters. *BMC Neuroscience 13* (2012), 13–19.
14. Scholl, P. M., van Laerhoven, K., Gordon, D., Scholz, M., and Berning, M. jNode: A sensor network platform that supports distributed inertial kinematic monitoring. In *Proceedings of the Ninth International Conference on Networked Sensing Systems* (2012).
15. Spüler, M., Bensch, M., Kleih, S., Rosenstiel, W., Bogdan, M., and Kübler, A. Online use of error-related potentials in healthy users and people with severe motor impairment increases performance of a p300-BCI. *Clinical neurophysiology: official journal of the International Federation of Clinical Neurophysiology 123*, 7 (2012), 1328–1337.
16. Stoyanchev, S., Salletmayr, P., Yang, J., and Hirschberg, J. Localized detection of speech recognition errors. In *Proceedings of the Spoken Language Technology Workshop* (2012), 25–30.
17. Vi, C., and Subramanian, S. Detecting error-related negativity for interaction design. In *Proceedings of the Conference on Human Factors in Computing Systems* (New York, USA, 2012).
18. Vu, N. T., Kraus, F., and Schultz, T. Multilingual a-stabil: A new confidence score for multilingual unsupervised training. In *Proceedings of the Spoken Language Technology Workshop* (2010), 183–188.

Constructing Conceptual Knowledge Artefacts: Activity Patterns in the Ontology Authoring Process

Markel Vigo
University of Manchester
School of Computer Science
markel.vigo@manchester.ac.uk

Caroline Jay
University of Manchester
School of Computer Science
caroline.jay@manchester.ac.uk

Robert Stevens
University of Manchester
School of Computer Science
robert.stevens@manchester.ac.uk

ABSTRACT
Ontologies are complex knowledge representation artefacts used widely across biomedical, media and industrial domains. They are used for defining terminologies and providing metadata, especially for linked open data, and as such their use is rapidly increasing, but so far development tools have not benefited from empirical research into the ontology authoring process. This paper presents the results of a study that identifies common activity patterns through analysis of eye-tracking data and the event logs of the popular authoring tool, Protégé. Informed by the activity patterns discovered, we propose design guidelines for bulk editing, efficient reasoning and increased situational awareness. Methodological implications go beyond the remit of knowledge artefacts: we establish a method for studying the usability of software designed for highly specialised complex domains.

Author Keywords
Ontologies; knowledge representation; semantic web; activity patterns; authoring tools; complex domains.

ACM Classification Keywords
H.5.m Information Interfaces and Presentation (e.g. HCI): Miscellaneous; I.2.4 Knowledge Representation Formalisms and Methods: Semantic networks

INTRODUCTION
Ontologies define a domain of interest by describing entities and their logical relationships. A number of fields including healthcare, genetics, chemistry and geography have successfully adopted ontologies to represent the entities in these domains [11]. We can illustrate how an ontology describes a field of interest by showing an excerpt from the Wine ontology [27]; according to this ontology we can say that wine is a potable liquid made in a region using at least one variety of grape. Using the Web Ontology Language, OWL [28], authors can formalise the knowledge stated in that natural language sentence using logical axioms that establish relationships between classes of objects (Wine, PotableLiquid, Region and WineGrape) using OWL constructs (subClassOf) and properties (locatedIn and madeFromGrape) as shown in Figure 1. The strict semantics of OWL, in conjunction with an automated reasoner, allow implicit knowledge to be inferred from the asserted ontology. These facilities help ontology builders construct robust and flexible knowledge representations for use in a range of application settings [11].

```
Class: Wine
    SubClassOf: food:PotableLiquid,
    locatedIn some Region,
    madeFromGrape min 1 owl:Thing
```

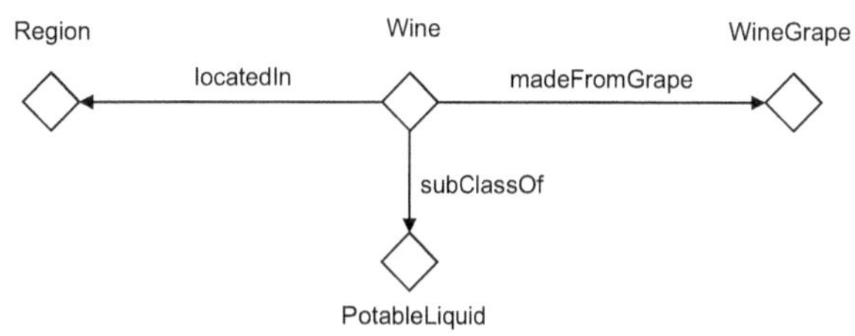

Figure 1. OWL syntax of the entities that define *Wine* and their visual representation below. Diamonds indicate individuals of a class.

Ontologies are employed for a variety of purposes, but are particularly useful for the definition of terminologies, which are frequently used in the biomedical domain for data descriptions. An exemplar is the SNOMED Clinical Terms terminology [20], which defines more than 300 000 medical concepts, and is mandated for use in around 60 countries. Similarly, the Gene Ontology [21] has three sub-ontologies containing more than 40 000 classes. It has been used to describe the functional attributes of gene products of many species, amounting to millions of annotations. The Gene Ontology also drives many analysis tools in biology [14]. These large, often complex, logical descriptions of a field of interest are key to much data analysis and are increasingly used to describe the wealth of Linked Open Data [2]. For instance, ontologies constitute a core technology of the British Broadcasting Corporation (BBC) website [3], which delivers information —including archival audio content— to around 40 million unique users per week. To support this activity, we must develop tools that reliably support the creation, maintenance and use of ontologies, by a wide range of users.

Despite their success and significance, ontologies are known to be complex to create and maintain, which hinders adoption, particularly by novices. This complexity has a number of dimensions:

CHI 2015, April 18 - 23 2015, Seoul, Republic of Korea

ACM 978-1-4503-3145-6/15/04 ...$15.00.
http://dx.doi.org/10.1145/2702123.2702495

- Cognitive complexity: description logics are difficult to understand [19] and consequently a steep learning curve is required to sufficiently master them [31].
- Size: ontologies can be large artefacts containing hundreds of thousands of axioms. Exploring, navigating and adding even a single axiom to an ontology can cause disorientation and confusion to a user [24].
- Expertise: ontologies are often used to model specific phenomena such as genes, nanoparticles, or amino acids. This requires domain experts to work together with computer scientists —a common practice, but one that can generate tensions between those playing different roles [18].
- Reasoning: because of the complexity of description logics, the logical justifications used to explain inferred knowledge or consistency problems in the ontology are often difficult to understand, let alone to correct [10].

One of the key factors contributing towards the acceptance of a new technology is the availability of tools to create high quality artefacts. Ontology authoring tools have seen many improvements over recent years, and Protégé in particular has become a popular integrated ontology development tool [5, 30]. However, primarily because little is known about how ontology authors tackle their tasks, the ontology engineering community has thus far largely ignored the question of whether existing tools are adequate to support authors. As a result, and as suggested by the analysis of the literature below, the interfaces of existing tools might not be well-suited to the intended tasks.

Background

The literature covering the usability of ontology authoring tools is scarce: seminal work in the realm of knowledge representation systems indicates that adequate reporting of errors and explanation of inferences are key to building usable tools [15]. Heuristic evaluation has often been used to assess the suitability of ontology authoring tools. These heuristics comprise questions to check whether particular types of functionality are implemented, e.g. "Is it possible to use multiple inheritance?", or cover aspects of usability, e.g. "Is there a good overview of the ontology?" [7]. Other work suggests that implementing faceted browsing, faceted viewing and inline editing would make semantic authoring tools more usable [12]. In a previous paper we proposed a framework [23], constructed around the strategies reported by ontology authors in an interview study, to evaluate ontology authoring tools based on a number of design recommendations, such as the inclusion of situational awareness mechanisms, efficient ontology population methods and search capabilities, amongst others. The conclusion of both this and previous studies using heuristics and quality frameworks, is that current tools have severe usability problems.

The direct participation of end users in the evaluation of knowledge engineering tools is also scarce. In a study of non-expert users, participants were asked to carry out basic tasks including ontology loading, and entity addition, modification and removal [13]. Tool efficiency, user attitude and aspects of learnability were measured using questionnaires. Another study, which involved authors tackling more difficult tasks including, adding subsumptions, equivalence and range axioms, also used questionnaires to measure the effectiveness, efficiency, and user experience of tools [8]. In an interview study with expert ontology authors we found that individuals employ sophisticated strategies to mitigate the weaknesses of tools [24]. Based on these strategies, we proposed a set of design insights to improve sensemaking, exploration, ontology building, debugging and evaluation tasks. The studies above involving users agree that tools are difficult to use and that no tool meets all the functional requirements of users. However, the results need to be handled with care. Ideally, they should be complemented (and corroborated) with objectively collected data to mitigate the cognitive biases that might have been introduced due to self-reporting.

To date, there is little work investigating how ontology authoring tools are actually used. In a recent study, Wang *et al.* analysed the ontology editing history of the online version of Protégé, using data mining techniques to predict the authoring event that is going to occur next [29]. In this instance, however, little is said about the tasks or activities of users.

A key contribution of this paper is the method we employ to identify the activity patterns of users. *A priori* we know very little about how users deal with conceptual knowledge artefacts and we ignore how the activities are exhibited. We collect event data via an instrumented Protégé, combine this with eye-tracking data, and use a data-driven approach to isolate core activities and their implementation details. We argue that this approach is generalisable to other situations in which individuals must deal with data of a complex nature, including exploration of big linked data, spreadsheet use and other forms of programming. The remaining contributions of the paper are as follows:

- We build a version of Protégé that logs interaction data to enable posterior analysis. The tool is openly available for the community —see §*Instrumenting Protégé*.
- We run the first study in which interaction and gaze data are used together to identify the authoring activities. This methodological contribution goes beyond the construction of knowledge artefacts, with potential application to studying the usability of highly specialised complex software whose users are typically experts —see §*Study*.
- We provide details about how the three main activities of editing, reasoning and exploring are realised. This study establishes a baseline for the exploration of how these activities are linked across different settings, tasks, types of users and ontologies —see §*Results*.
- We articulate the core activities and behaviours as design guidelines that authoring tools should support to improve the ontology engineering process. —see §*Discussion*.

INSTRUMENTING Protégé

Surveys indicate that Protégé is the preferred authoring tool of the vast majority of ontology authors, with reported uptake figures of around 68% in 2007 [5] and 74% in 2013 [30]. While we must be very careful about generalising our results beyond the realm of Protégé, it is safe to say that the outcomes of using Protégé in user studies are relevant to a majority of ontology authors.

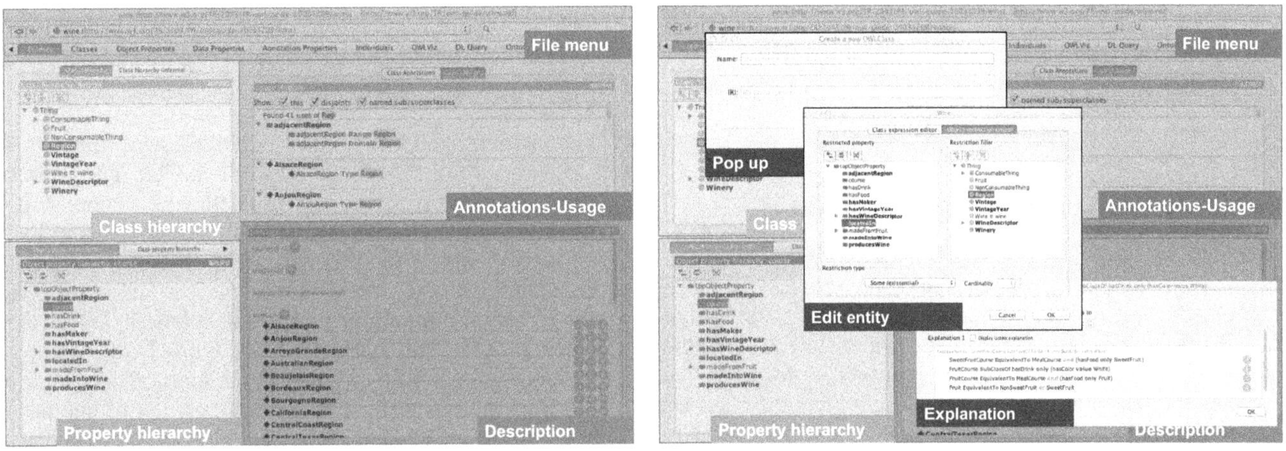

Figure 2. Core areas of interest defined in Protégé (left); Pop-up areas of interest defined in Protégé (right).

We modified the source code of Protégé 4.3 so that the tool logged the events triggered by users[1]. We classify these as *interaction events*, *authoring events* and *environment events*. Events occur in different areas of the Protégé user interface as highlighted by Figure 2 (left). At the top, the *file menu* contains a number of functionalities that can be reached by navigating the menus. In addition to running the reasoner and customising the views of Protégé, these drop-down menus typically provide redundant functionalities to those offered in the remaining areas. This area also contains a number of tabs that display different views of the ontology. On the left side, the *class hierarchy* and the *property hierarchy* contain expandable treeviews that represent the hierarchy of classes and properties as defined by subsumption axioms. On the top-right side, in the annotations-usage area, *annotations* are used to provide metadata for ontologies and their entities, and often show comments, label synonyms or authoring metadata about items in the hierarchies. *Usage* shows a list of axioms in which the latest selected entity appears. At the bottom right, the *description* area contains a list of the axiomatic descriptions for the latest item selected in either of the hierarchies; in addition, a number of functionalities to create and modify such entities can be invoked, for instance, a pop-up to set restrictions (see the *Edit entity* dialogue in Figure 2, right).

Interaction Events

Interaction events are logged as applying to either asserted hierarchies, entities and descriptions, or to inferred ones. The former are explicitly authored by the user, whereas the latter are built by the reasoner.

- *Hierarchy expanded*[2] causes the class hierarchy and property hierarchy to display child nodes of the clicked item.
- *Hierarchy collapsed* hides all the displayed subsumed classes or properties of a particular item.
- *Entity selected* indicates the selection of an item in any of the hierarchies.
- *Description selected* means an item contained in the description area is selected.

[1]The UI of the following versions including Protégé 5.0 is consistent with the version we instrumented.

[2]Protégé provides different ways of accomplishing certain events. For brevity, we describe how they most often occur in the study.

Authoring Events

- *Class/property addition* is typically carried out by typing the name of a new entity in the textbox of the *Pop-up* window —see the leftmost dialogue in Figure 2, right.
- *Entity edited:start* records that the dialogue for establishing relationships between entities, or modifying existing ones, has appeared. If we want to assert that all objects of the Wine class belong to a particular Region, the *Edit entity* dialogue provides two options: one, adding OWL statements using Manchester syntax in a textbox (writing locatedIn some Region in the class expression editor); or two, selecting, in the hierarchy, the restricted property (locatedIn), the restriction filler (Region) and setting existential (∃) as the type of quantifier.
- *Entity edited:finish* indicates that the editing is finished.
- *Entity renamed* is the action of modifying the original name of an entity in a hierarchy by typing the new name in a pop-up text box.
- *Entity deleted* removes the selected entity.
- *Entity dragged* moves an entity to another location.
- *Convert into defined class* turns a given class's restrictions from necessary into *necessary and sufficient* conditions.
- *Set property* defines the characteristics of a property by clicking on a set of checkboxes.

Environment Events

- *Run reasoner* invokes an automated reasoner. The results show whether any class is unsatisfiable or the ontology is inconsistent (i.e. there is a logical contradiction in the ontology), and any inferred knowledge is exposed.
- *Get explanation* shows the axioms that led to a given inference, including the unsatisfiability or inconsistency of any constructs —see the rightmost dialogue in Figure 2, right.
- *Load ontology* loads an OWL file into the environment.
- *Back* moves the focus to the previous view.
- *Undo* reverts the ontology to the state before the last modification was made.
- *Save* saves the current state of the ontology.

We report a thorough description of our instrumented version of Protégé, which includes more events and functionalities in addition to the ones above [25]. Generated log files (see an excerpt below) contain a timestamp, the name of the event, and the object of the event.

```
1: 1390228276585,Element edited:finish,StEmilion subclass of:
Bordeaux and madeFromGrape value CabernetSauvignonGrape
2: 1390228277786,Save ontology,wine.owl
3: 1390228280204,Reasoner invoked,HermiT 1.3.8
4: 1390228280647,Mouse entered,Class hierarchy
5: 1390228282910,I_Entity hovered,Burgundy
6: 1390228283049,I_Entity selected,Burgundy
7: 1390228283661,I_Hierarchy expanded,Burgundy
```

This excerpt shows that the user added a property madeFromGrape and a filler to that property CabernetSauvignonGrape to the class of StEmilion wines (line 1); that, the ontology is saved (line 2); and the reasoner is invoked (line 3). When the reasoner is finished the user enters the class hierarchy (line 4), selects an inferred class (line 6) and finally expands the inferred hierarchy under Burgundy.

STUDY

Participants

Sixteen participants (11 male) between 22 and 47, median age 32.5, took part in our study. They had a background in computer science, and worked both in academia and industry. We used snowball sampling to contact possible candidates and invited any who reported to be knowledgeable about OWL and Protégé to participate. Participants completed a questionnaire containing 5-point Likert scales on the following: "Assess your expertise with OWL"; "Assess your expertise with Protégé"; "Assess your knowledge about potato varieties" (to ascertain the familiarity of participants with the domain of the tasks), where 1 indicated 'Novice' and 5, 'Expert'.

Experimental Design

The overall goal was to construct an ontology of potatoes to drive a 'potato finder' application. Participants were asked to carry out the following tasks of increasing difficulty:

1. Classify the potatoes by cropping times.
2. Import a file containing descriptions of potato yields. Represent the yields of each kind of potato and classify by combinations of yield and cropping time.
3. Add in a representation of culinary role (i.e. preferred way of cooking). Build at least two classes that combine the three axes (culinary role, yield and cropping time).

Participants were told not to start from scratch, but to adopt the persona of a 'jobbing' ontologist given an OWL ontology to extend and maintain. No explicit instructions were given on how to accomplish the tasks, but because participants were experts, we expected them to exhibit a repertoire of activities, including the invocation of the reasoner and the establishment of restrictions on classes. Participants were given a printed table with the necessary information —cropping time, yield or skin colour— to build the potato ontology. We also provided them with an OWL file containing 13 subclasses of various potato varieties and another one with a small hierarchy of cropping times for potatoes, which also removed some of the burden of large amounts of editing. There was no fixed time specified in which to complete the tasks, but participants were free to stop at any time. Participants filled out a post-test questionnaire about the perceived difficulty of each task using a 5-point Likert scale, where 1 indicated 'easy' and 5, 'difficult'.

Apparatus

The instrumented Protégé was deployed on a Windows 7 laptop with a Tobii X2-60 eye-tracker installed. The areas of interest (AOIs) correspond to those defined in Figure 2. It must be noted that the AOIs are not necessarily static as their arrangement and layout changes depending on the view being used, and users do often switch views. There are 8 different views on the default Protégé installation. While there is a general view (the one shown in Figure 2), the other views specialise in particular aspects of the ontology: classes, properties or queries. Thus, when users switch to another view or a pop-up dialogue appears, the AOIs are redefined accordingly. Video and audio were also recorded; completion times were logged during observation of the video recordings.

RESULTS

A median of 4 was obtained for both the questions regarding OWL and Protégé expertise, which confirms that participants were tending towards being experts, whereas a median of 1.5 for expertise about potatoes suggests little knowledge about the domain. Participants perceived an increasing level of difficulty in the tasks: $Mdn = 1$ and $M = 1.4$ for task 1, $Mdn = 2$ and $M = 2.1$ for task 2, and $Mdn = 2$ and $M = 2.5$ for task 3. A Kruskal-Wallis test indicates that these differences are significant, $\chi^2 = 12.19, p < 0.005$. Median completion times were 10min 42s for task 1, 12min 11s for task 2 and 18min 37s for task 3. Again, the Kruskal-Wallis test suggest that these differences are significant, $\chi^2 = 10.65, p < 0.005$. Reasoning time was included in completion times; the impact of delays was negligible as the aggregated median time for reasoning across participants was just 560 ms.

Log Data Analysis

The logs of participants' interaction with Protégé show 9 210 events of the types mentioned in §*Instrumenting Protégé* and around 55K mouse hovering events. Figure 3, on the left hand side, shows the distribution of frequencies of the events. The top three events alone (*Entity selected*, *Description selected* and *Entity edited:start*) account for the vast majority of events (56%). On the other hand, the 8 events that are less frequently triggered —those at the bottom of the long tailed distribution— account for just 3.5% of all the events. If we analyse event frequency by event category we find that interaction events account for 65% of events, followed by authoring events (30%) and environment events (5%). 83% of the interaction events are on asserted entities, whilst 17% are on inferred entities. If we consider interaction events individually, the ratio of inferred events to the total number of events (inferred+asserted) shows that 13% of entity selections, 9% of description selections, 34% of hierarchy expansions and 36% of hierarchy collapses occur on the inferred entities.

We compute the correlations between completion times and the frequency of events in each task using Spearman's correlation test. For task 2 we find there is a strong positive relationship between completion time and the number

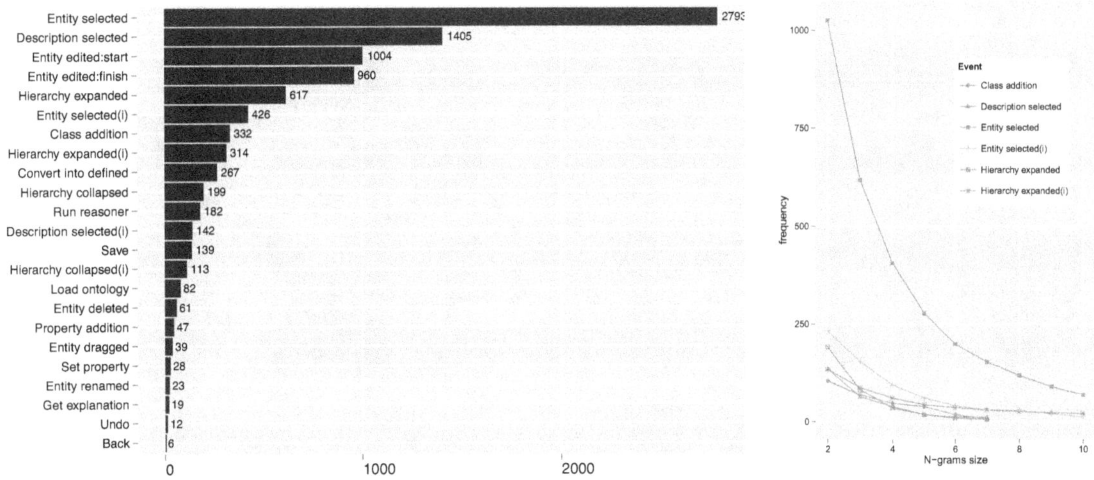

Figure 3. Log data of all participants: frequency of events (left) and frequency of N-grams of the same consecutive event (right) — (i) indicates inferred.

of selected entities $\rho = 0.76, p < 0.002$, and expansion $\rho = 0.67, p < 0.007$ and collapse $\rho = 0.63, p < 0.02$ of the asserted hierarchies. Interestingly, the more times explanations are requested ($\rho = 0.61, p < 0.03$) and the reasoner is invoked ($\rho = 0.48, p < 0.06$) the longer it takes to complete a task. Similar relationships are found for task 3 where there is a strong positive correlation between completion time and reasoner invocation ($\rho = 0.72, p < 0.003$) as well as with the number of times an entity has been renamed ($\rho = 0.63, p < 0.02$). Even if the correlations of the same event do not hold between tasks (except for the invocation of the reasoner), the strong correlations between completion time and number of selected entities, and the times the hierarchy is expanded and collapsed suggest that it took longer for participants to complete tasks because navigating in the asserted hierarchy kept them busy. Also, since the reasoner had to be run to classify entities, there are at least two explanations of why it takes longer to complete tasks for those who run the reasoner more often: (i) it might be a symptom of a trial and error strategy for not achieving the classifications enunciated by the tasks; (ii) it may be indicative of a particular authoring style in which participants run the reasoner at each modification in order to limit the spread of errors [24].

We define authoring patterns as common sequences of events. In order to identify such sequences we carry out an N-gram analysis of the events in the log files using the *tau* package [4] for the R statistical computing environment. A preliminary analysis shows there are many repeated N-grams of the same event. This is particularly illustrative of the events shown on the right hand side of Figure 3. In this case, an N-gram of size 3 means there are 3 consecutive occurrences of the same event: e.g. *class addition, class addition, class addition*. Figure 3 depicts that higher N-grams are less frequent. However, surprisingly, there are around 100 N-grams of size 10 for the entity selection event and a high number of size 3–6 N-grams for the rest of the depicted events. It is worth highlighting that all of these events (except *class addition*, which requires text entry) are performed using a mouse click. This facilitates triggering the same consecutive event without much effort. The high number of N-grams containing consecutive entity selections and class expansion events (either asserted or inferred) indicates that a great deal of activity occurs in the class and property hierarchy areas. Results also suggest that adding entities and navigating the class hierarchy is a highly repetitive and monotonous task. Another observation reveals that for N-grams > 3, more consecutive expansions occur in the inferred hierarchy than in the asserted.

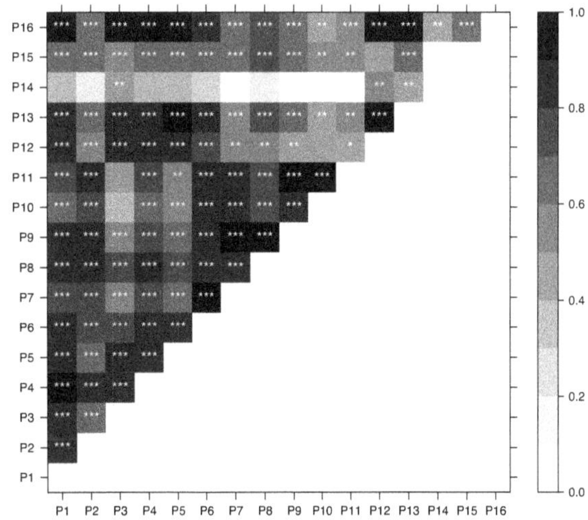

Figure 4. Mantel tests on transition matrices: * stands for $p < 0.001$, ** $p < 0.01$ and * $p < 0.05$, where correlations $r > 0.45$.**

Informed by the work of Thimbleby *et al.* [22] we build an adjacency matrix for each participant, where each cell contains the number of transitions from state S_i to state S_j, and where the states are those events described in §*Instrumenting Protégé*. These transition matrices can be considered the fingerprint of each participant and enable us to identify the similarity of the participants' interaction by comparing the matrices. One way of discerning the similarity between fingerprints is by computing correlations between transition matrices using Mantel's test[3]. An analysis of fingerprints on an

[3]Mantel's test is used in ecology to compare the genetic distance between organisms.

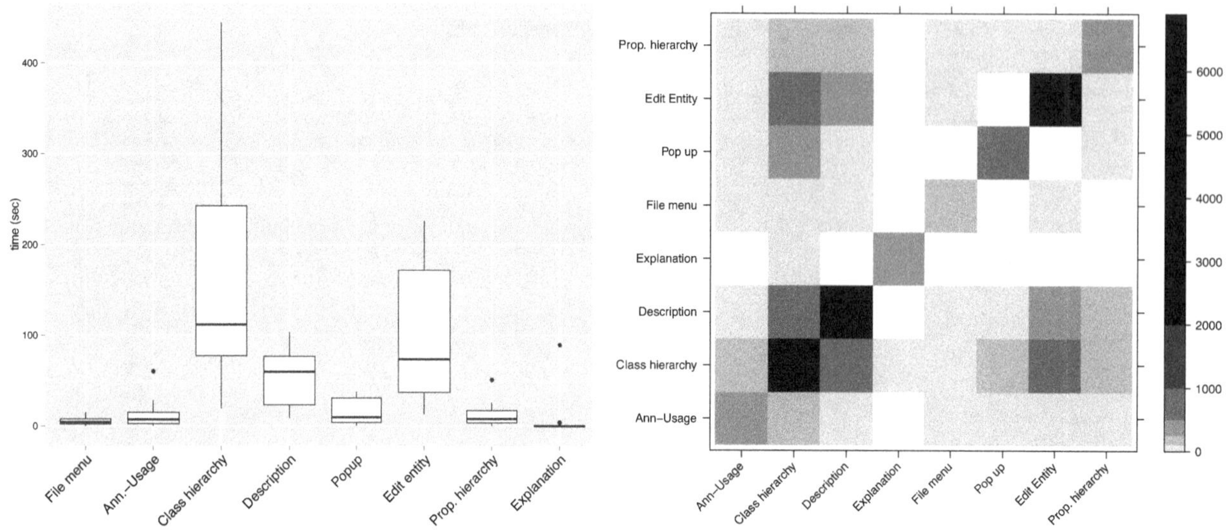

Figure 5. Eye-tracking data: distribution of aggregated dwell times on AOIs (left); matrix of consecutive transitions between AOIs (right).

individual basis yields an almost linear correlation for the majority of participants across the three tasks ($r = 0.73$ on average across all users), which suggests consistency of behaviour at an individual level. Similarly, results in Figure 4 show that the inter-user behaviour is very similar, which suggests the presence of patterns. However, it can also be seen that not all participants have common patterns, which may be indicative of different authoring styles.

Eye-Tracking Data Analysis

We collected 21 304 fixations in the defined areas of interest (AOI). The Shapiro-Wilk normality test indicates that the number of fixations and the aggregated dwell time on AOIs are not normally distributed, $W = 0.63, p \backsim 0.00$ and $W = 0.69, p \backsim 0.00$ respectively. We therefore apply a Friedman test to see if differences in the number of fixations and aggregated dwell time on the AOIs is statistically significant. Indeed, the Friedman test reveals a significant effect of AOI on dwell time, $\chi^2(7) = 80.932, p \backsim 0.00$. Post-hoc pairwise comparisons using Wilcoxon signed-rank test (with Bonferroni correction) indicate there are significant differences between all AOIs, except for *Property hierarchy* and *Annotations*. There is also a statistically significant difference in the number of fixations on the AOIs, $\chi^2(7) = 82.247, p \backsim 0.00$. Post-hoc pairwise comparisons using the Wilcoxon signed-rank test (with Bonferroni correction) suggests all differences are significant.

Table 1 shows the number of fixations and the overall dwell time on each AOI, while the boxplots on the left side of Figure 5 depict the distribution of dwell time on each AOI across all participants. The data suggest that the class hierarchy gets by far the greatest number of fixations (43%) and receives attention from participants 45% of the time. With the exception of the *Edit entity* dialogue (both 26% of the fixations and dwell time) and the description area (17% of the fixations and 15% of dwell time) the remaining areas obtain only a small number of fixations.

The matrix on the right of Figure 5 conveys the frequency of transitions between different areas. In other words, it shows

	File menu	Ann. -Usage	Class hierarchy	Desc.	Pop-up	Edit entity	Property hierarchy	Expl.
Fixations	314	722	9061	3557	883	5579	791	397
Dwell time	73.75	173.96	2318.29	766.79	227.99	1351.05	172.18	93.14
Mdn	4.11	6.85	111.61	60.05	9.45	73.69	7.85	0
SD	4.45	15.87	130.98	32.92	14.71	79.07	13.67	23.83
Max	14.59	60.26	444.53	103.23	37.60	226.36	51.01	89.36
Min	0	0.43	19.48	8.80	0.15	13.03	0.35	0

Table 1. First two rows: number of fixations and aggregated dwell time on each AOI. Below, descriptive statistics of dwell time across participants. All times are reported in seconds.

where the participants look in t_i based on where they were looking in t_{i-1}. While it is expected that cells at the diagonal of the matrix will get the higher number of fixations —it is likely that if there is a fixation in a given area the next fixation will be in the same area— there are also some unexpected findings. First of all, the matrix is (almost) symmetric, which indicates that frequencies are similar in both directions: i.e. fixating first on the class hierarchy and then on the description area is equally as likely as fixating on the description area and then looking at the class hierarchy. Secondly, there are some symmetric transitions not located on the diagonal, which stand out because of their higher frequency:

- From the class hierarchy to the description area.
- From the class addition pop-up dialogue to the class hierarchy.
- From the *Edit entity* dialogue to the class hierarchy.
- From the *Edit entity* dialogue to the description area.

Again, these findings emphasise the centrality of the class hierarchy and its role as a pivotal element in most activities.

From Events to Activities

The analysis of log and eye-tracking data alone yields a number of interesting findings about how repetitive the authoring process is and how most activities occur around the class hierarchy. In order to deepen our understanding of common authoring activities, we conducted N-gram analysis with log data and eye-tracking data merged as follows:

```
1395152087431,eye,Class hierarchy
1395152088065,eye,Class hierarchy
```

```
1395152090012,log,EntitySelected
1395152090589,log,EntitySelected
1395152091213,eye,Description
1395152091483,log,EntitySelected
1395152092605,log,EntitySelected
1395152093684,log,EntitySelected
1395152094896,log,HExpanded
```

The analysis of log data has already shown that participants exhibit similar behaviours (see Figure 4), as described in in §*Log Data Analysis*. However, the high frequency of the same events occurring consecutively initially obscures some common activities. The eye-tracking data also contains a high number of consecutive fixations in the same AOI, as shown by the diagonal of the matrix in Figure 5. To facilitate the analysis we merge the sequences of consecutive events. We illustrate this merging in the following log file shown, where the 'M' before events stands for 'multiple':

```
1395152088065,eye,M_Class_hierarchy
1395152090589,log,M_entity_selected
1395152091213,eye,Description
1395152093684,log,M_entity_selected
1395152094896,log,HExpanded
```

Using this merged data, the method used to identify the activities was to compute N-grams > 3 increasing the N-gram size one at a time until the output of the computation only yielded concatenation of repeated and smaller N-grams. Then, we selected the atomic N-grams as the representative ones and removed their permutations. The analysis of N-grams reveals that interaction can be classified into three main types of activity: editing, reasoning and exploration. Figure 6 depicts these activities, where an arc between states indicates a transition, and its value gives the probability that the transition is about to happen, while a dashed arc means there may be a gaze event in between two interaction events. These gaze events are typically fixations on the class hierarchy and the description area. For instance, the transition between *Run reasoner* and *Select entity* in Figure 6 (right) indicates that 41% of the time after the reasoner has been invoked, participants select an entity in the class hierarchy right after looking at the class hierarchy and/or at the description area.

Exploration

There are several activities that suggest participants are exploring the class hierarchy. Most notably, Figure 6 (left) shows that participants expand the asserted class hierarchy after loading an ontology, presumably to check the arrangement of the class hierarchy and the features of classes in the description area. The expansion of the asserted class hierarchy is often followed (48% of the time) by the repeated selection of different classes while participants look at their descriptions, and then finally settle on one. Interestingly, exploration of the inferred class hierarchy differs from exploration of the asserted one in several ways. Firstly, the goal of the exploration of the inferred hierarchy is not the selection of a description (for a later modification), but the observation and checking of the inferred class hierarchy and the features of its elements (which may have changed after running the reasoner). Secondly, exploration of the asserted class hierarchy entails expanding the hierarchy until a desired depth level is reached and then selecting and observing a number of items at that level; this suggests that participants may have a clear idea of the location of the classes for which they are looking. By contrast, the exploration of the inferred class hierarchy suggests more uncertainty, as participants expand the hierarchy multiple times, select and check the features of multiple classes and then again, expand the class hierarchy. This finding, together with the higher number of consecutive N-grams on the expansion of the inferred class hierarchy (see Figure 3, right), provides evidence for the exploratory nature of the navigation of the inferred hierarchy. Exploration of the asserted hierarchy is about familiarisation with the ontology and finding a specific location to add or modify an entity, while exploration of the inferred one is to check the state of the ontology.

Editing

The repetitiveness of editing classes is demonstrated by the number of times (362, an average of 22.6 per participant) the editing activity shown in Figure 6 (centre) is found. This four-step activity entails selecting an entity, which is followed by the selection of another one 37% of the time, and the selection of a description 29% of the time. As denoted by the dashed arcs, a fixation on the class hierarchy or on the description area is common in such transitions. If a description is selected it is likely to be modified (63% of the time) and followed by another selection of an entity 59% of the time.

Whilst editing, participants select entities in the class hierarchy and either look at their descriptions, or look for other entities in the class hierarchy. After the desired entity has been selected, it is modified by adding properties to classes or establishing restrictions on the class relationships. The high probability that these events occur consecutively, along with the frequency with which this activity is performed, indicates that entities were modified in batches. This can be explained by the fact that the tasks mostly consisted of adding restrictions to 13 classes that represented potato varieties.

Reasoning

We uncovered a number of patterns of activities before the reasoner is run, and a number after the reasoning process has finished. As depicted in Figure 6 (right), saving the current ontology occurs before the reasoner is invoked 40% of the time; after converting a class into a defined one, and looking at the class hierarchy, the reasoner is run 17% of the time. There are two key activities that occur after running the reasoner: 41% of the time participants observe the consequences of reasoning on the asserted hierarchy and the description area, then select one or more classes, and check their descriptions. Since the description area shows the inferred features of classes, this behaviour may indicate that participants are checking whether the reasoner had consequences for the features of classes, in addition to classifying classes. To check classification, participants expand the inferred class hierarchy and make selections on inferred entities, which occurs 30% of the time after the reasoner has been run.

How Activities Connect to Each Other

Once the main activities are identified we are able to detect them programmatically. Consequently we can reconstruct the authoring process, which can roughly be described as

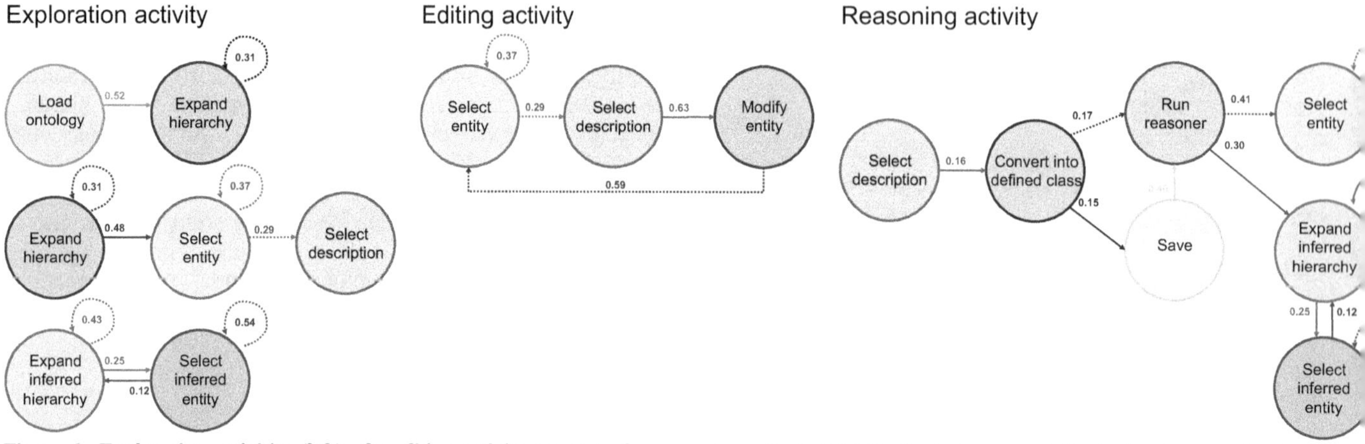

Figure 6. Exploration activities (left); the editing activity (centre); the reasoning activity (right). Dashed arrows indicate fixations on the class or description area between states.

an initial exploration of the ontology, a burst of modifications combined with exploration, and exploration after reasoning. Since activities (as opposed to events) have clear boundaries, activity completion times can be measured. We find that exploring the inferred hierarchy after reasoning takes longer with each task (from $Mdn = 4.56$s in task 1 to $Mdn = 16.27$s in task 3) perhaps because of the increased complexity. On the other hand, the editing activity stays stable (from $Mdn = 9.48$s in task 1 to $Mdn = 8.88$s in task 3). We can also identify different authoring styles: some participants run the reasoner every time they add a defined class; others only run it once all defined classes have been defined; others follow hybrid approaches.

DISCUSSION

Identification of Authoring Activities

The number of consecutive class additions, and the strong patterns found for editing activities, indicate that ontology authoring is highly repetitive and is carried out in batches: first classes and properties are added, then these are edited by adding properties to classes, and establishing restrictions on relationships. While the mouse event driven interface of Protégé certainly *enables* users to perform these monotonous tasks, correlations in §*Log Data Analysis* suggest that exploring the asserted hierarchy to place a new entity is a source of delay.

The class hierarchy receives the attention of users 45% of the time and most of the action occurs within its boundaries. Findings in §*Eye-Tracking Data Analysis* indicate that users' attention centres here when they add new classes and edit existing entities on pop-up dialogues, suggesting that the class hierarchy acts as an external memory of the ontology. This means that the decision making process for adding names to new entities and making modifications is based on the current state of the class hierarchy. Alongside the class hierarchy, the description area also plays an important role across all activities. When users explore the class hierarchy, seek the location of a class to be modified, or run the reasoner, their gaze fixates on the class hierarchy and the description area (see Figure 6). This behaviour suggests that the class hierarchy plays the role of an index containing pointers to extended information; this information is then accessed by looking at the container of the features of each element, i.e. the description area.

Even if reasoning engines have improved over the years, they (or their interaction with Protégé) sometimes show unstable behaviour that causes the authoring environment to freeze. The observed activity of saving the current ontology before running the reasoner might therefore be a strategy to prevent information loss. Those participants who ran the reasoner more often tended to be those who took longer to complete the tasks. Frequent reasoning may also be due to a particular authoring style, or an indicator of a 'trial and error' strategy for debugging [24].

We found that navigation of the inferred class hierarchy tends to be of an exploratory nature, and occurs to check the state of the hierarchy. By contrast, navigation of the asserted hierarchy is more directed —users know what they are looking for— and focuses on finding the specific location of a class to which a modification is planned. The direct relationship between a greater number of class hierarchy expansions and higher completion times might be explained by unsuccessful directed search. Similarly, exploring the hierarchy right after the ontology is loaded and checking the description of its elements suggests a strategy of becoming familiar with the ontology.

Design Recommendations

We enumerate a set of design recommendations that cater for authors' information needs, as expressed by the activities identified above.

- **Support bulk editing**: Authoring tools should provide bulk editing functionalities to add entities, and to establish restrictions on these entities —this is especially useful when building ontologies from scratch. This may be through including spreadsheet functionalities, and/or allowing authors to upload CSV (or similar) files as a mechanism to populate ontologies; such features and tools do exist, but these are not part of Protégé by default.
- **Place editing features close to the class hierarchy**: Because the class hierarchy appears to play the role of an external memory, functionality for editing ontologies should

be placed closer to the class hierarchy, and ideally the authoring environment should include recommendations for establishing restriction on entities, and suggestions for the names of those being added based on lexical patterns [17].

- **Show entity descriptions close to the class hierarchy**: The class hierarchy also plays the role of an index that users navigate when they wish to obtain information about the features of entities, which they must then read in the description area. While Protégé allows the description and class hierarchy to be juxtaposed, this is not the default; these areas should be merged rather than scattered, allowing details of entities to be hidden and shown on demand, and avoiding a division of attention across the screen.
- **Anticipate reasoner invocation**: As saving the ontology is a good predictor of running the reasoner, this could be used to anticipate the invocation of the reasoner in the background to save time (reasoning can be a lengthy process).
- **Automatic detection of authoring problems**: The 'trial and error' authoring strategy, which is operationalised as the concatenation of editing and reasoning activities, is used for debugging and indicates authoring difficulties [24]. Detecting this strategy automatically opens up new avenues to problem pre-emption.
- **Make changes to the inferred hierarchy explicit**: In order to check the (sometimes unexpected) consequences of running the reasoner, users engage in a detailed exploration of the inferred class hierarchy, which is time consuming and may be prohibitively difficult in large ontologies. This occurs because the changes made to the ontology as a result of reasoning are not made explicit by Protégé, and therefore they have to be actively sought. Authoring tools should give explicit feedback about the consequences of reasoning, without obliging users to perform a manual exploration of the class hierarchy. There could, for example, be an area for containing notifications produced by a tool that computes the semantic difference of the ontology before and after reasoning [9].

Methodological Considerations

The uptake figures of Protégé as the preferred environment to build ontologies indicate that it is an authoring environment used by the vast majority of authors (around 70%). However, our study contains some confounding factors that should be taken into account when assessing its external validity. There is the question as to whether the relatively small number of expert users, educated in computer science, are representative of novice authors, or those from other domains. Our findings are naturally most applicable to the population studied (i.e. OWL and Protégé experts), but we used an accessible domain to minimise the effect of domain expertise.

It is difficult to say to what extent the activities we found are generalisable to the ontology authoring process, and to what extent they are particular to the tool used, and the tasks carried out. We suggest that the identified activities will occur in other tasks, although their periodicity and the way in which activities are connected may vary. That is, sometimes there will be less reasoning and more editing, but the activities will still be present. We establish a baseline for future work that will include running studies in the wild, where the activity of users will be monitored on real projects, and running studies with different user groups, including novices.

Implications Beyond Knowledge Artefacts

Studying usability in highly-specialised domains requires the investment of significant resources, in terms of familiarisation with the domain and acquiring a minimum level of knowledge [6]. The identification of typical tasks is fundamental to informing usability walkthroughs. Our method, which is domain agnostic, facilitates the identification of activities by allowing them to emerge from the data. This methodology will thus have applications in highly-specialised complex software domains such as bioinformatics, e-health or design.

Previous work investigating the construction and curation of complex structured data has primarily explored the workarounds individuals employ when carrying out information management tasks in the fragmented landscapes of databases and spreadsheets [26]. End-users are able to publish complex data such as online spreadsheets, JSON, RDF and Bibtex files, provided that they have the appropriate development environment [1]. These studies, including those in which the authoring patterns of software programmers are discussed [16], conclude that the demands of users often exceed the capabilities of tools and, as a result, users develop sophisticated authoring strategies to mitigate the limitations.

Often, identifying such strategies relies on qualitative enquiry methods, which are able to provide rich information, but do not scale, and may be subject to experimenter or recall bias. Here we describe a bottom-up method for identifying user activities, unknown *a priori*, when they deal with complex information structures. Whilst this does not necessarily provide the same depth of information as a qualitative study, it provides potentially greater breadth, and supports a more ecologically valid design, as participants are free to engage in the tasks without interruption. We propose that this approach is useful not only for identifying the authoring strategies carried out by those who construct complex conceptual knowledge artefacts, but also those used for the construction of other complex artefacts of the kinds mentioned above.

CONCLUDING REMARKS

Understanding the activities performed by ontology authors is important, not only to make sense of the authoring process, but also to build tools that provide better support for engineering complex knowledge artefacts. Following an emergent, data-driven approach, we identify common authoring activities, discover how the user interface of the most popular current tool introduces inefficiencies into the authoring process, and propose a set of design guidelines that address these issues. Implications of this work go beyond the realm of ontology authoring; we suggest that the method we employ is generalisable to other scenarios in which users must deal with domain specific software and complex structured data.

ACKNOWLEDGMENTS

The instrumented version of Protégé and datasets are openly available at `http://owl.cs.manchester.ac.uk/whatif/`. The research was funded by the EPSRC (EP/J014176/1).

REFERENCES

1. Benson, E., and Karger, D. R. End-users publishing structured information on the web: An observational study of what, why, and how. In *Proc. of CHI '14* (2014), 1265–1274.
2. Bizer, C., Heath, T., and Berners-Lee, T. Linked data - the story so far. *International Journal on Semantic Web and Information Systems 5*, 3 (2009), 1–22.
3. British Broadcasting Corporation. BBC ontologies. Retrieved from `http://www.bbc.co.uk/ontologies`.
4. Buchta, C., Hornik, K., Feinerer, I., and Meyer, D. tau: Text analysis utilities. Available at `http://cran.r-project.org/web/packages/tau/`.
5. Cardoso, J. The semantic web vision: Where are we? *IEEE Intelligent Systems 22*, 5 (2007), 84–88.
6. Chilana, P. K., Wobbrock, J. O., and Ko, A. J. Understanding usability practices in complex domains. In *Proc. of CHI '10* (2010), 2337–2346.
7. Duineveld, A., Stoter, R., Weiden, M., Kenepa, B., and Benjamins, V. WonderTools? a comparative study of ontological engineering tools. *International Journal of Human-Computer Studies 52*, 6 (2000), 1111–1133.
8. Dzbor, M., Motta, E., Buil, C., Gomez, J. M., Goerlitz, O., and Lewen, H. Developing ontologies in OWL: An observational study. In *OWL: Experiences and Directions Workshop* (2006).
9. Gonçalves, R. S., Parsia, B., and Sattler, U. Categorising logical differences between OWL ontologies. In *Proc. of CIKM '11* (2011), 1541–1546.
10. Horridge, M., Bail, S., Parsia, B., and Sattler, U. The cognitive complexity of OWL justifications. In *Proc. of ISWC '11*, vol. 7031 of *LNCS*. 2011, 241–256.
11. Horrocks, I. Ontologies and the semantic web. *Communications of the ACM 51* (2008), 58–67.
12. Khalili, A., and Auer, S. User interfaces for semantic authoring of textual content: A systematic literature review. *Web Semantics: Science, Services and Agents on the World Wide Web 22* (2013), 1 – 18.
13. Lambrix, P., Habbouche, M., and Pérez, M. Evaluation of ontology development tools for bioinformatics. *Bioinformatics 19*, 12 (2003), 1564–1571.
14. Martin, D., Brun, C., Remy, E., Mouren, P., Thieffry, D., and Jacq, B. Gotoolbox: functional analysis of gene datasets based on Gene Ontology. *Genome Biology 5*, 12 (2004), R101.
15. McGuinness, D. L., and Patel-Schneider, P. F. Usability issues in knowledge representation systems. In *Proc. of the AAAI'98* (1998), 608–614.
16. Piorkowski, D. J., Fleming, S. D., Kwan, I., Burnett, M. M., Scaffidi, C., Bellamy, R. K., and Jordahl, J. The whats and hows of programmers' foraging diets. In *Proc. of CHI '13* (2013), 3063–3072.
17. Quesada-Martínez, M., Fernández-Breis, J., and Stevens, R. Lexical characterization and analysis of the BioPortal ontologies. In *Artificial Intelligence in Medicine*, vol. 7885 of *LNCS*. 2013, 206–215.
18. Randall, D., Procter, R., Lin, Y., Poschen, M., Sharrock, W., and Stevens, R. Distributed ontology building as practical work. *International Journal of Human-Computer Studies 69*, 4 (2011), 220–233.
19. Rector, A., Drummond, N., Horridge, M., Rogers, J., Knublauch, H., Stevens, R., Wang, H., and Wroe, C. OWL pizzas: Practical experience of teaching OWL-DL: Common errors & common patterns. In *Proc. of EKAW '04*, vol. 3257 of *LNCS*. 2004, 63–81.
20. Spackman, K. A., and Campbell, K. E. Compositional concept representation using SNOMED: towards further convergence of clinical terminologies. In *Proc. of the AMIA Symposium* (1998), 740.
21. The Gene Ontology Consortium. Gene Ontology: Tool for the Unification of Biology. *Nature Genetics 25* (2000), 25–29.
22. Thimbleby, H., Cairns, P., and Jones, M. Usability analysis with Markov models. *ACM Transactions on Computer-Human Interaction 8*, 2 (2001), 99–132.
23. Vigo, M., Bail, S., Jay, C., and Stevens, R. Overcoming the pitfalls of ontology authoring: Strategies and implications for tool design. *International Journal of Human-Computer Studies 72*, 12 (2014), 835–845.
24. Vigo, M., Jay, C., and Stevens, R. Design insights for the next wave ontology authoring tools. In *Proc. of CHI '14* (2014), 1555–1558.
25. Vigo, M., Jay, C., and Stevens, R. Protégé4US: Harvesting ontology authoring data with Protégé. In *The Semantic Web: ESWC 2014 Satellite Events*, vol. 8798 of *LNCS*. 2014, 86–99.
26. Voida, A., Harmon, E., and Al-Ani, B. Homebrew databases: Complexities of everyday information management in nonprofit organizations. In *Proc. of CHI '11* (2011), 915–924.
27. W3C Consortium. The Wine Ontology. Retrieved from `http://www.w3.org/TR/owl-guide/wine.rdf`.
28. W3C OWL Working Group. OWL 2 Web Ontology Language Document Overview, 2012. `http://www.w3.org/TR/owl2-overview/`.
29. Wang, H., Tudorache, T., Dou, D., Noy, N. F., and Musen, M. A. Analysis of user editing patterns in ontology development projects. In *On the Move to Meaningful Internet Systems: OTM 2013 Conferences*, vol. 8185 of *LNCS*. 2013, 470–487.
30. Warren, P. Ontology users' survey – summary of results. Tech. Rep. KMI-13-1, Knowledge Media Institute, 2013.
31. Warren, P., Mulholland, P., Collins, T., and Motta, E. The usability of description logics. In *Proc. of ESWC '14*, vol. 8465 of *LNCS*. 2014, 550–564.

Helping Users Bootstrap Ontologies: An Empirical Investigation

Yuhao Zhang, Tania Tudorache, Matthew Horridge and Mark A. Musen
Stanford Center for Biomedical Informatics Research
1265 Welch Rd., Stanford, CA-94305, USA
{zyh, tudorache, horridge, musen}@stanford.edu

ABSTRACT
An ontology is a machine processable artifact that captures knowledge about some domain of interest. Ontologies are used in various domains including healthcare, science, and commerce. In this paper we examine the ontology bootstrapping problem. Specifically, we look at an approach that uses both *competency questions* and *knowledge source reuse via recommendations* to address the "cold start problem"—that is, the task of creating an ontology from scratch. We describe this approach, an implementation of it, and we present an evaluation in the form of a controlled user study. We find that the approach leads users into creating significantly more detailed initial ontologies that have a greater domain coverage than ontologies produced without this support. Furthermore, in spite of a more involved workflow, the usability and user satisfaction of the bootstrapping approach is as good as a state-of-the-art ontology editor with no additional support.

Author Keywords
Ontologies; Authoring; Competency Questions; Bootstrapping; User Study

ACM Classification Keywords
H.5.m Information Interfaces and Presentation (e.g. HCI): Miscellaneous; I.2.4 Knowledge Representation Formalisms and Methods: Semantic networks

INTRODUCTION
An ontology is a machine processable representation of a domain of interest. Ontologies are used in many diverse domains such as healthcare, science and commerce. Classes in an ontology represent concepts in a domain and are typically organized into a subsumption hierarchy. For example, an ontology describing movies, will likely describe a class `Movie`, along with more specific classes such as `ActionMovie` and `ThrillerMovie`. A `Movie` is described by some properties such as `title`, `releaseYear`, and `genre`, and may have relationships to other entities in the ontology.

CHI 2015, April 18 - 23, 2015, Seoul, Republic of Korea
Copyright 2015 ACM 978-1-4503-3145-6/15/04$15.00
http://dx.doi.org/10.1145/2702123.2702433

Ontology engineering, the process of building and maintaining an ontology, is a notoriously complex task, and creating an ontology from scratch can be particularly challenging. It requires both cognitive effort to conceptualize a domain, as well as expertise in knowledge representation to actually develop the ontology. Because of this, over the years, the ontology engineering research community has proposed several ontology engineering methodologies [1] that can be used to assist and guide people when creating ontologies.

A common first step in many ontology engineering methodologies is defining a set of *competency questions* [2] that the final ontology should be able to "answer". For example, in the Movie domain, an example competency question could be: *"What types of movies are there?"*. The main idea behind competency questions is to both scope the ontology and to validate the final ontology. Another common step is using existing (unstructured or semi-structured) knowledge sources to expand the initial set of seed concepts. These sources can be used in a manual fashion, where the ontology engineer draws inspiration from them, or they can be used in a semi-automated fashion, for example, as an input into an ontology learning from text algorithm [4].

Despite the fact that these various methodologies and techniques have been proposed by the research community, and arguments made for their utility, there is currently no system that combines the ideas of competency questions and knowledge source reuse for bootstrapping ontologies. In this paper, we, therefore, explore these ideas for use in a practical setting. We implement a technique that tackles the bootstrapping problem, and we validate this through a user study. Our novel approach first generates seed terms by parsing user-provided competency questions. It then recommends additional terms from external knowledge sources in order to enrich the ontology. To the best of our knowledge, we are the first to support and evaluate this kind of bootstrapping process. As a side contribution, we have developed a tool, called TermBuilder that implements the proposed technique.

DESIGN
In recent work, other researchers have identified design recommendations for improving ontology authoring [3]. Our bootstrapping technique follows their recommendations to support automated ontology population and seamless integration with external knowledge sources. In contrast to ontology learning systems [4], our system does not require any training data and it allows users to specify competency questions

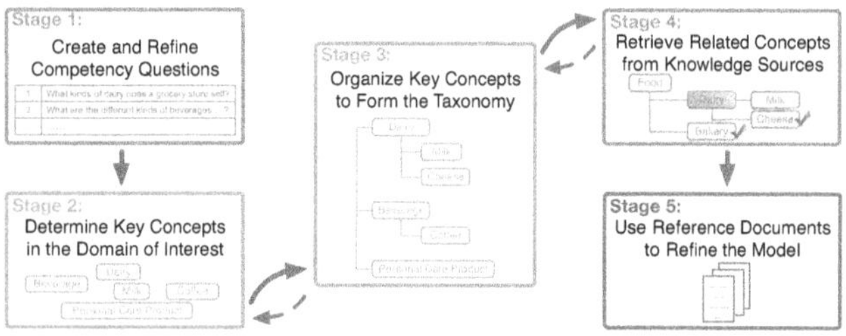

Figure 1. The workflow and the 5 stages for bootstrapping ontologies

in natural language rather than coming up with handcrafted seed terms as input.

The workflow of our ontology bootstrapping technique has five stages, and is shown in Figure 1. The workflow interweaves the seeding of the ontology using the competency questions (Stage 1, 2, and 3) with recommendations for additional terms from external sources (Stage 4 and 5).

Stage 1. Competency Questions Authoring Ontology developers start by listing the competency questions that the ontology should be able to answer.
Stage 2. Concept Extraction An algorithm is run that parses the competency questions syntactically, and extracts the seed concepts. These concepts are then presented to the user visually ranked by their occurrence frequency using varying font sizes and different color shades.
Stage 3. Hierarchy Management Users are able to add the relevant seed concepts in the class hierarchy in their appropriate positions (e.g., add `Cartoon` as a subclass of `Movie`).
Stage 4. Concept Recommendation Users select existing concepts in the ontology (for example, the recently created seed concepts), and the tool will recommend other related and relevant concepts by performing look-ups in general-purpose knowledge sources. Five types of recommendations are currently supported: `superclass-of`, `sibling-of`, `subclass-of`, `synonym-of` and `related-to`. We have evaluated several knowledge sources, and found that WordNet provides the best qualitative results with very little noise, and hence it is the one we are using.
Stage 5. Reference Document Recommendation We present the user with free text search results from Wikipedia and the general Web using the selected seed concepts as keywords. The search results provide additional reference documents that the user may use to further enrich the ontology.

USER STUDY

In order to investigate how users respond to our proposed bootstrapping technique and workflow we carried out a user study. The study evaluates the system as a whole, without isolating any part of it, and focuses on: **(1) Utility**: Does the technique help users build initial ontologies that are more detailed and have a better domain coverage than ontologies built without the technique?, **(2) Learnability**: Can users easily learn to use the technique? and, **(3) User Satisfaction**: Do users perceive the technique to be easy and pleasant to use?

The main part of the study consisted of the participants building two ontologies, with one ontology being built *without* bootstrapping tool support, and the other ontology being built *with* bootstrapping tool support. We chose two domains to be modeled (one for each ontology): Grocery ($\mathcal{D}1$) and Transportation ($\mathcal{D}2$). We chose these domains with the following considerations: (1) they are familiar to most people, (2) they are uncontentious as opposed to more complex domains, such as genetics, and, (3) we speculated that the effort required to identify the important terms in each domain is similar. All the experiment materials are available online.[1]

For building an ontology *without* bootstrapping tool support, participants used WebProtégé—a generic Web-based ontology editor. We chose WebProtégé as: (1) it is in wide use,[2] and (2) it supports ontology developers with varying levels of expertise, including ontology authoring neophytes.

For building an ontology *with* bootstrapping tool support, participants used TermBuilder—our implementation of the previously described workflow for bootstrapping ontologies. A detailed description of TermBuilder is available online.[3]

Participants

We recruited 12 participants (6 female participants) using convenience sampling. All participants (1 PhD student, 5 postdocs, 3 research scientists, and 3 software engineers) work in our department (a biomedical informatics research group). Participants self-reported their ontology authoring experience: 5 had no experience at all, 4 had an intermediate-level of experience, and 3 had an expert-level of experience. All participants were new to TermBuilder and WebProtégé. Each participant received a $20 gift card.

Materials and Methods

All experiments were conducted independently in the same environment (using a Mac desktop computer and keyboard, OSX 10.9.4, 2.66 GHz, 8GB RAM and Chrome v37.0). A facilitator (one of the authors) with full understanding of the study was in charge of presenting materials, recording times and answering questions, when necessary. All sessions were videoed for later analysis. Each participant completed three parts to the experiment:

PART 1 [*Tool Introduction*] The following background materials were given to the participant in sequence: (1) a *Participant Information Sheet* with background information about the study; (2) an *Ontology Background Knowledge Sheet* containing introduction and examples of ontology development; (3) a *Tool User Manual* with tutorials for using TermBuilder and WebProtégé to build ontologies.

PART 2 [*First and second ontology building sessions*] Participants were randomly assigned to one of the four groups shown in Table 1 (three participants per group). Each participant built two different ontologies from two different domains, $\mathcal{D}1$ and $\mathcal{D}2$. One ontology was built using TermBuilder, and the other ontology was built using WebProtégé. The order of domains and tools was specified

[1] `http://goo.gl/JjZXAx`
[2] `http://webprotege.stanford.edu` server hosts over 10,000 user-contributed or authored ontologies.
[3] `http://goo.gl/c7Fk6b`

Group	Session 1	Session 2
A	TermBuilder and $\mathcal{D}1$	WebProtégé and $\mathcal{D}2$
B	TermBuilder and $\mathcal{D}2$	WebProtégé and $\mathcal{D}1$
C	WebProtégé and $\mathcal{D}1$	TermBuilder and $\mathcal{D}2$
D	WebProtégé and $\mathcal{D}2$	TermBuilder and $\mathcal{D}1$

Table 1. Assignment of participants in different groups randomized by order of tools and domains.

according to their assigned group. For example, a participant in *Group A* first used TermBuilder to build an ontology from $\mathcal{D}1$, then she used WebProtégé to build an ontology from $\mathcal{D}2$. Before each session, the facilitator provided the participant with a *Task Description Sheet* containing a piece of stimulus text describing the domain to be modeled along with five example competency questions. Each ontology building session was limited to a maximum of 30 minutes in order to ameliorate problems caused by fatigue. However, we made it clear to participants that they could terminate the session at any time either because they deemed their ontology to be complete or for any other, unspecified, reason. For each session, we recorded the time spent building the ontology and the number of entities created.

PART 3 [*User feedback via questionnaire*] Following Part 2, each participant was asked to anonymously complete a short survey about their experience with TermBuilder and WebProtégé. The survey contained 5-point Likert-type questions designed to ascertain user satisfaction and perceived learnability of both WebProtégé and TermBuilder. It also contained questions about the perceived utility of the different TermBuilder modules. For each question, participants could provide free-text comments in order to explain their ratings.

RESULTS

Although 12 people participated in the study we discarded the results of participant P2 (a female medical expert). During the study P2 failed to interpret the task description correctly and populated her ontology with a large number of medical-domain (especially drug) classes—entities that do not belong to the grocery domain. We decided that this behavior was a breach of the study protocol and thus removed her from the results set and final analysis. All results can be found online.[4]

The median time to complete *Part 1* was 15 minutes; *Part 2* First session 30 minutes; and, *Part 2* Second session 21 minutes. All participants completed all parts of the experiment in full. The difference between the time spent in the first and second sessions is significant under a Mann-Whitney U test; $U = 91$, $p = 0.040$. As the experiment environment is identical in each session, this difference in times is most possibly caused by the fatigue effect. It is also worth noting that experiments for WebProtégé and TermBuilder are equally affected by this effect, since the assignment of the tools in the two sessions was randomized.

R1: Entity Creation We conducted a Mann-Whitney U test to compare the number of entities created with WebProtégé to the number of entities created with TermBuilder. We also calculated the effect size of the test (r). There was a significant difference between WebProtégé (Mdn = 60) and TermBuilder (Mdn = 97); $U = 25.5$, $p = 0.020$, r=0.45.

R2: Relevant Entity Creation A user-created entity was deemed to be *relevant* for the ontology, if the entity describes a concept in the domain modeled by the ontology. A modeling expert (one of the authors) performed a blind examination of the resulting ontologies in order to determine the number of relevant entities per ontology. We compared the number of *relevant* entities created with WebProtégé to the number created with TermBuilder. There was significant difference between WebProtégé (Mdn = 58) and TermBuilder (Mdn = 96); $U = 24.5$, $p = 0.016$, r=0.50.

R3: Non-given Relevant Entity Creation We define a *non-given relevant entity* to be an entity that is relevant for the domain, but is not explicitly mentioned in the supplied task description sheet. For example, when only "*Aeroplane*" is given in the Transportation domain task description sheet as subclasses of "*Aircraft*", the user also created "*Helicopter*" and "*Airship*" as subclasses. These two entities are also relevant to the domain. In terms of the number of *non-given relevant entities* per ontology, there was a significant difference between WebProtégé (Mdn = 35) and TermBuilder (Mdn = 78); $U = 18.5$, $p = 0.004$, r=0.59. There was also a significant difference in the rate at which participants created the *non-given relevant entities* (no. of entities/minute) between WebProtégé (Mdn = 1.38) and TermBuilder (Mdn = 3.62); $U = 16.0$, $p = 0.002$, r=0.62.

R4: Coverage We define the domain coverage of ontology to be the *number of reference competency questions that the ontology is able to "answer"*. In order to assess coverage by ontology, a modeling expert (one of the authors) performed a blind examination of the resulting ontologies. A Mann-Whitney U test shows a significant difference in the level of domain coverage of ontologies created with WebProtégé (Mdn = 8) and TermBuilder (Mdn = 10); $U = 29.5$, $p = 0.036$, r=0.45.

R5: Authoring Time A Mann-Whitney U test did not reveal a significant difference between the time spent using WebProtégé (Mdn = 23.5) and the time spent using TermBuilder (Mdn = 25).

Finally, Table 2 shows some of the results from the survey, including the *Users' perceived easiness of learning to use the tool* (EL) and the *User satisfaction* (US). Ratings were given on a 5-point Likert-typed scale, where 3 is neutral, 1 is strongly negative, and 5 is strongly positive. We computed both the median and interquartile range (IQR) for each measurement. A Mann-Whitney U test suggests that the difference between user's perceived easiness of learning (EL) to use WP and TB is significant; U=105.5, p=0.040, r=0.44. Moreover, no statistically significant difference is found between user satisfaction (US) of the two tools; U=70.5, p=0.991, r=0.02.

ANALYSIS

Summary

Results **R1** [Entity Creation] ($p = 0.020$), **R2** [Relevant Entity Creation] ($p = 0.016$), and **R3** [Non-given Relevant Entity Creation] ($p = 0.004$) are statistically significant (for $\alpha = 0.05$) and point to the fact that the workflow represented

[4]`http://goo.gl/8URRYs`

	TermBuilder		WebProtégé	
	EL	US	EL	US
Median	3.5	4	4	4
IQR	1	0.5	0.25	0.25

Table 2. The *Ease of learning to use the tool* (EL) and the *User satisfaction* (US) resulting from the questionnaires.

by TermBuilder produces ontologies that are more detailed than ontologies produced without tooling that supports the workflow. The workflow supported by TermBuilder encouraged participants to create new entities, that were not listed in the domain description, when compared with the traditional WebProtégé-based editing (**R3**). We note that the domain coverage measured by competency questions appears to increase significantly from WebProtégé to TermBuilder ($p = 0.036$). Furthermore, it appears that the workflow and tool, which is arguably more prescribed and requires more steps than the workflow used in a plain ontology editor, does not adversely impact the time taken to complete the task (**R5**) which, all things considered, is a positive outcome.

In essence, although using TermBuilder requires an understanding of the (somewhat involved) steps in the bootstrapping workflow, the fact that participants created richer ontologies using TermBuilder than they did with WebProtégé in the allotted time, suggests that the bootstrapping workflow and, indeed, TermBuilder brings benefits to this whole process.

Domain Coverage Measured By Non-given Terms

In terms of the number of *non-given relevant entities*, there is a significant difference between WebProtégé and TermBuilder ($p = 0.004$). These differences also suggest that the bootstrapping workflow encouraged participants to build ontologies that have a better domain coverage. It is arguable that the differences may stem from specifics of the bootstrapping workflow: Participants were able to easily bootstrap their ontology development with the seed concepts extracted from the competency questions, and then add further entities as they explored the knowledge sources and the recommended document resources (Steps 4 and 5). Ultimately, we believe that the bootstrapping workflow creates a snowball effect in the development process that boosts both efficiency and domain coverage.

Learnability and User Satisfaction

As shown in Table 2, participants' perceived learnability of TermBuilder is slightly lower than that of WebProtégé (with a median of 3.5 compared to 4). This result is understandable if we consider that users have only simple interactions (typing, drag-and-drop) when using WebProtégé, whereas using TermBuilder requires developers to follow the five-stage workflow. Since a rating of 3 is neutral, this result reveals that participants hold fairly positive attitudes toward the learnability of TermBuilder. User comments support this claim: One commented that "*I referred to the manual mainly because I did not recall all the steps (for TermBuilder). Once I did the step, it was quite easy*" (P5). Moreover, it is worth noting that the learnability of the technique could still be improved, as one participant wrote: "*Once I reviewed the tutorial and practiced the steps once or twice, the steps were very easy to repeat thereafter to build the ontology.*" (P6)

On the other hand, we see that self-reported user satisfaction (US in Table 2) for TermBuilder is positive. Moreover, participants were similarly satisfied with both setups (medians of 4) and no significant difference is found between the results of WebProtégé and TermBuilder. This, combined with the above discussion about learnability, points to the fact that users perceived the overall experience of using TermBuilder to be as satisfactory as using WebProtégé, even though the workflow of using TermBuilder is more involved and more difficult to learn compared to WebProtégé.

Further, the higher IQRs of the ratings for TermBuilder suggest that the attitude of the users toward TermBuilder compared to WebProtégé is more scattered. When we linked the participants' self-reported levels of expertise with their comments, an interesting connection is observed: While intermediate-level developers enjoyed the convenience with which TermBuilder provided them with, a novice participant commented: "*I found using TermBuilder more complicated*" (P3), and an expert participant wrote that "*I feel limited by WordNet*" (P7).

CONCLUSION

Ontologies are complex artifacts that are very hard to build. We present a technique for bootstrapping ontology development by combining competency questions with recommendations of knowledge reuse, and we evaluate it empirically. The user study shows that the technique helps ontology developers build more detailed ontologies that have a better coverage of the domain compared to a setup with no additional support. Even though the workflow is more involved, the usability and user satisfaction of the demonstrated technique are as good as the ones of a state-of-the-art ontology editor with no additional support. We believe that such bootstrapping techniques will play an important role in expanding the adoption of ontologies and opening up the field to new communities.

ACKNOWLEDGEMENTS

This work is supported in part by grants GM086587 and GM103316 from the US National Institutes of Health.

REFERENCES

1. Corcho, O., Fernández-López, M., and Gómez-Pérez, A. Methodologies, tools and languages for building ontologies. where is their meeting point? *Data & knowledge engineering 46*, 1 (2003), 41–64.
2. Ren, Y., Parvizi, A., Mellish, C., Pan, J. Z., van Deemter, K., and Stevens, R. Towards competency question-driven ontology authoring. In *The Semantic Web: Trends and Challenges*. Springer, 2014, 752–767.
3. Vigo, M., Jay, C., and Stevens, R. Design insights for the next wave ontology authoring tools. In *Proceedings of the 32nd annual ACM conference on Human factors in computing systems*, ACM (2014), 1555–1558.
4. Wong, W., Liu, W., and Bennamoun, M. Ontology learning from text: A look back and into the future. *ACM Computing Surveys (CSUR) 44*, 4 (2012), 20.

A Spreadsheet Model for Handling Streaming Data

Kerry Shih-Ping Chang and Brad A. Myers
Human-Computer Interaction Institute
Carnegie Mellon University
Pittsburgh, PA 15213 USA
{kerrychang, bam}@cs.cmu.edu

ABSTRACT
We present a spreadsheet model for working with streaming data. Our prototype tool presents techniques to let the user stream data from web services and web input elements to a spreadsheet without preprogramming those sources into the tool. Spreadsheet cells record metadata about where and when the data came from, allowing the user to view and manipulate streaming data using temporal information. Starting and pausing a data stream in the spreadsheet can be controlled programmatically using values computed by spreadsheet cells, making the spreadsheet program highly dynamic and interactive. We demonstrate the range of our design with a series of examples highlighting its ability to create different kinds of applications that process real-time data from the web using simple spreadsheet formulas.

Author Keywords
Spreadsheets; streaming data; web services; end-user programming; live programming

ACM Classification Keywords
H.4.1. Information Systems Applications – Spreadsheets

INTRODUCTION
Much data analysis work nowadays uses real-time data such as market prices, geo-locations of people and vehicles, or social network feeds. Tools that allow easy, ad-hoc use of streaming data sources could be very useful for people such as data analysts, emergency first responders, or even casual users who want to explore real-time web data. For example, one might want to monitor weather alerts from National Weather Service along with real-time searches for Twitter feeds in the alert areas for emergency events, or to monitor item auction prices on eBay to see the trends and guess the right time and price to bid. Currently, using real-time web data requires programmers to writing complex code that streams the data from the providers and dynamically manipulates the collected data. Commercial data analysis or visualization software can let users play with built-in data sources but often lacks customizability in terms of adding new data sources and using them in an ad-hoc manner.

CHI 2015, April 18 - 23 2015, Seoul, Republic of Korea

ACM 978-1-4503-3145-6/15/04...$15.00.
http://dx.doi.org/10.1145/2702123.2702587

This work extends our system called Gneiss[1] [3] (see the next section for an overview) that lets users create web applications by linking web UI elements to spreadsheet cells. In this paper, we describe a spreadsheet model that lets users work with streaming data from web data sources. Our spreadsheet model has several innovations: first, it presents techniques that allow users to stream any fields from arbitrary REST JSON web services without needing a developer to preprogram those sources into the tool (which is often a requirement in prior end-user mashup or spreadsheet tools such as [5,6]). Second, it introduces a design for spreadsheet cell "metadata" which describe other attributes of a cell's value and can be used to manipulate spreadsheet data. In this work, each cell automatically records metadata of its value's provenance and fetched time, allowing users to view or manipulate streaming data in the spreadsheet using temporal information, such as getting the daily maximum and minimum values. Lastly, Gneiss allows streaming to be paused and restarted using conditions computed live from spreadsheet data using formulas. These features make the created spreadsheet program very dynamic and interactive.

To show the generalizability of our model, we demonstrate how the same mechanism that handles streaming data from web services can be used for collecting user data in web input elements such as textboxes on web pages. A spreadsheet column can be set to pull data from a web UI element either when the input element changes or when triggered by live conditions. The data will be saved as a data stream in the spreadsheet, making the spreadsheet work as a backend database for the web application.

Combining all these features, this paper contributes a novel spreadsheet model for using streaming data, where custom real-time applications require only a few spreadsheet formulas that otherwise would require writing complex code.

BACKGROUND
Our prior system called Gneiss [3] introduced a spreadsheet environment for using web service data and creating inter-

[1] Gneiss (pronounced the same as "nice") is a kind of rock. Here it stands for Gathering Novel End-user Internet Services using Spreadsheets.

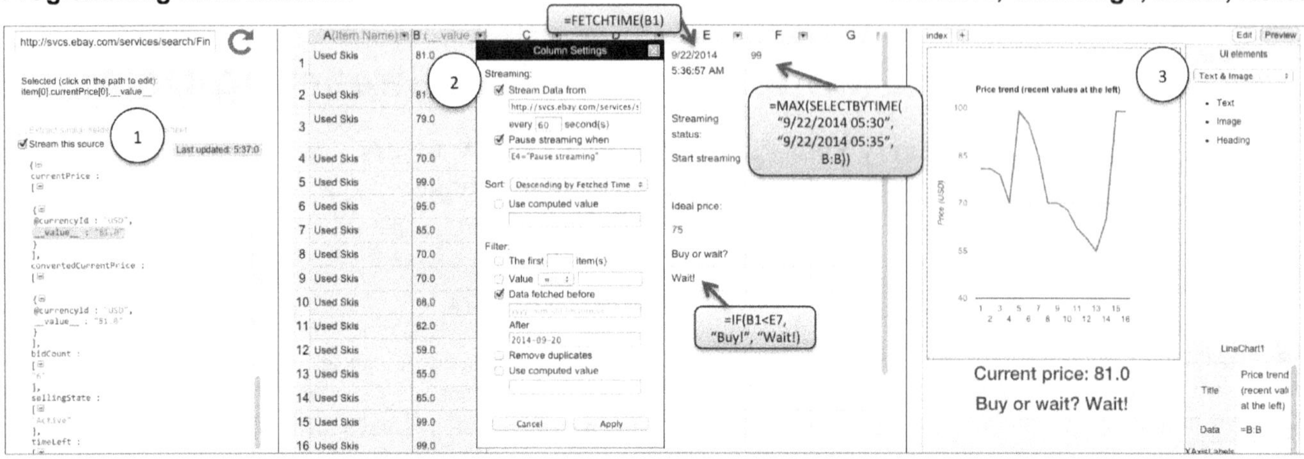

Figure 1: A screenshot of our tool. Here the user creates a real-time application that streams the name and price of a product on eBay to the spreadsheet (column A and B) every 60 seconds. Each streamed cell records when its data is retrieved (E1) and this temporal information can be used in sorting and filtering, or in spreadsheet formulas (F1) to select cells.

active web applications. Gneiss contains three panes (see Figure 1): at the left (1) is a "source pane" that let users load data from arbitrary REST web services returning JSON data; at the center (2) is a spreadsheet that holds the data to be shown in a web application, and supports arbitrary computations using that data and sorting and filtering rules; at the right (3) is a web interface builder where web pages can be created interactively. Data flow is two-way between the spreadsheet and a web service as a spreadsheet cell value can be referenced in a web API (entered in the URL textbox at the top of the source pane) using the syntax `{{cellName}}` which will invoke the web service whenever the cell's value changes. In the web interface builder on the right (3), the user can create UI elements and visualizations through drag-and-drop, and assign properties of UI elements to be computed from spreadsheet cells. UI element properties can be referenced in the spreadsheet using the syntax `UIID!PropertyName`. This enables two-way data flow between the spreadsheet and the web interface builder, thus allowing the creation of web applications that can interactively retrieve and present backend data.

Our work here extends Gneiss by providing a spreadsheet model for working with *streaming* data. The previous Gneiss system did not handle data streams nor did it support cell metadata that allow spreadsheet data to be manipulated based on the time fetched.

RELATED WORK

Some conventional spreadsheet tools have pre-programmed formulas or widgets that pull real-time data from external sources, such as the GoogleFinance formula in Google Spreadsheets or Microsoft Excel's web query. These tools by default do not support creating data streams – they update individual cells with latest values from the sources but do not preserve past sequences of data. Woo et al. [6] extend Excel to collect and process sensor data. Sensor values are stored on a server and streamed to a spreadsheet to use in formulas or visualizations. ActiveSheets [5] is another Excel extension for streaming data. It provides more controls of how and what data should be streamed, such as letting users create new streams using formulas or pause a stream using a button. However, neither system supports manipulating streaming data using temporal information of when the data are retrieved. They also require data sources to be preprogrammed into the server. Forms/3 [2] is a spreadsheet programming tool for creating graphical interfaces. It has a time model for storing and retrieving GUI I/O events, but it does not deal with data sources. There are other languages that support using streaming data, such as Microsoft's StreamInsight [1] for creating streaming applications in C#. In contrast, our work extends the spreadsheet metaphor, because it is already familiar to many end-users.

KEY FEATURES

Here we describe the key novel features in our tool for handling streaming data.

Create a Data Stream in the Spreadsheet

Figure 1 shows a screenshot of our tool's interface. Our tool supports REST web services returning JSON data. The user can enter a web API at the top URL bar in the source pane and view the return data below. In our tool, arbitrary web services can be turn into a streaming source if the checkbox "Stream this source" is checked. The system then starts to send the web service request every 3 seconds (configurable) and updates the source pane with the latest return data. We use a roll-up text animation when replacing old values in the return data to show that they have been refreshed. Unchecking the checkbox stops the streaming. The last updated time of the data is shown in a blue label next to the streaming checkbox.

To create a data stream in the spreadsheet, the user selects a desired field in the return data and drags it to the top cell of a spreadsheet column. The system then starts to stack the column with the latest values of the field pulled from the web service. By default the values are sorted descending by time, so the newest value appears at the top of the column. Using this mechanism, the user can easily stream multiple fields from one or multiple web services in a spreadsheet.

Manipulate Streaming Data using Temporal Information

Streaming data are inherently time-series data, and so the ability to view or manipulate streaming data in the spreadsheet by time is essential. To enable this, we designed each spreadsheet cell to have metadata that describe attributes of its value. The metadata are by default not visible but can be exposed through formulas and be used to manipulate, sort and filter spreadsheet cells (note that cell metadata in our tool are different from user comments in conventional spreadsheets as they are set and maintained automatically by the system). In our spreadsheet model, each streamed cell stores not only its display value but also metadata about its provenance and fetched time, allowing data to be viewed and manipulated using its value, source and temporal information. For example, a streamed column can be filtered to show only the data retrieved today, sort them descending by value and filtered to show only the top 5 rows, to view only the 5 highest values of the day. Our tool applies sorting and filtering rules *dynamically* in the spreadsheet – they are re-evaluated every time when new data are retrieved. So in the above example, the column will update continually to display the 5 highest values. Sorting and filtering rules of a column are controlled by a dialog box (Figure 1 at 2) that is brought up by clicking on the arrow button at the top of the column. By default, columns extracted from the same streaming source are sorted and filtered together and are highlighted in the same color when the dialog box is open.

As mentioned earlier, cell metadata can also be accessed through spreadsheet formulas. We provide a new formula `FETCHTIME(cellName)` that returns the retrieval time of a streamed cell. The return value is in standard ISO 8601 format and can be used with conventional spreadsheet time functions. We provide another formula `SELECTBYTIME(startTime, endTime, range)` that returns an array of values in `range` that are streamed between `startTime` and `endTime`. The `SELECTBYTIME` formula can be easily used together with many conventional spreadsheet formulas that process a set of values. For example, suppose column B in the spreadsheet holds latest news streamed from a news data source. The formula:

```
=COUNTIF(SELECTBYTIME("2014-09-21 9:00",
"2014-09-21 10:00", B:B),"*White House*")
```

returns the number of news articles fetched between 9-10am on September 21st, 2014 that contain the phrase "White House".

Control Streaming Timing

Our model also allows the user to set when it should pull data from a streaming source. To do so, the user opens the column setting dialog box of a streaming column. There she can set the tool to pull data periodically every *x* seconds (for example, "60 seconds" in Figure 1 at 2). She can also choose to pause a stream when a given condition is true (if the condition is not specified, the stream pauses immediately). For example, in Figure 1, the user selects the "Pause streaming when" checkbox and enters "E1='Pausing streaming'" as the condition, then our tool will pause streaming from the source if cell E1 becomes "Pause streaming", and restarts streaming when E1 becomes other values. This feature also allows the user to create applications that dynamically stream data from different sources.

Stream Data from Web Input Elements

Our spreadsheet model can also be applied to stream data from web input elements such as textboxes or forms. The user can set a column to pull data from a web input element by checking on the "Stream data from" checkbox in the column setting dialog box, and setting the input element to be the streaming source. For example, entering `TextBox1!Value` as the streaming source sets the column to stream the value of `TextBox1`. By default, the column pulls data from an input element whenever its value changes. The user can further use the "pause" mechanism described earlier to start streaming only when certain condition is true. For example, using `Button!State!="clicked"` as the pause condition makes the column stream data from `TextBox1` only when `Button` is clicked. Like spreadsheet cells storing data streamed from web services, cells storing data streamed from web input elements also have the same metadata and can be manipulated by retrieval time. This feature also enables our spreadsheet to be used as a form of database for a web application, as it stores input values as streams in the spreadsheet.

Save and Close a Spreadsheet

The user can save her spreadsheet on the server and decide whether to save the streaming data after she closes the spreadsheet. By default, the streamed data are stored on the server's database, and all streaming stops when the spreadsheet is closed. All streaming restarts when a spreadsheet is opened. The user can also choose to remove all streaming data on the server when closing the spreadsheet, or to keep streaming even when the spreadsheet is closed (although our server has a limit for how much data can be stored in the database[2]). As described in [6], the web pages created in the web interface builder can also be exported as a web application running on the server.

IMPLEMENTATION

Our tool is implemented as a web application that contains a client-side spreadsheet tool and a backend server. All streaming data are stored in the backend server for better performance. Based on the data selection rules that the user sets in the spreadsheet (such as filtering), when a new data value arrives, the server selects the appropriate data and returns them to the frontend. We use node.js and MongoDB in the backend, and ConstraintJS [4] in the frontend.

---

[2] We use MongoDB as the database. See its limitations at http://docs.mongodb.org/manual/reference/limits/

DEMONSTRATIVE EXAMPLES

Here we use two examples to demonstrate our tool's ability to create real-time applications that use live streaming data requiring only a few simple lines of spreadsheet code.

Auction Price Tracker

Online auction marketplaces such as eBay let customers bid on an item. The price of an item could change as bids are added or if the seller adjusts the base price. Using our tool, the user can create a real-time price tracker. Suppose the user wants to monitor the price of a product, see its highest and lowest value daily, and get notified when the price is below a threshold (Figure 1 shows a screenshot of a similar example).

The user first uses eBay's FindAPI to get information about the desired product. In the source pane she sets the tool to stream data from eBay and extracts the name and price field from the return data to spreadsheet columns A and B using drag-and-drop. The tool starts to stack data streamed from eBay to columns A and B, with the latest data in the top row. To get the highest price value of today, she enters

```
=MAX(SELECTBYTIME("2014-09-21 00:00:00",
    "2014-09-21 23:59:59", B:B))
```

in cell D1 (as September 21st is the date of today). She then enters the same formula with dates replaced with September 22nd in D2, selects both D1 and D2, and drags the selection down to D7 to fill in D1 to D7 with the highest value each day in the week of September 21st, using the familiar "auto-fill" mechanism in spreadsheets. She similarly fills in E1 to E7 with the daily lowest price. Finally, she enters a price threshold in cell F1 and enters `=IF(B1<F1, "Bid!", "Wait")` in cell F2 to remind herself when to make a bid. In the web interface builder, she creates a web page that has two graphs: one visualizing column B (the price trend, shown in Figure 1 at 3), and another graph showing columns D and E (the daily high and low values) in real-time, along with a text label showing the current price (B1) and another text label showing if she should make a bid (F2).

Real-time Weather Alerts based on Locations

Suppose a user works in a company that has an internal web service tracking current locations of company trucks and wants to create an application that monitors the weather condition at a truck's current location to alert the driver of issues such as if the atmosphere visibility becomes too low. The user first sets column A to stream GPS coordinates of a truck from the company web service and sort the data descending by time, thus the most recent coordinates are in cell A1. To retrieve weather data of the truck's current location, the user uses Yahoo's Weather API, replaces the query value to refer to cell A1 and streams the visibility field from the return data to column B. Cell B1 thus becomes the atmosphere visibility reading of the truck's current location. The user can then use an `IF` formula to check B1's value and see if it is below a certain threshold.

As mentioned earlier, our tool also allows the user to pause a data stream programmatically. Suppose the user stores the location of the truck's destination in cell C1. She can then set the pause condition to be `A1=C1`, so the streaming stops when the truck arrives at its destination.

CONCLUSIONS AND FUTURE WORK

This work contributes a model for using streaming data in spreadsheets. It includes techniques to let users stream data from web sources to a spreadsheet without writing conventional code, a design for spreadsheet cell metadata to let users manipulate spreadsheet data using temporal information, and ways to dynamically control when to pull new data using the spreadsheet language and interaction techniques. Based on this model, our prototype tool provides a live environment for dealing with live streaming data. For future work, we would like to support more types of streaming data sources, such as streaming web APIs (like Twitter's) and mobile sensors. We are interested in exploring more usage of cell metadata, such as to assist people in integrating data from multiple sources or editing a collaborative spreadsheet. We will also run a formal user study evaluating the full Gneiss system.

ACKNOWLEDGEMENT

This research was funded by the NSF under grant IIS-1314356. Any opinions, findings and conclusions or recommendations expressed in this material are those of the authors and do not necessarily reflect those of the NSF.

REFERENCES

1. Ali, M., Chandramouli, B., Goldstein, J., and Schindlauer, R. The Extensibility Framework in Microsoft StreamInsight. *Proc. ICDE*, IEEE (2011), 1242–1253.
2. Burnett, M., Atwood, J., Walpole Djang, R., Reichwein, J., Gottfried, H., and Yang, S. Forms/3: A First-order Visual Language to Explore the Boundaries of the Spreadsheet Paradigm. *J. Funct. Program. 11*, 2, Cambridge University Press (2001), 155–206.
3. Chang, K.S.-P. and Myers, B.A. Creating Interactive Web Data Applications with Spreadsheets. *Proc. UIST*, ACM (2014), 87–96.
4. Oney, S., Myers, B., and Brandt, J. ConstraintJS: Programming Interactive Behaviors for the Web by Integrating Constraints and States. *Proc. UIST*, ACM (2012), 229–238.
5. Vaziri, M., Tardieu, O., Rabbah, R., Suter, P., and Hirzel, M. Stream Processing with a Spreadsheet. In R. Jones, ed., *ECOOP 2014 – Object-Oriented Programming SE - 15*. Springer Berlin Heidelberg (2014), 360–384.
6. Woo, A., Seth, S., Olson, T., Liu, J., and Zhao, F. A spreadsheet approach to programming and managing sensor networks. *Proc. ISPN*, ACM (2006), 424–431.

TextAlive: Integrated Design Environment for Kinetic Typography

Jun Kato **Tomoyasu Nakano** **Masataka Goto**
National Institute of Advanced Industrial Science and Technology (AIST), Tsukuba, Japan
{jun.kato, t.nakano. m.goto}@aist.go.jp

ABSTRACT

This paper presents TextAlive, a graphical tool that allows interactive editing of kinetic typography videos in which lyrics or transcripts are animated in synchrony with the corresponding music or speech. While existing systems have allowed the designer and casual user to create animations, most of them do not take into account synchronization with audio signals. They allow predefined motions to be applied to objects and parameters to be tweaked, but it is usually impossible to extend the predefined set of motion algorithms within these systems. We therefore propose an integrated design environment featuring (1) GUIs that designers can use to create and edit animations synchronized with audio signals, (2) integrated tools that programmers can use to implement animation algorithms, and (3) a framework for bridging the interfaces for designers and programmers. A preliminary user study with designers, programmers, and casual users demonstrated its capability in authoring various kinetic typography videos.

Author Keywords

Kinetic typography; animation; creativity support tool; integrated design environment; live programming.

ACM Classification Keywords

H.5.2. Information interfaces and presentation (e.g., HCI): User interfaces – GUI; D.2.6. Software Engineering: Programing Environments – Integrated environments.

INTRODUCTION

Kinetic typography, a technique for moving and reshaping text in a video, is widely used in music, narrative, and commercial videos to deliver text information in a dynamic way. It can deliver the emotional feeling associated with a text in addition to the text's literal meaning [17]. When it is used in music and narrative videos, text is animated in synchrony with vocal music or speech. The animated text augments the listening experience with visual effects, helping listeners better comprehend what is being vocalized.

Kinetic typography videos have been produced with general-purpose tools for creating animations (e.g., Adobe Flash or After Effects [1]). While such tools provide a fine granularity of control over the animations, producing the final result takes long time even for the experienced user because manual synchronization of the text animation and audio is tedious. In addition, general tools do not provide any guidelines to help novice users produce convincing effects. Tools specifically designed for making kinetic typography videos (e.g., ActiveText [18] or Kinedit [7]) provide predefined templates of effective animations, from which the user can choose. Such domain-specific tools, though, have had a certain limitation in their flexibility. That is, the programming needed to create new animation templates has to be done in separate development environments.

With the goal of pushing forward the state of the art in kinetic typography design, we present TextAlive, a graphical tool that allows interactive editing of kinetic typography videos (Figure 1). While tools for designers and programmers have usually been designed separately, TextAlive is designed to benefit both. We therefore call it an integrated design environment (an integrated *development* environment is one designed only for the programmer). Thanks to its duality for the designer and programmer, its research contribution is three-fold. First, from an input pair consisting of audio and text information, TextAlive can automatically compose a playable kinetic typography video that serves as a concrete starting point for the designer. It also provides interactive user interfaces for editing the video in synchrony with the audio signals. Second, TextAlive allows live programming of animation templates with its built-in development environment that provides continuous graphical feedback to the programmer. Third, its unique framework allows the programmer to easily extend its GUI so that the programmer or designer can intuitively debug or customize the parameters of animation templates.

The remainder of this paper is organized as follows. Related work is introduced to highlight our research contribution. Next, the design and implementation of TextAlive's interaction for the designer and programmer are introduced.

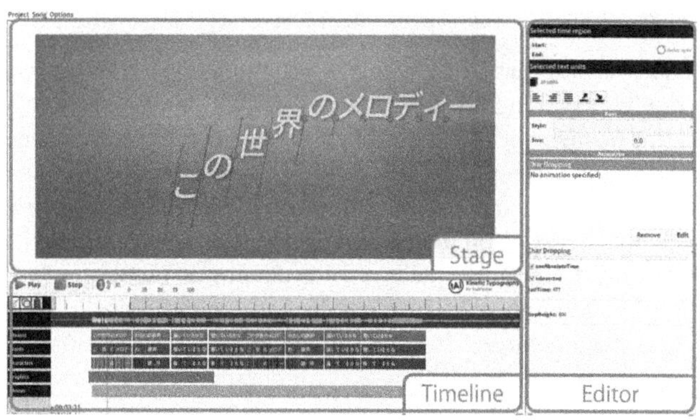

Figure 1. Overview of the TextAlive system.

CHI 2015, April 18 - 23 2015, Seoul, Republic of Korea

ACM 978-1-4503-3145-6/15/04...$15.00
http://dx.doi.org/10.1145/2702123.2702140

Then, the results of a preliminary user study are discussed. Finally, the conclusion and future work are presented. For better understanding, readers are encouraged to see the demonstration video and/or visit http://textalive.jp to try out the system before further reading.

RELATED WORK

Tools for Creating Kinetic Typography

Various tools for creating kinetic typography videos have been proposed. However, they focus on graphical aspects of creating videos. To our knowledge, none of them deals with audio signals synchronized with the videos. This is because their primary use of kinetic typography is for augmenting text-based communication. TextAlive, in contrast, aims to augment audio listening experience with dynamic graphical representation of text information. Prior work on editing time-series multimedia includes synchronized editing of transcription and narration [21]. This is a complementary technique and can be integrated into TextAlive.

The existing tools for kinetic typography videos target programmers, designers, or casual users, not all three. TextAlive is built on top of these. For instance, a framework to help programmers create kinetic typography videos by writing Java source code has been proposed [16]. TextAlive shares some concepts with this framework, such as the hierarchical structures of phrases, words, and characters for representing text information. The ActiveText [18] and Kinedit [7] systems allow designers and casual users to input text, choose animations from several templates, and edit their parameters by using sliders and other standard GUIs. TextAlive also provides similar features. A combination of natural language processing (NLP) and heuristics enables the extraction of emotional information from text and automatic generation of the associated videos [20]. While the existing techniques benefit from NLP, they do not allow user interaction, which is essential if the user is to express his/her creativity.

The existing tools have limitations because of their targeting certain users. While tools for designers and casual users provide interactive GUIs, they typically force the user to use a predefined set of motion algorithms and do not allow any extensions to be implemented. The tools for programmers, on the other hand, have extendibility based on their APIs, but their development environments are usually equipped with text-based user interfaces and do not provide interactive feedback on the source code changes.

There is a visual programming environment that overlays code elements on top of the animation and allows binding a set of elements to text units [3]. Each element represents one typography property (font size, color, style, or scaling), and the set of elements affects the properties of nearby text in a way that depends on the distance between a set element and a text unit. It does not allow precise control of properties, nor does it provide any abstraction, preventing reuse of the created animations. Instead of using visual programming, TextAlive integrates text-based programming into a graphical tool. It provides more precise and flexible control over the text animation and an abstraction of an animation template that is reusable not only by the programmer but also by designers and casual users.

Tools for Creating Animations

While this work focuses on text animation, it is closely related to prior work on tools for general animation. Adobe Flash and After Effects [1] are professional tools used to create various kinds of animation. The user specifies key frames for objects, and the system smoothly interpolates the motion between the frames. These tools have good support for direct manipulation, such as visualizing object trajectories and using drag-and-drop to change the motion or seek time periods. Compared with these professional tools, TextAlive has a limited, or rather focused, GUI for editing text animations synchronized with audio signals, including a timeline interface. The user does not specify key frames, but rather timings of each text unit being vocalized. The timing information is then passed to animation templates that output fluid motions. TypeMonkey [2] is a plug-in for After Effects that has additional user interfaces for choosing text animations from templates and editing their parameters for the purpose of making kinetic typography videos. While it reduces the pain of key-framing, it still requires manual synchronization of the animation and audio. In addition, it has the same issue as other tools for kinetic typography: the limited number of templates restricts the user's expressivity.

Tools that let casual users make animations, such as Microsoft PowerPoint and Movie Maker, do not require key-framing. However, the resulting motions are usually limited to those following simple trajectories. In particular, various sketching interfaces allowing the casual user to create animations have been proposed. K-Sketch [4] allows users to specify the motion of objects by drawing trajectories, which is implemented as our "Trace Path" animation. Draco [15] is a sketch-based tool to animate multiple objects. We also target casual users who make animations of multiple objects (text units) but with more finely grained control for each object. In addition, TextAlive integrates a programming environment that allows authoring of reusable animation templates.

Tools for Live Programming

Live programming [19] is a technique to provide the programmer with continuous feedback about the program being developed. It aims to get rid of the gulf of execution by providing a seamless programming experience with regard to writing code, executing the program, and debugging it.

Live programming in TextAlive is inspired by Victor's demo [23] that allows the programmer to dynamically rewrite parameters of graphical applications during their execution. In our system, the programmer can simply click the "update" button, and there is no need to re-launch the entire program and reconfigure the parameters. It allows the programmer to rewrite the logic of animation templates without losing their parameter information. VisionSketch [13] uses a similar technique, where the logic of image processing algorithms can be dynamically replaced, but it does not preserve the state information when the logic is updated. Subtext [6] continuously revalidates the program without explicit compilation. It updates the program output upon the typing of each character in the source code editor. We intentionally avoided such implicit revalidation and kept the "update" button because the implicit revalidation flushes the screen very often and is distracting.

Professional tools for animation are typically equipped with scripting engines. Adobe Flash and Adobe After Effects, for example, have a built-in scripting engine to control the properties of objects. Some tools meant for casual users, such as Microsoft PowerPoint, also allow such scripting. While most scripting engines allow conversational programming, these tools do not have decent support for bridging the activities of writing code and running the program. On the other hand, Juxtapose [12] is capable of generating a slider bound to a variable value, and Unity allows the programmer to extend its GUI for runtime parameter tuning. Within these environments, GUI widgets bridge that gap between the

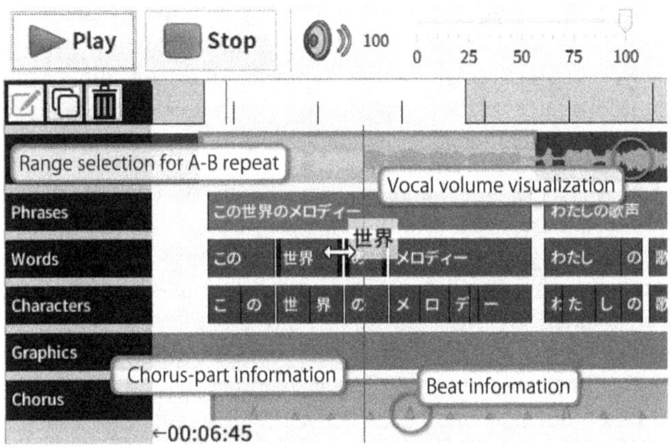

Figure 2. Timeline interface.

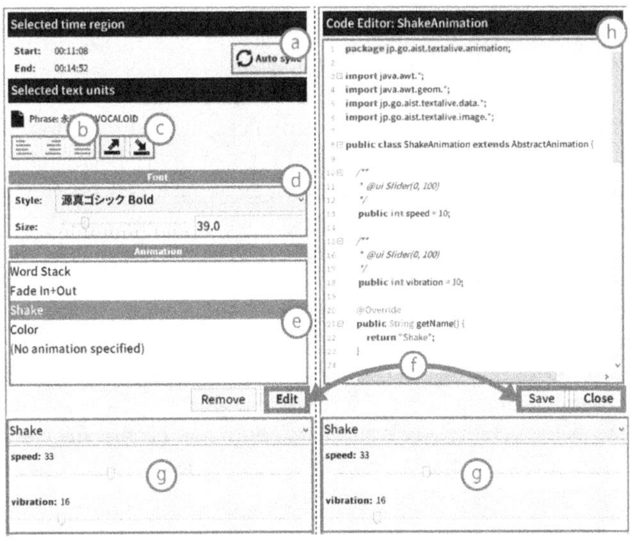

Figure 3. Editor interface and integrated source code editor; the user can switch between them by clicking the buttons (f).

static definition and the runtime behavior of the program. TextAlive takes the same approach, balancing the variety of widgets (more than Juxtapose) and the lines of code (less than Unity). Moreover, TextAlive is specialized for animation authoring. For instance, a set of APIs is provided for easily animating text units. The Stage interface can visualize object trajectories calculated from the user code. Whereas the prior work intended for game development has such visualizations [23, 9], TextAlive uses the trajectories not only for visualization but also for seeking time periods.

TEXTALIVE: AN INTEGRATED DESIGN ENVIRONMENT

This section introduces the interaction design of TextAlive. The first subsection describes interactive editing of kinetic typography videos by designers or casual users. This sort of editing does not require prior knowledge of kinetic typography or programming. The second subsection describes live programming of animation templates by novice programmers. These days, it is not uncommon for the designer to have programming skills. For instance, programming skills in scripting are required to precisely control many objects when using existing tools such as Adobe After Effects [1]. In TextAlive, programming abilities enable designers and casual users as well as programmers to control not only the currently present objects on the screen but also their later reuse and customization.

Interactive Editing of Kinetic Typography Videos

TextAlive can automatically create a kinetic typography video when given an audio file and its transcription. Whereas the existing tools require the user to create a video from scratch and to spend much time on manual synchronization of audio and text, TextAlive significantly reduces the effort required. The composed video can be interactively edited so that it matches the user's style.

Automatic Video Composition and Timing Correction

The user first inputs a pair consisting of a song and its lyrics or a narration and its transcription. Then, the system estimates the timings of each *character* in the text being vocalized [8]. Through this process, not only *characters* but also *words* that consist of characters and *phrases* that consist of words and correspond to one line in the original text come to have timing information about the starting and ending of the vocalization. The system then assigns a default animation template to each *text unit* (a character, word, or phrase) and synthesizes a playable video. If a song is provided, its chorus parts are detected and assigned a more gorgeous animation template (explained in the implementation section). Beat information is also analyzed, and the result is visualized on the Timeline (Figure 2). After this automatic synthesis, the video is shown on the Stage interface (Figure 1), and it will always be playable by clicking the "play" button in the Timeline interface. Any operation described hereafter can be carried out interactively so that the video can be instantly updated.

TextAlive cannot always estimate correct parameters. If there is an error in the estimation, the timing information can be interactively corrected in many ways before being saved for use the next time the same pair of audio and text is loaded. For instance, text units in the Timeline can be drag-and-dropped to instantly fix their timing information. Drawing a rectangle in the Timeline selects multiple text units that overlap the rectangle. Chorus parts are highlighted in the bottom row of the Timeline, and clicking them selects the text units vocalized during the chorus. Once the text units are selected, the "align left," "center," "right," and "justify" buttons in the Editor interface (Figure 3b) can be used to fix their timings collectively. Timing information can also be copied and pasted (Figure 3c), and this is quite useful for groups of text units with the same structure, such as repeating chorus parts.

The seek bar in the Timeline visualizes the sequential changes in vocal volume information extracted from the original audio signals, thereby helping the user to estimate correct timings visually. The seek bar allows one to select a specific time region. While a region is selected, the "play" button plays the corresponding part repeatedly, allowing one to concentrate on correcting the timing and editing the animation of the specific part. Automatic synchronization estimating the timings of the text units contained in the selected region can be applied again by clicking "auto-sync" in the Editor interface (Figure 3a).

Font and Animation Template Assignment

An automatically created video does not at all reflect the user's intention. To make it his/her own, the user selects text units in the Timeline and changes their properties, including fonts, and animation templates with the Editor interface (Figure 3d, e). As in timing correction, property changes can be collectively made on multiple text units. For instance, when a phrase is selected, changes in the font style and size are applied to all of the characters in the phrase.

Predefined animation templates allow novice users to create aesthetic kinetic typography. To avoid implausible visual effects, they are not always applicable to every type of text unit: phrases, words, and characters have different sets of assignable animation templates. In addition, multiple templates can be assigned to a single text unit at the same time. For example, "Sliding Animation" can be assigned to a phrase, and "Hopping Animation" can be assigned to the characters in that phrase. "Karaoke Animation" that changes the text color before/after vocalization can also be assigned to the characters (Figure 4). Combinations of different

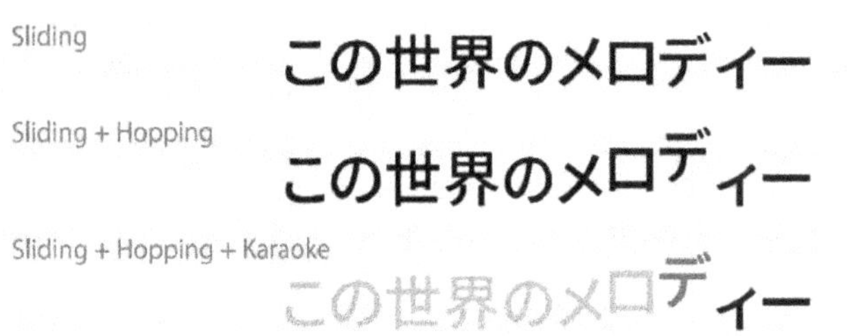

Figure 4. A simple example of kinetic typography effects generated from different sets of preset animation templates.

templates that can be assigned to suitable types of text units allow flexible yet effective kinetic typography design.

Animation Customization

Each animation template has parameters for customizing its appearance, and these parameters can be interactively manipulated with the GUI widgets shown on the Editor (Figure 3g) or the Stage. These widgets are dynamically generated by the template implementation, which is described in detail in the next subsection. They appear when the corresponding template is selected in the Editor interface.

While the Stage can usually show only the current frame of interest in the video, it would be desirable that the user can instantly see how an object's motion is affected by parameter tuning. To make this possible, the trajectories of the selected text units can be visualized on the Stage (Figure 1). The trajectories can be used to seek time periods in the way shown in prior work [5].

Live Programming of Animation Templates

While each animation template can be customized to meet the user's needs, it still limits the resulting animation to a certain extent. General tools for creating animations are often equipped with scripting engines with which the animation of lots of objects can be controlled in a mathematically precise way. Such scripting, though, typically does not allow later reuse because it lacks an abstraction mechanism. There is not much graphical feedback while the user is writing code either.

TextAlive aims to address this issue by enabling "live programming" of animation templates: the user can seamlessly go back and forth between editing animation and implementing templates (Figure 3f). The implementation can be updated by just one click and there is no notion of compilation or execution. The program that creates the animations continues running virtually. The update process updates not only the behavior of the text units but also the GUI widgets specific to the template (Figure 3g). These widgets help the programmer debug the template and help the user interactively customize it.

Implementation of Animation Templates

To read the implementation of an existing animation template, the user selects the template and clicks the "edit" button in the Editor interface. TextAlive then shows the code editor, with which the source code written in Java can be edited (Figure 3h). Each template is defined as a Java class that implements a specific Java interface. The template implementation can be updated by clicking the "update" button, which instantly updates animations of the text units that use the template. This update can be done at any moment, such as during the playing of a song or when the user is observing the motion of text units. To create a new template, the user can either click the "new" button or change the class name in the source code of any existing template and click the "update" button.

Updating running software is generally called a hot swap. It replaces existing objects using old code with dynamically generated new objects using new code. Since such a process simply discards the state information of the old objects, the state information (in our case, customized parameters of an animation template) usually needs special care, such as by the programmer writing some code to store and restore it. TextAlive handles this transparently, which frees the programmer from having to write boilerplate code and allows him/her to concentrate on the algorithm.

Implementation of GUI Widgets for Each Template

As discussed in *Animation Customization*, each template has dedicated GUI widgets to customize its appearance. "Sliding Animation," for instance, has a box of radio buttons to select its horizontal alignment and a slider to control its sliding angle. In order to implement a GUI widget, the programmer should declare a Java public field and write a comment block right before the field declaration in the source code. The comment should be written in a simple format: "*@ui WidgetName([options])*." The generated GUI widget is bound to the public field; GUI operations on the widgets change the field values.

The widgets are not only meant to help designers and casual users manipulate the parameters intuitively. They can also help the programmer debug and test the template during the development process. For instance, the programmer can temporarily create a box of radio buttons for switching between multiple implementations having a similar effect and check which one works best. Once he/she knows which one is best, he/she removes the radio buttons and publishes it for other users.

Below is the list of preset GUI widgets available in the current implementation of TextAlive (Figure 5). Other widgets can be easily added by writing Java source code.

@ui Slider(min, max) shows a slider to change the value of the corresponding integer field between *min* to *max*.

@ui Check() shows a check box to switch between true and false values of the corresponding boolean field.

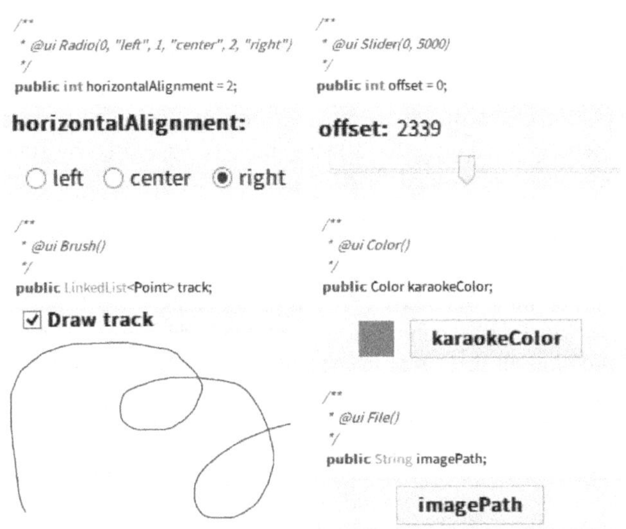

Figure 5. Comments and GUI widgets generated from them.

@ui Radio("label1", v1, "label2", v2, …) shows a box of radio buttons used to select a value.

@ui Color() shows a button with a colored rectangle so that the user can choose a color with the color picker dialog.

@ui File() shows a button used to choose a file whose path is stored in the corresponding String field.

@ui Track() shows a check box used to enable/disable drawing a path by dragging the mouse on the Stage. When a path is drawn, its data is represented as a list of (x, y) coordinates and stored in the corresponding List field. This is used to implement the "Follow Path" animation template that makes text move along the specified path.

IMPLEMENTATION

This section introduces the current implementation of the TextAlive system. It first gives an overview of the system along with the techniques used in the implementation, and then it explains the system in more detail. The first subsection explains how the creation of plausible kinetic typography videos is supported, and the second explains how a live programming experience is provided.

Overview

The architecture of TextAlive is shown in Figure 6. It is currently implemented with Java 7 (64-bit) and tested on a personal computer with a Windows 8.1 (64-bit) OS. Input sound files should use the MPEG-2 Audio Layer III format for playback in the system and are converted to the monaural MS WAV format using FFmpeg for further audio signal processing. Input text is written in a natural language (either Japanese or English) and is converted into a series of phoneme information by using MeCab, open-source software for morphological analysis and part-of-speech tagging.

The audio signal is synchronized with the corresponding phoneme information [8] by attaching timing information to the phrases, words, and characters of the original text. If the input sound file is a song, the beat information and the chorus

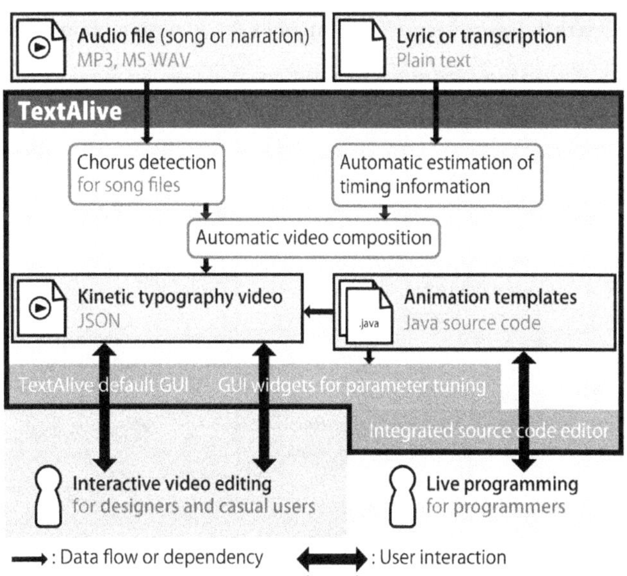

Figure 6. Software architecture of the TextAlive system.

part are detected [10]. This information is referenced for automatic video composition. The Java source code of animation templates is dynamically compiled with the Eclipse Compiler for Java and loaded into the Java VM with the Java Reflection API. In order to store and restore the state information of the animation templates, a text-based JSON format is used as a temporary backup. The animation data is also saved as a JSON file (Figure 9).

Implementation for Kinetic Typography Design

Automatic Video Composition
Given the automatically estimated parameters, TextAlive automatically assigns animation templates to text units and generates a playable kinetic typography video. By default, it

```
public class BasicCharHopAnimation extends AbstractAnimation {
  /**
   * @ui Slider(0, stageHeight)
   */
  public int hopHeight = 60;

  /**
   * @ui Slider(0, 1000)
   */
  public int hopTime = 200;

  public void animate(long time) {

    // Check current time.
    Char c = (Char) getAssignedUnit();
    if (time < c.startTime || (time > c.endTime + hopTime
        || hopTime == 0)) {
      return;
    }

    // Make this char hop!
    float progress = Math.min((float)(time - c.startTime)/hopTime, 1f);
    c.rendering.tx.translate(
        0, (float) -hopHeight * Math.sin(progress*Math.PI));
  }
}
```

Please note that some non-informative lines of code are omitted. The entire code is contained in the supplemental material.

Figure 7. Example implementation of an animation template.

```
// Calculate rendering parameters.
for each text unit,
  reset its rendering parameter.
  for each assigned animation,
    call animation.animate(time).
// Render text.
for each phrase,
  transform the coordinate system.
  for each child word,
    transform the coordinate system.
    for each child character,
      transform the coordinate system.
      render the character
      with the specified parameters.
// Do some pixel-based ops if needed.
for each text and graphic unit,
  for each assigned animation,
    call animation.background(time).
    call animation.foreground(time).
```

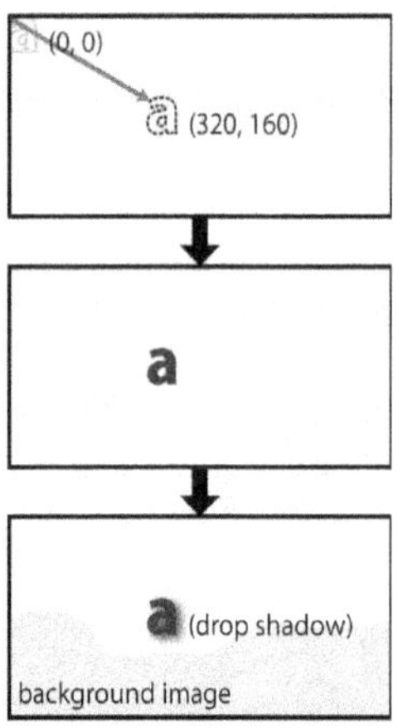

Figure 8. Pseudocode for rendering each frame.

simply assigns the "Sliding Animation" to all phrases and the "Karaoke Animation" to all characters. If the input sound is a song, phrases in the chorus part are assigned the "Sliding and Rotating Animation" and characters in the chorus part are additionally assigned "Hopping Animation" so that the chorus part looks more prominent than the other parts.

The strategy that defines how to assign animation templates is currently written as Java source code and can be easily customized. We plan to implement a GUI for choosing and implementing new strategies.

Text Animation
In a lot of kinetic typography videos, phrases, words, and characters have their own motion algorithms independent from the others. In order to animate text information in a human-readable way, characters often keep their positions relative to each other and are aligned horizontally or vertically. Multiple words are often organized into a phrase that is prevented from overlapping with other phrases. Such motion algorithms can be described in a simple and clean way by using the coordinate system relative to the parent text units (e.g., characters to words and words to phrases).

Given the characteristics of text animation, each text unit holds its timing information (when it starts and ends being vocalized), a list of assigned animation templates, a font name, and one or more characters contained in the unit. Each animation template is required to implement a method named *animate(time)* whose argument is the current time. An example implementation is shown in Figure 7. The template has access to its assigned text unit, and the *animate* method modifies the rendering parameters of the text unit. The parameters include font color, an alpha compositing rule (how to blend the text graphic with the existing pixel values), and an affine transform matrix (a three-by-three matrix that defines how to transform the text graphic and includes translation, rotation, and scaling) relative to the parent text unit. Since the *animate* method can be called with any *time* value at any time, the method is usually expected to be a pure function – in other words, it should return a value without modifying the state of the animation template object.

While changing the rendering parameters can reshape the appearance of the text unit as a vector graphic, there are kinetic typography effects that cannot be supported by such reshaping and instead demand pixel-based operations. They include adding blur or shadows to the text graphics. To support such effects, an animation template can implement *background(graphic context, time)* and *foreground(graphic context, time)* methods that render graphics behind and in front of the text units. Since these methods are called after rendering all text units in the off-screen buffer by using the *animate(time)* method, they have access to the pixel-based representation of the text units.

TextAlive plays and renders the video in a 30-frames-per-second format. The pseudocode for rendering each frame is shown in Figure 8. Graphic units are optional units that hold the start and end times as well as a list of animation templates mainly used for rendering the background or foreground to complement or emphasize text information.

Trajectory Rendering

Trajectory rendering allows the user to see the past and future motion at a glance. The same procedure as used for rendering frames is repeatedly called without actually using rendering graphics, and the absolute time-series positions of the selected text units are visualized as their trajectories.

The trajectory can also be used as an interface to seek time periods. Since the system knows the correspondence between a specific point in the trajectory and timing, the current mouse position can easily be converted into timing information by finding the closest point in the trajectory. When the trajectory is not straight-forward, though, following the closest point sometimes results in a big jump in time, which is not desired. To avoid this problem, the distances between the mouse position and the next or previous point in the trajectory are calculated.

Implementation for Live Programming Experience

Hot-swap for Updating Animation Templates

Animation templates are represented by Java classes that are compiled and dynamically loaded into the Java VM when TextAlive launches. After the user edits their source code, the corresponding classes are recompiled and the resulting Java bytecode is reloaded into the VM.

Such a process, i.e., replacing classes without restarting the VM, is called a hot-swap. A general hot-swap simply replaces an old class definition with a new one and is not sufficient for updating animation templates. If the updating process only updated the class definition, existing objects with old definitions would not be updated. To see the updated motion, the user would need to remove the objects, re-assign the animation template, and reconfigure parameters.

To avoid such hassle, TextAlive automatically extracts state information from old objects, creates new objects with the updated implementation, and makes its best effort to restore the state information. Before a hot-swap, a backup of the state information of the existing objects is created by calling the Java Reflection API to serialize all public fields of each object. It is used after the hot-swap to construct objects with the updated class definition, in effect replacing the old objects. The process of restoring state information is identical to that of loading videos, which is described later.

Static Code Analysis for Generating GUI Widgets

The GUI widgets for customizing animation templates are generated by static code analysis upon compilation of the class definition. The widgets can collectively change the values of multiple variables (i.e., the same parameters of multiple animation template objects) when multiple text units are selected in the Timeline.

Each comment that begins with *@ui* and is located right before a public field declaration is parsed and divided into the widget class name and its options. The option values are evaluated using a subset of the Java programming language, thereby providing dynamic parameters to widgets. The language supports simple mathematical calculations and read-only access to useful parameters such as the resolution of the video (the size of the Stage). For instance, a slider with the maximum value of the height of the Stage can be generated by writing *"@ui Slider(0, stageHeight)"* as shown on line 17 of Figure 7.

Saving and Loading Videos

TextAlive saves a kinetic typography video in plain text JSON format. It consists of a hierarchical architecture of phrases, words, and characters. Each text unit has the vocalization start and end times and a list of information about the assigned animation templates. Unlike phrases and words, characters are also saved with their font name and size. Each animation template is represented by its name and the customized parameters. Figure 9 shows an example of a JSON object of a video.

Loading videos is exactly the reverse of saving them, except for the chance of animation templates being updated. If an animation template has an updated definition, one or more public fields might be added or removed. To construct an animation template object with an updated definition, TextAlive makes its best effort to maintain the state information; newly added fields have their default values, and old values of removed fields are simply discarded.

PRELIMINARY USER STUDY

We conducted a preliminary study to gain user feedback on the TextAlive system and to investigate the capabilities, limitations, and potential of our interaction design. Seven users with varying levels of expertise in authoring videos and programming graphical applications participated in the study. They were asked to use the system and to create a kinetic typography video with one favorite song or narration. They were asked to compare their use of the system against their prior experience on tools for creating videos and graphical applications.

Participants

Seven participants aged 23 to 30 years old (mean 27) took part in the study. Each was paid $30 for their participation.

P1-4 are designers and casual users (two females and two males). P1 is an amateur singer who has used Adobe After Effects [1] to create a simple slide show for her music video; P2 is an amateur illustrator who has no prior experience in

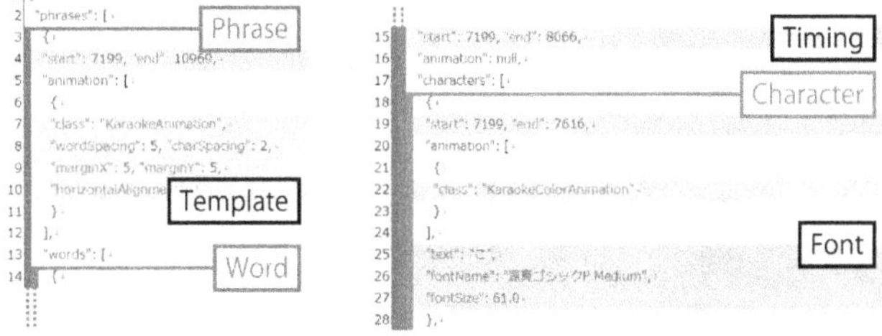

Figure 9. JSON-formatted text for saving the animation.

creating videos; P3 is an amateur disk jockey who has extensive experience in mixing music and recording narrations for Rakugo (a traditional form of Japanese storytelling) but no video authoring experience; P4 is an interaction designer who has used Motion, Final Cut Pro, openFrameworks, and Unity [22] for creating videos.

P5-7 are programmers and are all male; P5 has a small amount of experience creating demonstration videos for his software; P6 is an experienced user of Adobe After Effects (> 2 years) and has created music videos; P7 has a hobby of writing songs and has created music videos with AviUtl, which is freeware for casual video authoring.

Experimental setup

All participants used a standard set of laptop computers with a full HD (1920 x 1080 pixels) display and a mouse (Figure 10). Some of the participants brought their headphones or earphones; others used earphones we provided. The TextAlive system occupied the entire screen during the study. The experiment followed the steps described below and took 2-3 hours for each participant.

Pre-experiment questionnaire: Each participant was asked to fill out a form asking his/her experience in authoring songs, narrations, videos, and programming.

Introduction and demonstration: Each participant was given a 5-15 minute introduction to the TextAlive system by the instructor. The instructor then demonstrated the timing correction, font and animation template assignment, and animation customization using the GUI widgets. For the programmers (P5-7), the instructor also demonstrated the use of the integrated source code editor to modify and create an animation template.

Kinetic typography design: Each participant was given 2 hours maximum to create a kinetic typography video of his/her favorite subject with the system. The participant was allowed to bring data of a song, narration, or image to be used in the video or could choose from a list of the songs we prepared. Since it is usually impossible to create a video for an entire song or narration in 2 hours, the participant was asked to work on his/her favorite part of the song or narration. During this open-ended task, the participant was free to ask any questions about the usage of the system, including how to use the preset animation templates and APIs for implementing animation templates. The participant was allowed to end the study when he/she was satisfied playing with the system.

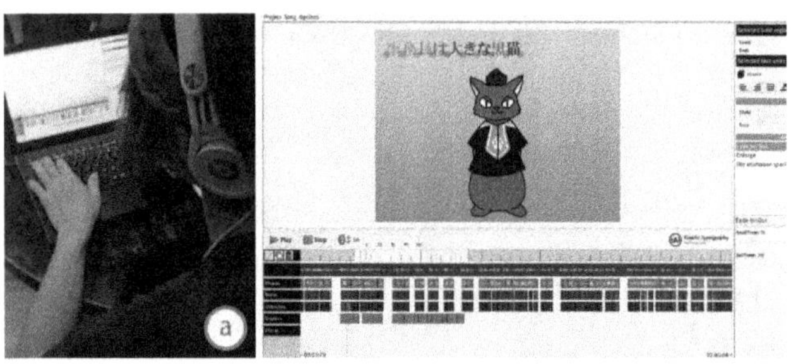

Figure 10. Setup of the user study. (a) A participant using our system. (b) A screenshot taken during the study.

Post-experiment questionnaire: Each participant was asked to fill out a form asking five questions about the usability of the system (selected answers on a 7-point Likert scale), and three questions about the good and bad points of the user interface.

Results and Lessons Learned

All participants could successfully create kinetic typography videos for their favorite part of a song or narration, some of whose screenshots are shown in Figure 11. Two participants used a song we prepared, while the others used their favorite song or narration. The results of the post-experiment questionnaire consisting of the mean, standard deviation, and percentage of positive responses (>4 on a 7-point Likert scale) are shown in Table 1.

Everyone who participated in the study was positive about how suitable TextAlive is for authoring kinetic typography videos (Q5). There were no answers representing negative impressions of the TextAlive system on Q1-3, but there were several neutral answers (= 4 points). The neutral answers were found to come from non-critical reasons such as the participant not being enthusiastic enough in creating kinetic typography videos (P1) and practical reasons that can be addressed by making minor revisions to the system such as adding keyboard shortcuts to frequently used commands (P7). Those who used the live programming feature (P5 and P7) indicated they felt the need for technical support in order to use the system. Their negative answers stem from the programming experience described later.

Automatic video composition was useful for both novice and experienced users: All participants liked the automatic video composition feature a lot. P7 commented *"automatically estimating timing information and synthesizing a playable video is extremely useful, reducing the effort always needed for existing tools I have used."* P3 commented *"it is nice that we no longer need to create but just edit the video."*

The abstraction of phrases, words, and characters was welcomed: Participants with prior experience of creating videos with text information such as subtitles (P1, P4, P6) especially favored the hierarchical abstraction, enabling assignment of different animation templates to each phrase, word, and character. P1 noted that *"the capability of modifying the properties of each character is very useful."* This feature is often missing from existing video authoring tools.

The abstraction of animation templates suggested potential applications: While animating text in a specific time period requires manual parameter tuning in existing authoring tools, animation templates in TextAlive adapt the animation to fit in the period. This allows the user to almost instantly animate text in synchrony with sound. P3 and P4 expressed their desire to play "text jockey" during their live disc jockey performances. P3 also foresees using it for Rakugo storytelling.

No need to stop the video, enabling a fluid experience: Many users appreciated that almost every operation on the system interactively updates the resulting video. P5 commented that *"there was no need to pause or stop the video. With TextAlive, I could select the time region of interest and play the video continuously while editing it. The only exception was when I got too tired to listen to the same part of the song."* P6 appreciated that *"animation templates can be edited in-place (without launching external editors.)"*

Having a variety of animation templates counts: P6 appreciated that the system allows novice users to create good looking videos simply by choosing animations from a list of preset templates. P1 and P7 requested more variety of templates. P4 wrote that *"more variety of animation templates would make TextAlive more appealing, but too many templates might overwhelm the user."* Actually, P3 and P7 complained that the current combo box for choosing an animation template is not informative enough. They commented that more detailed explanations or graphical previews would be desirable. In addition, P6 pointed out the difficulty of predicting the result of combining multiple animation templates, suggesting that we provide preset combinations of animation templates.

The Timeline interface is at the heart of synchronizing audio and video: All users appreciated the usability of the Timeline interface dedicated to timing correction. P1, P2 and P5 especially appreciated the wave-form visualization of vocal sound and the visualization of beat information. In addition, P1 and P5 requested snapping to the beat information while moving or resizing text units in the Timeline.

The Stage interface should allow (more) direct manipulation: P3 appreciated that most of the interfaces for customizing appearance of the selected units are gathered in the Editor interface. On the other hand, P2 commented that most of the

#	Question	The TextAlive system Mean	SD	%
1	I would like to use it frequently.	5.57	1.20	5/7
2	I found it unnecessarily complex.	2.71	1.02	0/7
3	I thought it was easy to use.	4.86	0.75	4/7
4	I needed technical support to use it.	3.29	1.74	2/7
5	I thought it is suitable for authoring kinetic typography videos.	5.57	0.75	7/7

Table 1. Results of the post-experiment questionnaire.

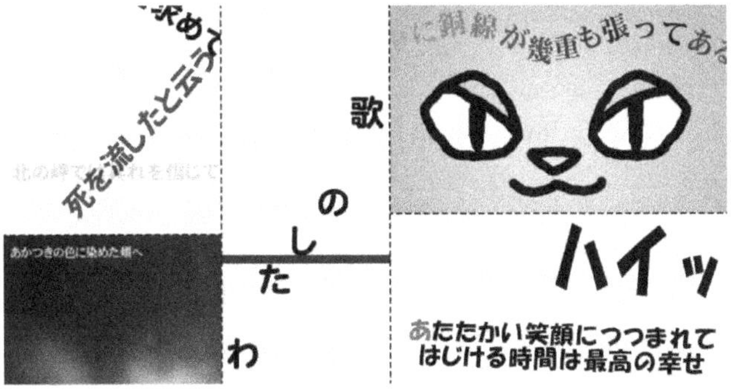

Figure 11. Screenshots of kinetic typography videos in various styles created by the participants (selected and trimmed.)

preset animation templates only use the widgets in the Editor interface and the animation templates should make more use of the Stage interface for their customization. Currently, the "Follow Path" animation is the only preset template that allows the user to interact with the Stage to interactively update the tracing path. P1, P3 and P4 requested that simple animations should be customized by direct manipulation on the Stage, e.g., allowing drag-and-drop of text units to fix their positions at a certain timing. However, it is not straightforward to support direct manipulation of objects whose motion is defined by a combination of multiple algorithms. Since each animation template transforms the coordinates and does not know how the other templates are implemented, the parameters for the template to move the assigned unit to the mouse cursor position cannot be easily retrieved. The process is identical to finding a set of parameters for an unknown function that returns a specific value. Similar problems in physical simulations have been addressed by introducing novel interaction techniques that might be applicable to our case [11]. More improvements to the sketching interaction might also be helpful, as has been indicated in prior work [15].

Programming ensures extendibility but needs training: Users who tried the programming interface (P5-7) all appreciated the extendibility of TextAlive, but at the same time, found it difficult to learn in 2-3 hours. P5 hesitated to use the feature. P7 commented that *"the live programming feature allows fine adjustments of animation but requires prior knowledge, making me procrastinate in its use for some time."* However, he was the most active person to create animation templates by the end of the experiment and also commented that *"the changes in code could be instantly applied to the video, which is nice."* P6 appreciated how easy it is to provide GUI widgets for tweaking parameters. Given that the live programming feature itself is not considered harmful, more software engineering effort to support more "learnable programming" [24] is desired.

CONCLUSION

We have described TextAlive, a tool for creating kinetic typography videos. It can automatically estimate the timing of each character being vocalized. Instead of providing a blank canvas and forcing the user to create videos from scratch, TextAlive analyzes a given pair of audio and text information and creates a playable and editable video. The video serves as a foundation on which the user can create his/her own video. The user interface for interactive editing of the video synchronized with audio signals was highly appreciated by the participants of the user study who had various professional backgrounds. The capability of editing animation templates by writing programs ensures the extendibility of the TextAlive system as a tool that can continue to evolve through use. While the user study confirmed its usefulness, its learning curve should be gentler, and more software engineering help provided.

Although the number of websites for sharing videos and audio files is increasing and more people are getting involved in creating new media content, it is still not easy to create videos synchronized with audio. Music videos on such websites typically feature the artists and illustrations. The lyrics are often placed in the safe area near the edges of the video or are not rendered on the video at all. Kinetic typography is effective at expressing the message of a song or narration visually. The tool described in this paper enhances the expressiveness of casual users by enabling them to create kinetic typography videos. While its current implementation is limited to placing objects on a two-dimensional plane, we are working on an extension to three-dimensional space.

TextAlive is available online at http://textalive.jp. Currently, many songs and narrations and their lyrics and transcriptions are available on the Internet. Preprocessing such information allows the user to create kinetic typography videos without first wading through the synchronization process. Corrected timing information can be shared with others, enabling crowdsourcing of such timing information. Animation templates can also be easily shared with others, meaning that the integrated design environment can be extended cooperatively. While this study focused on the experience of users with different backgrounds, the proposed interaction design enables various forms of collaboration (e.g. programmer with designer, designer with end user, etc.). Investigating such interactions would make an interesting follow up.

ACKNOWLEDGMENTS

This work was supported in part by JST, CREST.

REFERENCES

1. Adobe After Effects. http://www.adobe.com/products/aftereffects.html.
2. aescripts + aeplugins. TypeMonkey. http://aescripts.com/typemonkey/.
3. Chao, C. M. and Maeda, J. Concrete programming paradigm for kinetic typography. In *Proc. IEEE VL 1997*, 446-447.
4. Davis, R. C., Colwell, B. and Landay, J. A. K-Sketch: a "kinetic" sketch pad for novice animators. In *Proc. CHI 2008*, 413-422.
5. Dragicevic, P., Ramos, G., Bibliowitcz, J., Nowrouzezahrai, D., Balakrishnan, R. and Singh, K. Video browsing by direct manipulation. In *Proc. CHI 2008*, p.237-246.
6. Edwards, J. Subtext: uncovering the simplicity of programming. In *Proc. OOPSLA 2006*, p.505-518.
7. Forlizzi, J., Lee, J. and Hudson, S. The Kinedit system: affective messages using dynamic texts. In *Proc. CHI 2003*, 377-384.
8. Fujihara, H., Goto, M., Ogata, J., and Okuno, H. Lyric Synchronizer: automatic synchronization system between musical audio signals and lyrics. *IEEE Journal of Selected Topics in Signal Processing*, 5(6), 2011.
9. Fukahori, K., Sakamoto, D., Kato, J. and Igarashi, T. CapStudio: an interactive screencast for visual application development. *Ext. Abstracts CHI 2014*, 1453-1458.
10. Goto, M, Yoshii, K., Fujihara, H., Mauch, M. and Nakano, T. Songle: A web service for active music listening improved by user contributions, In *Proc. ISMIR 2011*, 311-316.
11. Ha, S., McCann, J., Liu, C. K. and Popovic, J. Physics storyboards. *Computer Graphics Forum 32*, 2 (*Proc. EG 2013)*, 133-142.
12. Hartmann, B., Yu, L., Allison, A., Yang, Y. and Klemmer, S. Design as exploration: creating interface alternatives through parallel authoring and runtime tuning. In *Proc. UIST 2008*, 91-100.
13. Kato, J., Sakamoto, D. and Igarashi, T. VisionSketch: Integrated support for example-centric programming of image processing applications. In *Proc. GI 2014*, 115-122.
14. Kazi, R., Chevalier, F., Grossman, T. and Fitzmaurice, G. Kitty: Sketching dynamic and interactive illustrations. In Proc. UIST 2014, 395-405.
15. Kazi, R., Chevalier, F., Grossman, T., Zhao, S. and Fitzmaurice, G. Draco: bringing life to illustrations with kinetic textures. In *Proc. CHI 2014,* 351-360.
16. Lee, J., Forlizzi, J. and Hudson, S. The kinetic typography engine: an extensible system for animating expressive text. In *Proc. UIST 2002*, 81-90.
17. Lee, J., Jun, S., Forlizzi, J. and Hudson, S. Using kinetic typography to convey emotion in text-basesd interpersonal communication. In *Proc. DIS 2006*, 41-49.
18. Lewis, J. and Weyers, A. ActiveText: a method for creating dynamic and interactive texts. In *Proc. UIST 1999*, 131-140.
19. McDirmid, S. Living it up with a live programming language. In *Proc. OOPSLA 2007*, 623-638.
20. Minakuchi, M. and Tanaka, K. Automatic kinetic typography composer. In *Proc. ACE 2005*, 221-224.
21. Rubin, S., Berthouzoz, F., Mysore, G. J., Li, W. and Agrawala, M. Content-based tools for editing audio stories. In *Proc UIST 2013,* 113-122.
22. Unity. http://unity3d.com/.
23. Victor, B. Inventing on Principle (2012). http://vimeo.com/36579366.
24. Victor, B. Learnable Programming (2012). http://worrydream.com/LearnablePrgramming/.

Power, Empowerment and Open Source Usability

Mikko Rajanen & Netta Iivari
Department of Information Processing Science, University of Oulu
P.O. BOX 3000, 90014 Oulu, Finland
firstname.lastname@oulu.fi

ABSTRACT
Open source software (OSS) projects are often seen as participatory and egalitarian settings where people collaboratively develop software to serve their needs as well as the needs of others. In this paper, however, we argue that power and politics also characterize OSS development, and that this has serious implications for OSS usability. The existing Human–Computer Interaction (HCI) research on OSS usability has already shown that power and politics play a role; this study offers a theoretical treatment of the matter. A theoretical framework on power and empowerment is utilized in analyzing empirical data on OSS usability as well as the existing body of knowledge on the topic. With the help of this framework, HCI research can address the aspects of power and empowerment in OSS usability in a more systematic and comprehensive manner.

Author Keywords
Open source software, usability, power, empowerment

ACM Classification Keywords
H.5.m. Information interfaces and presentation (e.g., HCI): Miscellaneous.

INTRODUCTION
Open source software (OSS) development has become popular in recent years, and many widely used solutions are OSS (e.g., Wordpress, Mozilla Firefox, Mozilla Thunderbird, OpenOffice). OSS is software of which the source code is available for anyone to use, modify or redistribute. OSS projects, however, may vary widely in nature. For example, they range from small one-man projects—created by the developer for his or her own use—to very large projects with thousands of developers and millions of users (e.g., Linux). Some OSS projects may even involve companies [13], while most OSS projects consist of only one or very few developers [22]. OSS development relies on individuals who are motivated to develop solutions for their personal needs, but who also voluntarily offer their solutions for use and further development by others. The community development model and the basic values of OSS development, such as gift giving, reciprocity, and sharing, motivate developers to do this [39, 40]. This discussion positions OSS projects as participatory and egalitarian settings where people collaboratively develop software to serve their own needs as well as those of others.

CHI 2015, April 18 - 23 2015, Seoul, Republic of Korea

ACM 978-1-4503-3145-6/15/04…$15.00
http://dx.doi.org/10.1145/2702123.2702441

However, this image of egalitarianism is not the whole picture. Less attention has been paid to the other side of the coin: to the aspects of power and politics that are intertwined with any human activity, including OSS development. In a sense, this has already been acknowledged in the existing Human–Computer Interaction (HCI) research on OSS usability, as researchers have encountered numerous problems when trying to introduce and ensure usability or User Experience (UX) in OSS development. UX and usability are at the heart of HCI research and practice, which strive for high quality systems for users. Existing HCI research has already hinted that OSS culture, ideology and philosophy may hinder work on usability and UX (henceforth collectively referred to as "usability"). Studies have indicated that it may be challenging to integrate heavy-weight usability methodologies with OSS development, given the latter's background of voluntary developers "scratching their own itch" [8, 10, 29]. It has been pointed out that meritocracy is standard in OSS projects, and that one attains status and reputation by being competent in technical development (e.g., [2, 28, 38]). Usability practitioners should be capable of demonstrating their merits and contribution to the overall development, too [4, 5, 6, 28, 38]. However, these merits and contribution are not necessarily valued by OSS developers [4, 5, 6, 28, 38]. Usability practitioners may need to utilize a variety of lobbying, persuasion, and allying strategies in order to succeed [6, 28, 32, 33]. All this indicates that power and politics indeed play a role in OSS development. However, theoretical treatment of the matter is limited in HCI research, even though the phenomenon has been empirically observed in numerous studies. This paper addresses this gap by presenting a comprehensive theoretical framework on power and empowerment [16] through which to make sense of the power dynamics involved in the field of OSS usability. Moreover, the framework indicates ways in which the "power-weak", meaning the usability specialists, may be empowered to influence decision outcomes [16], in this case design decision outcomes. It is hoped that this will also provide a valuable contribution for the OSS usability literature.

In this paper, we look at OSS development as an intriguing community-based phenomenon. Organizational science theorists have also long considered this type of OSS development as a specific way of organizing; in other words, as something more than a mere OSS license [40]. The focus of this paper is on small-to-medium sized OSS development projects that are volunteer-driven and do not have company or foundation involvement. This type of project forms the majority of OSS projects [22]. Very large OSS projects and those with company involvement may more closely resemble commercial software development in business organizations, regarding which there is already plenty of HCI research (e.g., [15, 20]). Company involvement in particular may increase this resemblance, as companies, if involved, tend to offer their usability resources and methods to the projects [2, 4, 5, 8, 38]. Nevertheless, while usability professionals have been shown to experience difficulties in both OSS and commercial settings, there are also clear differences between these settings that have implications for how usability professionals are able to have an impact on the software. The main differences can be summarized in terms of the timing of the usability development activities (in OSS, usability specialists tend to become involved much later, as usually the development starts by developers "scratching their own itch") and the management of the projects (e.g., budget and human resources allocated to usability activities). In small-to-medium sized OSS projects without company involvement, all development is conducted on a voluntary basis, and this also applies to usability activities. In this kind of situation, OSS developers can very easily dismiss the work of usability specialists. In commercial software development, the situation should be a bit better, as resources are allocated and spent on usability work, and there likely is a decision-maker overseeing to ensure that the resources are not wasted. This decision-maker may also be easier to locate and contact in a commercial software development context.

This paper is structured as follows. The next section reviews research on the role of power and politics in OSS development. The third section presents a four-dimensional model of power and empowerment to be used as a sensitizing device in the analysis. The fourth section presents the methodology of our empirical studies. The fifth section presents the empirical findings, which reveal that power struggles are evident as regards OSS usability, and suggest avenues of empowerment. The final section discusses the implications of these findings and identifies limitations and paths for future work.

POWER AND EMPOWERMENT IN OPEN SOURCE SOFTWARE DEVELOPMENT

This section will review literature that has already indicated important issues as regards power and politics in OSS development. While there is a lack of research explicitly addressing this issue, interesting findings on the topic can still be pinpointed as having implications for OSS usability. Altogether, it is important to remember that there is indeed a long history and important ideological underpinnings in regard to OSS development. The free software movement was launched in 1983 as a social and political movement to advocate what were seen as basic freedoms for software users: freedom to run software, freedom to study software, freedom to change software in any way that the user finds necessary, and freedom to distribute copies of software with or without changes to it [17, 24]. These freedoms promote progress in technology, since much of the wasteful duplication of programming can be avoided, and effort can instead go into advancing the state of the art [17, 24]. The term "open source" was coined to rebrand the free software movement so that it would be more appealing to the commercial software industry. The Open Source Initiative was founded in 1998 to promote this new term and to advocate the open source principles (opensource.org). The members of the free software movement objected to the open source approach, and felt that by concentrating only on the openness of the source code, the important philosophical and social values regarding the basic freedoms of software users were ignored (gnu.org). Despite these differences, however, open source and free software communities share many core values [17, 36].

An OSS development project is characterized as a loosely bonded community united by strong common values, and work is organized usually by one or a few coordinators [24]. An OSS community is often depicted as an onion model, with different layers representing levels of involvement in the community. In a typical OSS community, there is a lead developer or a small group of developers forming the core team that controls the overall architectural design and course of the project [12, 27]. These developers form the core of the onion. They are often supported by "committers", who have direct write access to the project's source code, but are required to ask permission for major modifications before committing a change. "Contributors" are external developers and users who send bug reports and minor fixes for errors in the code. They do not have power to upload their modifications to the official source code repository of the project. The outer layer of the onion consists of end users, who do not participate in the community, but only use the software [1]. It is these end users in particular whose interests the usability specialists aim to represent. However, the onion layers as described above also indicate the power of decision participants in each layer. End users, as well as usability specialists representing them, are very likely remain on the outer layer of the onion, which has been a concern for HCI researchers addressing the topic [4, 5, 28, 38].

However, not all OSS projects are the same, even when considering power and decision making in OSS development. There are many variables that may have an effect, such as the age and size of the project. Usually, at the beginning of a project, the founder of the project makes all decisions and rules regarding who can contribute and what will be included in the software. Later, she or he may relinquish some or all of her or his power to other developers, typically based on their merits. Linux, however, is a famous example of a long-term project where the initial developer still retains his rights to make final decisions, even though there are responsible persons for many areas of the code base. On the other hand, the Apache HTTP Server represents a project of which the founder is no longer in control, but that has achieved close to democratic decision making through a board of directors [23]. Hence, structures and leadership vary among OSS development projects, but smaller OSS development projects tend to have an informal, shallow, and meritocratic structure where contributors whose contributions are seen as being important or innovative are given developer or core developer status, by agreement of the developers or community as a whole. [1, 24, 34]

From the point of view of an OSS developer, "scratching one's own itch" and ideological issues have already been mentioned as motivational factors for taking part in OSS projects. A further key motivational factor is the status, fame, reputation, and recognition that a contribution can create for a developer [1, 34]. It has been pointed out that in order to become an accepted contributor or even an acknowledged member, there are joining scripts to be followed in OSS projects, implying that a developer may have to provide, for instance, *feature gifts*—whole modules or features as his contribution [41]. On the other hand, it is still up to the decision makers to assess the value of the contribution and the contributor, which often leads to a situation where only small part of the provided code is merged into the project [21, 23, 35]. Although OSS development is strongly transparent and visible for all, there remains a strong notion of ownership [1, 17]. Decisions makers typically have their own—often unwritten—vision of the project, and others are obliged to follow it. Even though OSS licenses usually allow anyone to release an alternative version of the software, there is significant prestige motivation to get one's own code contributions accepted to the original version and to become a member of the development team [1, 21, 27].

Interestingly, it is not only the software that it controlled by OSS developers: studies have also identified a surprising amount of control exercised in OSS projects in other ways [11, 14, 21]. Various kinds of governance configurations have been identified [11]. Depending on the configuration, management may be centralized, development process defined and conflict resolution managed. Different control modes and mechanisms have also been found in OSS projects: in addition to outcome control, behavioral control, clan control and self-control mechanisms are in use [11, 21]. Certain rules and procedures are expected to be followed, and peer pressure and self-criticism prevail in OSS development [21]. It has been even argued that the openness of OSS projects enables a continuous monitoring of people and their work that can be seen as an exercise of disciplinary power, in the sense of the Panopticon that Foucault often brought up in his work [21]. All this indicates that power and politics feature in OSS development, too. However, there are other disciplines within which power and politics have gained a much more thorough treatment. The following section discusses some findings from these disciplines.

THEORETICAL FRAMEWORK

In Information Technology (IT) research, power issues have already been addressed. It has been argued that one should inquire into the dominance, power, marginality and exclusions that take place in IT development and use [7]. The nature of IT development should be understood as conflicted and political [19], and the influential role of organizational politics and conflicts needs to been acknowledged. Studies [9, 19] have highlighted conflicts between users, developers and managers as widespread. HCI research has also contributed to this area by indicating that there is potential for power struggles between usability specialists and developers (e.g., [3, 15, 20, 26, 37]), including in the OSS development context [4, 5, 28, 38].

However, although widely studied topic, power is a very complex concept drawing on a multitude of definitions and approaches [16]. To make sense of and to reveal the diversity that can be associated with the concept, Hardy and Leiba-O'Sullivan [16] propose a four-dimensional model of power and empowerment. Table 1 captures the four dimensions of power and the conditions of empowerment in relation to each dimension.

This framework reveals power as a multifaceted concept that theorists have approached in various ways. The framework discusses the mainstream, critical, and Foucauldian approaches to power. In the first dimension, power is exercised through the use of different kinds of resources to influence decision making, while in the second dimension, power is exercised by controlling access to decision making. These two dimensions represent the mainstream approach to power, whereas the third dimension focuses on the legitimation of power through cultural and normative assumptions. Power is here used to ensure that conflict never arises, but that the oppressed remain satisfied with the current situation. The background to this view is in the critical research tradition. Finally, the fourth dimension relies on the Foucauldian notion of power, which maintains that power is embedded in the very fabric of the system we are all living in and cannot escape from. This system heavily constrains what and how we see and think: people are prisoners of this prevailing system, although some derive greater advantages in it than others. The framework also identifies the conditions of empowerment that emerge as regards each dimension.

	First dimension	Second dimension	Third dimension	Fourth dimension
Power of A over B	Management of resource dependencies	Management of decision-making processes	Management of meaning	None; power is embedded in the system
Interaction between A and B	Overt conflict	Overt or covert conflict	Apparent cooperation	
Reason for B's failure to influence outcomes	B is aware of the issue and able to get it to the decision arena, but is unable to use power effectively to influence outcomes	B is aware of the issue but unable to get it to the decision arena	B is unaware of the issue and thus has no will to resist it	Both A and B are prisoners of the prevailing discourses of power, although A may derive greater advantage from them
Requirements for empowerment of B	Acquisition of resources and ability to mobilize them	Ability to gain access to the decision arena	Consciousness-raising and "delegitimation" strategies to create will to resist	Empowerment in the sense of freedom from power effects is not possible, although local struggles may produce more positive experiences

Table 1. Empowerment and the Dimensions of Power [16: 462]

This theoretical model will be used as a means of making sense of our empirical data on OSS usability. Various theoretical frameworks were considered before selecting this one; the final selection was based on four considerations. First, this framework clearly has an established position in the research literature, indicated by numerous citations. Second, it has already been utilized in IT research, albeit not in the OSS development context. Third, it provides a comprehensive approach to power and empowerment, as it includes four dimensions of power based on a wide review of power-related research spanning several decades and different disciplines. Fourth, the framework enables us to reveal interesting issues in the OSS context, and was easy to apply to our data. To sum up, this framework provides a comprehensive and easily applicable lens for our analysis.

RESEARCH DESIGN

The research design of this study utilizes constructive research approaches [25], specifically the Design Science approach, which has been developed and extensively discussed within IT research [18]. This approach aims to develop new or improved ways to achieve human goals [25, 18]. An artifact is developed and evaluated for its purpose. This research is part of a larger research program aiming to find ways for usability specialists to offer their expertise to OSS development. Within this research program, suitable methods for introducing usability activities into small-to-medium sized OSS development projects have been experimented with by 14 different student usability teams doing usability work in OSS case projects over 7 years. The authors of this paper guided the student usability teams in organizing usability interventions with different strategies, methods and outcomes in OSS projects across different domains, communities and cultures. The student usability teams communicated with their allocated OSS projects and tried to introduce usability activities for them. The students conducting these usability activities had backgrounds from at least two previous courses on usability evaluation methods (e.g., heuristics evaluation and usability testing), user-centered design, and user interface design in both theory and practice. Each student usability team consisted of three to five students working 200–300 hours each in planning the usability activities, carrying them out in an OSS project, communicating with the OSS project, following up on the impact of these usability activities, collecting empirical data, and writing project reports.

In this paper, we analyze the data collected from five OSS case projects (henceforth, Cases 1, 2, 3, 4 and 5). These empirical cases and their usability interventions are briefly introduced as follows. Case 1 was developing a media application, targeted at non-technical end users without programming skills or interest. The project was started in 2004 and had a total of about 30 developers. The usability team observed this OSS project for five months in 2007, while conducting heuristic evaluations, cognitive walkthroughs and usability testing. The usability team reported the findings in the form of a report, which was sent to the core developers and mentioned in a post in the main discussion forum of the community. Case 2 was developing a game targeted at non-technical end users. This project, started in 2003, had a total of 15 developers. The usability team observed this OSS project for five months in 2008, while performing heuristic evaluation and usability testing. The usability team was in close contact with the lead developer regarding their findings and possible redesign solutions, and also participated in discussions in the project's IRC channel. After the evaluations, the usability team wrote a usability report, and this time included suggestions for changes to fix the identified usability problems. Case 3 was developing 3D content creation software targeted at end users with 3D content creation skills but without skills or interest in programming. The project, started in 2002, had a total of 40 more or less active developers. The usability team observed this project for six months in 2009, while carrying out usability testing and heuristic analysis and writing several reports about usability problems and their suggestions for changes to fix those problems. These reports were made available on the usability team's blog and advertised in the project's IRC channels and discussion forums. Case 4 was developing media center software, with target users of ordinary people. The project started in 2003 and had about 20 active developers. The usability team observed this OSS project for five months in 2009, while performing heuristic evaluations and usability testing. A results report was again sent to the OSS developers by email. Finally, Case 5 was developing a game targeted at non-technical end users without programming skills. This project started originally in 1995, and the development team had changed many times since then. This project had 20 currently active developers with commit rights. The usability team observed this OSS project for four months in 2010, while conducting heuristic evaluations using game usability heuristics and usability testing. The usability team wrote preliminary and final usability reports about the usability issues and their suggestions for changes to the user interface to fix them. The final usability report was delivered to the wiki of the OSS project. In addition, the usability team submitted code patches and level design work, including new user interface menus and a new tutorial for the game.

The collected empirical data included both usability teams' deliverables and online material specific to each OSS project case, including websites, discussion forum posts, IRC discussion logs, commit messages and emails. The student usability teams' deliverables consisted of different kinds of usability reports as well as project management-related documents (see the case descriptions). These data are versatile and useful, and enabled us to conduct our analysis from the viewpoint of power and empowerment using the framework by Hardy and Leiba-O'Sullivan [16]. This framework was adopted after the data collection; it did not guide the data collection process. Thus, the collected material was examined using the selected theoretical framework as a sensitizing device years after the data collection. First, instances representing power-related issues were inductively identified from the data through a data-driven analysis. Next, the concepts from the theoretical framework were employed to make sense of the identified instances. Each case project was examined from the viewpoint of usability work and what it entailed in the given case, its effectiveness in the OSS project, and the contributing factors to this effectiveness or lack of it. The data was further analyzed from the point of view of the power and empowerment of the usability specialists. In the analysis, the second dimension of power (management of the decision-making process [16]) proved to be the most salient and easily applicable one for making sense of power and empowerment in regard to OSS usability. Hence, it was utilized as a lens and in the following section; the discussion is narrowed to the empirical findings concerning power and empowerment in the sense of this second dimension [16]. However, this does not mean that the other dimensions are not relevant. Our empirical findings hint at their relevance, together with the existing literature on the matter. This will be discussed further in the last section.

EMPIRICAL INSIGHTS

Power of A over B: Management of decision-making processes

Using the terminology of the framework on power and empowerment [16], we labeled "OSS developers with commit rights", or committers, as *A* and "usability team" as *B* in our data. In all the examined cases, the usability team conducted both expert usability evaluations and empirical usability tests. Thereafter, they analyzed the data and crafted results reports that were delivered to the OSS project in question. After the delivery, the project committers reacted to the provided solutions in different ways depending on the case. Thus it was possible for us to examine in more detail some power-related issues arising in the projects, which are reported below.

Interaction between A and B: Overt or covert conflict

There may be both overt and covert conflicts between A and B [16]. Our findings align with this: we have examples of both in our data. In Case 1, members of the project expressed some hostility towards usability overall. This could be identified in discussions in the project's forums. Some users expressed criticism towards the user interface of the application, and offered certain usability improvement suggestions. The comments were disregarded by the developers, who commented that the application "is not meant to be for girlfriends". Interestingly, the project stated on its website that it wanted to target "non-technical end users", but "girlfriends", and usability for them, were apparently beyond that scope.

In Case 3, had firm opinions among the developers regarding the user interface could be identified. Some had very strong opinions about how the user interface should compare with competitive commercial alternatives; specifically, that the user interface should not resemble these alternatives in any shape or form. User critique of the user interface of the application and usability improvement suggestions offered via the project's communication channels had been disregarded by the core developers. One of the core developers even commented to the usability team that usability was not something that would apply to this type of professional and complex system. This is an example of an overt conflict between the core developer and the usability team that offered their help.

In Case 5, the usability team concentrated their efforts on improving a tutorial that was found to be incomprehensible and frustrating for novice users. The usability team streamlined the tutorial, cut the amount of data and descriptions presented to users, and polished the tutorial with an innovative new design. This new version performed well in usability tests and the developers and the community overall were enthusiastic about it. However, the creator of the original tutorial reverted it almost back to the previous version in the next major release. This is an example of a developer in covert conflict with a usability team. The usability team was totally unaware that the developer was unhappy with the outcome of the work of the usability team, and no public notification was provided of the change of the tutorial back to the previous version. Moreover, it seems that the community and the other developers were not even informed about the issue, while the original creator of the tutorial had the power to make such a unilateral decision. The usability team was naturally unable to react to this change in any way.

Reason for B's failure to influence outcomes: B is aware of the issue but unable to get it to the decision arena

In all the examined projects, the main issue at stake in the intervention concerned the usability team's ability to gain access to the decision-making arena. In some projects there were successes, while in others there were clear failures. In OSS development, it is argued that even if the decision making is truly transparent (e.g., happens via a public mailing list) and accessible by everyone (e.g., anyone can post), actual decision makers may not care about alternative opinions and turn a deaf ear to suggestions. Further, the decision-making process and channels are often not visible to newcomers, including usability specialists. This may be due to the core developers' desire to control the decision-making process and channels, or it may be simply because decision making in the OSS community is ad hoc in nature, and there are no processes or official channels. In the following we offer some examples from our data that show that the usability team was unable to access the decision arena, or were unable to influence decision making there despite having access.

In Case 1, the usability team sent the summary of usability findings to the developers by email, which was recognized as the main method of communicating within this community. This was the first contact between these developers and the usability team. The purpose of this approach was to mimic the way the software patches are submitted in OSS projects, where somebody writes the patch, which is then shared with the community, and the core developers either accept it into the main branch or reject it. Based on the OSS literature, it was reasoned that it would be important to fit the usability contributions into the existing procedures of the project's development. However, the work of the usability team had no impact. At first, no answer was received from the core developers. The same report was then posted to the discussion forum of the project, upon which one of the core developers answered there that they were discussing the document internally and could comment on it later. However, there was subsequently no answer or further communication, and there are no signs of changes in the OSS that could be traced back to the usability team's intervention.

A validation test was conducted in Case 4, which involved a similar kind of OSS project and approach by the usability team, and the result was similar. The results report was sent to the developers by email. The developers replied they had received the report, but there was no further communication from their side, and the report was not mentioned in the project's discussion forums, chat, or mailing lists. Further, the OSS in question has not been changed according the results reported. These cases together indicate that the power in OSS development is in the hands of the core developers. Their exercise of power has in these instances turned out to influence negatively the usability interventions. The problem is not related to gaining access to the decision-making arena, but to having an impact there.

In Case 3, by contrast, the project did not have one specific communication channel or small group of persons to contact. The decision-making core developers could not be reached just by sending email to the project's mailing list or discussion forum. In this case, the usability team documented their activities and results in open source fashion on a website, which was promoted in community forums and IRC channels and offered to several community news sites for publication. However, there was not much traffic generated, because the posts about the usability activities and their results were quickly buried beneath other discussions and news. This case is an example where the usability team did not even catch the attention of the decision-making core developers, and hence the usability team did not gain access to the decision arena and consequently was unable to influence the OSS.

Requirements for empowerment of B: Ability to gain access to the decision arena

The cases described here also include some successes, in the sense of the usability team becoming empowered to improve the usability of the OSS. This section discusses these successes. In Case 2, initial contact between the usability team and the developers consisted mainly of exchanging emails with the most active leading core developer. This core developer was initially not even sure of what usability meant, but he welcomed help from the usability team regardless, with the idea that any kind of contribution to the OSS project and community is potentially helpful. As the relationship continued, the usability team changed their communication strategy to chatting in the IRC channel with the whole community and introducing the concept of usability, different usability methods, potential benefits of improving usability, and potential risks of poor usability, as outlined in the usability cost-benefit literature (see [30]). On the whole, the community seemed to become interested in the usability effort and to appreciate the help provided by the usability team. After the evaluations, the usability team wrote a report and sent it by email to the core developers. The core developers included the suggestions outlined by the usability team as part of the changes to be made to the next version of the OSS. Later on, it was evidenced that these changes indeed were made. Moreover, the lead core developer later contacted the usability team and asked for another usability evaluation to be done for their new major version of the OSS. He even expressed a wish that the usability team would become a close-knit part of the development team. This case offers an example of a usability team gaining access to the decision arena of an OSS project and truly having an impact there. It can be stated that they were empowered to make changes to usability of this OSS. It seems that, in this case, they succeeded in convincing the core developers as well as the community of the value and importance of usability, which was previously an unfamiliar concept to them.

Case 5 is another success story. In this case, the usability team, after their evaluations, wrote preliminary and final usability reports; the former was delivered to the mailing list of the project and the latter to the community wiki. Even the preliminary report sparked an active discussion among the developers and the community, and the developers also actively commented on the final report. Moreover, the usability team submitted code patches and designs, including new user interface menus and a new tutorial. These contributions received a positive reception and were accepted into the code repository of the project. The developers acknowledged and were grateful for the quality of the usability reports and the work of the usability team. Additionally, the work of the usability team was referenced in several commit messages, one of which explicitly asked for additional input from the usability team. In this case, one member of the usability team even gained commit rights to the project: he was invited to become a member of the development team. This was achieved through his work in the usability team, through his contributions to code and design, through his active participation in discussions in the community IRC channels, and through his skills as an active user of the software. Hence, in this case one member of the usability team was truly empowered to access and affect design decision making in the project.

CONCLUDING DISCUSSION

The study was motivated by the lack of theoretical work on power in the context of OSS usability, while the existing HCI research has already indicated that current OSS culture, ideology and philosophy may hinder usability work, and that it may be challenging to integrate usability with voluntary, meritocratic OSS development. However, a thorough theoretical treatment of the power and politics involved with usability in OSS development is lacking in HCI research, although the phenomenon has been empirically observed. This paper attempts to address this gap by presenting a theoretical framework on power and empowerment [16] through which to make sense of the power dynamics involved with OSS usability This section summarizes and discusses the main empirical findings derived from the second dimension of power in the theoretical framework—management of the decision-making process [16]—followed by a discussion of the implications of the other three dimensions of power. The section concludes by suggesting theoretical and practical implications of this study. Table 2 below encapsulates the main empirical findings.

Table 2 indicates that in our data, the main challenge for the usability teams was to gain access and have an influence on decision making in the OSS projects. In three cases (1, 3, and 4), no influence was observed, while in two cases (2 and 5) the usability team succeeded in having an impact on the OSS in question. In two of the unsuccessful cases (1 and 4), gaining access to the decision arena (i.e., contacting the core developers through email) was not a problem, but having gained this access, usability contributions were still denied or "silenced to death." Even in one of the successful cases (5), the tutorial that the usability team had successfully developed was silently deleted after a while, which eventually turned a successful case into a partial failure.

	Second dimension of power
Power of OSS developers over usability specialists	Management of decision-making processes: accessing the arena, having an influence there
Interaction between OSS developers and usability specialists	Overt or covert conflicts: usability contributions denied, silenced to death or silently deleted
Reason for usability specialists' failure to influence outcomes	Usability specialists are aware of the issue and sometimes able to get it to the decision arena (gain contact with committers), but if so they are unable to influence the outcomes
Requirements for empowerment of usability specialists	Ability to gain access and have influence in the decision arena: through gaining commitment rights or gaining contact with and convincing the committers (see also [28, 32, 33])

Table 2. Empirical Findings on Empowerment and the Second Dimension of Power [16: 462] in OSS Usability

	First dimension	Third dimension	Fourth dimension
Power of OSS developers over usability specialists	Management of resources: (time, effort) expertise and status (see also [4, 5, 6, 28])	Management of meaning: the value of usability and usability specialists	None, power is embedded in the system: all parties are prisoners of the Panopticon
Interaction between OSS developers and usability specialists	Overt or covert conflict: usability specialists may be asked to not enter into OSS projects or their contributions may be denied, silenced to death or silently deleted	Apparent cooperation: usability specialists allowed to work, but usability contributions do not have influence on the OSS (e.g., silenced to death or silently deleted)	Local struggles among and between usability specialists and OSS developers
Reason for usability specialists' failure to influence outcomes	Usability specialists have time and effort at their disposal, but they may be unable to acquire the other resources (expertise and status)	Usability specialists are not even aware of how their work is treated	All parties are prisoners of the Panopticon, although committers may derive greater advantage from it
Requirements for empowerment of usability specialists	Acquisition of the resources: through showing the value of usability work and convincing the committers (see also [4, 5, 6, 28, 32, 33] or through becoming committers	Consciousness-raising and "de-legitimation" strategies to create will to resist: usability specialists are to make their problematic position visible, question this and convince the community for change	Empowerment in the sense of freedom from power effects is not possible although local struggles may produce more positive experiences also for usability specialists

Table 3. Empowerment and the First, Third and Fourth Dimensions of Power [16: 462] in OSS Usability

In Case 4, due to the more complicated project structure and numerous communication channels, the usability team did not even gain contact with the decision-making core developers. Hence, the empowerment of usability specialists seems to require that they first gain access to the decision arena and then also become able to influence the decision makers there. Another option is that usability specialists succeed in gaining commit rights in the OSS project (i.e., become decision makers themselves), which occurred in one case (5). However, we do not recommend that all usability specialists strive to achieve this, as it would require great investment from usability specialists, who often do not possess sufficient technical knowledge and skills.

Turning to the other dimensions of power, our own empirical data offered some findings on these issues (see Table 3) in addition to the existing body of knowledge, which offers further insights. For the first dimension of power—management of resources [16]—we argue that this takes a different form in OSS development than in commercial or company contexts, because OSS resources are immaterial and nobody in the community has direct decision-making power or control over labor (although some developers may be paid [13]). On the other hand, it can be argued that the core developers have indirect power over resources through their power to plan and decide the time and contents of the next releases [31]. Even though usability specialists may have time and effort at their disposal for usability work (as opposed to commercial software development, where resources are limited by the management), they may lack other kinds of resources. They may lack the required status, merit, expertise or other types of capital in the eyes of the OSS developers [4, 5, 6, 28], and thus end up in overt (Cases 1 and 3) or covert (Case 5) conflict with developers. OSS projects operate as meritocracies, and without status and merit usability specialists may be barred from entering an OSS project altogether (e.g., some instances in Cases 1 and 3) or they may have their usability contributions denied (Cases 1 and 3), silenced (Cases 1, 3 and 4) or deleted (Case 5). In order to empower usability specialists, so that their work can have an impact, they must convince the members of the OSS project in question of the value of their contribution (Cases 2 and 5). Usability specialists have to either convince the committers of the merits of usability work (Cases 2 and 5) or become committers themselves (Case 5).

The third and fourth dimensions of power were also found to be highly relevant concerning OSS usability, though more empirical research on these dimensions in the context of OSS usability is needed. The third dimension of power concerns the management of meaning: those who are powerful define how things should be seen and perceived. In our context of usability, an example could be a belittling attitude to the concept, as in some instances in Cases 1 and 3. However, the exercise of this power is very subtle: on the surface there is no evidence of conflict. In the case of OSS usability, this means that usability specialists may be allowed to do their work (which applies in any case to a voluntary OSS project where the software is freely available), but their contributions may remain ignored (e.g., silenced to death or silently deleted, as in Cases 1, 3, 4 and 5).

In some cases the usability team was not aware of how the OSS developers and the community perceived usability, and whether their usability contributions were valued or not (e.g., some instances in Cases 1, 3 and 4). For usability specialists to succeed, it is essential that they become aware of the underlying meanings and values that may hinder their work, and prepare for these. They should also subsequently make others aware of the issues, and convince others of their harmful nature. This may involve various kinds of lobbying, persuasion, and allying strategies [6, 28, 32, 33, 38] relying on, for example, usability cost-benefit literature (e.g., [30, 31]) or even encouragement to rebel.

The fourth dimension of power relies on Foucauldian notions of power that maintain that power is embedded in the very fabric of the system in which we live and from which we cannot escape. This applies to both OSS developers and usability specialists, who can both be seen as prisoners of the complex control and surveillance system inherent in an OSS environment, which encourages extensive peer pressure and self-control [11, 21]. It is likely that OSS developers derive more advantages from the overall system than usability specialists, but through local struggles, usability specialists may also be able to challenge the existing discourses and derive more positive experiences. However, this entire system and the societal discourses circulating around it deserve a much more thorough empirical inquiry.

This study contributes to the HCI research by offering new insights on the relationships between power, empowerment and usability work in the OSS development context. This should help HCI researchers to address these aspects of power and empowerment in OSS and other development contexts. The utilized framework addressed the multidimensional concept of power in a comprehensive manner, and indicated numerous ways through which usability specialists might become empowered. The value of the theoretical framework was illuminated in its ability to map both empirical data from the present study and extant OSS usability literature. This study can be considered as an intermediate step towards greater insight into this complex topic. There remain several complex and unexplained issues regarding power and politics in OSS usability. This paper brings us one step closer to understanding what is going on with regard to the participation of usability specialists in OSS development. This study can also be seen as addressing a gap in critical research: the study touches upon dominance, power, marginality, and exclusion in IT development, which has been called for in IT research [7, 19] and is badly lacking in HCI research [20].

Regarding implications for practice, this study should indicate to usability practitioners that, when aiming to introduce usability into OSS development, power and politics must be taken seriously into account. Because it is entirely up to the decision makers of the OSS project to assess the value of contributions and contributors, usability specialists cannot remain neutral experts outside of the power struggles and politics of OSS projects. By becoming aware of these different dimensions of power, usability work can be better adapted to the particular OSS project at hand, therefore minimizing the possibilities of conflict and failure to influence outcomes. Usability specialists need to gain access to and influence in decision arenas. They also need to acquire and deploy valued types of resources in order to succeed. They may even need to take part in the management of meaning in the project: to initiate consciousness-raising and legitimation campaigns that aim at challenging established, negative notions of usability.

Further empirical research remains necessary to see how these suggestions play out in practice, however. The ways in which power manifests in OSS projects with different structures and cultures should be investigated in more detail, as well as the crucial role of the core developers. Further, as stated earlier, in order to become an accepted contributor or even an acknowledged member in an OSS community, a potential contributor may have to provide feature gifts [41] in order to gain essential access and influence, but it is an open question what these feature gifts could be in the case of usability work.

REFERENCES

1. Aberdour, M. Achieving Quality in Open Source Software. *IEEE Software, 24,* 1 (2007), 58-64.
2. Andreasen, M., Nielsen, H., Schrøder, S. and Stage, J. Usability in Open Source Software Development: Opinions and Practice. *Information Technology and Control 25,* 3A (2006), 303-312.
3. Aucella, A. Ensuring Success with Usability Engineering. *Interactions May + June* (1997), 19-22.
4. Bach, P. M and Carroll, J. M. Characterizing the Dynamics of Open User Experience Design: The Cases of Firefox and OpenOffice.org. *JAIS 11,* 12 (2010).
5. Bach, P., DeLine, R. and Carroll, J. Designers Wanted: Participation and the User Experience in Open Source Software Development. *Proc. CHI 2009* (2009).
6. Bach, P. and Twidale, M. Social participation in open source: what it means for designers. *Interactions 17, 3* (2010).
7. Beck, E. P for Political. Participation is not enough. *Scandinavian Journal of Information Systems 14,* 1 (2002), 77-92.
8. Benson, C., Müller-Prove, M. and Mzourek, J. Professional usability in open source projects: GNOME, OpenOffice.org, NetBeans. *Ext. Ab. CHI2004* (2004).
9. Butler, T. and Fitzgerald, B. A Case Study of User Participation in the Information Systems Development Process, *Proc. ICIS* (1997), 411-426.
10. Bødker, S., Nielsen, L. and Orngreen, R. Enabling user-centered design processes in open source communities. In *Proc. HCII, Part I, LNCS 4559* (2007), 10-18.

11. Di Tullio, D. and Staples, D.S. The Governance and Control of Open Source Software Projects. *Journal of Management Information Systems 30,* 3 (2013), 49-80.
12. Feller, J. and Fitzgerald, B. A Framework Analysis of the Open Source Development Paradigm. *Proc. ICIS 2000* (2000), 58-69.
13. Fitzgerald, B. The Transformation of Open Source Software. *MISQ 30,* 3 (2006), 481-493.
14. Gallivan, M. J. Striking a balance between trust and control in a virtual organization: a content analysis of open source software case studies. *Information Systems Journal 11,* 4 (2001), 277-304.
15. Gulliksen, J., Boivie, I., and Göransson, B. Usability professionals – current practices and future development. *Interacting with Computers 18,* 4 (2006).
16. Hardy, C. and Leiba-O´Sullivan, S. The power behind empowerment: Implications for research and practice. *Human Relations 51,* 4 (1998), 451-483.
17. Himanen, P. *The hacker ethic and the spirit of the information age*. WSOY Helsinki (2001).
18. Hevner, A.R., March, S.T. and Park, J. Design research in information systems research. *MIS Quarterly 28,* 1 (2004), 75-105.
19. Howcroft, D. and Wilson, M. Paradoxes of participatory practices: the Janus role of the systems developer. *Information and Organization 13,* 1 (2003), 1-24.
20. Iivari, N. *Discourses on 'culture' and 'usability work' in software product development.* Acta Universitatis Ouluensis, Series A, Scientiae rerum nat. 457, (2006).
21. Ikonen, H., Iivari, N. and Hedberg, H. Controlling the use of collaboration tools in open source software development. *Proc. NordiHCI* (2010), 236-245
22. Krishnamurthy, S. Cave or community?: An empirical examination of 100 mature open source projects. *First Monday* (2002).
23. de Laat, P. Governance of open source software: state of the art. *Journal of Management & Governance 11,* 2 (2007), 165-177.
24. Ljungberg, J. Open Source Movements as a Model for Organizing. *European Journal of Information Systems 9,* 4 (2000), 208-216.
25. March, ST., and Smith, G.F. Design and natural science research on information technology. *Decision support systems 15, 4* (1995), 251-266
26. Mayhew, D. Strategic Development of Usability Engineering Function. *Interactions 6,* 5 (1999)
27. Mockus, A., Fielding, R.T. and Herbsled, J. A Case Study of Open Source Software Development: The Apache Server. *Proc. ICSE* (2000), 263-272.
28. Moghaddam, R., Twidale, M. and Bongen, K. Open source interface politics: identity, acceptance, trust, and lobbying. *Extended Abstracts of the CHI2011* (2011)
29. Nichols, D. and Twidale, M. The Usability of Open Source Software. *First Monday 8,* 1, (2003).
30. Rajanen, M. Different approaches to Usability Cost-Benefit Analysis. *Proc. ECITE 2006* (2006).
31. Rajanen, M. *Applying Usability Cost-Benefit Analysis – Explorations in Commercial and Open Source Software Development Contexts.* Acta Universitatis Ouluensis, Ser. A, Scient. rerum nat. 587 (2011).
32. Rajanen, M., Iivari, N. and Anttila K. Introducing Usability Activities into Open Source Software Development Projects – Searching for a Suitable Approach. *Journal of Information Technology Theory and Application 12,* 4 (2011), 5-26.
33. Rajanen, M., Iivari, N. and Keskitalo, E. Introducing usability activities into open source software development projects: a participative approach. Proc. *NordiCHI 2012* (2012), 683-692.
34. Raymond, E. *The Cathedral & the Bazaar: Musing on Linux and Open Source by an Accidental Revolutionary.* O'Reilly & Assoc. (1999).
35. Robbins, J. Adopting open source software engineering (OSSE) practices by adopting OSSE Tools. In *Feller et al.* (2005), 245-264.
36. Rolandsson, B., Bergquist, M. and Ljungberg, J. Open source programmer's strategies to cope with ideological tensions. *Proc. OLKC 2009* (2009).
37. Rosenbaum, S., Rohn, J., Humburg, J. A Toolkit for Strategic Usability: Results from Workshops, Panels, and Surveys. *Proc. CHI. 2000* (2000), 337—344.
38. Terry, M., Kay, M. and Lafreniere, B. Perceptions and Practices of Usability in the Free/Open Source Software (FOSS) Community. *Proc. CHI 2010* (2010), 999-1008.
39. von Hippel, E. Innovation by User Communities: Learning from Open-Source Software. *MIT Sloan Management Review 42,* 4 (2001), 82-86.
40. von Hippel, E. and Krogh, G. Open source software and the "private-collective" innovation model: Issues for organization science. *Organization science, 14*,2 (2003), 209-223.
41. Von Krogh, G., Spaeth, S., & Lakhani, K. R. Community, joining, and specialization in open source software innovation: a case study. *Research Policy, 32*,7 (2003), 1217-1241.

Digital Collections and Digital Collecting Practices

Rebecca D. Watkins[1,2], Abigail Sellen[3], Siân E. Lindley[3]

Cardiff University[1]
Cardiff, UK
watkinsrd@cardiff.ac.uk

University of Southampton[2]
Southampton, UK

Microsoft Research[3]
Cambridge, UK
{asellen, sianl}@microsoft.com

ABSTRACT

Reference is increasingly made to 'digital collections', yet this term encompasses accumulated digital objects of varying form, purpose and value. We review social science literature on material collections and draw from in-depth interviews with 20 people in the UK in order to offer a clearer understanding of what constitutes a digital collection and what does not. We develop a taxonomy that presents three distinct types of digital collection and demonstrate ways in which the affordances of digital environments may facilitate or impede meaningful practices of acquisition, curation and exhibition in each case. Through doing so, we present a framework for design in support of collecting practices and the development of more meaningful and valued digital collections.

INTRODUCTION

Although reference is increasingly made to people's 'collections' of digital content [e.g. 26, 20], little attention has been paid to what is specifically meant by the term 'collection' in such instances. The description 'digital collection' is often used in a very broad sense, to encompass large quantities of accumulated digital 'stuff' of varying form, purpose and value. However, within social science scholarship the term 'collection' holds a more specific meaning and is used to describe groups of acquired possessions with distinct characteristics, including clearly identified boundaries, selectiveness and perceived unity. We identify a need to better understand what constitutes a digital collection (and what does not), and to recognize how practices of digital collecting compare to practices of material collecting.

To address this need, we draw from multiple in-depth interviews with 20 people in the UK, which explored their use, management and experience of digital possessions, and later the notion of digital collections more specifically. In reflecting upon our research findings we are able to (1) distinguish between digital collections and other types of digital accumulations, (2) introduce a taxonomy of three distinct types of digital collection which involve different experiences, values and collecting practices and are experienced and valued differently, and (3) demonstrate ways in which the affordances of digital environments may facilitate or impede meaningful practices of acquisition, curation and exhibition. In doing so, this paper contributes to HCI by moving towards a clearer vocabulary for discussing digital possessions, and by presenting a framework that can guide HCI design in facilitating particular types of digital collecting practices.

CHI 2015, April 18 - 23, 2015, Seoul, Republic of Korea

ACM 978-1-4503-3145-6/15/04...$15.00
http://dx.doi.org/10.1145/2702123.2702380

BACKGROUND AND RELATED WORK

Material Collections: A Review

In order to frame our findings, we firstly review the understanding of collections adopted within the social sciences. Prior to the 1980s little academic research explored collecting. However, a wealth of literature on the topic has since emerged within, but not limited to, the disciplines of material culture studies, museum studies, consumer research, anthropology, sociology and social psychology. Whilst a comprehensive review of this, now fairly extensive, literature is beyond the scope of this paper, we identify key themes within prior discussions of material collections.

Within this body of work, collections are considered to be a group of possessions with very particular characteristics, although there is disagreement as to what these are. While much debate surrounds the exact definition of collection, one that is widely cited is that of Belk et al. [7, p.180], which is as follows:

"The selective, active, and longitudinal acquisition, possession, and disposition of an interrelated set of differentiated objects (material things, ideas, beings, or experiences) that contribute to and derive extraordinary meaning from the entity (the collection) that this set is perceived to constitute."

Although it is noted that it is not only physical objects that can be collected, prior work has studied collecting almost exclusively in relation to physical objects. From the above definition it is clear that collecting doesn't encompass all accumulations of objects and in particular great pains have been taken to distinguish collecting from the passive accumulation and unselective hoarding of objects [6, 8]. Collections are distinct in that collectors are highly selective, employing boundaries that distinguish what is and isn't appropriate for inclusion [4, 8, 9] and following the rule of 'no two alike', avoiding duplicate objects [11].

The objects included in collections are highly varied, including naturally occurring objects such as insects or shells, manufactured or 'orchestrated' collectables [21] such as Beanie Babies or

Pokémon cards, mundane everyday objects like beer cans and nutcrackers [4], and rare and valuable objects such as fine art and vintage cars [12]. Whilst objects included in collections are highly varied, they are typically non-necessities valued primarily for some reason other than their utility or economic value [4, 6, 7]. Collections are recognized to become treasured possessions, highly interwoven with people's sense of self, an important point of self-reflection, extension and expression [3, 4, 7, 8].

For many collectors the process of collecting is a pleasurable leisure pursuit and takes precedence over the collectibles themselves. Collectors often describe the thrill of the hunt and the pleasure of discovering a new addition to their collection [2, 4, 8]. Thus beyond 'having' a collection, 'being' a collector and 'doing' collecting are also important. Although acquisition is the most frequently discussed collecting practice, curating collections by organizing, storing, caring for and maintaining them, and exhibiting collections by displaying them to oneself and to others are also important collecting practices [4, 6, 11, 12]. Thus beyond acquisition, collecting involves a complex range of practices which involve a level of controlling, ordering, classifying, managing and ultimately dominating the collection; indeed Akhtar [1, p.40] proposes that "the collector reigning over his empire of inanimate objects begins to feel like a demigod."

Although we are limited to only a brief review of collecting literature here, it becomes quickly evident that perhaps the aforementioned difficulty in arriving at an agreed definition of the term lies in complexity and diversity not only in objects collected but also in collectors and collecting. Problems arise from attempting to encompass a range of highly distinct phenomena under the label 'collections' when motivations, practices and meanings are recognized to differ significantly.

For example, it has been acknowledged that collecting is not always intentional and does not always involve striving towards series completion [4, 7, 8]. Pearce [28, p.158] states that *"collections can creep up on people unawares until the moment of realization: it suddenly dawns on a woman that the old clothes at the back of the wardrobe constitute an important group of Mary Quant or Carnaby Street dresses, which then in her mind becomes a collection to which she may actively add."* However in many accounts, striving towards a perfect collection is key, with collectors aiming for completion or closure and even competing to have the 'best' collection [4, 11]. Perhaps the most commonly discussed motivation for collecting is mastery, success or competence; here collecting is an opportunity to demonstrate our knowledge, skill and tenacity to ourselves and to others through the successful pursuit of difficult to obtain objects [4, 6, 7, 8].

In other accounts however, collecting is not about pursuit and achievement but about discovering objects incidentally and unexpectedly. For instance, Grasskamp [1983, cited in 4, p.63] proposes that *"The art of collecting demands the element of surprise; the collector should not be allowed to know right from the outset what lies in store when he decides for instance to collect radios, even though it is clear that it is only radios he is going to collect."* Indeed Belk [4] discusses collecting as a vehicle of modern hedonism, a source of pleasure, desire and fantasy; it has also been described as a series of 'treasure hunts' [Lehrer, 1990, cited in 7]. Such accounts of collecting, defined by suspense, anticipation, excitement and discovery, differ significantly from those in the previous paragraph whereby collections have clear boundaries and an explicit end-goal.

Thus, the literature on collecting shows significant variation in collections, experiences and practices. Prior efforts to bring order to this variance are limited. Scholars have drawn distinctions between the types of objects that form collections. Pearce [29], for instance, draws on factors such as low grade material vs. quality material, unique vs. common, craft-made vs. mass produced. Others compare the types of collectors that build them. Danet and Katriel [11] contrast Type A and Type B collectors, the former having certain affective criteria for choosing items for a collection with the aim of improving it; the latter using cognitive criteria to choose items with the aim of improving their knowledge rather than the collection's beauty; similarly, Belk [4] distinguishes between taxonomic and aesthetic collectors. However, these efforts do not sufficiently account for the variance in accounts of collecting described above. We believe there may be value in building a deeper understanding of the key configurations of collecting, which could simultaneously account for distinctions in the nature of the collection, practices of collecting and the experience of the collector, and aim to do so in this paper.

Digital Collections: A Need for Research

In addition to this objective, we intend to broaden the focus of research on collecting. Collecting has long been a practice built around material objects, but might we see collections, collecting and collectors in the digital realm too? As people accumulate large quantities of digital objects, questions are raised about the meaning and value that these goods hold, and evidence suggests they may become meaningful objects to which individuals feel strongly attached. Prior research has explored the opportunities and challenges for meaningful possession that digital goods imply [13, 23, 24 25, 26, 34], but has not explicitly considered whether these items may be seen as collections.

Indeed, where the term 'digital collection' is used in HCI research [20, 26] it is not with reference to the scholarly understanding of collection summarized above. Prior HCI work has tended to consider how users may amass, archive and curate digital "stuff" for other purposes [e.g. 17, 19, 20], rather than for the sake of collecting as understood here. For instance, within work on archiving the emphasis is on effectively storing existing digital possessions for future use [17], as opposed to actively amassing a selection of digital objects as an end in itself.

This paucity of work on digital collections extends beyond HCI, and consequently Belk [5] identifies digital collections as an area about which little as known. Limited prior work indicates that collecting may be much transformed where digital content is concerned. Siddiqui and Turley [31] propose that the majority of accumulated digital content is not regarded as meaningful or self-defining, whilst Belk [5] has speculated that collections may become less selective in the digital realm since we are able to create, acquire and keep large amounts of digital stuff, relying on searching and sorting to provide coherence and unity. Thus whilst digital collections have yet to receive substantial empirical exploration, there is some indication that digital collecting may take on new and distinct forms. However, we lack a substantial understanding of how these practices might unfold. Do people collect digital objects? What might a digital collection consist of? How might digital collections compare to material collections? These are the research questions we aimed to explore.

RESEARCH DESIGN

Over a 2 year period (June 2012-July 2014) multiple in-depth interviews took place with 20 people in the UK in order to explore the ways in which they experienced, used and managed their digital possessions. This study adopted an emergent design, involving an iterative process of data collection, analysis and interpretation that enabled a gradual narrowing of the study's focus and aim, with emerging themes explored in increasing depth.

Participants

We conducted 41 interviews with 20 individuals (aged 17-80, 12 women and 8 men). Our aim was not to produce a 'representative sample', but to select participants who would generate a breadth of experiences. Screening questions asked via email and telephone calls enabled participants to be selected purposively. Participants spanned generations and life-stages and had diverse backgrounds. Our emphasis, however, was also on heterogeneity within participants' engagement with technology and in particular with digital objects. For instance participants included an ex-IT worker who described herself as a 'techie', a computing student specializing in hacking, an experienced beauty blogger and an avid MMORPG gamer, alongside participants who described themselves as having a fairly functional relationship with technology and worried they would have little to say on the matter. Sampling purposively in this way produced highly varied accounts of digital possessions, but nevertheless significant themes began to emerge within participants' stories.

Data Collection, Analysis and Interpretation

In unstructured, in-depth interviews, lasting between one and three hours, participants were asked to tell the first author about their digital possessions and where possible to show them (via laptops, mobile phones, tablet devices, gaming consoles, etc.). The aim was to cover areas key to participants' relationships with their digital possessions, rather than imposing an a priori set of topics. Participants were prompted to elaborate, where necessary, in order to produce rich, descriptive accounts. All interviews were transcribed in full, and subject to hermeneutic analysis [32, 33], moving between ideographic analysis of individual interview transcripts and cross-case analysis in which common themes were identified across participants' accounts.

Up to three interviews were conducted with each participant over a two year period, in order to understand and document changes over time. An iterative process of data collection, analysis and interpretation meant that where prominent themes began to emerge the researcher was able to prompt participants to elaborate on these subjects in greater depth in later interviews. For instance, in follow up interviews participants were asked to discuss those digital possessions that they might consider a 'collection'. Often participants would list content and ask whether the researcher would consider this a collection – a question that was never answered directly and always met by the question 'Do *you* consider it to be a collection?' Thus interviews were guided by emic rather than etic definitions of collection; care was taken not to assess during the interview whether content discussed would fit scholarly definitions of collecting, but to discuss fully all content that participants described as such. Data collection concluded once a point of theoretical saturation was reached. In total over 68 hours of interview data was collected, with an average of over 3 hours spent with each participant.

A TAXONOMY OF DIGITAL COLLECTIONS

During the interviews participants described a range of digital content as collections, including (but not limited to) objects in videogames, digital photographs, social media profiles, eBooks, digital music, and blogs. Participants' colloquial use of the term 'collection' often encompassed broader types of accumulated and gathered content than would conform to established theoretical definitions. Using this theoretical lens we point to two kinds of practices that participants referred to as collections but which do not fit established understandings, before focusing in the rest of the paper upon those practices which adhere more closely to a strict definition from the existing literature.

Firstly, in existing definitions, a collection consists of externally produced content that must be acquired, whether it is mass produced (e.g. trading cards), produced by another individual (letters written by a celebrity) or naturally occurring (e.g. shells). Personally-created content does not fall under this rubric. Therefore while it is common, for example, for people to refer to their 'photograph collections' (both digital and material), individuals' role in producing rather than acquiring these photographs distinguishes these digital accumulations from digital collections. Likewise, tweets, blog posts or Facebook pages might be classed as content that has been created or crafted, rather than collected. Using established definitions, then, user-generated content, which is considered in discussions of personal digital archives [17, 20] and online exhibitions [16], are not collections.

Secondly, a collection is considered as an end in itself, whether this perception emerges during or following its assembly. A group of objects that is gathered simply to serve as a means to another end, and continues to be valued only for this purpose, would not be classed as a collection. A common example within participants' accounts was Pinterest boards whereby, consistent with previous research [19], 'pins' were gathered as resources to aid in the achievement of tasks such as decorating a home or planning a wedding. Although such a board might come to be valued as a collection that is an end in itself, this was not found to be the case for our participants. Similarly, participants described completing collecting tasks in videogames, gathering items out of necessity to progress within the game. In both cases, the objects in question are regarded as resources for some other purpose, rather than collected for their own sake.

Having argued that some digital accumulations are more usefully understood as distinct from collections, we now consider digital collections present in participants' accounts that are more consistent with established theoretical definitions. Using the lens of collecting developed in prior work, we consider digital collections to consist of sets of acquired objects that are selective, have distinct boundaries, are valued for their unity, and may be actively added to. However, as with material collections, we found digital collections, collectors and collecting practices to be highly varied. We identify three key 'types' of digital collection (pursued, evolving and emerging), outlined in Figure 1 and described in greater depth below. As previously noted, prior work has not brought coherence to the varied accounts of collecting in the literature. Here we highlight common configurations of collections (their boundaries, desired end-state and meaning), collectors (their experience), and collecting (practices of acquiring, and later curating and exhibiting collections), which presents a novel contribution in itself.

Pursued collections draw the clearest parallels with existing literature on material collections. Both the boundaries and the desired end-state of a pursued collection are clear, whether defined by the market or by individuals. Objects outside of these boundaries are likely to be rejected from inclusion in the collection, whilst objects within these boundaries are actively sought. The collector enjoys the thrill of the hunt, with each successful acquisition producing feelings of achievement and mastery. Indeed, pursuing such collections provides a sense of purpose, and the collection itself becomes a symbol of the collector's skill, knowledge and competence, particularly when objects are rare or difficult to obtain. Pride is taken in this collection, and there may be a desire to display it in a prominent way that recognizes its status. Whilst a great deal of literature on material collections falls into this category, pursued digital collections occurred least frequently in our data, and were most evident in videogames.

An example of a pursued collection comes from Richard, a 22 year old sales executive and regular Xbox gamer from Cardiff, who described his car collection in racing videogame Forza 3.

"[I had] *one from each manufacturer. And the highest level one from each manufacturer I could get. So literally I had a whole garage that could beat anything. So if my mate came on and said 'let's race with Ferraris' for example, my Ferrari would be upgraded to such a level where there's no Ferrari he could have picked that would've beaten me."*

Although some players might strive to collect every car in the game, or perhaps every car by a particular manufacturer, Richard aimed to own one 'top' car from each manufacturer that was fully upgraded. Thus his collection had both clear boundaries and a defined end goal that was actively pursued. Richard strove towards his ideal collection for almost a year, earning in-game currency by racing less expensive, less desirable cars in order to finally afford his perfect collection. Time was then spent upgrading the performance of each car by purchasing new and better car parts and tuning the engine for better performance. It became evident that Richard's collection was highly selective; although there were a number of other cars in his Forza garage, only the 'top spec' cars were considered part of his collection. Additionally he adhered to the 'no two alike' rule [11]; where he received an in-game prize of a car that he already possessed he gifted this duplicate to a friend. Richard discussed his car collection with pride; it was difficult to build and represents his skill at racing within the game. However, as we shall see, the ease of acquiring many digital items meant such collections were uncommon.

		Pursued Collections	Evolving Collections	Emerging Collections
Example		*Richard strives towards a pre-defined, 'unbeatable' car collection in videogame Forza, actively pursuing new additions to his collection & eventually reaching a point of completion*	*Ben is continually discovering new songs and albums to add to his evolving iTunes collection, but has no desire for, or vision of, a completed collection*	*Wendy does not consider her eBook purchases as 'collecting', however as they accumulate they come to be perceived as a collection*
Collection		*Characteristics* Clear boundaries and envisaged end state	*Characteristics* Clear but flexible boundaries and no/ vague envisaged end state	*Characteristics* Loose boundaries, no envisaged end state
		Meaning Collection represents collector's skill and knowledge	*Meaning* Collection holds autobiographical value, may represent taste	*Meaning* Holds autobiographical value, and may represent taste
Collector		*Experience* Achievement and mastery, as well as a sense of purpose	*Experience* Experiences feelings of excitement and anticipation	*Experience* Act of collecting itself is passive
Collecting		*Acquisition* Goal driven and purposeful 'hunt' for desired additions	*Acquisition* Anticipation and excitement as new additions are discovered, often unexpectedly	*Acquisition* Objects are acquired without collection in mind
		Post-Acquisition Collection may be curated and/or exhibited	*Post-Acquisition* Collection may be curated and/or exhibited	*Post-Acquisition* Collection may be curated and/or exhibited

Figure 1. Taxonomy of digital collecting configurations.

Evolving collections, in contrast, have more flexible boundaries and are not pursued by individuals striving towards a perfect collection, but rather evolve gradually as new additions are discovered. Here there is a sense of excitement and discovery since there is no way of knowing what the next addition to the collection might be or when and where it will be discovered. Rather than skill, these objects represent collectors' personal taste and interests, and may hold autobiographical value. An example of this comes from Ben, 41, a graphic designer from Cambridge who DJs in his spare time and possesses large collections of records, CDs and mp3s. His collection of digital music stored within iTunes, which he estimates to be worth over a thousand pounds, has been continually evolving for almost a decade but not towards a pre-defined end state. Rather, Ben is continually discovering new music to add to his collection.

"I'll make lists of stuff I hear on the radio, then go and download that [...] *If I hear something through Spotify I like, I'll tend to*

email the name of the track and the author to myself and then go and buy that at home. [...] [I tend to delete] *things that I listened to again and didn't think they were that great the second time around, or maybe I just lost interest in that particular type of music. And in some instances, there was a particular genre of music I didn't listen to as much, and I got myself an external hard drive and then took all of that particular type of music off iTunes and then put it on that hard drive"*

Discovering new music is key to Ben's account, and whilst he could continue to listen to these tracks via Spotify he feels it is important to add these songs to his collection. Whilst his collection is extensive it is carefully curated, with meaningful categories imposed and less favoured items either deleted or removed and stored separately. Ben explains that his digital music collection prompts reminiscence as songs and playlists remind him of past DJ slots and music events. Thus we see that Ben's evolving digital music collection is similarly highly valued, yet differs significantly from Richard's pursued car collection in Forza in meaning, practice and experience.

The third category, ***emerging collections***, is distinct from pursued and evolving collections in that this kind of collection initially emerges as a by-product of some other activity. The majority of collections seem to begin as emerging collections; as noted by Belk [4] and Pearce [28], objects may only later be recognized as a collection to which items are then more actively added (at which point the collection becomes an evolving or pursued collection). Emerging collections are perhaps the most overlooked category of collection in material collection literature, although exceptions do exist. Shankar [30] illustrates that even when not actively 'collected', accumulated record collections become important and symbolic archeological representations of music consumption over time. Another example might be a traveler who comes to see the stamps on their passport as a meaningful collection representing countries visited, but does not actively travel abroad with the primary aim of adding new stamps to this collection. Emerging collections were most prominent in our participants' accounts of their digital collections.

An example comes from Alice, a 30 year old PR consultant and mummy blogger who studied English Literature at university and remains an avid reader. Indeed, one of the bedrooms in her home has been converted into a library. Having recently received a Kindle e-reader as a gift, Alice is a convert; while she still loves owning and displaying physical books she can't deny the convenience offered by eBooks. Alice considers both her eBooks and material books as collections (although her material books are more highly prized), yet she does not purchase eBooks with the primary intention of adding them to her collection. Rather she downloads eBooks to read, and later reflects on them as an accumulated collection that summarizes her e-reading history. However we shall see that Alice perceives this collection as less significant than her material books since exhibition is problematic.

Summary of Framework

To summarise our argument so far, our participants' meaningful digital collections can be organised into three key 'types'. These are exemplified by the three examples provided, however a range of other digital objects were also discussed as collections. The taxonomy presented in Figure 1 presents a useful framework in acknowledging that distinct types of collections exist, which are associated with highly varied meanings, experiences and practices. The same type of object may fall into different categories, depending upon how it is used and interpreted; indeed, collections may transition between the categories presented here, as meanings and practices change. Emerging collections may become evolving collections as individuals come to actively acquire new additions, and evolving collections may become pursued collections, as more explicit boundaries are established and a clearer end goal envisaged. It is worth noting that these categories apply not only to digital collections; much of the literature on material collections falls into one of the above collection types. Thus, our taxonomy presents a framework for imposing order on prior literature. We shall see in the following section, however, that a number of issues arise which make the types of highly meaningful, sacrilised collections described by Belk [4], Pearce [28] and others difficult to achieve in the digital realm.

DIGITAL COLLECTING PRACTICES

In our analysis it became quickly evident that many of the practices that have been documented as making material collections so precious can be difficult or problematic in digital collecting. Here we review some of the most prominent distinctions that emerged in practices of acquiring, curating and exhibiting digital collections, drawing from the three examples provided above (collections of digital music, digital cars and eBooks).

Acquisition

The pleasure of adding to material collections is such that people may delay their completion by extending boundaries, or begin new collections [4]. Acquisition is typically discussed as active and goal-driven, with much pleasure found in the thrill of the hunt, or as driven by anticipation and the thrill of discovery. To what extent might acquiring digital goods afford the same thrills?

Thrill of the Hunt

Existing work on material collecting describes the experience of the 'thrill of the hunt'. Where collections are pursued, complex practices of acquisition present a challenge that is relished, since it provides an opportunity to demonstrate skill and knowledge, and to experience a rewarding sense of achievement. Belk [4, p.89] proposes that "rarity is prized because it is not enough to succeed if everyone else succeeds as well". Collecting must be moderately difficult in order to be satisfying and generate pride.

However, in digital collecting, the hunt for new additions rarely presents an adequate challenge. A key advantage of many digital goods is their ease of acquisition; these items are infinitely reproducible and never 'beyond reach' or out of stock (unless artificial scarcity is employed). An exception within participants' accounts was collections within videogames, echoing the findings of Molesworth and Watkins [23] that a sense of achievement is gained through accumulating and crafting digital possessions within videogames. This is evident in Richard's pride when describing his unbeatable car collection within Forza, a collection he had built up through hard work and skill. During his interview he discussed desired cars he was working towards, alongside the satisfaction felt with each new acquisition. Richard's account illustrates that the thrill of the hunt can be experienced in the digital realm if acquisition presents a significant challenge.

Notably, within our dataset this experience was limited to videogames. Objects that were easily acquired did not provide a sense of achievement and did not represent skill, knowledge or status. For instance, a large record collection would likely involve significant commitment to searching for and acquiring rare records but, in contrast, participants noted that finding and downloading a song is not difficult and nothing to be proud of. Ben's CD and record collections were until recently given pride of place in his home, and he enjoyed their visibility. He is proud of his collection of CDs and records, which took significant effort to achieve, something that is not the case with his digital music collection:

"I was quite proud that that was up there actually in my living room so other people could see it [...] *I think with records they're so much harder to get, well they are nowadays anyway, there's certain records that are super hard to get hold of now* [...] [people] *may see this record and go 'wow you've got that on vinyl.' Whereas, you know, they may well have that on iTunes* [laughs] *they're not that bothered about their iTunes version of it, they would really like a seven inch record of this particular piece of music* [...] *It's to do with the effort of finding it. It's a super rare piece of music, extremely hard to find, you know, you'd have had to dig through a whole pile of crates in a record shop to get it."*

The effort involved in building Ben's physical music collection grants it an elevated status that has warranted practices of display. He explains that this collection would be difficult to replace since it contains rare and valuable items that would be difficult to find again. In contrast, his collection of music within iTunes is more replaceable – although he would be upset to lose it, it would be fairly straightforward to repurchase these mp3s. Practices of acquisition may shape the meaning of digital collections; so easily acquired are Ben's mp3s that they do not demonstrate skill and consequently do not warrant display or evoke pride.

Thrill of the Find

In contrast to the thrill of the hunt, evolving collections are characterised by the thrill of the find. Here additions are not actively sought, but are discovered and added to the collection. Hence the chance of discovery is key; McCracken [22, p.93] notes that when their acquisition is uncertain "collectibles make it possible once again to dream", whilst Belk [4] found that travelling to new places offered collectors the additional excitement of potentially discovering new objects. Might practices of digital collecting offer the same sense of excitement and anticipation emerging from the chance of discovery?

Becky, a 17 year old student from South Wales, has recently begun collecting old vinyl records. Becky's description of searching for records illustrates the anticipation of finding new records and taking them home to add to her collection – each visit to a car boot sale or charity shop is filled with potential for discovery.

"It's kind of exciting because I love seeing a box of loads of records and just choosing which ones I want. Like, I love just looking through them all, and the smell of them as well. Yeah, it's just quite an enjoyable experience, I could sit and just look through vinyls, not even wanting to buy any [...] *I'm always excited to go home and play it and just to listen to it, especially when it's someone I haven't heard of or I've never heard their music before"*

Evident in Becky's account of record collecting was a desire to acquire more, however there was also a desire to acquire new additions in a particular way. Whilst she recognizes that she could have more easily acquired records via platforms such as eBay she prefers the enjoyable experience of visiting places where she might unexpectedly stumble across an exciting new addition to her collection. Thus the practice of collecting emerges as perhaps more important than the collection itself, producing feelings of excitement and anticipation. In contrast, in her account of searching for digital music it appears that acquisition is simply a functional, rather than enjoyable, practice.

"It's not as exciting as buying a record, 'cause a lot of the time I'll have heard of the person. I never really, like, some way or another I've heard of that person that I'll be downloading new music from, whereas a lot of the vinyls, 'cause they're so old I haven't heard of a lot of the artists [...] *you can download it straight away, whereas you buy a vinyl you have to wait until you get home to play it, it's not, you can't just instantly hear it, so it's a bit more of an experience"*

Becky feels there is less opportunity for serendipitous discovery during her current practices of acquiring digital music, whilst the opportunity for instant gratification produces less sense of the pleasurable anticipation that makes record collecting so appealing. However, Ben points out that in purchasing music from iTunes there is the potential to discover new and exciting music:

"There's a really good feature on iTunes actually, so that if you put a search in for a piece of music, and you start to play it, there's a list that appears at the bottom of album covers, and that shows you what other people have bought [...] *So that helps to expose you to new music* [...] *I've bought absolutely piles of music through that feature, just because it's exposed me to stuff"*

Similarly, Alice describes herself as addicted to the Kindle Store which she browses for new eBooks, waiting for best prices and discovering new content. Whilst digital collections may lack the element of chance evident in Becky's account of record collecting, due to lack of scarcity, browsing for digital music and eBooks can remain an enjoyable experience with the anticipation of either a bargain or the discovery of new, exciting items.

Curation

Beyond acquisitional aspects of collecting, what curatorial practices might people engage in in terms of caring for, managing and ordering digital collections in meaningful ways? Typically items in material collections are placed out of use, indeed they are valued "not because of any inherent use value but precisely for their non-use value" [4, p.62]. The suggestion that the stamps in their collection should be used to post a letter would, to a stamp collector, seem absurd. However, even prized digital collections remained in use by our participants. Digital music collections were listened to, collections of eBooks were read and Richard's treasured collection of cars competed in races. We might speculate that practices other than removal from use signify a collection's meaning in the digital realm, such as storing objects together and separately from other items, and organizing them in personally meaningful ways. However, participants did struggle to bring order to digital collections in a way that recognized their elevated status and even their unity. We propose that where individuals are unable to perform such curatorial practices the meaning of digital collections can be eroded.

Organizing

The ways in which possessions are stored and organized enables people to mark, maintain or transform their meaning. Collectors are acknowledged to engage in a series of rituals to mark their collections as sacred. For instance they may separate them from more mundane artefacts, display them prominently or provide them with special care and attention [4, 7,15]. However our participants struggled to order their digital collections in meaningful ways. Whereas in previous work, acts of organizing material possessions are seen to produce and stabilize categories of meaning [14], it became evident that participants rarely organized their digital collections since such practices were often performed instead by software. Often there is limited choice as to how collections can be organized; for instance Richard explained that although he can choose to sort his cars in Forza by manufacturer or racing class, he is unable to impose his own classifications. He would not, therefore, be able to separate his prized collection of high spec cars from the functional cars in his Forza 'garage'.

Eve, a 35 year old artist and postgraduate student, explained that she carefully orders her record collection thematically, grouping what she perceives to be similar music together and storing some of her least favored records separately. Through this act of separating she recognizes and enforces distinctions in meaning, and explains that since her sizable collection of records "can be overwhelming, the way you personally want to organise things is really important to kind of make sense of it." Such practices became difficult in managing her digital music collection, however.

"the thing I don't like about iTunes, with this whole alphabetical organising thing, that means you can't hide stuff so easily. So say the album you want to hide begins, or the group begins, with A, they're there every time you open up your iTunes"

Eve feels that iTunes doesn't enable her to organize her digital music collection as she desires, and consequently she feels that she has less control over it than her record collection. This lack of control became particularly evident to her when she changed computers, meaning that her digital music collection moved to an updated version of iTunes where its prior order was changed.

"You get a new version of the software and it's mixed it all up, you regret that kind of having to re-organise it all or put it all back to how you used it before, and if you can't use it the way you used it before that's really frustrating. [...] *with a digital collection of music, because of the way you upgrade it and it organises things, it organises things differently, I don't really feel it's mine in a way* [...] *when you open up your computer and your collection of music isn't organised the way it was when you last opened it, that kind of makes the feeling of ownership not quite as... you don't feel you own that* [...] *I've got quite a substantial amount of music on my laptop, so I guess in a way I do have a collection, but it doesn't feel quite like it because I don't have this way of organising it in the way I'd like."*

In contrast to feelings of control, mastery and dominance associated with material collecting [4, 7, 8], here we see that Eve is struggling to achieve any real sense of control over a collection that she is unable to impose any meaningful or lasting order over.

Uniting

Often collections of content were bound to particular contexts or devices and participants had difficulties moving content around. For instance, videogame content was left behind on old consoles and within previous versions of games, whilst some participants struggled to move music collections between devices. Gregson [15] describes collections as perhaps the most enduring of possessions, however here we see that digital collections may not persist outside of certain contexts. For instance, Richard explains that when he purchased Forza 4, the more recent iteration of the videogame, he had to leave behind his treasured collection of cars; he was unable to transfer his collection to the new version of the game. In Forza 3 Richard had accumulated a total of 100 cars including a top car from each manufacturer, however in Forza 4 he has only 14. He talks about 'losing' these cars (even though they are still accessible in the old game) and explains that although he has tried to rebuild his collection in the newer version of the game the cars never feel quite the same since he feels that they do not have the same history. Richard's 'loss' made him less motivated to collect cars in the later iteration of the game; he plans to simply focus on the racing aspect of the game instead.

Other participants described similar instances. Becky, for example, explains that after receiving a new laptop for Christmas she is struggling to transfer her old content to her new device due to broken USB ports. She has uploaded some content to Facebook (photos) and sent others via email (e.g. CVs) with plans to re-download them onto the new laptop, however the majority of content (including her digital music collection) is left behind on her old device. She explains that she doesn't know how to transfer this data, and therefore this collection is effectively 'trapped' on her old computer and iPod. Becky is unable to connect the iPod to her old laptop since the USB ports are broken, but worries that if she plugs it into her new device it will sync automatically to the (empty) iTunes library and that she will lose her music. Consequently Becky is planning to purchase a new iPod to store her new music.

"I think I'll have to get a new iPod, because I think if I plugged mine in now all my old music would go [...] *I don't want to risk putting it on my old iPod, I'd rather get a new one for my new music and keep my old iPod for all the old music.* [...] *it would be annoying because they wouldn't be all, you can't access them all at once, you'd have to keep changing iPods"*

Becky is struggling to unite old content with new content. Similarly Richard explains that he is unsure how to unite his iTunes library with music purchased from the Google Play Store on his phone. Prior work indicates that keeping track of digital possessions across platforms can become problematic [24, 25]. Here, participants struggled to move their collections from device to device or videogame to videogame, and consequently we observed trapped collections left behind and fragmented collections spread across locations. Participants, even 'digital natives' such as Becky, lacked the technological understanding necessary to unite their collections as meaningful wholes.

Exhibition

Social scientists have long recognized that in displaying objects we both communicate to others aspects of who we are (or would like to be perceived to be) and reaffirm our own sense of self. In Shankar's [30] study of record collections, he proposes that records (and we might speculate also, books, films and other collections) may become an archaeological record of our past consumption, telling us something about who we are and who we once were, and communicating this information to others. Might digital collections serve the same self-reflective and self-presentational purpose? How do people exhibit their digital collections to themselves and others?

Self-Reflection

Reflection on digital collections in their entirety was largely absent from participants' accounts; it seemed that their digital collections often disappeared when not in use. Often these collections were not stored and displayed in an enduring way that facilitated easy reflection. For instance, Alice explained that she enjoyed browsing her library of material books, sometimes flicking through books and reminiscing. Her book collection represents her taste in literature, but also holds significant autobiographical value; books she studied at University contain annotations and remind her of a period in her life. Alice's eBooks, on the other hand, were described as disappearing into the depths of her Kindle after reading and were rarely reflected upon.

"I think when I've finished a book on the Kindle, it is probably just archived and discarded and I doubt that I'd look at it again, whereas I've got loads of bookshelves upstairs with all my books on [...] *I love my books. And I do like going and browsing, like sometimes I'll pick up a book that I read say ten years ago and re-read it if I remember I really enjoyed it, so I think that's where the relationship's different. Although I know what I've got on my Kindle I don't view it so much as a possession afterwards, once it's been read* [...] *I'd like to have the ability to read it on the Kindle just for the ease and practicality, but then I'd like to have the actual physical book to put on my bookshelf to keep, and to remind me that it's there"*

Consistent with prior work [26, 10], it becomes evident that Alice's eBooks simply don't have the presence of her material books, which through being stored and displayed prompt acts of browsing, reminiscing and reflecting. In contrast, her eBook collection only presents itself when summoned, via an e-reader which displays one or a few items at a time. Similarly, Richard explained that whilst it is easy to scroll through each car in his collection, he has no way to view the entire 'garage' as a whole. Current design seems to enable easier engagement with single digital possessions than collections. It can be difficult to grasp the scale of digital collections in their entirety, as they lack the presence that makes collections ideal candidates for self-reflection.

Displaying to Others

Displaying collections to others is key in many accounts of material collecting; Belk [4] proposes that when collections are presented to others the collector is in essence presenting themselves for evaluation. Prior research indicates that digital objects may communicate meaning to others, expressing skill, status and group membership [18]. However, digital objects present both challenges and opportunities for display. Hogan [16] illustrates that the digital realm may provide opportunities for enduring and highly visible exhibitions via social media, however, digital objects are not always characterized by enduring visibility. Participants described their material music, book and film collections as a talking point amongst friends, but digital collections were less socially visible. For instance, Richard had little opportunity to show his car collection to others, even when playing online.

"They can see how many races you've won, what level you are and whatever else. How much money you've got. But they can't see how many cars you've got or anything like that. And if you've downloaded a car that they don't own it just shows as a stock shaped car, it doesn't show the visual part of it, it's just a black shape driving around"

Furthermore, Eve notes that where friends can see her collection of digital music, her inability to organize and exhibit as desired results in a less meaningful or representative display.

"Every time I open iTunes, say if somebody else is there, they can see alphabetically what I've got, but it's not necessarily my favourite albums, whereas if I had a way of organising them, so like, if my favourite albums came up first, then it'd be more representative of the music I like. [...] *there should be some personal decisions there about how you display them."*

Here we see that digital collections not only lack social visibility, but where exhibition is possible, lack of curation can make such displays less meaningful. Material collections are often discussed in terms of identity, extending the self and shaping the self-definition of a collector [3, 4, 7]. Where digital collections are not viewed by oneself or by others they may become less clearly interwoven with the collector's sense of self.

DISCUSSION

We shall now consider in turn each of the research questions the study sought to answer. Firstly, do people actively collect digital objects? Prior research has discussed digital possessions at a broader level [24, 25, 26], and we have noted that where the term 'digital collection' is used in HCI it tends to refer to accumulated digital 'stuff' rather than collections as a distinct phenomenon. Digital accumulations may take a variety of forms; from digital clutter which simply accrues unintentionally (e.g. emails, metadata, browsing histories) to more carefully curated digital archives (e.g. folders of photographs and work documents). However in this paper we have demonstrated that digital collections present a distinct type of digital possession. Digital collections consist of sets of *acquired* digital objects that are *selective*, have *distinct boundaries*, are valued for their *unity*, and are often *actively added to* by the user. However, there are different types of digital collection, just as research on material collections points to variance. We have identified three kinds of digital collection, which share some, yet not all, of the characteristics of physical collections. We have defined these as *pursued*, *evolving* and *emerging*, and have shown that collecting practices as well as the meaning and value attributed to collections varies across these types. Thus, people do actively collect digital objects, and distinguishing these digital collections from other digital accumulations moves the HCI community towards a clearer vocabulary for discussing digital possessions.

Secondly, what might a digital collection consist of? We have focused on three examples discussed by participants: digital music, digital cars within a videogame and eBooks. However, these examples are illustrative rather than exhaustive and our research participants identified a broader array of digital objects that might be considered collections. Thus, consistent with prior work on material collections, we identify collections by the way they are experienced by the user and the performance of collecting practices, rather than by particular categories of object. Further work might extend the understanding offered here by focusing on specific contexts (quantified self systems, virtual worlds).

Finally, how might digital collections compare to the material collections previously documented? What is clear from this work is that individuals can both enjoy and attach importance to their digital collections, yet the tools at hand often fail to provide adequate support for the full range of value and meaning that they might otherwise derive from them. The analysis presented above presents a number of implications for design in support of collecting practices and more valued digital collections. In doing so, it extends prior work on how design may enable more meaningful relationships with digital possessions [e.g. 24, 25, 26].

A first set of implications relates to practices of acquisition and the subsequent value attached to digital objects by users. While recommender systems present opportunities for surprise and novelty, the nature of acquisition in the digital world means that, outside of videogames, there is little opportunity for the challenging pursuit of digital goods, a factor that has been linked to experiences of mastery, success and competence in material collecting. *Making things challenging to acquire by demanding a level of skill, knowledge or effort may enhance the value of collections.* Examples of how this might be accomplished in the digital realm include a mobile app developed in a zoo setting, where collecting was tied to physically visiting exhibits [27]. Likewise, attending a concert could unlock exclusive content on an mp3. Alternatively, design for challenging acquisition could draw on uniqueness and rarity. For instance, 'first edition' eBooks may retain unique covers and resist changes to their appearance brought about by software updates, developing a dated appearance that sets them apart from others and makes visible the fact that the collection contains unusual, rare, or difficult to obtain items.

A second set of implications involves *designing more flexible tools for managing digital collections, enabling users to mark their elevated status by separating them from other possessions and to impose their own structures of meaning*. Many applications impose organizational schemes that can undermine individuals' sense of control over their digital collections, and make it difficult for users to organize collected items across applications, devices and platforms. The result of this is trapped and fragmented collections, which make it difficult for users to maintain the entirety of their collections, and their existing order, as they shift across technologies. An approach that recognizes the importance of curatorial work in conferring meaning, and the persistence of a whole collection, may increase the stability and endurance of digital collections, and enable a greater sense of control and mastery on the part of the collector.

Finally, the findings point to the fact that, like physical collections, digital collections can and do play a role in personal reflection and public identity. This could be better supported by *providing ways to view collections in their entirety, and to produce more enduring, socially visible exhibitions.* Crucial here is underpinning ways for users to create a public face for their collections, whether this means more visibility in the digital realm, or more opportunities for display in the physical world. New kinds of displays, appliances, and even wearables could allow for the showcasing of collections. In increasing the visibility of digital collections, we may enrich the personal and public meanings they come to hold, and consequently their self-expressive and self-reflective value. Furthermore, we build on Odom et al's [25] suggestion that digital patina could be used to signify provenance and so play a role in personal reflection. A digital good might indicate that, for example, it was downloaded whilst on holiday or gifted by a friend, thus building an autobiography of use and underpinning a greater level of personal meaningfulness.

While the recommendations provided so far speak to digital collections in general, we can also draw on the taxonomy we have proposed to understand how design might differentially support collecting practices for pursued, evolving and emerging digital collections. In designing for pursued collections, for instance, we could draw on the importance of a clearly defined end goal and offer users the option to construct a template for an ideal "set" of objects that they hope to acquire. In contrast, evolving collections are characterised by a desire for surprise and novelty and might benefit from creative recommendations. Furthermore, design may have the potential to transition collections between categories by shaping collection practices. For instance, transition from an evolving to a pursued collection might be supported by enabling users to impose clearer boundaries and to envision a perfect collection, whereas transition from an emerging to evolving collection could be supported by design for surprise and novelty. Furthermore, we may aid recognition of other accumulated possessions as emerging collections by providing tools for curation and exhibition that can help shape their perceived value.

Conclusion

This paper advances emerging work on digital possessions by defining digital collections as distinct from other types of digital accumulations such as digital archives and clutter. We use the lens of collecting in the physical world to explore how the digital world is different, and how existing tools may undermine the value users seek from collections and the drive to collect. We highlight the challenge of acquisition, the imposition of the user's own meaning structures, and the potential for self-expression and personal reflection as key factors that could be better supported. Further, our analysis leads us to introduce a taxonomy of three distinct types of digital collection which can further inform HCI design by facilitating relevant collecting practices for each type, as well as for transitions between them.

REFERENCES

1. Akhtar, S. *Objects of Our Desire: Exploring our Intimate Connections with the Things around Us*. New York: Harmony Books, 2005.
2. Baker, S.M. and Gentry, J.W. Kids as collectors: a phenomenological study of first and fifth graders. *Advances in Consumer Research 23*, (1996), 132-137.
3. Belk, R.W. Possessions and the extended self. *Journal of Consumer Research 15*, 2 (1988) 139-168.
4. Belk, R.W. *Collecting in a Consumer Society*. Psychology Press, 1995.
5. Belk, R.W. Extended self in a digital world. *Journal of Consumer Research 40*, 3 (2013), 477-500.
6. Belk, R.W. "Ownership and Collecting," in Randy O. Frost and Gail Steketee, eds., Oxford Handbook ofHoarding and Acquiring, Oxford: Oxford University Press (forthcoming).
7. Belk, R.W., Wallendorf, M., Sherry, J.F. Jr. and Holbrook, M.B. Collecting in a consumer culture. In Belk, R.W. (Ed.), *Highways and Buyways: Naturalistic Research from the Consumer Behavior Odyssey* (pp. 178-215). Association for Consumer Research, 1991.
8. Belk, R.W., Wallendorf, M., Sherry, J.F. Jr., Holbrook, M.B. and Roberts, S. Collectors and collecting. Advances in Consumer Research, 15 (1988), p.548-553.
9. Bianchi, M. Collecting as a paradigm of consumption. *Journal of Cultural Economics 21*, (1997), 275-289.
10. Brown, B. A. T., Geelhoed, E., Sellen, A. J. (2001). The use of conventional and new music media: Implications for future technologies. INTERACT. Tokyo, Japan.
11. Danet, B. and Katriel, T. No two alike: play and aesthetics in collecting. *Play and Culture 2*, 3 (1989), 255–71.
12. Dannefer, D. Rationality and passion in private experience: modern consciousness and the social world of old-car collectors, *Social Problems 27*, (1980), 392–412.
13. Denegri-Knott, J., Watkins, R. and Wood, J. Transforming digital virtual goods into meaningful possessions. In M. Molesworth and J. Denegri-Knott (Eds.), *Digital Virtual Consumption* (pp. 76-91). Oxford: Routledge, 2012.
14. Douglas, M. and Isherwood, B. *The World of Goods: Towards an Anthropology of Consumption*. 2nd ed. London: Routledge, 1996.
15. Gregson, N. *Living with Things: Ridding, Accommodation, Dwelling*. Sean Kingston Publishing, 2007.
16. Hogan, B. The presentation of self in the age of social media: distinguishing performances & exhibitions online. *Bulletin of Science, Technology & Society*, 30, (2010), 377-386.
17. Kaye, J. et al. 2006. To have and to hold: exploring the personal archive. In *Proc. CHI 2006*, 275-284.
18. Lehdonvirta, V., Wilska, T. and Johnson, M. Virtual consumerism: case habbo hotel. *Information, Communication & Society 12*, 7 (2009), 1059-1079.
19. Linder, R., Snodgrass, C. and Kerne, A. Everyday ideation: all of my ideas are on Pinterest. In *Proc. CHI 2014*, ACM Press (2014), 2411-2420.
20. Lindley, S., Marshall, C.C., Banks, R., Sellen, A. and Regan, T. Rethinking the web as a personal archive. In *Proc. WWW 2013*, 749-760.
21. Martin, P. *Popular Collecting and the Everyday Self: The Reinvention of Museums?* London: Leicester Press, 1999.
22. McCracken, G. *Culture and Consumption: New Approaches to the Symbolic Character of Consumer Goods and Activities.* Bloomington: Indiana Univ. Press, 1988.
23. Molesworth, M. and R. D. Watkins. Adult Videogame Consumption as Individualized Episodic Progress. *Journal of Consumer Culture.* (Forthcoming)
24. Odom, W., Sellen, A., Harper, R. and Thereska, E. 2012. Lost in translation: understanding the possession of digital things in the Cloud. In *Proc. CHI 2012*, ACM, 781-790.
25. Odom, W., Zimmerman, J. and, Forlizzi, J. Teenagers and their virtual possessions: design opportunities and issues. In *Proc. CHI 2011*, ACM Press (2011), 1491-1500.
26. Odom, W., Zimmerman, J., Forlizzi, J. Placelessness, spacelessness, and formlessness: experiential qualities of virtual possessions. In *Proc. DIS 2014*, ACM Press (2014), 985-994.
27. O'Hara, K., Kindberg, T., Glancy, M., Baptista, L., Sukumaran, B., Kahana, G., & Rowbotham, J. (2007). Collecting and sharing location-based content on mobile phones in a zoo visitor experience. CSCW, 16(1-2), pp. 11-44.
28. Pearce, S.M. The urge to collect. In Pearce, S.M. (Ed), *Interpreting Objects and Collections* (pp. 157-159). Routledge: New York, 1994.
29. Pearce, S.M. *Collecting in Contemporary Practice*. London: Sage, 1998.
30. Shankar, A. *Identity and Consumption: An Interpretive Study of People and Their Record Collections*. Unpublished doctoral thesis, 2002.
31. Siddiqui, S., & Turley, D. Extending the self in a virtual world. *Advances in Consumer Research 33*, 1 (2006), 647–648.
32. Spiggle, S. Analysis and interpretation of qualitative data in consumer research, *Journal of Consumer Research 21* (December 1994), 491–503.
33. Thompson, C. Interpreting consumers: a hermeneutical framework for deriving marketing insights from the texts of consumers' consumption stories, *Journal of Marketing Research, 34* (November 1997), 438–55.
34. Watkins, R. & Molesworth, M. Attachment to digital virtual possessions in videogames. *Research in Consumer Behavior 14*, (2012), 153-171.

Medium, Access, and Obsolescence: What Kinds of Objects are Lasting Objects?

Jane Gruning, Julia Bullard, and Melissa Ocepek
The University of Texas at Austin
School of Information
1616 Guadalupe St., Austin, TX, USA
jane.gru@gmail.com, julia.a.bullard@gmail.com,
mgocepek@utexas.edu

ABSTRACT
This paper presents findings from a field study of records managers that provides context for understanding how people see objects on varying media as long-lasting objects (or not). Part of the mandate of the profession of records management is long-term preservation of digital and paper records. At the site of the fieldwork for this study, research participants' tasks primarily consisted of examining individual case files to determine if the files should be kept or destroyed under the relevant rules set by higher-level management according to legal requirements. Close observation of work practices showed that application of records management rules varied depending on the medium of the records, despite the policy that records on varying media are equal in importance. The results of the study suggest that the perceived accessibility and obsolescence of digital objects deserve more attention in the exploration of the place of digital objects in human lives over the long-term.

Author Keywords
Digital preservation; ethnography; field study; obsolescence; digital objects; records management.

ACM Classification Keywords
H.5.m. Information interfaces and presentation (e.g., HCI): Miscellaneous.

INTRODUCTION
Digital objects can be "lost" in a variety of ways: time and use damage physical storage media, hardware necessary for access becomes obsolete and difficult to acquire, and software necessary for display is replaced by new versions incompatible with old file formats. Solutions that exist for these problems are mostly designed for institutional-level implementation in cultural heritage institutions such as archives and museums. The loss of digital objects, however, is a part of everyday life for individuals as well. Recently, researchers in HCI have begun to examine the potential of digital objects as long-lasting personal possessions [14, 19, 20, 24]. Related studies have investigated how digital objects might become "cherishable" [13], or "heirlooms" [23]. An overlapping body of work examines differences (and similarities) in how people interact with digital and physical objects [18, 26, 27, 28]. It is unsurprising that these two strands of investigation tend to overlap; clearly people have no difficulty considering some types of physical objects as both precious and long-lasting, but they currently seem much less likely to value digital objects in the same way [13]. These studies have raised questions such as, "What are the important differences between digital and physical objects?" Or, to take a phenomenological approach, "What are the differences in our experiences of digital and physical objects, and how do those differences in experience relate to the ways that we value those objects?" Theses kinds of questions apply to human interactions with computers in a variety of settings including both the home and the workplace, although motivations for keeping objects vary across those settings.

The Job of Keeping Things
The nine studies mentioned above were conducted in home environments, excepting one that investigated the personal archiving practices of academics [18]. Although there is a long tradition of studying the workplace in HCI [e.g., 2, 15, 33], we make a comparison to work that has been done in home environments because those studies focus on lasting objects in a way that is also central to the study described below. This paper sheds new light on the issue of lasting digital objects by examining human behavior in a particular type of work environment, one in which very long term storage of both digital and physical objects is part of the job. As opposed to a home environment, this setting adds the element of rules for interactions with digital and physical objects. Misinterpreting or breaking those rules can have consequences beyond the personal life of the person interacting with the object.

CHI 2015, April 18 - 23 2015, Seoul, Republic of Korea

ACM 978-1-4503-3145-6/15/04 $15.00
http://dx.doi.org/10.1145/2702123.2702238

Records management is the "field of management responsible for the efficient and systematic control of the creation, receipt, maintenance, use and disposition of records..." [16]. While definitions of the term "record" vary, the following definition is typical: "information in a fixed form that is created or received in the course of individual or institutional activity and set aside (preserved) as evidence of that activity for future reference" [27]. Large corporate, governmental, and non-profit organizations use records management to control, organize, and destroy records. In practice, the job of a records manager is to provide guidance for his or her organization regarding the retention and destruction of records created by the organization. This guidance is based on legal requirements that determine how long organizations must retain various types of records, and may range from development of organizational policy down to advising individual employees on recordkeeping practices. Proper practices are determined by records managers as they interpret how legal requirements apply to the records of the organization, but are typically implemented by individual members of an organization as they go about their daily work. For example, when employees at the Arthur Andersen accounting firm shredded documents and deleted emails in an attempt to destroy evidence of illegal activities prior to the Enron Corporation financial scandal, they were breaking laws that govern records management, and most likely acting against the records management policies of their organization.

The research described here was part of a field study in which multiple researchers examined records management practices at four research sites using ethnographic techniques of observation and interview. The kinds of tasks described above, of setting organizational policy and providing guidelines for recordkeeping, were typical for records managers at most of the sites investigated in this study. One site was quite different: this was an office within the state Department of Children and Family Services (or DCFS[1]), a state agency charged with regulating child care and protecting children, elderly adults, and people with disabilities. At this site, four records clerks (supervised by a manager) applied records management rules for retention and destruction of records on a large scale. Instead of setting policy, the clerks applied it – and instead of applying it as an incidental part of their jobs, applying records management policy was their primary task. In their daily work practices, the clerks made decisions about how broad, organization-wide policies should be applied in many individual cases. The records the clerks handled were case files created by case workers in offices around the state, which were sent to external long term storage facilities once they were not in regular use. During our fieldwork, the research site office was beginning a multi-year project. The purpose of the project was to sort through stored records, identifying and destroying records that were past their destruction dates, so that the state was not paying to store records that it was no longer required to retain. This paper discusses findings from that site, and their implications for human interactions with technology.

[1] The actual name of the state department has been replaced with a common name for this type of department in several states for purposes of confidentiality. Names of participants have also been changed.

We first provide background on the records management policies regarding records medium. Then we review HCI findings on how media type changes perceptions of objects, particularly in cases of long-lasting objects. The paper then describes the office in which we completed our fieldwork and the work practices there, as well as how those practices varied depending on the medium and accessibility of the record. We then explore potential reasons for these differences. Finally, we describe the potential implications of our findings for technology design.

LITERATURE REVIEW

Records Management and Medium

The shift from paper to digital as the primary medium of creation for business records demanded a statement from the field of records management about the status of digital records. The leading records management professional organization, ARMA International, takes the perspective that medium is not a limiting characteristic in the determination of what kinds of objects can be records. This perspective is reflected in the definition of records management provided by ARMA: "any recorded information, regardless of medium or characteristics, made or received and retained by an organization in pursuance of legal obligations or in the transaction of business" [11]. ARMA additionally specifies that retention schedules, which determine for how long records must be kept, apply equally to records on varying media. "Each record listed on a records retention schedule specifies a specific period of time that the record is retained. *This retention applies whether the record is on paper or residing on magnetic or optical media (hard disk, floppy disk, tape, CD, etc.)...*" (emphasis in original) [12]. It is not clear, however, that everyday human interactions with records actually align with these guidance statements.

This issue has also been examined by scholars in the field of archival science [10, 32], as archival institutions are often the eventual recipients of records determined to have long-term value by records managers. Duranti has done extensive work on the authenticity of records with a specific focus on electronic records [5, 6, 7, 8], and is cited in the ARMA documentation. Her work has primarily had the aim of guiding policy rather than investigating human behavior. For instance, in findings from the first phase of the InterPARES project[2], she and Thibodeau determined that "the medium is not a relevant factor in assessing a record's authenticity," and that transfer of a record from one medium to another does not affect the authenticity of the record [9]. In this study, we explore how policies about records medium are applied in work practices.

Human-Computer Interaction

Unlike the archival science examinations of differences between media mentioned above, which are concerned with the properties of records as one kind of object, many HCI studies closely inspect how people's perceptions of and interactions with objects vary depending on the medium of an object. HCI studies of home archiving practices and differences between digital and physical objects uncovered that participants were concerned about the stability of digital objects and did not necessarily think about them as things that would continue to exist long-term. In one such study, Odom et al. explored the possibility of passing down digital objects from one generation of a family to the next in their investigation of home use of three devices designed to encourage "people to think more concretely about how digital materials might be inherited in the future" [23, p. 337]. They noted that, "...families described a general distrust over the longevity of their personal computers, which led them to create extensive backups on physical media (e.g., CDs or DVDs). Tensions also emerged with this approach, namely due to doubts over how long these media would last..." [p. 342]. In addition to concerns about the life span of digital objects, three interrelated themes from this literature speak specifically to the ways in which people live with digital objects over time: *deep storage, hybrid objects*, and *experiencing digital objects*. These interrelated themes reflect insights into in-the-moment interactions with digital objects that may be important for how we perceive those objects both in the present and over the long term.

Deep Storage

In a study designed to explore home archiving practices, Kirk & Sellen noted that one way their participants kept important objects was in "deep storage," in which objects were both "out of sight and out of mind" [20, p. 32]. "We observed many instances where old digital content and items of sentiment were stored away on various innocuous storage media, such as floppy disks, CDs, and hard drives in PCs, thus rendering them, in some ways, invisible" [p. 33]. Additionally, the authors noted that participants had to explicitly intend to access digital objects on external storage media in order to interact with them; objects that participants kept in this way lost the reminding function that both physical and digital objects have been shown to provide in some situations [1, 22]. They were functionally invisible unless participants sought them out [20].

Odom et al. built on this notion in their exploration of the idea of digital heirlooms [23]. They noted that heirlooms were used infrequently, but that "practices surrounding heirlooms were bound up with having them present and ensuring their safekeeping" [p. 341] over long periods of time. Support of this basic form of interaction with digital heirlooms, they argued, would require "the artful design of technologies that can be put away," that is, "new storage systems that are extremely robust and can handle sporadic use" [p. 345]. This is an implicit recognition that digital objects, which require a device for access, cannot currently be "put away" safely.

Hybrid Objects

Kirk & Sellen's study focused on objects "that people were deliberately archiving... cherished objects of sentimental value that are consciously or intentionally kept" [20, p.9], similar to the way that the DCFS as an organization was purposefully keeping certain records. Kirk & Sellen developed a medium-centric taxonomy based on the types of objects that their participants were actively keeping, dividing these objects into three types: physical (e.g., diaries, furniture, paintings), digital (e.g., photos, emails), and hybrid (e.g., music, home movies). The hybrid category contained objects that were "physical instantiations of media content such as cassette tapes, video tapes, CDs and vinyl records" [p. 14]. Although it was not explicitly stated in the definition of the category, from the description provided it was clear that these objects were storage media (some digital, some not) that were separate from devices used to access the objects on that media. Objects stored on media that is contained within an access device, such as a hard drive in a personal computer, were instead included in the "digital" category of the taxonomy. It was the objects or content contained on these media that were important rather than the hybrid objects themselves: "the actual VHS or tape cassettes used for storage held no sentimental value whatsoever, but the content was considered to be very precious" [p. 14]. This content was what became invisible in deep storage.

Why should these hybrid objects be set apart? A detour into a phenomenological examination [4, 34] of how people experience digital objects as compared to physical objects provides insight into this question. As Kirk & Sellen noted, much of the content stored within hybrid objects could quite easily be transferred to a PC [20, p. 14]. That content is made up of digital objects, in that they are inscriptions on a storage medium that can be read by a computer. The taxonomy of digital, physical, and hybrid objects reflects differences in interaction: external storage media (hybrid objects) hold a place somewhere in between physical objects, which are immediately accessible to anyone close enough to touch them, and digital objects, which must be

[2] InterPARES (International Research on Permanent Authentic Records in Electronic Systems) is an SSHRC-funded project focused on the long-term preservation of authentic digital records (http://www.interpares.org/).

accessed through a device. External storage media physically represent the potential presence of digital object(s), without providing direct access. Although it is the content (the digital objects that are potentially accessible from the hybrid object) that is important, when the hybrid object is separated from the access device it becomes the only experientially available representation of those "content" objects. The hybrid object is opaque. The difference between objects on external storage media and digital objects that are stored within an access device is in the relationship between access and physical presence, which may be more important than has been previously acknowledged.

Experiencing Digital Objects

The importance of the ways in which people experience digital objects, as contrasted with experiencing physical objects, was also reflected in statements made by participants in home archiving studies. For instance, participants said that digital objects are not "solid" [13] and that they lack "physicality" [28]. Golsteijn et al. found that some of their participants did not think of digital objects as objects, because that term "implies a concrete, often physical, thing, which led them to select digital objects that were in fact, according to the classification used here[3], hybrid or physical objects" [13, p. 4]. As they are typically experienced in daily life, digital objects do not match expected notions of materiality as associated with physical objects. Although a physical inscription on a storage medium is a necessary component of a digital object, it is not the form of that object with which we typically interact. Instead, our interactions with digital objects as seen on a screen are mediated by keyboards, mice, game controllers, or at the very least the screen itself. The physical form of a digital object supports the object and is required for its existence, but is not the primary form of the object for computer users. For them, the object is instead what is on the screen, and that is not directly tangible. As one participant put it, "There is less physicality in the computer hard drive than having something on paper, which might fade, but you will still have an image" [28, p. 164]. This quote illuminates the important contrast in how object accessibility is related to materiality for digital and physical objects. With a paper document, the presence of the object means that the content is fully accessible. But with digital objects it is possible to have possession of the object as it physically exists on a storage medium without being able to access the object. These differences in the ways people experience physical objects and objects saved on external storage media proved to be central to interpreting clerks' actions at the DCFS office.

[3] Golsteijn et al. applied Kirk & Sellen's object taxonomy in their study.

METHODS

Four researchers individually observed work practices at the DCFS site four times each over a period of two months in 2013, for a total of 39.5 hours. Observation sessions were three to four hours long, averaging 3.5 hours per observation. For each observation session, a researcher shadowed one participant, observing work practices, interactions with colleagues, and the work environment as a whole. During observations, researchers took detailed notes and audio-recorded conversations between multiple participants. Photographs, hand-drawn maps of offices, and copies of forms used in work practices supplemented these notes and recordings. After observations were complete, researchers conducted eight short (1/2 hour) interviews with participants, asking follow-up questions and checking interpretations of data.

Four clerks and two managers, ranging in age from their twenties to their fifties, were employed at the DCFS office during the fieldwork and all were included in observations. Participants were Latino/a, African-American, and white. Three participants were female and three were male. One clerk had a college degree; the rest did not. Clerks were trained for their positions on the job and were not required to have previous records management experience. The clerks all worked in the same large room in cubicles with half-height walls (see Picture 1 below). The manager worked in the same room but had full-height cubicle walls.

Picture 1. One clerk's desk, with boxes sitting against the cubicle wall waiting for processing.

During the time when researchers were active in the field, they took notes on themes that arose during observations and while reviewing notes, and held meetings to discuss data. Post-fieldwork, researchers used ATLAS.ti qualitative coding software to code their own and others' notes, thereby confirming or rejecting the potential themes that arose during observations, and ensuring that themes were prevalent across observations by different researchers. The theme of the medium of the records, and variances in participant behavior related to records medium, was strongly present in researcher notes from the DCFS.

FINDINGS

In their work, the clerks dealt only with paper records and what they called "memorabilia," a catch-all term used to refer to all non-paper records, such as cassette tapes, CDs, DVDs, floppy disks, VHS tapes, and even photographs. Any external storage media in a case file was considered memorabilia. Born digital records created by case workers were housed in the digital records management system used by the department (Case Control), and were not the responsibility of the clerks. However, digital records that existed on storage media and were included in a case file were under the clerks' purview. Clerks used Case Control to verify the status of the case that they were reviewing (whether it was open or closed, had been merged with another case, and it's destruction date). Case Control also showed the physical location of the case files, whether a file contained memorabilia, and the names of the individuals involved with the case. The primary comparison of media in this environment was between paper media and non-paper media, or memorabilia (including hybrid media). The most crucial characteristic of memorabilia in this situation was whether it was directly accessible, like a photograph (similar to paper documents), or if it was opaque and unreachable without an access device. These concerns strongly echo concerns raised about hybrid objects in the home context [20]. Despite the wide variety of the media on which records were stored, decisions about how long records should be kept were not supposed to be influenced by the medium of the records.

The clerks used a document created by the larger records management division of the DCFS agency, the Case Processing document, to process case files. This document outlined the steps clerks should take in making decisions about keeping and destroying records. The Case Processing document was the primary embodiment, for the clerks, of the rules that they followed. Although the clerks themselves were likely not aware of ARMA policy (not having been educated as records managers), the Case Processing document that the clerks used was indeed created to reflect ARMA's medium-neutral rules: it made no distinctions between records on the basis of medium. Similarly, the agency's retention policies, which the Case Processing document was intended to enact, were also not medium-specific. The agency's retention policies were based on laws regarding records retention and were reflective of a general agreement within the profession of records management that retention policies should be based on the content of the records rather than their medium.

What is Long-term?

The clerks kept records that the state had a continued responsibility to retain, and the state was required to retain some of these records for an extremely long time. The clerks stored these "forever" records in a box labeled "4712." Boxes were typically labeled with the year during which the records within them could be destroyed (their destruction date). The year 4712 was a year that the clerks had decided was so outlandishly far off that it was an adequate representation of "forever." As one of the clerks said of a file, "We are going to end up storing this one until we are all long dead." Forever records were typically either adoption or conservatorship records. Other kinds of records handled by DCFS records management pertained to foster care and child protective services more generally.

As the records that were going to be stored the longest (and therefore under the responsibility of the state the longest), forever records were the most important. Any memorabilia associated with these were converted by an external contractor to digital form and stored in Case Control. This was an added expense and was not necessarily done for records whose destruction dates were in the foreseeable future. A different calculus of risk, expense, efficiency, and responsibility was carried out in those cases, which are discussed below.

Reconciliation Project: To Keep or Destroy

During the time period of the observations, the clerks were engaged in a large-scale project called the IMR, or Iron Mountain Reconciliation Project (Iron Mountain is a company that the state contracted for long-term records storage). Several clerks had been hired specifically to work on this project. The essential task of the project was to determine whether each case file should be kept or destroyed, and subsequently move it to the proper location as determined by the keep/destroy decision. Sometimes these decisions were extremely simple and only involved matching the case in front of the clerk with the case in the Case Control system, which allowed the clerk to confirm the destruction date. If there was a case number written on the outside of the file, the case was marked as closed in Case Control, and the case's destruction date had passed, the clerk would separate any memorabilia from the paper file and set paper and memorabilia aside for destruction. However, keep/destroy decisions could easily become complicated, requiring a more thorough investigation of the contents of case files.

In the absence of a case number the clerks would have to try to identify the case by the names of the individuals in the file, which could be difficult because of name changes or the existence of multiple individuals with the same name in the system. An additional complication was that cases that might initially appear to be closed (based solely on the birth-date of the youngest child in the case) could have been merged with other cases, which happened frequently when there were multiple cases within one family. For instance, a case involving an older sibling might be closed when that child turned eighteen, "aging out" of the system, but it would often instead be merged with a case involving a younger sibling, because it contained documentation that was relevant to that latter case.

The clerks knew that the records in their care were very serious for the people represented in those records, and they sympathized with those people. The records sometimes represented abuse cases in which the state had the responsibility to protect the victims. One clerk, Louisa, said of the records, "sometimes I can't believe that someone could be that cruel. I mean some of the stuff you read will tear your heart out." Louisa also mentioned that once, while in a different position within the DCFS, she encountered a young man who was trying to get disability benefits and needed his records to do so. Unfortunately, his records could not be found, and the man therefore could not receive disability benefits. As Max, one of the managers, said, "I think that some of these kids that phase out of our system... the only records that we have [are] really the records of their life, I mean there's no parents involved..." In these cases, the DCFS could be the only reliable source of personal history for the people represented in the records. These were the records that the clerks were making keep/destroy decisions about on a daily basis.

Picture 2. Stacks of boxes in the DCFS office. The gray bins contain memorabilia that will be destroyed.

Despite the potential significance of those decisions, however, they were decisions that the clerks made hundreds of times in a week. The IMR project was projected to take at least two years, or possibly as long as four. One clerk mentioned that he had heard there were 60,000 boxes that had to be checked as part of the project. Shipments of fifty boxes were delivered multiple times a week and were stacked in the office, immediately outside of the clerks' cubicles (see Picture 2 above). Tensions in the office rose and fell with the level of the boxes, which were a visible reminder of the amount of work to be done, and could grow threateningly high if the clerks got behind schedule. Each day, the clerks turned in a productivity report detailing the number of boxes processed that day.

The clerks' decision-making processes (as they determined which records should be kept and which could be destroyed) have important implications for how people interact with objects of varying media. As discussed above, clerks often had to closely examine paper files to determine the keep/destroy status of a record. The following sections discuss how the necessity for investigation played out when the records were stored on memorabilia rather than paper.

Accessible Memorabilia

Although memorabilia was often interspersed in paper files, sometimes it would be stored in boxes with other memorabilia of the same media, separately from its associated paper files. In this situation, it was easy for an object to be disassociated from its case number, which often meant additional investigative work for the clerks. Two of the clerks, Lance and Daryl, were sometimes assigned the task of handling these "media" boxes, as they were known. During one observation, Daryl spent several hours going through boxes of DVDs that had been enclosed in manila envelopes (on which case numbers and other information might be written). Occasionally, there would be confusion in determining the correct keep/destroy decision as in the case discussed in the conversation below, when the information in Case Control did not match the information on the envelope. In such instances, Daryl would have to ask a manager, Ashley, for assistance.

> Ashley: What did you find?
> Daryl: This has a case number, but...
> A: Ok. Go ahead and open it. [He does.] Which box was that in?
> D: [Recites the box ID number.]
> A: Is that the same number? Oh, no it's a different one [They are looking at her computer.] It's here... but not in Case Control. If it had been merged, it would be here. You could see the child's name, but it's not here... unless she changed her name.

They ended up accessing the DVD on Ashley's computer, and saw an interview with a child whose name allowed them to determine which case the DVD was associated with.

Later, Daryl encountered a similar problem and attempted to resolve it without involving Ashley, but had trouble accessing the DVD on his computer.

> Daryl: That's not good.
> Observer: What's going on?
> D: I don't know. It's not loading the DVD. I don't know if it's the DVD drive or...

He and Ashley were able to access the DVD on her computer. Despite the fact that he could not access it on his computer, because there was an available access device in the office, Daryl did check the DVD. However, if a clerk came across external storage media in a file that was not accessible by any device currently available in the office, that might end investigation for that file and lead to a destroy decision. The next section describes how clerks could use inaccessibility as an indicator for a destroy decision.

Technological Obsolescence

Media obsolescence leading to inaccessibility was considered to be potentially a good enough reason to determine that a non-paper record was a destroy record, as discussed in an interview with Daryl.

> Daryl: I have come across a couple floppy disks, I've never had to insert them, and even if I did we don't even have slots for them anymore.
> Interviewer: You don't have floppy drives.
> D: So, that's a pretty good sign that that's going to be destruction.
> I: Yeah.
> D: We can just toss that right away.
> I: Just because it's –
> D: – And the same with VHS tapes, if it's that old, like, that's just a good sign that it's not active anymore.

With paper records, while apparent age contributed to the categorization of the records as destroy records, it was never the deciding factor. A clerk might note the obvious age of some paper records he or she was dealing with when pulling a hardened rubber band or rusted paper clip off of a folder, but this was not a legitimate reason to abandon the normal process for checking the age of the records – the rules for case processing required that destruction decisions be made based on the destruction date for the case as listed in Case Control. The clerk would still look for further evidence of age within the informational content of the record (a process the clerks referred to as "doing research"). The decision tree below (Figure 1) describes the decision-making process with a focus on how the medium of the records could influence that process.

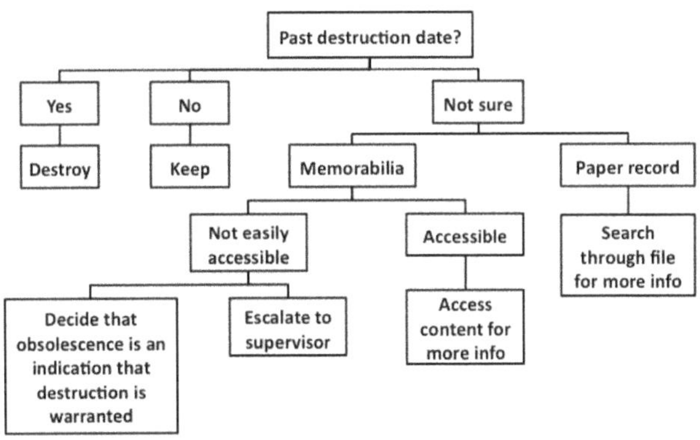

Figure 1: Simplified decision tree for the keep/destroy decision-making process.

Time spent on work tasks and progress towards the larger goal of completing the IMR project were ever present factors in the clerks' decision-making processes. Issues of time and progress combined to form the pressure of efficiency.

The clerks' awareness of the potential consequence of the records manifested as the responsibility they felt to do research into the contents of the records to accurately determine destruction dates. When we began our field work, Ashley was the manager in charge of the office. She left the DCFS after we had been observing the office for one week, and was replaced by Max, a manager from another DCFS office. After Ashley's departure, the clerks revealed that they had concerns about some of her policies. They felt that these policies did not align with agency guidelines for their work, and did not fully meet the responsibilities of the office with regards to the records, as discussed in the following quote drawn from a conversation between all four of the clerks.

> Daryl: Honestly I think she was just telling us... whatever, to get stuff out.
> Marcela: Well that's what I'm saying that's why they can't believe that we're already through with phase one, and we went through it that quickly... Well that's because, she basically told us, why are we doing research, just toss it. All the ones from '95, toss 'em. But the destruction date, if you look on the paper it says 2013, and we're only in February.

The clerks were concerned because Ashley had instructed them not to do research into the cases, in the interests of efficiency. However, they did not feel that this was in line with agency policy. Ashley also told them to destroy all files with a destruction date of 2013, despite the fact that 2013 files with a December date should not have been destroyed for another eleven months – directly contradicting the Case Processing guidelines which required that destruction decisions be based on the destruction date assigned to a record. The clerks were concerned that they might be held responsible for any improper records destruction that had occurred during Ashley's tenure (a concern that did not to our knowledge bear out). This conversation starkly illustrates the conflict between the pressures of responsibility for records and the clerks' efficiency at their jobs. While Ashley's directives against doing research applied equally to paper and non-paper records, this example shows that the clerks' speed in checking records was at issue in evaluations of their work, and doing research on non-paper records was more time consuming than doing research on paper records because of issues of accessibility.

Because the rules that the clerks followed did not mention medium as a potential issue, clerks were left without specific guidance to follow when they encountered obsolete and inaccessible media. The records management policy that medium was not a significant factor in designations of objects as records, while intended to elevate digital records to the status of paper records, instead had an opposite effect in this case. Material differences between the two types of records forced the clerks into a difficult choice, as illustrated in Figure 1. Efficiency pressures implicitly discouraged clerks from involving a supervisor in investigating inaccessible media, thereby encouraging clerks to use obsolescence as a reason to destroy a record.

DISCUSSION

Unclear dating in documents complicated the routine keep/destroy decisions of records management work. Complicated keep/destroy decisions required the clerks to do research, which was relatively simple with paper documents, took slightly more effort with records on accessible storage media, and was difficult (and expensive) to do with records on obsolete media. When records resisted investigation due to technological obsolescence, we saw clerks make one of two decisions: to defer the issue to their supervisor, or to interpret the lack of accessibility as grounds to destroy the record (Figure 1). The evidence in these records, which may have legal, financial, and personal weight, is then lost. Accessibility was clearly central in determining which records were investigated and which were not, but what other possible explanations exist for this apparent privileging of paper records over non-paper records?

Materiality

Because materiality is central to the experience of interacting with objects, it goes hand in hand with a phenomenological approach to investigating those interactions. The recent material turn in HCI [31] has taken many forms [29]. In line with this focus, we examine "the materiality of technological things as they are used and incorporated into everyday contexts and practices" [29, p. 119]. Observations at the DCFS showed that the specific material nature of the memorabilia required separate procedures from paper records. Paper files and memorabilia had to be separated for destruction, due to differing destruction processes for each type of record. Paper and external storage media also have diverging environmental requirements for safe long-term preservation (differing acceptable temperature and humidity ranges), which meant that when they had been properly processed for storage they would be kept in separate boxes (although it was not unusual for more hastily processed files to contain memorabilia). These differences in the materialities of paper and external storage media required differentiations between the two types of records in work practices. Max would question the clerks about how many reconciliation boxes had been completed and how many media boxes had been completed, highlighting how the varying material natures of each type of record caused them to be dealt with separately in daily work processes, despite their purportedly equal nature as records. This, combined with the different experiences of interacting with digital and physical objects as discussed above, made it difficult for clerks to treat the two types of objects as equal records.

Background Expectations

When examining users' attitudes towards technologies, it is necessary to consider not only the current contexts of actions but also past experiences, as these together help to shape users' understandings of the contexts in which they act. Winograd & Flores describe this situation: "...the world is encountered as something always already lived in, worked in, and acted upon. World as the background of obviousness is manifest in our everyday dealings as the familiarity that pervades our situation..." [34, p. 58]. Although they emphasize the importance of background expectations of users, Winograd & Flores acknowledge that we cannot ever expect to understand and represent those expectations completely, and of course details of users' backgrounds are not often available to designers. However, it would be unwise to ignore users' background understandings entirely, and there are some broad types of experiences with which most computer users would be familiar.

Because many computer users have been interacting with computers from childhood, they have experienced multiple shifts in computing technology. These shifts often render digital objects inaccessible as access and storage devices wear out or are disposed of, or software becomes obsolete. Daryl's statements above about floppy disks that "we don't even have slots for them anymore" and "if it's that old, like, that's just a good sign that it's not active anymore," suggest that he has had experience with technological obsolescence in the past, and that that experience is affecting decisions he makes in the process of his work. This is likely to be true not only of the other clerks in our study, but also of many of the participants in the home archiving studies. Even in the context of the DCFS, when clerks knew the potential importance of the records saved on obsolete storage media, the inaccessibility of the medium made the objects seem easier to relinquish. In the home context, dismissing invisible digital objects on opaque storage media may be even easier to do.

Previous research into the subject of differing interactions with physical and digital objects has not, to this point, put a major emphasis on issues of technological obsolescence and access. Findings from this study suggest that these aspects of the subject require further investigation. To encourage thinking of digital belongings as belongings that are worth investing in emotionally, it will be necessary to support people in thinking of those belongings as objects that have the potential to be long-lasting.

Regular experiences that occur over a long period of time are likely to affect peoples' expectations for different kinds of objects. This applies not only to digital objects, but also to our understandings of categories of objects such as "records." The paper record is the traditional form of the record and is therefore the standard for that form. Clerks were likely basing their expectations for the "recordness" of objects on their experiences of paper records. The ways in which records on other media were different from paper records could make them seem less legitimate as records. For instance, the ease of access to the information in the paper record is likely to reinforce its primacy as the most legitimate medium for records. Anyone who is literate and knows the language in which a paper record is written is able to access that record if it is in front of them. Paper records do not require additional translation in the form of software and hardware, as digital records do.

DESIGN IMPLICATIONS

This study suggests that there is a basic aspect of human interactions with technology that is likely to affect how and whether people consider digital objects as objects that potentially can exist for a long period of time – technological obsolescence. Although recent work in HCI [17, 21] has discussed obsolescence in somewhat different contexts from the ones described here, and there are important connections between problems of obsolescence and the focus on sustainability in HCI [30], this issue has not yet been thoroughly investigated. It has been similarly understudied in the history of technology [3], and while a focus on obsolescence is quite central to the study of digital preservation within cultural heritage institutions, that work generally focuses on pushing back against obsolescence for the purposes of preservation rather than understanding how users anticipate and react to it in their daily lives. Our findings reinforce the suggestion [23] that technologies specifically designed to last even when accessed infrequently would support users in thinking of digital objects as long-lasting and valuable possessions.

Our argument is not that external storage is inherently bad; for instance, similar issues could occur with old files that are associated with obsolete software. In that case, the bridge between the base inscription on external storage media or hard disk and the visual object on the screen has collapsed. The hardware-software stack is missing one or more essential connecting pieces. The issue instead is that the eventualities of obsolescence, and the expectations they engender in users, should be taken into consideration.

Technological obsolescence is not the only critical issue in examining interactions with digital objects over the long-term. We have also argued that closely considering the variances in how people interact with digital and physical objects will help in understanding differences in how they value those objects. These variances may be partially due to the different ways we experience the two types of objects as material. Not only do the distinct material natures of digital and physical objects often require contrasting treatment (as in storage requirements at the DCFS), but they also force differences in interactions. The user is always separated from the physical medium on which a digital object is stored, and interaction with that object is mediated through an access device. In contrast, physical objects are interacted with in a very direct, immediate, and tangible experience.

CONCLUSIONS

Despite the disparate settings of the HCI studies of home archiving and our study's location in a workplace, there are similarities in the examination of interactions with digital and physical objects, and the idea of preserving objects for future use by others. In this study, participants faced similar questions to home PC users in deciding whether older digital objects were valuable. These were questions such as: Do I have any indication of what the objects are (perhaps a label on storage media)? Is the hardware and software that would be needed to access the objects available to me? Are the objects potentially important to me or someone I care about? Will it make a difference to anyone if I do not try to retrieve these objects?

In the end, however, paper records seemed to have a legitimacy in the eyes of our participants that non-paper records did not have; non-paper objects were not long-lasting objects for them in the way that paper objects were. We have argued that this was related to their expectations for different kinds of records (technological obsolescence and paper as the traditional records medium), as well as differences in how paper and non-paper records were materially experienced. Although further research is needed to determine differences and similarities across various settings, the similarities between the issues our participants faced and those discussed in the home archiving studies support the idea these problems are relevant in a broad variety of situations.

ACKNOWLEDGMENTS

We thank the Institute of Museum and Library Services Laura Bush 21st Century Librarian Program for its generous funding of this research (Award #RE-02-12-0009-12), as well as Diane Bailey not only for her implementation and organization of the project, but for generously sharing her knowledge of and experience with ethnographic methods. Thanks also to Ramona Broussard, our excellent research partner in observing work practices at the DCFS, and Melanie Feinberg for her comments on an early version of this paper.

REFERENCES

1. Barreau, D., & Nardi, B. A. Finding and reminding: File organization from the desktop. *SIGCHI Bull. 27,* 3 (1995), 39–43.
2. Boardman, R., & Sasse, M. A. "Stuff goes into the computer and doesn't come out": a cross-tool study of personal information management. In *Proc. SIGCHI Conference on Human Factors in Computing Systems* (2004) (pp. 583–590). New York, NY, USA: ACM.
3. Campbell, S. M. On the absence of obsolescence. *IEEE Annals of the History of Computing 31,* 4 (2009), 118–120.
4. Dourish, P. *Where the action is: The foundations of embodied interaction.* MIT Press, Cambridge, MA, USA, 2001.
5. Duranti, L. Reliability and authenticity: The concepts and their implications. *Archivaria 1,* 39 (1995).
6. Duranti, L. Concepts and principles for the management of electronic records, or records management theory is

archival diplomatics. *Records Management Journal 20,* 1 (2010a), 78–95.

7. Duranti, L. From digital diplomatics to digital records forensics. *Archivaria 68,* 68 (2010b).
8. Duranti, L., & MacNeil, H. The protection of the integrity of electronic records: An overview of the UBC-MAS research project. *Archivaria 1,* 42 (1996).
9. Duranti, L., & Thibodeau, K. The concept of record in interactive, experiential and dynamic environments: The view of InterPARES*. *Archival Science 6*, 1 (2006), 13–68.
10. Galloway, P. Preservation of digital objects. *Annual Review of Information Science and Technology*, Vol. 38 (2003), 549–590.
11. *Generally Accepted Recordkeeping Principles*. ARMA International. 2014. Retrieved from http://www.arma.org/r2/generally-accepted-br-recordkeeping-principles.
12. Ginn, M. L. (Ed.). *Retention Management for Records and Information*. ARMA International, Lenexa, KS, USA, 2009.
13. Golsteijn, C., van den Hoven, E., Frohlich, D., & Sellen, A. Towards a more cherishable digital object. *Proc DIS 2012,* ACM Press (2012), 655–664.
14. Gulotta, R., Odom, W., Forlizzi, J., & Faste, H. (2013). Digital artifacts as legacy: Exploring the lifespan and value of digital data. *Proc. CHI 2013,* ACM Press (2013), 1813–1822.
15. Hughes, J. A., Randall, D., & Shapiro, D. Faltering from Ethnography to Design. In *Proc. CSCW 1992,* ACM Press (1992), 115–122.
16. *International Standard on Records Management*. ISO 15489-1:2001. Geneva, Switzerland: ISO.
17. Jackson, S. J., & Kang, L. Breakdown, obsolescence and reuse: HCI and the art of repair. *Proc. CHI 2014,* ACM Press (2014), 449–458.
18. Kaye, J. "Jofish," Vertesi, J., Avery, S., Dafoe, A., David, S., Onaga, L., … Pinch, T. To have and to hold: Exploring the personal archive. *Proc. CHI 2006,* ACM Press (2006), 275–284.
19. Kirk, D. S., Izadi, S., Sellen, A., Taylor, S., Banks, R., & Hilliges, O. Opening up the family archive. *Proc. CSCW 2010*, ACM Press (2010), 261–270.
20. Kirk, D. S., & Sellen, A. On human remains: Values and practice in the home archiving of cherished objects. *ACM Trans. Comput.-Hum. Interact. 17,* 3 (2010), 10:1–10:43.
21. Lomas, D., Kumar, A., Patel, K., Ching, D., Lakshmanan, M., Kam, M., & Forlizzi, J. L. The power of play: Design lessons for increasing the lifespan of outdated computers. *Proc. CHI 2013,* ACM Press (2013), 2735–2744.
22. Malone, T. W. How do people organize their desks?: Implications for the design of office information systems. *ACM Trans. Inf. Syst., 1,* 1 (1983), 99–112.
23. Odom, W., Banks, R., Kirk, D., Harper, R., Lindley, S., & Sellen, A. Technology heirlooms?: Considerations for passing down and inheriting digital materials. *Proc. CHI 2012,* ACM Press (2012), 337–346.
24. Odom, W., Sellen, A., Harper, R., & Thereska, E. (2012). Lost in translation: Understanding the possession of digital things in the cloud. *Proc. CHI 2012,* ACM Press (2012), 781–790.
25. Odom, W., Zimmerman, J., & Forlizzi, J. Teenagers and their virtual possessions: Design opportunities and issues. *Proc. CHI 2011,* ACM Press (2011), 1491–1500.
26. Odom, W., Zimmerman, J., Forlizzi, J., Choi, H., Meier, S., & Park, A. Investigating the presence, form and behavior of virtual possessions in the context of a teen bedroom. *Proc. CHI 2012,* ACM Press (2012), 327–336.
27. Pearce-Moses, R. Record. *A Glossary of Archival and Records Terminology*. Society of American Archivists, 2005.
28. Petrelli, D., & Whittaker, S. Family memories in the home: Contrasting physical and digital mementos. *Personal Ubiquitous Comput., 14,* 2 (2010), 153–169.
29. Pierce, J., & Paulos, E. Electric materialities and interactive technology. *Proc. CHI 2013,* ACM Press (2013), 119–128.
30. Remy, J.C. & Huang, E. Addressing the Obsolescence of End-User Devices: Approaches from the Field of Sustainable HCI. In Hilty, L.M., Aebischer, B. (eds.) ICT Innovations for Sustainability. Springer (2014), 257 - 267.
31. Robles, E., & Wiberg, M. Texturing the "Material Turn" in Interaction Design. In *Proc TEI 2010,* ACM Press (2010), 137–144.
32. Rothenberg, J. *Avoiding technological quicksand: Finding a viable technical foundation for digital preservation*. No. 77, Council on Library and Information Resources (CLIR), Washington, DC, USA, 1998.
33. Sellen, A., & Harper, R. *The Myth of the Paperless Office*. MIT Press, Cambridge, MA, USA, 2001.
34. Winograd, T., & Flores, F. *Understanding computers and cognition: A new foundation for design*. Ablex Corporation, Norwood, NJ, USA, 1986.

Things That Make Us Reminisce: Everyday Memory Cues as Opportunities for Interaction Design

Doménique van Gennip[1,2] **Elise van den Hoven**[1,2] **Panos Markopoulos**[2,1]

Faculty of Design, Architecture and Building
University of Technology, Sydney
domenique.vangennip@uts.edu.au
elise.vandenhoven@uts.edu.au

Department of Industrial Design
Eindhoven University of Technology, the Netherlands
p.markopoulos@tue.nl

ABSTRACT
Interactive devices can support personal remembering to benefit well-being. These designs require insight into what brings the past to mind, and how people relate to such cues. Prior work focused on mementos in the home; instead, this paper presents a diary and interview study of involuntary memory cueing in everyday life. Data was collected from fifteen adult individuals, using sentence completion diaries, combined with debriefing interviews. Qualitative analysis of the data showed that these participants were relying on everyday physical objects like food items for cueing memories during everyday life, locations and (repeated) activities, while digital items and photos were shown to be less frequent stimulants. Meaningful relations to memory cues can be partially explained from a memory cueing perspective. We discuss how design for remembering can benefit from our insights, through careful trade-offs in timing, exposure to cues, and supporting a process of personal attachment with items invoking memories.

Author Keywords
Interaction Design, Memories, Memory cueing, Remembering, Diary study

ACM Classification Keywords
H.5.m. Information interfaces and presentation (e.g., HCI): Miscellaneous.

INTRODUCTION
In everyday life we often remember our past: sometimes by deliberate effort, and sometimes because thoughts, people or elements in our environment remind us. Think of using social media to view and share family stories, or reminiscing while taking a walk in the park. Such reminiscing and reflecting on autobiographical memories has clear mental benefits, as remembering is vital to our self-image, personal identity, how we express ourselves, and relate to others [8]. These activities based on memories, and by extension the elements in the environment that trigger such memories, help us feel well and balance emotional needs [6, 30]. Stimulating beneficial remembering in daily life thus can be a worthwhile goal, as underlined by recent attention within the field of interaction design [e.g., 17, 30]. People have long used mementos for this purpose, and capture (for example) photographs to use as memory cues later on [30]. Interactive devices can support reminiscing using captured images and other data as memory cues, provided design efforts are based on a solid understanding of what makes people remember their past, how this colors their experience, and whether such interactivity is appropriate at a given time.

Figure 1. Examples invoking memories: Photo of a trip on Facebook; Thunderstorm; Boboti dish; Transistor radio.

Digital items stand a lesser chance of evoking memories and emotions compared to physical items due to lesser salience, often captured and stored but not reviewed [31]. People put meaningful items on display, and vice versa tend to attach meaning to items available in their environment. Personal mementos are increasingly stored digitally and are becoming more numerous due to lower perceived cost of capture, which also reduces chances of finding it again to help remembering [30]. When people were asked to indicate valuable items during home visits, digital mementos were often overlooked [20, 27]. Digitalization of personal media can reduce opportunities to evoke memories without effort [31], or as Schwarz argues do the opposite as we may frequently come across files when looking for

CHI 2015, April 18 - 23 2015, Seoul, Republic of Korea.
Copyright 2015 ACM 978-1-4503-3145-6/15/04...$15.00.
http://dx.doi.org/10.1145/2702123.2702460

something else [29]. The latter would alter our relation to those memories to become more casual as memory-related items would involuntarily cue us more often (beyond direct control over such exposures, which may be undesired).

This raises the challenge of how to assist the revisiting of personal digital items. We believe that if such revisiting (involuntary or otherwise) can influence wellbeing (as shown for positive memories [6]), this challenges designers to do (or refrain from doing) so sensibly. Good design of supportive devices can make a difference, provided that people's experiential needs are met. Still, empirical understanding to inform design lacks in two ways [17, 32]. First, the relation between cueing medium (e.g., digital or physical) and resultant remembering experience is not clearly understood. It is not evident whether the representation of a memory cue (e.g., photo, audio, writing) influences cueing of a memory, and how we think about this memory [15]. Some forms may stimulate a more positive remembering experience than others, perhaps because certain ways of cueing allow more freedom to imagine the event and emotions as desired. If photographs of an event do not support someone to relate to their own experience at the time (e.g., a photo may depict a different feeling), would another representation be more suitable for a device to adopt for experiential reliving? Second, the way this knowledge can be applied to actual interactive designs needs refinement.

In this work, we look into remembering experiences as cued by stimuli such as mementos, public images, and particular spaces (see Fig.1). We aim to relate memory cues with the memories and meaning within individuals' lives, and casted a wider net compared to earlier works focusing on a home context [20, e.g., 27]. Our focus is on external stimuli (in contrast to internal stimuli such as thoughts, which we cannot design or modify), as these external cues provide an opportunity for design to appropriate for everyday remembering. In addition, we discuss perceived differences between digital and physical items as cues. We argue this focus on digital, involuntary memory cues is warranted given the accumulation in people's archives and potential for appropriation by interactive devices. This work adds insight on involuntary memory cueing and related trade-offs to enable future design work to contextualize and explore this challenge.

RELATED WORK

Memory & cues in cognitive psychology

Remembered events of our life can differ in specificity: lifetime periods (e.g., being a teenager), general events lasting days to months, or event-specific knowledge for events lasting up to hours at most [8]. Memories come to our awareness based on intentional effort (e.g., seeing a vase and then trying to remember how you got it), or involuntarily (e.g., remembering your neighbor gave you a vase upon seeing that vase) [4]. Involuntary memories thus need some way of invocation, whether taking a cue from (for example) thoughts, activities, or external items.

Based on diary studies, Berntsen finds involuntary cueing happens between one to five times per day. Cues are most often external (e.g., objects), some internal, with only a small amount of sensorial cues (e.g., sound, smell) or having no identifiable cues [4]. Despite limited understanding of the cueing process, some correlation between a memory and a potential cue is assumed [8]. Distinctiveness, recency, frequent rehearsal, or relation to a highly emotional event may improve a perceived item's ability to cue a memory [4]. However, other mental processes interact to modulate a cue's effects: one can see a photo frame many times without becoming aware of related memories. Such selective recall illustrates that motivations matter, as does recent activation of related memories [e.g., 4]. During mundane activities (e.g., cooking) some people are more likely to be involuntarily triggered, perhaps because they are open to stimulation [e.g., 4, 28].

Personal collections as memory cues

Items are able to stimulate vivid re-experience of the past [10]. Because interactive devices can stimulate similar functions via cues (e.g., display of photos, old messages, audio recordings), it is relevant what types of cues people relate to. People actively shape their environment to support and portray their identity through curation of items reminiscent of past memories, with the goal of keeping things around as symbols of the self [e.g., 10, 20]. This behavior, known as autotopography [27], shows the complex relations between objects and the self. The popularity of everyday objects as mementos is "by the virtue of what the owner has invested in them, be it time or emotion," and such meaning develops over time through cultivation, selection, and how items relate to others [27].

Such cultivation practices are harder to support with digital mementos not being present in the everyday environment. Not surprisingly those are mentioned infrequently in studies of personally relevant memory objects [20, 26, 27]. However, this belies that there is an ever-increasing use and reliance on digital capturing of memory cues (i.e., digital photos, social network communication, email). The ease or even automaticity of digital capturing has grown the collections people keep, as reflected in the life logging movement [30]. However, this 'cue hoarding' has led to too many cues with too little relevance as filtering gets less attention [30]. Work on digital legacy, inheritance and memorials highlights people may at times be confronted to deal with vast and often unstructured digital collections [e.g., 13, 22]. These issues raise questions on what kind of items would be considered beneficial as memory cues, and at which moments this cueing might be done (if at all). Such changed practices fundamentally alter the way we remember and support recollection [31], and the changing landscape begets answers on how design can best support this trend.

Memory cues in interaction design

We would like to highlights several works that have tapped into the opportunities provided by interaction design for involuntarily cued reminiscing. Smell is rare but noticeable as involuntary cue, and offers a strong ability to bring back memories if a device would be aware of personally meaningful odors [24]. It is noticeable several works employ a tactic of random selection for serendipitous effects. Pensieve explored the use of digital mementos by using earlier social media posts as emailed prompts for reminiscing [9]. 4Photos, a dinner table photo displaying device [23], aimed to start dinner conversation by presenting random photos from social network streams. A similar tactic was employed by Cueb to support parent-teenager communication through random display of digital photos on tangible objects [12]. Meerkat and Tuba also went for serendipitous presentation of digital media in the home, abdicating user control in favor of surprise [14]. Knowing what to present and when requires keen understanding of what is personally meaningful, questions of interest in this work.

Petrelli *et al.* [27] argue reflective value of a memento comes out of reencountering and re-evaluating our disposition towards an item and its related memories (although this evaluative process happens in the mind, and is not evident to interactive devices). Echo uses this principle to encourage reflection on cues captured earlier [18]. Data Souvenirs does similarly by placing ambiguous digitally augmented objects in the home environment that upon seeing may stimulate reflection [1].

Knowledge gap

Notwithstanding the above illustrations of how understanding memory, cueing, and interaction design can support remembering our past, questions remain. As some of the related work reveals, additional understanding of what is of value, and when people would (not) appreciate being cued is needed. Despite an increasing interest in memory cues, and effects on recollection [e.g., 15], the effect of cue attributes on remembering remains ambiguous and is often not directly addressed. Contradictory to the studies quoted above, van den Hoven *et al.* [16] found that a no-cue condition compared to several types of cues gave rise to richer recollection of a past event. This appears to suggest interactive devices might also miss out on intended effects using such cues (e.g., photos on phones). We argue this ambiguity impedes successful design of interventions to support everyday remembering.

This is why it is valuable to look into memory cues from a design perspective. What kind of items cue memories in everyday life, as opposed to lab studies or just the home environment? Memory retrieval may largely be an involuntary process, but cues could be in the surroundings for voluntary reasons (e.g., a photo frame deliberately put somewhere). To which cues do people attach value, and for what reason? Is there a difference between digital and physical memory cues for the remembering experience?

This work qualitatively explores what elements in daily life cue a remembering experience, similar to the more quantitative approach in studies using diaries for data gathering [4, 28] and qualitative accounts of home visits [e.g., 10, 20, 27]. We were interested in items as memory cues and the related remembering experiences and meaning these items take on. Besides a general interest in the kind of memory cues encountered, we were especially interested in digital memory cues (if encountered). We believe our findings contribute towards successful designing for remembering support systems by further unpacking the relation between items and cued memories, and by outlining opportunities for future work through elucidating dimensions and trade-offs that designers may consider.

STUDY METHOD

This study explored the relation between memory cues and reminiscing in everyday life, in which diaries and debriefing interviews were used for data collection. We were interested in the type of cues and related memories, and how people relate to these cues. Involuntary memory cueing is a fleeting cognitive phenomenon quickly forgotten if not captured shortly after being cued. Akin to earlier work on involuntary memories [4, 28], participants were asked to record involuntary memories themselves in a diary as soon as they became aware of such a memory being cued. Self-reports provide a good account when initiated by a participant while the cued memory is still fresh, because reporting need not rely on retrospection (as might the case with other methods like experience sampling where delays between event and report are inevitable), at the cost of some subjectivity as interpretation may differ between participants [7]. Diary entries also provided input for debriefing interviews, which expanded on and added qualitative insight to themes found across diary entries.

Participants

Fifteen adults participated (another 5 started but did not complete). They were recruited via personal networks of the authors and university notices, via social network posts, emails, flyers, and in person. Participants were told the purpose of the study was to learn about the various ways people may be reminded of their past by encountering things in daily life. All respondents were included to maximize diversity, and no rewards were given for participation. Participants were aged 24 to 66 (M=39 years), 11 were female (73%), and most were affiliated to the university of the first author as postgraduate student or staff. Living situations varied from single, with flatmates, divorced (with children), to complete families. Half were born in Australia, others had been there for at least one year and had comparable to native language skills.

Diaries

Participants were handed a paper diary to record involuntary memories and related cues (see Fig. 2). They were instructed to 'write down things you encounter throughout the day that remind you of something about your own past, and perhaps made you go back to that moment for a while.' This phrase was chosen to satisfy a focus on external memory cues, while trying to be open. It was explained to participants that 'things' could refer to all modalities. People logged their responses via sentence completion, with three questions to be completed per entry: 'I remembered..,' 'Because I noticed..,' and 'This made me feel..' This format garners free responses with a minimum of guidance necessary for the study interests. Participants kept the diary for a minimum of ten days, although it was allowed to keep the diary longer if the first ten days proved unfruitful (e.g., due to forgetting or not (realizing) being cued). Diary entries were transcribed prior to interviews, with unclear and interesting entries marked for further questioning. Diaries were contrasted with earlier entries to help grounding of early findings.

Figure 2. Example of a completed and filled in diary.

Interviews

Three to seven days after handing in the diary an interview was held to aid interpretation of the diary, and discussed reminiscing practices and perspectives. The semi-structured interview elaborated on diary entries and how significant these listed memory cues were to the participant, how important reminiscing and reflection is in their life and in what way items play a role, and how they perceive differences (if any) between physical and digital mementos. The interviews were held in a quiet space on campus and lasted up to one hour.

Analysis

Data from 15 participants have been used (see Fig.3), including interview data for one participant who withheld her diary because she thought that its content was too personal for her to share, and another person handed in a diary but was not available for an interview. In total, 208 diary entries were used. Seven diary entries did not relate to a past memory and were excluded (e.g., observations about in-the-moment events). Entries based on involuntary internal cueing (i.e., thoughts), although infrequent and not the focus here, were left in. Qualitative thematic analysis aimed for data reduction through quantitative summaries of diary entries and identified recurring themes through inductive coding of the data, using a single coder [cf. 5]. Entries were coded twice: first in a directive approach on summative measures as in earlier work to enable comparison (i.e., categorizing as objects, or smells, or people, etc.) [4], and second, entries were clustered based on emergent affinity which allowed finer grained categorization and contrasts (i.e., not just objects as category, but split into tools, souvenirs, clothing, etc.). Further measures per entry included memory valence (positive/ambivalent/negative), memory specificity (lifetime periods/general events/event-specific knowledge [8]), and whether the participant controlled the exposure to a memory cue (as interpreted by the coder via entry text).

Interviews were transcribed and all relevant statements (i.e., excluding elaborations on tangential matters) were printed and cut into separate paper strips. These strips from all participants were clustered by similarity into a hierarchical structure to support examination. Recurring themes emerging across interviews, and diverse views on these themes were used as the basis for organization and analysis. Together with the diary clusters this provides the structure for our insights into what role memory cues play in people's lives, how people relate to their past, and what potential role HCI can play.

FINDINGS

We give an overview of the data, and discuss several themes that emerged during analysis, and relate the findings to our research questions. When relevant, findings will be contrasted with earlier work. Quotes from diaries are marked (P2-d), interview quotes show (P2-i).

What cues memories?

Quantitative overview of diary entries

We would like to give a brief quantitative impression (although our qualitative findings do not depend on these). The median number of reported cued memories was 11 (range: 2-37). This study limited itself to externally cued memories, while other studies included internal cues (e.g., thoughts) and those reported a slightly higher average of recorded memories [4]. Following a categorization similar to Berntsen, most cues relate to physical objects (52%), locations (14%), activities (9%), people (9%), digital items (e.g., photos or social media; 10%), and 7% other (e.g., sensory, feeling, wording). Objects were mentioned more often compared to ~17% in earlier work on involuntary memories using diaries [e.g., 4, 28]. This bias towards objects may result from our request for external cueing..

Valence showed strong dominance of positive (51%) compared to negative (21%) and ambivalent feelings (27%). In prior diary studies a higher percentage of negative memories surfaced (positives were similar), perhaps due to inclusion of internal memory cueing [4]. The cued memories related to event-specific knowledge in 45%

of entries, with 40% cueing general events, and 15% related to lifetime periods. Both measures showed variance between participants, which may either be genuine, due to style and specificity of writing, or due to a low number of entries for some. Our data is inconclusive on this aspect. For half of the cues reported on participants had some control over the exposure to a cue by means of ownership and/or deliberately seeking out these stimuli. This was clearly the case for categories such as tools, souvenirs, (digital) photos and websites visited. Other categories related to locations, music, social events, and social media did not give much control over exposure to cues.

[I remembered] *breakfast in my childhood - my father made breakfast every day, and we always had a porridge as part of our breakfast, which he was very particular about cooking*	[I remembered] *sitting with my dad while he talked about 'how' to do things*
[Because I noticed] *I still love to cook & eat porridge for breakfast – but my porridge is from the supermarket. My dad bought a special mix from the health food shop*	[Because I noticed] *I was sitting explaining what the plumber was doing with my friend's son*
[This made me feel] *connected back to my childhood, which was very happy and the routines + care of my father, which always gave me lots of safety + love.*	[This made me feel] *very happy, teary*

Figure 3. Two examples of typical diary entries.

Objects as cues

Physical things proved the most common memory cues. While incidence of objects was higher compared to other diary studies, this was not the case for all participants. Some participants perceived less sensitivity to objects: *"The nature of the diary led me to believe that physical objects were the cause of my memories, but what I found was that it was actions that made me remember things,"* (P8-i) according to a participant who noted not keeping a lot of things around in his home.

The kind of objects varied widely, with tools, clothing, souvenirs, gifts, books, decorative pieces, images, and food being the main subcategories. Not every object may bring back memories, but for those that do there is usually a story in which the object played a (minor) role and has since become a signifier for this story: *"[I noticed] My transistor radio! I listen to the ABC through the day - sport, news, and classical music! [I remembered] my father listening to his transistor radio all day as he carried it about with him around the house & garden (...) [This made me feel] fond + proud of my dad, and happy for everything that he taught me"* (P3-d). This entry illustrates that an object often cues memories not because of itself, but rather because it, or the cued memory, relates to other people. A part of the memories reported relate only to the participant, but the majority involved a social relation. This can range from rather mundane (e.g., acquaintances having the same cutlery set) to teddy bears that played a role in significant periods of someone's intimate relationships.

Photos as cues

With few exceptions people display photographs around the house, as told during interviews, but entries were infrequent for photos as cues. Most participants were active users of the camera function on their mobile phones. An interesting aspect of this use is the occasional glancing at taken photos people engage in whenever they have some time to kill. Recent and not so recent photos are flicked through ever so often for relaxation purposes.

Practices and values on personal photographs differ widely between people, as some take less and attach less value to images, whereas others appreciate photography as a hobby and enjoy having aesthetically pleasing examples around. Therefore, photos (and other items) in the home can take on a position beyond memory cue as a medium of expression of (family) identity, a conclusion similar to Kirk *et al.* [20]. Photographs may be a familiar sight and did not capture attention with related memories. When prompted, people could report on related events, but in daily life such items appear to be no constant source of involuntary memories: *"we do have lots of photographs around, but those in the living room weren't the ones stimulating memories. (...) It's nice to have some pictures around the house. I would be sorry if I'd lost them"* (P11-i).

Digital versus physical cues

Digital cues account for a small amount of entries, with social media posts most prevalent (e.g., photos posted by others). These photos were not deliberately sought by participants but rather appeared in the digital environment people frequent. All participants mentioned digital photos although only one diary entry listed a digital photo as cue. Perhaps people realize memory cueing more with physical than with digital items, including photographs. An example of such different perceptions is this quote by a male participant on family photos: *"I don't really pay much attention to the computer-stored ones. For me family pictures in frames around the house are important."* This seems in contrast with a later quote on digital photos: *"When the laptops are on there is a rotation of family pictures on them. And I do enjoy the process of seeing 'm come up."* (P11-i). Family pictures in frames take on extra meaning given their placement in the home. Digital media, when merely stored and not put to use as a background image or otherwise, as a result could be valued less. This finding, while not original [19, 25], appears robust across participants.

A majority expressed preference for physical compared to digital items as mementos. The following quote summarizes the opinions well: *"Things... you can feel and touch something. (...) Whereas with the digital (...) there is something removed about that, in a sense."* (P3-i). One participant explicitly mentioned his preference for digital media given that voluntarily bringing back memories feels equal to him, but physical things can be a practical burden (he kept hardly any himself).

Participants felt that digital media, such as photos taken on a phone, were lower in perceived value and usefulness, almost ephemeral. Such qualities have merit: digital snapshots are considered well suited to share with others as a means of keeping in touch. Preservation is not a big topic for some of the interviewees, with one participant mentioning she lost digital images by giving away an old phone to a friend and not feeling too bothered about the fact. A somewhat paradoxical case of preservation is seen in another participant's efforts to complete his life's timeline on Facebook by scanning and uploading old pictures. Despite considerable effort to make sure *"his story is told"* (P15-i), he mentioned not feeling much attachment to this result. In case of losing it (e.g., due to demise of Facebook), he would still have the memories, as well as the original photos. The tendency to ascribe lower value to digital mementos is generalizable [25, 27]. It appears positive values derived from digital media are less evident.

Locations as memory cues

Locations, and actions in specific locations, were reported on frequently. Most entries related to earlier experiences in the same environment, but just similarity was enough in some cases to invoke memories. For example, a sandy beach and high temperatures were distinct enough to cue memories of another beach far away in time and space. In other cases it was not so much the location as the opportunities afforded, such as the ability to go somewhere at a ferry terminal. The latter example could be described as reflective, similar to motivations to go to a park that later sparks many related memories.

This study provides no clear perspective on whether a location as a whole is the cue, or rather something specific within this environment. For example, in an entry noted at a beach a low moon reflected in the ocean, triggering a participant's memory of *"going in the ocean at night for the first time a couple of weeks ago. [This made me feel] excited: keen on going swimming at night soon again"* (P17-d). Being in the same place may evoke a similar state of mind and makes it likely some aspect pulls past events to the surface, making it difficult to retrospectively tell if it really was just that element as cue. Another entry underlines this by pointing to the column portico of a university building upon returning there. The act of going back, and taking that familiar walk, contributed to the sense of nostalgia before seeing the distinctive portico.

Activities as memory cues

Activity was often named as a cue for events in which a similar action had been performed. A few participants realized that for them it often wasn't specific items that brought back memories but rather it was doing something similar as in the past. For one person, aware of his proclivity to remember by doing, it became part of his practice (and tendency not to take many photos): *"When doing things, you get a déjà vu: what you were seeing, smelling, and feeling as well. [...] An image... I'd think 'oh, yeah, that was really, really good,' but doing something engages that whole process of remembering."* (P8-i).

Why do activities cue memories? When trying to fit groceries in a bicycle bag, a participant was reminded of previous times she faced the challenge. Without an immediate challenge present, it is less straightforward: *"When I swim in the morning, I always remember my boyfriend. [Sporting] became part of something we did together (...) and then you think about a person and it becomes a habit"* (P4-i). We argue it may be repetition, and through this the accumulation of meaning that aids remembering of events in which the activity took place. Although mundane activities like cleaning and cooking were mentioned as well, it appears sports provide a unique opportunity through the repetition and relation to values in life. This diary entry captures it well: *"[I noticed] how good I felt after going for a jog, and arguably during the jog. [I remembered] how good I felt when I was more active. (Used to run frequently). [This made me feel] good, proud that I have restarted the regime."* (P1-d).

Food related cues

Eating and food-related materials came up often, and included ingredients, making food, related tools, and sharing a meal (see Fig.2). Although not mentioned often within HCI [23], food is one category where items, activities, social gatherings and accumulated meaning combine. Food-related cues prompted memories on social gatherings, past events, people's preferences, and the relationship with family members: *"[I remembered] cooking with my mother – as a child living at home, [Because I noticed] her handwriting on a recipe I was about to use that evening. [This made me feel] a little sad – that I can no longer call her & chat about day-to-day things. That she is no longer with us."* (P9-d). Like activities, food and its social practices appear to accumulate meaning over time and as such the repetition makes for a stronger memory. The cooking example indicates dishes can be specific to an event or a period and take on a role as signifier for those moments, presumably cementing its ability to cue memories later.

Which memory cues are valuable?

While our focus was on involuntary cueing, discussions on valuable items as cues centered on practices in the home as the place for storage and display of items for their related memories and/or aesthetics. We found a relationship between the perceived need of access to related memories and item placement. For some, items were deliberately put on display to serve as signifiers of positive moments and self-attributes. These items thus served to display and cue positive attributes of identity: *"it's like each of those things paint a stroke in your own painting"* (P4-i). This desire to have the home reflect identity is found with nearly all participants, and echoes prior work [e.g., 10, 20, 27]. This highlights that the need for reminiscing ties into perspectives on the past, and how it relates to the present.

An item's relation to the present may morph over time as it may take on new meaning after influential events, and remain valuable partly because of this. For example, a hand-knitted scarf once received as a gift from a friend since lost has come to signify personal growth: *"it's ultimately a symbol of rejection [in the past]; it's also a symbol of love. (...) And when you keep things of your own failures around, it keeps you humble. (...) It encourages you to keep growing"* (P4-i). Such tokens of important life events relate to complex emotions. Other work on digital remains and heirlooms corroborate these findings [20].

Meaning develops over time for many personal items, as these things get put on display, get used, scarred, or fall out of use and are reencountered after a while. A good example is a story on a bike that a participant uses to go to work daily, which was bought years ago and has since accompanied him around the world: *"... I need to replace a few things. So I think 'do I get a new bike? Or do I replace the components?' And I replaced the components, because of the memories I think, and probably as a keepsake."* (P8-i). Other people illustrated similar stories that showed a gradual attachment over time as an item played a small part in their life. This complements other work on personal belongings that emphasize the beneficial role of a repeatedly observed (or used) factor for investment of meaning [20, 27].

DISCUSSION

In the reported study, we investigated involuntary memory cueing to inform design for remembering. Our findings show that a broad range of external stimuli can trigger remembering experiences. We found physical items took precedence as involuntary memory cues; environments such as parks and beaches got frequent mention, as did activities. The latter is not often discussed, perhaps because activities are not typically thought of as a cue for earlier events. Yet, psychology studies on involuntary memory cues back up our findings for these kinds of cues [e.g., 4, 28].

The use of self-reports throughout the day brought in reports beyond the personal and curated. However, for personal items people were able to relate stories and histories in which these items played a role. Meaningful items are often put on display (e.g., photos to display family bonds) or, like inherited dinner plates, are "honoring through use" [20]. Indeed, when discussing personal memory-related practices in the home, our findings dovetail with earlier ethnographic accounts [10, 20, 27], although these works oriented towards voluntary memories, and employ a broader sociological perspective [cf. 20].

In earlier involuntary cueing work there was no attention to the media representation of a cue, so no comments were possible on digital cues [e.g., 4, 28]. We did categorize these, and found digital items were not common as involuntary cues. Most participants who use digital social media were able to remember instances of reminiscing invoked this way. Browsing photos on a phone gave no diary entries, but was mentioned by several participants as a pleasant activity. It may be that participants regarded this as a voluntary act, while the focus here was on involuntary cues. Alternatively, if digital media are encountered involuntarily as on social media, these are able to foster reminiscing, but for self-managed material this value may be overlooked due to accessibility (e.g., participants mentioned storage and management burden). Photos on phones may lower the bar, being within easy reach.

Despite intent to focus on digital cues, this study does not make clear whether there is a difference in remembering experience for cues that could be both digitally and physically presented. Our findings suggest ability to cue extends to a wide variety of items, but availability to be observed is key (which may explain the prevalence of physical items in the responses). This question of representation is in need of future attention, because if remembering experiences differ depending on the way a memory cue is presented this has implications for future devices that support remembering using cues.

Some methodological limitations apply. Using diaries enabled self-reports directly after being cued. However, some people wrote in the diary a while after because they felt burdened carrying it around. Such practices may introduce retrospection on memories invoked earlier or leave ephemeral and quickly forgotten memories unreported. Diaries were then filled out upon coming home, perhaps around dinnertime, which may have primed food-related entries. Future studies could employ a staged capturing of data (e.g., noting keywords, with full descriptions added later) to ease reporting.

Observed differences between participants might be attributed to different task interpretations. In particular, some felt restricted to physical observations and, for example, excluded music as cue. This may partly explain the higher count of objects in our data compared to other work [4], and could have reduced the number of digital cues. However, comparing is difficult, as those did not specify involuntary memory cues as digital. Furthermore, we suspect some filtering took place on what was recorded. While unexpected when relying on someone's awareness of being involuntarily cued, some participants might have discarded cued memories that did not feel very personally relevant, which may bias our findings.

Although we stressed people to not look for things that reminded them of personal memories, and rather rely on involuntarily cueing, we could not control for this other than retrospectively asking about their motivations to note certain entries. While responses suggest entries were indeed based on unintentional invocation of memories, in many instances in the home items were deliberately put on display to serve as occasional reminders and evidently did so, blurring the line on intentionality.

It needs acknowledgement that memory cueing is not a straightforward process and a cue can via cascading thoughts lead to a memory that may no longer be recognized as brought about by the original cue. The act of writing in the diary (or remembering to do so later) may equally modify one's perspective on the original cueing event and related memories. This modifying aspect is relevant to consider for interactive devices, but here it can be seen as a potential influence outside our control.

The remainder of this section relates implications and opportunities for interaction design to support reminiscing, which are described as dimensions of trade-offs to consider. These dimensions are timing, exposure, and the process of becoming a meaningful memory cue.

Timing: moments for presenting cues

Reminiscing and reflection are not activities people set out to do for a while, according to participants. A reflective mood will certainly increase the odds, but it is rather something that comes up while doing another task (e.g., doing laundry, cooking, riding a bike). Depending on cognitive demands, a task may allow the main activity to move to the periphery of attention [2]. Opportunities for reminiscing can be facilitated by augmenting existing interactions that are prone to mind wandering. Making food was indicated as an example of such a low-key activity, and a device could capitalize on the opportunity to inspire positive reminiscing. Facilitation is certainly challenging because it may be hard to steer the wandering mind, but such suggestive devices embedded into everyday activities have potential to tap into moments when people say they enjoy thinking about their lives.

To engage people in reminiscing via designed cueing requires sensitivity to opportune moments. By definition involuntary cueing is unsolicited, but devices that aim to do so would benefit from a way to sense (un) desirability, or alternatively, provide the means for people to indicate in retrospect whether they appreciated the experience of being cued. Over time, a system may be able to learn from such feedback. Other technical means may be available to sensing appreciation (e.g., facial expressions, time spent looking at an item). Similarly, user activity could be classified as relaxed and open to interruption, or in a state of flow. The opposite end on this spectrum would entail no cueing is commenced without prior voluntary action.

Exposing a cue: what and how

A key element for any system is to find out which available items relate to a valued memory for someone, and in which way these items are best presented. Finding out about perceived value (whether of an item-as-cue or a related memory) could be done in advance through explicit inquiry, or retrospectively through feedback. One issue for automated gathering of such knowledge is that meaning of an item is idiosyncratic and perhaps ambivalent, as our findings indicate. While (for example) number of interactions may be a telling signifier (e.g., how often a song was played), a system may not know why. Previous work has sidestepped this issue by considering random viewing as a way of achieving serendipity [e.g., 9, 14].

Next comes the question of which form this exposure should take. While our data suggests a related memory is a stronger indicator of appreciation than the cueing itself, our findings leave room for exploration of this cueing manifestation. Remembering through action is worthwhile for further investigation. We imagine interactions can be leveraged not just as means to access content, but also be conducive to reminiscing. If a device is aware of reminiscence-prone activities, there may be opportunities to reminisce on earlier events through stimulation of activities. Relating to positive memories could stimulate similar experiences, as seen with the jogging example.

People expressed no need to consider the past all the time. Potential overexposure is important to consider for interactive devices as digital devices enable us to frequently encounter many mementos: we can quickly retrieve any old item, whenever we want, which may change how we develop relations with these mementos [29]. It is a contrast with the normally hidden shoeboxes of old, and explorations building on this theme [e.g., 11]. Frequent interaction with the past can have adverse effects, both for painful memories and the inability to move on with one's life, as pointed out by two participants familiar with depression. There is equal value in forgetting as part of a healthy memory system, and indiscriminate invocation of unpleasant memories can adversely affect people's wellbeing [3]. Still, we believe that when done right, designs can engage with the process of reflecting on meaningful events of the past [e.g., 21].

Process of becoming meaningful as a cue

Can meaning be designed for or cultivated through design? This is a design challenge we seek to contribute to. The study presented in this paper was concerned with existing items that had the ability to bring back memories without being designed explicitly for that goal. Based on our findings we note that memories and meaning do not form a straightforward relationship with an item. This sometimes tangential relationship can be idiosyncratic [27]. For example, the scarf discussed earlier symbolizes a lost friendship, but this symbol could have been another item. We speculate everything might be able to become a memory cue depending on how people relate to it, but some designs may be better suited to bring back memories. The scarf's handmade materiality may be such a design element that signifies emotional investment, a quality harder to replicate in digital media. Therefore, especially for digital devices that could cue memories, we believe a very relevant question is how it can be designed to become meaningful.

The notion that meaning develops over time is interesting to investigate in future designs, and echoes similar findings by Petrelli *et al.* [27]. Repeated exposure and engagement with potential memory cues seems important, and such investment of time hampers digital cues to pick up meaning. Compared to physical cues, digital ones get comparatively less exposure in everyday life, if going by our results (although Schwarz points at a different trend [29]). If repetition is key to accrue meaning, designs could explore ways in which meaning develops and grows over time (e.g., through repeated exposure). If indeed how people come to relate to something is more relevant than what the thing is, we should consider how we could foster a relationship between a personal memory and a cue. Designing for this process and facilitation of reminiscing and reflective thought appears a veritable direction of inquiry. This is different from designing an item to be able to cue an autobiographical memory, and rather may use items to facilitate the process.

Whether such accrual of meaning is deliberately sought via interactions with someone (e.g., by repeated exposure) or, as per the opposite, that increasing meaning is derived from usage data (e.g., how often an item is revisited), is a design decision to be made. It relates to the other dimensions by focusing on what could become valuable if given time. As an example, our findings suggest items that relate to social connections would be likely to become regarded as valuable, if this connection is indeed seen as such.

Limits to what technology could accomplish

The aforementioned dimensions all require trade-offs to be made considering the desirability of involuntary cueing from a user's perspective. For example, obtrusiveness of cueing relates to insensitive timing and/or misjudging exposure to a cue for an undesired memory. Whether a system can be successful depends on how well it is able to understand the context of its use and how well it adapts to such knowledge. The challenge is to judge this desirability within the means of technology, and handle the cases where it cannot adequately know in an appropriate manner.

Getting the necessary understanding may depend on machine learning algorithms that may or may not be sufficiently capable to do so given hard to measure data such as personal attachment to an item or openness to consider one's past. The latter issue implies a fully involuntarily experienced system may be imperfect, and a balance with some voluntary interactions could serve people's needs better (e.g., using retrospectively marking of certain cues as desired or not). Furthermore, there are aspects that are hard to prepare for with a technological system, as shown in earlier work on inheritance of digital data [e.g., 13, 22]. However, the ways imperfect moments play out are malleable. We believe designers should acknowledge the limitations of technology by not relying extensively on it and rather opt for a dialogue, similar to how physical items, their meaning, and visible (dis) placement form a dialogue with their owner through manipulation of place (e.g., hiding things).

Reflections on HCI research for remembering

Having made the argument that meaningful connections between items, the self and memories are forged over time, this has implications for design research. Careful study of designed interventions should consider the effects of repeated user engagement, and would therefore benefit from longitudinal evaluation. Most of the design examples discussed in this text were studied for a limited period of time (as are many not discussed here), perhaps falling short of the time necessary to become related to at a deeper level. Because passage of time may alter our perspective on earlier events, remembering experiences after two years can yield different insights from doing so after one month, the former closer to a real life use case. An emphasis on longitudinal evaluation can thus provide necessary insight on designing for remembering support.

CONCLUSIONS

We believe understanding what makes people remember their past and how this colors their experience is important to inform designs that aim to support everyday remembering. Our work contributes to the literature by integrating diary self-reports with follow-up interviews to further our understanding about the relation between involuntary memories and the things that cue such memories, and how people relate to particularly meaningful items. The findings illustrate memory cueing happens everywhere: meaningful cues are not limited to the home, nor should its study be limited to that environment.

Repeated encounters in daily life, in which the item may be tangential to the task at hand, provide opportunities for items to take on meaning. Such practices do not easily extend to digital items, although nowadays many potential cues are digital. While physical items can be put on display or used for common tasks (e.g., inherited cutlery), we believe this proves a challenge for digital items to be used for everyday remembering as these are often not encountered on a regular basis (or serendipitously for that matter). Even though easy capture of media for future recall seems a problem solved – too well perhaps [29, 30] – our work addressed how these items are currently encountered and can be used as support for reminiscing and wellbeing.

Considering our insights we can now state what we believe to be effective practices for interaction design to support everyday remembering. Integrating with common activities that stimulate the mind to wander provide opportunities for reminiscing through design; involuntary cueing can lead to surprise revisiting of memories, including undesired ones. Designs should allow for some control over (non) exposure to certain cues. Meaningful connections grow over time: designs can support this process. Evaluation of HCI designs for remembering can benefit from a longitudinal focus.

ACKNOWLEDGEMENTS
We would like to thank all participants for their time and contributions. This study was approved by the UTS Ethics Committee (#2012000570), and supported by STW VIDI grant number 016.128.303 of The Netherlands Organization for Scientific Research (NWO) and a UTS PhD Scholarship, both awarded to Elise van den Hoven.

REFERENCES
1. Aipperspach, R., Hooker, B., and Woodruff, A. Data Souvenirs: Environmental psychology and reflective design. *International Journal of Human-Computer Studies 69*, 5 (2011), 338–349.
2. Bakker, S., Hoven, E., van den, and Eggen, J.H. Peripheral interaction: characteristics and considerations. *Personal and Ubiquitous Comp*, (2014).
3. Bannon, L.J. Forgetting as a feature, not a bug: the duality of memory and implications for ubiquitous computing. *CoDesign 2*, 1 (2006), 3–15.
4. Berntsen, D. *Involuntary Autobiographical Memories*. Cambridge University Press, 2009.
5. Braun, V. and Clarke, V. Using thematic analysis in psychology. *Qual. Research in Psy 3*, 2 (2006), 77–101.
6. Bryant, F.B., Smart, C.M., and King, S.P. Using the Past to Enhance the Present: Boosting Happiness Through Positive Reminiscence. *Happiness Studies 6*, (2005), 227–260.
7. Carter, S. and Mankoff, J. When participants do the capturing. In *Proc. CHI '05*, ACM Press (2005), 899–908.
8. Conway, M.A. and Pleydell-Pearce, C.W. The construction of autobiographical memories in the self-memory system. *Psychological review 107*, 2 (2000), 261–287.
9. Cosley, D., Sosik, V.S., Schultz, J., et al. Experiences With Designing Tools for Everyday Reminiscing. *Human–Computer Interaction 27*, (2012), 175–198.
10. Csikszentmihalyi, M. and Rochberg-Halton, E. *The Meaning of Things*. Cambridge University Press, 1981.
11. Frohlich, D. and Murphy, R. The Memory Box. *Personal and Ubiquitous Comp 4*, 4 (2000), 238–240.
12. Golsteijn, C. and Hoven, E., van den. Facilitating parent-teenager communication through interactive photo cubes. *Personal and Ubiquitous Computing 17*, 2 (2013), 273–286.
13. Gulotta, R., Odom, W., Forlizzi, J., and Faste, H. Digital artifacts as legacy: exploring the lifespan and value of digital data. In *Proc. CHI '13*, ACM Press (2013), 1813–1822.
14. Helmes, J., O'Hara, K., Vilar, N., and Taylor, A.S. Meerkat and tuba: design alternatives for randomness, surprise and serendipity in reminiscing. In *Proc. INTERACT'11*, Springer-Verlag (2011), 376–391.
15. Hoven, E., van den and Eggen, B. The cue is key: Design for real-life remembering. *Zeitschrift für Psychologie 222*, 2 (2014), 110–117.
16. Hoven, E., van den and Eggen, J.H. The effect of cue media on recollections. *Human Technology 5*, 1 (2009), 47–67.
17. Hoven, E., van den, Sas, C., and Whittaker, S. Introduction to this Special Issue on Designing for Personal Memories: Past, Present, and Future. *Human–Computer Interaction 27*, 1-2 (2012), 1–12.
18. Isaacs, E., Konrad, A., Walendowski, A., et al. Echoes from the past: how technology mediated reflection improves well-being. In *Proc. CHI '13*, ACM (2013), 1071–1080.
19. Kalnikaite, V. and Whittaker, S. A saunter down memory lane: Digital reflection on personal mementos. *International Journal of Human-Computer Studies 69*, 5 (2011), 298–310.
20. Kirk, D.S. and Sellen, A.J. On human remains: Values and practice in the home archiving of cherished objects. *ACM TOCHI 17*, 3, Article 10 (2010), 43 pages.
21. Massimi, M. and Baecker, R.M. A death in the family: opportunities for designing technologies for the bereaved. In *Proc. CHI '10*, ACM (2010), 1821–1830.
22. Moncur, W. and Kirk, D.S. An emergent framework for digital memorials. In *Proc. DIS '14*, ACM Press (2014), 965–974.
23. O'Hara, K., Helmes, J., Sellen, A.J., et al. Food for Talk: Phototalk in the Context of Sharing a Meal. *Human–Computer Interaction 27*, 1 (2012).
24. Obrist, M., Tuch, A.N., and Hornbaek, K. Opportunities for odor: experiences with smell and implications for technology. In *Proc. CHI '14*, ACM Press (2014), 2843–2852.
25. Petrelli, D. and Whittaker, S. Family memories in the home: contrasting physical and digital mementos. *Personal and Ubiquitous Comp 14*, 2 (2010), 153–169.
26. Petrelli, D., Hoven, E., van den, and Whittaker, S. Making history: intentional capture of future memories. In *Proc. CHI '09*, ACM Press (2009), 1723–1732.
27. Petrelli, D., Whittaker, S., and Brockmeier, J. AutoTopography: what can physical mementos tell us about digital memories? In *Proc. CHI '08*, ACM (2008), 53–62.
28. Schlagman, S., Kvavilashvili, L., and Schulz, J. Effects of age on involuntary autobiographical memories. In J.H. Mace, ed., *Involuntary Memory*. Blackwell, Malden, MA, 2007, 87–112.
29. Schwarz, O. The past next door: Neighbourly relations with digital memory-artefacts. *Memory Studies 7*, 1 (2014), 7–21.
30. Sellen, A.J. and Whittaker, S. Beyond Total Capture: A Constructive Critique of Lifelogging. *Communications of the ACM 53*, (2010), 70–77.
31. van Dijck, J. *Mediated Memories in the Digital Age*. Stanford University Press, 2007.
32. Whittaker, S., Kalnikaite, V., Petrelli, D., et al. Socio-Technical Lifelogging: Deriving Design Principles for a Future Proof Digital Past. *Human–Computer Interaction 27*, (2012), 37–62.

Curatorial Agents: How Systems Shape Our Understanding of Personal and Familial Digital Information

Rebecca Gulotta
HCII
Carnegie Mellon University
rgulotta@cs.cmu.edu

Alex Sciuto
School of Design
Carnegie Mellon University
sciutoalex@cmu.edu

Aisling Kelliher
School of Design
Carnegie Mellon University
aislingk@andrew.cmu.edu

Jodi Forlizzi
HCII
Carnegie Mellon University
jforlizzi@cs.cmu.edu

ABSTRACT
As people increasingly turn to digital channels to share, store, and reflect on their lives and experiences, the processes by which they manage the diverse collection of information generated over the course of their lives are changing. These processes, once a matter of hands-on curation and personal meaning making, are now deeply rooted in interactions with digital systems. In this work, we drew from prior research from personalization, memory, and information management to create four interactive, provocative systems. Through sessions with 12 adults from Pittsburgh, PA we used a combination of these systems and interviews to examine how systems might play a role in the near and long term resurfacing of personal and familial digital information. Findings point to an opportunity to create systems that can openly mediate the curation and transmission of digital content, and ways to draw meaning from the differences between how systems and people recall and represent their experiences.

Author Keywords
Research through design; memory; digital legacy; identity; reflection; curation; metadata; personalization; agency

ACM Classification Keywords
H.5.m. Information interfaces and presentation (e.g., HCI): Miscellaneous.

INTRODUCTION
Managing digital information is a well-documented problem; it is far easier to generate information than it is to derive meaning from it. Though it is clear that people value some of the digital information and media they create through their interactions with digital systems [4, 25], it is less clear how to identify significant pieces of that information and how to make sense of vast, heterogeneous archives. Prior research has studied relationships with physical objects, and existing practices with digital content, to better understand how users and systems might work together to identify that which is meaningful [32, 34]. However, the idiosyncratic, fragmented nature of people's digital records and their management strategies makes it difficult to develop prescriptive solutions [19, 20].

CHI 2015, April 18 - 23 2015, Seoul, Republic of Korea

ACM 978-1-4503-3145-6/15/04...$15.00
http://dx.doi.org/10.1145/2702123.2702297

Looking forward, managing digital archives may be further complicated by the integration of records that span years, generations, and owners. The prevalence of digital media and information has already begun to uncover questions about how they might be integrated into existing practices related to death and dying [26] and whether they will hold value to future generations [15]. More broadly, there may be cultural and societal value in building systems that can archive and derive meaning from multigenerational records [11]. As such, it is worthwhile to explore how records that span generations might be integrated into the experiences of those left behind, even many years into the future. If people's digital records are to endure past their lifetimes, considering how people will make use of or contribute to those records in their own lives becomes significant.

In this paper, we explore these issues and focus on the implications of the nascent, but developing, capabilities for digital systems to analyze and make judgments about the information that they capture. We place special emphasis on how these types of systems, and the questions they elicit about user and system agency, intersect with concerns about the management of long-term collections of heterogeneous digital data. Drawing methodologically from technology probes [18] and reflective design [39], we developed four interactive systems (Fig. 1) to provoke discussions with participants about the role that both systems and people play in the process of curating and deriving meaning from digital records that are diverse with regards to their source, temporal context, and meaning.

Through sessions with 12 adults from Pittsburgh, PA we utilize these systems to investigate how digital systems might make sense of unwieldy, diverse collections of digital information. In addition, this work explores the complex nature of how people feel about digital systems interpreting and making judgments using their digital information. The findings from this work expose nuances regarding the discrepancies between system and human memory, the ability for systems to act as mediators for personal digital

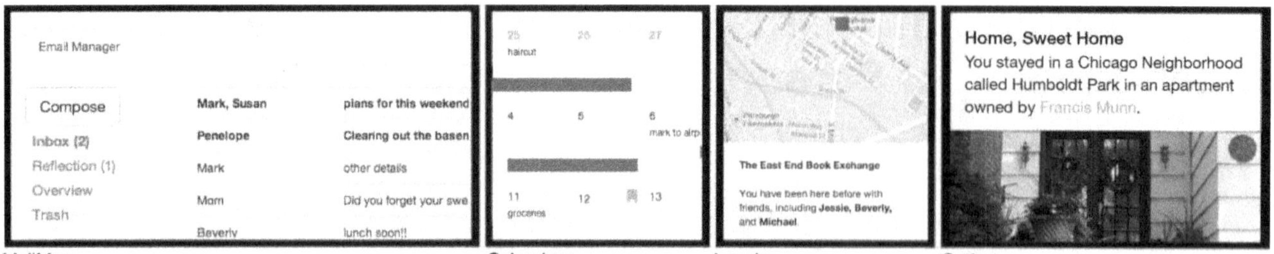

MailMem *Calendera* *Locale* *Gather*

Figure 1: Images from each of the systems developed as probes for this work: *MailMem*, *Calendera*, *Locale*, and *Gather*.

content passed down to future generations, the ways in which people sometimes use personalization systems to reflect on their own identities, and the opportunity to use metadata as a way to engage people in thinking deeply about what information is captured by digital systems. Based on these findings, this paper contributes a collection of design recommendations for the creation of systems that enable more meaningful interactions with heterogeneous digital records.

RELATED WORK

Research on personalization systems helps to articulate the complex feelings people have about being profiled and tracked by digital systems [1]. Studies in advertising reveal that most people do not feel comfortable with personalization, and this discomfort increases with knowledge about how this process works [43]. Giving people control over how information is collected reduces concerns [42]. However, this differs for recommendations (such as those for music or media) that are not framed as advertising; in these cases transparency can positively influence how people perceive the system [40].

Personalization has also been studied within the context of personal information management. Responding to the complexity associated with managing fragmented pieces of information, researchers have developed systems that provide users with the ability to add metadata and develop their own personal categorizations [10]. This research advances the notion that a person's subjective understanding of a digital item may be a useful mechanism for finding it later [5]. More recently, there has been a push to think of information fragmentation as a valuable aspect of personal digital information and, more broadly, as to how people understand and develop their digital identities [23].

Within human-computer interaction, researchers have developed systems aimed at enabling people to archive, reflect on, and revisit their information, memories, and media. Work in this area suggests that digital systems may be a valuable way for people to engage with the desire to communicate information about their lives to others [23], a process that is an integral part of how individuals develop a narrative about their life's experiences as they age [6]. In addition, everyday reminiscence, as embodied in digital systems, offers an opportunity for people to examine the context, meaning, and value of the parts of their lives that they choose to document [8]. Personal informatics systems, like activity trackers, offer people the ability to think broadly about how their digital information reflects their behaviors and practices [22]. Additionally, there is a large body of lifelogging work that suggests that information captured through lifelogging tools aids in the process of identity construction [30]. However, despite the potential of these systems, prior work highlights the challenges of tying the capabilities of digital media and information to existing reflection and management practices [35, 47]. In addition, this work also exposes unanswered questions about how systems can impact recalling and remembering [17].

It is also often the case that people will collaboratively manage digital information. Frequently, multiple members of a family will jointly manage the media, artifacts, and documents in a home. This is a long-standing practice; the objects in a home typically often reflect the relationships of people to whom they are connected [21]. Family members also sometimes collectively manage digital or intangible artifacts and information. For example, parents regularly take on the management of the digital photographs that reflect the lives of their family members and children [46]. This practice seems likely to increase as people become the owners of multigenerational collections of digital records. Looking beyond the family, collaborative information management is an integral part of creating repositories of cultural information. The development of these repositories represents an opportunity to understand how digital systems can reflect the needs and values of cultural groups and institutions [7].

A growing body of literature challenges the idea that computers should indiscriminately remember and safeguard digital information. With human memory, remembering is a reconstructive process that is influenced by a host of internal and external factors [3, 36]. Though they have complex implications, forgetting and misremembering can be an integral part of how people construct their identities, create life narratives, and contextualize their life experiences [2]. In recent years, technologists have integrated this understanding of human memory to reconsider how people and systems might work together to make sense of large quantities of digital information [9, 38, 47]. This is not to say that the loss of digital content is inconsequential; but rather instead, it is worth reflecting on the idea that forgetting and subjective remembering may have a valuable place in how digital systems operate [27].

STUDY DESIGN

Provocation and Engagement Through System Design

This related work highlights an opportunity to examine how systems might help people make sense of digital records and, subsequently, how those systems will influence practices related to legacy, information management, and meaning making with digital records. Building on this research, we developed four interactive systems – *MailMem*, *Calendera, Locale*, and *Gather*. These systems took the format of focused, but low-functionality websites, each of which enabled us to explore a number of questions derived from our larger research goals. Methodologically, our approach for the development, orientation, and use of these systems draws from reflective design [39], technology probes [18], and user enactments [33]. In line with these methods, we developed the systems as a way to provoke and inspire discussion with participants about issues that might otherwise be hard to imagine or articulate.

System Dimensions and Concepts

The systems were built around four dimensions — topic, generativity, agency, and time. These dimensions were chosen based on our goals for the study and on prior work in this area [14, 15, 47], which highlighted issues and opportunities for meaningful reflection with digital information. These dimensions were also drawn from related work in personalization [1], legacy making [44], and slow technology [31]. Each system represents a variation on all four of the dimensions to some degree.

In addition, all of the systems utilize metadata as a design material. Metadata is the information that describes, annotates, or adds onto digital data [13]. Though there is a fluid relationship between what is referred to as 'data' and that which is described as 'metadata', in this work we are centrally interested in metadata as a way to examine the relationship between digital systems and the people that use them. As such, we are concerned with two categories of metadata: (1) person-generated metadata, such as comments on a Facebook post, and (2) system-generated metadata, such as the number of times a song has been played.

Topic

The first dimension was the topic of the information held by the system. Existing systems created to help people reflect on their digital information are often not designed in a way that expresses or embraces individual variations in the meaning of that information. We selected topics that reflect aspects of a person's life that are often represented by digital data, such as familial relationships, exploring both new and familiar places, and shared experiences.

Generativity

The second dimension was generativity, or the extent to which the system generated novel presentations using existing data and metadata. Though each of the probes generates new representations of content to some degree, we were interested in exploring how users perceive the differences between systems that generate new ways of looking at existing digital information and those that more faithfully represent a user's digital content.

Agency

The third dimension was agency, or how the user and the system each influence the selection and representation of information. This dimension was, in some cases, built into the ways that the participant could interact with the system. In addition, for each system, we presented participants with a number of scenarios about how it would work, varying the degree to which the people could exercise agency about capturing and sharing the information held therein.

Time

The fourth dimension was time. This dimension is represented in the systems through several variations, most saliently through a decision about when the content is presented to users and the time periods represented by that content. In addition, the systems were designed to elicit conversations about how the information embodied therein might impact the remembrance of someone's life and how that information might evolve in meaning over time.

System Building

The systems were low-functionality websites, a format that reflects how these services would be used if they were real, working systems. Each was pre-populated with specific information that related to a scenario we developed. Though all of the data presented to participants, including emails, familial records, and location data, was fabricated for the study, participants were asked to imagine that the information presented was their own, a technique drawn from design research methods such as user enactments [33].

Protocol

Study sessions took place in a lab on our campus styled to look and feel like a contemporary home. It contains a kitchen and a living room separated by a room divider. Upon arriving at the lab, participants took part in an open-ended interview. Interview questions covered participants' assessments of what information was being captured by digital systems; their use of digital systems to deliberately generate digital content and data; the extent to which they engage with personalized services; and their perception of how computers make assessments about their life and experiences.

After the interview was completed, we introduced the participants to the systems one at a time. Participants were asked to think of their interaction with the systems as thought exercises. We made it clear that we did not intend to develop these systems further and that we were not interested in their usability or commercial viability. The interactions were instead framed as an opportunity to deeply consider the implications of the systems themselves. For each, we explained a basic scenario that provided context for the information held in the system and asked participants to imagine that the information therein was their own. We then provided them with as much time as they wanted to explore each system. Afterwards, we asked participants questions and provided them with an opportunity to ask their own questions. On average, sessions lasted about an hour and fifteen minutes and participants were compensated for their time.

SYSTEM DESCRIPTIONS

MailMem

MailMem is an email system that identifies meaningful email threads and then presents them to users in their inbox (Fig. 2). Participants were asked to imagine that the system was capable of selecting conversations that it had assessed as being meaningful or unusual. This process included an analysis of metadata collected by the system, such as the number of times an email had been viewed, the presence or absence of media, and the number of replies, in addition to a rudimentary, simulated semantic analysis of the content itself. We described how *MailMem* would unpredictably and periodically unearth these conversations and present them to the owner of the inbox, which allowed us to experiment with both time and agency.

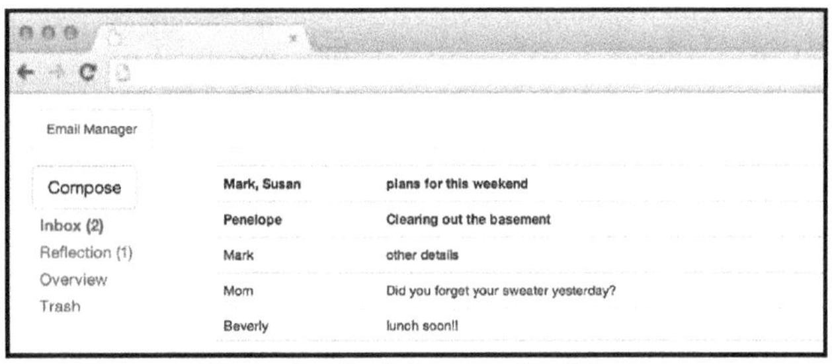

Figure 2: The inbox for *MailMem*.

For the study, participants were presented with a set of conversations marking the end of a relationship, shown in Figure 3. The graph is scaled to reflect the volume of communication between two people and the red lines indicate particular emails being highlighted by the system.

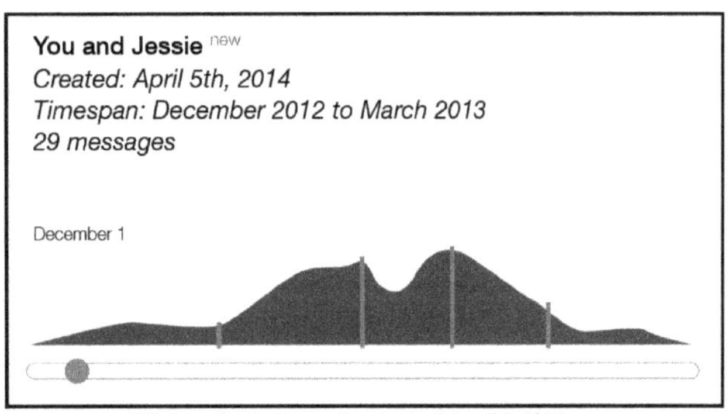

Figure 3: A thread selected by *MailMem*.

MailMem was positioned to explore how the differences between one's memory of an occurrence and the system's interpretation of that occurrence influence the process by which a person composes a life story or narrative [28]. In addition, this work was partly inspired by prior research exploring how to use email archives as a way to illustrate social connections and to identify interesting content held within [16, 45]. In contrast to these systems, however, the primary goal of *MailMem* was not to expose participants to information about their social networks or to help them gain a broader understanding of their communication patterns.

Instead, this system was designed to provoke conversations about systems using and interpreting information captured through their use. We chose to frame this system around an emotionally charged topic in order to talk with participants about how predictive and adaptive systems might operate given the deeply personal information sometimes held in digital systems.

Calendera

Calendera is a calendar that integrates records from one's forbearers into the user's monthly view of their schedule and was developed to explore how systems might be involved in deriving meaning from multigenerational records. These multigenerational micro-remembrances are signaled using a golden bookmark, pictured in Figure 4. *Calendera* contained three bookmarks, revealing content that was a mixture of public information (such as immigration records) and information that systems could capture but that is likely not publicly available (family photographs, music listening habits). While these micro-remembrances are integrated into a calendar, this format was used primarily as a tool to introduce the idea of routinely reflecting on digital records from past generations.

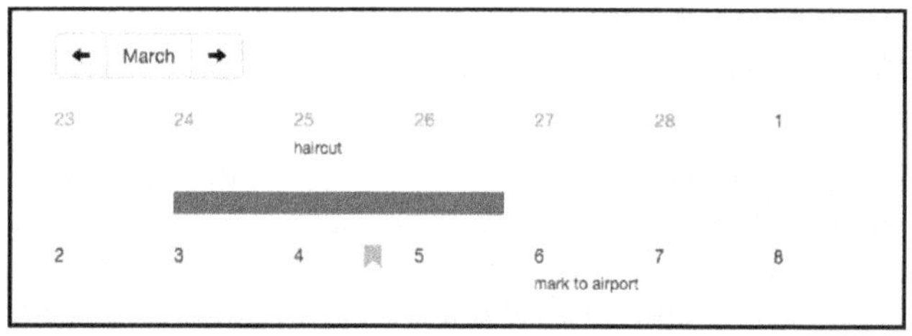

Figure 4: *Calendera* with a bookmark showing that there is information available about the owner's family.

During study sessions, participants were asked to imagine that *Calendera* had access to generations of digital records from which it could pull out pieces of information that it identified as interesting or meaningful. For our study, we created three micro-remembrances (Fig. 5): photographs from a parent's first trip to New York City, publicly available immigration records documenting the user's grandparents' arrival in America, and information about the user's dad's favorite music album.

Extending work on everyday reminiscence [8], our goal was to explore how the personal remembrance of a loved one can evolve over time and how being exposed to their digital records might influence the process of reflecting on their life. *Calendera* also provoked speculation about how a system would make judgments about what was meaningful and how the original owner of the content would be involved in the process of passing it on. Additionally, as a variation on the time dimension, *Calendera* explores how, in the future, digital systems might make use of extant digital content from one's family members.

This was the first day your dad ever listened to **The Beatles**. He went on to listen to Abbey Road over 200 times over the course of his life. **Listen now? ▶■**

Public immigration records tell us that it was around this time when your grandparents arrived in America at Ellis Island.

Lang	Herbert	87
•	Emma	84

Figure 5: Two micro-remembrances for *Calendera*.

Locale

Locale explores how systems might incorporate contextual information into a person's digital records. It is a map-based system that combines information about where a person has been with information captured from his or her own records and from external, publicly available sources such as Twitter and Facebook. *Locale* (Fig. 6) displays a map on which particular locations have been highlighted. If a location is clicked, it displays information about that location, the user's history at that location and, in some cases, external information about that place.

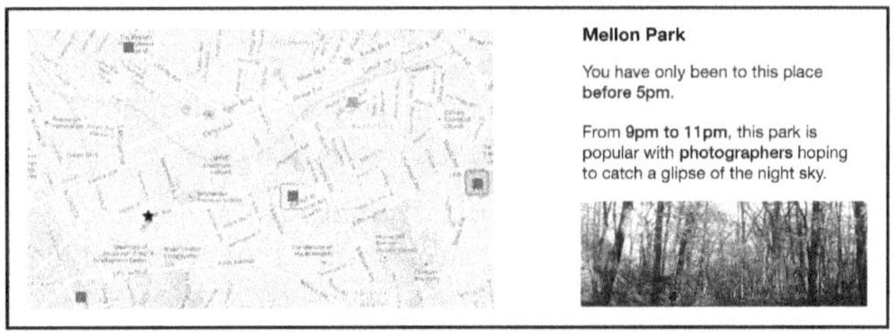

Figure 6: Location information and context in *Locale*.

Participants were asked to imagine that this map, the locations on it, and the information presented to accompany those locations, reflected their own experiences. Given that scenario, we provided them with time to explore the map and each of the pieces of information embedded therein.

Though *Locale* displays location data, it was not created to explore location-based records and reminiscence. These topics have been explored by prior work [24, 41]. Instead, the goal was to explore how information contributed by a user, and also autonomously by digital systems, might be used to identify meaningful places, events, and experiences from one's past. In addition, we wanted to investigate how people felt about systems acting on their behalf to provide additional context to their experiences and records.

Gather

Gather was developed to investigate how people react to systems creating new representations of their memories and experiences. This system combines heterogeneous information in the form of an assemblage to tell a story about a time in one's life. Assemblages are curated from data captured from a variety of sources tied to the user about whom the assemblages are created.

We asked participants to explore an assemblage generated for a trip to Chicago. As seen in Figure 7, the system utilized a number of different types of information for this assemblage including travel records, photographs taken on the trip, credit card expenditures, and location information captured from social network posts. When describing this system to participants, we indicated that the system would do this autonomously, running in the background and revealing these assemblages as it finds, curates, and generates them. Unlike the other systems, *Gather* allows users to add notes to the system-generated representations.

Figure 7: An assemblage from *Gather*.

Building on existing work that explores how digital information and collage can be used for storytelling [12, 48], the goal of *Gather* was to probe participants to think about the potential existence of systems that could autonomously generate new representations of one's experiences. This system was designed to investigate how participants felt about systems generating a representation that might differ from their recollection, or present a new perspective on an event from their past.

PARTICIPANTS

We recruited twelve participants (6 female and 6 male) from Pittsburgh, Pennsylvania. Participants were recruited using reddit.com, craigslist.com, and a local neighborhood email list. The participants in our study ranged in age from 21 to 85, with an average age of 42 and a standard deviation of 22. Participants held a wide range of occupations: activist, artist, caregiver, graduate student, writer, legal assistant, analyst, and retiree. They had varying levels of technical proficiency; experience levels ranged from people who primarily use the computer for email to people who are highly engaged with digital systems.

DATA ANALYSIS

Study sessions were captured using a voice recorder and were transcribed by the researchers. Those transcripts were then coded using an iterative, open-coding scheme. When completed, the coding scheme contained 63 codes distributed across seven broader categories.

FINDINGS

Our findings offer unique points of reflection on the design dimensions and on the broader themes embodied in the systems themselves: how systems might be employed to make sense of large, diverse collections of digital information and how people feel about digital systems interpreting and making judgments about that information. In what follows, we outline four themes that emerged from our findings: 1) the influence of digital systems on the process of remembering one's life; 2) perceptions of how systems will act as mediators of personal information across time and generations; 3) the ways in which personalization systems act as a lens through which people can better understand how and when digital systems capture information about them; and 4) the role that metadata might play in helping people engage with the deliberate and automatic accumulation of digital information.

Memory and Recollection

A focal point of discussions with participants centered on an issue of user and system agency: how a person remembers aspects of their life and how those experiences might be interpreted and represented by digital systems. Highlighting their own agency with regards to their interactions with digital systems, several conversations reflected a sense that while systems have control over the process by which information is collected and curated, the data collected by those systems is the product of a person's decision to engage with digital services like email and social networks. Many of the participants remarked that they expected that systems would soon be able to make more sophisticated judgments with their digital information, based in part on their experiences with existing personalization systems, such as those embedded into Netflix and Amazon.

Nearly all of the participants acknowledged that systems might someday be able to create meaningful representations of their experiences. Though they stated that a system's interpretation of their experiences might differ from their own, they felt that the system representation nevertheless had value. In supporting that idea, several people pointed to the variable nature of human memory and suggested that the information held by systems may be tied to a different reflection of the ground truth of a person's experiences. Reflecting on how *Gather* might be able to support the process of looking back at one's experiences, P9 said, "*Well memory is very, you know, variable and changeable. I think sometimes you remember things one way and that's not the, it's not like you're trying to be weird or whatever you just forget that that's what happened.*" Another participant, P5 added to this idea by emphasizing that systems may be able to draw from a wider view of one's experiences that are not based in their immediate context: "*And at a certain time, I don't think we have enough sense of our own history to, I don't think we have a sense that we are living in history enough to make decisions about what's important.*"

This is in line with previous work that suggests that given the scale of the archives we generate, system-selected content has the possibility of being just as meaningful as that which we select ourselves [37]. This finding potentially extends that idea to that of system-generated curation and meaning making, and encourages the consideration of how systems might work with people to engage in meaning making with diverse collections of data. Given this finding, we can begin to consider how to develop systems that frame this process in a way that provides users with the ability to participate in the authoring or safekeeping of these representations. Additionally, this finding points to the potential limitations of the idea that a well-designed system must feature an alignment of a user's mental model and the designer's mental model as embodied through the system as it is presented to users [29]. Instead, we can rework that idea to account for adaptive, analytical systems like these, that are being understood and utilized by users in a way that is productive but that may differ from the designer's goal.

This finding about memory and recollection also introduces broader questions related to how people's perceptions of the validity and value of system representations of their experiences may shift if digital, centrally held records become one of the primary ways in which people's lives are remembered. That is, if one's legacy is based in digital records, does that change how they view differences between what they remember and how their experiences are represented by a digital system? P4, drawing from his understanding of human memory as he used *MailMem* said: "*It's insulting. 'Cause most of the time, I forget the things I want to forget on purpose and I remember the things the way I want to remember them...*" Indeed, the mechanisms by which people forget and remember play a valuable role in how they create a life narrative and craft a legacy.

Systems as Multigenerational Mediators

Interacting with systems that integrated multigenerational records and delayed reflection into everyday systems, like *Calendera and Gather,* allowed participants to reflect on the use of systems to transfer content across generations. There was a great deal of divergence on this topic, stemming in part from the complex nature of people's relationships with their family. As such, this finding highlights how the topic and context of one's memories and experiences may impact the ability for systems to help people engage with those parts of a person's life in a way that is meaningful to them. In addition, this finding points to a number of ways in which time changes how people perceive the value of digital media and information.

Seven of our participants felt as though there was value in a system that could capture and make use of multigenerational information. P1, one of our older participants, described how a digital system might be able to address an issue present in her life – the desire to pass things down to her children and grandchildren at a time when those things would have meaning to them: "*[There] is a time in many people's lives when you've got so many other things going on, information that I give my grandchildren today is not something that is going to be very compelling to them at this point in their lives. But they'll probably say 'oh I wish I [remembered] that.' So if there is [a] way of retaining that over a period of time without having stacks of paper that they might not even be able to access."* In this way, systems can support, and perhaps enrich, the process of crafting a legacy by leveraging their inherent ability to archive information.

P6, reflecting on *Calendera*, described these concerns from the perspective of the receiver of an older family member's records: "*There are times I am rather upset of myself for not taking advantage of what was available, i.e. my grandfather. My mom's dad came from Poland. I should've sat down with that man some time and said, 'Grandpa, tell me about Poland. Tell me what you did'. But because the age where you are, on a timeline, I go to school, I go out with friends, at that age was appropriate, as opposed to stop, and talk to my grandfather."* These comments show that these types of systems may influence the perception of the value of records and how they are utilized and understood across one's life.

Six of our participants noted that there is some inherent strangeness associated with utilizing digital systems to communicate information between loved ones. Several of our participants felt uncomfortable with the idea that any system would engage in unsolicited curation of information related to their family life. P5, projecting into the future, described his reservations: "*I guess I would want to tell my kid [things] that I would want them to know. I wouldn't want the computer to like slurp something out of my email, you know. But I would want to say – 'Oh, hey, this was something important...' I want to share that, I want to make sure it's this family lore that exists, but I would want to consent to that*." These issues are interesting when they are considered in the broader context of how systems are already being integrated into existing practices around reflection, remembrance, and legacy making. Extending those ideas, this finding inspires speculation into how people might react to the need for more sophisticated means of passing down information as a part of a personal legacy.

Systems as Mirrors

Conversations with participants revealed that existing commercial personalization systems provide an opportunity for people to consider what information is being collected and how it is being used. Several of our participants described having observed content that they believed had been personalized based on information collected by about them, though it is not clear that all of the examples were indeed cases in which content was being personalized as the mechanisms behind that process can be difficult to uncover.

More strikingly, these personalizations also prompted the participants to consider the nuances of their lives that were not being captured or correctly interpreted by digital systems and the role that their own agency played in this process. Describing this experience, P9 said *"I'm pretty complex in my interests and what I like and I'm sure I could be pigeonholed to some degree but there's a part of me that's like, 'so, guess what, I happen to like Ella Fitzgerald from the 50s and this music from the 90s, and I also just downloaded Lana Del Ray'. What are you going to do with that?"* The point here is not that there are deficiencies in how personalization systems operate. Instead, we are interested in how users are interpreting the often opaque information presented by systems as part of a process of defining and exploring their own identity. This speculation about personalized content may also be a way of establishing a greater sense of agency as people understand the implications of increased tracking online.

Trying to contextualize the information about oneself that is interpreted by digital systems also calls forth a question about how systems might make use of sensitive information. While interacting with the systems, six of our participants raised concerns about the ways in which systems that leverage the data and metadata they contain could negatively impact their personal wellbeing and their relationships with other people. For example, P8 described her concerns: *"I don't want other people to know about my family. Like my dad is a racist... I don't want computer programs to analyze that because I already know that."* Given her strained relationship with her family, she was concerned that she might be exposed to information that would be difficult or hurtful. In addition, she was leery that a system could misrepresent the degree to which certain information and people are connected to her life. Clearly, the topic of the information being presented made a significant impact on its significance to the user.

P4 described a similar concern, in which the system exposes aspects of life that do not support the process of moving forward from difficult circumstances. "*Plus, say you have a bad life. Bad things happen to you, no one cares what happens to you... if you're reminded about the things that happen all the time, it can, it's always thrown in your face, it can be upsetting."* These concerns illustrate the potential implications of systems making judgments about people's experiences. That is, as we build systems designed to make sense of large collections of information, it is important to consider how the representations produced by systems may influence personal wellbeing and the ways in which people define their identities.

Metadata as a Gateway

Reflecting on the use of metadata as a design material, our findings also highlight how we might build systems that use metadata to help people make sense of large collections of heterogeneous data collected over the course of one's life. When reflecting on the systems in the study, participants expressed divergent perceptions of what types of data were meaningful to them and what they speculated might have value to future generations. What was meaningless to one person could be a source of great inspiration and recollection for another. For example, P2 questioned the value of location information: *"To keep track of the different places you've been. And what you did there. I'm not too sure how useful this kind of information would be,"* while others described ways in which they might benefit from looking back on where they'd been, especially as they transition to a different part of their life.

This finding challenges existing notions about how people might manage large-scale digital information. Although users may have a preference for systems that don't combine heterogeneous information [23], these types of systems may be an entry point for users to think about what information holds value to them and could also function as a starting point for discussions with family members about how best to treat digital records in the context of one's legacy. In addition, this finding illustrates the potential for metadata and personalization systems to help people curate records in a way that is personally meaningful.

Participants also described more advanced ideas about how systems that leverage data and metadata might help them engage with the mechanisms by which systems and people might work together. P5, talking about his perceptions of what role systems should play in creating reflective experiences said: *"To what extent does a computer have a responsibility to tell me about my past?"* As it stands, most people do not feel as though they have a great deal of involvement in the process by which systems collect information about them. However, it is clear that people are curious about the processes by which this happens and increasing the transparency and user agency built into those systems may facilitate better human-system interaction.

DISCUSSION

These findings highlight a number of issues regarding the ways in which digital systems are becoming a part of how people generate, organize, and revisit digital information. In this section, we discuss these implications, and reflect on the design and use of the four provocative systems.

One of the salient threads in this work is the way in which the increased capabilities of digital systems to capture and interpret information have created a situation in which both the system and the user can exercise agency over how digital data is utilized. Indeed, as systems begin to take on the role of curator or steward, people are shifted to a role in which they are responsible for a different collection of tasks – interpreting the ways in which the information is represented by systems, carrying out the wishes of those who have passed away, and deciding how the system interpretation is to be integrated into one's cultural and familial practices related to death, dying, and remembrance.

This focus on agency is also tied to concerns about the potential for a system to negatively impact the people whose information it captures and the future generations of people who reflect on that information. To a system, information does not have an inherent connection to the human values that shape how it will be understood by its recipients. But when we consider the breadth of information that is collected over the course of one's life, it is impossible to separate that information from the story it tells about that person. There is, therefore, a clear need for mechanisms and practices that can mediate the process of understanding and integrating these stories into the evolving remembrance of a person who has passed away.

Furthermore, it is important to consider how an increased ability for systems to curate and derive judgments from digital information raises concerns about the privacy of the information being used by the systems and the intentions of the original owner of that information. Even if this type of technology were to stay at its current level of sophistication, it would be difficult to articulate how a person's information should be used once they have passed away and to convey that responsibility and expectation to future generations that are increasingly removed from the original owner of that content. Of course, this technology will continue to advance, raising a host of questions about how people can make decisions about what future generations will do with the information people leave behind.

The systems used in this study played an integral role in helping participants conceptualize potential future capabilities of digital systems and to provide context about scenarios that will not be possible for many years. However, it seems important to note that, in this work, the strength of this method was a result of using those systems in conjunction with a flexible protocol that allowed for the participants and the researchers to imagine what the future of this technology might look like and how those ideas might impact our own notions of family and history.

DESIGN OPPORTUNITIES

Below, we discuss design opportunities that are derived from the findings of this work and a broader consideration of the implications of those ideas, ordered along a spectrum from near-term opportunities for system development to farther reaching ideas for future investigation.

Exposing System Interpretations

Prior work [2, 27] has suggested that we might reintroduce aspects of human memory and forgetting into the creation of digital systems in order to shift thinking about how information is used and reflected upon. On a practical level, outside of specific systems (like Snapchat), this is a provocative idea that might be difficult to encourage because it represents a direct challenge to a common understanding of how computers are supposed to work. As we examine the role that forgetting may play in digital systems, it is worthwhile to consider an intermediate step: providing people with information about how their actions are being interpreted by systems with the goal of fostering more productive relationships with digital systems. In addition, there may be a complementary opportunity for systems to learn from how people respond to system interpretations of their information.

Using Time as a Contextual Variable

An opportunity exists to build systems that help situate digital information in a time in a person's life when it would be most evocative, meaningful, or relevant. Participants discussed how time impacts the meaning, representation, and interpretation of digital information. This phenomenon extends well beyond digital data and artifacts, but is particularly interesting in the digital world given the possibility of automating the process of stewarding and passing on digital content. For example, one can imagine an application that allows people to set aside content that will later be unlocked once the recipient or inheritor has reached some milestone or part of their life. Though this form of information management would impact the way in which its owner understands that information, it offers both the curator and the receiver an opportunity to reflect on that process.

Closing the Gap in Multigenerational Records

An opportunity exists to expose meaningful threads present in collections of digital content. Participants consistently expressed interest in passing on records to future generations and in reflecting on records from those who have passed away. However, this presents a number of challenges related to helping people make use of content, such as that which you might inherit, some of which might not be directly relevant to one's life. That is, can we leverage existing or future technologies to make sense of and draw out themes from familial archives? This work might include the creation of a system that identifies particular shared experiences across different members of one's family, like battling with depression or taking trips across the country. In the absence of technology that can automatically identify and reveal these shared life experiences, there is an opportunity to help people assemble shared representations of their experiences or craft personalized recollections of their own experiences.

LIMITATIONS

A limitation of this work is that we had a small sample size of participants, derived entirely from people living in the United States. Talking with twelve people makes it difficult to identify the extent to which group differences are representative of larger trends. In addition, although several of our participants were citizens of other countries, we did not explicitly explore how western values may have shaped the information captured through our interviews and provocative systems. In both cases, these limitations expose rich areas for future work: (a) understanding how stage of life and other aspects of one's life influences legacy making with digital data and (b) exploring how cultural differences around technology use and remembrance may intersect to augment existing practices.

CONCLUSION

This paper draws from prior research from personalization, memory, and information management to create four interactive, provocative systems that were used to understand people's perceptions regarding access to and management of personal and familial digital information. We found that these systems can have an influence on the process of curating a legacy and deriving meaning from digital records, and that, employed in the right contexts, they are viewed as beneficial in managing information across time and generations. Our future work will explore how digital information and systems might be designed to support these important life processes.

ACKNOWLEDGMENTS

We would like to thank Will Odom, John Zimmerman, Queenie Kravitz, Steven Dow, Joy Chen, Alyson Youngblood, and all of our friends and colleagues at the HCII and the School of Design. Also, thank you to the reviewers who provided pivotal feedback for this work and to the participants who contributed to this work. This work was funded by an NSF grant - #0750271 - and by the HCII.

REFERENCES

1. Awad, N.F. & Krishnan, M.S. (2006). The personalization privacy paradox: An empirical evaluation of information transparency and the willingness to be profiled online for personalization. *MIS Quarterly 30*(1), 13 – 28.
2. Bannon, L.J. (2006). Forgetting as a feature, not a bug: the duality of memory and implications for ubiquitous computing. *CoDesign 2*(1), 3 – 15.
3. Bartlett, F.C. (1935). Remembering. *Scientia.*
4. Belk, R. (2013). Extended self in a digital world. *Journal of Consumer Research (40)*3, 477 – 500.
5. Bergman, O., Beyth-Marom, R., & Nachmias, R. (2008). The user-subjective approach to personal information management systems design: Evidence and implementations. *JASIST 59*(2), 235 – 246.
6. Bruner, J. (2004). Life as narrative. *Social Research 71*(3), 691 – 710.
7. Christen, K. (2009). Ara Irititja: Protecting the past, accessing the future – Indigenous memories in a digital age. *Museum Anthropology 29*(1), 56 – 60.
8. Cosley, D., Sosik, S.S., Schultz, J., Peesapati, S.T., & Lee, S. (2012). Experiences with designing tools for everyday reminiscing. *HCI 27,* 175 – 198.
9. Djick, J. (2008). Digital photography: Communication, identity, memory. *Visual Communication 7*, 57 – 78.
10. Dourish, P., Edwards, W.K., LaMarca, A., Lamping, J., Peterson, K., Salisbury, M., Terry, D.B., & Thorton, J. (2000). Extending document management systems with user-specific properties. *ACM Transactions on Information Systems 18*(2), 140 – 170.
11. Friedman, B., & Nathan, L.P. (2010). Multi-lifespan information system design: A research initiative for the HCI community. *CHI,* 2243 – 2246.
12. Frohlich, D.M., Rachovides, D., Riga, K, Bhat, R. & Frank, M. (2009). StoryBank: Mobile digital storytelling in a development context. *CHI,* 1761 – 1770.
13. Greenberg, J. (2003). Metadata generation: Processes, people, and tools. *Bulletin for the American Society of IST, 29*(2).
14. Gulotta, R., Odom, W., Faste, H., & Forlizzi, J. (2014). Legacy in the age of the internet: How digital systems influence how we are remembered. *DIS,* 975 –984.

15. Gulotta, R., Odom, W., Faste, H., & Forlizzi, J. (2013). Digital artifacts as legacy: Exploring the lifespan and value of digital data. *CHI,* 1813 – 1822.
16. Hangal, S., Lam, M.S., & Heer, J. (2011). MUSE: Reviving memories using email archives. *UIST, 75 – 84.*
17. Hoven, E. van den & Eggen, B. (2003). The design of a recollection supporting device: A study into triggering personal recollections. *HCI International*, 1034 – 1038.
18. Hutchinson, H., Bederson, B.B., Druin, A., Plaisant, C., Mackay, W., Evans, H., ...Westerlund, B. (2003). Technology probes: Inspiring design for and with families. *CHI,* 17 – 24.
19. Jones, W. (2004). Finders, keepers? The present and future perfect in support of personal information management. *First Monday, (9)*3.
20. Kaye, J., Vertesi, J., Avery, S., Dafoe, A., David, S., Onaga, L., Rosero, I., & Pinch, T. (2006). To have and to hold: Exploring the personal archive. *CHI,* 275 – 284.
21. Kirk, D.S. & Sellen, A. (2010). On human remains: Values and practices in the home archiving of cherished objects. *TOCHI, 17*(3).
22. Li, I., Dey, A., & Forlizzi, J. (2011). Understanding my data, myself: Supporting self-reflection with ubicomp technologies. *UbiComp,* 405 – 414.
23. Lindley, S., Marshall, C.C., Banks, R., Sellen, A., & Regan, T. (2013). Rethinking the web as a personal archive. *WWW,* 749 – 760.
24. Lindqvist, J., Cranshaw, J., Wiese, J., Hong, J. & Zimmerman, J. (2011). I'm the mayor of my house: Examining why people use foursquare – a social-driven location sharing application. *CHI,* 2409 – 2418.
25. Marshall, C.C., Bly, S., & Brun-Cottan, F. (2006). The long term fate of our digital belongings: Toward a service model for personal archives. *Archiving Conference,* 25 – 30.
26. Massimi, M. (2010). Thanatosensitively designed technologies for bereavement support. *CHI,* 2951 – 2954.
27. Mayer-Schonberger, V. (2011). Delete: The Virtue of Forgetting in the Digital Age. *Princeton University Press.*
28. McAdams, D.P. (2001). The psychology of life stories. *Review of General Psychology* 5(2), 100 – 122.
29. Norman, D. (2002). The Design of Everyday Things. *New York: Basic Books.*
30. O'Hara, K., Tuffield, M.M., & Shadbolt, N. (2009). Lifelogging: Privacy and empowerment with memories for life. *Identity in Information Society.*
31. Odom, W., Banks, R., Durrant, A., Kirk, D., & Pierce, J. (2012). Slow technology: Critical reflection and future directions. *DIS,* 816 – 817.
32. Odom. W., Pierce, J., Stolterman, E., & Blevis, E. (2009). Understanding why we preserve some things and discard others in the context of interaction design. *CHI,* 1053 – 1062.
33. Odom, W., Zimmerman, J. Davidoff, S., Forlizzi, J., Dey, A.K., & Lee, M.K. (2012). A fieldwork of the future with user enactments. *DIS,* 338 – 347.
34. Petrelli, D. & Whittaker, S. (2009). Family memories in the home: Contrasting physical and digital mementos. *UbiComp,* 153 –169.
35. Sas, C. & Dix, A. (2009). Designing for reflection on experience. *CHI EA,* 4741 – 4744.
36. Schacter, D.L. (2003). The seven sins of memory: How the mind forgets and remembers. *Mariner Books.*
37. Sellen, A., Fogg, A., Aitken, M., Hodges, S., Rother, C., & Wood, K. (2007). Do life-logging technologies support memory for the past? *CHI,* 81 – 90.
38. Sellen, A. & Whittaker, S. (2010). Beyond total capture: A constructive critique of lifelogging. *TOCHI,* 70 – 77.
39. Sengers, P., Boehner, K., David, S., & Kaye, J. (2005). Reflective design. *Proceedings of the 4th Decennial Conference on Critical Computing.*
40. Sinha, R. & Swearingen, K. (2002). The role of transparency in recommender systems. *CHI,* 830 – 831.
41. Sra, M & Schmandt, C. (2013). Spotz: A location-based approach to self-awareness. *Persuasive,* 216 – 221.
42. Toch, E., Wang, Y., & Cranor, L.F. (2012). Personalization and privacy: a survey of privacy risks and remedies in personalization-based systems. *User Modeling and User-Adapted Interaction*, 203 – 220.
43. Turow, J., King, J., Hoofnagle, C.J., Bleakley, A., & Hennessy, M. (2009). Americans reject tailored advertising and three activities that enable it. *Technical Report, Annenberg School for Communication.*
44. Unruh, D.R. (1983). Death and personal history: Strategies of identity preservations. *Social Problems 30*(3), 340 – 351.
45. Viegas, F.B., boyd, d., Nguyen, D.H., Potter, J., & Donath, J. (2004). Digital artifacts for remembering and storytelling: Posthistory and social network fragments. *Hawaii International Conference on System Sciences.*
46. Whittaker, S., Bergman, O., & Clough, P. (2010). Easy on that trigger dad: a study of long term family photo retrieval. *UbiComp,* 31 – 43.
47. Whittaker, S., Kalnikaite, V., Petrelli, D., Sellen, A., Villar, N., Bergman, O., Clough, P., & Brockmeier, J. (2012). Socio-technical lifelogging: Deriving design principles for a future proof digital past. *HCI, 27*(1-2).
48. Xiao, J, Zhang, X., Cheatle, P., Gao, Y., & Atkins, B. (2008). Mixed-initiative photo collage authoring. *Multimedia,* 509 – 518.

Improving Multilingual Collaboration by Displaying How Non-native Speakers Use Automated Transcripts and Bilingual Dictionaries

Ge Gao[1,2], Naomi Yamashita[1], Ari Hautasaari[1], Susan R. Fussell[2]

[1]NTT Communication Science Labs
2-4 Hikaridai, Seika-cho, Soraku-gun,
Kyoto, Japan
naomiy@acm.org,
ari.hautasaari@lab.ntt.co.jp

[2]Department of Communication
Cornell University
Ithaca NY 14850 USA
[gg365, sfussell] @cornell.edu

ABSTRACT
Conversational grounding, or establishing mutual knowledge that messages have been understood as intended, can be difficult to achieve when some conversational participants are using a non-native language. These difficulties in grounding can be challenging for native speakers to detect. In this paper, we examine the value of signaling potential grounding problems to native speakers (NS) by displaying how non-native speakers (NNS) use automated transcripts and bilingual dictionaries. We conducted a laboratory experiment in which NS and NNS of English collaborated via audio conferencing on a map navigation task. Triads of one NS guider, one NS follower, and one NNS follower performed the task using one of three awareness displays: (a) a no awareness display that showed only the automated transcripts, (b) a general awareness display that showed whether each follower was reading the automated transcripts and/or translating a word; or (c) a detailed awareness display that showed which line of the transcripts a follower was reading and/or which words he/she was translating. NS guiders and NNS followers collaborated most successfully with the detailed awareness display, while NS guiders and NS followers performed equally across conditions. Our findings suggest several ways to improve systems to support multilingual collaboration.

Author Keywords
Awareness Display; Collaboration; Multilingual; Automated Speech Recognition (ASR); Translation.

ACM Classification Keywords
H.5.m. Information interfaces and presentation (e.g., HCI): Miscellaneous.

CHI 2015, April 18 - 23 2015, Seoul, Republic of Korea

ACM 978-1-4503-3145-6/15/04...$15.00.
http://dx.doi.org/10.1145/2702123.2702498

INTRODUCTION
Globalization makes collaboration in modern organizations increasingly multinational and virtual [16]. As people with different national backgrounds and geographical locations work together, a multilingual context arises in which collaborators speak "a cocktail of languages [18]".

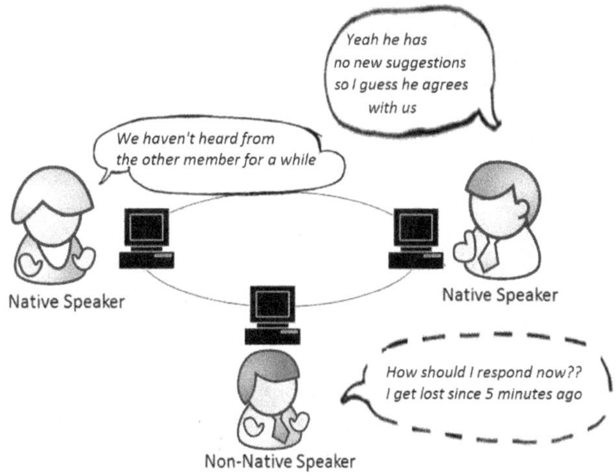

Figure 1. Grounding is hard to achieve during multilingual communication: Non-native speakers sometimes cannot express the problem they encountered, and native speakers may not realize anything is wrong.

In most multilingual collaborations, people use a common language, such as English [12]. Due to differences in fluency, multilingual teams may encounter communication problems that rarely happen within monolingual teams [21][25][27]. For example, non-native speakers (NNS) of English may need extra time to process information and generate speech, but there are few cues for the native speakers (NS) about the reason for the delay [21]. As a result, a NS may wrongly conclude that more information is required or fail to provide the information necessary to make the message clear. Such problems can be especially severe during multiparty audio conferencing due to the lack of visual cues [14][32]. NNS report that audio conversations are hard to follow when many people are

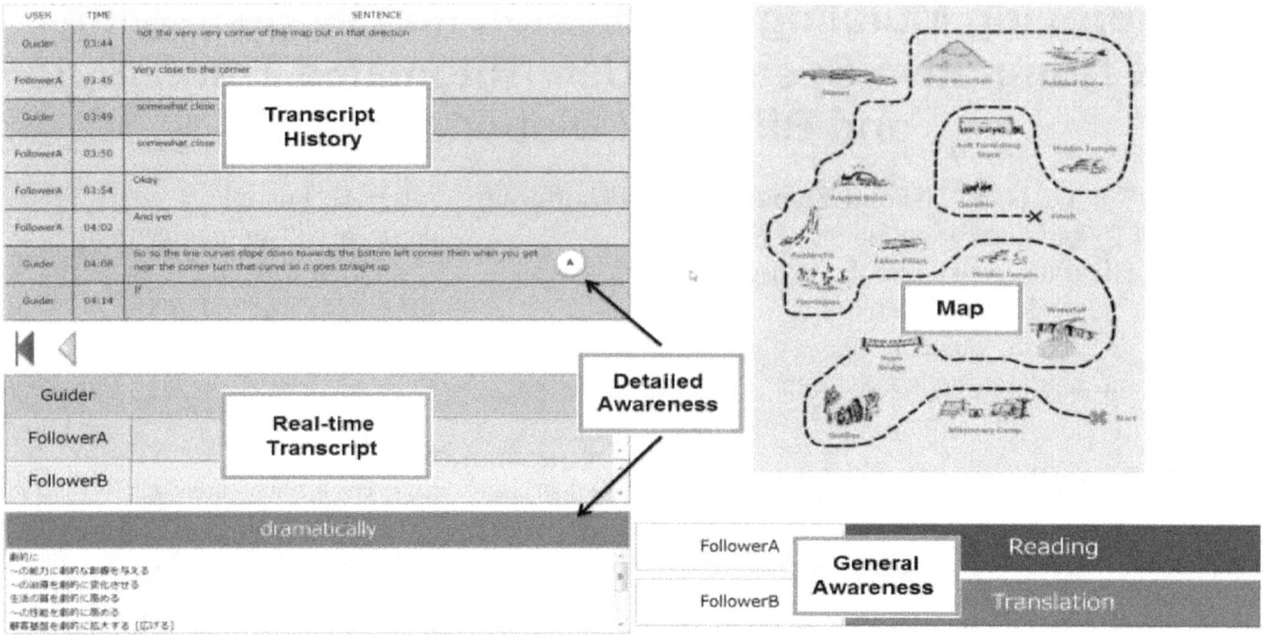

Figure 2. The task interface for NS guider in the detailed awareness display condition. The *general awareness display* (bottom right) signaling whether each follower was reading the automated transcripts and/or translating a word was available to NS guiders in both detailed and general awareness conditions; the *detailed awareness display* showing which line of the transcripts a follower was reading and/or which words he/she was translating was available only in the detailed awareness condition. Followers' interfaces showed the map without the prescribed route, the transcript history and the real-time transcript.

talking, but NSs may have little awareness of NNS's difficulties in understanding [32].

To address these problems, tools such as automated speech recognition (ASR) and translation have been adopted to support multilingual collaboration [14][19][29][32]. This line of work shows the potential of automated transcripts and translation in helping NNS follow group conversations, but overlooks the fact that collaboration is by nature a "joint activity" [7]. Previous work indicates that NS are motivated to make their utterances clearer for NNS addressees [3][14], but little research has been done to help NS assess how well their messages have been understood by NNS partners.

In this paper, we propose a low cost, automated way to signal potential grounding problems in multilingual conversations: providing awareness as to potential points of confusion. Previous studies [14][19][29][32] have shown that when NNS cannot easily express the problems they are experiencing, they try to solve them by checking automated transcripts and/or bilingual dictionaries. These simple behaviors can provide fellow team members with useful cues about points of confusion.

We test this idea in a laboratory study in which triads of two NS and one NNS performed a map navigation task via audio conferencing. The map guiders (all NS of English) were given one of three awareness displays: (a) a *no awareness display* in which the automated transcripts were present but there were no cues about what followers were doing with them; (b) a *general awareness display* that showed whether a follower was looking at the automated transcripts or using the bilingual dictionary; and (c) a *detailed awareness display* that showed where a follower was looking in the transcripts and/or what word he or she was looking up in the bilingual dictionary. We predicted that the more detailed display would facilitate grounding between the NS guider and the NNS follower but would have no effect on grounding between the NS guider and the NS follower.

As predicted, grounding with NNS followers was better when NS guiders had a detailed awareness display. Type of display had no effect on grounding with the NS follower. Guiders with the detailed awareness display were more sensitive to problems encountered by NNS followers, they adjusted their speech to address these problems, and task performance was significantly better than with the other two types of displays. The results add to our understanding of remote multilingual collaboration and suggest new tools to support these collaborations.

RELATED WORK AND HYPOTHESES

In this section, we first review literature on problems of grounding during multilingual collaboration. We then describe how techniques from the literature on awareness displays might be adapted to the context of multilingual communication. We describe how displaying two specific behaviors of followers – use of automated transcripts and looking up words in a bilingual dictionary – might be useful to display to NS guiders and outline our hypotheses.

Problems of Grounding in Multilingual Collaborations

Grounding, or establishing that a message has been understood as intended, is important for successful interpersonal communication [7]. Whether or not a message has been properly grounded is often detected on the basis of cues or evidence received from conversational partners [8]. Partners provide both positive evidence that grounding has occurred (e.g., related next turns, back-channel responses such as "uh huh", or nodding) and negative evidence suggesting grounding has not occurred (e.g., questions or requests for confirmation). When a listener provides little positive or negative evidence of grounding, speakers may have difficulty assessing whether common ground has been established [7].

Differences in fluency may create challenges for the grounding process. For example, research has shown that NNS give fewer responses because of the heavy cognition load of processing a second language [27][28]. In multiparty conversation in particular, NNS may have serious difficulties following others' speech while simultaneously generating their own messages [32]. Further, studies of turn-taking in multilingual groups show that NNS tend to avoid interrupting talk between NSs [25]. Finally, NNS may provide confusing feedback to NS, because they use discourse markers and/or gestures in different ways. For example, NNS use back-channel responses and nodding to express acknowledgement much less often than do NS [13][21][31].

Using Awareness Display to Support Grounding

Much HCI and CSCW research has examined the usefulness of awareness displays for communication and collaboration. This work has shown that awareness of others' activities facilitates a wide range of tasks, including remote assistance (e.g., [2][15][20]), collaborative writing (e.g., [4][11]), collaborative software development (e.g., [5]), collaborative gaming (e.g., [6][24]), and other types of teamwork (e.g., [9][23]). For example, Gergle and colleagues [15] showed that when instruction-givers in a collaborative puzzle task were given a display showing the actions the instruction-follower was taking, they were able to use this awareness information to ground their messages more effectively. They could tell when instructions were misunderstood (i.e., the follower had selected the wrong piece or placed it in the wrong location) or not understood at all (i.e., the follower had not selected a piece) and craft a message to address the problem.

In the case of multilingual conversations, awareness of the NNS' cognitive processes – as evidenced in his/her use of automated transcripts of spoken speech into text and/or bilingual dictionaries – could facilitate grounding by showing the speaker when and what kinds of clarifications are needed. For example, in our study, we ask triads to perform a map task. One NS serves as the "guider" and provides directions; one NS and one NNS serve as "followers" and try to draw the route on their individual maps. When a follower spends longer than usual reading the transcript, this may provide evidence of confusion. When a follower is using the bilingual dictionary, this can provide evidence that some words have not been understood. In this way, the display provides evidence about comprehension without the need for explicit verbal feedback.

Awareness displays can vary in their specificity, ranging from a general impression of what someone is doing to revealing their specific actions. With automated transcripts, for example, we could show general information that the follower is reading the transcripts or specific information about which line he or she is reading. Similarly, we could show that a follower is using the bilingual dictionary or we could reveal which word he or she is looking up.

There are tradeoffs between general and specific displays along a number of dimensions including privacy, cognitive load, and informativeness. For task coordination, several studies have found that abstract displays are better than specific displays (e.g., [9][24]). At the same time, the work on shared visual spaces [15][20] suggests that detailed information about what a partner is doing facilitates grounding. In our study, we expect that detailed displays will be superior to general displays because they pinpoint the nature of the follower's difficulties in understanding messages. Thus, we hypothesize that:

H1a. NS guiders will be able to ground their messages more effectively with NNS followers when they have a detailed awareness display vs. no awareness display.

H1b. NS guiders will be able to ground their messages more effectively with NNS followers when they have a detailed awareness display vs. a general awareness display.

H1c. NS guiders will be able to ground their messages more effectively with NNS followers when they have a general awareness display vs. no awareness display.

In our task, we examine triads consisting of one NS guider, one NS follower, and one NNS follower. While it seems unlikely that native speakers would need to use the automated transcripts or bilingual dictionary, the presence of the display may nonetheless influence the grounding process. Thus we ask:

RQ1: How does type of awareness display affect conversational grounding between NS guiders and NS followers?

Task Performance

Problems in grounding messages in multilingual teams can lead to problems in collaboration and performance. In Li's [22] study, for example, English NS pairs and Chinese-English pairs used English to finish a medical information exchange task. The NS pairs were more successful than the multilingual pairs at exchanging information, in part because Chinese listeners didn't provide feedback when they did not understand their partners. A number of other studies have found worse task performance in multilingual vs. monolingual teams using a variety of tasks (e.g., [10][26][30]). Thus, by improving the grounding process, we anticipate that awareness displays will improve task performance.

H2a. NNS followers will perform better on the map task when NS guiders have a detailed awareness display vs. no awareness display.

H2b. NNS followers will perform better on the map task when NS guiders have a detailed awareness display vs. a general awareness display.

H2c. NNS followers will perform better on the map task when NS guiders have a general awareness display vs. no awareness display.

In addition, we ask:

RQ2: How does type of awareness display affect NS followers' task performance?

Effects of Awareness Displays on the Guider's Cognitive Load

Both the general and the specific awareness displays add information to the guider's interface that is not present in the no awareness display condition. This might increase the guider's perceived workload because there is more for them to attend to, but it might also reduce workload by making it easier to figure out how to ground messages. Therefore we ask,

RQ3: How does type of awareness display affect NS guiders' self-reported cognitive workload?

METHOD

Overview

We conducted a laboratory experiment in which triads consisting of one NS guider, one NS follower and one NNS follower collaborated on a map task using audio conferencing. We manipulated the type of display provided to the guider using a between-groups design. In the *no awareness display condition*, the NS guider saw the automated transcripts but had no cues about what followers were doing with them. In the *general awareness display condition*, the NS guider saw whether each follower was reading the transcripts and/or translating words. In the *detailed awareness display condition*, the NS guider saw which line each follower was reading in the transcript and/or which English word he or she was translating into Japanese. We measured followers' ratings of the quality of the guiders' instructions, how successfully followers completed the map task, and how much cognitive work load the guiders experienced.

Participants

A total of 57 individuals participated in this study. Of these, 38 (6 female) were monolingual native English speakers who currently live in Japan but grew up in English speaking countries and received education in English. Their mean age was 40.57 years (SD = 10.69).

The rest of the participants (N = 19) were native Japanese speakers (6 female) who grew up in Japan and received education in Japanese. Their mean age was 36.16 years (SD = 9.57). They spoke English as a second language but were not fluent (M = 3.58, SD = .88 on a scale of 1-7).

Participants were randomly assigned to triads consisting of a NS guider, an NS follower, and an NNS follower. Triads were then randomly assigned to display condition (5 no awareness display, 7 general awareness display, 7 detailed awareness display).

Materials

Task. We modified two HCRC map navigation tasks [1] for use in this study. One task was used to introduce participants to the technology; the other was used for the experiment itself. Each HCRC map task consists of a guider map and a follower map. The guider's map shows a prescribed route around a set of landmarks. The original follower's map shows some but not all of the landmarks and has no route on it. We modified the original follower's map to create a second follower map matched in the number and type of differences from the guider map, so that each follower would need to independently ground messages with the guider. The labels of landmarks on one of the follower maps were translated into Japanese by a native Japanese speaker.

Surveys. Participants completed an online pre-experiment questionnaire that collected their demographic information (age, gender, country of birth, native language). This survey also asked participants to rate their English fluency on a 7-point scale (1= not fluent at all, 7= very fluent).

Participants completed a second online questionnaire at the end of the study that was customized to their experimental role. The survey included a manipulation check to confirm which type of awareness display was given to the guider in each group. The follower survey also included four questions asking about the quality of the guider's instructions (e.g., "The guider provided appropriate assistance based on my needs"). Responses were on a 7-point scale (1 = strongly disagree, 7 = strongly agree). The guider survey included four questions adapted from the NASA Task Load Index [17]. Participants rated their mental demand, temporal demand, effort, and frustration during the task on a scale of 1 = low to 7 = high.

Interview. We developed an open-ended interview protocol for NS guiders. We asked them whether they ever adjusted the way they gave instructions based on the follower's response. If they said yes, we followed up with questions about how and why they made these adjustments.

Software and Equipment

Speech recognition tool. Participants' speech was automatically transcribed into text using Dragon Naturally

Speaking (DNS). Participants went through a training session before the study started. The time delay required to generate transcripts was between 1-3 seconds.

Eye tracker. A Gazepoint3 (GP3) Eye Tracker was used to trace followers' eye movements in the automatic transcripts. The accuracy of the GP3 is between 0.5 to 1 degree of visual angle, with a 60 Hz update rate. It can capture 25 cm (horizontal) × 11cm (vertical) of eye movement with ±15 cm range of depth movement. The eye-tracker was positioned on the side of the screen and calibrated for each participant. When a follower was reading the transcript, the information was delivered to the awareness display in less than 0.5 sec.

English-Japanese bilingual dictionary. An electronic bilingual dictionary based on Eijiro Translation was set within the interface for NNS followers, allowing them to translate English to Japanese by clicking on a word in the transcript. The information was delivered to the awareness display with a delay of less than 0.5 sec.

Task interface for the guider. The interface for the guider included 4 main components (Figure 2): the map, the real-time transcript, the transcript history, and the awareness display. The *map* (top right) area showed the landmarks and route that the NS guider had to describe to two followers during the navigation task. The *real-time transcript* (middle left) showed the current utterance being generated by DNS, with a 1-3 second delay. This transcript was replaced by a new transcript as new utterances were spoken. The *transcript history* (top left) showed the full conversation history.

The *awareness display* area (bottom right) varied as a function of awareness display condition. In the *no awareness display* condition, no information about what the follower was reading or translating was shown on the guider's interface. In the *general awareness display* condition, the display showed whether each follower was reading the transcript and/or using the bilingual dictionary. A blue light came on when the eye-tracker recognized that a follower was reading the transcript. A red light came on when the translation module recognized that a follower was translating a word.

In the *detailed awareness display* condition, the display gave further information on how each follower was using transcript (top left) and/or bilingual dictionary (bottom left). Once the eye-tracker recognized that a follower was reading the transcript, the follower's icon showed up on the transcript to indicate which line he/she was reading. Once the translation module on the follower's side recognized that he/she was translating a word, the word showed up in red at the bottom left of the interface.

Task interface for the follower. The interface for the followers included three components: the map with no route information on it, the real-time transcript, and the transcript history. No awareness display was provided to the followers.

Equipment. Participants were seated at Sony Vaio laptops with 1.7 GHz CPU and 4GB memory, equipped with three 27 inch monitors. Participants wore headsets with a microphone to communicate with each other as well as receive instructions from the experimenter.

Procedure

Participants were assigned into triads consisting of a NS guider, an NS follower and an NNS follower. They then went through a 20-minute training session that included speech training for DNS and calibration on the eye tracker.

After the training and calibration, the experimenter introduced the study and explained the task and the interface assigned for their condition (no awareness vs. general awareness vs. detailed awareness). They then completed a 10-minute practice task using one of the HCRC maps to familiarize them with the interface. The NS follower and the NNS follower then collaborated with the same guider at the same time on a second HCRC map task. During the task, they used the same awareness interface they were assigned for the practice task and in the same roles (guider vs. follower).

After completing the map task, participants completed the post task survey and guiders were interviewed about how they coordinated their messages with the needs of the NNS follower. Interviews were transcribed by a native English speaker and imported into NVivo10 for analysis. We then identified interview segments focusing on whether and how guiders tailored their assistance to NNS followers for use in our qualitative analysis.

MEASURES

We collected three types of measures: a manipulation check to ensure guiders were aware of which awareness display they had used, survey items measuring quality of the guider's instructions and cognitive workload, and objective task performance.

Manipulation check. Participants' perception of the type of display they used was assessed by a multiple-choice question asking them to identify all information available on their interface (automated transcripts, automated translation, map, awareness display that shows whether a follower was reading transcripts and/or translating, and awareness display that shows detailed content of what each follower was reading and/or translating).

Quality of guider's instructions. The four questions about the quality of the guider's instructions formed a reliable scale (Cronbach's α = .84) and were averaged to create a measure of each follower's perception of the quality of the guider's instructions.

Route accuracy. We scored the route each follower drew using the system developed by Diamant and colleagues [10].

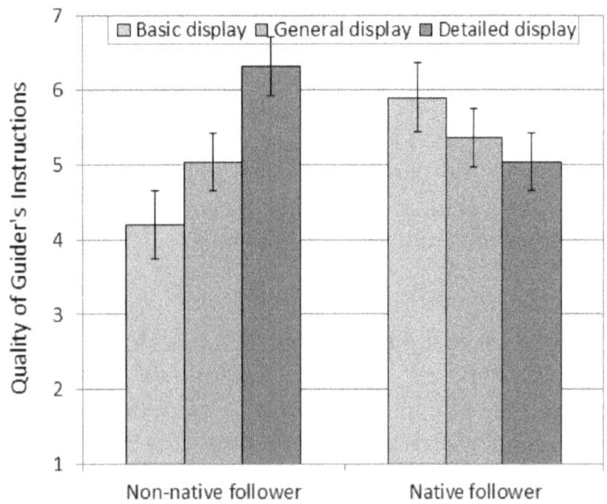

Figure 3. Mean rating of the quality of guider's instructions (on a scale of 1-7) by display type with non-native and native English followers (error bars represent standard errors of the mean)

Each guider-follower dyad earned one point every time they hit the correct landmark in the right order, but got zero points if they hit a wrong landmark or went to the landmark in the wrong order. Route accuracy was calculated as the total score of hitting correct landmarks.

Guider's workload. The four NASA-TLX questions [17] (mental demand, temporal demand, effort, and frustration) formed a reliable scale (Cronbach's α = .83) and were averaged to create a measure of the guider's workload.

RESULTS

To explore our hypotheses and research questions, we conducted a series of ANOVAS as well as qualitative analysis of the interview data. For quantitative measures collected from the followers, we used 3 (type of the awareness display: basic vs. general vs. detailed) × 2 (language background: NNS vs. NS) Mixed Model ANOVAs, nesting participants within groups. For quantitative measures collected from the guiders, we used a One-Way ANOVA to test the effect of display type. Since demographic variables in all models were not significant, we do not discuss them further.

Manipulation Check

Our manipulation check on the perception of display type showed all participants (100%) correctly perceived the type of display guiders used during the task.

Quality of Guider's Instructions

Our first set of hypotheses is about the quality of guiders' instructions. We hypothesized that NS guiders would be able to ground their messages with NNS followers most effectively when using the detailed awareness display (H1a, H1b) and least effectively when using the no awareness display (H1c). As shown in Figure 3, the results were consistent with H1a and H1b but not H1c.

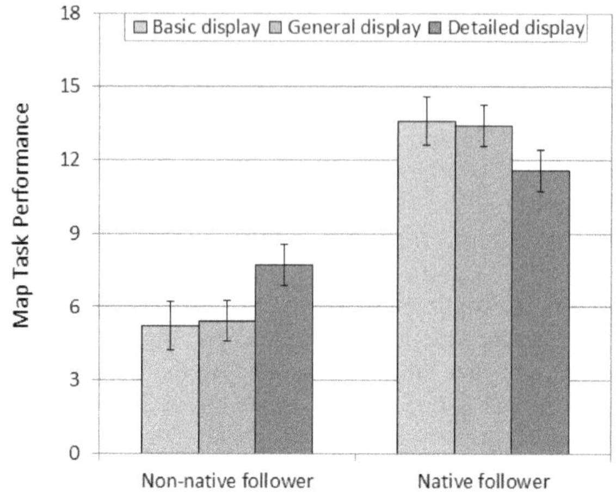

Figure 4. Mean map task performance (on a scale of 0-17) for non-native and native English followers by type of awareness display (error bars represent standard errors of the mean)

An ANOVA of the form outlined above showed a significant interaction effect between display type and follower's language background on the rating of the quality of guiders' instructions ($F [2, 32] = 6.29, p < .01; \omega^2 = 0.23$). The main effects of display type ($p = .47$) and language background ($p = .29$) were not significant.

To test our hypotheses, we ran pairwise comparisons among the three display types separately for NNS followers and NS followers. Consistent with H1a and H1b, NNS followers perceived the guiders' assistance to be better when guiders used the detailed awareness display (M = 6.32, SE = .39) vs. the general awareness display (M = 5.04, SE = .39; $F [1, 32] = 5.48, p < .05$; Cohen's d = 3.28) or the no awareness display (M = 4.20, SE = .46; $F [1, 32] = 12.43, p < .01$; Cohen's d = 5.39). However, contrary to H1c, there was no difference between the general and no awareness display conditions ($F [1, 32] = 1.93, p = .17$).

RQ1 asked about the effects of the guiders' awareness displays on NS followers. NS followers' ratings of the guiders' instructions did not differ significantly between conditions (for the detailed display, M = 5.04, SE = .39; for the general awareness display, M = 5.36, SE = .39; for the no awareness display, M = 5.90, SE = .46). (For detailed vs. no displays, $F [1, 32] = 2.06, p =.16$; for detailed vs. general displays, $F [1, 32] = 0.34, p =.56$; for general vs. no displays, $F [1, 32] = 0.81, p =.37$.)

Map Task Performance

Our second set of hypotheses addressed task performance. We hypothesized that NNS followers would draw the most accurate paths when guiders had a detailed awareness display (H2a, H2b) and the least accurate paths when guiders had no awareness display (H2c). See Figure 4.

An ANOVA of the form outlined above indicated a significant main effect of the follower's native language on map task performance ($F [1, 32] = 86.33, p < .001; \omega^2 =$

0.70). NNS followers hit fewer landmarks correctly (M = 6.11, SE = .51) than did NS followers (M = 12.87, SE = .51). The main effect of display type was not significant (p = .95), but there was a significant interaction between display type and follower's language background (F [2, 32] = 4.22, p < .05; $\omega^2 = 0.15$).

Pairwise comparison between the three display types showed that in support of H2a and H2b, the paths drawn by NNS followers were most accurate when guiders had the detailed awareness display (M = 7.71, SE = .84) vs. the general awareness display (M = 5.43, SE = .84; F [1, 32] = 3.74, p = .06; Cohen's d = 2.71) or the no awareness display (M = 5.20, SE = .99; F [1, 32] = 3.77, p = .06; Cohen's d = 2.73). Contrary to H2c, there was no significant difference between the general and no awareness displays (F [1, 32] = 0.03, p =.86.)

With respect to RQ2, the accuracy of path drawn by NS followers was equally good when guiders had a detailed awareness display (M = 11.57, SE = .84), general awareness display (M = 13.43, SE = .84), or no awareness display (M = 13.60, SE = .99). (For detailed vs. no displays, F [1, 32] = 2.45, p =.13; for detailed vs. general displays, F [1, 32] = 2.47, p =.13; for general vs. no displays, F [1, 32] = 0.02, p =.90.)

Guider's Workload

RQ3 asked how the workload experienced by NS guiders varied as a function of the type of awareness display provided. A one-way ANOVA of display type on self-reported workload showed no significant effect of display type (F [2, 18] = 0.77, p = .48). There were no significant differences between how much workload guiders reported when using the detailed awareness display (M = 4.29, SE = .47), general awareness display (M = 4.31, SE = .47), or no awareness display (M = 3.50, SE =. 56).

Insights from Interviews with Guiders

After they completed the task, we conducted open-ended interviews with each guider to ask whether and how they adjusted the way they gave instructions based on the followers' responses.

NS guiders reported three issues about coordination management: difficulties interpreting NNS' status from audio feedback, adjusting guidance based on NNS followers' use of the transcripts, and adjusting guidance based on NNS followers' use of the bilingual dictionary.

The first theme that ran through the interviews of all NS guiders concerned their problems understanding how to ground their messages based on NNS followers' verbal feedback. Guiders reported that it was hard to determine whether NNS followers understood an instruction because NNS followers were less vocal than NS followers.

There wasn't a lot of input from the non-native follower, so I was not sure if he is following or not. I assumed that he was following. [G13, no awareness display]

In the beginning I first thought that maybe the non-native follower understood very well and that is why she was quiet, but then I realized that is not true. Her map too is different [from mine], even if she didn't speak. [G17, detailed awareness display]

The second point that emerged from the interviews was that guiders adjusted their instructions based on the NNS followers' use of the automated transcripts. Guiders with both awareness displays reported that they modified the way they gave instructions upon seeing that a NNS follower was reading transcripts, but the way that they did so depended on the type of awareness display. For guiders with general awareness displays, seeing that a NNS follower was using the transcripts seemed to initiate a verbal rephrasing of the last steps presented.

If he was reading something on the transcript, he couldn't understand something [from the audio]. I would reconfirm [the path just described] ... So even if he said ok, I made sure that it is ok. [G18, general awareness display]

When I tried to explain what my map looked like, the native speaker responded quickly. The Japanese speaker needed time to process the information, so I wasn't sure if he understood what I said... or not. So rather than asking "do you understand, do you understand?" I would check the status of the [NNS follower's] reading, and also I was saying different words in case the transcript didn't work correctly. Hoping that he could pick it. [G2, general awareness display]

In contrast, with detailed awareness displays, guiders were able to make adjustments to their speech that took into account the specific utterances that the NNS followers found problematic.

When the non-native follower was reading transcript, I was slowing down and clarifying ... [based on] his physical position on the transcript, and if he was behind the native speaker. I think I also probably used more words, for example northwest or top-left, to give [the speech recognition] more choice to transcribe the words [G9, detailed awareness display]

I did try to make use of the reading information, to track, to clarify. [G11, detailed awareness display]

Guiders in both the general and detailed awareness display conditions also reported that they made adjustments to their instructions based on NNS followers' use of the bilingual dictionary. However, the strategies they used differed between display conditions. With the general display, they couldn't pinpoint the exact word that was unclear, but they were sensitive to the possibility that translating would take some time and slowed their speech accordingly:

When the red button is on, I slowed down or used a different word. ... if I say a sentence and notice the red color, I just say again in case there is any difficulty. [G1, general awareness display]

When the non-native speaker was translating ... I would slow down a little bit, because I felt that it was time consuming. [G4, general awareness display]

With the detailed display, guiders identified specific words that were problematic for their NNS followers and tried to use alternative words in their future utterances. In some cases such as G10 below, guiders used the absence of translation as a cue that the NNS follower knew a term.

I check the translation to see what words he had hard time with. Like, I tried not to use "diagonal", because I didn't think he knew that word, he translated it. So I just tried to use other words like "curvy". I didn't know if he knew curvy, but he didn't look it up, so maybe he knew. [G10, detailed awareness display]

First time I saw he couldn't understand "vertical" and from that on I tried to use "vertical" less and use north/south lines instead. So I try to change my vocabulary, although I am sure I still used vertical a few times but I tried to use it less. [G12, detailed awareness display]

Finally, we asked guiders whether they attended to the NS followers' use of transcripts and all reported that they did not because they could communicate successfully with the NS follower through audio communication alone.

DISCUSSION

In this study, we provided participants three types of displays that delivered different amounts of awareness information. Our findings indicate that providing NS guiders with detailed awareness displays best supports the grounding between the guiders and their NNS followers. In the rest of this discussion, we connect our study with previous work on awareness and grounding. Specifically, we consider cues used by NS guiders to support grounding with NNS followers, and trade-offs between general and detailed displays.

Cues Used by NS Guiders to Support Grounding

Both ratings of the guiders' instructions and NNS followers' task performance show that type of awareness display affects conversational grounding between NS guiders and NNS followers. Specifically, a detailed awareness display led to better communication and performance than either a general awareness display or no awareness display.

Our three types of displays intentionally provided different types of cues that could be useful to the grounding process. The no awareness display was similar to regular audio conferencing. The general awareness display offered additional cues of whether the follower was reading transcripts and/or translating words. The detailed display further indicated which line of transcripts the follower was reading and/or which words the follower was translating from the bilingual dictionary.

From the interviews, it is clear that guiders believed that the effectiveness of their instruction improved as the richness of the awareness information increased. NS guiders using the no awareness display reported that they tried to guess the NNS follower's level of understanding based on limited audio feedback. Given that the NNS followers often provided little verbal response, guiders may not have been able to accurately detect when to slow down and/or how clarify their instructions.

The general awareness display showed whether the NNS follower was requesting language-related help from the system, and the guiders believed that this information helped them adjust their instruction. However, as can be seen from the followers' ratings of the guiders' instructions, which showed no significant difference between this display condition and the no display condition, their adjustments probably did not meet the needs of the NNS followers. The interviews provide some suggestions why this might be the case. For example, guiders assumed that if a NNS follower was reading the transcript, he or she was reading the last instruction. But this would not address actual problems in grounding if the NNS followers had fallen behind in the conversation. In future work, we plan to examine the accuracy of speakers' assumptions about the grounding process as a function of different types of awareness cues.

The detailed awareness display provided concrete information that was directly linked to the on-going grounding process. This display serves similar functions as the shared visual space examined by Gergle and colleagues [15]. However, it's worth noting that displaying how NNS followers use transcripts and/or a dictionary may bring extra support compared to a display of shared visual space. In our task, for example, giving the guiders a view of the NNS follower's path on the map might also have helped them identify grounding problems, though a shared view alone is less clear as to which part of the message needs clarification (e.g., which words were misunderstood).

Trade-offs between General and Detailed Displays

Our results suggest that at least for audio conversations between native and non-native English speakers, grounding and performance will be better with detailed awareness displays. This finding is consistent with some previous work, such as that of Gergle and colleagues [15]; but contrasts with other work, such as that of Dabbish and Kraut [9]. It is therefore important to examine the trade-off between using general and detailed awareness displays.

The trade-offs between general and detailed awareness displays revolve around two issues: a) what tasks the display was intended to support and b) the richness of information required to accomplish that task. In both this study and Gergle and colleagues' study [15], the central purpose of collaboration is for an information-giver to convey instructions to an information-receiver and ensure that grounding has occurred. To accomplish such tasks, the information-giver needs cues that are rich enough to infer whether the information-receiver has understood the message, and if not, what kind of grounding problem has occurred. For situations in which grounding is primary, our results suggest detailed awareness displays may be best.

In other settings, the primary goal may be something other than conversational grounding, for example, appropriate timing of interruptions [9]. To accomplish this type of task, it may be more important for the interrupter to know whether the interruptee is busy or not than to know precisely what he or she is doing. Thus, there is little benefit to providing the additional information in a detailed awareness display.

An additional factor to consider is people's privacy preferences. For example, some people may not want others knowing precisely which words they need to look up but be more open them knowing that they are using a dictionary. We plan to explore this issue in our future work.

DESIGN IMPLICATIONS

Our findings suggest several ways that collaboration tools might be enhanced to facilitate the detection, repair, and prevention of grounding problems in multilingual teams.

Displaying NNS's Behaviors for Detecting Grounding Problems

The most direct design implication is that designers of tools to support multilingual collaboration should include detailed awareness displays. Guiders relied on these detailed displays to detect and repair grounding problems, and NNS followers reported that the instructions were better in the detailed display condition than in the general or no awareness display condition. For collaboration systems that have speech recognition and/or bilingual dictionary modules embedded in them already, it should be relatively straightforward to implement detailed awareness displays. For other types of tasks and systems, designers may need to create new mechanisms for detecting and displaying awareness of NNS difficulties in grounding messages.

Helping NS Interpret NNS's Behaviors

Further, the NS guiders' descriptions of how they used the awareness display indicate a design space for facilitating the repair of grounding problems. When the display showed the NNS follower was translating a word, for example, NS guiders reported that they would rephrase the instruction with what they thought was simpler word. However, it might actually be more effective for the NS to keep using the same word, given that NNS already looked up what it meant. In other words, NS's adjustments and NNS's needs may not match.

One way to address this mismatch between the grounding needs of NNS listeners and NS' perceptions of these needs is for the system to help interpret the data collected by awareness tools and generate recommendations to the NS about how to clarify their messages, perhaps on data from the conversation itself or from theories of second language learning. An automated system of this type might also help address possible privacy concerns caused by directly sharing NNS behaviors with their NS partners.

Learning from Different NNS's Behaviors to Prevent Grounding Problems

A related recommendation is for systems to collect general information about potential points of confusion in the grounding process, including specific words or grammatical structures that are difficult for non-native speakers to understand. For example, if a system is used by many different multilingual collaborations, it could collect data on which words are often looked up in the bilingual dictionary and which are not, or which kinds of messages NNS listeners spend a long time looking at in the automated transcripts and which they never look at. Based on this data, system might both provide suggestions to the NS about how to better phrase his or her messages and automatically provide translations to the NNS of words and phrases that are frequently problematic for other NNS.

CONCLUSION

We conducted a laboratory experiment in which NS and NNS of English collaborated via audio conferencing on a map navigation task using one of three awareness displays (no awareness vs. general awareness vs. detailed awareness). We found that NS guiders and NNS followers collaborated most successfully using the detailed awareness display. Specifically, NS guiders grounded their messages with NNS followers most effectively when the detailed awareness display was provided. NNS followers also performed best on the map task with the detailed awareness display. In interviews, NS guiders stated that they modified instructions to make grounding easier based on the cues they received about NNS' problems grounding the messages. Our findings suggest several ways that future collaboration tools might better support multilingual teams.

ACKNOWLEDGMENTS

This research was funded in part by National Science Foundation grant #1318899. We thank Leslie Setlock for editorial assistance and the NTT development team for their technical support.

REFERENCES

1. Anderson, A., Bader, M., Bard, E., et al. (1991). The HCRC Map Task Corpus. *Language and Speech, 34,* 351-366.
2. Bardram, J. E., Hansen, T. R., & Soegaard, M. (2006). AwareMedia- A shared interative display supporting social, temporal, and spatial awareness in surgery. *Proc. of CSCW 2006,* 109-118.

3. Beebe, L.M., & Giles, H. (1984). Speech-accommodation theories: A discussion in terms of second-language acquisition. *International Journal of the Sociology of Language, 46,* 5-32,
4. Birnholtz, J., & Ibara, S. (2012). Tracking changes in collaborative writing: Edits, visibility, and group maintenance. *Proc. of CSCW 2012,* 809-818.
5. Carter, J., & Dewan, P. (2010). Are you having difficulty? *Proc. of CSCW 2010,* 211-214.
6. Cheung, V., Chang, Y. L. B., & Scott, S. D. (2012). Communication channels and awareness cues in collocated collaborative time-critical gaming. *Proc. of CSCW 2012,* 569-578.
7. Clark, H.H. (1996). *Using Language*. Cambridge Press.
8. Clark, H. H., & Brennan, S. E. (1991). Grounding in communication. In L. B. Resnick, J. M. Levine, & S. D. Teasley, (Eds.). *Perspectives on Socially Shared Cognition* (pp. 127-149). APA Press.
9. Dabbish, L., & Kraut, R. (2008). Awareness displays and social motivation for coordinating communication. *Information Systems Research, 19,* 221-238.
10. Diamant, E.I., Fussell, S. R., & Lo, F. L. (2008). Where did we turn wrong? Unpacking the effects of culture and technology on attributions of team performance. *Proc. CSCW 2008*, 383-391.
11. Dourish, P., & Bellotti, V. (1992). Awareness and coordination in shared workspaces. *Proc. of CSCW 1992,* 107-114.
12. Feely, A. J., & Harzing, A. W. K. (2003). Language management in multinational companies. *Cross-Cultural Management: An Intl'l Journal, 10,* 27-52.
13. Fung, L., & Carter, R. (2007). Discourse markers and spoken English: Native and learner use in pedagogic settings. *Applied Linguistics, 28,* 410-439.
14. Gao, G., Yamashita, N., Hautasaari, A., Echenique, A., & Fussell, S. R. (2014). Effects of public vs. private automated transcripts on multiparty communication between native and non-native English speakers. *Proc. of CHI 2014,* 843-852.
15. Gergle, D., Kraut, R. E., & Fussell, S. R. (2013). Using visual information for grounding and awareness in collaborative tasks. *Human-Computer Interaction, 28,* 1-39.
16. Gibson, C. B., & Gibbs, J. L. (2006). Unpacking the concept of virtuality: The effects of geographic dispersion, electronic dependence, dynamic structure, and national diversity on team innovation. *Administrative Science Quarterly, 51,* 451-495.
17. Hart, S. G., & Staveland, L. E. (1998). Development of NASA-TLX: Results of empirical and theoretical research. *Advances in Psychology, 52,* 139-183.
18. Henderson, J.K. (2005). Language diversity in international management teams. *International Studies of Management and Organization, 35,* 66–82.
19. Ishida, T. (2011). *The language grid.* Springer Press.
20. Kraut, R. E., Fussell, S. R., & Siegel, J. (2003). Visual information as a conversational resource in collaborative physical tasks. *Human Computer Interaction, 18,* 13-49.
21. Li, H. Z., Yum, Y., Yates, R., Aguilera, L., Mao, Y., & Zheng, Y. (2005). Interruption and involvement in discourse: Can intercultural interlocutors be trained? *J. Intercultural Communication Research, 34,* 233-254.
22. Li, H. Z. (1999). Grounding and information communication in intercultural and intracultural dyadic discourse. *Discourse Processes*, *28*, 195-215.
23. Lim, B. Y., Brdiczka, O., & Bellotti, V. (2010). Show me a good time: Using content to provide activity awareness to collaborators with Activity Spotter. *Proc. of GROUP 2010,* 263-272.
24. Reynolds, L., Birnholtz, J., & Lee, A. (2012). The effect of communication channel and visual awareness display on coordination in online tasks. *Proc. iConference 2012*, 120-128
25. Rogerson-Revell, P. (2008). Participation and performance in international business meetings. *English for Specific Purposes, 27,* 338-360.
26. Setlock, L. D., Fussell, S. R., & Neuwirth, C. (2004). Taking it out of context: Collaborating within and across cultures in face-to-face settings and via instant messaging. *Proc. CSCW 2004,* 604-613.
27. Takano, Y., & Noda, A. (1993). A temporary decline of thinking ability during foreign language processing. *Journal of Cross-Cultural Psychology, 24,* 445-462.
28. Tange, H., & Lauring, J. (2009). Language management and social interaction within the multilingual workplace. *J. Communication Management, 13,* 218-232.
29. Wang, H. C., Fussell, S. R., & Cosley, D. (2013). Machine translation vs. common language: Effects on idea exchange in cross-lingual groups. *Proc. of CSCW 2013,* 935-944.
30. Wang, H-C., Fussell, S. R. & Setlock, L. D. (2009). Cultural difference and adaptation of communication styles in computer-mediated group brainstorming. *Proc. CHI 2009,* 669-678.
31. Wong, J. (2000). The token" yeah" in nonnative speaker English conversation. *Research on Language and Social Interaction, 33,* 39-67.
32. Yamashita, N., Echenique, A., Ishita, T., & Hautasaari, A. (2013). Lost in translation: How transmission lag enhances and deteriorates multilingual collaboration. In *Proc. of CSCW 2013*, 923-934.

Effect of Machine Translation in Interlingual Conversation: Lessons from a Formative Study

Kotaro Hara
Department of Computer Science
University of Maryland
College Park, MD 20742 USA
kotaro@cs.umd.edu

Shamsi T. Iqbal
Microsoft Research
One Microsoft Way
Redmond, WA 98052 USA
shamsi@microsoft.com

ABSTRACT
Language barrier is the primary challenge for effective cross-lingual conversations. Spoken language translation (SLT) is perceived as a cost-effective alternative to less affordable human interpreters, but little research has been done on how people interact with such technology. Using a prototype translator application, we performed a formative evaluation to elicit how people interact with the technology and adapt their conversation style. We conducted two sets of studies with a total of 23 pairs (46 participants). Participants worked on storytelling tasks to simulate natural conversations with 3 different interface settings. Our findings show that collocutors naturally adapt their style of speech production and comprehension to compensate for inadequacies in SLT. We conclude the paper with the design guidelines that emerged from the analysis.

Author Keywords
Multilingual communication; Spoken language translation; Automatic speech recognition; Machine translation

ACM Classification Keywords
H.5.3 [Group and Organization Interfaces]: Computer-supported cooperative work

INTRODUCTION
Language barrier is the primary challenge for effective cross-cultural communication in education, health care, and business collaboration [6,14,15]. In the U.S., for example, roughly 40 million foreign-born individuals constitute the total population [19], and many of whom do not use English as their first language. Despite the increasing need for a solution, language remains "the biggest barrier to intercultural collaboration" [26].

Though human interpreters can bridge the communication gap between people with different languages, the service is accessible only to a privileged few because of its cost and availability. For example, international organizations like the United Nations pay a freelance interpreter over $600 per day [27]. As a result, only a handful of spoken encounters between humans are interpreted [7].

CHI 2015, April 18 - 23 2015, Seoul, Republic of Korea
Copyright 2015 ACM 978-1-4503-3145-6/15/04...$15.00
http://dx.doi.org/10.1145/2702123.2702407

Automatic spoken language translation (SLT) has been expected to address the problem since its first appearance in the 1980s [21,22]. Decades of research has advanced the state-of-the-art, and some claim that it is usable in limited domains [7,12]. Despite the increasing interests in SLT, however, little research has paid attention to how people interact with the added complexity of speech recognition, translation, and speech synthesis. Consequently, we know little about how the system can be designed to support this complex exchange while still maintaining the flow of a conversation.

To better understand user experience of SLT systems, we conducted two sets of formative studies. We invited 8 pairs of French speakers and German speakers, and 15 pairs of English speakers and German speakers to hold cross-lingual conversations using our translator application. We collected and analyzed survey responses and interview recordings. Our main research questions were: what are the overall impressions on quality and challenges in using the translator tool? Do people adapt the way they use the system, and, if so, how? What interface components facilitate/disrupt their conversations?

Our findings suggest that, while SLT systems do not produce perfect results due to limitations in state-of-the-art speech recognition and machine translation, people naturally adapt to imperfect translation systems by changing the way they speak and comprehend speech. However, recurrent translation problems can cause frustration. Problems also arise from lack of information about when to speak and when to wait. Other issues necessitate a mix of speech and text to correctly convey an intended message, which then has a higher probability of being interpreted correctly.

This paper offers design guidelines for SLT systems with a focus on HCI. In the following sections, we first provide background on simultaneous interpretation, speech recognition, and machine translation technologies. Next, we review prior work on computer-mediated communication. Finally, we describe the user studies and present the quantitative and qualitative results.

TRANSLATION VS. INTERPRETING
The difference between "translation" and "interpreting" is blurred in computer science literature. "Translation" often refers to transfer of meaning from text to text, whereas

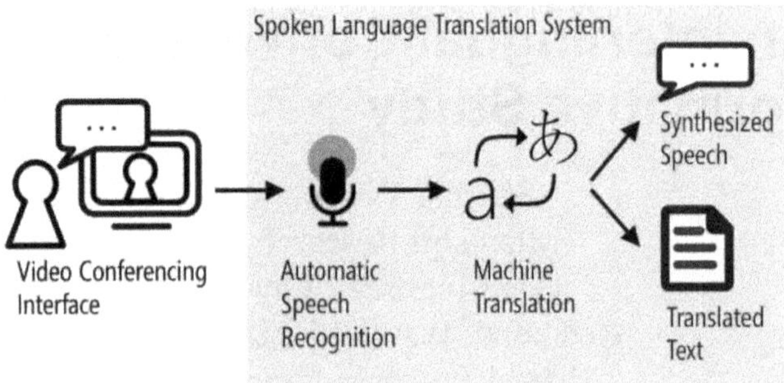

Figure 1. We used a translator application that has an interface similar to typical video conferencing tools (*e.g.,* Microsoft Skype, Google Hangout), but with a *spoken language translation (SLT)* system on background. In general, a translation system comprises *automatic speech recognition (ASR)*, *machine translation (MT)*, and *text-to-speech (TTS)* components, so does our system.

"interpreting" often refers to conversion from speech to speech [10]. Historically, computer science scholars use "translation" indiscriminately regardless of medium [7]. Our translator application performs simultaneous interpreting (*i.e.,* interpreting in nearly real-time). Unless otherwise mentioned, we use the term "interpretation" and "translation" interchangeably to indicate the automatic simultaneous interpretation of spoken language.

RELATED WORK

Spoken Language Translation

Outcome of decades of research on SLT technology is starting to enable people to overcome language barriers. The technology generally comprises 3 components: automatic speech recognition (ASR), machine translation (MT), and text-to-speech (TTS) (Figure 1). ASR transcribes human speech in real-time [5,12]. MT translates transcribed speech into another language [7,11,16]. Though ASR and MT are not perfect yet, they are expected to improve over time [7]. Translation can then be delivered in a form of synthesized speech and/or by text. Despite the extensive work on development and evaluation of translation quality, there is limited research on how people interact with the technology [26].

Cross-cultural Computer-mediated Communication

ASR and MT not only empower monolinguals, but they can also benefit greater audience such as second language speakers [9,17,23]. Research shows that MT enables non-native speakers to produce more ideas in brainstorming tasks with native speakers in text-based conversation [23]. Previous work reported benefits of presenting real-time transcription of English conversation between native and non-native speakers: changes in speaking behavior of native speakers (*e.g.,* better enunciation) and textual information both help non-native speakers to better comprehend conversation [9,17]. The work, however, only discusses the effect of each component in cross-cultural communication, and does not discuss the effect of SLT as a system.

Figure 2. The user interface of the translator application. Users can hear each other's voice. Users can choose to display transcribed text and translated text in a closed caption. Users can also choose to turn on TTS, so they can hear translated speech.

Effective MT-mediated communication requires solutions for hurdles posed by the technology [8,25,26]. Yamashita *et al.* found that MT-mediated chat imposes extra difficulties of building common ground between multiple parties due to mistranslation and peoples' lack of awareness thereof [25,26]. This not only hinders effective mutual understanding, but also reduces perceived quality of communication [8].

The aforementioned work, however, primarily focuses on text-based interaction, and limited HCI research exists for conversation with SLT. The most relevant to our work is the evaluation of NESPOLE! by Constantini *et al.*, in which the authors evaluated success rate of negotiation tasks using a multi-modal speech-to-speech translation system [3]. Though they uncovered effect of issues such as word sense ambiguity in interaction, they did not investigate important characteristics such as adaptation in speech production. Their push-to-talk interface also makes it hard for us to understand the difficulty of turn-taking in MT-mediated natural conversation. Thus, our goal is to reinforce the findings from the previous work and contribute to extend the body of HCI research on MT-mediated conversation.

SYSTEM DESCRIPTION

We used a video conferencing system with real-time SLT to evoke characteristics of MT-mediated conversation. The translator application allows two users to communicate face-to-face remotely like modern videoconference clients (*e.g.,* Microsoft Skype, Google Hangout). As a user speaks, the system recognizes and translates his/her utterance. Translation is then conveyed to another user via synthesized audio (*i.e.,* TTS) and/or text in a closed caption (CC), just like any other SLT systems (Figure 1).

Users can choose to turn CC or TTS on or off (in the study sessions, the experimenter controlled the setting). Note that a user's speech can be heard by their partner. Both parties could hear TTS. CC was displayed at the bottom of the interface (Figure 2). It displayed both transcribed text and the corresponding translation. CC was updated when the next utterance got translated and was ready to be displayed, similar to news captions and movie subtitles.

STUDY

Our goal was to understand how using the translator system in an interlingual conversation affects the interaction between two collocutors speaking in two different languages.

Participants

Potential users of an SLT system include not only pairs of monolingual speakers without a common language, but also pairs of second language learners who share a common second language where one side has much better understanding of one language. To study a diverse usage scenario, we conducted two studies with different groups of participants. The first group in the study consisted of French-German (Fre-Ger) pairs who spoke either French or German, but not both, so both sides had limited to no knowledge of each other's language. The second group in the study consisted of English-German (Eng-Ger) pairs who spoke either English or German as their primary language. This group represented a situation where both sides know a common language, but one side hesitates to speak in his/her second language and would prefer communicating in their native language. All participants could speak English reasonably well.

Participants in both groups were recruited via cold-calling, listserv, and word-of-mouth in rolling basis. Groups such as local English/German/French speaking meet-ups and schools were emailed and called. We also emailed employees of the authors' organization. While most pairs of participants did not know each other, four pairs in Fre-Ger pairs were colleagues or friends. Although participants were convenientce samples of local residents of any gender/age, we believe this did not negatively affect the validity of the study given its explorative nature. We considered reporting the results of two studies separately, but we decided to describe them in parallel to compare responses from the two groups.

Experimental Design

The study was a 3x3x2 (*Interface* x *Round* x *Language*) mixed design in-lab study. *Interface* condition (*i.e.,* (CC, TTS) = (on, on), (on, off), and (off, on)) and *round* (round 1 to 3) were within-subject factors; and *Language* (French and German, or English or German) was a between-subject factor. Changing between three *interface* settings—TTS only, CC only and both—allowed us to see the tradeoffs between the naturalness of the exchange (speech to speech), speed of exchange (speech to text), and reinforcement of the same information through two modalities (speech and text). *Round* was defined as a set of three task trials, and each of them included one of the three interface conditions. We considered *round* as a separate variable in our analysis as we wanted to see how user experience and adaptation change with increasing exposure to the system.

Task

Each pair of participants was asked to work on a story telling task, and each participant conversed in their own language (Video Figure). The objective was to collaboratively generate a fictional story. This task was inspired by prior work (*e.g.,* conversation in a second language with ASL [9]) and adapted from a conversation study in [13]. We did not ask participants to follow a strict turn taking protocol, but we suggested them to take turns so both parties could contribute to story formation.

Starting Sentence							
English	Olivia was practicing for the dance-off.						
French	Olivia s'entraine pour le concours de danse.						
German	Olivia trainierte für den Tanzwettbewerb.						
Word List							
English	swim	pig	plane	dance	smile	drink	doctor
French	natation	cochon	avion	danse	sourire	boisson	médecin
German	schwimmen	Schwein	Flugzeug	Tanz	Lächeln	Getränk	Arzt

Table 1. An example of starting sentence and a word list. English sentence and key words were translated into French and German.

Our task allowed free form speech, just like a normal conversation. However, we provided a starting sentence to initiate a task and so a conversation was more controlled than a random conversation (Table 1). To make it easier for participants to keep a conversation going, we provided 7 keywords relevant to the starting sentence, which participants could optionally use in the conversation. The English starting sentences and keywords were translated into German and French by translators hired from oDesk (www.odesk.com). Each task consisted of different starting sentences and corresponding keywords.

This task was appropriate for our study as it has important properties that map to normal conversations. (i) Building coherent narrative for explaining one's thought and sharing knowledge is a common and important task in daily life. (ii) The task requires effective conversational turn taking. (iii) The task has a clear objective without being restrictive in the required answers. To create starting sentences and keywords, we gathered inspiration from a web site that lists words for family games. We used the "easy" sets for Catchphrase, Charades, and Pictionary on the web site of http://www.thegamegal.com/printables/.

Procedure

Each study session comprised (i) task introduction, (ii) a practice task in English, (iii) 9 conversation tasks, and (iv) a final story telling task in English (*i.e.,* without translation) as a baseline. On arrival to the study location, each participant was asked to fill out an informed consent form and was provided a brief overview of the study by a member of the research team. Then, they were given a practice conversation task in English in order to familiarize themselves with task itself without using the translator tool.

We then placed participants in two separate rooms to have interlingual conversation using the translator application. Each participant was asked to wear a headset. A researcher sat in one of the two rooms and initiated a video call using a computer in the room, and a participant in the other room was instructed to respond to the call via the interface. Once the call was established, the researcher asked a participant in the same room to start the conversation using a staring sentence. The researcher stopped the conversation at a natural stop point after 2-4 minutes.

We exposed participants to all the interface settings in story telling tasks (*i.e.,* CC, TTS, and CC&TTS). Our goal was to observe and explore participant variation in how they use the application and obtain their opinions on interface condition preference (*e.g.,* do they prefer to have TTS or not). One round consisted of 3 story telling tasks using different interface settings. To minimize ordering effects, we permuted the orders of exposure. We repeated the tasks for 3 rounds. After each task and round, participants were asked to fill out a survey.

After the 9 main tasks were completed, we asked participants to work on another story telling task in English to assess how easy/difficult the task was when there was no real-time translation involved. The session ended with a post study questionnaire asking about their overall impressions and preference of conditions. A brief interview was held in which participants could suggest what interface elements they thought would have helped improve the interaction.

Data and Measures

In addition to in-situ observation, we collected the following data to conduct post-hoc analysis.

Survey responses. To analyze perceived usability of the system (*e.g.*, how successful a conversation was) and participants' preference towards interface settings, we asked participants to fill out surveys after each task, each round and at the end of a session. The surveys in each trial and round had Likert scale questions. Each survey had an optional free-text response space where participants could comment on, for example, their experience, suggestions for interface improvements, and specific problems with ASR and MT.

Conversation log. The translator tool collected conversation logs with the following data: (i) transcribed text, (ii) translated text, and (iii) a record that synthesized audio were sent to clients. All events were time stamped, and computation time was recorded where appropriate. However, we lost logs for 30 out of 72 (41.7%) Fre-Ger conversations and 47 out of 135 (34.8%) Eng-Ger conversations due to technical issues. We thus limited ourselves from drawing conclusions from these data.

Video recording and transcript. We also recorded and transcribed each session with a camcorder positioned over the user's shoulder in order to perform a post-hoc video observation. This allowed us to understand users' behaviors and interaction issues through the observation.

DESCRIPTIVE STATISTICS

We invited two groups of pairs to our in-lab study: 8 Fre-Ger pairs (16 participants, 6 female, *Avg. age*=32.9, *SD*=13.2) and 15 Eng-Ger pairs (30 participants, 15 female, *Avg. age*=46.0, *SD*=13.2). Participants self-reported their language proficiency in 5 point Likert scale where 1 is "not proficient at all" and 5 is "very proficient" (Table 2). All participants except for one English speaker had experience in using a video conferencing tool (*e.g.,* Skype), and the most common use case was conversation with friends followed by business, family, school, and game.

	French-German (N=16)		English-German (N=30)	
	French	German	English	German
Average Age (yr)	31.3 (13.5)	34.5 (13.6)	49.4 (14.2)	42.7 (11.7)
English Proficiency	4.8 (0.5)	4.9 (0.4)	4.9 (0.3)	4.7 (0.5)
German Proficiency	1.8 (0.9)	4.9 (0.4)	1.3 (0.6)	5.0 (0.0)
French Proficiency	4.8 (0.5)	1.5 (0.8)	1.1 (0.4)	1.1 (0.3)
Application use cases	Friends (40), business (18), family (12), school (8), game (2)			

Table 2. Participants' language proficiency and experience in using a video conferencing tool. All participants rated proficiency for their own language more than proficient. All participants had experience in using some video conferencing tool except for one English speaker in the Eng-Ger group.

On average, storytelling tasks in Fre-Ger group and Eng-Ger group lasted 2.6 min (*SD*=0.4 min) and 2.7 min (*SD*=0.4 min) respectively.

We first quantitatively analyzed participants' survey response from each task and each round to grasp how participants perceived the usability of the system and how (if ever) they adapted to using SLT. We then moved on to results from a content analysis to further investigate how participants felt while using the translator application.

STATISTICAL ANALYSIS

We used mixed models to analyze the participants' response. We first transformed the ordinal Likert scale data with aligned rank transformation to satisfy the normality assumptions [24]. The results were then analyzed by 3x3x2 (*Interface* x *Round* x *Language*) mixed model (*i.e.,* restricted maximum likelihood model)[1]. We used mixed models instead of traditional repeated measure ANOVA to incorporate subject variability. A critical value $\alpha = 0.05$ was used to assess significance. We omit descriptions of insignificant interactions and main effects, unless there was possible trend (*i.e., p*<0.10). Contrast tests with pairwise comparisons were protected against Type I error using a Bonferroni adjustment.

Overall Interface Preference

We asked participants to rank three *Interface* conditions (*e.g.,* (CC, TTS) = (on, off)) from "1" (least preferred) to "3" (most preferred) based on which one they liked/disliked after each round. We allowed ties in the ranking (*e.g.,* people could score everything as 1).

[1] There were only 2 *Interface* levels CC and CC&TTS for one question that asked about subjective speech recognition accuracy. Thus we used 2x3x2 mixed model for analysis.

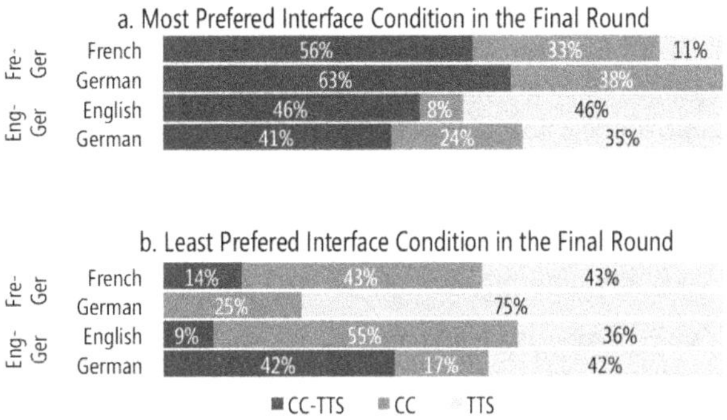

Figure 3. Participants' interface setting preference distribution after the final round of a study session. (a) About a half of participants liked CC&TTS. There were very few participants who liked TTS in the Fre-Ger group, but relatively more participants liked TTS in the Eng-Ger group. (b) Many disliked TTS only condition in the Fre-Ger group. Noticeably more German participants disliked CC&TTS condition.

There were no interaction effect or main effect of *Round* suggesting overall preference did not dramatically change over time. Given this, the preference from a single round provided a good picture of which interface condition was preferred by which language group. Therefore, we show the demography of the most preferred and least preferred interfaces for the final round in Figure 3.

In the Fre-Ger group, there was a significant interaction effect between *Interface* and *Language* ($F_{2,112}$=6.18, p<0.01) suggesting that interface preference differs between French and German speakers. Though we cannot strongly argue with the presence of interaction, it seems both disliked TTS only condition, which suggests the presence of a closed caption is crucial for this group (Figure 3).

Significant main effects of *Language* ($F_{1,28}$= 4.38, p<0.05) and *Interface* ($F_{2,224}$=6.967, p<0.01) were observed in the Eng-Ger group. Some English speakers ranked all conditions as "1", and thus the overall ranking of English speakers was significantly lower than that of German speakers. It indicates the quality of the experience was equality unsatisfactory for all *Interface* conditions for these English speakers. CC&TTS was significantly preferred compared to CC (p<0.05) and TTS (p<0.01).

In general, CC&TTS was most preferred by participants (Figure 3.a), but some disliked it. Noticeably more German speakers disliked CC&TTS compared to other participants, most likely because their speech overlapped with synthesized speech more frequently than others as discussed in the next section.

Subjective Usability Rating

After each trial, we administered a survey with questions on the usability of the system. Each question was answered in a form of 5-point Likert scale, where 1 was "strongly disagree" and 5 was "strongly agree."

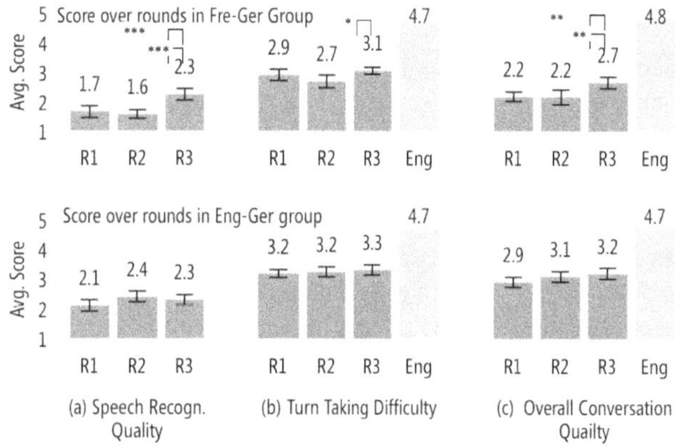

Figure 4. Change in average ratings for perceived usability over three rounds of a session. Likert scaling ranged from 1 to 5, where 5 is more positive. Scores for turn taking difficulty and overall conversation quality were compared to the scores from English conversation. Error bars represent standard errors. Statistical significance: *** $p < 0.001$; ** $p < 0.01$; * $p < 0.05$.

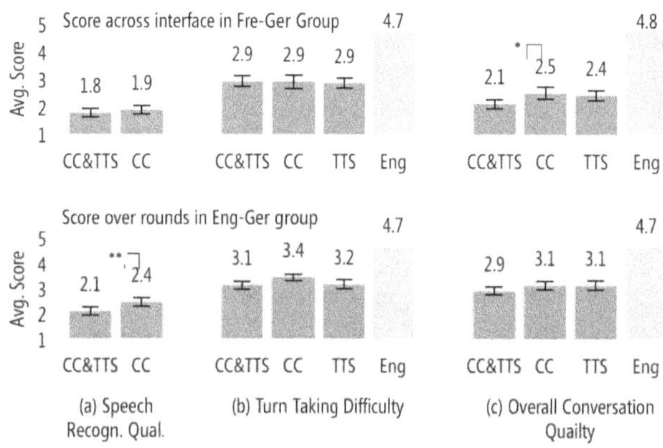

Figure 5. Average usability ratings for each interface condition. Likert scaling ranged from 1 to 5, where 5 is more positive. Perceived speech recognition quality was not assessed for tasks with the TTS only condition and English tasks because of the absence of a closed caption. Error bars represent standard errors.

Perceived quality of speech recognition. Automatically recognized speech was displayed in a closed caption in CC and CC&TTS conditions. Participants rated their agreement to: *"there were no noticeable errors in transcription."* Note that TTS condition was excluded from this analysis as closed caption was not displayed in this condition (*i.e.,* participants had no mean to assess the speech recognition quality). We observed a significant main effect of *Round* ($F_{2,70}$=10.774, p<0.001) to perceived quality of speech recognition in the Fre-Ger group. Contrast tests suggested that participants felt speech recognition quality in third round was significantly better than first (p<0.001) and second rounds (p<0.001), suggesting their speech style adjusted to the system. Figure 4.a shows the mean of raw scores for each round.

In the Eng-Ger group, we observed possible trend ($F_{2,140}$=2.622, p=0.076) of *Round* (Figure 4.a) as well as a significant main effect of *Interface* ($F_{1,140}$=9.197, p<0.01) on subjective speech recognition quality (Figure 5.a). Pairwise comparisons showed that participants felt the speech recognition quality of second round better than first round.

The results show that participants became used to the nuances of the system and learned *how they should speak* so the system could recognize their utterance. Note, however, the quality of the transcription in either group was far from perfect. We found that problems such as proper noun misrecognition and dialect act misclassification lowered the subjective scores; we discuss these issues further in the next section.

Participants in the Eng-Ger group felt that transcription quality in CC condition was significantly better than CC&TTS ($p<0.01$). A possible reason for the difference could be distraction in speech due to overlap with synthesized speech and resulting premature speech recognition.

Turn taking difficulty. We asked if participants felt turn taking was easy. The responses of participants in the Fre-Ger group showed a significant main effect of *Round* on turn taking difficulty ($F_{2,112}=3.123$, $p<0.05$). Pairwise comparisons showed that participants thought turn taking in third round was easier than second round ($p<0.05$). This suggests that participants became better at taking turns as they worked on more tasks.

We observed a significant main effect of *Interface* in the Eng-Ger group ($F_{2,224}=3.434$, $p<0.05$), but no difference between rounds. Participants in this group tend to prefer CC over CC&TTS ($p=0.069$) and TTS conditions ($p=0.062$) with regards to turn taking. Because TTS takes additional time for completion, participants, especially German speakers who understood their partner without translation, may have felt it was redundant and disrupted effective turn taking.

Figure 4.b shows the scores for turn taking difficulty in each round, and Figure 5.b shows the scores grouped by the interface condition. In both figures, we also show the turn taking difficulty scored in the English task that was performed at the end of the session. The results show that turn taking was harder in translation-mediated conversation compared to a normal remote conversation.

Overall quality of conversation. For each story telling task, we asked if participants agreed to a statement "*overall, we could hold a successful conversation.*" We found significant main effect of *Round* on overall success of a conversation in Fre-Ger pairs ($F_{2,112}=6.275$, $p<0.01$), and a possible trend in the Eng-Ger group ($F_{2,224}=2.615$, $p=0.075$). The responses from participants in Fre-Ger group also showed significant difference in rating between *Interface* conditions ($F_{1,112}=3.676$, $p<0.05$).

The contrast tests showed that third round was significantly more successful compared to first round ($p<0.01$) and second round ($p<0.01$) in the Fre-Ger group. Similarly, there was a trend that third round was more successful compared to first round ($p=0.058$) in the Eng-Ger group. Though some participants noted that they got used to using the application in early stage of a study session, the result suggest that it takes about two rounds (six tasks, which is approximately 16 min of conversation) to improve conversation quality.

Pairwise comparison revealed that participants in the Fre-Ger group rated perceived success higher in CC condition over CC&TTS condition ($p<0.05$) (Figure 5.c). Unexpectedly, we also observed a potential trend in preference of TTS condition over CC&TTS ($p = 0.058$). This was surprising, because the result contradicts with the overall interface preference, which was leaning towards favoring CC&TTS (Figure 3.b). This suggests that even conversation success is rated lower, participants wished to have both CC&TTS for as much information as possible to comprehend their partner's message.

Even though the quality of conversation was not as good as that of a remote conversation in English (Figure 4.c), we noted that, in the 2nd and 3rd rounds of the Eng-Ger group, the overall conversation quality was rated slightly above the neutral value of 3. However, the perceived conversation quality of the Fre-Ger group remained below 3 even after three rounds. In the next section, we discuss factors that may have affected the conversation quality.

Section Summary

The results suggest that despite limitations of the translator system, people do adapt their speaking styles as they get more familiar with these limitations. The results also suggest diverse preference in interface settings, highlighting the need of multimodal presentation (audio and text) of utterances as a fail-safe technique. Next, we contextualize the results by analyzing users' comments.

CONTENT ANALYSIS

To better understand *why* participants were satisfied or dissatisfied with the experience, we looked into their interview responses and free-text answerers in surveys. Interviews were recorded and transcribed by authors. Interview transcripts and survey responses were coded using a content analysis method; recurring themes were extracted in open coding step, then researchers developed a coding frame and combined similar themes to organize and identify findings [2]. Table 3 shows the final coding frame and number of participants who mentioned each theme. The remainder of this section will explain each theme in more detail together with exemplar quotes that represent participants' feelings.

Speech Recognition Errors

Among different types of speech recognition errors (*e.g.*, [18]), some were mentioned more frequently by participants in the current study: the system's inability to recognize *proper nouns* and *statement vs. question* classification.

	Fre-Ger (N=16)	Eng-Ger (N=30)	Overall (N=46)
Speech recognition errors			
Proper nouns	10 (62.5%)	16 (53.3%)	26 (56.5%)
Statement vs. question	2 (12.5%)	6 (20.0%)	8 (17.4%)
Translation errors			
Grammar and word order	6 (37.5%)	12 (40.0%)	18 (39.1%)
Idiomatic and colloquial expressions	6 (37.5%)	5 (16.7%)	11 (23.9%)
Comprehending imperfect messages			
Deciphering translated text	6 (37.5%)	11 (36.7%)	17 (37.0%)
Information from original speech	5 (31.3%)	10 (33.3%)	15 (32.6%)
Speech production and adaptation			
Closed caption as a feedback	10 (62.5%)	10 (33.3%)	20 (43.5%)
Adapting the way of speaking	14 (87.5%)	25 (83.3%)	39 (84.8%)
Repeat and rephrase	12 (75.0%)	17 (56.7%)	29 (63.0%)
Forgiving	6 (37.5%)	9 (30.0%)	15 (32.6%)
Difficulty in Turn Taking			
Latency	5 (31.3%)	15 (50.0%)	20 (43.5%)
Overlapping speech	4 (25.0%)	15 (50.0%)	19 (41.3%)

Table 3. Challenges identified using a translator tool coded from the user responses and number of participants who mentioned each theme.

Proper nouns. More than half of participants (56.5%) mentioned that the system did not recognize proper nouns (*e.g.*, a name of a person). For example, when a participant was asked to start a conversation with a starting sentence of *"Ava was planning a trip for the weekend,"* the name "Ava" could not be recognized.

"'Ava', there was no way it was getting 'Ava' no matter how many times I tried. So in German, when you say 'but,' it sounds very similar. So that's what it was picking up" – French-German Pair 4, German.

Unsuccessful recognition caused two problems: (i) it hindered participants from mutually agreeing on how to refer to a subject/object, and (ii) false recognition got translated into a different word(s) and changed the meaning of a speech. The issue, a case of an *out-of-vocabulary* problem [1,4], was severe primarily because of lack of effective adaptation techniques. Unlike other types of speech recognition errors (*e.g.*, incomplete utterance [18]), users could not fix the problem by repeating, rephrasing, or using simpler words.

Statement vs. question. Multiple participants (17.4%) mentioned that the speech recognition system did not correctly identify whether the utterance was a statement or a question. One participant noted:

"I found it really hard not to see or hear whether the translation is just making a statement or asking a question. And this was a total block in a conversation if you cannot make this decision"– E-G Pair 12, German.

The way one responds can change depending on the *act* of speech (*i.e.*, statement or question). For example, a response to "William likes tea" and "William likes tea?" could differ. Classifying a speech act is an open area of research [20] and there is no prescribed solution for a system to use.

Translation Errors

Translation errors affected quality of communication, and severity may have differed between interface conditions.

Grammar and word order. Some participants (39.1%) pointed out grammar and word orders were off. More interestingly, a participant noted that it affected a conversation more severely for the TTS condition.

"Because [...] German sentence structure is so different from English, [translated] sentence wouldn't make any sense when [TTS] said it, but when you see it on the screen, you can kind of reorganize the words in the way it supposed to go. And then it makes sense"– F-G Pair 3, German.

Trying to comprehend grammatically incorrect speech burdened one's working memory, but presence of a closed caption seemed to help. Some participants said "deciphering" a closed caption was their way of understanding their partner. This partially explains participants' preference towards CC and CC&TTS conditions (Figure 3).

Idiomatic and colloquial expressions. A participant's utterance did not get translated as they intended when it contained idiomatic and colloquial expressions. The challenge was mentioned by 23.9% of participants.

"Problem with me was that if you use a translator, it conveys the literal meaning but not the cultural one. Sometimes when you say some sentence in your own language, you can't translate it right way. In English, you need to find a different way to say that sentence" – F-G Pair 4, French.

People seemed to adapt and find workarounds to the problem where the system did not translate expression with non-literal meaning. For example, they rephrased and described their speech when their partner seemed confused. Though the problem may not be a showstopper, it certainly affected the quality of communication.

Comprehending Imperfect Messages

Although comprehending erroneous translation was hard, participants managed to understand their counterparts.

Deciphering translated text. Participants preferred settings where closed caption was available (Figure 3), and 37% noted that they could understand the meaning from text even there were some errors.

"[...] even if there are a lot of words that are switched in translation, it was still clear and the conversations made sense" – F-G Pair 5, French.

Because closed caption was a key for comprehending a message, its persistence on a screen was of great importance. Some participants complained about the design choice of the closed caption interface; when a person made consecutive utterances, the system removed a translated sentence and refreshed a closed caption with a new translation. Sometimes this happened too quickly that one could not finish reading the previous translation. One said with frustration:

"I disliked that the... translation sometimes, it flashes, and it's gone" – F-G Pair 8, German.

Information from original speech. 32.6% of participants mentioned that being able to hear their partner's voice was helpful. Original speech (i) maintained the feeling of talking to a human, and (ii) it allowed a participant to pick up information that was lost in translation.

"[Having partner's original voice] humanizes the relationships as well, because if you only get the robotic voice, I think it just cuts you off from the person you are engaged with. Whereas you talk, then it feels much more human relationship" – F-G Pair 1, French.

Another participant mentioned that original speech of their partner compensated for translation errors. For example, they could pick up basic words that were similar across languages. It even allowed participants to pick up proper nouns that were lost in speech recognition—a problem mentioned by more than half of participants.

"I know a couple of words 'nein' and 'ja', and a couple of other things from German. [...] I could pick up like 'Space Needle.' And there were a couple of words ... that I could pick up and help guide, like 'ok, is this what you mean?' as opposed to 'I don't know'" – E-G Pair 6, English.

Speech Production and Adaptation

To hold a successful conversation, participants adjusted the way they speak and how they interact with the system.

Closed caption as a feedback. A transcription of participant's own utterance helped them to see whether the system correctly recognized their utterance. Many of participants (43.5%) noted that it allowed them to adjust the way they spoke so that the system could recognize them well (*e.g.*, by speaking clearly).

"[Closed caption is useful] because you can see the mistakes better. Because people pronounce things differently than ... than it should be pronounced. If you see it, it's much easier to fix mistakes" – E-G Pair 4, German.

When both CC and TTS were on, recognized speech was displayed when TTS started. So when there were speech recognition errors, participants knew that translation was not going to make sense to their partner due to cascading errors. Participants identified a limitation of the design of the current system, which does not allow them to abort TTS. One participant said:

"I was seeing my own recognition in French, I started laughing because what was going to be sent was wrong. I saw very bad recognition. I knew I couldn't do anything, so I just had to wait for ... getting sidetracked by what you got or sometimes conversation totally getting fallen apart" – F-G Pair 7, French.

Adapting the way of speaking. Majority of participants (84.8%) mentioned that they adapted to the system and changed the way they spoke to accommodate the system. Main adaptation techniques included slowing down, enunciating, speaking louder, choosing simpler words, and constructing a simple sentence structure.

German: "I spoke more clearly, and a little bit slow." English: "Enunciate a little bit. Because we all have our own slung and we have a tendency to run words together, and software may not pick up" – E-G Pair 7, English & German.

However, sometimes speaking too slowly backfired. ASR uses a pause between speeches as a cue to segment an utterance; if there is too much of a pause, it misclassifies an intended pause as an end of a sentence consequently translating a premature utterance.

"I may have tried to speak slowly and clearly. Because [ASR] seemed bad. But it didn't do any good. Or it made the matter worse. [...] it didn't realize it was a pause (when he stopped between words to pronounce each word clearly)" – E-G Pair 11, English.

Repeat and rephrase. When their partners seemed lost, many participants (63.0%) found that not only repeating, but also rephrasing was a way to effectively fix the conversation.

"In normal conversation, you wouldn't just repeat it, but you would try to say it in a different way" – E-G Pair 8, German.

To request for repetition or rephrase, a listener used non-verbal cue as well as explicitly asking. One participant mentioned that she tried to convey that translation did not make sense via gesture and facial expressions.

Forgiving. Though they had to conform to the system and adjust the way they speak, about a third of participants (32.6%) said they did not feel uncomfortable because it was expected.

"My sentence became shorter, I pronounced more clearly, I was speaking ... I mean, if I were speaking to someone who's not a native German, and if I didn't have a translator, then I would also slow down, obviously. It was a similar experience to ... accommodate the machine" – G-F Pair 5, German.

This aligns with the behavior of people who hold inter-lingual conversation with a help of human simultaneous interpreter; when all parties are aware of the communication situation, people may be more cooperative and adapt their way of speech [10].

Turn Taking

System latency and overlap between participants' utterance and TTS distracted turn taking.

Latency. Many participants (43.5%) noted that latency, due to computation time of speech recognition, machine translation, and speech synthesis, disrupted the communication. Some also noted that waiting for TTS to finish speaking was cumbersome.

"The audio is slow and cumbersome, and, it kind of got in the way of the flow. I like the text better" – E-G Pair 4, English.

Some participants raised this as a reason for disliking CC&TTS condition. They knew what their partner had said from translated text, and did not want to wait for synthesized speech to finish playing.

Overlapping between speech and TTS. Nearly half of participants (41.3%) mentioned that their speech overlapped with translated TTS, which made it hard for them to speak.

"My partner and I would begin to speak then the translation from the previous statement would catch up, translation and speaker would then all be talking at the same time" – E-G Pair 4, English.

Speech overlap was caused by two reasons: (i) speaker's disfluency and (ii) forgetting the presence of TTS. The system treated speaker's disfluency (*e.g.*, "um…" in a sentence) as an end of a sentence and it prematurely started translating and synthesizing speech. Sometimes participants forgot the presence of TTS; a participant started speaking when they understood what their partner said before hearing the translation. As a result, their speech collided with TTS that was played slightly later. This was most prominent in German speakers in the Eng-Ger group because they understood their partners' English without translation.

Section Summary

The analysis suggests that speech recognition errors, translation errors, and difficulties in turn taking decreased the usability of the system. To deal with the imperfect system, participants adjusted the way that they speak, and comprehended messages not only from translation but also from CC and original speech. Some adaptation techniques were only available in some interface setting (*e.g.*, deciphering CC). Some problems were more severe because of the lack of adaptation techniques demanding some fallback options to mitigate the problems.

DESIGN GUIDELINES

We discuss design guidelines that emerged as a result of the analysis. Though they are not meant to be exhaustive, we believe they cover fundamental requirements for designing typical SLT systems.

Support Users' Adaptation for Speech Production

It is unlikely that MT and ASR will perform perfectly in the near future. However, system designers can help improve user experience by designing their application to support users' adaptation for speech production. The translator application suffered from incorrectly translating sentences with complex word structures and idiomatic expressions. Incorporating feedback mechanisms to let users know when translation is unsuccessful would allow them to effectively repeat and rephrase their utterance.

Participants found closed caption useful for identifying speech recognition errors and subsequently adjusting the way that they spoke. Nevertheless, because there were no clear indications of *why* the recognition failed, participants tried various adaptation techniques. Typical speech recognition software produces a *confidence* score for transcription accuracy and the information can be presented along with other information. Presenting *why* it had low confidence to its users allows them to better adjust the way they speak. For example, a user can slow down their speech if the system shows low speech recognition confidence with fast utterance speed.

Offer Fallback Strategies with Non-verbal Input

We found that some speech recognition problems were more severe due to the lack of effective correction techniques. System designers should consider offering alternative input methods to provide fallback options for problems such as *proper noun* recognition and *statement vs. question* classification. Allowing editable text-based input on top of speech input would mitigate the problem with ASR's out-of-vocabulary problem.

Support Comprehension of Messages

Closed captions helped participants comprehend imperfect translation; however, some were frustrated with it not persisting on a screen. Providing a history of translation on a screen could help one to comprehend a long message. Interface designers should consider how to show old transcriptions/translations on limited display of real estate.

Participants mentioned that their partners' original speech could be used to extract information lost during translation. For example, it allows one to pick up a proper noun in a sentence and conveys unspoken *feeling* in it. At the same time, some people may find it redundant. As there would be diverse preference for hearing/not hearing original speech, we recommend system designers to allow users to easily adjust the volume of original speech.

Support Users' Turn Taking

Increasing awareness of the system state would benefit turn taking. People can use information about *what* the system is currently doing to determine when they can safely speak and avoid speech overlap with TTS. Showing when recognition and translation are occurring is also useful as users can see if the system is passing premature utterance to the machine translation component or not.

Preference for having or not having TTS was polarized; some preferred having it to gain additional information, and others mentioned that it disrupted turn taking. To accommodate participants with different preferences, we suggest designers to make it easier to turn TTS on and off. Other potential design directions to reduce turn taking cost would be: (i) make TTS smarter to avoid it speaking while a user is speaking; (ii) simplify isolating TTS from the original users' voice (*e.g.*, ducking the volume of original voice, 3D audio effect to simulate different audio source position); (iii) allow users to abort ASR and MT to avoid immature translation due to speech collision.

LIMITATIONS AND FUTURE WORK

Our German participants in Eng-Ger group had reasonable English proficiency. This may have impacted their experience with the tool as they were able to comprehend what their partner said without the translation. However, we feel that studying this population is important as some of our potential users could be those who understand the other language, but prefer speaking in their own language.

Though we compared subjective usability scores between conditions with translation and without translation (*i.e.,* in English), the better control setting would have been a conversation with a human interpreter. We could not set up this control setting because participants were recruited in rolling basis and, as a result, we could not hire a human interpreter in a timely manner (in fact, a lack of no flexibly available human interpreter is one motivation for developing SLT). Future work should involve a human interpreter and compare the usability of SLT with quality of experience with human-interpreter-mediated conversation.

CONCLUSION

We have investigated the effect of spoken language translation on user experience in interlingual conversation. The statistical results from our study with 8 French-German pairs and 15 English-German pairs (a total of 46 participants) illustrated evidence of participants' adaptation and suggested preference of diverse interface setting. Content analysis contextualized *how* participants adapted to produce and comprehend speech, and *why* participants preferred one interface setting to another. The design guidelines based on the findings will contribute to the better design of spoken language translation systems.

ACKNOWLEDGEMENTS

We thank the Skype Translator team at Microsoft for many discussions and the feedback on this research.

REFERENCES

1. Bazzi, I. and Glass, J.R. Modeling Out-Of-Vocabulary Words For Robust Speech Recognition. Doctoral Dissertation. 2000.
2. Berg, B.L. and Lune, H. *Qualitative research methods for the social sciences*. Pearson Boston, 2001.
3. Costantini, E., Pianesi, F., and Burger, S. The added value of multimodality in the NESPOLE! speech-to-speech translation system: an experimental study. *IEEE ICMI*, (2002), 235–240.
4. Creutz, M., Hirsimäki, T., Kurimo, M., et al. Morph-based Speech Recognition and Modeling of Out-of-vocabulary Words Across Languages. *ACM TSLP. 5*, 1 (2007), 3:1–3:29.
5. Deng, L. and Huang, X. Challenges in Adopting Speech Recognition. *Commun. ACM 47*, 1 (2004), 69–75.
6. Feely, A.J. and Harzing, A.-W. Language management in multinational companies. *IJCCM 10*, 2 (2003), 37–52.
7. Fügen, C., Waibel, A., and Kolss, M. Simultaneous Translation of Lectures and Speeches. *MT 21*, 4 (2007), 209–252.
8. Gao, G., Xu, B., Cosley, D., and Fussell, S.R. How Beliefs About the Presence of Machine Translation Impact Multilingual Collaborations. *Proc. of CSCW* (2014), 1549–1560.
9. Gao, G., Yamashita, N., Hautasaari, A.M.J., Echenique, A., and Fussell, S.R. Effects of Public vs. Private Automated Transcripts on Multiparty Communication Between Native and Non-native English Speakers. *Proc. of CHI* (2014), 843–852.
10. Gile, D. *Theoretical components in interpreter and translator training*. . John Benjamins Publishing Company, 2009.
11. Hamon, O., Fügen, C., Mostefa, D., et al. End-to-end Evaluation in Simultaneous Translation. *Proc. of ECACL* (2009), 345–353.
12. He, X. and Deng, L. Speech-Centric Information Processing: An Optimization-Oriented Approach. *Proc. of the IEEE 101*, 5 (2013), 1116–1135.
13. Janssen, C.P., Iqbal, S.T., and Ju, Y.-C. Sharing a driver's context with a caller via continuous audio cues to increase awareness about driver state. *J. of E. Psychology*, (2014).
14. Kale, E. and Syed, H.R. Language barriers and the use of interpreters in the public health services. A questionnaire-based survey. *PEC 81*, 2 (2010), 187–191.
15. Morita, N. Negotiating Participation and Identity in Second Language Academic Communities. *TESOL Quarterly 38*, 4 (2004), 573–603.
16. Nakamura, S., Markov, K., Nakaiwa, H., et al. The ATR multilingual speech-to-speech translation system. *IEEE Trans. on ASLP 14*, 2 (2006), 365–376.
17. Pan, Y., Jiang, D., Picheny, M., and Qin, Y. Effects of Real-time Transcription on Non-native Speaker's Comprehension in Computer-mediated Communications. *Proc. of CHI* (2009), 2353–2356.
18. Prasad, R., Kumar, R., Ananthakrishnan, S., et al. Active error detection and resolution for speech-to-speech translation. *IWSLT*, (2012), 150–157.
19. Singer, A. Contemporary Immigrant Gateways in Historical Perspective. *Daedalus 142*, 3 (2013), 76–91.
20. Stolcke, A., Coccaro, N., Bates, R., et al. Dialogue Act Modeling for Automatic Tagging and Recognition of Conversational Speech. *Comp. Ling. 26*, 3 (2000), 339–373.
21. Takezawa, T., Sugaya, F., Yokoo, A., and Yamamoto, S. A new evaluation method for speech translation systems and a case study on ATR-MATRIX from Japanese to English. *Proc. of MTS.* (1999), 299–307.
22. Waibel, A., Jain, A.N., McNair, A.E., Saito, H., Hauptmann, A.G., and Tebelskis, J. JANUS: a speech-to-speech translation system using connectionist and symbolic processing strategies. *ICASSP*, (1991), 793–796 vol.2.
23. Wang, H.-C., Fussell, S., and Cosley, D. Machine Translation vs. Common Language: Effects on Idea Exchange in Cross-lingual Groups. *Proc. of CSCW* (2013), 935–944.
24. Wobbrock, J.O., Findlater, L., Gergle, D., and Higgins, J.J. The Aligned Rank Transform for Nonparametric Factorial Analyses Using Only Anova Procedures. *Proc. of CHI* (2011), 143–146.
25. Yamashita, N., Inaba, R., Kuzuoka, H., and Ishida, T. Difficulties in Establishing Common Ground in Multiparty Groups Using Machine Translation. *Proc. of CHI* (2009), 679–688.
26. Yamashita, N. and Ishida, T. Effects of Machine Translation on Collaborative Work. *Proc. of CSCW* (2006), 515–524.
27. AIIC-UN Agreement rates (viewed Sept 2014). http://aiic.net/page/275/aiic-un-agreement-rates-last-update-july-2014/lang/1.

Supporting the Modern Polyglot - A Comparison of Multilingual Search Interfaces

Ben Steichen, Luanne Freund
University of British Columbia, Vancouver, Canada
{ben.steichen, luanne.freund}@ubc.ca

ABSTRACT
The unrelenting rise in online user diversification has generated tremendous new challenges for search system providers. Among these, the need to address multiple user language abilities and preferences is paramount. The majority of research on multilingual search has so far focused on improving retrieval and translation techniques in cross-language information retrieval. However, less research has focused on the human-computer interaction aspects of multilingual search, particularly in terms of multilingual result display interfaces. To address this research gap, this paper presents a comparison of 5 different search interface designs for multilingual search. We analyze and evaluate these interfaces through a crowd-based experiment involving 885 participants. Our results show that the common approach of interleaving multilingual results is in fact the least preferred, whereas single-page displays with clear language separation are most preferred. In addition, we show that user proficiency and search content type play an important role in user preferences, and that different interfaces elicit different user behaviors.

Author Keywords
Multilingual Search; Multilingual Interfaces; Evaluation; Human–Computer Information Retrieval; Crowd-Sourcing;

ACM Classification Keywords
H.5.m. **[Information interfaces and presentation (e.g., HCI)]**: Miscellaneous; H.3.3 **[Information Search and Retrieval]**: Search process; H.5.2 **[User Interfaces]**: Evaluation/methodology;

INTRODUCTION
According to the latest estimates by the International Telecommunication Union, there are now in excess of 2.7 billion Internet users, up from only 1 billion users in 2005.[1] The biggest contribution towards this growth comes from areas outside of the native English-speaking world, with Asian markets now accounting for over 48% of all Internet users.[2] This globalization of the online population gives rise to tremendous new challenges for adapting online services to increasingly diverse user needs, abilities, and preferences, particularly in web search.

One of the most pressing challenges lies in supporting online users' individual language skills. In particular, while the diversity of native languages among Internet users is increasing, the number of polyglot users, i.e. those who are proficient in more than one language, is also on the rise. For instance, on average 94.6% of secondary education pupils in the European Union learn English in general programs, and 64.7% learn two or more languages.[3] This growth of polyglots is equally evident throughout the world, as it is estimated that there are many more people who know English as a second language than there are native speakers.[4] This development has also directly led to new multilingual online behaviors. For instance, a recent survey showed that the majority of polyglots frequently use multiple languages during their daily online browsing and searching [16]. This is in part a result of some languages being massively underrepresented in terms of web content with respect to their user base. For example, it is estimated[5] that while 55% of all websites are in English, Chinese-language websites only account for 4%, despite 22% of Internet users being from China.[2] Given the high likelihood that the diversity of language content and the polyglot user base will continue to increase, there is a pressing need for more sophisticated information access solutions, which can address the needs of these users.

Additional challenges exist to personalize such systems to individual users and situations. For example, multilingual users have varying levels of proficiency in different languages, which may affect their interactions with systems and content. Further, the type of content being searched (e.g. general web content vs. news) may have an effect. Each of these factors may play an important role in determining what and how information should be retrieved and presented to each individual user, as suggested in [16].

Despite the trend towards Internet polyglotism, web information access systems tend to emphasize distinctions between languages, often requiring users to switch between

CHI 2015, April 18–23, 2015, Seoul, Republic of Korea.

http://dx.doi.org/10.1145/2702123.2702541

[1] www.itu.int/en/ITU-D/Statistics/Pages/stat/default.aspx
[2] www.internetlivestats.com/internet-users/#byregion
[3] epp.eurostat.ec.europa.eu/statistics_explained/index.php/Foreign_language_learning_statistics
[4] www.britishcouncil.org/learning-research-english-next.pdf
[5] w3techs.com/technologies/overview/content_language/all

versions of the system or conduct separate searches in order to retrieve results in more than one language. This extra effort reduces the likelihood that multilingual searches are conducted, and may result in less relevant content being found. In the long run, reliance upon such systems undermines the growing linguistic and cultural diversity of the Internet. To address these shortcomings, there has been significant progress in developing systems that can retrieve information across language barriers, i.e. cross-language search systems that allow users to search for documents in a language that is different from the original query language. However, the human-computer interaction aspects of multilingual search have received comparably less attention. In particular, there is a lack of direct comparisons of different multilingual search result displays.

The goal of this paper is to compare and evaluate the most common interface designs for multilingual search, in order to provide a better understanding of the respective user preferences and behaviors. Specifically, we aim to answer the following research questions:

- (RQ1) Which interface designs are preferred by multilingual users?
- (RQ2) Do factors such as language proficiency, type of content, or the particular languages involved influence preferences?
- (RQ3) Do different interfaces induce different user behaviors?

Through a crowd-based experiment involving 885 participants, this paper provides the first comparative analysis of commonly used multilingual search interface designs, and provides novel insights and guidelines for the design of these interfaces.

RELATED WORK

Multilingual Search Interfaces

In the field of Multilingual Search, much research has been conducted on *cross-language information retrieval*. Significant progress has been made in recent years on both translation and retrieval effectiveness, through focused campaigns such as the *Cross-Language Evaluation Forum*[6]. In comparison, the human-computer interaction aspect of such systems has received less attention, although notable exceptions include the works by Petrelli et al. [14], Oard et al [11], Marlow et al. [10], and Peters et al. [13], as well as the interactive CLEF (iCLEF) campaigns[7] (e.g. [12][8]).

Petrelli et al. [14] investigated different interaction paradigms for query elicitation and translation, by comparing a 'delegate' mode, i.e. fully automated query translation, to a 'supervised' mode, i.e. users choose/edit the translation. Through a number of studies, they showed that a compromise between the two, i.e. automated translation with user-editing capabilities, was the most effective and satisfactory approach. Similarly, studies by Oard et al. [11] found that query translation aids were generally considered advantageous to the user's interaction experience. Marlow et al. [10] investigated the effect of language ability on the use of Google Translate during multilingual search. Results showed that for unfamiliar languages, users made substantial use of automated translations, whereas for familiar languages, they tended to write their own translations and focused on webpages in the original language.

In terms of the result display, there are two commonly used approaches in multilingual information retrieval. One is to aggregate results from all languages into a single merged list. These 'Interleaved' lists can be generated using round-robin (e.g. as offered by the now removed Google Translated Foreign Pages feature), or based on collection size or relevance feedback [5]. The other approach is to use a 'Tabbed' interface, as presented in [2][8], where results are split by language and presented to users on separate tabs. Similar to these, the system in [7] allows users to switch between languages using tabs, while also affording a tab that displays *All documents* (the merging strategy for this interleaved list is not specified). Most recently, some prototypes have been developed to display results in separate 'Panels' for each language (e.g. 2lingual[8], ollito[9]).

While all these systems allow users to search across multiple languages, direct comparisons of the affordances and limitations of these designs are lacking. In this paper, we undertake this task, by conducting a comparative user study on different designs.

Monolingual Aggregate Search

While there has been relatively little research in terms of multilingual result display interfaces, several related works in the field of (monolingual) 'Aggregate Search' have investigated the general problem of displaying aggregate content from multiple source collections.

In the work by Bron et al. [6], a 'Tabbed' display is compared to a 'Blended' display in the digital library domain. In the 'Tabbed' display, results from each collection are presented separately arranged in labeled tabs, similar to 'Tabbed' multilingual search interfaces in [2][8][7]. In the 'Blended' display, results from all collections are displayed in a single list similar to the 'Universal Search' style[10] that is now commonly used by web search engines, whereby results from different search collections are shown in contiguous blocks (e.g. news results, followed by image results, followed by web

[6] CLEF - now *Conference and Labs of the Evaluation Forum* - www.clef-initiative.eu/

[7] nlp.uned.es/iCLEF/

[8] www.2lingual.com/

[9] www.ollito.com/

[10] googlepress.blogspot.ca/2007/05/google-begins-move-to-universal-search_16.html

results). User studies showed that the 'Blended' interface was particularly useful for exploring multiple sources simultaneously, while users found the 'Tabbed' display more useful to zoom in and focus on a single source.

Sushmita et al. [17] compared a 'Blended' to a 'Non-Blended' aggregate search interface in the monolingual web search domain. While the 'Blended' interface was similar to that used by Bron et al. [6], the 'Non-Blended' interface presented results from each source in separate panels similar to the abovementioned 'Panel' display. Results showed that while both interfaces had similar click frequencies, users bookmarked slightly more pages in the 'Blended' design.

Similarly, Thomas et al. [18] compared four different aggregate interfaces in the government metasearch domain. In addition to 'Tabbed', 'Blended', and 'Side-By-Side' interfaces similar to the 'Tabbed', 'Blended', and 'Panels' interfaces used in [6] and [17], they also investigated a 'More Results' interface, which contained a side-section on the main results page (i.e. the page showing results from the main source) that pointed to additional results from other sources. Their findings showed that users preferred interfaces that provided more information up-front, and that the 'More Results' interface was least preferred because no indication was given as to which other sources had relevant results.

It is important to note that unlike multilingual search interfaces, aggregated search interfaces typically focus on Image, News (which is also typically accompanied by images), and Video (e.g. [6][17]), which are much more visually salient verticals and hence easier to distinguish from web results. It is thus of interest to investigate whether findings from aggregated search interfaces would still hold in multilingual search.

Summary of Notable Interface Techniques

From the related work, we identified five commonly used techniques for displaying results from different languages or collections, namely *Tabbed*, *Interleaved*, *Panels*, *Side-Bar*, and *Universal Search*. In the context of multilingual search, in this paper:

- *Tabbed* refers to interfaces that present results from each language using separate tabs (e.g. as shown in [2][8][7][6][18]);
- *Interleaved* refers to the approach of interleaving multilingual results in a single ranked list (e.g. as in [5][7] and Google Translated Foreign Pages);
- *Panels* refers to interfaces that present results in separate panels for each language (e.g. 2Lingual, Ollito, and the 'Non-Blended' interfaces in [17][18]);
- *Side-Bar* refers to the approach of splitting 'main' and 'additional results' (e.g. as shown in the 'More Results' interface in [18]); and
- *Universal Search* refers to the approach of displaying contiguous blocks of results in different languages (e.g. the 'Blended' interfaces in [6][17][18])[11].

EXPERIMENTAL SETUP

Based on the typical approaches identified in the related work, we implemented five multilingual search interfaces. These implementations [12] are representative, since they contain all characteristics of their respective interface approach discussed above.

Interfaces Used in the Study

Each of the interfaces used in the study are connected to the same back-end for web retrieval and translation (Bing Search API[13] and Microsoft Translator[14]), and only vary in terms of front-end result arrangement and interaction design.[15] These APIs are representative of the state-of-the-art in Web search and Machine Translation, which ensures a realistic experimental setup of real-world scenarios in practice, sufficient for the purpose of this study.

Tabbed Interface

As shown in Figure 1, the *Tabbed* interface provides a series of tabs allowing users to switch between their different languages, which are specified prior to the search session. The results page presents a single, monolingual ranked list, and users can choose to navigate further down/back up the list using 'next' and 'previous' buttons. The user can also choose to switch to a different language tab, at which point the query is translated and results are retrieved and displayed in that language.

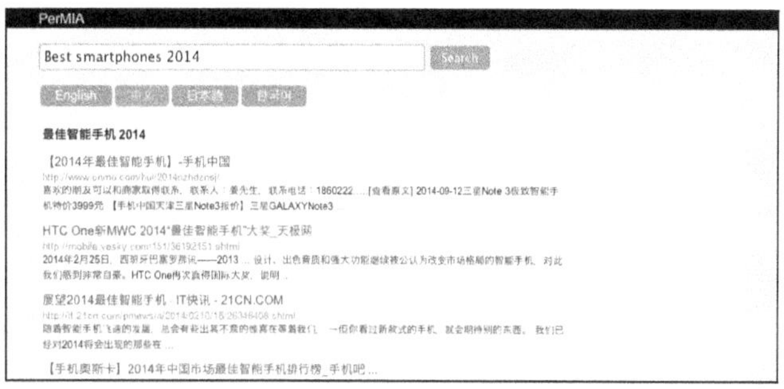

Figure 1. Tabbed Interface

---

[11] We refer to this technique as *Universal Search* rather than *Blended* to better distinguish it from the *Interleaved* interface, which is technically *Blended* too.

[12] Live demo: http://www.cs.ubc.ca/~steichen/PERMIA/ - note that the feature for users to manually edit translations was not included in the study shown in this paper, as we aimed to minimize variables and distractions from a pure comparison of different layouts.

[13] datamarket.azure.com/dataset/bing/search

[14] datamarket.azure.com/dataset/bing/microsofttranslator

[15] When participants selected a right-to-left scripted first language (e.g. Arabic or Hebrew), the interface displayed mirrored layouts of the figures shown in this section.

In the example shown in Figure 1 the user has entered the English query 'Best smartphones 2014', and has then chosen to view Chinese results, which are retrieved using the translation'最佳智能手机 2014'.

Side-Bar Interface

As shown in Figure 2, the *Side-Bar* interface also uses tabs, and additionally contains a small side-bar section, which displays results in the user's other languages. Since the idea for this interface is to convey a split between 'main' and 'additional' results, only titles of the results are displayed in the side-bar. In the example shown, a user has chosen German ('Deutsch') as the current focus language, which displays German results in the main area on the left. On the right hand side, additional results in English and French (this user's other languages) are displayed. The top of the main result area, as well as each side bar box displays the query in the respective language.

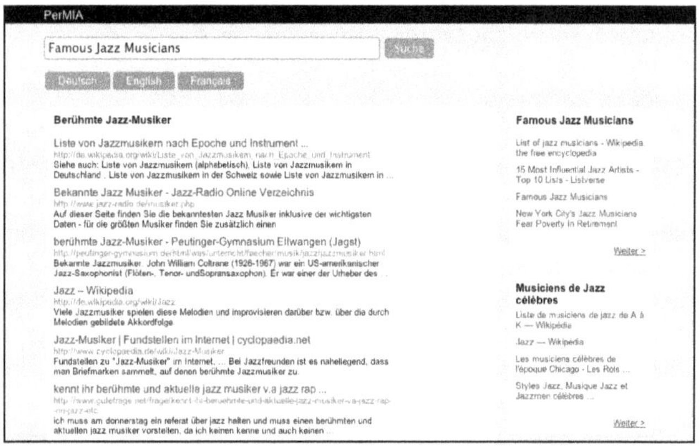

Figure 2. Side-Bar Interface

Panels Interface

The *Panels* interface (see Figure 3) displays results using equal-sized panels. Checkboxes allow users to select/deselect the languages that they wish to be displayed.

In order to show an overview of all languages on a single screen (i.e. above the fold), the number of results per language depends on the number of chosen languages. If a single language is chosen, the interface is similar to the *Tabbed* interface, showing a list of the top 12 results for the selected language only. When two languages are chosen, two result lists with 6 results each are displayed side-by-side. When 3 or more languages are selected, the interface displays panels that are split horizontally and vertically, with 4 results each in case of 3 languages, or 3 results each if more than 3 languages are displayed (as shown in Figure 3). This decreasing number of results per language ensures that the same number of results is displayed for each configuration. Each panel is headed by the query translated into the appropriate language, and the results within each panel can be navigated with 'previous' and 'next' buttons.

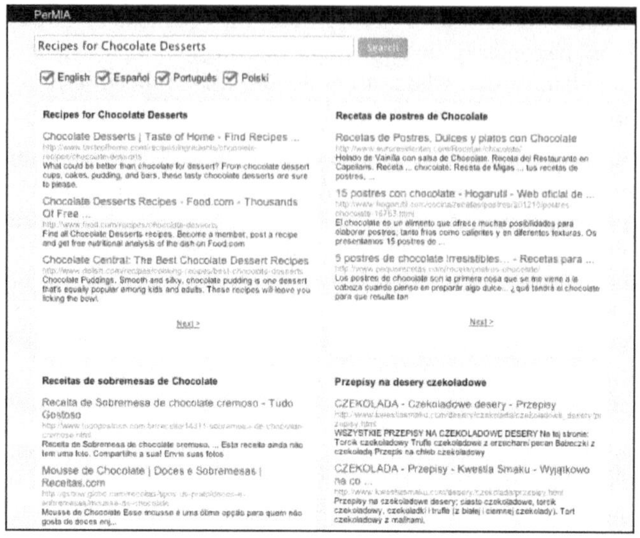

Figure 3. Panels Interface

Interleaved Interface

The *Interleaved* interface presents a single merged ranked list, with results from different languages being interleaved through a simple round-robin approach. For example, in Figure 4 results are shown in the following order: French-Russian-Norwegian (which is the order of language proficiency indicated by the user). In this case of 3 chosen languages, the result list displays a total of 4 results per language per page. Checkboxes allow users to select/deselect results in specific languages, and all query translations are shown together above the merged result list.

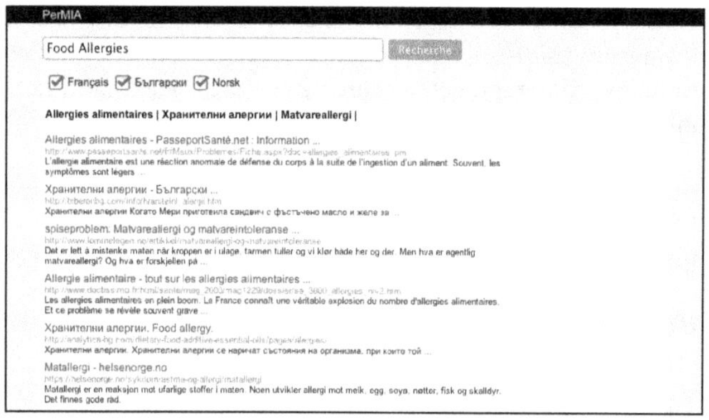

Figure 4. Interleaved Interface

Universal Search Interface

The *Universal Search* interface (see Figure 5) also presents a single ranked list. However, rather than interleaving results, this interface presents contiguous blocks of results, in decreasing order of language proficiency. For example, in Figure 5 a batch of 4 Finnish results is followed by a batch of 4 Dutch results, etc. Checkboxes allow users to select/deselect their languages, and all query translations are shown at the top of the list.

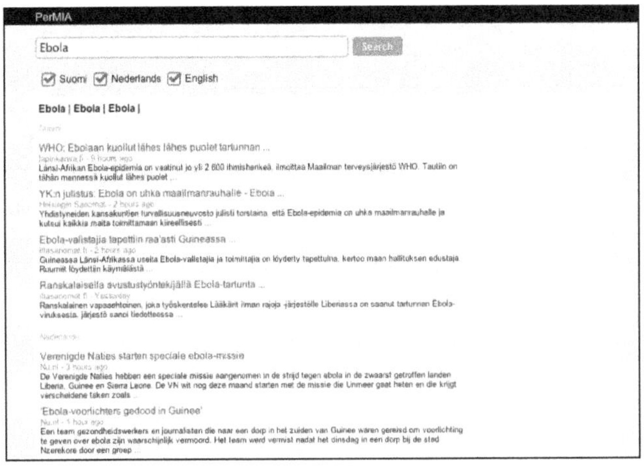

Figure 5. Universal Search Interface

Participant Recruitment

We conducted a crowd-based user study using the Crowdflower[16] platform. Participants were required to have 'some proficiency'[17] in at least two out of a set of 32 languages (which are all the languages supported by the Microsoft Bing and Translator APIs). In addition, only participants using desktop or laptop computers were recruited (future studies may specifically focus on mobile devices). To reduce noise and increase quality, only Tier 3 contributors [18] were invited for participation. Each participant was paid 10 cents, and the average user completion time was approximately 6 minutes.

Search Queries

Since the goal of our study was to compare different results display designs, it was necessary to ensure that while layouts varied, all other variables remained fixed, such as the search queries and their translations. In particular, we did not want preferences for a particular interface to be influenced by result relevance or better query translations. We therefore controlled the queries and manually verified query translations. This setup thus ensured that participants were presented with the same content, with the only variable being the layout of this content. To provide an unbiased and diverse set of topics, our queries were taken from the CLEF 2008 Ad Hoc Track [1] and Google Trends[19], as shown in Table 1.

To test for the effect of different content types (i.e. to answer RQ2), some queries were used to retrieve general Web content, whereas other queries (regarding current events) were used to retrieve News content[20]. This was based on our hypothesis that these broad distinctions might elicit different preferences (e.g. News searches particularly favoring displays that provide an overview of diversified viewpoints).[21] To avoid source mixing, each query returned results from one source only - either Web or News.

Query	Type
Decorating Children's Rooms	Web
Recipes for Chocolate Desserts	Web
Bordeaux Wine Guides	Web
Famous Jazz Musicians	Web
Youth Employment in Europe	Web
Food Allergies	Web
Diabetes	Web
Best smartphones 2014	Web
Ukraine	News
Gaza	News
Ebola	News
FIFA World Cup	News

Table 1. Queries used for the study

Procedure

After giving their informed consent, participants were first asked to provide demographic information regarding their country of origin and country of residence, as well as the languages in which they had some proficiency. Participants were also asked to indicate their levels of proficiency in the selected languages on a 5-point scale with labeled ends, where 1 indicates 'elementary proficiency' and 5 indicates 'native or bilingual proficiency'.

Participants were then shown a pair-wise comparison of results for one of the queries using two of the five interfaces (counterbalanced across participants overall) embedded in the Crowdflower interface.[22] Participants were free to click on any of the results, or use any other functionality (e.g. switch language using buttons, see more results, etc.), although the search box and the search button were disabled (to reduce variables and minimize distractions as discussed previously). The search boxes in the interfaces were pre-filled with the same query, drawn from the queries shown in Table 1. We asked users to indicate what they found to be 'the most interesting' result in each of the interfaces. Users were then asked to indicate which interface they preferred (or No Preference) and why (open question).

As noted in [9], first impressions or short interactions are crucial in human decision-making and preference judgments. Our study thus focused on relatively short interactions to gauge user interface preferences, as opposed to evaluating lengthy interactions with a fully operational multilingual search system. This setup minimizes

[16] www.crowdflower.com

[17] Having 'some proficiency' was defined as 'you must have some reading/writing ability' in the language.

[18] Described as '... the highest performance contributors who account for 7% of monthly judgments and maintain the highest level of accuracy ...' – www.crowdflower.com

[19] www.google.com/trends/

[20] Using the 'source' property in the Bing Search API

[21] Future studies may also investigate other, more fine-grained topic distinctions (e.g. health, technology, etc.)

[22] Following the technical approach of [20].

distractions posed by operational factors, such as the quality of the ranking algorithm or the query translations.

As a quality control mechanism, users were asked to indicate what the topic of the search was, by selecting one correct answer out of five topics from a pre-existing list. We also asked users to describe the search topic in the languages they claimed to speak. We then manually verified these responses and discarded spam entries. Although noise is unlikely to be completely eliminated due to the nature of self-reported data, we believe the control exercised in this study is sufficient for quality assurance.

Participant responses to the demographic questions and their interface preferences were collected through the Crowdflower interface. In addition, all interactions with the interface were logged by the search system, including language choices, checkboxes/tabs, and result clicks.

Data Analysis

We used the Bradley-Terry model [4] for the statistical analysis of preferences. Given a number of independently sampled pairwise comparisons (in our case preference judgments between pairs of interfaces), the Bradley-Terry model generates an overall 'ability estimate' for each item using transitivity, which can be interpreted as a generalized overall 'interface preference score'. These values not only allow an overall ranking of the different interfaces, but also provide odds ratios of preferences between any pair of items, which can then be converted to a more interpretable value that indicates the 'probability that one interface is preferred over the other' (thereby answering RQ1). For this analysis, we used the BradleyTerry2 package for R [19], which generates overall ability scores, as well as statistical significance testing between the 'ability' of pairs of items.

Note that a Bradley-Terry model allows for the specification of model factors to examine the effect and its statistical significance of study factors (analogous to factors in standard regression or ANCOVA). In order to answer RQ2, we specified proficiency ratings, the content type (Web vs. News), and a user's first language as model factors. For proficiency, we first ran a model using the actual value, followed by a 'high' vs 'low' model (using a median split) for ease of presentation. All reported results are corrected using Bonferroni corrections for Type I errors.

To analyze users' behaviors (to answer RQ3), we ran chi-square tests on result clicks, as well as choices of 'most interesting results', again correcting pairwise comparisons using Bonferroni corrections.

RESULTS

A total of 1220 participants took part in the study, of which responses were retained from 885 after filtering out invalid entries using the quality control mechanism discussed above. In the following sections, we provide an overview of participant demographics, followed by an analysis of user preferences and user behaviors.

Participant Demographics

A total of 76 countries of origin (see Figure 6), and 69 countries of current residence were reported by our participants. As required by the study, all users were proficient in at least two languages. In addition, 193 participants (21.8%) indicated that they were proficient in three languages, 48 participants were proficient in four languages (5.4%), and 9 participants (1%) indicated they were proficient in more than four languages.

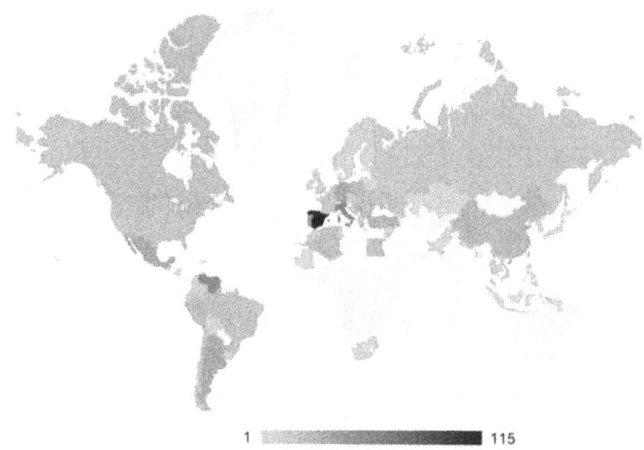

Figure 6. Map of participants' countries of origin - color tones reflect the number of participants from each country

In terms of users' first language (i.e. their most proficient language - L1 hereafter), 31 different languages were reported, with the most common languages being Spanish (32.1%), English (13.6%), Arabic (6.4%), Portuguese (6.1%), Italian (6.0%), and Chinese (5.1%)[23] (see Figure 7).

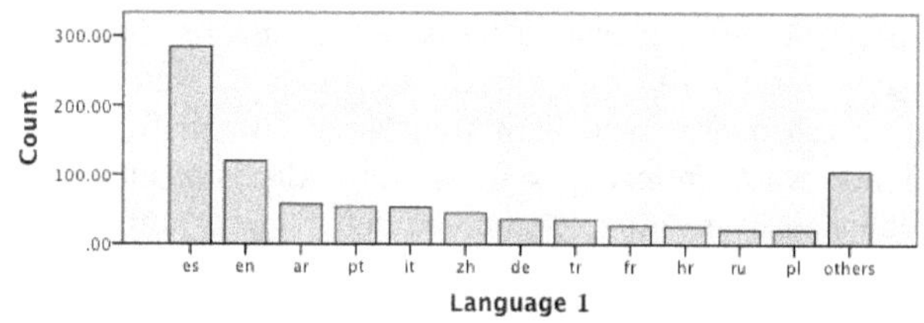

Figure 7. Overview of participants' L1

For L2 (i.e. their second most proficient language), 25 different languages were reported, with the vast majority of participants (71.2%) indicating English as their second language, followed by French (8.4%), and Spanish (4%) (see Figure 8).

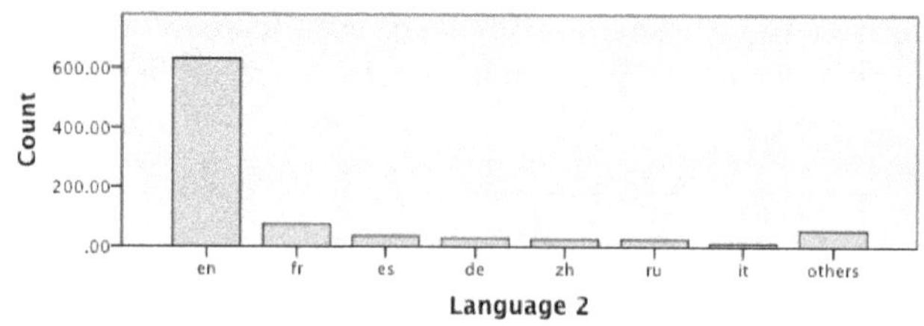

Figure 8. Overview of participants' L2

---

[23] note that we merged results for 'Chinese Simplified' and 'Chinese Traditional'

For people who indicated 3 or more languages, the most common language for 'L3' was English (33.6%), followed by French (18.8%) and German (12.8). For 'L4', the most common languages were French (26.3%), Spanish (19.3%), and Italian (10.5%).

Since L1 was participants' strongest language, the proficiency level for this was most dominantly 5 (i.e. native or bilingual language – 89.8%) or 4 (7.6%). For L2, there were great variations in terms of proficiencies, as shown in Figure 9. Lastly, users' third and fourth language proficiency levels were predominantly 3 or lower.

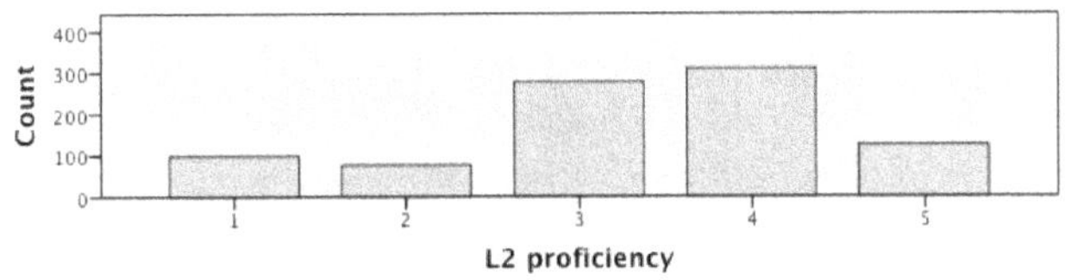

Figure 9. Overview of L2 proficiency levels (1=elementary proficiency, 5=native or bilingual proficiency)

Results for User Preferences (RQ1)

Recall that the primary research question addressed in the study is to find out what type of multilingual search result display is most preferred by multilingual users. To answer this question, we ran a Bradley-Terry test using the set of 885 preference judgments. As shown in Figure 10, there are indeed significant differences between interfaces, with the *Panels* interface having the highest overall 'preference score' (i.e. highest 'ability estimate'), and the *Interleaved* interface having the lowest.

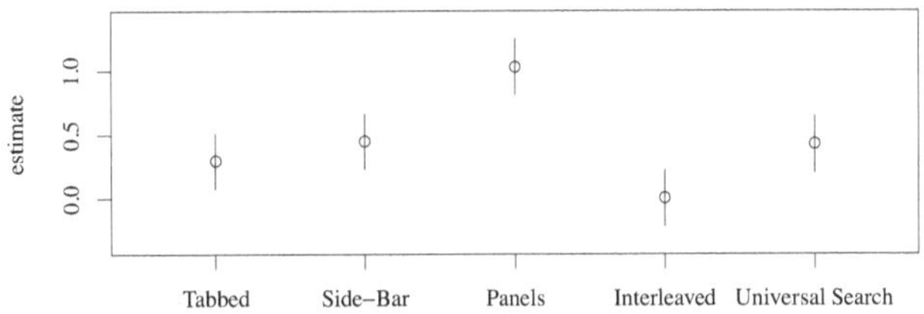

Figure 10. Overall comparison of the 5 interfaces. Ability estimates are generated from the Bradley Terry model, illustrating overall preferences for each interface

We found that the preference for *Panels* is statistically significantly higher than all other interfaces (p<.001), and the preference for *Interleaved* is statistically significantly lower than all interfaces (p<.001), except *Tabbed.*

	Tabbed	Side-Bar	Panels	Inter-leaved	Univ. Search
Tabbed		46.23%	32.48%	57.35%	46.81%
Side-Bar	53.77%		35.88%	**62.00%**	50.58%
Panels	**67.52%**	**64.12%**		**73.65%**	**64.66%**
Interleaved	42.65%	38.00%	26.35%		38.56%
Univ. Search	53.19%	49.42%	35.34%	**61.44%**	

Table 2. Direct comparisons between interfaces (generated using Bradley-Terry ability estimates) – bold numbers indicate that the interface in the left column is statistically significantly preferred over the corresponding interface in the top row

As shown in Table 2, the probability of choosing the *Panels* interface over the *Interleaved* interface is 73.65%. Similarly, the probability of choosing the *Universal Search* interface over the *Interleaved* interface is 61.44%.

Influences of Proficiency, Language, and Content Type on User Preferences (RQ2)

First, we tested for an effect of level of proficiency on interface preference. In this analysis, we found that there was indeed a statistically significant effect (p<.001) of a user's proficiency level in their L2.[24]

When splitting participants into either having a 'high' or 'low' proficiency in their second language (defined as proficiency levels of 5/4 and 3/2/1 respectively, based on a median split), we found that users with high proficiencies in their L2 significantly preferred the *Universal Search* interface over the *Interleaved* interface, and preferred it almost to the same extent as the *Panels* interface (see Figure 11 top figure). By contrast, for users with a low proficiency in their L2 (Figure 11 bottom figure), the *Universal Search* interface is no longer better than the *Interleaved* interface.

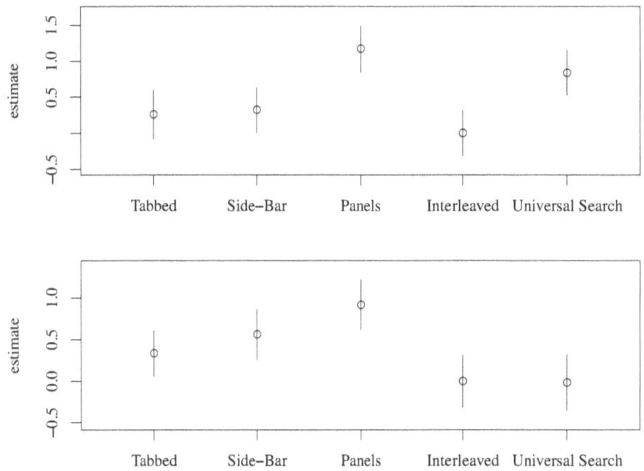

Figure 11. Interface preferences for participants with 'high' (top) and 'low' (bottom) proficiencies in their L2.

Secondly, we tested for an effect of the particular languages in which users were proficient, especially in terms of first languages. While we did not find a statistically significant effect, there were several trends suggesting that the user's first language may have some influence on interface preferences.[25] In particular, we found that users with right-to-left scripted first languages *highly* preferred the *Panels* interface, with all other interfaces being equally

[24] The majority of participants who were proficient in a third/fourth language indicated low proficiencies in them. Since there is little variation in L3 and L4 proficiencies, we did not perform separate tests for these.

[25] which may also be related to general cultural differences, as discussed in [15].

dispreferred. This may be a result of the majority of these users receiving both right-to-left (i.e. Arabic or Hebrew) and left-to-right (e.g. English) results, suggesting that the *Panels* interface provides better support for such 'mixed' script direction scenarios. Given the low number of participants for many language groups, however, there may have been insufficient power to show any statistically significant differences. While this study was explicitly aimed at gathering overall preferences from a diverse range of participants, a future study could focus on a few select languages to better elicit such effects. Similarly, we did not find an effect of the number of languages in which a user was proficient (e.g. two, three, four).

Lastly, we analyzed whether differences in content types influenced interface preferences. Results showed a statistically significant difference between Web and News content ($p<.01$). In particular, for News search, the preference for *Side-Bar* increased significantly, becoming statistically significantly preferred over the *Tabbed* and *Universal Search* interfaces (in addition to being preferred over the *Interleaved*). By contrast, for Web searches, the *Side-Bar* Interface was not preferred over *Tabbed*, *Universal Search*, or *Interleaved*.

User Behavior (RQ3)

Recall we were interested in whether different interfaces would lead to i) different choices (in terms of language) for the 'most interesting result', and ii) different click behaviors. Note that we do not assume more/less choices or clicks in a particular language to be more/less desirable or optimal. The goal here is to simply compare behaviors induced by different interfaces, in order to gain a better understanding of the different designs.

'Most interesting result' analysis

We first ran chi-square tests to analyze whether variation in interface design was associated with differences in the language of results chosen as 'most interesting', i.e. whether they were participants' L1, L2, etc. We found a significant difference between interfaces ($p<.001$), with participants choosing more results in their L1 when using the *Tabbed* and *Side-Bar* interfaces (see Figure 12). Conversely, the *Panels*, *Interleaved*, and *Universal Search* interfaces were associated with a significantly more 'diversified' selection of results in terms of languages.

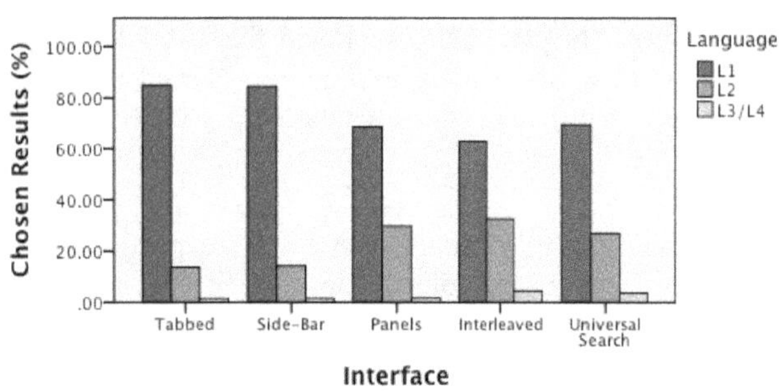

Figure 12. 'Most interesting result' selections by language (L1 vs. L2 vs. L3/L4)

Result clicks

The analysis of clicks (i.e. users clicking on a search result) showed a very similar pattern, with statistically significant differences between interfaces ($p<.001$). In particular, very few clicks were performed in a language other than participants' first language in both the *Tabbed* and *Side-Bar* interfaces (see Figure 13). Conversely, the *Panels*, *Interleaved*, and *Universal Search* interfaces led users to many more clicks in their other languages.

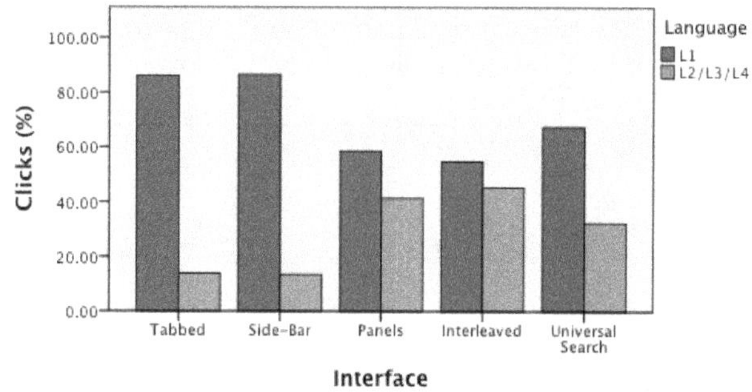

Figure 13. Result clicks by language (L1 vs. L2/L3/L4)

SUMMARY & DISCUSSION

The analysis of users' preferences, result choices, and click behaviors has shown that there are significant differences between different multilingual search interface designs. In this section, we will summarize key findings, provide further insights and recommendations based on participants' open-text comments, and discuss implications for these designs.

The Panels interface was most preferred over all other interfaces, while the Interleaved interface, most commonly used in multilingual search applications, was least preferred. Many participants considered the search results in the *Panels* interface to be more organized, easier to navigate, and easier to read. In contrast, users mentioned that the *Interleaved* interface was confusing, and that the unorganized languages made it harder to navigate and even tiring. These findings suggest that multilingual search interfaces should be designed to provide clear divisions between results in different languages. In particular, the preference for the *Panels* design is much stronger than previous research findings in monolingual aggregate search. This suggests that the inherent saliency differences between traditional verticals (e.g. between web and image results) help users in the separation of results, whereas multilingual results require additional structuring. Indeed, a possible reason for the negative results and comments on the *Interleaved* interface may be that users frequently needed to 'code-switch' between languages without any structure, nor language indication, which may have increased the cognitive load. A potential solution for this may be to use labels, icons, colors, or flags (although flags are generally regarded as bad practice in the localization community), which can be explored in future studies.

The degree of separation afforded in a Tabbed design seems to be too extreme - participants criticized the *Tabbed* interface for not showing what other results were available, and requiring too much clicking. This finding suggests that the *Tabbed* interface provides insufficient context to users and requires extra effort in switching between languages. These results are consistent with previous studies on monolingual aggregated search interfaces [18], which suggested that aggregate interfaces should show information about available information 'up-front' as much as possible. The fact that the *Tabbed* interface is dispreferred to all other interfaces (except *Interleaved*, of which the specific deficiencies are discussed above) also suggests that multilingual users are, in general, in favor of interfaces that show multiple languages on a single screen. This is possibly due to the increased information breadth of the other interfaces, as participants found them more varied, diverse, and providing a more complete overview.

Universal Search is the preferred design if only a single list is to be presented (e.g. to avoid drastically changing modern web search engine interfaces), particularly for users with high second language proficiency. These participants identified as positive features the simplicity of this design and the clear separation of languages in a single list. However, participants with low proficiency in their second languages dispreferred both single-list designs, i.e. *Universal Search* and *Interleaved*, to all others. This is potentially caused by the degree of language separation being insufficient for such users. This suggests that the *Universal Search* interface is well-suited only to users with high second language proficiencies, and that single-list designs should be avoided altogether for users with low second language proficiencies.

Preferences for the Side-Bar interface were similar to those of the Tabbed interface, even though *Side-Bar* provided additional information in other languages in a manner similar to the *Panels* interface. A likely cause for this result is that many participants mistook the side-bar for an advertising area, and they consciously chose to ignore these results, hence judging this interface to be less useful. While this seems to be the case for the Web searches, for News searches, however, the *Side-Bar* interface was actually preferred over the *Tabbed* interface, and came close to the *Panels* interface in terms of preference score. Participants mentioned that this interface was clean, and allowed them to focus on one language while being aware of/not missing others. This finding suggests that the *Side-Bar* design may be more effective for particular types of search tasks associated with news search, such as surveying and comparing multiple perspectives on a particular news story. Furthermore, it is possible that the performance of the *Side-Bar* interface may be improved significantly by making it clear to users that the side-bar results are in fact additional results in other languages (e.g. through explicit labeling at the top of the side-bar, or by moving the side-bar to a different location altogether). This may make the *Side-Bar* a viable option for quickly adding multilingual features to modern web search engine interfaces.

Many participants chose to select results in a language other than their first language as the 'most interesting result' – this result confirms the findings from [16] that polyglot users frequently acquire information in different languages. In particular, participants commented positively on the inclusion of multilingual functionalities regardless of the interface, saying there are more choices overall - not just results from one country - and that sometimes the results are more relevant and current in one language than in others. Although our results have shown that users often click on results in non-primary languages, it may not be the case that every user actually benefits from diversified multilingual results (e.g. for a simple fact finding task, multilingual results may not be necessary, and can be detrimental to the search process under some circumstances). Depending on the goal of the system designer and the user's information needs, this aspect of stimulating certain user behaviors may be explored in future studies that specifically focus on task and query types.

Lastly, *interface designs influence user behaviors* - we found that given different interfaces, more/less result clicks and choices in non-primary languages were generated. This difference may be influenced by the perceived ranking position, which is an unavoidable artifact intrinsically associated with all interface designs. For example, the low diversity for the *Tabbed* interface is intuitive, since it requires a user interaction (language tab switching) to view results in languages other than L1. For *Side-Bar*, the low diversity may indicate that users ignored the extra results (mistaking them for advertisements). Meanwhile, the greatest diversity of selected results was obtained using the interface designs preferred most (*Panels*) and least (*Interleaved*). This finding suggests that diversity is valued when the user is aware of and feeling in control of it, as in the *Panels* design, but not when it is imposed upon the user by the system. Although we do not make any assumptions about more/less clicking in (non-)primary languages being an advantage/disadvantage, our findings, however, may be useful to inform those aiming to build systems that maximize/minimize click diversity if so desired.

CONCLUSION & FUTURE WORK

This paper presents the first direct comparison of multilingual search result display designs with several informative key findings and recommendations (discussed above), thereby providing a significant contribution to the development, improvement, and deployment of systems that aim to better support the ever-increasing number of global polyglot users.

Using the most common designs in both multilingual information retrieval and monolingual aggregate search, our crowd-based evaluation has shown that participants particularly like an interface that presents results from different languages in separate 'Panels' on the same screen, and that language separation is generally preferred over the common approach of interleaving results. Also, our results have shown that the user's proficiency and search content type play a role in user preferences, and that different interfaces elicit different user behaviors.

In future work, we intend to conduct studies that specifically focus on different types of search tasks (e.g. fact finding, information gathering) and topics (e.g. business, health, technology) to determine which benefit most from linguistic diversity in search results, as well as which languages are preferred for which tasks and topics. In a more *personalized* multilingual search system (as proposed in [16]), user preferences and contextual factors could then be integrated into each of the interfaces, for example, through a reorganization of panels in the *Panels* interface, by slotting the most relevant languages higher up in the *Universal Search* interface, or by dynamically selecting the number of results per language.

Lastly, while the specific focus of this paper was to elicit user preferences without potential distractions posed by an operational interactive multilingual search system, such as the quality of the ranking algorithm or the query translations, it can be argued that some issues (e.g. confusing the side-bar with advertisements) may be overcome if given user familiarity. This speculation can be verified in future studies, e.g. through the evaluation of a fully functional interactive retrieval system involving simulated work tasks [3] that require users to enter their own queries.

ACKNOWLEDGEMENTS

This research is supported by the National Research Fund Luxembourg and cofunded under the Marie Curie Actions of the European Commission (FP7-COFUND).

REFERENCES

1. Agirre, E., Nunzio, G.M.D., Ferro, N., Mandl, T., and Peters, C. CLEF 2008: Ad Hoc Track Overview. *Evaluating Systems for Multilingual and Multimodal Information Access*, (2009), 15–37.
2. Amato, G., Debole, F., Peters, C., and Savino, P. The MultiMatch Prototype: Multilingual/Multimedia Search for Cultural Heritage Objects. *Research and Adv. Technol. for Digital Libraries*, (2008), 385–387.
3. Borlund, P. The IIR evaluation model: a framework for evaluation of interactive information retrieval systems. *Information Research 8*, 3 (2003).
4. Bradley, R.A. Paired comparisons: Some basic procedures and examples. *Nonparametric Methods 4*, (1984), 299–326.
5. Braschler, M. Combination Approaches for Multilingual Text Retrieval. *Information Retrieval*, *7*, 1-2 (2004), 183–204.
6. Bron, M., van Gorp, J., Nack, F., Baltussen, L.B., and de Rijke, M. Aggregated Search Interface Preferences in Multi-session Search Tasks. *Proc. of 36th Int. ACM SIGIR Conf. on Research and Development in Information Retrieval*, (2013), 123–132.
7. Capstick, J., Diagne, A.K., Erbach, G., Uszkoreit, H., Leisenberg, A., and Leisenberg, M. A system for supporting cross-lingual information retrieval. *Inf. Process. & Manage. 36*, 2 (2000), 275–289.
8. Clough, P., Al-Maskari, A., and Darwish, K. Providing Multilingual Access to FLICKR for Arabic Users. *Evaluation of Multilingual and Multi-modal Information Retrieval*, (2007), 205–216.
9. Gladwell, M. *Blink: The Power of Thinking Without Thinking.* Back Bay Books, New York, 2006.
10. Marlow, J., Clough, P., Recuero, J.C., and Artiles, J. Exploring the effects of language skills on multilingual web search. *Proc. of 30th European conf. on Advances in information retrieval*, (2008), 126–137.
11. Oard, D.W., He, D., and Wang, J. User-assisted query translation for interactive cross-language information retrieval. *Inf. Proc. & Manage. 44*, 1 (2008), 181–211.
12. Peinado, V., Artiles, J., Barker, E., and Lopez-Ostenero, F. FlickLing: a Multilingual Search Interface for Flickr. *Working Notes - CLEF Workshop*, (2008).
13. Peters, C., Braschler, M., and Clough, P. *Multilingual Information Retrieval: From Research To Practice, chapt. 4,* Springer Science & Business Media, (2012).
14. Petrelli, D., Levin, S., Beaulieu, M., and Sanderson, M. Which user interaction for cross-language information retrieval? Design issues and reflections. *J. Assoc. Inf. Sci. Technol., 57*, 5 (2006), 709–722.
15. Reinecke, K. and Gajos, K.Z. Quantifying Visual Preferences Around the World. *Proc. of SIGCHI Conf. on Human Factors in Computing Syst.*, (2014), 11–20.
16. Steichen, B., Ghorab, M.R., Lawless, S., O'Connor, A., and Wade, V. Towards Personalized Multilingual Information Access - Exploring the Browsing and Search Behavior of Multilingual Users. *Proc. of int. conf. on User Modeling, Adaptation, and Personalization*, (2014), 435-446.
17. Sushmita, S., Joho, H., Lalmas, M., and Villa, R. Factors Affecting Click-through Behavior in Aggregated Search Interfaces. *Proc. of 19th Int. Conf. on Inf. and Knowledge Management*, (2010), 519–528.
18. Thomas, P., Noack, K., and Paris, C. Evaluating Interfaces for Government Metasearch. *Proc. of 3rd Symp. on Inform. Interac. in Context*, (2010), 65–74.
19. Turner, H. and Firth, D. Bradley-Terry models in R: the BradleyTerry2 package. *Journal of Statistical Software 48*, 10 (2012).
20. Zuccon, G., Leelanupab, T., Whiting, S., Yilmaz, E., Jose, J.M., and Azzopardi, L. Crowdsourcing interactions: using crowdsourcing for evaluating interactive information retrieval systems. *Information Retrieval 16*, 2 (2013), 267–305.

New Interaction Tools for Preserving an Old Language

Beryl Plimmer[1,2], Liang He[2,3], Tariq Zaman[4], Kasun Karunanayaka[2], Alvin W. Yeo[4], Garen Jengan, Rachel Blagojevic,[5] Ellen Yi-Luen Do[2]
University of Auckland[1], CUTE Center, National University of Singapore[2], Carnegie Mellon University[3], ISITI, Universiti Malaysia Sarawak, Malaysia[4], Massey University, New Zealand[5]
beryl@cs.auckland.ac.nz, lianghe@andrew.cmu.edu, zamantariq@gmail.com, kasun@mixedrealitylab.org, alvin@isiti.unimas.my, susilanatasya@gmail.com, R.V.Blagojevic@massey.ac.nz, ellendo@acm.org

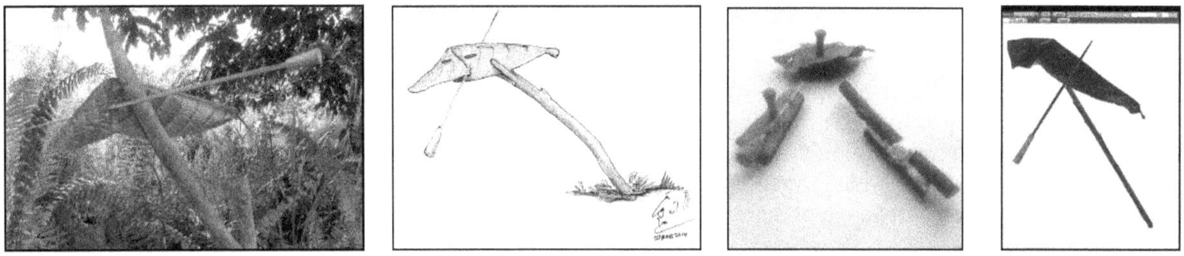

Figure 1 Oroo' sentence "I have left a hunted boar (or part of it) for you in this direction" a) in jungle, b) sketched by a Penan artist, c) tangibles of symbols d) made in application with tangibles

ABSTRACT
The Penan people of Malaysian Borneo were traditionally nomads of the rainforest. They would leave messages in the jungle for each other by shaping natural objects into language tokens and arranging these symbols in specific ways – much like words in a sentence. With settlement, the language is being lost as it is not being used by the younger generation. We report here, a tangible system designed to help the Penans preserve their unique *object writing* language. The key features of the system are that: the tangibles are made of real objects; it works in the wild; and new tangibles can be fabricated and added to the system by the users. Our evaluations show that the system is engaging and encourages intergenerational knowledge transfer, thus has the potential to help preserve this language.

Author Keywords
TUI; fabrication; capacitive tangibles; preservation of language

ACM Classification Keywords
H.5.2 [Information Interfaces and Presentation]: User Interfaces - Interaction styles

CHI 2015, April 18 - 23 2015, Seoul, Republic of Korea

ACM 978-1-4503-3145-6/15/04...$15.00
http://dx.doi.org/10.1145/2702123.2702339

INTRODUCTION
The Penan village of Long Lamai is nestled in the rainforests of Malaysian Borneo about 300km from the coast close to the Indonesian border. It is an example of a tribe that has successfully transitioned from a nomadic lifestyle to a self-reliant settled community. The village consists of about 100 families, each with their own home and gardens. Access to the village is by river: the villagers' small outboard powered boats ply the river from Long Banga, the local airstrip and hub, to Long Lamai in about 90 minutes. The village has a primary school, church, micro-hydro dam, gravity-fed running water and a telecentre. The telecentre, developed in liaison with Universiti Malaysia Sarawak, provides Internet access via VSAT (a satellite communications systems) and WiFi that is accessible in the centre of the village. A 3G mobile tower was set up recently. Many of the villagers have laptops and mobile phones.

The community settled in Long Lamai in the mid-1950's. This has brought many advantages, such as education for all children and better access to medical care. However, it has also resulted in the loss of traditional knowledge, in particular, Oroo', the focus of this project. Oroo' is the object writing [14 p25] language used by earlier generations to leave messages for each other in the jungle. The elders realized that Oroo' will be lost if they do not find ways to preserve and teach it to the younger generations.

Research engagement with the community has shown that only those over 60 who lived the nomadic life during their youth have a full command of the language [37]. This means that only a few individuals hold the key to retaining this language which is an integral part of their culture.

Similar challenges of preserving language and culture are evident in many parts of the developing world [28].

The Oroo' uses physical artefacts to create messages. The symbols are constructed from materials at hand: leaves, sticks, and vines, folded or carved and put together in specific spatial arrangements to convey messages such as "I have left a hunted boar (or part of it) for you in this direction" (Figure 1). Short stories consisting of many symbols are common. In many cases, sticks are used as a signpost and direction indicator and the other symbols are tucked into notches cut into the stick. Messages can also be left on the jungle path.

The goal for the community is to retain Oroo' as a living language that can evolve to incorporate new symbols. The elders have observed their children's fascination with computers. The elders are keen to exploit this and also learn about computers from the youngsters. Thus the community's goal is to have a software tool that will:

- Assist with preserving and maintaining Oroo' writing;

by

- Being engaging for the old and young alike so people are motivated to use it;
- Encouraging intergenerational knowledge transfer by being an enjoyable collaborative environment [31].

The language tokens (words) are instantiated with physical objects (such as sticks and leaves). With a tangible user interface these objects can be augmented to become tangibles. Hereby the system can closely match the real world context [20]. Furthermore, tangibles are known to be effective for playful educational experiences [22].

Thus, the research question addressed in this project is "how can tangible interfaces be used to support children's learning of indigenous object writing?" To answer this question we must design a system that is intuitive for users with low literacy and computer skills. It must work 'in the wild' and support the users by allowing them to add new tangibles. Yet at the same time it must be engaging, fun and educational for the old and young alike.

Most tangible research projects have been lab-based and the tangibles are designed and built by the researchers. They use camera input or sensors to detect the position of the tangibles. In this scenario, the system must literally work in the rainforest and members of the community must be able to add new tangibles to the system so that the language can grow and evolve. For example new objects have recently been designed for 'school' and 'church'.

The research design draws on aspects of ethnography, participatory design, education design research and iterative software development. The system presented here has evolved through iterative design, implementation and evaluation. We contribute a novel system which encourages learning engagement using tangible and touch interaction. Furthermore, the system supports users' addition of new tangibles taking advantage of the affordance of tablet computers and the spirit of bricolage [7].

The structure of this paper is as follows. Next, we provide a background to tangible interaction. Following this, we describe our approach, the technical aspects of the project, the evaluations, and finish with a discussion and conclusions.

BACKGROUND

Tangible interaction has been explored for many years and in many contexts [9, 10, 25, 34]. This section provides an overview of the motivation for tangible interaction and the demonstrated benefits it brings [22]. It then focuses on research into tangibles on capacitive displays.

The ability to manipulate objects is a skill acquired very early in life. Using tangibles for computing operations takes advantage of this existing skillset [32]. Tangibles lower the level of interaction abstraction allowing users to apply their natural tool-based skillset to the digital environment. An integral part of this interaction is the rich sensory feedback users receive from tangibles in the form of visual, tactile and proprioception stimulus. In essence, tangibles combine the advantages of the physical and digital worlds by allowing digital information to be manipulated, controlled, and represented by physical objects [13].

Using physical objects is an intuitive way to explain things to others, to teach and learn at the same time [22]. Tangibles have been shown to increase explorative behaviour [6], reduce conflicts in cooperation [21, 26], encourage prolonged engagement [8, 15] and act as a useful aid to problem solving in comparison to standard graphical user interfaces [35]. Tangibles have also been used to aid in the preservation of indigenous oral stories [18, 29]. They have proved useful to encourage language learning with toddlers [12] and to aid learning programming [30].

Cameras were used to sense the tangibles in most early tangibles research – this approach is unsuitable for the environment of this project. We must adopt technology and techniques that will work in a remote rural environment [2]. There have been a number of projects that have explored using tangibles on capacitive tablets [3, 16, 27, 36]. These tangibles work by transmitting an electrical charge from the user through touch points on the tangible to the capacitive display [1]. The capacitive display detects the tangible as finger touches, and then a recognizer is used to distinguish between the tangibles.

SmartSkin is an early system that used capacitive sensing with a mesh shaped antenna to detect hands and objects [23]. Conductive materials were attached to blocks in patterns to allow objects to be identified. Yu et al. [36] present three tangible technologies for use on capacitive touch surfaces: spatial, frequency and hybrid. Their spatial tangibles employ touch point patterns for object identification. Frequency tangibles use a modulation circuit (with a power source) to generate touches of varying frequency. The hybrid tangible combines the spatial and frequency technologies. Chan et al. [5] introduce stackable tangibles, sliders and dials for capacitive screens. The stackable tangibles are able to sense changes in capacitance when blocks are placed on top of them – this in turn modifies the touch point pattern for identification. CapWidgets [16] are tangible dials designed for mobile capacitive screens. GaussBricks [17] also uses a tablet interface but this is supplemented by magnetic sensing of the bricks.

OUR APPROACH

We conducted a field-based participatory design project using tangible technology, and evaluated these with families to understand how tangible technology might provide a way of engaging younger members of an indigenous community with their traditional writing.

To our knowledge no research has explored learning tools suitable for object writing systems such as Oroo'. Furthermore while tangible user interfaces (TUIs) have been explored for verbal language learning and programming, they have not been investigated in the context of this type of language. In addition, the goal of having a tool that functions in the wild governs the equipment and interaction design choices.

This project blends a number of methodologies: ethnography [11], where the researchers work in the community, education design research [4] that builds on constructivist theories of learning, participatory design protocol [24] in which the users are active participants in the research, and iterative software development that focuses on user experience [19]. All engagements with the Long Lamai community follow an agreed protocol with co-authorship and approval of the community.

We report here three rounds of design, evaluation and redesign. The key parts of the project are designing a system that will work in the wild and support the addition of new tangibles. There are two aspects to adding tangibles – the community being able to fabricate their own tangibles, and being able to interactively add these new tangibles to the system.

The first prototype was developed by the researchers as a proof-of-concept. It was shared with three elders individually and with their input, a second prototype was produced. This was then evaluated with a group of elders, a family group and at a community meeting. From these interactions the third prototype requirements were specified and subsequently developed. This prototype was evaluated more formally with 6 family groups.

SYSTEM DESIGN AND IMPLMENTATION

This section describes the technology behind the project. As there have been three rounds of development, we focus on the final prototype noting where appropriate changes made between prototypes. The software is written in HTML5 & JavaScript. It can be run directly from a compatible browser (Safari or Chrome) or saved as an app onto the user's home screen. A multi-touch tablet is required for the computer interface, we have tested on iPad, Android and Windows devices. In this section, we first describe the interaction design and tangible fabrication. This is followed by a description of the software and recognizer.

Interaction design

The software is designed so that the interaction is natural and intuitive. In particular, it must be suitable for the older members of the community (over 60): the only people fully conversant with Oroo'. Many of these people are otherwise illiterate and have had little exposure to computers. At the same time the software must be appealing and fun for young children so that the community's goals of retaining the language and supporting intergenerational knowledge transfer are met.

The system consists of the tangibles as shown in Figure 3, a multi-touch display and supporting software. To make an Oroo' in the system, the user presses a tangible onto the display (Figure 2a). An image of the symbol, the same size as the physical symbol is displayed directly under the tangible. The image can be moved by touching it and dragging it to a new location (Figure 2b). It can be rotated with two fingers (Figure 2c). To delete an image, it is dragged off the side of the screen (Figure 2d). Thus, the system supports add, change and delete with very simple and intuitive interactions.

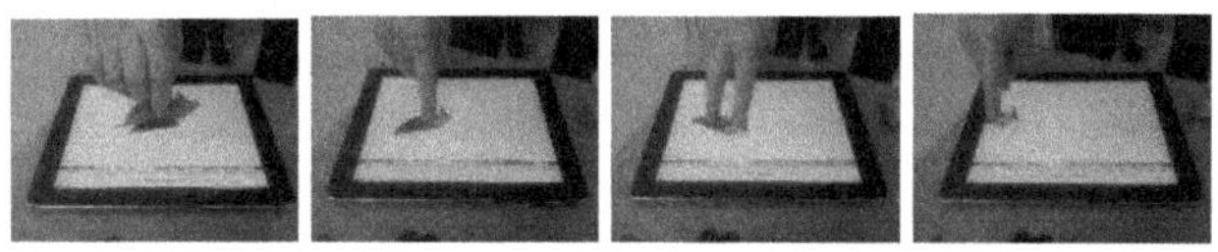

Figure 2 Interaction: a) add a symbol b) move c) rotate d) delete

Although registration of a tangible is required only once, we have also designed simple interaction for this. To register a tangible, the user first adds its pre-prepared image to the system by selecting the image file (from the standard file dialogue) and assigning it a name. When they select the image from a dropdown list in the menu bar (Figure 4) it is displayed. They associate the image to the tangible by aligning the tangible with the image and pressing the tangible onto the screen. The touch points are visualized to the user as feedback and when the user presses 'set', the association between the tangible and image is stored.

Tangibles

A tangible is constructed with a baseplate, capacitive touch tips, conductive clay, handles and the Oroo' symbol (Figure 3). The baseplate is a piece of rigid material that does not interfere with the electrical circuit. A baseplate can be of any shape, it has three 7mm diameter holes set in a unique irregular triangle. The holes house capacitive pen tips. Air-dry modeling clay is then used as a conductive medium to join the tips, hold the Oroo' symbol in place and provide a grip for the user. Depending on the shape of the symbol, a handle made of a metal screw covered in clay may be added to the top of the baseplate.

Figure 3 Tangible construction (from top left): a) pen tips with clay inside, b) conductive clay, c) MDF tangible baseplate with screw handle d) underside of the baseplate with pen tips in holes, e) a completed tangible.

Constructing tangibles that sense reliably has required considerable experimentation and extends the tangible design described in [27]. The materials, physical arrangement and construction all contribute to reliability. We found that the best materials for the baseplate are MDF (medium-density fireboard) or plywood – acrylic materials such as Perspex, hold a surface charge that interferes with the touch detection. Air-dry children's modeling clay is used as conductive material to glue the components together. However, the clay does not make suitable touch-points for the screen as it has too much friction; capacitive pen tips are a better medium. Metal screws covered in clay suffice as handles.

The tangibles are identified by the geometry of the touch-points (see Recognizer section below). It is best if these touch points are set close to the extremities of the baseplate in a triangle. Some of our initial baseplates had the three points in a straight line: it is more difficult to get contact with the surface on all three points with this arrangement because it is not stable. Furthermore, we found that the affordance of an obvious handle means that the users do not need to be instructed on how to hold a tangible. A handle also reduces the likelihood of unintended finger touches on the screen when pressing a tangible onto the surface.

When constructing a tangible, care must be taken to have an effective electrical circuit between the touch-points and handle. To keep the connection between the pen tip and clay, a small ball of clay is placed into the tip, but care must be taken not to make the tip stiff because then it is more difficult to have all three points in contact with the surface simultaneously. We experimented with adding various materials to the clay or inside the pen tips (such as copper wire, and iron crumbs), but none of these provided better connectivity and some were counterproductive.

Images

An image of the symbol is shown on the display when the tangible is recognized. New images can be added to the software. The process for this is to take a photo of the symbol. Off-the-shelf photo editing software is used to remove the background and scale the image to the right size for the display resolution.

To simplify the first-time user experience, a set of default images are automatically downloaded when the application is installed. New images can be added via the menu 'choose file' button (Figure 4).

Software

The software is built in KineticJS, which is an HTML5 Canvas JavaScript framework. The framework supports images as objects with multiple methods and properties including rotate and move. After download, the software is designed to be used offline so it can be used anywhere in the village or in the surrounding jungle. A set of default images is included in the install. Subsequently client-side storage is used. For the first and second prototypes, we adapted the browser's LocalStorage mechanism to store the tangibles' images. However, this has very limited capacity, so the third prototype uses a Javascript Database.

Figure 4 shows the software menu. The top-left dropdown list contains a list of all available images. Those that have a tangible registered to them are marked with a tick. To add new images, the software allows users to choose a file, associate a name with it and set the size of the image. The "Clear" button clears the canvas and the "Reload" reloads the software from the server.

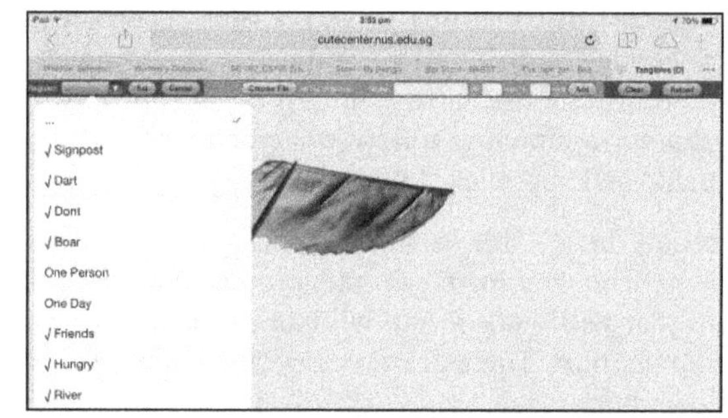

Figure 4 User Interface showing available images

When a tangible is recognized on the surface (see below for recognizer), the image associated with the tangible is retrieved from the database. The position and orientation of the image is computed so that it will lie directly under the tangible and the image is then displayed in that place.

The system also supports finger-touch image move, rotate and delete. We considered using the tangibles as interaction devices for these actions. However, a finger touch maps naturally to the real world experience of repositioning a physical symbol. Also, we found that while press actions are reliable with the tangibles, move and rotate are not; it is hard to maintain the contact of all three points while moving the tangible. The first two prototypes included move and delete. Rotate was added to the third prototype. Scaling of the images was discussed during the second prototype evaluation but the users considered it unnecessary.

Recognition

There are two steps to the recognition: first registering a tangible by recording its unique touch pattern (the triangle arrangement of pen tips) and associating this with an image; second, matching tangible interactions to existing registered tangibles.

We initially implemented a recognition algorithm based on [3] but found it was overly complex for the problem space. Three touch points are more than sufficient for the number of tangibles required therefore we use simpler triangulation techniques.

For registration, the image is displayed at a fixed offset and orientation on the display. The tangible's three touch point positions are recorded relative to the image position. The recognition algorithm calculates the distances between each pair of touch points, the centre of the triangle and angles of the triangle. The point which creates the biggest angle of the triangle is found. This largest angle is used to re-orientate the image later. The position and orientation of the touch points links the tangible to the image. Note this algorithm requires the points to form an irregular triangle for the orientation to work correctly.

To recognize a registered tangible, the same computation of relative points is executed. By traversing through the list of registered tangibles, the recognizer compares the distances to find a match. An error tolerance of 4mm is allowed. If a match is found, the recognizer calculates the translation of the tangible from its originally registered location by comparing the centre of the original tangible and the centre of the new touch points. Finally, the algorithm calculates the relative orientation compared to the original position by comparing the position of the largest angle relative to the centre of the triangle.

EVALUATION

Three rounds of evaluation were carried out. The first 2 were conducted on our first visit to the village. The third was on a subsequent visit a month later. Each round assessed different aspects of the research question. The first evaluation focused on whether the community elders felt that the tangible system could meet the basic requirement of aiding the preservation of Oroo'. In the second evaluation, we had people of various ages interact with the system. Thus, we were able to assess whether it was engaging to different user groups and informally observed knowledge transfer. The final evaluation concentrated on the efficacy of the system as an intergenerational collaborative environment. All community participants in the 3 rounds were Penans from the village.

First round

The first prototype had a default set of three pseudo symbols simply to provide a point of discussion (Figure 5). Other tangibles could be added by the process described above. Three members of the community explored this prototype.

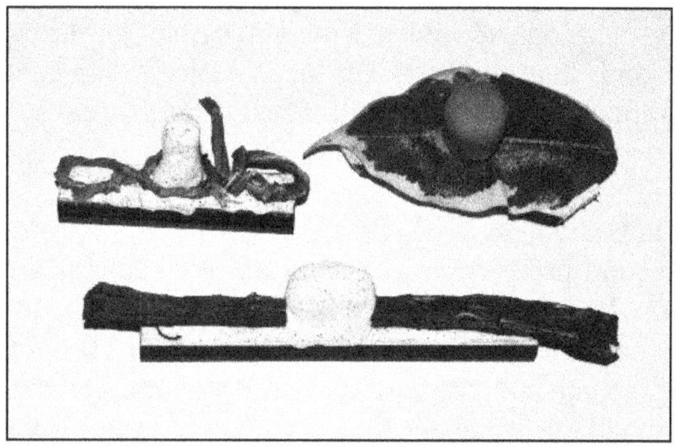

Figure 5 First prototype tangibles from top left: twisted grass, leaf and stick.

Individually, each was given a short demo with the default tangibles and then used the system to explore its functionality. While they could not make Oroo' from the pseudo symbols, they were able to place, move and remove symbols. They then made a new tangible with our guidance. A discussion followed about the potential of the system.

The first participant was, Garen, the village elder who has been instrumental in much of the research carried out with the community. His first reaction was of awe, followed by "We can make Ooro' with this". It was followed by lots of questions such as "Can they be recorded in a database? Labelled?"

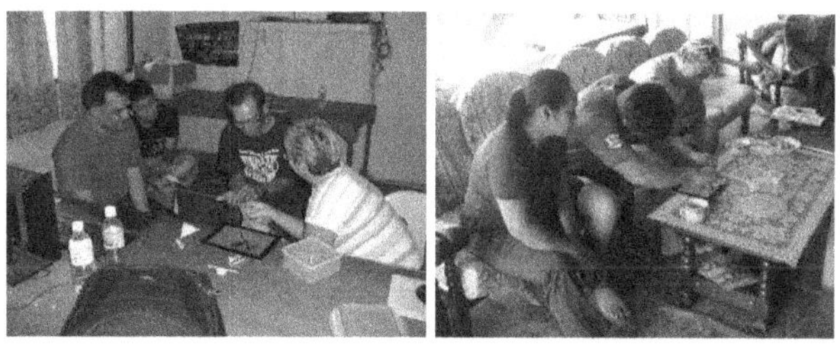

Figure 6 First round sessions 1 & 2

Figure 7 Flower image added to system and used to make a bouquet

Garen then took us to the second participant's home. She too was captivated and quickly called her adult son over to participate. He made his own tangible with a flower and made a bunch of flowers (Figure 7). They were both very interested in this approach. The final person to evaluate this prototype was an artist who is currently illustrating Oroo' (Figure 1b). He too was immediately captivated.

The participants' consensus from this first evaluation was that the system was excellent and could be used for Oroo'. However, in order to be more realistic, the tangibles needed to be made of actual symbols. Two of the participants had, with our guidance, added a new tangible to the system suggesting that this part of the system is adequate. In preparation for the next round, Garen made 4 real symbols and we reused the grass from the previous round (Figure 8).

Second Evaluation

The second prototype was technically the same as the first but now had 5 real symbols as exemplars. Three different groups evaluated the next prototype: a group of 3 elders, a family group and the villagers at a community meeting. This round tested again the suitability of the system for Oroo' and how people of various ages engaged with the system.

Figure 8 Second round tangibles from left to right: boar, signpost, don't, 3 days and dart.

Figure 9 Family group in second round.

The 3 elders, were age from 40 to 70. After a demo, they quickly started making different Oroo's. All three used the tangibles and discussed among themselves how they could be useful. They were intrigued with the technology and said they could see the system being very useful.

Surprisingly we learnt two new things about Oroo' during this session. First, the twisted grass – representing 3 days – could only be used with a person symbol, which we did not have. Also, the position of the different parts of the symbol on the signpost is meaningful. For example, placing the 'boar' on the top of the signpost has a different meaning to tucking it in one of the notches further down, and how tightly a symbol is tucked into a notch is also significant. These titbits of information were new to the researcher who had been working with the village documenting the language for 18 months.

After some discussion, it was decided that, with the 10 most regularly used symbols, the tool would provide an excellent base for evaluating whether the system is effective as a collaborative environment to teach Oroo' to children.

Later, the headman, his wife, son and son's friend tried the system. Their engagement and delight was evident (Figure 9). We observed everyone actively participating and enjoying the experience. Also, there was a lot of collaboration and teaching going on between the adults and children. They discussed the symbols and the way they fit together to make Oroo', all the while using the system to demonstrate the language.

The final session of this evaluation was a community meeting in the evening. About 25 members of the village were present with a balance of young and old, and genders (Figure 10). We placed the iPad in the middle of the floor and people gathered around. After a short demo, people used the system for the next hour. There was a lot of interaction between the people directly using the system and those observing. There was laughter while adding boar and dart symbols at different orientations and moving the dart around to pierce the neck, heart, eyes, tail, etc. Basically, the amusement was on where the dart should hit the boar for an effective kill.

Figure 10 Community meeting in second round.

Finally, there was a general discussion about what was required for the next prototype. There was agreement that the 10 symbols identified by the elders would provide an excellent platform to teach the basics of the language. For the interaction, the only change requested was to include finger touch rotate.

A bug in the recognizer meant that sometimes the image was rotated 180 degrees. While this obviously needed fixing, it also made us more aware of the importance of spatial relationships and orientation in the language. We also decided that the triangular base-plates worked best.

The participation of these various groups, established that the system was easy to use as well as engaging for people of different ages and that it represented Oroo' closely enough to emulate real Oroo'. We also defined the requirements of the third prototype as: fix the recognizer, add finger touch image rotation, and add the identified 10 basic symbols to the software as the default set.

Third evaluation

After completing the third prototype with the 10 default symbols, we returned to test it with the Long Lamai community. As we had learnt that realistic symbols are very important, the first step was to get Garen to make a set of appropriately sized symbols (Figure 11a) that were attached to the tangible bases. The set of tangibles used in this evaluation can be seen in Figure 11b.

Figure 11 Third round: a) making symbols b) symbol set with representations for people, objects, geographic features, directions, time and conditions.

The focus of this evaluation was on the engagement and intergenerational knowledge transfer goals. If these goals are met, the system will help with retention of the language. With the approval of the village headman (as required under the protocol of engagement), 6 family groups were recruited to participate in the study. The user study was based on standard methodologies but was more naturalistic than a lab study.

Each of the 6 family groups that participated in the study consisted of a child accompanied by their parent(s) or an adult relative, and in one case a child who had been a participant in an earlier group. We selected adults who know the Oroo' language. The children, 4 male, 2 female, were aged 7 to 16.

Most of the adults had used the system on our previous visit, we updated them on the project and checked that they remembered how to use it. They were given a few minutes to practise adding, moving, rotating and deleting symbols.

Following this, the adult and researcher together pre-tested the child's knowledge of the 10 Oroo' symbols. They were shown images of the symbol on a computer screen and asked to name the symbols they knew (see Table 1).

The adults were then asked to teach the symbols to the child using the Tangibles, and to use them with the software to make Oroo' stories. Later, we encouraged the child to use the system to make their own Oroo' stories. At the end of the session (about 60 minutes) we retested the child on the symbols (Table 1) and interviewed the adults.

Three sessions were conducted in the telecentre and the other three, at the family's home. Since most of the families are busy with agricultural activities during the day, the experiments were conducted between 6pm and 9pm. All sessions were video recorded and photographed. A member of the community was on hand to translate as required and took notes in Penan during the session; the notes were later translated to English for analysis.

RESULTS

In this section, we first report on the intergenerational knowledge transfer and then engagement. We refer to people involved in each group as G*n*[**F**ather|**M**other|**C**hild] e.g. G1F is Group 1's Father; G5C is Child in Group 5 .

The goal of intergenerational knowledge transfer was accomplished as the children all learnt a number of symbols during the session (see Table 1). Recall that the prototype includes the 10 most common symbols. In the pre-test, one child knew 2 symbols, the others knew none. In the post-test the mean was 8 correctly identified symbols.

Our first group (G1) included father, mother and son (Figure 12a). During the post-test G1C correctly remembered 9 symbols out of 10. G1F retaught the forgotten symbol. The 4th group (Figure 12b) the teachers were G1F & G1C while the student G4C was the nephew and cousin of G1. G4C, born and raised in the city was visiting Long Lamai with his parents. During this session we asked G1C to teach the Oroo' symbols to G4C. After introducing all the symbols, G1C asked G4C to repeat the names by looking at the tangibles; he correctly remembered 6 symbols. We observed how the children worked together well and noted that G1C had retained knowledge of the symbols he had learnt 2 days earlier, and how to put them together to make an Oroo' story.

Participant	Gender	Age	Symbols identified	
			Pre-test	Post-test
G1C	M	8	0	9
G2C	M	7	0	6
G3C	F	8	2	5
G4C	M	8	0	8
G5C	M	12	0	10
G6C	F	16	0	10
Mean			0.33	8

Table 1: Child pre-tests and post-tests of Oroo' symbols

Some adults taught the symbols one by one and then asked the child to repeat the names of the symbols and check for retention of earlier symbols. Then they taught the child how to make a story using the system. One father commented "I first went briefly through the symbols. Taught him how to use the tangibles and then asked him to create a story. After a few minutes we both were working on creating stories together". In another case, the adult came up with the story "I'm going to the river and I'm alone. It takes me one night to go there and I'm hungry," for the child to make.

One adult first taught the child the natural materials that are used to make the symbols (such as different types of leaves). Then he taught the child how to bend, fold and connect components and how different transformations of materials can create different symbols (e.g. the same leaf folded differently can be a 'wild boar' or 'I'm hungry'). He also checked the child's understanding of the symbols before teaching the Oroo' stories. After this, they used the tangibles and software to make stories.

Another adult integrated the symbol teaching and story making together. Showing the child a symbol, explaining its meaning he told the child when it is used. He asked questions while forming a story with the symbols.

After the teaching, the children used the system together with adults to form more complex Oroo' stories. Figure 14 shows 2 of the stories constructed during this phase.

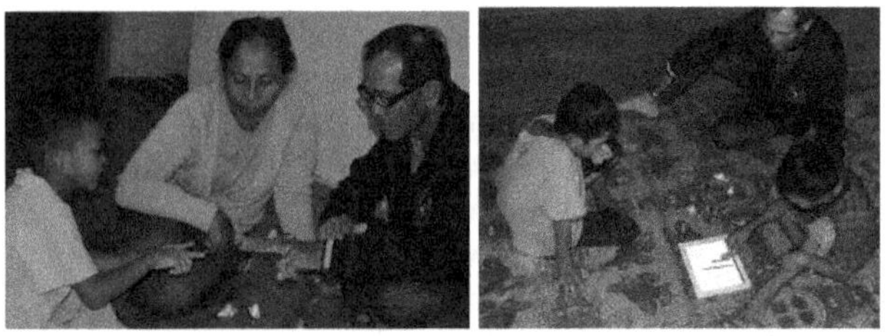

Figure 12 Group 1 and 4 in Evaluation 3

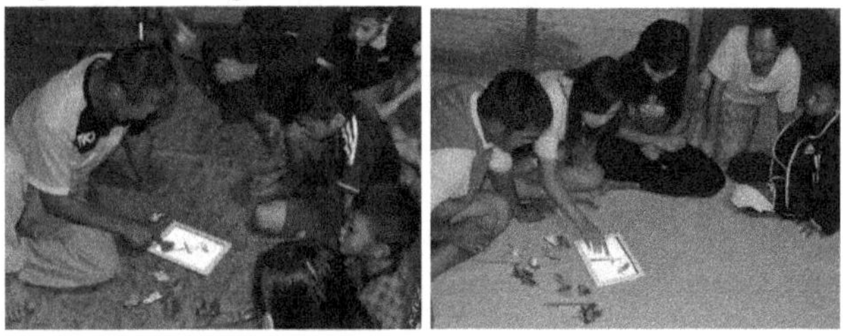

Figure 13 Groups 5 and 6 in evaluation 3.

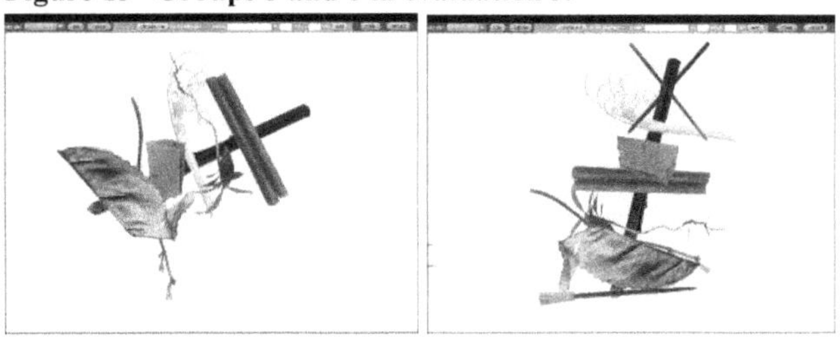

Figure 14 Oroo' stories made by children.

Engagement and enjoyment are central to all successful learning. We were pleased to observe that the children and adults alike were fully engaged and having fun. The tangibles provided them a platform to interact. For most of the participants using a tablet was a new experience. Just as with the adults in the earlier evaluations, the appearance of Oroo' symbols on the screen was magic for the children. Most used the system as if playing a game. While the adults were teaching, the children were eager to learn the symbols quickly, remember them and wanting to play with the software and tangibles as soon as possible.

In the one child-to-child session, we observed both children appeared to really enjoy themselves. They worked with little guidance while G1C taught and then they made stories together.

During the interviews at the end of the sessions the adults commented on the engagement aspects of the system.

G1F "I think this system is really good because children always love to play games and they learn very fast by playing. I feel they use this system as playing a game".

G2F "I'm excited to see this kind of system. It's nice and I think it is perfect. It is helpful".

G3F went a step further and said this tool works much better with the children than the old method of going to the jungle and teaching the Oroo's. He said "This is easy. It is fun using this system. Children do not want to go to the jungle and learn this stuff. I think after using the system they would like to go to the forest and try out the same things in real life".

However, G5F still believes the best way to teach the Oroo's is to go to the jungle and learn them by practice but he also doubted that the younger generation would go to the jungle unless there is a need. He said that apart from farming activities, the younger members of the community rarely go to the jungle now.

DISCUSSION

The overarching goal of this project is to provide a software tool that will aid in preservation of the Penan's sign language. This is accomplished by providing a highly engaging environment where intergenerational knowledge transfer can take place.

Preservation of indigenous languages and culture is urgent as the two-edged sword of globalization impacts small communities across the world [28]. Many of the endeavors focus on oral stories and story-telling rituals. Oroo' is not a language of storytelling nor is it primarily an oral language – it is *written* in that it takes a physical form and purpose it more functional. Few of these languages still exist, for example most of the tribes of Borneo had a similar language but only the Penan still remember theirs.

We witnessed a high level of engagement from both adults and children. This heightened engagement is consistent with other tangible research [8, 15]. The evaluations validated that knowledge transfer occurred between adults and children and that the system is also suitable for children working together. Tangible interfaces are known to function well as collaborative environments [21, 26].

Our evaluation does not demonstrate that the system results in more learning or higher engagement than the adults simply teaching the children at home without the system. This would require a comparative evaluation which is outside the agreed protocol of engagement between the researchers and community. Several adults commented that it's unlikely their children would engage in traditional ways of learning the Oroo' language. However, they are enthusiastic about using our system as they found the tangibles engaging and interesting for children and thought it shows great potential to keep the Oroo' language alive.

Another alternative would be a standard computer game. The evidence from existing research is that people learn more when using tangibles [22]. This is because tangibles engage more of the user's senses. The tangibles require more manipulation that a standard interface thus engaging the user's kinesthetic and proprioception. As well as this the manipulation may also create sound. In this case, the tangibles also provide richer textures to see and touch, and natural materials retain their smell. So all of the users' senses are more richly stimulated than with a standard computer system [13].

One of the adults in the third evaluation study suggested making the tangibles from artificial materials. He noted that natural materials such as leaves dry and decay and are not long lasting. He asked if we could find appropriate artificial materials, the tangible would look real and could be used for a longer period of time. Artificial flowers and trees are a viable source of realistic looking durable symbols (we have found the range of different artificial plants available is quite staggering).

Artificial materials would certainly be longer lasting. However, the sensory experience would lose some of its richness. For example, the fact that natural materials decay is integral to this language. The rate of decay of a leaf is well understood by these people: they know whether an Oroo' is a few hours, a day or a week old simply by glancing at it.

The way that the tangibles are designed means that it is easy to replace the symbol. One could imagine taking the system into the rainforest and getting the children to seek out the appropriate materials, and then craft them into the symbols. The symbols could then be attached with the appropriate bases and used in the system. Likewise, as the community becomes more familiar with the system they can, at any time add new symbols, thus expanding the vocabulary. However, for convenience they can also have symbols made from artificial materials.

We found that it is important the symbols are realistic – but the image does not need to match the tangible. Many of the signs can be made with different types of leaves – it is the folding or arrangement that is significant. Having a different leaf to the image did not cause a problem. However the mismatch disrupts the magic of having the exact symbol appear below the tangible. More investigation into the cognitive effects of the degree of match between the physical and virtual symbol would be interesting.

There was a range of suggestions for future enhancements. One suggestion was to implement the rules of Oroo' language in the next prototype. As we understand it, there are rules for the placement of the Oroo' signs on the signpost including order of symbols, place, and orientation. As an example, one elder demonstrated the importance of how the notches are made on the signpost. A possibility would be to use other tangibles for marking different types of notches.

These rules and subtleties of the language are not well documented. The system has already helped to uncovered language rules. Although this was not the aim of the current project, an area to explore is how such a system could be used to automatically capture the rules and nuances of the language.

CONCLUSIONS

The comments made during the evaluations suggest a high level of acceptance and enthusiasm for the system. These are perhaps best summarized by a comment from G1M. She said "Most of the adults of the community see the need to preserve the Oroo' language. This system will definitely help fill this space".

The tangibles are a core part of this system. We have extended tangible interaction research to realize a system that works in the wild and allows the user to dynamically add new tangibles. The core functionality of the system could be applied in many other scenarios, for example geometry games. The system could also be extended to automatically guide users and check results.

Unexpectedly the system revealed details about the Oroo' language unknown to the researcher documenting the language. This suggests that tangibles can have a role in discovery of knowledge. One area worthy of exploration is to extend the system so that it learns the language rules automatically.

The last word we give to one of the parents. He said "New technologies are coming to the village. Previously we didn't have the Internet, laptops or smart phones but now people are using them. Tablets will also be popular in Long Lamai in the near future. From the child's point of view, they are learning Oroo' symbols fast and remembering what they learn. The system seems really effective therefore, I think it will perfectly fit in to the community."

ACKNOWLEDGEMENTS

This research is supported by the National Research Foundation, Prime Minister's Office, Singapore under its International Research Centre @ Singapore Funding Initiative and administered by the Interactive & Digital Media Programme Office. And was carried out with the aid of a grant from the Information Society Innovation Fund ISIF Asia and Universiti Malaysia Sarawak under Postdoctoral Fellowship program.

REFERENCES

1. Barrett, G. and Omote, R., Projected-capacitive touch technology. Information Display, 26, 3, (2010) 16-21.
2. Bidwell, N. J., Reitmaier, T., Marsden, G., & Hansen, S., Designing with mobile digital storytelling in rural Africa. In *Proc* Chi2010, ACM, (2010), 1593-1602.
3. Blagojevic, R., and Plimmer, B. CapTUI: Geometric Drawing with Tangibles on a Capacitive Multi-touch Display. In P*roc* INTERACT. (2013), 511-528.
4. Bogdan, R. C. and Biklen, S. K. Qualitative research in education. An introduction to theory and methods. Allyn & Bacon, MA, USA, 2010

5. Chan, L., Müller, S., et al, CapStones and ZebraWidgets: sensing stacks of building blocks, dials and sliders on capacitive touch screens. In *Proc* CHI 2012, ACM, (2012) pp. 2189-2192.
6. Chipman, G., Fails, J. A., Druin, A. and Guha, M. L., Paper vs. tablet computers: a comparative study using Tangible Flags. In *Proc* IDC, ACM (2012), 29-36).
7. Do, E. YL, Gross, MD. Environments for Creativity: A Lab for Making Things, ACM C&C (2007) 27-36
8. Druin, A., Montemayor, J.et al, Designing PETS: A personal electronic teller of stories. In *Proc*eedings CHI 1999, ACM (1999), 326-329.
9. Fitzmaurice, G. W., Buxton, W., An empirical evaluation of graspable user interfaces: towards specialized, space-multiplexed input. In *Proc* CHI 1997, ACM (1997), 43-50.
10. Fitzmaurice, G. W., Ishii, H. and Buxton, W. A. (1995, May). Bricks: laying the foundations for graspable user interfaces. In *Proc* CHI 1995, ACM (1995), 442-449.
11. Geertz, C. The interpretation of cultures: Selected essays Basic books, Vol. 5019, 1973.
12. Hengeveld, B., Hummels, et al, Tangibles for toddlers learning language. In *Proc* TEI (2009), pp. 161-168.
13. Ishii, H., Tangible bits: beyond pixels. In *Proc* TEI, ACM, (2008), xv-xxv
14. Jensen, H. Sign, symbol and script: An account of man's efforts to write. London: Allen & Unwin. 1970
15. Karime, A., Hossain, et al, A., Magic stick: a tangible interface for the edutainment of young children. In *Proc* ICME 2009. IEEE (2009), 1338-1341.
16. Kratz, S., et al. CapWidgets: tangible widgets versus multi-touch controls on mobile devices. In *Ext Abstracts* CHI'11 ACM, 2011, (1351-135).
17. Liang, R. H., Chan, L., et al., GaussBricks: magnetic building blocks for constructive tangible interactions on portable displays. In *Proc* CHI 2014, ACM (2014), 3153-3162
18. Martínez, C., Digital Ayoyote Rattle: The Design of a Portable Low-Cost Digital Media System for a Mediated XicanIndio Resolana, *In Proc IKTC*, 2011, pp 88-97
19. Mayhew, D. J., The usability engineering lifecycle. In CHI'99 Extended Abstracts, ACM, (1999) 147-148.
20. Nielsen, J. 10 Usability Heuristics for User Interface Design. Nielsen Norman Group: Evidence-Based User Experience Research, Training, and Consulting. (1995)
21. Olson, I. C., Leong, Z.A., et al., It's just a toolbar!: using tangibles to help children manage conflict around a multi-touch tabletop. In *Proc* TEI, ACM, (2011), 29-36.
22. Price, S. and Marshall, P. (2013). Designing for learning with tangible technologies. Handbook of Design in Educational Technology, 288.
23. Rekimoto, J., SmartSkin: an infrastructure for freehand manipulation on interactive surfaces. In *Proc* CHI 2002, ACM, (2002), 113-120.
24. Schuler, D., and Namioka, A., Participatory design: Principles and practices. L. Erlbaum Associates, 1993.
25. Shaer, O. and Hornecker, E., Tangible user interfaces: past, present, and future directions. Foundations & Trends in HCI, 3,1–2, (2010). 1-137.
26. Schneider, B., Jermann, P., et al, Benefits of a tangible interface for collaborative learning and interaction. IEEE Trans on Learning Technologies, 4.3, (2011). 222-232.
27. Sia, C. and Tan, H., Little Chef: A Mergence of Kinesthetic and Digital Play, IDC 2014 Demos.
28. Simons, G. F. and Lewis, M. P. The world's languages in crisis. Responses to Language Endangerment. New directions in language documentation and language revitalization, (2013), 142, 3.
29. Smith, A., Reitsma, L., et al, Towards Preserving Indigenous Oral Stories Using Tangible Objects. In Culture and Computing, IEEE, (2011) pp. 86-91 IEEE.
30. Suzuki, H. and Kato, H., AlgoBlock: a tangible programming language, a tool for collaborative learning. In *Proc* of 4th European Logo Conference, (1993), 297-303.
31. Ullmer, B. and Ishii, H., The metaDESK: models and prototypes for tangible user interfaces. In *Proc* UIST, ACM, (1997), 223-232. ACM.
32. Ullmer, B. and Ishii, H., Emerging frameworks for tangible user interfaces. IBM systems journal, 39,3.4, (2000), 915-931.
33. Voida, A. and Greenberg, S., Console gaming across generations: Exploring intergenerational interactions in collocated console gaming. Universal Access in the Information Society, 11:1, (2012), 45-56.
34. Wellner, P., The DigitalDesk calculator: tangible manipulation on a desk top display. In *Proc* UIST, ACM, (1991), 27-33).
35. Xie, L., Antle, A. N. et al, Are tangibles more fun?: comparing children's enjoyment and engagement using physical, graphical and tangible user interfaces. In *Proc* TEI, ACM, (2008), 191-198.
36. Yu, N. H., Chan, L. W., et al, TUIC: enabling tangible interaction on capacitive multi-touch displays. In *Proc* CHI'91, ACM, (1991), 2995-3004.
37. Zaman, T., Jengan, G., et al. Signs, Concepts and Representation: Experiences in Documentation of Penan Indigenous Knowledge, In *Proc* 4th Regional Conference On Local Knowledge, Kuching, Malaysia., 2014

Mixed-Initiative Approaches to Global Editing in Slideware

Darren Edge[1], Sumit Gulwani[2], Natasa Milic-Frayling[3], Mohammad Raza[3], Reza Adhitya Saputra[1,4], Chao Wang[1], Koji Yatani[1,5]

[1] Microsoft Research Beijing, China
[2] Microsoft Research Redmond, USA
[3] Microsoft Research Cambridge, UK
[4] University of Waterloo Waterloo, Canada
[5] University of Tokyo Tokyo, Japan

{daedge, sumitg, natasamf, a-moraza, chaowa}@microsoft.com, radhitya@uwaterloo.ca, koji@iis-lab.org

ABSTRACT

Good alignment and repetition of objects across presentation slides can facilitate visual processing and contribute to audience understanding. However, creating and maintaining such consistency during slide design is difficult. In order to solve this problem, we present two complementary tools: (1) StyleSnap, which increases the alignment and repetition of objects by adaptively clustering object edge positions and allowing parallel editing of all objects snapped to the same spatial extent; and (2) FlashFormat, which infers the least-general generalization of editing examples and applies it throughout the selected range. In user studies of repetitive styling task performance, StyleSnap and FlashFormat were 4-5 times and 2-3 times faster than conventional editing, respectively. Both use a mixed-initiative approach to improve the consistency of slide decks and generalize to any situations involving editing across disjoint visual spaces.

Author Keywords

Presentations; visual consistency; layout editing; snapping; programming by example; least-general generalization.

ACM Classification Keywords

H.5.2. Information interfaces and presentation: User Interfaces.

INTRODUCTION

Designing, delivering, and watching slide presentations are common aspects of professional life. As a modular authoring medium, slides constrain the problem of visual communication and afford flexibility in restructuring and reuse. However, this same modularity can result in weak connections between slides that are also visually inconsistent.

The theory of *processing fluency* proposes that aesthetic pleasure is based on perceptual processing, with high fluency associated with positive evaluations such as agreement [33]. For slide design, audience negativity toward visual disorder (e.g., clutter, inconsistency, misalignment) has been argued to result directly from reduced processing fluency [1].

*CHI 2015, April 18 - 23 2015, Seoul, Republic of Korea. Copyright is held by the owner/author(s). Publication rights licensed to ACM.
ACM 978-1-4503-3145-6/15/04...$15.00
http://dx.doi.org/10.1145/2702123.2702551*

Nancy Duarte, author of "Slide:ology" [10], recommends the reuse of slide layouts to help the audience anticipate where content will appear next (i.e., to increase processing fluency through repetition). Garr Reynolds, author of "Presentation Zen" [34], also recommends repetition, but of "certain design elements" rather than whole slide layouts. The use of slide templates, copied slide elements, and temporary grids can all help to avoid inconsistency problems, whether within slides (nonaligned elements appearing randomly placed), between slides (misaligned elements "jumping" on transition), or across the deck (related elements lacking consistent styling).

However, creating and maintaining visual consistency across slides is difficult when the desired layouts and styles are not known in advance. During the design of slide visuals, making systematic changes one element at a time is both repetitive and tedious. Ad-hoc changes also make it difficult to refactor content using slide templates. Lack of support for the consistent redesign of elements repeated across slides is thus a major contributing factor to low processing fluency.

To address both the consumption problem of processing fluency and the authoring problem of repetitive styling, we present two complementary tools: (1) *StyleSnap*, for the automatic alignment of object edges within and across slides; and (2) *FlashFormat*, for the systematic restyling of related objects. Both are *mixed-initiative systems* [19] in which users collaborate with intelligent services to achieve their goals.

The intelligence of StyleSnap is through progressive hierarchical clustering of each of the four object edge positions (offsets from the left and top slide edges), in ways that increase alignment both within and across slides without introducing object overlaps or image distortions. Following an automated snapping process, the user can independently unsnap, merge, and style the resulting groups of objects that have been snapped to the same slide extent (i.e., all four corresponding edges share the same position values).

Conversely, the intelligence of FlashFormat comes after the user has directly supplied some examples of the repetitive edit they wish to apply more generally. It infers the *least-general generalization* [32] of the example edits through the attribute values shared among all edited objects and the transformation performed on the edited objects. The next application of FlashFormat always extends the current edit to the smallest set of objects that can be generalized to by allowing the unshared attributes to vary freely.

Since StyleSnap increases the number of shared attribute values throughout a slide deck (via both snapped object positions and propagated style changes), prior use of StyleSnap means that fewer example edits are required to cover all of the variance in the set of objects to be edited with FlashFormat. The two tools are thus complementary, although each has substantial value in standalone use.

In this paper, we first present a literature review on snapping and formatting, as well as the tools available in commonly used graphical systems. We then present an examination of a PowerPoint slide-deck corpus, showing how the use of such templates in practice restricts their ability to create and maintain consistency. In the following sections, we describe the design and implementation of two tools—StyleSnap and FlashFormat—that address the limitations of conventional templates. We also present a user study of each, demonstrating their superiority over existing approaches in task performance time and user preferences. We then report the lessons learned from both systems and discuss improvements for future mixed-initiative editing systems. These are relevant to the category of slideware augmented in this paper, as well as to any visual software that requires consistent styling across multiple pages (e.g., word processor documents), grids (e.g., spreadsheets), frames (e.g., editing of video overlays), or repeated visual spaces of any kind.

Overall, this work offers the following contributions:

1. Two approaches to selecting objects for systematic editing, based on: (a) similarity of objects' spatial extents as determined by clustering of their edge positions (StyleSnap); and (b) similarity of objects' attribute values as determined by the least-general generalization of example edits performed on other objects (FlashFormat).
2. Two approaches to editing objects simultaneously in order to reach a state of consistency, based on (a): snapping misaligned object edges into a reduced number of aligned positions, without introducing artifacts (StyleSnap); and (b) applying the least-general generalization of example edits to all objects selected for editing (FlashFormat).

RELATED WORK

Microsoft PowerPoint remains the most popular application in the category of "slideware". It has a wealth of existing presentations available online, rich tools for the analysis of its XML-based documents, and an add-in framework for augmentation of its feature set. Therefore, in the development and evaluation of our tools, we take PowerPoint as representative of slideware as a whole.

Alignment of Document Objects

Snapping is a commonly used technique to guide objects into a state of alignment [5]. For example, PowerPoint 2013 provides visual line-guides and snapping behavior to support object alignment within a slide, as well as the traditional snapping of object edges to an underlying grid whose resolution can be customized. Object snapping can be extended in several ways, such as adaptively changing the snapping behavior based on user input [26] or adaptively inserting motor space to support differentiation of snap targets [4]. Other approaches have addressed mouse-free snapping on surfaces and tabletops by using control-display gain [13], multi-touch [14], pen input [15], and the non-dominant hand [40]. None of them focus on alignment across disjoint visual spaces of any kind.

Layout of Document Objects

One approach to achieving consistent, well-designed layouts is to allow the user to select from a range of predesigned "templates" and enter content accordingly. Instead of making layout changes on individual slides (which can create inconsistencies), the user makes changes on the template itself, automatically updating slides that adopt the template.

In PowerPoint 2013, templates are provided in a special view called the Slide Master. This view defines slide layouts and styles through *placeholders* which are also exposed when the user selects a layout for a new slide from a menu or when the user updates a slide to an alternative Slide Master layout. However, there are several usability problems with this approach. First, templates need to be selected in advance of slide creation rather than formed through exploration on slides. Second, directly editing a slide object that is linked to a placeholder removes the ability to restyle that object through the Slide Master, unless the slide template is manually re-applied. When inspecting either an object or a slide, it is not possible to determine whether the links to the placeholder are intact. That makes it difficult to anticipate the scope of changes that are possible through the slide templates. All of these specific problems belong to a more general category of risks that are known to reduce users' willingness to invest attention in abstraction use [6].

In the research domain, document analysis has been used to suggest layouts that satisfy criteria given by the user [24], such as logical structures of information to be visualized in presentation slides [38], or to support version management of multiple slide decks [9]. An alternative approach is to specify the structure of the desired document directly and allow the system to provide "styling as a service", as in the HyperSlides system for presentation prototyping [11].

One approach to automating layout is to consider it as a visual constraint satisfaction problem. Constraints express high-level relationships between objects (e.g., text referencing a picture) or geometric structures (e.g., the sizes of all textboxes are the same). These constraints can be described as rules [7, 16, 39]. A major challenge of such rule-based systems is to anticipate all required rules. Another approach is to consider layout automation as a problem of optimizing energy functions. This has been explored in the context of adaptive grids [20], focusing on the goodness of template fit and micro-typography aesthetics. The concept of "conditional shapes and groups" can help to generate more flexible constraint systems dynamically [36], as can combinations of constraint- and force-based approaches [2].

While such automated layout systems are good for content that would not otherwise be "designed" or is yet to be designed, our tools specialize in the restyling of existing presentation content with a high degree of user control.

Formatting of Document Objects

The Slide Master is a form of indirect editing in PowerPoint and similar slideware. Another is the Format Painter, which allows all non-spatial attributes of a source object to be copied and "painted" onto destination objects, thus supporting reuse of object formatting in the slide view.

Macros, batch processing, history brushes, and graphical search and replace [22] are further ways in which users can capture and reuse action sequences. EAGER [8] is an early work using programming-by-example principles [29] to support efficient text data entry but not visual style changes. Abstract object selection and restyling are also possible with interactive machine learning [12], by inferring the user's desired scope based on patterns of selection and deselection (e.g., for file selection [35] and friend selection [3]).

For document editing, the LAPIS text editor [27] supports intelligent group selection and simultaneous reformatting of strings. An extension supports intelligent find-and-replace operations in text documents, grouping different string selection candidates by literal and semantic similarities [28].

CORPUS ANALYSIS OF TEMPLATE USAGE

We wanted to understand the extent to which the apparent usability problems of Slide Master templates were evident in examples of presentations downloaded from the Web. We built a corpus of over 8000 presentations using Bing web searches specifying the "ext:pptx" filter. The resulting slide decks were drawn from many fields including business, government, science, technology, and education. We used the Open XML SDK 2.5 [30] to parse these presentations and extract statistics on slides and objects. Table 1 shows the results from the 7663 successfully processed files.

Slide Statistics	Mean (*SD*)
# of slides	28.2 (20.7)
# of slides with placeholders unmodified	19.0 (17.5)
# of slides with placeholders modified	5.7 (9.0)
# of slides without placeholders	3.5 (7.8)
Shape Statistics	**Mean (*SD*)**
# of objects per slide	5.3 (6.1)
# of objects created by user	3.9 (6.2)
# of objects from unmodified placeholders	1.1 (0.9)
# of objects from modified placeholders	0.3 (0.4)

Table 1. Statistics on the number of slides and objects in 7,663 PowerPoint files we collected from the Internet.

We found that 88% of slides (24.7 out of 28.2) on average contained placeholder objects created by the Slide Master. We also found that the proportion of objects per slide that could actually be restyled through the Slide Master (without first resetting the slide to restore broken links, which loses any custom layout and styling of placeholders) was only 21% (1.1 out of 5.3) on average. Thus, while the vast majority of slides (88%) have the potential to be updated via the Slide Master, due to user editing behavior the vast majority of objects (79%) still require manual editing.

We conducted a second analysis to understand the degree to which objects shared the same or similar *spatial extent* on slides, reflected as the same or similar edge offsets (distances from the left and top slide edges). For each deck, we first created a mapping from extents to objects, progressively varying the matching tolerance from 0 to 100 points in 10 points increments (28pt=1cm). In each iteration, we grouped objects across slides whose edges were all located within a matching region of an existing extent (e.g., for the tolerance of 0, we only grouped objects with identical extents).

This analysis revealed a strong skew resulting from many small, often single-element groups. With exact matching (a tolerance of zero points), the average number of position groups was 35 and objects in the largest position group occurred on 82% of slides. All groups in the upper quartile (top 9 groups of 35) had objects occurring on at least 5% of slides. Since these cannot all be placeholder objects (which only contribute 1.4 objects per slide), they are likely to come from copy-and-paste actions applied to ensure size, position, and style consistency for individual objects (and slides). When the tolerance was 60 points (about 2cm – a "near match" on all four object edges), the number of overall position groups halved (from 35 to 18). Objects in the largest position group occurred on 93% of slides and those in the upper quartile (top 5 groups of 18) had objects occurring on at least 11% of slides.

In conclusion, there is ample opportunity to increase the *positional consistency* of objects by mapping "near match" objects into the exact same extent. If such a system could be developed, it could also increase the *style consistency* of position groups by propagating style changes to all members of the associated group. Such a system would have a greater restyling power than the Slide Master while also offering *implicit object templates,* abstracted directly from slides, rather than *explicit slide templates* designed indirectly in a separate view. Many of the problems of template-based layouts could thus be avoided.

STYLESNAP

Following on from the previous corpus analysis, we designed a mixed-initiative tool called *StyleSnap* that can be applied whenever a slide deck has evolved into a state of misalignment or inconsistency. Our first goal was to develop a method to align objects across slides without introducing new problems, such as object overlap and image distortion. Our second goal was to develop a user interface that would allow a user to invoke StyleSnap, view the resulting groups of objects snapped to the same extent, then undo, merge, or modify these groups accordingly. Our implementation of these concepts was through an add-in for PowerPoint 2013. We now describe the high-level design of the StyleSnap user interface and details of the underlying snapping algorithm.

StyleSnap Interface

Figure 1 shows the result of pressing the "StyleSnap" button in the PowerPoint ribbon menu. A side pane appears showing the resulting position groups—groups of objects across slides that have been mapped to the same position and size as a result of clustering and snapping edge values for the four edge types. Each group is listed showing its color (matching the color of the highlight boxes added to the corresponding objects), the number of objects in the group, a "Style Painter" icon for manually adding objects to the group and merging groups with one another, and a checkbox indicating whether the group is currently in its "Snap" state. Only non-singleton object groups are snapped by default but the user can toggle snapping for both individual groups and for all objects. Snapped objects are designated with a solid border in their new extent; unsnapped objects with a dashed border in their original extent. If all objects were already in the same extent and unaffected by snapping, the Snap checkbox is disabled.

Clicking on any slide object or position group highlights the object, its position group in the side pane, and all other objects in the group. For efficient visual browsing of this position group, the system also gathers all slides containing highlighted objects and places them in a temporary "Selected" section at the start of the slide list, with other slides organized in an "Unselected" section (existing sections are recreated after StyleSnap tool use). The color of the highlight box of the selected group fully saturates for clear differentiation from the colors of other object groups. This visual feedback allows the user to confirm quickly whether the automatic snapping of the position group is desirable. When using the StyleSnap tool, any location, size, font, or other format changes to an object are propagated across all other objects in its group and made visible in real-time on all slides in the "Selected" section of the slide list.

The Style Painter is similar to the Format Painter but extends to position and size attributes. Activating the Style Painter for a particular group by clicking the corresponding icon means that the next selected object or position group will automatically be merged with the active group.

Clicking the "Apply" button saves the changes to the deck and reverts to standard editing. Clicking "Discard" undoes the changes and reverts the deck to its pre-StyleSnap state.

Snapping through Hierarchical Clustering

We wanted to enable "snapping" of objects into (a) fewer extents with (b) better alignment across slides. Each of these goals suggests a different approach. In order to reduce object extents, we could apply hierarchical clustering [18, 37] directly to object extents (since it does not require a prior choice for the number of clusters, unlike, e.g., K-means). However, this will not result in good cross-slide alignment if the extents of objects within slides are misaligned. There is also a sparsity problem—objects may all be sufficiently different and no two objects should be mapped to the same extent, even though any individual object edge may be close to the corresponding edges of many other objects.

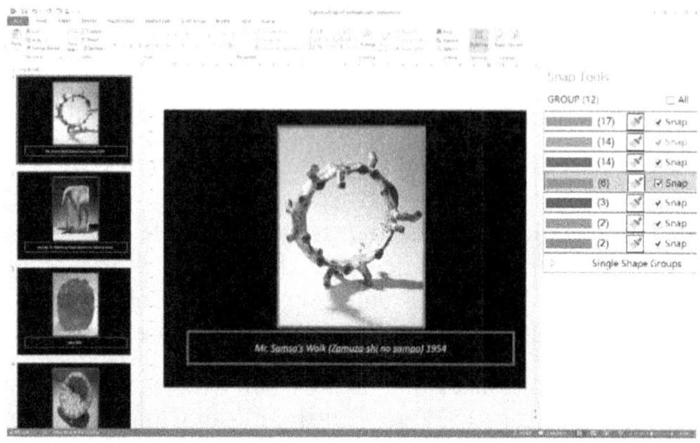

Figure 1. StyleSnap interface. The right pane shows all the groups whose objects are moved to the same position as a result of snapping. The user can manually undo and merge position groups, as well as simultaneously style all objects in the same group with real-time feedback in the slide list on the left.

This led us to a solution based on hierarchical clustering of individual object edges rather than object extents. We independently perform hierarchical clustering of all the left, top, right, and bottom edge positions of the objects within a presentation and then apply the results back to the objects. The result of such clustering for each of the four edge types is a hierarchy of depth N where N is the number of distinct edge positions. At level 1 there are N clusters of 1 edge position. At level N there is 1 cluster of N edges, all snapped to the modal edge position. From level 1 to level N, the algorithm merges the closest pair of clusters and snaps all edges in the new cluster to the new modal edge position.

We can determine the optimal clustering level for each edge type (left, top, right, and bottom) by an energy function that aims to balance similarity within and between clusters (i.e., to make close edge values the same while keeping distant edges separate). However, the naïve updating of object edge positions based on the optimum clustering of each edge type could easily cause problems in visual appearance:

1. *Object inversion*, since independent edge clustering does not respect relative positions of opposing object edges;
2. *Object overlap*, since initially separated objects can be moved into a state where their content regions overlap;
3. *Image distortion*, since images are especially sensitive to aspect ratio changes.

Given that we can identify and correct these problems only after position updates, our divide-and-conquer approach of clustering different edges independently is most suited to the agglomerative, bottom-up method of hierarchical clustering supported by the SLINK algorithm [37]. Overall, our snapping approach is summarized in Algorithm 1.

Systematic Performance Evaluation of Snapping

Snapping completes in several seconds, even for 500 objects (the 97th percentile in our PowerPoint corpus). In order to evaluate the degree to which automated snapping matches human judgments, we recruited two professional software engineers to test its accuracy and reliability across a range of typical slide decks: 80 presentations from our PowerPoint corpus, with varying numbers of slides (15–36; the lower and upper quartiles) as well as varying numbers of objects per slide (2.5–6.0 with mean 4.7).

Table 2 shows how the number of singleton position groups (a mean of 53.6) forms a long-tail, as expected from the earlier corpus analysis. Problems resulting from snapping are well controlled in both group types, limited to overly shrinking objects, creating inconsistencies among sets of slide objects that were previously consistent (e.g., in size, spacing, or alignment), and breaking spatial relationships between objects (e.g., by moving arrows within diagrams). Shrinkage can be dealt with by adding simple rules, but to address problems that arise from object relationships would require more complex rules or manual object grouping. Overall, on average only 4.5 position group modifications were required to reach a satisfactory state of alignment.

EVALUATION OF STYLESNAP

We conducted two user studies to evaluate the performance of StyleSnap against two alternative approaches to cross-slide alignment and styling: *Repeat Editing* and *Slide Master*. For the study tasks we selected a slide deck from our internet corpus with an average of 2 objects on each of 31 slides—one from a Slide Master template, one added manually—with a balance of title-and-bullets and image-and-caption slides.

Task: Cross-Slide Alignment of Misaligned Objects

There were 14 slides containing one picture and one textbox used as a caption, with no perfect alignment of any pair of objects. The task was to align all four object edges of groups of images with similar aspect ratios and make the caption format the same across all 14 slides. For consistency, we defined target object groups for the 14 images based on three aspect ratios: 9 portrait images, 4 landscape, and 1 panoramic. We also set the target text format to be 20pt Red Italic Arial.

Expert Performance Prediction

In order to predict the expert performance of each technique, we adopted an approach akin to Keystroke Level Modelling (KLM) by constructing a task model for each system and quantifying its time parameters through a user study. Since these models do not account for switching costs, they represent predicted lower bounds on task completion time.

***Repeat Editing*:** [*Start time* T_{re}] Make a duplicate of Slide 13 and use it as a layout guide to align content from Slide 14. Delete unwanted objects and slides. [*End time* T_{re}]

Reference task time = T_{re} × *13 slides*

***Slide Master*:** [*Start time* T_{sm1}] Open the Slide Master view and create a layout with content placeholders in the desired positions and aspect ratios. Close the Slide Master. [*End time* T_{sm1}] [*Start time* T_{sm2}] Go to Slide 13 and update it to the new custom layout. Delete unwanted objects [*End time* T_{sm2}]

Reference task time = T_{sm1} × *3 slide layouts (one per aspect ratio)* + T_{sm2} × *14 slides (apply new layout to each)*

Algorithm 1. Global snapping of object edge positions

1. **Cluster object edge positions in preparation for snapping**
   For each edge type *T* (left, top, right, bottom):
   a. Cluster edge positions using the SLINK algorithm
   b. Calculate the optimal clustering level L_T to minimize the following distance-based energy function:
      $$\alpha \sum_{c \in G}(C_g - C_{global}) + (1-\alpha)\sum_{g \in G}\sum_{s \in g}(l_s - C_g)$$
      (C_g, C_{global}, and l_s represent the centroid edge value of each cluster, the one of all objects, and the edge value of one object, respectively. α is the coefficient to determine weights for between-cluster and within-cluster similarities, set to 0.5)
2. **Apply snapping progressively, resolving overlaps and inversions**
   For $i = 1\ to\ N$ (number of adaptive steps, e.g., 20):
   a. For each edge type *T*:
      i. Apply the snapping associated with clustering at level $[(i/N) \times L_T]$ (where level 1 is no clustering) to objects that have not previously been inverted or overlapped.
   b. For each object O_i:
      i. If O_i is newly inverted or overlapped, reset to O_{i-1}.
   c. If no objects can be snapped further, move to (3).
3. **Resolve image distortion**
   For each snapped image object *I*:
   a. If its aspect ratio of *I* has changed by more than a threshold proportion (set to 0.1), shift the furthest-moved edge of *I* to return to the original aspect ratio, otherwise allow the change.

Position Groups of 2+ Shapes	Mean (*SD*)
# of position groups	10.3 (10.0)
# of position groups where snapping causes problems	0.7 (1.2)
# of merges among 2+ position groups required	0.8 (1.1)
Position Groups of 1 Shape (Singletons)	**Mean (*SD*)**
# of position groups	53.6 (33.7)
# of position groups where snapping causes problems	0.6 (2.5)
# of additions to 2+ position groups required	2.4 (2.8)

Table 2. Performance of StyleSnap auto-alignment on 80 decks.

***StyleSnap*:** [*Start time* T_{ss1}] Use the Style Painter to add the portrait image on Slide 28 to the position group of the portrait image on Slide 13. [*End time* T_{ss1}] [*Start time* T_{ss2}] Set the caption text to the target format. [*End time* T_{ss2}]

StyleSnap groups the captions into a single group and images into groups with 4, 4, 2, 1, 1, 1, and 1 objects. Reaching three position groups for these images requires a maximum of eight changes using the Style Painter (one object at a time).

Reference task time = T_{ss1} × *8 group changes (to make 3 groups)* + T_{ss2} *(applies to all captions at once)*

Procedure

We first explained and demonstrated each task before asking participants to repeat the procedure until they had mastered it. We used two such slides for our demonstration, with the task to make the layout and style of Slide 14 the same as Slide 13. We offered detailed instructions for each approach and allowed several timed trials until we did not observe large time variances. Participants' best times were recorded and used to calculate the reference task time (as is common when seeking to understand expert performance, e.g., in [40]).

We recruited 12 participants (6 male and 6 female, the average age of 25; PA1–PA12) from a local university. All were familiar with PowerPoint and fluent in English. We counterbalanced the condition order. Cash equivalent to $15 USD in local currency was offered as compensation.

Expert Performance Results

Table 3 summarizes the completion times of sub-tasks in each of the three techniques. Entering these times into our task models predicts the average expert performance to be 353, 322, and 107 seconds with Repeated Editing, Slide Master and StyleSnap, respectively. This prediction is highly promising and indicates that StyleSnap could substantially reduce the user effort of cross-slide alignment and styling. The results also show that updating any number of target slides with StyleSnap is comparable to refactoring a single slide with Slide Master, once the StyleSnap groups are correct and the Slide Master templates are created. Since 4.5 StyleSnap group merges are required to correct the snapping of a whole deck, on average, it also means that StyleSnap is about as fast at correcting alignment throughout this particular deck and refactoring 14 slides of a particular design (69s) as Slide Master is at creating a single template and refactoring just two slides (71s).

Novice User Performance Measurement

We also conducted a supplementary study with the same task set to measure the performance of novice users. The procedure was the same except that participants were asked to modify all 14 slides in each task. This study therefore offers realistic performance observations of the three techniques that account for the effects of learning and fatigue. From the expert performance prediction results, we had two hypotheses for this study: **[HA-1]** StyleSnap would be faster for global alignment than existing tools; and **[HA-2]** the perceived workload of global alignment tasks would be smaller with StyleSnap. StyleSnap training included 5-10 minutes of free exploration on a range of decks. Following the study tasks, participants completed a NASA-TLX questionnaire [17] for each approach. We recruited another eight participants for this study (5 male and 3 female, the average age of 25; PB1–PB8) from our research institute.

Novice User Performance Results

One-way repeated-measure ANOVA revealed a significant difference among techniques ($F_{(2,14)} = 90.8$, $p < .0001$, $\eta_p^2 = .93$), with *StyleSnap* faster than the other two ($p < .0001$ for both), shown in Figure 2, supporting HA-1. Analysis of NASA-TLX responses found seven significant pairwise results as shown in Table 4, partially supporting HA-2.

While the cost of both *Repeat Editing* and the *Slide Master* scale linearly with the number of target objects, the cost of StyleSnap scales only with the number of corrections to groups that contain target objects. The fewer groups that need to be corrected, the closer the performance of StyleSnap to a constant time cost, regardless of the number of objects.

StyleSnap Task for Expert Users: Completion Times	Mean (*SD*)
T_{re}: Refactor a target slide using Repeat Editing	25.2 (6.4)
T_{sm1}: Make a slide template using Slide Master	43.2 (9.6)
T_{sm2}: Refactor a target slide to a slide template using Slide Master	13.8 (2.1)
T_{ss1}: Find and add an object to a group using StyleSnap	11.5 (2.7)
T_{ss2}: Update all target slides using StyleSnap	15.2 (5.6)

Table 3. Sub-task completion time results in the expert performance user study.

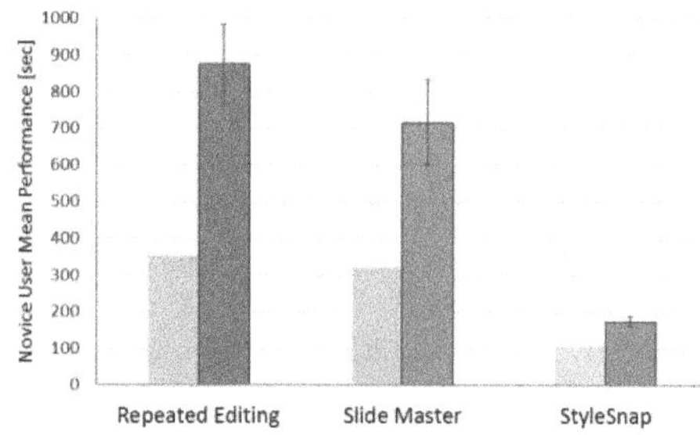

Figure 2. Predicted lower bounds on expert performance (bars without borders) and novice user mean performance time (bars with borders). Error bars represent 95% Confidence Intervals.

Qualitative Discussion

Participants in both studies unanimously preferred *StyleSnap* over *Repeat Editing* and *Slide Master* and many commented on how it would support their everyday authoring. The Slide Master was also widely criticized, e.g.: *"If we edit using Slide Master, we really don't know what the final result will look like. After we edit it we should go back to see the result... if is not satisfying we should go back again to the slide master view... If we use StyleSnap we can see the result directly"* (PA12).

The cost of automated snapping and manual modification was perceived to be relatively low. Participants described the "clustering" as *"very efficient... it really helps in saving time"* (PA4); *"really useful"* (PA8); *"a great idea... a simpler way to edit a lot of shapes"* (PA9). Participants also appreciated being able to edit all objects in a position group simultaneously: *"I can do quick edits for the whole content in the slides"* (PA5); *"You can do one 'style' and apply it everywhere fast"* (PA2).

The study also highlighted areas for improvement. Several participants expressed initial confusion about the meaning of colors and suggested the use of semantic descriptors, icons, or thumbnails to make the mapping clearer. One participant found the "shuffling" of the slide list distracting while another suggested a drag-and-drop mechanism for Style Painting. During free explorations of multiple decks, several participants expressed a desire for an algorithm that automatically identifies diagram-like collections of objects and groups them for StyleSnap alignment purposes.

StyleSnap Task for Novice Users: NASA-TLX Subjective Workload Results (in the format *median* [*lower quartile, upper quartile*])							
	Mental	Physical	Temporal	Performance	Effort	Frustration	Weighted overall
Repeat Editing (RE)	**25.0** [15.0,47.5]	**82.5** [70.0, 96.3]	**82.5** [73.8, 92.3]	**67.5** [62.5, 75.0]	**90.0** [73.8, 100.0]	**85.0** [78.8, 91.3]	**78.0** [73.3, 81.3]
Slide Master (SM)	**47.5** [40.0, 57.5]	**47.5** [33.8, 58.8]	**45.0** [27.5, 57.5]	**22.5** [8.8, 36.3]	**52.5** [25.0, 55.0]	**52.5** [36.3, 66.3]	**43.8** [35.8, 55.0]
StyleSnap (SS)	**30.0** [18.8, 66.3]	**22.5** [18.8, 31.3]	**17.5** [13.8, 21.3]	**15.0** [5.0, 16.3]	**27.5** [25.0, 33.8]	**20.0** [8.8, 30.0]	**25.0** [22.7, 29.3]
Friedman test: $\chi^2(2)$	0.077 (p = .96)	11.6 (p < .01)	13.6 (p < .01)	10.2 (p < .01)	13.1 (p < .01)	14.0 (p < .001)	15.5 (p < .001)
Pairs with p<.05	(none)	(none)	RE-SS	(none)	RE-SS, RE-SM	RE-SS, RE-SM	RE-SS, RE-SM

Table 4. NASA-TLX subjective workload results for novice users completing the StyleSnap task. Lower values are better.

The study also surfaced tensions in the design of StyleSnap, which is predicated on the value of object alignment and style consistency throughout a slide deck. As one participant explained, *"With StyleSnap I can easily design the layouts, especially if I want to change the same layouts, not manually edit the slides. But I think it will be difficult to change if on each slide the designs are different"* (PA8). A different approach is required to make repetitive changes to objects that do not share the same position—this is the purpose of the complementary FlashFormat tool that we present next.

FLASHFORMAT

StyleSnap supports aligning objects across slides in ways that increase processing fluency, but it is not applicable to repeated-object restyling when target objects are placed at different locations. FlashFormat offers the ability to apply global style changes with more flexible object selection.

FlashFormat is a programming-by-example system [29] that allows the user to perform repetitive formatting tasks in PowerPoint. The interface of FlashFormat is shown in Figure 3. It consists of only two buttons: "Start New Examples" and "FlashFormat". The user starts by clicking "Start New Examples" and then gives some examples of the formatting changes they would like to perform. When they click on "FlashFormat", the system infers the *least-general generalization* (LGG) from the given examples and applies the changes to the rest of the document ("FlashFormat-all").

In Figure 3b the user gives two examples of changing the color of diamond shapes to yellow, for which the system infers the LGG that changes all diamond shapes to yellow (Figure 3c). The inferred generalization depends on the given examples; for instance, to color yellow any object with underlined text, the user may give examples for different shapes and colors (e.g., white diamond, white rectangle, gray rectangle) containing underlined text.

The inference performed by FlashFormat is based on the XML specifications of objects (using the OOXML file format), and hence covers all properties expressed in this specification. The system is based on a domain specific language for expressing transformations of XML structures, and a synthesis algorithm for inferring LGG programs within this language. In this work, we focus on the interaction model and usability studies of the tool. The underlying inference algorithm builds on prior work in program synthesis [32].

An interactive and incremental generalization process

The user can guide the system to the desired generalization in an interactive and incremental fashion. Since the system is conservative in the inference of the generalization, the user can give additional (dissimilar) examples to express their intended selection criteria. For example, if the user wants to color all objects with underlined text and only gives examples of diamond shapes, then the system may infer a less general hypothesis: to color only diamond shapes containing underlined text. However, the system is designed to incrementally accept examples. At that point the user can give more examples through manual editing, and then

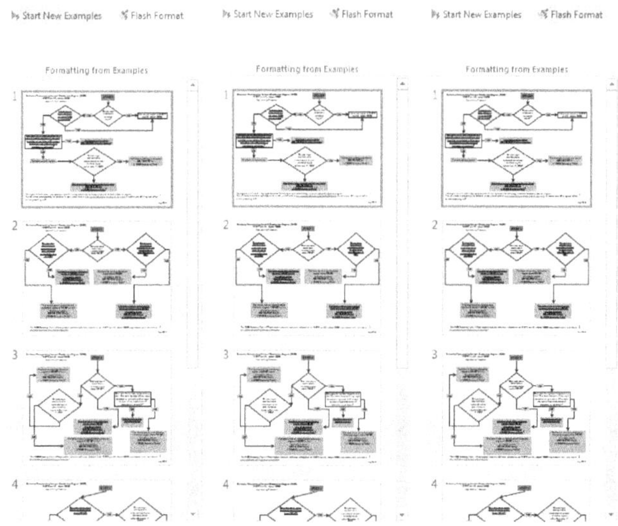

(a) (b) (c)

Figure 3. FlashFormat interface, illustrating the coloring of all diamonds to yellow: (a) the user clicks "Start New Examples"; (b) gives two examples of diamond shapes, changing the color; (c) clicks "Flash Format" to apply the least-general generalization from the example changes.

FlashFormat again; from added examples, the system will infer a more general transformation.

The user can also backtrack if the system does not infer the intended transformation. If the inferred generalization is not applicable to any other objects, then the system applies the transformation to the closest matching objects, according to a similarity measure on the XML specification of objects. If this inference is inaccurate, then the user can undo the changes using the standard "undo" feature, and provide more examples to guide the system in the right direction.

The system also supports a restricted application of the inferred transformations, allowing the user to verify the transformation before applying it globally. After giving examples, the user can select a set of objects or slides and then click "FlashFormat" to apply the transformation only to the selected objects or slides ("FlashFormat-selected").

EVALUATION OF FLASH FORMAT

We conducted a user study to examine the use of FlashFormat. We formulated three hypotheses: **[HB-1]** Users would be able to achieve their desired global restyling through FlashFormat; **[HB-2]** with the experience of using FlashFormat, users will develop a sense of which examples to give, and **[HB-3]** across a range of tasks, using FlashFormat would be faster than standard editing tools.

Tasks: Cross-slide Shape Restyling

We prepared a slide deck downloaded from the Internet. It contained flowcharts spanning five slides, using different shapes (rectangles and diamonds). Such diagrams are commonly encountered in slide presentations and cannot be restyled through the slide master because objects invariably occupy unique slide extents. Participants were asked to perform two changes specified by the experimenter, either with FlashFormat or manually (use of Format Painter was allowed in this condition). In order to create a balanced workload per task, we varied the number of objects to be restyled and the difficulty of giving examples. The participants were asked to make two systematic style changes in each trial but were not allowed to change any other visual attribute or text content of the objects. After this controlled task, participants were given another slide deck and asked to perform global restyling as they liked. They were encouraged to use FlashFormat to make changes and were given five minutes for this part of the study.

The interface used in the study did not include visual feedback before clicking the FlashFormat button. Our intention was to study how well participants could understand the behavior of LGG without being influenced by the feedback design and to test its effectiveness in a most basic form (any additional improvements on feedback would generally favor the performance of FlashFormat).

Procedure and Participants

We first explained FlashFormat with two examples of slide decks and asked participants to perform global restyling tasks. The slide decks included easy and difficult cases for FlashFormat. This pre-task session was intended to make participants knowledgeable about the system and able to perform restyling without help from the experimenters. We provided explanations that choosing *more, and more diverse examples* would lead to better results (referred to as "the golden rule"), but we did not force participants to do so. During each trial, we measured the performance time between the start of the task and the point when they confirmed all necessary changes on all specified objects. At the end of the study, participants were asked to describe their experience of FlashFormat, give suggestions for improvements, and fill out a questionnaire.

We recruited 12 participants (8 male and 4 female, with average age 25; PB1–PB12) from our research institute. All were familiar with PowerPoint and fluent in English, and none of them participated in the first study. The same compensation was offered to all participants in this study.

Results

Figure 4 shows the mean performance time for each number of objects with the two techniques. Times in the manual editing condition varied in the range of 90–100 seconds, whereas FlashFormat times were constant at about 40 seconds. Two-way repeated measure ANOVA revealed a significant main effect for technique ($F_{(1,11)} = 45.5, p < .0001, \eta_p^2 = .81$). The interaction between technique and task was also significant ($F_{(2,22)} = 4.40$, $p < .05$, $\eta_p^2 = .29$). The post-hoc analysis confirmed that the FlashFormat technique was significantly faster than the manual editing technique ($p < .0001$). This quantitative result demonstrates substantial improvements over existing editing tools and methods for global restyling, supporting our hypothesis HB-3.

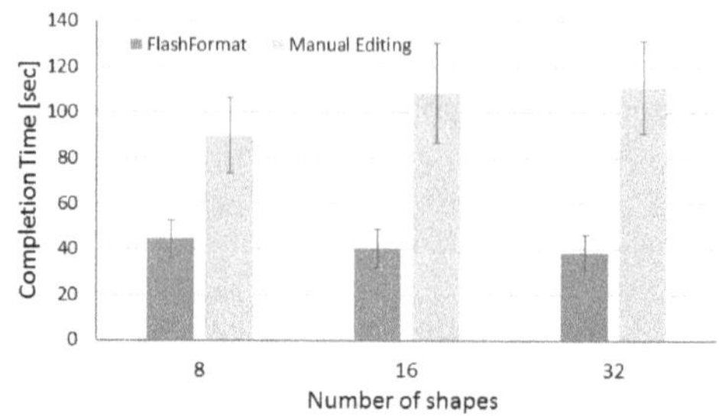

Figure 4. Mean performance time in the second study. The error bars represent 95% Confidence Intervals.

Questions	Mean response (*SD*)
I could always give appropriate examples to reach my desired end state.	5.1 (1.6)
I could anticipate the effects of FlashFormat before actually doing it.	4.6 (1.4)
It is necessary to anticipate the effects of FlashFormat to successfully use the tool.	5.8 (1.2)
It is annoying to repeatedly undo unwanted effects from FlashFormat.	4.3 (2.1)
I would prefer to use FlashFormat rather than make repetitive changes one-by-one.	6.5 (0.8)

Table 5. Responses of the post-experimental questionnaire. (1: strongly disagree – 7: strongly agree)

Table 5 presents the results of the questionnaire. Participants responded positively to their experience with FlashFormat, unanimously agreeing that FlashFormat was preferable to manual editing. As with StyleSnap, many participants commented on how it would support their regular authoring practices, especially with regard to diagram formatting. We further examined the qualitative study data to understand the reasons for these positive results.

Qualitative Analysis

In the pre-task session, participants exhibited a tendency to give one example, repeatedly FlashFormat-all until they reached the point of over-generalization, undo, and repeat. Thus, the participants did not follow the 'golden rule' of giving *more, and more diverse examples*, despite being reminded of it after each undo action. However, as the system repeatedly failed to produce their intended generalization from a single example, participants began giving more examples. At first, these were typically two examples given on the first two slides where they were applicable. However, we observed a gradual shift to a more systematic selection of diverse examples. Not only did participants learn to follow the golden rule through experience, they also learned what it means for examples to be diverse and how to give enough of them:

"Doing things automatically is good but sometimes I need to find out the differences of the shape, for example this is red and this is orange so I know I have to give two examples, one on the red and another on the orange, to let the system know that I want to change all the shapes no matter what the color is." (PB2)

"If you want to change the styles for all slides, you have to review all the slides first. For me it should be: first review all the slides, and then pick up all the different parts... different stuff in the same parts you want to change, and then change the different properties, and go ahead and FlashFormat and it should work." (PB8)

Overall, this suggests that repeated feedback from applying the LGG of self-selected formatting examples is sufficient to promote self-discovery of the optimum example-giving and generalization strategy. Our questionnaire results also support this, showing that participants agreed that they could provide examples and anticipate the effect. Thus, we concluded that HB-1 and HB-2 are also supported.

Nevertheless, the learning process could still benefit from additional guidance. One participant mentioned how before starting new examples, they *"always forget to press the button"* (PB12). Another participant described how, while giving examples, they *"sometimes feel lost about what to do next – should I choose more examples, or should I apply FlashFormat first?"* (PB1). Finally, several participants reported the need for better feedback, before and after applying FlashFormat-all, about which objects would be changed or had been changed already. Suggestions for improvements included highlighting the scope of objects that would be changed next, highlighting the differences of objects that share some attributes with the selected object to guide example selection, learning from multi-object examples where the relative changes are significant, and removing the need to press a start button. The latter could be done either showing a history of recently edited attributes that will be applied or suggesting multiple transformations from a single example.

Even without the suggested changes, the approach was assessed favorably against alternatives. Compared with the PowerPoint Format Painter, it was found to *"work more efficiently"* (PB3), to be *"much faster"* (PB12) and to be *"much more powerful"* (PB4) because it can *"work globally"* (PB4) and *"between slides"* (PB5) without overwriting all attributes (PB4). FlashFormat also *"has some features Slide Master does not provide"* (PB7), such as the ability to work on groups of objects that do not share the same location. In this respect, FlashFormat also surpasses the restyling power of StyleSnap, in which object groups are formed only by shared extents.

OVERALL DISCUSSION

We presented two complementary tools for automating global changes that can improve the visual consistency of slide decks. From the design and evaluation of these two tools we now synthesize limitations, lessons, and future work.

One limitation of the current work is our focus on the design of slide visuals only, and not of the underlying presentation material [23] or narrative structure [31]. While the balance of presentation preparation time should arguably be in favor of content and story, any time saved on styling slide visuals could conceivably be transferred to these other activities.

Another limitation is our sole use of PowerPoint for corpus analysis and prototyping. Since all slides and slideware are structurally similar, we expect our proposed solutions to generalize to other slideware and their associated slides. As for applications to other domains (e.g., vector-based graphical editing), this has not yet been demonstrated.

As we have already noted, StyleSnap does not preserve size and spacing constraints within a slide. Constraint-based reasoning, as used for single layout beautification [41], could provide a solution. Similarly, a limitation of FlashFormat is that imperceptible differences in attribute values are still viewed as differences by the system, leading to potential mismatches between user expectations and action outcomes.

Finally, we have evaluated our two tools independently rather than as a single system, such that we may evaluate their individual value. We hope to combine the functionality of the two tools into a single system in future work, taking into account the lessons discussed next.

Lesson 1: Suggest generalizations from single edits

One of the advantages of StyleSnap over FlashFormat is that users can confidently edit all of the objects in a position group at once rather than having to provide several examples first. One of the advantages of FlashFormat over StyleSnap is that object groups can be formed from any set of shared attributes, not just edge positions. Future work should investigate how to achieve both high predictability and flexibility from single examples. This could be achieved by suggesting multiple possible transformations after each edit, or suggesting snapping results for attribute values beyond edge positions (e.g., to create small, consistent sets of colors and font sizes) after each object selection. Users could thus make progress by incrementally applying such suggestions.

Lesson 2: Support state preservation as well as propagation

In both StyleSnap and FlashFormat, there were times when the user already had an example of their desired end state but were forced to recreate it for the benefit of the tool. In StyleSnap, this was because the snapped object groups represented the modal values of the clustered edges rather than the extent of a specified object. In FlashFormat, this was because only the edited attributes of an object contribute to the inferred example, and none of the other existing attributes. Future work should explore how to give examples of both the "change to" and "keep as" variety on a per-attribute basis, without requiring an enumeration of all object attributes.

Lesson 3: Show the scope of prospective changes

In StyleSnap, the real-time feedback from the combination of object highlights and the Selected slide section gave confidence to the user about the scope of their changes before and as they were making them. However, this feedback also created visual noise for dense slides and caused scrolling of the slide list for large numbers of selected objects. As literature suggests the importance of feedback in this type of systems [29], future work should explore alternative feedback strategies for tools like StyleSnap and FlashFormat.

Lesson 4: Incorporate design patterns and principles

StyleSnap makes the layout of objects consistent across slides, but it does not give any guidance about the desirability of those layouts. Similarly, FlashFormat can make large-scale changes easily, but provides no feedback about the desirability of those changes (e.g., considerations of the contrast between text and its background image following a global change to caption color). Future work should explore how to resolve aesthetic issues through assisted layout and styling that considers factors such as visual balance [25] and mood [21]. Supporting consistency, not just within sets of user-created visuals but also with external design patterns and principles, remains a significant research challenge.

REFERENCES

1. Abela, A.V. (2008). Advanced presentations by design. Pfeiffer.
2. Ali, K., Hartmann, K., Fuchs, G. & Schumann, H. (2008). Adaptive layout for interactive documents. SmartGraphics'08, 247-254.
3. Amershi, S., Fogarty, J. & Weld., D. (2012). Regroup: interactive machine learning for on-demand group creation in social networks. CHI'12, 21-30.
4. Baudisch, P., Cutrell, E., Hinckley, K. & Eversole, A. (2005). Snap-and-go: helping users align objects without the modality of traditional snapping. CHI'05, 301-310.
5. Bier, E.A. & Stone, M.C. (1986). Snap-dragging. SIGGRAPH'86, 233-240.
6. Blackwell, A.F. (2002). First steps in programming: A rationale for attention investment models. Human Centric Computing Languages and Environments, 2002.
7. Borning, A., Lin, R.K.H & Marriott, K. (2000). Constraint-based document layout for the Web. Multimedia Syst. 8(3), 177-189.
8. Cypher, A. (1991). EAGER: programming repetitive tasks by example. CHI'91, 33-39.
9. Drucker, S.M., Petschnigg, G. & Agrawala, M. (2006). Comparing and managing multiple versions of slide presentations. UIST'06, 47-56.
10. Duarte, N. (2008). Slide:ology: The art and science of creating great presentations. O'Reilly Media.
11. Edge, D. Savage, J. & Yatani, K. (2013). HyperSlides: dynamic presentation prototyping. CHI'13, 671-680.
12. Fails, J.A. & Olsen Jr., D.R. (2003). Interactive machine learning. IUI'03, 39-45.
13. Fernquist, J., Shoemaker, G. & Booth, K. S. (2011). "Oh snap"–helping users align digital objects on touch interfaces. INTERACT'11, 338-355.
14. Frisch, M., Kleinau, S., Langner, R. & Dachselt, R. (2011). Grids and guides: multi-touch layout and alignment tools. CHI'11, 1615-1618.
15. Frisch, M., Langner, R. & Dachselt, R. (2011). Neat: a set of flexible tools and gestures for layout tasks on interactive displays. ITS'11, 1-10.
16. Graf, W.H. (1998). Constraint-based graphical layout of multimodal presentations. Readings in intelligent user interfaces, Morgan Kaufmann, 263-285.
17. Hart, S. G., & Staveland, L. E. (1988). Development of NASA-TLX: results of empirical and theoretical research. Human mental workload, 1(3), 139-183.
18. Hastie, T., Tibshirani, R. & Friedman, J.J.H. (2001). The elements of statistical learning. Springer.
19. Horvitz, E. (1999). Principles of mixed-initiative user interfaces. CHI'99, 159–166.
20. Jacobs, C., Li, W., Schrier, W., Bargeron, D. & Salesin, D. (2003). Adaptive grid-based document layout. SIGGRAPH'03, 838-847.
21. Jahanian, A., Liu, J., Lin, Q., Tretter, D., O'Brien-Strain, E., Lee, S.C., Lyons, N. & Allebach, J. (2013). Recommendation system for automatic design of magazine covers. IUI'13, 95-106.
22. Kurlander, D. & Bier, E. (1988). Graphical search and replace. SIGGRAPH'88, 113-120.
23. Liu, Y., Edge, D. & Yatani, K. (2013). SidePoint: a peripheral knowledge panel for presentation slide authoring. CHI'13, 681-684.
24. Lok, S. & Feiner, S.K. (2001). A survey of automated layout techniques for information presentations. SmartGraphics'01, 61-68.
25. Lok, S., Feiner, S.K. & Ngai, G. (2004). Evaluation of visual balance for automated layout. IUI'04, 101-108.
26. Masui, T. (2001). HyperSnapping. HCC'01, 188-194.
27. Miller, R.C. & Myers, B.A. (2002). Multiple selections in smart text editing. IUI' 02, 103-110.
28. Miller, R.C. & Marshall, A.M. (2004). Cluster-based find and replace. CHI'04, 57-64.
29. Myers, B. A. (1992). Demonstrational interfaces: a step beyond direct manipulation. Computer 25(8), 61-73.
30. Open XML SDK 2.5. http://msdn.microsoft.com/en-us/library/office/bb448854.aspx
31. Pschetz, L., Yatani, K. & Edge, D. (2014). TurningPoint: narrative-driven presentation planning. CHI'14.
32. Raza, M., Gulwani, S. & Milic-Frayling, N. (2014). Programming by example using least general generalizations. AAAI.
33. Reber, R., Schwarz, N., & Winkielman, P. (2004). Processing fluency and aesthetic pleasure: is beauty in the perceiver's processing experience?. Personality and social psychology review, 8(4), 364-382.
34. Reynolds, G. (2012). Presentation Zen: simple ideas on presentation design and delivery. New Riders.
35. Ritter, A. and Basu, S. (2009). Learning to generalize for complex selection tasks. IUI'09, 167-176.
36. Schrier, E., Dontcheva, M., Jacobs, C., Wade, G. & Salesin, D. (2008). Adaptive layout for dynamically aggregated documents. IUI'08, 99-108.
37. Sibson. R. (1973). SLINK: an optimally efficient algorithm for the single-link cluster method. The Computer Journal 16 (1), 30-34.
38. Watanabe, T. & Hanaue, K. (2013). Composition support of presentation slides based on transformation of semantic relationships into layout structure. Multimedia Services in Intelligent Environments, 25, 155-181.
39. Weitzman, L. & Wittenburg, K. (1996). Grammar-based articulation for multimedia document design. Multimedia Systems, 4(3), 99-111.
40. Wigdor, D., Benko, H., Pella, J., Lombardo, J. & Williams, S. (2011). Rock & rails: extending multi-touch interactions with shape gestures to enable precise spatial manipulations. CHI'11, 1581-1590
41. Xu, P., Fu, H., Igarashi, T. & Tai, C-L. (2014). Global beautification of layouts with interactive ambiguity resolution. UIST'14, 243-252.

"For Telling" the Present: Using the Delphi Method to Understand Personal Information Management Practices

William Jones
Univ. of Washington
Seattle, WA USA
williamj@uw.edu

Robert Capra
Univ. of North Carolina
Chapel Hill, NC USA
rcapra@unc.edu

Anne Diekema
Utah State Univ.
Logan, UT USA
anne.diekema@usu.edu

Jaime Teevan
Microsoft Research
Redmond, WA USA
teevan@microsoft.com

Manuel Pérez-Quiñones
Virginia Tech
Blacksburg, VA USA
perez@cs.vt.edu

Jesse David Dinneen
McGill Univ.
Montreal, QC Canada
jesse.dinneen@mail.mcgill.ca

Bradley Hemminger
Univ. of North Carolina
Chapel Hill, NC USA
bmh@ils.unc.edu

ABSTRACT
Researchers have been studying personal information management (PIM) for many years, but little exists by way of practical advice for how individuals should manage their own information. We employed the Delphi Method to engage PIM researchers with expertise in a variety of relevant areas in a five-round extended dialog about PIM practices. Participants identified key everyday choices of PIM, suggested alternatives, and identified pros and cons of each alternative. Our contributions include: 1) a set of 36 PIM practices, along with pros, cons, and recommendations for or against each practice, 2) directions of future research and development including "near-future" improvements in tool support and 3) a detailed description of how we applied the Delphi Method to study PIM and how it might be used more widely in HCI research as a complement to more established methods of inquiry.

Author Keywords
Personal information management; PIM; Delphi Method.

ACM Classification Keywords
H.5.m. Info. interfaces and presentation (e.g., HCI): Misc.

INTRODUCTION
In many human endeavors practice proceeds of necessity, only occasionally to be informed and improved by principles elucidated from formal study. Such is true for personal information management (PIM), which is defined to be "the practice and the study of the activities people perform to acquire, organize, maintain, retrieve, use, and control the distribution of information items such as documents (paper-based and digital), webpages, and email messages for everyday use…" [16]. The phrase itself was coined less than 30 years ago [19], but people have been practicing PIM since ancient times. Logs, journals, ledgers, marginalia – even the proverbial string tied around the finger – are examples of PIM activity.

CHI 2015, April 18 - 23, 2015, Seoul, Republic of Korea
Copyright 2015 ACM 978-1-4503-3145-6/15/04 $15.00
http://dx.doi.org/10.1145/2702123.2702523

Though the practice of PIM is ancient, its importance has dramatically increased in modern times as, ever more so, the content of our perceptions and actions is mediated by information in one form or another. Frequent discussions of information overload, personal cloud-based storage, time and task management, privacy, security, etc. are testament to the practical importance of PIM in our daily lives.

Research has increased our understanding of how people manage information and the problems they encounter as they do. But each individual study is necessarily limited in scope and can only assess a small subset of the many situations of PIM activity and tool use that occur in the wild. As a result, few specific guidelines for the everyday practice of PIM have emerged from formal study. In this paper, we fill this gap using an application of the iterative Delphi Method [13, 20, 21, 23, 29]. Rather than studying people's PIM behavior, we study a different kind of participant: researchers who themselves study people in their daily practices of PIM. Drawing upon direct experience and observation across many studies, our participants considered:

1. Which of the many everyday practices of PIM had sufficient usage to warrant closer examination?
2. What considerations, costs, and benefits apply to each practice?
3. Which practices should be recommended or discouraged for information workers given reasonable assumptions about current tool support?

Our work makes several specific contributions:

- Using the Delphi Method, we identify a set of 36 PIM practices related to the capture and retention of personal information, how to find and organize personal information, task management, and the control for versions, clutter and fragmentation. For each practice we list relevant pros and cons and provide a recommendation for or against it. These practices and recommendations have immediate practical use for individuals and organizations to inform their day-to-day information management needs.

- We suggest directions for future research and development derived from outcomes of the Delphi Method. Many of the recommended PIM practices reflect work-around use of existing tools and so point to low hanging fruit for tool improvement. Additionally, practices where consensus was not achieved via the Delphi process point to areas where limited resources available for empirical research might be most fruitfully applied.
- We present details of an application of the Delphi Method and show how it can be used as a tool for human-computer interaction (HCI) research. We show how the method can be used to identify common user behaviors and practices in a domain (e.g., PIM). Where there is an achievable consensus among domain experts (e.g., PIM researchers), the Delphi Method provides an effective means to reach this consensus. And where not, the method makes explicit the reasons why not.

Just as the oracle at the eponymous site of ancient Greek civilization was used to foretell the future, the Delphi Method is a valuable way to achieve consensus among experts concerning likely futures in a given area such as HCI. However, the approach's consensus building process has broader application. It can, for example, be used to gather perspectives on past events or, as is the case for the work described in this paper, "for telling" a current situation of PIM practices. After a discussion of related work, we describe in detail how the Delphi Method was applied to study PIM, the practices that emerged from this process and wider applications of Delphi Method in the general study of HCI .

RELATED WORK

Personal Information Management

Previous research has explored PIM practices by looking at end-user behavior. These studies have shown that individuals differ dramatically in their tendencies to organize [10, 28]. For example, studies report a strong preference for navigation over search as the primary method for the return to personal files that endures notwithstanding the improvements in desktop search [1, 5, 24]. However, people are increasingly disinclined to invest in the organization of emails into folders for use in navigation [27], opting instead to use search as a primary method of return to email [17].

People keep their personal information in a wide variety of ways and according to best guesses of later use [11, 18], and tend to organize digital information by project [10]. Notwithstanding organizational efforts however, fragmentation of information, by tool and device, is a major concern [4, 14]. People often eschew the expressive freedom and flexibility of tags in favor of the familiarity and, we might say, universality of folders [6, 12]. Similarly, people often prefer to manage tasks and to-dos in an ad hoc manner using another universal form of information in our digital age – email [2, 3].

Some of these PIM studies have resulted in practical implications for people's everyday practices. For example, for efficient retrieval, people should keep fewer than 22 items in a folder [8] and use the icon view rather than the details view [9]. However, existing formal research addresses only a fraction of the choices people face in everyday PIM.

The work presented in this paper complements traditional PIM research by bringing together many of the researchers involved in these studies with the intent of being prescriptive concerning a broad range of everyday PIM practices. Through formal study and self-reflection, researchers acquire considerable practical knowledge concerning practices of PIM. The goal of our work is to enumerate these practices, and identify which are successful and which should be avoided given a particular user and circumstance. Codifying this knowledge has considerable practical value and offers a useful point of departure for additional study, especially into areas where researchers have not yet achieved consensus. Moreover, practices that work in spite of current tool support can carry implications for low hanging fruit that can be addressed with the next-generation of PIM tools.

The Delphi Method

We employ the *Delphi Method* [13, 20, 21, 23, 29], a widely-used process for achieving consensus. Noting the method's potential application to the study of human-computer interaction, Mankoff et al. describe it as a means of "collecting the views of people (typically, experts) through iterative dialog" [22]. The Delphi Method has been favorably contrasted with the use of focus groups. Rowe and Wright, for example, characterize the method as a way "to allow access to the positive attributes of interacting groups (knowledge from a variety of sources, creative synthesis, etc.) while pre-empting their negative aspects" [23].

The Delphi Method is perhaps most accurately regarded as an approach rather than a well-defined procedure. Although Linstone and Turoff have written extensively about the method over the years [20, 21], they avoid giving a detailed definition for the method, observing in one edited book that "if we were to attempt this, the reader would no doubt encounter at least one contribution to this collection which would violate our definition" [20]. Though consensus among experts is often an objective of its use, Turoff argues for the utility of the method even when consensus is not achieved, noting that the goal may be "to establish all the differing positions advocated and the principal pro and con arguments for those positions" [26].

Across the many variations in its application, four features characterize the Delphi Method: *statistical aggregation, anonymity*, *iteration*, and *controlled feedback* [23]. Statistical aggregation may be quite elaborate in studies involving a large number of participants. But the number of participants (often called *panelists*) can be quite small (e.g., 20 or fewer). In these cases, statistical aggregation may be a simple mean or median of participant responses or a tally of those for and against a position. Similarly, though anonymity can be critical in certain rounds of the Delphi process it is sometimes waived in other rounds to, for example, improve participation and compliance [29]. In our application of the Delphi Method we use different forms of statistical aggregation and we apply anonymity thoughtfully.

More essential for the Delphi Method are the features of iteration and controlled feedback. The Delphi Method involves one or more iterations in which the facilitator initiates the current round of discussion with a summary of results from the previous round. Consensus or an understanding of the differing positions is then given an opportunity to emerge. We iteratively use a number of distinctly structured rounds to collect controlled feedback from PIM researchers, as described in the next section.

METHOD

Our desire to build a picture of how PIM researchers understand present practices of personal information management arose at *PIM 2013* (http://pimworkshop.org/2013/) the sixth in a series of workshops concerning personal information management. In an afternoon breakout session, workshop attendees took turns sharing details of their own practices of PIM and discussing their observations from formal studies of PIM behavior. As discussion proceeded, an informal consensus emerged concerning the key challenges of PIM and notable alternatives for addressing each. As one person presented, other workshop participants would frequently offer, "I do that too!" or, "That's a lot like something I've seen participants do in my studies." To formalize this type of discussion and involve members of the larger PIM community, we decided to employ the Delphi Method.

Variations of the Delphi Method were used in five rounds grouped into two distinct phases, taking place from March through September 2014. In Rounds 1 and 2 of Phase 1, an effort was made to include PIM researchers with a wide variety of backgrounds in an open-ended dialog to collect notable instances of PIM behavior. Rounds 3, 4 and 5 of Phase 2 involved a smaller, select panel of participants who made a commitment at the outset to invest time to complete all three rounds.

Phase 1: Outreach

People employ a large number of practices in their everyday personal information management. The goal of Phase 1 of the study was to identify a manageable number of key PIM practices for closer consideration.

Participants for Phase 1 were recruited through broad announcement (e.g., email announcements to a PIM research mailing list) and active, direct solicitation of key PIM researchers by the authors. Twenty-seven researchers participated in Phase 1. A full list of participants can be found online at: http://pimworkshop.org/delphi_report.pdf.

Panelist	Affiliation
Nicholas Belkin	Rutgers University
Harry Bruce	University of Washington
Robert Capra	University of North Carolina
Mary Czerwinski	Microsoft Research
Anne R. Diekema	Utah State University
Jesse David Dinneen	McGill University
Michael Eisenberg	University of Washington
Thomas Erickson	IBM T. J. Watson
Ina Fourie	University of Pretoria
Daniel Gonçalves	University of Lisbon
Jacek Gwizdka	University of Texas
Bradley Hemminger	University of North Carolina
William Jones	University of Washington
David R. Karger	MIT
Diane Kelly	University of North Carolina
Barbara H. Kwaśnik	Syracuse University
Gary Marchionini	University of North Carolina
Gloria Mark	University of California
Manuel A. Pérez-Quiñones	Virginia Tech
Jaime Teevan	Microsoft Research
Amy Voida	Indiana University
Steve Whittaker	University of California

Table 1. Phase 2 PIM panel participants.

In **Round 1,** participants were asked to, "Please share a specific instance of a notable PIM behavior," and then, optionally, to provide details about the behavior including its intended benefits and rationale. They also provided circumstances through which they knew about the behavior, including, "I do this myself," "Observed in a formal study," or, "I've seen it informally in others." A Google form was used to collect the submissions anonymously into a spreadsheet. After submitting an instance, participants were given a link to the spreadsheet so they could see other submissions and encouraged to submit additional responses. Round 1 resulted in 102 PIM instances.

To serve as controlled feedback for the Round 2, the facilitators reviewed all the submitted instances and grouped them into four categories: 1) Organization, 2) Finding and re-finding, 3) Task management, and 4) Fragmentation.

Round 2 was structured as an asynchronous discussion about the four areas identified in Round 1. An editable Google Drive document was used to capture this conversation. For each of the four content areas, the facilitators seeded the document with a short prompt that described the main behaviors and choices that users face in that area, along with several open questions designed to stimulate discussion. For example, the prompt for the "Finding and re-finding" section read:

People appear to be using search ever more as a way to get back to their information – especially email messages. Still, recent studies indicate that navigation persists as a primary method for the return to files. How can search and navigation combine? When should people consider abandoning older ways of organizing (think use of email folders)? When should people opt for big "everything bucket" folders with minimal organization? When do/should people stick to organizations but use these in new ways (think search focused on file and folder names)?"

Participants were encouraged to read the prompts for each of the four areas and contribute their thoughts about the relevant behaviors and choices that users face, pros and cons of specific approaches, and successful alternatives. To support discussion, participants were given the option to identify themselves in their responses; all chose to do so.

Phase 2: Focused Deliberation

The results of Phase 1 were analyzed by the facilitators and resulted in 36 unique everyday practices of PIM (Table 2). These practices provided the nexus for focused deliberation by a select panel of PIM experts in Phase 2, which consisted of Rounds 3, 4, and 5.

Participants for Phase 2 were recruited in a highly coordinated and focused fashion. Facilitators nominated participants for Phase 2 based upon their existing PIM research. Altogether, Phase 2 had 22 panelists (Table 1), including the seven facilitators. 14 of these panelists had also participated in Phase 1. Other researchers were invited to participate as Phase 2 panelists but were unable to do so (including five of the researchers who participated in Phase 1).

In **Round 3** of Phase 2 participants were asked to anonymously complete a form to recommend or advise against one or more of the 36 PIM practices resulting from Round 2. Participants were also invited to enter comments for each item to explain their reasoning. At the end of Round 3, for each of the practices the facilitators wrote brief summaries that included: a short description of the practice, a list of pros and cons, a statement on whether there was consensus, and a list of outstanding questions for the practice.

In **Round 4**, these summaries were put into another editable Google Drive document with space left underneath each practice for participant discussion and contributions. Panelists were asked to review these summaries and then contribute to the discussion for at least two practices.

Finally, in **Round 5**, the facilitators used the discussions from the previous two rounds of Phase 2 to create consensus statements for each of the practices. A final report document was created with an introduction and the 36 consensus statements. Participants were asked to read and edit this draft report and make sure the statements were complete, substantive, and concise. During this round several statements were merged or split. After editing the draft report, panelists were asked if they were willing to endorse the report (all choose to do so), to highlight the practices they believed were particularly valuable, and to list up to five changes in PIM systems that they thought would be both impactful and reasonable to achieve in the near future.

Facilitators

Facilitators are essential to the Delphi Method, as they structure each round and provide the controlled feedback for iteration from one round to the next. The authors fulfilled the facilitator role throughout the study. As is sometimes done in Delphi studies [20], the facilitators, themselves each involved in PIM-related research, also participated in each round of the study. Their participation was anonymous or not, according the structure of a given round.

In any Delphi study, the facilitator must take care to insure that the controlled feedback is a balanced reflection of participant viewpoints. This is potentially a greater concern when facilitators are also participants. On the other hand, the seven facilitators represented a diverse set of viewpoints, drawn from very different organizations and backgrounds. We believe this diversity promoted balance in the controlled feedback provided in the transition from one round to the next. We concluded that it was better to support richer discussion by including the facilitators than to exclude the viewpoints of a number of PIM researchers.

RESULTS

The five-round application of the Delphi Method described above resulted in a list of PIM practices, each with a consensus statement, a list of pros and cons, and recorded vote of recommendation in favor or against. A list of the 36 practices is summarized in Table 2 and reported in detail at http://pimworkshop.org/delphi_report.pdf. In this paper, we present the details of the practices that were considered most valuable by the panelists, as expressed in the sign-off form of Round 5. These practices also garnered the highest proportion of "for" vs. "against" votes from Round 3.

Practices are presented in this paper to echo groupings created for Phase 2: 1) Information capture and retention for later use, 2) Finding and organizing information across applications, 3) Reminding and managing attention, tasks, and to-dos, and 4) Managing versions, controlling clutter, and combatting fragmentation.

The smaller set of practices that were "not recommended" by panelists are also listed, followed by a list of the desired near-future improvements panelists listed on the Round 5 sign-off form.

Category 1: Capture and Retention

This category deals with ways people capture and retain personal information for later use. Three practices in this category received 10 or more "most valuable practice" (or *MVP*) nominations each in Round 5 from the 22 panelists.

Take a picture with a smartphone: Smartphone photos are a very useful way to capture non-textual information, whiteboard meeting notes, or paper notes prior to disposal.

CATEGORY/PRACTICE	Round 5 MVP	Round 3 FOR	AGAINST
Information Capture and Retention for Later Use			
Take a picture with smartphone (e.g., of paper notes or whiteboard)	13	10	1
Email yourself notes, thoughts, tasks/to-dos	12	14	0
Keep a notes or "thoughts" file (e.g., as .txt or Word doc) for each project or topic	10	9	2
Use calendar events to represent the past and to support reflection of what has actually happened	9	6	1
Email information to others not only to share it with them, but also to serve a keeping purpose	6	7	2
Use a special-purpose note-taking tool (e.g., MS OneNote or Evernote)	5	5	2
Bookmark webpages that contain interesting/personally important information into folders	4	5	4
Use a sound recording device/app to record to-dos or notes on the go	1	3	8
Finding and Organizing Information Across Applications			
Organize information by project (one folder per project)	15	12	0
Use standardized file and/or folder names [also do this across devices]	12	8	2
Rely on search to find information	7	7	4
Store research papers in bibliographic management software	4	7	1
Structure subfolders according to standard sections of a document (e.g. academic folders match CV)	4	4	1
Organize information using a small number of large folders	3	7	4
Use tags to label files & folders in several different ways	3	5	1
Re-find by searching within the top level folder of a branch where a document is likely to be	3	5	2
Place keywords into file & folder names to aid later search-based retrieval	3	3	3
Let a "smart system" figure things out for me (e.g., "iPad hides structure which works fine for me")	1	1	9
Reminding, Managing Attention, Tasks/To-dos			
Use calendar events to represent the future and to remind of tasks and aid in completion	13	6	1
Use email inbox as to-do list (including flags as reminders, or maintaining a single "to-do" email)	9	10	1
Maintain a single, 'master' list of all tasks/to-dos	9	7	1
Keep windows and tabs open as a reminder to do something	9	6	2
Use leading characters in file and folder names to change display ordering (e.g., "aaa-", "zzz-").	7	9	2
Keep a simple to-do list in a generic application such as word processor or spreadsheet	7	6	2
Keep a simple paper-based to-do list (e.g., in a notebook or in note cards).	5	8	3
Duplicate critical task information across apps and devices (e.g., to-do as both email and calendar item)	5	4	3
Multi-task (e.g., do simple tasks while watching TV)	4	7	3
Use a special-purpose task management system (e.g.,Wunderlist, Things)	3	3	2
Use a desktop feature (e.g., Finder's 'sidebar') to organize currently active work items	3	2	1
Managing Versions, Controlling Clutter & Combating Fragmentation (esp. across devices)			
Store files in the cloud (e.g., Dropbox, OneDrive, Google Drive)	17	13	0
Add characters or words to file names to add context (e.g., "v1" or "final" at the end of a file name)	10	14	1
Archive old/inactive information into designated subfolder (e.g. "archive")	8	10	0
Store persona information (e.g., username and log-in details) in a single file	5	5	5
Use email as a file system (i.e., to store and access files across devices)	3	2	1
Avoid multiple devices; use a single device (e.g., laptop) no matter what	1	4	8
Use a dedicated version control system (e.g., Subversion, Git)	1	1	4

Table 2. PIM practices identified by panelists in the Delphi Method. Counts are always less than the number of panelists (22) because abstentions were allowed.

In some cases the image can be discarded after near-term use. However, some images may retain value for a much longer period of time, in which case it is necessary to ensure the image can be retrieved at a later date. The image can be stored within an existing organizational scheme, or embedded in a document, email, or webpage where the surrounding text supports search.

Pros: Quick capture of information. Facilitates distribution to a group.

Cons: Hard to search or re-find. For longer-term use, may require organization and/or annotation to support search.

Email yourself notes, thoughts, tasks/to-dos: People frequently email themselves personal notes, thoughts, and tasks. The practice is recommended and is effective because email is often available when information needs to be captured and the content is likely to be viewed again as long as it stays at the top of the user's inbox. But the value of these notes is only as good as the user's overall ability to manage email. Emailing notes to oneself could exacerbate feelings of being overwhelmed by email and add to email management overhead.

Pros: Can be done from any location/device with access to the Internet. Emails serve as reminders.

Cons: Contributes to overload of email inbox. Notes can get lost in one's flood of email.

Keep a notes or "thoughts" file for each project or topic: Keeping a notes or "thoughts" file is valuable because it is easy to forget items. Note taking produces a manageable record of precarious information items, thus preventing them from getting lost, and is also valuable to help synthesize and distill important ideas. The panelists widely endorsed the practice of keeping all the notes (e.g., thoughts, to-dos, and meeting notes) for a project together. However, there are many ways to accomplish this and the organization needs to be one that makes sense to each individual. When working on multiple projects with clear boundaries, keeping separate notes files for each project can be valuable. Such notes can be created as simple document files stored in project folders, or as emails with the project name in the subject line (sent to oneself and to project collaborators). Special purpose note-taking tools such as Evernote, TiddlyWiki, and Microsoft OneNote are recommended only for people with significant note-taking needs.

Pros: Reduces re-finding effort for people with projects that have clear boundaries.

Cons: Fragmentation of notes over multiple projects.

Category 2: Finding and Organizing

The next category of PIM practices deals with the organization of personal information, and how people use their organizations to find information in their own personal space. One MVP from this category is discussed below.

Organize information by project: Panelists indicated overwhelming support for the practice of organizing information by project (one folder per project). Maintaining a "Projects" folder with individual projects as subfolders is a structure that is easy to remember and supports re-finding by confining searches to a subset of folders. However, many panelists noted that the practice is not without limitations. Such an organizational structure is problematic when project boundaries change and when cross-cutting takes place among high-level folders. For example, two panelists mentioned their "Papers" folder is also a top-level folder like "Projects". More complex, matrix-like organizational structures could better support these situations, but are not widely implemented in current file systems. There was no consensus on how to resolve these issues, but one option that has worked for some is to create links among different folders.

Pros: Conceptually easy to identify project/folder. Ease of handling project (move, delete, backup, share, etc.)

Cons: Contents of projects might belong in multiple projects. Projects might grow into/from other projects.

Category 3: Task Management

Another set of PIM practices deals with how people organize their personal information to manage their attention, keep track of tasks and to-dos, and remind themselves of things. Some of the MVPs in this category include:

Use calendar events to remind of tasks, aid in completion, and to represent the future: For future intentions, a person's calendar can provide a simple kind of task management, not only for scheduled meetings and appointments, but also to set aside time for attending to tasks (e.g., "finish report"). People should consider setting aside blocks of time for personal tasks. They can often include in the calendar event description much of the information needed to complete the task (i.e., as text, links or attachments). However, it should be noted that these "meetings with self" (i.e., with the intention to complete a task) may be more easily missed or re-scheduled than meetings that involve others. To better insure task completion, therefore, this approach should be used as a supplement to other approaches for task management. Also, while effective for deadline-type scheduling, people who must manage a larger number of tasks or tasks with no fixed deadline might instead consider a more formal task management system.

Pros: Calendars are an effective, visible place to reserve time to work on tasks and to aid in reminding.

Cons: Not all tasks fit into the time/date model of calendars. Effort is required to re-schedule "missed appointments" to complete a task.

Maintain a single, "master" list of all tasks/to-dos: Many people could benefit from the ability to view all (or most) of their key tasks and to-do items into a single place as it allows them to see all of their commitments and prioritize across tasks. To minimize the overhead of maintaining the list, the master list should be accessible across devices and locations. Suggestions include: an online note taking tool (such as Evernote or OneNote), a file synced in the cloud, a draft email, or a paper notebook that is carried everywhere. People may also find it useful to limit the scope of their master list, including only key items rather than trying to create a complete, comprehensive list. Items on the master list might also serve as a reminder and a reference to other project-specific documents with more details.

Pros: Provides an overview of all tasks and allows user to get a big picture view of their task space.

Cons: List takes time to maintain and update. Sharing can be a problem; also, can be difficult to sync with calendar.

Use leading characters in file and folder names to change display ordering: This method can be used to bring important information to the top or to send old or inactive information to the bottom of a directory or folder display list (e.g., "aaa-", "zzz-"). This is a good technique for influencing the sorting order of a small number of files or folders in a directory display.

Pros: Quick way to move important files to the top and archived files to the bottom of file list.

Cons: Changing this organization scheme in large file sets could be labor intensive.

Category 4: Versions, Clutter and Fragmentation

The final category of PIM practices that we identified deals with how people manage multiple versions of documents to control file clutter and combat fragmentation. Three MVPs are discussed.

Store files in the cloud: Cloud storage services are a great method for accessing files from multiple locations or devices, for backups, and for collaboration. There are potential difficulties, however, with collaboratively managing and navigating the shared space. Users must also be aware of security and privacy risks and keep in mind that there may be regulatory and institutional policies and restrictions that apply in their particular cases. Some panelists recommended against storing confidential files in the cloud. As with any system, users are advised to make separate and regular backups of data stored in cloud storage. Cloud storage services can also create challenges with fragmentation of files and of users' online identities.

Pros: Great for collaboration. Good for backup and accessing files from multiple locations/devices.

Cons: Issues with collaborative management; privacy and security concerns; still need local backups.

Add characters or words to file names: Use of file names (especially by adding suffixes such as "-v1") is a simple way to keep track of versions. People working in collaboration should discuss guidelines for naming of files and folders (e.g. avoid spaces and special characters for better compatibility across platforms and applications) and conventions for representing versions of a shared document (i.e. for the "when" and "who" of a version). This discussion rarely happens, yet people are usually able to figure out the meaning of trailing characters even when different conventions are used (e.g., "v1", "v2", ... vs. author initials). Establishing a convention for which version is truly "current" can be very important. More formal version control systems (e.g., Subversion or Git) provide better support but require training and ongoing effort that few are willing to invest. Consequently, formal systems are not currently recommended. However, in the near future version control may increasingly be supported in more accessible ways via widely used storage applications such as Dropbox, Google Drive and One Drive.

Pros: a simple effective way to track versions, and in a group, who was the last person to work on a document

Cons: conventions are often jumbled and collaborators rarely discuss conventions ahead of time. File names may "lie" as in "-Final" and "-ReallyFinal".

Archive old/inactive information into designated subfolder: Archival of old/inactive information into a subfolder of a project folder (e.g., named "archive") is a practical way to reduce clutter and is a recommended practice for people who have an abundance of digital storage. For those who archive to reduce the use of active storage space, alternate plans should be considered – e.g., designate a parallel archival storage (cheaper, less accessible) for old information, but use an organizational scheme that parallels the active information. Alternatively, archive not only within projects, but also archive whole projects when they are completed.

Pros: simple way to get old information out of the way but still nearby and "available" just in case.

Cons: information archived is harder to find. Archival takes additional time and trouble.

Practices That Are Not Recommended

Among the practices discussed by our panel, several elicited strong negative reactions. We present them here as "not recommended" practices.

Not recommended: Avoid multiple devices; use a single device no matter what: Many people have needs to use multiple devices and it seems likely that the number of devices we manage will *increase* in the future. Utilizing cloud-based storage can help, and it will become increasingly important for device makers to provide a consistent user experience in accessing cloud-based information from different types of devices. Some users may find partial specialization of devices helpful (e.g. only do work on a work-issued laptop).

Not recommended: Use a dedicated version control system: Complex, dedicated version control systems like Git and Subversion are not ready for widespread use in PIM. However, simpler forms of version control are supported in services such as Dropbox and Google docs, which automatically save versions of files (up to a point) and allow users to access older versions if needed.

Not recommended: Let a "smart system" figure things out for me: Systems that eliminate, hide, or automatically classify data into folders may work in special circumstances (e.g. for music) or when information is "low stakes" (i.e. the costs of mistakes in organization are not so bad). But a kind of information such as photos or music may be "low stakes" to one person and very "high-stakes" another.

Not recommended: Use a sound recording device/app to record to-dos or notes on the go: Audio recording is fast, but most current systems do not have good support for indexing, searching, and retrieving information stored in audio form. Often this means that the ease of recording notes by voice is outweighed by the costs of retrieving the information at a later point. However, voice recording may be helpful to note the current state of work just before an interruption, as part of workflows that include a larger discipline to listen to the notes again, or within the context of existing services that convert speech to text.

Near-Future Recommendations

The final part of Phase 2 asked each panelist to list recommendations for changes to PIM systems that would be impactful and reasonable to achieve in the next five years. We collected 44 responses and grouped 37 of them to correspond to the categories of practice we have used elsewhere in this paper. These are discussed in greater detail below. The remaining seven were classified as "other," and include recommendations for "adding PIM to K-12 education", "improving security and privacy for data in the cloud", and "integrating voice input and analysis into more applications".

Capture and Retention

Two near-future recommendations related to the capture and retention of personal information. Panelists would like to see PIM systems extended to support the flexible addition of extra information to any application or document. This in turn could support more focused search and filter options. Additionally, panelists would like increased support for reflection in task management and calendar applications. A person could learn about their own practices through analysis of their captured personal information.

Finding and Organizing

Most (19) of the near-future recommendations related to the finding and organizing of personal information, with several focused specifically on improving file systems. A number of the recommendations in this category build on the suggestion to capture and retain additional metadata about files and folders, and suggest ways this metadata might be used. For example, it could be used to support customizable orderings of files and folders, or robustly link local and cloud-based information. Additionally, metadata that is common across files in a folder could be used automatically identify new candidates for inclusion in the folder and, more generally, to aid in the organization of information. Other common recommendations related to improving search support in file systems by, for example, providing people more control over the searches they issue.

Task Management.

Eight recommendations related to tasks, to-dos, and attention management. Common suggestions included easier capture of tasks, the ability to more effectively record and use notes via speech, and features to help in annotating folders. Panelists highlighted the need to integrate or cross-link to-dos with other information items. To accomplish tasks, panelists described needs to associate resources with to-do items. Desired associations included email and calendar, notes and projects, and the flexibility to integrate any other resources needed to carry out a task. One participant requested an easier way to break down larger tasks into smaller ones in order to get more work done (such as is done in *self-sourcing* [25]).

Versions, Clutter, and Fragmentation

Finally, eight recommendations focused on needs for improved synchronization of files across devices, version control, and cross-linking of information. The suggestions underscore problems users face managing information stored in different locations and devices. Panelists described needs not just for personal files, but also for sharing files with others. Panelists suggested developing versioning systems to help users maintain awareness of current file versions, and noted that a key aspect is the need for more usable version control systems. In cases where turn-taking is still the preferred means of collaborative authoring, for example, systems might more directly support the creation of snapshot versions (e.g., identified by the who, when and what was done) prior to transfer from one author to the next.

DISCUSSION

We have presented PIM practices identified through the Delphi Method related to the capture and retention of personal information, how to find and organize personal information, task management, and controlling for versions, clutter and fragmentation. We now discuss these findings in terms of the three contributions outlined in the Introduction: 1) the practical value of the recommendations, 2) the identification of specific areas for future research and development, and 3) use of the Delphi Method in for HCI research.

Practical Prescriptions for PIM

The list of 36 PIM practices we identified represents an important collection of practical advice for information workers. While some of these practices may be familiar to people within the HCI community, we nonetheless expect that most readers will come away with ideas for at least a few new practices to try, and we anticipate an even greater practical impact among the general public.

In addition to recommended practices, our findings also suggests practices to avoid. These practices shared traits of impracticality and inefficiency, and many evoked a fear of a potential loss of control. For example, using only a single device, while attractive to minimalists, is not feasible because no individual device can sufficiently reproduce every other device's functionality. It is better for people instead to face the challenges of a multi-device world directly, and some of the recommended practices suggest ways to do this (e.g., through increased reliance on cloud storage). Similarly, while it may seem attractive to use "smart" systems, we found that such systems are likely to meet a person's needs only in circumscribed domains where the items to be managed all share a small set of meaningful attributes (e.g., "artist", "album", "song", etc. for music) and a person's interactions with the items are predictable.

Future Directions for PIM Research and Development

In addition to having immediate practical use, our findings point to areas where PIM research and development efforts could have high impact. For example, many of the recommended practices illustrate ways people creatively appropriated their PIM tools, sometimes making work-around use of these, to meet their needs. Consider the recommended practices of using leading characters in filenames to effect order and of using subfolders to clear away clutter. While these are both good practices, their aims might be better met through file system improvements that allow a user to specify whether and how items should be shown in a display. Likewise, the recommendation to "Organize information by project (one folder per project)" might be better managed via explicit tool support. Relevant information (e.g., notes, component tasks, target completion date, and the desired state when done) could be associated with a project folder using metadata, making this information also available in other contexts.

In addition to better supporting existing behavior, areas where limited consensus exist suggest avenues for future exploration. Some of the "not recommended" practices, for example, may represent solutions that have not yet been perfected. For example, while panelists did not recommend existing text-oriented version control systems, they did see a near-future of version control where such systems will become easier to use and more directly meet the needs of their non-coding user (see, for example, early implementations in Dropbox, Google Drive, and Microsoft's One Drive). Likewise, as tool support improves and is better integrated into existing workflows, the use of sound or video may very well shift. Recordings may never take the place of active engagement in the lecture or meeting, but seem likely to eventually provide real value in support of task resumption or reminding where memories are partial and notes ambiguous.

The Delphi Method for HCI Research

We have shown that the Delphi Method provides a reasonably rapid, cost-effective means to achieve consensus among researchers with expertise in PIM concerning the current state of PIM practices. While the Delphi Method was recently used to better predict the future of HCI [22], we believe that the method also has significant utility when directed to the practical present of HCI. There are many areas in HCI where the Delphi Method could engage experts in a useful dialog "for telling" key choices, alternatives, and pros/cons for identified practices. Potential application areas of the method range from identifying the best-practices in web design, to facilitating a nuanced discussion of multi-tasking and how to interleave tasks.

The Delphi Method is complementary to more traditional methods of data collection, including interviews, surveys, observations, and focus groups. The Delphi Method, as used in this paper, is second order: rather than focusing on individuals practicing PIM, the focus was on researchers who observe, interview and survey individuals practicing PIM. However, as discussed in this section, the method's outcomes can suggest additional first order studies. In future work, we would like to engage samplings of people from the population targeted by the recommendations (i.e., information workers) in studies to selectively and directly assess the efficacy of the recommendations.

Limitations

Though variations of the Delphi process were used to establish consensus among PIM researchers concerning practices of PIM to recommend (with qualification) and to advise against, this consensus does not per se establish validity. In addition, although our panelists discussed many diverse research and personal experiences, there may be areas of PIM practice that were missed. Many practices recommended by the researchers (and observed in the participants of their studies) depend on existing tools and infrastructure, such as the near universal support of file and folder semantics. Other practices depend upon another universality of our digital world: Email (and related support for a digital calendar). Tool improvements that work to extend rather than replace these are likely to find the best reception (see, for example, [3, 7, 15]). But our focus on current practices limits our ability to observe entirely new ones.

As PIM research continues to shed light on how people do PIM and how they might do it better, the recommendations reached in this paper may ultimately prove wrong. Some may become dated as the tools and devices that support PIM improve. However, the recommendations represent the current consensus of experts in the field. We believe the Delphi Method will continue to be useful as an effective means to update our understanding of current PIM practices. In future work we plan to use the Delphi Method to understand people's PIM practices more deeply, including how the practices evolve over time and which combine well towards overall, coherent, sustainable strategies of PIM.

CONCLUSION

Given the existing variation in people's personal information management practices, it is unlikely that we will ever be able to determine the *best* practices of PIM of universal application. But an ongoing discussion of challenges, alternatives and the pros and cons of each may at least help individuals identify *better* PIM practices than they currently use, and allow them to consider the costs and benefits that apply in their adoption. As described in this paper, such a discussion can be structured and facilitated through applications of the Delphi Method.

We used the Delphi Method with a panel of PIM experts to elicit and assess 36 practices of PIM. The top-ranked "MVPs" in this set are worthy of consideration for immediate adoption. These practices relate to the capture and retention of personal information, how to find and organize personal information, task management, and the control of versions, clutter and fragmentation. Our findings also point to areas where PIM research and development efforts could have high impact.

This paper presents a detailed example how the Delphi Method can be used in HCI research as a complement to more established methods of inquiry. Rather than studying people's PIM behavior directly, we show that much can be learned through careful engagement of the researchers who themselves study people in their daily practices of PIM. The

Delphi Method should find useful application in other areas of HCI as well where it may serve to complement and catalyze existing research methods.

ACKNOWLEDGEMENTS

We appreciate the PIM researchers who made time in their busy schedules to participate in the Delphi process. We also thank Richard Neiman, M.D., for his identification of Delphi Method use among medical practitioners.

REFERENCES

1. Barreau, D. and Nardi, B.A. Finding and reminding: file organization from the desktop. *SIGCHI Bull. 27*, 3 (1995), 39–43.
2. Bellotti, V., Dalal, B., Good, N., Flynn, P., Bobrow, D.G., and Ducheneaut, N. What a to-do: Studies of task management towards the design of a personal task list manager. *Proc. CHI 2004*, 735–742.
3. Bellotti, V., Ducheneaut, N., Howard, M., and Smith, I. Taking email to task: The design and evaluation of a task management centered email tool. *Proc. CHI 2003*, 345–352.
4. Bergman, O., Beyth-Marom, R., and Nachmias, R. The project fragmentation problem in personal information management. *Proc. CHI 2006*, 271–274.
5. Bergman, O., Beyth-Marom, R., Nachmias, R., Gradovitch, N., and Whittaker, S. Improved search engines and navigation preference in personal information management. *ACM Trans. Inf. Syst. 26*, 4 (2008), 1–24.
6. Bergman, O., Gradovitch, N., Bar-Ilan, J., and Beyth-Marom, R. Folder versus tag preference in personal information management. *J. Am. Soc. Inf. Sci. Technol. 64*, 10 (2013), 1995-2012.
7. Bergman, O., Tucker, S., Beyth-Marom, R., Cutrell, E., and Whittaker, S. It's not that important: Demoting personal information of low subjective importance using GrayArea. *Proc. CHI 2009*, 269–278.
8. Bergman, O., Whittaker, S., Sanderson, M., Nachmias, R., and Ramamoorthy, A. The effect of folder structure on personal file navigation. *J. Am. Soc. Inf. Sci. Technol. 61*, 12 (2010), 2426–2441.
9. Bergman, O., Whittaker, S., Sanderson, M., Nachmias, R., and Ramamoorthy, A. How do we find personal files? The effect of OS, presentation and depth on file navigation. *Proc. CHI 2012*, 2977–2980.
10. Boardman, R. and Sasse, M.A. "Stuff goes into the computer and doesn't come out:" A cross-tool study of personal information management. *Proc. CHI 2004*, 583-590.
11. Bruce, H., Jones, W., and Dumais, S. Information behavior that keeps found things found. *Information Research 10*, 1 (2004).
12. Civan, A., Jones, W., Klasnja, P., and Bruce, H. Better to organize personal information by folders or by Tags? The devil is in the details. *Proc. ASIST 2008.*
13. Dalkey, N. and Helmer, O. An experimental application of the Delphi method to the use of experts. *Management Science 9*, 3 (1963), 458–467.
14. Jones, W. Finders, keepers? The present and future perfect in support of personal information management. *First Monday 9,* 3 (2004).
15. Jones, W., Hou, D., Sethanandha, B.D., Bi, S., and Gemmell, J. Planz to put our digital information in its place. *Proc. CHI 2010 Extended Abstract,* 2803–2812.
16. Jones, W. and Teevan, J. *Personal Information Management.* Univ.Washington Press, Seattle, WA, 2007.
17. Jones, W., Wenning, A., and Bruce, H. How do people re-find files, emails and web pages? *Proc. iConference 2014.*
18. Kwasnik, B.H. How a personal document's intended use or purpose affects its classification in an office. *Proc. SIGIR 1989*, 207–210.
19. Lansdale, M. The psychology of personal information management. *Appl. Ergon. 19*, 1 (1988), 55–66.
20. Linstone, H.A. and Turoff, M. *The Delphi method: Techniques and applications.* Addison-Wesley Reading, MA, 1975.
21. Linstone, H.A. and Turoff, M. Delphi: A brief look backward and forward. *Technological Forecasting and Social Change 78*, 9 (2011), 1712–1719.
22. Mankoff, J., Rode, J.A., and Faste, H. Looking past yesterday's tomorrow: Using futures studies methods to extend the research horizon. *Proc. CHI 2013*, 1629–1638.
23. Rowe, G. and Wright, G. The Delphi technique as a forecasting tool: Issues and analysis. *Int. J. Forecasting 15*, 4 (1999), 353–375.
24. Teevan, J., Alvarado, C., Ackerman, M.S., and Karger, D.R. The perfect search engine is not enough: A study of orienteering behavior in directed search. *Proc. CHI 2004*, 415–422.
25. Teevan, J., Liebling, D.J., and Lasecki, W.S. Selfsourcing personal tasks. *Proc. CHI 2014 Extended Abstract*, 2527-2532.
26. Turoff, M. Delphi and its potential impact on information systems. *Proc. Fall Joint Computer Conference (AFIPS 1971)*, 317–326.
27. Whittaker, S., Matthews, T., Cerruti, J., Badenes, H., and Tang, J. Am I wasting my time organizing email? A study of email refinding. *Proc. CHI 2011*, 3449–3458.
28. Whittaker, S. and Sidner, C. Email overload: Exploring personal information management of email. *Proc. CHI 1996.* 276-283.
29. Woudenberg, F. An evaluation of Delphi. *Technological Forecasting and Social Change 40*, 2 (1991), 131–150.

Privacy Concerns and Behaviors of People with Visual Impairments

Tousif Ahmed Roberto Hoyle Kay Connelly David Crandall Apu Kapadia
School of Informatics and Computing
Indiana University
Bloomington, IN, USA
{touahmed, rjhoyle, connelly, djcran, kapadia}@indiana.edu

ABSTRACT
Various technologies have been developed to help make the world more accessible to visually impaired people, and recent advances in low-cost wearable and mobile computing are likely to drive even more advances. However, the unique privacy and security needs of visually impaired people remain largely unaddressed. We conducted an exploratory user study with 14 visually impaired participants to understand the techniques they currently use for protecting privacy, their remaining privacy concerns, and how new technologies may be able to help. The interviews explored privacy not only in the physical world (e.g., bystanders overhearing private conversations) and the online world (e.g., determining if a URL is legitimate), but also in the interface between the two (e.g. bystanders 'shoulder-surfing' data from screens). The study revealed serious concerns that are not adequately solved by current technology, and suggested new directions for improving the privacy of this significant fraction of the population.

Author Keywords
Privacy; visually impaired people; wearable technology

ACM Classification Keywords
K.4.2 Computers and Society: Social Issues

INTRODUCTION
Visually impaired people face a variety of challenges in navigating a physical and social world that is often not designed with them in mind. Visual impairments include not only complete blindness, but also poor vision, such as the inability to read a newspaper with ordinary glasses.[1] In the United States alone, over 8 million people are visually impaired, and older people are especially affected — about 1 in 6 people over age 45 and 1 in 4 people over 75 years old [1].

One important challenge faced by visually impaired people is how to preserve their privacy and security in their daily lives. Sighted people are able to monitor their surroundings to protect themselves from privacy threats. For example, when using a mobile device in public, sighted people can obscure sight lines between the screen and nosy bystanders. When sharing a photo online (which, perhaps somewhat surprisingly, visually impaired people do as often as the average user [33]), sighted people can check that it does not include embarrassing or private content.

A wide variety of research has studied how technology can assist visually impaired people [7, 9, 26, 31, 34], often highlighting privacy concerns [16, 21, 27, 34]. Researchers have also studied security and privacy issues for visually impaired people in specific contexts such as Web authentication [17], CAPTCHAs [4, 13, 19, 25], and smartphone authentication [3, 11]. However, the unique privacy and security needs of the visually impaired are not sufficiently understood from a broader scope. We seek to explore how emerging sensor and camera-enabled mobile technologies could eventually enhance privacy in not only electronic settings, but also physical settings (e.g., bystanders overhearing private conversations) and the interface between the two (e.g., bystanders 'shoulder-surfing' data from screens). Before trying to develop solutions, however, we need to understand how visually impaired people manage privacy using existing techniques and what their remaining privacy needs are. Understanding the specific privacy concerns and behaviors of visually impaired people, as well as their commentary on existing and anticipated technologies, will inform and guide technical solutions to assist these users in enhancing their privacy.

Specifically, we seek to answer three main research questions:

R1: *What are the privacy concerns of visually impaired people?* We seek to understand their physical privacy concerns both in public and private spaces, including in the context of using electronic devices. We also seek to understand their concerns about privacy in virtual interactions, such as in online social networking and media-sharing websites.

[1]Blindness is "central visual acuity of 20/200 or less in the better eye with corrective glasses or central visual acuity of more than 20/200 if there is a visual field defect in which the peripheral field is contracted to such an extent that the widest diameter of the visual field subtends an angular distance no greater than 20 degrees in the better eye." [1] A person with a visual impairment cannot "recognize a friend at arm's length even when wearing glasses or contact lenses, or cannot read ordinary newspaper print even when wearing glasses or contact lenses, or reports poor or very poor vision even when wearing glasses or contact lenses, or is blind in both eyes." [1]

CHI 2015, April 18–23, 2015, Seoul, Republic of Korea .

http://dx.doi.org/10.1145/2702123.2702334

R2: *How do visually impaired people manage their privacy?* We seek to understand the existing privacy practices and behaviors of visually impaired people, again in the context of physical spaces, computing devices, and virtual interactions. We also seek to understand any existing assistive technology they use to enhance their privacy.

R3: *Which new technologies could offer enhanced privacy for visually impaired users?* We seek to understand how mobile and wearable computing technologies could enhance the privacy of the visually impaired, by both soliciting feedback on researcher-generated ideas and by collecting original suggestions from visually impaired people.

To answer these questions, we conducted an exploratory user study through semi-structured in-person interviews with visually impaired people (N=14). We explored their privacy concerns, needs, and behaviors in three main settings: physical, online, and at the interface between the two (e.g. privacy leaks that occur when using technology in public). We found that participants were aware of and concerned about privacy and security, and face a variety of risks. One recurring theme in their responses was that being forced to depend on other people, especially strangers, was a major privacy risk. We found that participants used a variety of techniques and technologies to try to manage privacy, but they repeatedly expressed a desire for better solutions. Moreover, assistive technologies themselves often created additional privacy risks. For example, screen-reading technology allows visually impaired people to access the web through their phones, but bystanders may also be able to hear; wearing headphones solves that problem, but muffles the sense of hearing, further reducing their ability to sense their surroundings [3, 27].

We now describe our work in detail. After reviewing related work, we describe our study protocol and procedure, and then present our major findings. We then discuss implications on the design and development of privacy-enhancing devices.

RELATED WORK

There is a large body of work on understanding the accessibility needs of visually impaired people in general, and some of this has highlighted the privacy implications of accessible devices. In their study on mobile device adoption, Kane *et al.* [16] report that visually impaired people have privacy concerns about using mobile devices in screen-reading mode. Naftali *et al.* [21] and Ye *et al.* [34] also find that people with visual impairments are concerned about eavesdropping when using screen readers and voice-to-text in public.

The work of Azenkot *et al.* [3] was one of the first to study the security and privacy threats and concerns of visually impaired mobile device users. They report that most users in their study were not aware of mobile device security threats, and none had enabled passcode locks on their phones. Most participants were also not aware of the threats of eavesdropping or shoulder surfing. They introduce an accessible non-visual authentication system that is designed to resist eavesdropping. Our work builds on theirs by including visually impaired participants who are not blind, which their paper suggested as an important direction for future work; we find that these participants were much more aware of and concerned about the potential for eavesdropping. We also study possible solutions to eavesdropping beyond authentication scenarios as well as privacy issues beyond mobile devices.

Shinohara and Wobbrock [27] discuss how simply having or using assistive devices may invite privacy-invading questions (e.g., "how did you lose your sight?") or behaviors (e.g., trying to give unwanted help). Our participants did not report concerns about stigma, but we did not specifically direct our interviews towards social issues. More research on the social consequences of assistive technologies is needed, since their success may depend on overcoming these social barriers.

In the context of the web, Sauer *et al.* [25] identify the top security challenges of blind users, including inaccessible CAPTCHAs, spam, keyloggers, and so on. Our participants brought up several of these like inaccessible CAPTCHAs and spam, but also identified other challenges like trying to practice good password management with a visual impairment, and accessibility of online privacy settings. Other work has studied usable authentication techniques for the visually impaired. Haque *et al.* [11] propose authentication using smartphone accelerometer sensors, and Azenkot *et al.* [3] propose authentication by tapping the phone. Kuber *et al.* [17] propose a web-based authentication system for blind users to keep their passwords safe from shoulder surfers, while several researchers [4, 13, 19, 25] have proposed usable CAPTCHAs for the visually impaired. In this paper we more broadly study privacy-enhancing concerns, behaviors, and tools used throughout everyday life, in addition to online concerns.

Outside the privacy domain, several papers have studied using wearable computing devices to enhance accessibility for the visually impaired. Velazquez *et al.* [31] present a number of prototypes of assistive devices for blind people, such as a wearable tactile feedback device called BrailleWatch, and a mechatronic shoe insole that vibrates to give navigational directions. Shilkrot *et al.* [26] present a handheld device to support reading text, while other researchers [7,9,34] have designed navigational tools for the visually impaired. Inspired by this work on accessibility, we focus here on how these devices could improve the privacy of visually impaired users.

METHODS

We interviewed visually impaired participants to investigate our research questions. The interviews were semi-structured and in person, to not only explore reports of participants' concerns and behaviors, but also to witness them ourselves.

Interview Preparation and Process

Each interview was conducted by two researchers, one of whom interacted with the participant while the other took notes. The audio of the interviews was recorded and later transcribed. After approximately half of the interviews were complete, one of the researchers analyzed the transcripts using an iterative coding process with initial coding and identified concepts [22, 24]. The two researchers discussed the identified concepts and developed a category of concepts based on our research questions. After each subsequent interview, they met to identify new concepts and added them to the list. This semi-structured interview design allowed us to pursue concepts identified from prior interviews and to adapt our questionnaire as needed. For example, several early participants reported concerns about medical records, so we added a question about this to our questionnaire.

We conducted separate interviews, with the exception of married participants who could choose to include their spouse in the interview, since spouses are mutually supportive and the presence of a spouse could improve recall of concerns and offer additional insight. We conducted interviews at places of participants' choosing, and provided transportation if needed.

Interview Protocol

We used the following categories of questions:

1. **Background.** We began by asking participants to characterize their degree and history of visual impairment, their current use of technology including assistive technologies, and the level of assistance that they require from others.
2. **Privacy concerns and behaviors.** We asked participants to describe their physical and virtual privacy concerns, and any privacy-enhancing behaviors they use. We also asked about specific topics, such as whether participants had any concerns about assistive devices, about people watching them, and about their comfort in requesting assistance.
3. **Novel ideas.** We introduced wearable devices, and gave a chance to try Google Glass. We then discussed our ideas for wearable assistive devices and asked whether they could help protect privacy. Finally, we asked if participants had anything to add, to identify unexplored areas.

Study Procedure

Recruitment and Enrollment

We recruited participants through Indiana University's disability services office, and through the Bloomington and Bedford (Indiana) chapters of the American Council of the Blind (ACB). They distributed our study ad to their members, and we recruited those who responded between July and September 2014. We also introduced our study at two ACB meetings.

Ethical Considerations

Our university human subjects ethics board approved our study. To obtain informed consent, we provided our information sheet via email so that participants could use accessibility tools. We also read the information sheet aloud if needed. Participants could skip any question, and we recorded interviews only after obtaining consent verbally or in writing.

Compensation

Each participant was compensated $15 at the end of the study.

FINDINGS

Participants

We interviewed 14 participants over a two month period. Table 1 summarizes their demographics, which included 5 men and 9 women, and a diverse range of ages from 18 to 70. Our participants included two married couples in which both partners were visually impaired, and three participants were married to sighted partners. The married couples chose to be interviewed jointly, while two of the three other married participants chose to have the sighted partners present. Two participants (P8 and P12) were both visually and hearing impaired. The interviews lasted between 25 and 100 minutes, with most about 45 minutes. Participants chose where to be interviewed, with most (N=7) choosing a public places, while others chose their home (N=5) or office (N=2).

Physical Privacy Concerns

We first discuss *concerns about physical privacy* (as opposed to those related to devices or the online world). We identified the following recurring themes: lack of independence, eavesdropping, embarrassment, and physical security concerns.

Lack of Independence

Visually-impaired people often need help from others, including strangers; they may need to ask bank employees to fill out financial documents, ask waiters to read the menu, or ask passersby to read street signs. These requests often involve revealing personal information to a stranger. In fact, most of the concerns that participants identified during our interviews seemed to result from this lack of independence, so we grouped them into the following subcategories.

Lack of accessibility. While many accessibility tools are available to access electronic documents, participants (N=9) expressed concerns about physical documents like letters and forms, especially ones with personal information. They reported receiving physical mail that they were unable to read on a daily basis. While some had devices that could scan and read content aloud, lack of standardization between documents frequently caused these tools to fail. Participants expressed concern about asking for assistance, since whether a document is sensitive is often not known *a priori*. P9 reported taking this risk because she did not have a choice:

> *I have to find out what a piece of paper says, so I have to ask someone to read it. It's a risk that you take.*

Filling out questionnaires and forms was another source of concern, for instance during visits to the doctor. P9 explained:

> *When you go to the doctor, there is a privacy issue. There are all these forms and they are never accessible, so somebody has to read them to you so you have to sign a document trusting that the person has read it correctly and completely to you.... Just because somebody takes you and gives you a ride to a doctor's office, they should not assume just because that person is a friend, that you want to share all of your health information with that friend.*

P3 expressed similar concerns about financial documents:

> *When I'm being asked to fill out paperwork at a bank, I can't do it so I have to ask the person to fill it out and have a verbal interview.*

Visually impaired people may need help reading restaurant checks or grocery bills. Cash transactions are particularly

ID	Age	Gender	Impairment	Device access method	Mobile device(s)	Assistive device(s)	Password management	Bank online?	Take photos?
P1	18-24	F	Low peripheral vision	Normal	iPhone	None	Save passwords	Yes	Yes
P2	18-24	F	Low vision, can see the shapes & outlines	Screen magnifier	iPhone, iPad	Magnifying glass	Memorize	Yes	Yes
P3	31-40	M	Low vision in one eye, blind in other	Screen magnifier, screen reader	iPhone	Ruby portable magnifier, portable reader	KeyChain	Yes	Yes
P4	31-40	F	Blind with light perception	Screen reader	iPhone	Braille displays, ebook players	Memorize, Braille	Yes	Yes
P5	31-40	M	Low vision, can see shapes	Screen reader	iPhone, iPad	iBook	Memorize	Yes	Yes
P6	41-50	M	Blind with light perception	Screen reader	iPhone	Victor Reader Stream	Store in text file	Yes	No
P7	41-50	F	Totally blind	Screen reader	iPhone	Victor Reader Stream, Ai Squared, Barcode Scanner	Change frequently	Yes	No
P8	51-60	M	Blind with light perception, hearing impaired	Screen reader, hearing aid	iPhone, landline	ZoomText, magnifier	Memorize	Yes	No
P9	51-60	F	Totally blind	Screen readers	iPhone	Braille embosser, color detector, electronic measuring tape, PenFriend, SignatureGuide, BrailleStylus, BrailleWatch, iPhone overlay	Braille	No	No
P10	51-60	M	Totally blind	Screen readers	Flip phone	DocuScan Plus Scanner	Memorize	Yes	No
P11	51-60	F	Totally blind	Screen readers	iPhone	DocuScan Plus Scanner, Prescription Reader	Braille	Yes	No
P12	51-60	F	Blind with light perception, hearing impaired	Screen readers, hearing aid	iPhone	OpenBook, Braille Printers, Braille Labels, Talking Timer	Save passwords, memorize	No	No
P13	61-70	F	Low vision, can see shapes	Screen readers	Landline	Barcode Reader, talking watch	Memorize	No	No
P14	61-70	F	Low vision in one eye, blind in other	Screen reader, magnifying tools	iPhone	CTC Scanner, Talking Calculator, Magnification Light	Memorize	Yes	Yes

Table 1. Summary of participant demographics and privacy behavior.

problematic since U.S. currency cannot be differentiated tactilely, so participants sometimes rely on others to identify bills. Although using debit or credit cards alleviates this problem, one participant mentioned that keypads on Point of Sale (POS) systems do not always have raised buttons, so she must ask strangers to enter her PIN — a potentially serious risk.

Finding items. It can be difficult for people with visual impairment to locate objects, and they often have to rely on others to find items in stores or even in their home. Requesting others' assistance in finding items can be uncomfortable, especially if the item is personal (e.g., a private medical item). P4 is learning to take photos for exactly this reason:

> *Once I learn to use the camera better I can take pictures of, like, boxes of unknown things that I have in my pantry that I don't know what they are anymore. It will read the barcode for me and tell me what it is and things like that.*

Navigation and transportation. Participants repeatedly raised challenges of navigation in the context of privacy, where the choice is sometimes asking a stranger for help and revealing private information, or maintaining privacy but risking physical harm. P12 struggles to find restrooms, especially in crowded places like airports. Others mentioned trying to navigate when routes change unexpectedly due to construction or maintenance. P3 once fell into an open manhole; he was using a cane, but by the time he had identified the hazard there was not enough time to avoid it. Assistive devices for navigation offer not only the prospect of improved privacy but also personal safety.

Eavesdropping

Eavesdropping was the next major category of privacy concerns indicated by participants (N=4), stemming from not knowing if other people are nearby. For instance, they mentioned concerns over giving out medical information in waiting rooms where others could be listening. P9 said:

> *I had gone to see a new doctor before, and they have to collect all of this private information from you about your health care and your lifestyles and everything. And, I actually had one of the attendants in the office; she came out to the waiting room, sat down and started filling out this paper. I said to her, 'I am assuming there is no one in the office but us right now.' Fortunately there wasn't, other than the person that had taken me to the office and that person was hard of hearing, so I let it go.*

Those who also have hearing problems felt even more exposed to eavesdropping, especially because they tend to speak loudly. P12 described her experience when donating blood:

> *They ask you some pretty private questions. It would be nice if there was a questionnaire that you can fill out independently, because they have to read it out to me. With me being hard of hearing they can't just whisper. That kind of bugged me. There's people on the other side of the little wall, that can probably hear everything that is going on.*

In these types of situations, participants reported either having to assume that there is nobody nearby, or asking a trusted person whether there is someone around.

Embarrassment

Some participants (N=3) reported embarrassing situations caused by not being able to sense the surroundings. P6 said:

> *One thing that bothers to me, and we encounter it so frequently. You can be standing there talking to somebody and one second you are talking to them and they answer you back. You keep on talking and they have since walked away. You were standing there jabbering, you don't know they have walked away. You look like fools.*

P4 mentioned a similar experience in her workplace:

> *There are a couple of people who work with us who are extremely shy people, so when I got on to them to at least*

> *say 'hi,' I was told that I was bullying them. I think I have no other way to know that they are in the room unless they say something. They don't have to talk to me, I just want to know that they are there.*

Shinohara and and Wobbrock [27] reported on similar struggles of their participants trying to stay connected to others in the workplace, especially while using assistive devices.

Physical Security Concerns

We found that physical security and safety were major concerns for some participants (N=4), and these in turn created privacy concerns: maintaining one's home free from intrusion has long been considered a basic tenet of privacy [28]. For example, most participants were extremely cautious with home security, like hesitating to open the door when someone knocks unless they were expecting someone or recognized the person's voice. P13 said she felt scared when her husband is not home, even though they have a security system. People with both visual and hearing impairments were even more concerned; for instance, P8 expressed difficulty in hearing responses from people outside his door. P12 explained:

> *Security is a big thing with me, being totally blind, being hard of hearing. After my first husband passed away, we immediately got security systems in the house. I have an intercom outside, that's why I knew you were coming. That's why I had the door open. It's a scary world, when you have dual sensory loss like I do.*

Some participants reported not feeling safe in public places. P13 and P14, who live with sighted spouses, specifically emphasized this concern. P13 expressed her feelings:

> *In public places, I get nervous if I am by myself, because I can't see very well. I don't usually go unless I am with someone. I don't like to be out by myself.*

Computing Privacy Concerns

Like other populations, people with visual impairments use devices like smartphones, tablets, laptops, and personal computers. In fact, many participants said that these devices help them communicate and achieve greater independence. However, these devices also create privacy risks because of the vast amounts of personal data they store, and poor visual acuity makes it harder to safeguard this information. In this section we describe privacy concerns shared by participants about using computing devices. Many of these have been previously studied [3, 4, 13, 25, 34], and our study suggests they are still problems that have not yet been solved.

Eavesdropping

Participants were concerned about people eavesdropping on their digital devices, either visually or aurally.

Visual eavesdropping. Many of our participants (N=5) were aware of the threat of visual eavesdropping ('shoulder surfing') and tried not to use their devices in public. In this regard, our results differ from those of Azenkot *et al* [3], who found that their participants were largely unaware of these risks. One key difference however is that they studied only blind users, whereas we included visually impaired people who were not completely blind; the latter population is particularly susceptible because they often use large fonts. For example, P2 and P3, who are partially blind and use magnifying tools, were especially concerned about shoulder surfing. P2 is a student and feels uncomfortable using screen magnification in class, because anybody in the room can see what she is doing. P3 is particularly uncomfortable at work:

> *Because I use screen magnifiers, what I'm looking at on the screen is very large and it is very easy for other people to see and read it even if they are not intending to. I try to be mindful of that. No matter where my desk is placed, the screen is visible to somebody walking by. So, I don't have any privacy here. At home it is similar with the person I live with. I trust them to be considerate, but I'm sure they see things that I don't realize they see.*

Aural eavesdropping. Many visually impaired people use accessibility features that read phone or computer screen content out loud. However, these features also create the risk of aural eavesdropping [3] of private information by bystanders, since visually impaired people may not be able to tell if bystanders are present. Generally, screen reader users are more concerned about aural eavesdropping, as has been reported in the literature [3, 21, 34]. We have found that those with both vision and hearing disabilities are more vulnerable to aural eavesdropping, as P8 explained:

> *I can't really see, so I depend on the audio. So, anybody in earshot can hear what my talking devices are saying. And because of my hearing aid I have to volume up a lot higher than most people would have. So, I have a concern of privacy there. I could use headphones but a lot of headphones are not compatible with hearing aids.*

Security of Computing Devices

Strong passwords are key for computer security, but participants (N=5) reported struggling with password management because of their disability. Some recorded their passwords in a computer file and used screen readers to retrieve them, but this creates aural eavesdropping risks. Typing in passwords securely is also difficult; P3's screen reader makes a generic 'click' sound for each keypress when entering a password instead of the sound for the actual key, which prevents eavesdropping but makes it hard to enter the correct password. Only one participant used password manager software, while others said they were not very accessible and expressed skepticism about their security.

Some participants (N=2) expressed frustration with visual CAPTCHAs and other online mechanisms that try to prevent access to bots but also make websites much more difficult for the visually impaired to access. In P7's words:

> *CAPTCHA's are extremely annoying. We can't see what's on the screen and sometimes the audio is such that you can't even hear it.*

Participants also felt that visual impairment left them more vulnerable to hacking. P6 shared:

> *My email account was hacked about a month ago twice within a two-week span. People started to get emails from*

> *an account claiming to be me. I dumped my previous email provider and went to a different provider. It's very much of a privacy concern for us because unlike a lot of people, we don't always have the means to verify whether accounts or privacy information has been compromised.*

Modern web browsers try to prevent some attacks like phishing schemes, but these features are not always accessible. For example, participants reported that screen readers interpret the URL in a browser by its display text rather than its contents, so it is difficult to identify a malignant URL. Other security cues like the lock icon verifying an encrypted connection are not easily confirmed by the visually impaired.

Technical Support

Like everyone, visually impaired people run into problems with their computing devices or need to learn how to use a new device, and require assistance either from technical support staff or from others. Some participants (N=5) reported concern about the privacy of the data on these devices, since it may be difficult for visually impaired people to verify that support staff are not accessing private information. P9 said:

> *When they were setting up my computer here and my laptop, I made sure that I had my work account separate than that of my personal account. The website person that helped me wanted to have remote access to my computer so that he could set up my account more quickly and I said no. I had a trainer before who had remote access to my computer and I wish I hadn't.*

Assistive devices themselves sometimes break down or do not work properly. P9 also complained:

> *These software are not foolproof and that is the frustrating part. So, sometimes I have to go find someone sighted to read it for me, either from my screen or hard copies of something. It's really frustrating.*

An additional complication is that the debugging information needed to diagnose a non-functional device is itself not accessible to a blind person. P9 noted that none of the accessibility tools installed on her computer worked until it was fully booted up, so she has no way to read errors during start-up.

Online Accessibility

Some participants (N=2) reported needing help accessing certain websites, creating privacy risks when private information is involved. P4 mentioned that a local bus operator's website is not accessible, so she gives her credit card number to someone else to buy tickets. P5's university website is not accessible, so he must ask someone to read his grades to him.

Privacy Concerns with Virtual Interaction

Like most users, visually impaired people share personal information online. Here we describe privacy concerns raised by our participants related to these virtual interactions.

Online Transactions

Many participants found online banking and shopping more accessible than visiting brick-and-mortar stores, but this was not a perfect solution because of concerns about the security of online transactions. These concerns mirror those of the broader population, especially among older adults (like many of our participants) [18]. P3's credit card information was recently stolen, making him more cautious and concerned about his online security. Others were sufficiently concerned about online security that they avoided it altogether. P12 said:

> *I am scared of online banking. I don't pay any kind of bills online, I don't even get bank statements online, everything is hard-copied.*

Social Media Privacy

Like most users, visually impaired people use social networking platforms such as Facebook, Twitter, and LinkedIn. In fact, the visually impaired people Facebook status updates more frequently than average, while sharing and commenting on just as many photos [33], in part because these platforms help overcome challenges in interacting with others [6]. However, these sites involve sharing personal information and raise many privacy concerns for sighted and visually-impaired users alike [10]. Here we focus specifically on challenges created or heightened by visual impairments.

Most of our participants (N=11) reported using Facebook or other social-sharing websites, though most do not post much because of privacy concerns. One challenge they mentioned is the notoriously volatile and complicated nature of Facebook's privacy settings [8, 20]. Many participants (N=6) reported difficulty in adapting to new systems, so changes to user interfaces are problematic. P7 expressed her frustration:

> *Facebook is constantly changing, for us one minute we can use it and the next minute we can't because they are always changing the site. If I can get into the settings and find what I want like the advertising part, I try to stop all of that.*

After posting content, it can be difficult for visually impaired users to confirm that the privacy settings are correct. P3 mentioned once trying to send a photo to specific friends and family but mistakenly made it public. He only realized this mistake when an unintended viewer commented on the photo.

Some applications help the visually impaired capture and manage photos [12, 15], but Adams *et al.* [2] report that blind users still face the risk of unintentionally sharing an embarrassing or sensitive image online. In our study, participants with low vision reported taking photos and magnifying them in order to see them. Only one completely blind participant (P4) takes photos. She was not concerned about sharing her photos because she avoids capturing any private images.

Privacy-Enhancing Behaviors

Participants used a variety of strategies to protect privacy.

Physical Privacy-Enhancing Behaviors

Most participants indicated that they address physical privacy concerns by requesting help from acquaintances. While some could depend on a sighted spouse to read their letters, for instance, others asked friends or acquaintances or relied on a scanner. Most participants mentioned that they were comfortable asking for help from a known person, including P2:

> *When it comes to reading out my credit card number, I have to ask friends who would not steal my stuff. I'd be pretty comfortable with that. It's about asking the right people.*

Some participants hired assistants to deal with their personal matters, although it was difficult to trust them at first. When P4 first hired an assistant, she tested the assistant with a financial transaction by placing extra money in an envelope and checking whether it was returned.

Although some participants were skeptical about online banking, P10 and P11 believe that online services are a solution to financial privacy. P10 explained:

> *Before the computers were invented we had people read our checkbook, which was kind of privacy invasion. Now we don't have to, fortunately; because of modern technology now we can do all those things ourselves.*

P11 added to her husband's argument:

> *Technology has come along and opened doors to blind people. Before, I used to hate to have someone fill out our checkbook, because you did not know if you could trust them. I felt that at that time you are taking a gamble, whereas now I can do it on my own and at least you now don't have to ask someone else.*

To prevent physical eavesdropping, most participants tried to be alone. They generally did not engage in personal activities in public, and if they felt that someone could overhear their personal information, they looked for a more private space.

Many participants have home security systems, and several even demonstrated them to us. P14 explained:

> *I put in a security system since I cannot recognize who is at the door, in case my husband was not home. I would not open the door unless I know their voice or I know they are coming. I put that in for the sole reason that I am blind. If anybody opens a door, it automatically tells me. I can push a button and the police will automatically come.*

Most participants used existing assistive technologies, including scanners or portable magnifiers to read documents. For labeling and finding items, they used bar-code scanners, PenFriends (which allows users to associate audio descriptions with a code on an adhesive label, and use a scanner to play back the description), color detectors, etc. For navigational help, most participants relied on canes or guide dogs. For money identification, they generally kept bills sorted and folded based on denomination, though some used smartphone applications. To identify items while shopping, some used smartphone apps like TapTapSee[2] to get an audio description of a photographed object (using a combination of computer vision and crowdsourcing).

Privacy-Enhancing Behaviors for Computing Devices

Participants reported several ways of preventing visual eavesdropping. Blind users reported using headphones to interact with their device, and either turned off their screens or used software to black it out (e.g., iOS Screen Curtain). In contrast, no partially impaired users used an auditory interface as a privacy-protecting mechanism, likely because the privacy benefits came at too high a cost (losing the visual channel).

To prevent aural eavesdropping, most participants used headphones, although this carries some risk: since visually impaired people rely on hearing in order to sense the environment, headphones leave them more vulnerable to other privacy and safety concerns (as Azenkot *et al* [3] also found). This caused many participants to avoid headphones, especially in situations involving social interactions. For example, during our interview with P9 in her office, she neither deactivated her screen-reader tool nor took other protective measures. Others simply reduced the speaker volume, and P8 and P9 felt screen readers play text so quickly that bystanders cannot understand what the screen reader tool is saying.

Most participants used caution with passwords. P2 memorizes long passwords, which she types rapidly to prevent anyone from seeing. P9 and P11 write their password in Braille. P6 stores his passwords in text files and changes them every three months. P12 stores some passwords in her browser's password management feature, but mostly types them manually. P3 discussed his struggle to find a good strategy:

> *I keep them either in Keychain in Mac OS X, or I also keep a list of passwords at home for personal things and [at the office] for work things. I keep that in a file on my computer. I have been trying to figure out what a good password utility to use is. I'm aware that keeping the list in the clear is not ideal. At home, my entire home folder is encrypted. When I'm logged in, it is unencrypted. If the computer was compromised, then the entire folder would be open.*

Privacy-Enhancing Behaviors for Virtual Interactions

Of our participants' concerns about virtual interaction, online transactions, and especially online banking, were the most severe. P6 changes his passwords more frequently for these sites so that nobody can steal his information. P3 mentioned concern ever since his credit card information was stolen:

> *I'm mindful when I create a public wish list that it's public. I'm mindful of browser history and passwords that I used to log in. The transactions themselves, particularly after the card was compromised. I am aware and concerned.*

While most (N=11) participants used online social networks, most were not very active, mainly sharing status updates, or others' photos or videos. P4 carefully checks privacy settings each time she shares on Facebook, while P3 is very selective about sharing any information. P12 echoed this strategy:

> *I am really cautious about what I post on there. I don't put anything like where I live, or if I'm going to be gone, for safety purposes.*

When deciding whether to share a photo online, those who have low vision problems magnify the image to see what is in it. Others add metadata to photos, like time and place, to help identify them later. P4, who is completely blind and just getting started with photography, avoids taking private photos, and in fact uses Facebook to identify them later:

[2]TapTapSee: `http://taptapseeapp.com/`

> *Since I have only had my iPhone for a week, I have only taken three photos. I put those three photos on Facebook and just let everybody describe them, so that I could figure out which photo it was, based on what time I posted them.*

New Technologies for Enhancing Privacy

Finally, our interviews explored technologies that could enhance the privacy and security of the visually impaired, with a focus on sensor-enabled mobile and wearable devices. After giving participants a chance to use Google Glass, we asked them for feedback on ideas that we had brainstormed ahead of time, and as well as for their own suggestions.

Feedback on our Ideas

In particular, we asked about seven specific features that a wearable camera-based device could implement.

1. Count the number of people nearby. Participants responded positively to this idea. P9 pointed out that knowing more about nearby people would be more helpful:

> *It would help you know how many people are around you when doing something private or a business interaction. However, how close are they? You'd have to know if they were within earshot or could see what you were doing.*

2. Detect and identify specific faces nearby. Some participants were very excited about this idea, like P3:

> *When I'm walking by people I don't know who I'm walking by. If I think I know, I might say 'hi,' which may be embarrassing. So I typically don't, which is unfriendly. It would be nice to be able to recognize who is coming towards me like other people.*

But P9 thought this would just create new privacy concerns:

> *If there's something that can identify people we have given up a lot of privacy. Not only can I identify people but someone can identify me. I would not want something that could identify someone automatically.*

3. Identify the room a user is currently in. This idea received mixed reviews. Some participants responded that they can already tell based on sound, while others liked this idea.

4. Assist with navigation. Most participants reported that any application that could aid them in navigation would be helpful. Some mentioned that the map applications on their smartphones are not very accessible. P5 explained:

> *In some areas, I want to know where Starbucks is. I'm looking for a GPS for blind people, to tell me how we can, by walking, go to a certain place. I use Google Maps sometimes. I try to memorize the directions and go to that place.*

5. Detect security cameras nearby. We thought visually impaired people might want a device to detect cameras, since sighted people can notice them and modify their behavior accordingly. P4 disliked this idea, saying that knowing about security cameras would make her feel paranoid. P6 and P7 liked it, saying that they want to be aware of anything that a sighted person is [27]. Other participants did not dislike the idea but felt it was not necessary, like P9:

> *I don't think about that since we are all living with cameras and I'm not out committing crimes.*

6. Prevent shoulder surfing. Participants were very receptive to ideas to prevent shoulder surfing. Some low vision participants suggested that Google Glass could magnify whatever they are looking at, which could prevent visual eavesdropping since the Glass display is more private than most devices [23] (though determined attackers could likely spy on the transparent display (in reverse) with a telephoto lens).

7. Organize photo albums. Most participants liked the idea of an automated tool to analyze and describe photos for them, whether they personally take the photos or not. P3 explained:

> *I have a lot of photos, I like taking them. More and more these days I look at photos and can't figure out what I'm looking at. It depends on the contrast, lighting, angles.*

Participant Ideas

We also solicited ideas from participants on using wearable devices to enhance privacy. Two ideas came up repeatedly in early interviews, so we incorporated them in later interviews. The first was to help find items using wearable devices; many participants said that existing locators were complex and expensive. P4 often drops belongings in laundry, so would like a device to help find items there. Others suggested barcode scanning on wearable devices to find items in stores. They also gave positive feedback about wearable devices that could read documents, as opposed to existing devices that are not as portable or convenient.

Another idea was a system to detect hazards and obstacles, like open manholes or warning signs. OrCam[3] identifies pedestrian signals at intersections, but participants felt that a more general version to identify other signs would be helpful.

DISCUSSION AND IMPLICATIONS

Our interviews made it clear that participants struggle with various types of security and privacy risks on a daily basis. Some of these are similar to the risks all people face but are heightened by visual impairments, whereas others are unique to the visually impaired. Participants expressed needs for better tools to protect privacy and security, and most were excited about the potential of mobile and wearable technology.

Assistive devices. Of course, a variety of assistive devices are already available to help the visually impaired. However, participants felt that many of them are too expensive, do not work well, or are not user friendly. P5, for example, felt learning to use an existing device is too time consuming, and found it easier and more cost-effective to hire an assistant. Wearable devices like Google Glass may help reduce cost and complexity, similar to how smartphones running user-installed apps have replaced multiple, dedicated devices such as audio recorders, GPS receivers, and cameras, providing a single integrated platform with lower cost and greater convenience.

Monitoring surroundings. A recurring theme throughout our interviews was the need to monitor surroundings, e.g., to know whether people are within earshot, to detect obstacles

[3] OrCam. `http://www.orcam.com/`

or hazards while walking, to locate and identify objects, and so on. These functions could be implemented as smartphone apps, but would require visually impaired users to take pictures manually, and only 5 of our 14 participants reported that they are able to take pictures. Head- or body-mounted cameras could be a viable alternative. Wearable cameras also could be 'always-on,' continuously analyzing the video feed and alerting the user whenever something unusual or suspicious is detected [29].

A key technical challenge would be how to recognize scene content. Unfortunately, while computer vision is progressing rapidly, state-of-the-art technology cannot perform these tasks accurately in unconstrained environments. One possibility is to use a combination of computer vision and crowdsourcing, which TapTapSee (reportedly) and Vizwiz [5] use to implement object detection on smartphones. For instance, computer vision could be used to detect potential hazards on a sidewalk, but then the relevant video frames could be sent to a sighted person (e.g., a friend or Mechanical Turk user) for verification. Of course, involving real people introduces the additional privacy challenges of allowing other people to see a person's wearable camera feed. This suggests that more work is needed on how to detect private content in images automatically, a problem that has recently been studied in the context of camera-based lifelogging [14, 30].

Another way of sidestepping the difficult computer vision problem is to incorporate data from non-visual sensors. For instance, instead of counting or identifying people using computer vision, one could exploit the fact that many people carry smartphones, so that Bluetooth signals could be used to estimate how many people are nearby as well as to identify certain people uniquely. GPS receivers and nascent indoor localization technology (like Apple's iBeacon) can be used to geo-locate users; systems could crowd-source reports of sidewalk hazards like construction zones and push notifications to visually impaired people who are nearby.

Feedback. Of course, an effective device would have to communicate information efficiently to the user, and a system that provides too many notifications could overwhelm and annoy the user. One solution would be to allow the user to provide privacy policies that could be executed automatically, depending on context. For example, a policy could turn off the screen and stop announcing emails if a bystander is nearby. Another policy could suppress all notifications in the home, except for emergencies like when an intruder is detected.

Limitations. Finally, we would like to acknowledge the limitations of our study and the opportunities for future work. Our participant sample was small, limited to one geographic area (southern Indiana), and restricted to those who chose to respond to an ad about privacy, so it is difficult to know how well our findings generalize to the greater population. Our participants were also older than average, and it is well-known that privacy concerns differ with age [18] (although the visually-impaired population itself is biased towards older adults, since 82% of the blind are over age 50 [32]). Studying privacy needs of younger populations (like teens and college students) would be interesting future work. In addition, our proposed solution space was biased towards wearable technologies, since we believe these may provide a hands-free, easy-to-use solution, although our participants did give their own feedback and alternative suggestions.

CONCLUSION

To better understand the privacy concerns and needs of visually impaired people, we conducted interviews with 14 visually impaired people. Our findings show that while the privacy concerns of people with visual impairments overlap with sighted people, there are also significant differences, due in part to their disability but also because of systems that were not designed with them in mind. Our participants were particularly aware of and concerned about these risks, and shared a variety of coping mechanisms to deal with them. They were generally excited about the potential for new wearable and mobile technologies to improve their privacy and independence. We hope that this research leads towards the implementation of some of these tools, which could have a major impact on the well-being of this underserved population.

ACKNOWLEDGMENTS

This material is based upon work supported in part by the National Science Foundation under grants CNS-1408730, CNS-1016603, CNS-1252697, and IIS-1253549, and by a Google Research Award. We thank Prerna Rustagi for helping us develop the initial Interview Protocol. We especially thank our participants, as well as Barbara Salisbury and Rita Kersh from the Bloomington and Bedford chapters of the American Council for the Blind, and Dorothy Lenard from IU Disability Services for Students, for helping us recruit participants.

REFERENCES

1. The lighthouse national survey on vision loss: The experience, attitudes and knowledge of middle-aged and older Americans. Tech. rep., The Lighthouse Inc, 1995.
2. Adams, D., Morales, L., and Kurniawan, S. A qualitative study to support a blind photography mobile application. In *International Conference on Pervasive Technologies Related to Assistive Environments* (2013), 1–8.
3. Azenkot, S., Rector, K., Ladner, R., and Wobbrock, J. Passchords: Secure multi-touch authentication for blind people. In *International ACM SIGACCESS Conference on Computers and Accessibility* (2012), 159–166.
4. Bigham, J. P., and Cavender, A. C. Evaluating existing audio CAPTCHAs and an interface optimized for non-visual use. In *SIGCHI Conference on Human Factors in Computing Systems* (2009), 1829–1838.
5. Bigham, J. P., Jayant, C., Ji, H., Little, G., Miller, A., Miller, R. C., Miller, R., Tatarowicz, A., White, B., White, S., and Yeh, T. Vizwiz: Nearly real-time answers to visual questions. In *ACM Symposium on User Interface Software and Technology* (2010), 333–342.
6. Brady, E., Morris, M. R., Zhong, Y., White, S., and Bigham, J. P. Visual challenges in the everyday lives of blind people. In *SIGCHI Conference on Human Factors in Computing Systems* (2013), 2117–2126.

7. Dakopoulos, D., and Bourbakis, N. Wearable obstacle avoidance electronic travel aids for blind: A survey. *IEEE Transactions on Systems, Man, and Cybernetics 40*, 1 (2010), 25–35.

8. Debatin, B., Lovejoy, J. P., Horn, A.-K., and Hughes, B. N. Facebook and online privacy: Attitudes, behaviors, and unintended consequences. *Journal of Computer-Mediated Communication 15* (2009), 83–108.

9. Fiannaca, A., Apostolopoulous, I., and Folmer, E. Headlock: A wearable navigation aid that helps blind cane users traverse large open spaces. In *Proceedings of the 16th International ACM SIGACCESS Conference on Computers & Accessibility* (2014), 19–26.

10. Gross, R., and Acquisti, A. Information revelation and privacy in online social networks. In *ACM Workshop on Privacy in the Electronic Society* (2005), 71–80.

11. Haque, M., Zawoad, S., and Hasan, R. Secure techniques and methods for authenticating visually impaired mobile phone users. In *IEEE International Conference on Technologies for Homeland Security* (2013), 735–740.

12. Harada, S., Sato, D., Adams, D. W., Kurniawan, S., Takagi, H., and Asakawa, C. Accessible photo album: Enhancing the photo sharing experience for people with visual impairment. In *SIGCHI Conference on Human Factors in Computing Systems* (2013), 2127–2136.

13. Holman, J., Lazar, J., Feng, J. H., and D'Arcy, J. Developing usable CAPTCHAs for blind users. In *International ACM SIGACCESS Conference on Computers and Accessibility* (2007), 245–246.

14. Hoyle, R., Templeman, R., Armes, S., Anthony, D., Crandall, D., and Kapadia, A. Privacy behaviors of lifeloggers using wearable cameras. In *ACM International Joint Conference on Pervasive and Ubiquitous Computing* (2014), 571–582.

15. Jayant, C., Ji, H., White, S., and Bigham, J. P. Supporting blind photography. In *International ACM SIGACCESS Conference on Computers and Accessibility* (2011), 203–210.

16. Kane, S. K., Jayant, C., Wobbrock, J. O., and Ladner, R. E. Freedom to roam: A study of mobile device adoption and accessibility for people with visual and motor disabilities. In *International ACM SIGACCESS Conference on Computers and Accessibility* (2009).

17. Kuber, R., and Sharma, S. Toward tactile authentication for blind users. In *International ACM SIGACCESS Conference on Computers and Accessibility* (2010).

18. Kwasny, M., Caine, K., Rogers, W., and Fisk, A. Privacy and technology: folk definitions and perspectives. In *CHI Extended Abstracts on Human Factors in Computing Systems* (2008).

19. Lazar, J., Feng, J., Brooks, T., Melamed, G., Wentz, B., Holman, J., Olalere, A., and Ekedebe, N. The SoundsRight CAPTCHA: An improved approach to audio human interaction proofs for blind users. In *SIGCHI Conference on Human Factors in Computing Systems* (2012), 2267–2276.

20. Liu, Y., Gummadi, K. P., Krishnamurthy, B., and Mislove, A. Analyzing Facebook privacy settings: User expectations vs. reality. In *Proceedings of the 2011 ACM SIGCOMM Conference on Internet Measurement Conference* (2011), 61–70.

21. Naftali, M., and Findlater, L. Accessibility in context: Understanding the truly mobile experience of smartphone users with motor impairments. In *International ACM SIGACCESS Conference on Computers & Accessibility* (2014), 209–216.

22. Renner, M., and Taylor-Powell, E. Analyzing qualitative data. Tech. rep., University of Wisconsin, 2003.

23. Roesner, F., Kohno, T., and Molnar, D. Security and privacy for augmented reality systems. *Communications of the ACM 57*, 4 (Apr. 2014), 88–96.

24. Saldana, J. *The Coding Manual for Qualitative Researchers*. Sage, Los Angeles, California, 2009.

25. Sauer, G., Holman, J., Lazar, J., Hochheiser, H., and Feng, J. Accessible privacy and security: a universally usable human-interaction proof tool. *Universal Access in the Information Society 9*, 3 (2010), 239–248.

26. Shilkrot, R., Huber, J., Liu, C., Maes, P., and Nanayakkara, S. C. A wearable text-reading device for the visually-impaired. In *CHI Extended Abstracts on Human Factors in Computing Systems* (2014), 193–194.

27. Shinohara, K., and Wobbrock, J. O. In the shadow of misperception: Assistive technology use and social interactions. In *SIGCHI Conference on Human Factors in Computing Systems* (2011), 705–714.

28. Solove, D. J. A taxonomy of privacy. *University of Pennsylvania Law Review 154*, 3 (Jan. 2006), 477–566.

29. Templeman, R., Hoyle, R., Kapadia, A., and Crandall, D. Reactive security: Responding to visual stimuli from wearable cameras. In *Workshop on Usable Privacy & Security for Wearable and Domestic Ubiquitous Devices* (2014), 1297–1306.

30. Templeman, R., Korayem, M., Crandall, D., and Kapadia, A. PlaceAvoider: Steering first-person cameras away from sensitive spaces. In *Annual Network and Distributed System Security Symposium* (2014).

31. Velázquez, R. Wearable assistive devices for the blind. In *Wearable and Autonomous Biomedical Devices and Systems for Smart Environment* (2010), 331–349.

32. Visual Impairment and Blindness, World Health Organization fact sheet 282, 2014.

33. Wu, S., and Adamic, L. A. Visually impaired users on an online social network. In *SIGCHI Conference on Human Factors in Computing Systems* (2014), 3133–3142.

34. Ye, H., Malu, M., Oh, U., and Findlater, L. Current and future mobile and wearable device use by people with visual impairments. In *SIGCHI Conference on Human Factors in Computing Systems* (2014), 3123–3132.

Participatory Design of Therapeutic Video Games for Young People with Neurological Vision Impairment

Jonathan Waddington
WESC Foundation
Exeter, Devon, EX2 6HA
jwaddington@wescfoundation.ac.uk

Conor Linehan, Kathrin Gerling, Kieran Hicks, Timothy L. Hodgson
University of Lincoln
Lincoln. LN67TS, UK
clinehan@lincoln.ac.uk

ABSTRACT
Neurological Vision Impairment (NVI) detrimentally impacts upon quality of life, as daily activities such as reading and crossing the road often become significantly impaired. Therapy strategies for NVI based on visual scanning of on-screen stimuli have recently been demonstrated as effective at improving functional vision. However, these strategies are repetitive, monotonous and unsuitable for use with children and young adults. This project explores the design of a game-based therapy programme that aims to support participant engagement and adherence. We first outline requirements for this software, before reporting on the iterative design process undertaken in collaboration with young people, therapists and teachers at a centre for vision impairment. Our work provides insights into the participatory design of games in collaboration with young people with special needs, and reflects upon the tension of balancing game challenge, therapy goals, and accessibility. Furthermore, it highlights the potential of games to empower special populations by providing a medium through which to communicate the subjective experience of specific impairments.

Author Keywords
Games; Vision; Rehabilitation; Therapy; Young People.

ACM Classification Keywords
K.4.2 [Computers and Society]: Social Issues – Assistive technologies for people with disabilities

INTRODUCTION
Neurological vision impairment, or vision impairment caused by injury to areas of the brain that are responsible for visual processing, often has a significant impact on functional vision, reducing an individual's independent living skills and negatively influencing quality of life [14, 34]. Fortunately, effective rehabilitation strategies are available that can help improve functional vision, and lead to improvements in independent living skills [19, 25, 30]. However, successful outcomes typically require months of adherence to daily routines that involve tedious repetitive tasks (e.g., repeatedly scanning images in a systematic manner to find a single geometric shape that differs from other similar distracting shapes) [25]. Adult stroke patients have previously demonstrated adherence to these types of interventions but this has not yet been demonstrated with children [34]. Indeed, these interventions are comparable to clinical assessment tools that have been criticized for being unsuitable and unreliable for use with young people [2]. Conversely, video games have been successfully used to improve excitement and commitment to therapy for young people with a range of conditions [12]. This paper reports on work that explores the use of game design as a means of engaging young people with vision therapy.

CHI 2015, April 18 - 23 2015, Seoul, Republic of Korea
Copyright 2015 ACM 978-1-4503-3145-6/15/04 $15.00
http://dx.doi.org/10.1145/2702123.2702261

In our work, we address the issue of designing vision-based games for people with vision impairment through a participatory design approach. Throughout the development process of our game, *Eyelander*, we involve young people with neurological vision impairment, and we solicit feedback from therapists. Our work makes three main contributions: (1) We present a novel game-based approach for functional vision rehabilitation, (2) we provide insights into the process of involving young people with vision impairment in the game design, and explore how their needs and abilities need to be considered throughout the design process to create appealing games, (3) we discuss challenges and opportunities to help inform the work of researchers and designers creating games for therapy and rehabilitation through a participatory design process.

Our work is a first inquiry into the design space of visual games for young people with vision impairment, with the goal of providing engaging tools for functional vision rehabilitation. In this context, providing a positive player experience is an important step toward prolonged engagement and improved therapy outcomes, potentially improving independent living skills and quality of life.

BACKGROUND
This section gives an overview of neurological vision impairment as well as common rehabilitation approaches. Furthermore, we discuss design efforts addressing people

with vision impairment, and give an overview of games for therapy and rehabilitation.

Rehabilitation for Vision Impairment

Neurological Vision Impairment

Neurological vision impairment (NVI) refers to a loss of visual function due to injury to areas of the brain concerned with visual processing. Typical causes of NVI include stroke and perinatal (i.e., immediately before or after birth) asphyxiation. The range of visual processes that can be affected by NVI is wide and they vary depending on the age of the patient, the aetiology of the injury and the neuroanatomy affected. Acquired NVI often leads to fear and isolation; it has a critical impact on skills of independent living such as reading and driving, and significantly affects wellbeing and quality of life. Young people with NVI caused by a perinatal injury will often have a more complex loss of visual perception, such as an impaired ability to see an object when it is placed on a complicated background or when it is not moving [20]. These young people may include those with additional complex needs such as cerebral palsy or learning impairments, but may also include those with no other cognitive or physical impairments [8].

Common rehabilitation approaches

Until recently, NVI was considered permanent. However, over the last two decades three broad strategies for rehabilitation have been proposed with varying degrees of effectiveness: substitution, restitution and compensation. *Substitution* involves using a physical device to substitute for a lost area of the visual field. Prismatic lenses can be worn on spectacles to direct the image in the blind visual field towards the healthy visual field [26]. *Restitution* aims to either restore function to the primary visual cortex or improve visual detection in nearby extra-striate visual pathways. This is typically undertaken with visual stimulation using extremely bright, high contrast stimuli [17]. *Compensation* aims to change behavior to compensate for lost visual function. This is typically achieved by developing efficient eye movement strategies during training with visual arrays and active scanning tasks [22, 25] (see figure 1). The current project focuses on building tools that teach and encourage compensatory strategies.

Designing Games for Vision Therapy

In order to understand the requirements of games for vision therapy we must consider existing research on designing video games for people with vision impairment, as well as research on using games for therapy and rehabilitation.

Designing video games for people with vision impairment

A growing body of research is beginning to focus on the development of video games that are accessible to players with vision impairment. Morelli et al. [23, 24] present a series of accessible versions of commercially available games (e.g., Nintendo Wii Sports Bowling and Tennis). In their games, the authors replace visual cues with auditory and tactile feedback. Following a similar approach, Rector et al. [27] explore the creation of an eyes-free yoga exergame that provides balance training for people with vision impairment and builds on audio cues to guide player movement.

In contrast, Eriksson et al. [9] present mini games that were designed for children who are blind and for players with less severe vision impairment, with the goal of encouraging children to practice the recognition of simple visual objects; results of user studies show that visual cues are considered helpful by players with a wide range of visual abilities. Likewise, Ching et al. [5] explore the inclusion of graphical content for players with vision impairment in their project Beachcomber. The game builds on touch- and audio-based interaction and includes high-contrast graphics; initial playtests suggest that players with vision impairment appreciate the graphical dimension of the game. Thus, existing work on video games for people with vision impairment show that it is possible to design video games that are accessible for players with vision impairment.

Games for therapy and rehabilitation

Recent years have seen much interest in the use of games technology to improve the engaging qualities of therapy programmes (see [16]). For example, Kato et al. [18] have demonstrated that games can be an effective means of increasing compliance [18]. Similarly, Achtman et al., found that games can help patients follow through with otherwise tedious therapy routines [1]. Games have been applied to teach sign language to deaf children [15], to support children with autism [11] and to provide cognitive training for children with Fetal Alcohol Syndrome [3].

There are a number of design lessons to take from these studies. Firstly, the justification for using games in therapy is typically based on the ability of games to improve participant motivation to engage with often-repetitive therapy tasks. In order to generate this type of motivation, games must present challenges to participants [29]. Goals are set through the game narrative and players aim to reach that goal by engaging in therapy appropriate behaviour. Secondly, when training a skill via game play, it is crucial that the target skill must form the basis of the core game mechanic [10, 13]. For example, if the therapy is designed to improve dynamic balance (i.e.,[10]), the principal way in which players interact with, achieve success in, and progress through, the game should be through measures of their ability to balance. Thirdly, a user-centered design approach that also takes into consideration the needs of therapists is essential [6].

Applying games in vision training and therapy

The use of games, a primarily visual medium, for the purposes of vision therapy presents a number of interesting opportunities. For example, there is some evidence that video games can encourage users of all abilities to follow through with tedious visual tasks [9]. Additionally, there is some evidence that video games have the potential to affect visual skills of participants of all abilities [1, 4, 11, 14]. For example, Li et al. [21] showed that playing video games has positive effects on how people with impaired spatial vision perform in functional vision tests. However, Achtman et al., [1] in a review article, concluded that there is little evidence that the use of commercially available games in therapy leads to improvements in vision that transfer to daily life. To facilitate this transfer, it seems crucial to develop games that strictly follow therapy requirements, rather than applying existing products.

While custom-designed video games appear a promising means of encouraging young people with NVI to participate in rehabilitation, there is no record in the literature of previous projects that have attempted to meet this goal. In this context, one of the core challenges of the work presented in this paper is translating therapy requirements into effective, yet engaging game mechanics that have the potential of eliciting the same type of visual (i.e., eye movement) behaviour as traditional therapy, while providing an enjoyable game experience.

Design Requirements

Interface and visual design
The use of a visual medium for the purposes of vision therapy presents notable challenges. Research on design for people with vision impairment typically focuses on the substitution of visual interface elements [23, 24] with stimuli that address other senses (e.g., hearing, touch). This approach is not appropriate in the context of vision therapy. Functional vision rehabilitation builds on the presentation of visual cues to encourage people with vision impairment to develop compensatory strategies such as eye and head movements to improve the effectiveness of visual scanning. To achieve this goal, players must complete search tasks using their visual skills, and displayed images should not be completely replaced with haptic or audio interface elements. The interface should be primarily visual, thus a standard PC, monitor and mouse will be used.

Requirements of vision therapy
Tools previously used for training compensatory visual scanning techniques are derived from stimulus arrays used in cognitive neuroscience experiments [25] (see figure 1). Simple geometric shapes are presented in white on a plain black background. Training requires the participant to passively view these stimulus arrays, searching with eye movements for a target stimulus in an array of distractors. The target typically differs from distractors on one physical dimension, such as size, shape or orientation. Each scanning task remains on-screen for 3 seconds. There is no mechanism for the participant to indicate whether or not they found the target stimulus. Each therapy session requires participants to carry out these scanning tasks for approximately 20 minutes and sessions must run 4-5 times per week for a number of months.

While adult stroke victims have demonstrated adherence to this intervention [25], due to its repetitive and passive nature it does not seem appropriate for use with young people. There is significant opportunity to use games design elements to improve the engaging qualities of these tasks. Indeed, simply improving the visual design and introducing interactivity would presumably help. A further complication is that there is little evidence to explain which specific features of search tasks are essential for successful therapeutic outcomes, and which are not. Thus, for pragmatic reasons, it seems necessary to replicate as much as possible in our game the functional characteristics of those original search tasks.

Therapy-appropriate game mechanics
When training a skill via game play, it is crucial that the target skill must form the basis of the core game mechanic [10, 13]. In our game, the core mechanic should involve the repetitive visual searching of an array of distractor stimuli in order to find a target, since this is the behaviour that is targeted by existing vision therapy. Notably, one of the core tasks in our participatory design process is exploring the tension between the design goals of *challenge* and *accessibility*. Vision therapy is inherently challenging for people with vision impairment. Games must also present game challenges for players in order to achieve their motivational qualities [30]. Both of these types of challenge have the potential to frustrate participants and players, and could lead to disengagement with the design process, or with the resultant game.

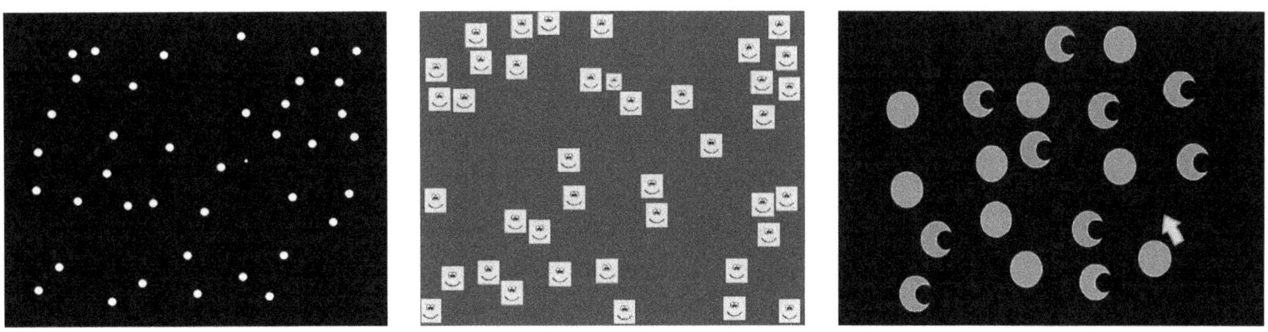

Figure 1. The original search task (left), an early version of the game (middle), and final version included in Eyelander (right).

End user adaptability

Due to the wide range of abilities observed with users of therapeutic games, it is essential to allow adaptability of game features based on player ability [10]. For example, through the process of developing game-based rehabilitation technology for adult stroke patients, Flores et al., [10] found that it was important to allow the user, carer, or therapist (as appropriate) the ability to adapt complexity of both the visual content and the cognitive challenges presented by the game. In addition, the game should allow the therapist, carer and player to track performance over time, in order to allow for intuitive judgments over whether progress is being achieved [7].

A PARTICIPATORY DESIGN APPROACH TOWARD DESIGNING GAMES AS VISION (RE)HABILITATION THERAPY FOR YOUNG PEOPLE

Due to the large number of requirements outlined above, it was not appropriate to begin the participatory process entirely from a blank slate. Rather, an initial prototype was developed, following the above guidelines, which formed the focus of sessions run with participants.

Initial Game Design

At the beginning of the design process, we focused on the development of a core mechanic that would allow us to integrate therapy requirements into *Eyelander*. This section focuses on the core mechanic. The theme and narrative of the game evolved throughout the design process and is described in the next section.

The core game mechanic, taken from previous research, required players to visually search arrays of coloured shapes in order to find specified target stimuli, and to click on those targets. Requiring players to make a click introduced interactivity, which is absent from the traditional search tasks, and supported the delivery of performance feedback. Correct clicks triggered both audio effects, and occasionally visual effects. The search tasks were framed by simple animations that introduced the concept of progression to the game, as a means for introducing challenge, goals and driving longer-term engagement. The player was presented with a goal for the play session (i.e. complete ten numbered levels) and medium term goals (i.e., a character climbing a ladder), which helped track progress.

Participants

We recruited three groups of participants for the iterative design sessions. Our first group included young participants with a diagnosis or presentation of NVI. We recruited four learners (3 female, 1 male), aged 15-18 from a specialist education center for learners with vision impairment. Two participants had a complex neurological presentation with suspected NVI and associated developmental delay, learning, speech and language difficulties. One participant had no light perception in the left eye and a right sided visual field loss caused by optic glioma. Our fourth participant had a confirmed diagnosis of cerebral palsy, left hemiplegia and suspected NVI. Two participants were legally blind and two had low vision.

A researcher met with this group of participants during fortnightly meetings over a three month period held in a familiar room at the centre. Each meeting lasted approximately half an hour, during which time participants were asked to play test the game and provide feedback on the game's visuals, controls and mechanics. While one of these participants gave consent to audio recording, two did not, and the fourth was non-verbal. Therefore, data from this group of participants was predominantly collected by observing behavior and note taking.

We recruited two further groups of participants for separate one-off design sessions. Our second group of participants included the therapy team that worked at the same specialist education center as our first group of participants, consisting of occupational, physical, and speech and language therapists (8 total) who had daily experience working with learners with NVI. We invited this group so that we could understand the concerns of gatekeepers, and also to come to solutions that our first group of participants may not have been able to provide alone. Our third group of participants consisted of three young people with acquired brain injury and suspected hemianopia who were part of a local community group. Each person in this group of participants had relatively minor cognitive and physical impairment.We felt that conversations with more cognitively abled participants would help us to corroborate and expand upon what we learned during observations with our first group of participants.

Data was collected from the second and third group of participants during two separate one-off design sessions that lasted approximately two hours. A researcher met with the second group of participants on the fourth week of the iterative design process, and with the third group of participants on the fifth week. A brief for the project was explained to each group, and participants were invited to play and observe the current iteration of the game at that time. After a roundtable discussion, each group collated a list of collectively agreed considerations and suggested amendments to the game. These findings were implemented gradually through the iterative design process.

Iterative Design Sessions

Observations are organized according to the requirements outlined above. The changes to game features implemented between the major iterations of the game are outlined in figure 2. These changes all emerged from findings of participatory design sessions.

Visual design of search tasks

Our first attempt at making the game more visually engaging was to add colours and smiley faces to the shapes displayed in the visual search task (see figure 1). While the range of different colours were appreciated, the additional

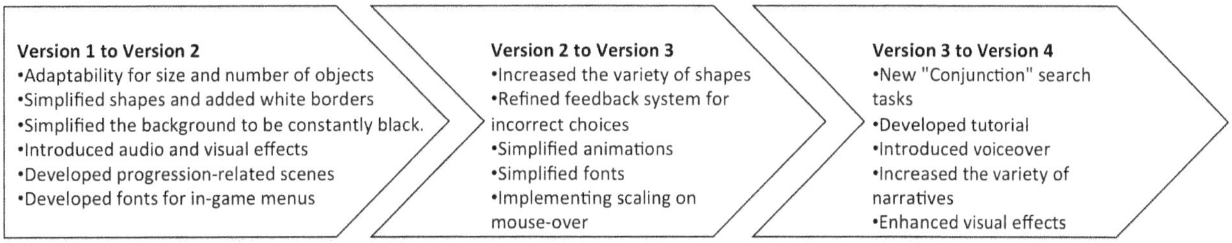

Figure 2. Flow chart describing the features designed and implemented across the major iterations through participatory design process.

detail of the smiley faces was either too difficult to see or queried negatively by participants ("What is that?"). We also found that the size of the shapes used in the original visual search task were too small for some of our participants to see.

In the next iteration we increased the average size of shapes and added an option to change the average size to "small", "medium" or "large". To increase contrast we kept a black background and added a white border around the edge of each shape. Engagement during this iteration dramatically improved. Negative feedback was rare from our first group of participants. However, they regularly requested more variety in shapes and colours. The original visual search task used lines, dots and squares. We increased the variety of geometric shapes through iterations, with the final version including rectangles, circles, squares, triangles, crescent moons and five-pointed stars.

Visual design of narrative scenes

The scenes that introduce narrative and illustrate player progress are more visually complex than the search tasks. We observed that these screens could pose a problem for some of our players. Specifically, persons with NVI can have difficulty with visually processing and identifying objects that they haven't seen before. To address this we added a number of features. Firstly, we introduced voiceovers for the level selection screen. When a player hovered the mouse cursor over a selectable level, a voiceover described the level in a short quirky phrase (e.g., "Barry the Alligator's Swamp") so that players have some prior information and preparation before they see the level. Secondly, when the player starts a level, only the avatar is visible on a black background. After a very brief period of time (500ms) we fade in the obstacle that they have to overcome e.g. lava rises from underfoot, and finally after another period of time (500ms) we fade in the background. This gives the player time to locate each of the key objects in the scene: the avatar, the obstacle, and the background rather than having to process the image all at once.

Visual design of menus

We attempted to introduce different styles of fonts to judge which participants might prefer. The participants in our first group were able to read all of the fonts, but during our meeting with the second group of participants (the therapy team), they recommended that we stick with a sans-serif (Arial) white font. We updated the font for the next iteration of the game and our first group of participants commented that the text was much clearer so we continued using the simple font.

Diversity in game mechanics

Our third group of participants, who were cognitively able, found some of the silly aspects of the game engaging (e.g. the stampede of angry cows), but felt that the game mechanics would get boring after time. These participants suggested new mechanics, such as having to remember a number of different shapes in a sequence that the player would have to find. While this seemed like a useful suggestion for the more cognitively able users, we were concerned that this might make the game inaccessible for those with cognitive impairment and may also be too different to the original visual search task and so might change the effect of the therapy. As a compromise we added more complex search tasks, where multiple groups of distractor shapes would be generated on the screen at any one time ("conjunction task"). This interaction demonstrated the difficulty involved in designing games for participants with a wide range of cognitive and physical ability. Games must be accessible for all users, while still challenging for those with more developed abilities.

Engagement

Three of the four participants in our first group played the game through to completion each session (111 search tasks; 20-30 minutes). Two of these participants were excitable throughout (e.g. observed bouncing on their seat, and clapping their hands when correctly identifying objects), and enthusiastically asked to play again when finished. On separate occasions we allowed these two participants to play through the game more than once, and they continued to play until the researcher ended the session after 45 minutes. One participant dropped out of the study after two sessions. This participant was non-verbal, so we were unable to discern the precise reason for disengagement. However, this person was clearly disinterested during play sessions, only completing 3 or 4 levels each play test before going back to his iPad or web browser.

Conclusions from iterative design sessions

One of the conclusions derived from the above interactions was that design features to support accessibility should be utilised during all sections of the game other than the search tasks. Although the therapy required players to use their visual skills to complete search tasks, it was not necessary for players to use their vision to perform other actions in the game such as selecting gameplay options from a menu. This was something that we missed in our initial requirements generation, due to the design goal of forcing participants to use their visual skills. This interaction also illustrated the usefulness of consulting experts in the therapy team. While participants were able to engage with the original designs (presumably with some difficulty), they did not have the knowledge or expertise to explain to us that there was a preferable solution. Participants can help us understand whether design features are acceptable, but may not be able to help identify solutions that we have not already considered.

A surprising finding was that even experts may not have a complete understanding of the subjective experience of vision impairment. During the session with the therapy team, some members asked how learners who were legally blind had coped with the game. They reacted with stunned silence when informed that the participants had been able to play the game to completion a number of times. Indeed, therapists seemed genuinely concerned that the visual media in the game would be too difficult, complicated or unfamiliar for participants with NVI to see, although others thought that more varied visual rewards could improve engagement. This illustrated the complexity involved in designing visual games for visually impaired people.

Final Game Design

Game mechanics and narrative

Core game mechanics remained relatively stable across iterations, due to the therapeutic requirement to strictly adhere to the formal components of the visual search task. However, through iterations, we focused on developing a coherent game narrative with which to frame the search tasks, with the intention of presenting a coherent and challenging goal, and helping participants to monitor their progress towards that goal. The final version is significantly more complex and rich than the original version, which simply had numbered levels and an animation of a character climbing stairs to denote progress.

When a player begins a new game they are presented with a brief narrative that frames the long-term goal for the session. The basic narrative is to help a character escape an island being engulfed in lava after a volcanic eruption. There are four additional scenarios that can occur, which impede the character's escape: stampeding angry cows, an invading UFO, a "naughty" panda, and a massive baby that blocks the character's path. Players are presented with a level selection screen illustrating the pathway through the levels from start to finish (see figure 3). Only the most recently unlocked level can be selected, and the player is given audio and visual cues when the cursor is over this target.

Figure 3. The island screen used to help participants track their progress through game sessions.

Each level begins with a simple animation that sets the goal for that level (i.e. overcome an obstacle such as a river of lava). Each visual search task begins with a description and visual presentation of the target shape that the player is asked to find. Targets are generated with randomly assigned features: shape, size, colour, orientation, and "blinking", and then placed at a random location on the screen. A group of distractor shapes are generated that differ from the target by one randomly chosen feature (again; shape, size, etc.), and are then placed at random locations on the screen such that they don't overlap. If the player selects the target shape on the first attempt they receive positive feedback through audiovisual effects and the game progresses. If the player selects a distractor on the first attempt nothing happens, and if they find the target after that the game progresses but does not give audiovisual feedback.

Once the player has completed the predetermined number of visual search tasks for that level they are rewarded through an animation of the character overcoming the obstacle that impeded progress earlier. After the player has completed a level they return to the level selection screen and can view their progress as visual cues mark where the player's character has already been and how well they performed (e.g. a gold star is displayed for finding all the target shapes first time on a level). Each successive level contains progressively more search tasks, and progressively more difficult search tasks. "Dummy" tasks (where the target shape does not appear) are added randomly with 10% chance from level 5 onwards, and the player must click the right mouse button to complete these tasks. At the end of the game the player is congratulated and presented with some feedback on how well they did and a high score table to compare with previous attempts.

End user adaptability options

We have developed three key options that can be changed depending on the varying visual, cognitive and physical abilities of players. These options include the average size of target shapes, the limit on the number of shapes displayed, and the time limit before a search task resets. The average size of shapes can be adapted to be "small", "medium", or "large", approximately equivalent to individual shapes covering 2%, 7% and 15% of the viewable screen area. Increasing the size of shapes was necessary for those participants with low vision to access the game, but decreasing the size of shapes can be useful for participants with extremely restricted visual fields. The option to limit the number of geometric shapes displayed during a search task can be adapted for those with impaired visual attention or an impaired ability to discriminate between multiple targets displayed at the same time (simultanagnosia). The time limit before a search task resets can be increased to give additional time to those players who require longer to process visual information or to physically move the mouse to respond.

Figure 4. Example output of the "heatmap" style automated assessment tool.

Automated assessment tool

We have also developed an automated vision assessment within the game, based on dividing the screen into a 4x4 grid that represents the participant's visual field limited by the size of the game screen. The automated assessment tool records the number of correct responses, incorrect responses, and response times to find targets in the game within each respective area on the 4x4 grid (not including "dummy" trials). As images are randomly distributed with a 2D uniform distribution on the screen during search tasks, it is possible to gather this data from each area of the grid if the player attempts enough tasks. The "heat map" generated from data recorded in this manner can help healthcare professionals assess the functional visual field of the player and pinpoint any problem areas (see figure 4). For example, if a player consistently makes "incorrect" responses on the left hand side or if they always take much longer to respond on this side, this may indicate a left visual field loss or impaired spatial attention. This assessment was not possible in the previous tools for visual search training, which did not have an interactive element. Visual field assessment of young people with NVI is notoriously difficult to perform. Collecting data over the rehabilitation period in this manner could help inform healthcare professionals about those problem areas and whether the training has been effective at improving the response to targets displayed in those areas. However, it is still necessary to assess whether functional vision skills learned in-game can translate to other activities of daily life.

Formative Longer Term Study

Since one of the core goals of the project is to promote longer term engagement with the therapy, we found it valuable to include within the participatory design process, a formative playtest with the prototype that ran over a number of consecutive days with the same participant. This participant was a 20 year old female, with a diagnosis of right sided hemianopia and no perception of light from the left eye, with very minor cognitive and physical impairments. She had a very constricted visual field but moderate visual acuity in her remaining visual field.

This participant played the game for four consecutive days one week, followed by two consecutive days the following week, with the first week closely matching the expectations of the final therapy programme. Observations during these sessions provide a number of interesting insights. Firstly, the participant always turned the music and audio off after the first level, reporting that it was "okay" but could get distracting and annoying. Secondly, the game was played through to completion every time, representing 20-30 minutes of game play. This is an encouraging result in light of the goal of player retention. However, it must be noted that different behaviour may have occurred if the participant was not being observed by the researcher. Thirdly, the participant sometimes adopted a head turn slightly to the right, presumably so that a larger area of her functioning visual field was facing the screen. It is currently unclear whether this is therapy appropriate behaviour, as emphasis in previous rehabilitation studies has focused on investigating eye movements only and not gaze. As the game is designed to promote effective eye movement strategies but eye movements are not measured directly it is possible that players may develop other behaviours to complete the game that are not therapy appropriate.

Interestingly, the heat map recorded on the first day of play gave a good indication of the participant's visual field, which is characterized as a thin band of vision from the midline to 45-60° left of the midline. The largest number of missed shapes and longest reaction times were on the far right, whereas all the shapes just left of the middle were found first time. This is an early indication that our automated assessment tool may prove useful in giving feedback on functional vision to players, carers and healthcare professionals.

Over the first four days both the participant's response time and the percentage of targets found continued to improve from 3.24s and 86% respectively to 2.30s and 99%. There was a dip in accuracy at the start of the second week but this improved on the final day when the participant had an average response time of 2.18s and found 95% of targets first time. These are encouraging results, although a controlled trial including measures of functional vision will be required to draw conclusions on the therapeutic effects of the training.

DISCUSSION

This paper outlines design requirements and presents the participatory design process of *Eyelander*, a video game to engage young people with NVI in functional vision rehabilitation. In this section, we discuss the implications of our findings for the design of video games for persons with vision impairment, we reflect on the role of challenge in game design for therapy and rehabilitation, and we highlight areas in which our findings can be generalized beyond game development for children and teenagers.

The Design of Interactive Interventions for Vision Rehabilitation

Visual simplicity and accessibility vs. visual appeal

The most important advantage of involving end-users in the design process of *Eyelander* was that it allowed us to tailor the graphical design of the game to the abilities and preferences of the target audience. The resulting design is rather simplistic (see figure 1 and figure 3), but our results show that this ensures accessibility to a range of players. While players generally expressed a positive view on the visual design of *Eyelander*, feedback from other stakeholders (e.g., parents and therapists) revealed a challenge for game designers: persons without visual impairment expressed concerns regarding the visual appeal when comparing *Eyelander* to commercially available games. Communicating the importance of accessibility – and the implications for visual design – to these stakeholders therefore seems to be an important step to ensure system adoption, as we expect parents and therapists to function as gatekeepers regarding the introduction of games to support vision therapy.

Games as an opportunity to reveal player abilities

Much research on games for players with disabilities – particularly on games for persons with visual impairment – focuses on ways of designing around the disability to provide a positive player experience (e.g., [23, 24]). Due to the therapeutic background of *Eyelander*, it was not possible to follow this approach; while this raised concerns about the possibility of exposing player vulnerability through visually challenging play (as discussed in the following section), the design sessions also revealed the potential of the game to highlight player abilities in a positive context. In the case of NVI it is often difficult to develop a detailed understanding of the visual abilities of a patient as the effects of impairment are often complex and highly individual. *Eyelander* helped therapists understand the individual visual capabilities of patients by giving players a platform on which they could demonstrate visual competence. In this context, the fact that therapists expressed surprise regarding the abilities of some players highlights the potential of as a means of empowering players with disabilities by allowing them to share abilities with others through play.

Player Abilities, Therapy Goals, and Role of Challenge in a Participatory Design Process

A recurring theme during the participatory design process of *Eyelander* was the importance of designing for challenge in games. In this section, we discuss how in-game challenge and therapy-related challenges need to be consolidated, and we discuss the role of challenge in games in the context of participatory design with audiences with special needs.

In-Game challenge and challenges related to therapy

There are two distinct types of challenges presented by a therapeutic game to the player. Firstly, the therapeutic task itself will represent a challenge for the player to undertake. Therapy necessitates repetition of skills or behaviours that the player is not proficient or comfortable in performing. Secondly, in order to present engaging and meaningful experiences for players, games must present appropriate levels of game challenge to participants [32]. These in-game challenges are the central means through which games generate the motivation and engagement that is valuable in the context of therapy. Both of these types of challenge can function as a source of frustration for players, and have the potential to undermine the engaging qualities of the game. Designers of therapeutic games must consider and address both types of challenge simultaneously when defining in-game tasks.

Further complicating the design task, game and therapy requirements can sometimes be contradictory. The activities necessary for successful therapy are not always (or often) the most fun feature to be implemented into games. For example, we initially planned to develop a series of interconnected but distinct mini-games. Upon researching the neuroscience literature in more detail, and realizing that the mechanics behind visual therapy are not yet well understood, we realized that we could not justify the design of tasks that were significantly different than the basic visual search tasks that were previously therapeutically successful. In another example, playing the same game every day for a number of months is probably not what participants would choose to do. Nonetheless it is therapeutically necessary. Generally, therapy may involve overstraining patients and pushing them to work at the limits of their abilities, whereas games try to balance challenge and ability to allow optimal experience [29].

Participatory design and challenge

Additional problems can be introduced when using a participatory design approach to design games that offer adequate levels of challenge.

Challenge vs. game accessibility. As demonstrated in our work, engaging in a collaborative, iterative design process is crucial in understanding the types of challenges experienced by participants while playing a therapeutic game. Only through this process can the designer make an informed and compassionate decision on which of the frustrating or uncomfortable tasks that may be presented by the game are unavoidable and necessary, and which may be avoided or supported through accessible design techniques. Through our design sessions we quickly realized that we needed to make all of the game elements surrounding the search tasks as accessible as possible, while maintaining the inherently challenging nature of the search tasks.

Participatory sessions also led us to two further insights that contradicted initial assumptions. Firstly, young people who had been declared legally blind, and who therapists and teachers did not expect to be able to play anything other than a hugely simplified version of the game, actually displayed little problem in playing the game successfully. Thus, we were able to set the baseline challenge of the search tasks far higher than we initially expected. Secondly, we found that young people often did not mention when they found something really difficult, as long as they were in any way able to engage with it. Often it was necessary to consult with the therapy team to understand how to improve our designs as the young people simply refused to complain.

Exposing vulnerability when trying to design challenging experiences. One of the drawbacks to using a participatory design approach is the significant potential, as a by-product of the process of exploring and testing activities that participants find challenging, for the exposure of participant vulnerabilities. During design sessions we must ask questions of our participants regarding whether they can see the on-screen items and whether they can discriminate between different shapes, since this is the goal of the scanning task. Designers in this situation, as in any situation working with vulnerable participants, cannot avoid reminding participants of the limits of their abilities, something that has the potential to cause upset.

LIMITATIONS AND FUTURE WORK

While the focus of this paper is on the design process of *Eyelander*, a limitation in terms of assessing the effectiveness and the appeal of the proposed approach is the lack of a long-term user study to investigate player experience, engagement, as well as therapy outcomes. We intend to assess how feasible and effective this computer game could be as a rehabilitation strategy in a formal long-term study. Additionally, our approach strongly focuses on younger players; while our design focus was focused on young people, game-based visual rehabilitation may also be valuable for other persons, e.g., adults. In this context, it would be valuable to explore their preferences and needs in terms of game design.

CONCLUSION

Recent research suggests that video games can be an effective means of supporting therapy and rehabilitation. However, the success of games in this context depends largely on their potential to engage and motivate users. Designing enjoyable games is a challenging task, made significantly more complex when the manner through which participants perceive and interact with the game is significantly and qualitatively different to that of the designers. The participatory design process of *Eyelander* allowed us to explore how the involvement of young people with vision impairment can contribute to design of games to support vision (re)habilitation. One of the core challenges identified in this process, and one that must be dealt with in the design of any therapeutic game, lay in judging the balance between presenting the player with (necessary) therapeutic, and (motivating) game related, challenges, while ensuring that accessibility guidelines are considered and players are not unnecessarily frustrated. Furthermore, we found that the process of finding this balance was sometimes problematic, potentially exposing participant vulnerabilities. However, through playing the game in play test sessions, players were also able to demonstrate and communicate their specific visual abilities in ways that often stunned therapists and tutors who worked with them on a daily basis. This experience highlights one of the powerful benefits of games for special populations; they can help people to communicate to others the subjective experience of living with their specific impairment.

ACKNOWLEDGEMENTS

We acknowledge the time contributed by all participants. This work was supported by The WESC Foundation, the Technology Strategy Board, and the Medical Research Council of the United Kingdom, as part of a Knowledge Transfer Partnership (Ref: KTP008989).

REFERENCES

1. Achtman, R.L., Green, C.S., and Bavelier, D. Video games as a tool to train visual skills. *Restor Neurol Neurosci* 26, 4-5 (2008), 435-446.
2. Allen, L.E., Slater, M.E., Proffitt, R.V., Quarton, E. & Pelah, A.A. A new perimeter using the preferential looking response to assess peripheral visual fields in young and developmentally delayed children. *J. Am. Assoc. Pediatric Ophthalmology and Strabismus* 16, 3(2012), 261-265.
3. Bartle, D., Rossoff, S., Whittaker, D., Gooch, B., Kerns, K., and MacSween, J. Cognitive Games as Therapy for Children with FAS. In: *Proc. of SIGGRAPH 2010*, ACM (2010).
4. Castel, A.D.,Pratt, J., and Drummond, E. The effects of action video game experience on the time course of inhibition of return and the efficiency of visual search. *Acta Psychologica* 119, (2005), 217-230.
5. Ching, N., Wang, M., Ryan, M., Stevenson, R., and Andreallo, C. Beachcomber: A game for the visually impaired. In: *Proc. of FDG 2011*, (2011), 289-291.

6. Coyle, D., McGlade, N., Doherty, G., and O'Reilly, G. Exploratory Evaluations of a Computer Game Supporting Cognitive Behavioural Therapy for Adolescents. In: *Proc. of CHI 2011*, (2011), 2937-2946.
7. Csíkszentmihályi, M. (1990). *Flow: The Psychology of Optimal Experience.* New York: Harper and Row.
8. Dutton, G.N., McKillop, E.C.A., and Saidkasimova, S. Visual problems as a result of brain damage in children. *Br J Ophthalmol* 90, 8 (2006), 932-933.
9. Eriksson, Y., and Gärdenfors, D. Computer games for children with visual impairments. In: *Proc. of ICDVRAT 2004*, (2004), 79-86.
10. Flores, E., Tobon, G., Cavallaro, E., Cavallaro, F. I., Perry, J. C., & Keller, T. Improving patient motivation in game development for motor deficit rehabilitation. In *Proc ACE 2008,* ACM Press (2008) 381-384.
11. Gotsis, M., Piggot, J., Hughes, D., and Stone, W. SMART-Games: A Video Game Intervention for Children with Autism Spectrum Disorders. In: *Proc. of IDC 2010*, ACM (2010), 194-197.
12. Griffiths, M. (2003). The therapeutic use of videogames in childhood and adolescence. *Clinical Child Psychology and Psychiatry, 8, 547-554.*
13. Habgood, M. J., & Ainsworth, S. E. (2011). Motivating children to learn effectively: Exploring the value of intrinsic integration in educational games. *Journal of the Learning Sciences*, *20*, 169-206.
14. Han, L., Law-Gibson, D., and Reding, M. Key neurological impairments influence function-related group outcomes after stroke. *Stroke 33*, 7 (2002), 1920-1924.
15. Henderson, V., Lee, S., Brashear, H., Hamilton, H., Starner, T., and Hamilton, S. Development of an American Sign Language Game for Deaf Children. In: *Proc. of IDC 2005*, ACM (2005), 70-79.
16. Hernandez, H. A., Ye, Z., Graham, T. C., Fehlings, D., & Switzer, L. Designing action-based exergames for children with cerebral palsy. In *Proc CHI 2013*, ACM Press (2013), 1261-1270.
17. Kasten, E., Poggel, D.A., and Sabel, B.A. Computer-based training of stimulus detection improves color and simple pattern recognition in the defective field of hemianopic subjects. *J Cogn Neurosci* 12, 6 (2000), 1001-1012.
18. Kato, P.M., Cole, S.W., Bradlyn, A.S., and Pollock, B.H. A Video Game Improves Behavioral Outcomes in Adolescents and Young Adults With Cancer: A Randomized Trial. *Pediatrics* 122, 2 (2008), 305-317.
19. Kerkhoff, G., Münssinger, U., and Meier, E.K. Neurovisual rehabilitation in cerebral blindness. *Arch Neurol* 51, 5 (1994), 474-481.
20. Leat, S.J., Yadav, N.K., and Irving, E.L. Development of visual acuity and contrast sensitivity in children. *J Optom* 2, 1 (2009), 19-26.
21. Li, R.W., Ngo, C., Nguyen, J., and Levi, D.M. Video-Game Play Induces Plasticity in the Visual System of Adults with Amblyopia. *PLoS Biology* 9, 8 (2011).
22. Mannan, S.K., Pambakian, A.L., and Kennard, C. Compensatory strategies following visual search training in patients with homonymous hemianopia: an eye movement study. *J Neurol* 257, 11 (2010), 1812-1821.
23. Morelli, T., Foley, J., Columna, L., Lieberman, L., and Folmer, E. VI-Tennis: a Vibrotactile/Audio Exergame for Players who are Visually Impaired. In: *Proc. of FDG 2010*, ACM (2010), 147-154.
24. Morelli, T., Foley, J., and Folmer, E. VI-Bowling: A Tactile Spatial Exergame for Individuals with Visual Impairments. In: *Proc. of ASSETS'10*, ACM (2010), 179-186.
25. Pambakian, A.L.M., Mannan, S.K., Hodgson, T.L., Kennard, C. Saccadic visual search training: a treatment for patients with homonymous hemianopia. *J Neurol Neurosurg Psychiatry* 75, 10 (2004), 1443-1448.
26. Peli, E. Field expansion for homonymous hemianopia by optically induced peripheral exotropia. *Optom Vis Sci* 77, 9 (2000), 453-464.
27. Rector, K., Bennet, C.L., and Kientz, J.A. Eyes-Free Yoga: An Exergame Using Depth Cameras for Blind & Low Vision Exercise. In: *Proc. of ASSETS'13*, ACM (2013).
28. Reinhard, J., Schreiber, A., Schiefer, U., Kasten, E., Sabel, B.A., Kenkel, S., Vonthein, R., and Trauzettel-Klossinski, S. Does visual restitution training change absolute homonymous visual field defects? A fundus controlled study. *Br J Ophthalmol* 89, 1 (2005), 30-35.
29. Salen, K. and Zimmerman, E. Rules of Play: Game Design Fundamentals. MIT Press, Cambridge, 2004.
30. Schuett, S. The rehabilitation of hemianopic dyslexia. *Nat Rev Neurol* 5, 8 (2009), 427-437.
31. Smeddinck, J., Siegel, S., and Herrlich, M. Adaptive Difficulty in Exergames for Parkinson's disease Patients. In: *Proc. of GI 2013*, ACM (2013).
32. Sweetser, P., and Wyeth, P. GameFlow: A Model for Evaluating Player Enjoyment in Games. *Computers in Entertainment* 3, 3 (2005), Article 3A.
33. Treisman, A.M., and Gelade, G. A feature-integration theory of attention. Cognitive Psychol 12, 1 (1980), 97-136.
34. Warren, M. Pilot study on activities of daily living limitations in adults with hemianopia. *Am J Occup Ther* 63, 5 (2009) 626-633.

ColourID: Improving Colour Identification for People with Impaired Colour Vision

David R. Flatla[1], Alan R. Andrade[1], Ross D. Teviotdale[1], Dylan L. Knowles[2], Craig Stewart[1]
[1]University of Dundee
Dundee, Scotland, United Kingdom
[2]University of Saskatchewan
Saskatoon, Saskatchewan, Canada
d.flatla@dundee.ac.uk, alanribeiroandrade@gmail.com, r.d.teviotdale@dundee.ac.uk,
dylan.knowles@usask.ca, craig@craigsprojects.com

Figure 1. Left to right: "Grab the yellow pencil.", CVD simulation showing difficulty, our ColourNames, ColourMeters, and ColourPopper techniques.

ABSTRACT
Being able to identify colours is a fundamental human activity; colour identification helps us work, get dressed, prepare food, and keep safe. But for the 5% of the world with impaired colour vision (ICV), colour identification is often a challenge, resulting in frustration and confusion with sometimes dangerous consequences. Colour namer tools have been proposed as a solution, however these are often slow to use and imprecise. To address these shortcomings, we developed three new colour identification techniques (ColourNames, ColourMeters, ColourPopper) using a new colour name dictionary based on the largest colour naming experiment to date. We compared our techniques to colour namers using participants with ICV in desktop and mobile conditions, and found that ColourNames and ColourPopper resulted in ∼99% colour identification accuracy (10% higher than the colour namer), ColourMeters and ColourPopper were three times faster, and ColourPopper had lower perceived effort and was ranked significantly higher. With the benefits provided by our new colour identification techniques, people with ICV are one step closer to seeing the world like everyone else.

Author Keywords
Colour identification; impaired colour vision; colour vision deficiency; colourblindness; colour namers

ACM Classification Keywords
K.5.2. Social Issues: Assistive technologies

CHI 2015, April 18–23, 2015, Seoul, Republic of Korea.

http://dx.doi.org/10.1145/2702123.2702578

INTRODUCTION
Colour identification is a fundamental human ability we use on a daily basis. We use colour identification to tell the ripeness of fruit (e.g., green and yellow bananas), to coordinate clothing and jewellery, to determine whether meat is cooked ("Any pink in that chicken?"), and for diagnosing rashes and burns. In digital environments, colour identification helps us distinguish between visited (purple) and unvisited (blue) website links, read data from visualizations, and to find missing information in web forms (often marked in red).

However, for 5%-10% of the population who have impaired colour vision (ICV) [26], colour identification is often a challenge, and sometimes impossible. As shown in the two left images in Figure 1, people with inherited Colour Vision Deficiency (CVD – or colourblindness – a common form of ICV) often see one colour, but everyone else will call that same colour multiple names (e.g., brown, green, orange), leading to confusion and frustration [4], and sometimes danger (e.g., unnoticed sunburn or eating raw meat) [25].

To help address this problem, tools that identify colours on-screen and using mobile phone cameras (*colour namers*) have been developed, however they have two major limitations:

1. *Speed*: Colour namers typically provide colour identification for the colour under the cursor (desktop) or a crosshair in the center of the screen (mobile). This works when a person wants to know the colour of a specific item, but fails when the user needs to find an object with a specific colour (e.g., "Quick, grab the green folder!", "Cut the red wire!") or needs to get the general sense of the colour of something (e.g., "Is there any pink in that meat?", "Is this bread moldy?"). Compared to people with typical colour vision, people with ICV using colour namers will take much longer to answer these types of questions.

2. *Precision*: Colour namers condense numerical colour information (e.g., RGB values) to human-readable colour names, which is typically lossy (e.g., 24-bit RGB has 16.8 million colours, English only has 11 basic colour terms [2]). As a result. designers need to make decisions about the number of colour names provided by their colour namers, as well as the mapping from RGB to colour name. To solve this, *colour name dictionaries* are often used (e.g., X11 colour names), but currently-available colour name dictionaries contain colour names that are imprecise or difficult to understand (e.g., 'peru', 'papaya whip').

To address these two limitations, we first developed a new colour name dictionary based on the large set of colour-name pairs collected from the readership of the popular online comic, XKCD (`www.xkcd.com`), and refined by Heer and Stone [11]. This data set is based on over three million unique colour-name pairs, and reflects the commonly-accepted colour-naming conventions found in English (eleven basic colour terms: black, white, red, green, yellow, blue, brown, pink, purple, orange, grey) [2].

We then employed our new colour name dictionary to develop three new techniques to help people with ICV identify colours. First, we developed *ColourNames* – a direct extension of existing colour namers that tiles colour names across the entire screen. ColourNames (Figure 1, centre) replaces the physical search of colour namers with a visual search task – users scan with their eyes, rather than scanning physically. Second, we developed *ColourMeters* – a simplification of the ColourNames approach that replaces tiled colour names with a visualization using tiled colour meters. ColourMeters (Figure 1, centre right) replaces the high load of linearly reading English colour terms in ColourNames with scanning for simple visual patterns. Third, we developed *ColourPopper* – an extension of the ColourMeters technique that maximizes the popout effect of some visual patterns in ColourMeters. ColourPopper (Figure 1, right) replaces the ColourMeters visualization with a user-directed colour highlighting effect.

We evaluated our new techniques by comparing their performance to traditional colour namers in desktop and mobile colour identification tasks for people with inherited CVD. On the desktop, our techniques enabled almost 100% colour identification accuracy, and were two-three times faster than our test colour namer. ColourNames achieved 99.1% accuracy, with a mean completion time of 8.0s. ColourMeters achieved 94.5% and 5.7s. ColourPopper scored 98.6% and 5.2s. The colour namer performed worse than our techniques, with 90% accuracy and 15.7s mean completion time. Compared to our 100% accurate non-CVD control group (1.6s), the colour namer took 9.9 times longer, ColourNames took 5.0 times longer, ColourMeters took 3.6 times longer, and ColourPopper took (a relatively fast) 3.3 times longer. The mobile evaluation results supported some of these findings, with CVD participants ranking the mobile versions of ColourMeters and ColourPopper higher than a commercially-available Android colour namer, but ColourNames lower.

This paper presents three main contributions. First, we developed three new techniques for helping people with ICV identify desktop and environmental colours. Second, we evaluated these three techniques and showed that all three give people with CVD almost the same colour identification accuracy as people without CVD, and do it faster than existing colour namers. Third, we improved colour to name mappings for colour identification by adapting a previously-published colour-name dictionary to colour identification tools.

RELATED WORK

ICV: Impaired Colour Vision

Three causes of ICV have been identified in the literature: inherited ICV or Colour Vision Deficiency (CVD) [3], acquired ICV (typically as a factor of age) [5], and situationally-induced ICV (often due to lighting conditions) [8].

Inherited CVD is more common in males (8%) than females (0.5%) [4], and typically manifests as a reduction in the ability to discriminate along the red-green axis of colours [3], causing colours that only differ in their amount of red or green to be difficult to distinguish [25]. Acquired ICV has been identified in 64% of people over 65 years of age [5], and usually manifests as a reduction in discriminability along the blue-yellow axis of colours [21] as we age [14]. Acquired ICV can also be due to chemical exposure [16], disease [24], as well as other factors [30]. Situationally-induced ICV is less well-studied, but can be induced through variations in lighting, monitor settings, and eyewear colour [8]. Its manifestation is dependent upon the inducing situation, so can reduce colour discrimination along any axis (including luminance discrimination) [8].

Colour Name Dictionaries

Colour name dictionaries map numerical colour values to human-readable colour names. A commonly known colour name dictionary is the X11 colour names (`/usr/lib/X11/rgb.txt` in UNIX), which provides 752 colour-name mappings, and its related variants (CSS 3.0 and HTML 4.01 colours). Although assigning names to colours is an inherently subjective task, these dictionaries are typically created by small groups of people with little colorimetric training, so often introduce arbitrary decisions (e.g, the differences between 'grays' in X11 and web colours).

Some colour name dictionaries informed by colorimetric expertise exist, such as the NCS (`ncscolour.co.uk`), Pantone's colour sets [6], and the Munsell colour system [20] but the colour coordinates of these systems need to be converted into digital colour representations (e.g., sRGB) before they can be used in colour namers, and these transformations are often proprietary or result in out-of-gamut colours.

Another approach to generating colour name dictionaries is to distill a dictionary from colour-name pairs gathered from many people – present a colour, and get people to name it. One example is HP's multi-lingual Color Naming Experiment [19], which has been collecting colour names for several years. A more recent example is the XKCD Color Survey (`blog.xkcd.com/2010/05/03/color-survey-results`), which collected over five million named colours. Heer and Stone [11] processed this colour name set to allow colour-based editing and other image applications (more below).

There have also been attempts to automatically decompose colour spaces [15, 22, 1] into named regions, with applications in automatic image description [17, 18]. However this approach rarely generates the level of detail necessary to be helpful for colour namers (the names are either too simplistic or provide information not generally needed by people with ICV (e.g., describing the lightness of a colour, which usually presents no difficulties for people with ICV).

Existing Colour Identification Tools

Several tools have been developed for helping people with ICV identify colours. The Color Grab utility for Android (`play.google.com/store/apps/details?id=com.loomatix.colorgrab`) is a real time, colour namer that provides a general colour category (e.g., yellow) and a more specific name (e.g., lemon). We use Color Grab in the mobile evaluation of our techniques. The Colorblind Vision (Free) app (`play.google.com/store/apps/details?id=com.givewaygames.colorblind_ads`) has an 'Extract Color' feature that allows colour highlighting (similar to ColourPopper) for a user-specified colour by suppressing the saturation of all other colours. However, as people with inherited CVD have reduced discrimination along the red-green axis, they often perceive pinks/magentas and cyans/greens as grey. As a result, this feature does not help identify these colours, because they already appear grey to the CVD user. For this reason, we opted to not include this in our evaluations below. Chroma [27] is a Google Glass application for helping people with inherited CVD that features a colour highlighting mode that repaints all pixels of a user-selected colour to white, similar to the highlighting functionality of ColourPopper. However, by painting all the pixels white, the underlying subtleties (lightness, intensity, and hue variations) of the colour are lost. Colour visualization techniques (similar to ColourMeters) have also been proposed [23, 13, 12], however each of these is designed specifically for people with inherited red-green CVD. Our techniques are designed to help with general ICV – even monochromatic vision – and do not require specific information about the user's type of ICV.

THREE NEW COLOUR IDENTIFICATION TECHNIQUES

Aiming to address the limitations with existing colour naming tools, we developed three new techniques for helping people with ICV identify colours – ColourNames, ColourMeters, and ColourPopper. We describe these in detail in this section, beginning with a description of our adaptation of Heer & Stone's recently-published colour name dictionary [11] to use within two our tools. We demonstrate each technique using the image shown in Figure 2, top.

Colour Name Dictionary

Both ColourNames and ColourPopper rely on a colour name dictionary to identify colours that will be meaningful to the user. As identified above, esoteric colour names are probably not helpful for people with ICV (e.g., most people would have difficulty knowing what colours 'peru' and 'papaya whip' represent; a simple term such as 'pink' or 'orange' would likely suffice). Anecdotal evidence from some of our participants with CVD would suggest the same.

Figure 2. Demonstration image for our colour identification techniques (top). CVD simulation showing loss of red-green contrast (bottom).

We used the colour name dictionary generated from the XKCD Color Survey data by Heer and Stone [11]. This colour name dictionary is based on five million colour+name pairs (the largest collected to date). We used the software provided at `http://vis.stanford.edu/papers/color-naming-models` to find the most common human colour name for every RG565 colour (for a total of 65536 possible colours). This resulted in a set of 33 unique colour names, with the eleven English basic colour terms (white, black, red, brown, orange, yellow, green, blue, purple, pink, grey) comprising 83.3% of the entire RGB565 colour space. Upon further inspection of the colour names produced by the colour name dictionary, several were identified as simple modifiers (e.g., 'navy' modifying 'blue'). To help reduce the complexity of names produced by the colour name dictionary, we identified all of these cases and mapped the more complex name to their simplified forms according to Table 1. In addition to this, we also included 'teal' as a basic colour term as this colour (representing the blue-green set of colours) is often confused with grey by people with inherited CVD. These modifications increased the proportion of the colour space occupied by the eleven basic English colour terms (plus teal) to 94.7% of the entire RGB565 colour space.

lightpink → pink	peach (**light orange**) → orange
lightblue → blue	navyblue (**deep blue**) → blue
lightgreen → green	limegreen (**bright green**) → green
darkgreen → green	maroon (**dark red**) → red
darkteal → teal	cyan (**light teal**) → teal
darkpurple → purple	off white (**white**) → white

Table 1. Mapping used to reduce modified colour names to basic colour names (our interpretations of the modified names appear in bold).

ColourNames: Grid of Names

This technique was designed to increase colour identification speed by using visual search to replace physically scanning with the cursor or the mobile camera crosshair in existing colour namers. As physical search fully contains visual search (the eyes scan along with the cursor to read the colour names that appear), removal of the physical component of this search should increase colour identification speed.

ColourNames decomposes the incoming image (i.e., a desktop screenshot or mobile camera frame) into a tiled arrangement of small rectangles. The average RGB colour for each rectangle is calculated and converted to RGB565. The RGB565 colour is used to lookup its corresponding colour name from our colour name dictionary, and this name is drawn to the screen within its source rectangle. To provide room for more rectangles (more colour names), colour names are truncated to the first four characters. This technique is illustrated in Figure 3. The grid of rectangles can also be shown to help users target specific colours or regions.

Figure 3. ColourNames demonstration. Magnification may be necessary to see the names here, but are clearly readable in the implementation.

ColourMeters: Grid of Meters

Although ColourNames should allow faster colour identification than colour namers for people with ICV, ColourNames users still need to read and process each written colour name which might incur a high cognitive load. In addition, the names are English names, so English reading skills are required to use this tool – reducing its utility for those who do not speak English or are too young to read.

To eliminate the time required to read English colour names, we developed a second colour identification technique that uses the same rectangular grid as ColourNames, but presents a simple visualization of the average RGB value instead. This visualization takes the form of a meter or gauge; the angle of the meter represents the hue of the average RGB value, the meter's length represents the average RGB's chroma.

To determine the angle and length of the meter, the average RGB value is converted to CIE L*u*v* angular coordinates (LCH: Luminance, Chroma, Hue) [29]. Hue is the dominant wavelength of the colour and is represented in degrees, having values between 0° and 360°. Beginning at 0° (pinkish-red), the hue value increases through red, orange, yellow, green, blue, purple, and pink before wrapping around. Although we could map hue value directly to meter angle, this approach causes difficulties because the user will have difficulty distinguishing between meters that are 180° different (e.g., a meter pointing at blue (270°) will look identical to a meter pointing at yellow (90°) without a frame of reference). To overcome this difficulty, we divided the hue value by two to get a value between 0° and 180°. By flattening the hue angle in this fashion, we eliminated the ambiguity from using the full 360° of hue values, as the only two angles that are equivalent in this flattened case are 0° and 360°, which are already identical colours. We decided to make 0° horizontal and pointing to the right, with 180° also horizontal but pointing to the left. The meter rises from 0° to 90°, and falls from 90° to 180°.

To determine the length of the meter, we scaled the chroma of the average RGB value to the height of one grid rectangle. Due to the preponderance of low chroma colours (e.g., greys, tans) in the real world, we opted to scale the chroma by two and clamp it to the height of the rectangle to help identification of low chroma colours. Our ColourMeters technique is illustrated in Figure 4 (with no grid visible).

Figure 4. ColourMeters demonstration. Magnification may be necessary to see the meters here, but are clearly visible in the implementation.

ColourPopper: User-Selected Highlighting

By replacing textual colour names with a simple visualization, ColourMeters should increase colour identification speed. However, ColourMeters will likely require training before it can be used. To help overcome this, we noticed that the clustering of meters in ColourMeters would occasionally allow a 'popout' effect in which two indistinguishable colours (for someone with ICV) were different enough to have substantially different meters. This would allow the user to find the unique colour very quickly because its pattern of meters would 'pop out'. Taking this visualization technique forward, we designed our third colour identification technique – ColourPopper – to take full advantage of this popout effect.

By its very nature, popout allows particular data points to 'pop out' from the rest of the data allowing rapid and easy identification in visualizations [28]. To use this in ColourPopper, the user requests that a particular colour in an image or video frame be popped-out, and ColourPopper emphasizes all pixels with that particular colour name by suppressing the brightness and chroma of all remaining pixels. This technique provides the particular benefit of eliminating the scanning (either physical or visual) of all previous techniques, but at the cost of requiring the user to specify their desired colour.

ColourPopper Mechanism

To highlight a particular colour in a scene, the user selects a popout colour (using the buttons shown in Figure 5). Ten popout colours are provided by our tool – each corresponding to a single English human colour term: red, orange, brown, yellow, green, teal, blue, purple, pink, and grey. These align closely with the eleven basic colour terms identified by Berlin and Kay [2], with the specific addition of 'teal', and the removal of 'black' and 'white'. Teal was added because this colour often presents challenges for people with inherited CVD, and it occupies a reasonably large region in many colour space decompositions [11]. Black and white were removed because they comprise $< 1\%$ of the RGB565 colour space, so we decided that the added interaction time resulting from adding buttons for white and black was not worth the relatively small addition to colour identification.

To identify which RGB values map to these ten colour names, we modified the colour name dictionary described above by mapping those colours names that are not listed above (tan, olive, lavender, beige, magenta, salmon, mustard, mauve, yellowgreen) to the colour that is most perceptually similar. We determined perceptual similarity by determining the centroid of all RGB values belonging to a single colour term and then comparing the Euclidean distance between all centroids in perceptually-uniform CIE L*u*v colour space.

To cause a colour to popout, all pixels that map to that particular colour's English name remain unchanged, while all remaining pixels have their luminance and chroma reduced by scaling each by 0.1. Luminance and chroma scaling is performed in the angular representation of CIE L*u*v* colour space, but could similarly be done in HSB or other angular colour spaces. To convert from RGB to L*u*v*, we used the sRGB gamma function and primaries and a D65 whitepoint. We opted to not scale up the luminance and chroma of the highlighted colour, as this can lead to the colour being pushed out of the gamut of the display, which can adversely change the colour drawn to the screen due to gamut clipping.

Although the colour modifications performed by the highlighting effect could be calculated on demand, this would lead to unnecessary recalculation because the modifications are entirely deterministic. As such, we used a look-up-table (LUT) to reduce the number of calculations and to improve the runtime performance of the technique by loading the LUT onto the graphics processing unit (GPU) where fragment shaders parallelize the colour replacement process.

One LUT is required for each colour term identified above. To generate each LUT, we created every possible pixel colour and modified it according to the above algorithm (leave unchanged if it belongs to the desired colour term, otherwise suppress luminance and chroma). Each resulting pixel is then written to a 1024x64 pixel image that serves as the LUT for the desired colour term. When a highlight colour is specified by the user, ColourPopper loads the corresponding LUT as a texture into the GPU and fragment shaders are used to recolour each frame. ColourPopper results for 'green' with our sample image are shown in Figure 5.

Figure 5. ColourPopper demonstration highlighting 'green'.

DESKTOP IMPLEMENTATION EVALUATION

We conducted an in-lab user study to compare our proposed techniques to existing colour namer tools. Our study focused on the problem of identifying the 'odd one out' – identifying a single element from a larger set by colour identification.

Participants

We recruited 22 unpaid participants from a local university (mean=26.8 years, SD=7.3, 18 male). Eleven of these participants were previously diagnosed with inherited CVD and eleven served as non-CVD controls. We used the HRR Pseudoisochromatic Plate Test [9] to assess the colour vision of each participant, and found that four participants had mixed protan and deutan CVD, and seven had protan CVD. [1]

Stimuli & Task

To evaluate each colour identification technique, a 10x7 grid of coloured circles on a black background was presented to the participant (Figure 6). Sixty-nine of these circles were one colour (of varying luminance), and the remaining (randomly-selected) circle was another colour. The participant's task was to click on the circle that was the different colour. A rest screen between trials listed the two colour names for the next trial, which were also available during the trial.

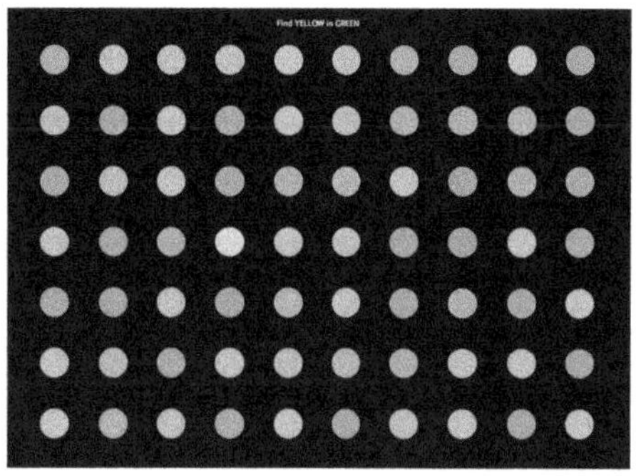

Figure 6. Field of coloured circles presented to the user. Task was to identify the specified colour (in this case, yellow) by clicking on it.

To properly evaluate each of our techniques, it was important that the colours presented are difficult for people with CVD to differentiate, but are still easily distinguishable for people with typical colour vision (to reflect the real world situation of a person with CVD trying to identify an object from a set of distractors by colour alone). Additionally, we wanted the different colours to have clearly identifiable names (e.g., 'green') to simplify the task for all participants.

To choose our evaluation colours, we selected colours from the X11 (red, dark red, dark orange [simplified to orange], yellow, green, blue, purple, pink, saddle brown [brown]) and W3C (green [dark green]) colour sets, as well as a mid-luminance grey (0x777777). By choosing colours from these colour sets rather than our own dictionary, we sought to reduce artificially favouring our techniques.

To select which pairs (target & distractor) of colours would be presented to the participants, we found the colour confusion line (line of indistinguishable colours) that intersects each colour listed above in CIE L*u*v* perceptually-uniform colour space for the two dominant types of inherited CVD (protan & deutan). The minimum Euclidean distances from the (u*,v*) coordinates for every other colour

[1] We recognize that this does not fit the expected pattern of 3/4 deutan, 1/4 protan [3] and are investigating this further.

to each line were then calculated. This resulted in two tables of distances (one protan, one deutan) that showed which pairs of colours were close to the same colour confusion line. By arbitrarily choosing a threshold maximum distance of 11.0 u*v* units, we identified five pairs of colours that should present difficulties for people with protan CVD (yellow+green, blue+purple, red+brown, grey+pink, darkRed+brown), and six pairs for people with deuteranopic CVD (grey+pink, darkRed+brown, red+orange, orange+green, darkRed+darkGreen, darkGreen+brown). Two pairs were shared between each set (grey+pink, darkRed+brown), leaving nine unique pairs of colours. We averaged the original luminance of each colour to reduce the chance of discriminating between the colours based on luminance differences, and generated luminance noise variations for each colour in each pair to further reduce any luminance contrasts. Each pair of colours is shown in Figure 7 along with protan and deutan simulations of the colour pairs.

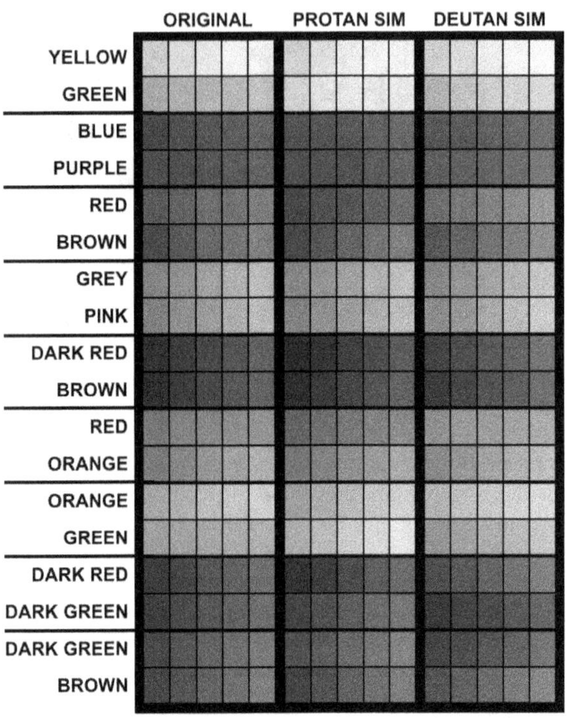

Figure 7. All pairs of colours used in the study with CVD simulations.

Colour Identification Techniques

For each presentation of coloured circles, participants had either a control (no assistance) or one of four colour identification techniques available to use:

- *Control*: This technique reflects the typical unassisted task of identifying the unique colour in a set of distractors.
- *ColourNamer*: This technique represents existing colour naming tools. To ensure the performance difference between this technique and our techniques was not due to differences in colour name dictionary, we used our dictionary to provide a human-readable English colour term for the pixel underneath the cursor. The colour name was provided to the right of the cursor, and moved with the cursor.
- *ColourNames*: This technique was used as described earlier, but with one modification. The base implementation of ColourNames described above is quite overwhelming – for the coloured circles shown in Figure 6, the default implementation provides 8162 colour names. Given the substantial load this would place on participants, we opted to use a modified version of ColourNames that identifies the location of each circle, and provides a single colour name for that circle. Although this modification may be highly optimized to the coloured circle task used in this evaluation, it allows a 'best case' evaluation of ColourNames.
- *ColourMeters*: This technique was used as described earlier, but with a similar modification as ColourNames – meters were only provided for the coloured circles.
- *ColourPopper*: This technique was used as described earlier. Popout colour selection was made via a horizontal row of buttons across the bottom of the screen (see Figure 5). The popout colour was reset to 'none' after each trial to force the participant to make a selection for every trial.

Procedure, Apparatus & Design

Participants were first given the HRR Plate Test, and were then introduced to the task. Participants with typical colour vision completed a single Control session, but participants with inherited CVD completed a session using each technique described above in counterbalanced order. A single session presented the participant with 22 coloured circle screens (trials) – two for each of the nine pairs of colours identified above (each colour in a pair was the target once), plus two protan and two deutan training screens at the beginning.

For each trial, we recorded the completion time, and whether the selected colour was the target colour. Once all 22 trials were completed for a given colour identification technique (Control, ColourNamer, ColourNames, ColourMeters, ColourPopper), participants completed the standard six responses of the NASA Task Load Index (TLX) [10] for the technique just completed. The entire study took about 30 minutes to complete for participants with CVD, and about 10 minutes for participants with typical colour vision.

The study was conducted under controlled lighting on a 1920x1080 LCD BenQ GL2450H monitor colour calibrated using a Spyder4Express, driven by a Windows 7 machine. The techniques and coloured circles presentation software was custom-built in Java using the `Processing.org` libraries.

The study used a one-way factorial design with a single factor (technique) with five levels (Control, Namer, Names, Meters, Popper). As CVD participants were presented with both protan and deutan pairs of colours, we selected results from the colour set that aligned with the type of CVD of the participant (as diagnosed by the HRR plates). We used both sets for participants with mixed protan and deutan CVD.

Dependent measures were mean completion time for the five CVD techniques and the non-CVD Control, mean accuracy for the same six conditions, and the CVD participant responses to the six TLX categories for each CVD technique.

Results

Accuracy

The nonCVD Control data serves as a baseline against which the performance of participants with CVD can be compared. As such, we conducted a one-way ANOVA across the six conditions identified above (NonCVD Control, CVD Control, CVD Namer, CVD Names, CVD Meters, CVD Popper). This identified a significant main effect of Technique (F_5=132.09, p<.001). Accuracy results are summarized in Table 2.

Technique	Mean Accuracy (s.e.)	Mean Completion Time (s.e.)
NonCVD Control	100.00% (0.00)	1.58 (0.16)
CVD Control	54.24% (8.20)	13.73 (4.90)
CVD Namer	90.00% (8.09)	15.67 (2.52)
CVD Names	99.09% (0.91)	7.97 (1.32)
CVD Meters	94.55% (4.55)	5.66 (0.76)
CVD Popper	98.59% (0.99)	5.19 (0.65)

Table 2. Mean accuracy and mean completion times ±s.e. for the non-CVD control and for CVD participants in the control condition, with the colour namer, and each of our three techniques.

As we are interested in the performance of all techniques, our post-hoc analysis comprised full pairwise t-tests, which resulted in 15 comparisons. We applied Bonferroni correction to get an adjusted alpha of (.05/15=.0033). We found that CVD Control had significantly lower accuracy than the Non-CVD Control and all colour identification techniques, and that the NonCVD Control, Meters, and Popper were significantly more accurate than Namer (all p<.05, adjusted). Importantly, there were no significant differences between any of our techniques and the NonCVD Controls.

These results are valuable for three reasons. First, they confirm the underlying premise of this research – that people with CVD have difficulty identifying colours. Second, they show that two of our techniques (Names and Popper) resulted in higher colour identification accuracy than the colour namer. Third, it suggests (through lack of significant differences) that our three techniques allow people with CVD to identify colours as accurately as people with typical colour vision.

Completion Time

As with Accuracy, we conducted a one-way ANOVA across the same six conditions. This identified a significant main effect of Technique (F_5=5.28, p<.001). Completion time results are summarized in Table 2.

We conducted another round of Bonferroni-corrected pairwise t-tests to determine where the completion time differences lie between techniques. The NonCVD Controls were faster than all other techniques and the Namer took significantly longer than Meters and Popper (all p<.05, adjusted).

These results are important for three reasons. First, they unfortunately show that our techniques do not enable participants with CVD to identify colours as quickly as people with typical colour vision, so more work is needed. Second, they show that two of our techniques (Meters and Popper) resulted in faster colour identification than the colour namer. Third, we see that CVD participants are willing to spend time to achieve higher accuracy (compare CVD Control and Namer completion times and accuracies in Table 2), suggesting that accuracy in colour identification is valuable.

Taking the accuracy and completion time results together, ColourPopper appears to be the only one of our tools that is both highly accurate (98.6%) and fast (5.2s).

Task Load Index

We performed one-way ANOVAs on each of the six measures of the NASA TLX [10] provided by CVD participants for each of the four techniques (plus the CVD Control condition) and followed this with post-hoc, Bonferroni-corrected t-tests when main effects were significant. All post-hoc results reported were significant at the adjusted .05 level (.05/10=.005). Results are summarized in Figure 8.

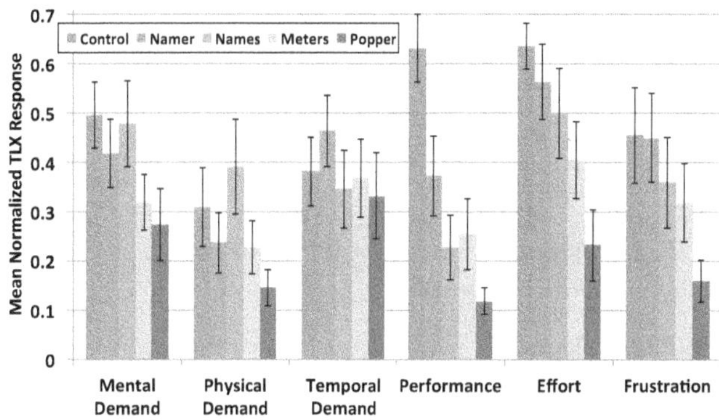

Figure 8. Mean TLX responses ±s.e. for CVD participants in the control and with each colour identifier.

Performance and Effort both had significant main effects of Technique (F_4=8.79, p<.001; F_4=4.41, p<.01). For Performance, post-hoc tests showed that our three techniques had higher perceived performance than the Control condition (all p<.05, adjusted). For Effort, post-hoc tests showed that Popper had lower perceived effort than both the Control and Namer conditions (both p<.05, adjusted).

These results suggest that our colour identification techniques help improve perceived performance over not having any tool (which is positive). In addition, Popper also has lower perceived effort than no tool, as well as the colour namer. Coupling these strong results with the overall pattern shown in Figure 8 (Popper lowest in every category), supports the accuracy and completion time results presented above – ColourPopper appears to be the strongest of our techniques.

Summary

Taken together the data shows that all colour identification techniques help people with CVD identify colours more accurately than with no assistance, with two of our techniques (Names and Popper) achieving almost perfect accuracy. The timing results show that this accuracy does not necessarily come at a cost, with Popper taking less time than all other techniques, although still not as quickly as people with typical colour perception. The TLX results show that our techniques help reduce the perceived effort of colour identification while improving perceived performance, again with special notice of Popper's strong scores across all of the TLX results.

MOBILE TOOLS

Given the relative success of our techniques in the desktop evaluation just presented, we implemented our techniques on a mobile platform and evaluated how well they supported people with CVD identify colours printed on paper samples.

Each tool (MobileNames, MobileMeters, MobilePopper) was implemented on a Samsung SM-T210 (Galaxy Tab 3), with a 1024x600 LED screen running Android version 4.1.2. Each system captured video frames from the built-in camera, and processed the image to either overlay colour information (MobileNames and MobileMeters) or manipulate the pixel colours via the ColourPopper LUTs described above. After processing, each frame was drawn to the screen to allow real time interactive colour identification.

MobileNames

Our mobile implementation of ColourNames utilized OpenCV libraries to overlay colour name information on each camera frame. This implementation was almost identical to the original ColourNames technique, except we opted to make the grid that identifies each individual colour naming rectangle visible. We found that the lines helped pilot testing participants properly align an individual naming cell with a target for which they wanted colour information.

MobileMeters

Our mobile implementation of ColourMeters also used OpenCV to overlay the meters as described for the original ColourMeters technique, and also displayed the individual meter cells. In addition to helping participants align the cell with a target, we also found that the grid helped reduce confusion because it provided an easily-accessible frame of reference for reading the angle of the meter. Without the grid, it was easy to get confused as the tablet was accidentally rotated during use (e.g,. the meters appear to be pointing up (yellow), but in reality are pointing to the right (red/pink) and the tablet has been rotated counter-clockwise 90°).

MobilePopper

Our mobile implementation of ColourPopper used OpenGL shaders to swap every pixel in the incoming camera video frame using the LUTs described in the ColourPopper section above. As the mobile screen was not large enough to clearly present all of the available LUTs as a row of buttons along the bottom of the screen, we opted to use a pop-up menu listing the available LUTs to allow the user to make this choice.

MOBILE IMPLEMENTATION EVALUATION

To evaluate the mobile versions of our techniques, we conducted an in-lab evaluation in which the CVD participants from the desktop evaluation used each mobile tool to identify coloured targets printed on plain paper.

Tools

Participants used the three Mobile tools just described (MobileNames, MobileMeters, and MobilePoppers), plus no tool (we call this condition 'Eyes'), and a commercially-available free Android colour namer tool (Color Grab v2.6.1 – described above). Each participant used each tool in counterbalanced order for each of nine stimuli.

Stimuli & Task

To provide carefully-controlled colours, we replaced the black background with a white background in the 18 colour pair stimulation screens from the Desktop Evaluation and printed them on white paper. As there were two for each pair (e.g., one blue in 69 purple, and one purple in 69 blue), we picked one representative from each pair that maximized salience for a co-author with typical colour vision, while minimizing salience for a co-author with CVD.

Sheets were shown to participants one at a time in randomized order, and the participant used each tool in counterbalanced order to see if they could identify the target colour. Participants were instructed to identify the target using each of the techniques with the aim of getting an overall impression of that technique's effectiveness for that colour pair. After each coloured sheet, participants ranked each of the five techniques according to how well it helped with colour identification for that colour pair (five being the lowest rank, one=highest).

Results

Figure 9 contains the mean rankings for each technique. We carried out a one-way ANOVA on these results and found a main effect of technique (F_4=7.90, p<.001). We carried out Bonferroni-corrected post-hoc t-tests to explore this main effect. Five techniques gives ten pairwise comparisons, giving an adjusted alpha of (0.05/10=0.005).

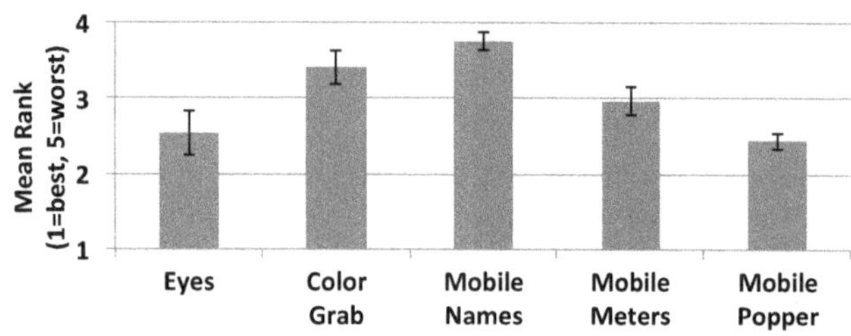

Figure 9. Mean rank ±s.e. for Eyes, Color Grab, and our Mobile tools.

We found that Mobile Names was ranked significantly worse (lower rank, higher number) than all other conditions except Color Grab, and Color Grab was ranked significantly worse than Eyes and Mobile Popper (all p<.05, adjusted).

Although less formal than the desktop evaluation, the findings from this study help refine some of our previous results. Once again, ColourPopper came out strong, with ColourMeters close behind. However, this study resulted in two surprises. First, ColourNames fared much worse in this study than would be expected from the desktop accuracy results. Many participants commented that ColourNames (with grid visible) was so visually 'busy' that it crowded out the actual image – a potential explanation for ColourNames' poor ranking. Second, Eyes fared much better in this study than in the desktop study for CVD participants. Our hypothesis is that despite our attempts at the contrary, the printed stimuli were in some cases actually distinguishable for our participants. In these cases, Eyes worked well, and the introduction of any of the mobile tools between the user and the stimuli likely resulted in the tools being rated poorly in these circumstance.

DISCUSSION

Summary & Explanation of Results

We found four main results:

1. ColourNames and ColourPopper allowed CVD participants to identify colours as accurately as their nonCVD counterparts, and more accurately than the colour namer.
2. ColourMeters and ColourPopper allowed CVD participants to identify colours more quickly than with the colour namer, but not as fast as nonCVD participants.
3. CVD participants perceived that their performance was higher with ColourNames, ColourMeters, and ColourPopper versus no tool, and that ColourPopper reduced their effort compared to no tool and the existing colour namer.
4. When tested on mobile versions of our techniques, CVD participants ranked ColourNames lowest, but ColourMeters and ColourPopper (and Eyes) highest.

The main reason for these results (ColourPopper is stronger than ColourMeters, which is stronger than ColourNames) is the progressive nature of their development; ColourNames built on colour namers, ColourMeters built on ColourNames, and ColourPopper built on ColourMeters. Overall, ColourMeters and ColourPopper appear to be the best candidates for future colour identification technology for ICV.

Strengths & Weaknesses of Each Technique

ColourNames is a simple extension of existing colour namers, that provided high accuracy and faster colour identification times than our desktop colour namer. This technique is arguably the easiest of our techniques to learn (little to no extension from colour namers), however ColourNames came out much worse in the mobile evaluation. One potential reason for this was that we turned the rectangular grids on in MobileNames, however MobileMeters also had the grid, but was not apparently penalized. Another possible explanation is that the grid actually offered little value in the MobileNames condition (in contrast to our pilot study findings), whereas the grid was valuable for providing a frame of reference in the MobileMeters condition. As such, participants may have penalized MobileNames for its unnecessarily cluttered screen.

ColourMeters had strong completion time and mobile ranking results, but had lower colour identification accuracy than our other tools (94.5% versus ~99% for ColourNames and ColourPopper). Upon closer inspection, we found that this lower score was attributable to a single CVD participant who scored a relatively low 50% accuracy. This may have happened due to confusion over how the technique works, highlighting the need for proper ColourMeters training. We did not remove outliers in the analysis presented above, but removing this single participant's data improves ColourMeter's accuracy to that of ColourNamers (99.1%), suggesting that with adequate training, ColourMeters is a valuable technique for helping improve colour identification.

Of all our techniques, ColourPopper was the fastest, had the lowest perceived load, had nearly 100% accuracy, and was highest ranked, but this technique has two major limitations. First, it required the designers (us) to determine the number of colour names ColourPopper supports, and we also had to decide which RGB colours map to which names. Fortunately, our colour name dictionary based on Heer & Stone's work [11] helped substantially with this, but there may be other use cases where our choices are not optimal. How to design ColourPopper to provide a dynamic number of colour highlighting options will be one focus in our future work.

Extensions & Future Work

The second limitation of ColourPopper is its required interaction for choosing a highlight colour. In our desktop implementation, users select the colour from a row of buttons along the bottom of the screen, and use a pop-up menu in the mobile version, but there are many more options which may prove much faster. Perhaps tracking menus [7] or contextual pie menus can provide some speed gains, but might prove cumbersome on touch-based mobile interfaces. Another option is simple voice input of just stating the name you want highlighted. This might work particularly well with ColourPopper on wearable transparent displays. We plan to explore reducing the interaction time of ColourPopper in the future.

In terms of wearable transparent displays, one of the central goals for future extensions of this work is moving our techniques to wearables. Both ColourPopper and ColourMeters offer promise for wearable platforms, which will allow our colour identification techniques to be used in a less cumbersome manner than our current mobile implementations. This extension will require revisiting our techniques for use in a wearable context, as well as evaluating our techniques in terms of real world colour identification (e.g., reading colour-coded subway maps, estimating fruit ripeness).

In spite of the slightly lower accuracy performance of ColourMeters (already discussed above), it offers potential value of a different nature than ColourPopper. First, it sometimes provides the popout effect of ColourPopper through texture patterns of its tiled meter visualizations. Second, unlike ColourPopper, ColourMeters does not require a colour name dictionary. This frees it from the limitations imposed by identifying colours by name in a particular language. ColourMeters offers the greatest promise for cross-cultural (and illiterate and preliterate) improvements in colour identification for people with ICV. Third, ColourMeters attempts to visually present raw colour information to the user. We contend that this might enable sub-sensory substitution when persistently used, in which over time, the user begins to 'see' colours (as mediated by the ColourMeters visualizations) and ceases to see the visualizations themselves. This would allow people with impaired colour vision to overcome their ICV entirely, resulting in a technologically-based 'cure' for ICV.

CONCLUSION

Colour identification helps in many day-to-day tasks such as preparing food, getting dressed, and being creative. However, for the 5-10% of the population with Impaired Colour Vision (ICV), colour identification is often frustrating and can lead to mistakes with potentially severe consequences (e.g., undercooking meat, misreading a wiring diagram). Colour naming tools have been developed to improve colour identification, but these tools are typically too slow for many common tasks and lack precision in the colour names they provide.

To address these problems, we developed three new colour identification techniques (ColourNames, ColourMeters, and ColourPopper) and evaluated them using desktop and mobile colour identification tasks with people with ICV. We found that ColourPopper offered the best performance overall, with ColourMeters close behind; both achieved nearly 100% colour identification accuracy in the best time. With the extensions we identify above, these two techniques can be even better, potentially becoming 'invisible aids' that allow people with ICV to experience the full range of colours.

ACKNOWLEDGMENTS

This work was supported by RCUK grant EP/G066091/1 "RCUK Hub: Inclusion in the Digital Economy".

REFERENCES

1. Benavente, R., Vanrell, M., and Baldrich, R. Parametric fuzzy sets for automatic color naming. *JOSA A 25*, 10 (2008), 2582–2593.
2. Berlin, B., and Kay, P. *Basic Color Terms: Their Universality and Evolution*. UCalifornia Press, 1969.
3. Birch, J. *Diagnosis of Defective Colour Vision*, 2 ed. Oxford University Press, 2001.
4. Cole, B. L. The handicap of abnormal colour vision. *Clin. & Exp. Opt. 87*, 4-5 (July 2004), 258–275.
5. Davies, I. R. L., Laws, G., Corbett, G. G., and Jerrett, D. J. Cross-cultural differences in colour vision: Acquired 'colour-blindness' in africa. *Personality and Individual Differences 25*, 6 (1998), 1153–1162.
6. Eisemann, L. *Pantone's Guide to Communicating with Color*. Grafix Press, Ltd., 2000.
7. Fitzmaurice, G., Khan, A., Pieké, R., Buxton, B., Kurtenbach, G. Tracking menus. In *Proc UIST* (2003), 71-79.
8. Flatla, D. R., and Gutwin, C. SSMRecolor: improving recoloring tools with situation-specific models of color differentiation. In *Proc CHI* (2012), 2297–2306.
9. Hardy, L. H., Rand, G., and Rittler, M. C. HRR polychromatic plates. *JOSA 44*, 7 (1954), 509–521.
10. Hart, S. G., and Staveland, L. E. Development of NASA-TLX (task load index): Results of empirical and theoretical research. *Adv. in psych. 52* (1988), 139–183.
11. Heer, J., and Stone, M. Color naming models for color selection, image editing and palette design. In *Proc CHI* (2012), 1007–1016.
12. Herbst, M., and Brinkman, B. Color-via-pattern: distinguishing colors of confusion without affecting perceived brightness. In *Proc ASSETS* (2014), 245–246.
13. Hung, P., and Hiramatsu, N. A colour conversion method which allows colourblind and normal-vision people share documents with colour content. Tech. rep., Konica Minolta, 2013.
14. Knoblauch, K., Vital-Durand, F., and Barbur, J. L. Variation of chromatic sensitivity across the life span. *Vision research 41*, 1 (2001), 23–36.
15. Lammens, J. M. G. *A computational model of color perception and color naming*. PhD thesis, State University of New York, 1994.
16. Lomax, R. B., Ridgway, P., and Meldrum, M. Does occupational exposure to organic solvents affect colour discrimination? *Toxic. Rev. 23*, 2 (2004), 91–121.
17. Mojsilovic, A. A method for color naming and description of color composition in images. In *Proc ICIP*, vol. 2 (2002), 789–792.
18. Mojsilovic, A. A computational model for color naming and describing color composition of images. *Trans. on Image Processing 14*, 5 (2005), 690–699.
19. Moroney, N. Unconstrained web-based color naming experiment. In *Proc Elec. Imag.* (2003), 36–46.
20. Munsell, A. H. *A Color Notation*. Munsell color company, 1919.
21. Pokorny, J., Smith, V., and Lutze, M. Aging of the human lens. *Applied Optics 26*, 8 (1987), 1437–1440.
22. Regier, T., Kay, P., and Khetarpal, N. Color naming reflects optimal partitions of color space. *PNAS 104*, 4 (2007), 1436–1441.
23. Sajadi, B., Majumder, A., Oliveira, M. M., Schneider, R. G., and Raskar, R. Using patterns to encode color information for dichromats. *IEEE Trans. Vis. Comput. Graphics 19*, 1 (2013), 118–129.
24. Schneck, M. E., and Haegerstrom-Portnoy, G. Color vision defect type and spatial vision in the optic neuritis treatment trial. *Investigative ophthalmology & visual science 38*, 11 (1997), 2278–2289.
25. Steward, J. M., and Cole, B. L. What do color vision defectives day about everyday tasks? *Optometry and Vision Science 66*, 5 (May 1989), 288–295.
26. Stone, M. *A Field Guide to Digital Color*. AK Peters, 2003.
27. Tanuwidjaja, E., Huynh, D., Koa, K., Nguyen, C., Shao, C., Torbett, P., Emmenegger, C., and Weibel, N. Chroma: A wearable augmented-reality solution for color blindness. In *Proc UbiComp* (2014), 799–810.
28. Ware, C. *Information Visualization - Perception for Design*. Morgan Kaufmann, California, USA, 2000.
29. Wyszecki, G., and Stiles, W. *Color science: concepts and methods, quantitative data and formulae*. Wiley-VCH, 2000.
30. Yates, J. T., Diamantopoulos, I., and Daumann, F.-J. Acquired (transient and permanent) colour vision disorders. *Operational Colour Vision NATO RTO Technical Report 16* (2001), 43–47.

TerraGuide: Design and Evaluation of a Multi-Surface Environment for Terrain Visibility Analysis

Matthew Oskamp[1], Christophe Bortolaso[1], Robin Harrap[2], T.C. Nicholas Graham[1]

[1] School of Computing
Queen's University
Kingston, Ontario, Canada
{7mao, christophe.bortolaso, nicholas.graham}@queensu.ca

[2] Department of Geology
Queen's University
Kingston, Ontario, Canada
harrap@queensu.ca

ABSTRACT

Terrain visibility analysis is a challenging task that is currently supported by complex digital tools with cumbersome interfaces. In this paper, we present TerraGuide, a novel multi-surface environment for exploratory terrain analysis. TerraGuide provides three tightly coupled displays including a real-time viewshed, a 3D panoramic view, and a helicopter view controlled by an optically tracked tablet. A user study compared these techniques and identified users' strategies in solving a complex terrain analysis problem. Users overwhelmingly adopted a bi-manual use of the tabletop viewshed and tablet-based helicopter techniques. This paper gives insight into how multi-surface environments can be designed to allow complementary use of and fluid switching between techniques.

Author Keywords

Multi-surface environment, digital tabletop; terrain analysis

ACM Classification Keywords

H.5.m. Information interfaces and presentation (e.g., HCI): Miscellaneous.

INTRODUCTION

Activities such as urban planning [23], military command and control [3,22], wildlife observatory design [10] and search and rescue [1] require line-of-sight analysis of physical geography. For example, an urban planner may wish to know the effect on the skyline of constructing a new apartment building, while a mobile systems engineer may wish to determine the highest-coverage locations for a set of cellular transmission towers. People find terrain analysis difficult because it requires them to construct a mental model of 3D geography from representations such as a 2D map [14].

CHI 2015, April 18–23, 2015, Seoul, Republic of Korea.

ACM 978-1-4503-3145-6/15/04...$15.00.
http://dx.doi.org/10.1145/2702123.2702480

Simple 3D visualization of terrain is not sufficient on its own, since terrain analysis problems may require an understanding of line-of-sight from multiple locations simultaneously. For example, picking the best location for a group of cell towers requires an analyst to understand the combined coverage of a set of candidate locations. In general, terrain analysis requires the analyst to answer questions such as "What places are visible from the given set of observation points?" and "How many places is the given location visible to?" [14]. Despite the development of new digital technologies for terrain analysis, universities can devote entire courses to this problem (e.g., [16]).

Traditionally, terrain analysis is performed using paper maps where contour lines and shading show terrain elevation. Acetate sheets are placed over the maps and are annotated using pens. More recently, Geographic Information Systems (GIS) use digital representations of maps, permitting special-purpose visualizations for terrain analysis. These include viewshed visualizations [17], line-of-sight tools [5], 3D panoramic views [10], and magic lenses [4]. Current GIS visualizations often suffer key usability problems, however, hindering their adoption. For example, the ABACUS military simulation tool [20] can

Figure 1. TerraGuide. The interactive tabletop provides the user with a 2D top-down view of a 3D terrain. Viewsheds show visibility from a source point. A secondary display shows a panoramic view. A hand-held tablet displays terrain in 3D.

show a 3D panoramic view from a given map location, but requires a multi-step dialogue box and several seconds to generate the view. Additionally, line-of-sight visualizations are typically decoupled from the underlying map view, making it difficult for users to move quickly between the map and the visualization [5,6,10].

In this paper, we address the problems of terrain analysis through a novel multi-surface environment. Our TerraGuide tool centres on a digital map presented on a digital tabletop surface, augmented by a large screen secondary display and a hand-held tablet (Figure 1). Three techniques aid with terrain analysis: a *viewshed* shows visibility in a cone drawn from the user's touch point on the table; a *panoramic view* provides a 3D first-person view on a separate display, and a *helicopter view* allows the user to see terrain in 3D on a handheld tablet positioned over the table. Previous systems have demonstrated visualizations similar to these; the novelty of TerraGuide comes from the real-time and fluid combination of these interaction techniques.

We have performed an exploratory study evaluating TerraGuide and its use. The first part of the study evaluated performance, user preference, user confidence and cognitive load in performing a simple analysis task with combinations of the different techniques. The second part determined the strategies that people used when performing a more complex task. Interesting results included that the use of the 3D panorama view worsened task completion time and did not improve error, yet increased participants' confidence in their analysis; that the viewshed technique was widely used for detailed analysis; and that the dominant strategy was bi-manual use of the viewshed and helicopter techniques.

Our central contribution is to show how interaction techniques on multiple surfaces can be designed to allow fluid, combined use of multi-surface techniques and easy change between these techniques. Our results are of interest both to designers of systems supporting terrain analysis and to designers of multi-surface environments in general.

The paper is structured as follows. First, we review the problem of terrain analysis. We then introduce TerraGuide and explain the principles behind its design. Finally, we report our study evaluating TerraGuide's multi-surface approach, and conclude with lessons for designers.

TERRAIN ANALYSIS

Tools to aid terrain analysis have evolved from paper maps to interactive, digital models. In this section, we describe what terrain analysis is and why it is complex, and report on existing terrain analysis tools.

Terrain and Visibility Analysis

Terrain analysis is the process of interpreting geographic features to predict the effect of the terrain on relevant operations. Within this domain, *visibility analysis* focuses on line-of-sight and visibility. Visibility analysis is used in siting communication towers [19], military planning [14], archaeology [29] and urban planning [23].

For example, terrain analysis is critical to military planning. The US Army field manual states, "*Weather and terrain have more impact on battle than any other physical factor, including weapons, equipment or supplies*" [28]. Analysis of terrain is useful in designing defensive positions (to ensure that all avenues of attack are covered), and in planning safe routes for mobile forces (reducing visibility to hostile forces.) [11]

Visibility analysis requires considerable expertise [14]. Tools used have become sophisticated, often leading to complex user interfaces [6]. University courses and certificates are offered on the subject of learning how to perform terrain analysis (e.g., [16]). Visibility analysis is a cognitively challenging process involving the projection a 2D map representation of the terrain into a 3D mental model [14]. The analyst then must mentally query their terrain model to answer questions such as "how much of the map do these cellular towers cover?", or "from what parts of the town is this new apartment building visible?"

Existing Techniques for Visibility Analysis

Existing visibility analysis techniques have been developed within specialized tools for military planning, and as part of more general geographic information systems (GIS). Techniques were initially developed around paper maps, more recently evolving to sophisticated digital tools.

Paper Maps and Contour Lines

A contour line on a paper map denotes terrain of equal elevation. Multiple contour lines on a map can convey the shape of the terrain. Features of contour lines such as line weight, colour, type, and numbers can show additional information such as the elevation as a number [26].

When trying to find a safe route for vehicles through a combat zone, a military planner might use a contour map overlaid with an acetate sheet. The planner draws the route on the acetate with a marker, using the contour lines to visualize the visibility of vehicles following the route. This requires an ability to extract a mental model of the terrain from the map representation, a cognitively demanding task requiring significant expertise [14].

Digital Maps and Tabletops

Digital maps have enabled powerful tools to assist terrain analysis. Using digital elevation models, algorithms can determine line-of-sight information and generate 3D models of terrain [14]. Digital maps allow for user interaction such as showing and hiding information layers (e.g. population) and changing the scale of the map [7].

Multi-touch tabletops have also been proposed for map-based tasks, bringing advantages of a large space over which to view the map, and natural support for collaborative discussion of the map's content [3]. Recent

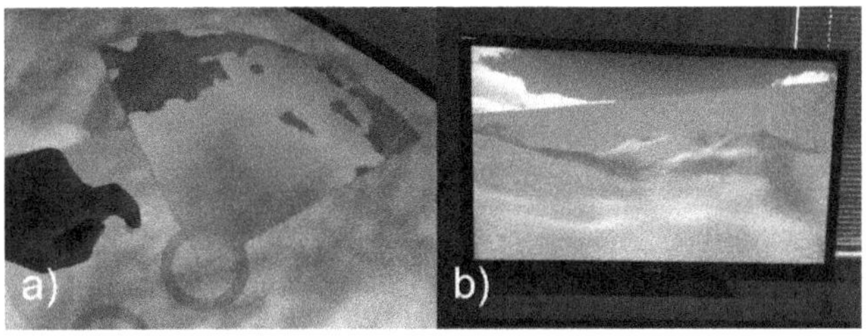

Figure 2. a) Colour-mapped elevation viewshed. b) The corresponding panoramic view.

tabletop tools such as Skyhunter [4] and DIGTable [15] allow users to explore the geographical properties of maps.

Mixed reality systems have been proposed to combine large displays with familiar physical devices for terrain analysis. Thumbles [18] provides physical pucks under robotic control to help with complex spatial layout problems such as telecommunication tower positioning. Thumbles is not intended to support general terrain analysis.

Interaction Techniques

Several interaction techniques have been developed for terrain visualization. The *viewshed* interaction technique shows what parts of the terrain are visible from a specific location on the map (Figure 2.a) [17]. Viewsheds are traditionally displayed as a 2D arc (pie slice) where visible terrain in shown in one colour and invisible terrain is shown in another colour. The viewshed tool provides answers to questions such as, "What places are visible from the given observation point?" and "How many places is the given observation point visible to?"

Viewshed tools in existing systems are typically cumbersome to use, requiring multi-step dialogues to specify and lengthy rendering times. For example, the viewshed tool in the popular GIS ArcGIS [30] takes seven parameters to operate, and depending on the task and computer hardware can take minutes to compute [10].

Panoramic views generate a 3D view of the terrain from a given perspective. 3D perspectives of digital terrains have been shown to give a better understanding of the shape of terrain and are generally preferred by users [10,13,24]. However, previous studies were performed with static images of 3D terrain and did not allow real-time updates. There has led to continuing debate on the types of analysis tasks that benefit from 3D perspectives [24].

Panoramic views and viewsheds can be complementary. For instance, when looking analyzing the Rocky Mountain landscape, Germino et al. found that 2D viewsheds were superior for quantifying the *dimensions* of a terrain (i.e. areal extent, relief, depth), while computer-generated 3D panoramic views at ground level performed better for representing the *composition* of a terrain (i.e. land cover, diversity, edge) [10]. The BUILD-IT system allows designers to view a virtual 3D representation of their workspace through a vertical display [8]. In the ABACUS military simulation tool, analysts can use the panorama tool to generate a soldier's first-person view [20]. Users must navigate a cumbersome dialogue to specify the desired view and then wait through a slow rendering phase.

Recent projects have used *tablets* to aid geospatial exploration and analysis. In Skyhunter, the user places a tablet on a tabletop to visualize seismic information corresponding to the geographic location underneath the tablet [4]. Tablets can act as Magic Lenses [2] to allow for the exploration of a 3D space or volume [25]. For example, the metaDesk [27] system uses a tethered arm-mounted magic lens to display a spatially contiguous 3D view of the MIT campus. Tablets have been shown to work well for exploring a 3D volume in combination with tabletops [25] when portability is important [4].

TERRAGUIDE

Existing digital tools for terrain analysis have made considerable advances over traditional paper-based approaches, allowing easier manipulation of maps using panning, zooming and providing visualizations such as viewsheds and panoramic views to aid analysis. However, existing systems fall short of integrating these tools in a fluid and fast experience. We have developed TerraGuide to explore how a multi-surface environment can allow users to easily combine different views of a terrain, allowing quick analysis where different interaction techniques are fluidly used in concert.

As shown in Figure 1, TerraGuide is composed of three surfaces: a large interactive tabletop, a vertical TV screen and a multi-touch tablet. The tabletop displays a top-down (planimetric) map. The user can move and rotate a number of viewshed widgets on the tabletop. A vertical display is located across from the user, and shows a panorama view from a first-person perspective. A tablet displays a *helicopter view,* showing parts of the terrain in a 3D view. We now describe the different views provided by the system, and how they are designed to fluidly work together.

Viewshed

TerraGuide includes a touch-based interactive widget implementing the viewshed visualization (Figure 2.a). The user places a viewshed anywhere on the terrain simply by touching and dragging it to the desired location on the 2D map. The viewshed can be rotated using a disk located around the widget. Viewsheds can be hidden (to reduce clutter) and revealed by tapping on the widget. In addition to visibility information, the viewshed displays elevation through a colour gradient. As in traditional terrain analysis applications, blue is mapped to low elevation, green to medium, and red to high elevation.

Unlike existing tools [10], TerraGuide's viewshed is rendered in real-time as it is dragged across the table. This is possible through a fast viewshed computation algorithm [17], and using an adaptive resolution where the viewshed is drawn in the best resolution possible while moving and high resolution while stable. This transforms how the viewshed can be used, allowing exploration of terrain visibility with simple dragging, as opposed to the careful planning of viewshed position required by traditional tools.

Panoramic View

In TerraGuide, the panoramic view is shown on a secondary display in front of the table (cf. vertical screen on Figure 1). It shows a 3D representation of the viewshed from a first-person perspective. The panoramic view shows the terrain from the origin of the viewshed, in the direction in which the viewshed is pointing. As the viewshed is moved or rotated, the panorama view updates in real-time. Points in the panorama view beyond the range of the viewshed are shown in grey fog to mimic distance limits in visibility, e.g., due to limits of human sight or transmission distance of a cellular tower.

Tablet-Based "Helicopter" View

A hand-held tablet shows a 3D view of the terrain in the style of a Magic Lens. Users can move the tablet over the table, and see the terrain as it appears from the perspective of the tablet's position and orientation. Moving and rotating the tablet changes the point of view of the 3D visualization that it displays. Intuitively, the tablet acts as a helicopter view, which the user can move around, to view the terrain from different angles.

The tablet view is synchronized with the tabletop, showing the terrain as it would appear if it rose in three dimensions from the table's surface. E.g., if the tablet is held obliquely to the table, it shows a panorama view similar to that of the secondary display. This allows quick exploration of terrain features by moving and rotating the tablet.

Rapid, Coupled Operation with Ease of Switching

The design of TerraGuide followed three principles. Views should be computed in real-time, allowing rapid exploration of the terrain without complex dialogues or noticeable rendering times. As discussed by Field et al. [9], the views on different surfaces should be tightly coupled, allowing them to be easily used in concert. In TerraGuide, all views are updated in real-time using simple interaction based on touch and hand motion. And finally, it should be easy to switch between views without loss of context or overhead of correlating information between the views.

As we have discussed, the views are coupled in two notable ways. First, the panoramic view is slaved to the last-used viewshed widget. A viewshed represents visibility and elevation information from the point of view of its origin. The panoramic view shows a first-person view of the terrain. As the widget is dragged or rotated, the panoramic view is updated. Therefore, a single touch-based drag or rotation controls both displays. This is significantly different from existing approaches where panoramic views are created explicitly using dialogues. Second, the tablet-based helicopter view is directly coupled to the map on the table, providing a 3D window onto the 2D table. Ease of switching between views is primarily supported by the tight coupling between the views, helping users retain context.

Implementation

TerraGuide was developed in C# using the Unity game engine. Views are synchronized using the Janus networking toolkit [21].

EVALUATION

TerraGuide was designed to allow people to fluidly move between different views represented on different surfaces, using whichever is most appropriate to their task. We intended that the combination of views and interaction techniques would enhance users' ability to perform terrain analysis tasks, and that the tight coupling of the views on the three surfaces would enable effective use of all three in concert. To determine whether these goals were met, we performed a user study consisting of two parts. The first assessed the effectiveness of combinations of the three techniques on task performance, user confidence and task load. The second involved an open-ended task to investigate users' strategies and preferences when using the three techniques together. This study led to interesting discoveries, such as that the overwhelmingly dominant strategy in the open-ended task involved the bi-manual use of the viewshed widget and the tablet helicopter view, and that the panoramic view increased users' confidence in their results, but did not improve their task performance.

Participants

We recruited 26 participants over the age of 18 (16 male, 10 female) from Queen's University. All participants regularly used touch devices. Part 1 took 25 minutes on average and part 2 took 15 minutes on average to complete.

PART 1: EFFECTIVENESS OF TERRAGUIDE TECHNIQUES

In the first part of the study, participants solved a simple terrain analysis problem using three different conditions: (1) viewshed only, (2) viewshed with panoramic view, and (3) viewshed with tablet view. They were trained on each condition with a practice map before starting the trials. Participants were instructed in how to use each technique and were allowed to practice until they felt comfortable using the system. Each condition was performed three times in a row on different maps for a total of 9 trials (12 including training). The conditions for task 1 were counter-balanced to reduce the impact of learning effects.

Task: Finding the Lowest and Highest Points

Participants were asked to perform a simple terrain analysis task, finding the highest and lowest points on a given terrain. To complete the task, participants dragged a red and a blue pin to what they thought was the highest and lowest locations on the map. Once satisfied with their placement of the pins, they indicated that the task was complete. Immediately after each trial they were asked to score their level of confidence in the correctness of their results. Participants completed questionnaires for each condition.

Measures

We assessed each condition based on: *completion time:* the time from the start of a trial until the participant specified he/she was done; *error:* the difference in heights between the participant's chosen points and the actual highest and lowest points on the map; *user confidence:* on a Likert scale ranging from 1 (no confidence) to 5 (fully confident); and *cognitive load:* measured through the NASA-TLX [12].

Apparatus

The interactive tabletop consisted of a 55" Sony television with a PQ Labs G4S infrared frame. The external vertical display was a Sony 46" television. A Microsoft Surface 2 provided the tablet view, which was tracked using four V100:R2 OptiTrack cameras.

Results

Our results compare the three conditions sets: viewshed alone (*ViewshedAlone*), viewshed and panorama view (*ViewshedPano*), and viewshed and tablet (*ViewshedTab*). We now summarize these results in terms of task completion time, error, confidence and cognitive load.

Task Completion Time

We defined completion time as the time it took each user to complete the task in seconds. A one-way within-subjects ANOVA was conducted with the factor of technique-set. The results indicated a significant effect on completion time, Wilk's Lambda=.68, $F(2,24)=5.76$, $p<.01$,

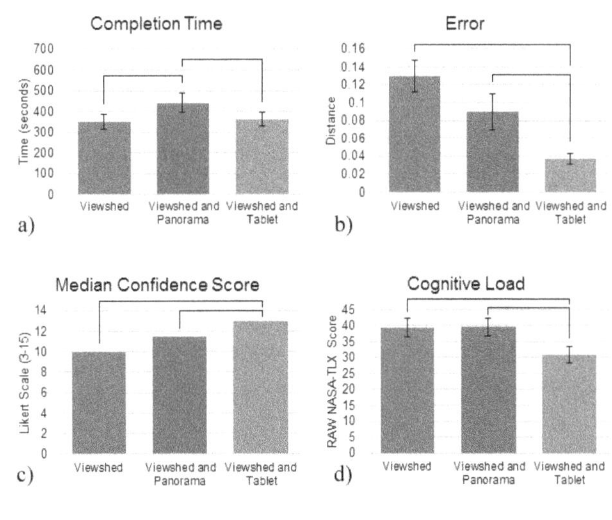

Figure 3. Graphs showing the techniques' performance in a) completion time, b) error, c) median confidence summing results of three trials, and d) cognitive load. Error bars show standard error and hats indicate significant difference.

multivariate $\eta^2=.32$.

A paired-samples *t*-test with a Bonferroni adjustment was conducted to evaluate effects on completion time. The mean completion time for *ViewshedPano* ($M=441.6$, $SD=231$) was significantly longer than *ViewshedTab* ($M=362.3$, $SD=164.2$, $d=.4$), $p<.03$, and *ViewshedAlone* ($M=353.1$, $SD=175.5$, $d=.4$), $p<.01$. I.e., participants were slower when using the *Panorama* view than when using the *Tablet* or *Viewshed* alone conditions (Figure 3.a). Cohen's *d* suggests a moderate effect size on this slow-down.

Error

A one-way within-subjects ANOVA was conducted with the factor of technique-set. The results indicated a significant effect on error, Wilk's Lambda=.42, $F(2,24)=16.4$, $p<.01$, multivariate $\eta^2=.58$. A paired-samples *t*-test using Bonferroni adjustment indicates that the mean difference in error when using *ViewshedTab* ($M=0.037$, $SD=0.03$) was significantly less than when using *ViewshedPano* ($M=0.09$, $SD=0.1$, $d=0.71$), $p<.02$ and *ViewshedAlone* ($M=0.13$, $SD=0.09$, $d=1.4$), $p<.01$ (Figure 3.b). Cohen's *d* shows a moderate to strong effect.

That is, using the tablet view together with viewshed, participants were able to find the highest point with significantly less error than when using the viewshed and panoramic view or the viewshed alone.

Confidence

Confidence was based on the participant's response to: *"Indicate the degree of confidence you have in the placement of your flags"*, using a scale of 1 (no confidence) to 5 (full confidence).

A Friedman test was conducted to evaluate differences in medians among the confidence levels when using *ViewshedAlone* ($MD=10$), *ViewshedPano* ($MD=11.5$), and *ViewshedTab* ($MD=13$). The test was significant, $\chi^2=18.24$, $p<.01$. The Kendal coefficient of concordance was .351, indicating moderate differences between the three conditions. Follow-up pairwise comparisons were conducted using a Wilcoxon test. The median confidence level for *ViewshedTab* was significantly higher than for *ViewshedPano* ($p<.02$) and *ViewshedAlone*, ($p<.01$). Also, participants were significantly more confident using *ViewshedPano* than *ViewshedAlone* ($p<.01$).

In sum, participants were more confident when using the panorama view and viewshed than when using the viewshed alone, and more confident yet when using the tablet and viewshed (Figure 3.c).

Cognitive Load

Cognitive load was based on NASA-TLX [12] scores for each of the technique sets. A one-way within-subjects ANOVA was conducted with the factor of technique set. A significant effect was found on cognitive load, Wilk's Lambda=.4, $F(2,24)=17.74$, $p<.01$, multivariate $\eta^2=.6$.

A paired-samples *t* test using Bonferroni correction indicated that the mean cognitive load for *ViewshedTab* (M=30.97, SD=13.3) was significantly lower than for *ViewshedPano* (M=39.53, SD=14.5, d=0.6), p<.01 and *ViewshedAlone* (M=39.38, SD=14.1, d=0.6), p<.01. Further, the Cohen's *d* suggests a moderate to high effect.

That is, participants' cognitive load was significantly lower when using the tablet and viewshed combination than when using the viewshed alone or the panorama view together with the viewshed (Figure 3.d).

Discussion

The results clearly show that the tablet plus viewshed condition outperformed the other two conditions. The presence of the tablet increased participants' confidence in their results, while reducing error and cognitive load. The use of the tablet had no effect on task completion time. This indicates that participants were able to successfully interpret terrain data using the tablet's "helicopter" view, and that any disadvantage in having to use two surfaces to solve the task was outweighed by the advantages the two views conferred.

Conversely, the presence of the panorama view did not enhance participants' performance. Compared to the viewshed alone, adding the panorama offered no improvement to error or cognitive load. Task completion time was worsened. Interestingly, participants' confidence in their results improved, despite the fact that their error did not improve.

With the viewshed alone, participants were able to complete the task as quickly (or quicker) than the other conditions, despite only approximately 10 minutes of training on what to them was a new interaction technique. This also implies that the viewshed is usable by non-experts.

PART 2: STRATEGIES IN REALISTIC TERRAIN ANALYSIS

In the second part of the study, participants were asked to use all three techniques (viewshed, panoramic view, and

Figure 4. User placing a watchtower (viewshed) to cover the red points of interest. Note the green point on the left of the viewshed indicating the point is in line-of-sight of the tower.

tablet) at the same time in a more complex terrain analysis task. The participants and apparatus remained the same as in part 1. Participants first familiarized themselves with the system by solving a sample task on a training map. They then completed the task six times on different maps.

Task: Watchtower Positioning

Participants were instructed to place three watchtowers around a terrain to cover six points of interest. This task required them to synthesize information over the entire map. As seen in Figure 4, a "watchtower" was represented by a viewshed widget and a "point of interest" was represented by a red circle on the terrain. The point of interest changed colour from red to green when it was in line-of-sight of a watchtower.

Procedure

Participants completed the task six times on six different maps. We video-recorded all trials. Following the session, participants completed a custom questionnaire to assess their preferences, and participated in a semi-structured interview.

We used an open coding process to analyze the videos and identify behaviours and events. Of the 26 participants, 25 videos were collected. One participant's video was not recorded due to technical difficulties. We randomly chose videos from 10 of the 26 participants for detailed coding, representing 22 minutes and 17 seconds of video. From these 10 videos, common strategies were determined. Two researchers performed less detailed video coding on the remaining 15 videos in order to identify instances of these common strategies. Conflicts were resolved through discussion between the researchers performing the coding.

Our detailed video coding followed the scheme showed on Table 1. Each action was coded over 3 dimensions: technique used, action type and the body part involved. Example events were *Viewshed 2 macro movement with left hand*, or *Panorama looked with head*. The action type dimension specifies the type of manipulation executed by users. For example, *Micro* and *Macro* distinguish between small versus large movements of a viewshed.

We coded interaction with the fourth map completed, allowing the participants enough time to have determined a preferred strategy. This map was difficult enough that it could not be solved moving around viewsheds randomly and hoping to find a solution by luck, but required actual analysis of the terrain.

Technique Used	Viewshed (1,2,3), Panorama, Tablet
Action Type	Micro, Macro, Rotate, Search, Still, Look
Body Part	Head, Left Hand, Right Hand

Table 1. Dimensions of coding scheme.

Strategy Name	Num. Users	Sweeping
Bi-manual viewshed/tablet alone	11	0
Table first then bi-manual viewshed/tablet	8*	8
Tablet first then bi-manual viewshed/tablet	6	1

Table 2. Number of participants using each strategy. *Two of eight participants put the tablet down to use the viewshed.

Results

Our detailed video coding revealed that participants took on average 2 minutes and 13 seconds to complete the task (*SD*=94 seconds). They switched frequently between techniques, on average 13 times throughout the task (*SD*=9). The table was used on average 6.6 times during the task (*SD*=4.3), or 71% of total time; participants physically interacted with the viewshed widgets for on average 59 seconds per trial (*SD*=41), representing 57% of their total time. The tablet was used 5.4 times on average (*SD*=3.9), or 28% of total time. Finally, the panoramic view was used 0.9 times on average (*SD*=2), representing 1% of total time.

Our results showed a dominant strategy of bi-manual use of viewshed and tablet. Minority uses involved first using the tablet for an extended period, or using the table first for an extended period, before switching to the combined viewshed/tablet strategy. The distribution of these strategies over participants is summarized in Table 2. With both the viewshed and the tablet, participants frequently adopted a sweeping motion, allowing real-time exploration of the terrain. Questionnaires showed a clear preference for tablet over the panoramic view. In the next section, we detail the strategies we observed and report participants' preferences.

Bi-Manual Viewshed and Tablet

23 of 25 participants adopted a bi-manual strategy, where they used the viewshed with one hand, and the tablet with the other, shifting their view between them. Figure 6 shows an

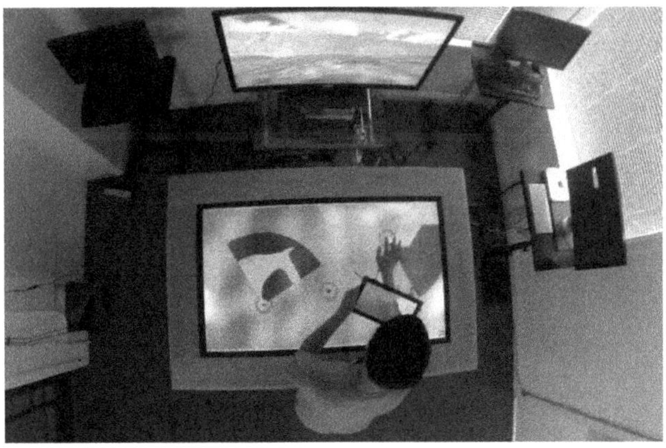

Figure 6. Participant demonstrating bi-manual use of the tablet and viewshed.

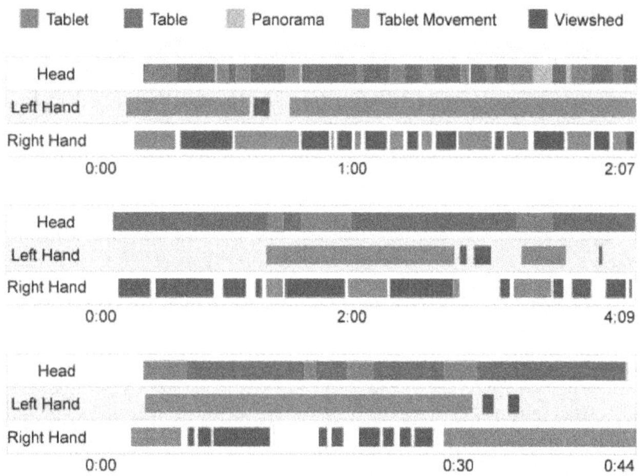

Figure 5. Strategies: a) Bi-manual; b) Table-first, then moving between tablet and viewshed – note two-handed use of tablet; c) Tablet-first, then bi-manual.

example of this strategy. Participants switched between attending to the viewshed and the tablet on average 12.1 times when performing the task. The table was used for intervals of 16.1 seconds on average, while the tablet was used in intervals of 6.5 seconds on average. An example of a video coded bi-manual strategy is shown in Figure 5a.

The remaining two participants used a variant of the bi-manual strategy. Rather than holding the tablet in their hands while interacting with the viewshed, they instead placed the tablet on the wooden edge of the table when using the viewshed, then picked the tablet up and used it with both hands, then put it down again to return to the viewshed. This variant moved back and forth between the interaction techniques, as with the truly bi-manual strategy.

The bi-manual approach allowed participants to see detailed visibility using the viewshed together with the 3D perspective of the tablet view. Participant 24 explained, *"I started off with the tablet, seeing where the points were. Then I tried a couple points with the viewshed, I'd see if I could actually see the points from where I thought I could with the tablet. If I couldn't, I'd either try fine-tuning it if I could, or I'd use the tablet again to see if there were any other points I could use."*

Table-First

Eight of 25 participants used a *Table-first* approach where they used the table for an extended period at the start of the task. On average, these participants used the table for 74 seconds before moving to the bi-manual strategy.

Some participants adopted this strategy in hope of completing the task without actually analyzing the terrain. Users swept the viewshed around, hoping for a solution. Participant 0 explained, *"I decided the distribution of the points where I would put the viewsheds, and then by chance see if I could get it, then if I couldn't, I would use the tablet to see if there is a mountain close by it could go on top of, or see why they're hidden."* Our map was sufficiently complex that this strategy did not work, forcing participants to change strategy (for 6 participants to bi-manual, and for two to the strategy of moving between tablet and viewshed, but holding the tablet in both hands when in use – an example of the latter strategy is shown in Figure 5b). Participant 10 explained: *"Initially I tried with just the viewshed, and then once I realized that it was really important to be able to see depth, I just started using the combination of the viewshed and the tablet."*

Tablet First

Six participants used a *Tablet First* strategy, involving an extended use of the tablet at the beginning of the task. These participants used the tablet for 15 seconds on average before switching to the bi-manual strategy (Figure 5c).

Participants reported that the tablet was easy to use and aided navigation through the terrain. Participant 0 stated, *"I liked the tablet because I could do a quick sweep of the terrain, and then I understood what I was looking at as a whole"*. Participant 16 said: *"The motion tracking made it really intuitive to use."* Participant 11 commented on the tablet's ease of use: *"The tablet was the best. It's a lot easier to see when you can just move the tablet around."* These comments are consistent with our findings from task 1 that the use of the tablet reduced users' cognitive load.

This strategy allowed users to get a big-picture view of the terrain. Participant 18 stated, "*[I used it] for getting a general lay of the land. It really helps in an intuitive sense to figure out where you have hills or valleys, where you are going to have the most occlusion."* Participants then moved to the bi-manual approach, already having ideas of potential locations for success and areas to avoid.

Panoramic View

These three strategies indicate the success of the viewshed and tablet views. The panoramic view, on the other hand, received minimal use, accounting for only 1% of the participants' time. In interviews, participants complained about discomfort when using the panoramic view. Participant 9 commented, *"I felt really dizzy"* and, *"It gave me a headache, and I felt that it was easier to see where I want to place my towers using the tablet"*.

The panoramic view was located in front of the participant, showing the terrain from the perspective of the viewshed. Therefore, the orientation of the panoramic view did not always match the orientation of the participant, requiring the participant to mentally reorient the view on the terrain to match that of the panoramic view.

Participants found that the tablet provided similar information to the panoramic view, but more effectively. 16 stated that they felt the panoramic view was not useful when the tablet was available. Participant 8 said, *"The tablet kind of made the panoramic view a little bit useless."* Participant 23 said, *"I could get all the information provided by the panorama on the tablet, but faster."*

Viewshed Sweeping

Nine participants displayed a *sweeping* behaviour with the viewshed where they made large circular movements around an area of interest. Nine participants used sweeping an average of 3.2 times each (*SD*=2.8). As shown in Table 2, all eight participants that used the *Table First* strategy also used the viewshed sweeping behaviour. One participant used sweeping during a *Tablet First* strategy. By taking advantage of the real-time nature of the viewshed widget, participants were able to quickly sweep the terrain to get a general sense of its elevation. Participant 0 explained, "*I would do a quick sweep with the viewshed, then I had a couple areas that I was interested in"*

Participant Preferences

Participants indicated their preferences through questionnaires. The majority felt that the viewshed alone would have been sufficient to carry out the task. When asked: "*Do you think you could have completed part 2 with the viewshed alone?*" 5 of 26 participants answered "*Yes*" and 21 answered, "*Yes, but longer*".

Participants overwhelmingly preferred the tablet to the panoramic view. When asked; "*If you had to choose one technique to use with the viewshed, which would you choose?*" 24 participants chose the tablet and two chose the panoramic view. When asked, "*Did you ever forget about a technique?*" 13 of 26 participants said they forgot about the panoramic view, two forgot about the tablet view and 11 did not forget any techniques. When asked, "*Was the panoramic view still useful when given the tablet to use?*" 16 replied with "No." These responses are consistent with the dominant adoption of the bi-manual use of the viewshed and tablet, and low usage of the panoramic view.

Participants believed the tablet to be the most efficient way to get a sense of the general topography. When asked "*To best understand the overall shape of the terrain I found it best to use...*" 17 of 26 participants specified the tablet, two chose the panoramic view and seven stated they used all three techniques. Similarly, when asked; "*Was there any technique that allowed you to perform the task quicker?*" 17 participants chose the tablet while nine indicated "*No.*"

IMPLICATIONS FOR DESIGN

TerraGuide is one of few multi-surface environments designed around a concrete application domain. As such, our experience in designing TerraGuide are of interest to other designers of multi-surface environments.

Where TerraGuide Succeeded and Failed

All users of TerraGuide were able to effectively use the three interaction techniques the system provides, and were able to successfully switch between the different surfaces implementing these techniques. Participants' comfort with attending to and manipulating multiple surfaces is convincingly demonstrated by the adoption of a bi-manual use of the tablet and viewshed by 23 of 25 participants (and where the other two participants used a variant on this strategy.) Participants moved fluidly and frequently between the tabletop and tablet. Rather than introducing a cognitive barrier, NASA TLX scores showed that the combined use of these two surfaces had a lower cognitive load than use of the viewshed alone.

Moreover, this combination of surfaces proved easy to learn. With only a few minutes of training, participants were able to use all aspects of the system to complete complex analysis tasks.

Our results also show that simply providing multiple surfaces supporting different interaction techniques is not a guarantee of success. Our panoramic view, as seen in study part 1, increased completion time with no commensurate decrease in error (although user confidence was increased). Study part 2 showed that given the choice, users prefer the tablet over the panorama because of its simplicity in navigation.

Over all, this indicates that systems based on optical tracking for movement and navigation like the tablet can provide significant benefit to task performance, error, and confidence, and are therefore worthy of consideration despite the complexity and cost of their implementation. Recently, optical tracking systems have become considerably less expensive, for example based on the consumer-priced Kinect camera [4].

Revisiting TerraGuide's Design Principles

We used TerraGuide to explore three design principles for systems supporting real-time spatial analysis: views should be computed in real-time, views should be tightly-coupled, and switching between surfaces should be easy. We now discuss insights from our experience with TerraGuide.

Views Should be Computed in Real-Time

One of our key technical advances over existing GIS systems is that views (particularly the viewshed and panoramic view) are computed in real-time, allowing rapid exploration of the terrain without complex dialogues or noticeable rendering times. This allowed participants to use both the viewshed and the tablet to perform *sweeping* actions over the terrain to gain a rapid overview of elevation and line-of-sight.

Thus, in addition to general streamlining of interaction, the real-time update of views enabled a new form of exploratory behaviour. Real-time updating was only possible because our viewshed computation was performed in low resolution when the viewshed was in motion. The benefit of sweeping must therefore be balanced with this lower fidelity while the sweeping is being performed.

Views Should Be Tightly-Coupled

We hypothesized that tightly coupling the views on different surfaces would simplify their use in combination. TerraGuide shows one example where this tight coupling was successful, and one where it was not.

Coupling the tablet's view to its physical position over the tabletop allows users to move between the table and tablet views rapidly, frequently, and with low cognitive overhead. The near unanimous adoption of bi-manual interaction shows that participants were able to effectively work with both views in concert. Conversely, participants struggled to interpret and use the panoramic view, whose use increased task completion time. The panoramic display was coupled with the position and orientation of the viewshed on the table, requiring users to mentally rotate the terrain to match these differing perspectives. Perhaps the panoramic view would have been more successful had it been controlled separately, rather than tightly-coupled with the viewshed.

Switching Between Views Should Be Easy

As we have discussed, participants made on average 12 switches between tablet and viewshed over their three-minute trials. This allays the fear that in multi-surface environments, users will be overwhelmed with too much choice, and with the overhead of switching between different devices. Ease of switching in this case is primarily a consequence of the tight coupling of the views, allowing users to switch between devices without loss of context, combined with the ease of holding the tablet in one hand while manipulating the viewshed in the other.

In sum, TerraGuide illustrates how these three design principles can lead to an effective use of multiple surfaces that leads to improved performance together with enthusiastic reception from users.

CONCLUSION

In this paper, we addressed problems of terrain analysis through a novel multi-surface environment consisting of three tools for terrain analysis: a real-time viewshed, a panoramic view, and a tablet-based helicopter view. The system exemplifies three design principles: views should display information in real-time, views should be tightly coupled, and switching between views should be easy.

We evaluated TerraGuide and its use as a multi-surface environment through a two-part user study. The results indicated that the tablet-based helicopter view allowed users to perform terrain analysis faster and with less error, while simultaneously lowering cognitive load and increasing confidence. The panoramic view, however, increased completion time with no improvement in error. We saw four strategies in the use of the techniques, including a near-unanimous adoption of bi-manual use of the tablet and tabletop.

Multi-surface environments are complex systems that enable powerful new interactions. Our three design principles led to the successful, effective use of multiple techniques that increased user performance. However, we discovered that simply presenting information on multiple interactive surfaces does not guarantee success.

ACKNOWLEDGEMENTS

We gratefully acknowledge the financial support of the SurfNet NSERC Strategic Network and the GRAND Network of Centres of Excellence.

REFERENCES

1. BC Search and Rescue Association, Rescue Techniques, 2014. [Online]. Available: http://www.bcsara.com/sar-groups/rescue-techniques/. [Accessed: 09-Sep-2014].
2. E. A. Bier, M. C. Stone, K. Pier, W. Buxton, and T. D. DeRose, Toolglass and magic lenses: the see-through interface, in *Computer graphics and interactive techniques*, (1993), 73–80.
3. C. Bortolaso, M. Oskamp, T.C.N. Graham, and D. Brown, OrMiS: a tabletop interface for simulation based training, *ITS '13*, (2013), pp. 145–154.
4. C. Burns, T. Seyed, F. Maurer, and M. Sousa, Multi-Surface Visualization of Fused Hydrocarbon Microseep and Reservoir Data, *GeoConvention*, (2012), pp. 2–5.
5. D. Caldwell and M. Mineter, Analysis and visualization of visibility surfaces, *GeoComputation*, (2003).
6. C. Davies and D. Medyckyj-Scott, GIS Usability: Recommendation Based on the User's View, *Int. J. Geogr. Inf. Syst.*, (1994), vol. 8, no. 2, pp. 175–189.
7. J. Detwiler, Internet Maps vs. Paper Maps, *The Pennsylvania State University*, 2014. [Online]. Available: https://www.e-education.psu.edu/geog863/print/book/export/html/1912 [Accessed: 09-Sep-2014].
8. Fjeld, M., Bichsel, M., and Rauterberg, M. BUILD-IT : a brick-based tool for direct interaction. *4*, 1, 205–212.
9. Fjeld, M., Lauche, K., Bichsel, M., Voorhorst, F., Krueger, H., and Rauterberg, M. Physical and Virtual Tools: Activity Theory Applied to the Design of Groupware. *CSCW 11*, 1-2 (2002), 153–180.
10. M. J. Germino, W. a. Reiners, B. J. Blasko, D. McLeod, and C. T. Bastian, Estimating visual properties of Rocky Mountain landscapes using GIS, *Landsc. Urban Plan.*, (2001), vol. 53, no. 1–4, pp. 71–83.
11. C. Grindle, M. Lewis, R. Glinton, J. Giampapa, S. Owens, and K. Sycara, Automating Terrain Analysis: Algorithms for Intelligence Preparation of the Battlefield, *Hum. Factors Ergon. Soc. Annu. Meet.*, (2004) vol. 48, no. 3, pp. 533–537.
12. S. G. Hart, NASA-task load index (NASA-TLX); 20 years later, in *Hum. Factors Ergon. Soc. Annu. Meet.*, 2006, vol. 50, no. 9, pp. 904–908.
13. John, M. S., Cowen, M. B., Smallman, H. S., & Oonk, The use of 2D and 3D displays for shape-understanding versus relative-position tasks, in *The Journal of the Hum. Factors Ergon. Soc.*, (2001), 79–98.
14. Y. J. Kim and C. M. Hoffmann, Enhanced battlefield visualization for situation awareness, *Comput. & Graph.*, (2003), vol. 27, no. 6, pp. 873–885.
15. K. Kobayashi, A. Narita, M. Hirano, K. Tanaka, T. Katada, and N. Kuwasawa, DIGTable: a tabletop simulation system for disaster education, in *Pervasive Computing*, (2008), pp. 57–60.
16. Nipissing University, GEOG 4106 Terrain Analysis, 2014. [Online]. Available: http://www.nipissingu.ca/calendar/Pages/Course.aspx?CourseName=GEOG-4106. [Accessed: 09-Sep-2014].
17. D. O'Sullivan and A. Turner, Visibility graphs and landscape visibility analysis, *Int. J. Geogr. Inf. Syst.*, (2001).
18. Patten, J. and Ishii, H. Mechanical constraints as computational constraints in tabletop tangible interfaces. *CHI '07*, (2007), 809.
19. S. Popelka and V. Vozenilek, Landscape Visibility Analysis and Their Visualisation, *ISPRS Arch.*, (2010).
20. Raytheon, ABACUS (Advanced Battlefield Computer Simulation). [Online]. Available: www.raytheon.com. [Accessed: 09-Sep-2014].
21. C. Savery and T.C.N. Graham, Timelines: simplifying the programming of lag compensation for the next generation of networked games, *Multimed. Syst.*, vol. 19, no. 3, pp. 271–287, Jun. 2012.
22. A. S. D. Scott, A. Allavena, K. Cerar, G. Franck, M. Hazen, T. Shuter, C. Colliver, and S. D. Scott, Investigating Tabletop Interfaces to Support Collaborative Decision-Making in Maritime Operations, 2010.
23. M. Sevenant and M. Antrop, Settlement models, land use and visibility in rural landscapes: Two case studies in Greece, *Landsc. Urban Plan.*, (2007), vol. 80, no. 4, pp. 362–374.
24. H. S. Smallman, M. St. John, H. M. Oonk, and M. B. Cowen, Information availability in 2D and 3D displays, *IEEE Comput. Graph. Appl.*, (2001) vol. 21, no. 4, pp. 51–57.
25. M. Spindler and R. Dachselt, PaperLens: Advanced Magic Lens Interaction Above the Tabletop, in *ITS '09*, (2009), p. 7.
26. J. C. Tracy, *Plane surveying: a text-book and pocket manual*. J. Wiley & Sons, (1907), p. 794.
27. Ullmer, B. and Ishii, H. The metaDESK: models and prototypes for tangible user interfaces. *Proceedings of the 10th annual ACM symposium on …*, (1997).
28. US Army, Field Manual, in *Operations*, Washington, DC: US Government Printing Office, (1982), pp. 100–5.
29. S. J. Winterbottom and D. Long, From abstract digital models to rich virtual environments: landscape contexts in Kilmartin Glen, Scotland, *J. Archaeol. Sci.*, (2006), vol. 33, no. 10, pp. 1356–1367.
30. ArcGIS. [Online]. Available: www.arcgis.com. [Accessed: 09-Sep-2014]

Lightweight Relief Shearing for Enhanced Terrain Perception on Interactive Maps

Wesley Willett
Inria / University of Calgary
wesley.willett@ucalgary.ca

Bernhard Jenny
Oregon State University
jennyb@geo.oregonstate.edu

Tobias Isenberg, Pierre Dragicevic
Inria
[tobias.isenberg,pierre.dragicevic]@inria.fr

ABSTRACT
We explore interactive relief shearing, a set of non-intrusive, direct manipulation interactions that expose depth and shape information in terrain maps using ephemeral animations. Reading and interpreting topography and relief on terrain maps is an important aspect of map use, but extracting depth information from 2D maps is notoriously difficult. Modern mapping software attempts to alleviate this limitation by presenting digital terrain using 3D views. However, 3D views introduce occlusion, complicate distance estimations, and typically require more complex interactions. In contrast, our approach reveals depth information via shearing animations on 2D maps, and can be paired with existing interactions such as pan and zoom. We examine explicit, integrated, and hybrid interactions for triggering relief shearing and present a version that uses device tilt to control depth effects. Our evaluation shows that these interactive techniques improve depth perception when compared to standard 2D and perspective views.

Author Keywords
Relief shearing; terrain maps; depth perception; interaction; plan oblique relief.

ACM Classification Keywords
H.5.2. Information Interfaces and Presentation:
User Interfaces—*Input devices and strategies.*

INTRODUCTION AND MOTIVATION
Topography and elevation are among the most important pieces of information on many maps, yet interpreting terrain from two-dimensional topographic maps is challenging for many users [21]. Traditionally, cartographers attempted to make terrain more accessible by using relief representations such as contour lines, shaded relief, and elevation coloring [11]. Most modern computational mapping tools still use these same representations or display terrain using 3D perspective views (e.g., Google Earth). These 3D views facilitate more immediate perception of the shape of terrain, but introduce occlusions and perspective distortions that complicate distance and elevation estimation. In addition, 3D views often require users to control the camera, which can be cumbersome and disorienting.

CHI 2015, April 18–23, 2015, Seoul, Republic of Korea.

ACM 978-1-4503-3145-6/15/04 ...$15.00.
http://dx.doi.org/10.1145/2702123.2702172

We explore *interactive relief shearing*, a set of non-intrusive, direct manipulation interactions (Figure 1) that expose depth and shape information in terrain maps using brief ephemeral animations. Based on this principle, we contribute a set of new, lightweight interaction techniques that use motion to enhance the perception of depth but remain compatible with the hardware and interaction techniques used for most 2D maps. We also describe two experiments in which we compared these techniques to existing interaction and rendering approaches. We find that relief-shearing animations improve users' ability to perceive depth, both when maps are animated automatically and when animations are connected to panning interactions. We also show that maps with interactive relief shearing help users make more accurate elevation judgments than either standard shaded relief maps or 3D perspective views.

BACKGROUND
Our work builds on prior research in relief rendering, 3D representation, and interaction.

Relief Rendering Techniques
Historically, communicating the shape and geometrical complexity of terrain in orthographic maps has been one of the biggest challenges faced by cartographers. In response, mapmakers have developed a range of techniques for representing elevation including contour lines, spot heights, shaded relief, and elevation coloring. Contour lines are difficult to read compared to other techniques [19, 21], but with training it is possible to extract absolute elevations by interpolating between lines. Spot heights and soundings, meanwhile, are useful for showing the elevations of select points but they cannot portray the continuity of the terrain surface [19]. Relief shading or

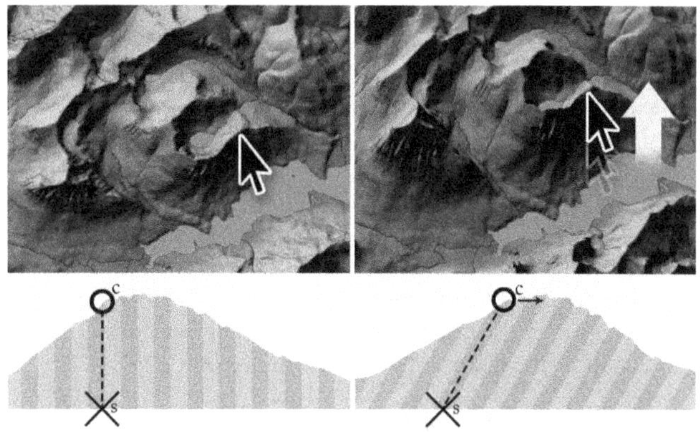

Figure 1. Using *explicit* interactive relief shearing, the user grabs a point on the map (left) and drags it upward (right). The base of the terrain model stays in place, but the model is sheared so that the selected point remains under the cursor, revealing the shape of the terrain. When released, the map animates back to the original un-sheared position.

"hill shading", a technique where terrain is shaded to simulate the highlights and shadows produced by a light source, is widely used on modern maps including many digital mapping services. This approach, pioneered by Swiss cartographers in the late 19th century and further refined and documented by cartographers like Eduard Imhof [11], uses natural visual cues to suggest the shape of the terrain. Similarly, elevation coloring (or "hypsometric tinting") uses color gradients to visualize terrain elevation. Colors may be modulated with illumination to more clearly illustrate shaded and illuminated terrain slopes. Relief shading and elevation coloring provide only relative elevation, but are easier and faster to read than contour lines and portray the terrain as a continuous surface [4, 19, 20].

Even for contemporary mapmakers, representing terrain in a map requires compromising between clearly conveying the shape of the terrain and communicating other information. For example, colorful stepped hypsometric tints can make elevation comparisons easier, but they also make it harder to use color elsewhere on the map. Imhof recommends a number of combinations of techniques appropriate for various map scales [11, chap. 14b]. However, even if contour lines, spot heights, relief shading, and hypsometric tinting are combined well it can still be difficult for many users of 2D maps to compare elevations or to understand the overall shape of terrain.

Alternatively, elevation information can be represented by applying projections that deviate from the traditional, orthographic top-down views—such as perspective, cylindrical, or oblique projections [12]. Mapmakers may also create views that distort the underlying map to emphasize specific terrain features [6, 13]. The panorama maps often used to show ski slopes are a common example of this technique. These types of maps are widely used and preferred by many map users—largely because the sides and edges of features more closely resemble what viewers see when looking at the actual terrain. Unfortunately, distorting or projecting terrain typically introduces occlusions which obscure portions of the map and can impede distance and area judgments.

Insights from Perceptual Psychology

While the problem of conveying terrain relief has been studied for several centuries, the mechanisms of 3D shape perception are barely starting to be fully understood. We now know that humans infer 3D shape from shading, gradients of texture, contour, binocular disparity (stereopsis), and motion [25]. Cartographers have extensively used—or experimented with [3]—all these cues except for motion, which has been mostly disregarded. Yet motion is known in perceptual psychology to be one of the most important sources of depth information. Depth information from motion can be inferred quickly, in less than a second [18], although findings remain controversial as to which of these cues is the most effective [26]. The extraction of 3D structure from motion has been given different names depending on the conditions under which it occurs [28], here we refer to the general phenomenon as *kinetic depth*.

Computer-Supported Map Exploration

Compared to early hand-drawn maps, computers dramatically expanded the range of possibilities for representing terrain relief. Maps can now be automatically generated, making it easier to explore more advanced relief rendering techniques. Dynamic animated and interactive displays as well as advanced input and output hardware also provide new opportunities for map rendering, but introduce new challenges for interaction.

2D Map Displays. Most applications that display 2D maps support a set of simple interaction techniques for navigation. Typically, navigation techniques are meant to emulate the way people examine paper maps: panning moves the map around, while zooming adjusts the map's distance to the user. On multitouch devices, most map applications let users pan, zoom, and rotate content using similar "drag" and "pinch" interactions. However, when terrain is displayed in map applications, relief information is just as difficult to extract as from traditional paper maps and depends heavily on graphical cues like shading.

3D Map Displays. Other map applications such as Google Earth offer dynamically rendered perspective views of terrain and 3D navigation techniques. This approach has several advantages for relief perception. First, perspective rendering can reveal terrain from viewpoints that make it easier for users to understand its shape. Second, interacting with 3D maps provides kinetic depth cues that can immediately reveal complex terrain structures.

However, 3D map displays also have a number of limitations. In particular, interacting with full 3D views can be more complicated than with 2D representations because it requires the user to manage more degrees of freedom [23]. In addition, 2D interactions do not translate into unambiguous movements in 3D space and complex 3D rotations can make it complicated to obtain the desired view. As a result, camera control can often distract users from their primary task. In response, prior research on 3D navigation has suggested adding constraints to reduce the number of degrees of freedom [23, 24]. Applications like Google Earth only allow users to control heading (rotation around z) and pitch (rotation around x), while Apple Maps and the web-based Google Maps default to toggling the pitch between a few fixed inclinations. Other research has focused on devising more direct 2D-to-3D interaction mappings (e.g, [2, 22]) which, while effective, remain more complicated than traditional map interactions.

Advanced Display and Input Hardware. Over the past few decades, researchers have also explored a number of display technologies for better conveying depth [16] including stereoscopic, autostereoscopic (3D without glasses), and volumetric displays. Stereoscopic displays have made their way to cinemas and home theaters, while autostereoscopic displays are now available on mass-market mobile devices like Nintendo's 3DS. These displays provide a vivid impression of depth and can heighten a user's sense of immersion. However, it does not appear that viewers are able to extract more information from stereopsis than from kinetic depth [25, 26]. While volumetric displays and other spatialized techniques seemingly outperform stereoscopic displays on depth judgment tasks [9], the technology remains bulky and expensive.

In summary, prior work in cartography has largely focused on 2D techniques for representing depth. More recent advances in 3D display technologies have led to an increased focus on reproducing realistic 3D views, often resulting in more com-

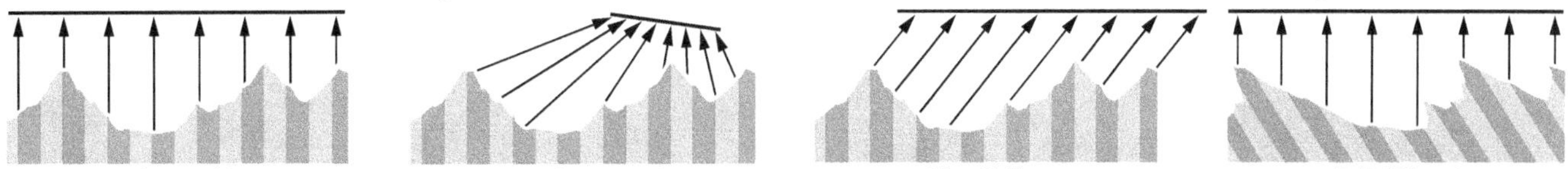

Figure 2. Projections for rendering terrain. Plan oblique relief and relief shearing create the same visual result, but differ in construction.

plex interactions. Meanwhile, kinetic depth, which perceptual psychology has shown to be a key element of 3D structure extraction, has not been used to its full potential. We explore a family of simple and lightweight interaction techniques that provide depth cues using kinetic depth and remain compatible with existing interactive maps.

INTERACTIVE RELIEF SHEARING

Our approach, which we refer to as *interactive relief shearing*, uses shearing animations that enhance depth perception for terrain maps. Interactive relief shearing provides many of the benefits of 3D views—users can view terrain from alternate angles that more closely resemble what they see in the real world and the maps provide kinetic depth information that improves perception of the terrain's shape. However, this approach also preserves many of the benefits of using 2D terrain maps—interactions remain simple and the map always returns to a standard orthographic view, making distance and area measurements easier.

Maps with *relief shearing* are identical to maps with *plan oblique relief* (Figure 2), a parallel projection technique in which the image plane is translated relative to the ground plane [12]. While Jenny and Patterson [12] coined the term *plan oblique relief* based on the concept of a translated image plane for ray-tracing, we achieve the effect by linearly shearing points in the model in x and y directions based on their elevation. Both techniques produce views in which low-elevation points remain near their original positions, but higher-elevation points are shifted laterally. This exposes the sides of terrain features and emphasizes ridges, saddles, and other terrain features that are less apparent in orthogonal 2D maps. Relief shearing is not a new invention and was used to great effect by 20th century cartographers like Erwin Raisz and Heinrich C. Berann [12]. However, constructing these maps manually was cumbersome and required considerable artistic talent, and thus the technique was not used often.

While Jenny and Patterson [12] used plan oblique relief to generate static maps, we couple shearing to user input. This allows users to interactively shear the underlying model and use kinetic depth cues to better understand the shape of the terrain. To create these views, we first overlay a 2D map image on top of a digital elevation model. When viewed from above using an orthographic projection, the map appears identical to the original image. However, users can now shear the model to expose the shape of the underlying terrain. In the simplest case, which we refer to as *explicit shearing* (Figure 1), a user grabs a point on the map and begins to drag. The selected point on the model's surface (c) follows the cursor, while the corresponding point at the base of the terrain model (s) remains fixed. As the cursor moves, we dynamically shear the model based on the angle between these two points, so that c always stays beneath the cursor, but the base does not move.

By grabbing and dragging at any point on the map, the user can quickly view the terrain from multiple angles. Shearing also provides motion parallax that enhances depth perception and helps users interpret the shape of the terrain. We shear the entire model (rather than locally deforming the terrain in the area of the drag) to ensure that motion can be interpreted consistently across the whole map.

Integrating Panning and Shearing

We have explored several variations of this basic interaction technique, focusing on interactions that add minimal overhead for the user and which are compatible with the kinds of maps typically used in desktop and mobile settings.

Explicit Shearing. As illustrated in Figure 1, explicit shearing varies the shear in direct response to user input. Grabbing and dragging on a point shears the map in the direction of the drag. When the map is released, the animation reverses and the point returns to its original position. Explicit shearing gives users direct control over the strength and direction of the shear and allows a user to hold terrain at a particular orientation for more detailed inspection. However, explicit shearing also adds a new interaction to the standard set (pan, zoom, and rotate) and requires an additional control or gesture to activate it. In our implementation, users can shear terrain by clicking and dragging with the right mouse button (on desktop machines) or by dragging after a long press (on touch-enabled devices). However, these interactions may conflict with existing uses of the same controls in other mapping tools.

Integrated Shearing. Because explicit shearing must be initiated directly by the user, it provides motion cues only when a user decides to shear. Moreover, it cannot be used while panning or zooming. To address this, we designed an even more lightweight approach, which we call *integrated shearing* (Figure 3) which integrates shearing with the existing panning interactions common on almost all 2D digital maps.

As before, grabbing and dragging a point on the map causes the model to shear in the direction of the cursor. However, when using integrated shearing, we also add an elastic force that pulls the *base* of the model towards the cursor. This force ensures that any time the cursor stops moving (even momentarily) the base of the model is pulled back into position beneath the selected point. The final result is identical to panning the map with the same cursor motion, but the intermediate shearing animation provides new kinetic depth cues with each interaction and helps users maintain peripheral and ongoing awareness of the terrain.

We model the elastic force as a simulated spring with $length = 0$ situated at the base of the model. One end of the spring (s_0) is anchored to the model directly below the initial press, while the other (s_1) follows the current position of the cursor (Figure 3). At each animation step, the elastic force of the spring tries to pull s_0 (and thus the entire base of the

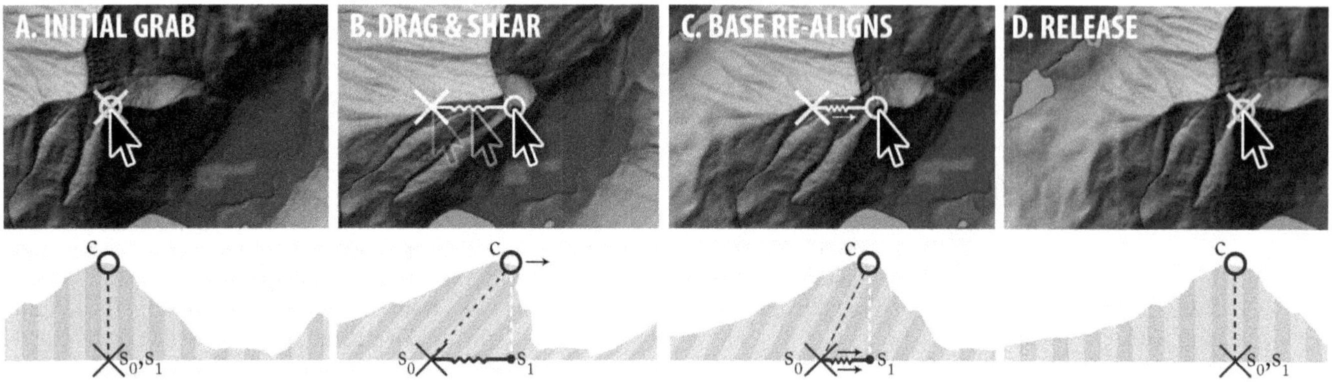

Figure 3. Using *integrated shearing*, the user grabs a point on the map (a) and drags it (b). This shears the model to keep the selected point under the cursor, while an elastic force pulls the map back into alignment (c). The final result (d) is identical to panning the map using the same motion.

model) back into alignment with s_1. We compute the velocity of the base at animation step t as:

$$v_t = k|s_1 - s_0| + Dv_{(t-1)}$$

where k specifies the spring constant and D specifies the drag coefficient. We then adjust the strength and direction of the shear to match the new angle between s_0 and c. While the cross-sectional diagrams in Figures 1 and 3 illustrate shearing in only one dimension, in practice, we model the spring in 2D and adjust the shearing in both x and y.

Integrated shearing produces motion that adapts smoothly to changes in panning speed and direction and intuitively feels like pulling the top of a jelly model. When released, the model elastically snaps back upright and may oscillate as it comes to rest—depending on the spring constant and drag coefficient used. In our experience, the oscillation produced by using a stronger spring and less drag provides a satisfying conclusion to panning operations, and the additional motion at the end helps persist the depth effect. These oscillations can also be triggered in response to zoom events, providing integrated depth cues as users zoom in and out.

Hybrid Explicit/Integrated Shearing. There is a clear trade-off between explicit and integrated shearing. Integrated shearing adds frequent peripheral depth information without adding any new interactions, but those depth cues are ephemeral and only last as long as the user is panning. Explicit shearing, by contrast, requires direct initiation but gives users more control over the persistence of depth cues and makes it possible to examine terrain from particular angles.

To help provide both peripheral cues and explicit manipulation of terrain, we can also combine explicit and integrated shearing into one *hybrid shearing* interaction. Hybrid shearing extends our integrated shearing model so that movement in a small radius around the selected point shears the model without panning. To achieve this, we allow the length of the spring (previously 0) to grow as long as the cursor stays inside the specified radius (Figure 4). As a result, small movements do not apply any elastic force and do not move the base. However, once the cursor leaves this area, the spring can no longer grow and further motion will cause the model to pan (as with standard integrated shearing).

Hybrid shearing supports both direct shearing and panning via one interaction. However, short pans become more difficult and—because the shearing behavior changes depending on how far a user drags—it can be harder for a user to predict what effect their interaction will have.

Shearing via Device Tilt. Panning and shearing can also be decoupled entirely and triggered using orthogonal input modalities. For example, on a handheld mobile device, we can use the tilt of the device to control shearing. This allows users to manipulate the map using the standard set of touch interactions, but simultaneously and independently adjust the shearing by varying the device's position and tilt. When holding the device, a user's passive body motion can also produce faint variations in the amount of shear, providing subtle depth cues even when she is not actively manipulating the map. This effect is related to, but different from, head-coupled parallax—where head tracking is used to control a virtual window into a 3D scene [8]. Although both techniques provide kinetic depth cues that can change based on the position of the device, tilt-driven shearing can produce views (e.g., oblique views of the sides of terrain features) that are not possible with head-coupled parallax.

Because tilt interactions require the user to actively hold and reposition the output device, they are impractical in some settings (e.g., desktop PCs). Also, while shearing and pointing use different inputs, it is possible for the two to conflict. For example, tilting the device can impede target acquisition by shearing the model and moving touch targets out from under a user's finger. In practice, however, we find that shearing by changing the device tilt tends to involve relatively small movements that are strongly coordinated with the user's body motion, making shearing behavior quite predictable.

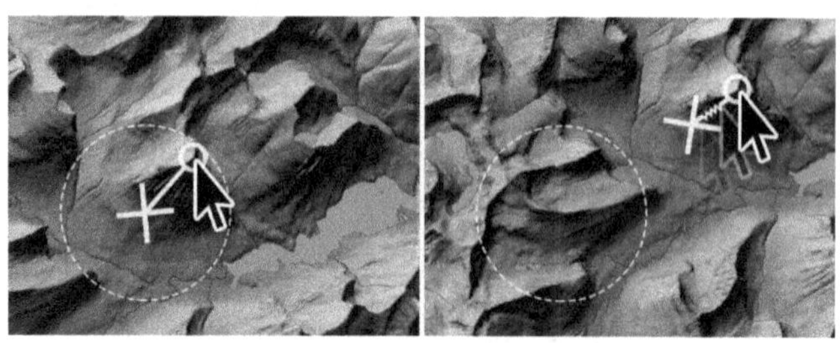

Figure 4. Using *hybrid shearing*, dragging within a small radius (left) shears the map and it snaps back to its original position when released (*explicit shearing* behavior). Dragging outside of this radius (right) shears and pans the map (*integrated shearing* behavior).

Shearing via Other Inputs. While we have focused on touch- and tilt-driven interactions, other input modes could also pair well with relief shearing. For example, using back-of-device interactions to shear and front-of-device interactions to pan could make it easier to perform both kinds of manipulations simultaneously. Face-tracking using on-device cameras [8] could also be an alternative to device tilt for controlling shearing on desktop devices.

Shearing Direction

When shearing is driven using direct touches or drags on the terrain, the dragged point should remain attached to the finger or cursor to preserve the impression of direct manipulation [10]. In our experience, this effect works well when a user drags on a topographically distinct high point on the map because the selected point appears to be pulled directly while the base of the map and terrain at lower elevations appear to lag behind (Figure 5-Left). This preserves the physical intuition of pulling from the top of an elastic model.

However, if a user drags from a low-elevation point, areas at high elevations will appear to move more quickly than the dragged point and may even occlude it, breaking that physical intuition. As a result, we have found it preferable to invert the shearing direction when interacting with a low point—treating the *top* of the model as fixed (rather than the base) and shearing points based on their distance below it. Low points then appear to be pulled directly, while the higher points lag behind (Figure 5-Right). This gives the sense of pulling on the same model, but from the bottom rather than the top.

In practice, the distinction between a low point and a high point can change when maps are zoomed to show small regions of terrain. For example, Figure 5 illustrates how a high alpine valley can appear to be a high point when zoomed out (as in view A), but then appear to be low point when the view is zoomed closer (view B). In our prototypes and evaluations, we address this issue by classifying each clicked point as either a local minimum or local maximum, based on the elevations of points in its immediate vicinity. We sample all elevations in a fixed radius around the selected point—performing the computation in screen space rather than model space to account for both the zoom level and the resolution of the elevation model. As Figure 5 illustrates, we assume a point is a local maximum (red) if more than half of the neighboring points are below it, and a local minimum (blue) otherwise.

IMPLEMENTATION

In order to explore the space of designs we have implemented several variants of our technique. The principal version is a Java application using OpenGL and based on software by Jenny *et al.* [14]. Our application overlays image files containing 2D maps or satellite imagery on top of digital elevation models and can be configured to use the explicit, integrated, or hybrid interaction models. We also implemented a variant for Windows tablets that uses touch input and data from the device's internal tilt sensor to control terrain shearing.

EXPERIMENTS

We conducted a series of experiments to assess the impact of our proposed interactive shearing techniques.

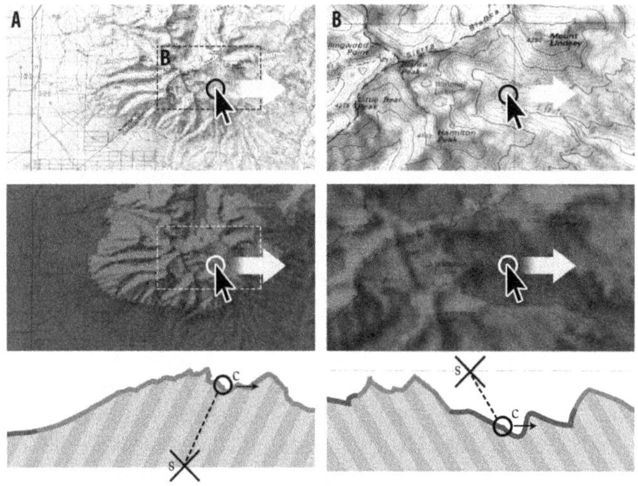

Figure 5. Shearing direction depends on the relative height of the target point. Dragging on a high point (left) shears the model in the direction of the drag using the bottom of the model as the baseline. Dragging a low point(right) uses the top of the visible model as the baseline for the shear. As illustrated here, same point can be either a local maximum (red) or local minimum (blue) depending on the zoom level.

Task Choice

Past experiments in the cartography literature have used a variety of tasks to assess participants' ability to parse and interpret terrain information. These include elevation-reading tasks in which participants must determine the height of a point, line-of-sight tasks in which participants are asked to mentally visualize the terrain between two points and determine if a clear line of sight exists, and comparison tasks where participants must compare heights, slopes, or distances between multiple points on a map (e.g., [4, 19, 20, 21]).

We use elevation comparison tasks, in which we present participants with a pair of points and ask them to determine which of the two points has the highest elevation. These taks have been widely used in prior studies of map-reading [19, 20] and we focus on them because they provide a strong indicator of whether or not a viewer understands the shape of the underlying terrain. Moreover, elevation comparisons are an implicit building block for other more complex map-reading tasks — such as determining elevation changes along a route or predicting visibility between locations.

Experiment 1: Depth Perception

In our first experiment, we sought to understand the extent to which animated shearing impacts viewers' ability to perceive depth on a map. We compared three different conditions:

Static. This condition showed elevation using traditional 2D techniques including contour lines and relief shading.

Animated Shearing. This condition used the same 2D techniques, but added a continuous animation that sheared the terrain in a clockwise circular pattern with a period of 1.5 seconds. This animation let users see all sides of the terrain and provided continuous kinetic depth cues.

Integrated. This condition used the same 2D cues as the other conditions, but participants could interactively pan and shear maps using *integrated shearing*.

The animated condition would be impractical in most real-world situations where the constant motion would make selection and direct interaction difficult. However, it provides very strong kinetic depth cues and allowed us to assess the overall impact of shearing animations on terrain perception. The interactive integrated shearing condition, meanwhile, allowed us to test whether participants were able to effectively access depth information by panning the map. We hypothesized that:

H1. Participants would be better able to discriminate depth when using an animated map rather than a static one.

H2. Participants would achieve similar depth discrimination when they interactively activated shearing as they did when shearing was animated.

Procedure. We used examples of three common types of real-world maps featuring varying degrees of relief and terrain complexity. The three maps included: a very detailed Swiss topographic map of the Bernese Alps with contour lines and shading; a US National Park Service map of the Glacier National Park with shading and hypsometric tints but no contours; and an urban terrain map of San Francisco from Google Maps that included shading. We overlaid the maps on digital elevation models drawn from the SRTM THIRD dataset[1].

For the elevation comparison tasks, we generated pairs of stimuli randomly according to a set of pre-defined criteria. We discarded points that fell within the outer 5% of the map in either x or y. We also ensured that points fell in the same area of the map and that the distance between them was less than 15% of the map height or width, whichever was larger. To create a continuum of both easy and hard tasks, we selected pairs with a range of different elevation changes between the higher and lower points. When selecting pairs, we eliminated pairs whose elevations were too similar or too far apart, and selected even numbers of pairs whose elevation differences fell into five discrete bins between the minimum and maximum differences. We tuned these elevation differences through a series of internal pilots to ensure that the task was sufficiently challenging to produce a high error rate, but that the most similar elevations were still possible to disambiguate.

At the start of each task, we displayed a white disk which hid the area of map where the new points would appear. This allowed participants to center their view before the task and reduced the need to visually search for the points once they were displayed. After one second, we removed the disk and participants were able to see the two stimulus points, one on the left (red) and one on the right (blue). We instructed participants to "quickly and accurately" determine which of the two points was the highest and press a key ("1" for left, "2" for right) to indicate the higher point. To reduce confusion with the keyboard mapping, we also labeled the physical "1" and "2" keys with red and blue marks that matched the colors of the points. To reduce confusion about which of the two points was the leftmost and which was the rightmost, we avoided pairs of points which were more than 60° from horizontal.

When contour lines are available, a viewer could spend a large amount of time comparing and tracing individual lines in order to determine the higher point. Because we wanted to assess participants' intuitive sense of the shape of the terrain

[1] http://geo.spectrumtelecom.ca/

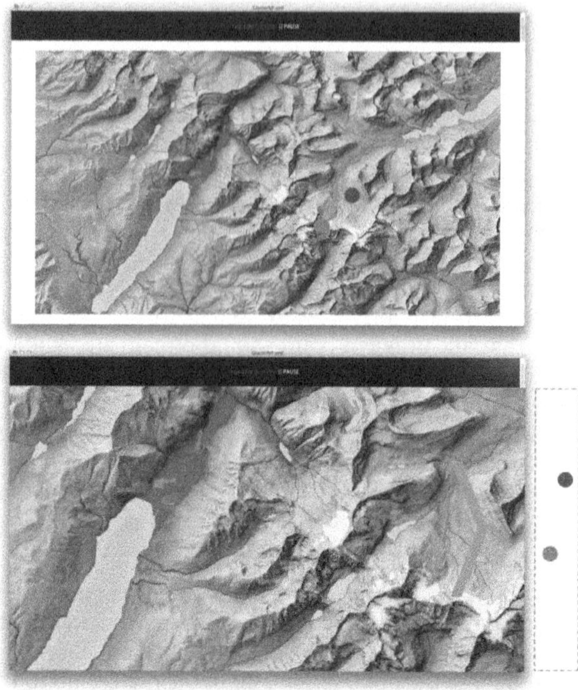

Figure 6. In Experiment 1 (top), participants could always see the entire map. In Experiment 2 (bottom) we increased the size of the map to necessitate panning, and placed all new pairs of points off-screen (simulated here) with an arrow showing their direction and distance. To improve legibility, this figure shows points at 4× their actual diameter.

and not their map reading ability, we chose to fix the amount of time available for the task and focus instead on the error rate. Therefore, we allowed participants to see each pair of points for only 4 seconds before fading out the map and points (participants could still answer after the map was hidden).

We used a within-subjects design in which each participant saw all combinations of maps and motion conditions and completed 45 trials for each (3 maps × 3 conditions × 45 tasks = 405 tasks). To help control for learning effects, we presented tasks in blocks of 15 and systematically varied the order in which maps and motion conditions were presented. Each participant received blocks of tasks in a unique, randomized order where we ensured that no two adjacent blocks used the same map or the same motion condition.

We used e-mail to recruit a set of 20 graduate student participants. Half of the participants were experts — cartographers and cartography students with prior training in map reading and experience with Geographic Information Systems (GIS). The other half had no GIS or cartography experience beyond basic map reading skills. Sixteen participants were male and four were female, with ages ranging from 23–33 ($mean = 27.8$, $SD = 2.8$). Participants self-administered the experiment in a controlled environment by following a set of printed instructions. An evaluator was present to monitor the experiment and answer questions from the participants. Each participant first completed a series of 45 training tasks (15 for each of the three motion conditions) using a fourth map not included in the actual study. Participants were encouraged to repeat the training if they felt they needed additional practice. Participants then proceeded to the main experiment—where they required

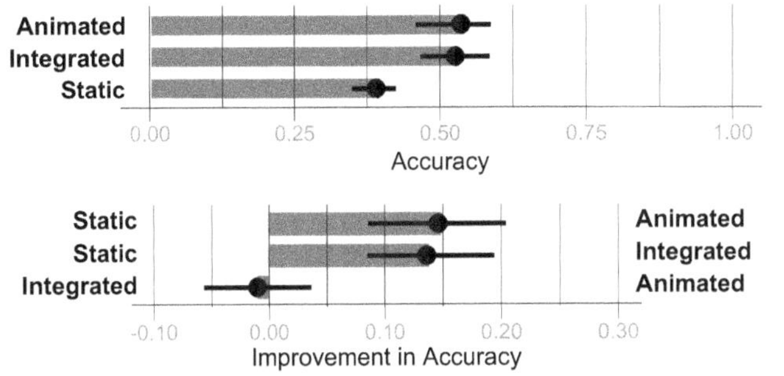

Figure 7. (Top) Mean accuracy across all participants by motion condition. Accuracy is normalized so that a score of 0 indicates a result equal to chance. (Bottom) Mean improvement in accuracy between conditions (right technique minus left technique). All error bars show 95% bootstrap confidence intervals.

an average of 36 minutes ($SD = 6$) to complete all 405 trials. Afterward, participants completed a short exit questionnaire. Each participant received a $15 gift certificate. Participants used a 24" display at 1920×1080 in a standard desktop setting. They interacted with the maps using a mouse and entered their inputs using a standard keyboard.

Results. We collected a total of 8,100 elevation judgments from our 20 participants. Due to increasing concerns in a variety of research fields about the use of null hypothesis significance testing [5, 7], we analyzed these results using estimation techniques and report effect sizes with confidence intervals rather than p-value statistics. This reporting methodology is consistent with recent APA recommendations [27].

To compare the three conditions, we computed an accuracy score $a = ((\frac{\text{correct responses}}{\text{total responses}} - 0.5)/0.5)$ for each participant in each condition. This score normalizes accuracy so that a 1 indicates a perfect performance while a 0 indicates a result equal to chance (e.g., randomly guessing). We then computed means and 95% bootstrap confidence intervals [15] across all participants (Figure 7-Top). These results showed that participants tended to be better at differentiating elevations in both the animated and interactive conditions than in the static condition. Pairwise comparisons between the conditions (Figure 7-Bottom) further illustrate that both animation and integrated shearing improved users' performance over the static condition. However, we saw very little difference in performance between the animated and integrated conditions.

These results confirm both of our initial hypotheses—showing that (H1) the presence of constant motion cues from animation improves depth discrimination, and (H2) that users are able to achieve similar improvement when motion cues triggered by their panning interactions. Expert users likely benefited more from the two motion conditions than non-experts did (Figure 8). However, non-experts still showed a clear increase in accuracy in both the animated and integrated conditions.

To check for the presence of learning effects, we computed mean accuracy scores for each participant for each of the 27 task blocks, then used those scores to perform a linear regression for $\textit{error rate} = a \times \textit{block number} + b$. The resulting model ($a = 0.006$, 95% CI [0.000, 0.011], $b = 0.438$, 95% CI [0.388, 0.487]) confirms that the accuracy of participants' responses did not change much as their familiarity with the maps and techniques increased.

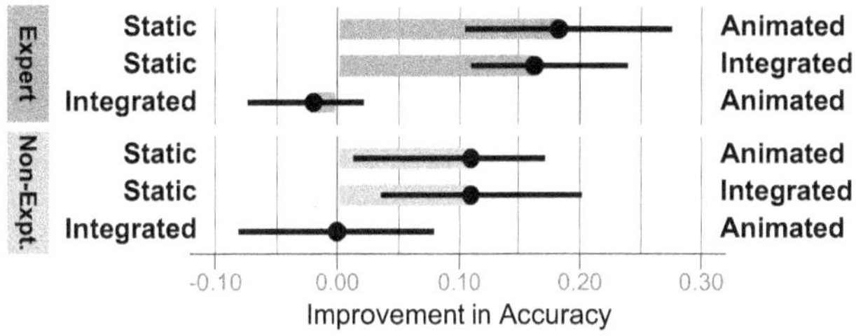

Figure 8. Mean improvement in accuracy between conditions (right technique minus left technique) for expert and for non-expert users. Error bars show 95% bootstrap confidence intervals.

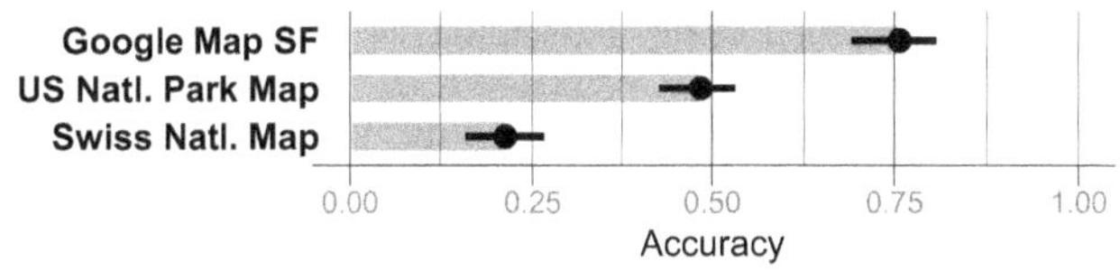

Figure 9. Mean accuracy for each map across all individuals. Accuracy is normalized so that a score of 0 indicates a result equal to chance. Error bars show 95% confidence intervals.

We also computed per-participant accuracies and confidence intervals for each map used in the study (Figure 9). We found that participants' judgments were much more accurate when using the topographically simple Google map than on the more complex National Park Service map. Participants were even less accurate when using the Swiss map, which was more detailed and had considerably more diverse terrain. This ordering held for nearly every single user in the study—regardless of expertise—and confirms that we indeed selected maps that spanned a range of difficulty levels.

Experiment 2: Depth Perception with Integrated Shearing

Based on the positive results of our first experiment, we conducted a second study in which we compared relief shearing against existing 2D and perspective techniques. This second experiment used the same basic elevation comparisons as Experiment 1 but situated them in a more realistic panning task. We also used a Microsoft Surface Pro 2 tablet with an 10.6" screen instead of a desktop PC, which allowed us to include a condition that used orientation sensors to control relief shearing. We compared five different interaction techniques:

Standard Panning. A standard 2D map with no motion cues.

Integrated. The integrated shearing technique.

Top-Down Central Perspective. This condition simulated the default perspective view available in applications like Apple Maps and Google Maps. The camera is fixed to show the terrain from directly above, but the perspective distortion provides some parallax depth cues, especially for steep terrain. We used a field of view of 60°.

Inclined Central Perspective. This condition simulated the inclined perspective views available in these same commercial tools. We set the field of view to 45°, oriented the camera to 30° from vertical, and configured panning so that it translated the camera parallel to the ground plane.

Device Tilt. In this condition, users could adjust the tilt of the device to shear the map independently of their panning.

We hypothesized that:

H3. Integrated shearing would improve depth perception when compared to standard panning (no motion cues).

H4. Integrated shearing would improve depth perception when compared to top-down perspective which provides more subtle parallax cues.

H5. Integrated shearing would improve depth perception when compared to inclined perspective which introduces pronounced depth compression effects.

We also included the more experimental *device tilt* condition to explore whether or not participants would actively vary tilt to manipulate the view, or if depth cues from their passive motion would be sufficient to improve their depth perception.

Procedure. Because Experiment 1 showed no evidence of learning effects or interactions between maps and motion conditions, we simplified Experiment 2 by reducing the number of maps. We used the Swiss map for training tasks and the US National Park Service map for the study itself.

To create realistic panning tasks we zoomed the maps to 2× the size of the viewport. For each task, we generated a pair of points off-screen with a large arrow indicating their direction and distance (Figure 6-Bottom). Participants needed to pan the view (using touch interactions) to reveal and then compare the points. We locked the tablet in landscape mode but allowed participants to physically tilt, turn, and rest the device however they wanted. We also asked them to indicate the higher point by tapping it directly, eliminating the need for a keyboard.

We selected points using the same criteria as in Experiment 1, but always ensured that the next point pair was not in the current view. Because participants could now indicate the higher point via touch, we also removed the restriction on the angle between points. Unlike the first experiment, we did not time-limit participants, but encouraged them to answer "quickly and accurately" and use less than 10 seconds per trial.

As in Experiment 1, we used a within-subjects design where each participant completed tasks using all of the interaction techniques (5 conditions × 60 tasks = 300 tasks). We presented tasks in blocks of 20 and systematically varied the order in which they were presented. We also included a series of 5 training blocks (10 tasks each) to introduce each technique.

We recruited 14 unpaid participants (8 female, 6 male), none of whom had taken part in our first experiment. Participants' ages ranged from 24–40 ($mean = 30.75$, $SD = 5.77$). Again, participants self-administered the experiment under the supervision of an evaluator, using a combination of printed and on-screen instructions. Participants took an average of 53 minutes ($SD = 13$) to complete the experiment.

Results. As in Experiment 1, we computed accuracy scores for each condition (Figure 10-Top) as well as pairwise differences between each condition. We found that participants had the highest accuracy scores when using *integrated shearing*. Furthermore, pairwise comparisons (Figure 10-Middle) show that participants were reliably more accurate when using *integrated shearing* than any of the other four conditions, confirming hypotheses H3–H5.

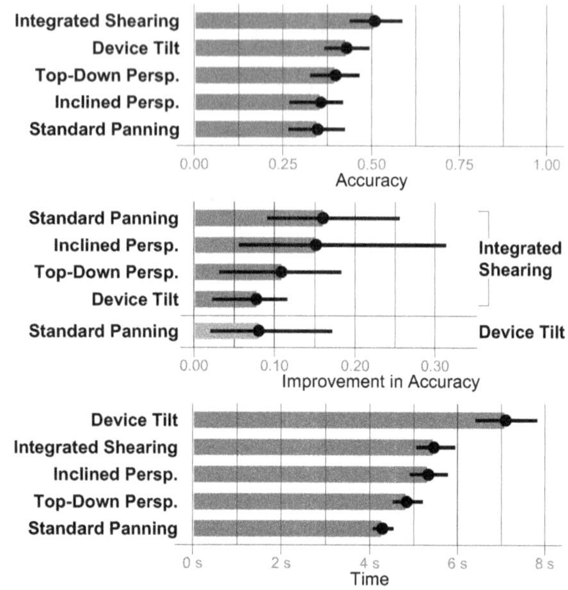

Figure 10. (Top) Mean accuracy across all participants by condition. Accuracy is normalized so that a score of 0 indicates a result equal to chance. (Middle) Mean improvement in accuracy between conditions (right technique minus left technique). (Bottom) Mean task completion times (in seconds). Error bars show 95% bootstrap confidence intervals.

Participants were also more accurate when using *device tilt* than when using standard panning, but device tilt was not clearly better than either of the perspective techniques. However, we observed that participants used device tilt much differently than the other techniques—often holding the tablet at extreme angles and attempting to align the stimulus points in order to compare them. As a result, participants tended to take substantially longer to complete tasks when using the device tilt shear (Figure 10-Bottom). Despite this, 8 of the 14 participants reported that they preferred *device tilt*, while 3 preferred *integrated shearing*, and just 1 preferred each of the other three conditions—although there was likely a novelty effect.

When kinetic depth cues are available, there may be a speed-accuracy tradeoff, since users can continue to extract information by moving the map and viewing the points from new orientations. However, with the exception of *device tilt*, participants spent only about 1 second longer in the motion conditions—even though we did not impose a time limit.

DISCUSSION

The results of these experiments indicate that using shearing to add subtle motion cues can improve users' ability to perceive depth in maps while adding little interaction cost. In particular, we found that integrated shearing, coupled to existing pan interactions, can help users discriminate elevations more accurately than standard shaded relief maps *or* perspective views. Next, we describe some of the benefits and trade-offs of interactive relief shearing, and examine several aspects of the technique that merit further exploration.

Benefits and Trade-offs of Interactive Relief Shearing

Using relief shearing to impart depth information on maps has a number of potential benefits, both when compared to traditional 2D maps and to other more-complex approaches.

First, **interactive relief shearing provides kinetic depth information that enhances 3D perception.** These cues make elevation discrimination and map-reading tasks that require depth judgment easier, especially when compared to traditional 2D maps. However, if no depth judgment is required, the animations may be distracting and could make interaction and distance estimation more difficult than they would be with a 2D map.

Second, **interactive relief shearing is primarily a 2D technique and is compatible with 2D map views.** As a result, our approach still facilitates 2D interaction and 2D visual judgment tasks that may be more difficult when using perspective views, stereo displays, and other approaches that attempt to approximate full 3D. Moreover, the motion is ephemeral and maps can rapidly revert to a standard 2D view. Conversely, relief shearing may still be less effective than full 3D views for tasks that require specific viewing angles—for example examining the profile of a mountain ridge or estimating slope steepness.

Third, **interactive relief shearing requires little new interaction** and can be coupled with existing operations like pan and zoom or controlled via an orthogonal input modality. *Integrated shearing*, in particular, provides depth cues without requiring users to learn any new controls or hidden gestures. Moreover, because these interactions rely on direct manipulation, they are likely to be easy to master. Coupling shearing to pan and zoom may be particularly beneficial for search and route-finding tasks that require depth discrimination and already entail extensive map manipulation. However, more complex versions of the technique such as *hybrid shearing* may increase the difficulty of panning. Pairing the depth effect with interaction also makes it less effective than stereo displays or physical models for situations where interaction is impossible or where the user needs continuous depth perception.

Finally, because it requires only a display and 2D input, **interactive relief shearing can be used on most modern PCs and mobile devices**. As a result, our approach is currently much more accessible than ones that rely on a stereo displays, head tracking, or other physical hardware. It could be easily implemented in modern web browsers and mobile devices with 3D graphics capabilities as well as forthcoming e-paper and electrowetting displays with higher refresh rates.

Interaction and Orientation

In addition to our formal experiments, one of the authors also used the the tablet version of our tool extensively over the course of a week-long backpacking trip through the Swiss Alps. During five days on trail, the author and several colleagues used maps augmented with explicit, integrated, and animated shearing to navigate and identify terrain features.

We found that shearing maps to view the profiles of terrain features was especially useful when attempting to match landmarks on a map to the surrounding real-world terrain. However, comparing profiles usually requires reorienting the map so that the face of the terrain feature in question can be sheared upwards. While it is often possible to reorient by physically turning the tablet, combining the device tilt and compass inputs to rotate and shear the map automatically could make matching landmarks even easier.

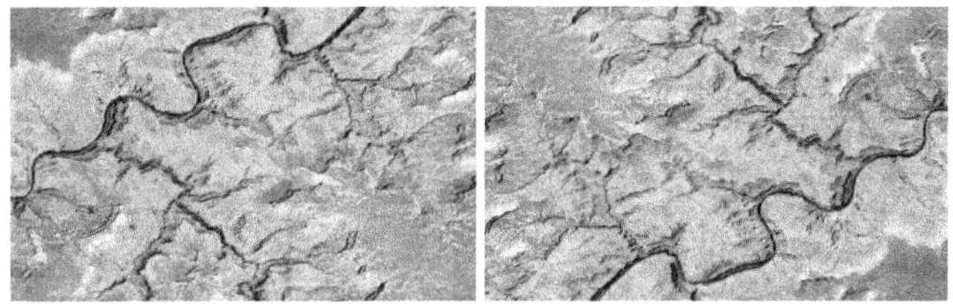

Figure 11. Canyon maps like this one (shown in its original orientation and rotated by 180°) are especially susceptible to the terrain reversal effect. Depending on motion, lighting direction, and other cues, the canyon can appear to be either concave or convex.

Animated Shear for Non-Panning Tasks

Integrated shearing when panning appears to add useful depth cues with little additional interaction cost. However, common digital mapping tasks like examining a route or set of search results can involve relatively little panning since the map is often automatically centered on the area of interest. In these cases it may be helpful to include a short shearing animation when the map is first presented. Such animations could also be triggered to help viewers re-situate when a map is changed significantly, e.g., when new pins or layers are added.

Interestingly, continuous shearing animations (like those used in Experiment 1) may also be useful in some cases when interaction is not necessary or when the map is being referenced indirectly or from a distance. For example, during our live deployment in Switzerland we found the continuous animations useful during long train trips—where the tablet was positioned on a table and could be used as a glanceable reference for multiple users. Our experience suggests that continuous motion may be useful for enhancing depth on ambient or public map displays intended for group viewing.

The Terrain Reversal Effect

In some cases, we have found that interactively shearing maps can trigger the "terrain reversal effect" [1, 11], in which the elevations on a map appeared to reverse—with high points like peaks and ridges appearing to be low and low points like canyons and valleys appearing to be high. This kind of reversal is well-documented in the cartography literature [11] and is known to occur on shaded-relief maps, especially when the light source or orientation of the map changes (as in Figure 11). The effect is likely the result of an underlying perceptual prior whereby the perceptual system tends to perceive ambiguous objects as convex rather than concave [17]. Because the size and speed of objects in a sheared projection do not change with depth, motion cues do not unambiguously indicate which areas are closer to the viewer and which are further away. As a result, motion from relief shearing animations can have two equally valid interpretations—for example, both a canyon and a ridge with the same elevation change could have identical motion profiles, depending on the orientation of the shear.

The reversal effect is highly individual. In our studies, a few participants experienced reversals on all orthographic maps (including static 2D versions) while many others experienced no reversals at all. However, in our experience, reversals seem to be less common if shearing is triggered using direct manipulation or device tilt—possibly because the sense of direct control makes it easier to interpret the resulting motion.

CONCLUSION

Our explorations show that interactive relief shearing can improve depth perception when compared to both traditional 2D maps and 3D perspective views. Our approach is simple, lightweight, and compatible with existing interaction techniques and could thus be a compelling addition to existing web-based mapping tools and mobile devices. Relief shearing animations may also be useful for adding depth cues to maps on public displays or in other applications where understanding the shape of the terrain is important, but complex interactions or advanced hardware like stereoscopic displays is impractical. Moreover, this work illustrates how lightweight, targeted interactions can make maps (as well as height maps and other 2.5D visualizations) even more usable and accessible—providing a richer sense of space while preserving simplicity.

ACKNOWLEDGMENTS

We thank our participants, Google for a Faculty Research Award, Tom Patterson for use of his Glacier National Park map, and Brooke Marston who helped administer the experiment and provided feedback on the paper.

REFERENCES

1. Bernabé-Poveda, M. A., and Çöltekin, A. Prevalence of the terrain reversal effect in satellite imagery. *International Journal of Digital Earth* (2015). To appear.
2. Bowman, D. A., Kruijff, E., LaViola, Jr., J. J., and Poupyrev, I. *3D User Interfaces: Theory and Practice*. Addison-Wesley, Boston, 2005.
3. Buchroithner, M. F., and Knust, C. True-3D in cartography—Current hard-and softcopy developments. In *Geospatial Visualisation*. Springer, Heidelberg/Berlin, 2013, 41–65.
4. Castner, H. W., and Wheate, R. Re-assessing the role played by shaded relief in topographic scale maps. *The Cartographic Journal 16*, 2 (Dec. 1979), 77–85.
5. Cumming, G. The new statistics: Why and how. *Psychological Science 25*, 1 (Jan. 2014), 7–29.
6. Degener, P., and Klein, R. A variational approach for automatic generation of panoramic maps. *ACM Transactions on Graphics 28*, 1 (Jan. 2009), 2:1–2:14.
7. Dragicevic, P., Chevalier, F., and Huot, S. Running an HCI experiment in multiple parallel universes. In *CHI Extended Abstracts*, ACM (New York, 2014), 607–618.
8. Francone, J., and Nigay, L. Using the user's point of view for interaction on mobile devices. In *Proc. IHM*, ACM (New York, 2011), 4:1–4:8.
9. Grossman, T., and Balakrishnan, R. An evaluation of depth perception on volumetric displays. In *Proc. AVI*, ACM (New York, 2006), 193–200.
10. Hancock, M., Cate, T., and Carpendale, S. Sticky tools: Full 6DOF force-based interaction for multi-touch tables. In *Proc. ITS*, ACM (New York, 2009), 133–140.
11. Imhof, E. *Cartographic Relief Presentation*. Esri Press, Redlands, CA, USA, 2007.
12. Jenny, B., and Patterson, T. Introducing plan oblique relief. *Cartographic Perspectives*, 57 (Spring 2007), 21–40.
13. Jenny, H., Jenny, B., Cartwright, W. E., and Hurni, L. Interactive local terrain deformation inspired by hand-painted panoramas. *The Cartographic Journal 48*, 1 (Feb. 2011), 11–20.
14. Jenny, H., Jenny, B., and Hurni, L. Interactive design of 3D maps with progressive projection. *The Cartographic Journal 47*, 3 (Aug. 2010), 211–221.
15. Kirby, K. N., and Gerlanc, D. BootES: An R package for bootstrap confidence intervals on effect sizes. *Behavior Research Methods 45*, 4 (Dec. 2013), 905–927.
16. Knust, C., and Buchroithner, M. F. Principles and terminology of true-3D geovisualisation. *The Cartographic Journal 51*, 3 (Aug. 2014), 191–202.
17. Langer, M. S., and Bülthoff, H. H. A prior for global convexity in local shape-from-shading. *Perception 30*, 4 (Jan. 2001), 403–410.
18. Loomis, J. M., and Eby, D. W. Perceiving structure from motion: Failure of shape constancy. In *Proc. ICCV*, IEEE Computer Society (Los Alamitos, 1988), 383–391.
19. Phillips, R. J., Lucia, A., and Skelton, N. Some objective tests of the legibility of relief maps. *The Cartographic Journal 12*, 1 (June 1975), 39–46.
20. Potash, L. M., Farrell, J. P., and Jeffrey, T. S. A technique for assessing map relief legibility. *The Cartographic Journal 15*, 1 (June 1978), 28–35.
21. Rapp, D. N., Culpepper, S. A., Kirkby, K., and Morin, P. Fostering students' comprehension of topographic maps. *Journal of Geoscience Education 55*, 1 (Jan. 2007), 5–16.
22. Reisman, J. L., Davidson, P. L., and Han, J. Y. A screen-space formulation for 2D and 3D direct manipulation. In *Proc. UIST*, ACM (New York, 2009), 69–78.
23. Shneiderman, B. Why not make interfaces better than 3D reality? *IEEE Computer Graphics and Applications 23*, 6 (Nov./Dec. 2003), 12–15.
24. Smith, G., Stuerzlinger, W., Salzman, T., Watson, B., and Buchanan, J. 3D scene manipulation with 2D devices and constraints. In *Proc. Graphics Interface*, CIPS (Toronto, 2001), 135–142.
25. Todd, J. T. The visual perception of 3D shape. *Trends in Cognitive Sciences 8*, 3 (Mar. 2004), 115–121.
26. Todd, J. T., and Norman, J. F. The visual perception of 3-D shape from multiple cues: Are observers capable of perceiving metric structure? *Perception & Psychophysics 65*, 1 (Jan. 2003), 31–47.
27. VandenBos, G. R., Ed. *Publication Manual of the American Psychological Assn.*, 6th ed. APA, Wash. D.C., 2009.
28. Vezzani, S., Kramer, P., and Bressan, P. Stereokinetic effect, kinetic depth effect, and structure from motion. In *The Oxford Handbook of Perceptual Organization*. Oxford University Press, Oxford, UK, 2014. In press.

An Evaluation of Interactive Map Comparison Techniques

María-Jesús Lobo
INRIA ; INRIA Chile (CIRIC)
maria-jesus.lobo@inria.fr

Emmanuel Pietriga
INRIA ; INRIA Chile (CIRIC)
emmanuel.pietriga@inria.fr

Caroline Appert
Univ Paris-Sud ; CNRS ; INRIA
caroline.appert@lri.fr

(a) `http://geobretagne.fr/sviewer/dual.html` (d) `http://storymaps.geo.admin.ch/storymaps/storymap1`

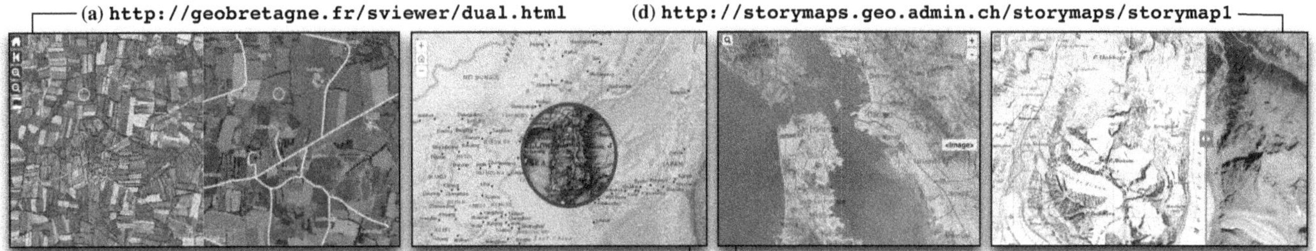

(b) `http://story.maps.arcgis.com/apps/StorytellingSwipe` (c) `http://mapstack.stamen.com`

Figure 1. The four main composition strategies: (a) synchronized juxtaposed views, (b) magic lens, (c) translucent overlay, (d) swipe.

ABSTRACT
Geovisualization applications typically organize data into layers. These layers hold different types of geographical features, describe different characteristics of the same features, or represent those features at different points in time. Layers can be composited in various ways, most often employing a juxtaposition or superimposition strategy, to produce maps that users can explore interactively. From an HCI perspective, one of the main challenges is to design interactive compositions that optimize the legibility of the resulting map and that ease layer comparison. We characterize five representative techniques, and empirically evaluate them using a set of real-world maps in which we purposefully introduce six types of differences amenable to inter-layer visual comparison. We discuss the merits of these techniques in terms of visual interference, user attention and scanning strategy. Our results can help inform the design of map-based visualizations for supporting geo-analysis tasks in many application areas.

Author Keywords
Geovisualization, Composite Visualization, Interference

ACM Classification Keywords
H.5.2 : User Interfaces - Graphical user interfaces.

General Terms
Human Factors; Design

INTRODUCTION
Geographic Information Systems (GIS) have applications in numerous domains, including: emergency response & management, transportation, environmental studies, weather forecast and climatology, urban planning, real-estate, hiking and traveling. Maps play a central role in these systems, as the primary means to display data to users. Maps are used as visual thinking and analysis tools, as well as visual communication tools. They take advantage of people's spatial reasoning abilities [35], serving four primary goals: exploration, confirmation, synthesis, and presentation to an audience [20].

GIS organize data into thematic layers that offer different perspectives on the real-world. Base maps can be schematic, showing only essential data that provide strong orientation cues such as administrative boundaries, relief and water bodies. Or they can use orthoimages, providing a more realistic – but possibly less useful [35] – background. Additional layers complement the base map. They can hold any type of geo-located data, ranging from cloud cover to road networks and live traffic conditions. Distinct layers may hold different types of features (e.g., roads, topographic contour lines), but may also show the same features, emphasizing different characteristics thereof (e.g., road type vs. traffic conditions).

GIS users often have to correlate data from several layers. Geovisualization tools must thus offer means to composite layers. Considering the simple case of one additional layer that features sparse content, as in many Web-based mashups, compositing can be as straightforward as placing the corresponding symbols on the base map. But when combining denser layers or comparing feature-rich maps of the same region, this simple method no longer works. More elaborate visual composition strategies [14, 9] are called for.

We identify and characterize techniques for the interactive composition of image layers in geovisualization applications (Figure 1). We empirically evaluate representative techniques on map comparison tasks using a set of 20 orthoimages and corresponding topographic maps, in which we purposefully introduced six types of differences with respect to the reference orthoimage. We present our operationalization strategy, and discuss the relative merits of these techniques in terms of visual interference, user attention and scanning strategy.

CHI 2015, April 18–23, 2015, Seoul, Republic of Korea.

http://dx.doi.org/10.1145/2702123.2702130

BACKGROUND AND MOTIVATION

Interface design for GIS is studied in two communities that approach the problem from complementary angles: Geographic Information Science & Human Computer Interaction.

The Geographic Information Science Perspective

Geographic Information Scientists investigate how to best render maps based on the properties of geographic features and on the styling strategy. Grounded in seminal work such as Bertin's *Sémiologie Graphique* [2], topics of active research include the process of map *generalization* [34] for multi-scale interfaces, and the static composition of layers or base maps of different nature [12]. The overall goal is to generate representations that best answer a given user demand. GI science is also increasingly investigating interactive cartography (see, e.g., [31, 32] for representative examples). User studies in GI science tend to rely on realistic experimental tasks and to yield mostly qualitative measures. Examples of such studies include assessing the legibility of alternative renderings and static composition strategies [27, 33]).

The Human-Computer Interaction Perspective

Human-Computer Interaction researchers focus on how users interact with maps such as, e.g., techniques to select specific items in dense sets [37], techniques to visualize offscreen content [10], and techniques to navigate more efficiently in both space and scale. The latter topic, termed multi-scale navigation, has received a lot of attention and is most closely related to our problem. Three main interface schemes exist [6]. *Classical pan & zoom* uses time multiplexing to present users with different views (possibly at different scales) on the map. Only one view is shown at a time, putting some burden on users' memory. *Overview + detail* interfaces use spatial multiplexing. They show both a detailed view and an overview of the map simultaneously, but in distinct presentation spaces, possibly causing problems of divided attention. Finally, *focus+context* interfaces seamlessly integrate detail and context views into a single display, minimizing problems of divided attention. Other problems arise, however, such as those due to spatial distortion, which is employed to achieve smooth transitions but can impede interpretation and target selection [1, 24]. User studies in HCI tend to rely on more abstract empirical tasks with more controlled conditions, yielding mostly quantitative measures (see, e.g., [1, 13, 23, 26, 28, 29]).

Recent developments include: PolyZoom [15], a technique that creates hierarchies of related windows displaying different regions of the same map at increasing zoom factors; JellyLenses [25], a locally-bounded magnification-lens technique that dynamically adapts its shape to match the geometry of objects of interest; and Mélange [8], a space folding technique that shows distant focus regions simultaneously.

Design and Evaluation of Map Comparison Techniques

The techniques mentioned just above provide users with multiple views on the same space (map or image) and can help them compare the content of these different views. But they are designed to show the *same region* at different scales, or different regions but of the *same map*. They are not adapted to our problem, which is to composite *heterogenous representations of the same geographical region at the same scale* so as to help users relate and compare features across them.

Map composition plays an essential role in geo-analysis tasks. It supports the exploratory visualization of geo-located data coming from multiple sources, unifying those data in a single representation. It can yield powerful insights, and it can help users identify patterns and anomalies [20]. Successful examples date as far back as 1854, when John Snow traced the source of a cholera outbreak to a water pump by plotting deaths on a map of London [16].

Geovisualization tools are now used in a broad range of application areas, by both professionals and lay users whose tasks often involve correlating data from different maps and layers [7, 21, 27]. Examples include emergency response & crisis management, where multiple data sources have to be correlated for damage assessment and coordination of field agents; studying the evolution of urban areas or melting glaciers; updating geographical databases such as ArcGIS[1] or OpenStreetMap[2], creating new content or adjusting the geometry of features by direct manipulation of map elements superimposed on the most recent orthoimagery. Building on top of initiatives such as OpenStreetMap, various tools also make it easy for a broad audience to make their own maps [7] by combining pre-rendered layers[3] (Figure 1-c) and even customizing the rendering of features with declarative stylesheets[4]. Thanks to these tools, map composition is actually no longer limited to professional cartographers.

As more and more data become available, and as the level of sophistication of geovisualization tools increases, designing efficient interactive composition techniques has become a critical issue. Such techniques should enable compositions of base maps and data layers that optimize the legibility of the end result and that ease inter-layer comparison. So far, this problem has received relatively little attention. Several techniques exist, some of them are even widely used (Figure 1), but at this point most are little more than ad-hoc designs whose strengths and weaknesses are not well-understood.

In their list of *research challenges for geovisualization*, MacEachren & Kraak advocate for a more human-centered approach [21], noting that: *"While visual representation remains a fundamental issue, the focus of both cartographic design and cartographic research now extends to problems in human-computer interaction and in enabling dynamic map and map object behaviors"*, further calling for *"[the development of] a better understanding of how ordinary users interact with geospatial displays [...] and formal methods for usability assessment applicable to geovisualization use"*. Our work makes contributions in this direction. We survey interaction techniques that enable image and map comparisons. We select 5 of them, characterize them in terms of composite visualization strategy [14], and report on a comparative eval-

[1] `http://www.esri.com/software/arcgis`

[2] `http://www.openstreetmap.org`

[3] `http://mapstack.stamen.com`

[4] `https://www.mapbox.com/tilemill`

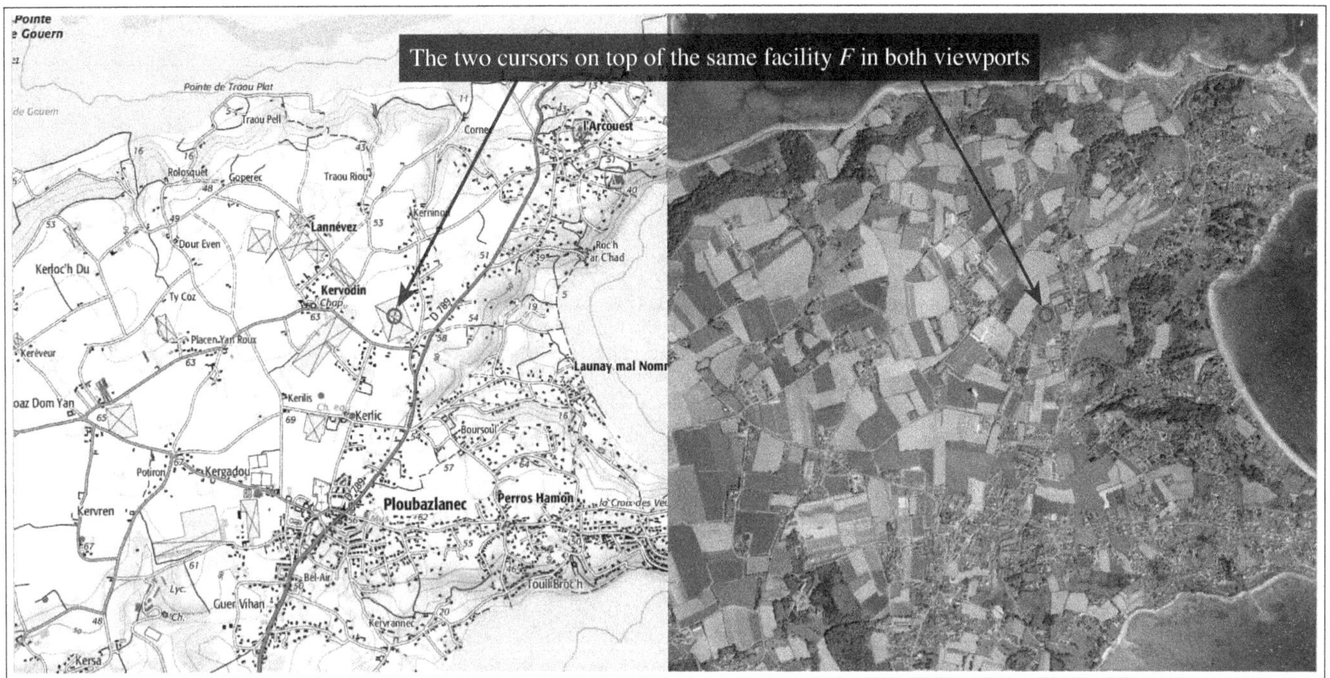

Figure 2. Technique JX: The two images are juxtaposed, showing the same geographical region in both viewports. Any pan and zoom action applies to both of them. Cursors are instantiated in each viewport. Their position is synchronized to help relate features in the two images.

uation of their performance on a set of 6 representative map comparison tasks. The tasks are based on an operationalization that favors external validity, involving a set of 140 customized real-world maps that we make available publicly.

MAP COMPARISON TECHNIQUES

We surveyed existing techniques by reading the literature, talking with GI science experts and reviewing prominent Web sites. A first observation is that those techniques do not only apply to geographical maps, but to any images that are spatially aligned. Some techniques are used in Medical Imaging to explore brain scans, in Exogeology to compare surveys of, e.g., planet Mars, made at different times or in different parts of the electromagnetic spectrum. The same applies to Astronomy, where comparisons also include looking at two images generated from the same FITS file (a high-dynamic-range format) using different transfer functions and color mappings.

Map and image comparison techniques predominantly employ two operators from Javed & Elmqvist's composite visualization design space [14]: juxtaposition and superimposition, which are called juxtaposition and superposition in Gleicher *et al.*'s taxonomy of visual designs for comparison [9]. As overview + detail interfaces for multi-scale visualization, juxtaposition uses spatial multiplexing, partitioning the screen in non-overlapping windows that each show one representation. As classical pan & zoom, the simplest case of superimposition, termed *blitting*, uses temporal multiplexing, overlaying the two representations and enabling users to toggle between them. More elaborate forms of superimposition employ adjustable translucence to show both representations simultaneously, an alternative termed *depth multiplexing* [11]. The following four techniques are the most commonly used in map and image comparison tools.

Juxtapose (JX)

As illustrated in Figures 1-a & 2, the two images can be juxtaposed, showing the same geographical region in both viewports. This technique does not cause any problem of visual interference, but suffers from problems of divided attention [11] as users have to repeatedly inspect each viewport. In addition, this technique can only display half the geographical area that superimposition techniques can show, requiring users to pan the view more often. Additional motor actions include moving the dual cursor to relate both views (Figure 5).

Translucent Overlay (OV)

Techniques that use a superimposition strategy can display a geographical region twice as large, but have their own drawbacks. The first technique consists in overlaying both maps and enabling users to adjust the opacity of the upper layer, so as to see the lower layer through it (Figures 1-c & 3). As the Macroscope [18], OV can cause significant visual interference depending on the maps' content and translucency settings, but it avoids the problems of divided attention from which JX suffers. Motor actions are limited to translucency control, enabling users to adopt a mostly vision-driven scanning strategy (Figure 5). Supporting image blitting is a simple matter of adding shortcuts to 0 and 100% opacity.

Swipe (SW)

Another popular superimposition technique consists in swiping between the two maps (Figures 1-d & 4). As with OV, the two layers are superimposed, but in this case both remain fully opaque. Users "swipe" (or push and pull) the upper layer above the lower one, revealing more of one or the other layer. This technique minimizes both divided attention and visual interference (Figure 5). However, even if, as with OV, motor actions are limited to a simple uni-dimensional control,

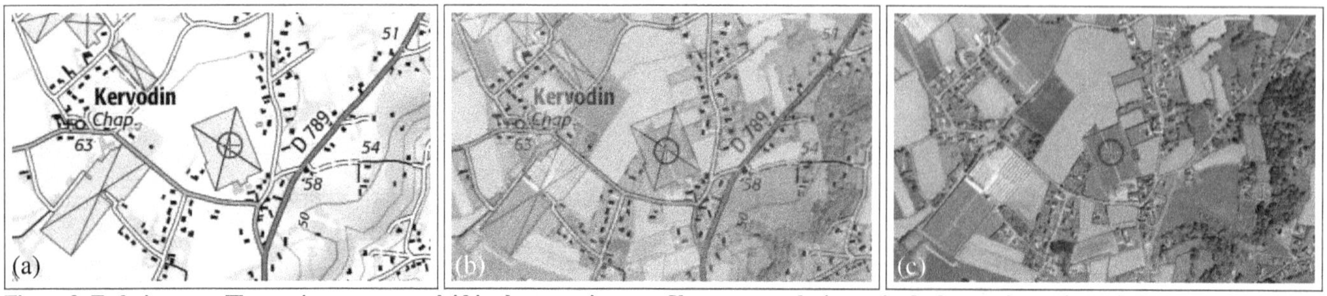

Figure 3. Technique OV**: The two images are overlaid in the same viewport. Users can see the image in the bottom layer *through* the image in the upper layer by adjusting the latter's opacity. (a) Upper layer fully opaque: only the topographic map is visible. (b) At 50% translucency (adjusted using the mouse wheel), the orthoimagery is made partially visible through the map. This time, the two representations of facility *F* (the same as in Figure 2, under the cursor) are spatially aligned. (c) Upper layer fully transparent: the orthoimagery is fully revealed.**

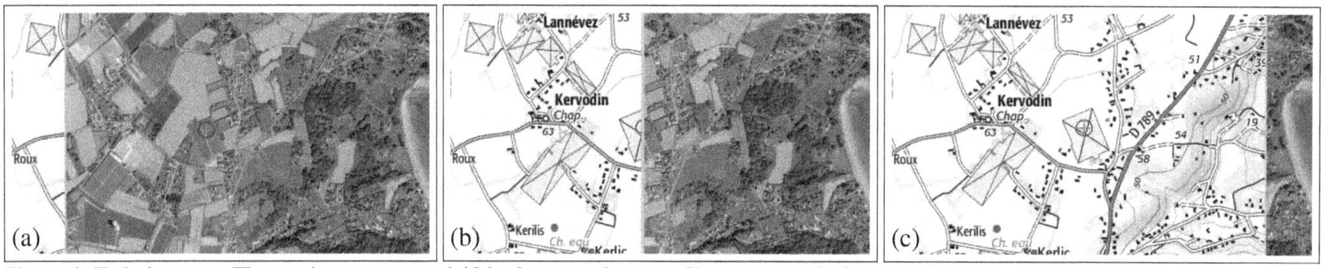

Figure 4. Technique SW**: The two images are overlaid in the same viewport. Users can see the image in the bottom layer by swiping horizontally. (a) Moving the separator to the left reveals more of the orthoimagery. (b) & (c) Moving the separator to the right reveals more of the topographic map. Comparing a feature such as facility *F* across the two layers requires moving the separator back and forth in its vicinity (b).**

the nature of the composition creates a stronger dependency between motor actions and visual scanning.

Blending Lens (BL)

Yet another strategy when the two images are superimposed consists of using a magic lens [3] to show the lower layer in a locally-bounded region around the cursor (Figure 1-b). Figure 6 shows a somewhat more elaborate variant called a Blending Lens [24]. This variant features a smooth transition between the lens' focus and the context thanks to a transparency gradient. As most of the upper layer remains fully opaque, providing a stable context, this technique does not suffer from visual interference as much as OV. There is no problem of divided attention. However, users have to place the lens directly on top of the region in which they want to compare the maps, which forces them to adopt a mostly motor-driven scanning strategy (Figure 5).

Offset Lens (OL)

The last technique, called OffsetLens, is a variant of the DragMag [36]. We identified it as a potentially interesting solution in the design space. OL combines the juxtaposition and nesting operators [14], trying to strike a balance between visual interference and divided attention. As illustrated in Figure 7, it follows the same general approach as BL, except that the two images are juxtaposed instead of being spatially aligned. This makes it possible to look at fully opaque renderings of the region of interest from both maps, minimizing visual interference compared to BL. However, OL reintroduces the problem of divided attention, though less so than JX since the distance between the two viewports is much smaller. As with BL, users have to adopt a mostly motor-driven scanning strategy (Figure 5). As a side note, a typical DragMag would not have the secondary viewport follow the lens automatically, and would allow users to manually reposition it independently. But this additional flexibility would impose more motor actions on users to minimize divided attention.

Specialized Techniques

Several other visual composition techniques exist, but were not considered in the following user study as they have a narrower scope and do not necessarily support general map comparison tasks. Böttger *et al.* [5] describe a technique that composites schematic metro maps with a distorted geographic rendering. Reilly & Inkpen [28] study morphing animations to keep track of entities between incongruent maps. Hoarau *et al.* [12] describe two techniques, *patchwork* and *camouflage*, for blending layers in mostly-static cartographic representations. Finally, WetPaint [4] enables users to scrape through

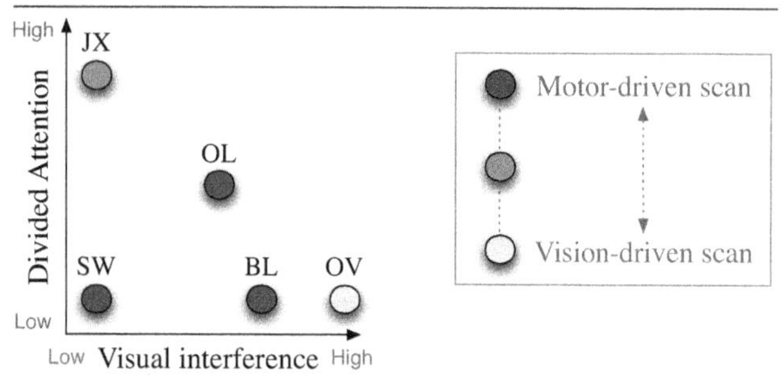

Figure 5. Coarse characterization of the techniques evaluated in the following study, in terms of visual interference and divided attention (which should both be minimized) and type of scanning. A motor-driven scanning strategy requires users to reposition elements on screen with their pointing device to compare different regions. A vision-driven strategy relies more on visual search and does not require so much interaction. This is a continuum: none of the techniques is either purely vision-driven or purely motor-driven.

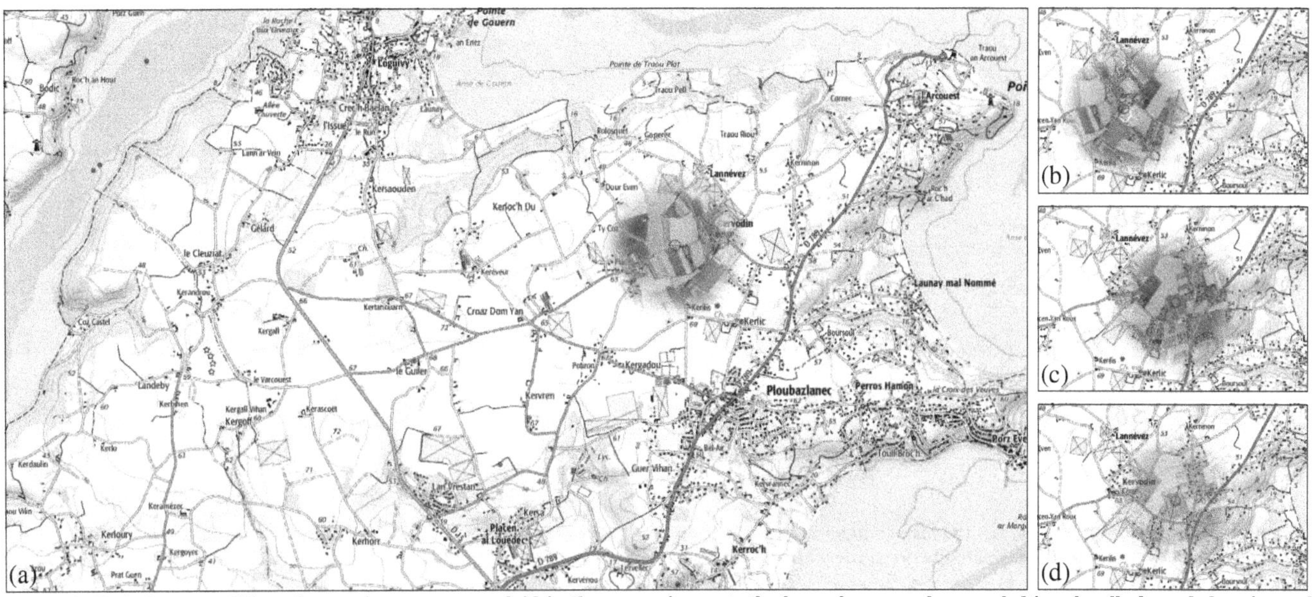

Figure 6. Technique BL: When the two images are overlaid in the same viewport, the lower layer can be revealed in a locally-bounded region only – instead of the entire viewport – using a Blending Lens. The lens *punches a hole* through the upper layer, revealing the lower layer. (a) & (b) The lens approaches from the left the same facility *F* as in previous figures. (c) The lens is centered above it, revealing its appearance in the orthoimagery. (d) The lens' translucency can be adjusted using alpha blending, so that both images are visible simultaneously, as with the overlay technique (OV).

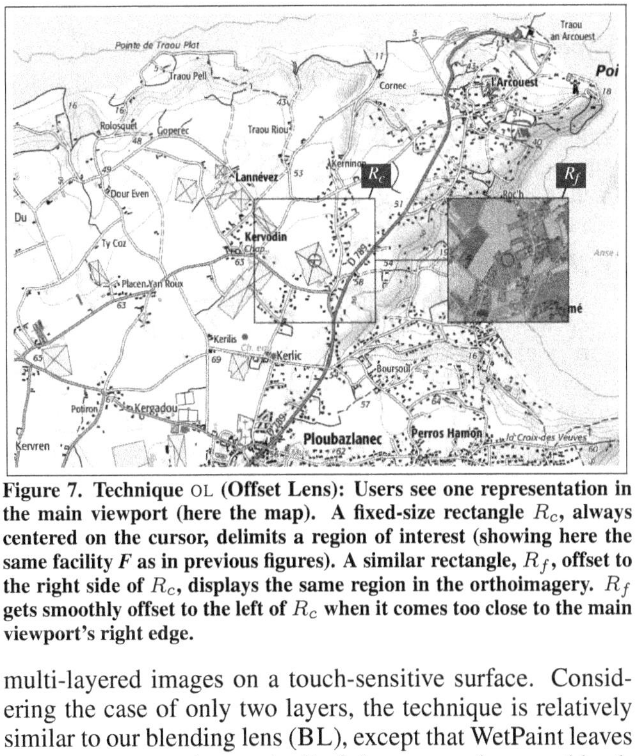

Figure 7. Technique OL (Offset Lens): Users see one representation in the main viewport (here the map). A fixed-size rectangle R_c, always centered on the cursor, delimits a region of interest (showing here the same facility *F* as in previous figures). A similar rectangle, R_f, offset to the right side of R_c, displays the same region in the orthoimagery. R_f gets smoothly offset to the left of R_c when it comes too close to the main viewport's right edge.

multi-layered images on a touch-sensitive surface. Considering the case of only two layers, the technique is relatively similar to our blending lens (BL), except that WetPaint leaves a temporary trace that gradually fades away, whereas a blending lens leaves no trace on its trail.

USER STUDY

To our knowledge, the five techniques introduced above have never been compared empirically on well-defined map comparison tasks. The following studies are related to our work, but try to answer other questions. Luz and Masoodian evaluated the readability of maps when translucent layers containing widgets (sliders) were superimposed on them [19], building upon Harrisson *et al.*'s study of the effect of transparent overlays on user attention [11]. WetPaint [4] was compared to OV on a path following task mixing satellite imagery and a schematic subway map. Plumlee & Ware compared zooming vs. multiple DragMags for multi-scale comparison tasks [26]. Finally, Raposo & Brewer [27] compared eight different topographic designs that statically overlay orthoimages and maps.

Our goal here is to better understand the strengths and weaknesses of comparison techniques based on their characterization in terms of visual interference, user attention and scanning strategy. To this end, we designed a controlled experiment in which users had to compare orthoimagery with topographic maps. We chose this particular configuration because it is representative of many scenarios [7], including map making (in, e.g., OpenStreetMap), cadastral & land management [17], and crisis management after a natural disaster, where satellite imagery can provide up-to-date views of the situation but is not sufficient on its own to perform analyses.

Maps

We used 1:25000 topographic maps (SCAN25) and the corresponding orthoimagery (ORTHO), both produced by IGN (*Institut National de l'Information Géographique et Forestière*, in France), to create 20 perfectly-aligned pairs amenable to comparison; see Figure 2 for a representative example. In each case, we used the orthoimagery as the reference image, and customized the map, purposefully introducing errors, as detailed below. This produced a total of 120 maps. All SCAN25 maps were manually edited in Adobe Illustrator, carefully removing features, introducing new ones, or modifying the geometry of existing ones so that those edits could not be detected without comparison to a reference. While using real maps in our study makes it much more challenging to control precisely all relevant factors, it is also essential in terms of external validity, as discussed later.

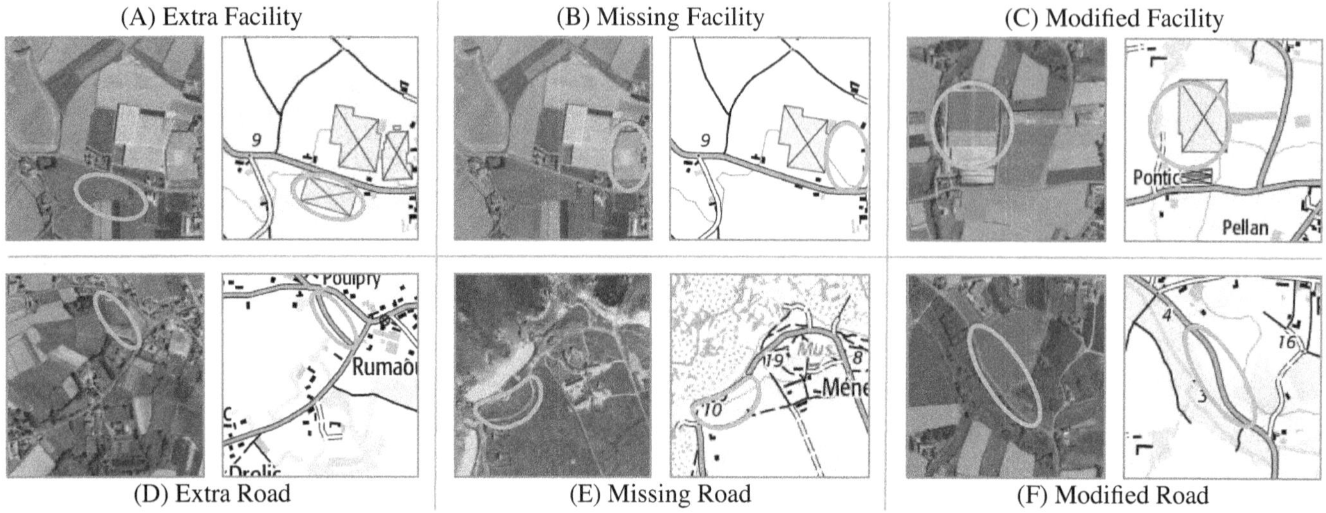

Figure 8. Six types of differences: (A) the map contains a facility not present in the orthoimage; (B) a facility in the orthoimage is missing on the map; (C) a facility shows a geometry mismatch between the map and the orthoimage. (D), (E) and (F) illustrate the same three differences for roads.

Tasks

Elias *et al.* observed that many queries require correlation of multiple maps, and identified three main user-task categories in their taxonomy [7]: familiarization (*"relating the primary features of a map to a context understood by the map user"*), evolution (*"[synthesis of] maps in a common category across time periods"*), fusion (*"synthesis of two maps from categories that are both unfamiliar to the user"*). Many of their examples involve some sort of geometric comparison performed on either lines or surfaces. We position our tasks at this latter level of abstraction, so as to make our findings as generalizable as possible (given the map types considered).

Our tasks test the *compare* objective primitive in Roth's taxonomy of primitives for interactive cartography and geovisualization [30]. These tasks are aimed at operationalizing comparisons performed on the two main map drawing primitives: surfaces and paths, using buildings and roads as representative instances, as detailed below. We believe the chosen tasks are reasonably close to actual comparison tasks such as, e.g., a cartographer updating an outdated topographic map from recent orthoimagery (photomapping).

We propose a set of 3 tasks, performed on 2 distinct types of geographic features: *road* (line), and large man-made *facility* (surface). There are thus 6 distinct types of differences, illustrated in Figure 8. All are separately instantiated on each of the 20 map pairs. To limit task difficulty, any facility involved in a difference is displayed as a gray polygon, at least $1cm^2$ on screen, with a black stroke and cross inside them (Figure 8-A). Modified facilities (Figure 8-C) can be either of the correct size, but offset in position (at least $1.5cm$), or they can have an incorrect size (by a factor of at least 1.5x). Roads to inspect are those painted orange (*routes départementales*). Missing roads (Figure 8-E) are always connected to an orange road at one junction, and are at least $3cm$ long. The distance between the modified segment of a road and the original one is at least $1cm$ (Figure 8-F). All these indications were explicitly given to participants. All 120 differences were evaluated in a pilot study, which helped us identify and replace a subset of trials that were too difficult to perform, no matter the technique used to achieve the task.

Hypotheses

Figure 5 summarizes the positioning of all five techniques considered in the experiment, with respect to how much divided attention and visual interference they cause relative to one another, and whether users' scanning strategy is predominantly motor- or vision-driven. This characterization of techniques led to the following hypotheses:

- *H1:* Techniques that superimpose images (BL, OV, SW) will perform better than those that juxtapose them (JX, OL) because problems of divided attention will be more detrimental to task performance than problems of visual interference, even more so given that the latter can be mitigated via interactive parameter adjustments.
- *H2:* This difference will be stronger for tasks that require precise geometrical comparisons (DIFF = *modified*) than for the other tasks (DIFF = *extra* or *missing*).
- *H3:* Vision-driven scanning should be more efficient than motor-driven scanning, implying that OV will perform best.
- *H4:* OL will provide a good compromise for tasks that do not require precise geometry comparison, as it tries to mitigate problems of divided attention and visual interference.

Participants and Apparatus

Fifteen unpaid volunteers (six females), daily computer users, age 20 to 37 year-old (average 28.5, median 28), served in the experiment. All had normal or corrected-to-normal vision and did not suffer from color blindness. We conducted the experiment on an HP workstation running Linux Fedora 19, equipped with a 3.2 GHz Intel Xeon CPU, 16GB RAM, and an NVidia Quadro 4000 driving a 27" LCD (2560x1440, 100 dpi). We used a standard HP optical mouse set to 400 dpi resolution and default system acceleration. The experiment was implemented in Java 1.7 using the ZVTM toolkit [22].

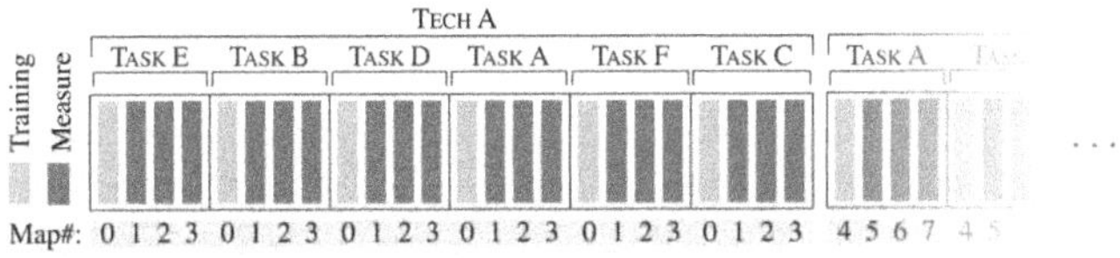

Figure 9. Counterbalancing example: blocking by TECH; the same 4 maps are used for all 6 tasks (1 training + 3 measures) in the same block.

Procedure

We followed a $[5\times2\times3]$ within-subject design with 3 primary factors: TECH ∈ [BL, JX, OL, OV, SW], and the type of task, decomposed into two factors: the type of feature GEOENT ∈ [*road*, *facility*], and the type of difference DIFF ∈ [*extra*, *missing*, *modified*]. Measures include task completion *Time* and incorrect selections, treated as *Errors*.

We grouped trials into 5 blocks, one per TECH. TECH presentation order was counterbalanced using a Latin square (5 orders). Within each TECH, trials were organized into 6 sub-blocks, one per task (GEOENT × DIFF). Task presentation order was counterbalanced independently for each block, using $15 \times 6 = 90$ orders randomly picked out from the $!6 = 720$ possible ones. Within each sub-block, participants performed 1 training trial followed by a series of 3 measures. Maps were grouped in batches of 4 per TECH, always presented in the same order. Using this counterbalancing strategy, illustrated in Figure 9, we ensured that every GEOENT × DIFF combination was performed on every map with every technique by 3 distinct participants. Proper counterbalancing is important: using real-world data means that we cannot fully control the content – and thus the complexity – of our maps and orthoimages. We thus have to handle this potential source of bias.

Participants could rest as long as they wanted between trials, but were asked to perform the task as fast as possible once a trial had started, while avoiding errors. To complete a trial, they had to put the mouse cursor on top of the difference (within 100 pixels from its center), and validate their answer by pressing the space bar. They were reminded about the type of difference before the start of each trial (DIFF+GEOENT, with the corresponding image pair from Figure 8) to avoid any confusion. After each series of 4 trials, participants had to call the experimenter, who asked them to rate the difficulty of the task with each technique using a 5-point Likert scale. The experimenter then made sure participants understood that the task was about to change, and what the new task was.

A correct answer was indicated by a large green tick mark; an incorrect one by a large red cross. To avoid participants rushing through the experiment, incorrect answers were counted as errors, but did not end the trial; participants still had to identify the right feature. To avoid participants getting stuck, we set a 90-second timeout for each trial. The average duration of the experiment was 75 minutes on average.

Results

A total of 1071 trials were successfully completed out of the 1350 performed, i.e., participants identified the difference within the 90s time limit in 79.3% of all trials. Figure 10 shows the distribution of successful trials that remain for analysis. We can see that, despite our initially-balanced

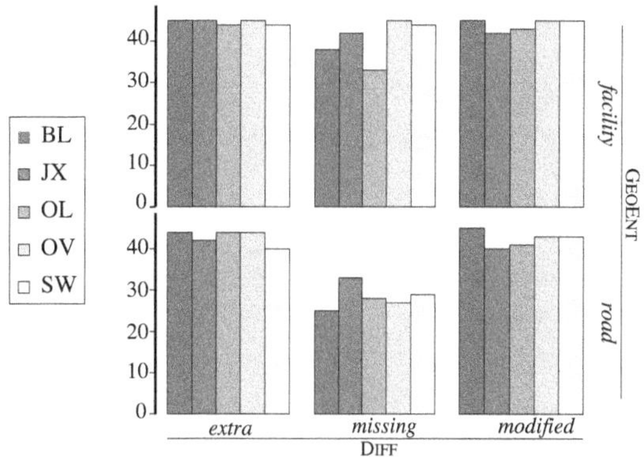

Figure 10. Number of successful trials per TECH × GEOENT × DIFF.

design, collected measures are not properly balanced among TECH × GEOENT × DIFF conditions. While successful trials are equally distributed among the different TECH conditions, their number is much lower in the *road* × *missing* than in all other GEOENT × DIFF conditions. Finding a missing road (Figure 8-E) was too difficult a task for some participants. In order to conduct analyses on datasets having approximately-equal sample sizes per condition, we filtered out all *road* × *missing* trials and considered the following two datasets:

- $D_{facility}$, containing the 642 successful trials in conditions GEOENT = *facility* and DIFF = {*extra*, *missing*, *modified*};
- D_{road}, containing the 426 successful trials in conditions GEOENT = *road* and DIFF = {*extra*, *modified*}.

In 43 of the 642 trials in $D_{facility}$, participants made at least one error before finding the right difference (error rate = 6.5%). An ANOVA on TECH × DIFF reveals that there is no significant effect on *Errors*, showing that no condition is more error-prone than others. On the contrary, both TECH and DIFF have a significant effect on *Time* ($F_{4,56} = 4$, $p = 0.005$, $\eta^2_G = 0.08$ and $F_{2,28} = 39$, $p =< 0.001$, $\eta^2_G = 0.28$, respectively). First, finding a missing facility (avg=22.6s) takes significantly longer than finding a modified facility (avg=15s), which takes significantly longer than finding an extra facility (avg=10s). Second, OV (avg=12s) is the fastest technique, significantly different from SW (avg=16s) and OL (avg=20s), but not from JX (avg=14s) and BL (avg=14s). OL is significantly slower than all other techniques. Finally, an ANOVA reveals a significant TECH × DIFF interaction effect on *Time*. Figure 11-a illustrates the results of post-hoc paired t-tests on the different pairs of conditions. For *missing* tasks, BL and OL perform much worse than the three other techniques, with no significant difference in-between those. However, for *modified* and *extra* tasks, the comparative performance between techniques changes. For *extra* tasks, BL and OL are the fastest techniques, although the difference is significant only for SW, which performs particularly poorly. For *modified* tasks, BL performs better than all other techniques. The difference is significant for all of them, except OV.

In 18 of the 426 trials in D_{road}, participants made at least one error before finding the right difference (error rate is 4.2%). As for $D_{facility}$, an ANOVA on TECH × DIFF reveals that there is no significant effect on *Errors*. Regarding *Time*, only TECH has a significant effect ($F_{4,56} = 2.8$, $p = 0.03$, $\eta^2_G = 0.06$). As shown in Figure 11-b, BL (avg=19s) is the fastest tech-

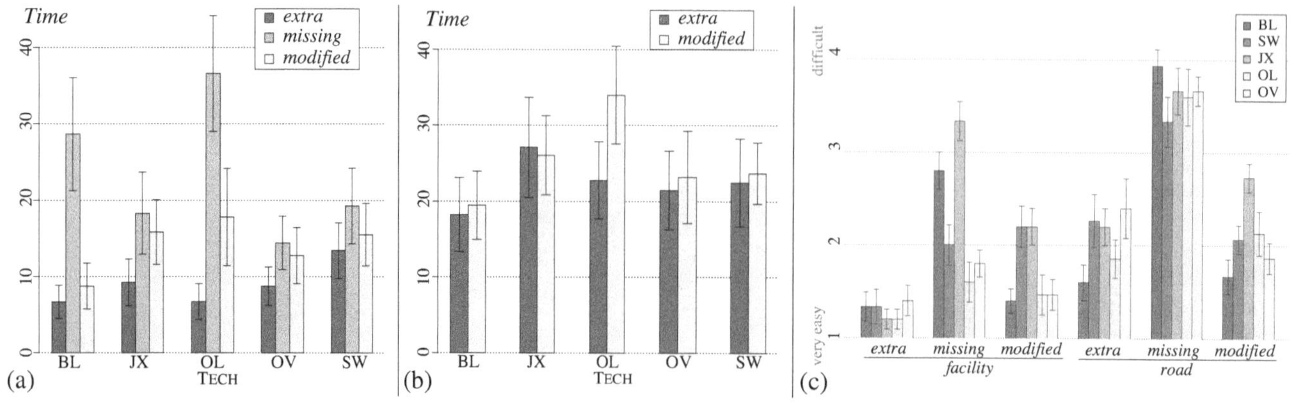

Figure 11. (a) *Time* per TECH × DIFF for GEOENT = *facility* trials (error bars represent the 95% confidence intervals). (b) *Time* per TECH × DIFF for GEOENT = *road* trials (error bars represent the 95% CIs). (c) Perceived *Difficulty* per TECH × TASK (error bars represent the standard errors).

nique, the difference being significant with OL (avg=28s) and JX (avg=26s), but not with SW (avg=23s) and OV (avg=22s).

Additional insights can be gained by performing an ANOVA on TECH × DIFF, without removing the *road* × *missing* trials that were filtered out in the above analysis. Results indicate that TECH ($F_{4,57.43} = 5.01, p = 0.0015$), DIFF ($F_{2,26.65} = 71.57$, $p < 0.0001$), and TECH × DIFF ($F_{8,108.3} = 6.31, p < 0.0001$) all have a significant effect on *Time*. OV is the fastest technique on average (avg=16s), followed by BL (avg=18s), JX (avg=20s), SW (21s) and OL (avg=25s). But BL is actually the best technique in the DIFF=*extra* and DIFF=*modified* conditions. However the difference with OV is significant only in the DIFF=*modified* condition.

Finally, Figure 11-c reports the perceived *Difficulty*, from 1 (very easy) to 5 (very difficult), of using a technique for completing each task (TASKs are the 6 GEOENT × DIFF combinations). An ANOVA reveals effects consistent with the measured quantitative performance. TECH has a significant effect ($F_{4,56} = 4, p = 0.006, \eta^2_G = 0.1461859$). OL, which performs the worst on average, was perceived as significantly more difficult to use than all other techniques, which do not significantly differ from each other. TASK also has a significant effect ($F_{5,70} = 69, p =< 0.001, \eta^2_G = 0.73$). Finding a missing road was rated as significantly more difficult than any other task. Finding a modified or an extra facility was significantly easier than other tasks (*extra* × *facility* being the easiest). Using BL, all tasks were perceived as easy or very easy, except for tasks in which DIFF = *missing*. Using OV, all tasks were considered as easy or very easy, except finding a missing road, which was rated as difficult, no matter the technique.

DISCUSSION

A first general observation is that, as expected, the three types of differences (DIFF) have a strong impact on task completion time: finding *missing* features takes longer than finding *modified* ones, which takes longer than finding *extra* ones. This observation can be explained by the strategy employed to find the three types of differences. It is important to recall that orthoimagery (ORTHO) was used as the reference image, with errors introduced in the topographic map (SCAN25). In the *extra* and *modified* conditions, participants would simply look at the different features on the SCAN25 map and compare them against ORTHO. Eligible features were quite easy to identify visually on SCAN25. But in the *missing* conditions, participants had to do the opposite: look for features in the ORTHO image and check whether they existed on the SCAN25 map or not. In this case, eligible features were less easy to identify, which partially explains the strong task completion time difference between *extra* and *missing* conditions in Figure 11-a. Finding *modified* features took longer than finding *extra* features because it involved more elaborate geometrical comparisons. Still, participants were faster at this than at finding *missing* features, as eligible features could be identified on SCAN25 maps, as in the *extra* conditions.

Regarding our hypotheses, *H1* is only partially supported. When comparing *roads*, BL, OV and SW do perform better than JX and OL indeed, but only significantly so for BL. Also, OL performs significantly more poorly than all other techniques. When comparing *facilities*, OV and BL are the two best techniques, along with JX. SW performs poorly overall, as discussed later. Thus, superimposition (as opposed to juxtaposition) does seem to be the right strategy, when combined with other properties. But it is not a determinant factor.

H2 is also partially supported. When looking for *modified* roads or facilities, the three techniques based on superimposition (BL, OV and SW) indeed perform consistently better than those based on juxtaposition (JX and OL). However, the task-time difference is not systematically significant. As for *H1*, our results provide empirical evidence only for specific techniques (BL); not for the whole class of superimposition techniques. Thus, our results only suggest that superimposition works best when looking for subtle differences, such as the path of a road portion being slightly different or a building's position being offset. Subjective ratings are in accordance with these quantitative measures (Figure 11-c), reflecting the higher difficulty of performing such comparisons on juxtaposed representations as opposed to aligned ones.

OV features the best overall task completion time, significantly shorter than those of SW and OL. *H3* is thus supported, though this should probably be attributed more to the low level of divided attention rather than to the vision-driven scanning strategy, since BL (which employs a more motor-driven strategy) performs as well – if not better – in many task conditions. This actually raises the question of whether a motor-driven scan could actually have positive side-effects. While it prevents users from performing fast visual searches, motor-driven scanning might actually help *structure* the exploration, making users less prone to performing random jumps between arbitrary locations, potentially reducing the number of revisits. Additional studies are required to confirm this.

H4 is rejected. By displaying the two representations closer together than JX does (thus limiting the amplitude of saccadic eye movements) while rendering both of them fully opaque (thus minimizing visual interference), we were expecting that OL would mitigate these two problems, but it does not.

As illustrated in Figure 5, techniques Translucent Overlay (OV) and Juxtapose (JX) can be seen as extreme points in the design space of composition techniques, with Blending Lens (BL), Offset Lens (OL) and Swipe (SW) trying to find compromises between those two extremes. OV is the most versatile technique, featuring good performance for all tasks. As expected, divided attention proved to be more detrimental than visual interference. While it looked promising, SW turned out to be surprisingly inefficient for most tasks. We tentatively attribute this poor performance to the tight coupling between motor actions and visual comparison, which forces users to adopt a very constrained scanning strategy if they want to avoid too many micro-swipes back and forth. OL was a DragMag-inspired [36] attempt at mitigating problems of both divided attention and visual interference, which failed for the most part, except for the identification of *extra* features. Somewhat surprisingly, BL turned out to perform quite well on both *extra* and *modified* tasks. Its bad performance in *missing* tasks is partly explained by the earlier-discussed higher difficulty of finding features in ORTHO images. Performance should improve drastically by allowing dynamic toggling of what layer is assigned to focus and context regions.

Validity

Many HCI experiments that involve techniques for interacting with maps are based on highly-abstracted experimental tasks [8, 15, 19, 23, 24, 28]. Even when seeking a higher-level of ecological validity, the base maps and overlaid features tend to be simplified, either in terms of rendering or layout, so as to minimize the influence of factors that would be otherwise difficult to control [4, 10, 13, 25, 26, 29, 37]. While this is a generally sound approach, our study warranted the use of real-world maps. Abstract representations, or even simplified maps, would have strongly altered the end-result of the different map composition strategies in terms of visual complexity, which would have significantly threatened the external validity of our experiment.

As a result, we had to address several potential threats to internal validity. First, orthoimagery and the corresponding topographic maps cannot easily be synthesized. We thus have to use actual maps, which entails that we cannot fully control the visual complexity of our base maps. As a consequence, we had to pay careful attention to our experiment design, so as to minimize this potential source of bias. In addition to the counterbalancing strategy we described earlier, we also tried to minimize differences between maps with respect to the particular geographical features considered. Some topographic maps were also customized by hand before the introduction of differences, changing the type of some roads so as to have a relatively equivalent length of eligible roads in all 20 map pairs. Producing these maps took significant effort, and we make them available to the community[5], both for the purpose of replication, and for possible use in other studies.

Another threat to internal validity is the lack of control over participants stumbling upon the correct feature earlier rather than later. While some operationalizations address this issue [23, 25, 15], these elaborate strategies rely on synthetic data and are incompatible with the use of real maps. But with 3 replications per participant per TECH × GEOENT × DIFF condition, and a total of 1071 successful trials analyzed over our 15 participants, this threat should be minimal.

Our focus on external validity does not mean that our findings generalize to the comparison of arbitrary types of images. As mentioned earlier, these techniques are used in a wide range of application areas. This includes astronomy and medical imaging, i.e., domains in which the two images are going to be visually much more similar than topographic maps and orthoimages are. Even in geovisualization, results may be different when comparing visually-similar maps. Indeed, the nature and impact of visual interference caused by the superimposition of such images is likely to be very different. Results might also differ in the case of topographic map & orthoimage comparison performed in highly-urbanized geographical regions, as we used maps of predominantly rural areas. Evaluating the influence of different map types would have required introducing additional factors such as object density. Doing so would have made the experiment's complexity unmanageable, and was left as future work.

SUMMARY

We characterized and evaluated five techniques for performing interactive map comparison, using real-world maps. The study's results suggest the following guidelines to UI designers: (1) Translucent Overlay (OV) is the best technique overall, which makes it a good choice when only one comparison technique should be provided to users. (2) Even if its overall performance is not as good as that of OV, Blending Lens (BL) performs as well as or better than OV when the task consists of identifying extra or modified entities. We tentatively attribute this to BL's mostly motor-driven scanning strategy, which helps structure inspection of candidate features in the upper layer. The combination of OV and BL should be favored by UI designers when possible, as the two are quite complementary. (3) Swipe (SW) and Offset Lens (OL) perform poorly. This is an interesting finding given that SW is a technique commonly encountered in Web mapping applications. Its use should probably be reconsidered.

ACKNOWLEDGMENTS

This research was partly supported by ANR project MapMuxing (ANR-14-CE24-0011-02). We wish to thank Charlotte Hoarau, as well as Sidonie Christophe and Guillaume Touya from IGN for sharing their GI science expertise with us.

[5]`http://ilda.saclay.inria.fr/mapmuxing/chi2015`

REFERENCES

1. Appert C., Chapuis O. & Pietriga E. High-precision magnification lenses. *CHI '10*, ACM (2010), 273–282.
2. Bertin J. *Semiology of Graphics*. University of Wisconsin Press, 1983.
3. Bier E. A., Stone M. C., Pier K., Buxton W. & DeRose T. D. Toolglass and magic lenses: The see-through interface. *SIGGRAPH '93*, ACM (1993), 73–80.
4. Bonanni L., Xiao X., Hockenberry M., Subramani P., Ishii H., Seracini M. & Schulze J. Wetpaint: Scraping through multi-layered images. *CHI '09*, ACM (2009), 571–574.
5. Böttger J., Brandes U., Deussen O. & Ziezold H. Map warping for the annotation of metro maps. *IEEE Computer Graphics & Applications 28*, 5 (2008), 56–65.
6. Cockburn A., Karlson A. & Bederson B. B. A review of overview+detail, zooming, and focus+context interfaces. *ACM Comput. Surv. 41*, 1 (2009), 2:1–2:31.
7. Elias M., Elson J., Fisher D. & Howell J. Do I Live in a Flood Basin?: Synthesizing Ten Thousand Maps. *CHI '08*, ACM (2008), 255–264.
8. Elmqvist N., Riche Y., Henry-Riche N. & Fekete J.-D. Mélange: Space folding for visual exploration. *IEEE TVCG 16*, 3 (2010), 468–483.
9. Gleicher M., Albers D., Walker R., Jusufi I., Hansen C. D. & Roberts J. C. Visual comparison for information visualization. *Information Visualization 10*, 4 (2011), 289–309.
10. Gustafson S., Baudisch P., Gutwin C. & Irani P. Wedge: Clutter-free visualization of off-screen locations. *CHI '08*, ACM (2008), 787–796.
11. Harrison B. L., Ishii H., Vicente K. J. & Buxton W. A. S. Transparent layered user interfaces: An evaluation of a display design to enhance focused and divided attention. *CHI '95*, ACM Press/Addison-Wesley (1995), 317–324.
12. Hoarau C., Christophe S. & Mustière S. Mixing, blending, merging or scrambling topographic maps and orthoimagery in geovisualizations? In *International Cartographic Conference* (2013).
13. Hornbæk K., Bederson B. B. & Plaisant C. Navigation patterns and usability of zoomable user interfaces with and without an overview. *ACM ToCHI 9*, 4 (2002), 362–389.
14. Javed W. & Elmqvist N. Exploring the design space of composite visualization. *PacificVis*, IEEE (2012), 1–8.
15. Javed W., Ghani S. & Elmqvist N. Polyzoom: Multiscale and Multifocus Exploration in 2D Visual Spaces. *CHI '12*, ACM (2012), 287–296.
16. Koch T. The map as intent: variations on the theme of John Snow. *Cartographica: Int. Jour. for Geographic Information and Geovisualization 39*, 4 (2004), 1–14.
17. Lee H., Lee S., Kim N. & Seo J. JigsawMap: Connecting the Past to the Future by Mapping Historical Textual Cadasters. *CHI '12*, ACM (2012), 463–472.
18. Lieberman H. Powers of ten thousand: Navigating in large information spaces. *UIST*, ACM (1994), 15–16.
19. Luz S. & Masoodian M. Readability of a background map layer under a semi-transparent foreground layer. *AVI '14*, ACM (2014), 161–168.
20. MacEachren A. M. The roles of maps. In *The Map Reader*. Wiley & Sons, 2011, 244–251.
21. MacEachren A. M. & Kraak M.-J. Research Challenges in Geovisualization. *Cartography and Geographic Information Science 28*, 1 (2001), 3–12.
22. Pietriga E. A Toolkit for Addressing HCI Issues in Visual Language Environments. *VLHCC '05*, IEEE (2005), 145–152.
23. Pietriga E., Appert C. & Beaudouin-Lafon M. Pointing and beyond: An operationalization and preliminary evaluation of multi-scale searching. *CHI '07*, ACM (2007), 1215–1224.
24. Pietriga E., Bau O. & Appert C. Representation-Independent In-Place Magnification with Sigma Lenses. *IEEE TVCG 16*, 3 (2010), 455–467.
25. Pindat C., Pietriga E., Chapuis O. & Puech C. Jellylens: content-aware adaptive lenses. *UIST '12*, ACM (2012), 261–270.
26. Plumlee M. D. & Ware C. Zooming versus multiple window interfaces: Cognitive costs of visual comparisons. *ACM ToCHI 13*, 2 (2006), 179–209.
27. Raposo P. & Brewer C. Comparison of topographic map designs for overlay on orthoimage backgrounds. In *International Cartographic Conference* (2011), 3–8.
28. Reilly D. F. & Inkpen K. M. Map morphing: Making sense of incongruent maps. *GI '04* (2004), 231–238.
29. Rønne Jakobsen M. & Hornbæk K. Sizing up visualizations: Effects of display size in focus+context, overview+detail, and zooming interfaces. *CHI '11*, ACM (2011), 1451–1460.
30. Roth R. E. An empirically-derived taxonomy of interaction primitives for interactive cartography and geovisualization. *IEEE TVCG 19*, 12 (2013), 2356–2365.
31. Roth R. E. Interactive maps: What we know and what we need to know. *Journal of Spatial Information Science*, 6 (2013), 59–115.
32. Slingsby A., Dykes J., Wood J. & Radburn R. Designing an exploratory visual interface to the results of citizen surveys. *International Journal of Geographical Information Science 28*, 10 (2014), 2090–2125.
33. Touya G. Social welfare to assess the global legibility of a generalized map. In *International Conference on Geographic Information*, Springer (2012), 198–211.
34. Touya G. & Girres J.-F. ScaleMaster 2.0: a ScaleMaster extension to monitor automatic multi-scales generalizations. *Cartography and Geographic Information Science 40*, 3 (2013), 192–200.
35. Tversky B. Some ways that maps and diagrams communicate. In *Spatial Cognition II*. Springer-Verlag, 2000, 72–79.
36. Ware C. & Lewis M. The DragMag Image Magnifier. *CHI '95 companion*, ACM (1995), 407–408.
37. Yatani K., Partridge K., Bern M. & Newman M. W. Escape: A target selection technique using visually-cued gestures. *CHI '08*, ACM (2008), 285–294.

Ethermap - Real-time Collaborative Map Editing

Thore Fechner
Institute for Geoinformatics
University of Münster
t.fechner@uni-muenster.de

Dennis Wilhelm
Institute for Geoinformatics
University of Münster
d.wilhelm@uni-muenster.de

Christian Kray
Institute for Geoinformatics
University of Münster
c.kray@uni-muenster.de

ABSTRACT
Real-time synchronization is increasingly available in web-based environments for editing textual data, and this has changed how groups of people collaborate. We present a novel approach for real-time collaborative editing of geo-data. We introduce Ethermap, an open source web-application that implements this approach and enables multiple users to map data concurrently. It supports synchronous and collaborative mapping in several ways: it visually highlights mapping activities, it allows for fine-grained reviewing of all changes, and it enhances text-based communication with cross-modal references to geo-objects.

We report on key results from a multi-tiered evaluation of Ethermap based on a user-study and on expert interviews. The concept of real-time collaborative editing was received favorably by users and experts. Participants of the study learned to use Ethermap quickly, and successfully completed a collaborative mapping task. Experts and users agreed that, given the right scenario (e.g., disaster mapping, teaching, planning), the approach could benefit the process of working on geo-data collaboratively.

Author Keywords
Collaboration; real-time; mapping; synchronous interaction

ACM Classification Keywords
H.5.3. Information Interfaces and Presentation (e.g. HCI): Group and Organization Interfaces

INTRODUCTION
With the rise of cloud-based computing, *real-time collaboration* has found its way into many web applications such as Google Docs, Cloud9 IDE, and Etherpad[1]. Real-time collaboration enables multiple users to simultaneously edit the same dataset while working on different devices and/or at different locations. Any changes in the shared workspace are immediately visible to all collaborators [16]. Real-time collaboration can thus lead to increased efficiency compared to standard approaches [12]. Real-time collaborative editors try to mimic the dynamic of working together at the same place and time. Conflicting changes can be resolved in real-time. In classic version control systems in contrast, this happens asynchronously. Version control is nevertheless an important tool for collaboration. It provides insights into data provenance and the history of datasets. In addition, it allows for inspecting changes and reverting to older versions, e.g., to remove errors or unwanted changes.

In this paper we investigate how to extend the process of non-blocking real-time collaborative editing to geo-data. We developed a web-based application called Ethermap that enables multiple users to simultaneously map/edit geo-data. The system supports this process by unobtrusively highlighting collaborative user activities, by a map history (version control) allowing for a detailed inspection of changes over time, by providing a functionality to easily follow other users' movements, and by a chat function that can directly reference geo-objects. A number of other features further contribute towards increasing user-awareness, such as color coding individual users and visualizing other users' work areas.

The design was informed by existing research in the area of multi-user collaboration environments [1, 16], single screen geocollaboration environments [20], and by geo-conference tools [4]. Current research in real-time collaboration is mainly focused on textual data. Occasionally, computer-aided design (CAD) systems [23] or graphics programs [29] are considered as well, but there is a lack of research investigating geospatial data. Usually, mapping tools are asynchronous and blocking applications that require sequential interaction. In multi-user scenarios, it is frequently the case that "same place work models" or remote presence systems are used [4], where one user "drives" the system and the others are merely "passengers". The interaction possibilities of the latter group are limited, as they often cannot interact with the data directly. They might also have to wait until a lock is released or a new version is made available. Real-time collaboration on maps removes these obstacles and thus challenges the very idea of what defines a map user, as every connected user can easily become a contributor at any time [8]. This is essential in scenarios where every edit counts, e.g., in crowd-sourced disaster mapping or urban planning as duplicates or conflicts are reduced, queues are eliminated, and efficiency is raised.

The main contributions of this paper are threefold: 1) a concept for non-blocking synchronous collaborative map editing tailored to specific properties of geo-data; 2) an in-depth evaluation of the concept; and 3) an open source application supporting this kind of interaction. In the remainder of this paper, we first review related work before introducing our approach

[1] `https://docs.google.com`, `https://c9.io`, `http://etherpad.org`, accessed 27.06.2014

CHI 2015, April 18–23, 2015, Seoul, Republic of Korea.

http://dx.doi.org/10.1145/2702123.2702536

and its implementation. We then report on how it was evaluated and discuss the results. The paper concludes by summarizing our main contributions.

RELATED WORK

The need for tools that support geospatial collaboration has been recognized by various parties, e.g., by Jankowski et al. [15] in 1997. They defined *collaboration* as the process of two or more persons working together on a single task. They used the term *cooperation* to refer to situations where persons are working on several tasks while only sharing the results. MacEachren coined the term *geocollaboration* [19] for collaboration focused on geospatial aspects. Geocollaboration scenarios can be placed in four distinct categories based on the spatial and temporal dimension: same time/same place, same time/different place, different times/same place, and different times/different places [10]. Each category differs in terms of the interactions it affords and how well it supports different tasks. Systems supporting synchronous distributed collaboration (same time / different place) are also called (distributed) real-time collaborative editing systems. Research investigating such systems is mainly focusing on code or text editors [12], but there is also work looking into graphics [29] and CAD [23].

Research targeting *synchronous* distributed collaboration on geo-data is comparatively scarce. Butt and Li [4] describe a prototypical geo-conferencing tool, where their primary focus is on supporting communication via whiteboard interaction. Unlike our approach, their application aims more at providing a presentation and discussion tool for geo-data rather than facilitating the editing of geospatial data. Chang and Li [6] propose an abstract model for real-time geocollaboration that incorporates technological, geospatial, and social aspects. Research in Participatory GIS (PGIS) is strongly linked to synchronous distributed geocollaboration, and can provide some convincing use cases for this approach, e.g., spatial decision support systems for groups [2], argumentation maps [28], and collaborative web mapping [3]. This aspect can also contribute to the democratization of GIS-based decision making [11]. The system most closely related to the work presented here is Cyclopath [27]. Cyclopath is an *asynchronous* computational geowiki that enables cyclists to map bike routes collaboratively. Ethermap differs from Cyclopath in that it enables synchronous and non-blocking collaboration across all functions, including those it shares with Cyclopath (e.g., version control and some user-awareness features).

Research in the area of synchronous multi-user editors in general suggests that creating awareness of other users in the workspace can greatly improve collaboration. Disadvantages arising from the lack of face-to-face communication can be reduced in this way [16]. These disadvantages include a limited field of view as well as the loss of gestures and facial expressions [5]. Different methods to increase awareness are well studied for software development and text editors. Usually they include real-time highlighting of changes, visualizations of the working areas of other collaborators, different colors for different users, and different means for communication (e.g., chat facilities) [1]. Drawing from work in this area, Ethermap uses such user-awareness methods and adapts them to the specific needs and properties of a map editor.

Version control systems are another important component contributing to successful collaborative work. They enable users to review the development of a document, to revert to a specific revision [13], and to evaluate authenticity. Version control systems such as Git and Subversion[2] are becoming increasingly popular means for collaboration [9]. They are often tightly integrated into text-based real-time collaborative systems (e.g., Google Docs and Etherpad). In contrast, tightly integrated version control for geo-data is an emerging field[3] [27]. For our prototypical implementation, we thus realized a version control system that is fully integrated with real-time collaborative editing of geospatial datasets.

Evaluating complex systems such as (distributed) real-time collaborative map editors is very challenging. Pinelle and Gutwin [26] surveyed how multi-user systems were evaluated in the past. They identified seven main methods: user observations, interviews, discussions, questionnaires, qualitative and quantitative work measures, and collecting archival material. Evaluation of such systems should not just focus on individuals but consider the increased complexity of real-time workflows with multiple concurrent users [24, 26]. Neale et al. [24] identified several relevant areas for evaluation of multi-user systems: usability issues (ease of use, effectiveness, efficiency, satisfaction), social and organizational impact, cooperative and collaborative factors, cognitive aspects, and the larger context of the system. Based on these observations and following recommendations by Butt and Li [4], we evaluated our approach in multiple ways. We first conducted a pre-study with a focus group that evaluated if certain features worked as intended (i.e., user-awareness, chat, version-control). We then carried out a user study focusing on usability, and interviewed experts to investigate collaborative or organizational issues.

APPROACH

The overall goal of our approach is to facilitate real-time collaborative map editing of geo-data between distributed users. Ethermap is the prototypical implementation of this concept, which is designed around the idea of quickly gathering, creating, and using geo-data together – thereby improving the process of collaboratively working on geo-data. Potential use cases for this approach include disaster mapping, participatory planning processes, and virtual town hall meetings. Real-time collaborative editing of geo-data could further enable novel application scenarios such as "pair" mapping (as in extreme programming, where two programmers work closely together). Generally, this approach can be beneficial in scenarios where awareness of other users is crucial, under time pressure, and where universal and equal access is essential. Real-time collaborative editing can also help to resolve conflicts through implicit coordination and to avoid double work

[2] `http://git-scm.com/`, `https://subversion.apache.org/`, accessed 12.09.2014

[3] cf. GeoGig `http://geogig.org/`, `https://github.com/blog/1772-diffable-more-customizable-maps`, accessed 28.08.2014

as contributors do not have to wait for others to finish working on a specific object before editing it.

The key challenge to overcome in realizing real-time collaboration on geo-data results from the distinct properties of such data (compared to other data types such as text). Firstly, geo-data is spatial, i.e., it extends to at least two dimensions, which makes is more difficult to navigate documents and to track changes. For example, whereas in texts, it may be feasible to show changes in-line with the old text being crossed out, this principle would not directly translate to geo-data, as the location of an object carries meaning. Secondly, geo-data is often layered to deal with different aspects related to a spatial area, multiple layers are superimposed. For example, it may be necessary to combine different layers encapsulating buildings, height profiles, and water bodies to assess flood risks.

Thirdly, geo-data is highly structured: in addition to spatial components, there is a (potentially large) number of non-spatial components, called attributes, which represent thematic aspects of a geo-object. For example, a two-dimensional polygon might represent a building, and several thematic attributes might describe its main use, its owner and value. Finally, geo-data can be very complex and might require extensive navigation when working with just a single object. For example, the geometry of a river may span multiple screens (depending on the zoom level) and contain thousands of points. The distinct properties of geo-data thus require adjusting principles and interfaces in real-time collaboration and the design of new ones to support collaboration.

Conflict resolution is a further area, where geo-data can pose significant challenges. Conflicts can arise easily when multiple users edit or map data, for example, in crowd-sourced projects dealing with geo-data such as OpenStreetMap (OSM) or the Humanitarian OpenStreetMap Team (HOT). OpenStreetMap is a project aiming at crowd-sourcing a map of the world, whereas HOT aims to support humanitarian actions and disaster response efforts. When conflicting versions appear in the system, OSM simply raises errors, while the HOT OSM Tasking Manager uses a soft locking mechanism that tries to focus work on a specific geographic area at a time.[4] However, conflicts can still arise, as contributors can leave the assigned geographic area easily by zooming and panning and then edit geometries outside, which potentially results in invalid and conflicting states. This can prevent collaborators from contributing, create frustration, and can also significantly reduce efficiency and scalability. Yet, time is often of the essence in scenarios requiring real-time collaboration, e.g., in disaster mapping or during participatory planning processes. Ethermap eliminates this problem by introducing real-time synchronization between all contributors.

In order to enable efficient real-time collaboration with geo-data, we propose a set of measures that account for the specific properties of geo-data. The approach is based on the

[4] `http://openstreetmap.org/`, `http://hot.openstreetmap.org/`, `http://tasks.hotosm.org`, accessed 17.09.2014

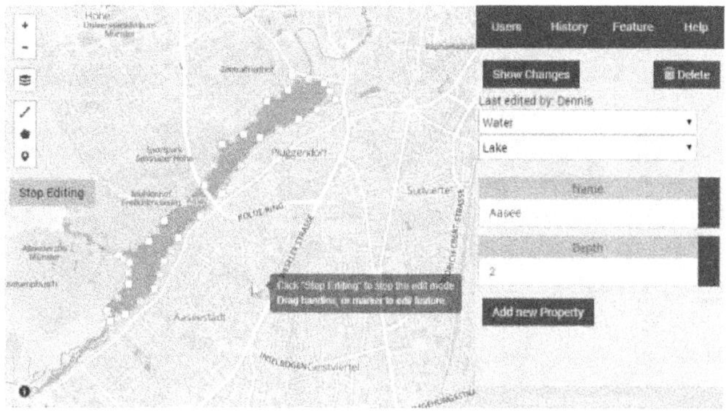

Figure 1: Ethermap web app: a map shows a geo-object being edited while a menu on the right displays its attributes.

principle of immediate and continuous real-time synchronization of all changes being made. The measures focus on raising user-awareness, facilitating communication, and the interactive exploration of changes. In the following paragraphs, we describe these measures as well as how they were realized in prototypical implementation (see Figure 1).

Real-time synchronization: The basic underlying principle is to enable users to create, edit, and delete simple geometries, such as points, lines, and polygons, while working in the same workspace and on the same data. Every time a feature is created or edited, the changes are immediately distributed to all users. This is essential to enable all users to edit any object at any time and thus to facilitate real collaboration [29]. Conflicts are not managed automatically, but the conflict resolution process is supported via the measures described below. In Ethermap, we achieved real-time synchronization via an optimized client-server architecture with push-based messaging to ensure that all users receive updates in real-time.

Raising user-awareness: In order to make users aware of the work of other collaborators, it is necessary to relay a number of aspects to them so that they can coordinate their activities. These include whether other people are currently focusing or working on a specific geo-object, who they are, what objects have been edited, and also which part of a potentially large map other users are working on at a particular time [17].

Ethermap realizes these functions in the following way: users are color-coded, and this color is used to highlight different actions they perform. When an object is updated, it is briefly highlighted in the color of the user who caused the change, and then it fades back to its original color. All information about currently connected users is displayed in a contextual menu (see Figure 2a). This menu can also be used to indicate the current work area of a particular user: clicking on a user's name will briefly highlight the bounding box of their current work area. In addition, it is possible to continuously "follow users around" by activating a "watch" function. Unless disabled, the map view of one user will then automatically follow the view of another user. This can be beneficial, e.g., when working in pairs where one person edits the geo-data while the other person checks if the changes are correct. If an object is currently being edited by a user, other users will

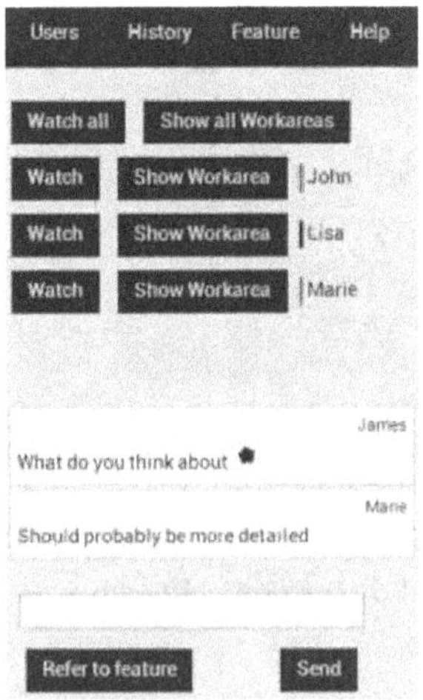

(a) Users tab: shows who is online; provides means to chat, and to show users' workareas.

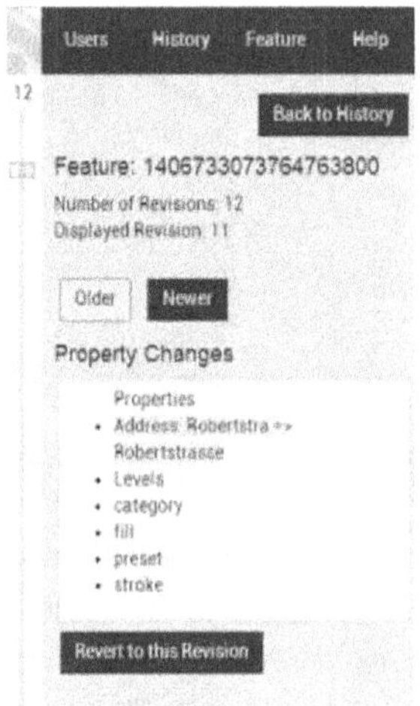

(b) History tab: supports browsing and reverting to revisions via slider or buttons.

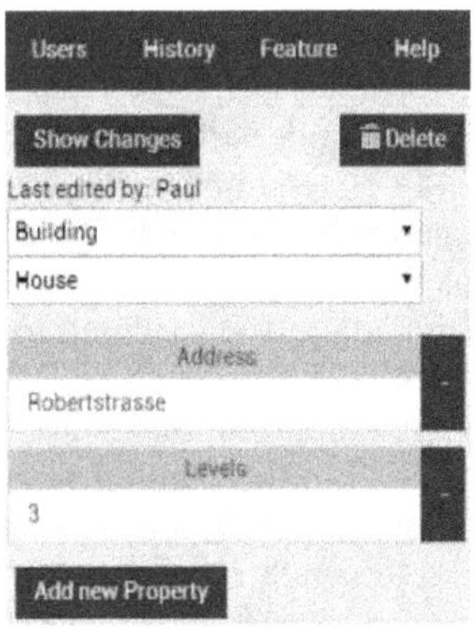

(c) Feature tab: shows the attributes of a geo-object and provides means to edit them.

(d) Global map history: shows aggregated changes to avoid cluttering the list.

Figure 2: Main views (tabs) of the contextual menu: user list, map history, feature attributes and feature history.

see a dashed outline in the color of the editing user. This helps reducing conflicts that might otherwise occur. If multiple users are editing the same object they are all displayed in the contextual menu of the application.

Facilitating communication: Establishing means to directly communicate with other users in the application is a requirement to collaboratively solve tasks [18]. The different means to raise user-awareness can facilitate implicit communication. Direct communication, e.g., via an online chat tool, enables users to explicitly discuss various aspects, to express opinions, and to ask questions. In the context of collaborative map editing, the domain of conversation is inherently spatial and also very complex (see the discussion at the beginning of this section). In addition, only a subset of geo-objects usually have meaningful names, which makes it difficult to refer to them verbally. We thus extended the chat with means to easily reference geo-objects and to navigate the potentially large map, which is known to improve communication [7].

In Ethermap, we realized this by including cross-modal references to geo-objects. Figure 2a shows a chat message that references a polygon. A reference is realized as an icon showing the symbol for the type of the geo-object (a polygon in the example case). Users can easily insert such references in a message by clicking on a button within the chat window and clicking on the geo-object afterwards. When a user clicks on a reference contained in a chat message, the map view automatically centers on the location of the corresponding geo-object while setting the appropriate zoom level.

Exploration of changes: When multiple users collaborate, it is important to keep track of what is being done by whom and when, and to provide means to revert to earlier states of the work. For example, how things have changed over time can help understand work processes and provenance. In the case of geo-objects, it can also document how the world has changed over time (e.g., after a disaster struck). The exploration of changes is subject to the similar constraints as the facilitation of communication. Due to the complex and spatial nature of the domain, it is necessary to extend the standard functionality of version control tools with means to easily reference and interact with geo-objects. Version control systems can be used in synchronous and asynchronous collaboration systems. Priedhorsky et al. [27] reported on an asynchronous version control system for geographic data, and OSM also provides rudimentary version control functionality.

Just like Cyclopath and OSM, Ethermap provides similar version control functions. However, Ethermaps' features can be used synchronously: all version control features are fully integrated into the real-time editing process. Any actions performed on the version history are thus immediately visible to all collaborators. In Ethermap, a continuous history feed records all changes made to the map. It encodes whether geometries and/or attributes were added, changed or deleted. The feed itself is displayed as a list, where subsequent actions of individual users are aggregated to avoid a cluttering of the history (see figure 2d). A click on an entry will center and zoom the map on the referenced geo-object. In addition to the overall map history, a more detailed overview is available for individual geo-objects. Different revisions can be visually inspected using either a simple GUI or textually via the history feed (cf. Figure 2b).

Changes are color-coded based on the type of the change to facilitate easy recognition. If attributes are added they are colored in green, changes are yellow, and deletions are displayed in red. Changes to the geometry of a geo-object are directly visible on the map. Geometry revisions are displayed in their original color (defined by the category of the geo-object). In addition to reviewing older versions, it is also possible to revert a geo-object to a previous revision.

IMPLEMENTATION

Ethermap (see Figure 1 for a screenshot) implements the approach described in the previous section. It supports the collaborative process through several functions that are inspired by related work and by the specific properties of geo-data such as non-linearity and multiple layers.

Ethermap was developed as a web-based application to keep the entry barrier low since this is one of the main challenges for open collaboration [22]. Furthermore, various successful web-based mapping platforms exists and the most common synchronous collaborative text editors are web-based as well. Ethermap was written in HTML5 and JavaScript. It uses well-known libraries and frameworks such as node.js for the server, socket.io for real-time messaging that is based on WebSockets. CouchDB is used as multi-version concurrency control database for storing JSON documents. The frontend (client) of Ethermap relies on Angular.js for easy modularization and Mapbox.js for map display and interaction. The latter integrates the "simplestyle specification"[5] that allows geo-objects to be rendered and styled according to their attributes. Data is exchanged and stored using the GeoJSON specification, a lightweight and widely used community standard.

Ethermap reuses the existing category system of OSM. Within this system, geo-objects can be classified and described according to informal standards. Example categories include buildings, landuses, and railways. The visual appearance of an object on the map (colors, line-width, etc.) is automatically derived from its category. For example, polygons categorized as a "building" are colored in red by default. Ethermap also automatically generates input fields for the appropriate attributes from these categories. For instance, buildings have an address and a number of levels, whereas roads have an attribute for the speed limit (see Figure 2c). Users can append custom attributes (as key/value pairs) to extend the default fields.

EVALUATION

As the review of the related work revealed, different evaluation methods should be used to assess the quality and usefulness of real-time multi-user applications [24, 26]. Therefore, we evaluated Ethermap using a multi-tiered approach. We first carried out informal user tests and a technical evaluation to assess the scalability and robustness of the approach. We then conducted a controlled user study to investigate collaborative aspects in more depth. We logged every user activity and followed up with a detailed questionnaire. In order to gain additional insights into the overall usefulness and the potential benefits and drawbacks of real-time collaborative map editing, we also carried out three semi-structured expert interviews.

User Study

The general goal of the user study was to gain insights into the usability of the approach, into usage patterns as well as into question how different aspects of the approach were being used.

Participants: 39 participants were recruited from university campus (most were students taking an introductory course on Geographic Information Systems). 17 participants were female, 12 male, and ten did not to state their gender. Their age ranged from 18 to 26 (mean = 20.6, SD = 1.7).

Scenario: The scenario used for the study was disaster-mapping, i.e., updating an existing map according to changes introduced by a disaster. Participants were tasked to collaboratively map flooded areas in an urban environment. We used official data from a recent flooding event, which was included in the application. Aerial images and OpenStreetMap data served as base data. We also provided means to overlay near-infrared images of the flooded area as this helps to identify them.

Procedure: Similar to the study by Butt and Li [4], a combination of logging user behavior and questionnaires was used to gather the data for the analysis. The user study was performed with two groups consisting of 20 and 19 participants each. After a ten minute introduction, participants were asked to start Ethermap by entering a user ID that we had previously been assigned randomly to each participant. Within Ethermap, an interactive tutorial repeated the task participants had to perform and reminded them about the available tools. As all participants were in the same room, they were invited to not talk to each other in order to simulate working from distinct places. After 15 minutes of actively mapping, the application closed automatically and switched to an online questionnaire. The embedded logging system recorded all interactions with Ethermap. The user IDs from the practical task were used to link the usage histories to the questionnaires.

Questionnaire: First questions captured demographic information and familiarity with mapping software as well as real-time synchronization. The questionnaire then focused on Ethermap's functionality and asked participants about real-time synchronization, user-awareness, and version control. In total, the questionnaire contained 27 questions: 12 questions used a seven point Likert scale (ranging from "strongly agree" to "strongly disagree"), eight were open questions (allowing for textual replies), and seven were yes-no questions. Free text answers were analyzed by categorizing the responses based on the given statements. Questions based on the Likert scale were analyzed by calculating the frequency of the given responses. We simplified the seven point Likert scale into a three point Likert scale as recommended by [21] with view to the relatively small sample size.

Results

The questionnaire started by asking the participants about their overall experience regarding geographic information systems as well as previous usages of real-time synchronized editors. 49% rated their experience with low to no experience at all. 28% selected medium and the rest rated themselves with a good or expert experience (24%). Out of these participants, 69% had never used real-time synchronized editors before, 8% were unsure and 23% had prior experience. Table 1 summarizes the participants' replies to key questions of the questionnaire.

Real-time synchronized map editing: Both groups created 268 geo-objects (93 lines, 10 markers, 141 polygons) with 972

[5] `https://github.com/mapbox/simplestyle-spec` accessed 28.08.2014

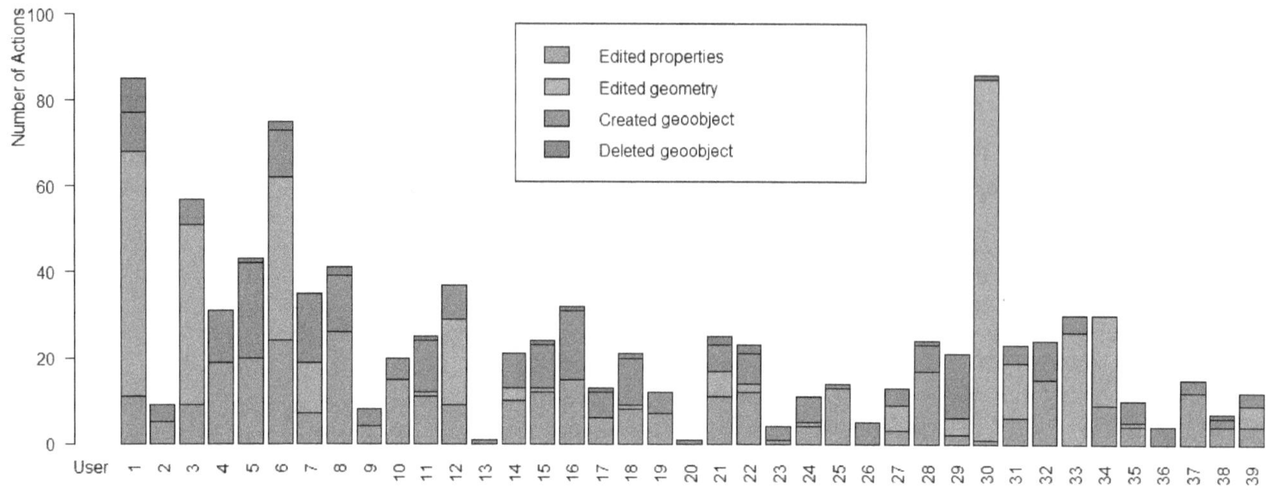

Figure 3: Histogram summarizing the number of logged actions performed by each user divided into four categories: edited properties, edited geometries, created and deleted geo-objects.

revisions in total. The revisions consists of 268 geo-object creations, 24 geo-object deletions, 344 geometry edits, and 336 attribute edits of the geo-objects. Figure 3 depicts the actions performed by the participants. Activity levels and dominant categories differed considerably between participants. We also observed different strategies of the participants: some users focused on editing geometries and properties, while others created objects and did not edit geometries afterwards. Four participants were particularly active: they performed over 55 actions (the average was 24.9 actions). Three users applied almost no changes to the map.

From the logged data, we identified three main collaborative patterns: 1) one participant applies edits while at least one other participant watches those edits; 2) multiple participants co-edit the same geo-object at the same time (within a few seconds); 3) multiple participants watch the same geo-object at the same time without applying edits. We define "watching" as an active selection of a geo-object. A geo-object is selected by clicking on it, which enables users to inspect/edit its attributes or the geometry. Pattern 1 occurred 31 times (on 25 geo-objects), while active co-edits (pattern 2) were more scarce: we logged nine separate instances on six different geo-objects. We counted as active co-edits only edits that occurred in quick succession (within a few seconds). The third pattern occurred 15 times on 13 geo-objects. We assume that users checked if further refinements were needed and that the simultaneous watching happened co-incidentally.

In total 29 geo-objects were created and edited collaboratively by two or more people: 23 geo-objects were edited by two users, five were edited by three different users, and one was edited by six users. Based on the results from the logging and the patterns we identified, we conclude that collaboration occurred mostly at the macro scale (mapping geo-objects in the same area) instead of at the micro scale (refinement of mapped geo-objects by collaborators).

Figure 4 shows the timeline of 15 minutes for an example geo-object, which was edited by six different people. Blue segments indicate that a user was in edit mode, and red ones indicate when changes were applied. The diagram highlights the complex nature of collaboration with different users performing different actions at different times (both concurrently and sequentially). At one point, for example, users 49, 77, and 26 were concurrently editing the geo-object, while user 50 simply watched the geo-object for a longer period of time without performing any actions.

41% of the participants stated that they stopped working on a geo-object when others applied edits, while 51% stated they did not. We assume that most of the users who did not stop their edits were actually observing edits of others, as only 9% of the geo-objects were actually *edited* by multiple users. This assumption is backed up by the high amount of views (705) where no edits were applied to the inspected geo-object. Based on this data we conclude that participants distributed the mapping tasks serendipitously among themselves and changed the work of others only sparsely. Overall, these results indicate that real-time synchronization is applicable for geospatial map editors and that users can successfully collaborate. Based on the questionnaire results participants thought that the task was performed more efficiently through the real-time collaboration.

User-awareness: Ethermap's user-awareness features were received well: 79% of the participants stated that they could recognize the presence of other collaborators well, 13% responded neutrally, while 8% responded negatively. 69% of the participants could easily detect changes, 28% could not, and 3% responded with a neutral answer. Participants stated which user-awareness functionality helped most with this in a free text answer. The most frequently mentioned ones were (in this order): colored highlighting, direct appearance of geo-objects within the viewport and through the history view. While the first two answers are directly linked and interdependent, the history view is a textual representation in

Question	Median	SD
I could easily recognize the presence of other collaborators.	6	1.54
I could easily detect changes by other users.	6	1.95
Different colors helped me identify which users had edited a geo-object.	4	1.64
Actions of other users did not interfere with my work.	4	1.64
I was satisfied with the speed of the editor.	7	1.61
A revision history is useful when jointly editing maps.	6	1.17
Real-time synchronization enabled me to complete the task more efficiently.	5	1.53

Table 1: Summary of Likert-scaled questions with answers ranging from 7 (strong agreement) to 1 (strong disagreement).

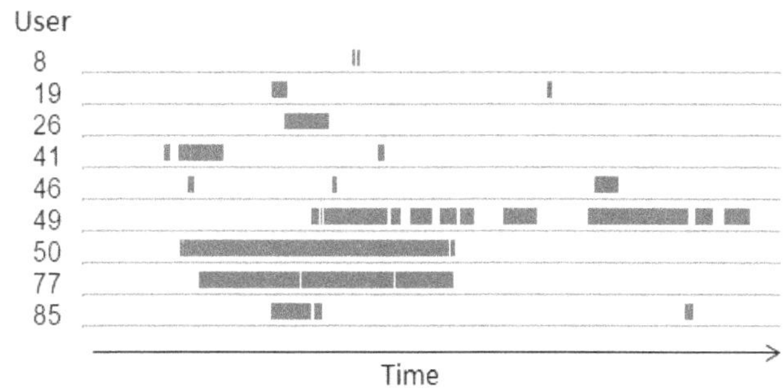

Figure 4: Chart displaying the actions performed on a single geo-object by different users. Each row corresponds to specific participant. Blue bars indicate when the geo-object was in edit mode, red bars indicate an actual edit/change.

the context menu. Even though visual highlights seemed to be important, 38% had a neutral opinion about color coded user-identification. The remaining 62% were evenly distributed in agreeing and disagreeing to the color coded user-identification.

When asked whether the actions of other users interfered with their own work, participants' answers were distributed evenly. 31% felt disturbed by the actions of other users, 33% had a neutral opinion, and 36% stated that other users' actions did not interfere with their work. The highlighting of geo-objects after changes was not perceived as particularly disturbing though: 56% found it useful, 26% had a neutral opinion, and only 18% disliked this feature. Half of the participants (51%) continued work on a geo-object even when other users were also editing the same object, while 41% stopped working on an object when others were editing it at the same time. 8% were unsure whether they stopped or not. 70% agreed real-time synchronization enabled them to complete the task more efficiently. 18% were unsure and 13% disagreed.

Users were thus able to recognize the presence of other collaborators, as well as changes others made to the map. The questionnaire revealed that 41% of the participants stopped editing a geo-object, that was currently also edited by someone else, which also confirms people's awareness of other users' actions. The actual awareness seemed to result mostly through highlighting changed geo-objects as well as the direct updates of the geometries within the viewport. Asked about "Watch" and "Show Workarea" functions most participants indicated that they did not use these functions to look at other users' activities. The functions to show the workarea of others or watch their actions were used sparsely (the "Watch" function was used 29 times in total; "Show all Workareas" was activated eleven times.). This might partially be due to the fact that we assigned random user IDs to anonymize participants as well as due to the difficulty to distinguish between "unique" colors for 20 (19) concurrently active users. Color coding and watch functionality might thus be more useful in scenarios with fewer participants and self-picked user names.

Communication: Another section of the questionnaire focused on the communication aspect of Ethermap. When asked why the chat was (not) used, the most common answer was that there was no need to communicate for the given task. Those who used the chat stated that it was used for asking or answering questions about the task. According to the questionnaire results, the "refer to geo-object" tool was used to ask questions about a specific geometry without having to textually describe it, and to spare collaborators the trouble of searching for the mentioned geo-object. Overall, 19 chat messages were sent by nine individual users. Four of those messages contained a reference to a geo-object within the map: three questions referenced a polygon asking if it marked a flooded area. One participant convinced other collaborators to edit existing geo-objects rather than creating new ones.

The last part of the questionnaire asked which features participants liked best/least. The real-time synchronization, the chat, and the simplicity/good usability of the editor received positive feedback. Negative comments pointed at too many collaborators working in the same area. Some people also found the history function too complicated. Overall, the user-awareness and communication functions seem to have worked: Online collaborators and status indicators for objects were successfully recognized by the users and informed user actions. Furthermore, communicating via chat messages and references to map geo-objects was received positively by the participants but rarely used in the our study.

Version control: Even though the map history was only used moderately – about two times per user on average (85 times in total; the history of individual geo-objects was opened seven times) – the questionnaire results showed that the map history was useful. The function to revert to previous states for individual geo-objects was not used. As participants started on an "empty" map they might have focused on adding data in order to cover the whole area affected by flooding rather than inspecting changes over time. As all participants were not familiar with disaster mapping, reviewing data and analyzing the mapping quality might also not have been as important to the users as creating new geo-objects. Other tasks, as for example, collaborating on planning processes could therefore result in different usage patterns.

Expert Interviews

Procedure

While the above study focused on investigating usability, interviews were used to gain insights into the subjective perspective of domain experts [14]. The interviews focused on the general usefulness of the Ethermap concept and on individual functions.

We used semi-structured interviews with a set of guiding questions allowing for enough space for open detailed statements of the interviewee [14]. All interviewed experts agreed to non-anonymous interviews. We selected our interview partners based on their background to capture different aspects such as innovative potential, usefulness in disaster management scenarios and productive use. Our first interview partner (I1) is the CEO of a not-for-profit company working on open source software in the geospatial domain. He also serves as innovation manager for a large commercial company developing mapping software. The second interviewee (I2) is the executive director of a group of volunteers supporting disaster response, and she is very familiar with current disaster mapping systems. The third expert (I3) is the head of product management at a medium-sized software company building custom solutions in the geospatial realm.

Before an interview started, Ethermap was demonstrated in a tutorial. Interviews lasted about 30-40 minutes. They were recorded and transcribed. The interviews were analyzed using a category system aggregating statements. Categories for the coding process were established based on the overall concept of Ethermap, interactive version control for geo-objects and methods regarding user-awareness.

Results

Real-time synchronized map editing: All three interviewees reacted positively to the overall concept of a real-time, synchronized map editor. I2 responded that they would normally use screen-sharing for real-time collaboration and only one person would be able to control the map. I2 further elaborated that real-time synchronization with a combined watch functionality is very useful, in particular for teaching purposes: *"For teaching there is certainly a huge benefit - on being able to edit in real-time. And also to better - working together."* In an initial familiarization phase new collaborators could watch how more experienced users work to learn from them (educational lurking [25]).

When asked about the efficiency when working simultaneously together, I1 responded that given the right scenario, the concept of Ethermap would definitely contribute to increase the productivity of all collaborators. Nevertheless, both I1 and I3 agreed that this could be very dependent on the specific use case. I1 further stated that real-time collaboration is only meaningful, if all persons *"are in the same context and [...] have a similar understanding of what has to be done"*. I2 agreed that real-time synchronization allows users to work better together, as usually editors have to include other mechanisms to prevent users from colliding with each other, which often result in restricting users.

In addition to the given use case of disaster management, interviewees identified further areas, that could benefit from real-time synchronization. They named teaching, planning, logistics, but also tourism and helpdesk applications as promising application areas. When asked about the current functionality of Ethermap and the integration of more complex GIS capabilities, I1 and I3 agreed that this is very use case specific. I1 stated: *"I think it's a very good idea to start with these simple features and then extend if necessary. So keep it simple as far as possible"*. However, the experts also pointed out that measuring (I1) or buffering tools (I2) could be helpful in discussions. Other feature requests were for example the need to get a quick overview of the existing attributes in the map. I2 reported: *"One feature I think would be useful, would be some sort of spreadsheet to view the attributes available for the geo-objects in an area"*. Overall, I1 and I2 agreed that many functions of a collaborative editor would benefit a lot from spatial filters. Examples would be the map history, geo-object attributes (I2), but also the user list (I1), which could be filtered based on the current map viewport (I2).

User-awareness and communication: Questions about user-awareness also resulted in positive feedback. I1 mentioned the importance of knowing where other collaborators are currently working on a map, and how active they are. This could inform organizers of the current focus or interest of collaborators. I2 also stated the usefulness of the user-awareness methods and compared them with positive collaboration experiences in GoogleDocs. I3 agreed that it is important for people to know that they are not working alone on a topic. Being able to see how many users are working on the same task would also impart a sense of relevancy (I3). In addition to methods to increase real-time user-awareness, I1 also mentioned that reviewing the activity on a timeline could be beneficial in order to know how the focus of the work has changed over time, or how up-to-date data is. However, allowing communication within the editor seemed to be one of the most important aspects for all interviewees. *"[...] I thought chatting about a specific object was really cool as well. Because it is an easy way to point them at an object if you had specific questions about it."(I2)* Even though I3 stated how important communication is, he explained that chatting is often only the first step, whereas a communication via voice would be even more beneficial.

Version control: Another aspect covered in the interview was the interactive version control. I2 reported on this subject that it was useful *"especially when you have new editors. Having an easy way to go back, and one: show the mistakes, and two: correct mistakes instead of redoing the work, you could just go back in time."* In addition to that, I3 stated that particularly in real-time scenarios where people are working under time pressure (e.g. disaster management), errors will occur. Having an "undo" tool is thus important. I1 also mentioned: *"To see what has happened to a geo-object and to see how it was edited, if it was refined somehow, or when did it pop up?"* is very important.

DISCUSSION

The multi-tiered evaluation of our approach aimed at assessing various key aspects of real-time synchronized map editing: the general usability of the approach, emerging usage patterns and further aspects pertaining to its use (user study) as well as the overall usefulness of the approach and individual functions (expert interviews). Overall, the outcomes of the evaluation provide strong evidence that the concept is technically feasible with a low entry barrier; that non-experts can grasp the underlying principle and learn how to use it in a short amount of time; and that the approach is perceived as useful by experts and non-experts. In the following, we briefly discuss the main areas targeted by our evaluation and report on limitations.

Usability and related aspects: Only three users did not map actively while 36 participants started mapping right after the introduction and tutorial. It is thus likely that the task of the study was easy to understand and to carry out using the prototypical application. Also, the basic concept of real-time synchronized map editing did not seem to pose a problem to participants. Though not all functions provided were used intensively – the version history and the chat in particular saw little use – feedback from participants and experts about the concept and the functions provided by the prototypical application was predominately positive.

Usage patterns and collaboration: As can be seen from Figure 3, usage patterns varied considerably across participants both in terms of number and type of actions. Collaboration occurred mostly on the macro scale (mapping geo-objects within the same area) rather than on the micro scale (refinement of mapped geo-objects). Figure 4 provides a example on what a collaborative refinement process on the micro level might look like. This could be an artifact of the task and the limited amount of time: participants might have focused on covering the largest possible area in the available time rather than on correcting details of the created geo-objects.

Nevertheless, people were aware of what their co-workers were doing, and seemed to use this information to serendipitously coordinate their work. 51% of the participants did not stop working on a geo-object when others applied edits, though "working" most likely included viewing an object according to the interactions logged during the study. These observations go along with some of the suggestions we received in the questionnaire: participants proposed to assign specific roles (such as "rough mapper","detailed mapper", or "only applying edits") to further improve coordination of the work. Color coding users according to such a role might be more useful than individual color assignments in case of many collaborators.

Usefulness and application scenarios: Based on the questionnaire results participants thought that the task was performed more efficiently through real-time collaboration. During the interviews, the domain experts commented positively on the overall concept as well. More specifically, the experts saw the version control feature and the chat function with direct geo-references as being very useful for real-time collaborative mapping. They also highlighted the "Watch" functions as great tools in a teaching context or for presentation purposes. Suggested improvements included voice chat, measurement tools, buffering, and spatial filtering. Considering the large number of map movement/zooming (265 times per participant on average), the latter function in particular has a substantial potential for improving efficiency.

The experts also pointed out that realizing the benefits of real-time synchronized mapping depends on the specific use case. Besides disaster mapping, they pointed out teaching, planning, logistics, tourism, and helpdesk scenarios as promising application areas. All these applications benefit from the immediate visibility of actions performed by others' and from the non-blocking nature of interaction, which is not afforded by asynchronous solutions. In addition, real-time synchronized mapping opens up new ways of collaborating and coordinating work. For example, using this approach the work practices of extreme programming – one person programming, while their partner looks over their shoulder to check their code as they type – can be translated to the geo-realm.

Limitations: The evaluation we performed is subject to a number of limitations. The number of participants and tasks was limited, so was the overall duration/execution time. The user study was performed with students who had some background in cartography, but little experience in active mapping and less so in disaster mapping. Our results for the communication aspects or "Watch" functionalities were limited by the type of the task and the study duration as well as by randomly assigned identifiers, which could have been an obstacle. It is also unclear how different group sizes could affect the outcome of the study. While users reported that the they were more efficient using Ethermap, a direct comparison study with an asynchronous system would be beneficial to validate these claims.

CONCLUSION

The main contributions of this paper are threefold. We proposed a concept for non-blocking synchronous collaborative map editing tailored to specific properties of geo-data. Based on this concept, we developed an open source application (Ethermap) that facilitates real-time collaboration on geo-data. We then used this prototypical implementation to carry out an in-depth evaluation of the concept, and we reported on key results we obtained. The overall concept of a real-time synchronized map editor was received favorably by users and experts alike. Unlike asynchronous systems (e.g., Wikis), Ethermap enables successful real-time collaborative group mapping, provides a common ground and understanding via continuous visual highlighting of geospatial edits, and supports cross-modal references to geo-objects in real-time conversations.

ACKNOWLEDGEMENTS

We would like to thank the participants of the user study, the domain experts we interviewed, and con terra GmbH (for funding part of the research reported here). We would also like to thank our anonymous reviewers for their feedback.

REFERENCES

1. Antunes, P., Herskovic, V., Ochoa, S. F., and Pino, J. A. Reviewing the quality of awareness support in collaborative applications. *J. Syst. Softw. 89* (Mar. 2014), 146–169.
2. Armstrong, M. P., and Densham, P. Cartographic support for collaborative spatial decision-making. In *Autocarto-Conference* (1995), 49–58.
3. Balram, S., and Dragicevic, S. *Collaborative Geographic Information Systems*. IGI Global, 2006.
4. Butt, M. A., and Li, S. Open source based online map sharing to support real-time collaboration. In *OSGeo J.*, vol. 10, FOSS4G (Jan. 2012), 10.
5. Carroll, J. M., Neale, D. C., Isenhour, P. L., Rosson, M. B., and McCrickard, D. Notification and awareness: synchronizing task-oriented collaborative activity. *Int. J. Hum. Comput. Stud. 58*, 5 (May 2003), 605–632.
6. Chang, Z. E., and Li, S. Geo-Social Model: A Conceptual Framework for Real-time Geocollaboration. *Trans. GIS 17*, 2 (Apr. 2013), 182–205.
7. Cherubini, M., and Dillenbourg, P. The effects of explicit referencing in distance problem solving over shared maps. In *Proc. of CSCW '07*, ACM Press (Nov. 2007), 331.
8. Crampton, J. Maps as social constructions: power, communication and visualization. *Prog. Hum. Geogr. 25*, 2 (June 2001), 235–252.
9. Dabbish, L., Stuart, C., Tsay, J., and Herbsleb, J. Social coding in GitHub. In *Proc. of CSCW '12*, ACM Press (Feb. 2012), 1277.
10. Ellis, C. A., Gibbs, S. J., and Rein, G. Groupware: some issues and experiences. *Commun. ACM 34*, 1 (Jan. 1991), 39–58.
11. Elwood, S. Critical Issues in Participatory GIS: Deconstructions, Reconstructions, and New Research Directions. *Trans. GIS 10*, 5 (Nov. 2006), 693–708.
12. Goldman, M., Little, G., and Miller, R. C. Real-time collaborative coding in a web IDE. In *Proc. of UIST '11*, ACM Press (Oct. 2011), 155.
13. Grishchenko, V. Deep hypertext with embedded revision control implemented in regular expressions. In *Proc. 6th Int. Symp. Wikis Open Collab. - WikiSym '10*, ACM Press (July 2010), 1.
14. Hopf, C. *5.2 Qualitative Interviews - ein Überblick*, vol. 55628. Uwe Flick, Ernst von Kardoff, Ines Steinke (Hrsgg.) Qualitative Forschung. Ein Handbuch. Reinbeck bei Hamburg., 2004.
15. Jankowski, P., Nyerges, T. L., Smith, A., Morre, T. J., and Horvath, E. Spatial group choice: a SDSS tool for collaborative spatial decisionmaking. *J. Geogr. Inf. Sci. 11*, 6 (Sept. 1997), 577–602.
16. Koren, I., Guth, A., and Klamma, R. Shared editing on the web: A classification of developer support libraries. In *Proc. of Collaboratecom 2013*, IEEE (Oct. 2013), 468–477.
17. Kraut, R. E., Gergle, D., and Fussell, S. R. The use of visual information in shared visual spaces. In *Proc. of CSCW '02*, ACM Press (Nov. 2002), 31.
18. Lanza, M., Hattori, L., and Guzzi, A. Supporting Collaboration Awareness with Real-Time Visualization of Development Activity. In *Softw. Maint. Reengineering (CSMR), 2010 14th Eur. Conf.*, IEEE (Mar. 2010), 202–211.
19. MacEachren, A. M. Cartography and GIS: facilitating collaboration. *Prog. Hum. Geogr. 24*, 3 (2000), 445–456.
20. MacEachren, A. M., Cai, G., Sharma, R., Rauschert, I., Brewer, I., Bolelli, L., Shaparenko, B., Fuhrmann, S., and Wang, H. Enabling collaborative geoinformation access and decisionmaking through a natural, multimodal interface. *Int. J. Geogr. Inf. Sci. 19*, 3 (Mar. 2005), 293–317.
21. Maurer, T. J., and Andrews, K. D. Traditional, Likert, and Simplified Measures of Self-Efficacy. *Educ. Psychol. Meas. 60*, 6 (Dec. 2000), 965–973.
22. Morgan, J. T., Gilbert, M., McDonald, D. W., and Zachry, M. Editing beyond articles. In *Proc. of CSCW '14*, ACM Press (Feb. 2014), 550–563.
23. Nam, T.-J., and Wright, D. The development and evaluation of Syco3D: a real-time collaborative 3D CAD system. *Des. Stud. 22*, 6 (Nov. 2001), 557–582.
24. Neale, D. C., Carroll, J. M., and Rosson, M. B. Evaluating computer-supported cooperative work. In *Proc. of CSCW '04*, ACM Press (Nov. 2004), 112.
25. Panciera, K., Priedhorsky, R., Erickson, T., and Terveen, L. Lurking? cyclopaths?: A quantitative lifecycle analysis of user behavior in a geowiki. In *Proc. of CHI '10*, ACM (2010), 1917–1926.
26. Pinelle, D., and Gutwin, C. A review of groupware evaluations. In *Enabling Technol. Infrastruct. Collab. Enterp. 2000.(WET ICE 2000). Proceedings. IEEE 9th Int. Work.*, IEEE (2000), 86–91.
27. Priedhorsky, R., and Terveen, L. The computational geowiki: What, why, and how. In *Proc. of CSCW '08*, ACM (2008), 267–276.
28. Rinner, C. Argumentation Mapping in Collaborative Spatial Decision Making. In *Collab. Geogr. Inf. Syst.* IGI Global, 2006, 85–102.
29. Sun, C., and Chen, D. Consistency maintenance in real-time collaborative graphics editing systems. *ACM Trans. Comput. Interact. 9*, 1 (Mar. 2002), 1–41.

Too Much Humanness for Human-Robot Interaction: Exposure to Highly Humanlike Robots Elicits Aversive Responding in Observers

Megan Strait[1,2], Lara Vujovic[2], Victoria Floerke[2], Matthias Scheutz[1], and Heather Urry[2]
Departments of [1]Computer Science and [2]Psychology
Tufts University, Medford MA 02155 USA
{megan.strait, lara.vujovic, victoria.floerke, matthias.scheutz, heather.urry}@tufts.edu

ABSTRACT

People tend to anthropomorphize agents that look and/or act human, and further, they tend to evaluate such agents more positively. This, in turn, has motivated the development of robotic agents that are humanlike in appearance and/or behavior. Yet, some agents – often those with highly humanlike appearances – have been found to elicit the opposite, wherein they are evaluated more negatively than their less humanlike counterparts. These trends are captured by Masahiro Mori's *uncanny valley hypothesis*, which describes a (uncanny) valley in emotional responding – a switch from affinity to dislike – elicited by agents that are "too humanlike".

However, while the valley phenomenon has been repeatedly observed via subjective measures, it remains unknown as to whether such evaluations reflect a potential impact to a person's behavior (i.e., aversion). We attempt to address this gap in the literature via a novel experimental paradigm employing both traditional subjective ratings, as well as measures of peoples' behavioral and phsyiological responding. The results show that not only do people rate highly humanlike robots as uncanny, but moreover, they exhibit greater avoidance of such encounters than encounters with less humanlike and human agents. Thus, the findings not only support Mori's hypothesis, but further, they indicate the valley should be taken as a serious consideration for peoples' interactions with humanlike agents.

Author Keywords

Human-robot interaction; uncanny valley; emotion regulation; situation selection/modification; attentional deployment; anthropomorphism; embodied conversational agents; virtual agents

ACM Classification Keywords

H.4 Information Systems Applications: Miscellaneous

CHI 2015, April 18 - 23 2015, Seoul, Republic of Korea

http://dx.doi.org/10.1145/2702123.2702415

INTRODUCTION

Based on the "like me" premise that people respond more positively towards agents similar to themselves ([27]), development of humanlike agents has been of growing interest to researchers in human-robot and human-computer interaction alike. For both robots and virtual agents, humanlike appearances and/or behaviors have been found to improve perceptions and increase rapport (e.g., [1, 9, 40]). Thus, by capitalizing on traits that are more familiar and intuitive to people, humanlike agents can offer more natural and effective interactions than their less humanlike counterparts [11].

However, agents that are "too humanlike" can produce the opposite effect. For instance, a recent exhibit by artist Tony Matelli – the Sleepwalker – was a highly realistic statue intended to depict a man "who is hopelessly lost" and "vulnerable"[1] amidst the open landscape of Wellesley College (see Figure 1). While the statue itself is obviously inanimate and therefore unable to do any physical harm, the unnerving nature of the statue's appearance resulted in a petition[2] that garnered over 1000 signatures for its removal – so that people "don't have to *confront him* as they go about their daily lives".

This response to the statue is consistent with Mori's uncanny valley hypothesis (UVH), which posits that people will generally respond with increasing affinity towards increasingly humanlike agents until a certain point. At that point, the degree of human likeness becomes "too much", evoking aversive responses instead of affinity [29]. This change in emotional responding is referred to as the *uncanny valley*. Though its nature and governing mechanisms continue to be of debate (e.g., [3, 8, 10, 17, 31]), there is substantial evidence confirming its existence (e.g., [14, 22, 24, 28, 33]). Moreover, the evidence extends beyond human adults to infants/children [21, 26] and even macaque monkeys [35], suggesting the general phenomenon is relatively pervasive, if not robust.

However, many question whether the uncanny valley presents a serious consideration for human-agent interactions. In particular, as the evidence to-date is primarily based on subjective evaluations, the bearing an agent's appearance may or may not have on a person's *behavior* remains unknown. Specifically, consistent with the UVH, highly humanlike

[1] `http://goo.gl/BxZBe6`
[2] `http://goo.gl/2ttL7m`

Figure 1. Artist Tony Matelli's *Sleepwalker* installation on the Wellesley College campus in Wellesley, MA. Photo credit: Megan Strait.

agents are often described as "eerie", "macabre", "unnerving" (e.g., [18]) – generally less likable than their less humanlike counterparts. But, could an agent's unnerving appearance be so emotionally motivating that it causes a person to act aversively (i.e., avoid interacting)?

In response to this questioning, reactions to Matelli's Sleepwalker would suggest yes. Though unintentional, its appearance nevertheless had significant consequences on how, and moreover, *whether* people would interact with it. For instance, proponents of the statue's removal report using strategies such as modifying its appearance (e.g., dressing it up) to "make him less intimidating", or even taking a different path to avoid the statue entirely. These are two examples – situation modification (dressing up the statue) and situation selection (taking a different path) of ways people regulate a significant emotional response (e.g., fear, apprehension, stress).

While emotions can be useful in certain situations (e.g., a fight or flight response to a dangerous stimulus), the stress elicited by an unnerving agent such as the Sleepwalker might not be particularly appropriate for students' daily lives on the campus surrounding the statue. Hence, regulatory mechanisms can be engaged to help modulate the emotions triggered by such a negative stimulus. According to the process model of emotion regulation (ER; [15]), there are five families of processes that help regulate aspects of the emotion generative cycle ([16]). For example, one can select the situations in which one puts themself (*situation selection*) based on the anticipated emotions resulting from the various contexts (e.g., selecting a different route around campus to avoid a stressful encounter with the Sleepwalker). Alternatively, if a person is already in a certain situation, one can change the emotion-provoking aspects (*situation modification*; e.g., dressing up the statue) or attend to different aspects of the environment (*attentional deployment*; e.g., averting one's gaze from the statue), thereby changing the emotional experience.

The implications of these effects and potential responses are particularly important to human-computer and human-robot interaction. If the Sleepwalker is any indication, an agent's appearance can thus pose particular interference with how and, moreover, *whether* a person interacts with it. Thus, while increasing human likeness has shown promise towards improving interactions, it also remains crucial to gain better understanding of the UVH. Hence, the purpose of the present study was to investigate whether the uncanny valley presents a serious consideration for human-agent interactions. Specifically, we wanted to determine whether highly humanlike robots can be so emotionally motivating that they evoke behavioral *aversion* in human observers.

To address this question, we observed subjects' *behavior* by looking at how often people choose to end encounters with highly humanlike agents versus less humanlike or human agents when given the opportunity, as well as their reasons for doing so. In our attempt to evaluate peoples' aversion to humanlike robots, we employed a modification of the button-press paradigm ([39]) for measuring relevant emotion regulatory mechanisms. Here we presented a series of pictures depicting humans and robots of varying human similarity (low, moderate, and high), with the option to press a button if the subject wished to stop looking at a given picture. In addition to the traditional subjective ratings of the agents' appearances, we collected the percentage of button presses and reaction times (RT) to measure the frequency and rapidity of attempts to end encounters with the various agents. We also recorded eye gaze behavior to index overt *attentional deployment*, as well as physiological indices of emotional responding (corrugator activity, heart rate, and skin conductance).

Hypotheses

Based on evidence that people who attribute negative valuations to a robot also report reduced interest in interacting with it (e.g., [34, 36]), we hypothesized that in order to regulate their emotional response, people would engage in *situation selection* or *modification* by ending encounters (pressing the button) more often and faster in response to highly humanlike robots than less humanlike robots or humans (**Hypothesis 1**). Further – while, based on [4, 27], we expected that greater human likeness might moderately increase interest in *not ending* some encounters (**Hypothesis 2a**) – for those that they terminate, we hypothesized they would report doing so due to being unnerved more so in response to the highly humanlike robots versus the other agents (**Hypothesis 2b**).

In addition, we hypothesized that – when the button press (situation selection/modification) is unavailable – people might engage other ER strategies, such as looking away from the unnverving content (**Hypothesis 3**). We specifically focused on *attentional deployment* as reflected in eye tracking, given that looking away from negative content has been observed in prior work examining other forms of ER (e.g., [6, 38]) and moreover, studies of the UVH using gaze behavior (e.g., [26, 35]) show reduced fixation in response to uncanny agents.

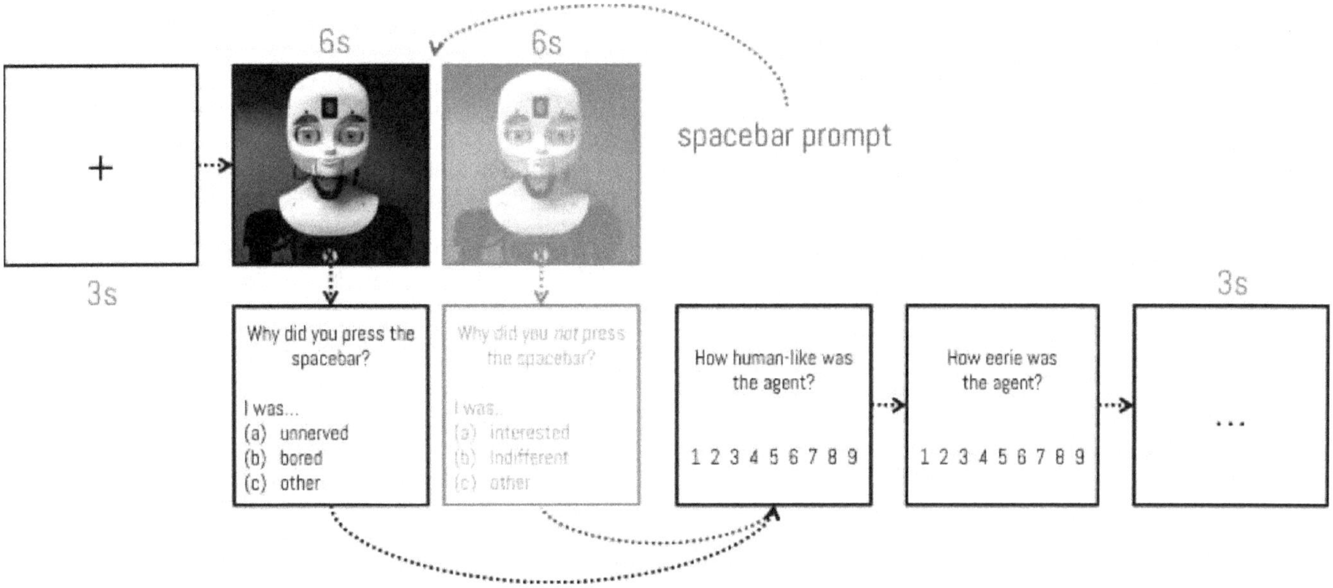

Figure 2. Trial structure: each trial began with a $3s$ fixation point, followed by presentation of an image for at least $6s$. At $6s$, subjects received the prompt: "You may now press the spacebar." If they did not press the spacebar, the image remained for $6s$ more. Otherwise, immediately upon pressing the button, the image was removed and the trial proceeded. After the viewing, subjects completed a series of self-report prompts.

MATERIALS AND METHODS

Based on Mori's UVH, we expected that highly humanlike agents may be so unnerving that people might be motivated to regulate their emotions via situation selection/modification and attentional deployment. To test our predictions, we conducted a fully within-subjects study in which we manipulated **human likeness** of the shown agents (four levels – robots with *low*, *moderate*, and *high* human similarity, and *humans*).

Procedure

Subjects viewed a set of 60 color pictures – each depicting a distinct (robotic or human) agent – selected from a subset of those tested in [37]. The images were obtained from various academic and internet sources and divided into the four *agent categories*. To help mitigate the influence of any one agent, we included 15 instances per category (see Figure 3). The specific agents were selected based on normative ratings showing people perceive these robots as having a low (M=1.80, SD=.13), moderate (M=2.57, SD=.32), or high (M=5.11, SD=.78), with the set of humans as having the highest (M=8.90, SD=.10), degree of human likeness on a nine-point scale (anchored from *machine-like* to *humanlike*).

The above set of 60 images were presented using E-Prime 2.0 (Psychology Software Tools, Pittsburgh, PA, USA) in an order randomized by subject. Each image was preceeded with a black fixation cross presented in the center of a white screen for $3s$. This was followed by the presentation of the image for between $6s$ to $12s$. Subjects were informed that, after $6s$ of viewing a given image, they could press the spacebar to remove the image from the screen. If the subject did not press the spacebar, the image would remain on the screen for six more seconds (for a maximum viewing duration of $12s$).

The purpose of this $6s$ delay was to impose a minimum encounter duration, during which participants could not modify the situation (via pressing the button). This allowed us to investigate whether people engaged in *attentional deployment* – an emotion regulatory strategy alternative to *situation selection/modification* – when the button pressing was unavailable.

Following the viewing, subjects were cued to select one of three reasons for either pressing (*unnerved*, *bored*, or *other*) or not pressing (*interested*, *indifferent*, or *other*) the spacebar. The choice of these options served to tease apart whether a stimulus creates a negative situation for the subject (being unnerved) or rather, whether a press response indicates boredom. The *other* option was included so that subjects were not presented with a forced choice, but instead could note that they chose to end or not end an encounter with an agent for reasons we did not anticipate. This screen remained present until a response was recorded, at which point, subjects were then prompted to enter the traditional ratings of how humanlike (vs. mechanical) and how eerie (vs. non-arousing) the given agent appeared. The rating screen also remained present until a response was recorded. Lastly, subjects were presented with a white screen showing a black ellipsis for $3s$ to provide a brief break between trials (see Figure 2).

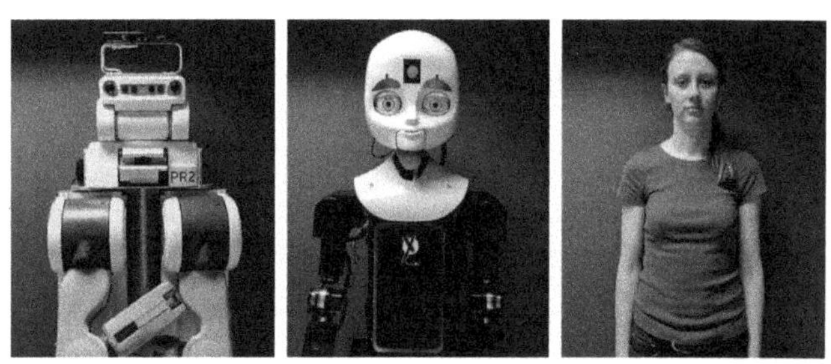

Figure 3. Exemplars of agent categories: robots with *low* and *moderate* human likeness (left and center, respectively), as well as a human (right).

Measures

Subjective ratings of the depicted agents' **humanness** and **eeriness** were used as a manipulation check that our agent categories (*low*, *moderate*, *high*, and *human*) were perceived as having significantly different degrees of human likeness and moreover, that the highly humanlike robots used fall within the proposed uncanny valley. As we used a fully-within subjects design, the ratings were averaged (by subject) across trials within each of the four agent categories.

In addition to the traditional ratings of the agents' appearances, subjects' button press behavior, bilateral eye tracking, and peripheral physiological data were collected using E-Prime 2.0, a Tobii T120 Eye Tracker (Danderyd, Sweden), and MP150 system (Biopac, Goleta, CA, USA) respectively. The details of these recordings and calculation of the dependent variables (DVs) of interest are detailed below.

Behavior

To represent the frequency at which subjects elected to end encounters, the percentage of trials on which subjects pressed the spacebar (**trials terminated**) was calculated within each of the four agent categories. On trials in which the button was pressed, we also calculated the mean **response time** (RT) to represent the speed at which subjects ended encounters.

In addition, we analyzed subjects' reported reasons for their behavior to understand why subjects pressed or did not press the spacebar. On trials in which the button *was pressed*, to determine whether subjects ended encounters due to a negative context associated with the agents' appearance, we calculated the percentage of terminated trials for which subjects reported each of the three responses: **unnerved**, **bored**, or **other**. On trials in which the button was *not* pressed, to determine why subjects elected to view the image for the full duration, we calculated the percentage of these trials for which subjects responded: **interested**, **indifferent**, or **other**.

Lastly, when button pressing was unavailable (during the first $6s$ of viewing), we analyzed subjects' eye gaze behavior to determine whether subjects engaged in *attentional deployment*. Specifically, we computed percentage fixation duration on three areas of interest (AOIs), operationalized as the amount of time subjects spent looking within the pre-defined AOIs for each image relative to total image viewing time. The three areas of interest included: the **agent**, defined as the agent's body and all contiguous, relevant parts (e.g., limbs, hair, clothing); the agent's **head**, defined as the portion of the agent that is clearly separable from a "torso"; and **eyes**, defined as the left/right eye and the area immediately between the two. Fixations within each AOI were identified using the Tobii fixation filter algorithm[3] and were averaged across trials for each AOI within each agent category.

Physiology

In addition to the above, *corrugator electromyography* (EMG), *electrocardiography* (ECG), and *electrodermal activity* (EDA) were sampled as these measures have been found to be sensitive to stimulus valence (e.g., [7, 20]). To index of facial expressive behavior using EMG, two $4mmAg/AgCl$ electrodes were placed in bipolar configuration over the left eye per [12]. Corrugator electromyography was sampled at $1000Hz$ and bandpass-filtered online ($5Hz$ to $3kHz$; $60Hz$ notch filter). Offline, the data were resampled to $400Hz$, rectified and smoothed with a $16Hz$ low pass filter, decimated to $4Hz$, and smoothed with a $1s$ moving average filter.

To measure heart rate, ECG was acquired continuously at $1000Hz$ via two disposable $Ag/AgCl$ electrodes (pregelled with 7% chloride gel and were placed under the left and right collarbones). Offline, the ECG signal was downsampled to $400Hz$ and band pass filtered from 0.5 to $40Hz$. Interbeat interval series were created by identifying R-spikes using automated ANSLAB algorithms. R-spikes that were not detected automatically, thus leading to an erroneously long period between successive R-spikes, were marked for inclusion by hand. Similarly, R-spikes that were identified incorrectly, thus leading to an erroneously short period between successive R-spikes, were removed by hand. Following such artifact correction, the interbeat interval series was converted to HR in beats per minute. HR data were decimated to $10Hz$ and then smoothed with a $1s$ prior moving average filter. Lastly, to index sympathetic activation of the autonomic nervous system, EDA was recorded with DC coupling and constant voltage electrode excitation at $31.25Hz$ via two disposable $1cmAg/AgCl$ electrodes (pregelled with 0.5% chloride isotonic gel and attached to the distal phalanges of the index and middle fingers on the non-dominant hand).

Participants

Sixty-two undergraduates participated in exchange for course credit. All procedures were approved by the Social, Behavioral, and Educational Research Institutional Review Board at Tufts University and subjects provided written, informed consent prior to participating. In anticipation of some loss in data due to issues with the equipment, artifacts, and/or missing values, we chose this sample size in order to achieve at least 50 useable observations in hypothesis testing. Due to equipment failure data were unavailable for two subjects, thus sixty subjects (28 male) with ages ranging from 18 to 28 years (M=19.13, SD=1.48) were included in our final sample.

RESULTS

We hypothesized that, in presenting images depicting agents varying in human likeness, the highly humanlike robots – more so than the less humanlike robots and humans – would be perceived so negatively that subjects would be motivated to regulate their emotions via early termination of their encounters. To test our hypotheses (as well as confirm our underlying assumptions), a repeated-measures ANOVA was conducted on each of the subjective ratings and behavioral DVs with *human likeness* as the IV (see Table 1).[4] The significant results are discussed below, with all post-hoc contrasts reflecting a Bonferroni-Holm correction for multiple comparisons.

[3] `http://www.tobii.com/en/eye-tracking-research/global/library/manuals/`

[4] Due to space constraints, the analyses and results of the peripheral physiological measures are not reported in this paper.

	n	Low	Moderate	High	Human	F	p	η^2
Subjective Ratings								
– *Humanness*	60	.18 (.14)	.33 (.17)	.68 (.17)	.99 (.03)	$F(2.50, 147.94) = 788.85$	$< .01$	.93
– *Eeriness*	60	.29 (.19)	.47 (.17)	.54 (.17)	.06 (.09)	$F(2.47, 145.74) = 219.31$	$< .01$	.82
Press Behavior								
– *Trials Terminated* (%)	60	.52 (.38)	.53 (.37)	.57 (.36)	.57 (.42)	$F(1.81, 106.79) = 1.76$	.17	.02
– *Response Time* (*s*)	42	1.49 (.80)	1.63 (.85)	1.39 (.51)	1.34 (.50)	$F(2.76, 113.29) = 2.00$	.12	.04
Rationale for...								
– Terminating (%):								
– *unnerved*	42	.26 (.29)	.39 (.32)	.47 (.31)	.04 (.15)	$F(2.50, 102.55) = 36.18$	$< .01$	.46
– *bored*	42	.62 (.32)	.46 (.32)	.39 (.30)	.88 (.21)	$F(3, 123) = 54.85$	$< .01$	.57
– *other*	42	.12 (.19)	.15 (.22)	.13 (.22)	.07 (.15)	$F(2.10, 86.42) = 3.19$	.04	.07
– Viewing (%):								
– *interested*	35	.60 (.34)	.63 (.32)	.70 (.30)	.35 (.36)	$F(2.66, 90.50) = 17.49$	$< .01$	.34
– *indifferent*	35	.39 (.34)	.31 (.34)	.24 (.27)	.60 (.36)	$F(3, 102) = 21.25$	$< .01$	.38
– *other*	35	.01 (.02)	.06 (.12)	.06 (.13)	.05 (.18)	$F(1.77, 60.27) = 1.55$	.22	.04
Gaze Behavior								
– Fixation Duration (%):								
– *agent*	56	.87 (.03)	.84 (.05)	.79 (.05)	.89 (.05)	$F(2.20, 121.09) = 102.91$	$< .01$	.65
– *head*	56	.33 (.05)	.50 (.06)	.57 (.06)	.64 (.07)	$F(2.48, 136.62) = 477.45$	$< .01$	.89
– *eyes*	56	.16 (.05)	.21 (.06)	.21 (.08)	.30 (.11)	$F(1.83, 100.75) = 97.66$	$< .01$	.64

Table 1. Descriptive statistics – number of observations and means (+/-SD) – for the dependent measures as a function of *agent condition* (*low*, *moderate*, *high*, and *human*), as well as inferential statistics (F, p, and *partial* η^2) from testing for main effects of human likeness.

For each ANOVA, the assumption of equal variance was confirmed using Mauchly's test of sphericity or otherwise adjusted. In cases of violation, the degrees of freedom and corresponding p-value reflect either a Greenhouse-Geisser or Huynh-Feldt adjustment as per [13]. We also note that only subjects who provided data in all conditions relevant to each particular test were included (e.g., analyeses of gaze behavior included only those who had non-zero fixations on each of the *agent*, *head*, and *eyes* AOIs). Thus, due to listwise deletion of subjects with missing data, the number of observations (and consequently the degrees of freedom) vary across tests.

Manipulation Check

To confirm the main assumptions of our study design, we first tested subjects' explicit ratings to determine whether our four-level manipulation of *human likeness* – robots with *low*, *moderate*, and *high* human similarity, and *humans* – elicited different attributions of *humanness* and *eeriness*. Specifically, we assumed the four levels would be perceived as having increasing human likeness from *low* (lowest) to *human* (highest). Further, we assumed these categories would elicit differentially negative evaluations, with the greatest eeriness attributed to highly humanlike robots and least to humans.

As expected, a repeated-measures ANOVA across all trials (regardless of whether subjects pressed the button) showed a main effect of *human likeness* on *humanness* ratings (F=788.85, p<.01, η^2=.93). All pairwise comparisons were significantly different (p<.01), confirming that subjects' attributions of human likeness were consistent with those assumed – increasing from agents categorized as *low* (M=.18, SD=.14), *moderate* (M=.33, SD=.17), and *high* (M=.68, SD=.17) in human likeness to *humans* (M=.99, SD=.03).

Similarly, *eeriness* ratings also showed a main effect of *human likeness* (F=219.31, p<.01, η^2=.78). Again, all pairwise contrasts were significant (p<.01) and consistent with assumptions. Specifically, the highly humanlike robots were rated highest (M=.54, SD=.17) and *humans* lowest (M=.06, SD=.09), indicating they were perceived as most and least eerie, respectively. Taken together, these results show that the pictures elicited the expected responding.

Hypothesis Testing

Hypothesis 1

To determine whether people end encounters with highly humanlike robots more frequently and faster than less humanlike robots and humans, we analyzed subjects' press behaviors: % of trials in which the button was pressed (*trials terminated*) and, in those (terminated) trials, the corresponding *response time* (s) to press the button. However, neither measure showed a significant main effect of human likeness (p=.17 and p=.12, respectively). That is, contrary to our expectations, subjects *did not* press the button significantly more frequently or quickly in response to highly humanlike robots than those of low or moderate human likeness and humans.

Hypothesis 2

Despite the non-significant effect of human likeness on termination rates and RTs between agent categories, we expected still that people would show distinct motivations for ending or not ending encounters with highly humanlike agents relative to all others. Specifically, when encounters with highly humanlike robots were *not* terminated, we hypothesized subjects would report doing so out of *interest* (vs. indifference) more so than in response to humans or robots with less human similarity. Conversely, when encounters with highly humanlike robots were indeed *terminated*, we hypothesized subjects would report doing so due to being unnerved (vs. bored).

H2a: Does greater human likeness elicit greater interest? To determine whether increasing human likeness increases

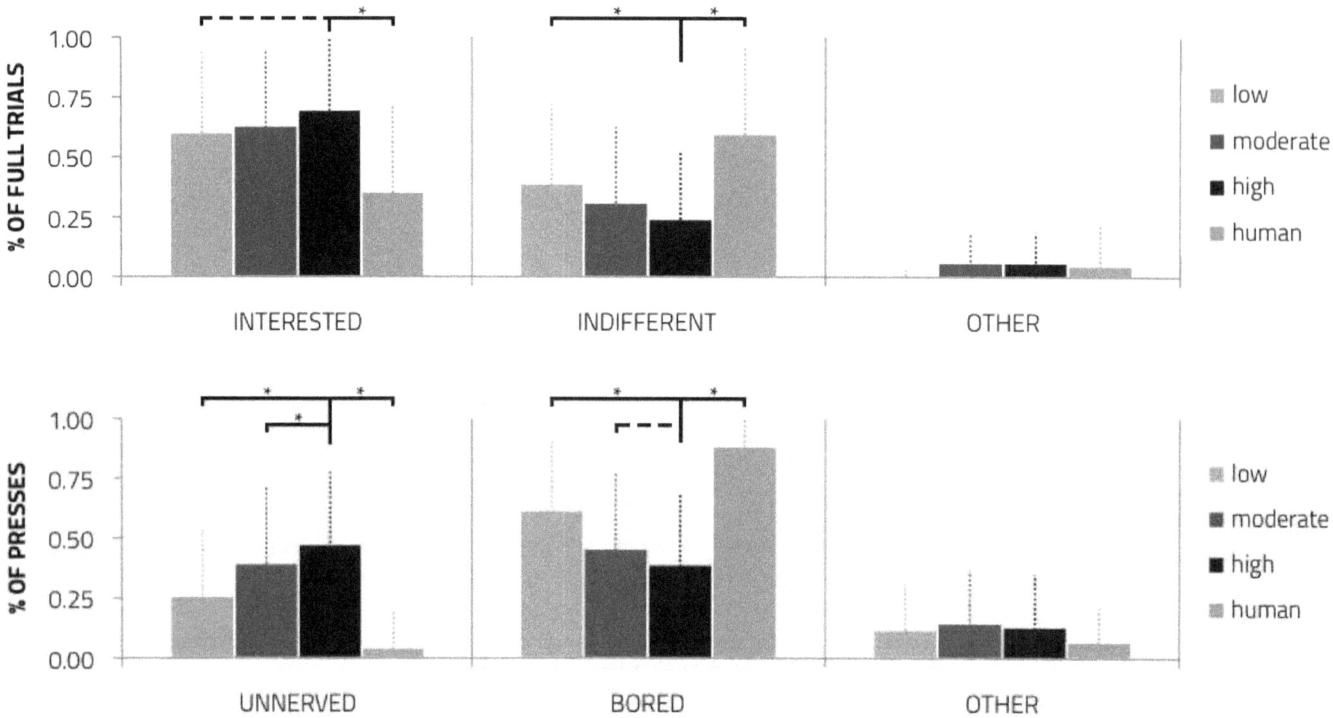

Figure 4. Response frequencies: mean percentage ($+/-SD$) of trials *viewed in full* due to being *interested*, *indifferent*, or *other* (top) and of *terminated trials* due to being *unnerved*, *bored*, or *other* (top) by human likeness category. Asterisks denote significance ($p < .05$) for planned contrasts (between highly humanlike robots and the three other agent conditions), with dashed lines denoting marginal significance ($p < .01$).

subjects' interest in *not* ending encounters with highly humanlike robots, we examined the frequency at which they reported being *interested*, *indifferent*, or *other* on trials that they viewed in full (see Figure 4, top). Repeated-measures ANOVAs showed a main effect of *human likeness* on both *interest* and *indifference* (F=17.49, p<.01, η^2=.34; F=21.25, p<.01, η^2=.38), but no significant effect on the frequency of "other" (p=.22), as reasons for not pressing the button.

As expected, subjects chose to *not* press the button out of indifference less often in response to robots of high (M=.24, SD=.27) versus low (M=.39, SD=.34, p<.01) human likeness. Conversely, they reported marginally greater interest in viewing highly humanlike robots (M=.70, SD=.30) relative to those low in likeness (M=.60, SD=.34, p=.08). However, subjects showed interest/indifference no more or less often in response to the highly humanlike robots than those with moderate human likeness (p=.18; p=.14).

More notably, on these trials where subjects *did not* press the button, they did so because they were more interested in robots – regardless of the degree of human likeness – than humans (M=.35, SD=.36, $p < .01$). Subjects also reported less indifference to robots (similarly, regardless of their human likeness) than humans (M=.60, SD=.36, p<.01).

H2b: Do people end encounters with highly humanlike robots because they are unnerved? To determine whether people ended encounters due to being unnerved more so by the highly humanlike agents relative to less humanlike or human agents, we examined the frequency at which they reported being *unnerved*, *bored*, or *other* on trials that they chose to terminate (see Figure 4, bottom). The analyses showed a main effect of condition on both responses of *unnerved* and *bored* (F=36.18, p<.01, η^2=.46; F=54.85, p<.01, η^2=.57).

As hypothesized, pairwise contrasts revealed subjects chose to press the button because they were unnerved more frequently in response to the highly humanlike robots (M=.47, SD=.31) relative to robots with low (M=.26, SD=.29, p<.01) and moderate human likeness (M=.39, SD=.32, p=.02), as well as humans (M=.04, SD=.15, p<.01).

Conversely, subjects chose to press the button due to boredom less often in response to the highly humanlike robots (M=.39, SD=.30) than to humans (M=.89, SD=.21, p<.01) and robots with low (M=.62, SD=.32, p<.01) and moderate (M=.46, SD=.32, p=.06) human likeness. There was also a main effect of human likeness on presses for reason of "other" (F=3.19, p=.04, η^2=.07); however, no pairwise contrast was significant ($p < .05$), even marginally ($p < .10$).

Although subjects did not terminate encounters with highly humanlike robots any more frequently than those with lesser degrees of human likeness or humans, these results show that their motivations for pressing (or not pressing) the button were nevertheless significantly different with respect to the highly humanlike robots. Importantly, they show that when people do end encounters with highly humanlike robots, they do so because they are unnerved more so than bored.

Hypothesis 3

To determine whether people used attentional deployment to help regulate their emotions *when button pressing was un-*

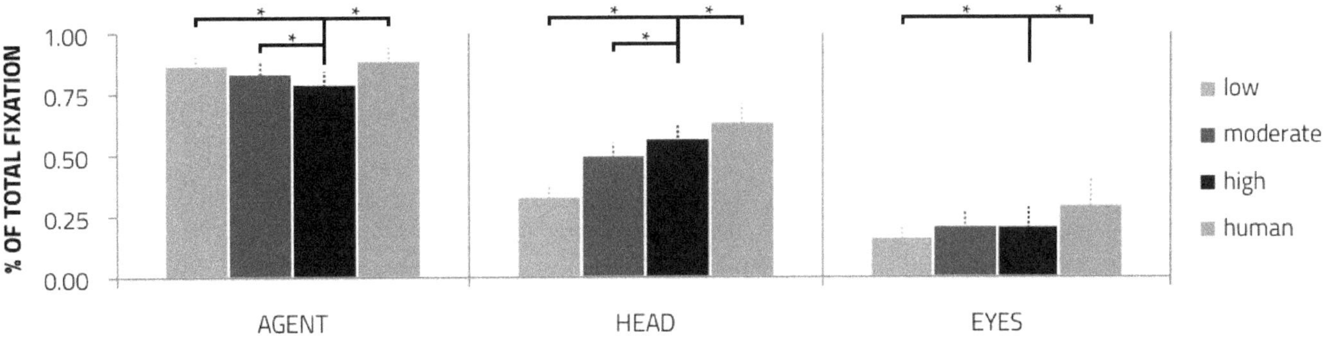

Figure 5. Gaze behavior: mean percent of *total fixation* (+/- one standard deviation) spent fixating on the *agent*, the agent's *head*, and the agent's *eyes* by human likeness category, and their planned contrasts (between highly humanlike robots and the three other agent conditions).

available, we analyzed how participants attended to the images as reflected by the mean percentage fixation duration on three AOIs out of total fixation (see Figure 5). The analyses show a main effect of *human likeness* on all areas of interest: the agent (F=102.91, p<.01, η^2=.65), and the agent's head (F=477.45, p<.01, η^2=.89) and eyes (F=96.67, p<.01, η^2=.64). With respect to the *agent* as a whole, post-hoc contrasts revealed a drastically lower (p<.01) duration spent fixating on the highly humanlike robots (M=.79, SD=.05) relative to the other agents (M_{low}=.87, SD=.03; $M_{moderate}$=.84, SD=.05; and M_{human}=.89, SD=.05).

As to what subjects fixated on within the agent's body, pairwise comparisons of the fixations on the *head* AOI showed significantly different (p<.01) and increasing durations with increasing human likeness: M_{low}=.33, SD=.05; $M_{moderate}$=.50, SD=.06; M_{high}=.57, SD=.06; and M_{human}=.64, SD=.07. Similarly, fixation on the *eyes* increased with increasing human likeness: M_{low}=.16, SD=.05; $M_{moderate}$=.21, SD=.06; M_{high}=.21, SD=.08; and M_{human}=.30, SD=.11. However, the contrast between robots with moderate versus high likeness was not significant.

These results show that increasing the realism of humanlike features (head and eyes) increases attention to such areas. Yet, the difference in overall fixation on highly humanlike robots (relative to the other agents) indicates that subjects use attentional deployment to avert their gaze away from these agents, thus facilitating regulation of the negative context.

DISCUSSION

Contrary to our expectations, subjects did not end encounters with highly humanlike robots any more frequently or faster than encounters with humans or robots with low and moderate human likeness (*H1*). Rather, differences in the use of ER strategies between encounters with highly humanlike versus those with less humanlike or human agents were only evident in their reasons for button pressing and gaze behavior.

Specifically, when subjects were able to *and did* end encounters with highly humanlike robots, they reported doing so more frequently because they were unnerved (*H2b*). For comparison, when subjects ended encounters with humans or robots of low/moderate human likeness, they did so more frequently due to boredom. This indicates that people engage in situation-targeted ER strategies (pressing a button to end an encounter), and with highly humanlike robots, they do so due to the negative context the agents' appearance creates.

In addition, when button-pressing was unavailable (the first 6*s* of image presentation), we observed evidence of gaze aversion. Specifically, despite subjects' tendency to fixate longer on salient humanlike features (the eyes and face) with increasing human likeness, they showed substantially lower overall fixation on highly humanlike robots relative to the three other agent categories (*H3*). This suggests that people attempt to avoid encounters with such robots, even when they do not have an explicit option to do so. Taken together, these observations show support for our second and third hypotheses, indicating that people are particularly averse to highly humanlike robots (as evidenced by their engagement of both situation-targeted ER and attentional deployment).

On the contrary, when subjects chose *not* to end encounters, human likeness did show a moderately positive effect (*H2a*) as evidenced by a marginal increase in interest and significant reduction in indifference towards robots of high (relative to low) human likeness. However, there was no gain in interest/reduction in indifference relative to the moderate likeness category and in general, subjects showed almost twice as much interest in robots (>60%) – regardless of their appearance – than humans (35%). This suggests the same degree of interest – with less negative consequences – can be achieved using robots of moderate (instead of high) human likeness.

Links to Existing Literature

Mori (1970/2012) hypothesized that people will (1) show increasing affinity towards agents with increasing human likeness up to a certain point – after which, the high degree of human similarity will (2) elicit aversion ([29]).

Prior research has confirmed the first part of Mori's hypothesis, with significant evidence of people responding more positively towards humanlike agents (both virtual and embodied) relative to those with less human likeness (e.g., [9, 30, 40]). Consistent with such findings, subjects here exhibited greater interest and less indifference in their rationale for *not pressing* the button in response to in highly humanlike robots (relative to robots with low and moderate human likeness).

Other work, using overt ratings of agent appearances (e.g., perceived *eeriness*) has shown support of the second part of

Mori's hypothesis with highly humanlike robots rated as more eerie than their less humanlike counterparts (e.g., [22, 24]). Consistent with such work, subjects here rated the highly humanlike agents as being the most eerie and humans the least.

Theoretical Implications

Here we found strong evidence that behavioral aversion was elicited by highly humanlike robots, as reflected by subjects' attempts to regulate their encounters. This included their rationale for ending encounters with highly humanlike agents, the frequency at which subjects reported being unnerved as a function of the human likeness manipulation, and their attentional deployment away from the unnerving agents.

Subjects' engagement of these emotion-regulatory behaviors (the situation-ending button press and gaze aversion) provide additional evidence of the uncanny valley's emotion elicitation. Furthermore, they underscore the negative implications for human-agent interactions which, prior to this investigation, had yet to receive much attention. That is, the highly humanlike robots (more so than the less humanlike and human agents) were so emotionally motivating that subjects averted their gaze from the stimulus and terminated their encounters.

The results also help to shed light on the link between gaze behavior and emotional responding with respect to the uncanny valley. In particular, the correspondance between press behavior, subjective ratings, and gaze lend further support to the conclusions of prior UVH studies using eye tracking data only. Specifically, in cases where overt ratings were unobtainable such as in studying young children [21, 26] and animals [35], this data confirms that lower fixations indicate greater behavioral and subjective aversion. In addition, subjects' increasing fixation on the agent's face and eyes with respect to agent category, suggests that relative human likeness may be reflected by attention to these humanlike characteristics.

Practical Implications

The development of humanlike robots and virtual agents has risen to the forefront of design goals for researchers in both human-robot interaction (HRI) and human-computer interaction, as such agents are increasingly intended for and deployed in social contexts. While there are numerous demonstrations of the benefits of increasing an agent's human likeness in prior work, the current findings suggest that the design of such agents should be done with great care.

Though the stimuli used in the present study were both innocuous and fleeting, participants nevertheless showed significant aversion to the encounters, however brief. Revisiting the Sleepwalker example: it was a statue, and thereby incapable of actively harming any onlookers. Similarly, the static, image-based stimuli here conferred no possibility of danger to participants and furthermore, were presented for only a matter of seconds. Yet, in both cases, the discomfort caused by the agents' appearances was sufficient to influence peoples' behavior via engagement of emotion-regulatory strategies such as situation selection/modification.

These reactions indicate that there may be a limit to the efficacy of increasing human likeness, and moreover, serious consequences if an agent's appearance goes "too far". Not only do these findings suggest an agent can be "too humanlike", but further, they show that an agent's appearance can significantly affect a person's behavior (such that he/she will avoid the encounter). Considering a more realistic interaction context such as an actual interaction with a physical robot – wherein there may be an actual possibility of danger (real or imagined) – such aversions might only be exacerbated.

Beyond the design of effective social agents, this also holds importance for effective evaluations as well. In the current task, we explicitly instructed people to end the situation if they wanted and by inquiring about the reasons for ending a situation, we further cued them to consider that they might do so if they became upset or bored. But in a actual human-agent interactions (whether in-the-wild or in-the-lab), explicit cues regarding opportunities and reasons for regulating ones emotions are rare. Thus, the situation – wherein a participant is discomforted by an agent but is not given the opportunity to regulate their emotional response – presents a potential confound in investigations that do not consider the adverse effects of an agent's appearance and/or behavior.

Limitations & Future Directions

Our approach to investigating the uncanny valley contributes a novel and simple laboratory task to assess the emotionally-motivated behavioral outcomes that follow from encounters with highly humanlike robots. In particular, the use of behavioral indices to monitor attentional deployment and situation-targeted ER strategies augments traditional methods that typically rely on a small set of self-report measures to study the UVH. This contribution is significant because it uncovers the behavioral impacts associated with the UVH, and furthermore, it sheds light on interpretations of eye tracking data with regard to the uncanny valley. That said, while we are confident that the present study was well-suited to address our primary goals, the approach also has its limitations, which serve to underscore important avenues for future research.

One significant limitation to consider is the use of static, image-based stimuli rather than actual embodied agents. At present, due to the cost and accesibility of physical robots, images are the only practical means of evaluating perceptions across a multitude of real agents. With 15 examples per agent category, broad inferences can be drawn regarding a general theoretical construct (human likeness). Whereas, the alternative (one physical representative agent per category) limits any inferences and their extensibility to those few agents used. However, the image-based stimuli are limiting as well. Specifically, due to their simplicity, the findings hold little bearing on how people might respond to interactive, moving, and/or embodied agents. Based on subjects' aversion despite the harmlessness of the photographed agents (relative the their physically-imposing embodiment), we speculate that the aversive behaviors will only be exacerbated in actual human-robot interactions. However, exactly how the observed effects transfer warrants additional investigation.

In addition, this study's participant sampling was also limited. Specifically, it was fairly homogenous – drawing entirely from undergraduates, most of whom are young women, at an American university. As such, there may be gender-based and/or cultural differences in perceptions of and emotional responding towards the robots that we did not capture in the present work. For instance, prior research indicates that men and women respond to robots in substantially different manners, with men showing more positive responding to robots than women [19, 32]. Other work has shown evidence that peoples cultural background also has a significant influence on perceptions of robots, with Americans showing the most positive responding [5].

There may also be individual differences amongst participants that further influence how they perceive and respond to humanlike robots. For example, Walters et al. showed that in general, people exhibited greater preference for robots with a more humanlike appearance. However, individual differences showed substantial disagreement with the overall effect: specifically, introverts and participants with lower emotional stability showed greater preference for a more mechanical appearance [40]. More recent findings have shown the similar personality characteristics can predict sensitivity to the uncanny valley [23, 25]. If prevalent within a given sample population, this could potentially bias or skew the results. Thus, subsequent work should draw on broader population to obtain more diverse demographics.

Finally, one question to consider is how to facilate peoples' emotion regulation when the interaction is unavoidable. In the present work we explicitly instructed people to end the situation if they wanted. But in actual interaction contexts, the need to continue interacting with an agent (e.g., to accomplish a collaborative task) might outweigh the motivation to terminate. In this case, it may be of benefit to consider robot-centric strategies to help modulate aversion arising due to its appearance. For instance, the agent's use of gaze aversion (e.g., [1, 2]) or polite speech (e.g., [36]) are two behavioral mechanisms shown to improve perceptions of the agent. Thus, should a person be tasked with interacting with an agent that they find to be "too humanlike", such efforts may have promise towards yielding better emotional outcomes.

CONCLUSIONS

We sought to determine whether the uncanny valley presents a serious consideration for human-agent interactions. Specifically, we investigated whether highly humanlike robots could be so unnerving that they motivate people to avoid them. To do so, we appropriated a simple laboratory task to observe whether subjects engaged in the emotion regulatory strategies, situation selection/modification, by deciding to end encounters with agents of varying human likeness. We also monitored subjects' gaze behavior, as an indication of attentional deployment and further evidence of overt aversion. Our results indicate that people attempt to avoid unnerving encounters with highly humanlike robots (via both situation-targeted strategies and attentional deployment) more so than encounters with less humanlike or human agents. Overall, the current study provides further support of Mori's hypothesis and its relevance to human-robot and human-computer interaction. Should these findings replicate, they provide validation of the valley's emotion elicitation as originally described.

ACKNOWLEDGEMENTS

We are grateful to the research assistants – John Budrow, Alice Chan, Kara Cochran, Melissa Hwang, Chris Martin, Jacob Merrin, Victoria Powell, Rachel Ribakove, and Anoushka Shahane – of the Emotion, Brain, & Behavior Laboratory at Tufts University for helping with data collection and processing; and – Brendan Fleig-Goldstein and Maretta Morovitz – of the Tufts Human-Robot Interaction Laboratory for helping with the literature review. We are also acknowledge Jeffrey L. Birk (now at Columbia University) and Philipp C. Opitz (now at the University of Southern California) for help on the conceptualization and implementation of the study. This research was funded by and conducted at Tufts University.

REFERENCES

1. Andrist, S., Pejsa, T., Mutlu, B., and Gleicher, M. Designing effective gaze mechanisms for virtual agents. In *Proceedings of CHI* (2012), 705–714.
2. Andrist, S., Tan, X. Z., Gleicher, M., and Mutlu, B. Conversational gaze aversion for humanlike robots. In *Proceedings of HRI* (2014), 25–32.
3. Bartneck, C., Kanda, T., Ishiguro, H., and Hagita, N. Is the uncanny valley an uncanny cliff? In *Proceedings of RO-MAN* (2007), 368–373.
4. Bartneck, C., Kanda, T., Ishiguro, H., and Hagita, N. My robotic doppelgänger – a critical look at the uncanny valley. In *Proceedings of RO-MAN* (2009), 269–276.
5. Bartneck, C., Suzuki, T., Kanda, T., and Nomura, T. The influence of peoples culture and prior experiences with aibo on their attitude towards robots. *AI & Society 21*, 1-2 (2007), 217–230.
6. Bebko, G., Franconeri, S., Ochsner, K., and Chiao, J. Look before you regulate: differential perceptual strategies underlying expressive suppression and cognitive reappraisal. *Emotion 11* (2011), 732–742.
7. Bradley, M. M., Codispoti, M., Cuthbert, B. N., and Lang, P. J. Emotion and motivation i: defensive and appetitive reactions in picture processing. *Emotion 1*, 3 (2001), 276.
8. Brenton, H., Gillies, M., Ballin, D., and Chatting, D. The uncanny valley: does it exist. In *Proceedings of HCII* (2005).
9. Broadbent, E., Kumar, V., Li, X., Sollers, J., Stafford, R. Q., MacDonald, B. A., and Wegner, D. M. Robots with display screens: a robot with a more humanlike face display is perceived to have more mind and a better personality. *PloS one 8*, 8 (2013), e72589.
10. Burleigh, T. J., Schoenherr, J. R., and Lacroix, G. L. Does the uncanny valley exist? an empirical test of the relationship between eeriness and the human likeness of digitally created faces. *Computers in Human Behavior 29*, 3 (2013), 759–771.
11. Duffy, B. R. Anthropomorphism and the social robot. *Rob. & Aut. Systems 42*, 3 (2003), 177–190.

12. Fridlund, A. J., and Cacioppo, J. T. Guidelines for human electromyographic research. *Psychophysiology 23*, 5 (1986), 567–589.

13. Girden, E. R. *ANOVA: Repeated measures*. No. 84. 1992.

14. Gray, K., and Wegner, D. M. Feeling robots and human zombies: mind perception and the uncanny valley. *Cognition 125*, 1 (2012), 125–130.

15. Gross, J. J. The emerging field of emotion regulation: an integrative review. *Rev. Gen. Psy. 2* (1998), 271–299.

16. Gross, J. J., and Thompson, R. A. Emotion regulation: conceptual foundations. *Handbook of Emotion Regulation 3* (2007), 24.

17. Hanson, D., Olney, A., Prilliman, S., Mathews, E., Zielke, M., Hammons, D., Fernandez, R., and Stephanou, H. Upending the uncanny valley. In *Proceedings of AAAI* (2005), 1728.

18. Ho, C.-C., and MacDorman, K. F. Revisiting the uncanny valley theory: Developing and validating an alternative to the godspeed indices. *Computers in Human Behavior 26*, 6 (2010), 1508–1518.

19. Kuo, I. H., Rabindran, J. M., Broadbent, E., Lee, Y. I., Kerse, N., Stafford, R., and MacDonald, B. A. Age and gender factors in user acceptance of healthcare robots. In *Robot and Human Interactive Communication, 2009. RO-MAN 2009. The 18th IEEE International Symposium on*, IEEE (2009), 214–219.

20. Lang, P. J., Greenwald, M. K., Bradley, M. M., and Hamm, A. O. Looking at pictures: Affective, facial, visceral, and behavioral reactions. *Psychophysiology 30*, 3 (1993), 261–273.

21. Lewkowicz, D. J., and Ghazanfar, A. A. The development of the uncanny valley in infants. *Developmental Psychobiology 54*, 2 (2012), 124–132.

22. MacDorman, K. F. Subjective ratings of robot video clips for human likeness, familiarity, and eeriness: An exploration of the uncanny valley. In *Proceedings of CogSci* (2006), 26–29.

23. MacDorman, K. F., and Entezari, S. O. Individual differences predict sensitivity to the uncanny valley. *Interaction Studies* (2015).

24. MacDorman, K. F., Green, R. D., Ho, C.-C., and Koch, C. T. Too real for comfort? uncanny responses to computer generated faces. *Computers in Human Behavior 25*, 3 (2009), 695–710.

25. MacDorman, K. F., Vasudevan, S. K., and Ho, C.-C. Does japan really have robot mania? comparing attitudes by implicit and explicit measures. *AI & society 23*, 4 (2009), 485–510.

26. Matsuda, Y.-T., Okamoto, Y., Ida, M., Okanoya, K., and Myowa-Yamakoshi, M. Infants prefer the faces of strangers or mothers to morphed faces: an uncanny valley between social novelty and familiarity. *Biology Letters 8*, 5 (2012), 725–728.

27. Meltzoff, A. N. 'like me': a foundation for social cognition. *Dev. Sci. 10*, 1 (2007), 126–134.

28. Mitchell, W. J., Szerszen, K. A., Lu, A. S., Schermerhorn, P. W., Scheutz, M., and MacDorman, K. F. A mismatch in the human realism of face and voice produces an uncanny valley. *i-Perception 2*, 1 (2011), 10.

29. Mori, M., MacDorman, K. F., and Kageki, N. The uncanny valley [from the field]. *IEEE Robotics & Automation 19*, 2 (2012), 98–100.

30. Riek, L. D., Rabinowitch, T.-C., Chakrabarti, B., and Robinson, P. How anthropomorphism affects empathy toward robots. In *Proceedings of HRI* (2009), 245–246.

31. Rosenthal-von der Putten, A. M., and Kramer, N. C. How design characteristics of robots determine evaluation and uncanny valley related responses. *Computers in Human Behavior 36*, 0 (2014), 422–439.

32. Schermerhorn, P., Scheutz, M., and Crowell, C. R. Robot social presence and gender: Do females view robots differently than males? In *Proceedings of HRI*, ACM (2008), 263–270.

33. Seyama, J., and Nagayama, R. S. The uncanny valley: Effect of realism on the impression of artificial human faces. *Presence 16*, 4 (2007), 337–351.

34. Stafford, R. Q., MacDonald, B. A., Jayawardena, C., Wegner, D. M., and Broadbent, E. Mind perception and attitudes towards robots predict use of an eldercare robot. *Int. J. Soc. Rob. 6*, 1 (2014), 17–32.

35. Steckenfinger, S. A., and Ghazanfar, A. A. Monkey visual behavior falls into the uncanny valley. *PNAS 106*, 43 (2009), 18362–18366.

36. Strait, M., Canning, C., and Scheutz, M. Investigating the effects of robot communication strategies in advice-giving situations based on robot appearance, interaction modality and distance. In *Proceedings of HRI* (2014), 479–486.

37. Strait, M., and Scheutz, M. Measuring users' responses to humans, robots, and human-like robots with functional near infrared spectroscopy. In *Proceedings of RO-MAN* (2014), 1128–1133.

38. van Reekum, C., Johnstone, T., Urry, H., Thurow, M., and Schaefer, H. Gaze fixations predict brain activation during the voluntary regulation of picture-induced negative affect. *Neuroimage 36* (2007), 1041–1055.

39. Vujovic, L., Opitz, P. C., Birk, J. L., and Urry, H. L. Cut that's a wrap! Regulating negative emotion by ending emotion-eliciting situations. *Frontiers in Psy. 5* (2014).

40. Walters, M., Syrdal, D., Dautenhahn, K., Te Boekhorst, R., and Koay, K. Avoiding the uncanny valley: robot appearance, personality and consistency of behavior in an attention-seeking home scenario for a robot companion. *Autonomous Robots 24*, 2 (2008), 159–178.

Look Like Me: Matching Robot Personality via Gaze to Increase Motivation

Sean Andrist,[1] **Bilge Mutlu,**[1] **Adriana Tapus**[2]
(1) University of Wisconsin–Madison, Madison, WI, USA; (2) ENSTA-ParisTech, Palaiseau, France
sandrist@cs.wisc.edu; bilge@cs.wisc.edu; adriana.tapus@ensta-paristech.fr

ABSTRACT
Socially assistive robots are envisioned to provide social and cognitive assistance where they will seek to motivate and engage people in therapeutic activities. Due to their physicality, robots serve as a powerful technology for motivating people. Prior work has shown that effective motivation requires adaptation to user needs and characteristics, but how robots might successfully achieve such adaptation is still unknown. In this paper, we present work on matching a robot's personality—expressed via its gaze behavior—to that of its users. We confirmed in an online study with 22 participants that the robot's gaze behavior can successfully express either an extroverted or introverted personality. In a laboratory study with 40 participants, we demonstrate the positive effect of personality matching on a user's motivation to engage in a repetitive task. These results have important implications for the design of adaptive robot behaviors in assistive human-robot interaction.

Author Keywords
Human-robot interaction (HRI); gaze; personality; motivation; compliance; similarity-attraction

ACM Classification Keywords
H.1.2 **Models and Principles**: User/Machine Systems—*human factors, software psychology*; H.5.2 **Information Interfaces and Presentation**: User Interfaces—*evaluation/methodology, user-centered design*

INTRODUCTION
Technologies with robotic features and social competence have long been envisioned as integrating into the working and living environments of people. In recent years, this vision has started to become reality, with the development and commercialization of social robotic products such as Jibo[1] and Pepper[2] that serve as family companions in homes, Baxter[3] and Hospi[4]

[1]http://www.myjibo.com
[2]http://www.aldebaran.com/en/a-robots/who-is-pepper
[3]http://www.rethinkrobotics.com
[4]http://news.panasonic.net/archives/2013/1105_24824.html

CHI 2015, April 18–23, 2015, Seoul, Republic of Korea.

ACM 978-1-4503-3145-6/15/04 ...$15.00.
http://dx.doi.org/10.1145/2702123.2702592

Figure 1. A socially assistive robot guiding a user in a puzzle-solving task.

that work alongside people in organizations such as factories and hospitals, and Autom[5] that takes on the role of a personal weight loss coach. Moving forward, social robots are expected take on even larger roles in areas such as education, collaboration, and rehabilitation.

In the area of rehabilitation, social robots hold great promise for improving the quality of life of the elderly, individuals with physical impairment, and those with cognitive disorders. Social robots envisioned for use in these contexts are referred to as *socially assistive robots* [11]. The purpose of these robots is to assist users by providing information, motivation, and feedback in order to increase compliance with an exercise regimen, take medication on a schedule, perform repetitive tasks for physical or cognitive therapy, and so on. Socially assistive robots are currently being developed to work as caregivers alongside doctors, nurses, and physical therapists [20]; therapy aids for children with autism [12, 39]; and as companions in nursing homes [10, 26].

Patient compliance with treatment for chronic diseases in the U.S. is often below 50%; over half of patients do not take their medication correctly [33]. Following a stroke, one of the most effective rehabilitation methods is for patients to repeatedly exercise the affected limb(s), an activity patients find quite difficult to keep up without a therapist present [9]. A powerful way of improving motivation and compliance in such settings is through nonverbal behaviors and adapting behaviors to the patient's characteristics. Socially assistive robots are particularly engaging in such scenarios due to their physical embodiment and ability to employ nonverbal cues.

[5]http://myautom.com

Gaze is a particularly important nonverbal cue in social interactions that robots have at their disposal [8]. Research in human-robot interaction (HRI) has investigated the positive outcomes achievable through a robot's gaze behavior, including increasing the robot's competence in conversations with people [1, 30, 29], enabling joint attention and referential communication [17, 41], and improving upon the robot's ability to hand objects to people [27]. To be truly effective, the robot must be able to *adapt* its behaviors in two ways. First, it must adapt to the unique characteristics of its user, and second, it must adapt to changes in user needs and behaviors throughout an interaction and across multiple interactions.

In this paper, we investigate how robots may achieve the first form of adaptation and present the design and evaluation of gaze behaviors for socially assistive robots that enable the robot to match the personality of the user, thereby more effectively motivating users to repeatedly engage in a therapeutic task. We focus on the extroversion dimension of the Big Five personality model [19] as it is the most accurately observable dimension of personality expressed by nonverbal behaviors over short timescales [25]. We also demonstrate the importance of taking the user's intrinsic motivation into account when attempting to motivate and increase compliance.

BACKGROUND

Three threads of research inform this work, including previous work on socially assistive robots, previous work on adapting technologies to the characteristics—especially personality—of users, and social-science research on the relationship between nonverbal behaviors, personality, and motivation.

Socially Assistive Robots

Prior work has established that the mere presence of a robot can positively affect user compliance in an array of contexts. In previous work where participants were recruited for a weight-loss program, Kidd found that adherence to the program was shortest when participants tracked their progress with pen-and-paper, longer with a computer interface, and significantly longer when reporting their progress to a robot [21]. Even a very simple robot—a Roomba vacuum cleaner robot augmented with a facial display—has been shown to be capable of helping people with medication compliance [42]. Social facilitation theory [28] provides some explanation for the effectiveness of robots in these contexts; the presence of an embodied humanlike robot increases motivation in the same way that the presence of other people increases an individual's drive and enhances their performance in tasks in which the individual is skilled. The robot's physical embodiment and shared physical context create an opportunity for strong engagement between the robot and the user.

To improve effectiveness, the robot must relate to the user with praise and feedback on their actions. Previous research has examined the positive effects of relational discourse—including praise and feedback—in an exercise coach robot leading elderly participants in physical and cognitive exercises [10]. Relational agents have also been found to be effective for delivering health communication and health behavior change interventions to older adults, especially those with low functional health, reading, or computer literacy [2].

Previous research has investigated the ability of social robots to provide cognitive therapy to users, such as older adults with mild cognitive impairments that need help planning and executing everyday activities [3]. Robot therapists for the elderly have also been employed to play memory enhancing music games with their users [45]. For individuals suffering from dementia and/or other cognitive impairments, socially assistive robots have been shown to improve, through social interaction, the cognitive abilities of their users, and thus their quality of life [46]. Robots are also educationally useful interventions to improve social interactions for individuals with Autism Spectrum Disorders (ASD) [32].

Socially assistive robots are capable of providing physical therapy for users without needing to make physical contact. Individuals who have recently suffered a stroke may benefit from the use of robots in this domain. Previous work has investigated the influence of robot coaching styles designed to enhance motivation and encouragement on post-stroke individuals during motor task practice [49]. In other prior work, a robot asked healthy users to engage in physical exercises similar to those used during standard stroke rehabilitation, such as repeatedly lifting and moving books or pencils. Participants were asked to perform the tasks for as long as they wished. Researchers manipulated the interaction style of the robot and found that extroverted participants preferred and complied more with a robot that challenged them rather than one which focused on nurturing praise [44]. In subsequent work, the robot adapted its behavior to match each participant's preferences in terms of therapy style, interaction distance, and movement speed [43]. In that work, as well as in research presented in the next section, it is shown that adaptation is key to creating positive interactions, especially in assistive contexts. The present work aims to further this research by presenting personality-expressing gaze behaviors and demonstrating that they must be targeted to the personality of users.

Adapting to Users

Previous research in HRI has demonstrated the benefit of a robot adapting to its users. In prior work in which a robot provided cooking help to participants in a kitchen, researchers found that adaptive dialogue—in which the robot adapted the content of its speech depending on the expertise of the user—improved information exchange and social relations, especially when users were under time pressure [47]. Previous research with children investigated the use of adaptive empathic behaviors (e.g., encouraging comments and offering help) for a chess-playing robot [24]. Children responded positively to the robot when the empathic behaviors were employed adaptively, rather than randomly. Previous work has also investigated the positive effect in eliciting user compliance of matching a "playful" or a "serious" robot (conveyed through the robot's speech) to a playful or serious task [14].

Adapting to user personality has been more widely studied in HCI. For example, previous research shows that computer interfaces can be manipulated to exhibit an extroverted or introverted personality through the use of language, pictures, and sounds, and that introverted users will perform tasks faster when using introverted software [36]. This result follows from the theory of *similarity-attraction* which predicts that a person will be attracted more to others who match their personalities than to those who mismatch [22]. In the same way, matching the personality of a synthesized voice, expressed through pitch, prosody, and so on, to user personality positively affects users' feelings of social presence, especially in extroverts [22]. Emotion matching is also important in computer interfaces. In a study of emotional speech generation for car interfaces, it was found that when the emotion expressed by the car voice (energetic or subdued) matches the emotional state of the driver (happy or upset), drivers have fewer accidents, attend more to the road, and speak more to the car [31]. Our research in socially assistive robots parallels these efforts by following similarity-attraction theory to match the gaze behaviors of the robot to the personality of the user.

Nonverbal Behaviors, Personality, and Motivation

Nonverbal behaviors, especially gaze, have long been recognized in social-sciences literature as useful tools in persuading others to comply with requests or demands. A number of theories have been proposed to explain this phenomenon, including speech accommodation theory, demand theory, and arousal intimacy theory [40]. According to *speech accommodation theory*, people may change their communication behaviors when interacting with others and convergence toward the style of the partner should produce a positive attitude in the partner and thus lead to compliance. According to *demand theory*, nonverbal behaviors can function as demands (e.g., staring as a demand for a response), producing a level of arousal that targets can alleviate by complying with any implicit or explicit demands. In *arousal intimacy theory*, nonverbal behaviors are predicted to produce compliance because they produce greater perceptions of intimacy between the source and target, leading to compliance when the target experiences positive arousal. Each of these three theories predicts a strong relationship between nonverbal behaviors and compliance.

A large amount of previous research has empirically demonstrated the positive effect of gaze on compliance. When a collector of money for charity engaged in mutual gaze with possible donors, rather than looking at the collecting tin, they were more successful in receiving donations [4]. Nonverbal behavioral cues, such as gaze, gesture, and proxemics, are sometimes referred to as *immediacy* cues [6]. Students are more likely to comply when they perceive their teachers as moderately to highly immediate, and are more likely to choose to reject requests made by nonimmediate teachers [5]. Similarly, attraction and dominance increase compliance and cues of such are often expressed through nonverbal cues like gaze [34]. Gaze is also closely tied to personality, with extroverts commonly engaging in significantly more mutual gaze with their conversational partners than do introverts [37].

In addition to nonverbal behaviors and personality, attempts to increase compliance in others must take into account a person's motivation, which can vary not only in magnitude but also in orientation [38]. The most basic distinction in motivation orientation is between intrinsic, which refers to doing something because it is inherently interesting or enjoyable, and extrinsic, which refers to doing something because it is accompanied by external pressure or control. In the current work, we use socially assistive robots to create extrinsic motivation in users, but also take into consideration the intrinsic motivation that those users have to complete the task.

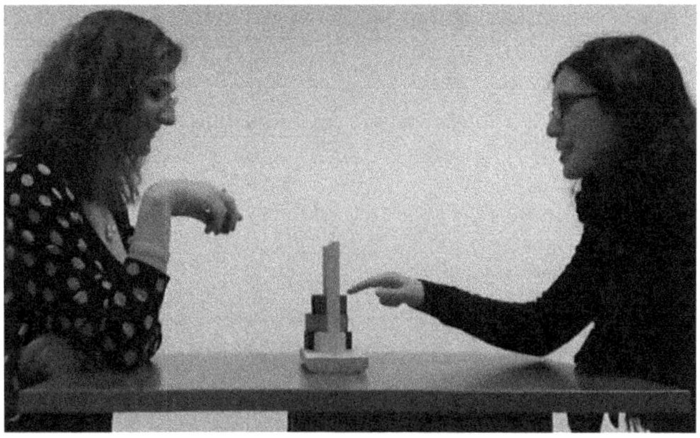

Figure 2. Setup of the human-human data collection study. The participant on the right (instructor) is providing extrinsic motivation to the participant on the left (worker) to complete the puzzle.

DESIGNING PERSONALITY-EXPRESSING GAZE

In order to develop adaptive gaze behaviors for a socially assistive robot to employ, we first sought to understand the relationship between gaze and personality, focusing particularly on extroversion, in a motivational context. In this section, we present a human-human data collection study we conducted in order to inform the design of personality-expressive gaze behaviors. We also present an online validation study we conducted to confirm that the designed robot gaze behaviors express the intended personality.

Data Collection and Modeling

To understand the relationship between gaze and personality in a motivational task, we sought to answer the following questions. How do people use their gaze when attempting to motivate others and increase compliance? What is the relationship between their use of gaze and their respective personalities? To answer these questions, we conducted a human-human data collection study with four participant dyads, obtaining more precise measurements of gaze behavior than what is traditionally presented in the social-sciences literature. We chose the Tower of Hanoi puzzle for participants to complete collaboratively. The goal of this puzzle is to move a number of colored blocks from one location to another while following some simple rules. This task was chosen for its mix of cognitive (solving the puzzle) and physical (actually moving the pieces around) elements, mapping well to tasks commonly used in physical and cognitive rehabilitation. The task can also be broken down into two repeating phases common to rehabilitation activities: (1) the actual execution of the task, which we will refer to here as the *in-task phase*, and (2) the time between tasks when the therapist must provide encouragement to persist with the task, which we will refer to here as the *between-task phase*.

Participants filled out the Big Five inventory prior to participation to determine their position on the extroversion-introversion spectrum [19]. The Big Five questionnaire con-

Worker Compliance & Mutual Gaze

Outcome	Compliance			Instructor Gaze toward Partner (%)		Worker Gaze toward Partner (%)	
Measure	Time (s)	Puzzles Done	Blocks Moved	In-Task Phase	Between-Task Phase	In-Task Phase	Between-Task Phase
Dyad (Instructor–Worker)							
Extroverted–Extroverted	1369	18	541	7.66	14.74	5.20	11.91
Introverted–Introverted	703	14	352	3.79	8.57	2.74	8.68
Extroverted–Introverted	320	9	227	5.31	10.53	1.77	8.97
Introverted–Extroverted	295	7	121	1.91	4.39	4.94	14.74

Table 1. Results from the human-human data collection on worker compliance in each dyad, as well as the amount of partner-directed gaze for all participants.

tains 44 items on a five-point rating scale that ask the participant to rate their agreement or disagreement with statements about their own personality and activities. Eight of these items contribute to the extroversion dimension of the participant's overall personality score. These items have good internal reliability (Cronbach's α = .88). Participants scoring lower than 2.5 on the extroversion dimension were labeled as introverted, and those above 2.5 were labeled as extroverted.

In each dyad, one participant was assigned to be the *instructor* and the other the *worker*. Each of the four dyads covered one of the four possible combinations of participant personality and role. The experimenter first explained the puzzle to the instructor without the worker present. Next, the instructor practiced solving the puzzle with the experimenter. The instructor was required to successfully solve the puzzle a number of times in front of the experimenter to prove that they were comfortable with the task. Then, the instructor was asked to carry out the following procedure: (1) explain the task to the worker, (2) monitor the worker as they complete the task, (3) provide encouraging feedback during the puzzle solving, (4) motivate the worker to keep working between puzzle tasks, and (5) correct workers when they make a mistake. The worker was told by the experimenter that everything would be explained by the instructor, but that they were welcome to work on the task for as long as they wished and that it was up to them to decide when they would like to stop.

The two participants sat at a table facing each other, with the puzzle between them (Figure 2). Over-the-shoulder view cameras recorded the gaze of each participant, and a side camera with wide-angle view was used for recording the entire task. The compliance of the worker to the instructor was measured in three ways: (1) total time spent solving puzzles, (2) total number of puzzles completed, and (3) total number of puzzle pieces moved. Worker compliance in each dyad, as well as the percentage of each participant's attempt to engage in mutual gaze with their partner, is presented in Table .

Gaze Lengths (Mean (Standard Deviation))

Personality	Extroverted		Introverted	
Phase	In-Task	Between-Task	In-Task	Between-Task
Partner	2.66 (0.80)	3.91 (1.22)	0.57 (0.19)	1.59 (0.39)
Puzzle	4.04 (2.12)	1.01 (1.26)	11.65 (11.17)	6.21 (8.14)

Table 2. Means and standard deviations of gaze fixations (in seconds) to the partner and to the puzzle for extroverted and introverted participants, divided into in-task and between-task phases of the interaction.

All videos were coded for participant gaze behavior. Participant gazes were recorded and labeled for two targets: the other participant and the shared workspace. The mean and standard deviation of these gaze lengths are presented in Table .

We observe three trends from the data. First, extroverts seem to be attempting to engage in more mutual gaze with their partner than do introverts. This relationship between extroversion and gaze behavior has been similarly demonstrated in previous research, including a study of dyadic interviews in which it was found that extroverts gaze at their interviewer more than introverts do [18]. Second, there is more mutual gaze between puzzle phases when the instructor is attempting to motivate the worker to solve more puzzles and much less mutual gaze during the actual puzzle completion. Third, there is some preliminary indication that personality matching is an effective strategy for increasing compliance, as personality-matching dyads exhibited longer time-on-task than the mismatching personality dyads. This point is explored further in the experimental evaluation presented later in this paper.

The results presented in Table are used to generate two models of gaze behavior for robots, one to express an extroverted personality and the other to express an introverted personality. The presented means and standard deviations are used to create normal distributions of gaze lengths that the robot draws from when planning and executing gazes toward the user and toward the task space. In an expression of the extroverted model, the robot gazes into the face of the user more, while the introverted model generates more gaze toward the task space. In both models, more gaze is generated toward the user in the motivational between-task phase than in the in-task phase, which involves monitoring the user's actions. For example, an extroverted robot drawing from the distributions in Table might generate a four-second gaze toward the user in a between-task phase, followed by a one-second gaze toward the task space. This sequence of long user fixations and short task fixations—randomly generated according to the distributions—would repeat until the start of the next in-task phase. At this point, the extroverted robot might generate a four-second gaze toward the task space followed by a two-and-a-half-second gaze to the user. This cycle of gaze shifts would repeat throughout the in-task phase.

Implementation

Following the data collection and analysis from human dyads, we next designed and implemented a system to allow a robot to take on the instructor role in the same puzzle completion scenario. We implemented the system on the Meka robot platform (Figure 1). We use the Robot Operating System (ROS) to handle the execution and communication amongst each of the system components described below (Figure 3).

Tracking the participant and task state—A depth camera mounted in Meka's chest was used for face tracking. A small amount of noise is added to the tracking output so that the robot's gaze does not remain motionless when gazing toward

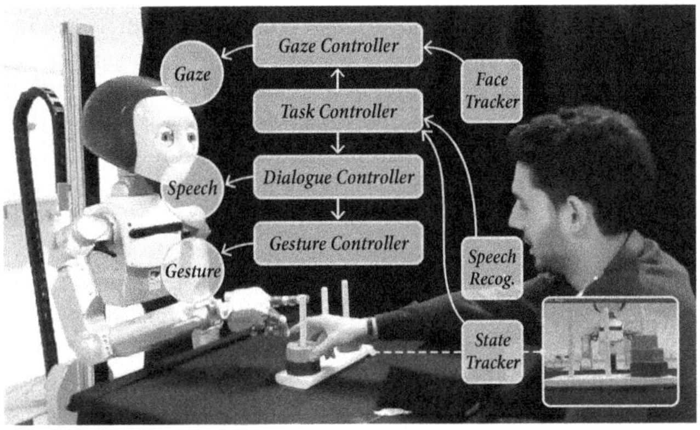

Figure 3. The implementation of the socially assistive robot. Participant face location, speech, and task state are tracked and passed to the dialogue controller, task controller, and gaze controller. These controllers determine the gaze, speech, and gestures of the robot. Rounded squares, circles, and rounded rectangles denote sensing, output, and control modules, respectively.

the user's face. For puzzle tracking, a separate webcam is placed on the table and focused on the puzzle. Color blob tracking is employed to determine the current locations of each of the different colored puzzle pieces. Google speech recognition is utilized for capturing the user's requests for help and requests to terminate the task.

Task controller—This component manages the flow of the overall scenario. It keeps track of the current task phase (in-task or between-task) and continuously solves the puzzle from the current state so the robot can provide hints and help when requested. The robot can provide general strategies or suggest moves to make in completing the puzzle. If the user makes five bad moves in a row or does not make a move for ten seconds, the robot automatically provides help. The robot also randomly provides positive feedback when it detects that the user has made a good move. Providing these hints and feedback has been shown in previous work to positively affect people's motivation to engage in a task [48].

Generating robot behavior—Depending on the current phase of the scenario (introduction, in-task, between-task, closing), the dialogue controller generates the robot's speech appropriately. If a request for help is detected, the dialogue controller generates the response speech and the gesture controller generates a pointing gesture to the appropriate puzzle piece. The gaze controller generates gaze shifts according to the personality being expressed and the current phase of the interaction. The values in Table are used to create distributions that the robot draws from when planning and generating gaze shifts toward the puzzle or toward the user. When gazing toward the puzzle, the robot looks toward blocks that are in motion, creating a stronger sense of responsiveness and lifelikeness.

Model Validation

After implementing the system, we conducted an online study to determine if the extroverted and introverted gaze behaviors generated by the gaze controller would actually be perceived as such. We filmed four one-minute videos of the robot interacting with a human user in the Tower of Hanoi scenario. In two of the videos, the robot utilized the extrovert model of gaze behaviors, with the other two videos depicting the robot utilizing the introvert model. This study used a within-participant design; all four of the videos were shown to each participant in a random order. Following each video, participants rated the perceived extroversion of the robot on six five-point rating scales which have also been used in previous research to rate the perceived personality of robots [23].

Participants in this study were recruited using Amazon's Mechanical Turk. We recruited 30 participants (15 Female, 15 Male) with a mean age of 34.9 (SD = 8.5). Standard IP-filtering techniques were employed to limit participation to the United States and prevent multiple participation. In order to eliminate participants that were not focusing on the videos, we asked participants to indicate the color of the robot's head (blue) at the end of the study, discarding data from participants who failed to provide a correct answer. We also tracked the amount of time that the browser window containing the video stimulus remained in focus on the participant's computer. Eight participants failed the color question and/or unfocused the stimulus window for a majority of the study time and were therefore eliminated from analysis, leaving 22 participants.

We analyzed the effect of the robot's gaze behavior on participant ratings of the robot personality using repeated-measures analysis of variance (ANOVA). Results indicated that participants did perceive a difference in the personality of the robot in the way that we intended. The extroversion rating of the robot was significantly higher in the extrovert gaze behavior condition (M=3.79, SD=0.54) than in the introvert gaze behavior condition (M=3.53, SD=0.59), $F(1,84) = 5.09, p = .027$. This result is supported by previous work which demonstrated that participants can accurately recognize a robot's intended personality based on its verbal and nonverbal behaviors [23].

EXPERIMENTAL EVALUATION

The validation study showed that the gaze manipulations indeed resulted in differential perceptions of the robot's personality. Next we present a more comprehensive study of the effect of using these personality-expressing gaze behaviors in motivational interactions with human users. The goal of this study was to test the effect on compliance of matching or mismatching the robot's personality with that of the user.

Hypotheses

Three hypotheses were developed that predict the effect of matching the personality of the robot—expressed through gaze—to the personality of users, as well as the potential effect of users' intrinsic motivation.

Hypothesis 1—Matching the robot's personality to the user's personality will improve the user's subjective ratings of the robot's performance.

This hypothesis follows from similarity-attraction theory, which predicts that a person will be more attracted to others who match their personality than to those whose personalities do not match [22]. Thus, we predict a strong interaction effect between user personality and robot personality.

Hypothesis 2—Matching the robot's personality to the user's personality will improve compliance with the robot's requests to engage in the task for a longer period of time.

This hypothesis also predicts a strong interaction effect between user personality and robot personality and follows from similarity-attraction theory. Previous work in socially assistive robots found a similar interaction effect on compliance between user personality (extrovert or introvert) and robot therapy style (challenging or nurturing) [44]. Our own data collection, which we presented earlier, also lends some preliminary support for this hypothesis, as the two personality-matching dyads participated in the puzzle task longer than both personality-mismatching dyads.

Hypothesis 3—The user's intrinsic motivation for the task will interact with the personality-matching effect on compliance. Users with low intrinsic motivation will be more affected by personality-matching than users with high intrinsic motivation.

If a user has high intrinsic motivation for the puzzle-solving task, they would inherently find the task interesting or enjoyable and thus would not respond to external motivation attempts from a socially assistive robot [38].

Participants

We recruited 40 participants for this experiment (16 Female, 24 Male) from a university campus. Participant ages ranged from 20 to 58 (M = 30.6, SD = 9.4). For feasibility purposes, all participants were healthy adults without need of physical or cognitive therapy, a strategy that has been employed in previous research on socially assistive robots [44]. Participants' countries of origin included France, the United States, China, Romania, and Tunisia, and came from both technical and non-technical backgrounds. The experiment was implemented in both English and French (including the script of both the experimenter and the robot), and participants were allowed to choose the language with which they were most comfortable (10 chose English, 30 chose French).

Study Design & Procedure

The study followed a 2×2 between-participants study design, with participant personality (extrovert or introvert) and robot personality (extrovert or introvert) comprising the two factors. The study contained four total conditions representing each of the four personality combinations, with ten participants recruited for each of these conditions. The robot's gaze behavior was the only difference between robot personality conditions; experimenter instructions and the content of robot speech were held constant for all conditions.

All participants were asked to complete and submit the Big Five personality inventory prior to participation to determine their position on the extroversion-introversion spectrum [19]. These items, as in the human-human task, took the form of five-point rating scales. We used a median split to separate participants into two groups. All participants with an extroversion score less than or equal to 3.0 were labeled as "introverted," with participants scoring higher than 3.0 labeled as "extroverted." Participants were also asked to complete and submit a questionnaire to assess their global motivation toward activities in their life. This questionnaire contains 28 items assessed on a seven-point scale, with constructs for both intrinsic motivation and extrinsic motivation [15].

Participants were randomly assigned to interact with either the extroverted or introverted robot. After receiving informed consent, the experimenter introduced the participant to the Meka robot and explained the task. Participants were told that they would be completing the Tower of Hanoi puzzle under the supervision of the robot, and that the robot would provide all the necessary instructions for the rules and for progressing through the various stages of the puzzle. Participants were seated in front of the robot, facing it at eye-level, with a table between them. The physical Tower of Hanoi puzzle was placed on the table between the robot and participant (as illustrated in Figure 1). The participant was clearly instructed that it was their decision as to when they wanted to terminate the interaction and that they could indicate this to the robot at any time they wished. A headset microphone was used for capturing the speech of the participants, while the robot's speech was projected through its own speakers.

The experimenter then started the system implementation and left the participant to interact with the autonomous robot. After initial introductions, the robot carefully explained the goal and rules of the puzzle and asked the participant to complete it. After the participant's first successful completion, the robot explained that it would be asking the participant to complete the same puzzle several times and reminded the participant that it was up to them to decide when they would like to stop. During the execution of each puzzle task—the *in-task phase*—the robot monitored the task and provided help if the participant got stuck or explicitly asked for help. Following the successful completion of each puzzle—the *between-task phase*—the robot first provided positive feedback and then asked the participant if they would like to continue. If the participant agreed, the robot indicated a new puzzle goal and asked the participant to begin another iteration of the task.

Three levels of difficulty were implemented for the puzzle. The easiest difficulty required the solution of the three-disk version of the puzzle; the medium difficulty used four disks; and the hardest difficulty involved five disks. The least number of disk movements that can be made for each level of the puzzle are 7, 15, and 31, respectively. When the participant completed the puzzle eight times at the same difficulty level (starting with the easiest), the robot asked them to increase the difficulty by adding another disk. If a participant reached the hardest difficulty level, they stayed at this difficulty until they decided to terminate the interaction.

When the participant indicated that they wished to terminate the interaction, the robot thanked and instructed them to fill out a follow-up questionnaire at a computer nearby. Once participants finished this final questionnaire, the experimenter returned and thanked them once again for their participation.

Measures

The study included three objective measures of participant compliance: total time spent working on the task, total number of puzzles solved, and total number of disks moved across all instances of the puzzle. The follow-up questionnaire contained several seven-point rating scales for assessing the performance of the robot. Five items from this questionnaire were combined into a single construct of *perceived robot performance*,

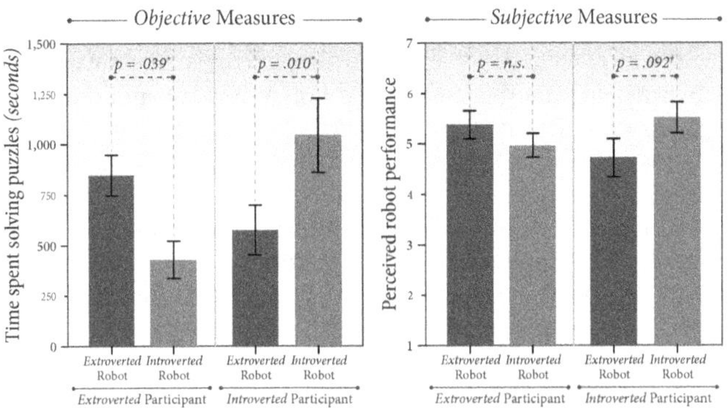

Figure 4. Left: objective results of compliance for total participation time. A personality matching effect predicted by similarity-attraction theory was found. Right: subjective results of perceived robot performance. Introverted participants reported a marginal preference for the introverted robot. (*) and (†) denote $p < .05$ and $p < .10$, respectively.

including questions about the robot's skills as an instructor and motivator, as well as questions relating to the usefulness of the robot's information and advice. This construct was found to have good internal reliability (Cronbach's $\alpha = .75$).

The follow-up questionnaire also included open-ended questions about why the participant chose to participate for as long as they did and why they chose to eventually terminate the interaction. In order to obtain a more task-specific measure of intrinsic motivation, these open-ended responses were coded for explicit mention of the participant's inherent desire to solve the puzzles, without mention of any external motivation coming from the robot.

Results

Analysis of the data was conducted using a between-subjects analysis of variance (ANOVA). Participant personality, robot personality, and the interaction of both were modeled as fixed effects. Participant gender, language (English or French), and previous experience with robots (yes or no), were found to be non-significant covariates on all measures and are not discussed further. Participant background (technical or non-technical) was found to have a significant effect on some measures and it has been retained as a covariate in the statistical model. A Bonferroni correction was employed to control for the experiment-wise error in multiple comparisons.

Compliance—Regarding the measure of total participation time, there was no main effect of either participant personality, $F(1,35) = 0.75, p = .39$, or robot personality, $F(1,35) = 0.16, p = .69$. A significant interaction effect was observed, $F(1,35) = 14.80, p < .001$, with a significant effect of extroverted participants participating longer with the extroverted robot, $F(1,35) = 5.97, p = .039$, and for introverted participants participating longer with the introverted robot, $F(1,35) = 8.97, p = .010$. Participant background also had a significant main effect on participation time, with non-technical participants participating for longer than those from technical backgrounds, $F(1,35) = 7.31, p = .011$.

On the total puzzles solved measure, there was no main effect of either participant personality, $F(1,35) = 0.36, p = .55$, or robot personality, $F(1,35) = 0.57, p = .45$. We found a significant interaction effect, $F(1,35) = 8.07, p = .007$, with a significant effect of extroverted participants solving more puzzles with the extroverted robot, $F(1,35) = 6.51, p = .031$, but no significant effect among introverted participants $F(1,35) = 2.16, p = .30$. Participant background did not have a significant effect on this measure, $F(1,35) = 0.51, p = .48$.

On the measure of total disks moved across the entire interaction, there was no main effect of either participant personality, $F(1,35) = 0.14, p = .71$, or robot personality, $F(1,35) = 1.72, p = .20$. Our analysis found a significant interaction effect, $F(1,35) = 5.42, p = .026$, with a significant effect of extroverted participants moving more disks with the extroverted robot, $F(1,35) = 6.65, p = .028$, but no significant effect among introverted participants $F(1,35) = 0.52, p = .94$. Participant background was not found to have a significant effect on this measure, $F(1,35) = 1.03, p = .32$.

Perceived Robot Performance—On the subjective rating of the robot's performance, there was no main effect of either participant personality, $F(1,35) = 0.25, p = .62$, or robot personality, $F(1,35) = 0.58, p = .45$. We found a significant interaction effect, $F(1,35) = 4.70, p = .037$, with no significant effect among extroverted participants, $F(1,35) = 0.99, p = .66$, and a marginal preference among introverted participants for the introverted robot, $F(1,35) = 4.27, p = .092$. Participants with a non-technical background also expressed marginally higher ratings of the robot's performance, $F(1,35) = 3.10, p = .087$. Results for compliance and perceived robot performance are visually presented in Figure 4.

Motivation—We conducted a regression analysis on the effect of the participant's reported global intrinsic motivation (collected in the pre-test survey) on all measures of compliance. No significant results were found for any of the measures. However, significant effects were observed for the task-specific measure of intrinsic motivation, in which we coded participant responses to the open-ended question: "Why did you participate for as long as you did?" Participants who indicated an inherent interest in solving the puzzle, rather than participating because of the presence of the robot and its feedback, were labeled as having high intrinsic motivation. Twenty-seven participants (14 extroverts, 13 introverts) were found to have high intrinsic motivation. We observed a three-way interaction effect between this measure of intrinsic motivation, participant personality, and robot personality on the compliance measure of total participation time, $F(1,34) = 5.62, p = .006$. Among participants with high intrinsic motivation, there was no significant effect of personality among extroverted participants, $F(1,34) = 1.43, p = .24$, or introverted participants, $F(1,34) = 2.08, p = .16$. However, among participants without high intrinsic motivation, extroverted participants participated for significantly longer with the extroverted robot, $F(1,34) = 15.84, p < .001$ and introverted participants participated for significantly longer with the introverted robot, $F(1,34) = 19.44, p < .001$. The results involving intrinsic motivation are visualized in Figure 5.

DISCUSSION

The goal of the experimental evaluation was to test the effectiveness of matching a socially assistive robot's personality—

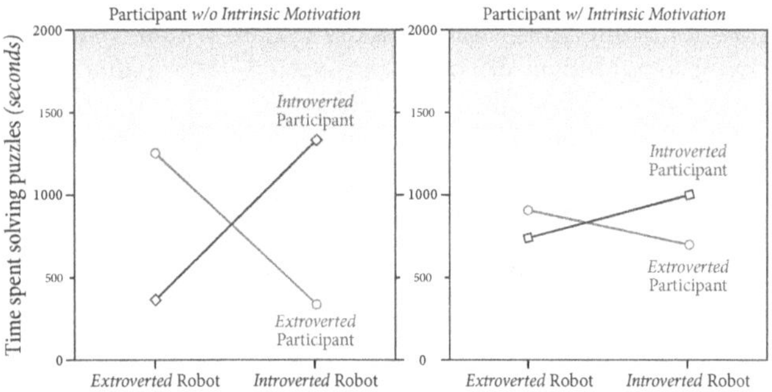

Figure 5. The interaction effect on compliance predicted by similarity-attraction theory is only present for participants that were not found to have high intrinsic motivation for the task.

as expressed via our designed gaze behaviors—to that of the participant in a repetitive task requiring persistent motivation from the robot. The robot's personality was manipulated purely through its gaze behavior, gazing much more toward the participant when expressing an extroverted personality and much more toward the task space when expressing an introverted personality. These behaviors were validated in an online study to express their intended personality, and we were interested in whether an extroverted and introverted robot would elicit more compliance and positive subjective perceptions from extroverted and introverted participants respectively.

Our first hypothesis predicted that, in line with similarity-attraction theory, participants would give higher subjective ratings to the performance of a robot that matches their personality. This hypothesis was partially supported in the experiment, in that introverted participants reported a marginal preference for the introverted robot behaviors. Extroverted participants reported no difference in ratings. Introverts may have been more consciously sensitive to the behaviors of the robot, as previous work has shown introverts have a superior detection rate and perceptual sensitivity than extroverts [7]. In a study involving the rating of other people, previous work has also found that introverts preferred other introverts on the measures of "reliable friend" and "honest and ethical," while extroverts were ambivalent in these measures [16].

The experiment provided support for our second hypothesis, which predicted that participants would comply more with robots that matched their personality. On the measure of total participation time, both extroverts and introverts exhibited significantly greater compliance with the personality-matching robot. However, in the measures of total puzzles solved and total disks moved, only extroverts exhibited significantly greater compliance with the personality-matching robot. Previous work in HCI has shown a similar result in that matching a synthesized voice's personality to a user's personality improved feelings of social presence, but only for extroverts [22].

Our third hypothesis predicted that the intrinsic motivation of participants and the personality-matching effect would interact. We found some support for this hypothesis, but not from the pre-test survey asking participants to rate their intrinsic motivation towards tasks in general. Instead, when we coded participants' open-ended responses to a post-study interview question asking why they participated for as long as they did, we found that some participants were more intrinsically motivated to solve the puzzles, whereas others were more extrinsically motivated by the robot. When we split the participants into these two groups, we found a significant interaction between intrinsic motivation and personality matching. For both extroverts and introverts, the personality-matching robot was most effective in motivating those who were not highly intrinsically motivated to solve the puzzles. We note, however, that splitting our population into groups with intrinsic and extrinsic motivation resulted in relatively small sample sizes and that follow-up work with a larger participant population must be carried out to more conclusively establish this relationship.

Design Implications

This work further demonstrates the importance of designing social technologies that can adapt to user characteristics. We have shown that a robot that matches the personality expressed by its gaze behavior to the personality of its user can improve compliance and subjective perceptions of the robot's performance. These outcomes are particularly critical for socially assistive robots that must motivate their users to engage in physical or cognitive exercises, especially when these exercises are repetitive or boring. Social theories such as similarity-attraction must be leveraged and further studied in human-robot interaction, as they can have powerful implications for the effectiveness of these interactions. We believe that the results presented in this work also extend beyond socially assistive robots and point to similar design considerations for embodied agents—including both robots and virtual agents—in other domains, such as education and companionship.

Limitations & Future Work

A significant limitation of the current work is that the study population was comprised of healthy adults all under the age of 60. This choice was made for the purposes of feasibility in testing a novel idea for socially assistive robots, similar to what has been done in previous work in this domain [44]. We expect our findings to hold for the targeted populations that need socially assistive robots, such as the elderly or post-stroke patients, but this expectation should be tested in future work.

The gaze model presented in this work has a number of limitations due to certain simplifications, including the small sample size it was generated from, the fidelity of included gaze targets, and the specificity to a single task in a controlled environment. These simplifications were necessary and the resulting model was sufficiently detailed for this initial effort and evaluation, but future work should seek to build more sophisticated models that overcome these limitations. While we observed participants in our study to gaze almost exclusively toward either each other or the task space, more complex interactions in less controlled environments will need to take into account more possible gaze targets. More sophisticated models will also need to dynamically adjust to the task state. In our work, we differentiate between on-task and between-task times, but future work will need to include finer-grained task analyses.

We chose to median-split our populations from both the modeling and the evaluation studies to establish "introverted" and "extroverted" groups in order to investigate the effect of matching/mismatching personality categories with balanced sampling. To address the potential limitations of this simplification, future work must model extroversion as a continuum, and the robot should dynamically adjust its behaviors to match the user's location on this continuous spectrum.

In this work, we presented two models of gaze behavior that can exhibit either an extroverted or introverted personality. Previous work has also shown that some aspects of the Big Five model of personality, including extroversion, neuroticism, and openness, have consistent correlations with a person's gaze behavior, as measured by fixation frequencies and durations [35]. However, previous research has also demonstrated that personality and nonverbal behavior are not always linked in simple ways [13]. Personality can be expressed differently in different contexts, group compositions, cultures, and combinations, and this richness should be taken into account in future work to align robot behaviors with user personalities. Additionally, future socially assistive robot systems should detect user characteristics such as personality *in-situ*, rather than requiring the user to explicitly provide this information, e.g., by filling out a questionnaire before using the system.

CONCLUSION

In this paper, we presented the design and evaluation of gaze behaviors for socially assistive robots that allow the robot to match the extroversion dimension of personality to the user, thereby more effectively motivating users to repeatedly engage in a therapeutic task. These robot behaviors were designed by analyzing the gaze behavior of participants in a human-human data collection study, and were validated in an online study to express either an extroverted or introverted personality. The evaluation also demonstrated the importance of taking the user's intrinsic motivation into account when attempting to produce external motivation and increase compliance. In general, socially assistive robots offer a particularly powerful way of improving motivation and compliance in rehabilitation settings due to their physical embodiment and ability to use nonverbal communication channels. By effectively taking advantage of these abilities and designing methods for adapting to the characteristics of their users, these systems can dramatically improve the quality of life for people in need.

ACKNOWLEDGMENTS

This work was supported by the Chateaubriand Research Fellowship. We thank Catherine Steffel for her editing help.

REFERENCES

1. Andrist, S., Tan, X. Z., Gleicher, M., and Mutlu, B. Conversational gaze aversion for humanlike robots. In *Proc HRI'14* (2014), 25–32.
2. Bickmore, T. W., Caruso, L., and Clough-Gorr, K. Acceptance and usability of a relational agent interface by urban older adults. In *Proc CHI'05 Extended Abstracts* (2005), 1212–1215.
3. Bruno, B., Mastrogiovanni, F., and Sgorbissa, A. Functional requirements and design issues for a socially assistive robot for elderly people with mild cognitive impairments. In *Proc RO-MAN'13* (2013), 768–773.
4. Bull, R., and Gibson-Robinson, E. The influences of eye-gaze, style of dress, and locality on the amounts of money donated to a charity. *Hum Relat 34*, 10 (1981), 895–905.
5. Burroughs, N. F. A reinvestigation of the relationship of teacher nonverbal immediacy and student compliance-resistance with learning. *Commun Educ 56*, 4 (2007), 453–475.
6. Christophel, D. M. The relationships among teacher immediacy behaviors, student motivation, and learning. *Commun Educ 39*, 4 (1990), 323–340.
7. Davies, D. R., Matthews, G., Stammers, R. B., and Westerman, S. J. *Human performance: Cognition, stress and individual differences*. Psychology Press, 2013.
8. Emery, N. The eyes have it: the neuroethology, function and evolution of social gaze. *Neurosci Biobehav R 24*, 6 (2000), 581–604.
9. Eriksson, J., Matarić, M. J., and Winstein, C. Hands-off assistive robotics for post-stroke arm rehabilitation. In *Proc ICORR'05* (2005), 21–24.
10. Fasola, J., and Mataric, M. J. Using socially assistive human–robot interaction to motivate physical exercise for older adults. *Proc IEEE 100*, 8 (2012), 2512–2526.
11. Feil-Seifer, D., and Mataric, M. J. Defining socially assistive robotics. In *Proc ICORR'05* (2005), 465–468.
12. Feil-Seifer, D., and Matarić, M. J. Toward socially assistive robotics for augmenting interventions for children with autism spectrum disorders. In *Experimental Robotics* (2009), 201–210.
13. Gifford, R. Personality and nonverbal behavior: A complex conundrum. 2006, 159–179.
14. Goetz, J., Kiesler, S., and Powers, A. Matching robot appearance and behavior to tasks to improve human-robot cooperation. In *Proc RO-MAN'03* (2003), 55–60.
15. Guay, F., Mageau, G. A., and Vallerand, R. J. On the hierarchical structure of self-determined motivation: A test of top-down, bottom-up, reciprocal, and horizontal effects. *Pers Soc Psychol B 29*, 8 (2003), 992–1004.
16. Hendrick, C., and Brown, S. R. Introversion, extraversion, and interpersonal attraction.
17. Huang, C.-M., and Mutlu, B. Robot behavior toolkit: generating effective social behaviors for robots. In *Proc HRI'12* (2012), 25–32.
18. Iizuka, Y. Extraversion, introversion, and visual interaction. *Percept Motor Skill 74*, 1 (1992), 43–50.
19. John, O. P., and Srivastava, S. The big five trait taxonomy: History, measurement, and theoretical perspectives. vol. 2. 1999, 102–138.
20. Kang, K. I., Freedman, S., Mataric, M. J., Cunningham, M. J., and Lopez, B. A hands-off physical therapy assistance robot for cardiac patients. In *Proc ICORR'05* (2005), 337–340.

21. Kidd, C. D. *Designing for Long-term Human-robot Interaction and Application to Weight Loss*. PhD thesis, 2008.

22. Lee, K. M., and Nass, C. Designing social presence of social actors in human computer interaction. In *Proc CHI'03* (2003), 289–296.

23. Lee, K. M., Peng, W., Jin, S.-A., and Yan, C. Can robots manifest personality?: An empirical test of personality recognition, social responses, and social presence in human–robot interaction. *J Commun 56*, 4 (2006), 754–772.

24. Leite, I., Castellano, G., Pereira, A., Martinho, C., and Paiva, A. Modelling empathic behaviour in a robotic game companion for children: an ethnographic study in real-world settings. In *Proc HRI '12* (2012), 367–374.

25. Lippa, R. A., and Dietz, J. K. The relation of gender, personality, and intelligence to judges' accuracy in judging strangers' personality from brief video segments. *J Nonverbal Behav 24*, 1 (2000), 25–43.

26. Marti, P., Bacigalupo, M., Giusti, L., Mennecozzi, C., and Shibata, T. Socially assistive robotics in the treatment of behavioural and psychological symptoms of dementia. In *Proc BioRob '06* (2006), 483–488.

27. Moon, A., Troniak, D. M., Gleeson, B., Pan, M. K., Zeng, M., Blumer, B. A., MacLean, K., and Croft, E. A. Meet me where i'm gazing: how shared attention gaze affects human-robot handover timing. In *Proc HRI'14* (2014), 334–341.

28. Mumm, J., and Mutlu, B. Designing motivational agents: The role of praise, social comparison, and embodiment in computer feedback. *Comput Hum Behav 27*, 5 (2011), 1643–1650.

29. Mutlu, B., Kanda, T., Forlizzi, J., Hodgins, J., and Ishiguro, H. Conversational gaze mechanisms for humanlike robots. *ACM TiiS 1*, 2 (2012), 12.

30. Mutlu, B., Shiwa, T., Kanda, T., Ishiguro, H., and Hagita, N. Footing in human-robot conversations: how robots might shape participant roles using gaze cues. In *Proc HRI'09* (2009), 61–68.

31. Nass, C., Jonsson, I.-M., Harris, H., Reaves, B., Endo, J., Brave, S., and Takayama, L. Improving automotive safety by pairing driver emotion and car voice emotion. In *Proc CHI'05 Extended Abstracts* (2005), 1973–1976.

32. Nikolopoulos, C., Kuester, D., Sheehan, M., Ramteke, S., Karmarkar, A., Thota, S., Kearney, J., Boirum, C., Bojedla, S., and Lee, A. Robotic agents used to help teach social skills to children with autism: the third generation. In *Proc RO-MAN'11* (2011), 253–258.

33. Osterberg, L., and Blaschke, T. Adherence to medication. *New Engl J Med 353*, 5 (2005), 487–497.

34. Peters, P. Gaining compliance through non-verbal communication. *Pepp Disp Resol L J 7* (2007), 87.

35. Rauthmann, J. F., Seubert, C. T., Sachse, P., and Furtner, M. R. Eyes as windows to the soul: Gazing behavior is related to personality. *J Res Pers 46*, 2 (2012), 147–156.

36. Richter, L. A., and Salvendy, G. Effects of personality and task strength on performance in computerized tasks. *Ergonomics 38*, 2 (1995), 281–291.

37. Rutter, D., Morley, I. E., and Graham, J. C. Visual interaction in a group of introverts and extraverts. *Eur J Soc Psychol 2*, 4 (1972), 371–384.

38. Ryan, R. M., and Deci, E. L. Intrinsic and extrinsic motivations: Classic definitions and new directions. *Contemp Educ Psychol 25*, 1 (2000), 54–67.

39. Scassellati, B., Admoni, H., and Matarić, M. Robots for use in autism research. *Annu Rev Biomed Eng 14* (2012), 275–294.

40. Segrin, C. The effects of nonverbal behavior on outcomes of compliance gaining attempts. *Commun Stud 44*, 3-4 (1993), 169–187.

41. Staudte, M., and Crocker, M. W. Investigating joint attention mechanisms through spoken human–robot interaction. *Cognition 120*, 2 (2011), 268–291.

42. Takacs, B., and Hanak, D. A prototype home robot with an ambient facial interface to improve drug compliance. *J Telemed Telecare 14*, 7 (2008), 393–395.

43. Tapus, A., and Mataric, M. J. Socially assistive robots: The link between personality, empathy, physiological signals, and task performance. In *Proc AAAI Spring Symposium: Emotion, Personality, and Social Behavior* (2008), 133–140.

44. Tapus, A., and Matarić, M. J. User personality matching with a hands-off robot for post-stroke rehabilitation therapy. In *Experimental Robotics* (2008), 165–175.

45. Tapus, A., Tapus, C., and Mataric, M. The role of physical embodiment of a therapist robot for individuals with cognitive impairments. In *Proc Ro-Man'09* (2009), 103–107.

46. Tapus, A., Tapus, C., and Mataric, M. J. The use of socially assistive robots in the design of intelligent cognitive therapies for people with dementia. In *Proc ICORR'09* (2009), 924–929.

47. Torrey, C., Powers, A., Marge, M., Fussell, S. R., and Kiesler, S. Effects of adaptive robot dialogue on information exchange and social relations. In *Proc HRI'06* (2006), 126–133.

48. Vallerand, R. J., and Reid, G. On the causal effects of perceived competence on intrinsic motivation: A test of cognitive evaluation theory. *J Sport Psychol 6*, 1 (1984), 94–102.

49. Wade, E., Parnandi, A., Mead, R., and Matarić, M. Socially assistive robotics for guiding motor task practice. *Paladyn 2*, 4 (2011), 218–227.

The Social Impact of a Robot Co-Worker in Industrial Settings

Allison Sauppé and Bilge Mutlu
Department of Computer Sciences, University of Wisconsin–Madison
1210 West Dayton Street, Madison, WI 53706, USA
asauppe@cs.wisc.edu; bilge@cs.wisc.edu

ABSTRACT
Across history and cultures, robots have been envisioned as assistants working alongside people. Following this vision, an emerging family of products—collaborative manufacturing robots—is enabling human and robot workers to work side by side as collaborators in manufacturing tasks. Their introduction presents an opportunity to better understand people's interactions with and perceptions of a robot "co-worker" in a real-world setting to guide the design of these products. In this paper, we present findings from an ethnographic field study at three manufacturing sites and a Grounded Theory analysis of observations and interviews. Our results show that, even in this safety-critical manufacturing setting, workers relate to the robot as a social entity and rely on cues to understand the robot's actions, which we observed to be critical for workers to feel safe when near the robot. These findings contribute to our understanding of interactions with robotic products in real-world settings and offer important design implications.

Author Keywords
Computer-supported collaborative work; human-robot collaboration; collaborative robots; technology adoption; manufacturing; sociality; social cues; design guidelines

ACM Classification Keywords
H.5.3 Group and Organization Interfaces: Computer-supported collaborative work; **K.4.3 Organizational Impacts**: Computer-supported collaborative work

INTRODUCTION
While robots have long been envisioned as ubiquitous assistants that work in day-to-day human environments, the primary use of robotic technologies have been in factories and field settings for automating repetitive work or performing tasks that are inaccessible or dangerous for humans [19]. The last decade, however, has seen significant growth in the introduction of robotic products into homes and workplaces for tasks such as cleaning and delivery [6, 16]. One recent example is the emerging use of *collaborative manufacturing robots* in industrial settings, which is poised to drastically change how work is done in small- and medium-sized manufacturing facilities. Figure 1 shows such a robot working collaboratively with a human worker on a manufacturing task.

CHI 2015, April 18 - 23 2015, Seoul, Republic of Korea
Copyright is held by the owner/author(s). Publication rights licensed to ACM.
ACM 978-1-4503-3145-6/15/04$15.00
http://dx.doi.org/10.1145/2702123.2702181

Figure 1. A collaborative manufacturing robot (right) working alongside a human operator (left) on a manufacturing task.

Unlike robots designed for automation and unsafe work, collaborative robots are designed to work alongside humans and to interact and collaborate with their users, potentially changing how people perceive and interact with robotic technologies. Research in HCI has proposed different roles that computer technologies play, including "tools," "media," and "social actors," that accordingly shape people's perceptions of and responses to these technologies [4]. Computer technologies that display aspects of human language, offer interactivity, and play roles that have traditionally been filled by humans elicit attributions of sociality and social responses [18]. We expect collaborative robots that play a "co-worker" role to also be perceived as social entities, although little is known about the potential social impact of the introduction of these technologies to industrial settings on individuals and organizations.

Previous research on the impact of the introduction of robotic technology into other types of human environments, such as hospitals [13, 16, 20] and the home [5, 6, 21, 22, 23] has shown that robots significantly change people's perceptions regarding their social relationships and trigger a process of sense-making that results in the application of specific schemas, such as "collaborator," "social entity," or merely "novelty." While we expect similarities in how the introduction of robots affects people's perceptions of work across different domains, a better understanding of these effects in the manufacturing domain is necessary to draw guidelines to inform the design of robots for these settings. Furthermore, among the different robotic technologies that have been introduced into human environments, collaborative manufacturing robots uniquely play a role that has traditionally been played by humans—that of a "co-worker"—making people's interactions with them a relevant and important topic of study for HCI and CSCW research.

In this paper, we present findings from an ethnographic study of the integration of one particular collaborative robot at three manufacturing facilities, focusing on worker perceptions of the robot and their work together. At each site, we conducted fly-on-the-wall observations of the robot, its environment, and those around it as well as interviews with multiple stakeholders. We analyzed data from these observations and interviews using Grounded Theory. Among the many themes that emerged from this analysis, we report on findings and propose design guidelines regarding the *sociality* of the robot. In the remainder of the paper, we introduce prior work on the social impact of technologies as well as the shift robotic technologies are currently undergoing. Next, we present the details of our study, including the robotic platform we focused on, details about study sites we visited, and the methods we used for data collection and analysis. We conclude the paper by outlining our findings and discussing their implications for the design of future technologies that may function as social agents in manufacturing settings.

BACKGROUND

Collaborative robots in manufacturing settings follow a long trend of technologies—from desktop computers to virtual agents—that are perceived by human users as having social qualities. These robots also represent a shift from the traditional use of robots in manufacturing settings for safe and efficient industrial automation. In the paragraphs below, we briefly review prior literature on the perception of prior technologies as having sociality, the introduction of robots into day-to-day human environments and their perceived sociality, and the recent shift in industrial use of robotic technology.

Perceived Sociality of Technologies

The design of computer technologies follow metaphors that shape the way their users perceive and interact with them. Fogg [4] proposed "tool," "media," and "social actor" as three such metaphors that respectively result in perceptions of computers as providing new abilities, conveying content, and playing social roles. When computers follow the metaphor of a social actor, particularly displaying aspects of human language, offering interactivity, and playing roles that humans play, their users "mindlessly" apply social rules and expectations despite explicitly acknowledging that these machines have no social qualities [18]. Even computers that minimally follow this metaphor elicit attributions of gender, ethnicity, personality, and expertise to them, displays of politeness and reciprocity toward them, and disclosure of information when they divulge information first [15, 18].

When computer technologies are designed to more closely follow the metaphor of a social actor, as speech interfaces, virtual agents, and social robots do, people's interactions with them more closely resemble human-human interactions [1, 11, 17]. Research on embodied conversational agents (ECA) has demonstrated that people employ dialogue strategies from human-human conversations, such as greetings, farewells, small talk, and insults, and display elements of a human conversational style, such as disfluencies, in their interactions with ECAs that engage in social dialogue with them [1, 11].

While the design of robotic technologies vary in how closely their designs follow the metaphor of a social actor, we expect much of these attributions and responses to be present in people's interactions with them. For example, users of robots designed with minimal cues for sociality, such as the Mars Rover, perceive the robot as a social actor, identifying with the unique qualities and abilities of the robot, as well as a social resource for the human team [24].

Robots in Day-to-Day Environments

The last decade has witnessed the widespread introduction of robotic technologies into day-to-day environments. Prior work has studied how these products changed workplace and domestic practices and how their users perceived them. Studies of the use of the robotic vacuum cleaner Roomba in domestic environments found that users attributed lifelike characteristics, such as personality, gender, intentions, and feelings, to their cleaning [5, 6, 23] and developed a sense of unique ownership and intimacy with their products that led them to promote their robots in their social networks [23].

Robotic technologies have also been introduced to organizations, most prominently to perform transportation and delivery tasks at hospitals. Prior work studying the effects of the introduction of these robots on work and social practices found differences in how different groups responded to and worked with the robot [13, 16, 20]. Hospital workers whose jobs were less demanding benefited from the help that the robot provided and perceived the robot more positively, while others who worked in a more demanding environment found the robot to be a burden and a disruption to their social environment due to the robot's inability to recognize and adapt to those demands [16]. Based on their familiarity and experience with the robot, different stakeholders applied different cognitive frames to the robot, including "alien," "machine," "worker," and "colleague" [13]. Prior work has also examined how people interact with robots integrated into organizations and the broader social processes involved in these interactions. A study of the deployment of a snack-delivery robot in a university building found that users develop social relationships with the robot and that individual interactions with the robot result in a "ripple effect" in the social environment, engaging non-users in these interactions and promoting socializing [12].

Robots in Manufacturing

Driven mainly by the automative industry, the use of robots in manufacturing has traditionally focused on efficient, reliable, and precise production [3], resulting in robots that are unsafe for and caged off from human workers [9]. Recent advances in technology and methods for robot control have enabled a new class of robots that are safe for human workers and flexible enough to be integrated into human-robot work-cells [10, 14]. While the growing introduction of these robots into manufacturing settings is expected to drastically change work practices, worker perceptions of the robot, and the design of the work environment in these settings, no studies to date have examined these changes. A significant gap exists in our understanding of the effects of the integration of collaborative robots into manufacturing settings and of people's interactions with and perceptions of these technologies. This paper presents a study that aims to close this gap, focusing on worker perceptions of and interactions with the robot, and draw guidelines for the design of future collaborative technologies for manufacturing.

STUDY OUTLINE

To better understand how collaborative robots are affecting the work practices and perceptions of manufacturing employees, we conducted an ethnographic study at three manufacturing plants that had acquired a particular robotic platform. Below, we describe the platform we studied, the study sites we visited, our data collection methods, and the analysis of our data.

Robotic Platform

We focused our study on companies that owned the Baxter[1] robot, developed and manufactured by Rethink Robotics, examples of which can be seen in Figure 2. Baxter was released after beta testing in October of 2012. Unlike traditional manufacturing robots that are expensive, dangerous, and highly specialized, it is designed to be affordable at a price point of $25,000 USD, safe to operate around humans, and trainable for a variety of tasks using a visual programming interface.

The robot's design follows a humanoid morphology, including two manipulator arms and a screen used as a "face" through the display of eyes, and is the standing height of a human. The robot itself is 3 ft (0.914 m) tall, but deployed robots are often mounted on a platform that raises its height to be between 5 ft 10 in (1.778 m) and 6 ft 3 in (1.905 m).

The robot's hardware and software is optimized primarily to perform *pick and place* tasks. In these tasks, Baxter acquires an object or objects using either one or both of its "hands," i.e., grippers attached to the end of its arms, from a bin or a moving conveyor belt. The object(s) are then deposited in another bin or a workbench. The robot might be integrated with nearby systems with which it can communicate. For example, the robot might pick a finished product from the moving conveyor belt of an assembly line and place it in a shipping container. After the product is appropriately placed and stacked in the container, the robot would communicate to the assembly line that it is ready to pick and place the next product.

Study Sites

We recruited three manufacturing companies, each of which owned at least one Baxter robot, to participate in our study. Below are brief descriptions of the companies.

[1] www.rethinkrobotics.com/products/baxter/

Company 1 is a small family-owned business of about 40 employees. It specializes in plastic injection molding and produces plastic parts for different clients. These parts are often components of products that the company's clients manufacture or assemble.

Company 2 is a small business of about 50 employees. It produces and sells components used for securing electrical connections and is known for its outdoor waterproof electrical components.

Company 3 is a large international company of several thousand employees spread out across multiple facilities that produce office furniture. Four of these facilities have purchased a single Baxter. We included one of these facilities with approximately 150 employees in our sites.

Each company had owned their robot for four to eight months at the time of our visit. In addition to phone and e-mail correspondence over several months, the first author spent four days at Company 1, two days at Company 2, and one day at Company 3 conducting fieldwork. All sites were located within the continental United States.

Workspace Setup

The robot was integrated into its own *work-cell*—an area defined by its resources and the equipment dedicated to a single task—at each site visited (see Figure 2). Below, we give brief descriptions of Baxter's work-cell at each site.

At *Company 1*, Baxter was assigned to move and automatically bag stacks of medical cups. In this setup, a traditional industrial robot was responsible for moving finished medical cups from the plastic injection molding machine to a conveyor belt, which moved stacks of finished medical cups toward Baxter, which then picked up a stack and placed it in the automatic bagging machine. After placing two stacks in the machine, Baxter sent a signal to the bagging machine to place the two stacks in a bag and deploy a new bag. Periodically, an operator gathered completed bags and packaged them in a larger shipping box. Operators and maintenance staff also attended to the robot when problems arose.

At *Company 2*, Baxter set up plastic tubes to be filled with a silicone material for waterproofing wires. A hopper of tubes gradually dispensed tubes into a second container and eventually onto a line that moved the tubes towards Baxter. Baxter then picked up a tube in each hand and placed them in a second machine to be processed. After processing, the second machine deposited the completed tube into a bucket. Operators were responsible for periodically filling the hopper with more tubes and replacing the filled buckets. Operators and maintenance staff attended to the robot when problems occurred.

At *Company 3*, Baxter was set up in a separate area for maintenance workers to retrain it for a new task. During our visit, the robot was being trained to package hardware for furniture, such as brackets, into a box. The maintenance worker arranged the hardware to be boxed to the right of Baxter in a particular configuration, flat pieces of cardboard to stack between hardware to the left of Baxter, and the box to package the hardware in front of Baxter. When activated, Baxter picked up each

Figure 2. Examples of a collaborative robot at work packaging medicine cups at Company 1 (top) and moving plastic tubes at Company 2 (bottom).

piece of hardware individually and placed it in the box. At predefined points, Baxter used its left hand to acquire a piece of cardboard and place it on top of the hardware currently in the box. Then, additional hardware was added. In the targeted workflow, the box and hardware would be delivered to Baxter via a conveyor belt, and the completed box would continue down the conveyor belt. An operator would be responsible for periodically giving Baxter additional flat pieces of cardboard.

Method

During the course of the study, we collected data on a number of different facets of the integration of the robot into the manufacturing environment, including motivations for purchasing a collaborative robot, the process of integrating it to the existing manufacturing workflow, organizational changes to accommodate the use of the robot, and worker perceptions of and interactions with the robot. In this paper, we focus on the design elements and factors that shaped worker perceptions of and interactions with the robot, including the robot's appearance, its social behavior, and its introduction into the work environment.

Fly-on-the-Wall Observations

We conducted fly-on-the-wall observations of activities around and involving the robot at both Company 1 and Company 2. While Company 3 had a collaborative robot that had previously been deployed at an assembly line, they had decided to re-train the robot in a separate area for a new task. While we did observe that the robot was located in a separate area for retraining at Company 3, we did not have the opportunity to see the robot being trained. Experiences about the retraining process were instead gathered from interviews. We also observed nearby human-operated work-cells to better understand what made the robot's work-cell unique. At Company 3, data collection also included observations of the setup of the human-operated work-cells and interviews about how the robot was or would be integrated into these tasks.

At each site, observations focused on the robot and its surrounding environment, including how the robot was completing its task, the robot's interactions with nearby equipment, how the robot reacted to unexpected situations, and how workers interacted with the robot. Observations also included understanding the more general environment of the company, including how workers interacted with one another and the organizational structure of the company.

Interviews

In addition to the fly-on-the-wall observations, we conducted semi-structured interviews with key stakeholders at each site, including *management*, *maintenance*, and *operators*. While there were differences in the task Baxter was assigned at each site, the roles and experiences of the stakeholders was uniform, allowing us to consider the same organizational roles across all three sites. Below, we describe the organizational roles of these stakeholders and their involvement with the robot.

Management staff included employees who were responsible for decisions regarding obtaining the robot, for setting and overseeing company goals, or for high-level human-resource issues. These employees had varying degrees of interaction with the robot, including helping with troubleshooting work-cell problems or contacting technical support, depending on the company's size. However, management relied on maintenance staff for the integration of and troubleshooting with the robot. Management staff were asked questions concerning the size, organization, and mission of the company; the demographics of their workforce; the decision-making process behind purchasing the robot; and the effect of the robot on various metrics, such as productivity and profit.

Maintenance staff included employees who handled the upkeep and troubleshooting of machines in the manufacturing environment. Additionally, these employees were responsible for the integration of the robot, programming the robot, training other employees on using the robot, and troubleshooting the robot as necessary. These employees were often the first to handle day-to-day issues with the robot and its work-cell. Maintenance staff were asked questions concerning their roles and responsibilities at the site; how they prioritized their work; their involvement with the integration of the robot; what skills they acquired during integration; their interaction with the robot; and troubleshooting the robot.

Operators included employees who worked at one or more workstations at the manufacturing facility. Although different operators might be assigned to a particular workstation at different times, each operator was solely responsible for meeting the quota at their workstation, and often developed a unique workflow for that particular workstation. Operators typically resolved minor troubleshooting tasks, but would contact maintenance staff when additional help or expertise was necessary. One operator was always assigned to work alongside and monitor the robot. These employees were not trained on how to program the robot, but they knew how to handle common mistakes in the work-cell and how to reset the robot if necessary. Some operators were assigned to work alongside the robot every day, while others only worked with the robot every other day. Operators were asked questions concerning their previous manufacturing experience; whether they had prior experience completing the robot's task manually; their perceptions and interactions with the robot; and their process for troubleshooting problems that the robot encountered.

Across the three sites, we interviewed a total of 17 informants, including six managers, eight maintenance employees, and three operators. The interviewees were identified from among employees suggested by the authors' contacts at each site, workers observed during fly-on-the-wall observations, and employees mentioned during previous interviews. The interviews started with the researcher seeking and obtaining informed consent and proceeded with a semi-structured interview involving an initial set of questions at Company 1 and growing sets of questions at Company 2 and Company 3 that built upon knowledge from previous site visits. The interviews were captured as written field notes and audio recordings. Each interview was approximately 30 min in length (M = 27 min, 22 sec; SD = 5 min, 33 sec), and employees received a $5 USD gift-card to a local coffee shop as compensation.

Analysis

A Grounded Theory approach [7] was used to analyze textual data obtained from field notes and interview transcriptions. We first conducted an open coding process in which codes were assigned to significant events or references. Open coding was completed for all field notes and transcriptions. To establish inter-rater reliability, a second researcher then used provided codes to code 10% of the data. The inter-rater reliability showed substantial agreement between the primary and secondary coders (82% agreement, Cohen's κ = .79). Next, axial coding was used to identify phenomena, such as repeated events or interactions, among the codes. In total, 11 axial codes were developed that relate to worker perceptions of and interactions with the robot. Finally, we used a selective-coding process to understand the relationships among axial codes.

FINDINGS

In this section, we present the main findings from our analysis that provide insight into the experiences of various stakeholders with the robot. Figure 3 provides a visual summary of the four themes that emerged from our analysis. We support each theme with observations or quotes from interviews where applicable, indicate stakeholder perspectives with labels "MG" for "Management," "MT" for "Maintenance," and "OP" for

Summary of Results

Operator-Robot Relationship
Operators view their relationship with the robot as humanlike, while maintenance and management view the robot as equipment.

Attribution of Human Characteristics
Operators believed the robot has personality and intent. The robot also inspired a range of emotional responses in operators.

Social Interactions with the Robot
Operators engaged in a number of social interactions with the robot. All staff desired a speech channel for social and troubleshooting purposes.

Responses to the Robot's Design
The robot's physical appearance helped nearby workers feel safe. The robot's eyes provided insights into the robot's status and next action.

Figure 3. An overview of our analysis of the resulting themes and how those themes manifested in our data. The collaborative robot's integration at three manufacturing plants yielded four main themes for employee-robot sociality.

"Operator," and indicate company affiliation with "C" followed by the number corresponding to our earlier descriptions.

Operator-Robot Relationship

A prominent theme that emerged from our analysis was the differential perceptions of the robot by operators and by maintenance and managerial staff. Operators who worked directly with the robot regularly characterized their relationship with the robot in collegial or personal terms, referring to the robot as their "work partner" (OP2C2) or "friend" (OP1C2). Even other operators who worked at nearby work-cells perceived these relationships as unique, one operator noting that her co-worker at a nearby station often referred to the robot as her "son" due to their ability to communicate and work well with each other.

> **OP1C2:** People call him my son. They don't like [the name] "Baxter" and think it's funny how much I like working with him, that I understand him.

Although operator-robot relationships were usually cordial, operators also characterized their relationships with the robot in negative, yet familial or relational, terms.

> **OP3C3:** He [the robot] just has a hard time doing work a lot. Especially when he goes down, I'm like "What's up?" ... Feels like babysitting my grandkids.

> **OP1C2:** Sometimes I write down on my [time] sheet "Baxter was not a team player today."

Operators also noted that they talked about the robot as a "friend" outside of work with their acquaintances. Some operators reported that their friends sometimes asked "how the robot was doing" (OP2C2).

While operators characterized their relationship with the robot in collegial and personal terms, maintenance and management staff viewed working with the robot to be similar to working with other industrial equipment. These employees often referred to the robot as "monotonous" and "error prone," describing their interactions with the robot as involving "fixing it" when problems arose.

Figure 4. The robot from Company 2, dressed up in a wig and jester hat. Previously, the robot was adorned with a rainbow clown wig.

We believe that these differences result from different formative experiences with the robot. Maintenance and management staff indicated that the initial demonstrations of the robot during its acquisition had set high expectations that were challenged during the integration process due to difficulties with enabling the robot to quickly and reliably sense its environment. Addressing these difficulties required these employees to iteratively create a static and predictable work environment for the robot and the intelligent sensing features of the robot to be underutilized. This gradual shift away from the initially-envisioned use-cases may have disillusioned these employees and resulted in perceptions that were similar to those of other equipment. While some operators had worked with the robot during this transition period, they had little knowledge of why the robot was transitioned into a more static environment, potentially maintaining their initial frames of the robot.

> **MT1C1:** It [Baxter] is easy to program, it's the precision of everything else [around Baxter] that's difficult.

> **MT2C1:** Our biggest thing is to tie Baxter into the bagger, tie Baxter into the conveyer, and tie Baxter there; and again it comes down to inputs, outputs, and there's not a lot of versatility. ... Right now, I have to sit here meticulously and program every little spec of dust where vision would be boom, boom, boom.

Even operators showed awareness of the differences in how they perceived their relationship to the robot compared to how maintenance and management staff did, as expressed in the following excerpt:

> **OP1C2:** He [MT3C2] likes to come tinker around. It's like his little toy. I'm like "Don't touch anything! You'll screw him up."

Attribution of Humanlike Characteristics

Our analysis revealed a second theme that centered around the operators attributing humanlike characteristics, such as personality and intent, to the robot. Operators frequently described Baxter as having personality traits, such as "cheerful" (OP1C2), "happy" (OP1C2, OP2C2), "fun" (OP2C2, OP3C3), and "perky" (OP1C2), as illustrated in the following excerpt:

> **OP2C2:** Yeah, he's a lot of fun to be around. He can improve my day.

At Company 2, the robot's physical appearance had been altered to include a wig and jester hat (see Figure 4). Operators at this site felt that the robot's new appearance fit well with its perceived personality, as described below:

> **OP1C2:** To me, it totally fits him. ... So if he's in a good mood, it fits him. Or sometimes he has an attitude, "Whatever," you know? That look is just him.

Operators also described the robot and its actions as triggering a range of feelings, reporting feeling happy or pleased while working with the robot—sometimes more so than with a human co-worker—as illustrated in the excerpt below.

> **OP3C3:** Yeah, it can be nice to work by him when I just want a quiet day and he's working well. Lot less hassle then trying to tell someone you don't want to talk.

Other times, operators reported feeling upset or angry with the robot for its actions and expressing resent towards the robot for its mistakes. An operator expresses stress and frustration in the following excerpt:

> **OP1C2:** If he's [the robot is] having a bad day, that...is...very frustrating. Cuz there's no numbers getting out on my job or his job, he's just a mess. ... It's a little stressful.

Some operators believed that the robot expressed intent in its actions, most commonly when the work-cell or the robot malfunctioned, particularly when the operator had just left the work-cell moments before. For example:

> **OP1C2:** I know that [the robot makes mistakes] and I understand that, so certain things don't bother me. Now sometimes, if I have 8 hours of that, and I'm like, that's when I think he knows what he's doing on purpose, or he's beeping, and as soon as I turn my back to look at him, he stops, I turn around again he beeps, and I'm like, "Really Baxter? Are you doing that on purpose? Cuz you're driving me nuts!"

As a result, these operators expressed the need for someone to watch or supervise the robot in their absence. They felt that supervision might help prevent the robot from making a mistake as well as allow mistakes to be corrected promptly. This feeling is illustrated in the excerpt below:

> **OP1C2:** I'm going to use the bathroom. If something weird happens, I'm only going to be gone 30 seconds. Sometimes I want to get someone to watch him, like he's a kid.

Finally, regardless of the type of emotions the robot regularly elicited, all operators reported that the robot inspired interest. Even if some operators were initially reluctant to work with the robot, they eventually became engaged with the robot. Operators reported asking maintenance staff questions and suggesting improvements in Baxter's programming, how the

Figure 5. Two operators working near the robot. The vantage point of the operators makes it difficult to monitor the robot's status. Additionally, the tasks the operators are completing requires their visual attention.

work-cell should be organized, and how to optimize the way operators interacted with the robot. For example:

> **OP3C3:** I noticed it didn't search so good sometimes, ... so I told them [maintenance] to see if they could make it better.

Social Interactions with the Robot

Another prominent finding from our analysis was that operators reported having a wide range of social interactions with the robot. The most pertinent day-to-day interaction for operators was listening to the sound of the robot's work to monitor the robot's activities. Many work-cells are not designed in such a way that nearby operators can visually monitor the robot, as illustrated in Figure 5. Even when the the design of the work-cell allowed visual monitoring, directing attention toward the robot would mean taking attention away from their own work. Thus, operators learned to interpret the sound and rhythm of the robot's work in order to identify patterns of mistakes that demanded their attention. For example, no sound may indicate that the work-cell had shut down, the sound of objects being incorrectly placed may suggest that a part of the cell had shut down and the robot continued to operate, and the sound of the robot acquiring new missing objects may indicate that the objects that the robot would later acquire were not being reliably moved toward the robot. The excerpts below provide examples of the practices that operators developed to interpret the sound of the robot's work.

> **OP1C2:** Now I don't look, I mostly listen. He's like a child, if he's been quiet for too long, I know something's wrong. ... We've developed an understanding.

> **OP2C2:** I mean maybe just because I'm accustomed to working with him everyday, maybe now I can anticipate the problems a little bit more. I know what's going on.

Operators also reported sometimes finding themselves talking to the robot. These expressions were often musings while trying to understand why the robot had stopped working. At other times, operators were upset with the robot and were admonishing it or yelling at it out of anger or frustration, as illustrated in the excerpts below.

> **OP1C2:** I find myself just wondering aloud sometimes when something is wrong, hoping he'll give me an answer.

> **OP3C3:** Sometimes he really tees me off, and I let him know it.

While operators reported already engaging in social interactions with the robot, they and some maintenance staff expressed a desire for the robot to display more social behavior. These employees appreciated the robot's use of its eyes to convey sociality (discussed in the next theme), but felt that the robot could be more socially interactive, for example, by making small talk. Operators explained that although their work required them to focus on their workspace, they frequently engaged in small talk with one another during shifts to help pass the time and establish and maintain relationships. They wished that the robot could similarly engage in basic small talk, mimicking the sociality of working with other nearby operators during shifts where operators are assigned work with the robot and no other operators are nearby, as shown in the excerpts below.

> **OP3C3:** They're [humans are] quicker and I need somebody to talk to. I couldn't teach him to talk. ... I tried to teach him to deal cards but that didn't work either.

> **OP2C2:** It would be nice if he could just shoot the breeze.

> **OP1C2:** I want it to say "Good morning, [informant's name], my favorite co-worker" and display a little bouquet of flowers.

Maintenance staff agreed with operators that the addition of speech to the robot would be beneficial, but for other reasons. The robot's work-cell can stop for a variety of reasons, including equipment malfunction, the lack of a necessary material or object, or a problem with the robot. Unsure of how to remedy the situation, operators often turn to a nearby maintenance worker for help. In such situations, neither operators nor maintenance workers usually have sufficient context for diagnosing the problem, requiring them to check many different components of the environment. Maintenance staff believed that the addition of speech capabilities to the robot may enable verbal troubleshooting, such as providing specifics on the problem (MT2C1) or giving step-by-step instructions on how to correct the problem (MT3C2, MT6C3).

> **MT3C2:** It would be nice if Baxter could fix his own problems, but I would settle for him telling us how to do it.

> **MT5C3:** I started working here long after he [the robot] got here, and sometimes I have no clue what to do [to fix him]. Him helping would be good.

Workers also suggested that the robot's face, which doubles as a screen, could provide more information. Employees felt that the screen could offer redundant information in addition to the speech content. Manufacturing plants often contain background noise that might at times grow progressively louder. While employees believed that speech would be the easiest way to communicate with the robot, the addition of using the screen as an information display would provide employees with an alternative channel of communication should speech be impaired by the environment.

Responses to the Robot's Design

The last theme that emerged from our analysis was worker responses to the robot's appearance, focusing on two features: the robot's overall form and its eyes. Both elements of the robot's design were considered important for staff to feel comfortable working near the robot. Workers described the humanlike design of the robot as "familiar," giving them a sense of security and comfort when working in close proximity to the robot. This familiar design was in stark contrast with many industrial robots that are distinctly non-human and dangerous to be around. In the excerpt below, a maintenance worker highlights that this familiar design provides the robot with predictability.

> **MT4C2:** I like that it looks kinda like a human. ... It's familiar, ya know? I feel like I know what to expect.

Two other employees described the robot not as humanlike, but still as bearing a resemblance to other lifelike forms, specifically to a "praying mantis" due to the way it arms rotate. These employees still felt that this appearance induced feelings of safety when compared to other industrial robots, as illustrated in the excerpt below.

> **MT3C2:** Those arms, they remind me of a, what is it? Praying mantis? Yeah. Still, looks very calm, deliberate.

Employees also expressed a preference toward the dark-gray-and-red color and the industrial design of the robot. Compared to traditional industrial robots, employees felt that the robot's design suggested a friendly and non-threatening, even a "playful," interaction, as indicated below.

> **OP1C2:** Yeah, I'm like [to my friends], "He's like a Rock 'em, Sock 'em robot!" That red, it's so playful.

At Company 2, the addition of the wig and jester hat shown in Figure 4 further emphasized the humanlike appearance of the robot, adding to its "personality."

One particularly well-liked design element was the robot's eyes. The robot was equipped with a screen for a face, which displayed a pair of graphical "eyes." The face or the eyes served no sensing purpose (i.e., vision capabilities) but instead provided a way for nearby workers to understand the robot's current status in a "natural" way that did not require additional training, as expressed by a managerial employee below.

> **MG5C3:** I like them [the eyes]. ... Because, I love that, I mean, it, because it's the nonverbal communication. ... I think that it's just natural.

These eyes were pre-programmed to follow the trajectory of its arms, allowing employees to better anticipate where the robot's hands were likely to move next. As illustrated in the excerpt below, this feature was considered particularly useful for new employees who might still be learning about the task.

> **MG1C1:** They [new employees] don't usually understand what the robot will do next, where it will go... This [the eyes], this helps them get it.

The robot also had a set of pre-programmed facial expressions: "confused" for when it is has trouble completing a task, "sad" for when the robot has given up on a task, and "surprised" for when a human had entered the workspace of the robot.

> **MG1C1:** They [the operators] know what the "surprise" look is, they know what the "sad" look is, they...they know it.

Employees noted that the robot's eyes and facial expressions were particularly useful when glancing at the robot from farther away. At a distance, the robot's eyes and facial expressions provided some context as to its otherwise indiscernible task status.

Additionally, employees felt that the robot's eyes conveyed intelligence. This perceived intelligence gave employees who worked in or around the robot's work-cell confidence in the robot's actions and intentions, as expressed by the maintenance worker below.

> **MT4C2:** The eyes make him seem smart. Like he knows what he's doing.

DISCUSSION AND DESIGN IMPLICATIONS

The themes that emerged from our analysis suggest two key implications for the design of collaborative robots: the importance of designing for sociality and the need to support a diverse set of relationships between the robot and different stakeholders. Additionally, these implications can be extended to other types of agentic technologies, including speech-based and embodied virtual assistants, such as a speech-based task guidance system building on its prior relationship with its user. Below, we discuss the implications of our work, the limitations of our study, and our plans for expanding this research.

Designing for Sociality

Many of our results highlight the importance of sociality in a robot playing the role of a co-worker. We did not expect the social elements of the robot's design or social relationships people established with it to be important factors in its integration into a manufacturing environment, due to our naive presumption that there is little need for sociality in completing manufacturing tasks. Workers across three organizations in our study repeatedly brought up sociality in characterizing their relationship with the robot, in discussing the characteristics of the robot, and in suggesting improvements for the robot. Our observations suggest that this desire for increased sociality stems from current social practices operators engage in amongst one another during their own work, such as two operators at adjacent workstations engaging in small talk.

The design of future collaborative robots for manufacturing settings must take into account the benefits of supporting worker expectations of sociality to improve work practices as well as the social environment in these settings. Although they offer the same safety and flexibility benefits as Baxter does, many collaborative robots are designed only as single robotic arms with little or no elements to support sociality. Our results indicate that social features that are already included in Baxter's design, such as its overall humanlike morphology and the behaviors displayed by its eyes and face, not only provide workers with a positive experience by eliciting feelings of safety and comfort but also improve manufacturing work by communicating cues that are necessary for successful coordination. However, increased sociality has the potential to create false expectations that may risk worker safety. Although collaborative robots are becoming increasingly safe for nearby workers, designers must strive to match the perceived safety of the robot with its actual safety. Future designs of collaborative robots must build on the success of these features and further expand their use of design elements that support sociality while understanding and balancing this increased sociality against the expectations and the needs of its users.

Based on our findings, we believe that future designs could improve the robot's sociality to achieve two design goals. First, collaborative robots must be designed to support and enrich the social environment in the organizations to which they are introduced. We found that social interactions and relationships are key elements of collaborative work even in task-oriented, safety-critical settings such as manufacturing. Supporting expectations for basic conversational skills, such as greeting co-workers and nearby operators at the beginning and end of their shifts, might enhance the social environment in these settings. Second, collaboration by definition requires a coordination of actions for which communication and social cues are critical. Therefore, future collaborative robots must be designed with the necessary communicative functions to facilitate this coordination. For example, basic language capabilities could be added to allow workers to ask the robot questions such as "What's wrong?" when there is a problem or to seek guidance from the robot in addressing it by asking "How do I fix it?" Additionally, future designs could draw on the cues that workers currently rely on to monitor the robot, such as the sound of its operation or the direction of its gaze, to support this implicit form of communication.

Supporting Different Relationships

We found that different stakeholders made different attributions to the robot, maintenance and management staff perceiving the robot in more mechanical terms and operators viewing it as an agent with whom they can build a relationship. These different attributions resulted in different behaviors toward the robot and different characterizations of relationships with it.

Prior studies of the introduction of technology into organizations found similar differences in the responses of different stakeholders to the technology. For instance, studies of the introduction of delivery robots into hospitals found varying perceptions among stakeholders based on worker familiarity and time spent with the robot [13], on the organizational role and gender of the workers [20], and on the workload of and emotional demands on the workers [16]. The design recommendations made by these studies included creating different behaviors that are better suited to the communication needs and context of different stakeholders, such as employing subtle light displays to alert high-workload employees at an oncology unit and using entertaining, pre-recorded voices that contribute to the cheerful social environment of a postpartum unit [16].

The design of future collaborative robots for manufacturing settings must similarly accommodate different perspectives and interactions with the robot. For instance, future designs could draw on the social elements of the robot's design to improve the robot's sociality for maintenance and management staff to help reshape perceptions of the robot from industrial equipment to a more sociable co-worker. Social behaviors could be built into the types of interactions that these stakeholders are engaged in, such as integration, programming, and troubleshooting. While many existing collaborative robots including Baxter are equipped with capabilities for interactive programming, such as learning from demonstration, these capabilities could be augmented to include conversational elements for input and feedback.

Limitations

While our findings offers many interesting insights into the integration of collaborative robots into manufacturing settings, our study has limitations that point to follow-up studies and analyses and future research directions. First, many of our results highlight the importance of sociality in worker interactions with and perceptions of the robot, which in large part might have been shaped by the robot's humanoid form [2]. However, prior work suggests that people's responses to robots are shaped by a broader set of design elements, such as how the robot's appearance matches its task [8]. Future work should examine worker interactions with collaborative robots with different morphologies, such as robotic arms, performing different types of tasks. Second, our study sites included some of the very first manufacturing facilities to own and use collaborative robots, who as early adopters, might have experienced integration issues that may become a rarity as the technology and integration practices mature. A smoother integration process might change some of our observations, such as the mechanical view that maintenance and management staff had of the robot. Future studies that focus on the integration process could clarify the role of integration problems (or lack thereof) on worker perceptions of collaborative robots.

CONCLUSION

The introduction of collaborative robots into manufacturing organizations is poised to revolutionize how work is done in industrial settings and how workers adapt to and interact with a robot "co-worker." To better understand these changes and guide the future design of these technologies, we conducted an ethnographic study at three manufacturing sites located in the continental United States that were early adopters of a particular type of collaborative robot. We conducted fly-on-the-wall observations and interviews at each site with different stakeholders, including managerial employees, maintenance staff, and operators. Our Grounded Theory analysis found four main themes of interest: (1) the close, social relationship that operators built with the robot, (2) attributions of positive and negative humanlike characteristics to the robot, (3) the wide range of social interactions that workers had with the robot for troubleshooting and coordinating work, and (4) worker responses to the morphological and behavioral characteristics of the robot's design.

Drawing on our findings, we recommended that future designs augment the social capabilities of collaborative robots, specifically to support the coordination necessary to perform manufacturing work and to enrich the social environment in the workplace. We also suggested that future designs accommodate the expectations and needs of different stakeholders, such as improving the social capabilities of the robot not only for immediate collaborators, but also for workers who have less frequent and different types of interactions with the robot. These improvements will help manufacturing organizations to more smoothly integrate collaborative robots into their work practices and the social environment. The findings of this study contribute to our broader understanding of interactions with robotic products in real-world settings, and these recommendations offer designers concrete guidelines for better supporting work and improving user experience in these settings.

ACKNOWLEDGMENTS

We would like to thank our contacts at the study sites for their cooperation, Brandi Hefty, Jieni Peng, Marley Crews-Hill, Chris Ward, and Catherine Steffel for their contributions to data analysis and writing, and National Science Foundation awards 1149970 and 1426824 for financial support.

REFERENCES

1. Bickmore, T., and Cassell, J. Social dialogue with embodied conversational agents. In *Advances in natural multimodal dialogue systems*. Springer, 2005, 23–54.
2. Breazeal, C. Emotion and sociable humanoid robots. *Int J Hum-Comput St 59*, 1 (2003), 119–155.
3. Brogårdh, T. Present and future robot control development—an industrial perspective. *Annu Rev Control 31*, 1 (2007), 69–79.
4. Fogg, B. J. Persuasive computers: Perspectives and research directions. In *Proc. CHI '98* (1998), 225–232.
5. Forlizzi, J. How robotic products become social products: An ethnographic study of cleaning in the home. In *Proc. HRI '07* (2007), 129–136.
6. Forlizzi, J., and DiSalvo, C. Service robots in the domestic environment: A study of the Roomba vacuum in the home. In *Proc. HRI '06* (2006), 258–265.
7. Glaser, B. G., Strauss, A. L., and Strutzel, E. The discovery of grounded theory: Strategies for qualitative research. *Nurs Res 17*, 4 (1968), 364.
8. Goetz, J., Kiesler, S., and Powers, A. Matching robot appearance and behavior to tasks to improve human-robot cooperation. In *Proc. ROMAN '03* (2003), 55–60.
9. Hirschfeld, R., Aghazadeh, F., and Chapleski, R. Survey of robot safety in industry. *Int J Hum Factor Man 3*, 4 (1993), 369–379.
10. Kock, S., Vittor, T., Matthias, B., Jerregard, H., Kallman, M., Lundberg, I., Mellander, R., and Hedelind, M. Robot concept for scalable, flexible assembly automation: A technology study on a harmless dual-armed robot. In *Proc. of ISAM* (2011), 1–5.
11. Kopp, S., Gesellensetter, L., Krämer, N. C., and Wachsmuth, I. A conversational agent as museum guide–design and evaluation of a real-world application. In *Proc. IVA '05* (2005), 329–343.
12. Lee, M. K., Kiesler, S., Forlizzi, J., and Rybski, P. Ripple effects of an embedded social agent: A field study of a social robot in the workplace. In *Proc. CHI '12* (2012), 695–704.
13. Ljungblad, S., Kotrbova, J., Jacobsson, M., Cramer, H., and Niechwiadowicz, K. Hospital robot at work: Something alien or an intelligent colleague? In *Proc. CSCW '12* (2012), 177–186.
14. Matthias, B., Kock, S., Jerregard, H., Kallman, M., Lundberg, I., and Mellander, R. Safety of collaborative industrial robots: Certification possibilities for a collaborative assembly robot concept. In *Proc. ISAM '11* (2011), 1–6.
15. Moon, Y. Intimate exchanges: Using computers to elicit self-disclosure from consumers. *J Consum Res 26*, 4 (2000), 323–339.
16. Mutlu, B., and Forlizzi, J. Robots in organizations: The role of workflow, social, and environmental factors in human-robot interaction. In *Proc. HRI '08* (2008), 287–294.
17. Nass, C., and Lee, K. M. Does computer-generated speech manifest personality? An experimental test of similarity-attraction. In *Proc. CHI '00* (2000), 329–336.
18. Nass, C., and Moon, Y. Machines and mindlessness: Social responses to computers. *J Soc Issues 56*, 1 (2000), 81–103.
19. Shibata, T. An overview of human interactive robots for psychological enrichment. In *Proc. of the IEEE*, vol. 92 (2004), 1749–1758.
20. Siino, R., and Hinds, P. J. Robots, gender & sensemaking: Sex segregation's impact on workers making sense of a mobile autonomous robot. In *Proc. ICRA '05*, vol. 3 (2005), 2773.
21. Sung, J.-Y., Christensen, H. I., and Grinter, R. E. Robots in the wild: Understanding long-term use. In *Proc. HRI '09* (2009), 45–52.
22. Sung, J.-Y., Grinter, R. E., Christensen, H. I., and Guo, L. Housewives or technophiles?: Understanding domestic robot owners. In *Proc. HRI '08* (2008), 129–136.
23. Sung, J.-Y., Guo, L., Grinter, R., and Christensen, H. "My Roomba is Rambo:" Intimate home appliances. In *Proc. UbiComp '07* (2007), 145–162.
24. Vertesi, J. Seeing like a rover: Embodied experience on the mars exploration rover mission. In *Proc. CHI '08 Extended Abstracts* (2008), 2523–2532.

Robots, Pancakes, and Computer Games: Designing Serious Games for Robot Imitation Learning

Benjamin Walther-Franks[1], Jan Smeddinck[1], Peter Szmidt[1], Andrei Haidu[2], Michael Beetz[2], Rainer Malaka[1]

[1]Digital Media Group, [2]Artificial Intelligence Group
TZI, Universität Bremen

{bwf, smeddinck, piotr, haidu, beetz, malaka}@tzi.de

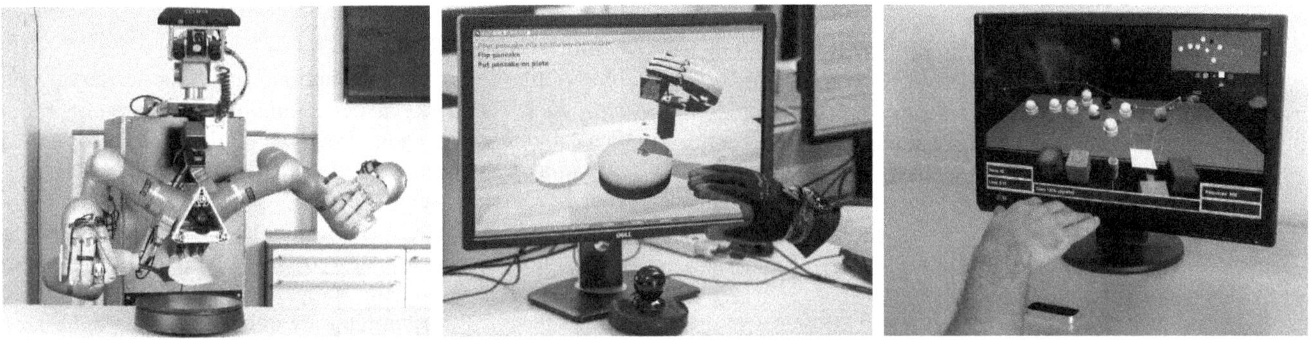

Figure 1: Many robot manipulation tasks (left) are learnt best by observing humans. Human motion can be demonstrated using virtual environments (center). Data acquisition with motion-based games makes demonstrating a fun activity (right).

ABSTRACT
Autonomous manipulation robots can be valuable aids as interactive agents in the home, yet it has proven extremely difficult to program their behavior. Imitation learning uses data on human demonstrations to build behavioral models for robots. In order to cover a wide range of action strategies, data from many individuals is needed. Acquiring such large amounts of data can be a challenge. Tools for data capturing in this domain must thus implement a good user experience. We propose to use human computation games in order to gather data on human manual behavior. We demonstrate the idea with a strategy game that is operated via a natural user interface. A comparison between using the game for action execution and demonstrating actions in a virtual environment shows that people interact longer and have a better experience when playing the game.

CHI 2015, April 18 - 23 2015, Seoul, Republic of Korea

ACM 978-1-4503-3145-6/15/04...$15.00
http://dx.doi.org/10.1145/2702123.2702552

Author Keywords
Programming by demonstration; human computation games

ACM Classification Keywords
H.5.2 User Interfaces; H.1.2 User/Machine Systems; I.2.9 Robotics; K.8.0 [Personal Computing]: General - Games.

INTRODUCTION
HCI has moved from focusing mainly on desktop interaction to ubiquitous interaction and in particular to embodied computer artifacts. With the advent of robots in our homes, computation is moving beyond the classical understanding of human-computer interaction. The future of household robots envisions active and intelligent companions in our everyday lives with many concepts exploring anthropomorphic robots like the NAO robot [24]. Researching the humanoid form factor is important, since it is likely to be accepted by humans when they are to "live" in the same environment [13]. Besides the familiar appearance of the robot, human-like robot behavior fosters human-robot interaction and cooperation, as it requires less adjustment and learning effort by the human. Even though the degrees of freedom of the robots' limbs and joints may allow for other non- or even super-human movements, it is often a better choice to let robots act in a way that corresponds to the mental models of their users. However, programming robots to master everyday activities in a human-like fashion has proven to be a huge challenge [3]. Today, robots can only solve tasks in a narrow range of

conditions. Many seemingly mundane everyday tasks are only vaguely described and show a high level of variation. The artificial intelligence vision of understanding common sense knowledge needed for everyday activities has been unsolved for decades [19].

In recent years, prototypical solutions for household tasks have been built, for instance robots making pancakes [3] or baking cookies [5]. The necessary knowledge for solving such tasks in various environments has to be fed into the systems through knowledge acquisition and machine learning in labor- and cost-intensive processes. Since most humans are experts at such tasks, there is great potential in acquiring this knowledge for robots from human sources. If people perform the required movements, such as those for making a pancake, they can be tracked, analyzed, and then used to build models for the motion of the robot's arms and hands [20,23]. In this imitation learning approach to robot programming, the challenge lies in collecting large amounts of movement data from humans solving some problem while conditions vary systematically. Obviously this is tedious work. It is difficult to motivate people to move pans on a stove over and over again with all sorts of pan sizes and stove heights.

Using virtual environments in which the user interacts with simulated task contexts, human motion data can be generated by recording user input [16]. The advantage being that a virtual world is fully observable and demonstration is unconcerned with real world constraints or safety issues. Games can increase the motivation for performing menial tasks in such environments, potentially increasing the number of demonstrations and thus the amount of -and variation in- motion data. They also offer further benefits for imitation learning: in games, objectives can be introduced to influence players' behavior, such as eliciting their best performance. Moreover, well-balanced challenge in games increases the players' resistance to frustration. This ability to design for task failure is highly important for robot programming, and games are an easy and controlled means of eliciting data on failing behavior.

In this paper we present a human computation games approach to knowledge acquisition tools for imitation learning. Engaging people as experts of everyday activities to perform actions in an embodied game raises the motivation of demonstrators and encourages them to deliver high quality data. Freedom in game design allows for tailoring player behavior to generate desired outcomes and allows obtaining varied human motion data from successful or, equally important, unsuccessful actions.

We present a sample application using a tower defense game with full-hand motion input. The users were highly motivated to play and thus contribute their embodied knowledge. With this setup, the data acquisition for programming a robot is translated to an HCI problem of game interaction and player experience. Our study shows 1) that performing tasks in-game provides a better self-reported experience than demonstrating them in a non-game virtual environment and 2) that motion data has the quality required for successful use in robot imitation learning

With this paper we not only contribute a successful design of a free-hand motion control serious game but also demonstrate a design approach of how to leverage existing game design knowledge for increasing the effectiveness of motion data acquisition tools. Moreover, this paper is a contribution to human-robot interaction for humanoid robots in home environments. We propose to use *gameful interaction* [8] as a means for building more realistic and acceptable robotic companions.

RELATED WORK

Robot Programming

Imitation is the behavior where an individual observes and reproduces another's action. *Imitation learning* or robot *Programming by Demonstration* (PbD) [4] (also called *Learning from Demonstration* [2]) is a means of learning and developing new skills by observing how they are performed by others. It is a technique for enabling robots to autonomously perform new tasks. When observing either success or failure examples one can reduce the complexity of search spaces for learning, by either beginning the search from the observed successful solution (local optima), or by eliminating the failures from the search space.

The PbD learning problem can be separated into two fundamental phases: *gathering* examples and *deriving* policies [2]. Focusing on the gathering phase there exists a large variety of techniques for executing and recording demonstrations, ranging from human operators moving robots around which then record their own enacted movements over recording teleoperation commands to observing demonstrators execute behaviors with their own body. Furthermore, the control levels may vary from low-level actions for motion control, over basic high-level actions (action primitives) to complex behavioral actions.

In the work of Haidu et al. [11] the authors learn a failure detector model to allow a robot to recognize the point where the current action will lead to a failure. The data used for learning is collected from a virtual environment by running multiple episodes (success and failure cases) of the given action. The virtual environment built on a robotic simulator with a realistic physics engine, resulting in precise, realistic data. Having a virtual scenario gives the advantage of a fully observable world; one can completely represent the motion and the states of all simulated objects. Even if the motion sequences are comparatively simple, they can contain valuable information (e.g. for low-level motion control).

Other researchers have also been employing simulation environments [25]. While the results in terms of accuracy of the gathered data are promising, these simulators have not been designed to appeal to the general public, to be operated by naïve users, or to support motivation by introducing game mechanics beyond the playful appeal of an interactive virtual world. In order to gather large amounts of varied data that can be used to build large-scale behavior models, such simulations must be able to run on consumer hardware and feature motivational structures to animate players to perform multiple actions.

Human Computation Games

Introducing playful and gameful elements [8] to collective intelligence applications has been a hot topic in a new emerging field over the last years: *Human computation* (HC) *games* (HCG) are a form of collective intelligence where participants are not paid but voluntarily contribute data or chunks of knowledge in game-based interaction. HC is similar to crowdsourcing, where traditional human workers are replaced with members from the public, but differs in that in HC human computers (usually also from the public) replace digital computers in domains where these struggle [21]. The first prominent examples of such *games with a purpose* [27] were used for image labeling tasks. It was shown that very simple casual games motivated a large number of users and that it was possible to aggregate their individual contributions into concerted collective intelligence. In recent years, human computation games have been developed for further labeling tasks [14], computational biology [6], question answering [1], and for many other use-cases [28].

Human Computation Games for Robot Programming

In an effort to structure human computation game design approaches, Krause and Smeddinck [14] name four categories: *Identification* (of a task that can be turned into a HC application), *Motivation* (design mechanisms for motivating members of the public to contribute time and effort), *Observation* (design methods for enacting solutions in the application and for observing the approach taken by each member of the crowd) and *Evaluation* (design methods for aggregating, analyzing and interpreting the potentially large numbers of crowd contributions); or IMOE in short. Notably, this structure is akin to the general steps of gathering (IMO) and deriving (E) in PbD. Accordingly, we argue that PbD is a special case of human computation and thus approaches from human computation games are likely applicable to PbD. Both communities can profit from research that aims at combining their approaches that have so far been discussed in almost entirely separate sub-communities. While crowdsourcing has established itself for PbD, it is rarely embedded in game contexts (see [10] for a recent overview).

Looking into the categories of typical HC tasks as part of the considerations on *identification*, Krause and Smeddinck describe four categories, each one taking advantage of a specific human ability: aesthetic judgment, making intuitive decisions, contextual reasoning, and free interaction with the physical world (mentioned as *embodiment issues*). The latter offers a matching category for the application domain of the study presented in this paper (harnessing hand movements and actions). Embodied human knowledge is implicitly at hand for humans but hard to be formalized explicitly, making this category a strong candidate for human computation. So far, however, most human computation games do not consider embodied human knowledge that is used in physical interactions with the environment. Some approaches exist in mapping applications [18,26]. However, they require substantial physical effort by all human contributors and capture a gross measure of human body location instead of intricate details of human embodied interaction.

Approaches from related areas, such as gamification, have investigated matching game mechanics to generalized tasks. Flatla et al. [9] tackle gamification for calibration tasks such as screen calibration or respiration chest strain sensor calibration. They developed a design framework for identifying calibration types and the basic tasks behind them, and how to match these tasks to basic game mechanics. Using this framework they designed three calibration games, and were able to show increased user motivation. They also discuss differences in the data quality between standard and gamified calibration. However, their approach has not yet been linked to the related area of PbD and they did not focus on embodied interaction.

DESIGN APPROACH: KITCHEN TOWER DEFENSE

The primary design goal is to motivate people to demonstrate manual tasks by transforming the experience of performing mundane manual actions (physical or simulated) into a more enjoyable activity. We lay out our strategy before discussing how target and source domains can be mapped.

Design Strategy

Our design strategy to reach this goal is situated toward the "Gaming" and "Whole" ends of the two dimensions Gaming/Playing and Parts/Whole of the design space [8].

Gaming vs. Playing

Playful tools for motion data acquisition based on simulated virtual environments have been explored in the robotics community [11,16]. They offer the benefits of a fully observable world and safety from real world constraints. However, embedding this in a rule-based game system as opposed to a mere playful environment has two distinct advantages. First, task demonstration can be designed into the game mechanics in order to pose tasks more implicitly, directed via game rules and level design. Second, the addition of game *aesthetics* [12] such as challenge and narrative can improve the experience; while the enjoyment of baking virtual pancakes will diminish over time, a well-designed game can captivate for hours.

Parts vs. Whole

Designing for the stated goal can involve either (whole) HCG or introducing game design elements (parts) into motion data acquisition tools. The latter can be achieved either by adding game elements to an existing application (gamification) or by adding purposeful elements to an

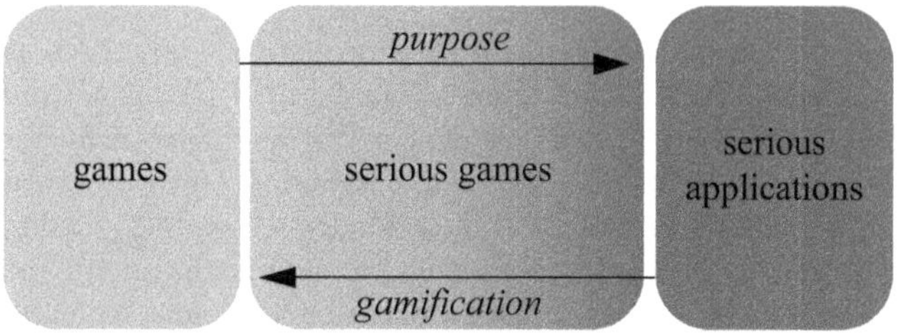

Figure 2: Serious games: increasingly purposeful games versus increasingly gamified applications.

existing game. This decision can be modeled as a third (if not fully orthogonal) dimension in the design space.

Games vs. Serious Applications

This axis reaches from one extreme, namely adding increasingly more game elements to a "serious" application, to an opposite extreme, which begins with full-fledged games that are augmented by an increasing number of "serious" elements (Figure 2). Our approach is situated toward the "games" end of this spectrum, in order to capture ordinary people and their sense of what constitutes a game. While gamification can be successfully used to increase motivation to perform otherwise boring or laborious tasks [9], we opted for creating a full game experience that uses established game mechanics for the following reasons: The approach enabled us to use whole game concepts to leverage existing design knowledge on working game mechanisms. Moreover, it increases the likelihood to create long-term motivation rather than short-lived engagement common in swiftly designed casual games. Furthermore, once a reliable game design is found for extracting a certain class of human behavior it can be used for a whole range of task domains, e.g. all workbench-based manipulation tasks.

Task Domain

Cooking is a good example of an embodied everyday activity. It includes complex and diverse manual activities that are easy to perform for (many) people but are hard to describe in a formal or algorithmic way. In robotics, cooking simulators are being investigated for knowledge acquisition [3,5,11,16]. We chose cooking as a paradigmatic scenario for an activity in the household and demonstrate how human computation games that go beyond the playfulness of simulator tools can help to gather data from ordinary persons who have no experience in robotics.

The first step in designing a game around a task domain is to identify the characteristic of the domain. We can identify four characteristics of cooking:

Characteristic 1: An enclosed, planar workspace

Characteristic 2: Well-defined manual actions

Characteristic 3: Actions operate on objects within the workspace

Characteristic 4: Active management of events

Note that these are valid for a number of worktop-based activities, such as crafts (e.g. sewing) or deskwork. The next step is to select an existing game archetype that matches these characteristics best.

Game Domain

The selection of a suitable game genre has to result in a good mapping from actions in the game domain to the desired actions in the task domain. Turn-based strategy (TBS) games reflect the above-mentioned properties very well. The player has a "godlike" position of a commander with an overview of a confined terrain or map. This relates well to *characteristic 1*, since players are able to see the available objects and the according contextual action space. TBS players perform various manipulation actions (relating to *characteristic 2*) that change the events enfolding on this map. Such actions can be recorded and their execution parameters and the contextual variables can be used for imitation learning. When enacted and chained to complex behaviors such as building up a base or city, or directing units, the manual actions operate on available objects (relating to *characteristic 3*). This results in information about workspace organization, object alignments and positioning. Lastly, in TBS, the player has control over the pace of the events unfolding via turn advancement. Relating to *characteristic 4,* the turns help with the challenging problem of chunking action sequences, which is needed for interpreting the overall user action sequences. Moreover, the game genre is suitable for embodied control with real hand gestures, which is important since we are interested in the actual trajectories of the player's arms and hands.

Other popular game genres, such as action or adventure, are focused on steering an avatar through expansive game-worlds (violating *characteristic 1*), and interaction with the game world occurs via the avatar as a mediator (violating *characteristic 2*) rather than the player manually interacting with it. Real-time games that are not turn-based lead to higher time pressure (violating *characteristic 4*), which could also have a negative influence on the resulting data.

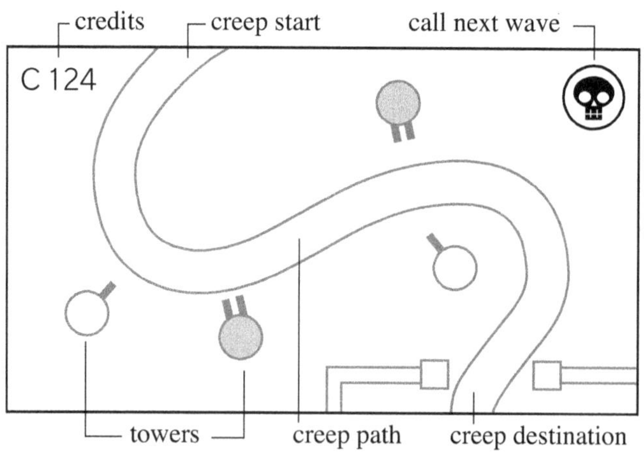

Figure 3: Schematic view of a typical level of a tower defense game with respective game elements.

intention	actions
build	*pick* type + *pick* site
upgrade	*pick* tower + *pick* upgrade
move	*pick* tower + *pick* site
demolish	*pick* tower + *pick* demolition

Table 1: General tower defense game intentions and actions.

intention	actions
place	*pick* pan + *place* on stove
add	*pick* bowl + *pour* batter
move	*pick* bowl + *place* bowl
turn	*pick* spatula + *lift* pancake + *flip* pancake

Table 2: Task intentions and actions in pancake making.

In this light we chose *tower defense games* (TD) as the game domain (Figure 3). In TD, players have to create and manage defensive structures against hordes of intruders invading their territory (also called *creeps*). These typically arrive in waves, whose arrival can be managed by the player to a certain degree. Game mechanics involve a simple (typically single-currency) economy in which construction costs are balanced against "revenue" earned by defeating enemies.

Mapping Actions

Having established a game genre that matches task domain characteristics, it is necessary to define the exact mapping from task actions to game actions. In order to arrive at a mapping we must consider the asymmetry in requirements: from the game domain we only require strict adherence to *intentions*, while a correct rendition of the task domain *actions* is crucial for gaining the right motion data. We thus need to map task domain actions to game domain intentions (Table 1). Since cooking is an activity for which a vast amount of behavior can be identified, we chose pancake making as a well-defined example also used in related research [3,11,16]. We assume a simplified procedure that uses ready-made pancake batter, reducing the task to few simple actions (Table 2). As there is no way of further operationalizing the mapping procedure, the last step is down to creative design. For the example of pancake making, we chose a mapping that relates action intentions semantically: building is conceptually related to moving things, an upgrade adds functionality, and constructions are demolished by turning them over (Table 3).

Control Interface

The goal is to tap the embodied knowledge on manual behavior that humans are not used to describing explicitly, but can better recall implicitly given a task context (e.g. describing the procedure of operating clutch, gearstick and accelerator versus performing the act of driving). This requires interfaces with as little mediation and indirection as possible. Task simulators for recording human motion thus employ virtual hand manipulation techniques using full-hand trackers. Since glove interfaces incur obtrusiveness, the best solutions for a broad audience are outside-in hand tracking systems, i.e. camera-based solutions. High-fidelity full-hand trackers have reached consumer level of maturity and support the prospects of success of outsourcing embodied manipulation knowledge acquisition through full-hand interaction games.

3DFEND: FREE-HAND CONTROL TOWER DEFENSE

As a result of these design considerations we developed *3DFEND*, the first free-hand 3D TD. The story of the game is a micro-narrative in a style found in many casual games (Figure 4). Players defend earth against hordes of robot aliens by constructing a defense system via hand motions. While input is 3D, the game follows the typical planar TD logic, i.e. creeps move along two-dimensional paths, along which towers can be placed. A large platform provides the stage on which towers can be constructed. Players operate on objects on the stage through tools, not directly via cursor. Creeps advance over the stage from left to right.

Game Controls

Free-hand control is implemented as a simplified virtual hand metaphor [7]. This takes the form of a 3D cursor to which palm translation and orientation are mapped directly. Fingers are not used, since robust low-latency tracking is not solved in the category of hand trackers under consideration. Balloon cords, shadows, and a map overlay provide depth cues. Tool selection occurs if the cursor collides with the tool before a certain timeout, which is animated with a blend to white. Figure 5 gives an overview of the interface configuration; please refer to the video figure for a more immediate illustration of the controls.

A 3D toolbar at the bottom of the screen offers three construction modules for three different tower types, a nano bot container, and a relocation/demolition tool. Tools are selected by the above procedure. Each of the four basic controls involves compound manual actions (Table 3).

Build Turret

The player can choose one of the three construction modules and place it on the stage: after a construction time of one second, the turret is ready. Constructing a turret costs different amounts of energy credits, depending on type.

intention	actions
build	*pick* construction tool + *place* on site
upgrade	*pick* upgrade tool + *pour* nano-bots
move	*Pick* demolish tool + *place* on new site
demolish	*pick* demolish tool + *lift* turret + *flip* turret

Table 3: The basic game controls of 3DFEND.

Far in the future, a wormhole opened in proximity to earth. A hostile alien race is sending troops through the wormhole. The nations of earth have sent you, the player, to construct a defense in space. As the enemy is entirely unknown, you must quickly match their strategy with specialized defense systems. Fortunately, destroyed aliens set free energy that you can harness and use to improve your defenses.

Figure 4: The game background story of 3DFEND.

Upgrade Turret
The player can choose the upgrade tool and pour *nano bots* on constructed turrets. Turrets upgrade continuously, depending on the amount of nano bots received. Upgrading costs energy credits.

Move Turret
The player can use the relocation tool to move a tower by using it like a spatula on constructed towers, once on the spatula they can be placed elsewhere on the stage.

Demolish Turret
In the same manner, lifting it with the demolition tool and turning it by more than 90° can demolish a turret. The player receives a percentage of the tower construction cost as energy credits.

A heads-up overlay provides data on the game state: current wave, lives remaining, credit costs, and resources. A 3D button on the top center can be used to call for the next wave when the player is ready.

Gameplay

Apart from the unique free-hand interaction described above, 3DFEND has the typical dramaturgy of a tower defense game: creeps move over the stage from left to right along a highlighted path. Players must build towers along the way that automatically fire at the creeps lest these reach the portal on the far right end of the stage, in which case the player loses life points. Building towers costs energy credits that can be replenished through harvesting destroyed enemies or demolishing unused towers. With each wave, creep health and number increases. Starting with the fifth wave, creeps gain a shield that increases in power with each wave. Bullet towers are ineffective against shielded enemies, while laser turrets diminish shields quickly but are ineffective otherwise. Rocket turrets diminish both enemy shield and health, but are slow and expensive. With increasing enemy numbers and power, players will need to upgrade towers to manage the incoming hordes. They will need to figure out the ideal configuration of tower count, position and level to defeat the incoming enemies.

Implementation

3DFEND was implemented using the Unity3D game authoring environment. For a hand tracker we used the *Leap Motion* sensor [17], which was integrated into Unity using the SDK plug-in.

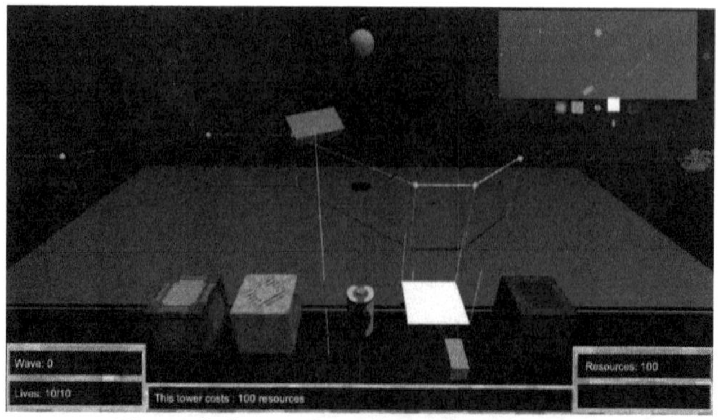

Figure 5: Screenshot of the 3DFEND game.

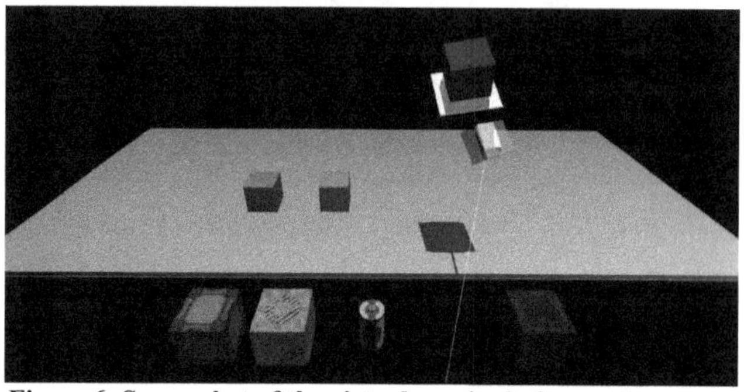

Figure 6: Screenshot of the virtual manipulation environment.

EXPERIMENT

We conducted a formal experiment to evaluate our claim that HCG can be used to increase motivation for demonstrating manual actions for robot imitation learning. Two hypotheses coin this statement:

H1. Demonstrating manipulation tasks in a game environment provides a better experience than following instructions in a playful environment.

H2. The manipulation data recorded in a game environment has at least the level of quality as motion data recorded in a playful non-game environment.

Study Design

The study design compares following explicit instructions to perform virtual manipulation tasks with performing the same tasks implicitly while playing a game. It uses a within-subjects design with an alternating order of treatments. The independent variable is *activity evocation type* with the conditions *virtual manipulation environment with instructions (VE)* and *game.*

For the *VE* condition, a virtual environment was created (Figure 6). It features the same basic manipulation controls but no game elements, namely: enemies, game overlay, or animations. Instructions were administered via text overlay. Participants were asked to place a cube, move a cube, pour on a cube, and flip a cube, and repeat this twice with varying locations. On completing these 12 actions the treatment was terminated. Attention was paid not to introduce any bias by framing (e.g. by using the words "game" or "virtual environment"): both conditions were introduced neutrally by declaring them as "prototypes".

The *game* condition consisted of playing a prototype of 3DFEND for at least 15 minutes. Pre-tests showed that twelve actions is a typical number for 15 min gameplay. Players were alerted when this time was over, but were allowed to terminate gameplay on their own accord.

Measures
To measure the subjective *player experience* we used the competence, autonomy, presence/immersion and intuitive controls subscales of the Player Experience of Need Satisfaction (PENS) questionnaire [22]. Since the scenario at hand focuses on single-player experience we dropped the relatedness scale. An interview complemented the assessment of the participant experience.

In PbD, data on demonstrating motions is used to build a model for robot behavior. It is hard to quantify what makes "good" motion data for PbD. Based on the experience gained in previous work [5,11,16], three aspects of motion data were identified to operationalize *data quality* for the purposes of assessing H2.

- A large amount of completed actions is a basic requirement for motion data for use in PbD; The VE condition as representative of state-of-the-art motion data acquisition was designed for a high frequency of demonstration samples.
- Cursor speed, height, and angle can serve as simple characteristics for comparing manipulations between this baseline and the proposed alternative.
- Spill in the pour action serves as an indicator for the precision of operation (accuracy was less consequential in the place and turn actions).

Participants
We recruited 16 participants (13 male, 3 female) from the academic milieu. Participant ages ranged from 24 to 32 (M =26.8, SD=2,32). Out of all participants, 11 considered themselves regular gamers (more than 1 hour of playing computer games a week) and all but one had experience with games and motion input in games.

Setup and Procedure
Participants sat at a table with a 24" screen and a Leap Motion sensor. First, participants were asked to fill out a demographics questionnaire. After introducing participants to the experiment procedure, they were trained on the basic controls (without instructions or game) until they felt competent and comfortable to proceed. Next they were exposed to both treatments in turn. After each treatment they were asked to fill out the questionnaire. Finally, a short interview was conducted.

Results
We used two-sided repeated measures Student's t-test on the collected data. Due to logging problems with the move action we only report on the three other actions.

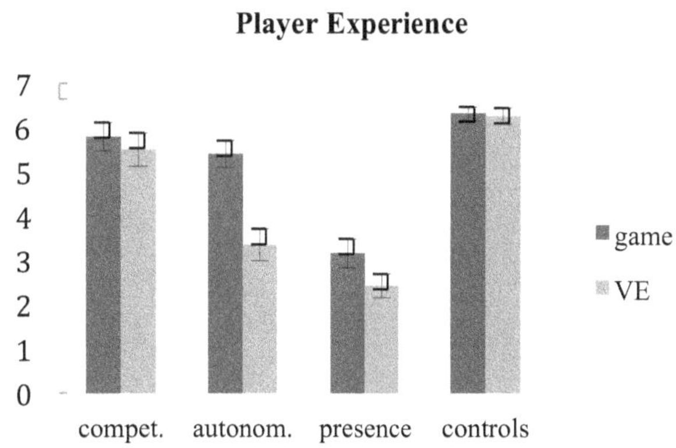

Figure 7. Player experience (PENS subscales). Error bars indicate the standard error of the mean (SEM).

Player Experience
Figure 7 displays score means and SEM of the four PENS scales for player experience. While no significant differences in the subjective assessment of *competence* (p=0.27) or *intuitive controls* (p=0.69) can be made out, both *autonomy* (p<0.01) and *presence/immersion* scored significantly higher for the game condition (p=0.02).

15 participants voluntarily extended their gameplay, on average playing the game for 30 minutes 26 seconds (VE instructions took 5 minutes 46 seconds on average).

Participant's comments showed a clear subjective preference of the game version. Some comments after the game condition were: *"I want to finish the round! What was the highest high score yet?", "Where can I buy the game and where can I buy the sensor?", "Can I play again?", "The game is so much fun".* Comments of the users after and during the VE condition were along the lines of: *"Do I have to do all of this?"* and *"What, again?".*

Beside these general comments the participants also provided feedback on the graphics, the interface and the tracking system: The users would like to see more advanced and appealing graphics, more accurate hand tracking and grasping. Some of these improvements would certainly further improve the experience and usability of the system. However, the goal of our study was to establish 3DEFEND in an initial version with simple methods and tools.

action	game	VE
place	14,56	6,13
pour	16,63	4,94
turn	2,94	3,00

Table 4. Mean number of completed actions.

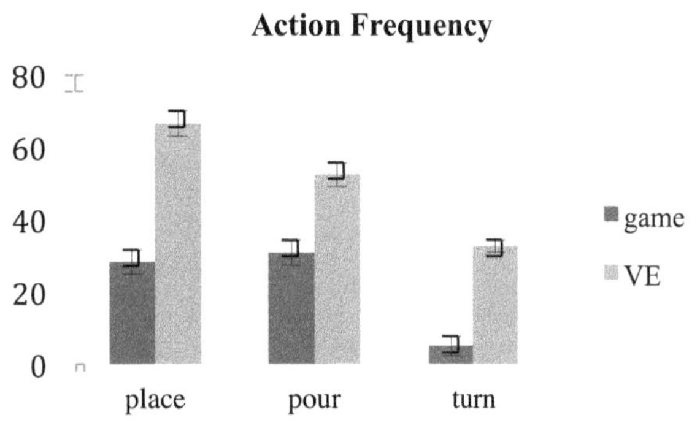

Figure 8. Action frequency of the main control actions (completed actions per hour). Error bars indicate SEM.

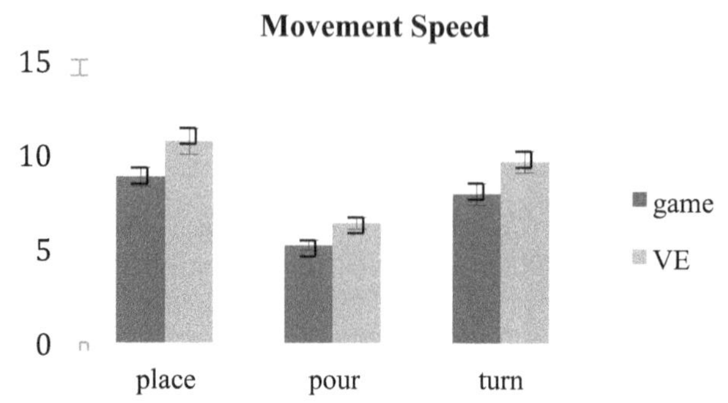

Figure 9. Movement speed in the main control actions (game units per second). Error bars indicate SEM.

Motion Data

Figure 8 shows the action frequency means extrapolated from the measured data. Significantly fewer occurrences can be measured for all actions under the game condition ($p<0.01$). The small number of turn actions under the game condition shows that game mechanics need better balancing so that these controls are more frequently used.

Figure 9 shows movement speed means per action. Movement was significantly slower for all actions ($p_{place}<0.01$, $p_{pour}<0.01$, $p_{turn}=0.01$) in the game condition. Pour height ($p=0.73$) and turn height ($p=0.15$) did not differ significantly between the conditions; neither did the pouring orientation ($p_x=0.62$, $p_y=0.36$, $p_z=0.69$).

There was significantly less content spilled in the pour action in the game condition than under instructions in the VE (5.4% versus 20.8%, $p=0.01$).

ANALYSIS

Our game provides a better experience regarding autonomy and presence. Combined with the observed motivation of participants, this supports H1 that demonstrating manipulation tasks in a game environment provides a better experience than following instructions in a playful environment. This has a direct effect on the amount of motion data that can be acquired. While games are less efficient than instructions (in our example only half as many actions per time range), the willingness of players to spend more time playing and thus demonstrating more than makes up for this: Despite lower frequency our game totaled the same amount or more actions (Table 4). The motion from both conditions had the same spatial characteristics; the same actions can be discerned from the data. However, in the game condition, manipulation speed was slower and more precise (for the pouring action). A likely explanation, corroborated by interview responses, is that players care more about the outcome of actions in the game. Such effects have been observed in other studies comparing user behavior in games with comparable non-game contexts [9]. The difference in spilling illustrates this best. When actions have outcomes that affect players this motivates them to act more carefully: Spilling valuable nano-bots wastes credits, while the VE did not penalize spill. Thus, regarding H2 we can assess that the quality of the motion data resulting from the game condition is at least the standard of the baseline VE condition. High player motivation and thus longer demonstration sessions can compensate the lower frequency of actions. Taken together with similar observations in related work we can surmise that the higher task accuracy is a strong indicator for the motivational background increasing task performance and thus quality of motion data for PbD.

DISCUSSION

We have established a HCG for collecting data on embodied knowledge of everyday activities that can be used for programming manipulation robots. In the following we touch points of discussion regarding controls, game design, and experiment design and reflect the chosen approach.

Free-hand Controls

As a first exploration of HCG for robot imitation learning and for the first 3D TD available, controls were sufficient and very usable. As suggested by participants, the free-hand controls for virtual action demonstration can be further improved. With a more literal virtual hand that includes tracked fingers, grab and release gestures could replace tool/object activation via timeout, resulting in more fluent and efficient interaction that better replicates the real world activity. Advances in camera-based low-latency hand tracking will also improve the controls. A stereoscopic display would provide better depth perception, which was an issue for some participants despite depth cues.

Physics Simulation

Game engine physics are not optimized for fully realistic simulation of physical processes. For practical use, game-based knowledge acquisition tools such as 3DFEND require more realistic simulation engines. Related research problems such as enabling interactive simulation at real-time frame rates are complementary to the problems under investigation in this work and are being researched in the robotics and computer graphics communities. Actual PbD tools will thus integrate insights on HCG for imitation learning with state-of-the-art physics simulation.

Game Design

3DFEND is the first free-hand control 3D tower defense game and still in prototype stage. Game design was minimalist, and game mechanics, assets and story should be improved in further iterations. Also, proper balancing is essential in order to make sure that no "game-breaking" strategies emerge and frequency distribution of the various actions is even. However, player feedback confirmed that the prototype was sufficient for exploring a HCG approach to acquiring motion data for PbD.

Experiment

The control condition of our experiment presented participants with instructions for basic manipulation without motivation or context. We abstracted from the task domain cooking in order to provide a generalizable, neutral counterpart to the game scenario. This includes two design choices that might have affected the aspects of experienced presence and autonomy, respectively. The first is that a context can give such scenarios intentions: baking virtual pancakes is likely more motivating and likely increases presence over moving cubes. The second is that purely following instructions subdues the creative potential and experienced autonomy of playful virtual task exploration—different players might develop different action strategies to reach the same goal. However, without the guiding effect of game mechanics and narrative, it is very difficult to control action frequency in such free designs. We leave exploring the effects of these design nuances for future work.

Scalability and Extendibility

We have illustrated that the chosen game design approach works for the cooking subtask of making a pancake. This can be easily scaled and extended to other task domains with similar characteristics. Strategy is a game genre with huge variation. For TD, more tower types, different levels, varied enemy resistances and tactics are only a few examples of how game design can model more diverse and complex actions.

Embodied Human Computation Games

HCG can incorporate embodied knowledge by capturing intricate details of motion behaviors through modern natural user interfaces. The mapping of game intentions to task domain actions is a flexible design decision. However, with embodiment issues, the mapping of user input to actions, also discussed for PbD [2], can be very direct, requiring less complex methods in the *deriving* step. Thus marrying HGC for embodied task knowledge and imitation learning is an especially promising approach.

Toward a Framework for Manual Behavior HCG

In order to bring insights gathered in our design process into a tentative framework for choosing game archetypes for manual action demonstration human computation games, we formulate questions for designers to consider.

Can every part of the game world be reached within a short time space? Large-scale locomotion is distinct to strategies of manual behavior. To capture the latter, the former should be avoided. In most tower defense games, the game world can easily fit into 1-4 screens.

Do game controls require many degrees of freedom (DOF)? High-DOF game controls might be more difficult to match than low-DOF controls. In the tower defense example, the simple click-and-select controls gave us more freedom in matching manual actions.

Can game time constraints be managed (e.g. turns, waves)? Full real-time game world simulation can be limiting, as manual actions often have a different time scale than the game world. Managed time constraints such as in turn-based gameplay gives more leeway in matching task and game domain time scales.

CONCLUSION

HCI paradigms will change dramatically in the future when the hardware moves from current display-dominated interfaces to active agents such as household robots. Programming such companions for everyday activities requires new methods for acquiring knowledge about highly variable environments and the tasks they have to perform in them. With 3DFEND we established a human computation games approach for harvesting embodied knowledge on "workbench" manipulation tasks. Our study shows that this embodied human computation game motivates users to voluntarily contribute data for imitation learning. We mapped a set of typical manual actions to a tower defense game that could easily be extended to other task domains. Our work shows that gameful human computation approaches with consumer hardware motion-based input can generate motion data for understanding human manual behavior. It provides a basis for future work on mappings from the task domain to the game domain.

REFERENCES

1. Aras, H., Krause, M., Haller, A., & Malaka, R. (2010). Webpardy: Harvesting QA by HC. In *Proc. HCOMP 2010*, (pp. 49–52). ACM.
2. Argall, B. D., Chernova, S., Veloso, M., & Browning, B. (2009). A survey of robot learning from demonstration. *Robotics and Autonomous Systems*, *57*(5), 469–483.
3. Beetz, M., Klank, U., Kresse, I., Maldonado, A., Mosenlechner, L., Pangercic, D., Ruhr, T., & Tenorth, M. (2011). Robotic roommates making pancakes. In *Proc. Humanoids 2011*, (pp. 529–536). IEEE.
4. Billard, A., Calinon, S., Dillmann, R., & Schaal, S. (2008). Robot programming by demonstration. In B. Siciliano, & O. Khatib (Eds.) *Springer Handbook of Robotics*, chap. 60, (pp. 1371–1394). Springer.
5. Bollini, M., Tellex, S., Thompson, T., Roy, N., & Rus, D. (2013). Interpreting and executing recipes with a cooking robot. In J. P. Desai, G. Dudek, O. Khatib, & V. Kumar (Eds.) *Experimental Robotics*, vol. 88 of *Springer Tracts in Advanced Robotics*, (pp. 481–495). Springer.

6. Bonetta, L. (2009). New citizens for the life sciences. *Cell, 138*(6), 1043–1045.
7. Bowman, D. A., Kruijff, E., LaViola, J. J., & Poupyrev, I. (2004). *3D User Interfaces: Theory and Practice*. Addison-Wesley.
8. Deterding, S., Dixon, D., Khaled, R., & Nacke, L. (2011). From game design elements to gamefulness: Defining "gamification". In *Proc MindTrek 2011*, (pp. 9–15). New York, NY, USA: ACM.
9. Flatla, D. R., Gutwin, C., Nacke, L. E., Bateman, S., & Mandryk, R. L. (2011). Calibration games: Making calibration tasks enjoyable by adding motivating game elements. In *Proc. UIST 2011*, (pp. 403–412). ACM.
10. Forbes, M., Chung, M. J., Cakmak, M., & Rao, R. P. N. (2014). Robot programming by demonstration with crowdsourced action fixes. In *Proc. HCOMP 2014*, (pp. 67–76). AAAI Press.
11. Haidu, A., Kohlsdorf, D., & Beetz, M. (2014). Learning task outcome prediction for robot control from interactive environments. In *Proc. Intelligent Robots and Systems*. IEEE/RSJ.
12. Hunicke, R., LeBlanc, M., & Zubek, R. (2004). MDA: A formal approach to game design and game research. In D. Fu, S. Henke, & J. Orkin (Eds.) *AAAI Workshop Challenges in Game Artificial Intelligence*. AAAI Press.
13. Kanda, T., Ishiguro, H., Imai, M., & Ono, T. (2004). Development and evaluation of interactive humanoid robots. *Proceedings of the IEEE, 92*(11), 1839–1850.
14. Krause, M., & Smeddinck, J. (2012). Human Computation: A New Aspect of Serious Games., (pp. 1027–1047). In *Handbook of Research on Serious Games as Educational, Business and Research Tools: Development and Design*. IGI Global.
15. Krause, M., Takhtamysheva, A., Wittstock, M., & Malaka, R. (2010). Frontiers of a paradigm: Exploring human computation with digital games. In *Proc HCOMP 10*, (pp. 22–25). ACM.
16. Kunze, L., Haidu, A., & Beetz, M. (2013). Acquiring task models for imitation learning through games with a purpose. In *Proc. IROS, 2013*, (pp. 102–107). IEEE.
17. Leap Motion, Inc. http://leapmotion.com (last visited on 2015-01-07).
18. Matyas, S., Matyas, C., Schlieder, C., Kiefer, P., Mitarai, H., & Kamata, M. (2008). Designing location-based mobile games with a purpose: Collecting geospatial data with CityExplorer. In *Proc. ACE 2008*, (pp. 244–247). ACM.
19. McCarthy, J. (1968). Programs with common sense. In *Semantic Information Processing*, vol. 1, (pp. 403–418).
20. Pollard, N. S., Hodgins, J. K., Riley, M. J., & Atkeson, C. G. (2002). Adapting human motion for the control of a humanoid robot. In *Proc. ICRA 2002*, vol. 2, (pp. 1390–1397). IEEE.
21. Quinn, A. J., & Bederson, B. B. (2011). Human computation: A survey and taxonomy of a growing field. In *Proc. CHI 2011*, (pp. 1403–1412). ACM.
22. Ryan, R. M., Rigby, C. S., & Przybylski, A. (2006). The motivational pull of video games: A Self-Determination theory approach. *Motivation and Emotion, 30*(4), 344–360.
23. Schaal, S. (1999). Is imitation learning the route to humanoid robots? *Trends in Cognitive Sciences, 3*(6), 233–242.
24. Shamsuddin, S., Ismail, L. I., Yussof, H., Ismarrubie Zahari, N., Bahari, S., Hashim, H., & Jaffar, A. (2011). Humanoid robot NAO: Review of control and motion exploration. In *Proc. ICCSCE*, (pp. 511–516). IEEE.
25. Toris, R., Kent, D., & Chernova, S. (2014). The robot management system: A framework for conducting Human-Robot interaction studies through crowdsourcing. *Journal of Human-Robot Interaction, 3*(2), 25+.
26. Tuite, K., Snavely, N., Hsiao, D. Y., Smith, A. M., & Popović, Z. (2010). Reconstructing the world in 3D: Bringing games with a purpose outdoors. In *Proc. FDG 2010*, (pp. 232–239). ACM.
27. von Ahn, L., & Dabbish, L. (2008). Designing games with a purpose. *Commun. ACM, 51*(8), 58–67.
28. Yuen, M.-C., Chen, L.-J., & King, I. (2009). A survey of human computation systems. In *Proc. CSE*, vol. 4, (pp. 723–728). Los Alamitos, CA, USA: IEEE.

Medium, Access, and Obsolescence: What Kinds of Objects are Lasting Objects?

Jane Gruning, Julia Bullard, and Melissa Ocepek
The University of Texas at Austin
School of Information
1616 Guadalupe St., Austin, TX, USA
jane.gru@gmail.com, julia.a.bullard@gmail.com, mgocepek@utexas.edu

ABSTRACT
This paper presents findings from a field study of records managers that provides context for understanding how people see objects on varying media as long-lasting objects (or not). Part of the mandate of the profession of records management is long-term preservation of digital and paper records. At the site of the fieldwork for this study, research participants' tasks primarily consisted of examining individual case files to determine if the files should be kept or destroyed under the relevant rules set by higher-level management according to legal requirements. Close observation of work practices showed that application of records management rules varied depending on the medium of the records, despite the policy that records on varying media are equal in importance. The results of the study suggest that the perceived accessibility and obsolescence of digital objects deserve more attention in the exploration of the place of digital objects in human lives over the long-term.

Author Keywords
Digital preservation; ethnography; field study; obsolescence; digital objects; records management.

ACM Classification Keywords
H.5.m. Information interfaces and presentation (e.g., HCI): Miscellaneous.

INTRODUCTION
Digital objects can be "lost" in a variety of ways: time and use damage physical storage media, hardware necessary for access becomes obsolete and difficult to acquire, and software necessary for display is replaced by new versions incompatible with old file formats. Solutions that exist for these problems are mostly designed for institutional-level implementation in cultural heritage institutions such as archives and museums. The loss of digital objects, however, is a part of everyday life for individuals as well. Recently, researchers in HCI have begun to examine the potential of digital objects as long-lasting personal possessions [14, 19, 20, 24]. Related studies have investigated how digital objects might become "cherishable" [13], or "heirlooms" [23]. An overlapping body of work examines differences (and similarities) in how people interact with digital and physical objects [18, 26, 27, 28]. It is unsurprising that these two strands of investigation tend to overlap; clearly people have no difficulty considering some types of physical objects as both precious and long-lasting, but they currently seem much less likely to value digital objects in the same way [13]. These studies have raised questions such as, "What are the important differences between digital and physical objects?" Or, to take a phenomenological approach, "What are the differences in our experiences of digital and physical objects, and how do those differences in experience relate to the ways that we value those objects?" Theses kinds of questions apply to human interactions with computers in a variety of settings including both the home and the workplace, although motivations for keeping objects vary across those settings.

The Job of Keeping Things
The nine studies mentioned above were conducted in home environments, excepting one that investigated the personal archiving practices of academics [18]. Although there is a long tradition of studying the workplace in HCI [e.g., 2, 15, 33], we make a comparison to work that has been done in home environments because those studies focus on lasting objects in a way that is also central to the study described below. This paper sheds new light on the issue of lasting digital objects by examining human behavior in a particular type of work environment, one in which very long term storage of both digital and physical objects is part of the job. As opposed to a home environment, this setting adds the element of rules for interactions with digital and physical objects. Misinterpreting or breaking those rules can have consequences beyond the personal life of the person interacting with the object.

CHI 2015, April 18 - 23 2015, Seoul, Republic of Korea
Copyright is held by the owner/author(s). Publication rights licensed to ACM.
ACM 978-1-4503-3145-6/15/04 $15.00
http://dx.doi.org/10.1145/2702123.2702238

Records management is the "field of management responsible for the efficient and systematic control of the creation, receipt, maintenance, use and disposition of records..." [16]. While definitions of the term "record" vary, the following definition is typical: "information in a fixed form that is created or received in the course of individual or institutional activity and set aside (preserved) as evidence of that activity for future reference" [27]. Large corporate, governmental, and non-profit organizations use records management to control, organize, and destroy records. In practice, the job of a records manager is to provide guidance for his or her organization regarding the retention and destruction of records created by the organization. This guidance is based on legal requirements that determine how long organizations must retain various types of records, and may range from development of organizational policy down to advising individual employees on recordkeeping practices. Proper practices are determined by records managers as they interpret how legal requirements apply to the records of the organization, but are typically implemented by individual members of an organization as they go about their daily work. For example, when employees at the Arthur Andersen accounting firm shredded documents and deleted emails in an attempt to destroy evidence of illegal activities prior to the Enron Corporation financial scandal, they were breaking laws that govern records management, and most likely acting against the records management policies of their organization.

The research described here was part of a field study in which multiple researchers examined records management practices at four research sites using ethnographic techniques of observation and interview. The kinds of tasks described above, of setting organizational policy and providing guidelines for recordkeeping, were typical for records managers at most of the sites investigated in this study. One site was quite different: this was an office within the state Department of Children and Family Services (or DCFS[1]), a state agency charged with regulating child care and protecting children, elderly adults, and people with disabilities. At this site, four records clerks (supervised by a manager) applied records management rules for retention and destruction of records on a large scale. Instead of setting policy, the clerks applied it – and instead of applying it as an incidental part of their jobs, applying records management policy was their primary task. In their daily work practices, the clerks made decisions about how broad, organization-wide policies should be applied in many individual cases. The records the clerks handled were case files created by case workers in offices around the state, which were sent to external long term storage facilities once they were not in regular use. During our fieldwork, the research site office was beginning a multi-year project. The purpose of the project was to sort through stored records, identifying and destroying records that were past their destruction dates, so that the state was not paying to store records that it was no longer required to retain. This paper discusses findings from that site, and their implications for human interactions with technology.

[1] The actual name of the state department has been replaced with a common name for this type of department in several states for purposes of confidentiality. Names of participants have also been changed.

We first provide background on the records management policies regarding records medium. Then we review HCI findings on how media type changes perceptions of objects, particularly in cases of long-lasting objects. The paper then describes the office in which we completed our fieldwork and the work practices there, as well as how those practices varied depending on the medium and accessibility of the record. We then explore potential reasons for these differences. Finally, we describe the potential implications of our findings for technology design.

LITERATURE REVIEW

Records Management and Medium

The shift from paper to digital as the primary medium of creation for business records demanded a statement from the field of records management about the status of digital records. The leading records management professional organization, ARMA International, takes the perspective that medium is not a limiting characteristic in the determination of what kinds of objects can be records. This perspective is reflected in the definition of records management provided by ARMA: "any recorded information, regardless of medium or characteristics, made or received and retained by an organization in pursuance of legal obligations or in the transaction of business" [11]. ARMA additionally specifies that retention schedules, which determine for how long records must be kept, apply equally to records on varying media. "Each record listed on a records retention schedule specifies a specific period of time that the record is retained. *This retention applies whether the record is on paper or residing on magnetic or optical media (hard disk, floppy disk, tape, CD, etc.)...*" (emphasis in original) [12]. It is not clear, however, that everyday human interactions with records actually align with these guidance statements.

This issue has also been examined by scholars in the field of archival science [10, 32], as archival institutions are often the eventual recipients of records determined to have long-term value by records managers. Duranti has done extensive work on the authenticity of records with a specific focus on electronic records [5, 6, 7, 8], and is cited in the ARMA documentation. Her work has primarily had the aim of guiding policy rather than investigating human behavior. For instance, in findings from the first phase of the InterPARES project[2], she and Thibodeau determined that "the medium is not a relevant factor in assessing a record's authenticity," and that transfer of a record from one medium to another does not affect the authenticity of the record [9]. In this study, we explore how policies about records medium are applied in work practices.

Human-Computer Interaction

Unlike the archival science examinations of differences between media mentioned above, which are concerned with the properties of records as one kind of object, many HCI studies closely inspect how people's perceptions of and interactions with objects vary depending on the medium of an object. HCI studies of home archiving practices and differences between digital and physical objects uncovered that participants were concerned about the stability of digital objects and did not necessarily think about them as things that would continue to exist long-term. In one such study, Odom et al. explored the possibility of passing down digital objects from one generation of a family to the next in their investigation of home use of three devices designed to encourage "people to think more concretely about how digital materials might be inherited in the future" [23, p. 337]. They noted that, "...families described a general distrust over the longevity of their personal computers, which led them to create extensive backups on physical media (e.g., CDs or DVDs). Tensions also emerged with this approach, namely due to doubts over how long these media would last..." [p. 342]. In addition to concerns about the life span of digital objects, three interrelated themes from this literature speak specifically to the ways in which people live with digital objects over time: *deep storage*, *hybrid objects*, and *experiencing digital objects*. These interrelated themes reflect insights into in-the-moment interactions with digital objects that may be important for how we perceive those objects both in the present and over the long term.

Deep Storage

In a study designed to explore home archiving practices, Kirk & Sellen noted that one way their participants kept important objects was in "deep storage," in which objects were both "out of sight and out of mind" [20, p. 32]. "We observed many instances where old digital content and items of sentiment were stored away on various innocuous storage media, such as floppy disks, CDs, and hard drives in PCs, thus rendering them, in some ways, invisible" [p. 33]. Additionally, the authors noted that participants had to explicitly intend to access digital objects on external storage media in order to interact with them; objects that participants kept in this way lost the reminding function that both physical and digital objects have been shown to provide in some situations [1, 22]. They were functionally invisible unless participants sought them out [20].

Odom et al. built on this notion in their exploration of the idea of digital heirlooms [23]. They noted that heirlooms were used infrequently, but that "practices surrounding heirlooms were bound up with having them present and ensuring their safekeeping" [p. 341] over long periods of time. Support of this basic form of interaction with digital heirlooms, they argued, would require "the artful design of technologies that can be put away," that is, "new storage systems that are extremely robust and can handle sporadic use" [p. 345]. This is an implicit recognition that digital objects, which require a device for access, cannot currently be "put away" safely.

Hybrid Objects

Kirk & Sellen's study focused on objects "that people were deliberately archiving... cherished objects of sentimental value that are consciously or intentionally kept" [20, p.9], similar to the way that the DCFS as an organization was purposefully keeping certain records. Kirk & Sellen developed a medium-centric taxonomy based on the types of objects that their participants were actively keeping, dividing these objects into three types: physical (e.g., diaries, furniture, paintings), digital (e.g., photos, emails), and hybrid (e.g., music, home movies). The hybrid category contained objects that were "physical instantiations of media content such as cassette tapes, video tapes, CDs and vinyl records" [p. 14]. Although it was not explicitly stated in the definition of the category, from the description provided it was clear that these objects were storage media (some digital, some not) that were separate from devices used to access the objects on that media. Objects stored on media that is contained within an access device, such as a hard drive in a personal computer, were instead included in the "digital" category of the taxonomy. It was the objects or content contained on these media that were important rather than the hybrid objects themselves: "the actual VHS or tape cassettes used for storage held no sentimental value whatsoever, but the content was considered to be very precious" [p. 14]. This content was what became invisible in deep storage.

Why should these hybrid objects be set apart? A detour into a phenomenological examination [4, 34] of how people experience digital objects as compared to physical objects provides insight into this question. As Kirk & Sellen noted, much of the content stored within hybrid objects could quite easily be transferred to a PC [20, p. 14]. That content is made up of digital objects, in that they are inscriptions on a storage medium that can be read by a computer. The taxonomy of digital, physical, and hybrid objects reflects differences in interaction: external storage media (hybrid objects) hold a place somewhere in between physical objects, which are immediately accessible to anyone close enough to touch them, and digital objects, which must be

[2] InterPARES (International Research on Permanent Authentic Records in Electronic Systems) is an SSHRC-funded project focused on the long-term preservation of authentic digital records (http://www.interpares.org/).

accessed through a device. External storage media physically represent the potential presence of digital object(s), without providing direct access. Although it is the content (the digital objects that are potentially accessible from the hybrid object) that is important, when the hybrid object is separated from the access device it becomes the only experientially available representation of those "content" objects. The hybrid object is opaque. The difference between objects on external storage media and digital objects that are stored within an access device is in the relationship between access and physical presence, which may be more important than has been previously acknowledged.

Experiencing Digital Objects

The importance of the ways in which people experience digital objects, as contrasted with experiencing physical objects, was also reflected in statements made by participants in home archiving studies. For instance, participants said that digital objects are not "solid" [13] and that they lack "physicality" [28]. Golsteijn et al. found that some of their participants did not think of digital objects as objects, because that term "implies a concrete, often physical, thing, which led them to select digital objects that were in fact, according to the classification used here[3], hybrid or physical objects" [13, p. 4]. As they are typically experienced in daily life, digital objects do not match expected notions of materiality as associated with physical objects. Although a physical inscription on a storage medium is a necessary component of a digital object, it is not the form of that object with which we typically interact. Instead, our interactions with digital objects as seen on a screen are mediated by keyboards, mice, game controllers, or at the very least the screen itself. The physical form of a digital object supports the object and is required for its existence, but is not the primary form of the object for computer users. For them, the object is instead what is on the screen, and that is not directly tangible. As one participant put it, "There is less physicality in the computer hard drive than having something on paper, which might fade, but you will still have an image" [28, p. 164]. This quote illuminates the important contrast in how object accessibility is related to materiality for digital and physical objects. With a paper document, the presence of the object means that the content is fully accessible. But with digital objects it is possible to have possession of the object as it physically exists on a storage medium without being able to access the object. These differences in the ways people experience physical objects and objects saved on external storage media proved to be central to interpreting clerks' actions at the DCFS office.

[3] Golsteijn et al. applied Kirk & Sellen's object taxonomy in their study.

METHODS

Four researchers individually observed work practices at the DCFS site four times each over a period of two months in 2013, for a total of 39.5 hours. Observation sessions were three to four hours long, averaging 3.5 hours per observation. For each observation session, a researcher shadowed one participant, observing work practices, interactions with colleagues, and the work environment as a whole. During observations, researchers took detailed notes and audio-recorded conversations between multiple participants. Photographs, hand-drawn maps of offices, and copies of forms used in work practices supplemented these notes and recordings. After observations were complete, researchers conducted eight short (1/2 hour) interviews with participants, asking follow-up questions and checking interpretations of data.

Four clerks and two managers, ranging in age from their twenties to their fifties, were employed at the DCFS office during the fieldwork and all were included in observations. Participants were Latino/a, African-American, and white. Three participants were female and three were male. One clerk had a college degree; the rest did not. Clerks were trained for their positions on the job and were not required to have previous records management experience. The clerks all worked in the same large room in cubicles with half-height walls (see Picture 1 below). The manager worked in the same room but had full-height cubicle walls.

Picture 1. One clerk's desk, with boxes sitting against the cubicle wall waiting for processing.

During the time when researchers were active in the field, they took notes on themes that arose during observations and while reviewing notes, and held meetings to discuss data. Post-fieldwork, researchers used ATLAS.ti qualitative coding software to code their own and others' notes, thereby confirming or rejecting the potential themes that arose during observations, and ensuring that themes were prevalent across observations by different researchers. The theme of the medium of the records, and variances in participant behavior related to records medium, was strongly present in researcher notes from the DCFS.

FINDINGS

In their work, the clerks dealt only with paper records and what they called "memorabilia," a catch-all term used to refer to all non-paper records, such as cassette tapes, CDs, DVDs, floppy disks, VHS tapes, and even photographs. Any external storage media in a case file was considered memorabilia. Born digital records created by case workers were housed in the digital records management system used by the department (Case Control), and were not the responsibility of the clerks. However, digital records that existed on storage media and were included in a case file were under the clerks' purview. Clerks used Case Control to verify the status of the case that they were reviewing (whether it was open or closed, had been merged with another case, and it's destruction date). Case Control also showed the physical location of the case files, whether a file contained memorabilia, and the names of the individuals involved with the case. The primary comparison of media in this environment was between paper media and non-paper media, or memorabilia (including hybrid media). The most crucial characteristic of memorabilia in this situation was whether it was directly accessible, like a photograph (similar to paper documents), or if it was opaque and unreachable without an access device. These concerns strongly echo concerns raised about hybrid objects in the home context [20]. Despite the wide variety of the media on which records were stored, decisions about how long records should be kept were not supposed to be influenced by the medium of the records.

The clerks used a document created by the larger records management division of the DCFS agency, the Case Processing document, to process case files. This document outlined the steps clerks should take in making decisions about keeping and destroying records. The Case Processing document was the primary embodiment, for the clerks, of the rules that they followed. Although the clerks themselves were likely not aware of ARMA policy (not having been educated as records managers), the Case Processing document that the clerks used was indeed created to reflect ARMA's medium-neutral rules: it made no distinctions between records on the basis of medium. Similarly, the agency's retention policies, which the Case Processing document was intended to enact, were also not medium-specific. The agency's retention policies were based on laws regarding records retention and were reflective of a general agreement within the profession of records management that retention policies should be based on the content of the records rather than their medium.

What is Long-term?

The clerks kept records that the state had a continued responsibility to retain, and the state was required to retain some of these records for an extremely long time. The clerks stored these "forever" records in a box labeled "4712." Boxes were typically labeled with the year during which the records within them could be destroyed (their destruction date). The year 4712 was a year that the clerks had decided was so outlandishly far off that it was an adequate representation of "forever." As one of the clerks said of a file, "We are going to end up storing this one until we are all long dead." Forever records were typically either adoption or conservatorship records. Other kinds of records handled by DCFS records management pertained to foster care and child protective services more generally.

As the records that were going to be stored the longest (and therefore under the responsibility of the state the longest), forever records were the most important. Any memorabilia associated with these were converted by an external contractor to digital form and stored in Case Control. This was an added expense and was not necessarily done for records whose destruction dates were in the foreseeable future. A different calculus of risk, expense, efficiency, and responsibility was carried out in those cases, which are discussed below.

Reconciliation Project: To Keep or Destroy

During the time period of the observations, the clerks were engaged in a large-scale project called the IMR, or Iron Mountain Reconciliation Project (Iron Mountain is a company that the state contracted for long-term records storage). Several clerks had been hired specifically to work on this project. The essential task of the project was to determine whether each case file should be kept or destroyed, and subsequently move it to the proper location as determined by the keep/destroy decision. Sometimes these decisions were extremely simple and only involved matching the case in front of the clerk with the case in the Case Control system, which allowed the clerk to confirm the destruction date. If there was a case number written on the outside of the file, the case was marked as closed in Case Control, and the case's destruction date had passed, the clerk would separate any memorabilia from the paper file and set paper and memorabilia aside for destruction. However, keep/destroy decisions could easily become complicated, requiring a more thorough investigation of the contents of case files.

In the absence of a case number the clerks would have to try to identify the case by the names of the individuals in the file, which could be difficult because of name changes or the existence of multiple individuals with the same name in the system. An additional complication was that cases that might initially appear to be closed (based solely on the birth-date of the youngest child in the case) could have been merged with other cases, which happened frequently when there were multiple cases within one family. For instance, a case involving an older sibling might be closed when that child turned eighteen, "aging out" of the system, but it would often instead be merged with a case involving a younger sibling, because it contained documentation that was relevant to that latter case.

The clerks knew that the records in their care were very serious for the people represented in those records, and they sympathized with those people. The records sometimes represented abuse cases in which the state had the responsibility to protect the victims. One clerk, Louisa, said of the records, "sometimes I can't believe that someone could be that cruel. I mean some of the stuff you read will tear your heart out." Louisa also mentioned that once, while in a different position within the DCFS, she encountered a young man who was trying to get disability benefits and needed his records to do so. Unfortunately, his records could not be found, and the man therefore could not receive disability benefits. As Max, one of the managers, said, "I think that some of these kids that phase out of our system... the only records that we have [are] really the records of their life, I mean there's no parents involved..." In these cases, the DCFS could be the only reliable source of personal history for the people represented in the records. These were the records that the clerks were making keep/destroy decisions about on a daily basis.

Picture 2. Stacks of boxes in the DCFS office. The gray bins contain memorabilia that will be destroyed.

Despite the potential significance of those decisions, however, they were decisions that the clerks made hundreds of times in a week. The IMR project was projected to take at least two years, or possibly as long as four. One clerk mentioned that he had heard there were 60,000 boxes that had to be checked as part of the project. Shipments of fifty boxes were delivered multiple times a week and were stacked in the office, immediately outside of the clerks' cubicles (see Picture 2 above). Tensions in the office rose and fell with the level of the boxes, which were a visible reminder of the amount of work to be done, and could grow threateningly high if the clerks got behind schedule. Each day, the clerks turned in a productivity report detailing the number of boxes processed that day.

The clerks' decision-making processes (as they determined which records should be kept and which could be destroyed) have important implications for how people interact with objects of varying media. As discussed above, clerks often had to closely examine paper files to determine the keep/destroy status of a record. The following sections discuss how the necessity for investigation played out when the records were stored on memorabilia rather than paper.

Accessible Memorabilia

Although memorabilia was often interspersed in paper files, sometimes it would be stored in boxes with other memorabilia of the same media, separately from its associated paper files. In this situation, it was easy for an object to be disassociated from its case number, which often meant additional investigative work for the clerks. Two of the clerks, Lance and Daryl, were sometimes assigned the task of handling these "media" boxes, as they were known. During one observation, Daryl spent several hours going through boxes of DVDs that had been enclosed in manila envelopes (on which case numbers and other information might be written). Occasionally, there would be confusion in determining the correct keep/destroy decision as in the case discussed in the conversation below, when the information in Case Control did not match the information on the envelope. In such instances, Daryl would have to ask a manager, Ashley, for assistance.

> Ashley: What did you find?
> Daryl: This has a case number, but...
> A: Ok. Go ahead and open it. [He does.] Which box was that in?
> D: [Recites the box ID number.]
> A: Is that the same number? Oh, no it's a different one [They are looking at her computer.] It's here... but not in Case Control. If it had been merged, it would be here. You could see the child's name, but it's not here... unless she changed her name.

They ended up accessing the DVD on Ashley's computer, and saw an interview with a child whose name allowed them to determine which case the DVD was associated with.

Later, Daryl encountered a similar problem and attempted to resolve it without involving Ashley, but had trouble accessing the DVD on his computer.

> Daryl: That's not good.
> Observer: What's going on?
> D: I don't know. It's not loading the DVD. I don't know if it's the DVD drive or...

He and Ashley were able to access the DVD on her computer. Despite the fact that he could not access it on his computer, because there was an available access device in the office, Daryl did check the DVD. However, if a clerk came across external storage media in a file that was not accessible by any device currently available in the office, that might end investigation for that file and lead to a destroy decision. The next section describes how clerks could use inaccessibility as an indicator for a destroy decision.

Technological Obsolescence

Media obsolescence leading to inaccessibility was considered to be potentially a good enough reason to determine that a non-paper record was a destroy record, as discussed in an interview with Daryl.

> Daryl: I have come across a couple floppy disks, I've never had to insert them, and even if I did we don't even have slots for them anymore.
> Interviewer: You don't have floppy drives.
> D: So, that's a pretty good sign that that's going to be destruction.
> I: Yeah.
> D: We can just toss that right away.
> I: Just because it's –
> D: – And the same with VHS tapes, if it's that old, like, that's just a good sign that it's not active anymore.

With paper records, while apparent age contributed to the categorization of the records as destroy records, it was never the deciding factor. A clerk might note the obvious age of some paper records he or she was dealing with when pulling a hardened rubber band or rusted paper clip off of a folder, but this was not a legitimate reason to abandon the normal process for checking the age of the records – the rules for case processing required that destruction decisions be made based on the destruction date for the case as listed in Case Control. The clerk would still look for further evidence of age within the informational content of the record (a process the clerks referred to as "doing research"). The decision tree below (Figure 1) describes the decision-making process with a focus on how the medium of the records could influence that process.

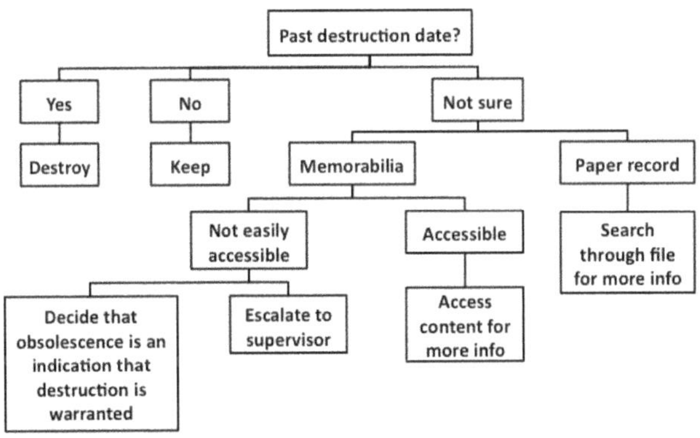

Figure 1: Simplified decision tree for the keep/destroy decision-making process.

Time spent on work tasks and progress towards the larger goal of completing the IMR project were ever present factors in the clerks' decision-making processes. Issues of time and progress combined to form the pressure of efficiency.

The clerks' awareness of the potential consequence of the records manifested as the responsibility they felt to do research into the contents of the records to accurately determine destruction dates. When we began our field work, Ashley was the manager in charge of the office. She left the DCFS after we had been observing the office for one week, and was replaced by Max, a manager from another DCFS office. After Ashley's departure, the clerks revealed that they had concerns about some of her policies. They felt that these policies did not align with agency guidelines for their work, and did not fully meet the responsibilities of the office with regards to the records, as discussed in the following quote drawn from a conversation between all four of the clerks.

> Daryl: Honestly I think she was just telling us… whatever, to get stuff out.
> Marcela: Well that's what I'm saying that's why they can't believe that we're already through with phase one, and we went through it that quickly… Well that's because, she basically told us, why are we doing research, just toss it. All the ones from '95, toss 'em. But the destruction date, if you look on the paper it says 2013, and we're only in February.

The clerks were concerned because Ashley had instructed them not to do research into the cases, in the interests of efficiency. However, they did not feel that this was in line with agency policy. Ashley also told them to destroy all files with a destruction date of 2013, despite the fact that 2013 files with a December date should not have been destroyed for another eleven months – directly contradicting the Case Processing guidelines which required that destruction decisions be based on the destruction date assigned to a record. The clerks were concerned that they might be held responsible for any improper records destruction that had occurred during Ashley's tenure (a concern that did not to our knowledge bear out). This conversation starkly illustrates the conflict between the pressures of responsibility for records and the clerks' efficiency at their jobs. While Ashley's directives against doing research applied equally to paper and non-paper records, this example shows that the clerks' speed in checking records was at issue in evaluations of their work, and doing research on non-paper records was more time consuming than doing research on paper records because of issues of accessibility.

Because the rules that the clerks followed did not mention medium as a potential issue, clerks were left without specific guidance to follow when they encountered obsolete and inaccessible media. The records management policy that medium was not a significant factor in designations of objects as records, while intended to elevate digital records to the status of paper records, instead had an opposite effect in this case. Material differences between the two types of records forced the clerks into a difficult choice, as illustrated in Figure 1. Efficiency pressures implicitly discouraged clerks from involving a supervisor in investigating inaccessible media, thereby encouraging clerks to use obsolescence as a reason to destroy a record.

DISCUSSION

Unclear dating in documents complicated the routine keep/destroy decisions of records management work. Complicated keep/destroy decisions required the clerks to do research, which was relatively simple with paper documents, took slightly more effort with records on accessible storage media, and was difficult (and expensive) to do with records on obsolete media. When records resisted investigation due to technological obsolescence, we saw clerks make one of two decisions: to defer the issue to their supervisor, or to interpret the lack of accessibility as grounds to destroy the record (Figure 1). The evidence in these records, which may have legal, financial, and personal weight, is then lost. Accessibility was clearly central in determining which records were investigated and which were not, but what other possible explanations exist for this apparent privileging of paper records over non-paper records?

Materiality

Because materiality is central to the experience of interacting with objects, it goes hand in hand with a phenomenological approach to investigating those interactions. The recent material turn in HCI [31] has taken many forms [29]. In line with this focus, we examine "the materiality of technological things as they are used and incorporated into everyday contexts and practices" [29, p. 119]. Observations at the DCFS showed that the specific material nature of the memorabilia required separate procedures from paper records. Paper files and memorabilia had to be separated for destruction, due to differing destruction processes for each type of record. Paper and external storage media also have diverging environmental requirements for safe long-term preservation (differing acceptable temperature and humidity ranges), which meant that when they had been properly processed for storage they would be kept in separate boxes (although it was not unusual for more hastily processed files to contain memorabilia). These differences in the materialities of paper and external storage media required differentiations between the two types of records in work practices. Max would question the clerks about how many reconciliation boxes had been completed and how many media boxes had been completed, highlighting how the varying material natures of each type of record caused them to be dealt with separately in daily work processes, despite their purportedly equal nature as records. This, combined with the different experiences of interacting with digital and physical objects as discussed above, made it difficult for clerks to treat the two types of objects as equal records.

Background Expectations

When examining users' attitudes towards technologies, it is necessary to consider not only the current contexts of actions but also past experiences, as these together help to shape users' understandings of the contexts in which they act. Winograd & Flores describe this situation: "...the world is encountered as something always already lived in, worked in, and acted upon. World as the background of obviousness is manifest in our everyday dealings as the familiarity that pervades our situation..." [34, p. 58]. Although they emphasize the importance of background expectations of users, Winograd & Flores acknowledge that we cannot ever expect to understand and represent those expectations completely, and of course details of users' backgrounds are not often available to designers. However, it would be unwise to ignore users' background understandings entirely, and there are some broad types of experiences with which most computer users would be familiar.

Because many computer users have been interacting with computers from childhood, they have experienced multiple shifts in computing technology. These shifts often render digital objects inaccessible as access and storage devices wear out or are disposed of, or software becomes obsolete. Daryl's statements above about floppy disks that "we don't even have slots for them anymore" and "if it's that old, like, that's just a good sign that it's not active anymore," suggest that he has had experience with technological obsolescence in the past, and that that experience is affecting decisions he makes in the process of his work. This is likely to be true not only of the other clerks in our study, but also of many of the participants in the home archiving studies. Even in the context of the DCFS, when clerks knew the potential importance of the records saved on obsolete storage media, the inaccessibility of the medium made the objects seem easier to relinquish. In the home context, dismissing invisible digital objects on opaque storage media may be even easier to do.

Previous research into the subject of differing interactions with physical and digital objects has not, to this point, put a major emphasis on issues of technological obsolescence and access. Findings from this study suggest that these aspects of the subject require further investigation. To encourage thinking of digital belongings as belongings that are worth investing in emotionally, it will be necessary to support people in thinking of those belongings as objects that have the potential to be long-lasting.

Regular experiences that occur over a long period of time are likely to affect peoples' expectations for different kinds of objects. This applies not only to digital objects, but also to our understandings of categories of objects such as "records." The paper record is the traditional form of the record and is therefore the standard for that form. Clerks were likely basing their expectations for the "recordness" of objects on their experiences of paper records. The ways in which records on other media were different from paper records could make them seem less legitimate as records. For instance, the ease of access to the information in the paper record is likely to reinforce its primacy as the most legitimate medium for records. Anyone who is literate and knows the language in which a paper record is written is able to access that record if it is in front of them. Paper records do not require additional translation in the form of software and hardware, as digital records do.

DESIGN IMPLICATIONS

This study suggests that there is a basic aspect of human interactions with technology that is likely to affect how and whether people consider digital objects as objects that potentially can exist for a long period of time – technological obsolescence. Although recent work in HCI [17, 21] has discussed obsolescence in somewhat different contexts from the ones described here, and there are important connections between problems of obsolescence and the focus on sustainability in HCI [30], this issue has not yet been thoroughly investigated. It has been similarly understudied in the history of technology [3], and while a focus on obsolescence is quite central to the study of digital preservation within cultural heritage institutions, that work generally focuses on pushing back against obsolescence for the purposes of preservation rather than understanding how users anticipate and react to it in their daily lives. Our findings reinforce the suggestion [23] that technologies specifically designed to last even when accessed infrequently would support users in thinking of digital objects as long-lasting and valuable possessions.

Our argument is not that external storage is inherently bad; for instance, similar issues could occur with old files that are associated with obsolete software. In that case, the bridge between the base inscription on external storage media or hard disk and the visual object on the screen has collapsed. The hardware-software stack is missing one or more essential connecting pieces. The issue instead is that the eventualities of obsolescence, and the expectations they engender in users, should be taken into consideration.

Technological obsolescence is not the only critical issue in examining interactions with digital objects over the long-term. We have also argued that closely considering the variances in how people interact with digital and physical objects will help in understanding differences in how they value those objects. These variances may be partially due to the different ways we experience the two types of objects as material. Not only do the distinct material natures of digital and physical objects often require contrasting treatment (as in storage requirements at the DCFS), but they also force differences in interactions. The user is always separated from the physical medium on which a digital object is stored, and interaction with that object is mediated through an access device. In contrast, physical objects are interacted with in a very direct, immediate, and tangible experience.

CONCLUSIONS

Despite the disparate settings of the HCI studies of home archiving and our study's location in a workplace, there are similarities in the examination of interactions with digital and physical objects, and the idea of preserving objects for future use by others. In this study, participants faced similar questions to home PC users in deciding whether older digital objects were valuable. These were questions such as: Do I have any indication of what the objects are (perhaps a label on storage media)? Is the hardware and software that would be needed to access the objects available to me? Are the objects potentially important to me or someone I care about? Will it make a difference to anyone if I do not try to retrieve these objects?

In the end, however, paper records seemed to have a legitimacy in the eyes of our participants that non-paper records did not have; non-paper objects were not long-lasting objects for them in the way that paper objects were. We have argued that this was related to their expectations for different kinds of records (technological obsolescence and paper as the traditional records medium), as well as differences in how paper and non-paper records were materially experienced. Although further research is needed to determine differences and similarities across various settings, the similarities between the issues our participants faced and those discussed in the home archiving studies support the idea these problems are relevant in a broad variety of situations.

ACKNOWLEDGMENTS

We thank the Institute of Museum and Library Services Laura Bush 21st Century Librarian Program for its generous funding of this research (Award #RE-02-12-0009-12), as well as Diane Bailey not only for her implementation and organization of the project, but for generously sharing her knowledge of and experience with ethnographic methods. Thanks also to Ramona Broussard, our excellent research partner in observing work practices at the DCFS, and Melanie Feinberg for her comments on an early version of this paper.

REFERENCES

1. Barreau, D., & Nardi, B. A. Finding and reminding: File organization from the desktop. *SIGCHI Bull. 27*, 3 (1995), 39–43.
2. Boardman, R., & Sasse, M. A. "Stuff goes into the computer and doesn't come out": a cross-tool study of personal information management. In *Proc. SIGCHI Conference on Human Factors in Computing Systems* (2004) (pp. 583–590). New York, NY, USA: ACM.
3. Campbell, S. M. On the absence of obsolescence. *IEEE Annals of the History of Computing 31*, 4 (2009), 118–120.
4. Dourish, P. *Where the action is: The foundations of embodied interaction*. MIT Press, Cambridge, MA, USA, 2001.
5. Duranti, L. Reliability and authenticity: The concepts and their implications. *Archivaria 1*, 39 (1995).
6. Duranti, L. Concepts and principles for the management of electronic records, or records management theory is

archival diplomatics. *Records Management Journal 20*, 1 (2010a), 78–95.

7. Duranti, L. From digital diplomatics to digital records forensics. *Archivaria 68*, 68 (2010b).
8. Duranti, L., & MacNeil, H. The protection of the integrity of electronic records: An overview of the UBC-MAS research project. *Archivaria 1*, 42 (1996).
9. Duranti, L., & Thibodeau, K. The concept of record in interactive, experiential and dynamic environments: The view of InterPARES*. *Archival Science 6*, 1 (2006), 13–68.
10. Galloway, P. Preservation of digital objects. *Annual Review of Information Science and Technology*, Vol. 38 (2003), 549–590.
11. *Generally Accepted Recordkeeping Principles*. ARMA International. 2014. Retrieved from http://www.arma.org/r2/generally-accepted-br-recordkeeping-principles.
12. Ginn, M. L. (Ed.). *Retention Management for Records and Information*. ARMA International, Lenexa, KS, USA, 2009.
13. Golsteijn, C., van den Hoven, E., Frohlich, D., & Sellen, A. Towards a more cherishable digital object. *Proc DIS 2012*, ACM Press (2012), 655–664.
14. Gulotta, R., Odom, W., Forlizzi, J., & Faste, H. (2013). Digital artifacts as legacy: Exploring the lifespan and value of digital data. *Proc. CHI 2013*, ACM Press (2013), 1813–1822.
15. Hughes, J. A., Randall, D., & Shapiro, D. Faltering from Ethnography to Design. In *Proc. CSCW 1992*, ACM Press (1992), 115–122.
16. *International Standard on Records Management*. ISO 15489-1:2001. Geneva, Switzerland: ISO.
17. Jackson, S. J., & Kang, L. Breakdown, obsolescence and reuse: HCI and the art of repair. *Proc. CHI 2014*, ACM Press (2014), 449–458.
18. Kaye, J. "Jofish," Vertesi, J., Avery, S., Dafoe, A., David, S., Onaga, L., ... Pinch, T. To have and to hold: Exploring the personal archive. *Proc. CHI 2006*, ACM Press (2006), 275–284.
19. Kirk, D. S., Izadi, S., Sellen, A., Taylor, S., Banks, R., & Hilliges, O. Opening up the family archive. *Proc. CSCW 2010*, ACM Press (2010), 261–270.
20. Kirk, D. S., & Sellen, A. On human remains: Values and practice in the home archiving of cherished objects. *ACM Trans. Comput.-Hum. Interact. 17*, 3 (2010), 10:1–10:43.
21. Lomas, D., Kumar, A., Patel, K., Ching, D., Lakshmanan, M., Kam, M., & Forlizzi, J. L. The power of play: Design lessons for increasing the lifespan of outdated computers. *Proc. CHI 2013*, ACM Press (2013), 2735–2744.
22. Malone, T. W. How do people organize their desks?: Implications for the design of office information systems. *ACM Trans. Inf. Syst., 1*, 1 (1983), 99–112.
23. Odom, W., Banks, R., Kirk, D., Harper, R., Lindley, S., & Sellen, A. Technology heirlooms?: Considerations for passing down and inheriting digital materials. *Proc. CHI 2012*, ACM Press (2012), 337–346.
24. Odom, W., Sellen, A., Harper, R., & Thereska, E. (2012). Lost in translation: Understanding the possession of digital things in the cloud. *Proc. CHI 2012*, ACM Press (2012), 781–790.
25. Odom, W., Zimmerman, J., & Forlizzi, J. Teenagers and their virtual possessions: Design opportunities and issues. *Proc. CHI 2011*, ACM Press (2011), 1491–1500.
26. Odom, W., Zimmerman, J., Forlizzi, J., Choi, H., Meier, S., & Park, A. Investigating the presence, form and behavior of virtual possessions in the context of a teen bedroom. *Proc. CHI 2012*, ACM Press (2012), 327–336.
27. Pearce-Moses, R. Record. *A Glossary of Archival and Records Terminology*. Society of American Archivists, 2005.
28. Petrelli, D., & Whittaker, S. Family memories in the home: Contrasting physical and digital mementos. *Personal Ubiquitous Comput., 14*, 2 (2010), 153–169.
29. Pierce, J., & Paulos, E. Electric materialities and interactive technology. *Proc. CHI 2013*, ACM Press (2013), 119–128.
30. Remy, J.C. & Huang, E. Addressing the Obsolescence of End-User Devices: Approaches from the Field of Sustainable HCI. In Hilty, L.M., Aebischer, B. (eds.) ICT Innovations for Sustainability. Springer (2014), 257 - 267.
31. Robles, E., & Wiberg, M. Texturing the "Material Turn" in Interaction Design. In *Proc TEI 2010*, ACM Press (2010), 137–144.
32. Rothenberg, J. *Avoiding technological quicksand: Finding a viable technical foundation for digital preservation*. No. 77, Council on Library and Information Resources (CLIR), Washington, DC, USA, 1998.
33. Sellen, A., & Harper, R. *The Myth of the Paperless Office*. MIT Press, Cambridge, MA, USA, 2001.
34. Winograd, T., & Flores, F. *Understanding computers and cognition: A new foundation for design*. Ablex Corporation, Norwood, NJ, USA, 1986.

Investigating the Dexterity of Multi-Finger Input for Mid-Air Text Entry

Srinath Sridhar[1] **Anna Maria Feit**[2] **Christian Theobalt**[1] **Antti Oulasvirta**[2]

[1]Max Planck Institute for Informatics
{ssridhar,theobalt}@mpi-inf.mpg.de

[2]Aalto University
{anna.feit,antti.oulasvirta}@aalto.fi

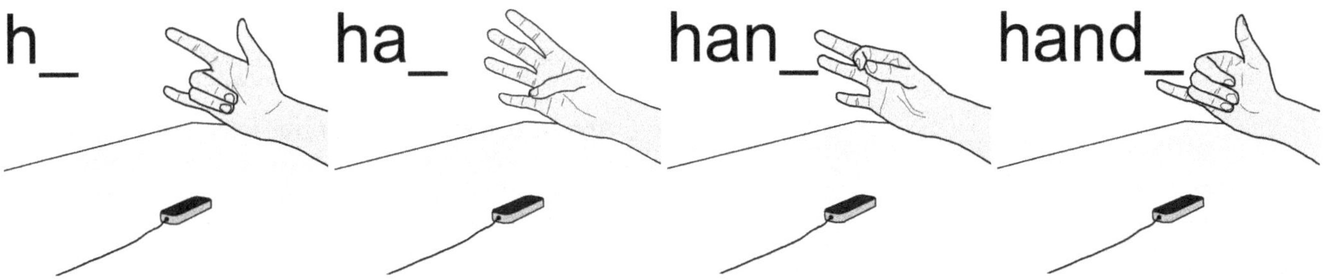

Figure 1. We investigate the dexterity of using multiple fingers for mid-air input. The paper reports performance and individuation characteristics of fingers and deploys them to the design of a mid-air text entry method using multi-objective optimization. Here we show an example of the word 'hand' being typed using one of our automatically obtained designs.

ABSTRACT

This paper investigates an emerging input method enabled by progress in hand tracking: input by free motion of fingers. The method is expressive, potentially fast, and usable across many settings as it does not insist on physical contact or visual feedback. Our goal is to inform the design of high-performance input methods by providing detailed analysis of the performance and anatomical characteristics of finger motion. We conducted an experiment using a commercially available sensor to report on the speed, accuracy, individuation, movement ranges, and individual differences of each finger. Findings show differences of up to 50% in movement times and provide indices quantifying the individuation of single fingers. We apply our findings to text entry by computational optimization of multi-finger gestures in mid-air. To this end, we define a novel objective function that considers performance, anatomical factors, and learnability. First investigations of one optimization case show entry rates of 22 words per minute (WPM). We conclude with a critical discussion of the limitations posed by human factors and performance characteristics of existing markerless hand trackers.

Author Keywords

Mid-air interaction; freehand input; Fitts' law; text entry

ACM Classification Keywords

H.5.m. Information Interfaces and Presentation (e.g. HCI): Miscellaneous

CHI 2015,, April 18 - 23, 2015, Seoul, Republic of Korea

ACM 978-1-4503-3145-6/15/04...$15.00
http://dx.doi.org/10.1145/2702123.2702136

INTRODUCTION

This paper investigates an emerging category of input enabled by progress in computer vision-based hand tracking: *input by free motion of the hand involving any and all fingers*. Until recently, computer vision-based input was limited to gross movements of the arm and a few basic hand poses like pinching [3, 39]. However, recent methods can track full hand articulation using a single camera (*e.g.* [21, 27]). Leveraging the hand's capacity "directly" without intermediary devices like joysticks or buttons has always appealed to HCI researchers. With its many degrees of freedom, and fast and precise movements, the hand is the most dexterous of the extremities [12, 19]. Furthermore, freehand motion could provide an always-on input method, as only a camera is required. The method could alleviate the known input limitations of wearable or mobile devices.

Our goal is to inform the design of *high performance input* using multiple fingers in mid-air. High performance is decisive in activities like text entry, virtual reality, command selection, and gaming. However, previous work has focused on eliciting intuitive multi-finger gestures from users [23, 26]. This leaves out many issues, including performance characteristics of gestures involving single and multiple fingers simultaneously. To push the field forward, designers need to know some key factors affecting performance: How fast can users move their fingers? Can all fingers be moved independently and accurately? What are their movement ranges? How to combine fingers with different properties in one gesture?

Our work focuses on chord-like motions in mid-air as shown in Figure 1. These are easy-to-perform and familiar gestures, and among the few gesture categories that current computer vision sensors can reliably track. In this input gesture, there is no external target like a button (cf. most previous work on mid-air text entry [1, 20, 25, 35]). The involved fingers are extended or flexed at a single joint to a discriminable end posture. Although this input method *can* be used with visual feedback, it allows for eyes-free input after memorization.

We extensively study the dexterity of single fingers in a target selection task. Users were asked to move a finger quickly and accurately between two *angular targets* (*e.g.* from a neutral resting position to the maximum position "down"). We assess each finger separately to report on three critical factors:

- **Speed and accuracy** of angular motions of fingers measured by Fitts' law models [17].
- **Individuation** of fingers, as measured by the so-called Schieber index [33]. It captures the extent to which non-instructed fingers remain still when a finger is moved.
- **Comfortable motion ranges** of fingers reported by users.

The results afford several insights. First, we report performance characteristics of each finger. The data show differences of up to 50% in movement times. Second, we asked users to move fingers *comfortably* and report on their motion ranges when using computer vision tracking. Third, to our knowledge, this is the first paper to report individuation indices for joints in HCI. For the middle and ring finger, coactivation can be so high that input may be compromised by false activations. In contrast, coactivation of other fingers while moving the thumb is virtually non-existent. We argue that individuation is a critical consideration in multi-finger input in mid-air which lacks physical resistance.

Our second contribution is to propose how to use this data in the design of high-throughput gesture sets. While our study considered only single joints, we attempt to apply our findings in the design of *multi-finger* input. The approach builds on literature in motor learning and assumes that multi-finger performance is limited by the *slowest* joint [13, 32]. Moreover, we exploit the fact that individuation constraints do not apply if co-dependent fingers participate together in a gesture. The benefit of these two assumptions is that the derivation of models to inform hand gestures is significantly less expensive than a study that tried to look at *all* combinations of fingers. Even with only three discretization levels per joint such an approach would have to cover roughly 10^{10} gestures. Finally, we use our findings to construct a proof-of-concept objective function called PALM to optimize text entry in mid-air. PALM considers performance (P), anatomical comfort (A: *i.e.* individuation), learnability (L), and mnemonics (M) to optimize multi-finger gestures. First investigations of a text entry method optimized for one-handed input show entry rates of 22 WPM. However, we note that users' performance was limited by brief training times, individuation constraints, and relatively limited performance of the tracker.

To summarize, this paper informs the design of high-performance input methods in mid-air by

1. providing ready-to-use models and look-up tables on performance, individuation and movement ranges of fingers, and
2. showing the applicability of the results by proposing an extension to multi-joint gestures and exploring its use in the multi-objective optimization of mid-air text entry methods.

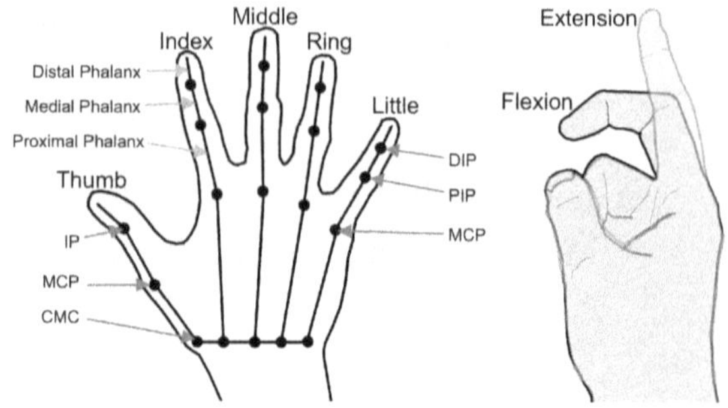

Figure 2. Left: Aspects of human hand anatomy with bones (green) and joints (blue). Right: We focus on *flexion-extension* of the five fingers.

BACKGROUND: CHARACTERISTICS OF FINGER MOTION

Our investigation of multi-finger input is informed by hand anatomy, the degrees of freedom of its joints, the performance of finger motion, and the limitations posed by dependencies on finger movement.

The Kinematic Skeleton

The skeleton of the human hand has 27 bones, the interfaces of which form the wrist and finger joints [12, 32] (Figure 2 shows a simplified skeleton). Together, this results in more than 25 degrees of freedom (DOFs) for the hand. In this paper, we focus on a subset of these DOFs. Finger movement (*flexion–extension* and *abduction–adduction*) is controlled by extrinsic muscles in the arm and intrinsic muscles in the hand. All joints except the Metacarpophalangeal (MCP—Index, Middle, Ring, and Little), and carpometacarpal (CMC—Thumb) have one DOF each. As humans we can describe hand gestures with terms like *thumbs up* or *v sign*. However, a formal representation is needed for study and use in computer vision-based input. We use a *kinematic skeleton* [24] to parametrize gestures. The hand skeleton configuration Θ can be specified by angles of the joints connecting the bones, *i.e.* $\Theta = [\theta_1, \theta_2, \ldots, \theta_i]^{\mathrm{T}}$, $\theta \in \mathcal{R}$.

Movement Performance

Finger movement performance can be quantified by movement time MT which is the time it takes for an end-effector to reach a target from a given distance. Fitts' law has been highly successful for predicting MT with traditional input devices [17]. It estimates the upper bound of pointing performance achievable after practice. Given a target of width W and distance D, Fitts' law states that the MT to reach the target is given by $MT = a + b\log_2(D/W + 1)$. Fitts' law has also been used previously to quantify performance differences in fingers, wrist, and forearm [4, 7, 15, 18, 28]. However, in this work, we use *angular* motions at joints instead of translation [14]. Considering the angular target width α_W and distance β_D, we get:

$$mt_\theta = a_\theta + b_\theta \log_2\left(\frac{\alpha_D}{\beta_W} + 1\right). \quad (1)$$

To acquire the a and b parameters, we conduct an experiment that employs a unidimensional pointing task. We address speed–accuracy trade-off in this task by using *effective* width $\bar{W}$ and distance $\bar{D}$.

Inter-Finger Dependencies
Movements of the hand act over multiple joints which makes coactivation of non-contributing joints common [12]. For example, many people cannot move their ring finger without coactivated movement of the little finger. More generally, coactivation is known to be larger among the metacarpophalangeal and the proximal interphalangeal joints [12, 33]. Hand gestures should minimize the extent of *unintended coactivation* of non-instructed fingers. Coactivations can be hard to inhibit and can cause recognition errors.

Schieber [33] proposed an *index of individuation* that indicates how independently an instructed finger can be moved from all others. The index was modeled for monkeys and humans [10]. A fully independent finger does not involve coactivation of other fingers during its activation, or vice versa. The individuation index is widely known in neuroscience, but largely disregarded in HCI. In order to compute it for every finger, the position of the non-instructed digit is plotted as a function of the instructed digit's position. The resulting trajectories are typically linear and the slope of a line fitted to these data points serves as a measure for the *relative coactivation*: the extent to which a non-instructed finger moves relative to the instructed finger. Given the coactivation C_{ij} of finger i during the movement of finger j, the individuation index of j is

$$I_j = 1 - [(\sum_{i=1}^{n} \mid C_{ij} \mid -1)/(n-1)], \qquad (2)$$

where $n = 5$ is the number of fingers. $I_j = 1$ indicates perfectly individuated movement, and $I_j = 0$ if all non-instructed fingers move simultaneously with j. The original study of individuation was reported for fingers, but it can be extended to multiple *joints* used in multi-finger input.

EXPERIMENT: FINGER DEXTERITY
Our experimental method is based on the reciprocal selection task used in Fitts' law studies [17]. As shown in Figure 3, users move a finger between two targets. Instead of extrinsic targets (*e.g.* buttons), the target here is a joint angle. Visual feedback is provided on a monitor with high refresh rate. In contrast to most Fitts' law studies, we track not only the endpoints of movements but the full motion of the hand. This allows us to quantify three aspects of the dexterity of finger motion: performance (speed and accuracy), individuation (unwanted motion of non-instructed fingers), and comfortable motion ranges. In addition, the data allow us to look at the range of individual differences.

We chose to focus on six joints spanning seven degrees of freedom (see Figure 3). This selection is motivated by the capabilities of present-day trackers and our pursuit of studying joints that could be a "class" of input motions. We conducted a pilot study of the Leap Motion sensor[1] and learned that individuated motions of interphalangeal joints are not well tracked, except for the thumb. Therefore, we decided to focus on the flexion/extension of the MCP joints of the fingers and the CMC joint of the thumb, which intuitively correspond

[1] `https://www.leapmotion.com/`

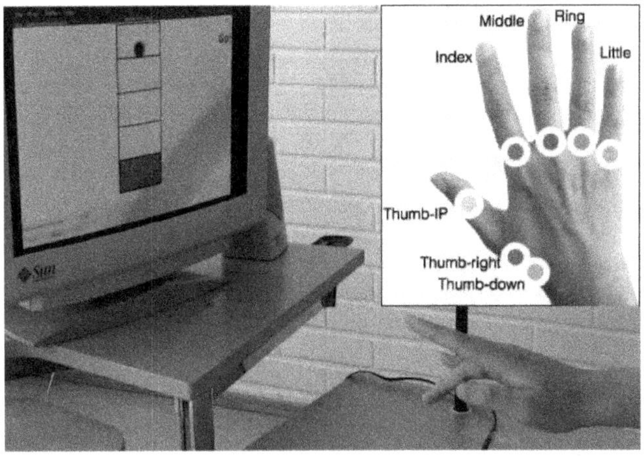

Figure 3. The experiment investigates the dexterity of six joints that can be reliably tracked with the Leap Motion sensor. The user is asked to move a finger between two target angles indicated on a display. Full hand motion was tracked. The color coding for joints is used in the Results section. Note that the CMC joint of the thumb is a special case, as it can be independently moved in two directions.

to "up" and "down" movements when the hand is in a neutral pose. Moreover, we included the IP joint of the thumb which was the only interphalangeal joint that could be moved *and* tracked well. Figure 3 also shows our naming convention and color coding used in the rest of the paper. For the thumb we use Thumb-Down and Thumb-Right to denote "up-down" and "left-right" movement of the CMC joint.

Participants
The study was conducted with 13 participants (8 male and 5 female) at two different locations. All participants were right-handed and had an age ranging from 22 to 32 (mean 27). Due to technical issues, one of the participants completed only 4 of the 7 joint conditions. The experiment took 1.5–2 hours per participant. Participants from one location were compensated with cinema vouchers. The trials were carried out under controlled lighting conditions with no distractions.

Experimental Design
The experiment followed a 7×4 within-subjects design with 7 DOFs and 4 index of difficulty (ID) conditions. To minimize order effects, the DOFs and ID conditions were randomized for each participant. Pre-trial practice was employed and breaks were provided after the trial for each joint.

Task, Materials, and Procedure
The task was a unidimensional target selection task. Participants had to move a pointer up and down between two targets on a screen and were instructed to move as fast and accurately as possible without moving non-instructed fingers too much. Control occurred by angular motions of joints that were linearly mapped to a pointer on the display. A trial would start from a comfortable neutral pose. The target region turned green when the pointer reached it and the user had to change direction to select the previous target again. In each condition, users had to perform 50 repetitions. Auditory feedback was given in the form of a low-frequency click. Throughout, participants placed their hand in a horizontal position over the sensor with their arm resting on a support.

Because of anatomical differences, we determined the movement range of each user experimentally, and used it to determine concrete target widths and distances for each user. Therefore, we first recorded the user-specific angular limits of each joint at the beginning of each task. We asked the participants to flex and extend the joint without moving the other fingers too much. The corresponding movement range was then uniformly divided into 2, 3, 4, and 5 bins. This gave us the same four unique IDs for every user: 1, 1.6, 2 and 2.3. Over all discretization levels there were 10 different target pairs for each joint, resulting in $7 \times 10 = 70$ conditions.

Apparatus

The joint angles were tracked using the Leap Motion by transforming its output to a kinematic skeleton. The software for tracking and display of the task ran on a fast desktop computer (3.1 GHz Intel i7 at one place, 3.1 GHz Intel i5 at the other). We showed visual feedback on high refresh rate monitors (112 Hz CRT and 120 Hz LCD respectively) and the Leap Motion was capable of tracking at up to 100 Hz.

Analysis

Performance: The design and evaluation of the Fitts' law task was done according to [36]. Movements with a movement time or distance beyond 3 SD of the median were excluded. Accuracy was adjusted to allow an error rate of 5%, a rate common in high-performance tasks such as text entry. Based on the remaining movements, we determined the *effective* target width $\bar{W}_{5\%}$ and distance $\bar{D}_{5\%}$ which was used to compute the effective index of difficulty (ID_e) of each task: $ID_e = log_2(\frac{\bar{W}_{5\%}}{\bar{D}_{5\%}} + 1)$. This indicates the actual difficulty of the performed task and captures the speed–accuracy trade-off. To account for individual differences, we cluster the effective IDs into 5 equally sized bins and compute the average movement time within each bin. For this purpose, we excluded data points with an effective ID of 3 SD beyond the median. Least-squares linear regression was then used to determine the slope and intercept of the Fitts' law model.

Individuation: We followed the protocol described in [33] to determine individuation indices. We first plotted, separately for each user, the normalized angle of every *non-instructed* joint as a function of the normalized angle of an instructed joint. The resulting 500 trajectories were then averaged by taking the median. Outliers beyond 3 SD of the median were excluded. The slopes of the resulting data were determined by least-squares linear regression. While linear movement trajectories were the norm, there were a few outliers where a linear relationship could not be determined. We observed two reasons: (1) Problems in tracking the joint angle (Figure 5 (b)) and (2) drifting of fingers, a phenomenon in which the non-instructed joint gradually changes its angle due to fatigue, inattention, or corrective behavior (Figure 5 (c)). To account for this, we excluded models with a fit of $R^2 < 0.5$. As suggested by Schieber, we averaged the *absolute* value for each slope, to generalize the relative individuation over all participants. These values were then used to compute the individuation index. In the next section, we report findings for performance, individuation, and movement ranges.

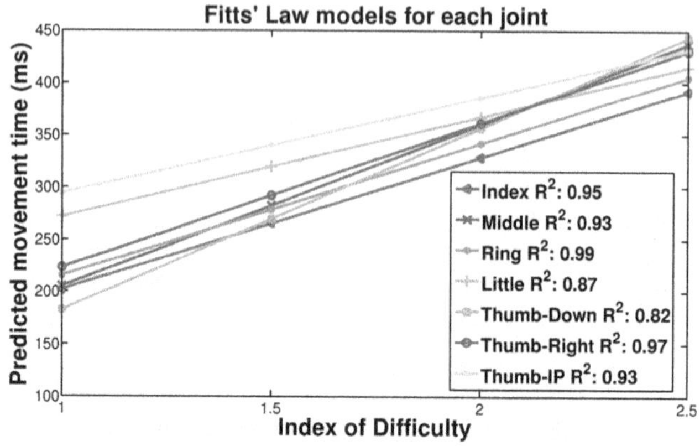

Figure 4. Performance models for each joint as given by Fitts' law. Overall, Index is the fastest, while Thumb and Little finger are the slowest.

Joint	Intercept a	Slope b	R^2
Index	75.140	126.77	0.95
Middle	49.940	155.03	0.93
Ring	88.450	126.79	0.99
Little	176.52	95.510	0.87
Thumb-Down	8.1900	174.26	0.82
Thumb-Right	84.590	138.44	0.97
Thumb-IP	202.73	91.590	0.93

Table 1. Fitts' Law models for each joint, given by intercept and slope.

RESULTS

Performance: Fitts' Law Models

Fitts' law models and fitness scores for the joints are given in Table 1. The R^2 values range from high (0.82) to excellent (0.99). One-way repeated measures ANOVA showed statistically significant differences among the joints for MT: $F(6, 60) = 3.3$, $p < 0.05$. Overall, Index had the highest performance, while Thumb-IP was the worst.

More subtle differences can be observed by looking at the cross-over points of the slopes in Figure 4. The Index finger was the fastest for most part of the ID range. However, for small IDs, corresponding to large neighboring targets, Thumb-Down outperformed Index. We also observe that for small IDs, MTs are spread for the different fingers (difference of 112 ms, $ID = 1$) while they become more condensed for larger IDs (51 ms, $ID = 2.5$). In other words, there is more variation for "easy" movements.

Significant individual differences could be observed. Differences in MT for the same joint were as large as 418 ms. The top performance was 91 ms for $ID = 1$, while the worst user performed at a speed of 509 ms per movement $ID = 1$.

Individuation: Schieber Indices

Table 2 provides an overview of the findings. We report aggregate indices per finger and by finger-pair coactivation.

Individuation Index: The individuation index for each finger can be found in the second column of Table 2. The values range from 1 for perfect individuation to 0 for perfect coactivation. Thumb-IP was found to be the most individuated joint, while Thumb-Down seemed to be the one with the highest coactivation. The individuation indices of the MCP joints showed only marginal differences.

Instructed Joint	Index of Individuation	Relative Coactivation						
		Index	Middle	Ring	Little	Thumb-Down	Thumb-Right	Thumb-IP
Index	**0.819**	1	0.24	0.20	0.19	0.29	0.11	0.06
Middle	**0.817**	0.16	1	0.41	0.14	0.20	0.11	0.07
Ring	**0.808**	0.16	0.20	1	0.36	0.15	0.22	0.06
Little	**0.806**	0.18	0.35	0.29	1	0.14	0.12	0.08
Thumb-Down	**0.792**	0.12	0.12	0.10	0.08	1	0.69	0.14
Thumb-Right	**0.853**	0.07	0.09	0.10	0.09	0.27	1	0.26
Thumb-IP	**0.889**	0.11	0.13	0.11	0.09	0.12	0.12	1

Table 2. Individuation index and relative coactivation describe the involuntary motion of joints. The individuation index is an aggregate that describes the independence of a finger when averaged over all other fingers (1 = perfect individuation). Relative coactivation denotes the movement of an non-instructed joint when the instructed joint (each row) is moving. A value of 1 denotes that the two joints always move together.

Joint	Min° (SD)	Max° (SD)	Range (SD)
Index	48.39 (12.25)	−21.19 (8.70)	69.58 (11.81)
Middle	37.58 (11.95)	−18.69 (8.02)	56.27 (12.54)
Ring	44.66 (8.320)	−12.24 (7.70)	58.90 (11.46)
Little	39.47 (15.78)	−20.81 (8.64)	60.28 (14.89)
Thumb-Down	27.31 (1.680)	−6.280 (6.54)	33.58 (7.130)
Thumb-Right	22.18 (10.53)	−11.99 (8.43)	31.32 (12.59)
Thumb-IP	62.97 (12.94)	−27.41 (4.37)	90.38 (13.93)

Table 3. Angular limits and movement range of each joint. The table shows values averaged over all users together with standard deviations.

Relative Coactivation: While the individuation index provides an elegant way to summarize the independence of each finger, greater insight is provided by the *relative coactivation* of joints, which denotes the movement of an non-instructed finger when the instructed finger is moved. In Table 2, we present the relative coactivation averaged over all users. It ranges from 0 to 1, where 1 is perfect coactivation, *i.e.* the non-instructed finger moves exactly along with the instructed finger. Note that the value range is the opposite to the individuation index, where 1 is better. We observe that Thumb-Down is closely correlated with Thumb-Right, explaining why it has the lowest individuation index. This indicates that the two DOFs of the thumb's CMC joint cannot be reliably distinguished and should be combined when implementing thumb movements for gestural input. Particularly high values were also observed for the movement of Ring during instructed movement of Middle, and the other way around (Figure 6). Thumb-IP shows low values throughout all joints which explains the good individuation index.

Comfortable Movement Ranges

The average angular limits and movement range for each joint are given in Table 3. The values represent joint limits that are comfortable for the user in this setting and reachable without moving the other joints too much. One-way repeated measures ANOVA (subjects with missing data excluded) showed statistically significant differences between movement ranges: $F(6,60) = 39.19$, $p < 0.0001$. We observe that the CMC joint of the thumb has the smallest movement range in both movement directions (34°and 31°). The range of the MCP joints is twice that, and Index has the largest range (70°). Thumb-IP has overall the largest movement range with an average of 90°.

Observations on Individual Differences

Large differences among users were observed. Some users were able to keep their non-instructed finger nearly static (slope close to 0), while others moved them to a large extent along with the instructed joint (slope $= 0.4$). Figure 7 shows the coactivation of Index relative to Middle. Movement strategies vary too, resulting in a positive slope (moving along with the instructed joint) or even a negative slope (moving opposite to the instructed joint). If a joint could not be kept static, users either moved it along with the instructed joint or opposite to it. Attempts at "counteracting" movement like this were also observed in the original work by Schieber [33]. It may represent a strategy for preventing non-instructed fingers from moving along instructed digits. This suggests that these strategies are applied unconsciously.

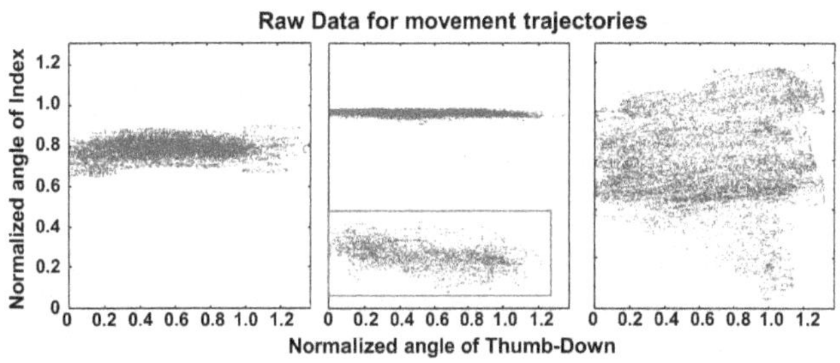

Figure 5. Raw data for movement of Index relative to instructed movement of Thumb-Down. Left (a): Example of high individuation, Middle (b): Tracking errors (red box), and Right (c): "drifting finger".

We also observed what we denote as the *drifting finger effect*: the position of non-instructed fingers may change gradually over time for some users, as they "forget" to keep the finger still. For some users, this poses no problem, they are able to produce the exact same movement over and over (Figure 5 (a)). We show raw data of this "drifting finger" problem in Figure 5 (c). Due to user-specific differences like this, the linear model of Schieber does not always fit to a user's motion. On average, an R^2 of 0.77 (SD 0.14) was found, ranging from 0.5 to excellent fits of 0.99. As discussed above, we excluded the data where no sufficient linear relationship could be found. On average, this amounted to excluding data from 4 users per joint-joint condition.

Finally, despite our efforts to ensure the ergonomics of the posture and to provide enough breaks, some users complained about fatigue, especially with their wrist or arm getting tired. This suggests that these motions are tiring even if they do not require the use of large forces.

APPLICATION TO TEXT ENTRY

The results of the study offer a nuanced picture of the two characteristics of finger motions. The performance and independence of fingers differ and are inter-connected in sub-

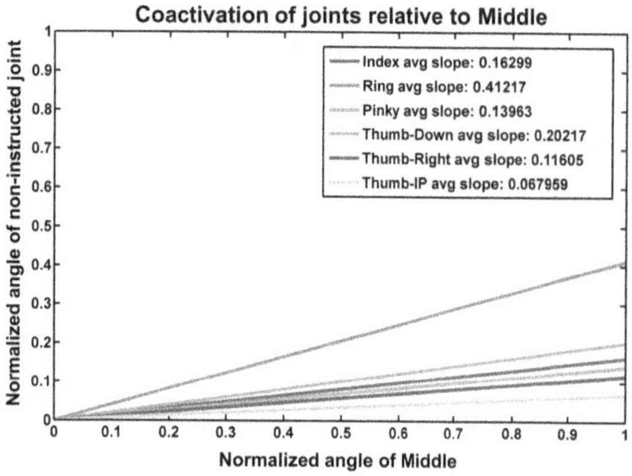

Figure 6. Average coactivation of all joints relative to the instructed movement of the middle finger. The slopes are the average of the absolute values over all users.

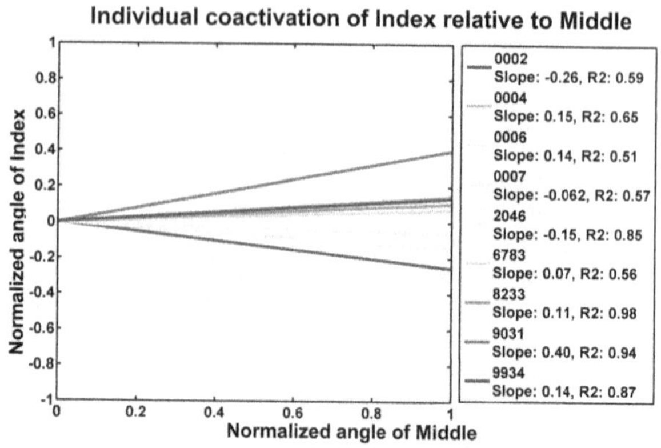

Figure 7. Differences among users (denoted by four digit user ID) in the movement of the index finger relative to the middle finger. A positive slope indicates that it follows the instructed joint, negative slope that it moves in the opposite direction.

tle ways. In this section, we present a proof-of-concept that shows how to use the results to design multi-finger gestures for a high-performance input task. We chose to focus on text entry by mapping *static mid-air hand postures* to letters. We use the terms 'gesture' and 'posture' interchangeably in this section to denote static postures. Mid-air input is a promising input modality for emerging devices like smartwatches and heads-up displays [20]. In contrast to previous mid-air text entry methods which used *extrinsic* key targets or handwriting gestures [1, 20, 25, 35], we focus on chord-like gestures controlled by angular motions. Although more complex than single finger input, it has been shown that a large number of chords can be memorized [34] and used for text entry (*e.g.* [9, 16]), as well as on multitouch displays [2].

Since the space of possible posture-letter mappings is (exponentially) large, we follow an optimization approach (*e.g.* [8, 40]). We outline a novel objective function called PALM that optimizes mappings for four objectives. In addition to performance and individuation constraints, it considers learnability and mnemonics. The outcomes can be used to enter text with any hand tracker and gesture recognizer. Our approach has four main steps, which serve as a roadmap for designing tasks other than text entry: (1) Discretizing Joint Angles, (2) Generalizing to Multi-Joint Gestures, (3) Formulating an Objective Function, and (4) Optimization.

Step 1: Discretizing Joint Angles

We first need to select the number of discretization levels of angular motion that each joint can afford. This is determined by the robustness of the hand tracker and by performance data we obtained. Our estimate for angular discretization when using the Leap Motion is between 2 and 5 levels per joint angle. For each joint, an integer from 0–k is used to represent the current joint angle, where k is the highest level. Thus, the posture of the hand can be compactly represented using a string of numbers which we call a *bin address*. For instance, the posture corresponding to the letter 'h' in Figure 1 can be denoted by the string [0,0,1,1,0] (using 5 joints). We also define a neutral pose for the hand, which is a comfortable position, and calibrate such that it corresponds to the bin address [0,0,0,0,0].

Step 2: Generalizing to Multi-Joint Gestures

Since the findings from our study are for single joints, we make two assumptions to generalize to multi-joint gestures. First, to estimate movement time (MT) for gestures involving multiple joints, we assume that it is bounded by the performance of the slowest contributing joint. We base this on evidence that movement of arm joints are timed so that all joints reach their final positions simultaneously [13, 32]. Thus, we estimate the time for a multi-joint gesture as the maximum over each of the MTs of all joints involved. Formally, we define time for moving from one posture to another as,

$$MT = \max\{mt_{\theta_i}\}, \theta_i \in \Theta, \tag{3}$$

where mt_θ corresponds to the movement time of one joint as given in Equation (1).

Second, to estimate individuation constraints of a multi-finger gesture, we extend the individuation index of Schieber to take into account the fact that coactivation between fingers is not an issue when those fingers are used in the same gesture. The middle finger, for example, has a poor individuation index, which is mainly dominated by the relative coactivation of the ring finger. A gesture involving both fingers can therefore be performed with higher individuation than a gesture involving only one of the fingers. To this end, we define the coactivation C_{iG} of a joint i relative to a gesture (or posture) G as the maximal coactivation of i relative to any joint j involved in the gesture: $C_{iG} = \max_{j \in G} C_{ij}$. Then, following the original Equation (2), we compute the individuation index for any multi-joint gesture as

$$I_G = 1 - [(\sum_{i=1}^{n} |C_{iG}| - |G|)/n - |G|], \tag{4}$$

where $|G|$ denotes the number of actively involved joints, and n is the total number of joints.

Step 3: Objective Function Formulation

Our design task is to maximize the *usability* U of a letter assignment, *i.e.* the mapping of each character in a character set to a unique posture (gesture) of the hand. To characterize U, we formulate a multi-term objective function for mid-air text entry called PALM which addresses four factors affecting mid-air text entry with multiple fingers: Performance, Anatomical comfort (individuation), Learnability, and Mnemonics. In addition to performance and individuation, we formalize learnability and mnemonics based on existing literature.

Usability U is thus defined as a weighted sum of four normalized (*i.e.* $\in [0,1]$) terms[2]. Formally, we write our usability objective as

$$U = w_p\,\hat{P} + w_a\,\hat{A} + w_l\,\hat{L} + w_m\,\hat{M}, \tag{5}$$

where the positive weights w_p, w_a, w_l, and w_m set by a designer sum up to 1. The remaining terms in the objective function are described below in turn.

Performance Term (P)
Our performance score P is measured in words per minute (WPM). Following previous work on keyboard optimization [8, 40], we use Fitts' law models to predict the time $mt_{k\ell}$ to articulate a joint from letter k to letter ℓ by computing the movement time as described in Equation (3).

We then compute WPM with 5 % error rate as:

$$P = 60/(\sum_k \sum_\ell f_{k\ell} mt_{k\ell}) \times 5, \tag{6}$$

where $f_{k\ell}$ is the frequency of bigram $k\ell$.

Anatomical Comfort Term (A)
For each gesture, we use Equation (4) to estimate how well it individuates. An index of 1 corresponds to perfect individuation where none of the non-instructed joints moves along with the joints involved in the gesture, a value of 0 would mean that all fingers move to the same extent, even if they are not part of the gesture. Thus, $\hat{A}$ takes the value of the individuation index.

Learnability Term (L)
Learnability is an important factor to consider for any activity involving rapid and careful articulation of multiple joints. To develop a score for learnability of a gesture, we build on some prevalent theories of motor learning that view learning as a *hierarchical combination of primitives* [22]. According to this view, the brain simplifies multi-dimensional motor control by collapsing it into a few dimensions. Practicing a complex gesture gradually increases hierarchical organization and decreases reliance on feedback. This has two consequences. First, the fewer DOFs a gesture involves, the easier it will be to learn. For instance, gesturing with one finger is easier to learn than a gesture using three fingers. We name the number of involved DOFs u_{dofs}. Second, if the involved digits involve the same *end posture*, it will be easier to learn because the articulations can be represented with a single learning primitive. For example, it is easier to extend all digits by 40° than to extend some by 20° and others by 40°. We denote the number of DOFs for which a target angle is defined in a gesture by u_{targets}. Our learnability score combines these two aspects:

$$L = 1 - \sum_k (0.5\,\hat{u}_{\text{targets, k}} + 0.5\,\hat{u}_{\text{dofs, k}}). \tag{7}$$

[2]Normalized variables are marked with a hat.

Mnemonics Term (M)
Studies of human memory suggest that categorization, chunking, and mnenomics help forming more durable long-term memory traces among otherwise unrelated materials [38]. Our mnemonics score M considers the memorability of a letter assignment *as a whole*. We call a *mnemonic set* a set of similar gestures, such as gestures that all have a neighboring finger. To identify finger mnemonics, we build on a recent study of multi-finger chord gestures that showed a positive effect on learning [38]. We take the mnemonic principles presented there and extend them from three fingers to five. In particular, we include the following mnemonics rules: neighboring fingers (*e.g.* thumb and little finger together), base (*e.g.* thumb or index with other fingers), and single finger.

The M-score considers two aspects: (1) the proportion of gestures belonging to a mnemonic set m_{coverage} and (2) how *few* mnemonic sets are required m_{sets}, which is the inverse of the proportion of all mnemonic sets being in use. We define $M = 0.5\,(m_{\text{coverage}} + m_{\text{sets}})$. M thus rewards designs where a large proportion of gestures belong to a few mnemonics sets. While our learnability score L looks at motor learning "from scratch", this score focuses on the benefit of the set consisting of easily recognizable gestures.

Step 4: Optimization
To optimize the multi-term objective function we use techniques from multi-dimensional Pareto optimization [29]. Instead of searching for a global optimum in a single run, we use a multi-start local search method. Local search starts from a random position in the search space and randomly samples its neighborhood. When search converges, we store the incumbent to a file and restart search. A similar approach was used in a previous paper addressing a multi-objective task [8]. Our implementation reaches reasonable designs in minutes while good ones take about one day on a cluster computer.

DESIGN CASES
This section presents mappings optimized for fast performance, learnability, as well as for different character sets. Apart from this, we present solutions with multiple discretization levels for the joint angles. This demonstrates how the approach can be used across varying design interests. Finally, we present a preliminary evaluation of one of our designs.

Before discussing the designs, we report our experiences regarding the value of optimizing for all four objectives of PALM. To learn if performance and individuation are compatible design goals, we optimized for P, A, and P+A goals separately. The results showed that the benefit of optimizing for only one of the goals is negligible. In other words, performance and individuation may not always be competitive goals for design. The P-only design has fewer multi-joint gestures, whereas both A-only and P+A have more gestures involving neighboring fingers. This encouraged further exploration of the multi-objective design space.

Table 5 lists all outcomes along with two alternative text entry methods: Engelbart's chording keyboard [9] and a fingerspelling method (American Sign Language). Words per minute is predicted considering expert motor performance

Bin Address	Character	Bin Address	Character
0,1,0,0,0	_	1,1,0,0,0	n
1,0,0,0,0	a	1,0,0,1,0	o
0,0,1,0,1	b	0,0,0,1,1	p
1,1,0,1,0	c	0,1,1,1,1	q
0,1,1,1,0	d	0,1,0,1,0	r
0,0,0,1,0	e	0,1,1,0,0	s
1,1,1,1,0	f	0,0,1,0,0	t
0,1,0,0,1	g	0,0,0,0,1	u
0,0,1,1,0	h	1,0,0,1,1	v
1,0,1,0,0	i	1,0,0,0,1	w
0,1,1,0,1	j	0,0,1,1,1	x
1,1,0,0,1	k	0,1,0,1,1	y
1,1,1,0,0	l	1,0,1,0,1	z
1,0,1,1,0	m		

Table 4. FASTTYPE was optimized favoring Performance. The bin addresses describe each gesture, see text for explanation. Observe how commonly occurring letters like 'a' are assigned to easy postures such as flexing the thumb.

only, using Equation (6). Due to space limitations we report the full mapping only for FASTTYPE in Table 4. Please see the supplementary material for the remaining mappings.

Standard Character Sets: NUMPAD is a solution that maps the numbers from 0–9 to postures formed by the 5 joints, one per finger. Each joint angle is discretized into 2 levels. The predicted performance for this mapping is the highest at 113.0 WPM due to the small character set. FASTTYPE is a solution with the letters *a–z* (including space), and 5 joints each with 2 discretization levels. This mapping was optimized for typing speed and uses chord-like movements with a predicted performance of 54.7 WPM. We show this mapping in Table 4. In the table, we use the concept of bin address as explained earlier. The joints are ordered from Thumb to Little. For example, [0,0,0,0,1] would mean flexing Little but keeping the rest in a neutral pose. BALANCETYPE, a variant with balanced weights for the four objective function weights had a predicted performance of 50.1 WPM.

Extended Character Sets: FULLTYPE is optimized to map all letters of the alphabet, numbers, and special characters for a total of 48 characters. The predicted performance was 50.7 WPM with 5 joints and 5 discretization levels per joint. While this mapping has a good predicted performance, we hypothesize that it is hard to perform because of 5 discretization levels for joint angles. Finally, THREETYPE optimizes a full keyboard to the three fingers with the highest individuations: Thumb, Index, Middle. It, too, assumes 5 discretization levels which is presently impossible with our tracker and would require a long time to learn.

We also represented fingerspelling in American Sign Language using our bin address notation. For the represented mapping, our objective function predicts an entry rate of 43.9 WPM which is surprisingly close to the empirically observed rate of 40–45 WPM for experienced practitioners [30].

First Observations on User Performance: FASTTYPE

In order to estimate if the predicted performance is indeed achievable with mid-air text entry, we conducted a preliminary evaluation of FASTTYPE with 10 users. We followed a word-level paradigm previously used by Zhai *et al.* [5]. Here, a randomly sampled word is practiced until performance peaks. The benefit of this is that the upper boundary of entry performance can be estimated even without having to learn the full gesture set.

Method: 10 right-handed participants took part in the experiment (9 male, 1 female; ages from 21 to 39, mean 26). The experiment took 1.5–2 hours and all participants were compensated. We randomly sampled 4–8 character strings from the Enron Email Dataset [37] for the stimulus. Each contained 1–2 frequently entered words and also included the space character. A task consisted of repeatedly entering a word. At the beginning, participants were allowed to practice the word by going through the gestures for all letters and exploring the fastest transitions between each gesture. As soon as they could memorize the mapping of the corresponding letters, the task started. The task was terminated by the experimenter when a performance plateau could be observed.

Prototype: We built a prototype that allowed users to enter text, and recorded performance of typed words. Our gesture recognizer used joint angle data from the Leap Motion, and used a combination of dwell times and signal peak detection to detect when users made a particular posture which was converted to text. A custom-built application displayed information to the user as well as recorded data for analysis. The hardware used was identical to the first experiment.

Result: Overall, the 10 users entered 53 words at an average peak performance of 22.25 WPM (SD 8.9). For analyzing the peak performance of each word, we extracted the top 3 repetitions with an error rate less than 15% (measured by Damerau-Levenshtein distance). Three words had to be excluded due to this restriction. The remaining words were typed with an average error rate of 2.3% (SD 0.04). A one-way ANOVA on WPMs showed a statistically significant difference among users: $F(9, 49) = 7.68$, $p < 0.001$. Average peak performances ranged from 13 WPM to 38.1 WPM. This large performance range clearly shows the influence of individual differences in performance, individuation and anatomical limitations found in our first experiment. While these results serve as a first exploration of PALM, further detailed studies are needed to validate the effectiveness of our model.

DISCUSSION

The results presented in this paper deepen the understanding of multi-finger input in mid-air. The findings show that multi-finger input has potential for high throughput. While it was known previously that differences existed in performance and individuation between fingers, they were not quantified in a setting that is representative of modern computer vision-based input. Our results were obtained by adapting the familiar methodology of Fitts' law studies along with a measurement of individuation adopted from motor control research. This is in contrast to existing work in gesture design that has considered elicitation methods to learn about user preferences, intuitiveness, and social acceptability [23, 26, 31].

In a proof-of-concept, we demonstrated the applicability of our results by computationally optimizing a mid-air text entry method. Based on prior work on motor performance [13, 32], we extended our findings from single fingers to multi-

Mapping	Character Set	Joint Discretization	Weights (PALM)	Objective values (PALM)	Predicted WPM
NUMPAD	0–9	2, 2, 2, 2, 2	0.30, 0.30, 0.05, 0.05	0.27, 0.03, 0.22, 0.22	113.0
FASTTYPE	*a–z*	2, 2, 2, 2, 2	0.50, 0.10, 0.10, 0.30	0.53, 0.03, 0.18, 0.50	54.7
BALANCETYPE	*a–z*	5, 5, 5, 4, 4	0.25, 0.25, 0.25, 0.25	0.42, 0.02, 0.19, 0.17	50.1
FULLTYPE	0–9, *a–z*	5, 5, 5, 5, 5	0.20, 0.20, 0.20, 0.20	0.41, 0.14, 0.19, 0.33	50.7
THREETYPE	*a–z*	5, 5, 4	0.40, 0.40, 0.20, 0.00	0.38, 0.01, 0.28, 0.00	65.1
Fingerspelling	*a–z*	4, 3, 3, 3, 3	0.25, 0.25, 0.25, 0.25	0.51, 0.02, 0.28, 0.80	43.9
Engelbart's Chord Kbd	*a–z*	2, 2, 2, 2, 2	0.25, 0.25, 0.25, 0.25	0.58, 0.03, 0.17, 0.69	49.0

Table 5. An overview of optimized mappings and predicted WPM. The bottom part shows predictions for two existing methods.

joint gestures. The P and A terms of PALM are based on the empirical results, whereas the L and M terms are derived from prior work on human memory and motor learning [22, 38]. While further evaluation is needed to prove the validity of these assumptions, we show how our findings can serve in the search for good solutions among millions of designs.

To analyze the outcomes, we built a prototype and explored the performance for one of the optimized mappings which showed an entry rate of 22 WPM. While the performance predicted by Equation (6) was surprisingly close to the observed performance in fingerspelling, FASTTYPE falls short of the predicted rate of 54.7 WPM. As Equation (6) only predicts expert motor performance, this can be partially attributed to the lack of training and limited tracker performance. However, further evaluation is needed to investigate learning over time and cognitive effort involved in mid-air input.

CONCLUSION AND FUTURE WORK

In this paper, we investigated the dexterity of fingers for mid-air input. The results provide insights into the performance of individual fingers and their coactivation. The findings suggest that mid-air input is a promising input modality, but there are limitations to the capacity of the human hand.

The physiology and cognitive skills of humans pose two critical constraints that future work should consider. First, the learnability of gestures is a pragmatic obstacle for multi-finger input. If a gesture set for text entry is prohibitively time consuming to learn it will affect large-scale adoption. With PALM, we propose a method to optimize for learnability. However, further evaluation is needed to investigate the influence of the L and M term on performance and learnability, and evaluate the involved models. Second, the effect of fatigue in multi-finger input is not fully understood yet. Users in both our studies reported discomfort in their arm and wrist.

The technological challenges of hand tracking without markers pose additional constraints to mid-air input. Despite much progress, markerless hand and finger tracking is still a challenging problem. We restricted our study to 6 joints since even commercial sensors like the Leap Motion could not reliably track certain finger joints. Our evaluation showed that users were limited in their speed by errors in tracking all joint angles under fast motion. We assume that some of these issues arise from assumptions about finger individuation used by the tracker.

A notable omission in our investigation is appropriate feedback for mid-air input. While no visual feedback is needed for our text entry method, it is unknown if proprioception alone suffices to perform fast and accurate mid-air gestures. As an alternative, tactile feedback was shown to improve performance on touch screens [11] and new technologies such as UltraHaptics [6] provide a way to bring non-contact haptic feedback to mid-air input.

This paper has contributed empirically derived models of performance factors involved in mid-air input and a proof-of-concept approach to design. Our optimizer allows finding designs that strike desirable trade-offs in this demanding design landscape. Although our final evaluation of mid-air text entry fell short of the performance predicted by our Fitts' law model, the result is promising and justifies further research. We believe that when the outstanding human and technological issues are solved, this category of input can achieve performance that is currently seen only for physical keyboards.

Acknowledgments: This research was funded by the ERC Starting Grant projects CapReal and COMPUTED (637991), and the Academy of Finland.

REFERENCES

1. Amma, C., Georgi, M., and Schultz, T. Airwriting: Hands-free mobile text input by spotting and continuous recognition of 3D-space handwriting with inertial sensors. In *Proc. ISWC* (2012), 52–59.
2. Bailly, G., Müller, J., and Lecolinet, E. Design and evaluation of finger-count interaction: Combining multitouch gestures and menus. *Int. J. Hum.-Comput. Stud.* (2012), 673–689.
3. Bailly, G., Müller, J., Rohs, M., Wigdor, D., and Kratz, S. ShoeSense: a new perspective on gestural interaction and wearable applications. In *Proc. CHI* (2012), 1239–1248.
4. Balakrishnan, R., and MacKenzie, I. S. Performance differences in the fingers, wrist, and forearm in computer input control. In *Proc. CHI* (1997), 303–310.
5. Bi, X., Smith, B. A., and Zhai, S. Multilingual touchscreen keyboard design and optimization. *Human–Computer Interaction 27*, 4 (2012), 352–382.
6. Carter, T., Seah, S. A., Long, B., Drinkwater, B., and Subramanian, S. UltraHaptics: multi-point mid-air haptic feedback for touch surfaces. In *Proc. UIST* (2013), 505–514.
7. Crossan, A., Williamson, J., Brewster, S., and Murray-Smith, R. Wrist rotation for interaction in mobile contexts. In *Proc. MobileHCI* (2008), 435–438.

8. Dunlop, M., and Levine, J. Multidimensional Pareto optimization of touchscreen keyboards for speed, familiarity and improved spell checking. In *Proc. CHI* (2012), 2669–2678.
9. Engelbart, D. C., and English, W. K. A research center for augmenting human intellect. In *Proc. of Fall Joint Computer Conference* (1968), 395–410.
10. Häger-Ross, C., and Schieber, M. H. Quantifying the independence of human finger movements: comparisons of digits, hands, and movement frequencies. *J. Neuroscience 20*, 22 (2000), 8542–8550.
11. Hoggan, E., Brewster, S. A., and Johnston, J. Investigating the effectiveness of tactile feedback for mobile touchscreens. In *Proc. CHI* (2008), 1573–1582.
12. Jones, L. A., and Lederman, S. J. *Human Hand Function*, 1 ed. Oxford University Press, 2006.
13. Kaminski, T., and Gentile, A. Joint control strategies and hand trajectories in multijoint pointing movements. *Journal of Motor Behavior 18*, 3 (1986), 261–278.
14. Kondraske, G. An angular motion Fitt's law for human performance modeling and prediction. In *Proc. IEEE EMBS* (Nov. 1994), 307–308 vol.1.
15. Langolf, G. D., Chaffin, D. B., and Foulke, J. A. An investigation of Fitts' law using a wide range of movement amplitudes. *Journal of Motor Behavior 8*, 2 (1976), 113–128.
16. Lyons, K., Starner, T., and Gane, B. Experimental evaluations of the twiddler one-handed chording mobile keyboard. *Human-Computer Interaction* (2006).
17. MacKenzie, I. S. Fitts' law as a research and design tool in human-computer interaction. *Human-Computer Interaction 7*, 1 (1992), 91–139.
18. Malik, S., Ranjan, A., and Balakrishnan, R. Interacting with large displays from a distance with vision-tracked multi-finger gestural input. In *Proc. UIST* (2005), 43–52.
19. Mao, Z.-H., Lee, H.-N., Sclabassi, R., and Sun, M. Information capacity of the thumb and the index finger in communication. *IEEE Trans. Biomedical Engineering 56*, 5 (May 2009), 1535 -1545.
20. Markussen, A., Jakobsen, M. R., and Hornbaek, K. Vulture: A mid-air word-gesture keyboard. In *Proc. CHI* (2014), 1073–1082.
21. Melax, S., Keselman, L., and Orsten, S. Dynamics based 3D skeletal hand tracking. In *Proc. i3D* (2013), 184–184.
22. Mitra, S., Amazeen, P. G., and Turvey, M. T. Intermediate motor learning as decreasing active (dynamical) degrees of freedom. *Human Movement Science 17*, 1 (1998), 17–65.
23. Morris, M. R., Danielescu, A., Drucker, S., Fisher, D., Lee, B., schraefel, m. c., and Wobbrock, J. O. Reducing legacy bias in gesture elicitation studies. *interactions 21*, 3 (2014), 40–45.
24. Murray, R. M., Li, Z., and Sastry, S. S. *A Mathematical Introduction to Robotic Manipulation*, 1st ed. CRC Press, Inc., 1994.
25. Ni, T., Bowman, D., and North, C. AirStroke: Bringing unistroke text entry to freehand gesture interfaces. In *Proc. CHI* (2011), 2473–2476.
26. Piumsomboon, T., Clark, A., Billinghurst, M., and Cockburn, A. User-defined gestures for augmented reality. In *INTERACT 2013*, no. 8118. Jan. 2013, 282–299.
27. Qian, C., Sun, X., Wei, Y., Tang, X., and Sun, J. Realtime and robust hand tracking from depth. In *Proc. CVPR* (2014).
28. Rahman, M., Gustafson, S., Irani, P., and Subramanian, S. Tilt techniques: investigating the dexterity of wrist-based input. In *Proc. CHI* (2009), 1943–1952.
29. Rao, S. S., and Rao, S. *Engineering optimization: theory and practice*. John Wiley & Sons, 2009.
30. Ricco, S., and Tomasi, C. Fingerspelling recognition through classification of letter-to-letter transitions. In *Proc. ACCV*. 2010, 214–225.
31. Rico, J., and Brewster, S. Usable gestures for mobile interfaces: evaluating social acceptability. In *Proc. CHI* (2010), 887–896.
32. Rosenbaum, D. A. *Human motor control*. Academic Press, 2009.
33. Schieber, M. H. Individuated finger movements of rhesus monkeys: a means of quantifying the independence of the digits. *J Neurophysiology 65*, 6 (1991), 1381–91.
34. Seibel, R. Data entry through chord, parallel entry devices. *Human Factors: The Journal of the Human Factors and Ergonomics Society 6*, 2 (1964), 189–192.
35. Shoemaker, G., Findlater, L., Dawson, J. Q., and Booth, K. S. Mid-air text input techniques for very large wall displays. In *Proc. GI*, Canadian Information Processing Society (2009), 231–238.
36. Soukoreff, R. W., and MacKenzie, I. S. Towards a standard for pointing device evaluation, perspectives on 27 years of Fitts' law research in HCI. *Intl. J. of Human-Computer Studies 61*, 6 (Dec. 2004), 751–789.
37. Vertanen, K., and Kristensson, P. O. A versatile dataset for text entry evaluations based on genuine mobile emails. In *Proc. of MobileHCI* (2011), 295–298.
38. Wagner, J., Lecolinet, E., and Selker, T. Multi-finger chords for hand-held tablets: recognizable and memorable. In *Proc. CHI* (2014), 2883–2892.
39. Wilson, A. D. Robust computer vision-based detection of pinching for one and two-handed gesture input. In *Proc. UIST* (2006), 255–258.
40. Zhai, S., Hunter, M., and Smith, B. A. The Metropolis Keyboard - an exploration of quantitative techniques for virtual keyboard design. In *Proc. UIST* (2000), 119–128.

Myopoint: Pointing and Clicking Using Forearm Mounted Electromyography and Inertial Motion Sensors

Faizan Haque, Mathieu Nancel, Daniel Vogel
Cheriton School of Computer Science, University of Waterloo, Canada
{fwhaque, mnancel, dvogel}@uwaterloo.ca

ABSTRACT
We describe a mid-air, barehand pointing and clicking interaction technique using electromyographic (EMG) and inertial measurement unit (IMU) input from a consumer armband device. The technique uses enhanced pointer feedback to convey state, a custom pointer acceleration function tuned for angular inertial motion, and correction and filtering techniques to minimize side-effects when combining EMG and IMU input. By replicating a previous large display study using a motion capture pointing technique, we show the EMG and IMU technique is only 430 to 790 ms slower and has acceptable error rates for targets greater than 48 mm. Our work demonstrates that consumer-level EMG and IMU sensing is practical for distant pointing and clicking on large displays.

Author Keywords
pointing; large displays; electromyography;

ACM Classification Keywords
H.5.2. Information interfaces (e.g., HCI): User Interfaces.

INTRODUCTION
Using a bare human hand for distant pointing and clicking is advantageous [9]: hand movement can be used for pointing, and finger movement for "dwell-free" clicking. However, tracking hand and finger positions with enough fidelity in a large physical space across various environmental conditions remains challenging. For example, computer vision is susceptible to occlusion and lighting, and without additional markers, vision-based tracking of hands at arbitrary orientations over a large area is difficult.

An arm-mounted inertial measurement unit (IMU) provides motion and orientation tracking suitable for pointing with minimal environmental interference, but detecting a click requires additional sensing. On-body computer vision is one approach [4], but inter-finger occlusion and lighting interference remain problematic. Sensing hand poses through muscle activation using Electromyography (EMG) eliminates occlusion and lighting issues and can be reliable, non-invasive, and portable [7, 8]. Previous work combining EMG and IMU for cursor control has focused on gesture detection and recognition algorithms, not user interaction [3, 10].

We present Myopoint, an EMG and IMU pointing and clicking technique using a consumer Myo arm band device (`http://www.thalmic.com`). Myopoint translates and extends a relative pointing technique developed for ideal hand tracking by Vogel and Balakrishnan [9]. We extend their interaction language for activation, clicking, and clutching; we provide a tuned pointer-acceleration transfer function; and we develop input filtering techniques to compensate for involuntary hand movements when clicking and false posture recognition from fast arm movements. To evaluate Myopoint, we replicate Vogel and Balakrishnan's experiment and use their data as a between-subjects benchmark. We show that Myopoint is only 430 to 790 ms slower over the tested range of index of difficulty (3.37 to 7.98 bits) with a 15% error rate for 48 mm targets and 5% for 144 mm targets. Our work demonstrates that consumer-level EMG and IMU sensing devices are practical for fundamental pointing input.

CHI 2015, April 18–23, 2015, Seoul, Republic of Korea.

ACM 978-1-4503-3145-6/15/04...$15.00
`http://dx.doi.org/10.1145/2702123.2702133`

RELATED WORK
Vogel and Balakrishnan [9] evaluated device-free pointing and clicking using absolute ray-casting and position-based relative cursor control. They found relative had lower error rates and comparable selection times when clutching was minimized. They used a high-quality Vicon motion tracking system with hand-mounted reflective markers – reasonable for a laboratory, but impractical for real-world use. We translate their relative technique to a practical real-world device and use their experiment results as an ideal upper bound on for relative performance comparison. Note that subsequent barehand pointing research has not changed relative pointing interaction — the focus has been evaluating un-instrumented tracking (e.g. [1]) or using barehand input for other purposes.

IMUs measure relative motion that can made suitable for relative cursor control. Glove mounted IMUs require physical buttons for clicking [2] or extra finger-mounted IMUs for gestural clicking [6]. Kim *et al.*'s Digits [4] is a gloveless wrist-mounted system combining a vision tracking system for hand postures and an IMU for arm motion. They demonstrate a basic pointing and clicking application without evaluation. The wrist-mounted device is bulky and using computer vision means inter-finger occlusion and lighting interference remain.

Recent work exploring EMG for interaction suggests an alternative method for clicking. Saponas *et al.* develop EMG classification techniques for recognizing finger grip gestures un-

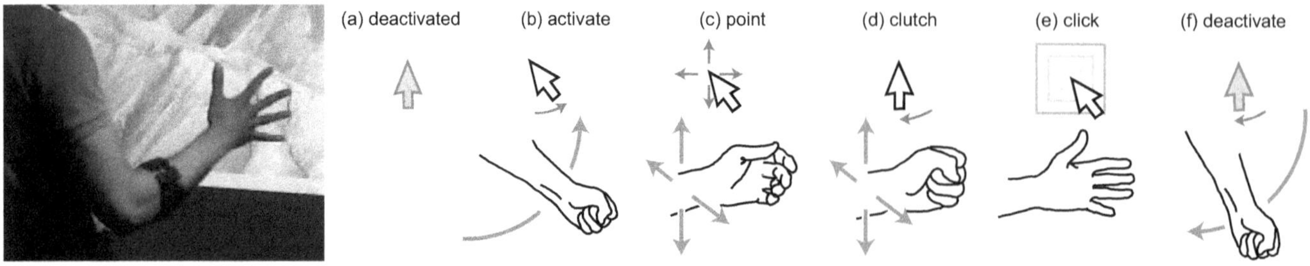

Figure 1: Myo armband (left) and Myopoint interaction (right): (a) initially deactivated; (b) activate by raising clenched fist and releasing; (c) point by moving arm with relaxed hand; (d) clutch with clenched fist; (e) click by spreading all fingers; (f) deactivate by lowering clenched fist and releasing.

der load [7] and pinch-gestures [8] and demonstrate EMG for discrete event input. Xiong *et al.* [10] and Forbes [3] report on mouse input techniques combining arm-mounted EMG and IMU. Forbes combines continuous EMG and IMU for cursor control, while Xiong at al. use IMU for cursor control and EMG postures for mouse control modes and events. Both projects are focused on classification algorithms, not interaction — no human performance evaluations are conducted. There has been no systematic design or validation of a combined EMG and IMU gloveless pointing technique.

MYOPOINT

The Myopoint pointing and clicking technique is built for commodity EMG and IMU sensors. We use a Myo armband, a low-cost consumer device. It may be less sensitive than lab-based EMG and IMU sensors, and it uses proprietary EMG classification and IMU fusion, but we consider these design constraints to develop a real-world pointing technique.

Myo Device

The Myo is a 40 mm wide, 11.5 mm thick, 95 g band worn on the upper forearm. Eight dry electrodes are arrayed around the arm on elasticised segments for EMG sensing and the IMU is a 3-axis gyro, accelerometer, and magnetometer. When placed on the arm, a one-step calibration compensates for handedness, electrode offset, and inter-person EMG differences. During use, on-board processors classify EMG sensor data to determine if the hand is at rest or forming one of 5 hand postures. IMU data is fused and filtered to provide forearm orientation and acceleration. EMG posture events are sent with minimal lag and IMU state is updated at 60 Hz.

Relative Pointing Interaction Technique

Despite its capabilities, the Myo is not originally intended for pointing and clicking. Myopoint translates and extends Vogel and Balakrishnan's *Relative Pointing with Clutching* technique [9]. We also use a neutral 'safe hand' for pointing cursor control (Fig 1c) and a clenched fist 'Grip Clutch' to disengage from the cursor (Fig 1d). Detecting fine finger movements to enable Vogel and Balakrishnan's AirTap click technique is not yet possible on the Myo. We use a finger spread posture to click (Fig 1e). Spreading is a 'click down' and releasing is a 'click up'.

We extend Vogel and Balakrishnan's work by adding activation and deactivation gestures to address Midas touch. Saponas *et al.* [7] used a non-dominant fist to delimit every dominant hand EMG posture. Myopoint is designed to be single-handed and used for longer periods of time, so we use a combination of EMG pose and arm orientation to activate and deactivate the pointing mode. Raising the arm with a clenched fist and releasing activates pointing (Fig 1a). Clenching the fist while lowering the arm and releasing deactivates (Fig 1f). Since a fist is also used for clutching, this does not interfere with cursor position and extends the metaphor of "clench to clutch" to "clench and drop to deactivate." Saponas *et al.* [7] stress the importance of visual feedback for EMG interaction. We translated Vogel and Balakrishnan's audio and visual feedback and extend the 'dangling cursor' clutch visualization to also fade out when Myopoint is deactivated.

Vogel and Balakrishnan use a scaled version of the Windows XP pointer acceleration function tuned for their motion tracking system and absolute hand position sensing. The Myo has different device characteristics and reports relative forearm orientation velocity in rad/s. Following guidelines from Nancel *et al.* [5], we designed a new pointer acceleration function to transform v_{arm} (rad/s) to v_{cursor} (mm/s):

$$v_{cursor} = v_{arm} \times \left(58.28 + \frac{5060.14}{1 + e^{-1.45 \times (vel_{arm} - 1.66)}}\right)$$

Although the Vicon technique also supports wrist movement, it is primarily tuned for forearm movement like Myopoint.

Correction and Filtering

Combining EMG and IMU input together can produce side-effects such as tense EMG hand postures causing unintended IMU arm movement, and fast IMU arm movement causing unintentional EMG pose recognition. We minimize these side-effects with three correction and filtering techniques conservatively tuned to avoid blocking intended clicks. In our experiment, these are logged to assess frequency.

Click position correction – The 'finger spread' hand posture reduces side-effect movement when clicking, but when performed quickly, unintentional movement can make the cursor "jump" when forming the posture (click-down) or releasing (click-up). To avoid this, we implemented a corrective mechanism built on the observation that people slow down just before clicking. When a click-down or -up posture is detected, we examine recent movement and use a cursor location corresponding to minimum velocity. Based on pilot studies, we examine a 250 ms window for click-down and 500 ms for click-up. In both cases, we ignore 25 ms preceding the click posture due to EMG lag. When clicking on targets, the click-up window often overlaps the click-down window so both have the same corrected cursor location. This increases click stability while still enabling dragging. Since the correction occurs after unintentional motion, the cursor may appear to jump back. This visual jump could be avoided by buffering cursor movement, but the extra lag would impair usability. We found that once people understood the system was correcting click positions, they ignored the visual jump and simply expected click events to occur where they intended.

Movement-induced false positive posture filtering – Moving the arm quickly or extending it very far can activate forearm muscles leading to false-positive hand postures recognized by the EMG system. Since users briefly slow down before clutching or clicking, we use speed thresholds above which click and clutch postures are ignored. Based on pilot data, we use a threshold of $V_{ignore} = 1.0$ rad/s to reduce unwanted events while keeping false negatives to a minimum.

Unlikely posture sequence filtering – When quickly switching from 'fist' to 'neutral' the EMG recognizer can misclassify the final 'neutral' posture as a 'finger spread'. This causes an unintentional click-down immediately after a clutch release. People are unlikely to perform these events so rapidly, so we ignore click-downs within 250 ms after a clutch release.

EXPERIMENT

We evaluate Myopoint accuracy and speed using a near-replication of Vogel and Balakrishnan's experiment design, task, and large display [9]. Our intention is to give more substance to our comparison than usual high-level discussions using summative data. Using their original data, a between-subjects comparison can benchmark Myopoint performance.

Participants and Apparatus

We recruited 7 'expert' participants from Thalmic Labs who use the Myo daily (for purposes other than pointing) and 7 participants from the general public. Since the Myo device is unfamiliar, balancing for expertise (EXP) is important. All 14 participants (1 female) were right-handed and none had experience with the Myopoint technique or distant pointing. Participants stood 2m from a 4.6 by 1.4m (3840 by 1200 px) front-projected display with two side-by-side HD projectors. Vogel and Balakrishnan used a 5.0 by 1.7 m (6144 by 2304 px) display. Our display width is smaller, but above the maximum target distance of 4.02 m and our 0.83 px-per-mm density is comparable to their 0.81 density.

Task and Stimuli

Like Vogel and Balakrishnan, we had sets of a Transition Task followed by a Sequence Task. In both tasks, the current target was rendered as a blue circle on a black background and the next target rendered as a blue outline.

Transition Task – This simulates transitioning to the pointing technique. After the cursor and target appear at controlled locations, the participant activates the technique and selects the target. The initial cursor position relative to the target is controlled. Note that Vogel and Balakrishnan use a synthetic activation technique, we use our real Myopoint activation.

Sequence Task – This simulates continuous pointing usage. Immediately after selecting the transition target, the participant selects a sequence of 6 more targets at controlled distances and randomized directions. Participants had to successfully select each target before the next would appear. After the sequence task, the participant used the deactivation gesture to simulate a transition back to a non-pointing task.

Design and Protocol

We used the same three levels of D and W as Vogel and Balakrishnan: D = 4020, 2680, 1340 mm; W = 144, 48, 16 mm (index of difficulty, ID = 3.37 to 7.98 bits). This is a repeated measures mixed design where TASK, D, and W are within-subjects and TECH is between-subjects. TECH = *Myopoint* or *Vicon*, where Vicon is Vogel and Balakrishnan's complete data set for their Relative Pointing with AirTap technique.

Participants first completed the default Myo calibration, then a 5 minute Myopoint learning session, then 1 block of practice trials, and then 3 blocks of measured trials. Each block had 3 sections of tasks, one section for each width (W was held constant throughout a section). The order of width sections was Latin square balanced for measured blocks. Each section had 3 sets of the two consecutive tasks: one target selection in the Transition Task followed by 6 selections in the Sequence Task. All target distances were presented randomly an equal number of times within each section and task. Participants could rest between sections and a 5 minute rest between blocks was enforced. Participants did not report substantial fatigue during the 45 to 60 minute experiment.

In summary, the experimental design was: 3 blocks $\times$ 3 sections of target widths $\times$ 3 sets of tasks: Activation Task (1 target) followed by Sequence Task (6 targets) = 36 task sets per participant (36 targets selected in Activation Task, and 216 targets selected in Sequence Task).

Results

Trials were successful if both click-down and -up were inside the target, otherwise the trial is an error. Requiring down and up on target is more stringent than Vogel and Balakrishnan's error analysis, but we feel more realistic.

Initial analysis revealed 207 click-down errors occurring within the first 300 ms of a trial, i.e. after a successful release event. We consider these click-down events misclassified as it is unlikely that users spread, then relaxed their hand to click twice within 300 ms. To correct for this, we ignore all click-downs occurring within 300 ms after a click-up. This removes 357 errors including the ones above. It also removes 81 click-downs used for successful trials, which likely were lucky erroneous clicks. For consistency, we remove these trials. Fig. 2b illustrates the reduction in error from this post hoc "300ms filter". Below we discuss how this 300 ms rule could form a real time filter.

Error trials were excluded from time statistics and Fitts' models (17.9% of trials, on par with 18.4% in the Vicon study). Median times were used to compensate for non-normal time distribution (flagged by the SAS JMP REML normality test). Multi-way ANOVA was used with post-hoc Tukey tests.

Error Rate

We found a significant effect of W ($F_{2,26} = 33.12$, $p < 0.0001$) on ERROR. As expected, error increased as W decreased (.05, .15, .37, all significantly different) (Fig. 2b). Between-subject

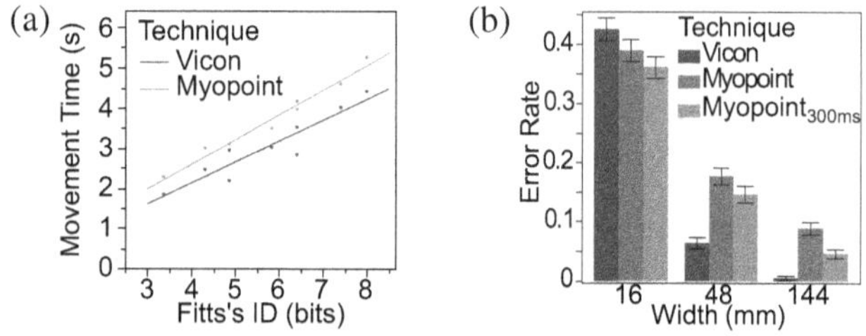

Figure 2: (a) time by ID; (b) error rate by W (*Myopoint* bar is without the "300ms filter", $Myopoint_{300ms}$ is with it, error bars are SEM).

analysis of TECH reveals no main effect but there is an interaction between TECH and W ($F_{2,193} = 6.42$, $p = .002$). Post-hoc tests did not find significantly different error rates between techniques for the same W, and the Vicon error rate for 48 mm targets is not significantly different than Myopoint or Vicon for 144 mm targets. For targets above 48 mm, Myopoint error rate is an encouraging 15.4% and for 144 mm, it is a practical 4.6%. Note that error rates reported in Vogel and Balakrishnan are lower since only click-down errors are considered.

Selection Time

We fit Sequence Task data for both TECHS to Fitts' models. The models have similar slopes with Myopoint slower by 430 to 790 ms in the considered ID range (Fig. 2a).

$$\text{Myopoint} \quad R^2 = .97, \quad MT = 171.59 + 609.36 \times ID$$
$$\text{Vicon} \quad R^2 = .87, \quad MT = 28.93 + 528.32 \times ID$$

Clutching and Activation/Deactivation

We calculated the mean time spent clutching, pointing, and (de)activating in all TASKS and TECHS. A between subjects ANOVA showed a significant effect of TASK ($F_{1,24} = 14.52$, $p = .0008$) and TASK × TECH ($F_{1,24} = 10.74$, $p = .0032$) on Clutch Time. Significantly more time was spent clutching in the Transition Task (363.6 ms) than in the Sequence Task (127.99 ms); this effect is increased with Vicon (491.88 and 53.67 ms), while the difference is not significant with Myopoint (235.32 and 202.32 ms). Note only Myopoint has a real activation technique, the median time to activate is 1816 ms, and 1140 ms to deactivate. High (de)activation speed was not emphasized to participants, so these are comfortable baselines.

Experts (E) and non-experts (NE)

Between-subject analysis revealed no significant effect of EXP on MT. There was a significant effect of EXP ($F_{1,12} = 7.24$, $p = .0197$) on ERROR: 15% for E, 23% for NE. This is explained by an interaction effect with W ($F_{2,96} = 16.19$, $p < 0.0001$): the only significant difference between E and NE is with 16 mm targets: 25% for E, 49% for NE. Fitts models (E: $MT = 90 + 594 \times ID, R^2 = .96$ and NE: $MT = 252 + 624 \times ID, R^2 = .95$) reveal a mostly constant difference. This suggests experts are more efficient at forming hand postures.

DISCUSSION

Some degradation in performance when moving from a Vicon to a consumer-level EMG and IMU armband is expected. Considering the Vicon as an ideal upper bound, Myopoint performance is quite good. Myopoint is slower for technical reasons: clicking with the hand spread posture is slower than small finger movements with AirTap, and despite our filtering, correction, and transfer function, very fast or careless clicks can still cause cursor jumps and participants were sometimes cautious. Further tuning may help.

Correction and Filtering – From our logs, the click position correction converted what would have been errors to successful selections 32 times per click down (0.9% of trials) and 316 times per click up (8.9% of trials). Our movement-induced false positive filtering was invoked 605 times (17.1 % of trials) and our unlikely posture sequence filtering rejected 225 false click events (5.4 % of trials). The data indicates our filtering corrects unintended movements symptomatic of any forearm-mounted EMG+IMU device. The thresholds may change, but we believe our algorithms would apply to other devices. The misidentified clicks within 300 ms of a previous spread pose suggest a simple additional filter.

CONCLUSION AND FUTURE WORK

Our work demonstrates that distant pointing interaction is practical for consumer-level EMG and IMU sensing. As future work, we are applying Myopoint to smartphones and head-mounted displays and are exploring panning and zooming techniques already prototyped in ideal, but impractical tracking environments. The intention is that by using consumer input devices as a practical constraint, we can translate, extend, and validate lab-based interaction technique research.

ACKNOWLEDGEMENTS

Funded in part by NSERC Engage 453380 2013.

REFERENCES

1. Brown, M. A., Stuerzlinger, W., and Filho, E. J. M. The performance of un-instrumented in-air pointing. In *Proc. Graphics Interface* (2014), 59–66.
2. Dipietro, L., Sabatini, A., and Dario, P. A survey of glove-based systems and their applications. *IEEE Trans. on Sys, Man, Cybernetics 38*, 4 (2008), 461–482.
3. Forbes, T. *Mouse HCI Through Combined EMG and IMU*. MSEE thesis, University of Rhode Island, 2013.
4. Kim, D., et al. Digits: Freehand 3d interactions anywhere using a wrist-worn gloveless sensor. In *Proc. UIST*, ACM (2012), 167–176.
5. Nancel, M., et al. High-precision pointing on large wall displays using small handheld devices. In *Proc. CHI*, ACM (2013), 831–840.
6. Perng, J., et al. Acceleration sensing glove. In *3rd Symp. on Wearable Computers* (1999), 178–180.
7. Saponas, T. S., et al. Enabling always-available input with muscle-computer interfaces. In *Proc. UIST*, ACM (2009), 167–176.
8. Saponas, T. S., et al. Making muscle-computer interfaces more practical. In *Proc. CHI*, ACM (2010), 851–854.
9. Vogel, D., and Balakrishnan, R. Distant freehand pointing and clicking on very large, high resolution displays. In *Proc. UIST*, ACM (2005), 33–42.
10. Xiong, A., et al. A novel HCI based on EMG and IMU. In *2011 IEEE International Conference on Robotics and Biomimetics (ROBIO)* (2011), 2653–2657.

Joint Estimation of 3D Hand Position and Gestures from Monocular Video for Mobile Interaction

Jie Song[1], Fabrizio Pece[1], Gábor Sörös[1], Marion Koelle[1,2], Otmar Hilliges[1]
[1]ETH Zurich, [2]University of Passau
{jsong|fabrizio.pece|gabor.soros|otmar.hilliges}@inf.ethz.ch, marion.koelle@uni-passau.de

ABSTRACT
We present a machine learning technique to recognize gestures and estimate metric depth of hands for 3D interaction, relying only on monocular RGB video input. We aim to enable spatial interaction with small, body-worn devices where rich 3D input is desired but the usage of conventional depth sensors is prohibitive due to their power consumption and size. We propose a hybrid classification-regression approach to learn and predict a mapping of RGB colors to absolute, metric depth in real time. We also classify distinct hand gestures, allowing for a variety of 3D interactions. We demonstrate our technique with three mobile interaction scenarios and evaluate the method quantitatively and qualitatively.

Author Keywords
mobile interaction; gesture recognition; machine learning

ACM Classification Keywords
H.5.2 User Interfaces: Input devices and strategies

INTRODUCTION
We are currently witnessing how ultra-mobile devices such as smartwatches and head-worn displays (HWDs) are rapidly becoming commoditized. However, how the user will interact with these ever richer forms of virtual information is becoming a pressing issue. Current commercial offerings, such as Google Glass, Epson Moverio, or other AR research prototypes commonly leverage smartphone technologies such as touchscreens or acceleration sensors for user input. This limits interaction mostly to manipulations of *2D* content – rather than *3D* information embedded into the real world.

Natural user interface (NUI) research has enabled rich, contactless 3D input using hands, fingers and the full body. NUI is now synonymous with depth sensing technologies such as Kinect or the LeapMotion controller. Most available depth sensing technologies are based on either a stereo setup or a combination of a single camera and some form of active illumination such as structured light or time-of-flight. These dependencies set hard lower bounds on the size, weight and the power consumption of such devices. Hence, most depth sensing technologies are currently prohibitive in wearables.

CHI 2015, April 18 - 23, 2015, Seoul, Republic of Korea
Copyright ©2015 ACM 978-1-4503-3145-6/15/04...$15.00
http://dx.doi.org/10.1145/2702123.2702601

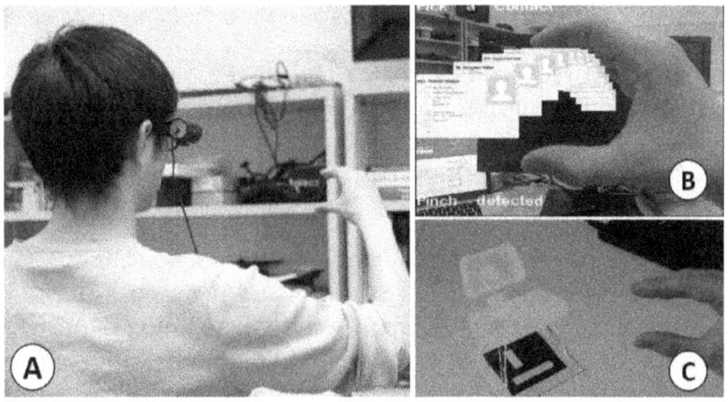

Figure 1. Joint classification of gesture and regression of metric depth from a single head-worn camera for spatial interaction. (A) User wearing a monocular RGB camera attached to AR glasses. Depth-aware gestures allow for rich interactions. (B) Invoking a contacts app by gesture and selecting a contact card by depth (C) Simultaneous control over discrete and continuous parameters in 3D apps.

At the same time almost all wearable computing devices and HWDs are equipped with RGB cameras for image capture. We leverage these and propose a novel machine-learning based algorithm that *jointly* recognizes gestures and estimates the 3D position of hands. In contrast to previous work [2], where instrumentation of the camera is required to obtain depth information, our technique uses *only* the built-in RGB camera, and hence is suitable for off-the-shelf, unmodified mobile devices, including compute-limited HWDs.

Our technique successfully copes with variation in gesture execution, and varying lighting conditions. To achieve this, we take a data-driven machine learning approach similar to those presented in [2, 13] but extend this framework to a hybrid classification-regression scheme, capable of learning a mapping from 2D images to 3D hand positions plus gestures.

RELATED WORK
Ultra-mobile interfaces have seen a lot of interest recently. In particular, researchers have tried to extend the input capabilities of small-screen devices such as smartwatches by adding touch sensitive wristbands [10] or by leveraging the skin for user input [3, 9]. Others have attempted to enable more free-form, in-air gestures using finger- [14] or wrist-worn [5] sensors. These approaches all require hardware modification, which allow for richer input but add bulk and power draw.

Researchers have also looked into expanding the input capabilities of emerging HWDs (e.g., [12]) but do not provide sensing solutions and rely on external infrastructure. More unconventional solutions to the mobile input problem include sensors placed on the tongue [11], behind ears [8], or on cheeks [12]. All these approaches require the user to wear

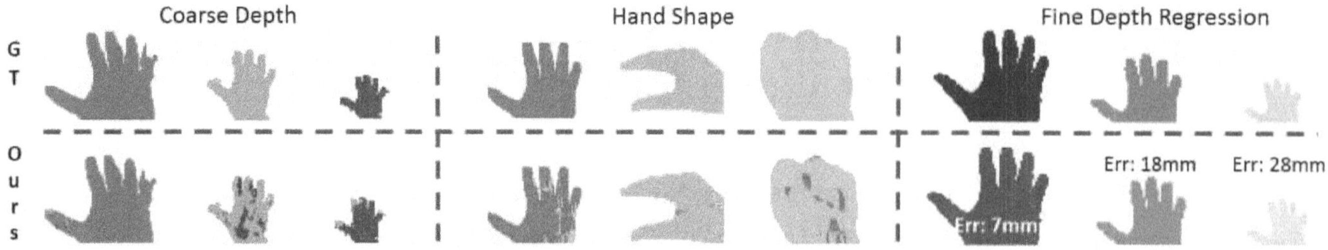

Figure 2. Classification-Regression pipeline overview. Top row: ground truth (GT) data used for training. Bottom row: posteriors outputted at each level by the forests. Left: Coarse depth classification. Middle: Hand-shape classification. Right: Fine-grained depth regression (average depth per hand shown at different depth). The inset shows the error in mm compared to the ground truth.

specialized sensor electronics and might not be feasible in real-world scenarios. Song et al. [13] recently introduced a data-driven gesture recognition approach that enables mid-air interaction on unmodified portable devices. However, the type of interactions are limited to 2D gestures.

Our approach leverages machine-learning techniques to jointly infer hand shape (gestures) and hand position in 3D from only monocular RGB imagery. Estimating depth from single images is ill-posed and a hard problem. Although several approaches exist that try to estimate surface normals or scene depth from single images. These methods rely on associating still images and ground-truth depth pairs, to then derive coarse scene depth [4, 7]. These approaches make use of complex and computationally costly algorithms, infeasible for interactive scenarios on mobile devices.

SPATIAL INTERACTION FOR WEARABLE COMPUTING

In this section we introduce our machinery for joint *classification* of discrete hand gestures and *regression* of scene depth of hands. Similarly to our work, Fanello et al. [2] learn a direct mapping between infrared intensity and depth measurements, to predict per-pixel depth values. Relying on infrared intensity fall-off, this requires mounting of IR illuminants and an IR pass filter, and as such, renders the camera unusable for other purposes while also increasing power draw.

Our method is similar to those proposed in [2, 13]. In [13] several randomized decision forests (RFs) are combined to enable the recognition of discrete 2D hand shapes or gestures. We extend [13] to jointly detect hand shapes and to regress the average hand depth. Together with the hand's centroid this gives full 3D hand position. This allows users of HWDs to interact with rich 3D graphics in a natural and direct fashion. The method relies only on 2D RGB camera imagery and works on completely unmodified mobile devices.

Cascaded Random Forests

The pipeline in [13] consists of simple image processing steps and three cascaded RF classifiers to detect i) coarse depth ii) hand shape and iii) hand parts. Our pipeline (see Fig. 2) is similar but differs in important aspects. We briefly compare our technique to the original algorithm:

Hand Segmentation

We use the same skin color segmentation method as [13] which is robust enough under normal lighting conditions. In this step the main importance is to keep the hand contour as complete as possible, whereas false positives (background noise) are handled later in the pipeline.

Coarse Depth Classification

After background segmentation we classify the image into three coarse layers of depth [2, 13]. For our purposes we are only interested in close range interaction (i.e., arms reach). By experimentation, we found that 90mm to 390mm measured from a head-worn camera to the center of the palm is a comfortable range for most users. We divide this global range into three smaller intervals: $90-150$mm, $150-240$mm and $240-390$mm (Fig. 2, left). Note how the interval ranges increase with distance. This is due to perspective effects causing the change in appearance of the users hand to decrease with distance from the camera.

This layer serves two purposes. First, it removes most of the noise coming from the simple segmentation method. Second, it constrains the variation in terms of hand appearance that the steps further down the pipeline have to deal with, as prior work has shown that classifying the scene into canonical depth regions helps in subsequent, more fine-grained depth estimation [6]. This means that overall we can use shallower trees, resulting in reduced memory footprint (as was the main goal in [13]). Analogously, this approach also allows us to increase the predictive power of the RF ensemble while keeping the memory footprint constant, for example to solve a more difficult task, as is our intention with this work.

Given an input image I with associated pixels x and a segmentation S, the forest at the top layer infers a probability distribution $p(l|x, S)$ over the three coarsely quantized depth ranges and an additional noise class, where $l = \{close, middle, far, noise\}$ are the labels. This per-pixel distribution (Fig. 2, left) is forwarded to the next layer.

Shape Classification

At the next level we evaluate each pixel x in I again to compute a gesture probability distribution $p(c|x, S)$, where c is the label for different hand shapes or gestures, in our case $c = \{splayed\_hand, pinch, closed\_hand\}$ for the three gestures. The predicted posteriors are combined:

$$p(c|x, S) = \sum_{l=1}^{L} w_l p_l(c|x, S) \quad (1)$$

Here the output posterior p is the weighted sum over the estimates p_l of the forests trained on the three gesture classes. The weights w_l are the posterior probabilities estimated by the first layer. Note that this means we need to run all shape classification forests simultaneously. In practice this is not a problem as the trees at depth 15 are relatively shallow. Finally we pool, and average, the probabilities across the image to attain a single value $p(c|S)$ (Fig. 2, middle).

Depth Regression

At the final level we switch from classification to regression forests. Here the goal is to map from an input pixel x in I to an absolute depth value (Fig. 2, right). Note that in contrast to the previous level here we only run one forest per gesture (they are trained only on examples of one hand shape). The continuous value $y(x|S)$ is attained as

$$y(x|c,S) = \sum_{l=1}^{L} w_l y_l(x|c,S) \quad (2)$$

Where l is the coarse depth level and weights w_l are again the posteriors from the first layer.

Prediction and Features

For prediction we follow [13] as closely as possible, with the predictions for $p(l|x,S)$, $p(c|x,S)$ and $y(x|c,S)$ are all done in a similar fashion. We pass individual pixels down several decision trees, forming an ensemble or forest. At each split node we evaluate a split function, passing the pixel to its left or right child, until it reaches a leaf node. The classification forests at the first two levels simply store learned, discrete probability distributions in their leaf nodes and output the mode. For regression, the distributions are multi-modal, and outputting the mean can lead to poor performance. Hence, we store a small set of distributions and perform a median filter over a small patch of pixels around x, resulting in the final depth prediction $y_l(x)$ (Fig. 2, right). We use the same binary split criteria and visual feature responses as in [13].

Training

Both the tree structure and the final probability distributions are learned from annotated training data. In the case of RFs, this is done by randomly selecting multiple split candidates and offsets and choosing the one that splits the data best. The quality metric for the split thereby is typically defined by the information gain I_j at node j. For the classification levels we use the Shannon-Entropy $E(S)$ of the empirical *discrete distribution* of coarse depth values and hand shapes, respectively, to compute I_j (cf. [2, 13]). For the regression forest, $E(S)$ is the differential entropy of the empirical *continuous density* $p(y|S)$, modeled as a 1D Gaussian. Thus $E(S)$ reduces to $E(S) = log(\sigma_s)$, where σ is the the Gaussian variance.

Our training data (cf. Fig. 2) consists of ground-truth images attained from a Creative Senz3D depth camera. We use simple depth thresholding and connected component analysis to attain clean segmentation of the hand. We also keep the segmented depth map for training of the regression forest. We record training data for the different hand shapes separately so that labeling can be automated. In addition we add artificial noise to the binary segmentation in the fashion of [13].

For coarse depth classification we train a single tree of depth 8 using 8K training images. This tree achieves an average

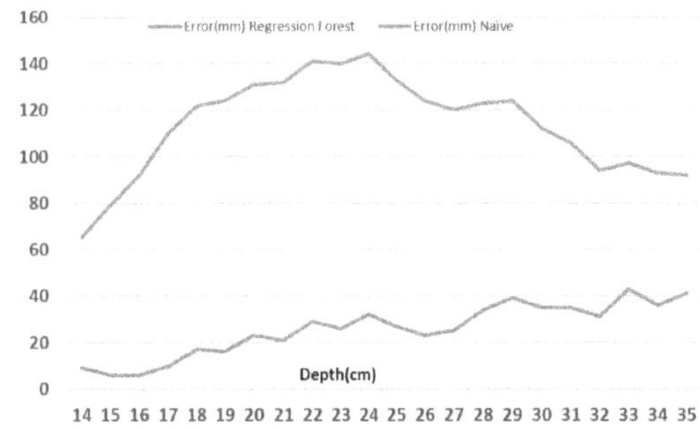

Figure 3. Error vs. ground-truth as a function over depth. Blue is our method (avg. avg. 24mm) and orange is the Naïve method (avg. 87mm).

classification accuracy of 90.1% in half-test-half-train cross-validation. For each gesture in the second layer we use 4K images for training, totaling 12K training data. Using this data we train three trees of depth 15 achieving an average accuracy of 95.3%. For regression, we train one forest per coarse depth interval and per gesture, each consisting of 6 trees ($3 \times 3 \times 6 = 54$ trees in total). Each tree is trained to depth 16 using 4K training images. As we only execute one of the regression forests at a time, the algorithm still runs in real time.

SYSTEM EVALUATION

We have conducted a number of experiments to asses the accuracy of the algorithm. We compare our output to two separate data sources. First, we compare against the ground-truth (GT) data acquired from a Creative Senz3D camera as a baseline. We also compare to a naïve depth estimation technique based on raw hand size. This naïve baseline is calibrated offline and per user by moving the hand repeatedly to and away from the camera. We record min and max pixel counts and corresponding depth values. At runtime we simply interpolate the depth between these two values. While not a very robust method this actually works reasonably well in particular with constant hand shape and linear motion along z.

Fig. 3 plots the error of the two depth estimates as function of distance from the camera, compared to the GT depth value. Our technique compares favorably to the naïve method and also tracks the GT data well. The accuracy of our approach can also be assessed qualitatively. Again, our technique performs significantly better than the naïve approach (cf. Fig. 4).

The experiments so far were conducted using a single gesture. A more realistic scenario is evaluated in Fig. 5. Here we show depth estimates data over $2K$ frames and under gesture variation. The plot is divided into three areas corresponding to the different gestures. Our method tracks the GT closely, with small recurring spikes. These can be traced back to the boundaries between the coarse depth levels. One could detect and filter these, alternatively one could train the regres-

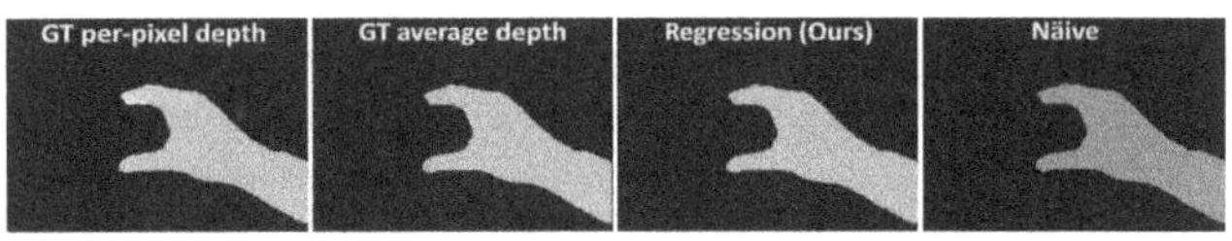

Figure 4. Qualitative Results compared to GT.

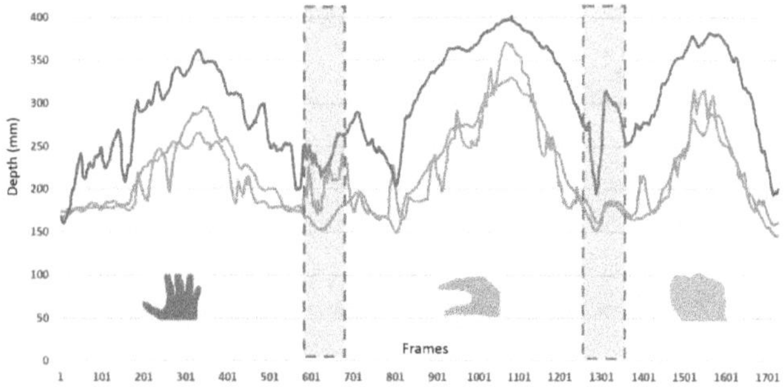

Figure 5. Depth estimation under gesture variation. GT (green) is tracked closely by Ours (orange). Naïve (blue) is significantly worse.

sion forests with training data that has more overlap across the depth boundaries. In contrast, the naïve technique systematically over and undershoots the GT and exhibits a much larger avg error (17.3mm vs. 81.1mm). A t-test reveals that this difference is statistically significant ($p = 0.001$).

APPLICATION SCENARIOS

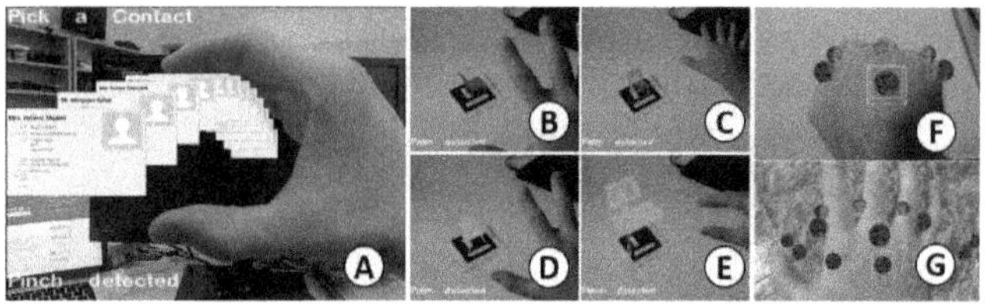

Figure 6. Application scenarios. See text and video figure.

We have built a variety of proof-of-concept demonstrators. These are illustrated in Fig. 6 and the accompanying video. The main advantage of our technique is that it can recover gesture and hand position simultaneously. This allows users to control discrete and continuous inputs jointly. For example, gestures and depth may be used to invoke and browse linear list controls. For instance, to find and select a contact card (Fig. 6, A). Similarly, in an AR furniture application a flat hand may be used to switch 3D models and the pinch gesture may be used to control size of the model (see Fig. 6, B–E). Finally, our approach could also be used to control a spatial, hierarchical 3D menu, where the x, y position of the hand is used to browse entries, z is used to select levels of the hierarchy, and gestures confirm the final selection (Fig. 6, F+G). A promising area for future work could be to combine our input with a trajectory based menu system akin to [1].

DISCUSSION AND CONCLUSION

We have presented a method to jointly estimate 3D hand positions and gestures for 3D input on HWDs. Additionally, we have demonstrated its feasibility quantitatively and qualitatively. However, our method also has clear limitations. First, it is not a general purpose depth estimation technique, but is only trained to recover depth for hands and only at close range. Furthermore, we currently only regress a single, average depth value per hand. This clearly affords less fidelity than what commercial depth cameras produce – albeit at the cost of size and power consumption. However, this depth estimate, when combined with the x, y position of the hand's centroid into a 3D position, is often what an application programmer is interested in. Alongside the possibility to detect gestures this already enables exciting interaction possibilities. For future work we are interested in experimenting with estimating depth for individual parts of the hand such as fingertips versus the palm [13]. Given that the method operates on hand shape only it is unclear whether this could be extended to per-pixel depth but offline methods [6, 7] suggest that there is room for further research and improvement.

REFERENCES

1. Bau, O., and Mackay, W. E. Octopocus: A dynamic guide for learning gesture-based command sets. In *Proc. ACM UIST* (2008), 37–46.
2. Fanello, S. R., Keskin, C., Izadi, S., Kohli, P., Kim, D., Sweeney, D., Criminisi, A., Shotton, J., Kang, S. B., and Paek, T. Learning to be a depth camera for close-range human capture and interaction. *ACM Trans. Graph. 33*, 4 (2014), 86:1–86:11.
3. Harrison, C., Tan, D., and Morris, D. Skinput: Appropriating the Body As an Input Surface. In *Proc. ACM CHI* (2010), 453–462.
4. Karsch, K., Liu, C., and Kang, S. B. Depth extraction from video using non-parametric sampling. In *Proc. of ECCV* (2012), 775–788.
5. Kim, D., Hilliges, O., Izadi, S., Butler, A. D., Chen, J., Oikonomidis, I., and Olivier, P. Digits: Freehand 3D interactions anywhere using a wrist-worn gloveless sensor. In *Proc. ACM UIST* (2012), 167–176.
6. Ladicky, L., Shi, J., and Pollefeys, M. Pulling things out of perspective. In *Proc. IEEE CVPR* (2013), 89–96.
7. Ladicky, L., Zeisl, B., and Pollefeys, M. Discriminatively trained dense surface normal estimation. In *Proc. of ECCV* (2014), 468–484.
8. Lissermann, R., Huber, J., Hadjakos, A., and Mühlhäuser, M. Earput: Augmenting behind-the-ear devices for ear-based interaction. In *ACM CHI Extended Abstracts* (2013), 1323–1328.
9. Ogata, M., Sugiura, Y., Makino, Y., Inami, M., and Imai, M. SenSkin: Adapting Skin As a Soft Interface. In *Proc. ACM UIST* (2013), 539–544.
10. Perrault, S. T., Lecolinet, E., Eagan, J., and Guiard, Y. Watchit: Simple Gestures and Eyes-free Interaction for Wristwatches and Bracelets. In *Proc. ACM CHI* (2013), 1451–1460.
11. Saponas, T. S., Kelly, D., Parviz, B. A., and Tan, D. S. Optically Sensing Tongue Gestures for Computer Input. In *Proc. ACM UIST* (2009), 177–180.
12. Serrano, M., Ens, B. M., and Irani, P. P. Exploring the use of hand-to-face input for interacting with head-worn displays. In *Proc. of ACM SIGCHI* (2014), 3181–3190.
13. Song, J., Soros, G., Pece, F., Fanello, S., Izadi, S., Keskin, C., and Hilliges, O. In-air Gestures Around Unmodified Mobile Devices. In *Proc. ACM UIST* (2014), 319–329.
14. Yang, X.-D., Grossman, T., Wigdor, D., and Fitzmaurice, G. Magic finger: Always-available input through finger instrumentation. In *Proc. ACM UIST* (2012), 147–156.

zSense: Enabling Shallow Depth Gesture Recognition for Greater Input Expressivity on Smart Wearables

Anusha Withana, Roshan Peiris, Nipuna Samarasekara, Suranga Nanayakkara
Augmented Senses Group, International Design Center,
Singapore University of Technology and Design, Singapore
{anusha | roshan_peiris | nipuna | suranga}@sutd.edu.sg

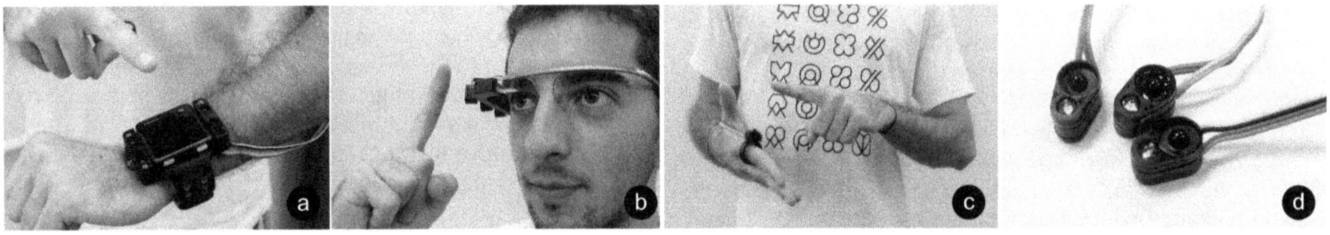

Figure 1: Shallow depth gesture recognition with *zSense*: a), b) Extending interaction space of a smartwatch and a smartglass, c) Enabling gesture interaction on a smart ring, d) *zSense* Sensor-emitter modules.

ABSTRACT
In this paper we present *zSense*, which provides greater input expressivity for spatially limited devices such as smart wearables through a shallow depth gesture recognition system using non-focused infrared sensors. To achieve this, we introduce a novel Non-linear Spatial Sampling (NSS) technique that significantly cuts down the number of required infrared sensors and emitters. These can be arranged in many different configurations; for example, number of sensor emitter units can be as minimal as one sensor and two emitters. We implemented different configurations of *zSense* on smart wearables such as smartwatches, smartglasses and smart rings. These configurations naturally fit into the flat or curved surfaces of such devices, providing a wide scope of *zSense* enabled application scenarios. Our evaluations reported over 94.8% gesture recognition accuracy across all configurations.

Author Keywords
Shallow Depth Gesture Recognition; Interacting with small devices; Smart Wearables; Compressive Sensing

ACM Classification Keywords
H.5.2 User Interfaces: Input devices and strategies

INTRODUCTION
The recent unveiling of smart wearable technologies has led to an increased demand for devices such as smartwatches[1], smartglasses[2], smart rings [24] and other body-worn accessories [25]. These compact devices often have to compromise between reduction of form factor and sophistication of interactions [30]. Among potential solutions, mid air gestures have been one of the leading frontiers [19, 10, 27] as it extends the interaction space beyond the device's surface area. However, many existing approaches [22] require significant processing power, physical space and energy resources that are extremely limited in compact devices. In addition, for smaller devices, shallow depth or close proximity gestures are more desirable [6]. As such, *zSense* focuses on providing greater input expressivity on these spatially limited devices.

In *zSense*, we introduce a non-linear spatial sampling (NSS) technique for shallow depth gesture recognition based on the compressive sensing principle [3, 21] and spatial light modulation [9]. The *zSense* system consists of infrared (IR) sensors and emitters that can be arranged in many different configurations (Figure 2). For example, the number of these units can be as minimal as one sensor and two emitters. NSS technique enables us to overcome the challenges faced by gesture recognition systems for small form factor devices due to following key features:

Spatially efficient non-focused gesture sensing: Typical non-focused gesture sensing requires a relatively larger separation between sensors [8] compared to *zSense*. In the current implementation, five expressive gestures could be detected from a single sensor and two emitters located within a $15mm$ space.

Low energy consumption: In *zSense*, the effective ON time of emitters are minimal due to a modulated spatial lighting pattern. For example, in the current implementation, emitters are on for only 8% of the time. This significantly

[1] `http://goo.gl/G7USq6`, `http://goo.gl/olfxj9`

[2] `http://goo.gl/2nZVEh`

CHI 2015, April 18–23, 2015, Seoul, Republic of Korea.
Copyright © 2015 ACM 978-1-4503-3145-6/15/04 ...$15.00.
http://dx.doi.org/10.1145/2702123.2702371

reduces the energy consumption compared to existing systems.

Low processing power: The effective data throughput of *zSense* is $1.2kBps$ (with three sensors) or $0.2kBps$ (with one sensor), which generates significantly less amount of data that is needed to be further processed.

Low cost: System uses low-cost off-the-shelf components and standard microprocessors without requiring any special hardware.

With these capabilities, *zSense* enables a broad application space leveraging on limited space and energy available in small scale smart devices. These devices and their unique form factors support different configurations of *zSense* to recognise expressive gestures with high accuracy. For example, embedding only two emitters and one sensor on the curved surface of a ring (Figure 1c) enables recognition of five gestures with over 91% accuracy. This, for example, could be paired with a smartglass to play a game on the go. Three sensors and emitters can be embedded on the narrow space between the screen and the edge of a smartwatch (Figure 1a) to recognize seven gestures with over 91% accuracy. Furthermore, the elongated surface on the temple of a smartglass can be embedded with three sensors and three emitters to recognise eight gestures with over 90% accuracy.

In the next few sections, we introduce the concept and theoretical background of *zSense*; different sensor-emitter configurations; details of the prototype implementation; user evaluation; and application possibilities. The contributions of this paper can be summarized as,

- Introduction of a non-linear spatial sampling (NSS) approach for shallow depth gesture recognition and development of a theoretical framework for *zSense*
- Exploration of various spatial arrangements of *zSense* configurations and identifiable gestures
- Prototype implementation of *zSense*, verification of its performance through user studies and a discussion of application space.

RELATED WORK

Extending the interaction space on smart devices has been a widely researched topic. Computer vision technologies such as 2D cameras [10], markers [4, 26] and commercial depth cameras[3] have been frequently used in the literature due to its ability to track gestures relatively robustly in real time [2]. Harrison et al., in OmniTouch [12] presents a wearable sensor-projection system to enable interaction on everyday surfaces. Here the authors use a depth camera attached to the shoulder to identify various gestures or surfaces for interaction. In [17], the authors use similar depth camera tracking system to provide around the device interaction to investigate free-space interactions for multi scale navigation with mobile devices. However, such computer vision based approaches generally operate by capturing the whole interaction space frame by frame, and processing each frame to identify gestures. As such, these technologies require high computational processing power, high energy for operation and generally a large setup which makes these technologies less desirable for spatially constrained application domains. Furthermore, since camera based systems have a minimum focusing distance, near-device (shallow depth) gestures are not recognisable.

Magnetic field sensing is another frequent technique that has been used to extend the interaction space around mobile devices [18, 1, 7]. Works such as [13] and [16] use external permanent magnets to extend the interaction space around the mobile device. Both works use the inbuilt magnetometers of the device to detect the magnetic field changes around the device as input to the system. Here, [13] uses a magnet on the finger for gestural input and [16] introduces new unpowered devices for interaction. However, the magnetic sensing approach requires instrumenting the user, generally having the user wear a magnet on the finger tip.

Almost all mobile devices are equipped with sound sensors. As such, TapSense [14] is a technology that uses the embedded sound sensor to classify various sounds. It allows the user to perform different interactions by interacting with an object using the fingernail, knuckle, tip, etc. Skinput [15] on the other hand uses the human body for acoustic transmission. Here, the authors introduce a sensor embedded armband to identify and localise vibrations caused by taps on the body as a form of input.

Infrared is another common technology that has been used to extend the interaction space with mobile devices. In SideSight, authors use arrays of infrared sensors attached on the two sides of a mobile device to provide multi-"touch" interaction when placed on a flat surface [5]. Similarly, in [23], authors use infrared beams reflected from the back of your hand to extend interactions with a smart wristwatch. Here, the users interact with the wristwatch by using the back of your hand as an input touch pad.

Additionally, infrared technologies have often been used for mid air gesture sensing as well. In Mime [8], authors introduce a 3D gesture sensor that uses a three pixel infrared time of flight module combined with a RGB camera. Here, the authors introduce tracking 3D hand gestures with the time of flight module, that is combined with the images from the RGB camera to perform finer shape based gestural interactions. However, in Gesture Watch [20], the authors use infrared proximity sensors on a wrist worn device combined with hidden Markov models to recognise gestures for interaction with other devices. The use of infrared in this context requires to light up the whole interaction space [5, 20] which generally requires relatively high energy for the scope of spatially constrained applications. In addition, capturing and processing the whole interaction space would require relatively high computation power [20]. Similarly, Mime [8] operates at a high sampling rate which increases the processing power required for the system.

Our main goal with *zSense* is to develop a low power, low processing overhead and a spatially efficient gesture sensing

[3] `http://goo.gl/wjFcjn`

technology for wearable devices. As such, even though technologies such as depth cameras provide extremely accurate sensing, such technologies require a vast amount of processing power due to the amount of information captured by the camera. Some other technologies such as magnetic sensing requires instrumenting the user's fingers or sound sensing requires a high processing power. In contrast, in *zSense*, we propose NSS to spatially modulate the sensing environment such that a minimal and only required amount of information can be captured for sensing. As such, NSS minimises the required number of sensors and emitters for gesture sensing on devices with limited space. This significantly reduces its power and processing requirements and improves its spatial efficiency.

ZSENSE CONCEPT

zSense concept is based on optimising space, power and cost while being able to recognize a reasonable number of expressive gestures. To this end, we adapted compressive sensing and spatial light modulation to propose the concept of Non-linear Spatial Sampling (NSS) for gesture recognition.

Non-linear Spatial Sampling (NSS)

Computer vision based gesture recognition systems require a high sensor density since each spatial location is mapped to a pixel sensor (linear sampling). Similarly, other approaches such as IR based systems, equally sample the space with a high number of sensors (high density) [5, 20]. In *zSense*, we use a significantly less amount of emitters with relative spatial displacements (linear or angular) between each other, and temporally modulate the emitters with different lighting patterns. Each sensor records separate measurements of reflected light from a target per each modulating pattern. Since sensor values represents a cumulative sum of the reflected light from a spatial light pattern, recorded data carries spatial information of the target. Therefore this non-linear spatial sampling (NSS) scheme enables *zSense* to minimize the number of sensors and the number of emitters needed, leading to reduced power and signal processing requirements.

zSense Configurations

Any *zSense* system must have at least two IR emitters coupled with one or more sensors. The spatial arrangement of sensors and emitters is a key factor in determining the modulated spatial illumination pattern and the quality of the captured signal. Therefore, selecting an appropriate spatial configuration is vital to *zSense*'s operation. In addition, the accuracy and the number of recognizable gestures increases with the number of sensors and emitters. For smaller devices, a trade off is required for the accuracy and the number of desirable gestures at the design stage.

In *zSense*, we use spatial configurations of emitters to implement NSS. This can be achieved by a linear displacement or an angular displacement. Linear configurations can be achieved in two axes (displacement along front facing axis of emitters will not change the spatial pattern), and angular as the relative angle. In this paper, we describe three configurations to demonstrate these three variations using a linear displacement along one axis (Figure 2a), linear displacements

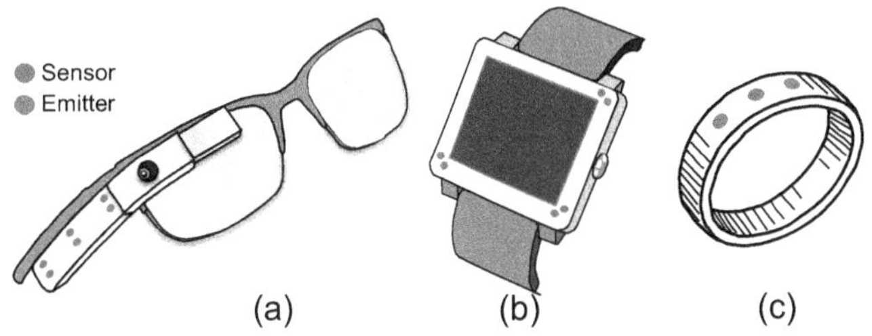

Figure 2: Selected set of spatial configurations: a) One axis linear displacement (3S3E linear), b) Two axes linear displacement (3S3E triangular), c) Angular displacement (1S2E angular).

along two axes (Figure 2b) and angular variations (Figure 2c). These configurations naturally support flat and curved surfaces.

One Axis Linear Displacement (3S3E Linear): This configuration is studied using three sensors and three emitters arrangement as shown in Figure 2a. This arrangement makes sense for devices with an elongated flat surface such as temple of a smartglass or a tie-pin.

Two Axes Linear Displacement (3S3E Triangular): This configuration is shown in Figure 2b where sensor units are arranged in a triangular shape. This configuration supports devices with a flat surface (such as a smartwatch frame) to perform simple gestures along either axis of the device.

Angular Displacement (1S2E Angular): This is ideal when the space available for interaction has a curved surface, such as buttons, earrings, finger rings etc. For example, Figure 2c shows a configuration where two emitters and a sensor are mounted on a ring. NSS is achieved by leveraging the form of the ring where curvature of the surface introduces an angular displacement between the sensor and emitters in opposite directions.

Gesture Space

We use *Form* based categorisation [29] to name the surface gestures. *Form* describes the gestures that are differentiated with pose and motion and is further divided into six categories, in which we have selected *static pose*, *dynamic pose* and *static pose and path*. These gestures are shown in Figure 3.

Static pose paths shown in Figure 3c can be performed in symmetrical mirror images in case of the sensors are place symmetrically, for an example, swipe far (Figure 3G5) and swipe close (Figure 3G6) can be performed from right to left and left to right. In the same manner, diagonal swipe (Figure 3G7) can be from left to right and right to left. Circular gesture (Figure 3G8) can be clockwise or anti-clockwise.

Gesture Set

Within the gesture space described above, we select a set of gestures (Table 1) based on the following criteria.

Applicability: We include most commonly used gestures such as swipes to be studied across all the considered configurations.

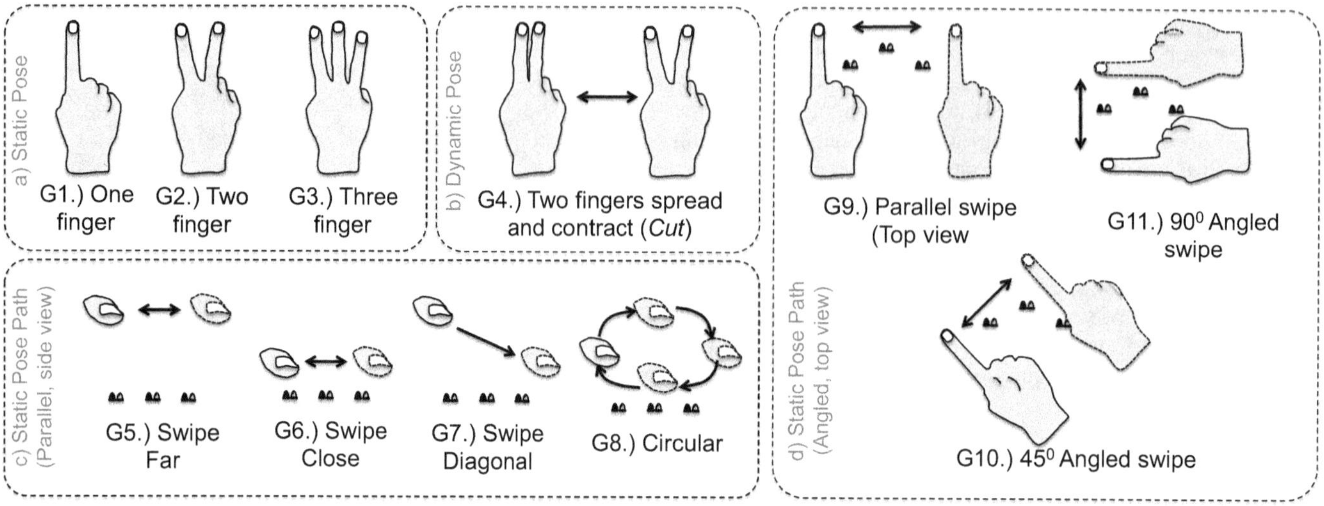

Figure 3: Set of gestures examined in the paper: a) Three *static poses*, b) One *dynamic pose*, c) four basic *static pose paths*, d) three angular variations in the direction of *static pose paths*.

Spatial Configuration		Static Pose	Dynamic Pose	Pose Path
3S3E	Linear	G1,G2,G3	G4	G5R,G6R,G7R G8CCW, G8CW
	Triangular	G1,G2,G3	G4	G7R, G10,G11
1S2E	Angular	G1,G2	G4	G5L,G7R

Table 1: Set of selected gestures and configurations.

Uniqueness: Gestures were selected to reflect unique features, such as poses, pose path, and dynamic poses. Only one iteration of mirrored gestures were selected (i.e. swipe left and swipe right are symmetric and only one of them is selected).

Relevance: Gestures with special relevance to a given configuration has been selected. For example, angled swipes (G10 and G11 of Figure 3) are only relevant to non linear arrangements, and only included as such.

Theory of Operation

We derived a generalised mathematical model to explain the principle of *zSense* operation. This model helps to make initial design choices in a *zSense* based gesture recognition system, by simulating it for various spacing and choice of components.

Received Intensity Model: Let us consider a *zSense* setup with m number of emitters, n number of sensors and a point target T at location $\vec{T_l}$. Figure 4a shows a simplified configuration of a reference emitter E_i ($i = 0, 1, 2, ..., m-1$) at location $\vec{E_{li}}$ directed at $\vec{E_{di}}$ and sensor S_j ($j = 0, 1, 2, ..., n-1$) at location $\vec{S_{lj}}$ directed at $\vec{S_{dj}}$. Let us take a ray received at sensor S_j, r, reflected from point target at $\vec{T_l}$, emitted from the emitter E_i. In order to calculate the received intensity at S_j, let's take optical characteristic-radiation pattern of emitter and sensor gain profiles to be, $I_i(\theta)$ and $G_j(\beta)$ respectively for the ith emitter and j^{th} sensor.

The received intensity $f_{i,j}(\vec{T_l})$ at the sensor S_j from a ray emitted by emitter E_i with reference intensity W_i and reflected at target point T_l can be calculated using inverse-square law as,

$$f_{i,j}(\vec{T_l}) = \frac{I_i(\theta_{(i,\vec{T_l})})G_j(\beta_{(j,\vec{T_l})})W_i}{16\pi^2(|\vec{T_l}-\vec{E_{li}}|^2|\vec{S_{lj}}-\vec{T_l}|^2)} \quad (1)$$

where
$\theta_{(i,\vec{T_l})} = \cos^{-1}\frac{(\vec{T_l}-\vec{E_{li}})\cdot\vec{E_{di}}}{|\vec{T_l}-\vec{E_{li}}|}$ and $\beta_{(j,\vec{T_l})} = \cos^{-1}\frac{(\vec{T_l}-\vec{S_{lj}})\cdot\vec{S_{dj}}}{|\vec{T_l}-\vec{S_{lj}}|}$

Note that $|\vec{E_{di}}| = |\vec{S_{dk}}| = 1$ since they are unit vectors and we assume the target to be radiating isotropically, and ignore the Lambert's cosine coefficient due to radial fall-off [8].

From equation 1, for each sensor-emitter combination, we can construct sensor-emitter cross intensity matrix with $m \times n$ dimensions, where each element $f_{i,j}(\vec{T_l})$ represents the power intensity received by j^{th} sensor due to the illumination by i^{th} emitter reflected by a target point at a given location $\vec{T_l}$.

Spatial light modulation pattern can be created by turning ON and OFF m emitters with p number of different patterns; where $p \leq 2^m - 1$. These patterns can be represented in a $p \times m$ matrix Λ, where each row represents a pattern and an element in a row, $\lambda_{i,j}$, represents whether the emitter is on or off using binary 1 or 0 in the given pattern.

Based on the pattern matrix Λ and sensor-emitter cross intensity matrix F, we can now compute the cumulative measured intensity matrix $A_{\vec{T_l}}$, with dimensions $p \times n$.

$$A_{\vec{T_l}} = \Lambda \times F \quad (2)$$

Any member of $A_{\vec{T_l}}$, $\alpha_{k,j}(\vec{T_l})$, contains a measured intensity at j^{th} sensor by the cumulative sum of different ray compo-

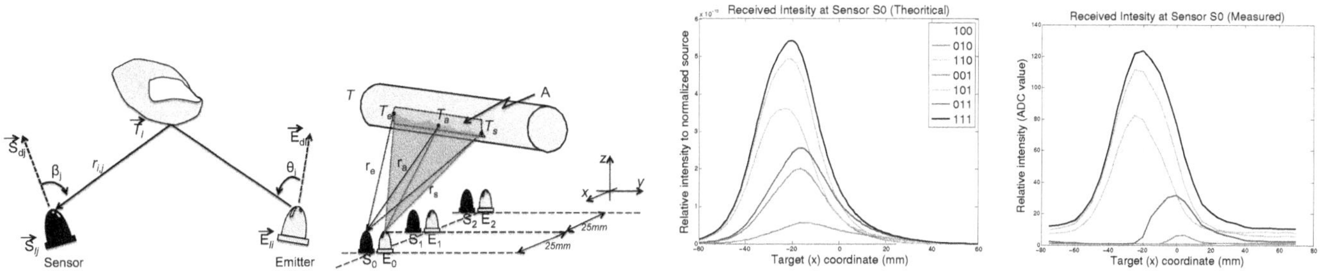

(a) (b) (c) (d)

Figure 4: a) Configuration of a ray (r) emitted from emitter E, at location $\vec{E_l}$, reflected from a point T at location $\vec{T}$, received at a sensor S at location $\vec{S_l}$. Unit vectors $\vec{E_d}$ and $\vec{S_d}$ represent the directions of the emitter and sensor respectively. θ and β represents the existing and incidence angles of the ray r, b) Equally spaced linear configuration of three sensor-emitter units with IR rays reflecting from a cylindrical target, c) Profiles of the simulated values from one sensor, d) Measured values for the same sensor with same configuration and conditions.

nents emitted by different emitters, reflected from target point $\vec{T_l}$ according to the kth SLM pattern.

$$\alpha_{k,j}(\vec{T_l}) = \sum_{i=0}^{i=m-1} \lambda_{k,i} f_{i,j}(\vec{T_l}) \quad (3)$$

Usage of Theoretical Model: In order to demonstrate the theoretical model and its practical significance, we compared the experimental measurements with model-based simulations. For this purpose, we implemented 3 sensors and 3 emitters ($n = 3, m = 3$) configuration as shown in Figure 4b. We use off the shelf emitter, Optek technologies OP293[4], with emission angle of half power at $\pm 30^0$. Sensor used is Osram SFH203FA[5] half sensitivity angle $\pm 20^0$. We estimated the normalized $I_d(\theta)$ and $G_s(\beta)$ for emitter and sensor respectively to best fit the shape and parameters given in the data-sheet as follows,

$I_d(\theta) = \frac{1}{9\sqrt{2\pi}} e^{\frac{-\theta^2}{162}}$ and, $G_s(\beta) = \frac{1}{1+|\frac{\beta}{20}|^3}$

Due to the linear arrangement and the symmetry along $y = 0$ plane, we can assume each sensor-emitter units (i.e. S_0, E_0) are co-located along the line intersecting $y = 0$ and $z = 0$ planes. In the practical setup, each sensor unit was $25mm$ apart along the x axis.

We used a cylindrical rod with diameter $15mm$ as the target to imitate a human finger. In order to calculate the total reflected energy towards a given sensor i from the pattern k, we integrate over the complete reflective area of the target, A as shown in figure 4b. However, considering the symmetry of the target about $y = 0$ plane, the average reflected intensity will be representative of a point target T_a, lying on the $y = 0$. In order to easily compare the calculated and measured values at individual sensors, we kept the target constantly at $z = 50mm$ from the sensor plane ($y = 0$), and move it along the x axis in $5mm$ steps, taking 100 readings per sensor per pattern. Location of S_1E_1 is considered as the origin.

Three emitters E_i for $i = 0, 1, 2$ create a total of 7 patterns (i.e. $p = 7$). This is done by sequentially switching ON a single IR (001) to all three IR's (111). These patterns resulted in a measurement matrix A of 7×3, corresponding to 21 total measurements (i.e. 7 measurements from each of the 3 sensors) per any given $\vec{T_l}$ target point. As can be seen from Figure 4c and 4d, simulated values and measured values are correlated. Due to the space limitation, we only show the measured and simulated values of the received pattern for one sensor corresponding to each of the 7 emitted patterns. From the simulation, one can observe that once target displacement exceed 25mm (Figure 4c and 4d), curves get extremely converged. This span depends on the sensor directionality G_s and emitter relative radiant pattern I_d. Therefore, according to the choice of sensors and emitters, this model would be helpful to simulate the gesture sensitive area. In our prototype, we chose $25mm$ to be the ideal sensor-emitter unit displacement because we used the same sensors and emitters described above.

IMPLEMENTATION

zSense prototype is implemented using off the shelf IR sensors (SFH203FA) and emitters (OP293) and expected to work with maximum of 3 sensors and 3 emitter configurations. Sensor-emitter pairs are designed as single modules which can be plug into the main electronics unit.

Prototype

Figure 5a shows the block diagram of the *zSense*'s electronics unit. Sensors and emitters are driven using a commonly available Arduino Pro Mini[6] (16MHz, 5V) microprocessor to create the SLM pattern, which is modulated at 38kHz to reduce background noise. Figure 5b, 5c, 5d shows SLM patterns generated by linear 3S3E configuration. Patterns shown are (0,1,1), (1,0,0), (1,0,1) respectively. They were shot as the IR light reflected on a vertically standing sheet of white paper along the horizontal sensor line using an IR camera.

IR sensor input is amplified by a current to voltage converting amplifier (ST TL074 op-amp) followed by a phase lock amplifier (using TL074) to get a high signal to noise ratio (SNR). This significantly reduces the noise from external sources such as florescent lights. Our experiments were carried out directly under fluorescent lights, and the observed

[4]`http://goo.gl/d428fz`
[5]`http://goo.gl/sxTdLR`

[6]`http://arduino.cc/en/Main/ArduinoBoardProMini`

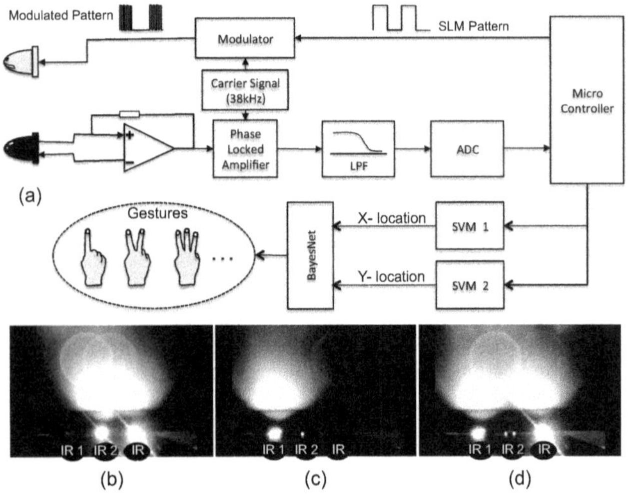

Figure 5: a) Prototype hardware block diagram, b),c),d) Three different SLM emitter patterns, (0,1,1), (1,0,0), (1,0,1)

effect was minimal. We have tested the system outdoors and the performance reduced only when the sensors were exposed to direct sunlight. We digitize the amplified signal using MCP3204 analog to digital converter (ADC) and transmit the data to the computer. ADC needs $10us$ conversion cycle, therefore each emitter pattern kept ON for $10us$ per sensor. Measurements from different patterns are combined into one data frame, and averaged over 10 frames. These frames were transmitted to the computer at rate of $50Hz$. This reduced acquisition rate contributes to low power consumption. Total emitter power consumed by *zSense* with 3S3E is $16.8mW$ and 1S2E $4.2mW$. Amplification and ADC stages consume about $3mW$ per sensor. Resulting total power for 3S3E to be $29mW$ and 1S2E to be $7.2mW$ (excluding microprocessor). Power saving mechanisms such as sleep modes can be introduced to save the power even further.

Software Classifier

A software classifier was implemented as a two stage process with two Support Vector Machines (SVMs) and a BayesNetwork algorithm provided by the Weka Toolkit [11]. First stage estimates the finger locations and second stage determines the exact gestures.

In the first stage, *zSense* module sends the measured IR light level of each sensor for each pattern as a 8 bit (ADC reading) numerical value. These readings are fed into the two Multi class SVMs which are trained to estimate vertical and horizontal level of the finger location respectively. Additionally, the number of fingers are determined by the same classifiers. For example, we trained two SVM classifiers using a rig to estimate 5 vertical (first classifier) and 5 horizontal levels (second classifier) for 1 finger, 2 vertical and 1 horizontal levels for two fingers and a single point for three fingers.

In the second stage, 20 consecutive finger locations are fed into a multinomial Naive Bayes classifier to determine the corresponding gesture.

EVALUATION

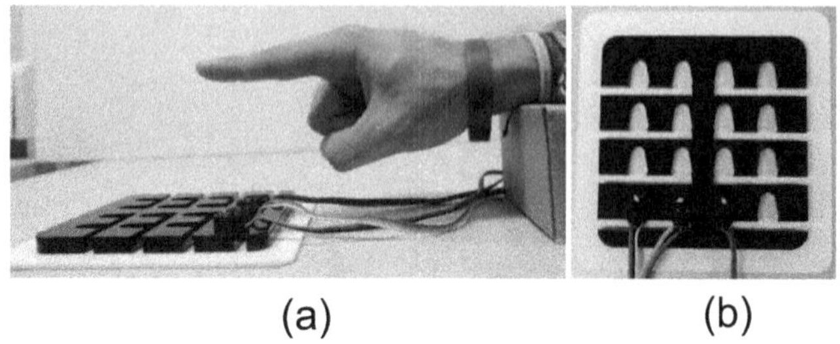

Figure 7: a) Side view of the study setup showing arm rest position and sensor grid, b) Top view of the sensor grid

The main objective of the experiment was to assess whether the current implementation of *zSense* is sufficiently accurate so as to ensure that future user studies with *zSense* enabled applications will yield unbiased data. Another goal of the study is to mix and match different gestures to different configurations, so that, in future, designers can use the findings of this paper as a key to create gesture interfaces using *zSense*. We describe the gesture set that was tested, the study method and the results.

Method

Twelve (11 males and a female, age with min = 23, max = 36, mean = 28.3) participants took part in the study. All of them were right-handed and used their dominant hand to perform the gestures.

The experiment was conducted in three separate sessions, studying 3S3E linear, 3S3E triangular and 1S2E angular configurations respectively. For each session, the selected set of gestures were performed as shown in the table 1. In order to keep the relative sensor-emitter locations consistent between users and configurations, we used a grid assembly as shown in Figure 7.

Before starting each trial, the experimenter demonstrated the intended gesture to the subject. The subject was then given a few test trials to practice the gesture. Order of the sessions were counterbalanced and the gestures were randomized to eliminate bias. Subjects were instructed to only bring the finger to the sensitive region of *zSense* at the start of the gesture and to remove it once they finished. Since *zSense* can identify the presence of a finger, start and end point of the gesture were identified automatically. Participants were allowed to take a rest anytime during the study and average duration for the study was 40 minutes including the training and evaluation phases.

Training phase: During the training session, participants were briefed about the gestures they had to perform. In addition, they were instructed to adjust their gestures in order to capture variations of the same gesture. During the training session, we captured 20 instances of each gesture. For each gesture, finger location sequence was identified using two Support Vector Machine (SVM) models. Finger location training (i.e. training SVM modes) is not required for individual users. Therefore the two SVMs were trained by the experimenter before the user study.

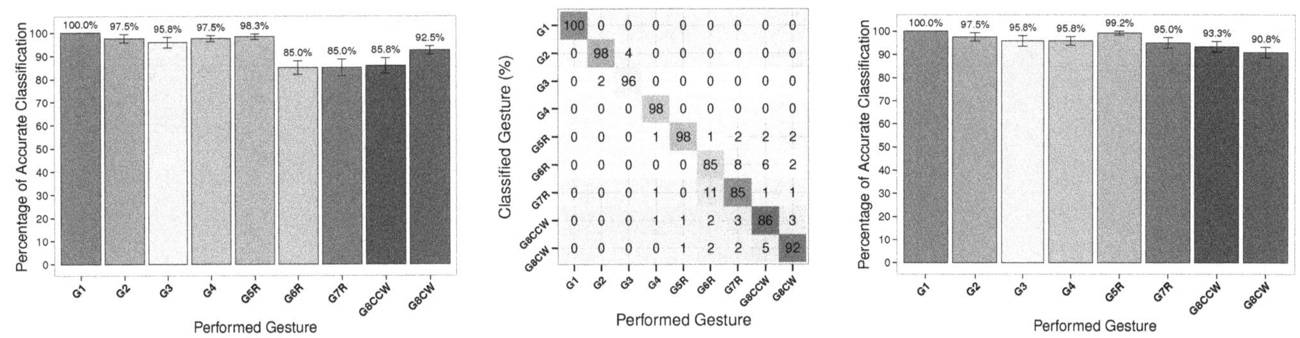

(a) (b) (c)

Figure 6: Evaluation results for session 1 (Linear arrangement of *zSense* modules): (a) Classification accuracy for all 9 gestures in the session, (b) Confusion matrix between gestures, (c) classification accuracy after G6R is removed from the gesture set.

Evaluation phase: During the evaluation phase, participants were requested to perform 210 gestures. This corresponds to 21 gestures (9 in session 1, 7 in session 2 and 5 in session 3) and each gesture having 10 repetitions. We use this to calculate the accuracy of each gesture per each user with a BayesNet classifier.

Results

Accuracy Measures: The accuracy for each gesture is measured as a percentage of number of correctly classified gestures of that type. Our results showed that the accuracy of overall gesture recognition (all the gesture across all of configurations) is at 94.8% (SD=8.3%). In addition, mean percentage of confusion (false positives) are at 0.81% (SD=1.69%, max=10.8%). Results are discussed separately for each session.

Session 1: Linear Arrangement: Session 1 used three sensor and emitter units in a linear arrangement (Figure 2a) with $25mm$ space between them. We tested 9 gestures in this arrangement: one finger (G1), two fingers (G2), three fingers (G3), Cut (G4), Left to Right Swipe far (G5R), Left to Right Swipe close (G6R), Left to Right Swipe diagonal (G7R), Clockwise circle (G8CW), Counterclockwise circle (G8CCW). Short form of the name given within the brackets refer to the gesture number given in Figure 3 followed by letters to indicate the direction the gesture is performed. Figure 6a shows the average accuracy of classified gestures by 3S3E linear arrangement. All the gestures have accuracy over 85%, leading to overall accuracy result 93.05% (SD=9.61%).

Left to Right Swipe close (G6R, 85.0%, SD=10.0%) and Left to Right Swipe diagonal (G7R, 85.0%, SD=12.4%) had the least accuracy percentages. Using the confusion matrix shown in Figure 6b, it is evident that 10.8% of G6R is misclassified as G7R and 7.5% vice versa. One cause for the high confusion between close and diagonal right swipe (G6R and G7R) is most of the participants tends to follow a steep diagonal angle, so that the finger reaches close to the sensors in mid sweep. A solution to this problem would be either eliminate one of the gestures or be more specific in the instructions given to users.

At the post-hoc analysis, we removed the gesture G6R from the gesture data set and reclassified the data. Figure 6c shows the accuracy of the reduced gesture. Student's t-test reveals a significant improvement in G7R ($p < 0.01$) and G8CCW ($p < 0.05$). Average accuracy reduction in G8CCW was not statistically significant. Removing G6R can be justified because G6R is performed closer to the screen, where this might be confused with alternative technologies such as capacitive hover sensing.

Session 2: Triangular Arrangement: In session 2, three

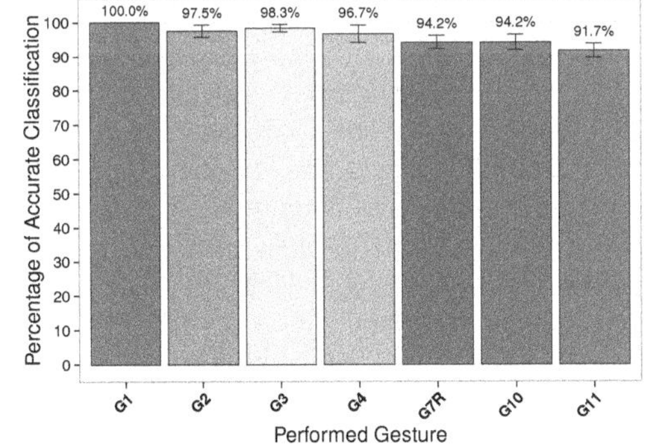

Figure 8: Classification accuracy of the gestures used in session 2 (Triangular arrangement of *zSense* modules)

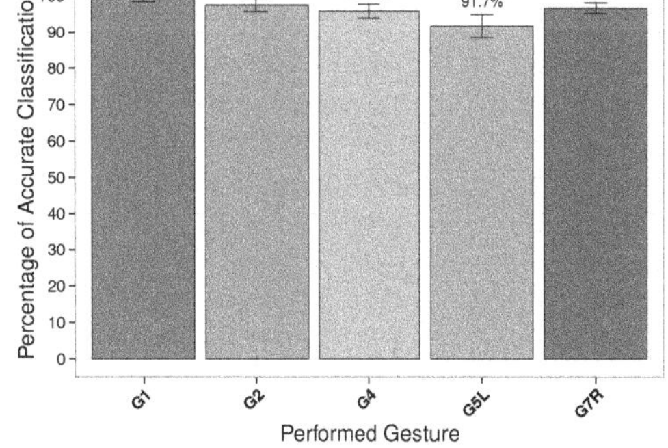

Figure 9: Classification accuracy of the gestures used in session 3 (Angular arrangement of *zSense* modules)

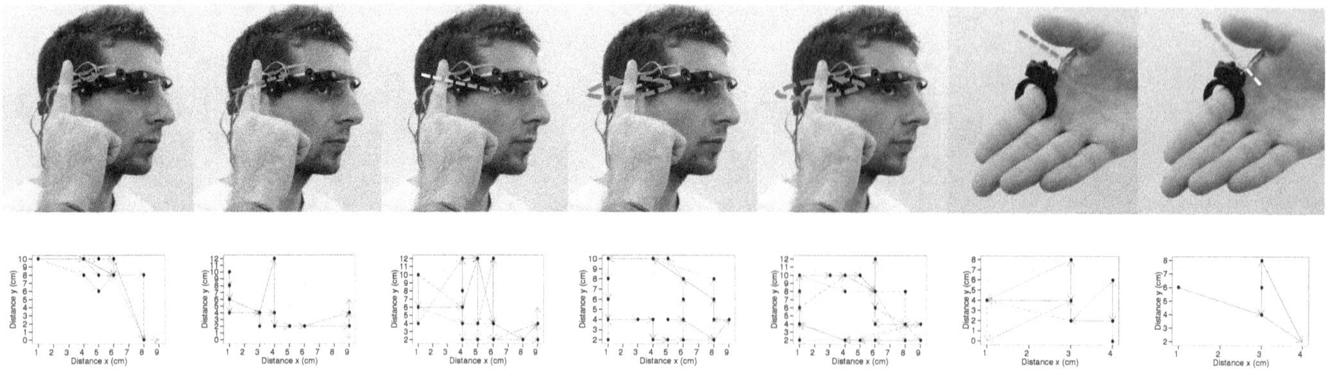

(a) G5R (b) G6R (c) G7R (d) G8CCW (e) G8CW (f) G5L (g) G7R

Figure 10: Detected $x - y$ finger locations of different static pose path gestures by *zSense* for five different instances

sensor-emitter units were arranged in a triangular configuration as shown in (Figure 2b right ($25mm$ spacing along the edges). We selected 7 gestures in this arrangement (Figure 3): one finger (G1), two fingers (G2), three fingers (G3), Cut (G4), Left to Right Swipe diagonal (G7R), 45^0Angled swipe (G10) and 90^0 Angled swipe(G11). Figure 8 shows the accuracies of each of the gestures in 3S3E triangular arrangement. All the gestures have accuracy over 91%, leading to overall accuracy of 96.0% (SD=6.77%). G11 (45° angled gesture) has the least accuracy at 91.7% (SD=7.18%).

Session 3: Angular Arrangement: For the session 3, one sensor and two emitters (at an angle of 30^0) in a linear arrangement was used (Figure 2c1). In this session the following 5 gestures were analysed: one finger (G1), two fingers (G2), three fingers (G3), Cut (G4), Right to left swipe close(G5L) and Left to Right Swipe diagonal (G7R).

Gestures used in this session had an overall classification accuracy of 96.2% (SD=7.15%). Least accurate gesture was Left right swipe close (G5L) with mean percentage accuracy 91.7% (SD=11.15%). Results are shown in the figure 9.

DISCUSSION

We discuss the various aspects related to the concept, implementation and the evaluation of the *zSense*. We hope that these insights will help other researchers in the field to design spatially limited devices with greater input expressivity.

***Implications of results*:** *zSense* is meant as a technology that provides greater input expressivity for devices with limited space, processing power and energy. We utilise non-linear spatial sampling to minimise the number of sensors and emitters required to identify shallow depth gestures. In this paper, we presented *zSense* configurations with a single sensor and two emitters capable of identifying five expressive gestures and two, three sensors - three emitter configurations capable of identifying eight and seven gestures with overall gesture recognition accuracy of 94.8%. From the evaluation results, we can conclude *zSense* is capable of identifying a significantly high amount of gestures with very few sensors and emitters, leading to high *gesture to sensor-density ratio*. Since the overall power consumption of NSS approach is lower, and the amount of data collected is smaller, *zSense* can be used as a durable and power efficient gesture recognition system in battery powered embedded systems.

***Training Process*:** The current version of *zSense* requires two stages of training. First stage is trained per configuration and used to estimate finger location. This stage is required once for each configuration and does not depend on the individual user. Second stage is trained per user to extract gestures. However, the second level training is required by individual users. This is required to be performed only once at the beginning which also allows the user to familiarise with the new gestures.

***Position Accuracy*:** *zSense* utilizes the non-linear spatial sampling in extracting a valid spatial representation of the finger location with minimal number of sensors. Sensitive region of *zSense* is very shallow with a resolution of about 20mm displacement between two adjacent detectable finger locations. A slight movement of fingers could lead to inaccurate estimation of a point. However, this does not affect *zSense*'s performance since multiple consecutive locations traced by a finger are able to counterbalance between accurate and erroneous location estimates and identify the correct gesture. This can be seen from Figure 10, where $x - y$ locations (of 5 instances) of different *static pose paths* are shown. These extracted $x - y$ locations were sufficient for a simple classifier to accurately identify the exact gestures. Gesture recognition accuracy can be improved even further by selecting only the required gestures as shown in Figure 6c.

***Configuration-Gesture Relationship*:** *zSense* concept allows various configurations based on the number of sensors, emitters and their spatial displacement. Specific configuration can be chosen depending on the form factor of a particular device. For example, curved surface of a ring naturally provide the angular configuration required in 1S2E configuration of *zSense* (Figure 2c) and is able to recognize five expressive gestures with high accuracy. Similarly, 3S3E triangular configuration can be embedded on devices with flat squarish surfaces, such as a smartwatch (Figure 1a), enabling seven recognisable distinct gestures. The 3S3E linear configuration (Figure 1b), fits into devices with an elongated surfaces and able to distinguish eight gestures with high accuracy. Adding more sensors-emitters would not significantly contribute to the accuracy of gesture detection but would increase the interactive area.

zSense Application Space

Three potential application prototypes (Figure 11) are described here to demonstrate the broad application space of *zSense*. We hope these explorations will help peers in the field to inform future designs of expressive input capabilities on spatially limited devices.

***Extending interaction space of a Smartwatch*:** Integrating smartwatch with 3S3E triangular configuration can improve the interaction in two different ways. Firstly, it enables eyes-free interactions. For example, one can control a music application through swipe gestures without looking at the device, which is a useful feature when users attention is required for another task such as jogging. Secondly, gestures can add new possibilities to address the limitations of interactions. For example, playing a mobile game on a smartwatch could be difficult due to the limited space (fat-finger [28]), however, with *zSense*, one can use static poses and dynamic poses along with pose paths to trigger different aspects of the game (i.e. in a FPS game, G4 to shoot, G2 and G3 to change weapons). The smartwatch prototype is shown in Figure 11a, 11b.

***Enabling gesture interaction on a ring*:** We integrated the 1S2E configuration on the rim of a ring as shown in Figure 11c, 11d, 11e. The ring is able to sense five gestures, four of which can be easily performed with the thumb, enabling it as a private and personal gestural interface as proposed in [6]. Figure 11c shows a usage scenario of the ring interface as a slide controller. Additionally, Figure 11d shows how both hands can be used to interact using static poses (G1, G2) and dynamic pose (G4). Interacting directly with a glass can lead to fatigue over prolonged time. With *zSense*, arm can be kept in a relaxing position as shown in Figure 11e.

***Clip-on pin as a flexible and portable gesture interface*:** Figure 11f, 11g, 11h shows a clip-on pin prototype that uses the 3S3E linear configuration of *zSense*. This can be used as a flexible and portable mediating interface for other smart devices such as smartglasses, mobile phones, PDAs, etc. For example, it enables complex pose paths such as G8CW, G8CCW, that can allow fast scrolling a web page or a photo library through continuous cyclic gestures. It can can be attached to the pocket, collar and sleeves as shown in Figure 11f, 11g, 11h) to perform different gesture interactions according to the context.

LIMITATIONS OF THE CURRENT SYSTEM

Gestures identifiable through *zSense* depend on the spatial configuration and can be chosen based on the form factor of a particular device. For example, we observed that sensitive area is too narrow to perform G8 in both 3S3E triangular and 1S2E angular cases. Also, we observed that complex gestures such as G3 create significant ambiguities. As discussed under results, there is a high ambiguity between G5R and G6R.

In addition, sensing space of *zSense* is limited to 15cm from the sensors and only capable of accurately recognizing the finger gestures as opposed to high-resolution hand/finger/body gesture recognition provided by systems such as (Leap motion (LM), MS Kinect (MSK). However, LM/MSK uses focused sensing, which requires gestures to be performed from a certain distant from the sensor. This would be not desirable for applications that require subtle and private interactions. Since *zSense* uses non-focused sensors, it can detect very close proximity gestures.

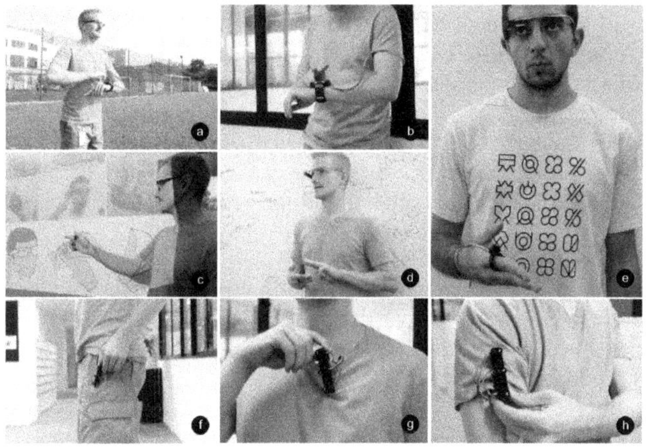

Figure 11: Application Space of *zSense*

zSense is unable to detect the precise location of user fingers with high accuracy. This is because, *zSense* was developed as a gesture sensing technology, which, detects a sparse *set* of finger locations to identify the gesture through a machine learning algorithm. Therefore, within its intended domain of gesture sensing, *zSense* works with high accuracy for gesture sensing applications. However, in our future steps, we intend to focus on the accuracy of the of the finger locations which would enhance and enrich the application scope of *zSense*.

Furthermore, since the current prototype of *zSense* uses IR sensors, limitations posed by IR technology persist in *zSense*. Current prototype utilizes noise resilient amplification techniques (i.e. phase lock amplification) to reduce the background noise to a minimum level. Even then *zSense*'s performance would be negatively affected by direct sunlight. However, through our experience with the system, we identified that this effect can be avoided by simply shading the sensors from direct sunlight. Additionally, the current version of *zSense* was developed using off-the-shelf components. However, by using surface mount components, customized printed circuit boards, etc., the system can be made much smaller and can be used in a more integrated manner.

CONCLUSION

In this paper we described *zSense*, a novel technology that effectively enables shallow depth gesture recognition on spatially limited devices such as smart wearables. We presented a non-linear spatial sampling (NSS) scheme which minimizes the sensor density, processing power and energy consumption required. The current implementation of *zSense* consumes less power ($1S2E < 8mW$, $3S3E < 30mW$) and requires less processing capabilities (throughput rate $1S2E = 0.2kBps$, $3S3E = 1.2kBps$). Our evaluations reported overall gesture recognition accuracy of 94.8% across three main configurations. This coupled with *zSense*'s ability to be used in different configurations, depending on the device form factor (as discussed), enhances its application scope with smart devices such as smartwatches, smartrings, smartglasses. Furthermore, the scope of *zSense* can be extended to mobile phones, tablets and other ubiquitous devices.

ACKNOWLEDGMENT

This work was supported by the International Design Center of the Singapore University of Technology and Design. Also, we thank all study participants for their time and valuable feedback.

REFERENCES

1. Ashbrook, D., Baudisch, P., and White, S. Nenya: Subtle and eyes-free mobile input with a magnetically-tracked finger ring. In *Proc. of CHI '11* (2011), 2043–2046.
2. Bailly, G., Mller, J., Rohs, M., Wigdor, D., and Kratz, S. ShoeSense: A new perspective on gestural interaction and wearable applications. In *Proc. of CHI '12* (2012), 1239–1248.
3. Baraniuk, R. G. Compressive sensing. *IEEE signal processing magazine 24*, 4 (2007), 118–121.
4. Bencina, R., Kaltenbrunner, M., and Jorda, S. Improved topological fiducial tracking in the reacTIVision system. In *IEEE CVPR Workshops* (2005), 99–99.
5. Butler, A., Izadi, S., and Hodges, S. Sidesight: multi- touch interaction around small devices. In *Proc. of UIST '08* (2008), 201–204.
6. Chan, L., Liang, R.-H., Tsai, M.-C., Cheng, K.-Y., Su, C.-H., Chen, M. Y., Cheng, W.-H., and Chen, B.-Y. FingerPad: Private and subtle interaction using fingertips. In *Proc. of UIST '13* (2013), 255–260.
7. Chen, K.-Y., Lyons, K., White, S., and Patel, S. uTrack: 3d input using two magnetic sensors. In *Proc. of UIST '13* (2013), 237–244.
8. Colao, A., Kirmani, A., Yang, H. S., Gong, N.-W., Schmandt, C., and Goyal, V. K. Mime: Compact, low-power 3d gesture sensing for interaction with head-mounted displays. In *Proc. of UIST '13* (2013), 227–236.
9. Duarte, M., Davenport, M., Takhar, D., Laska, J., Kelly, K., and Baraniuk, R. Single-pixel imaging via compressive sampling. *IEEE Signal Processing Magazine 25*, 2 (2008), 83–91.
10. Gustafson, S., Bierwirth, D., and Baudisch, P. Imaginary interfaces: Spatial interaction with empty hands and without visual feedback. In *Proc. of UIST '10* (2010), 3–12.
11. Hall, M., Frank, E., Holmes, G., Pfahringer, B., Reutemann, P., and Witten, I. H. The WEKA data mining software. *ACM SIGKDD Explorations Newsletter 11*, 1 (2009), 10.
12. Harrison, C., Benko, H., and Wilson, A. D. OmniTouch: Wearable multitouch interaction everywhere. In *Proc. of UIST '11* (2011), 441–450.
13. Harrison, C., and Hudson, S. E. Abracadabra: wireless, high-precision, and unpowered finger input for very small mobile devices. In *Proc. of UIST '09* (2009), 121.
14. Harrison, C., Schwarz, J., and Hudson, S. TapSense: enhancing finger interaction on touch surfaces. In *Proc. of UIST '11* (2011), 627–636.
15. Harrison, C., Tan, D., and Morris, D. Skinput: Appropriating the body as an input surface chris. In *Proc. of CHI '10* (2010), 453–462.
16. Hwang, S., Ahn, M., and Wohn, K.-y. MagGetz: customizable passive tangible controllers on and around conventional mobile devices. In *Proc. of UIST '13* (2013), 411–416.
17. Jones, B., Sodhi, R., Forsyth, D., Bailey, B., and Maciocci, G. Around device interaction for multiscale navigation. In *Proc. of MobileHCI '12* (2012), 83–92.
18. Ketabdar, H., Roshandel, M., and Yksel, K. A. Towards using embedded magnetic field sensor for around mobile device 3d interaction. In *Proc. of MobileHCI '10* (2010), 153–156.
19. Kim, D., Hilliges, O., Izadi, S., Butler, A. D., Chen, J., Oikonomidis, I., and Olivier, P. Digits:freehand 3d interactions anywhere using a wrist-worn gloveless sensor. In *Proc. of UIST'12* (2012), 167–176.
20. Kim, J., He, J., Lyons, K., and Starner, T. The gesture watch: A wireless contact-free gesture based wrist interface. In *Proc. of ISWC '07* (2007), 1–8.
21. MacKenzie, D. Compressed sensing makes every pixel count. *What's Happening in the Mathematical Sciences*, July (2009), 114–127.
22. Mitra, S., and Acharya, T. Gesture recognition: A survey. *IEEE Transactions on Systems, Man and Cybernetics, Part C (Applications and Reviews) 37*, 3 (May 2007), 311–324.
23. Nakatsuma, K., Shinoda, H., Makino, Y., Sato, K., and Maeno, T. Touch interface on back of the hand. In *proc. of SIGGRAPH '11* (2011), 39:1–39:1.
24. Nanayakkara, S., Shilkrot, R., Yeo, K. P., and Maes, P. EyeRing: A finger-worn input device for seamless interactions with our surroundings. In *Proc. of AH '13* (2013), 13–20.
25. Olberding, S., Yeo, K. P., Nanayakkara, S., and Steimle, J. AugmentedForearm: Exploring the design space of a display-enhanced forearm. In *Proc. of AH '13* (2013), 9–12.
26. Rekimoto, J., and Saitoh, M. Augmented surfaces: A spatially continuous work space for hybrid computing environments. In *Proc. of CHI '99* (1999), 378–385.
27. Ruiz, J., Li, Y., and Lank, E. User-defined motion gestures for mobile interaction. In *Proc. of CHI '11* (2011), 197.
28. Siek, K. A., Rogers, Y., and Connelly, K. H. Fat finger worries : How older and younger users physically interact with PDAs. In *Proc. of INTERACT '05*, Springer Berlin Heidelberg (2005), 267–280.
29. Wobbrock, J. O., Morris, M. R., and Wilson, A. D. User-defined gestures for surface computing. In *Proc. of CHI'09* (2009), 1083–1092.
30. Xiao, R., Laput, G., and Harrison, C. Expanding the input expressivity of smartwatches with mechanical pan, twist, tilt and click. In *Proc. of CHI '14* (2014), 193–196.

Providing Adaptive Support in an Interactive Simulation for Learning: an Experimental Evaluation

Samad Kardan, Cristina Conati
Department of Computer Science
University of British Columbia, Vancouver, Canada
{skardan, conati}@cs.ubc.ca

ABSTRACT

Recent rise of Massive Open Online Courses (MOOCs) with unlimited participants, makes employing learning tools such as interactive simulations all but inevitable. Interactive simulations give students the opportunity to experiment with concrete examples and develop better understanding of concepts they have learned. However, some students do not learn well from this relatively unstructured form of interaction, suggesting the provision of adaptive support as a way to address this issue.

This paper presents a formal evaluation of this approach. We describe the process of designing an intervention delivery mechanism for adding adaptive support to an exploratory interactive simulation. The experimental evaluation of the adaptive version of the simulation indicates that the adaptive support provided to students significantly improved their learning performance. Quantitative and qualitative evaluations of users' acceptance of the system are generally positive but pinpoint areas for improvement.

INTRODUCTION

Advances in HCI continuously aid the creation of novel interfaces to support education and training. For example, interactive simulations are increasingly used as exploratory/open-ended environments for learning different subjects (e.g., physics and math [18,21]). These exploratory educational simulations (ESims hereafter) are designed to foster exploratory and active learning, by giving students the opportunity to proactively experiment with concrete examples of concepts and processes they have learned in theory. However, it has been shown that some students may not learn well from this relatively unstructured and open-ended form of interaction, because they lack skills needed to explore effectively [9,10]. Hence, students may benefit from having additional guidance when they interact with an ESim (e.g., [9,19]).

In this paper, we evaluate an approach to provide this guidance adaptively, based on the real-time evaluation of whether a user's interaction behavior with an ESim is conducive to learning or not. The test-bed for our research is the AIspace CSP applet [1], an interactive simulation that illustrates the workings of the AC3 algorithm for constraint satisfaction problems. This applet is part of AIspace, a publicly available suite of interactive simulations for a variety of AI algorithms that is routinely used in AI courses both in our university and elsewhere. There is extensive positive feedback from students when these applets are used for in-class demonstrations, and formal studies on the CSP applet have shown that it both fosters learning and motivates students [1]. These studies, however, also showed that not all students leverage at best the functionalities available to explore the AC3 algorithm mechanics. We hypothesize that the CSP applet's effectiveness could be further enhanced by providing guidance on how to use these functionalities to those students who need it. To investigate this hypothesis, we devised a new version of the CSP applet that provides *adaptive interventions* designed to provide such guidance.

The adaptive version of the CSP applet (adaptive-CSP henceforth) leverages a user modeling approach proposed in [11,12] to determine in real time if/when a user needs help in using the applet and why. In this paper we introduce a mechanism that, by relying on this user model, selects which interventions to deliver at any given point of the interaction. We illustrate the design process we used to understand how to deliver the interventions in an effective and unobtrusive manner, and present a user study aimed at evaluating the resulting adaptive interventions by answering the following research questions:

- Do the adaptive interventions added to the CSP applet increase the applet's effectiveness in fostering student learning?
- Do users have a positive impression of the interventions, in terms of relevance, usefulness, noticeability, and unobtrusiveness?

Our results provide positive answers to both questions. This work contributes to the general area of intelligent learning

CHI 2015, April 18 - 23 2015, Seoul, Republic of Korea.

ACM 978-1-4503-3145-6/15/04...$15.00.
http://dx.doi.org/10.1145/2702123.2702424

environments. In this area, there is extensive evidence that real-time personalized support can increase user learning during structure problem solving tasks, where feedback can be provided based on a clear definition of correctness for the student behaviors [22,25]. There is much more limited evidence for providing support for *open-ended exploration* in ESims, due to the more unstructured nature of the interaction which makes it difficult to define a priory how student behavior relates to learning. Our work contributes to fill this gap, and shows encouraging evidence that personalized support to open exploration with ESims, provided by helping students understand how to use the simulation's functionalities at best, can increase the pedagogical effectiveness of these educational tools.

In the rest of this paper, we first discuss the related work. Next, we introduce the original CSP applet, followed by a brief description of the user modeling approach leveraged by the adaptive version. Then we describe the process of adding adaptive interventions to the applet, the study we conducted to evaluate their effectiveness, and its results. We conclude with a summary of findings and future work.

RELATED WORK

Providing adaptive support to students is an important part of Intelligent Tutoring Systems (ITS), where this support is intended to partially replace the guidance a student would receive in a one-to-one tutoring setting [24]. There is ample evidence that adaptive support can be beneficial in ITSs that target problem solving and other pedagogical activities where there is a well-defined set of solutions/behaviors that the ITS can target. For example, Westerfield et al., showed the effectiveness of personalized feedback on errors the students make in an ITS that provides step-by-step training on assembling a computer mother board [25]. Stamper et al., [22] used a data mining approach to generate automatic solicited hints for an algebra tutor, and showed that the tutor performed better compared to a non-adaptive version in terms of both number of problems solved and overall learning. AutoTutor, an ITS that provides adaptive feedback on answers to physics questions, was successfully evaluated in [8]. It should be noted that this ITS includes a simulation that helps find the answers but no support is given on how to use it.

On the other hand, providing adaptive support for exploratory learning environments such as ESims is in early stages of research [16]. One defining characteristics of these environments is that there is usually no definition of correct behaviors. Students can explore the environment as they like. This makes it difficult to judge a priori and track which ensemble of user interaction behaviors should be the target of adaptive support [23]. Most of the work done so far on designing and evaluating adaptive feedback for learning environments that include interactive simulations has dealt with the challenge by limiting the exploratory nature of the interaction. For instance, the simulations developed by Johnson [7] provide feedback on how to behave in pre-defined cultural/language-related scenarios with clear definition of correct answers/behaviors. CTAT-VLab [2] provides help on well-defined steps required to run a scientific experiment. Science Assistments [6] provides feedback on the specific problem of controlling for variables in experimental design. Thus, although [7], [2] and [6] add some form of adaptive feedback to interactive simulations, the feedback targets pre-defined behaviors that help students find correct answers/solutions in the instructional domain. In contrast, in our work we designed and evaluated adaptive support for a more open-ended exploratory interaction, with no prior definition for correct actions/solutions. The support aims to help students use the simulation to explore the underlying algorithm effectively, not find a correct answer/solution.

The work closest in nature to ours is eXpresser, a simulation environment for learning algebra, which leverages a set of predefined feedback strategies to provide both unsolicited and solicited feedback to students based on the student's interactions [16]. A preliminary qualitative assessment of this feedback resulted in modest positive ratings for student perception, but no quantitative study has been published so far [16]. Thus, our work is the first (to the best of our knowledge) to provide a rigorous evaluation of an adaptive support mechanism for open-ended exploration in an ESim. Moreover, while in eXpresser a significant amount of manpower has been spent on defining the behaviors to be tracked in student model and the feedback strategies, in our work both adaptive interventions and the user model activating them are generated by mining the user interaction data with minimal human involvement.

THE AI SPACE CSP APPLET: ORIGINAL VERSION

A CSP consists of a set of variables, variable domains, and a set of constraints on legal variable-value assignments. Solving a CSP requires finding an assignment that satisfies all constraints. The CSP applet illustrates the Arc Consistency 3 (AC-3 [20]) algorithm for solving CSPs represented as networks of variable nodes and constraint arcs (see Figure 1). AC-3 iteratively makes individual arcs consistent by removing variable domain values inconsistent with a given constraint, until all arcs have been considered and the network is consistent. Then, if there remains a variable with more than one domain value, a procedure called domain splitting is applied to that variable in order to split the CSP into disjoint cases so that AC-3 can recursively solve each case.

The CSP applet demonstrates the AC-3 algorithm dynamics via interactive visualizations on graphs using color and highlighting (Figure 1). The applet provides several mechanisms for the interactive execution of the AC-3 algorithm on a set of available CSPs. These mechanisms are accessible through the applet's toolbar (see top of Figure 1), or through direct manipulation of graph elements. The user can perform seven different actions: (1) Fine Step: use the fine step button to see how AC-3 goes through its three basic steps (selecting an arc, testing it for consistency, removing domain values to make the arc consistent); (2) Direct Arc Click: directly click on an arc to apply all these steps at once; (3) Auto AC: automatically fine step on all arcs one by one using the auto arc consistency button; (4) Stop: pause auto arc consistency; (5) Domain Split: select a variable to split on, and specify a subset of its values for further application of AC-3 (see pop-up box in the left side of Figure 1); (6) Backtrack: recover alternative sub-networks during domain splitting; (7) Reset: return the graph to its initial status.

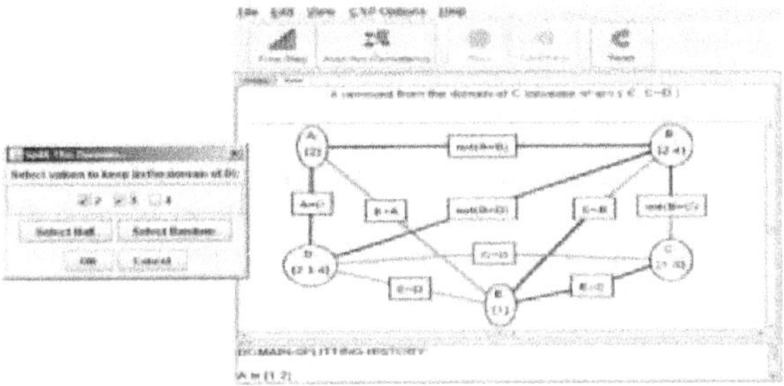

Figure 1. The CSP applet with an example CSP problem

The CSP applet is the product of an extensive process of iterative design and evaluation, and formal studies have shown that it can foster learning [1]. However, because the available affordances make it relatively easy to progress through a given task (e.g., finding a solution for a CSP problem), some students might not learn at best with this tool if they fail to use the available affordances to understand the underlying AC-3 processes. To address this issue, we have developed a new version of the applet that provides adaptive interventions designed to help these students use the simulation's functionalities more effectively.

In the next section, we briefly summarize the user modeling approach we leverage to determine in real-time during interaction if and why a user needs an intervention, proposed in [12]. The two following sections introduce the mechanism we designed to generate and deliver these interventions in the CSP applet.

MODELING STUDENT LEARNING IN THE CSP APPLET

The user modeling approach used in the adaptive-CSP applet consists of two phases: *Behavior Discovery* and *User Classification* (Figure 2). In *Behavior Discovery* (Figure 2-top), data from existing interaction logs is preprocessed into feature vectors where features consist of statistical measures that summarize the user's actions in the interfaces (e.g., action frequencies and time interval between actions). Each vector summarizes the behaviors of one user. A clustering algorithm then groups these vectors according to their similarities, thus identifying users who interact similarly with the interface. Next, association rule mining is applied to each cluster to extract its common behavior patterns, i.e., rules in form of X→ *c*, where X is a set of feature-value pairs and *c* is the predicted cluster for the data points to which X applies (Table 1 shows samples of these rules, which will be further explained in the next section).

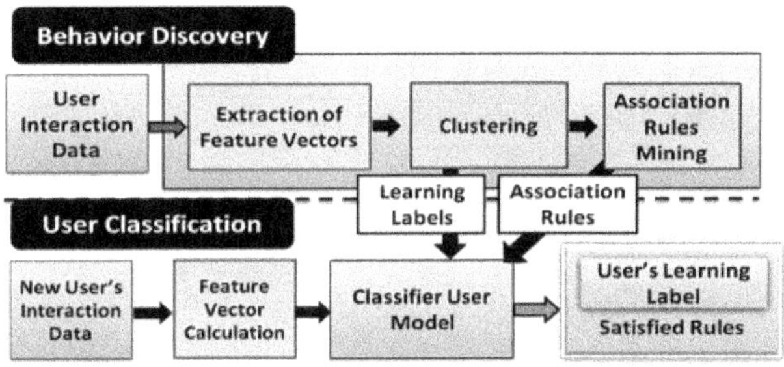

Figure 2. The user modeling framework

Clusters are then analyzed to identify how they relate to student learning performance. Thus, the *Behavior Discovery* phase generates groups of users who are associated with different levels of learning performance, as well as sets of interaction behaviors typical of each group.

The *User Classification* (Figure 2-bottom) phase uses the clusters and class association rules extracted in the *Behavior Discovery* phase to build an online classifier user model. This classifier assesses in real-time the (possibly evolving) learning performance of a new user by (*i*) incrementally building a feature vector based on the interface actions seen so far; (*ii*) classifying this vector in one of the available clusters. Note that the classification can change over time depending on the evolution of the user's interaction behaviors.

We built the user model for the adaptive CSP applet by applying *Behavior Discovery* to a dataset of 110 users obtained from two previous studies on this simulation [12,13]. From this dataset, the Behavior Discovery generated two clusters of users that achieved significantly different learning levels, labeled as High Learning Gain (HLG) and Low Learning Gain (LLG) groups from now on. Learning level was measured using pretest and posttest scores collected in the original studies, and a standard measure of learning performance (Percentage Learning Gain, or PLG), calculated as follows:

$$PLG = \begin{cases} \frac{PostT-PreT}{Max-PreT} \times 100 & if\ PostT - PreT > 0 \\ 0 & otheweise \end{cases} \quad (1)$$

where *PreT* and *PostT* are the student's test scores and *Max* is the maximum possible score.

Table 1 shows a subset of behavior patterns (association rules) discovered for each cluster of this dataset. A total of four and fifteen rules were found for the HLG and LLG respectively. We evaluated the accuracy of the classifier built from the HLG and LLG clusters and the corresponding association rules via 10-fold cross-validation on the available dataset. The classifier achieved an accuracy of 78.2% after observing only the first 25 percent of the interactions, indicating that this user model can be reliably used to trigger adaptive interventions from the early stages of the interaction.

Rules for HLG cluster:
Rule1: Auto AC frequency = Lowest
└ **Rule2:** Auto AC frequency = Lowest **and** Fine Step frequency = Lowest
Rule3: Direct Arc Click pause average = Highest
Rules for LLG cluster:
Rule4: Backtrack frequency = Highest **and** Direct Arc Click pause average = Lowest
Rule8: Auto AC frequency = Highest **and** Direct Arc Click frequency = Lowest
Rule 10: Reset frequency = Highest

Table 1. A selection of representative rules for HLG and LLG clusters in the CSP dataset

ADAPTIVE INTERVENTIONS FOR THE CSP APPLET

In addition to assigning a "label" to the user, the CSP's user model also returns the satisfied association rules causing that classification decision (Figure 3). These rules represent the distinctive interaction behaviors of a specific user so far, including a subset of behaviors associated with high learning (effective), as well as a subset of those associated with low learning (suboptimal). The adaptive interventions evaluated in this paper are designed specifically to target these behaviors (i.e., reinforcing the effective behaviors and discouraging the suboptimal ones).

For instance, rule 8 in Table 1 indicates that low learners show very high frequency of *Auto AC* actions, while rarely using the *Direct Arc Click* (DAC) action (values for behavior's frequency and latency are binned based on a mechanism described in [12]). A possible explanation of why both these behaviors are associated with limited learning is that they identify users who are not very engaged in the exploration process because they prefer to (*i*) run the algorithm to completion instead of stepping through it; (*ii*) leave to the applet the selection of the next arc to work on, rather than being proactive in choosing it.

Thus, this rule identifies two possible interventions (*intervention items* from now on) that address these suboptimal behaviors exhibited by low learners: (*i*) discourage excessive use of the Auto AC; (*ii*) encourage higher usage of DAC. Table 2 summarizes all behavior patterns (i.e., the intervention items) identified by the association rules that were generated in the *Behavior Discovery* phase.

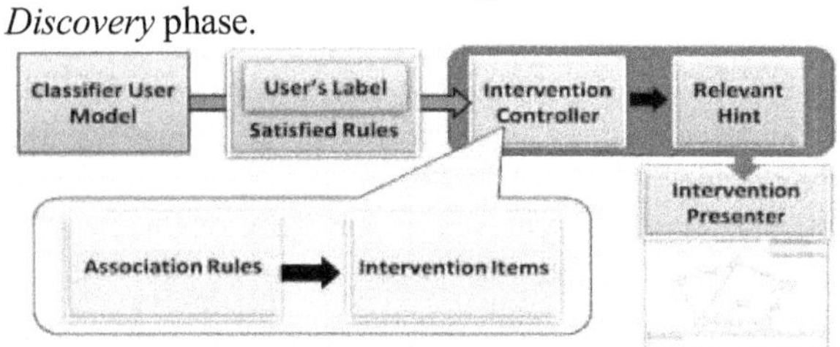

Figure 3. The intervention mechanism

The intervention mechanism in the CSP applet consists of two components: intervention controller and intervention presenter (Figure 3). Intervention controller selects the next intervention to be given and intervention presenter delivers the respective hint. The process of providing adaptive interventions starts by identifying which of the items in Table 2 are relevant at any given point of a user's interaction with the applet (intervention controller in Figure 3). More specifically, when a user is classified as LLG, the intervention controller identifies which detrimental behaviors they should stop performing and/or which beneficial behaviors they should adopt, based on the association rules that caused the classification.[1] For instance, if the user is being classified as LLG, and one of the association rules activated says that the frequency of the *Direct Arc Click* action is lower than a threshold (e.g. Rule 8 in Table 1), then the intervention controller marks the *DAC_fr* intervention in Table 2 as relevant. This intervention entails prompting the user to perform more Direct Arc Click actions.

Intervention Code	Intervention Description
DAC_fr	Using Direct Arc Click more often
DAC_PA	Spending more time after performing Direct Arc Clicks
Reset_fr	Using Reset less frequently
AAC_fr	Using Auto Arc-consistency less frequently
DS_fr	Using Domain Splitting less frequently (only when appropriate)
FS_PA	Spending more time after performing Fine Steps
BT_fr	Using Back Track less frequently (only when appropriate)
FS_fr	Using Fine Step less frequently
Reset_PA	Spending more time after performing reset for planning

Table 2. Description of hints

There may be several intervention items that are relevant given a user's behaviors at any given point of their interaction with the CSP applet (*active* intervention items from now on). To avoid confusing or overwhelming the user, in this version of the adaptive applet we decided to deliver one intervention at a time, chosen based on a ranking that reflects the relevance of the behaviors being targeted for learning. More specifically, the intervention controller gives each intervention item a score calculated as the sum of the weights of the association rules which triggered that item. The weight of a rule in turns indicates its importance in classifying a user as a high or low learner. At each hinting opportunity, the intervention controller chooses the intervention item with the highest score among the active items. The next section illustrates the design and rationale behind the mechanism that delivers interventions (intervention presenter in Figure 3) while trying to maximize effectiveness and minimize intrusiveness of the process.

[1] Potential causes of the suboptimal interaction (e.g., lack of needed skills, cognitive overload, etc.) are not revealed by our approach. In this respect, our model and resulting hints are rather shallow. They attempt to correct the behaviors, but cannot do anything to address their causes.

DELIVERING THE ADAPTIVE INTERVENTIONS

Our first design principle is to deliver adaptive interventions incrementally, following well established practices in the Intelligent Tutoring Systems literature [15]. Thus, each selected intervention item is first delivered with a textual hint that prompts or discourages a target behavior, followed when needed by a textual hint that reiterates the same advice, accompanied by a related interface adaptation that can help the user follow the advice (e.g., highlighting relevant interface items).

Delivering adaptive interventions also requires deciding whether the interventions should be subtle or forceful. Subtle interventions are in the form of suggestions that can be easily ignored by the user. Forceful interventions make the user follow the related advice by reducing or eliminating user's options for the next action. We decided to try the subtle approach for the adaptive-CSP applet because, although with this approach the user can easily decide to ignore the system's suggestions (even when they are appropriate), it has the very desirable advantage of being less intrusive than the forceful approach. Therefore, from a usability point of view, it makes sense to try and see whether subtle adaptive interventions can already improve the effectiveness of the CSP applet. The general mechanism to deliver subtle incremental adaptive interventions in the CSP applet works as follows:

(*i*) Each intervention item selected for delivery (*target item* in the rest of this section) is first presented as a textual hint message shown in a box at the upper right corner of the applet, as shown in Figure 4a (level-1 hint). This message is phrased as a suggestion for behaviors to be adopted or avoided. For instance, a level-1 textual hint for the DAC_fr intervention item in Table 2 is "*Do you know that you can tell AC-3 which arc to make consistent by clicking on that arc?*" which aims to promote the *Direct Arc Click* action. In order to draw user's attention to the new message, the hint box first appears in the center of the screen, and then quickly moves to the upper right corner of the applet.

(*ii*) After receiving a level-1 hint on the *target item*, the student is given some time to change her behavior accordingly (a *reaction window* equal to 20 actions). During this time, the user model will keep updating the feature vector describing the user interaction behavior, its classification, and the ranked list of active intervention items (excluding the *target item*); delivering any of them as needed. To avoid overwhelming the user with hints, a maximum frequency of one hint per ten actions is enforced.

(*iii*) At the end of the time window, based on the updated feature vector, the user model determines whether the user has followed the hint for the *target item* or not. If at this point the preconditions for the adaptation rule that generated the level-1 hint for the *target item* are still satisfied, then the user has not followed the hint and the *target item* is selected for delivery again.

(*iv*) In this case, a level-2 hint is delivered, consisting of both a text message as well as highlighting the relevant interface elements that can help the user follow the hint. Figure 4b shows an example of level-2 hint for the DAC_fr intervention item. The text messages in level-2 hints are more detailed than that of level-1 hints. The first part of a level-2 hint reiterates the level-1 hint with a slightly different wording, while the second part provides a justification for the suggestion and, if relevant, mentions the highlighted elements of the interface. For instance, in Figure 4b, the arcs of the displayed CSP graph that can be selected via Direct Arc Click are highlighted in yellow. The phrase "relevant arcs" in the hint message is highlighted similarly to create a visual link between the text and the change in the graph. The highlight effect is automatically removed as soon as the user performs a relevant action (e.g., user clicks on an arc for the DAC_fr intervention). The highlights can also be manually toggled using the "hide/show highlights" button at the bottom of the hint box (see Figure 4b).

(a) (b)

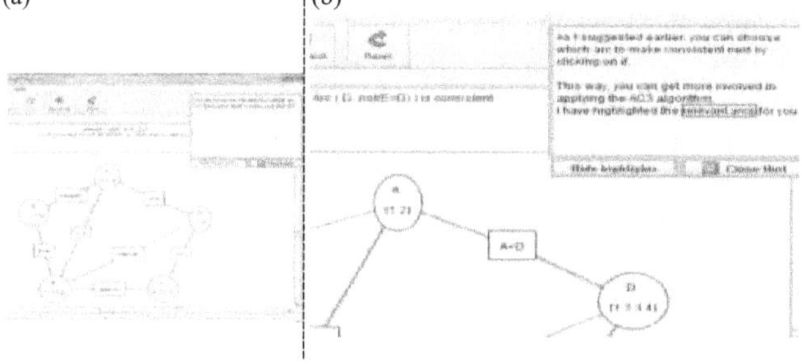

Figure 4: Sample Level-1 and Level-2 hints

(*iv*) If the user's behavior during the reaction window following a level-2 hint shows that s/he did not follow the system's suggestion, the corresponding intervention item will be put back on the list of active items and, if selected, it will be delivered starting again from a level-1 hint.

The hint delivery mechanism described above is the result of an iterative design and evaluation process based on three different pilot studies. All these studies had a similar setup: participants first studied a textbook chapter on the AC-3 algorithm, and then used the CSP applet to solve two CSPs, while their gaze was tracked with a Tobii T120 eye-tracker. A follow-up questionnaire and interviews were administered to gain a qualitative evaluation of relevant aspects of the interaction.

The first pilot was a Wizard-of-Oz during which an experimenter triggered the interventions based on a set of adaptation rules similar to those described earlier. The goal of the study was to pilot test the general two-level hints approach in terms of visibility, intrusiveness and follow rate of the interventions, and involved 6 second and third year computer science students.

Participants generally did not find the hint messages intrusive and they rated them as useful. The interviews however, uncovered various issues with visibility: for the textual hints, subjects reported that sometimes it was hard to notice when a new message appeared. For the highlights provided in the level-2 hints (which in that version were based on bolding the relevant interface elements), some participants did not notice them at all; others saw them but failed to make the connection with the textual hint. These observations were supported by the gaze data collected with the eye-tracker.

The final design presented in this section is the result of changes we made to the original design to address these issues, tested with two subsequent pilot studies. More specifically:

- Visibility of new textual hints was increased by adding the motion and change in initial positioning of the hint box as described earlier.
- Visibility of the highlights for level-2 hints was increased by testing two alternative ways to emphasize the target elements, namely yellow highlighting vs. blinking (increase in attentional draw [5]). Yellow highlighting proved to be the preferred and more effective method based both on user's feedback as well as gaze data.
- The connection between the level-2 hint messages and the related interface changes was emphasised by both mentioning in the hint text that the relevant elements are highlighted, as well as using the same highlight effect on the keywords in the text.

The last two pilots were also used to (*i*) evaluate ways to give user control over displaying the interface changes by adding the "hide/show highlights" buttons (Figure 4b); (*ii*) adjust the thresholds controlling the hint delivery rate.

USER STUDY

To investigate the effectiveness of the intervention mechanism, we conducted a user study that tested the following hypothesis:

H1: Under similar conditions, participants who work with the adaptive-CSP applet (i.e., receive adaptive support) will have a higher learning performance compared to ones that work with the original CSP applet (control condition).

Procedure

The experiment was a between-subjects design, fitting in a single session lasting at most 2 hours. There were two randomized experimental conditions: in the *Control* condition participants worked with the original CSP applet; in the *Adaptive* condition participants used the adaptive-CSP applet.[2]

During the study each participant: (1) studied a textbook chapter on the AC-3 algorithm[3]; (2) wrote a pre-test on the concepts covered in the chapter; (3) watched an introductory video on how to use the main functionalities of the CSP applet; (4) used the CSP applet to solve three CSPs; (5) took a post-test analogous to the pre-test; and (6) took a questionnaire on aspects relevant to both groups (described below). Participant in the Adaptive condition took an additional questionnaire on aspects specific to the adaptive-CSP applet. The study ended with a follow up interview that solicited explanations for user ratings.

Study Materials

The study tests involved items selected from a standard bank of homework questions used in the introductory AI course at a university in North America. They required students to apply knowledge of different aspects of the AC-3 algorithm on selected CSP networks. The maximum possible score for both tests was 25 based on existing marking schemes.

All study participants took a post-questionnaire (*general questionnaire* from now on) in which they rated the following three statements (using a Likert scale from 1: strongly disagree to 5: strongly agree):

- I felt more confident answering the post-test questions compared to the pre-test questions (*improved confidence*)
- I think I did better in the post-test compared to the pre-test (*perceived learning*)
- I found the applet helpful in understanding the AC-3 algorithm (*helpfulness of the applet*)

The additional questionnaire administered to participants in the Adaptive condition (referred to as *intervention questionnaire*) included 18 items on different elements of the intervention mechanism, also ranked on a 5-point Likert scale. Pairs of similar statements were provided to evaluate hint messages and highlights in terms of *relevance*, *usefulness*, *noticeability*, *intrusiveness*, and *annoyance*:

- In general, the [hint messages | highlighting of the interface items] were appropriate given my behavior (*relevance*).
- The [messages displayed in the hint box | highlighting of the interface items] were useful for me (*usefulness*).
- I easily noticed the [new messages displayed in the hint box | highlighting of the interface items] (*noticeability*).
- I found the [hint box | highlighting of the interface items] intrusive (*intrusiveness*).
- I found the [hint box | highlighting of the interface items] annoying (*annoyance*).

It should be noted that, in our first pilot, we did not have items for annoyance, because we thought intrusiveness would capture a user's negative perception of how the interventions interfere with their work. However, some

[2] It should be noted that this design does not fully isolate the contribution of the hints from the adaptive delivery component. We did plan to have a third condition with hints triggered randomly, but we could not recruit enough users with the right background for a 3-way study. We chose not to use this random condition as control because we used it in our pilots and user feedback indicated irritation with it. Thus we felt that it would not be a good control due to its intrusiveness.

[3] This is all the instruction participants get on the AC-3 algorithm. Hints in the adaptive condition did not provide additional instruction on the algorithm.

participants who rated the hints as intrusive commented in follow-up interviews that they did not perceive these interruptions as negative; therefore a new set of items targeting annoyance was added.

The remaining 8 items focused on specific attributes of each element of the intervention mechanism. These items are not discussed in this paper due to space constraints. Screenshots of all the relevant intervention elements were provided in the questionnaire to facilitate recollection.

Study Tasks

The three CSP problems used in the study task were selected to provide incremental coverage of all relevant aspects of the AC-3 algorithm, as well as different outcomes. The first CSP had one solution that could be found without domain splitting. The second CSP had no solution and required one domain splitting to reach this conclusion. The third problem had 3 solutions, which required multiple domain splitting and backtracking activities to be found.

Participants were given an instruction sheet indicating that they needed to report the outcome of using AC-3 on each of the problems. They were given a minimum of 15 minutes for working on this activity, but no maximum time limit.

Study Participants

Thirty eight university students (11 female) participated in the experiment. We selected the number of participants by performing a power analysis [14] a priori on the parameters of our experimental design, defined to detect large effect size of $d = 1.0$ in terms of performance with 0.8 power.

Participants were selected such that they did not have any knowledge on solving constraint satisfaction problems beforehand (a new concept); however they had the computer science pre-requisite knowledge necessary to learn this concept (e.g., basic graph theory and algebra). We used flyers, email, and social media to recruit participants with these prerequisites at a North American university.

RESULTS FOR PERFORMANCE MEASURES

We looked at the impact of study condition on three different measures of performance: *learning performance* from pretest to posttest, as measured by the Percentage Learning Gain (PLG) defined in equation 1; *task performance,* which is a score out of 10, given based on the number of correct solutions found for the three CSP problems using the applet (including identifying the CSP with no solution); *task time*, i.e., the time in minutes spent working on the three CSP problems using the applet; Summary statistics for the three performance measures and pretest for each condition are shown in Table 3.

An independent samples t-test on the pretest scores of the two conditions found no significant difference ($t(36) = .189$, $p = .851$, $\eta^2 = .001$), indicating that the random assignment of participants to conditions was successful in generating two groups with comparable initial knowledge.

In addition to studying the impact of experimental conditions on our performance measures, we are also interested in verifying whether the impact is moderated by a student's initial knowledge, as measured by pretest. Thus, we ran a moderated multiple regression analysis [4] for each of our performance measures, with that measure as the dependent variable. Independent variables (IV) are condition (coded as -1 for Control and 1 for Adaptive), pretest and the interaction between condition and pretest. This interaction is calculated by first centering pretest (by subtracting the sample mean) and then multiplying pretest and condition together. Alpha level is set to 0.05, and Pearson r is reported to show the effect size (small for .1, medium for .3, and large for .5 [3]). Models are adjusted for family-wise error by applying the Bonferroni correction. Data screening did not suggest problems with assumptions of normality and linearity. The multicollinearity assumption was not violated in any of the models (based on Variance Inflation Factors [17]). For each independent variable, we report both standardized regression coefficient (β) and squared semipartial correlation (sr^2).

Measure	Pretest		PLG		Task Performance		Task Time	
Condition	Cont.	Adapt.	Cont.	Adapt.	Cont.	Adapt.	Contr.	Adapt.
Mean	9.66	9.37	28.59	54.29	8.58	8.42	18.32	18.37
Std. Dev.	5.553	3.696	19.045	24.784	2.434	2.364	3.198	5.756

Table 3. Descriptive Statistics for the performance measures

Results on learning performance

The overall regression model significantly predicted PLG, $F(3, 34) = 7.435$, $p = .001$, $R^2 = .396$, adjusted $R^2 = .343$. There was a significant Pretest×Condition interaction, $\beta = -.296$, $t(34) = -2.048$, $p = .048$, $sr^2 = .075$, with a medium effect size ($r = .331$). The interaction accounts for an additional 7.5% of the variance in PLG. There was also a significant main effect for condition $\beta = .517$, $t(34) = 3.878$, $p < .001$, $sr^2 = .267$, with a large effect size ($r = .554$), however the main effect for pretest was not significant ($\beta = .128$, $t(34) = .886$, $p = .382$, $sr^2 = .014$).

The main effect for condition shows that the difference in learning performance of the two groups in the study is significant; with the Adaptive condition having greater learning performance compared to the Control condition (the average standardized difference is 1.034 which is slightly more than one standard deviation). This confirms our hypothesis H1.

The interaction effect indicates that the effect of condition on PLG is moderated by pretest. To better qualify this finding, we plotted the effect of condition on PLG at three different levels of standardized pretest scores (z-scores) labeled as high (z=1), average (z=0), and low (z=−1); (Figure 5). The line equations are derived from the standardized β values. As shown in Figure 5 the effect of condition on PLG is highest for the low pretest group and decreases as pretest performance improves, i.e., the interventions are most effective on the students with lower initial knowledge. This is very encouraging for us because these are the students who need the most help.

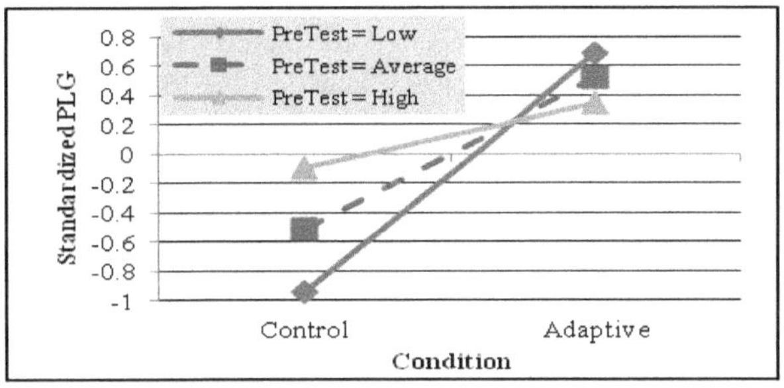

Figure 5. Interaction between Pretest and Condition

Results on task performance and completion time

The regression models with the aforementioned IVs, did not significantly predict task performance, $F(3, 34) = 1.650$, $p = .196$, $R^2 = .127$, adjusted $R^2 = .050$ or task time, $F(3, 34) = .554$, $p = .649$, $R^2 = .047$, adjusted $R^2 = .038$. These results indicate that condition did not significantly explain the variance of task performance or task time, i.e., the two conditions are not significantly different in terms of these two measures. The fact that participants in the Adaptive and Control conditions performed equally well in the task with the CSP applet, while achieving very different results for learning gain, confirms that unaided interaction with the CSP applet can lead students to find solutions without obtaining a clear understanding of the process.

Given the system design and study results, we think the students in the adaptive condition learned more because the hints help them correct some of the suboptimal ways in which they use the applet to explore the AC-3 algorithm. Although we do not have hard data to support this intuition, post-hoc interviews provide some insights on how the hints affected user behaviors. Students reported that hints helped them to "control their pace thus understand the process better", "explore more actions", "direct their focus".

RESULTS ON INTERVENTIONS ACCEPTANCE

Success of any adaptive support mechanism highly depends on the users' perception of its quality. To gauge this perception, in this section we will look at both objective and subjective indicators: respectively, the actual follow rate for the hints and post-questionnaires ratings.

Actual hint follow rate

For every hint received by a user in the Adaptive condition, we check the user model after the reaction window to see if the user is still showing the behavior that triggered the hint. If the user was not showing that behavior, the hint is marked as followed and vice versa. Table 4 shows the descriptive statistics for the number of hints given in total, at level 1 and level 2, along with the follow rate for each. One participant did not receive any hints, and thus s/he is not included in this analysis as well as in the analysis of subjective measures in the next section.

	N	Min	Max	Mean	Std. Dev.
Number of Hints	18	1	15	7.06	4.65
Level-2 Hints	18	0	8	1.56	2.09
Follow rate Level-1 (%)	18	16.67	100	62.96	32.95
Follow rate Level-2 (%)	10	0.0	100	73.33	37.84
Follow rate overall (%)	18	16.67	100	64.44	31.65

Table 4. Descriptive Statistics for Hints

As shown in Table 4, the overall average follow rate is 64.4 percent, indicating a relatively good acceptance of the adaptive suggestions. Notably, the average follow rate for hints increases from 63 percent for level-1 hints to 73.3 percent for level-2 hints. This validates the 2-level design of our interventions.

Analysis of post-questionnaire ratings

We first compare the user ratings on the general post-questionnaire items, which were filled by both the control and adaptive conditions. Then, we discuss the ratings provided by participants in the Adaptive condition for a selected set of items from the interventions questionnaire.

User Ratings for the General Questionnaire

We used Mann-Whitney U tests to compare the ratings of the three items in the general post-questionnaire. The distributions in the two groups did not differ significantly for Improved Confidence (Mann–Whitney $U = 150.50$, $n_1 = n_2 = 19$, $P = .322$ two-tailed), Perceived Learning (Mann–Whitney $U = 142.50$, $n_1 = n_2 = 19$, $P = .223$ two-tailed), and for Helpfulness of the applet (Mann–Whitney $U = 171.50$, $n_1 = n_2 = 19$, $P = .766$ two-tailed). The ratings were generally positive for all three items across conditions (see Figure 6). The positive ratings reflect the value of the CSP applet for visualizing the steps of the AC-3 algorithm compared to studying examples in the textbook, as revealed by the follow up interviews (e.g., It is "much easier to learn" from the applet, I could "see the outcomes in real time" and "step-by-step", I easily "learned from my mistakes").

Notably, however, there is a mismatch between the relatively high perceived learning for the Control condition, and their actual learning performance. Possibly, perceived learning is positively influenced by their task performance, which as illustrated in the previous section was as good as that of the students in the Adaptive condition. The mismatch between perceived and actual learning is concerning because these students will not feel the need to explore more problems to improve their learning, if left to their own devices.

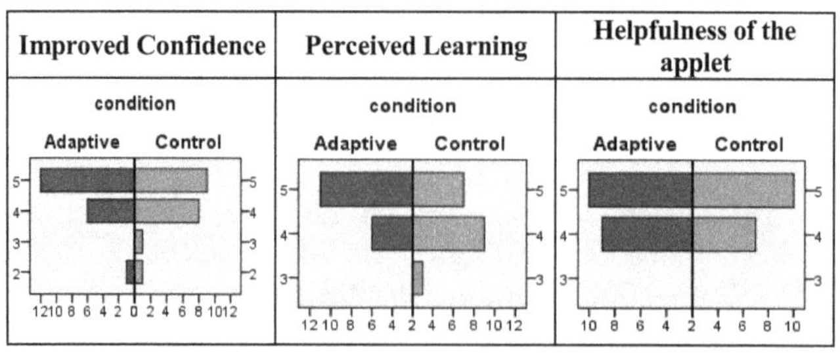

Figure 6. User ratings of the general items (5: most positive)

User Ratings for the Interventions Questionnaire
In this section we report user ratings for items on the Intervention questionnaire that evaluated hint messages and highlights in terms of *relevance*, *usefulness*, *noticeability*, *intrusiveness*, and *annoyance* (as described in the *Study Materials* section). Due to the fact that highlights were only present for the level-2 hints, and only 8 of the 18 participants received a level-2 hint with highlights, we report ratings for hint messages and highlights separately.

To simplify the analysis in the following discussion we combined the "agree" and "strongly agree" ratings as *agree-all* and "disagree" and "strongly disagree" ratings as *disagree-all*. Using this aggregation, the rating distribution of the mentioned items for the hint box were: *relevance* (67% agree-all, median = "agree"), *usefulness* (44% agree-all, median = "neutral"), *noticeability* (100% agree-all, median = "agree"), *intrusiveness* (27% agree-all, median = "disagree"), and *annoyance* (39% agree-all, median = "neutral"). The majority of the users (over 67%) found the hints relevant to their behavior, whereas 28% found them irrelevant. Usefulness received fewer negative ratings, with only 22% reporting that they did not find the hint useful, however there were more neutral ratings, resulting in fewer users agreeing over usefulness (44%). Based on post interviews, one prominent reason given for negative rating of usefulness and relevance was the nature of the textual hints. Some users reported expecting the hints to give more explicit help on how to solve the problem at hand, rather than telling them how to use the applet, possibly because they focused on getting the job done (e.g., "I wanted to find the solution and the hints kept telling me to slow down") as opposed to trying to improve their understanding of the AC-3 algorithm, which is the task that is supported by the intervention mechanism.

Our design decision to increase the prominence of the appearance of the hint box (to ensure new hint messages are not missed), succeeded in improving noticeability of these hints, reaching 100% of agree-all rating, at the expense of only a small increase in ratings for intrusiveness (28% agree-all, which is 6% higher than the analogous ratings from the first pilot). Compared to the results from our pilot studies, a higher number of users rated the hint box as annoying. In the follow-up interviews, the majority of students who reported annoyance, indicated that the reason for it was receiving hints that they did not agree with repeatedly (i.e., beyond a level-2 hint). This happens when a user insists on not following a hint, and this hint stays ranked high in the list of active intervention items, indicating high relevance for learning. These negative ratings are mirrored by the actual follow rate of repeated hints. We found a trend showing that the follow rate for repeated hints is lower than that of hints given up to level 2. We cannot judge from the available data to what extent hints given repeatedly were actually justified (recall that the user model is not 100% accurate), but regardless our results indicate that we should consider reducing the number of repeated hints in future versions of the applet. In the interview, none of the users attributed their annoyance to the animation used for appearance of the hint box, which provides further positive feedback on the current design of the hint box.

Ratings for the corresponding questionnaire items for highlights were generally more positive than for the hint box, with the exception of noticeability: *relevance* (88% agree-all, median = "agree"), *usefulness* (75% agree-all, median = "agree"), *noticeability* (88% agree-all, median = "agree"), *intrusiveness*, and *annoyance* (0% agree-all, median = "disagree" for both items). Positive ratings for highlights show an effective balance between noticeability and intrusiveness/annoyance.

DISCUSSION AND FUTURE WORK

In this paper, we present the formal evaluation of user-adaptive interventions designed to guide students in learning at best through open-ended exploration of an educational interactive simulation called AIspace CSP applet. There is extensive evidence that not all students can learn well from interactive simulations, due to the rather unstructured and open-ended nature of the interaction that they support. Our work is the first to show formal results on the effectiveness of providing support for open-ended exploration in an interactive simulation. An additional contribution of our work is that support is provided via strategies that are automatically learned from previous learner interaction data.

We described a mechanism for selecting adaptive suggestions based on the output of a user model that identifies in real-time if a student is learning well from the CSP applet and, if not, why. We also described the design process that generated a 2-level subtle method of delivering interventions using both text messages and interface highlights. A formal evaluation of these interventions against the original version of the CSP applet shows very encouraging results for both users learning and their perception of the system, but also provides valuable insights for further improvements.

Students in the two experimental conditions performed similarly in terms of time on task and task performance, but students in the adaptive condition learned significantly more than students in the control condition. Furthermore, the effect of interventions on learning is even more pronounced for students with lower levels of initial knowledge. In terms of users' acceptance of the intervention mechanism, there was a positive attitude towards the applet in general and users followed 64.4% of the recommendations given to them. The users' ratings of the interventions were generally positive; however they indicate that the number of repeated hints should be reduced, since that was a source of annoyance for users. Thus, we are planning to further investigate how to strike the right balance between providing hints when they are needed and not overwhelming the user. We also plan to investigate having a third condition in a new study where hints are given in a fixed manner to better isolate the effect of getting any hints from receiving them adaptively. We will also work on adding adaptive interventions to other applets in the AIspace suite of adaptive simulations in order to test the generalizability of our approach. Finally, we are aware of the limitations of a lab setting study and plan to make the applet available online and use remote logging for further analysis of its performance.

ACKNOWLEDGEMENTS

This work has been partially supported by the Institute for Computing, Information and Cognitive Systems (ICICS) at the University of British Columbia.

REFERENCES

1. Amershi, S., Carenini, G., Conati, C., Mackworth, A.K., and Poole, D. Pedagogy and usability in interactive algorithm visualizations: Designing and evaluating CIspace. *Interacting with Computers 20*, 1 (2008), 64–96.
2. Borek, A., McLaren, B.M., Karabinos, M., and Yaron, D. How Much Assistance Is Helpful to Students in Discovery Learning? In U. Cress, V. Dimitrova and M. Specht, eds., *Learning in the Synergy of Multiple Disciplines*. Springer Berlin Heidelberg, 2009, 391–404.
3. Cohen, J. *Statistical Power Analysis for the Behavioral Sciences.* Lawrence Erlbaum, 1988.
4. Cohen, J., West, S.G., Aiken, L.S., and Cohen, P. *Applied Multiple Regression/Correlation Analysis for the Behavioral Sciences.* Lawrence Erlbaum, Mahwah, N.J, 2002.
5. Gluck, J., Bunt, A., and McGrenere, J. Matching attentional draw with utility in interruption. In *Proc. CHI '07*, (2007), 41.
6. Gobert, J.D., Montalvo, O., Toto, E., Sao Pedro, M., and Baker, R.S.J. d. The Science Assistments Project: Scaffolding Scientific Inquiry Skills. In *Proc. Intelligent Tutoring Systems*, (2010), 445–445.
7. Hussain, T.S., Roberts, B., Menaker, E.S., et al. Designing and developing effective training games for the US Navy. *The Interservice/Industry Training, Simulation & Education Conference (I/ITSEC)*, NTSA (2009).
8. Jackson, G.T., Olney, A., Graesser, A.C., and Kim, H.J. AutoTutor 3-D Simulations: Analyzing user's actions and learning trends. In *Proc. the 28th annual meeting of the Cognitive Science Society*, (2006), 1557–1562.
9. De Jong, T. Technological Advances in Inquiry Learning. *Science 312*, 5773 (2006), 532–533.
10. Van Joolingen, W.R., De Jong, T., and Dimitrakopoulou, A. Issues in computer supported inquiry learning in science. *J. of Computer Assisted Learning 23*, 2 (2007), 111–119.
11. Kardan, S. Data Mining for Adding Adaptive Interventions to Exploratory and Open-Ended Environments. In *Proc. UMAP 2012,* Springer Berlin / Heidelberg, 2012, 365–368.
12. Kardan, S. and Conati, C. A Framework for Capturing Distinguishing User Interaction Behaviours in Novel Interfaces. In *Proc. the 4th Int. Conf. on Educational Data Mining*, (2011), 159–168.
13. Kardan, S. and Conati, C. Exploring Gaze Data for Determining User Learning with an Interactive Simulation. In *Proc. UMAP 2012,* Springer Berlin / Heidelberg, 2012, 126–138.
14. Lenth, R.V. *Java Applets for Power and Sample Size.* 2006. http://www.stat.uiowa.edu/~rlenth/Power
15. Maloy, R.W., Verock-O'Loughlin, R.-E.A., Edwards, S.A., and Woolf, B.P. *Transforming Learning with New Technologies.* Pearson, Boston, 2013.
16. Mavrikis, M., Gutierrez-Santos, S., Geraniou, E., and Noss, R. Design requirements, student perception indicators and validation metrics for intelligent exploratory learning environments. *Personal and Ubiquitous Computing*, , 1–16.
17. O'brien, R.M. A Caution Regarding Rules of Thumb for Variance Inflation Factors. *Quality & Quantity 41*, 5 (2007), 673–690.
18. Perkins, K., Adams, W., Dubson, M., et al. PhET: Interactive Simulations for Teaching and Learning Physics. *The Physics Teacher 44*, 1 (2006), 18–23.
19. Ploetzner, R., Lippitsch, S., Galmbacher, M., Heuer, D., and Scherrer, S. Students' difficulties in learning from dynamic visualisations and how they may be overcome. *Computers in Human Behavior 25*, 1 (2009), 56–65.
20. Poole, D.L. and Mackworth, A.K. *Artificial Intelligence: Foundations of Computational Agents.* Cambridge University Press, 2010.
21. Salajan, F.D., Perschbacher, S., Cash, M., Talwar, R., El-Badrawy, W., and Mount, G.J. Learning with web-based interactive objects: An investigation into student perceptions of effectiveness. *Computers & Education 53*, 3 (2009), 632–643.
22. Stamper, J., Eagle, M., Barnes, T., and Croy, M. Experimental Evaluation of Automatic Hint Generation for a Logic Tutor. *Int. J. Artif. Intell. Ed.22*, 1 (2013), 3–17.
23. Ting, C.Y., Zadeh, M., and Chong, Y.K. A decision-theoretic approach to scientific inquiry exploratory learning environment. In *Proc. Intelligent Tutoring Systems*, (2006), 85–94.
24. VanLehn, K. The Behavior of Tutoring Systems. *Int. J. Artif. Intell. Ed. 16*, 3 (2006), 227–265.
25. Westerfield, G., Mitrovic, A., and Billinghurst, M. Intelligent Augmented Reality Training for Assembly Tasks. In *Proc. Artificial Intelligence in Education,*(2013), 542–551.

Interactive Cloud Experimentation for Biology: An Online Education Case Study

Zahid Hossain [1,3], Xiaofan Jin [3], Engin W. Bumbacher [2], Alice M. Chung [3], Stephen Koo [1]
Jordan D. Shapiro [3], Cynthia Y. Truong [3], Sean Choi [1], Nathan D. Orloff [3]
Paulo Blikstein [2,1], Ingmar H. Riedel-Kruse [3]
[1]Department of Computer Science, [2]School of Education, [3]Department of Bioengineering
Stanford University
{zhossain, ingmar}@stanford.edu

ABSTRACT
Interacting with biological systems via experiments is important for academia, industry, and education, but access barriers exist due to training, costs, safety, logistics, and spatial separation. High-throughput equipment combined with web streaming could enable interactive biology experiments online, but no such platform currently exists. We present a cloud experimentation architecture (paralleling cloud computation), which is optimized for a class of domain-specific equipments (biotic processing units - BPU) to share and execute many experiments in parallel remotely and interactively at all time. We implemented an instance of this architecture that enables chemotactic experiments with a slime mold Physarum Polycephelum. A user study in the blended teaching and research setting of a graduate-level biophysics class demonstrated that this platform lowers the access barrier for non-biologists, enables discovery, and facilitates learning analytics. This architecture is flexible for integration with various biological specimens and equipments to facilitate scalable interactive online education, collaborations, research, and citizen science.

Author Keywords
Remote Experimentation; Cloud Computing; Biology; Automation; Education; Cloud Experimentation; Cloud Lab

ACM Classification Keywords
K.3.1 Computers and Education: Computer Uses in Education; J.3 Computer Application: Life and Medical Sciences; B.4.0 Hardware Input/Output and Data Communications: General

INTRODUCTION AND MOTIVATION
Interacting with biological systems via experiments is important for academia, industry, and education, but many access barriers exist that are related to training requirements, cost, safety and logistics. Consider, for example, a computational scientist lacking the hands-on wet lab training to test her own hypotheses experimentally, in which case the final data is of primary focus while the actual act of performing the experiment is merely logistical. Similarly, access barriers arise in life-science education where traditional teaching labs are too costly or time consuming [30], or where online courses [19] do not include lab sections [15, 48]. On the other hand, citizen-science and crowd-sourcing projects have demonstrated how non-scientists can make relevant scientific contributions [18, 41], especially when users can design experiments that are centrally executed in batch by a technician [32]. Hence, enabling many more people to directly interact with microbiology in various contexts by designing and executing biology experiments while abstracting away the skills required for their actual execution would be very powerful.

In this paper we introduce the concept of *interactive cloud experimentation* for biology, which enables multiple users to execute live biology experiments over the Internet by efficiently sharing the necessary resources (Fig. 1) seamlessly. This abstracts away the complex logistics of experimentation and allows users to rather focus on the data analytics, which enables a broader interdisciplinary participation in life- science research and education. The notion is similar to the well-established framework of cloud computing. Ongoing advances in life-science technology [31, 37, 44, 49] are continuously pushing the boundaries of high-throughput experimental technologies with the required automation and parallelization capabilities but they are rarely designed to be accessed remotely and shared across multiple users concurrently. Our proposed *cloud experimentation* aims to enable high-throughput technologies to be shared across many users over the Internet concurrently while allowing iterative interactions, i.e. a user will be able to make changes to her experiments based on the current state of the investigation. This strategy is also critically distinct from previous remote experimentation efforts in the academia [25, 28, 34], which were primarily designed for real-time feedback control of one instrument by a single user. We are not aware of any fully automated cloud or remote labs for biology, although various educational remote labs exist in other science and engineering disciplines [9, 22, 26, 27]. Few "cloud lab" companies have emerged recently that execute biology experiments in a centralized location [5, 1, 4]. As of the writing of this manuscript, none enables users to run experiments online interactively (mailing DNA samples to be cloned and mailed back has a very different quality of interactivity than what we provide). But according to these companies' website in-

CHI 2015, April 18 - 23 2015, Seoul, Republic of Korea
Copyright 2015 ACM 978-1-4503-3145-6/15/04?$15.00
http://dx.doi.org/10.1145/2702123.2702354

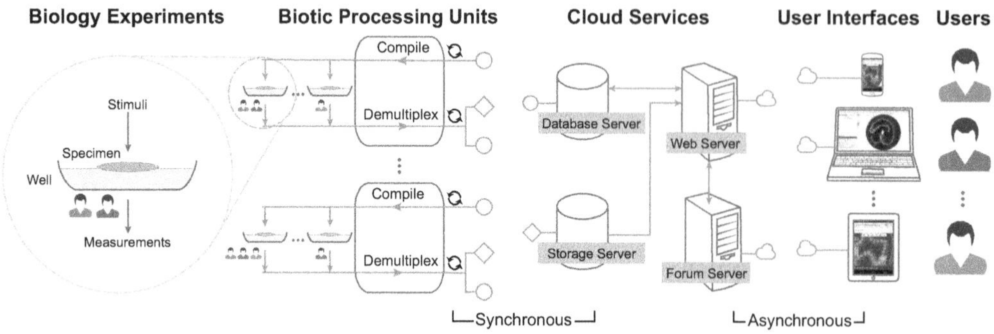

Figure 1. We developed a general architecture for a *cloud experimentation* system that allows multiple users to optimally share high-throughput equipment online to run many interactive biological experiments in parallel and to collaborate. Experiments are carried out in wells and can be shared by multiple users. Many such experiments are executed in parallel on a individual Biotic Processing Units (BPUs), multiples of which operate autonomously and synchronously with two clock cycles. One clock polls the central server for a set of currently scheduled instructions that are multiplexed from several users; the BPU then compiles and executes these instructions. On the other clock cycle, the BPU takes experimental readings (for example, imaging a well or measuring the current temperature) and demultiplexes these data for different users before sending them back to the central database (state data) and storage server (bulk data). Priority is given to one clock when both cycles overlap, based on the specific type of experimentation. Users access the system over the Internet without the need to book a time slot, and they can perform interactive experiments, i.e., change the experimental instructions multiple times throughout the course of the experiment. The web server provides the user interface for experimentation, while the forum server hosts social networking services (chat capabilities, a question and answer forum, etc.). Overall, this architecture is optimized to coordinate asynchronous user actions with synchronous equipment cycles, which enables a convenient user experience while optimally utilizing parallelized equipment at the same time.

teractive experimentation is envisioned for the future, which argues for additional relevance of our present work.

We propose a general systems architecture for *cloud experimentation* for biology that can scale to large numbers of users and diverse applications in a cost - and logistics - effective manner (Fig. 1). We prototyped this architecture as a "mini-cloud," which served as a lab component for a graduate-level biophysics class and conducted a user study within both research and educational contexts. During this study, we assessed the effectiveness, general logistics, and HCI aspects of our system, particularly focusing on answering the following questions: (i) Can *cloud experimentation* be successfully integrated in education? (ii) Does it enable true open-ended research, especially by lowering access barriers for non-biologists? We then discuss limitations of the present system followed by some practical lessons learned, and scalability issues. Finally we allude on how such a system can be leveraged for learning analytics and discuss future directions. The novelty of our work was not in the individual parts but in the whole combination of existing technologies to derive the aforementioned system. The key contribution was to implement and analyze the first end-to-end use-case of a truly interactive biology cloud lab for education. This work is targeted toward a broad audience of engineers, biophysicists, educators, and learning researchers.

System Architecture and Biotic Processing Unit (BPU)

Biological investigations are diverse (Fig. 1), and unlike general purpose computing, there exists no clear basis (e.g. binary 1s and 0s) for executing all types of experiments. Therefore, we adopted a domain-specific philosophy [46] to design conceptual high-throughput hardware - *Biotic Processing Unit* (BPU) - to handle only a specific type of experiment with a specific set of instructions. Swapping out this hardware allows execution of different types of experiments. The goal then is to design a general architecture of a cloud system that can exploit and integrate these hardware under a common platform using a set of protocols while maintaining some key properties: 1) *scalable*, 2) *time-shared* and 3) *available* at all times, meaning that users can access and run experiments anytime without having to book a time slot. In this section we will mainly discuss the design criteria of the key hardware component of our system – *Biotic Processing Unit* (BPU) – and how it interacts with the central servers.

At the backend, experiments are executed in multiple BPUs, and we formally define one of these as an automated hardware that houses a specific set of biological specimens in one or more isolated compartments, termed *wells* (Fig. 1). Each of these *wells* is shared among one or more users, who collaboratively run an independent experiment where the stimulus and measurements can be characterized by the dimensionality of the corresponding spaces. Similar works in the past [28, 34], though different engineering disciplines, have mostly shared their piece of hardware by requiring a user to book a time slot in advance. This approach is not suitable for biology as a single experiment may require an extended period. An alternative approach could be batch-processing, whereby all the experimental instructions from all the users can be aggregated and run concurrently without any further interactions with the user, although it is desirable that users are able to run experiments in several interactive cycles. We enable this interactivity by defining a time scheduling protocol that is carried out jointly by the central server and a microcontroller inside a BPU.

Time Scheduling

To achieve both interactivity and concurrent execution of experiments, we let users provide instructions in discrete *blocks*, where each *block* consists of a small sequence of instructions that need to be performed at a future time. Critically, the instructions within a single *block* can be executed in any order, i.e a *block* is a declarative program [33]. A user is allowed to add *blocks* at any time as well as edit or delete any existing *block* that has not been executed yet. Total time ordering of the instructions is achieved by scheduling these *blocks* at different points on a time line. With this restriction, a BPU is then able to aggregate *blocks* from all the users that pertain to a certain time and interleave them in a way that is optimal for a batch execution by the BPU, which may involve a complex actuation sequence of various parts. We term the life time of a single experiment as an *experimental session*.

Microcontroller
A microcontroller must be integrated within each BPU because the instructions, which must be domain specific like the BPU itself, need to be interpreted at the BPU site. This microcontroller may operate *synchronously* with two independent clock cycles (Fig. 1). The first clocks polls the central server to find appropriate instruction *blocks* from different users, interprets them, and executes them as discussed earlier. The second clock acquires the measurement data (output) from the various *wells* and demultiplexes them for different users before sending them back to the storage server (Fig 1).

Cloud Services and UI
Users submit experimental instructions in *blocks*, which needs to be performed at a future time, interactively through a web application that communicates with central database server asynchronously. Instructions from several users are queued in this database server until BPUs are ready to poll in a synchronous manner as discussed earlier. This buffering aspect of the database server helps connect the asynchronous user interactions in the frontend with the synchronous BPUs at the backend (see Fig 1). The current state of the experiment, which resulted from executing past instructions, are relayed to the user whenever they are available. Note that the frontend UI also need to be domain specific, although not as specific as the BPU since, for example, a single UI can control a large class of experiments involving stimuli and measurements via multidimensional spatiotemporal arrays (such as chemical pipetting and time-lapse imaging, respectively). We omit discussion related to user and data management as any standard framework for these purposes can be adopted.

Practical Implementation of the Architecture

Biology
In order to assess the practical utility of this cloud architecture, we implemented a mini-cloud system for educational purposes that allowed students in a graduate-level biophysics class to execute open-ended biology experiments like real scientists. We named our system *Jagadish* after the Bengali polymath Sir Jagadish Chandra Bose who had worked extensively in both wireless communication [16, 21] and biology [17]. In this section we discuss our implementation at a broader level while we welcome the reader to see the appendix and supplementary material for all the details. This implementation also permitted instructors to perform learning analytics [10, 11, 14]. We selected the chemotactic response of the slime mold *Physarum polycephalum* (Fig. 2, SOM1) as our experimental paradigm. *P. polycephalum* is a single-celled, multi-nuclei, cytoplasmic organism that forms active and dynamic tube networks to search for food [6, 7, 35, 42, 43, 50]. These interesting macroscopic growth and foraging phenotypes represent both multicellular behavior and development [36], inspiring many questions for further investigation in areas ranging from basic biology and biophysics to abstract computation [6].

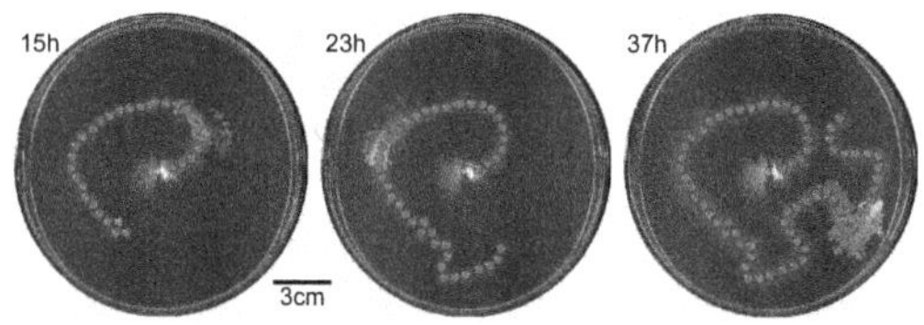

Figure 2. The spatiotemporal chemotactic response of the slime mold *P. polycephalum* (yellow) to an oatmeal solution trail (red) offers a scientifically interesting experimental paradigm with high-dimensional input/output spaces. Food trails of liquid oatmeal pipetted onto an agar surface lead to growth behavior in which *P. polycephalum* follows the trail at a speed on the scale of 1 cm/h. Once the organism encounters one or more food sources, it optimizes its branches in terms of path length and fault tolerance. During this process, the organism sends pulsating fluid flows at a frequency of approximately 0.5 min^{-1} throughout this network, achieving both mass transport and global communication. Note how *P. physarum* follows the trail through sharp turns while occasionally deviating from the trail. See SOM1 for animation. This experiment was executed automatically by the BPU implementation in Fig. 3.

Prototype BPU
To automate these experiments with *P. polycephalum*, we built a BPU that carries out automated liquid handling and imaging tasks to support multiple experiments inside standard Petri dishes (Fig. 3A; SOM2 and Methods for details). In this system, each Petri dish represents a *well* that houses a single experiment that can be shared by multiple online users. The input space in this case is the spatiotemporal dispensing of liquid oatmeal solution, which prompts the chemotactic response of *P. polycephalum*, while the output space is primarily a time-lapse sequence of images that captures these responses. The oatmeal solution is dispensed by a motorized gantry, which we prototyped using a Lego NXT robotics kit, that positions a liquid pipettor (Fig. 3B) on top of a regular flatbed scanner. Standard plasticware and Petri dishes containing various liquids and biological materials are placed on this scanner, which carries out time-lapse imaging of the specimens from below. One BPU fits six Petri dishes (90 mm in diameter) or five standard rectangular plastic wells (85 mm x 127 mm). Imaging rate and resolution were set to 6 images/h at 300 DPI. A Lego NXT robotics kit combined with a Raspberry PI mini-computer board [3] served as the controller for this BPU. For the backend, we stacked three such BPUs into an enclosed regular computer server rack (Fig. 3D). Multiple hardware and software fail-safe mechanisms were implemented to ensure reliability and long-term durability for a 10-week deployment in a classroom.

Backend Servers
We implemented a scalable backend server (Fig. 4A) to connect these BPUs (Fig. 3) to the Internet. The backend server system consists of a web server, a database server, a chat server (to allow discussion among collaborators and communication with the system administrator), and a storage server (primarily for bulk data, such as time-lapse images captured by the scanner). The entire software stack is open- source. Each BPU, which houses multiple experiments concurrently,

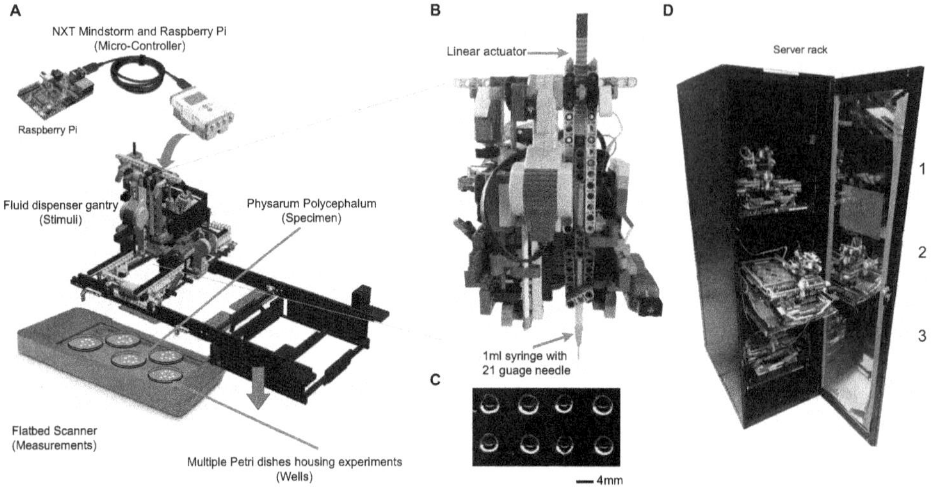

Figure 3. We developed an instance of a BPU for automated fluid handling and imaging to execute versatile biology experiments. (A) A Lego-based gantry for positioning a pipette (stimuli) in the x, y, and z planes is placed atop a flatbed scanner (measurements). Biological materials are housed in standard plasticware (*wells*) placed on this scanner. A Raspberry Pi device combined with an NXT robotics kit controller forms the microcontroller component of the BPU, communicating with the central server, compiling instructions on the fly, and demultiplexing the raw scanned image data for appropriate users (Materials and Methods). The small size and the built-in WiFi capabilities of Raspberry Pi also enable wireless operation of the BPU inside a controlled environment. (B) The Lego-actuated pipettor is made from a standard syringe that reliably pipettes volumes on the order of $10\ \mu$L. (C) Example of eight successive water droplets dispensed and imaged by the BPU. (D) A standard computer server rack provides housing for three BPUs (1-3).

polls the database server synchronously at a regular interval of 10 min before compiling and executing all pending pipetting instructions from several users in parallel.

User Interactions

A system admin would start an experimental session by preparing Petri dishes (6 to 18 depending on the size of the dishes) that are inoculated by *P. polycephalum* at the center unless a special initial condition was specified by a student ahead of time. For example, towards the end of the course, one student requested the system admin to start his experiments with multiple tiny isolated pieces of *P. polycephalum* instead of one at the center (discussed in details later). Experiments pertaining to a single student were distributed across multiple BPUs to ensure there are other experiments to continue with in an event of a catastrophic BPU failure. Students were notified through emails along with secret keys, unique for each student, once all experiments were loaded. A student could then access her experiments using the given key, which she could optionally change later, from her account's homepage (see Fig 4A). This experimental session would last two to three days in which time there would be no further manual intervention. During this time students were able to manipulate and investigate the states of their experiments concurrently through a web based UI (discussed below) at any time and place without having to book a time slot. All experimental data were archived when the session expires and students were able to investigate these later at any time using the same UI.

We developed the frontend UI as a cross-platform web application (Fig. 4, SOM2-4 for details). After selecting an experiment from the dashboard (Fig. 4A), the user is directed to the web interface (Fig. 4B), which is essentially a time-lapse movie player showing the selected Petri dish. The user can now select various UI elements (Fig. 4C) to play back and investigate the collected time-lapse data interactively (Fig. 4D) as well as program new *blocks* of instructions based on the current state of the investigation. All experimental instructions are *visually programmed*, i.e., liquid stimuli are drawn as desired output pattern directly onto the time-lapse images, where stimuli can be dispensed as single drop at a time or as a trail of fluid (Fig. 4B): a *temporal brush* leads to a trail that grows incrementally over time instead of dispensing all of the liquid at once. Being a web application, our UI runs on most systems, including mobile phones (Fig. 4E, SOM4). We implemented adaptive streaming of time-lapse images to account for slow Internet speed and display size. Finally, we also added a live chat capability and a collaborative editor (similar to Google Docs) to allow discussion and collaborative experimentation among multiple users. In this implementation we allowed users to optionally set their own experiments to be viewable publicly, i.e. other users can look at the results but not necessarily modify anything.

USER STUDY

We evaluated our implementation of a *cloud experimentation* system in the light of its utility in education and research (mostly qualitatively as it is the first of its kind) by integrating it into an interdisciplinary graduate-level biophysics course titled, "Biophysics of Multicellular Systems and Amorphous Computing." The course objective was to learn modeling approaches for understanding multicellular biological pattern formation. During this user study we automatically logged every user interaction (i.e., position and timing of mouse click as well as any other data entry) in the backend database server upon full written consent of the students. The frontend UI sent a small packet of ping data to the backend server every second as long as the experiment page was in the foreground or the user interacted with the system in some way, allowing us to compute session times more reliably. Users were able to

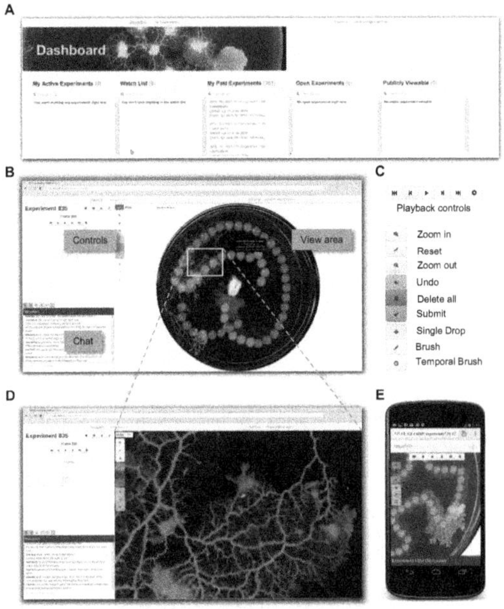

Figure 4. The frontend web-based UI allows the user to program instructions through visual programming, to analyze experimental data remotely, and to collaborate with other users. (A) The dashboard view displays five lists of experiments, enabling easy navigation through all past and currently running experiments owned by the user as well as access to experiments made open or publicly viewable by other users. (B) The desktop interface allows the user to perform experiments (e.g., program timing and position food drop placements), browse and magnify the data, and chat with other users. This layout was optimized for experiments with *P. polycephalum* (Fig. 2). (C) The relevant user interaction control buttons from (B). (D) The user can zoom-in and pan on high-resolution images provided by the server on demand (in contrast to a simple digital zoom). (E) Mobile UI with a customized layout for small displays. See SOM2-4 for more detail.

interact with 30 UI elements; we logged each element according to the timestamp, IP address, browser type, experiment identification number, image sequence visible on the screen, and exact viewing geometry (window size, image size, zoom level, center of image on the window). These logs enabled us to reconstruct log-in activity as a movie based on a set of very compressed data (see Fig 7C).

We carried out three one-on-one interviews with each student: an initial interview at the end of week 2 (out of 10 weeks), an interview in the middle of the term (week 5), and an exit interview during week 10. We also collected written feedback and bug reports with every homework. During the second interview, we learned that the students wanted a system feature that allowed them to view each others' experimental data, but not necessarily interact with it. We immediately implemented this critical design feature.

Cloud Experimentation for Education

From an educational point of view we were particularly interested in whether this platform could serve as a wet-lab component to enrich a theory course. Eleven online experimentation sessions were conducted over 10 weeks (Fig. 5A). Each session lasted 2-3 days, during which each student ran 2-6 experiments concurrently; the system was robust throughout the course. Four graduate students enrolled from different backgrounds: two from bioengineering, one from electrical engineering, and one from applied physics. The latter two students had no prior biology wet-lab experience. This small student population allowed us to follow each student closely (aided by the data-logging capabilities of the system itself), to collect feedback multiple times during the course, and to conduct post-interviews. This provided us with an in-depth understanding of how, in essence, such a system could aid education and research without having to deal with complexities due to scale in an initial deployment.

The system was integrated into this course in three main phases: familiarization and guided homework (2 weeks), hypothesis iteration (4 weeks), and final project (2 weeks). Students spent the first two weeks exploring and becoming accustomed to *P. polycephalum* and the UI, ran experiments and measured the growth rate and fractal dimension of *P. polycephalum* (Fig. 5B) [29] . All students reported that they found the UI to be fairly intuitive and simple, with the exceptions of a few minor bugs and confusing UI elements that were fixed immediately. During the second phase, students were asked to develop and test experimental hypotheses, for examples, whether *P. polycephalum* can be made to split into two parts, or whether it can distinguish between different-sized food sources (Fig. 5A, SOM5a-c). During the final project phase, students worked in pairs on one of these hypothesis with the goal of bringing quantitative experimental data and biophysical modeling together; we will discuss one of these projects in depth in the next section (Fig. 6).

Student feedback indicated that compared to conventional labs, this *cloud experimentation* platform lowered the threshold of entry to biology experimentation in three major ways. First, it empowered non-biologists to perform real experiments without concerns about wet-lab training and safety. For example, the electrical engineering and the physics student respectively stated: *"It was a matter of playing around"* and *"...if you really require me to take one month to train for it, then I would probably just skip that [class]."* All students reported that their initial system contact was easy yet unstructured and exploratory while they worked through the guided homework (Fig. 5B). These initial playful interactions led to more systematic self-driven explorations that gave rise to different qualitative hypotheses. Second, the system abstracted away all of the wet-lab details and allowed the students to concentrate on experimental strategies and data analysis; as expressed here: *"When I worked in a wetlab, I would have to prepare a whole bunch of agar plates, ...cleaning a whole bunch of stuff, ...lots of like chemical mixing so you get the right concentration. .... that's pretty time consuming stuff that is sort of logistical, so it's nice to not have to do it."* Third, the system provided a critical convenience by allowing students to remain continually engaged with their experiments from any place at any time: *"To place a droplet every 30 minutes, you would have to be up 24 hours, you could not even take a nap."* The logged user interaction data confirmed that students ran experiments through mobile phones while on the move and sometimes even past midnight.

A pressing question in educational research is whether computer simulations can substitute for real experiments [12, 15,

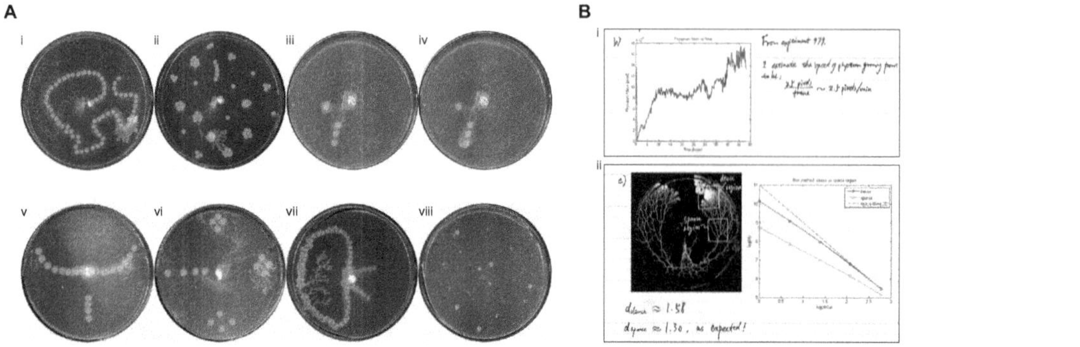

Figure 5. Integrating our *cloud experimentation* system into a lecture-based course on the biophysics of multicellular systems empowered biology experimentation by abstracting away hands-on skills and logistics. (A) Examples of experiments carried out by students throughout the course. The students progressed from initial open-ended, playful exploration of broad behavioral aspects, to developing more specific hypotheses about the observed behaviors, to setting up experiments to test these hypotheses. (i) How well does *P. polycephalum* follow a path and make sharp turns? (ii) How does *P. polycephalum* travel between islands of food? (iii-iv) How does *P. polycephalum* decide where to go when presented with different numbers of food droplets (in this case, three versus one)? (v-viii) Changes in the experiments carried out by one student throughout the course. See SOM5a-c. (B) Sample homework from students. (i) Quantification of apparent area (growth) of *P. polycephalum* over time. (ii) Computing the fractal dimension from binarized *P. polycephalum* images via the box-counting method.

24, 30, 38, 45, 52]. In interviews, the students expressed a clear preference for the latter. First, real systems have implicit narratives attached to them through which students can be more appreciative of and connect more naturally to the system; knowing that something is real changes student motivation. As one student expressed *"Well, it's real, that's why it is so exciting! And so, then you're genuinely interested in asking more questions. So, I think you learn a lot more."* Second, real systems promote open discovery, especially in the context of biology. This context can also lead to unexpected experimental observations (see next section, Fig. 6A), which would not be possible in a virtual environment (e.g., PhET [38]). Ultimately, each instructional medium (conventional lab, virtual lab, online lab) has its own benefits [45], whereas combined or hybrid approaches normally achieve better learning gains [15, 20]. Hence, an exciting future research area is how to achieve optimal synergy between *cloud experimentation* and existing educational media [15].

Cloud Experimentation for Research

Can *cloud experimentation* enable key aspects of the scientific process and lead to genuine scientific advancements? Our evidence suggests a positive answer: The applied physics student who had no prior wet-lab or biology experience, went through multiple hypotheses and exploratory phases throughout the course (Fig. 5Av-viii). During this process, he observed that *P. polycephalum* often does not stop growing even when all food stimuli are depleted (Fig. 5Avii). This observation led him to run a controlled experiment with two Petri dishes, one with and one without food. He then made the unexpected observation that a tiny isolated fragment of *P. polycephalum* moved across the dish in a "worm"-like, random, self-avoiding path. The student emailed a screen shot (Fig. 6A) to the system administrator with the text *"... I've attached the picture of an example of what I mean here - you probably did it by accident last time but it gave birth to a worm-like small strain of physarum moving around which is really interesting and potential more suitable for modeling!"* During the remainder of the course this student (together with another student) employed several more rounds of experimenting and modeling to explore this initial observation and to understand how the branching dynamics and morphology of the organism changes over time and with the organism's size (mass) (Fig. 6B-D). The student asked the system administrator to setup experiments with smaller fragments of *P. polycephalum* of varying size. The administrator fulfilled this request (Fig. 5Aviii), which went beyond the experimental paradigm intended for the course. The student was particularly struck by his observation that organisms with smaller masses had fewer branches (Fig. 6Ci), which seemingly went against the notion of "self-similarity across scales" in fractals [29] that had been discussed earlier in the course. The students' models iterated from symmetric (Fig. 6Cii) to probabilistic (Fig. 6Ciii) branching models, and eventually developed a dynamic model with several phenomenological rules (Fig. 6Civ), such as the model would conserve mass and branch tips would grow as long as there is mass available, otherwise growth stalls and tips shrinks to the last branching point when stalled for too long, thereby providing mass for other growing tips. This model generated visually realistic dynamic morphologies with multiple simultaneously expanding and retracting branches (Fig. 6D). The students also noted limitations in their model, for example that the ratio of retraction and outgrowth rates did not match with the experimental data. In order to go beyond a visual comparison, the students also compared the fractal dimension of *P. polycephalum* fragments versus total mass (Fig. 6D, SOM6) between the model and the experimental data, and obtained quantitative agreement [15].

To assess the novelty of these findings, including modeling, we conducted a literature search that failed to uncover any direct reports of this behavior (see Appendix for details on this literature search). While we suspect that the mass-dependent morphology of *P. polycephalum* may be known [7, 23], no publication has discussed this feature or reported systematic investigations of its dynamics. The students will publish a more detailed analysis of their model separately. This case study aptly demonstrates that the logistic abstraction offered by *cloud experimentation* enables individuals without biol-

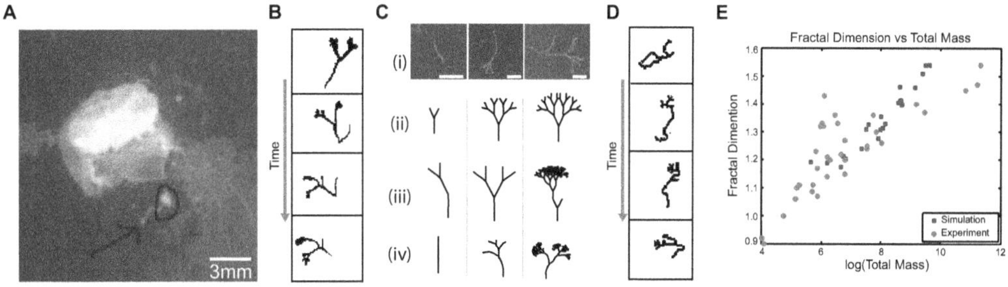

Figure 6. Chance observation by one student and subsequent iterative biophysical model development and experimental testing represent genuine discovery and the scientific method. (A) Email attachment by student sent to the system administrator illustrating the observation that small pieces of *P. polycephalum* behave like a "worm" rather than a fractal (arrow and circle drawn by student). (B) Experimental time sequence of medium sized *P. polycephalum* demonstrating branching dynamics and morphology. (C) The modeling approach taken by this student (jointly with another student) as part of their final project. (i) *P. polycephalum* data at slightly different scales. The student was particularly struck by his observation that organisms with smaller masses had fewer branches, which seemingly went against the notion of "self-similarity across scales" in fractals that had been discussed earlier in the course. Scale bars, 3 mm. (ii-iv) Models developed by students of increasing mathematical complexity and visual correspondence with experimental data: (ii) Static symmetric bifurcation model. (iii) Static random bifurcation model. (iv) Dynamic growth-retraction model that also includes conservation of total mass. (D) Time sequence of model (iv) for medium-sized fragments captures realistic branching dynamics and morphologies (compare to B). See SOM6. (E) In order to go beyond a visual comparison, the students compared the fractal dimension of the *P. polycephalum* fragments and total mass between the model (blue) and the experimental data (red), and obtained reasonable quantitative agreement.

ogy training to perform meaningful experiments. Critically, our system empowers users to iterate computational models side-by-side with experiments. This achievement matches design principles where educational researchers have recently advocated to "selectively expose" students only to learning-relevant features, while technical aspects are hidden unless needed to accomplish the learning goal [13].

LIMITATIONS

Any cloud experimentation system is necessarily limited to a specific sub-set of possible biology experiments, due to the biological material present and the restricted state and measurement space of the automation. In other words, the equivalence of Turing completeness for biology experimentation is not obvious. For example, in our implementation of the BPU, the user was restricted to study *physarum* chemotaxis to oatmeal solutions, and there was no mechanism for providing an alternative stimulus such as shining light patterns to study phototaxis. Furthermore, while backend servicing is inherent to all cloud systems, biological systems would typically require extra care. For example, *physarum* experiments were loaded manually at the beginning of an experimental session but in principle this type of bottleneck can be mitigated by automating the loading process itself as BPUs are domain specific.

DISCUSSION AND CONCLUSION

The primary goal for this project was to understand the effectiveness and potential of *cloud experimentation* for biology, and we share some practical lessons for future implementations: (1) Building and utilizing such cloud systems requires integrating diverse expertise ranging from biology, mechatronics, database, web interfaces, education, and more. A modularized approached with well-defined and minimal I/O interfaces between modules enables parallel development and upgrading of individual components. Parallel modules (such as multiple BPUs) provide overall robustness against component failure, and we propose distributing experiments from the same user across multiple BPUs. (2) Constructing and maintaining the BPU and it's biological content is the most challenging of those modules as specimens must be stable and responsive to defined stimuli over a long time, while all other components (electronics, web servers, etc.) are straightforward by today's standards. Thus, we recommend to first identify a suitable BPU and experimental specimen, assess and test their robustness and logistics towards the desired application, and only then implement any of the other components. (3) Any (online) experiment has limitations, but users will likely request additional features. We suggest that the developers and system administrators aim to be (reasonably) flexible, especially while these cloud systems are under development, and the UI should allow to request extra features. For example, we allowed the users to request different placements and sizes of *P. polycephalum* seeds on the dish by emailing a sketched image to the administrator. (4) There are many open questions regarding what constitutes an optimal UI for performing experiments online. For example, during our study users were online only for very short bursts of time, rendering our chat ineffective for inter-user communication; an online Q/A forum, similar to Piazza or Stackoverflow [47], would have been a better choice. Hence critical UI features should be user tested well in advance, while a few non-critical ones can be beta-tested during the actual usage.

The proposed *cloud experimentation* architecture is scalable as BPUs are independent of each other and more BPUs can be added easily on demand, while failure of one does not effect any other. For example, In our implementation, we had a single BPU failure during the 10 weeks user study, which we were able to recover within 2 hours while the rest of the system was still live. Even though BPUs are domain specific, one can easily run different types of experiments that happen to fall within the state space of a BPU. For example, we employed the same prototype BPU to run gene induction experiments on 24-well plates where users could program instructions using a simple scripting language (data not shown).

Tools for Learning analytics [40] come for free with *cloud experimentation* as we were able to track every student's activ-

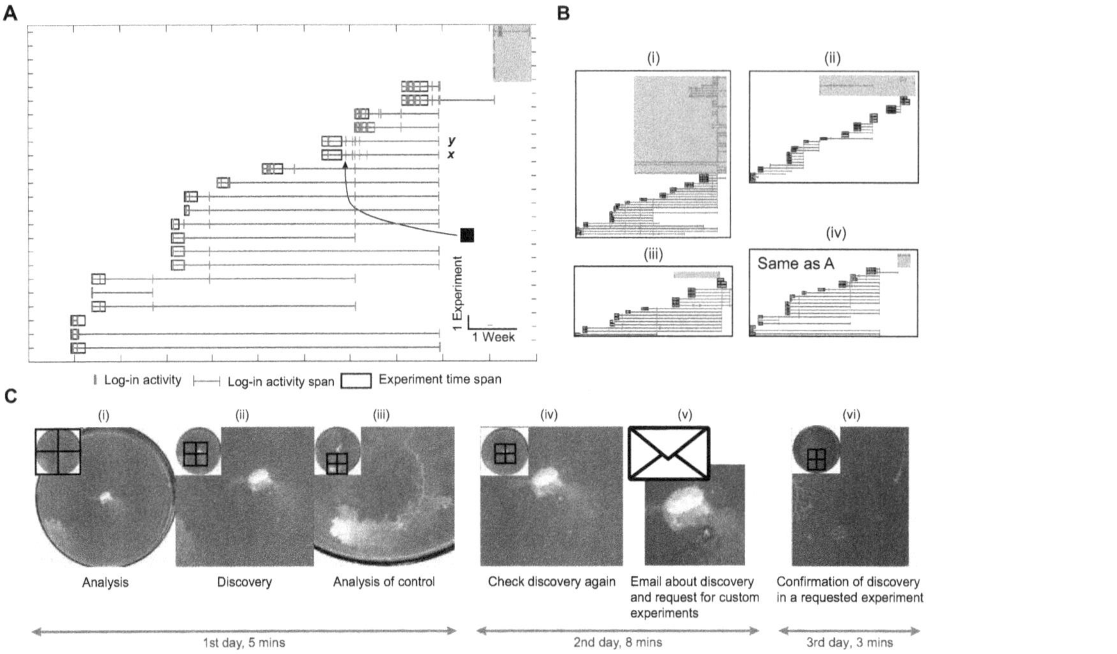

Figure 7. Rich user interaction data can be mined with visualization for student assessment and learning research. (A) The coarsest level of visualization in which the interaction history (experimentation and data analysis) of a single student is shown over the entire course in chronological order. Red ticks, log-in activities; horizontal blue line, first to last log-in activities for a particular experiment; pink background, log-in activities on experiments belonging to other students. (B) Comparison of user history for all four students revealed substantial differences in user history (Biv is the same as A). (C) Complete visual reconstruction of what a student did and saw on the UI enabled us to investigate how discoveries (Fig. 6) came about (see full movie in supplementary material SOM7). (i-ii) Student zooming in when the small-scale behavior of *P. polycephalum* was first seen (experiment marked with an x in (A); session is marked with a black box). (iii) Immediate switching to concurrently running a control experiment (marked y in (A)) and zooming indicates that the student is searching the available data for similar behavior. (iv) Logging back into the original experiment for re-analysis followed by (v) emailing the system administrator with an attached image. (vi) The student notices similar behavior in the custom setup experiment on day 3, confirming discovery. See SOM7 for full animation.

ities in full detail as demonstrated in Figure 7. An instructor could potentially use these activity logs to visualize emerging patterns, for example Figure 7A,B reveals that one student was very keen at looking back to this previous results as well as others' result before starting his own experiments. Figure 7C demonstrates how we were able to reconstruct the exact sequence of actions made by a student in form of a video from just logged data that gave us an intriguing window into the moment the physics student made his first "worm like" observation. Thus the application of *cloud experimentation* in learning analytics is clear and we intend to provide a detailed study in a separate paper.

Wide adoption of *cloud experimentation* depends on the availability of suitable BPUs and interest groups of early adopters (most likely educators). Much existing (automated) life-science equipments do not lend themselves directly as BPU, since stimuli and measurement are often not integrated within one machine (such as separated liquid-handling robots [31] and motorized microscopes [37]), or equipment control is closed during a run (such as real-time PCR machines [51], which do integrate stimulation and measurement, but where protocols cannot be altered during a run). BPUs can be developed at the high-end professional level as well as at the do-it-yourself scale. The presented Lego BPU is itself functional as a mini-cloud, and is supported by increasingly low-cost robotics, such as those used for 3D printers. The do-it-yourself and open source communities have made significant contributions to larger development efforts [2]. We ultimately envision horizontal evolution of BPUs to address diverse applications, and that great value is placed on designs that are simple, easy to assemble, and modular, which over time will lead to higher-throughput and lower-cost systems. For universality, BPUs ultimately need to be coupled (e.g. output of one BPU is fed as input to another), and a lot of future work will hinge on accomplishing this in a scalable manner. Since many biological applications occur at sub-mm scales, even massively parallel BPUs in the future would require only small footprints and researchers have already demonstrated how micro-organisms could be interacted with remotely in form of *Biotic Games*, housed in small micro-fluidic chambers [39]. Reasonably strict protocols for BPUs and UIs will support this development. We speculate that early adoption will come from educational applications, with primary life-science research following later, since educational experiments can be less sophisticated, include a much larger and homogeneous user base, and no novel discoveries must be made during the use of the platform. For the foreseeable future, these cloud systems may remain local (such as within a school), although an educational school supply company could offer a central service similar to that offered by some remote labs in engineering education.

In summary, we have developed a system architecture for biology *cloud experimentation* that is optimized for sharing parallelized high-throughput equipments among many users over the Internet in a *scalable* manner. The main distinguishing features compared to previous work in other engineering disciplines [9, 22, 25, 26, 27, 28] are that all experiments are *interactive* and are *available* all the time to the users seamlessly, while they executed in a high-throughput manner using time-sharing at the backend. Our key contribution was to successfully implement this architecture and analyze its utility for applications in education and true biological discovery. We also discussed future directions for further development along this line and deployment scenarios along with possibilities in learning research. BPU building instructions and open source software are included (SOM8; SOD1; SOS1) for implementation and further development.

ACKNOWLEDGEMENTS

This work has been supported in part by Stanford BioX IIP, Stanford VPOL grants, Lemann Center for Educational Entrepreneurship and Innovation in Brazil, NSF Cyberlearning (NSF 1324753), NSF Bifocal Modeling (NSF 1055130), SIGF, BioX graduate student fellowship and REU. We like to thank J. Grayson, G.I. Lee and P. Floyd.

Author Contribution

Idea: IRK; Hardware: ZH, IRK, JS; Software: ZH, SK, SC; Study design and evaluation: ZH, IRK, EB, PB; Study execution: ZH, XJ, AC, IRK; Supporting: JS , CT, NO; Writing: ZH, IRK.

REFERENCES

1. Emerald Cloud Laboratory. http://emeraldcloudlab.com (last accessed: 19th Dec 2014).
2. OSHWA: Open Source Hardware Association. http://www.oshwa.org (last accessed: 10th July 2014).
3. Raspberry Pi. http://www.raspberrypi.org (last accessed: 10th July 2014).
4. Synthego. http://www.synthego.com (last accessed: 19th Dec 2014).
5. Transcriptic. https://www.transcriptic.com (last accessed: 19th Dec 2014).
6. Adamatzky, A. *Physarum machines: computers from slime mould*, vol. 74. World Scientific, 2010.
7. Alim, K., Amselem, G., Peaudecerf, F., Brenner, M. P., and Pringle, A. Random network peristalsis in physarum polycephalum organizes fluid flows across an individual. *Proceedings of the National Academy of Sciences 110*, 33 (2013), 13306–13311.
8. Alparslan, E., and Fuatince, M. Image enhancement by local histogram stretching. *IEEE Transactions on Systems Man and Cybernetics 11* (1981), 376–385.
9. Alves, G. R., Ferreira, J. M., Muler, D., Erbe, H., Hine, N., Alves, J. B. M., Pereira, C. E., Chiang, L., Herrera, O., and Sucar, E. 2005 IEEE Conference on Emerging Technologies and Factory Automation. In *2005 IEEE Conference on Emerging Technologies and Factory Automation*, IEEE (2005), 1023–1030.
10. Baker, R. S., and Yacef, K. The state of educational data mining in 2009: A review and future visions. *JEDM-Journal of Educational Data Mining 1*, 1 (2009), 3–17.
11. Berland, Matthew and Baker, Rachel and Blikstein, Paulo. (in press) Learning Analytics in Constructivist, Inquiry-based learning environments. *Technology, Knowledge, and Learning*.
12. Blikstein, P. Connecting the science classroom and tangible interfaces: the bifocal modeling framework. *Proceedings of the 9th International Conference of the Learning Sciences, Chicago, IL.* (2010).
13. Blikstein, P. Gears of our childhood: Constructionist toolkits, robotics, and physical computing, past and future. In *Proceedings of the 12th International Conference on Interaction Design and Children*, IDC '13, ACM (New York, NY, USA, 2013), 173–182.
14. Blikstein, P. Multimodal learning analytics. In *Proceedings of the Third International Conference on Learning Analytics and Knowledge*, ACM (2013), 102–106.
15. Blikstein, Paulo. (in press) Bifocal Modeling: Comparing Physical and Computational Models Linked in Real Time. *Playful Learning Interfaces*, 317–352.
16. Bose, J. C. On the determination of the wave-length of electric radiation by diffraction grating. *Proceedings of the Royal Society of London 60*, 359-367 (1896), 167–178.
17. Bose, J. C. *Comparative electro-physiology: a physico-physiological study*. Longmans, Green, and Co., 1907.
18. Cooper, S., Khatib, F., Treuille, A., Barbero, J., Lee, J., Beenen, M., Leaver-Fay, A., Baker, D., Popović, Z., and Players, F. Predicting protein structures with a multiplayer online game. *Nature 466*, 7307 (Aug. 2010), 756–760.
19. Cooper, S., and Sahami, M. Reflections on stanford's moocs. *Communications of the ACM 56*, 2 (2013), 28–30.
20. de Jong, T., Linn, M. C., and Zacharia, Z. C. Physical and Virtual Laboratories in Science and Engineering Education. *Science 340*, 6130 (Apr. 2013), 305–308.
21. Emerson, D. The work of jagadis chandra bose: 100 years of millimeter-wave research. *Microwave Theory and Techniques, IEEE Transactions on 45*, 12 (Dec 1997), 2267–2273.
22. Esche, S. K., Chassapis, C., Nazalewicz, J. W., and Hromin, D. J. 32nd Annual Frontiers in Education. In *Conference on Frontiers in Education*, IEEE (2002), T2E–1–T2E–6.
23. Fessel, A., Oettmeier, C., Bernitt, E., Gauthier, N. C., and Döbereiner, H.-G. Physarum polycephalum percolation as a paradigm for topological phase transitions in transportation networks. *Physical review letters 109*, 7 (2012), 078103.

24. Finkelstein, N., Adams, W., Keller, C., Kohl, P., Perkins, K., Podolefsky, N., Reid, S., and LeMaster, R. When learning about the real world is better done virtually: A study of substituting computer simulations for laboratory equipment. *Physical Review Special Topics-Physics Education Research 1*, 1 (2005), 010103.
25. Fujita, J., Cassaniga, R., and Fernandez, F. Remote laboratory. In *Industrial Electronics, 2003. ISIE'03. 2003 IEEE International Symposium on*, vol. 2, IEEE (2003), 1104–1106.
26. Gomes, L., and Bogosyan, S. Current Trends in Remote Laboratories. *IEEE Transactions on Industrial Electronics 56*, 12, 4744–4756.
27. Gravier, C., Fayolle, J., Bayard, B., Ates, M., and Lardon, J. State of the art about remote laboratories paradigms-foundations of ongoing mutations. *International Journal of Online Engineering 4*, 1 (2008).
28. Hesselink, L., Rizal, D., and Bjornson, E. Cyberlab: Remote access to laboratories through the world-wide-web. *Retrieved September 26*, 2005 (2000), 27–39.
29. Kim, S.-H. Fractal dimensions of a green broccoli and a white cauliflower. *arXiv preprint cond-mat/0411597* (2004).
30. Klahr, D., Triona, L. M., and Williams, C. Hands on what? the relative effectiveness of physical versus virtual materials in an engineering design project by middle school children. *Journal of Research in Science Teaching 44*, 1 (2007), 183–203.
31. Kong, F., Yuan, L., Zheng, Y. F., and Chen, W. Automatic liquid handling for life science a critical review of the current state of the art. *Journal of laboratory automation 17*, 3 (2012), 169–185.
32. Lee, J., Kladwang, W., Lee, M., Cantu, D., Azizyan, M., Kim, H., Limpaecher, A., Yoon, S., Treuille, A., and Das, R. Rna design rules from a massive open laboratory. *Proceedings of the National Academy of Sciences* (2014), 201313039.
33. Lloyd, J. W. Practical Advantages of Declarative Programming. In *Joint Conference on Declarative Programming, GULP-PRODE*, vol. 94 (1994), 94.
34. Macías, M. E., and Méndez, I. elab-remote electronics lab in real time. In *Frontiers In Education Conference-Global Engineering: Knowledge Without Borders, Opportunities Without Passports, 2007. FIE'07. 37th Annual*, IEEE (2007), S3G–12.
35. Nakagaki, T., Yamada, H., and Hara, M. Smart network solutions in an amoeboid organism. *Biophysical chemistry 107*, 1 (2004), 1–5.
36. Niizato, T., Shirakawa, T., and Gunji, Y.-P. A Model of Network Formation by *Physarum* Plasmodium: Interplay Between Cell Mobility and Morphogenesis. *Biosystems 100*, 2 (2010), 108–112.
37. Pepperkok, R., and Ellenberg, J. High-throughput fluorescence microscopy for systems biology. *Nature Reviews Molecular Cell Biology 7*, 9 (2006), 690–696.
38. Perkins, K., Adams, W., Dubson, M., Finkelstein, N., Reid, S., Wieman, C., and LeMaster, R. Phet: Interactive simulations for teaching and learning physics. *The Physics Teacher 44*, 1 (2006), 18–23.
39. Riedel-Kruse, I. H., Chung, A. M., Dura, B., Hamilton, A. L., and Lee, B. C. Design, engineering and utility of biotic games. *Lab on a Chip 11*, 1 (2011), 14–22.
40. Romero, C., and Ventura, S. Educational data mining: a review of the state of the art. *Systems, Man, and Cybernetics, Part C: Applications and Reviews, IEEE Transactions on 40*, 6 (2010), 601–618.
41. Seung, S. EyeWire. https://eyewire.org, last accessed: 18th September, 2014.
42. Tero, A., Takagi, S., Saigusa, T., Ito, K., Bebber, D. P., Fricker, M. D., Yumiki, K., Kobayashi, R., and Nakagaki, T. Rules for biologically inspired adaptive network design. *Science 327*, 5964 (2010), 439–442.
43. Tero, A., Yumiki, K., Kobayashi, R., Saigusa, T., and Nakagaki, T. Flow-network adaptation in physarum amoebae. *Theory in Biosciences 127*, 2 (2008), 89–94.
44. Trietsch, S., Hankemeier, T., and Van der Linden, H. Lab-on-a-chip technologies for massive parallel data generation in the life sciences: A review. *Chemometrics and Intelligent Laboratory Systems 108*, 1 (2011), 64–75.
45. Triona, L. M., and Klahr, D. Point and click or grab and heft: Comparing the influence of physical and virtual instructional materials on elementary school students' ability to design experiments. *Cognition and Instruction 21*, 2 (2003), 149–173.
46. Van Deursen, A., Klint, P., and Visser, J. Domain-specific languages: An annotated bibliography. *Sigplan Notices 35*, 6 (2000), 26–36.
47. Vasilescu, B., Filkov, V., and Serebrenik, A. Stackoverflow and github: associations between software development and crowdsourced knowledge. In *Social Computing (SocialCom), 2013 International Conference on*, IEEE (2013), 188–195.
48. Waldrop, M. M. Education online: The virtual lab. confronted with the explosive popularity of online learning, researchers are seeking new ways to teach the practical skills of science. *Nature 499*, 7458 (2013), 268–270.
49. Whitesides, G. M. The origins and the future of microfluidics. *Nature 442*, 7101 (July 2006), 368–373.
50. Wohlfarth-Bottermann, K. Oscillatory contraction activity in Physarum. *Journal of Experimental Biology* (1979).
51. Wong, M. L., and Medrano, J. F. Real-time pcr for mrna quantitation. *Biotechniques 39*, 1 (2005), 75.
52. Zacharia, Z. C., Olympiou, G., and Papaevripidou, M. Effects of experimenting with physical and virtual manipulatives on students' conceptual understanding in heat and temperature. *Journal of Research in Science Teaching 45*, 9 (2008), 1021–1035.

Mining Memories: Designing a Platform to Support Social Media Based Writing

John Sadauskas
Arizona State University
699 S. Mill Ave.
Tempe, AZ 85281
john.sadauskas@asu.edu

Daragh Byrne
Carnegie Mellon University
5000 Forbes Avenue,
Pittsburgh, PA 15213
daraghb@andrew.cmu.edu

Robert K. Atkinson
Arizona State University
699 S. Mill Ave.
Tempe, AZ 85281
robert.atkinson@asu.edu

ABSTRACT
Many teens struggle with school writing and particularly in identifying personally relevant topics, which motivate writing improvement. However, a wealth of potential topics is available through their social media data. We explore the design of Sparkfolio, a prewriting support tool that aims to help students successfully prepare meaningful writing topics from their own social media content. This web-delivered tool was evaluated with 46 teen users in the context of their high school English class. Findings demonstrate that the use of social media can enhance the quality of written outcomes, as Sparkfolio users had significantly greater gains than a control group.

Author Keywords
Social Media; Education; Storytelling; Creative Writing

ACM Classification Keywords
H.5.2 [User Interfaces]: User-centered design; K.3.1 [Computer Uses in Education]: Computer-assisted instruction

INTRODUCTION
Over the past decade, the social web has enabled new and profound ways to document and examine our everyday experiences. Through platforms like Facebook, Flickr, Instagram and Twitter, we now have large, long-term and intimate archives of ourselves authored as short, succinct multimedia-narratives or 'status updates.' Teens are among the most deeply immersed in these platforms [17] and this creates an exciting opportunity space to enhance the educational experiences of students by connecting instructional content to communication technologies.

Several recent studies highlight how social platforms positively enhance instruction by creating forums for discourse and engagement, by supporting digital collaboration, and by offering mechanisms for formal and informal mentorship [3]. These classroom interventions typically either directly co-opt or create simple non-technical extensions to these platforms (e.g. using Facebook Groups to coordinate assignments). Rarely are social media tools adapted; rarer still are purpose-designed solutions for social participation, engagement or exchange found within the classroom. Consequently, there are many unrecognized opportunities to enhance the classroom by leveraging these social platforms and their content [24].

CHI 2015, April 18 - 23, 2015, Seoul, Republic of Korea.

http://dx.doi.org/10.1145/2702123.2702383

When employed in curricular contexts, the use of social content mainly explores the development and sharing of new content rather than creative re-use of students' existing multimedia. The re-examination of past, personal content could inspire new instructional scenarios for civic and social education, art making, and in our case, English instruction. In particular, the efficacy with which teens regularly narrate their experiences online ought to connect strongly to literacy and creative writing education. However, a strong perception remains that using social media, and especially Facebook, is antithetical to educational use, particularly as social networking is often seen as a vehicle for procrastination and distraction from core curricular content [3].

This raises fundamental questions about introducing social media re-use within instructional settings: *How can social data be re-used in education scenarios such that it enhances student outcomes but minimizes the potential for distraction?* To address this, we prepared and evaluated an online tool, named Sparkfolio, which was designed to support English personal creative writing in K-12 settings. Through this prewriting support scenario, we explore how socially documented experiences can help identify writing topics, overcome creative blocks, and highlight self-efficacy in writing via previously authored social narratives. Our goal is to illuminate students' natural storytelling abilities, positively affect their writing self-confidence, and ultimately motivate writing improvement.

We begin this paper by describing prior work in the area and motivate the need for a social media based approach to prewriting. Next, we describe two probative studies that led to design recommendations for our tool. Following an overview of the implemented online platform, we present findings from an evaluation with 46 high school students using the tool over a four-week period. We conclude with a discussion of the primary contributions of this work: 1) evidencing the utility of social media in enhancing student motivation for writing and writing quality; 2) highlighting the advantages of tool support in mediating social media based writing and 3) the potential to enhance engagement and learning through personally relevant social content.

BACKGROUND

As modern communication becomes increasingly digital in the age of the Internet, adolescents in particular have embraced this paradigm shift, cited by many as "digital natives" [21] due to their frequent, enthusiastic use of technologies such as social media, instant messaging, SMS, and email [17]. Through these channels, American teenagers regularly engage in informal writing activities [15], and as teen cell phone ownership continues to increase [17], many are able to engage in these writing activities anytime and anywhere. Despite being deeply engaged in writing practice through text-based communication via digital devices, this does not necessarily translate to increased academic writing proficiency among adolescents, as in 2011, only 27% of 8th and 12th grade students scored as "proficient" or higher in writing [26]. One reason for this disconnect is that students view their digital activity as "being social" rather than "writing" [15]. Furthermore, writing involves complex cognitive processes [12] and is especially daunting for adolescents [14]. This is particularly because they are self-conscious about their academic abilities [1] and tend to believe they are born with them rather than seeing possibilities for acquiring and developing them [19]. Hence, the act of writing has a strong affective component [12,19,20]. Self-beliefs impact one's actions [19], and so in the case of writing, negative self-views can result in low quality work which in turn affirms negative self-beliefs, and the cycle repeats.

With this in mind, many efforts have been made to intrinsically motivate students to write by allowing them to choose topics that are personally meaningful [2]. Students themselves provide support for this approach, reporting "they are motivated to write when they can select topics that are relevant to their lives and interests, and report greater enjoyment of school writing when they have the opportunity to write creatively" [15].

One particularly effective instructional strategy for improving adolescent writing involves prewriting—the gathering, planning, and organization of ideas before beginning a first draft [11]. Although the practice is constantly employed by professional writers, school-age students tend to spend little to no time prewriting prior to starting first drafts [6], even when prompted by a teacher [4]. Thus, focusing on structured prewriting strategies is especially beneficial for adolescents [11], including the use of visual tools such as graphic organizers to externalize their thoughts [22]—which can reduce cognitive load while organizing ideas and drawing connections [13].

However, an additional problem lies in combining personally relevant topics with prewriting strategies, particularly with struggling adolescent writers. While choosing their own writing topics appeals to adolescents [2,15], actually deciding on one can be challenging and even intimidating. Given boundless options, they often do not know where to start [22] and struggle with developing initial general ideas to workable, specific ones [2]. While teachers can work with students one-on-one and provide structured questions for teasing out an idea [2,22], a teacher cannot conference with every student. Moreover, if the aim is for the student to select a topic that is personally meaningful, a teacher cannot make that choice—it must be the student. One approach to addressing this problem involves "mining memories" [2], a practice in which students are encouraged to keep a log of topics that interest them as a bank of potential ideas for future writing [22], typically cultivated over time through frequent brainstorming sessions and freewriting. Yet, this method requires a significant time commitment from both teachers and students and is typically paper-based, making months' worth of work easy to misplace. Hence, while approaches such as mind maps, one-on-one conferencing and idea logs are available, for many students, the stumbling block of finding the spark for a relevant topic remains.

One possible solution to these challenges is the use of technology to support prewriting, but most existing computational writing tools instead focus on subsequent portions of the writing process (drafting and revising) and the use of natural language processing to evaluate writing quality [24]. Few systems (if any) approach writing from a content perspective [24]—i.e. supporting personally relevant idea generation. Rather than helping students generate engaging ideas, most frameworks assume a topic is already chosen and address how to organize it. This is largely because it is easier to have computers analyze language patterns than to mimic creative human thought.

However, social media, smartphones, and digital media have made it very easy to archive one's life events [7], and using these technologies, adolescents regularly document their lives and thoughts via status updates, photos, and videos [15,16]—essentially "authoring" stories every day—stories that matter to them, stories they share because they want to. Furthermore, lifelogs and social media data have proven effective in seeding other narrative forms [7].

DESIGNING SOCIAL MEDIA BASED WRITING

Thus, within this work, we explore the potential of social media based writing to empower students to better writing outcomes. Our hypothesis is that grounding this creative exercise in personally relevant topics, drawing on past personal experiences to stimulate recall, and repurposing previously authored content toward new applications will lead to increased writing quality and motivation. By leveraging content authored previously by the writer, this can potentially highlight that they have valid ideas worth sharing with peers and can provide a supportive framework during topic selection. However, using social media in this context simultaneously yields both opportunities and challenges; it would provide a vast collection of potential ideas, but making sense of this large volume of disparate content could quickly become unbounded and overwhelming for a struggling teen writer. Hence, in exploring the use of social media in this context we consider the following research questions:

RQ1: Does the use of social media data as inspiration for writing during the prewriting process improve adolescents' writing quality and writing motivation in comparison to those who do not?

RQ2: How should social data be leveraged in a computational tool for students to enhance their personally relevant written outcomes while minimizing distraction (overwhelming, procrastination, etc.)?

To balance the (sometimes competing) needs of teachers and students during prewriting, we conducted two design studies to explore the utility of social media as a dataset for prewriting support: first, a probative study assessed teacher and student needs in prewriting; next, a series of design workshops with teen writers were carried out. Principle outcomes are summarized below.

Needs Assessment

One-on-one interviews with six middle/high school English teachers and focus group interviews with 14 high school students were first conducted [22]. Discussions with teachers explored needs, challenges and best writing instruction practices; use of technology in classrooms, and social media as a tool for writing. The six English teacher participants (4 female, 2 male) all work in schools in the American Southwest, and range in age (31-54 years), years of teaching experience (4-28), and grades taught (6-12). Student focus group topics included: students' experiences with writing; their social media/technology use; and social media based writing. The 14 students (4 female, 10 male; aged 13-18; grades 8-12) participated in three focus groups (3-5 students per group). Students were recruited from two high schools in the American Southwest, both of which emphasize the integration of technology into instruction. All sessions were audio-recorded, transcribed, iteratively coded for emerging categories and themes, and conceptualized using Grounded Theory [8]. Outcomes were ultimately synthesized into two main categories (justification for a social media based writing approach, and design recommendations for such applications) as summarized below; more details can be found in [22].

Both students and teachers agreed that *student self-confidence is a major challenge* in writing instruction. One teacher shared that many students come to school *"saying 'I'm a bad writer,' and they don't have any confidence in their writing...[they've] made a decision that reading is boring and writing is too hard*". 10 out of the 14 student participants self-described as "*okay*" or "*bad*" writers, including several students in AP/Honors English. This implies a disjoint between students' actual abilities and self-confidence. Yet, and consistent with [15,16], teachers and students affirmed that *teens are constantly engaged in social media writing activities*, particularly via smartphones, which they "*always*" and "*constantly*" keep within reach. Teens also reported that they appreciate having a large audience for their thoughts, and being able to share with them at any moment through social media, and—in agreement with [10,23]—that the instant validation of their posts and photos from friends and family positively impacts their self-views, encouraging them to continue to share [22]. Finally, as supported by [2,15], teachers find success in using *personally relevant topics to ease students into writing*, and students feel this makes writing *"easier"* and allows them to *"play to their strengths"* [22].

Overall, students were especially interested in *"seeing all of [their online] activity in one place,"* allowing them to *"learn about themselves"* and *"reflect"* while looking for writing ideas. However, teachers confirmed that students often do not know where to begin with a writing assignment. Even given the option of choosing their own topic, students claim they "*don't have anything interesting to write.*" In agreement with [11,14], teachers cited *"scaffolding"* (walking students through the writing process) as the most effective strategy for addressing this issue, specifically providing structured questions for generating personally relevant ideas: "*I give them various questions based on experiences they've had in the past...memories that are funny or things where they have a lot of emotion."* ;*"When they can map out all of their ideas in some way...it really helps them to see that there's lots of ideas to choose."* Once a topic is chosen, teachers typically continue to aid students in *"narrowing [the topic] down"* to a usable idea: *"you've got this huge monstrosity and you want to pick just a slice...I don't want to hear about your entire day at Disneyland...I want to hear about a moment in time."* Teachers emphasized the importance of a scaffolded workflow guiding students from initial idea to a specific topic and then to a formal, organized plan and highlighted the value of several popular mechanisms to flesh out and organize ideas in preparation for a draft including *"mind maps,"* and *"graphic organizers."*

Design Workshops

Based on design insight gathered from the student/teacher interviews, a low fidelity prototype of the tool was prepared. This initial prototype was presented to teenagers as part of a participatory design session. The wireframe design included two principle features. First, a constrained review model only displays five social media items at a time. This was designed to avoid overwhelming students and unbounded exploration. Second, it includes a flexible planning tool intended to integrate familiar graphic organizer techniques, solicit rich descriptions and scaffold toward a structured writing plan. Focus groups were conducted with 21 students (12 female, 9 male) in four sessions. All participants were eleventh-grade students recruited from one of the same high schools (see Needs Assessment). The interactive wireframe was displayed and students were asked—without any prior explanation—how they would expect or want to interact with each screen. This aimed to explore the expectations, affordances and intuitiveness of the two approaches. Directed feedback, as well as open-ended discussion, was solicited. Focus group responses were audio-recorded, transcribed, and iteratively coded via Grounded Theory, following the same methodology as described previously [8,22]. Student responses were positive and enthusiastic, with little (if any) negative feedback. Findings were organized around the two principle areas of interest: the constrained approach and the digital organizer.

Constraint During Ideation: Students were particularly receptive to the use of constraint. They felt viewing all of one's data at once (as in a timeline or exploratory interface) would be *"overwhelming", "distracting"* and run the risk of bringing *"the procrastination level to a new point"* during prewriting. They noted that by only using five items, it *"doesn't overload you"* with too much content. While constrained review is atypical for social media review, participants were in favor of it in this context. They expressed interest in using this method for their own writing and believed it would effectively aid peers in choosing personally relevant writing topics while avoiding distractions.

Scaffolding A Writing Plan. Participants felt the writing organizer would meet the needs of a wide variety of students and learning styles. They immediately recognized the graphic organizer approach and included writing elements. One student appreciated that it was *"like doing a web [planning diagram]. I love doing those...I'm a very visual person, so that's probably why I like it."* At the same time, students who prefer text-based planning felt it was *"a lot like an outline."* Students believed the workflow would need to help scaffold their writing planning without being prescriptive and that it should be flexible to the preferences of the individual student. For example, some students favored the preparation of highly detailed writing plans and wanted to be able to include multiple layers of detail and specificity. Other students (consistent with [4,6]) preferred not to construct detailed plans: *"I don't like to prewrite. I've never prewritten."* Another added: *"I just write out [lists of] ideas."* A third student shared that once she has a basic plan (a list of 1-2 words for each idea to include), *"I just start writing."* Nevertheless, students admitted that successful writing requires at least some level of planning, as *"you need to have somewhere to begin rather than just staring at a blank piece of paper."* They also acknowledged that instructors often require them to write detailed outlines they do not always feel are valuable to their writing process: *"You don't want to make [students] fill out extra details if they're just ready to start writing." "Everyone is different,"* another student echoed, *"so if you feel confident enough, you should be able to just start writing."* Finally, asked when a user ought to be "finished" with a writing plan, students unanimously answered: *"when you want to be."*

Design Recommendations

Inspiration and Planning: Both students and teachers were very receptive to the use of personally relevant social media to support ideation and planning as part of prewriting. The use of constraint during the presentation and review of social content was seen as an effective strategy to avoid overwhelming students.

Flexible planning: Students noted that they used prewriting/ planning methods to varying degrees and had a variety of preferences for their application and use. While teachers strongly favored every student using an organizational method, students strongly believed that they should be able to proceed directly to writing a draft when they already had clear topics for their writing and felt confident about their ideas. This predicates the need for a flexible approach to writing organization that would facilitate scaffolding toward a well-developed writing plan while also catering for a wide range of preferred prewriting strategies.

IMPLEMENTATION AND EVALUATION

The design research and its outcomes were leveraged in the preparation of an online tool to support student writing via personally relevant social media, following which a 46-student trial was conducted in an 11th grade English class.

Implementation

The application, named Sparkfolio, is realized as a web-delivered application, allowing students flexible and ubiquitous use from any Internet-enabled device. It offers the ability to: import and automatically organize social multimedia from a variety of sources; to revisit and re-find social content to seed ideas for personal writing; to assemble social media into a lightweight narrative and to develop that narrative into a fully-formed writing plan by adding relevant details. It offers a carefully designed experience intended to increase writing quality and motivation. In subsequent sections, we describe this approach, design considerations, and the functionality prepared in more detail.

Content Aggregation: Users are able to connect their social media accounts and import their data from three platforms: Facebook, Twitter and Instagram. Once connected, the application performs an initial import of content but periodically synchronizes with their feeds to include new content. Users can also manually initiate this update. For Facebook, the application imports their: friends and associated metadata; photo albums; location check-ins; photos; their status updates; and photos they were tagged in. For Instagram, the tool will parse the full history of the user's timeline, importing both videos and photos. Media liked by the user and the accounts they follow are also imported. Finally, for Twitter, the user's personal timeline is parsed to a maximum of 3200 status updates (imposed by the API), along with "tweets" the user has been mentioned in and/or favorited, and their list of followed accounts. In addition to content authored by the user, content they have acted on (replies, re-shares, likes) is imported, after which, content is denoted as one of five media types: text, photo, video, place or person. Metadata on authorship and social activity and engagement for each item (number of "likes," comments, replies, or shares by other users) is also stored.

Content Re-experience: Constraint is deliberately designed into the ideation phase for the tool, using the familiar metaphor of playing cards. It compiles imported social media into a "deck" of cards, with each "card" representing a single post (e.g. a tweet, status update, or photo). When presenting content, a constrained "hand" of five of these idea cards is dealt (see Figure 1). Given that the user does not know what will satisfy their information need, it also avoids user-driven search as the primary means to identify relevant content within their archive. The card metaphor is extended to offer five suits of cards, namely text, photo, video, locations, and people. At each draw, the user can decide which of the five results they wish to "hold" before clicking a "redraw" button to replace unwanted cards. Users are free to redraw as many times as they like until they find a set of cards to use as a starting point for a writing piece. Associated with enhancing creativity, the topic of constraint is of particular interest in this context [18], as it is intended to encourage students to weigh and evaluate each option for latent relationships for more considered outcomes.

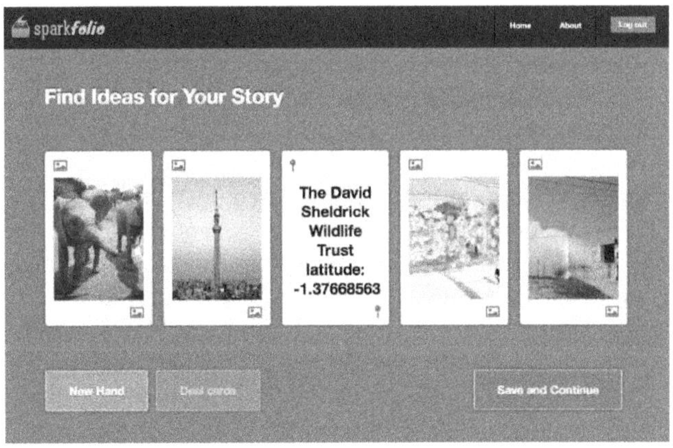

Figure 1. A constrained layout shows 5 social media cards to help inspire writing topics from personally relevant content.

Narrative Development: Once students have found their idea or source material, a new challenge lies in developing it into a well-formed first draft. A common solution is to use graphic organizers to scaffold toward a draft by organizing thoughts and applying rich descriptions appropriate for the assigned writing genre. The tool incorporates a variant of these classroom strategies to guide students from their initial "idea cards" toward a well-conceived writing plan (see Figure 2). During the planning process, students sort and organize their selected cards. Based on the relevant genre (e.g. personal story, explanation, persuasive piece), students are encouraged to add relevant details through iterative research-based prompts (e.g. [9]). For example, if students are writing a personal story, they are cued to add story elements such as an Exposition, Conflict, Climax, and Resolution. Each element can then be 'fleshed out' with questions prompting additional details specific to the story element (e.g. people involved, emotional responses to the situation, etc.). This encourages reflection on the media through established story development methods toward a complete and well-formed story plan.

Figure 2. Final graphical organizer designed to assist story planning and organization.

Export for Writing: Once a plan is completed, it is saved and can be accessed and revised at any later date. The user can also export it as a richly described PDF. The exported plan is organized as a nested bullet-point summary of chosen media, their arrangement, and descriptive annotations. This enables portability of the developed plan for subsequent development into a fully-formed narrative.

Evaluation

Writing Quality: Sparkfolio was evaluated in a study involving 46 eleventh-grade English students, each of whom were enrolled a two sections of a large, block-style English class (at one of the Needs Assessment schools) taught by a two-teacher team (60 students per section, 120 total). Student participation was based on their own (and their parents') interest, using a standard recruitment script. The 46 participants were randomly assigned to three experimental groups: a) the "My Media" group, who used self-authored social media post data while planning with Sparkfolio; b) the "Network Media" group, who used only data from posts authored by their friends while planning with Sparkfolio (and no self-authored data—similar to the social media content they would review through a timeline); and c) a control group who did not use Sparkfolio. Assignment to the conditions was purely random; students were automatically assigned as they registered for the tool, with the first assigned to My Media, the second to Network Media, the third to Control, the fourth to My Media, etc. Participants wrote three personal narratives during the course of the four-week experiment. A first, pretest personal narrative was written prior to the introduction of Sparkfolio—all participants wrote this narrative however they felt most comfortable. Next, Sparkfolio was introduced, and participants were then asked to write two additional personal narratives within their assigned conditions. They were given two 20-30 minute sessions per each treatment narrative for in-class prewriting (during which My/Network Media prewrote with Sparkfolio while Control prewrote by hand). My/Network Media students were also free to log onto and use Sparkfolio outside of class, and the Control group was free to prewrite (without Sparkfolio) outside of class as well. Writing prompts were selected based on state standards and personal narratives were scored with a nationally-adopted holistic writing evaluation rubric [25]. This rubric was chosen because it is the "officially" adopted writing quality instrument used on all standardized tests for the state in which the study occurred. The rubric considers multiple facets of writing (ideas & content, organization, voice, word choice, sentence fluency, and conventions) and assigns a single holistic score from 1 to 6, with scores of 1 and 2 indicating that the writing "falls far below" grade-level standards, 3 indicating that the writing "approaches" the standards, 4 "meets" the standards, and scores of 5 and 6 "exceed" the standards [27]. Thus, the outcome variable of interest in assessing writing quality was the rubric-based change in holistic writing quality from the first (pretest) narrative to the third (second treatment) narrative. Student outcomes were independently assessed using this rubric by a teacher with 10 years' experience, who was very familiar with the instrument, and had used it for several years with her own students' writing. She had no knowledge of the study's purpose or design, Writing samples were additionally anonymized, randomly sequenced, and contained no information on experimental group or the order that papers were written in. In addition to the writing quality measures, the Writing Dispositions Scale (WDS) [20] was administered to all 46 participants as a pre/posttest to measure the change in writing motivation. The pretest was administered before Sparkfolio was described or used and the posttest was completed after submission of the final personal narrative. The primary dependent variable was the change in writing motivation—the change in the mean scaled response for all items of the WDS. Finally, the System Usability Scale (SUS) [5] was administered, including open response items to qualify scaled responses.

RESULTS

Perception of the Tool

Students received Sparkfolio well with a mean SUS score [5] of 2.39 (on a 0-4 scale; *SD*=0.53), particularly responding to its ease of use (*M*=2.53), ability to quickly learn the system (*M*=2.73) and their confidence in using it (*M*=2.53). They felt it *"helped [them] remember events that happened in the past,"* aiding in the identification of personally relevant topics, and enjoyed *"the ideas that came from bringing up old posts."* Overall the tool was viewed as supportive as *"it helped promote ideas and create a full story from beginning to end."* There were slight differences between the two conditions with My Media having a mean scaled score of 2.50 and Networked Media's lower score of 2.27, but this difference was nonsignificant.

Social Media Data

All 46 users imported content into the system (15 My Media, 15 Network Media, 16 Control.) A mean of 5,514.09 (*SD* = 4127.42) items were imported per user, of which 1,986.82 (*SD* = 1,669.08) were explicitly authored by the user, 10.51 (*SD* = 10.58) represented tagged locations, and 1,089.60 (*SD* = 789.32) were friends listed in their social networks. 32 users had Twitter accounts, 36 users had Facebook accounts and 37 users had Instagram accounts. Twitter users authored a mean of 1,338.81 items imported over 1.46 years. 342.76 were replies, indicating the users were actively engaged in discussions on Twitter with peers and the content was typically text-based (1,231.23 items) but a small amount of media content was also posted (40.5 photos). They had large social networks with an average of 463.14 friends and regularly engaged with their content, 'liking' 492.06 items and 'retweeting' 504.20 items. Overall, their posts contained limited location metadata, with only 9.11 places being tagged. Instagram had much lower use, with only 127.51 items posted over a 1.12-year period. These tended to be images, but 2.32 videos were also posted. Instagram users liked a mean of 20.92 items and had smaller networks of 51.97 people. Place metadata was also only sparsely applied, with an average of 0.86 locations per user. Finally, Facebook users posted an average of 1162.42 items over a 3.12-year period. Like Twitter, these were primarily status updates (880.31 text-based items) but users had also uploaded a large volume of photo content (282.11 items on average). As with all other platforms, place-based metadata was low (3.38 locations tagged). The social network size was the largest among all of the platforms; 858.28 Facebook friends were found on average. Mean content available for review was as follows. For My Media: 625.46 text; 257.13 photo, 12.06 place, 1209 people; and 2.73 video items. For Network Media: 2332.13 text; 604.5 photo, 13.5 place, 929.25 people; and 0.19 video items.

Identifying Writing Topics and Story Composition

My Media users (2,106.4) averaged half the amount of content as Network Media counterparts (3,880.13 items). As noted above, this was primarily distributed across text (MM: 60.1%; NM: 13.8%), photo (MM: 15.6%; NM: 70.7%), and people content (MM: 23.9%; NM: 12.3%).

Users in the My Media condition needed to review half the amount of content to identify writing topics. My Media users issued an average of 244.13 redraws, from which they viewed an average of 1,049.20 items, 552.53 of which were unique. Network Media users issued a substantially higher number of redraws (441.73) where they saw an average of 1,890.60 items, of which 1,065.47 were distinct. While Network Media had half the amount of content to review, it was presented randomly, giving an equal chance of identifying prospective content and so the more involved review phase is in part attributable to the increased volume of content but also the lowered utility of content (which was not authored explicitly by the user) in this creative exercise.

Both groups each prepared 26 stories using a total of 130 items of media from their archives. The distribution of media across 'suits' is presented in Table 1. Interestingly, despite lower relative distribution of photo-based content in the My Media condition, the group showed a very strong affinity for this content in their final selections. 70.8% (92 of 130 items) of media selected was photographic. Text and people content was included to a lesser degree (18 and 16 items from 130 respectively.) However, while photo content was abundant for Network Media (70.7% of available archive) it was less preferred (66 of 130 items selected or 50.8% of selections). In this condition, the use of text and place based content doubled. This is indicative of differences in the fluencies and affordances of self-authored and peer-authored content in story development.

Exploration	*Text*	*Photo*	*Place*	*People*	*Video*
My Media	13.8%	70.8%	3.0%	12.3%	0.0%
Network Media	29.2%	50.8%	7.7%	12.3%	0.0%

Table 1. Social Media Content Type Used in Stories

Story Planner Use

The total number of story plans created by participants did not widely differ between groups, and consequently this difference was nonsignificant. The My Media group created a mean of 1.73 stories (SD = .59) and the Network Media group created a mean of 1.40 (SD = .83). While participants were asked to create at least two story plans (one for each treatment narrative), participants varied in their readiness and prewriting processes for each assignment. While strongly encouraged to use all Sparkfolio's features for both treatment narratives, some participants simply felt they were confident and ready to start writing first drafts as soon as they received writing prompts (and before logging into Sparkfolio). While encouraged to use both the idea cards and planner to build upon and structure their initial ideas, participants were not forced to do so.

Furthermore, open responses on the usability survey and one-on-one conferences indicated that Network Media users tended to find their data (authored by others) more difficult to work with than My Media users (who used self-authored data). For example, one Network Media user shared, *"Most of the stuff that would come up on the cards was things I would never want to write about, some even completely irrelevant to me."* Another said her cards *"were all old, irrelevant pictures of random people."* In contrast, My Media participants felt Sparkfolio *"helped bring ideas and thoughts to the table"* and was *"beneficial because I got to use pictures to help me think about the things in the past."*

The trend of the My Media group viewing Sparkfolio as more useful than Network Media was extended to the number of total detail nodes created on planners as well as the planner total word count. My Media created almost twice as many (M = 18.80) as Network Media (M = 11.20). While this difference was nonsignificant, it agrees with the number of story plans results. Additionally, the My Media group wrote more than twice as many words on their planners (M = 210.20) as the Network Media group (M = 95.33). This difference was significant at the .05 level: $F(1, 28) = 4.259, p < .05$, with a large observed effect (f = .39).

Writing Motivation

The My Media (M = .06; see Table 2) and Control (M = .03) groups increased and Network Media decreased (M = -.07). This Network Media decrease can be partially supported by qualitative comments, as Network Media participants tended to report more difficulties finding useful social data than the My Media group (see above). However, these between-group differences not only represent less than .1 of a Likert point, but were also nonsignificant.

Planning Mode	*M*	*SD*	*N*
My Media	.06	.37	15
Network Media	-.07	.36	15
Control	.03	.41	16
Total	.01	.38	46

Table 2. Change in Overall Writing Motivation

Writing Quality Improvement

An ANOVA with experimental group as a between-subject factor and pretest writing quality scores as the dependent variable was nonsignificant, indicating that there were no significant differences in writing ability between the three groups as they began the study. Furthermore, as shown in Table 3, the two treatment groups increased in writing quality from pretest to posttest and the Control group decreased. My Media had the greatest increase (M = .27), followed by Network Media (M = .07). Although the Control group had the greatest change from pretest to posttest, it was a decrease (M =-.38). These results pose the question as to why the Control group decreased in writing quality. Participants from all three groups commented during the study that completing three writing assignments of the same genre during a four-week period was challenging, and so the Control group's decrease can be attributed to the assumed decreased enthusiasm by the third assignment. However, it is also important to note that both My Media and Network Media still increased in writing quality. It can thus be argued that Sparkfolio not only maintained participants' interest despite the multiple assignments, but also actually resulted in improved writing quality under these circumstances. Furthermore, an *a priori* orthogonal contrast between the two treatment groups and the Control group was significant, $F(1, 43) = 5.139, p < .05$, with a medium-to-large observed effect ($f = .35$).

Planning Mode	*M*	*SD*	*N*
My Media	.27	.59	15
Network Media	.07	.96	15
Control	-.38	.72	16
Total	-.02	.80	46

Table 3. Change in Overall Writing Quality

A multiple regression analysis provided further validation of these results. Using the forward selection method, the analysis investigated whether gender, treatment/no treatment, mean authored social media posts per day, or total social media activity accurately predicted the change in writing quality. In the resultant linear regression model, the treatment variable was the sole predictor included, and was significantly related to the change in writing quality, $F(1, 44) = 5.198$, $p < .05$. With $R = .33$ and $R^2 = .11$, approximately 11% of the variance of the sample's change in writing quality can be accounted for by a linear prediction model with treatment as the sole predictor. These results imply that the treatment was, in fact, effective; those who used Sparkfolio had significantly greater gains in overall writing quality than participants in the Control group, regardless of their genders and social media usage.

DISCUSSION

Writing Quality and Motivation

Most notable among the results is the validation of Sparkfolio's efficacy in enhancing writing quality outcomes, as those who used it had statistically significantly greater gains in writing quality compared to the Control group. This justifies the writing approach explored within this work, particularly the use of personally relevant social media data during prewriting. However, while the difference in writing quality gains between the My Media and Network Media groups was nonsignificant, it is worth noting that self-authored data appears to be more useful and efficient in increasing writing quality compared to data authored by others. My Media participants had higher gains in writing quality (four times the Network Media group's gain). My Media users also reviewed half as many idea cards as the Network Media group, suggesting that using one's own media was "twice" as efficient as using data authored by others. This trend was also reflected in story planner data, as My Media users created nearly twice as many story detail nodes and wrote more than twice as many words on their planners as the Network Media group. With four times the writing quality gain, half the idea selection effort, and twice the output on story planners, it was clear that My Media users had a more positive experience overall than Network Media users.

Complexities of Self-Motivation

While results suggest that utilizing adolescents' social media data during prewriting empowers higher quality writing, there was little impact on writing motivation. We assumed that engaging students with personally relevant content as a foundational resource for writing would provide a framework that affirmed self-efficacy and enticed students. This effect (or lack thereof) may be reflective of larger, open challenges for K-12 writing instruction and education [12,19,20] but may also be a product of the short time frame of the studies conducted. A four-week evaluation is unlikely to produce noticeable effects on students' long-term motivation. Additionally, students did not receive feedback or grading on the final products until after the trial was completed. Rapid (and positive) iterative feedback may have fostered the gains in motivation and increased feelings of self-efficacy. Nevertheless, it is somewhat encouraging that writing motivation largely remained stable among students during the introduction of this new tool and process for writing. Broadly, we note a need to more fully explore and assess the affective implications of social media based writing through longer-term evaluation.

Inspiring Prewriting: Media Availability

Our intent was to support students in identifying personally relevant writing topics through social media. This predicates the need for rich and relevant content to be available through social platforms, and we know from the data imported from the 46 participants that certainly longer-term multimodal content (typically 1 to 3.5 years' worth) is at the disposal of teens for creative production in this context. For Facebook, the average user had over 3 years of content and over 1,000 personally narrated moments available to them. Additional social sources enriched this dataset, and users brought in another 1,338.81 items from Twitter (excluding replies - 996.05) and 127.51 items from Instagram, over a 1.5- and 1-year period respectively. Twitter users are much more engaged in regular authoring (approx. 17.63 per week; 13.12 excluding replies), adding considerably more content than Facebook users (approx. 7.16 items per week) in a shorter span of time.

Inspiring Prewriting: Media Fluency

While rich content is definitely available to teens via social data, it begs the question, *what content is most useful?* The benefit of personal content is clear from the outcomes between the two treatment conditions. Students working with timeline/network content had to perform double the number of 'redraws' to identify a prospective topic. While some of this content may be relevant, such content is likely to be sparsely found. We anticipate that it is more cumbersome to creatively re-use this content, requiring reframing to view one's self through the lens of others.

Clearly, not all content is created equal. Not only does authorship, but also the modality of the media plays a role in composing writing ideas. We observed that 'people' and 'places' infrequently populated story outlines. This questions whether contextual information has as much value as social content (text and photos) within ideation. Inherently broader and more thematic, contextual information may not ground writing ideas in the way that more specific content can. Additionally, both treatment conditions strongly favored visual media, despite the availability of higher volumes of text-based content. We expect this is because photos allow versatility that text does not. Photos are rich, expressive and can simultaneously convey an array of experiential information. They can be interpreted in a variety of ways and more easily juxtaposed with other media, allowing students to more readily adapt meanings to fit within the context of a narrative plan. In general, text content is more narrowly focused, and thus more difficult to situate within a nascent topic.

While there is a wealth of social content and context information available, the resources that will most empower students to more creative outcomes is a key consideration. Noting the different fluencies of social media prompts the question, would displaying *only* photo content reduce the potential for inspiration and the quality of outcome? By tailoring the media presented to those most suited to the writing context, we anticipate there is the potential to further enhance the writing inspiration phase.

Use of Constraint

A key design decision in the user interface approach was a constrained presentation of media explicitly aimed at reducing distraction in ideation. Given the large volume of social media available, it avoided overwhelming students with a vast review of large social media datasets. This approach shifts the burden away from the user by removing the opportunity to exhaustively review a 'stream' of social data. Logged data indicates that under this paradigm students are still reviewing a large volume of their content in order to identify topics, but they do so by refreshes or "redraws." By presenting only five items at a time, users do not need to look for associations at large within the archive, but instead do so only for the currently presented items. This visual arrangement inherently frames content as possible pieces of a narrative, juxtaposing them to encourage examination of possible relationships and latent meaning. This makes the process reflective rather than interrogative. Further, there were neither reports of an overwhelming experience nor procrastination from students who used the tool. We anticipate that this reflective approach not only contributed to overall increases in quality, but also to the observed increases in organization and planning found within the two groups who used the tool, compared with the Control group.

Computer Mediated Review

Nonsignficant results indicate that regardless of experimental condition, the two treatment groups had minor, but equivalent, gains in the organization of their writing (while the Control group had no gains). This suggests the tool's utility in enhancing and planning organization. Our approach is to heavily mediate this process and employ "technology to manage technology." While a simpler, less sophisticated approach likely has merit (e.g. simply asking students to manually review social timelines) this would likely introduce other complexities into the classroom. Design research highlighted shared concerns around procrastination, disruption and exhaustive interrogation. Moreover, a less mediated approach would place a burden on the instructor to conceive and manage the process for students, as well as guiding them in repurposing their social data into a well-formed narrative. Demonstrated by our process, by working with the stakeholders involved, well-documented and research-based organizational strategies can be successfully embedded in digital tools to offer self-guided and self-paced strategies for student success. This enables students more opportunities to develop self-efficacy and become less reliant on the teacher for support.

The Value of Social Media in the Classroom

We have highlighted that creative reuse of socially documented experiences can help students identify writing topics, organize thinking and improve the quality of their writing through a mediated process. Despite the potential of such support tools and the possible impact of reusing social data in education contexts, there are relatively few explorations in this space. However, social media is a medium in which students are deeply immersed and regularly engage. We hope the encouraging outcomes of this preliminary study will also call attention to this rich opportunity space. Our outcomes demonstrate the potential for enhancing and personalizing learning experiences by increasing the relevance and personal connection to learned content. We note that successful interventions require crafted solutions that blend the requirements of multiple stakeholders (institutional, instructor, and student), that negotiate the perception of technology and that creatively intertwine media, reuse and mediated process; this presents a fertile arena for future design research and human-centered inquiry.

FUTURE WORK

Sparkfolio will be the subject of several future evaluations in adolescent writing. We will next examine how the tool impacts student writing quality in longer-term, larger-scale deployments. Future work will also explore improved interactive and content-based methods for identifying prospective story content from social media, e.g. by mining social metadata, or via improved recommendations. Additionally, we plan to examine this approach within other writing genres (e.g. argumentative) and for other candidate populations (e.g. undergraduates, creative professionals).

CONCLUSION

Despite their constant engagement in digital communication via social media, adolescents are generally averse to academic writing. However, it stands to reason that leveraging their own personally relevant, informally authored social media content in a writing classroom would foster intrinsic motivation and deeper engagement, ultimately improving writing quality. It was with this mind that Sparkfolio was developed, and through its constrained ideation and scaffolded planning, it has been validated as a sound approach for improving writing, as Sparkfolio's users had statistically significantly higher gains in writing quality than a control group in a preliminary evaluation. These results imply that utilizing one's own social media data holds powerful potential in personalizing learning, particularly in offering opportunities for making personally relevant connections in learning environments, a design space that is still relatively unexplored.

ACKNOWLEDGEMENTS

We thank the teachers, students, school administration, and district technology team for their participation in this work.

REFERENCES

1. Anderman, E.M. and Maehr, M.L. Motivation and Schooling in the Middle Grades. *Review of Educational Research 64*, 2 (1994), 287–309.
2. Atwell, N. *Lessons That Change Writers.* Firsthand, Portsmouth, NH, USA, 2002.
3. Aydin, S. A review of research on Facebook as an educational environment. *Educational Technology Research and Development 60*, 6 (2012), 1093–1106.
4. Berninger, V., Whitaker, D., Feng, Y., Swanson, H.L., and Abbott, R.D. Assessment of Planning, Translating, and Revising in junior High Writers. *Journal of School Psychology 34*, 1 (1996), 23–52.
5. Brooke, J. SUS: A "Quick and Dirty" Usability Scale. In P.W. Jordan, B. Thomas, B.A. Weerdmeester and I.L. McClelland, eds., *Usability Evaluation in Industry*. Taylor & Francis, Bristol, PA, USA, 1996, 189–194.
6. Burtis, P., Bereiter, C., Scardamalia, M., and Tetroe, J. *The Development of Planning in Writing.* Wiley, Chichester, England, 1983.
7. Byrne, D., Kelliher, A., and Jones, G.J.F. Life Editing: Third-Party Perspectives on Lifelog Content. *Proceedings of the 2011 annual conference on Human factors in computing systems (CHI '11)*, ACM (2011), 1501–1510.
8. Charmaz, K. Grounded Theory. In J.A. Smith, ed., *Qualitative Psychology: A Practical Guide to Research Methods*. Sage Publications, London, 2003, 81–110.
9. Danoff, B., Harris, K., and Graham, S. Incorporating strategy instruction within the writing process in the regular classroom: Effects on the writing of students with and without learning disabilities. *Journal of Literacy Research 25*, 3 (1993), 295–322.
10. Ellison, N.B., Steinfield, C., and Lampe, C. The Benefits of Facebook "Friends:" Social Capital and College Students' Use of Online Social Network Sites. *Journal of Computer-Mediated Communication 12*, 4 (2007), 1143–1168.
11. Graham, S. and Perin, D. A meta-analysis of writing instruction for adolescent students. *Journal of Educational Psychology 99*, 3 (2007), 445–476.
12. Hayes, J. A new framework for understanding cognition and affect in writing. In M. Levy and S. Ransdell, eds., *The science of writing: Theories, methods, individual differences, and applications*. Erlbaum, Mahwah, NJ, USA, 1996, 1–27.
13. Kellogg, R.T. Effects of topic knowledge on the allocation of processing time and cognitive effort to writing processes. *Memory & cognition 15*, 3 (1987), 256–266.
14. De La Paz, S. and Graham, S. Explicitly teaching strategies, skills, and knowledge: Writing instruction in middle school classrooms. *Journal of Educational Psychology 94*, 4 (2002), 687–698.
15. Lenhart, A., Arafeh, S., Smith, A., and Macgill, A.R. *Writing, Technology and Teens.* Washington, DC, USA, 2008.
16. Lenhart, A., Purcell, K., and Zickuhr, K. *Social Media & Mobile Internet Use Among Teens and Young Adults.* Washington, DC, USA, 2010.
17. Madden, M., Lenhart, A., Duggan, M., Cortesi, S., and Gasser, U. *Teens and Technology 2013.* Washington, DC, USA, 2013.
18. Moreau, C.P. and Dahl, D.W. Designing the Solution: The Impact of Constraints on Consumers' Creativity. *Journal of Consumer Research 32*, 1 (2005), 13–22.
19. Pajares, F. Self-Efficacy Beliefs, Motivation, and Achievement in Writing: A Review of the Literature. *Reading & Writing Quarterly 19*, (2003), 139–159.
20. Piazza, C.L. and Siebert, C.F. Development and Validation of a Writing Dispositions Scale for Elementary and Middle School Students. *The Journal of Educational Research 101*, 5 (2008), 275–286.
21. Prensky, M. Digital Natives, Digital Immigrants Part 1. *On the Horizon 9*, 5 (2001), 1–6.
22. Sadauskas, J., Byrne, D., and Atkinson, R.K. Toward Social Media Based Writing. *Proceedings of the 15th International Conference on Human-Computer Interaction - DUXU/HCII 2013, Part II, LNCS 8013*, Springer (2013), 276–285.
23. Valkenburg, P.M., Peter, J., and Schouten, A.P. Friend networking sites and their relationship to adolescents' well-being and social self-esteem. *Cyberpsychology & behavior: The impact of the Internet, multimedia and virtual reality on behavior and society 9*, 5 (2006), 584–590.
24. Vojak, C., Kline, S., Cope, B., McCarthey, S., and Kalantzis, M. New Spaces and Old Places: An Analysis of Writing Assessment Software. *Computers and Composition 28*, 2 (2011), 97–111.
25. Official Scoring Guide: Arizona's Instrument to Measure Standards - Holistic Rubric Based on 6 Traits of Writing. *Arizona Department of Education*, 2010.
26. *The Nation's Report Card: Writing.* Washington, DC, USA, 2011.
27. Assesssment: AIMS Writing. *Arizona Department of Education*, 2013. http://www.azed.gov/standards-development-assessment/aims/aims-writing/.

Wait-Learning: Leveraging Wait Time for Second Language Education

Carrie J. Cai[1] **Philip J. Guo**[1,2] **James R. Glass**[1] **Robert C. Miller**[1]

[1]MIT CSAIL
Cambridge, MA USA
{cjcai, glass, rcm}@mit.edu

[2]University of Rochester
Rochester, NY USA
pg@cs.rochester.edu

ABSTRACT
Competing priorities in daily life make it difficult for those with a casual interest in learning to set aside time for regular practice. In this paper, we explore *wait-learning*: leveraging brief moments of waiting during a person's existing conversations for second language vocabulary practice, even if the conversation happens in the native language. We present an augmented version of instant messaging, WaitChatter, that supports the notion of wait-learning by displaying contextually relevant foreign language vocabulary and micro-quizzes just-in-time while the user awaits a response from her conversant. Through a two week field study of WaitChatter with 20 people, we found that users were able to learn 57 new words on average during casual instant messaging. Furthermore, we found that users were most receptive to learning opportunities immediately after sending a chat message, and that this timing may be critical given user tendency to multi-task during waiting periods.

Author Keywords
Wait-learning; Micro-learning; Second language learning.

ACM Classification Keywords
H.5.2. User interfaces: User-centered design; K.3.1. Computer Uses in Education: Computer-assisted instruction

Figure 1: WaitChatter presents vocabulary exercises in the *learning panel* while the user awaits an IM response. Here, the user is being quizzed on a word and must enter the second language (L2) translation given the native language (L1) prompt. The word is highlighted in the chat history because it appeared in the context of the conversation.

INTRODUCTION
Learning a second language requires significant time and effort on a recurring basis. Living in a country where the language is spoken is often necessary to reach fluency, yet many language learners do not have the time to dedicate years of their lives to immersive instruction. Even for those who attempt to learn informally, the busyness of daily life makes it difficult to schedule regular time for practice. Learners must maintain the *executive motivation* [12] necessary to study the second language on a repeated basis.

Despite the struggle to find time for learning, there are countless moments in a day that go wasted, due to suboptimal scheduling or necessary waiting [19]. Recent work on *micro-learning* has explored ways to distribute traditional language study into many micro moments throughout a person's daily life [16]. In this work, we extend micro-learning and introduce the notion of *wait-learning*. The novelty of this approach lies in the targeted use of time that users would ordinarily spend waiting. The proposed benefit is that learning during wait time will minimize the likelihood that learning is perceived by learners as intrusive or time-consuming.

Due to inherent difficulties in predicting whether someone is waiting based purely on tracking their activities [19], we turn to an activity that necessarily involves waiting *within* the activity itself. Instant messaging (IM) offers a powerful opportunity for wait-learning due to its semi-asynchronous nature. Because messages being typed are unseen by the conversant and can be revised before being sent, a user must often wait for a brief moment in anticipation of a response, with no guarantee that the other party will in fact reply [28].

CHI 2015, April 18–23, 2015, Seoul, Republic of Korea.

ACM 978-1-4503-3145-6/15/04 ...$15.00.
http://dx.doi.org/10.1145/2702123.2702267

In this paper, we explore the notion of wait-learning with WaitChatter (Figure 1), an extension of instant messaging that presents vocabulary exercises while the user awaits an IM response. The interaction is asymmetric, meaning that the user can engage in learning without any knowledge of this activity by the other party. Based on findings from a wizard-of-oz exploratory study [7], we designed and implemented the WaitChatter system as an extension of Google Chat in the Chrome web browser. Through a two-week field study in which 20 participants used WaitChatter on their personal computers, we find that users are most receptive to learning in the moments after sending a chat message. We also show that wait-learning can facilitate learning. On average, participants learned 57 new vocabulary words over the course of two weeks, while exchanging on average 170 chats per day.

The main contributions of this paper are:

- the central idea of *wait-learning*, an extension of micro-learning that leverages wait time for education
- a system that implements wait-learning by presenting learning exercises at automatically-detected moments of waiting during instant messaging
- a naturalistic evaluation that suggests users are most receptive to wait-learning in the moments after sending a chat message

BACKGROUND AND RELATED WORK

Our research on wait-learning extends existing work on micro-learning to use wait time for education. It also builds upon prior research on instant messaging and interruptions.

Micro-Learning and Contextual Micro-Learning

Based on growing evidence that spaced exposure [11] and continued exposure [30] to second language vocabulary result in greater learning gains, recent work on *micro-learning* [16] has explored methods to distribute learning into small units throughout a person's day-to-day life. Micro-learning has largely been implemented in the form of *contextual micro-learning*, through mobile applications that provide opportunities to learn contextually relevant vocabulary based on surrounding objects [5], location [10, 14] and text [29].

Spaced exposure has been posited to benefit learning, even in the absence of context [11]. Due to low interactivity, certain instructional elements that can be reasonably learned in isolation may be more appropriate for micro-learning. For example, the study of vocabulary, computer terminology, and chemical symbols are posited to impose a lower cognitive load in comparison to learning algebra, which has more interactive parts [26].

Prior work on contextual micro-learning has tended to focus more on *what* the user is learning rather than *when* to present these learning opportunities. However, several researchers have aimed to make use of the transition time between tasks to present learning opportunities. Lernschoner [16] activates a learning program whenever the learner's computer screen becomes idle. MicroMandarin [14] and Vocabulary Wallpaper [10] leveraged moments while users are visiting certain locations to present location-sensitive vocabulary, though even these studies tended to focus more on the content delivered rather than the timing of those deliveries.

Micro-Waiting during Instant Messaging

Prior research suggests that even micro-diversions during frequent activities could be perceived as disruptive if the user feels that regular tasks are being delayed [29]. Beyond micro-learning, our work on wait-learning specifically targets moments when users would ordinarily spend waiting.

Research on *mobile micro-waiting* suggests it is difficult to use activity information alone to predict idleness, possibly because users may be more receptive to content delivered during fleeting intervals of idle time *within* an ongoing activity [19]. In one study on in-home interruptability, participants rated watching television as both a high and low engagement activity depending on their goals [27].

During instant messaging, waiting often occurs within the activity itself. Unlike email and face-to-face communication, instant messaging conversations range from rapid exchanges to long periods of time passing between messages [23]. Due to its semi-asynchronous nature, users frequently use waiting breaks between conversation turns to attend to other informal activities [18]. Prior work has explored ways to reduce the attention cost of multi-tasking, such as by predicting interruptability [2, 15] and examining how IM notifications affect other tasks [9]. While these examples aim to decrease time wasted, our work instead makes use of this time by encouraging users to engage in learning while waiting for a response.

Attention and Interruption

Although wait-learning aims to leverage idle time, previous work on interruptability suggests that the detailed manner and timing of delivery can still cause significant differences in task performance and levels of frustration [1]. Because our minds dynamically allocate and release resources throughout task execution [20], the timing of information delivery relative to a user's ongoing task may affect interruption cost [4].

Because decreases in workload tend to be larger at boundaries corresponding to larger chunks of a task [4, 22], a system that presents information during IM should differentiate between the many boundaries that might exist, favoring those that represent more salient breaks in workflow [4]. In one study on face-to-face communication, users processed additional information best when presented with small batches of information, and when the user was not speaking [24].

WAITCHATTER DESIGN AND IMPLEMENTATION

In order to explore and empirically validate wait-learning as it applies to instant messaging, we developed WaitChatter (Figure 1) as an extension of Google Chat that runs in the Web browser when a Gmail page is in view. The client is packaged as a Chrome extension with a Python-based server backend.

User Interface Design

A central design challenge is the small amount of space available for designing interactions. Because instant messaging is intended to be the main task, with learning as a secondary

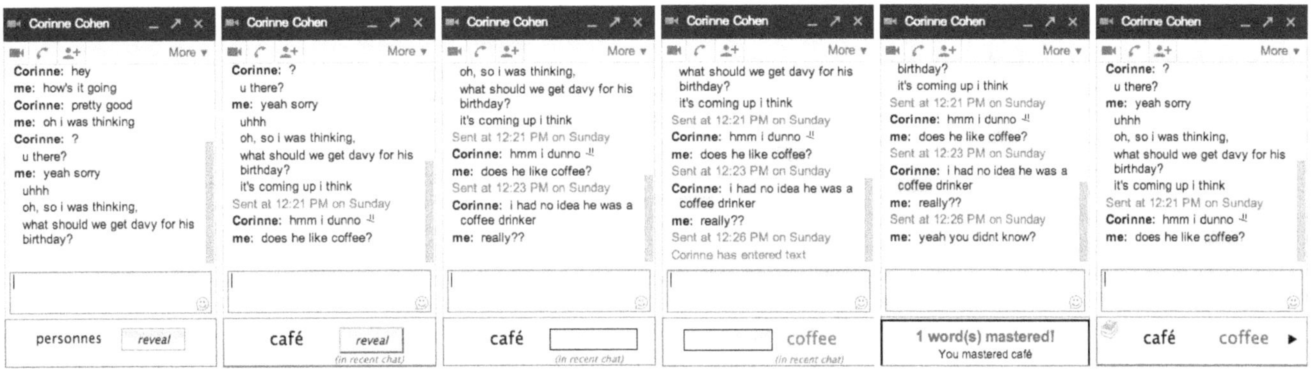

(a) Study Mode for a non-contextual word. (b) Study Mode for a contextual word. (c) Quiz Mode at easy level (translate to L1). (d) Quiz Mode at difficult level (translate to L2). (e) Mastery panel slides up when word is learned. (f) Clicking the arrow fetches the next exercise.

Figure 2: WaitChatter teaches words during automatically detected wait-moments. Here are components of the user interface.

benefit, user interface elements should not demand a substantial context switch away from the IM conversation.

Based on findings from an exploratory study [7], the learning panel is situated directly below the chat input box to minimize the visual and motor effort of switching between chatting and learning activities. To avoid user concern over whether chat conversants can view WaitChatter content, we keep the exercises within the learning panel, but highlight a keyword inside the chat history if it is selected and presented for learning.

Vocabulary exercises appear and remain on the learning panel for 10 seconds, during which the user can either do the exercise or ignore it by doing nothing. If the user has not interacted with the exercise for 10 seconds, it fades away. To minimize disruption, the learning panel remains present at all times regardless of whether an exercise is present. After the user completes an *initial* exercise, he can fetch a *follow-up* one by clicking the right arrow (Figure 2f) or hitting the right arrow key on the keyboard. This functionality allows the user to continuously learn more words during longer wait times.

A vocabulary word is displayed in *study mode* (Figure 2a, 2b) the first time it is presented for learning, and in *quiz mode* (Figure 2c, 2d) during subsequent exposures. In study mode, the L2 (second language) vocabulary word is shown alongside a button which the user can click to view the L1 (native language) translation. Once a learner reveals the new word, the user is asked to indicate whether he or she already knew that word. If not, the word is added to the learner's *vocabulary list*, a growing list of words that the user did not already know but has been exposed to via WaitChatter. In quiz mode, the user is shown the L2 word and provides the L1 translation if the exercise is at the *easy* level (Figure 2c), or the reverse if the exercise is at the *difficult* level (Figure 2d). Users can submit a blank response if they don't remember the word.

Vocabulary

WaitChatter aims to support the learning of second language vocabulary. We limit our implementation to nouns because, in addition to being closely tied to the meaning of a conversation, nouns are also typically acquired before verbs and are easier to translate automatically because they are less context-dependent. A related system [29] also focused on nouns for similar reasons.

Findings from a prior study indicate that contextual and non-contextual vocabulary serve complementary roles in learning, balancing needs across language levels, and that users may benefit from a combination of the two [14]. Although that study examined context with respect to location relevance, in WaitChatter the IM conversation itself provides a ripe opportunity for in-context learning. The nouns in WaitChatter are either drawn from a built-in word list (*non-contextual*, Figure 2a), or selected on-the-fly from words used by either conversant in the IM conversation (*contextual*, (Figure 2b). *Non-contextual* words could in theory be drawn from a number of sources, such as a word bank seeded by the learner or teacher.

For each chat message exchanged during an IM conversation, WaitChatter determines whether an adequate *contextual* word exists. First, it identifies nouns in the chat message using the Senna part-of-speech tagger [8]. Then, each noun is translated on-the-fly using Google Translate. To maximize the chances that the word is translated correctly in context, WaitChatter sends both the word and the entire chat message to Google Translate, and considers an L1/L2 pair *accepted* only if the L2 word appears in both translation results. To mitigate against inaccurate results, a dictionary icon (Figure 2f) is displayed which the user can click to see the word's dictionary definition. For privacy reasons, WaitChatter logs only the length of a chat message and the L1/L2 pair displayed in an exercise, but not the content of the chat message itself.

Because exercises can only be displayed during appropriate wait-learning moments (described below), WaitChatter keeps a running set of *accepted* contextual L1/L2 pairs, for which the L1 word is still within the visible part of the chat history (*viewport*) but not yet displayed for learning. Once the word scrolls off the viewport, WaitChatter discards the L1/L2 pair from being considered for learning.

Vocabulary Scheduling Algorithm

WaitChatter uses the Leitner schedule [17] for scheduling the order of learning exercises. The Leitner schedule is based on the principle of *spaced repetition*: given that humans exhibit a negatively exponential forgetting curve [13], repetitions should occur at increasingly spaced intervals so that they are encountered just as they are about to be forgotten.

We define each flashcard in the system as an L1/L2 pair. WaitChatter maintains a set of five unlearned flashcards and a *correct count* for each flashcard, which represents the number of correct responses to that flashcard. This count is incremented when the learner answers the flashcard correctly and decremented if not. Flashcards with a correct count of n are displayed every nth Leitner session, so that better known cards are reviewed less frequently. In WaitChatter, flashcards are displayed at the easy level when the correct count is below three, and at the difficult level otherwise. A flashcard is "learned" and retired when its correct count reaches four (Figure 2e), opening up a slot for a new card to be added.

In WaitChatter, the Leitner algorithm was modified to enable a combination of contextual and non-contextual words. First, if an opportunity arises for a new card to be added, WaitChatter picks a contextual word if one is available. If no contextual word can be found, WaitChatter shows the next unused non-contextual word at random from the same Leitner session. To capitalize on contextual opportunities, any word already on the vocabulary list that re-appears in the context of the conversation is prioritized to be displayed at the next wait opportunity, regardless of the Leitner state.

During pilot studies, some users indicated a preference for seeing new words over repeatedly seeing old ones. To maximize engagement, we rotate words within the same Leitner session whenever a word is ignored so that learners are unlikely to ignore the same stale word consecutively. Furthermore, if a new slot becomes available during a *follow-up* exercise, WaitChatter will display the newly added flashcard at the next *initial* exercise than showing it immediately, and instead display the next flaschard in the Leitner schedule. Since follow-up exercises are requested by the user whereas initial exercises are not, we display new flashcards during initial exercises with the intent of maximizing engagement.

Detecting Waiting Opportunities

Results from an exploratory study [7] identified two situations in which a user may be waiting during an instant messaging conversation: 1) waiting for the conversant to start responding, and 2) waiting for the conversant to finish responding. Figure 3 shows these two types of waiting opportunities in the flow of a typical conversation.

The first case, which we name *i_sent*, occurs after a user has sent a chat message and is waiting to see whether his conversant will respond. Because a common IM behavior is to type a sequence of short chat messages as part of one conversational turn [18, 21], an exercise that is naively delivered immediately after a chat is sent may interrupt a follow-up message that the user is in the midst of composing. For this reason, WaitChatter waits for an additional amount of *hesitation time* after a message is sent, and subsequently triggers a learning exercise only if the user has not typed more. We used 1.5 seconds of hesitation time to balance against the user tendency to

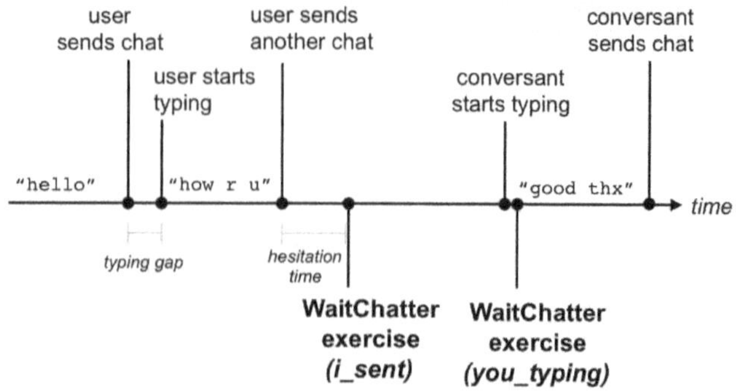

Figure 3: Detection of waiting opportunities in WaitChatter.

leave the chat window after sending a message. According to a prior study [2], the probability that the message window is still in focus is approximately 60% after 1 second, and drops to approximately 50% within 5 seconds.

The second case, which we name *you_typing*, occurs when the conversant has started typing a response but has not yet sent the message. In Google Chat and other similar instant messaging applications, users see an indicator (i.e. "Corinne is typing...") which signals that the conversant has started typing. WaitChatter triggers an exercise when the indicator appears in the user's chat window and the user is not typing. In both *i_sent* and *you_typing*, the exercise is only triggered if the cursor focus is still inside the chatbox.

The creation of an exercise requires server-side interaction, a round-trip process that results in a small but unpredictable delay. WaitChatter will cancel an exercise before it is displayed if it detects that the user has typed between the time that the browser requested an exercise and received a server response.

EVALUATION

To evaluate WaitChatter and the extent to which wait-learning can help second language acquisition, we ran a two-week field study in which participants used WaitChatter in Google Chat on their personal computers during their normal instant messaging activities.

The questions our study sought to answer are:

- Learning: To what extent can users learn vocabulary using WaitChatter?
- Timing: What are the best times to present learning exercises for the purpose of wait-learning?

Vocabulary

For ease of user recruitment, our implementation of WaitChatter teaches Spanish and French, but could be extended to other languages. Non-contextual vocabulary were drawn from high frequency English nouns as measured in the British National Corpus.[1] The words were translated to Spanish and French using Google Translate, after which two native speakers manually reviewed the word list for inaccurate translations and highly ambiguous words. The final non-contextual word lists consisted of 446 words in each language.

[1] http://www.natcorp.ox.ac.uk/

Procedure

Participants first met with a researcher to have WaitChatter installed on their personal computers. They were then given a walkthrough of how WaitChatter could be used. Participants used WaitChatter as they pleased for the next two weeks. During the study, WaitChatter prompted participants to indicate whether or not they already knew a word the first time it appeared. Known words were not added to the user's vocabulary list. At the end of two weeks, participants returned to complete a post-study questionnaire, semi-structured interview, and vocabulary quiz. The quiz tested all vocabulary the user had been exposed to (but didn't already know) while using WaitChatter, and was divided into two parts: participants translated from L1 to L2 in the *recall* quiz, and from L2 to L1 in the *recognition* quiz. Within each part, the order of questions was randomized. Users were asked not to guess.

Timing Variation

To better understand how the timing of exercises may affect the learner's capacity to engage in learning, we exposed each participant to two versions of our application: the *detected_wait* version uses the *i_sent* and *you_typing* waiting opportunities as described above. The *random* version displays prompts at random whenever WaitChatter determines that a user has been actively instant messaging. We define a user's instant messaging activity as *active* if the Gmail page is in focus, has had keyboard or mouse activity within the last 30 seconds, and contains at least one open chat window which had keyboard activity within the last 5 minutes. Because a user may be waiting for an instant messaging response while engaged in nearby tasks on the same page, we consider moments when the Gmail page is in focus even though the chatbox is not as viable candidates for wait-learning, so long as the user is active as defined above. We also require at least one chatbox to be open because an open chatbox indicates the likely presence of an ongoing conversation [2].

Each participant used the *detected_wait* and *random* versions on alternating days. To ensure that users are exposed to WaitChatter prompts at approximately equal frequencies on the *detected_wait* and *random* versions, the desired frequency on a *random* condition day was determined by calculating the cumulative frequency, which is the number of exercises shown per time active, from the user's previous *detected_wait* condition days. On *random* days, this desired frequency was used every second the user was active to probabilistically determine whether an exercise should be shown.

We examined three metrics: whether the learner responded to the exercise, the time taken to respond, and users' subjective impression of how well the exercises integrated into the flow of their activities. We define response time as the time between a prompt being displayed and the user's cursor focusing into the answer box. To capture subjective impressions, users were asked to complete a daily survey with two 7-point Likert scale questions: 1) "In the past day, [WaitChatter] exercises appeared at good moments within the flow of my daily activities", and 2) "I enjoyed using [WaitChatter] today." The survey was sent via email every evening, instructing users to complete it once they finish chatting at the end of the day.

Participants

21 participants were recruited by emails sent through university department, dorm, and foreign language course email lists. We selected only those who were regular users of Google Chat in the web browser, desired to learn or were currently learning Spanish or French, and were not traveling for more than 2 days of the two-week study period. One participant was dropped midway through the study because they stopped instant messaging and completing the daily surveys after the sixth day. Participants were given a $30 gift card for their time, and also entered into a raffle for one $100 gift card.

The 20 participants who completed the study included 12 males and 8 females, ages 19 to 35 (mean=25.5). They consisted of mostly undergraduate and graduate students (17 out of 20), as well as two alumni working in industry and one research scientist. Eleven chose to learn French and nine learned Spanish. Ten users had prior formal education in the language ranging from elementary school (2) and middle or high school (6) to university-level classes (2). Eight of the participants had studied the language informally through using language learning software, traveling in a foreign country, or talking to friends. Six participants had never studied the language before, either formally or informally. The participants typically use Google Chat on their computers "Several times an hour" (9) or "Several times a day" (11), mostly for social reasons or to chat with labmates about research.

RESULTS AND DISCUSSION

Overall, we observed 47393 instant messages exchanged by the 20 participants, who communicated with a total of 249 friends. Users exchanged an average of 170 chats per day.

Learning

In just two weeks of casual usage, participants were on average able to recall 57 new words, equivalent to approximately four words per day. Participants were on average exposed to 106.7 words, 87.7 (sd=64.8) of which they didn't already know. Among those, approximately 40-60% of words were cognates. In post-study quizzes, users translated 57.1 words (66%) correctly to L2 and 80.2 words (92%) correctly to L1. In quiz translations to L2, 15% of wrong answers appeared to be spelling errors or near-misses. The user who was exposed to the most new words (256) translated 161 correctly to L2 and 232 correctly to L1. The most infrequent chatter (55 chats per day) learned 17 new words. These results suggest that down time during instant messaging can serve as a viable channel for learning, at least for bite-sized information.

Some participants wished old words they had already mastered could be revived after a few days so that they wouldn't be as easily forgotten. Because there was no limit on the number of times a learner could continuously fetch more exercises, it was possible for a user to "learn" a flashcard in a single sitting. A spacing algorithm that incorporates temporal effects, such as that described in [25], could be used in the future to improve long term retention.

Usage Patterns

During post-study interviews, users reported behavior that resembled episodes in which they were learning while waiting.

For example, participants said they tended to complete exercises *"while waiting for people to respond," "while the other person is thinking,"* or *"when it was unpredictable how long my friend would be gone for."*

Users indicated that they were most likely to interact with WaitChatter during a *continuous but casual* IM conversation. They were least likely to engage with exercises if they were having a particularly time-sensitive conversation or if the nature of the conversation was serious or work-related. As one user put it, *"The best times are when I'm talking continuously with one person, but we're not having a very heated conversation. Just like hi, how are you, and when the material is more light."* Thus, WaitChatter usage seemed to occur during periods of "outeraction" [23], when people communicate for the purpose of maintaining social connection and awareness, rather than for specific information exchange.

High-usage participants indicated that they frequently used the "fetch more" feature to complete a long sequence of exercises if the conversation was particularly sporadic: *"At some points I needed to wait for the other person to respond. The longer they take, the more words I would go through."* Others were more likely to use WaitChatter to complete only one or two exercises in the transition time *between* chatting and a primary task. Because instant messaging is itself a common break-time activity, IM functioned as a bootstrap for learning when the main task did not require high mental effort: *"If I'm doing something else at the same time like packing and stuff, I might hear the ping, read the reply, do a word or two, get up and go back to what I was doing."*

Overall, we found that people tend to fill their wait time by doing casual tasks, and that wait-learning in many ways served as a timely replacement for those alternative downtime activities: *"There were definitely times when I would keep clicking the arrow because whatever's on TV was really boring."* Another user remarked, *"Maybe I'm just chatting and looking at Facebook. Instead I would use WaitChatter because it's more productive."*

Responsiveness to Timing Conditions

We first measure the amount of time between messages during IM conversations to understand the extent to which learning exercises can be feasibly completed during this time. We found that the time between the user sending a message and receiving a message from the conversant (Figure 4) exhibits a distribution with a peak and a long tail, similar to responsiveness distributions reported in a prior IM study [2]. This intermessage distribution includes instances in which the conversant has started composing a message before the user has sent his message. The time taken to complete an exercise was short (median=1.83 seconds), well within the median intermessage time (11 seconds). However, because intermessage time is most commonly short (mode=4 seconds), particularly during conversations with frequent exchanges, it is reasonable that learning exercises be lightweight.

To understand how the user's ability to respond to exercises could be affected by different timing conditions, we looked at the following measures: whether the user responded to the exercise, and the time taken to respond, as defined in the Timing Variation section above. For each user, data on the first *detected_wait* condition day and the first *random* condition day were excluded from analysis to avoid novelty effects. Furthermore, because follow-up exercises are requested by the user whereas initial exercises are not, we focus our analysis only on initial quiz exercises.

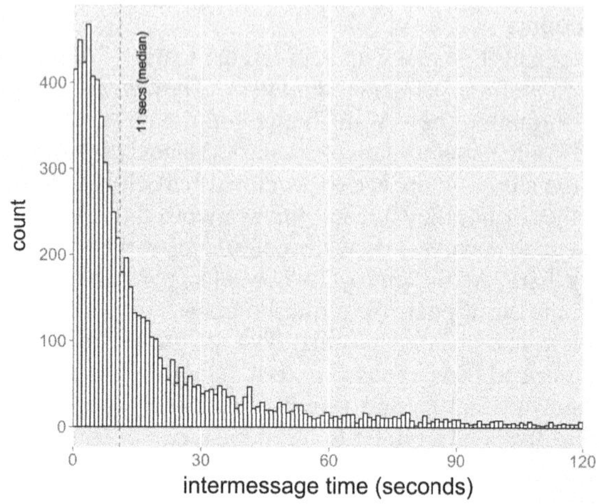

Figure 4: Histogram of intermessage time: the time between the user sending a message and receiving a message from the conversant. Bin size is 1 second.

Because *i_sent* and *you_typing* exercises occurred only while the user had cursor focus inside the chatbox, we subdivided exercises on the *random* condition days into *random_inside*, when the chatbox had focus, and *random_outside*, when the chatbox did not have focus. We compared *i_sent* and *you_typing* only to *random_inside* trials. In all cases, the user had been actively instant messaging as defined in the Timing Variation section above. Table 1 displays a summary of conditions.

Whether the learner responded

We found that 43.5% of the exercises received a response in the *random_inside* condition, whereas only 31.2% received a response in the *random_outside* condition. A generalized linear mixed effects analysis with the Timing condition (*random_inside* and *random_outside*) as the fixed effect and Participant as a random effect found that *random_outside* deliveries were significantly less likely to receive a response ($p<0.0001$). This analysis excludes one participant who did not receive any *random_outside* exercises. Consistent with a prior study [2] which found that chat window focus may be a strong indicator for chat responsiveness, our results imply that this applies to learning interactions as well.

Comparing *i_sent*, *you_typing*, and *random_inside*, we found that response rate was highest for *i_sent* (49.1%), followed by *random_inside* (44.5%) and *you_typing* (41.2%). In a generalized linear mixed effects analysis, p-values were 0.0085 (*i_sent*>*you_typing*), 0.0498 (*i_sent*>*random_inside*, and 0.397 (*you_typing*=*random_inside*), of which only the

Condition	Day Shown	Condition Requirement
i_sent	detected_wait (odd days)	1.5 seconds after user sends a chat, provided he has not started typing again
you_typing	detected_wait (odd days)	"[conversant name] is typing..." indicator appears and user is not typing
random_inside	random (even days)	Chat window is in focus
random_outside	random (even days)	Chat window is not in focus

Table 1: Summary of conditions.

first passed the Bonferroni-corrected threshold of 0.0167 (*i_sent*>*you_typing*).

The relatively low response rate in the *you_typing* condition could be due to a number of factors. *you_typing* moments may occur when users are visually focused on another screen, even if the cursor is focused inside the chatbox. Conversely, *random_inside* prompts that happen to be delivered mid-typing are likely to be noticed, and could conceivably be attended to before the exercise disappears. Moreover, as chat messages tend to be short [21], users may already be receiving a response by the time they are able to attend to the exercise.

Time to respond

As shown in Figure 5, response time for the *random_inside* condition (mean=3973 ms, sd=792) was faster than that of the *random_outside* condition (mean=4888, sd=1282). A paired t-test found this difference to be significant ($F(1,16)=13.24$, $p<0.005$). This analysis excludes three participants who did not respond to any *random_outside* exercises. The longer time to respond in the *random_outside* condition could be due to the mental cost of switching from another activity, or the extra distance traveled to reach the answer box.

Comparing *i_sent*, *you_typing*, and *random_inside* (Figure 6), we found that *i_sent* had the fastest response time (mean=3628, sd=637), followed by *random_inside* (mean=4009, sd=792), and *you_typing* (mean=4209, sd=969). A repeated measures ANOVA showed a significant effect of condition ($F(2,38) = 4.00$, $p<0.05$). Post-hoc Bonferroni tests revealed that learners were significantly quicker to engage with prompts delivered during the *i_sent* condition than those presented during *random_inside* ($p<0.05$). Users were also quicker to engage with *i_sent* than *you_typing*, a difference that was marginally significant ($p=0.05$).

Results suggest that exercises appearing during *you_typing* were not easier to process while conversing, despite occurring at a detected wait moment. It is possible that, during *you_typing*, users are already in the midst of planning their next message, or concentrating on what their friend will say in their response. The mental resources released may be small due to a large carryover of information being actively maintained in short-term memory, which is characteristic of low-level task boundaries or non-boundaries [4]. Conversely, *i_sent* occurs almost immediately after the user has finished typing, and may thus be more consistent with moments of lower mental workload because it occurs between the completion of one subtask and the beginning of the next [22].

During the study, it appeared that in the *random_inside* condition, many users responded quickly to an exercise even if it appeared while they were typing. We thus examined response times depending on the number of keystrokes remaining in the message being composed (Figure 7). We split these instances into two equally sized groups, and found that the response time of prompts arriving just before the user sent a chat (within the last 8 keystrokes) is lower (median=2216ms, sd=2248) than those arriving earlier (median=3446ms, sd=2175). This result suggests that exercises arriving immediately prior to message completion may receive fast engagement, possibly because the user is almost done typing and has mentally queued up the exercise.

Lastly, we evaluate the 1.5 second hesitation time that WaitChatter used to ensure the user was not typing a followup message before it delivered a learning exercise in the *i_sent* condition. Due to missing log data for some users, we report preliminarily on the seven users for whom we had a full set of millisecond-accurate data, including all times they pressed the enter key. We limit our analysis to events where the user

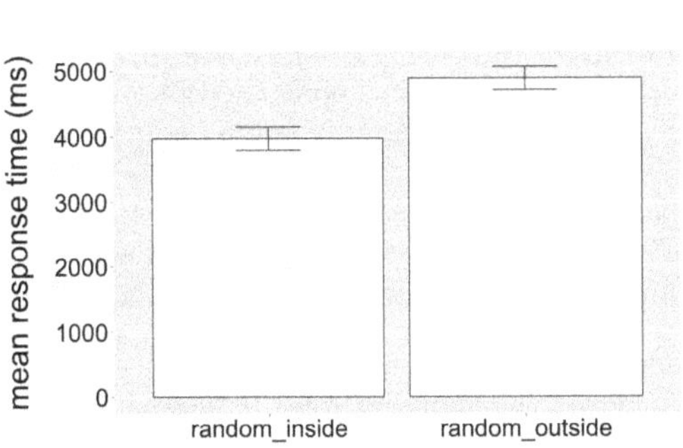

Figure 5: Mean response times for *random_inside* and *random_outside* exercises. Error bars show SE of the mean.

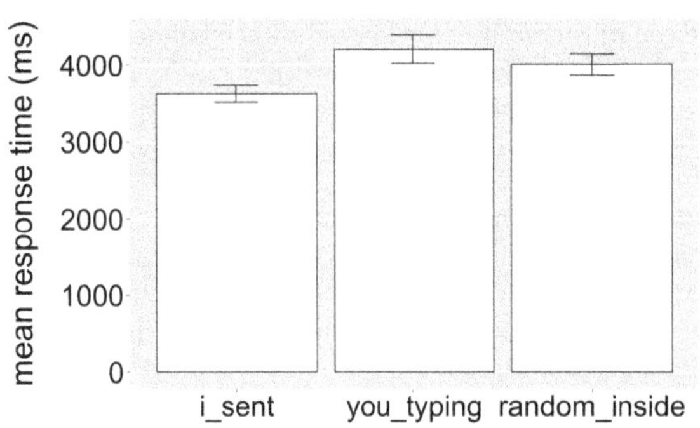

Figure 6: Mean response times for *i_sent*, *you_typing*, and *random_inside*. Error bars show SE of the mean.

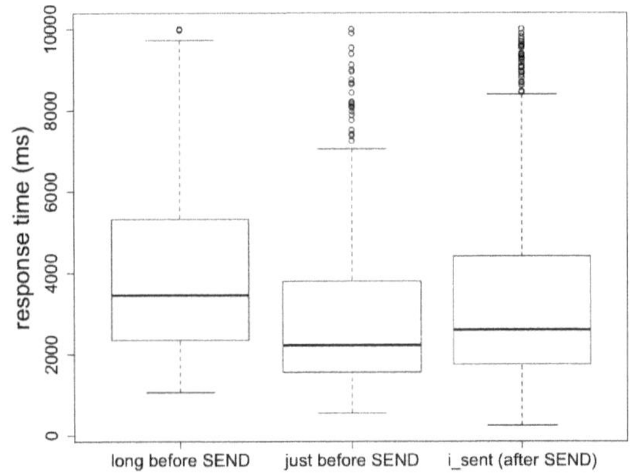

Figure 7: Box plots of response times to exercises arriving just before a chat is sent ($\leq$ 8 keystrokes left), compared to longer before a chat is sent ($>$ 8 keystrokes left).

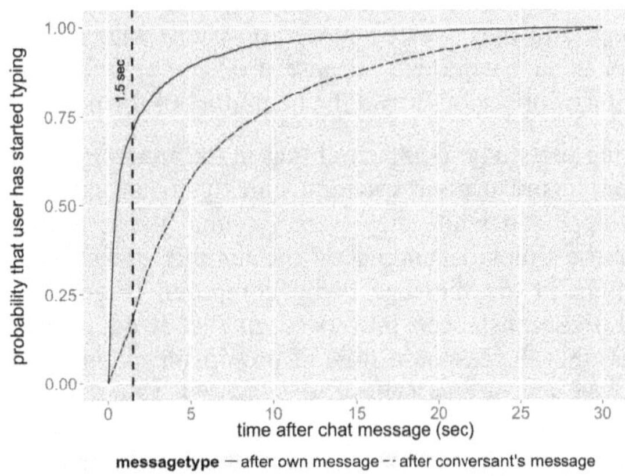

Figure 8: If the user has started typing within 30 seconds of sending a chat, there is a 70% chance that this re-typing occurs within 1.5 seconds. In contrast, if the user starts typing within 30 seconds after *receiving* a chat, there is only a 18% that it occurs within 1.5 seconds.

re-started typing within 30 seconds, based on prior research findings that 28-30 seconds is a typical amount of time between conversational turns [3]. Among these instances, 70% occurred within WaitChatter's hesitation threshold of 1.5 seconds, making it a reasonable estimate (Figure 8). Nevertheless, the hesitation threshold ought to be balanced against the user tendency to leave the chat window after sending a message. A more lenient implementation of WaitChatter might set the hesitation threshold to be even lower than 1.5 seconds.

Perception of Time and Disruption

Because WaitChatter specifically makes use of wait time, we were interested in how users perceived the time and effort they spent on learning, as compared to alternative learning methods. Here, we report on results from the post-study questionnaires and interviews related to this question.

Perception of Time Spent

As shown in Figure 9, responses to 7-point Likert scale questions (1=strongly disagree, 7=strongly agree) indicated that users found WaitChatter very enjoyable (mean=6.15). They also felt that they would continue using WaitChatter if they could (mean=6.15), and would engage in vocabulary practice more frequently than they would otherwise (mean=6.6). On the last question, 15 out of 20 participants submitted a rating of 7.

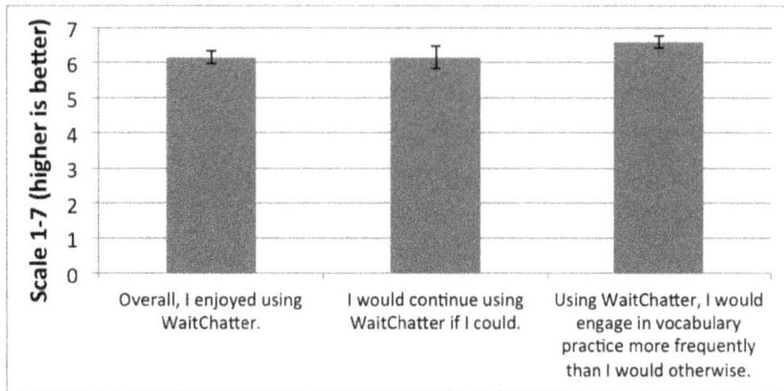

Figure 9: Post-study questionnaire results, with standard error bars.

During interviews, nearly every participant expressed that WaitChatter felt less time-consuming compared to other channels of learning because they did not need to set aside time for learning. As one user stated, "*The key thing is that I didn't feel like I was taking extra time out of my day to dedicate to learning vocabulary words. It was just sort of time that would be wasted otherwise.*" Another compared it to typical break-time activities: "*Some people play Angry Birds, but for me, I would play with [WaitChatter]. At least I'm learning some French words.*"

Many contrasted WaitChatter to language courses and software, which they felt required a conscious effort to schedule time for learning. One person commented, "*With Duolingo you have to think 'I have to go do this now', whereas with [WaitChatter] it's already done for you, spoonfed to you.*" Another said, "*With this I never had to make time or put away things to the future. Whereas learning from Rosetta Stone, you have to schedule time.*" Most who had used vocabulary-learning mobile applications indicated that they eventually gave up, citing time as a major factor.

Several users noted that the little time required to complete a WaitChatter exercise ironically encouraged them to interact more with it overall. One person described the low time commitment as follows: "*It's just like, here, literally just take 2 seconds!*" Another appreciated the regularity of exposure: "*You're just constantly getting new words. It might be a slower rate overall [compared to classes], but it's neat in the aspect that you're always chugging along, learning new vocabulary.*" These comments suggest that user engagement could hinge more on the perceived than the actual time spent.

Perception of Disruption

Overall, participants felt that WaitChatter integrated well into their daily lives because they already instant message regularly: "*I already have gmail open and I'm always chatting with people anyway.*" Furthermore, the ease of access was key to their frequent usage: "*It being so close to the chatbox made me do it more. If it was a separate thing it wouldn't be as easy – an extra click away is a large amount of effort.*"

In the 7-point Likert scale questions sent daily (1=strongly disagree, 7=strongly agree), users on average felt that the exercises "appeared at good moments within the flow of my daily activities" (mean=5.45, sd=1.05) and that they "enjoyed using WaitChatter today" (mean=5.61, sd=1.02). A Wilcoxon Signed-rank test found no significant difference between user ratings on *detected_wait* versus *random* condition days, for either question (p=0.71 and p=0.57).

During interviews, users indicated that they did not notice systematic differences in the timing of exercises, and that the appearance of exercises almost never felt disruptive because they always had the option to ignore them: *"It was just a matter of choice. Subconsciously I would see that a word has appeared. Sometimes it would pique my interest and I would look at it, but if not I just wouldn't look at it so it wasn't really disrupting anything."* These findings are consistent with the notion that interruptions which do not occlude the primary task are perceived to be less mentally demanding and less annoying [6]. Unlike pop-up notifications, the learning panel was in a persistent self-allocated space, making it potentially less distracting even in cases when timing was sub-optimal.

Some users reported feeling frustrated when they could not attend to the exercise in time because they were still typing a long message. Hence, while users did not perceive the timing of appearances to be intrusive, they may be less tolerant of the premature disappearance of an exercise.

LIMITATIONS AND FUTURE WORK

One limitation of this study design was that the frequency of surveys may have been too coarse-grained to capture more transient impressions. We sent the survey only once a day to prevent the frequency of the survey itself from negatively impacting user experience. Future studies may consider sampling user impressions closer in time to the user's actual encounter with learning exercises. In addition, we alternated timing conditions on a daily basis to balance the frequency of exercises. While it is possible that more frequent switching could better mask the conditions, users expressed during the interviews that they did not detect a noticeable pattern in the timing of exercises.

Furthermore, our implementation was limited to vocabulary learning. Some users wished the system could additionally teach sentence structures and phrases. It remains to be seen whether more complex structures can be taught in a way that still preserves the bite-sized nature of wait-learning. For example, a more sophisticated system could present more complex exercises when users actively fetch more exercises, indicating that they are open to learning more, or when the waiting period is particularly long.

DESIGN IMPLICATIONS

The timing and manner in which learning components appear during waiting opportunities can have important implications for actual end-user use. In the following sections, we consider four implications related to the use of wait time for education.

Engaging Prior to Context-Switching

Learning exercises should be delivered immediately at the start of or prior to waiting, rather than times that are well into the waiting period. Because users are likely to attend to other tasks while waiting, they may be less likely to engage in learning once they have already shifted attention to other default waiting activities. Results from our user study indicate that educational prompts delivered right after the user has sent a message tend to receive the fastest engagement, and that this may be true even if exercises are presented within the last few keystrokes while the user is still typing.

Multiplexing the Learning Component

To ensure a non-intrusive user experience, learning components should appear in a way that allows the user to be sufficiently informed of the arrival of a learning opportunity without losing interactivity with their main task. Participants in our study found WaitChatter to be non-intrusive even when exercises appeared amidst typing, citing their degree of control and ability to ignore prompts as primary reasons.

Extending Engagement with Optional Continuations

Because the system could be imperfect in predicting when a user is interruptable, educational prompts should serve as an entryway to further learning. If a prompt is well-timed and the user chooses to interact, this opportunity should be capitalized to encourage continuation of learning. In WaitChatter, the right-arrow enabled users to fetch more exercises if their waiting period was particularly long, and in some cases generated momentum such that the user continued fetching until she had reached a particular learning goal.

Using Micro-Structures to Complement Micro-Waiting

Because expected time commitment may affect engagement more than actual time spent, learning exercises designed to capture user attention during waiting periods should be bite-sized and low-pressure. Users reported that a core benefit of WaitChatter was that it demanded very low time commitment, which ironically invited more frequent usage. In line with prior research on education [26], our research suggests that, beyond vocabulary flashcards, general learning tasks which impose a low cognitive load and can be reasonably learned in isolation may be more appropriate for wait-learning.

CONCLUSION

In this paper, we introduced the idea of wait-learning and evaluated a system that offers wait-learning opportunities in IM. We found that exercises displayed at the beginning of a potential waiting period receive higher engagement, and that exercises should be optional and demand a low cognitive load to minimize intrusiveness. While this work investigated the effectiveness of wait-learning within a single medium (IM), the general classes of measures that were investigated – the amount learned during wait time and the timing of learning opportunities – occur in other situations and generalize to other potential forms of wait-learning. In the future, it would be beneficial to investigate wait-learning in other media contexts and educational domains, enticing even the busiest users to engage in life-long learning.

ACKNOWLEDGMENTS

We thank Max Goldman and the members of the UID group at MIT CSAIL for all their help and feedback. This work was funded by Quanta Computer and MIT Lincoln Laboratory.

REFERENCES

1. Adamczyk, P. D., and Bailey, B. P. If not now, when?: the effects of interruption at different moments within task execution. In *CHI '04*, ACM (2004), 271–278.
2. Avrahami, D., Fussell, S. R., and Hudson, S. E. Im waiting: timing and responsiveness in semi-synchronous communication. In *CSCW '08*, ACM (2008), 285–294.
3. Avrahami, D., and Hudson, S. E. Communication characteristics of instant messaging: effects and predictions of interpersonal relationships. In *CSCW '06*, ACM (2006), 505–514.
4. Bailey, B. P., and Iqbal, S. T. Understanding changes in mental workload during execution of goal-directed tasks and its application for interruption management. *TOCHI 14*, 4 (2008), 21.
5. Beaudin, J. S., Intille, S. S., Tapia, E. M., Rockinson, R., and Morris, M. E. Context-sensitive microlearning of foreign language vocabulary on a mobile device. In *Ambient Intelligence*. Springer, 2007, 55–72.
6. Böhmer, M., Lander, C., Gehring, S., Brumby, D. P., and Krüger, A. Interrupted by a phone call: exploring designs for lowering the impact of call notifications for smartphone users. In *CHI '14*, ACM (2014), 3045–3054.
7. Cai, C. J., Guo, P. J., Glass, J., and Miller, R. C. Wait-learning: leveraging conversational dead time for second language education. In *CHI'14 Extended Abstracts*, ACM (2014), 2239–2244.
8. Collobert, R., Weston, J., Bottou, L., Karlen, M., Kavukcuoglu, K., and Kuksa, P. Natural language processing (almost) from scratch. *The Journal of Machine Learning Research 12* (2011), 2493–2537.
9. Czerwinski, M., Cutrell, E., and Horvitz, E. Instant messaging: Effects of relevance and timing. In *People and computers XIV: Proceedings of HCI*, vol. 2, British Computer Society (2000), 71–76.
10. Dearman, D., and Truong, K. Evaluating the implicit acquisition of second language vocabulary using a live wallpaper. In *CHI '12*, ACM (2012), 1391–1400.
11. Dempster, F. N. Effects of variable encoding and spaced presentations on vocabulary learning. *Journal of Educational Psychology 79*, 2 (1987), 162.
12. Dornyei, Z., and Ottó, I. Motivation in action: A process model of l2 motivation. *Working Papers in Applied Linguistics* (1998), 43–69.
13. Ebbinghaus, H. *Memory: A contribution to experimental psychology*. No. 3. Teachers college, Columbia university, 1913.
14. Edge, D., Searle, E., Chiu, K., Zhao, J., and Landay, J. A. Micromandarin: mobile language learning in context. In *CHI '11*, ACM (2011), 3169–3178.
15. Fogarty, J., Hudson, S. E., Atkeson, C. G., Avrahami, D., Forlizzi, J., Kiesler, S., Lee, J. C., and Yang, J. Predicting human interruptibility with sensors. *TOCHI 12*, 1 (2005), 119–146.
16. Gassler, G., Hug, T., and Glahn, C. Integrated micro learning–an outline of the basic method and first results. *Interactive Computer Aided Learning 4* (2004).
17. Godwin-Jones, R. Emerging technologies from memory palaces to spacing algorithms: approaches to secondlanguage vocabulary learning. *Language, Learning & Technology 14*, 2 (2010).
18. Isaacs, E., Walendowski, A., Whittaker, S., Schiano, D. J., and Kamm, C. The character, functions, and styles of instant messaging in the workplace. In *CSCW '02*, ACM (2002), 11–20.
19. Isaacs, E., Yee, N., Schiano, D. J., Good, N., Ducheneaut, N., and Bellotti, V. Mobile microwaiting moments: The role of context in receptivity to content while on the go.
20. Kahneman, D. *Attention and effort*. Citeseer, 1973.
21. Ling, R., and Baron, N. S. Text messaging and im linguistic comparison of american college data. *Journal of Language and Social Psychology 26*, 3 (2007), 291–298.
22. Miyata, Y., and Norman, D. A. Psychological issues in support of multiple activities. *User centered system design: New perspectives on human-computer interaction* (1986), 265–284.
23. Nardi, B. A., Whittaker, S., and Bradner, E. Interaction and outeraction: instant messaging in action. In *CSCW '00*, ACM (2000), 79–88.
24. Ofek, E., Iqbal, S. T., and Strauss, K. Reducing disruption from subtle information delivery during a conversation: mode and bandwidth investigation. In *CHI '13*, ACM (2013), 3111–3120.
25. Pavlik, P. I., and Anderson, J. R. Using a model to compute the optimal schedule of practice. *Journal of Experimental Psychology: Applied 14*, 2 (2008), 101.
26. Sweller, J., Van Merrienboer, J. J., and Paas, F. G. Cognitive architecture and instructional design. *Educational psychology review 10*, 3 (1998), 251–296.
27. Takemae, Y., Chaki, S., Ohno, T., Yoda, I., and Ozawa, S. Analysis of human interruptibility in the home environment. In *CHI'07 Extended Abstracts*, ACM (2007), 2681–2686.
28. Tree, J. E. F., Mayer, S. A., and Betts, T. E. Grounding in instant messaging. *Journal of Educational Computing Research 45*, 4 (2011), 455–475.
29. Trusty, A., and Truong, K. N. Augmenting the web for second language vocabulary learning. In *CHI '11*, ACM (2011), 3179–3188.
30. Webb, S. The effects of repetition on vocabulary knowledge. *Applied Linguistics 28*, 1 (2007), 46–65.

Masters of Control: Behavioral Patterns of Simultaneous Unit Group Manipulation in StarCraft 2

Eddie Q. Yan
Electrical Engineering
UCLA
eddieyan101@ucla.edu

Jeff Huang
Computer Science
Brown University
chi@jeffhuang.com

Gifford K. Cheung
Information School
University of Washington
giffordc@uw.edu

ABSTRACT
Most user interfaces require the user to focus on one element at a time, but *StarCraft 2* is a game where players often control more than a hundred units simultaneously. The game interface provides an optional mechanism called "control groups" that allows players to select multiple units and assign them to a group in order to quickly recall previous selections of units. From an analysis of over 3,000 replays, we show that the usage of control groups is a key differentiator of individual players as well as players of different skill levels—novice users rarely use control groups while experts nearly always do. But players also behave differently in how they use their control groups, especially in time-pressured situations. While certain control group behaviors are common across all skill levels, expert players appear to be better at remaining composed and sustaining control group use in battle. We also qualitatively analyze discussions on web forums from players about how they use control groups to provide context about how such a simple interface mechanic has produced numerous ways of optimizing unit control.

Author Keywords
video games; skill; control groups; player behavior

ACM Classification Keywords
K.8.0 Personal Computing: Games

INTRODUCTION
Games are interesting to study because of how they are free to evolve independently from and also influence conventional software interfaces [15]. Many competitive video games are currently growing in popularity. Often referred to as electronic sports, or esports, these games are defined by competitive international tournaments that draw millions of spectators with prize pools reaching millions of dollars [18]. Esports are also characterized by being entertainment not only for the player, but also for the spectator [4, 18]. In this work, we focus on a unit grouping interface feature in a popular esport title, *StarCraft 2*, a real-time strategy (RTS) game. *StarCraft 2*, like many other esports, present players with an intricate and demanding task that favors rapid context switching and mastery of the game interface.

Players of competitive games strive to excel in a structured environment, where those who find an edge are rewarded with wins and better ratings. The growing competitive landscape for videogames has motivated game developers to implement features in support of professional and amateur players who play not just for entertainment, but to improve their skills and strategies. In RTS games, these features include sophisticated ranking systems that automate player matchmaking in online ranked games and the ability to record gameplay as sequences of commands performed by each player. For many games, a near-complete record of game state, user keystrokes, and mouse clicks are available from players at a wide variety of skill levels in the form of files known as "replays."

These games provide an ideal case for exploring how the behaviors of expert players have been optimized to efficiently multi-task and strategize. *StarCraft* and other real-time strategy games require skilled players to control and manage hundreds of units at once, from soldiers in battle to resource harvesting units to production buildings and builders. While novice players struggle to keep up as they jump around the map, better players use an interface feature called control groups to bind groups of units to single keys, and thus can issue commands to numerous units quickly. We aim to understand the characteristics of control group use among players of different skill levels in *StarCraft 2*.

The main contributions of our work include a quantitative and qualitative analysis of a variety of player control group behaviors at different skill levels. These behaviors include warmup, producing units, and rebinding units under both normal and pressured situations. We also investigate control group habits among players and use our understanding of control group behaviors to build two classifiers: one for player skill and another for identifying expert players. Finally, we discuss the characteristics of control groups that we consider relevant to theories in human-computer interaction and interface design.

CHI 2015, April 18–23, 2015, Seoul, Republic of Korea.

http://dx.doi.org/10.1145/2702123.2702429

RELATED WORK

Analysis of Gameplay Data and Player Skill

Many other modern multiplayer video game titles ship with the ability to record gameplay data and incorporate matchmaking features for players. Halo: Reach is an example of such a game and has been studied extensively in [8, 13]. As in Huang et al. [8], we explore the explanatory power of gameplay data for user skill. Like Halo: Reach, *StarCraft 2* also has built-in skill estimation capabilities that are used for matchmaking, which we relate to the features defined in *Metrics and Features*.

StarCraft 2 replay data has been studied previously to identify which characteristics explain a player's skill level [19]. Several features that were highly relevant to player skill were identified, including the "Perception-Action Cycle" (PAC), and actions per minute (APM). In this paper, we narrow down on the actions encompassed in the APM metric from an alternative perspective. We also extend this work by using our data to build a trinary classifier of player skill following the binary classifiers introduced in Thompson et al. [19]. In addition to the variation of replay data with player skill levels studied in Thompson et al., we also consider the variation between players at a similar skill level.

Weber and Mateas demonstrated a process for opponent modeling through data mining by analyzing *StarCraft: Brood War* replays [20]. We demonstrate a process of identifying players from anonymous replays which can enhance opponent modeling as it enables the focused study of a particular player's game to predict strategy.

In this paper we investigate whether it is possible to identify online players using their control group configurations as a practical application of understanding individual control group usage differences. This is similar to the question posed by Lauradoux [11] about identifying chess players from their in-game behaviors extracted from replays.

Understanding Task Transfer in the Real World

The predecessor to *StarCraft 2*, *StarCraft: Brood War*, has been used as a proxy for real world situations to improve communication, collaboration, and understanding in the process of collaborative task transfer [10]. In Kirsh and Rebotier [10], the effectiveness of methods such as annotated stills and annotated video in "passing the bubble" (switching control from one player to another in the middle of a match) was evaluated by measuring win/loss rates, game score, and knowledge of the game.

In our work, we investigate the differences among novice users (those uninitiated or potentially on the receiving end of the task transfer) and expert users (those potentially generating the information to facilitate task transfer). Our results suggest that task transfer is more awkward in the case of expert-to-expert task transfer, whereby each expert has already developed his or her own unique signature of gameplay that may be difficult to consciously modify.

Keystroke-Level Models

Keystrokes have been studied more generally in software applications. Regarding user identification, past work on keystroke-level modeling (KLM) has shown that skilled individuals develop characteristic patterns of input when typing text on a keyboard or tapping characters via a telegraph [12]. In Leggett et al. [12], digraph latencies were demonstrated to be promising features for both static and dynamic identity verification of users performing tasks using a keyboard. We relate this to players of an RTS game by investigating whether professional gamers also tend to develop distinctive styles of keyboard use. However, our analysis focuses on features that are subtly different from those used in KLM (see *Metrics and Features*).

For KLM-based analysis of interfaces, two of our major concepts promise to be especially relevant for time-pressured use cases [6]. First, we show that there is a marked distinction between experts and novice performance during time periods of high time-pressure. A KLM analysis of general user interfaces should anticipate similar drop-offs from novice users in the "heat of battle." Second, we investigate the idea of warmup actions in *StarCraft*, a concept that is especially interesting when applied beyond games. The idea of meaningless key presses is not addressed by the KLM model. The typical KLM analysis of an interface is based on the expectation that each key press is either meaningful or erroneous. However, in a game where victory or defeat are defined by micro-second precision, we find that meaningless warmup actions are applied regularly and that the best players are those who start keying without purpose and are able to seamlessly transition that rhythm of tapping from meaningless to meaningful game actions. This implies that the traditional KLM model can deeply benefit from a closer look at the relationship among habit, tempo, expertise, and meaningless actions.

CONTROL GROUPS

The class of commands we focus on in this analysis are those that apply to control groups. Control groups are commonly referred to within the RTS community as "unit bindings" or more colloquially as "hotkeys." This naming occurs because control groups are used by players to efficiently control and manage diverse groups of units within the game. Control groups are generally referred to and accessed via keys {0–9} on the keyboard and store selections of units within the game. This ability is important as during a game players can only issue commands to their *current selection*, a single buffer containing references to units currently controlled by a player. In order to control a unit not currently selected, players must update their current selection to include the desired unit before issuing commands.

Control groups are convenient because they allow users to rapidly switch their current selection to previously defined selections of units. Players can modify control groups by adding ("binding") additional selected units to a control group number or by replacing its selection with the current selection of units. Players can also recall the units assigned to a specific control group, which will update their current selection with the units assigned to the selected control group. Use of control groups is not required to play *StarCraft 2*, as players can simply manually select units each time using the mouse, but allows for faster context switching and command execution within the game. An example of a control group mapping is shown in Figure 1.

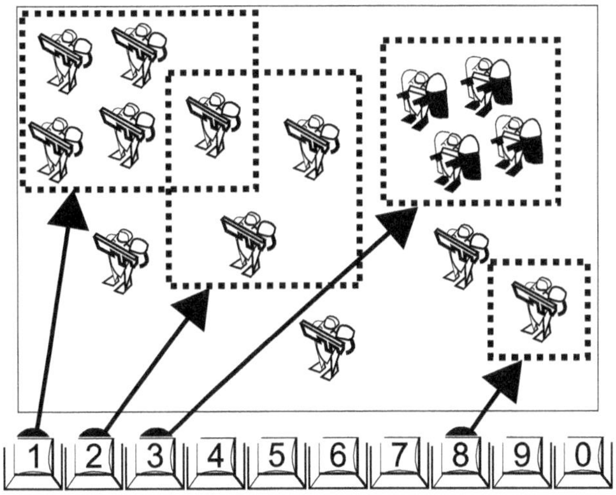

Figure 1: Control groups are bound to keyboard keys 0–9 and represent groups of units. Different groups can include the same units, or no units at all.

Comparisons to Other Applications

Control groups match a familiar interface design pattern: they are a set of buffers that can be updated, reset, and recalled. These interfaces are present in many applications outside of games. The ubiquitous copy-and-paste clipboard matches this pattern. Just as control groups allow a user to manage multiple sets of data, Microsoft's Office Clipboard history allow users to set and recall multiple clipboard items. Researchers continue to innovate on this clipboard: Faure et al. [5] introduce a keyboard-based interaction technique for navigating clipboard history via a long pressed Ctrl-V followed by repeatedly pressing the letter V to cycle through the items. This technique maps almost directly onto focus-cycling shortcuts in *StarCraft 2*. Other applications with a similar model include: desktop window managers where adding and removing windows from workspaces is analogous to adding and resetting control groups; advanced text editors such as Emacs with buffers and marks; and the group functionality in vector-based image programs (e.g. Adobe Illustrator, Microsoft Powerpoint).

METHOD

We use a mixed-methods approach involving quantitative analysis of data from replay collection websites, and qualitative analysis from online discussion forums about control group use. Using these two methods allows us to not only find out large-scale patterns of control group use, but also why players behaved in a particular way.

Quantitative Analysis

Replays of *StarCraft 2* games were retrieved from two sources and included player information that allowed us to discern the skill level of the source players.

To investigate how differences in player skill affect control group use, we examined data from players of three different skill levels {novice, proficient, expert}. We consider players in the bronze and silver leagues (roughly 0–30th percentile) of Blizzard's rating system as the novice class. We consider players in the platinum and diamond leagues together (roughly 60th–90th percentile) as the proficient class and players in the grandmaster league (top 0.5% of players and above) as the expert class.

For the novice and proficient classes, we downloaded replays from a popular replay aggregator website, GGTracker. We also collected other replays of players in the gold and master leagues from GGTracker, but these were excluded in our classification of player skill to avoid the problem of trying to classify players in adjacent leagues[1]. Players upload replays to aggregator websites such as GGTracker to share them with others, or to access the analytics of replay data (e.g. actions per minute, resources collected, etc.) that such websites provide. Replays representing the expert class were obtained from season 2 of the 2013 World Championship Series (WCS) tournament replay pack released by Blizzard [1].

Inclusion criteria for the replays obtained from GGtracker website:

- The replay has two players (1 versus 1 mode)[2]
- Both players have a profile located at us.battle.net[3]
- Both players must be a member of the expected league during the collection[4]
- Both players must have usernames not consisting entirely of I's, |'s, or l's [5]
- The match length must be at least 300 seconds (≈420 in game seconds)[6]

[1]Attempting to separate adjacent leagues of skill rating into distinct classes adds to the difficulty of the classification problem due to players are between adjacent leagues. We adopt Thompson et al.'s approach [19] and avoid differentiating between adjacent leagues.

[2]We are estimating 1v1 ratings; Blizzard's rating system assigns a different rating for each mode of gameplay e.g. 2v2, 3v3, etc.

[3]Different regions have separate ranking systems, and therefore potentially different definitions of leagues.

[4]We used the "Highest Career Finish" provided by the player's `battle.net` profile and replay metadata to determine this.

[5]A common tactic to obscure one's identity is to use a "barcode" username e.g. `lIlIlIlIlIlIlI`. While we demonstrate a classifier that is capable of de-anonymizing expert players, we avoid replays from barcodes because of the difficult in establishing truth labels to evaluate classification performance.

[6]We wish to avoid shorter games that may only exhibit transient control group behavior.

Inclusion criteria for the player data obtained from the 2013 WCS Season 2 replay pack:

- The player has at least two recorded matches in the same replay pack
- The player has an identifiable name (same as above)

In total, 3,316 replays representing 138 expert players, 800 proficient players (platinum: 400, diamond: 400), 802 novice players (bronze: 401, silver: 401) as well as 400 gold and 400 master league players were included in this analysis. We consolidated aliases or variations of usernames of known players. The data was parsed from the replay files using the sc2reader Python library [9].

Metrics and Features

We consider metrics to explore based on the variety of user behavior they expose. Studies on KLM have examined features such as digraph latencies [12] or the amount of time it takes a user to perform a specified command (e.g. keystroke or mouse click) [3]. However, input for *StarCraft 2* and many other video games is often flexible in terms of individual keystroke sequences. That is, commands involving control groups can be repeated, executed out of order, or sometimes not at all with no direct influence on the outcome of the game. For example, players have the freedom to essentially select a control group as many times as they want, as this does not affect the game unless an additional command is issued. In considering the freedom that such interface flexibility confers upon the users, we choose to invert the concept of latency used in KLM and consider the frequency of control group commands instead. This frequency is computed based on real time as opposed to game time (real seconds are longer by a factor of 1.4).

Our qualitative analysis indicates that *StarCraft 2* players often choose to assign units of different types in habitual yet distinct ways. For example, one player may always choose to bind production structures to control group 5 whereas another may always choose control group 3. Considering these tendencies, it seems appropriate to consider frequencies for each of the control groups separately, as control group usage may depend on how often the units bound to a control group need to be selected.

We also distinguish between the types of commands that can be issued to control groups so that a different set of command rates is obtained for setting a control group to the current selection, another for adding the current selection to a control group, and another for recalling the selection specified by a control group. This differentiation is potentially useful again because of the freedom players have in executing control group commands—how often players repeatedly rebind or update a control group is user dependent.

Together, these combinations yield 30 features per player per game, as we consider three types of control group commands: add, set, get, with 10 possible key bindings {0–9} per command. Each feature was therefore the frequency that a specific control group and action combination was used in the game. These features are used for the classification tasks described later in the paper.

Defining Battles and Warmup

Some additional constraints were implemented to observe how players used control groups when in battle and during the warmup phase.

For our analysis, we defined battles as multiple units dying within a short period of time to include both small skirmishes and large engagements, both of which can tax a player's attention. To detect battles, we segmented the replay into periods of 10 in-game seconds (about 7 real seconds) and recorded the number of units owned by a player that were killed by an opposing player. Segments with more than two unit deaths were treated as times in which battles occurred. The window size and threshold on unit deaths were decided by reviewing replays at a variety of skill levels and was intended to capture as wide of a range of battles as possible. Peacetime is defined as the set of time windows that were not detected as battles. In some cases, replays were excluded from peacetime vs. battle analysis as either no battles were detected in them or because the replays had corrupted data. Players are excluded from the boxplots shown later in the paper if their ratios of command rates involve a divide by zero.

For battles and peacetime, we considered two subsets of control group use. We studied how often players selected the structures used to produce and upgrade units (macro) in and out of battle and also how often players modified or rebound their control groups, e.g. to manage newly produced units during battles and peacetime.

We define the warmup period as the first 120 in-game seconds ($\approx$86 real seconds). During this time period, players have only a few units to control. Still, players can choose to bind these units to control groups and rapidly cycle through them to warmup. We compared their warmup to their non-warmup (120+ seconds until the end of the game) control group usage.

Qualitative Analysis

Additionally, we conducted a qualitative analysis of control groups through a phenomenological lens that prioritizes the personal experience of the players as they reported in online discussions. This analysis was conducted in parallel to the data modelling to validate our choices of quantitative features and to inform our interpretations of the data and how to generalize our findings. The quotations throughout this paper are from this analysis and are used to illustrate the context of the features.

We collected forum posts about control group usage from the online social website Reddit. 50 posts with 776 total comments were analyzed via grounded theory [17] (Figure 2). A technical report comprising the data and coding scheme from the qualitative analysis is available online at `http://hci.cs.brown.edu/StarcraftReport.pdf`. All of the quotes listed as forum posts in this paper are taken from this collection.

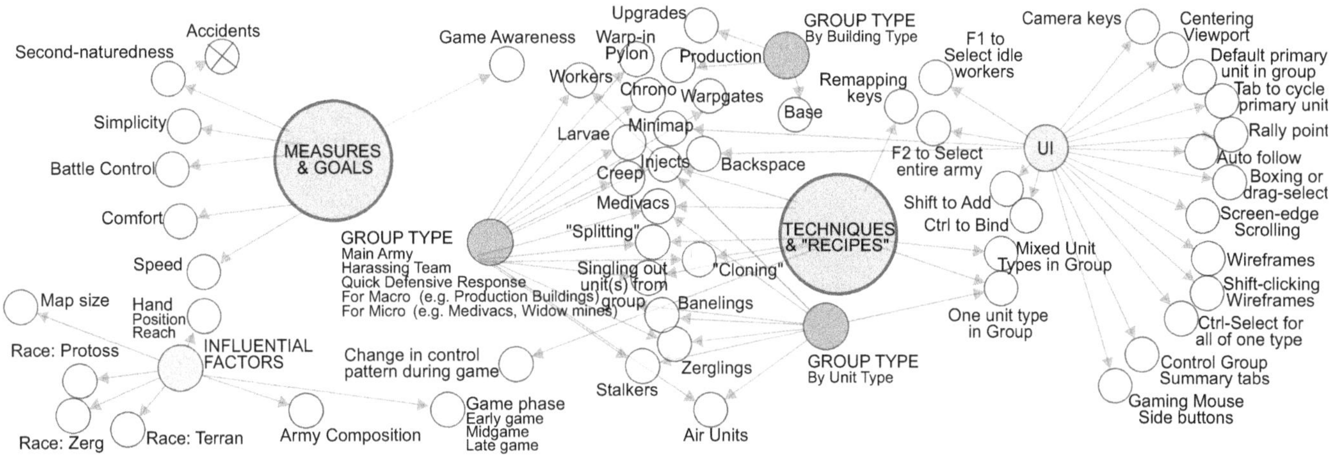

Figure 2: Diagram of themes and selected sub-categories from our qualitative analysis. This graph was manually created during the analysis. It shows major themes of habit, high technical skill, and diversity in technique.

DIFFERENCES BETWEEN SKILL LEVELS

Warmup

"Something that really made me play better was spamming, getting your hands warm and fast will make it possible in the later stages of the game for you to multitask and just play alot faster. Also try tapping between armies, scouting units, bases even if nothing is really going on. The worst thing you can do is just to sit and watch ur base with 0 APM when nothing is needed to be done." —P1

Figure 3 shows the relationship between warmup and non-warmup control group use. The ratio between warmup control group use and non-warmup control group use peaks in players below the expert class. In the lower leagues, a few players bind units to control groups at the start of the game and then stop using them entirely. Other players, and in greater number, exhibit similar behavior: they use control groups more than three times as frequently during the warmup phase than they do outside of it. This result could be attributed to less skilled players who attempt to mimic the behavior of expert players at the beginning of the game by spamming excessively yet lack the ability to sustain the control group use rates thoughout the game as their attention is taxed. These players may be attempting to integrate control groups into their play (see warmup trends in Table 1) but have not yet sufficiently mastered them.

"I constantly spam [control groups] 5 and 6 checking my queens energy and only stop when I'm moving guys or building units." —P2

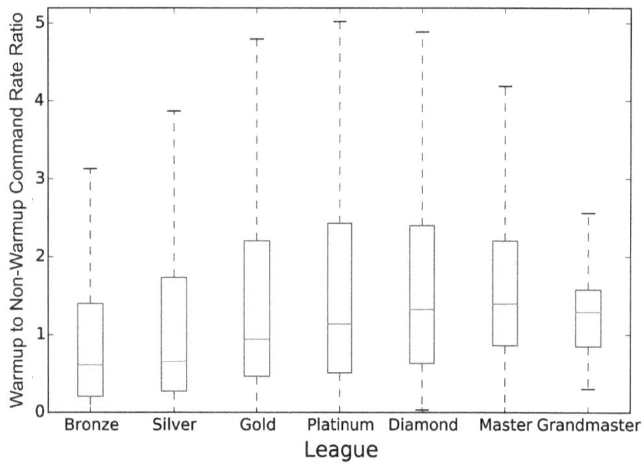

Figure 3: Warmup to non-warmup control group usage ratio at different skill levels. Some lower-skilled players use control groups at the beginning of the game but stop using them later. Expert players show the most consistent usage throughout the game.

Aggregate Control Group Use

Overall, we find that players at higher skill levels tend to use control groups more frequently. Distributions of aggregate control group use are shown in Figure 4 and steadily move towards greater control group usage with increasing skill. We find that in both the novice and proficient classes, there remains a substantial proportion of players who essentially do not use control groups at all. Within the expert class, everyone uses control groups to some extent, with the majority executing around two control group commands per second.

War and Peace, Macro and Micro

To gain a better understanding of control group usage and its relationship to player skill, we focused on finer-grained features that represent two distinct control group usage: macro and micro. Macro actions maintain the player's economy to keep income and production optimal: continually ordering new workers, buildings, and attack units. Micro actions optimize the effectiveness of individual units as they scout, position, harass, and fight. We investigate these features in two different forms of time-pressure in the game: battle and peacetime. Because it is

League	Median Warmup Command Rate	Median Non-Warmup Command Rate
Bronze	0.012	0.020
Silver	0.023	0.052
Gold	0.125	0.143
Platinum	0.307	0.229
Diamond	0.782	0.482
Master	1.377	0.901
Grandmaster	**2.360**	**1.907**

Table 1: Median warmup and non-warmup command rates (in units of commands/second). As skill ratings increase, warmup and non-warmup command rates increase. Players at higher skill levels seem better at sustaining control group usage throughout the game.

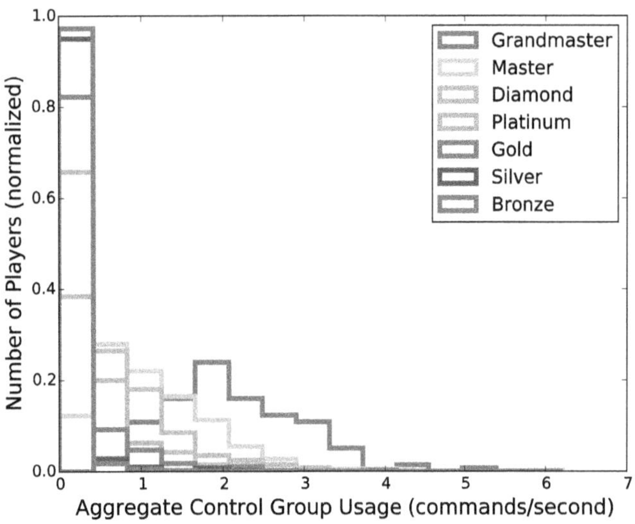

Figure 4: Distribution of control group usage among the leagues. A significant proportion of players in the novice classes do not use control group commands at all. Increasing rates of control group usage are seen with increasing skill ratings up to the expert class, where the average is around two commands per second.

easy to neglect unit production and resource harvesting during battle, the ability to maintain economic efficiency (macro) while using units appropriately during battle (micro) is a trait of a skilled player.

Use of Control Groups to Produce Units Under Pressure

"Get a macro rotation.... Every time you warp in, check money, check supply... Every time you start a colossus [a unit that requires 8 food supply], ... build a pylon [a building that provides 8 supply]" —P3

Battles require a lot of focus from players as they try to manage dozens of fighting units. More skilled players are still able to multi-task during these battles and continue to execute macro commands. In replays, expert players show the most frequent use of control groups to select production structures both in and out of battle, with lower usage rates in the lower leagues (Figure 5). Interestingly, the median event rate for expert players in battle is quite close to that of master league players during peacetime. Performing excessive or spamming selections of production structures can be helpful to monitor queues as it can ensure that the idle time of buildings is minimized. In the quote above, P3 habitually checks his different units and buildings in rotation. He also has trained himself to pair the training of an expensive unit with the construction of the food supply that it consumes. This allows him relegate some of his macro work to pure reflex.

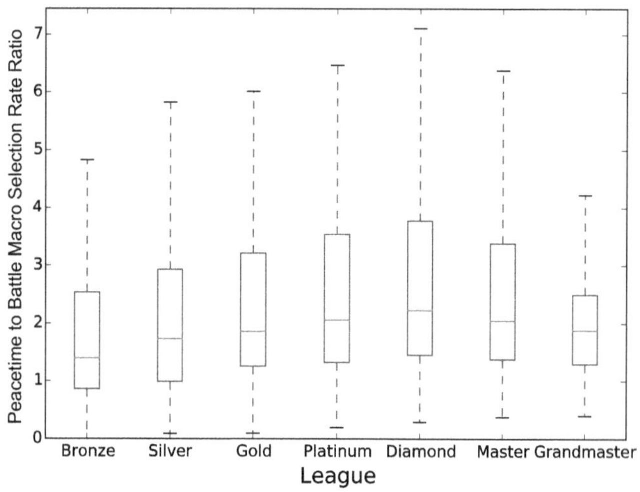

Figure 5: Ratios of macro selection rates via control groups during peacetime vs. battle. Nearly all players perform macro control group actions more frequently during peacetime.

League	Median Peace Selection Rate	Median Battle Selection Rate
Bronze	0.011	0.002
Silver	0.036	0.020
Gold	0.114	0.058
Platinum	0.216	0.098
Diamond	0.422	0.161
Master	0.752	0.317
Grandmaster	**1.332**	**0.712**

Table 2: Median macro selection rates during peacetime and battle (in units of commands/second). As skill ratings increase, production structure selection rates increase. Many expert players select production structures via control groups in battle as often as players in lower leagues do during peacetime.

Rebinding Control Groups in Battle

"want to reinforce [your army in the middle of a battle]? [Press these keys:] 1->s->zzzzzzzzz->shift+control+left click [eggs]->shift+[army control group] Blam .... the reinforcements will pop out immediately under your control. This is VITAL to Zerg play" —P4

StarCraft 2 is a fast-paced game, and during battles the number of units bound to a player's control groups can diminish rapidly as units are eliminated from the game. Unless they are given explicit orders, newly produced units do not automatically join these groups. To maintain these groups, skilled players rebind their control groups by either setting them to new selections of units or adding additional units to them. In the replay data, these actions can be connected to player skill.

We find that players rebind units most in the expert class both in and out of battle, and that players in the grandmaster and master leagues have the most similar rebind rates (compared to themselves) in and out of battle (Figure 6). This suggests that higher skilled players are more vigilant about managing newly produced units, and that lower skilled players are distracted by battles so they perform fewer rebinds than during peacetime.

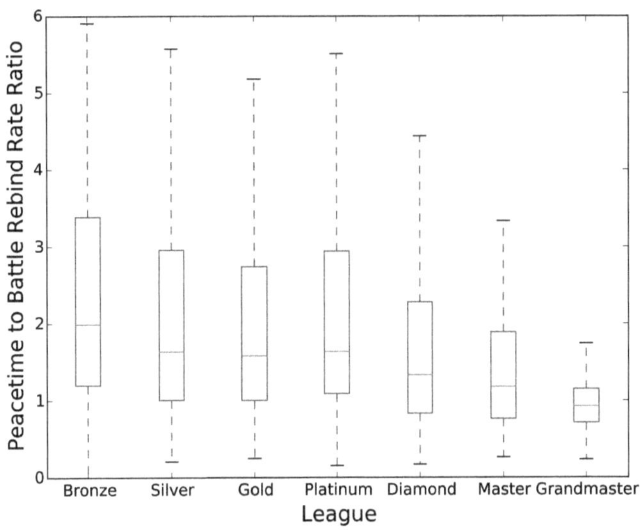

Figure 6: Ratio of control group rebind rates during peacetime vs. battle. Most expert players rebind control groups as frequently in battle as during peacetime. Players are able to better match their peacetime rebind rates in battle with increasing skill.

League	Median Peace Rebind Rate	Median Battle Rebind Rate
Bronze	0.006	0.000
Silver	0.010	0.000
Gold	0.019	0.004
Platinum	0.027	0.009
Diamond	0.037	0.022
Master	0.054	0.047
Grandmaster	**0.088**	**0.097**

Table 3: Median control group rebind rates during battle and peacetime (in units of commands/second). Rebind rates are highest in the expert class.

CONTROL GROUP HABITS

Our qualitative analysis found that players use control groups because they want to execute commands faster, to improve their ability to focus, grow a greater awareness of game events, and precisely manipulate game units. These mastery goals require interface control to become habitual and unobtrusive, and players practice heavily with the goal of making it natural to them.

As they improve, players develop a personal and routinised control style that fits their game strategy (race, opponent race, play style) and their physical needs (left/right-handedness, hand span). This relationship is maintained in two ways. Players configure their control to better execute their style of play; they depend on that configuration to keep them focused on their preferred style.

Frequently Used Keys

"Whatever you're comfortable with and can get to quickly. I basically don't use control groups past 5, simply because it's further away." —P5

The default keyboard shortcuts in *StarCraft 2* are heavily biased towards the left half of a QWERTY keyboard. Given this arrangement of shortcuts, we expected and found that keys {1–5} are the most frequently used while keys {6–9, 0} were less frequently used. This corresponds with our qualitative analysis which shows that players prioritize the closer keys to maximize their physical comfort when they expect to click on the keys for certain control groups at a high rate. Conversely, players will assign units to far away keys if they plan to recall them only on occasion.

How Habit Uniqueness Changes with Skill Level

Naturally, expert players are dissimilar or distant from players in the novice or proficient classes simply because experts tend to use control groups more frequently. However, this leads to a follow-up question: since experts use control groups more frequently, do they use them in similar ways? Or, are their styles of use unique?

Comparing player to player distances at different skill levels answers this question. We consider the Euclidean distance between players computed from the features described previously as a perspective on how similar two players are in their control group habits (Table 4). From the perspective of our features, expert players have the *most* distinct control group habits. This trend also appears in lower skill levels: the average distance between two gold players is also less than the average distance between two diamond players, and so on.

SKILL CLASSIFICATION

Classifying Skill from Control Group Usage

Our findings show that control group features contain predictive information about the skill levels of players. Applying this knowledge, we constructed machine learning classifiers using the support vector machine (SVM) implementation provided by the scikit-learn Python library [16].

League	Mean	Median	SD	Min	Max
Bronze	0.076	0.036	0.188	0.000	2.317
Silver	0.118	0.057	0.204	0.000	1.710
Gold	0.261	0.139	0.283	0.000	1.818
Platinum	0.396	0.254	0.379	0.002	2.853
Diamond	0.581	0.500	0.390	0.006	2.861
Master	0.754	0.676	**0.430**	0.039	**3.801**
Grandmaster	**0.955**	**0.914**	0.378	**0.096**	2.452

Table 4: Player to player distance statistics at different skill levels (in units of commands/second). The higher the skill level of players, the greater the distance becomes between any two players. This trend suggests that as skill level increases, players tend to diverge in terms of their control group usage habits.

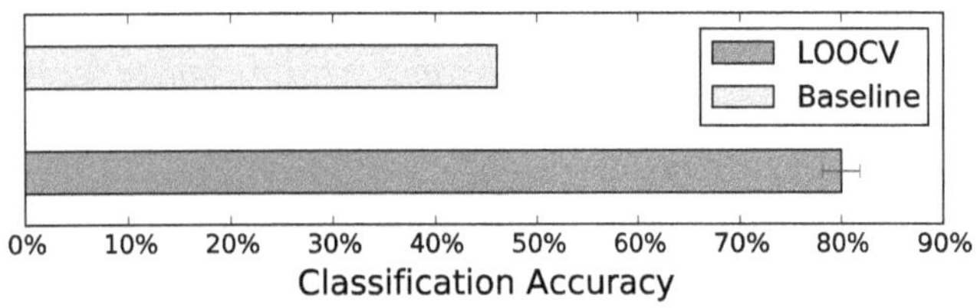

Figure 7: Skill level classification performance of {novice, proficient, expert} players estimated via LOOCV compared to baseline classification performance from choosing the most frequent class. Here, the error bar represents the 95% confidence interval for LOOCV accuracy.

Data was scaled before training and testing of the classifiers to have zero mean and unit variance by the preprocessing function for SVMs provided by the scikit-learn library. In the case of skill level classification, players who appear in multiple replays had their data averaged together such that each player is only represented once during the process. This averaging is done to help avoid "twinning" of the data [7], where cross-validation produces an overly optimistic estimate of accuracy due to highly similar instances of data being present in both the training and testing set. The default implementation of multi-class classification (one-against-one) in scikit-learn was used. The performance of our classifiers was evaluated using leave-one-out cross validation (LOOCV).

With an SVM-based classifier, we were able to achieve a LOOCV classification accuracy of 80.0% (95% CI 78.1%-81.9%) in the case of the trinary problem {novice, proficient, expert} compared to a baseline accuracy of 46.1% when choosing the most frequent class (Figure 7).

The results show that control group usage patterns have considerable predictive power to classify the skill level of players. The trinary classification performance when estimating players as {novice, proficient, expert} is comparable to the binary classification performance in [19]. This classifier enables a rapid (requires only a single match) and coarse estimation of skill that can supplement existing methods of matchmaking or skill estimation for online players. Instead of undergoing a series of placement matches to estimate player's initial skill rating, our method can be used to match players at a similar skill level after a single game.

Individual Variation and Expert Player Identification

"You just have to worry about doing the same thing every time, regardless of the situation, so it becomes muscle memory and a reaction. ... whatever you're doing needs to be consistent every time so it can be written in your memory and you yourself will become consistent." —P7

Our features show that players in the expert class tend to develop unique patterns of control group use. Additionally, the intra-cluster distance (distance between two points generated by the same player in two different matches) was on average significantly lower (mean = 0.359, SD = 0.272 commands/second) than the inter-cluster distance (distance between two players). Therefore, expert players not only tend to develop unique patterns of control group use, but also they remain reasonably consistent from game to game. In other words, expert players have signatures of control group behaviors that can be used to identify them.

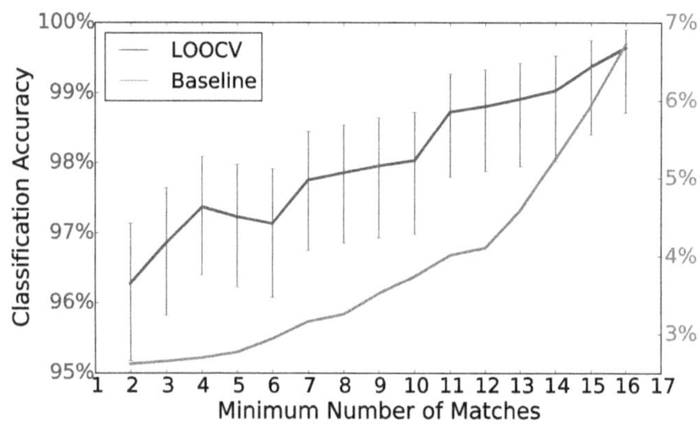

Figure 8: Classification performance of identifying expert players from control group features estimated via LOOCV compared to baseline classification performance. Here, error bars represent the 95% confidence intervals for the LOOCV accuracy. The minimum number of matches is an additional inclusion criteria for players.

Since our data includes expert players with varying number of examples (number of matches played), we consider our LOOCV classification performance as we increase the minimum number of matches required for a player to be included. With a minimum of 2 matches required per player, we were able to achieve a LOOCV classification accuracy of 96.3% (95% CI 95.2%–97.1%) compared to a baseline accuracy of 2.6% when choosing the most frequent class[7]. In general, classification performance improved as the number of games required for a player to be included was increased (Figure 8). As we increased the minimum number of games to 16 matches required per player, we were able to achieve a LOOCV classification

[7]Due to the relatively high value of $\hat{p}$ in these cases, we compute the 95% CI using the Wilson interval recommended and defined according to Brown et al. [2]

accuracy of 99.6% (95% CI 98.7%–99.9%) compared to a baseline accuracy of 6.7%.

Experts are particularly concerned with hiding their identity when sparring on public ranked matches as it prevents opponents from gaining advantages by studying replays and understanding one's unique tendencies, strengths, and weaknesses. At the time of writing, more than 70 out of the top 100 ranked players in the world were using a barcode username to obscure their identities. Our performance shows that accurate and rapid identification of experts is possible using our features. As online tournaments for esports increase in popularity as qualifying stages for larger events, we believe that the ability to identify players or detect mismatches in identity will become increasingly valuable.

"Professional gamers are known to study the replays of an opponent before an important match, much like a chess grandmaster preparing for a match." —Weber and Mateas [20]

DISCUSSION: HABIT, WARMUP, AND TIME-PRESSURE

Many players practice gaming competitively, optimizing the user interface so to be as unique and idiosyncratic as themselves. This nature is reflected in narrow tasks such as rebinding new units into one's existing control groups. Doing so is not considered a creative or playful task in-game, yet personalization exists. Qualitative reports show multiple ways to do this one task and our replay data accurately fingerprints these users. The same tendencies are found in other games, but also in the repeated, habitual interactions for all software.

If these affordances in games reward practice, personalization, routinisation, and warming-up, interaction designers can look for similar affordances elsewhere. *StarCraft* allows players to warmup without consequences. Warmup sequences can be employed that are harmless and valid (the user interface responds to each warm-up command giving subtle cues that they are doing the right thing). How might an air traffic controller warm up when he starts his work? Perhaps, like the *StarCraft* player, he needs to go through the motions of selection, de-selection, binding, rebinding; or in the controller's case, when he arranges his flight strips, his communications equipment, how is he creating and maintaining a tempo of readiness?

Our findings about these habits explore several points: is spamming to warm up, defined as useless keystrokes to engage muscle memory, a form of practice that enables players to regain skill with an interface rapidly? Does staying active in periods of idle time improve performance when our abilities are taxed? The most frequently used keys are similar across players, but experts can still differ significantly from each other in their total control group command rates. Community norms such as using the first few control groups for armies also exist. Therefore we interpret this variation to be a result of personal spamming habits throughout the game. That is, does one player prefer to repeat the sequence "1,2,4" throughout the game while another repeats "1,3" over and over again? How frequently do they do so? It is not clear that spam actions, when ingrained to the point of habit, can be easily unlearned or adjusted.

The consistency that exists among the usage patterns of expert players is interesting because these players are not executing the same strategy (e.g. build orders) without fail for sixteen games in a row in a tournament setting. They are constantly forced to adapt their play to their opponent's race, style, and tendencies, yet the same usage patterns hold. This behavior suggests that experts shoehorn their control groups to their current build order and composition, perhaps as away of coping with the need to play quickly. If control group use were defined by game events and outcomes, (e.g. only checking on an army when being attacked, selecting production only when idle), we would see little consistency among players. Our results lead to the hypothesis that the relationship between habit and performance is cyclic: experts are capable of sustaining consistently high performance because of their control group habits, and their control group habits exist as a result of this consistent performance. Overall, our work speaks to the power of habit and importance of adaptation in the face of diverse and time-pressured situations.

We see promising future work in finding the value in meaningless warmup actions that, in actuality, allow users to exercise familiarity and to establish a routine or flow that they will then apply towards the real work that they intend to do. Software interfaces that do not afford warmup may themselves be obstacles to work they are meant to accomplish.

Returning to our related work, we can also comment on task transfer. We have identified features that should be addressed. Because experts are so personalized in their style, we cannot expect two expert-level users to transfer tasks without a drop in performance. Instead, we might expect wasted time as experts have to "wipe the slate clean." Alternatively, if two experts are similar in their personalization style, we may predict a smoother transition, meaning that in organizations where we have enough experts, our classifier can save time in transitions between job-shifts by recommending the best replacements for outgoing experts.

Furthermore, our work informs a time-critical perspective of interaction design [6] (and also, [14]'s concept of automatic negative affect). This is not limited to formal crisis management. Even everyday interactions have "peace"-time and "battle." A brother who is coordinating a plane ticket purchase with his and his sister's family is under pressure when is given only minutes to secure a good price. His expertise at navigating the purchase, researching, and communicating is taxed. Here we may understand that a user who has had less practice with the booking interface would have trouble multi-tasking, dealing with the micro-level intricacies of flight booking while processing the demands of his family. As we have found, habit, expertise, and time pressure are deeply intertwined.

CONCLUSION

We introduced a set of features in game replay data to describe control group use, then provided a broad overview of how players use control groups at various skill levels and a qualitative context for these trends. In addition, we showed that players at higher skill levels diverge in terms of their habits despite following overall usage trends. We then demonstrated applications for these features, including the rapid classification of player skill and the identification of expert players, the latter of which has significant implications for professional gamers. Finally, we turn to implications of these features on the area of interaction design in general, identifying a connection with warming-up, task transfer, and time-critical interactions.

As an optional user interface component for organizing units, control groups may seem to the outside observer to be nothing more than programmable keyboard shortcuts. However, when players are issuing commands as fast as they can physically do so and their human motor abilities reach their limits, mastery of control groups through habitual play extend the players' capabilities so they can perform menial tasks like managing their economy in the midst of battle. These findings offer guidance towards other interactive scenarios where our human abilities are taxed (even if for one, critical moment) and additional capacity may come from minor details in the user interface.

ACKNOWLEDGMENTS

The authors would like to thank the contributors of the sc2reader (Graylin Kim et al.) and GGTracker (David Joerg et al.) projects. The authors would also like to thank Robbie Nakamura of teamliquid.net for providing guidance on expert player identities.

REFERENCES

1. Blizzard. Wcs season 1 and 2 replays. `http://media.blizzard.com/sc2/replays/WCS-Season1-and-2-Replays.zip`. Accessed August 30, 2014.
2. Brown, L. D., Cai, T. T., and DasGupta, A. Interval estimation for a binomial proportion. *Statistical Science 16*, 2 (2001), pp. 101–117.
3. Card, S. K., Moran, T. P., and Newell, A. The keystroke-level model for user performance time with interactive systems. *Commun. ACM 23*, 7 (July 1980), 396–410.
4. Cheung, G., and Huang, J. Starcraft from the stands: understanding the game spectator. In *Proceedings of CHI* (2011), 763–772.
5. Faure, G., Chapuis, O., and Roussel, N. Power tools for copying and moving: useful stuff for your desktop. In *Proceedings of CHI* (2009), 1675–1678.
6. Fields, B., Wright, P., and Harrison, M. Time, tasks and errors. *ACM SIGCHI Bulletin 28*, 2 (1996), 53–56.
7. Forman, G., and Scholz, M. Apples-to-apples in cross-validation studies: Pitfalls in classifier performance measurement. *SIGKDD Explor. Newsl. 12*, 1 (Nov. 2010), 49–57.
8. Huang, J., Zimmermann, T., Nagapan, N., Harrison, C., and Phillips, B. C. Mastering the art of war: How patterns of gameplay influence skill in halo. In *Proceedings of CHI* (2013), 695–704.
9. Kim, G. sc2reader. `http://sc2reader.readthedocs.org/`, 2011.
10. Kirsh, D., and Rebotier, T. Passing the bubble: Cognitive efficiency of augmented video for collaborative transfer of situational understanding. Tech. rep., DTIC Document, 2003.
11. Lauradoux, C. Show me how you play and I will tell you who you are. In *Atelier Protection de la Vie Privée* (Soreze, France, June 2011).
12. Leggett, J., Williams, G., Usnick, M., and Longnecker, M. Dynamic identity verification via keystroke characteristics. *International Journal of Man-Machine Studies 35*, 6 (1991), 859 – 870.
13. Mason, W., and Clauset, A. Friends ftw! friendship and competition in halo: Reach. 375–386.
14. Norman, D. A. Emotional design. *Ubiquity 2004*, January (Jan. 2004), 1–1.
15. Pagulayan, R. J., Keeker, K., Wixon, D., Romero, R. L., and Fuller, T. User-centered design in games. *The human-computer interaction handbook: fundamentals, evolving technologies and emerging applications* (2003), 883–906.
16. Pedregosa, F., Varoquaux, G., Gramfort, A., Michel, V., Thirion, B., Grisel, O., Blondel, M., Prettenhofer, P., Weiss, R., Dubourg, V., Vanderplas, J., Passos, A., Cournapeau, D., Brucher, M., Perrot, M., and Duchesnay, E. Scikit-learn: Machine learning in Python. *Journal of Machine Learning Research 12* (2011), 2825–2830.
17. Strauss, A., and Corbin, J. *Basics of Qualitative Research: Techniques and Procedures for Developing Grounded Theory.* SAGE Publications, 1998.
18. Taylor, T. *Raising the Stakes: E-sports and the Professionalization of Computer Gaming.* Mit Press, 2012.
19. Thompson, J. J., Blair, M. R., Chen, L., and Henrey, A. J. Video game telemetry as a critical tool in the study of complex skill learning. *PLoS ONE 8*, 9 (2013), e75129.
20. Weber, B., and Mateas, M. A data mining approach to strategy prediction. In *Computational Intelligence and Games, 2009. CIG 2009. IEEE Symposium on* (Sept 2009), 140–147.

Cooperative Game Play with Avatars and Agents: Differences in Brain Activity and the Experience of Play

Daniel Johnson, Peta Wyeth, Madison Clark, Christopher Watling
Queensland University of Technology
Brisbane, Australia
dm.johnson|peta.wyeth|m15.clark|christopher.watling@qut.edu.au

ABSTRACT
The current study sought to identify the impact of whether teammates in a cooperative videogame were controlled by other humans (avatars) or by the game (agents). The impact on player experience was explored through both subjective questionnaire measures and brain wave activity measurement (electroencephalography). Play with human teammates was associated with a greater sense of relatedness, but less competence and flow than play with other computer-controlled teammates. In terms of brain activity, play with human teammates was associated with greater activity in the alpha, theta and beta power bands than play with computer-controlled teammates. Overall, the results suggest that play with human teammates involves greater cognitive activity in terms of 'mentalising' than play with computer-controlled teammates. Additionally, the associations between subjective measures of player experience and brain activity are described. Limitations of the current study are identified and key directions for future research are discussed.

Author Keywords
Videogames; cooperative play; Player Experience; EEG.

ACM Classification Keywords
K.8.0 [Personal Computing]: General – Games.

INTRODUCTION
Much gameplay is inherently social. We compete against others, we play in teams, we can collaboratively apply individual skills to defeat an opponent or we can work as a group to overcome challenges. In some contexts these teammates and rivals are our friends, in many situations they are strangers, and quite often they are system-controlled game characters. With such an abundance of gaming experiences that embed this type of interactivity at their core, the level of research interest in the area is growing. Research has examined motivations for playing games with other people [28, 36] and the types of social interaction that occur within the context of social play [36].

CHI 2015, April 18 - 23, 2015, Seoul, Republic of Korea
Copyright 2015 ACM 978-1-4503-3145-6/15/04…$15.00
http://dx.doi.org/10.1145/2702123.2702468

The increasing number and diverse range of people playing videogames together, pulls into focus the need to better understand how, and in what contexts, these interactions improve player experience and potentially influence player wellbeing. Research has shown that videogame play with other people fosters social interactions both in and around games [21], it enhances feelings of social presence, engagement and fun [13], and promotes a sense of relatedness within both cooperative and competitive contexts [28]. Despite the importance of both social and co-operative play within games, and research that broadly examines social interaction across a range of game genres, it has been noted that social play has been largely neglected in evaluations of player experience [6], with a majority of this research continuing to focus on solo gameplay [13].

In examining more explicitly the social aspects of player experience, our interest is focused on the way in which interactions with other characters within a game influence engagement. This paper explores the extent to which the player experience differs when we play with other humans (avatars) as opposed to playing with system-controlled characters (agents). Theories on why people react differently to avatars and agents can be associated with the role that cognitive social functions play [7]. In our interactions with technology we often develop a disposition to treat an entity as a rational agent, possessing particular beliefs, desires, and intentions, in order to interpret and predict its behaviour [7]. It seems likely that this process of 'mentalising' might have an effect upon our interactions with avatars and agents in a videogame. Our expectations of opponents or teammates may be influenced by our perceptions of the characteristics they bring to the game experience.

The current study is designed to explore the differing impact of cooperative play with avatars (human controlled) and cooperative play with agents (AI controlled). The study examines these differences in the context of a complex and in-depth cooperative gameplay task. Following prior physiological investigations of brain wave activity during play [20], we were interested in assessing the impact of player experience both via subjective measures and also via more objective biometric measures (specifically, brain activity measured through electroencephalography or EEG).

PLAYER EXPERIENCE

There is promising research focused on the rigorous and systematic analysis of the gameplay experience. While originally focused on individual motivations such as challenge and curiosity [13], more recent research has considered interpersonal motivations and contexts such as competitive and cooperative interaction [13, 15].

Self-Determination Theory (SDT) is an approach to motivation that is primarily concerned with the potential of social contexts to provide experiences that satisfy universal needs (competence, autonomy and relatedness) in people [27]. People are more likely to be motivated to undertake activities that satisfy these needs and positive impacts on wellbeing are likely to result. Research has established videogames as an activity that satisfy self-determination related needs in players [23].

Although in-game agents may be capable of fulfilling a role otherwise played by a human (for example, as an ally in a first-person shooter mission), research has demonstrated that the player experience differs significantly. Weibel and colleagues [35] reported that believing that the in-game opponent was another human player increased the degree of presence, flow and enjoyment reported by participants. Cairns and colleagues [1] found that in a series of competitive tasks, participants' experienced greater immersion with human opponents compared to computer-controlled opponents. Similarly, research has demonstrated that participants who believed they were interacting with a human controlled avatar reported more fun, excitement, engagement and social presence than those who believed that they were interacting with a computer-controlled agent [15]. Spatial presence, engagement and anticipated threat have been shown to be higher when playing against a human opponent (either friend or stranger) than when playing against a game-controlled agent [24]. Overall the weight of evidence supports that playing a videogame with or against human players elicits more positive psychological experiences than playing the same game with or against computer-controlled agents [13].

Challenges in Measuring Player Experience

Analysis of the player experience, typically relies on analysing player response during a game [22] or player self-report after the game [1, 11, 14]. A number of survey measures have been developed with the aim of measuring player experience. Many of the relevant measures focus specifically on the experience of videogame play, including the Player Experience of Need Satisfaction [28] and the Game Experience Questionnaire [10]. However, subjective report through interview or questionnaire is not an effective means of gaining direct insight into player responses during gameplay [15].

Protocols involving observational analysis, while providing a rich source of behavioural data, are time consuming and subject to bias [15]. Additionally, techniques such as think-aloud used in observational contexts can prove invasive and distract from the gameplay experience. The use of physiological measures provides an avenue for examining a player's emotional response during gameplay, without the issues related to rigor and bias associated with observational analysis.

Using Biometric Measurements to Understand Player Experience

Researchers have used electroencephalography (EEG), electrocardiography (ECG), electromyography (EMG), galvanic skin response (GSR) and eye tracking, as well as magnetic resonance imaging, to assess player responses in games [7, 13, 16, 20, 26]. These measures are often used in concert with interviews, questionnaires and video analysis. Electroencephalography, which is the recording of electrical potentials of the brain, is used to measure emotion, cognition and attention, has been used in conjunction with the Game Experience Questionnaire (GEQ) and the MEC Spatial Presence Questionnaire (SPQ) to measure player experience [18, 20]. EEG has also been used in conjunction with ECG, which measures heart rate and interbeat intervals, and the profile of mood states (POMS) survey to examine the relationship between physiological responses and mood [26]. A study of the impact of audio on player experience employed the GEQ in combination with GSR, a measure of the electrical conductance of the skin, and EMG, which measures facial muscle movement [19]. Mandryk and colleagues [16] used GSR, ECG and EMG in combination with interviews and questionnaires. Ravaja and colleagues [24] used only biometric (EMG, GSR and ECG) measures in conjunction with events in games to determine players' emotional reactions.

A significant number of studies have collected biometric data as players compete against AI opponents either in a first person shooter [4] or sports game [15] context. Only one study [13] has examined measures of physiology in the context of cooperative, rather than competitive gameplay.

A small number of researchers have examined people's physiological responses within a social play context in terms of investigating differences associated with whether the opponent was controlled by the computer or other human players. A study that used functional magnetic resonance imaging (fMRI) to measure brain activity demonstrated significantly greater brain activation in an area known for mentalising when players believed they were playing against a person rather than a computer [7]. The same study found that playing a competitive computer game (stone, paper, scissors) against a human opponent versus the computer ''felt'' distinctly different, and that playing against the human opponent felt more like interacting with another person whose actions one could ''go along with''. Mandryk, and colleagues [16] investigated physiological responses (GSR, EMG and heart rate) when people played an ice-hockey videogame against a friend or against the computer. The results reveal that players exhibited significantly greater GSR and EMG activity when they played against their friend than when they played against the computer. In this study subjective measures corroborated this data; with players reporting feeling a greater degree of fun, excitement and engagement, and less boredom while playing the game with another human player than while playing with a computer. Research has also demonstrated that playing against a human elicits higher arousal as measured by cardiac interbeat intervals, as well as more positively valenced emotional responses elicited via self report, when playing a human (friend or stranger) in comparison to playing against a computer based opponent [25].

Lim and Reeves [13] have conducted research into the affective nature of avatar and agent interactions within both a competitive and a cooperative context. The competitive task involved competing with an opponent in a duel; the cooperative task was relatively simple and involved trading in-games items. Heart rate and skin conductance were measured and game players were asked to respond to questions about emotional valence and feelings of presence. The study showed that players exhibited greater physiological arousal when their collaborator was perceived as being a human avatar rather than a computer-controlled agent, and when the gaming task was competitive rather than cooperative [13]. Apart from this study, little is understood about the physiological impact of whether a teammate is an avatar or an agent in the context of cooperative play. There has been no research that examines how players respond when engaging with teammates (either avatar or agent) during relatively complex cooperative activity.

How Electroencephalography Relates to the Player Experience

Electroencephalography is the recording of the electrical activity of the cerebral cortex via electrodes that are placed on the scalp. The change in the electrical activity that is observed in the EEG wavelets is suggested to be the summated postsynaptic potentials of neuronal activity [31]. The rhythmicity of the voltage fluctuations of the EEG is jointly controlled by the cortical tissue as well as the thalamus [5]. Cortical arousal levels can be determined from examining the frequency spectrum of the voltage fluctuations. A spectral analysis converts the EEG signal from the time domain to the frequency domain (via a Fourier Fast transformation). The amount of power ($\mu Volts^2$) contained in predetermined frequency bands is then calculated. The fundamental frequency bands for spectral analyses are: delta (0.5-4 Hz), theta (4-8 Hz), alpha (8-13 Hz), beta (13-30 Hz), and gamma (36-44Hz).

Increases and decreases in these particular frequency bands are indicative of different neurobehavioural states. For instance, increases in the alpha and theta power bands are indicative of lower levels of arousal [31]. Furthermore, increases in activity in the theta band have been associated with daydreaming, creativity, working memory tasks and emotional processes [20]. Increases in beta activity are indicative of cognitive processes, information processing, problem solving and decision making [2, 20] and activity in the gamma power band are indicative of increased mental concentration and high level information processing [20]. While beta and gamma activity have been associated with attentional processes, the functional significance of the alpha component in EEG remains uncertain [3]. While synchronisation in the alpha frequency range is typically taken to be a marker of cognitive inactivity, (i.e., 'cortical idling'), there is work to suggest that alpha is associated with greater task demands [2, 3].

Within the context of studies that have used EEG to better understand individual gameplay experiences the following findings across the power bands have been reported:

- *Delta*: increases with negative affect and tension [18]; increases with immersion [20]; and decreases with boredom and flow [20];
- *Theta*: increases with immersion [20]; increases with challenge or engagement [30]; and decreases with boredom and flow [20];
- *Alpha*: increases with negative affect and tension [11]; and decreases with positive mood [26];
- *Beta*: increases with feelings of spatial presence [18];
- *Gamma*: increases with feelings of spatial presence [18].

COOPERATIVE PLAY STUDY

The current study was designed to further contribute to the developing understanding of the impacts of social play. We sought to explore the impact of type of partner (agent or avatar) on the cooperative play experience. We measure the play experience both subjectively (Player Experience of Need Satisfaction, flow) and objectively (EEG). A secondary aim of the study was to contribute to knowledge regarding how subjective and objective measures of the play experience align. Based on previous research, the following hypotheses and research questions were derived.

H1: We expect participants to experience greater relatedness when playing with other humans (that is, higher relatedness as measured by the PENS in the avatar than the agent condition).

RQ1: How does the experience of playing cooperatively with humans (avatars) vs AI partners (agents) impact on flow, presence/immersion, competence and autonomy?

RQ2: How does the experience of playing cooperatively with humans (avatars) vs AI partners (agents) impact on brain activity?

RQ3: How does the subjective experience of play relate to brain activity?

Participants

A snowball procedure was used to gather the sample of study participants. The study was advertised via university courses, email and social media. All participants were over the age of 18 years and had an interest in videogames. No other selection criteria were applied to participant selection. The research protocol received Ethical and Health and Safety approval from the university.

Measures

Demographic information

The demographic information collected included participant age and gender. Game experience demographic data, such as participants' general gaming experience and experience with first-player shooter games was collected on a seven point Likert scale (range 1 "extremely inexperienced" to 7 "extremely experienced"). Participants were also asked how many hours they had previously played the game used in the study (Payday: The Heist (Overkill software).

Physiological arousal

Physiological arousal levels were measured via electroencephalography (EEG). The EEG was recorded with a NeuroSky MindSet headset which records a single channel of EEG data which is sampled at 512 Hz. The data is recorded from the participant's forehead (at approximately the Fp2 site from the 10-20 electrode placement system) and is referenced to the participant's earlobe on the same side. The MindSet is a non-invasive headset worn like a normal audio headset and uses a dry contact electrode system that does not require skin preparation.

Player Experience of Needs Satisfaction questionnaire

The Player Experience of Needs Satisfaction questionnaire (PENS) [28] is a self-report measure of an individual's gameplay experiences consisting of 21 items responded to on a seven-point Likert scale (scored 1 "do not agree" to 7 "strongly agree"). The items are then combined to form five subscales, which are: competence (perceived efficacy playing the game), presence (sense of physical, emotional and narrative presence), autonomy (sense of freedom and independence), intuitive controls (perception of the in-game controls), and relatedness (connectedness within the game). The intuitive controls subscale was not included in the analysis of the current study, as the means by which the game is controlled did not change between conditions. Higher scores on each scale indicate greater positive experiences. The items that corresponded to a particular subscale were averaged to create the PENS subscales. The initial validation of the PENS was performed in experimental contexts with participants who may or may not have been experienced video game players and in a non-experimental context with a sample of MMO players [28]. The PENS has since been used successfully in a variety of settings and with various videogames [11, 23, 28].

Game Experience Questionnaire

The Game Experience Questionnaire (GEQ) [10] is a self-report measure of an individual's experience during gameplay. The GEQ measures a number of aspects of videogame play (e.g., immersion, tension, challenge) however in the present study we were particularly interested in the players' experience of flow and so only that subscale was employed. Flow is measured with five items on a five-point Likert scale (ranging from 1 "not at all" to 5 "extremely"). The five items were averaged to create the GEQ flow subscale. The flow subscale of the GEQ has been successfully used in a variety of settings [6, 12, 19].

Videogame stimulus

The videogame "Payday: The Heist" (Overkill Software) was chosen for use in the study as it offers an equivalent cooperative experience whether playing with other humans or with other computer-controlled teammates. The game level utilised in the study was the 'First World Bank' heist. The level objectives include: locating and subduing the bank manager, burning a floor with thermite, and drilling through a security gate, eliminating security guards and police officers, and taking hostages. The difficulty level was set to easy to reduce barriers to access for players unfamiliar with the game and to minimise any time spent waiting to re-join the game if the players' character was eliminated by enemies.

Figure 1. Laboratory - showing seating for two participants.

Procedure

All participants completed the study in groups of four. Upon arrival at the lab (see Figure 1) participants signed a consent form and had the MindSet EEG headset correctly placed on their heads by one member of the research team. It was explained to participants that they would be playing the game once with their three teammates being controlled by the other participants in the room and once with their three teammates being controlled by the game system. In an attempt to reduce the effects of playing the game in a non-naturalistic setting, participants were told to focus on having fun while playing the game and not to worry unduly about their performance. All participants received standardized instructions.

Prior to the gameplay participants completed a questionnaire including demographics and questions about their previous experience playing videogames. A two-minute baseline was taken at the beginning and end of the experiment session. During this time the computer screen went black and participants were encouraged to stare at the screen and relax. Then participants watched a 5 minute video of the game. The 7 minute acclimation period also allowed participants to adjust to the novelty of wearing the headsets. Participants then completed an 8-minute play session (either playing co-operatively with the three other participants in the room – the 'avatar' condition; or playing co-operatively with three computer-controlled teammates – the 'agent' condition) after which they completed a questionnaire related to their gameplay experience (the PENS and the GEQ flow subscale). Participants then completed a second 8-minute play session (whichever condition they had not yet played – avatar or agent teammates) and completed the same questionnaire relating to their play experience. The order of conditions was counterbalanced between sessions. EEG data was collected throughout both play sessions.

The eight-minute time limit was chosen as it allows players to play a significant amount of the campaign, while not being overly fatiguing. Participants were not allowed to communicate with one another during the experiment and no participant was able to view another participants' computer screen. The game was played on a PC with a 27-inch monitor and using a mouse and keyboard. Participants were provided with a tip sheet showing the games controls.

Physiological Data Treatment

The physiological data was inspected for artefact and any epoch that contained movement artefact was excluded from the analysis. A spectral analysis was then performed on the EEG data with the Acqknowledge software (BIOPAC Systems, Inc., California). The absolute power (μV2) was determined for each 10 second epoch for the frequencies of alpha (4-8 Hz), theta (8-13 Hz), beta (13-30 Hz), and gamma (36-44Hz). The absolute power for each 10 second epoch was then averaged for each frequency within both of the conditions.

Design

A within-subjects design was utilized to test the study hypotheses. The effect of the study condition (avatar or agent) was assessed by the outcome variables, which were: EEG (theta, alpha, beta, and gamma absolute power levels), PENS (competence, autonomy, relatedness, presence subscales), and the GEQ (flow subscale).

Statistical Analyses

The subscale reliabilities were evaluated with Cronbach's alpha coefficient. All outcome measures were examined for their distributional properties. The PENS and GEQ had normal distributions and a within-subjects multivariate analysis of variance was used to test hypothesis 1 (that participants would experience greater relatedness when playing with human controlled teammates than computer-controlled teammates) and RQ1 (How does the experience of playing with human controlled teammates differ from playing with computer controlled teammates in terms of flow, presence, competence and autonomy?). All of the EEG variables were found to have non-normal distributions. As a result, a series of non-parametric tests (Wilcoxon signed-rank) were used to explore RQ2 (How does brain activity differ when playing human as opposed to AI controlled teammates?). Data from 55 of the 72 participants was available for the EEG analyses owing to technical issue (a non-responsive computer) or the participant adjusting the headset and affecting the EEG signal quality. Spearman's Rho correlation coefficients were calculated to allow exploration of RQ3 (How does the subjective experience of play relate to brain activity?)

RESULTS

Characteristics of the Sample

In total, 72 participants took part in the study. The average age of the participants was 20.95 years (SD = 2.69; range = 18-31), with four fifths of the participants being male (80.6%). All participants had some degree of experience with videogames and more specifically, with first person shooter videogames. Game experience was measured on a 7-point Likert scale (scored 1 "extremely inexperienced" and 7 "extremely experienced"). The participants' mean rating of their experience with videogames 5.96 (SD = 1.01) and with first person shooter videogames was 5.34 (SD = 1.43) indicated a reasonably experienced sample. In total, 10 of the 72 participants reported having prior game experience with the videogame used in the study; having previously played the game on average for 3.82 hours (SD = 16.19).

PENS and GEQ analyses

Cronbach's alphas indicated acceptable scale reliabilities for all subscales (see Table 1). Regarding the first hypothesis and research question one, the within-subjects multivariate analysis of variance was performed on the dependent variables from the PENS subscales and the GEQ flow subscale with the avatar and agent conditions (n = 72). Using the Wilk's criterion, the dependent variables were found to differ significantly between the two conditions ($F(5,64) = .77$, $p = .01$). The means, standard deviations (SD), and univariate test between the avatars and agent conditions for the PENS and GEQ subscales are shown in Table 1. The PENS competence score was significantly greater for the agent condition than the avatar condition. There was also a marginally significant difference for the flow subscale such that participants reported greater flow in the agent than the avatar condition (the decision was made to cautiously interpret the marginal result on the basis of the small sample size and potential theoretical relevance of the findings). In contrast, the PENS relatedness score was significantly higher for the avatar condition than the agent condition.

	Avatar		Agent			
Variable	Mean (*SD*)	α	Mean (*SD*)	α	*F*	p^b
Competence[a]	5.08 (1.19)	.81	5.38 (1.10)	.85	**8.44**	**.01***
Autonomy[a]	4.39 (1.22)	.84	4.44 (1.21)	.84	0.20	.66
Relatedness[a]	3.36 (1.37)	.77	3.00 (1.24)	.65	**4.37**	**.04***
Presence[a]	3.82 (1.29)	.90	3.71 (1.13)	.87	1.72	.19
GEQ Flow	3.80 (0.93)	.85	3.95 (0.93)	.91	3.13	.08+

Table 1. Means, standard deviations, reliability and significance test between conditions for the PENS and GEQ

[a] PENS. [b] Bonferroni adjusted. * < .05, + < 0.10

	Median Value				
Variable	Avatar	Agent	*Z*	*p*	*r*
Alpha abs. power	7.92	6.33	**-1.98**	**.04***	.27
Theta abs. power	18.38	14.46	-1.85	.07+	.25
Beta abs. power	6.23	6.12	-1.71	.09+	.23
Gamma abs. power	1.96	1.82	-1.54	.12	.21

Table 2. Median values and significance tests between the Avatar and Agent conditions for the EEG data with effect size

* < .05, + < 0.10

EEG analyses

The EEG data was averaged across the two 8-minute gameplay conditions. All of the EEG variables were found to have non-normal distributions and therefore we have presented median values in Table 2 and used non-parametric tests [33]. Regarding the second research question, a series of Wilcoxon signed-rank tests were conducted comparing the avatar condition and the agent condition for each of the absolute power bands (n = 55). Table 2 displays the median values and the Wilcoxon signed-rank test results including effect size (r). It can be seen that the median alpha absolute power was significantly higher in the avatar than the agent condition. A marginally significant difference between conditions for the theta and beta absolute power bands was found such that the median values for both power bands were higher in the avatar than the agent condition.

Associations between subjective experience and brain activity

To examine the third research question a set of Spearman's Rho correlation coefficients were calculated on the study variables from the avatar condition (see Table 3) and another set of correlations were performed on the agent condition variables (see Table 4). Correlations were found within the subscales of the PENS and GEQ as well as among the EEG power bands. These relationships are outside of the scope of the current paper and are not interpreted. As shown in Table 3, none of the EEG power bands for the avatar condition significantly correlated with any of the subscales from the PENS or GEQ.

	1.	2.	3.	4.
1. Alpha absolute power	-			
2. Theta absolute power	**.96****	-		
3. Beta absolute power	**.89****	**.78****	-	
4. Gamma absolute power	**.68****	**.56****	**.89****	-
5. PENS Competence	-.17	-.21	-.23	-.25
6. PENS Autonomy	.08	.01	.06	.03
7. PENS Relatedness	.10	.05	.12	.10
8. PENS Presence	.06	-.02	.04	-.01
9. GEQ Flow	.10	.11	-.01	-.03

* < .05, ** < 0.01

Table 3. Spearman's Rho correlation coefficients between the EEG, PENS, and GEQ variables for the avatar condition

	1.	2.	3.	4.
1. Alpha absolute power	-			
2. Theta absolute power	**.83****	-		
3. Beta absolute power	**.95****	**.74****	-	
4. Gamma absolute power	**.59****	**.51****	**.89****	-
5. PENS Competence	.14	.08	.09	-.04
6. PENS Autonomy	.18	.12	**.32***	**.32***
7. PENS Relatedness	-.05	-.04	.09	.20
8. PENS Presence	.25	.22	**.36****	.26
9. GEQ Flow	.08	.06	.10	.06

* < .05, ** < 0.01

Table 4. Spearman's Rho correlation coefficients between the EEG, PENS, and GEQ variables for the agent condition

As shown in Table 4, three significant correlations were found between the subjective measures of the play experience and EEG power bands in the agent condition. The EEG variables of Beta and Gamma were significantly and positively correlated with the PENS autonomy subscale. The EEG variable of Beta was also significantly positively correlated with the PENS presence subscale.

DISCUSSION

Few published studies have looked at how the subjective experience while playing a cooperative videogame varies as a function of whether teammates are human (avatars) or AI controlled (agents). Even fewer have explored how brain activity varies in relation to social videogame play. Additionally, understanding of how brain activity relates to the subjective experience of play is still developing. The current study provides evidence of differing subjective experiences associated with social play as well as differences in brain activity patterns. It also contributes further knowledge regarding the brain activity patterns associated with specific subjective play experiences.

Subjective Experience of Play

We confirmed our first hypothesis, with participants showing a greater sense of relatedness when playing cooperatively with humans-controlled teammates than with AI-controlled teammates. While on the face of it this is unsurprising, it is encouraging given that the PENS measure of relatedness is based on self-determination theory [28] and hence, feelings of relatedness experienced during gameplay can be expected to contribute positively to overall wellbeing. Our own research has supported this connection, showing links between feelings of relatedness during videogame play and emotional, psychological, social and total wellbeing [34]. Hence, the findings of the current study further contribute to the developing understanding that videogame play can positively influence wellbeing and more specifically, that playing with others can lead to beneficial feelings of relatedness. This finding is particularly interesting given that the game used in the current study is a first-person shooter in which players are tasked with robbing banks. While this type of game is often presented in mainstream media as potentially harmful, these results suggest that regardless of their content, such games can foster a social connection between players.

With respect to our first research question, regarding the impact of social play on the subjective experience of play (flow, presence, competence and autonomy), we found differences in competence and flow. Participants' experience of greater competence when playing with agents may well reflect that the AI controlled teammates performed more effectively than the human participants in our study. If the AI controlled teammates were better (than the human controlled teammates) at supporting each other and the player (for example reviving each other when downed, providing covering fire etc.), then participants may have been able to perform better themselves when playing with AI teammates as a result of being better supported in their goals and actions. This would naturally result in greater feelings of competence. Again, the measure is based on self-determination theory [28] and hence, these feelings of competence can be expected to also contribute positively to wellbeing. It may also be that the pattern of results relating to flow is partially explained by the results in terms of competence. The greater competence experienced by players in the agent condition may reflect a better match between the challenge experienced by participants and their skill level. Given that flow is more likely to occur when challenge and skill are appropriately matched, the AI-teammates may have facilitated a play experience with the right level of challenge for participants' to experience flow.

The finding that participants experienced greater flow in the agent condition than in the avatar condition may suggest that participants were more distracted, and hence less able to experience flow, when playing with human teammates. There are several potential causes of distraction in the avatar condition relative to the agent condition. Firstly, it may be that humans are more distracting as teammates because they are more unpredictable than AI teammates or more likely to take unusual or erroneous actions while AI teammates are less distracting as a function of being more likely to stay on task during play. Even if not more distracting per se, it may be that human teammates cause greater information processing for players as a function of the tendency for 'mentalising' as identified by Gallagher and colleagues [7]. In the present study it seems likely that players are more likely to 'mentalise' in terms of evaluating their human teammates' actions and to think about their teammates goals and motivations around the in-game task, as well as (conversely) thinking about how their human teammates are evaluating the player's actions, goals and motivations. This additional information processing load may, in turn, make flow less likely. That greater information processing (associated with mentalising) is occurring during play with human teammates is further supported by our EEG results (described below).

The finding that participants experienced greater flow when playing with AI-teammates than with human teammates is in contrast with the findings of Weibel et al. [35] who found greater flow during play with other human players. However, Weibel and colleagues' [35] study involved participants playing a role-playing game with a large part of the in-game task being competitive, in contrast, the current study involved purely cooperative play of a first-person shooter. It seems likely that the differing features of the games or the competitive versus cooperative mode of play caused this differing response in terms of flow.

Brain Activity

Overall, the results show that participants exhibited greater activity in the alpha, beta and theta bands when playing with human teammates than with AI teammates. The most intuitively interpretable of these findings is the greater activity in the beta band. As described, beta activity is associated with cognitive processes, decision-making, problem solving and information processing [18, 20]. Broadly, this indicates that, in the current study, when playing with other humans, participants are processing more information. In part, the additional information being processed is likely related to the process of 'mentalising' in the form of evaluation of human teammates' thoughts, beliefs, desires and intentions. While a player might accept their AI teammates' behaviour for the pre-programmed behaviour that it is, observations of human teammates' behaviour are likely to naturally lead to consideration of their motivations and strategies and attempts to predict their behaviour. Conversely, it is likely that when playing with human teammates the player is more likely to devote thought to how they are being perceived by others or to undertake social comparison. Players are likely to be more self-conscious and/or aware of their performance as part of a team when playing with other humans. This interpretation is further supported by the lowered competence and flow when playing with humans.

Furthermore, the greater social experience that comes from play with human teammates also likely leads to greater information processing because of the potential for communication and connection. For example, doing something amusing or impressive in the game in the presence of other human players is likely to be more interesting or engaging than doing the same action in the presence of AI teammates. It is possible to amuse, impress or otherwise engage with human teammates in a way that it is not possible with AI teammates. Overall, play with human teammates is likely to involve interpretation of the actions of others, thoughts about the mental state of others, processing related to social interaction and processing related to the in-game task. In contrast, play with AI teammates is likely to be largely limited to processing related to the in-game task. As a result, greater information processing would be expected when playing with human teammates in comparison to AI teammates.

As described in the introduction, the extant literature suggests that findings related to theta band activity are less clear-cut than with other brain activity bands. In broader EEG research, theta activity appears to be associated with daydreaming, creativity, working memory tasks, and emotional processes [17]. In research specific to videogames, connections have been made between theta activity and challenge or engagement [30]. Although challenge was not directly assessed in the current study, as described above, it is feasible that since participants' experienced greater competence when playing with AI teammates they were more challenged when playing with human teammates. Hence, the greater theta activity may reflect greater challenge. More broadly, the greater theta activity may reflect that when playing with human teammates there is greater opportunity for creativity, more working memory activity and greater experience of engagement. Further research assessing a broader range of subjective experience measures and/or manipulating levels of challenge or opportunities for creativity is needed to explore these links.

The finding that participants exhibited greater activity in the alpha band when playing with AI teammates (in comparison to human teammates) can be interpreted in two ways. Alpha activity has been associated with task demands [2, 3]. As described above, the greater competence experienced by participants when playing with AI teammates, may reflect that play with human teammates was inherently more challenging or demanding. It may also be that the 'mentalising' associated with playing with human-teammates also makes the task more demanding. The process of trying to predict the behaviour of others and identify their thoughts and intentions may distract from the primary task or simply make it more difficult. However, greater alpha activity has also been associated with mental idleness or cortical inactivity. In that case, it may be that participants were less mentally active when playing with human teammates either because they felt less need to contribute when there were other humans to share the load or because they felt more need to contribute and manage the team when playing with AI teammates. However, this interpretation does not fit with the larger pattern of results in the study (particularly the greater information processing, challenge and creativity suggested by the greater activity in the beta and theta bands). It seems most likely that the greater activity in the alpha band is associated with relatively greater task demands when playing with human teammates.

Subjective Experience of Play and Brain Activity

In terms of associations between the subjective play measures and brain activity, three significant correlations were found in the agent teammate condition. Firstly, greater activity in the beta band was associated with increased feelings of presence. This aligns with Nacke's [18] finding of greater activity in the beta band with feelings of spatial presence. In the current study this finding seems likely to reflect an increase in information processing associated with presence. As the player becomes more involved and engaged with the game there is an associated increase in cognitive activity. Similarly, the associations between activity in the beta and gamma bands and feelings of autonomy likely reflect that autonomy involves freedom, choice and decision-making. These characteristics of autonomy involve greater information processing and would be expected to result in greater activity in these bands.

It is interesting to note that these relationships (between the subjective experience of play and brain activity) only emerged in the agent condition. Looking at the pattern of results as a whole, the explanation for the lack of connection between the subjective experiences measured in the present study and brain activity in the avatar condition could be related to our findings around 'mentalising'. It may be that the greater information processing associated with human teammates (e.g., thinking about teammate motivations, goals, etc.) moderated the relationships between brain activity and the components of the subjective play experience that were measured.

Limitations and Future Research

The current study provides important insight regarding the impact of social play on the subjective experience of play and associated brain activity. However, some key questions could not be answered by the current study. A limitation of the current study was the recording of only one location of EEG activity compared to prior studies that have used multiple electrode locations to analyse brain wave activity [18, 20]. The EEG headset used in the study records EEG activity from approximately the Fp2 location and frontal recording sites are more susceptible to eye blink artefact. Eye blink artefact has been shown to increase absolute power levels of delta and theta power bands [8, 9]. Additionally, the functional significance of EEG activity from other scalp locations (i.e., parietal, temporal, occipital) in terms of differences between cooperatively videogame play with humans and AI partners cannot be addressed with the current data. Previous research suggests there are differences of cortical activity levels between various cortical regions [32] and the two hemispheres of the brain assessed as frontal midline theta [29] with videogame play. Future research could seek to examine these regional differences with cooperatively videogame play with humans and AI partners.

Because of a desire to avoid participant fatigue resulting from long study sessions while also incorporating gameplay sessions long enough to allow the participant to properly experience the game, we were not able to test all possible conditions or include all relevant measures of the subjective experience of play. Specifically, we were not able to ensure that the task-related performance of the AI and human controlled teammates was equivalent. This could be achieved by including a condition in which participants believe they are playing with human teammates when they are actually playing with AI teammates (or alternatively, a condition in which participants believe they are playing with AI teammates when they are actually playing with other humans). This would allow insight regarding the impact of the social component of play without the possible confound of humans performing less well than AI teammates (or vice versa). However, this would not solve the challenge of the partly artificial nature of the avatar condition in the present study. This could separately be resolved by allowing participants to verbally communicate with one another while playing the game.

In the present study, we chose to focus on the PENS measures of competence, autonomy, relatedness and presence and the GEQ measure of flow. However, many of the findings can potentially be linked to other components of subjective experience such as challenge and negative affect. Future research incorporating a broader range of measures will further contribute to this developing body of knowledge. Additionally, the failure of some of our equipment meant that we lost biometric data for a number of participants. This meant that our sample size (and associated statistical power) was reduced for analyses involving brain activity. To this end, the effect size of many of our results was relatively small. Future research should seek to confirm our findings with a larger sample. Finally, given this area of research is relatively new and somewhat exploratory we chose to interpret some marginally significant findings. It will be important to confirm the pattern of results found in the current study in future work.

CONCLUSIONS

These findings extend previous work in terms of exploring EEG in the context of a complex collaborative videogame task. While previous research has explored simpler collaborative tasks and solo or competitive tasks with other biometric measures, the current study shows a clear link between complex collaborative tasks and brain activity. Broadly, the study provides clear evidence of a differing subjective experience when playing with human teammates than with AI teammates and an associated difference in brain activity. Social play is associated with greater information processing which is likely a function of 'mentalising' related to considering and trying to predict other players' thoughts and intentions. The process of 'mentalising' seems to be associated with activity in the beta and possibly also the theta band.

In terms of the connections between EEG and subjective measures of the play experience, some trends are beginning to emerge. The current study aligns with Nacke's prior research [18, 20] in terms of showing a link between activity in the beta band and the experience of presence. The study also provides important initial evidence of a link between activity in the beta and theta bands and the experience of autonomy while playing. Overall, the findings further support the contention that biometric measures are an informative and valuable compliment to traditional subjective assessments of the videogame player experience. In terms of the impacts of social play, there is clear evidence that cooperative videogame play with human teammates leads to greater feelings of relatedness between people. Considered in tandem with findings linking feelings of relatedness and wellbeing, these results contribute to a growing body of evidence showing the benefits of videogame play.

ACKNOWLEDGMENTS

We thank all the participants for their time, the Young and Well Cooperative Research Centre for partially funding this research and Lennart Nacke for his review and help with revisions of this paper.

REFERENCES

1. Cairns, P., et al., Who but not where: The effect of social play on immersion in digital games. *IJHCS 71*, 11 (2013), 1069-1077.
2. Cole, H. and W.J. Ray, EEG correlates of emotional tasks related to attentional demands. *International Journal of Psychophysiology 3*, 1 (1985), 33-41.
3. Cooper, N.R., et al., Paradox lost? Exploring the role of alpha oscillations during externally vs. internally directed attention and the implications for idling and inhibition hypotheses. *J. Psy-phys 47*, 1 (2003), 65-74.
4. Drachen, A., et al. Correlation between heart rate, electrodermal activity and player experience in first-person shooter games. *ACM SIGGRAPH Symposium on Video Games* 2010, ACM (2010), 49-54.
5. Fisch, B.J. and R. Spehlmann, *Fisch and Spehlmann's EEG primer: basic principles of digital and analog EEG*. (1999), Amsterdam: Elsevier Health Sciences.
6. Gajadhar, B., Y. De Kort, and W. Ijsselsteijn, *Shared fun is doubled fun: Player enjoyment as a function of social setting*, in *Fun and Games*. (2008): Eindhoven, Netherlands. p. 106-117.
7. Gallagher, H.L., et al., Imaging the intentional stance in a competitive game. *Neuroimage 16*, 3 (2002), 814-821.
8. Gasser, T., L. Sroka, and J. Mocks, The transfer of EOG activity into the EEG for eyes open and closed. *Elec-enceph. & Clin. Neurophys 61*, 2 (1985), 181-193.

9. Hagemann, D. and E. Naumann, The effects of ocular artifacts on (lateralized) broadband power in the EEG. *Clinical Neurophysiology 112*, 2 (2001), 215-231.
10. IJsselsteijn, W., Y. De Kort, and K. Poels, The Game Experience Questionnaire: Development of a self-report measure to assess the psychological impact of digital games. *Manuscript in Prep* (2008).
11. Johnson, D. and J. Gardner, *Personality, motivation and video games, OzCHI.* (2010), ACM press. p. 276-279.
12. Johnson, D., et al., *Personality, genre and videogame play experience*, in *Proc. Int. Conf. on Fun and Games.* (2012), ACM press: Toulouse, France. p. 117-120.
13. Lim, S. and B. Reeves, Computer agents versus avatars: Responses to interactive game characters controlled by a computer or other player. *IJHCS, 68*, 1-2 (2010), 57-68.
14. Lucas, K. and J.L. Sherry, Sex Differences in Video Game Play: A Communication-Based Explanation. *Communication Research 31*, 5 (2004), 499-523.
15. Mandryk, R.L., M.S. Atkins, and K.M. Inkpen, *A continuous and objective evaluation of emotional experience with interactive play environments*, in *Proc. CHI.* (2006), ACM: Montreal, Quebec, Canada. p. 1027-1036.
16. Mandryk, R.L., K.M. Inkpen, and T.W. Calvert, Using psychophysiological techniques to measure user experience with entertainment technologies. *Behaviour & Information Technology 25*, 2 (2006), 141-158.
17. Mitchell, D.J., et al., Frontal-midline theta from the perspective of hippocampal "theta". *Progress in Neurobiology 86*, 3 (2008), 156-185.
18. Nacke, L.E., *Wiimote vs. controller: electroencephalographic measurement of affective gameplay interaction*, in *Proc. Int. Conf. on the Future of Game Design and Technology.* (2010), ACM: Vancouver, British Columbia, Canada. p. 159-166.
19. Nacke, L.E., M.N. Grimshaw, and C.A. Lindley, More than a feeling: Measurement of sonic user experience and psychophysiology in a first-person shooter game. *Interacting with Computers 22*, 5 (2010), 336-343.
20. Nacke, L. E., Stellmach, S., & Lindley, C. A. Electroencephalographic Assessment of Player Experience: A Pilot Study in Affective Ludology. Simulation & Gaming, 42, 5 (2010), 632–655.
21. Olson, C.K., Children's motivations for video game play in the context of normal development. *Review of General Psychology 14*, 2 (2010), 180-187.
22. Pasch, M., et al., Movement-based sports video games: Investigating motivation and gaming experience. *Entertainment Computing 1*, 2 (2009), 49-61.
23. Przybylski, A.K., C.S. Rigby, and R.M. Ryan, A motivational model of video game engagement. *Review of General Psychology 14*, 2 (2010), 154-166.
24. Ravaja, N., et al., Phasic emotional reactions to video game events: a psychophysiological investigation. *Media Psychology 8*, (2006), 343-367.
25. Ravaja, N., et al., Spatial presence and emotions during video game playing: Does it matter with whom you play? *Presence, 15*, 4 (2006), 381-392.
26. Russoniello, C.V., K. O'Brien, and J.M. Parks, EEG, HRV and Psychological Correlates while Playing Bejeweled II: A Randomized Controlled Study. *Studies in health technology and informatics 144*, (2009), 189-92.
27. Ryan, R.M. and E.L. Deci, Self-determination theory and the facilitation of intrinsic motivation, social development, and well-being. *American Psychologist 55*, 1 (2000), 68-78.
28. Ryan, R.M., C.S. Rigby, and A.K. Przybylski, The Motivational Pull of Video Games: A Self-Determination Theory Approach. *Motivation and Emotion 30*, 4 (2006), 344-360.
29. Salminen, M., et al. Frontal EEG asymmetry in the study of player experiences during competitive and cooperative play. In *Proc. of IADIS Int. Conf. Game and Entertainment Technologies* (2009).
30. Salminen, M. and N. Ravaja, Oscillatory brain responses evoked by video game events: The case of Super Monkey Ball 2. *CyberPsy & Beh 10*, 3 (2007), 330-338.
31. Sanei, S. and J.A. Chambers, *EEG Signal Processing.* 2008, Chichester: John Wiley & Sons, Ltd.
32. Schier, M.A., Changes in EEG alpha power during simulated driving: a demonstration. *International Journal of Psychophysiology 37*, (2000), 155-162.
33. Tabachnick, B.G. and L.S. Fidell, *Using Multivariate Statistics.* 5th ed. 2007, Boston: Pearson.
34. Vella, K., D. Johnson, and L. Hides. Positively playful: when videogames lead to player wellbeing. In *Int. Conf. on Gameful Design, Research and Applications* 2013, ACM (2013).
35. Weibel, D., et al., Playing online games against computer- vs. human-controlled opponents: Effects on presence, flow, and enjoyment. *Computers in Human Behavior 24*, 5 (2008), 2274-2291.
36. Yee, N., Motivations for Play in Online Games. *CyberPsychology & Behavior 9*, 6 (2006), 772-77.

Examining Game World Topology Personalization

Sauvik Das
Carnegie Mellon University
sauvik@cmu.edu

Alexander Zook
Georgia Institute of Technology
a.zook@gatech.edu

Mark O. Riedl
Georgia Institute of Technology
riedl@gatech.edu

ABSTRACT
We present an exploratory analysis of the effects of game world topologies on self-reported player experience in Computer Role Playing Games (CRPGs). We find that (a) players are more engaged in game worlds that better match their self-reported preferences; and (b) player preferences for game topology can be predicted based on their in-game behavior. We further describe how in-game behavioral features that correlate to preferences can be used to control procedural content generation algorithms.

Author Keywords
Games; Player Modeling; Procedural Content Generation

ACM Classification Keywords
H.5.m. Information interfaces and presentation (e.g., HCI): Miscellaneous.

INTRODUCTION
Personalizing game content can increase the enjoyment and reduce the frustration of players to the effect of improving player experience [1]. Furthermore, understanding how in-game behavior relates to player preferences can enable adaptive games automatically tailored to a player's preferences based on behavioral cues. It therefore seems possible to adaptively personalize game content from in-game behavioral cues to increase enjoyment with a game.

In this paper, we examine whether personalizing game world topologies increases user engagement with a Computer Role-Playing Game (CRPG), and whether in-game behavior can predict a player's topological preferences so that a system can adaptively personalize the game world topology based on that behavior.

CRPGs require players to take on the role of a story character and embark on a number of quests. The spatial nature of game content in CRPGs make them ideal for investigating the relationship between in-game behavior and preferences for the topological factors of the game world such as size, shape, and linearity. Indeed, studies have found that exploring non-linear worlds are important to CRPG players [7]. Given this perceived importance of game space, we address the following research questions: (1) How does game world topology affect user experience? and (2) Can we predict player preferences for different world topologies based on their in-game behavior?

CHI 2015, April 18 - 23 2015, Seoul, Republic of Korea

ACM 978-1-4503-3145-6/15/04?$15.00
http://dx.doi.org/10.1145/2702123.2702473

Figure 1. Screen capture of our CRPG game being played.

We ran an exploratory, within-subjects study where participants played several versions of the same CRPG, differing only in the size, shape and linearity of the world topology. We collected in-game behavioral traces for each player, along with their ultimate topological preference. Using a ridge logistic regression, we were able predict the topological preferences for 13 of our 16 participants, and found that players seemed to be more engaged when they played in worlds aligned with their topological preferences. We further speculate how world topology features can serve as variables that can be procedurally adjusted according to in-game behaviors to personalize game play experiences.

THE GAME
We created a simple CRPG game for the purposes of this study. The game included a turn-based battle system, the ability for player characters to accumulate "experience points" to become stronger, items for players to gather, an annotated world map to help players navigate through the virtual space, and rare spawns for players to hunt and slay. Slaying these rare spawns provides players with special treasure, a mechanic that mimics the style of many CRPGs that reward players for engaging in challenging tasks. Treasure chests located in side areas reward players for exploration. Items rewarded for combat provided players with incentives to engage in combat. See Figure 1 for a screenshot of the game.

We also implemented several basic measures to avoid player confusion. To ensure that players always had an idea

Recorded Behavior Category	Description
Distance From Path (2)	The average and standard deviation of the avatar's closest distance from the path.
Unique Areas (4)	The number of unique areas the player's visited in a world. Further sub-divided into the number of unique plot areas, main path areas and sidepath areas visited.
Area Visits (4)	The average number of visits/revisits across all plot, main path and sidepath area.
Battles (4)	The number of battles initiated, won, lost and fled.
Time (3)	The amount of time spent in the game, spent exploring and average amount of time to finish plot events.
Rare Spawns (2)	Number of Rare Spawns found and killed.
Items (2)	Number of items used and number of unique items acquired.

Table 1. Behavioral features and feature categories recorded for every playthrough. Parenthesized numbers indicate the number of features recorded in a particular category. Twenty-one behavioral features were collected in total.

of what to do next in the story, we provided a map of the game world (see Figure 2). This map annotated the player's current location, the main regions for plot events, the primary path between plot events, and side paths not essential to story progress. The next plot point players had to visit was clearly indicated with an arrow. Additionally, our interface offered instructions on how to progress to the next story event and players were given an in-game tutorial that provided basic instruction on movement in the world and the meaning of various interface elements.

During each playthrough we recorded 21 behavioral features (see Table 1). Examples include all of a player's movements, total time in game, and enemies slain.

METHODOLOGY

We recruited 16 participants to play our CRPG, fourteen of who were male. All participants were computer savvy and all 16 reported playing games regularly. Thirteen participants were college students, one was a post-doc, and the remaining two were management professionals.

Participants played through three worlds. The first world was a baseline world of moderate size and linearity. The second and third worlds were presented in randomized order across subjects. They represented relative extremes in the size and linearity of the world according to our parameter space: one was large with many branching side paths ("big"), and one was compact ("small"). The story and playable game mechanics were constant across all three worlds. To ensure baseline story quality, we implemented a simplified version of a sidequest in the widely acclaimed Playstation game *Final Fantasy 7*.

Upon completing the third and final world, participants were prompted to enter a total order ranking of the three worlds they had played. Participants knew in advance that they would be asked to rank the worlds they played.

RESULTS

The random ordering of the big and small worlds created two groups of players: *"Big First"* and *"Small First"*. Eight participants were randomly assigned to each group. Whenever the ordering of worlds impacted a particular analysis, we compared participants within their own groups. Participants took 45 minutes on average to complete the study (s.d. 14.8 minutes), with a range of 27 to 83 minutes.

Player World Preferences

Among the sixteen participants, seven ranked the big world first (most liked), seven others ranked the small world first and the remaining two ranked the baseline world first. The two participants who ranked the baseline world first also ranked the small world over the big world. Additionally, among the fourteen participants who chose the small or big world as their favorite, ten rated the baseline world second and the opposite topological extreme as their least favorite.

We did not find that the ordering of worlds significantly affected participants' reported preferences for world

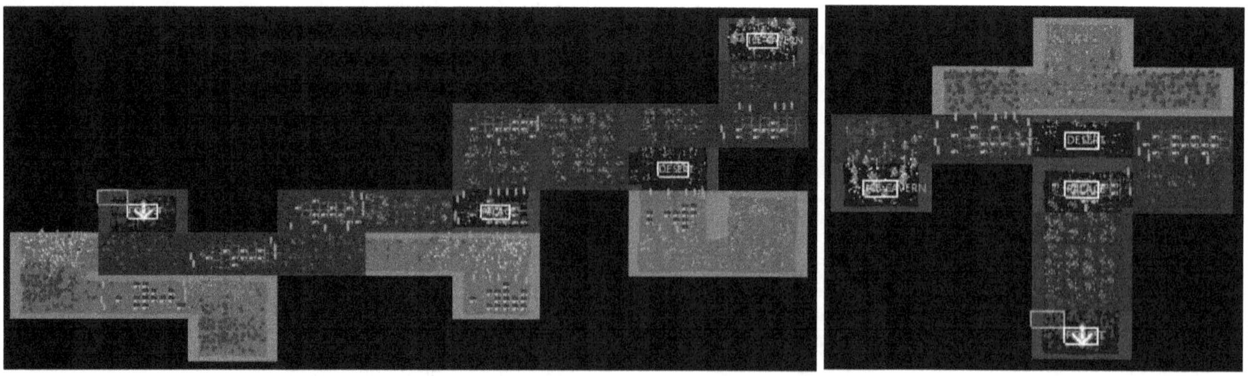

Figure 2. Maps of the "big" world (left) and "small" world (right) used in the experiment. Areas highlighted in blue contain plot points, areas highlighted in red are direct paths between plot points, and areas highlighted in green are sidepaths. An arrow graphic depicts the player's next destination, and the green square shows the current location.

Feature	Preference for Big world	Preference for Small world
Opened Treasure Boxes	0.93	1.08
Rare Spawns Found	0.47	2.14
Avg Visit Per Area	2.88	0.35
Unique Items Acquired	3.40	0.29

Table 2. Odds ratios for the ridge-logistic regression model.

topology. Among the eight players in the *Big First* group (players who played the big world first), four players ranked big over small and the remaining four players ranked small over big, whereas among the eight players in Small First group, five preferred small over big and the remaining three preferred big over small. According to a Fisher's Exact Test, these differences were not found to be significant (p=1, odds ratio=0.61).

These results suggest that players have clear preferences for CRPG world topologies—those participants who preferred either the big or small worlds generally rated the opposite extreme as their least favorite. Some preferred large, sprawling worlds, while others preferred small, compact worlds. In the following analyses, we group the two participants who ranked the baseline world first with those that ranked the small world first to allow comparison between the two major preference categories. We chose this grouping because both players who ranked the baseline world first ranked the small world over the big world. Using this categorization, 7 players preferred the big world and 9 preferred the small world.

Behavior-based Preference Prediction

To test whether in-game behavior relates to world topology preference, we modeled participants' binary world preference (big or small) on a subset of their behavioral features collected in the baseline world (which was always presented first). We started with the 21 behavioral data features and found the most predictive feature subset using the Wrapper feature subset selection algorithm in the WEKA machine learning toolkit [2,3]. To mitigate the effects of overfitting, we limited the number of features Wrapper considered at one time to four, so that we had many more observations than variables (16 vs. 4).

Using the reduced data set of four features found by Wrapper, we built a ridge logistic regression predictive model. We chose to use a logistic regression for classification to obtain coefficient estimates that can intuitively explain the relationship between the selected behavioral variables and topological preference. We chose a ridge-based approach shrink coefficient estimates and mitigate the effects of overfitting given our small dataset. Without the coefficient shrinkage provided by a ridge-based approach, regression models can provide extreme parameter estimates for small datasets [2]. The final variables selected, along with their odds ratio is shown in Table 2. For the "Unique Items Acquired" feature, an odds ratio of 3.40 for big world preference means that for every additional unique item a player acquired, our model predicted that the player is 3.4x as likely to prefer the big world.

Using leave-one-out cross validation, our ridge logistic regression model accurately predicted the preferences of 13 out of the 16 participants (81.25% predictive accuracy).

The three misclassifications were all players who preferred the large world, but were predicted to prefer the small. Examining the odds ratio suggests where our model erred. We note that a higher propensity to open treasure boxes and find rare spawns was indicative of a preference for the *small* world, which seems odd. This artifact may be a result of our model confounding topological preferences for propensity for exhaustive exploration—i.e., the obligation to *explore* the whole world, but not necessarily *wanting* to explore. Thus, the three users who were misclassified enjoyed exploring large, open worlds but were confused with users who felt obligated to explore the world. These edge-cases highlight the need for future mixed-methods research to tease apart behavior that indicates enjoyment from behavior that indicates un-enjoyed obligation.

In summary, these results indicate that player behavioral traces can accurately predict CRPG topological preferences.

World Topology and Player Engagement

Finally, to answer the question "Is there value in personalizing game world topologies?", we explored the effects of topological preferences on in-game engagement. We divided players into two groups: (i) those who preferred the big world and (ii) those who preferred the small. Then, controlling for ordering effects, we compared players' relative activity levels in both worlds.

We operationalized engagement as higher overall activity within the world (e.g., more battles initiated, more time spent exploring, more treasure gathered, more sidepaths explored). To control for the effects, on behavior, of world presentation order and world topological differences, we compared players within their own order group (Big First or Small First) and separately within the big and small worlds. Then, we sub-divided players within each of the four populations into two further subgroups based on their preference for the big or small world: **b**ig world first, **b**ig world preferred (BB, n=4), **b**ig world first, **s**mall world preferred (BS, n=4), **s**mall world first, **b**ig world preferred (SB, n=3), **s**mall world first, **s**mall world preferred (SS, n=5). Our analysis is based on a qualitative comparison of engagement features, as the number of users in any given bucket is too small for standard statistical comparisons.

We compared the means of engagement features in both the big and small worlds, and observed how the means of the big and small preference groups varied across both worlds. If personalized game world topology positively influences engagement, we would expect that the BB and SB groups—who prefer the big world—should be more engaged than BS and SS in the big world, and vice versa for the small

	Big World				Small World			
	Big First		Small First		Big First		Small First	
	Big Pref	Small Pref	**Big Pref**	Small Pref	Big Pref	**Small Pref**	Big Pref	**Small Pref**
Mean Unique Sidepaths	**60**	25	**50**	38	10	**29**	8	**15**
Mean Opened Treasures	**30**	14	**22**	20	3	**4**	1	**7**
Mean Battles Initiated	**29**	21	**35**	24	6	**11**	12	**14**
Mean Time Spent Exploring	**8**	3	**7**	4	1	**2**	1	**3**

Table 3. Comparison of engagement feature means in the big and small worlds, with means computed within ordering and preference groups. Bolded columns represent groups where topology aligns with preference, where we should see higher values.

world. Table 3 illustrates the general trends seen across the full feature set using a subset of features for brevity (Table 3). We found that preference for big worlds corresponds to greater activity in big worlds, and preference for small worlds corresponds to greater activity in small worlds.

In summary, we believe that there is value to personalizing CRPG topologies—our players seemed to be more engaged when playing in worlds that aligned with their topological preferences. However, as our small sample size ruled out strict statistical comparison, we note that these results do not provide conclusive proof that players are more engaged in game worlds aligned with their topological preferences.

MAPPING TO GAME CONTENT

There remains the problem of "closing the loop"—or mapping player behaviors back to configurable elements of game world topology.

We believe that procedural content generation [4,5,6] techniques can close the loop by feeding in-game behaviors to automated content generation algorithms. For example, Hartsook et al. [4] describe a system that generates game levels to optimize a topology given target values for (a) the maximum space between significant story events, (b) the minimum space between story events, and (c) the frequency of side-branches. These variables can easily map to our behavioral features—for example changing the number of sidepaths depending on how much time a player spends exploring or reducing the length of the main path if the player seems to transition through story events quickly.

DISCUSSION & CONCLUSION

Overall, we found some support for the following three assertions: (1) players have clear and distinct preferences for world topologies; (2) player behavior in a baseline, neutral world can predict preferences for world topology; and (3) players exhibit greater engagement in worlds aligning with their topological preferences.

It seems, therefore, that topological personalization is both valuable and feasible, and that game designers should consider employing adaptive topological personalization to maximize user engagement with their CRPG. Indeed, we outlined one way that such personalization could be achieved by directly mapping player behavior traces to procedural-content generation algorithm parameters.

Still, there remains a wealth of direction for future work. The present study is lacking in its small sample size, but has provided us with a theoretical grounding to implement a real-time procedural topology generator to "close the loop"—or, map player behaviors to real-time changes in the game world. In future studies, we plan to evaluate this real-time topology generator in a controlled experiment. We also plan to explore varying combinations of parametrically adaptable aspects of the game (e.g., story) to provide a richer understanding of the relative contributions of different game content to player experience.

ACKNOWLEDGEMENTS

We would like to thank Ken Hartsook for assisting with implementing our game engine, and Boyang 'Albert' Li and Stephen Lee-Urban for providing helpful feedback.

REFERENCES

1. Charles, D., Kerr, A., McNeill, M., et al. Player-Centered game design: Player Modelling and Adaptive Digital Games. Proc. Digital Games Research Conf., (2005).
2. Hair, J.F., Jr., Anderson, R.E., Tatham, R.L., and Black, W.C. Multivariate Data Analysis with Readings, Prentice-Hall, Englewood Cliffs, New Jersey.
3. Hall, M., Frank, E., Holmes, G., Pfahringer, B., Reutemann, P., and Witten, I.H. The WEKA Data Mining Software: An Update. SIGKIDD Explorations (2009)
4. Hartsook, K., Zook, A., Das, S., and Riedl, M.. Toward Supporting Storytellers with Procedurally Generated Game Worlds. Proc. IEEE CIG, IEEE (2011).
5. Shaker, N., Yannakakis, G., and Togelius, J. Towards Automatic Personalized Content Generation for Platform Games. Proc. AIIDE'10 (2010).
6. Sorenson, N., and Pasquier, P. Towards a Generic Framework for Automated Video Game Level Creation. Applications of Evolutionary Computation (2010).
7. Weber, B.G., Mateas, M., and Jhala, A.H. Using Data Mining to Model Player Experience. EPEX'11 (2011)

The Use of Games as Extrinsic Motivation in Education

Chris Preist[1] and Robert Jones[2]

[1]University of Bristol
Department of Computer Science
Merchant Venturers Building
Woodland Road, Bristol, BS8 1UB, England
chris.preist@bristol.ac.uk

[2]Games Faction
Electric Works
Sheffield Digital Campus
3 Concourse Way, Sheffield, S1 2BJ England
robjones@gamesfaction.com

ABSTRACT

This paper presents results of a controlled trial using a clash-of-clans style game as an extrinsic motivator to encourage revision in 15-16 year olds preparing for a maths exam. The trial demonstrates a statistically significant improvement in performance among those using the game. We discuss differences between our work and a previous trial that showed no performance improvement from an extrinsically linked educational game, and present hypotheses as to why the game structure we used may be effective within our chosen deployment environment.

Author Keywords
Education; gamification; motivation; extrinsic; intrinsic;

ACM Classification Keywords
H.5.m. Information interfaces and presentation (e.g., HCI): Miscellaneous.

INTRODUCTION

The role of games, both traditional and computer-based, has long been recognised in education. As a result, significant research has been conducted on the use of game mechanics in motivating and engaging students [3]. One approach is to adopt game-like mechanics such as points, badges and leaderboards to support a learner's progress and contribution through a series of learning tasks, by providing virtual rewards as a motivator. For example, badges have been shown to successfully increase engagement in an online course environment while maintaining quality of contribution [2]. A second approach is to interweave some form of enjoyable game playing with learning. There is clear evidence that in some cases this approach can lead to significant improvements, though simply designing a game is not enough and overall results are mixed [6]. Evidence suggests that care must be paid to the game design and deployment to ensure that an appropriate educational framework [6], approach to psychological motivation [7] and pedagogical environment [4] is used. Specifically, Habgood and Ainsworth [4] demonstrated through a controlled study of primary school children learning arithmetic that children using an intrinsically integrated game improved their performance to a statistically significant level compared to a control group, while a third group using a version of the game that required answering maths questions between game levels did not. This provides evidence in support of two hypotheses: (i) Intrinsically integrated games are more effective educationally than extrinsically integrated games. (ii) Extrinsically integrated games are not effective educationally.

However, intrinsic integration in educational games has certain practical disadvantages. Firstly, it is challenging to design a game that is intrinsically integrated, requiring expertise both in education and effective game design. Secondly, such a game will necessarily tend to be integrated with a specific set of concepts within a subject area, and will not naturally generalise to other concepts and subjects. Thirdly, if it is to be used outside a classroom environment it must compete for attention against other activities, including other computer games. A game which is not intrinsically integrated can be developed and deployed in a way which avoids these disadvantages – however, if the second hypothesis listed above is correct and it will have no educational value, then it is simply not worth doing.

While accepting that the first of the two hypotheses is likely to be true, in this paper we present evidence that challenges the second. We hypothesise that extrinsically integrated games can be effective if designed differently, and/or are deployed in different environments from those studied in [4]. Specifically, their extrinsic game design has the potential to be perceived as strongly controlling of participants, interrupting gameplay between levels with questions that must be answered to continue. A review of educational games [8] has shown that educational games are often not more motivating than traditional classroom techniques, and argues that this may be because of the demotivating effect of perceived control, even when engaged in something otherwise potentially enjoyable [1].

In this paper we present a design and deployment of an extrinsically integrated educational game that is intended to be perceived as less controlling of participants. We present

CHI 2015, April 18 - 23 2015, Seoul, Republic of Korea Copyright is held by the owner/author(s). Publication rights licensed to ACM. ACM 978-1-4503-3145-6/15/04...$15.00
http://dx.doi.org/10.1145/2702123.2702282

experimental evidence that our game does indeed result in improved performance by learners. We then consider possible reasons why an extrinsic approach might be effective in the deployment environment we have used, and finally consider the wider implications of this for educational games.

APPROACH

We use an approach based on the popular free-to-play (F2P) game business model used in games such as Clash of the Clans and FarmVille. In the F2P model, players have access to a fully functional version of the game free of charge, but have the option of making micropayments to speed up play or access virtual goods. Our game sought to encourage revision (review and practice of material) among pupils aged 15-16 preparing for their Mathematics GCSE, a national exam taken by all pupils aged 16 in the UK educational system.

Our gaming environment has a similar structure, but replaces the role of micropayments with a virtual currency earned by taking revision tests at any time within the game. Participants use the system in their own time, and are free to choose how much they do so. They are also free to choose whether and when to play the game and when to participate in revision activities. However, participation and success at the revision activity results in the earning of resources which can be used to speed up game play in the game itself – in the same way that certain 'speed-up' resources can be purchased for real money and used in free-to-play games to improve the game play experience.

We are interested in understanding if this motivational structure has advantages over traditional approaches to revision, and so compare it to a revision question generator without associated game play.

THE STUDY

The software system[1] used in our study consists of two parts:

(i) A revision quiz generator for Maths GCSE.

The quiz generator uses 30 different question templates covering the full Edexcel GCSE syllabus. These were designed by identifying the different question types used in past papers. They are instantiated with random values to give a potentially infinite number of specific questions. For example, one question template is to solve a quadratic; the parameters of it are generated randomly. The interface is straightforward: A window appears on the screen containing a question and 4 buttons below it contain possible answers. The user clicks on one, and proceeds to the next. They are presented with 5 random questions (each a different template), and then given their score.

[1] An appendix containing example questions and screenshots from the system is available at : http://www.bris.ac.uk/engineering/people/chris-w-preist/publications.html

(ii) A Clash-of-the-Clans style game.

The game mechanism used is a simplified version of Clash of the Clans – a real-time strategy game which combines resource gathering with combat. In our version, players build a town by spending resources to create new buildings, improve existing ones, and to hire and train soldiers. The three resources they need – food, gold, and wood – are generated by farms, mines and sawmills that they have built. Barracks can be built to train troops, and walls, turrets and other features can be added to the town.

Like F2P games, creation and upgrading of buildings, and creation and training of troops, takes time, with higher level upgrades taking longer. A timer is displayed showing how long is remaining before the action is completed. An additional resource, knowledge, can be expended to reduce or eliminate this wait. However, while in F2P games this additional resource is gained only through the payment of money, in our game it is gained through completion and successful answering of revision quizzes generated by the revision quiz module. At any point in the game (except in mid-combat) a player can choose to take quizzes to gain knowledge resources. There are 25 combat stages for the player to complete, which are unlocked 5 at a time.

Players advance in level by gaining experience points (XP). These can be gained by creating and upgrading buildings and troops, completing quizzes and successfully completing a combat stage. The player's level determines the maximum upgrade level of buildings and troops available to them. There are also a number of 'achievements' the player can choose to pursue, and these lead to a reward of additional resources. Only quiz-based achievements lead to additional knowledge resource.

The game interface is close to that used by Clash of the Clans. The town is displayed in the centre of the screen. Information bars at the top and bottom display current resources and XP/Level. The top bar also includes menus allowing the player to make game actions, and a separate button allowing them to take a quiz to earn knowledge. Apart from the existence of this button, no prompting is given to take the quiz.

Experimental procedure

A class of year 11 students (age 15-16) preparing for UK GCSE Mathematics exams was briefed on the aims of the study, shown the prototype system and given the option to participate. All 32 students (14 female, 18 male) chose to do so. The students then took a pre-test and (as in [4]) were randomly assigned to 3 groups ensuring the spread of ability in each group was identical. The GAME group (11 subjects, 6F, 5M) were provided with access to the game, the QUIZ group were provided access to the revision quiz generator only (11 subjects, 4F, 7M), and the CONTROL group (10 subjects, 4F, 6M) were provided with neither. They were told that they would be tested again in 3 weeks. During this period, usage data was collected by the software. A post-test was then administered, followed by a questionnaire. Both tests had a maximum score of 27. The questionnaire used multiple-choice options to collect data such as self-reported estimates of time spent gaming in a week and revision techniques used, and Lickert scales to collect data on attitude to and engagement with the software. Open questions were used to collect further qualitative data on opinions and usage, and a class discussion and debrief was conducted to finish.

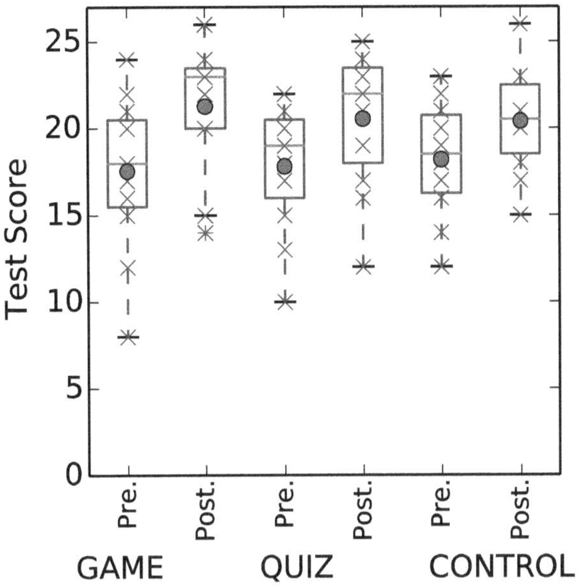

Figure 1: Test scores (out of 27) of individual students in each cohort, before and after the 3-week trial. Circles give the mean.

RESULTS

Figure 1 shows the test results of the three cohorts, before and after the 3-week trial. The change in mean/median score of the three groups is as follows: GAME (3.72/4), QUIZ (2.55/3), CONTROL (2.20/2). Figure 2 shows the change in score of each participant between the pre-test and the post-test. We apply the non-parametric Robust Rank Order (RRO) test[2] to determine statistical significance.

GAME v CONTROL: Ù = 2.234, (P<2.5%) DM= 0.49
GAME v QUIZ: : Ù = 1.676, (P<7.5%) DM = 0.40
QUIZ v CONTROL: Ù = 0.340, (P>>10%) DM = 0.15

Hence the distributions of GAME and CONTROL differed significantly, and that of GAME and QUIZ differed weakly significantly, with the improvement in performance of the GAME group dominating that of QUIZ and CONTROL. Though QUIZ shows a slight dominance over CONTROL, this is not to a significant level.

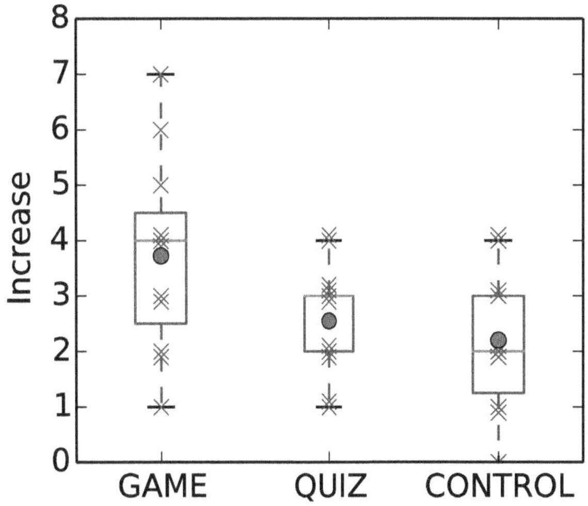

Figure 2: Score increase in the 3 groups.

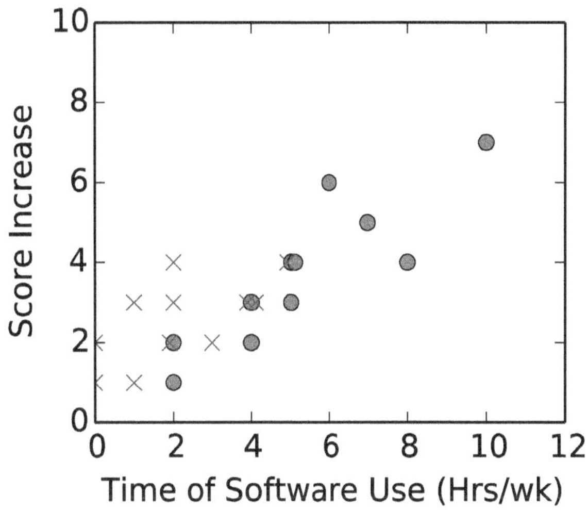

Figure 3: Usage time plotted against increase in score, for individuals in QUIZ (blue crosses) and GAME (red dots) groups. GAME includes both game and quiz usage.

Figure 3 plots the time spent using the software by individuals in the GAME and QUIZ groups against their score difference between the two tests. As can be seen, users of the QUIZ software used it less (median weekly usage = 2 hours) than users of the GAME software (median weekly usage = 5 hours). The RRO gives Ù = 4.446, showing that this is significant (P<0.5%). GAME students who used the software for a low number of hours (≤ 5) consistently achieved a score increase less than or equal than those in the QUIZ group who used the software for a similar time. It is likely that such students chose to play the game with relatively little use of the 'premium' speed-ups available through use of the revision features.

[2] The Robust Rank Order Ù test is an extension of the Wilcoxon-Mann-Whitney U test, and has been shown to be more reliable for small sample sizes over discrete variables [5]. Like the Wilcoxon-Mann-Whitney U, it is non-parametric so makes no *a priori* assumption of distribution pattern. The Dominance Measure, DM, provides a measure of effect size ranging from -1 to 1, with 0 being no effect and 1 being complete dominance in rank order.

In the questionnaires and the debrief sessions, students in the GAME group reported that their use of the software replaced gaming time rather than other activities (including revision outside the game). While this is self-reported, and therefore cannot be considered reliable, it is corroborated by the fact that those students who stated that they game for 10+ hours a week in the initial questionnaire were more likely to engage with the software for longer.

Some students also voiced dissatisfaction that the GAME and QUIZ simply told them which answers were incorrect without explaining why. Hence future versions of the software could incorporate more explanatory mechanisms. However, the GAME group self-reported a slight increase in revision activity outside the game. It may be that test marking without explanation acts as a motivator for further independent study, and so may have some benefits.

DISCUSSION

Despite the arguments and experimental evidence against extrinsic linking of games and education, our results have shown some positive benefit of this approach. We now consider potential explanations for this by considering differences between our situation and that of [4].

Though both experiments were focused on maths, ours is with an older age range, revising rather than learning new material. Students were working at home in their own time, rather than in a classroom environment, and were able to choose if, when and how to use the game provided. In particular, they were able to freely choose when and how much to use the quiz to earn extra points in the game.

Settling down to tasks such as revision requires a certain exercise of will even for highly motivated students. It is possible that interweaving it with gameplay made this easier. Furthermore, the nature of the interweaving would mean that the act of revision would take place for short periods, interspersed by gaming 'breaks'. This is in line with the commonly recommended revision technique of revising for short periods often, rather than for extended periods. Hence it may be that the game structure naturally encourages students to adopt a more effective strategy with less exercise of will on their part. Further research to explore this would be of value.

Deci et al. [1] demonstrate that extrinsic rewards often undermine intrinsic motivation when used in education. The undermining they demonstrate occurs only when such rewards are experienced subjectively as controlling of behaviour, and therefore undermining of an individual's perceived self-determination. We hypothesise that students engaged in our study do not experience GAME rewards as controlling of behaviour because (i) if, when and how-much is entirely self chosen; (ii) the game itself is self-chosen and can be enjoyed without any revision activity in the same way that an F2P game can be played without payment; (iii) it may feel like part of the game rather than an educational action carried out to receive a reward; (iv) the rewards themselves are 'micro-rewards' for small acts of effort or results, rather than the larger and more public rewards discussed by Deci. Furthermore, it is deployed to support revision, which is an educational activity fundamentally associated with the extrinsic motivation of passing an exam. Whether F2P based motivation systems do undermine intrinsic motivation, and if not then why not, is a key area for further research.

If such research proves supportive of this approach then it offers a promising and relatively low-cost means of turning what may be a source of distraction in the home environment into a motivator to revise. A system with 'knowledge rewards' could be integrated into a suite of existing F2P games alongside traditional payment mechanisms, allowing students to play on their existing favourites, interweaving revision activities with a pleasurable pastime. Games companies could offer credits to schools to use in this way as an act of corporate social responsibility – an approach that may be particularly effective if targeted at schools in areas of deprivation.

CONCLUSION

We have provided experimental evidence that, in certain deployment environments, games used as extrinsic motivators through an F2P style mechanism can have a positive impact on educational performance. Further research is necessary to corroborate this and to understand the underlying psychology of what is happening – and, in particular, if it has a longer term impact on intrinsic motivation. If this confirms the initial positive results, this presents a promising low-cost means of supporting revision.

REFERENCES

1. Deci, E. L., Koestner, R., and Ryan, R. M. "Extrinsic rewards and intrinsic motivation in education: Reconsidered once again." *Review of Educational Research*, *71*(1), 1-27,2001.
2. Denny, P. "The Effect of Virtual Achievments on Student Engagement." *Proc. ACM CHI 2013*, 763-772.
3. Dondlinger, M. J. (2007). "Educational video game design: A review of the literature." *Journal of Applied Educational Technology*, *4*(1), 21-31.
4. Habgood, M. J. and Ainsworth, S. E. "Motivating children to learn effectively: Exploring the value of intrinsic integration in educational games." *Journal of the Learning Sciences*, *20*(2), 169-206, 2011.
5. Feltovich, N. "Nonparametric tests of differences in medians: comparison of the Wilcoxon–Mann–Whitney and robust rank-order tests." *Experimental Econ, 6(3),* 273-297, 2003.
6. Linehan, C., Kriman, B., Lawson, S., and Chan, G. "Practical, appropriate, empirically-validated guidelines for designing educational games." ACM CHI 2011, 1979-1988.
7. O'Rourke,E., Haimovitz, K., Ballweber, C., Dweck, C., and Popovic, Z. "Brain Points: A Growth Mindset Incentive Structure Boosts Persistence in an Educational Game." ACM CHI 2014, 3339-3348.
8. Wouters, P., van Nimwegen, C., van Oostendorp, H., & van der Spek, E. D. "A meta-analysis of the cognitive and motivational effects of serious games." *Journal of Educational Psychology*, *105*(2), 249, 2013.

Exploring Cyberbullying and Other Toxic Behavior in Team Competition Online Games

Haewoon Kwak
QCRI
Doha, Qatar
hkwak@qf.org.qa

Jeremy Blackburn
Telefonica Research
Barcelona, Spain
jeremyb@tid.es

Seungyeop Han
University of Washington
Seattle, WA, USA
syhan@cs.washington.edu

ABSTRACT
In this work we explore cyberbullying and other toxic behavior in team competition online games. Using a dataset of over 10 million player reports on 1.46 million toxic players along with corresponding crowdsourced decisions, we test several hypotheses drawn from theories explaining toxic behavior. Besides providing large-scale, empirical based understanding of toxic behavior, our work can be used as a basis for building systems to detect, prevent, and counter-act toxic behavior.

Author Keywords
MOBA; online video game; toxic playing; team competition; cyberbullying; crowdsourcing; League of Legends; trolling

ACM Classification Keywords
J.4 Computer Applications: Social and Behavioral Sciences—*Sociology, Psychology*; K.4.2 Computers and Society: Social Issues—*Abuse and crime involving computers*

INTRODUCTION
With the remarkable advances from isolated console games to massively multi-player online role-playing games (MMORPG), the online gaming world provides yet another place where people interact with each other. The main reasons that researchers pay attention to online games are 1) that the purpose of actions is relatively clear, and 2) that actions are quantifiable. A wide range of predefined actions for supporting social interaction (e.g., friendship, communication, trade, enmity, aggression, and punishment) reflects either positive or negative connotations among game players [47], and they are unobtrusively recorded by game servers. These rich electronic footprints enable and encourage research of social dynamics [22, 28, 47].

There is no end to the growth of online gaming in sight. For example, in 2011 the First Dota 2 International Tournament had a prize pool of $1,600,000. In 2014, the prize pool started again at $1.6M, but, a *crowdfunding* mechanism brought it up to just under $11M. For comparison, the winners of the 2014 International received $5M ($1M for each team member), while the winner of the 2014 US Open Men's tennis tournament received $3M. In other words, video games have reached a level of sophistication and competitiveness that not only can gamers make a living playing them, they can make quite a comfortable living.

CHI 2015, April 18 - 23 2015, Seoul, Republic of Korea

http://dx.doi.org/10.1145/2702123.2702529

While the widely adopted game design element of competition increases enjoyment [52], it has also led to an increasing concern about negative behavior. In online gaming, negative behavior, such as cyberbullying [46], griefing [26], mischief [31], and cheating [10] are often grouped together and called *toxic behavior*. Unfortunately, the definition of toxic behavior is often unclear [16] due to differences in expected behavior, customs, rules, and ethics across games [53]. Such ambiguity and subjective perception of griefing make griefers themselves sometimes fail to recognize what they did [34].

To make matters worse, since online games are very popular in the younger generation [5], instances of cyberbullying can cause far reaching problems. In general, cyberbullying is associated with depression, anxiety, and has been shown to result in drastic actions such as suicide in several well publicized cases [6]. With the amount of time and energy players invest into games, victims of toxic behavior are likely to feel emotional effects that persist to the real-world.

In this paper, we make use of a large-scale dataset capturing millions of instances of toxic behavior perpetuated by hundreds of thousands of accused toxic players from the League of Legends (LoL)[1], the world's most popular online game [4]. The richly detailed cases are augmented by crowdsourced decisions on whether or not the accused was in fact toxic. Drawing from sociology and psychology literature, we explore toxic behavior through the lens of competitive online games.

BACKGROUND
In this section we begin with a basic description of LoL and the Tribunal, its crowdsourcing platform for addressing toxic behavior. We highlight the differences between LoL and other online games from the perspective of team formation, the goal of the game, and the common game modes. We then move on to how Riot Games attempts to detect toxic players and which behavior is considered toxic. Lastly, we explain how the Tribunal system works.

League of Legends as a Team Competition Game
The League of Legends (LoL), a Multiplayer Online Battle Arena (MOBA), is arguably the most popular online game in the world. The developer, Riot Games, recently announced

[1] http://www.leagueoflegends.com

there are 67 million players per month, 27 million players per day, and over 7.5 million concurrent players at peak times [2]. LoL is an online team competition game whose goal is to penetrate and destroy the enemy's central base, called the Nexus. In contrast to massively multiplayer online role-playing game (e.g., World of Warcraft), LoL is a match-based team competition game, where a single match usually takes around 30 to 40 minutes. Although LoL provides a few different modes of matches, all the modes are competitions between two teams. In the most popular game mode, each team has five members. A player is given the option to form a team with friends before the match. Otherwise, the player is randomly assigned to a team with strangers who have similar skill levels.

Player Reports on Toxic Behavior

After a match, players see a scoreboard as in Figure 1. In Figure 1, (A) is the match summary, (B) lists players who played the game together, and (C) is a chat window. Users can report toxic players by clicking the rightmost red button in (B). Each player can submit one report for every other player per game. We stress that player reports can only be submitted *after* the match is completed, and at a later date reviewers vote as described in the next section. Therefore, player reports are not considered a strategic element during the match itself.

Figure 1. LoL scoreboard after a match

When reporting, players choose from several predefined categories of toxic playing: assisting enemy team, intentional feeding [suicide], offensive language, verbal abuse, negative attitude, inappropriate name, spamming, unskilled player, refusing to communicate with team, and leaving the game/AFK [away from keyboard]. Detailed explanations of each type of toxic playing are given in [3]. Each report is submitted under one category. We further classify these categories as either cyberbullying (offensive language and verbal abuse) or domain specific toxicity (the remaining categories).

While most of categories are self explanatory, two of the domain specific categories need additional explanation: intentional feeding and leaving the game. Intentional feeding indicates that the player died to the opposing team on purpose, often repeatedly. Leaving the game/AFK refers to instances when a user is inactive through the entire match. These two categories of toxic behavior usually make the opposing team stronger due to the game's design.

To understand the motivation behind intentional feeding and leaving the game, we present one common scenario where such toxic play happens. A LoL match is concluded when the Nexus of one team is destroyed. If one team is obviously at a disadvantage during the game, the team may give up the match by voting to "surrender". However, surrender is accepted only when at least four out of five players on the same team agree to do so. When the surrender vote fails, players who voted for surrender may lose interest in continuing the game. Then, they might exhibit extreme behavior, such as intentional feeding or leaving the game/AFK, in an attempt to force the game to finish earlier or convince other players to cast a vote for surrender.

LoL Tribunal as a Crowdsourcing System

The LoL Tribunal is a crowdsourcing system to make decisions on whether reported players should be punished or not. Only players that are reported more than a few hundred times are brought to the Tribunal [11]. Once this threshold is reached, up to 5 randomly selected matches that an accused player was reported in are aggregated into a case. Reviewers, who are LoL players with enough time invested to be considered "experts," are then presented with a rich set of information about the case. They see the full chat logs from each match, the performance (similar to the end score board) of each player in the game, the duration of the match, and the category (and optional comments) that the player was reported for. To ensure an unbiased result, all players are anonymized in the match data. We note that among 10 predefined categories of toxic behavior, the Tribunal excludes reports of unskilled player, refusing to communicate with team, and leaving the game.

It is known that about 100-150 reviewers cast votes for a single case [11], and a majority voting scheme is used to reach a verdict. Guilty verdicts can result in a ban for 1 week, a few months, and sometimes longer suspensions/permanent bans. E.g., professional players have received lengthy, career impacting suspensions due to Tribunal decisions [1].

DATA COLLECTION

We collect all information available in the Tribunal: player reports, the crowdsourced decision, and detailed match logs. This rich collection is the basis for our quantitative analysis.

Early studies on moral behavior in sports largely depend on self-reports [41], but they suffer in quality and scalability from bias in the human recall process [35]. Furthermore, self-reports in particular can be influenced by social desirability, the tendency to behave in a way that is socially preferable [29]. In this sense, reports submitted by 3rd parties, as in the Tribunal, are more reliable since they eliminate the bias of self-report.

Another widely used method is asking individuals about hypothetical situations, but it also has the same social desirability bias, and additionally has limitations due to the specificity of scenarios and scalability [42]. Our huge collection of witness reports on *observed* toxic behavior helps address these problems. Furthermore, crowdsourced decisions offer an even more objective viewpoint on reported toxic behavior.

Riot Games divides the world into several regions and maintains dedicated servers for each region. We focus on three highly active regions, North America (NA), Western Europe (EUW), and South Korea (KR) by considering representativeness of cultural uniqueness and familiarity to the authors. Although a player may connect to servers operated in different regions, a further distance between a player and a server usually results in increased latency in Internet connections, sacrificing the quality of responsiveness and interactiveness of online games. We thus reasonably assume most players connect to the servers corresponding to their real-world region for the best quality of service.

In April 2013, we collected about 11 million player reports from 6 million matches on 1.5 million potentially toxic players across three regions. We collect all available data from the servers and summarize it in Table 1. We first note that the KR portion of our dataset is smaller than other regions because the KR Tribunal started in November 2012 but the EUW and NA Tribunals started in May 2011. Next, since player reports are internally managed, it is not easy to measure our dataset's completeness. However, as reviewers can see their past votes and final decisions at a later time, it makes sense that no votes or reports are removed from servers and we have what amounts to a complete picture of the Tribunal.

	NA	EUW	KR	TOTAL
Player	590,311	649,419	220,614	1,460,344
Match	2,107,522	2,841,906	1,066,618	6,016,046
Report	3,441,557	5,559,968	1,893,433	10,898,958

Table 1. Summary of our dataset.

RESEARCH QUESTIONS AND HYPOTHESES

In this section we formulate our research questions on how a toxic player behaves as well as how other players react to the toxic player.

At its core, LoL is a team competition game. Although competition against human opponents provides a high degree of player enjoyment [54], it can also result in toxic behavior. The potential for toxic behavior can be further exacerbated by the anonymous aspects of LoL, as people do not feel accountable for their toxic behavior when anonymous and can actually increase their aggressive behavior [17]. We present several compelling theories from sociology and psychology that describe the "whys" of toxic behavior. Our large-scale dataset gives the opportunity to apply these theories "in the wild."

We begin with an explanation of the bystander effect and the vague nature of toxic playing. Next, we discuss the concepts of in-group favoritism and out-group hostility with respect to competition. We then describe how intra-group conflict emerges in a team competition environment like LoL and some related theories which indicate a socio-political effect on how toxic behavior is both expressed and perceived. Finally, we consider the effects of team-cohesion on performance, which can provide insights into what might trigger toxicity in online games in particular.

Bystander Effect and Vague Nature of Toxic Playing

Our first research question is focused on how actively people report toxic playing. It is essential to understand the effectiveness and design implications of a system for counter-acting toxic playing, such as the Tribunal.

RQ1a: How active are players in reporting toxic behavior?

This research question is heavily related to the social psychology concept of the bystander effect [9], which describes the tendency for observers to avoid helping a victim, particularly when they are immersed in a group. Considering LoL's anonymous setting with ephemeral teams, the bystander effect can influence how other players react to a toxic player. If the bystander effect is valid in this setting, then most players in a match will *not* report the toxic player even though they directly witnessed the abuse. We explore how actively players report their observation of toxic behavior via our dataset.

Interestingly, the bystander effect is known to be mitigated with explicit pleas for aid [33]. We can thus draw a testable hypothesis.

HYPOTHESIS 1.1. *If there is a request asking to report toxic players, the number of reports is increased.*

RQ1b: How does the vague nature of toxic playing affect tribunal decisions?

Additionally, players have different perceptions on the severity of toxic behavior and thus sometimes fail to recognize its presence [34]. This vague nature of toxic playing might affect both reporting and reviewing. We expect that different perceptions between players who report toxic behavior and Tribunal reviewers will result in a number of pardons.

In-group Favoritism and Out-group Hostility

The next question we explore is related to the team-based, competitive gameplay of LoL.

RQ2: What is the difference between reporting behavior of the toxic player's teammates and his opponents?

In-group favoritism is simply the tendency of people to favor in-group members (e.g., teammates) over similarly likable out-group members (e.g., opponents) while *disliking* out-group members when compared to similarly dislikable in-group members [51]. This is also related to homophily [37], which is the tendency for similar individuals to form relationships.

Deindividuation theory explains how an individual loses the concept of both self and responsibility when immersed in a crowd [21], which provides a possible mechanism behind in-group favoritism. This foundation meshes with the unique characteristics of computer-mediated communication (CMC): anonymity and reduced self-awareness [15, 48].

Reicher et al. [43] proposed the Social Identity Model of Deindividuation Effects (SIDE) as a way of explaining effects that classic deindividuation theory could not. In short, they discovered that simply being part of an anonymous crowd was insufficient impetus for displaying anti-normative behavior. Instead, in-group identity alone becomes relevant only in comparison to a relevant out-group. In other words, both anonymity *and* context drive deindivduation.

Even though the groupings in LoL are ephemeral and mostly anonymous, the two teams are in direct competition and only one team can win: the thrill of victory or the agony of defeat is shared by all members of a team. This configuration catalyzes group identification and provides clear cut divisions of in- and out-groups in a context that is *driven* by out-group hostility; i.e., players are literally attempting to defeat the opposing team. Thus, we expect to see empirical evidence of in-group favoritism in reporting of some toxic behavior that equally affects both teams.

HYPOTHESIS 2.1. *For toxic behavior that affects both teams equally, in-group members (teammates) are less likely to submit reports when compared to out-group members (opponents).*

Intra-group Conflicts and Socio-political Factors

Although we expect to find evidence of in-group favoritism and out-group hostility, the team competition setting of LoL might also lead to substantial intra-group conflict. Intuitively, it is easy to blame overall team performance on a single poorly performing player. Unlike the aforementioned concept of in-group favoritism, the poorly performing player does not affect both teams equally because he makes the opponent team relatively stronger. Thus, he becomes a target to blame.

According to the classification scheme of human society introduced by Tönnies [49], teams in LoL are closer to task-oriented associations (Gesellschaft) than the social community associations (Gemeinschaft). In task-oriented associations, the relationship among players is somewhat impersonal and social bonding does not necessarily exist. Thus, toxic players might not feel a sense of a team and feel no qualms about harassing teammates who are hurdles to winning rather than recognizing enemies for beating his team.

While it is difficult to make direct conclusions about intra-group conflict, LoL players are generally segregated by what amounts to socio-political regions. The large world-wide user-base of LoL makes it feasible to study regional differences of such intra-group conflicts. Thus, leading to our next research question.

RQ3: What is the impact of socio-political factors on toxic behavior?

There are several studies to support that the degree to which bullying occurs is influenced by socio-political factors [8, 14]. Chee reports on a unique Korean gaming culture called *Wang-tta* [14]. In the context of gaming, *Wang-tta* describes the phenomenon of "isolating and bullying the worst game player in one's peer group." *Wang-tta* is thought to be modeled after the similar Japanese term *Ijime* [8] which describes the comfort members of collectivist societies feel from similarity and the abuse thrust upon those that are different.

Conversely, other socio-political regions such as North America and Western Europe tend to be individualistic, with a focus on relying on ones' self [27]. In such socio-political regions, while bullying of poorly performing players certainly occurs, there is less ingrained hostility towards another player's poor individual performance [39]. For example, consider the counterpart to the cliché "there's no 'I' in team," "well there ain't no 'WE' either." There is simply more focus on *my* performance as opposed to *our* performance. If there are in fact socio-political factors at play, then we would expect to see this reflected in reports on toxic behavior from different regions, leading to a testable hypothesis.

HYPOTHESIS 3.1. *Due to a more group-success oriented socio-political environment, cyberbullying offenses are less likely to be punished in Korea than in other regions.*

Collectivist societies such as Korea and Japan have a desire towards similarity, while differences are a source of disparagement [39]. In addition, collectivism, by definition, places more emphasis on cooperation, the group goal, and a sense of belonging than individualism does [18, 50]. That is, deliberately harming the group is anathema to the highly held social value of cooperation and is met with intense derision. Thus, we propose the next two hypotheses from the perspective of reporters and reviewers.

HYPOTHESIS 3.2. *Reports on toxic behavior that largely affects the result of the match are more often submitted in Korea than in other regions.*

HYPOTHESIS 3.3. *Reports on behavior that largely affects the result of the match are more likely to be punished in Korea than in other regions.*

Team-cohesion and Performance

The cohesion-performance relationship in sports has been studied for decades. Several studies have confirmed a moderate but significant effect of cohesion on performance, with the effect varying according to the type of sport, the mechanism of team building, and the gender of players [13, 38]. More generally, Felps et al. discuss how a single negative member can bring group-level dysfunction [25]. The negative member violates interpersonal social norms and thus can lead to negative emotions and reduced trust among teammates. These psychological states then trigger defensive reactions and influence the overall functioning of the group. Intuitively, toxic behavior is likely to have a negative effect on team-cohesion, and thus performance, leading to our next research question.

RQ4: What is the relationship between toxic behavior, player reports, and team performance?

Weiner proposes attribution theory which states that individuals are likely to search for causal factors of failure, considering even innocuous factors as significant [55]. Naquin and Tynan present a similar concept, the team halo effect [40], which describes the tendency of people to give credit for success to the team as a collective, but to blame other people for poor team performance.

The underlying cognitive process is known as counterfactual thinking [44], which is when we create a mental simulation built on events that are contrary to the facts of what really happened. If an individual deduces a high likelihood of changing the outcome to a more positive one via the mental simulation, then the difference between simulation and reality is identified as the causal factor for the negative outcome.

Generally speaking, counterfactual thinking helps us accurately identify causal factors of outcomes, but it can be biased by numerous factors [23], such as the halo effect. For example, if one player makes a poor decision, then a toxic player might imagine what would have happened if that decision was not made, attributing the current state of the match to that singular incident regardless of any mistakes he or other players might have made. Similarly, after the match is completed, a negative outcome and counterfactual thinking might lead bullied players to seek revenge on toxic players as a defensive reaction to perceived victimization and a method by which to gain some emotional satisfaction [20].

Since theory indicates negative outcomes trigger both toxic behavior and attempts to punish said toxic behavior, but reviewers of Tribunal cases are unbiased, we propose the following hypotheses.

HYPOTHESIS 4.1. *More reports come from matches where the accused was on the losing team.*

Also, such aggressive reporting might be likely to be pardoned.

HYPOTHESIS 4.2. *There are more cases pardoned when the accused was on the losing team than on the winning team.*

RESULTS

Bystander Effect and Vague Nature of Toxic Playing

First, we look into how actively people report toxic playing. When toxic play occurs in LoL, either 4 players (allies of the toxic player) or 9 players (all players but the toxic player) are exposed. For instance, if a toxic player is verbally abusive or uses offensive language in the ally chat mode, it is only visible to his allies. However, he can also use the all chat mode, exposing all 9 players to toxicity. For the other categories, all players are exposed in essentially the same manner.

Figure 2 plots the distribution of reports per match depending on the type of behavior reported for each region. Across all regions, the mean and median number of toxic reports per match are 1.812 and 1, respectively[2]. I.e., no more than 2 players per match report toxic playing on average. Overall, intentional feeding matches have the highest number of reports—about 50% of cases have more than 1 report, with over 60% for KR and EUW in particular—but the majority of matches have less than 3 reports. This is extremely low compared to the number of exposed players. I.e., on average, LoL players do not actively report toxic players.

To test *[H1.1] If there is a request asking to report toxic players, the number of reports is increased*, we look for situations where a request to report is sent to players on the enemy team; i.e., those that are not negatively affected by the toxic player, yet are likely to recognize his behavior and react if a plea is made. An explicit request sent to the opposite team when

[2]Every match in our dataset has at least one player report, as only players that have been reported appear in the Tribunal.

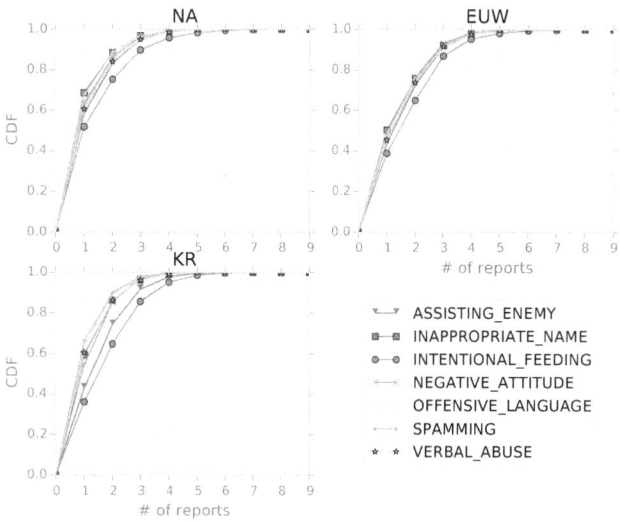

Figure 2. Distribution of the number of reports per match.

intentionally feeding or assisting the enemy satisfies this condition.

To test this, we define two dichotomous variables: 1) whether an explicit request exists, and 2) whether members of the opposite team report intentional feeding or assisting the enemy. We set the former variable to 1 when the word "report" appears in all chat, and 0 otherwise. We then create a 2×2 matrix of these variables. A Chi-Square test with Yates' continuity correction reveals that the percentage of reporting by enemies significantly differs with the existence of explicit requests ($\chi^2(1, N = 580{,}480) = 194552.9$, $p < .0001$).

Surprisingly, through the odds ratio we discover that the probability of opponents reporting is 16.37 times higher when allies request a report. This supports H1.1: explicit requests to report toxic players highly encourage enemies to report toxic players *even if toxic behavior is beneficial to the enemies.* In other words, we find the bystander effect is neutralized via explicit requests for help. This is interesting because opposing players can benefit from toxic playing, and their typical behavior of not reporting is changed due to explicit requests. This finding suggests that interaction design should actively encourage players to report others' toxic playing.

We next explore the possible impact of the vague nature of toxic playing on reporting and reviewing. First, we look into an association between the recognizability of toxic playing and the number of reports. Among the 7 types of toxic playing in LoL, intentional feeding and assisting the enemy team are, generally speaking, much more concrete expressions of toxicity than other types. The average number of reports per match for these two categories is higher than that for other types, as shown in Table 2. Both categories are consistently the first and the second ranked in terms of the average number of reports per match across all regions. A Kruskal Wallis test revealed a significant effect for category of toxic behavior on the number of reports per match ($\chi^2(6) = 117{,}399.1$, $p < .0001$). Further post-hoc statistical testing using the pairwise

Wilcoxon test with Bonferroni correction showed a significant difference between categories ($p < .0001$).

A.E	I.N	I.F	N.A	O.L	S	V.A
1.876	1.602	2.091	1.696	1.691	1.769	1.740

Table 2. Avg. number of reports per match for each type of toxic playing.

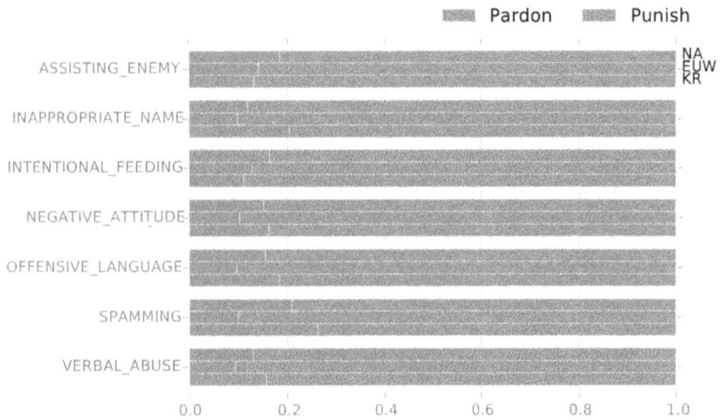

Figure 3. Proportion of decisions according to categories of toxic playing.

Second, we look at how many reported toxic players are pardoned in Figure 3. Since players come to the Tribunal only after a few hundred reports against them, we do not expect to see a 50/50 punish/pardon ratio. We obtained records for 477,383 punishments (80.9%) and 112,930 pardons (19.1%) for NA, 559,449 (86.0%) and 90,966 (14.0%) for EUW, and 187,253 (85.0%) and 32,929 (15.0%) for KR across all categories of toxic playing. The highest pardoned ratio we found for a specific category[3], spamming, is 26.1% in KR. Being reported means that *players* regard it as toxic playing, and a pardon means that *reviewers* do not regard it as toxic. Therefore, a 26% pardoned rate shows that different perceptions exist: for 1 in 4 cases, reviewers do not find the player toxic. This high pardoned ratio confirms the impact of the vague nature of toxic playing in reviewing as well as in reporting.

In-group Favoritism and Out-group Hostility

Our next research question is understanding the difference between reporting behavior of the toxic player's teammates and his opponents. To test *[H2.1] For toxic behavior that affects both teams equally, in-group members (teammates) are less likely to submit reports when compared to out-group members (opponents)*, we carefully revisit the definition of in-group favoritism. The key concept of in-group favoritism is "similarly" likable or unlikeable members from the same group are more favorable. We find this kind of relatively "neutral" toxic behavior from reports of inappropriate name. The inappropriate name of a toxic player is visible to all players equally, and thus the impact of the inappropriate name is neutral to both teams.

In Figure 4 we plot the number of matches reported for each category of toxic behavior per region. As we hypothesized,

[3]When multiple reports per accused player per game are submitted, we use the most common report type.

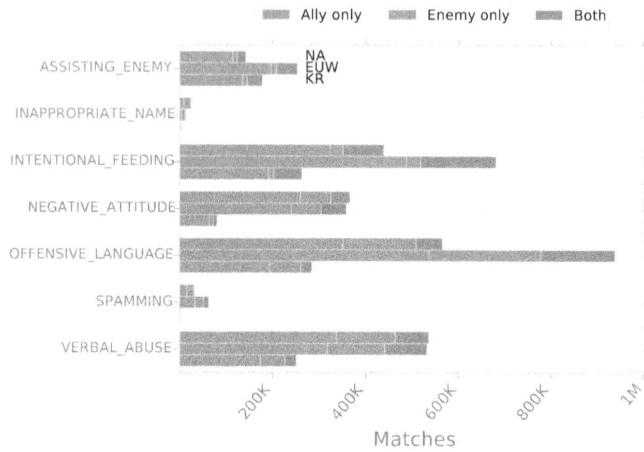

Figure 4. Number of matches that report each category of toxic behavior.

the only category in which the number of reports from enemies is higher than from allies is inappropriate name (ally only: 16,339, enemy only: 23,966, across regions). This indicates that allies are more forgiving, and thus less likely to report, than opponents in cases where the toxic player's offense is neutral to both teams. This is exactly what in-group favoritism describes, and thus H2.1 is supported.

Intra-group Conflicts and Socio-political Factors

We now explore our next research question on the relationship between intra-group conflicts and socio-political factors. Figure 4 shows the number of matches that are reported due to each category of toxic behavior. The horizontal bar for each category divided into three parts shows the number of matches reported by ally-only, enemy-only, and both, respectively from left to right. For instance, about 200 thousand matches are reported by ally-only due to assisting enemy, 12,106 matches by enemy-only, and 44,927 matches by both in EUW. We find that most reports come from allies rather from enemies as evidences of intra-group conflicts.

In Figure 4, offensive language is the most reported toxic behavior in LoL and is highly reported by allies. The chat feature is designed for exchanging strategies and sharing emotions, and thus serves to foster a sense of belonging in the team. In practice, however, it becomes a channel for toxic players to harass other ally players [32].

We additionally note that Riot Games disabled the all chat by default in newly installed clients since April 2012, while the Tribunal began in May 2011. Although players can easily turn the all chat option on in the game configuration by one click, we expect that it decreases the verbal interaction across teams after April 2012. To confirm that this is not the reason that players are likely to report allies rather than opponents for verbal abuse or offensive language, we look into the temporal trend of the toxic reports for those two reasons. We divide toxic reports by a fixed-size time window, defined as 1,000 consecutive numeric identifiers of the toxic reports. We compute the proportion of toxic reports that come from allies to those from opponents in each time window and find that the number of reports by allies is consistently higher than those by opponents, although it varies over time. This shows that frequent intra-group conflicts through chat are not artificial effects of the user interface.

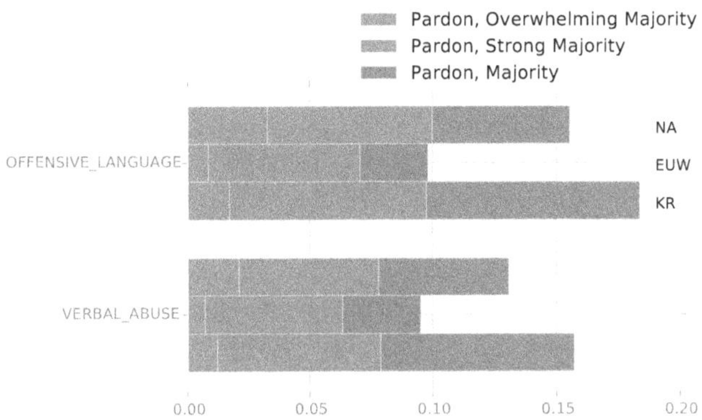

Figure 5. The percentage of cyberbullying reports that result in pardons for each region.

To test *[H3.1] Due to a more group-success oriented socio-political environment, cyberbullying offenses are less likely to be punished in Korea than in other regions*, we examine the rate of pardons for cyberbullying offenses in the different regions.

Figure 5 plots the percentage of cyberbullying reports (offensive language and verbal abuse) that result in pardons for each region. 17.1% of such reports are pardoned in KR, compared to 14.3% in NA and 9.7% in EUW. A Chi-Square test with Yates continuity correction reveals the effect of region on pardons in those categories is significant ($\chi^2(2, N = 3{,}108{,}172) = 24123.3, p < .0001$). Thus H3.1 is supported.

As we reviewed in previous section, a likely explanation for this is due to the *Wang-tta* concept in KR. Particularly invasive in gaming culture, *Wang-tta* probably leads to reviewers empathizing not with the cyberbullying victim, but rather the alleged toxic player who verbalized his displeasure with the victim's performance.

To test *[H3.2] Reports on toxic behavior that largely affects the result of the match are more often submitted in Korea than in other regions*, we compare the percentage of reports for intentional feeding or assisting enemy across regions since such toxic behavior directly contradicts the group-success goal.

We find support for H3.2 by looking at the mean and median of reports for assisting enemy or intentional feeding coming from teammates (1.482 and 1, 1.714 and 2, and 1.75 and 2 for NA, EUW, and KR, respectively). A Kruskal-Wallis test reveals the effect of region on reports coming from teammates is significant ($\chi^2(2) = 31175.43, p < .0001$). A post-hoc test using Mann-Whitney tests with Bonferroni correction confirms the significant differences between NA and EUW ($p < .0001, r = .129$), between NA and KR ($p < .0001, r = .148$), and between EUW and KR ($p < .0001, r = .02$).

We move on to testing *[H3.3] Reports on behavior that largely affects the result of the match are more likely to be punished in Korea than in other regions*. We plot the percentage of punish decisions for behavior that directly affects the result of the match for each region in Figure 6. While such offenses are heavily punished in each region (over 80%), we do find a difference. Korean reviewers are more likely to perceive assisting enemy and intentional feeding as severe toxic playing with much higher levels of agreement than other regions (for Punish, Overwhelming Majority, KR: 48%, NA: 27%, EUW: 24%), which is affirmative support for H3.3. A Chi-Square test with Yates continuity correction reveals the effect of region on the percentage of Punish, Overwhleming Majority in those categories is significant ($\chi^2(2, N = 1{,}955{,}297) = 83593.08, p < .0001$).

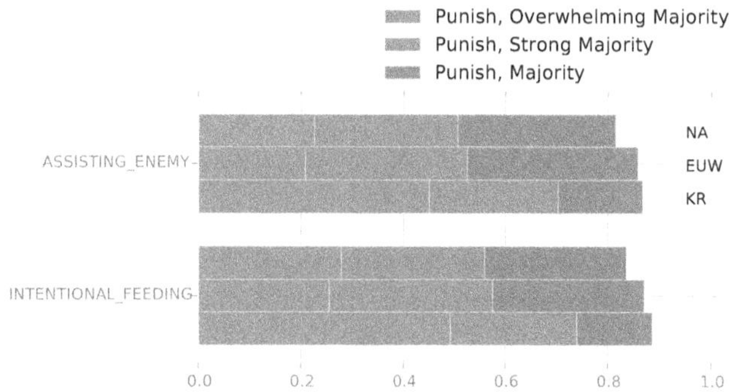

Figure 6. The percentage of reports for behavior that directly affects the result of the match for each region that results in a punishment.

Team-cohesion and Performance

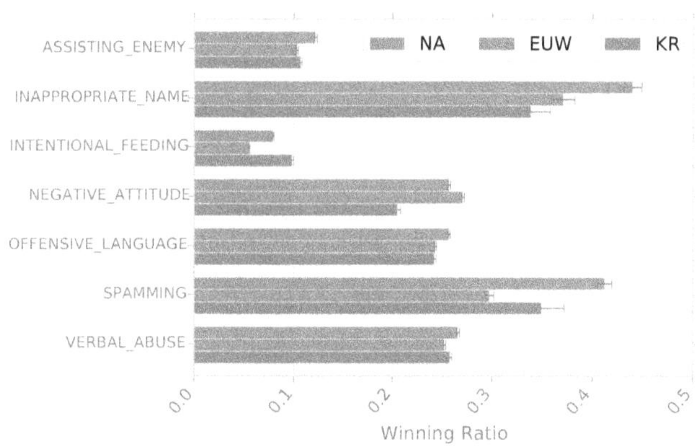

Figure 7. The winning ratio for each category of toxic behavior with 95% confidence interval.

To test *[H4.1] More reports come from matches where the accused was on the losing team*, we plot the winning ratio with 95% confidence interval for the different categories of toxic play reported in Figure 7. From the figure, it is immediately apparent that winning ratio is clearly below than 50%, even though LoL uses a match making system similar to Elo ranking [24] that attempts to match players in a manner where there is a 50% chance of winning for each team. In particular, we see that the winning ratio for intentional feeding and assisting the enemy are extremely low (under 15% for both). Therefore, more reports come from losing teams so that the observed winning ratio is less than 0.5. H4.1 is supported.

As we mentioned in the research question section, lower team cohesion leads to lower performance. Or, a poor performance might trigger toxic behavior like cyberbullying and also might be a cause for the high number of reports involving a losing team. Cyberbullying offenses are explained by attribution theory in that when a toxic player recognizes a poor performance (e.g., even though the match is not decided, his team is losing) he looks for someone other than himself to place blame. Related to this, for example in the spamming category, players that were on the losing side of the match might attempt to attribute the loss to a another member of the team and attempt to punish him via the reporting system.

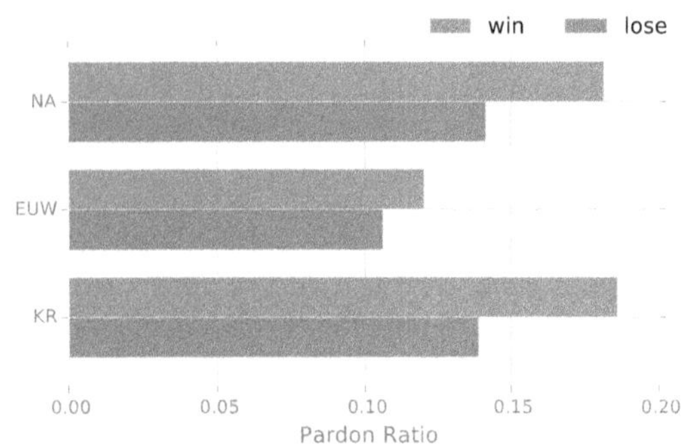

Figure 8. Pardoned ratio when losing vs. winning

To test *[H4.2] There are more cases pardoned when the accused was on the losing team than on the winning team*, we plot the pardoned ratio when the accused toxic player was on the winning or losing side. Figure 8 plots the breakdown of pardon and punish decisions as a function of whether the accused toxic player was on the winning or losing side. If people regard somewhat innocuous factors as significant reasons of defeat and report it as toxic behavior, the pardoned ratio for defeats will be higher than that for wins. As seen in Figure 8, by contrast, we find that the proportion of being pardoned by crowds when losing is less than that when winning. Thus, H4.2 is *not* supported, and in fact the opposite is the case.

DISCUSSION AND CONCLUSION

In this work we explored toxic playing and the reaction to it via crowdsourced decisions using a few million observed reports. Our large-scale dataset enables an opportunity to explore several compelling theories from sociology and psychology that discuss the "whys" of toxic behavior.

We first showed that there is relatively low participation in reporting toxic behavior and reconfirmed the impact of anonymity in CMC and cyberspace. This finding underlines the difficulties in relying solely on voluntary player reports. For example, in Facebook there is a button to report a comment that violates cyber-etiquette. The low degree of participation for social control we found raises a fundamental question about the design considerations of such report-based systems: if relatively few "victims" voluntarily report such behavior, how effective can it truly be? Interestingly, our finding that an explicit request to report toxic behavior significantly increases the likelihood of reporting indicates that actively encouraging reporting should be considered in the design of systems to address toxic behavior.

Next, we examined the vague nature of toxic behavior. This issue is repeatedly observed in online games [34]. With over 10% of cases being pardoned in the Tribunal, it is clear that crowdsourcing using experienced players is useful in protecting innocent victims who are wrongly reported by other players due to poor gaming skills or aggressive (but not toxic) linguistic behavior. The Tribunal could further improve the quality and efficiency of crowdsourced workers via several proposed mechanisms for quality control in crowdsourced systems and augmentation with machine-learning solutions [11].

We then moved on to how group setting might influence reporting behavior. We quantitatively show that in-group favoritism and out-group hostility increase or decrease the willingness to report. This is rooted in competition among players. Since competition is a common game design element for enjoyment [52], our findings are applicable to most online games. Even though a given game might not have a form of team competitions, sense of belonging is frequently derived from a small group of players, called guilds or parties in MMORPGs [22]. In a broad sense, homophily can appear not only in an explicit group but also in an implicit group [37]. The current work portends possible bias of observed reports in such settings.

Most online games allow interactions between players. In this environment toxic playing is a serious issue that degrades user experience. Our work offers understanding of toxic playing and its victims based on LoL data, but much of the mechanics involved are typical game elements not unique to LoL. We also believe that with the growing trend of gamification (e.g., as applied to citizen science) our findings have broader application than traditional entertainment gaming. In fact, some gamified citizen science projects have already experience low level toxicity [7]. As designers and scientists import more and more gaming elements into their systems, they will most assuredly be accompanied by less desirable elements of gaming culture, such as toxic behavior.

We also see similarities between LoL and online communities. Online communities, e.g., Reddit, allow anonymous user identities. They use unique user names which are not linked to real identity. Although there are differences between forms of toxic playing and cyberbullying in online communities, the disconnect between real and virtual world is a common root that both cyberbullying and toxic playing stem from.

Beyond gaming, our work deepens understanding of team conflicts in general. This has great potential because teams are an essential building block of modern organizations. Also, in the current globally distributed workspace, collaboration through an electronic channel is pervasive. This often results in a goal-oriented group that lacks *social* connections. Such settings can accelerate the tendency to blame others, further escalated by the individuals' unfamiliarity with remote partners [19]. Competitive games in general, and the LoL Tribunal in particular, are thus a valuable asset to capture group conflicts in the virtual space and test effective treatments for them. We believe that solutions for toxic play in team competition online games could have huge impact for real-world scenarios, and not just virtual spaces.

For the overall CHI community, while ethnography is traditionally considered as one of the best methods to understand people, we show that studying human behavior with big data and testable hypotheses works well. We hope that this helps accelerate the discovery of big data's value by the CHI community.

Caveats and Limitations

Although our findings confirm several theories on cyberbullying and toxic behavior, we note that there are limitations and caveats that must be considered. First, although there is reason to believe that gamers generally behave the same in-game as they do in the real-world [12], the fact remains that our dataset is drawn from a game. At minimum, this means applying our results to other domains must be done carefully [30]. Further, our findings are from LoL in particular, and there are domain specific concerns that might not be present in other games even within the same genre. For example, SMITE is currently the 3rd most popular MOBA in the market, but completely lacks an all-talk chat mode. Additionally, SMITE and Dota 2 (the 2nd most popular MOBA) both have integrated voice communication, which might intensify or soften cyberbullying with feelings of social presence.

Next, the social network structure among players, "friend" relationships, is not considered in this work due to lack of data. We thus do not incorporate social relationship among specific players in building our hypotheses. As recent studies reveal that playing together with friends influences performance and toxicity [36, 45], we believe that more detailed data including players' social networks would enable testing of more sophisticated hypotheses.

Finally, although our dataset is large-scale and quite rich, it is anonymized and thus prevents us from knowing how toxic players behaved before and after the matches were aggregated into their case and a decision being made. We also lack knowledge of how other players in the game typically behave. Thus, while we were able to provide significant support for several theories, there are questions for which answers continues to elude us.

ACKNOWLEDGMENTS

This material is based on research sponsored by DARPA under agreement number FA8750-12-2-0107. The U.S. Government is authorized to reproduce and distribute reprints for Governmental purposes notwithstanding any copyright notation thereon.

REFERENCES

1. IWillDominate Tribunal permaban & eSports competition ruling. http://goo.gl/2qHH4I.
2. Player tally for League of Legends surges. http://goo.gl/YxjSjb.
3. Reporting a player. https://support.riotgames.com/hc/en-us/articles/201752884-Reporting-a-Player.
4. Riot Games' League of Legends officially becomes most played pc game in the world. http://goo.gl/iqrru6.
5. Riot Games releases awesome League of Legends infographic. http://goo.gl/bDKLnO.
6. Suicide of Megan Meier. http://goo.gl/MHgLJG.
7. To anyone who seen the recent popular post about a game called Foldit. This is why you should avoid it. http://redd.it/2n97b1.
8. Aggression, R., and Roles, P. M. Cyberbullying in Japan. *Cyberbullying in the Global Playground: Research from International Perspectives* (2011), 183.
9. Barlińska, J., et al. Cyberbullying among adolescent bystanders: role of the communication medium, form of violence, and empathy. *Journal of Community & Applied Social Psychology 23*, 1 (2013), 37–51.
10. Blackburn, J., et al. Branded with a scarlet "C": cheaters in a gaming social network. In *WWW* (2012).
11. Blackburn, J., and Kwak, H. STFU NOOB! predicting crowdsourced decisions on toxic behavior in online games. In *WWW* (2014).
12. Boellstorff, T. *Coming of age in Second Life: An anthropologist explores the virtually human*. Princeton University Press, 2008.
13. Carron, A. V. Cohesion and performance in sport. *Journal of Sport & Exercise Psychology 24* (2002), 168–188.
14. Chee, F. The games we play online and offline: Making Wang-tta in Korea. *Popular Communication 4*, 3 (2006), 225–239.
15. Chen, V. H.-H., Duh, H. B.-L., and Ng, C. W. Players who play to make others cry: The influence of anonymity and immersion. In *ACE* (2009).
16. Chesney, T., et al. Griefing in virtual worlds: causes, casualties and coping strategies. *Information Systems Journal 19*, 6 (2009), 525–548.
17. Christopherson, K. M. The positive and negative implications of anonymity in Internet social interactions:"on the Internet, nobody knows you're a dog". *Computers in Human Behavior 23*, 6 (2007), 3038–3056.
18. Cox, T. H., Lobel, S. A., and McLeod, P. L. Effects of ethnic group cultural differences on cooperative and competitive behavior on a group task. *Academy of management journal 34*, 4 (1991), 827–847.
19. Cramton, C. D. The mutual knowledge problem and its consequences for dispersed collaboration. *Organization science 12*, 3 (2001), 346–371.
20. Denant-Boemont, L., Masclet, D., and Noussair, C. N. Punishment, counterpunishment and sanction enforcement in a social dilemma experiment. *Economic theory 33*, 1 (2007), 145–167.

21. Diener, E. Deindividuation, self-awareness, and disinhibition. *Journal of Personality and Social Psychology 37*, 7 (1979), 1160.
22. Ducheneaut, N., et al. The life and death of online gaming communities: A look at guilds in World of Warcraft. In *CHI* (2007).
23. Einhorn, H. J., and Hogarth, R. M. Judging probable cause. *Psychological Bulletin 99*, 1 (1986), 3.
24. Elo, A. E. *The rating of chessplayers, past and present*, vol. 3. Batsford London, 1978.
25. Felps, W., Mitchell, T. R., and Byington, E. How, when, and why bad apples spoil the barrel: Negative group members and dysfunctional groups. *Research in organizational behavior 27* (2006), 175–222.
26. Foo, C. Y., and Koivisto, E. M. I. Defining grief play in MMORPGs: player and developer perceptions. In *ACE* (2004).
27. Hofstede, G. H. *Culture's consequences: Comparing values, behaviors, institutions and organizations across nations*. Sage, 2001.
28. Huang, Y., et al. Functional or social?: exploring teams in online games. In *CSCW* (2013), 399–408.
29. Kavussanu, M., and Ntoumanis, N. Participation in sport and moral functioning: Does ego orientation mediate their relationship? *Journal of Sport and Exercise Psychology 25* (2003), 501–518.
30. Keegan, B., et al. Sic transit gloria mundi virtuali?: promise and peril in the computational social science of clandestine organizing. In *WebSci* (2011).
31. Kirman, B., et al. Exploring mischief and mayhem in social computing or: how we learned to stop worrying and love the trolls. In *CHI EA* (2012).
32. Kwak, H., and Blackburn, J. Linguistic analysis of toxic behavior in an online video game. In *EGG workshop* (2014).
33. Latane, B., and Darley, J. M. *The unresponsive bystander: Why doesn't he help?* Appleton-Century Crofts New York, 1970.
34. Lin, H., and Sun, C.-T. The "White-Eyed" player culture: Grief play and construction of deviance in MMORPGs. In *DiGRA Conference* (2005).
35. Marsden, P. V., and Campbell, K. E. Measuring tie strength. *Social forces 63*, 2 (1984), 482–501.
36. Mason, W., and Clauset, A. Friends FTW! friendship and competition in Halo: Reach. In *CSCW* (2013).
37. McPherson, M., Smith-Lovin, L., and Cook, J. M. Birds of a feather: Homophily in social networks. *Annual review of sociology* (2001), 415–444.
38. Mullen, B., and Copper, C. The relation between group cohesiveness and performance: An integration. *Psychological bulletin 115*, 2 (1994), 210.
39. Naito, T., and Gielen, U. Bullying and Ijime in Japanese schools. In *Violence in Schools*. Springer, 2005.
40. Naquin, C. E., and Tynan, R. O. The team halo effect: Why teams are not blamed for their failures. *Journal of Applied Psychology 88*, 2 (2003), 332.
41. Ommundsen, Y., Roberts, G., Lemyre, P., and Treasure, D. Perceived motivational climate in male youth soccer: Relations to social–moral functioning, sportspersonship and team norm perceptions. *Psychology of Sport and Exercise 4*, 4 (2003), 397–413.
42. Paulhus, D. L. *Measurement and control of response bias*. Academic Press, 1991.
43. Reicher, S. D., Spears, R., and Postmes, T. A social identity model of deindividuation phenomena. *European Review of Social Psychology 6*, 1 (1995), 161–198.
44. Roese, N. J. Counterfactual thinking. *Psychological bulletin 121*, 1 (1997), 133.
45. Shores, K. B., He, Y., Swanenburg, K. L., Kraut, R., and Riedl, J. The identification of deviance and its impact on retention in a multiplayer game. In *CSCW* (2014).
46. Smith, P. K., et al. Cyberbullying: Its nature and impact in secondary school pupils. *Journal of Child Psychology and Psychiatry 49*, 4 (2008), 376–385.
47. Szell, M., Lambiotte, R., and Thurner, S. Multirelational organization of large-scale social networks in an online world. *PNAS 107*, 31 (2010), 13636–13641.
48. Thompson, P. What's fueling the flames in cyberspace? a social influence model. *Communication and cyberspace: Social interaction in an electronic environment* (1996), 293–311.
49. Tönnies, F. *Gemeinschaft und gesellschaft*. Springer, 2012.
50. Triandis, H. C., et al. Individualism and collectivism: Cross-cultural perspectives on self-ingroup relationships. *Journal of personality and Social Psychology 54*, 2 (1988), 323.
51. Turner, J. C. Social comparison and social identity: Some prospects for intergroup behaviour. *European journal of social psychology 5*, 1 (1975), 1–34.
52. Vorderer, P., Hartmann, T., and Klimmt, C. Explaining the enjoyment of playing video games: The role of competition. In *ACE* (2003).
53. Warner, D. E., and Ratier, M. Social context in massively-multiplayer online games (MMOGs): Ethical questions in shared space. *International Review of Information Ethics 4*, 7 (2005).
54. Weibel, D., et al. Playing online games against computer- vs. human-controlled opponents: Effects on presence, flow, and enjoyment. *Computers in Human Behavior 24*, 5 (Sept. 2008), 2274–2291.
55. Weiner, B. A cognitive (attribution)-emotion-action model of motivated behavior: An analysis of judgments of help-giving. *Journal of Personality and Social Psychology 39*, 2 (1980), 186.

Computer-Enabled Project Spaces: Connecting with Palestinian Refugees across Camp Boundaries

George Yerousis[1], Konstantin Aal[2], Thomas von Rekowski[2], David W. Randall[2], Markus Rohde[2], Volker Wulf[2]

[1]Birzeit University
PO Box 14, Birzeit
West Bank, Palestine
gyerousis@birzeit.edu

[2]University of Siegen,
57068 Siegen, Germany
[konstantin.aal, thomas.vonrekowski, dave.randall, markus.rohde, volker.wulf]@uni-siegen.de

ABSTRACT

Come_IN computer clubs are an established approach to support inter-cultural and inter-generational learning in German neighborhoods. We explore the adaptation of the come_IN concept to the Palestinian context as a means to bridge the social and economic divide that has plagued West Bank society for a period of more than six decades. Social exclusion, political conflicts and prolonged military occupation have kept the refugee camps in a perpetual state of marginalization. In this paper we report on our work in Al Amari– a Palestinian refugee camp adjacent to the city of Ramallah. We examine how the computer club enables the emergence of social ties among residents of the camp and university students acting as tutors. Even though the ties are small-scale and informal, they have the potential to generate new and wider opportunities for exchange that may eventually support more social integration between the camp's marginalized population and the wider Palestinian population.

Author Keywords

Learning; Computer Club; Communities; Integration; Empowerment.

ACM Classification Keywords

K.4.m. Computers and Society: Miscellaneous.

INTRODUCTION

In this paper, we report on, and evaluate, attempts to introduce the come_IN computer club concept to a marginalized community, a refugee camp, in the West Bank in Palestine. Over the past 65 years, West Bank refugee camps have developed into marginalized dwellings with populations of up to 25.000 inhabitants. Over the years, a growing population of refugees has produced new socio-economic problems, which we can characterize as entailing a social and 'digital' divide, as a result of a complex relationship with the rest of the Palestinian population and the wider geo-political situation.

CHI 2015, April 18 - 23 2015, Seoul, Republic of Korea
Copyright is held by the owner/author(s). Publication rights licensed to ACM.
ACM 978-1-4503-3145-6/15/04...$15.00
http://dx.doi.org/10.1145/2702123.2702283

Computer clubs have long been aimed at the so-called 'digital divide', and have generally been seen as bridging a socio-technical problem (see e.g.[10]). As Helsper [8] has pointed out in the context of the UK, the socially disadvantaged are the very people who are likely to be digitally disadvantaged. She estimates that this 'dual exclusion' means that the disadvantaged are seven times less likely to engage with the Internet than others. Seven years after its establishment in Germany (see e.g. [20]), aiming to address issues of exclusion in a specifically multicultural context, the come_IN network has extended its reach to this different and more complex socio-economic context. Whilst the German computer clubs engage with children and parents of mainly German and Turkish origin, come_IN clubs in Palestine cater to deeply marginalized refugees whose daily struggle is to live and survive in poor and precarious living conditions. The extension of the come_IN network into Palestine came as a result of a research-driven cooperation and partnership between Siegen and Birzeit Universities.

By leveraging and appropriating ICT, we suggest that Palestinian refugees may be empowered to become more resourceful and knowledgeable agents of positive and meaningful change in their communities. Bridging the digital divide could also help them forge closer linkages among themselves – across different camps, villages, and cities – promoting their integration into society and allowing them to positively engage in the Israeli-Palestinian conflict-to-peace transformation process [1] (See [24] for description of more overtly political activity).

In this paper, we examine the establishment of a community-based learning space in the Al-Amari refugee camp. The paper contributes to an existing literature on community informatics and HCI4D by examining efforts to foster community integration in a particularly difficult and 'socially disorganised' setting. We describe how a diverse team of young university student volunteers was mobilized to plan, articulate, and run a technology-based youth mentoring program in the club. The tutors had to learn to tackle numerous problems as a result of the unique social, cultural, and political context of the refugee camp. As a team they had to overcome challenges (e.g. limited resources) and make sure that the program stayed relevant. Furthermore, we describe how the volunteers utilized their capabilities, often exploring new topics that are not related to their university studies to try to positively engage a wider base of in-camp children in the program and to sustain their level of interest. We also discuss how the social relevance of the technology program in the clubhouse helped the in-camp community to embrace it. The 'learning experience' we describe here, entails a great deal more than skills acquisition and rather problematizes functional or goal-driven approaches to educational technology in a context such as this, even when value-based. The benefits that accrued from the efforts we describe could not have been entirely anticipated, and neither could some of the problems we encountered.

STATE OF THE ART

While there is ample and seminal research investigating the positive implications of computer-supported community-based learning spaces in diverse urban and rural settings, little attention has yet been paid to contexts in which the targeted underprivileged communities are "forced" refugees living in isolated but open quasi-temporary enclaves.

Learning by designing, cultivating a community of learners, fostering respect and trust, and encouraging youth to build on their own interests were the guiding principles (set forth by MIT's Media Lab) by which the first Computer Clubhouse was established in Boston in 1993 [18]. Grounded in the fields of education, developmental and social psychology, and cognitive science, the Computer Clubhouse model has grown to a network of more than 100 active youth community learning centers across 20 countries around the world [26].

Consisting of six computer clubs spread across four cities, the come_IN network in Germany is inspired by the original clubhouse concept but follows a fundamentally different approach by focusing on cross-cultural interaction between the members. Mainly located in elementary schools, the intercultural community spaces were established to foster learning, social networks, and integration in German neighborhoods with a substantial Turkish migrant population [20, 22]. As a result of cooperation between Birzeit and Siegen Universities, the first come_IN computer club was established in the Jalazone refugee camp. Weekly project activities targeting school-age youngsters have captured the attention of Jalazone parents as well as teachers from the two UNRWA (United Nations Relief and Works Agency) schools serving the camp community [1].

There are relatively few studies dealing with computer supported learning and community building under the specific conditions of Palestinian refugee camps. Wahbeh [24] analyzed a number of cases that involve students and teachers in public, private and UNRWA schools in the West Bank, where institutions like the Intel Club performed training courses for young people. These computer labs were not connected to the Internet due to budgetary reasons, so the pupils had to rely on both the clubs and Internet cafés to use the computers and otherwise access the Internet for doing their homework.

The digital divide between the students in a camp and those outside is still obvious. The term "digital divide" was defined by Mehra [12] as "the troubling gap between those who use computers and the internet and those who do not." To narrow this divide and to empower students in a refugee camp, Sawhney [19] hosted storytelling workshops over a period of three years. The young people in refugee camps have stories to tell and reflect a lot on "their identity, heritage, environment, and life experience" [ibid]. Storytelling can also be used to work through intractable conflicts; this enables people with traumatic social experiences to digest these experiences and learn to live with the events. Working with a Palestinian- Israeli group, Bar-On [4] demonstrated in a similar manner that storytelling often helps in dealing with painful events.

Asthana & Havandjian [3] conducted a hermeneutic exploration of "how young people in refugee camps in Palestine appropriate and reconfigure old and new media in the process of creating personal and social narratives. Focusing on Palestinian identity and selfhood, the project explores how and in what specific ways children and young people engage with media forms to express their ideas of politics, citizenship, and democratic participation." [2] For them [Palestinian refugee camp youth], citizenship is as much about consensus as it is about 'conflictual' engagement [13, 14]. Youth empowerment in Palestine was also addressed by Hart, exploring "the challenges of promoting the participation of children and youth in the face of immense political, physical, social and cultural constraints." [7]

Nevertheless, and despite this work, no evaluation has been conducted relating specifically to the potential of intercultural and inter-generational computer clubs in refugee camps – in particular long term forced camps. In this paper we focus on a second come_IN computer club established in the Al Amari refugee camp. We specifically analyze the emergence of social ties between the camp population and the tutors from Birzeit University as a fundamental feature of the 'learning experience'.

RESEARCH SETTING

The continuous provision of humanitarian services to West Bank refugee camps over a period of sixty years has not significantly alleviated a chronic state of isolation, exclusion, and poverty among the refugee population.

While the Palestinian Authority (PA), the West Bank government, maintains the rule of law in cities, refugee camps remain devoid of enforceable laws and regulations and are sometimes regarded as places of illegitimacy. Refugee camp communities often rely on their own internal actors to resolve their grievances and conflicts. Urban Palestinians generally anticipate negative interactions with refugee camp residents due to perceived differences in behavior, morals, values, and attitudes. As a result, refugee camp spaces are regarded by many Palestinians as probable hostile places.

Al-Amari: A Palestinian refugee camp in the West Bank

A total of 59 refugee camps are administered by the United Nations Relief and Works Agency (UNRWA) in the West Bank, Gaza, Syria, Jordan and Lebanon. Six and a half decades after its establishment as one of the first temporary encampments for those who were forcefully displaced and rendered homeless during the 1948 Arab-Israeli war, Al-Amari refugee camp remains the confined living space of some 12,061 Palestinian refugees [16].

Located at the southwestern urban periphery of the West Bank's city of Ramallah, Al-Amari refugee camp is a hostage to the complex and unstable political and military situation characterized by historical conflict between Israel and Palestine (see e.g. [6]; [9]). There can be no doubt that the ongoing conflict has been punctuated with prolonged periods of suffering in the camps and elsewhere (see also [2] and [21]).Though the camp falls within the Palestinian Authority (PA) controlled territories and is adjacent to Al-Masyoun- a very affluent Ramallah neighborhood- it continues to be an underdeveloped enclave under the humanitarian responsibility of the UNRWA. Rudimentary aid services (limited by resources) are provided to the camp residents, encompassing basic education, essential health care, and microfinance for income-generation purposes.

Al-Amari refugee camp's internal power structure is characterized by a complex tapestry of non-state actors- unlike the situation in other PA controlled areas- and which includes the popular committee of camp services, political factions – mainly Fatah, the women's activity center, youth activity center, tribal council (conciliation committee), and UNRWA services administration – with the popular committee being the most salient actor.

The scarcity of gainful employment opportunities and the absence of thriving economic enterprises within the camp are manifested in a high unemployment rate (8% higher than in the rest of the occupied Palestinian territories [15]) and a persistent dependence on civil service employment in the Palestinian Authority, UNRWA jobs, and irregular daily-wage labor. Unregulated vertical and horizontal residential expansion has led to a further increase in cramped and crowded camp conditions giving rise to overall poor hygiene.

In Al-Amari, it turns out that almost all of the schools after-school activities are planned and run by an active youth community center, located inside the camp. The Palestinian Child Center (PCC) is a community outreach non-governmental organization that caters to school-age youngsters up to grade twelve. This center is seen as the only safe and productive place for in-camp school kids to participate in meaningful extra-curricular after-school activities. The center's director and two administrative staff have full-time day jobs and run the center's day-to-day activities as volunteers in the afternoon. Much of the support network of the center consists of visiting volunteers who are working for international organizations on short-term assignments. Unfortunately, the capacity building activities that they carry out in the camp are short-lived and often end abruptly as the volunteers' work with their affiliate organizations comes to an end or when the foreign volunteers' visas expire. This has caused many of the youth programs at the center to become fragmented, thus undermining their desired outcomes and overall impact.

Figure 1: Al-Amari refugee camp's poor housing conditions

RESEARCH METHOD

For better insights into the daily routines and practices of a refugee camp, Participatory Action Research (PAR) by Kemmis & McTaggert [11] was the chosen methodological framework. We were active agents in the whole process of establishing and operating the computer club (choosing the right partner and location, preparing the sessions and manage the work with the volunteers and children). In accordance with Tacchi et al's [23] views on 'ethnographic action research' we adopted conventional observational strategies to guide our research and the action research framework to link those observations back to the planning of activities. Observations were conducted over a period of 52 months, from the foundation of the first computer club in May 2010 to September 2014. The first author visited both clubs once a week and was accompanied by the other authors during their visits to the West Bank; at least every six months with a total stay of 16 weeks. During these visits, our researchers attended, observed and took part in the weekly club sessions. In meetings and workshops with the local tutors they tried to deepen their understanding of the situation in the refugee camp. Every evening and after the sessions, extensive documentation was written pertaining to the respective day; over 90 pages of protocols were collected.

In 2013, a native speaker carried out 13 semi-structured interviews and informal talks with the children from both computer clubs. The aim here was to triangulate with other observational data already collected and to get a better sense of the motivational elements that contribute to participation. It was felt that this number of interviews was adequate for those purposes. Children were asked about their experiences in the weekly sessions, their relationship with the tutors, and the influence of the club in their life. Additionally, the tutors wrote detailed protocols from the weekly session and collected feedback sheets from the children. The close relationship between the tutors and the computer club members helped to gain reliable perspectives on the club sessions and further project ideas. Other materials (e.g. drawings, project results, 3D-prints) were documented and collected for analysis.

EMPIRICAL FINDINGS

Sourcing a computer club hosting partner

The second computer club opened one year after the first one in Jalazone refugee camp. Exploring the potential of different refugee camps was the primary rationale behind setting up the second club. Al-Amari refugee camp was suggested by the Jalazone's popular camp committee. The reasoning was that both popular committees have previously had contact through playing soccer games.

Acting on their suggestion, the team of researchers visited Al-Amari on numerous occasions, discussing the computer club concept with the main actors. The team also talked to parents and spoke with children playing in the area. In-camp kids immediately provided the team with visions of how a computer clubhouse might look like while parents elaborated on expectations of possible functions and modes of operation. Not surprisingly, some parents expressed concerns regarding children's possible negative encounters with outsiders while others raised the issue of gender segregation, voicing their preference for keeping the sexes separate. Most people that we talked to feared that the computer club might potentially resemble the undesirable Internet cafés in which children could engage in unsupervised computer use (e.g. playing violent games, watching pornography).

There was, even so, some institutional support. In the Jalazone refugee camp, members of the popular camp committee had established a small non-governmental organization, 'Dima for Innovation', in order to bring new donor projects to the camp community and to host our first computer club. In Al-Amari, the Palestinian Child Center (PCC) – a relatively independent organization – showed interest and provided compelling evidence to suggest why they would be the most capable partner to host the computer club and to provide available personnel to facilitate the sessions. Connecting and working with reputable academic institutions was a key driver for the PCC to engage in the project. In a memorandum of understanding it was agreed that the academic partners would procure the hardware and source the mentoring team of volunteers to run weekly sessions for a period of one year, while the PCC would enable the physical environment by allocating the needed space. The PCC's genuine interest quickly materialized as the administration took the necessary steps to dedicate a room on the second floor of the building as the working space for the project. Previously, the room had been used as a neglected storage space for zero-value old computers and a few non-functional pieces of musical and office equipment. The PCC rehabilitated the room by painting the walls and adding some used tables and chairs.

Hardware architecture

After two years of usage, the thin client-based hardware configuration in Jalazone was functioning well and proved to be easy to maintain. We decided, therefore, to use the same system configuration for the new computer club in Al-Amari. The decision was also influenced by the relatively low initial investment cost of the thin client system along with the low total cost of ownership. Furthermore, the inability of the thin clients to fully function as a stand-alone computer station without the host computer makes them less prone to theft. Peripherals were also procured including a projector, a monochrome laser printer, and a flatbed scanner – the same equipment as in the Jalazone computer club. Expecting no more than 20 children to actively participate in the weekly sessions – as was the case in sessions taking place in the club in Jalazone – the initial plan was to encourage the participants to work on projects in groups of 2 or 3. The assumption was that twelve computer stations would be more than enough to serve all the participants.

Figure 2: One of the first girls-only sessions

However, children in the first instance did not want to work in groups, which meant there was a shortage of machines. Student volunteers tried to accommodate the children by bringing a few mini-laptops that Birzeit University (BZU) provided for this project (Figure 2) to the sessions. The mini-laptops were procured by BZU as part of an annual technology summer camp program for school-age children. In turn, this meant the laptops had to be shuttled back and forth between Al-Amari and Jalazone as needed. Furthermore, volunteers had to provide their own laptops for the children to use on a number of occasions. Children were unexpectedly demanding with regard to screen size and colour.

While the project coordinator was in the process of setting up the computer club in Jalazone, the community leaders had demanded that local ISP provide free Internet to the club. In Al-Amari, it happened that one of the camp's residents worked for a local ISP and, following a request from the PCC, his company provided a 1-year complimentary Internet access with a connection speed of 8 MB. The main ADSL line was installed in the PCC's administration office, and Internet access to the clubs' room was made available via a wireless repeater device. The student volunteers were able to replace the main wireless connection with a wired one and connect the two host computers to the Internet (Figure 3).

Figure 3: Internet connection in the computer club

Recruiting University student volunteers

Undergraduate Birzeit University students, working as volunteers, are the main driving force of the computer club weekly sessions and the mentoring that they deliver to the in-camp children remains a crucial factor in maintaining continuity of the program. The volunteer selection and screening process was extensive, and at many times the coordinator had to go through numerous iterations of students in order to source committed and capable volunteers.

The selection and screening process

Birzeit University requires every student to participate in a 120-hour mandatory community-service program. At the start of every fall and spring semester undergraduate students are recruited to become part of the new active mentoring team. The semi-formal selection process entails a simple "expression of interest" signup form followed by a face-to-face interview during which the student applicants are given the chance to talk about their interests, talents, previous volunteering work, and availability. Students who are residents of Al-Amari camp and are passionate about bringing meaningful positive change to their community are typically selected from the shortlist. After a second interview, 5-8 volunteers are chosen from the shortlist and are assigned to work in the computer club.

The case of one of our students, Sujood, a student of the Architectural Engineering department, indicates why the computer clubs were attractive for students. She had frequently participated in on-campus community service activities offering support for students with physical disabilities. However, she had dedicated less and less time in what had become to her *"monotonous on-campus volunteering work."* After a few months of working in the club in Al-Amari, Sujood describes the challenges that she encounters in the camp as *"a golden opportunity [to leverage her experiences in the refugee camp] to learn new skills and to sharpen existing ones."*

Exchange of experiences between volunteers

As the new university semester begins, a new round of selection processes is initiated. The successful candidates attend a "handover" workshop that is carried out in the refugee camp during which the alumni mentors pass over all important and relevant information and experiences to the new student volunteers (new mentors). We found that conducting such workshops is important for ensuring a seamless handover of responsibilities and an effective communication of the lessons learned to successive mentors. Maintaining continuity in the work is vital. To help boost and sustain their level of engagement and motivation, laptops are provided to each of the volunteers and are handed over to the successive mentors during the handover session.

Group dynamics workshops take place on a bi-monthly basis during the course of the work with the computer clubs. These workshops are designed to bring up, discuss, and mitigate important issues related to the work of the volunteers. A substantial amount of time in the workshops is spent on reflection regarding past work and future planning of activities in the computer club, while capitalizing on and re-using past practical experience and knowledge. Personal safety issues in the camps were a frequent subject of discussion. As Sujood said during one of the workshops, *"When you arrive to the refugee camp, make sure you are walking in groups. Never wonder alone in the camp alleys."*

Implications of location

The close proximity of Al-Amari to the city of Ramallah makes it easily accessible by public transportation. As a result, almost all of the students who volunteered to work in the computer club were residents of Ramallah and its nearby villages. This was not the case in the Jalazone refugee camp; almost all of the volunteers working there were in-camp residents. Jalazone refugee camp is perceived to be dangerous because it borders the Israeli settlement of Beit El with frequent clashes erupting between Jalazone youngsters and the IDF [1]. Sourcing student volunteers from outside of Jalazone camp was difficult, as the journey to and from the refugee camp was perceived to be unsafe and to present unpredictable difficulties. Conditions are no more secure in the camp itself, where volunteers reported verbal harassment by groups of young people, and on one occasion even a physical attack.

Many of the newer student volunteers have already participated in volunteering opportunities such as assisting disabled students around campus or offering occasional support to caregivers in senior homes off campus. For them, even so, doing community service work in a refugee camp setting can be overwhelming as they find themselves immersed in trying to gain ground-level perspective of the socio-political intricacies involved.

Participants

Weekly face-to-face mentoring sessions in Al-Amari took place in the afternoon with a typical duration of an hour and a half. 5th and 6th grade children assemble in the computer club, sometimes more than 20 at one time, and meet with the group of university student volunteers. A specific challenge here was the absence of any wider perspective on the part of the children, allied to the pressures of their family and community existence. They preferred to tell personal stories grounded in immediate experience, such as of a family wedding that they attended with their parents, a football game that they participated in, or at one time, how the school's principal made jocular threatening remarks about the consequences if they did not attend a pre-planned in-school after-school activity. The large weekly fluctuation in the number of participants made it difficult to work continuously on their chosen projects.

Computer club projects

Children gather in groups of 2 or 3 and work alongside a student volunteer. They brainstorm and agree on a project that they will plan and execute. Projects typically last for 6-8 weeks and are created and developed using a common set of technology tools agreed upon in advance. A more detailed description of three projects can be found in what follows.

Scratch

The first few sessions after the clubhouse's opening were part of a Scratch project. Since no training material was available in the Arabic language, the research team developed a Scratch guide in close collaboration with the volunteers, after an introduction in the first club in Jalazone. The training material evolved over the whole course of the Scratch project and was adjusted based on experiences with the children (e.g. many pictures, easy language).

In the beginning the children worked individually to complete specific tasks assigned to them by the student tutor. Some tasks were designed to allow the children to explore Scratch's environment and user interface, while others were meant to introduce basic programming concepts, such as conditional or looping blocks. Later on, and as the sessions progressed, children were asked to come up with a simple game and attempt to create it using Scratch. Here, children agreed to work in groups of two, as they felt more confident of their ability to develop the game as a group. They continued to work in groups from this point onwards. At the end of the Scratch program, children presented their projects and received small gifts and certificates of participation.

Electric projects building kit

The IT Center of Excellence at Birzeit University had previously purchased 10 electricity-learning kits [27] for a technology summer camp. The research team was able to utilize these kits, especially adjusted to fit the needs of children. Working in groups of 2, the children completed hands-on experiments that were designed to introduce the basic laws of electricity and magnetism. Based on the detailed training material, the children managed to tinker with components of the kit without receiving help from the volunteers. Later in the sessions, children created projects ranging from solar powered devices to a simple piano. Solar-powered devices were put together utilizing some learning kits that were provided to the research team by the PCC.

Figure 4: Children working with electricity kit

3D printing

A simple 3D printrbot printer was brought to the clubhouse by a visiting team of two researchers from Siegen University. For a period of 6 weeks, children explored and tinkered with cubeteam [28], an online-tool to build models out of cubes. The research team created an open world, where the children worked collaboratively. They wanted to see the printer in action and take home their 3d creations on the same day after the session. As a result, they preferred to create simple objects that took little time to design and print. As one group of children came up with the idea to create names of children and print them, all the other groups followed suit. They also printed other things rooted in immediate experience such as a truck with a rocket on it or a mosque. After some sessions, the children wanted to go one step further in designing and printing by using round shapes, but the software's limitations prevented any shape other than cubes being printed.

Club Sessions

The weekly sessions follow the principle of informal learning with no fixed curriculum: starting with a time slot to play games, subsequent round-table discussions about the actual project and then project-related work. Facilitated by a university student volunteer, the session starts with the children gathering around a U-shaped set of tables and are given the chance to bring up an issue (often related to their community) that they think is important to them. Several times during the course of our work with the children, sessions took place out of the normal computer club working space - two times in open space inside the refugee camp as the children were developing solar-powered projects. The participants frequently asked questions about the volunteers' academic fields of study and at many times asked to visit the university. On one occasion, we were able to arrange for one of the children to come to Birzeit University and interact with the student volunteers as they were meeting to discuss and test the next technology tool that they wanted to utilize in the sessions.

When the project started, the PCC requested that we hold two sessions per week - one for the boys and another for the girls. In contrast, the administration of the Jalazone club had told us they wanted no separation; girls and boys would attend the same club session. All of the in-camp tutors at Al-Amari suggested separate sessions and for about 2 months, the student volunteers went to Al-Amari twice a week. As it happened, however, children were not willing to accept this gender segregation (with girls coming into the boys sessions and vice versa), so the frequency was reduced to once weekly sessions in which both girls and boys participated.

The continuity of the club sessions was also impacted by the uncertain political context. In early August of 2014, a young Palestinian man, resident in the Al-Amarai camp, partaking in protests near the settlement of Psagot was shot and killed. The individual was a close relative of Shahd - a 6th grade girl who diligently attended the computer club sessions. The killing galvanized thousands of people from the camp and the surrounding area as they marched in a monumental funeral procession. The clubhouse session had to be cancelled and the mentoring team visited Shahd's parents to offer condolences as the camp community mourned for 3 straight days. In early September of 2014, a 2nd resident of the Al-Amari was shot dead. The planned computer club session had to be cancelled yet again as tensions in and around the camp escalated.

Focusing on shared experiences

The precarious and often hostile circumstances in the camps are difficult for outsiders to grasp. For children with almost no exposure to the outside world, it is not surprising that their ideas about worthwhile activities are grounded in the immediacy of their experiences. Developing project ideas that were both educationally worthwhile and deemed to be relevant by the children was not easy. This epistemological gap inflected much of the planning. Nevertheless, and with much effort, we have seen at least on one occasion that the children and their mentors were able to develop individual and collectively shared values for project ideas through bringing up shared life experiences. In the next sub-section we describe how a mentor helped them to design and print architectural projects (instead of their initial desire to draw Barbie dolls in cubeteam and print them in 3D.)

Project idea shaped by socio-political shared experiences

Sujood describes the first few sessions working with the refugee children in Al-Amari camp as both fulfilling in terms of helping under-privileged communities and a learning experience for herself, as she had to explore and use new technologies and software as part of the mentoring sessions. Her own experiences prior to volunteering unsurprisingly shaped her commitments

Her parents had moved to the vibrant city of Ramallah in 2009 during the "Fayyadism" reform era to capitalize on the surging economic growth that has been reshaping the city and has opened up diverse and high-paying employment opportunities. Their relocation took place a month after prime minister Salam Fayyad issued "Palestine - Ending the Occupation, Establishing the State" - a 36-page work plan outlining his vision to establish a de facto Palestinian State as an "independent, democratic, and modern Arab state" and setting objectives and activities to "stimulate economic recovery and develop an enabling environment for business and investment."

Her parents' old house in Jenin is a few kilometers away from the Jenin refugee camp - the site of the worst conflict during the second intifada. Sujood was 9 years old when the camp saw the demolition of a huge portion of its infrastructure and the deaths of both 50 residents and 23 members of the IDF.

At BZU, Sujood became immersed in conceptualizing and designing modern structures for her architectural engineering classes. However, while brainstorming with Al-Amari camp children to come up with ideas for 3D design and printing projects, childhood memories of her life in Jenin were evoked and, coupled with her love of creative design, prompted her to ask her group of children to think about how they wanted to re-shape their poor living conditions. They all discussed the idea of re-building in-camp houses as a way of living a happy life. The 3D project that she and 3 twelve-year old girls conceived of and agreed upon entailed the design and 3D-print of a model of a shiny new house with a star-like roof structure (the star was meant to symbolize a happy new life)

Figure 5: Children and mentors discuss project ideas (left) Preliminary sketch of their 3D design and printing project (right)

The inception of the project's idea was partially inspired, she reported, by her graphic memories of the destruction of Jenin's refugee camp and the re-building efforts that took place afterwards and partly by her desire to see Al-Amari camp children live and thrive in spacious and healthy environment. From the children's point of view, the project was an imaginary house that the three of them wanted to live in as a replacement of their existing home.

Perceived fear of stigmatization

Active student tutors and their co-tutors come from diverse backgrounds and different study fields spanning numerous colleges across Birzeit University. While there are a handful of Birzeit University students who are residents of Al-Amari, only one of them - Hanin - jumped on board the group of volunteers in order to help run the weekly sessions. Even though she was born in the camp and was brought up there, this computer science student tended to - whenever possible - avoid mentioning Al-Amari refugee camp as the place of her domicile. Instead, she preferred to identify herself as a resident of the wider city of Ramallah because of the stereotypical negative connotation associated with the label "refugee camp resident" (bint al-mukhayyam) that she thinks could potentially limit her future endeavors and constrain her career opportunities.

Bissan is another student volunteer who is studying information technology at Birzeit University and lives in Qaddoura refugee camp. Situated on the sprawling outskirts of the city of Ramallah less than 1 km away from Al-Amari, Qaddoura refugee camp came into existence in 1948 but remains to this day unrecognized as an official UNRWA camp. In a discussion about the reluctance of university students who are residents of Al-Amari to join the mentoring team, Bissan believes that university male students who are residents of the nearby Al-Amari camp, are proud of their Palestinian identity and possess a heightened sense of nationalism but at the same time are concerned that their "camp resident" labeling might stigmatize them and hinder them from blending into the social structure of the university, considering that the overwhelming majority of its students are members of middle-class and urban elite families.

Positive interpersonal relationships

After spending a few weeks working on their projects - Scratch, for example - children sometimes got frustrated and wanted to give up as they found themselves unable to build sophisticated games. The volunteers discussed this issue and decided to bring new fun activities to some of the sessions. One idea was to bring a cake and celebrate the birthday of one of the children or one of the volunteers if it coincided with the day of the session. Volunteers took pictures with the children as they sang together and extinguished birthday candles. Photos were later posted and shared on Facebook. Another idea, suggested by one of the children, was for the team of volunteers to visit her house in the camp. The volunteers accepted the invitation, and the visit to Waad's house turned into a learning experience in expressive art. The child's father was a self-taught artist. He showcased his art creations and took time to tell the volunteers the story behind each of his oil paintings.

As time progressed and computer club sessions continued to take place on a weekly basis, more interpersonal relationships emerged. When the club house sessions would end, a few children would accompany the volunteers as they walked to the exit of the camp, chitchatting on the way about friends, family, and school and on one occasion one of the children invited some of the volunteers to have dinner at her parents' houses. "*Children [refugees] are children. They want to play their favorite sport and attend school,*" notes Amani, a computer systems engineering student and one of the volunteers who we interviewed. She explained that she had never been in a refugee camp before she started tutoring children in the computer club. After a full semester of working with the camp children, Amani said that she could no longer sense the social disparity between the in-camp children and those of her neighborhood.

DISCUSSION

Community anchor institutions

In-school computer clubhouses that are part of the German come_IN network are relatively straightforward to set up and manage as they benefit from the schools' existing infrastructure and leverage their in-house expertise. Equally, and even allowing for cultural differences between migrant communities and the host community, there is a shared knowledge of the wider world provided for by extensive and stable Western infrastructure (associated, for instance, with schooling). Adapting the same model to the West Bank refugee camps' context is challenging as unique material and socio-economic characteristics come into play. The schools in Al-Amari refugee camp are part of UNRWA's humanitarian aid system that was set up in 1949 to provide educational, health, and social services to Palestinian refugees. The UNRWA schools, however, could neither host the computer club nor offer any support due to financial constraints, centralized decision-making and bureaucratic inertia.

Local NGOs such as the children centers substituted for the schools as a host site for the computer clubs. However, these NGOs are often strongly aligned with the political structures in the camp - in both cases as parts of the Fatah movement. In Jalazone, the computers in the club were sometimes used for political purposes (e.g. designing and printing political handouts, promoting political messages on Facebook) [1]. In Al-Amari the PCC had a more independent stance. The children and youth centre pre-existed the computer club and already had a good reputation as a safe and trusted place.

Political Issues

Anchor institutions are sometimes held to be a vital part of community regeneration and development (see e.g. the Nettercenter at the University of Pennsylvania [29]). They, it is argued, enable communities to 'build from strength'. Here, however, weak community anchor institutions within the camp limited the options for possible hosting of the computer club, and geo- political factors seemed to disrupt the continuity of the sessions on a regular basis. The computer club that the research team established in the Jalazone refugee camp in mid 2012 exemplifies many of the difficulties. The camp is adjacent to Beit El – an Israeli settlement and active military outpost that - according to a '*Peace Now*' report – stands on private Palestinian land [17].

Whatever one's stance on Arab- Israeli conflict, the fact is that the Jalazone clubhouse sessions had to be frequently cancelled as violent clashes erupted between in-camp youngsters who threw stones and burnt tires, and the IDF who responded with the firing of tear gas, rubber-coated bullets

Fortunately, Al-Amari does not directly border any Israeli settlements and the assumption is was that clubhouse sessions would less likely be interrupted as a result of violent confrontations with the Israeli army. However, this assumption turned out to be false (see above).

Mutual benefit for the volunteers and children

Community work is mandatory for every student of Birzeit University; most students, understandably, choose easy tasks (e.g. planting trees). Like most Palestinians from mainstream urban society, the volunteers working in the computer club never had visited a refugee camp before and very rarely knew anyone living in there. Our project in Al Amari allowed the students to explore a refugee camp relatively close to Ramallah and positioned in a fairly safe location. Running the club helped them to understand the conditions and situation of refugees, who are often living next door to their villages or urban neighbourhoods in very different circumstances. The children benefited from the mentoring program by getting the opportunity to work and learn together with the student volunteers. In the hostile refugee camp environment, academic role models are uncommon; the volunteers can be seen as new role models – establishing a link between camp and university. There is a very real sense in which mutual learning went on. Students became a great deal more aware of the conditions under which refugees often have to live and of the challenges associated with that. Children were exposed to points of view, and experiences, that they all-too-rarely experienced otherwise.

CONCLUSION

As Baumer and Silverman [5] have noted, CHI has seldom dealt with 'when not to design' and has failed to deal on a systematic basis with the prospect that computer solutions may do more harm than good. Our point is precisely that understanding how technology is contextually appropriated over a period of time is one way to deal with the complex issue of how technology, culture and educational experience may intersect in difficult and fragmented circumstances.

Connecting volunteers with an academic background and children from refugee camps has been shown to positively impinge on both partners: children may extend their perspective over the boundaries of the refugee camp while acquiring new skills and contacts; the student volunteers gain insights about the reality of the refugee camps and gain a better understanding the needs and struggles of the camp inhabitants. This is evidently not a function of sophisticated technological development but of a mutual learning process concerning the conditions of life experienced within a community and the possibilities for engagement, possibilities, which exist but are constrained by context. While the regularity of the computer club sections, for instance, is severely impacted by the political context, the shared activities still seem to create social ties and elements of common practice both within the group of student volunteers and also among children in the camp. These joint activities over time have an impact on collective identity and have a beneficial effect on perceptions of a stigmatized group.

Stevens et al. [22] assumed that computers and their potential social attributes could serve as an attractor to motivate actors to work on common projects. The appeal of computers definitely plays an important role in bringing together the children and convincing the head of PCC to join our efforts. However, the students may be less strongly motivated by the challenges of computing. Tutoring the computer club in Al Amari offered a relatively safe way to gain experiences with the refugee camps' population – a population which is strongly marginalized in the Palestinian society.

ACKNOWLEDGMENTS

The research for this paper has been supported by the German Federal Foreign Office. We are indebted to Irina Shklovski for invaluable suggestions for improvement. We also want to thank Adham Swedan, Birzeit University, for taking the photos printed here and the other volunteers for supporting us in the computer clubs. We would particularly like to thank Kai Schubert for his crucial work in establishing these computer clubs.

REFERENCES

1. Aal, K., Yerousis, G., Schubert, K., Hornung, D., Stickel, O., and Wulf, V. Come_in@palestine: adapting a german computer club concept to a Palestinian refugee camp. In Proc. CABS 2014, ACM Press (2014), 111-120.
2. Al-Husseini, J. UNRWA and its needs. Position Paper by Ibrahim Abu-Lughod Institute of International Studies. Birzeit University, (April 2011).
3. Asthana, S. and Havandjian, N.R. Youth Media Imaginiaries in Palestine: A Hermeneutic Exploration. *European Scientific Journal 9*, 10 (2014).
4. Bar-On, D. and Kassem, F. Storytelling as a Way to Work Through Intractable Conflicts: The German-Jewish Experience and Its Relevance to the Palestinian-Israeli Context. Journal of Social Issues 60, 2 (2004), 289-306
5. Baumer, E. and Silberman, M. 2011. When the implication is not to design (technology). Proceedings of CHI'2011. pp 2271-2274
6. Chomsky, N. and Pappe,I. 2010. Gaza in Crisis: Reflections on Israel's War Against Palestinians. London: The Penguin Group
7. Hart, J. Empowerment or Frustration? Participatory programming with young Palestinians. *Children Youth and Environments 17*, 3 (2007), 1–23.
8. Helsper, E. 2008. Digital Inclusion: An Analysis of Social Disadvantage and the Information Society. Department for Communities and Local Government. London, UK.
9. Khalidi, R. 2007. The Iron Cage. Oxford: OneWorld Publications
10. Light, J.S. 2001. Rethinking The Digital Divide. Harvard Educational Review, Vol. 71 (4), 709-734
11. McTaggart, R. and Kemmis, S. *The action research planner.* Deakin university, 1988.
12. Mehra, B., Merkel, C., and Bishop, A.P. The internet for empowerment of minority and marginalized users. *New Media & Society 6*, 6 (2004), 781–802.
13. Miessen, M. *„Die Gewalt der Partizipation: Räumliche Praktiken jenseits des Konsensmodells "*. Eurozine, 2007.
14. Mouffe, C. Artistic activism and agonistic spaces. *Art & Research 1*, 2 (2007), 1–5.
15. Palestinian Central Bureau of Statistics. Press Release on International Refugee Day. Ramallah, (20 June, 2013)
16. PASSIA. Palestinian Refugees: Endless Injustice. Palestinian Academic Society for the Study of International Affairs (March 2014).
17. Peace Now Settlement Watch team. Breaking the Law in the West Bank – One Violation Leads to Another: Israeli Settlement Building on Private Palestinian Property (March 2007). Retrieved September 1, 2014 from http://peacenow.org.il/eng/sites/default/files/Breaking_The_Law_formal%20data_March07Eng.pdf
18. Resnick, M., Rusk, N., and Cooke, S. The Computer Clubhouse: Technological Fluency in the Inner City. In High Technology and Low-Income Communities 1998, MIT Press (1998), 266-286.
19. Sawhney, N. Voices beyond walls: the role of digital storytelling for empowering marginalized youth in refugee camps. ACM Press (2009), 302.
20. Schubert, K., Weibert, A., and Wulf, V. Locating computer clubs in multicultural neighborhoods: How collaborative project work fosters integration processes. *International Journal of Human-Computer Studies 69*, 10 (2011), 669–678.
21. Shabaneh, G. Education and Identity: The Role of UNRWA's Education Programmes in the Reconstruction of Palestinian Nationalism. *Journal of Refugee Studies, 4*,25 (2012), 491-513.
22. Stevens, G., Veith, M., Wulf, V. Bridging among Ethnic Communities by Cross-cultural Communities of Practice. In Communities and Technologies 2005. Springer, 2005, pp 377-396
23. Tacchi, J., Slater, D. and Hearn, G. 2003. Ethnographic Action Research: A User's Handbook. UNESCO
24. Wahbeh, N. ICT and Education in Palestine: Social and Educational Inequalities in Access to ICT
25. Wulf, V., Aal, K., Abu Kteish, I., Atam, M., Schubert, K., Rohde, M., Yerousis, G. & Randall, D. (2013, April). Fighting against the wall: Social media use by political activists in a Palestinian village. In *Proceedings of the SIGCHI Conference on Human Factors in Computing Systems* (pp. 1979-1988). ACM.
26. Intel Computer Clubhouse Network. http://www.computerclubhouse.org/locations
27. Electricity learning kits. Jumbo Trading. http://jumbotrading.com/
28. Cubeteam. https://cubeteam.io/
29. Anchor Institutions Tool. https://www.nettercenter.upenn.edu/anchortoolkit/what-anchor-institution

Transnationalism, Indigenous Knowledge and Technology: Insights from the Kenyan Diaspora

Kagonya Awori, Frank Vetere, Wally Smith
Department of Computing and Information Systems,
Microsoft Centre for Social NUI
The University of Melbourne, Australia
sawori@student.unimelb.edu.au, {f.vetere, wsmith}@unimelb.edu.au

ABSTRACT

Our paper investigates how current digital technologies are sufficient, or insufficient, in supporting Kenyan transnationals in practising indigenous knowledge. We first outline a view of indigenous knowledge, and then apply it to a study of Kenyan diasporans living in Australia. The findings are framed as nine techniques for sustaining displaced practising of indigenous knowledge. These appropriations suggest directions for technology innovation, providing design considerations for technologies that translate, formulate and support indigenous knowledge in transnational contexts.

Author Keywords

Traditional knowledge; indigenous knowledge; Transnational HCI;

ACM Classification Keywords

H.5.m. Information interfaces and presentation (e.g., HCI): Miscellaneous.

INTRODUCTION

Transnational HCI is principally concerned with how technologies are designed, used and appropriated across different geographies and cultures [24, 29]. Related to this, but with a different focus, studies of *indigenous knowledge* (IK) within HCI investigate technologies that support indigenous communities in sustaining their ways of living and knowing when they are physically or generationally separated from their indigenous land and wider community (e.g. [14, 21]). In this paper we explore the nexus of these two areas and investigate how existing digital technologies support transnationals in sustaining their IK. Based on previous research that highlights the inconsistencies that arise when indigenous knowledge systems are designed from western logics [6, 27], we posit that an understanding of the transnational indigenous user of technology offers a valuable perspective on how technology can connect or marginalise users with indigenous ways of knowing. We investigate how existing technologies connect or isolate indigenous transnationals wishing to sustain indigenous knowledge in a diaspora community.

Our approach is to start by proposing a definition and perspective on indigenous knowledge. We then apply this lens to generate findings from an ethnographic study conducted with Kenyan transnationals in Australia. Based on these findings, we develop insights for the HCI community in the following ways: articulating a nexus between indigenous knowledge and transnational HCI, and thereby articulating a focus on the indigenous transnational user; offering an indigenous lens to technology design that can be used as a framework to motivate IK research and design; and identifying gaps that technology can fill in order to better support the practise of indigenous knowledge among indigenous transnationals.

CHI 2015, April 18 - 23 2015, Seoul, Republic of Korea

ACM 978-1-4503-3145-6/15/04...$15.00
http://dx.doi.org/10.1145/2702123.2702488

BACKGROUND

Technology and transnationalism

Transnational HCI concerns the ways 'social and cultural interconnectedness and mobility across space, time and geography' impact technology use and design [24]. Areas of investigation include observing how pervasive and ubiquitous technologies gain new forms and uses when transported to new places (e.g. [15]). Significant theoretical questions have been raised about how transnationals appropriate technology, and the interplay of new technologies with mobility, hybridity, identity, culture, and local-global interconnectedness[24]. These studies offer insights into how to design for people who are highly mobile, and yet remain 'anchored', culturally and socially, both to their countries of migration and their countries of origin [29].

Specific projects in transnational HCI have examined, for example: the use of mobile technology by Thai retirees across distributed homes in different countries [29]; the use of technology by diaspora Ghanaians to connect with foreigners in the diaspora [7]; how Kenyans use technology to communicate within rural, urban, peri-urban and diaspora settings [20]; and, how online gaming in urban China becomes socially and culturally situated [15].

Technology and Indigenous Communities

In a different area of research, a variety of technologies, e.g. [17, 25], have been designed specifically to facilitate the collection, translation, validation, preservation and dissemination of indigenous knowledge (IK). While this produces valuable records, the approach has often been critiqued as being unfavourable to IK's growth and sustenance [22, 28]. Agrawal [2] and others argue that the attempt to collect and preserve IK assumes that IK is easily 'collectable' and 'preservable'. This 'scientisation' of IK tends to consider IK as a commodity that can be abstracted and decontextualized, and that its significance can be readily maintained outside of the socio-physical environment of the indigenous community.

This is not to deny the significance of archiving. For example, the preservation of audio recordings of endangered languages, the storage of video archives of ritual ceremonies, or the creating a digital herbarium of an indigenous people's flora are all important. These become collections that can be recreated, studied or referred to, and additionally be actors in the future generation of IK. However, they are not the entirety of IK, nor are they immediately valuable to indigenous communities themselves. There is therefore an opportunity and a need for technology design to move beyond managing indigenous data, and into supporting the nurturing of IK.

Indigenous Data and Indigenous Knowledge

In the field of knowledge management in western organisations, collections of images, numbers, words and sounds arising from observation or measurement are most accurately considered as data, where data is understood in contrast with more meaningful information and knowledge [13]. When such collections are derived from indigenous communities, this paper similarly refers to them as *indigenous data*. While indigenous data is important and serves various purposes - scholarly, ceremonial, scientific, commercial, and entertainment – it is primarily an abstraction at a particular time and location. In contrast *indigenous knowledge* arises from social and physical interactions amongst the people, and with their environment. Indigenous knowledge is retained and refined through time by an indigenous community in order to sustain its unique identity. This knowledge makes up the community's ways of being, living and knowing[4, 21].

While this view of knowledge as being social, materially grounded and situated, is not new to HCI [12], few IK technologies reflect this perspective. Nevertheless there are a few notable examples of technologies that attempt to cultivate indigenous knowledge: a mobile knowledge sharing platform that allows *in situ* community members to create a media rich visual representation of their environment [14]; a reality game that allows users to practise indigenous knowledge within digital representations of their indigenous environment[21] ; and the use of indigenous objects to enable the learning of IK within a mixed-reality space [18].

It is within this shift – from preserving indigenous data to cultivating indigenous knowledge – that this paper positions itself. This shift not only views knowledge as a social, physical and situated process, but also aims to mediate the indigenous ways of interacting with, developing and negotiating knowledge. We explore these issues in the context of a diaspora community, where cultural dispersion and social isolation often accentuate the challenges of practising IK. But first we clarify our perspective on indigenous knowledge.

THE THREE "P"S OF KNOWLEDGE

In developing a view of IK, it is important to emphasize that it does not stand in opposition to scientific/western knowledge. In a critical analysis of this supposed dichotomy, Agrawal [1] contrasts the two knowledge groups across three themes – substantive, methodological/epistemological, and contextual - and concludes that no clear divide exists between them.

Also, while IK can be viewed as a 'complete body of knowledge, know-how and practices maintained and developed by peoples through generations'[17], its inseparability from the indigenous community carries with it the uniqueness of each of these communities. Indigenous communities are not all similar, and consequently, not all forms and definitions of IK are identical.

Additionally, IK may be viewed as both a product of the knowledge of an indigenous community, e.g. indigenous languages, artefacts and practices, and as an approach to understanding how knowledge is created, shared, stored and developed among indigenous communities. IK brings an indigenous perspective to how we approach and respond to knowledge, particularly the knowledge of indigenous communities. Our intention is to understand how an indigenous view of knowledge may influence the design of technologies intended for indigenous users. We begin by explicating an indigenous view of knowledge that proposes three important foci: *people*, *place* and *practise*.

Practise as knowledge

According to epistemologies applied by indigenous communities, knowledge is acquired though lived experiences and primarily involves face-to-face interactions with other people [10]. Meaning is gained through situated socio-physical interactions with nature, people and objects. These interactions are not only oral or written, but bodily - movement, gesture, voice, dances, stories, performances, rituals, pitch, smell, texture, sound, role- based interactions etc. This view echoes the phenomenological view of knowledge as embodied - meaning is gained by being in and interacting with the world; the mind gains meaning of the world by virtue of the body being in that same world [8].

This indigenous epistemology is well illustrated in a study involving a 3D visualisation tool with an indigenous community in Namibia [14]. When asked to identify his house from a bird's eye representation of his village, one respondent replied, "*I have never been on my roof, so how should I know how it looks like?*" The respondent determined that he could not possibly know what his roof looked like because his body had never been on the roof. Knowledge of a place or activity was only possible by being in and interacting with that place, or actually performing that activity.

People as knowledge

Many indigenous communities apply the aphorism "*I am because we are*" to the way they live, be and know; the individual is not at the centre of the world, instead the community has primacy in terms of identity and knowledge[19].

Knowledge is seen as belonging to the entire community. However, access to knowledge and the enactment of knowledge varies within and between communities. Some community members have privileged access to certain knowledge depending on their role within the community. For example, among the Maori, the role of 'official knowledge bearer' is assigned to particular members [10]. This means that members of the Maori tribe have to interact with these living repositories of knowledge in order to learn particular skills, histories, and practices. Another example is from the Penan community, where the youth embarked on knowledge sharing journeys with the elderly in order to learn essential life skills like cooking, hunting, and fishing [25]. In rural Namibia, villagers often described their wisdom in terms of social relationships with key members of their community [4].

For these indigenous communities, knowledge is viewed as being shared, applied and contained in and through people. This has a consequence on the approaches that tend to make knowledge abstract and remove it from an identifiable voice/body.

Place as knowledge

The relationship that indigenous communities have with their ancestral place of settlement (i.e. the land on which they believe they first settled) is paramount in understanding indigenous knowledge. For example, it is common in African countries for each ethnic community to have a clearly identifiable land area from which they believe to have originally settled. In many instances, the ancestral land of an ethnic community remains the land on which it is the largest occupant of in the country. These spaces therefore become rich environments of indigenous knowledge due to the high concentration of people from one ethnic community, living their indigenous practices *in situ*. Even community members who live beyond ancestral lands (e.g. within a city) may still maintain a connection to the ancestral land, and this connection is "resilient, highly variable, with dynamics of its own, and not just dependent on personal choice" [11].

The relationship to the ancestral home is transcendental and perpetual, and facilitates an understanding of a community's ancestral land as more than a place of settlement. Instead, the ancestral land plays several roles: it is a place of identity[11]; an active participant in the socio-physical interactions of the community – an actor in the process of knowledge construction[4]; a keeper of knowledge, with whom interactions are necessary in order to acquire that knowledge[21]; a sacred gift to be cared for and respected; and a determinant of what and how knowledge interactions and exchanges can take place[21]. The ancestral place acquires a pedagogical role in their expression of indigenous knowledge.

A STUDY OF TRANSNATIONALISM, INDIGENOUS KNOWLEDGE & TECHNOLOGY

To explore the significance of the P-P-P view of IK, as described, we conducted an ethnographic field study of 8 Kenyan diasporans living in Melbourne, Australia. The aim was to study people in a geographical dispersed diaspora while attempting to practice IK from their distant homeland. This provided a site of study within the nexus of transnationalism and IK. The focus, for each participant, was on understanding how transnationalism challenges the way indigenous knowledge is practiced in the diaspora, and on how technologies play a critical role in negotiating these challenges.

We are interested in how technologies are culturally appropriated, specifically how 'people adapt and make technology their own', and the new ways in which technology gains meaning depending on the social, political and economic context of use[16]. Cultural appropriation does not merely examine how western technologies are domesticated in their indigenous cultures, but in the ways that technology 'is framed and articulated, that is, transformed, not as a technical artefact but as a cultural object.'[16].

While a diaspora community is different from an indigenous community, we applied our P-P-P lens to study Kenyan transnationals for three main reasons. Firstly, we are interested in matching an investigation of IK with a view that reflects an indigenous epistemology. Previous researchers [27] and [6] have highlighted the inconsistencies that arise when IK systems are designed from western logics. We therefore find it fitting to apply an indigenous view of knowledge (the P-P-P lens) when investigating the sustenance of IK by indigenous communities. Secondly, as previously stated, transnational HCI allows us to examine how information flows might connect or isolate developed and developing nations[29]. We were therefore motivated to investigate how current technology connects or isolates members from developing nations who live in developed nations, and yet desire to maintain an active connection/identity to their countries of origin. Lastly, we intend that investigating a diaspora community offers insight into how, and why, IK is practised when community members are separated, physically or generationally, from both their ancestral home and the wider ethnic community.

For these reasons, we conducted a study with Kenyans living in Melbourne, Australia. Our goals for research were threefold: to understand the motivations for sustaining IK in the diaspora; to understand the workarounds employed to practise IK; and to identify technology appropriations applied in order to continue practising IK.

Method

We conducted interviews with eight Kenyan women living in Melbourne, Australia. Our choice to investigate women was motivated by a respect for the customs of the traditional communities we intended to study. In indigenous communities, access to knowledge is often gender based. Our primary researcher (the first author in this paper) is a woman thus to study only allowed wider and easier access to both participants and the activities under investigation. Our primary researcher is also Kenyan, and familiar with the structure of Kenyan society and its bearing on our participants. Our existing relationships with technology research organisations in Kenya, and the ease of access to participants for future *in situ* studies further motivated our interest in the Kenyan diaspora. As advocated in [9], we considered our primary researcher's sentiments, understandings and familiarity with the participants as contributing to the research we undertook. For example, interviews were conducted both in English and Kiswahili, following a norm amongst Kenyans to code-switch between the two languages. Code-switching allowed for colloquialisms, phrases, sayings, and commonly understood norms to be expressed by the participants and understood by the researcher, thereby allowing for nuanced user requirements to be collaboratively generated.

Recruitment was by snowball sampling, thus half our participants knew each other. This proved advantageous in that the stories that recurred in our data were enriched and clarified through multiple viewpoints. Our primary research method was interviews, which were conducted at the residences or workplaces of the participants and lasted between one to three hours. In addition, pictures of traditional artefacts were taken in order to glean a richer understanding of how IK is transported and developed in places of migration.

Analysis of the data involved transcribing audio recordings of interviews while translating the Kiswahili parts into English. The data was then analysed through a P-P-P lens, where we interpreted how the social, physical and situated characteristics of IK were manifest in the reports participants. We identified the actions, interactions and workarounds employed by participants when attempting to sustain IK, sometimes during interaction with the people and places of their homeland. The identification of relevant elements in the data was motivated by asking how the development of IK related to people, place and practise. Under these three foci, we identified nine techniques for sustaining IK used by these Kenyan diasporans. The techniques all relate in some sense to combinations of people, place and practice, but we present them here as falling principally under one of those themes. The techniques identified were considered by the researchers as being highly relevant to the circumstances and intentions described by all participants, though not all reported using them.

Description of participants

All participants were women between the ages of 25 to 60, and had lived in Australia for between three and fifteen years. All were either employed or owned their own businesses. To note, we used the term traditional knowledge interchangeably with indigenous knowledge, as the former term was more meaningful to the participants. Table 1 briefly presents the demographic profiles of the eight participants. The next section discusses findings from the ethnographic study.

FINDINGS

We present our findings by first describing the motivations of our participants for sustaining IK in the diaspora, including an unexpected interest from the youth in IK. We then discuss the accommodations and workarounds made, with and without technology, to sustain IK through connections to people, place and practise. The gaps in what technology currently appears to offer, as we later discuss, present opportunities for improvements and new innovations.

Motivations: Identity, values and belonging

A key motivation for sustaining IK was the desire to construct a Kenyan identity amid the multiple other cultures that participants interacted with. There was a recurring concern that "Kenyans assimilate easily and forget their culture" (*Lucy*). Therefore, in order to sustain their Kenyan identities, including particular ethnic identities within the Kenyan nation, participants participated in activities such as attending Kenyan social events, maintaining active use of their national and/or ethnic languages, cooking Kenyan meals daily or occasionally, and keeping abreast with Kenyan news.

Participant	Age (yrs)	Description
Ann	25 to 30	Social worker; Has lived in Australia for 6 years; Last visited Kenya 10 years ago.
Shangazi	55 to 60	Nurse and business owner; Married with two children aged 25 and 29; Lived in Australia 15 years; Last visited Kenya in March 2014. Visits each year.
Baraka	25 to 30	IT consultant; Lived in Australia 3 years; Has not visited Kenya since being in Australia, plans to travel at the end of the year.
Lucy	40 to 45	Teacher; Married with two children aged 7 and 16; Lived in Australia for 8 years; Last visited Kenya 10 years ago. Visits Kenya about every decade.
Senge	40 to 45	Trainer, Business owner; Married with two children who are in their early twenties; Has lived in Australia for 10 years; Last visited Kenya 3 years ago.
Mariamu	40 to 45	Business owner; Married with three children (16 – 27 years of age); Has lived in Australia for 12 years; Last time in Kenya was in January 2014, visits approx. every 1.5 years.
Dada	35 to 39	Accountant; Married with three children, all under 8 years of age; Has lived in Australia for 8 years; Last visited Kenya 3 years ago.
Binti	25 to 30	PhD student and lecturer; Has been in Australia for over 5 years; Last visited Kenya a year ago.

Table 1: Summary of Participants (all names are pseudonyms)

There was a recurring perception that children were losing values due to living in new environments. Videos and documentaries about traditional communities were used to cultivate the learning of these lost values. We also observed that interactions and engagements around traditional activities provided a special site for the teaching of "traditional values". For instance, cooking of intricate traditional foods was coupled with storytelling where the cooking activities acted as prompts to pass on values that the teacher had learnt while cooking, and were reference points for the learner to understand a traditional value.

Another reported motivation for sustaining IK was to show belonging. The story below illustrates this:

> *"I remember when he first spoke to his future mother-in-law. His wife had called her mum in Kenya so that she could introduce her to the guy she planned to marry. He talked to the future mother in law on the phone in his limited Kikuyu language, blundering endlessly along the way but he persisted. Then the mother asked the daughter, "Is that man a Kikuyu really? You have to teach him the language if he wants to talk to me." Shangazi*

In this instance, the man in question needed to show the mother-in-law that he was a "true Kikuyu". This could only be demonstrated by the degree to which he could speak the Kikuyu language fluently. This pushed him to learn the language from his fiancé, in order to achieve a sense of belonging and approval from his future mother-in-law. This sentiment recurred across the participants, with many of them stating, "*Mkosa mila ni mtumwa*" (He/she without a culture is a slave).

We found a strong desire by the younger participants (aged <30 years) and the children of older participants (reported indirectly), to learn about their ethnic background and to practise aspects of their culture. One of the drivers of these interests was a feeling of having "missed out" on aspects of their ethnic or national background. This missing out was felt to be a result of having been physically or generationally separated from the place and people of their ethnic community.

Moreover, the knowledge sought by the youth was not only reserved to skill and language acquisition, but also about having an alternative reference point for everyday questions and activities. As summarised by *Ann*:

> *"I want to know the roots. Our roots, back at home. I don't feel bad that I cannot speak my ethnic language. I don't have sleepless nights about it. But when I am asked about my ethnic background, I can't say anything, and that is why I feel as though I lack and I would love to know more about that. Growing up, we weren't exposed to that... the things I do right now, would they be accepted? Would the elders give me a leso at my wedding?"*

According to *Ann*, her ethnic community, the *Taita*, only give a *leso* (a clothing item similar to a sarong) to women who the village elders or community members consider honourable.

There was also a preference for interactive experiences. In the case of learning about "the roots", there was a preference for interactions involving music, artefacts and activities. According to *Ann*, while many technology applications she had come across for learning IK often relied heavily on storytelling, other media within her environment, like video conferencing and interactive public displays, could offer more memorable and engaging experiences.

Limits of current digital technologies

A multitude of social media applications and communication tools were used by participants to connect with the Kenyan and/or ethnic community. Common examples were Whatsapp, Viber, Skype, phone calls, forums, YouTube and email. These were used to facilitate various interactions, for example finding out what locally unavailable item could be replaced in a traditional recipe; organising life events with other Kenyans, e.g. birthdays and weddings; keeping up with news via Kenyan YouTube channels and online newspapers; teaching children Kiswahili via Kenyan- produced animations on YouTube e.g. TingaTinga tales; and crowd sourcing for information about a particular ethnic community or a particular practice.

While these technologies were found useful to an extent, the following findings indicate their limitations and opportunities for improvement, by describing the various related workarounds and techniques for sustaining IK that go beyond what is readily possible with these technologies of connectivity.

Interactions with people holding IK

Following the P-P-P lens, the first category of techniques to sustain IK are those that concerned connecting to people holding IK.

Physical encounters with people in the homeland

When searching for IK there was a desire to meet physically with elderly members of the ethnic community who were perceived as legitimate sources of IK. The story below exemplifies this:

> *We did a bit of Googling, my husband and I, but we did not get much from there about our ethnic community. So we have purposed that next time we go to Kenya we have to look for old men, old Kikuyu men to explain to us those processes because we realise we do not know them."Mariamu*

Such a meeting needed to be face-to-face given the importance of the people to be met, i.e. the elders of the village. Moreover, non-verbal interactions and feedback between the elders and the audience, constitute the learning that takes place in these physical encounters with knowledge bearers. Thus *Mariamu* preferred physical meetings with the elders given the wealth of learning it would offer and also an opportunity to sustain a relationship with the elders and her village.

Flying in experts

The converse of visiting elders in the homeland, was to arrange for visits to the diaspora. Our study revealed instances where elders, religious leaders and ethnic community members from Kenya, were flown out to Australia in order that they could chaperon a traditional ceremony.

> *"I hadn't paid attention to what the songs meant when I attended weddings in Kenya. At my wedding here, we had a lady from Kenyan who taught us the traditional songs of my tribe. Her and my mum arranged us accordingly, as per our customs, and we performed the traditional ceremony of wooing the bride out of the house."Lucy*

Here, knowledge experts were sought and brought in to guide the performance of a traditional ceremony.

Physical meetings among learners

Another technique of sustaining IK through its relation to people, was to create spaces and events for those in the Melbourne diaspora to meet with each other and to share their learning. Three participants were involved in launching and running a language school in Melbourne for children from the Kenyan community to learn Kiswahili. The school doubled up as a space of social interaction, where the children could meet, engage and practise their language.

Participants expressed pride in setting up a regular language school, as it was a visible means of passing "something down" to their children, and it gave them another reason to meet with each other. As noted by *Shangazi*, the school was also a physical avenue to the past as it brought connections to her childhood and reminded of the Kiswahili poems she used to sing.

Cultural apprenticeships

A related technique for sharing IK among those in the Melbourne diaspora can be described as cultural apprenticeships. Here members arrange to meet physically for the sharing of specific knowledge. A frequent site for this kind of exchange was during learning of highly embodied practices, such as the preparation of traditional meals. The story below exemplifies this:

> *"One of my friends said that before she leaves Melbourne in two weeks she has to come over for me to show here how to cook chapatis. I told her I could explain it to her over the phone but she has refused! I have explained to her before how to do it over the phone, but she said every time she tried cooking them, they were hard. So she insists on coming to do it with me." Shangazi*

Despite the availability and use of digital media to pass on knowledge, we observed a preference to 'learn by doing' in the presence of others.

Maintaining a connection to the places where IK is performed

The second category of techniques for sustaining IK are those that attempted to connect with the places of IK.

Visiting the homeland

Connections to Kenya and to participants' ancestral homes were maintained primarily by regular trips to those physical places. The need for these trips went beyond visiting friends and relatives, and included the need to connect with the places of IK. The prevalence of this technique confirms the importance of sustaining IK and reminds us of the limits of technologies to fully substitute.

Being there through digital connectivity

However a range of digital technologies were used for a secondary kind of connection to place. This was reported in the use of, for example, phone calls, Skype calls, Whatsapp groups, diaspora forums and Facebook pages. While these technology-mediated always involved connections to people, and very often to practices as well, it was clear in the testimony of participants that part of the value was in connection to the places of IK.

For example, in one reported case, to create a more immersive sense of 'being there' multiple channels of connection were used in tandem. *Baraka* watched a one-way live feed of a wedding ceremony online. SMS messaging was used to communicate with her family members who she was watching live. Additionally, she performed actions in unison with the wedding attendees, despite a 10-hour time difference; eating when they ate, and singing and dancing along to the traditional ceremonies being performed at the wedding.

Extending places of origin

We also observed how the connection to ancestral place was enlivened in the country of migration of the participants. We call this extending the place of origin, where the activities that would have been carried out in Kenya, are practised as they would have been, but in Australia. This is clearly also relates to the notion of IK through practice. But here we refer to the way the place of the homeland is felt to extend to the periphery of the diaspora. As described by *Senge*:

> *"Australia feels more or less like Kenya. After some time you forget that you are not in Kenya. I have brought my Kenya here." Senge*

By sustaining several IK practices in her life in Melbourne e.g. food, language, religious practices, community, radio, *Senge* was able merge her connection to Kenya with her current physical place. She augmented her indigenous practices from her place of origin to her place of migration. HCI provides some examples where the lived world of indigenous users has been virtually merged with their indigenous home. For example, Digital Songlines [21] which is a game that allows the indigenous user to be immersed in a virtual world that closely resembles his/her own ancestral land. By simulating place, Digital Songlines provided a means through which users could invoke knowledge about their indigenous land, the fauna and flora, and the events that transpired on the land. Similarly, *Senge* cooked Kenyan meals daily, listened to Kenyan news and music, used artefacts from her country of origin and maintained use of her traditional languages, in order to recreate her home of origin into her new home.

Enacting the practise of IK

The third category of techniques for sustaining IK are those concerned with the direct adoption of practices that embody and depended on IK.

Pre-learning indigenous practices

One technique occurred before participants left Kenya. Knowing that they were to migrate, they deliberately learned new aspects of IK that they would need in their new life. For example, *Mariamu* decided to learn how to braid her children's hair before moving to Australia, where she anticipated that she would not have easy or immediate access to the practice:

> *"I am undoing my hair now so that it can be redone by a friend, into an African hairstyle I like. I used to do this for my daughters when they were younger.. I learnt it in Kenya because I knew I was moving here. And here, the salons do not know what to do with our hair." Mariamu*

What is additionally interesting here is the bodily literacy *Mariamu* acquired in order to braid hair. However, *Mariamu* stated that because she no longer did her daughters' hair, she had forgotten the indigenous skill. The bodily literacy of hair braiding could not be sustained without practice.

Re-enacting Traditional Ceremonies

Once out in the diaspora, a key technique in which IK is nurtured through focus on practices, is the re-enactment of traditional ceremonies. Participants used online searches to source detailed information about how to perform them. However, the internet was largely perceived as lacking in legitimate sources. Consequently, information was sourced from peers, or notable books written about pre-colonial Kenya, the period before the western colonisers' subjugation of indigenous ways of knowing and living. These provided reference points from which traditional ceremonies were re-enacted into the life events of the participants, e.g. birth ceremonies and weddings. As illustrated below:

> *"When he was born, the men did the itega (A traditional ceremony to celebrate the birth of a baby) for him. We got a goat, which is apparently supposed to be cooked by the men only. So my friends and I just sat here while the men were cooking and doing everything. I did not even know that is a traditional thing! Some people had been reading the book Facing Mount Kenya, and that is how they became aware of how things used to be done before... So we re-enacted all that." Dada*

As described by *Shangazi*, the practise of IK, e.g. speaking the Kikuyu language, proved a sense of belonging to the ethnic community. Videos and pictures facilitated the amassing of evidence of belonging as they captured the practise of traditional ceremonies and life events.

DISCUSSION

In the previous section we have reported the motivations and techniques of eight Kenyan diasporans living in Melbourne for sustaining the IK of their homeland. The desire to know one's roots, and to know the real reason behind a traditional practice, performance, saying or ceremony, from a legitimate source, recurred in our data. This was true for all of our participants, and was reportedly strong in the young of their communities who are interested in interacting with the elderly, in order to learn about day-to-day ways of living. This finding encourages us to take seriously the opportunities for new technologies of exchange between people of different exposure and experience of IK. This first requires attention to the kinds of activities of exchange currently sought and enacted within a cultural diaspora, this being the focus of the present study.

In the present study, then, we have sketched a people-place-practise view of IK, and demonstrated how it can be used as a lens to identify nine specific techniques for sustaining IK in the group of Kenyan diasporans. Most of these techniques involve at least some use of digital technologies of connectivity, though some do not. Collectively they are presented as evidence about the current gaps and opportunities for digital technologies to support the maintenance of IK in diaspora communities. As such, they provide directions for technology innovation, and speak to possible considerations when designing technologies that translate, formulate and support the P-P-P of IK. In this section, we will discuss some of the design considerations that are inspired by the appropriations and non-appropriations that were observed.

It is important to recall that while the appropriations have been framed here through the categories of people, place and practise, no distinct boundaries exist between the three; i.e. practise cannot be separated from people, or people from place. Also, we are working under the premise, admittedly contentious, that while indigenous communities are distinctive, and their uniqueness carries with it unique ways of knowing and living, there are similarities that can be abstracted across indigenous knowledges. The people, place and practise lens is offered as a potential source of commonality that provides a reusable framework to inspire technology designs.

Based on the evidence of this small study, connected technologies were used largely to facilitate searching, and often a kind of crowd sourcing, for resources on IK, through platforms like Whatsapp and Facebook. Principal targets for learning were family and friends in Australia, those in Kenya and other countries in the diaspora. Similar to [29], we observed that "communication technologies are also information technologies". Meaning that the technologies used for communication with other people e.g. Whatsapp and Facebook, were seen as sources of IK; they facilitated communication with people who might be bearers of knowledge, or links to those who are. Phone calls were a popular means of communication when seeking IK from those in Kenya. Youtube proved a popular channel for keeping up with Kenyan news, music, dances, comedy, and learning Kiswahili. Video recording and live streams were used to record or participate in traditional ceremonies performed during life events like birth and marriage. News collection sites were popular, in particular http://www.kenyamoja.com/, due to its curation of all major television channels, radio stations, and entertainment blogs in Kenya. Technology also allowed for the live streaming of life events, such as weddings, where activities could be carried out with remotely located participants at the same time. Remote observers used props available to them to participate in the ceremony they were viewing via the live stream. Two-way communication was facilitated by phone messaging, which was preferred because it did not disrupt the activities in the observed place, and also supported a one-to-one intimacy. This viewing, augmented with two-way communication and synchronous participation of live activities, gave the remote participant a feeling of "actually being there".

Applying a P-P-P lens to these observations, revealed gaps where current technologies in use were not able to support the needs of the participants for IK. Perhaps one of the biggest gaps can be summarised through the continued desire and reliance on physical meetings where it might be thought that digital exchange could contribute. Physical meetings, that underpinned techniques like apprenticeships and pre-learning, allowed learners to acquire knowledge found in taste, observation, feel and located interactions. Indigenous community members not only communicate knowledge verbally, but also highly utilise the non-verbal sounds, ululations, silences, changes in tone and resonance, mime, and body and gestural movements that constitute their languages [6, 26]. We observed that the cooking of intricate dishes and activities like hair dressing, involved knowledge in the form of feel of the food or hair, smell of the food, rhythm of hand movements when plaiting hair, change of texture of the food while it is cooking etc. Additionally, *Baraka* and *Shangazi* attempted to use phone calls to give instructions on how to prepare traditional foods. However, our participants expressed difficulty in translating bodily literacies into a form that is afforded by phone calls and videos. By extension, we can infer that common knowledge sharing tools, e.g. YouTube and phone calls, unsatisfactorily translate the gamut of literacies indigenous communities use to share and nurture knowledge. These observations and the more general inference resonate with other research. As noted by [3], the inability of videos to capture the relationships with the place and artefacts, hidden or revealed in sound, movement or feeling hinders valuable expression of IK practices. This motivates a need to understand how audio-visual technology design can transport, engage and enliven interactions and artefacts, in everyday activities like cooking, and when the parties concerned are dispersed, i.e. between the diaspora and *in situ*. In another study[5], a traditional healer critiqued the use of video cameras when teaching about local herbs. The healer preferred to teach by walking with the student and participating in particular activities, tasks which he found cumbersome if done with a video camera.

The flying in of experts, planned physical encounters and the creation of special meeting spaces also speaks to the need to cater the participants' varied levels of exposure and experience of IK. For example, *Mariamu* was involved in a dowry ceremony for her niece. This involved her flying from Melbourne to Adelaide three times to meet the families of her niece's fiancé. *Mariamu* had previously understood the dowry ceremony to be about selling the bride. However, by taking part in the ceremony and having to physically meet the groom's family, she learnt otherwise. Traditionally, the groom was not allowed to pay the full price at once, and was meant to do so bit by bit every year to ensure the families of the couple met regularly, and maintained a relationship throughout the marriage of their children. Participation in the dowry ceremony further prompted *Mariamu* to travel to her home in rural Kenya, so that she could understand the dowry ceremony from the perspective of "the old men of the village". This presents an interesting challenge as it pushes for a consideration of not only the situatedness of life events, but the need for participants to customise or build their own memories, learnings and experiences of such events. IK life events, while largely communal, are at the same time an assembly of defined roles, persons and actions, each with a need for a personalised experience of the whole. The balance between mediating IK practices for the whole and at the same time for the one presents a significant consideration for IK design.

CONCLUSION

Through a people-place-practise lens, we have identified nine techniques to sustain IK used by a group of Kenyan diasporans living in Melbourne. We contend that an the evidence of how existing technologies are appropriated, or not appropriated, within these nine techniques can inform the design of new technologies for IK exchange (as discussed in [23]). By seeking to identify areas where current arrangements and technologies do not suffice in sustaining IK, our work invites the design of new technologies that can fill these gaps. This represents a move away from analysing the surface use or non-use of technologies from a Euro-American perspective, to understanding and designing for the less visible, but more significant, influence of people, place and practise. Moreover, examining the practise of IK among transnationals in the diaspora is a new space for technology research and design. The indigenous transnational user offers unique requirements, including the need to cater to multiple connectedness, i.e. to places of origin and places of migration; technologies that can be dissimilar due to diverse users e.g. *in situ* elders and urban diaspora, and yet fulfil the same desire to cultivate IK; and technologies that can transport, personalise and replicate people, place and practise such that IK is cultivated in remote locations.

In conclusion, though focusing only on a small group of Kenyan women, our study offers a window into understanding the challenges faced by other globally dispersed cultural groups who similarly desire to develop IK in their places of migration. We hope that this paper will motivate more research in the areas of IK and transnational HCI, and that more nuanced technologies may be designed to cultivate and share IK.

ACKNOWLEDGMENTS

We thank all the participants that took part in this study.

REFERENCES

1. Agrawal, A. Dismantling the Divide Between Indigenous and Scientific Knowledge. *Development and Change*, *26*, 3 (1995), 413-439.
2. Agrawal, A. Indigenous knowledge and the politics of classification. *International Social Science Journal*, *54*, 173 (2002), 287-297.
3. Bidwell, N., truna aka j.turner, Holdsworth, J. L. and Shay, C. M. Heritage & Habitus: Designing to Support Situated, Living Knowledge. *In Proc. Mobile HCI 2007*, (2007).
4. Bidwell, N. J., Winschiers-Theophilus, H., Koch Kapuire, G. and Rehm, M. Pushing personhood into place: Situating media in rural knowledge in Africa. *International Journal of Human-Computer Studies*, *69*, 10 (2011), 618-631.
5. Bidwell, N. J. and Winschiers-Theophilus, H. Audio pacemaker: walking, talking indigenous knowledge. *In Proc. SAICSIT*, ACM (2012), 149-158.
6. Bidwell, N. J. Moving the Centre to Design Social Media for Rural Africa. *AI&Soc: Journal of Culture, Communication & Knowledge, Springer*, October (2014).
7. Burrell, J. and Anderson, K. `I have great desires to look beyond my world': trajectories of information and communication technology use among Ghanaians living abroad. *New Media & Society*, *10*, 2 (2008), 203-224.
8. Dourish, P. *Where the action is: the foundations of embodied interaction*. Cambridge, Mass. ; MIT, 2004., 2004.
9. Dourish, P. Reading and Interpreting Ethnography, In *Ways of Knowing in HCI*.Springer New York, (2014), .
10. Duncker, E. Cross-cultural usability of the library metaphor. *In Proc Joint Conference on Digital libraries (JCDL '02)* 2002, 223-230.
11. Geschiere, P. and Gugler, J. Introduction: the urban–rural connection: changing issues of belonging and identification. *Africa*, *68*, 03 (1998), 309-319.
12. Harrison, S., Sengers, P. and Tatar, D. Making epistemological trouble: Third-paradigm HCI as successor science. *Interacting with Computers*, 23, 5 (2011), 385-392.
13. Hislop, D. The objectivist perspective on knowledge, In *Knowledge management in organizations : a critical introduction*. Oxford University Press, 2005., (2005).
14. Jensen, K. L., Winschiers-Theophilus, H., Rodil, K., Winschiers-Goagoses, N., Kapuire, G. K. and

Kamukuenjandje, R. Putting it in perspective: designing a 3D visualization to contextualize indigenous knowledge in rural Namibia. *In Proc. of DIS'12*, ACM Press (2012), 196-199.

15. Lindtner, S., Mainwaring, S., Dourish, P. and Wang, Y. Situating Productive Play: Online Gaming Practices and Guanxi in China. *In Proc. Interact*, Springer Berlin Heidelberg (2009), 328-341.
16. Lindtner, S., Anderson, K. and Dourish, P. Cultural appropriation: information technologies as sites of transnational imagination. *In Proc. CSCW*, ACM (2012), 77-86.
17. Lodhi, S. and Mikulecky, P. Management of indigenous knowledge for developing countries. *In Proc. Communication and management in technological innovation and academic globalization*, WSEAS (2010), 94-98.
18. Martinez, C., Kemp, R., Birchfield, D., Campana, E., Ingalls, T. and Gkisedtanamoogk. Culturally sensible digital place-making: design of the mediated xicanindio resolana. *In Proc. TEI*, ACM (2010), 161-168.
19. Mkabela, Q. Using the Afrocentric Method in Researching Indigenous African Culture. *Qualitative Report*, *10*, 1 (2005), 178-189.
20. Oduor, E., Neustaedter, C., Judge, T. K., Hennessy, K., Pang, C. and Hillman, S. How technology supports family communication in rural, suburban, and urban kenya. *In Proc. Human Factors in Computing Systems*, ACM (2014), 2705-2714.
21. Pumpa, M. and Wyeld, T. G. Database and Narratological Representation of Australian Aboriginal Knowledge as Information Visualisation using a Game Engine. *In Proc. Information Visualisation* (2006), 237.
22. Ratuva, S. Commodifying cultural knowledge: corporatised western science and Pacific indigenous knowledge. *International Social Science Journal*, 60, 195 (2009), 153-163.
23. Rogers, Y. and Marsden, G. Does he take sugar?: moving beyond the rhetoric of compassion. *Interactions*, 20, 4 (2013), 48-57.
24. Shklovski, I., Lindtner, S., Vertesi, J. and Dourish, P. Transnational times: locality, globality and mobility in technology design and use. *In Proc. 12th ACM international conference adjunct papers on Ubiquitous computing - Adjunct*, ACM (2010), 515-518.
25. Siew, S.-T., Yeo, A. and Zaman, T. Participatory Action Research in Software Development: Indigenous Knowledge Management Systems Case Study, *In Human-Computer Interaction. Human-Centred Design Approaches, Methods, Tools, and Environments*.Springer Berlin Heidelberg, (2013), 470-479.
26. Thiong'o, N. w. *Decolonising the mind : the politics of language in African literature*. London : J. Currey ; Portsmouth, N.H. : Heinemann, 1986.
27. Verran, H. *Science and an African logic*. Chicago : University of Chicago Press, 2001., 2001.
28. Verran, H., Christie, M., Anbins-King, B., Van Weeren, T. and Yunupingu, W. Designing digital knowledge management tools with Aboriginal Australians. *Digital Creativity*, 18, 3 (2007), 129-142.
29. Williams, A., Anderson, K. and Dourish, P. Anchored mobilities: mobile technology and transnational migration. *In Proc. of DIS'08*, ACM Press (2008), 323-332.

Collective Intelligence in Computer-Mediated Collaboration Emerges in Different Contexts and Cultures

David Engel
Massachusetts Institute of Technology
Cambridge, USA
dengel@mit.edu

Anita Williams Woolley
Carnegie Mellon University
Pittsburgh, USA
awoolley@cmu.edu

Ishani Aggarwal
Tilburg University
Tilburg, Netherlands
ishaniaggarwal@gmail.com

Christopher F. Chabris
Union College
Schenectady, USA
chabris@gmail.com

Masamichi Takahashi
Fuji Xerox Co., Ltd.
Kanagawa, Japan
masamichi.takahashi@fujixerox.co.jp

Keiichi Nemoto
Fuji Xerox Co., Ltd.
Kanagawa, Japan
keiichi.nemoto@fujixerox.co.jp

Carolin Kaiser
University Erlangen-Nuremberg
Nuremberg, Germany
carolin.kaiser@gfk-verein.org

Young Ji Kim
Massachusetts Institute of Technology
Cambridge, USA
youngji@mit.edu

Thomas W. Malone
Massachusetts Institute of Technology
Cambridge, USA
malone@mit.edu

ABSTRACT
Collective intelligence (CI) is a property of groups that emerges from the coordination and collaboration of members and predicts group performance on a wide range of tasks. Previous studies of CI have been conducted with lab-based groups in the United States. We introduce a new standardized online battery to measure CI and demonstrate consistent emergence of a CI factor across three different studies despite broad differences in (a) communication media (face-to-face vs online), (b) group contexts (short-term ad hoc groups vs long-term groups) and (c) cultural settings (US, Germany, and Japan). In two of the studies, we also show that CI is correlated with a group's performance on more complex tasks. Consequently, the CI metric provides a generalizable performance measure for groups that is robust to broad changes in media, context, and culture, making it useful for testing the effects of general-purpose collaboration technologies intended to improve group performance.

Author Keywords
Collective intelligence; group performance; online collaboration; cross culture; factor analysis; outcome metrics.

INTRODUCTION
Recent research on group performance demonstrates that there is a single statistical factor for groups, just as there is for individuals, that predicts how well a group will perform on a wide range of different tasks [43]. This factor, called *collective intelligence* (CI), depends not only on the characteristics of the individuals in the group but also on how they work together. In a sense, therefore, this factor focuses on processes that are critical for using computers to help groups of humans interact.

CHI 2015, April 18 - 23, 2015, Seoul, Republic of Korea
Copyright 2015 ACM 978-1-4503-3145-6/15/04...$15.00
http://dx.doi.org/10.1145/2702123.2702259

An important type of research in human-computer interaction and computer-supported cooperative work involves empirically studying how well various kinds of computer tools help groups of people work together cooperatively. Typically, this is done by choosing a specific task and evaluating how well groups perform the task with (and sometimes without) the computer tools. However, the generalizability of such studies is always limited by the nature of the specific task chosen.

But imagine that we had some general way of measuring the ability of a group to work together, regardless of the type of task involved. Or, more precisely, what if we could measure the performance of a group working together on a carefully chosen set of tasks and then use these measurements to statistically predict how well the group would perform on a very wide range of other tasks?

Here we introduce a generalizable measure of team collective intelligence which can do just this. For example, web conferencing systems can be used to support groups performing many kinds of tasks, but it isn't obvious how to pick the tasks to use for testing such systems. Our collective intelligence test battery provides a carefully chosen set of tasks, which can be used to test the effects of such systems on group performance, and a statistical basis for using these results to predict performance on a much wider range of other tasks.

In this paper, we explore the generality of our newly designed computer-based measure of collective intelligence [8,43]. We meta-analyze three data sets to test the degree to which the CI factor emerges not only across different tasks, but across communication media (face-to-face vs. online), group contexts (short-term ad hoc groups vs long-term groups) and cultures (US, Germany, Japan) making this test battery generalizable to a variety of settings.

BACKGROUND

Measuring Collective Intelligence

We are increasingly reliant on groups in a growing number of domains in our daily lives. Decisions in healthcare, science, law enforcement, national security, transportation, and public policy, to name just a few, are all increasingly made by groups of highly networked individuals, and their performance is driven not only by their individual skills, but also by their ability to collectively collaborate and coordinate. However, until recently, we have lacked good tools to evaluate the degree to which groups can consistently perform at a high level.

By contrast, in research on individual performance, over the last century psychological researchers have devised effective tools for predicting who is likely to perform at a high level across many domains and over time. Cognitive psychologists have repeatedly demonstrated that a single statistical factor—often called "general intelligence" or "g"— emerges from the correlations among individuals' performance on a wide variety of cognitive tasks [6,38] and is highly predictive of individuals' future performance. Recently, Woolley et al. [43] applied the same statistical techniques used in individual intelligence research to measuring the intelligence of groups. The researchers first gave 192 groups a wide range of tasks that required qualitatively different collaboration processes for successful accomplishment [24]. In a factor analysis of all the groups' scores, the first factor accounted for 43% of the variance in performance. This is consistent with the 30–50% of variance typically explained by the first factor in a battery of individual cognitive tasks [4]. In individuals, this factor is called "intelligence" or "*g*". For groups, Woolley et al. referred to it as "*collective intelligence*" or "*c*," and it is a measure of the general effectiveness of a group on a wide range of tasks. The *c* factor also predicted how the groups performed on more complex tasks at a later point in time, above and beyond the predictive ability of the average individual intelligence of group members. Woolley et al. also showed that a group's collective intelligence was positively affected by the proportion of women in the group, the group members' social sensitivity, and their equal participation in group discussion.

The emergence of a single collective intelligence factor is itself a somewhat surprising outcome. The null hypothesis of any factor analysis is the emergence of as many factors as there are scores entered into the analysis. In other words, a test battery including five tasks should yield five roughly equivalent factors, unless there is a common force driving performance across some or all of them. And indeed, in the history of research on teams, much attention has been given to the *different* demands of different sorts of tasks, and the development of taxonomies to articulate the different ways groups would need to collaborate to successfully accomplish them. This would suggest that teams that perform well on one kind of task would not necessarily perform well on others. However, the emergence of a single dominant collective intelligence factor strongly suggests a central mechanism or set of mechanisms driving team performance across many domains. This has important implications for designing technological systems to support group work, as those that will enhance these key underlying collective abilities will have a much more profound effect on collaboration more generally.

This approach to conceptualizing and measuring intelligence in groups builds and improves upon traditional approaches to investigating intelligence and performance in team settings in two important ways. First, the relationship between team cognitive ability and performance has been previously examined as the aggregate of individual member intelligence. Individual intelligence has been shown to be a moderate predictor of team performance in lab-based settings, but the correlation of team average cognitive ability and performance becomes much smaller in field settings [7,18,26]. One probable explanation for this lack of explanatory power is the attempt to conceptualize *team* ability by aggregating *individual*-level measurements, which loses information in generalizing across levels of analysis [32].

Second, the vast majority of team research measures performance on a single task, whereas most teams in real world settings need to perform a multitude of tasks to operate effectively. Thus, a more robust method for capturing what constitutes team collective intelligence, utilizing uniquely team-level information and observation of performance on a variety of tasks will improve our ability to predict which teams are likely to consistently perform at a high level in the future.

Though the existence and emergence of a general collective intelligence factor in teams has been empirically supported [43], the existing work relies on U.S. lab-based samples involving groups of strangers collaborating face-to-face for a few hours. Indeed, recent research examining CI in a small sample of distributed groups raised questions about whether a single CI factor exists in such settings [1]. This is an important issue to explore, as work in organizations, both traditional and online, usually involves individuals with an ongoing relationship with each other and/or a common institution, collaborating both face-to-face and via media, from around the globe. Will a collective intelligence factor emerge in settings with these characteristics? Or will features of the culture, context, or the relationships among members create so much variance or randomness in how groups perform different tasks that a collective intelligence factor will not emerge?

Group Collaboration Online vs. Face-to-Face

Well over half of all employees in organizational settings have at some point worked in online teams [22]. Online teams are used in almost all industries and in a variety of areas, such as software development, customer service, sales and R&D [3,11,23].

A commonly addressed issue in online group collaboration is the lack of nonverbal and social cues during interaction. Early media characteristics theories suggested that the lack of cues in computer-mediated communication (CMC) makes it inferior to face-to-face communication in facilitating social interactions and conveying more complex, equivocal messages [5][36]. According to this view, technologies that do not offer the transmission of nonverbal cues cannot adequately support the processing of socioemotional and richer content, thereby inhibiting group members from engaging in further interaction. When group members collaborate on a task, limited interaction can potentially prevent them from exchanging necessary information to perform tasks effectively.

However, this so-called "cue-filtered-out" perspective, which claims face-to-face collaboration is better than text-based CMC, has been broadly challenged. In particular, Walther's social information processing theory provided a major counterargument to the early theories, by positing that with time, individuals are able to adapt to the lack of nonverbal cues, and engage in social and relational communication online just as well as face-to-face [42]. In addition, in some cases, text-based computer-mediated communication has been argued to be "superior" to face-to-face in that it gives individuals more agency and control in self-presentation by selectively transmitting cues that portray them in a positive light [21].

In spite of this, when a group works together online only, the group's ability to perform tasks may reflect not only their collective intelligence but also the degree to which members utilize and adapt to online collaboration tools (e.g., chat, real-time collaborative editing software) in task performance. Groups may differ in their experience with a given medium, which may emerge as a potential factor that creates variation in groups' performance independent of their collective intelligence [1]. Given these arguments, it is not clear whether a general collective intelligence factor will emerge to describe a group's performance capability regardless of communication media that support the group collaboration.

Group Collaboration in Short-Term Ad Hoc Groups vs Long-Term Groups

Woolley et al. [43] found the initial evidence of collective intelligence in groups of strangers gathered for a lab study. Would this finding apply to groups with ongoing work relationships? Literature that provides a basis for the linkage between time and group collaboration suggests mixed scenarios. On one hand, it is plausible to think that long-term groups may have an advantage in developing rules of coordination compared to ad hoc short-term groups. Ad hoc groups, without a stabilized work routine, may require more time for coordination, which can hurt performance [39]. In addition, long-term groups may be able to develop more trust among members of the group, promoting smooth information sharing and knowledge transfer [19]. Thus, one may expect greater consistency in performance across different types of tasks and thus the emergence of collective intelligence for long-term groups.

On the other hand, there can be a downside to longer tenure in groups. Groups can fall into habitual routines that they apply in inappropriate situations [9]. In addition, groups with ongoing relationships are subject to relational factors biasing information exchange such that members seek information only from someone they know and have access to [2]. This may lead to inconsistencies in how the same group performs different tasks, reducing the degree to which a CI factor would predict performance across domains. Therefore, one may imagine that collective intelligence emerges in a more consistent fashion in task-oriented short-term groups as they focus on a given task under time constraints, preventing existing relationships and prior assumptions about group members from affecting task-oriented interaction.

Group Collaboration across Cultures

Culture influences what social norms individuals recognize and what behaviors they believe they should or should not engage in when collaborating with others [30,41]. Culture is a multi-dimensional construct, and a number of competing frameworks have been proposed for thinking about how cultures differ from one another [12] (see [25] for a review). Some view cultural differences in terms of core values, which are stable across individuals, situations, and time [13][29], whereas others take a systems perspective, seeing culture as a dynamic system shaped by sociocultural artifacts such as symbols, discursive routines, and social institutions and structures [15]. We acknowledge that both psychological processes and sociocultural practices shape culture, resulting in both commonality and variability within a national culture. While not every member of one national culture thinks and behaves alike during group collaboration, culture has been considered an undeniable factor that explains differences in understanding of groups and collaboration [12][34].

To understand possible sources of cross-cultural differences in collective intelligence, if any, we discuss two dimensions that have been demonstrated to be particularly relevant to computer-mediated group communication, and potentially relevant to collective intelligence: individualism vs. collectivism [13], and high- versus low-context cultures [10].

Individualism-collectivism is an analytical dimension that captures the relative importance people accord to personal interests and to shared pursuits. Individualism is the condition in which personal interests are accorded greater importance than are the needs of groups [13,41]. Individualists look after themselves and tend to ignore group interests if they conflict with personal desires. Collectivism, on the other hand, occurs when the demands and interests of groups take precedence over the desires and needs of individuals. Collectivists look out for the well-being of the groups to which they belong, even if such actions sometimes require that personal interests be disregarded.

High-vs. low context culture is an additional distinction that often parallels individualism-collectivism [10]. A high-context culture is one in which people are deeply involved with each other. As a result of intimate relationships among people, a structure of social hierarchy exists, individual inner feelings are kept under strong self-control, and information is widely shared through simple messages with deep meaning. A low-context culture is one in which people are highly individualized, somewhat alienated, and fragmented, and there is relatively little involvement with others. Society in general imposes less on individuals' lives, and communication between people is more explicit and impersonal.

It is conceivable that notions of collective intelligence developed based on Western samples (made up of largely individualistic and low-context cultures) would not generalize to high-context, collectivistic cultures such as those found in East Asia. We might observe less variance in general in how more collectivistic teams perform, given their commitment to the group, making the notion of a predictive measure of collective intelligence one that has less utility for teams in collectivistic societies. Or, if we employ a traditional approach of convening lab-based groups of strangers, we might find in high context cultures a difficulty for such groups to "gel" enough to exhibit a consistent level of performance across tasks. Thus the degree to which notions of collective intelligence will generalize at all to high context, collectivistic samples remains an open question.

The difficulties of extending the collective intelligence construct to high context, collectivistic cultures may be even greater when groups collaborate online. Other research has predicted and found that high-context, collectivistic cultures, such as those in East Asia, place more value than do low-context cultures on feedback and social cues that may be reduced or eliminated in some forms of computer-mediated communication. For example, Chinese collaborators have been shown to engage in dramatically less communication when conversations are computer-mediated than face-to-face, compared to American collaborators who exhibit little to no reduction in communication between the two modes [35]. By contrast, improvements to computer mediated communication, such as multi-party chat, emoticons, and audio-video chat, which enhance communicators ability to convey and respond to context, are much more broadly embraced by high-context, collectivistic cultures than low-context, individualistic cultures [14]. Taken together, this suggests we might see a much weaker or less consistent collective intelligence factor emerge in online teams from high-context, collectivistic cultures (e.g., Japan) compared to their low-context, individualistic counterparts (e.g., Germany, US).

METHODS

Test Design

Following the protocol outlined in Woolley et al. [43], we adapted the original collective intelligence test battery into an online tool that enabled us to administer the test in a standardized way to all groups, whether working face-to-face or online. All members could see the input of others in the real-time. Even in settings where all group members were collocated and could communicate freely, they worked together through the browser-based platform. Figure 1 shows a screenshot of the interface.

Expanding on the work from Woolley et al.[43], we aimed to develop a battery of tasks that span a wide and comprehensive range of group processes. Consequently, we chose the initial set of tasks based on well-established taxonomies of group tasks as those developed by McGrath [24] and Larson [17] together with other basic types of task groups proposed by researchers in cognitive psychology and artificial intelligence [28,33,37]. The design of the specific tasks and task groups was strongly inspired by the

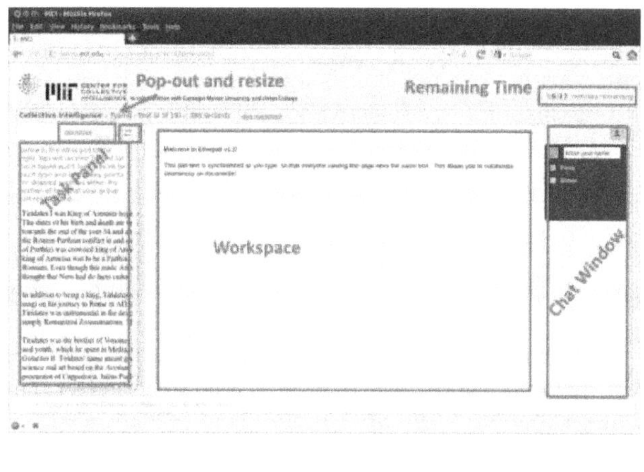

Figure 1: The online testing interface. The current task and instructions are displayed on the left hand side. The instructions can be popped out into a separate window. An integrated chat window on the right allows the groups to coordinate their efforts. The workspace in the center is a synchronized Etherpad that allows collaborative editing.

Task Group	Process	Summary
Typing (TY)	Executing	Create a copy of either a text or a long list of numbers as accurately as possible.
Detection (DE)	Sensing	Study a large grid of images or words and answer questions about them such as naming the most frequent object in that grid
Memory (ME)	Remembering	Collectively remember enough about videos, images or words to answer specific questions
Judgment (JG)	Choosing	Make a judgment such as estimating how a larger population of people would rate a slogan or an image
Brainstorming (BS)	Generating	Come up with as many words for a specific pattern, uses for an object (e.g. a brick) or equations following some constraints
Matrix Solving (MS)	Choosing	Solve matrix puzzle problems
Unscramble Words (SC)	Choosing	Figure out what word is represented in a set of letters which have been randomly shuffled around

Table 1:Tasks used in our Collective Intelligence (CI) test battery, the group process tested and a brief explanation.

set of tasks used in the original study of collective intelligence [43]. The tasks in the online battery fall into five general categories of group ability:

a) *Generating:* Requires the generation of new information

b) *Choosing:* Groups have to jointly pick one answer among a set of possible choices. The question can either have one objectively correct answer or be based on subjective ratings.

c) *Executing:* Requires careful coordination of psychomotor skills of team members such as joint typing.

d) *Remembering:* Groups need to remember features of previously presented information requiring them to distribute their attention during the presentation phase and later integrate their knowledge, similar to ideas explored in transactive memory research [11].

e) *Sensing:* Requires groups to recognize patterns in a noisy stimulus that is calibrated to exceed the capabilities of an individual.

We aim to have little overlap between task groups with respect to the specific group ability or process they are measuring. We avoided more complex, composite tasks since for those, the intertask correlations could stem from similarities between the tasks, instead of an underlying factor driving performance across all of them. Table 1 provides a brief explanation of the tasks deployed in the different task groups.

Most of these task groups contain several similar tasks in order to create a reliable index of the category. For example, the Memory task group contains a video memory task in which the members as a group need to remember certain features of a short movie clip, an image memory task where the group has to memorize a picture or a set of pictures and a word memory task in which the objective is to reproduce a previously presented and memorized list of words. We also aim to include both verbal and nonverbal operationalizations of each task group.

We are reporting meta-analyses of data from three studies conducted over a timespan of two years. Between the times when the studies were conducted, we not only evolved the tool but also improved several of the tasks. The subsets of tasks that were used in each study differ slightly, due to this evolution, and to specific restrictions such as language, time constraints, and concerns about possible cheating.

Given differences in timing of administration and cultural setting, there were minor differences in the specific task combinations the groups had to solve and differences in the wording especially across different languages. However, this does not inhibit our ability to explore the main question of our study, which is to what degree does group context and culture affect the emergence of a collective intelligence factor? Japan and Germany are particularly interesting contrasts for our purposes as they are on opposite ends of the cultural spectrum in terms of individualism/collectivism and high/low context.

CI Battery Administration and Scoring

The group members were assigned to groups either at random or according to a pre-existing team membership (as described for each specific study below.) We provided each person with an anonymized login ID that they used to login to our testing server and join their group. Once all group members were logged in, our system started the administration of the tasks. The system continuously provided a collaborative environment for online task solving where group members were presented with the task instructions, a joint workspace and a chat interface (see Figure 1). The system recorded answers and interactions, and moved the group members simultaneously through the tasks according to pre-specified time allocations.

After the teams had completed the online battery, we downloaded the results and scored the tasks with the help of a semi-automated script. As mentioned above, some of the task groups contained multiple subtasks (e.g. the memory task group containing a video, an image and a word memory task). We combined these tasks by averaging the normalized subscores.

Finally, we conducted a principal component analysis to explore the factor structure of the scores in each study. The score of a group on the first factor is what constitutes the group's collective intelligence (CI) score.

Samples and Measures

The three studies took place in different settings, different cultures, and different languages; included groups with varying lengths of working relationships; and contained different modes of communication between the group members. All groups completed our online, browser-based test described above which was the basis for their CI score.

Study 1: United States

The first study contained 68 groups of 4 people that were recruited from the general population in the Boston area using online advertisements. The team members were compensated for their participation. All groups were invited to a lab setting where they completed a one-hour battery of tests as a team. Participants were randomly assigned to groups. Approximately half of the groups worked online and communicated solely through the text-based chat window provided by our online tool. The other half were allowed to communicate normally while seated around a table to work on the battery of tasks. After completing the online collective intelligence test, all teams also participated together in the Desert Survival Situation task [16]. The Desert Survival Situation task is a well-established team exercise where a group is asked to imagine a hypothetical scenario of a plane crash in a desert and to rank 15 items salvaged from the crash in order of their importance to the group's survival. The task requires an intense level of group interaction and a synergistic integration of various pieces of information, making it a suitable criterion task for collective intelligence. Other results from this study were reported by Engel et al. [8], and further details about the study procedure are reported there.

Study 2: Germany

In the second study, we recruited 116 groups of 2–5 students from a class on innovation management that was attended by students from the fields of business studies, economics, computer science, and engineering at a German university. The groups were intact teams that worked together on an extra-credit project for which they had to invent and prototype a smartphone app in the area of social service, education or nutrition. Their participation in our study was voluntary but was incentivized by a raffle of monetary prizes among all groups that completed the test battery. The team members knew each other and had previously worked together in the same configuration for earlier group assignments in the class. The groups were furthermore allowed to self-select their mode of communication while completing the CI battery, ranging from (a) face-to-face communication, through (b) ad hoc voice and video communication of their own choosing, to (c) the text chat facility built into our testing platform. For purposes of analysis, we considered teams communicating primarily by text, voice or video chat to be "online" and those that were primarily co-located to be "face to face." To reduce potential confusions and noise due to different levels of comfort with English, we had native German speakers translate the user-interface and the tasks in the battery into German before administration.

Study 3: Japan

In the third study, we recruited 25 groups of 4 persons through a temporary staffing agency in Japan and invited them to a lab setting to participate. They were compensated for their participation in a shortened battery. The setting restricted them to only communicate through the chat interface in our system. Native speakers translated the battery and the interface into Japanese. Because of time constraints in administering the battery and concerns about the translation of some of the verbally intensive tasks, we selected and administered only a subset of five task groups in this context.

RESULTS

1. A general Collective Intelligence factor emerges consistently in groups performing collaborative tasks in different cultural settings

In examining the subtests of any test of general intelligence, researchers want to see a small to moderate average pairwise correlation, which indicates an underlying relationship among the tests but sufficient independence that each is capturing unique variance. The pattern of pairwise correlations among the groups of tasks in the CI battery is displayed in Table 2. We see there an average pairwise correlation of 0.32 among the subtests of the collective intelligence battery for the US groups, of 0.23 for the Japanese groups, and of 0.37 for the German groups.

Next, we analyzed the factor structure underlying the group scores. The scree plot in Figure 2 shows the amounts of variance explained by each of the factors. Although the settings, methods of communication, and cultural norms differ substantially among the three studies, there is a striking similarity among the factor structures. Similar to classical results for individual intelligence tests, the first factor explains about 40% or more of the variance in all settings. Confirmatory factor analyses support the conclusion that a one factor model is the best fit for the data. In the U.S. sample: $\chi^2 = 28.36$, $p = .37$, RMSEA = .01. AIC = 56.36; in the German sample: $\chi^2 = 15.09$, $p = .37$,

		TY	BS	MS	ME	DE	SC
United States	BS	.46					
	MS	.53	.53				
	ME	.42	.27	.45			
	DE	.35	.31	.28	.22		
	SC	.25	.51	.40	.23	.24	
	JG	.19	.29	.20	.29	.05	.30
Japan	BS	.00					
	MS	.35	.43				
	ME	.21	.26	.04			
	DE	.22	.52	.16	.07		
	SC	.01	.40	.15	.25	.19	
Germany	BS	.45					
	MS	.46	.35				
	ME	.45	.48	.19			
	DE	.22	.28	.05	.25		
	SC	.41	.40	.20	.41	.17	
	JG	.19	.24	.20	.18	.07	.14

Table 2:Pairwise correlations for each task group for each study. See Table 1 for task group abbreviations. Correlations > .20 are significant at $p < .05$ in U.S. and Germany samples; > .40 in Japan sample. *Note:* The JG subtest was not included in the Japan study.

RMSEA = .03, AIC = 43.09; and in the Japanese sample: $\chi^2 = 9.18, p = .42$, RMSEA = .03, AIC = 33.18.

A second observation that is of interest when we compare these studies is the congruence of the loadings of the different task groups on the main collective intelligence factor. Coefficients of congruence are useful for comparing the similarity of factor patterns [40]. Lorenzo-Seva and ten Berge [20] suggested "a value in the range .85–.94 corresponds to a fair similarity, while a value higher than .95 implies that the two factors or components compared can be considered equal." In the current samples, the loadings produce congruence coefficients that range from $r_{congruence}$=.94 (Japan:German sample) to $r_{congruence}$=.99 (German: US sample).

2. The Collective Intelligence factor is consistent across communication media and group contexts

In the US setting, we randomly assigned groups to two conditions [8]. In the *online* condition, group members were not able to see each other, and they communicated solely via the provided chat interface. In the *face-to-face* condition, subjects were seated around a conference table and could communicate freely by speaking to each other. By holding all other factors constant, such as test administration, subject pool, and location, this study

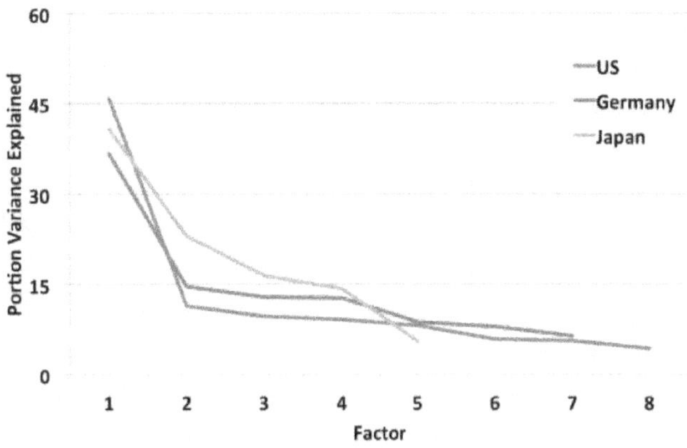

Figure 2: Scree plot of the variance explained by the factors in the three studies. The first factor explains around 40% of the variance while the next factors explain significantly less. The number of factors is equivalent to the number of task groups in the analysis. The German dataset had the highest variance in group sizes and modes of communication, which contributed to the slightly reduced variance explained by the first factor. The Japanese study contained only a subset of five task groups, which leads to the reduced number of factors.

allowed us to take a clearer look at the influence of communication on group performance. In the German setting, as noted above, groups had a history of working together and were able to self-select which mode of communication to use. Figure 3 shows the scree plot of the two datasets, comparing modes of communication.

The CI factor emerges clearly across communication media, group contexts (i.e., short-term ad hoc vs. long-term) and cultures, explaining about 40% or more of the variance in all cases. This supports the generality of the metric for studying groups across various modes of communication, group contexts, and cultural settings.

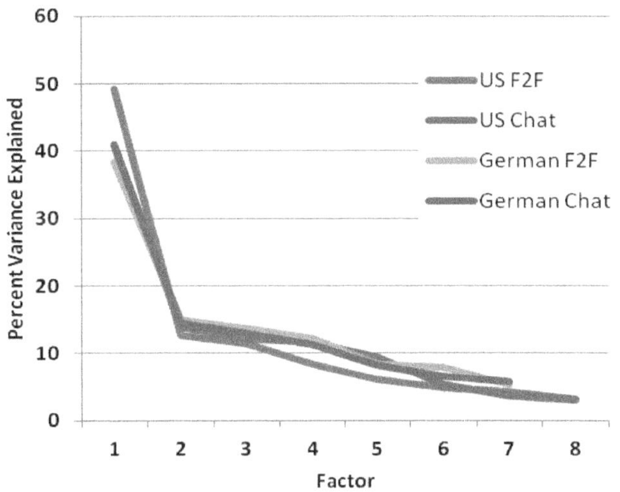

Figure 3: Scree plots of the U.S. and German samples comparing culture and communication media.

3. Collective Intelligence is correlated with performance on complex tasks

In two of our samples, groups worked on other projects or complex tasks as a criterion task, in addition to completing the collective intelligence battery. Their performance on these tasks was moderately correlated with their collective intelligence scores.

In the U.S. lab-based study, both the online and face-to-face teams participated together in the Desert Survival Situation at a later time in the same lab session. Groups completed the task using the same mode of communication that was used to complete the collective intelligence battery.

Analyses of group performance scores on the Desert Survival Situation demonstrated that groups' CI scores were a strong positive predictor of performance on the task ($b = .24$, $p = .058$), controlling for communication media.

In the German student teams, the project descriptions and prototypes were rated by 47 other students along the following dimensions: Novelty, Added Value, Innovativeness, Creativity, Interestingness, Business Relevance and New Thinking. There was a significant positive correlation between the average scores received by student raters and the team's CI scores: $r = .25$ ($p = .008$). While smaller than the relationship between CI and performance observed in lab-based studies, it is comparable in size to other relationships between standardized tests and performance in longer-term, multi-faceted situations, such as between SAT scores and individual college grade point average (GPA): $r = .23$ ($p < .01$) [27]. It is also substantially higher than the average correlation of individual intelligence and group performance found in meta-analyses of field studies: $r = .14$, ($p > .05$) [7]. Though we did not have the data to evaluate it here, prior studies have documented a weak relationship between aggregate individual intelligence and collective intelligence, suggesting the former is not a proxy for the latter [43]. Taken together, the results support the criterion validity of our battery as a measure of collective intelligence, which accounts for reasonable variance in team performance both within and outside laboratory.

It is also noteworthy that CI, as measured using the battery of various tasks, is also a much stronger predictor of student team performance than any of the single tasks in the CI battery alone (average $r = .12$) except for the most highly correlated task ($r = .27$). Had we attempted to gauge team performance capability with the use of a single task, as is common in most lab studies, we would have likely done poorly, since all but one of the tasks correlated less with the project score than did the composite CI measure, and it is not possible to know in advance which task will correlate most highly. This demonstrates the advantage of the composite CI score over traditional ways of measuring group performance by using a single task only. Our measure of collective intelligence is more robust against noise than are single tasks, in part because it more reliably measures the underlying factor that drives group performance.

SUMMARY & CONCLUSION

We have presented a meta-analysis of three studies investigating the emergence of a general collective intelligence factor in groups working together on a wide array of tasks in our online testing environment. The studies were conducted in three different cultural settings (US, Germany and Japan), in three different languages, using slightly different subsets of tasks and different modes of communication. However, the factor structure that emerges is highly congruent across all three studies. These results suggest some underlying similarities in the basic interaction patterns supporting human group performance, despite differences in communication modes, group contexts, and cultural settings.

While we have shown that the concept of CI is general, questions remain as to whether CI emerges in similar ways across various modes of communication, group contexts, and cultural settings. For example, Woolley et al. [43], in their lab studies with US ad hoc groups interacting face to face, found that CI was positively correlated with group members' average social sensitivity and equal distribution of conversational turn-taking. Engel et al. [8] validated the role of these factors in CI for groups working online. An important question that future research should pursue is whether these factors are as important for groups with ongoing working relationships and for groups in other cultures. For example, groups with ongoing working relationships may have already established a system of who knows what and who does what, in which case distribution of turn-taking is likely to be a manifestation of variance in roles and expertise domains. Thus, in some cases, unequal distribution may demonstrate greater specialization and efficient coordination in long-term groups, which can affect collective intelligence.

In cultures where power distance is considered more natural such as East Asian countries, distribution of participation may not vary as much as in their western counterparts, thereby having limited role in affecting CI. National cultures characterized as high-context cultures may also have higher social sensitivity than low-context cultures on average; thus, the role of social sensitivity in CI may be limited by a ceiling effect. While the current study did not allow us to explore these possibilities, future research can tease out the effects of group contexts and cultural settings on the process of CI emergence.

In addition, we did not have access to individual intelligence scores or grades for the individual participants in these studies, and were not able to determine the correlation between them or the relative contributions of individual intelligence versus collective intelligence to group performance. Earlier work on the topic demonstrated a relatively weak correlation between the two [43]. However, the utility of the concept of collective intelligence does not rely upon its distinctiveness from individual intelligence, so much as its ability to capture underlying patterns of behavior in the group driving performance across different domains. These patterns can be influenced by a range of individual differences, including general intelligence and social ability, as well as a host of group-level norms, routines, and even collaboration technologies, the latter being of greatest interest to us here.

In closing, we believe that our results have important implications for designers of collaboration technologies. In particular, they support the idea that researchers can use collective intelligence tests to measure the effects of various kinds of general-purpose group collaboration tools, such as email systems, web conferencing software, and social media, on group performance. The CI battery provides a carefully chosen set of tasks to use for testing the effects of such tools on group performance. For instance, a researcher with two versions of a web conferencing system could have groups take our collective intelligence test after randomly assigning the groups to use either version A or version B while doing the test. If the groups using version A perform better, then the researcher has a statistical basis for predicting that groups using version A would perform better on a wide range of other tasks, too. This, therefore, provides an economy of effort in testing tools to facilitate online collaboration in a wide variety of settings.

ACKNOWLEDGMENTS

This work was made possible by financial support from the National Science Foundation (grant numbers IIS-0963285 ACI-1322254, and IIS-0963451), the U. S. Army Research Office (grant numbers 56692-MA and 64079-NS) and Cisco Systems, Inc. through their sponsorship of the MIT Center for Collective Intelligence. We wish to thank Geena Chen, Nada Hashmi and Lisa Jing from MIT, and Sabine Schlick and Lucas Calmbach from University Erlangen-Nuremberg for their help with data collection.

REFERENCES

1. Barlow, J.B. and Dennis, A.R. Not as smart as we think: A study of collective intelligence in virtual groups. *Proceedings of Collective Intelligence 2014*, (2014).
2. Borgatti, S.P. and Cross, R. A relational view of information seeking and learning in social networks. *Management Science 49*, 4 (2003), 432–445.
3. Carmel, E. *Global Software Development Teams: Collaborating across Borders and Time Zones*. Prentice Hall, Upper Saddle River, NJ, 1999.
4. Chabris, C.F. Cognitive and neurobiological mechanisms of the law of general intelligence. In M.J. Roberts, ed., *Integrating the Mind: Domain General versus Domain specific Processes in Higher Cognition*. Psychology Press, Hove, UK, 2007, 449–491.
5. Daft, R.L. and Lengel, R.H. Organizational information requirements, media richness and structural design. *Management Science 32*, 5 (1986), 554–571.
6. Deary, I.J. *Looking Down on Human Intelligence: From Psychometrics to the Brain*. Oxford University Press, New York, 2000.
7. Devine, D.J. and Philips, J.L. Do smarter teams do better: A meta-analysis of cognitive ability and team performance. *Small Group Research 32*, 5 (2001), 507–532.
8. Engel, D., Woolley, A.W., Jing, L.X., Chabris, C.F., and Malone, T.W. Reading the mind in the eyes or reading between the lines? Theory of Mind predicts collective intelligence equally well online and face-to-face. *PLoS ONE 9*, 12 (2014).
9. Gersick, C.J. and Hackman, J.R. Habitual routines in task-performing groups. *Organizational Behavior and Human Decision Processes 47*, (1990), 65–97.
10. Hall, E.T. *Beyond Culture*. Anchor Press--Doubleday, New York, 1976.
11. Hertel, G., Konradt, U., and Orlikowsi, B. Managing distance by interdependence: Goal setting, task interdependence and team-based rewards in virtual teams. *European Journal of Work and Organizational Psychology 13*, (2004), 1–28.
12. Hinds, P. and Reinecke, K. Advancing Methodologies for Cross- Cultural Studies of Collaborative Systems. *Proceedings of the Companion Publication of the 17th ACM Conference on Computer Supported Cooperative Work*, ACM Press (2014), 323–326.
13. Hofstede, G.H. *Culture's Consequences, International Differences in Work-related Values*. Sage, Beverly Hills, CA, 1980.
14. Kayan, S., Fussell, S.R., and Setlock, L.D. Cultural differences in the use of instant messaging in Asia and North America. *Proceedings of the 2006 20th Anniversary Conference on Computer Supported Cooperative Work*, ACM Press (2006), 525–528.
15. Kitayama, S. Culture and basic psychological processes: Toward a system view of culture: Comment on Oyserman et al. (2002). *Psychological Bulletin 128*, (2002), 89–96.
16. Lafferty, J.C., Pond, A.W., and International, H.S. *Desert Survival Situation*. Human Synergistics International, 1987.
17. Larson, J.R. *In Search of Synergy in Small Group Performance*. Psychology Press, New York, NY, 2009.
18. Lepine, J.A., Hollenbeck, J.R., Ilgen, D.R., and Hedlund, J. Effects of individual differences on the performance of hierarchical decision-making teams: Much more than g. *Journal of Applied Psychology 82*, 5 (1997), 803–811.
19. Lewis, K. Knowledge and performance in knowledge-worker teams: A longitudinal study of transactive memory systems. *Management Science 50*, (2004), 1519–1533.
20. Lorenzo-Seva, U. and Ten Berge, J.M. Tucker's congruence coefficient as a meaningful index of factor

similarity. *Methodology: European Journal of Research Methods for the Behavioral and Social Sciences 2*, 2 (2006), 57–64.

21. Markus, M.L. Electronic mail as the medium of managerial choice. *Organization Science 5*, 4 (1994), 502–527.
22. Martins, L.L., Gilson, L.L., and Maynard, M.T. Virtual teams: What do we know and where do we go from here? *Journal of Management 30*, 6 (2004), 805–836.
23. McDonough, E. An investigation of the use of global, virtual, and colocated new product development teams. *Journal of Product Innovation Management 18*, (2001), 110–120.
24. McGrath, J.E. *Groups: Interaction and Performance*. Prentice-Hall, Englewood Cliffs, NJ, 1984.
25. Myers, M., D. and Tan, F., B. Beyond models of national culture in information systems research. In *Advanced Topics in Global Information Management*. Idea Group Inc (IGI), 2002, 14–29.
26. Neuman, G.A., Wagner, S.H., and Christiansen, N.D. The relationship between work-team personality composition and the job performance of teams. *Group & Organization Management 24*, (1999), 28–45.
27. Noftle, E.E. and Robins, R.W. Personality predictors of academic outcomes: Big five correlates of GPA and SAT scores. *Journal of Personality and Social Psychology 93*, 1 (2007), 116–130.
28. Nye, J.L. and Brower, A.M. *What's Social about Social Cognition? Research on Socially Shared Cognition in Small Groups*. Sage, Thousand Oaks, CA, 1996.
29. Oyserman, D., Coon, H.M., and Kemmelmeier, M. Rethinking individualism and collectivism: Evaluation of theoretical assumptions and meta-analyses. *Psychological Bulletin 128*, 1 (2002), 3–72.
30. Probst, T.M., Carnevale, P.J., and Triandis, H.C. Cultural values in intergroup and single-group social dilemmas. *Organizational Behavior and Human Decision Processes 77*, 3 (1999), 171–191.
31. Ren, Y. and Argote, L. Transactive memory systems 1985–2010: An integrative framework of key dimensions, antecedents, and consequences. *The Academy of Management Annals 5*, 1 (2011), 189–229.
32. Rousseau, D.M. Issues of level in organizational research: Multi-level and cross-level perspectives. In L.L. Cummings and B. Staw, eds., *Research in Organizational Behavior*. JAI, Greenwich, CT, 1985, 1–37.
33. Russell, S.J. *Artificial Intelligence: A Modern Approach*. Prentice Hall, Upper Saddle River, 2010.
34. Scissors, L., Shami, N.S., Ishihara, T., Rohall, S., and Saito, S. Real-time collaborative editing behavior in USA and Japanese distributed teams. *Proceedings of the SIGCHI Conference on Human Factors in Computing Systems*, ACM Press (2011), 1119–1128.
35. Setlock, L.D., Fussell, S.R., and Neuwirth, C. Taking it out of context: Collaborating within and across cultures in face-to-face settings and via instant messaging. *Proceedings of the 2004 ACM Conference on Computer Supported Cooperative Work*, ACM Press (2004), 604–613.
36. Short, J., Williams, E., and Christie, B. *The Social Psychology of Telecommunications*. Wiley, New York, 1976.
37. Smith, E.E. *Cognitive Psychology: Mind and Brain*. Pearson/Prentice Hall, Upper Saddle River, N.J, 2007.
38. Spearman, C. General intelligence, objectively determined and measured. *American Journal of Psychology 15*, 2 (1904), 201–293.
39. Tschan, F. Ideal cycles of communication (or cognitions) in triads, dyads, and individuals. *Small Group Research 33*, 6 (2002), 615–643.
40. Tucker, L.R. *A Method of Synthesis of Factor Analysis Studies*. Department of the Army, Washington, D.C., 1951.
41. Wagner, J.A. and Moch, M.K. Individualism-collectivism: Concept and measure. *Group & Organization Management 11*, 3 (1986), 280–304.
42. Walther, J.B. Interpersonal effects in computer-mediated interaction: A relational perspective. *Communication Research 19*, 1 (1992), 52–90.
43. Woolley, A.W., Chabris, C.F., Pentland, A., Hashmi, N., and Malone, T.W. Evidence for a collective intelligence factor in the performance of human groups. *Science 330*, (2010), 686–688.

Google+ Communities as Plazas and Topic Boards

Michael J. Brzozowski
Google, Inc.
Mountain View, CA, USA
zozo@google.com

Phil Adams
Cornell University
Ithaca, NY, USA
pja22@cornell.edu

Ed H. Chi
Google, Inc.
Mountain View, CA, USA
edchi@google.com

ABSTRACT
Researchers have recently been focusing on understanding online communities in social networks that offer easy access to new audiences. How do online communities function within these social networks? In this work, we conducted a mixed-method study of public Google+ Communities and found two major types evident in both how users talk about them and how they appear to use them: *plazas* to meet new people, and *topic boards* to discuss common interests. This reflects two common motivations users cite in describing Communities: "meeting like minded people" and "finding great content". We characterize these two types of Communities within Google+ using mixed methods including surveys, interviews, and quantitative analytics, and expose differences in user behaviors between them.

Author Keywords
Online communities; Online social networks; Google+

ACM Classification Keywords
H.5.3. Information Interfaces and Presentation (e.g. HCI): Group and Organization Interfaces

INTRODUCTION
For decades, online communities have provided a way for users to connect around their interests, ask questions, and provide support to one another. Before the Web, dial-up bulletin board systems and the WELL (Whole Earth 'Lectronic Link) community in 1985 [8] pioneered many community practices. Many forms of online communities flourished, including Usenet news, mailing lists, and web forums focused on specific topics such as health.

Recently, online communities have been coupled with online social networks (OSNs) such as Facebook, LinkedIn, and Google+, allowing users to interact with both their friends or contacts they follow, as well as fellow members of a community. This coupling enables us to examine the relationship and the differences between these two forms of social interaction. On one hand, communities enable users to circumvent the graph to reach others who share their interests. On the other, social network users may already be destined to connect to others who share their cultural identity and values [12], so communities in an OSN may simply reflect existing ties.

Here we are interested in exploring how the combination with OSNs has changed the nature of online communities. We perform this work in the context of a relatively new social network, Google+[1], which is built around a directed social graph. In Google+, a user follows someone by adding them to one of his or her *Circles*; this action need not be reciprocated. The Google+ social graph is thus a hybrid of symmetric and asymmetric edges [24] just like Twitter, but with a higher clustering coefficient [13], reflecting a hybrid use to connect both with one's friends and with interests. In October 2013, Google announced the Google+ OSN has 300 million 30-day active users [7].

Google+ Communities[2] launched in December 2012, marketed as "for all the people you ought to know" [6]. Communities can be designated by their creator as *Public* or *Private*. Public Communities and their contents are visible to everyone, while Private Communities' contents are only shown to members. Additionally, the owner of a Community may elect to require new members to ask permission before joining. Users can find Communities from within Google+ by searching for topics, by scanning a list of system-selected "recommended" Communities, by receiving an invitation from someone they follow, or by following a link shared by someone they follow.

Our main research questions focus on the understanding of Communities within the Google+ OSN:

1. Why do people join Communities in Google+? Do their motivations align with prior studies of other online communities?
2. To what extent are Communities used as meeting places for new friendships to form? Are Google+ Communities used as a way to connect with new people?
3. Since the directed Google+ graph already affords following users' interests, how likely are people to be following fellow Community members?

In our study, we used a combination of several methods, including surveys, interviews, and quantitative analytics, to achieve some understanding of these questions. First, we coded 167 free-form responses from our survey to ascertain why respondents used Communities, and we interviewed 12 subjects in depth. Then we obtained a snapshot of the public membership rosters of 429,693 Public Communities

CHI 2015, April 18–23, 2015, Seoul, Republic of Korea.
ACM 978-1-4503-3145-6/15/04.
http://dx.doi.org/10.1145/2702123.2702600

[1] plus.google.com
[2] plus.google.com/communities

in Google+ with more than two members, and analyzed the graph density and engagement metrics of those Communities.

We found most active users describe their motivations for joining Google+ Communities to be finding like-minded people and finding relevant content. Further analysis of Communities suggests these uses are supported by two main archetypes: *plazas* and *topic boards*. Many large public Google+ Communities fall somewhere on this spectrum. The findings suggest that successful communities can come in either flavor, but the prevalence of common interest forums suggest new ways of supporting these different types of communities in OSNs.

In the rest of this paper, we will first present a very brief overview of the rich history of online community research. Then we will outline the methods and results of the survey and interview studies. Next, we go into details of quantitative analyses of graph density and engagement metrics of a wide variety of communities. We further discuss the implication of these findings, and conclude by summarizing our findings.

RELATED WORK

An *online community* is a virtual community whose members interact with each other primarily via the Internet [25]. It's a simple information system where any member of the community can post content for other members to see and react to. Some communities restrict their membership, or have moderators with the ability to remove inappropriate content or people.

Many online forums have developed into communities of practice (COP) [29, 25], in which users are bounded by not just a common topical interest but also a common pursuit. Members in these COPs collaborate and help each other to improve their skills [25]. For example, members in many photography communities in Google+ often share tips, advice, and results of their work and failures with each other.

Understanding User Behaviors in Online Communities

Much has been written about building online communities—*e.g.*, how to bootstrap and maintain them, how to form social norms and regulate behavior, and how to encourage commitment and increase engagement. Kraut *et al.* offer a comprehensive synthesis of this research [10].

Sociologists distinguish two types of connections people have with the groups they join. In *common bond* groups, members feel more connected with each other than the group; in *common identity* groups, members feel more associated with the group identity than with other members [20]. An analysis of Flickr groups maps these categorizations into "social" and "topical" groups, respectively, finding that "social" groups have more comments per member [5].

Ridings and Green found that "information exchange" is the most common reason people join online communities, followed by either social support or friendship [22]. Wang *et al.* suggested that "informational support" is a key reason people joined a breast cancer support group, but "emotional support" from fellow members was a key reason they stayed [27].

OSNs and Communities

Online social networks (OSNs) developed much later than online communities, within the last 10–15 years. In OSNs, the focus is not on joining existing communities, but rather, finding specific friends or contacts to follow. Usually they feature a personalized stream of posts that does not focus on any one topic in particular, but is an aggregation of all posts made by contacts that the user follows. This leads to more sociality, but also much more complex social relationship structures.

For example, recent analysis of Twitter's follower graph suggests it exhibits properties of both a social and an information network [14], as users follow a mix of friends, celebrities, and news sources. To deal with this, Google+ users commonly engage in selective sharing to target posts at particular audiences who might be interested in them [9, 28].

Facebook Groups is one of the first combinations of online community features with an OSN. Park *et al.* found that Facebook Groups serve four primary needs: socializing, entertainment, status-seeking, and information [19]. Our notion of plazas and topic boards matches well with the two socializing and information uses of Facebook Groups. Other work has explored Facebook Groups being used for personal support (*e.g.*, with breast cancer) [1] and political advocacy [30].

In general, a common theme in online communities research is the categorization of online communities—indeed, Lazar and Preece contribute a clustering of classification schemes into four groups: (1) by community attributes (*e.g.*, social support); (2) by the software platform affording the community; (3) by connection to in-person communities (*e.g.*, a church group); and (4) by social boundedness [11]. Such classification is blurred by the evolution and overlapping of traditionally separate online spaces, *e.g.*, Groups and Communities being added to Facebook and Google+.

Following on this prior research, we wish to understand the blurring of the boundary between OSNs and online communities. We focus on understanding communities and their common use cases amongst Google+ users, and extending the categorization work to focus on two specific use cases that appear to be common in Google+ Communities. Do users see these communities as places to meet people, or to learn about a topic of interest? As relationships and interests are articulated by the graph in an OSN, we can also ask: Do users tend to join communities in which they socialize with other members they already know?

METHODS

We employed a mixed-methods approach since we are focused on understanding a wide variety of user behaviors at different granularities within Google+ Communities. Each successive method below refines the research questions we explore in earlier stages.

1. **Survey**: To understand how people perceive Google+ Communities, we deployed a short preliminary survey on Google+ and in key Communities. This provided a first broad understanding of how users perceive the Communities feature within Google+, including their initial use cases.

2. **Interviews**: Informed by the findings from the survey, we conducted a set of followup interviews, which provide for a closer look at why users behave the way they do in these Communities, what their intentions are, and how their goals manifest as actual behavior.
3. **Examining Google+ Communities**: To empirically measure the some motivations we saw in surveys and interviews, we analyzed activity data from Public Communities and the publicly visible portion of the Google+ follower graph. We identified outlier Communities to examine by hand. This provided a broad validation of trends that we found from the survey and interview studies.

SURVEY

In March 2013 we posted a short survey in English soliciting potential participants for future interviews. We reached respondents via snowball sampling: we posted on Google+ and in a few key Communities focused on discussing users' experience with Google+, and people reshared it on the network 110 times. We received 818 responses from 61 countries; the US, UK, Canada, India, and Germany were the most common, together covering 75% of respondents.

In addition to a few demographic questions, we asked those who confirmed they used Communities a single free-response question: "Briefly, what's your impression of Google+ Communities?" One of the authors then applied open coding to a randomly-selected 167 of these responses by hand.

Why People Use Communities

Fifty-nine of these responses were coded as describing why the respondent used Communities as follows:

Content

Forty (68%) of these respondents mentioned using Communities to find content around their interests. R160 said, "It's been very helpful to organize some of the things that I'm interested in."

R27 elaborated that it provides an alternative to using Circles:

> Communities are great to find shared intetests *[sic]* without having to circle people. ... It also gives more room for discussions as people you are normally [not] connected with can find the post in a community and engage with you.

People

Twenty-seven (46%) of these respondents described the opportunity to "find like-minded people" or "meet people". While topical interests are often mentioned as a common trait used to find like-minded people, the responses in this category focused on actually finding or meeting *people*, rather than just getting interesting *content*. These are not typically random strangers, but people who share a common interest.

Some explicitly described the opportunity to *meet* new people. R21 said, "They provide a wonderful opportunity to meet and share with people having similar interests." R180 commented, "It further facilitates the process of meeting new people with similar interests, and condenses down to a forum where everyone can participate."

Others used vaguer terms like *find* and *connect*. R65 remarked, "I think this is a great tool to find people with related interests." "They seem like a good way to connect with people with similar interests", said R39.

In contrast to R27, R25 described using them as a way to find new people to follow: "Great way to find posts relating to a specific topic and people worth circling."

Relationship to the Circles Network

Another 27 respondents opined on the relationship of Communities to the broader Google+ OSN.[3] This was somewhat controversial; ten people commented that they felt that discussion topics were now fragmented between their Circles graph and Communities. R120 described a pressure to join Communities to remain connected to content they were previously following:

> ...when they hijack conversations from the larger public community I don't like that. Say you have not joined every community that has to do with your main interest. Now the people who used to be in your stream have diverted their posts from the regular Public stream to a community. As far as I see, they're just gone. The person is still posting, and probably feels that their posts are still public (if it's a public community) but only those who have joined the community already will see the posts.

Meanwhile, another six commented that they preferred this separation.[4] Google+ users employ selective sharing in part to avoid "spamming" uninterested people [9]. For example, R129 and R128 use Communities to target posts at specific audiences:

> I like granularity to my interests so I can keep my specific nerdly things separate. My ukulele people don't want to hear about yarn or Ingress or writing or drawing. I like the separation. (R129)
>
> I do love how the focus on certain aspects of one's interests can be segregated from one's main stream. I can get specific questions answered, discuss favorite topics, and not dilute my main stream with posts I don't want to share with everyone. (R128)

Summary

Two dominant motivations for Google+ Communities use emerged, covering 83% of those who described why they used Communities (49 respondents)[5]: a place for interesting content beyond the Circles graph (both to receive content and to post it), and to find or meet like-minded people; this is consistent with [22]. There still appears to be a large group of respondents who are more interested in meeting people than in merely getting access to interesting content.

[3] Other responses included: 88 describing general sentiment toward Communities, 30 citing specific frustrations, and 25 feature requests.
[4] The remainder of comments in this category related to details of the UI implementation and integration into Google+.
[5] Other uses mentioned included: 10 connecting an existing real-life group, 7 learning about a topic, and 6 having a place for discussion.

As we only had one author coding responses, and recruited through snowball sampling, it's not appropriate to infer the precise prevalence of these attitudes in the general population. However, we can still have reasonable confidence that a majority of respondents expressed one of these two uses[6].

There's certainly a lot of overlap between these respondents—we coded eighteen (30%) as motivated by both content and people. Other, less prevalent, uses cited by respondents included learning and discussion, organizing an existing offline group, and connecting friends or family.

We explored these uses in more depth with interviews and data analysis.

INTERVIEWS

To get a sense of how people connected with each other in Communities, we conducted twelve one-hour interviews with Communities users in the United States who specifically reported having met someone in a Community. We sampled respondents recruited via both snowball sampling in key Google+ Communities and a broader user research panel. Participants were eight men and four women ranging in age from 18–60 from across the continental US.

Interviews were semi-structured, conducted by the same author, and video was reviewed by a second author. We derived themes from an *ad hoc* analysis of interview notes, agreed upon by two of the authors. Quotes were verified from interview videos.

Finding Communities

Participants articulated a variety of motivations for joining Communities, mirroring earlier findings from our survey. All expressed a desire to follow an interest and get quality content. Ten of the twelve specifically said they wanted to interact with other people around a shared interest.

Although they had joined as many as 50 Communities, none of these participants paid regular attention to more than five Communities. Of those five, they report typically feeling a strong connection to just one or two favorite Communities.

Some participants reported discovering Communities by seeking them out to indulge an interest. The Communities participants seemed to report the greatest sense of belonging to, however, tended to be those they received an invitation to from someone they admired or respected.

Orientation

First impressions can make or break a new member's engagement with online communities [2]. Some members were surprised to discover Communities that fostered collective participation [25]:

> Joining a Community doesn't cost anything; you don't have to invest anything. So even if there were just interesting links and pictures, that'd be cool. I was looking just to see what was out there. But I found something more than that—something cool: at the end of each month everyone votes on a pattern and the next month everyone knits it. (P9)

Some Communities felt particularly tight-knit, supporting the use case of meeting new people. This quality is often readily apparent to newcomers:

> I'm kind of surprised by the kind of and level of camaraderie that's immediately there... When new people come in people really latch onto them and find out about them—where do you live, what do you do, what's your lifestyle like. It really is like a family... there's just such support and interest. (P4)

Several participants reported that moderators played a large role in setting a tone for the Community. P12 said, "The mods are pretty good about making sure people play by the rules. You see the mods jumping in and letting people know." P5 added: "The photography communities all have really great mods, they're good about making sure people aren't posting junk and aren't posting other people's work."

When a "Group" Becomes a Community

Several participants articulated two distinct types of Communities: those that felt more intimate and private, and those that felt more like larger groups of people who merely subscribe to the same interest streams.

> To me, the distinction between a private community and a public community is very clear. I like both, but you can tell the difference. My private[7] one is smaller, they curate who comes in, and it feels like a community and I've made friends there. The big ones (Chromebook, for example) are active and I'll comment, but they are really like larger interest-based groups. (P10)

Another described the use of a Private Community as a place to seek support:

> ...and then there's my private community for really personal stuff. It's for eight people I've met through G+ where if I really need to talk about hard things, this is where I do it. Most of the communities I've been invited to are interest-based, topical. Not special purpose like this. (P11)

P12 was a member of a Community that organized group workouts over video Hangouts. The small-group interaction added a sense of belonging:

> I thought it was pretty cool how [Jennifer] in one of the workouts was paying enough attention to the itty bitty little screens to say, "keep going [Michael]!". That makes it not just me sweating on my own in [Indiana], but part of a community.

Summary

Interviews revealed the importance of first impressions and moderator actions to set the tone for the types of interactions

[6]Even if up to 22% of responses were mis-coded, 36/59 would represent a majority of the sample ($p < .05$).

[7]The Community described here is actually Public but members must ask to join it.

a Community will afford. Participants also perceived a difference between large "interest-based" groups and more intimate communities. Interestingly, the moderators' engagements with the community foster a sense of intimacy and collectiveness.

EXAMINING GOOGLE+ COMMUNITIES

A significant portion of our survey respondents and interview subjects reported finding like-minded people in Communities, while others were driven more by the content. Likewise there appears to be disagreement about the extent to which people want Communities integrated with their social network. While many users *report* the desire to foster connections, we set out to *empirically* measure how likely people are to "know" others within their Communities.

To quantify this, we turn to the Communities themselves. We obtained snapshots of the member rosters of public Google+ Communities and public Circle edges[8] in August 2013. Again, the Google+ social graph is directed: an *edge* represents one user following another by adding that user to a Circle, an action that need not be reciprocated[9]. All of this data is publicly visible to Google+ users. After discarding empty Communities, we found 429,693 communities with two or more members.

The size of Communities appears to follow a power law, with many small Communities and few very large ones. This is common in networks [16], and suggests many people feel empowered to experiment with creating their own Communities. Our informal observations suggest there are many tiny communities that reflect closer ties to a creator who was experimenting with starting a community. Thus, smaller communities likely reflect existing ties.

Dunbar proposed that humans can maintain at most 100–200 personal relationships, which has been reflected in the sizes of pre-industrial villages, businesses, and militaries throughout history [3]. We saw 17,896 Communities with more than 150 members, and a wide variety of Communities that exceed this by an order of magnitude: 2,449 Communities in our dataset had over 1500 members. Clearly, at these sizes one cannot be expected to know everyone in the Community.

Edge Density

To explore the extent to which people connect with each other in Communities, we examine the number of edges between members of the same Community. The more *dense* a Community's graph is, the more likely members are to follow one another.

Only about 15% of the public Communities that *could* have any circle edges between members actually *do*, suggesting that Communities may be augmenting the social graph by providing access to people they would not be following otherwise and perhaps helping users break out of the "filter bubble" created by their networks [18].

[8]Google+ privacy settings allow users to make some edges private. Such edges are not included in this analysis.

[9]Reciprocal edges are not distinguished in this analysis; they're simply counted as two following edges.

The maximum possible number of edges E in a Community with M members is $E_{max} = M(M-1)$, a scenario where every member follows every other member. This theoretical ceiling is fairly elusive; no community with more than three members had more than $0.5E_{max}$ edges.

We fit a linear[10] regression model to Communities with two or more members:

$$E \sim 1.812 \log M + .117M + \left(2 \times 10^{-7}\right) E_{max} - 1.651$$

The model's R^2 value is 0.52, which is not a great fit, suggesting that the number of edges observed in a Community is not merely a function of its size, and some other hidden factors describe the likelihood of edge connection.

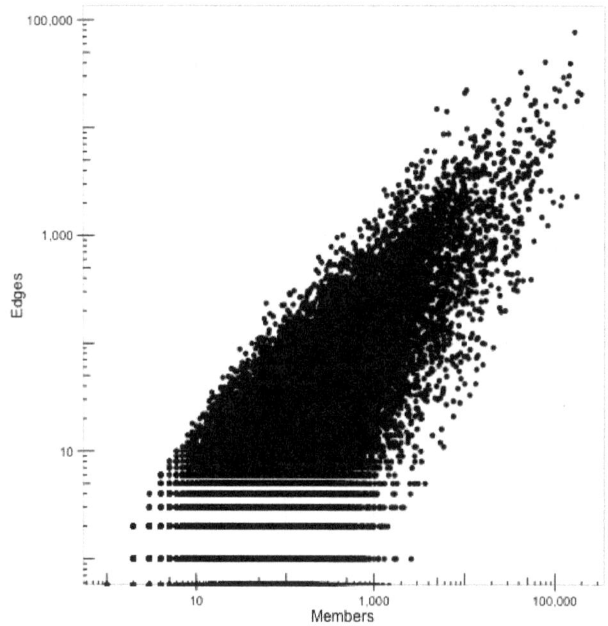

Figure 1: Number of internal edges in Public Communities v. number of members.

Figure 1 shows the relationship between members and edges. As communities scale up in membership, the number of edges increase on a log scale: that is, $\log E \sim \log M$. If the probability of any two people being connected with an edge is relatively constant, then we might expect E to correlate with the upper bound of edges possible, approximating $M(M-1) \approx O(M^2)$. However, the number of edges does not keep pace. Therefore, in general, as Communities become larger, the likelihood of any two members being connected drops, reflecting our intuition about large communities being less personal.

The Outliers

Since Community edges are not merely a factor of their size, there must be at least one other factor that explains graph density. To explore this, we evaluated the Communities with the

[10]We also fit a log-linear regression model but it had a lower R^2 value.

largest residuals from this model—that is, the ones with surprisingly *many* or surprisingly *few* edges given the prediction from our model. Note that this naturally biases our analysis away from tiny Communities with few members. This suggests a spectrum model where the more (or less) residual edges a Community has, the more likely it is to behave like these extremes. Communities in the middle could exhibit characteristics of both, or neither.

We coded the top 30 on each side for the analysis that follows; for brevity only the top 10 on each side are listed in Tables 1 and 2. We found these extreme outlier Communities tended to exhibit common characteristics. Those with surprisingly many edges we call *Plazas*, while Communities with surprisingly few edges as *Topic Boards*. This is an admittedly arbitrary cutoff; we selected a sufficiently small group to so we could inspect them all by hand.

We heard in interviews that moderators play a large role in setting the tone for a Community. One of the key tools they have for defining their Communities and setting members' expectations is the "About this Community" descriptions, which prospective members can see when previewing a Community, and which remains readily accessible at the top of the Community's home page. We use these descriptions and an inspection of recent public activity in these Communities to describe how they function.

Plazas: Communities with Surprisingly Many Edges

Table 1 lists the Communities with the largest residuals from the model. Plazas fall into roughly two categories: meeting places and communities of practice.

Meeting places: Online communities can provide a sort of "virtual third place" for people seeking social interaction [26]. There appear to be a number of Communities providing this sort of "neutral ground" [17] where people who do not necessarily have a rich online social graph can meet others. Some communities make this explicit in its description:

> Quero Ser Círculado *[I Want To Be Circled]* is a community that aims to group people to exchange ideas, make new friends and posts, is a great community for those who are new users of Google Plus. Because as everyone knows, when you're young, have few friends, and nobody shares or comments on your posts, stream completely still, it is very annoying. It's different here.

Common identity can be a powerful means of defining a community [21], and some plazas quite literally define themselves by shared identity. Eu Acredito em Deus! ("I believe in God!") invites members who self-identify as Christians: "JESUS this is your community, we created it because we love you and we are forever grateful for everything." Other Communities define themselves by national identity, like the simply-named Indonesia Community, which "is open to anyone who loves Indonesia".

Others, like Google+ Discuss, are targeted at new users looking to "chat about Google+" while meeting other newcomers. Meanwhile, others appear to target audience as wide as possible, like Earth, which invites users: "You live on Earth? Join!"

Communities of practice: A number of these dense Communities are also focused around the craft of photography and other arts (*e.g.*, painting, sculpture). Many of them bear hallmarks of communities of practice [29, 25], serving as a virtual space for people wishing to practice the same craft. For example, Light Box explicitly encourages members to critique others' work if they wish to receive feedback on their own: "provide a short opinion/critique/vote on 15 eligible photos in the Voting pool...for each photo you submit". The moderators of Landscape Photography "highly encourage you to promote your own work and contribute to the knowledge of the other community members", while The Photo Community bills itself as "our neo-Montmartre".

There are also a few examples of communities of practice around online marketing, such as Hội +1 Google Plus ("+1 Google Plus Club"), a Community that specializes in search engine optimization and encourages members to share best practices.

These Communities often invite new members to introduce themselves, often through a dedicated category of posts, as seen in The Photo Community, HDR Photography, and Light Box.

For these communities of practice, one factor driving density may be the practice of sharing circles [4]; before Google+ added Communities, there were already informal communities of photographers following each other. It's possible that many of these edges existed before the formalized Communities did, and these Communities may be a reflection of existing clusters in the graph. This practice continues; TOP Photos on G+ has a category for members to share circles of photographers they like.

Topical networking: Of the top 30 Plazas, 26 are either *Meeting places* or *Communities of practice*. The remaining four are content-focused Communities that bear explicit calls to connect with other members. For example, Science on Google+ describes itself as

> a community moderated by scientists, for all people interested in science, both professionals and the general public. The primary goal of this community is to bring real scientists to the public, for science outreach. A secondary and long-term goal is to create an environment that fosters interdisciplinary collaborations; thus, enabling and promoting cloud collaboration between scientists.

Topic Boards: Communities with Surprisingly Few Edges

Table 2 lists the ten Communities with the most negative residual edges—that is, those with significantly fewer edges than expected given our model. The 30 most negative Communities were all content-focused Communities we call *Topic Boards*. We draw this distinction in that these Communities make comparatively less effort to define their members by anything other than a topic of interest or to facilitate meeting people.

True devotees of *Harry Potter* or *Twilight* might self-identify as fans, and indeed, their respective Communities describe themselves as "for fans of Harry Potter on Google+" or "the

Community	Members	Edges	Residual	Type
Landscape Photography	164,645	77,515	52,810	Community of practice: photography
Google+ Discuss	77,034	40,925	30,706	Meeting place: new users
The Photo Community	41,464	32,614	27,401	Community of practice: photography
Hội +1 Google Plus (*+1 Google Plus Club*)	10,371	22,240	20,990	Community of practice: marketing
Hội Cần ++++++++++++++ (*Need +++ Club*)	9,883	20,924	19,733	Community of practice: marketing
HDR Photography	146,459	39,729	18,283	Community of practice: photography
Light Box	48,949	23,362	17,138	Community of practice: photography
Q.S.C - Quero Ser Círculado (*I Want To Be Circled*)	20,802	17,875	15,338	Meeting place: Brazil
TOP Photos on G+	4,838	14,892	14,308	Community of practice: photography
Photoshop and Lightroom Users	30,632	18,089	14,300	Community of practice: photography

Table 1: The ten Communities with the most positive residual edges (surprisingly many edges) according to our model.

Community	Members	Edges	Residual	Type
Harry Potter	173,564	2,326	-24,026	Interest: media
Gaming	120,247	2,289	-14,691	Interest: hobby
Forever Twilight	115,343	1,895	-14,280	Interest: media
Fitness & Weight Loss	94,599	2,048	-10,829	Interest: health
Joke of the Day	194,860	20,481	-9,932	Interest: humor
The Hunger Games	82,405	1,235	-9,783	Interest: media
Dogs	87,738	2,641	-9,183	Interest: hobby
Android	174,236	17,768	-8,709	Interest: technology
The Walking Dead Circle	71,053	1,470	-7,871	Interest: media
Cakes & Baking - The Cadbury Kitchen	58,245	886	-6,625	Interest: hobby

Table 2: The ten Communities with the most negative residual edges (surprisingly few edges) according to our model.

place where Twi-Hards can come". However, they generally lack explicit calls to get to know other members or to interact with each other. It's unclear whether an interest in *Harry Potter* is as deeply rooted a part of one's identity as nationality or religion.

Topic boards promise rich streams of content focused on specific topics. For example, Gaming describes itself as "a bonanza of gaming news, reviews and discussion". Joke of the Day offers "funny quotes, jokes, memes, photos, and good humor!". This provides a way for members to find content around a topic of interest without much effort or expectation of engagement.

Topic boards also provide members with an audience for specific interests. Cakes & Baking invites members to "share and discover the most delicious recipes imaginable". Dogs describes itself as "a place to share your dog pictures, stories, and experiences".

Summary

In general, plazas tend to define themselves by declaring *who* belongs there, while topic boards tend to define *what content* belongs there. However, this is not a rigid binary categorization, but rather a spectrum, with some Communities bearing characteristics of both sides.

Also, while there are lots of photography communities of practice, topicality doesn't necessarily determine a place on the spectrum. For example, while The Hunger Games is a topic board focused around the popular teen novels, the Chinese-language Community Google+ ShuPíng ("Google+ Book Review") is a denser plaza of people invited to "share wonderful book reviews [and] recommend good books" .

User Engagement Analysis

Given these two types of Communities we believe to be qualitatively and measurably different, we next collected a set of metrics on per-user engagement in the 30 Communities with the most positive and 30 with the most negative residuals. For these 60 Communities, we measured and compared their total number of members, posts, and comments. None of these metrics are normally distributed, so we report the medians and apply a Mann-Whitney test to each pair. The data is summarized in Table 3.

Median of...	Topic boards	Plazas	p
Members	69,839	25,451	***
Edges	2,265	16,898	***
Posts	17,506	27,103	
Comments	49,706	39,092	
Posts/member	0.26	0.79	***
Comments/member	0.80	1.26	*
Comments/post	2.7	1.4	**

*** $p < .001$; ** $p < .01$; * $p < .05$

Table 3: Median values for basic metrics of the 30 topic board and plaza Communities we identified.

Membership size: In general, topic boards are larger than plazas ($p < .001$), as seen in Figure 2a. This makes sense: it's hard to scale a plaza. But despite their larger size, Figure 2b shows topic boards tended to have fewer edges between

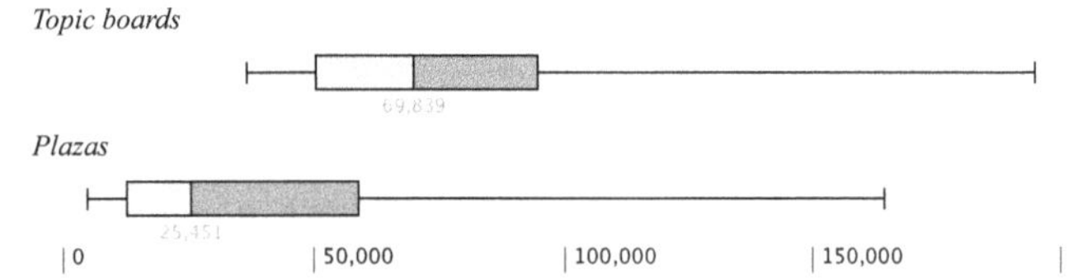

(a) Members

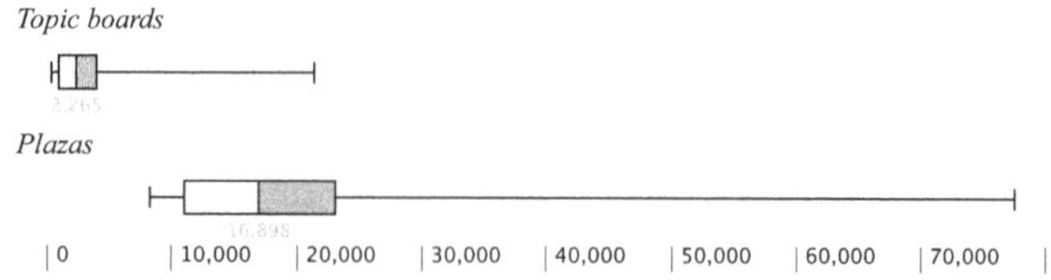

(b) Edges

Figure 2: Distributions of members and edges for the topic boards and plazas in our sample

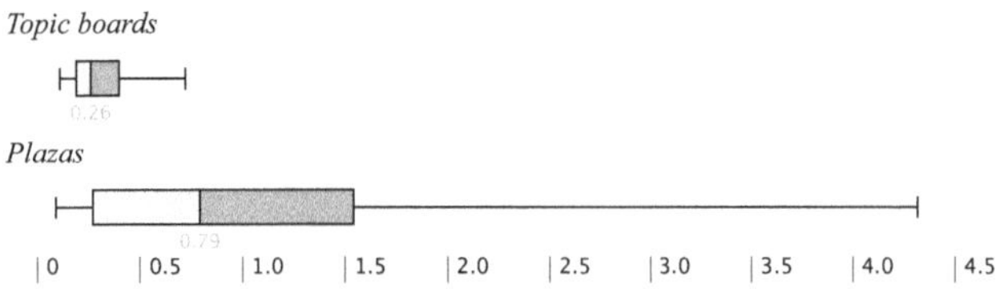

(a) Posts per member

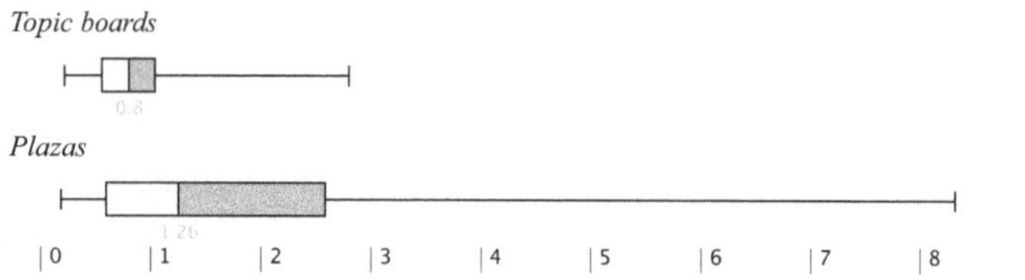

(b) Comments per member

Figure 3: Posts and comments per member in topic boards and plazas in our sample

members ($p < .001$), reflecting the extremes of the spectrum we are sampling.

Activity per member: Both topic boards and plazas can generate lots of posts; the difference between them was not significant ($p = 0.4$). However, Figure 3a shows that plazas see significantly more posts per member ($p < .001$), suggesting that individual users are more likely to post in the Community, or more likely to post more. Likewise, plazas see significantly more comments per member ($p = 0.025$; see Figure 3b), consistent with findings in [5].

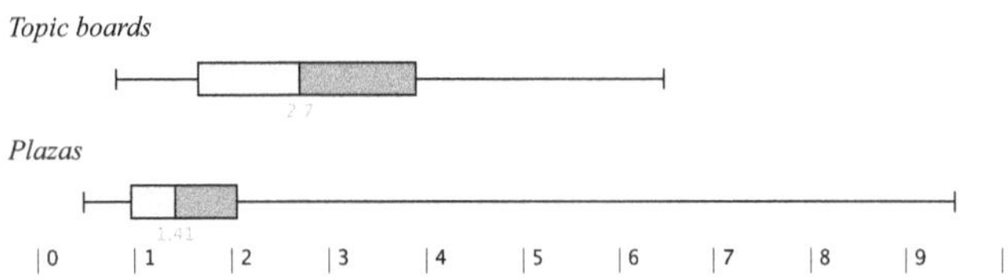

Figure 4: Comments per post in topic boards and plazas in our sample

Activity per post: Topic boards are hardly engagement wastelands, though; they tend to see more comments per post than plazas do ($p = 0.006$; see Figure 4). Therefore, while individual people may not contribute as often, for sufficiently large Communities *someone* is likely to see and comment on a post, even if it is a different *someone* each time. Sites like Digg have demonstrated this diffuse attention can effectively crowdsource evaluation of a high volume of content [31].

This pattern can help us partially distinguish between identity-defined plazas and identity-claiming topic boards. Table 4 shows four Communities—two plazas defined by religion and nationality, and two topic boards that describe themselves as for fans of specific novel series. The two plazas on the top have more posts per member and fewer members than the two topic boards on the bottom.

An analysis over the same engagement metrics revealed no significant differences between communities of practice and

	Posts/member	Members
Plazas		
Eu Acredito em Deus!	0.99	46,917
Indonesia	0.83	24,386
Topic boards		
Harry Potter	0.22	173,564
Forever Twilight	0.19	115,343

Table 4: Comparing plazas and topic boards claiming identity

meeting places. This agrees with survey and interview data in grouping these two Community styles together as plazas.

DISCUSSION

We presented a framework for understanding different forms of Google+ Communities. This division of Google+ Communities into plazas and topic boards parallels Park *et al.*'s work on uses and gratifications in Facebook Groups [19]. Their categories of *socializing* (*e.g.*, peer support, meeting interesting people, talk about things with others, *etc.*) and *self-status seeking* (*e.g.*, pressure to participate, make myself look cool) map well onto plazas, while *entertainment* and *information seeking* categories similarly fit topic boards. We extend this by showing these uses correspond to the prevalence or absence of edges observed within a Community.

Indeed, one possible explanation for this phenomenon may be that people are more likely to invite friends to plazas than topic boards. Each of these invites would increase the number of edges apparent inside the Community. While we did have anecdotal examples from interviews to suggest this, we did not have access to invitation logs to verify it.

Another way to understand the two styles of Google+ Communities is via the lens of *social awareness streams* [15]. Communities users driven by connecting with others may be similar to Naaman *et al.* 's "meformers", while those driven by content or an audience to share content with may be "informers". It is unclear the extent to which users can be strictly separated into one of these two motivations, and it's possible the same users may be "informers" in some Communities and "meformers" in others.

Of course, this is not meant to be a strict dichotomy, but rather a spectrum. New Communities could become a densely-knit plaza or a popular topic board. Moderators help guide successful Communities toward their desired outcome.

Plazas reflect a scaled-up version of the desire to form connections with like-minded people articulated by our respondents in the survey and interviews. While greatest intimacy is afforded by smaller, more exclusive (and sometimes Private) Communities, and there may be a multitude of such dense Communities present, they don't appear in our list of extreme plazas because they're not large enough to have many residual edges.

At first glance it may seem that plazas are more compelling for users, especially given the potential for online communities to provide a social support net [1] or virtual "third place" [26], and the importance of common identity and interpersonal bonds in driving online community participation [21].

But not everyone wants to deeply connect with like-minded strangers online—some just want to get interesting content, or an audience to share their passion with. Topic boards are just as successful, since they provide a platform for people to get their content seen by others who share their interests, and they provide content that sparks interaction.

Obviously, deep personal ties can form even in ostensibly very topic-focused online communities [23]. Indeed, while users may enter a Community as a lurker with a topical interest, they may form bonds with other members as they begin to identify with the group. While we didn't have enough data to quantify this, we suspect that plazas may make this easier.

Implications

We see evidence that communities may provide an opportunity for people to form edges in an OSN. Some Communities explicitly encourage this behavior, and some appear to have unusually high graph density, suggesting that the Community itself may be a good source of contact recommendations.

However, people appear split on the extent to which their Communities should be integrated into their social graphs. Some prefer to keep their social network distinct from their interests, while others build bonds in Communities with the people they follow. This may suggest there is no "one-size-fits-all" approach to situating communities within an OSN, and that for some communities, nudges to follow fellow members outside the community may not be effective.

In any case, graph density is not necessary for lively activity within Communities. But it tends to afford a different type of activity: a smaller, more active core of members posting rather than a larger, diffuse crowd contributing more comments collectively on posts.

Finally, we propose that comparing graph density to a regression model based on its size is an easily implemented metric that could automatically detect whether a Community is trending towards becoming a plaza or a topic board. This could provide guidance to moderators to help steer a Community's development, trigger adaptations in UI affordances, or suggest Communities for people who specifically want to meet others.

Limitations

There are some obvious limitations to our work, which was conducted on Google+, arguably a unique environment among OSNs. However, as mentioned above, our findings parallel existing work on Facebook [19] and Twitter [15], suggesting the patterns we observe may apply to other online community environments as well.

Our surveys and interviews were sourced through snowball sampling, which may bias responses somewhat towards more active users of Communities; lurker behavior is beyond the scope of this study. Also, they were conducted in English, which may limit global generalizability.

Another limitation is that the quantitative analysis considers only Public Google+ Communities on Google+, and in obtaining edge graph, membership, and activity data we are limited to only Public data. However, in interviews and surveys participants may choose to discuss Private Community activity. Since popular Public Communities are exposed in a variety of ways to potential members, Communities can form without existing edge ties. On the other hand, we expect Private Communities to behave differently, since typically users cannot see Private Communities unless they've been explicitly invited to them by a member.

Future Work

A natural extension is to evaluate the temporal ordering of edge creation and community joins to see in which Communities members actually followed each other after joining. This would paint a clearer picture of under what conditions Communities actually foster people meeting each other. A temporal analysis could also reveal whether Communities evolve into plazas or topic boards. Is it inevitable that sufficiently large plazas must become more topic board-like?

Another question is whether overall Community density is perhaps less important than membership in smaller, dense components within each community. Perhaps large topic boards contain a core component of tightly-knit members and a periphery of disconnected lurkers.

ACKNOWLEDGMENTS

We gratefully acknowledge Lichan Hong for technical advice. We thank Laura Granka and Dan Russell for helpful conversation, and our anonymous reviewers for their feedback and suggestions. We are also grateful to our survey respondents and interview subjects for their participation.

REFERENCES

1. Bender, J. L., Jimenez-Marroquin, M.-C., and Jadad, A. R. Seeking support on facebook: a content analysis of breast cancer groups. *Journal of medical Internet research 13*, 1 (2011).

2. Burke, M., Kraut, R., and Joyce, E. Membership claims and requests: Conversation-level newcomer socialization strategies in online groups. *Small group research 41*, 1 (2010), 4–40.

3. Dunbar, R. *How Many Friends Does One Person Need?: Dunbar's Number and Other Evolutionary Quirks*. Faber & Faber, 2010.

4. Fang, L., Fabrikant, A., and LeFevre, K. Look who I found: Understanding the effects of sharing curated friend groups. In *Proc. WebSci 2012*, 137–146.

5. Grabowicz, P. A., Aiello, L. M., Eguiluz, V. M., and Jaimes, A. Distinguishing topical and social groups based on common identity and bond theory. In *Proc. WSDM 2013*, 627–636.

6. Gundotra, V. Google+: Communities and photos, 2012. googleblog.blogspot.com/2012/12/google-communities-and-photos.html.

7. Gundotra, V. Google+ hangouts and photos: save some time, share your story, 2013. googleblog.blogspot.com/2013/10/google-hangouts-and-photos-save-some.html.

8. Hafner, K. *The well: A story of love, death & real life in the seminal online community*. Avalon Publishing Group, 2001.

9. Kairam, S., Brzozowski, M., Huffaker, D., and Chi, E. Talking in circles: selective sharing in Google+. In *Proc. CHI 2012*, 1065–1074.

10. Kraut, R. E., and Resnick, P. *Building successful online communities*. The MIT Press, 2012.

11. Lazar, J., and Preece, J. Classification schema for online communities. In *Proc. of the Association for Information Systems Americas Conference* (1998), 84–86.

12. Lazarsfeld, P. F., and Merton, R. K. Friendship as a social process: A substantive and methodological analysis. In *Freedom and control in modern society*, M. Berger and T. Abel, Eds. Van Nostrand, New York, 1954.

13. Magno, G., Comarela, G., Saez-Trumper, D., Cha, M., and Almeida, V. New kid on the block: exploring the Google+ social graph. In *Proc. IMC 2012*, 159–170.

14. Myers, S. A., Sharma, A., Gupta, P., and Lin, J. Information network or social network?: The structure of the twitter follow graph. In *Proc. WWW Companion* (2014), 493–498.

15. Naaman, M., Boase, J., and Lai, C.-H. Is it really about me?: Message content in social awareness streams. In *Proc. CSCW 2010*, 189–192.

16. Newman, M. E. The structure and function of complex networks. *SIAM review 45*, 2 (2003), 167–256.

17. Oldenburg, R. *The great good place: Cafes, coffee shops, bookstores, bars, hair salons, and other hangouts at the heart of a community*. Da Capo Press, 1997.

18. Pariser, E. *The filter bubble: How the new personalized Web is changing what we read and how we think*. Penguin, 2011.

19. Park, N., Kee, K. F., and Valenzuela, S. Being immersed in social networking environment: Facebook groups, uses and gratifications, and social outcomes. *CyberPsychology & Behavior 12*, 6 (2009), 729–733.

20. Prentice, D. A., Miller, D. T., and Lightdale, J. R. Asymmetries in attachments to groups and to their members: Distinguishing between common-identity and common-bond groups. *Personality and Social Psychology Bulletin 20*, 5 (1994), 484–493.

21. Ren, Y., Kraut, R., and Kiesler, S. Applying common identity and bond theory to design of online communities. *Organization studies 28*, 3 (2007), 377–408.

22. Ridings, C. M., and Gefen, D. Virtual community attraction: Why people hang out online. *Journal of Computer-Mediated Communication 10*, 1 (2004).

23. Rood, V., and Bruckman, A. Member behavior in company online communities. In *Proc. GROUP 2009*, 209–218.

24. Schiöberg, D., Schneider, F., Schiöberg, H., Schmid, S., Uhlig, S., and Feldmann, A. Tracing the birth of an OSN: social graph and profile analysis in Google+. In *Proc. WebSci 2012*, 265–274.

25. Shirky, C. *Here comes everybody: The power of organizing without organizations*. Penguin, 2008.

26. Soukup, C. Computer-mediated communication as a virtual third place: Building Oldenburg's great good places on the world wide web. *New Media & Society 8*, 3 (2006), 421–440.

27. Wang, Y.-C., Kraut, R., and Levine, J. M. To stay or leave?: The relationship of emotional and informational support to commitment in online health support groups. In *Proc. CSCW 2012*, 833–842.

28. Watson, J., Besmer, A., and Lipford, H. R. +Your circles: sharing behavior on Google+. In *Proc. SOUPS 2012*, 12:1–12:9.

29. Wenger, E. *Communities of practice: Learning, meaning, and identity*. Cambridge University Press, 1998.

30. Woolley, J. K., Limperos, A. M., and Oliver, M. B. The 2008 presidential election, 2.0: A content analysis of user-generated political facebook groups. *Mass Communication and Society 13*, 5 (2010), 631–652.

31. Wu, F., and Huberman, B. A. Novelty and collective attention. *PNAS 104*, 45 (2007), 17599–17601.

Gender and Tenure Diversity in GitHub Teams

Bogdan Vasilescu[†§*], **Daryl Posnett**[†], **Baishakhi Ray**[†], **Mark G.J. van den Brand**[§], **Alexander Serebrenik**[§], **Premkumar Devanbu**[†], **Vladimir Filkov**[†*]
[†]University of California, Davis and [§]Eindhoven University of Technology
[*]vasilescu@ucdavis.edu, filkov@cs.ucdavis.edu

ABSTRACT

Software development is usually a collaborative venture. Open Source Software (OSS) projects are no exception; indeed, by design, the OSS approach can accommodate teams that are more open, geographically distributed, and dynamic than commercial teams. This, we find, leads to OSS teams that are quite diverse. Team diversity, predominantly in offline groups, is known to correlate with team output, mostly with positive effects. How about in OSS?

Using GITHUB, the largest publicly available collection of OSS projects, we studied how gender and tenure diversity relate to team productivity and turnover. Using regression modeling of GITHUB data and the results of a survey, we show that both gender and tenure diversity are positive and significant predictors of productivity, together explaining a sizable fraction of the data variability. These results can inform decision making on all levels, leading to better outcomes in recruiting and performance.

Author Keywords

Open source; gender; diversity; productivity; GitHub.

ACM Classification Keywords

H.5.3. [Information Interfaces and Presentation (e.g. HCI)]: Computer-supported cooperative work

INTRODUCTION

Because of the world-wide demand for talented and skilled labor, hiring in STEM (Science, Technology, Engineering, and Math) fields has become increasingly almost entirely meritocratic, and largely blind to demographic factors. This is certainly true for software engineering; as a result, both commercial and open source software teams can be very diverse. What are the effects of this on the project as a whole? Indeed, demographic similarity enhances mutual trust (and thus, arguably, team effectiveness), while demographic diversity may lead to stereotyping, cliquishness, and conflict [20,43]. However, a team's social diversity seems to improve its technical performance [24].

CHI 2015, April 18 - 23, 2015, Seoul, Republic of Korea.
Copyright held by authors. Publication rights licensed to ACM. 978-1-4503-3145-6/15/04$15.00. http://dx.doi.org/10.1145/2702123.2702549

Software development teams can be *diverse* in various ways, *e.g.*, w.r.t. gender, experience, nationality, and coding language preference; some teams can be more diverse in one attribute and less so in others. Diversity attributes may also interact (*e.g.*, in some nations, female professionals may face more obstacles), which complicates analysis and study. Team diversity has been studied in physical ("meat-space") settings; however, data is hard-won in such settings. Smaller sample sizes make it difficult to effectively control for confounds. Data requirements for such effective controls, however, increase exponentially with the number of dimensions studied (one aspect of the "curse of dimensionality" [22]). Thus, studies of effects of diversity in teams (given the ineluctable confounds) require data on a great many teams, with sufficient variance along all co-variates of concern.

GITHUB, a social coding platform, has attracted millions of developers and thousands of Open Source Software projects.[1] All commits, issues, code changes, pull-requests etc. are archived and publicly available. GITHUB has become the new standard for comprehensive studies of social and technical organization and achievement [16, 37, 39, 41, 60]. Evidently, this is an attractive setting in which to study the relationship of diversity to performance. The scale of GITHUB is especially relevant when considering the role of women, who are very underrepresented in programming.[2] With a large enough dataset, however, the effect of increased gender diversity becomes noticeable. Additionally, since all data in GITHUB is historical (*i.e.*, archived), it is possible to study the effects of tenure, or one's length of time with a project and with GITHUB. However, the reliance on *volunteers* in OSS projects complicates matters; volunteers come and go, leading to team turn-over. Team turnover can certainly influence performance, and will confound the effects of diversity. The constructs of "team" and "team turnover" clearly also depend on the observation time-scale. In a healthy project, some rate of turnover is in fact desirable, as "new blood" brings in new abilities and ideas [21]. Arguably, turnover *will* affect observed diversity in GITHUB OSS teams, and must be considered carefully.

In this paper, using GITHUB data, we explore several questions: How diverse are online teams with respect to gender and tenure? Does gender diversity depend on tenure? On

[1] OSS depend on distributed volunteers' efforts whereas commercial software is much more centralized, and depends more on paid groups of programmers [23]; in both, the quality can be high [8].

[2] Especially so, it seems, in OSS projects: A 2013 FLOSS Survey [49] indicates 10% females; all earlier surveys [19] agree on merely 1–5%. Industry reports slightly higher numbers, *e.g.*, Google with 17% female technology employees.

team size? And how do gender and tenure diversity relate to outcomes like productivity? Remaining mindful of various confounds, we claim the following contributions.

(1) We collected a data set comprising thousands of projects from GITHUB, capturing or inferring the contributions, gender, and tenure of each recorded participant. We also ran a survey on GITHUB, to get a sense of how participants assess and value team composition and diversity.

(2) We use statistical modeling to analyze the relationship of gender and tenure diversity to productivity, when controlling for team size and other confounds. We find that *both gender and tenure diversity have a significant, positive effect on productivity*, gender across all team sizes and tenure for teams larger than 10. Together, these two explain 1–2.5% of the data variance, depending on team size.

(3) Models of turnover, or team change over time, in those teams reveal a negligible effect of gender diversity. Tenure has a large negative effect on turnover, while tenure diversity has a small, positive effect of turnover.

RELATED WORK

Background and Theory

The relationship between team diversity and team outcomes has been studied extensively over the past 40 years (see, *e.g.*, [31, 54] for recent reviews). Understood broadly, diversity arises from any attribute that differentiates people [66]. Attributes can be demographic (*e.g.*, age, gender, culture, ethnicity), functional (*e.g.*, role, tenure, expertise), or subjective (*e.g.*, personality). While there is ample literature on the matter (mostly from offline groups), different studies report different results. Some report significant positive correlations between diversity and performance (*e.g.*, [24]), while others report that diversity negatively impacts team outcomes (*e.g.*, [64]). Meta-analyses have tried to rationalize these contradictions by examining how effects are mediated by context (*e.g.*, group type, group size, or task complexity [31, 54]), research design, or sample characteristics [54].

However, despite the apparent contradictions between the different studies regarding the effects of diversity in workgroups, the literature tends to agree on three analytical frameworks: *similarity-attraction theory* (SA) [12], *social identity and social categorization theory* (SIC) [55], and *information-processing theory* (IP) [52]. According to SA, people prefer working with others similar to them in terms of values, beliefs, and attitudes [66]. SIC postulates that people tend to categorize themselves into specific groups, and categorize others as outsiders. Members of one's own group are then treated better than outsiders [55]. Due to greater perceived differences in values, norms, and communication styles between groups than within groups, SA and SIC explain why work-group heterogeneity can lead to confusion, stress, and conflict [31]. Both perspectives suggest negative effects of diversity on team outcomes. In contrast, IP treats diversity as positive: bringing to the table a mixture of cultural/educational backgrounds, and access to different networks and broader information can enhance a team's creativity, adaptability, and problem solving skills (*e.g.*, [33, 64]).

How team members react to diversity depends on the extent to which member characteristics are salient, and the effects are moderated by time [24, 30, 68]. As a team forms, members may well form durable first impressions of their new team-mates based on salient personal characteristics (typically demographic features), and as a result engage in social categorization [68]. However, as time passes and team members engage in meaningful interactions, the effects of surface-level diversity weaken and the team can better leverage its members' different cognitive frameworks and value sets (*i.e.*, their information-processing approaches), thus improving the team's efficiency and decision making processes [30]. Therefore, during a team's life-span, different phenomena related to the team's experience and size may arise, causing the effects of diversity to vary.

Diversity in OSS Teams

In task-oriented online communities (*e.g.*, OSS), group dynamics are substantially different than offline. First, in OSS geographic (and cultural) dispersion represents the norm, as members rarely meet in person; instead, collaborators on OSS projects assemble in online communities, and coordinate their activities through distributed communication channels (*e.g.*, email lists). Second, OSS teams are fluid, *i.e.*, they tend to form and dissolve organically around the task at hand. Third, since OSS contributors are often volunteers, teams face high turnover [50]. Finally, OSS communities generally exhibit a core-periphery structure [23], in which a small group of developers drives the work (the *core*), and a larger and more loosely coupled group of contributors (the *periphery*) supports the core by reporting issues, submitting patches, or contributing documentation. These characteristics make OSS teams less tangible than their offline counterparts: interactions between members are typically limited to online channels, and it can be hard to tell precisely who is on a team and who is not. Diversity attributes may, therefore, operate differently in OSS than in offline groups [40].

In particular, demographic characteristics such as ethnicity or gender become less salient in OSS [48]. Instead, OSS communities typically function as meritocracies [26], with sustained, high-quality contributions being the main drivers behind impression formation, reputation building, and trust [6, 16, 39]. For example, on social coding sites such as GITHUB, a very large fraction of members' actions within and across projects is more readily observable. This level of transparency, available without any personal interaction, allows one to make rich inferences about the commitment, work quality, or community significance of others [16, 17], and use these rather than demographics to form impressions.

The idea of OSS as meritocracy [26], widely-accepted, suggests that despite their great diversity (making them susceptible to SA or SIC), OSS teams should benefit from diversity. Diverse OSS teams should be able to reconcile and exploit their differences for the greater (*i.e.*, the project's) good, as IP suggests. However, all is not well in the meritocratic state of OSS. For example, the "hacker" culture tends to be male-dominated and unfriendly to women [58, p.194], who are underrepresented at not more than 10% of the all developers [19, 49]. Moreover, recent results[3] report active discrimination towards women in OSS, leading to the so-called "impostor syndrome": despite being knowledgeable

[3]FLOSSPOLS Deliberable D16 Gender, retrieved from `http://flosspols.org/deliverables.php` in Sep 2014

and professionally well-settled, women consider themselves to be disqualified or frauds. Moreover, sexist behavior in OSS is said to be "as constant as it is extreme" [44].

Very few authors have studied effects of diversity on team outcomes in online volunteer communities or OSS. Daniel *et al.* [18] studied effects of diversity on community engagement and market success in a sample of 357 SourceForge projects. They found that while diversity based on developers' reputation and role positively influences market success and community engagement, diversity of spoken language and nationality has a negative impact on community engagement, and a positive impact on market success. Chen *et al.* [13] studied diversity of experience and interests among members of Wikipedia Projects. They found that experience diversity increases group productivity and turnover up to a certain threshold, beyond which group productivity remains high but members are more likely to withdraw. In contrast, interest diversity increases productivity and decreases member withdrawal. In a similar context, Wang *et al.* [63] observed that members with very different tenure than the overall group tenure were more productive, but also more likely to withdraw early. To our knowledge, we are the first to consider effects of *gender* diversity in OSS communities.

Gender and Tenure Diversity in GitHub Teams

We choose to study gender and tenure diversity in GITHUB project communities. GITHUB (2008) has become the largest code host in the world, with many popular OSS projects (*e.g.*, the Linux kernel, Ruby on Rails, Bootstrap, Django, jQuery, and Homebrew) residing there. We chose GITHUB for our study because it: (i) is the largest ecosystem of its kind; (ii) has a wealth of trace data available [29]; and (iii) is known to promote women in technology through a number of initiatives, such as the Passion Projects, a series of talks aimed at providing female developers and engineers with role models, or the 2013 partnership with the Ada Initiative, offering free private repositories to women learning to write OSS. We are interested in effects of gender and tenure diversity on two project group outcomes: *productivity*, understood as the amount of work accomplished by each community of developers over time, and *turnover*, understood as the rate of change in each community over time.

Hypotheses

Gender is known to influence group outcomes [1, 42, 51] using the mechanisms explained by SA, SIC, and IP. Gender diversity brings different attitudes, perspectives, and values to a group. For example, while men are known to exhibit more task-oriented behaviors, women are said to show more socio-emotional behaviors [15], increasing a group's "ability to integrate divergent solutions while discouraging interpersonal and competitive conflict" [51]; this social orientation of women in teams is speculated to reduce the risk for egocentric listening and social loafing, and to allow for more effective teamwork [51]. As a consequence, diverse groups will be better equipped to handle uncertainty and take decisions, making them more productive (IP). On the flip side, gender diversity in a male-dominated "hacker" culture such as OSS may trigger discrimination towards women and sexism [44] (SIC), which in turn may lead to disengagement by women and perpetuation of the male dominance (SA).

The starting point for our exploration of gender diversity is the study of Rogelberg and Rumery [51]. The authors studied team decision quality, time on task, and interpersonal cohesion for 96 four-person teams having all five possible gender ratios (from all-male to all-female). The task, a winter survival exercise where each team had to rank order the most important 12 items salvaged from a plane crash, was determined to be male-oriented after pilot testing. The authors found that gender diversity significantly affected team decision quality (but not time on task nor interpersonal cohesion), with lone-female teams (*i.e.*, three men and one woman) performing the best. That is, despite the male orientation of the task, all-male teams were outperformed by the more gender-diverse lone-female teams. Apesteguia *et al.* [1] reported similar findings in a recent study of three-person teams competing in an online business simulation game: again the more gender-diverse teams (two men, one woman) performed the best. In both studies teams consisted of students. Since neither studies considered larger teams, it is hard to reason whether increasing gender diversity or rather simply having women on teams would be responsible, in general, for the reportedly positive effects on team outcomes. Given the previous argument based on IP, and supported by the parallel between the male-orientation of the task of Rogelberg and Rumery [51] and the known male-dominance of OSS, we posit, more generally, that:

H1. Gender diversity has a positive effect on productivity.

The socio-emotional behavior and non-aggressive strategies attributed to women in teams [42, 51] could imply a more positive attitude towards teamwork and collaboration in gender diverse projects. As all male-groups tend to be overaggressive and competitive [2], the presence of women may moderate over-competitiveness, reducing conflicts and improving communication and collaboration [51]. All other things aside, projects with a more welcoming community should exhibit less turnover, or:

H2. Gender diversity has a negative effect on turnover.

Tenure refers to the amount of experience accumulated by each group member. Highly tenured developers are more likely to be part of a project's core team (*i.e.*, to have committer status, the highest trust level in a typical OSS project), and to take part in decision making. Newcomers, or less tenured developers, are at the other end of the scale. Although typically not as experienced, they are very motivated to provide contributions by reputation building [36] and their desire to learn [67]. Mixed-tenure OSS communities will have more opportunities to leverage the energy and experience brought forward by juniors and seniors, respectively [13, 18], and will be more productive. The presence of tenured, senior developers will set the example for newcomers that increasing rewards can be obtained through sustained participation and contribution [18], and will create mentoring opportunities [47]. In turn, motivated by example [16, 28], newcomers may expend more efforts to prove themselves and build reputation [36]. Following this logic we test:

H3. Tenure diversity has a positive effect on productivity.

Tenure diversity tends to be associated with differences in attitudes, views, or approaches to tackle a particular problem [18]. For example, tenured developers may have a preference for more mature technologies, while newcomers may be more willing to experiment with newer, less proven, libraries or APIs. In the extreme, as tenure diversity in a project team increases, newcomers and seniors may find insufficient common ground, leading to communication breakdown and conflict [13], which may lead to higher attrition [46]. Since tenure-diversity-based conflicts have already been reported for Wikipedia Projects [13], a community comparable to OSS [45], we test whether:

H4. Tenure diversity has a positive effect on turnover.

METHODS AND DATA

We followed a mixed-methods approach with a sequential exploratory strategy [25]. First, we conducted a survey of GITHUB contributors to obtain insights in the way team collaboration and diversity are being perceived. Following it, to assist in interpreting the qualitative findings, we assembled a longitudinal dataset of GITHUB developers and projects, on which we modeled productivity and turnover outcomes using a variety of statistical models.

GITHUB's pull-based development model imposes a different definition for *project* than in traditional OSS. On GITHUB, to facilitate scaling up, typically only a small group of developers (*the core*) have access to the main repository and can push their changes directly. All other contributors, if any, work in isolation in their local copies of the repository (*forks*), and submit their contributions back for review and integration via *pull requests*. Therefore, a project on GITHUB consists of a base repository and all its forks (and transitively all their forks). We adopt this definition since measuring the activity of a repository independently of its forks will underrepresent the activity of all of them as part of a single project [34].

Survey

We selected 4,500 GITHUB contributors stratified according to gender (as inferred by `genderComputer` [59], *i.e.*, male, female, or unknown; see *Inferring gender* below) and number of projects contributed to (one project—the majority of contributors; many projects—7 or more, distributional outliers; and few projects—between 2 and 6), randomly selecting for each combination of gender and number of projects 500 individuals with known email addresses in our GHTorrent-based data set. We contacted all of them by email and invited them to participate in the survey. Participation was voluntary and confidential, and was expected to take about ten minutes. We received 816 responses to the survey and 236 automatic replies. Ignoring the latter, we achieved higher than 19% response rate, slightly exceeding the 15–17% response rates reported in comparable studies [4,57].

Among the respondents, 199 (24%) indicated their gender as "female", an underrepresentation as at least one third of the invitations had been sent to women ("female" inferred by `genderComputer`). Age ranged from 14 to 66 (median 29; mean 30); IT experience ranged from zero (*e.g.*, a student, a manager, and an individual not working in tech) to 44 years (median 8; mean 10.5). The largest group of respondents reside in the USA (264), followed by Germany (52), France (42) and Canada (34). To evaluate the representativeness of the respondents group, we aggregate the country information to the macro-regional level (Africa, Asia, Australia and New Zealand, Eastern and Southern Europe, Latin America, North America, Western and Northern Europe). A χ^2 test comparing the macro-regional distribution of our respondents with those reported in a previous study of GITHUB users [56] reveals no differences w.r.t. the known general GITHUB population ($p > 0.9$).

Our first observation after analyzing the responses relates to perceptions of teams. Two-thirds of respondents indicated they consider themselves as part of a team when working on a repository. Women (76%) score higher than men (63%), in adherence with their more socio-emotional behavior in teams [42, 51]. When asked who else they consider part of their team, respondents could indicate multiple answers related to the kind of activity (*e.g.*, committing or issue reporting), frequency, and organizational aspects. The most popular answer was "everyone who does something in this repository (*e.g.*, pushes code, submits pull requests, reports issues)" (44%). Differences between answers by men and women were not statistically significant (χ^2 $p \simeq 0.97$).

Another observation relates to perceptions of diversity attributes. We asked whether they are aware of certain aspects of other team members (*e.g.*, age, gender, hobbies, political views, programming skill, real name, and social skills). 98% of those that answered this question indicated they are aware of the *programming skills* of at least some team members. This makes programming skills the most visible diversity aspect we considered, hardly surprising as GITHUB contributors can be expected to interact in their software development roles. In addition, almost half of respondents to this question (48.6%) indicated they are aware of the *gender* of most of their teammates. This salience of gender among team members on GITHUB contradicts earlier claims of obscurity of gender in OSS [48] and goes against the purely meritocratic model of OSS. Discrimination and sexism in OSS *can* happen if gender is so salient, and they *do* happen, as discussed in the previous section. This suggests that gender diversity in GITHUB teams may have more intricate effects than hypothesised above. Finally, as expected, hobbies and political views (3% are aware for most team mates; 17%—for some team mates) are the least visible diversity aspects.

Lastly, respondents greatly differed in perception of importance of diversity. Some maintain that OSS development is "more about the contributions to the code than the 'characteristics' of the person" (40, male, N America), and that "any demographic identity is irrelevant" (26, female, N America) since "code sees no color or gender" (34, male, W&N Europe). In contrast, *e.g.*, awareness of the only woman on the team of other team members' views on diversity makes her "feel more welcome and eager to work since the stereotype threat isn't prevalent" (29, female, W&N Europe), while diversity is being perceived as a "source of creativity" (42, male, N America). Unfortunately, not all diversity-related experiences are positive, *e.g.*, forcing a 23-year old N-American female respondent to create a fake GITHUB-handle to masquerade as male or to quit a project; the latter experience has also been reported by a 40-year old N-American female. A 38-year old N-American female summarized her experiences as mostly positive, in particular on projects she leads; for other projects "interactions are usually positive too, with occasional sexism, but nothing more than one encounters in the rest of life".

Overall, we draw several conclusions from the survey and carry these into the subsequent analysis. First, *participants recognize team-members as those who make any type of contribution to the project.* Second, *team members are quite aware of certain aspects of other team members, including gender and technical skill.* Finally, *diversity appears to matter to contributors, but the perceived effects appear to vary.*

Data Set

Assembling a *diversity* GITHUB data set, with precise gender, location and tenure information, is challenging. First, on a GITHUB profile page personal information fields (*e.g.*, name, location) are free-text entries, thus often noisy; gender data is missing altogether. Second, some developers use multiple accounts, making it difficult to accurately measure their contributions. Finally, the OSS population, with the typically heavy-tailed workload distributions [62] (few very active projects/contributors and many much less active ones) require careful data filtering and preprocessing.

Preprocessing and Filtering

Our data collection process starts from the MySQL GHTorrent dump [29] dated 1/2/2014. GHTorrent is an offline persistent mirror of GITHUB's event streams, containing all user events, including commits, comments, pull requests, etc.

We then cleaned and filtered this data set as follows: (i) we unified different accounts used by the same contributor (see unmasking aliases below); (ii) we only considered activity between January 1, 2008 00:00 and January 2, 2014 23:59; (iii) we removed inactive projects (*i.e.*, having strictly less than 100 commits in total, and strictly less than 90 days of history between their earliest and latest recorded events, be it commits, pull requests, issues, or comments); (iv) since we are interested in effects of diversity on *team* outcomes, we excluded very small projects (*i.e.*, having less than four contributors, two of which committers, throughout their history); and (v) since we could not infer gender for all contributors (see the following subsection) and in order to compute gender diversity reliably, we further excluded projects for which we could not infer gender for at least 75% of contributors. Table 1 presents basic statistics about our data set. The effects of steps (ii)–(v) are denoted by "post filter". We stress the drastic but necessary reduction in number of projects during filtering. Even though our sample is restricted to only 1% of the initial projects, this step is paramount to ensuring sufficient variance in the data set along all co-variates of concern.

Unmasking Aliases

Recognising all the different accounts (or aliases) a person may have used when contributing to an online community (process known as identity merging or unmasking aliases) is essential to attributing contributions accurately, yet an ever-recurring challenge when analyzing OSS trace data [27, 35, 61]. On GITHUB, the committer's name and email address are set locally in each developer's git client, rather than globally at GITHUB level. Hence, due to variations in these attributes across devices or time, commits may not be attributed properly to the relevant GITHUB accounts. Furthermore, to account for "unknown" committer aliases encountered while processing events from GITHUB's API without losing data, GHTorrent assigns the corresponding commits to artificial aliases not linked to actual GITHUB accounts. This phenomenon is far from negligible: in the GHTorrent dump we analyzed, approximately 23% of all users have been labeled as "unknown".

Attribute	Total	Post filter	Min	Med	Mean	Max
Repo's	6,818,042					
Projects	2,605,486	23,016				
Commits	76,478,208	10,735,308	100	211	466.4	150,380
Pull req's		1,827,391	0	11	79.4	135,557
Issues		697,913	0	4	30.3	22,905
Comments		2,633,614	0	11	114.4	102,813
Contrib's	2,677,443	671,301	4	10	29.1	13,230
Females		9,292	0	0	0.96	300
Males		157,965	0	8	22.9	9650

Table 1. Basic statistics about our GITHUB data set.

To link the different aliases belonging to the same GITHUB contributors as well as deal with the issue of "unknown" aliases (an artifact of GHTorrent), we devised a series of heuristics inspired by those of Bird *et al.* [5] and Vasilescu *et al.* [62].[4] We stress that we have been as conservative as possible when deciding if two aliases belong to the same person, as the false positives count (*i.e.*, aliases incorrectly merged) would otherwise likely increase significantly [27]. For example, if multiple aliases share the same well-formed and non-fictitious email address, then we merge them, since email addresses are considered individual. Otherwise, if email addresses differ, then we only merge aliases for which we have collected sufficient evidence that they belong to the same person, from their first and last names, usernames, email address prefixes and domains, or locations. Even so, with a conservative approach to unmasking aliases, we determined that more than 170,000 users in our data set had used more than one alias (2,917,942 before; 2,677,443 after, 91.7%), with a median of 2, a mean of 2.4, and a maximum of 14. Moreover, using these heuristics we linked more than half of the "unknown" users to actual GITHUB accounts. Each unique account after unmasking aliases contained activity and personal data aggregated from all its aliases.

Inferring Gender

For each GITHUB contributor we infer gender based on their name and, if available, country, following the approach of Vasilescu *et al.* [59]. This approach combines a number of transformations, diminutive resolution, and heuristics (*e.g.*, users from Russia with surnames ending in *-ova* are female), with female/male frequency name lists collected for thirty different countries. Country data is indeed an essential ingredient to inferring a person's gender from their name (the classical example is Andrea, a common male first name in Italy, but a common female one in many other countries). In absence of country information, this gender inference approach seeks agreement between all country name lists available that report on a given name. The reported precision of `genderComputer` is 93% [59].

[4] Our code, too involved to be presented here, is available online at `https://github.com/bvasiles/ght_unmasking_aliases`.

On GitHub, registered users can choose to disclose their name and location in their profiles, but these fields are unstructured and often noisy, if not absent altogether. For example, only 40% of all users identified after unmasking aliases filled in what we consider reliable entries (*i.e.*, at least two parts separated by space) in their name fields. Location descriptions are also not readily trustworthy. Since not all include actual geographic data (*e.g.*, city names, latitudes/longitudes, or postcodes), to identify countries we combine information obtained from the Bing Maps API with information derived using our custom set of heuristics.[5] Following this process we identified countries for 12.6% of all users. Then, using Vasilescu *et al.*'s `genderComputer` [59], we could infer gender for 873,392 (32.6%) GitHub contributors: 91% male, 9% female. These numbers confirm an underrepresentation of women on GitHub, but comparable proportions to those reported for OSS (*e.g.*, [19,49]) or Stack Overflow [59].

We stress that while the fraction of users for which we could identify gender seems low (32.6%), it represents 80% of those who disclosed their names, the best we could hope for using any name-based technique, be it automatic or manual. Among the remaining 20% without any gender inferred, manual inspection of a small sample revealed missing country data as the main cause of ambiguity.

Measures

Using the methodology described above we assembled a longitudinal dataset of GitHub projects, in which each observation contains the composition, characteristics, and outcomes of a project's team of contributors for each quarter in the evolution of the project. We measure quarters as 90-day intervals starting from the earliest recorded commit in each project's history, such that data for the last quarter included is not incomplete, *i.e.*, there is at least one commit on the end date of this last quarter or later. In line with the study of diversity in Wikipedia projects of Chen, Ren, and Riedl [13], we also stress that a longitudinal approach is crucial: diversity may affect turnover, which in turn affects team composition, which affects diversity.

Response variables

Productivity: We measure team productivity by the number of commits by team developers recorded in either the main repository or any of its forks in a given quarter. Commits are the most encompassing form of coding contribution to a GitHub project and a representative facet of developer productivity in OSS [18]. Clearly, not all commits are created equal, some have different length and quality, and only some commits to forks are integrated in the main repository. Therefore, their number is insufficient to quantify the total contribution of a team in a project, or even to quantify their energy expenditure while doing so. However, commits are a reasonable representative, or sample, of the overall activities developers undertake while working on a project, hence a reasonable estimate of team productivity.

Turnover: As discussed earlier and as supported by our user survey results, we define each project's team as the set of contributors active in a given quarter, where activities can be either commits, pull requests (merged or not), issues, or comments, recorded in the project's main repository or any of its forks. To capture turnover in project teams we use the fraction of the team in a given quarter that is different with respect to previous quarter (*i.e.*, the turnover ratio).

Independent variables

Gender diversity: We measure team gender diversity using the Blau index [10], defined as $1-\sum_{i\in\{m,f\}} p_i^2$, where p_i are the fraction of male and female team members. The Blau index is a well-established diversity measure for categorical variables (*e.g.*, [13,33]). If teams contain members for which we could not infer gender, the measure only considers the fraction of the team for which we could infer gender.

Tenure diversity: Different kinds of tenure are accessible for GitHub developers: (i) account tenure, capturing global GitHub *presence*; (ii) commit tenure, capturing global GitHub *coding experience*; or (iii) project tenure, capturing local *project experience*, not restricted to coding. We select commit and project tenure as the most appropriate measures of coding experience and of project expertise, respectively. Note that while GitHub commit tenure is restricted to coding experience *within* GitHub, other, perhaps more appropriate, measures of coding experience *outside* GitHub are unavailable. To measure commit tenure for a GitHub contributor w.r.t. a given quarter, we compute the number of days since her earliest ever recorded commit (in any GitHub repository) until the end of that quarter. Commit tenure is not available for all team members, since not everyone will have been committer, in this or other projects. To measure project tenure for a GitHub contributor, we compute the number of quarters since her earliest recorded event in the current project until the end of that quarter. Project tenure is available for all team members. Commit and project tenure are orthogonal measures: a team can be diverse w.r.t. commit tenure, if it has a mix of novice and expert coders, but homogenous w.r.t. project tenure, if all contributors formed the team at the same time. Since tenure measures are numerical variables, we measure tenure diversity using the coefficient of variation, defined as the ratio between the adjusted standard deviation and the mean.

Control variables

Team size: The number of contributors per project team in a given quarter. Larger team sizes are likely associated with increased productivity and increased turnover. However, given a small overall number of women involved in OSS projects, we expect the impact of gender diversity to be more visible for smaller teams.

Project forks: The number of forks part of a project. Since activity in forks is more likely to be limited (both in time and in amount) compared to a project's main repository, the number of forks is expected to have a negative effect on team productivity, and a positive effect on turnover.

Quarter index: The index of each 90-day interval in a project's history, starting with 1. Time is known to have a moderating influence on the effects of diversity [64]: as group members continue to interact, they have more time to adjust to differences between them.

Overall project activity: The overal total commit count.

[5] `https://github.com/tue-mdse/countryNameManager`

Project age: The difference between the maximum index and the index of the 90-day interval during which the first commit was recorded, w.r.t. 1/1/2008 (newer projects have smaller values), starting with 24. Controls for changes in environment as GITHUB grows with time: later projects and their teams may have experienced a different culture.

Tenure median: To represent the "average" project or commit tenure as opposed to tenure diversity, we also include the project median tenure and the commit median tenure.

Comments: The number of GITHUB comments left by the team members during a given quarter on commits, pull requests, or issues. Reflects a project's social activity (not covered by our productivity measure).

Statistical Modeling

We wish to capture the variation in several outcomes with respect to the basic control measures and diversity indices described above. Our dataset contains a large number of projects and, within each project, consists of multiple time windows. Mixed effects models are often used in this context in order to capture measurements from within the same group, *e.g.*, within the same project, as a random effect. Similarly, they are used longitudinally, to measure the variance between time points. In our case we have both, so we use two random effect terms, the project and time window in which the measurement was taken. For the time window we model only the intercept as a random effect. However, as we do not expect that projects will respond to different team sizes in the same way, *e.g.*, some types of projects may benefit greatly from the addition of a new team member, while others less so, we include team size as a random slope within the project. All other variables were modeled as fixed effects. We tested the inclusion of random team size slope within time windows but the additional random effect was not significant. We used multiple linear mixed-effects models, as implemented in the functions *lmer* and *lmer.test* from the *lme4* [3] package in R.

Due to the varying (*i.e.*, unstable) behavior of the fitted coefficients in the models over the full range of team sizes, we decided it was appropriate to use *piecewise*, or *segmented* regression models. In those models, the range of a variable is split at structural breakpoints and multiple, piecewise linear models are fitted, one for each segment. Additionally, as we are interested in increased effects of diversity on OSS outcomes, we further required at least one female committer over the life of the project. This better corresponds to our hypothesis of increasing diversity, when some diversity is already present, versus adding a woman to an all-male team. Coefficients are considered important if they were statistically significant ($p < 0.05$). Their effect sizes are obtained from ANOVA analyses. We evaluate models using the sum of squares goodness of fit measure, while insisting on coefficient stability across models, in the segmented regression.

RESULTS

To assess the effects of our controls and diversity predictor variables on productivity and turnover we used mixed effects, multiple linear regression models. We filtered the data and retained a subset of it that both allowed for the calculation of all measures and was homogenous enough to yield stable models, as described in the Data section above. The variables that upon examination showed a log-normal distribution (*e.g.*, counts) were log-transformed, as indicated. A number of different measures that were highly correlated were excluded from the models. We note that our models were driven by our hypotheses, and were all based on the full complement of variables and confounds that we started with, concordant with good statistical modeling practice [53].

Productivity

To model productivity, we used *segmented regression* due to the instability of the fitted model coefficients when a single model was used over the whole range of team sizes. The results of three models, one for small teams (< 11), the second for medium-sized teams (11 to 30 members), and a third, for large teams (> 30), are given in Table 2. In addition to the three model coefficients, given in the left columns of the three pairs of model columns, the table shows the sum of squares, a measure of variance explained, for each variable. The significance is indicated by stars. We note that the project coefficients and the sum of squares are not comparable across the three models, but only within each model.

As expected, the number of committers and the other controls play a dominant role in explaining the variance in the data. The effect of gender diversity is positive, highly significant, and stable over all team size ranges. Its contribution to explaining the data variance is sizable for those team sizes. Thus, ***H1*** is confirmed. Likewise, looking at the commit tenure diversity coefficient, we see it is positive and significant for medium and large teams, partially confirming ***H2***.

Turnover

The turnover models are given in Table 3. We did not observe an effect instability with respect to team size in the turnover models, hence we did not use segmented regression. As with the productivity models, the number of committers and the other controls play a dominant role in explaining the variance in the data. For turnover, gender diversity is not significant in the model, thus we could not confirm a relationship between increasing gender diversity and the tendency for team composition to change. Therefore, ***H3*** is not confirmed. Both tenure diversity measures, however, are significant and contribute significantly and positively to the variance explained by the model. Therefore, ***H4*** is confirmed. Additionally, the interaction with median tenure across the team is also significant; we discuss this further in Section 4.

DISCUSSION

In the first set of models, we find that gender and tenure diversity have very significant, positive effects on productivity, across different team size segments, when controlled for other effects. These effect sizes are small compared to the controls: together, the two explain between 1% and 2.5% of the total sum of squares (variance). This falls into the range of small, but reportable effects (0.01 or greater in Cohen's criteria [14], which admittedly are not without fault [38]). Their small sizes were expected since the majority of the variance is explained by the big, technical players: total commits, project age, team size and number of committers. The effects, however, are stable (remain significant) across different team sizes. A plausible interpretation of our results is, then, that given strong known technical confounds, there is

	Small Teams		Medium Teams		Large Teams	
	Coeffs (Errors)	Sum Sq.	Coeffs (Errors)	Sum Sq.	Coeffs (Errors)	Sum Sq.
(Intercept)	−0.16281 (0.04003)***		0.05540 (0.02247)*		0.10205 (0.02667)***	
scale(log(total_commits))	0.82962 (0.00772)***	3127.67***	0.92775 (0.01961)***	487.19***	0.84236 (0.03348)***	122.99***
scale(log(proj_age + 0.5))	−0.08517 (0.00760)***	696.09***	−0.15728 (0.01785)***	94.50***	−0.13490 (0.02363)***	26.06***
scale(log(num_team))	0.34781 (0.00742)***	388.06***	0.13788 (0.01216)***	14.09***	0.24916 (0.03403)***	6.01***
scale(log(total_committers))	−0.35371 (0.01068)***	874.25***	−0.16661 (0.02288)***	37.08***	−0.07542 (0.04020)	4.68
scale(log(forks + 0.5))	−0.11534 (0.00915)***	33.53***	−0.16243 (0.01951)***	9.75***	−0.14167 (0.03411)***	1.78***
scale(log(num_comments + 0.5))	0.06840 (0.00626)***	24.18***	0.08385 (0.01588)***	3.85***	0.07763 (0.02582)**	1.47**
scale(proj_tenure_med)	0.05559 (0.00770)***	24.64***	0.00500 (0.01651)	0.30	0.02607 (0.02667)	0.67
scale(proj_tenure_div)	−0.04899 (0.01126)***	7.37***	−0.10813 (0.01940)***	6.49***	−0.09226 (0.02208)***	1.97***
scale(commit_tenure_med)	−0.02622 (0.00754)***	12.80***	0.05927 (0.02100)**	0.00**	0.14005 (0.03104)***	0.50***
scale(commit_tenure_div)	0.01395 (0.00750)	0.53	0.07525 (0.02195)***	5.17***	0.12343 (0.03316)***	2.18***
scale(gender_div)	0.03137 (0.00564)***	8.59***	0.03765 (0.01043)***	2.20***	0.03992 (0.01522)**	0.84**
scale(proj_tenure_med):scale(proj_tenure_div)	0.01554 (0.00933)	1.00	0.02166 (0.02226)	0.16	0.05869 (0.02828)*	0.72*
scale(commit_tenure_med):scale(commit_tenure_div)	0.00622 (0.00498)	0.43	0.00045 (0.00966)	0.00	0.01893 (0.01190)	0.29

***$p < 0.001$, **$p < 0.01$, *$p < 0.05$

Table 2. Productivity Models, log (number of commits) is the response. Team size segments: Small < 11; 10 < Medium < 30; 30 < Large.

	Diversity	
	Coeffs (Errors)	Sum Sq.
(Intercept)	−0.26408 (0.07017)***	
scale(log(total_committers))	0.32924 (0.01120)***	708.47***
scale(log(forks + 0.5))	0.04446 (0.00883)***	244.04***
scale((proj_age + 0.5))	−0.00526 (0.00788)	49.17
scale(log(total_commits))	−0.44783 (0.00819)***	2415.86***
scale(log(num_team))	0.19782 (0.00753)***	773.27***
scale(commit_tenure_med)	0.02439 (0.00741)**	92.86**
scale(commit_tenure_div)	0.07222 (0.00741)***	274.39***
scale(proj_tenure_med)	−0.21963 (0.00758)***	933.91***
scale(proj_tenure_div)	0.28548 (0.01191)***	169.13***
scale(gender_div)	0.00756 (0.00528)	2.25
scale(log(total_committers)):scale(log(forks + 0.5))	0.01607 (0.00497)**	4.10**
scale(commit_tenure_med):scale(commit_tenure_div)	−0.04586 (0.00465)***	24.12***
scale(proj_tenure_med):scale(proj_tenure_div)	0.09921 (0.00910)***	42.80***

***$p < 0.001$, **$p < 0.01$, *$p < 0.05$

Table 3. Turnover Models, developer turnover is the response.

a small but notable effect of gender and tenure diversity on productivity in online software teams.

The relative effects of gender and tenure vary with team size. As gender diversity increases, team productivity increases. The coefficient and the size of the effect are roughly the same across the three separate team size ranges. The positive effect is not surprising in light of prior work on online [13] and offline groups [24]. Our findings align more with IP [52] than the other theories discussed in the background section; this suggests that merit matters more than demographics in OSS. In general, in OSS projects the existence of latent social structures (communities) corresponding to code modules has been documented [7]. Thus, project participants are arguably acutely aware of others in their smaller community, and are more attuned to reacting to changes within those smaller groups. On average, our results across team sizes point to the equitable distribution of gender diversity across the communities, over time, resulting in a scalable diversity effect, which we observe. The productivity of programming teams as a function of size is a complicated issue [11, 65]; however, one can reasonably expect that the effects of size in this data are modulated by software modularization and the organization of teams into task-oriented groups.

We now consider diversity in commit tenure and project tenure. Recall that commit tenure measures experience across *all* of GITHUB, not just the specific project under consideration; thus, it reflects the experience diversity of the individuals in the team. On the other hand, project tenure diversity reflects the diversity of experience of project members *within the project.* Thus, it is entirely possible for a project to be highly commit-tenure diverse and not very project-tenure diverse (and vice-versa). The effects of both types of diversity tend to grow with team sizes. Commit-tenure diversity has no significant productivity effect for smaller teams. This is consistent with the theory that introducing "new blood" benefits any project, and more so the bigger ones. In contrast, project tenure diversity is negative and significant, indicating that a lot of per project diversity is counterproductive. This suggests that project diversity increases co-ordination effort, perhaps arising from conflicts between vested interests (long tenure) and newcomers.

The second model shows that turnover (rate of change in project staff) is not effected by gender diversity, since its coefficient is not significant. So, higher diversity does not effect a change in team composition. These models do show significant effects of tenure on turnover, however. In particular, median project tenure (not tenure diversity) has a substantial negative effect on staffing changes, *i.e.*, the higher the median tenure in the project, the less likely it is there will be people joining or leaving the project. This is consistent with the notion that more experienced teams will persist, and attrition will be lower. The project and commit tenure diversity effects are both positive: more diverse teams experience more staffing changes. This is due to, perhaps, people preferring teams with more homogeneous experience.

THREATS TO VALIDITY

Any empirical study is subject to a number of threats to validity. Validity of extraction of information from GITHUB can be threatened in a way similar to digital trace data [32] or put in a "peril" by concerns related to mining Git repositories in general [9], or specifically GITHUB data [34].

We attended to the threats identified above; *e.g.*, our "post filter" steps discussed earlier removes projects with too few commits (Peril II [34]) and also one-person projects (Peril V [34]). The threat of misrepresenting individual contributions, related to generated-data reliability [32], was addressed by combining contibutions of the different aliases of an individual, and in forks of the same project. However, despite best efforts, our measures of productivity (number of commits) might be an underestimation, since the project history might have been rewritten (Perils 4 and 7 [9]). Furthemore, to reduce the threats related to analysis tools [32] we have opted, whenever possible, for techniques and approaches empirically evaluated in previous studies: *e.g.*, the gender inference tool has been evaluated previously [59], the Blau index is a common diversity measure [13,33], and temporal aggregation, concern raised before [32], is done per quarter as common in diversity studies [13,18,63].

CONCLUSION

Our study suggests that, overall, when forming or recruiting a software team, increased gender and tenure diversity are associated with greater productivity. This finding is consistent with information processing theory [52]: a diverse team, comprised of women and men, and more and less experienced people, brings different perspectives together, thus improving outcomes. The benefits of experience diversity have a limit, though, as higher tenure diversity may increase attrition. This negative effect appears to be mitigated, however, when more experienced people are present.

Currently, however, women programmers are in the minority in OSS and other technical teams. Our study suggests that on a larger, economic and societal scale, added investments in educational and professional training efforts and outreach for female programmers will likely result in added overall value. Such efforts may have to be coordinated with efforts to remove existing barriers standing in the way of women's equitable integration in programming teams. To the best of our knowledge this is the first work that provides empirical evidence that productivity and turnover of software development teams are effected by team diversity.

ACKNOWLEDGEMENTS

Many thanks to survey participants for their time and interest, and to reviewers for their helpful remarks. BV, AS, and MvdB gratefully acknowledge support from the Dutch Science Foundation, project NWO 600.065.120.10N235. VF, PD, DP, BR, and BV gratefully acknowledge support from the US Air Force Office of Scientific Research, project FA955-11-1-0246.

REFERENCES

1. Apesteguia, J., Azmat, G., and Iriberri, N. The impact of gender composition on team performance and decision making: Evidence from the field. *Manage. Sci. 58*, 1 (2012), 78–93.
2. Aries, E. Interaction patterns and themes of male, female, and mixed groups. *Small Group Behavior* (1976).
3. Bates, D. M. *lme4: Mixed-effects modeling with R*, 2010.
4. Begel, A., and Nagappan, N. Usage and perceptions of agile software development in an industrial context: An exploratory study. In *ESEM*, IEEE (2007), 255–264.
5. Bird, C., et al. Mining email social networks. In *MSR*, ACM (2006), 137–143.
6. Bird, C., et al. Open borders? immigration in open source projects. In *MSR*, IEEE (2007), 6.
7. Bird, C., et al. Latent social structure in open source projects. In *FSE*, ACM (2008), 24–35.
8. Bird, C., et al. Does distributed development affect software quality?: An empirical case study of Windows Vista. *CACM 52*, 8 (2009), 85–93.
9. Bird, C., et al. The promises and perils of mining git. In *MSR*, IEEE (2009), 1–10.
10. Blau, P. M. *Inequality and heterogeneity: A primitive theory of social structure*, vol. 7. Free Press NY, 1977.
11. Brooks, F. P. *The mythical man-month*, vol. 1995. Addison-Wesley Reading, MA, 1975.
12. Byrne, D. E. *The attraction paradigm*. Personality and psychopathology. Academic Press, 1971.
13. Chen, J., et al. The effects of diversity on group productivity and member withdrawal in online volunteer groups. In *CHI*, ACM (2010), 821–830.
14. Cohen, J. *Statistical Power Analysis for the Behavioral Sciences*. Lawrence Erlbaum Associates, 1988.
15. Croson, R., and Gneezy, U. Gender differences in preferences. *J. Econ. Lit.* (2009), 448–474.
16. Dabbish, L., et al. Social coding in GitHub: transparency and collaboration in an open software repository. In *CSCW*, ACM (2012), 1277–1286.
17. Dabbish, L., et al. Leveraging transparency. *IEEE Software 30*, 1 (2013), 37–43.
18. Daniel, S., et al. The effects of diversity in global, distributed collectives: A study of open source project success. *Inform. Syst. Res. 24*, 2 (2013), 312–333.
19. David, P. A., and Shapiro, J. S. Community-based production of open-source software: What do we know about the developers who participate? *Information Economics and Policy 20*, 4 (2008), 364–398.
20. de Gilder, D., and Wilke, H. A. M. Expectation states theory and the motivational determinants of social influence. *Eur. Rev. Soc. Psychol. 5*, 1 (1994), 243–269.
21. de O. Melo, C., et al. Interpretative case studies on agile team productivity and management. *Inform. Software Tech. 55*, 2 (2013), 412–427.
22. Domingos, P. A few useful things to know about machine learning. *CACM 55*, 10 (2012), 78–87.
23. Ducheneaut, N. Socialization in an open source software community: A socio-technical analysis. *CSCW 14*, 4 (2005), 323–368.
24. Earley, C. P., and Mosakowski, E. Creating hybrid team cultures: An empirical test of transnational team functioning. *Acad. Manag. J. 43*, 1 (2000), 26–49.
25. Easterbrook, S., et al. Selecting empirical methods for software engineering research. In *Guide Adv. Empir. Softw. Eng.* Springer, 2008, 285–311.
26. Feller, J., and Fitzgerald, B. A framework analysis of the open source software development paradigm. In *ICIS*, Association for Information Systems (2000), 58–69.
27. Goeminne, M., and Mens, T. A comparison of identity merge algorithms for software repositories. *Science of Computer Programming 78*, 8 (2013), 971–986.
28. Gould, R. V. The origins of status hierarchies: A formal theory and empirical test. *Am. J. Sociol. 107*, 5 (2002), 1143–1178.
29. Gousios, G. The GHTorent dataset and tool suite. In *MSR*, IEEE (2013), 233–236.
30. Harrison, D. A., et al. Beyond relational demography: Time and the effects of surface-and deep-level diversity on work group cohesion. *Acad. Manag. J. 41*, 1 (1998), 96–107.

31. Horwitz, S. K., and Horwitz, I. B. The effects of team diversity on team outcomes: A meta-analytic review of team demography. *J. Manag. 33*, 6 (2007), 987–1015.
32. Howison, J., et al. Validity issues in the use of social network analysis with digital trace data. *JAIS 12* (2011).
33. Jackson, S. E., and Joshi, A. Diversity in social context: a multi-attribute, multilevel analysis of team diversity and sales performance. *J. Organ. Behav. 25*, 6 (2004), 675–702.
34. Kalliamvakou, E., et al. The promises and perils of mining GitHub. In *MSR*, ACM (2014).
35. Kouters, E., et al. Who's who in Gnome: Using LSA to merge software repository identities. In *ICSM* (2012), 592–595.
36. Lakhani, K. R., and Von Hippel, E. How open source software works: "free" user-to-user assistance. *Research Policy 32*, 6 (2003), 923–943.
37. Lee, M. J., et al. GitHub developers use rockstars to overcome overflow of news. In *CHI*, ACM (2013), 133–138.
38. Lipsey, M., et al. Translating the statistical representation of the effects of education interventions into more readily interpretable forms. Tech. Rep. NCSER 2013-3000, U.S. Dept of Education, Institute of Education Sciences, 2012.
39. Marlow, J., et al. Impression formation in online peer production: activity traces and personal profiles in GitHub. In *CSCW*, ACM (2013), 117–128.
40. Martins, L. L., et al. Virtual teams: What do we know and where do we go from here? *J. Manag. 30*, 6 (2004), 805–835.
41. McDonald, N., and Goggins, S. Performance and participation in open source software on GitHub. In *CHI*, ACM (2013), 139–144.
42. Michailidou, A., and Economides, A. Gender and diversity in collaborative virtual teams. *Computer Supported Collaborative Learning: Best practices and principles for instructors* (2007), 199–224.
43. Molleman, E., and Slomp, J. The impact of team and work characteristics on team functioning. *Hum. Factors Ergon. Manuf. 16*, 1 (2006), 1–15.
44. Nafus, D. 'Patches don't have gender': What is not open in open source software. *New Media & Society 14*, 4 (2012), 669–683.
45. Oreg, S., and Nov, O. Exploring motivations for contributing to open source initiatives: The roles of contribution context and personal values. *Comput. Hum. Behav. 24*, 5 (2008), 2055–2073.
46. O'Reilly III, C. A., et al. Work group demography, social integration, and turnover. *Admin. Sci. Quart.* (1989), 21–37.
47. Preece, J., and Shneiderman, B. The reader-to-leader framework: Motivating technology-mediated social participation. *AIS Trans. Hum.-Comput. Interact. 1*, 1 (2009), 13–32.
48. Riordan, C. M., and Shore, L. M. Demographic diversity and employee attitudes: An empirical examination of relational demography within work units. *J. Appl. Psychol. 82*, 3 (1997), 342.
49. Robles, G., et al. FLOSS 2013: A survey dataset about free software contributors: challenges for curating, sharing, and combining. In *MSR*, ACM (2014), 396–399.
50. Robles, G., and Gonzalez-Barahona, J. M. Contributor turnover in libre software projects. In *Open Source Systems*. Springer, 2006, 273–286.
51. Rogelberg, S. G., and Rumery, S. M. Gender diversity, team decision quality, time on task, and interpersonal cohesion. *Small Group Research 27*, 1 (1996), 79–90.
52. Salancik, G. R., and Pfeffer, J. A social information processing approach to job attitudes and task design. *Admin. Sci. Quart. 23*, 2 (1978), 224–253.
53. Simmons, J., et al. False-positive psychology undisclosed flexibility in data collection and analysis allows presenting anything as significant. *Psychol. Sci. 22*, 11 (2011).
54. Stahl, G. K., et al. Unraveling the effects of cultural diversity in teams: A meta-analysis of research on multicultural work groups. *J. Int. Bus. Stud. 41*, 4 (2010), 690–709.
55. Tajfel, H. Social psychology of intergroup relations. *Annu. Rev. Psychol. 33*, 1 (1982), 1–39.
56. Takhteyev, Y., and Hilts, A. Investigating the geography of open source software through GitHub, 2010.
57. Tao, Y., et al. How do software engineers understand code changes?: An exploratory study in industry. In *FSE*, ACM (2012), 51:1–51:11.
58. Turkle, S. *The Second Self: Computers and the Human Spirit*. MIT Press, 2005.
59. Vasilescu, B., Capiluppi, A., and Serebrenik, A. Gender, representation and online participation: A quantitative study. *Interacting with Computers* (2013), 1–24.
60. Vasilescu, B., et al. StackOverflow and GitHub: Associations between software development and crowdsourced knowledge. In *SocialCom*, IEEE (2013), 188–195.
61. Vasilescu, B., et al. How social Q&A sites are changing knowledge sharing in open source software communities. In *CSCW*, ACM (2014), 342–354.
62. Vasilescu, B., et al. On the variation and specialisation of workload–A case study of the Gnome ecosystem community. *Empir. Softw. Eng. 19*, 4 (2014), 955–1008.
63. Wang, L., et al. Searching for the goldilocks zone: trade-offs in managing online volunteer groups. In *CSCW*, ACM (2012), 989–998.
64. Watson, W. E., et al. Cultural diversity's impact on interaction process and performance: Comparing homogeneous and diverse task groups. *Acad. Manag. J. 36*, 3 (1993), 590–602.
65. Weyuker, E. J., et al. Do too many cooks spoil the broth? using the number of developers to enhance defect prediction models. *Empir. Softw. Eng. 13*, 5 (2008), 539–559.
66. Williams, K. Y., and O'Reilly, C. A. Demography and diversity in organizations: A review of 40 years of research. *Res. Organ. Behav. 20* (1998), 77–140.
67. Ye, Y., and Kishida, K. Toward an understanding of the motivation of open source software developers. In *ICSE*, IEEE (2003), 419–429.
68. Zellmer-Bruhn, M. E., et al. When and how do differences matter? an exploration of perceived similarity in teams. *Organ. Behav. Hum. Dec. 107*, 1 (2008), 41–59.

Offline Strangers, Online Friends: Bridging Classroom Gender Segregation with WhatsApp

Preeti Mudliar
Xerox Research Centre, India
preeti.mudliar@xerox.com

Nimmi Rangaswamy
Xerox Research Centre, India
nimmi.rangaswamy@xerox.com

Prestige Technology Park – II
Etamin - 3, 4th Floor, Wing - A
Marathahalli-Sarjapur ORR
Bangalore – 560103

ABSTRACT
Mobile Instant Messaging (MIM) apps such as WhatsApp are heralding new communication behaviors amongst students in peri-urban India. From an ethnographic study of a co-ed engineering college, we describe and analyze the role of WhatsApp in both engendering and balancing the ripples caused by cross gender communication. Through in-depth interviews and immersive participant observations in both physical as well as digital spaces, we show how WhatsApp emerges as the backbone of student interactions in a gender segregated academic environment. In analyzing social conditions and identifying structural features of WhatsApp that led to its bottoms up appropriation, our study presents possibilities for educators and designers aiming to create technology enabled collaborative spaces between people otherwise hemmed in by social norms from reaching out to one another.

Author Keywords
Mobile Instant Messaging, WhatsApp, Indian Youth, Cross Gender Communication

ACM Classification Keywords
H.1.2 [Human Factors]

INTRODUCTION
Student life in a restrictive gender-dissociative environment can be full of intrigue. While social norms divide girls and boys into separate spaces in the classroom and render taboo any cross-gender interaction that is not strictly necessary, instant messages from mobile phone apps often vault over, slide under, percolate, and infiltrate through the restrictions - even as they allow surface appearances of conformity to remain mostly unthreatened and undisturbed. More crucially, these messages bind the classroom into a cohesive singular unit – at least in the digital space. As a communication tool embedded in the opposing dualities of the private and the public characteristic of a mobile phone, Mobile Instant Messaging (MIM) services such as Whatsapp allow students to cross over the social wires that fence their interactions into largely homosocial territories. In their research on the adoption of instant messaging (IM) by teens, Grinter and Palen [8] suggest that the choice of technology as a means of communication depends on a number of non-technological factors and propose that technology be studied as a feature of the very culture in which it is being used. We look at WhatsApp as a site that acts as a surreptitious agent of change by students to co- create and structure their peer interactions with the opposite sex through both personal as well as group messaging efforts.

CHI 2015, April 18 – 23, 2015, Seoul, Republic of Korea.
Copyright 2015 ACM 978-1-4503-3145-6/15/04…$15.00.
http://dx.doi.org/10.1145/2702123.2702533

Our discovery of the importance of WhatsApp in regulating student interactions with the opposite sex was incidental and not part of a deliberate research plan. A semester-long study that sought to understand student life and the learning choices they make in an engineering college in the peri-urban outskirts of Bengaluru city, yielded serendipitously the role of WhatsApp in initiating friendship, developing assurances, and supporting the maintenance of these relationships as integral to student life. After establishing the crucial role the MIM was playing in facilitating communication amongst students, we delved deeper into examining WhatsApp enabled communication.

We were guided by the following questions in our investigation: 1. Why did students turn to WhatsApp in bridging gender interactions? 2. How does this digital channel encourage students to nudge cultural boundaries to form and maintain cross gender friendships? 3. What is the kind of communication enacted on WhatsApp groups that allows for gender boundaries to be bridged?

Our research suggests that WhatsApp creates a low-risk environment to facilitate new cross-gender interactions while simultaneously reflecting and affirming accepted norms governing gender behaviors. We discuss how rapid student migration to WhatsApp complemented by the app's affordances, propelled tentative cross-gender digital exchanges that soon grew into full-fledged conversations.

Interestingly, these conversations were seldom replicated in the offline world even when students had been co-present in the same classroom for over two years. We then illustrate the enactment of group communication on WhatsApp to explain how the technology is used to order online student relations in an offline gender segregated classroom.

India is no stranger to mobile messaging. It is one of the earliest adopters of SMSs and is familiar with group SMS culture [15]. Due to the value proposition of SMS, literate people have been more connected with texting as compared to phone calls. Hence, WhatsApp's increasing adoption seems in line with user skills and comfort already developed with SMS as an affordable communication channel. WhatsApp is by no means a unique application and competes with other MIMs such as WeChat, Viber, Telegram, and Hike that offer similar features. Although the participants in our study were aware of other MIMs and were even present on some of them, they stated a clear preference for WhatsApp owing to its popularity amongst their friends. A study of WhatsApp users, [4] found that while economic considerations made WhatsApp a very attractive proposition, it was the social influence from friends that spurred user adoption. Our study too found a similar adoption pattern. We found social influence driving WhatsApp adoption so strong that one of our respondents was accessing WhatsApp on a shared family laptop by installing Bluestacks (an app player that enables Android apps to run on Windows and Mac laptops) because she could not afford a smartphone!

RELATED LITERATURE

WhatsApp describes itself as "Simple. Personal. Real Time Messaging." [10]. As a cross-platform MIM app, it facilitates 'free' exchange of messages by drawing from the user's existing mobile Internet plan. Its features support exchange of text, audio, and video messages. It also allows users to see each other's presence on the app through 'timestamp' information that reveals when a user was 'last seen' on the app. However, in recent privacy changes, Whatsapp allows users to restrict access to information such as the last seen timestamp, and their profile picture. The app hit headlines in February 2014 when it was acquired by Facebook in a US$19 billion deal. Academic papers on WhatsApp are trickling in and taking cues from O'Hara et al [13] and the exploration of 'faithfulness' in friendship, we turn the spotlight on changing gender interactions made possible through WhatsApp as a channel of communication.

Youth and Text Messaging

The relationship that young people share with their mobile phones and the messaging practices that they engage with have allowed researchers to comment on various aspects of this phenomenon. Viewing text messaging as a social practice that is symbolic to the rituals of gift exchange, Taylor and Harper [18] demonstrated the ways in which teens enacted friendships and rivalries with one another. Further insights on the text messaging were provided by Grinter and Eldridge [9] on the nature and purposes of everyday conversations that teens carried via text messaging that comprised 'chatting', 'coordinating communications', and 'planning activities'. Studying IM practices amongst teens, Grinter and Palen [8] attempted to locate what drew teenagers to IM, their collaborative use, and the nature of its embeddedness in their domestic routines. Ito's work [11] on Japanese youth's relationship with their mobile phones provides insightful data on the way young people use mobile phones depending on the power dynamics of the spaces that they are in. More recently, Ames [2] described the ways in which Stanford students engaged with social expectations and exhibited techno-resistance to expectations of mobile multitasking with respect to their phone use.

While these studies provide a wealth of insights, research in developed countries takes for granted the availability and functionality of seamless, perpetual and functional ICT infrastructures to understand communication behaviors and practices amongst their participants. Thus, Walton, et al [19] provide a welcome contribution with their examination of phone and mobile media sharing relationships between youth in a low income settlement in Cape Town. Given that there is very little by way of scholarly literature on digital media and youth behaviors from the developing world and especially India, we turn to broader sociological work to contextualize our primary data and analysis.

Friendships amongst Indian Youth

It is no gainsaying to suggest powerful cultural socialization asserting a major influence on what are considered to be 'correct' gender interactions among young person living in India [14]. Studies examining the posturing that accompanies friendships and masculinities in south India comment on the aggressive socio-sexual posturing in public life [16] and how inter-generational changes in are dealt through friendship in providing a space for the negotiation of cultural hierarchies, both old and new [12]. Heterosocial interactions amongst Indian youth are often formed and conducted under a cloud of cautiousness. While the boys are often privy to more liberal norms of conduct, girls bear the brunt of safeguarding the 'family honor' by ensuring that they are never publicly seen interacting with boys outside of their families beyond what is strictly necessary. Thus, not only does gender socialization proceed in ways that constrain female sexuality [5,7], but more pertinent to our study it is also facilitated by societal institutions such as educational institutes that seek to control female sexuality [3]. We found similar perpetuations of gender socialization in our fieldwork through practices such as gender segregated seating in classrooms.

Digital channels of communication create and organize a set of "possibilities and interdictions" [6] that are leveraged for sociability in culture specific ways. What interests us is how the digitally smart applications and messaging technologies offer a means to communicate and to create content. Messaging technology becomes part of the palette of meaning and content production that may push conventional

relationships to be experienced differently WhatsApp then is a "…site of encounter where friends perform and experience small but frequent acts of commitment and faithfulness… in essence, part of the way they live and dwell together even when apart…" [13]
How then does WhatsApp fit in a milieu of new and emerging interplay of low digital infrastructures and cross-gender cultural interactions?

METHODOLOGY

We conducted a semester-long qualitative study that included observations and interviews at an engineering college - anonymized as School of Information Technology (SOIT), to understand the teaching and learning context of engineering students and their daily college life. Below, we describe the field and detail our methodological approach.

Field Site

SOIT, a private institution is affiliated with a major state public university. It offers engineering courses in six disciplines and enrolls about 1500 students every year. Founded in 2008, SOIT is a very new institution and is located on the outskirts of Bengaluru. Though a part of Bengaluru city limits, the college is located in a small town that is witnessing sudden rise in real estate prices as a result of the city's rapid expansion. The town is linked to major state highways and its accessibility makes it an attractive choice for students from Bengaluru and surrounding towns. In terms of academic reputation, SOIT is not a premier institution. However, its students value the quality of teaching at the institute due to the reputation of the institute's senior professors who were earlier affiliated with a prestigious local engineering college.

Following the pattern of engineering education in most Indian states, students at SOIT too gained admission to the college on the basis of their performance in an annual common entrance test. Students said that their low ranking on the test meant that SOIT was one of the places where they could hope to be admitted. Students from outside Bengaluru, especially those living in the girls' on campus dormitories had a rather interesting basis for choosing SOIT. Most of these girls belonged to two small towns in Karnataka state and were drawn to the institution because a couple of SOIT's professors hailed from these towns. The girls revealed that their parents felt safe sending them to SOIT due to the professors' affiliation to their respective hometowns. Some girls also mentioned that their parents insisted they share a room with girls from their own hometowns with whom their families already had longstanding relations. Thus overall, SOIT has a mixed social milieu of students belonging to cosmopolitan Bengaluru city and students from nearby urban and rural towns as well as small towns from neighboring states of Karnataka.

Data Collection

The fieldwork was primarily conducted by the first author. She was introduced to students by professors as a researcher from a corporate research lab, interested in learning about engineering student life through observations and interviews. The first author built rapport with students by inviting questions about herself and her research agenda. Her prior experience as a journalist in India and her student days pursing a PhD in America generated curiosity. She was approximately 10 years older to students and leveraged her previous experience in a reputed Indian university as a media studies professor to build rapport with students - leading to extended dialogues even after fieldwork was completed. The first author's presence among students was thus framed by her identity as a reasonably but not significantly older Indian woman, a former journalist & university professor, and a fresh PhD from abroad, now home.

Our data collection spanned a variety of sources : 1) Participant observation in classrooms where the first author was accompanied by another colleague in the early stages of the study totaling to approximately 350 hours of observing 109 third-year students (n=109) belonging to two streams - computer science (CS) and electronic and computer engineering (ECE). 2). Interview sessions with students were conducted both individually as well as in groups with 53 students (n =53). 3) and preliminary surveys on student demographics and technology use and access with 109 students (n = 109). 4) We "hung out" in a variety of spaces (i.e. hallways, labs, and cafeteria) that helped in building rapport with the students. 5) The first author also sought the permission of the college authorities and moved into the on campus dormitory for a period of eight days in order to better understand the life of students who chose to live in the campus dormitories. Though access was limited to the girls dormitories, this stay served as a period of intensive field immersion facilitating in-depth observations through participation in the routine of hostel life and more freewheeling interactions with students that took the form of both recorded as well as informal conversations. 6) Lastly, the first author, also embedded herself in a class WhatsApp group to observe the activity and interactions of the students in their digital 'hangout' space.

The class WhatsApp group especially, carries great significance for students at SOIT. Of the two classes that we were observing, one class refused to grant access to their group citing privacy concerns in admitting an outsider into their class' online space. We fared significantly better in our attempt to gain access to the group of the second class owing to a good rapport with the popular students of the class. These 'popular' students facilitated our access to their WhatsApp group by signaling their acceptance of us and our research agenda. This access was again negotiated by the first author who explained the research interest for observing their WhatsApp activity. We then asked the group administrator to post our request on the class group and secure the consent of all members. The members responded with their agreement on the group and once everyone's consent was gathered, the first author was added with the understanding that her role would be that of a silent observer with permission to report data for research purposes while protecting the anonymity and confidentiality of all participants. All student names used in this paper to report data have been suitably anonymized.

While the group had been in existence since August 2013 and we continue to be a part of it, the reported findings are a result of a 45-day observation from April 15- May 30 2014. These observations were buttressed with follow up questions to students about their activity thus resulting in greater clarity about the group's activity. Most of the conversation in the group took place in English with occasional use of the local language – Kannada. Finally, though we did not announce any compensation for student participation in the beginning or during the study, we provided all participants Flipkart gift vouchers of Rs. 250 each (~US$ 4) at the end of fieldwork.

Analysis

Our analysis was primarily guided by the constant comparative method [17]. Transcriptions of both interviews and WhatsApp group activity along with observation notes were repeatedly read by the first author. The insights from these readings were shared and discussed with students during their lunch break and free lecture hours to seek opinions on the way the first author was interpreting their WhatsApp use. This constant interpretive process led to the emergence of conceptual categories that were analyzed in tandem with the structural features of WhatsApp to formulate final categories. The second author contributed her insights on these categories based on her experience of studying the SNS use of Indian youth. The categories were further developed by reading relevant literature that helped reflect and refine on the final categories. Finally, we arrived at themes from these categories that would best help us communicate the findings of our research.

FINDINGS

We begin our findings by describing some salient socio-cultural features of SOIT that help locate in context the emergence of WhatsApp as a popular channel for cross-gender communication:

Gendered Socio-spatial Classroom Arrangements

One of the most striking features of classrooms in SOIT is the neat gender segregation of students. In some classrooms, the seating was split in the middle with the girls and boys occupying one half each of the room, while in others, a few groups of boys and girls were scattered around the classroom. Whatever the seating arrangements, the unwritten norm dictated that boys and girls never sat together or shared the same bench. This segregation was also observed in lab sessions as well as college wide sessions that took place in a large seminar hall. Moreover, we observed this pattern even during the college fest when the environment was much more casual and informal and had mixed gender teams competing for various events ranging from dumb charades, song and dance contests, speech and debate et.al.

One woman professor we frequently interacted with opined that segregated seating was a desirable norm to have and that it was nothing more than an extension of what students were used to in school. During the course of our conversation, she cautiously joked that this was a slightly controversial topic. She said, *"Students join college fresh out of their plus twos (high school in India). Their behavior is still childish (sic). This seating (segregation) is actually a way of giving disciplinary respect to the teacher. If they sit together, it may give rise to some complications."* We probed further about why mixed sex seating could be controversial and undisciplined. To this, the professor referred to the years that we (the authors) had spent abroad in the United States and sought to differentiate our social contexts from SOIT's. She said, *"We are different from the western world. We are more cultural and religious and it is best we follow tradition."*

"We are Brothers and Sisters"!

The emphasis on segregated seating was not entirely unwelcome by students and we received a range of responses when we invited students to comment on seating arrangements. While some students shrugged and accepted it as an extension of the norm from their primary and high school days, some students reported that though there was no formal diktat on mixed sex seating, a few professors had reprimanded boys and girls who were seated together during class thus deterring others from doing the same. Recalled one student, *"Even if you say hi (to an opposite sex member), that's a big issue in the class."*

The restrictive seating norms at SOIT reflect the quality of face-to-face interactions that students had with the opposite sex. Girls who struck friendships with boys said they were often the target of gossip while boys who mingled and spoke to girls were often at the receiving end of their male classmates' ire. Suresh an ECE student who found no reason to hold back from interacting with girls shared his experience, "*There would have been absolutely no problem if everybody spoke to everybody else in my class, but imagine in a class of 50 I am the only one talking to girls. The boys got really jealous of me and spread rumors about me and the girls. I did not let it bother me. I continued making friends and eventually the boys got bored. I mean how many girls can they pair me off with so they gave up."* Karan who is Suresh's closest friend in SOIT echoed his views, *"Boys who speak to girls are envied. We get every possible nicknames. We are also approached by boys who are romantically interested in certain girls and questioned on our interaction with those girls. We are then asked to facilitate contact with them."* Jagan who has been in a steady relationship with his classmate Sarita since the first semester said, "*The teasing did bother me for some time and we (Sarita and he) even had fights about it, and then we stopped caring."* On her part, Sarita said, "*Gossiping about girls who speak to boys is common, but you realize how hurtful it is only when you find yourself targeted."*

Even if the majority of students did not go on to form the kind of bonds that allowed casual and frequent face-to-face interaction with members of the opposite sex, the daily rhythm of college life was often punctuated with tentative cross-gender exchanges for functional purposes. For instance, one of the major reasons meriting a boy approaching and speaking to a girl face-to-face in the college, was for lecture notes. Girls were commonly perceived to be more diligent than boys about attending classes and maintaining notes. Occasions such as a boy missing a lecture or examinations often meant that notes taken by the 'studious' girls would be much sought after by others in the class. Not only was an interaction around class notes often regarded as a legitimate reason for a boy and girl to interact, but it also acted as a safe alibi to further any latent romantic feelings. Said Karan, *"Everyone knows that girls are academically more diligent. They tend to attend classes and be attentive resulting in good notes. Before examinations, I generally field a lot of phone calls from the other boys in the class and they would plead with me to get notes from the girls because they were frightened to do it themselves."*

Eventually even if friendships grew out of these occasional interactions around classroom notes, both boys and girls were quick to dub their opposite sex friends as purely platonic and firmly labeled their relation as - "She is my sister" or "He is like a brother to me." Youth in India often characterize their heterosocial friendships with peers as that of a brother or a sister to protect themselves from gossip and teasing by their peers and avoid scrutiny from the society at large [1]. Once, Jhanvi who was scrolling through her contact lists to help us identify the administrator of the class group halted at a photograph of a boy with his arm around a girl. We asked her if the girl was the administrator's girlfriend. Horrified, Jhanvi corrected us, *"Oh no, she is like a sister to him."* Jhanvi herself engaged in face-to-face interactions with only one boy in her class – Shashi, who was in a steady relationship with one of her classmates. Predictably, she also dubbed him as her brother. Jhanvi's interactions with Shashi began when he approached her for notes since both he and his girlfriend had missed a few classes. As these interactions progressed to firmer friendship, Jhanvi now labels their relationship as that of a 'brother and a sister'.

WhatsApp as a Techno-social Infrastructure at SOIT

For an engineering institute, SOIT offers both students as well as its instructors minimal information technology infrastructure. Although it does not have a campus wide wireless network, it has two computer labs available to students during designated working hours only. The library also has about five computers that are accessible during college hours. Since the students are usually attending classes during this time, the computers are not really used. SOIT has a website, but it does not offer students any semblance of an academic digital presence such as a student portal or a classroom management system. Most of the administration and teaching is conducted through offline means. Information relevant to students is communicated via notice boards that are located at strategic points around the college premises. The onus of being informed is thus placed on the students who are required to walk up to the notice boards and sift for relevant information from among many other notices that are pinned to the board. Mobile phones are not allowed in the classrooms and many students store their phones in small shared lockers in the college. Despite this, some students carry mobile phones to class and we observed a few students surreptitiously texting during lectures.

In the survey that we conducted to gather demographic and communication information, 68 out of 109 students reported WhatsApp as a primary means of communication with their friends. Students also reported a very high dependence on mobile phones for their communication needs. They typically had pre-paid mobile connections and subscribed to Internet 'net packs' spending on an average Rs. 50/- (.9$) per month for 1 GB of data at 3G speed. For students who lived on campus, dependence on mobile internet was especially high. While a culture of sharing resources such as laptops and pre-paid Internet data cards existed, most students who lived on campus, reported complete dependency on mobile internet for their daily usage as the college did not provide for Internet or laptop facility in the hostels. The 'free' messaging service that WhatsApp afforded was thus a big draw for the students given that economic considerations was a prime driver in their choice of communication [3]. Access to internet connectivity, via mobile enabled Internet, laptops and desktops though fairly prevalent was not a given for everyone due to reasons of affordability. Even for students who were living off campus with their families, sometimes Internet access was possible only at the local cybercafé. Some students had access to a desktop and Internet at home, but could not afford a smartphone. Such students generally relied on their friends to keep them updated not only about important school-related information that was shared on WhatsApp, but also the 'fun' stuff that was being circulated on the group.

A group of boys that we spoke to reported that only one amongst them (Omar) had access to an Internet connected smartphone where WhatsApp could be accessed. When they met in college, Omar's phone was often passed around amongst his friends who wanted to catch up on the latest exchanges that were taking place on the class WhatsApp group. Omar's friend Suresh said, "*We are very interested in our WhatsApp group. Omar shows us all the videos and photos that are shared there. His phone is usually with one of us in college and we pass it around to catch up on the previous night's activity on the group.*"

If Omar's friends get by with circulating his phone around, then for Surekha, this dependency was trying enough to make attempts to become independent at accessing WhatsApp even without a smartphone. Using Bluestacks [2], Surekha now accesses WhatsApp even though she is tethered to her laptop. She said, *"I feel if I am not on WhatsApp, I miss out on a lot. Of course, my friends would keep me in the loop about everything, but I wanted to experience and be a part of WhatsApp myself. I have a laptop that I share with my family and we have wired Internet connectivity at home so a friend helped me download Bluestacks through which I can now access WhatsApp. When I go home from college in the evenings, I use WhatsApp and participate in all of the group as well as interpersonal conversations with my friends.*

The Digital Bridge of WhatsApp

To illustrate the role that WhatsApp plays in connecting students across the chasms of gender segregation, we return to Jhanvi's friendships with the boys in her class. As mentioned previously, Shashi was the only boy Jhanvi interacted with face-to-face. However, he was not the only male classmate that she considered her friend. Jhanvi was friends with at least four other boys in her class and though they had never interacted in person, she reported that she shared a lot of intensely personal thoughts with them on WhatsApp. How do these friendships begin amidst the social barriers of cross gender interaction?

The Mobile Number

Noting the growing popularity of WhatsApp amongst their peer group, Jhanvi's classmate – Rajesh decided that it would be a good idea to form a WhatsApp group for their class. In the beginning, the group was only composed of Rajesh and his own friends, but slowly as more people in the class began to get on to WhatsApp, Rajesh began adding his classmates to the group. With growing numbers, the group began to see increased activity in the form of forwards and jokes that students shared on the group. Not only that, the group was also a phone directory of sorts with every member's phone number visible to other members of the group. Additionally, WhatsApp notifies all members every time a member joins or leaves a group. Where earlier mobile numbers would have remained private except when explicitly shared with one another, group membership now meant that numbers were rendered visible to all members. Jhanvi said that her friendship with the boys began when some of them messaged her on WhatsApp. These messages were innocuous and were limited to exchanging helloes in the beginning. However, they soon progressed to long conversations that took place after college hours. Interestingly, most WhatsApp friendships at SOIT are initiated by boys and we did not come across any girl who had or at least admitted to 'friending' a boy on WhatsApp.

Laughing at the way gender interactions in her class play out, Jhanvi said, *"Yes, we do sit separately in class, but actually we are very friendly with each other even though we don't interact directly. I speak face-to-face only with Shashi, but on WhatsApp I am constantly in touch with Vijay and Sanath. In class, we act as if we don't know each other, but once we go home, we regularly ping each other. Our conversation usually begins with wishing each other "good morning" or "good evening" and asking each other how the day had been. Even if I do speak face-to-face, with them, it will be very business-like. Perhaps exchanging pen drives or notebooks. But on WhatsApp, we chat like friends. If they notice that I am not smiling in class, they message to ask why I was sad or if I don't come to class, they message to know the reason for my absence. We don't have these conversations face-to-face. There is this one boy who I have never spoken to directly. We have been classmates for three years now, but on WhatsApp he has asked me for my notes nearly eight times this semester. I take a picture of my notes and share it with him on WhatsApp, but we have never ever spoken to each other."*

Vijay agrees with Jhanvi's experience. He said, *"I feel you can get to know girls on WhatsApp. I generally begin by asking them how their day went or I ask them for their notes. From there on, the conversation could progress to asking about who their favorite actor is or their favorite film. With such questions, I can get to know the person and then we can see if our interests match and if there is potential for furthering the friendship."* We asked Vijay why he could not have the same conversations with a girl directly and he said, *"It is not that we don't talk to girls directly, but it is infrequent. In class we don't have time. They are sitting on one side and we sit on the other. I am ready to talk, but I feel the girls might feel awkward if I approach them so I ping them on WhatsApp."*

Maya who has a mixed gender friend group in college disagrees with Vijay's view. She said, *"I really wonder about why boys find it difficult to speak to us. They make no attempts to be friends. I find it very weird that the boys ping me and attempt to speak to me on WhatsApp, but not face-to-face."*

While some students such as Maya find the hesitancy exhibited by boys to speak to them face-to-face strange, many others welcome the opportunity that WhatsApp allows them to have at least some kind of interaction with the opposite sex. This opportunity mostly begins with membership in the class WhatsApp group that facilitates access to everyone's mobile number.

Group Formation

The lack of communication between boys and girls at SOIT was in some ways also responsible for the formation of a WhatsApp group. According to the group administrator of the WhatsApp group that we were observing, this communication also impacted class unity. Said Resham, *"There was hardly any communication in our class between us. We would only smile at each other with no conversation. I was really upset about this because I wanted our class to have unity and be a more interactive place where we also did fun things such as celebrate each other's birthdays. The idea for forming a class WhatsApp group actually came from Facebook. In our second semester, we formed a class group on Facebook, but it was largely inactive. We would only post the class timetable there. I realized a lot of people were using WhatsApp to talk to their friends, so I decided to form a group to get my classmates to talk to each other. I felt that WhatsApp would work more than Facebook."*

Resham also said that the communication in the group took time to take off. From a class with around 55 students, the group currently has 50 members although the number of students regularly active on the group is around 32. Resham is satisfied by the number of people who are active and said, *"We can't force people to be interactive and not everybody will even be interested. In the beginning there were very few members so the group was not as active as it is these days. People were only sharing funny pictures on the group. But as more people joined, the conversations increased. Now boys and girls even address each other by names and have conversations about things such as class happenings, and national politics. We all tease each other and it has helped break the ice. I think it has really helped us bond as a class."*

Echoing Resham, Shanti said, *"I am older to the other students in the class and because I had to repeat a year, I barely knew anyone when the semester began. However, all that changed when I was added to the class group. I am naturally gregarious and I began interacting with a lot of people in my class after chatting with them on WhatsApp. I began private messaging with some of the boys too, but we don't speak much face-to-face. At the most they will greet me in class and ask if I had breakfast, but on WhatsApp we constantly message each other and converse on many things. It is a little strange, but I think it is a mix of ego and shyness that prevents boys from talking to us in person. So at least they converse with us on WhatsApp."*

Gender and Event-based Group Splintering

Typically, every student was a part of at least four WhatsApp groups that were directly connected to SOIT. While most members were part of their class groups, the online space was not completely devoid of gender segregation. In both the classes that we observed, girls and boys were also part of 'girls' and 'boys' class groups on WhatsApp. These groups were formed with a view to replicate the real world homosocial interactions that the students were used to when with their own genders. However, most of the girls we spoke to reported very little activity on the girls' only group. In contrast, the boys reported more usage. We asked Satish an ECE student why he felt the need for a 'boys-only' group and he said, *"That is to maintain decency. Decency in the sense that there are no language constraints and we can be as colorful as we want. We cannot be this liberal if girls are also present"*

Aniket, a final year student had another take on the need for a boys-only group and pointed to the topical preferences for discussion of each gender. He said, *"In our class the boys group came into being because there was a lot of discussion about cricket on the class group. And then suddenly one day the girls started discussing about the sarees they would wear for the traditional day celebrations. We felt it was better if such things were discussed amongst interested parties. It so happened that only boys were in favor of cricket discussions and only girls were in favor of sarees discussions so that is when the split happened though we all are very active in our common class group. Sometimes, the gender specific groups are handy to have."*

While gender distinctions were responsible for the creation of some groups, other groups were formed on the basis of certain events or shared interests and routines. For instance, students who went on a three-day class trip to a nuclear power plant formed a group to share photographs and trip memories. Other groups included a 'dormitory-WhatsApp' group or 'college-fest committee' group. Similarly, students belonged to other SOIT-related groups such as 'bus-groups' depending on which college bus route they traveled on. The function that these groups served varied from exchange of information such as: "no water in hostel today" to sharing 'forwards', jokes, puzzles, and an easy way to coordinate outings.

Conflicts and Resolutions

Even as WhatsApp lead to increased interaction amongst boys and girls that was largely welcomed by both genders, it was not always smooth sailing. The existing gender tensions that were rooted in offline realities were often mirrored and sometimes even exacerbated online. Groups witnessed their fair share of stormy interactions with members sometimes quitting the group in anger. Interestingly, most conflicts that spilled into the class WhatsApp groups were usually heterosocial and interpersonal in nature. We were privy to one such incident that took place after we were granted access to the group. The incident involved Shanti and Rupesh and an altercation they had in the college canteen. Their offline quarrel quickly escalated to an online conflict that was conducted on the class WhatsApp group. Their interaction on the group spiraled into name calling and ended only when a fellow classmate intervened and asked members to maintain decorum on the class group. The quarrel ended with both Shanti and Rupesh quitting the group although both rejoined a couple of days later. We spoke to Shanti after the incident and she said, *"I have known Rupesh for about five months now. We were talking in the cafeteria and he began calling me an 'aunty'. I responded by calling him a 'child'. Later in the evening when we all began chatting on the class group, I again teased him by calling him a child and he responded by saying something insulting about my character. I reacted very angrily as it wasn't warranted on his part. That is when Kshitja intervened and made a general request to everyone to keep things peaceful. I was very angry and left the group and so did Rupesh."*

Such interactions are revealing about the gender tensions that exist amongst students. With tentative friendships between boys and girls, misunderstandings often flare into serious conflicts that result in both parties putting an end to any further interaction with each other. Shanti said that the result of the conflict was that her interaction on the group has become much more muted. She said, *"I feel I should be careful about what I post on the group so I don't message too much. Plus, Rupesh and I don't talk to each other anymore on WhatsApp or face-to-face."* Another student Rani had a similar experience as Shanti. Rani is a very frequent user of WhatsApp, but a lurker on the class group. She said, *"Before I joined the group, a boy made a hurtful comment about me. My friends who were in the group stood up for me. I did join the class group after that, but prefer not participating in the conversations. I am much more active in the WhatsApp group that I have created with seven of my other class friends. I feel more at ease there."*

We found that whenever conflicts took place on the groups, the aggrieved parties immediately left the WhatsApp group automatically broadcasting their unhappiness to all the other members because of WhatsApp's group activity notification feature. However, this leave taking was rarely permanent. Not only were quitters usually persuaded by other members to return, but they would also willingly return and continue their participation on the group.

Enacting Group Communication on WhatsApp

Until now, we focused on the gendered nature of WhatsApp use owing to the social norms that are reflected in the student culture at SOIT. We now explain the enactment of communication on WhatsApp groups such that it transforms a gender segregated classroom into a group with a sense of community owing to its online activities.

What is in a Name?

One of the ways in which the group expressed its identity as a singular unit was by changing the group name to reflect the collective sentiments of its members. While the usual name of the group remained 'ECE B' to signal that they were electronics and communications engineering students belonging to section 'B', the name was changed at intervals to mark incidents of significance to members. For instance, the class welcomed us as an observer of their WhatsApp group not only by individually typing "welcome Ma'am" messages, but also by changing their group name to "Welcome Ma'am" followed by two emoticons of a girl and a pair of hands joined together in a *namaste* – the traditional Indian greeting. This group name remained in force for a couple of days after which the group reverted to its usual name of 'ECE B'. Similarly, the group changed its name to "Vote maadi" (cast your vote) followed by emoticons of a finger pointing and a smiley exhorting members to vote in the general parliamentary elections in India. The group also changes its name to wish members on their birthdays. Typically, a member's birthday is observed on the group by changing the name to "Happy Birthday – Name".

The name changes also reflect the pride members feel in belonging to their class. Recently, Resham changed the group name to 'ECE B Riders'. When asked the reason for the name change, Resham spoke about how the organizing committee for the college fest had maximum representation from her class. She said, *"I was really proud at the efforts my classmates were putting in organizing the college fest. I changed the name to 'ECE B Riders' because I felt we were the coolest class around."* Every member in the group has the freedom to change the name and Resham said that there had never been any conflicts or dispute about name changes. Generally, name changes were followed by members signaling their approval of the change by responding with various emoticons such as 'clapping', 'thumbs up', and 'smileys'. Overall, it contributed to members feeling that their class was a cohesive unit that functioned well as a group.

Group Content

We found the communication between members on the group could be categorized into three main sections. We discuss each of them in the following sections:

Small Talk

One of the important kinds of content that members exchange with each other on the group is small talk. This usually takes the form of good morning messages that begin early in the morning before members leave for college. One 'good morning' message fetches similar 'good morning' responses from at least five to six other members. This is often a ritualistic start to the WhatsApp exchanges on the group for the day. We asked members about their opinion on these messages and wondered if some members viewed them as spam. Surekha who is a lurker on the group, but enjoys the group enough to access it from her laptop in the absence of a smartphone said, *"I don't think the messages are spam. In fact the days that I don't attend college, I feel like I belong to the class because of the messages."*

The group generally remains inactive during college hours when classes and restrictions on phone use limit any WhatsApp group activity. Thus, most activity on the group begins in the evenings. The activity for the evening is preceded by good evening messages. These messages are then followed by queries about what was had for dinner. Amidst all of this, members begin conversations by posting forwards that generally take the form of puzzles and jokes. When we asked members where they got this content from, they all revealed that the content came to them through membership in other WhatsApp groups. For instance, Shanti shared a love story on the group lasting over five episodes. She would post one episode every day and her post was eagerly awaited by other members who would plead with her to share the complete story. We asked Shanti about this and she said, *"I got the story from my school WhatsApp group. I restricted myself to one episode per day because I knew they were enjoying the story and I liked maintaining the suspense in the tale."*

Sharing content such as stories, puzzles, and jokes acted as an icebreaker for the day and often progressed to a lot of mutual teasing and laughter amongst members. After sharing a puzzle with the group, Tina declared that she would gift a BMW car to whoever cracked it. Ever since, Tina is often teased with numerous demands for fancy cars by her classmates. Badgering Resham, the group administrator, for a party on the slightest pretext is another common practice and leads to a lot of laughter in the group.

Academic Discussion

While small talks helps in maintaining a spirit of light heartedness in the group, it is often also the site where important academic information is exchanged. Members post queries such as *"What did I miss in class today? Was it a lot?"* A query such as this is usually followed by a list of topics that were taught with reassuring messages such as *"Don't worry. It is easy you will catch up."* Sometimes, queries are more specific such as *"Can anyone tell me how to write interfacing programs in record?.. programs on rhs, lhs what to write?"* This particular message was followed by a few members posting photographs of their notes on the groups as examples of the way interfacing programs were written.

A common practice that members indulge in is to share images of their notes with the group. As a mobile application that supports sharing of text, image, video, and voice, WhatsApp's diverse features are a major attraction and it is very easy for members to post requests for class notes on the group if they are missing sessions. In response, within seconds, whoever has the information takes a picture of the content using the mobile phone camera and shares it with the rest of the group. Easy dissemination of images is a crucial feature of WhatsApp and enables members to catch up on notes they may have missed. It also helps in updating everybody in the group about notices that are displayed on the college board. Said Ragini, *"The college board is often cluttered with a lot of notices and it is easy to miss information. If one of us spots something important, then we take a picture and share it on the group. All of us remain updated on important information this way."*

"Class/College Activities

Another major role that the WhatsApp group plays in the life of the students is of being a natural online extension of the activities that form a part of their college life. Members frequently use the group to discuss, laugh, and even vent at the quirks of different professors and class happenings. One particular professor was a favorite for discussion on the group due to his quirks that brooked little disobedience from students. Members often created funny memes using his photographs and shared them on the group. They reported that such practices not only helped them cope with the vagaries of college life, but also helped the group maintain their bond with each other.

In one particularly memorable incident, the students decided to mass bunk a class having returned from a class trip the previous night. It resulted in the college sending an SMS to the parents informing them about their ward's behavior. This created a fair amount of angst amongst the students and led to animated discussions on the group. While the students said that their parents did not take the SMS from the college seriously, shrugging it as a part of college life, the students felt that it was completely unfair on the part of the college to inform their parents of their absence from class. Needless to report, the WhatsApp group activity on the day the SMS was sent to the parents made for some entertaining observations as each student gave free vent to their feelings about their college.

DISCUSSION

This paper attempts to locate student's experiences in interacting with the opposite sex in an environment of gender segregation. Leveraging the popularity of a MIM, students found that not only could they make tentative attempts at friendship, they could also transform their segregated classroom into a group with a perceptible sense of community. Though students seldom broke through the online screen to pursue their interactions in the real world, the forging of equations in a low risk digital environment benefited the students by providing avenues for learning about each other, collaborating for exchange of notes and information, as well as serving as a space for entertainment. We detailed the enactment of communication on the group and illustrated the transformation of a classroom of strangers to an online community of friends. This transformation was aided by various communicative instances such as small talk, frequent changing of the group name, and discussion about class and college activities.

Our observation and analyses reveal that WhatsApp is an empowering medium for our participants who could use it to subvert the traditional diktats of social norms regulating heterosocial peer friendships in the face of institutionalized social disapproval. Here, the ubiquity of the mobile phone coupled with the privacy of an MIM liberated students and created an alternative space where they could get to know one another. As with any human interaction, communication could sometimes turn hostile and reproduce the offline realities of tentative acquaintanceship with one another. Largely, though students felt that they were better off with such a technology at their disposal.

LIMITATIONS

We acknowledge that student behaviour on the WhatsApp group may have been modified due to our presence. However, our constant offline contact with the students helped alleviate any concerns they may have had though we did not hear of any concern directly or through the grapevine. Instead, students reassured us that they were continuing with their usual activities on the group. Our research is also limited to one engineering college in Bengaluru. While we do not claim generalizability, we believe that our study provides insights into how a mobile app facilitates cross gender interaction constrained by real world social norms.

CONCLUSION

Our paper provides an insight into how WhatsApp is steadily making inroads into the lived experiences of students who otherwise are not the primary beneficiaries of the new wealth of globalizing India. Their non-elite educational background and the peri-urban cultural milieu create further constraints in entering into an open friendship with the opposite sex. It is here that we see the subversive role of WhatsApp in transforming a restricted offline environment into a fluid digital space that allows exploration of friending opportunities and easy communication.

ACKNOWLEDGMENTS

Our thanks to the students and staff at SOIT for their generosity in making this research possible. Thanks to Rinku Gajera and Om Deshmukh for their assistance with fieldwork. We thank our anonymous reviewers and AC for their thoughtful suggestions and reviews. Finally, Amit Trivedi and Amitabh Bhattacharya for music and lyrics.

REFERENCES

1. Abraham, L. Bhai-behen, true love, time pass, friendships and sexual partnerships among youth in an Indian metropolis. In *An International Journal for Research, Intervention and Care,* (2001). 337-353.
2. Ames, M.G. Managing mobile multitasking: The culture of iPhones on Stanford campus. In *Proceedings of CSCW'13,* ACM (2013), 1487-1498.
3. Chanana, K. Hinduism and female sexuality: social control and education of girls in India. In *Sociological Bulletin, 50,* (2001), 37-63.
4. Church, K. and de Oliveira, R. What's up with WhatsApp? Comparing mobile instant messaging behaviors with traditional SMS. In *Proceedings of MobileHCI'13,* ACM (2013), 352-361.
5. Das, V. (1998). Femininity and the orientation to the body. In *Socialization, Education and Women,* Chanana, K, Ed. Orient Longman (1988), 193-207.
6. De Certeau, M. (1984) The Practice of Everyday Life, Berkeley: University of California Press.
7. Dube, L. *Women and Kinship: Comparative Perspectiveson Gender in South and South-East Asia*, United Nations University Press, (1988).
8. Grinter, R.E. and Palen, L. Instant messaging in teen life. In *Proceedings of CSCW'02,* ACM (2002), 21-30.
9. Grinter, R.E. and Eldridge, M. Wan2tlk?: Everyday text messaging. In *Proceedings of CHI'2003,* ACM (2003), 441-448.
10. http://whatsapp.com
11. Ito, M. Mobile phones, Japanese youth, and the re-placement of social contact. In Ling, R. and Pederson, P. (eds) In *Mobile Communication and Renegotiation of the Public Sphere.* Springer (2005), 131-148.
12. Nisbett, N. Friendship, consumption, morality: practising identity, negotiating hierarchy in middle-class Bangalore. In *Journal of the Royal Anthropological Institute, 13,* (2007) 935-950
13. O'Hara, K.,Massimi, M., Harper, R., Rubens, S., Morris, J. Everyday Dwelling with WhatsApp. In *Proceedings of CSCW'* 14, ACM Press (2014).
14. Osella, C & Osella, F. Friendship and Flirting: Micro-Politics in Kerala, South India Author(s): *The Journal of the Royal Anthropological Institute, 4, 2* (1998), 189-206
15. Rangaswamy, N and Cutrell, E. 'Re-Sourceful Networks: Notes from a Mobile Social Networking Platform in India', *Pacific Affairs*, Fall, 2012
16. Rogers, M. Modernity, 'authenticity', and ambivalence: subaltern masculinities on a South Indian college campus. *Journal of the Royal Anthropological Institute 14*, 79-95. (2008).
17. Strauss, A. and Corbin, J. *Basics of qualitative research: Techniques and procedures for developing grounded theory.* Thousand Oaks, CA: Sage Publications, 1998.
18. Taylor, S.A. and Harper, R. Age-old Practices in the 'New World': A study of gift-giving between teenage mobile phone users. In *Proceedings of CHI'02,* ACM (2002), 439-446.
19. Walton, M., Hassreiter, S., Marsden, G., and Allen, S. Degrees of sharing: Proximate media sharing and messaging by young people in Khayelitsha. In *Proceedings of MobileHCI'12,* ACM (2012), 403-41.

Online Inspiration and Exploration for Identity Reinvention

Oliver L. Haimson
Dept. of Informatics
Univ. of California, Irvine
Irvine, CA, USA
ohaimson@uci.edu

Anne E. Bowser
iSchool
University of Maryland
College Park, MD, USA
abowser1@umd.edu

Edward F. Melcer
NYU Polytechnic School of Engineering
Brooklyn, NY, USA
eddie.melcer@nyu.edu

Elizabeth F. Churchill
eBay Research Labs[1]
San Jose, CA, USA
churchill@acm.org

ABSTRACT
Self-representation online can be difficult for those who are in life transitions that involve exploring new identity facets and changes in personal style. Many desire to tailor their online representations for different audiences. Social media site profiles and sharing settings offer varying levels of anonymity, privacy, and thus safety, but these settings are often opaque and poorly understood. To understand the complex relationship between identity, personal style and online self-representation, we examine how people explore and experiment with new styles in public and in private online settings during gender transition. We present the results of interviews with transgender people who have recently reinvented their personal style, or are planning to do so in the near future. We find that people explore new styles in online settings to craft possible or ideal future selves. When involving others, people engage intimate and unknown others, but often avoid weak ties. Our results indicate that to account for changing identities, social media sites must be designed to support finding inspiration and advice from strangers and style experimentation with close friends.

Author Keywords
Online identity; social curation sites; social networking sites; identity transitions; transgender; LGBTQ.

ACM Classification Keywords
H.5.3. Information interfaces and presentation (*e.g.*, HCI): Group and Organization Interfaces: Collaborative computing, Web-based interaction.

INTRODUCTION
Online self-representation is highly dependent on perceived audience [3, 30]. An online space's social composition (*i.e.*, the mix of people from different social categories, including friends, acquaintances, strangers, only the user, *etc.*) affects how many and what types of risks a person is willing to take when exploring dimensions of self and identity. Social networking sites' affordances, such as privacy, disclosure settings, level of anonymity allowed, *etc.*, not only shape the way people behave on these sites [2], but impact online self-presentation during identity changes [23].

Personal identity is constructed and communicated materially through clothing, accessories, and other personal style artifacts [11]. People wittingly or unwittingly craft or participate in "looks," projecting identity to an audience through self-expression [31]. Others interpret a person based on these looks, which are deemed reflective of explicit and intentional "signaling" choices [22, 32, 35], and develop assumptions about membership in particular social roles and categories, including gender [31]. Fashion items are, thus, a "technology for managing identity" [27:105]. They are used to strategically signal role and identity stability (*e.g.*, "signature items" that are cherished and repeatedly worn) or change (*e.g.*, wearing more expensive items to reflect an income change). In McCracken's words, "clothing can also be used to mark and even to effect the *transition from one cultural category to another*" [31:60, italics are ours] as a result of significant life experiences and/or changing life contexts [9, 13]. Of course, changing one's identity is more complex and involved than just wearing a new outfit, a type of identity management that may be superficial, temporary, and ad hoc [22]. Progressive identity changes that challenge social norms involve a commitment to ongoing change through experimentation and exploration, and can be fraught with anxiety as well as excitement [15, 33].

Our research sought to understand how people craft new personal styles in times of identity change, how style changes and identity changes are intertwined and inform each other, and how such changes are represented online. We elected to focus on a group of individuals who deviate from assumed "everyday" occurrences or theoretical norms, which can reveal deep insights about practices overall [38]. In this paper, we detail the experiences of a group of transgender individuals who have recently changed, or plan to change in the near future, their gender and personal style. Transgender people specifically were chosen as the focus of this study because of the constant, active, dynamic negotiations that this group faces around personal style. Particular challenges arise as transgender people explore their personal identities and in the process confront entrenched cultural views regarding the binary nature of sex and gender (male/female; man/woman), assumed stability of gender from birth, and cultural norms of style and signaling.

CHI 2015, April 18 - 23 2015, Seoul, Republic of Korea.

ACM 978-1-4503-3145-6/15/04...$15.00
http://dx.doi.org/10.1145/2702123.2702270

[1] now at Google

We address the role of online resources for inspiration and experimentation, and the navigation of online social spaces where exploration and experimentation of new styles may be intentionally or unintentionally shared with others. Broadly, we are interested in elucidating the complex and dynamic relationship between style and online identity. Although gender identity is much more complex than clothing and appearance, we intentionally narrowed our focus to style as one important facet of identity reinvention.

Specifically, we ask: How do people find inspiration for an emerging personal style during times of deep personal change? How do they envision and craft possible/ideal selves? With whom and how do they communicate their ideal selves? How do they socially manage iterative changes that challenge assumptions about gender and style? How do online services and other tools help and hinder this process?

We find that uncertainty around identity, social roles, and category membership can lead to playful and meaningful, but also occasionally stressful, engagement with available resources for inspiration. We also find that when identity is shifting, highly faceted, and/or highly situated, clothing and accessory choices are more consciously maneuvered and can be more challenging. Items become symbolically laden with questions of whether they are or are not representative and communicative of past, current, future, or ideal self and identity. Further, people engage in collaborative, social ways of discovering inspiration for emerging selves and crafting possible/ideal selves during identity changes, both online and offline. When involving others, such processes require substantial emotional labor [25] and constant consideration of privacy, safety, and intimacy, whether online or offline. Importantly, we find that sociality around personal style changes includes close friends and anonymous strangers, but not acquaintances or weak ties as typically found in networks on social networking sites like Facebook and Twitter [10].

In the following sections, we provide background and then describe results from ethnographically-inspired interviews focused on transgender people in online spaces. This work provides important insight into the ways that people find inspiration and interact with others online when crafting selves during identity changes. We intentionally give voice to a diverse group of people, whose experiences are often lumped together under the label "transgender," by articulating their differences as well as commonalities.

BACKGROUND

Our work contributes to HCI and CSCW literature on faceted and changing identities [3, 9, 13], gender identity and social media [*e.g.*, 23], and social curation sites [17, 21, 28, 39], as well as transgender studies and queer theory [5, 24, 34, 36]. Researching the experiences of transgender people as they find inspiration and engage in experimentation online allows us to better understand the differences between sociality in different online venues. This work also highlights how online identity exploration leads to formation of future selves not only for transgender people, but for those undergoing a variety of identity changes (*e.g.*, transition from college to a professional career, moving to a different geographical location). This work also applies to non-binary transgender people and others who experiment with personal style, seek style inspiration online, and work toward possible/ideal future selves.

Changing and Faceted Identities

Identity and image matter, and managing complex identities can be difficult. Many life changes and circumstances bring about changing or multifaceted identities. People inhabit different social roles, defined by different responsibilities, activities, and products [13, 18]. As such, people craft selves in ambiguous, complicated ways as different social roles take precedence and proscribe a person from simply being one singular "themselves" [26]. Instead, identities are "multiple, fraught with tension and contradiction, and asserted in specific performative contexts" [26:306]. Although gender change certainly exemplifies the complexities of identity, it is not only transgender people who must negotiate complex identities. Past research has focused on shifting and faceted identities of teenagers [3], and those transitioning from college to work [9].

Transgender Identities

Transgender is a term that refers to "people who move away from the gender they were assigned at birth, people who cross over (trans-) the boundaries constructed by their culture to define and contain that gender" [34:1]. That said, some suggest transgender is complex and perhaps misleading as an identity category, because many who are described by the definition above do not self-identify as transgender [36]. Most importantly though, a person's relationship to their gender is what matters here, not necessarily physical characteristics or changes. Our sample includes nine people who identify as transgender: eight people who transitioned from one gender to another, and one self-identified "polygender" person who plans to transition to female in the future. Following [23], we use "trans" for the remainder of this paper to refer to the broad transgender population.

Gender norms are culturally constructed, and these ideals regulate and constrain everyone, trans or not, as they express gender along with other aspects of identity [5]. However, trans people face additional challenges, as they must adapt to living as a gender different from their gender assigned at birth, which they have spent many years being culturally mandated to perform. The risk of failing to "pass," and uncertainty around how others recognize one's gender, leads to further marginalization and stigmatization [19]. In such gender "failures," others may assume that trans people are merely "performing" a gender, implying a lack of authenticity [5]. Instead, trans people express gender identity, as we all do, through gender performativity, Butler's notion that gender identity arises through a process of iteration and reconstruction of cultural gender norms [5]. Butler's concepts allow us to express the differences between participants' experimental or provisional selves, which are recognized and experienced as gender performance, and asserted gender identities, which reveal gender as performative [5]. Much of the vulnerability

	Pseudonym								
	Marcus	Alex	Kieran	Donna	Jasmine	Lydia	Amelia	Elisha	Shallie
Gender	Male	Male	Male	Female	Female	Female	Female	Female	Poly-gender
Race/Ethnicity	White	African American / White	Pacific Islander / African American	White	Hispanic / White	White	White	Hispanic / Latino	White
Age	28	17	17	30	23	44	23	22	25
Full-time status*	FT	FT	FT	FT	FT	FT	PT	FT	NT
Length of time living full-time	2 months	2 years	not disclosed	not disclosed	3 years	2 months	N/A	5 months	N/A
U.S. Region	Mid-Atlantic	California	California	California	West	South	West	South	New England
Residential setting	Small city	Small city	Small city	Large city	College town	Suburb	College town	Large city	Small city / suburb

*Full-time status categories include FT (Living full-time in a gender different from their birth sex), PT (Living part-time in a gender different from their birth sex), and NT (Not yet living in a gender different from their birth sex). Categories modified from [20].

Table 1. Personal Characteristics of Participants.

and anxiety expressed by participants results from a lived / true identity (performative) being read by others as a mere performance that lacks authenticity [24].

Gender transition, like many identity changes, is an iterative, non-linear process that has no prescribed beginning and end. Identity exploration is exciting and can be fraught with personal styles explored and discarded potentially at a rapid rate. During and after gender change, gender identity presentation is managed using what Garfinkel calls "management devices," a constant string of strategies, improvisations, and learning-as-one-goes-along that enable performing a new gender [16]. We find that many of these management devices are learned online. Since online identity carries different expectations around authenticity, certain online contexts may afford a degree of reprieve from stigma.

Because personal style, gender, and identity are so closely entwined, style and fashion, and even the daily act of wearing clothing, can be especially complicated for trans people. Cultural norms around gender and gender identity [5] are inscribed into products and "reinforce existing cultural assumptions" [7:54], which makes consumption and dress difficult for those with complex or changing gender identities. Media and products "embody messages about who we can be," and because such products are implicitly gendered, "who we can be," *i.e.*, our ideal self, also must be decidedly gendered and dependent on cultural assumptions [7:52]. The gendered nature of products and cultural norms around gender constrain gender expression and serve as an important backdrop for this work.

METHODS

We conducted in-depth interviews with nine participants representing a diverse subset of the trans population (see Table 1). Participants were recruited via several methods: in person at the 2014 San Francisco Trans March ($N = 3$), trans-focused Facebook groups ($N = 2$) and reddit forums ($N = 2$), and through the first author's personal network ($N = 1$). We recruited people who expressed they had reinvented their personal style during gender transition, were currently doing so, or planned to in the near future. We interviewed both transmen and transwomen, but in the later stages of our research focused more on recruitment of transwomen after discovering that style tends to change more drastically when moving from male to female than vice versa. We also skewed toward seeking out participants who were just beginning or had not yet begun their transition. This way, participants would be presently engaged in seeking inspiration for a current style reinvention, rather than recalling a transformation that occurred in the past. Each participant received a $50 Visa gift card as compensation for their time.

Prior to interviews, we built rapport and trust with participants via email exchanges and/or in-person meetings. Interviews were semi-structured and conversational to allow themes to emerge that were most important to participants and that they were comfortable sharing. Thus, topics discussed varied to some extent among participants. General areas covered in all interviews were identity and personal style, style influences, and use of social media for style inspiration with an emphasis on social curation sites[2]. Interviews were conducted in July and August 2014 and lasted on average 72 minutes ($SD = 15$, range: 41-86). Interviews were conducted in the format desired by / feasible for each participant, and included video chat ($N = 4$), phone ($N = 2$), in-person ($N = 2$), and instant message text chat ($N = 1$). All non-text interviews were either audio or video recorded and transcribed. Interviews included two interviewers, one of whom took detailed notes throughout.

[2] A social curation site is a type of social media site that allows users to curate content collections and interact socially with other users through traditional social media interactions (*e.g.*, liking, commenting, following, sharing) [21].

Following each interview, the researchers present conducted a debrief session in which we identified insights and possible emerging themes. Debriefs were audio-recorded and transcribed for later analysis. We engaged in data triangulation by following up on social media materials that participants recommended. The first author kept detailed memos throughout the interview process to document emerging insights and themes.

Interviews transcripts were analyzed primarily using a grounded theory approach of inductive open coding [8]. This inductive approach was used along with a deductive analysis of *a priori* themes, namely the use of social media and social curation sites for style inspiration, as found in previous literature [17, 28]. We met weekly throughout the analysis process to discuss themes that surfaced from the data. We then collaboratively organized codes into larger themes including inspiration, experimentation, and formation of possible/ideal selves. We reread all debriefing sessions and memos and determined that they were in line with the themes that had emerged from the interview data. Interview data was then re-visited and organized according to the dominant themes.

RESULTS

Reinvention practices included formulating possible/ideal selves, seeking inspiration and understanding, curating items for possible/ideal selves, and engaging in active experimentation and exploration. These practices may occur sequentially, but more often happen concurrently and iteratively. In what follows we describe participants' experiences with style reinvention practices in a variety of online settings, and how their narratives demonstrate the ways that online sociality is situated and contextual. Importantly, style reinvention also happened in offline contexts in tandem with the online experiences we describe here. While a full description of offline practices is beyond the scope of this paper, we interweave some anecdotes to highlight the relationship between online and offline identity reinvention and the inability of truly separating the two. We begin by asking: *How do people craft possible/ideal selves?*

Possible/Ideal Selves

An important part of making any identity change is imagining the future self that may be possible. For example, Alex half-jokingly described his future self: *"I'm gonna hit that dad phase, and I'm gonna like build decks and wear nothing but Hawaiian shirts."* Similarly, Amelia described her desire to wear more revealing clothing after her body changes: *"I would wear clothing that's considered more stylish. I can't wear it now because it's more revealing than I can do."*

However, some versions of an imagined future self are not possible, and thus fall under the category of "ideal selves." The feasibility of an imagined future self depends on the existence and obstinacy of barriers, which may be practical (*e.g.*, lack of access to healthcare or finances), psychological (*e.g.*, fear, anxiety), and/or social (*e.g.*, social pressure to dress in accordance with age or social role). For those early in the transition process, practical barriers sometimes made ideal selves feel impossible. Shallie, for instance, experienced financial difficulty receiving the therapy necessary to move forward with their transition: *"Main thing I want to start doing is getting into therapy and that should probably be starting sometime early next year, once I rearrange my insurance plan."* At the beginning of her transition, Jasmine experienced psychological barriers to embodying her ideal self. The most difficult part of changing her style was *"realizing that I had permission to do it."* Lydia, on the other hand, experienced social barriers to her ideal self. She described her strong desire to dress in goth or fetish attire, but felt it was not *"appropriate for someone my age that was well known to people."*

Regardless of whether or not a future self was considered out of reach, all participants imagined or actively curated collections of items online representing possible or ideal selves. Such curation entails seeking inspiration, browsing and exploration, and active experimentation. All participants were actively engaged in seeking out inspiration and resources online, and all discussed the role of others, both intimate and unknown, in this process. In the next section we discuss this in detail, asking the question: *Where and how do people find inspiration and resources for style during identity changes?*

Finding inspiration

Online resources and spaces such as social curation sites, social networking sites, forums, and support groups act as places of inspiration during identity transitions [39]. Importantly, reported online interactions with others were often anonymous. Participants privately browsed content, followed unknown inspirational others, and anonymously sought advice or other resources on online forums and support groups. We demonstrate how such resources are used in concert and in practice, and how each are navigated and managed in the identity transition process.

Online search, though not inherently social, is an important way to privately find style inspiration and resources for new personal styles, as well as a space for experimentation. For example, Elisha was unsure about what would be appropriate to wear to a restaurant described to her as being "dressy casual," leading to a Google search: *"I actually, I searched 'dressy casual' on Google. You know, it's the simplest way to get things done, it seems."* Similarly, Shallie used Google search to find items or outfits for their transition: *"A lot of it just comes from Google Images. Just like, 'Okay. XYZ outfit. Boop, you get stuff.'"* Online search is both a way to find inspiration and a lightweight way to experiment with new personal styles.

Social media, including social curation sites, social networking sites, and other online social content sources were an important source of inspiration for emerging personal styles. Many participants described using social curation sites to find ideas for personal style.

> *"I browse Pinterest for ideas sometimes... When I look at the pictures I often find myself thinking, 'Oh wow! I would have never thought those would look so nice together'"* – *Amelia*

"Once I discovered the Internet years ago, ... I really started to look for fashion inspiration. And nowadays, a lot of what I find are on Pinterest, which is a huge outlet for fashion right now, looking through that and comparing looks to things I already own to try and figure out what I can piece together." – Lydia

Several participants found information and style inspiration from feeds showing content from people that they "followed" on sites like Tumblr and YouTube.

"And then I'll look at it and I found... a set of black nails. I think it was on Tumblr and they were matte black with shiny black French tips. And I was like, 'I finally found something that I like.'" – Jasmine

"There are people that I follow on YouTube that I get some good ideas from regarding trans issues, transitioning, stuff like that." – Shallie

Shallie elaborated on the ways that YouTube in particular was an important source of inspiration, because of its highly visual nature, the access to inspiration from other trans people rather than the broader population, and because the format made it feel like the people from whom they sought advice and inspiration spoke *directly to* them.

"The people who do it well do create that sort of intimate personal relationship with their subscribers. Instead of going, 'Hello everyone,' they sort of go, 'Hello you,' and it feels a lot more friendly that way...Video I think is probably the best way to do it, 'cause we're very much a visual species. Being able to see things in addition to... as well as hear them makes things a lot more palatable." – Shallie

In this way, anonymous yet personalized online interactions fill an information-need gap when style advice and inspiration from friends is unavailable and/or perceived as socially risky.

Although many items discovered are fun and/or symbolic of the ideal self in development, for many items found online, additional discussion needs to take place. One example is clothing. Most clothing is inherently gendered; gender identity is asserted simply through the act of wearing certain accessories or items of clothing. Because trans bodies often do not conform to standard masculine and feminine clothing sizes and because bodies in transition can change rapidly and extensively, deeper exploration is pursued. Off-the-shelf, standard-size-conforming brands frequently do not fit [14]. Such discussions can be sensitive, and require either intimacy or anonymity. Our participants found anonymous forums like reddit ideal for crowdsourcing information and advice about clothing and makeup in order to find items for their new personal styles that also are likely to fit.

"I mean [reddit is] comfortable because it's anonymous, tons of people. I guess it's most helpful for sourcing resources for tiny bodies particularly for menswear, or a lot of times it's hard to find men's pants styles that will actually fit... You can crowdsource those kinds of questions instead of just having to do trial and error everywhere. So that's been helpful. I've tried a couple of things online that I probably wouldn't have known about otherwise." – Marcus

"That's a major source of information for me. I subscribe to all of the subreddits related to transgender topics. I've gone on the makeup subreddits as well as the fashion advice." – Amelia

Others employed crowdsourcing within trans-specific online support groups on sites like Facebook and Tumblr, which for some offered a sense of home and belonging.

"I use Tumblr a lot. It's a blogging website. And it's got a really, really big LGBT community. It's like a home, you know? I'll go there, and I'll look for... well now, I'm at the point in my transition where I can spread tips and information and helpful advice, the kind of stuff that I would've wanted when I was 12 years old and thinking I was a freak." – Alex

"There are a few different Facebook groups that I'm a part of that I'll be like, 'Oh, what's a stylish flat?' ... or, 'What type... Who makes good bras for people with wide chests, but small tits?' and stuff like that." – Donna

Our participants were clear about drawing inspiration from others in offline contexts, as well as from online sources. Strangers in public were an important source of inspiration, as Amelia described: *"When I look for ideas of what to wear, I generally think of the women I saw outside that day that wore things I liked."* Retail store clerks were another important source of inspiration for participants, providing information about how to wear and size women's clothing. Close friends helped participants by taking them shopping, answering questions and giving advice about particular types of clothing and accessories and places to shop, and offering support. Family was also an important source of style inspiration. However, because many participants did not have supportive families, they instead silently observed family members to learn about style. Kieran learned much of his masculine dress style from his cousins and brother, without making them aware that he was gathering inspiration from them. While participants may not have felt comfortable seeking inspiration from acquaintances, strangers in public and retail clerks offered the anonymity that made such gathering of information possible, while close friends and family members' intimacy and proximity did the same.

Gathering inspiration and advice from online sources allowed participants to better imagine their possible or ideal future selves, and understand how they might become that person. We next examine another important step in the "becoming" process by asking: *How do people curate items for possible/ideal selves?*

Curating Items for Possible / Ideal Selves

Much of the search, exploration, or advice-seeking behavior described above resulted in ideas for possible and ideal future selves. As part of this exploration process, people created curated collections of things that struck them as interesting, useful, and/or potentially representative of their future self.

Content Curation on Social Curation Sites

Collages and other visual collections of images have long been an important practice for self-reflection. Previous research showed that people used personal websites as digital collages, particularly during major life changes, often constructing multiple websites to represent incompatible identities [32].

For many participants, social curation sites were a fundamental space for *crafting* possible or ideal selves through the curation of items found through inspiration searches and explorations. Specifically, the websites used by our participants for social curation of personal style items include Pinterest, Polyvore, Etsy, and Wantworthy. Such sites allow for search but also discovery. Items collected on social curation sites are "visual reminders of the ideal self," which help people to learn about themselves, motivate change, and make "unfamiliar activities seem achievable" [28:2418-2419].

Participants in our study illustrated social curation sites' importance during identity changes. Items can be selected for inspiration without limits of money, fit, or geography, allowing for representation of an ideal self that may not necessarily be feasible [32]. These are not shopping lists; they are social identity waypoints in a space of exploration.

"So yeah I have my own boards, there's a style one, it's just an easy way to... 'inspiration board' sounds kind of corny, but it's just an easy way to remember ideas or remember styles or remember oh, that way too expensive pair of shoes that I kind of lust after." – Marcus

"Or whatever I find on Pinterest, I'm like, 'I really like that. I will definitely, eventually, purchase or make something like that,' and then I never do. But it's nice to have just in case." – Jasmine

Participants often faced financial barriers to obtaining the items that they imagined their future self would wear, leading them to curate collections of items that they loved but may never buy. As Marcus explains, *"Yeah, I totally put idealized things on there even if they're inconceivably expensive or inaccessible or whatever."*

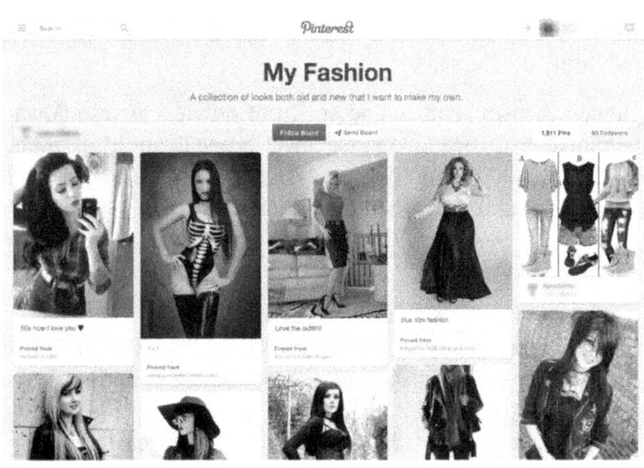

Figure 1. Lydia's Pinterest board of "looks both old and new that I want to make my own" (used with permission).

Many participants stated that they curated collections of items that they felt would make them stand out too much to incorporate into their current wardrobe, or just simply would not look good. Curating such items online allowed participants to enjoy a creative space to play with such styles, which was not always feasible offline. Jasmine described curating a board of colorful items that she loved but knew would not look good on her. For instance, one dress made her think, *"I would love to wear this dress in yellow, but that makes me look like I have jaundice."* Several other participants described liking brightly-colored or showy items, but feeling that they would draw too much attention to themselves if they wore such items. Similarly, Lydia curated a board including items that were not only too expensive, but she felt were too "over-the-top" to wear in her day-to-day life (see Figure 1). She stated, *"I may not have the funds or time to get all of the pieces on there, but you know, what I've shared with people and the looks that I've formed on there that I have yet to wear in real life all represent me, as diverse or over-the-top as some of them are."*

Interestingly, several of our participants curated collections of clothing and accessories that they desired for possible or ideal selves, but did so mentally in their mind, *not* on social curation sites. Yet even these imaginings were influenced by social curation sites: mental collections often consisted of items found on social curation sites and were organized in a similar fashion. Elena explained, *"I should probably get around to making one, that way I can just keep things organized, but I usually just keep things in my head."*

Amelia, an active Pinterest browser, also engaged in curation processes of items for an ideal or possible self, but stated that she did not feel knowledgeable enough about women's fashion to curate her own board online. Instead, she kept a mental collection of items, despite being aware of the ability to curate private collections online. Mental curation, a desirable alternative to online curation for participants, made items more accessible and required less expertise, thus reducing barriers to crafting future selves.

Engaging Others in Social Curation

While much curation and exploration is conducted alone, many participants sought or would like to seek input from others. Although Jasmine and Donna were the only participants who had collaboratively used social curation sites, many others expressed desire to do so in the future, especially to share items with a small group of close friends. According to Alex, *"That'd be kinda rad. So like, a group of people on there? You'd have to add people into it? That'd be rad! Yeah!"*

Offline, close friends were an important source of inspiration, understanding, and experimentation for many participants. Close friendships gave participants the comfort and safety to explore emerging identities through clothing. Jasmine and Donna described close friends who were available for in-person advice and style ideation. Donna explains, *"Mostly I choose people in person that I am close friends with, and because I am such an open person ... it's really easy for me to seek in-person advice about things from other people and I have a large community of people that are like me in part..."* The comfort in intimate friendships allowed an open dialogue that was useful in curating items for future selves.

However, despite participants' desire to engage in similar experiences with close friends online, understanding how to share content among a small group of intimate others was not easy. Most were not aware that this functionality existed, which may explain why few had used social curation sites collaboratively. Others had difficulty using collaborative features. For instance, Donna described loving Etsy, but having difficulty using the site socially: *"I find their feature for sharing with your friends really confusing. I don't know. It's really random, and in general, their favorite lists and all that stuff, isn't really accessible. I'm having a hard time with it. But I'm friends with one of my trans lady friends on there, but I'm not sure that the way that they share what your friends are buying is really as helpful as it seems like it would be."*

Drawing from the closeness, comfort, and safety found in offline friendships during identity changes, it is important for social curation sites to enable shared and collaborative collections in an intuitive, easy-to-use manner. Our participants' experiences curating items for possible / ideal selves both online and mentally highlight the ways that social curation sites are an important space for crafting of self during identity transformations. The act of pulling together items allows people to more fully imagine future selves as possible, or if impossible, allows important identity work to take place.

We next examine the ways that our participants engage in active experimentation with and exploration of new styles. We ask, *In what settings and with whom do people experiment with emerging new styles and identities?*

Active Experimentation

Inspiration and understanding for new styles is important, but perhaps even more vital to new identity construction is the ability to experiment with those new styles. Identity change requires space in which to explore new possible selves, and much of this playful work is done online.

Anonymous online environments enable identity reinvention by allowing people to explore different identities [4, 32, 35], and are also important spaces for experimentation with new emerging styles. However, this identity work is more than "play"; it is serious, and can be used to aid transformation and identity reinvention in the real world [35]. Online technologies, such as avatars and anonymous forums, allow people to discover the differences between societal identity constructions and their own desires to construct and assemble identities [27]. Gender in particular is often explored and experimented with in online settings, such as virtual worlds [4] and online forums [15]. Identity reinvention, including reinvention of gender identity, can and does happen in online spaces.

In keeping with these findings, online spaces allowed participants to experiment with their new identities anonymously and privately through lightweight social interaction with strangers. Shallie, a gamer, engaged in online experimentation with new style through female avatars in virtual worlds: *"It's a way for me to experiment playing, experimenting with being another sex... I always find opportunities to do something like that very rewarding."*

Most of participants' online sites of style and identity experimentation (*e.g.*, reddit, Tumblr, blogs, forums, games, virtual worlds), with the notable exception of Facebook, allowed participants to remain anonymous, which led to the private and safe space necessary to embody new identities. In such anonymous spaces, one's imagined audience [30] consists of unknown others. Sites of experimentation allowed varying degrees of anonymity. For instance, when interacting in trans-specific groups on Facebook, participants used their name and personal profile. However, even these profiles were often anonymous in the sense that many were new or ancillary profiles and sometimes, as in Lydia's case, removed completely from one's pre-transition persona: *"About a year ago, as I was getting through therapy, and you know not hating myself, is when I started my Facebook page. I had no public identity, no online presence pre-transition."* Additionally, the majority of trans-specific groups on Facebook are private and are made up mostly of people whom are not part of one's Facebook friends list or network of intimate others. Thus, participation in Facebook groups is still somewhat anonymous, and can sometimes provide the privacy and safety needed for exploration.

Just as participants reported finding inspiration and understanding for style from observing unknown others, strangers in online and offline contexts are an important audience for experimentation during style reinvention. Unknown others offer anonymous and private observation or interaction that cannot occur when interacting with intimate others or acquaintances. This anonymity can allow important space for people to ask private or potentially embarrassing questions and/or to experiment without fear of recourse.

For instance, Lydia explored her new self in written form through a blog that was part of a website for her local trans support group. She expressed clearly how this was a process of developing comfort with her own "voice:" *"And I basically vented in a blog there for about a year until I felt comfortable enough, having processed a lot of stuff, and I have no idea if anyone ever looked at or read that thing. But it represented a safe place for me to explore in."*

Participants also engaged in complicated decisions regarding how to represent their iterative, emerging selves to networks on social networking sites. Elisha transitioned her Facebook profile picture gradually, as a way of carefully managing her online identity as her style changed: *"And then I changed my picture. And then a couple, about a month ago, I put a picture and that is overtly feminine of me. I was wearing a dress and flats. So I guess that was my second real coming out."*

Shallie, who maintained separate Facebook lists for family (whom were not aware of Shallie's trans identity) and friends, imagined a future time, post-transition, when faceted Facebook lists would no longer be necessary: *"Well, honestly, if I'm out about that, there's nothing really else that I need to hide... So I probably wouldn't even need those privacy blocks anymore."*

Offline, active style experimentation allowed participants to explore the materiality of their emerging identity and how items physically look and feel on the body, and to concretely embody possible future selves. While much offline style experimentation took place alone in private, public settings also provided an audience for participants to anonymously explore new styles. This led to positive anticipatory and actual experimentation for Jasmine, who made subtle changes to her wardrobe to publicly experiment with identity through personal style. Yet public spaces also engendered vulnerable, anxious feelings and invoked careful risk calculations; Elisha described *"shaking like a leaf"* the first time she went out wearing women's jeans, and several participants spoke about fear for safety. The comfort and safety in relationships with intimate others allowed participants to understand through close observation, interaction, and mutual experimentation what it might be like to embody a new style. Many participants described a particular close friend or a small group of friends who experimented alongside them as they explored a new style. During the beginning of Marcus's transition, a close friend was also exploring masculine style. They shopped together as a way of experimenting with masculine fashion: *"She and I sort of became tie buddies. We did a lot of scouring vintage shops and stuff for ties. I feel like we both sort of got into that together."* When involving others in offline experimentation, like in online contexts, participants chose to involve unknown others in public settings, and intimate others such as friends and family, but not acquaintances.

In sum, during identity change, active experimentation allows people to try out new possible selves without commitment while carefully managing fears and anxieties about trans identities. Importantly, experimentation with new styles and identities allows people to embody possible future selves, thus building the bridge from inspiration to possibility. Presenting themselves as their new gender allowed participants to explore how it felt to be female, or be male, in different settings and for different audiences. Experimentation with intimate and unknown others helps people to become more comfortable in their new identity, opening them up to express this new identity among acquaintances or in public. The exploration process helped people to understand whom their ideal self is, and how that self may be possible. Clothing, accessories, and the physical artifacts of gender, along with one's online presentation including those items, transforms a future self from an imagined, aspirational identity to a real, lived, material identity. Once a person makes that step, identity is no longer being experimented with: it is being asserted.

DISCUSSION

For participants in our study, online interactions were key to supporting exploration around shifting style identities. They found resources on a range of sites, including social media platforms and forums (*e.g.*, Tumblr, reddit, YouTube) and social curation sites (*e.g.*, Pinterest, Etsy). But participants' experiences highlight that the type of sociality desired when finding inspiration and engaging in experimentation during identity change is different than the sociality typically found in online social networking sites like Facebook and Twitter. On social networking sites, one's network contains many acquaintances and loose ties [10]. Conversely, our participants found inspiration, understanding, and an audience for experimentation from close friends and from strangers, while avoiding experimentation under the gaze of acquaintances. Though one's network on social networking sites certainly includes close friends and may also include strangers, it is the large body of loose ties that makes identity change uncomfortable. Close friendships allow the comfort and intimacy needed to ask private and potentially embarrassing questions and try out new looks that may expose vulnerabilities. Strangers allow the anonymity to explore these same types of questions and styles.

We show that the right mix of social, anonymous, and private inspiration and exploration allowed participants to craft new visions of possible or ideal future selves. These ideal selves have as much to do with online identity management as with style. Although most participants discussed management tactics for sharing with others, some expressed an ideal future when faceted sharing would no longer be necessary, such as Shallie's expectation of merging their faceted Facebook lists in the future. Thus, an ideal self is not just a coveted body or a collection of clothing and accessories that convey a particular image. An ideal future self may also involve the expectation that faceted identities will one day coalesce to create a "true self" that is impeccably and easily managed online.

Yet such an ideal self for some includes either an erasure or a hiding of past 'selves,' while for others it is assumed that previous 'selves' will easily be incorporated into the ideal future self. This denies the social "face" and accountability work that caused our participants fear and anxiety. The work of managing multiple audiences in multiple temporalities that are constantly moving and changing is why participants avoided weak ties, whom, it was feared, may be critical, may require explanation work and/or may cause social complications. Such multifurcation results in an extreme form of impression management [18], where instead of a front stage and a back stage, there exist many stages with different-sized, shifting audiences and overlapping performance times.

Much has been written about the work of managing social information flows online (*e.g.*, through privacy settings) [1, 23, 37], and many social media sites do make some affordances for faceted identities. However, the complexities of self-presentation online for those who must make a conscious effort to do the work of both exploring and projecting a fluid self *en route* to an ideal self is still not effectively designed for. Change management is not just personal; it is public, and involves constant reassessment and negotiation of self in relation to others. Tools to support changing identities on websites are currently nonexistent or clunky. As an example,

Facebook's "lists" allow people to limit posts to only certain audiences. These features have been shown to be challenging for users [23, 37], but in addition to this, they do not account for the temporality of posts. Just because someone is on one's "Close Friends" list today, does not mean that one would want that person to view certain posts that occurred in the past (*e.g.*, pre-transition).

We have shown that online spaces such as social curation sites are great places to find inspiration for those who are reinventing their style as part of an identity change. To support style exploration, content sharing, and self-presentation online during identity changes, social media sites must design for the complexities of both social networks and human experiences.

DESIGN IMPLICATIONS

We highlight the disconnect between the potential of social curation sites to be an important social space during style reinvention, and the current capacity of these sites to support such interactions. Most participants did not use social curation sites in a social way, as they did with other social media sites, despite a desire to curate item collections with friends or strangers as part of their identity change.

Social interactions that include friends and strangers while excluding acquaintances, which we show that people desire during identity changes, is in line with the sociality that other researchers found common on social curation sites [6, 39]. For instance, Pinterest is driven by connections based on common interests, not on existing social connections [6, 39]. Although profiles are only sometimes anonymous, social curation sites do not pressure their users to present a true, authentic self the way that social networking sites like Facebook do [12, 23]. Because social interactions take place outside of one's core social network, and due to the lack of emphasis on static, authentic identity, social curation sites are an important place to reinvent style during identity transitions. Similar to virtual worlds as "identity workshops" where people can explore identities with little consequence [4], social curation sites can be spaces to explore identity and gender presentation through fashion.

Although the types of interactions and connections that happen on social curation sites are conducive to identity change, these sites are not designed to support such interactions. Pinterest, for instance, actively encourages users to "find your Facebook friends and follow them on Pinterest," assuming a uniformity between one's Facebook network and Pinterest network. Because social curation sites are important spaces for exploration and inspiration during identity change, we argue that such sites should design for users facing identity changes. To do so, designers must understand the important ways that networks on social curation sites are different than those on other social networking sites, and design specifically for the types of networks and interactions fundamental to social curation sites. We recommend several design improvements.

First, collaborative sharing, with ability to control privacy to share only with a specific group of people, should be at the forefront when users create collections. Private, collaborative collections facilitate the sharing of sensitive information and style experimentation that emerges during identity transitions. Although different social curation sites currently exhibit different levels of ease of collaboration and privacy controls, important omissions remain in each. Lack of features for collaboration and privacy hinder users' ability to find inspiration for and experiment with new personal styles, thus limiting social curation sites' use as spaces for identity change.

Next, although it is not appropriate to import entire friends lists from sites like Facebook and Twitter into social curation sites, interfacing with particular communities on other social media sites may be a powerful way to support identity changes. A collaborative Pinterest board, for example, viewable and editable only by those who are part of a particular trans support group on Facebook, would be an innovative way for group members to collect visual and concrete examples of items recommended from one person to another. Many sites employ algorithms that make recommendations based on shared interests, but few allow people to recommend items to each other based on shared experiences.

Finally, in order to further support individuals during identity changes, social curation sites could implement highly personalized, social ways to share items. Participants found much value in YouTube as a place to find resources, not only because of the visual engagement of videos, but because the platform allows people to speak directly to each other in a personal manner. Collections of items on social curation sites are another visual way of sharing with others, but social curation site interfaces often lack the personal touch that gives the impression of one person talking *directly to* another person, rather than to an audience. Whether by embedding videos or allowing for text chat, social curation sites should make sharing personal.

CONCLUSION

This research explores the practices in which people engage when embarking on style reinvention during gender transition and the social contexts and networks in which these practices happen. We show that people engage in collaborative, social ways of discovering inspiration and crafting selves during identity changes. However, the sociality around style and identity reinvention involves close friends and anonymous strangers, but *not* acquaintances and weak ties as typically found in online social networks. Much work has focused on single site analyses. By focusing on the personal practices of participants we offer an analysis that shows how varied online tools and resources (*e.g.*, online search, social media sites, *etc.*) are used in concert. Future research could expand on a number of our findings and provocations. For instance, a longitudinal study of people's online and offline behavior as they change identity would provide a deeper understanding of online self-presentation and the role of online spaces and networks in identity change. Additionally, future research should further examine the barriers to representing marginal identities online, especially in light of Facebook's recent efforts to enforce the use of "real names" on user profiles [29].

ACKNOWLEDGMENTS

We thank our participants for sharing their experiences with us. Thank you to Colleen Jankovic, Gillian Hayes, members of STAR, and our anonymous reviewers for their generous help and support with this paper. This research was conducted during an internship at eBay Research Labs; we thank eBay.

REFERENCES

1. Acquisti, A. and Gross, R. Imagined communities: Awareness, information sharing, and privacy on the Facebook. *Privacy Enhancing Technologies*. Springer, 2006, 36–58.
2. boyd, d. Social network sites as networked public: Affordances, dynamics, and implications. *Networked Self: Identity, Community, and Culture on Social Network Sites*. Routledge, 2010, 39–58.
3. boyd, d. and Heer, J. Profiles as conversation: Networked identity performance on Friendster. *Proc. HICSS* (2006).
4. Bruckman, A.S. Gender Swapping on the Internet. *Proceedings of INET* (1993).
5. Butler, J. *Bodies That Matter: On the Discursive Limits of "Sex."* Routledge, 2014.
6. Chang, S. *et al*. Specialization, homophily, and gender in a social curation site: Findings from Pinterest. *Proceedings of CSCW* (2014).
7. Churchill, E.F. Sugared puppy-dog tails: Gender and design. *interactions*. 17, 2 (2010), 52-56.
8. Corbin, J. and Strauss, A. *Basics of Qualitative Research: Techniques and Procedures for Developing Grounded Theory*. Sage, 2008.
9. DiMicco, J.M. and Millen, D.R. Identity management: Multiple presentations of self in Facebook. *Proceedings of GROUPS* (2007).
10. Ellison, N.B. *et al.* The benefits of Facebook "friends:" Social capital and college students' use of online social network sites. *J of CMC.* 12, 4 (2007), 1143–1168.
11. Entwistle, J. *The Fashioned Body: Fashion, Dress and Modern Social Theory*. Polity, 2000.
12. Facebook. "Maintain an authentic personal account," 2014. *https://www.facebook.com/help/206559146047897*
13. Farnham, S.D. and Churchill, E.F. Faceted identity, faceted lives: Social and technical issues with being yourself online. *Proceedings of CSCW* (2011).
14. Fashion industry, retailers and the gender binary: *http://bigstory.ap.org/article/fashion-industry-retailers-and-gender-binary*. Accessed: 2014-07-31.
15. Gagné, P. *et al*. Coming out and crossing over: Identity formation and proclamation in a transgender community. *Gender & Society*. 11, 4 (1997), 478–508.
16. Garfinkel, H. Passing and the managed achievement of sex status in an "intersexed" person. *The Transgender Studies Reader*. Routledge, 2006.
17. Gilbert, E. *et al.* "I need to try this!": A statistical overview of Pinterest. *Proceedings of CHI* (2013).
18. Goffman, E. *Presentation of Self in Everyday Life*. Doubleday Anchor Books, 1959.
19. Goffman, E. *Stigma: Notes on the Management of Spoiled Identity*. Simon and Schuster, 2009.
20. Grant, J.M. *et al. Injustice at Every Turn: A Report of the National Transgender Discrimination Survey*. NCTE & NGLTF, 2011.
21. Hall, C. and Zarro, M. Social curation on the website Pinterest.com. *Proceedings of ASIST* (2012).
22. Hebdige, D. *Subculture: The Meaning of Style*. Routledge, 1979.
23. Haimson, O.L. *et al*. Disclosure, stress and support during gender transition on Facebook. *Proc. of CSCW* (2015).
24. Hines, S. and Sanger, T. *Transgender Identities: Towards a Social Analysis of Gender Diversity*. Taylor & Francis, 2010.
25. Illouz, E. *Cold Intimacies: The Making of Emotional Capitalism*. Polity, 2007.
26. Kondo, D.K. *Crafting Selves: Power, Gender, and Discourses of Identity in a Japanese Workplace*. University of Chicago Press, 2009.
27. Liao, C. Virtual fashion play as embodied identity re/assembling: Second Life fashion bloggers and their avatar bodies. *Reinventing Ourselves: Contemporary Concepts of Identity in Virtual Worlds*. Springer, 2011.
28. Linder, R. *et al.* Everyday ideation: All of my ideas are on Pinterest. *Proceedings of CHI* (2014).
29. Lingel, J. and Gillespie, T. One Name to Rule Them All: Facebook's Identity Problem. *The Atlantic*, 2014.
30. Marwick, A.E. and boyd, d. I tweet honestly, I tweet passionately: Twitter users, context collapse, and the imagined audience. *New Media & Society* 13, 1 (2011), 114–133.
31. McCracken, G.D. *Culture and Consumption: New Approaches to the Symbolic Character of Consumer Goods and Activities*. Indiana University Press, 1990.
32. Schau, H.J. and Gilly, M.C. We are what we post? Self-presentation in personal web space. *Journal of Consumer Research*. 30, 3 (2003), 385–404.
33. Schouten, J.W. Selves in transition: Symbolic consumption in personal rites of passage and identity reconstruction. *J Consumer Rsrch*. 17, 4 (1991), 412–425.
34. Stryker, S. *Transgender History*. Seal Press, 2009.
35. Turkle, S. Cyberspace and Identity. *Contemporary Sociology*. 28, 6 (1999), 643–648.
36. Valentine, D. *Imagining Transgender: An Ethnography of a Category*. Duke University Press, 2007.
37. Wang, Y. *et al*. A Field Trial of Privacy Nudges for Facebook. *Proceedings of CHI* (2014).
38. Yin, R.K. *Case Study Research: Design and Methods*. SAGE Publications, 2013.
39. Zarro, M. *et al.* Wedding dresses and wanted criminals: Pinterest.com as an infrastructure for repository building. *Proceedings of ICWSM* (2013).

Unequal Representation and Gender Stereotypes in Image Search Results for Occupations

Matthew Kay
Computer Science & Engineering | dub, University of Washington
mjskay@uw.edu

Cynthia Matuszek
Computer Science & Electrical Engineering, University of Maryland Baltimore County
cmat@umbc.edu

Sean A. Munson
Human-Centered Design & Engineering | dub, University of Washington
smunson@uw.edu

ABSTRACT
Information environments have the power to affect people's perceptions and behaviors. In this paper, we present the results of studies in which we characterize the gender bias present in image search results for a variety of occupations. We experimentally evaluate the effects of bias in image search results on the images people choose to represent those careers and on people's perceptions of the prevalence of men and women in each occupation. We find evidence for both stereotype exaggeration and systematic underrepresentation of women in search results. We also find that people rate search results higher when they are consistent with stereotypes for a career, and shifting the representation of gender in image search results can shift people's perceptions about real-world distributions. We also discuss tensions between desires for high-quality results and broader societal goals for equality of representation in this space.

Author Keywords
Representation; bias; stereotypes; gender; inequality; image search

INTRODUCTION
Every day, billions of people interact with interfaces that help them access information and make decisions. As increasing amounts of information become available, systems designers turn to algorithms to select which information to show to whom. These algorithms and the interfaces built on them can influence people's behaviors and perceptions about the world. Both algorithms and interfaces, however, can be biased in how they represent the world [9,34]. These biases can be particularly insidious when they are not transparent to the user or even to the designer [28]. The information people access affects their understanding of the world around them and the decisions they make: biased information can affect both how people treat others and how they evaluate their own choices or opportunities.

One of the most prevalent and persistent biases in the United States is a bias against women with respect to occupational choices, opportunities, and compensation [20,26]. Stereotypes of many careers as gender-segregated serve to reinforce gender sorting into different careers and unequal compensation for men and women in the same career. Cultivation theory, traditionally studied in the context of television, contends that both the prevalence and characteristics of media portrayals can develop, reinforce, or challenge viewers' stereotypes [29].

CHI 2015, April 18–23, 2015, Seoul, Republic of Korea.

ACM 978-1-4503-3145-6/15/04...$15.00.
http://dx.doi.org/10.1145/2702123.2702520

Inequality in the representation of women and minorities, and the role of online information sources in portraying and perpetuating it, have not gone unnoticed in the technology community. This past spring, Getty Images and LeanIn.org announced an initiative to increase the diversity of working women portrayed in the stock images and to improve how they are depicted [27]. A recent study identified discrimination in online advertising delivery: when searching for names, search results for black-identifying first names were accompanied by more ads for public records searches than those for white-identifying first names, and those results were more likely to suggest searches for arrest records [34]. These findings raise questions about the possible impacts of this discrimination and how to design technology in consideration of issues such as structural racism.

Despite efforts to address some of these issues, there has been limited public effort to measure how online information sources represent men and women. Further, we do not know how people perceive these biases when they view information sources, or the extent to which it affects their choices or perceptions about the world. For example, are gender distributions in search results representative of those in the real world – and if not, how does that affect people's perceptions of the world?

In this paper, we begin to address these gaps through four studies characterizing how genders are represented in image search results for occupations. We evaluate whether and how these biases affect people's perceptions of search result quality, their beliefs about the occupations represented, and the choices they make. In a series of studies on existing image search results, manipulated search results, and people's perceptions of these results, we investigate the following phenomena:

- *Stereotype exaggeration*: While gender proportions in image search results are close to those in actual occupations, results for many occupations exhibit a slight exaggeration of gender ratios according to stereotype: e.g., male-dominated professions tend to have even more men in their results than would be expected if the proportions reflected real-world distributions. This effect is also seen when people rate the quality of search results or select the best image from a result: they prefer images with genders that match the stereotype of an occupation, even when controlling for qualitative differences in images.

- *Systematic over-/under- representation*: Search results also exhibit a slight under-representation of women in images, such that an occupation with 50% women would be expected to have about 45% women in the results on average. However, when evaluating image result quality, people do not systematically prefer either gender: instead, stereotyping dominates, and they prefer images that match a given occupation's gender stereotype.
- *Qualitative differential representation*: Image search results also exhibit biases in how genders are depicted: those matching the gender stereotype of a profession tend to be portrayed as more professional-looking and less inappropriate-looking.
- *Perceptions of occupations in search results*: We find that people's existing perceptions of gender ratios in occupations are quite accurate (R^2 of 0.72), but that manipulated search results can have a small but significant effect on perceptions, shifting estimations on average ~7%.

This last point contributes to the broader motivation of this work: not only to contribute to an understanding of how everyday information systems – here, image search results – both reflect and influence perceptions about gender in occupations, but also to characterize a possible design space for correcting or adjusting for differences in representation. We do not take a stance on whether or how designers and system builders should address gender inequality and its effects in their systems, but we believe that designers should be aware of inequalities in their systems and how those inequalities can affect perceptions. We particularly note two overriding design tensions in this space: the desire to improve perceived search result quality, and societal motivations for improving equality of representation.

In the remainder of this paper, we review motivating work and our specific research questions. We then describe four studies and their answers to these research questions before discussing the implications for designers and society.

BACKGROUND AND MOTIVATION

The Internet and large data sets create many new opportunities for engaging with data and using it in communication and to support decision making. They also come with challenges and pitfalls. A recent White House report noted that biases in data collection and presentation can lead to flawed understandings of the need for and use of public services, and that this can lead to discrimination in who receives those services [8].

In the studies presented in this paper, we investigate the prevalence and risks of gender-based stereotyping and bias in image search results for occupations. Our research questions were guided by prior work in stereotyping and biases, the role of media in forming, perpetuating, or challenging these, and contemporary discussions of the effects of stereotypes and biases information environments.

Stereotypes and bias

A stereotype refers to a belief that individuals in a group – e.g., gender, occupation, race, ethnicity, or particular background – generally have one or more traits or behaviors. People make use of stereotypes to explain their own or others' behaviors [14,35], to justify actions or decide how to act [4,35], and to define group boundaries [35]. While accurate stereotypes may be useful for making decisions in the absence of more specific information, inaccurate stereotypes can be harmful. Belief that one's group performs poorly at a task can lead to lower performance (stereotype threat [32]). Stereotyped expectations about someone's behavior can also lead them to behave in that way, a self-fulfilling prophecy [32,38], and expectations about one's own abilities can influence aspirations and choices, such as beliefs about what career path one should follow [6,7].

Bias arises when an individual, group or process unfairly and systematically treats an individual or group favorably or unfavorably. Stereotypes about abilities or character are a common source of bias [17], often to the disadvantage of a particular race, sexual orientation, or gender. For example, stereotypes about gender and parental roles can systematically limit women's career advancement [13,15,16].

Effects of stereotypes and bias in the media

The portrayal of women and racial/ethnic minorities in television and other media has received considerable attention as both a possible source of stereotypes and opportunity to challenge them [11]. Exclusion of these groups can imply that they are "unimportant, inconsequential, and powerless" [11]. Their inclusion offers specific examples whose implications depend on how they are portrayed, and these portrayals can reinforce or challenge stereotypes. Unfortunately, portrayals often reinforce negative stereotypes, for example by showing racial/ethnic minorities as criminals, victims of criminals, and in low-status service jobs [11].

Cultivation theory predicts that television's portrayal of the world affects people's beliefs about reality [10,31]. Portrayals, or the lack of portrayals, can affect whether people believe that people like them commonly participate in an occupation, or their perceived self-efficacy for that role [11,31]. Researchers studying television commercials find that women are less likely to be portrayed as workers and that they exaggerate gender-occupation stereotypes [5]. They express concern that such portrayals may perpetuate stereotypes. Cultivation theory has also been found to predict how people perceive risks after experiencing them in a video game [37], and playing a sexualized female character reduces female players' feelings of self-efficacy [3].

Stereotypes and bias in information systems

Like media and other built systems or environments, computer systems have bias. Friedman and Nissenbaum describe biased systems as those that "systematically and unfairly discriminate against certain individuals or groups of individuals in favor of others" [9]. They describe three categories: pre-existing bias (arising from biases present in individuals or society), technical bias (arising from technical constraints), and emergent bias (arising in real use, in which a system is mismatched for the capabilities or values of its users). They argue: "freedom from bias should be counted among the select set of criteria according to which the quality of systems in use in society should be judged."

Search engines have been studied and received popular attention for bias in their results, both for what they index and present overall [19,36] and what they present to particular users [28]. People tend to rely on search engines' selection and ordering of results as signs of quality and relevance [21,22], and so biased search results may affect people's choices and beliefs. Scholars have previously noted bias in which geographic locations are indexed and listed [36]. Others express concern that search autocomplete features could perpetuate preexisting biases, noting that suggestions varied between different religious groups, and sexual and racial minorities received more negatively framed questions as suggestions [2]. As illustrated by these examples, a search engine which has neither algorithms that systematically favor one group nor designers with a particular bias can still perpetuate preexisting societal biases: a representative indexing of biased source material will produce results that contain the same biases.

More recently, Getty Images and Sheryl Sandberg's Lean In Foundation announced an effort to improve the depiction of working women in stock photos. They argue that existing images support stereotypes of working women as sidelined, sexualized, or in supporting roles, and that these depictions hurt women's career aspirations and prospects [12,24,27].

RESEARCH QUESTIONS

Motivated by these concerns and questions about them, we conducted a series of studies to evaluate bias in image search results. Pre-existing biases that affect the images available for image search systems, and algorithms designed to represent available content, may lead to biased result sets, which in turn affect people's perceptions and choices among the search results. We specifically focus on gender representation in image search results for occupations. We choose the portrayal of occupations because it is a topic of societal importance that has recently received attention and efforts to ameliorate biases. While efforts such as the partnership between Getty Images and Lean In may make more diverse or positive images available, and particularly to those who access the Lean In collection, many people turn to major search engines when looking to illustrate a topic, and so we focus our attention on the image search results for a major search engine.

To the discussion of the bias in computer systems, we contribute an assessment of the current extent and form of several forms of stereotyping and differences of representation present in image search results: *stereotype exaggeration*, *systematic over-/under-representation*, and *qualitative differential representation*. We also explore the effects of these biases on perceptions of the occupations in question. We designed four studies to answer these research questions:

- Study 1: How does the prevalence of men and women in image search results for professions correspond to their prevalence in actual professions? Are genders systematically over- or under-represented across careers, and is there stereotype exaggeration in gender proportions?
- Study 2: Are there qualitative differences in *how* men and women are portrayed in the image search results?
- Study 3: Do biased image search results lead people to perpetuate a bias in image search results when they choose images to represent a profession (i.e. through stereotype exaggeration)? Are there systemic over- or under-representations of women in preferred results? How do differences in representation affect people's perceptions of the search result quality?
- Study 4: Do differences in representation in image search results affect viewers' perceptions of the prevalence of men and women in that occupation? Can we shift those opinions by manipulating results?

For all studies, we recruited turkers/participants[1] from Amazon's Mechanical Turk microtask market. We required that they be from the United States (as our occupation prevalence data is specific to that population) and, for studies 2-4, required them to have the Masters qualification.

STUDY 1: GENDER PROPORTIONS IN RESULTS COMPARED TO ACTUAL PROPORTIONS

In this study, we sought to characterize the extent to which the prevalence of men and women in image search results for professions correspond to their actual prevalence in those occupations. As a gold standard for actual prevalence of men and women by occupation, we used estimates from the US Bureau of Labor and Statistics (BLS) [5]. We did not use all occupations, but removed occupations that:

- Presented difficult polysemy problems: for example, occupations that are listed as conjunctions of multiple occupations in the BLS, such as "Musicians, singers, and related workers", are difficult to reduce to a single search.
- Had non-obvious search terms: for example, "Miscellaneous media and communication workers".
- Are typically referred to using gender-specific terms: for example, "tailor" and "seamstress"

[1] We use "turkers" for studies 1 and 2, where they were asked only to label data, and "participants" for studies 3 and 4, where their opinions and perceptions were solicited.

Most of the remaining terms had straightforward translations from BLS categories into search terms for a worker in that occupation (for example, we mapped "Nurse practitioners" in the BLS database to the search term "nurse practitioner"). Some categories required limited interpretation (e.g., we translated "Police and sheriff's patrol officers" into "police officer"); for these terms, all three authors had to agree on a corresponding search term for the category to be included. This left us with 96 occupations having an entry in BLS and a corresponding search term.

We then downloaded the top 100 Google Image search results for each search term (from July 26–29, 2013). For each image, turkers were asked to indicate whether there were no people, one person, or more than one person in the image. They were also asked whether the people were women, men, children, or of unknown gender (and to check all that apply).[2] We had three turkers label each image.

Results

Representativeness of filtered dataset

A requirement of this study was to obtain a representative dataset of images of individuals in different occupations with properly labelled gender. This required some filtering to ensure that images had correctly labelled genders, depicted only people of that gender, and were generally images of people in the first place. To label gender, we took the majority label for each image, and dropped those images from the results which did not have majority agreement. We then dropped entire search terms which:

- Had less than 80% of the images labelled with majority agreement (two terms failed this criterion: firefighter and baker; notably, firefighter had only 64% agreement, largely because most of the images were dark silhouettes of uniformed firefighters with ambiguous gender, frequently labeled as "male" by some turkers).
- Had few images containing only one gender or that mostly depicted workers with clients/patients. For example, hairdresser was dropped since too many of its images contained both hairdresser and client, making it difficult to determine which gender label corresponds to which. We considered asking turkers whether the person in question has the given occupation; however, this implicitly asks them to decide if a person of that gender *could* be a hairdresser (thus potentially subject to gender stereotypes related to that profession, which would bias our labelled data set), so we opted to filter occupations with multiple genders in the majority of images.
- Had too few people in the image results; e.g., dishwasher largely returned images of dishwashing machines.
- Corresponded with a common name (e.g., baker returned many results of people with the surname Baker).

[2] As the BLS uses only binary gender classifications, we also restricted labels to binary gender classification here.

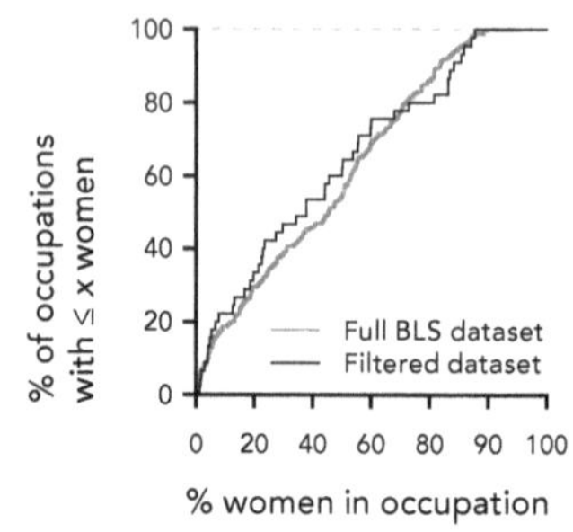

Figure 1. Comparison of empirical cumulative distribution functions of gender distributions in the full set of BLS occupations and our filtered dataset, showing similar distribution.

This second filtering process left us with 45 occupations. To ensure that all levels of our filtering (from the initial selection of search terms down to the filtering of labelled images) had not biased the representativeness of our final selection of occupations in terms of gender or ethnicity, we conducted a series of Kolmogorov-Smirnov tests comparing the gender and ethnicity distributions of the filtered 45 occupations to the entire set of 535 occupations in the BLS (using bootstrap p values; unlike the traditional KS test this allows for non-continuous distributions and ties). We did not find evidence that our filtered dataset significantly differed from the set of occupations in the BLS in terms of gender distribution ($D_{45,535} = 0.0997$, $p = 0.765$), distribution of Asian people, ($D_{45,535} = 0.0901$, $p = 0.814$), distribution of Black or African American people ($D_{45,535} = 0.1021$, $p = 0.729$), or distribution of Hispanic or Latino people ($D_{45,535} = 0.1423$, $p = 0.315$). Note the close correspondence of empirical cumulative distribution functions for the gender distribution in the filtered dataset versus the full BLS dataset in Figure 1 (plots for ethnicity showed similar correspondence).

Misrepresentation of genders in search results

We ran several models to assess the possibility of systematic differences of representation in depictions of occupations in image search results compared to the known proportions in the BLS. The purpose of these models was to assess the presence of two potential forms of quantitative differences in representation.

The first is that gender proportions are exaggerated according to stereotypes for each career (*stereotype exaggeration*). For example, if stereotyping occurs in image results, we would expect a profession with 75% males in the BLS to have more than 75% males in the image results. The second possibility is that there is a *systematic overrepresentation* of one gender, across all careers, in the search results.

Stereotype exaggeration by career

To assess whether men or women were over- or underrepresented according to stereotypes for careers, we ran two logistic regression models: a stereotyped and a nonstereotyped model. The *stereotyped model* regressed the logit of the proportion of women in the search results on the proportion of women in BLS (exhibiting an s-curve characteristic of the logit of a proportion and indicative of stereo-

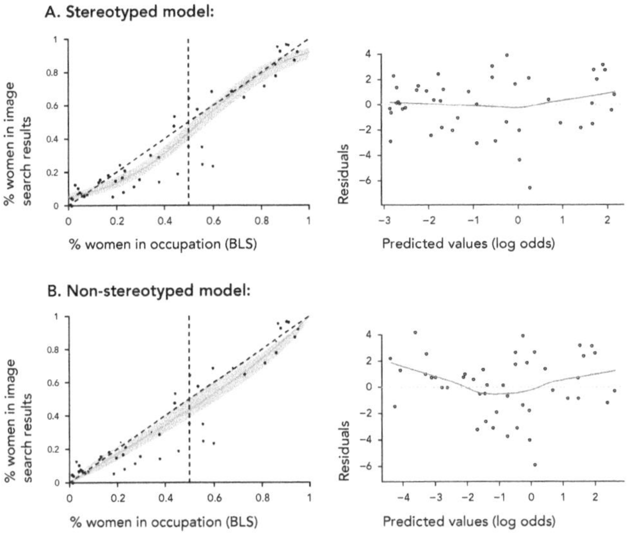

Figure 2. Stereotyped (A) and non-stereotyped (B) models of image search gender distributions compared to actual distributions. Note the improved fit of the stereotyped model, suggesting stereotype exaggeration in search results.

typing: extreme gender proportions in the BLS are pulled even more to the extremes in the search results). The *non-stereotyped model* regressed the logit of the proportion of women in the search results on the logit of the proportion of women in BLS, thus not exhibiting an s-curve. While both models can account for a systematic over-representation of one gender across careers, only the stereotyped model can account for the pulling at the extremes characteristic of stereotyping by the typical gender of a career.

We found some evidence for stereotype exaggeration: the stereotyped model had qualitatively better residual fit (Figure 2). Vuong's closeness test for model fit also suggested that the stereotyped model had better fit ($z = 1.55$, $p = 0.06$). This stereotyping effect can be seen as the overall s-shape of the data compared to a line with slope = 1 (we would expect a line with slope = 1 if the data did not exhibit stereotype exaggeration).

Systematic over-/under- representation across careers

We can estimate overrepresentation of a gender across careers from our logistic regression model by testing to see if the coefficient of the intercept is significantly different from 0 when the x-intercept is set to 50% women in the BLS. Indeed, we find that the intercept does have a significant effect in this model (estimated effect: −0.26, 95% confidence interval: [−0.45, −0.07], $t_{43} = -2.68$, $p < 0.05$);[3] this effect can be seen in Figure 2 as a dip in the predicted proportion of women in the search results at (50%, 50%). This effect corresponds to an odds ratio of approximately 0.77 (95% CI: [0.64, 0.93]); this means that in a profession with 50% women, we would expect about 45% of the images to be women on average (95% CI: [38.9%, 48.2%]).

The particular combination of stereotype exaggeration and underrepresentation of women that we see – slight pulling at the extremes and slight bias towards male images – combine to affect male- and female-dominated professions differently. In male-dominated professions (lower-left quadrant of Figure 2A) both effects amplify each other, so a higher proportion of males appear in search results than are in the BLS. By contrast, in female-dominated professions (upper-right quadrant of Figure 2A) these two effects essentially cancel each other out, leading to a similar proportion of women in the search results as are in the BLS.

STUDY 2: DIFFERENCES IN QUALITATIVE REPRESENTATION

Search results can be biased even when their gender proportions are representative. For example, in reviewing the images collected for Study 1, we identified many examples of sexualized depictions of women who were almost certainly not engaged in the profession they portrayed; we dub this the **sexy construction worker problem**, as images of female construction workers in our results tended to be sexualized caricatures of construction workers. We wished to assess whether images that better match the stereotypical gender of a profession were systematically portrayed as more or less professional, attractive, or appropriate. Note that while there are many interesting differences to unpack here, our primary focus is on assessing these characteristics so that we can control for them in subsequent analysis.

Methods

We used the top 8 male and female images from each profession, as these images will be used again in study 3, below. Initially, we piloted a study in which people were asked to give 5 adjectives describing the person in each image, but found that this task was too difficult. We therefore opted to select 8 adjectives derived from our pilot results and our research questions: attractive, provocative, sexy, professional, competent, inappropriate, trustworthy, and weird. We then had turkers indicate on a 5-point scale (strongly disagree to strongly agree) whether they felt each adjective described the person in the picture. Each turker could rate each image at most once, though no turker could rate more than 600 images. Each image was rated by at least 3 turkers.

Results

At a high level, we found that images showing a person matching the majority gender for a profession tend to be ranked as slightly more professional-looking and slightly less inappropriate than those going against stereotype.

Adjective ratings

One would expect that men and women rate images differently; however, this is not our focus here, so we have attempted to factor out these differences. We conducted a series of mixed-effects ordinal logistic regressions to model how turkers rated images for each adjective. We included

[3] This test was carried out using the stereotyped model, but we note that a similar test carried out on the non-stereotyped model yielded similar results and confidence intervals.

the turker's gender, the image gender, and their interaction as fixed effects; we included the turker and the image as random effects.[4] This allows our models to account for (for example) situations where women systematically rate men as more attractive than men do. We used the coefficients of the image effect in each model as a normalized rating for that adjective. These ratings have the effects of turker, turker gender, image gender, and their interaction factored out and are all approximately standard normally distributed.

Stereotyping bias in qualitative ratings

We hypothesized that images matching the typical gender of a given profession might be portrayed differently from images that do not match the typical gender of that profession (as in the sexy construction worker problem). To assess the whether this was the case, we ran linear mixed-effects regressions, each with one of the adjective ratings derived above as the independent variable. Each model included *image gender*, the *image gender proportion in BLS* (the % of people in the BLS matching the gender of the image; e.g. for a male image of a construction worker, this would be the % of construction workers who are male according to the BLS), and the interaction of these two terms as fixed effects. The models also included the occupation as a random effect. As noted above, we are primarily interested in these factors as controls in Study 3 (below), so we only summarize two high-level trends in the results here.

First, adjectives like professional ($F_{1,623.6} = 36.6$, $p < 0.0001$), competent ($F_{1,630} = 28.4$, $p < 0.0001$), and trustworthy ($F_{1,627.8} = 33.8$, $p < 0.0001$) had significantly higher ratings when the proportion of people in the BLS matching the gender of the image was higher. Second, adjectives like inappropriate ($F_{1,635.2} = 20.4$, $p < 0.0001$) or provocative ($F_{1,635.12} = 4.38$, $p < 0.05$) had significantly lower ratings when the proportion of people in the BLS matching the gender of the image was higher. In other words, we again we see an effect of stereotyping exaggeration: images matching the gender stereotype of a profession tend to be slightly more professional-looking and slightly less inappropriate than those going against stereotype. The reason for this effect is unclear: it may be that these images are rated less professional/appropriate because of raters' biases against images going against their stereotypes for those professions. However, it may also be that these depictions are of lower quality – examples of the sexy construction worker problem, where depictions against stereotype are not true depictions of the profession at all.

STUDY 3: PERCEPTIONS OF SEARCH RESULTS

Having described the bias present in image search results for careers – stereotype exaggeration and differences in representation – we next turn our attention to whether these differences affect people's appraisals of the quality of search results and, in a hypothetical task, what image they choose to represent an occupation. This is not a purely abstract problem: a textbook publisher recently recalled a math textbook after discovering they had selected an image from a pornographic film for the cover [18].

We generated synthetic sets of image search results for each occupation, in which the gender balance was manipulated by re-ranking images from the original search results. Each synthetic result had a different gender distribution, with 8 images in each result. For each search term we generated up to 7 synthetic results: all men, all women, equal proportions, proportions from Google search, proportions from the BLS, the reverse of the proportions from Google search, and the reverse of the proportions in the BLS.

To ensure that the proportion of women in the BLS for a given search term does not influence the proportion of images in the synthetic results for that search term, synthetic subsets (other than equal) were only included if their corresponding reversed subset could also be included (for example, if we had enough women to make a synthetic search result with 6/8 images of women, but not enough men to make a synthetic search result with 6/8 images of men, neither synthetic result was included). This ensures that if gender has no effect on the probability of an image being selected, the baseline probability of two images of different gender being selected for any occupation will be the same: ⅛ (regardless of the gender ratio in that occupation).

To generate a subset with *k* women, we selected the top *k* female images from our labelled dataset (in the order they appeared in the original Google image search results) and the top *8-k* male images. The images were displayed to participants in the order they appeared in the original search results. Participants could view one result set per occupation. This was to prevent participants from realizing that we manipulated the gender proportions of the search results, as they might if they saw multiple synthetic results for the same occupation with very different gender distributions.

On viewing a result set, we asked participants to select one image to illustrate the occupation for a hypothetical business presentation. We then asked them to describe how well the image results matched the search term (the occupation), in a drop down from 1 (very poor) to 5 (very good), and to describe why they rated as they did.

Image Selection Results

We used logistic regression to model the probability that a given image is selected as the best result by a participant. Our model included *image gender*, the *image gender proportion in BLS* (see explanation under Study 2), *participant gender*, and their interactions. We also included all of the image adjective ratings to control for differences in qualitative representation. Results are shown in Table 1.

[4] While we have used worker and image as random effects here and elsewhere in the paper, where estimable we have also compared results with fixed effects models and found similar effects. We believe random effects to be more appropriate here as some workers have completed only a small number of tasks.

	Est.	SE	z	p	
(Intercept)	−2.661	0.273	−9.737	<0.0001	***
% image gender in BLS	0.928	0.414	2.244	0.0248	*
female image	0.239	0.360	0.663	0.5072	
male participant	0.041	0.393	0.104	0.9173	
professional	−0.089	0.082	−1.082	0.2794	
attractive	−0.028	0.080	−0.35	0.7262	
inappropriate	−0.018	0.109	−0.168	0.8662	
provocative	−0.312	0.166	−1.877	0.0606	.
sexy	−0.021	0.087	−0.244	0.8076	
competent	0.448	0.104	4.298	<0.0001	***
trustworthy	−0.046	0.090	−0.513	0.6078	
weird	−0.485	0.111	−4.355	<0.0001	***
% image gender in BLS × female image	−0.222	0.585	−0.38	0.7037	
% image gender in BLS × male participant	0.003	0.594	0.005	0.996	
female image × male participant	0.011	0.512	0.021	0.9836	
% image gender in BLS × female image × male participant	−0.175	0.832	−0.21	0.8333	

Table 1. Factors affecting image selection in Study 3. Coefficients are on a logit scale. Note the stereotype effect: greater *% image gender in BLS* is associated with higher probability that an image is selected.

Over-/under- representation and participant effects

We found no evidence of systematic over-/under- representation of either gender (there were no significant effects of image gender). Neither were there significant effects of participant gender (suggesting men and women generally judge the best search result in the same way), nor any significant interactions with either of these factors.

Stereotype exaggeration

As with the gender distributions in the search results themselves, we found evidence of stereotyping when people choose image results: *image gender proportion in BLS* had a significant effect on the probability of an image being selected; i.e., an image matching the majority gender proportion of its occupation was more likely to be selected. We believe this is consequence of stereotype matching: an image matching a person's stereotype for that gender is more likely to be selected as an exemplar result.

Search Result Quality Rating Results

We saw very similar effects influencing quality rating. We ran a mixed effects ordinal logistic regression to model *quality rating* based on *proportion of women in BLS, proportion of women in the synthetic search result, participant gender*, and their interactions. We included the adjective rating of the selected image (as possibly the most salient in judging search quality) in the synthetic search result to control for differences in qualitative representation. We also included *participant* and *search term* (occupation) as random effects. Results are in Table 2.

Over-/under- representation and participant effects

As above, we found no significant over-/under-representation effect: in an occupation with 50% women, we would not expect an all-male search result to be rated differently from an all-female search result (estimated difference = −0.41, SE = 0.47, $z = -0.87$, $p = 0.38$). As above, there were no significant effects of participant gender.

	Est.	SE	z	p	
% women in BLS	−2.978	1.344	−2.22	0.0268	*
% women in search result	−2.255	0.889	−2.54	0.0112	*
male participant	0.156	0.871	0.18	0.8581	
professional	−0.039	0.186	−0.21	0.8324	
attractive	0.160	0.180	0.89	0.3748	
inappropriate	0.411	0.243	1.69	0.0911	.
provocative	−0.491	0.329	−1.49	0.1357	
sexy	−0.053	0.209	−0.25	0.8016	
competent	0.506	0.227	2.23	0.0257	*
trustworthy	−0.392	0.219	−1.79	0.0732	.
weird	−0.509	0.218	−2.33	0.0199	*
% women in search result × % women in BLS	5.321	1.699	3.13	0.0017	**
% women in search result × male participant	−0.595	1.221	−0.49	0.6261	
% women in BLS × male participant	−0.525	1.359	−0.39	0.6992	
% women in search result × % women in BLS × male participant	2.036	2.325	0.88	0.3812	

Table 2. Factors affecting search result quality ratings in Study 3. Coefficients are on a logit scale.

Stereotype exaggeration

We again saw a stereotype exaggeration effect, manifested here as a significant interaction between *proportion of women in BLS* and *proportion of women in the search result*: in male-dominated occupations, search results with more males are preferred; in female-dominated occupations, search results with more females are preferred.

Viewed from the perspective of this task, these results make sense: we asked people to select the best search result (or to rate the quality of all results), and they tended to prefer images matching their mental image of each profession, both in qualitative characteristics and in expected gender. This reflects the strong sense that people have of expected gender proportions in a broad spectrum of occupations, which we explore in more detail next. This also emphasizes an important tension between possible broader societal goals in manipulating gender as a design dimension in search results versus end-users' quality expectations, an issue we discuss in detail at the end of this paper.

STUDY 4: PERCEPTIONS OF GENDER PROPORTIONS IN OCCUPATIONS

Finally, we sought to understand whether and how gender proportions in image search results can affect people's perceptions of the *actual* prevalence of men and women in different occupations, both to understand how existing (stereotype-exaggerating, misrepresented) results might be affecting people's perceptions of gender proportions and how feasible manipulating gender distributions in image search might be as a method for affecting those perceptions. This gets at a primary motivation of our paper: opening up gender proportions as a design dimension in image search.

Given the many possible day-to-day influences on perceptions of the prevalence of genders in different fields, we

	Est.	SE	df	*t*	*p*	
(Intercept)	0.074	0.021	103.6	3.51	<0.001	***
% women in manipulated search result	0.070	0.024	206.3	2.90	<0.01	**
perceived % women in occupation before manipulation	0.803	0.033	211.8	24.57	<0.001	***

Table 3. Effects of the manipulated search result and a person's pre-existing opinion of % women in an occupation on their opinion after seeing the manipulated result (Study 4).

chose to collect people's baseline perceptions, wait two weeks, show them a synthetic image search result set for the same career, and then immediately ask them their perceptions of prevalence.

We asked each participant the demographics information we used in studies 2 and 3. Then for each career we asked what percent of people working in that career in the US are women, alongside three distraction questions: what education they believe is typical for someone in that career, whether they believe the career was growing, and how prestigious they think it is. Participants could answer for as many careers as they wished.

After two weeks, each participant received an email thanking them for their prior participation and inviting them to participate in a new round of tasks; we limited access both in the script that managed our tasks and using an assigned qualification on Mechanical Turk. For each profession to which they had previously responded, we returning participants to view a synthetic search result and complete the image search task from study 3; on the next page we re-asked the four questions from the first page: typical education for the career, percent women, whether the career was growing, and its prestige.

Results

Perceptions absent influence

People's initial perceptions of gender proportions in occupations are quite good. We assessed the correlation of their existing perceptions to real-world proportions using a mixed-effects linear regression with *gender proportions in BLS* as the fixed effect and *participant* as a random effect. The marginal pseudo-R^2 of this model was 0.717 ($F_{1,297.71} = 870.21, p < 0.0001$).

Perceptions after influence

After exposure to search results with manipulated gender proportions, estimates shifted slightly in the direction of the manipulated proportions. We ran a linear mixed-effects regression to predict perceived gender proportions, with *initial perceived gender proportion* and *manipulated search gender proportion* as fixed effects and *participant* as a random effect. Both fixed effects were significant: while a person's original perceptions of an occupation dominated their opinion two weeks later; approximately 7% of a person's subsequent opinion on average was determined by the result set they were exposed to (p < 0.01, see Table 3).

While this only shows short-term movement due to manipulated search results, cultivation theory suggests that long-term, ongoing exposure to such results might shift perceptions over time. This suggests that there may be value in considering gender distribution as a more deliberate design dimension in image search results, as we discuss next.

DISCUSSION

Our results provide guidance on the short-term effects of possible changes to search engine algorithms and highlight tensions in possible designs of search algorithms.

As a design space, what other kinds of search results could we design and what might be the consequences?

There are two sets of adjustments that can be made: adjusting the gender distribution, and adjusting the distribution of qualitative image characteristics within genders (e.g. increasing the proportion of female construction worker results that are rated as professional or competent to correct for the sexy construction worker problem). Taking the former as a starting point, we outline three possible (amongst many) ways of adjusting search results: 1) exaggerating, or continuing to accept, exaggerated gender stereotypes; 2) aligning the gender balance of results to match reality; or 3) balancing the genders represented in results.

These models also surface several design tensions in this space. In particular, we might ask if our goal is to improve perceptions of search result quality, or to advance a broader social agenda to shift perceptions of gender equality in various professions. While potentially at odds in the short term (e.g., highly stereotyped results might be highly rated but not have desirable societal effects), cultivation theory also suggests these goals may not be as contrary over the long term if perceptions can be shifted to match a broader goal of equal representation (as, at least in the short term, Study 4 suggests is possible). We discuss how these motivations interact in more detail for each proposed model. We do not wish to come down on any side of these issues, but wish to advance an understanding of how the choices people make in designing algorithms can (and *already do*) define a design space that explicitly or implicitly affects these issues.

1. Stereotype model. Exaggerate gender stereotypes. This might improve subjective assessment of quality over baseline results if the dominant gender is already represented as professional and appropriate, so would likely not require correcting for qualitative differences (simplifying the technical problem). This would also give more exemplars for the selection task. At the same time, continuing to portray careers as more gender-segregated than they are, or even further exaggerating gender imbalances, has the disadvantage of potentially influencing people's perceptions of occupation gender distributions over time to be less accurate and reinforcing stereotypes that can shape and limit career aspirations and treatment.

2. Reality model. Correct the slight stereotype exaggeration and underrepresentation of women seen in the data so that gender distributions better resemble the BLS. So long as we can select images of the non-dominant gender that have high professionalism and low inappropriateness, this would at least better represent the reality of the profession while having little effect on the perceived search result quality or the selection task. Over the long term, exposure to such results might improve people's estimations of real-world gender proportions in occupations. This also represents only a small perturbation to existing results, and may not even require adjustments to distributions to account for qualitative differences in representation due to how close the existing search proportions are to actual BLS proportions.

3. Balanced model. Adjust the gender proportions in occupations to be equal or closer to equal. This may impair the selection task by giving fewer gender exemplars. However, if this is paired with corrections for qualitative differences in representation so that portrayals of the non-dominant gender are similar to the dominant one (particularly for professionalism), we do not believe it would significantly degrade people's overall perceptions of the quality of the results. This model exposes a tension between a desire for results perceived as high-quality and possible societal goals for advancing equal representation. While the short-term effects on perceived search result quality would likely be negative, both cultivation theory [31] and the results of study 4 predict that this could, in the long term, shift people's perceptions towards a less gender-stereotyped view of these professions. Along with that long-term shift, a possible result may be that perceptions of quality shift back as people begin to perceive gender proportions as more equal.

Feasibility of Manipulating Representation

Automatic gender classification of images of people is an outstanding problem. While state-of-the art classifiers perform well under certain circumstances, they have historically focused on straight-on images of a single face, typically without visual occlusions, uneven lighting, or complicated backgrounds [25]. However, recent studies on gender classification on images collected in the wild [1,30] or of only partial features [23] strongly suggest that automated solutions will soon reach or surpass the accuracy of human annotators. Meanwhile, automated human labelling of these images would not be much more costly than the data collection processes used in this paper, and would provide ground truth data for future automated approaches.

Limitations and Future Work

We have focused here on search results absent personalization or other additional context (such as time of year or location) that may affect results shown to users in real-world tasks. While the businessperson making a slide presentation might be seeking an accurate depiction of a given profession, other users with different goals might prefer caricatured or inaccurate portrayals, such as the sexy construction worker. We also do not address the cause of the biases and misrepresentation found (e.g., are these due to actual prevalence in webpages, or due to the ranking algorithms used by Google?). Future work might try to tease these effects apart, and to investigate these phenomena in other types of image search, such as on photo sharing sites and in social media. To aid in replication, **our data and code are available online**: https://github.com/mjskay/gender-in-image-search.

CONCLUSION

Academics and the technology community have raised concerns about potential biases in search engines and in stock photos. We contribute an assessment of gender representation in image search results and its effects on perceived search result quality, images selected, and perceptions about reality. We find that image search results for occupations slightly exaggerate gender stereotypes and portray the minority gender for an occupational less professionally. There is also a slight underrepresentation of women. This stereotype exaggeration is consistent with perceptions of result quality – people believe results are better when they agree with the stereotype – but risks reinforcing or even increasing perceptions of actual gender segregation in careers.

Addressing concerns such as these in search engines and other information sources, however, requires balancing design tensions. For example, maintaining perceived search quality and accurately representing available materials may be at odds with supporting socially desirable outcomes and representing either real-world distributions of careers or idealized distributions of careers. We hope to advance a constructive discussion on gender representation as a design dimension (explicit and implicit) in information systems.

ACKNOWLEDGEMENTS

We thank Gilbert Bernstein and Benjamin Mako Hill for their valuable feedback on this work.

REFERENCES

1. Arigbabu OA; Ahmad SMS, Adnan WAN, Yussof S, Iranmanesh V, Malallah, FL, Gender recognition on real world faces based on shape representation and neural network. *ICCOINS* 2014.
2. Baker P, Potts A. "Why do white people have thin lips?" Google and the perpetuation of stereotypes via auto-complete search forms. *Crit Disc St* 10(2): 187-204.
3. Behm-Morawitz E, Mastro D. The Effects of the Sexualization of Female Video Game Characters on Gender Stereotyping and Female Self-Concept. *Sex Roles* 2009; 61(11-12): 808-823.
4. Bodenhausen GV, Wyer RS. Effects of stereotypes in decision making and information-processing strategies. *J Pers Soc Psychol* 1985; 48(2): 267.
5. Bureau of Labor Statistics. Labor Force Statistics from the Current Population Survey, Section 11. 5 February 2013. http://www.bls.gov/cps/aa2012/cpsaat11.htm.Coltrane S, Adams M. Work–family imagery and gender stereotypes: Television and the reproduction of difference. *J Vocat Behav* 1997; 50(2): 323-347.

6. Correll SJ. Gender and the career choice process: The role of biased self-assessments. *Am J Sociol* 2001; 106(6): 1691–1730.
7. Correll SJ. Constraints into preferences: Gender, status, and emerging career aspirations. *Am Sociol Rev* 2004; 69(1): 93-113.
8. Executive Office of the President. *Big Data: Seizing Opportunities, Preserving Values.* May 2014.
9. Friedman B, Nissenbaum H. Bias in computer systems. *ACM T Inform Syst* 1996; 14(3): 330-347.
10. Gerbner G, Gross L, Morgan M, Signorielli N. Living with television: The dynamics of the cultivation process. *Perspectives on media effects* 1986: 17-40.
11. Graves SB. Television and Prejudice Reduction: When Does Television as a Vicarious Experience Make a Difference? *J Soc Issues* 1999; 55(4): 707-727.
12. Grossman P. New Partnership with LeanIn.org. *InFocus by Getty Images. http://infocus.gettyimages.com/post/new-partnership-with-leaninorg.*
13. Halpert JA, Wilson ML, Hickman JL. Pregnancy as a source of bias in performance appraisals. *J Organ Behav* 1993.
14. Haslam SA, Turner JC, Oakes PJ, Reynolds KJ, Doosje, B From personal pictures in the head to collective tools in the word: how shared stereotypes allow groups to represent and change social reality. In C McGarty, VY Yzerbyt, R Spears (eds.). *Stereotypes as explanations: The formation of meaningful beliefs about social groups* 2002. Cambridge University Press, 157-185.
15. Heilman ME. Description and prescription: How gender stereotypes prevent women's ascent up the organizational ladder. *J Soc Issues* 2001; 57(4): 657-674.
16. Heilman ME. Okimoto, TG. 2008. Motherhood: A potential source of bias in employment decisions. *J Appl Psychol* 2008; 93(1): 189-198.
17. Hilton JL, & Von Hippel W. Stereotypes. *Annu Rev Psychol* 1996; 47(1): 237-271.
18. Hooper B. Porn star appears on cover of Thai math textbook. *United Press International. http://upi.com/5031410787947*
19. Introna L, Nissenbaum H. Defining the web: The politics of search engines. *Computer* 2000; 33(1): 54-62.
20. Jacobs J. *Gender Inequality at Work.* Thousand Oaks, CA: SAGE Publications, 1995.
21. Kammerer,Y, Gerjets P. How search engine users evaluate and select Web search results: The impact of the search engine interface on credibility assessments. *Libr Inform Sci* 2012; 4: 251–279.
22. Keane MT, O'Brien M, Smyth B. Are people biased in their use of search engines? *Commun ACM* 2008; 51(2): 49-52.
23. Khorsandi R, Abdel-Mottaleb M. Gender classification using 2-D ear images and sparse representation. 2013 IEEE *Workshop on Applications of Computer Vision* (WACV), 461-466.
24. Lean In Foundation. Getty Image Collection. http://leanin.org/getty.
25. Makinen E, Raisamo R. Evaluation of Gender Classification Methods with Automatically Detected and Aligned Faces, *IEEE T Pattern Anal* 2008; 30(3): 541-547.
26. Massey D. *Categorically Unequal: The American Stratification System.* NY: Russell Sage Foundation, 2007.
27. Miller CC. 10 February 2014. LeanIn.org and Getty Aim to Change Women's Portrayal in Stock Photos. *New York Times,* B3. *http://nyti.ms/1eLY7ij*
28. Pariser E. *The Filter Bubble: What the Internet Is Hiding from You.* 2011. Penguin Press.
29. Potter WJ. Cultivation theory and research, *Hum Commun Res* 1993; 19(4): 564-601.
30. Shan C. Learning local binary patterns for gender classification on real-world face images, *Pattern Recogn Lett* 2012; 33(4), 431-437.
31. Shrum LJ. Assessing the Social Influence of Television A Social Cognition Perspective on Cultivation Effects. *Commun Res* 1995; 22(4): 402-429.
32. Spencer SJ, Steele CM, Quinn DM. Stereotype threat and women's math performance. *J Exp Soc Psychol* 1999; 35(1): 4-28.
33. Snyder M, Tanke ED, Berscheid E. Social perception and interpersonal behavior: On the self-fulfilling nature of social stereotypes. *J Pers Soc Psychol* 1977; 35(9): 656–666.
34. Sweeney L. Discrimination in online ad delivery. *Commun ACM* 2013; 56(5): 44-54.
35. Tajfel H. Social stereotypes and social groups. In Turner JC, Giles H. *Intergroup Behaviour* 1981. Oxford: Blackwell. 144–167.
36. Vaughan L, Thelwall M. Search engine coverage bias: evidence and possible causes. *Inform Process Manag* 2004; 40(4): 693-707.
37. Williams D. Virtual Cultivation: Online Worlds, Offline Perceptions. *J Commun* 1996; 56(1): 69–87.
38. Word CO, Zanna MP, Cooper J. The nonverbal mediation of self-fulfilling prophecies in interracial interaction. *J Exp Soc Psychol* 1974; 10(2): 109–120.
39. X Tang, K Liu, J Cui, F Wen, X Wang. IntentSearch: Capturing User Intention for One-Click Internet Image Search, *IEEE T Pattern Anal* 34(7): 1342-1353.
40. Zha ZJ, Yang L, Mei T, Wang M, Wang Z, Chua TS, Hua XS. 2010. Visual query suggestion: Towards capturing user intent in internet image search. *ACM T Multim Comput* 2010; 6(3): a13.

Finding the Adaptive Sweet Spot: Balancing Compliance and Achievement in Automated Stress Reduction

Artie Konrad[1,2], Victoria Bellotti[2,1], Nicole Crenshaw[3,2], Simon Tucker[2], Les Nelson[2], Honglu Du[2], Peter Pirolli[2], and Steve Whittaker[1]

[1]UC Santa Cruz
1156 High Street, Santa Cruz, CA
{akonrad, swhittak}@ucsc.edu

[2]Palo Alto Research Center
3333 Coyote Hill Rd.,
Palo Alto, CA
{bellotti, stucker, lnelson, hdu, pirolli}@parc.com

[3]UC Irvine
Irvine, CA
crenshan@uci.edu

ABSTRACT

Automated coaching systems offer a convenient, cost-effective way to reduce stress, which can be a serious health issue. However, one concern with such systems is *compliance*; users fail to achieve daily stress reduction goals because goals are too easy or too difficult. To address this, we built DStress (Design for Stress), a theoretically grounded system that sets adaptive goals in three coaching dimensions: Exercise, Meditation and Accessibility. DStress modifies goal-difficulty based on the individual's immediately previous performance. In a 28-day deployment with 65 users, DStress reduced scores on one direct measure of stress almost in half, significantly more than two other non-adaptive coaching strategies. However, on a second direct stress measure, no improvement was found. There were also no improvements on other indirect stress measures. Analysis of 2842 user-generated reports suggests our findings were the result of DStress balancing compliance against the degree of challenge of the goals it would set.

Author Keywords

Stress reduction; mental health; compliance; behavior change.

ACM Classification Keywords

H.5.m. Information interfaces and presentation (e.g., HCI): Miscellaneous.

INTRODUCTION

The majority of healthcare coaching systems target physical health, but mental well-being is increasingly seen as critical [16,27,32]. Stress is an unavoidable fact of life. Mild stress can be adaptive, but chronic stress profoundly affects individual and societal health [43]. Chronic stress increases mortality, morbidity, immunosuppression, anxiety, depression, and absenteeism [9,34 ,38]. Job stress alone is estimated to cost the U.S. economy more than $300 billion a year [43]. We describe the design and evaluation of an adaptive, personalized healthcare system that addresses stress.

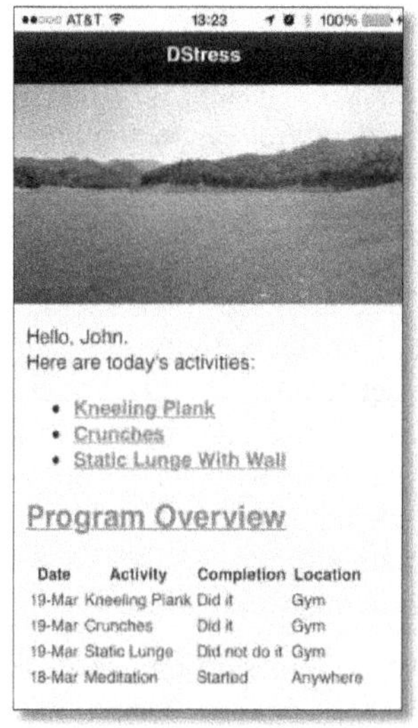

Figure 1. The DStress system. Program overview and activities for the day.

Two successful approaches to stress reduction are *physical exercise* and *mindfulness meditation*. These are effective when implemented under expert supervision, but they require costly personalization to ensure compliance [4,15]. This has prompted calls for new approaches to provide *simple*, *accessible*, *scalable*, and *sustainable* regimens that meet user needs [8]. Computational methods show significant promise as a class of solutions. In a 2000 survey, 91% of respondents said they wanted access to computational interventions. These are cheap, highly convenient and users need not worry about perceived social stigma of interacting with professionals [18].

But while automated mental healthcare systems are affordable and private, they have limitations. One common problem is *compliance,* where users fail to persist with proposed health-enhancing behaviors. A review of 46 computerized interventions for anxiety and depression, found the median completion rate was only 56% [47]. Recent work on mental and physical health indicates that compliance failure can result from lack of personalization. [16] improved compliance with an online mental health intervention by emphasizing personalization among other strategies. [13] investigated goal-setting strategies for fitness, but found it hard to design effective programs from

CHI 2015, April 18–23, 2015, Seoul, Republic of Korea.

ACM 978-1-4503-3145-6/15/04…$15.00.
http://dx.doi.org/10.1145/2702123.2702512

national recommendations. Participants stated that recommended activities often did not fit personal goals or expertise. This is a major limitation of many commercial health programs (e.g. [1,22]) and national recommendations (e.g. [40,45]).

However, designing effective personalized systems is complex. Prior research on behavior change shows an apparent paradox. On the one hand, people need to be given challenging activities [29]. On the other, if activities are *too* difficult, this demotivates as goals are seen as unattainable [5].

How then might we design stress reduction systems that avoid this apparent paradox? Building on successful approaches to physical well-being [6,28] we designed an *adaptive* system, DStress (see Figure 1), which *modifies goal difficulty depending on participants' immediately previous performance*. Incorporating behavior change theory [29] participants are given successively more challenging stress reducing activities. If they succeed in these activities, this should motivate. But participants who fail on an activity are immediately given an easier goal. Succeeding on this easier goal should re-establish self-confidence and thus motivation, increasing the probability that they will persist with the system [5]. This adaptive mechanism aims to optimize system compliance while still maintaining a challenging level of difficulty so that users experience the greatest reductions in their stress.

We address compliance in two other ways. A second critical system design feature is that we support stress reduction via both Exercise and Meditation dimensions. By providing *multiple strategies* for success, we counter a different critique of current physical healthcare systems; that they are overly simplistic [19,39]. A final more pragmatic design dimension is Accessibility. Users have to be provided with goals they can achieve in *multiple contexts*. Suggesting a fitness goal that requires users to always attend a gym may restrict their ability and willingness to attempt that exercise. Thus the Accessibility dimension complements the Exercise dimension by adjusting the location of workouts, if the user is having trouble making it to the gym.

We conducted a one-month field trial deployment comparing our adaptive stress coaching system, DStress, with non-adaptive versions of the system, to address the following questions:

- *Stress*: Does DStress actually reduce stress?
- *Adaptivity*: Does adaptivity reduce stress more than non-adaptive approaches?
- *Compliance versus Achievement*: We also explore underlying mechanisms for achieving stress reduction. Is simple compliance sufficient or must users also carry out tasks that present a challenge?

We show that an adaptive approach can lead to greater stress reduction. However, compliance alone is insufficient, with participants only receiving well-being benefits when they successfully tackled activities that were optimally challenging.

RELATED WORK

Behavior Change Theory

There are many behavior change theories. Some focus on the capacity to control behavior, e.g. the *Theory of Planned Behavior* [2], and Bandura's *Self-Efficacy Theory* [5]. The *Transtheoretical Model of Behavior Change* [41] considers behavior change as a series of stages. *Goal-Setting Theory* describes different types of goals and predicts which are most motivating [29]. Goffman's *Presentation of Self in Everyday Life* has been applied to coaching systems that exploit social motivations (e.g. [14]). We focus on Goal-Setting Theory and Self-Efficacy Theory because they address our concerns of adapting goal difficulty to optimize challenge and maintain self-confidence, as we shall discuss.

Goal-Setting Theory: Difficult is Better

Goal-Setting Theory (GST) proposes a linear positive relationship between goal difficulty and the effort put into achieving that goal [35]. Also, specific goals elicit more effort than abstract goals, e.g. "do 20 push-ups," as opposed to, "do your best" [29]. In Goal-Setting Theory, goals represent a discrepancy between a person's current state and the state they seek to achieve. According to the theory, achieving a goal confers satisfaction by closing that gap and more challenging goals are more motivating because they require more effort to achieve than easier goals.

Self-Efficacy Theory: Easier is Better

Self-efficacy is the belief in one's ability to succeed in a given situation [5]. If people observe themselves failing at a desired goal, their confidence in their ability to succeed in that situation drops. Past achievement is critical to influencing behavior change, so Self-Efficacy Theory holds that *successful completion* of planned goals is more important than the goal itself [7]. So less challenging goals are therefore more desirable because, by effortlessly realizing these goals, participants feel confident that they can achieve future goals and therefore remain compliant.

Technology to Support Health

The past few years have seen the emergence of many healthcare-coaching technologies (see [26] for a review). The vast majority of these systems are designed to address physical health, e.g. providing social persuasion to motivate exercise [44]. There has been less research on systems built to support mental health and stress, although new research is emerging [23]. For example, [36,37] suggest "just in time" coping techniques when the user exhibits elevated stress and negative mood. [31] designed a wearable biofeedback device to help monitor and self-regulate stress. [30] built a smartphone application that detects stress from changes in speech production. Many of these mental health systems are therapy-based (invoking Cognitive Behavioral

Therapy or Positive Psychology) [16,27,32]. There has also been interest in mindfulness-based design for mental health [46]. However, with the exception of [16], [27] and [32] very few mental health systems have been designed to address underlying issues with compliance.

Coaching Strategies

Some systems employ *predetermined* coaching strategies that profile the user along different dimensions to set goals that remain fixed regardless of user achievement. For instance, Chick Clique, Houston, and Ubifit set personalized goals but these are not continually reevaluated in line with user progress [12,13 ,44]. Another example is the Mobile Lifestyle Coach where users earn "lifestyle points" for exercising and eating healthily. Users attempt to earn the same predetermined number of lifestyle points each day [17].

While predetermined strategies are simple to implement, they may be problematic from a compliance perspective. If a user surpasses a predetermined easy goal, they may lose motivation (following Goal-Setting Theory), or if goals are too difficult users might lose self-efficacy (following Self-Efficacy Theory). Adaptive systems attempt to avoid these scenarios by providing goals that dynamically adjust to users' progress, encouraging them to persist with the coaching system.

Adaptive systems´ are more complex to implement, however. Some rely on 'embedded' professionals to evaluate progress and set new personalized goals. For example, some systems log health information that is continually reviewed by a healthcare practitioner who provides feedback and adjusts goals [25,48]. Automated approaches that don't rely on professionals are less common but becoming popular. For example in online learning, adaptive and intelligent web-based educational systems (AIWBES) tailor lessons to the development of the student. Systems like ELM-ART and ActiveMath, adapt the content and sequence of the curriculum to the individual [10]. In adaptive coaching for health, systems like Fish'n'Steps, SMS Coach, and "Laura" assess disposition and user performance to tailor appropriate goals [6,19 ,28]. Goals are adjusted depending on current progress.

While these systems provide adaptivity, one user critique is that they often provide limited strategies for success. Users of SMS Coach, for instance, frequently reported that they wanted multiple variables to be considered to help change their behavior, as well as more diverse feedback [19]. Participants in Obermayer's smoking cessation study desired messaging that was more tailored to their individual challenges [39]. So, like a real coach, an automated, adaptive system should be flexible along multiple dimensions to meet user needs.

Accessibility has been shown to be important in past medical research. For example, accessibility of soap stations encourages handwashing compliance among nurses [24]. Adaptive systems also need to be accessible to provide coaching that fits a user's lifestyle [14,47]. For instance, if it were more convenient to join friends on a bike ride than to go for a walk, Fish'n'Steps users would not get any credit for their exercise [28]. Thus, adaptive systems must be flexible enough to provide goals that can be achieved in different contexts.

Finally, recent review articles argue that the majority of automated health systems are not based on theory [11,42]. In some systems that do claim theoretical motivations, the specifics of how theory informs their design are never discussed (e.g. [20]). Systems that are informed by theory can address the bottlenecks in behavior change, resulting in more effective interventions [13,42].

Finding the Adaptive Sweet Spot

We designed DStress to address these limitations and adaptively select goals derived from behavior change theory. By balancing Goal-Setting Theory and Self-Efficacy Theory we aim to design a program that is the best of both worlds. Our objective is to maximize compliance by balancing goals that are not too difficult (maintaining self-efficacy) and not too easy (maintaining motivation). DStress does this by adapting difficulty based on the user's past performance. These daily adjustments occur in three different coaching dimensions: *Exercise*, *Meditation*, and *Accessibility*. Furthermore, each of these dimensions is *complementary* and *reinforcing*. Compliance with meditation provides greater relaxation to recover from physical exercise. The Accessibility dimension adjusts convenience of exercise location to induce greater compliance with the Exercise dimension. We seek to evaluate our multidimensional approach as well as the influence of our adaptive mechanisms on compliance, achievement, and ultimately stress.

METHOD

We developed and evaluated three versions of a coaching system; an adaptive DStress, a non-adaptive *Easy* version, and a non-adaptive *Difficult* version. The Easy version was intended to maximize one aspect of compliance by presenting straightforwardly achievable activities. The Difficult version was meant to motivate another aspect of compliance with challenging activities. The DStress version was designed to balance ease and challenge, and our overall goal was to determine which of the three systems most reduced stress.

Participants

We recruited 77 participants through Facebook and an internal database of participants. We also used a snowball-recruiting scheme where participants could recommend others. They were paid $15 for starting the study, and another $35 for completing. People who recruited friends that completed the study received an additional $10 per person up to a maximum of $50 dollars. Participants were first screened to confirm they were physically capable of performing the exercises in this study using the Physical

Activity Readiness Questionnaire. Four participants were removed who did not pass this screening. Eight dropped out because of unexpected surgery, international travel, busyness at work, or because they ceased communication with the research team. This left 65 (42 female) aged 19-59 (M=31.12, SD=9.29), of which 45 used iPhones, 16 used Androids, and 1 person used another type of smartphone. Participants were randomly assigned to a group and each group was assigned an Easy, Difficult, or DStress version of the system. Participants were blind to which group they were in and were not informed that there were different groups. There were 24 participants in the Easy (16 female, age M=31.75, SD=9.26), 22 in the Difficult (13 female, age M=31.68, SD=8.94) and 19 in the DStress group (13 female, age M=29.68, SD=10.04).

The DStress System

DStress is a web-based coaching system (see Figure 1) that runs in a browser, making it accessible from any smartphone. The system provides information about a participant's stress-related activities program (exercise, meditation), details about how to execute activities, methods for logging progress with activities, reminders about activities and logging, and a record of past activities. To manipulate accessibility we also provided participants with information about *where* to carry out their activity.

Users log-in to access their personalized program of activities for the day. There are three types of days: exercise, meditation and rest. On *exercise* days, exercises are presented as clickable links to detailed instructions on how to perform each one and how many repetitions and sets to do. They are presented with a recommended *location* (either the gym or a convenient place, such as at home). On exercise days, users receive one upper body exercise, one lower body exercise, and one circuit training exercise. If the day is a *meditation* day, DStress presents a link to instructions and how many minutes to meditate that day. And on *rest* days, users do no exercise or meditation.

Users can click a link on the home screen to see their entire *program overview*. This also displays all previous activities and which ones were completed. Users can also see the day's scheduled activity to help with planning. Users can browse activities further in the future which are titled as "Exercise", "Meditation" or "Rest" days without details, since the specifics are determined adaptively based on user performance.

After completing activities, users click a link to *report* how they did. On exercise days, DStress asks whether users made it to the gym. And for each exercise users report whether they completed it successfully ("*Complete*"), started but didn't finish ("*Start*"), or didn't start the exercise ("*Fail*"). The same responses are collected for meditation days allowing users to report progress against the day's goal (number of meditation minutes).

Each morning at 9am users receive an automatic email reminder to complete the day's activities with a link to login to DStress. And at 8pm, if users have not yet reported their progress for the day, they are emailed a reminder to log their activities.

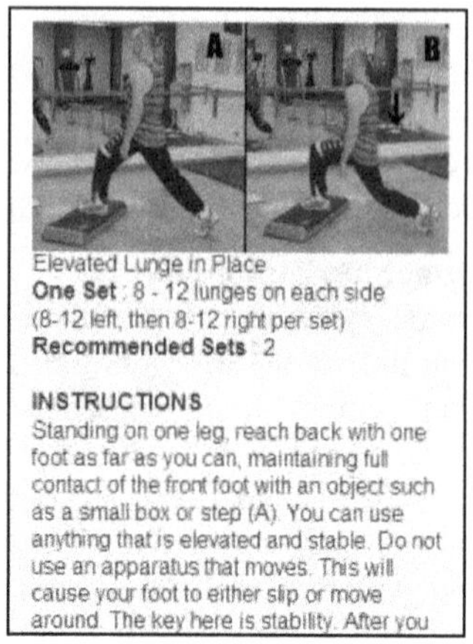

Figure 2. DStress stress reduction exercise. Elevated lunge instructions.

Procedure

We wanted to assess changes in stress level as a result of using DStress. Participants therefore took an online *pre-test* survey to measure baseline stress along with demographics. They then worked with the system for 28 days, after which they took a *post-test* survey with the same scales. Comparing the pre and post surveys allowed us to measure stress reduction. Participants took the surveys a day before their first activity and a day after their last activity. We emphasized the importance of reporting daily progress, regardless of whether participants completed activities, to ensure we had sufficient data to analyze. Next we describe the three coaching dimensions (Exercise, Meditation and Accessibility), which adapted to the individual for the DStress group, followed by the predetermined schedules for the other two groups.

Exercise

We worked with three certified trainers to develop 46 exercises in total. Example exercises include: Wall Pushups, Standing Knee Lifts, Squats, and Burpees. Figure 2 shows the Elevated Lunge exercise with instructions. Each exercise was independently rated for difficulty from 1 to 10 by at least 2 of the trainers (most were rated by all three and trainers were generally consistent in their evaluations). The difficulty ratings for each exercise were averaged and rounded to the nearest whole number to establish clear difficulty levels for scheduling purposes. This yielded exercises ranging in difficulty from 1 to 8.

When Participants logged-in, a link explained: how to warm up with light cardio and stretching; perform exercises with safety and good form; and cool down afterwards. The trainers also iteratively developed detailed instructions for each exercise, which we pre-tested on colleagues with very little exercise experience. Each description prescribed the number of repetitions to be completed (typically 8-12) and the number of times to complete the exercise (typically 2 sets) to standardize the exercises (see Figure 2). Some exercises required equipment usually found in a gym, but we developed equipment-free versions of these for home deployments. Exercises were always scheduled for Mondays, Wednesdays, and Fridays.

Meditation

Meditation days were designed to both reduce stress and allow recuperation to maximize exercise benefits. Meditation days fell in between exercise days (on Tuesdays, Thursdays, and Saturdays) with Sundays being a rest day with nothing scheduled. On Meditation days, participants practiced mindfulness meditation for varying lengths of time. A member of our research team has previous experience as a meditation teacher. He developed simple standard instructions, centered around observing one's thoughts with moment-to-moment awareness, labeling them as "thoughts" without judging them, and attending to breathing when the mind wanders. These instructions were piloted to ensure that participants were clear about what they should do.

Accessibility

We expected that the burden of travelling to the gym would be an important component affecting compliance [24]. So the adaptive version of DStress adjusted the proposed location for each workout based on past performance. To accomplish this, for each exercise that required equipment, a non-equipment version was created that worked the same muscle groups, was rated at the same level of difficulty, and that could be completed wherever was convenient. This gave us both more Accessible and less Accessible versions when creating exercise schedules. Location was not specified for Meditation, since any calm place is acceptable.

We now describe the monthly schedule for the three groups. Two were predetermined (Easy, Difficult) and one was adaptive (DStress).

Easy Condition

The Easy group received exercises that were rated as easy, but slightly increased in difficulty throughout the study. Participants received exercises with difficulty ratings of 1 for the first half of the study, and then those rated 2 for the last half. Their meditation days followed a similar pattern; they were asked to meditate for 5 minutes for the first half of the study, then 10 minutes for the last half. Thus, both exercise and meditation schedules had a slight increase across the study so that activities were easy but still had some variety (to be more realistic as a stress reduction program). Lastly, so that the Accessibility dimension would also be easy in this condition, participants were told that all exercises could be completed anywhere convenient.

Difficult Condition

The Difficult group received exercises that increased in difficulty to be challenging to participants. Since there were 12 exercise days, and 8 difficulty levels rated by the trainers, we chose the difficulty to increase across the 12 days as follows:

Level: 1, 2, 2, 3, 4, 4, 5, 6, 6, 7, 8, 8.

Meditation days increased similarly in 5-minute increments:

Minutes: 5, 10, 10, 15, 20, 20, 20, 25, 30, 30, 35, 40, 40.

Thus, both exercise and meditation increased steeply across the study. As in the Easy condition, both were non-adaptive, i.e. they did not depend on user performance. So that the Accessibility dimension would also be more demanding in this condition, participants were told to complete all exercise activities at the gym.

DStress Condition

The DStress group received exactly the same exercise, meditation, and accessibility schedule as the Difficult group, except that the system adapted to their performance. For example, if an individual successfully completed all three exercises that day, then they would advance to the next level along the same trajectory as the Difficult group. Thus, if a DStress user completed all exercises, did them all at the gym, and completed all meditations, they would progress through the levels at exactly the same rate as the Difficult group. The difference was in how DStress adaptively handled non-completions.

If a user did not complete an exercise or meditation level, they were given an easier level. If they completed this lower level, advanced again to the higher level, and were unable to complete this level a second consecutive time, the system locked onto the lower level indefinitely. This was because we didn't want users continually cycling back and forth to a level that was too difficult. The system therefore attempted to preserve self-efficacy and only presented exercise or meditation at the previous successful level. However, at any point, if the user reported that they did *more* exercise or meditation than was suggested, then the system advanced once again to the higher level to be more motivating. Meditating or exercising beyond what was suggested was taken as an indication that participants had mastered the lower level and were ready to advance.

If a user did not complete a specific exercise, then the next exercise day the system reduced the difficulty of all three exercises in the activity following guidance from our certified trainers. The rationale is that if users struggle with exercises in one area of their body, instead of increasing difficulty in other areas (risking potentially more failure), the system should step back altogether to offer a better chance of strengthening the weak link. For incomplete meditations, the system also stepped down meditation minutes the next meditation day.

For accessibility, our goal for DStress was to provide an adaptation for travel convenience. Initially DStress suggested that participants perform the exercises at the gym. If, however, a DStress user reported not getting to the gym, then the next exercise day the system adapted by providing a workout that could be completed wherever was convenient. If this was completed, as with exercise and meditation difficulty, the system then ramped back up and next proposed a gym workout. A second failure to get to the gym locked the system in non-gym mode until the user reported going to the gym. In this way, DStress adapted

Accessibility based on user performance, to balance self-efficacy and motivation.

Although DStress users generated reports reliably, if they failed to report progress on any day (16% of occasions), there was no information to drive adaptation, so the three dimensions remained unchanged. In contrast the other two groups progressed through the schedule regardless of their reported actions. All three dimensions (Exercise, Meditation, Accessibility) were treated independently so if a user stepped up or down in one dimension, this would not affect the schedules of other dimensions.

Data Collected

Progress reports: We collected daily progress reports from participants, allowing us to assess compliance and difficulty level achieved for each of the three dimensions (Exercise, Meditation and Accessibility).

Stress Measures: Because there is no universal measure for stress, we include DASS, PSS, and CHIPS scales which assess both direct and indirect aspects of stress across different time intervals. *Direct* measures probe participants' perceived stress, whereas *indirect* measures assess related manifestations such as physical symptoms, depression or anxiety. All stress measures were administered at both pre-test and post-test.

- *Perceived Stress Scale (PSS):* 10-item scale assessing perceived stress levels over the past month that provides a *direct* stress measure.
- *Depression, Anxiety, Stress Scale (DASS):* 21-item short version of the original 42-item scale, chosen to reduce survey burden on participants. Measures negative emotional states of depression, anxiety and stress in three independent 7-item sub-scales which are not typically combined. Participants assess emotional states over the past week. The Stress sub-scale *directly* measures stress. The Anxiety and Depression sub-scales are *indirect* measures because they are comorbid with stress [3].
- *Cohen-Hoberman Inventory of Physical Symptoms (CHIPS):* 33-item scale measuring concerns about physical symptoms over the past 2 weeks. Included as an *indirect* measure because stress is often manifested in such symptoms [33].

To exclude possible confounds, at pretest we measured body mass and exercise frequency, and at posttest we measured perceptions of system usability.

- *Body Mass Index (BMI):* Calculated from height and weight and is a measure of a person's body shape (a rough proxy for body fat percentage).
- *Godin Leisure-Time Exercise Questionnaire (GLTEQ):* 4-item scale measuring the frequency of physical activity during one's leisure time.
- *System Usability Scale (SUS):* 10-item scale designed to check whether perceived system usability was interfering with the ability to perform and record daily exercises. We wanted a brief survey, so we selected just two items (questions 1 and 8): "I think I would like to use this system frequently" and "I found the system very cumbersome to use."

These scales all demonstrate good psychometric properties such as discriminant and convergent validity and test-retest reliability in multiple populations.

STUDY HYPOTHESES

We had four research hypotheses (RHs) concerning compliance, difficulty, and stress reduction.

RH1- Superior Outcome with Adaptivity

The DStress group should show the greatest improvements on our direct and indirect stress measures due to higher compliance rates.

RH2- Exercise and Meditation Compliance

DStress' adaptive multi-dimensional approach should induce more exercise and meditation compliance than the other non-adaptive groups.

RH3- Compliance Benefits for Accessibility

Compliance should be greater for exercise activities overall if the location can be adapted to be convenient instead of the gym default. Adapting the location occurs when the user is having difficulty getting to the gym, and should increase self-efficacy, and consequently, compliance.

RH4 - Differences in Difficulty

The Difficult group should complete more difficult levels than DStress, and DStress more than Easy in the Exercise and Meditation dimensions. DStress adapts to failure by presenting easier exercises, reducing average completed difficulty level.

FINDINGS

First we analyze potential confounds to our results. We then present pre- and post-test survey results to determine effects on stress measures, followed by analysis of user-generated reports to examine compliance.

Manipulation Check

We confirmed there were no initial group differences at baseline that could confound our results. There were no baseline group differences in *Age* (p=.73), *Gender* (p=.80), *Body Mass Index* (BMI: p=.71), *Exercise Frequency* (GLTEQ: p=.65), *Perceived Stress* (PSS: p=.82), *Depression (DASS)* (p=.63), *Anxiety (DASS)* (p=.92), *Stress (DASS)* (p=.17), or *Physical Health Symptoms* (CHIPS: p=.32). At post-test there were no group differences in the *System Usability* questions. All three groups were above neutral in their desire to use the system frequently, and below neutral in finding the system cumbersome (except the Easy group which was slightly above neutral).

	Pre Stress	Post Stress	Difference
Easy	17.33	15.08	-2.25
Difficult	17.64	15.00	-2.64
DStress	21.79	12.32	-9.47***

Table 1. DStress reduces stress more than other conditions for DASS. Mean DASS Stress scores and difference scores before and after working with the three system versions. Highest possible score is 42, and lower scores indicate less stress (***p<.001)

Survey Data

Stress Measures

To compare effects of the three system versions on our stress measures, we ran a MANOVA with one between-subjects factor: Condition (Easy, Difficult, DStress) and one within-subjects factor: Time (pre-test, post-test). The dependent variables were the following self-report scales: Perceived Stress Scale (PSS), Depression, Anxiety, and Stress (separate subscales of DASS), and Physical Symptoms (CHIPS). Using Pillai's trace, the main effect for pre-test vs. post-test was significant, V=.33, $F(5,58)$=5.63, p<.001, η_p^2=.33, showing that overall the intervention improved the combined stress measures, for the three groups combined. More interestingly, we also found a significant interaction effect of Time by Condition, V=.29, $F(10, 118)$=1.96, p=.04, η_p^2=.14, with a medium to large effect size. Univariate tests of this interaction indicated that this was caused by the Stress subscale of the DASS ($F(2, 62)$=4.37, p=.02). A simple main effects analysis showed that the DStress group reduced DASS Stress (p<.001), while the Easy group (p=.24) and the Difficult group (p=.11) did not. Table 1 shows the pre-test and post-test means of DASS Stress for each group. However, we did not find evidence that the DStress group improved more on *all* stress measures. Aside from DASS Stress, there were no group interactions for the other scales (PSS: $F(2, 62)$=.36, p=.70, CHIPS: $F(2, 62)$=1.47, p=.24, DASS Depression: $F(2, 62)$=1.92, p=.16, DASS Anxiety: $F(2, 62)$=.72, p=.49).

Progress Report Data

To understand why one direct measure of stress was reduced by DStress but not the Easy and Difficult groups, we analyzed user progress reports to examine compliance. Users reported on their progress 2842 times (84%) out of 3380 possible reports. There were no significant differences between the groups in number of reports generated.

Difficult Group Less Compliant for Exercise and Meditation

Compliance is assessed by program adherence, so both completing and starting an exercise were considered compliant. A person is no less compliant simply because they are not strong enough to finish an exercise. We therefore defined compliance as percentage of *Starts* and *Completes* from the total number of user generated reports (omitting the no-reports which provide no information).

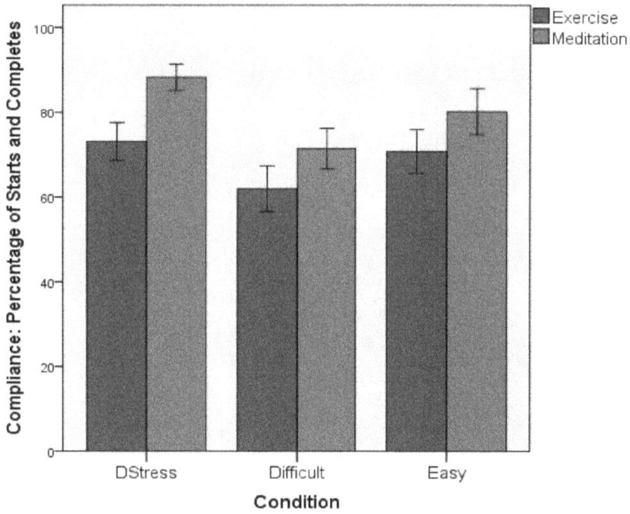

Figure 3. Compliance is greater for DStress and Easy conditions for exercise and meditation. Compliance is represented by percentage of Starts and Completes. Error bars are 1 standard error in all figures.

We carried out a one-way MANOVA to compare the effects of Condition (Easy, Difficult, DStress) on both Exercise and Meditation compliance. Using Pillai's trace, the main effect for Condition was significant, V=.17, $F(4, 124)$=2.96, p=.02, η_p^2=.09, showing group differences in overall compliance. Univariate ANOVAs revealed group differences in both Exercise, $F(2, 62)$=4.66, p=.01, η_p^2=.13 and Meditation dimensions, $F(2, 62)$=5.34, p=.01, η_p^2=.15. Figure 3 shows the compliance percentages of Exercise and Meditation for each group. Using Tukey's HSD, post-hoc tests revealed that for Exercise, the DStress group was significantly more compliant than the Difficult group (p=.02) but not the Easy group (p=.82). The Easy group was trending toward more compliance than the Difficult group (p=.052). Likewise in the Meditation dimension, the DStress group was significantly more compliant than the Difficult (p=.01) but not the Easy group (p=.63), and the Easy was trending toward more compliance than the Difficult group (p=.054). So, for both Exercise and Meditation, the DStress and Easy groups had comparable levels of compliance, while the Difficult group was less compliant than both of them.

Accessibility: DStress More Compliant at Home than at Gym

For each user-generated exercise progress report, we collected data on whether the system proposed gym or non-gym (wherever convenient) exercises. For the DStress group, the system proposed 444 gym exercises (M=23.37, SD=8.58), and 240 non-gym exercises (M=12.63, SD=8.58). Also, we wanted to test our prediction that adapting the exercise location to the individual would improve compliance for the DStress group. We assessed compliance within the DStress group only. We excluded Difficult and Easy groups because for them accessibility was confounded with difficulty levels.

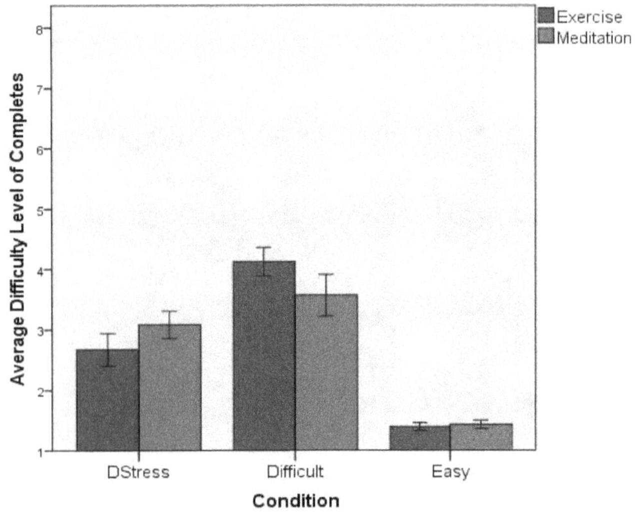

Figure 4. Achievement is greater for Difficult condition. Average difficulty level for exercise and meditation completions by condition. Length of meditation (in minutes) was converted to levels from 1 to 8 for depiction purposes.

We first compared compliance of proposed gym exercises with compliance of proposed non-gym exercises. DStress only proposes a non-gym workout if the user reports exercising at a non-gym location for the prior workout. Thus the system is adapting when proposing non-gym workouts versus the default gym workouts. A paired t-test of compliance percentages for proposed non-gym vs. proposed gym exercises showed differences, $t(16)=3.04$, $p=.01$, $d=.74$ with greater compliance for non-gym proposed exercises ($M=.84$, $SD=.20$) than gym exercises ($M=.69$, $SD=.19$). Higher compliance might represent an advantage of the system learning when a person has entered a busy moment in time (and is unable to make it to the gym). Also, proposing a non-gym workout after previously presenting gym workouts might increase user self-efficacy as the location becomes more convenient. This encouragement might also contribute to compliance. However, these results do not distinguish whether the increased compliance rates for non-gym exercises were generated from the adaptivity of DStress, or whether non-gym exercises in general encourage more compliance than gym exercises due to added convenience.

The Difficult Group Succeeded with Harder Tasks

We examined the effects of difficulty, exploring what difficulty levels participants had completed across the different conditions. For Exercise, a one-way between subjects ANOVA comparing the effects of Condition (Easy, Difficult, DStress) on Level (exercise difficulty) found significant differences in average exercise level completed, $F(2, 62)=40.95$, $p<.001$, $\eta^2=.57$. Post-hoc tests revealed that the Difficult group completed higher levels than DStress ($p<.001$) and Easy groups ($p<.001$). Also DStress completed more difficult exercises than the Easy group ($p<.001$). These differences support our predictions.

A one-way between subjects ANOVA also revealed group differences in Meditation level completed, $F(2, 62)=19.74$, $p<.001$, $\eta^2=.39$. Post-hoc tests show that the Easy group meditated for fewer minutes than both DStress ($p<.001$) and Difficult groups ($p<.001$). However, contrary to our prediction, there were no differences in the Meditation levels completed between DStress and Difficult groups ($p=.43$). It may be that the meditation schedule for the Difficult group became more challenging to participants quicker than the exercise schedule, resulting in lower meditation completions. Alternatively, a difficult exercise goal might be inherently more motivating than a difficult meditation goal that, in a sense, requires "non-doing". Figure 4 shows mean difficulty levels of Exercise and Meditation completed by group. Minutes of meditation was converted to difficulty level (1 to 8) for depiction purposes.

DISCUSSION

Our results are highly encouraging adding to our emerging knowledge about automated coaching systems for well-being, and to our understanding of compliance. A large-scale month-long intervention showed that a system that combines adaptivity on multiple dimensions (Exercise, Meditation, Accessibility) reduces scores on one direct measure of stress by almost 50%. We were also successful in exploring theory led design, teasing apart opposing predictions from behavioral theory, informing the ongoing debate about the role of theory in healthcare systems [11,13,14,20,42]. The study also extends our empirical understanding of how different designs encourage compliance, as well as the importance of achievement on system efficacy.

Easy tasks and adaptivity led to better compliance than difficult tasks. Furthermore, compliance was greater for adaptive non-gym proposed workouts than non-adaptive default gym workouts. But we show that compliance alone does not guarantee stress reduction, as only the adaptive DStress group showed reduced DASS Stress scores. Stress reduction with DStress seemed to result from adaptively balancing compliance *and* achievement. Increasing difficulty irrespective of individual performance may reduce self-efficacy and exceed limitations in ability. In contrast, providing simple tasks may not be as effective at inducing health benefits.

Our exercise program here comprised only resistance training but to support multiple success strategies, future designs might include other forms of exercise including running, swimming, or tennis. Social activities may also be beneficial [26]. Combining different physical activities in cross training might provide benefits consistent with the multiple strategies for success observed here. Similarly, other forms of meditation such as Transcendental Meditation, walking meditation, or guided imagery might provide successful alternatives to those who find mindfulness doesn't suit them. Furthermore, if an activity is started but incomplete, the system might suggest easier activities that can be supplemented that day, to maximize benefit and rapidly support self-efficacy. While DStress provided different strategies for reducing stress (Exercise and Meditation), these activities occurred on predetermined days, whereas offering multiple options on the same day might add another layer of flexibility.

Our adaptive approach was complex to implement, as we defined appropriate sets of exercises with qualified exercise coaches. Future designs might exploit pre-existing graded exercise programs to expedite this step. Another issue with our approach is reporting costs. While reporting was designed to be lightweight, the requirement to do so is an imposition on users. Future work might explore more automated, lightweight ways to record progress. GPS might track whether a participant went to the gym and an accelerometer might sense compliance. Physiological responses might help track exercise and meditation activity levels, suggesting a need for easier or more challenging activities. We might also aim to measure stress levels automatically to allow dynamic monitoring of program efficacy, although we are aware that such measures are currently under development [30,31].

There are limitations to this work. DStress reduced DASS Stress scores while the other system versions did not. However there were also inconsistencies across our scales. Why for instance, did DStress reduce one direct measure of stress (DASS) but not the other (PSS)? One explanation is that our DASS stress finding might have been statistical error. While this result was highly significant ($p<.001$), it is possible that the other non-significant measures were more accurate. An alternative explanation stems from the time scale of the probe question. The PSS probes stress over the past month, while the Stress subscale of the DASS probes it over the past week only. Stress reduction may have been more pronounced in the last week of the study compared to baseline, than over the entire study compared to baseline. Administering stress measures over multiple time points during a future study (or employing physiological sensors) would assess the time scale of benefits to resolve these inconsistencies. Furthermore, PSS measures the degree of stress attributed to situations in one's life, whereas DASS Stress measures psychological tension and irritability. It's also possible that DStress was more effective at reducing appraisals of psychological rather than external sources of stress.

The indirect stress measures such as physical symptoms (CHIPS) and the Depression and Anxiety subscales of DASS, may be less sensitive to exercise and meditation than the direct measures. Alternatively, differences on these other measures may take longer to emerge than the 28-day deployment we explored here.

DStress almost halved DASS stress scores in a month-long field trial setting. But compliance becomes a greater issue over longer periods of time [21]. Longer-term studies with adaptive systems should explore whether DStress promotes longer lasting changes of behavior and stress reduction. In addition, our study provided multiple success strategies, so further research must determine whether exercise, meditation or a combination of both was most effective for stress reduction.

We also need to examine further issues around compliance. Goal-setting theory predicts that the DStress group would be more compliant than the Easy group because they were doing more difficult, motivating exercises while maintaining self-efficacy. We did not find this. It may be that in this context, self-efficacy overshadows the motivations of more challenging exercises. We were also unable to determine whether the increased compliance rates for non-gym exercises in DStress can be attributed to adaptivity or only to the convenience of the location. And since our adaptive components were not manipulated, exercise compliance was simultaneously influenced by both accessibility and task difficulty. Future research may help to tease apart difficulty from accessibility, as well as location convenience from adaptability.

Our results suggest important practical and theoretical directions for computational systems to promote well-being. We designed an automated health system to address multiple facets of compliance, by providing personalization that is driven by theory. By achieving balance between self-efficacy and goal-setting theories, DStress provided an effective coaching strategy for reduced stress.

ACKNOWLEDGMENTS

We wish to thank the certified coaches who helped us generate the exercise content. And thanks too to our participants who were daring enough to try something new. This research was partially supported by NSF grant IIS-1321102 and NSF grant IIS-1346066.

REFERENCES

1. 4 Minute Abs. http://www.4minuteabs.com/
2. Ajzen, I. From intentions to actions: A theory of planned behavior. *Springer Berlin Heidelberg* (1985), 11-39.
3. Antony, M. M., Bieling, P. J., et al. Psychometric properties of the 42-item and 21-item versions of the Depression Anxiety Stress Scales. *Psychol Assess*, *10*,2, (1998). 176-181.
4. Astin, J. A. Stress reduction through mindfulness meditation. *Psychother Psychosom 66*,2 (1997), 97-106.
5. Bandura, A. Self-efficacy: toward a unifying theory of behavioral change. *Psychol Rev*, *84*,2 (1977), 191-215.
6. Bickmore, T. W., Caruso, L., & Clough-Gorr, K. Acceptance and usability of a relational agent interface by urban older adults. *Ext Abstracts CHI'05,* ACM Press (2005), 1212-1215.
7. Bodenheimer, T., Lorig, K., et al. Patient self-management of chronic disease in primary care. *JAMA, 288,*19 (2002), 2469-2475.
8. Bower, J. L., & Christensen, C. M. Disruptive technologies: catching the wave. *Harvard Bus Rev,* (1995), Jan-Feb, 43-53.

9. Brenner, M. H. Mortality and the national economy. *The Lancet 314,*8142 (1979), 568-573.
10. Brusilovsky, P., & Peylo, C. Adaptive and intelligent web-based educational systems. *IJAIED 13*,2 (2003), 159-172.
11. Cole-Lewis, H., & Kershaw, T. Text messaging as a tool for behavior change in disease prevention and management. *Epidemiol Rev*, *32*,1 (2010), 56-69.
12. Consolvo, S., Everitt, K., et al. Design requirements for technologies that encourage physical activity. *Proc CHI'06,* ACM Press (2006), 457-466.
13. Consolvo, S., Klasnja, P., et al. Goal-setting considerations for persuasive technologies that encourage physical activity. *Persuasive'09*, ACM Press (2009), 1-8.
14. Consolvo, S., McDonald, D. W., & Landay, J. A. Theory-driven design strategies for technologies that support behavior change in everyday life. *Proc CHI'09,* ACM Press (2009), 405-414.
15. Cramer, S. R., Nieman, D. C., & Lee, J. W. The effects of moderate exercise training on psychological well-being and mood state in women. *J Psychosom Res 35*,4 (1991), 437-449.
16. Doherty, G., Coyle, D., & Sharry, J. Engagement with online mental health interventions: an exploratory clinical study of a treatment for depression. *Proc CHI'12,* ACM Press (2012), 1421-1430
17. Gasser, R., Brodbeck, D., et al. Persuasiveness of a mobile lifestyle coaching application using social facilitation. *Persuasive'06,* Springer (2006), 27-38.
18. Graham, C., Franses, A., et al. Psychotherapy by computer. *Psychiatr Bull*, *24*,9 (2000), 331-332.
19. Haug, S., Meyer, C., et al. Continuous individual support of smoking cessation using text messaging: a pilot experimental study. *Nicotine Tob Res 11*,8 (2009), 915-923.
20. Hurling, R., Catt, M., et al. Using internet and mobile phone technology to deliver an automated physical activity program. *J Med Internet Res, 9*,2 (2007), e7.
21. Ice, R. Long-term compliance. *Phys Ther 65,*12 (1985), 1832-1839.
22. Insanity. http://www.beachbody.com/
23. Isaacs, E., Konrad, A., et al. Echoes from the past. *Proc CHI'13,* ACM Press (2013), 1071-1080.
24. Kaplan, L. M., & McGuckin, M. Increasing handwashing compliance with more accessible sinks. *Infect Control 7,*8 (1986), 408-410.
25. Kim, S. I., & Kim, H. S. Effectiveness of mobile and internet intervention in patients with obese type 2 diabetes. *Int J Med Inform 77,*6 (2008), 399-404.
26. Klasnja, P., & Pratt, W. Healthcare in the pocket. *J Biomed Inform 45,*1 (2012), 184-198.
27. Lederman, R., Wadley, G., et al. Moderated online social therapy. *TOCHI 21*,1 (2014), 1-26.
28. Lin, J. J., Mamykina, L., et al. Fish'n'Steps: Encouraging physical activity with an interactive computer game. *UbiComp'06*, ACM Press (2006), 261-278.
29. Locke, E. A., & Latham, G. P. Building a practically useful theory of goal setting and task motivation. *Am Psychol 57,*9 (2002), 705-717.
30. Lu, H., Frauendorfer, D., et al. StressSense: Detecting stress in unconstrained acoustic environments using smartphones. *UbiComp'12,* ACM Press (2012), 351-360.
31. MacLean, D., Roseway, A. & Czerwinski, M. MoodWings: A Wearable Biofeedback Device for Real-Time Stress Intervention. *PETRA'13*, ACM Press (2013), 66-73.
32. Matthews, M., & Doherty, G. In the mood: engaging teenagers in psychotherapy using mobile phones. *Proc CHI'11,* ACM Press (2011), 2947-2956.
33. McFarlane, A. C., Atchison, M., et al. (1994). Physical symptoms in post-traumatic stress disorder. *J Psychosom Res*, *38,7* (1994), 715-726.
34. McKee, G. H., Markham, S. E., & Scott, K. D. (1992). Job stress and employee withdrawal from work. In J. C. Quick (Eds.), *Stress & Well-Being At Work.* (pp. 153-163). Washington, D.C.: APA
35. Mento, A. J., Steel, R. P., & Karren, R. J. A meta-analytic study of the effects of goal setting on task performance: 1966–1984. *Organ Behav Hum Decis Process 39,*1 (1987), 52-83.
36. Morris, M., & Guilak, F. Mobile heart health: project highlight. *Pervasive Comput, 8,*2 (2009), 57-61.
37. Morris, M. E., Kathawala, Q., et al. Mobile therapy: case study evaluations of a cell phone application for emotional self-awareness. *J Med Internet Res 12*,2 (2010), e10.
38. O'Leary, A. Stress, emotion, and human immune function. *Psychol Bull 108,*3 (1990), 363-382.
39. Obermayer, J. L., Riley, W. T., et al. College smoking-cessation using cell phone text messaging. *J Am Coll Health 53*,2 (2004), 71-78.
40. President's Council on Fitness, Sports & Nutrition. http://www.fitness.gov/about-pcfsn/our-history/
41. Prochaska, J. O., & DiClemente, C. C. The transtheoretical approach. *Handbook of Psychotherapy Integration, 2* (2005),147-171.
42. Riley, W. T., Rivera, D. E., et al. Health behavior models in the age of mobile interventions: are our theories up to the task? *Transl Behav Med 1*,1 (2011), 53-71.
43. Rosch, P. J. The quandary of job stress compensation. *Health and Stress, 3* (2001), 1-4.
44. Toscos, T., Faber, A., et al. Chick clique. Ext Abstracts *CHI'06,* ACM Press (2006), 1873- 1878.
45. US Surgeon General. http://www.surgeongeneral.gov/
46. Vidyarthi, J., & Riecke, B. E. Interactively mediating experiences of mindfulness meditation. *Int J Hum Comput Stud 72,* 8-9 (2014), 674-688.
47. Waller, R., & Gilbody, S. Barriers to the uptake of computerized cognitive behavioural therapy. *Psychol.Med 39,*5 (2009), 705-712.
48. Walters, D. L., Sarela, A., et al. A mobile phone-based care model for outpatient cardiac rehabilitation. *BMC Cardiovasc Disord 10,*1 (2010), 1-8.

SoberDiary: A Phone-based Support System for Assisting Recovery from Alcohol Dependence

Chuang-Wen You†, Kuo-Cheng Wang‡, Ming-Chyi Huang⊔, Yen-Chang Chen‡, Cheng-Lin Lin*, Po-Shiun Ho‡, Hao-Chuan Wang◇, Polly Huang*, Hao-Hua Chu‡
†Intel-NTU CCC Center, ‡Dept. of Computer Science and Information Engineering, and *Dept. of Electrical Engineering, National Taiwan University, Taipei, Taiwan
⊔Taipei City Psychiatric Center, Taipei City Hospital Songde Branch, Taipei, Taiwan
◇Dept. of Computer Science, National Tsing Hua University, Hsinchu, Taiwan
cwyou@ntu.edu.tw, r01922030@csie.ntu.edu.tw, mch@tpech.gov.tw, b98902090@csie.ntu.edu.tw, {b99901156, b00902097}@ntu.edu.tw, haochuan@cs.nthu.edu.tw, phuang@cc.ee.ntu.edu.tw, hchu@csie.ntu.edu.tw

ABSTRACT
Alcohol dependence is a chronic disorder associated with severe harm in multiple areas, and relapsing is easy, despite treatment. This study proposes SoberDiary, a phone-based support system that enables alcohol-dependent patients to self-monitor and -manage their own alcohol behavior, and remain sober in their daily lives. We tested SoberDiary in a real-life 12-week user study involving 27 clinical patients. The quantitative and qualitative results revealed that SoberDiary helped patients self-monitor and -manage their alcohol-use behavior, and reduced their total alcohol consumption as well as the number of heavy drinking days. Compared with patients who received standard treatment alone, this study demonstrated SoberDiary successfully complemented current alcohol treatment in reducing patients' alcoholic cravings and dropout rate over 3-month study period. Follow-up interviews further revealed the sophisticated use practices and value of SoberDiary.

Author Keywords
Mobile support system; recovery from alcohol dependence.

ACM Classification Keywords
H.4.m. Information Systems Applications: Miscellaneous

INTRODUCTION
Alcohol dependence is a debilitating psychiatric disorder, and is associated with maladaptive and destructive behavior. Characterized by persistent, compulsive, and uncontrolled drinking, it leads to marked impairment, distress, and substantial interpersonal and social problems. Up to 50% of patients treated for alcohol dependence relapse within 2 years following treatment, even after achieving abstinence [12].

CHI 2015, April 18–23, 2015, Seoul, Republic of Korea.

ACM 978-1-4503-3145-6/15/04 ...$15.00.
http://dx.doi.org/10.1145/2702123.2702289

Therefore, developing a rational approach for enhancing relapse prevention is crucial for alcohol-dependent patients who experience cravings or the desire to resume alcohol use once they have achieved abstinence [15]. This study proposes a phone-based support system that helps alcohol-dependent patients stay sober in their daily lives after completing alcohol withdrawal treatment.

Previous researchers have developed self-monitoring techniques [19] and cognitive behavioral therapy (CBT) [19] to engage or motivate patients to self-manage triggers or challenging life events. To self-monitor their drinking behavior, psychiatrists ask patients to keep a drinking diary, so that they can find triggers by reviewing their diary. Because of memory recall errors, patients might easily forget or record the time or amount of alcohol consumption incorrectly. Furthermore, patients are reluctant to invest effort into maintaining a drinking diary. To extend the well-proven treatment of CBT, recent studies [6, 10, 20] have identified cellphones as a platform. However, these systems either have not incorporated breathalyzers to facilitate the self-monitoring of patients' drinking behavior during the study [10, 20], or they did not provide real-time feedback that visualizes patients' progress on their phones [6]. Furthermore, these studies have evaluated the patients' sobriety performance based on telephone-based surveys [10, 20], or excluded alcohol-dependent patients [6]. By contrast, SoberDiary uses a Bluetooth breathalyzer (Figure 1) to assist patients in self-monitoring their drinking behavior by taking breath alcohol tests and providing real-time feedback to their progress, to raise users' awareness of alcohol use. Various support functions are also provided, so that patients can appropriate them to better manage their emotions and become more sensitive to triggers.

This study involved the use of a phone-based support system, SoberDiary, to help alcohol-dependent patients maintain sobriety in their daily lives once they have completed alcohol withdrawal treatment. By carrying a Bluetooth breathalyzer that is wirelessly connected with the SoberDiary application installed on their phones, patients can perform breath alcohol tests to self-monitor their own alcohol use. To motivate behavioral change, SoberDiary also records personal progress and achievements in maintaining sobriety for patients review. SoberDiary also incorporates the principles of the 12-step program [19] to enable patients to learn the concepts associated with each step, thereby promoting self-fulfillment to recognize the values and beliefs of the community and the self. All test results and momentary feedback sampled by the SoberDiary client are used to provide appropriate recommendations for reducing alcohol cravings, and is uploaded to a backend server to enable continuous patient monitoring.

The contributions of this paper are the design, prototype, and evaluation of SoberDiary. A 12-week real-life study involving 27 alcohol-dependent patients using SoberDiary was conducted. The quantitative results revealed that the participants using SoberDiary were able to self-monitor and -manage their alcohol-use behavior, and reduced their total alcohol consumption and the number of heavy drinking days following intervention. The qualitative results, obtained from participant interviews, revealed how patients appropriated SoberDiary in their regular lives to assist them in staying sober. Compared with patients who received the standard treatment alone, this study demonstrated SoberDiary effectively complemented current alcohol maintenance treatment in reducing patients' alcoholic cravings and dropout rate over 3-month study period.

DIFFICULTIES IN STAYING SOBER IN DAILY LIFE

This section provides an explanation on the challenges for alcoholics in maintaining sobriety after completing treatment at hospitals/centers and returning to normal life. First, we define the following terms used in this article:

- A *standard drink* (or *drink*) [11] is a unit of alcohol used to quantify the amount of alcohol intake. In the United States, a drink is 14 g of pure alcohol, approximately equivalent to the amount of alcohol in one regular beer containing 5% alcohol (approximately 340 mL).
- A *lapse* occurs when patients consume any alcoholic beverage containing approximately one drink of pure alcohol.
- A *relapse* occurs when male (female) patients consume more than six (four) drinks per day.

After completing withdrawal treatment, patients need to revisit the hospital regularly to attend follow-up maintenance programs. To monitor their alcohol use in daily life, psychiatrists ask patients to maintain a drinking diary, so that patients can identify triggers by reviewing them. However, patients tend to forget to record drinking behavior easily, or recall the time or amount of alcohol consumption incorrectly, thereby failing to maintain their drinking diary accurately and consistently. Without the drinking diary, psychiatrists can provide only limited recommendations to patients to improve their sobriety outcomes during each revisit.

The lack of a continuing maintenance program further degrades the efficacy of CBT [19], which can highlight triggers and coping strategies for relapse prevention. When patients return to their lives, alcohol cues (e.g., alcohol beverages in convenience stores or alcohol cravings triggered by emotions; for instance, stress might trigger alcohol use). Without continuing care to assist them in learning relapse prevention or alcohol management skills, they are bound to relapse easily when facing cues or craving alcohol. These observations suggest that alcohol treatment professionals cannot rely only current approaches, and a complementary treatment modality to improve the efficacy of relapse prevention is required.

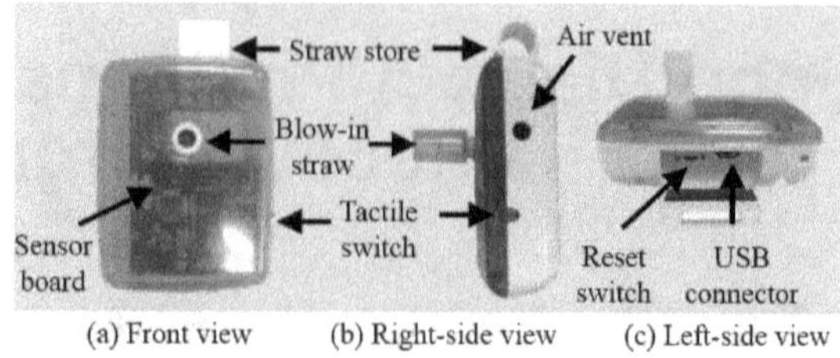

Figure 1: Photos of the Bluetooth breathalyzer.

SOBERDIARY DESIGN

The SoberDiary system contains three components: (1) a portable Bluetooth breathalyzer, (2) a phone application, and (3) a backend server, which are described as follows.

Portable Bluetooth Breathalyzer

Figure 1 shows the front and left and right sides of the breathalyzer, which measures patients' breath alcohol concentration (BrAC). During each breath test, alcohol absorption on the alcohol gas sensor [4] causes the electrical resistivity of the sensor to vary, altering the voltage output of the sensor. According to the voltage-to-BrAC lookup table learned from a calibration process, a BrAC reading is interpolated and returned through a built-in Bluetooth module.

SoberDiary Phone Application

The SoberDiary application provides various supporting functions that (1) enable users to self-manage addictive behavior, (2) suggest proper relapse prevention skills to reduce alcohol cravings, and (3) promote self-fulfillment. Relapse prevention [16] involves complex interactions with lifestyle factors (e.g., lifestyle imbalance or stress), intrapersonal factors (e.g., personal mental or physical status), and interpersonal factors (e.g., social relationships). To develop skills for staying sober, multiple behavioral theories were used to influence patients' behavior from various aspects [19] in this study (i.e., self-efficacy theory [21], CBT [19], and self-determination theory [10]). According to self-efficacy theory [21], self-monitoring increases patient awareness of risky situations and behaviors, enhances patients' self-efficacy and competence, and enables them to build the relationships and skills necessary for relapse prevention and sustaining abstinence. However, self-monitoring can be difficult to maintain without adequate support. Therefore, the SoberDiary application also includes CBT modules enabling cognitive behavioral theories [19] to emphasize triggers and coping strategies for relapse prevention and functional modules based on self-determination theory [10], to internalize the motivation for recovery when patients feel that they are able to maintain recovery (competence), perceive the decision to abstain from alcohol use as resulting from free will (autonomy), and feel support from others in their recovery efforts (relatedness). In the next section, the application is described.

Backend Server

A backend server receives behavioral data uploaded from patients' phones for future analysis and continuous monitoring. To provide information on sobriety outcomes, the server tracks the rankings of peers' achievements in alcohol recovery. To facilitate the management of patients participated in this study, a monitoring web service was used to monitor all data uploaded by patients continuously, and provide researchers and psychiatrists with a daily summary including the details of patients who did not perform adequately.

SOBERDIARY PHONE APPLICATION

The four modules of the SoberDiary application are the (1) user interface, (2) supporting functional module, (3) app use logging, and (4) behavioral data store, as follows.

User Interface

A simple user interface with three full-screen main pages—test, statistical, and self-fulfilling pages—was designed. Patients switch between these pages by using three buttons located at the bottom of the screen. When patients launch the application, they view the test page for self-administering breath alcohol tests. After a test is conducted, a summary appears instantaneously on the statistical page. To facilitate social sharing and learn positive self-fulfilling concepts, patients can switch to the self-fulfilling page. Mood sampling can be initiated by tapping the menu key. The designs for each page are described in the following subsections.

Supporting Functional Module

Four functional blocks—alcohol use detection, progress feedback, a self-fulfilling guide, and mood sampling—are included to assist patients in maintaining abstinence, described as follows.

Alcohol use detection

Continuous patient monitoring [21] was identified as crucial for relapse prevention, and has long been absent from current alcohol treatment. To reduce the effort required to complete the tests allocated daily, we divided a day into three time slots: (1) a morning slot from 0:00 to 12:00, (2) an afternoon slot from 12:00 to 20:00, and (3) an evening slot from 20:00 to 24:00. Patients are required to perform at least one test in each slot to complete the alcohol-screening task and are asked to complete at least two slots per day.

To ensure that a sufficient amount of air from the deep lung accumulates in the sample chamber, a pressure sensor monitors whether patients exhale air into the sample chamber for longer than an empirical threshold (i.e., a 5-s exhalation process in this study). To prevent cheating, patients are asked to perform the test with their face in view of the phone's camera. During the 5-s exhalation process, the application captures three photos of the patient's face. After the test, the final BrAC value is extracted by calculating the median of all samples. Finally, a questionnaire appears, and patients record their momentary emotion and craving indices by responding

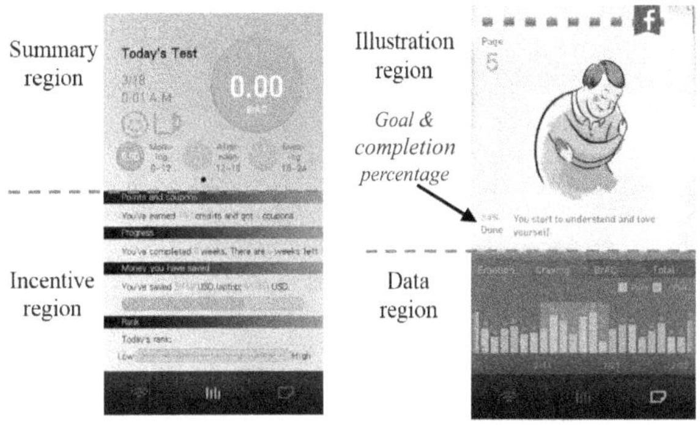

(a) Statistical page (b) Self-fulfilling page

Figure 2: Screenshots of the SoberDiary phone application.

to a visual analogue scale (VAS) on the screen. To encode the indices in numeric values, 10- and 5-point Likert scales are used for their momentary indices, respectively.

Progress feedback

Figure 2(a) shows a screenshot of the statistical page, which visualizes patients' personal progress, and motivates them with achievements and rewards based on contingency management therapy [18]. The top of the statistical page provides a summary, and the bottom lists incentives. The summary region visualizes personal test results to enable patients to review their recent alcohol use on a daily dashboard. The dashboard shows the BrAC value as well as the craving and emotion indices of the latest test, and shows whether patients have stayed sober in the morning, afternoon, and evening slots. Each slot is represented in one of three possible state colorings: (1) the *sober* state, encoded in green, indicating that the patient passed all tests; (2) the *drinking* state, encoded in red-orange, indicating that the patient failed a test; and (3) the *missing* state, encoded in dark gray, indicating that the patient missed a test.

To provide positive feedback to patients, the incentive portion shows the rewards earned and their performance in the recovery process. Based on contingency management therapy [18], a reward is shown to motivate patients to continue using the application (i.e., the number of coupons earned). To encourage competition among participating patients, SoberDiary also showed patients' rankings among all patients according to the average number of credits that all of the patient participants have accumulated since the study began.

Self-fulfilling guide

Figure 2(b) shows the self-fulfilling page, which enables patients to recognize positive self-fulfilling concepts. The self-fulfilling page also consists of two separate parts: the top half displays sobriety goal sentences with drawing illustration, and the bottom half provides visualization of the patient's emotion, craving and drinking behavior. The sobriety goal sentences come from Alcoholics Anonymous (AA), which proposed the principles of the 12-step program [19] to delineate the recovery process from alcohol dependence. This process comprises 12 steps to guide patients in promoting their self-fulfillment and staying sober, as shown in the

(a) Alcohol is the worst enemy. Don't let it master you. Never give up!

(b) You have been eager to step on the road to abstinence for a long time. You are on the way to achieve the goal and getting better and better.

(c) Do not wait for your ship to come in – swim out to it.

(d) You are aware that you are getting better through failure. Treasure each day that you stay sober.

Figure 3: Screenshots of drawings (a)—(d) displayed in the top half of the self-fulfilling page.

subcaptions of Figure 3. The last eight steps were omitted from the figure because of space limitations. To encompass the self-fulfilling aspects of the alcohol recovery process, a self-fulfilling guide is presented in the illustration part, containing 12 pages depicting each step. These 12 steps appear in the order specified according to the 12-step principle, with durations distributed evenly over the alcohol recovery process. When a step begins, the application shows a new page with a colored drawing in the illustration part, along with the goal sentence and a completion percentage for slots in the period of the step shown below the drawing.

The bottom part contains four tabs: the emotion index, the craving index, and the daily BrAC values are plotted as three respective bar charts, and these trends are overlaid aggregately as a line graph in different tabs. By reviewing the self-fulfilling summary, patients can recall relapse prevention skills learned during treatment, and recognize positive self-fulfilling concepts described in the goal sentence. When they observe abrupt behavioral changes in the collected data, they can record their feelings by using voice recordings to remind themselves of the cause of those feelings in the future.

Mood sampling

The mood sampling block samples emotions and triggers to identify participants' negative thoughts based on CBT treatment. Because negative moods (e.g., stress) trigger alcohol cravings, they may cause patients to turn to alcohol for relief. To prevent negative moods, identifying and addressing negative feedback is crucial. Using their smartphones, patients can record triggers of their negative moods when experiencing symptoms of depression and anxiety through an ecological momentary assessment (EMA) [13].

App Use Logging

To analyze how the participants used the SoberDiary application in this study, we designed the app use logging module to record their click/scroll streams with timestamps. All streams are uploaded to the backend server once daily. To calculate the application use time associated with one of the four supporting functions, the monitoring services on the server label each action as belonging to each supporting function, and then aggregate the duration of the individual use of a function in each session to calculate the total use time of a specific function.

Behavioral Data Storage

The behavioral data consist of BrAC values, the testing time, sampled emotions, triggers, and corresponding timestamps. To provide continuous monitoring, the collected behavioral data are sent to the server immediately after patients complete testing, or they are uploaded in a batch when patients launch the application.

SOBERDIARY PROTOTYPE

As shown in Figure 1, we fabricated a plastic case (7 cm $\times$ 5.8 cm $\times$ 2.5 cm) to hold a customized Arduino-compatible sensor board, equipped with a microcontroller [1], a digital pressure sensor [2], a Bluetooth module [3], and an alcohol sensor [4]. The microcontroller samples the ADC voltage output of the pressure and alcohol sensors, to detect when patients blow air into the chamber, and to measure the alcohol concentration in the exhaled air. The sensor board is powered by a lithium-ion battery, which can be recharged approximately every 10 days by using a USB. Three color LEDs are used to inform patients whether the sensor is running (red LED on), low in battery power (yellow LED blinking), or charging (green LED on).

After calibrating the breathalyzers by using a standard alcohol-breath test simulator [5], the resultant accuracy was +/- 0.05 mg/L of breath alcohol within the range of 0 to 0.5 mg/L, and within 10% of the range of 0.5 to 0.75 mg/L. This is a suitable accuracy level for the classification of each patient's BrAC values into three categories. However, to reduce the impact of mouth alcohol [7], the final screening threshold was set at 0.068 mg/L in this study, slightly higher than the original screening threshold of 0.05 mg/L. Three categories were defined: the sober class, representing measured BrAC values lower than 0.068 mg/L; the lapse class, representing measured BrAC values in the range of 0.068 to 0.25 mg/L to detect lapses in alcohol use; and the relapse class, representing measured BrAC values greater than 0.25 mg/L to detect relapses in alcohol use. The SoberDiary application communicates with the Bluetooth breathalyzer through Android Bluetooth APIs. An SQLite database (i.e., the behavioral data storage) is used to store the patients' BrAC test results and momentary feedback locally on the phone. The backend server records the breath alcohol test results, momentary feedback, and application use logs from all patients in a MySQL database hosted on an Apache server.

USER STUDY

We conducted a real-life 12-week user study involving 27 alcohol-dependent patients who tested the SoberDiary system. To demonstrate the feasibility of using SoberDiary to self-monitor patients' alcohol use behavior, this study quantitatively evaluated patients' self-monitoring adherence and measured differences between SoberDiary-detected and TLFB-recalled drinking days. To further explore how well SoberDiary complements current treatment in a real-world setting, we follow the quasi-experimental design to compare

Name	*Intervention* *Avg (Std)*	*Control* *Avg (Std)*
Craving index (9)*	2.9 (2.7)	1.4 (2.0)
# of heavy drinking days (day)	53.1 (35.1)	70.3 (26.4)
Total alcohol consumption (drink)	1239.1 (1524.0)	1406.1 (1061.0)

Table 1: Variables assessed in baseline medical reviews. The maximal values of craving index is indicated by numbers in parentheses. Significant differences of craving index between two groups are indicated by the "*" symbol ($p < .05$).

the data from 27 patients in this study with another data from other 20 participants who only received standard treatment in an ongoing project (i.e., a surrogate measure of sobriety outcome improvement contributed by standard treatment). Finally, this study also qualitatively evaluated how well SoberDiary helped patients self-monitor and -manage their drinking behavior to maintain sobriety.

Participants

We recruited participants through hospital referrals and advertisements. To screen participants, we conducted structured interviews to determine their eligibility according to the inclusion and exclusion criteria. We explained the goal of the study, and asked eligible participants to provide informed consent.

For the intervention group, we recruited 27 participants (i.e., 23 men and 4 women) aged from 31 to 58 years. The average age and standard deviation (std) were 42.7 years and 7.4 years, respectively. Eight participants were unemployed, and the others were engineers, salespeople, or clerks, or were self-employed. All participants were clinical patients who had completing withdrawal treatment and passed a screening test at Taipei City Psychiatric Center (herein referred to as TCPC). To compensate for the cost of revisiting the hospital for follow-up assessments, patients were reimbursed US$6.5 for each revisit. Depending on the frequency and conformity of the requested SoberDiary usage, each patient was also rewarded with a maximum of four restaurant coupons (approximately US$6.5 in value) per week.

For the control group, we leveraged the data from 20 participants (i.e., 20 controls comprising 16 men and 4 women) from another ongoing project from June to September of 2013. All controls collected ground-truth drinking data by using the timeline follow-back (TLFB) method [11]. Similarly, all of the controls were clinical patients who had passed the same inclusion and exclusion criteria as those used to recruit the intervention group. Each control was reimbursed US$6.5 for each revisit. The age distribution of the controls ranged from 28 to 53 years, and the average and std were 42 and 7.44, respectively. The occupations of the control group were similar to those of the intervention group.

Table 1 lists the variables assessed using baseline medical reviews, including the participants' self-assessed craving index, the number of heavy drinking days, and total alcohol consumption, as recalled by the participants over 12 weeks before the study. Based on the responses, the participants exhibited various unique alcohol addiction behaviors. One-tailed t-test results revealed no significant differences between these two groups, except for a significantly higher craving index (p = .01) of the intervention group, indicating that the participants in the intervention group had a higher alcohol craving compared with the control group.

We provided a Bluetooth breathalyzer to each participant in the intervention group, and the breathalyzer was paired with every smartphone. We also installed the SoberDiary application on all smartphones and asked participants to use them as their primary phones during the study.

Procedure

The procedure for the intervention group consisted of three parts: (1) a pre-study medical assessment, (2) a 12-week real-life study with SoberDiary, and (3) post-study interviews.

The purpose of the pre-study medical assessment was to collect the baseline craving index and alcohol consumption and compliance. Recent alcohol consumption and compliance were measured using the TLFB method in the baseline assessment and clinical assessments (described later in this subsection) of follow-up medical reviews, obtained from participants' self-reports. The structured drinking diary recorded the type and amount of alcohol consumed per day in grams of pure alcohol. To teach the intervened patients how to use the phone application and breathalyzer, they all attended a 30-min training session teaching them how to operate the SoberDiary application and the breathalyzer.

During the 12-week real-life study, the intervened patients used the SoberDiary application for recovery from alcohol dependence. To collect ground truth data and address questions related to application use, the intervened patients were required to attend scheduled medical reviews held during Weeks 1, 2, 4, 8, and 12 at the TCPC. Each medical review consisted of a clinical assessment session and a technical support session.

Clinical assessment session: The intervened patients underwent medical care, typically available in hospital-based alcohol treatment services, in Weeks 1, 2, 4, 8, and 12. Intervened patients were asked to complete the questionnaires assessing the craving index in the final medical review in Weeks 4, 8, and 12. When intervened patients lapsed, they were encouraged to resume abstinence.

Technical support session: We asked intervened patients to report any problems related to application use, and tested the breathalyzer's accuracy in Weeks 1, 2, 4, 8, and 12. We provided rewards (i.e., restaurant coupons) to each intervened patient. When they failed to attend the scheduled medical reviews, follow-up telephone calls were made to arrange another appointment. A maximum of three contact attempts were made to ensure the retention of each intervened patient.

For the post-study interviews, we randomly selected 8 participants from the intervention group who completed the 12-week study. For each selected participant, an audio recorder was set up to record a 45-min semi-structured interview that inquired into the intervened patients' daily application use behavior, opinions toward each supporting function of Sober-

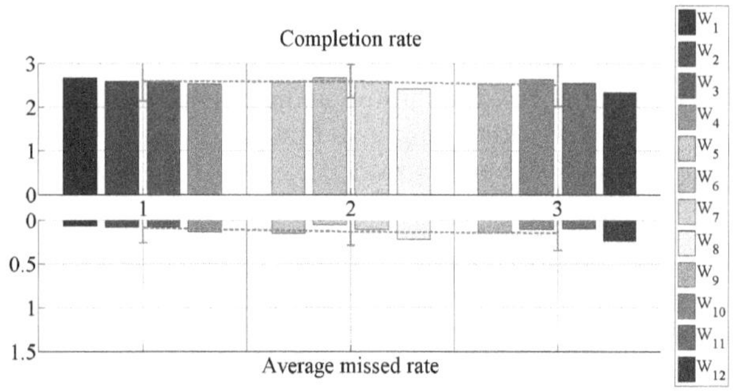

Figure 4: The completion rate (top) and the average missed rate (bottom) from W_1 to W_{12}. The red dotted lines show the trends in three months.

Diary, notable behavioral changes, and influences on social interactions after using SoberDiary. Data saturation [22] was reached after 8 participant interviews in the intervention group (5 men and 3 women, aged 33-58 years with average and std of 48.88 years and 8.36 years, respectively).

For the control group, all controls underwent baseline and follow-up medical reviews (identical to those for the intervened patients) simultaneously, without the SoberDiary intervention. The procedure was identical to that used in the intervention group, except for the absence of the 30-min training sessions at baseline and all technical support sessions in the follow-up reviews.

Quantitative Results

After collecting data from the participants, a quasi-experimental research method was used to determine how the participants' use of SoberDiary affected their drinking behavior. Data from medical reviews and the SoberDiary application were compared for consistency, and used to justify abstinence by observing whether patients using SoberDiary exhibited a lower average drinking amount and fewer average heavy drinking days compared with 20 controls. The drinking behavior monitored using the TLFB method was compared with that monitored using SoberDiary. Statistical methods were used to analyze the application logs and interpret application-use behavior.

The evaluation metrics derived from the variables measured using medical reviews were *total alcohol consumption* and the *number of heavy drinking days* measured both 12 weeks before and in the ith month during the study. By contrast, the evaluation metrics for the ith month derived from SoberDiary-monitored data are as follows. The *completion rate* measured the average daily number of tests (or slots) completed by the participants. The *missed rate* measured the average daily number of tests (or slots) missed by participants, because patients were required to complete at least two tests in two time slots per day. The *application-use time* measured the average time a participant spent using SoberDiary daily.

The statistical methods for analyzing the data are as follows. We used repeated measures ANOVA as the statistical test to check whether or not completion rate, missed rate, and application-use time exhibit significant trends over 3-month period. We used independent samples t-test and paired t-test as the statistical tests to compare the means of measures between two groups and the means of variables between baseline and final assessments on controls or intervened patients, respectively.

Drinking days	M_1 *(84 slots in 28 days)*		M_2 *(84 slots in 28 days)*		M_3 *(84 slots in 28 days)*		*Monthly average*
	Avg	*Std*	*Avg*	*Std*	*Avg*	*Std*	*Avg*
detected	3.22	4.65	3.96	6.41	2.71	5.59	2.90
recalled	2.81	5.23	3.21	6.00	4.90	8.69	3.22
diff	2.41	4.08	2.65	4.74	3.43	5.69	2.44

Table 2: The number of drinking days detected by SoberDiary (i.e., the second row) or recalled using TLFB (i.e., the third row) and the difference between detected and recalled drinking days (i.e., the fourth row) in the ith month. The monthly average (i.e., the last column) of the difference between detected and recalled drinking days is calculated by averaging the absolute values of the difference.

Results of patients' self-monitoring behavior

The top (bottom) graph in Figure 4 shows the participants' average completion rate (average missed rate), which was high (low) at 2.6 (0.12) tests per day, and showed no significant change over the months ($F(2, 68) = .24$, $p = .79$ for completion rate and $F(2, 68) = .72$, $p = .49$ for missed rate). The high completion rate and low missed rate showed that most participants were able to conform to the twice-a-day SoberDiary self-monitoring in their daily life.

Differences between SoberDiary-detected and TLFB-recalled drinking days

To examine whether SoberDiary generated feedback that reflected the participants' drinking days accurately, Table 2 lists the differences between the SoberDiary-detected and TLFB-recalled drinking days. The columns in Table 2 enable a comparison between the number of drinking days detected by SoberDiary and those recalled using the TLFB method at the ith month. Subtracting the number of drinking days recalled using TLFB (i.e., the *recalled* row) from that detected by SoberDiary (i.e., the *detected* row) yields the data for the *diff* row, which is the absolute value of signed difference between SoberDiary-monitored and TLFB-recalled drinking days. The average diff was small (i.e., 2.44 days per month). Several possible explanations for the reporting inconsistencies between the SoberDiary-detected method and the TLFB-recalled method are provided in the following section.

How well SoberDiary complements current maintenance treatment

Total alcohol consumption and the number of heavy drinking days in the intervention group decreased significantly by 94.4%, and 86.5% ($p < .01$ for both two variables), respectively, which were comparable to the reductions of 93.3% and 88.6% of total alcohol consumption and the number of heavy drinking days in the control group ($p < .01$ for both two variables), respectively. Because both groups received the standard maintenance treatment for abstinence, participants in both groups showed significant reductions in total alcohol consumption and the number of heavy drinking days.

After completing treatment, the intervened patients reported fewer cravings, and the craving index significantly decreased by 59.0% (p = .001). By contrast, the craving index for the controls slightly increased by 53.8% (p = .09). The dropout rate in the intervention group was 22% (i.e., 6 of 27 intervened patients), which was nearly significantly lower than 45% (i.e., 9 of 20 controls) of the control group (p = .051). Although both groups showed comparable significant reductions in sobriety outcomes, the intervention group showed lower dropout rate than the control group. In other words, this study shows that SoberDiary successfully complements current maintenance treatment in reducing patients' alcoholic cravings and dropout rate in the 3-month follow-up program. Furthermore, 5 intervened patients expressed that they were very willing to continue using SoberDiary after the 3-month study period.

Application-use behavior

Regarding the daily application-use time for each participant in each week, the average use times were 15.3 min, 16.4 min, and 13.7 min per day in Months 1, 2, and 3, respectively. The application-use time increased moderately in M_2, but decreased slightly in M_3 ($F(2, 68) = .38$, $p = .68$). This indicated that the incentives offered to motivate patients to continue using this application were effective.

Qualitative Findings

Data for the qualitative findings were retrieved from the audio recordings of the semi-structured interviews with 8 intervention participants. We manually transcribed the recorded audio from the intervention-patient interviews, and coded the transcriptions to identify salient themes. We organized the emerging themes and findings as follows.

Self-administered monitoring improved self-efficacy

The participants' beliefs on self-efficacy produced effects in cognitive development, and determined how they behave. We found that participants underwent a process of adopting the self-monitoring function of SoberDiary to identify self-efficacy. All interviewees responded that they were able to complete two test slots in a day, and to fit the test time into their working schedules.

My working hours are not from 9:00 AM to 5:00 PM. Because I am a consultant, I spent more time reading reports after conference calls with my colleagues abroad from 10:00 PM to midnight. Therefore, I often slept late, at 2:00 or 3:00 AM. [...] So, I usually performed the tests before going to the bed early in the morning and after finishing my lunch and dinner. (P17)

Four interviewees commented that requiring tests in two arbitrary time slots in a day (e.g., one early in the morning and one late in the evening) could create a cheating window of opportunity that was sufficiently long for the body to potentially metabolize a certain amount of alcohol, resulting in undetected drinking.

I thought that even completing all three test slots in a day is not enough [to close the cheating gap]. The night slot starts at 8:00 PM, and ends at midnight. There are 12 hours [of a window] until 8:00 AM the next day. So, if I complete a test for the night slot, and immediately start drinking or at midnight, can SoberDiary detect this alcohol use at 8:00 AM the following morning? (P16)

Among these four interviewees, two interviewees reported higher levels of alcohol cravings immediately after completing withdrawal treatment. Specifically, they commented a craving for strong alcoholic drinks such as whiskey. However, they wanted to achieve good results on SoberDiary by attempting to prevent SoberDiary from catching them drinking. This motivated them to gradually learn and exploit this cheating window by drinking at a controlled amount (i.e., they partially relieved their craving and still passed the next SoberDiary test).

When you fail a test, it is just like ... a kid doing something wrong (Uneasy laugh), and being caught by SoberDiary that I drank alcohol again. [...] I thought a good part of SoberDiary for me was to remind me not to drink too much. If I drank too much, I would fail the [morning] test after I woke up. So, I control myself ... I mean only to drink a small amount of alcohol to relieve my cravings. Meanwhile, I can still pass the test tomorrow morning. (P13)

Although the proposed system presented a window of opportunity for participants to cheat, exploiting this window requires that participants be aware and control the amount of alcohol intake, such that sufficient time exists for their body to dissipate the alcohol and pass the next test. The participants commented that they avoided situations where they risked out-of-control drinking.

In the beginning of the study, I might have cheated the system to pass the tests. But later, I felt that it is important to be determined, and that I should not continue cheating the system. So, I gradually controlled my behavior. [...] Now, I think I am more capable of controlling my drinking behavior. For example, I usually attended parties invited by my colleagues before using SoberDiary. Now, I would be more aware of these occasions, which trigger alcohol use, and know how to refuse such invitations. (P34)

Many participants gradually learned how to control their alcohol intake. This increased perceived control over their drinking behavior helped participants improve their personal efficacy to stay sober through the efficacy-activated processes [21].

Coupons and performance ranking encouraged routine application usage, but was ineffective to alter determination

Two incentives to motivate participants' continuous use of SoberDiary were (1) restaurant coupons, and (2) the application showing each participant's ranking in a group. Seven interviewees responded that the reward coupons had an effect on encouraging them to spend more time exploring and using the various application functions.

Sometimes, I did care how many coupons I earned. [...] These coupons were ... mental and material encouragements for myself. I would click through buttons to use different func-

tions. As I clicked the buttons, I might have accumulated more coupons. This is just like self-encouragement. (P5)

In addition, SoberDiary generated competition among patients [19] by ranking each participant's performance in a group. All of the interviewees responded that they cared for their standing, because they did not want to finish with a low rank, suggesting a poor sobriety outcome.

I wanted to maintain the above-middle ranking. [Ranking] served as a reminder to me. For example, this was like when I took exams (in class). If I was ranked 10th on this exam and dropped to the 30th on the next exam, it made me realize that ... I should work harder. (P34)

The findings revealed that both restaurant coupons and performance ranking motivated participants' continuous and routine use of SoberDiary. However, routine usage did not help strengthen participants' determination or competence in staying sober, which is the essential construct of self-determination theory [10]. Six interviewees shared similar thoughts, as shown in the following:

I didn't think the ranking information made me more determined to keep up with sobriety. Keeping up with sobriety is more about self-regulating drinking behavior. I cared about my ranking because I felt ashamed to lose to other participants. (P13)

Experience reflection and goal setting enhanced determination

Most participants suggested that coupon rewards and performance ranking were not sufficiently strong incentives to affect their determination to stay sober. Instead, the participants found the application's self-filling guide to be more effective in strengthening determination compared with the coupons and ranking system. Six interviewees provided a similar response.

The goal sentence [in the application's self-fulfilling guide] for each week gave me a weekly target. It informed me which stage I was currently on. Because I might not know what should be achieved in these 12 weeks. The only thing I knew was that I wanted to maintain sobriety, but didn't know how long I should take to achieve these goals. [...] I thought this [stepwise] self-fulfilling guide, other than suggestions from psychiatrists or clinical psychologists, is an information source for understanding how well you performed. (P17)

The weekly goal sentences in the self-fulfilling guide were designed to appear repeatedly as a part of the routine SoberDiary usage. They reminded participants of the course of action they could conduct for alcohol recovery. The weekly goal sentences provided them with positive behavior principles, and enhanced their determination to fight the cravings. Four interviewees responded that the scenarios in these goal sentences were connected to their past experiences of struggling with alcohol.

Some sentences made me realize that I have been through the same scenarios before. I thought my job was good, but why couldn't I do or keep my job properly? Because of alcohol use, I could not show up regularly for work. Then, my boss became less willing to interact with me. These events occurred again and again. Finally, I quit my job. (P18)

Because these goal sentences touched on their experiences, many participants commented that they remembered these goal sentences so well that these goal sentences helped them engage in more self-reflection on events in their daily life.

I remembered some sentences or ... keywords in sentences. It's easy to relate my experiences to these sentences. These sentences described... to be determined to maintain sobriety. And another one was ... your health conditions or life would be better if you continue to stay sober, and so on. [...] Furthermore, one day, when I watched a movie, I was deeply impressed by a line in the movie "Respect yourself" (i.e., the principle behind the goal sentences of Week 7). Once you decide to participate in this study to maintain sobriety, you should respect yourself. That is, I am doing this not for others, but for myself. This is about self-discipline, not about doing it for someone else. (P34)

Frequent self-reflection helped participants raise their self-determination and self-discipline to better handle cravings.

During the third week, I remembered that something had happened suddenly. That thing ... made me unable to focus on staying sober. I can't remember what happened. But I read the sentence on the third page of the self-fulfilling guide, and realized that ... it was my own responsibility to solve this problem. I should be actively accountable for solving this, not counting on other people's help. (P16)

Present SoberDiary results as a way to communicate with family members

For most participants, their uncontrollable and repeated abuse of alcohol in the past had seriously harmed their family relationships. Even after medical treatment, their family members still remained skeptical and suspicious regarding the truthfulness of their words, and that they had stopped drinking. Two interviewees expressed sadness that their words had lost their family's trust completely.

In place of their words, many participants presented the breathalyzer's results and our coupon rewards as a way to communicate with their family members that they were expending effort and progressing toward sobriety.

I think those rewards (i.e., coupons) are an extra for me. The most crucial point for me was that SoberDiary proved that I didn't drink alcohol. First, I proved to my family that ... after wasting 20 years on drinking alcohol ... with the help of [my psychiatrist], I provided proof that I really did not drink anymore. (P18)

After using SoberDiary, I felt that I had more interactions with my parents. Actually, I felt that they would be even happier that I performed the tests in their presence. It seemed that I was actively proving that I don't drink alcohol. (P08)

Because the family members felt greater confidence because of the application and the breathalyzer results compared with the participants' words, two participants responded that

SoberDiary had helped them reestablish trust and improve family communication.

DISCUSSION

One interesting observation is that the requirement for participants to engage in self-administered alcohol screening and monitoring appears to produce positive influence on their drinking behaviors and attitudes in more than one way. Some of the ways that SoberDiary produces impacts are not fully calculated or intended at the design stage.

Consideration of Alcohol-Screening Frequency

There are several ways to cheat the SoberDiary system. For example, patients may purchase another breathalyzer for pretesting, whereby they would not use the SoberDiary breathalyzer until they had passed the pretest by using the pretest breathalyzer. Increasing the frequency of alcohol screening from twice to three or four times daily may rectify such issues. However, remembering and performing additional tests would necessitate additional effort, and place a greater burden on users. The goal and purpose of SoberDiary is not to burden patients with frequent breath tests, but to raise their awareness of their alcohol-use behavior, which is evidenced in the interviewee responses. Increasing awareness is believed to be a relatively apparent mechanism how SoberDiary influences the patients.

Constructive Cheating

What's less apparent yet noteworthy is that allowing people to cheat may still be constructive and can be useful to transforming their attitudes and behaviors toward reducing alcohol consumption. On the one hand, cheating certainly discredited the results of SoberDiary. However, our interviews revealed the other side of cheating. Cheating suggested that participants cared and were actively engaged in SoberDiary. It is a signal that they wanted to do well, such as having a good standing in their group and presenting positive results to family members, even when they lacked full capability to control their drinking behavior.

By keeping participants engaged in SoberDiary, they will have more opportunities to learn how to control their drinking behavior, as suggested in this study. For the higher level goal of design, some space or flexibility for participants' constructive cheating may help control the drop-out rate. High dropout rate is certainly not a desirable outcome for this sort of system. While it is important in the design of behavior modification applications to ensure the accountability of logged behaviors, we believe that there exists a design space on how to leverage the positive aspect of cheating toward the benefit of the participants by keeping them engaged.

Alternative Stakeholders to Manage SoberDiary in the Process of Alcohol Treatment

In this study, the SoberDiary system was managed by researchers from National Taiwan University and National Tsing Hua University, who closely collaborated with psychiatrists from TCPC. Because participants trusted medical specialties of psychiatrists (i.e., medical specialists), they tended to respect feedback or recommendations made by the SoberDiary system. Furthermore, patients who have established long-term psychiatrist-patient relationships felt responsible for maintaining sober to adhere to expectations from psychiatrists. For example, P13 expressed *"If I drank alcohol and failed a test, I felt sorry to [the psychiatrist]"*. Therefore, to integrate the SoberDiary system into future alcohol withdrawal treatment, finding reputable institutes/organizations to manage the SoberDiary system should be crucial for properly transferring SoberDiary to a supervising representative of psychiatrists. Future studies are required to explore ways to collaborate medical institutes/organizations with psychiatrists to manage the SoberDiary system and evaluate impacts on the efficacy of patients' sobriety outcomes.

Reasons Causing Inconsistencies between System-Detected and Human-Recalled Sobriety Outcomes

In this study, SoberDiary-detected drinking days were compared with TLFB-recalled drinking days to measure the accuracy of sobriety outcomes with SoberDiary use. The reasons attributed to inconsistencies between these two data sets are as follows: (1) Participants made memory recall errors, leading to over-reporting or under-reporting lapses/relapses in each revisit. For example, patients tended grossly exaggerated the number of drinking days as the time between two successive hospital revisits increased to 1 month; and (2) breathalyzers might be subject to a false or missed detection because of the slow recovery of the sensor, the morning breath problem (i.e., residual mouth alcohol not yet metabolized), or substances (e.g., certain cold medicines) containing alcohol. Based on interviewee feedback, they may eat foods or take nighttime cold medicines containing alcohol, which would influence the screening outcomes.

Difficulties in conducting randomized controlled trials

Randomized controlled trials (RCTs) are the gold standard for demonstrating the efficacy of medical interventions. However, we faced difficulties in recruiting clinical patients for the control group because they expressed strong desires to be in the intervention group during the screening phase. When clinical patients found out that they were in the control group (not using the SoberDiary application), they tended to refuse to participate. As a results, this study was based on the quasi-experiment design to explore how well SoberDiary helped patients self-monitor and -manage their drinking behavior to maintain sobriety and complemented with deeper qualitative interviews to draw useful results and valuable insights. In our next study with a different setup, we are accumulating the number of controls and will be able to use the randomized controlled trial to further validate the efficacy of SoberDiary.

RELATED WORK

Previous research on designing technology-based intervention applications for managing recovery from substance dependence has addressed habitual smoking [14], alcohol abuse [6, 10, 20], and drug use [17]. To prolong participation in continuing care for adults who drink frequently or alcohol-dependent patients, researchers have devised technology-based services [6, 10, 20] to explore how technology can help patients maintain abstinence. However, these systems have either evaluated patients' sobriety outcomes based on inaccurate long-term recall data collected through telephone surveys every 4 months [10, 20], or they excluded alcohol-dependent patients from the study [6]. By contrast, SoberDiary provides a Bluetooth breathalyzer and various supporting functions for patients to self-monitor their alcohol use.

Numerous health-related phone sensing projects have been conducted to facilitate health data collection or enhance the health of users through persuasion, such as Playful Bottle [8], which encourages office workers to drink healthy quantities of water, and the UbiFit Garden system [9], which promotes physical activity by using on-body sensing and personal displays on phones, Based on the design concepts learned from these related studies, we devised SoberDiary to incorporate the various concepts of persuasive feedback, to motivate alcohol-dependent patients to stay sober. Furthermore, this study evaluated SoberDiary by recruiting clinical patients, and we undertook the difficult task of facilitating self-monitoring and -managing behavior.

CONCLUSION

This study presented a novel phone-based support system that enables alcohol-dependent patients to self-monitor and -manage their alcohol use after alcohol withdrawal treatment. The results of this 12-week user study with 27 clinical alcohol-dependent patients revealed that patients using SoberDiary reduced their total alcohol consumption and the number of heavy drinking days. The themes identified in a qualitative study showed how patients appropriated SoberDiary in their regular lives to assist them to stay sober. Compared with patients who received standard treatment alone, this study demonstrated SoberDiary effectively complemented current alcohol maintenance treatment in reducing patients' alcoholic cravings and dropout rate over 3-month study period.

REFERENCES

1. Atmel 8-bit AVR RISC-based microcontroller. `http://www.atmel.com/devices/atmega328.aspx`.
2. Bosch BMP085 Digital Barometer. `https://www.sparkfun.com/products/11282`.
3. EGBT-045MS Bluetooth Module. `http://www.e-gizmo.com/KIT/egbt-04.htm`.
4. MR 513 type alcohol sensor. `http://www.futurlec.com/Alcohol_Sensor2.shtml`.
5. Guth Model 2100, Alcohol Breath Test Simulator. `http://www.guthlabs.com/product.asp?item_id=184`.
6. Alessi, S.M., Petry, N.M. A Randomized Study of Cell-phone Technology to Reinforce Alcohol Abstinence in the Natural Environment. *Addict. 108*, 5 (2013), 900-909.
7. Caddy, G.R., Sobell, M.B., and Sobell, L.C. Alcohol Breath Tests: Criterion Times for Avoiding Contamination by "Mouth Alcohol". newblock *Behavior Research Methods & Instrumentation 10*, 6 (1978), 814818.
8. Chiu, M.-C., Chang, S.-P., Chang, Y.-C., et al. Playful Bottle: A Mobile Social Persuasion System to Motivate Healthy Water Intake. In *Proc. UbiComp 2009*, ACM Press (2009), 185-194.
9. Consolvo, S., McDonald, D.W., Toscos, T., et al. Activity Sensing in the Wild: A Field Trial of UbiFit Garden. In *Proc. CHI 2008*, ACM Press (2008), 1797-1806.
10. Gustafson, D.H., Shaw, B.R., Isham, A., et al. Explicating an Evidence-based, Theoretically Informed, Mobile Technology-based System to Improve Outcomes for People in Recovery for Alcohol Dependence. *Subst Use Misuse 46*, 1 (2011), 96-111.
11. Litten, R.Z., and Allen J.P. (Eds). *Measuring Alcohol Consumption: Psychosocial and Biochemical Methods.* Humana Press, 1992.
12. McKay, J.R., Franklin, T.R., Patapis, N., et al. Conceptual, Methodological, and Analytical Issues in the Study of Relapse. *Clin Psychol Rev 26*, 2 (2006), 109-127.
13. Moskowitz, D.S, and Young, S.N. Ecological Momentary Assessment: What It Is and Why It Is a Method of the Future in Clinical Psychopharmacology. *J Psychiatry Neurosci 31*, 1 (2006), 13-20.
14. Obermayer, J.L., Riley, W.T., Asif, O., et al. College Smoking-cessation using Cell Phone Text Messaging. *J Am Coll Health 53*, 2 (2004), 71-78.
15. Petrakis, I.L. A Rational Approach to the Pharmacotherapy of Alcohol Dependence. *J Clin Psychopharmacol 26*, (2006), Suppl 1:S3-S12.
16. Donovan, D.M., and Marlatt, G.A. *Relapse Prevention: Maintenance Strategies in the Treatment of Addictive Behaviors (Second Edition).* The Guilford Press, 2007
17. Natarajan, A., Parate, A., Gaiser, E., et al. Detecting Cocaine Use with Wearable Electrocardiogram Sensors. In *Proc. UbiComp 2013*, ACM Press (2013), 123-132.
18. Higgins, S.T., and Petry, N.M. Contingency Management: Incentives for Sobriety. *Alcohol Res Health 23*, 2 (1999), 122-127.
19. Volkow, N.D. *Principles of Drug Addiction Treatment: A Research-Based Guide (2nd Ed.).* DIANE Publishing Company, 2011.
20. Gustafson, D.H., McTavish, F.M., Chih, M.A., et al. Smartphone Application to Support Recovery from Alcoholism: A Randomized Clinical Trial. *JAMA Psychiatry 71*, 5 (2014), 566-572
21. Bandura, A. Self-efficacy. In *Encyclopedia of human behavior Vol. 4.* Academic Press (1994), 71-81.
22. Corbin, J., and Strauss, A. *Basics of Qualitative Research: Techniques and Procedures for Developing Grounded Theory 3e.* SAGE Publications, 2008.

Solutionism, the Game: Design Fictions for Positive Aging

Mark Blythe, Jamie Steane
Northumbria University
Newcastle, UK
mark.blythe / jamie.steane
@northumbria.ac.uk

Jenny Roe
Stockholm Environment Institute
University of York,
York, UK
jenny.roe@york.ac.uk

Caroline Oliver
COMPAS
University of Oxford
Oxford, UK
caroline.oliver@compas.ox.ac.uk

ABSTRACT

This paper reports a qualitative study of thriving older people and illustrates the findings with design fiction. Design research has been criticized as "solutionist" i.e. solving problems that don't exist or providing "quick fixes" for complex social, political and environmental problems. We respond to this critique by presenting a "solutionist" board game used to generate design concepts. Players are given data cards and technology dice, they move around the board by pitching concepts that would support positive aging. We argue that framing concept design as a solutionist game explicitly foregrounds play, irony and the limitations of technological intervention. Three of the game concepts are presented as design fictions in the form of advertisements for products and services that do not exist. The paper argues that design fiction can help create a space for design beyond solutionism.

Author Keywords
Design fiction, well being, older people.

ACM Classification Keywords
H.5.m. Information interfaces and presentation

DESIGN FICTION

The speed of technology development is now such that directors like Terry Gilliam feel that their science fiction films are already dated by the time they come out [20]. It feels as if we are "living in the future" (ibid) and it is perhaps for this reason that there is so much interest around Design Fiction [e.g 29, 43, 7, 26, 24, 13, 2]. But there are many questions as to the value of design fiction and speculative design. Although Dunne and Raby insist that their critical and speculative designs are not art, Bardzell and Bardzell [2] point out that if there is a difference it is not evident in the designs themselves but rather in the surrounding discourse. However there are also similarities in the discourse around art and speculative design. An analysis of fifteen years worth of art gallery press releases by Rule and Levine identified a distinctive argot they characterize as International Art English where "an artist's work inevitably interrogates, questions, encodes, transforms, subverts, imbricates, displaces" [35]. Similarly speculative design according to Dunne and Raby's latest book seeks to question, challenge, provoke, expose, explore, trouble, disturb and disrupt [13]. The evaluations in Dunne and Raby's speculative design are presented in terms of refined taste, the examples cited are either "close" or distant to their "interests". Timothy Archibald's Sex Machines for instance, are praised but the authors note "it is a shame the machines are so phallic and so mechanical" [13, p. 162] the criteria for approval or legitimacy then is that expert practitioners such as themselves do or do not like it. Much as early literary critics constructed canons of the best that has been thought and said Dunne and Raby in this book are the arbiters of what is provocative and what is cliché.

CHI 2015, April 18–23, 2015, Seoul, Republic of Korea.
Copyright 2015 © ACM 978-1-4503-3145-6/15/04...$15.00.
http://dx.doi.org/10.1145/2702123.2702491

Bardzell et al propose a range of interpretive strategies for close readings of critical and speculative designs [3]. But there is little agreement about how to evaluate design fiction and definitions of what design fiction is are still forming. The first use of the term appears in science fiction writer Bruce Sterling's 2005 book *Shaping Things* where he remarks that he has been "making design fiction for years", going on to define it in terms of plausibility: "the core distinction is that design fiction makes more sense on the page than science fiction" [38.p30]. Julian Bleecker developed the notion of a diegetic prototype where a design is understood in the context of a story [1]. Wakkary and colleagues propose design fiction as a "material reflection" where scenarios, sketches and illustration are "materials of thought for design" [47]. Sterling most recently defined it "as the deliberate use of diegetic prototypes to suspend disbelief about change." [40]. This places an emphasis on artifacts that belong to imagined worlds, examples include the steampunk artifacts discussed by Tanenbaum et al [43].

Design fiction is a still evolving form but the various definitions agree that it allows for a greater emphasis on social and political contexts than traditional concept design or scenario development. This paper employs design fiction to mitigate against the tendency towards what Morozov has called "solutionism" in HCI. Solutionism has been characterized as solving problems that don't exist or proposing technological quick fixes for complex social, political and environmental problems [31]. Design fictions have been used previously as a means of responding to solutionism through "imaginary abstracts" which frame concept designs in fictional academic studies to consider whether actually building prototypes would answer any research questions or not [7]. This paper reports findings from a study of thriving older people and approaches the findings through a "solutionist game". The game was devised to generate design concepts in response to data while stressing that there is no technological "silver bullet" for any of the issues addressed. The final section presents research based design fictions in the form of advertisements for products and services that do not exist.

FLOURISHING EIGHTY AND NINETY YEAR OLDS

For the first time in human history the old are beginning to outnumber the young and in the UK there are now more people over sixty than under eighteen [1]. A sixty five year old today can look forward to around twenty more years of life (ibid). The oldest "baby boomers" (those born between 1946 and 1964) have already begun to retire and the youngest are in their fifties so this generation can anticipate a longer retirement than any other. This is often treated as a crisis but the starting point for this project was not needs or problem centered. Over the past twenty years there has been a remarkable shift of focus in the field of Psychology. Many academics and practitioners have begun to study not mental illness but mental health. This kind of focus on positive affect and emotion is relatively new.

Perhaps the most familiar concept in Human Computer Interaction (HCI) from this emerging field is Csikszentmihalyi's "flow". This state of intense absorption and the conditions in which it occur have been cited in many studies. But Csikszentmihalyi also studied creativity and motivation and this work has informed more general theories of wellbeing and happiness. In 2002 Martin Seligman became the President of the American Psychological Association and pointed out that psychologists had been studying psychosis, neuroses, depression and other forms of anguish for over a hundred years with little success in developing treatments. He argued that the field should focus attention on people who were thriving and happy and see what could be learned from them. Seligman called this approach "positive psychology". This is perhaps an unfortunate term as it connotes "positive thinking" and snake oil salesman. There are a great many scams which suggest that thinking positive thoughts will result in good things happening: if we believe we are going to be successful then we will be, if we imagine ourselves owning some fabulous object then somehow the universe will deliver it to our door. This kind of "positive thinking" is nothing whatever to do with positive psychology, nevertheless there is much skepticism around the new approach. Psychologists like Czikszentmihalyi, Gottman and Seligman have all written popular self help books that can arouse the suspicion of academics. Findings on the benefits of optimism have been caricatured as "cheer up and you'll be happier" and Seligman has been attacked in journalistic polemics that argue positive thinking is ruining America [15]. So it must be stressed that positive psychology is not positive thinking, A range of empirical studies have been undertaken over the last decade which have deepened our understanding of well being [36,37]. Researchers in HCI are increasingly applying these theories of well being in their work [e.g. 44, 30].

Seligman's P.E.R.M.A. theory provides an overarching framework which summarizes current understandings of well being as constituting more than just happiness [37]. The PERMA acronym breaks down like this: P, is for positive affect such as optimism; E, is for engagement in Csikszentmihalyi's sense of flow; R is for relationships, Seligman often challenges audiences to think of the last time they were happy, suggesting that they probably were not alone; M is for meaning, this is something larger than oneself, it might be a faith tradition, a political cause or the march of science; and finally A is for achievement and mastery [37]. Seligman advocates PERMA as a model for flourishing and thriving. Our study follows the broad approach of positive psychology in studying older people who are not lonely or depressed but rather flourishing.

This study then is in the vanguard of work which overturns the notion of old age as pathology. Definitions of successful ageing have been articulated to include: physical health and independent functioning, life expectancy, mental and psychological health and cognitive function, as well as a variety of psycho-social factors to capture life satisfaction and wellbeing, including psychological characteristics, resources and social networks [2, 6]. The study extends work on the psychosocial aspects of successful ageing, adding to lay perspectives [33] by learning from self-identifying 'flourishing' older people.

THE STUDY

We recruited fourteen people over eighty who self identified as being happy e.g. *"Yes, I'm a happy soul."* (Roger) . We used a combination of targeted sampling and snowballing techniques [32] in order to recruit thriving individuals. Following the insight that strong relationships are important to wellbeing [37] we specifically targeted institutions where strong communities might be expected - a home for retired actors, a nunnery and a Jewish care home. Within specific care home contexts, we began by interviewing managers and asking them to identify thriving residents. The manager and staff of the Jewish care home immediately identified Theo. "*Oh, Theo is brilliant.* [...] *he strides out down the corridor, a big grin on his face saying hello to absolutely anybody and everybody, passing the time of day.* (Manager). In this way we recruited from a range of residencies including: independent home owners, residents of care homes, a nunnery and visitors to a day care centre. There was a mix of backgrounds in terms of both ethnicity, gender, religious and socio-economic group. This then was a deliberately unrepresentative, targeted sample [34] of diverse but thriving individuals.

Location	Participants and Ages
Private Residences	Vera (91 and Eric 89); Doris (89) Bill (80) Stephen (96) Elizabeth (84) Lillian (96)
Home for Retired Actors	Annabel and Phyllida (Manager and Trustee) Mildred (93) Howard (79) Roger (87)
Enclosed Nunnery	Extern Nun and Mother Abbess (interviewed) 6 resident nuns aged (59-104)
Jewish Care Home	Manager, 2 staff (interviewed) and Theo (93)
Day Care Centre	Alvita (86), Jacinta (93), Rosi (89)

Table 1: Location of Interviews, Participants and ages

We conducted in-depth interviews lasting between one and two and a half hours. The interview was semi structured and questions attempted to elicit "a day in a life" and also "a life in a day" focusing on the participants biography. Questions began with daily, weekly and yearly routines and then worked backwards through the decades to the participants' earliest memories.

The data analysis was conducted within the broad tradition of grounded theory. The two most common forms of qualitative data analysis in social science are content analysis and grounded theory [34]. In a content analysis data are sorted into categories drawn from existing theory, for example it would have been possible to sort the data into the PERMA categories. Grounded Theory approaches rather generate categories by summarizing data, grouping those summary categories and attempting to identify connections, There is much confusion in HCI about grounded theory [16] and naïve reviewers sometimes declare that an approach is or is not an application of it although there is no single agreed method. Following the publication of *The Discovery of Grounded Theory* [21] there was an academic spat between its authors - Glaser and Strauss - that resulted in two camps [45]. Strauss with Corbin proposed a prescriptive set of coding procedures involving open, axial and selective coding [40]. They also allowed for the use of existing theory and literature as "sensitizing concepts". Glaser was less prescriptive about coding but insisted that no other theory should be consulted [45]. But social scientists recognize a range of approaches under the broad umbrella term of grounded theory [9]. Another aspect of the approach which may cause misunderstanding in HCI is the word "theory". The "theory" generated by this approach is seldom if ever a predictive model, it is rather a rich description of phenomena [9]. The data here were analyzed using a grounded theory approach with Seligman's work included as sensitizing concepts – things to look out for.

FINDINGS: POSITIVE AGING

All interviews were transcribed and coded into the following "axial codes" or broad themes – attitudes, ties, challenges, agency, little worlds. All italicized quotes are from audio transcriptions of interviews. All names have been changed in order to preserve anonymity.

Attitudes: Tradition, Values, Standards, and Work

Each of the participants conveyed a strong "attitude" in the sense of a broad orientation to life. This was most obvious with the nuns whose orientation to the world was a matter of religious faith. The Actors were also very serious about their vocation, taking acting so seriously it was not possible to provide amateur dramatics *"if you did that here, they would be crucified!"* (Phyllida). Amongst the participants who lived alone there was also strong attitudes based on tradition and continuity. Doris, a widowed working class woman living in her own terraced home, ran the Darby and Joan club as her Mother had done till she died at the age of 86. Doris's sister, Vera also felt her Mother's values and lasting influence, saying she would *"do for anybody"*. For many of the participants, voluntary work was very important. Vera did voluntary work for a York Cancer charity until ill health prevented such a regular time commitment. Elizabeth volunteered her time and skill in knitting and sewing for friends and neighbours. Doris annually baked over fifty Christmas cakes for various friends and charities. Bill, a retired builder, had renovated, with a retired joiner, the working man's club they belonged to. There were then strong attitudes and values throughout the cohort.

When Howard first arrived at the actor's home he had been "self neglecting" - neither washing nor looking after his own basic needs. The manager of the Actors Home pointed out that it was the other residents who helped him recover from this decline by saying. *'You know, you can't come downstairs in your jamas and your boxer shorts, we have a code of dress in this house"*(Annabel). Howard had transferred from another care home which he described as "*a prison*", the improvement in health and appearance was immediate and marked on joining the Actor's home. Eric had early onset dementia but his wife Vera was also determined that standards of dress would not slip telling him he couldn't go out "*in those trousers and that jumper*". Standards were shared and important across the groups.

Many of the participants were fastidious about housework and undertook it with a sense of the values instilled in childhood. Alvita washed her curtains with the same regularity her grandmother had. Many of the participants upheld what might be described as a rigorous work ethic. The nuns' schedule involved punishingly early starts and days where every hour was accounted for. Though Bill was in his eighties he did odd jobs for his friends and neighbors such as cutting their lawns. These acts reflected a philosophy of life, evident in this reflection on what happened to a friend of his who used to help him with jobs at the weekend: *"he was a very fit bloke, but once he moved that was it, he just deteriorated and within a very short time he was in a nursing home.* [...] *he just deteriorated because he didn't do anything* (Bill). There is an almost causal relationship in Bill's narrative between stopping work and decline. But this work ethic was not considered as punishing, Bill enjoyed work: "*I do, I love it,"* Many of the retired actors continued to do paid work, taking parts in film, TV and radio. Bill and many of the other participants might agree then with Noel Coward that "work is more fun than fun".

Although the participants upheld quite strict values and traditions they were not necessarily solemn. Here Mildred describes breakfast in the Actor's home: *"it's absolutely disgraceful, somebody of my age giggling, but I'm afraid we do see the funny... And the gentleman who is the other side of the table, he is very bad tempered at times and it absolutely kills us! [Laughter].* Their attitude to life and work was serious but they did not take themselves seriously.

Challenges: Conflict, Change Trauma and Achievement

Although we have described the participants as thriving this is not to say that they were in good health or that they suffered no disability. Howard had undergone surgery on his spinal column. Roger had Parkinson's disease and suffered from tremors, he was sighted in only one eye and struggled to read. Stephen was registered blind, Lillian suffered severe arthritis in her hands and could also only see from only one eye. Theo describes his various ongoing health issues in typically comic fashion here: *"You see, I'm like an old car and the tyres go and then the engine pops and then the steering doesn't exactly work and then eventually the headlights go, and that's it.* [Laughter]*."*

Stephen's wife had suffered from dementia before she died. He described the care she received as "*horrific*". Elizabeth reported ongoing conflict with her carers: "*I don't let them put me to bed, I don't want to be going to bed when they can come, which can be any time"*. Some participants had experienced loneliness. Howard noted that "*it's not easy to get to know somebody of 94*". Lillian, who had recently moved into warden controlled sheltered housing observed that it becomes harder to make friends as you get older because people get set in their routines. And yet the participants were remarkably resilient in the face of difficulty and change.

The most dramatic change in the lives of the nuns came the year before when they left the abbey where their order had been based for over a hundred and fifty years. The six surviving nuns left a large Victorian abbey in seven acres of grounds to move into a six bedroom detached house. Most of the nuns in the order are over eighty and it is sometimes argued that moving the very elderly can be extremely traumatic if not fatal though there is little evidence for this. The extern nun observed that the oldest sister who is 104 coped with the move "*brilliantly*". She had lived in the abbey for eighty years and the last day was traumatic "*as she was leaving she said "oh the last time I'll see this statue" or whatever*" But she settled into the new house quickly, Sister Peter noted that she still had the same people around her, the "*bits and pieces she had before*" and she was enjoying a new view of the front garden and the people coming and going. Although the built environment is clearly very important to any older person, life for the nuns continued in the modern detached house much as it had done before in the grand and imposing abbey.

Perhaps the most traumatic change endured by these participants was bereavement. Stephen had recently lost his wife: *"After 59 years, waking up in a lonely bed is perhaps the worst"* (Stephen). Since his wife died Stephen had not undertaken the long journey to visit their children, Doris had also lost her husband though he died when she was just forty-five and she never remarried. "*No... Never been kissed or cuddled since* [laughter]*."* Many of the participants had endured some form of trauma in the form of serious illness and abrupt change of circumstances. But all participants were resilient in the face of change. The trustee of the Actors studio thought actors were particularly "good at change". During a rebuild the residents were moved about the building as work was done and they complained that they didn't know where things were. One of the residents remarked to another: *'Oh darling come on, it's like being on tour. You go to another town and you've got to get the hairdresser's and you've got to find the theatre, the manager's office, it's pretty much like that.' And the person said, 'Well, I wouldn't know, I only every played the West End!* [laughter]*'* (Phyllida). In the face of change then there was a strong sense of community and identity but also resilience and agency.

Agency: Stubbornness, Abstinence, Exercise, Routine

When Mildred was a child recovering from Tuberculosis she began a lifelong habit of walking every single day which she kept up as a resident of the Actors home. When Stephen found himself isolated after the death of his much loved wife he started going to cafes so that he wouldn't be alone. After a fall Theo was told that he would not walk again, he grinned as he declared "*But I do!*" taking evident delight in proving the doctors wrong through his determined engagement in physiotherapy. There was then a strong sense of personal agency in all of the participants.

Many of the participants could be described as "stubborn" in one way or another and exhibited this quality in both the questions they answered and the questions they avoided. At the end of the "day in the life" biography the participants were asked to rate themselves on a scale of one to ten on terms drawn from the positive psychology literature.

Several of the participants avoided these questions or answered without giving numbers. Theo best expressed his determination to engage with the research on his own terms when he told us we were too young too really understand, *"you don't think about 1 to 10s and things, you just live! You just carry on living!"* Some participants also self identified as stubborn but it should be emphasized that this was considered to be a positive trait.

The Manager of the Actors Home was well aware of how stubborn the residents were. When a Health visitor advised that a resident needed a walking frame Annabel said: *'Look for an alternative, it is not going to happen.'* The Health visitor subsequently explored alternatives. Doris was persisting with Donna Tartt's eight hundred page novel *The Goldfinch* even though it was: *"blooming awful; me niece brought me it. I've been trying since Christmas and it's supposed to be a bestseller. [...] I want to finish it and it's all about this blooming painting"* According to polls The Goldfinch was one of the most unfinished books of that year making Doris's determination all the more remarkable. Lillian also carried on reading when the reading got tough. She was partially sighted in one eye only and could no longer read the text in paper books. However she bought a kindle and found she could enlarge the text and turn pages with arthritic hands more easily.

Strong self determination was evident in the life stories of many of the participants. Bill had emigrated from Ireland to London as a young man and gone to Kings Cross wishing to leave the capital but not knowing where he should go. "*I saw up in print, 'York', and I'd never even heard of it, but I went over to the ticket place and said,* [...], *'I'll have a single ticket to York."* Strong will was also evident in health regimes. Eric. Bill and Roger had all been smokers as younger men but quit around forty years ago, all of them said it was "*easy*". As well as being self disciplined around cigarettes and alcohol most of the participants exercised regularly. Bill began his day by doing leg kicks, jogging on the spot and touching his toes twenty times, he happily demonstrated this regime for the first author who, though about half his age, was entirely unable to match it.

Many of the participants observed very regular routines. Even where participants denied having a routine it was clear that there was much order and repetition of activity: *"I don't have a routine as such, I just have different things to do nearly every day"* [Bill]. Such routines have been seen as creating structure and purpose during the week to avoid 'stagnation' in free floating time [32].

Ties: relationships, family, community and class

Each of the participants described strong ties to family, friends and larger communities. Bill's son lived in the house next door to him. Jacinta's son was cleaning her house while she was being interviewed in the day care centre. Jacinta noted: "*it's their duty to take care of me now*". [Jacinta}. But this was exceptional, none of the other participants spoke of duty and stressed that they did not want to be "a burden" on their relatives. The network of family and friends was clearly important to all of them but the relationships were framed as being of reciprocal benefit.

The nuns formed their own enclosed community but they were visited regularly by family so they had *"good friends, good family, and God*" (Sister Peter). The nuns were perhaps the strongest community, sharing the same beliefs and backgrounds. In the Jewish community there was also shared "common ground"; many of the residents were not religious but nevertheless shared important cultural referents. Similarly the actors shared a professional ethos and had often worked together in the past. The relationships then were resonant and meaningful.

Vera and Eric had been married for over fifty years. Gottman notes that all marriages entail conflict but successful ones are defined by effective strategies of "repair", e.g. an apology or even something silly like pulling a face [22]. After an argument Eric would *"put his arm around me and say - come on let's forget about it."* [Vera] This repair strategy no longer worked as Eric would forget that they were having an argument. Vera said she got irritable because of this and also regretted the decline in their sex life over the last two years. However she knew he didn't "*mean it*" and the relationship remained strong.

Vera's sister Doris had lived on the same street of terraced houses for fifty years but the character of the neighborhood had changed dramatically with most houses now primarily temporary student accommodation. The turnover of residents was high and most people did not know their neighbors. Doris however would make a point of saying hello and getting to know new people. This meant that should she need a letter posting or a loaf of bread picking up she could ask passing neighbors. Many of the participants made a point of going out and talking to people, if only by sitting outside their houses.

In some respects each of the participants lived in their own "little world". In a recent biography the actor Simon Callow reflects on Charles Dickens' characterization of the theatre as a "little world" noting "his stress is on the noun, not the adjective: he sees the theatre as an entire world, consistent with itself." [8p.82]. We use the phrase in that sense in the following final section and stress the vital importance of the networks that make up such little worlds.

Little Worlds: Religion, Sport, Work

The research team was struck by the ways in which the Actor's home and the Jewish Retirement home did and did not look like other care homes they had visited. There were certain institutional features common to both: handrails on stairs, stair lifts, long corridors with doors at either side. But in the Actor's home the walls were decorated with old playbills, black and white publicity shots of movie stars who were past or present residents; the library contained three shelved walls of books all about acting and actors -

with many of the biographies about the people living there. In the dementia wing there were "memory boxes" full of mementos of previous plays, films and TV shows that the residents had been in. There were Jewish symbols and names on all of the doors to rooms. There was a synagogue and a "tree of life" sculpture in the garden. The managers of the Jewish care home described it as a "*community within a community*" with support from Jewish schools and synagogues. Similarly the house that had become a nunnery was both like and unlike an ordinary domestic residence. There were religious icons all over the house, the front room was furnished with chairs facing an alter, the kitchen featured a huge cross at one end of the room, the table was laid with the simple provisions that the nuns ate daily. These sites were in Dickens' sense "little worlds" complete and consistent with themselves.

Sport could also function as a self contained little world. Stephen was an expert on cricketing history and had been a member of the Yorkshire County Cricket club for over sixty watching games from a box with eight to ten friends. Similarly Bill was a boxing enthusiast with a dedicated boxing TV channel and an encyclopedic knowledge of the sport. He also watched fights in the working man's club he went to and, like Stephen, discussed the "greats" of past and present sporting figures. Doris was similarly passionate about sport *"I love sport on the telly, any sport, any. Rugby...I always sit up on a Saturday night and watch Match Of The Day, always."* These sporting enthusiasms were inherently social, even when watched alone, and part of the pleasure was, of course, discussing the matches with other fans. Although the researchers knew little to nothing of any of these sports the participants enthusiasm was infectious.

For some participants religious ritual was a deeply important aspect of their world: "[prayer] *and Mass are the things that we hang our whole life on,*" (Sister Peter). Some participants observed religious practice although they did not necessarily believe in God: *"I used to go to the synagogue with my two grandsons a lot, every Saturday morning, and it was like a social there and it was very good, but I don't go now"*. (Theo). Others found meaning in church attendance though they were not necessarily orthodox, as with Bill: "*to me, all churches are the house of God, and they are all talking about the same person, so I don't mind.*" (Bill). Doris volunteered to clean the church every weekend; even though she did not consider herself "*right religious*" faith endured: *"I think whatever you do in this world is God, anything that you do that's nice.*" In this sense there was a meaning to her activities, to use Seligman's terms, larger than herself.

Many of Seligman's PERMA characteristics were evident in the lives of the participants but they were embedded in a range of complex "little worlds". The grounded theory resulted in what might be described as a Little Worlds theory of Positive Aging. This does not contradict Seligman, it confirms previous studies but emphasizes the complex contexts in which well being occurs. As Bruno Latour notes: "An individual is not an atom but extends as far as all the entities that it perceives and with which it is in relation." [28]. Well being is not a property of an isolated individual, it is a phenomenon that occurs in a network or, a little world.

SOLUTIONISM: THE BOARD GAME

In recent years there has been a move away from broad and general "implications for design" [11] towards the development of research prototypes [16], concept designs e.g. [42] and design fictions [1, 39]. However Morozov [31] recently castigated HCI for "solutionism" i.e. devising solutions for problems that don't exist or proposing technological "silver bullets' for complex social, political and environmental problems (ibid). The "BinCam" is Morozov's favorite example of solutionism. This research prototype featured a phone in the lid of a bin that sent photographs of the contents to Facebook so the user's friends could see if recycling was happening or not. The idea was pilloried in the press as Orwellian and generated a furious media and academic backlash not least form Morozov. The goal of a research prototype is not to produce new products but rather new knowledge. The controversy then makes BinCam more rather than less interesting as a research prototype. Morozov argues that "the geeks" think "the internet" will save the world, an understandable though ungenerous caricature [31]. It is unlikely that the makers of Bincam ever thought it would save the world, more likely they thought it would be interesting, and it was. The term "impressionism" was initially a pejorative used to dismiss the paintings it described. But it was adopted as a general description of the school perhaps because it indicated the strengths as well as the limitations of the style. Similarly "solutionism" is a derogatory term but perhaps it should also be embraced to indicate very clearly an acknowledgement of the limitations of HCI work.

While acknowledging that ageing populations present complex social, political and environmental problems we nevertheless see value in relating findings from studies like this to questions of design. The following sections propose concepts and design fictions derived from a "solutionist" game. We adopt the label "solutionist" to indicate that we are very well aware that they will not solve the complex issues around ageing populations and to acknowledge that the design fictions may, like many real consumer products, address problems that do not really exist.

Card games are very frequently used to generate design ideas. Brian Eno's "Oblique Strategies" cards for example ask provocative questions like "what would your best friend do?" to inspire new thinking. Inspiration cards have also been used in HCI research [e.g. 23, 27]. Cards developed by Vines et al featured data quotes and "questionable concepts" – provocative concept designs to elicit feedback during participatory design sessions with older people. A card game called "solutionism" was developed for student brainstorms by the first author. The cards consisted of four "suits" representing: an issue, a user, a motive and a technology, which players combined in order to "solve the world's problems and make everybody happy" [42]. For this project the first author developed a solutionist board game to encourage players to move from data to design.

The game consisted of a board that players moved tokens around featuring various age associated predicaments and occasional positive qualities, e.g: arthritis, boredom, deafness, isolation, heart condition, regret, wisdom and so on. Players then took data quotation cards from five different stacks based on the categories described in the last sections: attitude, challenges, agency, ties and little worlds.

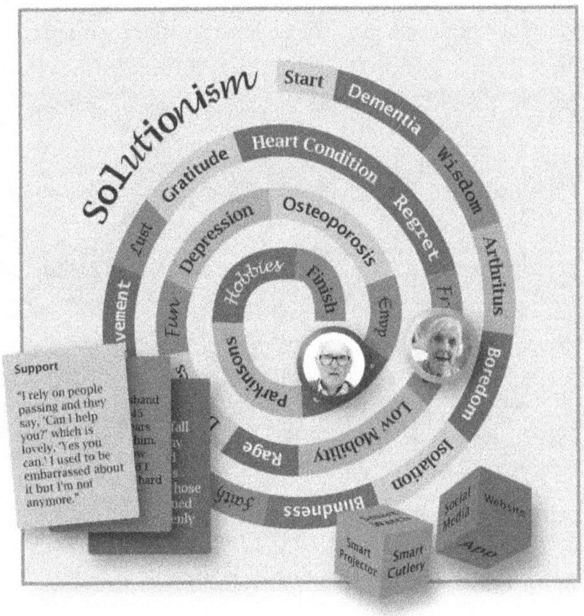

Figure 2. Solutionism, The Board Game

To move around the board players threw a technology dice. One contained general technologies like apps or robots, the other suggested technologies around the "internet of things" e.g. smart chair, smart crockery and so on. To reach the finish, players had to generate ideas and draw them on postcards, they then pitched the ideas to the other players and moved one space for each idea they came up. Players were awarded bonus points if other players liked the idea. In presenting each idea the players first read out the quote and specified the technology and the challenge. In this way the team became more familiar with the data than they would have if it were presented in more traditional formats like a slideshow.

The game was intended to stress that the team were creating fictions rather than proposals and the focus was on questions rather than solutions. The board game emphasized play and irony, underlining the fact that there is no quick "technological fix" for the complex social, political and environmental phenomena surrounding aging populations

The games were played by the project team which included a sociologist, a psychologist, designers and an entrepreneur. As with most brainstorming activities, quantity was stressed over quality and the rule of thumb that it takes 93 bad ideas to produce 3 good ones [40] was observed to apply here. The game was played twice and on both occasions a large number of ideas were generated. Although two of the team members were unfamiliar with this kind of brainstorming activity some of the most interesting ideas came from them and the competitive element seemed to spur players on. Some of the ideas were frivolous but some were considered worth developing further. The game was fun and we suggest it could be adapted for play with any qualitative data set. The following section illustrates the range of solutionist concepts that emerged.

Solutionist Concept Designs

The following ideas were rejected but perhaps retain some value in illustrating the findings. For example: a "homing walking stick" was suggested in response to Mildred's insistence on walking every day and the care staff's fears that she might leave the grounds and get lost. In response to a quote about the importance of ties a "biographical mirror" was proposed to augment the user's reflection with images of people who are important to them. In response to a quote from Phyllida on the importance of small daily "light touch" interactions in the actor's home "Anonyment" was suggested as a system which allowed the delivery of anonymous compliments e.g. nice scarf! "Skill share" was a response to the many quotes about voluntary work, here Chinese students of English would Skype over iPads with care home residents to practice English. One response to Stephen's enthusiasm for talking to strangers in cafes was a "conversation cup" for cafes where users could indicate their interests and look for matches. A quote from Doris saying that people in care homes would "*get up and about*" if someone just "*gave them a duster*" prompted the notion of a "time limited chair" that would register the length of time a person had spent sitting and gradually tip them up onto their feet. Instances of isolation and neglect prompted a "rate your relations" system that would allow older people to rate carers, family and friends. An "instant timebank" would allow people to volunteer for ten or fifteen minutes at a time.

Three of the concepts were chosen for further development as design fictions in the form of advertisements for services and products that don't quite exist yet.

DESIGN FICTIONS

Two recent Interactive Media Design graduates were briefed to create advertisements for "The Pavillion" a "Social Watch" and "Vintage Volunteers".

More and more care homes are being set up around communities of interest. There are for instance, homes for retired academics, vicars, army personnel and homes for gay and lesbian people [24]. The Pavillion was imagined as a themed care home for cricket fans. Amongst the "little worlds" described was Stephens group of eight to ten people in their seventies and eighties who would book a box at a local cricketing venue where they would watch four day long cricket matches. Stephen stressed that it was important to him "*because they are kindred spirits in so much as they're all retired businessmen of one kind or the other and we get on very, very well together and we have a lot of laughs.*" (Stephen). It was not simply the pleasure of watching the sport that was important but the company of similarly minded friends who could discuss the play and the history of the game. Similarly Bill was a boxing enthusiast who lit up when talking about classic fights and fighters "*I've been to Manchester, The Barbican, seen him box there, seen him fight for the World Title in Manchester and the pictures there of him there...* [points to pictures on mantlepiece]. *That's him up there with Mickey Duff; he used to be, he was a big man in boxing.*" These self referential little worlds of sport suggested sport themed care homes as well as other specialized institutions.

The Pavillion was imagined as a specialist home aimed at cricketing fans like Stephen. A large video screen or projection would be displayed on one wall of a communal area made up to look like a box at a cricketing ground. Clearly this home would not be for everybody and hellish to those uninterested in sport.

Figure 3. The Pavillion

We consider the Pavillion a useful fiction because it indicates a large design space, based not on age, but "homophily", the tendency to be drawn to and bond with people who are similar to ourselves. The design fictions here took the form of adverts in order to suggest a wide sector of themed care catering to many specialized tastes, e.g. Sherlock Holmes enthusiasts, KISS fans and so on.

Many of the participants remarked that it was harder to make new friends the older they got. Stephen had developed the strategy of going to cafes to combat loneliness after his wife's death, but it was not always easy to strike up or maintain conversations "*You can't have long conversations with total strangers really in cafes because they're usually in twos or threes anyway and being on your own, you're a bit of an oddball.*" Quotes such as this led to ideas like the Social Watch. The earlier "conversation cup" idea was rejected because it was recognized that the odds of two people eager to talk about cricket being in the same cafe were probably slim. But the "social watch" was conceived as a smart watch app where users could register interests and find like minded people in a city. A user might, for example, discover that there is a poker club about to meet in the park. It is possible that such a system might serve as a "ticket to talk" or at least to make an approach easier.

Figure 4 . Social Watch

The fiction, though undoubtedly solutionsist was considered useful because it illustrates homophily, as a useful concept for independent older people as well as those in care settings.

Voluntary work was important to many of the participants. Vera volunteered for a cancer charity for 22 years noting that she "*got great pleasure out of it because my mum had cancer and that gave me interest.*" Ill health meant she had given up this regular commitment but she helped friends and neighbours where she could. Similarly Elizabeth could not engage in regular voluntary work anymore but "*if somebody said, 'Will you shorten these trousers for me?' or something, then if I could I would. Somebody would ring up and say, 'Can you make me a cake? We're having a stall...' I do.*" Although Bill had slowed down and was not "*doing points*" for neighbours, as he had done, or large projects like the club renovation, he remained happy to work "*if you're outside I will come out and if there's something I can do to help you then I will.*". Comments such as these led to a range of "solutionist" concepts, amongst them, Vintage Volunteers.

This built on the idea of the instant timebank but added the twist that it should be exclusively aimed at older people. The fictional advert for the Vintage Volunteers service shows a digital notice board with various time dependent requests for help. For example – Can someone go to the shop for me? Could someone walk my dog? The passing older person accepts the job by activating the screen with their bus pass (in the UK those over sixty five get a free bus pass).

Figure 5: Vintage Volunteers

This was considered to be a useful fiction not because it was provocative or critical but because it is a resonant illustration of the findings around the vital importance of meaningful work in positive aging.

DISCUSSION

It is sometimes claimed that provocative concept designs, questionable concepts or design fictions are just "bad designs". But to insist on "good design" in such contexts is to demand a truly solutionist approach. To solemnly suggest purely design based solutions for ageing populations is clearly preposterous. Nevertheless the challenges around ageing populations are real and it is important to explore the emerging design space.

Although the Solutionist games were played with a degree of irony they ensured that the research team incorporated findings and insights from the fieldwork into their thinking. During the game the designers became players who knew very well they were engaged in make believe: producing fictions. Sterling suggests that we are going to see more and more design fictions and it is certainly becoming more and more popular in HCI. Why design fiction and why now? Fiction has been defined as a means of providing resolution for conflicts at the level of fantasy that cannot be resolved in real life [14]. Perhaps what makes "design fiction" such a useful term is the insistence on its status as fantasy. In this sense design fiction may mitigate against the tendency towards solutionism and the hope that there are technological quick fixes for the challenges we face.

CONCLUSION

This paper makes three contributions. The first is the study of thriving ninety year olds which suggests that well being is not the property of an individual but rather achieved within networks. The second is the "solutionist" board game which we suggest could be applied to any qualitative study as a means of generating design concepts informed by data and research insights. The third contribution takes the form of research based design fictions addressing the challenge of positive aging. We consider their value to be in indicating the broad shape of the design space to be explored. We have argued that fiction can create a space for design beyond solutionism.

REFERENCES

1. AgeUK (2014) Later Life in the United Kingdom. http://www.ageuk.org.uk/Documents/EN-GB/Factsheets/Later_Life_UK_factsheet.pdf?dtrk=true
2. Baltes P., & Baltes M., (1990). Successful aging: perspectives from the behavioral sciences. New York: Cambridge University Press.
3. Bardzell, J., and Bardzell, S. (2013). What is "critical" about critical design? Proc. of CHI'2013. ACM:
4. Bardzell J., Bardzell S., and Stolterman E., (2014). Reading critical designs: supporting reasoned interpretations of critical design. In Proc. of (CHI '14).
5. Bleecker, J.(2009). "Design Fiction: A Short Essay on Design, Science, Fact and Fiction". webeditionpdf
6. Bowling, A. and Dieppe, P. (2005). "What is successful aging and who should define it?" British Medical Journal. 331 (7531): 1548–1551.
7. Blythe M. (2014) Research through design fiction: narrative in real and imaginary abstracts. In Proc of (CHI '14). ACM, New York, NY, USA, 703-712
8. Callow S., (2012) *Charles Dickens and the Great Theatre of the World.*. Harper press
9. Charmaz, K. (2006) *Constructing Grounded Theory*. Sage, London, 2006.
10. Csikszentmihalyi M. (2014) *Flow and the Foundations of Positive Psychology*: The Collected Works of Mihaly Csikszentmihalyi. Springer.

11. Dourish, P. (2006) Implications for design. In *Proc. CHI '06*, ACM , 541-550.
12. Dourish, P. & Bell, G. (2013). "Resistance is futile": Reading science fiction alongside ubiquitous computing. Personal Ubiq. Comput., Springer-Verlag, May
13. Dunne A., and Raby F. (2013). *Speculative Everything: Design, Fiction, and Social Dreaming*. The MIT Press.
14. Eagleton, T. (1996) *Literary Theory* (2nd ed.). Wiley Blackwell, Hoboken, NJ,
15. Ehrenreich B., (2010) *Bright-sided: How Positive Thinking is Undermining America*, Picador USA.
16. Furniss D., Blandford A., and Curzon P.. (2011). Confessions from a grounded theory PhD: experiences and lessons learnt. In Proc of (CHI '11). ACM
17. Gaver W. (2012) What Should We Expect from Research Through Design. CHI 2012 pp 937-946
18. Gaver , W., Beaver, J., and Benford, S. (2003) Ambiguity as a resource for design. In *Proc. CHI '03*, ACM (2003), 233-240.
19. Gaver, W., Boucher, A., Pennington, S. and Walker, B. (2004). Cultural probes and the value of uncertainty. *Interactions*, 6 (5), 2004, 53-56.
20. Gilliam T. (2014) http://www.sfx.co.uk/2014/03/14/the-zero-theorem-terry-gilliam-interview/
21. Glaser, B. and Strauss, A. (1967) *Discovery of Grounded Theory: Strategies for Qualitative Research.* Aldine Publishing Company, Chicago, 1967.
22. Gottman J and Silver N (2000) *The Seven Principles for Making Marriage Work.* An Onion Paperback
23. Halskov, K. and Daslgaard, P. (2006) Inspiration Card Workshops. In Proc. DIS '06, ACM Press (2006), 2-11.
24. Kirman B., Linehan C., Lawson S., and O'Hara D., (2013) CHI and the Future Robot Enslavement of Humankind: a retrospective. In Proc of CHI'13 ACM
25. Independent. *The. The Only Gay (Retirement home) in the village*. 31.6.2013
26. Linehan C., Kirman B., Reeves S., Blythe M., Tanenbaum J., Desjardins A., and Wakkary R., (2014). Alternate endings: using fiction to explore design futures. In Proc of CHI '14 ACM
27. Lucero, A. and Arrasvuori, J. (2010) PLEX Cards: A Source of Inspiration When Designing for Playfulness. In Proc. Fun and Games '10, ACM Press (2010), 28-37.
28. Latour B. (2013) From Aggregation to Navigation. A few Challenges for Social Theory. CHI 13 Keynote address. Paris. 2003
29. Markussen T., and Knutz E. (2013). The poetics of design fiction. In Proc of DPPI '13. ACM
30. Marshall K., Thieme A., Wallace J., Vines J., Wood G., and Balaam M., (2014) Proc of DIS 14 Vancouver.
31. Morozov E. (2013) *To Save Everything Click Here: Technology, Solutionism and the Urge to Fix Problems That Don't Exist.* Allen Lane Penguin Books.
32. Oliver, C. 2008. Retirement Migration. Paradoxes of Ageing. New York: Routledge
33. Phelan E., Anderson L., Lacroix A., Larson E. (2004) Older adults' views of "successful aging"—how do they compare with researchers' definitions? J Am Geriatr Soc;52: 211-6
34. Robson C. (2002) *Real World Research.* Blackwell Publishing, Oxford.
35. Rule A. and Levine D., (2014) International Art English. http://canopycanopycanopy.com/contents/international_art_english
36. Seligman M.E.P. (2002) Authentic Happiness: Using the New Positive Psychology to Realise Your Potential for Lasting Fulfillment Simon and Schuster
37. Seligman M.E.P. (2011) Flourish: A Visionary New Understanding and Well Being. Nichoals Brealey Publishing
38. Sterling B. (2005) Shaping Things. MIT Press. Cambridge Massachusetts
39. Sterling B. (2009) Design Fictions. Interactions. Vol 16. Issue 3.
40. Sterling B. (2013) Patently untrue: fleshy defibrillators and synchronised baseball are changing the future. *Wired* (2013, Oct. 11).
41. Strauss, A., Corbin, J., (1990): *Basics Of Qualitative Research: Grounded Theory Procedures And Techniques*. London, Sage.
42. Steane J. (2014) *The Principles and Processes of Interactive Design.* Bloomsbury.
43. Tanenbaum, J Tanenbaum K., and Wakkary R. (2012). Steampunk as design fiction. In Proc of CHI '12. ACM, New York, NY, USA, 1583-1592
44. Thieme, A., Balaam, M., Wallace, J., Coyle, D. and Lindley, S. Designing wellbeing. *Proc. DIS '12*. ACM (2012), 789-790.
45. Thulesius H., (2005) Grounded Theory. Wikipedia. http://en.wikipedia.org/wiki/Talk:Grounded_theory
46. Vines J., Blythe M., Lindsay S., Dunphy P., Monk A., and Olivier, P. (2012). Questionable concepts: critique as resource for designing with eighty somethings. In Proc of CHI '12.
47. Wakkary R., Desjardins A., Hauser S., and Maestri L. (2013). A sustainable design fiction: Green practices. TOCHI. Volume 20 Issue 4, September 2013

Design Considerations for Patient Portal Adoption by Low-Income, Older Adults

Celine Latulipe
University of North Carolina at Charlotte
clatulip@uncc.edu

Amy Gatto
Wake Forest School of Medicine
agatto@wakehealth.edu

Ha T. Nguyen
Wake Forest School of Medicine
nguyen@wakehealth.edu

David P. Miller
Wake Forest School of Medicine
dmiller@wakehealth.edu

Sara A. Quandt
Wake Forest School of Medicine
squandt@wakehealth.edu

Alain G. Bertoni
Wake Forest School of Medicine
North Carolina, USA
abertonie@wakehealth.edu

Alden Smith
Greene County Health Care
dsmith@greenecountyhealthcare.com

Thomas A. Arcury
Wake Forest School of Medicine
tarcury@wakehealth.edu

ABSTRACT
This paper describes the results of an interview study investigating facilitators and barriers to adoption of patient portals among low-income, older adults in rural and urban populations in the southeastern United States. We describe attitudes of this population of older adults and their current level of technology use and patient portal use. From qualitative analysis of 36 patient interviews and 16 caregiver interviews within these communities, we derive themes related to benefits of portals, barriers to use, concerns and desired features. Based on our initial findings, we present a set of considerations for designing the patient portal user experience, aimed at helping healthcare clinics to meet U.S. federally-mandated 'meaningful use' requirements.

Author Keywords
technology barriers; elderly populations; eHealth; low-income populations; patient portals

ACM Classification Keywords
H.5.m. Information Interfaces and Presentation (e.g. HCI): Miscellaneous

INTRODUCTION
As part of the American Recovery and Reinvestment Act, healthcare providers across the U.S. are under a mandate to implement patient portal systems. These systems do not just need to be put in place: providers must demonstrate 'meaningful use' by significant percentages of their patient population in order to qualify for the financial incentives provided by the law [3]. This federal mandate impacts all communities, but those where there are significant populations of older, low-income, adults may be particularly affected. Older adults consume vastly more medical resources of community health clinics than other age groups (and in rural communities make up a larger proportion of the patients, because younger people often migrate to urban areas), so older adult's adoption and use of patient portals is the most critical in terms of the potential to actually see economic and health care benefits. These benefits will only be realized if the portals are used effectively. In this research, we are focusing on lower-income older adults because there are more health care issues among lower-income populations, due to lack of insurance coverage and less access to preventative healthcare. This is the population that has the most to benefit from effective use of patient portals. However, we suspect that this population has the most barriers to adoption and use of patient portals.

Our team has conducted in-depth interviews with patients and caregivers in this demographic to understand the barriers to adoption of patient portals in these communities. We focus on perceived and actual barriers to adoption as well as the perceived benefits of use and actual benefits accruing to patients already using the portals. We find that lack of familiarity with technology and lack of technology-related skills are prevalent barriers, while security and privacy fears are a consistent concern. We also find that among some of our interview population there is a general lack of interest in learning about technology. Based on our findings, we provide an initial set of design considerations that may be useful for patient portal designers and IT staff deploying these systems.

BACKGROUND
The field of Human-Computer Interaction (HCI) has lately turned its attention to healthcare informatics. There is mount-

CHI 2015, April 18–23, 2015, Seoul, Republic of Korea

ACM 978-1-4503-3145-6/15/04 . . . $15.00
http://dx.doi.org/10.1145/2702123.2702392

ing evidence that applying techniques of User-Centered Design (UCD) to eHealth applications is not only beneficial, but necessary [19]. Many of the inquiry-based techniques of interviewing and surveying are already common in community-based health inquiry, and we apply those techniques here. Interdisciplinary research that crosses computing, social science, and medicine has much to offer, both in gathering requirements and in designing new systems. As an example, a recent study showed that patients with Type-2 Diabetes are interested in having social computing systems that can leverage the social network to help motivate them towards healthy behaviors [20]. Pang et al. performed qualitative interviews to understand how friends and family members share information and health updates about a chronically ill patient, noting that synchronous video conferencing was not as useful or desirable as expected in this situation because of contextual and privacy issues [24]. Pratt et al. applied a Personal Information Management (PIM) lens to consider how patients manage all of the data they receive and collect while interacting with the healthcare system as a whole, and they demonstrate the significant challenges that patients face in managing and integrating this information [25]. Evidence shows that health information technology in general is having positive impacts on patient outcomes [8] and these examples demonstrate the diverse ways in which HCI can help to identify, contextualize and address healthcare technology issues [13].

Personal Health Records

Some HCI and healthcare informations researchers investigate user experiences with Personal Health Records (PHR), a broader classification of systems of which patient portals are one type. Many PHR systems are commercially available apps that are patient-controlled and independent of the healthcare provider. While the work of Baird et al. showed that the intention to use such PHR systems is high, their survey demographic was middle-income, educated, graduate students, which is not representative of the population as a whole [7]. Kim et al. demonstrated that in the case of patient-initiated PHR systems, most older adult patients do not keep the systems up to date, even when they have regular, weekly access to technical assistance with the system [14]. The work of Liu et al. is particularly relevant as they showed that patients and caregivers face numerous issues in PHR adoption including dealing with software complexity, medical terminology and concerns about security and data accuracy [17]. Tang et al. posit that education is one of the keys to increasing adoption of PHR systems that are patient-managed [29].

The Patient Portal Mandate & Meaningful Use

Beginning in 2015, providers who do not comply with Stage 2 of the Meaningful Use mandate will lose portions of the Medicaid and Medicare reimbursements that they are due. This requires that at least 5% of patients actively view and download information through their primary care provider's patient portal and that at least 5% of patients use the secure messaging feature of their portal during the measurement period [2]. This means that healthcare clinics must invest in patient portal systems and patients at each clinic need to learn about, register for, and actually make use of the portal. While meeting this mandate may be easy in affluent, well-educated communities, it seems likely that there will be particular difficulties in meeting the meaningful use requirements in less affluent communities. The mandate does include exemptions for counties where more than 50% of the population does not have internet access with bandwidth higher than 7Mbps, but determining which counties fit this criteria is difficult. Our work investigates rural and urban communities where a significant portion of the population is low-income and elderly.

Patient Portal Adoption

Research related to adoption issues around patient portals has surged, likely spurred on by the federal mandate and the meaningful use specifications. Ruland et al. presented the CONNECT system, a patient portal deployed in Norway, and discussed numerous user experience issues, including a clear tradeoff between data security and user friendliness [26]. Wilson et al. showed that Technology Acceptance Models (TAM) [23], can be usefully applied to predict whether patients will adopt systems such as patient portals [30]. In a survey of existing literature related to technology adoption by patients, Or and Karsh found that most studies focused on patient demographic and health condition variables or prior experience with technology, while not enough focused on the human-computer interaction variables or the organizational or environmental variables that could impact adoption [22].

Klein studied patients' behavioral intention (BI) and factors, such as technology self-efficacy, to predict likelihood of adoption of patient portal systems. He found that greater technology self-efficacy and personal innovativeness positively impacted BI, as did having a chronic health condition. Patients were also more likely to express intention to use patient portals provided by primary care physicians than those provided by specialists [15]. Wilson and Vance developed a model to predict patient portal adoption and found that incorporating facilitating factors such as prior use of offline health systems, structural need for health services, age and chronic health conditions all led to better adoption predictions than just using behavioral intention [31].

In a focus-group study by Zickmund et al., factors that were associated with interest in using a patient portal included dissatisfaction with healthcare provider communication and inability to access medical information and records, while factors associated with disinterest in the portal included usability issues and the possibility of reduced face-to-face contact with the provider [33]. Goel et al. conducted a telephone survey with urban patients to inquire about reasons for enrolling or not enrolling in a patient portal and found that lack of information and motivation were the most important factors preventing enrollment (63% of respondents); negative attitudes toward the portal was another critical factor (30% of respondents); while technological obstacles accounted for only 8% of respondents who had not enrolled [10]. They did not find any age, gender or educational differences, although they did find that African-American respondents were less likely than white respondents to express interest in self-management features offered by the patient portal.

Technology Adoption by Sub-Population

Greysen et al. have investigated how functional impairment impacts internet use among older adults and found that this had negative implications for meaningful use of patient portals [11]. Yagil et al. also found that using everyday technologies generated stress for older adults, which also suggested a potential barrier to patient portal adoption and use [32].

Ancker et al. have investigated how disadvantaged populations use patient portals, based on system access logs of more than 74,000 patients at a Federally Qualified Health Center in New York City [4]. They found good adoption of the system by low-income participants, but small persistent racial disparities in both likelihood to be offered an access code and likelihood to actually use the system. Thus, income itself did not appear to be a limiting factor in adoption of patient portals, but may have a modifying influence in combination with other demographic factors. However, these results may not generalize to rural populations.

Fruhling reports on a qualitative study of e-Health users in rural Nebraska and reports that usability and clarity were important in the development of such systems, and also noted that security and privacy issues were a major concern with this population [9]. However, the study offered no comparison to urban populations.

Research Gaps

The synthesis of research described shows that there is knowledge about eHealth technology adoption by different sub-populations, and knowledge about patient portal adoption gleaned from modeling behavioral intention based on various criteria. Our work adds to this literature by providing a deep understanding of the factors that impact adoption for low-income, older adults. Unlike most of the previous work, our approach is unique in that it details attitudes of both patients and caregivers. In addition, our focus is on the sub-population most likely to benefit from use of patient portals: lower-income, older adults, who tend to have significant chronic health issues. In examining this sub-population, we have interviewed a broad mix of races, genders and ethnicities, ensuring that our results are generalizable to low-income, older adult populations across the US. We have also included participants from both urban and rural areas, allowing further generalization from our results.

INTERVIEW STUDY

Our interview study was aimed at gaining an understanding of the IT environment among low-income, older adults living in urban and rural communities, the information seeking behaviors of such patients and their caregivers, their technological access and abilities, their knowledge, perceptions and use of network technology, eHealth and patient portals.

Participants

We conducted interviews with 52 individuals: 36 patients and 16 caregivers. Participants were recruited from four North Carolina counties: Forsyth County, the location of Wake Forest School of Medicine, and Caldwell, Greene, and Robeson

Table 1. High-Level Interview Participant Demographics

Category	White	African Amer.	Amer. Indian	Other/ Mixed	Hispanic
Patients	13	13	3	7	7
Caregivers	5	6	2	3	3
Totals:	18	19	5	10	10

Table 2. Patient Participant Demographics

Age	Male	Female	Rural	Urban
55-64 (13)	7	6	5	8
65-74 (13)	5	8	9	4
75+ (10)	5	5	7	3
Totals (36):	17	19	21	15

Counties, the locations of three health centers in the Community Partners Healthnet network. The health centers include an urban academic health center and three rural Federally Qualified Health Centers (FQHCs). These counties represent variation on the urban-rural continuum [1], such that two (Forsyth, Caldwell) are in metropolitan areas with a population of 250,000 to 1 million, one (Robeson) is a nonmetropolitan area with an urban population of 20,000 or more, and one (Greene) is a nonmetropolitan county with an urban population less than 2,500.

Table 1 shows the participant demographics for patient and caregiver participants. More specific demographics of our patient interview participants, including their education level, is broken down by age group in Table 2. For the purposes of this study we define 'caregiver' as a friend, family member or other individual who helps a patient look after themselves. Caregivers may be involved in transporting the patient to health care appointments, checking on medications, picking up prescriptions, helping to research treatment options, helping to pay for health care or file insurance claims and helping the patient with exercise and diet. Table 3 shows the breakdown by age, education level, gender and location of caregivers who participated in interviews. In at least some cases, the caregivers we interviewed are elderly and/or suffering from chronic health conditions themselves.

Methodology

Data collection was completed between October 2013 and June 2014, by three trained interviewers. The goal of this study was to recruit patients and caregivers that were racially and ethnically diverse, but representative of the population of older, low-income adults. The research team followed best practices for recruiting community participants for qualitative healthcare related studies [6]. Patients and caregivers were recruited based on recommendations from clinic partners. Investigators reviewed lists of potential participants and selected individuals that reflected the desired diversity in gender and ethnic group, as well as geographic distribution, household income, and educational attainment. One hundred and ninety-two patients were mailed a letter detailing the study and then received a follow-up phone call. Fifty three refused to participate, for reasons including no interest and lack of time, 88 did not respond, and 11 were added to a wait-list. All patients who were contacted were asked to identify their

Table 3. Caregiver Participant Demographics

Age	Male	Female	Rural	Urban
unknown (2)	0	2	2	0
<55 (4)	0	4	4	0
55-64 (6)	0	6	3	3
65-74 (3)	1	2	1	2
75+ (1)	0	1	0	1
Totals (16):	1	15	10	6

primary caregiver. These caregivers were then contacted as potential participants in the study. We also contacted several other potential patient and caregiver participants referred to us through our network of contacts.

The patient and caregiver interview was designed to elicit use of technology and electronic patient information management systems to manage chronic conditions by patients and their caregivers. First, participants were asked about their general health, self-management strategies, and health care quality. Second, participants were asked about their health literacy. Third, participants were asked about their background with technology and any technology experience. This included questions about the accessibility of computers and the internet and environmental and community factors that affected technology usage. Fourth, participants were asked about the benefits of using electronic health information systems to manage their health. This included e-health literacy, training to use patient portals, and privacy and security concerns they had about health information being available via the internet. Lastly, participants were asked about their individual use of their patient portal. This included facilitators and barriers to patient portal use, strategies to expand use, and concerns.

Interviewers met participants at a location of the participants' choice, usually in their homes, but sometimes at their healthcare center. The interviewers explained the study, and obtained signed consent. Participants received a $20 incentive upon completion of the interview. In-depth audio recorded interviews ranged in length from thirty minutes to two hours.

Data Collection and Analysis

Data analysis was based on a systematic, computer assisted approach [5] using Atlas.ti. Interview transcripts and interview notes constituted the raw data and varied from brief responses to longer narratives. The interviews were edited for accuracy and identifying information was removed in this process. For interviews conducted in Spanish, the interviews were simultaneously translated and transcribed. Data analysis began with the collection and ongoing reflection on interview content through listening to interview recordings and reading the interview transcripts. The research team reviewed each interview and recorded themes, patterns and issues that arose in those narratives [18]. This information was shared and discussed by the entire research team. The transcribed interviews were then coded in a two-step process, based on the use of coding dictionaries created by the team. Tags in the coding dictionaries reflected themes present in the interviews as well as concepts from the conceptual framework and research literature. During an initial training period, the research team members practiced coding interviews to reach agreement on assignment of codes. Each transcript was coded by two research team members and any differences were resolved through discussion. This double coding throughout data processing was a check on completeness and drift from the original code definitions.

RESULTS

Descriptive Statistics

Tables 1, 2 and 3 show the demographics of our different participant populations. This sample is, by design, diverse, and segments of the older adult population in North Carolina are represented. Ethnic minorities are well represented. While our patients participants are diverse in gender, our caregiver participants are predominantly female.

Portal Usage

Of the 36 patient participants, only five had already accessed and made use of their patient portals. These patients are all in relatively low-income households, vary in age range, but all have at least a high school diploma. Of the 16 caregivers we interviewed, three had used their own patient portals, though none had used patient portals on behalf of the patients they cared for. The three caregivers using their portals were all younger than 65 and two had university degrees while the third had only some high school education.

Socio-Technological Environment

Most of the participants we interviewed were aware that there is internet service available in their communities, and this was true across urban and rural participants. However, three rural participants could not answer questions about whether there was internet service available in their communities. More than half of our patient participants had computers, laptops or tablets (20 patients had some kind of computer while 16 patients had none). However, not all of the patients with computers had home internet access, indicating that some of these devices may not be effectively in use. The percentage of caregiver participants who use the internet was much higher, with 14 of the 16 caregivers having home internet access.

We had a few participants who talked about having computers that were not 'plugged in' or 'not set up yet.' For example, caregiver C9 (a female in her 70s) mentioned a computer that she had just acquired (but not yet set up) on the advice of family members. She had plans to get it set up and then sign up for internet service. This demonstrates that some elderly patients are being nudged into using technology by their family members, but this process can be slow.

Many of our patient participants and a few of our caregiver participants had no interest in technology at all. For example, P1, a rural patient, did not own a computer or have internet access at home. When asked if it was possible to get access to the internet in his community, he replied:

> The fact is, I don't feel like I need to know. That's one reason I don't be going in to check on it. For what little business I have going on I don't need to know that stuff.

Similarly, caregiver C11 expressed a complete lack of interest in technology. These examples demonstrate elderly patients and caregivers who would be unlikely to become users of a patient portal.

For urban participants, internet access is easily available. For example, P17 described the socio-economic situation and how it relates to internet access in his community:

> The people that's in the neighborhood that buys the homes – we're in a subdivision and they're running $120K to $150K. [...] So, I don't say that they have any issues with getting that. The cable's all available. All of it's available if they want it.

Similarly, P23 noted the difference in wireless networks visible to her depending on what part of the city she is in:

> Here in this area [...], it's become a sort of depressed area...And so what I have discovered – and this is a thing that I know by looking at my wireless networks – what's available besides me. So on any given day on this street, I can see up to ten...Whereas in other areas, I'll see so many, I can't even list them.

P23 noted that people can access computers and the internet at the Urban League. She then described a situation with her cousin using these computers:

> I had dragged my cousin up there to - the woman I gave a computer to. Her sons gave her a computer. And she just won't grasp - you know? But, she was willing to go up there [to the Urban League] and use the public computers to do her own internet searches. So I notice that people who are somehow afraid to have it in their own hands, in their own home, will go there.

This also reflects that some people are simple lacking confidence with respect to technology. For example, when asked what keeps him from using a computer, P11 responded:

> Like overall I don't have trust in myself. I don't think I can do it.

For the participants who do regularly use the internet, there appeared to be a dichotomy between using it for work versus leisure. C7, a caregiver participant who is older than 70, noted that she uses the internet to play games and to video chat with her grandchildren, thus falling into the leisure use category. P36, a rural patient, falls into the former category and described his internet usage this way:

> I really use the internet for things that I really need and when I need to do something for work. I am not the type of person that uses it for leisure.

Similarly, one of the rural caregivers we interviewed, C4, used the internet extensively for her work, reporting that she and her husband are heavy users of technology:

> I have a laptop, and we carry that with us when we travel, so when we're in motel rooms we can access the internet...At home, we have just the regular traditional standalone computer, high speed so we can download things very quickly. I use that basically for email and I'm the publicity person for [organization], so we have our fundraisers. I send out all the info to the websites and papers and things like that...

There appears to be no lack of internet service available in the communities our patient and caregiver participants are living in, but only about half of the elderly population we interviewed are actively engaged with computing technology and the internet. Those who are engaged use technology for work purposes, for communication and to play games.

We also asked participants about their perceived health literacy levels and, as expected, responses to this were varied, ranging from participants with high perceptions of health-literacy, to those with very low confidence in their health literacy skills.

THEMATIC ANALYSIS

Patient Portal Benefits

The five patients and three caregivers who had already used their patient portal systems were more likely to identify specific uses and benefits. The patients and caregivers who had not yet used a portal could only guess at the benefits of a patient portal, often repeating back the words and features the interviewer used to describe the system.

Convenience

Caregiver C2, who had used her own patient portal, noted how it would be very convenient for her and her mother if her mother's providers offered the portal and they could access it from other doctor's offices. She also noted that being able to fill out forms online was easier for her and she felt that if she could use it for her mother then she would not have to write out all of her mother's medications, because she already has them on her computer and she could simply copy and paste them into the portal when filling out forms:

> It was really easy to log into, to fill out your information whenever I set mine up. It was easy to answer the doctor's questions instead of waiting there and answering a stack of paper: I'd prefer to answer online and it would go quicker; my hand gets tired of writing. Especially with my mom having a long list of medicines – I already have it typed into the computer; I can just copy and paste instead of typing it. So that would be helpful...

Caregiver C15, who looks after her husband's elderly parents, could see how a patient portal would make it easier to bring medical staff up to speed in case one of her in-laws had a medical emergency, noting:

> It would be good, for example, if I have to take him or her to the hospital, not to have to come or talk to the doctor for them to send their records, I could just open it there and say "look, this is their medical history and this is what they have", or if I have to go with another doctor, just to open it and show him what they have...

This caregiver pointed out that the ability to share accurate medical information could result in fewer prescriptions that could react with one another.

Digital Archiving and Analysis

The patients already using their portals could give some very specific examples of ways that the system had already been helpful to them. Many of these benefits related to the way a patient portal acts as an archive of health information and even provides ways for patients to conduct their own analyses of lab results over time. For example, in response to a question about whether they would rather call or use the patient portal to ask their doctor a question about a non-pressing medical concern, P16 responded:

> I'd rather message him 'cause he'd message me back, and then I'd have it in writing and I can sit there and study it. If I call him, and he get to talking, and I done forgot half of it by the time [laughter] the phone call is over, I will be in as bad of shape as I was when I started.

This highlights the fact that information provided through the portal is archived, and can be referenced as needed, mitigating the need for a patient to remember the details.

P21, who suffers from short term memory loss, noted two important benefits of the patient portal. First, he explained that sending a message (as opposed to calling on the phone) forces him to get his thoughts together:

> You've got to think about what you're saying when you write it down, you know, so it's more concise.

Second, he noted that the information on the patient portal is:

> ...great for reinforcement of what the doctors told you. I can't remember what he told me, so I can get on and look it up and it's in print and I can understand that.

This also supports the notion that the digital archiving aspect of the patient portal is a real benefit for elderly patients, who may have issues with memory function. Similarly, P5 noted that she really likes being reminded of upcoming appointments and that she can look up information that she has forgotten, also noting memory issues:

> Well just the fact that they remind me and notify me of when my appointments are and the fact that they give me the information and it's there where I can see it and I won't forget it, maybe. Because I tell you what, you can tell me but not everything – I can't remember everything.

When asked about whether the system helps her keep track of her medical information, P19 replied:

> Yes. Because I'm constantly comparing my lab results to the previous ones, which they do the chart or the graph on there – either one – and it's just very easy.

This demonstrates that in addition to just archiving, the portal allows patients to conduct their own analysis of past and present health results. P23, who hadn't accessed her portal, mentioned this as a potential benefit:

> So, again, this would be me trying to assess my status. How high have I come – how high have I progressed from point A to now. That would be of interest to me. How is it different? You know?

Another benefit of using the portal that was highlighted was the way test results were available quickly and were contextualized. For example, P27 explained:

> ...when I go into the laboratory I have a battery of tests run I can quickly access them and see the values and see what the acceptable ranges are, and then if I have a question or a concern I can immediately email my doctor...

Neutral Communication Medium

Participant P35 hypothesized that a patient portal system might provide a more neutral medium for delivering difficult news or difficult to hear advice. Similarly, C8 felt that he would be able to say things to the doctor through the portal that he wouldn't say in person:

> .. I'd probably have something to say to him [the doctor], and it's a lot easier than to say it to his face because he'd run the other way.

These examples illustrate that communication mediated through a patient portal may allow patients to discuss issues which could be awkward to discuss face-to-face.

Patient Portal Concerns and Barriers

Privacy and Security

The most frequent concern noted by potential patients and caregivers regarding the idea of patient portals was that of privacy and security. While many of the participants understood that the system was password protected, they still felt that their information would be at risk. For example, P6 noted that having her information on the computer was a main factor in preventing her from wanting to use a patient portal:

> I just don't want no information about me discussed on other computer, internet, anything. I will talk to him face to face, discuss whatever my issues are or he can send me a letter, but I wouldn't participate in it.

This demonstrates a lack of understanding that medical records are already stored on networked computers, but shows that privacy of medical information and lack of security of online systems is a critical concern.

A number of patient participants were more pragmatic about their privacy, noting that they did not really care if someone found out about their medical issues, but still had concerns around issues of identify theft. For example, P17 noted:

> If you're sick, you're sick. I don't want everybody and his brother knowing it, but if somebody stole an e-mail where I said I had cancer, well, what are you going to do with that? Who cares? It's not like you got my social security number and my house address.

While P36 was not worried about other people finding out about his health issues, he expressed a concern that the information available on patient portals could be used by insurance companies to deny coverage, which could have a negative financial impact on his family:

> Instead what worries me are material things they can get from you but an illness is something that comes and

> many times comes with age. So it is concerning that others may be able to find things they may be able to use to create you problems or to reject you for something; that will be my only concern, nothing else.

Provider Face Time

Patients expressed a fear that use of the patient portal could eventually replace face-to-face visits with their healthcare provider and this was seen as a potential negative consequence of signing up. P17 expressed this concern, noting:

> I do things 'cause I have to with the e-mail, but I'm still old-fashioned enough that I prefer face-to-face. I don't even like discussing much on health issues with a doctor by phone. [...] But, there's anything really major about my health, I want to face-to-face.

P16, who used his patient portal, had similar misgivings. He noted that he preferred face-to-face communication and had concerns about the patient portals replacing this, but as an actual user of the portals, seemed resigned to it:

> ...I like to talk to the doctor personally. You can get a better understanding. You can read the face and see what they're telling you. If it's not right, you can tell that also... But, as you were saying, using the portals and all that, sometimes you might not be able to talk to him face-to-face, and you have to use the portals. So, you have to learn how to live with that, too.

These comments suggest that some patients may have strong misgivings about the future of this technology.

Lack of Interest

Fifteen of the 36 patient participants had not used a patient portal and expressed no interest in trying one. Many of these patients fell into a category of much older patients and they felt that they were too old to learn how to use a computer, the internet or a patient portal. For example, P33 noted:

> I think I could learn, but I don't think I want to take up the time to mess with it. I told you I ain't got but a few years or days or what.

P34 noted similar reasons for his lack of interest in the portal:

> Because of my age for one thing. Remember it would be hard probably to catch on to it too. Because when you get 79 you don't remember as you used to.

These comments demonstrate that lack of interest in technology appears linked to age, and the absence of computing technology during formative and working years for many elderly patients. We also noted that the patients in our survey with lower levels of schooling were less likely to own computers and less likely to know how to use them. This ties in to our next theme, which is technology.

Lack of Technology

Patient P9 noted his lack of a computer as the reason he would not be able to get on to the patient portal, but this tied into a lack of interest:

> I can't. I ain't got one [computer] anyway! I dont have one. That's what keeps me from – if I had one but I don't have one... And don't want to get one. Ain't nothing but a headache for me, really.

In a similar situation, P31 noted that she would not be able to access a patient portal because her computer is not working:

> My computer's messed up...and until I can get a better one, I'm just stuck.

If the main barrier to using computers was affordability, patients and caregivers who don't own their own computers could go to public computing facilities such as libraries or community centers. However, it seems that for many patients, the absence of computers in their homes is due to lack of ability, confidence and interest. For such patients, using computers at the library is unlikely to be of interest.

Usability Issues

A few patients also discussed usability issues, such as system complexity. Many of these concerns appeared to relate to the difficulty of initially logging on to the system. P17 had observed his wife use her patient portal and he commented about how difficult it was to use:

> And that's a [mess] getting into their website. It is a [mess]. It is not even kosher as far as it's just way too difficult. And that's probably is the reason why I haven't just fooled with going here.

Similarly, caregiver C1, who looks after her mother, talked about the need for easy to remember passwords, suggesting:

> Like a password, an easy password. For a senior citizen, where they would know maybe four letters.

Medical Language

Caregiver C12, who used her own patient portal once, expressed a concern about how seeing medical information in writing can be scarier than hearing it explained to you:

> ...these words were so – I mean it just made it seem like you've got so much wrong with you...

This demonstrates that for some patients, reading medical information may be too stressful. In this case, C12, who worked as a nursing assistant, noted that she had no interest in going back onto the portal after that experience.

Desired Features

Many of the patient and caregiver participants who had not already used a patient portal suggested features that are already part of most patient portals, such as the ability to look at lab results, schedule appointments, send questions to the healthcare provider and renew prescriptions.

Complete Medical Records

One of the features requested both by those who had already used their portal and those who had not, was access to their complete medical record, or at least a fully detailed medical history. P19, who used her patient portal, noted this as the only drawback she could see:

> I'd say my only drawback is medical history. I like a lot more detail than they can probably put on there...

This desire for full information was reiterated by several participants; when P12 was asked if she would sign up for a patient portal at her doctor's office if it was offered, she replied:

> I believe I would. Because it would be interesting to see some of the things [...] written in my medical records.

These comments reflect a strong curiosity about doctor's notes, comments and diagnoses among patients.

Contextualized Medical Advice

The other type of feature that many patient participants mentioned was the provision of information related to their medical conditions, daily tips or encouragement messages to help them stick to a diet or exercise regimen, and a dictionary of medical terms. For example, patient P31 noted:

> I think if a person has like have my trouble with walking and stuff [...] if they haven't got it on there, they need more of that to be able to encourage a person to walk.

Similarly, P19 expressed an interest in having more helpful medical information available through the portal:

> Maybe if there was like a dictionary there that when something is a term you don't understand [...] something if you click it will give you a little bit...

While some patient portals did have this information available, it seemed that what would be most helpful to these patients is customized healthcare information, contextualized to the information in their lab results on the portal.

Technical Assistance

The patients and caregivers who had already been on the patient portals typically found them easy to use and had no concerns about technical assistance. But patients and caregivers who had not been on the portals felt that having really good technical assistance would be necessary. Some participants were unclear about how they would go about getting help using a portal if they ran into problems. C1 suggested that she would call the computer company, which demonstrates a lack of understanding of the difference between hardware and software. Other patients were interested in having training videos available to watch before trying to use the patient portal. As an example, C4 advised:

> If someone had done a little video or something and said, "Okay, you do this and this and then here you can do this," people would, I think, be more receptive.

DISCUSSION

The five patients and three caregivers who are already using their patient portals seem quite happy with the systems and the features provided. While this is a small number of portal adopters, it suggests that the systems must have at least basic usability and functionality. Of the 31 patient participants who were not already using a portal, fifteen expressed no interest in trying to use one. Our findings suggest that both lack of technological experience and lack of access to technology (which appeared to be linked to age and education level) are major factors contributing to this lack of interest. This suggests a deeper social issue that clinics and the federal government must contend with. If many older low-income adults do not have the education and inclination to use technology in general, it is problematic to expect them to use patient portals. For patients who fit this profile, any potential benefits of using patient portals are completely overshadowed by the costs to them in terms of the amount of effort they would have to expend to sign up and use these sites. This represents a significant barrier for clinics which need to meet the federally-mandated meaningful use guidelines for patient portals. This finding supports the evidence found by Goel et al., who found that lack of motivation and negative attitudes were dominant factors in adoption rates of portals, though we found lack of technology to be linked to this and also prevalent [10].

Most patients interviewed described their communities as having internet available, most often through a television cable company or the phone company. Even patients that had very little computer knowledge were able to report that they knew that the internet was available. Thus the 'digital divide' does not reveal itself with respect to internet availability in North Carolina [12]. Of the 36 patients interviewed, half used the internet and most knew that it was available. However, half of them had no experience of actually using the internet directly, and so the digital divide does reveal itself in terms of internet usage. One patient participant mentioned having had the internet in the past but not being able to afford it at the time the interview was conducted, and it is possible that some of the other participants who do not have internet also could not afford it, but would not want to say so. It seems that income may be a factor that could prevent some patients and caregivers from using patient portals, because even if internet service is available, it may not be affordable for the lowest income patients. This fits with research conducted by Ancker et al. who found that income appeared to be a modifying factor, but not a main issue preventing adoption [4].

Trust issues appear to be another important barrier that will prevent some patients from signing on to patient portals. Even those who can see the potential benefits may be hesitant to sign in and use the system due to concerns about the privacy of their health and personal information. The information sent through patient portals is typically encrypted and is more secure than email, but none of the participants we interviewed mentioned this distinction and we surmise that most are unaware of it. Moyer et al. found that while many patients expressed willingness to use email to converse with their doctors, few of them mentioned any concerns about the security of such email correspondence, despite the fact that most email is unencrypted [21]. The lack of trust relates to the threat of hackers engaging in identity theft or of unethical healthcare employees accessing information that our participants only expect to be seen by their doctors.

Face-to-face communication with doctors was also an important issue that arose throughout our interviews. We saw evidence that some patients feared the use of portals would be a replacement for face-to-face visits. This is similar to the findings of Zickmund et al. who found this possibility to be related to disinterest in using patient portals [33]. This concern must be addressed in the marketing of the portals.

Design Considerations

Our findings point to some ways to make patient portals more palatable to low-income, elderly patients and caregivers. These could help patients and caregivers who are interested, but have misgivings or a lack of technological know-how. We focus here on the design considerations arising from our findings that add to the many design considerations (such as the need to address privacy concerns and ease the login process, and the need for clear helplines) already published in the literature.

Audio Lexicon and Lab Results: Written medical language can be frightening to patients because they may not recognize written terms that they are actually familiar with. Providing audio versions of terminology could address this. In addition, allowing doctors to record a simple audio message to explain lab results could be more personal and less intimidating for patients than a typed explanation.

Video Training: Many of the older patients seemed to indicate that they would want training before using the system, and videos seemed to be the preferred medium. This makes sense, given issues such as poor eyesight for reading and the lower rates of literacy among low-income, older adults.

Advice & Encouragement: Patients are most likely to trust medical advice from their own provider. Doctors in a practice could create a set of common advice and encouragement messages for patients to be made available with lab tests or other medical reports posted on the portal.

Some of these design considerations will immediately seem problematic to many HCI researchers. Adding audio features to the system will increase the complexity and lead to other usability issues, and providing videos is great, as long as everyone's device can handle the video codec. We are not suggesting that these design considerations are absolute requirements, and they do clearly introduce design trade-offs. It is our hope that these considerations may prompt portal designers to consider how best to address the needs of older adult patients.

In terms of promoting the patient portal, clinics should be emphasizing to patients that the system is *not* meant to be a replacement for face-to-face patient-provider appointments. And in fact, the portal can be a way to increase personalized attention for patients. If doctors are going in to the portal system and typing notes to explain test results to a patient, it could be just as easy for a doctor to record a message and relay the information that way, if the system would allow it. This more personal mode of delivery could, through a word of encouragement from the doctor, provide comfort to patients digesting important medical information at home.

Finally, it is important to consider addressing those patients for whom technology is strange and intimidating. Providing patient portal training at community centers and libraries could help older adults who have no computer experience get access to the portals. If it is necessary to get these patients using portals the benefits to them will have to outweigh the high costs of learning how to use technology. It is important to make sure that such patients are not left behind if clinics mandate use of the portals. Patients without any computing experience would need a lot of help getting on to the system, and this would require a heavy investment on the part of the healthcare providers. It is unclear how effective such a strategy could be and whether it would be worth the investment.

CONCLUSION

We have presented a detailed qualitative study that outlines the potential benefits and barriers of a patient portal system, from the perspective of low-income, elderly patients and their caregivers in North Carolina. This is an important perspective, as this population presents a significant challenge for healthcare providers who must implement patient portals and meet the federal government's meaningful use guidelines. Our results show that lack of technological experience, disinterest in technology, lack of trust in electronic systems and economic factors all present barriers to adoption of patient portals for some portion of this population. However, some elderly patients are using portals and finding important benefits related to convenience and archiving of information.

ACKNOWLEDGMENTS

This work was supported by Grant R01 HS021679 from the Agency for Healthcare Research and Quality.

REFERENCES

1. Rural-urban continuum codes, 2013. `http://www.ers.usda.gov/data-products/rural-urban-continuum-codes.aspx#.VAW_UmRdW-S` [Online; accessed 2-Sept-2014].
2. Step 5: Achieve meaningful use, 2014. `http://www.healthit.gov/providers-professionals/step-5-achieve-meaningful-use-stage-2` [Online; accessed 2-Sept-2014].
3. Ahern, D. K., Woods, S. S., Lightowler, M. C., Finley, S. W., and Houston, T. K. Promise of and potential for patient-facing technologies to enable meaningful use. *American Journal of Preventive Medicine 40*, 5 (2011), S162–S172.
4. Ancker, J. S., Barrón, Y., Rockoff, M. L., Hauser, D., Pichardo, M., Szerencsy, A., and Calman, N. Use of an electronic patient portal among disadvantaged populations. *Journal of General Internal Medicine 26*, 10 (2011), 1117–1123.
5. Arcury, T. A., and Quandt, S. A. Qualitative methods in arthritis research: sampling and data analysis. *Arthritis & Rheumatism 11*, 1 (1998), 66–74.
6. Arcury, T. A., and Quandt, S. A. Participant recruitment for qualitative research: A site-based approach to community research in complex societies. *Human Organization 58*, 2 (1999), 128–133.
7. Baird, A., North, F., and Raghu, T. S. Personal health records (phr) and the future of the physician-patient relationship. In *Proceedings of the 2011 iConference*, iConference '11, ACM (2011), 281–288.

8. Buntin, M. B., Burke, M. F., Hoaglin, M. C., and Blumenthal, D. The benefits of health information technology: a review of the recent literature shows predominantly positive results. *Health Affairs 30*, 3 (2011), 464–471.
9. Fruhling, A. Perceptions of e-health in rural communities. *Patient-Centered E-Health* (2008), 157–167.
10. Goel, M. S., Brown, T. L., Williams, A., Cooper, A. J., Hasnain-Wynia, R., and Baker, D. W. Patient reported barriers to enrolling in a patient portal. *Journal of the American Medical Informatics Association 18*, 1 (2011), 8–12.
11. Greysen, S., Chin, G. C., Sudore, R., Cenzer, I., and Covinsky, K. Functional impairment and internet use among older adults: Implications for meaningful use of patient portals. *JAMA Internal Medicine* (2014).
12. Hoffman, D. L., and Novak, T. P. Bridging the racial divide on the internet. *Science 280*, 5362 (1998), 390–391.
13. Kellermann, A. L., and Jones, S. S. What it will take to achieve the as-yet-unfulfilled promises of health information technology. *Health Affairs 32*, 1 (2013), 63–68.
14. Kim, E.-H., Stolyar, A., Lober, W. B., Herbaugh, A. L., Shinstrom, S. E., Zierler, B. K., Soh, C. B., and Kim, Y. Usage patterns of a personal health record by elderly and disabled users. In *AMIA Annual Symposium Proceedings*, vol. 2007, American Medical Informatics Association (2007), 409–413.
15. Klein, R. An empirical examination of patient-physician portal acceptance. *European Journal of Information Systems 16*, 6 (2007), 751–760.
16. Kumar, S., and Aldrich, K. Overcoming barriers to electronic medical record (EMR) implementation in the us healthcare system: A comparative study. *Health informatics journal 16*, 4 (2010), 306–318.
17. Liu, L. S., Shih, P. C., and Hayes, G. R. Barriers to the adoption and use of personal health record systems. In *Proceedings of the 2011 iConference*, iConference '11, ACM (2011), 363–370.
18. Luborsky, M. R. *The identification and analysis of themes and patterns.* Sage Publications, Inc, 1994.
19. Mauro, A., and de Quiros, F. G. B. Patient-centered e-health design. *Patient-Centered E-Health: Medical Info Science Reference* (2009).
20. Milewski, J., and Parra, H. Gathering requirements for a personal health management system. In *CHI '11 Extended Abstracts on Human Factors in Computing Systems*, CHI EA '11, ACM (2011), 2377–2382.
21. Moyer, C. A., Stern, D. T., Dobias, K. S., Cox, D. T., and Katz, S. J. Bridging the electronic divide: patient and provider perspectives on e-mail communication in primary care. *The American Journal of Managed Care 8*, 5 (2002), 427–433.
22. Or, C. K., and Karsh, B.-T. A systematic review of patient acceptance of consumer health information technology. *Journal of the American Medical Informatics Association 16*, 4 (2009), 550–560.
23. Pai, F.-Y., and Huang, K.-I. Applying the technology acceptance model to the introduction of healthcare information systems. *Technological Forecasting and Social Change 78*, 4 (2011), 650–660.
24. Pang, C. E., Neustaedter, C., Riecke, B. E., Oduor, E., and Hillman, S. Technology preferences and routines for sharing health information during the treatment of a chronic illness. In *Proceedings of ACM CHI 2013*, ACM (2013), 1759–1768.
25. Pratt, W., Unruh, K., Civan, A., and Skeels, M. M. Personal health information management. *Communications of the ACM 49*, 1 (2006), 51–55.
26. Ruland, C. M., Brynhi, H., Andersen, R., and Bryhni, T. Developing a shared electronic health record for patients and clinicians. *Studies in health technology and informatics 136* (2008), 57.
27. Simon, S. R., Evans, J. S., Benjamin, A., Delano, D., and Bates, D. W. Patients attitudes toward electronic health information exchange: qualitative study. *Journal of Medical Internet research 11*, 3 (2009).
28. Sun, S., Zhou, X., Denny, J. C., Rosenbloom, T. S., and Xu, H. Messaging to your doctors: Understanding patient-provider communications via a portal system. In *Proceedings of ACM CHI 2013*, CHI '13, ACM (2013), 1739–1748.
29. Tang, P. C., Ash, J. S., Bates, D. W., Overhage, J. M., and Sands, D. Z. Personal health records: definitions, benefits, and strategies for overcoming barriers to adoption. *Journal of the American Medical Informatics Association 13*, 2 (2006), 121–126.
30. Wilson, E. V., and Lankton, N. K. Modeling patients' acceptance of provider-delivered e-health. *Journal of the American Medical Informatics Association 11*, 4 (2004), 241–248.
31. Wilson, E. V., and Lankton, N. K. Predicting patients use of provider-delivered e-health: The role of facilitating conditions. *Patient-centered e-health* (2009), 217–229.
32. Yagil, D., Cohen, M., and Beer, J. D. Older adults coping with the stress involved in the use of everyday technologies. *Journal of Applied Gerontology* (2013), 0733464813515089.
33. Zickmund, S. L., Hess, R., Bryce, C. L., McTigue, K., Olshansky, E., Fitzgerald, K., and Fischer, G. S. Interest in the use of computerized patient portals: role of the provider–patient relationship. *Journal of General Internal Medicine 23*, 1 (2008), 20–26.

BaseLase: An Interactive Focus + Context Laser Floor

Jörg Müller[1,2] Dieter Eberle[2] Constantin Schmidt[2]
[1]Department of Computer Science, Aarhus University, Denmark
[2]Quality and Usability Lab, Telekom Innovation Laboratories, TU Berlin, Germany

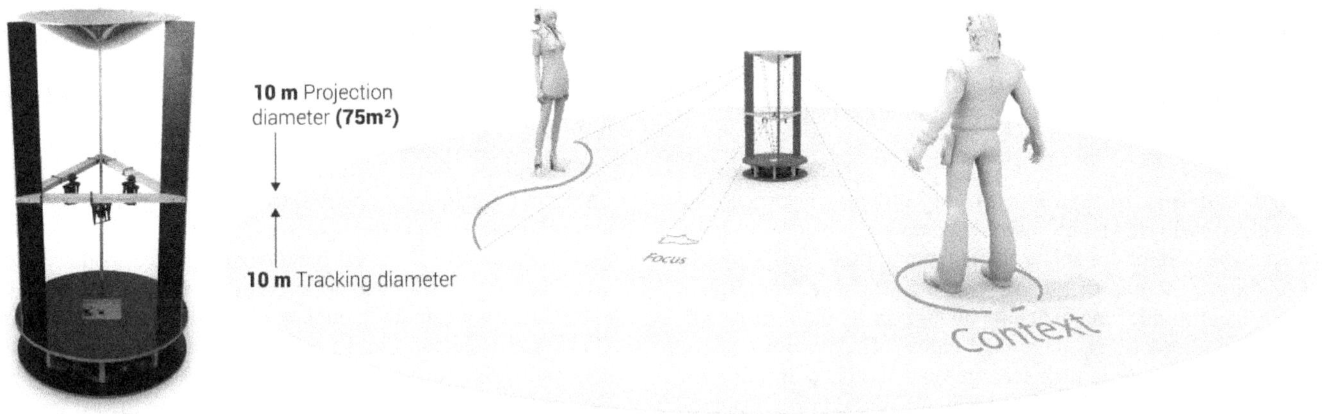

Figure 1. BaseLase is an interactive laser floor display, especially suited for large, and possibly public, spaces. BaseLase covers a very large projection area ($75\,\mathrm{m}^2$) with a low resolution context projector, while providing three movable high-resolution focus spots. Users can interact with feet, hands, and full-body, being sensed via depth cameras.

ABSTRACT
We present BaseLase, an interactive laser projected focus + context floor display. In order to provide a transportable system that works in areas where there are no ceilings, we provide an integrated unit (1.3 m height) that stands on the floor. One unsolved challenge for laser projectors is to cover large projection areas while providing high resolution at the same time. Our focus + context laser projector solves this problem. BaseLase can cover a large context area in low resolution, while providing three movable high-resolution focus spots. We provide a convex mirror design that enables the laser to reach a large area ($75\,\mathrm{m}^2$) with low resolution while decreasing the beam dispersion compared to spherical or parabolic mirrors. This hyperboloidal mirror shape approximately equalizes the point size on the floor independent from the projected location. We propose to add a number of planar mirrors on pan-tilt units to create dynamic zones of high resolution that can adjust to the user behavior. We provide example applications for BaseLase and report on user experience in preliminary trials.

INTRODUCTION
Public displays are rapidly appearing in many public places, for uses such as social gaming [19] or political participation [9]. Most of these displays are installed vertically, so that they compete for precious estate with shop windows and other signage, and are naturally limited in size.

CHI 2015, April 18–23, 2015, Seoul, Republic of Korea

ACM 978-1-4503-3145-6/15/04..$15.00.
http://dx.doi.org/10.1145/2702123.2702246

Floor displays can potentially be very large [3] and enable users to walk through the content. Such displays also offer the advantage that the floor is often not used for other information. Furthermore, many pedestrians look at the floor regularly [26].

Interactive floor projections today are mostly realized using video projectors. Using such projectors, area filling raster graphics can be projected in high resolution on the floor. However, the projected light is distributed to the entire projection surface, such that these displays suffer from limited size and/or limited brightness. In cases where the displayed content covers a small fraction of the entire surface (such as vector graphics without area fill), laser projectors are able to achieve higher brightness in larger areas by concentrating the provided light on the actual content.

In this paper, we propose to use laser projection for large interactive floor displays. In order to prevent the laser beams from crossing the eye level of users, and to remove the need for ceiling mount, we provide an integrated unit (1.3 m height) that stands on the floor.

One unsolved problem for laser projectors is how to cover large display areas while providing high resolution at the same time.

Our main contribution is the design of a focus + context laser projector to address this problem. In order to enable the laser to reach the entire area, we use a convex mirror mounted above the laser. Convex mirrors have the problem that the laser beam is widened, and thus the resolution is decreased.

We propose a mirror design that decreases the widening of the beam compared to spherical or parabolic mirrors. Our mirror shape is optimized such that for the entire projection area the projection point has approximately the same size. In order to create focus areas, we propose to add a number of planar mirrors on pan-tilt units to create dynamic zones of high resolution that can adjust to user behavior.

Thus, we present to our knowledge the first focus + context laser projector. It can cover a very large projection area from a small build height. At the same time, it provides multiple movable high-resolution spots, e.g., for text projection.

SCENARIO

Clara and Ben are tourists strolling downtown streets one evening, exploring a new city. When they come across a large plaza, they notice some halos surrounding their feet. They are standing on a map of the area, where a fisheye lens around their feet provides many details on their immediate surroundings, like attractions, shops and cafes. The portions of the map not surrounding their feet are only sketched broadly, but the entire map covers more than $70\,\mathrm{m}^2$ of the plaza. As they are walking around the map, they can obtain detailed information on different areas of the city. They decide which sight they are interested in, and tap on it with their feet to obtain some more information. They tap on a button to confirm they would like to navigate to this site. Upon this action, a school of fish appears around their feet and slowly starts to swim into the direction they need to go. When they leave the plaza down one street, the fish disappear, but they reappear on crossings that are also equipped with BaseLase to show them the way. The fish are swimming faster as they cross a street and the traffic light is about to turn red, and slower to notify them of some interesting vistas along the way. Because BaseLase supports a large projection area, only a limited number of units are needed along the way.

RELATED WORK

Interactive Public Displays

Interactive Public Displays are often installed outdoors [23, 19] or in large indoor spaces. In such areas, vertical displays are often integrated in an ecosystem of other content, and may be overlooked or ignored [13, 20]. Because pedestrians look at the floor regularly [26], it may be an interesting alternative placement for displays.

Interactive Floors

Top projection systems like iFloor [16] usually use a video projector and cameras mounted on the ceiling. iFloor for example was installed in a library, and users could move a cursor by walking around. One benefit of top projection systems is that sensitive equipment is out of reach, and occlusions between users are minimized. The main limitation is that they are only applicable when ceiling mount is feasible, and that there may be self-occlusion issues for both projection and tracking. Commercial deployments have used short throw projection to remove the need for ceiling mount[1]. The resulting interactive floor is however still relatively small.

One solution to the occlusion issues is to use a diffusely transparent floor and project and/or sense from below. The iGamefloor [12] used a diffuse transparent glass floor with back-projection and diffuse illumination based camera tracking from below. Multitoe [3] uses FTIR, diffuse illumination, and back-projection to create a high-resolution sensing and displaying interactive floor. GravitySpace [7] uses the high-resolution FTIR sensing floor to track users and their poses. Back-projected systems solve the occlusion problem and can provide high-precision input. Their main drawback are the high installation costs for the floor and the room needed below.

An alternative to projection and camera based systems are lights and sensors embedded into floor tiles. Orr [21], for example, integrated pressure sensors into floor tiles to identify users. Paradiso [22] used piezoelectric wires to detect foot position and pressure and doppler radars to detect upper-body kinematics with audio feedback. The tactile luminous floor [11] consists of 360 tiles of 66cm that integrate pressure sensors and lights for interactivity. Rogers [25] used LEDs and a pressure mat embedded into floor tiles to influence passers-by to take the stairs instead of the elevators. Dalton [10] integrated LEDs in carpet tiles and also used the LEDs as input to determine whether they are covered by users' feet. Such integrated floor tiles can lower the installation costs compared to back-projection and solve the occlusion problem compared to top-projection. Their main drawback is that the currently achievable resolution is relatively low, and most floor sensors can only sense the users' feet.

In this paper, we propose laser projection on floors as an alternative to video top- or back-projection and interactive floor tiles. Laser projection has the benefit of achieving potentially very large displays, especially when the content covers a relatively small percentage of the projection area. Our mirror design also enables an integrated mobile unit containing the entire system.

Interactive Laser Projection

Laser projectors are less frequently used in HCI compared to video projectors. Among the few examples of interactive laser projectors are the works by Cassinelli. The Camera-less Smart Laser Projector [8], for example, uses a laser that is controlled by galvanometers (further used as galvos) simultaneously as a display and 3D-position sensor. A non-imaging photodetector is used to measure the reflection of the laser beam at any point in time. By drawing circles, the system can measure the shape of the object the laser is reflecting from.

Laser projectors like other projectors face a dilemma between providing a large display area or maintaining high resolution. BaseLase solves this dilemma.

Focus + Context Screens

In HCI, there are two different meanings associated with focus + context. In focus + context visualizations, like fish-eye views [17], usually a display with constant resolution over the entire display area is used. More screen real-estate is used for portions of the content (e.g., a map) where more detail is needed. This *focus* region can usually be moved relative

[1] http://www.gesturetek.com/cube/introduction.php

to both the virtual content and the physical display. In contrast, Focus + context screens [4] provide a smaller area with physically higher resolution for detailed information, while simultaneously providing a very large area of lower resolution on a screen. Usually, the high resolution area is movable relative to the virtual content, but not to the physical screen. BaseLase is a focus + context display in the latter sense. In [4], such a display is presented in an desktop context, where the focus area is provided by a desktop display, while a projection around it enlarges the display area with lower resolution. The Escritoire [2] is a tabletop system using two video projectors. One projector creates a high-resolution *foveal display*, while the second projector covers the entire table area in much lower resolution. Lee [18] presents a system for tracking interactive surfaces (like touch surfaces or tablet computers) while a projector projects on them. They present an application where a tablet computer is used as a magic lens, providing high-resolution focus on a map display, while the video projector provides the context area. Illumiroom [15] combines a TV with a wide-angle projector that provides contextual content around the television. They provide numerous visual illusions, such as focus + context screen, peripheral flow, color augmentation, texture displacement, lighting or physical interactions.

A number of focus + context systems have been presented, mostly in the desktop or tabletop area. We provide 1) the first focus + context laser projector that 2) uses the same projector for both focus and context display, which 3) provides movable focus areas, and 4) is a floor display.

Omnidirectional Displays

The Pinch-the-Sky Dome [5] uses a video projector projecting upwards through a wide-angle lens on a dome. Such wide-angle lenses enable surround projection, but the resolution of the video projector is distributed to the entire dome surface and thus comparatively low, and significant distortions are introduced that need to be corrected in software. More recently, RoomAlive [14] proposed integrated camera-projector units that can be combined to make an entire room interactive. PlayAnywhere [27] uses a short-throw projector together with IR illumination and a wide-angle camera to create a mobile system that can be placed on arbitrary tables to make them interactive. The setup allows the creation of projection areas from a relatively low height, but the use of the video projector limits the projection size, and the projection is only to one side of the projector. The ubiquitous cursor [28] used projection on a hemispherical mirror to provide the cursor location when the cursor is travelling between displays (such as from a PC to the TV).

The work most related to our system is the Everywhere Displays projector (ED) [24]. It consists of a video projector with a movable mirror mounted above that can steer the projected image to arbitrary surfaces in the environment, including floors and walls. The system includes an environment model that is used to undistort the projected image when the projector projects on a surface at an oblique angle. The system also adjusts the focus of the projector according the distance to the projection surface. At oblique angles, the entire projection area can not be in focus, but the system works satisfactorily "up to 30° of inclination". ED further includes a camera, and the authors worked on enabling gestural interaction through computer vision.

The main difference to our system is that ED can only project on one surface in the environment at a time, because of the inertia of all moving parts and their thus relatively slow motion compared to galvos. In contrast, our system can project on the entire environment simultaneously while providing multiple high-resolution focus spots, similar to ED. Further, because our system uses a laser, it does not have focus issues.

BASELASE

Our system is an interactive focus + context laser floor display. BaseLase can project in two different resolutions: The context projection covers the area of up to 5 m radius around its center which results in approx. 75 m^2 of low resolution images while there are multiple focus areas that are smaller but can project images at high resolution. The projector itself has a height of 1.3 m and a diameter of 0.7 m. The system is able to detect and track users through depth cameras, and can thus let them interact with the projection.

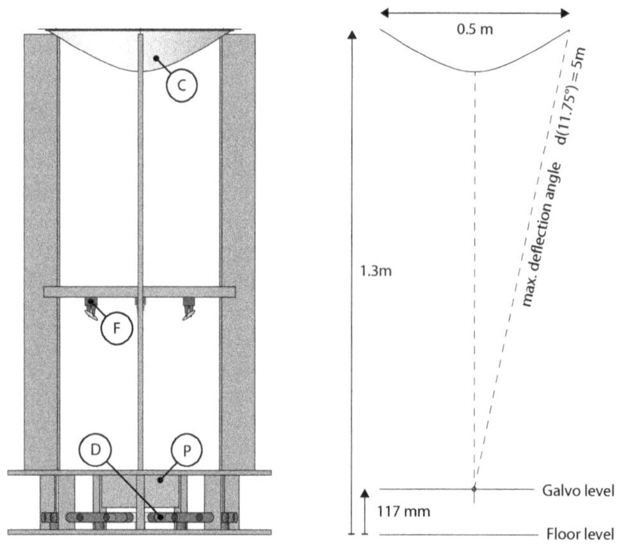

Figure 2. Left: projector construction, right: main dimensions

Figure 2 shows the components of BaseLase. There is the actual laser projector (P) that generates the images and deflects them over the context mirror (C) and the three focus mirrors (F), which allow us to create up to three focus areas simultaneously. On the bottom, there are depth cameras (D) that track the users.

When BaseLase detects a user it can generate feedback that is then projected on the ground using either the context mirror, one or multiple focus mirrors, or both, depending on the situation. The setup is designed to explicitly detect feet close to the ground but the user can also interact with hands and the whole body.

Laser Projector

The central issue of the curved mirror is the increase of the width of the laser beam, and the narrower the beam the smaller the increase. In order to have greater control of the laser beam, we decided to build a custom laser projector. A custom projector enables us to easily replace the laser source with a narrower beam width and more power in the future. We can also design the laser projector to fit in the frame of the unit. Furthermore, it allows us to pick the components that fit our needs best, such as galvos with larger angles resulting in the possibility to use a larger mirror and increasing the projection area, and also picking a low-power laser source to safely experiment during the developing phase. Finally, it gives us the possibility to run the projector from a battery source and overall results in a cheaper price than a commercial laser projector. In summary, we have built a compact and cost-efficient prototype that helps us study the possibilities of such a projection unit.

The projector is a unit of 3 different parts: a laser, galvos and electronics. The laser source is a low-power bright green laser pointer with $< 5\,\mathrm{mW}$. It generates a coherent laser ray of 1.5 mm diameter and diverges $< 1\,\mathrm{mm}$ on a distance of 1 m. This point is directed at three fast rotating mirrors mounted on galvos. Each galvo is controlled by an analog voltage which adapts the orientation of the attached mirror in a linear manner to the applied voltage. Two galvos are placed perpendicular to each other to deflect in two orthogonal directions achieving an X-Y projection plane. The third galvo guides the ray either into a light trap or onto the other galvos allowing us to interrupt the laser line to project separate objects. When the third galvo moves the ray into the light trap, another galvo counter-acts this movement to prevent motion of the point within the image. The controlling signals are generated by a sound card which we modified to allow DC current. We subsequently designed a circuit that subtracts the DC offset of the audio signal and outputs a 5 V signal and its inverted opposite to make use of differential signaling. These signals are fed to the galvo amplification board, subtracted by each other, and amplified to a higher voltage and current to power the galvos.

MIRROR DESIGN

Common galvos have a rather small scan angle (e.g., 20°). To project big pictures, it is necessary to place the projector far away from the projection plane. In case of a floor projection this could mean high above ground or very far from the projection. In outdoor scenarios, for example, both are rather difficult or even impossible to accomplish. Assuming a laser projector has a rather high scan angle of 60°, one would need to mount the projector 8.6 m above the floor to achieve a projection area that is similar to our setup. One way to decrease this distance is to position the projector on the ground facing upwards to a mirror which then reflects the laser rays to the ground. A planar mirror facing the projector would halve that distance if the projector is close to the ground. Using a planar mirror with a radius of 0.25 m in 1.3 m height like BaseLase a projection area with only 0.5 m radius would be achieved. Projecting in a flat angle from a large distance introduces severe occlusion problems. Uneven floors also lead to distortions when projecting at a very flat angle. To further increase the projection area while keeping the mirror in a realistic size we decided to use convex mirror (similar to a surveillance mirror). Using such a mirror the projector can cover a 10 m diameter surface. The main downside of a convex mirror is a spread laser beam.

Mirror Shape

First we tested the reflection over a standard spherical surveillance mirror with a diameter of 0.6 m. For close distances the laser beam was quite small and sharp but with larger distances the laser beam was heavily distorted in radial direction. To understand this effect better we implemented a simulation to generate and analyze different mirror shapes.

For all further analyzed mirror shapes we defined the following requirements for comparability:

1. Mirror radius should not exceed 0.25 m, and height 1.3 m
2. A ray of 0° off-axis should deflect to 0 m and a ray with the max. angle should deflect to 5 m, which is our maximum projection distance ($d(0°) = 0\,\mathrm{m}$ and $d(max\ \alpha) = 5\,\mathrm{m}$)
3. Radial point size $p(\alpha)$ should be as independent of projection distance and as small as possible, $p(\alpha)' \approx 0$

Common mirrors are often spherical or parabolic. The simulation shows that both types do not comply with the requested design because they break requirement 3 (see Figure 4). Even in the case of a perfect fitting spherical mirror (Requirement 1 and 2) the beam would be 120 times larger than the originally emitted ray. A conical mirror does not allow projecting very close to the projector and at 5m distance simultaneously.

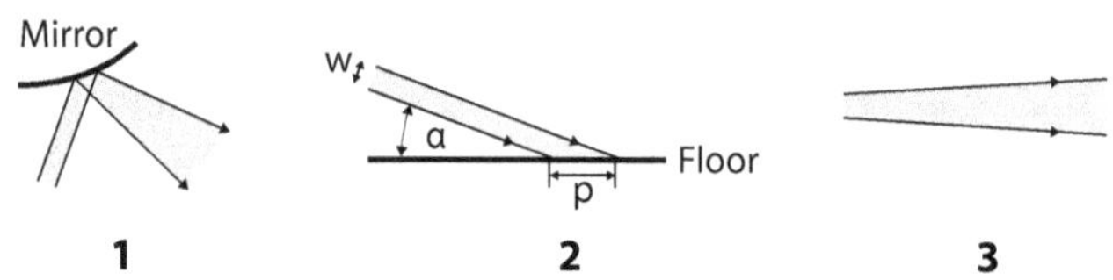

Figure 3. Increase of ray width due to 1) curved mirror 2) incidence angle 3) ray divergence.

Since these generic shapes did not result in a satisfactory mirror shape for our projector, we manually generated a shape that complied with all requirements. The main problem is to keep the point size independent of the distance (requirement 3). There are three factors that have an impact on the beam expansion. For a simplified understanding of the laser, its ray can be interpreted as two parallel rays with an offset of the laser ray width (w). When these two rays hit a curved mirror surface both will reflect to different directions due to the different surface normals at the reflection points (Figure 3 (1)). Another issue results from the incidence angle. The steeper the angle the bigger the point becomes on the floor (2). Also the laser is diverging, which means that, unlike assumed in the simplification, both border rays are not completely parallel (3). The sum of each of these factors makes it difficult to design a parametric mirror shape. In the simulation we emulate a diverging laser with the diameter of d.

We send two rays that represent the border of the laser beam and let them reflect at the mirror to the ground. The distance between these two points on the floor produces the point size p . Then the simulation calculates the point size for a given angle and mirror shape considering all effects that we mentioned previously (Figure 3). For a given mirror shape the mapping between *distance* and the *ray widening* is recorded (Figure 4). After a few unsuccessful trials with classical optical shapes like segments of spheres or parabolas, we started an iterative process to generate the mirror shape from very small linear segments. We optimized the shape to comply with our 3 requirements in an acceptable manner.

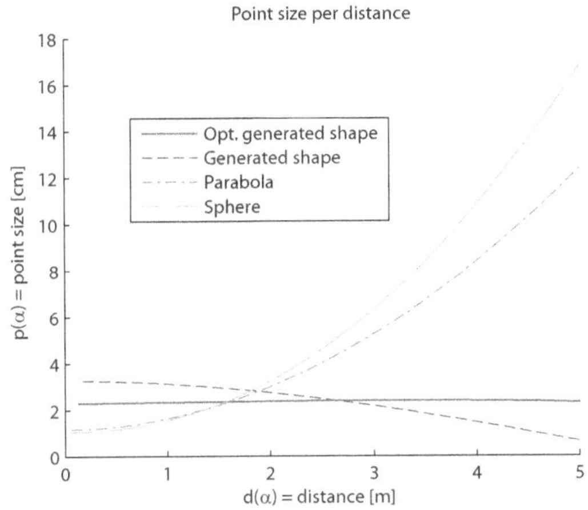

Figure 4. Laser point size on the floor after deflection over the context mirror for different mirror shapes. A laser diameter at source of $1.5mm$ with $< 1mm$ divergence per meter is assumed.

For the first generation we used a linear mapping from ray angle to the distance where the laser should hit the ground. As visible in Figure 4, for the resulting shape (Generated shape) the point size on the floor decreases for higher distances. We optimized the shape until achieving the point size shown in Figure 4 (Opt. generated shape).

The optimized generated shape appears similar to a hyperbola. We fitted a hyperbola to that shape using a regression for conic section like ellipses and hyperbolas[2]. The resulting parameters for 3339 points are $a^2 = 86.01048, b^2 = 190.0683$ in the formula for a hyperbola $\frac{y^2}{a^2} - \frac{x^2}{b^2} = 1$ with a normalized sum of squared residuals of $6.73 \cdot 10^{-12}\ m^2$.

MIRROR FABRICATION

Traditional flat mirrors are made of glass with a silver or aluminum coating on the backside. Curved mirrors are either ground and polished glass like *Zerodur*[3] or thermoplastics like Polystyrene, PMMA or ABS coated similarly. Of course metal blocks or plates can be milled or formed and finally polished as well.

BaseLase requires a very specific mirror shape. Since it was only a prototype, we wanted to minimize costs. Blocks of optical glass or metal are very expensive. Plates of metal are much cheaper but only few companies offer CNC metal spinning for small numbers of items. Afterwards these parts would also need polishing, which can be expensive. So the most realizable and low-cost process to produce such a shape for this projector is to use a thermoplastic with a metalization to achieve a reflective surface. To thermoform a plate of plastic, we needed a tool (positive shape) that defines the mirror shape. The heated thermoplastic is pressed onto that tool by a vacuum (vacuum forming). After cooling the material keeps the shape.

For our mirror we milled a tool for thermoforming out of polyurethane as shown in Figure 5 (1). This is a default material for tooling in industry for thermoforming. In a subsequent process we vacuum formed black high-gloss polystyrene plates over this milled shape (2). Finally, we used a sputtering process to deposit an aluminum layer on the polystyrene (3).

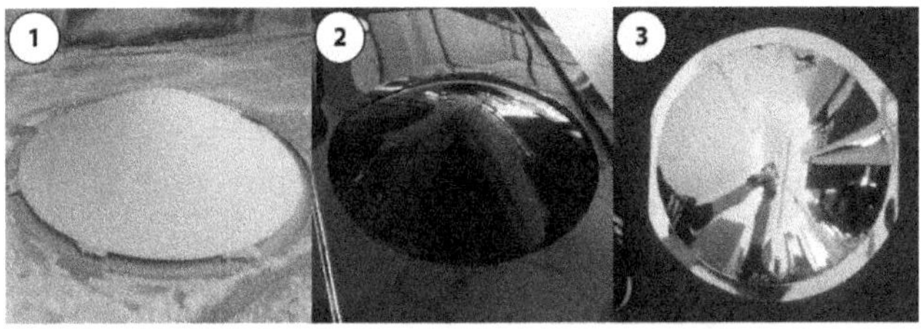

Figure 5. 1) Vacuum forming tool, 2) mirror body before and 3) after metalization

FOCUS MIRRORS

There are three small pan-tilt units attached at the outer region of the frame. These units each control a small flat mirror that can deflect the laser to a specific area which we call *focus area*. Unlike the curved context mirror, the laser ray is not widened by the flat mirrors. This shape makes it possible to project high-resolution pictures in those specific focus areas. The pan-tilt unit is designed to keep the mirror centered at a fixed position independent of its orientation. By rotating around the center it is easier to calculate the projection matrices to achieve the desired projection on the floor. Two servos rotate the mirror around two axes as shown in Figure 6 (1). The first servo turns the whole pan-tilt unit around the vertical axis which goes through the center of the mirror. The second axis is perpendicular to the first traversing the mirror's left and right side. Both axes intersect in the center of the focus mirror.

To remove the perspective distortion, the inverse physical projection is applied to all points. The physical projection matrix is obtained through simulation by shifting the projector to a virtual position shown in Figure 6 (2).

SURROUND TRACKING

To be able to track users all around the projector, seven depth cameras (Asus Xtion Pro) are installed within the base of the frame. Because of their horizontal field of view of 58°, seven of these cameras are needed to cover the whole area around the projector with minimal overlapping as shown in Figure 7 (1). Figure 7 (2) shows that the cameras are tilted by 22.5° so

[2]http://nicky.vanforeest.com/misc/fitEllipse/fitEllipse.html

[3]http://www.schott.com/advanced_optics/english/products/zerodur-extremely-low-expansion-glass-ceramic/index.html

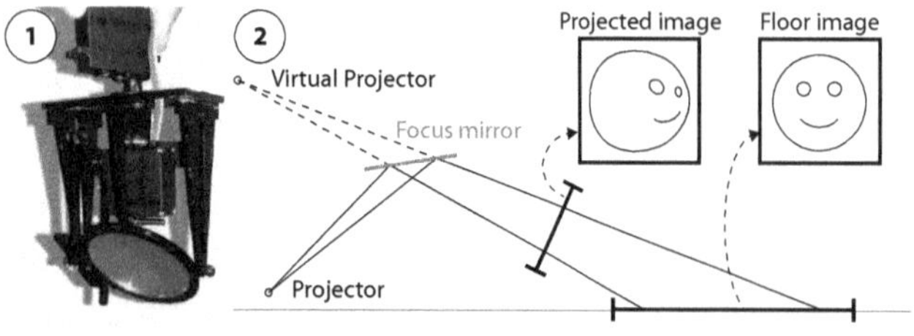

Figure 6. 1) Focus mirror, 2) projection through the focus mirrors

that the bottom of the frustum is parallel to the ground plane because their vertical field of view is 45°. This simplifies the tracking of the feet, because we can assume that the feet are always on the bottom of the depth image regardless of the distance between the user and the camera.

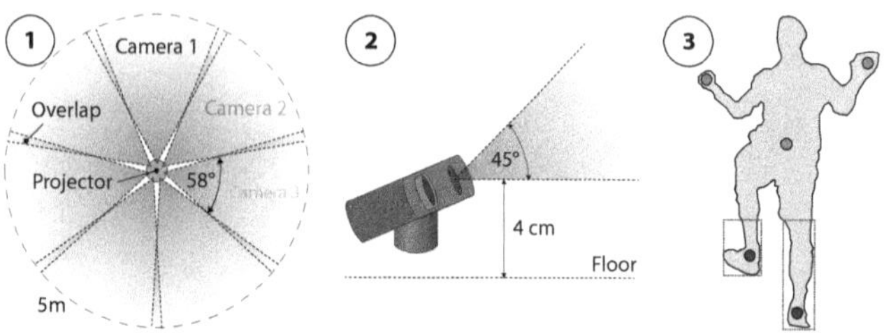

Figure 7. Camera alignment 1) top view, 2) side view, 3) debug view that shows the tracked elements: user contour, hands, feet and center position, bounding box around feet for hover detection.

For the general user tracking OpenNI and NITE are used. They allow simple access to the users' contours and skeletons for accessing the users' hand and feet positions as shown in Figure 7 (3). The user contour in the depth image is further utilized to detect the feet and especially whether the feet are on the ground or not. Thus, we are able to detect tap and hover events. For this, a contour finding algorithm is applied to the bottom part of the depth image. Each resulting contour is interpreted as a foot and the distance from the lowest part of that contour to the ground is interpreted as the height above ground.

Because the cameras have some overlapping areas, a single user can be detected by two cameras at the same time. To prevent this problem, a handover of users between cameras was implemented. If a user is on the left border of a camera's depth image, then the camera on the left checks if there is also a user on its right border. If that is the case, then we assume that both cameras track the same user, and thus we merge the data of these cameras to a single user. The resulting user data is the sum of the data from each cameras weighted by the coverage of the user.

PROJECTION PIPELINE

Drawing pictures on the ground requires a multi-stage pipeline. At first the drawable objects are sorted to minimize the trajectories between objects. The first object to be drawn is selected randomly. After that the object that is closest to the previous one is selected. Also special blanking points are added in between objects which tell the projector to move the laser into a light trap so that the line is interrupted. Because of the galvos' inertia, effects like overshooting and undershooting can happen. To prevent undershooting some points are repeated multiple times, thereby increasing the time the galvos spend for that point. The amount of repeats is decided by the angle between the previous and the next line. The larger the angle the more repeats are needed. To prevent overshooting, some points are added in close distance to the final point so that the galvos can decelerate. Additionally there are also new points that are added between longer distances, to ensure that a straight line stays a straight line after the projection due to the curved mirror shape. Finally, the image is projected.

Until this step in the pipeline the pictures were handled in world positions and now they need to be converted into sound volume values which represent angles for the galvos. The mapping between the sound volume and the angles is linear. We set the volume of the sound card to 100% and kept it constant. This way we only had to calibrate a global scale once. During the design of the mirror shape, we simulated the mapping between angles of the rays that we cast to the mirror and distances where the laser point hits the floor. We used the inverse of this mapping to fit a polynomial that we then applied to all world positions based on their distance from the projector in order to get angles. Our API provides a function where a focus mirror can be selected to draw a shape at certain position in world coordinates. The focus mirror is then automatically moved to point at the center of the drawn shape. Furthermore, the laser is automatically steered over the focus mirror instead of the context mirror. To undistort the focus images, we simulated the projection of a square on the ground using the current focus mirror's orientation. We then calculated a mapping between the real and the simulated projected square using OpenCV's *cvGetPerspectiveTransform()* function. The inverse of this mapping was then applied to the projected image in order to achieve an undistorted image on the ground.

LIMITATIONS

Occlusion is one major problem of BaseLase due to the flat projection angle. For top projection, occlusion is mainly self-occlusion due to the large torso. In contrast, with BaseLase users mostly occlude content for other users with their legs. People may not be aware that they occlude content for others. Because legs are relatively thin, only a small slice of the projection is occluded. While BaseLase is certainly not suited for crowds or dancefloors, according to our experiences, up to 10 users seem feasible. In particular, in using the silhouette, natural personal space management seems to lead users to avoid occlusions. In addition, it is more obvious where the projector is and what its line-of-sight is compared to ceiling-mounted projectors, so users simply adjust their locations such that they can see the projector. Possible solutions for occlusions include 1) monitoring occlusions via depth cameras and moving content (e.g., buttons) when necessary and 2) using multiple overlapping projectors.

Sunlight is the second major problem for BaseLase. Every projector creates contrast by brightening up a surface, competing with the ambient light. With strong ambient light, contrast may be low. Also the surface color, texture and reflectivity has an impact on the picture. The surround tracking uses depth cameras utilizing structured IR light to sense depth. In case of a strong ambient IR light source like the sun, the tracking may not function properly. Both issues can be addressed by using a brighter laser source and depth cameras which are less susceptible to sunlight.

In the current implementation, BaseLase is best suited for contexts where ceiling mount is difficult but with little sunlight. This may be because the ceiling is too high or does not provide structures to attach the projector, e.g., in big halls and lobbies. Another reason may be that the ceiling is too low to achieve a satisfactory projection size e.g., in shopping malls and hallways. While outdoor use is currently only feasible in the evening and at night, future versions might make daytime outdoor deployment possible.

A more minor issue, the number of focus mirror limits the number of focus areas. If every user gets an assigned focus mirror, the number of focus mirrors can be too small. To reduce this problem, groups of users can be detected to use one focus area per group. Like with ultra short throw projectors, the steep incidence has an impact on image distortions when the surface is uneven.

PROJECTION TECHNIQUES & APPLICATIONS

The combination of context and focus projections enables a number of interesting projection techniques that we discuss in this section.

Dynamic High Resolution Insets and Magic Lenses

The focus mirrors can be used to create high resolution insets in the context projection, much like focus + context displays. In contrast to most existing focus + context displays, these high resolution insets are dynamic, and they can be moved to wherever higher resolution is needed. One possible example is a map that provides dynamic information. The broad outline of the map could be displayed as low resolution vector graphics. Then, on some parts of this display, high resolution text insets may be provided by the focus mirrors. These areas can also be dynamic, e.g., when the map is moving around, or when some dynamic items like cars are shown on the map in higher resolution. These areas may also show information different from that shown by the context projection, and be controllable by users, much like Magic Lenses [6]. Such a display could also show templates for street painters and sprayers. The overall image could be displayed in low resolution, and the part that is currently being painted in high resolution.

Projecting Outside of the Context Area

The focus mirrors also allow to project outside of the area covered by the context mirror. When no user is in the tracking area of the system, attracting texts and animations can move around in a larger area attempting to attract users into the context area. For example, footsteps could walk from farther distances towards the context area in the hope that passers-by might follow them. An evacuation situation is another scenario where projecting outside the context area would be useful. The focus spots could project moving arrows on the evacuation routes outside the context area. Within the context area, an evacuation map could be displayed.

Projecting on Users and Objects

Finally, the focus mirrors can also be used to project on users' bodies and objects in the scene. One possible application could be a display for traffic accidents or crime scenes. The display could be placed at the site of the accident and used to interactively create annotations on the road and vehicles or objects. The annotated image could be automatically synchronized with remote investigators, who could also create annotations from their personal computers. One can also imagine more fun applications. For example, the floor might show images of insects crawling around, and these can then also crawl up the feet and legs of users.

INTERACTING WITH BASELASE

In this section, we discuss three interaction paradigms we implemented for BaseLase. BaseLase offers direct interaction with the users' feet, indirect interaction with hands through a cursor, and indirect interaction through the users' silhouette projected on the ground, as shown in Figure 8.

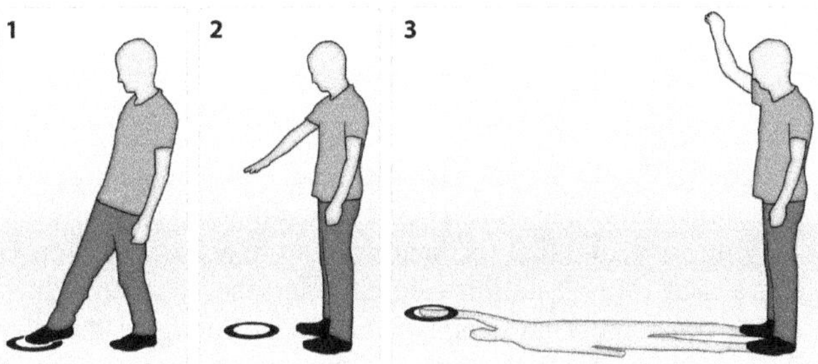

Figure 8. Interacting with BaseLase through 1) *tapping*, 2) *hand cursor* and 3) *silhouette*.

Direct Interaction with Feet

Users can step and tap on items to select them, while our vision based implementation cannot distinguish between stepping and tapping, as does Multitoe [3]. Thus, we cannot distinguish activation vs. walking, and non-interactive areas need to be provided for walking. Similar to Multitoe, we use jump for invoking menus.

Direct interaction with feet provides the advantage that input and output are co-located, much like with a touch device. Inherent downsides of this approach are 1) feet are used for standing, requiring users to change their posture and/or balance for interaction, 2) legs are heavier than arms, making quick interactions more difficult, and 3) feet are even bigger than fingers, rendering the *fat finger problem* even more grave.

Indirect Interaction with Hands through a Cursor

As an alternative to direct interaction with the users' feet, we implemented indirect interaction with the hands. In order to enable this, the user needs to be represented in the interface, such that the user can interact via this representation. In our implementation, the user's hand is tracked and mapped via a mapping function to movements of a cursor on the ground. We tried two different mapping functions. The first mapping function simply projects the hand position vertically to the ground. The second mapping function projects the cursor to a position in front of the user (same position as with the silhouette, see below). The second mapping function provides a much bigger reach without walking around, and a more comfortable head position. Users do not need to look straight down.

Indirect Interaction through the Users' Silhouette

We also implemented a representation of users through their silhouette. It is often easier for users to recognize and control their own silhouette than a cursor [19]. In our implementation, users' silhouettes are always oriented towards the projector, minimizing occlusions.

If users interact with their hands, a natural delimiter (like tapping) is not available. Possible delimiters (e.g., for selecting items) include dwell time, using a dimension that is not used for controlling the cursor (e.g., hand height), separate modalities (e.g., speech), crossing, dynamic gestures (e.g., Pigtail), or dedicated poses (e.g., touching one's hip with a hand) [1]. Because our foremost objective is immediate usability, we decided for dwell as delimiter. This option, however, enables inadvertent activations, when the user dwells over an item inadvertently.

Interaction with hands provides the main advantages that users are free to use their feet for balancing and walking while they interact, and that the hands are more agile than feet. Using a user representation can also increase users' reach, because the representations may be shown far from the users. The main disadvantages are that there is no natural delimiter (like tap), and that interaction is indirect, i.e., input and output are not at the same location.

APPLICATIONS

We implemented two example applications for our projector to show its potential.

Jump Ball

First we implemented a game where users can repel a ball by jumping close to it. The playing field is a circle of 4.5 m radius and to prevent the ball from stopping inside the projector there is also an inner circle of 0.35 m radius. If the ball collides with either of the boundary circles, it bounces physically. On two opposing sides, there are goals which are drawn as circles. If the ball moves into that circle, the other team gets a point. While everything game related is drawn using the context mirror, both scores are displayed in the focus areas to see the score more clearly. There is no limit of users that can play the game simultaneously as long as they do not occlude each other and as long as they stay within the tracking area of the cameras which is up to 5 m away from the projector.

Street Painting

As a second application we implemented a drawing application where users have a cursor that draws a line along the way when it is moved. This application is mainly intended to experiment with different interaction methods with BaseLase. Users are able to open a menu when jumping. In the menu they can select how the cursor is moved. They can switch between 1) foot position, 2) hand position orthogonal projected on the ground, and 3) silhouette projected on the ground where their right hand is the cursor (see Figure 8). The menu is represented with three circles where the currently selected mode is a smaller circle. When users hover over one of the circles, a high resolution icon is shown above the circle that describes the mode. Those icons were 1) a shoe, 2) a hand, and 3) a silhouette of a human. To switch to a different mode users hold the cursor over the circle for a dwell time of two seconds. To close the menu, users jump again.

PRELIMINARY USER EXPERIENCES

In order to explore the interaction paradigms presented in Figure 8, and to explore interaction with BaseLase in general, we conducted a qualitative user study. Our 12 participants were between 24 and 50 years old ($\mu = 31.3$) and 5 were female.

Menu Selection

For direct interaction with feet, we were interested in comparing different delimiters. With the *foot dwell* method, whenever the foot crossed an interactive area (e.g., button), a dwell time visualization was shown. The item was selected after 2 s. With the *tap* method, items were selected when a foot transitioned from hover state to foot down state within an interactive area. This tap method is much cruder than the one used in [3], because our foot detection cannot distinguish between the ball and the heel touching the ground.

For indirect interaction with hands, we were interested in different mappings from hand movements to cursor movements. With *orthogonal* projection, the cursor was shown vertically below the users' hand. With *frontal* projection, the cursor was shown in front of the user, at the same position where the cursor was shown in the *silhouette* condition. In the *silhouette* condition, the silhouette of the user was shown on the ground towards the projector. A cursor was attached to the users' hand. All methods except *tap* used dwell time to select the button.

In the first part of the study, users had to select a specific button in a menu of three buttons. The users were instructed to explore how to interact in each mode. If they did not discover how to select objects within 1 min, we provided hints. Users rated each condition on a 7-point Likert scale regarding A) how easy the method was to understand (7 being very easy), and B) how well users were able to select items (7 being very well).

Drawing

In the second part of the study a simple painting application was presented where users could draw continuous lines. We tested four different conditions: painting with the 1) *foot* position, 2) hand position *orthogonal*, 3) hand position *frontal*, and 4) *silhouette*. The first task was to draw a square, and the second to draw a predefined Euler path in the form of a house. The drawings were saved and are shown in Figure 9.

Participants rated how precise they were able to draw in each mode on a 7-point Likert scale (7 being very precise).

Results

For the *silhouette* condition, no users needed explanation, followed by *frontal* (1), *foot dwell* (1), *orthogonal* (2), and *tap* (5). Silhouette was rated as easiest to understand ($\mu = 5.67$), followed by foot dwell ($\mu = 5.33$), frontal ($\mu = 4.67$), tap ($\mu = 4.67$) and orthogonal ($\mu = 4.33$). Foot dwell was rated as easiest to select items ($\mu = 6$), followed by silhouette ($\mu = 5.75$), tap ($\mu = 5.58$), orthogonal ($\mu = 5.42$) and frontal ($\mu = 5.33$). A Friedman test revealed a significant effect of condition on both questions ($\chi^2(5) = 14.03, p < 0.05$ and $\chi^2(5) = 15.35, p < 0.05$). Post-hoc tests using Wilcoxon tests with Bonferroni correction revealed no pairwise differences for either question. After the drawing task, users felt they could draw most precisely in the frontal condition ($\mu = 4.17$), followed by silhouette ($\mu = 4.08$), orthogonal ($\mu = 4$) and foot ($\mu = 3.92$).

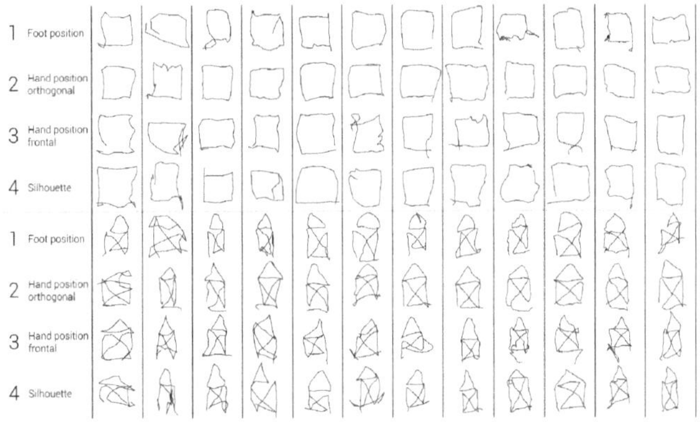

Figure 9. Drawings resulting from the user study. *Hand position orthogonal* seems to result in slightly more accurate drawings.

Users were very quick to understand how the silhouette works (P2: "Ah, I see - myself!"). With the other conditions, they had some difficulties to understand how to control the cursor. In particular, as the hands were often hanging down or sometimes in the pockets, users did not realize that they could control the cursor with their hands. In particular in the orthogonal condition, they sometimes had difficulties understanding whether the cursor was controlled with the hand, foot, or other body parts. Also, in the silhouette and frontal condition, it was a slightly easier for them to see the feedback, because they did not have to look straight down. For drawing, some users preferred to draw by walking around (foot, orthogonal) rather than moving their arms (silhouette, frontal), because they felt to have greater control. Some users found the silhouette to get in the way visually when drawing.

Discussion

As shown in [3], tapping is a very intuitive and efficient way to select items on floors. With the possibilities of depth cameras (no distinction between heel and ball), tap and foot dwell seem to be close alternatives, where both alternatives do not allow users to walk over interactive elements without activating them. Foot dwell was rated as easier to understand, but a combination of tap and foot dwell might be possible.

Our results also show that silhouette and hand cursor might be promising alternatives to interaction with feet. Silhouette needed less explanation, and was rated as easy to understand and easy for selecting items. Especially when immediate usability is premium, and it is difficult to render strong affordances (e.g., due to the low resolution of the laser projector), silhouette can be beneficial. With cursor representations, a frontal cursor seems to be easier to see and understand. Designers should choose freely between these three interaction paradigms, weighing their benefits and drawbacks in light of their particular applications' requirements.

FUTURE WORK

We plan to improve the safety for future iterations of the project. Our current prototype is safe in particular because it uses a low-powered laser source. Commercial laser projectors rated for audience scanning make sure that the laser always moves sufficiently quickly such that the maximum energy that can enter users' eyes is always on a safe level. We plan to implement such a constraint in BaseLase. Safety could be also be increased by detecting faces and/or eyes and preventing the laser from projecting onto them, or by decreasing the height of the system.

Currently the projector has three bars that hold the context mirror and block thin vertical stripes of the projection. In future versions, we would like to use a cylindric acrylic glass that holds the context mirror. This would also protect the projector from environmental influences like rain.

A higher quality laser source with higher brightness and a smaller beam diameter would greatly increase image quality. This would also allow us to experiment with even larger projection ranges. Higher quality galvos could allow us to project more detailed images. Finally, we are very interested in mounting BaseLase on an autonomous robotic platform to have a self-driving interactive floor that can adjust to the surrounding situation.

CONCLUSION

In this paper, we have presented an interactive laser projected focus + context floor display. It covers a large display area in low resolution through a convex mirror design that approximately equalizes the point size for the entire display area. At the same time, the display provides multiple movable high-resolution focus spots. We introduced interaction with hands and full body on floors through cursors and silhouettes as an alternative to direct foot based interaction.

Our design is able to cover entire plazas with very few display units and does not require a ceiling mount. We believe that focus + context laser projectors provide an interesting alternative to conventional projectors, especially on floors but potentially also on other surfaces where very large display areas from a small projector distance are important.

ACKNOWLEDGEMENTS

This project has been supported by the European Institute of Innovation and Technology. We would like to thank Alvaro Cassinelli, Konrad Tollmar, Robert S. Brewer, Yuka Nagashima, and the FH Potsdam for their help.

REFERENCES

1. Accot, J., and Zhai, S. More than dotting the i's — foundations for crossing-based interfaces. In *Proc. of CHI'02*, ACM (2002), 73–80.
2. Ashdown, M., and Robinson, P. Escritoire: A personal projected display. *MultiMedia, IEEE 12*, 1 (2005), 34–42.
3. Augsten, T., Kaefer, K., Meusel, R., Fetzer, C., Kanitz, D., Stoff, T., Becker, T., Holz, C., and Baudisch, P. Multitoe: high-precision interaction with back-projected floors based on high-resolution multi-touch input. In *Proc. of UIST'10*, ACM (2010), 209–218.
4. Baudisch, P., Good, N., and Stewart, P. Focus plus context screens: combining display technology with visualization techniques. In *Proc. of UIST'01*, ACM (2001), 31–40.
5. Benko, H., and Wilson, A. D. Pinch-the-sky dome: freehand multi-point interactions with immersive omni-directional data. In *CHI EA '10*, ACM (2010), 3045–3050.
6. Bier, E. A., Stone, M. C., Pier, K., Buxton, W., and DeRose, T. D. Toolglass and magic lenses: the see-through interface. In *Proc. of SIGGRAPH'93*, ACM (1993), 73–80.
7. Bränzel, A., Holz, C., Hoffmann, D., Schmidt, D., Knaust, M., Lühne, P., Meusel, R., Richter, S., and Baudisch, P. Gravityspace: tracking users and their poses in a smart room using a pressure-sensing floor. In *Proc. of CHI'13*, ACM (2013), 725–734.
8. Cassinelli, A., Zerroug, A., Watanabe, Y., Ishikawa, M., and Ängeslevä, J. Camera-less smart laser projector. In *SIGGRAPH Emerging Technologies* (2010).
9. Dalsgaard, P., and Halskov, K. Designing urban media façades: cases and challenges. In *Proc. of CHI'10*, ACM (2010), 2277–2286.
10. Dalton, N. S. Taptiles: LED-based floor interaction. In *Proc. of ITS'13*, ACM (2013), 165–174.
11. Delbrück, T., Whatley, A. M., Douglas, R., Eng, K., Hepp, K., and Verschure, P. F. A tactile luminous floor for an interactive autonomous space. *Robotics and Autonomous Systems 55*, 6 (2007), 433 – 443.
12. Grønbæk, K., Iversen, O. S., Kortbek, K. J., Nielsen, K. R., and Aagaard, L. Igamefloor: a platform for co-located collaborative games. In *Proc. of ACE'07*, ACM (2007), 64–71.
13. Huang, E. M., Koster, A., and Borchers, J. Overcoming assumptions and uncovering practices: When does the public really look at public displays? In *Pervasive Computing*. Springer, 2008, 228–243.
14. Jones, B., Sodhi, R., Murdock, M., Mehra, R., Benko, H., Wilson, A., Ofek, E., MacIntyre, B., Raghuvanshi, N., and Shapira, L. Roomalive: Magical experiences enabled by scalable, adaptive projector-camera units. In *Proc. of UIST'14*, ACM (2014), 637–644.
15. Jones, B. R., Benko, H., Ofek, E., and Wilson, A. D. Illumiroom: peripheral projected illusions for interactive experiences. In *Proc. of CHI'13*, ACM (2013), 869–878.
16. Krogh, P., Ludvigsen, M., and Lykke-Olesen, A. " help me pull that cursor" a collaborative interactive floor enhancing community interaction. *Australasian Journal of Information Systems 11*, 2 (2007).
17. Lamping, J., Rao, R., and Pirolli, P. A focus+ context technique based on hyperbolic geometry for visualizing large hierarchies. In *Proc. of CHI'95*, ACM (1995), 401–408.
18. Lee, J. C., Hudson, S. E., Summet, J. W., and Dietz, P. H. Moveable interactive projected displays using projector based tracking. In *Proc. of UIST'05*, ACM (2005), 63–72.
19. Müller, J., Walter, R., Bailly, G., Nischt, M., and Alt, F. Looking glass: a field study on noticing interactivity of a shop window. In *Proc. of CHI'12*, ACM (2012), 297–306.
20. Müller, J., Wilmsmann, D., Exeler, J., Buzeck, M., Schmidt, A., Jay, T., and Krüger, A. Display blindness: The effect of expectations on attention towards digital signage. In *Pervasive Computing*. Springer, 2009, 1–8.
21. Orr, R. J., and Abowd, G. D. The smart floor: A mechanism for natural user identification and tracking. In *CHI EA '00*, ACM (2000), 275–276.
22. Paradiso, J., Abler, C., Hsiao, K.-y., and Reynolds, M. The magic carpet: physical sensing for immersive environments. In *CHI EA '97*, ACM (1997), 277–278.
23. Peltonen, P., Kurvinen, E., Salovaara, A., Jacucci, G., Ilmonen, T., Evans, J., Oulasvirta, A., and Saarikko, P. It's mine, don't touch!: Interactions at a large multi-touch display in a city centre. In *Proc. of CHI'08*, ACM (New York, NY, USA, 2008), 1285–1294.
24. Pinhanez, C. The everywhere displays projector: A device to create ubiquitous graphical interfaces. In *Proc. of Ubicomp'01*, Springer (2001), 315–331.
25. Rogers, Y., Hazlewood, W. R., Marshall, P., Dalton, N., and Hertrich, S. Ambient influence: Can twinkly lights lure and abstract representations trigger behavioral change? In *Proc. of Ubicomp'10*, ACM (2010), 261–270.
26. Schrammel, J., Mattheiss, E., Döbelt, S., Paletta, L., Almer, A., and Tscheligi, M. Attentional behavior of users on the move towards pervasive advertising media. In *Pervasive Advertising*, J. Müller, F. Alt, and D. Michelis, Eds., Human-Computer Interaction Series. Springer London, 2011, 287–307.
27. Wilson, A. D. PlayAnywhere: a compact interactive tabletop projection-vision system. In *Proc. of UIST'05*, ACM (2005), 83–92.
28. Xiao, R., Nacenta, M. A., Mandryk, R. L., Cockburn, A., and Gutwin, C. Ubiquitous cursor: A comparison of direct and indirect pointing feedback in multi-display environments. In *Proc. of GI'11* (2011), 135–142.

Ergonomic Interaction on Touch Floors

Dominik Schmidt[1], Johannes Frohnhofen[2], Sven Knebel[2], Florian Meinel[2], Mariya Perchyk[2], Julian Risch[2], Jonathan Striebel[2], Julia Wachtel[2], Patrick Baudisch[1]
Hasso Plattner Institute
Potsdam, Germany
[1]{first.last}@hpi.de, [2]{first.last}.student@hpi.de

Figure 1: We argue that touch floors have bad ergonomics as they are designed for being used while standing, which causes fatigue, especially in combination with looking down. We thus propose allowing users to operate touch floors in other poses. Based on a series of studies, we have created a simple view manager that supports users in switching poses by re-layouting screen content.

ABSTRACT

The main appeal of touch floors is that they are the only direct touch form factor that scales to arbitrary size, therefore allowing direct touch to scale to very large numbers of display objects. In this paper, however, we argue that the price for this benefit is bad physical ergonomics: prolonged standing, especially in combination with looking down, quickly causes fatigue and repetitive strain. We propose addressing this issue by allowing users to operate touch floors in any pose they like, including sitting and lying. To allow users to transition between poses seamlessly, we present a simple pose-aware view manager that supports users by adjusting the entire view to the new pose. We support the main assumption behind the work with a simple study that shows that several poses are indeed more ergonomic for touch floor interaction than standing. We ground the design of our view manager by analyzing, which screen regions users can see and touch in each of the respective poses.

CHI 2015, April 18 - 23 2015, Seoul, Republic of Korea
Copyright is held by the owner/author(s). Publication rights licensed to ACM.
ACM 978-1-4503-3145-6/15/04…$15.00
http://dx.doi.org/10.1145/2702123.2702254

Author Keywords

Ubicomp; Smart Rooms; Interactive Floor; GUI; Multi-touch; Ergonomics.

ACM Classification Keywords

H.5.2. [Information Interfaces and Presentation]: User Interfaces–Input devices and strategies, interaction styles.

INTRODUCTION

The main appeal of touch floors (e.g., [1,11,26]) is that they allow creating interaction spaces of *arbitrary* size, while maintaining the affordance of direct touch. This makes touch floors different from touch tables, tablets, etc. whose size is limited by arm's reach—even interactive walls, which can be arbitrarily long, are limited in height. Touch floors thus open new opportunities as they can be designed to scale direct touch to handle substantially bigger problems [1]. Working on bigger problems, however, not only requires space—it may also require users to interact for longer periods of time.

In this paper, we argue that interaction for longer periods or time can be an issue, because of the particular form factor of touch floors: prolonged standing, especially in combination with looking down, quickly causes fatigue and repetitive strain. The hydrostatic blood pressure in the legs increases over time, causing discomfort [10]. Even worse, users find themselves continuously looking down, increasing the risk of neck pain, a milder form of which is also known to notebook computer users, as their screen position also makes users look down [5].

We propose addressing floor ergonomics by allowing users to operate touch floors in poses that are less prone to fatigue, such as sitting or lying. As illustrated by Figure 2, we argue that floors naturally afford multiple poses—unlike most existing direct touch form factors (e.g., tabletops require sitting, interactive walls require standing).

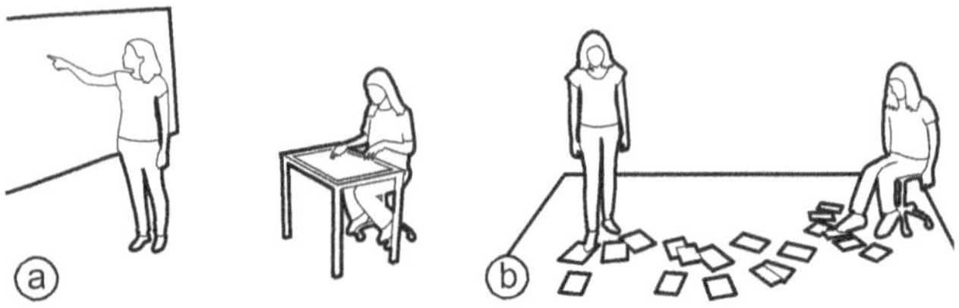

Figure 2: Unlike (a) other touch devices, such as wall displays or tabletops, (b) we argue that touch floors allow users to assume a range of poses.

CONSTRUCTING A POSE-AWARE VIEW MANAGER

To help users work in any pose, we propose the concept of a "pose-aware" view manager with the following functionality. (1) Such a system should support users in accessing their content in their current pose. (2) Since any pose gets tiring after some time (see Study 1) users will *change* poses periodically, relieving whatever tension the previous pose has caused. The pose-aware view manager should allow users to continue their interaction seamlessly whenever such a pose switch occurs.

We construct our pose-aware view manager in three steps:

Step 1: We verify that at least some of the other poses afforded by touch floors are indeed less fatiguing than standing. We do this in the form of a simple user study. The study also tells us *which* out of many possible poses work best, thus should be supported by our view manager.

We use the same study to also extract the first set of parameters we need for constructing our pose-aware view manager, which is the *scale* at which users would like to view content for each possible pose.

Step 2: We determine the remaining parameters we need for our view manager, which is *where* to place content. Direct touch interaction requires users to see *and* touch content. By intersecting the two we determine candidate regions for each pose.

Step 3: Based on these findings, we present our pose-aware view manager, which we termed *PoseUI* (Figure 1).

CONTRIBUTION

In this paper, we make two main contributions. (1) We argue that touch floors afford interaction in various other poses than standing. We verify this assumption in a simple study in which we find that *several* of the poses afforded by touch floors are less fatiguing than standing. (2) We present a simple pose-aware view manager that allows users to continue their interaction seamlessly when they switch between poses. We build this view manager on a careful analysis of the necessary parameters, in particular scale and placement of content.

RELATED WORK

This work builds on interactive floors, research in ergonomics, direct-touch tabletop UIs, and automatic UI layouting.

Interactive Floors

Interactive floors are part of the ubiquitous computing vision, that is, computers being integrated into the environment, thus becoming invisible [24]. Researchers have explored floors from different perspectives, for example, as part of immersive environments for virtual [7] and augmented realities [18], as unobtrusive sensing platform (e.g., for pose detection [4]), and for interactive installations (e.g., to support collaboration in public space [15] or for gaming [11]). In addition, recent work has proposed precise direct touch manipulation for interactive floors [1] and floors as platform for tangible UIs [19].

Ergonomics

Research in ergonomics on other devices and form factors suggests that changing poses relieves fatigue (e.g., [10,21]) and recommends work equipment that encourages frequent pose change [16].

Direct-Touch Tabletop UIs

Interactive floors share major UI design challenges with direct-touch tabletops, particularly with respect to multi-user collaboration, content orientation, occlusion, and reach [20].

To allow for interacting with objects beyond a user's physical reach, researchers have proposed a range of techniques, such as temporarily moving target icons closer to the user [3], switching between absolute and cursor-based input [8], or interacting with a scaled-down world-in-miniature view [22].

To avoid occluding information, *Display Bubbles* dynamically wrap content around physical objects placed on a table [6]. Vogel and Balakrishnan automatically show callouts to make information visible that would otherwise be obscured by the user's hand and arm [23].

Automatic UI Layouting

A simple layout adaptation is implemented by *Lean and Zoom*, which detects the user in front of a laptop computer leaning forward and zooms the UI accordingly to meet half-way [12]. *SUPPLE*, in contrast, automatically pre-renders UI layouts for devices with varying constraints, using models of the user and the device and treating interface generation as an optimization problem [9]. *Cassowary* is a linear solver that maintains layout constraints of interactive UIs [2].

STEP 1: TOUCH FLOORS AFFORD OTHER POSES THAT ARE LESS FATIGUING THAN STANDING

The primary objective of this user study was to validate our assumption that some of the poses afforded by touch floors are indeed more ergonomic than standing.

At the same time, this study provides a first basis for our pose-aware view manager in that (1) it tells us which poses are worth supporting (2) it allows us to determine at what scale users would like to view content in each pose.

Task

Participants performed a repetitive direct touch task (i.e., the game "whack-a-mole" shown in Figure 3). Each participant performed this task in each of the eight different poses shown in Figure 4. Note how some poses allowed users to interact using their hands, others using their feet.

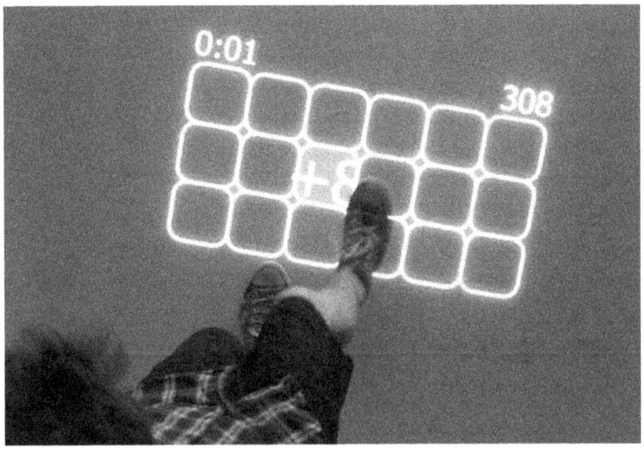

Figure 3: Participants performed a repetitive "whack-a-mole" direct touch task, i.e., they tried to touch/tap highlighted buttons as soon as they appeared.

For each trial, participants made themselves comfortable in the respective pose; they were allowed to use pillows if they preferred. Participants then rotated and scaled the game board so that they could reach it comfortably; we logged these settings. We intentionally initialized interfaces to too small a scale, forcing participants to tediously scale up their interface by repeatedly pushing a button. This approach, however, allows us to interpret the resulting scales as a lower bound for scale, which is one of the required parameters for our pose-aware view manager.

Participants then performed the whack-a-mole task for 60 s. At the end of a trial, participants rated the pose using a questionnaire (two ratings: one referring to the first seconds and one rating referring to the end of the 60-second period).

We used a within-subjects design (i.e., each participant interacted in all eight poses). The order of these poses was counterbalanced.

The study was designed to establish *lower bounds* on ergonomic issues. While 60 s are a comparably short amount of time, one would expect any fatigue effects found to be amplified during prolonged use.

Participants

We recruited eight participants (two female) from our institution. They were between 21 and 26 years old ($M = 22.1$ yr, $SD = 1.7$ yr).

Figure 4: Every participant performed the study task in each of these eight poses.

Results: Fatigue

Figure 5 shows the median fatigue rating for each pose. For the beginning of each trial, participants rated only one pose as less tiresome than standing (pose "sitting cross-legged", bold outline) on a scale from 1 (effortless) to 7 (tiresome). For the end of the 60 s trial, participants rated *four* poses as less tiresome (bold outlines). A Friedman test showed significant differences in pose ratings for the beginning of a trial ($\chi^2(7) = 18.63$, $p < 0.01$) as well as for the end of a trial after 60 s ($\chi^2(7) = 15.27$, $p < 0.05$).

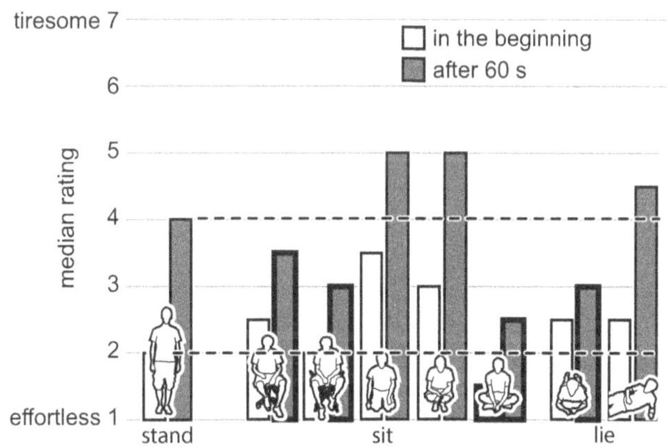

Figure 5: Participants rated "sitting cross-legged" as less tiresome than standing upright in the beginning of a task. After 60 s, four poses had better rating than standing (bold outlines).

For four participants, standing was their highest rated pose *in the beginning*. However, standing was rated highest only for one participant after 60 s. As illustrated by Figure 6, all but one pose received the highest rating from at least one participant. We assigned fractional points for draws.

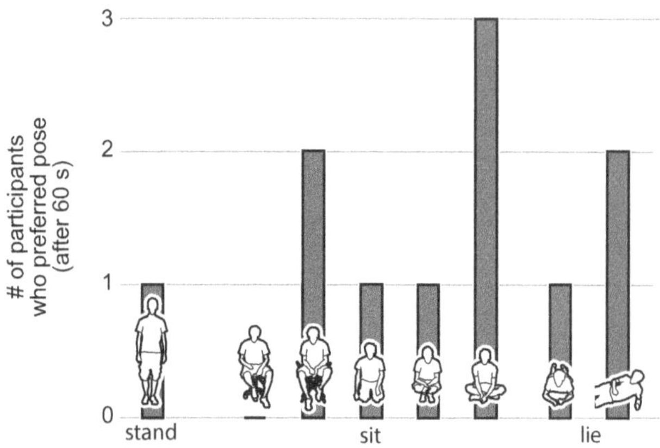

Figure 6: All but one pose received the highest rating from at least one participant (we assigned fractional points for draws).

Discussion: These findings support our main hypothesis: touch floors indeed afford other poses that are more ergonomic than standing.

The findings also inform our design of a pose-aware view manager, in that they tell us which poses should be supported. If we choose to support the poses that cause less fatigue than standing (which is four of them) as well as poses favored by at least one user (which surprisingly is all but one, Figure 6), the answer is that *all* tested poses should be supported by a pose-aware view manager.

Results: Scale

Figure 7 shows how participants scaled their interfaces for the respective pose. As expected there was a significant main effect of pose onto scale ($F(7,42) = 5.73$, $p < 0.001$).

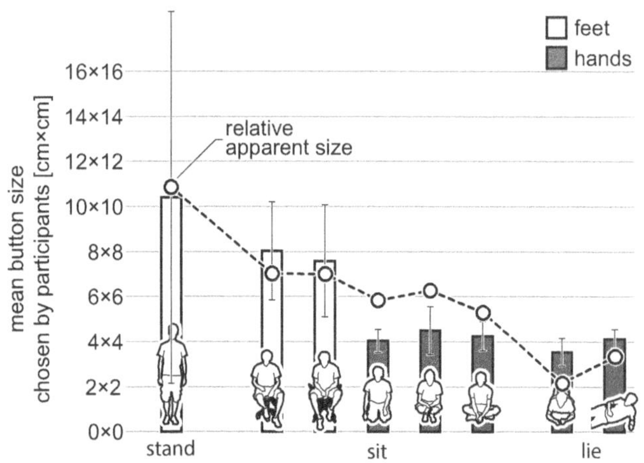

Figure 7: Mean button sizes chosen by participants (error bars: ±1 std. deviation): they seemed to maintain the apparent UI size, i.e., scaled the interface relative to standing.

Discussion: As expected, there was a positive relationship between participants' head height and scale of the interface. A correlation of 0.87 ($p < 0.01$) suggests that participants might try to scale content so as to *appear* to them at a certain size across pose. We calculated the apparent size as 1 / distance (between eyes and floor).

Poses that let participants interact using their feet resulted in larger buttons than those that let participants interact using their fingers. This is expected, based on the different accuracy levels of hands and feet in direct touch [1,13].

Figure 7 shows a reasonably good fit for the three poses that let users interact using their feet as well as for the two lying poses, in which participants used their hands to interact. For sitting poses, in contrast, it seems that the higher accuracy of finger touch allowed participants to make the interface smaller than suggested by apparent size. While this worked well for our study task, scaling below the apparent size might not be desirable for other tasks, such as reading text or performing visual search.

These findings suggest that document scale may be approximated by means of head height and whether users use feet or hands to interact. This suggests that a pose-aware view manager may not have to fully capture the user's pose; instead, we might obtain a good approximation by only tracking the vertical position of the user's head and determining whether a pose affords foot or finger touch.

STEP 2: WHERE TO PLACE CONTENT ACROSS POSES

Now that we know how to scale content across poses, our next step in constructing our pose-aware view manager is to determine *where* to place content for each pose.

Direct touch interaction requires users to see *and* touch content. In this section we model both for each of the eight poses used earlier. For each pose, we then intersect visible and touchable regions, obtaining candidate regions for direct touch.

What Users Can See

Figure 8 shows how we approximately model what users can see in a given pose. We use the simple metric of how long it would take a user to see a documents placed at a certain location. Our model distinguishes three areas.

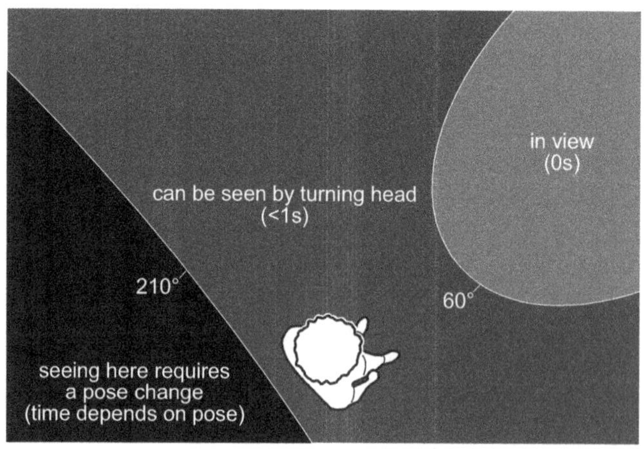

Figure 8: Our simple model of what users can see

1. "In view" We compute this area by casting a cone-shaped 60° spotlight [14] from the point between the user's eyes.

2. "Can be seen in 1s by turning head" We determine this area using a 210° cone (60° maximal eye + 150° lateral neck rotation [17]).

3. "Seeing here requires a pose change." The time it takes to see a document here depends on the user's pose (e.g., is longer for sitting vs. standing).

In addition, some areas are occluded by the user's body and thus not visible. We will handle these later when we determine what users can touch.

To get a sense for what areas can be seen in each pose, we created the simple real-time visualization shown in Figure 9. It tracks the user using an optical motion capture system (*OptiTrack,* naturalpoint.com), then uses the GPU to calculate the visibility of each pixel based on shoulder orientation and incident angle of gaze.

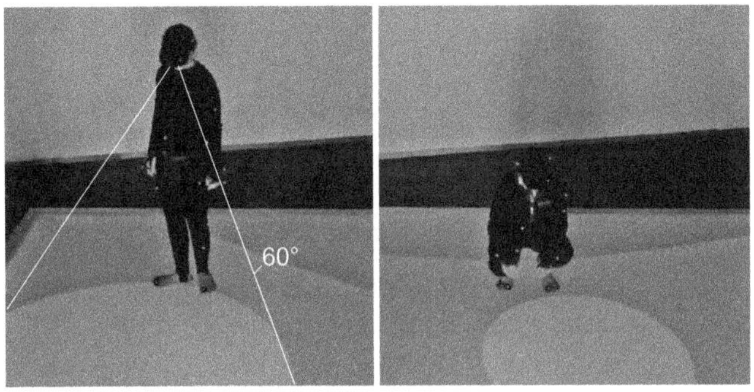

Figure 9: Our simple real-time visualization allows us to get a sense for what users can see from which pose.

For our pose-aware view manager, we want content to be visible without requiring a pose change. Figure 10 shows the resulting models, which we obtain by simply removing the area that users can only see by means of a pose change.

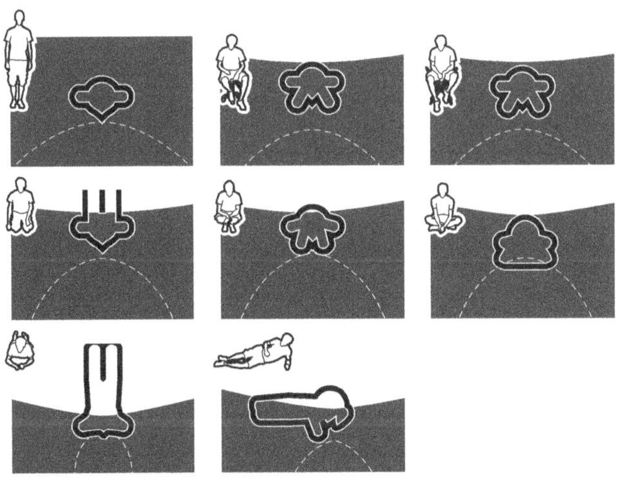

Figure 10: What users can see for each pose. Standing users can turn and walk around without changing pose. Thus, we do not prune the visible space for standing.

We are making one exception though: standing users can turn around and walk around without changing their pose, making it easy to access content anywhere—a big strength of this pose (and probably the reason it has been so popular in the related work, e.g., [1,11,26]). We reflect this in that we do *not* prune the space for standing and instead consider all screen space to be acceptable for placing content.

What Users Can Touch

To determine what users can touch in each pose, we conducted another simple study. We recruited eight participants (two female) from our institution between 22 and 32 years old (M = 26 yr, SD = 3.7 yr) and between 165 and 180 cm tall (M = 173.4 cm, SD = 5.9 cm). Their arms were between 52 and 66 cm (M = 59 cm, SD = 4.5 cm), their legs between 92 and 105 cm (M = 99.8 cm, SD = 4.3 cm) long. As shown in Figure 11, we placed them on a study interface consisting of a 5 cm × 5 cm button grid and asked them to show what areas they could touch, using their left, their right hand, their left foot, and their right foot. We had them repeat this for each of the eight poses in counterbalanced order.

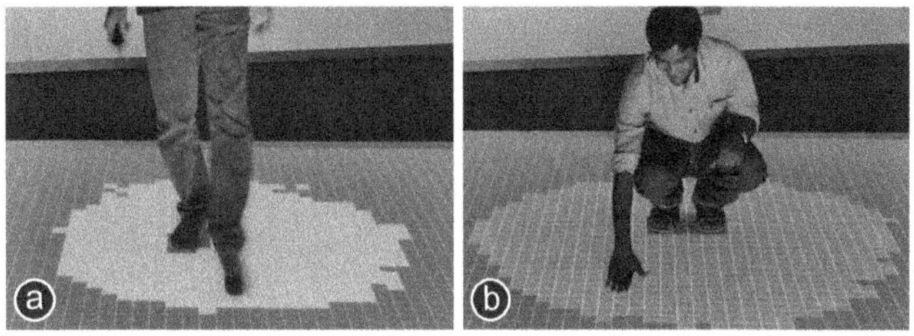

Figure 11: We asked participants to indicate areas they could touch in different poses using their hands and feet, for example, (a) left foot (standing) and (b) right hand (crouching).

Figure 12 shows the participants' touch outlines for feet and hands. Areas that could be reached by at least *two thirds* of participants are filled green for feet and blue for hands. As before, we make an exception for standing and include the entire screen space for placing content.

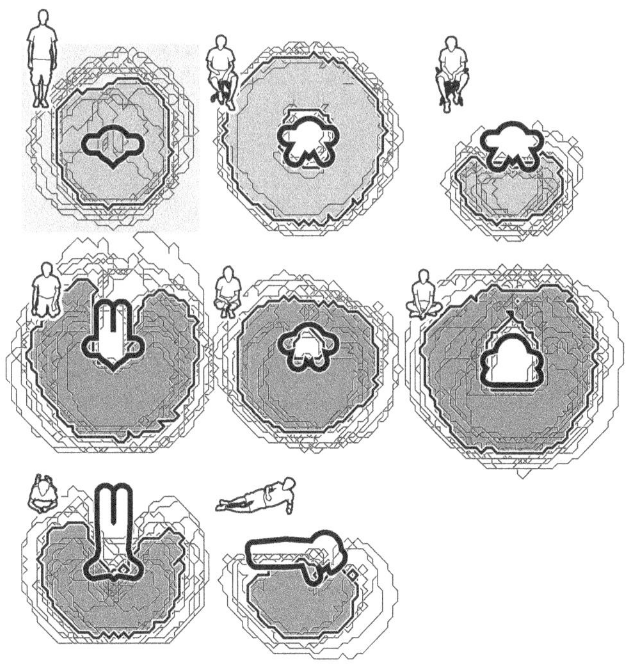

Figure 12: Areas participants could touch in different poses using feet (green) and hands (blue). Standing allows users to reach any location on the floor without changing pose.

Direct Touch: What Users Can See *and* Touch

Figure 13 shows the resulting direct touch areas for each pose as the intersection of what users can see with what they can touch.

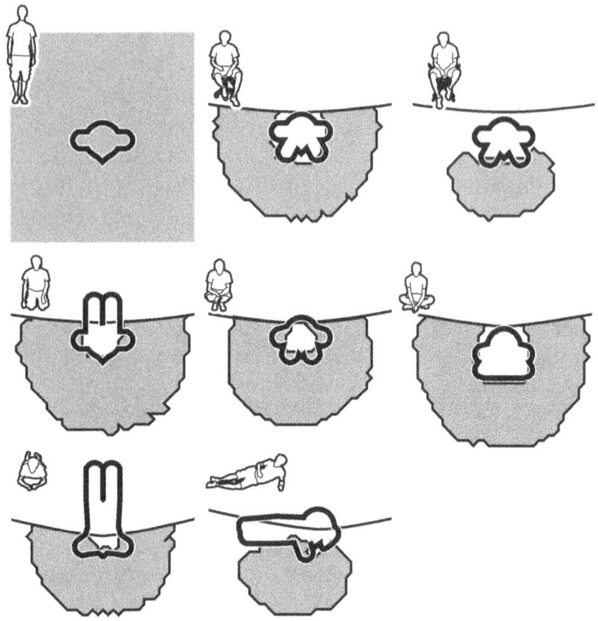

Figure 13: Direct touch is possible where what a user can see intersects with what a user can touch. Standing takes on a special role as users can move without additional effort.

We now have all necessary information (scale and placement) for placing content with respect to any of the eight poses.

STEP 3: A POSE-AWARE VIEW MANAGER

Based on the findings from Steps 1 and 2, we created a simple pose-aware view manager. It rearranges the user's documents to match the new pose after a pose change.

Prototype Framework

When the user changes pose, the system's objective is to select all relevant documents, scale them to the target scale, and arrange them into the target direct touch area with the goal to make all documents that users could see and touch in the previous pose visible and reachable in the new pose.

To enable this, we created the following hardware setup. In order to detect pose changes, a pose-aware system has to continuously monitor the users' pose. Pose recognition on interactive floors is a well-understood problem (e.g., FootSee [25], GravitySpace [4]); we thus simply used an optical motion capture system. For our first prototype we used a full-body tracking suit; based on insights from Study 1, we simplified the tracking set-up to a single rigid body marker on the users' shoulder for our second prototype. All prototypes run on a 360 cm × 260 cm back projected touch floor [1] with software written in C++ and some components running on the GPU.

V1: Optimized Layout at the Expense of Spatial Memory

Based on this hardware setup, we created a first prototype. This version used a "per-document" approach to pose change as illustrated by Figure 14: when the user changed pose, the system selected only those documents currently in reach (determined based on Figure 13; for standing, we chose to include all documents at most two steps away). The system then not only scaled documents according to the scales determined in Study 1 (Figure 7) but also rearranged them to best fit into the direct touch area of the target pose. It did so by moving documents individually.

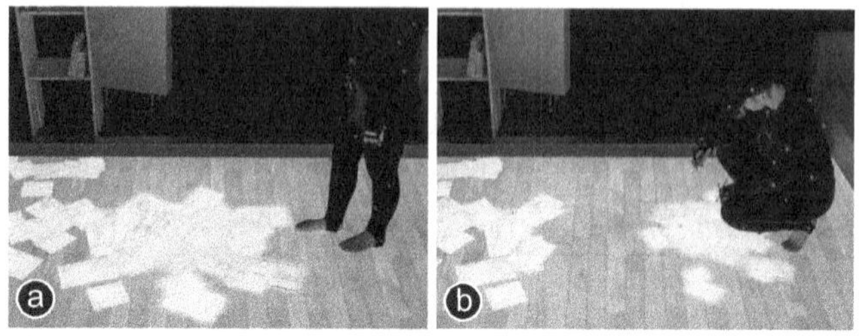

Figure 14: First version re-laid out documents individually, invalidating users' spatial memory by breaking up groups.

This approach worked well in the sense that it maximized the number of documents users could reach in the new pose. On the other hand, the approach performed poorly in that the re-layout severely affected the neighborhood relationships between formerly adjacent documents, even breaking up clusters. This severely affected users' spatial memory. In addition, and arguably more important, the rearranged layout offers no visual cue *how* it was rearranged. As a matter of fact, most neighborhood relationships are still intact—there is just no obvious way for users to tell.

Based on this experience, we redefined our design objectives by complementing our objective of an optimal layout with a second objective reflecting the desire to minimize impact on spatial memory. Any re-layout has the potential to disorient users [3]. We thus created a second, improved version of our view manager that minimizes change.

V2: Preserving Spatial Memory

Figure 15 illustrates the redesigned version of our view manager, which we termed PoseUI.

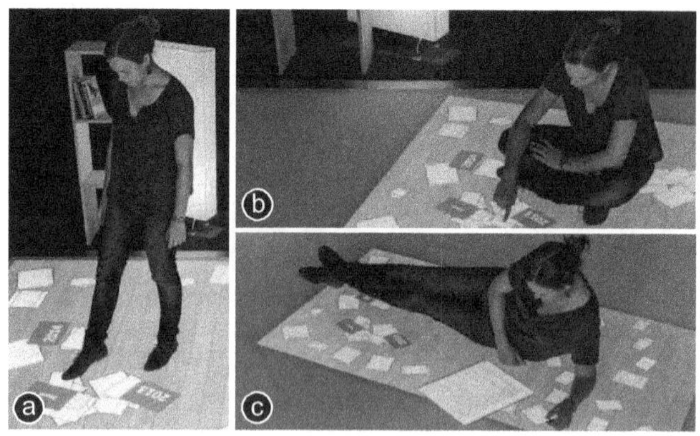

Figure 15: (a) This user is sorting documents for her tax return. Initially, she stands. (b-c) As she sits or lies down, PoseUI positions documents optimally for these poses.

Like the previous version, PoseUI arranges documents so that the user can still see and reach the same documents in the new pose. Compared to its predecessor, however, we made eight changes in order to better preserve users' spatial memory. We describe these changes in the following.

1. Simplified Transformation

Where the previous prototype moved documents individually, PoseUI applies a single global transformation (translation, scale, rotation) to all documents at once. This obviously limits the level of optimization the document layout can achieve, especially when the shape of the direct touch area of the target pose differs from the shape of the previous pose (e.g., sitting cross-legged vs. on folding chair). However, most direct touch layouts look similar in that they form an abstract crescent shape, so in the typical case the simplified transformation works well.

Figure 16 shows how PoseUI places content for a rectangular region building on the parameters determined earlier in this paper. If we use our 360 cm × 260 cm touch floor as an arbitrary reference, we see that some poses can almost accommodate the space as a whole, trivializing the layout question even with our simple transform-as-a-whole approach. After this scale-adaptation, however, some of the poses offer access to much fewer documents. Particularly the two chair-based poses offer access to very few, thus may be less suitable for manipulating large collections of documents.

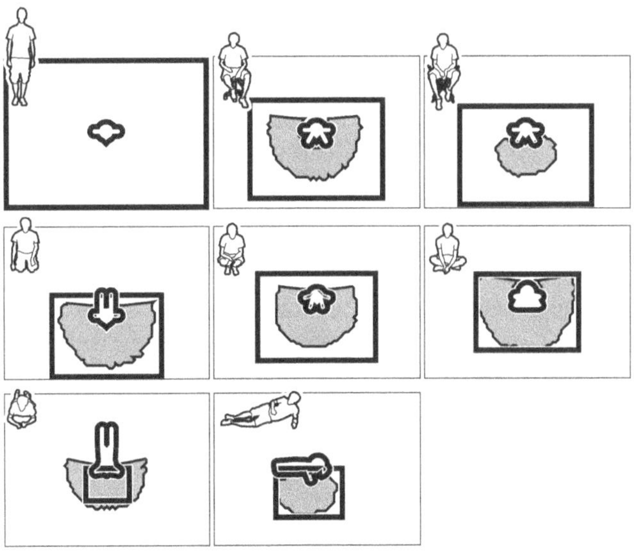

Figure 16: PoseUI applies a single global transformation including the entire floor area with all its content.

2. Visually Explained Transformation

The approach of transforming the layout already makes the layout in the new pose much easier to understand. In order to allow users to *instantly* grasp how the layout was adapted, PoseUI transforms the background image behind the documents along with the documents (here we gave it the texture of hardwood floor); we will refer to it as *backdrop*.

The backdrop in the version shown in Figure 17 was chosen to be of rectangular shape—a particularly good choice in that the rectangular outline of the backdrop already contains the transformation's three parameters translation, rotation, and scale (minus symmetries), so that it allows users to read these transformation parameters intuitively from the outline of the backdrop alone.

Figure 17: PoseUI transforms the entire floor imagery alongside with the documents, which helps users to understand the current layout information.

By scaling the backdrop along with the documents, all documents now stay on top of the same spot of the backdrop throughout all transformations. The backdrop and especially its frame thereby serve as landmarks, allowing users to locate familiar content at intuitively named locations such as "the top right corner of the hardwood floor", leveraging spatial memory.

3. Resolving Clipping at the Edge of the Screen

The simplified translation, rotation, and scale transformation is obviously less flexible and thus can lead to parts of the backdrop ending up off-screen. To prevent documents from becoming inaccessible, PoseUI pushes documents together at the edge of the screen. To help users understand the effect, PoseUI *bends* the backdrop in these border regions, as illustrated by Figure 18. This way, documents again remain positioned at their spot in the backdrop, helping the backdrop serve as landmark, leveraging spatial memory.

Figure 18: PoseUI bends the backdrop where pushed outside the screen.

4. Resolving Occlusion by Physical Objects

Similarly, transforming the space during pose change can make it clash with objects placed on the floor, such as furniture. To prevent documents from becoming inaccessible, PoseUI pushes out content from underneath such objects.

Early versions of our algorithm resolved occlusion by pushing out each document towards the closest edge of the occluding object (similar to *Display Bubbles* [6]). Unfortunately, this locally stretched the layout by an infinite factor, piling up documents very densely *towards* the occluding objects, while it spread documents out only very loosely *along* the perimeter. This distortion obfuscated neighborhood relationships and once again made it hard to tell which documents belong together.

We therefore redesigned our approach to occlusion resolution. As shown in Figure 19, the improved version produces space for the occluding object in the form of a *cut*. Along the edges of this cut, the floor bends up, similar to how it behaves at the edges of the screen. If the cut runs through a document, the document stays whole and moves to the closest sides, which keeps the documents readable. If the occluding object moves or is moved, the effect animates with the object slicing up the backdrop, resealing the cut behind it.

Figure 19: PoseUI prevents documents from being occluded by physical object by cutting the virtual floor and bending it up on both sides.

The main benefit of the cut is that it better preserves neighborhood relationships. It fully preserves neighborhood relationships along the cut; neighborhood relationships across the cut can still be reconstructed to a certain extent by measuring along the cut.

The underlying algorithm creates a raster of vertices surrounding the cut-to-be, which are moved outwards following a function parameterized by the size of the occluding object; this function defines the shape of the cut. We implemented our algorithm as shader to allow for fast update rates.

5. Using "Borrowed" Space

If content and thus the backdrop are scaled down, additional space is created that is void of documents. PoseUI marks this "borrowed" space by showing a pattern visual distinct from the backdrop (here gray linen cloth).

In order to maximize users' performance, PoseUI allows users to use borrowed space for the task at hand, i.e., users can place and manipulate documents in that space (Figure 20a). At the same time, the visual distinction is designed to clarify the nature of borrowed space: when the user stands up, this space will go away and documents placed here will be "scooped up" against the edge of the screen (Figure 20bc). Borrowed space thus serves as a temporary cache.

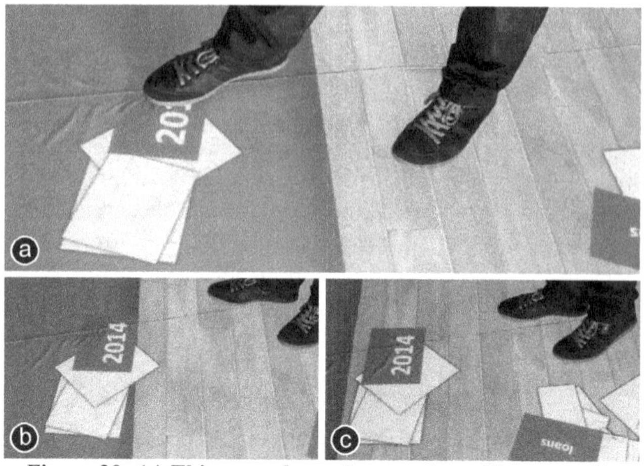

Figure 20: (a) This user places documents on "borrowed" space. These documents do not follow layout transformations, but are (b, c) "scooped up" once the backdrop moves across.

6. Layout Consistency Over Time

PoseUI uses the following two-step algorithm to prevent distortions from accumulating and to keep the layout consistent across any series of pose changes. Whenever the user changes pose, PoseUI computes the target layout by first restoring the backdrop to its rectangular shape, which undoes any distortion caused by screen edges and occluding objects. It then applies the transformation of the target layout and renders it. This approach keeps documents anchored with respect to the backdrop at all times.

PoseUI uses any return to the standing pose as an opportunity to reset the backdrop to its default position, i.e., to scale and rotate the backdrop such that it aligns with the physical screen. This resolves any backdrop clipping from previous poses and maximizes the amount of visible content.

7. Supporting *Navigational* Pose Changes

So far, we talked about pose changes exclusively as a means to optimize ergonomics. However, pose changes obviously also are users' primary means for navigating towards desired content. Similar to how laptop users lean forwards to see content in detail and backwards to get an overview [12], touch floor users may walk towards content or squat in order to view specific content in detail (Figure 21a); they may get up in order to obtain an overview.

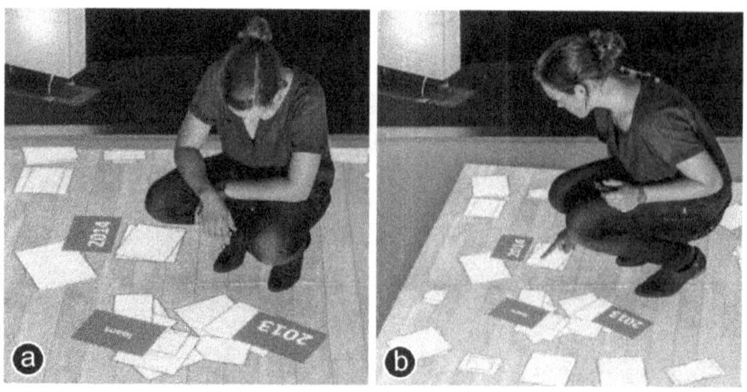

Figure 21: When a user (a) squats the system assumes the purpose is to inspect content in detail, thus not adjusts the view. (b) By marking the pose change as an ergonomic change (here using a wireless presenter), screen content adapts.

Such *navigational* pose changes occur more frequently than ergonomic pose changes. PoseUI therefore handles the distinction by letting users manually mark when a pose change is an *ergonomic* pose change. The problem of triggering events on touch interfaces is well understood (e.g., trailing widget [8]); in the shown version, we simply used the button on a wireless presenter. As a side effect, the explicit mechanism allows users to make content follow them as they pace across the floor (Figure 22b).

Figure 22: This user enjoys wandering around while interacting, which is supported by PoseUI.

8. Supporting Multiple Concurrent Users

When PoseUI sees multiple users, its default assumption is that these users collaborate on a single big task—as afforded by the size of touch floors. It therefore continues to provide a single shared backdrop with all documents.

Sometimes, however, users are more effective working in parallel on separate subtasks. PoseUI supports this by creating multiple backdrops, each of which forms a view onto the same set of documents (Figure 23). Moving a document in one of these views thus also moves that document in the other view.

In the particular implementation of PoseUI, prototype, we invoke this "forking" process manually: when one of multiple users indicates a pose change, PoseUI provides a separate view for this user.

Figure 23: As the user on the right sits down, PoseUI clones the view, allowing each user to work independently.

As illustrated by Figure 1, PoseUI partitions space in the form of a Voronoi tessellation, i.e., all users are assigned the screen area that is located closest to them. This oftentimes generates overlap between the views, which PoseUI resolves the same way it handles clipping at the end of the screen, i.e., by bending the involved backdrops. Note how the concept of backdrops and borrowed space naturally extends to multiple users.

CONCLUSION

In this paper, we proposed improving the ergonomics of touch floor interaction by allowing users to interact in and across multiple poses. We used a three-step design process: (1) Our first study challenged the status quo, which is that touch floors are used almost exclusively for standing users. (2) Our first and second study determined the parameters for touch interaction in different poses. (3) Based on these results we presented a simple view management system called PoseUI that allows users to seamlessly continuing their task across poses. The main design objective behind PoseUI was to minimize the impact of pose change on users' spatial memory.

As future work, we plan on creating a complete GUI/NUI framework for touch floors, replacing the "documents" we used in this paper with the complexity of GUI/NUI components they are supposed to stand in for.

REFERENCES

1. Augsten, T., Kaefer, K., Meusel, R., et al. Multitoe: High-Precision Interaction with Back-Projected Floors Based on High-Resolution Multi-Touch Input. In *Proc. UIST'10*, 209–218.
2. Badros, G.J., Borning, A., and Stuckey, P.J. The Cassowary Linear Arithmetic Constraint Solving Algorithm. *ACM Trans. Comput.-Hum. Interact. 8*, 4 (2001), 267–306.
3. Baudisch, P., Cutrell, E., Robbins, D., et al. Drag-and-Pop and Drag-and-Pick: Techniques for Accessing Remote Screen Content on Touch- and Pen-Operated Systems. In *Proc. INTERACT'03*, 64–57.
4. Bränzel, A., Holz, C., Hoffmann, D., et al. GravitySpace: Tracking Users and Their Poses in a Smart Room Using a Pressure-Sensing Floor. In *Proc. CHI'13*, 725–734.
5. Breu, F.X., Guggenbichler, S., and Wollmann, J.C. A Survey of Ergonomic Issues Associated with a University Laptop Program. *Journal of Education and Human Development 1*, 2 (2008), 1–15.
6. Cotting, D. and Gross, M. Interactive Environment-Aware Display Bubbles. In *Proc. UIST'06*, 245–254.
7. Cruz-Neira, C., Sandin, D.J., and DeFanti, T.A. Surround-Screen Projection-Based Virtual Reality: The Design and Implementation of the CAVE. In *Proc. SIGGRAPH'93*, 135–142.
8. Forlines, C., Vogel, D., and Balakrishnan, R. HybridPointing: Fluid Switching between Absolute and Relative Pointing with a Direct Input Device. In *Proc. UIST'06*, 211–220.
9. Gajos, K.Z. and Weld, D.S. SUPPLE: Automatically Generating User Interfaces. *IUI*, (2004), 93–100.
10. Grandjean, E. *Fitting the Task to the Man*. Taylor & Francis/Hemisphere, 1989.

11. Grønbæk, K., Iversen, O.S., Kortbek, K.J., et al. iGameFloor - A Platform for Co-Located Collaborative Games. In *Proc. ACE'07*, 64–71.
12. Harrison, C. and Dey, A.K. Lean and Zoom: Proximity-Aware User Interface and Content Magnification. In *Proc. CHI'08*, 8–11.
13. Holz, C. and Baudisch, P. The Generalized Perceived Input Point Model and How to Double Touch Accuracy by Extracting Fingerprints. In *Proc. CHI'10*, 581–590.
14. Karmakar, S., Pal, M.S., and Majumdar, D. Application of Digital Human Modeling and Simulation for Vision Analysis of Pilots in a Jet Aircraft: a Case Study. *Work 41*, (2012), 3412–3418.
15. Krogh, P.G., Ludvigsen, M., and Lykke-Olesen, A. "Help Me Pull that Cursor" - A Collaborative Interactive Floor Enhancing Community Interaction. In *Proc. OZCHI'04*.
16. Lueder, R. and Noro, K., eds. *Hard Facts about Soft Machines: the Ergonomics of Seating*. CRC Press, 1994.
17. NASA. Anthropometry and Biomechanics. In *Man-Systems Integration Standards (NASA-STD-3001)*. 1995.
18. Raskar, R., Welch, G., Cutts, M., et al. The Office of the Future: A Unified Approach to Image-Based Modeling and Spatially Immersive Displays. In *Proc. SIGGRAPH'98*, 179–188.
19. Schmidt, D., Ramakers, R., Pedersen, E., et al. Kick-ables: Tangibles for Feet. In *Proc. CHI'14*, 3143–3152.
20. Shen, C., Ryall, K., Forlines, C., et al. Informing the Design of Direct-Touch Tabletops. *IEEE Comp. Graph. and App. 26*, 5 (2006), 36–46.
21. Sjogaard, G. and Jensen, B.R. Low-level Static Exertions. In *The Occupational Ergonomics Handbook*. 1999, 247–259.
22. Stoakley, R., Conway, M.J., and Pausch, R. Virtual Reality on a WIM. In *Proc. CHI'95*, 265–272.
23. Vogel, D. and Balakrishnan, R. Occlusion-Aware Interfaces. In *Proc. CHI'10*, 263–272.
24. Weiser, M. The Computer for the 21st Century. *Scientific American 265*, 3 (1991), 94–104.
25. Yin, K. and Pai, D.K. FootSee: An Interactive Animation System. In *Proc. SCA'03*, 329–338.
26. Epidémik. http://www.cite-sciences.fr/epidemik, Aug. 14th, 2013.

Display Blindness? Looking Again at the Visibility of Situated Displays using Eye Tracking

Nicholas S. Dalton
Pervasive Interaction Lab,
The Open University,
Milton Keynes, UK
sheep.dalton@open.ac.uk

Emily Collins
UCL Interaction Centre
University College London
London, UK
e.collins@ucl.ac.uk

Paul Marshall
UCL Interaction Centre
University College London
London, UK
paul.marshall@ucl.ac.uk

ABSTRACT
Observational studies of situated displays have suggested that they are rarely looked at, and when they are it is typically only for a short period of time. Using a mobile eye tracker during a realistic shopping task in a shopping center, we show that people look at displays more than would be predicted from these observational studies, but still only short glances and often from quite far away. We characterize the patterns of eye-movements that precede looking at a display and discuss some of the design implications for the design of situated display technologies that are deployed in public space.

Author Keywords
Public displays;eye tracking;display blindness; space

ACM Classification Keywords
H.5.m. Information interfaces and presentation (e.g., HCI): Miscellaneous

INTRODUCTION
Public and situated display technologies are increasingly common in many urban spaces. These include advertising displays on bus stops, interactive screens providing information to tourists or shoppers, and large screens in transport hubs showing travel information as well as news and advertising content.

Situated display research has also been prominent in HCI, ranging from studies of community displays in cafes and village shops [30] to large interactive games in public spaces [24] and techniques to allow users to interact with different configurations of display and personal technologies.

Despite this significant interest in the potential of situated display technologies in both the commercial and research worlds, observational studies that have assessed the engagement of passers-by with them in real world settings such as shopping centers or university buildings [12, 23] have suggested that they are actually rarely attended to. Müller et al. [23] characterise this phenomenon as 'display blindness', drawing a parallel with the 'banner blindness' effect seen with online advertising. They suggest that passers-by deliberately don't look at displays because they expect them to show advertising content that is of little interest. Huang et al. [12] suggest, on the basis of extensive observational studies in public settings, that people pay only very brief attention to displays, if at all. They also suggest that displays at eye height are most effective at attracting attention with those placed higher getting significantly fewer glances, that video content tends to be more successful at attracting attention than text, animated text or still images, and counter intuitively, that in some situations smaller displays attract more attention than large ones. Huang et al. also discuss the role of the surrounding context in mediating the attention of passers-by, suggesting that objects in the vicinity sometimes serve to catch people's attention, which then moves to the display. They also observed that even when potential audiences are "captive" – for example, on an escalator moving towards a display – they still pay little attention to it.

Huang et al.'s and Müller et al.'s work has been very influential in public display research, with much subsequent research focusing on interaction techniques or representations that maximize the likelihood of attracting attention [20, 21] or suggesting that displays in public spaces need to blend representations of useful information in with existing advertising content in order to increase people's interest in the technology [2].

The study presented in this paper was motivated by two developments that have occurred since the seminal work of Huang et al. [12] and Müller et al. [23]. Firstly, displays have changed significantly, with much larger displays becoming available in a variety of form factors and the emphasis of advertising on digital displays has changed from the provision of information about brands (e.g. giving information about the price of a holiday) to the provision of aesthetic content designed to evoke positive affective experiences associated with brands (such as showing a video of a tropical beach with the logo of a brand (e.g.[6])). Secondly, mobile eye tracking technologies have become commercially available, making it possible to study

CHI 2015, April 18 - 23 2015, Seoul, Republic of Korea

ACM 978-1-4503-3145-6/15/04...$15.00.
http://dx.doi.org/10.1145/2702123.2702150

people's looking behaviors in much greater detail than was possible in the earlier observational studies (e.g. [8]).

The goal of the study was to use mobile eye tracking to determine whether, given the changes described above, the display blindness phenomenon still occurs in complex real world environments and what factors are associated with passers-by being most likely to look at displays.

RELATED WORK

Interactive and non-interactive digital displays are becoming a ubiquitous part of many urban environments [2, 6, 12, 20], and have been found to increase customer traffic and create a more welcoming atmosphere in retail contexts such as shopping centres [6]. While the use of displays varies across different situations, the effectiveness of all public displays relies on the assumption that they will be noticed and attended to [23]. However, it has been suggested that this often does not occur in real world contexts such as train stations, department stores and university campuses [12]. Even when they do attract glances, these are usually very brief. This has been termed 'display blindness' [23] (named after the 'banner blindness' effect seen with web page adverts) and may be because participants expect them to feature uninteresting content such as advertisements. In an extensive observational study of a variety of situated displays, Huang and colleagues [12] suggest that glances at public displays are both rare and typically brief (usually less than the 800ms, which would imply that a glance was intentionally directed [19]).

However, certain features of the display itself or the surrounding environment may make 'display blindness' less likely to occur. Previous research has highlighted that animations or videos, bright colours and text (rather than icons) appear to be most successful in catching an individual's attention and encouraging attention to or interaction with a display [12, 16, 21]. Müller et al. [20] summarise work on visual perception, which suggests that bottom-up features of visual stimuli that indicate need for immediate action are most likely to capture attention. These include the abrupt appearance of new objects, luminance contrast changes and stimuli that seem to loom towards the observer. They also cite Itti et al. [13] who propose a model of Bayesian surprise for bottom-up visual attention that also includes expectations of encounters in the world based on prior experience. A different perspective is presented by Rothkopf et al. [28], who criticise these and other findings, which are based on participants viewing stimuli under controlled laboratory conditions and in the absence of a realistic task. They argue that both task and context determine gaze patterns.

In addition to the influence of different kinds of display content on noticability, researchers have also investigated the effects of the spatial and social context of displays. Location in particular, has received substantial attention, as where the display is positioned will influence how it is viewed and, if appropriate, interacted with [1]. One possibility is that longer engagement periods will be associated with areas in which people are likely to be waiting rather than quickly passing through, such as corridors [5, 11]. However, Huang et al. [12] found limited benefits of having such "captive audiences" on looking at screens. They also suggest that smaller displays positioned at eye height encourage more glances than larger displays or those that are positioned higher and that other objects in the vicinity of displays, such as product displays, can attract attention that can then move to the display.

More complex spatial influences, have mostly been investigated with large, interactive installations, such as CityWall [26], or CoCollage [7]. For these kinds of displays, not only does the display itself need to be noticed by passers-by, but they also need to realise it has interactive capabilities and feel comfortable taking part in the interaction (cf. [18]), which is sometimes difficult to achieve [10, 24]. One possibility is to ensure the display is visible to the largest area possible, in particular to those entering the space rather than leaving it [1] Getting a display noticed and encouraging engagement can further influence its visibility through influencing the social dynamics of those around it. Groups of people forming around the display can create a 'honey pot' effect [4], drawing the attention of others.

Despite the high levels of interest in public display technologies, and their ubiquity in many urban environments, there has been a paucity of work that has used eye tracking to understand attention to them. It has long been acknowledged that the location and duration of fixations, as well as more general eye movements can provide a strong indication of how much attention is being paid to particular aspects of an environment or stimulus [19]. Ravnik and Solina [27] who used a display-mounted gaze tracker in a clothes store suggested that 35% of customers who walked past it looked at it for an average period of 0.7s, a significantly higher proportion than might be expected from Huang et al. and Müller et al.'s studies. However, as this system worked by tracking people's faces rather than their eyes, it may have over-estimated the number of looks.

The development of mobile eye tracking technology has greatly expanded the potential for eye-tracking studies in complex real world environments [8]. The few public display studies that have collected mobile eye tracking data have tended to focus on general browsing behaviour in contexts such as museums. However, some have studied eye movements to digital displays on public transport systems [9], reporting a high level of attention being paid to these displays irrespective of content. Although these findings are useful in establishing the utility of such displays on public transport, it is unlikely that the same patterns of engagement would be evident in other contexts; those travelling are likely to be actively searching for an activity to occupy their time or travel information and may be motivated to view the displayed content in a way that those walking through a shopping centre, for example, may not be. Schrammel et al.[29] conducted a study of participants' eye movements while walking through a shopping street, finding most held a relatively steady gaze in the horizontal middle of the field of view, with a greater orientation to the direction of the shops, which were located to the right of the street. However, research has shown gaze to be highly influenced by the demands of the task (e.g. [8]), making the instruction to simply walk through the street potentially not representative of the motivations of individuals who naturally find themselves in this situation.

The goal of the study presented in this paper was to understand if and when participants in a realistic shopping task in a shopping centre would look at public displays. The organisation of the study is described in the next section.

METHODOLOGY

An ecologically valid in the wild experiment was planned using a mobile eye tracker to record what participants looked at while shopping in a large shopping centre.

Setting

The study was conducted in a large shopping centre (approximately 175,000m^2) in London, UK, which comprises two department stores, a cinema, a supermarket and more than 400 stores and restaurants. It was chosen because it provides an environment with many advertising and information displays (see figure 2), which ensured that participants would pass multiple displays during their shopping task. The centre is spread over three floors. Displays of different sizes are positioned on plinths in the corridors between shops, attached to walls at different heights and are positioned in some shops and shop windows. While many of the displays show advertising content, others are designed to support wayfinding or provide information about the stores, cafes and restaurants within the centre. The study was conducted on weekdays between 10am and 7pm when the shops in the centre were open.

Equipment

A Tobii Glasses mobile eye tracker was used in the study (see figure 1). This comprises a pair of 75g glasses and a 200g recording pack joined by a data cable. These are not significantly heavier than a normal pair of glasses and participants reported that they were unobtrusive. The system recorded a 640x480 pixel movie at 30 frames per second with a recording angle/visual of view of 56° horizontal and 40° vertical. Following calibration, the embedded firmware performs an internal calculation to match the participant's eye movements to the captured video of the scene in front of them. Following recording, Tobii software was used to output video files that superimpose coloured circles onto the video which represent where the eye fixation points (see Figure 2). These were used in the analysis.

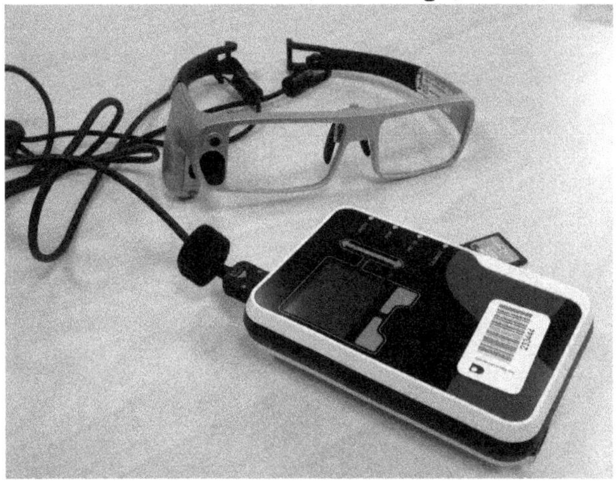

Figure 1: Tobii Glasses Mobile Eye Tracking System

Participants

24 participants were recruited for the study, two of whom were excluded from the analysis because they followed a route that didn't go past any displays (straight to a bookshop, where they read books for the duration of the study) leaving 22. Of the 22 participants included in the analysis, 10 were male and 12 female and all right handed. 12 participants reported being unfamiliar with the shopping centre, five somewhat familiar and five very familiar. Ages ranged from 19 to 73. 50% of the participants were British and the rest came from other countries covering 5 continents.

Procedure

The participants were told that the study would investigate what people look at when shopping. No mention was made that displays were the focus of the study.

Participants were paid £10 for participation but were told that there would be a prize draw after the study where one of the participants would receive a gift up to the value of £100. Their task was to find one or more items to spend the money on if they won the draw, which would be paid for by the experimenters. This design was to create an ecologically valid in the wild shopping task, where the participants were focused on shopping for items that were of genuine interest to them.

Participants were met near an entrance to the centre. After reading an information sheet that described the aims of the project they signed a consent form. They were then introduced to the Tobii eye tracking glasses and a calibration procedure was carried out, which typically took less than one minute. The participants were then asked to shop for their gift anywhere in the shopping centre. The shopping task took approximately 15 minutes, after which participants were fully debriefed on the aims of the study, filled in a small demographic questionnaire and were paid.

Analysis

Tobii Studio software was used to convert the eye movements to a fixation point overlaid on the video of the scene – (see the red dots in figure 2). The software can automate much of the process of matching eye fixations to

Figure 2: Typical video recording showing eye fixation point in red circle. Potential screens in rectangles

the visual environment. However, automation does not function in the complex spatial environments of a shopping centre. We coded fixations using Anvil software [15] to assist the post-recording analysis process. This was a time consuming process (cf. [14]) taking approximately one day to code each 15 minute video.

We began by focusing on the time that each participant spent wayfinding. Wayfinding [3] was the process of navigating from one location to another in the shopping centre.. During wayfinding, the participants were in motion, engaging in collision avoidance, collecting visual information from the environment, and making decisions about possible destinations. Participants typically only stopped to inspect potential items to purchase. Huang et al. [12] also observed participants when they were 'captured': not in motion, but for example, queuing for a service. During this study none of the participants queued, but some were 'captured' when they stood on moving escalators.

For the duration of the periods of wayfinding, we coded whenever a digital display was available in the video captured by the eye tracker. Each display was given a unique code so that we were able to identify how many times each was fixated on. Figure 2 shows a period when 3 displays (marked as A, B and C) were visible (the red dots denote eye fixations). In the figure, two vertical portrait displays are visible, one in the foreground (B) and one in the background (C). There is also a larger display (A) above eye height, which is also typical of those viewed by our participants. We also coded when participants looked at a display, which we operationalized as two or more consecutive fixations intersecting with the display. If the head moved between fixations (as it often did), then the second fixation would not occur at the same coordinate in the video, but would rather move to compensate for the head movement. We were quite conservative in our coding: for example if the eye followed the edge of a display (as it often did), but did not move to the screen, then this was not categorized as looking at a display.

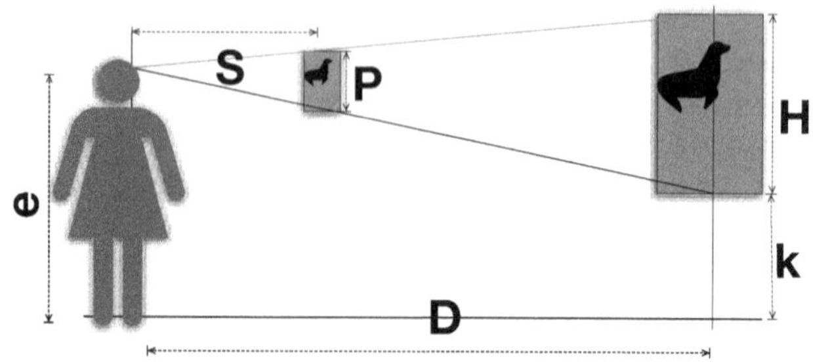

Figure 3: geometry permitting participant's distance to a display to be derived from image measurements

A further code was introduced to record when one of the visible displays noticeably flickered (a large luminance contrast change), which Müller et al. [20] had predicted might attract attention to a display.

The coding was carried out by the first author and seven of the videos were independently coded by a second coder. The inter-rater reliability was calculated through Anvil to give a Cohen's kappa of 0.7.

Distance

We reasoned that if a display was at a fixed height (K in figure 3) above the ground and of a known height (H) in meters, then a measurement of the height of the display in pixels (P) on the video could then be used to estimate the horizontal distance of the participant from the display (D). This was fixed regardless of participant's eye properties (the camera geometry dominated) and would only be weakly influenced by the height of the participant (e). That is if H, S and K are fixed or known, then D is a function of P (see figure 3). In the laboratory we conducted a calibration experiment using the eye tracker. From our calibration experiment we confirmed that the distance from the observer to the screen was a function of the reciprocal of the height in pixels of the screen and our measurements, which gave an R^2 correlation of 0.996 for the relation between screen measurement in pixels and the distance to display. From this we could determine the distance between a display and the participant using only video information.

This distance to screen measure was calculated whenever a screen was first coded as having been looked at. Figure 2 shows a typical participant looking event. A video screenshot image of the first intersection was recorded and the screen dimensions were measured from this (effectively P is the height of the orange box in figure 1). These dimensions could then be used to compute the distance (D) of the participant from the display at the point the display was first noticed. While this could only be done for the eye-height level displays we felt this would give useful objective data for the distribution of 'first view' distances.

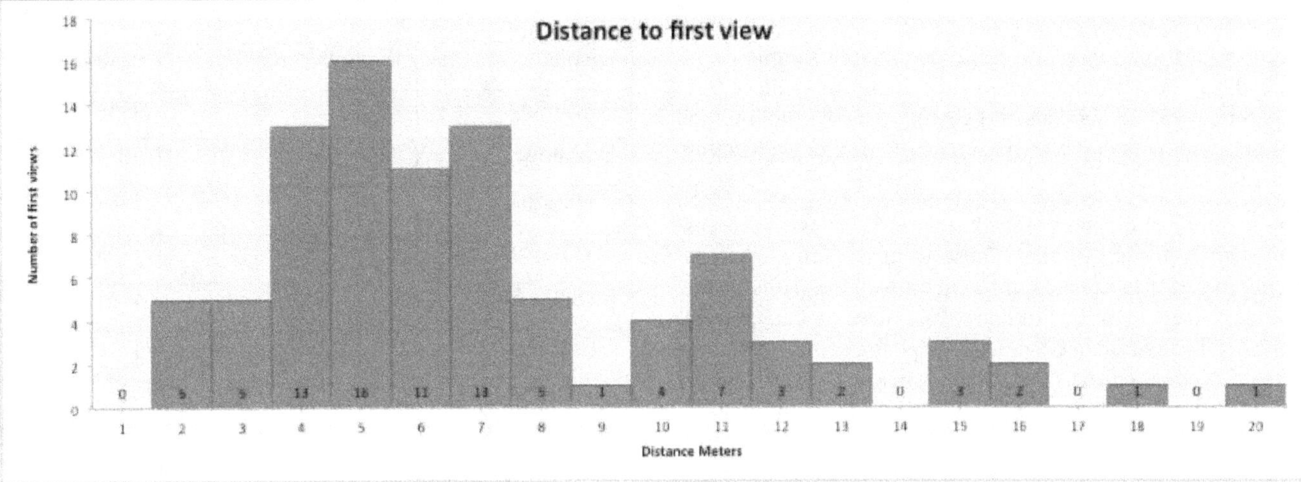

Figure 4: Histogram of frequency of distance to first glance at a display

Due to the nature of the error in pixel measurements, the distance to closer screens could be more accurately measured (+/- 0.2m) than those that were further away, which could be +/- 1.0 m. The histogram of these first view distances is presented in Figure 4.

Comparative viewing data

As well as the above analysis, analysis was conducted of a one minute sample of each video to identify what other environmental features participants attended to whilst wayfinding. A one-minute sub-sample was drawn from the mid-point of the recording, or from the period of wayfinding chronologically closest to the mid-point if the participant was not actively wayfinding at this point. During this one-minute sample **all** of the participant's fixations were exhaustively coded. On average 103 separate fixations were recorded per 1 minute period (min 64, max 124). The fixations were coded as being on: a digital display (looking at a digital display as described), signage (looking at non-digital signage), large text (typically reading the names of shops), architecture (looking at walls, floors, pillars, beams, ceilings or any other architectural feature), people, and products (looking at specific products or into shops). This one-minute sample was used to give some comparative context to the longer wayfinding periods spent collecting only data on digital displays.

RESULTS

Overview

Participants spent a total of 3 hours 43 minutes wayfinding. Each participant engaged in a wayfinding segment for an average of 9 minutes 43 seconds (s.d. 3 minutes 36 seconds). Across all participants, 337 Digital displays were potentially visible for a total of 59 minutes (26% of wayfinding time), giving an average of 2 minutes 36 seconds (s.d. 1 minute 20 seconds) display visibility per participant. Digital displays were potentially noticeable for an average episode of 3.48 seconds (s.d 1.29 seconds) before moving out of the frame (if multiple displays were visible, then this onset of this period was from the first frame any display was visible and the offset was last frame any display was visible.

Participants each fixated on an average of 16 displays (s.d.= 9, min 3, max 33). The mean period spent fixating on displays during wayfinding was 4.9 seconds (s.d. 2.9 seconds). Each display was fixated on for a mean of 0.318 seconds (s.d. 0.261). While this looks very brief it is informative to compare this with the average time spent looking at other items. From the one-minute mid-wayfinding samples, the mean duration spent looking at different categories of environmental features was also low (see table 1), with the longest non product time being on architectural features. During exhaustive samples participants spent 3.3% of their wayfinding time looking at digital displays.

Category	% of total wayfinding looking time	Average duration of fixation (seconds)
Architecture	38.2%	0.517(∂=0.460)
People	12.7%	0.379(∂=0.247)
Products	39.4%	0.498(∂=0.424)
Signage	1.1%	0.491(∂=0.381)
Large text	5.3%	0.416(∂=0.263)
Digital displays	3.3%	0.340(∂=0.267)

Table 1: Percentages of time looking at all categories of environmental features during 1-minute exhaustive samples

While this is a small proportion of their time it is consistent with the amount of time spent looking at non-digital signage. The longest recorded time looking at a digital display was 2.1 seconds, with most participants looking for maximum of 0.8 seconds. No participant was observed walking up to or attempting to interact with any of the displays, although some were interactive. The duration of fixation for digital displays in the one-minute sample (0.34 seconds) is consistent with the time found over the entire experiment (0.318 seconds) suggesting that the one-minute samples are reasonably representative of the wayfinding periods.

The majority of displays looked at were 55" plasma screens arranged as portrait plinths. These were typically arranged facing, but just to the side of the main walking paths of the shoppers (see item B in figure 2). These displays were typically located at eye-height, except for some occasions when they were on the floor above or below the participants and visible via an atrium space. Contrary to Huang et al.'s [12] finding that few displays above eye height were attended to, of the 285 distinct observations 72 (25%) of the displays observed were above eye height and 13 (5%) below eye-height. The screens above eye height were large multi-display screens in portrait orientation (see A in figure 1).

Proportion of looks at different displays

Our participants began from the same starting location. As they began walking they had a choice of turning either left or right. In both directions, displays were present on both upper and lower levels of the shopping centre. We decided to take the opportunity to count the number of times a display was looked at against the number of times the participant was in the view field of the display. We picked the 12 displays that were most commonly walked past in the early part of the participant's journey. As the participants continued they would encounter further displays but less frequently.

Table 2 represents the numbers of times that these 12 displays were walked past and as well as actual views as a percentage of possible views. The percentage of times that many of these displays were fixated on was very high given if 'display blindness' is assumed to be a similar phenomenon to banner blindness, although not all displays were viewed as often, and one not at all. For example, display B is a large above-eye display (see A in figure 1), which was fixated on by the majority of participants who walked past it (60%). Display E, which was fixated on by many of the participants who walked past it was an approximately 2m high display on a shop front that was edge-on to the primary flow of most participants. Plinth F, which was fixated on by nearly half of those who walked past it was directly in front of an escalator. It should be noted that displays H-L were all located on a less used route leading to the anchor store, in the centre and were walked past proportionally less than the other displays.

Distance

We captured video pixel measurements for each eye-height display of a known size at the point when a display was first fixated on by a participant. We excluded images in which the display was partly occluded, above or below eye-height or if the display was of an unknown dimension. This produced 92 measurements for all participants.

Display	Looked at	Passed	% looked at
A (Plinth)	7	16	44%
B (Above)	9	15	60%
C (Plinth)	3	13	23%
D (Plinth)	4	15	27%
E (Shop front)	7	15	47%
F (Escalator)	7	15	47%
G (Plinth)	2	5	40%
H (Plinth behind Escalator)	0	5	0%
I (Upper Right)	0	2	0%
J (Plinth)	2	3	40%
K(Plinth)	1	1	100%
L (Plinth)	1	4	25%

Table 2: proportion of participants who noticed a display

From this analysis we discovered that participants first viewed the 55-inch plinth screens (see figure 4) at an average distance of 8.03 meters (28ft) (s.d. 8.99m). The maximum distance we observed a participant looking at the screen was beyond 42 m.

We make two main observations from the distance data. Firstly if an observer was standing near to the display it would be unlikely that they could accurately notice a user observing the screen at a range of eight meters. This may account for the disparity between our findings and those of Huang et al. [12] and Müller et al. [23]. Secondly, 50% of the participants looked at the display for the first time from quite far away, at a distance greater than 8m. We noticed that participants viewed large text (typically reading the name of the shop) at quite large distances as well. It is likely that that shop name signage has already evolved to be readable at the kinds of distances from which people make shopping route-choice decisions.

Qualitative analysis

To further understand how the gaze patterns were influenced by the environment we performed a qualitative analysis of the events leading up to each time a display was fixated on to give a more qualitative understanding of what led to it being looked at. This produced 11 different categories of precursors to looks at a display (see table 3), with only six examples classed as "uncategorised". These uncategorisable examples were principally due to lack of saccade and fixation information prior to the look (e.g. blinking).

Overall, 360 precursors to looking events were coded, the largest category being that of 'looking back' (27%). That is,

Look back (look again)	98	27.2%
Architecture	86	23.9%
Scan and hit	66	18.3%
People (honeypot)	44	12.2%
Bright display	19	5.3%
Dark display	15	4.2%
Screen flickered	9	2.5%
Eye lead from products	7	1.9%
Revelation	6	1.7%
Path block	4	1.1%
Uncategorised	6	1.7%

Table 3: events preceding noticing a display

quickly looking back at the display once it has already been glanced at. This seemed to be the eye tracking equivalent of Müller's et al.'s 'landing effect' [22], where people first walk past an *interactive* display, before walking back to use it. This might be due to users needing time to comprehend the information displayed or possibly that they were re-looking at the display as a way of triangulating their position in space.

The second most common precursor to a look at a screen was where the saccade pattern followed some feature of the building's architecture or interior design (vertical pillar, floor, or most commonly ceiling) before moving to a display. For the smaller vertical plinth displays, following lines of perspective would frequently lead to these displays being looked at from quite far. Due to their position, the larger landscape displays, were often looked at after the saccade pattern following the edge of the ceiling lead the eye to the display.

18% of gazes on a display followed a large rapid eye movement, including turning the head and ending with the gaze fixating on one of the displays. We have called these 'scan and hit'. These events had the largest saccade distances prior to the display discovery.

Another theme that links to one established prior to observation is the 'honeypot effect' [4]. We generalized this to any event where the eye was drawn to the display by the proximity of another person or group of people near that display. We noticed no occasion where the other person was overtly looking at or interacting with the display themselves, thus this is a more subtle example of the honeypot effect that has previously been described. In our study this preceded 12% of all fixations on displays.

For 'bright display' events there was high contrast between the luminosity of the display and that of the surroundings. This made the display stand out against the darker background (e.g., when a display was shaded by having an escalator above it). These comprised approximately 5% of the display looks. On occasion the displays could also be very dark with very bright surroundings, we found that 4% of displays discovery events happened when this occurred. Collectively these contrast events occurred 9% of the time.

It might be expected that large changes in the visual field, such as high luminance changes on a screen might be attention grabbing (cf. [20]). However, of the 52 observed examples of a large change, only 9 led the participant to look at the screen and a look following a flicker only comprised 2.5% of the overall looking events, This seems to contradict the intuition that moving and changing displays should 'catch the eye'.

Among the smallest saccades distances away in a display was discovered after looking at a product (2%). These precursors to a fixation were typically with displays within the shop rather than in the larger way-finding area; given the visual separation between product and displays this is not surprising. Related to this were a number of what we term 'revelation' events. These were where the eye was drawn to a display following the screen suddenly becoming visible following one or more people standing or walking in front of it and then moving away to reveal it. These accounted for 1.7% of screen fixation events.

A similar low-frequency event (1.1%) was when the display blocked the path of a participant's movement. At this point the display was normally very large and in front of the participant and it would be difficult for them to ignore it.

LIMITATIONS

Before discussing the implications of these findings it is necessary to highlight some of the limitations of eye tracking systems. Huang et al. [12], cite Müller et al. [19] in suggesting that any dwell time under 800ms is not under conscious control. Our data suggest that nearly all (96%) of participants' gazes in the environment were under this 800ms threshold but this does not mean that they were not processing any perceptual information or that they were not conscious of features in the environment, only that they were not typically consciously choosing to look at the displays (e.g., reading the text of an advert).

A further limitation is that the algorithmically generated 'fixation' produced by the Tobii software, which is a cluster of small saccades, is not designed to work with mobile eye tracking data, where head movements, etc. make the algorithmic calculation of a fixation point very challenging. Our approach in coding the data was to go through frame-by-frame, and to only count a gaze behaviour if two or more consecutive fixations were on the same object. This meant that the fixation had to be on the object itself, and if the head moved between fixations (as it often did), then the second fixation would not occur at the same coordinate in the video, but would rather move to compensate for the head movement.

The Tobii glasses also have a visual error of 1°, which means that the accuracy of a fixation decreases as object distance increases. At the distances where most displays were viewed, this translates into an error of 9-13cm, but there is a potential error of 73cm at the upper range. Because of this potential error, we were quite conservative in our coding: for example if the eye followed the edge of a display (as it often did), but did not move to the screen itself, then this was not categorized as looking at a display.

The use of mobile eye tracking in public also raises questions about the validity of participants being overly self-conscious during the experiment and changing their behaviour. Our participants did informally report that after wearing the glasses for a short time, they ceased to be overly self-conscious. This would seem to be supported by examples in our data of what can only be described as "checking out" other shoppers. However, it is probably intrinsic to any eye tracking study that some kind of increased self-consciousness is inevitable. Participants were still unaware of the focus of our study and therefore we believe that our findings are still of value to researchers interested in public displays.

DISCUSSION

This study builds on the initial work of Huang et al. [12] and Müller et al. [23] using the new approach of mobile eye tracking to test, augment and challenge the phenomenon of 'display blindness'. Here we discuss each of our main findings, introducing some implications for design and future work on public displays.

Participants were not 'blind' to the displays

Previous studies that took an observational approach to study whether passers-by look at situated displays in real world environments have suggested that people rarely look at them and when they do it is for only a short period, a phenomenon that has been described as 'display blindness' [23]. Our findings suggest that this term may exaggerate people's lack of engagement with situated displays, as all but one of the displays were looked at by a sizeable proportion of the participants.

Reasons for this disparity would seem likely to be related to the challenges of observing when a passer-by is and is not looking at something. It is probable that the previous observational studies were only able to identify a subset of glances at the displays. A second possibility is that changes in the size, design, placement or content of displays (cf. [6]) since initial studies of situated displays were carried out mean that they are more effective in attracting attention.

However, confirming Huang et al.'s [12] observations, participants rarely looked at displays for long: typically around a third of a second. This suggests that most glances at displays were reflexive and simply an aspect of navigating through the busy shopping centre, rather than intentional [19]. However, they were still of a timescale that would enable participants to perceive and cognize information from the display (e.g. [8]). The phenomenon of looking and then looking back at the displays would seem to suggest that something on the display attracted the attention of the participant, who then looked back at it to pick up more information.

This has implications for the design of situated display technologies, as if designers want to grab people's attention, and particularly encourage them to engage with *interactive* displays, then they might need to do so in a way that uses a very simple representation that is easy to perceive and understand in a short space of time. Similarly, if the goal is to convey some information to the passer-by, then it needs to be represented in a format that can be apprehended and understood very quickly. Many of the displays that we saw in the shopping center seemed to be designed to create more of an aesthetic experience than to convey information [6], in which respect they may have been more successful in adding to the generally pleasant and visually interesting design of the centre.

Displays were often looked at from far away

Using simple geometric calculations we were able to estimate the distance at which some of the displays were first glanced at. This proved to be from further away than might have been expected: looking at the graph in figure 4, there is a peak of first glances at around 11 meters and then a larger peak at around 5 meters. This goes some way to explaining the previous underestimation of the proportion of looks at displays in observational work [12, 23], as it would be very difficult to determine from this distance what passers-by are looking at without access to a mobile eye tracker. Again, this finding has implications for the design of situated displays in the wild. If the first glance at a display is from 5 or 11 meters away, then any information on the display will need to be able to be perceived from this distance, which will significantly limit the font size of any text used or the complexity of any graphical representation.

Context matters in attracting glances to a display

Huang and colleagues [12] described how objects such as products in the vicinity of displays could attract the attention of passers-by, which would then move to the displays themselves. Our eye-tracking study supports and adds detail to this finding. In particular, our participants were seen to look at displays following looks at architectural features, with fixation patterns often following lines such as ceilings or wall edges to the displays. Participant's attention also seemed to be attracted to the displays by the proximity of other people: this is like the 'honey pot' effect described by Brignull and Rogers [4], but nearby people did not need to be particularly engaged with the display. Architects and interior designers might be able to use these findings in considering where the optimal location might be to position a display, for example at the end of a long piece of furniture or at the end of a line projected from some architectural feature. Researchers and interaction designers may also be able to use the proximity of people to a display, not only to attract their attention, but to attract the attention of others in the environment who might be further away. Again to design elegant interaction techniques that work robustly in a busy environment such as a shopping center will present many challenges.

Higher and bigger displays seem to attract at least as much attention as smaller displays at eye height

Huang et al. [12] suggested that displays positioned at eye height received more looks than displays that were positioned higher and that larger displays seemed not to attract more glances than small ones. Neither of these findings held in our study. Although, we do not have enough data for inferential statistics, the large displays in the shopping center that were positioned high above people's heads seemed if anything to attract more looks than the smaller eye height plinth displays. Two possible explanations for this disparity are that Huang et al.'s observational approach may have underestimated the number of glances at larger displays from further away. A second explanation is that the displays in the shopping center showed different kinds of content to the displays observed by Huang and colleagues. Many of the images of displays visible in their paper seem to be relatively heavy on text, which might be difficult to read from below. As described by Dennis and colleagues [6], there is now more of an emphasis in retail contexts on "atmospherics": using displays and other features of the environment to create a pleasing and interesting atmosphere to generate positive associations with brands rather than to provide information. Where the displays were used to provide information, messages were typically short, and used very large fonts.

Static luminance differences seem more important than luminance changes

We had anticipated that the kinds of visual changes that might be expected to require immediate action [2, 20], such as large variations in luminance, or that would be characterized by a model of Bayesian surprise [13] might attract attention. However, we found limited evidence for this, with most significant changes in the luminance of displays being ignored. A possible explanation for this comes from alternative models of human gaze deployment that suggest a much stronger role for both task and context in determining where people look [8, 29]. The environment of the shopping center was visually very busy, and the participants were engaged in a realistic shopping task, so bottom-up visual salience might have had less of an effect than it would have done in a calmer visual environment, or one where participants were engaged in some other task.

Where luminance did seem to have an effect was where the brightness of displays seemed to grab participants' attention when they scanned around the space with large head movements. We characterized these as "scan and hit", and suggest that it was the relative brightness of the displays that led to the gaze settling on them. A similar phenomenon, but without large head movements was observed whereby bright displays against relatively dark backgrounds and dark displays against relatively bright backgrounds seemed to 'pop out' and attract more looks than other displays. This is, however, quite speculative and further work would be required to validate this finding. If it is found to generalize, then designers might think more explicitly about the relationship between a representation on a display and the visual context around it.

CONCLUSION

There is a significant amount of work in HCI research on the design of different display technologies, particularly interactive displays to be used in public spaces. It is premised on the idea that people will actually notice these displays, pick up information from them and choose to interact. The 'display blindness' effect seemed to suggest that this premise may be questionable [12, 23]. By using mobile eye tracking, we have been able to uncover more detail about exactly when people do look at interactive displays and have presented a more nuanced perspective than 'display blindness', which should aid designers and researchers in developing new mechanisms to attract and hold their attention (cf. [1, 2, 10, 17, 20, 21, 25]) and to encourage them to interact with these devices.

However, this study has only investigated the engagement of people engaged in a shopping task with situated displays in a single retail context. Significantly more work needs to be carried out to understand the relative contribution of task and context on patterns of looking at displays and other kinds of situated technologies in a variety of real world environments (cf. [29]).

Observational studies in real world environments have questioned the extent to which people look at situated displays. In this study, we have used mobile eye tracking to demonstrate that people in a shopping center do look at displays more than had initially been thought, but only for short period of time, and often from quite far away. A qualitative analysis of what precedes looking at a display has allowed us to categorize different patterns of behavior that may be of use to researchers and designers who seek to develop situated technologies for public spaces.

ACKNOWLEDGEMENTS

Emily Collins was supported by a grant from ICRI Cities. Many thanks to Ruth Dalton for her insightful comments on this paper.

REFERENCES

1. Akpan, I., Marshall, P., Bird, J., and Harrison, D. Exploring the effects of space and place on engagement with an interactive installation. In *Proc. CHI 2013,*, ACM Press (2013), 2213–2222.
2. Alt, F., Schneegaß, S., Schmidt, A., Müller, J., and Memarovic, N. How to Evaluate Public Displays. In *Proc. PerDis 2012*, ACM Press (2012), 17:1–17:6.
3. Arthur, P. and Passini, R. *Wayfinding: people, signs, and architecture.* 1992.
4. Brignull, H. and Rogers, Y. Enticing people to interact with large public displays in public spaces. In *Proc. INTERACT*, (2003), 17–24.

5. Churchill, E.F., Nelson, L., and Denoue, L. Multimedia fliers: Information sharing with digital community bulletin boards. In *Proc. C&T 2003,* Springer (2003), 97–117.

6. Dennis, C., Brakus, J.J., Gupta, S., and Alamanos, E. The effect of digital signage on shoppers' behavior: The role of the evoked experience. *Journal of Business Research 67*, 11 (2014), 2250–2257.

7. Farnham, S.D., McCarthy, J.F., Patel, Y., et al. Measuring the impact of third place attachment on the adoption of a place-based community technology. In *Proc CHI 2009*, ACM Press (2009), 2153–2156.

8. Hayhoe, M. and Ballard, D. Eye movements in natural behavior. *Trends in Cognitive Sciences 9*, 4 (2005), 188–194.

9. Höller, N., Schrammel, J., Tscheligi, M., and Paletta, L. The Perception of Information and Advertisement Screens Mounted in Public Transportation Vehicles- Results from a Mobile Eye-tracking Study. In *Proc. 2nd Workshop on Pervasive Advertising*, (2009).

10. Houben, S. and Weichel, C. Overcoming interaction blindness through curiosity objects. In *Proc. CHI'13 Extended Abstracts*, ACM Press (2013), 1539–1544.

11. Houde, S., Bellamy, R., and Leahy, L. In search of design principles for tools and practices to support communication within a learning community. *ACM SIGCHI Bulletin 30*, 2 (1998), 113–118.

12. Huang, E.M., Koster, A., and Borchers, J. Overcoming assumptions and uncovering practices: When does the public really look at public displays? In *Proc. Pervasive Computing*. Springer, 2008, 228–243.

13. Itti, L. and Baldi, P.F. Bayesian surprise attracts human attention. *Advances in Neural Information Processing Systems*, (2005), 547–554.

14. Jacob, R.J. and Karn, K.S. Eye tracking in human-computer interaction and usability research: Ready to deliver the promises. *Mind 2*, 3 (2003), 4.

15. Kipp, M. and others. Spatiotemporal Coding in ANVIL. *LREC*, (2008).

16. Kukka, H., Oja, H., Kostakos, V., Goncalves, J., and Ojala, T. What makes you click: exploring visual signals to entice interaction on public displays. In *Proc. CHI 2013*, ACM Press (2013), 1699–1708.

17. Marquardt, N., Ballendat, T., Boring, S., Greenberg, S., and Hinckley, K. Gradual engagement: facilitating information exchange between digital devices as a function of proximity. In *Proc. ITS 2012*, ACM Press (2012), 31–40.

18. Michelis, D. and Müller, J. The audience funnel: Observations of gesture based interaction with multiple large displays in a city center. *Intl. Journal of Human–Computer Interaction 27*, 6 (2011), 562–579.

19. Müller, H.J. and Rabbitt, P.M. Reflexive and voluntary orienting of visual attention: time course of activation and resistance to interruption. *Journal of Experimental Psychology: Human Perception and Performance 15*, 2 (1989), 315.

20. Müller, J., Alt, F., Michelis, D., and Schmidt, A. Requirements and Design Space for Interactive Public Displays. In *Proc. MM 2010.*, ACM Press (2010), 1285–1294.

21. Müller, J. and Krüger, A. *MobiDiC: context adaptive digital signage with coupons.* Springer, 2009.

22. Müller, J., Walter, R., Bailly, G., Nischt, M. and Alt, F. Looking glass: a field study on noticing interactivity of a shop window. In *Proc. CHI 2012,* ACM Press (2012), 297-306.

23. Müller, J., Wilmsmann, D., Exeler, J., et al. Display blindness: The effect of expectations on attention towards digital signage. In *Proc. Pervasive Computing*. Springer (2009), 1–8.

24. O'Hara, K., Glancey, M. and Robertshaw, S. Collective play in an urban screen game. In *Proc. CSCW '08*, ACM Press (2008), 67-75.

25. Ojala, T., Kostakos, V., Kukka, H., et al. Multipurpose interactive public displays in the wild: Three years later. *Computer 45*, 5 (2012), 42–49.

26. Peltonen, P., Kurvinen, E., Salovaara, A., et al. It's Mine, Don'T Touch!: Interactions at a Large Multi-touch Display in a City Centre. In *Proc. CHI 2008*, ACM Press (2008), 1285–1294.

27. Ravnik, R. and Solina, F. Audience measurement of digital signage: Quantitative study in real-world environment using computer vision. *Interacting with Computers 25*, 3 (2013), 218–228.

28. Rothkopf, C.A., Ballard, D.H., and Hayhoe, M.M. Task and context determine where you look. *Journal of Vision 7*, 14 (2007), 16.

29. Schrammel, J., Mattheiss, E., Döbelt, S., Paletta, L., Almer, A., and Tscheligi, M. Attentional behavior of users on the move towards pervasive advertising media. In *Pervasive Advertising*. Springer, 2011, 287–307.

30. Taylor, N., Cheverst, K., Fitton, D., Race, N.J., Rouncefield, M., and Graham, C. Probing communities: study of a village photo display. In *Proc. OzCHI*, ACM Press (2007), 17–24.

Detecting User Intentions at Public Displays from Foot Positions

Bernd Huber
Technische Universität München, Munich, Germany
berndbhuber@gmail.com

Joong Ho Lee
Korea Institute of Science and Technology, Seoul, Korea
yap153@gmail.com

Ji-Hyung Park
Korea Institute of Science and Technology, Seoul, Korea
jhpark@kist.re.kr

ABSTRACT
Foot positions are features of how humans express their intentions during conversations. This inspired us to investigate the usage of foot expressions during interactions with computers. We conducted an observational study to determine how foot positions correlate with the intentions of users at public displays. Using our findings, we performed a case study to demonstrate the usefulness of adapting content according to the intentions detected based on foot positions. Our results are valuable for researchers designing context-aware public displays.

Author Keywords
Affective Computing; Public Displays; Subconscious Interaction.

ACM Classification Keywords
H.5.2 [Information Interfaces and Presentation]: User Interfaces - Interaction styles. : Miscellaneous

INTRODUCTION
Consider an interactive display situated at a bus station that always provides the content that users want to view but without requiring explicit inputs. For example, it might provide information rapidly to passing users who are in a hurry or entertainment to a waiting user, thereby serving the community. Public display research aims to use contextual awareness to communicate content effectively via public displays, by capturing the attention of users and motivating more users to interact with the display, while also considering the public nature of interaction. Recent research suggests that personal device design paradigms are ineffective for distracted users of public displays, which may explain the low usage rate for the systems deployed at present [6].

Predicting the intentions of users is a powerful tool for satisfying their needs. Body language detection can be used to automatically interpret user behavior and react accordingly; for example, gaze can be used to predict the level of attention and proxemics can be used to measure user awareness. However, public display users exhibit complex behaviors. For example, in-observance or the maintenance of social roles represent new challenges when sensing and interpreting human behavior. Furthermore, distractions in public places may cause gaze to be insufficient to determine the true focus of a user's attention.

CHI 2015, April 18 - 23 2015, Seoul, Republic of Korea
Copyright 2015 ACM 978-1-4503-3145-6/15/04$15.00
http://dx.doi.org/10.1145/2702123.2702148

Feet have not been considered previously in public display interactions, although they express people's interests when interacting with others [11, 12]. The present study provides new insights into the potential for sensing the intentions of public display users. Analyzing user foot positions can make public displays adaptive to context, encouraging more users to interact.

RELATED WORK

User Model Investigation
In public display settings, user models are based on observations in real-world settings, e.g. *CityWall* is focused on the social behavior of the audience [3], where the design objectives focus mostly on attracting, engaging, and motivating users.

Hall's proxemics theory of interpersonal spatial relationships is used widely to build user models [4]. One of the first systems proposed in this domain was the *Interactive Public Ambient Display*, which interpreted proximity and body orientation as direct signals to facilitate display content adaptation [14]. Both modalities were combined to model the user's interest and the content displayed became more detailed and personalized as the user's interest increased. Similarly, the *Proximity Toolkit* combined proximity and the head orientation to control a multimedia application [8].

Design Factors in Proxemics
The ephemeral nature and the wide range of information that can be presented on ubiquitous computing displays, as well as the possibility of animation, may be combined more effectively when the user's affective state is considered. This has led to numerous design suggestions in ubiquitous computing [9]. A previous approach [1] tried to tackle these design challenges by producing a multimedia display that uses human proximity, orientation, identity, and movement to control a display.

Foot Detection Systems
The unavoidable relationship between feet and human body movements makes feet an appealing medium for interaction, which has led to investigations of their use in a variety of settings. *GravitySpace* is a touch sensor-based system for group

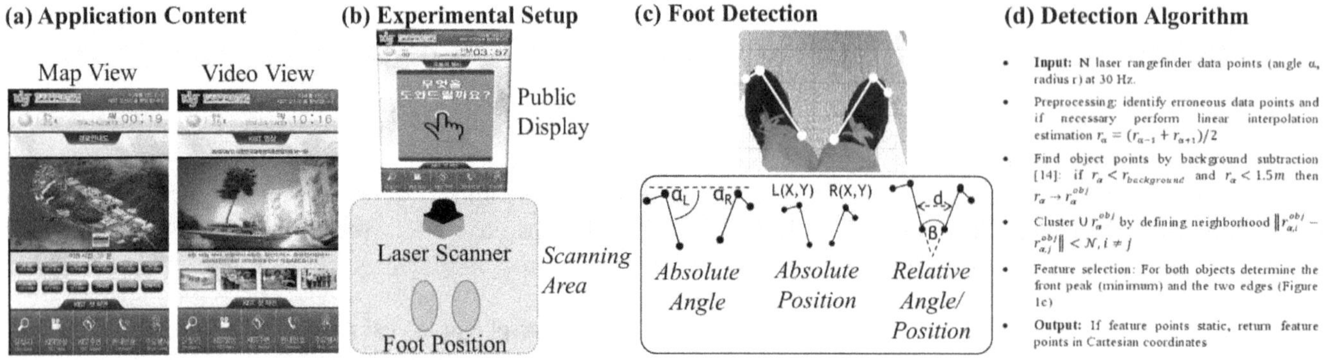

Figure 1: (a) Content of public display application. (b) Experiment setup with laser scanner at the bottom of the display. (c) Foot feature points detected by the laser scanner at the front peak and the two edges. (d) Foot detection algorithm based on background subtraction.

collaboration [2], which employs pressure sensors that are attached to the floor to estimate the pose of users and to predict input events. Foot positions have also been investigated based on their relationship to the direction of gaze in a laboratory setting [13]. In a public space, foot positions were first introduced as a user intention measure in [7]. We extend this direction of research by presenting a foot position adaptive system.

METHODS

Foot Scanner

A two-dimensional depth map of the floor in front of a display is required to detect foot positioning. In the present study, we used a *Hokuyo URG* laser range-finder, installed at the bottom of the display, invisible to users (Figure 1b). We developed an algorithm using background subtraction (Figure 1d), to detect three feature points for each foot for foot angle and proximity detection (Figure 1c). An evaluation revealed an overall angle accuracy of $\sigma = 7.4°$ and $\mu = 6.0°$, and a foot proximity accuracy of $\sigma = 4.3cm$ and $\mu = 3.5cm$.

Display Setup

A 40-inch multi-touch display with an attached *PQ-Labs* infra-red touch frame and with the foot scanner was placed next to a magazine holder and a water dispenser to attract the attention of those passing by. The display was deployed in the entrance lobby of a research institute, where there was a counter desk for visitor registration. Visitors come to the counter to ask for directions and may use the lobby as waiting area.

Public Display Content

The public display application developed for this setup was an information system that provided a detailed map of the institute's campus and the surrounding neighborhood, an entertainment function with a video collection related to recent research findings, and a contact list for staff at the institute. Furthermore, the institute's server provided a daily event schedule. A touch trigger symbol was displayed as the default screen and the system switched back to this default screen after 15 seconds of inactivity (Figure 1b). At the bottom of the display, a bar with menu buttons could be used to retrieve the desired content.

User Model

Public display information systems provide information to passers-by about the local environment. Depending on the content selected, the user's motivation is an external goal, or the tool itself may be a goal. Therefore, the target design of the public display must address two problems. First, users who need information should be able to find it easily and unused functionality must not interfere. Second, entertainment content should be delivered at a lower interaction threshold during casual usage in order to motivate more users to interact with the system [10]. Thus, we performed an observational study and a case study to test the possibility of foot positions fulfilling these needs.

APPROACH

This project aimed to bridge the gap between sensing technology and real-world public display settings by detecting user intentions based on the measurement of foot positions. To address the goals of context-aware public displays, we considered two hypotheses.

H1. *The intentions of public display users can be measured based on the position and orientation of their feet.*

H2. *The adaptation of the public display content to the intentions users based on foot positions helps the display to meet the needs of users. This adaptivity supports rapid information searches and motivates users to interact with these systems.*

OBSERVATIONAL STUDY: FOOT POSITION AS INDICATOR OF USER INTENTIONS

Experiment Description

The foot position data, which were combined with video recordings and a touch log, formed the basis of the observational results. The data-set produced comprised two types of user intentions and the captured foot positions. The foot position features were defined using the angle of each foot and their relative positions. A foot position was logged automatically when it was static and < 1.5 meters from the screen. Data from groups of users were sorted out. To simplify the model, we omitted the user's understanding of the interface's content and functionality from this study.

User intentions were classified manually using the video recordings and the touch log of the display. Interactions were labeled as *information search* if users first retrieved directional information and left afterwards. Interactions were labeled as *casual interaction* if users first selected entertaining content, or if entertaining content was selected after retrieving directional information. This mapping corresponds to the purpose of the display to the user and the urgency of the information being accessed. The mapping was motivated by foot position theory in conversations, which states that foot positions differ depending on the purpose of the conversation to the person.

This study design focuses on users in *direct interaction* [10]. According to the foot position theory, there needs to be a basic physical collaboration between the public display and user in order to cause some alignment related to the user's intention. Therefore, these potential users were omitted; however, we consider that other modalities such as proximity are more suitable methods in the case of peripheral interactions. The labeled data were classified using a support vector machine (SVM) classifier. The SVM had a C-SVC type configuration and it used a radial basis function with three degrees. It was trained and tested using a repeated random sub-sampling validation process.

Results

We collected data from 115 samples over the course of one working week, i.e., 9 AM to 7 PM from Monday to Friday. The average duration of one recorded foot position was 9 seconds and the average duration of one interaction was 11 seconds. We classified 55 of the 115 samples as *information search* and 50 as *casual interaction*. Figure 2a shows the average confusion matrix produced when the SVM algorithm was applied to the 115 samples. The SVM algorithm was trained with feature data (two foot angles and their positions) from 30 recorded samples, and tested using the 25 remaining samples from information search interactions and 30 from casual interactions. The user intention detection accuracy using foot positions was determined as 84.4% with an F-measure of 0.83.

Discussion

The results show that user intentions can be detected with high accuracies using foot position measurement. If a user requests specific information, their feet are oriented toward the screen. If the interaction is casual, their feet point away from the screen, thereby indicating their intention to leave. As seen by the information gain (IG) of large (Angle 1) and small (Angle 2) angles and relative proximity, all foot features contribute to the classifier. Figure 2c shows samples of the foot positions that were captured frequently from interacting users.

CASE STUDY: ADAPTING THE CONTENT OF AN INTERACTIVE PUBLIC DISPLAY BASED ON FOOT POSITIONS

Experiment Description

We conducted a case study to determine the suitability of public display content adaptation based on user intentions, where the content of a public display was adapted automatically according to the foot positions of users. The system was modified to classify foot positions using the trained SVM algorithm at the beginning of an interaction session. The interaction model was based on adapting the content to the foot positioning of users when they approached the public display. The content was selected to meet the objectives of optimizing the interaction times during information searches and increasing the attention of users during casual usage. Navigation information popped up for users who were classified as requiring specific information. An entertainment video collection about recent research findings was shown when casual usage was detected. After the system detects the first static foot position of an interacting user, further new foot positions of the same user were filtered out by the system. A time threshold in the system determined the end of a session.

In order to interview users, we positioned ourselves outside the entrance lobby where the display was located to ensure that the users did not feel that they were being observed. We approached them only after their interaction with the system was clearly finished. We then performed a qualitative analysis of the user interviews and the content- and interaction-related feedback that we captured. The interaction times and foot position data were also used as quantitative references.

Results

Over the course of 10 days, quantitative and qualitative data were collected from 27 users (average age = 35 years, female users = 16). The perceived usefulness of the system was high and users who required specific information agreed that they could find the information they needed quickly. During casual usage, the average interaction time increased significantly (p¡0.05) to 19 s compared with 10 s in the observational study. The average interaction time for information searches dropped significantly (p¡0.05) to 8 s. Overall, 70% of the users thought that the content had changed due to their proximity. The user intention classification accuracy based on foot positions was 88.8%, which was similar to the results obtained in the observational study.

Discussion

Based on a previous study on attention models [5], we assumed that users who searched for information would be less satisfied if the wrong content was shown. In our setting, some users searched for a specific location, whereas others simply passed by, waited in the waiting area, or used the system out of curiosity.

The adapted content was beneficial for users in both categories. The longer interaction duration and the high content rating during casual usage suggest that the attention of users was increased. Thus, their threshold for interacting with the system may have been reduced by adapting the content [3].

(a)

	A (Predicted)	B (Predicted)
A (Actual)	92.0% (23/25)	08.0% (2/25)
B (Actual)	23.3% (7/30)	76.7% (23/30)

Accuracy: 84.4%, F = 0.83

(b)

	Information Search		Casual Interaction		
	σ	μ	σ	μ	IG
Angle 1	28.5	58.6	23.8	39.4	0.34
Angle 2	12.6	84.2	34.7	81.7	0.12
Rel. Prox.	9.8	10.2	16.7	22.4	0.22
Abs. Prox.	12.2	79.9	8.2	80.4	0.01

(c) A. Information Search B. Casual Usage

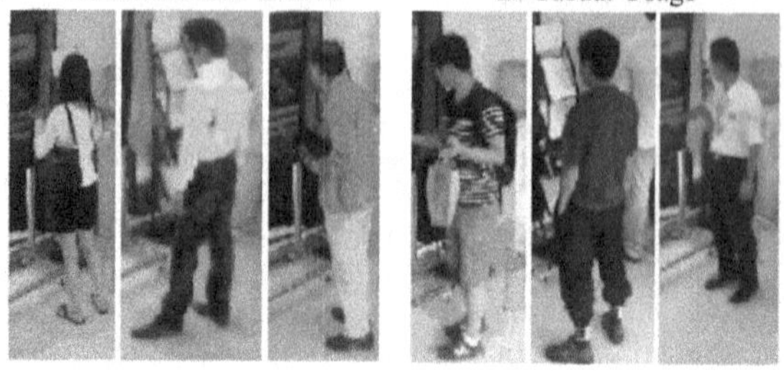

Figure 2: (a) Resulting confusion matrix of SVM algorithm applied on labeled foot position data. (b) Raw foot position data. (c) Frequently occurring foot positions for each user intention.

The lower interaction time and high perceived usefulness during information searches also suggests that the content provided was appropriate for users in this category.

DESIGN IMPLICATION

In the present study, we considered subconsciousness of foot positions as a novel design factor. That the majority of users thought the display adapts to proximity indicates the subconsciousness of foot positioning. Distractions and social roles can play a subsidiary role for such subconscious signals, suggesting the design for these signals in public systems.
IG comparison of absolute proximity and foot position features suggests integration of both measures in a more complex user model. While proximity can be used to approximate user behavior, foot positions may be used to detect nuances in intention and purpose.
More generally, when designing adaptive public displays, the risk for the worse case, that users stop interacting due to adaptation failure, should be minimized. Despite automatic content selection, an additional graphical user interface may provide users with the feeling of control over the system in any case.

FUTURE WORK AND CONCLUSION

Our findings make a significant contribution to the measurement of user intentions in public display environments. Foot positions are easy to detect and a foot position detection system may encourage interaction through adaptive content. Therefore, foot positions are an important modality for detecting the intentions of public display users and their use could facilitate beneficial and effective interactions with public displays. To further enhance our user model, we plan to integrate other body language indicators such as gaze direction. Comparisons of different indicators of subconscious and conscious interaction modalities will help us to further understand user behavior, which is important for the generalization of the user model.

ACKNOWLEDGEMENTS

This work was supported by a grant from the KIST Institutional Program.

REFERENCES

1. Ballendat, T., Marquardt, N., and Greenberg, S. Proxemic interaction: designing for a proximity and orientationaware environment. In *Proc. ITS*, ACM Press (2010), 121–130.
2. Bränzel, A., Holz, C., Hoffmann, D., Schmidt, D., Knaust, M., Lühne, P., Meusel, R., Richter, S., and Baudisch, P. Gravityspace: tracking users and their poses in a smart room using a pressure-sensing floor. In *Proc. CHI*, ACM Press (2013), 725–734.
3. Brignull, H., and Rogers, Y. Enticing people to interact with large public displays in public spaces. In *Proc. INTERACT*, vol. 3 (2003), 17–24.
4. Hall, E. T., and Hall, E. T. *The hidden dimension*, vol. 1990. Anchor Books New York, 1969.
5. Horvitz, E., Kadie, C., Paek, T., and Hovel, D. Models of attention in computing and communication: from principles to applications. *Communications of the ACM 46*, 3 (2003), 52–59.
6. Huang, E. M., Koster, A., and Borchers, J. Overcoming assumptions and uncovering practices: When does the public really look at public displays? In *Pervasive Computing*. Springer, 2008, 228–243.
7. Huber, B. Foot position as indicator of spatial interest at public displays. In *Extended Abstracts of CHI*, ACM Press (2013), 2695–2700.
8. Marquardt, N., Diaz-Marino, R., Boring, S., and Greenberg, S. The proximity toolkit: prototyping proxemic interactions in ubiquitous computing ecologies. In *Proc. UIST*, ACM Press (2011), 315–326.
9. Marquardt, N., and Greenberg, S. Informing the design of proxemic interactions. *IEEE Pervasive Computing 11*, 2 (2012), 14–23.
10. Michelis, D., and Müller, J. The audience funnel: Observations of gesture based interaction with multiple large displays in a city center. *Intl. Journal of Human–Computer Interaction 27*, 6 (2011), 562–579.
11. Morris, D. *Bodywatching: A field guide to the human species*. Cape, 1985.
12. Morris, D. *Peoplewatching*. Random House, 2002.
13. Quek, F., Ehrich, R., and Lockhart, T. As go the feet...: on the estimation of attentional focus from stance. In *Proc. ICMI*, ACM Press (2008), 97–104.
14. Vogel, D., and Balakrishnan, R. Interactive public ambient displays: transitioning from implicit to explicit, public to personal, interaction with multiple users. In *Proc. UIST*, ACM (2004), 137–146.

A Diary Study on Combining Multiple Information Devices in Everyday Activities and Tasks

Tero Jokela
Nokia Technologies
P.O. Box 1000, FI-33721
Tampere, Finland
tero.jokela@nokia.com

Jarno Ojala
Tampere Univ. of Technology
P.O. Box 589, FI-33101
Tampere, Finland
jarno.ojala@tut.fi

Thomas Olsson
Tampere Univ. of Technology
P.O. Box 589, FI-33101
Tampere, Finland
thomas.olsson@tut.fi

ABSTRACT
As people possess increasing numbers of information devices, situations where several devices are combined and used together have become more common. We present a user study on people's current practices in combining multiple information devices in their everyday lives, ranging from pragmatic tasks to leisure activities. Based on diaries and interviews of 14 participants, we characterize the usage practices of the most common devices, including smartphones, computers, tablets, and home media centers. We analyze 123 real-life multi-device use cases and identify the main usage patterns, including Sequential Use, Resource Lending, Related Parallel Use, and Unrelated Parallel Use. We discuss the practical challenges of using several information devices together. Finally, we identify three levels of decisions that determine which devices are used in a particular situation, including acquiring, making available, and selecting the devices for use.

Author Keywords
Information devices; smartphones; tablets; multi-device; device ecologies; mobile use; user study.

ACM Classification Keywords
H.5.m. Information interfaces and presentation (e.g., HCI): Miscellaneous.

INTRODUCTION
Visions of ubiquitous computing have long predicted an evolution from single-device computing towards computing with multiple devices. Weiser [19] envisioned a future of multiple computers of different scales per user, all interconnected by a ubiquitous network. Norman [14] proposed families of information appliances, specialized to perform specific activities and capable of sharing information among themselves, as a solution to the complexity of personal computers. In line with these predictions, people today own and use increasing numbers of interconnected devices with diverse form factors. First smartphones and then tablets have established themselves as new device categories alongside personal computers. Some conventional devices such as televisions and cameras have become connected to the Internet and gained capabilities to provide access to many of the same applications and services as computers. Emerging industry trends, including wearable devices, connected cars, and the Internet of Things, suggest continuing increase in the number and diversity of devices in the future.

While this development towards computing with multiple devices offers many new opportunities, it has also created a need for interfaces, applications, and services that better support multi-device use. Today, many popular applications and services can be accessed with a range of devices with different screen sizes and form factors. A session of use can be saved and closed on one device and re-opened and continued on another device. Cloud services support centralized management of device families, including device settings and installed applications, and file hosting services allow accessing and synchronizing content between devices. Recent web browsers provide a common usage history across all devices and allow moving browser tabs between devices. A multiplicity of technologies has been developed for presenting visual or audio information through other devices, for example, using one device to show pictures on the screen or to play music through the speakers of another device. Attempts to harmonize software and hardware platforms and tools across device categories aim to make it easier to develop applications that support multiple devices.

While a wide variety of different technologies have been proposed to support multi-device use, only a few studies have addressed how people actually use multiple information devices together in their everyday lives. Of these studies, many are relatively old, pre-dating the emergence of modern smartphones, tablets, and cloud services. In this paper, we present a recent diary study on how people today combine multiple information devices in everyday activities and tasks. Based on diaries and interviews of 14 participants, we characterize the evolving usage practices of the most common devices, including

CHI 2015, April 18 - 23 2015, Seoul, Republic of Korea
Copyright 2015 ACM 978-1-4503-3145-6/15/04...$15.00
http://dx.doi.org/10.1145/2702123.2702211

smartphones, computers, tablets, and home media centers. We analyze 123 user-reported cases of multi-device use and identify the main usage patterns, including Sequential Use, Resource Lending, Related Parallel Use, and Unrelated Parallel Use. We discuss the practical challenges of owning and operating several information devices together. While most of the earlier studies have been based solely on user interviews, our study is additionally grounded on user diaries reporting real-life use cases recorded in real contexts of use over a time period of one week. Also, while most of the earlier studies have focused on information work related use, our study explores a range of different use cases from pragmatic tasks to leisure activities in various mundane contexts of use. The objective of our study is to provide qualitative insights into real-life practices of multi-device use. The results inform the design of future interfaces, technologies, and applications that better support multi-device use.

RELATED WORK

A wide variety of systems, user interfaces, and interaction methods have been proposed to support computing with multiple devices. These include device binding methods that allow connecting several devices to operate together, ranging from virtual methods (such as scanning for available devices in the proximity) to physical methods (such as synchronous user actions, spatial alignment, and use of auxiliary devices) [18]. Similar techniques have also been developed to support transferring content objects or application windows between screens, including transfers between devices within hand's reach and between devices at longer distances from each other [13]. Migratory interfaces [1] provide techniques for moving application windows between devices. Solutions have also been developed for managing and switching tasks in multi-device computing environments [2]. Beyond single-user systems, a broad range of multi-user systems that support collaboration with multiple devices have been developed, addressing different physical scales and types of social interaction [17].

In addition to the development of methods and solutions to support multi-device use, a number of studies have addressed how people actually use multiple devices in real life. Several reasons and motivations for using multiple devices have been identified [15, 3]. Different devices suit different tasks, social situations, and physical environments. Estimated effort to set up the device is an important consideration in selecting which device to use, especially for short tasks. No single device may have all the functions or data needed, forcing the use of multiple devices. Additional devices can also be used as data or battery backups. Sometimes personal preferences and habits may influence the decision to use different devices for different tasks.

Practices and workflows in using multiple devices have been found to vary between different individuals and professional groups [3, 9, 16]. People tend to divide tasks between devices, assigning each device a specific role within the workflow [5, 3, 16]. In addition to serial patterns of multi-device use [9], also parallel patterns have recently become more common [16, 4, 12].

Accessing and managing content across devices has been observed to be one of the key concerns in multi-device environments [15, 3, 16, 12]. People have been found to assemble their own personal patchworks of solutions by combining multiple different tools and approaches, often in creative ways. Conventional solutions include manual synchronization and mirroring between devices, dedicating a certain device for certain kind of information, portable storage devices such as USB memory sticks, e-mailing content items to oneself, and network drives. More recently, various cloud-based storage and synchronization solutions have increased their popularity. In addition to content, other kinds of data such as interaction histories should also be synchronized between devices [15, 3, 8].

In mobile use, managing different device configurations may require significant physical effort and planning [15]. People have been observed to address this problem by adopting different strategies, including development of stable habits, making just-in-case preparations for potential situations, and doing careful advance planning. A Mobile Kit refers to a stable set of multiple personal devices kept together and carried while traveling [11]. Jung, et al. [7] suggest examining the set of digital devices that a person uses as an ecology of interactive artifacts, in order to understand how people experience and strategize the use of interactive artifacts and the development of their ecologies over time.

While a number of studies have addressed how people use multiple devices in real life, they are still relatively few given the broadness of the topic. Further, several of the earlier studies have been made before the availability and widespread adoption of modern smartphones, tablets, and cloud services. Therefore, there is room for an updated view into how the new extended ecologies of devices and services are managed by users. Most of the earlier studies have also focused on technologically advanced users and use cases related to information work. We believe our study addressing diverse groups of users and exploring beyond work-related use is useful in broadening the understanding of the evolving practices and needs in multi-device use.

OUR STUDY

Objectives

In this study, we were interested in how people today combine multiple information devices in their everyday activities and tasks. For the purposes of this study, we defined an information device as any device that can be used to create or consume digital information, including personal computers, smartphones, tablets, televisions, game devices, cameras, music players, navigation devices, and wristwatch computers. In particular, we were interested in the following three research questions related to multi-device use: (1) What devices do the participants have and what are the roles of the different devices in their personal device ecologies? (2) In which situations do they combine multiple information devices and what kinds of practices do they have for multi-device use? (3) What kind of challenges and problems they face in multi-device use? Overall, based on a qualitative analysis, we aimed at creating a rich picture of the current and emerging practices and challenges in using multiple information devices together, in order to support the development of future multi-device interfaces, technologies, and applications.

Participants

We recruited a total of 14 people living in Southern Finland to participate in the study by posting an advertisement on local mailing lists and social media groups. We selected a diverse group of people who owned multiple devices and actively used them for a wide range of different applications and services. Six of the participants were female and eight male. Seven of the participants were students (age M=24.4, SD=2.8 years), while the other seven were professionals working in different fields (age M=35.6, SD=6.7 years). Regarding education and professional background, four participants had their primary background in information technology. The remaining ten participants represented a wide variety of other professions, including graphic and industrial designers, a medical doctor, a goldsmith, a teacher, and a management assistant. Despite not being pure technologists, the participants were fairly advanced users of information technology: on a scale between 1 and 7 (1=novice, 7=expert), the participants rated their familiarity with information technology above average (M=5.6, SD=0.8). The participants received small rewards for their participation.

Method

The study consisted of three phases: an initial briefing session, a one-week self-reporting period, and a final interview. All the briefing sessions and interviews were individual with the participant and one or two researchers present. Five briefing sessions were held over the phone – other briefing sessions and all interviews were made face-to-face, either in a meeting room in our laboratory or in the participant's place of study or work. The purpose of the briefing session was to provide the participant with necessary information and materials for the self-reporting period. After introducing the participant to the scope and the objectives of the study, the researcher gave the participant a workbook for the self-reporting period and explained the contents of the book.

The main part of the workbook was a diary where the participant was asked to report all situations and tasks where they used multiple information devices together. We asked the participant to keep a complete diary for at least three days (two working days and one non-working day) during the study period, but we also encouraged them to report any interesting situations that occurred on the other days. For each situation, the participant was asked to report the context of use, overall course of events, devices that were used, practices for and motivations of using multiple devices, frequency and importance of the situation, as well as satisfaction with the course of events and possible problems. The researcher emphasized the importance of filling in the book as soon as possible after the event occurred. In addition to the diary, the workbook included other tasks, where the participant was asked to provide information about their devices, the tasks they were used for, and the contexts they were used in. The participant was also asked to describe the typical set of devices that they carried with them in mobile situations, as well as their ideal multi-device setup. The purpose of these tasks was to help the participant to prepare for the interview by collecting information about their device ecology and practices, and reflecting them in real contexts of use (for example, at home or at the workplace).

The participant then started the one-week self-reporting period during which they filled in the workbook. At the end of the period, the researchers tentatively analyzed the workbooks to prepare for the semi-structured interviews. We asked the participant to bring with them the devices they carried on a typical work day. The interview started by asking about the participant's devices and their use, followed by a detailed discussion of two or three different situations that the participant had reported. Specific questions were asked about various topics, including sharing of content between devices, maintaining multiple devices, and obtaining new devices. At the end of the approximately one-hour interview, the participant was asked to summarize the main benefits and drawbacks of using multiple devices. The interviews were audio recorded and photographs of the participant's devices and their use were taken when considered relevant.

For each interview, the researcher who made the interview wrote notes about it based on the audio recordings. Three researchers then analyzed the data and built an Affinity Diagram [6] in a series of interpretation sessions. Based on interpretative content analysis, the notes were grouped based on similarity. The groups were then further clustered to broader categories that were identified from the data and jointly revisited, discussed, and refined. The diary data was separately analyzed and the reported use cases were categorized into different patterns of multi-device use based on a bottom-up data-driven categorization. This was done to develop an understanding of different patterns of multi-device use based on the collected data rather than to prove any a priori hypothesis. The categorization scheme was primarily based on the roles and the configuration of the devices as well as the user's motivations for multi-device use. Finally, based on the data from the other tasks in the participants' workbooks, we constructed matrices describing relationships between devices, tasks, and contexts of use.

RESULTS

We begin by giving an overview of the participants' device ecologies, describing the most common devices and their practices of use. We then present an analysis of the collected multi-device use cases and identify the main usage patterns, including Sequential Use, Resource Lending, Related Parallel Use, and Unrelated Parallel Use. Finally, we highlight various practical challenges related to owning and using several devices together and discuss the problem of selecting which devices to use.

Device Ecologies

On the average, each participant was actively using 7.9 information devices in their everyday life. Four participants had mainly Apple devices, while the remaining 10 had a more balanced mixture of devices from different manufacturers. In addition to their personal devices, seven participants also had devices provided by their employers. Not surprisingly, the most commonly used devices by the participants were smartphones, computers, tablets, and home media centers (Fig. 1).

All participants (14/14) had a smartphone; two participants had two smartphones, a work phone and a personal phone. The smartphone was the only device that every participant said they used every day. Several participants commented that smartphone was their most important device and their everyday life depended on it. *"[P7] I am hooked on my [smartphone]. There is no life without it. I use it for everything. ... It is my most important device that I use the most."* As the participants carried their smartphones almost always with them, the phones allowed them to be reached and kept them up to date anywhere they went. The smartphones were used for a wide variety of different tasks, including calendar, e-mail, messaging, phone calls, web browsing, social media, music, and calculator. Smartphones were also commonly used for taking pictures and for several participants, the phone was their primary camera. However, the use of smartphones was focused on retrieving and entering small amounts of information and the smartphones were not considered capable of handling large amounts of information or complex tasks. While many applications and services had smartphone versions, they often lacked features or did not work properly.

All participants (14/14) also had laptop computers and more than half of them (8/14) had several laptops in their use. Nearly half of the participants (6/14) also had a desktop computer. As computers were replaced by other devices in consumption and entertainment oriented tasks, their use was increasingly characterized by more complex tasks, which included entry of long texts, creation of complicated content, detailed work, and handling large amounts of content. These tasks were often related to work or studies, and they were described as important but serious and somewhat boring. *"[P13] My laptop is my trusted companion, which I use for all important things: school and work."* The participants considered their computers as their most powerful devices that provided options beyond what their other devices could offer. Computers were also regarded as fallback devices that the participants turned to when their other devices failed. Sometimes computers formed a link between devices that could not otherwise communicate with each other. Among modern smartphones and tablets, the participants felt that their computers were like legacy devices from the old world but they simply could not manage without them. *"[P6] After I got the tablet, my laptop feels really ancient, somehow it is awfully old-fashioned. But certain things you just cannot do without it."*

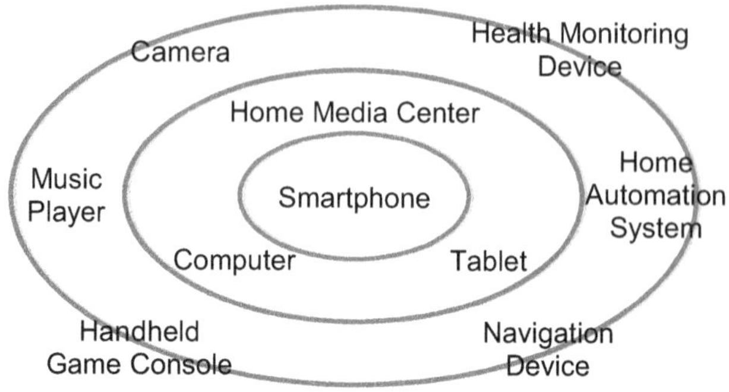

Figure 1. Most commonly used devices.

Almost all participants (12/14) actively used tablets [12] and two participants had several tablets. The two participants who did not use tablets had tested them but considered that they did not have use for a tablet as other devices (especially smartphones) served the same purposes. The tablets were primarily used for searching for and consuming content and for entertainment, such as reading, playing games, and watching videos. Some participants considered tablets as smartphones with larger screens. Compared to laptops, the tablets were considered to be more lightweight and instantly available for use. Two common patterns of use were observed: 1) a shared family tablet at home for multiple purposes; 2) a personal tablet that was partly replacing a laptop in mobile use. However, tablets were not considered suitable for entering long texts or doing complex or detailed work. One participant described this limitation also as an advantage since it forced him to focus on the essential. In general, tablets were still looking for their role and their use involved more experimentation than the use of the other devices.

For the purposes of this study, we defined Home Media Center to consist of a TV or other large screen together with game consoles, Home Theater PCs (HTPCs), and other media appliances connected to it. All participants had some kind of a Home Media Center system. The Home Media Center was the heart of social entertainment at home. It provided the largest screen in the household supporting collective viewing of and sharing of TV programs, movies, games, music, and personal photos and videos. Video consumption was dominated by on-demand Internet services and local content providers. Lack of ready-made solutions supporting all content sources led the participants to build custom solutions, which were often PC based.

In addition to these four most commonly used devices, the participants reported using a variety of other devices. Of the other devices, the most common were digital cameras, which were used in pre-planned situations where high quality photographs and videos were desired. Other devices included music players, handheld game consoles, navigation devices, health monitoring devices, and home automation systems.

The smartphones were considered the most personal devices and were rarely shared, with only a few exceptions such as a child playing games on a parent's phone or a wife taking a photo with her husband's phone. Sharing tablets and computers was more common, and within families, all devices were in principle shared. Still, most devices had a clear primary user and others used the device only randomly. The primary user had their services and applications configured and often always running on the device. *"[P5] All of our devices are shared. But I use primarily some devices and my husband uses other devices, because on those you always have the web pages, files, and apps you need already opened."* Some participants also expressed a desire to keep some of their devices private. *"[P6] I have tried to keep the tablet to myself, but of course [my daughter] can use it as well if she wants. But some devices you just want to keep to yourself."*

Patterns of Multi-Device Use

The participants reported a total of 111 situations and tasks in which they had used multiple information devices together during the one-week diary period. Initial analysis of the data indicated that 23 of the situations involved several separate instances of multi-device use and therefore these situations were split into multiple cases. On the other hand, 12 situations were rejected, either because the description of the situation was too unclear or because the situation did not involve use of multiple information devices (for example, there was only one information device used). Eventually, the preliminary analysis resulted in a total of 123 cases of multi-device use.

Fig. 2 illustrates the categorization of these multi-device use cases into the main patterns of use. On the highest level, multi-device use can be divided into Sequential Use and Parallel Use. In Sequential Use, the participant changed the device during the task. In Parallel Use, the participant used several devices simultaneously. Of the multi-device use cases analyzed in the study, 37% were Sequential Use while the remaining 63% were Parallel Use.

The cases of Parallel Use can be further divided into three subtypes: Resource Lending, Related Parallel Use, and

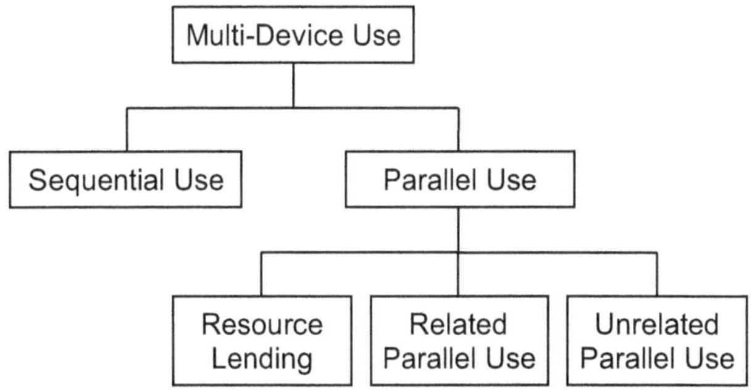

Figure 2. Patterns of multi-device use.

Unrelated Parallel Use. In Resource Lending, the participant's task focused on a single device, but the device borrowed some resources from other devices. In Related and Unrelated Parallel Use, the participant used several devices simultaneously. The difference is that in Related Parallel Use, the participant was working on a single task and all devices were involved in this task, while in Unrelated Parallel Use, the participant was working on multiple tasks simultaneously and different devices were involved in different tasks. Of the cases of Parallel Use analyzed in the study, 43% were classified as Resource Lending, 44% as Related Parallel Use, and 13% as Unrelated Parallel Use.

In general, the participants' motivations for using multiple devices could be divided in two broad categories. First, in 83% of the cases, the participant voluntarily decided to use multiple devices, for example, in the hope of improved performance, efficiency, or convenience of use. Second, in the remaining 17% of the cases, the participant was forced to use several devices, for example, because of technical limitations or errors, or because the original device used to start the task had become unavailable.

In the following subsections, we discuss each pattern of multi-device use as well as related motivations and behaviors in more detail.

Sequential Use

In Sequential Use (Fig. 3.a), the participant changed the device during the task. The participant could change the device once or several times in a sequence.

In 68% of the Sequential Use cases analyzed in the study, the user voluntarily changed the device. We observed several reasons that triggered the participant to switch devices. A common reason was a transformation in the character of the task, which made the participant to consider another device better suited for the task and to change the device. *"[P7] I googled the phone number of my physiotherapist with the tablet and called with my phone."* Another common reason was a change in the physical environment or the social context, which resulted in another device deemed more appropriate for the task. *"[P1] In the bus, I was browsing with my phone and found an interesting page about teacher's copyrights. At work, I*

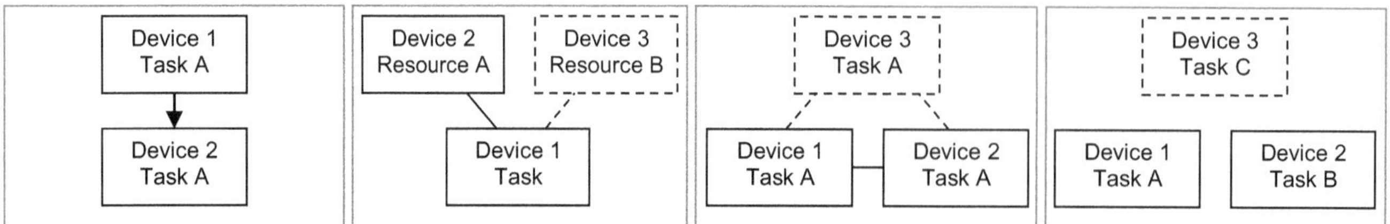

a) **Sequential Use:** Changing the device during the task.

b) **Resource Lending:** Borrowing resources from other devices.

c) **Related Parallel Use:** All devices involved in a single task.

d) **Unrelated Parallel Use:** Devices involved in different tasks.

Figure 3. Different patterns of multi-device use.

continued reading the page with my laptop." Often, both the task and the context changed at the same time. In these cases, there was typically a workflow consisting of a sequence of clearly separate steps, each done at a different location. *"[P13] I searched for a recipe with my laptop. Then I moved to the kitchen, opened the recipe with the tablet, and started cooking."* There were also a few cases in which the task and the physical and social context remained unchanged, but the participant still decided to change the device. In these cases, the participant's initial evaluation of the task proved incorrect as more information was learned about the task, ultimately resulting in a device change. *"[P13] When meeting the other members of the project group, I tried to browse the course materials with my phone, but finally switched to my laptop because the phone was too slow and the display too small."*

The dilemma of whether to change the device or not can be illustrated with Fig. 4.a. The horizontal axis represents the progression of a task, while the vertical axis represents the user effort. Each device requires an initial setup effort, represented by the y-intercept of the line, before it can used to work on the task. Each device also has certain efficiency, represented by the slope of the line. As illustrated in Fig 4.b, the efficiency of the device may change as the characteristics of the task change. In order to switch the device (Fig. 4.c), the user has to do additional effort. While the person may gain improved performance after the switch, it may take a long time to outdo the switching effort. The problem may be further complicated by the difficulty of predicting the future evolution of the task.

In 32% of the Sequential Use cases, the user was forced to change the device. The most common reason was technical problems that prevented continuing with the original device [9]. *"[P6] I opened the electronic messaging system of my daughter's school with my tablet and tried to reply to a message, but a scrolling text field did not work with the tablet. I mailed the text I had entered to myself and continued with my laptop."* Overall, technical problems were the reason for using multiple devices in 25% of the Sequential Use cases. Other reasons that forced the user to change the device included the original device running out of battery or the need to access content that was stored on another device.

We observed a variety of different methods of moving a task from one device to another. It was common that the devices and applications did not support any way of moving the task from one device to another, or the user was unaware of or unwilling to use them. In these cases, the user just started the task from the beginning with the new device and manually copied information from the old device to the new one as necessary. However, in many cases it was possible to save the task on a network resource, for example, on a cloud service or a network disk, and to reopen it with another device. Other less common approaches were to send a message, typically an e-mail, to oneself, or to use a physical medium such as a USB stick or memory card to transfer the task.

Parallel Use

In Parallel Use, the participant used two or more devices simultaneously. The cases of Parallel Use can be further divided into three subtypes: Resource Lending, Related Parallel Use, and Unrelated Parallel Use.

Resource Lending

In Resource Lending (Fig. 3.b) use cases, the participant's activity primarily focused on a single device, but this device borrowed some resources from other devices.

Common examples of Resource Lending included borrowing the input and output capabilities of another device. For example, the screen of another device could be used to display visual information or speakers to play audio. *"[P6] I connected my laptop to my TV to watch an episode of a TV series."* Alternatively, the input devices of one device could be borrowed to provide input for another device. *"[P8] I controlled my home theatre system with an app installed on my phone."* In some cases, both input and output capabilities of another device were borrowed and all interaction took place through another device. *"[P2] I used my laptop to organize messages and music on my phone."* In addition to input and output capabilities, another common resource shared between devices was the network connection. *"[P2] In the bus, I used the hotspot feature on my phone to connect my laptop to the Internet."* Resource Lending was almost exclusively done using direct wireless connections between devices. Other approaches included traditional cables and docking stations as well as lending resources through a cloud service.

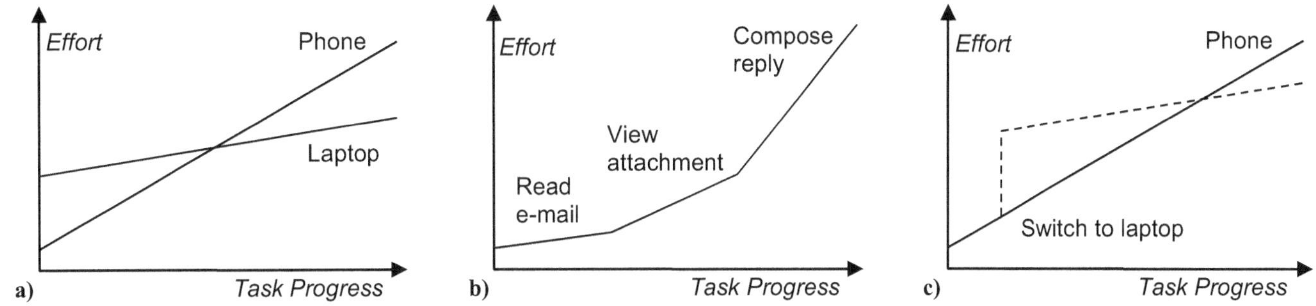

Figure 4. a) Different devices have different setup efforts and task efficiencies. b) Changing task characteristics may influence device efficiency. c) Switching devices requires additional effort that may exceed the benefits.

Related Parallel Use

In Related Parallel Use (Fig. 3.c), the participant was working on a single task using two or more devices. All devices were involved in the same task.

In most cases, the motivation for using multiple devices in parallel was to have multiple views to the task, dedicating different devices to different content or applications. A common situation was that a participant was using another device to view additional information when watching video content with a home media center. *"[P5] While watching a movie on TV, I opened the IMDB page with my phone."* In other cases, a participant was viewing instructions on one device while working on a task on another device. *"[P1] I installed software on my phone and looked at instructions on my computer."* The participant could also work on a new document on one device, while having the source documents open on the other devices. *"[P10] While making a project presentation with my laptop, I had my notes open on my tablet."* Sometimes, there simply were several documents that needed to be viewed in parallel. *"[P10] I displayed CAD drawings on my laptop and images on my tablet."* A second device could also be used for simple auxiliary tasks, for example, to access the dictionary. *"[P8] While watching TV, I checked the translation of a word with my phone."*

Another common category of cases of Related Parallel Use was situations where the participant was collaborating with remote persons over a real-time communication link. One device, typically a phone, was then assigned for handling the communication, while other devices were used for accessing related content and applications. *"[P8] My friend called me and asked me to the movies. I checked my calendar and information about the movie with my laptop while talking on the phone."* Other less common motivations for Related Parallel Use included speeding up a computationally complex task like 3D graphics rendering by using multiple devices as well as various technical reasons which forced the use of several devices.

In most cases, the participants used two devices together. However, in a few cases the participants had built more sophisticated device configurations which involved Parallel Use of three or more devices. *"[P4] While watching sports on TV, I have live statistics open on a laptop. At the same time, I can do real-time betting on my tablet or phone."* In practically all cases, the devices provided no technical support of any kind for Related Parallel Use. The participants had to manually connect and transfer information between the devices.

Unrelated Parallel Use

In Unrelated Parallel Use (Fig. 3.d), the participant was working on several tasks simultaneously using several devices. Different devices were involved in different tasks.

In cases of Unrelated Parallel Use, there was typically a primary foreground task and a secondary background task. Typical examples of background tasks included watching videos or listening to music. *"[P10] I listen to music with my phone while doing homework with my laptop or tablet."* In a few cases, the participant was working on two equal tasks in parallel, for example, when the participant received two simultaneous phone calls. *"[P1] I was talking with my mother on my personal phone, when my girlfriend called to my work phone."* There were also a few cases where technical restrictions required the participant to use different devices for different tasks. While different devices were involved in different tasks, in some situations coordination between the devices would have been beneficial. *"[P6] I was listening to a net radio with my laptop, when I received a phone call. I would have wanted to turn down the laptop volume when the phone rang."*

The participants reported relatively few cases of Unrelated Parallel Use. It is possible that the participants did not recognize many common situations as Parallel Use of multiple devices, as the unrelated parallel tasks may not always be conscious. For example, carrying a phone in order to be reachable by voice calls or messages when working on other tasks with other devices (undoubtedly a very common case) could be classified as Unrelated Parallel Use.

Deciding Which Devices to Use

Owning multiple devices creates the problem of choosing which devices to use in a specific situation. In our analysis of multi-device use cases, we identified three levels of decisions which determined which devices to use: 1) deciding which devices to acquire, 2) deciding which of your devices to make available in a specific context, and 3) deciding which of the available devices to actually use. Each level of decisions narrowed the available options until finally the devices to use were left. The participants' device selections determined the pattern of multi-device use: the decision to change device resulted in a Sequential Use pattern, while the decision to use two or more devices simultaneously resulted in a Parallel Use pattern.

Regarding acquisition of new devices, most participants said that interoperability with their current devices was a major factor when considering which new devices to obtain. On the other hand, other factors such as price or curiosity to try and opportunity to learn new devices and systems often overrode it. The level of influence the participants had over the acquisition decisions varied: the participants had more control over devices they purchased for their personal use than over devices that were provided to them by their employers. Overall, the participants could not fully control their device environments as they were constrained by the choices of other people and organizations, such as their employers, educational institutions, clients, and friends.

For fixed devices, the decisions on which devices to make available in specific contexts primarily related to the physical locations of the devices, for example, in which room to place the device at home. For mobile devices, the decisions related to which devices to take with you in mobile situations. Regarding the mobile devices, we observed similar practices as Oulasvirta, et al. [15]. Most participants had a fixed Mobile Kit [11] of devices they took with them every day. Heavier devices such as laptops and special devices such as USB drives were taken based on expected need. In addition to computing devices, the participants carried with them a wide variety of auxiliary devices such as chargers, headsets, cables, and memory sticks.

Decisions on which of the available devices to use in specific situations were based on several criteria. The device characteristics that were considered included both user interface capabilities (such as display size, pointing device, and the level of multi-tasking support), technical capabilities (such as processing power, storage capacity, network connection, and camera quality), and physical characteristics (such as the size and weight of the device). For tasks requiring entry of long texts, the text entry capability, especially availability of a physical QWERTY keyboard, strongly influenced the device selection. *"[P4] I won't write any long texts with a virtual keyboard. I want the good old physical QWERTY."* As already discussed in section Sequential Use, another major factor influencing the decision on which device to use was the easiness of starting to use the device. If the required content was available only on certain devices, the participant was forced to use those devices. People had also developed different habits of using certain devices for certain tasks or in certain contexts of use. Finally, the participants also considered the context of use, including both social aspects (such as acceptability of using a certain device in a certain social situation) as well as physical aspects (such as the available space). *"[P13] As I met new persons, I did not want to hide behind the [laptop] screen, as we were supposed to work together and be social."*

Accessing Content Between Devices

Being able to access any content on any device was the most commonly requested feature to support multi-device use by the participants. For transferring individual content items between devices, sending e-mail to oneself was still common, but also direct network transfers between devices over WiFi or Bluetooth were used. Traditional physical methods of memory sticks, cables, and DVDs had largely been replaced by wireless or cloud-based solutions, but were still used as fallbacks when more advanced solutions failed to work, especially between systems of different owners.

The participants utilized cloud storage services (for example, Dropbox, Google Drive, and iCloud) for a wide variety of purposes, including storing and accessing personal content from any device, and synchronizing and making backups between devices. Cloud storage services were also used for other purposes, such as sharing and collaborating between people and for temporary storage. Using several services in parallel was common as this allowed the participants to grab free storage space from every service and reduced the risk of being tied to a single service provider. It was also common to dedicate different services to different purposes or content types, for example, using one service for personal content, another for work, and a third for collaboration with others.

While the participants utilized cloud storage services in many ways, they also raised many concerns about cloud storage and did not trust the cloud as the only storage solution [16], especially for important content. Accessing content in the cloud was considered slow and sometimes unreliable, particularly over wireless networks. *"[P5] Accessing [cellular] networks sometimes causes problems in certain areas. It is really infuriating."* To address this problem, one participant used different wireless network operators on different devices to be able to always select the best working network. A few participants were concerned about privacy and security risks, for example, of storing personal photographs or work-related content in the cloud. Another source of concern was the persistence and possible discontinuation of cloud services. Finally, many current cloud services were considered complicated and poorly integrated with native applications.

Device Maintenance and Energy Management

Participants with large collections of information devices had to do significant amounts of maintenance work to keep their devices up to date and running. However, half of the participants (7/14) said that this was not a major problem as the software updates were so easy to do. *"[P8] All [devices] have automatic updates and I just have to accept them."* Other participants (6/14) considered the need to maintain a large amount of devices as troublesome and would have preferred more automated solutions. Maintenance responsibility was often concentrated on a particular person in a social network, for example, the husband in a family. These people typically enjoyed the maintenance task and considered it as a positive challenge. *"[P4] Device maintenance in our family is my responsibility. ... I like to do it. I take it as a challenge. Updating the devices of my parents and my mother-in-law are my responsibility, too."*

Another challenge related to the use of multiple devices was managing the energy and charging the batteries of portable devices. The battery concerns were mainly related to smartphones and most participants (9/14) said they were frustrated with the battery lives of the current smartphones. Other devices were considered to have reasonably good battery lives – tablets, in particular, were praised for their long battery lives.

DISCUSSION

In general, the participants wanted all their devices to seamlessly work with each other. However, in practice, they continuously encountered problems in multi-device use, especially between devices from different ecosystems. Common problems included connecting and transferring information between devices, incompatible content formats, web pages that did not work on all devices, and applications and services that were not available for all devices. The participants often had to resort to common core functions, such as e-mail, to work around interoperability problems. Plenty of work still remains to be done to realize the visions of smooth and effortless multi-device computing.

Today, most of the commercial support for multi-device use is aimed towards supporting patterns of Sequential Use, for example, moving sessions between devices. Also, traditional forms of Resource Lending, such as displaying pictures on the screen of another device, are well supported. However, the results of our study indicate that also patterns of Related Parallel Use were common among the participants. This finding is supported by other recent studies [16, 4, 12]. Still, the devices and systems used by the participants provided practically no support for Related Parallel Use.

Being able to access any content with any device was the most commonly requested feature to support multi-device use by the study participants. While the participants utilized cloud storage services in many ways, it was obvious that the current services were not adequate as the only storage solutions. A wide range of user concerns should be addressed in future storage solutions, including capacity, cost, privacy, security, performance, reliability, persistence, and complexity. As suggested by one of our participants, one potential direction to explore might be more direct sharing of content between devices, in order to provide improved reliability and performance and lower cost: *"[P10] Information between devices currently flows through the cloud, but when the devices are close to each other, why it couldn't pass directly between the devices?"*

The participants described that in the modern world of smartphones and tablets, the PC felt like a legacy device from the old world. Some participants had tried to completely replace their computers with smartphones and tablets. However, it was clear that while smartphones and tablets had taken over many simple tasks traditionally done with computers, in their current form they could not fully replace computers in more demanding tasks. The main problems were related to limited text-entry capability, inaccurate pointing devices, and restricted multi-tasking capability. This calls for "reinventing the PC" in the age of multi-device computing, that is, developing multi-device solutions that are capable of handling the large, complex, and detailed tasks that currently require the use of a personal computer. Interestingly, the limited multi-tasking capabilities of current tablets and smartphones already seem to encourage the use of multiple devices to overcome them.

As the participants purchased new devices, they sometimes recycled their old devices for others to use. However, often the old devices were gradually left unused, partly because the limitations of current systems to support multi-device use promote the use of a single device. Over time, this resulted in large collections of unused devices. Multi-device ecologies might provide opportunities to extend the life of old devices. The old devices could adopt more specialized or supporting roles in the device ecology, for example, an old tablet could be permanently attached to the kitchen wall to support cooking activities, or an old computer could be used as a home server.

Generalizability of Results and Future Work

As we wanted to gain insights into the current practices and behaviors in combining multiple information devices, we decided to approach the topic though a detailed analysis of a limited number of subjects and cases, emphasizing qualitative research methods. While this approach provided us with a rich picture of the current practices and the underlying motivations and needs, it is not possible to statistically estimate the frequency of the observed behaviors in the overall population. In order to validate the results, a quantitative study, such as a survey or a logging study, with a larger sample would be useful.

It should also be noted that the study results reflect current practices – future devices and technologies may enable new practices, as can also be seen when comparing these results with the earlier similar studies. Also, while the participants represented a rather diverse sample in terms of occupations, they were still relatively advanced users of technology with generally high level of education living in a western country. Different user groups in different parts of the world might display different behavior. Another possible future direction could be more focused studies addressing specific user groups, applications, or contexts of use.

CONCLUSION

We have presented a user study on people's practices in combining multiple information devices in their everyday lives, ranging from pragmatic tasks to leisure and entertainment activities. Based on diaries and interviews of 14 participants, we have characterized the usage practices of the most common devices, including smartphones, computers, tablets, and home media centers. We have analyzed 123 real-life cases of multi-device use and identified the main usage patterns, including Sequential Use, Resource Lending, Related Parallel Use, and Unrelated Parallel Use. Additionally, we have observed three levels of decisions that determine which devices are used in a particular situation, including acquiring, making available, and selecting the devices for use. We have also discussed the practical challenges related to owning and operating several information devices together, including content access, maintenance, and energy management.

While the participants wanted all their devices to seamlessly work with each other, in practice they continuously encountered problems in multi-device use. Of the multi-device use patterns, Sequential Use and Resource Lending were relative well supported by current devices and systems, but there was little technical support for Related Parallel Use even though it was found to be common among the study participants. Current cloud-based storage solutions were found to have several weaknesses in supporting multi-device use. Finally, improved support for multi-device use might also provide opportunities to extend the life of old devices by allowing the old devices to take more specialized or supporting roles in the device ecology.

ACKNOWLEDGMENTS

We thank Prof. Kaisa Väänänen-Vainio-Mattila, Guido Grassel, and Petri Piippo for contributing to the planning of the study and for their valuable comments.

REFERENCES

1. Bandelloni, R., and Paternò, F. Migratory user interfaces able to adapt to various interaction platforms. *Int. Journal of Human-Computer Studies* 60, 5-6 (2004), 621-639.
2. Bardram, J. Activity-based computing for medical work in hospitals. *ACM Transactions on Computer-Human Interaction* 16, 2 (2009).
3. Dearman, D. and Pierce, J. It's on my other computer!: computing with multiple devices. In *Proc. CHI '08*, 767-776.
4. Google. The New Multi-Screen World Study. https://www.thinkwithgoogle.com/research-studies/the-new-multi-screen-world-study.html
5. Grudin, J. Partitioning digital worlds: focal and peripheral awareness in multiple monitor use. In *Proc. CHI '01*, 458-465.
6. Holtzblatt, K., Wendell, J. B. and Wood, S. *Rapid Contextual Design.* Morgan Kaufmann, 2004.
7. Jung, H., Stolterman, E., Ryan, W., Thompson, T. and Siegel, M. Toward a framework for ecologies of artifacts: how are digital artifacts interconnected within a personal life? In *Proc. NordiCHI '08*, 201-210.
8. Kane, S., Karlson, A., Meyers, B., Johns, P., Jacobs, A. and Smith, G. Exploring cross-device web use on PCs and mobile devices. In *Proc. INTERACT '09*, 722-735.
9. Karlson, A., Iqbal, S., Meyers, B., Ramos, G., Lee, K. and Tang, J. Mobile taskflow in context: a screenshot study of smartphone usage. In *Proc. CHI '10*, 2009-2018.
10. Karlson, A., Meyers, B., Jacobs, A., Johns, P. and Kane, S. Working overtime: patterns of smartphone and PC usage in the day of an information worker. In *Proc. Pervasive '09*, 398-405.
11. Mainwaring, S., Anderson, K. and Chang, M. Living for the global city: mobile kits, urban interfaces, and Ubicomp. In *Proc. UbiComp '05*, 269-286.
12. Müller, H., Gove, J. and Webb, J. Understanding tablet use: a multi-method exploration. In Proc. *MobileHCI '12*, 1-10.
13. Nacenta, M. *Cross-display object movement in multi-display environments.* PhD thesis, University of Saskatchewan, 2009.
14. Norman, D. *The Invisible Computer.* MIT Press, 1999.
15. Oulasvirta, A. and Sumari, L. Mobile kits and laptop trays: managing multiple devices in mobile information work. In *Proc. CHI '07*, 1127-1136.
16. Santosa, S., and Wigdor, D. A field study of multi-device workflows in distributed workspaces. In *Proc. UbiComp '13*, 63-72.
17. Terrenghi, L., Quigley, A. and Dix, A. A taxonomy for and analysis of multi-person-display ecosystems. *Personal and Ubiquitous Computing* 13, 8 (2009), 583-598.
18. Uzun, E., Saxena, N. and Kumar, A. Pairing devices for social interactions: a comparative usability evaluation. In *Proc. CHI '11*, 2315-2324.
19. Weiser, M. The computer for the 21st century. *Scientific American* 265 (1991), 94-104.

Spatially-aware or Spatially-agnostic? Elicitation and Evaluation of User-Defined Cross-Device Interactions

Roman Rädle[1*], Hans-Christian Jetter[2*], Mario Schreiner[1], Zhihao Lu[3], Harald Reiterer[1], Yvonne Rogers[3]
[1]HCI Group, University of Konstanz, Konstanz, Germany
[2]Intel ICRI Cities, University College London, London, United Kingdom
[3]UCL Interaction Centre, University College London, London, United Kingdom
{Roman.Raedle,Mario.Schreiner,Harald.Reiterer}@uni-konstanz.de
h.jetter@ucl.ac.uk, zhihao.lu.13@alumni.ucl.ac.uk, y.rogers@ucl.ac.uk
[*] First two authors contributed equally to this work

ABSTRACT
Cross-device interaction between multiple mobile devices is a popular field of research in HCI. However, the appropriate design of this interaction is still an open question, with competing approaches such as *spatially-aware* vs. *spatially-agnostic* techniques. In this paper, we present the results of a two-phase user study that explores this design space: In phase 1, we elicited gestures for typical mobile cross-device tasks from 4 focus groups (N=17). The results show that 71% of the elicited gestures were *spatially-aware* and that participants strongly associated cross-device tasks with interacting and thinking in space. In phase 2, we implemented one *spatially-agnostic* and two *spatially-aware* techniques from phase 1 and compared them in a controlled experiment (N=12). The results indicate that spatially-aware techniques are preferred by users and can decrease mental demand, effort, and frustration, but only when they are designed with great care. We conclude with a summary of findings to inform the design of future cross-device interactions.

Author Keywords
Cross-device interaction; user-defined gestures.

ACM Classification Keywords
H.5.2. User Interfaces: Evaluation/methodology.

INTRODUCTION
Cross-device interaction between multiple mobile devices is an increasingly popular field of research in HCI [5,8,16,17,18,22,26]. It can be regarded as the latest incarnation of Weiser's vision of ubiquitous computing [35] in which user experiences truly begin to *cross* devices [8] and the co-located devices can be easily joined to create *ad-hoc device communities* [13]. Ideally, users experience such a community as a single seamless and natural UI (or even a "symphony of devices" [8]) that is flexible in terms of use and is not restricted to a few possible configurations or predefined sequences of use [13,26].

CHI 2015, April 18 - 23 2015, Seoul, Republic of Korea
Copyright 2015 ACM 978-1-4503-3145-6/15/04...$15.00
http://dx.doi.org/10.1145/2702123.2702287

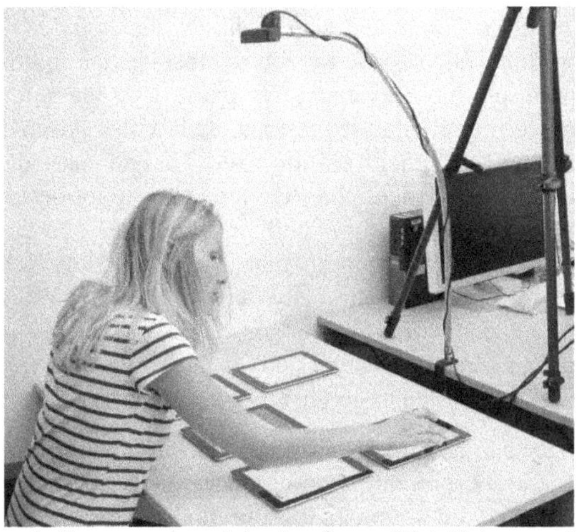

Figure 1. Our experimental setup for multi-tablet cross-device interaction.

Applications of cross-device interaction have become increasingly diverse, ranging from collaborative photo sharing or brainstorming with smart phones [17,18] to multi-tablet active reading [4,5] and sensemaking [8]. User studies have shown that multi-tablet systems can be successfully used in the wild [5] and that users can effectively manage cross-device interactions with 5 to 10 devices [8]. However, many questions remain unanswered: How should cross-device interaction between mobile devices be designed so that they are easy to learn and easy to use? What role should increasingly popular technologies for sensing spatial configurations and detecting mid-air gestures play in their design? Should interactions follow a traditional, yet robust, non-spatial model, e.g., menu-based selection of devices [8]? Or should systems sense locations and use gestures to make cross-device interactions more like familiar non-digital interactions [7]?

These questions are especially important because our devices are still rather limited in terms of sensing their mutual spatial relations [8] without the use of expensive or custom-built sensing hardware such as rooms equipped with motion tracking systems [19]. However, such spatial information could enable interfaces to easily grow across nearby devices and annex them in natural ways [11,25], ideally as a byproduct of natural use in space (e.g., by putting tablets on a table, moving them around, placing them side-by-side, making pick-and-drop gestures between them [26]). Only very recently have new low-cost sensing solutions based on overhead depth cameras such as HuddleLamp [26] become available; these solutions can track not only the positions and movements of off-the-shelf mobile devices on tables but also above-the-table hand gestures. The availability of these new technologies calls for more research on *spatially-aware* vs. *spatially-agnostic* interactions, particularly since the necessary sensing technology was still considered futuristic and far beyond the state of the art just one year ago [8].

We therefore conducted a two-phase user study to better explore the design space for future cross-device interaction with multiple mobile devices. In phase 1 of the study, we conducted four elicitation sessions, each with a group of 4-5 participants. In each session, we elicited user-defined gestures for 19 typical cross-device tasks, ignoring current technological restrictions and leaving the question of *spatially-aware* vs. *spatially-agnostic* interaction to users. In phase 2, we used a low-cost tracking system to implement one *spatially-agnostic* and two *spatially-aware* techniques that were suggested in phase 1 and evaluated them in a controlled experiment with 12 participants.

In the following sections, we introduce previous and related work and report on our two-phase user study and its results. We conclude by summarizing our findings in the form of design recommendations for future cross-device systems.

BACKGROUND AND RELATED WORK

Today, performing tasks across multiple devices is often tedious [7], but new UIs promise to achieve a more natural use of multiple devices [4,8] through (1) new interaction techniques, (2) better sensors, and (3) user-defined gestures.

(1) Cross-Device Interaction Techniques

We differentiate between three main categories of cross-device interactions: *synchronous gestures*, *spatially-agnostic interactions*, and *spatially-aware interactions*.

Synchronous Gestures – Chen et al. propose a multi-tablet system for single-user reading activities that uses synchronous "conduit" interactions to move information between devices [4,5]. These interactions employ temporal simultaneity and sequences to express directed cross-device actions. For example, users might first designate a target by touching a device with their non-dominant hand, and then use their dominant hand (which offers more precision) to tap the item to be transferred. This approach is loosely based on Hinckley's and Rekimoto's pioneering work that suggested synchronous gestures such as device bumping [12], pen-based stitching [11], or synchronous tapping [29] to exchange content or create multi-device tiled displays. Similarly, Lucero et al. used synchronous touch-based "pinching" across phones to create multi-device huddles in [17,18].

Spatially-Agnostic Interactions – In contrast, Hamilton and Wigdor's multi-tablet system Conductor uses traditional menus with color-coded device names to select the tablets to share information with or to chain tasks across them [8]. Thus, in Nacenta et al.'s terminology [22], Conductor's referential domain for selecting devices is "non-spatial". However, Hamilton and Wigdor's own experimentation and user study revealed that keeping track of multiple, often very similar devices can represent a surprisingly significant challenge, and also that users extensively used spatial configurations of tablets for categorical organization [8]. Therefore, it is possible that a non-spatial (or *spatially-agnostic*) interaction might diminish the benefits of cross-device interaction: It could create a mismatch between the spatial referential domain in which the user's intention is expressed and the non-spatial way in which the interaction technique requires the user to select a destination device [22]. In other words, although menus are a robust and familiar way to select items that have no clear spatial relation, they might seem cumbersome for the purpose of selecting one out of many devices from a spatial configuration.

Spatially-Aware Interactions – An alternative involves spatially-aware interaction techniques that use real-world spatial configurations as the referential domain – for example, hyperdragging or pick-and-drop of objects between laptops and table surfaces [28] and flicking/throwing objects within AR settings [33], tabletops [27], or from phones towards large displays [6]. Throwing and flicking techniques are also frequently named by participants in gesture elicitation studies for multi-display interactions (e.g., [15,31]), including our own elicitation study in this paper. This popularity of spatial referential domains resonates with user studies that have observed how important space and spatial configurations are as meaningful cognitive resources during knowledge work in offices [14] or sensemaking on large screens [1]. However, in our elicitation study, participants also raised concerns about the accuracy of throwing and flicking and the danger of inadvertently sending content to the wrong device. This is particularly relevant in mobile cross-device interactions in which the target screens are relatively small and/or far away. More reliable spatially-aware techniques include world-in-miniature or radar views that allow target regions or devices to be selected in a top-down map-like representation of the environment [3,27,36]. User studies on tabletops have revealed that these approaches can be more accurate (albeit slower) than flicking [27].

(2) Sensing Space and Proximity

To achieve spatially-aware cross-device interactions, it is necessary to accuratly track the current positions of all devices. One solution involves a camera-based motion capturing system [19], a typically expensive method requiring to instrument rooms, devices, and users; this is generally considered futuristic in the context of present-day mobile scenarios [8]. A low-cost alternative is using the front facing cameras of mobile devices to track positions by detecting fiducial markers on the ceiling [16]. Lucero et al. equip mobile phones with sensors for radio trilateration [17], and Marquardt et al. combine this with overhead depth cameras [20] to sense locations. This approach is further improved by Rädle et al.'s HuddleLamp, which enables tracking of uninstrumented tablets and phones using only an overhead depth camera [26]. Due to its low-cost and ready availability, we chose HuddleLamp for the experiment in phase 2 of our study.

(3) Elicitation of User-defined Gestures

Nielsen et al. propose gesture elicitation studies for the design of intuitive and ergonomic gestural interfaces and to avoid arbitrary gesture sets that are optimized for reliable recognition by technology rather than for ease of learning and use by humans [24]. Similarly, Nacenta et al. find that user-defined gestures are preferred by users and are also easier to remember [23]. Wobbrock et al. successfully elicited multi-touch gestures for typical tasks from non-technical users [37]; since then, many similar studies have explored connecting phones, public displays, and tabletops [15], for diagram editing with multi-touch and pen [10], for multi-display environments [31], for active tokens querying big data [32], or for skin input [34]. As we describe below, our work substantially differs from this research in two respects: First, we are not primarily interested in a single, ideally "optimal" gesture set, but rather in a wide variety of user suggestions and deep insights into users' underlying thinking and metaphors. Second, we do not stop at eliciting gestures, but additionally evaluate them in a controlled experiment to learn more about their cognitive and ergonomic properties during repeated use. To our knowledge, only [10,24,33] have pursued this approach, but in domains other than cross-device interaction.

PHASE 1: GESTURE ELICITATION STUDY

Phase 1 of our study sought to elicit user-defined cross-device gestures during the course of 4 focus groups. We explain why we decided on this rationale and why and how our methodology differs from traditional gesture elicitation.

Overview and Rationale

To learn more about users' ideas, preferences, expectations, and mental models for cross-device gestures, we decided to prompt users with typical cross-device tasks and then elicit suggestions from them for the corresponding cross-device interactions. In order to reduce bias and increase their creativity, we primed them with a video showing the latest cross-device techniques; the participants were then asked to be imaginative and to ignore any technological restrictions they might know about. We also avoided commenting on the feasibility of their suggestions during the discussions.

Three main topics guided this first phase of our study:

1.) One great advantage of *synchronous gestures* such as SyncTap [29], conduit [4], bumping [12], stitching [11], and pinching [17] is that they only need built-in sensors. However, these gestures must be learned and executed by the users across screens in the correct sequence and timing. How "intuitive" are such synchronous gestures, and would users – rather than designers – suggest them themselves?

2.) *Spatially-agnostic interactions* such as device selection menus are familiar from GUIs and likely to be suggested by users (see "legacy bias" discussed in [21]). However, as described above, non-spatial selection is also potentially cumbersome [22]. Would users be aware of this limitation, and what would their suggestions and opinions be?

3.) *Spatially-aware interactions* such as throwing or flicking are popular suggestions in gesture elicitation studies (e.g., in [15,31]). They are fast and efficient [27], both because they employ an open-loop control paradigm [22] and because they make use of the user's natural understanding of space and physical movement. However, they are also less precise than other spatially-aware interactions (e.g., the top-down world-in-miniature or radar view representations in [3,27,36]) that offer closed-loop control [22] with higher accuracy but slower interactions [27]. We wanted to learn about users' preferences and opinions on this issue and to see whether they would identify speed and precision as important criteria.

Reducing Bias with Partners, Production, and Priming

To reduce bias, we did not introduce our three guiding topics of interactions to the users; we only applied them afterwards to categorize the users' suggestions, to analyze their verbal comments and opinions and their feedback on questionnaires. We also decided against a traditional gesture elicitation study (as in [37]), instead opting for an approach similar to Morris et al.'s proposal to reduce legacy bias through *partners*, *priming*, and *production* [21].

We used *partners* – i.e., focus groups of up to 5 partners in each session – to collect as many different suggestions, comments, and explanations as possible. By enabling partners to fruitfully build upon one another's ideas and asking them to decide on a single preferred interaction, we hoped to facilitate more reflection and discussion and to elicit more diverse opinions about the designs. Similar to [20,33], our sessions therefore contained an element of co-creation instead of pure elicitation. As a result, we received many novel and elaborate suggestions, including details on physical input and visual output.

We also employed *production* and *priming* [21]. *Production* was promoted by requiring groups to produce at least 3 proposals for each task before choosing their favorite, in an attempt to move beyond a few simple, legacy-inspired techniques. *Priming* was implemented by showing each group an introductory video that depicted a variety of the latest cross-device interactions in order to reduce the group's bias towards legacy-inspired GUI interactions. In addition, users were encouraged to perform their suggestions with physical props such as tablets, pens, and paper so that they would think about the capabilities and affordances of mobile form factors instead of technological restrictions. Nevertheless, we still followed a strict formal procedure during elicitation with carefully selected materials, questionnaires, and tasks.

Task Set

An initial set of tasks was extracted from cross-device systems and elicitation studies in the literature [4,8,15,26,31,32]. This initial set of 22 tasks was intended to represent the most typical and relevant cross-device tasks. In a pilot study, we then identified redundant tasks and those tasks that were too complex for non-technical users to understand. After removing these tasks, the final set contained 19 tasks (see Table 1).

T#	Function	Object	Source	Destination	Distance
1	Move	File	Tablet	(Tablet)	In reach
2	Move	File	Tablet	(Tablet)	Far
3	Move	File	(Tablet)	Tablet	Far
4	Move	File	Phone	(Tablet)	In reach
5	Move	File	Phone	(Tablet)	Far
6	Move	File	(Tablet)	Phone	Far
7	Copy	File	Tablet	(Tablet)	In reach
8	Copy	File	Tablet	(Tablet)	Far
9	Copy	File	(Tablet)	Tablet	Far
10	Expand	View	Tablet	(Tablet)	In reach
11	Duplicate	Screen	Tablet	(Tablet)	In reach
12	Duplicate	Part of Screen	Tablet	(Tablet)	In reach
13	Duplicate	Screen	Tablet	(Tablet)	Far
14	Duplicate	Part of screen	Tablet	(Tablet)	Far
15	Open	File	Tablet	(Tablet)	In reach
16	Open	File	Phone	(Tablet)	In reach
17	Connect	Keyboard	-	Tablet	In reach
18	Copy	All files	(All tablets)	Tablet	Far
19	Copy	All files	(All tablets)	Phone	Far

Table 1. Set of 19 tasks used for the elicitation study.

Tasks 1-9 represent typical cross-device object movements. Tasks 10-14 deal with stitching and duplicating screens. Tasks 15-19 are miscellaneous tasks such as pairing a wireless keyboard with a tablet or copying all files from all other devices to the personal device. In the table, "source" and "destination" define the devices involved and the direction. Parentheses mean that a remote device, e.g., "(Tablet)", is not held in the hands of the users and is not lying directly in front of them. A distance of "in reach" means that the device is within an arm's length, while "far" means that users have to stand up and walk to reach it.

During the study, we prompted each group with one task at a time. Each prompt was an animation that first showed the starting point and then the outcome of the task. To avoid bias, the animation did not show any user interactions. For example, one prompt first showed two tablets lying on a table, with an object on the screen of the first tablet. Then it showed this object disappearing and appearing on the screen of the second tablet, without hinting at any possible user interaction.

Participants and Groups

We recruited 17 participants (7 female) through mailing lists and posters on a university campus. The age of participants ranged from 18 to 43 years (mean=26.4, SD=7.2). All participants had several years of experience with using a smart phone (mean=3.9, SD=2.7). 13 participants also had experience with using a tablet (mean=2.2, SD=1.1). After reviewing the pool of participants, we manually assigned them to four groups to avoid overly heterogeneous focus groups. Group A (n=4) were undergraduate students in computer science. Group B (n=4) were researchers in computer science or professional software developers. Group C (n=5) and Group D (n=4) were students from non-technical subjects such as comparative literature, anatomy, neuroscience, linguistics, architecture, and financial risk management.

Procedure

In each session, the group sat around a table with various switched-off tablets, sheets of paper, and marker pens (in case participants wanted to demonstrate or sketch their suggestions). After the introductory video was shown, the recording of the elicitation began, and the following procedure was repeated for each of the 19 tasks: First, the animated prompt for the task was shown on a projector or large screen. Second, the group was asked to think of corresponding interactions and discuss them with their fellow group members. The groups were asked to produce at least 3 different interactions. Third, the group chose one favorite interaction for the given task. Finally, each group member filled out a questionnaire with 7-point Likert scales on the understandability of the task, their personal agreement with the group's selected favorite, and how difficult it had been to propose an interaction. After the 19 tasks, there was a debriefing and a closing discussion. Participants were given post-test questionnaires with 7-point Likert scales to determine whether they had always understood what they had been asked to do and whether they had felt that they could express their ideas during the session. Each session lasted between 1.5 and 2 hours, and participants were compensated for their time with £20.

Results & Discussion

The questionnaires revealed that participants had no problems understanding what they needed to do ($\bar{x}$=6.76, SD=0.75) or expressing their ideas ($\bar{x}$=6.06, SD=1.25). The agreement and difficulty ratings of each task revealed high overall agreement ($\bar{x}$=5.99, SD=1.15) and low to neutral difficulty ($\bar{x}$=3.57, SD=1.67). Unsurprisingly, the tasks with lowest agreement and highest difficulty were tasks 3, 9, 18, and 19, all of which involved retrieving objects from one or multiple sources outside one's reach. However, there were no indications of more general problems with the study's design, its social setting, or the difficulty of the task set.

Synchronous, Spatially-Aware, and Spatially-Agnostic

After the analysis and thematic coding of the video recordings, we took the favorite gestures from each group and all tasks (19 tasks × 4 groups = 76 favorites) and categorized them: 12 favorites (15.8%) were *synchronous gestures* (e.g., bumping devices), 10 favorites (13.2%) were *spatially-agnostic interactions* (e.g., selecting a target device from a menu of devices by name), and 54 favorites (71.1%) were *spatially-aware interactions* (e.g., flicking an item to a remote device).

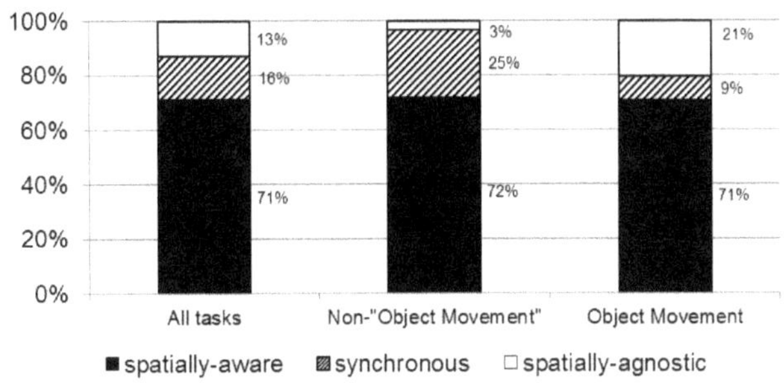

Figure 2. Categorization of favorites.

We checked whether the predominance of *spatially-aware interactions* was due to the many cross-display object movement tasks in the task set (tasks 1-9, 18, 19) by excluding them. For the non-"object movement" tasks (10-17), *spatially-aware interactions* were again the most popular at 71.9%, *synchronous gestures* were second at 25%, and *spatially-agnostic interactions* third at 3.1% (Figure 2). This clearly indicates how strongly participants associated cross-device tasks with interactions in space and how much their thinking and suggestions were of a spatial nature. Although they were already familiar with some of the *spatially-agnostic* or *synchronous* cross-device techniques that are popular today, *spatially-aware interactions* still seemed to be the most appealing, even for non-"object movement" tasks.

Synchronous gestures were most popular for task 10 "expanding view to other device" (4 of 4 groups) and task 17 "pairing keyboard and tablet" (2 of 4 groups). In general, participants seemed to use *synchronous gestures* when they wanted to refer to the device itself or the entire screen, but not for cross-device object movement tasks. For such object movement tasks, only 4 favorites (9.1%) were *synchronous gestures* (mostly similar to the "conduit" gesture [4]), while 20.5% were *spatially-agnostic* (Figure 2). Overall, *synchronous gestures* seemed to be most important in the context of expanding screens or pairing devices, but were not popular for object transfer tasks.

We were surprised that *spatially-agnostic interactions* were almost as popular as *synchronous gestures* for all tasks and twice as popular for object movement tasks (20.5%). They were particularly popular in Group C, which had a heterogeneous, non-technical background. While this could be seen merely as a case of strong legacy bias [21], it also hints at the ongoing importance and great practical relevance of more traditional menu-based interactions for cross-device interaction (e.g., as demonstrated in [8]). This also resonates with the surprisingly good performance of menu-based techniques that we observed later in phase 2.

Suggestions for Spatially-Aware Interactions

We further analyzed the 54 favorites involving spatially-aware interactions. 25 favorites (46.3%) entailed open-loop flicking/throwing gestures between devices. Participants discussed their potential limitations with regard to precision and control. For example, Group D addressed the problem of inadvertently sending content to the wrong person or device in a room with 4 or 5 other tablets. Group C also discussed the idea that imprecise flicking might result in content ending up on the wrong tablet, and Group A brought up the problem of how to flick content between two devices when a third device is situated between them.

Groups B and D suggested a *slingshot metaphor* instead of merely flicking/throwing. Inspired by games like Angry Birds, they suggested that direction and the force/distance of flicking could be better controlled when an item is first pulled back from its current position with a finger on the touch screen and then launched in the opposite direction when the finger is lifted. They also considered additional visual output during aiming, such as highlighting the prospective target device to allow more control; the slingshot would thus become an intermittent or closed-loop control paradigm rather than an open loop [22].

Another suggestion involved using visual proxies to represent remote devices on the local screen. This was suggested in 18 (33.3%) of the 54 spatially-aware favorites. For example, Group A suggested that all remote devices be represented as bubbles on the edges of the local screen. These bubbles would appear where the imaginary line between the center of the local device and the center of the remote device intersected with the local screen's boundaries and could be used as proxy targets for drag-and-drop or flicking to remote devices. Alternatively, Group C suggested an overhead map or radar view containing live representations of all devices at their current locations as proxy targets (similar to [3,27,36]).

Conclusions and Input for Phase 2

Given the significant role that both *spatially-aware* and *spatially-agnostic* interactions played in participants' suggestions, we decided to further explore such techniques in phase 2 of our study. We decided to implement the two spatially-aware techniques (*edge bubbles* and *radar view*) that users suggested to address the problem of insufficient control in open-loop flicking/throwing. Furthermore, given that *spatially-agnostic* interactions played a greater role than *synchronous gestures* in object movement, we also decided to implement a non-spatial *menu*-based technique to compare the two types of approaches.

PHASE 2: INTERACTION TECHNIQUES & PROTOTYPE

For phase 2 of our study, we integrated the *edge bubbles*, *radar view*, and *menu* techniques from phase 1 in a prototype application for multi-tablet sensemaking. The application prototype enabled users to use tablets to search a database with a few hundred text documents for keywords and to read the documents found. Users could highlight parts of the document in different colors, annotate documents, and copy relevant parts of a document into a summary document. For the experiment, we focused on three cross-device operations between a local tablet and a remote tablet: 1.) duplicating the current view of the document on the local tablet onto a remote tablet, 2.) selecting a piece of text from the current document on the local tablet and copying it to a remote tablet, and 3.) selecting an object on the local tablet and moving it to a remote tablet. To enable a fair comparison, we ensured that these operations had equivalent functionality, so that all three were possible with all three interaction techniques. Based on the observations in [8], we also assigned a unique color to each tablet. This color was always visible on the edges of the screen to facilitate identification and selection.

Figure 3. Menu cross-device interaction.

Interaction Technique 1: Menu

In our experiment, the spatially-agnostic *menu* technique represented the many suggestions of traditional GUI techniques from phase 1. These were particularly popular in Group C and have also been used in recent publications [8]. First, the object to move or copy must be identified on the local tablet, and its "Share" button must be pressed (Figure 3A+B). This opens a context menu for selection of the destination tablet from a horizontal list of rectangles representing the remote tablets 1-4 by their color (Figure 3C). Please note that they are ordered by an internal ID number and *not* by their spatial location, since their locations are unknown in a spatially-agnostic technique. By tapping one of the rectangles, a remote tablet is selected as the target, and the object is moved or copied there (Figure 3D). Figure 3 shows an example of moving an object. To copy text or duplicate a view, the necessary interactions are almost the same. In the first case, a "Copy" button appears next to the currently selected text; for duplication of the view, there is a "Share" button that is permanently shown in the bottom right-hand corner of the screen.

Figure 4. Radar view cross-device interaction.

Interaction Technique 2: Radar View

Following the suggestions from phase 1 (particularly from Group C for task 2), we included the *radar view*, a spatially-aware technique similar to [3,27,36] that displays a top-down map instead of just a list. The map shows color-coded rectangles as visual proxies for all devices at their current real-world locations from an overhead perspective and is updated in real-time when devices are moved (Figure 4C). To open the map and select a destination device, the text or object to move or copy is dragged and dropped onto the "Open Radar" button in the bottom right-hand corner of the screen. Tapping on one of the colored rectangles in the map then selects the corresponding remote tablet as the destination device and closes the *radar view*. To duplicate the current view, users need only press the "Open Radar" button and select a tablet without dragging text or an object onto it.

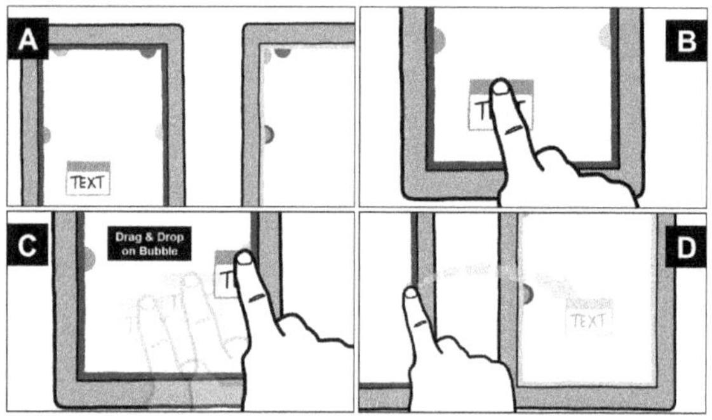

Figure 5. Edge bubbles cross-device interaction.

Interaction Technique 3: Edge Bubbles

Edge bubbles is another spatially-aware technique mainly based on suggestions made by Group A for tasks 1, 2, 5, 6, 8, and 9. Colored semi-circles around the edges of the screen serve as visual proxies for remote devices; similar to off-screen visualization techniques [2], they indicate direction in which the remote devices are located (Figure 5A). The distance to a device is mapped to the radius of its bubble. The locations of the bubbles are defined by imaginary lines between the center point of the local device and the center points of the target devices in the real world. Each bubble is located where this imaginary line intersects with the edges of the local screen. The positions of the bubbles are updated in real-time and thus always reflect changes in the physical configuration of devices. Dragging and dropping an object onto one of the edge bubbles moves the object to the corresponding target device. Tapping an edge bubble duplicates the current view from the local device on the remote device or copies selected text to it.

PHASE 2: COMPARATIVE EVALUATION

Our comparative evaluation of *menu*, *radar view*, and *edge bubbles* was inspired by Nielsen et al., who suggest the evaluation of user-defined gestures in experiments to test them for cognitive and ergonomic quality [24]. Consequently, we tested these interaction techniques in order to 1.) learn more about ergonomic aspects (e.g., memory and stress) and 2.) to better understand the benefit of spatially-aware visual proxies of devices in comparison to spatially-agnostic menus. To this end, we designed the study as a controlled laboratory experiment with a within-subjects design and an independent variable *interaction technique* with three within-subjects factors: *menu*, *radar view*, and *edge bubbles*. The order of the three aforementioned tasks *Duplicate View*, *Copy Text*, and *Move Object* was kept constant, but the interaction techniques were systematically counterbalanced for each task using a balanced Latin Square. The dependent variables were the task completion time and subjective measures (ranking of techniques by preference, how much users liked a technique, mental demand, effort, and frustration level). Additionally, a questionnaire with two open-ended questions asked for ideas to improve the interaction techniques and suggestions for other cross-device interaction techniques. In order to achieve a high degree of external validity, we chose realistic tasks as part of a typical sensemaking procedure; as described above, the study prototype was a fully functional sensemaking application. To achieve higher internal validity, each task was repeated 48 times per condition.

Participants

12 participants (7 female, 5 male) were recruited to take part in the experiment. The mean age was 24.3 years (SD = 2.5, min = 20 years, max = 28 years). 11 participants were right-handed and 1 participant was left-handed. None of the participants had color vision deficiency and thus there were no problems with the color-coding employed. We only chose participants without a background in a computer science-related field. 8 participants were students from non-technical subjects such as economics or law, 2 were research assistants (in political science and physics), 1 was a kindergarten teacher, and 1 was an occupational therapist.

Apparatus

Figure 1 shows the physical setup of the experiment. As a working surface, we used a conventional office desk (1.2×0.8m). Five Apple iPads (9.7″ diagonal) were provided as tablet devices; as illustrated in Figure 1, these were situated in a U-shaped starting configuration that could be altered by participants in course of the study. The remote tablets to the left and right of the local tablet were comfortably within an arm's length and were therefore considered to be "in reach" according to Table 1. The other two tablets could only be reached by leaning forward and reaching out to them. The symmetric layout was chosen to account for the different handedness of participants. Each remote tablet was labelled with a number (Figure 1).

To track the positions of the tablets for the spatially-aware interaction techniques *radar view* and *edge bubbles*, we used the HuddleLamp vision tracking of [26]. This system tracks devices with sub-centimeter precision at a rate of 25 frames per second. A Creative Senz3D RGB-D camera was set up at a height of 78cm, which provided a tracking region of 102cm×57cm. We preferred HuddleLamp over our lab's motion capturing system because it allowed us to avoid augmenting devices with passive markers that might distract participants during the tasks. In addition, we used actual tracking data to update the *radar view* and *edge bubbles* in real-time in order to expose users to the limited accuracy, reliability, and noise in real-world tracking settings.

The application running on each tablet was implemented in HTML5/JavaScript for Safari Mobile. Tablets were wirelessly connected to the tracking system to continuously receive location and orientation data for all tablets from a Web socket connection.

Task Design

The study consisted of the three tasks *Duplicate View*, *Copy Text*, and *Move Object*, and each task consisted of three conditions: *menu* (M), *radar view* (RV), and *edge bubbles* (EB). For each trial, users were prompted with a number between 1 and 4 to indicate the destination device. The trial was noted as successful when the target device was correct; otherwise, an error was noted.

In each condition, participants repeated the cross-device interaction 48 times (each remote tablet was the target device 12 times). The sequence of numbers was randomized to avoid learning effects. Participants were asked to perform the cross-device interaction quickly and without errors. In total, there were 12 participants × 3 tasks × 3 interaction techniques × 48 repetitions = 5184 trials, with 432 trials per participant. *Duplicate View* and *Copy Text* always used the center tablet as the source device and the different tablets 1-4 as destinations. It was also necessary to confirm the end of each trial by closing the duplicated view or deleting the copied text on the remote device. The *Move Object* task began with the center tablet as the source device and one of the tablets 1-4 as the destination device. The destination tablet was then used as the source device in the next trial, and so forth.

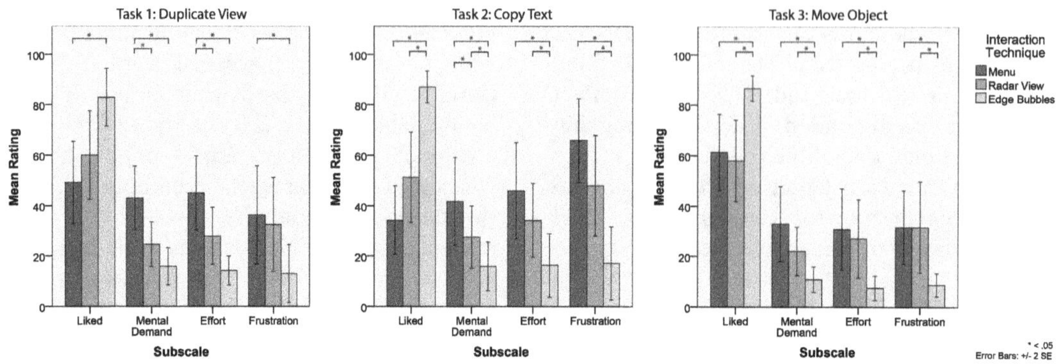

Figure 6. Subjective ratings *Liked, Mental demand, Effort, Frustration* for each task.

Procedure

After signing a consent form and filling out a demographic questionnaire, the participants were introduced to the first task in their assigned first condition. We did not include a training phase due to the simplicity of the task and the many repetitions. After participants had completed the task for the first condition, they were introduced to the next condition until all 3 conditions of this task were completed. After the task, participants were asked to rank the three interaction techniques in order from most favored to least favored. They also rated each interaction technique in a questionnaire with four subscales: *Liked* (scale from 0 to 100; 0: did not like it, 100: liked it), *Mental demand, Effort,* and *Frustration* (all subscales from NASA TLX [9]; 0: low, 100: high). Two open-ended questions at the end of the questionnaire asked for the reason for the ranking and for possible improvements to any of the interaction techniques. This procedure was repeated for each of the three tasks. Each session lasted about 1.5 hours, and participants were compensated for their time with €12.

PHASE 2: RESULTS & DISCUSSION

In the data analysis, Kendall's W coefficient (exact method) was used for the ranking of interaction techniques. The analysis of task completion time was conducted using repeated-measures ANOVAs with post-hoc pairwise comparisons (all Greenhouse-Geisser corrected). The subjective ratings were analyzed with Friedman's Tests and Wilcoxon Signed Rank Test was used for post-hoc comparisons. All post-hoc tests were Bonferroni corrected. Figure 6 shows the subscales *Liked, Mental demand, Effort,* and *Frustration* for tasks 1-3.

The ranking for tasks 1-3 was significant with a Kendall's $W_{T1} = .361$ ($\chi^2(2) = 8.67, p < .05$), $W_{T2} = .72$ ($\chi^2(2) = 17.17, p < .001$), and $W_{T3} = .65$ ($\chi^2(2) = 15.50, p < .001$). For all tasks, cross-device interactions were ranked in the following order: M_{EB} (T_1: 1.3, T_2: 1.1, T_3: 1.1), M_{RV} (T_1: 2.2, T_2: 2.2, T_3: 2.3), and M_M (T_1: 2.5, T_2: 2.8, T_3: 2.6) (values from 1 "most favored" to 3 "least favored"). The statistical analysis revealed that the order of the mean rankings from most favored to least favored for each task was consistently *edge bubbles*, *radar view*, and *menu*. The spatially-aware techniques proved to be favored by users even after many repetitions, and the popularity of spatially-aware techniques during the elicitation study in phase 1 was clearly reflected in the results of phase 2. However, as we show in the following section, it is not possible to generalize this to all spatially-aware techniques.

Spatially-aware interactions are not always better

For all tasks 1-3, an ANOVA revealed a statistically significant difference between interaction techniques in terms of task completion time (T_1: $F_{1.88,20.69} = 22.69$, $p < .001$, *partial* $\eta^2 = .67$, T_2: $F_{1.45,15.98} = 56.04$, $p < .001$, *partial* $\eta^2 = .84$, T_3: $F_{1.82,20.04} = 24.95$, $p < .001$, *partial* $\eta^2 = .69$). All Friedman's Tests revealed statistically significant differences between interaction techniques for each of the subjective ratings *Liked, Mental demand, Effort*, and *Frustration* for all tasks 1-3 (Figure 6).

The spatially-aware *edge bubbles* outperformed *menu* in task times for tasks 1 & 2 and consistently scored higher than the non-spatial *menu* on the *Liked* subscale for tasks 1-3. Surprisingly, (also spatially-aware) *radar view* was outperformed by *menu* in terms of task time in task 3 and never scored significantly higher than *menu* on the *Liked* subscale. The differences between the two spatially-aware techniques are also visible in the higher *Mental Demand* and higher *Frustration* for *radar view* than for *edge bubbles* in tasks 2 & 3. Moreover, for all tasks, the task times for *radar view* were significantly higher than for *edge bubbles.* It seems that, despite its popularity among users, spatial awareness alone does not lead to enhanced user performance and better usability.

A potential explanation for why *edge bubbles* is clearly superior to *radar view* in our experiment is the cognitive load of mentally mapping the virtual proxy objects on the screen to their real-world counterparts. To use the *radar view*, users must locate the destination tablet on the map. This requires mentally switching from the natural egocentric view of the environment to a top-down view. This switch can be demanding, as we all know from using street maps or floor plans. Some mobile map applications try to facilitate this by automatically rotating the map so that it matches the egocentric orientation of a user. Research shows that such automatic rotation reduces users' mental load in comparison to the "north-up" alignment [30]. Similarly, *edge bubbles* indicates the directions and distance of other tablets without the need to mentally switch between an egocentric and a non-egocentric view. This resonates with user comments that *edge bubbles* "[...] are very intuitive because proximity and direction are clear and natural [...]"; the bubbles were considered "immediately appealing" and the "most intuitive".

The mental load of switching seems to diminish the benefits of the *radar view* in relation to the *menu*. This becomes evident in the absence of significant differences between the techniques in terms of *Frustration* in all tasks. Moreover, while the *radar view* helps users to identify devices faster when the spatial configuration is unknown or very dynamic, the performance of *menu* improves after users have internalized the mapping of colors to tablets over time. Using the *menu* only requires a sequential scanning of a one-dimensional list of colored objects, whereas the *radar view* still requires users to mentally switch between egocentric and top-down views. This explains why *menu* was faster than *radar view* in task 3 and the lack of differences between the interactions in *Mental Demand* for task 3 and *Effort* for tasks 2 & 3.

SUMMARY OF FINDINGS FROM PHASES 1 & 2

In the following section, we summarize our results and discussions from phases 1 and 2 in four findings that can inform the design of future cross-device interaction.

1.) Phase 1 has clearly revealed that users expect cross-device interactions to be *spatially-aware* (71.1% of all suggestions). In phase 2, the spatially-aware *edge bubbles* technique outperformed other techniques in a controlled experiment and was the most favored technique, even after many repetitions. We therefore recommend *spatially-aware* interactions for future mobile cross-device interactions, in particular because low-cost technologies such as [26] can now provide the necessary sensing.

2.) However, as shown in the experiment, *spatially-aware techniques* must be designed with care. The *edge bubbles* technique succeeded because of its directness of interaction and a spatial representation that did not require mentally switching between an egocentric and a top-down view. Top-down views such as radar views and maps [30] seem to introduce a cognitive load that can entirely diminish their advantages over simple *spatially-agnostic* menus.

3.) *Spatially-agnostic interactions* such as menus were popular for cross-device object movements (20.5% of suggestions), particularly for tasks involving one or multiple remote devices as sources. Their performance can be good or even equivalent to that of maps or radar views when the number of devices is small and their spatial configurations are not changing rapidly.

4.) *Synchronous gestures* were popular (25% of suggestions) for tasks concerned with expanding views or pairing devices, or whenever users wanted to refer to the device itself or its entire screen. They seem to be inherently suitable for pairing tasks but were only suggested in very few cases for cross-device object movement (9.1%).

LIMITATIONS & FUTURE WORK

A limitation of our study is its focus on two-dimensional device configurations on a desk. The results are therefore not generalizable to other spatial configurations such as handheld devices or see-through tangible lenses. Additional work is needed to study cross-device techniques for more complex 3D device configurations.

Moreover, the different results for *edge bubbles* and *radar view* demonstrate how difficult it can be to generalize findings for all spatially-aware techniques. Different visual representations of space (e.g., egocentric or top-down) clearly had a great impact on user performance and usability. These differences must be investigated in further research in the future.

CONCLUSION

We have presented the results of a two-phase study exploring the design space of mobile cross-device interactions. First, we described our results from a gesture elicitation study in which 71% of the elicited cross-device interactions were *spatially-aware*. We discussed how participants strongly associated cross-device tasks with interacting and thinking in space. Based on the users' suggestions, we implemented two spatially-aware interaction techniques and one spatially-agnostic technique, comparing them in a controlled experiment. The results showed that spatially-aware techniques, when designed with care, are preferred by users and can decrease their mental demand, effort, and frustration during mobile cross-device interactions.

REFERENCES

1. Andrews, C., Endert, A., and North, C. Space to Think: Large, High-Resolution Displays for Sensemaking. *In Proc. CHI '10*, ACM Press (2010), 55–64.
2. Baudisch, P. and Rosenholtz, R. Halo: a technique for visualizing off-screen objects. *In Proc. CHI '03*, ACM Press (2003), 481–488.
3. Biehl, J.T. and Bailey, B.P. ARIS: an interface for application relocation in an interactive space. *In Proc GI '04*, Canadian Human-Computer Communications Society (2004), 107–116.
4. Chen, N., Guimbretiere, F., and Sellen, A. Designing a multi-slate reading environment to support active reading activities. *ACM Transactions on Computer-Human Interaction 19*, 3 (2012), 1–35.
5. Chen, N., Guimbretière, F., and Sellen, A. Graduate student use of a multi-slate reading system. *In Proc. CHI '13*, ACM Press (2013), 1799–1808.
6. Dachselt, R. and Buchholz, R. Natural throw and tilt interaction between mobile phones and distant displays. *In Prof. CHI EA '09*, ACM Press (2009).

7. Greenberg, S., Marquardt, N., Ballendat, T., Diaz-Marino, R., and Wang, M. Proxemic Interactions: The New Ubicomp? *interactions 18*, January (2011).
8. Hamilton, P. and Wigdor, D.J. Conductor: enabling and understanding cross-device interaction. *In Proc. CHI '14*, ACM Press (2014), 2773–2782.
9. Hart, S. and Staveland, L. Development of NASA-TLX (Task Load Index): Results of empirical and theoretical research. *Human mental workload*, North Holland Press.
10. Heydekorn, J., Frisch, M., and Dachselt, R. Evaluating a User-Elicited Gesture Set for Interactive Displays. *M&C 2011*, Oldenbourg Verlag (2011), 191–200.
11. Hinckley, K., Ramos, G., Guimbretiere, F., Baudisch, P., and Smith, M. Stitching: pen gestures that span multiple displays. *In Proc. AVI '04*, ACM Press (2004).
12. Hinckley, K. Synchronous gestures for multiple persons and computers. *In Proc. UIST '03*, ACM Press (2003).
13. Jetter, H.-C. and Reiterer, H. Self-Organizing User Interfaces: Envisioning the Future of Ubicomp UIs. *Workshop Blended Interaction (in conjunction with CHI '13)*, University of Konstanz (2013).
14. Kidd, A. The marks are on the knowledge worker. *In Proc. CHI '94*, ACM Press (1994), 186–191.
15. Kray, C., Nesbitt, D., Dawson, J., and Rohs, M. User-defined gestures for connecting mobile phones, public displays, and tabletops. *In Proc. MobileHCI '10*, ACM Press (2010), 239–248.
16. Li, M. and Kobbelt, L. Dynamic tiling display: building an interactive display surface using multiple mobile devices. *In Proc MUM '12*, ACM Press (2012).
17. Lucero, A., Holopainen, J., and Jokela, T. Pass-them-around: collaborative use of mobile phones for photo sharing. *In Proc CHI '11*, ACM Press (2011).
18. Lucero, A., Keränen, J., and Korhonen, H. Collaborative use of mobile phones for brainstorming. *In Proc. MobileHCI '10*, ACM Press (2010), 337–340.
19. Marquardt, N., Diaz-Marino, R., Boring, S., and Greenberg, S. The proximity toolkit: prototyping proxemic interactions in ubiquitous computing ecologies. *In Proc. UIST '11*, ACM Press (2011).
20. Marquardt, N., Hinckley, K., and Greenberg, S. Cross-device interaction via micro-mobility and f-formations. *In Proc. UIST '12*, ACM (2012), 13–22.
21. Morris, M.R., Danielescu, A., Drucker, S., et al. Reducing legacy bias in gesture elicitation studies. *interactions 21*, 3 (2014), 40–45.
22. Nacenta, M., Gutwin, C., Aliakseyeu, D., and Subramanian, S. There and Back Again: Cross-Display Object Movement in Multi-Display Environments. *Human-Computer Interaction 24*, 1 (2009).
23. Nacenta, M.A., Kamber, Y., Qiang, Y., and Kristensson, P.O. Memorability of pre-designed and user-defined gesture sets. *In Proc. CHI '13*, ACM Press (2013).
24. Nielsen, M., Störring, M., Moeslund, T.B., and Granum, E. A Procedure for Developing Intuitive and Ergonomic Gesture Interfaces for HCI. In A. Camurri and G. Volpe, eds., *Gesture-Based Communication in Human-Computer Interaction*. Springer Berlin Heidelberg, Berlin, Heidelberg, 2004, 409–420.
25. Pierce, J.S., Mahaney, H.E., and Abowd, G.D. *Opportunistic Annexing for Handheld Devices: Opportunities and Challenges*. Georgia Institute of Technology, 2003.
26. Rädle, R., Jetter, H., Marquardt, N., Reiterer, H., and Rogers, Y. HuddleLamp : Spatially-Aware Mobile Displays for Ad-hoc Around-the-Table Collaboration. *In Proc. ITS '14*, ACM (2014).
27. Reetz, A., Gutwin, C., Stach, T., Nacenta, M., and Subramanian, S. Superflick: a natural and efficient technique for long-distance object placement on digital tables. *In Proc. GI '06*, Canadian Information Processing Society (2006), 163–170.
28. Rekimoto, J. and Saitoh, M. Augmented surfaces: a spatially continuous work space for hybrid computing environments. *In Proc. CHI '99*, ACM Press (1999).
29. Rekimoto, J. SyncTap: synchronous user operation for spontaneous network connection. *Personal and Ubiquitous Computing 8*, 2 (2004), 126–134.
30. Seager, W. and Fraser, D.S. Comparing physical, automatic and manual map rotation for pedestrian navigation. *In Proc. CHI '07*, ACM Press (2007).
31. Seyed, T., Burns, C., Costa Sousa, M., Maurer, F., and Tang, A. Eliciting usable gestures for multi-display environments. *In Proc. ITS '12*, ACM Press (2012).
32. Valdes, C., Eastman, D., Grote, C., et al. Exploring the design space of gestural interaction with active tokens through user-defined gestures. *In Proc. CHI '14*, ACM Press (2014), 4107–4116.
33. Voida, S., Podlaseck, M., Kjeldsen, R., and Pinhanez, C. A study on the manipulation of 2D objects in a projector/camera-based augmented reality environment. *In Proc. CHI '05*, ACM Press (2005).
34. Weigel, M., Mehta, V., and Steimle, J. More than touch: understanding how people use skin as an input surface for mobile computing. *In Proc. CHI '14*, ACM Press.
35. Weiser, M. The Computer for the 21st Century. *Scientific American 265*, 3 (1991), 94–104.
36. Wigdor, D., Shen, C., Forlines, C., and Balakrishnan, R. Table-centric interactive spaces for real-time collaboration. *In Proc. AVI '06*, ACM Press (2006).
37. Wobbrock, J.O., Morris, M.R., and Wilson, A.D. User-defined gestures for surface computing. *In Proc. CHI 09*, ACM Press (2009), 1083–1092.

Weave: Scripting Cross-Device Wearable Interaction

Pei-Yu (Peggy) Chi *
Computer Science Division, UC Berkeley
peggychi@cs.berkeley.edu

Yang Li
Google Inc.
yangli@acm.org

ABSTRACT
We present Weave, a framework for developers to create cross-device wearable interaction by scripting. Weave provides a set of high-level APIs, based on JavaScript, for developers to easily distribute UI output and combine sensing events and user input across mobile and wearable devices. Weave allows developers to focus on their target interaction behaviors and manipulate devices regarding their capabilities and affordances, rather than low-level specifications. Weave also contributes an integrated authoring environment for developers to program and test cross-device behaviors, and when ready, deploy these behaviors to its runtime environment on users' ad-hoc network of devices. An evaluation of Weave with 12 participants on a range of tasks revealed that Weave significantly reduced the effort of developers for creating and iterating on cross-device interaction.

Author Keywords
Scripting; cross-device interaction; wearable computing; mobile computing, UI tools; gesture-based interaction.

INTRODUCTION
Mobile and wearable computing gadgets are flourishing. For example, smartphones have become an all-purpose computing device for our everyday activities; smartwatches provide glanceable information and instant access to a set of frequent tasks; and smart eyewears such as Glass [13] enable users to navigate private content and receive prompt assistance in their peripheral vision. Each of these devices offers a distinctive form factor, and input and output capabilities that are designed to seamlessly blend into users' existing artifacts and daily activities.

To allow users to fully leverage a multi-device ecosystem in their lives—a vision of ubiquitous computing [31]—it is important to combine the unique strengths of each device and to enable rich and fluid interaction behaviors across devices [6,23]. Prior work has investigated a variety of behaviors that can be formed by orchestrating a smartphone and a watch [4]. Existing commercial products have begun to support basic cross-device behaviors, such as browsing an image gallery on the phone with a watch remote [14] or navigating media on the TV with a phone [12].

However, programming cross-device wearable interaction remains challenging. To create an interaction behavior that spans multiple wearable and mobile devices, developers have to design and implement based on the varying input and output resources and preferred interaction styles of each individual device. Developers also need to distribute user interfaces and synthesize user input and sensing events across devices. Realizing these tasks manually involves many low-level details such as dealing with device-specific constraints, communication and synchronization across devices, which is technically challenging and effort consuming. It distracts developers from concentrating on their interaction behaviors and results in a system that is often difficult to maintain and adapt to new types of devices or device combinations that might be available at runtime.

To address these issues, prior work has investigated tool support for creating cross-device interaction. In particular, Panelrama introduced mechanisms for automatically distributing a web interface across multiple displays based on the specified preferences of each UI segment and the screen real estates of target displays [32]. XDStudio provided a GUI builder for visually authoring a distributed user interface in a simulated or an on-device mode [25]. However, there is still a lack of high-level support for developers to easily handle interaction events that are synthesized from user input and sensed physical events across multiple devices, which is crucial for creating rich cross-device wearable interaction as shown previously [4]. Moreover, few have considered abstractions and mechanisms for accessing wearable devices regarding their affordances, such as glanceable and shakable natures. These properties are unique aspects of programming cross-device wearable interaction.

In this paper, we propose *Weave*, a framework that allows developers to easily create cross-device wearable behaviors by scripting. Weave provides a web-based development environment (see Figure 1) where developers can author interaction scripts and test them based on a set of simulated or real wearable devices anywhere and any time. Weave also provides a runtime environment that allows Weave scripts to run in users' ad-hoc network of wearable devices

CHI 2015, April 18–23, 2015, Seoul, Republic of Korea
ACM 978-1-4503-3145-6/15/04.
http://dx.doi.org/10.1145/2702123.2702451

* This work was done while the author was an intern at Google.

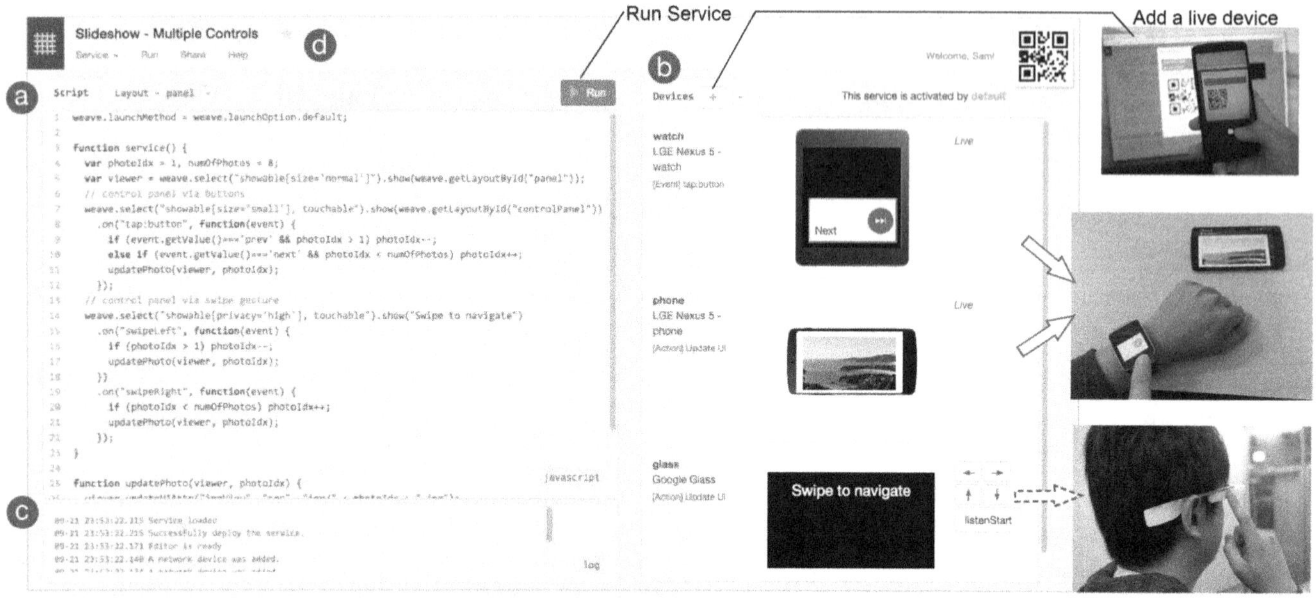

Figure 1. The Weave authoring environment. Developers can (a) script cross-device behaviors and specify associated UI layouts in the Edit Panel, (b) test these behaviors on emulators or live devices via the Test Panel, (c) debug the scripts by observing detailed output in the Log Panel, and (d) manage and share a script via the menu. In this figure, the Test panel contains two real devices, i.e., watch and phone, and one emulator device, i.e., glass. Alternatively, the glass emulator can be replaced with an actual Google Glass device.

and easily adapt to specific device configurations. Weave contributes a set of high-level abstractions and APIs that capture affordances of wearable devices and provide mechanisms for distributing output and combining sensing events and user input across multiple devices, using high-level clauses such as "select" and "combine". These APIs combined with Weave's integrated authoring and runtime support enable a new approach for programming event-based cross-wearable interactions, which allows developers to focus on target interaction behaviors rather than low-level implementation details.

RELATED WORK

Weave builds on prior work of cross-device interactions and tools for creating these behaviors. We review and discuss our relationship with the art in these areas.

Wearable & Cross-Device Interactions

Mobile and wearable devices equipped with lightweight sensors have introduced new possibilities for interaction modalities. Versatile commercial wrist-worn products and phones are able to track people's physical activities [9] and perform daily tasks such as automatic voicemail playback [1]. Eyewears enable users to blend digital content with the physical world [8], navigate content with eye blinks [20] or hand-to-face gestures [28], control remote objects [33], and track health status [19]. Wagner *et al.* studied how body-centric interaction techniques can be used to manipulate digital content in a multi-surface environment [30]. By locating the relative positions of hand-held devices to body joints, Chen *et al.* investigated techniques that allow users to retrieve virtual content by physical movement around the body, such as orienting devices [5].

To form rich behaviors based on limited but versatile I/O capabilities of each wearable device, prior work has investigated novel interactions beyond a single device. Studies have revealed that users tended to allocate a complex task across multiple devices based on the device form factors and functionalities [6,27]. Recently, Duet demonstrates a variety of intriguing behaviors, such as cross-device pinch gestures and finger knuckle and tip inference by fusing sensor input across a watch and a phone [4]. Existing commercial products have started to support cross-device behaviors such as using a watch as a remote to control content on a phone [14] or automatic task continuation when the user moves from a phone to a computer [1]. These scenarios inspired us to design high-level tool support for developers to design and create cross-device wearable interaction, which would otherwise be difficult to implement.

Prior work has extensively investigated cross-device interaction in a multi-display, multi-user environment [7,17,11]. In these situations, handheld devices are often used as a remote control to manipulate digital content on large displays [2,18]; physical distance (often referred as proxemics) and orientation relationships between devices are frequently used as cues in these scenarios [22,23]. We focus on a body-centric cross-device situation in which multiple wearable devices are intended to perform as an organic whole for the user, although Weave can be applied to addressing more general cross-device scenarios.

Tools for Creating Cross-Device Wearable Interactions

While cross-device wearable interaction is promising, it is extremely challenging to develop due to the complexity in combining multiple heterogeneous devices to form fluid interaction behaviors. To address this issue, prior work has developed several toolkits to simplify the distribution of UI content across devices. Yang and Wigdor developed Panelrama, a framework for distributing a web UI across multiple displays. Using linear optimization, Panelrama dynamically allocates each portion of the UI to a display based on its screen real estate and input modality [32]. Other approaches include designing high-level UI abstractions, e.g. [24,26], and runtime frameworks for distributing UIs to a dynamic environment, e.g., [10].

Sinha explored informal prototyping tools for iterative design of multidevice user interfaces, which are not aimed for generating functional systems [29]. Recently, Nebeling *et al.* developed XDStudio, a visual tool for interactively authoring cross-device interfaces [25]. With XDStudio, developers can design cross-device interfaces with simulated devices or directly on real devices. It also allows developers to specify how a UI should be allocated by authoring distribution profiles. Similar to XDStudio, Weave allows developers to test their scripts with simulated devices, real devices or a mix of them.

While prior systems provide tool support for distributing user content across displays, they are insufficient for creating complex cross-device wearable interaction in two ways. First, there is a lack of high-level support for event handling across devices especially for combining user input and sensing events from multiple devices. This is crucial for wearable interaction because a user action often involves a collaboration of multiple wearable devices that forms a compound event as shown previously [4]. We designed Weave to provide a set of high-level API mechanisms for easily synthesizing events across devices. Second, Weave allows developers to script based on abstractions of devices regarding their affordances and capabilities. These types of abstractions, which are not shown in previous work, greatly simplify the creation of wearable interaction and allow developers to focus on high-level target behaviors.

SCRIPTING CROSS-WEARABLE INTERACTION

We discuss how a developer creates cross-device wearable behaviors in Weave, which we refer to as a Weave service. A Weave service consists of an interaction script, based on JavaScript, and a collection of UI layout specifications in HTML. A Weave service runs across devices and stitches capabilities on these devices. To help us illustrate the use of Weave, assume a programmer, Sam, who wants to design and implement a "Smart Messenger" service that brings an incoming message to the user's attention and allows the user to easily play and respond the message using a combination of wearable devices.

Creating a Weave Service

To create a Weave service, Sam opens the Weave authoring environment by pointing a web browser to the Weave server (see Figure 1). This environment allows him to create a new service, edit an existing service, and later share a service such that users can discover and install it on their devices. The Weave authoring interface has three parts: On the left is the Edit panel where the developer can edit Weave scripts and describe UI layouts in HTML. On the right is the Test panel where the developer can specify a set of wearable devices, simulated or real, and test the Weave service on these devices. The Log panel at the bottom of the screen helps developers to debug their scripts.

Sam starts by describing the name of the service and how the service is supposed to be launched, e.g., in response to a notification or when the user manually invokes it. Here Sam specifies the service to be invoked by an incoming message (notification) (see Figure 2a). To show an incoming message on a device that is easily `glanceable` by the user and equipped with a speaker, Sam adds several criteria in Weave's `select` clause (see Figure 2b) and refers to the selected device by a variable `notifier`. Each device that is Weave-capable maintains a device profile that captures the device's I/O resources such that Weave can match these selection criteria at runtime. Sam also requires the device's input capability to be touch-sensitive, i.e., `touchable`, and detect two motion events, `shakable` and `rotatable`. These criteria will select a watch if it is available. In the following discussion, we use "watch" and `notifier` interchangeably.

Sam then specifies the content to show on the selected device in the *Layout* tab, which consists of a title message and two buttons (see Figure 3). The sender's name will be updated at runtime when the service is invoked (see Figure 2c). To show this UI on the `notifier` device, the developer simply uses `notifier.show(ui)` (see Figure 2d). Depending on what device is selected by Weave at runtime, the UI will be rendered by Weave differently to be consistent with device-specific UI guidelines.

To handle button touch events, Sam adds a callback function (see Figure 2e). Based on which button is tapped by the user, the service either plays the message or texts back the sender via the device that originates the button-tap event—`event.getDevice()`, i.e., the `notifier` device.

To playback the voice message automatically when the user intends to listen to the message privately by bringing a smartphone to the ear, Sam adds another behavior to the service. He selects a device that affords private playback and subscribes to the `listenStart` event (Figure 2f), which is a built-in sensing event fired by Weave's runtime environment when it detects a phone "listen" action triggered by the user. Similar to existing commercial products, we detect this activity based on the phone's proximity sensor and accelerometer.

While the message is playing on the phone, a text message will be shown on the original `notifier` device to prompt the user for available options: the user can shake the watch to replay the message on the phone, or rotate the watch to call back the sender. The developer adds two chained event

```
a)  1  weave.launchMethod = weave.launchOption.notification;
    2  function service(notif) {
b)  3    var notifier = weave.select(
    4      "showable[glanceability='high'], speakable,"
    5      + "touchable, shakable, rotatable");
    6    var ui = weave.getLayoutById("mainPanel");
c)  7    ui.updateUI("callerName", notif.caller.name);
d)  8    notifier.show(ui)
e)  9      .on("tap:button", function(event) {
   10        if (event.getValue() === "playMsg") {
   11          event.getDevice().play(notif.voiceMsg)
   12            .show(weave.getWidget("mediaPlayer"));
   13        } else if (event.getValue() === "text") {
   14          event.getDevice().startApp("Messenger",
   15            notif.caller.name);
   16        }
   17      });
f) 18    weave.select("speakable[privacy='high'], phoneable")
   19      .on("listenStart", function(event) {
   20        var phone = event.getDevice().play(notif.voiceMsg);
   21        notifier.show("Shake to reply / rotate to call back")
   22          .on("shake", function(event) {
   23            phone.play(notif.voiceMsg);
   24          }).on("rotate", function(event) {
   25            phone.call(notif.caller.num);
   26          });
   27      });
   28  }
```

Figure 2. The complete script of the Smart Messenger service.

```
<div id="mainPanel">
  <p>New voice message from
    <span id="callerName"></span>
  </p>
  <button value="playMsg">Play</button>
  <button value="text">Text back</button>
</div>
```

Figure 3. An example of a UI layout. This layout is referred by the script at Line 6 in Figure 2.

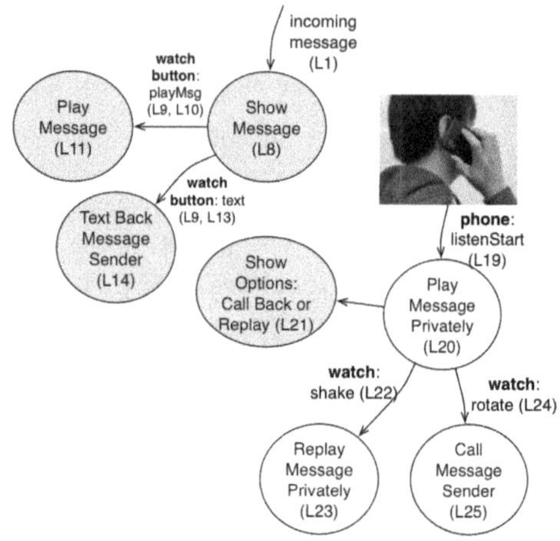

Figure 4. The interaction flow of the Smart Messenger. The shaded circles denote the watch's states and the plain circles for the phone's. The corresponding line of code is labeled.

handlers (Line 22 to 26) to respond to the motion events on the `notifier` device: `shake` and `rotate`. These options allow the user to continue the task with the watch while the user keeps the phone to the ear that is less accessible for further interaction. This example demonstrates that Weave allows developers to easily combine the strengths of multiple devices and distribute an interaction flow across devices to fulfill a task (see Figure 4).

Testing & Deploying a Weave Service

To verify if a service behaves as expected, Sam tests the service in Weave by running it on emulators, real devices, or a mix of them. Weave's authoring environment provides a collection of predefined emulators, which include typical wearable devices such as a watch, and several presets of common device combinations. These allow developers to test a service with minimal effort. Each emulator device allows a set of built-in events, such as `swipe` and `listenStart`, shown along the emulator in the *Test* panel (see the Glass emulator in Figure 1). Sam can tap on these events to trigger actions. He can also create new emulators that best characterize their target devices.

To add a real device to the test, Sam scans the QR code shown above the Test panel or in the dialog box via the + button (see Figure 1), using the Weave proxy running on a device. The screen of a registered device will be displayed in this panel, which is marked as *Live* in red. With actual devices, Sam can physically perform actions such as shaking the device or tapping the buttons. Any changes on a device's UI will be synced with its representation in the Test panel for the developer to monitor the output of multiple devices in real time. The *Log* panel at the bottom of the screen offers detailed information for debugging a service, including the event history and script outputs.

THE DESIGN OF THE WEAVE FRAMEWORK

We aim to provide a set of high-level abstractions for developers to easily program complex cross-device wearable interactions. A common pattern for modern UI development follows an object-oriented event-driven paradigm, where developers attach event handlers to a UI object (or a widget) that update the object accordingly when an event occurs. We are especially inspired by popular JavasScript library designs such as jQuery and d3 [3] that provide a high-level abstraction for programmers to manipulate UI components. One can easily select desired HTML elements to change their properties, e.g., `$(".target_class").css("color", "white")` changes the color of all the elements of `target_class` to white, or to handle user input events, e.g., the inline function of `$("button").click(function(){...})` will be invoked when any button is clicked by the user. Providing function calls based on high-level abstractions allows developers to focus on target behaviors rather than low-level operations, such as device specifications and network connection. Based on the unique challenges raised by programming cross-device wearable interaction, we designed Weave's scripting framework (see Table 1).

Selecting Abstract Devices

It is challenging for developers to cover various types of devices and their combinations that might occur at runtime. For example, some users may carry a smartwatch paired with a smartphone, while others may use an eyewear with a phone. Therefore, in addition to directly retrieving a device by its specific type, a framework should enable flexible selection of devices based on their high-level input and output capabilities so that a cross-device service can adapt to specific sets of devices that a user carries at runtime. As the earlier example shows, developers may choose to stream a message to a glanceable display, which at runtime could be a watch or an eyewear available on the network. With Weave, a developer selects target devices using the `select` clause with a selector of format "`CAPABILITY[PROPERTY='VALUE'],...`". Our framework returns a `WeaveSelection` object that includes one or more qualified devices to be operated. Developers can use multiple criteria at the same time to refine the selection. The following example selects devices with a small, glanceable display that detects rotation motion, which could be a smartwatch at runtime.

```
weave.select("showable[glanceability='high',
             size='small'], rotatable")
```

To select devices that can make phone calls, afford high privacy, and have a touch-sensitive display, developers may use the following criteria, with which Weave may find a smartphone and an eyewear at runtime.

```
weave.select("phoneable[privacy='high'], touchable")
```

In addition, our framework allows developers to easily select all the available devices using `weave.selectAll()`. Developers can also select devices of a specific type, e.g., `getDeviceByType("phone")`, or designed to be worn at specific body locations, e.g., `getDeviceByJoint("wrist")`, which is predefined in the device profiles. For fine-grained controls over device selection, developers can also directly fetch specific devices by their IDs, e.g., `getDeviceById("LGEphone")`. Finally, a negating operator allows the developers to exclude certain devices, such as `.not("speakable")` to select those without a speaker.

At runtime, Weave attempts to match these high-level criteria against devices that are available on the network. Each Weave-capable device runs on our runtime framework maintains a profile about its I/O capabilities, such as the display size or whether the device has a touchscreen, rotation sensor, or accelerometers. Analogous to conventional UI frameworks, each Weave device is treated as an interactive object in the context of a cross-device UI, which can be manipulated and registered to events.

Applying Actions to Devices

After specifying a selection, developers can apply actions to the device, such as providing output feedback. To show visual content on a device, `device.show(MESSAGE)` displays the message string in text, or developers can displays a UI layout defined as an HTML5 element in the Layout Panel using `device.show(weave.getLayoutById(LAYOUT_ID))`.

API	Description
Selecting Target Devices	
`.select(selector)`	Return a `WeaveSelection` object that includes all the matched device(s) on a local network based on the selector string.
Combining Multiple Devices	
`.all()`	Return a `WeaveSelection` object that each device in the selection will behave the same.
`.combine()`	Return a `WeaveSelection` object that encapsulates the devices in the selection as one virtual device.
Performing Output Actions	
`.show(panel)`, `.show(string)`	Render a UI panel or a string on the device or the `WeaveSelection` object.
`.play(filepath)`	Play a media file of the file path on the device(s).
`.startApp(appname)`	Launch the specified native app.
Handling Input Events	
`.on(eventType, handler)`	Attach an event handler for one or more events to the device(s).

Table 1. Weave's core APIs.

To realize a UI layout on devices with different form factors and interaction styles, Weave takes into account the design guidelines of specific devices. It adopts the concepts of responsive web design that adapts the UI elements to different I/O capabilities in order to provide optimal viewing and interactive experience [21]. Our engine distributes the UI based on HTML tags (e.g. `div`, `span`, `p`, `img`, and `button`) and their attributes in a layout specification. For a UI layout that contains a text string (e.g. "Launch Pad Options") and three buttons ("Maps", "Email", and "Calendar"), on a phone with a high-resolution display, Weave shows all these components on the same pane and distributes the buttons vertically. On a watch with limited screen real estate, Weave displays the components in a grid view with each as an interactive card—a design metaphor for commercial smartwatches [15]. Similarly, on an eyewear they are represented as a list of swipeable cards that users can swipe through and tap to select [16]. Developers can update the UI shown on a device referred to by an element `id` using `device.updateUI(ID, NEW_CONTENT)` for the inner content or `device.updateUIAttr(ID, ATTR, NEW_ATTR_VALUE)` for a certain attribute. These functions are useful for providing incremental feedback.

To fully leverage the functionality of each device, a Weave service can invoke native apps on the device from the script, using `device.startApp(APP_NAME)`. A service can also make a phone call using `device.call(PHONE_NUMBER)` and play a media file using `device.play(MEDIA_FILE)`.

Attaching Event Callbacks to Devices

Based on what UI elements and sensor events are available on a selected device, developers can add a callback function to the device to handle user input. For example, developers can easily program a remote control service that allows the user to launch an application on a target device (e.g., a smartphone) by selecting the app from a `launchList` on a different device (e.g., a smartwatch) (see Figure 5).

```
weave.select("showable[size='small'], touchable")
  .show(weave.getLayoutById("launchList"))
  .on("tap:li", function(event) {
    weave.select("showable[size='normal']")
      .not(event.getDevice())
      .startApp(event.getValue());
  });
```

Figure 5. The script snippet allows the user to launch an app on a "normal"-sized device by selecting it from a list on a "small"-sized "touchable" device.

When the user taps on a list item that corresponds to an app name, Weave executes the callback function. The `event` argument passed into the function stores detailed event information, including the corresponding value retrieved by `event.getValue()`, and the device that triggers this event accessed via `event.getDevice()`. In this example, the callback function launches the app designated by `event.getValue()` on a device that has a normal-sized screen and is not the device where the event is triggered.

Weave provides other useful built-in events including `shake`, `rotateCW`, and `rotateCCW` inferred from motion sensors, `listenStart` and `listenEnd` if the user approaches the device to his ear, and common touch events such as `doubleTap`, `longPress`, and `swipe`. Note that our framework is designed to support device selection chaining and event propagation so that developers can attach the above operations in sequence, such as showing UI, adding several event callback functions, and applying other actions.

Coordinating Cross-Device Behaviors

Leveraging the strengths of multiple devices can form rich interaction behaviors. However, it is challenging to coordinate the behaviors of multiple devices. For instance, developers might want to display an urgent message to all the devices at the same time to maximally acquire the user's attention. For another instance, developers might want to use the current orientation of a smartwatch to indicate a different mode for a tap event on a smartphone touchscreen, e.g., detecting a knuckle or a fingertip tap [4]. Programming event callbacks and UI output for a single device is often straightforward. But handling these tasks for multiple devices can be extremely complex. A framework should assist developers in fulfilling these tasks.

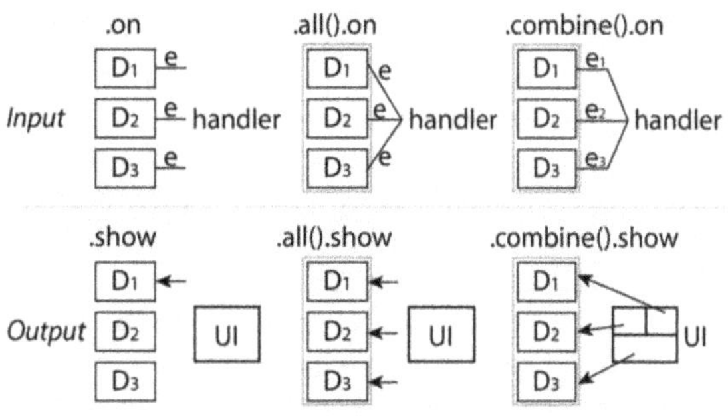

Figure 6. Weave coordinates multiple devices in three different modes (from left to right): default, `all`, and `combine` managing both input and output.

By default, when an event callback is attached to a selection (returned by `weave.select`) that includes multiple devices, Weave invokes the callback whenever one of these devices fires the event. Likewise, to execute an action on the selection, Weave selects a device in the selection that best matches the selection criteria, instead of performing the action on all the devices in the selection. On top of the default mode (which is similar to "any" device in a set), Weave provides two operators that can be applied to a selection for coordinating cross-device behaviors of these devices: `all` and `combine` (see Figure 6).

The `all` Operator

Developers can choose to enable multiple devices to behave simultaneously in the same way. One example is to broadcast the same message such that the message will be displayed on every device returned by `weave.select`. For coordinating input behaviors, the `all` mode requires a specific event to occur on all the devices in the selected set to invoke a callback function. For example, consider an interaction scenario that requires multiple users to physically bump their devices at the same time to form a user group. Realizing this scenario manually would require developers to collect the "shake" events from each device and compare their timestamps. To ease the development of this type of behaviors, Weave provides a high-level mechanism, i.e., the `all` operator, where developers can specify when and how devices should be synchronized. The code snippet in Figure 7 defines a callback function that is invoked when a shake event co-occurs on any two or more devices within a time range (500ms by default). In this snippet, each of the devices is required to have a display (`showable`), an accelerometer (`shakable`) for the shake event, and a speaker (`speakable`) for the audio output.

```
weave.select("showable, shakable, speakable")
  .all({minNumOfDevices: 2}) // at least 2 devices
  .show("Bump to join")
  .on("shake", function(event) {
    event.getDevices().show("Welcome to the group!")
      .play("audio/success.mp3");
  });
```

Figure 7. The `all` operator synchronizes the input and output of multiple devices and enables interaction scenarios such as bumping devices together to join a group.

The `combine` Operator

Weave introduces the `combine` operator that combines the input and output resources of multiple devices as an organic whole in which each device is allowed to perform a different part of a compound behavior. Via the `combine` operator, multiple devices within a selection essentially form a single virtual device that allows more diverse interaction behaviors.

Consider a cross-device slideshow scenario where a watch serves as a control panel for the user to go forward and backward through a list of images shown on a phone that can be viewed by others. To realize this scenario, developers apply the `combine` operator (Figure 8) to a selection of devices, e.g., a watch and a phone. Weave analyzes a UI layout that consists of an image viewer and two buttons and automatically distributes the buttons, which require minimum screen estate for "Previous" and "Next," to the watch and the image viewer, which requires higher resolution to be shown, to the phone. The distribution strategy is similar to Panelrama's [32] that primarily relies on preferred dimensions of each UI element. Note that an alternative script without using the `combine` operator is listed in Figure 1 (line 4-12) for comparison, which requires more variables to manage the device allocations for both the viewer and the control panel separately.

```
<div id="controlPanel">
 <button value="prev">Previous</button>
 <button value="next">Next</button>
 <img id="imageView" src="img/1.jpg"/>
</div>

var photoIdx = 1, numOfPhotos = 8;
weave.select("showable[privacy='low'], touchable")
  .combine().show(weave.getLayoutById("controlPanel"))
  .on("tap:button", function(event) {
    if (event.getValue()==="prev" && curPhoto > 1) {
      photoIdx --;
    } else if (event.getValue()==="next"
       && photoIdx < numOfPhotos ) {
      photoIdx ++;
    }
    event.getDevices().updateUIAttr("imageView",
      "src", "img/" + photoIdx + ".jpg");
  });
```

Figure 8. The `combine` operator distributes UI elements considering the screen estates and user interactions.

In addition to distributing a user interface, the `combine` operator allows developers to fuse different types of input events from multiple devices to create a new interaction mode. For example, Figure 9 shows a cross-device pinch gesture that invokes the callback function when a watch on the wrist detects a left swipe and the phone (assuming holding in hand) detects a right swipe at the same time.

```
weave.selectAll().combine()
  .on("swipeLeft[joint='wrist'],
     swipeRight[type='phone']", function(event) {
       event.getDevices().show("Pinch detected");
  });
```

Figure 9. The `combine` operator supports cross-device gestures as a new interaction mode.

Internally, Weave listens to element events of a compound (e.g., `swipeLeft` and `swipeRight`) on each device in the combination and triggers the callback when these events occur approximately at the same time. Weave maintains a global event pool to buffer and synthesize events from multiple devices. In general, `combine` creates an internal representation to manage the I/O of the combined devices. Weave encapsulates all these complexities for developers.

THE RUNTIME ARCHITECTURE

Weave employs a web-based architecture (see Figure 10) for creating and deploying services. Developers can access

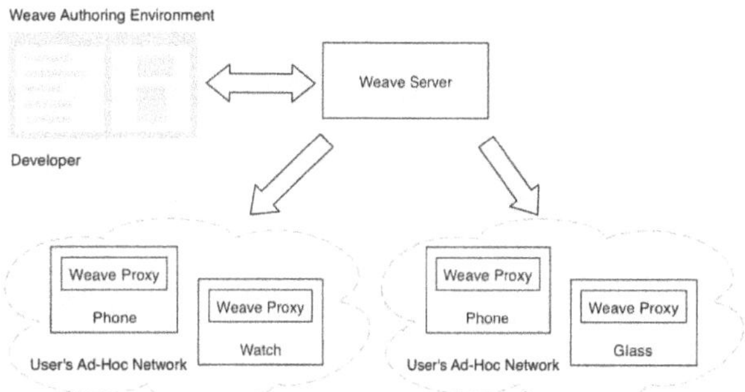

Figure 10. The architecture for creating Weave services.

Weave's authoring environment anywhere by pointing a web browser to the Weave server. Users can install a Weave service on their devices by accessing the Weave server using a Weave proxy.

A Weave proxy needs to be preinstalled and runs on each individual device. A Weave proxy serves two purposes. First, it provides tools for 1) generating a device profile that describes the capabilities of the device, 2) registering the device directly to the Test panel by scanning the QR code for developers to test a service on the device (see Figure 1), and 3) accessing the Weave server for searching and installing a service. A device profile is extracted automatically by analyzing the device resource (e.g. detecting available sensors), which can be refined by the owner using XMLs. Ideally the profile should come with the device, as it is specific and fixed to each type of device.

Second, a Weave proxy hosts a runtime environment for managing the ad-hoc network of wearable devices for a user and executing a Weave service on these devices (see Figure 11). To simplify the architectural design, Weave employs a client-server-based runtime architecture within each ad-hoc network. At any time, only one device on the

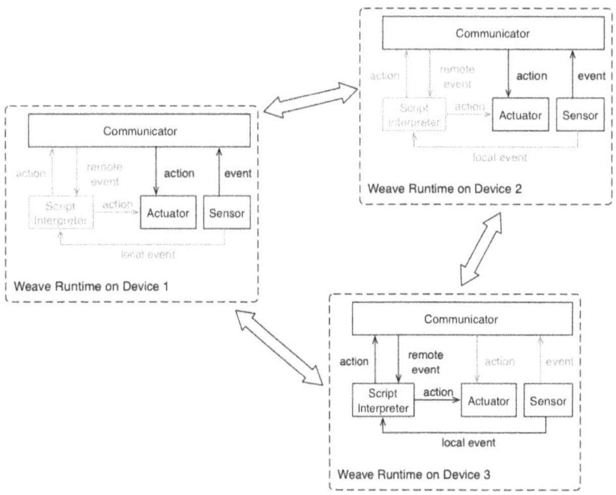

Figure 11. An illustration of Weave's runtime environment on a user's ad-hoc network. Here the network contains three devices, and Device 3 acts as the server for executing a script, and synthesizing events and distributing actions across devices.

network acts as the server that is responsible for executing the script and distributing the UI feedback and synthesizing events across devices. The runtime environment has four major components. The *Communicator* maintains connections with other devices on the ad-hoc network, and sends and receives events or actions between devices. The *Actuator* performs actions for updating the user interface on the device including playing audible or vibration feedback. The *Sensor* detects user input and sensor events on the device and sends the events to the *Script Interpreter*, which runs either locally on the device or remotely on another device on the network. The Script Interpreter executes a script and manages event callbacks and interaction states.

Any device can be added to the ad-hoc network or removed from it at runtime, as Weave promptly updates the device selection and status. When a server device leaves the network, another device on the network will succeed it as the server. This design allows flexible device configuration and stability in executing a cross-device service.

IMPLEMENTATION

The Weave web server is implemented based on Node.js to host the authoring UI. Weave's Script Interpreter executes scripts and HTML5-based UI layouts using a JavaScript engine. We have implemented and tested Weave proxies on three types of devices: the Nexus series of smartphones, Android Wear powered smartwatches such as Samsung Gear Live, and Google Glass.

The runtime server uses WebSocket and JSON to communicate with the Communicator running on each device. Note that since smartwatches such as Samsung Gear Live currently lack the web socket capability via Wi-Fi and only supports Bluetooth, they are paired with Android phones in order to connect to the server through the Wearable Data Layer API defined by the Google Play service. The Communicator on each device is responsible for redirecting traffic to a target device if the target device is not directly reachable from the server.

EVALUATION

To evaluate the usability of Weave's API framework design as well as the authoring environment as a whole, we conducted a user study with 12 participants. We hypothesized that Weave would allow developers to easily create a range of interaction behaviors across multiple mobile and wearable devices. We chose not to include a baseline condition (i.e., a control group) as our pilot studies showed that programming these interactions using the Android framework would take three hours at minimum.

Participants and Setups

We recruited 12 participants (2 females), aged between 20 and 48 years (Mean=28) from an IT company, including software engineers and interns. Participants were required to have moderate web programming knowledge and were selected randomly from volunteers via an internal study invitation. Participants had a varying programming background, ranged from 3 to 30 years (Mean=9 and SD=8). They had used two JavaScript tools on average, including jQuery, AngularJS, and Node.js. 9 out of 12 participants had mobile programming experience with Android phones, but only few had programmed wearable devices: two built basic Android Wear apps and one in Google Glass. Each participant was compensated with a $40 gift card for their participation.

The study was conducted in a quiet lab environment. A MacBook Pro running OS X and Google Chrome browser was connected to two 24-inch LCD displays of 1920x1200 pixel resolution. We provided an external mouse and keyboard. The set of mobile and wearable devices that are used in the experiment include two Android phones (Nexus 5 and Nexus), one Samsung Gear Live smartwatch that is powered by Android Wear, and one Google Glass eyewear.

Procedures and Tasks

To learn the framework, participants went through a tutorial and performed a practice task to create a single-device Launch Pad using Weave. Participants had the opportunities to learn different device selection criteria, specifying UI layouts in HTML, and adding callback functions to handle button taps. Participants also tested their service with emulators and real devices. The Weave API documentation was provided and available during the experiment. The learning phase was about 17 minutes on average. Participants were then asked to perform three programming tasks to create cross-device interactions using Weave.

Task 1: Modify the single-device Launch Pad created from the practice task to run a control panel on a glanceable device with three options (Maps, Email, and Calendar) and launch applications on a handheld device.

Task 2: Design a bump service that multiple users could join a group by physically shaking their devices at the same time. Provide both visual and audio feedback when successfully joined.

Task 3: Design a slideshow service that provides a panel on a small-size wearable for the user to browse a list of photos on a larger device—that is more viewable by others—by going forward or backward.

Participants could choose to test their scripts any time during the experiment. Finally, they were asked to answer a questionnaire, followed by a discussion with the experimenters. On average, the total duration of an entire user session lasted 80 minutes. We included some sample code from these tasks in Figures 5, 7 and 8.

EXPERIMENTAL RESULTS AND DISCUSSION

We discuss our observation about participants' coding strategies with Weave, their subjective feedback as well as opportunities for future work.

Code Analyses and Scripting Strategies

All the participants successfully scripted and tested the three tasks in the study. The average time of completing each task was 5, 11, and 18 minutes (SD=2, 3 and 6). The duration of Task 2 and 3 also included the time for participants to learn the `all` and `combine` operators. In general, participants were impressed by Weave's ease of use for development: P4 said, "*It was fast, easy to learn, and provided a way to unify cross platform devices with the same code. Would have taken a lot more time for me to do any of the tasks individually.*" Compared to programming with the Android framework, all the participants suspected that it would have taken them at least three hours to multiple days for a single task, as they would have to work on the environment setup (P1), specific APIs (P8), and details such as network or message passing (P5).

The average number of lines of code within the "`service`" function was 6 ([*min*, *max*]=[5, 9], SD=1), 6 ([3, 9], SD=2), and 16 ([12, 22], SD=3) for each task, excluding the comments and code for system log printouts. The range varied for several reasons. Since Weave supports the chaining of functions, developers showed different styles of coding: some preferred to align operators in several lines, some contracted into one, and some created variables to manage. For a relatively complicated task such as Task 3, some participants chose to create an inner function to improve code readability. These behaviors showed that participants retained their JavaScript coding styles when scripting with Weave. P8 explained: "*I could interact with them (the devices) via a common interface that was easy to pick up with basic HTML, JS, and CSS (due to selector-like syntax) knowledge.*" P12 summarized, "*jQuery-like API is straightforward to most JavaScript programmers.*"

We observed that participants had a similar coding strategy: they started by selecting a set of devices and confirming the selected devices were as expected, then modified UI outputs and attached event listeners, and finally designed the callback logic. Such a coding strategy suggested that Weave supported a top-down and modular development in handling output, input, and interaction logic.

Feedback on Development

Participants were very positive about developing with Weave. They found it easy to learn the framework (4.6 on a 5-point Likert scale, SD=0.5), script a target behavior (4.6, SD=0.5), test a behavior (4.1, SD=0.9) and deploy it to real devices (4.8, SD=0.5). Participants commented: "*It was a fun experience. It was quite simple.*" (P11); "*Definitely easier than any other model I am aware of.*" (P10).

Framework Design

Participants found the abstraction and selection of Weave easy to manage: "*The CSS-like selection with Weave was pretty intuitive and made device selection very manageable. I also liked that it abstracted away the specific interface for each of the devices by allowing me to specify things that apply to (e.g.) any shakable device.*" (P8), and "*I like the concept of defining sets of devices by their use and semantic attributes (glanceable, private...).*" (P2). The results also showed that Weave's event-based structure supported interaction flow designs. P12 explained "*The API allows developers to implement cross-device interactions in functional programming paradigm is innovative.*"

However, participants desired more controls over distributing UI layouts across devices while using the `combine` operator. Previous mechanisms such as "panel" in Panelrama [32] can be useful in our framework for adding more developer controls to automate UI distribution. Some also wanted to see how Weave could embed an existing widget or web plugin in interfaces (P6, P8), which can be enabled in the future.

Service Deployment and Testing

Participants were surprised about the ease of use and the speed for deploying a service in real-time: "*Testing was great and easy. I definitely liked the immediate deploy of the code to the devices*" (P3); "*It was surprisingly easy to deploy the apps*" (P2). P1 liked the live testing and "*write once and run multiple*".

However, the debugging feature was limited with the current system. Several participants explicitly mentioned the need of highlighting syntax errors (P6, P8), code completion (P9), and writing test cases (P4). On average, the experimenters offered little help to participants for completing these tasks. The only type of help that was provided (less than two times on average for a task) was on fixing syntax errors, such as missing closing marks and incorrect built-in event names.

Opportunities

Participants expressed strong interests in scripting cross-device interactions with Weave (4.6, SD=0.7). Participants were also interested in potentially including more devices for content retrieval and manipulation, such as a desktop or a laptop (P2, P8), and a TV or other large monitors (P7, P9, P12). Some expected to integrate other services such as online photo collection or games (P9). All in all, the developer feedback showed that Weave provides a powerful tool as "*It significantly shortens the time required to prototype new ideas on wearable devices.*" (P12). We drew most of our examples and tasks from recent cross-device literature and commercial products, since our evaluation primarily focused on lowering the technical threshold, i.e., "lowering the floor". In the future, we intend to explore further on how our tool can raise the ceiling for creating more sophisticated cross-wearable behaviors.

We also identified the weakness of our framework and opportunities for future work. Weave currently does not support specification of relative spatial relations that have been used in prior work [22,32,5]. This limitation can be addressed by enabling developers or end-users to specify these spatial relations on devices [25] or enhancing with more sensors [5]. In addition, we are experimenting with features that allow developers to create custom cross-device events using programming by demonstration, and support multi-user scenarios by adding user identifiers, e.g., enabling `device.owner` as a built-in variable.

CONCLUSIONS

We present Weave, a framework for developers to create cross-device wearable interaction by scripting. We contributed a set of high-level APIs, abstractions and integrated tool support. Our evaluation with 12 participants indicated that Weave significantly reduced developer effort for creating complex interaction behaviors that involve UI distribution and event synthesizing across multiple wearable devices.

REFERENCES

1. Apple Inc. Apple – iOS 8 – Continuity. https://www.apple.com/ios/whats-new/continuity/ (2014).
2. Boring, S., Baur, D., Butz, A., Gustafson, S., and Baudisch, P. Touch projector: Mobile Interaction through Video. In *Proc. CHI '10*, ACM Press (2010).
3. Bostock, M., Ogievetsky, V., and Heer, J. D3: Data-Driven Documents. IEEE Transactions on Visualization and Computer Graphics 17, (2011).
4. Chen, X., Grossman, T., Wigdor, D.J., and Fitzmaurice, G. Duet: Exploring Joint Interactions on a Smart Phone and a Smart Watch. In *Proc. CHI '14*, ACM Press (2014).
5. Chen, X., Marquardt, N., Tang, A., Boring, S., and Greenberg, S. Extending a mobile device's interaction space through body-centric interaction. In *Proc. MobileHCI '12*, ACM Press (2012).
6. Dearman, D. and Pierce, J.S. "It's on my other computer!": Computing with Multiple Devices. In *Proc. CHI '08*, ACM Press (2008).
7. Elmqvist, N. Distributed user interfaces: State of the art. In *Distributed User Interfaces*. Springer London, 2011, 1–12.
8. Feiner, S. and Shamash, A. Hybrid user interfaces: breeding virtually bigger interfaces for physically smaller computers. In *Proc. UIST '91*, ACM Press (1991).
9. Fitbit Inc. Fitbix Flex. http://www.fitbit.com/flex (2014).
10. Frosini, L. and Paternò, F. User interface distribution in multi-device and multi-user environments with dynamically migrating engines. In *Proc. EICS 2014*, ACM Press (2014).
11. Gjerlufsen, T., Klokmose, C.N., Eagan, J., Pillias, C., and Beaudouin-Lafon, M. Shared substance: developing flexible multi-surface applications. In *Proc. CHI '11*, ACM Press (2011).
12. Google Inc. Chromecast. http://www.google.com/chrome/devices/chromecast/ (2014).
13. Google Inc. Google Glass. https://www.google.com/glass/start/ (2014).
14. Google Inc. Android Wear: The developer's perspective. https://www.google.com/events/io/io14videos/ (2014).
15. Google Inc. UI Patterns for Android Wear. https://developer.android.com/design/wear/ (2014).
16. Google Inc. Google Glass – Patterns. https://developers.google.com/glass/design/patterns (2014).
17. Hamilton, P. and Wigdor, D.J. Conductor: enabling and understanding cross-device interaction. In *Proc. CHI '14*, ACM Press (2014).
18. Hartmann, B., Beaudouin-Lafon, M., and Mackay, W.E. HydraScope: Creating Multi-Surface Meta-Applications Through View Synchronization and Input Multiplexing. In *Proc. PerDis '13*, ACM Press (2013).
19. Hernandez, J., Li, Y., Rehg, J.M., and Picard, R.W. BioGlass: Physiological Parameter Estimation Using a Head-mounted Wearable Device. In *Proc. MobiHealth '14* (2014).
20. Ishimaru, S., Kunze, K., Kise, K., Weppner, J., Dengel, A., Lukowicz, P., and Bulling, A In the blink of an eye – Combining Head Motion and Eye Blink Frequency for Activity Recognition with Google Glass. In *Proc. AH '14*, ACM Press (2014).
21. Marcotte, E. *Responsive Web Design*. A Book Apart (2011).
22. Marquardt, N., Diaz-Marino, R., Boring, S., and Greenberg, S. The proximity toolkit: Prototyping Proxemic Interactions in Ubiquitous Computing Ecologies. In *Proc. UIST '11*, ACM Press (2011).
23. Marquardt, N., Hinckley, K., and Greenberg, S. Cross-device interaction via micro-mobility and f-formations. In *Proc. UIST '12*, ACM Press (2012).
24. Mayer, S., Tschofen, A., Dey, A. K., Mattern, F. User Interfaces for Smart Things - A Generative Approach with Semantic Interaction Descriptions. ACM Transactions on Computer-Human Interaction (2014), 21, 2, article 12.
25. Nebeling, M., Mintsi, T., Husmann, M., and Norrie, M. Interactive development of cross-device user interfaces. In *Proc. CHI '14*, ACM Press (2014).
26. Paternò, F., Santoro, C., Spano, L.D. MARIA: A Universal Language for Service-Oriented Applications in Ubiquitous Environment. ACM Transactions on Computer-Human Interaction (2009), 16, 4, article 19.
27. Santosa, S. and Wigdor, D. A field study of multi-device workflows in distributed workspaces. In *Proc. UbiComp '13*, ACM Press (2013).
28. Serrano, M., Ens, B.M., and Irani, P.P. Exploring the use of hand-to-face input for interacting with head-worn displays. In *Proc. CHI '14*, ACM Press (2014).
29. Sinha, A. K. Informally Prototyping Multimodal, Multidevice User Interfaces. Ph.D. Dissertation. UC Berkeley (2003).
30. Wagner, J., Nancel, M., Gustafson, S.G., Huot, S., and Mackay, W.E. Body-centric design space for multi-surface interaction. In *Proc. CHI '13*, ACM Press (2013).
31. Weiser, M. and Brown, J.S. The coming age of calm technology. Beyond calculation: the next fifty years, Copernicus (1997).
32. Yang, J. and Wigdor, D. Panelrama: Enabling Easy Specification of Cross-Device Web Applications. In *Proc. CHI '14*, ACM Press (2014).
33. Zhang, B., Chen, Y., Tuna, C., Dave, A., Li, Y., and Lee, E., Hartmann, B. HOBS: Head Orientation-Based Selection in Physical Spaces. In *Proc. SUI '14* (2014).

MultiFi: Multi-Fidelity Interaction with Displays On and Around the Body

Jens Grubert[1], **Matthias Heinisch**[1], **Aaron Quigley**[2], **Dieter Schmalstieg**[1]
[1] Graz University of Technology [2] University of St Andrews
jg@jensgrubert.de, heinischmatthias@gmail.com, aquigley@acm.org, schmalstieg@tugraz.at

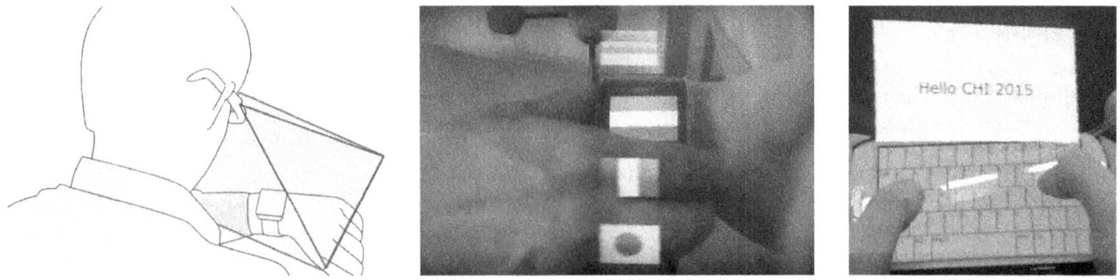

Figure 1: MultiFi widgets crossing device boundaries based on proxemics dimensions (left), e.g., middle: *ring menu* on a smartwatch (SW) with head-mounted display (HMD) or right: *soft keyboard* with full-screen input area on a handheld device and HMD.

ABSTRACT

Display devices on and around the body such as smartwatches, head-mounted displays or tablets enable users to interact on the go. However, diverging input and output fidelities of these devices can lead to interaction seams that can inhibit efficient mobile interaction, when users employ multiple devices at once. We present MultiFi, an interactive system that combines the strengths of multiple displays and overcomes the seams of mobile interaction with widgets distributed over multiple devices. A comparative user study indicates that combined head-mounted display and smartwatch interfaces can outperform interaction with single wearable devices.

ACM Classification Keywords

H.5.2 Information interfaces and presentation: User Interfaces - Graphical user interfaces

INTRODUCTION

Personal, public and ambient displays form a pervasive infrastructure around us. However, displays are typically unaware of each other and make little attempt to coordinate what is shown across them. The emergence of second-screen applications, screen mirroring and remote desktop access demonstrates the benefits of suitably designed coordination. In particular, when users carry multiple displays on and around their body, these displays form a space that can be leveraged for seamless interaction across display boundaries.

In this work, we introduce MultiFi, a platform for implementing user interface widgets across multiple displays with different fidelities for input and output. Widgets such as toolbars or sliders are usually specific to a single display platform, and widgets that can be used between and across displays are largely unexplored. This may come from the problems introduced by the variations in fidelity of input and output across devices. For input, we must accommodate different modes and degrees of freedom. For output, we must accommodate for variations in resolution and field of view. Both input and output affect the exactness of the user experience. Moving across devices can make the differences in fidelity apparent and introduce seams affecting the interaction.

MultiFi aims to reduce such seams and combine the individual strengths of each display into a joint interactive system for mobile interaction. For example, consider continuous navigation support, regardless of where a person is looking. Such navigation may employ a range of worn, handheld or embedded displays. Even if the navigation system is capable of switching among displays in a context-aware manner, the user will still need to contend with varying and uncoordinated fidelities of interaction.

MultiFi addresses the design problem of "interaction on the go" across multiple mobile displays with the follow-

CHI 2015, April 18–23, 2015, Seoul, Republic of Korea.
ACM 978-1-4503-3145-6/15/04.
http://dx.doi.org/10.1145/2702123.2702331

ing contributions: 1) We explore the design space of multiple displays on and around the body and identify key concepts for seamless interactions across devices. 2) We introduce a set of cross-display interaction techniques. 3) We present empirical evidence that combined interaction techniques can outperform individual devices such as smartwatches or head-mounted displays for information browsing and selection tasks.

RELATED WORK

Today's dominant handheld devices, such as smartphones or tablets, have a high *access cost* in terms of the time and effort it takes to retrieve and store the device from where it typically resides, such as one's pocket. This cost reduces the usefulness of a device for micro-interactions, such as checking the time or one's inbox.

Wearable devices such as a smartwatch (SW) or head-mounted display (HMD) lower the access cost to a wrist flick or eye movement. However, interaction with these always-on devices is encumbered by their low *fidelity*: limited screen and touch area, low resolution and poor contrast limit what users can do. Currently, HMDs require indirect input through touch devices, while high-precision spatial pointing is not yet commercially available. Recent research aims to improve the overall fidelity, investigating higher resolution and more immersive displays, improved touchscreen precision [24, 31] or physical pointing [10, 11].

A recurring topic for wearable displays is the extension of display real-estate using virtual screen techniques [14, 15, 29]. Recently, Ens et al. [13] explored the design space for a body-centric virtual display space optimized for multi-tasking on HMDs and pinpointed relevant design parameters of concepts introduced earlier by Billinghurst et al. [4, 5]. They found that body-centered referenced layouts can lead to higher selection errors compared to world-referenced layouts, due to unintentional perturbations caused by reaching motions.

Users with multiple devices tend to distribute tasks across different displays, because moving between displays is currently considered a task switch. For some forms of interaction, a tight spatial registration may not be needed. For example, Duet combines handheld and SW and infers spatial relationships between the devices based on local orientation sensors [9]. Similarly, Billinghurst et al. [7] combine handheld and HMD, but use the handheld mainly as an indirect input device for the HMD. Stitching together multiple tablets [21] allows for interaction across them, under the assumption that they lie on a common plane. Several other approaches combine larger stationary with handheld displays through spatial interaction [1, 6]. The large stationary displays make virtual screens unnecessary, but restrict mobility. The same is true for the work of Benko et al. [2], who combine a touch table with an HMD. Yang and Widgor introduced a web-based framework for the construction of applications using distributed user interfaces but do not consider wearable displays [32].

Figure 2: The extended screen space metaphor for showing a high resolution inlay of a map on SW inside a low resolution representation on a HMD.

Unlike prior work, we focus on the dynamic alignment of multiple body-worn displays, using body motion for spatial interaction.

INTERACTION BY DYNAMIC ALIGNMENT

MultiFi aims to reduce the access cost of involving multiple devices in micro-interactions by dynamically leveraging complementary input and output fidelities. We propose *dynamic alignment* of both devices and widgets shown on these devices as an interaction technique.

Dynamic alignment can be seen as an application of proxemics [16]: Computers can react to users and other devices based on factors such as distance, orientation, or movement. In MultiFi, dynamic alignment changes the interaction mode of devices based on a combination of proxemic dimensions. We focus on *distance* and *orientation* between devices. However, different alignment styles can be explored, which are location-aware, vary between personal and public displays or consider movement patterns.

Design factors

To better understand the design implications of dynamic alignment, we begin with a characterization of the most relevant design factors determined throughout the iterative development process of MultiFi.

Spatial reference frames encompass where in space information can be placed, if this information is fixed or movable (with respect to the user) and if the information has a tangible physical representation (i.e., if the virtual screen space coincides with a physical screen space) [12].

Direct vs. indirect input. We use the term direct input, if input and output space are spatially registered, and indirect input, if they are separated. As a consequence of allowing various spatial reference frames, both direct and indirect input must be supported.

Fidelity of individual devices concerns the quality of output and input channels such as spatial resolution, color contrast of displays, focus distance, or achievable input precision. We also understand the display size as a fidelity factor, as it governs the amount and hence quality of information that can be perceived from a single screen.

Continuity. The ease of integrating information across several displays not only depends on the individual display fidelities, but also on the quality difference or gap between those displays, in particular, if interaction moves across display boundaries. We call this *continuity of fidelity.* In addition, *continuity of the spatial reference frame* describes if the information space is continuous, as with virtual desktops, or discrete, e.g., when virtual display areas are bound to specific body parts [8]. Continuity factors pose potential challenges when combining multiple on and around the body displays. For example, combining touch screen and HMD extends the output beyond a physical screen of a SW, but not the input. This leads to potential interaction challenges, when users associate the extension of the output space with an extension of the input space.

Social acceptability of interactions with mobile, on and around body devices have been extensively studied [30], revealing the personal and subjective nature of what is deemed acceptable. This varies due to many factors including the technology, social situation or location. Dynamic alignment allows for some degree of interaction customization, allowing people to tailor their interactions in a way which best suits their current context, rather than having to rely on default device patterns which may be wholly unsuited to the context of use.

Alignment modes

For the combination of HMD and touch device, we distinguish three possible alignment modes (see Figure 3):

In *body-aligned mode*, the devices share a common information space, which is spatially registered to the user's body (Figure 3, left). While wearable information displays could be placed anywhere in the 3D space around the body, we focus on widgets in planar spaces, as suggested by Ens et al. [12]. The HMD acts as a low fidelity viewing device into a body-referenced information space, allowing one to obtain a fast overview. The touchscreen provides a high fidelity inset, delivering detail-on-demand, when the user points to a particular location in the body-referenced space. Also, in contrast to common spatial pointing techniques, the touchscreen provides haptic input into the otherwise intangible information space.

In *device-aligned mode* , the information space is spatially registered to the touchscreen device and moves with it (Figure 3, middle). The HMD adds additional, peripheral information at lower fidelity, thus *extending the screen space* of the touch screen, yielding a focus+context display.

In *side-by-side mode*, interaction is redirected from one device to the other without requiring a spatial relationship among devices (Figure 3, right). For example, if the HMD shows a body-referenced information space, a touch device can provide indirect interaction. The touch device can display related information, and input on the touch device can affect the body-referenced display. If the touch device is outside the user's field of view, the touch screen can still be operated blindly.

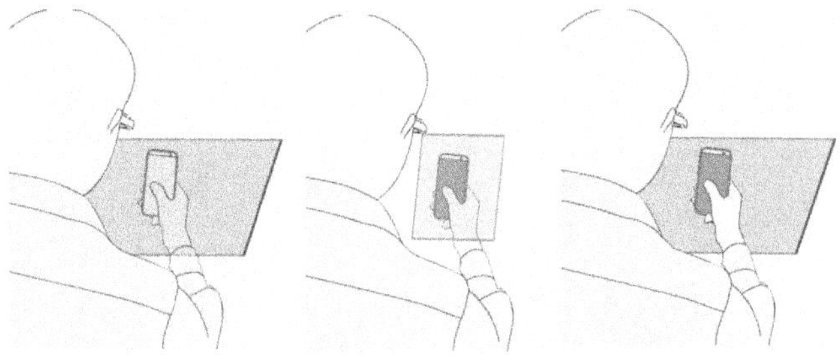

Figure 3: In body-aligned mode (left) devices are spatially registered in a shared information space relative to the user's body. In device-aligned mode (middle) the screen space of the touchscreen is extended. In side-by-side mode (right) devices have separated information spaces and do not require a spatial relationship.

Navigation

The principal input capabilities available to the user are spatial pointing with the touch device, or using the touch screen. Spatial pointing with the touch device is a natural navigation method in body-aligned mode. Once the alignment is recognized (the user's viewpoint, the handheld and the chosen item are aligned on a ray), the HMD clears the area around the element to let the handheld display a high resolution inset. This navigation method can be used for selection or even drag-and-drop in the body-referenced information space. However, extended use can lead to fatigue.

Spatial pointing in device-aligned mode can be seen as a more indirect form of navigation, which allows one to obtain a convenient viewpoint on the device-aligned information space. Navigation of the focus area will naturally be done by scrolling on the touch screen, but this can be inefficient, if the touch screen is small. Hence, users may mitigate the limitation of input to the physical screen with a clutch gesture that temporarily switches to body-aligned mode. At the press of a button (or dwell gesture), the information space can be fixed in air at the current position. Then users can physically select a new area of the information space by physical pointing, making it tangible again.

Focus representation and manipulation

An additional design decision is the representation shown on the higher fidelity display: The first option is to solely display a higher *visual level of detail.* For example, the user could align a touch screen over a label to improve the readability of text (Figure 2). The second option presents *semantic level of detail* [25], revealing additional information through a magic lens metaphor [3]. Here, the widget changes appearance to show additional information. For example, in Figure 4, the "Bedrooms" label turns into a scrollable list, once the borders of the

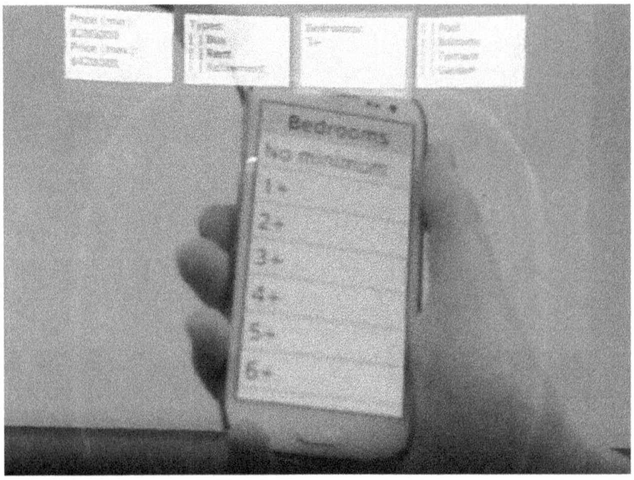

Figure 4: Spatial pointing via a handheld triggers a low fidelity widget on the HMD to appear in high fidelity on the handheld.

handheld and the label represenation in the HMD are spatially aligned. Similarly, in Figure 5 (bottom row), a handheld shows a richer variation of a widget group including photos and detailed text, once it is aligned with the low fidelity representation on the user's arm.

An interactive focus representation on the touch device can naturally be operated with standard touch widgets. In body-aligned mode, this leads to a continuous coarse-to-fine *cascaded interaction*: The user spatially points to an item with a low fidelity representation and selects it with dwelling or a button press. A high fidelity representation of the item appears on the touch screen and can be manipulated by the user through direct touch (Figures 2, 4, 5).

For simple operations, this can be done directly in body-aligned mode. For example, widgets such as checkbox groups may be larger than the screen of a SW, but individual checkboxes can be conveniently targeted by spatial pointing and flipped with a tap. However, holding the touch device still at arm's length or at awkward angles may be demanding for more complex operations. In this case, it may be more suitable to *tear off* the focus representation from the body-aligned information space by automatically switching to side-by-side mode. A rubberband effect snaps the widget back into alignment, once the user is done interacting with it. This approach overcomes limitations of previous work, which required users to either focus on the physical object or on a separate display for selection [11].

Widgets and applications

MultiFi widgets adapt their behavior to the current alignment of devices. For example, widgets can relocate from one device to the other, if a certain interaction fidelity is required. We have identified a number of ways how existing widgets can be adapted across displays. Here we discuss several widget designs and applications employing such widgets to exemplify our concepts.

Menus and lists: On a SW, menu and list widgets can only show a few items at once due to limited screen space. We use an HMD to extend the screen space of the SW, so users get a quick preview of nearby items in a *ring menu*, Figure 1, middle. Similarly, list widgets on an HMD can adapt their appearance to show more information once a handheld device is aligned, Figure 4.

Interactive map: Navigation of large maps is often constrained by screen space. We introduce two map widgets that combine HMD and touch screen. The first map widget works similar to the list widget, but extends the screen space of a touch display in both directions. Interaction is achieved via the touch display.

The second variant makes use of a body-referenced information space. The map is displayed in the HMD relative to the upper body, either horizontally, vertically or tilted (Figure 2). If the map size is larger than the virtual display space, the touchpad on the SW provides additional pan and zoom operations.

Arm clipboard: Existing body-centric widgets for handhelds [8, 23] rely on proprioceptive or kinesthetic memorization, because the field of view of the handheld is small. With an additional HMD, users can see where on their body they store through head pointing and subsequently retrieve information with a handheld device. If a list widget displays additional information on one side of the SW (overview+detail), we can let users store selected items on their lower arm (Figure 5). Aligning the handheld with one of the items stored on the arm automatically moves the item to the higher fidelity handheld. For prolonged interaction, the item can now be manipulated with two hands on the handheld. Through the combination of HMD for overview and touch enabled displays for selection and manipulation, body-referenced information spaces could become more accessible compared to previous approaches solely relying on proprioceptive memory [8, 23].

Text input: Using MultiFi text widgets, we have implemented a full-screen soft keyboard application for a handheld used with a HMD. The additional screen real estate on the handheld allows MultiFi to enlarge the soft keys significantly, while the text output is redirected to the HMD. As soon as a HMD is aligned, the text output area can relocate from one device to the other (see Figure 1, right). This results in two potential benefits. First, the larger input area could help speed up the writing process. Second, the written text is not publicly visible, hence supporting privacy.

IMPLEMENTATION

Software

The MultiFi prototype is based on HTML5, JavaScript, WebSockets for communication, three.js for rendering and hammer.js for touch gesture recognition. All client devices open a website in a local browser and connect to the Java-based application server. JSON is used to

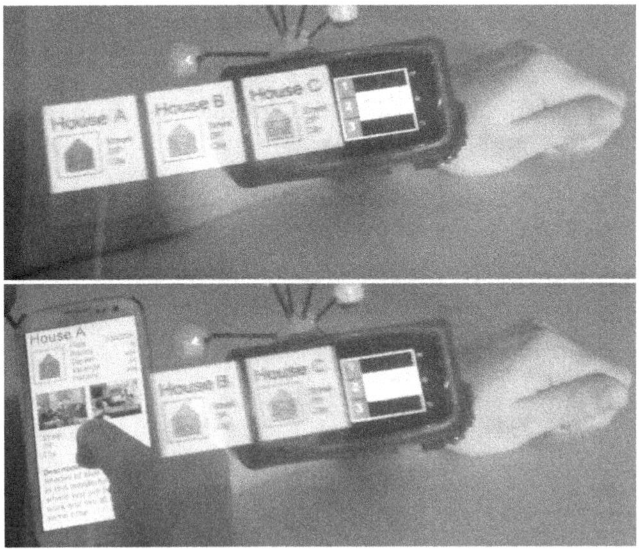

Figure 5: Arm clipboard with extended screen space for low fidelity widgets (top). Spatial pointing enables switching to high fidelity on a handheld (bottom).

encode the distributed messages, and tracking data is received via VRPN.

Widgets have potentially multiple graphical representations in replicated and synchronized scenegraphs and a common state which is shared via the central application server. For widgets that do not change their appearance and simply span multiple devices, multiple camera views on the same 3D scene are used (e.g., ring menu, map). Widgets that adapt their appearance (such as list items) use multiple synchronized representations. Interaction across devices relies on the known 3D poses of individual devices, shared via the central application server. For example, selection of an item in the HMD via a touch screen is realized through intersection from the touch point with the virtual HMD image plane.

As our system relies on the accurate registration between devices, calibration of individual components is required. Foremost, the HMD is calibrated via optical see-through calibration methods (using single or multiple point active alignment methods [17]). In addition, the image masks for the touch screen devices (i.e. the area that should not be rendered on the HMD) and thus their positions relative to their tracking markers have to be determined. For this the user manually aligns the touch screen with a pre-rendered rectangle displayed on the HMD (having the same size as the touch screen) which allows MultiFi to determine the transformation between the touch screen and the attached tracking target. Please note that these calibration steps typically have to be carried out only once for each user and device respectively.

Devices

We implemented a MultiFi prototype using a Samsung Galaxy SIII (resolution: 1280x720 px, 306 ppi, screen size: 107x61 mm) as smartphone, a Vuzix STAR 1200 XL HMD (resolution: 852x480 px, horizontal field of view (FoV): 30.5° vertical FoV: 17.15°, focus plane distance: 3 m, resolution: 13 ppi at 3 m, weight with tracking markers: 120 g) and another smartphone (Sony Xperia Z1 compact) as smartwatch substitute (resolution: 1280x720 px, cropped extent: 550x480 px, 342 ppi, weight with tracking markers: 200 g). We chose this approach to simulate next generation smartwatches with higher display resolution and more processing power. To this aim, we limited the screen extent to 40x35 mm to emulate the screen extent of a typical smartwatch. The HMD viewing parameters were matched with virtual cameras which rendered the test scenes used in the smartphone, HMD and SW.

Tracking

We used an A.R.T. outside-in tracking system to determine the 3D positions of all devices. This currently limits our prototype to stationary use in laboratory environments. Still, mobile scenarios could be supported by relying on local sensors only. For example HMDs with in-built (depth) cameras could be used to determine the 3D position of touch screens relative to the HMD [26]. Alternatively, in-built orientation sensors could track the touch screen and HMD positions relative to a body-worn base station (such as an additional smartphone in the user's chest pocket). Please note that the later approach would likely result in less accuracy and drift over time. This would need to be considered in the adaptation rules for widgets when spanning multiple devices.

USER STUDY

We conducted a laboratory user study to investigate if combined device interaction can be a viable alternative to established single device interaction for mobile tasks. For the study we concentrated on two atomic tasks: information search and selection. Those tasks were chosen as they can be executed on the go and underpin a variety of more complex tasks.

Experimental design

We designed a within-subjects study to compare performance and user experience aspects of MultiFi interaction to single device interaction for two low level tasks. We complemented the focus on these atomic tasks with user inquiries about the potential and challenges of joint on and around the body interaction. For both tasks, we report on the following dependent variables: *task completion time, errors, subjective workload* as measured by NASA TLX [19] as well as user experience measures (After Scenario Questionnaire (ASQ) [22], *hedonic and usability aspects* as measured by AttrakDiff [20]) and overall *preference* (ranking). The independent variable for both tasks was interface with five conditions:

Handheld: The Samsung Galaxy SIII was used as only input and output device. This serves as the baseline for a handheld device with high input and output fidelity.

Smartwatch (SW): The wrist-worn Sony Xperia Z1 compact was used as only input and output device. The input and output area was 40x35 mm and highlighted by a yellow border, as shown in Figure 2. Participants were notified by vibration if they touched outside the input area. This condition serves as baseline for a wearable device with low input and output fidelity (high resolution, but small display space).

Head Mounted Display (HMD): The Vuzix STAR 1200XL was used as an output device. We employed indirect input as in the SW condition using a control-display ratio of 1 with the touch area limited to the central screen area of the HMD. This condition serves as the baseline for a HMD with low input and output fidelity, which can be operated with an arm-mounted controller.

Body-referenced interaction (BodyRef): The content was displayed in front of the participant in body-aligned mode with additional touch scrolling. Selection was achieved by aligning the smartwatch with the target visible in front of the user and touching the target rendered on the smartwatch.

Smartwatch referenced (SWRef): The information space was displayed in device-aligned mode (Figure 9). All other aspects were as in BodyRef.

Apparatus and data collection

The study was conducted in a controlled laboratory environment. The devices employed were the ones described in the implementation section. The translation of virtual cameras for panning via touch in all conditions parallel to the screen was set to ensure a control-display ratio of 1. Pinch to zoom was implemented by the formula $s = s_0 \cdot s_g$, with s being the new scale factor, s_0 the map's scale factor at gesture begin and s_g the relation between the finger distances at gesture begin and end. While the system is intended for mobile use, here participants conducted the tasks while seated at a table (120x90 cm, height 73 cm, height adjustable chair) due to the strenuous nature of the repetitive tasks in the study. Null hypothesis significance tests were carried out at a .05 significance level, and no data was excluded, if not otherwise noted. For ANOVA (repeated measures ANOVA or Friedman ANOVA), Mauchly's test was conducted. If the sphericity assumption had been violated, degrees of freedom were corrected using Greenhouse-Geisser estimates of sphericity. For post-hoc tests (pairwise t-test or Wilcoxon signed rank) Bonferroni correction was applied. Due to space reasons not all tests statistics are reported in detail, but are available as supplementary material[1].

Procedure

After an introduction and a demographic questionnaire, participants were introduced to the first task (counterbalanced) and the first condition (randomized). For each condition, a training phase was conducted. For each task, participants completed a number of trials (as described in the individual experiment sections) in five blocks, each block for a different condition. Between each block, participants filled out the questionnaires. At the end of the study, a semi-structured interview was conducted and participants filled out a separate preference questionnaire. Finally, the participants received a book voucher worth 10 Euros as compensation. Participants were free to take a break between individual blocks and tasks. Overall, the study lasted ca. 100 minutes per participant.

Participants

Twenty-six participants volunteered in the study. We had to exclude three participants due to technical errors (failed tracking or logging). In total, we analyzed data from twenty-three participants (1 f, average age: 26.75 y, σ=5.3, average height: 179 cm, σ= 6, 7 users wore glasses, three contact lenses, 2 left-handed users). All but one user were smartphone owners (one less than a year). Nobody was a user of smartwatches or head-mounted displays. Twenty users had a high interest in technology and strong computer skills (three medium).

Hypotheses

One of our main interests was to investigate if combined display interaction could outperform interaction with individual wearable devices. We included Handheld interaction as a baseline and did not expect the combined interfaces to outperform it. Hence, we had the following hypotheses: *H1:* Handheld will be fastest for all tasks. *H2:* BodyRef will be faster than HMD and SW (ideally close to Handheld). *H3:* BodyRef will result in fewer errors than HMD and SW. *H4:* SWRef will be faster than HMD and SW (ideally close to Handheld). *H5:* SWRef will result in fewer errors than HMD and SW.

EXPERIMENT 1: LOCATOR TASK ON MAP

A common task on mobile mapping applications is to search for an object with certain target attributes [28]. We employed a locator task similar to previous studies involving handheld devices and multi-display environments [18, 27]. Participants had to find the lowest price label (text size 12 pt) among five labels on a workspace size of 400x225 mm. We determined the workspace size empirically, to still allow direct spatial pointing for the BodyRef condition. While finding the lowest price could easily be solved with other widgets (such as a sortable list view), our task is only an instance of general locator tasks, which can encompass non-quantifiable attributes such as textual opinions of users, which cannot be sorted automatically. Users conducted ten trials per condition. With 23 participants, five interface levels and 10 trials, there was a total of 23x5x10=1150 trials.

Task completion time and errors

The task completion times (TCT, in seconds), for the individual conditions can be seen in Figure 6. A repeated measures ANOVA indicated that there was a significant effect of interface on TCT, F(3.10, 709.65)=42.21,

[1] http://www.jensgrubert.wordpress.com/research/multifi/

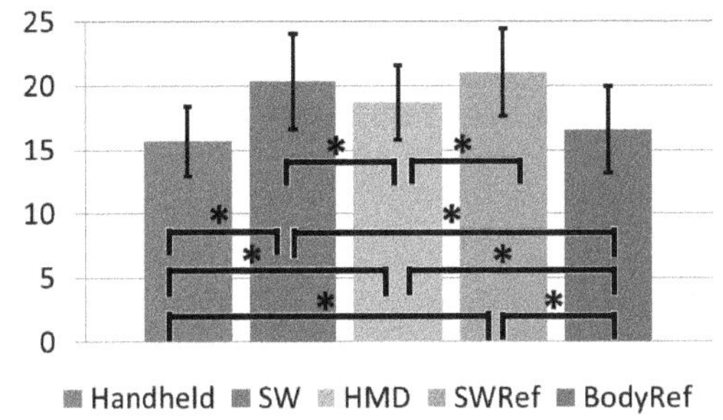

Figure 6: Task completion time (s) for the locator task.

p<.001. Post-hoc tests indicated that both Handheld and BodyRef were significantly faster than all remaining interfaces with medium to large effect sizes (see also Figure 6). HMD was significantly faster than both SW and SWRef. There were no significant differences between Handheld-BodyRef and SW-SWRef.

From 230 selections, eight false selections were made in the Handheld, HMD and BodyRef conditions. In the SW condition, 13 errors have been made, in SWRef five errors. No significant differences were found.

Subjective workload and user experience

Repeated measures ANOVAs indicated that there were significant effects of interface on all dimensions. Post-hoc tests indicated that BodyRef resulted in a higher mental demand than smartwatch (albeit with a small effect size). The handheld condition resulted in significantly lower subjective workload for all other dimension compared to most other interfaces. The analysis of the ASQ (repeated measures ANOVA and post-hoc tests) indicated that for Handheld ease of task was significantly higher than for SWRef. Analysis of AttrakDiff showed that all interfaces scored slightly below average for pragmatic quality (PQ), see Figure 7, and only a significant difference between HMD-SWRef could be found (but with a small effect size). For hedonic quality stimulation (HQ-S), the Handheld and SW interface were rated significantly lower than the other three conditions. Preference analysis showed that Handheld (MD=2, M=1.13, σ=1.13) was significantly more preferred than SW (MD=4, M=3.87, σ=1.10), Z=-4.25, p<.001.

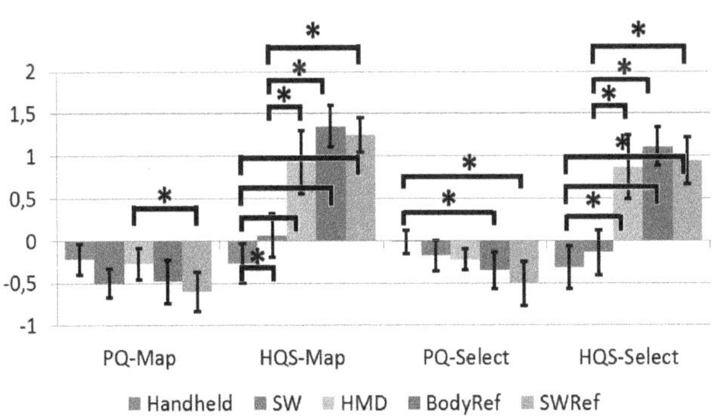

Figure 7: Pragmatic Quality (PQ) and Hedonic Quality Stimulation (HQS) measures (normalized range -2..2) for the locator task (left) and the select task (right).

Figure 8: The selection task for SWRef.

EXPERIMENT 2: 1D TARGET ACQUISITION

We employed a discrete 1D pointing task similar to the one used by Zhao et al. [33] (Figure 8). Participants navigated to a target (green stripe) in each trial using touch input (for Handheld, SW, HMD, SWRef) or spatial pointing (BodyRef). Final target selection was confirmed by a touch on the target region in all conditions. The participants were asked to use their index finger to interact with the touch surfaces. For each trial, the task was to scroll the background (Handheld, SW, HMD, SWRef) or to move the smartwatch towards the target (BodyRef) until it appeared on the *selection area.* Prior to each trial, participants hit a start button at the center of the screen to ensure a consistent start position and to prevent unintended gestures before scrolling. The target was only revealed after the start button was hit. After successful selection, the target disappeared. For BodyRef, participants returned to a neutral start position centered in front of them before the next trial. In the experiment design we fixed target width to 20 mm (0.5*width of the smartwatch), use the control window and display window sizes of the individual displays and use two target distances (short: 15 cm, long: 30 cm)[2]. The conditions were blocked by interface. Per condition, each participant conducted eight trials (plus two training trials). With twenty three participants, five interface levels, two target distances, two directions and eight trials per condition a total of 23x5x2x2x8=3680 trials were conducted.

Task completion time and errors

Task completion times are depicted in Figure 9. Repeated measures ANOVAs indicated that for both distances (15 cm, 30 cm) and smartwatch sides (towards and away from dominant hand) interface had a significant effect on TCT. The pairwise significant differences are depicted in Figure 9. Handheld was the fastest interface for both directions and distances. BodyRef was significantly faster than all remaining interfaces. No other significant effects of interface on task completion time were found.

Selection errors occurred when participants tapped outside the target region. The total number of errors for individual interfaces were as follows: Handheld:

[2]We fixed those parameters as the focus of the experiment was not on generating a new target aquisition model.

53 (M=.07, σ=.28), SW: 34 (M=.05, σ=.23), HMD: 223 (M=.30, σ=.77), BodyRef: 258 (M=.35, σ=.78), SWRef: 37 (M=.05, σ=.24). A Friedman ANOVA indicated that there was a significant effect of interface on error count ($\chi^2(4)$=231.68, p<.001). Post-hoc tests indicated significant differences between BodyRef and all interfaces except HMD, as well as between HMD and all interfaces (except BodyRef).

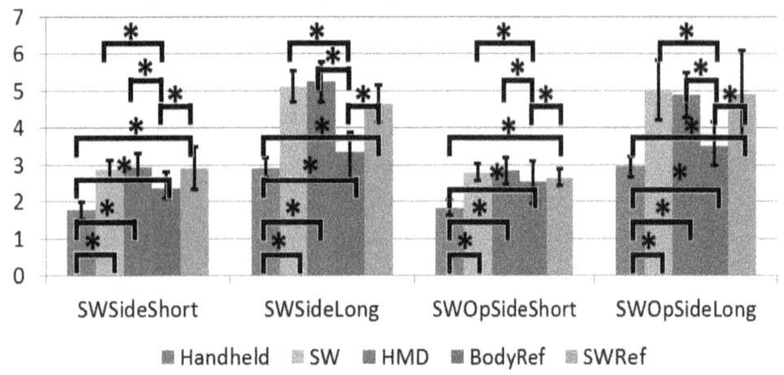

Figure 9: Task completion times (s) for the select task. SWSide: side on which smartwatch was worn, SWOpSide: opposite side.

Subjective workload and user experience

A repeated measures ANOVA indicated that there were significant effects of interface on all dimensions but temporal demand and performance. Post-hoc tests indicated that Handheld resulted in a significantly lower mental demand than most other conditions (except SW) and in a significantly lower overall demand than all conditions. BodyRef and SWRef resulted in significantly higher physical demands compared to Handheld and HMD (but not SW). Frustration was significantly higher for SW and SWRef compared to Handheld. Analysis of results of the ASQ indicated a significant difference between Handheld and SWRef for ease of task (Z= -3.36, p=.01). As in the locator task, all interfaces scored below average for PQ-S (see Figure 9). BodyRef and SWRef scored significantly lower than Handheld (indicated by repeated measures ANOVA and post-hoc t-tests). For HQ-S, the Handheld and SW interface were rated significantly lower than the other three conditions as in the locator task.

Qualitative feedback

In semi-structured interviews participants commented on potentials and limitations of the prototypical MultiFi implementation. Most participants (21) commented on the benefits of having an *extended view space* compared to individual touch screens with one participant saying "*Getting an overview with simple head movements is intuitive and natural*". Those participants also valued the fact that precise selection was enabled through the smartwatch with one typical comment being "*The HMD gives you the overview, and the SW lets you be precise in your selection*". Three participants highlighted the potentially lower *access costs* of MultiFi over smartphones, with one comment being "*I dont have to constantly monitor my smartphone*". In line participants felt that BodyRef interaction was fastest (even though this is not confirmed by the objective measurements). Five participants commented on the benefits of MultiFi over HMD only interaction highlighting the direct interaction or that they could "*take advantage of proprioception and motion control*".

Many participants (15) commented on the limitations of the hardware, specifically the quality of the employed HMD with a typical comment being "*The combined interfaces [SWRef, BodyRef] gave me trouble because of display quality*". Specifically, the employed HMD obscured parts of the users' field of view "*preventing the ability of glancing down (on the SW) without moving your head*". Another issue highlighted by 6 participants was the *cost of focus switching* which refers to the accommodation to different focus depths of the touch screen and the virtual HMD screen with a typical comment being: "*I have to focus on three layers, which is overwhelming: SW, HMD and real world*". This also led to *coordination problems across devices* as mentioned by 9 participants. Hence, some participants suggested not to concurrently use HMD and SW as output: "*Pairing the two devices is good, but use one as input, the other as output, not both as output, it's confusing*". Also, social concerns of spatial pointing were raised, "*I could not imagine this in a packed bus*".

DISCUSSION

The study results indicate that combined SW and HMD interaction in body-referenced information spaces can outperform individual wearable devices in terms of task completion time (*H2* holds) and that handheld interaction is not always fastest (H1 does not hold). However, this currently comes at the expense of higher workload and lower usability ratings. We see two major sources for this. First, compared to commercially available wearable devices, we used relatively heavy laboratory equipment (smartphone and HMD with separate retro-reflective markers). Participants mentioned that they would prefer the combined interaction more, if it were lighter. Second, we compared novel interaction techniques involving continuous spatial pointing with established touch screen interaction. Hence, we assume that both lighter devices and more training could mitigate these workload effects.

In the selection task, BodyRef and HMD resulted in a significantly higher error number than the other interfaces (H3 does not hold). Also, SWRef did not result in significantly less errors (H5 does not hold). For HMD, this could be explained by the indirect touch input combined with a smaller control window (SW area) compared to the larger display window. For BodyRef, it turned out that the outside-in tracking system for spatial pointing and our system architecture introduced an average end-to-end delay from user motion to display update of 154 ms (σ=36). A further video analysis revealed that users were tapping the SW repeatedly when they have reached the target area, even though they were informed to select as precisely as possible. While this is clearly a limitation of our current experimental system setup, we believe that future tracking systems will minimize delay, allowing more precise physical pointing.

Semi-structured interviews revealed that users generally preferred Handheld, as it was the most familiar device, had the largest touch input area and was most comfortable to use. BodyRef was preferred as it felt fast and separated target search via head pointing and selection via spatial pointing with the SW. User comments included "*Moving your head to get an overview is very intuitive*" and "*knowing where to move before you move makes it easier than other conditions*". Still, confirming spatial selection with the touchpad was not welcomed by all, "*I would prefer to just point with my fingers or eyes*".

SWRef performed (for both tasks) not better than individual devices, even though they are based on the extended screen space metaphor as the body-referenced condition (H4 does not hold). Subjective feedback in the semi-structured interviews indicated that participants could not efficiently use the SWRef condition due to the need for refocusing between the SW display (~40 cm distance) and the focus plane of the HMD (~300 cm). In addition, the HMD had a lower visual fidelity, which likely increased the effort for reading the labels. Some participants still favored the SWRef condition, specifically for the selection task. They indicated that the HMD gave them "*a peripheral awareness when the target approaches the smartwatch*". This hints that SW referenced display space extension could be beneficial, if the visual fidelity of the HMD and costs of display switching is considered in the design process. For example, instead of rendering a map continuously across displays without adjustments, individual map regions could be adjusted to be more readable across displays (or to avoid the need for actually reading the text on the HMD at all).

SW alone was least preferred due to cumbersome interaction with a small input and output area. Specifically, swiping motions were deemed inefficient. For example, in the select task, participants mentioned a lack of overview, "*I did not know when I passed the target*". HMD was preferred by some users, because they could keep their head and arm in comfortable positions and have a "lean back" experience. They mention it is "better than Google Glass as I can use the smartwatch as touchpad". One participant said: "I could imagine using this for presentations were I can see the slides in the HMD and keep eye contact with the audience when controlling the app with my smartwatch".

Revisiting MultiFi we see that the spectrum of *dynamic alignment* ranging from uncoupled individual devices to closely coupled spatially registered interaction is a key concept for supporting a broad range of mobile scenarios. It facilitates the idea that over time, users can develop individual preferences for multi-display interaction styles just like current touch interfaces offer multiple ways of interaction. The qualitative feedback in the study indicated that users could see benefits of MultiFi over individual device interaction in terms of *access costs* and *direct interaction*. Being able to directly interact within this view space through a touch screen distinguishes MultiFi from other approaches like mid-air interaction via depth-sensors, which lack the haptic feedback of touch screens and through this potentially result in a lower selection precision.

However, such benefits may come at an increased *coordination cost* across displays. Specifically, while we presented a first set of possible widgets, our study revealed that those widgets have to be designed carefully to be able to efficiently lower interaction gaps introduced by individual devices (such as focus distance and resolution differences). Simply extending the display space for widgets across displays without adapting their appearance and operation (as done with the SW referenced map) seems not to be enough to overcome interaction seams. This indicates the need for more research to further investigate the particulars of efficient cross display widgets for interaction on the go. For example, for the map widget we could imagine to further reduce the visual complexity on the low fidelity HMD by simply indicating the location of points of interest with details only appearing on the high fidelity display (as in the arm clipboard).

CONCLUSION AND FUTURE WORK

We have presented *MultiFi*, an interactive system that combines the strengths of multiple displays on and around the body. We explored how to minimize seams in interaction with multiple devices by dynamic alignment between interfaces. Furthermore, we discussed the implications for user interface widgets and demonstrated the feasibility of our concept through a working prototype system. Finally, we demonstrated that combined HMD and smartwatch interaction can outperform interaction with single wearable devices in terms of task completion time, albeit with higher workload.

In future work, we will explore the design concepts of combining multiple wearable and other displays within our conceptual framework. We also want to build a fully mobile prototype using only mobile sensors.

Acknowledgements

This work was supported by the EU FP7 project MAGELLAN under the grant number ICT-FP7-611526.

References

1. Beaudouin-Lafon, M., Huot, S., Nancel, M., Mackay, W., Pietriga, E., Primet, R., Wagner, J., Chapuis, O., Pillias, C., Eagan, J., Gjerlufsen, T., and Klokmose, C. Multisurface interaction in the wild room. *Computer*, 45(4), 2012: 48–56.
2. Benko, H., Ishak, E. W., and Feiner, S. Cross-dimensional gestural interaction techniques for hybrid immersive environments. *VR 05*. 2005, 209–216.

3. Bier, E. A., Stone, M. C., Pier, K., Buxton, W., and DeRose, T. D. Toolglass and magic lenses: the see-through interface. *SIGGRAPH*. 1993, 73–80.
4. Billinghurst, M., and Starner, T. Wearable devices: new ways to manage information. *Computer*, 32(1), 1999: 57–64.
5. Billinghurst, M., Bowskill, J., Dyer, N., and Morphett, J. An evaluation of wearable information spaces. *VRAIST 98*. 1998, 20–27.
6. Boring, S., Baur, D., Butz, A., Gustafson, S., and Baudisch, P. Touch projector: mobile interaction through video. *CHI 10*. 2010, 2287–2296.
7. Budhiraja, R., Lee, G. A., and Billinghurst, M. Using a hhd with a hmd for mobile ar interaction. *ISMAR 13*. 2013, 1–6.
8. Chen, X., Marquardt, N., Tang, A., Boring, S., and Greenberg, S. Extending a mobile device's interaction space through body-centric interaction. *MobileHCI 12*. 2012, 151–160.
9. Chen, X., Grossman, T., Wigdor, D. J., and Fitzmaurice, G. Duet: exploring joint interactions on a smart phone and a smart watch. *CHI 14*. 2014, 159–168.
10. Cockburn, A., Quinn, P., Gutwin, C., Ramos, G., and Looser, J. Air pointing: design and evaluation of spatial target acquisition with and without visual feedback. *IJHCS*, 69(6), 2011: 401–414.
11. Delamare, W., Coutrix, C., and Nigay, L. Designing disambiguation techniques for pointing in the physical world. *EICS 13*. 2013, 197–206.
12. Ens, B., Hincapié-Ramos, J. D., and Irani, P. Ethereal planes: a design framework for 2d information space in 3d mixed reality environments. *SUI 14*. 2014, 2–12.
13. Ens, B., Finnegan, R., and Irani, P. The personal cockpit: a spatial interface for effective task switching on head-worn displays. *CHI 14*. 2014, 3171–3180.
14. Feiner, S., MacIntyre, B., Haupt, M., and Solomon, E. Windows on the world: 2d windows for 3d augmented reality. *UIST 93*. 1993, 145–155.
15. Fitzmaurice, G. W. Situated information spaces and spatially aware palmtop computers. *CACM*, 36(7), 1993: 39–49.
16. Greenberg, S., Marquardt, N., Ballendat, T., Diaz-Marino, R., and Wang, M. Proxemic interactions: the new ubicomp? *interactions*, 18(1), 2011: 42–50.
17. Grubert, J., Tuemler, J., Mecke, R., and Schenk, M. Comparative user study of two see-through calibration methods. *VR 10*. 2010, 269–270.
18. Grubert, J., Pahud, M., Grasset, R., Schmalstieg, D., and Seichter, H. The utility of magic lens interfaces on handheld devices for touristic map navigation. *PMC*, 2014:
19. Hart, S. G., and Staveland, L. E. Development of nasa-tlx (task load index): results of empirical and theoretical research. *AIP*, 52, 1988: 139–183.
20. Hassenzahl, M., Burmester, M., and Koller, F. Attrakdiff: ein fragebogen zur messung wahrgenommener hedonischer und pragmatischer qualität. In: *M&C 03*. Springer, 2003, 187–196.
21. Hinckley, K., Ramos, G., Guimbretiere, F., Baudisch, P., and Smith, M. Stitching: pen gestures that span multiple displays. *AVI 04*. 2004, 23–31.
22. Lewis, J. R. Psychometric evaluation of an after-scenario questionnaire for computer usability studies: the asq. *SIGCHI Bulletin*, 23(1), 1991: 78–81.
23. Li, F. C. Y., Dearman, D., and Truong, K. N. Virtual shelves: interactions with orientation aware devices. *UIST 09*. 2009, 125–128.
24. Olwal, A., Feiner, S., and Heyman, S. Rubbing and tapping for precise and rapid selection on touch-screen displays. *CHI 08*. 2008, 295–304.
25. Perlin, K., and Fox, D. Pad: an alternative approach to the computer interface. *SIGGRAPH 93*. 1993, 57–64.
26. Rädle, R., Jetter, H.-C., Marquardt, N., Reiterer, H., and Rogers, Y. Huddlelamp: spatially-aware mobile displays for ad-hoc around-the-table collaboration. *ITS 14*. 2014, 45–54.
27. Rashid, U., Nacenta, M. A., and Quigley, A. The cost of display switching: a comparison of mobile, large display and hybrid ui configurations. *AVI 12*. 2012, 99–106.
28. Reichenbacher, T. Adaptive concepts for a mobile cartography. *JGS*, 11(1), 2001: 43–53.
29. Reichlen, B. A. Sparcchair: a one hundred million pixel display. *VRAIS 93*. 1993, 300–307.
30. Rico, J., and Brewster, S. Gestures all around us: user differences in social acceptability perceptions of gesture based interfaces. *MobileHCI 09*. 2009, 64:1–64:2.
31. Vogel, D., and Baudisch, P. Shift: a technique for operating pen-based interfaces using touch. *CHI 07*. 2007, 657–666.
32. Yang, J., and Wigdor, D. Panelrama: enabling easy specification of cross-device web applications. *CHI 14*. 2014, 2783–2792.
33. Zhao, J., Soukoreff, R. W., Ren, X., and Balakrishnan, R. A model of scrolling on touch-sensitive displays. *IJHCS*, 72(12), 2014: 805–821.

Form Follows Sound: Designing Interactions from Sonic Memories

Baptiste Caramiaux[1], Alessandro Altavilla[1], Scott G. Pobiner[2], Atau Tanaka[1]

[1]Department of Computing
Goldsmiths, University of London
{ b.caramiaux, a.altavilla, a.tanaka }
@gold.ac.uk

[2]School of Design Strategies
Parsons The New School of Design
New York, USA
pobiners@newschool.edu

ABSTRACT
Sonic interaction is the continuous relationship between user actions and sound, mediated by some technology. Because interaction with sound may be task oriented or experience-based it is important to understand the nature of action-sound relationships in order to design rich sonic interactions. We propose a participatory approach to sonic interaction design that first considers the affordances of sounds in order to imagine embodied interaction, and based on this, generates interaction models for interaction designers wishing to work with sound. We describe a series of workshops, called *Form Follows Sound*, where participants ideate imagined sonic interactions, and then realize working interactive sound prototypes. We introduce the *Sonic Incident* technique, as a way to recall memorable sound experiences. We identified three interaction models for sonic interaction design: *conducting*; *manipulating*; *substituting*. These three interaction models offer interaction designers and developers a framework on which they can build richer sonic interactions.

Author Keywords
Interaction Design; Sonic Interaction Design; Methodology; Gesture; Sound.

ACM Classification Keywords
H.5.5. Sound and Music Computing: Methodologies and techniques; H.5.2. User Interfaces: User-centered design; H.5.2. User Interfaces: Interaction styles; H.5.2. User Interfaces: Auditory-non speech feedback.

INTRODUCTION
Sound has a long history in Human-Computer Interaction, often as a supporting function in the user interface as a way to notify the user about their actions. An early example is the SonicFinder [17], that introduced auditory icons defined as "everyday sounds meant to convey information about computer events by analogy with everyday event". Sound as a medium for interaction has recently emerged through the discipline of Sonic Interaction Design [16] making use of continuous interaction between user actions and sound feedback to help in accomplishing a task while performing it. While this approach has found several promising applications; for example, in rehabilitation [3], sport [33], or music, few insights have been given to interaction designers to allow them to realize such interactions. In this paper, we propose a participatory approach to extract insights for novel and rich sonic interaction designs.

CHI 2015, April 18–23, 2015, Seoul, Republic of Korea.

ACM 978-1-4503-3145-6/15/04...$15.00.
http://dx.doi.org/10.1145/2702123.2702515

Sound can be thought of as an information medium, one that conveys clues about materials, substances and their environment, and reveals a sense of the physical dimensions of a space and its surfaces [2]. At the same time, sound is an affective medium evoking memory and emotion. High amplitude sounds, rich in low frequencies, can be physically felt by humans, as in the case of powerful sound systems [21]. Sound can even be used as a weapon using high frequencies and narrow beams [19]. Most importantly, sound is a temporal phenomenon and "exists in time: It is an inherently transient phenomenon" [17]. Listening becomes a critical activity for Gaver, who distinguishes *musical listening* from *everyday listening* [18], the former emphasizes musical qualities of sound while the latter focuses on causal and contextual aspects of a sonic event.

Sound is powerful in that it can provoke a visceral response and influence action. In cognitive neurosciences, couplings between the auditory and motor systems have been reported at the level of the brain [39]. The body is not passive in listening – human actions have been shown to have an effect on auditory perception [29]. Behavioral approaches of sound–action coupling have examined how a physical gestures can represent the sound it accompanies [27]. Considering environmental sounds, recent studies showed that corporeal representation of sound depends on the user's level of identification of the sound source [7]. This points out the possibility that sound sources, and possibly sounds themselves, can take on qualities we can think of as *affordances*, inviting accommodation, response, and possibly use, on the part of the beholder.

In this paper, we propose an approach for the design of sonic interaction where sound and the user's sonic experience serve as the starting point from which action–sound relationships are envisaged. We consider the perception–action loop as a fundamental design principle that facilitates forms of embodied interaction [8,10]. We introduce a methodology based on critical incident technique and workshopping to aid users in accessing memorable sound events, and use scenario building to aid them to prototype sonic interactions. Advanced interactive sound and gesture capture technologies are introduced to allow groups of participants to elaborate novel, functional action–sound relationships. From the insights we gained, we derive interaction models for continuous interaction with sound that could be useful for interaction designers to conceive rich sonic interactions for future products and interactive systems.

The paper is structured as follows. In the next section we review the state of the art in sonic interaction design and interaction models in HCI. We then present the workshop procedure and describe its evolution across four iterations. The Results section reports on outcomes from the workshops and insights they provide. The Discussion uses analysis of the results to frame our proposed interaction models for sound. We conclude by indicating how this research might inform the work of interaction designers and frame future research directions.

RELATED WORK

Sound as an interface

The use of sound in the user interface arises from the need to transmit information through a different medium than the visual (*sonification*). Sound HCI research has resulted in techniques such as audification (raw translation of data to sounds), earcons (audio messages made of short rhythmic sequences of pitched tones with variable timbre), auditory icons (sounds from everyday conveying information about events). For a review see [23]. Sound as a display for information communication has also been the core of the International Community for Auditory Display (ICAD) [26].

Sonic interaction design

Sonic Interaction Design (SID) brings together research and design works that use sound as an "active medium that can enable novel phenomenological and social experience with and through interactive technology" [16]. In this context sound is used to provide information about the nature of the interaction itself, helping the user to refine her actions under a given task [22]. SID also extends the use of sound in an interaction setting for non-task oriented and creative activities. For instance, previous works combined sound design and interaction design techniques to explore sonic augmentation of everyday objects [32,34].

According to Franinović et al. [15], a central element in SID "is the role that embodied action and perception plays, or how action can be guided by sound in a concrete, lived manner" based on theories of embodiment in cognitive sciences [38] and interaction design [10]. The authors added that embodied sonic interaction is a critical notion as "the body is continually navigating through space, attending to cross-modal phenomena [...]" ([15], p.43). Embodied actions are crucial in sonic interaction. However, the field lacks an operational framework for designers to realize such interactions.

Techniques for sonic interaction design

Techniques for teaching Sonic Interaction Design are broad and often exploratory. Such techniques are: performing soundwalks [13], listening exercises, cinema sound effects foley analysis [25], and the writing of sonic dramas [31]. Vocal sketching is a technique that uses the human voice as a sketching "tool" for interaction design [11] and, according to Rocchesso, can be thought of as an extension of bodystorming, or "physically situated brainstorming" [6].

Workshops, and processes of *workshopping* are gaining acceptance in HCI as a key methods in qualitative and user-centric research [36]. Franinović et al. [14] propose the workshop as a means to investigate sound in the design of everyday products and to set the methodological basis for this practice, which includes elements of auditory display, product interaction design and ubiquitous computing. A recent study by Houix et al. [24] proposed the use of a participatory workshop to generate prototypes using sounds associated to manipulations of physical objects and prototypes implementing certain gesture–sound relationships. There, the workshop was used as an exploration to test gesture–sound relationships in object manipulation. There is a need, therefore, to formalize some of the very subjective methods in sonic interaction design and to extract insight from them to be transferred to interaction designers wishing to create new products and systems that make robust use of sound as a central part of human-machine interaction.

Interaction Models

Interaction design research has provided a number of different frameworks through the notion of interaction models. Beaudouin-Lafon defines Interaction Model as "an operational description of how interaction proceeds" [5]. Examples of interaction models in HCI include the instrumental interaction from the same author [4] or the direct manipulation model by Shneiderman [35]. While several interaction models have been developed for computer-based interaction through graphical interfaces, interaction models for sonic interaction still remain to be proposed.

METHODS: WORKSHOPPING SONIC EXPERIENCE

We designed and delivered a series of participatory design workshops that focus on participants' memory and direct experience of sound in the everyday. We used a two-phase structure, Ideation followed by Realization, as a way to move from the description of an affective experience to the elaboration of a functioning interactive sound prototype. Since the design process is driven by sound through sonic memories, we called the series of workshops *Form Follows Sound* (FFS), in reference to the idiomatic "form follows function".

We carried out the workshop 4 times in an 8-month period, with a total of 43 participants of varying degrees of experience with sound and music:

- **New York**. A two-day workshop at Parsons The New School for Design. 15 participants (8 female and 7 male), aged 22 - 44. Participants' background included graphic and interaction design, theatre and dance performance, music.
- **Paris.** A two-day workshop at IRCAM Centre Pompidou as part of the European summer school, Human-Computer Confluence (HC2). 6 participants (2 female, 4 male), between 24 and 35 years old. Participants were from a wide range of fields including engineering, rehabilitation, music technology, physics, bioengineering, and art.
- **London.** A one-day workshop at Goldsmiths College. 9 participants (2 female and 7 male). Their background was various including art and technology, social science, film studies, sound design and computing.
- **Zurich.** A one-day workshop at the ZHdK academy of art as an activity within a teaching module in Sonic Interaction Design. Participants were 12 students (4 female, 8 male) aged between 20 and 24 years, with beginner's experience in sound design.

Phase 1: Ideation

Phase 1 of the workshop was called *ideation* as the goal was to generate ideas for action–sound relationships based on memories of sounds from participants' everyday lives. This phase does not involve technology.

Sonic Incident Technique

Critical incident technique is a set of procedures in psychology that elicit specific memories related to particular recent moments lived by the subject [12]. This technique has then been used in HCI as input for design [28] and in evaluation [20]. As a design input method, it facilitates participants recalling situations, describing why they may be atypical, and highlighting the desired normal operation of an interactive system.

With the *Sonic Incident,* we have adapted critical incident technique to specifically address sound-based memories and experiences. We start by asking workshop participants to remember a particular incident that occurred within the last two days for which the sound was memorable. We guided the participants by encouraging them to think of incidents where the situation was frustrating, surprising, or funny, in which the sound contributed to that situation being memorable. The participants were asked to describe the incidents, the reason why they remembered them, the situation they were in while they heard them, and finally how those particular sounds were related to themselves.

The participants were asked to write a text and/or graphical description of the sonic incidents. As text, it might be a narrative of the event, or a textual description of the sound. As drawings, they could be a pictorial representation of the sound, or a storyboard recounting the incident. In all cases, the exercise required participants, independent of their level of prior experience with sound, to represent the sound in its original situation in words or pictures, and in a non-technical way.

The participants then shared their sonic incidents with the group through vocalization, a standard technique from Sonic Interaction Design. Each participant imitated the sound using their voice and the rest of the group tried to guess what the original sound was. This provides an interesting converse to the text/image description of sound. It required the participant to describe a sound by using sound. The activity remained without technology, and, by using the voice, exploited an intuitive and corporeal mode of sound production.

Imagining sonic interaction

In this part of the workshop we asked participants to imagine possible gestural interactions with their sonic incidents. They did not need to be realistic, and rather could be situations in which they could act upon the sound through their movements, or conversely allowed themselves to be moved by the sound. For this activity, we adopted two strategies to invoke corporeal engagement with sound in different iterations of the workshop.

A first strategy was based on the actions in sound (Parsons workshop). We gave the following task "*To see what actions and reactions the sound may provoke in you or in the space around you.... getting from the sound itself to its effect and to the actions that may cause it.... Sketch this interaction between the sound and your actions ... and how do you think this can happen.*" This task encouraged participants to focus on sound and action, and to explore interaction beyond volitional control.

A second strategy encouraged participants to think about having agency over sounds from their sonic memories (Paris, London and Zurich workshops). We introduced the metaphor of "*Superpowers*" asking participants to imagine themselves as all-powerful beings who could create and act upon sounds. The task was: "*Imagine you have super powers and through action with your body, you can manipulate the sounds/situations described previously in the sonic incident. So, look at your sonic incident, and imagine what happens and how it happens. It doesn't have to be realistic.*" This version of the task intentionally introduced volitional control as a mode of sound/gesture interaction.

Phase 2: Realization

The second phase of the workshop was an activity where the participants created functioning technology prototypes to play out their imagined sonic interactions. We created breakout groups where each group selected one imagined scenario from the set of sonic incidents described in the ideation phase in order to implement it.

Gestural Sound Toolkit

We provided a hardware/software toolkit to realize gestural sound interactions (Figure 1). The toolkit includes gesture sensors, and software tools for motion data processing, mappings and sound synthesis. The system affords real time, continuous interaction where sound is sculpted and modified live as movement is performed.

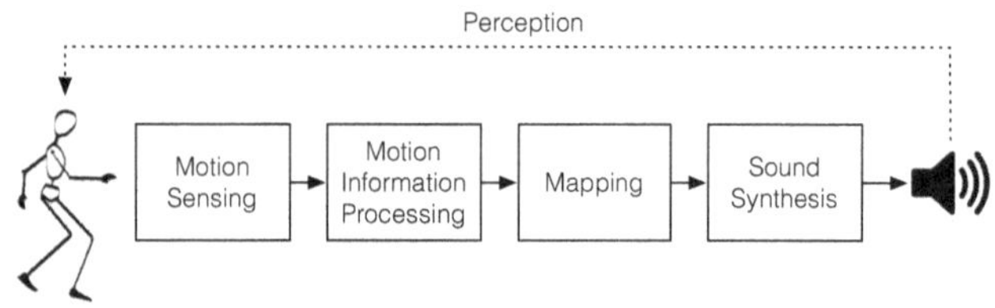

Figure 1. Architecture of the Gestural Sound Toolkit

The sensing hardware was chosen to minimize object-based affordance and cultural association [1,37]. To do so, we chose to use a small sensor to provide a suitable representation of the gesture, not too complex in order to be understood by the participants, non-specialist in motion sensing. We used the Axivity Wax[1], a miniature (the sensor is about the size of a thumbnail), low power wireless 3D accelerometer (see Figure 2) with a sampling rate of 100Hz.

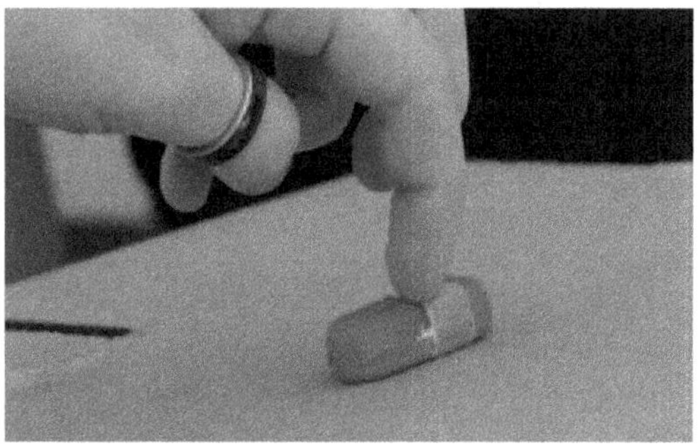

Figure 2. Sensing hardware used in the workshops

The software part of the toolkit was designed to allow participants with no background in interactive sound design, programming, or working with sensors to author forms of continuous sound manipulation through gesture. The software is a collection of high-level modules that can be freely linked to each other. These modules are the following:

- *Receiver module:* receives motion data from the sensing hardware.
- *Analysis modules:* analyze and process the accelerometer data. A Filter module can be used to reduce noise. The Energy module extracts gestural energy from the incoming signal. Velocity was calculated by computing the derivative. A Machine Learning module performs gesture recognition and neural network regression [9]. An Impact Detector, senses percussive gesture from the accelerometer signal.
- *Synthesis modules:* allow pre-recorded sounds (from the sonic incidents) to be played and manipulated. The toolkit integrates temporal modulation (scrubbing). A trigger module allows for triggering a sound from a sound bank. A manipulation module allows sound to be sculpted and modified live as movement is performed.

The toolkit uses the Max/MSP visual programming environment[2]. Our library is available online and open for contribution[3] and is based on the FTM[4] and MuBu[5] libraries. A screenshot is reported in **Figure 3**. This architecture allows sound selection, triggering, and most importantly continuous manipulation of amplitude, pitch, and effects, articulated from user or object movement as captured on the sensors. The sensors are mounted by workshop participants on part of the body, on objects, or in the environment, as imagined in their scenarios.

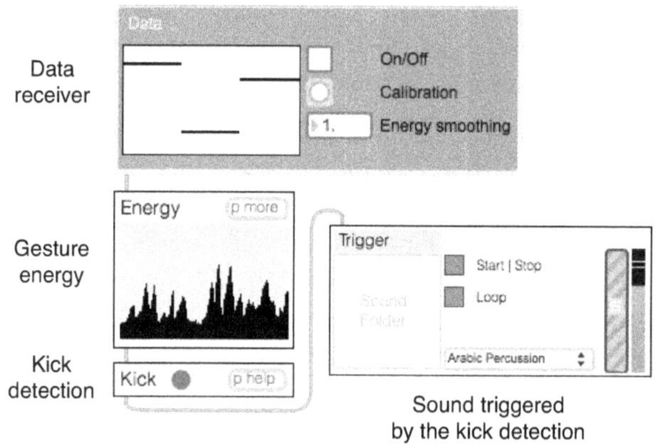

Figure 3. Gesture Sound Tookit software, showing modules which can be interconnected and reconfigured

Group Activity

The Gestural Sound toolkit was presented in a tutorial introducing general notions of gestural sound interaction followed by a short session where participants build simple interaction examples. With this basic guidance, each group created a storyboard of their chosen scenario and implemented using the toolkit. The participants were asked to define, find, or record sounds to be used, and define the actions or gestures involved in the interaction, and the consequences of these gestures on the sounds based on the imagined situation that has been chosen. This was done with minimal guidance from the workshop facilitators, who guided the participants in basic operation of the system and

[1] http://axivity.com/v2/index.php?page=product.php&product=wax3

[2] http://www.cycling74.com

[3] https://github.com/bcaramiaux/Gestural-Sound-Toolkit

[4] http://ftm.ircam.fr/index.php/Main_Page

[5] http://imtr.ircam.fr/imtr/MuBu

its technological constraints. The workshop ended with live performance and demonstrations of the final prototypes to the group, and a general discussion.

Data collection and analysis

All workshop activities were filmed. We collected graphical and textual descriptions from participants of their sonic incidents and scenarios. Two authors performed the analysis and annotated the videos against the graphical and textual descriptions. They then generated a table describing each step from sonic incidents (columns) to the realized project for each participant in each group (rows). This table was the basis to identify emerging interaction strategies. Finally, each participant completed a questionnaire at the end of his or her workshop.

RESULTS

Phase 1

This section presents results from the ideation phase of the workshop, participants' sonic incidents and imagined sonic interactions.

Sonic incidents

All participants across the four iterations of the workshop were able to describe one or two sonic incidents, with several describing more than three incidents.

Of the 61 total sonic incidents, and 57 were sounds produced by non-human events from the everyday. Of these, 20 sonic incidents referred to transport situations: "beep before tube's doors closing", "squeaking doors in the bus", or "bike hitting a manhole". 14 sonic incidents referred to domestic situations: "bubbling of oil while cooking", or "stormtrooper wake up alarm impossible to stop". Two other categories are: environmental sounds such as "wind" or "rain" happening in a particular situation such as "rain at the train station"; and electronic sounds such as "Skype ringing" while not being in front of the computer. Human-produced sonic incidents mostly involved social situations (8 sonic incidents) referred to such situation, for example "children playing football.

Every sonic incident involves a sound that was not produced by the participant but that happens in a situation in which the participant was an observer.

Interaction scenarios with sonic incidents

The second activity encouraged participants to imagine scenarios where they could actively interact with the sounds evoked in the sonic incident. We used two different strategies to invoke corporeal engagement with sound: 1) Sound interaction without volitional control, and 2) Volitional control using the superpowers metaphor.

From the set of 15 interaction scenarios generated by the first strategy, we took the textual description of the sound incidents and the subsequent interaction scenarios and traced their evolution.

- 9 scenarios are (graphical) **representations** of either the cause of the sounds or the actions on the sound on the participant. For example, reported Figure 4, a sonic incident was a "*Stormtrooper wake up alarm impossible to stop*" for which the interaction representation was a sketch with arrows pointing down and a pushing mechanism, an abstract view of the effect of the alarm on the participant.

Figure 4. Sketch of sonic incident: *Stormtrooper Alarm*, showing effect of being awoken by an alarm clock

- 3 scenarios described **reactions** of the participants after hearing the sound from the sonic incident. For example, a sonic incident was "*cats jumping after [the participant] steps on it"* and the interaction scenario was "*stepping on cat, cat reactions* [sound]*, my movements in reaction to the cat's reactions*" (Figure 5). These produced reaction scenarios kept the same situations in which the sonic incident occurred.

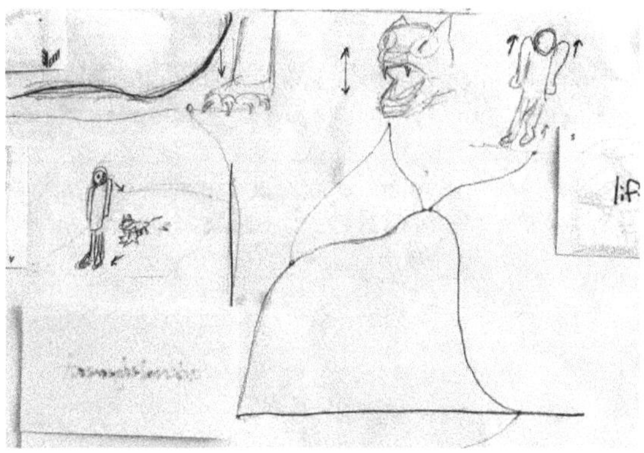

Figure 5. Sonic incident as reactions: *Stepping on Cat*, a series of reactions, first by cat, then of the user to the sound

- 1 scenario describes the **manipulation** of sound from body movements. The sonic incident was "*Squeaking ventilation in the workshop room*" and the imagined was a "*man controlling characteristics of sound by moving*"
- 2 are scenarios that are not related to the earlier sonic incidents. For example the sonic incident was "*Car's tires on wet asphalt*" and the imagined scenario was "*Springs connected together playing Jingle Bell*".

From the set of 26 interaction scenarios generated using the superpower strategy, we performed the same analysis, tracing the evolution from textual description to interaction scenarios. We observed differences across the scenarios imagined, finding that 22 scenarios involve both the sound and the situation in which the sound takes place in the corresponding sonic memories, while only 4 used just the sound, isolated from its initial situation. Of the former, we found differences in how the participants relate body movement to the sound material.

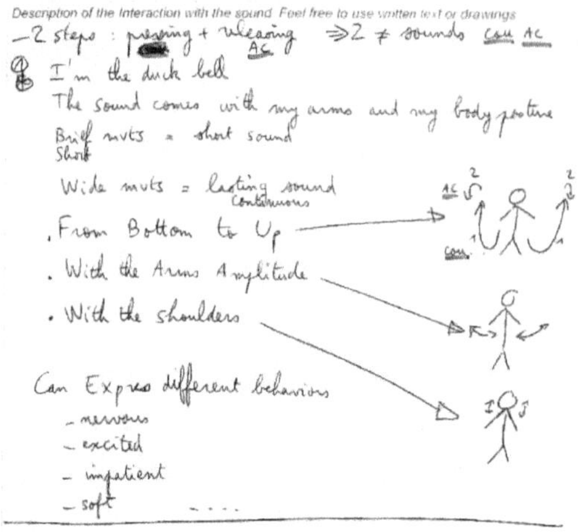

Figure 6. Substitution as interaction scenario: *Duck Honk*, user becoming the duck

- 3 scenarios described movements that **substitute** the sound or the cause of the sound. For example, a sonic incident was "*Duck honk on the bike that was inappropriate"* and the interaction scenario was "*Being the duck, limbs control different qualities of squeaking*" (Figure 6).
- 7 scenarios described gestures that **manipulate** sound parameters. For example, a sonic incident was "*Walking in the woods, snow cracks under his feet, breaking ground"* and the interaction scenario was "*Sound: Crack + Swoosh + thud; with actions: Crack/Crush by moving the fist + slide and stop using legs*" (Figure 7).

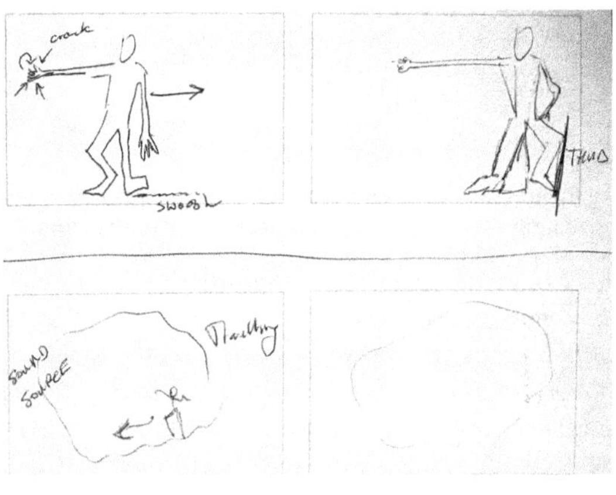

Figure 7. Manipulation in interaction: *Snow Cracks*, limb movements crushing snow, zooming into imagined actions

- 7 scenarios described movements that **conduct** sounds. This differs form the previous case by the existence of an explicit gesture vocabulary. For example, a sonic incident was "*Annoying sounds of neighbors' children playing"* and the interaction scenario was "*Transforming children's screams in music by conducting them as a musical conductor*".

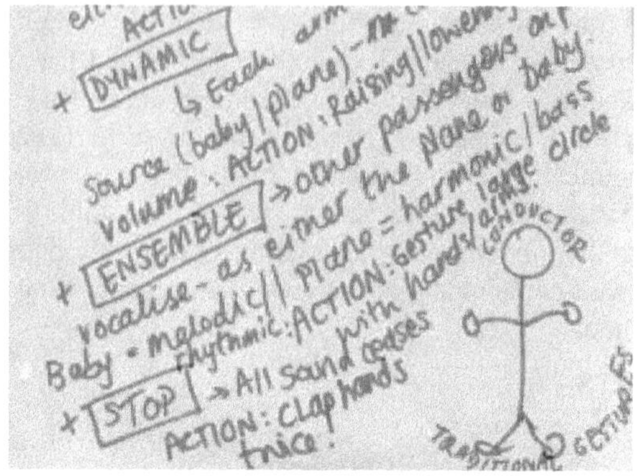

Figure 8. Reaction in interaction: *Laser Destroy Alarm* where a user's gesture conducts sound in reaction to sonic incident

- 3 scenarios described **reactions** of the participants after hearing the sound from the sonic incident (similarly to Workshop 1). For example, a sonic incident was "*Phone alarm + Clock alarm failing to wake her up"* and the interaction scenario was "*Destroying loud alarm with laser vision explosion*" (see Figure 8).
- The two last scenarios involved **unrelated relationship** to the actual sonic incident even if using the sound and situation. For instance, a sonic incident was "*Sizzling sound of oil in fraying pan"* resulted in the unrelated the interaction scenario, "*Sound to navigate through locations"*.

The strategy used in facilitating embodied sonic interaction, therefore had an impact on the action–sound relationships imagined by workshop participants in their interaction scenarios.

Phase 2

In the realization phase, each breakout group chose one scenario from their group to develop into a functioning prototype. They first created a realizable interaction scenario by storyboarding it, describing actions, sounds and interactions. They then recorded or searched online databases for sounds that approximated the sound of the incident. With this, they authored a movement/sound interaction using our hardware/software toolkit.

Despite the potential difficulty of working with interactive sound software, the high level abstractions and workflow of our gestural sound toolkit was generally well understood by the participants. During all the workshops, the participants were highly independent and asked for help from the facilitators only when they wanted a software feature that was not included in the toolkit, for instance a sound synthesis engine such as sine wave generator (IRCAM). This was facilitated by the modular architecture of the toolkit and also by working in breakout groups.

During the four workshops, 14 projects were realized. In 13 cases, participants produced fully working prototypes that were presented to the whole group, while in only one case participants were not able to complete a final implementation. In complement with this, only one project was realized without using sound material from the sonic incident activity in the first phase. Although all the 12 other projects made use of a recalled sound from sonic incidents, the final projects made different uses of the situation in which the sound from the sonic incident occurred.

There were two types of project – those that implemented a scenario, or part of a scenario, from the ideation phase, and others that implemented a scenario that used only the sound from the sonic incident and implemented a totally different situation and interaction than originally imagined.

Of the first type of project (8 total), an example includes: "*Hum of airplane revealed by baby crying*" and imagined "*conductor gestures, e.g. dynamic responding to raising/lowering hands*" as interaction mode. The prototype recognized three gestures. The first one triggers the hum of airplane, the second one start a baby crying, the last one stops the sounds. In this case, the participants found sounds in the Freesound[6] online sound database. During the demonstration, the participants placed the sensor on the hand. Accelerometer data was low-pass filtered to take out noise and then sent to the gesture recognizer. The recognized gesture was used as a selector for a sound in a playlists and subsequently played. This shows a conducting situation.

In another example, the sonic incident was "*vibration ring of phone on a shelf while sleeping*", which was characterized as "*wrong rhythm, it was like a call, instead it should have been like an alarm*". The imagined interaction was the "*Snooze action to fall asleep again and creating a sound that would suggest me as being awake while still sleeping".* The group implemented a scenario in which after the clock alarm is heard, moving (mimicking the movement in the bed) against the clock activates a "snoozy melody". Subtle movements change the speed of the melody played back to help waking up. When moving towards the clock, the alarm sound plays back to wake up the user. Here, participants substitute the alarm mode of operation through actions related to sleep.

Of the second type of project (4 total), examples include a sonic incident "*Sound of filling water bottle, changing*" where the participant represented the action linked to the sound as "*Bottle being filled with water*" changing the pitch. The implemented prototype gives different sound feedback (based on the recorded sound sample of water poured in a bottle) according to the position of the arms. This resulted in an application, the "Yoga corrector" that facilitates adapting body position during a yoga exercise according to sound feedback similar to the rising pitch of the filling water incident. The sensor was strapped on the arm or on the leg. They used the variations in orientation of the sensor to control the reading cursor and pitch transposition. This shows how participants manipulated sound parameters through their actions.

[6] http://freesound.org

From the 12 projects, of the two types, we found that the prototypes involved actions that conduct the sound, substitute to the sound cause or manipulate the sound. No interaction scenario from the first phase that involved actions in reaction to sounds was retained for implementation. Interestingly, all were from the workshops where the superpowers metaphor was used. We infer from this that the use of technology to realize scenarios has an effect on previously imagined action–sound relationships and is dependent on the metaphor (actions in sound or the metaphor of superpowers) used in the task from the first phase.

DISCUSSION

We have presented a series of workshops that investigate participatory and sound-centered methods for the design of sonic interactions. This approach proposes the sonic incident technique, and the notion of sonic affordances, as parts of an ideation process for generating ideas for embodied sonic interaction. Importantly, the methodology leverages on a non technology-centered approach for authoring action/sound relationships. From the proposed methodology, we highlighted three types of actions-sound relationships in the final prototypes: actions that conduct sounds, substitute the sound source, or manipulate sound parameters. Here we discuss the methodological contributions presented in this paper and we show that the workshops provide interaction models for sonic interaction design.

Sonic incidents and sonic affordances

The sonic incident technique was successful in facilitating users' thinking about sound in context. Participants tended to describe sounds that happen to them rather than sounds that they cause. The technique makes the participants aware of why sound was an important part of the incident, why they remember it and what would be the normal situation with this sound [28]. Each sound is thus contextualized in an idiosyncratic situation from participant's everyday life. Engaging the everyday of the participants is an important conceptual aspect of the technique as it can provide a context of use through the sonic incident itself. As such, sonic incident can be thought as a technique that could facilitate the design of situated interaction (as defined in [5]). With Sonic Affordance, we propose the notion that sound can invite action. It was explored in the second part of the Ideation phase of the workshops by asking participants to imagine corporeal engagement with the sonic incident.

The small, non-descript, sensing technology became a "non-object" that served a function without carrying a physical affordance. Objects afford user actions based on their form factor, shape, size, and textures. Similarly, sound can have prior cultural association, such as musical context in identifiable instrument sounds. By using a miniature sensor, the sensing technology itself did not offer physical affordances to influence the interaction imagined. By working with sound from the everyday, we minimized musical association that may have colored the resulting gestures. In so doing we were able to use the workshops to drive participants to focus on the affordances from the sound itself and not the interface used, hence, *Sonic Affordance*. The concept of a Sonic Affordance is useful as a way to think about the corporeal response that a sound may invite on the part of its beholder.

Participants in general were not accustomed to imagining interactive scenarios with sound. A critical aspect of the ideation process was therefore to aid the participants to think about acting in the situation of the sonic incident. Mentioning actions in relation to sound did not lead the participants to involve the body in the interaction. The metaphor of superpowers was more successful in generating physical action–sound relationships in the imagined sonic interactions. We used this metaphor in three workshops (Goldsmiths, IRCAM and Zurich), and interestingly faced questions about the meaning of the task. Participants were questioning from which perspective they have to imagine the interaction: "*Can I be the sound?*" or "*Am I listening to the sound?*".

Methodological contribution

In our workshop procedure, the ideation phase takes place without computers. This encourages participants to focus on sounds and their context, without influence of technology. Interactive technology is introduced only in the subsequent realization phase, after sounds, incidents, and scenarios have already been imagined. The sonic interactions imagined, therefore, were not technology-driven. The creation of the scenarios has been grounded in the concepts of sonic incidents, resulted affordances and imagined interaction scenarios.

Figure 9. Physical constraints in the use of the Gesture Recognition System, the sensor is placed on the foot

Workshop participants were able to take the sonic interactions imagined in phase 1 and implement them using our toolkit. They overcame limits in their own technical knowledge to nonetheless use machine learning techniques in their prototypes. They were also tactful in working around limitations and constraints of the technology. For example in one prototype, participants transformed the physical space, creating an obstacle course to walk through to more clearly send distinct foot gestures and slowing down the user's walk to aid the recognition module of the toolkit in distinguishing gestures to trigger different floor crackling sounds (Figure 9).

It was a challenge to present advanced sound programming and interaction authoring techniques as just one part of a workshop program. Given that the workshop participants had no prior experience with the Max/MSP software, we were mindful that the workshop not become a tutorial on use of that software. The library of high-level modules we designed is effective in giving access to powerful, reconfigurable sound interaction functionality in a highly accessible manner.

Emerging interaction models for sonic interaction design

In the three workshops where volitional control of sound was explicitly mentioned, the scenarios that were generated showed interaction scenarios involving movements that *substitute, manipulate,* and *conduct sounds*, and their technology implementations capture user movements that reflect this. We propose these action/sound relationships as interaction models for sound. More precisely, these interaction models are described as:

- **Substituting**: the movements substitute the cause of the sound or the sound itself. Possible actions are defined by the sound itself and not constrained by an interface. Then there is a direct modulation of some aspect of the sound (volume, brightness, playback speed) by the participant's actions.
- **Manipulating**: where movements manipulate the sound. The possible actions in interaction should be let to the choice of participant/user. They can be constrained by the interface. Then there is a direct modulation of the sound through the participant's actions, similar to the previous model.
- **Conducting**: there is a semantic relationship between the participants' gestures and the sound. The gestures should be free to be chosen by the user but they are, eventually, part of a finite set of gestures (a vocabulary). Then there is a direct relationship between a symbolic feature of gestures (what gesture, how it is performed) and the sound.

These three interaction models provide respectively unique operational descriptions that can be used by interaction designers or developers to build innovative sonic interfaces that respond to particular contexts. Further, interaction designers can use these models to characterize interaction according to descriptive (incorporating existing interaction techniques), generative (facilitating new interaction techniques) and evaluative (comparing techniques) powers [5] and therefore to enhance the specificity with which they respond to a given sonic interaction design problem.

These models enhance the design process by describing distinct approaches to the design of a sonic interface, establishing criteria that can be used in the early stage assessment of a sonic design problem. The substitution model focuses the designer on sound and its source; manipulation addresses controllable aspects of sonic artifacts, such as instrumental control; and finally conducting introduces the symbolic and semantic meaning of gestural interaction with sound.

The models are further distinguished by the way in which they can be evaluated: while conducting and manipulating may involve quantitative measures to compare interaction techniques (time completion, accuracy), substituting necessitates a qualitative explanation of the relevance of chosen actions to an associated sound, its cause and its context.

Innovation in sonic interaction design

Norman and Verganti [30] argue that human centered design tends to produce incremental innovations that are constrained by users' past experiences. They further argue that radical innovation requires technological change or meaning change. The work presented does not introduce technological change: accelerometer sensors are commonly available and gesture recognition algorithms in the toolkit had been developed in our prior research. Meaning change, however, is explicitly addressed, by encouraging participants to think about, discuss, and manipulate sound through our methodology. Our method aids workshop participants without specialist audio engineering or musical training to work with sound, representing a change in meaning of sound for those participants. The process identifies sonic incidents and translates them into embodied interaction concepts and prototypes. Differences in the emphasis in the task (volitional or non-volitional), led to different interaction scenarios and models. This method can be replicated, and leveraged, by designers to expand the meaning and utility of sound in consumer device interaction.

CONCLUSION AND FUTURE WORKS

In this paper we presented a series of four workshops that explore the rich potential of action–sound relationships and their use in designing interactive systems where sound is a fundamental part of the interaction. The workshop structure is comprised of ideation activities including the *Sonic Incident* technique as well as graphical, textual and vocalized sound representations; followed by realization activities including scenario building and prototyping. Participants generated final projects that implemented three principal interaction models: *conducting*, *manipulating* and *substituting*. These three interaction models can be operationalized by interaction designers and developers building innovative sonic interfaces and products.

Sound in the user interface has heretofore been made up mostly of sound bites, events and triggers. The sonic interactions of the sort presented here involve continuous interaction between physical action and sound, putting the user in an action–perception feedback loop. Each of the three models described above is the basis for an interaction strategy within this feedback loop, which can help designers build better sonic interfaces that respond to specific circumstances and contexts. Together, these methods and interaction models can help designers to address sound as a continuous and informative phenomenon in the interface rather than as a simple display mode for alerts.

The research presented in this paper will be useful for interaction designers to conceive future products that integrate sound in the interface in a robust and continuous fashion. The proposed interaction models are not limited to sonic applications and might be considered for interaction with other continuous phenomena, such as light, and moving image. These interaction models fit into interaction paradigms that go beyond the desktop to objects, environments, and sounds, in our everyday lives.

ACKNOWLEDGMENTS

The authors would like to acknowledge the support of the Provost's Office and the Parsons School of Design Strategies at The New School. The research has received funding from the European Research Council under the European Union's Seventh Framework Programme (FP/2007-2013) / ERC Grant Agreement n. 283771.

REFERENCES

1. Altavilla, A., Caramiaux, B., and Tanaka, A. Towards Gestural Sonic Affordances. *Proc. NIME'13*, (2013), 61–64.
2. Augoyard, J.-F. and Torgue, H. *Sonic Experience: A Guide To Everyday Sounds.* McGill-Queen's Press - MQUP, 2006.
3. Avanzini, F., De Götzen, A., Spagnol, S., and Rodá, A. Integrating auditory feedback in motor rehabilitation systems. *Proc. International Conference on Multimodal Interfaces for Skills Transfer (SKILLS)*, (2009), 53–58.
4. Beaudouin-Lafon, M. Instrumental interaction: an interaction model for designing post-WIMP user interfaces. *Proc. CHI*, (2000), 446–453.
5. Beaudouin-Lafon, M. Designing interaction, not interfaces. *Proc. Working Conference on Advanced Visual Interfaces AVI,* (2004), 15–22.
6. Burns, C., Dishman, E., Johnson, B., and Verplank, B. "Informance": Min(d)ing future contexts for scenario-based interaction design. Presented at BayCHI. 1995.
7. Caramiaux, B., Bevilacqua, F., Bianco, T., Schnell, N., Houix, O., and Susini, P. The Role of Sound Source Perception in Gestural Sound Description. *ACM Transactions on Applied Perception 11*, 1 (2014), 1–19.
8. Caramiaux, B., Françoise, J., Bevilacqua, F., and Schnell, N. Mapping Through Listening. *Computer Music Journal 38*, 3 (2014), 34–48.
9. Caramiaux, B. and Tanaka, A. Machine Learning of Musical Gestures. *Proc. NIME*, (2013), 513–518.
10. Dourish, P. *Where the action is: the foundations of embodied interaction.* The MIT Press, 2001.

11. Ekman, I., Rinott, M., and Box, P.O. Using Vocal Sketching for Designing Sonic Interactions. *Proc. DIS*, (2010), 123–131.

12. Flanagan, J.C. The critical incident technique. *Psychological bulletin 51*, 4 (1954), 327–58.

13. Franinović, K., Gaye, L., and Behrendt, F. Exploring Sonic Interaction with Artifacts in Everyday Contexts. *Proc. ICAD*, (2008), 1–4.

14. Franinović, K., Hug, D., and Visell, Y. Sound Embodied: Explorations of sonic interaction design for everyday objects in a workshop setting. *Proc. ICAD*, (2007), 334–341.

15. Franinović, K. and Salter, C. The Experience of Sonic Interaction. In S. Franinović, Karmen, Serafin, ed., *Sonic Interaction Design*. MIT Press, 2013, 39–75.

16. Franinović, K. and Serafin, S. *Sonic Interaction Design*. Mit Press, 2013.

17. Gaver, W. The SonicFinder: An Interface That Uses Auditory Icons. *Human-Computer Interaction 4*, 1 (1989), 67–94.

18. Gaver, W.W. What in the World Do We Hear?: An Ecological Approach to Auditory Event Perception. *Ecological Psychology 5*, 1 (1993), 1–29.

19. Goodman, S. *Sonic Warfare: Sound, Affect, and the Ecology of Fear*. MIT Press, 2009.

20. Hartson, H.R. and Castillo, J.C. Remote evaluation for post-deployment usability improvement. *Proc. Working Conference on Advanced Visual Interfaces AVI*, (1998), 22–29.

21. Henriques, J.F. The Vibrations of Affect and their Propagation on Night Out on Kingston's Dancehall scene. *Body Society 16*, (2010), 57–89.

22. Hermann, T. and Hunt, A. An introduction to interactive sonification. *IEEE Multimedia 12*, 2005, 20–24.

23. Hermann, T. *Sonification for Exploratory Data Analysis*. University of Bielefeld, 2002.

24. Houix, O., Gutierrez, F., Susini, P., and Misdariis, N. Participatory Workshops : Everyday Objects and Sound Metaphors. *Proc. CMMR*, (2013), 41–53.

25. Hug, D. Using a systematic design process to investigate narrative sound design strategies for interactive commodities. *Proc. ICAD*, (2009), 1–8.

26. Kramer, G., Walker, B., and Bargar, R. Sonification report: Status of the field and research agenda. *International Community for Auditory Display*, (1999).

27. Leman, M., Desmet, F., Styns, F., Van Noorden, L., and Moelants, D. Sharing musical expression through embodied listening: A case study based on Chinese Guqin music. *Music Perception 26*, 3 (2009), 263–278.

28. MacKay, W. Using Video to Support Interaction Design. *Tutorial CHI*, 2002.

29. Maes, P.-J., Leman, M., Palmer, C., and Wanderley, M.M. Action-based effects on music perception. *Frontiers in psychology 4*, 1 (2014).

30. Norman, D.A. and Verganti, R. Incremental and Radical Innovation: Design Research versus Technology and Meaning Change. *Design Issues 30*, 1 (2014), 78–96.

31. Pauletto, S., Hug, D., Barrass, S., and Luckhurst, M. Integrating Theatrical Strategies into Sonic Interaction Design. *Proc. Audio Mostly*, (2009), 1–6.

32. Rasamimanana, N., Bevilacqua, F., Bloit, J., et al. The Urban Musical Game: Using Sport Balls As Musical Interfaces. *Proc. CHI EA'12*, (2012), 1027–1030.

33. Roby-Brami, A., Van Zandt-Escobar, A., Jarrassé, N., et al. Toward the use of augmented auditory feedback for the rehabilitation of arm movements in stroke patients. *Annals of Physical and Rehabilitation Medicine 57*, (2014), e4–e5.

34. Rocchesso, D., Polotti, P., and Monache, S.D. Designing continuous sonic interaction. *International Journal of Design 3*, 3 (2009), 13–25.

35. Shneiderman, B. *Designing the User Interface: Strategies for Effective Human-Computer Interaction*. Reading, MA: Addison-Wesley, 1998.

36. Svanaes, D. and Seland, G. Putting the users center stage: Role playing and low-fi prototyping enable end users to design mobile systems. *Proc. CHI*, (2004), 479–486.

37. Tanaka, A., Altavilla, A., and Spowage, N. Gestural Musical Affordances. *Proc. SMC*, (2012), 318–325.

38. Varela, F.J., Thompson, E.T., and Rosch, E. *The Embodied Mind: Cognitive Science and Human Experience*. MIT press, 1991.

39. Zatorre, R.J., Chen, J.L., and Penhune, V.B. When the brain plays music: auditory--motor interactions in music perception and production. *Nature Reviews Neuroscience 8*, 7 (2007), 547–558.

Repurposing Conversation: Experiments with the Continuous Speech Stream

Donald McMillan **Antoine Loriette** **Barry Brown**
Mobile Life Centre, Stockholm University, Sweden
[don, antoine, barry]@mobilelifecentre.org

ABSTRACT
Voice interaction with mobile devices has been focused on hands-free interaction or situations where visual interfaces are not applicable. In this paper we explore a subtler means of interaction – speech recognition from continual, in the background, audio recording of conversations. We call this the 'continuous speech stream' and explore how it could be repurposed as user input. We analyse ten days of recorded audio from our participants, alongside corresponding interviews, to explore how systems might make use of extracts from this stream. Rather than containing directly actionable items, our data suggests that the continuous speech stream is a rich resource for identifying users' next actions, along with the interests and dispositions of those being recorded. Through design workshops we explored new interactions using the speech stream, and describe concepts for individual, shared and distributed use.

INTRODUCTION
The success of commercial speech interfaces – such as Apple's Siri, Google's Now, and Microsoft's Cortana – has highlighted new possibilities for speech interfaces, particularly on mobile devices. Yet HCI research into speech has been somewhat conflicted, with some claiming that HCI speech research is having a "middle-life crisis" [3], and that HCI researchers have been insufficiently opportunistic with new possibilities for speech interfaces. In this paper we attempt to explore one new approach for speech interfaces making use of always-on ambient sound recording as an input to system behaviour.

Using the "continuous speech stream" (CSS) we explore if and how systems could use speech recognition to pre-empt user actions, support activities without disrupting them, and draw on shared repositories of others' recognised speech. Most current commercial speech systems focus on a *dialogic* model of interaction, where users enter a dialogue with a system, where speech results are recognised for immediate system activity, with spoken responses, and the possibility for further dialogue. Yet recent advances in battery life and signal processing offer the possibility of systems that continually listen to natural conversation, and can conduct at least partial recognition on that speech to detect keywords, or even attempt transcription. With the opportunities of technologies such as smart watches or other wearable devices (such as the Motorola Hint earpiece), clear audio recording of everyday conversation is also easier to foresee (although with some serious privacy issues). Technically, this offers opportunities for systems that could modify and change their behaviour based on a users' implicit spoken interaction with others. For example, phones could automatically carry out actions based on spoken audio – searches could be opportunistically run and displayed on lock screens, adverts could be better based on user activities, and models of user behaviour could make use of richer descriptions of users' lives.

We explore currently available open source speech recognition software with which we were able to recognise keywords from a previous recorded corpus, suggesting potential for future implementation. The paper then moves on to study system opportunities for using a 'continuous sound stream' (CSS). We recorded day-long audio streams from ten participants, and manually partially transcribed the stream to explore pre-emptive system functions. Interviewing participants we explored possible automatic system actions from the CSS. Two design workshops produced a set of potential design concepts based around individual, collective and distributed use of the speech stream. In conclusion we discuss the relevance of our findings for speech as an interface more broadly.

BACKGROUND WORK
Automatic speech recognition (ASR) is broadly defined as the translation of spoken words, or an acoustic waveform containing speech, into a string of words [8]. In modern ASR speech is modelled as a mixture of acoustic and language properties [2]. The acoustic models attempt to move from audio samples of speech to potential phonemes being spoken, and from these phonemes to possible words. While speaker independent speech recognition is possible, acoustic model accuracy increases by up to three fold if they are trained on a specific speaker [26]. These have traditionally been implemented as Hidden Markov Models [20] however there is an increasing interest in using Deep Neural Networks [7] for greater accuracy and performance.

CHI 2015, April 18 - 23, 2015, Seoul, Republic of Korea.

ACM 978-1-4503-3145-6/15/04...$15.00.
http://dx.doi.org/10.1145/2702123.2702532

The language model provides the probability of a specific sequence of words occurring given a particular form of speech – such as news, lectures or conversation. This is used in conjunction with the output by the acoustic model to identify the spoken phrases which are most likely to be correct [8]. Constraining the vocabulary of the model is used to increase the identification rate for systems like telephone interfaces [4] and controlling subsystems in a car [13]. Larger, yet still constrained, models are used for tasks such as Internet search and calendar management [22]. The advantages of such a system are that with a tightly defined language model recognition rates can be greatly increased. Constraining the vocabulary can improve the accuracy between 50% and 80% [4].

A much more difficult task for speech recognition is to consider less constrained speech, such as inter-personal conversations, where the language model is expected to encompass the totality of the language being spoken and the speech itself is more natural in both content and context – meaning that the speech will contain fillers, such as 'um', words that run together, and the audio stream itself will include more background noise [2]. In such situations the error rate rises considerably – however it is improving with Kingsbury *et al* [11] reporting an accuracy of 32% in 2001 and Povey *et al*, reporting 55.7% in 2011 [19].

Speech in HCI

Speech has been used as an input in HCI in a number of ways. The most common are dialogic systems where the user interacts with the system as part of a conversation, such as Siri. These are now commonly available on consumer devices. There has been research on improving the interface for speech dictation, by making it more immediate and interactive [14] and controlling a traditional touch and click based UI using speech input has also been tried in systems such as SpeechAct [28].

Using speech as a secondary input for information retrieval, for example automatic transcription and indexing of voice mails [25] and meetings [24] has received considerable research. Beyond transcription, problems such as topic extraction, detection of conversational 'hot spots', and recording speaker decisions have been addressed [23]. Speaker diary recording and role recognition can provide information on the number of people in a conversation and show the flow of conversational control from one to the other. Speech audio can also be examined to label instances of fillers and laughter. Systems where the speech is used in the background are rare, however one such example is the Ambient Spotlight [10] where supporting documents were retrieved to match the current topic in an ongoing meeting. It is also possible to perform tasks such as 'mining' sociometric data [27] to understand the social connections of subjects. This has been done with continual listening on mobile devices to extrapolate the audio levels and sound characteristics of social activity and to detect patterns of social interactions between users [6].

Working with Recognised Speech

Building on work that process the audio into text, and annotating it with other features, it is also possible to employ natural language processing to analyse the text extracted. There are many approaches that can be used, in particular text summarisation approaches, covered in detail by Lloret & Palomar [15], which support extraction of key phrases and words from text. One simple approach is to extract the *subject* term from sentences. This can be done with a fairly high accuracy – over 90%.

THE CONTINUOUS SPEECH STREAM (CSS)

As noted by Aylett [3] there is an apparent divide between HCI practitioners and speech technologists – however they also note that there are opportunities to improve user experience by using speech technologies. One identified area of research that has had less focus is how a system might make use of users' conversations in the background. That is to say, using spoken conversations that are not directed at a device but that are picked up incidentally by listening to users' interactions with others.

Our interest in this was sparked by earlier research we conducted which used mobile phones to record audio and screen interactions with the phone. Even though our intent was to understand interaction with phones, we found that we also incidentally collected surprisingly legible person-to-person audio from conversations conducted around the phone. This led us to consider whether speech could be extracted from background audio and used as a resource for systems and applications. For example, could an application detect when a user might run a search on their phone from their conversation. This would require a speech recognition system that could detect *topical resources* from conversation, grammatical structures such as *objects, subjects,* and *nouns.*

Exploring the Technology

We conducted two tests – one based on previously recorded data of natural speech in the wild, and another on an open source speech corpus. The situational audio data we used in the first test was recorded by the microphone on a GoPro camera around the neck of a participant while in conversation recorded from a previous user trial. This audio was segmented into 2 - 10 second clips of speech, based on voice activity detection carried out using the Bob library [1]. Each of these clips was submitted to the, undocumented yet public, Google Speech API. Submitting our conversational clips, totalling 56 minutes of spoken audio, returned either an indication of no speech detected, or incorrectly recognised text. The clarity of speech in the audio for ASR needs to be much higher than could be processed from our source, which included environmental audio from the city as well as the speech. The very nature of the speech we were trying to recognise – spontaneous, bursty and often unstructured – was inherently difficult for ASR to transcribe accurately suggesting that a keyword spotting approach may provide better results.

For our second test we used an open source corpus of human speech, the VoxForge database (voxforge.org), with the Sphinx (speech.cs.cmu.edu) open source speech recognition system. We compared giving a list of keywords to the Sphinx recogniser (which were used in the recognition algorithm), with a keyword spotting system based on using Google Speech API and filtering the output to only include the keywords. This keyword list comprised of the 30 most common bigrams and trigrams (2 and 3 word phases) in the VoxForge dataset.

When processed through the Google Speech API we found 28% of the keywords in the source were detected, with a 83% precision. Using Sphinx gave performance in a range between a 63% detection rate with 24% accuracy and a 35% detection rate with 64% accuracy.

Speech recognition benefits greatly from one dedicated microphone per speaker, increasing the signal to noise ratio (SNR), which has a large impact on the accuracy of the recognition. Training on a particular speaker also increases accuracy, suggesting that a personal approach should be taken excluding others' speech. However, with the large amount of investment going into applications such as Google Now, Siri and Cortana, we are confident that the technical challenges for improving recognition of human-human communication are being met with advances in fields such as noise-robust and missing-feature ASR.

Defining the stream

While a CSS system could be possible, it is still beyond the publically available state of the art. To explore the design space we experimented with a two stage process for working with audio. In a working system ASR would provide a transcript of the spoken words and phrases. As noted above, the quality of the audio, volume of the speech and training on a particular person's voice has a great impact on the accuracy of the automatic speech recognition. Taking this into account we decided that only the owner of the device would have their speech transcribed, background conversations and conversation partners would be ignored in their stream. For the second stage we determined that natural language processing would be used to extract *subjects* and *objects* of speech, filtering out personal pronouns, for inclusion in the stream. We also decided to include *time phrases* and *numbers* wherever they appeared grammatically given their utility. Such processing of an ASR transcript we deemed to be computationally feasible. We note that the attributes of the ASR and the NLP stages could be tuned to include or exclude a number of attributes – grammatical, aural or statistical – however this definition was compatible with both our goals for design and privacy. Not providing a full transcription, not promising accuracy of recognition, not providing timestamps – all of these were to introduce ambiguity, uncertainty and therefor deniability into the system.

METHODS

For our experiment we had three research questions:

1. Can information be extracted from the continuous speech stream which is representative of the users day?
2. Are there common system actions (such as search) that could make use of terms from the speech stream?
3. What applications more broadly could we build that would make use of the speech stream?

Our first step was to obtain a collection of continuous speech streams, recorded from a variety of individual's ordinary days. Participants wore a lapel microphone mounted onto their clothing, with small digital audio recorders worn on the belt or in a pocket. We recruited ten participants who agreed to carry audio recorders over the period of a day, recording their spoken conversations. For privacy reasons we allowed participants to stop and start the recorder at will, and also offered to delete any sections from the audio that the participants did not want to share with us. This provided us with a small but rich dataset of naturalistically recorded speech. Six of our participants were recruited via a dedicated participant recruitment website and compensated with a cinema gift card, the remaining four were recruited from our extended social network. Participants ranged from an architect, an elementary school teacher, a brand consultant, a special needs carer and a mystery shopper. All participants were requested to inform those around them that they were recording and to wear the microphone openly during the day. Four participants recorded a day during which they were not working, six participants recorded a weekday comprising of work and after work.

The worn microphone setup meant that we did record talk that was not by the participants themselves, although for the experiment we focused on the speech of the main participant – simulating the accuracy enhancement of a speaker dependent system.

We manually simulated two technical stages – speech recognition and subject extraction. It was likely that our manual approach provided a much more accurate extraction that could be obtained automatically so we would be experimenting with a 'best case' scenario of speech recognition and language abstraction.

This produced a word list from the day for each participant, covering all the topics spoken about over this period. This let us provide a summary that could be used by our participants to reflect upon their day and the contents of the speech stream without having to read a complete transcription. These words also represent an automatic analysis of the speech stream that systems could potentially be built upon.

We interviewed the participants using the word list as prompts. This let us explore participants' reactions and how the list summarised their day by asking them to describe

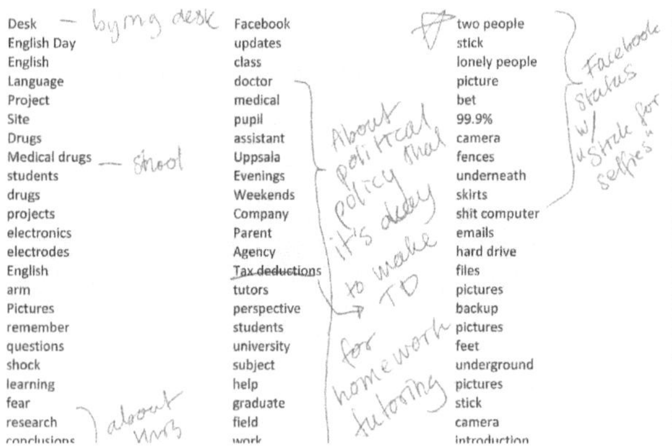

Figure1: Sample CSS annotated during participant interview

their actions and interactions first without, then with access to the list. We also explored any system actions they might want to be automatically performed on those words. We covered how the participants would feel about a system listening to their speech – and how this related to the recordings we were carrying out for the trial. We then discussed the participants experiences in using a mobile device in conversation, and the relationship between their spoken conversations and any actions they carried out on their phone (such as searches, diary entries or phone calls).

Lastly, for seven of the participants we asked them to look through a sample of other participants' word lists and to describe how they perceived the events taking place and the personality and demographic of the subject.

Trial results

The longest day recording was of 12 hours, with a mean of 7.4 and a median of 8.5. The number of words processed ranged from 287 to 1,405 words, and from 228 to 1,291 unique words (median 525, average 585) recorded and transcribed into the sample streams.

The transcribed items were then coded for topical and semantic content. An initial set of 500 randomly selected items was independently coded by two researchers using a data centric technique allowing for classifications to emerge from the data naturally. A coding scheme was then agreed upon containing 11 categories, into which all unique items were independently coded. Mismatches were discussed and resolved after the coding was completed.

The categories, with their percentage of unique keywords in parentheses, are *Action (7%), Body (6%), Communication (4%), Food (9%), Leisure (8%), Numbers (6%), People (15%), Place (11%), Items (10%), Time (7%), Work (12%), and N/A (7%).* Just from the initial spread of items we can see some patterns emerge. In talking about people they, understandably, each have their own names which are unique to our list and increase the size of that category. Work as well contains a lot of domain specific items.

Looking at the wordlists individually we can see contextual domination of categories, for example one participant who recorded a day of picnicking with friends had a wordlist containing 24% in food and leisure, a second participant on a workday in his architecture firm produced a list containing 23% work related terms, with a further 9% related to places. Our recruitment agent participant produced 32% on work and people, and one participant who recorded a romantic evening returned a list with 37% of the 1,405 items taken up with leisure, people and places.

We counted a total of 2,502 unique English words and while this is somewhat large for a speech recognition keyword dictionary, dictionaries in the thousands of words have been shown to be successful in recognition [17]. This suggests that building a keyword list for each user alongside a model of their speech would lead to increased precision over time. The word lists give an overview of what was talked about by the participants on these days.

Interviews

The interviews were conducted for between 40-90 minutes and explored their use of mobile devices, the interpretation of the stream with regards to their memory of the day in question, any likely straightforward system actions they would want to carry out on stream words, and their interpretation of the stream of another person. Participants were encouraged to annotate their CSS as they discussed their recorded day with us, the results of which can be seen in Figure 1. All the interviews were fully transcribed.

We look at the results of the interviews in five sections by topic. First we examine their experiences being recorded. In the second section we focus on *using the stream.* Following that we discuss the implications for and effects of *memory and recollection* and the different *activities and people* that the stream helps to identify. We finish this section with an analysis on how the *streams of others* are interpreted.

Experiences with being recorded

Due to the self-selection inherent in any trial such as this it may be unsurprising that the general consensus of the participants was that being recorded was not a great cause for concern. However, on reflection a number of our participants reported some lingering awareness of the recording taking place, with a couple reporting a change in their activity as a direct result. One participant consciously didn't say the name of a confidential client during the recording, even if he was working on this client's project for the whole day.

"I didn't say the name, because it is, the client is a secret client, but Oliver [his co-worker] said it all the time."

There was also some concern as to the projected image of themselves that would be produced by a transcript of everything they say in a day.

"I was a little apprehensive, because I thought, Oh God, everyone's going to know how stupid I am all the time."

But most of our participants reported some degree of normalisation to the process, with half of them reporting that in some way the recording device was forgotten at least

Action	Number	Examples
Search	53	Blister, Suits
Add to calendar	24	Sushi, happy birthday
Show map	1	Mariatorget
Remind later	23	Calligraphy, check email
Others	3	Skybar, Humlegarden

Table 1: Desired Actions Based on Wordlist

for part of the time. Most of our participants discussed the recording taking place with the people they were talking to throughout the day, partly as a way of explaining the visible lapel microphone and partly as a disclosure that the other party may be recorded – although the speech from anyone but the participant was not transcribed it was at least partly listened to in the production of the stream. Only one participant reported that they were requested to stop the recording, the reactions from others were mostly ambivalent.

It was also noted by our participants when reviewing their streams that the periods of time without any keywords, when they were working or alone, were longer than expected.

Using the Stream

Our initial design ideas for the use of the CSS centred around better supporting interaction with the mobile device during speech. We ask participants if there were any terms of the list that they would like to have their phone automatically process in some way – such as showing a search result from a term that was spoken. We also asked for items to potentially place in their calendar, for places that could be viewed on a map, for items to be reminded of, and lastly any for other automatic functions they would want to be performed based on an item in the list. An overview is shown in Table 1.

All of our participants expressed a hesitance to use their mobile devices in conversation. While they had all experienced the phenomena of either using their device or having another party use a mobile device in a conversation which they were a part of it was universally described as something that they didn't want to do – let alone encourage or make easier.

The concept of delayed interaction with the device, queuing up topics for later enquiry, was more acceptable to our participants. However, presenting the list of words and asking for likely actions resulted in a fairly small set of selected terms. Moreover, many of the terms that were selected for phone-based operation were ambiguous and it is difficult to see how they could clearly map to automatic actions. For example, "happy birthday" refers to a date that the participant would have wanted recorded in their calendar, but in the wordlist itself there is no record of when that date would actually be. That said, around 10 items were selected to be searched on per day by each participant, representing a potential use case.

Memory and Recollection

There has been a longstanding interest in systems that can help with memory formation, but also in recollection of events, notably with the work carried out using the SenseCam [9] – an automatic wearable camera. In the interview the participants were all asked to first describe their day including who they talked to and what they talked about, they were then given the same task with access to their personal ambient speech stream from that day. Every participant drew on the words to illustrate and narrate their day, describing events that they said they would have missed without the list of terms. However this was not a straightforward reading of the keywords and describing what had happened, there was considerable work done by the participants to reconcile what was placed in front of them with their memory of the day in question.

Again, this is similar to the SenseCam [9] studies, and our participants reported that they remembered more about their activities during the day simply as a result of the novelty of being recorded and taking part in the trial. Our participants also recalled more events when recreating their day through their stream than before they were exposed to it.

> *"I missed so much in my original summary of my day."*

Much of the stream was recognised and supported the participants' memories of the day in questions. There were three different types of supported recall that we noticed in our participants. The most simple was the recollection of an interaction that had been forgotten.

> *"...even ones that like 'enormous worm' and I was like what is that? But then I obviously remembered the funny moment."*

We also saw examples of participants correcting their memories in various ways. The order of events, as noted by Sellen, was something that was plastic in the memory of our participants. One participant reported surprise that a particular conversation happened on that day, and using this information was able to also correct her recollection of the person to whom she had told that particular story.

> *"Oh yeah, hang on, I think I was telling, was that that day?"*

The length of time certain topics were discussed was also something that we saw corrected as our participants re-interpreted their day through the lens of the keywords. One participant in particular reported a conversation over lunch where he was talking in derogative terms about his boss alongside discussing 'life, and everything' with his friend. When he examined the keyword stream of this particular conversation he was forced to re-evaluate the conversation:

> *"I cannot believe it. It's crazy, we talk so much about work."*

This could be that the more enjoyable, interesting and uncommon conversation topic became the most memorable part of the lunch, superseding the work conversation. This is also an example of how access to a record of the conversation caused a re-evaluation of the experience. Up until this point the conversation over lunch was described positively, a pleasant memory of a wide-ranging conversation with a friend. After the speech stream was interrogated this experience became one of reflecting on the amount of time and energy spent on work related topics even out-with the working environment.

> *"Oh, now I remember where 'delicious kids' came from [...] we were talking about eating their artwork, 'Delicious, kids.'"*

This final example shows the ambiguity of meaning in the CSS where the removal of large parts of the speech and timing has changed the meaning at first read.

Activities and People

We noted that certain terms were repeated by a number of the participants, on a global level these were related to their dominant activity from their work, study or hobby – individual words like *mascara* for the cosmetics brand manager or the word *facade* for the architect, or cooking topics for the school teacher (who cooked as a hobby).

These terms could also be used to identify conversational partners – participants talked about how particular topics went together with those they were talking about:

> *"I was back to Eva because of the botox [...] that was the discussion with Joel that always turns around the same thing."*

Conversations surrounding work were littered with jargon or codes for some while for others revolved around specific topics – yet for all the participants that used the recording device at work the identification of these portions of the stream was easy. They were also able to assign differing clusters of keywords to the same anecdote recited to different people. Specific pieces of information relating to activities were identified, with features such as starting times, durations and locations easily tied to a particular event – be that one in the planning stage, or one that took place on the day of the recording. A clear example of this was before meal preparation or eating, where the stream would contain numerous food related words.

Lastly, lists of options were also easily identifiable from the stream. The particular conversation pattern consisting of listing a number of options of the same genre for consideration by the other party produces a dense and informative section of the stream showing the options, then their narrowing until a choice is made.

These lists are different from the patterns of keywords that identify the pre-purchase activities of evaluating the relative merits of one purchase vs. another. This follows work in marketing which has discussed how products and advertisements can come to have an involvement in conversation [21]:

> *"if I'm talking about something to have a good offer come up [...] usually when I Google and those first sponsored links, I use a lot."*

Streams of Others

From the second round of interviews the participants were shown the stream of others, what was most interesting about this exercise was the manner in which our participants approached the problem of interpreting the partial streams of others.

> *"This must be a girl that right here. It's the first person. It looked like it's a person that is a bit stressed about the age because talking about Botox all the time and her legs."*

They worked to simultaneously build a model of the user who created the stream and to understand the context around the words presented to them through that model.

Lessons

From these wide ranging observations and analysis we distilled a number of important characteristics of the CSS to be fed back into our design dialog.

- Activities and interests were identifiable where prospective actions such as search were not.
- Both people and activities have identifying keyword clusters.
- Lists of options produced by planning future activities are easily recognizable.

DESIGN PHASE

While these interviews and the topic lists gave us some insight into the speech stream itself, our goal was to explore future design opportunities using the stream. Accordingly, we ran two design workshops based around the data. In the first we asked five professional designers (1 digital design team leader, two post-doctoral industrial designers and 2 junior designers) to generate design concepts, using the topic lists as input to imagined systems. This workshop involved: (1) reading through the word lists to understand the technology, (2) comments on the word list (3) concept generation around systems that could use the lists (4) discussion of possibilities for sharing lists. We selected stories from the interviews as prompts to the design, printed on cards, to seed the designs in the workshop. In the second design workshop we repeated this method ourselves, again going through the word lists and interview data to suggest potential systems drawing on the interviews and further refining the design concepts that arose in the first design workshop.

We categorized the concepts these workshops generated into three different categories based on who the stream of the user is shared with. *Personal* designs are those where the stream is kept between the user and the application or service provider. *Shared* designs are ones where a stream is published, uni- or bi-directionally. Lastly, *distributed* designs are those in which a large number of streams are aggregated, transformed or shared to provide a service.

Personal Stream Designs

We outline three sections of this area and give examples of applications of services in each to better make our case that the proposed ambient speech sensor stream is an interesting design proposal and worthy of future research and development.

Pre-Input

The first ideas we generated were around the use of these streams as a resource for pre-input, that is using the words heard in conversation to prepare for device use by either pre-launching applications, pre-searching for information or images, or preparing calendar entries for use when the user turns their attention to the mobile device. Terms used in speech could also be used for auto-complete fields used when entering text. For example, a navigation application could listen for addresses spoken and offer these as options when entering a destination address. Words spoken could also be used to manage the text entry dictionary on a phone keyboard, and to offer to autocomplete words that have been spoken recently.

Memory Aids

One of the most straightforward uses of this information would be in the area of memory aids, life logging and quantification of self. The amount of conversation taking place, the topics (work related or personal), and the counts of certain words can be used for a number of self-reflective purposes. The use of images recorded though out the day using a wearable camera as a memory aid have been shown to be successful [9], extending this to the conversations people have would be an interesting comparison. Such word counts and graphs can also be used in language learning, to quantify progress and suggest areas of vocabulary for further study. However in this space there are also more performative and playful applications for this technology that can be explored. Extending the language learning example to provide real time synonyms and antonyms could be used as an enabling technology for the production of amateur rap music, and – possibly more practically – the stream surrounding taking of a particular photo could be embedded within the photograph in tags, or even visualised to give additional context to the photo.

Qualified Self

While there has been recent interest in techniques for quantifying activity in an array of sense-able areas, in contrast the CSS offers possibilities for systems that can *qualify* that experience. We might call this the 'qualified self' – models and systems that make use of the concepts and terms spoken as part of our activity, rather than reducing this to what can be easily measured. So, for example, relationships can be examined for their qualitative attributes, such as the common topics of conversation and their similarities to other relationships, as well as their quantitative qualities of duration and frequency. A system could even offer suggestions for when a conversation became difficult, or was likely to engage with difficult topic areas. Since there is the potential with the CSS to track the semantics of activities one could also imagine a system attempting to intervene if a user started on activities they had declared they wanted to reduce. More playfully, we could imagine systems that record experiences to present personal collages of activity, or to expand ones social network through tracing and suggesting new activities.

Shared Stream Designs

Our second set of concepts focused on applications that could exploit sharing the stream with other users.

Awareness

We envisage two main ways in which the awareness of others can be enhanced using the ambient speech stream. First would be the active sharing of a length of time in the style of the "Glympse" (http://www.glympse.com) application for location sharing. A user could send the stream of their current situation to a loved one as part of an explanation of their lateness or to share a meeting with mutual friends with one who is not present. The second concept we explored was active reading, where the participants of a meeting or class could allow their streams to be accessible during that time to others on the class list. This would allow those arriving later to avoid topics that have been discussed, or prepare for what is currently under discussion in the room as they are arriving.

Subscription

The nature of the word lists we experimented with is that they condense and remove many details from what is spoken, which introduces some inherent ambiguity but also mediates some of the privacy concerns our participants had. This opens the possibility of subscriptions to the streams of famous people, giving a personal glimpse of their life that is filtered through the persona projected by them in the media. The sharing of not-so-famous people can also be envisaged, given the opportunity to self-publish feeds people could follow a group learning the same language for vocabulary tips or a fresh produce buyer for information on what is in season. Friends and family could also be subscribed to in order to increase awareness and connectedness, with simple filters set up to alert when two people are talking about the same topic or say each other's name for example.

Performance

The performative aspects of creating such a stream also offer opportunities for design. Along with the sharing of snippets of the stream from certain personal experiences such as birthdays or sports events and attaching them to other media users have the opportunity to manipulate their streams by altering their speech. This could be used in any number of ways, from showing your affiliation to a genre of music or a particular band to friendly, playful competitions to see who can manipulate their stream to match those generated by inputting the lines of a movie from their favourite character.

Distributed Stream Designs

Lastly, we discuss the opportunities afforded when a number of streams are shared and aggregated to provide a service. These are not only end user systems, but can provide value for the corporations producing or managing the streams.

Matching & Prediction

Chalmers [5] points out that the order and temporal structure of activities can provide a deep insight into the character of the user and pointers to predict use. While in that work the examples were generally confined to location, it is possible to expand this to include a historical vector of context built from the topics and keywords identified in an ambient stream. The main problem identified by Chalmers' was that sparsity of data could have a negative affect on the quality of recommendations. Using a corpus of many users' speech streams the comparison of vectors of topics and keywords would allow recommendations to be made of topics those with similar conversation trajectories had touched upon. This matching could also be used in a more playful, or possibly profitable, manner by introducing these sensors to the online dating community. An application could use the number of overlapping topics of conversation as a metric for the compatibility of a potential partner.

Perhaps the most obvious application for this sort of recommendation is advertising, in that the speech stream could be used to target or personalise advertisements. While few might be happy about advertisers having access to their private conversations, it might be possible to compensate a sample group who could be recorded. Through correlations with other data, such as websites visited, connections between the sample group's spoken topics and already widely tracked data could be found. We acknowledge that targeting advertising based on the contents of private conversations would be considered by many (ourselves included) as somewhat sinister, regardless of any potential benefits. We thus need to proceed with some caution around applications here, even if end users are properly informed or compensated.

Events tracking

A more straightforward application area is for the tracking and identification of events and users activities using their spoken conversation. So, one of the clearest signals in the word streams was before a visit to a restaurant where multiple food related terms could be detected in the stream. Similarly before activities (such as sport events) there would be a cluster of words related to the event itself. One obvious suggestion from this would be the possibility of offering suggestions or making recommendations for particular establishments at an appropriate time. With access to multiple users streams a system could even predict future congestion by multiple users attending the same event, or going to the same restaurant.

Similar to our earlier playful suggestion of being able to follow a friend or partner's stream we could imagine being able to follow the stream from a particular place. The text stream could aggregates the conversations taking place – providing for those who do attend a record of their interaction with a particular event and for those who are not in attendance a glimpse into the atmosphere through their projected experience of attending.

Talkthrough

One of the most interesting possibilities for even a small percentage deployment of such a system would be the ability to extract information on the topics of conversation in an area to form a new type of demographic. For advertisers this would lead to a new metric, the "*talkthrough*". It would allow those serving adverts to be alerted to the number of situations where keywords from their advertisement, be they the brand name or a other salient feature of the product, have entered the conversation of the viewer. Moreover, the detectable pre-purchase routines discussed earlier would allow advertisements to be specifically targeted to those who are in the market for a competing product and to track if that consumer considered, talked about, or even bought the alternative.

On a similar note, the action of polling an area or demographic for a sentiment could be augmented by allowing polling agencies to purchase the number of occurrences of certain words or phrases in a specific area or within a specific demographic group over a period of time. This could be used to measure statistics such as the dissemination of marketing campaigns or the political engagement of voters on a particular topic.

PRIVACY

There are a number of areas of concern in this regard when the deployment of the underlying technology that would enable the systems outlined above is considered. That our self-selected trial participants voiced some discomfort with being recorded suggests the problems that such systems might face with regards to the concept of being listened to at all times. However we note that systems listening continuously seems to be acceptable, at least to some, with this functionality now commercially available in both Android and iOS platforms. The recent release of commercial home appliances which continuously listen such as Amazon's Echo and The Ubi (theubi.com) not only signposts the acceptability of such listening services to consumers, but highlights the need for research in understanding the implications of their deployment. Confidential information being inadvertently disclosed during the use of this system was one such concern, with one of our participants modifying his speech to not include the name of a particular client. In mitigation of this risk a system could offer users control through word, concept filter or context [12] filtering, or by obscuring new or unexpected content in some way until it is approved.

There is considerable ambiguity in the keyword stream, so on one hand the potential for a user to be held accountable for a particular topic of conversation is lower than it would first appear. This, of course, is taking the continuous speech stream as an isolated data point. When combined with other sources of data it provides yet another point of triangulation. For example, the combination with location data and time could add enough context to a keyword to strongly suggest an action. The other side of the ambiguity of the stream is the potential for topics, or even errors in recognition, to be taken out of context causing concern and embarrassment:

"Porn [...] I think we were perhaps joking about something, but I can't remember exactly [...] I really wouldn't want to share that word with family."

This could be to do with the novelty of such close and continuous surveillance, however it has been shown that these concerns can drop over time – even among those opposed to such surveillance – as familiarity with the technology increases [18].

Broader Concerns

More broadly, the prototypes suggested here are in some senses personal surveillance systems. The use of the distributed system not to help pollsters and advertisers, but to alert government authorities to the people and places involved when 'subversive' discourse is taking place is easily envisaged. It is even possible that such technologies are already used by security services. For example, the electronic privacy information centre used a freedom of information request to obtain a list of 'trigger words' that the US department of homeland security uses as signs of terrorism. There are also organisations, such as Stratign (statigen.com), that sell GSM intercept systems that both break GSM encryption on calls and watch for particular 'trigger phrases' in speech or text. These concerns do not stop with official access to the data, the service provider using the data for a purpose unforeseen by the end user is another risk that must be mitigated.

The everyday speech of the user is more personal a resource than either location or app usage. Not only must the lessons learned in giving users graduated control of there exposure be applied in this area, the underlying implications that the device, and through it the service provider, is continuously listening must be dealt with honestly and openly if there is to be any chance of these technologies being accepted. We plan to include a participatory design phase in future work to better understand both users' current understanding of their aural privacy, and how we can design to empower them when it is threatened by emerging technology. The idea of control and empowerment of users through ensuring their understanding of logged location data and use data has been positioned [16], and expanding this work to more potentially invasive systems is also a goal for the future.

CONCLUSION

In this paper we have explored the design opportunities presented by a continuous speech stream. By manually producing 10 such naturalistic day-long streams we explored how the topics of everyday speech relate to the actions of our participants. We then, though a process of design workshops with designers, developed three areas for further research and application development. In future work we propose to move further on the exploration of these areas, starting with the Personal Stream area of applications. For applications of this sort it would be possible to conduct a real-time Wizard of OZ user test of any produced applications, exploring in detail how the pre-input and pre-search applications would be used either during or after conversations.

We have discussed the feasibility and practicality of deploying such a system, and while it may seem difficult to justify the development effort for any one of the applications outlined above, the opportunities presented when they are taken as a suite of possibilities are much greater. The possibility to track the spread and flow of conversation topics would give a new and exciting metric for the understanding of how topics, brands and idioms are placed in the public consciousness. By leveraging this against the consumer facing applications of this technology the expense of development and deployment becomes a much more attractive opportunity.

We have opened up the design space by projecting a very ambitious goal for speech technology, however with regards to the call for HCI researchers to bound their expectations of speech technology put forward by Aylett *et al* [3] we note that each of the designs for systems put forward above could be build upon a specific, and therefor more tractable, speech technology solution.

Despite the privacy and ethical concerns of an entity having access to a significant proportion of the conversations spoken by their users on a regular basis, the opportunities presented by speech recognition technologies go far beyond the simple dialog-based interactive systems that are the mainstream today. In this stream there is a possibility to get access to and provide much more reflective and personal services in a way we have rarely seen before. With such a personal, nuanced and malleable source – the day to day conversations of the user – the envisaged speech stream would enable whole new genres of services and applications from the playful to the powerful.

REFERENCES

1. Anjos, A., El-Shafey, L., et al. Bob: a free signal processing and machine learning toolbox for researchers. In *Proc. of the 20th ACM international conference on Multimedia* (2012),1449-1452 ACM.
2. Anusuya, M. A. K., S. K. Speech Recognition by Machine, A Review. *International Journal of Computer Science and Information Security*, 6, 3 (2010), 25.
3. Aylett, M. P., Kristensson, P. O., et al. None of a CHInd: Relationship Counselling for HCI and Speech Technology. In *CHI '14 Extended Abstracts on Human Factors in Computing Systems* (2014),749–760 ACM.
4. Boyce, S. and Gorin, A. User interface issues for natural spoken dialog systems. In *Proc. of The International Symposium On Spoken Dialog*, 96(1996), 65–68.

5. Chalmers, M. A Historical View of Context. *CSCW Journal*, 13, 3 (2004), 223-247.

6. Chon, Y., Lane, N. D., et al. Understanding the coverage and scalability of place-centric crowdsensing. In *Proc. of the 2013 ACM international joint conference on Pervasive and ubiquitous computing* (2013),3-12 ACM.

7. Hinton, G., Deng, L., et al. Deep Neural Networks for Acoustic Modeling in Speech Recognition: The Shared Views of Four Research Groups. *IEEE Signal Processing Magazine*, 29(2012), 82-97.

8. Jurafsky, D. and Martin, J. H. *Speech and Language Processing (2Nd Edition)*. Prentice-Hall, Inc., Upper Saddle River, NJ, USA, 2009.

9. Kalnikaite, V., Sellen, A., et al. Now Let Me See Where I Was: Understanding How Lifelogs Mediate Memory. In *Proc. of the SIGCHI Conference on Human Factors in Computing Systems* (2010),2045–2054 ACM.

10. Kilgour, J., Carletta, J., et al. The Ambient Spotlight: Queryless Desktop Search from Meeting Speech. In *Proceedings of the 2010 International Workshop on Searching Spontaneous Conversational Speech* (2010),49–52 ACM.

11. Kingsbury, B., Saon, G., et al. Robust speech recognition in Noisy Environments: The 2001 IBM spine evaluation system. In *Proc. of 2002 IEEE International Conference on Acoustics, Speech, and Signal Processing* (ICASSP) (2002),I-53-I-56.

12. Klasnja, P., Consolvo, S., et al. Exploring privacy concerns about personal sensing. In *Proc. of Pervasive Computing,* Springer (2009), 176-183.

13. Kuhn, T., Jameel, A., et al. Hybrid in-car speech recognition for mobile multimedia applications. In *Proc. of Vehicular Technology Conference*, 1999 IEEE 49th (1999),2009-2013 vol.2003.

14. Kumar, A., Paek, T., et al. Voice Typing: A New Speech Interaction Model for Dictation on Touchscreen Devices. In *Proc. of the SIGCHI Conference on Human Factors in Computing Systems* (2012),2277-2286 ACM.

15. Lloret, E. and Palomar, M. Text summarisation in progress: a literature review. *Artificial Intelligence Review*, 37, 1 (2012), 1-41.

16. Morrison, A., McMillan, D., et al. Improving consent in large scale mobile HCI through personalised representations of data. In *Proc. of the 8th Nordic Conference on Human-Computer Interaction* (2014),471-480 ACM.

17. Nouza, J. and Silovsky, J. Fast keyword spotting in telephone speech. *Radioengineering*, 18(2009), 665–670.

18. Oulasvirta, A., Pihlajamaa, A., et al. Long-term effects of ubiquitous surveillance in the home. In *Proc. of the 2012 ACM Conference on Ubiquitous Computing* (2012),41-50 ACM.

19. Povey, D., Burget, L., et al. The subspace Gaussian mixture model—A structured model for speech recognition. *Computer Speech & Language*, 25, 2 (2011), 404-439.

20. Rabiner, L. and Juang, B.-H. An introduction to hidden Markov models. *ASSP Magazine, IEEE*, 3(1986), 4–16.

21. Ritson, M. and Elliott, R. The social uses of advertising: an ethnographic study of adolescent advertising audiences. *Journal of Consumer Research*, 26, 3 (1999), 260-277.

22. Starner, T. E., Snoeck, C. M., et al. Use of Mobile Appointment Scheduling Devices. In *CHI'04 Extended Abstracts on Human Factors in Computing Systems* (2004),1501–1504 ACM.

23. Tur, G. and Mori, R. D. *Spoken language Understanding: Systems for Extracting Semaintic Information*. John Wiley, 2011.

24. Waibel, A., Schultz, T., et al. SMaRT: the Smart Meeting Room Task at ISL. In *Proc. of the IEEE International Conference on Acoustics, Speech, and Signal Processing* (2003), vol.754.

25. Whittaker, S., Hirschberg, J., et al. SCANMail: A Voicemail Interface That Makes Speech Browsable, Readable and Searchable. In *Proc. of the SIGCHI conference on Human factors in computing systems* (2002),275–282 ACM.

26. Woodland, P. C. Speaker adaptation for continuous density HMMs: A review. In *Proc. of the ISCA Tutorial and Research Workshop on Adaptation Methods for Speech Recognition* (2001).

27. Wyatt, D., Choudhury, T., et al. Inferring Colocation and Conversation Networks from Privacy-sensitive Audio with Implications for Computational Social Science. *ACM Transactions on Intelligent Systems and Technology*, 2(2011), 7:1–7:41.

28. Yankelovich, N., Levow, G.-A., et al. *Designing SpeechActs: Issues in Speech User Interfaces* (1995), 369–376 ACM Press/Addison-Wesley Publishing Co.

The CADENCE Corpus: A New Resource for Inclusive Voice Interface Design

Maria K. Wolters, Jonathan Kilgour
School of Informatics
University of Edinburgh, UK
maria.wolters|j.kilgour@ed.ac.uk

Sarah E. MacPherson
Human Cognitive Neurosciences
University of Edinburgh, UK
sarah.macpherson@ed.ac.uk

Myroslava Dzikovska, Johanna D. Moore
School of Informatics
University of Edinburgh, UK
m.dzikovska|j.moore@ed.ac.uk

ABSTRACT
Papers on voice interfaces for people with cognitive impairment or demenita only provide small snapshots of actual interactions, if at all. This is a major obstacle to the development of better interfaces. Transcripts of interactions between users and systems contain rich evidence of typical language patterns, indicate how users conceptualise their computer interlocutor, and highlight key design issues. In this paper, we introduce the CADENCE corpus and outline how it can be used to stimulate replicable research on inclusive voice interfaces. The CADENCE corpus is first data set of its kind to include rich data from people with cognitive impairment and free for research use. The corpus consists of transcribed spoken interactions between older people with and without cognitive impairment and a simulated Intelligent Cognitive Assistant and includes comprehensive data on users' cognitive abilities.

Author Keywords
Voice interfaces; spoken dialogue systems; dementia; cognitive impairment; repliCHI; assistive technology

ACM Classification Keywords
H.5.2. User Interfaces: Voice I/O

MOTIVATION
In this paper, we present a reusable data set for HCI research, the CADENCE corpus, a rich collection of multimodal interactions between an Intelligent Cognitive Assistant (ICA) that helps users interact with a simple calendar system and older people, people with mild cognitive impairment, and people with dementia. All interactions are stored in a format that allows others to query the data, add new layers of annotation, and reanalyse the data using different theoretical frameworks. The CADENCE corpus thus goes well beyond the emerging practice of providing access to raw data.

CHI 2015, April 18–23, 2015, Seoul, Republic of Korea.

ACM 978-1-4503-3145-6/15/04 ...$15.00.
http://dx.doi.org/10.1145/2702123.2702372

While many similar corpora exist in Computational Linguistics, including the MATCH corpus of interactions between younger and older people and a simulated appointment scheduling system [4], the CADENCE corpus breaks new ground. Like the MATCH corpus, it contains detailed information about the cognitive abilities of each participant (which most comparable corpora lack), but unlike MATCH, it is the first corpus to include people who have been diagnosed with dementia or mild cognitive impairment. Thus, the CADENCE corpus complements existing work on designing voice interfaces for people with cognitive impairment [10, 14, 18] which focuses on reporting findings, and provides almost no examples of actual interactions for others to (re)analyse.

The CADENCE corpus lends itself to two main types of HCI research, detailed quantitative or cognitive modelling of user actions and discourse analysis of system/user interactions. It can also be used to inform ethnographic studies, technology probes, and user requirements capture.

In the following sections, we summarise the original aims of the CADENCE project, describe the study that generated the corpus data, outline the content of the corpus, discuss limitations, and suggest avenues of further research.

CADENCE

Talking to Intelligent Cognitive Assistants
As people live longer, more older people are likely to develop a form of cognitive impairment [1]. Assistive technology can help these people lead lives that are as full and independent as possible [11, 17]. But no matter how well designed a piece of technology is, some people will still need help using it, in particular those who are prone to forgetting.

ICAs (e.g., [7, 10]) are systems for helping people complete a task successfully. Based on detailed observations, ICAs detect when help may be needed, and use prompts (mostly speech) to guide the user through the steps required to solve the problem that arose. They can be robots, avatars, or, as in our case, disembodied voices.

CADENCE is based on the stochastic COACH ICA framework [6, 7]. The main project goal was to develop guidelines for interactive ICAs that help older people use technology. To that end, we extended COACH with two new dialogue interactions. First, the ICA can ask yes/no questions in order to determine which ability is at the root of a problem. Second, the ICA can recognise and respond to the user's help requests.

Both interactions are designed to ensure the answers can be handled reliably by a speech recognition system. All user utterances are classified into one of four types: "confirm", "disconfirm", "ask_help" and "other". These types were derived from a high-level task analysis and reflect typical dialogue acts in voice interfaces. "Confirm" and "disconfirm" are responses to ICA queries, help requests ("ask_help") are general requests for context-appropriate help, and utterances that do not fall into these categories, such as social remarks or self-talk, are categorised as "other".

The aim of CADENCE was to investigate two key design choices for dialogues with the ICA, initiative and prompt design. In a *system-initiative* approach, the ICA intervenes when a potential problem is detected. With a *user initiative* approach, the ICA waits for the user to ask for help. We compared two *prompt design* options, neutral confirmations versus encouraging feedback. Since we hypothesised that preferred design choices depended on the presence of cognitive impairment, we recruited older people with and without cognitive impairment.

For the design of the CADENCE ICA, we consulted with older people, people with dementia, and informal caregivers of people with dementia. We found that orientation in time was highly relevant for many people, therefore we chose to build an ICA for a calendar system. The key design metaphor for the ICA that emerged was that of a supportive guide.

In order to make it easy for the ICA to observe the state of the calendar app's interface, we implemented our own app on an iPad 2 tablet. Its look and feel resembled normal computer and mobile calendars. It was pretested with older and younger people to ensure it was reasonably intuitive to use.

THE EVALUATION STUDY

The ICA design parameters were evaluated using a Wizard of Oz paradigm [3]. The human "wizard" translated all user utterances into one of the four specified utterance types. Based on this information and data from the calendar app, the ICA decided whether a prompt should be given, and if so, which one. The prompt was then generated automatically, approved by the wizard, and played to users using a highly intelligible computer-generated voice.

Tasks

Each participant interacted with two systems. Participants were divided into four groups (Table 1). Experimenters explained the ICA set up to participants showed a short video demonstration of the calendar system that covered basic functionality, and ensured appropriate breaks. A highly experienced cognitive psychologist worked with people with cognitive impairment.

Participants were asked to complete a simple and a complex task with each system. Complex tasks required more steps and a better understanding of the calendar app. Having looked up an appointment, participants were then asked to write down relevant details.

We developed two sets of tasks that were assigned to ICA 1 and ICA 2 using a Latin Square design. Each task began on the day view for the current date. For the simple task, the target appointment was in the previous or following week, and for the complex task, the target was several months prior to or after the current date.

Table 1. Groups of Systems and Number of Participants in Group. init.: initiative; +: encouraging, 0: neutral tone

	N (Impaired)	ICA 1	ICA 2
1	12 (2)	system init., 0	user init., +
2	11 (3)	system init., +	user init., 0
3	12 (3)	user init., +	system init., 0
4	10 (2)	user init., 0	system init., +

For each task, we measured task completion (completed, not completed, not attempted), task success (maximum score of 5 for simple, 6 for complex tasks), and task completion time. We also logged all page views and button presses.

After participants had interacted with an ICA, they were asked about their experience using a structured interview, which had been designed to be easy to follow for people with and without cognitive impairment. Participants with dementia were additionally debriefed during an informal interview.

Participants

The CADENCE corpus consists of data from 35 participants aged 50 or older without cognitive impairment (Control group) and 10 older participants with mild cognitive impairment or dementia (Impairment group). All participants with impairment were still well enough to live in the community. The sample size was chosen to support conclusions about the main hypothesis with a power of 0.8 for a medium effect size.

The Control group was recruited through a volunteer panel. Participants with impairment were recruited through the Scottish Dementia Clinical Research Network and had been diagnosed with Mild Cognitive Impairment or Alzheimers Disease by a clinician when joining the Network's register. Wilcoxon tests were used to determine whether differences between the participant characteristics of the two groups were statistically significant.

The mean age of control participants and those with impairment was 66 years (Control: SD=9, Impairment: SD=4). Eight of 10 participants in the impaired group were male (80%) versus 12 (34%) in the control group ($p < 0.001$). People with impairments had also spent fewer years in full-time education (Impairment: M=12, SD=3; Control: M=16, SD=3, $p < 0.05$).

All participants completed a dementia screen, the Addenbrooke's Cognitive Examination-Revised (ACE-R,[8]), and a set of four standard tests that assessed their current cognitive abilities. The tests assessed verbal working memory (digit span forwards and backwards [16]), speed of information processing (digit symbol coding [16]), immediate verbal recall (Logial Memory I [16]), and fluid and crystallised intelligence (Wechsler Abbreviated Scale of Intelligence [15]).

Scores on the ACE-R range from 0 to 100, with a score below 88 indicating possible dementia. Our participants with cognitive impairment fall well below that threshold. Participants in

Table 2. Cognitive Test Results. (**: $p < 0.001$ ***: $p < 0.0001$)

	Control	Impairment
ACE-R ***	97 ± 3	75 ± 13
WASI IQ ***	126 ± 9	92 ± 20
Logical Memory I**	$69\% \pm 13$	$38\% \pm 23$
Digit Span***	$61\% \pm 9$	$44\% \pm 10$
Digit Symbol***	67 ± 15	34 ± 17

Table 3. CAAFI Results (.: $p < 0.05$)

	Control	Impairment
Aversion .	2 ± 1	1 ± 1
Attitude	2 ± 1	1 ± 2
Familarity	-1 ± 1	-1 ± 2

the impaired group also score significantly worse on all four cognitive tests than participants in the control group. Results are summarised in Table 2. For ACE-R, WAIS IQ, and Digit Symbol Coding, we give scores; for Digit Span and Logical Memory I, we give percent correct.

We used the Computer Attitude, Aversion, and Familiarity Inventory (CAAFI, [12]) to assess participants' attitudes to technology. The CAAFI consisted of three scales, attitude to computers, aversion to computers, and familiarity with computers. Values range from -3 to 3, with positive values indicating a positive attitude, high familiarity, and low aversion. Overall, the two groups did not differ much. People with cognitive impairment were slightly more averse to computers (c.f. Table 3).

THE CORPUS

The CADENCE corpus consists of four components: participant information; task-related data; detailed transcriptions of the interactions between our 45 study participants and the CADENCE ICA; and a complete log of all system events during each interaction. The corpus is distributed under a Creative Commons Attribution NonCommercial ShareAlike 2.5 License.

The corpus is in NXT format [2]. NXT is a set of libraries and tools that provide for the native representation, manipulation, query and analysis of language data that has been annotated with multiple kinds of information. The free open source NITE XML toolkit is available for researchers who wish to work with NXT data sets. As it is based on XML, it can be read and parsed with a range of tools. It was designed to allow the annotation of speech data with different levels of granularity, from phoneme to speech act. Here, we use two levels of annotation, system events and words.

Participant information includes demographics, cognitive abilities, and attitudes to computers, as described above. Task data include completion, score, time taken, and number of steps required.

In addition to low-level information about the ICA's function, we record three types of events: Sensor, Wizard and Speaker. Sensor events capture information about button presses and page views. Wizard events include the start and end of an interaction, utterances recommended by the CADENCE system, and participant utterance types as entered by the wizard. Speaker events record the time and content of all system utterances.

System:	Have you found what you are looking for?
DF09:	Yes, thank you.
System:	You have finished the task.
DF09:	(hey)
System:	Please write down the answer.
DF09:	Well I am thank you, just be quiet.

Figure 1. Simple Task, System 1, DF09, female participant with cognitive impairment

All interactions between the ICA and our 45 participants were transcribed verbatim using the AMI transcription conventions [9], which were designed to facilitate training speech recognition systems and allow detailed discourse analysis. All filled pauses, hesitations, and nonverbal sounds are transcribed as they occur.

The corpus documents a total of 174 tasks, 34 of which come from people with cognitive impairment. Seven people with impairment completed all four tasks, one completed three, one two, and one person completed only one task. For healthy users, we logged a median of two dialogue acts per task; for users with impairment, we logged 5.5. An excerpt of a brief interaction for a simple task is given in Figure 1.

DISCUSSION

To the best of our knowledge, the CADENCE corpus is the only corpus that contains fully transcribed spoken interactions between older users with cognitive impairment and a (simulated) voice interface. We expect that data will also be useful to researchers who are interested in analysing verbal user feedback to auditory reminders (e.g., [13]). The corpus was produced as part of a larger study and is now distributed separately to stimulate further empirical research and analysis. It is therefore similar in origin and remit to the User-defined Interface Gestures data set, which is intended to stimulate work on interaction gestures [5].

The main challenge was to produce a coherent data set that allows other researchers to query and analyse time-aligned events, user speech, and system speech. Therefore, we captured as much information that would be relevant for the analysis of usage patterns as possible and used the NXT framework to provide an integrated representation of the different data streams.

Since the CADENCE corpus was collected within a controlled experiment, all interactions are limited by the original experiment design. Investigating how users would cope with the inevitable speech recognition and natural language understanding errors of a running system was also outwith the scope of the CADENCE study.

The corpus is not designed to be representative of the way older adults speak with computers. This would require a much larger sample, stratified by dialect, experience with technology, and socioeconomic status. Instead, it shows how early adopters, i.e., older people who are open to research and new technology, might interact with an ICA.

As participants with impairment were recruited through a research network affiliated with the UK National Health Service (NHS), NHS Ethical Approval was required. The conditions of approval prevent us from distributing speech files, which would have been a rich source of further data, because people who knew the participants would have been able to recognise them by their voices. Likewise, we only obtained permission to share transcripts of interactions, but not full transcripts of the interviews.

FUTURE WORK

The rich data recorded in the corpus offer many avenues for analysis for HCI researchers. We are currently annotating the corpus with a more detailed taxonomy of user speech acts, which covers instances of self talk, or cases where users deviated from simple yes/no answers—both of which are difficult to handle. On completion, the new layer of annotation will be made available to the HCI community as part of the corpus. Once analysis of the interview data is completed, we will also add information about participants' views of the systems.

Since the corpus is set up to allow multiple complex layers of annotation, we welcome further annotations by other researchers. For example, one layer might focus on a typology of usability issues with the underlying calendar app, while another layer might seek to classify situations where users tended to ask for help. We are happy to share details of the experiment set up with those who wish to extend the corpus.

ACKNOWLEDGMENTS

Funder: Leverhulme trust, Grant No. F/00 158/CP. We thank our collaborators Jesse Hoey and Marek Grzes and our research assistants Dashiell Oatman-Stanford and Ramune Margeviciute for their invaluable support. Corpus URL: `http://groups.inf.ed.ac.uk/match/Cadence/`.

REFERENCES

1. Alzheimer's Association. 2013 Alzheimer's disease facts and figures. *Alzheimer's & Dementia 9*, 2 (Mar. 2013), 208–245.
2. Carletta, J., Evert, S., Heid, U., Kilgour, J., Robertson, J., and Voormann, H. The NITE XML Toolkit: flexible annotation for multi-modal language data. *Behavior Research Methods, Instruments, and Computers 35*, 3 (2003), 353–363.
3. Dahlbäck, N., Jönsson, A., and Ahrenberg, L. Wizard of Oz Studies - Why and How. *Knowledge-Based Systems 6* (1993), 258–266.
4. Georgila, K., Wolters, M., Moore, J. D., and Logie, R. H. The MATCH corpus: a corpus of older and younger users interactions with spoken dialogue systems. *Language Resources and Evaluation 44*, 3 (Mar. 2010), 221–261.
5. Grijincu, D., Nacenta, M. A., and Kristensson, P. O. User-defined Interface Gestures. In *Proceedings of the Ninth ACM International Conference on Interactive Tabletops and Surfaces - ITS '14*, ACM Press (New York, New York, USA, Nov. 2014), 25–34.
6. Hoey, J., Plötz, T., Jackson, D., Monk, A., Pham, C., and Olivier, P. Rapid specification and automated generation of prompting systems to assist people with dementia. *Pervasive and Mobile Computing 7*, 3 (Dec. 2011), 299–318.
7. Mihailidis, A., Boger, J. N., Candido, M., and Hoey, J. The coach prompting system to assist older adults with dementia through handwashing: An efficacy study. *BMC Geriatrics 8*, 28 (2008).
8. Mioshi, E., Dawson, K., Mitchell, J., Arnold, R., and Hodges, J. R. The Addenbrooke's Cognitive Examination Revised (ACE-R): a brief cognitive test battery for dementia screening. *Int J Geriatr Psychiatry 21*, 11 (Nov. 2006), 1078–1085.
9. Moore, J., Kronenthal, M., and Ashby, S. Guidelines for AMI Speech Transcriptions. Tech. rep., Deliverable, AMI Project, 2005.
10. O'Neill, B., Moran, K., and Gillespie, A. Scaffolding rehabilitation behaviour using a voice-mediated assistive technology for cognition. *Neuropsychological rehabilitation 20*, 4 (Aug. 2010), 509–27.
11. Orpwood, R., Chadd, J., Howcroft, D., Sixsmith, A., Torrington, J., Gibson, G., and Chalfont, G. Designing technology to improve quality of life for people with dementia: user-led approaches. *Universal Access in the Information Society 9*, 3 (Aug. 2010), 249–259.
12. Schulenberg, S. E., and Melton, A. M. A. The Computer Aversion, Attitudes, and Familiarity Index (CAAFI): A validity study. *Computers in Human Behavior 24*, 6 (2008), 2620–2638.
13. Szymkowiak, A., Morrison, K., Gregor, P., Shah, P., Evans, J., and Wilson, A. A memory aid with remote communication using distributed technology. *Personal and Ubiquitous Computing 9*, 1 (2005), 1–5.
14. Turner, K. J., Gillespie, A., and McMichael, L. J. Rigorous development of prompting dialogues. *Journal of biomedical informatics 44*, 5 (Oct. 2011), 713–27.
15. Wechsler, D. *Wechsler Abbreviated Test of Intelligence*. Psychological Corporation, San Antonio, TX, 1999.
16. Wechsler, D. Wechsler Adult Intelligence Scale IV, 2009.
17. Wherton, J. P., and Monk, A. F. Technological opportunities for supporting people with dementia who are living at home. *International Journal of Human-Computer Studies 66*, 8 (Aug. 2008), 571–586.
18. Zajicek, M., and Khin Kyaw, Z. The Speech Dialogue Design for a PDA/Web Based Reminder System. In *Proc. 9th IASTED, Hawaii* (2005), 394–399.

Empirical Evidence for a Diminished Sense of Agency in Speech Interfaces

Hannah Limerick
Dept. of Computer Science
University of Bristol, UK
hannah.limerick@bristol.ac.uk

James W Moore
Dept. of Psychology
Goldsmiths, University of London
j.moore@gold.ac.uk

David Coyle
Dept. of Computer Science
University of Bristol, UK
david.coyle@acm.org

ABSTRACT
While the technology underlying speech interfaces has improved in recent years, our understanding of the human side of speech interactions remains limited. This paper provides new insight on one important human aspect of speech interactions: the sense of agency - defined as the experience of controlling one's own actions and their outcomes. Two experiments are described. In each case a voice command is compared with keyboard input. Agency is measured using an implicit metric: intentional binding. In both experiments we find that participants' sense of agency is significantly reduced for voice commands as compared to keyboard input. This finding presents a fundamental challenge for the design of effective speech interfaces. We reflect on this finding and, based on current theory in HCI and cognitive neuroscience, offer possible explanations for the reduced sense of agency observed in speech interfaces.

Author Keywords
Speech interfaces; voice commands; the sense of agency.

ACM Classification Keywords
H.5.m. Information interfaces and presentation (e.g., HCI): Miscellaneous.

INTRODUCTION
At ACM CHI 2014 Aylett et al. discussed the ups and downs of the relationship between HCI research and speech technology [1]. They argue that disillusionment within the HCI community with speech interfaces is partly due to a mismatch of expectations. Speech technologists have often presented speech interfaces as providing a *"natural means of communication"*, whereas in reality technical limitations such as high error rates, recognition latency and issues with ambient noise can reduce their effectiveness. Aylett et al. make a strong case for significant progress in tackling these limitations. However, they also recognise that substantial non-technical challenges remain. For example, Shneiderman has argued that *"speech is slow for presenting information, is transient and therefore difficult to review or edit, and interferes significantly with other cognitive tasks"* [9]. He further argues that our understanding of the human side of speech interactions is insufficient and that there is a need to address design challenges in speech interfaces by increasing this understanding.

CHI 2015, April 18 - 23 2015, Seoul, Republic of Korea

ACM 978-1-4503-3145-6/15/04...$15.00
http://dx.doi.org/10.1145/2702123.2702379

This paper provides new insight on one important aspect of the human side of speech interactions: the sense of agency. We focus on the sense of agency when interacting with voice command interfaces. The sense of agency can be defined as the experience of controlling one's own actions and, through this control, affecting the external world [2]. It is a crosscutting experience that links to concepts such as free will, causality and responsibility. In the context of HCI the importance of agency is illustrated by Shneiderman's 7th rule for interface design, which recommends that designers strive to create interfaces that *"support an internal locus of control"* [10]. This is based on the observation that users *"strongly desire the sense that they are in charge of the system and that the system responds to their actions"*.

Agency has been extensively studied in the field of cognitive neuroscience [4]. More recently Coyle et al. have applied methods developed in cognitive neuroscience to investigate peoples' sense of agency when interacting with computers [2]. They have shown, for example, that on-body interfaces can engender a greater sense of agency than keyboard interactions. A more detailed review of early HCI research on the sense of agency is also available in [6]. In this paper we describe two experiments comparing peoples' sense of agency in voice command and keyboard interfaces. Our aim is to determine if the sense of agency when interacting with speech interfaces is different to that experienced in more traditional input methods. Our results lead us to conclude that people experience less control over their environment when interacting via speech interfaces.

INTENTIONAL BINDING
Both of our experiments use intentional binding as an implicit metric for the sense of agency. Intentional binding is the name given to a temporal phenomenon that occurs when a person takes a voluntary action that causes an outcome [3]. In this case actions are perceived to happen later than they actually did, while outcomes are perceived as happening earlier. The overall effect is a binding, whereby the interval between an action and its effect is perceived as shorter than is actually the case (Figure 1).

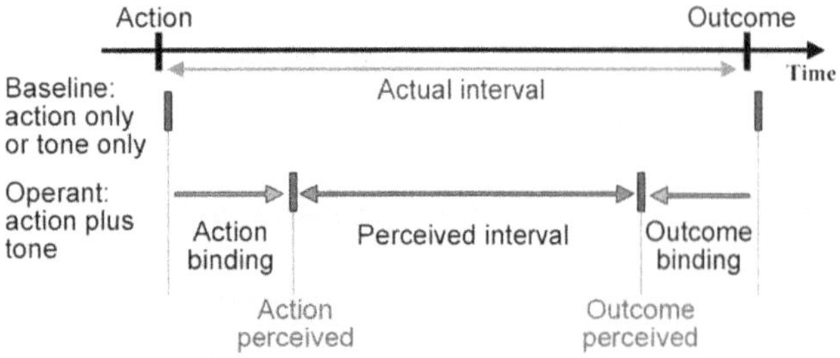

Figure 1: The intentional binding effect. Intentional binding = action binding + outcome binding.

Research has shown that for binding to occur, actions must be intentional and must lead to an outcome. Involuntary or unintended actions have the opposite effect, with the interval between actions and outcomes perceived as longer than the actual interval. Overall, there is a strong scientific consensus that intentional binding is a robust implicit metric for the sense of agency [3, 8]. Larger binding values correlate to a greater sense of agency. Other methods to assess agency do exist, e.g. fMRI studies or self-report questionnaires. Binding studies cost significantly less than fMRI studies, are more practical in most contexts, and provide an implicit means to investigate agency. A key advantage of the binding measure is its implicit nature, sidestepping issues with explicit measures (e.g. questionnaires) such as demand effects and introspection.

EXPERIMENT 1

This experiment compared participants' sense of agency for two action conditions: a key press and a voice command. Previous research has shown that the predictability of action-outcome relationships can have an impact on the sense of agency [8]. In order to remove voice recognition errors as a potential confound we required the recognizer to have a very low error rate. We implemented our voice interface using Sphinx 4 [11], an open source, hidden Markov model-based recognition system, with continuous recognition capabilities. Our task required recognition of just one word, "Go", so our grammar file contained only this word. This approach proved effective. In the study there was no block of trials with more than 4 errors (less than 10% error rate). Previous work shows that an error rate below 10% is unlikely to cause a confound [8].

Procedure

Coyle et al. [2] describe two methods for measuring participants' temporal perception in binding experiments: the Libet Clock and interval estimation methods. The Libet clock method offers a more detailed insight into the agentic experience and is the one applied here. Participants report their perception of time by recording the position of the hand on a clock that rotates at a rate of one rotation every 2560ms. In order to measure intentional binding, baseline and operant measures are taken for both actions and outcomes. In the operant blocks actions cause an outcome. For baseline blocks only an action or an outcome occur. Table 1 shows the full set of measures taken and the calculations used for intentional binding.

A within-subjects design was used, with one independent variable: action modality - voice command or key press. Figure 1 illustrates the procedure for individual trials. Participants watched a screen showing a Libet clock and used a footswitch to initiate trials. Once initiated, the clock hand started to rotate. For key press trials, participants pressed the 'enter' key on the keyboard as an action. For the voice command condition, participants said the word 'Go'. We used the end of the utterance as the point of action in the voice condition. In both conditions participants were asked to make an action whenever they were ready.

As is common in intentional binding experiments the outcome used in our experiment was a tone. A fixed action-outcome interval of 500ms was used to ensure sufficient time for word recognition by the voice recognizer. This is a slightly longer interval than is typically used in intentional binding experiments, but it is well within the interval range for which binding is expected [8].

Blocks of trials were completed for each input condition as outlined in Table 1. Each block included 40 trials, with mean values used to determine intentional binding using the calculations shown in Table 1. This resulted in a total of 320 trials per participant. The blocks for each condition were grouped together and the order of the input conditions was alternated for odd and even numbered participants. The

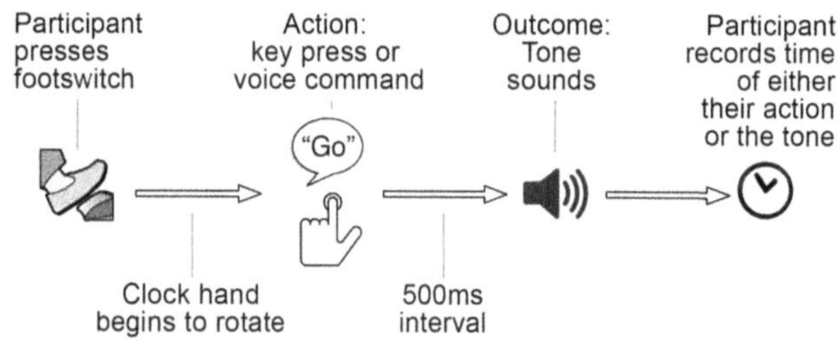

Figure 2: The procedure for trials in Experiment 1.

Measurement Blocks			
Block Type	**Action**	**Outcome**	**Participant report**
Action Baseline	Key-Press or Voice command	None	Perceived time of action
Action Operant	Key-Press or Voice command	Tone	Perceived time of action
Tone Baseline	None	Tone	Perceived time of outcome
Tone Operant	Key-Press or Voice command	Tone	Perceived time of outcome
Intentional Binding Calculations			
Action Baseline Error = actual time – perceived time			
Action Operant Error = actual time – perceived time			
Outcome Baseline Error = actual time – perceived time			
Outcome Operant Error = actual time – perceived time			
Action Binding = Action Operant Error - Action Baseline Error			
Outcome Binding = Outcome Baseline Error - Outcome Operant Error			
Total Binding = Action Binding + Outcome Binding			

Table 1. The temporal measurements, in milliseconds, and calculations used to estimate intentional binding.

	Action binding	Outcome binding	Total binding
Button	23.00ms (16.25ms)	22.57ms (34.28ms)	45.56ms (36.47ms)
Voice command	40.12ms (64.10ms)	5.78ms (39.16ms)	45.90ms (93.80ms)

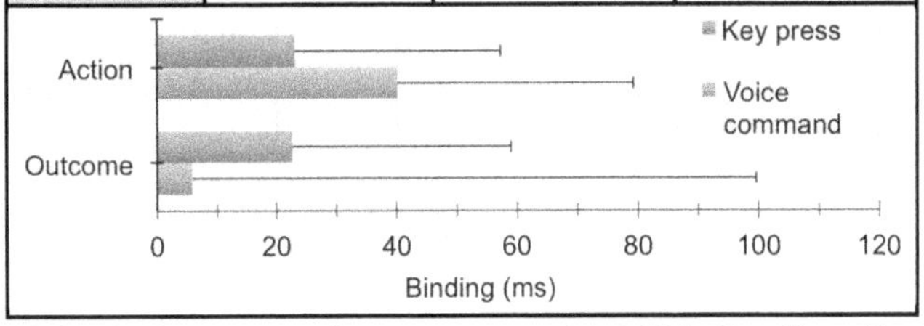

Table 2: the mean action, outcome and total binding times for Experiment 1. Standard deviations in brackets.

order of the blocks was randomised within the input conditions, but was balanced for odd and even participants.

Participants

14 participants, all right-handed and aged 20-40, took part. All had normal or corrected to normal vision and hearing. The study was approved by the University of Bristol ethics committee. All participants gave written, informed consent and received a £15 retail voucher for participating.

Results

Table 2 shows the mean action, outcome and total binding values for the key press and voice command conditions across 14 participants. The full operant and baseline measures and calculations for these binding values are included in Appendix 1 (see online auxiliary materials). To test if intentional binding occurred in either the key press or voice condition, we conducted separate 2x2 repeated measures analysis of variance on participants' perceived times for each input modality, with factors event (action vs. outcome) and context (operant vs. baseline). For the key press condition there was significant intentional binding: $F(1,13)=20.293, p<.001$. For the verbal command we did not find significant binding: $F(1,13)=3.112, p<.101$.

Analysis

Intentional binding is the shift of *both* the perceived action and outcome towards one another. This binding was present for the key-press condition, with a binding value consistent with prior literature. Binding was not found for the voice command. The mean action and outcome binding for the speech interface indicate that insufficient outcome binding occurred to elicit a significant overall binding effect.

Further analysis of the temporal measures in the voice condition revealed an important issue. Participants' action baseline error (see online Appendix) indicates that they perceived their speech action occurring 316ms before the point recorded by the computer. This is an unusually large baseline error for action estimation. Subsequent recordings suggest that saying the word "Go" takes ~300ms. Taken together this suggests that our participants perceived their speech actions as occurring at the beginning of their utterance, rather than at the end – the point we chose as the action reference point for the computer. In effect this means the action-outcome interval for the voice command was ~800ms, rather than the 500ms we intended. While intentional binding has been observed at intervals of 800ms, it is less likely than at 500ms [8]. It is thus possible that a longer action-outcome interval may explain the absence of binding in the voice condition.

	Action binding	Outcome binding	Total binding
Button	47.37ms (122.34ms)	47.75ms (117.11ms)	94.12ms (176.17ms)
Voice command	-5.70ms (94.90ms)	-4.36ms (34.51ms)	-10.06ms (95.44ms)

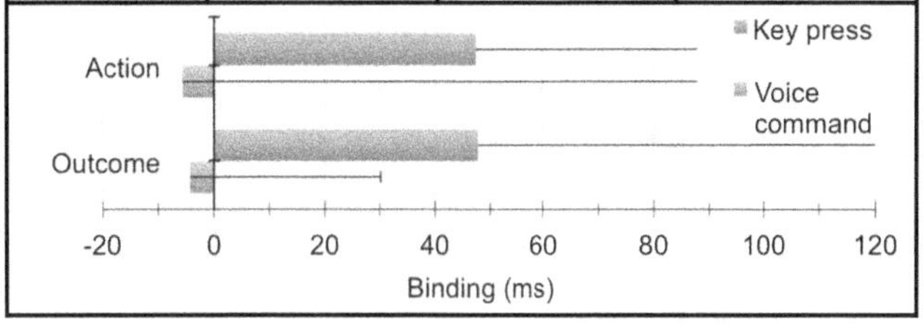

Table 3: the mean action, outcome and total binding times for Experiment 2. Standard deviations in brackets.

EXPERIMENT 2

To address our concerns with Experiment 1, a second experiment was conducted with two alterations. First, the 'StartSpeech' signal (a built-in component in Sphinx4 which indicates that speech has started) was used as the point of speech actions. This change addressed our observation in Experiment 1 that participants perceived their actions as occurring at the start of the utterance. Second, to address the possibility that a longer action/outcome interval resulted in no intentional binding for the speech condition, the action/outcome interval was shortened to 300ms. Aside from these changes the procedure was the same as Experiment 1.

Participants

Again we had 14 participants; all right-handed, aged 20-40, with normal or corrected to normal vision and hearing. The university ethics committee approved the study and participants received a £15 retail voucher. One participant was excluded from our analysis due to an equipment fault.

Results

Table 3 shows the mean action, outcome and total binding effects for the key press and voice command conditions. To test whether intentional binding was occurring, we again conducted separate 2x2 repeated measures analysis of variance tests on participants' perceived times for each input modality, with factors of event (action vs. tone) and context (operant vs. baseline). For the key press condition there was a trend toward significant intentional binding: $F(1,12)=3.496$, $p< .086$. Although the mean binding scores where higher than in Experiment 1, a large variance between participants rendered the score insignificant. For the verbal command we did not find significant binding: $F(1,12)=.144, p< .711$.

Analysis

Experiment 2 addressed a potential reason for the absence of intentional binding for voice commands in Experiment 1. We found that these alterations did not elicit intentional binding for voice commands. The key press condition showed a trend towards significance and given a larger sample size would likely be consistent with Experiment 1 and a wealth of prior intentional binding literature.

DISCUSSION AND CONCLUSION

Our results suggest that intentional binding does not occur for voice command interfaces. This in turn suggests that the sense of agency is lower for voice commands than for input techniques such as a keyboard. We believe this finding reveals an important underlying limitation of speech interfaces and presents a challenge for designers of speech interfaces. Users will experience a reduced sense of control over their environment when interacting via voice interfaces. Voice interfaces will feel less responsive and as a result users may experience a reduced sense of ownership or responsibility for the outcomes of their actions. Overall users will have a reduced sense that they are in charge of the system. In this context it is worth noting that the simplified speech interface used in our experiments allowed us to minimise recognition errors and latency. Therefore, even with continuing improvements in the technology underlying speech interfaces, the issue of a reduced sense of agency is likely to remain.

An obvious question that arises from our results is: Why do speech interactions provide a diminished sense of agency as compared to keyboard interactions? We are not yet in a position to offer definitive answers to this question. However we can offer two possible explanations, both of which have implications for designers.

One explanation from prior HCI research relates to the allocation of cognitive resources during tasks. It has been suggested that usability issues for speech interfaces are due to the fact that working memory is a cognitive resource that is shared between the processes of problem solving, recall and speech, and further that limb movements do not compete for the same cognitive resources [9]. This explains why humans find it difficult to speak and think at the same time, but can easily walk and talk simultaneously. This is interesting as recent research in cognitive neuroscience finds that increasing a person's cognitive working memory load reduces their sense of agency [5]. An implication of this finding is that voice command interfaces should only be deployed with care in situations that have high cognitive working memory loads, but also require users to maintain a strong sense of control.

An alternative explanation for a reduced sense of agency in speech interactions is based on a theory in cognitive neuroscience – cue integration. This theory holds that various cues surrounding actions and outcomes are integrated optimally and are weighted by their reliability to give rise to sense of agency [7]. This includes internal sensorimotor cues, e.g. proprioception, and contextual cues such as an intention to make a certain action. In [2] participants experienced significantly greater intentional binding for skin-based input than for keyboard input. The present study and [2] currently represent the only two investigations into agency and non-conventional input techniques. However from these we see a potential continuum arising. Skin-based input provides a greater sense of agency than keyboard input, which in turn provides a greater sense of agency than voice commands. It is possible that the graded degree of agency across these interfaces may be ascribed to the varying number of cues and/or the reliability of these cues. For speech interfaces the main agency cues available are auditory and proprioceptive. By comparison a keyboard offers a wider array of cues, including auditory, proprioceptive, visual and haptic. Over and above this, the skin-input modality provides further cues, through the body itself acting as the input device.

This explanation of the reduced sense of agency in our speech interface is intriguing, as it also offers a possible solution for designers. It suggests that the sense of agency in speech interfaces – or indeed any input modality - could be improved by offering users increased contextual cues (e.g. haptic feedback) regarding their interactions.

ACKNOWLEDGEMENTS

This research was funded by the Wellcome Trust Neural Dynamics PhD programme at the University of Bristol.

REFERENCES

1. Aylett, M.P., Kristensson, P.O., Whittaker, S. & Vazquez-Alvarez, Y. (2014) *None of a CHInd: relationship counselling for HCI and speech technology*. ACM CHI EA 2014. 749-60.
2. Coyle, D., Moore, J., Kristensson, P.O., Fletcher, P. & Blackwell, A. (2012) *I did that! Measuring users' experience of agency in their own actions*. ACM CHI 2014. 2025-34.
3. Haggard, P., Clark, S. & Kalogeras, J. (2002) *Voluntary action and conscious awareness*. Nature Neuroscience **5**(4) 382-85.
4. Haggard, P. & Tsakiris, M. (2009) *The Experience of Agency: Feelings, Judgments, and Responsibility*. Curr Dir Psychol Sci. **18**(4) 242-46.
5. Hon, N., Poh, J.H. & Soon, C.S. (2013) *Preoccupied minds feel less control: Sense of agency is modulated by cognitive load*. Consciousness and Cognition. **22**(2) 556-61.
6. Limerick, H., Coyle, D. & Moore, J.W. (2014) *The Experience of Agency in Human-Computer Interactions: A Review*. Frontiers in Human Neuroscience. **8**:643.
7. Moore, J.W. & Fletcher, P.C. (2012) *Sense of agency in health and disease: A review of cue integration approaches*. Consciousness and Cognition. **21**(1) 59-68.
8. Moore, J.W. & Obhi, S.S. (2012) *Intentional binding and the sense of agency: a review*. Conscious Cogn. **21**(1) 546-61.
9. Shneiderman, B. (2000) *The limits of speech recognition*. Commun. ACM. **43**(9) 63-65.
10. Shneiderman, B. & Plaisant, C. *Designing the User Interface: Strategies for Effective Human-Computer Interaction*. 2004.
11. Walker, W., Lamere, P., Kwok, P., Raj, B., Singh, R., Gouvea, E., Wolf, P. & Woelfel, J. (2004) *Sphinx-4: a flexible open source framework for speech recognition*.

To Beep or Not to Beep? Comparing Abstract versus Language-Based Multimodal Driver Displays

Ioannis Politis[1], **Stephen Brewster**[2]
School of Computing Science
University of Glasgow
Glasgow, G12 8QQ, UK
[1]I.Politis.1@research.gla.ac.uk
[2]Stephen.Brewster@glasgow.ac.uk

Frank Pollick
School of Psychology
University of Glasgow
Glasgow G12 8QB, UK
Frank.Pollick@glasgow.ac.uk

ABSTRACT
Multimodal displays are increasingly being utilized as driver warnings. Abstract warnings, without any semantic association to the signified event, and language-based warnings are examples of such displays. This paper presents a first comparison between these two types, across all combinations of audio, visual and tactile modalities. Speech, text and Speech Tactons (a novel form of tactile warnings synchronous to speech) were compared to abstract pulses in two experiments. Results showed that recognition times of warning urgency during a non-critical driving situation were shorter for abstract warnings, highly urgent warnings and warnings including visual feedback. Response times during a critical situation were shorter for warnings including audio. We therefore suggest abstract visual feedback when informing drivers during a non-critical situation and audio in a highly critical one. Language-based warnings during a critical situation performed equally well as abstract ones, so they are suggested as less annoying vehicle alerts.

Author Keywords
Multimodal feedback; warnings; audio; visual; tactile; speech; Tactons; urgency; recognition; response.

ACM Classification Keywords
H.5.2 [Information interfaces and presentation]: User Interfaces. - Auditory (non-speech) feedback; Haptic I/O; Voice I/O.

INTRODUCTION
Informing drivers has become easier with the availability of rich in-car displays. Car manufacturers use these displays to present drivers with a wide range of information, such as vehicle-related updates or collision warnings. Messages can be abstract, e.g. repeated pulses with no semantic association to the events signified [27] or more informative, e.g. speech, having a higher association to the event [29]. Additionally, such warnings can use any of the audio, tactile or visual modalities. Previous experiments have evaluated the performance of abstract versus more informative audio [11,18,25] or tactile cues [13]. However, no research has studied all multimodal combinations of these warnings and how their simultaneous presentation affects responses. This is important in order to provide guidelines on the effectiveness of these two types of messages and the best modalities to utilize for message display. Further, Speech Tactons, tactile patterns synchronous to speech [29], presented promising results when combined with speech warnings. However, they have never been tested in the driving context, which may affect performance.

In this paper, we address the above and present two experiments investigating responses to abstract versus language-based multimodal warnings varying in urgency in a driving simulator for the first time. Abstract warnings were repeated pulses along the audio, visual and tactile modalities, as well as all their bimodal and trimodal combinations. Language-based warnings were delivered in the same modalities and were speech, text or Speech Tactons. All warnings were evaluated in terms of recognition time of the cues' urgency and response time to high urgency cues.

CHI 2015, April 18 - 23 2015, Seoul, Republic of Korea
Copyright 2015 ACM 978-1-4503-3145-6/15/04...$15.00
http://dx.doi.org/10.1145/2702123.2702167

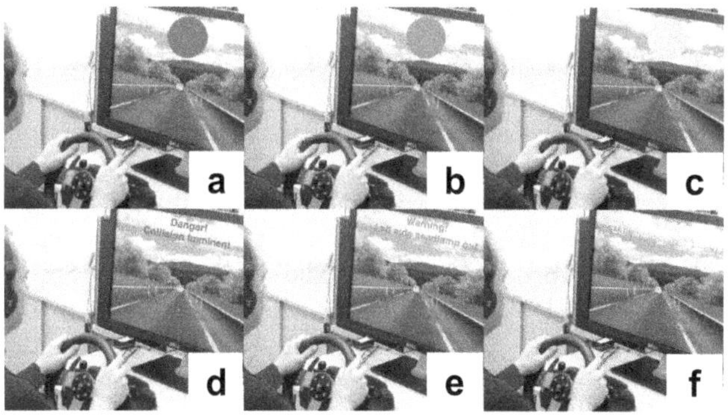

Figure 1: The experimental setup. The visual signals are Abstract L_H (a), L_M (b) and L_L (c) and Language-based L_H (d), L_M (e) and L_L (f).

In summary, we can derive the following guidelines from this work:

- Abstract cues have quicker recognition in a low criticality task, i.e. recognizing warning urgency with no critical event on the road;
- Multimodal cues including visuals are suitable for the same task, since participants rely on a visual interpretation of the cues;
- Multimodal cues including audio create quicker responses in a high criticality task, i.e. responding to a car in front braking sharply;
- Abstract and language-based cues have similar response times when a critical event is presented and can be used interchangeably. However, the use of language-based cues marginally improves driving performance;
- In high urgency situations, the use of warnings leads to a slight degradation of steering performance, but warnings are still suggested, since they improve response times.

RELATED WORK

Using multimodal warnings to alert drivers

Previous work has shown the utility of multimodal warnings to alert drivers to various situations on the road. Ho, Tan & Spence [19] used simple spatial vibrotactile cues, coming from the direction of an approaching threat, in order to decrease reaction times to a simulated critical event while driving. Ho & Spence [18] found advantages in reaction times when using a car horn sound and the words *"front"* or *"back"* indicating the direction of a threat. All sounds performed better when coming from the direction of a rapidly approaching vehicle (front or back), and, in this case, speech related messages led to shorter reaction times compared to car horn sounds. Ho, Reed & Spence [16] elaborated on these results by showing that reactions can be quicker when audio and tactile messages were delivered in combination, with a car horn sound used along with a simple vibrotactile cue.

Comparing unimodal messages in the audio, tactile and visual modalities, Scott & Gray [31] observed quicker responses to vibrotactile messages compared to simple visual cues and simple tones. Serrano *et al.* [32] verified the advantage of directional speech cues for identifying whether a presented road scene was hazardous or not. The above studies show the benefits of multimodal cues for driving, especially when the direction of the cues corresponds to the direction of the impending danger. However, the cues where either unimodal or bimodal in one case, and no systematic comparison between abstract and language-based cues was attempted. In our study, we used the benefits of directionality by presenting our warnings from the appropriate direction, in this case the front. We also compared all unimodal, bimodal and trimodal combinations of audio, visual and tactile cues, as well as abstract, i.e. repeated pulses, versus language-based messages, to explore fully the effectiveness of these different warning types.

Designing urgency in warnings

Other than alerting drivers, car warnings should reflect the urgency of the signified situation. There is a rich body of literature on how to design differently urgent abstract warnings. Edworthy, Loxley & Dennis [10] found that higher fundamental frequency, speed and pitch range increased the perceived urgency ratings for auditory warnings. Edworthy *et al.* [9] found shorter response times to highly urgent warnings compared to medium and low urgency ones. Marshall, Lee & Austria [23] showed that higher pulse duration and lower interpulse interval increased ratings of urgency of audio alerts. Gonzalez *et al.* [12] further described the influence of higher fundamental frequency, pulse rate and intensity to the ratings of urgency and annoyance of sound warnings. Pratt *et al.* [30] observed that pulse rate also increased the ratings of urgency for tactile alerts. Lewis & Baldwin [20] created a crossmodal urgency scale, where pulse rate (or flash rate for visual signals) was suggested as an effective means to vary urgency in all of these modalities. Increased sound intensity and frequency were effective for audio signals, while colours were used for visual ones.

In terms of language-based warnings, urgency, annoyance and alerting effectiveness have been investigated in the past. Baldwin & Moore [1] suggested the use of the word *"Danger"* to increase ratings of perceived urgency of speech. *"Warning"* and *"Caution"* showed intermediate results, while *"Notice"* was perceived as the least urgent. Higher S/N ratio increased ratings of urgency, regardless of the content of the messages. Baldwin [2] also observed lower reaction times to highly urgent words, presented with high signal intensity. Hellier *et al.* [15] demonstrated how urgently spoken signal words increased ratings of urgency compared to non-urgently spoken ones, which in turn had higher ratings compared to words spoken in a monotone manner. Edworthy *et al.* [8] showed that signal words spoken urgently are perceived as more urgent and appropriate.

Using all combinations of audio, visual and tactile modalities and the above guidelines, Politis, Brewster & Pollick [27] designed a set of abstract warnings. They consisted of repeated pulses, across three levels of urgency. It was found that perceived urgency increased and recognition time decreased, as modalities used increased from one, to two, to three. Using the same set of warnings, Politis, Brewster & Pollick evaluated the influence of a critical event, i.e. a simulated lead car braking, along with the exposure to the signals [28]. They found improved reaction times when the warnings accompanied such an event. Finally, using a set of language-based messages along three different urgency levels, Politis, Brewster & Pollick [29] found that when speech was accompanied by Speech Tactons the recognition of warnings' urgency and their perceived effectiveness improved. However, in [29] there was no driving task, which would increase ecological validity and is vital if the cues are to be used in real driving. In our study, we combine the use of abstract warnings from [27,28] and language-based ones from [29] to make a comparison across all combinations of audio, tactile and visual modalities, along three different urgency levels using a driving simulator. We evaluate the cues in terms of recognition and reaction times, providing new quantitative results for both high and low criticality driving tasks, which has not been attempted in the past.

Comparing Abstract and Informative Warnings

A direct comparison between some abstract and more informative warnings has been investigated. McKeown & Isherwood [25] experimented with more complex sound cues of varying content in order to alert drivers. They used abstract sounds, environmental sounds, Auditory Icons and speech. When participants were matching these sounds to the appropriate driving events, abstract sounds had the highest response times and lowest accuracy, while speech and Auditory Icons had the lowest response times and the highest accuracy. Speech was perceived as more pleasant and less urgent compared to the abstract sounds. McKeown, Isherwood & Conway [24] later compared repetitive pulses and a gunshot sound with the sound of screeching brakes and found lower response times when participants reacted to the latter, which had a higher association with driving. Although useful, the above studies only attempt comparisons in audio. We extend this by using all combinations of audio, visual and tactile cues to assess the influence of modality and designed urgency on response performance.

Cao *et al.* [6,7] used speech, abstract audio cues and visuals to present road obstacle warnings in a simulator. Speech combined with pictures led to high recall of the signified events when asked about them after the experiment, and low reaction times. The use of speech along with images was therefore suggested by the authors for tasks not requiring imminent responses, such as navigation. In more demanding situations, like low visibility and under fatigue, speech and images were also perceived as most useful. One of the limitations of these studies, as mentioned by the authors, is the relatively long utterances of the speech cues, some of which were as long as ten words. We address this in our study, by using speech cues whose text is between three and six words long.

More recently, there has been interest in evaluating audio and tactile signals whose intensity and location change with time. Gray [14] found low reaction times and high response accuracy to audio warnings with looming intensity, i.e. intensity increasing as the danger was approaching. These warnings outperformed abstract pulses and a car horn sound. Ho, Spence & Gray [17] confirmed the good results of looming intensity for audio, while no additional benefit of looming intensity was found in the tactile modality. Gray, Ho & Spence [13] however found decreased response times in the tactile modality compared to constant pulses, when looming intensity was combined with apparent motion towards the drivers' head, created by a vertical array of three tactors attached on the abdomen and activated in an upward manner. A variation of apparent motion was tested by Meng *et al.* [26] by activating vibrotactile cues first on participants' hands and then on their torso, creating a sense of cues moving towards the torso. This intervention produced lower response times compared to static cues, while looming intensity of vibration showed again no additional benefits. The above studies present an interesting application of varying audio and tactile intensity or location to alert drivers. Although not looming or moving, our warnings use changes in intensity, which increases with urgency.

The above work provides an indication of the potential of warnings with a stronger semantic association to the event signified compared to abstract ones. However, no attempt has been made to test the effectiveness of these warnings multimodally, something we address in our study. We compare abstract and language-based warnings, taking into account their designed urgency by evaluating our cues in three different urgency levels. Other than Edworthy, Walters & Hellier [11], who found no difference in perceived urgency between speech and non-speech audio warnings, no other study has directly compared these two types of alerts taking into account the designed urgency of the cues, identifying in this way the best modalities for each case.

WARNING DESIGN

In order to compare responses to abstract versus language-based warnings, cues from [28] and [29] were used, utilizing respectively repeated pulses and language-based messages and presented in all combinations of the audio, visual and tactile modalities: Audio (A), Visual (V), Tactile (T), Audio + Visual (AV), Audio + Tactile (AT), Tactile + Visual (TV), Audio + Tactile + Visual (ATV).

Abstract Warnings

The abstract warnings consisted of repeated tones and were similar to [28]. As in [28], three Levels of Designed Urgency (LDU) were created, indicating conditions varying in importance. L_H (Level High) signified situations of high urgency, such as an impending collision, L_M (Level Medium) situations of medium urgency, such as a broken headlamp and L_L (Level Low) situations of low urgency, such as an advertisement. There were 21 signals: 7 signals with the above modalities (A, T, V, AT, AV, TV, ATV) × 3 Levels of Designed Urgency. The warnings consisted of pure tones, colours or vibrations delivered as repeated pulses. Pulse rate increased as signals became more urgent, as in [20,28]. Warnings of the same urgency level had the same pulse rate, independent of modality. 8 pulses having 0.1 *sec* single pulse duration and interpulse interval were used for L_H, 5 pulses having 0.17 *sec* single pulse duration and interpulse interval for L_M and 2 pulses having 0.5 *sec* single pulse duration and 0.5 *sec* interpulse interval for L_L. All warnings had 1.5 *sec* duration. Auditory warnings were varied additionally in base frequency, as in [10,20,23]

(1000 Hz for L_H, 700 Hz for L_M and 400 Hz for L_L).Visual warnings were also varied in colour, in line with [20,28] (Red for L_H, Orange for L_M and Yellow for L_L [1]). A C2 Tactor from Engineering Acoustics[2] was used for the tactile warnings. Tactile warnings had a frequency of 250 Hz, the nominal centre frequency of the C2. The above warnings showed significantly different ratings of perceived urgency in [28] and were selected as good candidate abstract signals to convey differently urgent events multimodally.

Contrary to the fixed intensity of [28], we decided to decrease the intensity of audio and tactile cues as their designed urgency decreased for three reasons. Firstly, annoyance levels in [28] were higher in the tactile modality, an effect that was ameliorated by varying intensity as urgency decreased in [29]. Secondly the good recognition results achieved for language-based cues in [29] provided a good potential for a similar result for the abstract tones. Finally, we wished to have a fair comparison between abstract and language-based warnings and avoid any observed effects to be accounted on different intensities. Therefore, we used the intensity of speech cues of the same urgency level, described below, also in the abstract cues. Thus, in both audio and tactile cues, L_H messages had a peak of -1.9 *dBFS*, L_M had a peak of -11.1 *dBFS* and L_L had a peak of -16.5 *dBFS*. Simultaneous delivery of unimodal signals was used in the multimodal ones, to create a synchronous effect of sound, vibration, visuals and all their combinations.

Language-based warnings

The language-based warnings used were the best performing cues in terms of recognition accuracy from [29]. Three speech messages designed to convey three different urgency levels, L_H, L_M and L_L were used: *"Danger! Collision Imminent"* for L_H, *"Warning! Left side headlamp out"* for L_M and *"Notice! Call and win free tickets"* for L_L. All messages were recorded by a female voice actor, who in line with [15] was instructed to narrate the message of L_H in an urgent manner, as if a loved one was in imminent danger. The L_M message was spoken non-urgently, as if in a friendly conversation with nothing interesting about the situation and the L_L message was spoken in a monotone, deadpan manner. The L_H message was 1.7 *sec* long and had a peak of -1.9 *dBFS* and an average frequency of 377 *Hz*. The L_M message was 2.7 *sec* long, had a peak of -11.1 *dBFS* and an average frequency of 285 *Hz*. Finally, the L_L message was 3.7 *sec* long, had a peak of -16.5 *dBFS* and an average frequency of 202 *Hz*.

For the Speech Tactons, all stimuli designed were auditory, to be used with a C2 tactor. To construct the auditory cues, the fundamental frequency F_0 (pitch) of each sample of the speech recordings was obtained, which resulted in alternating pure tones for each utterance. Then, the changes in intensity of the original sound files were used in the tones. All tactile cues retained the rhythm and intensity variations of the original recordings. The resulting values of average frequency of all tactile cues never differed to the average frequency of the audio more than ±10Hz.

Finally, for the visual cues, the text of the warnings was displayed in the same colour as the abstract cues of the respective LDU (Red for L_H, Orange for L_M and Yellow for L_L). A possible limitation of this approach is that the effects of text meaning and text colour were not measured separately. However we chose to maintain a consistent colouring between abstract and language based visual cues for simplicity, in line with [20]. 21 different language-based cues were created, 7 cues with all modalities (A, T, V, AT, AV, TV, ATV) × 3 Levels of Designed Urgency. For all modifications, Praat[3] and Audacity[4] software were used.

In all, there were 42 different warnings, 21 abstract and 21 language-based ones[5]. These warnings were evaluated in two experiments, looking into how quickly and accurately participants would respond when exposed to them.

EXPERIMENT 1: RECOGNITION TIME

The first experiment evaluated how quickly and accurately participants were able to recognize the level of urgency of the presented multimodal warnings. A 7×3×2 within subjects design was used with Modality, Level of Designed Urgency (LDU) and Information as the independent variables and Recognition Time (RecT) and Recognition Accuracy (RecA) as the dependent variables. Modality had 7 levels (A, T, V, AT, AV, TV, ATV), LDU had 3 levels (L_H, L_M, L_L) and Information had 2 levels (Abstract, Language-based). There were the following hypotheses:

- RecT will be influenced by Modality (H_{1a}), LDU (H_{1b}) and Information (H_{1c});
- RecA will be influenced by Modality (H_{2a}), LDU (H_{2b}) and Information (H_{2c}).

Procedure

Twenty participants (10 female) aged between 20 and 38 years (M = 25.05, SD = 5.11) took part in this experiment. They all held a valid driving license and had between 1 and 20 years of driving experience (M = 6.05, SD = 5.23). There were two left handed participants and all reported normal hearing and normal or corrected to normal vision. They were either University students or employees.

[1] Red was *RGB*(255,0,0), Orange was *RGB*(255,127,0) and Yellow was *RGB*(255,255,0).

[2] http://www.atactech.com/PR_tactors.html

[3] http://www.fon.hum.uva.nl/praat/

[4] http://audacity.sourceforge.net/

[5] All warnings are available at http://goo.gl/XHViGY

The experiment took place in a University room, where participants sat in front of 27-inch Dell 2709W monitor and a PC running the simulator software (see Figure 1). In the software, a three lane road in a rural area was depicted, with a lead car maintaining a steady speed in the central lane. This simulator has been used in several previous research studies, e.g. [4]. As in [4], safety cones were placed on either side of the central lane, to reinforce lane keeping. Participants used a Logitech G27 gaming wheel and pedals to steer the simulated vehicle and to brake. Inputs were logged with a frequency of 50 *Hz*. Participants wore a set of Sennheiser HD 25-1 headphones and a wristband on their left wrist with a C2 Tactor attached on the inside of the band, in line with [29,30]. This simulated tactile feedback being presented by a smart watch. To cover any noise from the Tactor, car sound was played throughout the experiment. For two participants, sound and vibration were slightly adjusted to maintain comfortable intensities. Visual abstract cues were delivered through coloured circles that flashed in the top central area of the screen, and were sized 400×400 pixels (about 12×12 cm). Visual language-based cues were coloured text displaying each warning, which appeared once and for as long as the warning was uttered in the top central area of the screen, and were sized 200×800 pixels (about 24×6 cm). The visual cues did not obstruct the lead car and were designed to simulate a Head-Up Display. Abstract and language-based visual cues were also designed so as to occupy roughly the same area on the screen (about 144 cm^2). Figure 1 shows the setup and visual cues.

Participants were welcomed and provided with a brief introduction to the experiment. Afterwards, the participants were exposed to all the warnings as follows: first, a label with the text *"Level High (H) Warnings of HIGH urgency will follow"* appeared on the screen, then the 7 abstract warnings of L_H were played once to half of the participants, in the following order: A → T → V → AT → AV → TV → ATV and then the 7 language-based warnings of L_H were played in the same order of modality. Afterwards, a label with the text *"Level Medium (M) Warnings of MEDIUM urgency will follow"* appeared and then the 7 abstract warnings of L_M were displayed followed by the 7 language-based L_M ones, keeping the same order for modalities. Finally, a label with the text *"Level Low (L) Warnings of LOW urgency will follow"* appeared, followed by the 7 L_L abstract and then the 7 L_L language-based warnings as above. To the other half of the participants, first the language-based cues were played in each LDU and then the abstract ones, in the same manner as above. This procedure was chosen to minimize any order effects when presenting abstract and language-based cues, while still presenting them in a memorable way. The training lasted about 6 *min* for each participant. Participants were then asked to drive for 90 *sec*, to get accustomed to the simulator.

In the main part of the study, participants were presented with a driving scene, where they drove a simulated vehicle along a straight rural road following a car in front. Participants were able to steer the vehicle but did not use the accelerator pedal. The vehicle controlled by the participants maintained a constant speed of just above 70 *mph*. This speed was chosen in order to exceed the UK motorway speed limit (70 *mph*) creating a hazardous driving situation and requiring the drivers' attention. While steering the vehicle, the warnings were displayed to the participants in a random order and with a random interval of any integral value between (and including) 11–19 *sec*. These values were chosen to be similar with previous driving studies with repeated exposure to stimuli, e.g. [27]. Each stimulus was played twice. This resulted in a total of 82 stimuli (42 warnings × 2 presentations). Participants were asked to identify the urgency level of each stimulus by pressing one of three buttons on the steering wheel as quickly as possible. Buttons were labelled with letters (H, M or L) according to the urgency levels – topmost for L_H, middle for L_M, bottom for L_L. Participants were asked to maintain a central lane position. The whole experiment lasted about 30 *min* and participants were then prepared for the next experiment, which followed immediately.

Results

Recognition Time

All data for recognition time were analysed using a three-way repeated measures ANOVA, with Modality, Level and Information as factors. Mauchly's test showed that the assumption of sphericity had been violated for Modality and the interaction between Modality and LDU and Modality and Information. Therefore Degrees of freedom were corrected with Greenhouse–Geisser sphericity estimates.

There was a significant main effect of Modality ($F(3.01,102.33) = 103.34$, $p < 0.001$). Contrasts revealed that AV, ATV, V and TV warnings elicited significantly quicker responses compared to A and AT ($F(1,34) = 22.77$, $r = 0.59$, $p < 0.001$), which in turn had quicker responses compared to T ones ($F(1,34) = 106.78$, $r = 0.87$, $p < 0.001$). There was a significant main effect of LDU ($F(2,68) = 74.13$, $p < 0.001$). Contrasts revealed that L_H warnings were recognised quicker compared to the L_M and L_L ones ($F(1,34) = 89.05$, $r = 0.85$, $p < 0.001$). There was a significant main effect of Information ($F(1,34) = 37.55$, $p < 0.001$). Contrasts revealed that Abstract warnings were recognised quicker than Language-based ones (1.41 *sec* on average for Abstract vs. 1.57 *sec* for Language-based warnings, $F(1,34) = 37.55$, $r = 0.72$, $p < 0.001$). As a result hypotheses H_{1a}, H_{1b} and H_{1c} were accepted. See Figure 2 for Recognition Times across Modalities (a) and LDU (b).

There was a significant interaction between Modality and LDU ($F(7.28,247.60) = 2.63$, $p < 0.05$). Contrasts revealed that A warnings had slower recognition times compared to TV ones for L_M compared to L_H ($F(1,34) = 14.55$, $r = 0.55$, $p < 0.05$). Also, that although for TV warnings L_M cues were quicker than L_L in recognition, this effect was reversed for A ($F(1,34) = 4.73$, $r = 0.35$, $p < 0.05$). Finally, that AT warnings had quicker recognition times compared to T ones for L_H compared to L_M ($F(1,34) = 6.04$, $r = 0.39$, $p < 0.05$). There was a significant interaction between Modality and Information ($F(3.68,125.07) = 26.82$, $p < 0.001$). Contrasts revealed that for TV warnings Abstract signals were recognised quicker than Language-based ones, but this was reversed for A warnings ($F(1,34) = 11.87$, $r = 0.51$, $p < 0.05$). Also, while for AT warnings Language-based signals were recognised quicker than Abstract ones, this was reversed for T ($F(1,34) = 52.37$, $r = 0.78$, $p < 0.05$).

Recognition Accuracy

In all, there were 1512 participant responses and only 1 trial where a participant failed to respond. For the rest, 1366 responses were correct (90.4%) and 145 incorrect (9.6%). Data for recognition accuracy were treated as dichotomous (with values "correct" or "incorrect") and analysed with Cochran's Q tests. These revealed that participants made significantly more mistakes in modality T compared to all the rest of the modalities. Specifically, out of 228 trials for each modality, there were 80 mistakes for T versus 16 for A ($Q(1) = 47.63$, $p < 0.001$), 17 for V ($Q(1) = 46.69$, $p < 0.001$), 18 for AT ($Q(1) = 46.89$, $p < 0.001$), 9 for AV ($Q(1) = 63.81$, $p < 0.001$), 12 for TV ($Q(1) = 57.80$, $p < 0.001$) and 13 for ATV ($Q(1) = 54.08$, $p < 0.001$). Contrasts also revealed that there were significantly more mistakes in L_L compared to L_H and L_M. Specifically, out of 532 trials for each level, there were 80 mistakes for L_L versus 38 for L_H ($Q(1) = 16.04$, $p < 0.001$) and 47 for L_M ($Q(1) = 10.78$, $p < 0.001$). There was no significant difference in number of mistakes between Abstract and Language-based cues. Specifically, out of 798 trials for each type of Information, there were 88 mistakes for Abstract versus 77 for Language-based cues, $Q(1) = 0.83$, $p = 0.36$. As a result, hypotheses H_{2a} and H_{2b} were accepted and H_{2c} was rejected.

EXPERIMENT 2: RESPONSE TIME

The second experiment evaluated how quickly participants were able to respond to presented multimodal warnings of high urgency (L_H). Other than their response time to this task, two driving metrics suggested in studies such as [5,27] were used. These were the Root Mean Square Error (RMSE) of the vehicle's lateral deviation and steering angle. Lower lateral deviation and variation of the steering angle can indicate lower driver distraction [21,22]. Also, the variable Time was used to measure the effect of the warning presentation on participants' driving behaviour by comparing the metrics described above before and after the presentation of the warnings.

A 7×3×2×2 within subjects design was used with Modality, LDU, Information and Time as the independent variables. Response Time (ResT), Lateral Deviation (LatDev) and Steering Angle (SteAng) were the dependent variables. As in the previous experiment, Modality had 7 levels (A, T, V, AT, AV, TV, ATV), LDU had three levels (L_H, L_M, L_L) and Information had 2 levels (Abstract, Language-based).

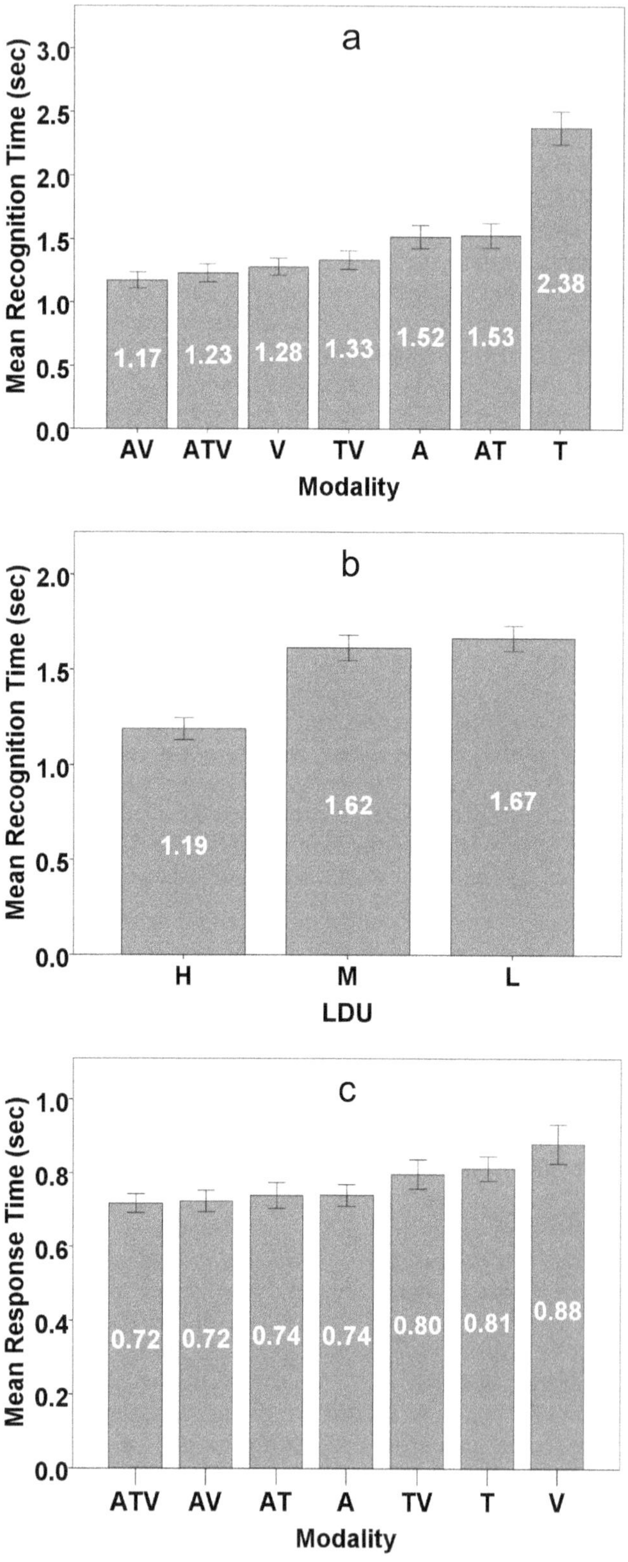

Figure 2: Recognition times for Experiment 1 across Modalities (a), Level of Designed Urgency (b) and response times for Experiment 2 across Modalities (c). Graphs are sorted by mean values. Error bars represent 95% Confidence Intervals.

Time had 2 levels: Before cue was presented and After cue was presented. There were the following hypotheses:

- ResT when reacting to L_H warnings and a car braking event will be influenced by Modality (H_{3a}) and Information (H_{3b});
- LatDev when reacting to L_H warnings and a car braking event will be influenced by Modality (H_{4a}), Information (H_{4b}) and Time (H_{4c});
- SteAng when reacting to L_H warnings and a car braking event will be influenced by Modality (H_{5a}), Information (H_{5b}) and Time (H_{5c});
- LatDev when exposed to L_M and L_L warnings without a car braking event will be influenced by Level (H_{6a}), Modality (H_{6b}), Information (H_{6c}) and Time (H_{6d});
- SteAng when exposed to L_M and L_L warnings without a car braking event will be influenced by Level (H_{7a}), Modality (H_{7b}), Information (H_{7c}) and Time (H_{7d}).

Procedure

Participants and equipment were identical to the previous experiment. It took place after participants completed the previous experiment and had a short break. Participants were presented with the same driving scene showing a vehicle maintaining a constant speed of just above 70 *mph*. Other than steering the vehicle, participants were able to respond by pressing the brake pedal. While steering the vehicle, the warnings were again displayed to the participants in a random order and with a random interval of any integral value between (and including) 11–19 *sec*. Each stimulus was again played twice, resulting in a total of 82 stimuli (42 warnings × 2 presentations). When there was a L_H warning, the vehicle in front started braking towards the participant vehicle along with the presentation of the warning. In case of an L_M or L_L warning, the vehicle in front continued driving and did not brake.

Participants were asked to maintain a central lane position throughout the experiment. They were instructed to respond by pressing the brake pedal as quickly as possible when there was a L_H warning presented along with the car in front braking. Finally, they were instructed to ignore the L_M and L_L warnings and not to respond to them. This process was chosen because responding to some warnings and ignoring others would create an increased workload for participants, requiring higher attention. Also, as shown in [28], the presentation of warnings along with a critical event resulted in quicker response times, which is desired in this situation. Finally, testing responses to L_H warnings was considered as more ecologically valid, since participants would not have to respond promptly to L_M and L_L warnings in a real setting.

Participants' ResT was calculated from the onset of the L_H stimulus and start of the braking event of the lead car, until the participant first pressed the brake pedal. Their LatDev and SteAng were logged for 4.7 *sec* (from 5.7 *sec* to 1 *sec* before any stimulus was displayed), forming their baseline value for driving performance. They were logged again for 4.7 *sec* immediately after the stimulus to assess the warning effects on driving. The value of 4.7 *sec* was chosen, since it was the duration of the longest of all cues (3.7 *sec*), increased by 1 *sec*. Thus, any effects occurring throughout the longest possible duration of a cue would be recorded.

For both LatDev and SteAng, the RMSE values were then computed from the logged values. As a result, out of the 82 overall trials, there were 28 values of ResT ([7 Abstract L_H cues + 7 Language-based L_H cues] × 2 presentations). Also, since LatDev and SteAng were logged in all cases (L_H, L_M and L_L cues), for each of the 82 trials there were two values for their LatDev (baseline value and value after the cue was displayed) and two values for their SteAng (baseline value and value after the cue was displayed). The whole experiment lasted about 30 *min* and participants were then debriefed about the purpose of both experiments and paid £6 for their participation.

Results

Response Time

Data for response times to L_H cues were analysed using a two-way repeated measures ANOVA, with Modality and Information as factors. Mauchly's test showed that the assumption of sphericity had been violated for Modality, therefore Degrees of freedom were corrected with Greenhouse–Geisser sphericity estimates. There was a significant main effect of Modality ($F(4.17,154.37) = 18.83$, $p < 0.001$). Contrasts revealed that ATV, AV, AT and A warnings caused quicker responses compared to TV and T ones ($F(1,37) = 7.46$, $r = 0.41$, $p < 0.05$), which in turn had quicker responses compared to T warnings ($F(1,37) = 6.92$, $r = 0.40$, $p < 0.05$). There was no significant effect of Information ($F(1,37) = 1.37$, $p = 0.25$). As a result, H_{3a} was accepted and H_{3b} was rejected. See Figure 2 for Response Times across Modalities (c).

Lateral Deviation and Steering Angle

Data for LatDev when reacting to L_H cues by braking were analysed using a three-way repeated measures ANOVA, with Modality, Information and Time as factors. Time had two levels: Before cue was displayed (baseline data) and After cue was displayed. There was a significant main effect of Time ($F(1,39) = 5.65$, $p < 0.05$). Contrasts revealed that LatDev was higher after the cues were displayed (0.47 *m* on average before the L_H cue and the car braking event vs. 0.51 *m* after the cue and the event, $F(1,39) = 5.65$, $r = 0.36$, $p < 0.05$). There was an effect of Information which approached significance ($F(1,39) = 4.00$, $p = 0.053$), suggesting that the average LatDev both before and after the exposure to Language-based cues may be lower compared to Abstract cues, but not significantly so. No other significant effects were observed.

Data for SteAng when reacting to L_H cues by braking were also analysed using a three-way repeated measures ANOVA, with Modality, Information and Time as factors.

As above, Time had two levels: Before cue was displayed (baseline data) and After cue was displayed. There was a significant main effect of Time ($F(1,39) = 26.63$, $p < 0.001$). Contrasts revealed that SteAng was higher after the cues were displayed (0.07 *rad* on average before the L_H cue and the car braking event vs. 0.08 *rad* after the cue and the event, $F(1,39) = 26.63$, $r = 0.64$, $p < 0.001$). There were no other significant effects observed.

Data for LatDev and SteAng when exposed to L_M and L_L cues without reacting were analysed using a four-way repeated measures ANOVA, with Modality, Level, Information and Time as factors. There were no significant effects observed. As a result, H_{4c} and H_{5c} were accepted and H_{4a}, H_{4b}, H_{5a} and H_{5b} were rejected. Further, H_{6a} - H_{6d} and H_{7a} - H_{7d} were all rejected.

DISCUSSION

Recognition Time and Accuracy

Results for recognition time showed an advantage of abstract cues when identifying the level of designed urgency (LDU). This can be partly explained by the fact that these cues were shorter in length overall. In studies like [6], speech cues also created longer response times compared to abstract ones. We note, however, that our task was an identification one, requiring recall of the cues' LDU. As will be discussed later, this is different to a simple response task, in which abstract and language-based cues performed similarly in our study. As a guideline, abstract multimodal cues can cause quicker identification compared to language-based ones in a non-critical task. Although we designed the speech cues so that the distinctive word describing their LDU (*Danger*, *Warning* or *Notice*) came first in the message, it seemed that the cue length still required more time to interpret compared to the short abstract pulses. Interestingly, language-based warnings performed better in terms of RecT compared to abstract ones in modalities A and AT, indicating that when there is sound conveying the information, speech can also be a good means to do so. However, our above guideline still holds, since the main effect showed better performance of abstract cues overall. In future work, even simpler language-based cues could be evaluated to compare their recognition time with abstract ones.

In terms of modalities, results are very similar to [28], where only abstract cues were used. As in [28], the visual modality seemed to play an important role in participants recognizing the cues' LDU, since the modalities with the shortest recognition times all included visuals. Other than V, all other better performing cues were multimodal, similar to studies like [27,28,29], where the presence of more modalities enhanced responses. The presence of V in the group of best performing modalities confirms the role of visuals when interpreting such messages. However, V alone cannot be recommended for critical situations as it has been shown that it suffers in terms of performance when a visual critical event occurs [27]. Also in our study, as will be discussed later, V cues performed worse when users were reacting to an imminent collision event. As a guideline, abstract cues including visuals can be used to quickly inform about non-critical driving events. Combining results of perceived annoyance in [28], which increases as modalities used increase, we recommend bimodal rather than trimodal cues for this case.

A disadvantage of unimodal tactile cues in terms of recognition time was found. As also mentioned by several participants, cues were harder to identify when not accompanied by sound and / or visuals clarifying their meaning. This was also found in [28], where only abstract cues were evaluated, indicating that this difficulty holds also when language-based cues are used. The results of recognition accuracy, where the T cues were the worst performing compared to all other modalities, also add to this observed disadvantage. Thus, we recommend avoiding the delivery of messages through vibration alone when recognition time is important, since this may slow down their interpretation.

Finally, recognition of L_H cues was quickest, confirming that they were conveying an increased level of urgency. This was again in line with [28] and showed that the design used was effective in conveying high urgency in both abstract and language-based warnings. Combined with the recognition accuracy results, where L_L cues performed the poorest, we are confident that the cues designed afford quick recognition in more urgent situations. In terms of low urgency situations, we conclude that cues should be used cautiously, since a driver response is not essential in such cases (e.g. for an advertisement) and combined with the low performance observed, it may also be disruptive.

Response Time, Lateral Deviation and Steering Angle

Results for response time were similar to [27], with warnings including audio creating quickest responses compared to the rest. With the exception of A, all warnings in the quickest performing group were multimodal. This is in line with [27], although in that study all best performing warnings were multimodal. This enhanced performance of warnings including audio could be attributed to the reliance on cues different than visual for reacting to a visual critical event. As shown in [27], visual cues can suffer in terms of response times when users were exposed to a critical event in the simulator. This was confirmed in our study, since unimodal visual cues performed the poorest and only when accompanied by sound or by sound & vibration did they create quick responses. As a guideline, sound is a viable means of creating quick responses in highly urgent situations. We note that the task used in this study was a response one, where participants did not have to evaluate the cues' content, but rather automatically react. In this way, we were able to assess performance of cues in the presence of an event requiring an imminent response, where identifying the cues' content may be less critical.

Interestingly, there was no difference in performance between abstract and language-based cues. This is an indication that the designed language-based warnings perform as well as the abstract ones in this case. This is in line with [11], where no difference was found in terms of how urgent abstract and language-based warnings were perceived. Although not a perception task, our study showed similar response results for these two types of warnings. It could be concluded that as long the cues' content is clear, the response to such high urgency warnings is more affected by the modality they are delivered in (multimodally and including audio) than by their content (language-based or abstract sounds). Considering the results of [29], where language-based cues received low annoyance ratings overall, these cues seem to present an advantage over abstract pulses in a critical situation. As will be described below, a trend towards better lane keeping performance when exposed to the language-based warnings is an additional indication of this possible advantage.

In terms of lateral deviation and steering angle, the results showed that the exposure to L_H cues led to higher values and poorer lane-keeping. This is in line with [27], where the presence of cues did not improve or slightly worsened these metrics. We confirm therefore that the presence of cues along with critical events can create a distraction to the driving task. This is expected, since it is an additional factor for the driver to address. It has also been confirmed by studies like [3], where a startling effect of beeping cues was observed, leading to degradation of driving metrics. Additionally, since there is a physical reaction to the cues with braking, some increase in the driving metrics values is justified. As long as this increase is not dramatic, and as long as the set of cues improves response performance compared to the absence of them, as has been shown to do in [27], this is a necessary drawback when exposed to critical warnings. This also suggests that the use of warnings should be scarce, unless they signify critical events.

As described earlier, there was marginally better overall driving performance with the language-based cues, however the results did not reach significance. Therefore, we cannot provide a definite guideline on their advantage in this case, but they seem to create a trend towards better lane keeping behaviour. This could be addressing the problem of beeping cues in [3], since speech may avert startling effects created by abstract sounds. This new finding could be further examined in future work, by investigating the use of less prominent speech cues in critical situations, or using abstract looming warnings found in studies like [17], where intensity in the cues changes with time.

The presence of L_M and L_L cues, which had to be ignored, did not disturb the driving metrics. This is an important finding, since non-critical warnings should not add additional burden to the main task of driving. Participants were very accurate in discriminating the L_H cues from the L_M and L_L ones and in reacting to L_H. In only one case out of 1120 trials did a participant mistakenly react to a L_M cue and in no case did anyone react to a L_L one. These are encouraging results for all the cues designed, showing their suitability for use in contexts of intermediate or low criticality, which may occur more frequently when driving.

Finally, we note that since the results of this study were acquired using a simulated driving task, their generalizability to a road situation should be investigated in the future.

CONCLUSIONS

This paper describes two experiments presenting the first evaluation of responses to abstract versus language-based multimodal car warnings of varying urgency. All multimodal combinations of audio, tactile and visual warnings were evaluated in the driving context. Two tasks were used; a recognition task, where the cues' urgency was identified with no critical event present, and a response task, where responses to high urgency warnings were measured in the presence of such an event. An advantage of abstract warnings and warnings including visuals in the recognition task was observed. Cues including audio performed better in the response task. In both tasks, multimodal cues were the best performing ones, with the exception of unimodal visuals for recognition and unimodal audio for response. Driving behaviour, although slightly worsened by all cues in the critical situation, was marginally better when using language-based cues compared to abstract ones. These results show the benefit of using abstract cues in non-critical situations and a possible advantage of language-based cues in a critical situation. The derived guidelines can aid car warning designers and extend available knowledge by directly comparing these different ways of informing drivers.

ACKNOWLEDGEMENTS
The study was partly funded by Freescale Semiconductor Inc., Automotive Microcontroller Product Group.

REFERENCES

1. Baldwin, C.L. and Moore, C. Perceived Urgency, Alerting Effectiveness and Annoyance of Verbal Collision Avoidance System Messages. *HFES Annual Meeting 46*, 22 (2002), 1848–1852.
2. Baldwin, C.L. Verbal collision avoidance messages during simulated driving: perceived urgency, alerting effectiveness and annoyance. *Ergonomics 54*, 4 (2011), 328–337.
3. Biondi, F., Rossi, R., Gastaldi, M., and Mulatti, C. Beeping ADAS: Reflexive effect on drivers' behavior. *Transportation Research Part F: Traffic Psychology and Behaviour 25*, (2014), 27–33.
4. Brumby, D. and Seyedi, V. An empirical investigation into how users adapt to mobile phone auto-locks in a multitask setting. *MobileHCI 2012*, ACM Press (2012), 281 – 290.
5. Brumby, D.P., Davies, S.C.E., Janssen, C.P., and Grace, J.J. Fast or Safe? How Performance Objectives

Determine Modality Output Choices While Interacting on the Move. *CHI 2011*, ACM (2011), 473–482.

6. Cao, Y., Mahr, A., Castronovo, S., Theune, M., Stahl, C., and Müller, C.A. Local danger warnings for drivers: The effect of modality and level of assistance on driver reaction. *Intelligent User Interfaces*, ACM Press (2010), 239–248.
7. Cao, Y., Theune, M., and Müller, C. Multimodal Presentation of Local Danger Warnings for Drivers : A Situation-dependent Assessment of Usability. *Professional Communication Conference (IPCC)*, IEEE (2010), 226–229.
8. Edworthy, J., Hellier, E., Walters, K., Clift-Mathews, W., and Crowther, M. Acoustic, semantic and phonetic influences in spoken warning signal words. *Applied Cognitive Psychology 17*, 8 (2003), 915–933.
9. Edworthy, J., Hellier, E., Walters, K., Weedon, B., and Adams, A. The Relationship between Task Performance, Reaction Time, and Perceived Urgency in Nonverbal Auditory Warnings. *HFES Annual Meeting 44*, 22 (2000), 674–677.
10. Edworthy, J., Loxley, S., and Dennis, I. Improving auditory warning design: Relationship between warning sound parameters and perceived urgency. *Human Factors 33*, 2 (1991), 205 –231.
11. Edworthy, J., Walters, K., Hellier, E., and Weedon, B. Comparing Speech and Nonspeech Warnings. *HFES Annual Meeting 44*, 22 (2000), 746–749.
12. Gonzalez, C., Lewis, B.A., Roberts, D.M., Pratt, S.M., and Baldwin, C.L. Perceived Urgency and Annoyance of Auditory Alerts in a Driving Context. *HFES Annual Meeting 56*, 1 (2012), 1684–1687.
13. Gray, R., Ho, C., and Spence, C. A comparison of different informative vibrotactile forward collision warnings: does the warning need to be linked to the collision event? *PloS one 9*, 1 (2014), e87070.
14. Gray, R. Looming Auditory Collision Warnings for Driving. *Human Factors 53*, 1 (2011), 63–74.
15. Hellier, E., Edworthy, J., Weedon, B., Walters, K., and Adams, A. The Perceived Urgency of Speech Warnings: Semantics versus Acoustics. *Human Factors 44*, 1 (2002), 1–17.
16. Ho, C., Reed, N., and Spence, C. Multisensory In-Car Warning Signals for Collision Avoidance. *Human Factors 49*, 6 (2007), 1107–1114.
17. Ho, C., Spence, C., and Gray, R. Looming Auditory and Vibrotactile Collision Warnings for Safe Driving. *Proceedings of the 7th International Driving Symposium on Human Factors in Driver Assessment, Training, and Vehicle Design.*, (2013), 551–557.
18. Ho, C. and Spence, C. Assessing the effectiveness of various auditory cues in capturing a driver's visual attention. *Journal of experimental psychology. Applied 11*, 3 (2005), 157–74.
19. Ho, C., Tan, H.Z., and Spence, C. Using spatial vibrotactile cues to direct visual attention in driving scenes. *Traffic Psychology and Behaviour 8*, 6 (2005), 397–412.
20. Lewis, B.A. and Baldwin, C.L. Equating Perceived Urgency Across Auditory, Visual, and Tactile Signals. *HFES Annual Meeting 56*, 1 (2012), 1307–1311.
21. Lindgren, A., Angelelli, A., Mendoza, P.A., and Chen, F. Driver behaviour when using an integrated advisory warning display for advanced driver assistance systems. *IET Intelligent Transport Systems 3*, 4 (2009), 390–399.
22. Liu, Y.C. Comparative study of the effects of auditory, visual and multimodality displays on drivers' performance in advanced traveller information systems. *Ergonomics 44*, 4 (2001), 425–42.
23. Marshall, D.C., Lee, J.D., and Austria, P.A. Alerts for In-Vehicle Information Systems: Annoyance, Urgency, and Appropriateness. *Human Factors 49*, 1 (2007), 145–157.
24. McKeown, D., Isherwood, S., and Conway, G. Auditory Displays as Occasion Setters. *Human Factors 52*, 1 (2010), 54–62.
25. McKeown, D. and Isherwood, S. Mapping Candidate Within-Vehicle Auditory Displays to Their Referents. *Human Factors 49*, 3 (2007), 417–428.
26. Meng, F., Gray, R., Ho, C., Ahtamad, M., and Spence, C. Dynamic Vibrotactile Signals for Forward Collision Avoidance Warning Systems. *Human Factors*, (2014).
27. Politis, I., Brewster, S., and Pollick, F. Evaluating Multimodal Driver Displays under Varying Situational Urgency. *CHI 2014*, ACM Press (2014), 4067 – 4076.
28. Politis, I., Brewster, S., and Pollick, F. Evaluating Multimodal Driver Displays of Varying Urgency. *Automotive UI 2013*, ACM Press (2013), 92 – 99.
29. Politis, I., Brewster, S., and Pollick, F. Speech Tactons Improve Speech Warnings for Drivers. *Automotive UI 2014*, ACM Press (2014), 1 – 8.
30. Pratt, S.M., Lewis, B.A., Penaranda, B.N., Roberts, D.M., Gonzalez, C., and Baldwin, C.L. Perceived Urgency Scaling in Tactile Alerts. *HFES Annual Meeting 56*, 1 (2012), 1303–1306.
31. Scott, J.J. and Gray, R. A Comparison of Tactile, Visual, and Auditory Warnings for Rear-End Collision Prevention in Simulated Driving. *Human Factors 50*, 2 (2008), 264–275.
32. Serrano, J., Di Stasi, L.L., Megías, A., and Catena, A. Effect of directional speech warnings on road hazard detection. *Traffic injury prevention 12*, 6 (2011), 630–635.

Lost in Email: Pulling Users Down a Path of Interaction

Benjamin V. Hanrahan
Xerox Research Centre Europe
6 chemin de Maupertuis Meylan, France 38240
ben.hanrahan@xerox.com

Manuel A. Pérez-Quiñones
Department of Computer Science
Virginia Tech, Blacksburg, VA 24061
perez@cs.vt.edu

ABSTRACT

In this paper we describe a study exploring why users spend more time in email than originally intended, which we call *getting lost in email*. To study this phenomenon, we implemented an IMAP logger that also dispatched diary entries to collect data for twenty participants over a two week period. Most participants reported *getting lost in email* during both short and long sessions. Our analysis suggests two primary factors in *getting lost*: the number of emails awaiting a reply and whether or not the session caused an interruption. We conclude that much of the problem around *getting lost in email* is in managing the tension between promptly responding to messages while limiting engagement with email.

Author Keywords

Email; Personal Information Management

ACM Classification Keywords

H.5.2 User Interfaces

INTRODUCTION

Email has been called one of the most successful computer applications [24]. It is considered to be a common, if not critical, part of everyday life for many, especially at work [23, 9]. As such it has a long history of research in its forty years of existence and there have been a number of enhancements proposed for the inbox [11, 6, 10], many of which center around email triage. However, calls for better tools have been reiterated recently [21] and email overload remains a problem, even with the latest tools [12].

In this paper we add to this body of research with our investigation into how email has the ability to draw its users down a path of interaction, almost against their will. We isolate a particular phenomenon we call *getting lost in email*. This is the process of becoming further distracted from the original intent of an email session, or a loss of agency over attention during an email session. This concept is similar to chains of diversion [15] and work on interruptions [7]. However, our work is more focused on email and the specific pull that it has on its users attention.

CHI 2015, April 18 - 23 2015, Seoul, Republic of Korea
Copyright 2015 ACM 978-1-4503-3145-6/15/04$15.00
http://dx.doi.org/10.1145/2702123.2702351

To investigate whether and how email users are *getting lost in email*, we ran a two phase study. The first was a survey of 52 email users, and the second was a two week usage and diary study with 20 participants. We find that our participants are becoming lost with fair frequency. They become lost by encountering a series of emails that require (or at least are thought to require) immediacy in their response. This takes email users down a path of interactions that is difficult to resist. This path causes users, unexpectedly, to enter into a longer session than they had anticipated.

We find that there are no reliable indicators given to users to predict the danger of becoming lost. Instead, the primary indicator of getting lost is the number of replies written and whether or not the session caused an interruption. Lastly, participants developed strategies to cope with getting lost, which shows both awareness of the problem and its nature.

RELATED WORK

Email is a ubiquitous tool, playing a central role in many work and personal activities. It is also a core application on many of our most familiar personal computing devices. As a result it has been the target of a large amount of research.

Several researchers have proposed redesigning aspects of email [1, 13, 3]. There have also been proposals to change the culture around email use. Chase et al. [5] proposed that users better manage sender expectations. Others have called for organizational training courses [18], or to put limits on email as a company or an individual [14]. Bradely et al. [4] found evidence for the efficacy of these types of approaches, when they found that infrequent checking reduced email stress. This is in contrast to the findings of Dabbish et al. [8], where it was found that email related stress was reduced with more frequent checking. While Wainer et al. [22] found that curiosity played heavily into the decision to attend to messages.

While email is certainly a place of work [2], increased engagement with email increases feelings of overload [19]. Other studies have also identified that email volume contributes to email stress, as well as worrying about email [16]. Along these lines, in our work we seek to understand some of the causes for increased email use.

METHOD

For phase 1 of our study, we recruited 52 participants from our university to complete a survey about their email practices and habits. This survey also requested volunteers for phase 2 of our study, which was a usage logging and diary study. 20 participants elected to participate in phase 2. In this paper we primarily report results from phase 2 of our study, but also include some comments from the survey in phase 1 in our results. Quotes from participants that only participated in phase 1 are labeled with an 'R', while participants that participated in both phase 1 and 2 are labeled with a 'P'.

Participants ranged from the ages of 23-37, with $\bar{x} = 25.6$ and $\sigma = 4.6$. 11 were graduate students, 1 was an undergraduate student, 1 was a stay at home parent, 5 were working professionals, and 2 did not report. Of the 20 participants, 14 filled out 215 diary entries. They received a $5 gift card for enrolling in our email study, and another if they completed over half of their diary prompts.

We logged participant's email usage using an IMAP logger of our own creation. The logger took a snapshot every 3 minutes (the minimum time required to complete the snapshot). We ignored any activity in folders that were labeled as *Junk* or *Spam*. We kept track of many aspects of the participants' email activity, including: their total number of messages; unread messages; new messages since the last session; messages in the inbox; and number of composed / replied to messages. For each session we tracked what messages they had read, deleted, composed, and replied to.

We classified participants as *active* when our tool detected any actions in the IMAP data (e.g. reading, writing, filing). This activity was detected by comparing snapshots, i.e. if they had moved an email, read an email, composed an email (we kept track of the *Drafts* folder) this would be reflected in IMAP status. Second, to determine the length of an active email session, we summed the 3 minute active slices. When our software detected the end of a period of activity, the software sent a request to complete a diary via SMS. This occured at most twice a day during typical work hours with at least four hours between prompts. This request contained a URL to a specific diary instance related to the usage session.

Each diary entry contained the following questions: *What did you do during your email session?; What prompted you to start your email session (if anything)?; What task, if any, was interrupted by email use?; Did you become further distracted by email related tasks?* The final question is how we determined if participants became lost during their email session.

RESULTS

Of the 14 participants in our study that completed diary entries, 9 (64%) reported that they *got lost in email*. Participants reported being lost in 23% (47/204) of all diary entries. This means, that in the email sessions that participants were *prompted* and *responded* to diary prompts, they reported *getting lost* 23% of the time.

Unexpectedly, participants reported *getting lost in email* during both short and long sessions. Figure 1 divides the sessions by length and shows the number of sessions where participants reported being lost versus not. The cases where participants reported being lost in short three minute (180 seconds) session only comprised 21% of the total number. This is in contrast to the proportion of sessions greater than or equal to 12 minutes (720 seconds), where participants reported becoming lost in 57% of the sessions. As a session becomes quite long, participants have a higher probability to get lost.

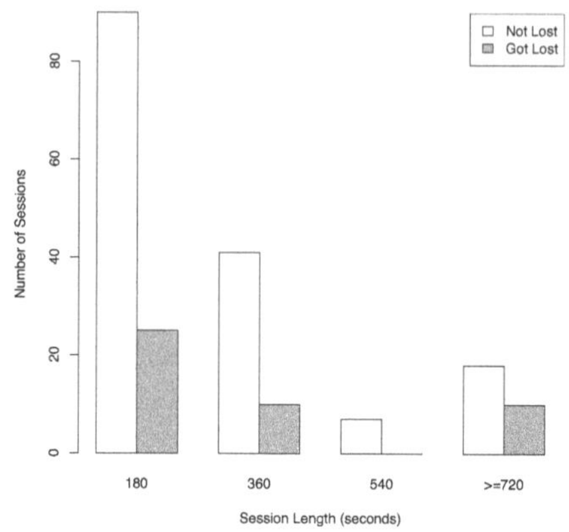

Figure 1. Different session lengths and how often they got lost.

We looked specifically at short sessions where participants reported getting lost and found that they often were falling into chains of diversion [15]. These chains took them outside of email and our ability to track their activity. So it seems that the short email sessions were part of longer chains of diversion. The following quotes are participants' description of what they did during short sessions where they reported getting lost.

> **P14**: *I read a couple emails, which had links to articles so I read the articles too.*

> **P2**: *The last time I was on my email though I responded to 3 emails and checked facebook since it was telling me I had some facebook messages.*

How Are Users Getting Lost?

In our analysis we chose to use a Binary Logistic Regression [17], as our dependent variable, *Got Lost*, was yes/no. In our model we included features related to the starting conditions for a session (i.e. number of unread mails, interrupted) and the subsequent actions (i.e. reading, moving). Table 1 shows the results of our analysis. Our model was found to fit significantly better than the null model using the likelihood ratio test ($p < 0.001$) with a log likelihood of $-91.29154(df = 12)$, and our model correctly predicted 79% of the responses. The most important variables, relative to the others within the model, are whether or not a participant was *Interrupted*, the number of *Replies* written, and the number of *Composed* messages written.

Examining the *Odds Ratios* for these three variables reveals their relationship to whether or not participants *Got Lost*. If a participant began the session because they were *Interrupted*, they were 3.025 times more likely to *Get Lost*. For each message that they replied to during their session, they were 2.54 times more likely to *Get Lost* (e.g. the more a participant replied to messages the more likely that they *Got Lost*). In contrast, for each message that a participant *Composed*, they were 0.5 times less likely to *Get Lost*. Perhaps, the purposeful act of going to email to compose a message creates a more focused path of interaction. As opposed to engaging

	β	SE	Odds Ratio	z-stat
Intercept	-1.320**	0.427	0.267	0.002
Interrupted	1.107**	0.420	3.025	0.008
Length	0.002**	0.001	1.002	0.003
Replies	0.933*	0.400	2.541	0.020
Composed	-0.684*	0.286	0.505	0.017
Read	-0.035	0.098	0.966	0.724
moved	-0.035	0.049	0.965	0.470
Inbox new	0.120*	0.058	1.127	0.037
Total emails	-0.0003*	0.0001	0.999	0.036
Total unread	0.0002	0.0002	1.000	0.494
To you	-0.069	0.276	0.934	0.804
Only to you	-0.111	0.286	0.895	0.698

Table 1. Binary logistic regression against getting lost (* $p <= 0.1$, ** $p <= 0.05$, *** $p <= 0.001$.)

with the list of emails and replying to them, which tends to pull participants towards further interactions.

Surprisingly, the number of emails read, new, or otherwise was not found to have a strong effect. This can be attributed to the large amount of noise that we observed in email. That is, of all of the email that our participants received, roughly a third (32%) of emails went unread. Keep in mind that this is not counting any of the spam or junk emails. Furthermore 73% of messages remain in the Inbox and were not acted upon.

Why are users getting lost?

Replying to messages was a strong correlate to *getting lost*. We found insight into why this might be in the various survey responses about what participants considered successful in their email habits. These responses make it clear that participants feel a clear pressure to *maintain an image of responsiveness* [20]. This pressure may lead them to reply to messages that they encounter during a session. Below are a series of example responses to a prompt about what was successful about their email practices that are representative of the value that participants put into responding promptly. These reponses show how participants compare themselves with others.

> **P19**: *I try to respond within a day. However, some people don't think that is quick enough. I also have emails well-organized into archive folders.*

> **R24**: *I read all my emails, unlike most people, so I don't miss out on anything.*

Awareness and Avoidance Strategies

The participants in our study were clearly aware of the problematic nature of email. The majority of the email strategies they reported were around the management of time instead of emails. Respondents go so far as to structure not only their email use to minimize their email time, but also structure their work day around email to avoid problematic usage. While, we reported in the previous section the clear evidence that users maintained an image of responsiveness, in these responses we see them defining success in email more as limiting the time spent. In this section we present responses to a survey prompt about what is unique about their email practices.

Some respondents mentioned how they structure their work day around email. This first response mentions how they take care to structure their access to email, so that they are not tempted to spend too much time reading everything that gets sent to them.

> **R42**: *I try not to check it in first hour of day. I check once I get engrossed in some other work. This way, I just read through them in a hurry. If I start my day by reading mails then I read a lot of them and go to their links also*

Another response mentions how this participant sets aside time several times a day to read and respond to email.

> **P9**: *[...] I also set aside time, several times a day, to read and respond to emails.*

Some users structure their email use in such a way as to help manage their time and attention spent on email. This participant mentions how they separate facets of their identity between email and Facebook.

> **P19**: *[...] I use emails almost only for work and use facebook messages for social messaging.*

Other respondents outlined the way in which they make more important messages more salient than others, helping them to direct their attention only to the most important messages.

> **R39**: *I flag emails that require action for later reference and act on email immediately so I don't forget to do it.*

Others, structure usage of email to avoid wasting time in email and to be efficient.

> **R35**: *[...] Usually I only deal with a particular piece of email once. It either gets filed, deleted, or responded to. Once I've responded to an email, I will file it away. [...]*

These various strategies show that the participants were aware of the potential issues with increased engagement with email and how they structured their email use to avoid these issues.

DISCUSSION

When we began this study, we imagined that it would be difficult to capture sessions where participants *got lost* in an email session. That we captured so many of these sessions speaks somewhat to the effectiveness of our method, but in a much larger part to the unexpectedly high frequency that participants found themselves doing more within email than they had anticipated. However, we acknowledge that our sample size was both limited in scope and diversity. That said, participants responded well to our method and none mentioned their privacy as a concern, only one participant dropped out due to costs associated with receiving text messages.

The raw count of email (unread or not) was not found to influence whether or not participants became lost. This seems to be due to the large amount of noise the participants received. Likewise, filing and deleting messages seems to be a relatively easy thing for our participants to do, as it was not found to cause users to become lost.

Instead we found that the number of emails awaiting a reply was a primary reason for becoming lost in email. Furthermore, sessions that began because of an interruption were also more likely to result in getting lost. Likely this is representative of a similar phenomenon, where the interruption is because of a notification for an email that requires a response. In both of these cases it is clear that email, particularly emails that require a response, have the ability to pull its users down a path of further interaction. This suggests that concern with email triage needs to be reexamined, as the participants in our study spent overwhelmingly more time in reading and writing email than managing messages. These findings were further confirmed by the strategies that were reported by our participants. These strategies show that much of the problem around email is in managing the tension between the perceived social responsibility of promptly responding to email and limiting ones engagement with email.

In the future we plan on running our study with a larger, more diverse sample and open sourcing the tools that we developed for this study.

REFERENCES

1. Bälter, O., and Sidner, C. L. Bifrost inbox organizer: Giving users control over the inbox. In *Proc. NordiCHI '02*, ACM Press (2002), 111–118.
2. Bellotti, V., Ducheneaut, N., Howard, M., and Smith, I. Taking email to task: the design and evaluation of a task management centered email tool. In *Proc. CHI '03*, ACM (New York, NY, USA, 2003), 345–352.
3. Bellotti, V., Ducheneaut, N., Howard, M., Smith, I., and Grinter, R. E. Quality versus quantity: E-mail-centric task management and its relation with overload. *Human-Computer Interaction 20* (2005), 89–138.
4. Bradley, A., Brumby, D. P., Cox, A. L., and Bird, J. How to manage your inbox: Is a once a day strategy best? In *Proc. of BCS-HCI '13*, British Computer Society (Swinton, UK, 2013), 20:1–20:6.
5. Chase, N., and Clegg, B. Effects of email utilization on higher education professionals. *International Journal of Technology and Human Interaction* 7, 4 (2011), 31–45.
6. Cselle, G., Albrecht, K., and Wattenhofer, R. Buzztrack: topic detection and tracking in email. In *Proc. IUI '07*, ACM Press (2007), 190–197.
7. Czerwinski, M., Horvitz, E., and Wilhite, S. A diary study of task switching and interruptions. In *Proc. CHI '04*, ACM (New York, NY, USA, 2004), 175–182.
8. Dabbish, L. A., and Kraut, R. E. Email overload at work: an analysis of factors associated with email strain. In *Proc. of CSCW '06*, CSCW '06, ACM (New York, NY, USA, 2006), 431–440.
9. Ducheneaut, N., and Bellotti, V. E-mail as habitat: an exploration of embedded personal information management. *Interactions 8*, 5 (2001), 30–38.
10. Faulring, A., Myers, B., Mohnkern, K., Schmerl, B., Steinfeld, A., Zimmerman, J., Smailagic, A., Hansen, J., and Siewiorek, D. Agent-assisted task management that reduces email overload. In *Proc IUI 2010*, ACM Press (2010), 61–70.
11. Freed, M., Carbonell, J. G., Gordon, G. J., Hayes, J., Myers, B. A., Siewiorek, D. P., Smith, S. F., Steinfeld, A., and Tomasic, A. Radar: A personal assistant that learns to reduce email overload. In *AAAI* (2008), 1287–1293.
12. Grevet, C., Choi, D., Kumar, D., and Gilbert, E. Overload is overloaded: Email in the age of gmail. In *Proc. of CHI '14*, ACM (New York, NY, USA, 2014), 793–802.
13. Gwizdka, J. Reinventing the inbox: Supporting the management of pending tasks in email. In *Proc. of CHI EA '02*, ACM (New York, NY, USA, 2002), 550–551.
14. Hemp, P. Death by information overload. *Harvard business review 87*, 9 (2009), 82–89.
15. Iqbal, S. T., and Horvitz, E. Disruption and recovery of computing tasks: field study, analysis, and directions. In *Proc CHI '07*, ACM Press (2007), 677–686.
16. Jerejian, A., Reid, C., and Rees, C. S. The contribution of email volume, email management strategies and propensity to worry in predicting email stress among academics. *Computers in Human Behavior 29*, 3 (2013), 991–996.
17. McCullagh, P., and Nelder, J. A. *Generalized Linear Models*. New York: Chapman & Hall, 1990.
18. McMurtry, K. Managing email overload in the workplace. *Performance Improvement 53*, 7 (August 2014), 13–37.
19. Sumeckia, D., Chipulua, M., and Ojiakoa, U. Email overload: Exploring the moderating role of the perception of email as a business critical tool. *International Journal of Information Management 31* (2011), 407–414.
20. Tyler, J. R., and Tang, J. C. When can I expect an email response? a study of rhythms in email usage. In *Proc of ECSCW'03*, Kluwer Academic Publishers (Norwell, MA, USA, 2003), 239–258.
21. Vacek, M. How to survive email. In *9th IEEE International Symposium on Applied Computational Intelligence and Informatics*, IEEE (May 2014), 49–54.
22. Wainer, J., Dabbish, L., and Kraut, R. Should I open this email?: inbox-level cues, curiosity and attention to email. In *Proc. of CHI '11*, ACM (New York, NY, USA, 2011), 3439–3448.
23. Whittaker, S., Bellotti, V., and Gwizdka, J. *Personal Information Management*. University of Washington Press, 2007, ch. Everything Through Email.
24. Whittaker, S., and Sidner, C. Email overload: exploring personal information management of email. In *Proc. CHI 1996*, ACM Press (1996), 276–283.

Balancing Boundaries: Using Multiple Devices to Manage Work-Life Balance

Rowanne Fleck[1,2], Anna L. Cox[1], Rosalyn A. V. Robison[3]

[1]UCL Interaction Centre
University College London
Gower Street,
London WC1E 6BT, UK
r.fleck, a.cox@ucl.ac.uk

[2]The HCI Centre
University of Birmingham
Birmingham
B15 2TT, UK
r.fleck@cs.bham.ac.uk

[3]Global Sustainability Institute
Anglia Ruskin University
Cambridge
CB1 1PT, UK
Rosie.robison@anglia.ac.uk

ABSTRACT
Information and communication technologies (ICTs) continue to give us increased flexibility about when and where we choose to work and the freedom to deal with home tasks whilst at work. However more use of ICT for work during non-work time has been linked with negative outcomes including lower work and life satisfaction and increased stress. Previous work has suggested that in order to reduce some of these negative effects, people should adopt technology use strategies that aid separation of their home and work lives. In this paper we report the results of a questionnaire study investigating work-life balance boundary behaviours and technology use. We find that people use multiple devices as a way of creating boundaries between home and work, and the extent to which they do this relates to their boundary behaviour style. These findings have particular relevance given the increasing trend for Bring Your Own Device (BYOD) policies.

Author Keywords
Life-work balance; boundary control; technology boundary work; device separation; Bring Your Own Device.

ACM Classification Keywords
H.5.m. Information interfaces and presentation (e.g., HCI): Miscellaneous.

INTRODUCTION
Previous research has found many positive and negative aspects of the effects of communication technologies on our work-life balance. Flexibility is one of the main benefits these technologies offer: they allow people to fit their work around other responsibilities [13] and reduce the cost for people in transitioning between work and non-work roles which can be very positive for people with multiple roles [6]. Being able to deal with home matters whilst at work is associated with job satisfaction [10] and people who make use of communications technologies outside normal work hours can feel more in control of and more productive in their work [3]. However, use of information technology has also been reported to cause blurring of the boundaries between work and non-work [10] and to allow work to intrude more into our private lives [4]. This can lead to negative spillover from one role to another, the perception of more job stress and a heavier workload [10, 11].

In order to reduce the negative impacts of ICT, previous research suggests that people should try to limit their use of work technologies at home, or adopt techniques for separating their home and work lives more [11] However, boundary theory posits that different people have different preferences for the extent to which they are willing to allow their work to intrude on their non-work time [1] and this might affect their use of technology [11]. To date there is limited research that considers the way people use technology to manage their boundaries; in particular, we are unaware of any work that considers the extent to which people make use of multiple devices as a means of managing their home/work boundaries or how this relates to their boundary preferences. Exploring whether they do this or not is timely given the increasing trend for Bring Your Own Device (BYOD) policies at work and school. These encourage employees or pupils to bring their own devices into work/school to use for work purposes, and could potentially cause problems for people in maintaining their preferred work/life balance [5].

Therefore, the aim of this research was to understand more about how people use one or more devices to integrate or separate their work and non-work activities, and how this relates to their overall boundary behaviour style. To address these questions we conducted a national survey of people in paid full or part-time work in the UK. Participants were asked about their technology device ownership and use for work/non-work purposes, and questions to determine their current boundary behaviour style. This research makes 3 contributions: *first*, drawing on literature from diverse sources, we define a specific situation that would benefit

CHI 2015, April 18 - 23, 2015, Seoul, Republic of Korea Copyright is held by the owner/author(s). Publication rights licensed to ACM. ACM 978-1-4503-3145-6/15/04…$15.00
http://dx.doi.org/10.1145/2702123.2702386

from HCI research that is not currently considered, that of the impact of multiple device usage on work-life boundary management; *second* we verify and expand on previous work around boundary behaviour styles; and *third* we are the first to present evidence that people use their devices to create and maintain boundaries between work and non-work in line with their preferred boundary behaviour style.

RELATED RESEARCH

According to Boundary theory, different people have different preferences for how much they like to separate or integrate their work with other aspects of their life [1]. It has been suggested that violations of these preferences can lead to stress [9]. However, the way that individuals *actually* manage their boundaries is determined by a number of factors beyond people's preferences, including the type of job a person is employed in, work-place attitudes and flexible working policies, their work role identification, their family situation and family role identification and their feeling of control over their job and their boundaries [8]. Based on interview studies of workers in North America, Kossek and Lautsch [7] identified three main boundary behaviour styles (flexstyles) that their participants adopted: 'Integrators' (who integrate work and non-work), 'segmenters' (who separate them, usually putting work or non-work first) and 'volleyers' (who are people who switch between an integration or segmentation behaviours depending on current demands). Within these three flexstyles they identified some people who were happy with, or in control of their boundary behaviours, and some people who did not feel in control of them. The resulting six categories are shown in Table 1 later. In subsequent research they developed a Work Life Indicator scale to organize people into these categories and found that higher perception of boundary control is related to better work-family outcomes for people across different boundary behaviour styles [8]. Also, in a study of mobile communications device adoption, Duxbury et al. [4] found that around half of their participants struggled to maintain their preferred boundary behaviours after adoption of a Blackberry device. Therefore not only is having good control of boundaries to fit your preferred boundary behaviour style important, the introduction of new ICTs can affect this.

Boundary work is the term given to describe the tactics people use in order to try to maintain their preferred boundary behaviours [9]. Kreiner et al. [9] identified four main ways in which people do this: behavioural, temporal, physical and communicative. Research has also suggested that people do boundary work using technology: e.g. For example, features of the technology can help people in managing boundaries: caller ID, different ringtones and voicemail can enable you to choose not to answer calls at an inappropriate time [2, 9].

Whilst the research above begins to explore the kind of technology boundary work people do, there is little research that considers the extent to which these tactics are used in practice, by whom, or how effective they are at enabling people to manage their work-life balance in a way that suits them. Park & Jex [11] suggested that creating rules around the use of ICTs at home for work related matters was linked to greater psychological separation from work, and that people with a separation preference were more likely to do this. However, Duxbury et al. [4] suggested that creating and maintaining such rules took a great deal of self-control and some people struggle to achieve this. Given the increase in number of devices people now use and their increasing functionality, people have more choice over whether to use all their devices to integrate home and work, or keep separate devices for each. Therefore the aim of this paper is to explore if and how people use multiple devices as a technology boundary work tactic. We hypothesise that people will use multiple devices in a way that matches their current boundary behaviour style.

METHOD

Participants

285 participants (157 male, 127 female, 1 preferred not to say) ranging in age from 18-69 took part in this research. Of these 201 reported they were in full-time paid employment, 47 part-time, 37 full or part-time self-employed, 4 part-time students and 5 other (multiple categories permitted). Participants were recruited via a web panel and selected to be a nationally representative sample of the UK working population, in terms of age, gender, and region. They were paid a small sum for their participation.

Measures

Participants were asked to list up to 10 digital technology devices they used on a regular basis, including those located at their workplace, and whether they used each device: entirely for work, mainly for work, partly for work and partly for non-work, mainly for non-work or entirely for non-work. To categorise people's boundary behaviour style, we used the Work Life Indicator developed by Kossek [8]: A 17 item, 5 factor scale which captures people's non-work interrupting work behaviours (e.g. I take care of personal or family needs during work), work interrupting non-work behaviours (e.g. "I regularly bring work home"), boundary control (e.g. "I control whether I have clear boundaries between my work and personal life"), work identity (e.g. "people see me as highly focused on my work") and family identity (e.g. I invest a large part of myself in my family life), measured using a 5 point Likert scale.

Analysis

$$\text{Device Separation Score} = \frac{3\times\text{devices used only for work} + 2\times\text{devices used mainly for work} + 1\times\text{devices used for both home and work} + 2\times\text{devices used mainly for non-work} + 3\times\text{devices used only for non-work}}{\text{Total number of devices used}}$$

We calculated a Device Separation score between 1 (integration) and 3 (separation) for each person as above, based on how they reported they used their devices. Values for the scores on the Work Life Indicator were calculated according to the instructions provided by the authors of the scale.

RESULTS

Use of Devices

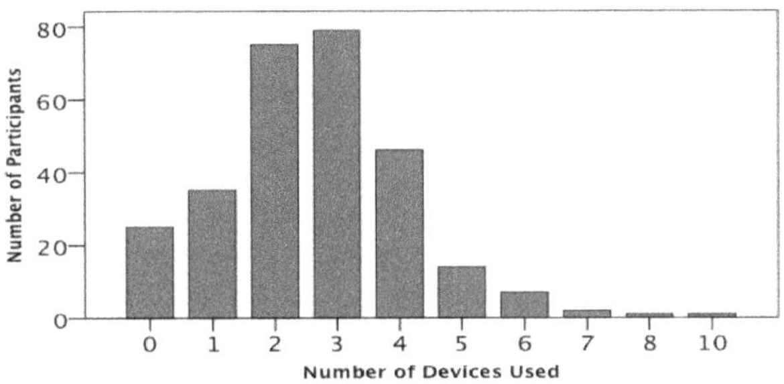

Figure 1: Number of devices people use

26 participants reported that they did not use any digital technology devices (such as mobile phones or computers) on a regular basis either at home or work (see Figure 1), and so were excluded from further analysis. The modal number of devices used by participants was 3.

Boundary Behaviour Styles

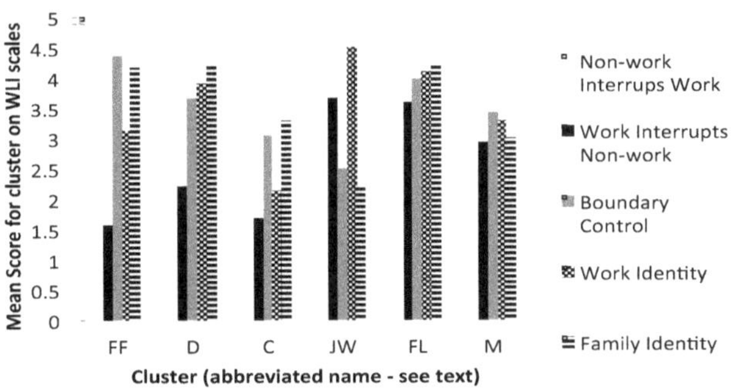

Figure 2: Mean scores of each cluster on WLI measures

Following Kossek et al. [8] we conducted a cluster analysis to discover participant's flexstyle [7]. We used SPSS's K-Means clustering with a Euclidean distance similarity index, and looked for a 6 cluster solution as suggested by this previous research. Figure 2 illustrates the mean scores for the final 6 clusters, which are described in more detail below. Table 1 illustrates how the six clusters that emerged fit with Kossek and Lautsch's qualitative flexstyle descriptions [7].

Fusion Lovers (FL) showed the highest total interruptions (i.e. non-work interrupts work + work interrupts non-work scores) of all groups and these were equal in both directions (i.e. they allowed a similar number of interruptions from work into non-work time and vice-versa). They also reported high boundary control, so can be considered high control integrators. ***Moderates (M)*** allow moderate interruptions in both directions and their perceived boundary control is just below average, so we consider them low control integrators. However their level of control is not as low as the reactor flexstyle would suggest, or the reactor cluster found by Kossek et al. [8] so we chose a new name for them.

One cluster, ***Job Warriors (JW),*** represented a small number of participants who showed moderate overall interruptions, but in contrast to all other clusters, more of these were work into non-work. They also reported a much higher work than family identity and low control.

Three clusters showed segmenter boundary behaviours: ***Family Firsters (FF)*** had low total interruptions, higher family identities than work identity and allow very little work to interrupt non-work time, though they do allow some interruptions from non-work into work time. They report the highest level of boundary control, suggesting these people are Family First separators. Kossek et al. [8] also found a group matching this description in their own cluster analysis. ***Dividers (D)*** interruptions were symmetrically low in both directions, had both high work and family identities and report feeling quite in control of this separation. Therefore, unlike the suggestion that segmenters tend either to put family or work first, this group of people seem to have equal loyalties to both home and work, but choose to keep them separate. We have named them after Kossek et al.'s [8] 'divider' group, found in their cluster analysis. Finally ***Captives (C)*** also report low interruptions in both directions, but with low control.

	Integrators	Volleyers	Segmenters
In control	Fusion lovers *fusion lovers*	Quality timers	Firsters (work or family) *family firsters* *dividers*
Low control	Reactors *moderates*	Job Warriors *job warriors*	Captives *Captives*

Table 1: Comparison of Kossek's Flexstyles (standard text) [7] with our resulting clusters (in italics).

Clusters and Device Use

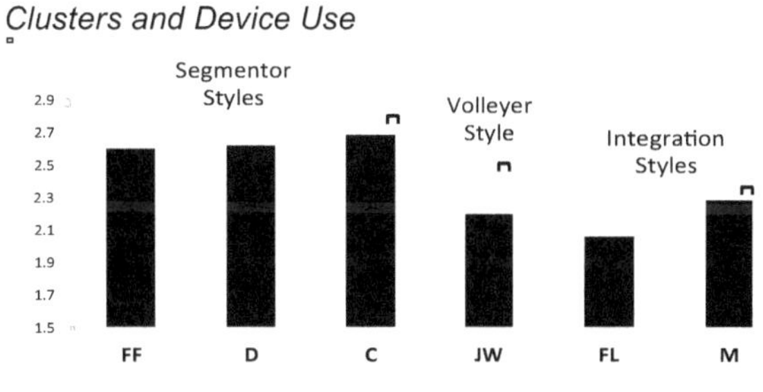

Figure 3: Device Separation Score across clusters.

To explore whether people's boundary behaviours are related to their technology boundary tactics, we looked at the total number of devices participants' used and device separation scores across clusters. The total number of devices owned did not differ significantly between clusters, however a one-way between groups analysis of variance suggested the device separation scores did: $F(5, 254)= 8.0$, $p<0.01$. As illustrated by Figure 3, those with segmentation behaviours had higher device separation scores than those with integrator behaviours. Post-hoc tests using Tukey HSD suggest this difference was significant for Fusion Lovers (M=2.05, SD=0.69) who had a lower score than Family Firsters (M=2.60, SD=0.52) Dividers (M=2.61, SD=0.48) and Captives (M=2.68, SD=0.51).

DISCUSSION

To discover our participants' boundary behaviour styles we clustered them based on their scores on the WLI developed by Kossek et al. [8] as this approach allows us to consider how a combination of variables important to work-life balance relate to technology use. We compared our resulting clusters to their qualitative flexstyle descriptions [7] and to their own cluster analysis based on the WLI [8]. We found some overlap in our clusters with theirs, but some differences, which we suggest are due to the different samples used: they used a sample of North American teleworkers, whereas we considered a representative sample of the whole UK working population. We found that using separate devices for home and work *is* something that our participants do, and that the extent to which they do it is related to their boundary behaviour styles. Therefore, whilst mobile ICTs become more multi-functional and offer easier integration of work and home in one device, our findings suggest not everyone chooses to do this: we found people with segmentation boundary behaviour styles were more likely to have separate devices for home and work, even though overall they used the same number of devices as those with integration behaviour styles. This could suggest that using separate devices creates more separation between home and work and decreases interruptions, and that it is an effective boundary management tactic. Alternatively, it could just be that people who prefer to segment their work and non-work lives are more likely to use device separation as a tactic. However, we measured boundary *behaviours* rather than preferences: some of our participants reported low levels of perceived control over their boundaries (in particular job warriors and captives) which has been linked to lower work-life outcomes [8]. Therefore, if they are unhappy with their current boundary behaviour style, being aware of this and adopting a different device separation tactic could help change their behaviour. For example, Job Warriors could benefit from using separate devices for home and work, or, if they are able, captives could try using their devices across home and work more. These findings also have implications for BYOD policies: whilst they may decrease cost and save people carrying multiple devices around, some people may want to buy a separate device for work/school in order to stay in control of their boundaries.

CONCLUSIONS

In this research we have highlighted the impact of multiple device usage on work-life boundary management as a topic that warrants further HCI research, especially given the growing trend for BYOD policies at work and school. We have verified and extended previous work on boundary behaviour styles, and have found evidence that people use their devices to create and maintain boundaries between work and non-work in line with their preferred boundary behaviour style.

ACKNOWLEDGMENTS

This research was funded by the EPSRC Digital Epiphanies project EP/K025392/1. Many thanks to Jon Bird, and UCLIC and CHI reviewers for comments on the drafts.

REFERENCES

1. Ashforth, B.E., Kreiner, G.E., and Fugate, M. All in a day's work: Boundaries and micro role transitions. *Academy of Management review 25*, 3 (2000), 472-491.
2. Battard, N., and Mangematin, V. Idiosyncratic distances: Impact of mobile technology practices on role segmentation and integration. *Technological Forecasting and Social Change 80*, 2 (2013), 231-242.
3. Diaz, I., Chiaburu, D.S., Zimmerman, R.D., and Boswell, W.R. Communication technology: Pros and cons of constant connection to work. *Journal of Vocational Behavior 80*, 2 (2012), 500-508.
4. Duxbury, L., Higgins, C., Smart, R., and Stevenson, M. Mobile technology and boundary permeability. *British Journal of Management 25,* 3 (2014), 570-588.
5. Grevet, C. Managing the work-home boundary in a BYOD culture. *Workshop on Socio-Technical Systems and Work-Home Boundaries. Mobile HCI'14* (2014).
6. Kirchmeyer, C. Managing the work-nonwork boundary: An assessment of organizational responses. *Human Relations 48*, 5 (1995), 515-536.
7. Kossek, E.E., and Lautsch, B.A. *CEO of me: Creating a life that works in the flexible job age*. Pearson Prentice Hall, (2007).
8. Kossek, E.E., Ruderman, M.N., Braddy, P.W., and Hannum, K.M. Work–nonwork boundary management profiles: A person-centered approach. *Journal of Vocational Behavior 81*, 1 (2012), 112-128.
9. Kreiner, G.E., Hollensbe, E.C., and Sheep, M.L. Balancing borders and bridges: Negotiating the work-home interface via boundary work tactics. *Academy of Management Journal 52*, 4 (2009), 704-730.
10. Nam, T. Technology Use and Work-Life Balance. *Applied Research in Quality of Life* (2013), 1-24.
11. Park, Y., and Jex, S.M. Work-home boundary management using communication and information technology. *International Journal of Stress Management 18*, 2 (2011), 133.

Working 9-5? Professional Differences in Email and Boundary Management Practices

Marta E. Cecchinato
UCL Interaction Centre
University College London
London, WC1E 6BT
m.cecchinato@cs.ucl.ac.uk

Anna L. Cox
UCL Interaction Centre
University College London
London, WC1E 6BT
anna.cox@ucl.ac.uk

Jon Bird
HCID Research Centre
City University London
London, EC1V 0HB
jon.bird@city.ac.uk

ABSTRACT
Technology not only brings benefits such as flexible working practices but can also have negative stressful consequences such as increasing email overload and the blurring of work-home boundaries. We report on an exploratory study that extends the current understanding of email usage by investigating how different professions at a university manage work and personal emails using different devices and how this impacts their work-home boundary management. Our findings lead us to identify two user groups: those with permeable boundaries (primarily academics) and those who have more rigid ones (primarily professional services employees) and that there are differences in when, where and how they manage their work and personal emails. In particular we find that some participants use *micro-boundary* strategies to manage transitions between work and personal life. Based on these novel findings we propose improvements of email software design to facilitate effective email, work-home boundary management, and micro-boundary practices.

Author Keywords
Email; work and personal email; email overload; cross-device interaction; boundary management; work-home interference.

ACM Classification Keywords
H.5.m. Information interfaces and presentation (e.g. HCI): Miscellaneous.

INTRODUCTION
As technology becomes increasingly embedded in our everyday life through a suite of devices, the way we work is changing. Over the past couple of decades email has brought numerous improvements to the way we communicate and work. However, there are also negative consequences: the increasing number of emails exchanged requires more time to read, respond to, file or delete, resulting in email-related stress, or 'email overload' [7], i.e. the lack of control felt when trying to deal with a growing number of emails. Furthermore, constant connectivity means people often feel they are expected to respond to emails at any time or anywhere [21] and this can lead to work interfering with home life. Such interference has been proven to have a negative impact on health, with a significant positive correlation between work interrupting non-work and psychological distress [18].

However, the differences in the way personal and work emails are managed are currently understudied. Most prior research has investigated the professional use of email, focusing on management strategies, e.g. [7,33], since the number of business emails sent daily is growing and is expected to increase from 100 billion in 2014 to 132 billion by 2017 [27]. Email management studies generally recruit participants from different professional groups to overcome the limitation of collecting data only from one type of work setting. Samples have ranged from university employees (faculty staff, students or admins), e.g. [3,6], to technology companies, e.g. [31,32], to a mixture of professions, e.g. [13,30]. However, this prior research has not focused on differences in email management in different working environments or how different strategies impact on work-home boundaries. A further limitation of email research to date is that it has concentrated on defining email practices for specific devices such as desktop computers, e.g. [10,33], or briefly outlining new uses of mobile phones with regard to emails, e.g. [20,23], but little research has compared email processing strategies on different devices or how they might result in work interfering with home life.

In this paper we report on an exploratory study that extends our current understanding of email usage by investigating how different professions manage work and personal emails using different devices and how this impacts their work-home boundary management. We make three contributions. First, we show that not just individual differences, but also professional context has a large impact on email practices: when, where and how people manage emails and the impact these have on work-home boundaries. Second, we describe the novel finding that some users rely on *micro-boundary*

CHI 2015, April 18 - 23, 2015, Seoul, Republic of Korea
Copyright is held by the owner/author(s). Publication rights licensed to ACM. ACM 978-1-4503-3145-6/15/04...$15.00
http://dx.doi.org/10.1145/2702123.2702537

email practices to support their transitions between work and personal life. These findings inform the third contribution, which are a set of recommendations to improve email software design to help users manage their email and work-home boundaries.

RELATED WORK

In this section we present relevant research in the three strands of literature our study draws from, in order to highlight the following three gaps that inform our research questions:

- Differences in the ways professional groups use email is understudied, with only two studies [8,32] directly investigating such differences.
- There is still little understanding of how people specifically manage email across devices, and across work and personal accounts.
- There is a need for an increased understanding of how boundary management practices – a field that is less considered in human-computer interaction (HCI) – are applied to devices and email accounts.

Differences in Email Management Styles

Findings in email management research are usually based on studies that have participants drawn from a variety of professional groups (academics, mixed professions and/or employees in the tech industry) to avoid bias. However, the studies do not typically contrast the email management practices of these diverse professional groups, implying there are no differences. One exception is found in Dearman et al. [8]: their interview study compared computer science researchers from industry with those from academia. Differences in email practices between the two professional groups were not reported, but it was found that industry users had clearer boundaries between personal and work devices, suggesting that it is the working environment that influences people's boundary management practices.

Work Email

Work email usage reflects both individual preferences and professional demands [6], and the level of seniority may have an impact [16]. Individual preferences include how often the user clears the inbox and files away emails, whether this is done automatically or manually and the frequency of occurrence [19]. Professional demands have been noticed when comparing managers with non-managers across 29 countries (n =13,877) [32]. Managers were found to have almost double the number of stored messages, and more than double the number of folders than non-managers, suggesting that job role partially accounts for the variance in filing style.

Personal Email

Research has shown that work emails are managed differently to personal emails, i.e. communicating with friends and relatives, and with organisations such as schools and businesses [3,13]. Differences include the software used to check email (desktop vs. web client), the types of emails received, and the email management strategies employed.

To the best of our knowledge, only two studies have explicitly compared work and personal email practices across the same sample. In 2013, Grevet et al. [13] used a mixed methods approach, combining interviews with screenshots to measure the size of each participant's email inbox. They recruited 19 participants with diverse job titles who used Gmail for both their work and personal accounts. They demonstrated that even though work email has doubled in size over the years, personal email accounts were found to be 5 times bigger than work ones, especially for the number of unread messages. Despite this huge growth of exchanged emails, Rector and Hailpern [28] found that only 12.37% of emails are actually critical (i.e. too important to miss).

Capra et al. [3] conducted a survey-based study (n=596) with university employees (both academics and professional services employees) to look at usage patterns across personal and work email accounts. Their findings suggest that there are strong individual preferences in both contexts and that email is an important boundary management artefact. They argue that email can increase boundary permeation between work and personal life. Despite recognising their importance, Capra et al. do not investigate the role of mobile devices in managing the boundary between work and personal emails.

Cross-Device Interaction (XDI)

Today, 58% of Americans own a smartphone and 89% use them to check emails [25]. However, the majority of email research focuses on how email is used on single devices such as desktop and laptop computers. As mobile technologies are becoming increasingly affordable and ubiquitous, workers have access to multiple devices (computers, smartphones, tablets). More research needs to investigate how email is managed across the suite of devices we now own and/or have access to. Research in email cross-device interaction (XDI) [29] is rather fragmented as it either looks at how users access and manage data across personal and work desktop computer/laptop devices, but not smartphones [8]; or how tasks are completed across computer and smartphone devices, without distinguishing between work and personal purposes [17].

Only two studies have reported the use of different devices to access emails: in [13] they were treated as anecdotes and hence not included in the analysis. However, a noteworthy study conducted in 2009 by Matthews et al. [20] directly explored how new generation phones like the iPhone 3G were used. They interviewed 21 members of a corporate research lab to uncover usage patterns. Even though they did not focus on cross-device interaction or specifically on email use, their results describe how smartphones were used in combination with computers. For example, their users preferred using their phone to triage messages in the inbox, while fully featured computers were used for reading and replying to emails. They also observed that smartphones were used to maintain awareness of information while away from a computer, e.g. checking for emails from remote collaborators. The ways in which people use mobile devices is evolving [9] and the usage scenario today looks very different from five years ago. Therefore we reconsider these findings in the context of today's use of mobile devices.

Boundary Management

Academic interest in mobile email use is not just limited to the HCI field, but is also a focus in the work-home conflict and boundary management literature where mobile technologies are seen as a facilitator of increased spill-overs between personal and work domains. Such spill-overs occur when "*the strain produced by stressors in one domain provokes stressful situations in another domain*" ([12] p. 15). Boundaries between work and home can be conceptualised along an integration/segmentation continuum [22]. At one end of the continuum are individuals who tend to have work and home domains fully integrated, where 'home' and 'work' are "*one giant category of social existence, for no conceptual boundary separates its contents or meaning*" ([22] p.567). At the other end are those for whom work and home are perceived as two completely separate worlds. These two positions constitute extremes and people are typically somewhere in between. As a result, daily repeated shifts occur between the various roles one has in different domains (e.g. employee and parent). These shifts are known as "micro-role transitions" [1] and an example of this is when a parent receives a phone call or email from their child's school whilst at work. People's email strategies partly define where they are positioned along the integration-segmentation continuum [3].

We are interested in understanding how people use their email practices to create and maintain boundaries between work and non-work and how they handle cross-domain interruptions. This is especially important because interference between work and personal life is positively correlated with stress, particularly when work permeates non-work [18].

RESEARCH QUESTIONS

Even though devices have been classified as being personal or work-related, or a mixture [8], there is still a lack of understanding about how users access and manage both personal and work emails across multiple devices, in particular mobile devices. We argue that there is a need for an updated view of mobile usage patterns, especially in the context of boundary management. There is also little evidence about how different professional groups manage emails within the same organisation, even though there are indications of its existence [32]. We argue that understanding current boundary practices in different groups is a crucial first step to finding effective ways of dealing with email overload. To address these gaps, we used semi-structured interviews and questionnaires to investigate the following research questions:

1) How do people manage personal and work email accounts across devices?
2) What are the boundary management strategies adopted for personal and work email accounts across devices?
3) Are there email and boundary management differences between two professional groups from the same organization?

METHOD

Following [3,8,13,20] we took a qualitative approach to gain an in-depth understanding of participants' email practices. In particular, this study was designed as an extension of Capra et al. [3], who also recruited university participants, but builds on it in three novel ways: first, we take a more qualitative approach; second, we consider cross-device interaction; and third, we compare different professional groups. As a result, in May 2014 sixteen interviews with university employees were conducted in participants' offices and labs, lasting between 30 and 60 minutes. Questions explored participants' device usage patterns for managing email, their feelings towards emails in relation to work-home interference, and their email management practices, especially in relation to devices used to access emails while working and when not working. Participants were asked to bring along any device they used to access email as a prompt to facilitate contextual explanations. They were also asked if they were willing to share screenshots of their inboxes on their various devices, however only five participants agreed. Following the interviews, participants were asked to fill out two surveys: the first one included email overload measurement scales [7,14], whilst the second one included the Work-Life Indicator scale [18] to measure boundary management strategies. All but one participant completed both post-interview surveys. We report findings from the second survey to triangulate our interview data but results from the first survey are not reported in this paper.

Materials

The Work-Life Indicator scale is comprised of five factors: Work Interrupting Non-Work (WINW), which measures one direction of boundary crossing; Non-Work Interrupting Work (NWIW), that measures the opposite direction of boundary crossing; Boundary Control (BC), which measures the perceived control over boundary crossing; Family Identity (FI), which measures the degree of identification with a family role; and Work Identity (WI) which measures the salience of an occupational career. The five factors capture different styles of managing the boundaries between work and non-work by identifying the relationship between cross-role interruption behaviour (WINW, NWIW), identity centrality (FI, WI), and perceived control of boundaries (BC). A total of 17 items are used to measure the factors, using a 5-point Likert scale, with 1=Strongly Disagree and 5=Strongly Agree.

Participants
We recruited 16 participants from two professional groups at a single large university in London, UK. Our convenience sample included nine academic and seven professional services employees. Academics included research associates and assistants, a lecturer, and a teaching fellow. Professional services employees included a department manager, a human resources (HR) manager, library assistants, an assistant study coordinator, a personal assistant, and a public relations administrator. Fourteen participants were employed full-time, one had two part-time jobs within the same university and one was employed part-time. Two participants had an additional part-time job or were involved in volunteering. Ages ranged between 20 and 54, and 11 participants were female. All participants owned a smartphone with a data package (except for one who relied on Wi-Fi only) and had access to computers at home and at work. The sample was recruited using a recruitment website, posters, opt-in mailing lists and word-of-mouth. They received a total of £17 for taking part in the study.

Analysis
Interview transcriptions were integrated with paper notes and the email inbox screenshots and analysed thematically [2]. The first level of analysis focused on email differences across devices and domains (work vs. personal). The second level looked at differences between professional groups and boundary management strategies across devices and email accounts. The Work-Life Indicator questionnaire data were analysed for differences between the professional groups.

FINDINGS

Work-Life Indicator Questionnaire
Results from the Work-Life Indicator questionnaire show a distinction in how the two professional groups manage boundaries between work and non-work. Figure 1 shows the mean scores for each professional group for each of the five factors of the scale. There is a notable difference between the two groups regarding the extent to which they allow work to interrupt non-work: the academics score much higher on this value than the professional services staff, suggesting that their boundaries are more permeable. Mann-Whitney tests showed a significant difference (z=-2.04, p=0.04) between professional services participants and academics for WINW. On average academics experienced greater WINW (M=3.62, SE=0.31) than professional services staff (M=2.33, SE=0.43) and this represents a large-sized effect (r=0.53). The difference between the two professional groups was not significant for NWIW (z=-0.41, p>0.05); FI (z=-0.89, p>0.05); WI (z=-1.37, p>0.05); nor for BC (z=-1.36, p>0.05).

This analysis provides evidence to suggest that there is a significant difference between the two professional groups in terms of how they manage their cross-role interruptions. Boundary theory suggests it is unlikely that profession is the only factor of influence and that personal preferences play a large role in the extent to which people are willing to allow their work to interrupt their non-work time [1] and this might affect their use of technology [24]. The interview data supports this and provides evidence that, in addition to professional differences, individual preferences also play a role in boundary management styles. We also find evidence that people use their devices and digital systems to create boundaries between work and non-work.

Boundary Management Styles Between Professions
We identified differences between the two professional groups in the way they perceive their job and therefore handle their work email outside office hours. Professional services participants were not required to take emails outside office hours, and some were not even allowed to.

"I'm quite fortunate in that my work doesn't require me to take it home and I've never been in the situation where I would need to check it outside of working hours until now." – P12, Female, Professional Services worker (PS).

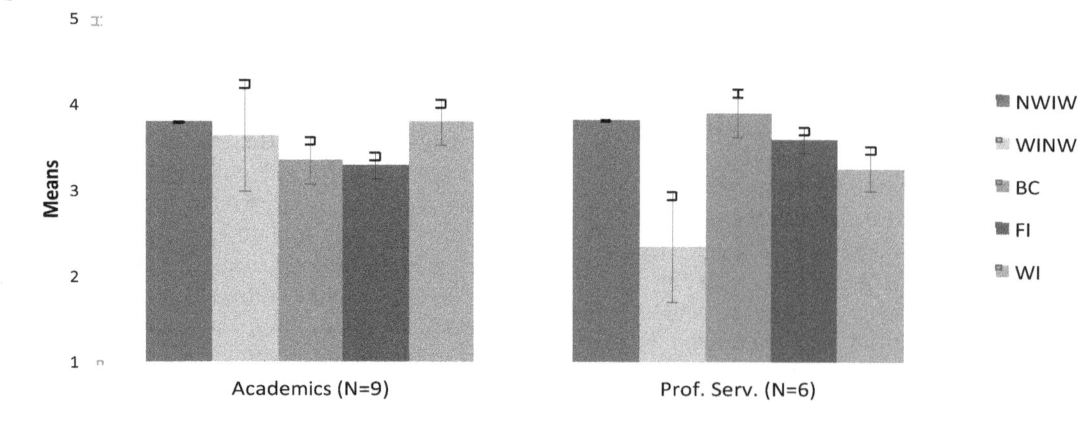

Figure 1: Mean values for the 5-factor Work-Life Indicator scale showing differences between the professional groups

Professional services participants occasionally checked their work emails during weekends or holidays as a way of maintaining awareness. Similarly, they checked their personal email accounts whilst at work, but as P13 explains, it was not viewed as a completely legitimate practice:

"In a way it's a demarcation [the fact that she cannot work from home] *but actually it's not* [...] *because I have my personal email even when I'm at work,* [whispers] *it's a little bit cheeky isn't it?"* – P13, Female, PS.

Conversely, the same situation is seen in a completely different manner by academics, who feel legitimized to check both personal and work accounts at all times.

"Some companies, they block your personal emails right? And I'm really glad I don't have that in case... you know, I really like that I can reply to a personal email and I don't need to have it so separately but then I also... if I can reply to personal stuff at work then I feel that I can reply to work stuff in my personal life." – P9, Female, Academic (A).

In interviews, academics described how theirs was not a typical office job and hence how the boundaries between work and personal life were blurred.

"I know it sounds a bit silly, but this job doesn't feel as much as a job and I don't mean it's not like hard work, but academia always feels a bit different." – P1, Female, A.

Although no significant difference was found in the survey between WINW and NWIW for academics, our interview data suggests that there is a symmetrical interference where work interrupts non-work and vice versa within academics. Rather than having clearly demarcated work hours, academics often reported that work and non-work are interweaved:

"The first check is probably right after I woke up, I will check everything that has come in the night [on the phone]. [...] *I will probably have another look once I'm outside the house, so during my commute time I will check once again. And once I'm in my office, I don't have any specific rule, it's really case by case.* [...] *Once I'm home* [...] *I have a second work shift after* [my son] *goes to bed until quite late in the night."* – P15, Male, A.

"In the back of my head I would like to not check my work emails in my personal time but I guess, realistically speaking, research is not really a 9 to 5 thing anyway. I guess if I had a job [where] *working happens between 9 to 5 and not outside that, then I would make more of an effort to not cross that boundary, but now it doesn't really fit with research I think."* – P9, Female, A.

In particular, one participant compared academia to other research jobs in industry, stressing the fact that email practices vary among professions and are influenced by company policies. While she was not allowed to take work emails outside the office in her previous industry research position, she now relies on being able to do so:

"I should say that when I was at [previous company] *I never checked email outside of work because I couldn't. It was only on my laptop, it wasn't allowed on my phone, I wasn't allowed to access it remotely and I very rarely checked on my laptop. So I only checked email going in the door at 8.30 in the morning until 5.30 at night and I never checked at home.* [...] *I have long commutes so for me, especially now that I work part-time and I have to leave early, if I can get my emails done there and back that's a real advantage."* – P1, Female, A.

Despite these general differences between professional groups, individual differences highlight how two of the professional services participants showed similarities to academics: the boundary between work and personal emails was not as clear for them and they reported this as a benefit. In one case an HR manager was able to better organise her work and her personal life as a result of allowing work to interrupt non-work time:

"I don't see looking at emails that are from home or vice versa as an interference at all in work-life balance. This is my life. So actually they balance it." – P14, Female, PS.

In the other case, a librarian underlined the positive benefits that mobile devices can bring to boundary management in the context of email:

"The environment is pushing you to have an imbalanced life towards of course work and that amazing smartphone is actually helping us not be unbalanced." – P7, Male, PS.

Email Management

Types of Account

All of our participants had at least two main email accounts, one of which they considered personal and the other work-related. They each had an Outlook account for their university job. A little more than a third of participants also had access to an additional work account, and reasons for this included:

- Having a second job;
- Needing to access a shared email account;
- Needing to access other features (e.g. Google Calendar, Google Documents);
- Needing to access social media (e.g. Facebook, YouTube);
- Archiving forwarded emails from a previous job account to which they no longer have access to.

Moreover, the majority of our participants had at least one additional personal account, mostly used for signing up to mailing lists and receiving promotional email that did not fall in the spam category but were still considered unwanted messages. We can summarise the motivations as:

- A desire for a different online identity (e.g. anonymous, full name, or nickname accounts);
- A management strategy to reduce email overload, expressed well in this quote:

"For example, if you apply online to something and then, you know, I don't want my email inbox to be uploaded with a lot of rubbish, then I use a different account, and I use that account just whenever I need it. [...] *Because then I don't want to be bombarded by all this commercial and promotion stuff."* – P14, Female, PS.

Email Accounts On Smartphones

Eleven respondents used their phone to check both personal and work accounts (all academics and two of the professional services staff). Five participants (the remaining professional services staff) accessed only their personal email account from mobile devices. Of the participants who accessed both work and personal accounts on their phone, five of them accessed the two types of account through separate applications. Of these five, four were Android users and the remaining owned an iPhone. Android users used two separate applications (one for work accounts and the other for personal accounts), while the iPhone user had two Internet browser bookmarks for the different accounts. When asked why, she explained that:

"I did used to have an app and then messages came up straight away but I would find that anytime that I would look at my phone I'd see messages unread and I'd always want to check and I don't always want to being doing that when I'm on my phone. Sometimes it's best not to know all the time if you have an unread message." – P6, Female, A.

Four participants, all of whom were academics, accessed both account types from the same application on their phone, signifying they did not separate their personal and work inboxes.

Email Accounts On Computers and Tablets

Three participants (of which one was a professional services participant) had personal email synchronised to the same desktop application they used to access work emails in the office. The majority of participants instead checked their personal account at work through a browser window or tab, which they always left open. Of these, only one participant (a professional services participant) also had notifications enabled for their personal account, as a Firefox plug-in. Three participants also anecdotally mentioned having a tablet: one did not use it for accessing emails (P15, Male, A); one used it to check both work and personal emails (P14, Female, PS); and another used it only to access personal emails (P10, Female, A).

Device Management

Checking Habits

Most participants used their phones primarily at home, when commuting, when socialising, at weekends and on holidays. Computers were mainly used in the office, or at home only if work had to be done. Only two participants did not use their phone at home to check emails, using instead a computer or a tablet. Respondents explained that it was faster to check on their phone because, along with always being at their fingertips, it helped fill up moments when one is bored, such as when commuting. One academic reported that using her smartphone meant she was: "*more in touch with what's going on more immediately than what I used to be before I got my new phone*" (P8, Female, A).

However, our interviews indicate that smartphones can intrude even in the most private of moments, and lead to work interfering with non-work, as highlighted by the questionnaire. For example, some participants use smartphones to check emails first thing in the morning when waking up and even in the bathroom:

"I get up, check my email, in bed, check my email on the toilet, check my email downstairs, maybe whilst I'm having breakfast, walk to work, generally don't check my email while I'm actually walking, when I'm waiting for the train, on the train, maybe in the lift getting up to work. Maybe then at work, then on the train on the way home, in front of the TV, during dinner, yeah, that's about everything I think." – P5, Male, A.

Smartphones vs. Computers

Overall, our participants were happy to use their smartphone for scanning through new emails and saw clearing their inbox as a way of dealing with an overloaded account.

"[On my phone] *I sometimes just look at my emails and delete all the* [spam] *ones at night so that I think 'oh when I go in in the morning then I won't have to do that at work and my inbox will be a bit more clear.'*" – P8, Female, A.

"I check my email very frequently [on my phone], *especially to get rid of all the spam."* – P5, Male, A.

In addition the majority of respondents explained they generally only reply on their phone if it is an urgent or quick matter, because they find "*having a little keypad is not very good for writing long things*" (P11, Male, PS).

While all academics accessed both work and personal email through their phone, only two professional services participants had both personal and work accounts on their mobile devices – the same ones who have permeable boundaries between work and non-work. Only two academics and one professional services participant used their phone to manage most of their emails, including replying, explaining that "*it's just quicker*" (P4, Female, A).

Notifications

We found a substantial difference in the way devices are used when we asked about notifications: while all but one had work email notifications enabled on their computers, more than half of our participants chose to not be interrupted by email notifications on their phone. In fact, they either disabled them completely; consciously disabled them during certain hours; disabled pop-up/sound notifications that would increase the number of interruptions; or limited them only for particular senders or specific accounts.

"No I turned [notifications] *off, it's really annoying* [...] *when I'm not at work I don't like being alerted about emails coming in. If I want to check my emails I'll check it, but I don't really like being alerted."* – P16, Female, A.

Interestingly, one participant, used her phone as a notification centre that triggered her to check directly on her computer while at work because *"it's a nice big screen and it's a nicer interface to sort of read the emails with"* (P8, Female, A).

Boundary Management Challenges

The interviews revealed situations where it was not possible to maintain clear boundaries between work and personal email, despite using devices for only one type of account or not checking emails at certain times. While weekends are generally considered personal time which require less checking "*'cause I know that most people are not at work*" (P16, Female, A), work emails might be dealt with as an exception for urgent matters, one participant explaining "*if I am on a deadline it can interfere*" (P4, Female, A).

P10 underlines a boundary management issue that can arise during holidays because not everyone has the same time off work:

"If I'm going on holidays not everybody is going at the same time and sometimes they really need something urgent and I feel they cannot wait." – P10, Female, A.

Similarly, working part-time can also force people to deal with work emails during non-work time:

"Our students, they aren't part-time and because I take Fridays and Mondays off, if they need something on a Friday then I don't check again until Tuesday, that's a long time for them to wait. So I guess it's like yes my life is carrying on in a different way but other people's lives they also have needs and I have a responsibility to them." – P1, Female, A.

Participants reported receiving complaints at home when work interrupted their personal life:

"It does irritate my partner. Like if we're in front of the TV and she's playing on a game on her phone and I check my work email then that would irritate her 'cause [...] she sees it like me being in work rather than spending time with her." – P5, Male, A.

Even when participants tried to keep personal and work email accounts separate there were two cases of interference between work and non-work, again suggesting individual differences. One participant used Gmail for their personal account, but also got work notifications because it is automatically linked to features used primarily for collaborative work (e.g. Google Documents). Another participant's work account received personal messages from her close family/friends who chose to use it "*because they know that I see it more often*" (P10, Female, A).

Cross-Device Issues

Despite continuous improvements in technology, users still experience problems related to cross-device interaction that are mostly a result of technical issues. For example, several respondents reported feeling frustrated when email applications on different devices did not synchronise properly (e.g. an email sent on one device was not shown in the sent folder on the other device).

Another issue raised was related to cross-device task completion. Users who relied on messages being marked unread as a strategy to remember to do something, had trouble keeping track of their inbox to-do list because when they scanned emails on their phone while travelling to work these messages would then be marked as read and they would then forget to act upon them once they arrived in the office.

"What I'll do on my phone is [...] *I'll go into my work email* [...] *at night time and then I'll say 'I'll sort all those tomorrow when I go to work' but because they're not marked as unread anymore, whenever I go to work I forget to reply to them because they're marked as read so I sort of feel I've handled them."* – P8, Female, A.

Other technical issues mentioned refer to tabs [11], a recently added feature in Gmail, which automatically sort new emails depending on the type of message. As of August 2014, the five tabs are: 'primary', 'social', 'promotions', 'updates' and 'forums'. Despite appreciating this feature on the web client, users lamented the extra work it involved on other platforms where the filtering system did not work:

"I think [Gmail tabs] *are good because generally the social stuff I'm not that interested in and the promotional stuff is mainly spam.* [...] *It's interesting because when I access my same account on my phone it doesn't have those filters, so it's just all in one block.* [...] *With the phone I need to delete things that are near the top* [...] *because that's getting in my way, whereas on the browser account because I've already filtered out those things I can just leave them there."* – P5, Male, A (an iPhone user with Gmail synced to Mail app).

"The online account creates three tabs, social, commercial, promotion, which is actually quite helpful for me, which I don't have here [Thunderbird] *but I use quite a lot there because it divides stuff so I just go on the social tab and delete most of the things, I go to the third tab and I delete most of the things."* – P7, Male, PS.

DISCUSSION

This study extends previous research by providing insights into how different professional groups in the same organisation manage work and personal emails using different devices and how this impacts the way they manage the boundary between work and non-work. Initial findings from this study were reported in [5]. By triangulating the interview data with the findings from the

Work-Life Indicator questionnaire, several novel findings come out of the study. First, we show that, other than just individual preferences, professional context also has a large impact on email practices: when, where and how people manage emails and the impact these have on work-home boundaries. Second, we find that some users rely on *micro-boundary* email practices to support their transitions between work and personal life.

Profession Influences Email and Work-Home Boundary Management

Our study confirms Dearman et al.'s [8] findings that working environment influences people's boundary management practices and extends them to different professional groups. We found that both professional services staff and academics allow non-work emails to interrupt work, for both convenience as well as emergencies. However, there is a significant difference between the two groups in the extent to which work email interferes with non-work: in the interviews, academics report having symmetrical interference between work and non-work, whereas professional services staff report having an asymmetry and work does not tend to interfere with non-work.

We found that professional services participants generally have a work culture that rigidly separates work and non-work. 'Working 9 to 5' means they do not need to access work emails in their private time and there are fewer work interruptions during non-work time. In contrast, academics do not consider themselves to have a 9 to 5 job and have more permeable boundaries between work and non-work. Academics often reported that they needed to be available for work during personal time, particularly if they worked part-time, and for some this also extended to when they were on holiday. A potentially negative consequence is that academics reported work interrupting non-work more often than professional services participants and this is supported by the results of the Work-Life Indicator questionnaire.

A few exceptions were found in the patterns of interference between work and non-work typical of professional service staff and academics. Two professional services participants reported having symmetrical interference more similar to academics; and two academics said that they did not allow work to interrupt non-work as much as their peers. These exceptions can be partially explained by a personal preference in how to manage work-home boundaries. This does not mean however, that the working environment does not influence their behaviour. P1 in particular illustrated the importance of organizational culture on email management when comparing her previous research job in industry, where she was not allowed to check work emails outside the office, with her current academic role, where she benefitted from being able to manage her emails on her commute to and from work.

In summary, we provide evidence that the symmetry of interference between work and non-work email management is a function of job type, which had previously only been hypothesised [18]. Capra et al. [3] also found an asymmetrical imbalance between work and personal life, but they did not distinguish between professional groups, nor did they consider the consequences of these interruptions. We found in our survey that work interfering with non-work led to complaints by other members of participants' households, and this was especially true for academics. This comes as no surprise, given that academics are known for having more challenging work-home boundaries compared to some other professions, due to the overarching work culture that goes beyond individual universities.

We also found that there is a difference in the way professional groups used smartphones to access their different email accounts. All academics used their privately-owned phone to check both personal and work accounts, supporting research that has argued that phones are sometimes considered both personal and work devices [8]. In contrast, only two professional services participants accessed their work email accounts on their phone. Participants had a tendency to use their devices in specific locations: smartphones were primarily used to access emails at home and on the move (e.g. on public transport), but usually not in the office; computers were primarily associated with work activities. The fact that only professional services staff restricted their email to personal accounts on their phones suggests that smartphones are considered differently between the two professional groups. In addition, confirming our finding that smartphones intrude even in the most private of moments, Pielot et al. [26] found that the number of emails received on smartphones is correlated with stress from receiving work emails after work. Moreover, we are able to confirm that Matthews et al.'s [20] findings are still valid after five years where people generally still use their phones to triage their email, and computers respond to messages, despite the fact that mobile behaviours are said to have changed over the course of that time [9].

Micro-Boundaries to Minimise Interruptions

Our study indicates how, in general, interviewed professional services participants are positioned towards the segmentation end of the work-home boundary continuum (i.e. have more rigid boundaries), while interviewed academics are placed more towards the integration end of the continuum (i.e. have more permeable boundaries). However, boundary management behaviours are context dependent and the pervasive nature of email and its accessibility across devices has increased the frequency of unexpected micro-role transitions, e.g. receiving a work email at home. We found these transitions can have negative consequences, such as participants reporting complaints in their household about their emails habits. The interviews show that, particularly within devices, users developed resilience strategies to help them minimise transitions between different work and home micro-roles and their associated negative effects. We describe these strategies as *micro-boundaries* and define them as:

A strategy to limit the impact of micro-role transitions caused by cross-domain technology mediated interruptions.

Examples of micro-boundary strategies in email management that emerged from our interviews include:

- Checking personal and work emails on the same device (computer or phone) but on separate applications, thereby limiting the temptation of checking work emails during non-work time;
- Deliberately removing work email from their phone during time off, e.g. when on holiday;
- Creating dedicated folders for one domain in another domain account with automatic filtering, i.e. functionality that is similar to Gmail tabs.

All but three participants kept personal and work accounts separated while at work and used micro-boundary practices to switch between the two domains. We hypothesise that people who are highly engaged in their work and therefore suffer more from high levels of work interrupting non-work (such as academics) could benefit from these practices. More work is needed to explore micro-boundary practices within other professional groups to extend the novel findings presented in this paper.

DESIGN IMPLICATIONS

Strategies to overcome the stressful effects of email need to take into account boundary management preferences and cross-device interaction, and be updated regularly to keep up with technological advancements. As a result of our findings, we propose a set of recommendations that rely on personalisation and customisation, as previously suggested by Cecchinato et al. [4], to minimise the negative consequences of email and support micro-boundary practices:

- *Setting contextual notifications based on locations and account type.*

Our results suggest that people have personal preferences about notifications depending on the type of account and where they are (e.g. home, office, commute). Jackson et al. [15] found that users react to 70% of emails within six seconds from being notified. By disabling notifications outside office hours (an example of micro-boundary practice) our users reduced the number of interruptions caused by email. Hence, we recommend creating smart-notifications that allow users to decide when to be notified and from which account, based on their location. This is especially important for users who prefer having all accounts synchronised to a single mobile application, because it would give them more control on when and where interruptions occur.

- *Automatically tagging email with device icons based on where they were first opened.*

Some participants complained that while at work they would forget to reply to emails which had originally been opened on a mobile device and thus got lost in the sea of messages. Enabling automatic tagging of emails with a device icon based on where they were first opened could enable users to re-arrange their inbox and address this issue.

CONCLUSION

We have extended previous work on work-home boundary management and cross-device interaction by investigating the email practices of two professional groups at the same university. Despite the small sample size, our study shows differences between professional groups in terms of email and boundary management practices, and the way these are carried out on multiple devices. We found that the symmetry of interference between work and non-work reflects job function. Interviewed professional services staff typically have 9 to 5 jobs with rigid boundaries defined around working hours; interviewed academics have more permeable boundaries and report significantly more interference between work and non-work, which other studies have shown can result in increased stress. We therefore propose that people with more permeable boundary management styles create micro-boundaries to help them reduce micro-role transitions between work and personal domains, for example, using separate email clients for work and personal emails.

Overall, implications from this study may have a significant impact in areas beyond both email and a university context. As a result, further work could be completed in this direction to investigate how micro-boundary practices differ between other professional groups. More generally, we propose a set of design recommendations and argue that new email client features should be implemented to reduce the negative effects of email.

ACKNOWLEDGMENTS

We thank Siân Lindley, Daniel Harrison and the reviewers for their helpful feedback. This work is funded by an EPSRC DTG studentship and supported by the EPSRC grant EP/K025392/1 Digital Epiphanies project.

REFERENCES

1. Ashforth, B., Kreiner, G., and Fugate, M. All in a day's work: boundaries and micro-role transitions. *Academy of Management review 25*, 3 (2000), 472–491.
2. Braun, V. and Clarke, V. Using thematic analysis in psychology. *Qualitative Research in Psychology 3*, 2 (2006), 77–101.
3. Capra, R., Khanova, J., and Ramdeen, S. Work and personal e-mail use by university employees: PIM practices across domain boundaries. *Journal of the American Society for Information Science and Technology 64*, 5 (2013), 1029–1044.
4. Cecchinato, M.E., Bird, J., and Cox, A.L. Personalised Email Tools: A Solution to Email Overload? *CHI'14*

Workshop on Personalised Behaviour Change Technologies, (2014), 1–4.

5. Cecchinato, M.E., Cox, A.L., and Bird, J. "I check my emails on the toilet": Email Practices and Work-Home Boundary Management. *MobileHCI'14 Workshop on Socio-Technical Systems and Work-Home Boundaries*, (2014), 1–4.
6. Dabbish, L., Kraut, R., Fussell, S., and Kiesler, S. Understanding email use: predicting action on a message. *Proc. of CHI*, (2005), 691–700.
7. Dabbish, L. and Kraut, R. Email overload at work: an analysis of factors associated with email strain. *Proc. of CSCW*, (2006), 431–440.
8. Dearman, D. and Pierce, J.S. "It's on my other Computer!": Computing with Multiple Devices. *Proc. of CHI*, (2008), 767–776.
9. Dery, K., Kolb, D., and MacCormick, J. Working with connective flow: how smartphone use is evolving in practice. *European Journal of Information Systems*, April (2014), 1–13.
10. Fisher, D., Brush, a. J., Gleave, E., and Smith, M. a. Revisiting Whittaker & Sidner's "email overload" ten years later. *Proc. of CSCW* (2006), 309–312.
11. Google Help Center. Inbox tabs and category labels. 2013. http://bit.ly/Zno8R4.
12. Greenhaus, J. and Parasuraman, S. A Work-Nonwork Interactive Perspective of Stress and Its Consequences. *Journal of Organizational Behavior 8*, 2 (1987), 37–60.
13. Grevet, C., Choi, D., Kumar, D., and Gilbert, E. Overload is Overloaded : Email in the Age of Gmail. *Proc. of CHI*, (2014), 793–802.
14. Hogan, B. and Fisher, D. A scale for measuring email overload. *Microsoft Research 7*, 9 (2006).
15. Jackson, B.T.W., Dawson, R., and Wilson, D. Understanding email interaction increases organisational productivity. *Communications of the ACM 46*, 2003, 80–84.
16. Kamsin, A., Blandford, A., and Cox, A. Personal task management: my tools fall apart when I'm very busy! *CHI'12 Extended Abstracts on Human Factors in Computing Systems*, (2012), 1369–1374.
17. Karlson, A., Iqbal, S., and Meyers, B. Mobile taskflow in context: a screenshot study of smartphone usage. *Proc. of CHI*, (2010), 2009–2018.
18. Kossek, E.E., Ruderman, M.N., Braddy, P.W., and Hannum, K.M. Work–nonwork boundary management profiles: A person-centered approach. *Journal of Vocational Behavior 81*, 1 (2012), 112–128.
19. Mackay, W. Diversity in the use of electronic mail: A preliminary inquiry. *ACM Transactions on Information Systems (TOIS) 6*, 4 (1988), 380–397.
20. Matthews, T., Pierce, J., Road, H., Jose, S., and Tang, J. No smartphone is an island: the impact of places, situation and other device on smart phone use. *IBM RJ10452. 10452*, 2009, 1–10.
21. Mazmanian, M. and Erickson, I. The product of availability: understanding the economic underpinnings of constant connectivity. *Proc. of CHI*, (2014), 763–772.
22. Nippert-Eng, C. Calendars and keys: The classification of "home" and "work." *Sociological Forum 11*, 3 (1996), 563–582.
23. Oulasvirta, A. and Sumari, L. Mobile kits and laptop trays: managing multiple devices in mobile information work. *Proc. of CHI*, (2007), 1127–1136.
24. Park, Y., Fritz, C., and Jex, S.M. Relationships between work-home segmentation and psychological detachment from work: The role of communication technology use at home. *Journal of Occupational Health Psychology 16*, 2011, 457–467.
25. Pew Research. Mobile Technology Fact Sheet. 2014. http://pewrsr.ch/OotDJE.
26. Pielot, M., Church, K., and Oliveira, R. De. An In-Situ Study of Mobile Phone Notifications. *Proc. of MobileHCI*, (2013), 233-242.
27. Radicati Group. Email Statistics Report, 2013-2017. http://bit.ly/1l2gJ2z.
28. Rector, K. and Hailpern, J. MinEMail: SMS alert system for managing critical emails. *Proc. of CHI*, (2014), 783–792.
29. Scharf, F., Wolters, C., Cassens, J., and Herczeg, M. Cross-Device Interaction. *AMBIENT 2013, The Third International Conference on Ambient Computing, Applications, Services and Technologies*, (2013), 35–41.
30. Soucek, R. and Moser, K. Coping with information overload in email communication: Evaluation of a training intervention. *Computers in Human Behavior 26*, 6 (2010), 1458–1466.
31. Sumecki, D., Chipulu, M., and Ojiako, U. Email overload: Exploring the moderating role of the perception of email as a 'business critical' tool. *International Journal of Information Management 31*, 5 (2011), 407–414.
32. Tang, J., Matthews, T., Cerruti, J., et al. Global differences in attributes of email usage. *Proceedings of the 2009 international workshop on Intercultural collaboration*, (2009), 185–194.
33. Whittaker, S. and Sidner, C. Email overload: exploring personal information management of email. *Proc. of CHI*, (1996), 276–283.

Inferring Employee Engagement from Social Media

N. Sadat Shami[1], Michael Muller[2], Aditya Pal[3], Mikhil Masli[1], Werner Geyer[2]
[1]IBM, 1 New Orchard Road, Armonk, NY 10504, USA
[2]IBM Research, 1 Rogers St., Cambridge, MA 02142, USA
[3]IBM Research, 650 Harry Road, San Jose, CA 95120, USA
{ sadat, michael_muller, apal, mnmasli, werner.geyer } @ us.ibm.com

ABSTRACT
Employees increasingly are expressing ideas and feelings through enterprise social media. Recent work in CHI and CSCW has applied linguistic analysis towards understanding employee experiences. In this paper, we apply dictionary based linguistic analysis to measure 'Employee Engagement'. Employee engagement is a measure of employee willingness to apply discretionary effort towards organizational goals, and plays an important role in organizational outcomes such as financial or operational results. Organizations typically use surveys to measure engagement. This paper describes an approach to model employee engagement based on word choice in social media. This method can potentially complement surveys, thus providing more real-time insights into engagement and allowing organizations to address engagement issues faster. Our results predicting engagement scores on a survey by combining demographics with social media text demonstrate that social media text has significant predictive power compared to demographic data alone. We also find that engagement may be a state than a stable trait since social media posts closer to the administration of the survey had the most predictive power. We further identify the minimum number of social media posts required per employee for the best prediction.

Author Keywords
Social media; employee engagement; workplace; work; office; workforce analytics; social analytics; language.

ACM Classification Keywords
H.5.3 [Information Interfaces]: Group and Organization Interfaces – *Computer Supported Cooperative Work.*

General Terms
Human Factors; Design; Measurement.

CHI 2015, April 18 - 23 2015, Seoul, Republic of Korea
Copyright 2015 ACM 978-1-4503-3145-6/15/04…$15.00
http://dx.doi.org/10.1145/2702123.2702445

INTRODUCTION
Workforce studies have attracted increasing attention in the CHI and CSCW tradition. Recent studies have focused on areas such as crowdwork and worker availability [e.g. 25, 34, 53], multitasking [e.g. 32, 33], use of cloud based tools [56], serendipitous interaction [6] etc. In addition to these studies of work practices and/or technologies, we have also seen an interest in larger-scale studies of employee experiences from social media [9, 21, 32, 48, 49, 60].

We continue the line of research inquiry that utilizes social media to better understand the employee experience. In this paper we focus on employee engagement, a concept that has gained attention in both behavioral and business domains. Employee engagement has received much interest in recent years [31] due to its perceived relationship with workers' relationship to their workplace, as well as improved financial and operational results for businesses [22, 23, 43]. Although there is no clear consensus on the definition of employee engagement, it could be regarded as "going the extra mile" in service of organizational goals [59]. Research on employee engagement has mostly been conducted in the organizational psychology field, but interest in understanding the employee experience has grown in CSCW and other fields [e.g. 9, 38, 49, 57]. Increasingly, researchers are finding relationships between employee experience and social media [9, 21, 32, 38, 49].

Employees are increasingly adopting social media, often spontaneously sharing their opinions and feelings about work related issues on internal social platforms [3, 12, 62], and are willing to have their social media content mined provided certain privacy conditions are met [21]. A survey conducted by global consulting firm McKinsey found that 65% of the companies they studied use social technologies [12]. Surveys of Microsoft employees conducted from 2008 to 2012 found gradual increase of social media usage among employees [3, 62]. Social media thus offers an opportunity to gain insights into employee engagement through the analysis of employee social media posts.

Currently, tools exist that allow textual analysis of employee social media content [e.g. 9, 49]. Most of these tools focus on sentiment analysis of employee social media chatter. We believe that other forms of linguistic analysis of social media could be possible. One analysis that could provide value to an organization is the ability to infer employee engagement from the words employees use in their social media posts. A real-time understanding of employee engagement achieved through mining social media text could allow an organization to respond to emergent employee issues more rapidly compared to the traditional way of collecting employee feedback through an annual employee engagement survey.

In this paper, we conduct an exploratory study of whether social media text can be used to improve a statistical model to predict employee engagement in a large multinational company. The paper is organized as follows. We first review related work on employee engagement measurement and how social media can enrich the measurement methods available to organizations for measuring employee engagement. We then outline our research questions and describe how we answered them. We conclude with a discussion of our findings, weaving together practical, theoretical, and design implications.

LITERATURE REVIEW AND RESEARCH QUESTIONS

Employee engagement

The importance of employee engagement has been stressed in both the academic and practitioner literature. For example, a study of 65 firms in different industries found that the top 25% on an engagement index had greater profitability, and more than double the shareholder value compared to the bottom 25% [30]. It has been reported that roughly half of all Americans in the workforce are not fully engaged, costing US businesses about $300 billion a year in lost productivity [26]. Engaged employees are more likely to be productive [43], associated with higher performance [41] stay with their current employer [22], and interact positively with clients [7]. Given the role employee engagement plays in organizational outcomes, a key issue is improving ways of measuring employee engagement so organizations can create action plans for improving it.

Surveys have been the primary instrument of measuring employee engagement. Among organizations with at least 100 employees in the United States over the last 15 years, the proportion conducting employee engagement surveys has grown from 50 percent to 60 percent [58]. Surveys allow an organization to obtain feedback from a large employee population [28]. Like any research instrument, surveys also have their limitations. Surveys take time to design and administer. Furthermore, the results are usually communicated 4-6 months after administration [29]. This delay between survey administration and release of results precludes the organization from acting on emergent issues that may be affecting employee engagement. A lengthy turnaround time can be perceived as inaction, potentially worsening the engagement of employees.

While researchers and practitioners alike agree that employee engagement is beneficial for organizations, there exist numerous definitions of employee engagement. Common to these definitions is that employee engagement has an organizational purpose, and connotes involvement, commitment, passion, enthusiasm, focused effort and energy [31]. For example, Harter, Schmidt, and Hayes define employee engagement as "the individual's involvement and satisfaction with as well as enthusiasm for work" [22]. Schaufeli et al. regard engagement as "a positive fulfilling, work-related state of mind that is characterized by vigor, dedication, and absorption" [45]. Schaufeli and Salanova [44] note that being fully absorbed in a role comes close to what Csikszentmihalyi calls 'flow' [13] or being present. They suggest that whereas engagement is a relatively persistent work state, flow is a more complex concept that involves momentary peak experiences that may occur outside of work.

Kahn placed the 'task' as central to engagement by noting that engagement is the simultaneous employment and expression of a person's "preferred self" in task behaviors that promote connections to work and to others, personal presence (physical, cognitive, and emotional) and active, full role performances [27]. He suggested that those that are psychologically present bring more of themselves to work, doing something *extra*. It is common to define employee engagement in terms of 'discretionary effort' [54].

Engagement behaviors include innovative behaviors, demonstrations of initiative, proactively seeking opportunities to contribute, and going beyond what is typically expected or required [31]. In this paper, we adopt the definition of employee engagement as "The extent to which employees are motivated to contribute to organizational success, and are willing to apply discretionary effort to accomplishing tasks important to the achievement of organizational goals" [59].

In conversation, employee engagement is sometimes conflated with employee satisfaction. Although correlated with engagement, satisfaction is characterized by a sense of well-being and pleasantness, which is at best related to moderate levels of activation and energy [31]. Being engaged involves psychological presence, activation, and extra behavioral energy which requires an investment on the part of the employee, whereas satisfaction requires nothing of the sort [31].

Measuring employee engagement

Employee engagement has traditionally been measured through surveys (see [1, 4] for reviews). Surveys are used with items intended to measure organizational antecedents and/or drivers of employee engagement, the engagement construct itself, behavioral outcomes of employee engagement, or combinations of all four [59]. Vance [55] provides a summary of the most common employee engagement measurement survey questions. We review a representative sample of survey approaches of engagement measurement by researchers and practitioners below.

Researchers have created survey instruments to measure employee engagement. The Utrecht Work Engagement Scale contains 17 items that measure the 'opposite' of burnout through the concepts of vigor, dedication, and absorption [46]. Mone and London define and measure employee engagement using the constructs of involvement, commitment, meaningfulness, empowerment, manager support, and loyalty [36]. Fine et al. measure employee engagement as satisfaction, commitment, and discretionary effort [17]. The Job Engagement Scale [41] contains 18 items measuring three broad areas of experience: physical, cognitive, and emotional. Additionally, there are several vendors that offer survey based measurements of employee engagement. For example, Gallup's G12 survey consists of 12 questions to measure engagement [23] and Kenexa's survey measures four individual elements: pride, satisfaction, advocacy and retention [59].

We believe social media can augment surveys to obtain a more real-time understanding of engagement. However, there are no published studies that describe a methodology of inferring engagement from social media text. One of the most common applications of social media text is sentiment analysis (see [16] for a review). Word usage in social media has also been used for predictions in many domains. For example, researchers have correlated word use on blogs with personality [19, 61]. See [20, 21, 52] for similar personality analyses based on Facebook and Twitter. The approach used by these researchers was to utilize collections of thematic dictionaries such as Linguistic Inquiry and Word Count (LIWC) [40] and calculate word counts for different dictionaries. They would then correlate these word counts with measures of individual personality as measured through a survey. Other domains where social media have been used to predict individual outcomes of interest include depression [10, 11], human values [8], well-being [47], and healthcare [e.g. 14, 15, 42].

Our approach in this study is similar to other researchers [e.g. 8, 11, 14, 47] that have treated survey data as a 'gold standard' and determined how well their social media based model predicts the outcome measured through the survey. If social media can reliably predict the engagement scores on a survey, it can be used by organizations to be aware of and respond to employee issues quicker than a survey. This leads us to our first research question:

> **RQ1:** *Can social media text improve the explanatory power of a model predicting employee engagement scores on a survey, in comparison to a model based on demographic characteristics alone?*

Engagement State vs. Trait

Employee engagement has been theorized in terms of three components. We will begin with a straightforward model of those components, and then we will consider some controversies and complexities.

Macey and Schneider proposed that employee engagement could be analyzed in terms of trait, state, and behavior (Figure 1) [31]. Traits were considered to be enduring predispositions, similar to personality attributes. These

Figure 1. Summary of the Macey and Schneider model of Employee Engagement [31].

attributes were experientially manifested as states, which could be measured indirectly through surveys. States would further manifest through observable and directly measurable behaviors.

However, the timecourse of the state-based aspects of engagement is controversial. Macey and Schneider considered state to be "relatively durable over time" [31]. In their formulation, engagement state appears to be a theoretical construct to bridge between long-term, unmeasurable traits, and directly-measurable behaviors. In contrast, Sonnentag et al. addressed the state aspect of engagement in a specifically time-limited form, through a diary study [50]. They concluded that 30-40% of the variance in engagement scores could be explained by within-persons factors during a single week. In another diary study, Breevaart et al. systematically modified the Utrecht Work Engagement Scale (UWES) [46] to anchor each question in the current day, and again found a time-varying component of engagement [5].

While Macey and Schneider hypothesized a "state" of engagement, they provided no evidence about its timeframe or duration. Diary studies have shown that engagement may change rapidly over time [5, 50]. In the prediction of engagement from social media, it is important to know the timeframe of an effective prediction. Therefore, we ask:

> **RQ2:** *Can the recency of social media posts used to predict engagement be used as evidence of it as a stable trait vs. a more temporary state?*

Research on predicting personality from social media suggests that individual tweets may not contain sufficient text to support stable characterizations [21]. Personality is, of course, a very complex topic, and it makes intuitive sense that a large amount of text might be needed to compute a linguistic pattern for particular personality types. As we have reviewed, engagement is also a complex concept, and so we ask a similar question in our domain:

> **RQ3:** *What is the minimum number of social media posts by an employee needed to make a reliable prediction about engagement?*

Finally, if social media can be used to predict engagement, then we want to know:

> **RQ4:** *Which linguistic dictionaries contribute to the prediction of engagement?*

METHOD

Dataset

Our study was conducted in a large multinational software, hardware and IT services company. Inside the company, there is an integrated social media platform available to all employees. The platform supports social media features that allow free form text such as status updates, blog posts, and online community forum posts. Only status updates had a character limit, which was 255 characters. For this study, we collected and anonymized 'public' social media content within the enterprise, where 'public' indicates that the posting was designated by their authors as viewable by all employees of the company. Table 1 summarizes the social media data, referred to as Dataset 1.

Like many other companies, an annual employee engagement survey is conducted in the company to better understand the employee experience and identify areas for improvement. In 2013, all regular employees of the company were invited to participate in the survey, and 258,289 responded, yielding a response rate of 62%. This is Dataset 2 in Table 1.

The dataset for our study consists of the intersection of Datasets 1 and 2, as summarized in Table 1.

Measures

Dependent variable: Employee Engagement Index

The dependent variable in our study is a measure of employee engagement consisting of a 3 question index that was adopted in the company based on [59]. These three questions represent pride ("I am proud to work for [company name]"), work experience ("For me, [company name] is a great place to work"), and advocacy ("I would recommend [company name] to a good friend as a place to work"). Each question was rated on a 5 point Likert agreement scale from 1=strongly disagree, to 5=strongly agree. The average of these 3 questions was the Employee Engagement Index. It had high internal consistency (Cronbach's alpha = 0.92). We treat this index as 'ground truth' of employee engagement in the company.

Independent variables

We wanted to predict employee engagement scores from the survey using a statistical model that incorporates employee social media word use along with several demographic characteristics, in order to demonstrate that social media linguistic variables derived from language dictionaries improve the predictive power of the model compared to using demographic characteristics alone.

- Language dictionaries: We utilized dictionaries from six *sources*, comprising 90 theme-specific *dictionaries* that contained a list of words that have been validated to be associated with constructs such as wellbeing, engagement, positive and negative emotion, power etc. These *sources* are Harvard's General Inquirer [18, 51]; Linguistic Inquiry and Word Count (LIWC) [40]; National Research Council's word-emotion association lexicon [35, 39]; Hyland's metadiscourse [24]; and an Experimental dictionary of employee engagement created within the company. Whenever there was a match between a word used by an employee on social media and a dictionary word, the score for an employee for that dictionary would get incremented by 1. Scores on each dictionary per employee were normalized by dividing the number of matches by the total word count in the social media posts by the employee within our study timeframe.

Dataset 1: Social Media	Dataset 2: Engagement Survey
1,009,308 records from 111,095 employees	258,289 records from 258,289 employees
Combined (Intersection of Datasets)	
68,353 aggregated records from 68,353 employees	

Table 1. Datasets in this study.

- Demographic characteristics: On an anonymous basis, we included three demographic variables to determine whether our language dictionaries provide additional explanatory power beyond what these demographic variables already contribute. These were country, rank, and whether the employee's job was being a seller. We assumed that each country might have a different mean level of engagement. Therefore, we included 42 dummy variables to represent the 43 countries in which there were at least 100 employees. These countries were distributed across Africa, Asia, Europe, North America, Oceania, and South America. We assumed that employees at different organizational levels might have different levels of engagement. Therefore, we included two dummy variables to distinguish among executive vs. high-ranked non-executives, vs. rank-and-file employees. We assumed that employees in direct sales jobs might think about engagement differently from other employees because of the client facing nature of their job. Therefore, we included a single dummy variable to distinguish between sales vs. non-sales job roles.

RESULTS

We analyzed the social media data in two distinct timeframes, using several distinct definitions of "data quality." In each timeframe, we considered the mean score on the engagement survey as "ground truth," and we predicted that mean score using SPSS multiple linear regression, organizing our predictors into a series of blocks. Each block addressed a different category of predictor.

Structure of the Regression Analysis

Table 2 presents a summary of the blocks of the multiple linear regressions. We considered the three classes of demographic variables to be a priori predictors, and so we *required* that these three classes of variables enter the regression model before we considered the effects of the linguistic dictionaries. We used the SPSS Enter method to insure this. The last block in the regression analysis added the 90 linguistic dictionaries from the 6 sources. We had no apriori hypotheses about which dictionaries would be most influential, so we included all 90 dictionaries within a

Block	Method	Predictor Category	Adjusted R-Square
1	Enter	**Country** (42 dummy variables)	.037, ns
2	Enter	**Rank** (2 dummy variables: Executive vs. High-non-executive vs. rank-and-file)	.032, ns
3	Enter	**Seller** (1 dummy variable: whether the employee was in a sales role)	.033, ns
4	Stepwise	**Dictionaries** from NRC [35, 39], General Inquirer [18, 51], LIWC [40], Hyland [24], and Experimental.	.483, p<.001

Table 2. Analytic structure of multiple linear regression, and regression results that contrast demographics (Blocks 1,2,3) vs. social media (Block 4). The models build from top to bottom: Thus, the R-Square in a row *j* includes the terms in rows *j-1* and above.

single SPSS Stepwise block. Our principal results are based on the outcome of this stepwise block.

For each employee, we combined all of their social media posts through the appropriate timeframe (see next subsection), and counted the number of word-matches for each dictionary.[1] This resulted in a single record for each employee, including their anonymized ID, their country, rank, seller-status, and number of posts in their individual dataset, followed by their scores on the 90 dictionaries. In practice, we divided each of the dictionary scores by the number-of-posts, so as to provide roughly equal weights or impacts across employees. Thus, the core question of **RQ1** (predictability) is addressed in the factors summarized in Blocks 1-4 of Table 2.

Timeframes: Trait and State Models

In **RQ2** we contrasted two timeframes for inferring engagement from social media. Under a "trait" timeframe, we assumed that engagement was a stable, time-invariant attribute of each employee [31]. For each employee, we combined all of their social media posts throughout 2013, and computed the dictionary scores on their whole-year snippet dataset. We fit a regression model to predict each employee's engagement index on the survey, based on the four blocks listed in Table 2, using the data from all of 2013. We considered this year-long analysis to be our "trait model."

In **RQ2**, we also considered the possibility that engagement might be a relatively transitory state [5, 50]. To assess this possibility, we separated our analyses into months. For each employee, for each month, we combined all of their social media posts. We did this for the six months in 2013 preceding the survey administration in early November – i.e., May, June, July, August, September, and October. Within each month, we fit a regression model to predict an employee's mean engagement score on the survey, based on the same four blocks listed in Table 2, using the data from the respective month. We considered these more limited-duration samples to be a series of "state" models.

The analyses of the trait model and the state models used the same factor structure, summarized in Table 2. However, the data used for the trait model were aggregated across all of 2013, whereas the data for each state model were aggregated from a single month in 2013.

Data Quality: Minimum numbers-of-posts

According to **RQ3**, there might be an unknown minimum number of posts that are required per employee to compute a stable dictionary score. We created an Inclusion Criterion, *k*, which specified the threshold number of posts required for each employee's data to be included in analysis. We computed separate models, distinguished by distinct values of *k*. The lowest value that we tested was *k*>=0 (include all employees). We then tried *k*>=5 (include any employee who had at least 5 posts within the timeframe). We continued with *k*>=10, *k*>=15, *k*>=20, and *k*>=25. Of course, higher values of *k* resulted in fewer employees being included in the model. We return to this issue in our account of RQ3, below.

Summary

We computed a total of seven regression models within each of seven timeframes. These regression results are identified in the legend in Figure 2.

Regression Outcomes

***RQ1**: Can Social Media Predict Engagement?*

Table 2 presents a summary of the analysis, presenting the conventional demographics-based approach (Blocks 1-3), as contrasted with the added predictive power from the linguistic dictionaries, based on social media (Block 4). Adding social media raised the predictive power from a non-significant adjusted R-square of .033 to a highly significant adjusted R-square of .483 ($p < 0.001$). Thus, the answer to **RQ1** is that social media can increase the ability to predict employee engagement.

[1] Unlike the other dictionaries, the LIWC dictionaries included wildcard suffixes for many words (e.g., "clear*" could be matched by any of "clears, cleared, clearing, clearance," etc.). For the LIWC dictionaries, we counted matches including wildcard expansions. The other dictionary sources (General Inquirer, Hyland, and Experimental) did not include wildcard expansions, and so we used simple word-matching for those dictionaries.

There are some important qualifications to that conclusion, which we explore in analyses of **RQ2** and **RQ3**, below.

RQ2: State vs. Trait

Figure 2 uses adjusted R-square values to summarize the regressions based on the models of Table 2. The models for the all-2013 Timeframe (Trait model) led to very low adjusted R-squares at all values of the Inclusion Criterion, *k*. The highest adjusted R-square for any of the Trait models was .11 (k>=20).

By contrast, some of the State models had much higher predictive power. The models for October (the month immediately preceding the survey) had much greater adjusted R-squares – as high as .483 (k>=15, p<.001). On the basis of this recency effect, we conclude that the Trait model of **RQ2** is not supported, and the State model of **RQ2** is supported. The social media posts that employees wrote immediately preceding the survey best predicted their scores on the engagement survey. We note that, if there was no state effect, then the trait analysis should have led to better results, because they combined textual data across 12 months, whereas the state analysis had data from only one month of data.

RQ3: Minimum number of posts

In **RQ3**, we considered whether there were a minimum number of posts per employee that is required for high data-quality or predictive power. The data in Figure 2 show that, for all Timeframes (including all-2013), adjusted R-square increased monotonically from k>=0 through k>=15. Thus, in answer to **RQ3**, 15 or more posts are required for stable dictionary-based scores. In our sample, the mean number of words per post was 71.86. Thus, the minimum number of words at k>=15 was 1078 words.

There is a trade-off. Applying a per-employee inclusion criterion leads to strong prediction (higher adjusted R-square), but at the cost of decreasing the number of employees in the dataset (the number of employees who have the required minimum number of posts). All of our monthly samples exhibited steep initial slopes in their long-tail distributions of number of posts per employee. The inclusion criterion of k>=15 reduced the October sample size from 8467 employees down to 159 employees; other months were similar. If we had used a less powerful inclusion criterion of k>=10 posts per employee (adjusted R-square=.244, p<.001), then the sample size would have been 330 employees for October. In this case, the minimum number of words per employee would have been 719 words. While this is a limitation, we note that HCI [37] and other disciplines such as marketing, clinical trials in medicine, and many of the social sciences make predictions on the basis of much smaller samples of the target population than our sample.

Recency Effects within a Month

The preceding month-by-month analysis established a recency effect for October, the month that immediately preceded the survey. Based on evidence that engagement can change from day-to-day [5, 50], we wanted to know if the recency effect was really a matter of a month, or a shorter timeframe. To answer this question, we hoped to repeat our month-by-month approach, now going week-by-week during the month of October. However, there were too few data within each week of October to compute weekly regressions at all of the values of the Inclusion Criterion, *k* (e.g. at k>=15, there are only 18 employees with sufficient data). At a future time, when there are more employees using social media frequently, we may be able to perform week-by-week analyses.

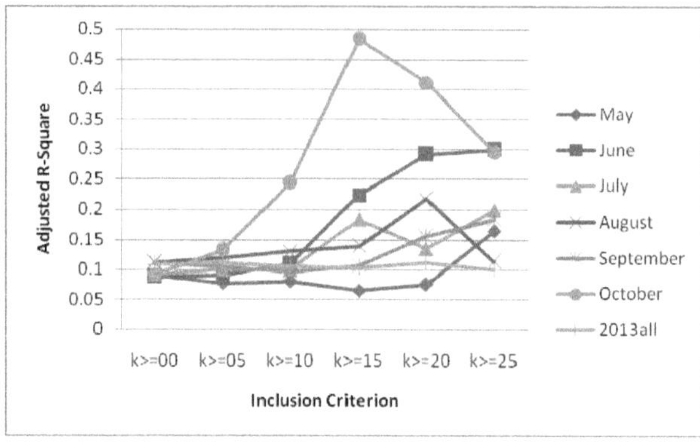

Figure 2. Predictive power (adjusted R-square) as a function of whole year and month-by-month Timeframe and Inclusion Criterion.

RQ4: Dictionaries used to Infer Engagement

The positive answer to **RQ1** (predictability), qualified by the answers to **RQ2** and **RQ3**, make it appropriate to answer **RQ4** (which dictionaries predict engagement?). In effect, we are asking: *Which topics are associated with high levels of engagement?* Table 3 shows the dictionaries that were selected by the Stepwise regression algorithm, in the order of selection in the model, under the strongest prediction parameters (recency/state timeframe and k>=15 data quality).

Engagement was positively predicted by posts that mentioned attitudinal or personal themes such as positive affect, optimism, and well-being. These themes connote feelings of positive attachment to work and co-workers. By contrast, engagement was negatively predicted by themes of vice, decrease, and economics. The negative association of engagement with themes of vice and decrease appears to be common-sense, and also desirable.

In the area of work and work practices, engagement was positively predicted by themes of time and striving. However, engagement was negatively predicted by a particular phase of time (future), as well as economics. Taken together, these coefficients suggest contextualization (time) of the current work effort (striving), but also perhaps some negative impact of anxiety about the future and about economic issues.

Dictionary (Source)	Coefficient	p <
Vice (GI)	-77.60	.001
Time (LIWC)	+39.51	.001
Positive affect (LIWC)	+18.13	.048
Try (GI)	+45.45	.006
Decrease (GI)	-297.40	.008
Future (LIWC)	-50.10	.001
Social (LIWC)	+23.64	.001
Engagement (HY)	+65.20	.001
Economics (GI)	-30.45	.001
Optimism (LIWC)	+64.31	.002
Wellbeing (GI)	+44.78	.001
1st-person singular (LIWC)	-16.41	.005
Exchange (GI)	-87.56	.045

Table 3. Dictionaries that predict engagement. For the sources of each dictionary: GI = General Inquirer [18, 51]. LIWC = Linguistic Inquiry and Word Count [40]. HY = Hyland [24].

With regard to relationships, engagement was positively predicted by themes of social relationships and textual evidence of engagement between writer and reader [51]. Correspondingly, engagement was negatively predicted by the use of first-person *singular* pronouns (but not first-person *plural* pronouns). The emphasis on social themes, and the intention to connect with a reader, suggests a strong social or collaborative component to workplace engagement. The negative association of first-person *singular* appears to be convergent with the social themes. We are more engaged when we work with others, and less engaged when we work alone.

DISCUSSION

Several studies have provided empirical evidence of the growing use of social media in the workplace [3, 12, 62]. Given the increased adoption of social by employees, we were interested to know if the text of social media posts could be used to infer employee engagement - a concept that has been associated with increased employee productivity and stronger customer experiences [2]. Although there are linguistic analyses of social media to answer other questions in CHI and CSCW [e.g. 8, 10, 11, 14, 21], there are no published studies that infer employee engagement from social media text. This study sought to explore the feasibility of employee social media text mining to infer the concept of employee engagement. We achieved this by showing that the words used in social media by employees can improve the predictive power of a statistical model over one based on demographic characteristics alone.

There are several implications that follow from our study. We describe them in terms of implications for organizations, theory, and the design of tools.

Implications for organizations

Our study shows the potential of social media text in the context of understanding the employee experience. Since social media can be updated on a daily or hourly basis by employees themselves, this provides much more immediate and timely data than a survey. Annual employee engagement surveys are a snapshot in time. By the time the survey is designed, administered, and analyzed, the results might be stale. Our results indicate that inferring employee engagement from social media might provide a more dynamic view of engagement compared to the static snapshot obtained through a survey.

Further, given the increasing usage of social media within the enterprise [3, 12, 62], if sufficiently developed and strengthened, organizations one day may consider a predictive model similar to ours to augment surveys. This would allow them to respond more quickly to problems, and potentially save considerable amounts of time, effort and money. As research has found, disengaged employees can cost organizations through lost productivity [26].

A limitation of our approach is that there is a minimum number of social media posts required per employee per month to achieve the results we obtained. This requirement may impede the application of our approach in organizations that do not have active participation in social media by their employees. Furthermore, it is unknown what the effects of our approach will be over time as employees realize that their social media content is being mined to infer engagement. Longitudinal studies are needed to demonstrate the long-term efficacy of our approach. Additionally, we did not test our model on held-out data. Our future work will involve training a machine learning classifier using our social media based model to predict engagement scores on a future engagement survey to validate the efficacy of our approach. Despite these limitations, our research shows early promise for using social media to infer employee engagement.

As is the case with any mechanism that attempts to infer personal characteristics from online activities, privacy is an important concern for organizations that intend to use predictive models like ours to infer employee engagement. Organizations should make all efforts to protect employee privacy by putting in place policies such as only analyzing social media after identity has been anonymized; only measuring engagement in the aggregate; and adhering to all guidelines regarding security of the system and data. Most importantly, organizations should be forthcoming in communicating to their employees how their social media traces are being analyzed and build a relationship based on trust so that employees continue to use social media as a platform for both self expression and conducting business.

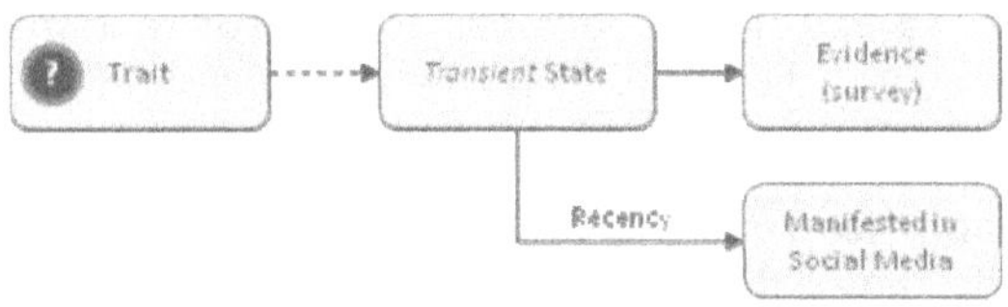

Figure 3. Proposed model of Employee Engagement

Implications for theory

In our test of timeframes (**RQ2**), we compared the Macey and Schneider assumption of static or enduring trait-like engagement [31] vs. the more dynamic state-like phenomena revealed by Breevaart et al. [5] and Sonnentag et al. [50]. While we did not conduct repeated measures of engagement, as in the diary studies of [5, 50], we were able to show a recency effect, suggestive of a relatively transient *state* of engagement which is reflected in both survey behaviors and social media postings. We modify the three-component engagement model of [31] (Figure 1) to propose the less direct relationship between engagement state, survey behavior, and social media text, as shown in Figure 3. We have tagged the Trait component of Figure 3 with a question mark, because our data provided no support for trait-like attributes. We hope that, with sufficiently rich social media data, we can work toward a more accurate model of the timeframe and recency attributes.

Our research shows that engagement is more of a temporary state than a permanent trait, suggesting that it may fluctuate at a rate higher than what a measurement strategy based solely on annual surveys can detect. Using the measurement approach in this paper, we may be able to take advantage of the more real-time nature of social media activity to complement survey-based measurement and provide a more complete understanding of engagement in the workplace.

Implications for the design of tools

Recent studies describe tools that can be used to analyze employee social media content [e.g. 9, 49]. We believe our method of inferring employee engagement could be incorporated into the design of such tools. One could imagine designing a widget in an organizational dashboard that displays scores of inferred employee engagement in near real-time. This can allow an organization to view the aggregated engagement of its (anonymized) employees along different demographic characteristics such as country of work, years of service, business unit, client facing vs. non client facing etc. Comparisons can be drawn to the overall company engagement score to identify issues and target action plans to improve workplace issues and thus improve engagement. Since the dashboard is only as good as the content employees decide to share, organizations may consider providing employees access to visualizations of engagement analytics as an incentive to participate. This may create a more transparent and open culture, and may encourage employees to express themselves on internal social media to influence organizational policies. This can give employees a voice in affecting organizational policies that affect them. Whether the organization acts on the data will ultimately determine how much employees can trust their employer with either feedback.

Quantifying and displaying engagement scores raises the possibility of manipulation or 'gaming'. However, social media language use in an enterprise context may be difficult to game. It is hard to fake the reality in an enterprise social network environment because one's identity is tied with content, and the network may keep one honest. Whether this assertion bears out is an extremely interesting direction of future empirical research. Additional future work could involve exploring if employee engagement exhibits patterns of social network based contagion, as well as determining if there is systematic variation in the use of specific language predictive of engagement across different geographies and cultures.

Our model depends on active participation by employees on social media. However, even with a relatively small sample of employees, we were able to predict engagement scores on a survey with high statistical confidence. As more employees become comfortable with social media, and a new generation of individuals already comfortable with social media joins the workforce, one assumes that the predictive power of our model can only increase.

CONCLUSION

This study provides several contributions. First, we show the value of social media as containing signals for inferring employee engagement, which can help organizations be more responsive to issues related to the employee experience. Ours is the first study to utilize social media as a method for inferring employee engagement. In this way, we extend the range of options available to organizations for measuring employee engagement by looking beyond traditional engagement surveys. Secondly, we inform the theoretical debate on employee engagement by addressing the temporal dimension of state engagement. By utilizing social media data to infer engagement, we have opened up a space not previously addressed in the literature. Thirdly, we empirically illustrate the conditions under which social media based inferences of employee engagement can be made. We demonstrate the minimum number of social media posts needed per employee to make a reliable prediction, and the dictionaries that are predictive of employee engagement. While our study is limited to a single company, we believe our findings can be valuable for other researchers and practitioners to build on.

ACKNOWLEDGMENTS

We thank Eben Haber for discussions on data quality, leading to the inclusion criterion in our analyses.

REFERENCES

1. Albrecht, S. L. *Handbook of employee engagement: Perspectives, issues, research and practice.* Edward Elgar, Cheltenham, UK, 2010.
2. Anderson, L. Employee Engagement and its Impact on Brand Value. *Performance Improvement Council* (2012).

3. Archambault, A. and Grudin, J. A longitudinal study of facebook, linkedin, and twitter use. In *Proc. CHI 2012*, ACM Press (2012).
4. Bakker, A. B. L. M. P. *Work engagement: A handbook of essential theory and research.* Psychology Press, New York, 2010.
5. Breevaart, K., Bakker, A. B., Demerouti, E. and Hetland, J. The measure of state work engagement: A multilevel factor analytic study. *European Journal of Psychological Assessment 28,* 4 (2012), 305-312.
6. Brown, C., Efstratiou, C., Leontiadis, I., Quercia, D. and Mascolo, C. Tracking serendipitous interactions: How individual cultures shape the office. In *Proc. CSCW 2014,* ACM Press (2014), 1072-1081.
7. Chalofsky, N. E. *Meaningful Workplaces: Reframing How and Where we Work.* Jossey-Bass, San Francisco, CA, 2010.
8. Chen, J., Hsieh, G., Mahmud, J. U. and Nichols, J. Understanding individuals' personal values from social media word use. In *Proc. CSCW 2014,* ACM Press (2014), 405-414.
9. Choudhury, M. D. and Counts, S. Understanding affect in the workplace via social media. In *Proc. CSCW 2013*, ACM Press (2013).
10. Choudhury, M. D., Counts, S. and Horvitz, E. Predicting postpartum changes in emotion and behavior via social media. In *Proc. CHI 2013,* ACM Press (2013).
11. Choudhury, M. D., Counts, S., Horvitz, E. J. and Hoff, A. Characterizing and predicting postpartum depression from shared facebook data. In *Proc. CSCW 2014,* ACM Press (2014), 626-638.
12. Chui, M., Manyika, J., Bughin, J., Dobbs, R., Roxburgh, C., Sarrazin, H. et al. The social economy: Unlocking value and productivity through social technologies. *McKinsey Global Institute* (2012).
13. Csikszentmihalyi, M. *Flow: The psychology of optimal experience.* Harper & Row, New York, 1990.
14. Culotta, A. Estimating county health statistics with twitter. In *Proc. CHI 2014*, ACM Press (2014).
15. Dredze, M. How Social Media Will Change Public Health. *Intelligent Systems, IEEE 27*, 4 (2012), 81-84.
16. Feldman, R. Techniques and applications for sentiment analysis. *Commun. ACM 56*, 4 (2013), 82-89.
17. Fine, S., Horowitz, I., Weigler, H. and Basis, L. Is good character good enough? The effects of situational variables on the relationship between integrity and counterproductive work behaviors. *Human Resource Management Review 20,* 1 (2010), 73-84.
18. General Inqurier. Retrieved May 26, 2014, from http://www.wjh.harvard.edu/~inquirer/
19. Gill, A. J., Nowson, S. and Oberlander, J. What are they blogging about? Personality, topic and motivation in blogs. In *Proc. ICWSM 2009*, AAAI Press (2009).
20. Golbeck, J., Robles, C., Edmondson, M. and Turner, K. Predicting Personality from Twitter. In *Proc. SocialCom 2011,* (2011), 149-156.
21. Gou, L., Zhou, M. X. and Yang, H. KnowMe and ShareMe: Understanding automatically discovered personality traits from social media and user sharing preferences. In *Proc. CHI 2014,* ACM Press (2014).
22. Harter, J. K., Schmidt, F. L. and Hayes, T. L. Business-unit-level relationship between employee satisfaction, employee engagement, and business outcomes: A meta-analysis. *Journal of Applied Psychology 87* (2002).
23. Harter, J. K., Schmidt, F. L. and Keyes, C. L. Well-being in the workplace and its relationship to business outcomes: A review of the Gallup studies. In C. L. Keyes and J. Haidt (Eds.), *Flourishing: The positive person and the good life* (pp. 205-224). Washington, DC: American Psychological Association, 2003.
24. Hyland, K. *Metadiscourse: Exploring interaction in writing.* Continuum, London, UK, 2005.
25. Irani, L. C. and Silberman, M. S. Turkopticon: interrupting worker invisibility in amazon mechanical turk. In *Proc. CHI 2013,* ACM Press (2013).
26. Johnson, G. Otherwise engaged. *Training 41,* 10 (2004).
27. Kahn, W. A. Psychological Conditions of Personal Engagement and Disengagement at Work. *Academy of Management Journal 33,* 4 (1990), 692-724.
28. Lawler, E. *High-Involvement Management. Participative Strategies for Improving Organizational Performance.* Jossey-Bass Inc. Publishers, 1986.
29. Lilienthal, P. If you give your employees a voice, do you listen? *The Journal for Quality and Participation 25*, 3 (2002), 38-40.
30. Macey, W. H. *Employee engagement: Tools for analysis, practice, and competitive advantage.* Wiley-Blackwell, Chichester, UK, 2009.
31. Macey, W. H. and Schneider, B. The Meaning of Employee Engagement. *Ind. and Org. Psych.,* 1 (2008).
32. Mark, G., Iqbal, S. T., Czerwinski, M. and Johns, P. Bored mondays and focused afternoons: The rhythm of attention and online activity in the workplace. In *Proc. CHI 2014,* ACM Press (2014).
33. Mark, G., Voida, S. and Cardello, A. "A pace not dictated by electrons": An empirical study of work without email. In *Proc. CHI 2012,* ACM Press (2012).
34. Mazmanian, M. and Erickson, I. The product of availability: understanding the economic underpinnings of constant connectivity. In *Proc. CHI 2014,* ACM Press (2014), 763-772.

35. Mohammad, S. and Turney, P. D. Crowdsourcing a Word-Emotion Association Lexicon. *Computational Intelligence 29,* 3 (2013), 436-465.

36. Mone, E. M. and London, M. *Employee engagement through effective performance management: A practical guide for managers.* Routledge, New York, 2010.

37. Muller, H., Sedley, A. and Ferrall-Nunge, E. Survey Research in HCI. In J. S. Olson and W. A. Kellogg (Eds.), *Ways of Knowing in HCI.* New York: Springer, 2014.

38. Neeli, B. K. A Method to Engage Employees Using Gamification in BPO Industry. In *Proc. ICSEM 2012,* IEEE Computer Society (2012), 142-146.

39. NRC word-emotion association lexicon. Retrieved May 26, 2014, from http://www.saifmohammad.com/WebPages/ResearchInterests.html.

40. Pennebaker, J. W., Chung, C. K., Ireland, M., Gonzales, A. and Booth, R. J. *The development and psychometric properties of LIWC2007.* Austin, TX, LIWC.Net (2007).

41. Rich, B. L., Lepine, J. A. and Crawford, E. R. Job Engagement: Antecedents and Effects on Job Performance. *Academy of Management Journal 53,* 3 (2010), 617-635.

42. Sadilek, A., Kautz, H. and Silenzio, V. Predicting Disease Transmission from Geo-Tagged Micro-Blog Data. In *Proc. AAAI Conference on Artificial Intelligence,* (2012).

43. Saks, A. M. Antecedents and consequences of employee engagement. *Journal of Managerial Psychology 21,* 7 (2006), 600-619.

44. Schaufeli, W. and Salanova, M. Work engagement: An emerging psychological concept and its implications for organizations. In G. S. W, D. D. Steiner and D. P. Skarlicki (Eds.), *Managing social and ethical issues in organizations* (pp. 135−177). Greenwich, CT: Information Age Publishing, 2007.

45. Schaufeli, W., Salanova, M., González-romá, V. and Bakker, A. The Measurement of Engagement and Burnout: A Two Sample Confirmatory Factor Analytic Approach. *Journal of Happiness Studies 3,* 1 (2002).

46. Schaufeli, W. B., Bakker, A. B. and Salanova, M. The Measurement of Work Engagement With a Short Questionnaire: A Cross-National Study. *Educational and Psychological Measurement 66,* 4 (2006), 701-716.

47. Schwartz, H. A., Eichstaedt, J. C., Kern, M. L., Dziurzynski, L., Lucas, R. E., Agrawal, M., Park, G. J., Lakshmikanth, S. K., Jha, S., Seligman, M. E. P. and Ungar, L. Characterizing Geographic Variation in Well-Being Using Tweets. In *Proc. ICWSM 2013,* (2013).

48. Shami, N. S., Nichols, J. and Chen, J. Social media participation and performance at work: a longitudinal study. In *Proc. CHI 2014,* ACM Press (2014), 115-118.

49. Shami, N. S., Yang, J., Panc, L., Dugan, C., Ratchford, T., Rasmussen, J. et al. Understanding employee social media chatter with enterprise social pulse. In *Proc. CSCW 2014,* ACM Press (2014), 379-392.

50. Sonnentag, S., Dormann, C. and Demerouti, E. Not all days are created equal: The concept of state work engagement. In A. B. Bakker and M. P. Leiter (Eds.), *Work engagement: A handbook of essential theory and research* (pp. 25-38). Hove: Psychology Press, 2010.

51. Stone, P. J. Thematic text analysis: New agendas for analyzing text content. In C. Roberts (Ed.), *Text analysis for the social sciences.* Hillsdale, NY: Erlbaum, 1997.

52. Sumner, C., Byers, A., Boochever, R. and Park, G. J. Predicting Dark Triad Personality Traits from Twitter Usage and a Linguistic Analysis of Tweets. In *Proc. ICMLA 2012,* IEEE Computer Society (2012), 386-393.

53. Teodoro, R., Ozturk, P., Naaman, M., Mason, W. and Lindqvist, J. The motivations and experiences of the on-demand mobile workforce. In *Proc. CSCW 2014,* ACM Press (2014).

54. Towers-Perrin. *Working today: Understanding what drives employee engagement,* Stamford, CT, 2003.

55. Vance, R. J. *Employee Engagement and Commitment: A Guide to Understanding, Measuring and Increasing Engagement in your Organization.* SHRM Foundation, Alexandria, VA, 2006.

56. Voida, A., Olson, J. S. and Olson, G. M. Turbulence in the clouds: challenges of cloud-based information work. In *Proc. CHI 2013,* ACM (2013), 2273-2282.

57. Webb, E. N. Gamification: When it works, when it doesn't. In *Proc. DUXU 2013,* Springer-Verlag (2013).

58. Wiley, J. W. *Strategic employee surveys: Evidence-based guidelines for driving organizational success.* Jossey-Bass, San Francisco, 2010.

59. Wiley, J. W., Herman, A. E. and Kowske, B. J. Developing and Validating a Global Model of Employee Engagement. In S. L. Albrecht (Ed.), *Handbook of Employee Engagement.* Cheltenham, UK: Edward Elgar Publishing, 2010.

60. Yardi, S., Golder, S. A. and Brzozowski, M. J. Blogging at work and the corporate attention economy. In *Proc. CHI 2009,* ACM Press (2009), 2071-2080.

61. Yarkoni, T. Personality in 100,000 Words: A large-scale analysis of personality and word use among bloggers. *Journal of Research in Personality 44,* 3 (2010).

62. Zhang, H., Choudhury, M. D. and Grudin, J. Creepy but inevitable?: the evolution of social networking. In *Proc. CSCW 2014,* ACM Press (2014), 368-378.

Mailing Lists: Why Are They Still Here, What's Wrong With Them, and How Can We Fix Them?

Amy X. Zhang
MIT CSAIL
Cambridge, MA 02139, USA
axz@mit.edu

Mark S. Ackerman
University of Michigan
Ann Arbor, MI 48109, USA
ackerm@umich.edu

David R. Karger
MIT CSAIL
Cambridge, MA 02139, USA
karger@mit.edu

ABSTRACT
Mailing lists have existed since the early days of email and are still widely used today, even as more sophisticated online forums and social media websites proliferate. The simplicity of mailing lists can be seen as a reason for their endurance, a source of dissatisfaction, and an opportunity for improvement. Using a mixed-method approach, we studied two community mailing lists in depth with interviews and surveys, and surveyed a broader spectrum of 28 lists. We report how members of the different communities use their lists and their goals and desires for them. We explore why members prefer mailing lists to other group communication tools. But we also identify several tensions around mailing list usage that appear to contribute to dissatisfaction with them. We conclude with design implications, discussing ways to alleviate these tensions while preserving mailing lists' appeal.

Author Keywords
mailing lists; email; online communities; discussion groups

ACM Classification Keywords
H.5.3. Group and Organization Interfaces: Asynchronous interaction; Web-based interaction

INTRODUCTION
Just four years after the invention of email, the first mailing list, MsgGroup, was created in 1971 to help Arpanet users discuss the idea of using Arpanet for discussion. In the 40 years since, mailing lists have become pervasive, helping communities share information, ask and answer questions, discuss issues, and build ties. More recently, alternative methods of group communication have emerged, including discussion forums, Q&A sites, and social networking sites. As other tools gained prominence, some believed that mailing lists would die out and be replaced [14]. But mailing lists continue to be widely used.

Despite ongoing use, mailing lists have changed little from their original design. There have been some modifications and advancements, but generally mailing lists are used much as in the 1970s. While mailing list development stagnated, newer applications and websites have introduced numerous collaborative curation features, including following, tagging, and social moderation. These new systems and their features have been studied extensively in recent years. Email clients have also undergone dramatic changes in the last 40 years, so that now many people access their email in new ways [7]. Though email access practices have shifted due to features like automatic filing, the mailing list model has not.

Given the continued pervasive use of mailing lists, the lack of new development or research surrounding them, and advances in our social computing systems, we believe that a closer study of mailing lists today could reveal significant room for improvement. We consider the following questions:

- What are the reasons people continue to use mailing lists in the face of modern social media tools?
- What are the problems and limitations of mailing lists that remain despite their continued use?
- How might we address these problems and limitations without ruining what makes mailing lists so attractive?

To gain insight into these questions, we studied the use of mailing lists by two communities through in-depth interviews. We augmented this qualitative examination with a survey of more members of these two lists as well as 28 additional mailing lists of varying community types. We explored the diversity of goals, expectations, and perceptions among community members subscribed to lists, and how this can leave many users dissatisfied. In more detail,

- We observed significant disagreement over the preferred types, quantity, and tone of email delivered over each list;
- We found that many users muzzled themselves and others posted too much, based on their perception of others' preferences—perceptions that were often wrong;
- In particular, we found that the wide variation in how users handle incoming email influenced their perception of how the list should be used, to the detriment of others; and
- We saw that despite these problems, many users considered the mailing list superior for group communication to both web forums and social media for a variety of reasons.

Given these findings, we explore a design space for allowing diverse users to *all simultaneously* use the same mailing list in their different preferred ways without negatively impacting users with different preferences. Our results suggest that mailing list users could benefit from *greater flexibility and control* in how they choose their audience and their incoming content, and this might encourage more contributions that the community finds valuable. We also find a need for *greater*

CHI 2015, April 18 - 23 2015, Seoul, Republic of Korea

http://dx.doi.org/10.1145/2702123.2702194

transparency and social awareness within mailing list systems to allow users to better know who their audience is and how their content is received.

BACKGROUND AND RELATED WORK

In the 1990s to early 2000s, there was a great deal of excitement over the potential of mailing lists to connect geographically dispersed people in scholarly and professional circles [10]. Studies found that lists allowed highly affective interpersonal interactions [17], encouraged reflection [10], and extended users' social capital [16]. However, even then there were problems, such as complaints about flaming, lurkers, off-topic threads, and information overload [26]. There was also frustration with the need for time-consuming administrative moderation to maintain quality discourse [4]. Some issues with mailing lists in that period simply reflected general problems of email overload [5, 28]. Given the inflexible design of mailing lists, users had no recourse except to unsubscribe when they felt overloaded [26]. Problems were magnified when the messages were deemed nonessential or served a different purpose than regular email, as was often the case for mailing lists [22]. This suggests mailing lists may have exacerbated email overload.

Much has changed since these studies, suggesting we should re-examine mailing lists in light of today's email clients and practices. Popular clients such as Gmail now have features such as threaded conversations and automatic filing and tagging, which may help with interruption fatigue and overload. However, this automatic handling may change the way users access their mailing list email to something more like news feeds [23] such as on Facebook or Twitter, where users can dip in occasionally to view content [2]. While much research has explored how email practices may affect the recipients of email [8], we also consider the perceptions and attitudes of *senders* of email, including how their expectations of how others receive their email can cause tensions.

Research on motivations within group discussion systems since the early 2000s have primarily focused on newer social media. Studies have looked at what content users share and why [6, 11], and what they self-censor and why [24, 27, 15]. Research has also looked into the motivations for participation specifically in online groups [21]. Research on Facebook Groups suggests that it is used for information sharing [25] as well as for socialization [20]. We extend this work by considering the ecology of options for group discussion today, specifically comparing users' perceptions of mailing lists with those of more modern systems. Additionally, we bring attention back to the study of mailing list communities so as to encourage innovation in this area. We address a gap in the research literature by considering how mailing lists could be improved given their simple design, and we reflect on how we might incorporate some of the features in modern social media without losing what makes mailing lists valuable.

DATA COLLECTION

We collected both interview and survey data. We used qualitative interview data to gain a deeper understanding of the two communities we studied. The surveys, which reached a larger user population and a more diverse set of mailing lists, let us triangulate our interview findings.

Interview Study

We began in May 2014 with in-person interviews of members of two mailing list communities, summarized in Table 1 and characterized in more detail in the next section. The mailing lists were chosen because they were well established in terms of age and integration into their respective communities, giving them a sizable membership, community participation ratio, and posting frequency that would allow for interesting dynamics to be observed. Our first mailing list, called DORM, is for members of a 300-person undergraduate dormitory of a mid-sized U.S. university. We interviewed 10 (4 female, 6 male, median age of 22) members, including 8 undergraduates and 2 residential advisors. Our second mailing list, called LAB, is for members, affiliates, and followers of a 1000-person technology research lab in a different mid-sized U.S. university. We interviewed 10 (1 female, 8 male, 1 other, median age of 30) members, including 1 professor, 2 administrators, 2 researchers, 4 graduate students, and 1 former graduate student. Potential interviewees were recruited by emailing the target list, by emailing related mailing lists, and by word-of-mouth. We selected interviewees to reach a diverse set of users in terms of affiliation to the community, length of time in the community, and level of usage, including those who used the list infrequently or were unsubscribed.

Interviews were conducted by the first author, lasted from 20 to 80 minutes, and were mostly open-ended to allow users to describe their experiences in detail. Before the interview, we asked interviewees to reflect on their experiences and bring two posts or threads that were memorable in either a good or bad way in order to ground our discussion. We began the interviews by asking users about the posts they brought as well as their inclination or resistance to contributing in those instances. We then asked general open-ended questions about the mailing list, such as their opinions and participation level. We also had interviewees bring their laptops and demonstrate their strategies for organizing their mailing list email within their email client. Finally, we asked users to compare their mailing list with other community discussion systems that they used and to imagine what the list would be like if migrated to such alternative systems.

We employed a grounded theory approach [3] to elicit themes from the interviews. The interviews were coded by the first author using standard qualitative coding techniques [18] to find concepts around what users liked about mailing lists, frustrating or rewarding experiences, and moments of doubt or self-censorship. The authors as a group iteratively discussed the codes and grouped them into themes. Some groupings were generated from concepts that seemed contradictory; these form the tensions that we will describe later. Others were generated from commonly-expressed explanations for behaviors and preferences.

Survey

Using the themes generated, we then built a survey to see whether our interview findings could be confirmed by a larger

	Interview	Survey	Subscribed*	Posters**	Membership	Archives	Posts/day***	Moderated
DORM	10	43	541	531	restricted	public	15.75(13.53)	No
LAB	10	108	4,147	708	unrestricted	public	6.45(5.25)	No

Table 1. The two mailing list populations studied in depth. *Number of subscribers in May 2014. **Posters refers to the number of unique contributors from June 2013 to June 2014. ***Average number of posts per day, followed by standard deviation, from June 2013 to June 2014.

subset of the two communities and by a more diverse set of mailing list communities. Our 4 page SurveyMonkey web survey combined multiple choice questions, free-response questions, and 5-point Likert scales. In addition to DORM and LAB, we surveyed 28 other mailing list communities. These communities were found by asking others to publicize the survey to mailing lists they used. We aimed to reach a diverse set of mailing list populations and selected communities of varying sizes and functions.

Our survey investigated users' attitudes towards and perceptions of their mailing list, which is why we relied on self-reported data. To build the survey, we took the themes from our interpretive analysis and constructed sets of questions, with some multiple choice responses taken from the codes extracted from the interviews. We asked users about their strategies for managing their mailing list email and characteristics of the list. We inquired whether they cared about things like missed email, irrelevant content, or high volume. We delved into how users felt about lengthy discussions and what gave them pause when considering posting. Finally, we asked users to rate potential changes to the list, including introducing hypothetical features and moving to alternative systems.

We screened out 74 people who completed the survey in under 4 minutes, completed less than half, or had a variance below 0.5 for answers to Likert scale questions, which had items of reverse valence. Of 415 remaining participants, 43 (37% male, 56% female, median age 21) were from DORM, 108 (67% male, 23% female, median age 27) were from LAB, and 264 (33% male, 65% female, median age 21) were from other lists. Some chose not to divulge their gender or age. The demographics for DORM and LAB respondents reasonably approximate those of the membership. We did note a slight skew in gender towards more female respondents; however, we were careful to consider this in our analysis and did not find reason to suspect it would alter our main findings. The total number of subscribers and unique contributors in the last year for DORM and LAB are shown in Table 1. We presume that some email accounts were inactive or were filtered into a spam folder, but expect the number of people actually reading the mailing list to be somewhere between the subscriber and unique contributor count. Thus, we believe the real response rate to be above 5% for both communities.

Our recruitment method of emailing the mailing list did not reach people who had left the list previously or did not check their email in time. This presents a non-response bias in our survey data, though we did take care to find and interview people who had left the list or did not check it frequently. We were able to reach these people by inquiring in person to members of both communities. We discuss potential biases in more detail below. Though we report numbers in the following sections to describe our survey results, these numbers

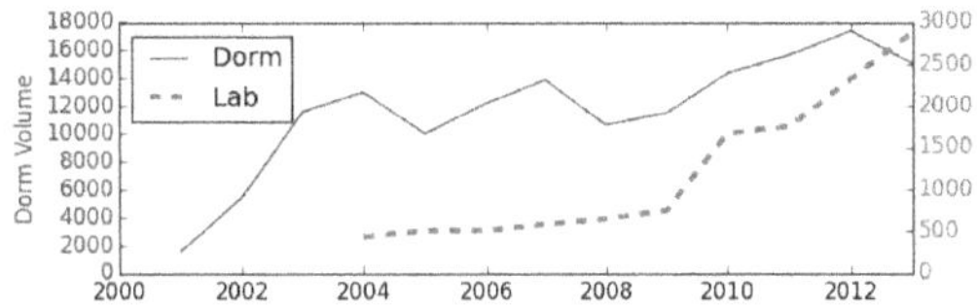

Figure 1. Total number of emails per year for DORM and LAB.

should be regarded as indicative due to our low response rate and potential biases. For the Likert scale questions, we report 1-2 as disagreeing with the statement, 3 as neutral, and 4-5 as agreeing.

THE MAILING LIST COMMUNITIES

We begin with a deeper look at the communities that we interviewed and surveyed.

The DORM Mailing List

As shown in Figure 1, the DORM mailing list was started in the fall of 2001 and increased in volume in the years since. The community of DORM is composed of primarily undergraduates and some residential advisors and staff that live together in dormitory housing. Students are randomly assigned to the housing community during their first years and stay until they graduate, so they generally know each other by name or face. Students are automatically added to the mailing list upon joining the community and removed when they leave, though they can unsubscribe at any time. As Table 1 shows, the number of unique posters over the year from June 2013 is quite close to the year's subscription number, meaning almost all users posted to the list. However, about 25% of the unique posters only posted once. Interviewees described the content as comprised mostly of publicity for events organized by students for other students, with event announcements appearing several times a day. This activity is so prevalent that students name it "pubbing." This may explain why only about 30% of the year's posts were replies. During our study, there were also many posts by graduating seniors selling items, highlighting the periodic nature of content driven by the school year cycle.

The LAB Mailing List

The LAB mailing list was started in 2004 and has since seen a considerable increase in volume, also shown in Figure 1. The LAB community is composed mostly of current and alumni graduate students and some faculty, research staff, administrators, and undergraduates that are members of a technology research institute. Graduate students are automatically added but can unsubscribe at any time. The list is public, so affiliates of the lab or interested parties may also be on the list. The volume is generally less than DORM and varies less. Interviewees described the list as a general-purpose list for the lab, with many job postings, housing listings, event announcements, and occasionally interesting discussions. As seen in Table 1, there are over 4,000 subscribers although only 708 unique people posted in a year's time, suggesting that there are many lurkers and dormant accounts on the list. Of the people who did post, 51% only posted once. At the other end, the most frequent poster on the list posted over three times as much as the next most frequent poster. This person was referenced many times by name in both interviews and surveys as a polarizing and outspoken list member.

We additionally surveyed 28 other communities, with 3 sports teams, 8 extracurricular or cultural clubs, 5 academic groups, 6 dorms, 1 sorority, 3 social clubs, and 2 neighborhoods. Though we reached communities of different sizes and functions, many of them were connected to a university or were comprised mostly of university students due to our method of convenience sampling. In a further section, we address the generalizability of our findings in light of our sample.

WHY ARE MAILING LISTS STILL IMPORTANT?

We first turn towards understanding why people still use mailing lists today in the face of modern communication systems. Following this section, we will address problems related to mailing lists before discussing potential fixes to these problems, keeping in mind the positives we explore here.

We asked users to rate how often they used different group communication systems, including mailing lists, Facebook Groups, Google+ Communities, subreddits, or discussion forums. We found that after mailing lists, the next most popular tool for group communication was Facebook Groups. When asked about the Facebook Groups they were on, interviewees overall said that there was generally little activity and that they checked them much less frequently than their mailing list emails, even if they checked Facebook several times a day. Some interviewees mentioned that DORM and LAB in fact had Facebook Groups, but that they had low membership and were mostly dormant. When we refer back to Figure 1, we can see that volume on both mailing lists has gone up substantially over time even during the growth of Facebook.

We asked users to imagine moving their mailing list to other systems and consider what would change. Overall, interviewees believed that moving their list to Facebook would result in less activity or discussion and preferred to continue using their mailing list. From the surveys, only a small minority of respondents liked the idea of moving their mailing list to a Facebook Group (13% agree, 15% neutral, 72% disagree). We found even lower percentages in favor of moving to a subreddit or a web forum (5% and 9% agree respectively). We now explore several differences we encountered in how people thought of email versus social media and how this played into their preference for mailing list communication.

Email is for Work, Social Media for Play

From the surveys, a majority of users thought that email was more professional than Facebook (61% agree, 25% neutral, 14% disagree). In a similar vein, interviewees associated discussion forums like Reddit with procrastination. When asked if the mailing list should move to Facebook, one user said:

> *I wouldn't be surprised if people start posting cat videos to this. [Facebook] has been a distraction for most people...When I look at* [LAB]*...I don't see it as a place to post cat videos.* –LAB

While interviewees overall felt that their mailing list content was more work-related than content on social media, many interviewees also agreed that some posts on the mailing list were not work-related. One interviewee who enjoyed reading discussions on the mailing list felt that these discussions would not thrive on Facebook, but they also did not quite fit with his perception of email as more work-related:

> *...it leaves the open discourse in an awkward split between personal conversation, Facebook Groups, and the part of email that's not all business-y.* –DORM

The overloading of email with different types of content has been described in prior work [8]. Overall few survey respondents minded that group discussions were going into their email (14% agree, 22% neutral, 64% disagree), though our data is biased in that users who unsubscribed were less likely to respond to our survey. Some interviewees, one of whom had unsubscribed, indicated that the discussions in their inbox distracted them from their work-related emails.

Email Feels More Private than Social Media

When explaining low activity on Facebook Groups, a number of interviewees said that social media somehow felt more public than mailing lists. This was interesting because it was technically untrue; both mailing list archives were public while a private Facebook Group would not be publicly visible. However, most interviewees of both groups were surprised to hear that the mailing list archives were public. We also found that both interviewees and those surveyed severely underestimated the number of people on their lists, echoing other research [1]. For instance, only 7% surveyed from LAB accurately estimated how many people were subscribed. Instead, the median guessed list size was 500-800 people, an order of magnitude less than the actual subscription count.

Some interviewees reasoned that the archives were harder to access and read, while it would be easier to scroll down a group's Facebook page. Also addressing public exposure, many interviewees commented that on Facebook people's identities were more tied to their messages because of the proximity of profile images and linked profiles:

> *There's a greater sense of [Facebook] being public...you can see everybody who's on there. It's very visible, very present. Whereas on email, you're sending it into the mystic...you don't see all the faces staring back at you.* –DORM

Greater Confidence that Email will be Seen

Many interviewees expressed the opinion that their mailing list emails were more likely to be seen than a social media post. This may be partly due to email's "push" model (see below) where emails are *delivered* to all recipients. In contrast, systems like Facebook that employ an opaque algorithm for displaying content make a mystery of who receives what:

> *Facebook plays games with what they show people and so there's no even clear notion of who it is that's seen what you're sending...[Email's] really the only mechanism where it comes with this feeling of it'll get seen.* –LAB

Despite the popularity of Facebook, many interviewees also mentioned knowing people in the community who were not on Facebook but used email; reaching these people clearly requires using email. Several interviewees also stated that they checked their email more often than they checked Facebook, with a majority of those surveyed agreeing (67% agree, 14% neutral, 19% disagree). Users might therefore sense that email delivery will be more timely than social media delivery. Like the privacy perception, this perception that mail will be seen and seen quickly can also prove false due to other recipients' filtering choices, as we shall explore later.

Email Management is More Customizable

Another difference between email and social media is that email, using the SMTP standard, is more readily customizable and viewable with many different interfaces. Many interviewees preferred to have the flexibility to set up custom filters, tags, or notifications. One interviewee expressed frustration with Facebook's interface, which is not customizable:

> *You only have the choice [on Facebook Groups]...I want to watch every message...or I don't. If you say yes, then...your cellphone [is] beeping every 5 minutes. If you say no, you're going to miss everything. There's no in between where once a day I can...see what's new.* –LAB

In the survey, a majority said that they enjoyed having the flexibility and power to organize their email the way they wanted (67% agree, 22% neutral, 11% disagree).

TENSIONS WITHIN MAILING LIST COMMUNITIES

We now turn to examining several tensions that we observed within the mailing list communities we studied that may lead to problems. To facilitate our exploration, we categorize the types of mailing list posts into *transactional* (events, sales, etc.) and *interactional* (discussion, humor, etc.) communication. These categories have been used for spoken discourse and found in prior mailing list studies [9]. We acknowledge that not all posts fit easily into one category and that some intended transactional posts become interactional.[1]

Breaking down the mailing list content more finely, we asked survey respondents to self-report how often certain types of posts occur and also how often they would *like* certain types of posts to occur. In Figure 2, we plot the difference for DORM and LAB. To validate our survey results, two people were employed to manually tag 100 random emails from May 2014 from each mailing list into one of 9 categories we chose, given the subject line and body of the email (Cohen's kappa = 0.698). After resolving disagreements through discussion, we found that with minor exceptions people's perceptions of how many emails they received of each category generally aligned with the normalized frequencies we found. For instance, our tagging over-reported the category of "interesting discussions" compared to survey respondents' perceptions. This may be because we could only safely tag all emails that were discussion-related, without knowing the context for whether it was interesting or annoying.

[1]For instance, our post to LAB soliciting participants for our survey turned into a multi-week, 70-post discussion on the ethics of using Amazon gift cards as a reward.

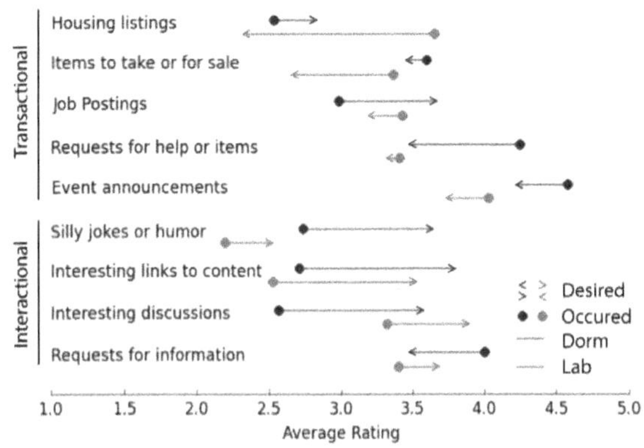

Figure 2. Survey results drawing an arrow starting from the number of times users stated a type of post occurred (circle) and ending at how often users would have liked for it to appear (arrow). Ratings are displayed as averages. Scale is 1–Never, 2–Once a month, 3–Once a week, 4–Once a day, 5–More than once a day.

	DORM
+	One of my favorite...types, is the sort of intellectual discourse...there was a golden time, where you had the right combination of people, you could get a good...intellectual discussion.
-	I personally am glad that [the discussion is] gone. I think it keeps [DORM] to be much more efficient.
	LAB
+	I sometimes wish there were more meaningful conversations about technology and less about logistics and so on. ...Those things show up a lot in talks but I don't think people discuss them enough.
-	...if I had to pinpoint an ideal level for me, personally, I don't know, maybe 10 to 15 percent less of what [the discussion level] currently is right now, would be great.

Table 2. Interview quotes expressing positive and negative feelings about interactional content on the two mailing lists.

Tension 1: Type and Quantity of Content

Our interviews revealed that often users, even within the same community, had different ideas about what their mailing lists should contain. For instance, we learned from the senior student interviewees of DORM that the mailing list used to have more discussions during their sophomore year, because of a certain set of outspoken seniors. Table 2 shows that interviewees disagreed on whether that was a good thing. Interviewees in LAB also disagreed on the optimum level of interactional content. When it came to more specific categories of email, such as the ones in Figure 2, interviewees also disagreed. Some interviewees were strongly in favor of more lighthearted humor or silliness on the mailing list while others were strictly against it. As another example, one interviewee spoke about job postings:

> *I think people will differ in that evaluation. I'm sure there's lots of people who actually appreciate the job postings and stuff whereas I'm not looking for a job.* –LAB

Some users acknowledged the tension between the two functions of the list:

> *The users of* [DORM] *are the types of people that don't really care about spammy stuff in their inbox ...Only upon reflection of what* [DORM] *used to be, do I stop and think like yeah, maybe that spammy stuff kind of pushed out more of that intellectual conversation...* –DORM

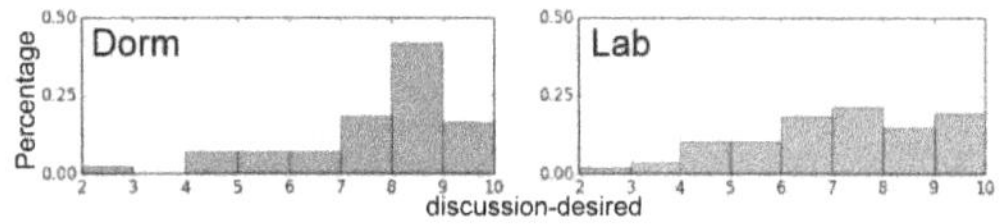

Figure 3. The *discussion-desired* measure, from 2–least desired to 10–most desired, for DORM and LAB.

When asked if the mailing list should stick to informational posts, a sizable minority of survey respondents agreed (24%). On the flip side, 34% wished the list had more discussions. Because these two questions were inter-related (Cronbach's alpha = 0.704), we added them together to create an overall *discussion-desired* measure. The average variance within the communities was 1.95, demonstrating a large spread of preferences. Figure 3 shows that while there was a general trend in both lists towards wanting more discussion, there appeared to be no one level of discussion ideal for even a large plurality of users.

Users also had very different ideas about how on-topic their list content should be. Some interviewees were sensitive to relevance and stated that they would leave the list if there were an increase in the number of irrelevant emails:

> *...I don't like getting email. Especially when it's not applicable.* –LAB

Other interviewees didn't mind irrelevant content because they wanted to feel more connected to the community and liked knowing what was going on, even if it didn't affect them. Some also appreciated serendipitous discoveries:

> *There's always that case that there's an event or something that I'm like, "...This is really cool." I never would have found that, if it wasn't for* [DORM]. *...To reduce those [types of posts] would be probably detrimental to those small instances.* –DORM

Interviewees additionally disagreed about whether replies to posts should appear on the list. The following two quotes are from different interviewees from LAB:

> *...You might as well just post it [to the list]. If they're not interested they can either skip over it, or quickly skim over it, or whatever.* –LAB

> *I despise it when people hit the reply to all button instead of the reply to button.* –LAB

This tension over appropriate content could cause backlash or the fear of backlash against certain posts or behaviors, leading to self-censorship, as we explore further in Tension 2. It also shows that attempts to improve mailing list designs cannot be one-size-fits-all, but should instead strive to give users more control of what they get.

Tension 2: Desire for Interaction vs. Hesitation to Post

As can be seen from the arrows in Figure 2, the desired occurrence is higher than perceived occurrence for most of the interactional content, while the opposite is true for transactional content. Despite this general desire for more interaction, we found paradoxically that *many users who wanted more discussions did not contribute to them.* One interviewee acknowledged the discrepancy between her actions and desires, saying:

> *I think it is kind of a Catch 22...I want more discussion but I also don't want to put myself out there...* –DORM

We found additional evidence of this in the surveys when we focused only on the respondents who said they wanted more discussion. Of the people who wanted more discussion, a majority of them had actually *never* participated in a discussion on the list (66%).

Though low levels of posting can be attributed to issues such as social loafing [12], we asked interviewees whether there were times when they wanted to participate in a conversation or had even written a post but did not send it. In these cases, users were *actively interested* in participating but were *deterred* for various reasons. We categorized the reasons that interviewees cited for why they self-censored their posts. Our survey then asked which of these categories gave respondents pause when posting. Though previous research has uncovered some similar deterrences [24, 27], a few stood out here. We report them for context and as motivation for some of our later design implications:

Spamming Large Audiences: Many interviewees stated that they were worried about spamming a large number of people. This was the most troubling of all the issues for LAB (62%) and the other communities that we surveyed (61%), but less so for DORM (43%) possibly because of the many event announcements on that list. One interviewee talked about the times he wrote long replies but never sent them, saying:

> *I'm not sure what it is that I would be losing if I hit that send button but...I felt...I'm just spamming people...and I'm only perpetuating inbox overload to people.* –LAB

Misinterpretation: This issue was the most troubling of the issues for DORM survey respondents (67%). Many interviewees from DORM said that they were hesitant to engage in discussions of controversial issues over email for fear of misspeaking and offending someone. This issue may have been more salient for DORM because members live in close proximity and all generally know each other. To them it felt difficult to craft a response that would be politically correct and not be misinterpreted:

> *Writing an email that is nuanced enough for* [DORM] *without pissing people off just like takes so long that it's not worth my time.* –DORM

Heated Arguments: People often expected that joining a discussion might lead to a heated argument they didn't want to get into. Interviewees from DORM and LAB could both name particular people on the list that they felt were "trolls"—people who could be counted on to spark controversy, leading to repetitive arguments. This was the second and third most problematic issue for LAB (50%) and DORM (57%) respectively.

> *...A couple times...I would feel like I had something to say and I would write this reply...I would spend a lot of time on it and then think this isn't worth it...it's just going to devolve into an age old argument of the same type that has happened over and over again.* –LAB

Appearing stupid: People from both communities were worried that they would be judged for appearing stupid. In LAB, this often translated to being afraid to talk about technical issues, for instance:

> *One thing that* [LAB] *is relatively devoid of is technical questions. You're keenly aware that the way...you'll ask a question signals an ignorance that you're afraid to show in* [Lab] *with such smart people.* –LAB

This was also the second most problematic issue for DORM (54%). One international interviewee said that she was embarrassed about her poor English and chose not to post questions, even when she really wanted help.

Summary: As can be seen, users were deterred from posting due to their fears of how their participation would be perceived by other members. We saw many users were afraid of spamming others with unwanted discussion, yet still a majority of people wanted to see more discussion. This highlights how these fears may sometimes be unfounded. Indeed many interviewees spoke of experiences where their participation resulted in positive outcomes. However, there were also times when users' fears were not unfounded, with arguments or harsh responses resulting. These conflicts may be exacerbated in part to differences outlined in Tension 1.

Tension 3: Push vs. Pull Access

The last tension is related to how users chose to access their email and how this may have affected their attitudes and actions on the mailing list.

Information access and exchange has often been differentiated as *push* versus *pull*. In push systems, senders actively "push" content to recipients, while in pull systems, senders make content available and recipients "pull" it at their leisure. There are two aspects of push systems that are often expected: recipients receive all messages, and they receive them in real-time. Neither of these expectations hold in pull systems, where recipients can ignore content or read it when they wish.

Traditionally, email is considered a push system while discussion forums and message feeds such as on Facebook, Twitter, or RSS are accessed more like pull systems. But while email *systems* are push-based, some users' email access *practices* have become more pull-based. For example, some now use automatic filing to divert mailing list email away from their inboxes to separate folders. The difference in behavior of these users versus users in the same community who access their mailing list in a traditional way may lead to tensions.[2]

A Pull Experience via Automatic Filing

A currently popular practice is filtering email into secondary folders that are then accessed less often. Many interviewees said that they had their mailing list email automatically filed into a separate folder. One interviewee, explaining the difference between his interaction with his main inbox and his mailing list folder said:

> *It does change your interaction. It's a lot less urgent. I perceive* [DORM] *as something that's less important. ...I want to check* [DORM] *so I'm going to open it and look at it. ...Whereas with my email inbox it's coming there. I need to check this.* –DORM

[2]A small part of our survey population (2%) also used digests to aggregate their list email, but we do not further focus on this group.

Another user had mailing list email come to his main inbox until Gmail began automatically filing it into a Forums tab:

> *Once Gmail made that change...most of my day is spent in the Important Email tab and I rarely look at the Forums tab. ...I think I skim* [LAB] *less not because of a disengagement from the list but just because the email client has suddenly hidden them...* –LAB

For some interviewees, filing the mailing list into a separate folder meant that occasionally they would forget to check it for an extended period. Others said that they purposefully checked the folder less often when they were busy.

> *It doesn't feel like I can't keep up perhaps because I don't want to be reading every single email.* –DORM

> *I treat it the same way that I would treat a...water cooler where you walk by and there's some colleagues talking...but you can't spend all day at the water cooler.* –LAB

In our survey, automatic filing was the most popular strategy for DORM and second most popular for all other communities (48% DORM, 17% LAB, 11% others). This difference may be due to the relatively high volume of emails that DORM receives. A majority of automatic filers reported that they did not mind missing email from the list (67% agree, 20% neutral, 13% disagree). A majority also reported that they read email from the list when they felt like it instead of when it arrived (70% agree, 15% neutral, 15% disagree). Additionally, many interviewees with this strategy stated that they did not mind irrelevant email or high volume from the mailing list specifically because the emails were being filed away.

A Push Experience without Automatic Filing

We observed a different attitude from the users who did not file their mailing list email separately from their normal email. These users had to go through each mailing list email just like any other email because it arrived in the same place. One such user noted problems that arose when he neglected to read his mailing list email:

> *...[there's] the risk of missing important mails when I allow many to go unread because the state of being read or unread is less signaling...* –LAB

In our survey, receiving content in the main inbox was the most or second-most popular way of dealing with mailing list email (23% DORM, 58% LAB, 68% others). In comparison to automatic filers, a smaller proportion of these users did not mind missing email from the list, with more than double the previous population disagreeing (50% agree, 31% neutral, 29% disagree). Far more users also disagreed with the idea that they read email when they felt like it instead of when it arrived (36% agree, 16% neutral, 48% disagree). Interviewees also expressed an inclination to unsubscribe if email became more irrelevant or volume started to increase, making it more difficult to maintain a casual relationship to the community or benefit from serendipity:

> *[Email] is something that I make an effort to stay on top of. I will unsubscribe from mailing lists if I think it's sending me too much email that's not relevant.* –LAB

Comparison
The survey data supported our association of automatic filing with pull-based and of manual handling with push-based behavior, though the numbers we report here should only be regarded as indicative. We found that automatic filers were more likely to completely miss email from the list (18% vs. 7%) and to not mind missing email from the list (67% vs. 50%). Automatic filers also were more likely to only read mailing list email when they felt like it, not when the email messages arrived (70% vs. 36%). On the other hand, users who had no filing strategy were more likely to read every message from the list (81% vs. 75%).

In the interviews with automatic filers, we found an expectation that others were accessing their email in the same way and would not mind additional email:

> *When...you get emails from someone, it doesn't take you that much time to just get rid of it. I think the people who really don't like spam already filter their* [DORM list]... *In which case my additional email really takes like three seconds of your time.* –DORM

An interviewee who did not have any strategy to differentiate his mailing list email had a very different thought-process when thinking of whether to post to the list:

> *When I'm thinking about sending an email to* [LAB], *I'm like, "Wow, does every single person related to* [LAB] *really need to get this email?" If that's not the case, I probably wouldn't send it.* –LAB

Our interviews suggest that how people access their list email may impact how they feel about the list as a whole and how they then act as senders on the list. For instance, people who automatically file may assume that emails are not time-consuming and in turn may send more emails, annoying or overwhelming fellow members, or send less relevant emails, contributing to Tension 1. Conversely, people who read email from their main inbox may be more wary about spamming and thus not contribute as much, in relation to Tension 2.

DISCUSSION

Design Implications

Our results suggest that a better group communication system would preserve the characteristics that people appreciate about mailing lists but also provide new features to alleviate the tensions we found. We note that many of our findings are not fundamentally tied to mailing lists but point to general preferences and tensions related to information exchange and communication within communities. Thus they also suggest design implications for many group communication systems including social media.

Indeed, the challenges we have identified in this work can be addressed from either end—by modifying a social media system to address the problems that lead some users to prefer mailing lists, or by modifying a mailing list system to address the problems perceived there. Enterprise social media systems such as Yammer are taking the former approach, and it is clearly important to extend our study to understand how the issues we have raised play out in those systems. For example, a *separate* social media system for work may be able to address the "Work vs. Play" concern we described for social media (but perhaps not the others).

But we believe that the second approach of "fixing mailing lists" has equal potential and may be far easier to undertake. For we benefit from the fact that the "user interface" for these systems is users' own email clients. This means that these (server-only) mailing list systems are much smaller and simpler than social media systems, so are easier for researchers to modify. And many robust open source implementations exist as starting points for experimentation. Furthermore, changes to these systems by definition will not change the user interface, reducing the disruptions that can discomfit users, and allowing them to preserve all the customizations they have adopted. But perhaps most importantly, mailing lists are not a monolith like social media systems. It is possible to build a new mailing list system and shift a single mailing list to it that its members can continue to read (in their traditional clients) with no disruption. Getting users to move (with the rest of their community) to a new social media system would be far more challenging.

For these reasons, we have developed a new mailing list system, Murmur, (http://murmur.csail.mit.edu/) that we are beginning to deploy and test.

Applying Social Media Ideas
To many of our users, mailing lists felt more professional than social media but still contained some content that did not quite feel work-related. This inspires us to consider how mailing lists could be designed to be something *in between social media and email* by continuing to stay within email technically while incorporating features from social media systems.

One issue we discussed is users' concerns about excessive volume—both as recipients who do not want it, and as senders who fear imposing it on others. We also found in Tension 1 that users in the same community often have different ideas about what their mailing list should contain. These issues may be exacerbated by the differences in email access strategies shown in Tension 3. One potential way to fix discrepancies in content type could be to split the list into two or more lists, but this was rejected by a sizable minority surveyed (38%), due to fears of it leading to less participation and splintering of the community (this experiment was actually attempted in the LAB list several years ago, and none of the sub-lists gained traction).

A different way to to address volume concerns and permit various preferences to coexist is to incorporate now-standard techniques from social media systems such as tagging (already explored in email in the Mail2Tag system [19]), social moderation, and collaborative filtering [13]. We've integrated these capabilities into Murmur, for example by using a blank reply as an up-vote and permitting tags in subject lines and replies. With this data, scoring and collaborative filtering can be used to decide which mailing list emails to forward to which individuals. We also provide a web interface to let users configure richer filtering of the list without giving up their preferred email clients.

Guaranteeing Delivery

However, introducing these social media techniques can damage one of the key appeals of mailing lists: users' "guaranteed delivery" sense that they know who will (and who will not) receive their posts. While no longer strictly true (as we saw in Tension 3), this notion was an appealing aspect of email to many of our interviewees.

Working within email gives us a useful way to address these concerns. Email's organizational capabilities are richer than many social media systems'. Instead of just choosing whether or not to show a post as social media streams do, we could use information from message content, tags, senders, and social moderation to route *all* messages to different *folders* specified by the user, who could access different folders at different times and frequencies. Instead of social media's "look now or it is gone forever," readers could fit reading to their own schedules. Importantly, no user would *have* to configure anything—the default behavior of delivering all list email would persist.

We must also be careful to respect users' desire for control over what they receive. Algorithms for curating feeds may introduce biases and may be difficult for users to comprehend. Thus, schemes with *explicit, transparent* filtering rules may be appealing for users who reject the opaque selection mechanisms provided by many of today's social media tools.

Limiting Delivery

On the flip side, we saw that many users were deterred from posting content welcomed by most users on the mailing list (Tension 2). Some of these deterrents were real (fear of trolls) and others were often imagined (concern that others wanted less volume). Just as we can help address the concerns of receivers by allowing them more accurate control over reception, there are opportunities to help senders more accurately control the way their information is sent. For example, we can give senders the ability to post their message to only a specific subset of friends (or random users) on the mailing list—who can then "up-vote" it and by doing so cause it to propagate to more list recipients. This can give the sender confidence that their email will hit many users only if it is interesting to many users. A small subset can also be asked to act as "friend-moderators", returning a message for corrections to grammar and tone before it spreads further. These friends can also act as "shielders," stripping the identity of a shy sender to protect them from trolls without introducing the problems of full anonymity. Murmur incorporates all these processes in the email environment using replies and forwards.

Of course, when we introduce ways for senders to limit their sending, we risk impacting the recipients who would like to receive more. There are interesting ways to address this. Borrowing from social media, we can permit users to "follow" specific users (with permission) and tags. Such followers would receive all content posted by the users or with the tags, overcoming excessive shyness by the senders. Also, while some of the aforementioned features to limit sending may make *receiving* these particular emails no longer deterministic, this may be a reasonable tradeoff if the sender would have chosen to not post otherwise.

Promoting Transparency

A common thread through our findings was a difference in people's perceptions of circumstances versus what they actually were. We discuss some potential ways to alleviate this with greater transparency. For users that were unaware of the general desire for more discussion, features such as up-voting could serve as feedback to encourage desired content. Tension 3 also uncovered differences in perceptions of how other users handled their email. To alleviate this, we could let users direct messages only to others who have not received too much email from the mailing list recently.

Finally, this study brought up privacy implications in that most people severely underestimated the number of subscribers to the list and most did not know that the list was public to join or had public archives. These issues need to be made clearer to the users so that they are aware of who their audience may be. Additionally, any changes to make archives more readable or searchable or allow them to be crawled could have negative effects if not properly revealed to users. Even though these changes may cause people to self-censor even more, we believe coupling them with some of the other features we have mentioned may mitigate effects.

This discussion only scrapes the surface of possibilities that are opened up by moving away from the opaque filtering algorithms provided by social media and instead giving both senders and recipients more transparent levers for controlling the delivery of information to them.

Limitations and Future Work

We examined only a student and a research-driven mailing list, and surveyed a convenience sample of other mailing list participants, many of whom were students or in academic roles. We did find the survey respondents for *Dorm* and *Lab* matched the demographics of the two primary communities we study, but in general we do not know our non-response bias. Generalization from our data should be done cautiously given how our data was collected. However, we believe our results generalize theoretically [3], in that they will be true for a large number of mailing lists and information environments. We do believe we found some significant groups of mailing list participants who share the perceptions, expectations, and frustrations that we have outlined. In addition, because most of the participants in our interviews and surveys were young enough to have spent many of their formative years using social media, their preference for using mailing lists over social media for group discussion is potentially more interesting than that of a general population.

Many populations were not included in this study—for example, work-related mailing lists. There, different factors such as workplace hierarchy and the culture around socializing may play an important role. As discussed, it would be interesting to contrast mailing list usage with regular email and real-time work communications such as Yammer. Similarly, we are curious how non-work systems might be enhanced or replaced by a real-time group chat interface, such as IRC. Several respondents mentioned using GroupMe for small group discussion, which does for SMS what mailing lists do for email. It would be interesting to study how our findings translate to text messaging and whether GroupMe could then support larger groups.

CONCLUSION

Many people still use mailing lists today to communicate within groups. There are now many new systems with new features for group communication, but they have not displaced mailing lists. We studied two mailing lists through interviews and surveys and surveyed 28 other mailing lists to understand why people continue to use them in the face of social media. We also uncovered important tensions within communities: we found that mailing list users within a single community *disagree on the types of content* the list should have; that despite wanting more discussion, *users self-censor* due to real and imagined concerns; and that *how users access* their mailing list email may alter their attitude towards receiving and posting messages. We also made a case for why simply moving to one of the new systems or building a new system outside of email may not be successful. From the issues we uncovered within current mailing list communities, we formulated design implications that could be introduced within mailing list systems in order to alleviate tensions.

ACKNOWLEDGEMENTS

Thank you to our participants who provided valuable insights. Thanks to those who read earlier versions of this work and to our anonymous reviewers for their helpful feedback. This material is based upon work supported by a Google Social Interactions Grant and the National Science Foundation Graduate Research Fellowship under Grant No. 1122374.

REFERENCES

1. Bernstein, M., Bakshy, E., Burke, M., and Karrer, B. Quantifying the invisible audience in social networks. *Proc. CHI* (2013), 21–30.
2. Chen, J., Nairn, R., and Chi, E. Speak little and well. *Proc. CHI* (2011), 217–226.
3. Corbin, J., and Strauss, A. *Basics of qualitative research: Techniques and procedures for developing grounded theory*. Sage, 2008.
4. Cubbison, L. Configuring listserv, configuring discourse. *Computers and Composition 16*, 3 (1999), 371–381.
5. Dabbish, L., and Kraut, R. Email overload at work. *Proc. CSCW* (2006), 431–440.
6. Ellison, N., Steinfield, C., and Lampe, C. The benefits of Facebook "friends". *JCMC 12*, 4 (2007), 1143–1168.
7. Fisher, D., Brush, A., Gleave, E., and Smith, M. Revisiting Whittaker & Sidner's "email overload" ten years later. *Proc. CSCW* (2006), 309–312.
8. Grevet, C., Choi, D., Kumar, D., and Gilbert, E. Overload is overloaded: Email in the age of Gmail. *Proc. CHI* (2014), 793–802.
9. Harrison, S. E-mail discussions as conversation: moves and acts in a sample from a listserv discussion. *Linguistik online 1*, 4 (1998).
10. Hyman, A. Twenty years of listserv as an academic tool. *The Internet and higher education 6*, 1 (2003), 17–24.
11. Kairam, S., Brzozowski, M., Huffaker, D., and Chi, E. Talking in circles. *Proc. CHI* (2012), 1065–1074.
12. Karau, S., and Williams, K. Social loafing. *Journal of personality and social psychology 65*, 4 (1993), 681.
13. Konstan, J., Miller, B., Maltz, D., Herlocker, J., Gordon, L., and Riedl, J. Grouplens. *Communications of the ACM 40*, 3 (1997), 77–87.
14. Lambert, G. Where do listservs fit in a social media world? *American Association of Law Libraries Spectrum 13* (2009), 8–13.
15. Lampe, C., Wash, R., Velasquez, A., and Ozkaya, E. Motivations to participate in online communities. *Proc. CHI* (2010), 1927–1936.
16. Matzat, U. Academic communication and internet discussion groups. *Social Networks 26*, 3 (2004), 221–255.
17. McCarty, W. Humanist: Lessons from a global electronic seminar. *Computers and the Humanities 26*, 3 (1992), 205–222.
18. Miles, M. B., and Huberman, A. M. *Qualitative data analysis: An expanded sourcebook*. Sage, 1994.
19. Nelson, L., Nairn, R., Chi, E., and Convertino, G. Mail2tag: Augmenting email for sharing with implicit tag-based categorization. *Proc. CTS* (2011), 23–30.
20. Park, N., Kee, K., and Valenzuela, S. Being immersed in social networking environment. *CyberPsychology & Behavior 12*, 6 (2009), 729–733.
21. Ren, Y., Kraut, R., and Kiesler, S. Applying common identity and bond theory to design of online communities. *Organization studies 28*, 3 (2007), 377–408.
22. Rojo, A., and Ragsdale, R. A process perspective on participation in scholarly electronic forums. *Science communication 18*, 4 (1997), 320–341.
23. Silberstein, A., Terrace, J., Cooper, B., and Ramakrishnan, R. Feeding frenzy: selectively materializing users' event feeds. *Proc. SIGMOD* (2010), 831–842.
24. Sleeper, M., Balebako, R., Das, S., McConahy, A., Wiese, J., and Cranor, L. The post that wasn't. *Proc. CSCW* (2013), 793–802.
25. Smock, A., Ellison, N., Lampe, C., and Wohn, D. Facebook as a toolkit. *Computers in Human Behavior 27*, 6 (2011), 2322–2329.
26. Talja, S., Savolainen, R., and Maula, H. Field differences in the use and perceived usefulness of scholarly mailing lists. *Information research 10*, 1 (2004).
27. Vitak, J. The impact of context collapse and privacy on social network site disclosures. *Journal of Broadcasting & Electronic Media 56*, 4 (2012), 451–470.
28. Whittaker, S., and Sidner, C. Email overload: Exploring personal information management of email. *Proc. CHI* (1996), 276–283.

Regulating Access to Adult Content (with Privacy Preservation)

Karen Renaud & Joseph Maguire*
School of Computing Science, University of Glasgow, Glasgow, UK
{karen.renaud,joseph.maguire}@glasgow.ac.uk

ABSTRACT
In the physical world we have well-established mechanisms for keeping children out of adult-only areas. In the virtual world this is generally replaced by self declaration. Some service providers resort to using heavy-weight identification mechanisms, judging adulthood as a side effect thereof. Collection of identification data arguably constitutes an unwarranted privacy invasion in this context, if carried out merely to perform adulthood estimation. This paper presents a mechanism that exploits the adult's more extensive exposure to public media, relying on the likelihood that they will be able to recall details if cued by a carefully chosen picture. We conducted an online study to gauge the viability of this scheme. With our prototype we were able to predict that the user was a child 99% of the time. Unfortunately the scheme also misclassified too many adults. We discuss our results and suggest directions for future research.

ACM Classification Keywords
H.1.2 User/Machine Systems: Human Factors

Author Keywords
Children; Protection; Access

INTRODUCTION
Automatically regulating access to adult content is challenging, especially if privacy is preserved [9]. The aim is to permit access to adults, but not to minors. In the physical world we effortlessly categorise people, in terms of age [24]. This makes it relatively easy for us to judge adulthood. When we are not sure, and being sure is a legal requirement, we may resort to identification. In the digital world, age-group classification without identification is challenging. While solutions exist (eg. German e-ID), they have not yet been widely accepted [19]. The concern is that society seems to be sleepwalking into using biometrics for this purpose [33]. Such widespread identification offsets the adult content provider's legal responsibility, but it also gives them a wealth of potentially sensitive information, something they might well abuse [49].

There is increasing concern from authorities across the world [33, 15], that children are accessing adult content online. Recent reports indicate that approximately 200,000 minors accessed age-inappropriate content in a single month [47], with the youngest being six years of age. Indeed, many minors claimed to have encountered pornographic images before the age of twelve [2]. The impact of such unrestricted consumption on developing minds should not be underestimated [11, 36, 47]. The existing mechanisms, are either ineffective or intrusive [51].

This paper explores a primary difference between adults and children that could be used to test for adulthood. Adults have lived longer and have accumulated more knowledge over the course of their lifetime [42, 38]. We propose to exploit these *knowledge differences* to achieve adulthood estimation without invading privacy. Our mechanism exploits this difference by testing the ability to label specially-chosen images correctly, essentially implementing a privacy-preserving access control mechanism. We first explain how we identified suitable images, and then how we used these images to judge the adulthood of experimental subjects in two iterations. We conclude by discussing our outcomes and presenting our suggestions for future developments. In summary, this paper's contributions are:

- The concept of knowledge-based regulation of access to adult content;
- Proven accuracy of the scheme based on two studies, using empirically validated images to perform adulthood estimation;
- Discussion of the implementation challenges and proposals for future work.

RELATED WORK
We first review existing mechanisms and then explain why we deployed images to test knowledge.

Existing Techniques
Parents use a variety of techniques to prevent their children from accessing adult content [33]: (1) education and

---

*School of Computing Science

CHI 2015, April 18–23, 2015, Seoul, Republic of Korea.

Include the http://DOI string/url which is specific for your submission and included in the ACM rightsreview confirmation email upon completing your ACM form supervision, (2) automated filtering on devices and/or (3) relying on content providers to prevent access.

Education alone is not entirely effective [30], judging by its efficacy in other contexts [22]. It could prove useful in conjunction with supervision. Nevertheless, while supervision may seem sensible it may have unintended consequences. Chirkov *et al.* argue that adolescents need to be allowed to express their autonomy, competence and relatedness in order to successfully come of age [10]. This suggests that parents and teachers should gradually relax control rather than tightening their grip if the child is to become a responsible adult.

Automated blocking and filtering of adult content is the second option [33]. A range of technical parental control tools can help parents to shield minors from age-inappropriate content [32], but the effectiveness of such solutions is debatable [6]. Unfortunately, many software solutions are ineffective because they either over- or under-block digital content [43]. These inaccuracies may be the result of guardians struggling with configuration options and user interfaces [7, 29]. Furthermore, Fleming *et al.* reported little difference in exposure to inappropriate material when blocking software was, or was not, installed [13]. A possible explanation is that minors are innovative enough to bypass such software. Moreover, there is also evidence that children resent their use, since they feel that the use of such software by their parents provides evidence of a lack of trust [28]. The reality is that the majority of guardians do not deploy automated filtering tools [31].

The previous two strategies are within the control of the guardian. When this is delegated to adult content providers, the deployed mechanism is usually either completely ineffective or overly intrusive. The ineffective approaches typically take the form of self-declaration, whereby individuals must declare their age or date of birth [52]. The process is elegant and effective at preventing *accidental* access. However, evidence suggests that many minors deliberately seek out, rather than accidentally stumble upon, adult content [13]. Livingstone *et al.* reported that 22% of surveyed 9-19 year-olds had purposefully accessed age-inappropriate content [25].

Some vendors go a step further, requiring a valid credit card, for example. This is based on the assumption that only adults can own a credit card but actually possession of such a token does not constitute proof of adulthood [39] especially since sufficiently motivated minors can easily obtain one [21].

The token-based technique crosses the invisible privacy boundary. Once privacy is violated, identification is carried out and age is established as a side effect. Vendors are able to gather far more information than is strictly required. Many other mechanisms, such as biometrics, also identify to authenticate. Biometrics seems an attractive alternative at first glance since pre-adolescent minors are smaller than adults, by and large, and this can easily be measured, especially as modern devices now routinely incorporate the requisite sensors. Unfortunately, the efficacy of the biometric-based approach has been questioned [49, 40]. Furthermore, there are genuine privacy concerns surrounding the collection and storage of biometrics belonging to minors without proper legislation mediating their use, and the storage and retention of such data [54, 14].

Another even more invasive solution is that of verifying identity by cross-referencing customer information such as name and address, date of birth with information held by other vendors or governments. This assumes that the other systems' data is accurate [39, 49] but there is evidence that such systems are easily manipulated by adolescents [48].

Based on this summary, we can conclude that the current range of third party mechanisms is unsatisfactory. They either present no bar to entry, or identify in order to establish adulthood, violating privacy. Moreover, many of these mechanisms introduce a substantial time lag into the access process which punishes adults instead of merely excluding children. The aim is to find a middle ground, something that estimates adulthood more effectively without identification. Such a solution would preserve the privacy of adult, or child, wanting to access adult content.

Using Images to Test Memory

There are two reasons for using images instead of simple questions to test knowledge. The first is that we inhabit the era of information being at everyone's fingertips, via search engines. If you ask someone a textual question they can search for the answer online — proving nothing more than an ability to search. If we use images to spark a memory it becomes harder for people to find the answer online.

The second reason is that people remember images better than the words than name them [27, 34, 35, 46]. Vision is the dominant human sense, being attended to before other modalities [37]. The sighted human effortlessly and almost subconsciously processes millions of images every day. Over time, an internal database of image forms and descriptors are accumulated, to support instantaneous recognition [46]. Lexical labels are linked with these objects, and every time the person interacts with the object and names it, that link gets stronger. Images appear to deliver two benefits: they are not as easy to search for, and they are more memorable than text.

We plan to use images in a recall-based context — not recognition as is the case with many psychological experiments proving the superiority of picture memory. Unlike recognition, recall requires provision of a lexical label from someone who is being cued by an image. There is evidence that people can label images they have seen before [8, 26]. Unfortunately, the labels are essentially proper nouns, and these are seldom descriptive, that can cause the memorial link between the name and the object to disappear or weaken over time [5]. There is also the "tip of the tongue" effect to consider [4, 18]. This, too, is particularly prevalent for proper noun labels. These labelling difficulties might impact the efficacy of our our proposed adulthood estimation mechanism, and we will return to this aspect in our discussion section.

Finally, it must be acknowledged that this mechanism excludes those with vision problems, and any deployment would have to be done in conjunction with some other mechanism to cater for those who cannot see the images well enough to label them.

DESIGN

The proposed mechanism acts to ensure that adults can access content but that minors are excluded. The concept is simple: an individual is presented with a grid of M images. They are required to label each image. The individual does not necessarily need to label all images correctly, but simply reach a threshold of N images to be classified as an adult. The expectation is that adults will be able to label at least N of M images but that minors will not. The mechanism does not effect identification, use biometric data or require the use of issued tokens, essentially preserving privacy.

The simplicity of this approach does not mean that achieving it is easy or simple. We faced two primary challenges in developing such a knowledge-based adulthood estimation mechanism: (1) finding the right set of images, and (2) delivering an accurate estimation.

(1) Image Identification

The first aim was to identify a set of candidate images for the proposed mechanism. The following *null* and *alternative* hypotheses were used to accept or reject a particular image:

$H1_0$: There is no difference between adults and minors when correctly identifying an image.

$H1_1$: There is a difference between adults and minors when correctly identifying an image.

(2) Estimating Adulthood

The challenge is that in estimating we inhabit the realms of probability. Hence we will make a judgement, and some of the time that judgement will be incorrect. We need to decide how many images to display, M, and how many of these the person should label correctly, N, to be judged an adult. The numbers chosen for N and M reflect the system's tolerance for error. The following hypotheses were tested:

$H2_0$: Adults will not have a different mean score than minors.

$H2_1$: Adults will have a higher mean score than minors.

$H2_2$: Adults will have a lower mean score than minors

The mechanism should judge adulthood to an acceptable level of accuracy. The classification of an individual can be categorised as a true positive, true negative, false positive or false negative. Table 1 illustrates the values of each, as a contingency table with the columns representing actual values and rows representing prediction values.

		Actual: *Adults*	Actual: *Minors*	
Prediction	*Adults*	True Positive	False Positive	*PPV*
Prediction	*Minors*	False Negative	True Negative	*NPV*
		Sensitivity	*Specificity*	*Accuracy*

Table 1. Contingency Table of Performance

Table 1 depicts the *sensitivity, specificity, positive predictive value, negative predictive value* and *accuracy.* The sensitivity (true positive rate) of the mechanism is the correct prediction of adults and the specificity (true negative rate) of the mechanism is its ability to exclude minors. The PPV, the positive predictive value, is the probability that the mechanism will correctly predict an adult. The NPV, the negative predictive value, is the probability that the mechanism correctly predicts a minor. PPV and NPV reflect the proportion of adults and minors in the sample and whether they are correctly assessed by the mechanism [1]. Lastly, accuracy is a measure of the true positives and true negatives in the population.

Delineating Children

Adults and children are generally defined in biological terms, with 18 years being the pivotal point as individuals enter adulthood on their 18th birthday. Different societies have different rules about people at various ages. In the UK people can marry at 16 and drink alcohol at 18, but in the US citizens have to be 18 to marry and 21 to drink alcohol. In some African countries marriage is allowed at 15, and in some European countries it is legal to drink alcohol at 16. Instead of focusing on 18 as a pivotal age, therefore, we should focus on the progression from childhood to adulthood, and the particular stage where they are most in need of protection.

The literature highlights the vulnerability of the 11-12 age group. This is when young people start spending less time with their families [23] and also start needing the support of adults outside the home [41]. If this is not provided at school they might well go online to get what they need. This is also the age when children, as a consequence of transferring from a relatively small primary school to a large secondary school, start to experience feelings of anonymity [44] and start interacting with the opposite sex [45] since they are embarking on puberty (earlier than in previous centuries, now to be expected at 11-12 [17]). Hence online anonymity is likely to appeal to them. At this age they start becoming more independent [3] and moving into adulthood and many are eager to embrace adult activities [20]. They need to be permitted increasing levels of autonomy to mature [10]. Parents and teachers therefore slowly relax controls to allow this. Unfortunately, the period of entering secondary school is when self-esteem decreases [53], and this only recovers when they settle properly into secondary school. Pre-adolescents are considered more vulnerable to abuse than older or younger children [12] and this reduced self-esteem might well be the reason for this vulnerability. Thus the 11-12 age group is a pivotal age, where efforts to enter the adult world need to be thwarted to protect them from that which they are not yet ready to deal with.

Finally, Fleming *et al.* [13] reported that younger adolescents were far less safety conscious when using the Web. Hence, in identifying images and testing our mechanism, we will focus on trying to distinguish between 11-12 year olds, and over 18s.

STUDY ONE

We started by identifying suitable images, then proceeded to test them in an estimation mechanism.

Identifying Images

An initial set of 104 images was gathered. Images were culled from various sources and aimed to include images of public figures and significant events, from the perspective of Western popular culture. The images within the set can be categorised, as follows: (1) Entertainment: music, film & television, (2) World Events, (3) Iconic Figures and (4) Politicians. Examples of images are: Michael Jackson, World Trade Centre, Dolly the Sheep and David Cameron.

Participants

60 minors and 74 adults participated. Participants aged 18 and over were recruited using traditional means, such as social networks and mailing lists. A number of schools were contacted in the United Kingdom, predominately Scotland and England, to obtain permission for their pupils to participate.

Procedure

The purpose of the survey was explained to the participant. The participant was then asked to complete a few simple questions pertaining to their nationality and age-range. Participants were then presented with each image and asked to label the image, i.e. identify the image content. The participants were asked to do this for each of the images in the initial set. The performance of each participant was analysed to determine if they had successfully identified the image or not. The label each participant submitted was analysed automatically using Levenshtein distance [16] to compensate for spelling errors.

Results

The survey was completed by all 134 participants, representing 60 minors and 74 adults. Adults scored higher on average (μ=54.32) than minors (μ=24.16) when labelling images within the initial set.

The next step was to identify those images that children struggle to label but that adults are able to label. The decision was taken to implement a threshold, as statistical analysis for all images was deemed unnecessary given certain images were easily identifiable by both groups. Consequently, images were selected when 75% more of adults correctly labelled it and only 25% or less of children correctly labelled it. The resulting 16 images were then statistically analysed using a Chi-Square test for association to determine if age-group was independent of performance. If performance for a particular image was not independent of age-group, it was deemed that $H1_0$ could be rejected and $H1_1$ accepted. In those cases were there were fewer than 5 participants in any of the contingency tables, used in the statistical analysis, a Fisher's exact test was used. The motivation for not using Fisher's exact test in all cases is that it may have been too conservative and lead to the rejection of viable images. Consequently, we deemed the Chi-square test adequate for the purpose of confirming image use and only defaulted to a Fisher's exact test when necessary.

The statistical analysis for each of the 16 images showed a strong association between adults and labelling performance when compared to minors. Consequently, in each case $H1_0$ was rejected and $H1_1$ was accepted and each image was added to the evaluation set.

Adulthood Estimation

The image identification stage pinpointed the image set for evaluation of the proposed mechanism. We could now proceed to test the mechanism. The image set of 16 images that emerged from the previous stage was used. The proposed mechanism was web-based and accessible from any device with a fully featured web-browser.

Participants

A total of 33 participants were recruited for the evaluation, comprising of 24 adults and 9 minors. Participants from the previous stage were excluded from this stage. A similar recruitment process to the previous stage was used.

Procedure

Participants accessed the system from a web browser. The first page provided information about the purpose of the investigation and what was expected. The participant was then asked for their actual age. The participant was than presented with six images and asked to label them. The system then predicted the user's age, based on the correctness of the image label, using Levenshtein distance [16] to compensate for spelling errors. The prediction was logged and participants thanked.

Results

The evaluation was completed by 33 participants, comprising 24 adults and 9 minors. Table 2 outlines the performance of the mechanism. The sensitivity of the mechanism, i.e. correct prediction of adults, is approximately 96%. The specificity of the mechanism, i.e. correct prediction of minors, is approximately 89%.

		Actual: *Adults*	Actual: *Minors*	
Prediction	*Adults*	23	1	*PPV* **≈96%**
	Minors	1	8	*NPV* **≈89%**
		Sensitivity **≈96%**	*Specificity* **≈89%**	*Accuracy* **≈92%**

Table 2. Mechanism Performance

An independent samples t-test was performed to determine if there was any difference in scores between adults and minors. Upon inspection of box-plots there were no outliers greater than 3 box-lengths from the edge of the box, but adult scores were not normally distributed, as assessed using a Shapiro-Wilk's test ($p < .05$). However, scores for minors were normally distributed, as assessed using a Shapiro-Wilk's test ($p > .05$), and there was homogeneity of variances for scores for adult and children, as assessed by Levene's test for equality of variances ($p = .870$). It thus became clear that a nonparametric test such as the Mann-Whitney U-test would be unsuitable due to the structure of the data, and the assumptions that this test makes. Consequently, the decision was taken to continue with the independent samples t-test. The reality is that adults scored higher (5.04 ± 1.197) than minors (1.78 ± 1.202). There was a statistically significant difference in mean scores between adults and minors, with adults scoring 3.26 (95% CI, 2.31 to 4.22) higher than minors, $t(31) = 6.968$, $p = < .001$.

The statistical analysis supported acceptance of H21 and rejection of $H2_0$ and $H2_2$. However, the small samples, unbalanced groups and the fact that one of the groups was not normally distributed, undermines the validity of our statistical analysis. Consequently, the data and analysis does not allow us to confirm or reject the hypotheses with any degree of certainty.

The aforementioned issues in the analysis could arguably be addressed using an alternative approach. A nonparametric equivalent to an independent t-test might well have produced stronger results. In this case, an acceptable alternative would have been a Mann Whitney U-test. However, nonparametric tests make assumptions about the structure of data. The Mann Whitney U-test, for example, requires the groups to be similarly structured. Given that this is not the case, we could only reasonably compare and report mean ranks rather than the scores themselves. Consequently, it was felt that adopting such an alternative approach would only serve to muddy the issue and limit subsequent discussions, as the focus would not be on mean scores but on ranks.

Discussion

The first study taught us lessons which fed into the next stage.

Image Identification: (1) Images of events appear to be unsuitable but images related to people can deliver the required distinctions if chosen carefully. (2) The best images for supporting adulthood-estimation are those that peak in the public media 15-20 years before the current date, and are then revisited from time to time so that they re-enter public consciousness.

Accuracy: (1) We should not ask participants to self-declare their age. In retrospect this was naïve. We ought to have two different sites for adults and children to use so that we are sure of the adulthood of the participant. (2) The first prototype used a challenge set comprising M=6 and N=2 to support a judgement. This might well set the bar too low.

STUDY TWO

Having learnt lessons from the first study, we commenced with our main study. We started with an image identification phase to identify a larger number of suitable images, then used these to trial a knowledge-based adulthood estimation prototype.

Image Identification

We expanded image topics beyond well-known people to also include images of vintage cars, old sweets and movies & television shows. We did not use images of widely publicised world events as the first study had shown these kinds of images to be suboptimal. We gathered a total of 481 images in categories: Famous People, Sweets, Cars and Film & Television Shows. The sweet name was obscured. It was, unfortunately, quite difficult to find suitable images of yesteryear's sweet wrappers. Car images depicted vintage cars with the logos and model names obscured.

The images used in the survey focused strongly on Western popular culture because we were exploiting people's exposure to images in public media and these are country-dependent, and we were going to test it primarily in the UK and the US. The main condition for an image to be considered suitable for use was whether adults, and not children, were likely to have been exposed to the image content (i.e. part of popular culture at least a decade ago).

Participants

As argued earlier, children under 13 years of age are considered to be most vulnerable. For this reason the image identification was carried out amongst S1 and S2 pupils (11 to 13 years of age) in two Scottish high schools. There was a total of 1601 participants, 1382 minors and 219 adults. A similar recruitment process was used as the previous study, with adults recruited using social networking services and mailing lists. Children were recruited by contacting various schools and obtaining permission from teachers.

Procedure
The first study asked participants to label all images. We could not realistically ask people to do this for all 481 candidate images. Moreover, the schools we contacted indicated that they could not allocate more than 5-10 minutes to this task, being under some pressure to complete their curriculum. We therefore decided to choose 30 images randomly to show to each participant. We did the same for adults and children.

We explained what the study was about, then collected demographics. We displayed 30 randomly chosen images, one at a time, and asked them to provide labels. Participants could also click on a button to pass. No cues were provided. Auto-fill in the label field was disabled. We recorded how long they took to label the images. We concluded by thanking them for their time and participation.

The system then determined the correctness of the labels. Participants' answers were compared to the correct labels for each image (both converted to lowercase, with punctuation and spaces removed). In case of the images of famous people, participants were expected to provide the name (eg. John Kennedy), not the role (eg. "President"), nicknames (eg. "JFK") or fictional character names in the case of actors (eg."Rocky"). A Levenshtein string distance algorithm [16] was used to accommodate spelling mistakes.

Results
1382 children and 219 adults participated in the image identification. The majority of child participants were born (1094) and raised (1114) in the UK.

When we examined the image labels it became clear that sweets and cars were unsuitable. Cars were too difficult even for adults to label. The Famous People and Film & TV categories delivered far better results since there was a clear divide between adults and children in terms of ability to label them. The mean score for children was 10% and for adults 26%.

Outcome
We realised that a timeout was not feasible when we considered the average labelling time. Web searching is so fast that we could not set any meaningful timeout period which would not also prevent people from typing in the answers they actually knew.

Since we were not able to test labelling of all images by all participants we had variable numbers of labels for our images, which barred reliable statistical testing. We thus decided that in order for an image to be considered suitable for use in the adulthood estimator it had to be labelled correctly by at least 50% of adults and by no more than 20% of children. This seemed to divide adults and children satisfactorily. A total of 44 images (9%) emerged from this stage.

Adulthood Estimation
To prepare the images we attempted to foil circumvention attempts, in this case searching for the image online. Since we could not feasibly prevent searching by implementing a timeout we decided rather to distort the images. The idea was to edit each image so that its content would still be recognisable to humans but not to software such as Google Image Search. Each image was edited using age-effect filter(old photography) as well as two artistic filters (ink outline and coloured pencil). However, for a few images this was not enough to deter an online image search. In this case, the images were edited using a texture filter (fissured) and an artistic filter (coloured pencil) which gave a very similar effect to that of age-effect filters combined with ink outlines and coloured pencil yet this indeed prevented an online image Search from returning any results. We disabled the right click and gave the images anonymous names.

Figure 1. Two faces, clear and distorted[50, 55]

Participants
For the purposes of the study three Scottish high schools were approached and asked to allow their first and second year pupils to participate in the survey. Adult participants were friends of those involved in the project but the majority of participants consisted of students from the University of Glasgow, both local and international. An invitation was also posted online.

Procedure
The experiment started with a page explaining what the study was about. Participants were instructed to label the images and to leave the label field blank if they could not. Demographics were collected, depending on whether this was the adult or child website.

Six *distorted* images were first displayed for labelling. The image set was randomised for each participant and no cues were provided.

One image in each set was a decoy image. Since many of our participants were children we did not want them to feel too discouraged by the process so the decoy image was one that they had a high probability of recognising. The correctness of the decoy image label was not used to judge adulthood. Depending on their performance, one of two things would happen:

- **Able to Make a Judgment:**
  If they labelled 4 or 5 images correctly it was likely that this was an adult (a Levenshtein string distance algorithm accommodated spelling errors.). If they got fewer than three correct (1 or 2), it was likely that this was a child. The next screen thus showed Challenge Set A again, *in the clear*, with the label fields pre-populated with the previously provided labels. They could then label the images again or re-submit initial labels.
- **Ambiguity:**
  If the system couldn't make a clear judgement a new set of images (Set B) was displayed. After they had labelled the new images, the first and second sets were displayed again, *in the clear*, in case this helped to jog their memory. They could change their initial labels.

The system concluded by telling the participant whether they had been judged adult or child, and thanked them for participating. A comment box was provided.

The reasoning behind this implementation was as follows. If we displayed 5 images then, based on the image identification results, we could expect adults to be able to guess 50% of these. This converts to ±3 images in the challenge set. If they identified four out of the five, they scored 80% and were classified as adult. If they identified only three, another set would be displayed. If they were able to identify three again (scoring 6 out of 9 = 67%), they would have passed the test and be classified as adult.

Children, based on our previous findings, only have a 1 in 5 chance of identifying images. If we presented them with 5 images we could expect them only to identify one or two of these. If by some fluke they managed to get three right in the first set, they would probably not be able to repeat that in the second set of images, and would be classified as a child.

Results

869 child participants aged 11 to 13 years participated with 356 adults participating. 79% of the adults were either British (31%) or American (48%). Child participants were mostly born (844) and raised (860) in the UK.

Accuracy:
Each participant was required to label at least 67% of the images correctly to be classified as adult. 99.7% of children were classified correctly when labeling distorted images and 99.08% when labeling in-the-clear images. At the same time, almost 34% of adult participants were classified correctly by the system when labeling distorted images and just over 43% when labeling the in-the-clear images.

		Actual		
		Adults	*Minors*	
Prediction	*Adults*	154	8	*PPV* ≈**95%**
	Minors	202	861	*NPV* ≈**81%**
		Sensitivity ≈**43%**	*Specificity* ≈**99%**	*Accuracy* ≈**83%**

Table 3. Mechanism Performance for Non-Distorted Images

The poor results with respect to the adults were unexpected so we posted a random sample of 20 images from our image set on CrowdFlower, a crowd sourcing website. We posted two jobs: (1) one with the images distorted and (2) one with the images in the clear. Each job collected responses from 100 participants. We had to remove three fraudulent responses from the first job, and four from the second[1], but we were left with a large enough number of reasonable attempts to draw conclusions about recognition rates. The recognition rate for the distorted images was 38.66% whereas the recognition rate with the clear images was 49.31%. These numbers are remarkably close to the percentages in our study (33.89% and 43.26%), given the differences between the two population groups. This gave us more confidence in the paucity of our adult responses, suggesting that this was not an anomaly caused by our sample.

Adults scored better than children with the distorted images (2.14 ± 1.70) vs (0.18 ± 0.02). The assumption of homogeneity was violated, as assessed by Levene's test for equality of variances ($p < .001$). Therefore a Welch t-test is reported. There was a statistically significant difference in mean scores between adults and children, with adults scoring higher than children, 1.91 (95% CI, 1.71 to 2.10), $t(325.119)=19.29$, $p< .001$.

With respect to the clear images, adults scored higher (2.59 ± 1.80) than children (0.39 ± 0.73). The assumption of homogeneity was violated, as assessed by Levene's test for equality of variances ($p < .001$). Therefore a Welch t-test is reported. There was a statistically significant difference in the scores between adults and children, with adults scoring higher than children, 2.20 (95% CI, 1.99 to 2.41), t (340.167) = 20.75, $p < .001$.

Timings:
We examined the timings of responses and discovered a significant difference between the times taken by children and adults labelling the distorted images ($p < 0.001$).

[1]These were nonsense responses, with labels such as x entered for all images

There was no significant difference between the times adults and children took to label the clear images, however. We will discuss the implications of this in the next section.

DISCUSSION

Accuracy

Our knowledge-based adult estimation mechanism detected 99% of child participants, using N/M being greater than 67%. Unfortunately, the mechanism also classified too many adults as children (false negatives). An analysis was subsequently performed to investigate how the false positive and negative rate would change if the minimum score, N, was reduced (shown in Table 4). The percentage values for both child and adult participants represent the proportion of each group classified as adult.

	% False Positives		% True Positives	
Min Threshold	Distorted	Clear	Distorted	Clear
20% (1 out of 5)	17.91	30.15	82.22	86.24
40% (2 out of 5)	4.45	9.2	64.44	72.47
44% (4 out of 9)	0.51	2.3	41.67	50.84
56% (5 out of 9)	0.3	1.61	38.06	47.75
60% (3 out of 5)	0.8	2.88	43.33	51.97
67% (6 out of 9)	0.3	0.92	33.89	43.26

Table 4. Tweaking Thresholds

The distortions might have deterred recognition. Some comments referred to this: *"It was really, really difficult to see who they were when the pictures werent clear"*. If the distortions made recognition difficult, it is indicative of the unfortunate yet inevitable tension between preventing circumvention and maximising accuracy. Still, this would not have made the adults fail the test, since we displayed the images in the clear too.

Adults took significantly longer to label the distorted images. What were they doing differently? Four different things might have happened when they examined the image: (1) they recognised the person, and knew the label; (2) they recognised the person but couldn't come up with label; (3) the distortions made it difficult to be sure; or (4) they did not know who the person was.

(1) does not explain the time lag. Using an online image search would be the natural thing to do if (2) were true. With no timeout this strategy might have been deployed. One of the comments confirms that this happened at least in one case *"I admit that I googled Lisa Kudrows last name, because I knew who she was but just could not remember the last name for whatever reason."*.

Was this a manifestation of tip-of-the-tongue syndrome [4]? Eight participant comments alluded to this eg. *"I think recognized the guy from Monty Python (first picture) but couldnt remember his name (not Michael Palin) and felt I shouldnt look it up."*.

If (3) were the case the time lag could simply be due to a participant spending some time examining the picture. There were three comments related to this, including: *"thank goodness there were clearer pictures later!"*. In this case circumvention resistance clearly impacted accuracy.

What about (4)? We used images that 50% or more of adults were able to label, but that is a probability, not a certainty. It could have been the case that the test was just too hard. They could have attempted a online image search, which would explain the time lag.

We believe that the images presented the adults with too much of a challenge. Those who knew enough about the depicted person to search probably found the name via a search engine. Some may have felt that this was cheating, but it is fairly safe to conclude that the combination of the hard to identify images, and the requirement for a pass rate of over 67%, probably led to the estimation mechanism delivering too many false negatives.

It might be reasonable to lower the minimum threshold to 40% (2 out of 5) or to 60% (3 out of 5). On the other hand, as more adults are correctly classified, so the number of false positives, in terms of children being classified as adults, increases (see Table 4). This is where context comes in. Some adult content is far more sensitive than other, as reflected by the different ratings applied to films, and the tolerance for error might well be aligned to the nature of the content being protected by the access control mechanism.

Foiling Circumvention Attempts

We used distorted images which would deliver no results if fed into image search engines. So we know that an online image search would not have delivered any results. Any adulthood-estimation mechanism has to contend with the ingenuous efforts of determined children. What would an enterprising child do if he or she were determined to access adult content and this mechanism was barring entry? The child could feasibly post the image onto a social networking site, asking others to identify it. This, of course, would take time and even a relatively long timeout could help to foil this tactic. Such a posting might also alert a responsible adult to the child's activities. They could also send the image to an older friend or sibling and ask for help in identifying it. When we rejected the idea of a timeout earlier that was because we couldn't prevent online searching with a timeout. It does seem more feasible to prevent children consulting other children with a timeout since that will probably take longer.

We should also implement some kind of mechanism to discourage repeat attempts. A doubling delay would be very effective — so that no further requests are accepted from a particular IP address for a certain period if the previous attempt failed.

Future Work

The primary challenge is addressing deployment-related issues. **The first** issue is bootstrapping the solution with a viable image set. Whereas a time-consuming collection and curating process was reasonable to support a research project, it is unrealistic in a real-life solution. Consequently, an automated process to collect and curate images is required. **Secondly,** such a process would have to incorporate some notion of periodic refreshing of the image set to tackle evolving public consciousness and improvements in online search tools. Furthermore, minors will adopt other strategies to defeat the mechanism, eg. creating online communities to exchange answers. Moreover, even if an automated process could rapidly deliver viable images, it would encounter difficulties related to the number of well-known personalities available for use. There is a finite number of individuals and events that can be used in this context.

Nevertheless, even if all the aforementioned issues are tackled and an evergreen image set *can* be created, **the convenience** of such a solution is debatable. The solution may seem viable when presented prior to consuming a lengthy 2-hour motion picture, but seems excessive if the user is consuming several short videos via YouTube, for example. These challenges would have to be overcome if this mechanism's potential is to be realised in practice.

If we are able to resolve the deployment challenges, two aspects of the current solution require attention. **(1) Setting N and M:** What should N and M be? This is likely to depend on the level of certainty required that the user is an adult. The required certainty will probably be linked to the content it is shielding, and we will consider this a matter for future research.

(2) Easing The Process for Adults: To ameliorate the tip of the tongue problem we could accept meta-data instead of a label. This would lead to greater complexity since even more spelling errors would have to be accommodated and it would slow the estimation process down. Moreover, search engines already help people to fix on a name given meta data, development in this area does not seem warranted.

CONCLUSION

In this paper we presented a knowledge-based mechanism for classifying an online user as either an adult or a child. The mechanism was able to correctly classify the a user as a child with 99% accuracy. It also currently delivers an unacceptably high rate of false negatives, barring far too many adults. It is a clear improvement over self-declaration, and, most importantly, does not violate the user's privacy.

It would be naïve to believe that we can craft a mechanism that uses one technique, in solo, to solve this tricky problem of adulthood estimation. Our desire for simplicity of purpose and solution cannot be satisfied in this case. There are some directions to take this research, which are certainly worth pursuing, since parents currently face unprecedented challenges in protecting their children.

Acknowledgements

We acknowledge the essential contributions of Charlene Low and Aga Kielbinska, who worked on the first and second phases of this project, respectively. Without their sterling work we could not have completed this project. We also thank our many participants and the teachers who made the evaluations possible.

REFERENCES

1. D. G. Altman and J. M. Bland. Diagnostic tests 2: predictive values. *BMJ: British Medical Journal*, 309(6947):102, 1994.
2. BBC3. BBC three survey reveals one in four young people first view porn at age 12 or under. `http://www.bbc.co.uk/mediacentre/latestnews/2014/porn-whats-the-harm.html`.
3. T. J. Berndt. The features and effects of friendship in early adolescence. *Child Development. Early Adolescence (Dec., 1982)*, 53(6):1447–1460, 1982.
4. R. Brown and D. McNeill. The "tip of the tongue" phenomenon. *Journal of verbal learning and verbal behavior*, 5(4):325–337, 1966.
5. D. M. Burke, J. K. Locantore, A. A. Austin, and B. Chae. Cherry pit primes brad pitt homophone priming effects on young and older adults' production of proper names. *Psychological Science*, 15(3):164–170, 2004.
6. M. Buzzi. Children and YouTube: Access to Safe content. In F. Cipolla-Ficarra, K. Veltman, D. Verber, M. Cipolla-Ficaeea, and F. Kammüller, editors, *Proceedings of the 9th ACM SIGCHI Italian Chapter International Conference on Computer-Human Interaction: Facing Complexity*, CHItaly, pages 125–131, New York, NY, USA, 2011. ACM.
7. M. Buzzi. What are your children watching on YouTube? In *Advances in New Technologies, Interactive Interfaces and Communicability*, pages 243–252. Springer, 2012.
8. C. B. Cave. Very long-lasting priming in picture naming. *Psychological Science*, 8(4):322–325, 1997.
9. D. Chaum. Security without identification: Transaction systems to make big brother obsolete. *Commun. ACM*, 28(10):1030–1044, Oct. 1985.
10. V. Chirkova, R. M. Ryan, Y. Kimc, and U. Kapland. Differentiating autonomy from individualism and independence: A self-determination theory perspective on internalization of cultural orientations and well-being. *Journal of Personality and Social Psychology*, 84(1):97–110, 2003.
11. J. Edgar and G. Rayner. Judge blames easy access to online pornography after boy, 12, rapes seven-year-old sister, 4 March 2014. The Telegraph.
12. D. Finkelhor and L. Baron. High-risk children. In D. Finkelhor and Associates, editors, *Sourcebook on child sexual abuse*. Sage, Newbury Park CA, 1986.
13. M. J. Fleming, S. Greentree, D. Cocotti-Muller, K. A. Elias, and S. Morrison. Safety in cyberspace adolescents' safety and exposure online. *Youth & Society*, 38(2):135–154, 2006.
14. A. M. Froomkin. The death of privacy? *Stanford Law Review*, pages 1461–1543, 2000.
15. F. Gilbert. Age verification as a shield for minors on the internet: A quixotic search? *Shidler Journal of Law Commerce & Technology*, 6, 2008.
16. M. Gilleland. Levenshtein distance, in three flavors. *Merriam Park Software: http://www. merriampark. com/ld.htm*, 2009.
17. P. D. Gluckman and M. A. Hanson. Evolution, development and timing of puberty. *TRENDS in Endocrinology and Metabolism*, 17(1):7–12, 2006.

18. T. H. Gollan, R. I. Montoya, and M. P. Bonanni. Proper names get stuck on bilingual and monolingual speakers' tip of the tongue equally often. *Neuropsychology*, 19(3):278, 2005.

19. M. Harbach, S. Fahl, M. Rieger, and M. Smith. On the acceptance of privacy-preserving authentication technology: The curious case of national identity cards. In E. De Cristofaro and M. Wright, editors, *Privacy Enhancing Technologies*, pages 245–264. Springer, 2013.

20. D. F. Jacobs. Juvenile Gambling in North America: An Analysis of Long Term Trends and Future Prospects. *Journal of Gambling Studies*, 16(2-3):119–152, 2000.

21. H. Kanda, Y. Osaki, T. Ohida, Y. Kaneita, and T. Munezawa. Age verification cards fail to fully prevent minors from accessing tobacco products. *Tobacco control*, 20(2):163–165, 2011.

22. D. Kirby. Sex and HIV/AIDS education in schools. *BMJ: British Medical Journal*, 311(7002):403, 1995.

23. R. Larson and M. H. Richards. Daily companionship in late childhood and early adolescence: Changing developmental contexts. *Child Development*, 62(2):284–300, 1991.

24. P. W. Linville. The complexity–extremity effect and age-based stereotyping. *Journal of personality and social psychology*, 42(2):193, 1982.

25. S. Livingstone, M. Bober, and E. Helsper. Internet literacy among children and young people: findings from the UK children, 2005. Go Online project `http://eprints.lse.ac.uk/archive/00000297(Accessed04/06/2010)`.

26. C. M. MacLeod. Forgotten but not gone: Savings for pictures and words in long-term memory. *Journal of Experimental Psychology*, 14(2):195–212, 1988.

27. S. Madigan. Picture memory. In J. Yuille, editor, *Imagery, memory, and cognition: essays in honor of Allan Paivio*, pages 65–89. Lawrence Erlbaum Associates, Hillsdale, NJ, 1983.

28. G. Mascheroni. Parenting the mobile internet in italian households: Parents' and children's discourses. *Journal of Children and Media*, (Published online: 02 Sep 2013):1–17, 2013.

29. L. A. McFarlin, K. J. Buffardi, and R. M. Schumacher. Usability impact on effectiveness of parental controls. In *Proceedings of the Human Factors and Ergonomics Society Annual Meeting*, volume 51, pages 1039–1043. Sage Publications, 2007.

30. F. Mishna, C. Cook, M. Saini, M.-J. Wu, and R. MacFadden. Interventions for children, youth, and parents to prevent and reduce cyber. *Campbell Systematic Reviews*, 2, 2009.

31. K. J. Mitchell, D. Finkelhor, and J. Wolak. Protecting youth online: Family use of filtering and blocking software. *Child abuse & neglect*, 29(7):753–765, 2005.

32. H. F. Odabaşi. Parents views on internet use. *Turkish Online Journal of Educational Technology*, 4(1), 2005.

33. Ofcom. Ofcom report on internet safety measures. strategies of parental protection for children online, 15 January 2014. `http://stakeholders.ofcom.org.uk/binaries/internet/internet-safety-measures.pdf`.

34. A. Paivio. *Imagery and verbal processes.* Holt, Rinheart & Winston, New York, 1971.

35. A. Paivio, T. Rogers, and P. Smythe. Why are pictures easier to recall than words? *Psychonomic Science*, 11(4):137–138, 1968.

36. J. Peter and P. M. Valkenburg. Adolescents' exposure to sexually explicit Internet material and sexual satisfaction: A longitudinal study. *Human Communication Research*, 35(2):171–194, 2009.

37. M. I. Posner, M. J. Nissen, and R. M. Klein. Visual dominance: an information-processing account of its origins and significance. *Psychological review*, 83(2):157, 1976.

38. C. J. Rathbone, C. J. Moulin, and M. A. Conway. Self-centered memories: The reminiscence bump and the self. *Memory & Cognition*, 36(8):1403–1414, 2008.

39. B. Reznikov. "Can I See Some ID?" Age Verification Requirements for the Online Liquor Store. *Shidler Journal of Law, Commerce & Technology.*, 4:5–13, 2007.

40. C. Roberts. Biometric attack vectors and defences. *Computers & Security*, 26(1):14–25, 2007.

41. R. W. Roeser, C. Midgley, and R. C. Urdan. Perceptions of the school psychological environment and early adolescents' psychological and behavioral functioning in school: The mediating role of goals and belonging. *Journal of Educational Pscychology*, 88(3):408–422, 1996.

42. D. C. Rubin. *Autobiographical memory across the lifespan.* MIT Press Cambridge, MA, 2002.

43. K. G. Schneider. *A practical guide to Internet filters.* Neal-Schuman Publishers, Inc., 1997.

44. R. G. Simmons and D. A. Blyth. *Moving into Adolescence: The Impact of Pubertal Change and School Context.* AldineTransaction, 2009.

45. R. G. Simmons, R. Burgeson, S. Carlton-Ford, and D. A. Blyth. The impact of cumulative change in early adolescence. *Child Development*, 58(5):1220–1234, 1987.

46. S. N. Singh, M. L. Rothschild, and G. A. C. Jr. Recognition versus recall as measures of television commercial forgetting. *Journal of Marketing Research*, 25(1):72–80, 1988.

47. A. Spence. 200,000 children are watching hardcore porn, 28 March 2014. The Times. `http://www.thetimes.co.uk/tto/news/medianews/article4047202.ece`.

48. B. Szoka. COPPA 2.0: The New Battle over Privacy, Age Verification, Online Safety & Free Speech, 24 May 2009. http://techliberation.com/2009/05/24/coppa-20-the-new-battle-over-privacy-age-verification-online-safety-free-speech/.

49. A. Thierer. Social networking and age verification: Many hard questions; no easy solutions. *Progress on point*, 14:1–33, 2007.

50. U.S. National Archives and Records Administration. Richard Nixon. `http://upload.wikimedia.org/wikipedia/commons/3/39/Richard_M._Nixon,_ca._1935_-_1982_-_NARA_-_530679.jpg`.

51. L. Wade. Facing the threat: Invading the body for national security. *Knowledge, Technology & Policy*, 17(1):74–80, 2004.

52. L. G. Walters. Method of age verification for electronic media. US Patent 6959861, 2003.

53. A. Wigfield, J. S. Eccles, D. MacIver, D. A. Reuman, and C. M. Midgley. Transitions during early adolescence: Changes in children's domain specific self-perceptions and general self-esteem across the transition to junior high school. *Developmental Pscyhology*, 27(4):552–565, 1991.

54. J. D. Woodward, N. M. Orlans, and P. T. Higgins. *Biometrics:identity assurance in the information age.* McGraw-Hill/Osborne New York, 2003.

55. World Economic Forum. Tony Blair. `https://www.flickr.com/photos/worldeconomicforum/3488873590/in/photostream/`.

Resilience Mitigates the Negative Effects of Adolescent Internet Addiction and Online Risk Exposure

Pamela Wisniewski, Haiyan Jia, Na Wang, Saijing Zheng, Heng Xu, Mary Beth Rosson, and John M. Carroll
College of Information Sciences and Technology, Pennsylvania State University
University Park, PA 16802, USA
{pamwis, hjia, nzw109, suz128, hxu, mrosson, jcarroll}@psu.edu

ABSTRACT
We cannot fully protect adolescents from experiencing online risks; however, we can aim to better understand how online risk experiences impact teens, factors that contribute to or prevent teens from exposure to risk, as well as factors that can protect teens from psychological harm *in spite* of online risk exposure. Through a web-based survey study of 75 adolescents in the US, we develop and empirically validate a theoretical model of adolescent resilience in the presence of online risks. We show evidence that resilience is a key factor in protecting teens from experiencing online risks, even when teens exhibit high levels of Internet addiction. Resilience also neutralizes the negative psychological effects associated with Internet addiction and online risk exposure. Therefore, we emphasize the importance of design solutions that foster teen resilience and strength building, as opposed to solutions targeted toward parents that often focus on restriction and risk prevention.

Author Keywords
Adolescent Online Safety; Internet Addiction; Risk; Resilience

ACM Classification Keywords
K.4.1 [Public Policy Issues]: Ethics, Human safety, Privacy

INTRODUCTION
Understanding adolescent online behaviors and experiences is critical to teens' safety and wellbeing. In 2011, Yardi and Bruckman [40] called for studies of what teens do online and what might be done to mediate their use of technology. Three years later, there remains a paucity of research in the CHI community that has focused specifically on understanding adolescents as online users, even though teens are often early adopters and heavy users of Internet and social media technologies. It is crucial for HCI researchers to invest resources in studies that examine how teens interact within online contexts, pinpoint the key challenges associated with their online activities, identify theories that can help to address these challenges, and design solutions that support teens as well as their families and friends in optimizing the benefits while navigating the risks associated with online technology use.

To help fill in this research gap, we conducted a web-based survey study of 75 US adolescents (13 to 17-years-old). Our intent was to study the negative effects (i.e. psychological and affective responses) that Internet Addiction and Online Risk Exposure might have on adolescents and to examine how teens' level of Resilience might mitigate the possible negative effects associated with these risks. ***Resilience*** is the ability to overcome negative effects associated with risk exposure, helping an individual cope with traumatic experiences [34]. It is an intrinsic capability but also a competence that can be acquired and developed [1]. Therefore, if resilience can reduce the negative effects associated with Internet Addiction and Online Risk Exposure, our research will provide researchers, educators, designers, and parents with new insights on how to help protect teens online. Further, we will gain a better understanding of how teens can protect themselves against online risk exposure.

In this paper, we first draw from past research on adolescent online safety to develop a theoretical framework of adolescent resilience in the presence of online risks. We then empirically validate the resulting framework through a quantitative survey study. Using path and mediation analyses [23], we confirmed the negative impact of Internet Addiction on Negative Affect. We also observed that Risk Exposure partially mediates the relationship between Internet Addiction and Negative Affect. Most importantly, we found that Resilience plays a key role in protecting teens, either neutralizing or reducing the negative effects of Internet Addiction and Online Risk Exposure. We discuss the key implications of our findings.

BACKGROUND
Many researchers interested in online safety for adolescents have investigated factors that influence teens' exposure to

CHI 2015, April 18 - 23 2015, Seoul, Republic of Korea
Copyright 2015 ACM 978-1-4503-3145-6/15/04...$15.00
http://dx.doi.org/10.1145/2702123.2702240

various online risks. A common perspective in these studies is what might be termed a "risk-adverse" view of adolescent online safety, where risk exposure is framed as the dependent variable of interest, with the presumption that minimizing exposure to such risks is the desirable outcome [38]. Few studies move beyond examining the factors that affect adolescent online risk exposure, for example to seeking to understand the negative effects that such exposure might have on teens or how one might mitigate the negative effects once risk exposure occurs [38].

To illustrate why a deeper analysis is needed, consider this contrast: Two teens view the same unwanted pornographic online content; one teen ignores the explicit sexual imagery while the other is traumatized. In both cases, it is unrealistic to believe that we (as parents, designers, researchers, and adults) could have prevented either teen from viewing such undesired content – that is, eliminating exposure to the risk. Thus, it becomes increasingly important to understand how and why such exposure negatively impacts some teens (and not others), as well as to explore protective measures for keeping teens safe online *in spite* of online risk experiences.

Researchers from EU Kids Online were among the first to explain that adolescent exposure to online risks does not necessarily equate to harm [9, 29]. They found that youth who reported having more psychological problems and/or lower self-efficacy tended to become more bothered when experiencing these online risks while other teens remained unbothered [9]. Yet, the authors admit that a key limitation of their study was their simplified, dichotomous treatment of resilience as being "not bothered" [9]. Our research draws from and builds on this prior literature, offering a more detailed examination of adolescent resilience in the presence of online risks. Our research therefore makes the following key contributions:

- Draws from developmental psychology to build a theoretical framework of adolescent resilience in the presence of online risk exposure;
- Operationalizes theoretical constructs with pre-validated psychological instruments for measuring Resilience and Negative Affect; and
- Empirically validates the resulting theoretical model to demonstrate relationships among Internet Addiction, Online Risk Exposure, Resilience, and Negative Affect for adolescents.

THEORETICAL FRAMEWORK

Adolescent Resilience Framework

We designed our study around a theoretical framework of ***adolescent resilience*** that was derived and validated by researchers in developmental psychology [34]. The framework has been useful in explaining outcomes related to a number of risky teen behaviors, including substance abuse, violent behavior, and sexual promiscuity. We are one of the first to apply the adolescent resilience framework to risky behaviors that are linked to Internet use. Research grounded on theories of adolescent resilience differs from the "risk-adverse" approach often taken in adolescent online safety research by "focusing on the assets and resources that enable adolescents to overcome the negative effects of risk exposure (p. 399)" [34], rather than trying to limit exposure to risk. Another way of understanding the contrast is that the resilience perspective leads to a focus on teen strengths rather than their deficits. A key point in this theoretical view is that both ***risk*** (negative influencing) and ***promotive*** (positive influencing) factors are seen as contributors to risk exposure and outcomes. Additionally, the outcomes associated with resilience theory are not simply whether or not teens are exposed to risk, but instead whether or not they are able to thrive *in spite* of it [34].

We are particularly interested in the ***protective model*** [34] of resilience in which promotive factors mitigate the effects of risk exposure on negative outcomes in two ways: First, a promotive factor can have a *protective-stabilizing effect* such that the presence of the factor neutralizes the effect of risk exposure on the negative outcome (i.e. moderating the relationship between risk exposure and a negative outcome so that it is no longer operative). Alternatively, it can have a *protective-reactive effect* where it diminishes the effect of risk exposure on a negative outcome but does not remove it. **Figure 1** illustrates the generalized theory summarizing the protective model of adolescent resilience [34]. In the following sections, we introduce the salient constructs of our theoretical model for online risk exposure as they map to the adolescent resilience framework [34].

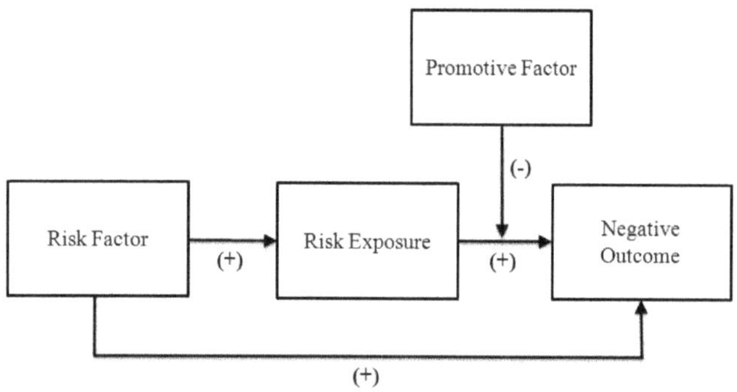

Figure 1: Protective Model of Adolescent Resilience

Online Risk Exposure

Adolescents encounter a number of different types of risks when they engage with others online. Online risks examined in past research studying adolescent online safety include teens becoming the victims of information breaches [27-28]; online harassment or cyberbullying [25, 30]; sexual solicitations [25, 32]; and exposure to pornography, violence, or other explicit content [25, 28-29]. Therefore, we define ***Online Risk Exposure*** as a culmination of these various negative online risk experiences. Online Risk Exposure as a construct is central to our research: We seek to understand the negative effects associated with Risk Exposure, factors that contribute to or limit Risk Exposure;

and especially factors that may protect teens from online risks once they have been exposed.

Negative Outcome: Negative Affect

The EU Kids Online studies [9, 29] conceptualized the negative outcome associated with a range of online risk exposures as whether or not youth were "bothered" by the experience; that is, the study operationalized Resilience as a dichotomous outcome variable [9]. We extend that earlier research by reframing resilience using the adolescent resilience framework [34] derived from developmental psychology; we also integrate the theoretically sound and clinically proven construct of Negative Affect to capture negative outcomes associated with Online Risk Exposure. ***Negative Affect*** is a psychological, self-reported measure of "distress and unpleasurable engagement that subsumes a variety of aversive mood states, including anger, contempt, disgust, guilt, fear, and nervousness (p. 1063)" [36]. The construct has been validated and widely used in social and behavioral psychology research [13, 36]. It is associated with anxiety, stress, poor coping, and health complaints [36], and has been deemed "clinically useful for identifying youth with anxiety and mood problems (p. 191)" [13]. Given the relevance of Negative Affect as a potential negative outcome of Online Risk Exposure, we adopt it as our dependent variable.

Risk Factor: Internet Addiction

We defined ***Internet Addiction*** as the problematic [26] or excessive use of the Internet to the point where it becomes a psychological dependence [5] that "displaces [teen's] social or personal needs in a way that they cannot control (p. 30) " [27]. Internet Addiction has been studied as a risk factor that contributes to negative, emotional and psychological responses, such as depression, loneliness and hostility in adolescents' online communication [35]. Studies have directly linked adolescent Internet users' compulsive or excessive use of the Internet to Negative Affect [5, 41]. However, even though Internet Addiction is seen as a pathologically problematic behavior [5, 41], it is not clear how addictive Internet use leads to these undesirable outcomes. We argue that teens' exposure to negative, Online Risk experiences may help to explain why excessive and problematic use of the Internet correlates with these negative psychological outcomes. Some studies have shown that compulsive Internet use influences the frequency with which adolescents are exposed to online risks [12, 26]; others indicate that experiencing online risks such as peer aggression and unwanted sexual material upset teen users and sometimes result in more severe, public health problems [10, 31]. Nonetheless, there is little evidence that relates Online Risk Exposure to the psychological well-being of teens; in particular there has been no empirical test of the potential mediation effect of Online Risk Exposure on the relationship between Internet Addiction and Negative Affect. Therefore, we propose that:

H1: *Online Risk Exposure mediates the relationship between Internet Addiction and Negative Affect.*

Promotive Factor: Resilience

Reducing the Negative Effects of Online Risk Exposure

Resilience "embodies the personal qualities that enable one to thrive in the face of adversity (p.76)" [8], and can be viewed as a measure of one's stress coping ability for reducing negative psychological outcomes, such as anxiety, depression, and other stress-related outcomes associated with negative experiences. Based on the protective model of resilience, a promotive factor can moderate the relationship between risk exposure and a negative outcome by either neutralizing the relationship between the two or weakening it [34]. For example, Héber et al. [20] found that Resilience played a protective role against post traumatic stress in the context of adolescent sexual abuse. Fincham et al. [16] similarly identified Resilience as a moderating factor which significantly reduced the effects of child abuse and neglect on symptoms of post traumatic stress.

Past research has confirmed a strong, negative correlation between Resilience and Negative Affect [2]. Yet, to date, we could not find any study that specifically used resilience theory to investigate a protective role for Resilience as a moderator in the relationship between Online Risk Exposure and Negative Affect. One study by D'Haenens et al. [9] found that adolescents who took more proactive approaches to coping with online risk experiences felt more empowered and less bothered by negative online experiences. Thus, applying resilience theory and the results of this related empirical study as our justification, we propose that:

H2: *Resilience moderates the relationship between Online Risk Exposure and Negative Affect by reducing the effect of Online Risk Exposure on Negative Affect.*

Reducing Risk Exposure for the Internet Addicted

Because resilience implies the presence of risk [6], researchers tend to consider resilience as consequential to risk and discuss the effect of resilience in terms of reducing negative outcomes after risk exposure (as we do in H2). However, this approach may oversimplify the role of resilience and overlook the interplay of risk and resilience over time. More recently, researchers have pointed out the need for examining risk and resilience at multiple stages, emphasizing their dynamic relationship through adolescents' development [7]. Resilience may have an "inoculation effect," where past negative experiences may help build resilience to experiencing future risks [34]. Previous, negative online experiences may facilitate the development of coping strategies, which can directly influence adolescents' future online activities and behaviors, including avoidance of or protection against online risk [24]. From a developmental point of view – considering risk exposure as part of a learning process –

resilience that develops through previous risk encounters may either reduce the possibility of exposure to risk in the future or reduce the negative impact felt in the present [24].

Research that has used Social Cognitive Theory and Protection Motivation Theory to study adolescent online behaviors provides theoretical support for the effects of resilience on risk protection. Scholars [18] have suggested that the self-perception of being able to anticipate, control, avoid, or cope with the potential risks can positively influence individuals' reaction to potential online risks. Such resilience can determine adolescents' decision as to whether or not they would be engaged with risky online activities [33]. Studies of online risk intervention [4] have shown that positive coping appraisals and previous safe behaviors can reduce online risk to which frequent teenaged Internet users are susceptible. Yet, empirical evidence is still needed to see if Resilience may effectively limit Online Risk Exposure of adolescents, especially in cases of Addictive Internet Use. Therefore, we also propose a moderation effect of Resilience as a *first-stage* moderator between Internet Addiction and Online Risk Exposure:

H3: *Resilience moderates the relationship between Internet Addiction and Online Risk Exposure by reducing the effect of Internet Addiction on Online Risk Exposure*

In summary, we propose to examine the mediating effects of Online Risk Exposure (H1) as well as the possible moderating effects of Resilience, both with respect to reducing Negative Affect in the presence of Online Risk Exposure (H2), and limiting Online Risk Exposure as a result of Addictive Internet Use (H3). **Figure 2** illustrates the corresponding two-stage (pre- and post-risk exposure) theoretical framework of adolescent resilience in online contexts. In our Methodology section, we will explain how we empirically validate this theoretical framework.

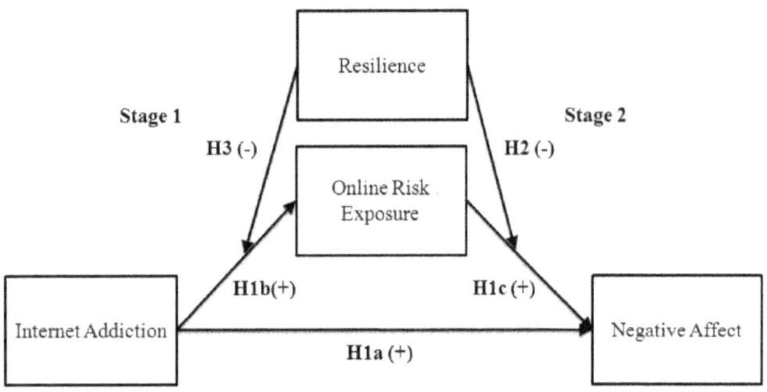

Figure 2: Theoretical Model of Adolescent Online Resilience

METHODOLOGY

Operationalizing Constructs

We used pre-validated measures to operationalize the majority of our constructs. All measures were based on 5-point Likert scales and indices were created based on standardized, average scores across all items. ***Negative Affect*** was measured by asking teen participants to indicate their degree of negative feelings and emotions based on 15 adjectives such as "sad," "frightened," and "ashamed" from Watson's Positive and Negative Affect Scales (PANAS) [36]. ***Internet Addiction*** was measured using six items from previous research [27]; for example, how often teens "felt bothered when [they could not] be on the Internet." ***Resilience*** was measured using the proprietary Connor-Davidson Resilience Scale (CD-RISC 10) [3], which we licensed from the authors [8]. It was comprised of ten items, for example, asking teens if they handled "painful feelings" effectively [3]. We created our own scale for adolescent ***Online Risk Exposure,*** working from a meta-review of the adolescent online safety literature to compile 16 items that probed unique yet common online risk experiences across four risk types (information breaches, online harassment, sexual solicitations, and exposure to explicit content; see **Appendix A, Table 2**). To encourage teen reporting, we minimized the implied severity of the risk categories by relabeling them in the survey to "information sharing," "online interactions," "online flirtations," and "online content," respectively. The four risk types were collapsed to create an overall measure of Online Risk Exposure because we found them to be highly intertwined, both conceptually and empirically.

Data Collection and Recruitment

We designed a web-based survey study using the Qualtrics survey platform. Because our target population consisted of minors (US-based adolescents between the ages of 13 and 17-years old), we obtained informed consent from both teens and a parent or legal guardian. Participation was incentivized with a $25 Amazon.com or Walmart gift card mailed to participants at their home address after survey responses were verified. We began recruitment during January 2014 and completed data collection May 2014. We first attempted to recruit teens through public high schools across the US but encountered too many barriers to entry. Therefore, we reached out via phone calls and emails to public libraries, YMCA's, non-profit organizations, government-funded children and youth service organizations, family-based community centers, churches, and after-school programs across the US. We also sent recruitment mailings though a contact database of parents based on birth announcements from the local vicinity, which is maintained by our university's psychology department. The majority of our participants were recruited from the state of Pennsylvania (74%); however, we had representation within 12 other states, including New York (8%), South Dakota (3%), Florida (3%), and others (12%).

Data Analysis Approach

To test our theoretical model, we leveraged path analysis techniques using IBM SPSS AMOS 22 [23]. Mediation effects and moderated mediation effects were analyzed using PROCESS, an SPSS macro for observed variable mediation, moderation, and conditional process modeling [19]. When examining the moderating role of Resilience, three path models and three moderated mediation models were examined, framing Resilience as: 1) a *second-stage* moderator (H2: Online Risk Exposure X Resilience → Negative Affect), 2) a *first-stage* moderator (H3: Internet Addiction X Resilience → Online Risk Exposure), and 3) as both a *first-stage* and *second-stage* moderator (**Figure 2**), respectively. In the Results section, descriptive statistics, path model, and mediation results will be reported.

RESULTS

Participant Profiles

Ninety-five teens originally registered to participate in our online survey study and completed the process of informed consent. However, we had a total of 75 complete survey responses from our participants, including 46 girls and 29 boys between the ages of 13 and 17-years old. The age distribution of teens was as follows: 13-years old (17%), 14 (31%), 15 (21%), 16 (17%), and 17 (13%). The majority of our participants were Caucasian (73%), 13% African-American, 5% Hispanic, 3% Asian, and 5% of reported being of "other" descent. Most of the teens lived in two parent homes with their mother and father (60%), while 17% reported living with their mother only, 18% reported living with one biological parent and one step-parent, and 5% reported having other living arrangements. We asked teens how frequently they used the Internet; 33% of teens reported being online several times an hour, 41% went online several times a day, 24% reported going online every day or almost every day, and 1% of teens reported going on the Internet once or twice a week. **Table 1** summarizes the scale reliabilities and descriptive statistics for all of the main constructs in our model.

Table 1: Scale Reliabilities and Descriptive Statistics

Construct	Cronbach's α	Mean	SD
Negative Affect	0.95	1.85	0.77
Online Risk Exposure	0.85	1.51	0.42
Resilience	0.91	3.56	0.76
Internet Addiction	0.78	2.46	0.80

Path Model Results

Mediation Model of Risk Exposure

First, the proposed mediating model (H1) of Online Risk Exposure between Internet Addiction and Negative Affect was tested. **Figure 3** shows the path model, indicating positive significant paths between Internet Addiction and Negative Affect (H1a); Internet Addiction and Online Risk Exposure (H1b), as well as Risk Exposure and Negative Affect (H1c). The indirect effect of Addiction on Negative Affect was also statistically significant at the $p = 0.05$ level. These combined findings confirm a significant, yet partial, mediation effect of Online Risk Exposure, providing support for our first hypothesis. Overall, this mediation model had fairly high explanatory power, explaining 28% of the variance in Online Risk Exposure and 28% of the variance in Negative Affect.

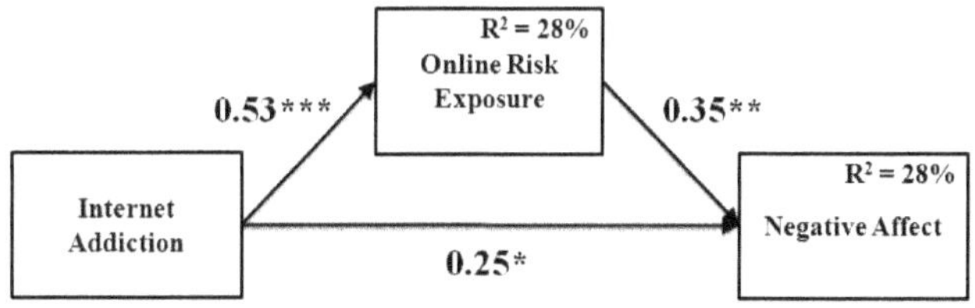

* *p-value < 0.05, ** < 0.01, *** < 0.001*

Figure 3: Effects of Internet Addiction and Risk Exposure

Moderated-Mediation Models of Resilience

Next, we iteratively tested the competing theoretical models of Resilience. We first tested Resilience as only a second-stage moderator between Online Risk Exposure and Negative Affect (H2), as this model is most consistent with resilience theory [34]. Second, we tested Resilience as only a first-stage moderator between Internet Addiction and Online Risk Exposure (H3). Third, we tested our proposed model of Resilience that includes the construct as both a first and second (two-stage) moderator (**Figure 2**). Fit statistics of all three models are included in **Appendix A, Table 3**. Only our proposed model of Resilience as both a first and second stage moderator indicated a good fit with the data; therefore, we present the results of our proposed model below.

As shown in **Figure 4**, our proposed model indicated a significant interaction between Internet Addiction and Resilience (H3; $p < 0.05$), which predicted Risk Exposure and a marginally significant interaction between Risk Exposure and Resilience (H2; $p = 0.07$), which predicted Negative Affect. The direct effect of Online Risk Exposure on Negative Affect became non-significant; the direct and indirect effects of Addiction also became statistically insignificant. This model yielded a good fit to the data (**Appendix A, Table 3**) and indicated high explanatory power, explaining 41% of the variance in Online Risk Exposure and 40% of the variance in Negative Affect.

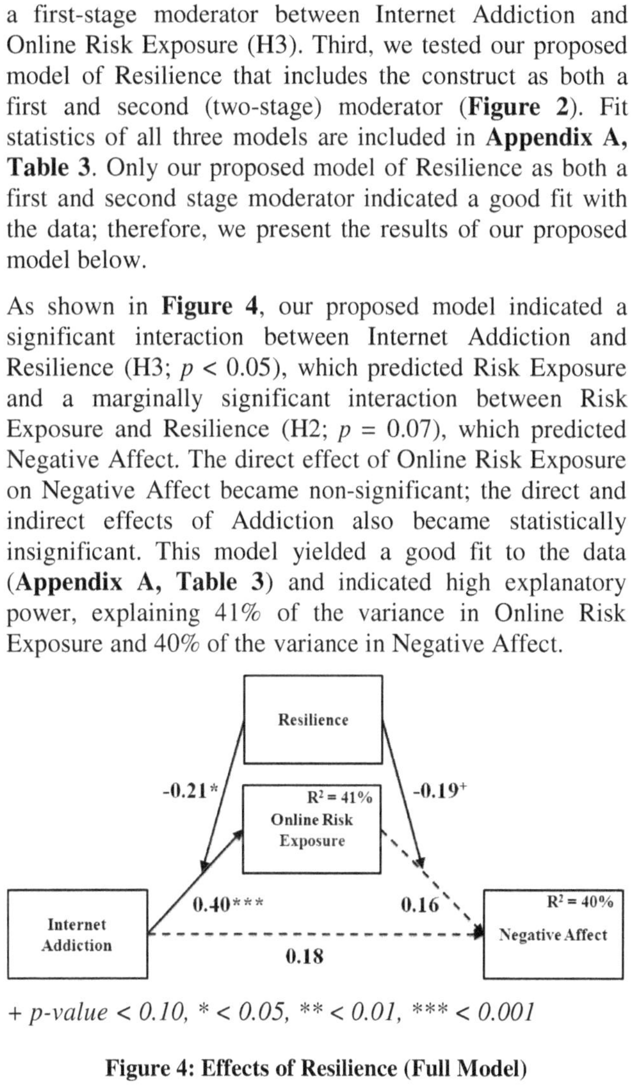

*+ p-value < 0.10, * < 0.05, ** < 0.01, *** < 0.001*

Figure 4: Effects of Resilience (Full Model)

In order to illustrate how Resilience moderated Online Risk Exposure (H2) and Internet Addiction (H3), we dichotomized (High/Low) each variable based on one +/- standard deviation from the mean and graphed the interaction effects [11]. **Figure 6** shows the marginally significant interaction between Online Risk Exposure and Resilience on Negative Affect. This pattern is consistent with adolescent resilience theory's ***protective-stabilizing model*** of a promotive factor on negative outcomes [34]. In the presence of frequent Risk Exposure, Resilience essentially neutralizes the negative effects of Online Risk Exposure on Negative Affect. However, we also see a strong main effect of Resilience, where teens who are more resilient tend to have lower levels of Negative Affect.

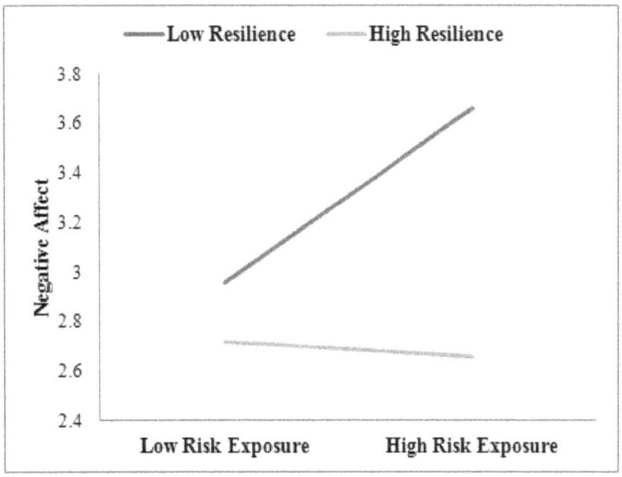

Figure 5: Protective-Stabilizing Effect of Resilience

Figure 7 shows the significant interaction effect between Internet Addiction and Resilience. The graph indicates that, as the level of Internet Addiction increases, a higher level of Resilience is likely to reduce, but not neutralize, the amount of Risk Exposure teens experience online.

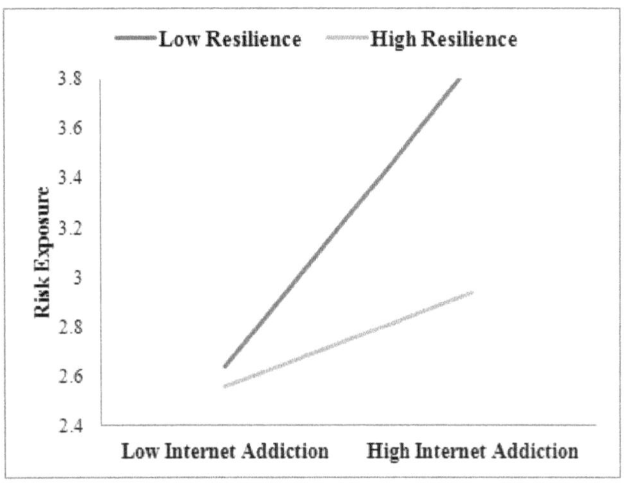

Figure 6: Protective-Reactive Effect of Resilience

This pattern is consistent with Resilience theory's ***protective-reactive model*** [34], where a negative outcome associated with risk is effectively reduced by the presence of a third factor. However, we observed this Resilience effect as a *first-stage* moderator (pre-risk exposure), instead of after risk occurs. This somewhat differs from resilience theory, and we will further consider the implications of this effect in our Discussion.

DISCUSSION

Overall, we found support for our main hypotheses. When Resilience was not in the model (**Figure 4**), Online Risk Exposure partially mediated the relationship between Internet Addiction and Negative Affect (H1): While Internet Addiction shows a significant direct effect on Negative Affect, Online Risk Exposure appears to be a key factor that helps explain the effect of Internet Addiction on Negative Affect. After testing three alternative theoretical models, we found that Resilience acts as a two-stage moderator (**Figure 5**) between Online Risk Exposure and Negative Affect (H2; marginal significance) and between Internet Addiction and Online Risk Exposure (H3). It reduces the effects of Internet Addiction on Online Risk Exposure (**Figure 7**) and neutralizes the direct effects of Internet Addiction and Online Risk Exposure on Negative Affect (**Figures 5 & 6**). Next, we will discuss the theoretical and practical implications of our findings.

Key Implications

Mediating Effects of Online Risk Exposure

While past studies often assume that adolescent online risk exposure leads to psychological problems [38], we provided empirical confirmation of a relationship between Online Risk Exposure and Negative Affect (H1c). However, we also found evidence suggesting that exposure to online risks helps explain why Internet Addiction can cause psychological problems for teens (H1). Practical implications of this finding include the importance of 1) identifying teens who suffer from severe Internet addiction; 2) being vigilant in interventions of Internet addiction that can limit risk exposure experienced by these higher-risk teens; and 3) treating psychological symptoms that arise due to addictive behaviors or negative online experiences. A key point to note is that overly restrictive parental rules for limiting teen Internet use do not address the underlying psychological dependence teens may have on the Internet. Therefore, limiting Internet use without otherwise helping teens meet their psychological needs for social interaction, acceptance, support, etc. may trigger deeper psychological issues.

Resilience in the Presence of Risk Exposure

Our findings include empirical evidence that adolescent resilience theory [34] can be applied to risks that teens experience online, not just to offline risks such as substance abuse, violent behavior, and sexual promiscuity. We found that resilient teens seem able to experience higher levels of online risk without incurring serious, psychological harm (H2). A key implication of this finding is a shift in research focus from an "abstinence-only," risk-adverse approach to adolescent online safety, to one that focuses on ways to help teens effectively cope when they do encounter online risks [24]. Especially in high-risk situations, resilience theory [34] and thus clinical interventions that build teen resilience [1], provide potential solutions for educating teens about Internet safety literacy and suggesting positive resources, such as proactive parenting strategies, community support, and evidence-based group interventions, to help protect high-risk teens from serious online risks.

Resilience as Risk Prevention

In addition to the widely established effect of resilience as a coping mechanism once risks occur (*second-stage*), our results show that resilience can also affect outcomes both pre- *and* post-risk exposure. Our findings confirmed that Resilience served to mitigate Online Risk Exposure as the negative effect of Addictive Internet Use (H3). In particular, the role of Resilience as a first-stage moderator in the two-stage moderated mediation model (**Figure 5**) suggests a new conceptualization of resilience as a form of *risk prevention*. This new view yields important theoretical and practical implications. First, it offers a more proactive way of reducing the negative outcomes of online risk (e.g., Negative Affect). Instead of relying on resilient coping to lessen the post-risk exposure harm or trauma, it suggests that resilience may also reduce the effects of Internet addiction on adolescents' psychology and emotions, perhaps by directly reducing their exposure to online risks. In other words, by cultivating the abilities to adapt to stress and adversity through minimal-risk experiences or practices of online safety behaviors, adolescents are likely to avoid risk events or become victimized when facing such harms and threats. Second, the new view suggests an alternative to the "over-protective, risk averse (p. 364)" approach that restricts online exploration entirely [33]. It highlights the benefits of allowing adolescents more freedom of exploration in their online communication, which will equip them with sufficient skills as well as resilience for navigating challenging situations in the future.

Practical Implications

Online systems should attempt to protect adolescents from excessive harm while still allowing them to engage online with others. Unfortunately, the current design solutions and strategies for promoting adolescent online safety often tend to focus on risk prevention, for instance by limiting Internet use and attempting to eliminate teens' exposure to online risks. This is contrary to research that suggests that teens make better online decisions when they have parents who are actively engaged in what they do online but yet allow them to engage online and learn from their online experiences [24, 37, 39]. For instance, direct intervention by parents through the use of parental monitoring software has been associated with fewer basic disclosures made by teens through social media; however, teens who experience high levels of direct intervention from their parents also tend to use SNSs less frequently and take fewer protective measures to ensure their online privacy [37]. Many parental monitoring packages often implement parental controls that limit when a teen can go online, block unwanted content, and otherwise prevent teens' from having negative online experiences. This preventative approach does little to help teens build resilience to the online risks that they will eventually encounter.

Thus, in addition to designing systems that support parental mediation of teens' online behaviors, we should also focus on design solutions that promote teen resilience so that teens can effectively and wisely protect themselves from online risks. Resilience can be promoted indirectly by supporting other factors that are known to contribute to teen resilience, such as heightened self-awareness [17, 21]. Thus, we support Yardi and Bruckman's [40] earlier proposal to use social translucence theory for implementing a semi-transparent "digital window" that facilitates visibility, awareness, and accountability between parents and teens. Yet, we extend this idea by encouraging designers to also give teens access to view their own digital footprints in order to form self-awareness of their potentially risky online behaviors and patterns. Providing teens a more transparent view of what strangers or friends of friends are able to see about them via social media, for example, may promote self-awareness that translates into resilient behaviors when online interactions escalate into risky situations.

Additionally, we can promote teen resilience directly through web-based educational or counseling programs that help build resilience [1] or through interface designs that empower teens to take protective measures upon encountering online risks. For example, Facebook provides a "Family Safety Center" that offers tips for teens to develop better online safety practices [14]. If popular social media platforms simultaneously offered highly visible yet simple safety features, such as the anonymous reporting of cyberbullying, sexual solicitations or sharing of inappropriate content, teens would be able to leverage these mechanisms to protect themselves online without requiring the intervention of their parents. Providing protective mechanism within interactive systems would allow teens to engage with others online and encourage them to effectively work through lower risk situations to build resilience for handling more severe online risks they may encounter in the future.

Limitations and Future Research

Before we conclude, we would like to discuss some of the limitations of our current study that can be used to inform the design of future research. First, the implied causal paths in our theoretical and empirical models are based on theory and validated through iterative model testing, which exhibits support for our hypotheses, good fit statistics, and high explanatory power. However, survey studies like this may not be the most ideal methodological approach to fully capture the causal effects and the interplay of the various factors. Future studies should investigate these underlying mechanisms through longitudinal studies or controlled experiments to confirm causality and long-term effects.

Second, our findings may be limited by our modest sample size (N = 75). We calculated the statistical power [15] associated with our model to assess the likelihood that we made any Type II errors (i.e. accepting the null hypothesis that no significant relationship existed between two variables when, in fact, it does). The current sample size is capable of detecting effect sizes greater than 0.18, and only one of our path coefficients fell slightly below this value (See **Figure 5**. H1; $\beta = 0.16$). This does not negate any of the statistically significant relationships in our model, but follow-up studies with a larger sample size would help confirm our findings. Thus, we plan to launch a national survey in order to further investigate the resilience effect in teens' online experiences.

Finally, in our future studies, we plan to explore the role of other protective factors beyond resilience that might also inoculate teens from the negative impact of online risk exposure. These factors include potential promotive assets possessed by teens [34] (e.g. social self-efficacy, coping skills, etc.) and external resources provided to teens [34] (e.g. parental mediation, family communication, etc.).

CONCLUSION

Instead of focusing on ways to limit adolescents' exposure to online risks, our study shows how teen resilience can act as a protective mechanism for reducing online risk exposure as an effect of Internet addiction and neutralizing the negative psychological effects of Internet addiction and exposure to online risks once it has already occurred. A key to adolescent online safety is to teach teens how to effectively cope with negative online experiences so that they can more readily benefit from the vast resources and beneficial social interactions the Internet can provide.

ACKNOWLEDGMENTS

First, we would like to thank Daniel F. Perkins for introducing us to the theory of resilience. Also, this research was supported by the U.S. National Science Foundation under grant CNS-1018302. Part of the work of Heng Xu was done while working at the U.S. National Science Foundation. Any opinion, findings, and conclusions or recommendations expressed in this material are those of the authors and do not necessarily reflect the views of the U.S. National Science Foundation.

REFERENCES

1. Alvord, M. K. and Grados, J. J. Enhancing Resilience in Children: A Proactive Approach. *Professional Psychology : Research and Practice*, *36*, 3 (Jun 2005 2005), 238-245.
2. Burns, R. A. and Anstey, K. J. The Connor–Davidson Resilience Scale (CD-RISC): Testing the invariance of a uni-dimensional resilience measure that is independent of positive and negative affect. *Personality and Individual Differences*, *48*, 5 (2010), 527-531.
3. Campbell-Sills L, S. M. B. Psychometric analysis and refinement of the Connor-Davidson Resilience Scale (CD-RISC): validation of a 10-item measure of resilience. *J Traumatic Stress*, *2007*, 20 (2007), 1019-1028.
4. Chai, S., Bagchi-Sen, S., Morrell, C., Rao, H. R., & Upadhyaya, S. J. Internet and online information privacy: An exploratory study of preteens and early teens. *IEEE Transactions*, *52*, 2 (2009), 167-182.
5. Chou, C., Condron, L. and Belland, J. C. A Review of the Research on Internet Addiction. *Educational Psychology Review*, *17*, 4 (Dec 2005 2005), 363-388.
6. Coleman, J. and Hagell, A. *Adolescence, Risk and Resilience: Against the Odds*. John Wiley & Sons, 2007.
7. Compas, B. E. and Reeslund, K. L. Processes of Risk and Resilience During Adolescence. In *Handbook of Adolescent Psychology*, (2009).
8. Connor, K. M. and Davidson, J. R. T. Development of a new resilience scale: the Connor-Davidson Resilience Scale (CD-RISC). *Depression and Anxiety*, *18* (2003), 71-82.
9. D'Haenens, L., Vandonink, S. and Donoso, V. *How to cope and build resilience*. EU Kids Online, 2013, http://eprints.lse.ac.uk/48115/1/How%20to%20cope%20and%20build%20online%20resilience%20%28lsero%29.pdf.
10. David-Ferdon, C. and Hertz, M. F. Electronic Media, Violence, and Adolescents: An Emerging Public Health Problem. *Journal of Adolescent Health*, *41*, 6, Supplement (2007), S1-S5.
11. Dawson, J. Moderation in Management Research: What, Why, When, and How. *J Bus Psychol*, *29*, 1 (2014/03/01 2014), 1-19.
12. Duerager, A. and Livingstone, S. *How can parents support children's internet safety?* , 2012, http://www.lse.ac.uk/media@lse/research/EUKidsOnline/EU%20Kids%20III/Reports/ParentalMediation.pdf.
13. Ebesutani, C., Regan, J., Smith, A., Reise, S., Higa-McMillan, C. and Chorpita, B. The 10-Item Positive and Negative Affect Schedule for Children, Child and Parent Shortened Versions: Application of Item Response Theory for More Efficient Assessment. *Journal of Psychopathology and Behavioral Assessment*, *34*, 2 (2012/06/01 2012), 191-203.
14. Facebook. *Family Safety Center*. 2014, https://www.facebook.com/safety.
15. Faul, F., Erdfelder, E., Lang, A. and Buchner, A. G* Power 3: A flexible statistical power analysis program for the social, behavioral, and biomedical sciences. *Behavior Research Methods*, *39*, 2 (2007), 175-191.

16. Fincham, D. S., Altes, L. K., Stein, D. J. and Seedat, S. Posttraumatic stress disorder symptoms in adolescents: risk factors versus resilience moderation. *Comprehensive Psychiatry*, *50*, 3 (May 2009 2009), 193-199.

17. Fonagy, P., Steele, M., Steele, H., Higgitt, A. and Target, M. The Emanuel Miller Memorial Lecture 1992 The Theory and Practice of Resilience. *Journal of Child Psychology and Psychiatry*, *35*, 2 (1994), 231-257.

18. Gabriel, I. J. and Nyshadham, E. A Cognitive Map of People's Online Risk Perceptions and Attitudes: An Empirical Study. In *Proc. Hawaii International Conference on System Sciences, Proceedings of the 41st Annual* (2008), 274-274.

19. Hayes, A. F. *Introduction to mediation, moderation, and conditional process analysis: A regression-based approach.* Guilford Press, 2008.

20. Hébert, M., Lavoie, F. and Blais, M. Post Traumatic Stress Disorder/PTSD in adolescent victims of sexual abuse: resilience and social support as protection factors. *Ciência & Saúde Coletiva*, *19* (2014), 685-694.

21. Hippe, J. Self-Awareness: A Precursor to Resiliency. *Reclaiming Children and Youth 12*, 4 (2004), 240-242.

22. Hooper, D., Coughlan, J. and Mullen, M. Structural Equation Modelling: Guidelines for Determining Model Fit. *Electronic Journal of Business Research Methods*, *6*, 1 (2008), 53-60.

23. IBM. *Structural Equation Modeling with IBM SPSS Amos.* 2014, https://www.hearne.com.au/getattachment/f36d4537-6943-4ac2-9ed2-645a329c39fb/White%20Paper%20-%20Structural%20Equation%20Modeling%20with%20IBM%20SPSS%20Amos.aspx.

24. Jia, H., Wisniewski, P., Xu, H., Rosson, M. B. and Carroll, J. M. Risk-taking as a Learning Process for Shaping Teen's Online Information Privacy Behaviors. In *Proc. Computer-Supported Cooperative Work and Social Computing* (2015).

25. Jones, L. M., Mitchell, K. J. and Finkelhor, D. Trends in Youth Internet Victimization: Findings From Three Youth Internet Safety Surveys 2000–2010. *Journal of Adolescent Health*, *50*, 2 (2012), 179-186.

26. Leung, L. and Lee, P. S. N. The influences of information literacy, internet addiction and parenting styles on internet risks. *New Media & Society*, *14*, 1 (2012), 117-136.

27. Livingstone, S., Haddon, L., Görzig, A. and Ólafsson, K. *Risks and safety on the internet: The perspective of European children.* EU Kids Online, 2011, http://eprints.lse.ac.uk/33731/.

28. Livingstone, S. and Helsper, E. J. Parental Mediation of Children's Internet Use. *Journal of Broadcasting & Electronic Media*, *52*, 4 (2008), 581-599.

29. Livingstone, S., Ólafsson, K., O'Neill, B. and Donoso, V. *Towards a better internet for children: findings and recommendations from EU Kids Online to inform the CEO coalition.*, The London School of Economics and Political Science, London, UK., 2012,

30. Mesch, G. S. Parental Mediation, Online Activities, and Cyberbullying *CyberPsychology & Behavior*, *12*, 4 (2009), 387-393.

31. Mitchell, K. J., Finkelhor, D. and Wolak, J. The Exposure Of Youth To Unwanted Sexual Material On The Internet: A National Survey of Risk, Impact, and Prevention. *Youth & Society*, *34*, 3 (March 1, 2003 2003), 330-358.

32. Rosen, L. D., Cheever, N. A. and Carrier, L. M. The association of parenting style and child age with parental limit setting and adolescent MySpace behavior. *Journal of Applied Developmental Psychology*, *29*, 6 (2008), 459-471.

33. Staksrud, E. and Livingstone, S. Children and online risk: powerless victims or resourceful participants? *Information, communication and society*, *12*, 3 (2009), 364-387.

34. Stevenson, F. and Zimmerman, M. A. Adolescent Resilience: A Framework for Understanding Healthy Development in the Face of Risk. *Annual Review of Public Health*, *26* (2005), 399-419.

35. van den Eijnden, R. J., Meerkerk, G. J., Vermulst, A. A., Spijkerman, R. and Engels, R. C. Online communication, compulsive Internet use, and psychosocial well-being among adolescents: a longitudinal study. *Dev Psychol*, *44*, 3 (May 2008), 655-665.

36. Watson, D., Clark, L. A. and Tellegan, A. Development and Validation of Brief Measures of Positive and Negative Affect: The PANAS Scales. *Journal of Personality and Social Psychology*, *54*, 6 (Jun 1988 1988), 1063.

37. Wisniewski, P., Jia, H., Xu, H., Rosson, M. B. and Carroll, J. M. "Preventative" vs. "Reactive:" How Parental Mediation Influences Teens' Social Media Privacy Behaviors. In *Proc. Computer-Supported Cooperative Work and Social Computing* (2015).

38. Wisniewski, P., Xu, H., Carroll, J. M. and Rosson, M. B. Grand Challenges of Researching Adolescent Online Safety: A Family Systems Approach. In *Proc. the Nineteenth Americas Conference on Information Systems* (2013).

39. Wisniewski, P., Xu, H., Rosson, M. B. and Carroll, J. M. Adolescent Online Safety: The "Moral" of the Story. In *Proc. CSCW 2014* (2014).

40. Yardi, S. and Bruckman, A. Social and technical challenges in parenting teens' social media use. In *Proc. Proceedings of the SIGCHI Conference on Human*

Factors in Computing Systems, ACM (2011), 3237-3246.

41. Yen, J.-Y., Ko, C.-H., Yen, C.-F., Wu, H.-Y. and Yang, M.-J. The Comorbid Psychiatric Symptoms of Internet Addiction: Attention Deficit and Hyperactivity Disorder (ADHD), Depression, Social Phobia, and Hostility. *Journal of Adolescent Health*, *41*, 1 (2007), 93-98.

APPENDIX A

Table 2: Item Wording for Online Risk Exposure Measures

Below are some possible experiences that you may have had online during the past 12 months. Please select how often these types of events have occurred. If you haven't experienced a particular event, select "Not at all." (Likert Scale: 1 = "Not at all," 5 = "Almost every day")

Information Breaches/Information Sharing

- Someone else shared my personal information or a photo of me that I didn't want him/her to post.
- I shared my personal information or a photo of myself that I later regretted sharing.
- I have been the victim of what I felt was an improper invasion of privacy or misuse of my information in some other way.

Online Harassment/Social Interactions

- I was treated in a hurtful or nasty way online ("Cyberbullied").
- Someone made rude or mean comments about me or threatened me in some way online.
- Someone tried to spread a mean rumor about me online.
- There are other types of negative and unwanted interaction that hurt my feelings, and made me feel embarrassed, or unsafe.

Sexual Solicitations/ Online Flirtation

- Someone I know sent me a sexual message ("Sexting").
- Someone I know asked me to send them a sexual message, revealing, or naked photo of myself.
- A stranger asked me to meet them offline.
- There are other types of sexually suggestive interactions that made me feel even a little uncomfortable.

Exposure to Explicit Content/ Online Content

- I saw online stories, images or videos that were pornographic (naked or sexual in nature).
- I saw online stories, images or videos that contained excessive violence.
- I saw online stories, images or videos of illegal or deviant (morally questionable) behavior.
- I saw online content that promoted self-harm (such as eating disorders, cutting, suicide, etc.).
- I saw other online content that made me feel uncomfortable some way.

Table 3: Goodness of Fit Statistics for Competing Theoretical Models of Resilience

Moderated-Mediation Model	Chi-square	DF	CMIN/DF	SRMR	CFI	RMSEA
First-stage only	17.1***	2	8.55	0.1	0.84	0.32
Second-stage only	14.51***	2	7.25	0.11	0.88	0.29
First and Second-stage	**3.21**	**2**	**1.61**	**0.02**	**0.99**	**0.09**

****p*-value < 0.001. ***Note:*** A fair to good model fit is characterized by a χ^2 that is not statistically significant ($p > 0.05$); *CMIN/DF* < 2; *CFI* > 0.95; and *RMSEA* < 0.10 [22].

Generation *Like*: Comparative Characteristics in Instagram

Jin Yea Jang, Kyungsik Han, Patrick C. Shih, and Dongwon Lee
College of Information Sciences and Technology
The Pennsylvania State University
{jzj157, kuh178, patshih, dongwon}@ist.psu.edu

ABSTRACT
The emergence of social media has had a significant impact on how people communicate and socialize. Teens use social media to make and maintain social connections with friends and build their reputation. However, the way of analyzing the characteristics of teens in social media has mostly relied on ethnographic accounts or quantitative analyses with small datasets. This paper shows the possibility of detecting age information in user profiles by using a combination of textual and facial recognition methods and presents a comparative study of 27K teens and adults in Instagram. Our analysis highlights that (1) teens tend to post fewer *photos* but highly engage in adding more *tags* to their own photos and receiving more *Likes* and *comments* about their photos from others, and (2) to post more *selfies* and express themselves more than adults, showing a higher sense of self-representation. We demonstrate the application of our novel method that shows clear trends of age differences as well as substantiates previous insights in social media.

Author Keywords
Teens; age difference; social media; Instagram

INTRODUCTION
Social media allows people to access, create, and interact with a wide range of information. Although this is true for people at all ages, teens' engagement in social media is especially high. Research has been conducted to understand teens in social media mainly in two ways. First, reports of ethnographic inquiries (e.g., interviews, observations, focus groups, etc.) found that teens spend a considerable amount of time interacting and socializing in online spaces, and use social media as a main channel to share their everyday life, learn something new and useful, and establish and reinforce social empowerment [5,7]. Teens also shift to new social platforms quickly to meet their fast changing priorities, and personal and social needs [1,5]. The second method utilizes quantitative analysis of real usage data. For example, in an analysis of a total of 100 users, [11] showed that teens express themselves and share personal stories online more than senior adults (over 60). They reported that teens use diverse social media sites and maintain multiple forms of communications, because each channel affords different ways of interacting with others. [13] analyzed interactions by a total of 160 users in a public online news community and found that teens maintain more social connections than the elderly (over 65).

Although these two approaches show many perspectives on how teens use and perceive social media compared to other age groups, very few empirical studies have been conducted using large datasets. Many studies are based on relatively small sample size (e.g., 5-30 users for qualitative studies and 100-300 for quantitative studies). As people create a huge volume of social media data everyday, we believe that there are novel opportunities to explore trends with large datasets. However, thus far, this attempt has found to be challenging, because most social media sites neither collect nor reveal users' age information.

In this paper, we introduce a novel method for identifying age information from user profiles. Recent research has shown the possibility of using a facial detection technique to extract the age information from users' photos [3]. We enhance this method using natural language processing of users' bio statements, which allowed us to collect a total of 27K teens and adults in Instagram. With this data, this paper aims at exploring the following question.

> *How do teens use and engage in Instagram compared to adults?*

Our contributions include: (1) demonstrating the possibility of leveraging a combination of textual and facial recognition methods to accurately detect users' age information, (2) extracting a large dataset for conducting comparative analysis of social media usage based on age differences, (3) identifying clear trends of age differences in social media that are otherwise unattainable using the qualitative and quantitative methods employed in previous studies. We close this paper by proposing future research opportunities afforded by our method.

STUDY DATA COLLECTION
We chose Instagram, because over 90% of Instagram users are under the age of 35, which is suitable for our target age groups of teens and adults[1]. We used the programming API[2]

CHI 2015, April 18 - 23 2015, Seoul, Republic of Korea
Copyright 2015 ACM 978-1-4503-3145-6/15/04...$15.00
http://dx.doi.org/10.1145/2702123.2702555

[1] http://www.businessinsider.com/instagram-demographics-2013-12
[2] http://instagram.com/developer/

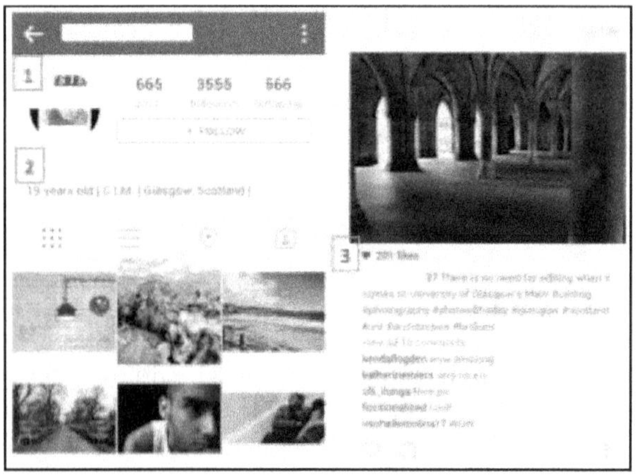

Figure 1. Screenshot of the user profile (anonymized) in Instagram, including (1) a profile image, # posts, followers, and followings; (2) bio; (3) # Likes, tags, and comments.

to extract users' all usage data. The data collection was done between April and May 2014. We first chose one random seed user and crawled followers of the seed user until we have 150K users. We then randomly chose 1K users from the pool of 150K and again crawled followers of them until we reached 2 millions of unique users. We used this two-step random-seed crawling process to minimize the bias in sampling a homogenous population. Overall, the dataset includes various pieces of user information such as name, the number of photos posted, the number of Likes, tags and comments in the photo, the number of followers and followings, and a bio description (Figure 1).

We define our target user populations as follows:

- *Teens:* people who are between 13 and 19
- *Adults:* people who are between 25 and 39

Classifying users to a specific age group was challenging, because most social media platforms including Instagram neither collect nor disclose users' age information. We propose a novel method that leverages two existing media contents (i.e., bio descriptions and profile images) with existing APIs. First, we applied textual pattern recognition algorithms to parse a list of patterns that specifically describe users' age in the bio (e.g., *"I am a teenager," "I am 17 years old," "I'm 23"*). Second, we used an online tool called Face++[3], which was designed to detect and provide the age and gender information of people presented in the photo. Face++ provides an API and has been utilized to extract age information in recent studies, and age verification showed a high accuracy (i.e., 96% accuracy in age range between 18 and 35 and 99% in ages over 35) [3].

Based on the users' bio descriptions, we identified 13,533 teens and 8,596 adults. To fill the gap between two groups, we analyzed the rest with Face++ and added 4,756 more adults, resulting in a total of 26,885 teens and adults for the analysis. Finally, we manually verified the age of all users to make sure the data accurately represented each group. A total of five people (two authors and three Turks) visited all users' Instagram page and checked their profile image, bios and posted photos. We only included users who achieved agreements among more than four raters for the analysis. Note that Face++ was only used for detecting adults but not teens in this study, because facial recognition was less accurate for people of a younger age range.

STUDY RESULTS

Difference in engagement

	Teens (13,533)		Adults (13,352)	
	Median	SD	Median	SD
# Photos	110	272	175	487
# Likes	3,293	29,851	2,150	24,829
# Tags	446	2,595	294	2,511
# Comments	175	1,016	35	1,023
# Followers	401	3,683	348	5,700
# Followings	286	2,045	272	2,699

Table 1. Summary of interactions & activities by two groups.

Table 1 shows the summary of Instagram activities for each group. Because all variables show a long-tailed distribution, we used the median value for the analysis. Because of our large and non-normalized datasets, to correctly measure the differences, we used eta-square (the effect size), denoted as η^2, which refers to the proportion of variance associated with each of the main effects, interactions, and error in an ANOVA study [12]. As a rule of thumb, $\eta^2 = 0.01, 0.13, 0.26$ are considered to be small, medium and large respectively. The results indicate all significant differences where teens post fewer photos ($\eta^2 = 0.02$, $p < 0.001$) but have more Likes ($\eta^2 = 0.04$, $p < 0.001$), tags ($\eta^2 = 0.01$, $p < 0.05$), and comments ($\eta^2 = 0.02$, $p < 0.001$) than adults.

	Teens (13,533)	Adults (13,352)
# Likes / # Photos	56.10	40.03
# Tags / # Photos	6.34	4.70
# Comments / # Photos	2.52	1.06

Table 2. The ratio of Likes, tags, and comments to photos.

We also measured the ratio of Likes, Tags, and Comments to Photos (Table 2). As a result, teens are likely to receive more Likes per photo than adults ($\eta^2 = 0.09$, $p < 0.001$). Teens add more tags ($\eta^2 = 0.01$, $p < 0.001$) per photo than adults. One of tagging motivations is to attract more views [2], and this implies that teens may want to make their photos and themselves more exposed to others than adults. Teens also have more comments ($\eta^2 = 0.07$, $p < 0.001$) per photo than adults, showing higher interactions in Instagram.

The result of teens having fewer photos than adults is quite unexpected and interesting; thus, we conducted additional analyses based on our sample. First, we hypothesized that teens may have limited resources to explore environments outside their daily activities. To test this, we identified latent topics from the tags of users' photos through an LDA analysis [4] using Mallet [9]. We used tags to infer photo

[3] http://www.faceplusplus.com/

content, because people tend to add tags that represent the photos they post [6]. We also obtained ground-truth tag topics from two popular websites (i.e., tagsforlikes.com and tagstragram.com) and then manually coded the types of photo topics from Mallet's output into those topics. Table 3 summarizes the 11 topics extracted from our dataset.

Topic	Tag examples
Arts/photos/design	photo, interior, architect, design, building
Entertainment	music, movie, pop, rock, song, star, dance
Fashion/beauty	makeup, model, fashion, jewelry, beauty
Follow/like	followme, followback, follow, tagsforlike
Foods	food, coffee, yummy, delicious, dessert
Instagram-tags	instagood, instalove, instadaily, instashare
Locations	nyc, boston, spain, brazil, dutch, europe
Mood/emotion	love, happy, depressed, bored, sad, great
Nature	sky, sun, ocean, beach, flower, sunset
Social/ people	family, girlfriend, friends, folks, gay, pets
Sports/wellness	hiking, biking, fitness, cleaneating, soccer

Table 3. LDA-discovered topics from all users (N=26,885).

We then calculated the ratio of topics that users in each group have in their photos, as presented in Table 4.

Topic	Teens (13,533)	Adults (13,352)
Arts/photos/design	4.59%	16.99%
Entertainment	11.34%	6.28%
Fashion/beauty	1.53%	4.20%
Follow/like	11.43%	2.22%
Foods	3.18%	3.13%
Instagram-tags	4.10%	3.22%
Locations	7.05%	24.89%
Mood/emotion	40.54%	14.21%
Nature	5.05%	9.04%
Social/people	4.50%	10.74%
Sports/wellness	6.69%	5.08%

Table 4. LDA-discovered topics from all teens and adults.

We found a clear difference between two groups in terms of topic types. On the one hand, for teens, more than half of photos are in the "Mood/emotion" and the "Follow/Like" topics. These topics are not necessarily tied to the content of photos but rather describe one's emotional status or intention to have more followers. On the other hand, adults show a high ratio in more diverse topics, including "Arts/photos/design," "Locations," "Mood/emotion," "Nature," and "Social/people." These topics imply more diverse contents in the photos, including photos that depict different facets of cities and countries around the world, photos of arts and design (where some of them were taken professionally), photos of a variety of people, and so on. This may be due to the fact that teens are financially and culturally dependent on their parents to venture outside of their daily activities compared to adults.

Second, previous studies found that many teens manipulate the content that they have shared; for example, removing photos [1,8]. To check this, we additionally collected the number of photos by teens and adults (13K each) in the 12-hour interval over 12 days (from December 26, 2014 to January 6, 2015). We then calculated the delta of photo counts in every two consecutive time slots and checked the number of users who removed their photos in 12 hours. As a result, given the same number of users for each group, more teens tend to remove photos than adults ($t(44) = 41.9$, $p < 0.001$; Figure 2), supporting our hypothesis.

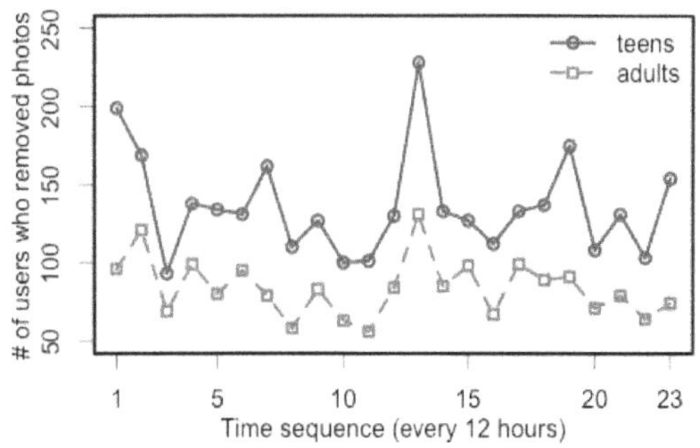

Figure 2. Number of users who removed photos (teens: 13K, adults: 13K).

Difference in self-representation

We extended our finding about teens' high engagement by analyzing their photos. We assumed that teens might post photos of themselves, namely "selfies," more than adults, because teens see social media as a place for self-representation [5,7]. To infer the photo content, we calculated the number of photos with tags and those with "selfie-tags" (we used #selfie and #me) as well as their ratio for each group. As a result, teens tend to post selfies more than adults ($\eta^2 = 0.08$, $p < 0.001$; Table 5).

	Teens (13,533)	Adults (13,352)
# Selfies / # Tagged-Photos	226,382 (12.8%)	99,782 (7.5%)

Table 5. Ratio of selfies for each group based on the tag analysis.

Our second approach to find out selfies was a photo content analysis. We verified photos posted by users in each group and calculated the percentage of selfies. With the randomly selected 1K users, we extracted around 56K photos from teens and 86K photos from adults. We manually checked all photos if they are selfies. On average, we found that teens have more selfies than adults ($\eta^2 = 0.05$, $p < 0.001$; Table 6). These results support the idea that self-representation is one of the motivations for teens to engage in social media over adults.

	Teens (1,000)	Adults (1,000)
Total # Photos	56,458	86,227
Total # Selfies	14,627 (25.9%)	14,823 (17.1%)

Table 6. Ratio of selfies from photos by randomly selected users based on the photo content analysis.

Lastly, we utilized the Linguistic Inquiry and Word Count (LIWC) [10] tool to parse words representing emotions in the bio descriptions. We randomly chose 8,596 teens and adults for the comparison of word per sentence (a level of expression) and words for follows (the number of words of "follow," "following," and "follows").

Table 7 shows the results with two insights. First, teens' bio contained more *word per sentence*, than adults ($\eta^2 = 0.06$, $p < 0.001$), indicating teens tend to be more verbose on their bio, which is a way of self-expression. Second, confirming the findings in Table 4 that teens add more photos in the *Follow/Like* topic, teens tend to use more words, "follow, following, or follows" in their bio descriptions than adults ($\eta^2 = 0.03$, $p < 0.001$). A qualitative analysis of teens' bio descriptions revealed that teens actively advertise others to follow them, which would also lead to gaining popularity, making friends, and making their photos more visible. For example, many teens post texts, similar to the following in their bios: "*Please follow me and I follow you.*"

	Teens (8,596)	Adults (8,596)
Word per sentence	16.11	10.62
Words for follow-words	2.39	1.44

Table 7. Scores of two attributes from the bio description. The higher result means more expressive and more words for follow-ships.

DISCUSSION AND CONCLUSION

The primary contribution of our work is the demonstration of a method that leverages existing tools (i.e., Instagram and Face++ APIs) and social media contents as a channel and triangulates findings about different age groups that can be difficult to observe using existing methods.

Our analysis shows an interesting trend that teens post fewer photos than adults. To explore reasons behind it, we further analyzed our dataset in two ways. First, the LDA-based topic analysis showed that over half of teens' photos were in "Mood/emotion" (40%) and "Follow/Like" (11%), while adults' photos were more evenly distributed across other topics. This result shows that teens tend to post topics related to themselves and focus on self-expression. Second, we found that more teens tend to remove photos than adults everyday, which substantiates some insights presented in previous studies. Many teens tend to manipulate their photo content to receive as many Likes as possible or sometimes remove some photos with too few Likes [1,8]. This may be because attention generated by Likes has become one way of establishing self-validation and self-worth[4], and teens want to show off their "coolness" to the public [5].

We also found that teens tend to have more Likes, tags, and comments and be more expressive about themselves in their profiles and photos. This shows that teens are leveraging social media as a "conversation space," and using Likes, tags, and comments to have conversations and interactions. This may be because teens are well aware of the intention of these activities as social signals and familiar with the technology and the "tagging culture" in online space, which reinforces teens' social practices [1].

Although our study shows many insights, we acknowledge some limitations that can be handled in future studies. First, errors may exist in the detection of age information even if we manually verified them. Many users provide additional social media links (e.g., Facebook, Twitter, etc.) in their profile. Future studies applying our method should obtain additional age information from those sites. Second, our results may only be limited to users in Instagram. We plan to extend our study to other social media sites to validate our method and compare results. Third, the age information from users' profiles could be obsolete when social media becomes more mature. A possible way to address this is to validate users' age information by comparing users' most recent selfies to their profile photos. This could potentially address the information obsolescence issue, but a future study to validate its accuracy will be necessary.

Our findings also ask for follow-up qualitative studies with some detailed questions that will give additional insights on teens in social media; for example, "Why do teens post fewer photos?," "What makes teens engage in Liking, tagging, and commenting?," "To what extent do teens and adults consider social media a conversation space?," etc.

Overall, we believe that our novel method opens up a new possibility of mining activities among different age groups in social media. We hope that this method can be used as a guide for researchers to better understand social phenomena and to formulate future research directions.

ACKNOWLEDGEMENTS

This research was in part supported by NSF CNS-1422215 award.

REFERENCES

1. Agosto, D. E., Abbas, J., & Naughton, R. Relationships and social rules: Teens' social network and other ICT selection practices. *JASIST 63,* 6 (2012), 1108-1124.
2. Ames, M., & Naaman, M. Why we tag: motivations for annotation in mobile and online media. *CHI 2007*, ACM Press (2007), 971-980.
3. Bakhshi, S., Shamma, D. A., & Gilbert, E. Faces Engage Us: Photos with Faces Attract More Likes and Comments on Instagram. *CHI 2014*, ACM Press (2014), 965-974.
4. Blei, D. M., Ng., A. Y., & Jordan, M. I. Latent dirichlet allocation. *JMLR 3*, (2003), 993-1022.
5. boyd, d. Why Youth (Heart) Social Network Sites: The Role of Networked Publics in Teenage Social Life. *MacArther Foundation Series on Digital Learning - Youth, Identity, and Digital Media*, (2008), 119-142.
6. Hollenstein, L., & Purves, R.S. Exploring place through user-generated content: Using Flickr tags to describe city cores. *Journal of Spatial Information Science 1*, 1 (2010), 21-48.
7. Ito, M., Baumer, S., Bittanti, M., et al. *Hanging Out, Messing Around, and Geeking Out: Kids Living and Learning with New Media.* MIT Press, 2009.
8. Madden et al. Teens, Social Media, and Privacy. *Pew Research Center*, 2013.
9. McCallum, A. K. "*Mallet: A Machine Learning for Language Toolkit*," 2002.
10. Pennebaker, J. W. & Francis, M. E. *Linguistic inquiry and word count (LIWC)*. Mahwah, NJ: Erlbaum, 1999.
11. Pfeil, U., Arjan, R., & Zaphiris, P. Age differences in online social networking - A study of user profiles and the social capital divide among teenagers and older users in MySpace. *Journal of Computers in Human Behavior*, 25 (2009), 634-654.
12. Tabachnick, B. G., & Fidell, L. S. *Using Multivariate Statistics* (5th ed.). Upper Saddle River, NJ: Pearson Allyn & Bacon, 2001.
13. Zaphiris, P., & Sarwar, R. Trends, similarities, and differences in the usage of teen and senior public online newsgroups. *TOCHI 13*, 3 (2006), 403-422.

[4] http://www.pbs.org/wgbh/pages/frontline/generation-like/

Investigating High School Students' Perceptions of Digital Badges in Afterschool Learning

Katie Davis
University of Washington
Mary Gates Hall, Suite 370
Seattle, WA 98195
kdavis78@uw.edu

Eve Klein
Pacific Science Center
200 2nd Ave North
Seattle, WA 98109
eklein@pacsci.org

ABSTRACT

This paper investigates high school students' perceptions of the opportunities and challenges of using digital badges to recognize and reward the skills and achievements they acquire in an afterschool science education program. Focus groups and usability tests were conducted with 10 students during the design of a badge system prototype for use in the program. We found that students recognized opportunities for personal empowerment in their use of badges, but also expressed concerns about sharing badges in various online contexts. The findings provide new insight into the values and goals that learners bring to discussions of digital badges in education. These insights hold relevance for designers of education-based badge systems as well as educators seeking to introduce badges into their practice.

Author Keywords

Digital Badges; Education; Gamification; Human Factors

ACM Classification Keywords

H.1.2. Human Factors; H.5.2. User Interfaces; K.3.1. Computer Uses in Education.

INTRODUCTION

Though once the purview of video games, digital badges are increasingly being used in non-gaming environments like MOOCs (e.g., edX), question and answer forums (e.g., oDesk), and consumer product purchases (e.g., American Express). There is growing interest in using badges to recognize and reward learning in a variety of education contexts, both formal and informal. As web-enabled digital icons containing metadata associated with specific learning goals, practices, and outcomes, digital badges represent an alternative credentialing system aimed not only at recognizing learning within particular settings, but also connecting learning across disparate settings [11].

CHI 2015, April 18–23, 2015, Seoul, Republic of Korea.

http://dx.doi.org/10.1145/2702123.2702413

Several major cities across the United States, including Chicago, Dallas, and Los Angeles, have implemented digital badges on a large scale across a variety of learning settings. However, the implementation of badges is growing considerably faster than research on their effectiveness at motivating, rewarding, and connecting learning [6]. In particular, we lack knowledge of students' attitudes toward badges in educational settings, insight that is critical to designing gameful systems that support learning [8].

This study examined high school students' perceptions of digital badges within the context of an afterschool science education program. We conducted focus groups and usability tests with students to inform the design of a digital badge system that recognizes the skills and achievements students acquire in the program (Figure 1). Our analyses identified specific ways that badges support student empowerment by putting them in control of their learning pathways. We also uncovered concerns that students expressed in relation to sharing badges outside the context in which they were earned. This investigation contributes new empirical findings that will support the design and implementation of badge systems in education.

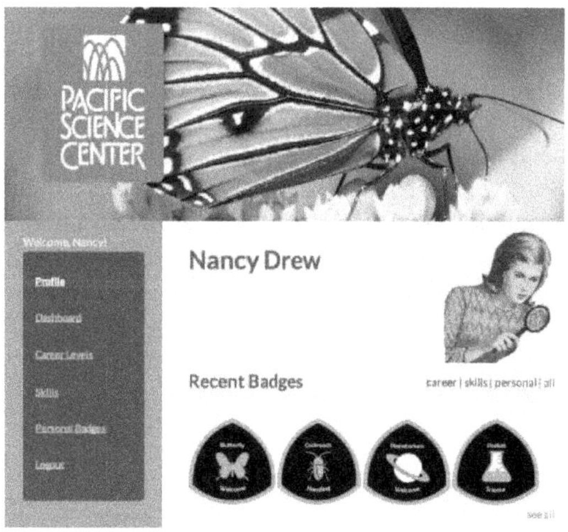

Figure 1. Badge system prototype developed to reward learning in an afterschool science education program.

PREVIOUS RESEARCH

Existing research on digital badges in education focuses on the motivational effects of badges within particular learning contexts. Denny [6] examined the impact of a badge-based achievement system on college students' engagement with an online learning tool. Badges increased the quantity of students' contributions and length of time they engaged without decreasing the quality of contributions. Students reported high levels of enjoyment and a preference for having badges incorporated into the online interface.

Abramovich et al. [1] examined the effects of using badges in an intelligent-tutor system for teaching applied mathematics to middle school students. The motivational effects differed across learners with different levels of prior knowledge. Researchers found a negative motivational effect of earning participatory badges (vs. skill badges) for learners with little prior subject knowledge. They suggest that designers of educational badge systems must take into account the characteristics of individual learners and how they might interact with different types of badge designs.

These studies provide insight into the motivational effects of badges *within* systems. However, an important part of current discussions about digital badges relates to their ability to facilitate connections *across* systems so that skills and achievements gained in one setting can be recognized and used to unlock future opportunities in another setting [2,9,11]. By facilitating such connections, badges have the potential to support the visibility of learning pathways that span multiple contexts. To this end, Mozilla, developer of the Firefox browser, has developed an open standard to support the interoperability of badge systems [5]. Rughinis [12] observes that this interoperability makes it possible for badges to serve as "boundary objects" [3] that help to negotiate meaning across contexts. Yet, he notes that considerable interpretative work is required to make sense of badge collections, raising challenges related to validating the credibility of badges earned in diverse contexts.

To summarize, initial research into badges suggests beneficial effects on learners' motivation levels, but the ratio between speculation and empirical evidence remains high. As badges are introduced into more learning environments, there is a need for research on the value that users ascribe to badges within and across systems. By focusing on users' experiences, the current study investigated the research question: "What are students' perceptions of the opportunities and challenges of using digital badges to recognize learning in afterschool settings?"

METHODOLOGY

The study took place in January-May 2014. Inspired by design-based research [7], focus groups and usability tests were conducted before, during, and after the design of a digital badge system prototype intended to recognize the skills and achievements that students gain by participating in an afterschool science education program. The iterative input from youth guided each stage of the design process and led to the articulation of two types of badges: those that are internal and those that are external to the program. Career badges were designed as a *within* system badge that mark students' progress through the various levels of the science program. Personal badges are another type of within system badge; students identify personal goals in the program and articulate corresponding badges that embody those goals. By contrast, skill badges were design as an *across* system badge documenting students' attainment of skills, such as public speaking, that would be of interest to external audiences like college admissions officers.

Context and Participants

Participants included 10 high school students in grades 9-12 who were current members of a science center-based youth development program intended to develop students' interest in science and promote their college and career readiness. Seven students took part in two focus groups (4 students in focus group #1, 3 students in focus group #2), and 6 students (3 of whom participated in focus group #2) took part in usability tests associated with the design of the badge system prototype.

Procedure

Focus groups were conducted during the design process as a method to elicit multiple viewpoints concurrently regarding students' pre-existing perspectives on and experiences with badges. Questions assessed students' prior knowledge of badging systems; their interest in earning digital badges to mark their progress in the program; and their thoughts on using science center badges in other contexts like college applications. Each group also went through a design exercise in which they were asked to consider the skills they gain in the program, and to identify one that might be a good candidate for a badge. This input guided the design and structure of the badge system prototype, which consisted of a website through which students could see their earned badges and track their progress in the program. The first usability test was conducted after completing the initial prototype. Students were invited to tour the badge website while narrating aloud their impressions as they encountered different design elements. The second usability test followed this format and was conducted after updating the prototype based on feedback from the first session.

Data Analysis

Data for the present analysis include verbatim transcripts of students' comments during focus groups and usability testing; researcher field notes; and collective notes recorded on chart paper during the focus groups. Two researchers worked collaboratively throughout the investigation to identify and document themes relating to participants' attitudes toward using badges inside and outside the science center. The themes were shared with the program staff and youth during and after the design of the badge system prototype. These "member checks" served as a means to validate the findings reported below by confirming that the themes identified by the researchers aligned with participants' lived experiences [10].

RESULTS

Empowering Learner Pathways

Consistent with earlier research, youth participants affirmed the motivational aspect of digital badges, which they related in particular to a sense of empowerment associated with earning and displaying badges online. In the usability testing, participants commented on the usefulness of the progress bar that shows their progress toward earning particular badges as well as their overall progress through the program (Figure 2). One student contrasted this digital monitoring mechanism with the paper-and-pencil system currently used in the program: "[The progress bar] really helps...Right now I feel like I've completed all my [level 2] stuff, but I'm not [sure]...I think I completed it but nothing's happening. No one is telling me what I'm supposed to do..." This quote illustrates the desire expressed by several youth to take more ownership over their experience in the program by monitoring their progress independently without having to ask an adult supervisor how they are doing or what they should be doing next. A digital badge system consisting of a personal profile page for each student empowers youth to manage their experiences in the program and inquire about next steps rather than waiting to be told what to do by a program coordinator. Remarked one student in a usability test: "I like that, how it's laid out where you can see the specific, 'Okay, here's what I need to do before moving on.'"

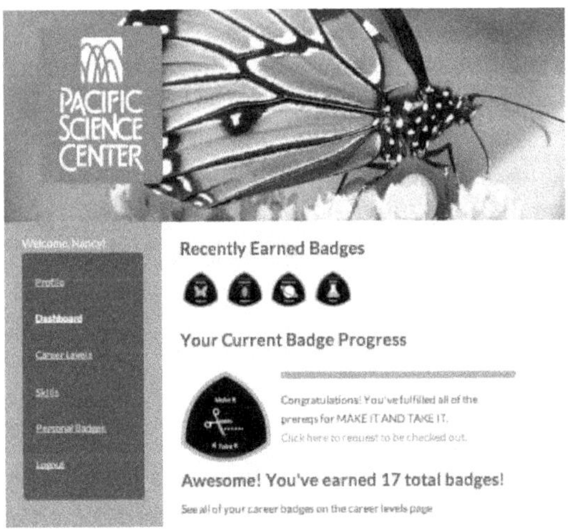

Figure 2. Dashboard page showing user progress.

In light of the fact that profile pages are visible to other program members, youth commented on the value of being able to look at their peers' progress as well as their own. One youth observed: "From where I am right now, I would definitely like [to see other people's profiles], so, if I had any questions on something I'm learning, I could see whoever knew, or who's an expert. I could ask them." This quote points to the value associated with being able to look at others' profiles in order to help youth visualize their own pathways to success in the program.

Consistent with the theme of personal empowerment, several of the focus group participants asked if—or assumed that—they would have the ability to self-assign badges for personally defined skills they felt they had gained. As a result of this input, designers developed a personal badge component that recognizes the individual goals and achievements of students.

Connecting Contexts

Though connecting skills and experiences across learning contexts is a major emphasis of Mozilla's open standard for digital badges, all but one student in the present study were uninterested in using badges to link their afterschool science activities more closely with their school lives. This sentiment is likely related to the fact that youth participants said they rarely talk to their friends or parents about what they do at the science center, and they do not typically consider or perceive topical connections across these contexts. Students value this separation because it allows them to carve out an experience distinct from their friends and family; they derive a sense of autonomy from knowing their participation in the afterschool program is theirs alone.

Similarly, with one exception, the teens expressed a resistance to linking a professional badging system to their personal social media profiles such as Twitter, Instagram, and Facebook. Several students alluded to the idea of not wanting to "brag" about their extracurricular accomplishments to their peers. They also said that constant online updates would likely get "annoying" to their friends. These sentiments reinforce earlier research showing that teens value the ability to keep certain of their social contexts separate from each other [4].

The one external connection that students unanimously endorsed was using badges to help gain access to college, or college credit. Students pointed to the opportunity for badges to recognize "soft" skills like public speaking and leadership that are difficult to measure and communicate to external audiences. One student commented on the value of being able to share these skills on a college application: "I think it would be a good idea if we could show colleges or other people things you know. But if it were just, 'Oh I have these badges on this one site,' and no one else uses it, it's not going to be as effective."

Embedded in the previous statement is the recognition that in order for badges to unlock opportunities such as college admissions, they must be widely available and recognizable as holding a particular value outside their original context. Indeed, all focus group participants raised concerns about standardization of digital badges. When a badge is awarded, it is necessarily based on the judgment of an individual or group of individuals. Students wondered how the rigor behind badges could be compared across institutions, and how the credibility of the awarder could be established.

DISCUSSION

The findings support and extend earlier work pointing to the potential for badges to motivate learners [1,6,11]. Students valued the ability to take control of and track their progress through the afterschool science program; examine their peers' progress in order to visualize future pathways; and use personal badges to shape an individualized learning experience. Collectively, these themes suggest that a key motivational element of badges is the empowerment that students experience when they are placed in control of their learning. This insight represents a new empirical contribution to our understanding of the potential of badges from the learner's perspective. Designers of educational badge systems can make use of this insight by seeking ways to design for personal empowerment, for example, by including a progress bar on users' profile pages and making it possible for users to design and create their own badges based on personal goals and achievements.

Proponents of digital badges celebrate their transportability, which is thought to help learners connect their skills and achievements across contexts [9]. However, the youth participants in the current investigation were not interested in using badges to connect their science center experiences with their school lives, and they did not want to share these experiences with their friends or family members. They did value the ability to use their badges in the college admissions process, but they raised concerns that such external audiences may find it difficult to assess the worth of a particular badge without some level of standardization in the badge awarding process.

These findings suggest that designers must take into account the values that students bring to discussions and uses of digital badges in education. Specifically, they must consider the particular contexts in which students do and do not wish to display their badges based on their specific educational, social, and personal goals.

CONCLUSION AND FUTURE WORK

The findings from this study provide new and needed insight into learners' perceptions of the opportunities and challenges of using digital badges in education. Students were attracted by the ability to take personal control of their learning, but they were wary of sharing their badges across social contexts they experience as distinct. Students also wanted to know that their badges would have value to external audiences like college admissions officers, suggesting the ongoing discussion among designers about standardization, validation, and credibility of badges is one that is also of importance to the badge earner [5,11].

In future work, we will use the insights gained from this study to further refine and implement a fully functional badge system for use in the science center program. Upon implementation, we will track students' evolving experiences with and perspectives on the badge system. The results will provide needed insight into whether the opportunities and challenges identified in the current study bear out as students use the badge system on a daily basis.

ACKNOWLEDGMENTS

The authors would like to thank the staff and students of the afterschool science program for their support of and participation in this research.

REFERENCES

1. Abramovich, S., Schunn, C., & Higashi, R.M. Are badges useful in education? it depends upon the type of badge and expertise of learner. *Education Tech Research Development 61,* 2 (2013), 217-232.
2. Antin, J. & Churchill, E. Badges in social media: a social psychological perspective. *SIGCHI 2011,* ACM (2011), 1-4.
3. Bowker, B. & Starr, S. *Sorting things out: classification and its consequences.* MIT Press, Cambridge. 2000.
4. boyd, d. *It's complicated: the social lives of networked teens.* Yale University Press, New Haven. 2014.
5. Casilli, C. Mozilla Open Badges: the ecosystem begins to take shape. 2012. http://carlacasilli.wordpress.com/2012/07/31/mozilla-open-badges-the-ecosystem-begins-to-take-shape/
6. Denny, P. The effect of virtual achievements on student engagement. *SIGCHI 2013*, ACM (2013), 763-772.
7. Design-Based Research Collective. Design-based research: an emerging paradigm for educational inquiry. *Educational Researcher 32*, 1 (2003), 5-8.
8. Deterding, S., Dixon, D., Khaled, R., and Nacke, L. From game design elements to gamefulness: defining "gamification". Proc. MindTrek '11, ACM (2011), 9-15.
9. Ito, M., Gutiérrez, K., Livingstone, et al. *Connected learning: an agenda for research and design.* 2013. http://dmlhub.net/sites/default/files/ConnectedLearning_report.pdf
10. Lincoln, Y. S., & Guba, E. G. *Naturalistic inquiry*. Sage, Beverly Hills. 1985.
11. Riconscente, M.M., Kamarainen, A., & Honey, M. STEM Badges: current terrain and the road ahead. New York Hall of Science. 2013. http://badgesnysci.files.wordpress.com/2013/08/nsf_stem badges_final_report.pdf
12. Rughinis, R. Talkative objects in need of interpretation: re-thinking digital badges in education. *SIGCHI 2013 Extended Abstracts,* ACM (2013), 2099-2108.

Piggyback Prototyping: Using Existing, Large-Scale Social Computing Systems to Prototype New Ones

Catherine Grevet and Eric Gilbert
School of Interactive Computing
Georgia Institute of Technology
cgrevet@gatech.edu, gilbert@cc.gatech.edu

ABSTRACT
We propose a technique we call *piggyback prototyping*, a prototyping mechanism for designing new social computing systems on top of existing ones. Traditional HCI prototyping techniques do not translate well to large social computing systems. To address this gap, we describe a 6-stage process for prototyping new social computing systems using existing online systems, such as Twitter or Facebook. This allows researchers to focus on *what people do on their system* rather than *how to attract people to it.* We illustrate this technique with an instantiation on Twitter to pair people who are different from each other in airports. Even though there were many missed meetings, 53% of survey respondents would be interested in being matched again, and eight people even met in person. Through piggyback prototyping, we gained insight into the future design of this system. We conclude the paper with considerations for privacy, consent, volume of users, and evaluation metrics.

Author Keywords
Social computing; large-scale systems; prototyping; evaluation; privacy; ethics; social interactions.

ACM Classification Keywords
H.5.3: Group and Organization Interfaces. Evaluation.

INTRODUCTION
We were contemplating building an app to introduce people waiting in airports (as illustrated in Figure 1). We quickly realized that attracting users would be a central challenge since the usefulness of the app rests on the fact that many others are also using it. How could we pair up people in airports unless many tens of thousands of users, at the very least, had opted-in? The uncertainty involved with scaffolding a social app to this scale could have stalled our project.

CHI 2015, April 18 - 23, 2015, Seoul, Republic of Korea.

ACM 978-1-4503-3145-6/15/04...$15.00
http://dx.doi.org/10.1145/2702123.2702395

Figure 1. Storyboard of the airport meet-up app we wanted to build to pair people while they wait.

Even massively funded and pioneering commercial systems (such as Google Wave[1] and Color[2]) have failed to achieve this critical mass of users. Thus, building the app was risky: it would cost significant engineering resources and ... what if no one used it? Did we have to build the system end-to-end just to see if we had a viable concept?

Of course, this is what *prototyping* is designed to solve. Prototyping can pinpoint fundamental flaws in interactive systems *before* a design team invests considerable energy building the system. Most HCI systems start as prototypes: they are designed and developed iteratively, and at increasing levels of fidelity. Unfortunately, existing HCI prototyping techniques do not translate well to social computing systems. For example, imagine if we had tried to "wizard-of-oz" [1] the airport meet-up app. We would have needed an entire team of "wizards" living the life of Tom Hanks in the movie "The Terminal." They would have each had to buy plane tickets (so they could get past security), and then set up camp for days in airports across the country. Then they would have met a participant when they received a match, presuming they had not been arrested first.

[1] http://googleblog.blogspot.com/2010/08/update-on-google-wave.html
[2] http://mashable.com/2012/10/17/color-shuts-down/

Our solution to these shortcomings was to develop a novel prototype technique: *piggyback prototyping*, a 6-stage prototyping mechanism for testing and iterating on new social computing designs. It works by coupling semi-autonomous bots to already successful large-scale social computing systems, such as Twitter. Piggyback prototyping overcomes the challenges of obtaining critical mass by leveraging existing social platforms. A piggyback prototype can focus on exploring *social interactions*, rather than *interface interactions*. Specifically, social interactions are those involving people directly interacting with each other. Such interactions can involve messaging or commenting, liking or up-voting, meeting face-to-face, sharing information to each other, etc. We are not using "the crowd" to add information or change the display of an interface, rather Piggyback Prototyping is used for systems in which people directly communicate with one another.

In this paper, we describe the mechanism and an example of deploying a piggyback prototype. We created a semi-autonomous bot that paired Twitter users who had checked-in to the same airport and told them to meet. We ended up forming 3,161 pairs, from which we received 576 tweet replies, 183 survey responses, and 8 participants who actually met in person. We learned that people would, in fact, meet others through our envisioned system, and more importantly, specifically how future design iterations could facilitate more meet-ups to occur.

This paper's contributions are threefold. First, we describe the steps of piggyback prototyping, illustrating along the way with examples. Second, we describe our experience using a piggyback prototype in a real-life project. Finally, we reflect on the scope, benefits, and limitations of the piggyback prototyping technique.

BACKGROUND

First we briefly review the history of prototyping in HCI. Then we describe the challenges faced by social computing systems and why traditional HCI techniques do not work for large-scale social systems.

A brief overview of prototyping

In HCI, a prototype is "a concrete representation of part or all of an interactive system" [1]. This is in contrast to an abstract representation, such as a verbal description. As such, prototypes can be manipulated. Their manipulation creates a vehicle for communication between designers, engineers, and users [1, 13]. The prototype should serve a well-defined function, such as prototyping the role of a new capability, the look and feel of an existing concept, or the implementation of how a system actually works [13].

Through the process of adapting and refining the prototype, it evolves. To allow for this flexibility, prototypes tend to be rough and sketch-like. Low-fidelity prototypes are a rapid prototyping technique: they are easy and quick [1]. Common methods for this are *paper prototyping* where an interface is literally drawn on paper [22], or *wizard-of-oz prototyping* where the interface is a curtain behind which a researcher responds to user input [1]. *Higher fidelity prototypes* require significant coding, but provide a more finished look [1]. Crafting a relevant prototype requires the skill of a domain expert.

Prototypes serve to elicit guidelines for future design improvements and they are evaluated in observational settings. To use Computer Science terminology, they are compared against "benchmarks of performance." These metrics are determined prior to a study and guide the tasks that users will be asked to perform [1]. Other forms of evaluation are less directed: the user creates meaning through interacting with the prototype such as with *probes* [7]. In addition, prototypes can also be viewed as essentials tools for generating design ideas and insights [16].

Prototyping social computing systems

Here we use "social computing systems" as a broad term for technologies that involve human-human interaction. We distinguish between two types of social computing systems: those for small groups, and those for larger crowds. Small-scale collaborative group systems can be prototyped with adaptations of traditional HCI techniques. Social computing research has many examples of these [9]. For example, "paratypes" are probes that can help understand the social context and social acceptance for a new technology [14]. When using a paratype, a researcher surveys reactions to the prototype as they go about their day-to-day activities. To our knowledge, however, there are no prototyping techniques for large-scale systems.

A simple search in the ACM digital library underlines this gap: only 4 papers from the CSCW conference contain the words "prototype" or "prototyping" in their title, as compared to 85 papers for CHI. If we naively align HCI work to CHI and social computing work to CSCW, it becomes apparent that prototyping techniques for social computing are scarce. This may be due to a number of challenges.

One major problem with large-scale social computing systems is the need to obtain critical mass [10]. To avoid this issue, some systems have foregone testing with people and opted instead with agent simulations [6] or simply proposed a prototype without evaluation [18]. In these approaches, it is not possible to evaluate the social affordances of the system. Others have created complete systems in the hope of attracting users to a polished product. Turkopticon, a tool for Amazon Mechanical Turk (AMT) workers, for example used bootstrapping by collaborating with an AMT employer to obtain their initial users [15]. At the time of publication, four years after the launch they had 7,000 installations [15]. Some may be lucky, such as Link Different, a social translucence tool for Twitter, which gained 144,232 users in two months thanks in part to media attention [8]. In both cases, obtaining critical mass was central to their efforts. This may not be the case for all projects.

Another challenge is determining evaluation metrics. Is a system that gets fewer than thousands of users a failure? Number of users is a common metric for commercial products, and we have also—we argue to our detriment—adopted

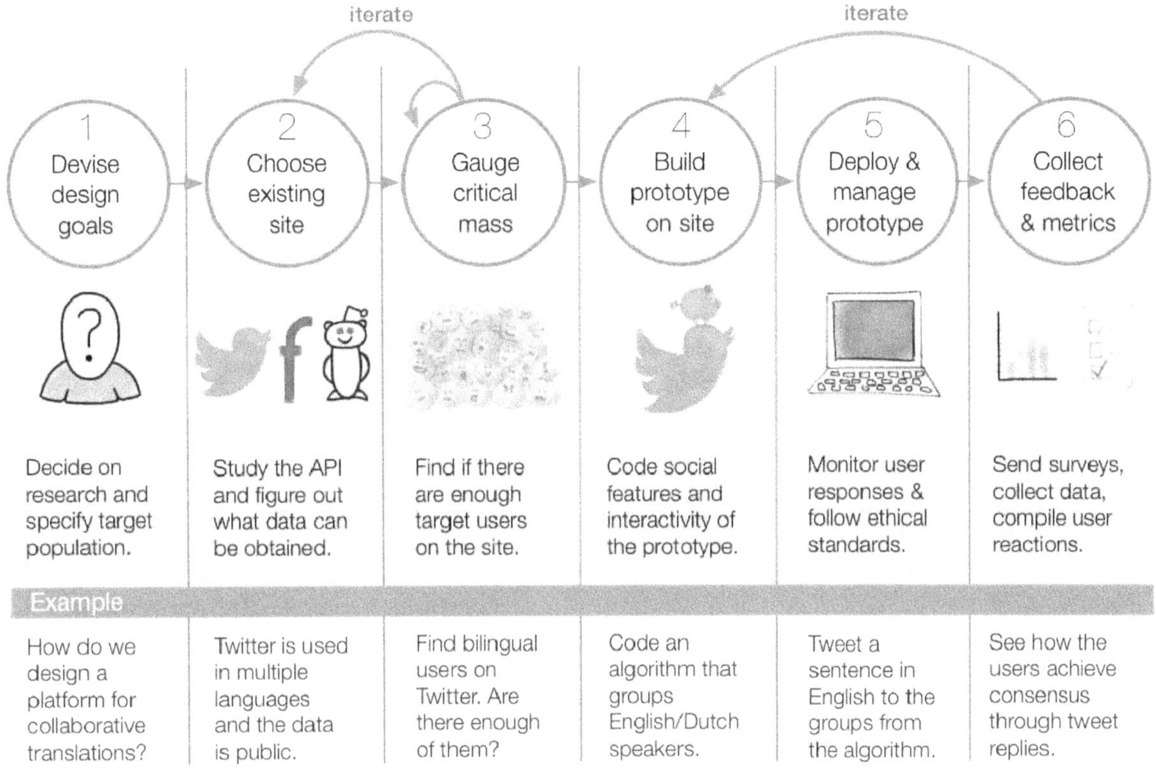

Figure 2. The 6 stages of piggyback prototyping: 1) Devise design goals, 2) Chose existing site, 3) Gauge critical mass, 4) Build prototype on site, 5) Deploy and manage prototype, 6) Collect feedback and metrics. Stages 3 and 6 are iterative, if critical mass is not present for the target population (3) or the deployment was not successful (6) previous stages may be modified and re-evaluated.

it as a standard for research. Would Turkopticon have been irrelevant if it only had 10 users? If achieving critical mass is our main measure of success, we are limiting the quantity and quality of social questions we can ask.

INTRODUCING PIGGYBACK PROTOTYPING

We next introduce the six stages of piggyback prototyping, a social computing system prototyping technique that utilizes existing social platforms to evaluate novel social interactions for large-scale systems. Piggyback prototyping is best suited to projects that require coordination between multiple people and that do not have access to readily available large-scale social data. We believe, for example, that a large variety of social matching systems could have been prototyped with this technique, such as organizing people for disaster relief, assisting a collaborative activity, matching people according to interests, and many others. Piggyback prototypes involve 6 stages, two of which distinguish it markedly from other techniques: a non-social pilot (stage 3 in Figure 2) and a social deployment (stage 4 in Figure 2). The evaluation of the prototype will likely involve mixed methods in which a researcher might craft a survey, plan an interview, collect log data, or compile user responses.

1. Devise design goals

The first step is to decide on the research goals and the desired social interactions. Figure 2 presents an example for a collaborative translation system, a system resembling the exiting site Duolingo[3]. We also suggest in this step to determine the target population for the prototype. This will be the basis for the next step and for planning the architecture of the prototype.

2. Chose existing site

There are many existing social platforms that could be used for piggyback prototyping—for example Twitter, Facebook, or Reddit. The researcher should consider the pros and cons of the different platforms. We recommend choosing a platform with public data and an API. In particular, three types of data shared on these platforms may have value to designers [11]:

People: User profiles contain a wealth of information such as demographics, interests, and network data. If it is possible to obtain a social graph, then systems that require this structure could be prototyped. In this case, the prototype might require some sort of massive scale snowball sampling [2] to get friends of friends to participate.

Things: The things that people talk about create vast amounts of content about current events, interests, and sentiments. A researcher could build a prototype that centers on topics. There exist off-the-self natural language process packages (such as NLTK[4]) and topic models that can provide enough accuracy to develop quite sophisticated tools.

[3] https://www.duolingo.com

[4] http://www.nltk.org/

Places: There are a number of sites where people broadcast their location (Twitter, Foursquare). These platforms may serve different purposes and motivations for publicly sharing geo-location information may be complex [3, 17, 24]. Understanding these intricacies will help align a prototype with user expectations.

3. Gauge critical mass

Finding critical mass on the chosen site for the target population is key. Critical mass is not an absolute value, but rather is specific to each project. If the goal is to match people based on topics, then enough people need to be talking about a given topic. We suggest gauging critical mass on the chosen site by testing the participant recruitment method without a social component. This pilot can be a simple message sent to users, or it may be a survey. This can help determine characteristics of the target population such as: demographics, behavioral patterns of the target population, and technical aspects such as the types of devices typically used by the participants.

As described in Figure 2, gauging critical mass is an iterative process. Using our experience as an example, we tried in previous work to recruit participants for a study about political discussions on Facebook. We initially planned on recruiting participants who shared a link to a political petition in a public Facebook post. We quickly observed hostility towards our requests via Facebook, which was not the case when we reached out on Twitter about the same topics. The *norms and expectations* were different, and we learned that Twitter was a better choice for our study. This example does not suggest that Facebook is not a viable site for piggyback prototyping. It may be just right for certain systems.

4. Build prototype on site

Once the site is chosen and proves to have enough potential participants for a viable study, the social aspects of the prototype can be built. This requires building a messaging infrastructure to reach out to the target population. A researcher could manually message participants, but this might not scale. Because of this, piggyback prototypes will generally be semi-autonomous: running code may find users and send them a template message, yet the researcher will still read every incoming response. Some prototypes might suggest that participants communicate with each other through the existing site. In the collaborative translation example from Figure 2, groups would communicate through Twitter replies. Other prototypes might ask participants to communicate through a low-fidelity interface. For example, Facebook users might be asked to collaborate with others on a simple and easily deployed message board.

There are two components that are well suited to be tested through a piggyback prototype:

Algorithms: piggyback prototyping can test social algorithms. Recommender algorithms and natural language processing are examples of such algorithms that are commonly used in social computing and that are particularly difficult to evaluate without critical mass. Since a prototype is rough, these tools need not be perfect. In fact, piggyback prototyping could help evaluate them in a live setting.

Interaction: this concerns the messages that are sent to users, the tools available to users through the prototype, and the means that users have to communicate with each other. Piggyback prototyping can help iterate on these aspects.

5. Deploy and manage prototype

Next, the researcher or designer deploys their prototype on the chosen site. Systems prototyped with this technique should strictly adhere to Internal Review Board (IRB) processes or corporate ethics boards if applicable, and *always* to ethical standards. Prototypes should not violate privacy and should only present minimal risk.

Obtaining consent

We worked closely with the IRB at our institution to conduct our study using piggyback prototyping (presented next). We highly recommend doing so. When we deployed our prototype, we obtained a *waiver of consent without need of documentation*. Our participants were aware that they were participating in a study, however, and they had an explanation of the study. Piggyback prototypes can work with documentation of consent as well, as long as the necessary critical mass of participants signs it. Full-disclosure on the research goals and obtaining consent may be prohibitive for some projects. Those studies fall outside the scope of piggyback prototyping.

The role of the researcher and self-presentation

Even though piggyback prototyping involves running code, it is not completely autonomous: the designer/researcher is still a central part of the prototype. They must present themselves as such to the participants with whom they interact. Moreover, similar to a wizard-of-oz prototype in which the researcher is part of the system, in piggyback prototyping the researcher must be deeply involved in the process. This means that the researcher needs to be available to conduct duties such as answer specific participant questions if appropriate, or to remove participants who have asked to be excluded or who behaved badly.

6. Collect metrics and feedback

The goal of prototyping in HCI is to evaluate a system in order to iterate on the design [1]. Participants of a piggyback prototype can be sent a follow-up survey to ask about their experience. They might even be interviewed, though the number of participants in this prototyping technique might get overwhelming. We propose that the metrics that can be obtained through piggyback prototyping are:

Engagement metrics

These are the data that can be obtained from the social platform and supporting ecosystem. For example, the number of clicks on the supporting documentation can serve as one indication of how many people saw the message.

Survey evaluations

The gauging critical mass survey and final survey are two entry points to ask users for their thoughts on the system.

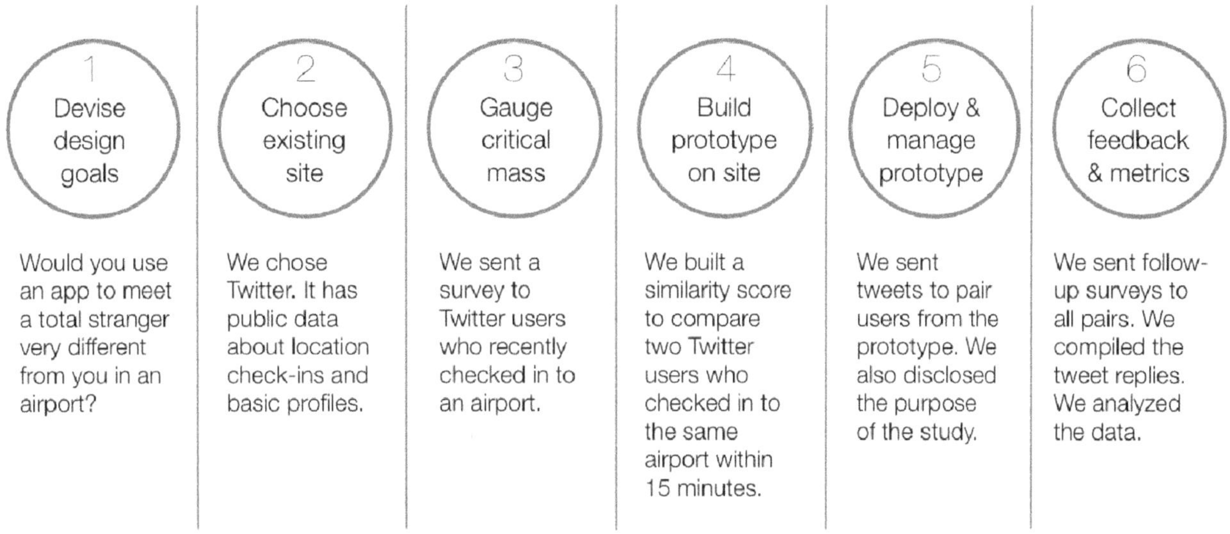

Figure 3. The 6 stages of piggyback prototyping used in our instantiation. We chose Twitter as our existing site and built a social matching algorithm that pairs users checked-in to the same airport, at the same time, who are different from one another.

These surveys could ask usability questions about their interactions, or could also ask behavioral questions.

EXAMPLES AMENABLE TO PIGGYBACK PROTOTYPES

We next present three short examples of existing systems that we believe could have been prototyped with piggyback prototyping, yielding informative research directions. These examples are commercial systems that have already proven their success by being viable commercial products. While we now know how users interact via these sites, it is an interesting thought exercise to apply piggyback prototyping to them.

Online dating: Can we prototype OkCupid?

Piggyback prototyping could help evaluate certain components of an online dating site such as the matching algorithm. What algorithm results in the most relationships formed? Who are people looking to meet? For example we could find people who tweet about being single, and about a sports team. Do those who root for the same teams end up getting along? The evaluation could ask whether they would be interested in seeing that person again.

Expert knowledge systems: Can we prototype Quora?

We could imagine studying a knowledge system across many people. For example we could find people interested in the same topic in subreddits and ask them to contribute to a shared document. Studying the design of this system has many important research contributions. Who contributes? What topics make the most sense for this? What incentives foster the best answers?

Co-location meet-ups: Can we prototype Foursquare?

People go about their daily lives in public places where they are in the presence of others with similar patterns, known as *familiar strangers* [19]. We could try to increase the social capital present in a city by pairing people who tend to tweet from the same location. How should these meetings occur? Does this indeed increase social capital?

OUR INSTANTIATION OF PIGGYBACK PROTOTYPING

We present an example of deploying the piggyback prototyping technique in a social matching context (see Figure 3). Before building an app, we wanted to explore the conditions under which people would meet face-to-face.

1. Our prototype goal: Will people meet strangers?

The goal of our prototype was to nudge people to meet others different from them in order to combat our natural tendency towards associating with people similar to us, called *homophily* [23]. Previous research on Political Blend, a system designed to introduce people of different political beliefs over coffee [5], showed indications that such meetings could be valuable. Yet, prototyping the system itself was challenging. Through piggyback prototyping, we can answer the following questions:

- Are people willing to meet strangers when prompted through social media?
- Are people willing to meet strangers despite not having much in common?
- What are the design considerations for a system that breaks homophily? What are the pitfalls?

2. Our selected existing social network: Twitter

We chose Twitter as an existing large social network. The Twitter API provided us with the ability to obtain public data including user location, social networks, and profile data. We chose U.S. airports as locations for introducing people since they have benefits such as: many diverse individuals might be collocated; engaging in a conversation with a stranger may be a pleasant way to pass time; and importantly airports have significant security procedures that may lower the risk of meeting a stranger. Furthermore, Airport check-ins on Twitter seemed like a viable route following the success of the TSATracker system which asks Twitter users for updates about security lines [21].

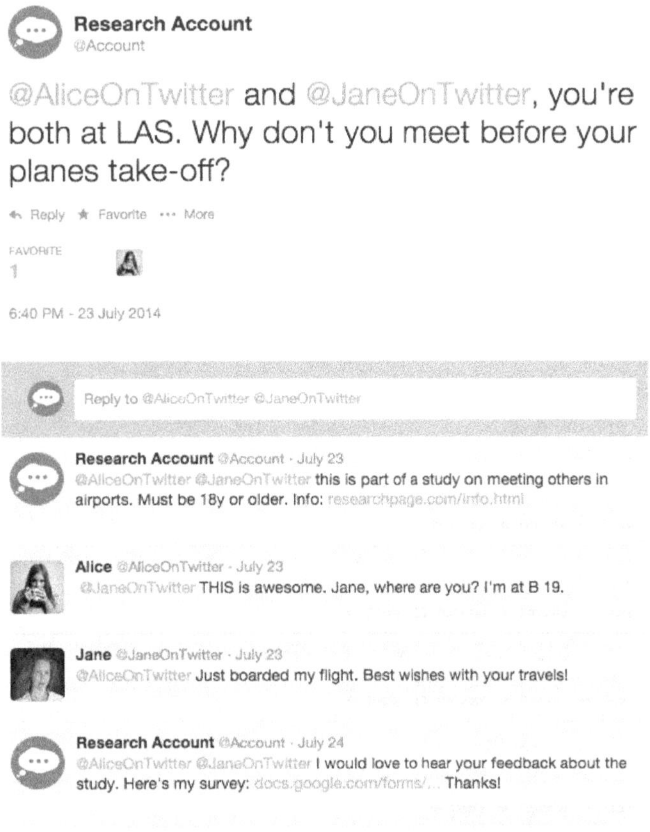

Figure 4. Screenshot of piggyback prototyping in action. Example replies on Twitter, the messages are actual replies from participants. All accounts, names, images, and times have been anonymized.

3. Did we find critical mass for airport check-ins? Yes.

We first conducted a formative survey for three purposes: 1) to determine whether people would be willing to meet strangers in airports; 2) to help us determine an expected response rate using airport check-ins on Twitter; and 3) to give us insights into the demographics of this population. The survey asked whether they had met a stranger today in the airport, whether they would use an app to meet strangers in the airport, as well as demographic questions to explore the diversity of the population.

We sent surveys to 1,512 Twitter users who checked in to a U.S. airport between December 2013 and Jan 2014. They received a request to fill out a survey about an app to introduce people in airports.

We obtained 213 responses with a response rate of about 14%. From their responses, we found that our target population was interested in meeting fellow travelers and that there was critical mass for users who checked-in within 15 minutes of each other. This was encouraging to pursue further down this road.

4. Our prototype algorithm

Once we had early evidence that some significant groups of people had interest in meeting strangers in airports and that it would be feasible, we prototyped the actual interaction in-

	Count	Rate
Visitors on info page	712	11.0 %
Tweets that got replies	576	9.0 %
Survey responses	183	3.0 %
Tweets favorited	61	1.0 %
Replies with location	31	0.5 %
Participants who met	8	0.1 %
Total	6,322	100%

Table 1. Engagement metrics for the social deployment. We paired 6,322 twitter users (which

volved with matching-users and prompting them to meet-up through Twitter.

For this prototype, we paired users based on their similarities and differences. We built a Twitter similarity classifier that is based on common known dimensions of homophily [4]: content of a user's tweets, their followers, and who they follow. We assigned our participant pairs to three user groups (high similarity, some similarity, low similarity) based on the obtained similarity score. These thresholds were obtained from formative data collection resulting from determining critical mass.

The implementation of this algorithm was done in Python with the Tweepy[5] module to connect to the Twitter API[6]. Through the Twitter Search API we searched for users who checked in to U.S. airports, then for each user we obtained their social graph and their last 20 tweets. Then, we created clusters of users per airport who checked in within the last 15 minutes. Within each cluster we computed the similarity score for each possible pair. We sent a matching tweet to those who were 1) most different, 2) most similar, and 3) finally if some pairs were left they were paired up. Our prototype consisted of approximately 1,000 lines of code, of which a significant proportion was the similarity algorithm.

5. Prototype deployment

We ran our prototype on weekdays from May to September 2014. We did not run it continuously during that period since we did not know what to expect from user responses or from Twitter – our account could have been blocked. We started by sending tweets manually, and eventually turned to a semi-automatic system when we found that most responses were positive. We stopped contacting those who requested it (such as not sending them our survey). This only concerned 10 pairs of the 3,161. All the follow-up surveys were sent manually. By monitoring our study closely, we could iterate on some aspects of our prototype:

First, we initially contacted participants as the primary author. This put the spotlight on the researcher's account since it was contacting thousands of users. Instead, we changed to

[5] http://www.tweepy.org/

[6] https://dev.twitter.com/

a more general research account. Our contact information was still available in the study documentation.

Second, we iterated on the message crafted for introductions [25]. Each pair (e.g. A and B) was sent the following prompt: "@A and @B you're both at CLT. Why don't you meet before your planes take-off?" The prompt was followed by a tweet containing the age limit of 18 for participation, and another tweet with information about the study. We got feedback that the tweet about having to be 18 years old was deterring so we included it in the same tweet as the information link. This streamlined the process by only sending two tweets (one to initiate the match and one with the study information).

6. Evaluation: survey instruments and other data

The day after we paired Twitter users, we sent them a link to a survey to ask them about their experience with the meet-up (see Figure 3 and Figure 4). In this survey, we asked them whether they did meet up or not. If they did meet up, we asked them questions on these three topics: inter-personal likeability [12], self-disclosure, and follow-up connections. Finally, we asked them how long the meet up lasted. In the cases where the participants were not able to meet up, they were asked why. We asked all participants if they would like to be matched again. Most of the questions were Likert scale.

In addition to the surveys, we also obtained data for our prototype through page views analytics and tweets we received back from our participants. This data was simply obtained from a Google Analytics script inserted on the documentation page residing on our lab server.

Did you meet this person in the airport?	● Yes	○ No
How long did you talk? (in minutes)		
Did you exchange contact information?	○ Yes	○ No
Would you like to be matched again with someone in the airport?	○ Yes	○ No

Figure 3. Survey questions for participants who did meet in the airport. They were also asked questions about interpersonal likeability and self-disclosure (not pictured here).

Did you meet this person in the airport?	○ Yes	● No
Why didn't you meet this person?		
Would you like to be matched again with someone in the airport?	○ Yes	○ No

Figure 4. Survey questions for participants who did not meet.

LESSONS LEARNED FROM OUR PROTOTYPE

The goal of our prototype was to see if people would meet face-to-face, and to gain design insight into a system that would prompt people to do so. We did see people meet and the engagement we got with the prototype was enough for us to develop insights into the design of a system in this context. The metrics are summarized in Table 1.

People were willing to meet strangers in airports

We sent a survey to 1,512 Twitter users who checked in to a U.S. airport between Dec. 2013 and Jan. 2014 and we obtained 213 responses. In this survey, we asked about whether they have talked to a stranger since they have been in the airport. Over half of the users who checked-in to an airport on Twitter had engaged in a conversation at the airport with someone they did not already know (56%). When asked if they would be interested in meeting strangers while they waited, 71 participants (32%) said "yes" and 112 participants (51%) said "maybe." Only 33 participants (15%) said that they would not be interested in meeting strangers. Of those who said they would not be interested in meeting someone while they waited, there were only 10 of them (21%) who would not use a social app in the airport. Others might install an app to get a coupon with someone while they wait (35%) or to play a social game (20%). These were key findings that allowed us to move forward.

Airport check-ins on Twitter had critical mass

Since December and January tend to be high travel seasons, we compared the critical mass from this period with a relatively low travel season (end of March, beginning of April) we found that most 15 minute time spans had at least two users checked in to a large airport in the U.S. We came to this finding after some trial and error since we did not know what to expect of people's airport check-in behavior. Since we wanted to pair two people, we determined that 15 minute windows was enough for critical mass of users to conduct our study.

Participants engaged with our prototype

From May to September 2014, we paired up 6,322 Twitter users (3,161 pairs) who had checked in to airports on Twitter and sent a follow-up survey the next day. We obtained 186 survey responses, of which 182 respondents had not met their match and 4 had met their match. We got 576 Twitter replies and we had 712 unique visitors to our study information page. Our pairing tweets were favorited 61 times. Of the replies we received, 31 had location or contact information. These data suggest that a rough social prototype like the one we deployed can lead to significant amounts of data that help gain insights on the intended interaction. The replied tweets can be analyzed to understand what is happening. The fact that the tweet was repeatedly favorited (61 times) is encouraging. And we obtained enough survey responses to gain a more in depth understanding, which we will talk about next.

An example exchange between participants is illustrated in Figure 4. Other tweet replies we received were:

"would've made my afternoon"

"haha safe travels! Hope you're not #theOnethatGotAway"

"I hope you're doing this for awhile it's such a cool idea!!"

"I would have participated had I not been so preoccupied with getting my luggage and search for tacos. Next time"

People actually met when prompted by our prototype

The day after participants were paired, we sent them a follow-up survey to ask about whether they met the other person or not, and what the meet up was like.

Missed connections

In the deployment, we saw a number of missed connections. 31 participants tweeted their gate or location information as a follow-up to our pairing tweet. We found that the reasons meetings did not occur were: participants saw our tweet too late; the participants were too far away from each other; the participants did not have enough time before their flight; social reason (such as traveling with a family member); some checked in to the airport even though they were not travelling; and finally some had arrived to the airport rather than waiting to depart.

Actual meetings

What is remarkable is that people actually did meet when prompted through our prototype. In total eight participants met thanks to our prototype. These meetings occurred between people who were highly different (according to our computed similarity score). Of the four reported meet-ups, the participants felt rather neutral about whether they could be friends with the person. This could be simply because a friendship needs more time to develop. Yet, most participants would be interested in being paired again (3 of the 4 pairs). Most meetings exchanged contact information (3 of the 4). One of the pairs, in fact one of the most different pairs, talked about topics that tend to be more controversial, such as religion and politics. In all cases, they talked about their jobs. Family and relationships, and general interests such as music and movies were also talked about in three of the meet-ups. The participants also reported that the meetings lasted 60 minutes in two cases, 30 minutes for one and 5 minutes for another.

Future design considerations

The goal of prototyping is to gain design insight about what would happen when a full system is built and deployed. From our instantiation of the prototype, we learned:

Opt-in system

Most missed connections might not happen if users initially signed up for the system and were thus expecting these prompts. The challenge with building an opt-in system is obtaining critical mass, this was the reason we did not go that route in the first place. Now that we have an idea that people are interested in meeting others while waiting in airports, we can build a complete system with more confidence about our design decisions.

In an opt-in system, we would have greater control in creating pairs that can meet. For example, we could take into account how much time travelers have until they board, and whether they are arriving or departing. Through this prototype, we were able to determine some of these issues that could be explicitly designed for in our next iteration.

Matching message

It was surprising to us that participants did not seem to need to know much about the other person to be willing to meet. While it might have been more motivating to know some common interests with the match, we did not see the lack of information about the match to be a large barrier. Perhaps a finding here is that people do not really care to look at the profile of the other person and are actually generally willing to meet a stranger no matter who that person is. A controlled comparative study using piggyback prototyping could more fully explore this. A priori, we thought the introductory message would be key, but it did not seem to matter much in our prototype.

Technical considerations

Finally, 66% of survey respondents used iOS devices and 24% used Android. This gives us an indication of how to prioritize the development for a future app in this space.

Limitations of this specific prototype

People have different attitudes towards meeting strangers and towards seeking diversity, some are more introverted and some are more extroverted [20]. We did not include a personality survey though it is likely that we got an extrovert crowd that was more willing to engage with a diverse group of people since we only got people who were interested in sharing their location publically. Furthermore, the computed similarity score was approximated from the data we can obtain from Twitter, which is noisy. This might be the case no matter what data is used to obtain a measure of homophily. However, a system in which we could ask for specific profile data may be more accurate.

CONSIDERATIONS WITH PIGGYBACK PROTOTYPING

As a prototype technique, a piggyback prototype is not meant to be a fully completed system. Rather it is rough and flexible: it should be easy to iterate on. As we described, the piggyback prototyping technique is a 6-stage process that provides a scaffolding mechanism for an iterative process for designing large-scale social computing systems. In our instantiation of piggyback prototyping, we learned about ideas that would improve our initial system like having it be opt-in for pairing people according to more fine-grained information. We hope to have shown how other researchers can also implement this approach.

Critical mass

Obtaining critical mass in any system is extremely complex and not well understood. Users might come because of good design, a well-timed product launch, or simply because of good luck. In our prototype, we knew from our formative survey and data collection that there were enough people checked-in at the same airport at the same time to pair them up. This step is necessary to make sure that a prototype will have enough users.

It is not because a prototype is successful that the resulting completed system will obtain critical mass. However, through this technique we hope to give researchers and designers more tools to consider projects that they might not have had resources to even start otherwise.

Volume of users

Piggyback prototyping concerns large numbers of users. This is unique to this prototyping technique compared to others used in HCI. As such, the evaluation of a piggyback prototype must be catered to this volume. We would argue that a quantifiable survey is more manageable than user interviews. This also means that the resources to manage the volume of participants must be considered. Participants may want information about the study or may personally message the researcher. While we only had two cases of participants emailing us for more information, we can imagine that this could quickly become difficult to manage if every participant had emailed us.

Choosing appropriate metrics

Our piggyback prototype made us reconsider the traditional evaluation metrics of social computing systems. We had many participants due to the fact that Twitter had many people checking in to airports, thus the fact that we had 6,322 users does not speak to the merit of our system. What does? We looked more deeply at survey results, engagement metrics and user responses to get a sense for the value of our system. Similarly, researchers who employ piggyback prototyping should determine for their project what metrics and feedback they would like to obtain.

What was important to us was to determine whether some people would meet up and whether those meet-ups were meaningful. Some might consider the four meet-ups we saw to be a limiting aspect of our study: "four is a small number, so the impact of the system is underwhelming." Yet, we saw that those meet-ups were highly successful from the survey responses despite the fact that the people paired up were highly different. This finding is surprising and significant enough to continue down this line of work.

Longitudinal studies using piggyback prototyping

There is a dilemma around the longitudinal aspect of piggyback prototyping. On the one hand, a script could constantly run to obtain data over a long period of time, as long as one does not get blocked from crawling the site. (That is, a site could interpret high levels of activity against it as an attack and shut the script down.) At the same time, one must consider possible user fatigue. To our knowledge, Twitter users who tag their location are not constantly bombarded with research requests. While this study shows that at the time of the study, a significant number of people welcomed our intervention, this could also be due to some novelty effect. If these requests were a more frequent occurrence, Twitter user behaviors may change. While we see promise in the feasibility of this technique, we are also aware that an overabundance of piggyback prototyping might drastically change behavior, and therefore the feasibility of the technique. This kind of reflexivity is present in most social systems.

Generalizing outside of Twitter

Our piggyback prototype was deployed on Twitter. This platform was ideal at the time of this study because it contained a large public dataset of location check-ins through its tight integration with geo-locating services such as Foursquare. We believe this platform could work for many other types of piggyback prototypes. Though we imagine that other platforms may be just as suitable. Facebook and Reddit are examples of platforms on which users can message each other, and thus provide an infrastructure for piggyback prototyping. Certain limitations (such as the current $1 cost to message a non-friend on Facebook) should be considered. Each project should consider the implications of the chosen existing site. If Twitter is widely popular and accessible today, it could be different tomorrow. Piggyback prototyping would still be feasible, but a careful understanding of available social platforms is necessary.

What falls outside the scope of piggyback prototyping?

Not all large-scale social computing systems can be prototyped with piggyback prototyping. Three types of projects may not be well-suited to this technique: 1) those that deal with sensitive or protected data, 2) those that cannot disclose the purpose of the study to the user, and 3) those that require anonymity. For example, if the researcher has access to private data like direct messages on Twitter, then that data should not be shared with other users. Or, if the system depends on anonymity, then leveraging existing non-anonymous social networks might make it difficult to evaluate in situ. Considerations for privacy are especially important and not always straightforward. For example, we suggested that piggyback prototyping could test social algorithms such as matching algorithms. However, some algorithms might reveal information from public data that most users would not have been able to find.

Biases and limitations

People who publicly share broadcast messages are a self-selected group. For example, they might be more extroverted or more narcissistic. Beyond how this might impact findings in our own study on location sharing, this bias must also be considered in most piggyback prototyping systems. Second, using certain sites may not be accessible to all researchers. For our study, we used a Twitter account that was first a personal account and then evolved into a study account. As such, Twitter's automated defenses did not block it. It is possible that an account specifically created for a piggyback prototype might exhibit behaviors that would get it blocked.

Towards a social toolkit

In HCI, a basic building block of software UI prototyping was the development of UI toolkits that contained modular pre-defined UI components that could quickly be assembled. Could we consider the social computing systems counterpart? If we compare piggyback prototyping to the Model-View-Controller paradigm, we could use existing social data as the Model and we prototype the View and the Controller parts to varying degrees. In our example of pairing users who checked in to Twitter, we emphasized a prototype of the

Controller. Others might choose to focus more on the View to prototype the visual aspect of the system. For example, Groupkit [9] provides a toolkit for video-conferencing, which facilitates the development of critical components (such as sessions) for these types of systems. Similarly, a toolkit for large social systems could be envisioned as follow-up to piggyback prototyping.

CONCLUSION

We developed *piggyback prototyping*, a prototyping technique for large-scale social computing systems. We described an example of using this prototyping technique to pair people checked-in to airports. The goal of this project was to see whether people would meet despite differences, yet we quickly realized that we needed a critical mass of users for the system to be useful. We took advantage of pre-existing critical mass on Twitter and deployed a prototype of our matching algorithm on top of Twitter. Through this we learned that travelers who shared their location on Twitter responded positively to social matching prompts. We were surprised that many were willing to meet in the context of our prototype. We found that piggyback prototyping addressed the shortcomings of HCI prototyping techniques when it comes to large-scale social computing systems: piggyback prototyping allowed us focus on *what people do on a social computing system* rather than *how to attract people to the system*.

REFERENCES

1. Beaudouin-Lafon, M. and Mackay, W. Prototyping Tools and Techniques. *The Human-Computer Interaction Handbook*. 2002. p. 1006-1031.
2. Biernacki, P. and Waldorf, D. Snowball Sampling: Problems and Techniques of Chain Referral Sampling. *Sociological Methods & Research*. 1981.10(2):141-163.
3. Cramer, H., Rost, M. and Holmquist, L.E. Performing a check-in: emerging practices, norms and 'conflicts' in location-sharing using foursquare. *MobileHCI*. 2011. p. 57-66.
4. DeChoudhury, M. Tie formation on Twitter: Homophily and structure of egocentric networks. *SocialCom: IEEE Conf. on Social Computing*. 2011.
5. Doris-Down, A., Versee, H. and Gilbert, E. Political blend: an application designed to bring people together based on political differences. *Communities and Technologies*. 2013. p. 120-130.
6. Foner, L. and Crabtree, I. Multi-Agent Matchmaking. *Software Agents and Soft Computing: Towards Enhancing Machine intelligence, Concepts and Applications*. 1997. p. 100-115.
7. Gaver, B., Dunne, T. and Pacenti, E. Design: Cultural probes. *Interactions*. 1999. 6(1): p. 21-29.
8. Gilbert, E. Designing social translucence over social networks. *CHI*. 2012. p. 2731-2740.
9. Greenberg, S. and Roseman, M. Groupware Toolkits for Synchronous Work. *Computer-Supported Cooperative Work: Trends in Software 7*. 1999.
10. Grudin, J. Groupware and social dynamics: eight challenges for developers. *Communications of the ACM*. 1994. 37(1): p. 92-105.
11. Guy, I., Jacovi, M., Perer, A., Ronen, I., Uziel, E. Same places, same things, same people? mining user similarity on social media. *CSCW*. 2010. p. 41-50.
12. Hancock, J.T., Toma, C.L. and Fenner, K. I Know Something You Don't: The Use of Asymmetric Personal Information for Interpersonal Advantage. *CSCW*. 2008. p. 413-416.
13. Houde, S. and Hill, C. What do Prototypes Prototype? *Handbook of Human-Computer Interaction Second Edition*. 1997. p. 367-380.
14. Iachello, G., Truong, K.N., Abowd, G.D., Hayes, G.R., Stevens, M. Prototyping and sampling experience to evaluate ubiquitous computing privacy in the real world. *CHI*. 2006. p. 1009-1018.
15. Irani, L. and Silberman, S. Turkopticon: Interrupting Worker Invisibility in Amazon Mechanical Turk. *CHI*. 2013. p. 611-620.
16. Lim, Y-K., Stolterman, E. and Tenenberg, J. The Anatomy of Prototypes: Prototypes as Filters, Prototypes as Manifestations of Design Ideas. *ACM Trans. on Computer-Human Interaction*. 2008. 15(2).
17. Lindqvist, J., Cranshaw, J., Wiese, J., Hong, J., Zimmerman, J. I'm the mayor of my house: examining why people use foursquare - a social-driven location sharing application. *CHI*. 2011. p. 2409-2418
18. McDonald, D., Gokhman, S. and Zachry, M. Building for social translucence: a domain analysis and prototype system. *CSCW*. 2012. p. 637-646.
19. Milgram, S., in *The Familiar Stranger: An Aspect of Urban Anonymity*. 1972.
20. Munson, S. and Resnick, P. Presenting Diverse Political Opinions: How and How Much. *CHI*. 2010. p. 1457-1466.
21. Nichols, J. and Kang, J-H. Asking questions of targeted strangers on social networks. *CSCW*. 2012. p. 999-1002
22. Rettig, M. Prototyping for tiny fingers. *Communications of the ACM*. 1994. p. 21-27.
23. Smith, J., McPherson, M. and Smith-Lovin, L. Social Distance in the United States: Sex, Race, Religion, Age, and Education Homophily among Confidants, 1985 to 2004. *Annual Review of Sociology*. 2014. p. 432-456.
24. Tang, K.P., Lin, J., Hong, J., Siewiorek, D. and Sadeh, N. Rethinking location sharing: exploring the implications of social-driven vs. purpose-driven location sharing. *Ubicomp*. 2010. p. 85-94.
25. Terveen, L. and McDonald, D.W. Social matching: A framework and research agenda. *ACM Trans. Computer-Human Interaction*. 2005. p. 401-434.

Situated Social Media Use: A Methodological Approach to Locating Social Media Practices and Trajectories

Thomas Hillman
Department of Education, Communication and Learning
University of Gothenburg
thomas.hillman@gu.se

Alexandra Weilenmann
Department of Applied IT
University of Gothenburg
alexandra.weilenmann@gu.se

ABSTRACT
In this paper we draw upon a number of explorations of social media activities, trying to capture and understand them as located, situated practices. This methodological endeavor spans over analyzing patterns in big data feeds (here Instagram) as well as small-scale video-based ethnographic studies of user activities. A situated social media perspective involves examining how social media production and consumption are intertwined. Drawing upon our studies of social media use in cultural institutions we show how visitors orient to their social media presence while attending to physical space during a visit, and how editing and sharing processes are formed by the trajectory through a space. We discuss the application and relevance of this approach for understanding social media and social photography in situ.

Author Keywords
Social media, social photography, Instagram, ethnography, methodology, trajectories, museum studies.

ACM Classification Keywords
H.5.m. Information interfaces and presentation (e.g., HCI): Miscellaneous.

INTRODUCTION
Social media use has emerged as a central topic in HCI. There has been a range of studies of different aspects of social media use. To a large extent these studies focus on the online environment, and draw heavily upon interview data and analyses of usage patterns. This approach has been facilitated by the relatively easy access to data of online social media interactions. Researchers can now create large databases that can be processed and analyzed, creating new opportunities for seeing patterns and trends in user behavior [13]. Big data approaches to social media uses hold great promise, although they have been criticized for resting on a 'mythology' that more data is always better and leads to new knowledge and higher accuracy [2]. This has provoked some researchers to define their work as "small data" studies [14], where the focus is on smaller sets of data from social media, often in conjunction with interviews or some form of qualitative content or linguistic analysis.

While a small data approach gives us more qualitative insight into social media practices, these studies usually tend to focus on post-production. That is, social media content (tweets, status updates, etc.) are analyzed and focus lies on online activities. Because of this, we have very little knowledge about the implications of social media use on the local context, and vice versa how local surroundings shape social media productions. This is where social media is used, where tweets are produced and shared, where photos are taken and edited as well as liked and commented. Recent advancements in mobile technologies have provided us with new possibilities to study social media practices in a more detailed fashion [3,11].

In this paper, we argue for a perspective on situated social media practices, that adds the local context to online social media use. We present results from a study, where we continue to explore located social media practices. This involves a set of methodological challenges. Seeing mobile social media use as a connective practice [7] we have developed our methods to incorporate both online social media activities and situated practices. This approach lets us answer a range of questions that have emerged from our empirical studies including: To what extent is there a connection between the 'online' narrative and the physical trajectory of a visit to a cultural institution? How is the orientation towards an online audience affecting the trajectories the visitors take in a designed exhibition space? How do visitors choose to structure their visit, compared to how they present it online? In this note we provide some answers to these questions, but we put emphasis on

CHI 2015, April 18–23, 2015, Seoul, Republic of Korea.

http://dx.doi.org/10.1145/2702123.2702531

methodology, exemplifying a range of topics that can be investigated with a situated social media approach.

STUDYING SITUATED SOCIAL MEDIA USE

During the past few years we have been involved in a number of projects looking at how visitors use their own mobile technologies and social media in science centers, museums and zoos. In these studies we have continually tried to get closer to the phenomenon by experimenting with different data collection techniques. This methodological endeavor spans across the analysis of patterns in big data e.g. Twitter and Instagram feeds, ethnographic examination of online interactions through social media, as well as small-scale video-recorded field ethnographic studies of user activities. We take our starting point in the field, where we explore how visitors orient to their social media presence while attending to physical space and the temporality of a visit.

Our approach is informed by methodological bodies of work with origins in other disciplines that are now well established within the CHI tradition, i.e. ethnographic fieldwork, online ethnography and social network analysis. In addition to these more established data collection methods we are also inspired by recent developments in the study of mobile device use. Researchers with an interest in understanding the organization of social interaction on the go are currently exploring new ways of collecting naturally occurring data of such interaction. For example, the iPhone in vivo study [3] records users' phone screen, and combines those screen capture videos with video analysis of users activities and interactions. Using similar data collection techniques, Licoppe and Figeac [11] have examined gaze switches between the device and the online environment, in order to learn more about the temporal organization of multiple involvements. This data collection approach holds much promise when it comes to understanding mobile device use, including the use of social media on the go.

In the next section, we show a few examples of the different types of data that we have collected as a part of our methodological experiments getting closer to the phenomenon of social media practices *in situ*. We draw upon material from two different cases. The first example is a study of the use of Instagram at a natural history museum [15]. The material collected for that study consists of instagrams from a group of invited Instagram users, who visited the museum and posted images on Instagram. These visitors were then interviewed, but we did not follow them walking through the museum. In the second example we provide data from a study of a group of three children who took photos and posted on Instagram as they visited a zoological garden. These three study participants were followed around the zoo, tracked by a GPS, and their phone screens and interactions were video recorded. In the following we discuss what we have learned from these different data collection approaches and how they can be combined to understand situated social media use.

SOCIAL MEDIA TRAJECTORIES

Our first step towards understanding social media use in situ involved an investigation of Instagram use at a museum. When examining the corpus of instagrams we noticed that several visitors had created narratives based on their museum visit and oriented to the audience in various ways [15]. Analyzing this material and creating a "heat map" for Instagram activity during museum visits leads us to consider *social media trajectories*, a concept that we define as the relationship between online activities and physical movements.

One particularly salient aspect of visitors' social media trajectories in the museum seemed to be the way they oriented themselves spatially while sharing instagrams from their visits. Some visitors chose to instagram a series of objects that are very close to each other in an exhibition space while others posted instagrams from locations at much greater distances from each other. For example, one visitor posted a collection of 16 instagrams from several different areas of the museum while concentrating his efforts in the fish and reptile galleries (Fig. 2). This visitor posted most of his instagrams both physically and temporarily close together at the beginning of the visit, then posted far more sporadically later on. These types of trajectories tell us a lot about the types of exhibits that are suitable and interesting to share online. It is easy to conclude that certain parts of a museum are very popular to share on social media whereas certain exhibits in the museum are rarely shared. However, what is most popular to share online does not necessarily reflect the most popular exhibits. There can be several reasons why things are not photographed, e.g. the extent of interactive elements, the light conditions, rules for taking photographs, etc.

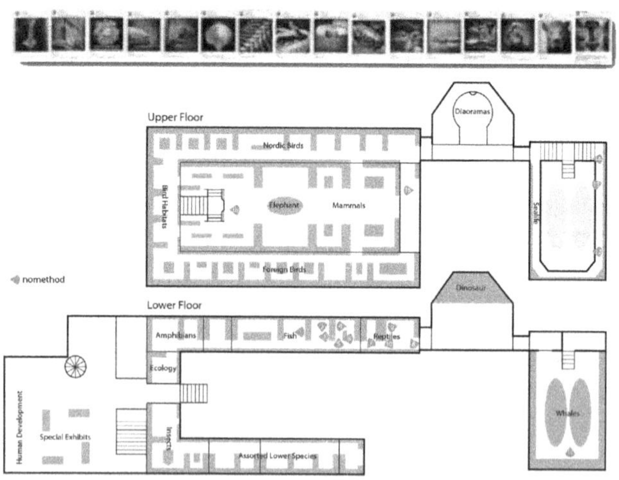

Figure 2: Locations of visitor @nomethod's collection of instagrams from a museum visit.

From this type of data collection approach where we did not follow the visitor while walking around the museum, we could not know if they actually posted the instagrams from the locations represented or posted them later. We still lack knowledge about the actual sharing circumstances and the practice of walking through a museum and choosing what to share. While visualizing the location where the instagrams were shared (Fig. 2) makes it possible to draw conclusions about the social media trajectories created within the museum space, we cannot necessarily say how these trajectories overlap with visitors' physical patterns of walking through the museum space. Therefore, as part of our next study we were interested in mapping the paths of visitors to their instagrams to give us some insight into the work of walking through a space and sharing objects. When conducting fieldwork at a zoo we tracked our study participants by GPS, and combined these traces with instagrams posted during the visit (Fig 3).

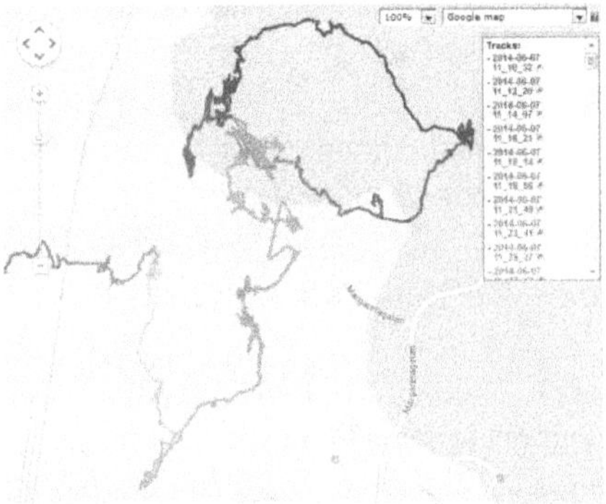

Figure 3: GPS tracking from a visit to the zoo, showing how long the visitors stayed in certain areas ("hot spots").

From this data we can discern certain hot spots in the zoo as we could at the Natural History Museum. However, because of the time stamps provided by the GPS, we can also learn to what extent the spots participants stayed in for an extended period of time correlate with their online activities. There can be many reasons why hot spots are created, for example a hot spot is created on the map where the study participants had a lunch break. In order to make sense of and analyze these types of trajectories, we need to combine them with other types of data, focusing on social media production and consumption *in situ*.

SOCIAL MEDIA PRODUCTION AND CONSUMPTION

In his studies of everyday photography conducted between 1940 and 1980, before the advent of the Internet connected cameraphone, Chalfen [4] recognized that amateur photographers were already orienting to an audience when taking their photos . Today, we have a completely different technological context, where pictures can be shared and consumed immediately. Many researchers have argued that today's widespread multimedia environments have allowed for a new set of practices where consumption and production practices merge [8]. In order to study this phenomenon more closely, we suggest an approach where we study photographic practices in the field.

Figure 4: Two young zoo visitors in front of an information sign while composing captions for their Instagram photos.

We can briefly exemplify with a case from the zoo field study. Two participants were taking photos of banded mongoose on their respective mobile devices. This photo taking was a collaborative and socially organized process. They discussed the search process (what animal to capture), how to do it (the need to zoom in and be quick) as well as assessing the quality of the images ("Look, didn't this turn out great?"). They then moved on to sharing these images online, checking information about the animal including how to spell its name correctly in the caption (Fig. 4), and agreeing on what smileys to include. A discussion about liking the recently posted instagrams then evolved, where the participants competed to be the first to like the images. They then went back to assessing the images, and continued to take some more, moving between producing and consuming. There were several cases like this where photographic and editing processes were collaboratively performed and editing choices were discussed. From this data we can see how consumption and production are no longer two distinct processes, rather they are inseparably intertwined and socially organized. In addition, our data shows how social media activities have now become an integrated part of what has been called co-visiting [6].

DISCUSSION

As new media technologies and applications allow for new practices we need to adapt existing techniques for studying these practice. Our methodological approach to studying situated social media use, including examining visitors' social media trajectories, has a number of implications. First, this approach opens up new opportunities for museum studies. Mapping out social media trajectories, gives us new opportunities to understand how visitors engage with museum content. The traditional approach to measuring visitor engagement has been to quantify time spent at an exhibit. This has lead to the common use of concepts such as "museum fatigue" derived from comparing the relative amounts of time visitors spend at exhibits [12]. Yet literature that uses time spent at an exhibit to measure visitor engagement has, to a large extent, neglected to detail the process of museum visiting [1]. Similarly, the practices we have described in this chapter suggest that we need to rethink the issue of "signs of engagement" and "dwell time" [6] with exhibits and also study content produced as part of the visit. By connecting situated activity to social media practices we can learn more about the impact of a museum's curated exhibitions on visitors' practices.

Second, a situated social media approach allows us to reach a new understanding of social media and social photography behavior, insight that can be valuable when designing new tools and services. We can briefly mention one such example here. Our results suggest that users have a number of strategies to deal with and play with time in their social media productions. However, the prevalent timeline metaphor forces linearity of use and visitors have to handle timelines when creating narratives. In Instagram, the focus of this paper, there is currently no way to reorder images after they have been posted. If we take users creations of narratives seriously we suggest that we should not force linearity on the user's experience, but instead allow users to rearrange how experiences are presented.

Another example of a design space that is opened up by this type of approach relates to social media trajectories. Our findings using a situated social media approach suggest that the way users represent their activities on social media is related to their walking paths through the environment. Using this approach we can learn more about production and editing, and examine whether our social media interactions are affected by our local interactions, and vice versa. Such knowledge has the potential to inform a range of HCI studies and applications dealing with the domains of e.g. storytelling [5,10], and trajectories [9].

CONCLUSION

In this paper we have presented the perspective of situated social media studies. We have shown a few examples from our studies of social media use in cultural institutions, drawing upon different methodological experiments in order to get closer to the phenomenon of social media practices *in situ*. This approach allows us to see how visiting, in this case a museum, science center or a zoo, has changed with the ubiquitous use of social media. An extra layer has been added to the visit that is now also about documenting the experience and sharing it with others. Studying situated social media use gives us access to the ways in which production and consumption of social media are linked and moves us closer to an understanding of social media use as a phenomenon that is not only played out online, but is situated in a particular context.

ACKNOWLEDGEMENTS

We thank our study participants as well as our colleagues Beata Jungselius and Igor Stankovic for their contribution to this work.

REFERENCES

1. Bitgood, S. Museum fatigue: A critical review. *Visitor Studies 12*, 2 (2009), 93–111.
2. Boyd, D. and Crawford, K. Critical Questions for Big Data. *Information, Communication & Society 15*, 5 (2012), 662–679.
3. Brown, B., McGregor, M., and Laurier, E. iPhone in vivo: video analysis of mobile device use. *Proc. of CHI 2013*, ACM Press (2013), 1031–1040.
4. Chalfen, R. *Snapshot Versions of Life*. Bowling Green State University Popular Press, 1987.
5. Chi, P.-Y. and Lieberman, H. Raconteur: integrating authored and real-time social media. *Proc. of CHI 2011*, ACM Press (2011), 3165–3168.
6. Heath, C. and Vom Lehn, D. Interactivity and Collaboration: new forms of participation in museums, galleries and science centres. In R. Parry, ed., *Museums in a Digital Age*. Routledge, 2010, 266–280.
7. Hine, C. Virtual ethnography. *The Sage Handbook of Research Methods*, (2000), 179.
8. Jenkins, H. *Convergence culture: Where old and new media collide*. New York University Press, New York, 2006.
9. Kanda, T., Shiomi, M., Perrin, L., et al. Analysis of people trajectories with ubiquitous sensors in a science museum. *Proc. IEEE Int. Conference on Robotics and Automation*, (2007), 4846–4853.
10. Kostoska, G., Fezzi, D., Valeri, B., et al. Collecting memories of the museum experience. *Proc. of CHI EA '13*, (2013), 247.
11. Licoppe, C. and Figeac, J. Direct video observation of the uses of smartphones on the move: Reconceptualizing mobile multi-activity. In A. de Souza e Silva and M. Sheller, eds., *Mobility and Locative Media: Mobile Communication in Hybrid Spaces*. Routledge, New York, 2015, 48–64.
12. Miles, R. and Tout, A. Impact of research on the approach to the visiting public at the Natural History Museum, London. *International Journal of Science Education 13*, 5 (1991), 543–549.
13. Rost, M., Barkhuus, L., Cramer, H., and Brown, B. Representation and Communication: Challenges in Interpreting Large Social Media Datasets. *CSCW*, (2013), 1–6.
14. Stephansen, H. C. and Couldry, N. Understanding micro-processes of community building and mutual learning on Twitter: a 'small data' approach. *Information, Comm. & Society*, (2014), 1–16.
15. Weilenmann, A. and Hillman, T. Instagram at the Museum : Communicating the Museum Experience through Social Photo Sharing. *Proceedings CHI 2013*, ACM (2013), 1843–1852.

Break It Down: A Comparison of Macro- and Microtasks

Justin Cheng*, **Jaime Teevan**†, **Shamsi T. Iqbal**†, **Michael S. Bernstein***
*Stanford University, †Microsoft Research
{jcccf,msb}@cs.stanford.edu, {teevan,shamsi}@microsoft.com

ABSTRACT
A large, seemingly overwhelming task can sometimes be transformed into a set of smaller, more manageable microtasks that can each be accomplished independently. For example, it may be hard to subjectively rank a large set of photographs, but easy to sort them in spare moments by making many pairwise comparisons. In crowdsourcing systems, microtasking enables unskilled workers with limited commitment to work together to complete tasks they would not be able to do individually. We explore the costs and benefits of decomposing macrotasks into microtasks for three task categories: arithmetic, sorting, and transcription. We find that breaking these tasks into microtasks results in longer overall task completion times, but higher quality outcomes and a better experience that may be more resilient to interruptions. These results suggest that microtasks can help people complete high quality work in interruption-driven environments.

Author Keywords
Crowdsourcing, microtasks, task breakdown, interruptions.

ACM Classification Keywords
H.5.m. Information Interfaces and Presentation (e.g., HCI): Miscellaneous

INTRODUCTION
Information tasks are often thought of as having a fixed structure. A task may be long and complex, or short and easy to complete, and this is assumed to be a property of the task. However, many large tasks ("macrotasks", e.g., transcribing a speech) can actually be transformed into number of smaller, more easily achievable components ("microtasks", e.g., separately transcribing the speech's individual sentences). There is evidence that information workers already implicitly break larger tasks down: people perceive tasks in segments [13], and mental workload dips at task boundaries, rising during individual subtasks [12]. Additionally, common tasks such as email are accomplished in short bursts of less than five minutes [2]. In fact, microtasking is prevalent in crowdsourcing, where a number of workflows have been developed that decompose large, seemingly complex tasks into microtasks for goals such as as taxonomy creation and copyediting.

CHI 2015, April 18–23, 2015, Seoul, Republic of Korea.

ACM 978-1-4503-3145-6/15/04 ...$15.00.
http://dx.doi.org/10.1145/2702123.2702146

By explicitly segmenting a macrotask into microtasks, larger, more overwhelming tasks can be done in smaller chunks of time. In crowdsourcing, microtasking has allowed crowd workers greater time flexibility [8]. The rising success of crowd work suggests that traditional information workers may stand to benefit from microwork structure [10], and enable people to complete large tasks in many brief moments when they feel productive but do not have a long, uninterrupted period of time [11].

To explore the trade-offs between microtasking and macrotasking, we conducted an experiment with 110 participants that compared performance on macrotasks with equivalent sets of microtasks. By looking at three simple but common task types (arithmetic, sorting, and transcription), we study how quickly and accurately participants were able to complete the task across macrotasks and microtasks. While breaking a macrotask into microtasks resulted in longer overall task completion times, it also yielded higher quality outcomes and easier work. We also find evidence that microtasks may be more resilient to interruption than macrotasks, suggesting that microtasking could be helpful for information workers, who tend to be interrupted often and have difficulty resuming their tasks afterwards [1]. Overall, our results suggest that microtasks may enable information workers to complete high quality work in short bursts of time that have previously been unproductive.

METHOD
To study the impact of breaking a task down from a macrotask into a set of equivalent microtasks, we manipulated three primary variables: *task type*, *task format*, and the presence of *interruptions*.

Task Type
We studied three types of tasks: receipt arithmetic, line sorting, and audio transcription. We selected these task types because they can be directly decomposed into microtasks, have clear correctness criteria, and are common in information work. Addition is a common activity in personal finance, sorting is implicit in ranking and selection tasks, and transcription is prevalent in crowdsourcing markets.

Arithmetic: Sum the cost of items from a scanned receipt.

Sorting: Sort seven lines of text. Each line contains a list of 10 numbers and should be ordered by the number of odd numbers in each list of numbers.

Transcription: Transcribe approximately 30 seconds of audio from an audiobook of Aesop's fables.

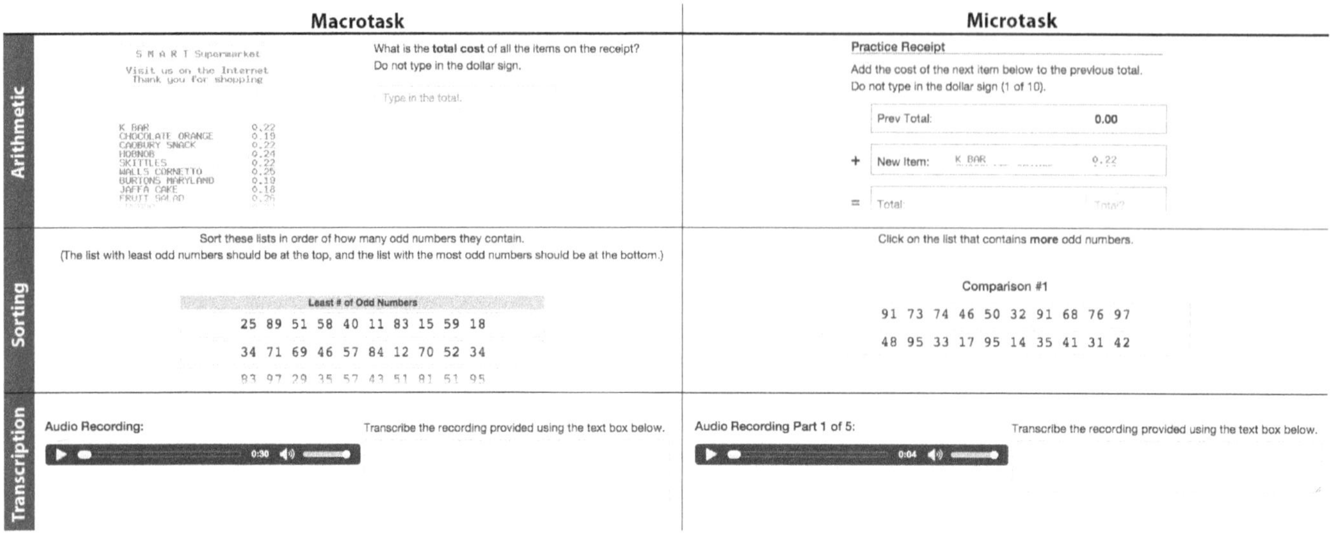

Figure 1. Screenshots of the three task types, showing both the macro- and microtask structure.

Task Format

While the three task types can be performed as complete macrotasks, each has also been explored in the crowdsourcing literature broken down into microtasks (Figure 1).

Arithmetic: In the macro version, participants were shown a receipt listing 10 items and their cost. They were then asked to sum the costs and enter the total. In the micro version, participants were shown a single line at a time and asked to add the cost of the displayed item to a running total.

Sorting: The macrotask showed seven lines of text and asked the participant to sort them by dragging and dropping each line into its new position. The microtask implemented a human-powered quicksort [7]. Participants compared pairs of lines, selecting the line with more odd numbers.

Transcription: The macro audio transcription task involved transcribing a complete 30 second audio clip. The microtask split the clip into five parts using prosodic pauses. Workers were then asked to transcribe each part individually. Similar crowdsourced approaches include Legion:Scribe [5], where different workers capture different parts of a clip in real-time.

Interruptions

In some conditions, we interrupted participants with distractor tasks as they worked. When interruptions occurred, they appeared eight times at random intervals, spaced roughly 10 seconds apart, without regard to where in the underlying task the participant was. The interruption task was modal; it blocked the interrupted task and had to be completed before that task could be resumed.

The interruption task required participants to add a pair of two-digit numbers and select an answer from a set of five possible choices. The choices were designed such that the incorrect options appeared similar to the correct answer. To stop participants from randomly selecting an answer, they were required to select the correct answer in order to continue. A pilot version that required participants to type their answer into a text box revealed similar results. Arithmetic tasks are commonly used in the literature to distract attention when studying interruptions [9, 1].

Experimental Design

The study followed a 3 (task type) $\times$ 2 (task format) $\times$ 2 (interruptions) design. The experiment was between-subjects with respect to task type and within-subjects with respect to task format and the presence of interruptions. Each participant was assigned a task type and completed four tasks of that type, performing the macro and micro versions, with and without interruptions. The order of these tasks was randomized. To familiarize participants with their assigned task type and the interruption task, participants initially completed a practice task with interruptions. After completing all trials, participants were asked if they preferred the macro- or microtask structure, and completed a NASA Task Load Index (TLX) assessment [3] to measure subjective mental workload. The entire process took under 30 minutes.

Measures

For each condition, we measured the total time it took to complete the task excluding the time spent on interruptions, and the average amount of time it took to complete each interruption task. To further control for external interruptions, we also tracked any loss of browser window focus during each task and excluded participants who left a task for more than ten seconds. We also measured the quality of work performed. For the receipt arithmetic task we measured the probability that the final answer was incorrect. For the sorting task, we measured the Kendall's tau distance of the submitted ranking from the correct one, and for audio transcription we measured the word error rate.

To calculate significance we used a linear mixed-effects model, with participant as a random effect. p-values were calculated using an F-test with a Kenward-Roger correction. A mixed-design ANOVA resulted in empirically similar results. Error bars in figures depict standard errors.

	Coef.	SE	df(num/den)	F	p-value
Task Time ($R^2 = 0.77$)					
(Arithmetic Macrotask)	55.2	11.8			0.00**
Task Type			2/181	59.8	0.00**
Sorting	29.7	17.6			0.00**
Transcription	134	16.2			0.00***
Microtask	18.9	9.30	1/377	13.3	0.00***
Interrupted	12.8	9.30	1/377	6.00	0.01*
Type × Micro			2/377	4.12	0.02*
Type × Interrupted			2/377	0.42	0.61
Microtask × Interrupted	-3.30	13.2	1/377	2.64	0.10^
Type × Micro × Interrupted			2/377	0.46	0.63
Task Error Rate ($R^2 = 0.37$)					
(Arithmetic Macrotask)	0.10	0.04			0.00**
Task Type			2/143	9.38	0.00**
Sorting	0.23	0.06			0.00**
Transcription	0.04	0.05			0.00***
Microtask	-0.05	0.05	1/377	15.3	0.00***
Interrupted	0.03	0.05	1/377	0.07	0.78
Type × Micro			2/377	0.79	0.46
Type × Interrupted			2/377	0.29	0.75
Micro × Interrupted	-0.02	0.06	1/377	0.01	0.93
Type × Micro × Interrupted			2/377	0.13	0.88

Table 1. A linear mixed-effects model for both task time and task error rate (^: p<0.1, *: p<0.05, **: p<0.01, ***: p<0.001). Some non-significant effects elided for space.

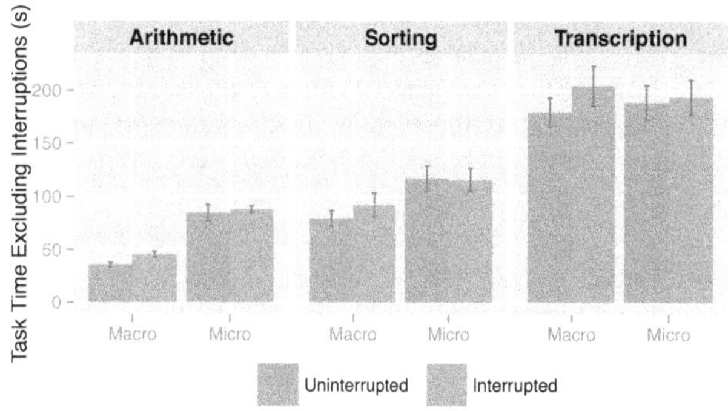

Figure 2. Microtasks incur a significant additional fixed cost. Interruptions cause an increase in task time for macrotasks but not microtasks.

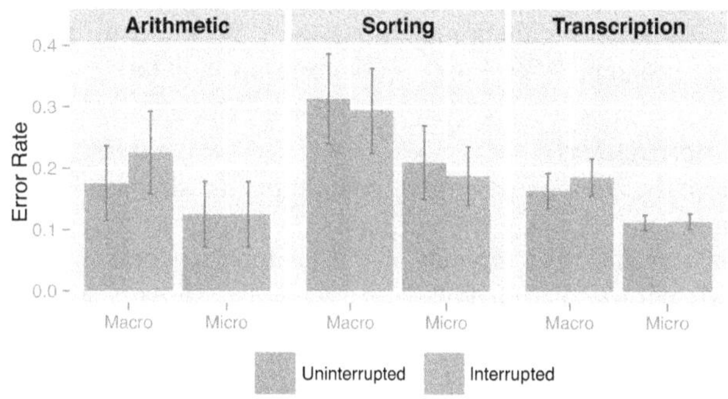

Figure 3. Microtasks significantly reduce task error rates for a task. The presence of interruptions does not impact task quality.

Participants

A total of 110 people participated in the experiment, with 42 in the arithmetic condition, 28 in the sorting condition, and 40 in the transcription condition. The experiment was conducted using an in-house microtasking platform that outsources crowd work to vendors, similar to CrowdFlower. We used the Clickworker vendor, with all participants from the United States. Empirically similar observations were obtained when testing each condition on Mechanical Turk. Participants were compensated $3.00 and repeat participation was disallowed.

RESULTS

Completing a task via microtasks took longer overall than completing it as a macrotask, but the microtask format led to fewer mistakes, an easier experience, and greater stability in the face of interruption. Table 1 shows the strength of the impact of task type, task format, and the presence of interruptions on task time (in seconds) and task error rate. The intercept corresponds to the arithmetic task in a macrotask format without interruptions.

Time

For the three task types that we studied, overall, completing the task via microtasks took longer than doing it as a macrotask (p<.001). For instance, the uninterrupted arithmetic task took approximately 42 seconds longer when broken down than whole (Figure 2). This was expected, as each task type requires some additional work when broken into microtasks to support the added structure (e.g., in the arithmetic task, participants enter many additional numbers to keep a running total in the microtask condition, but only a single number in the macrotask condition), and corroborates prior work showing that introducing breaks between microtasks increases overall completion time far beyond a continuous microtask workflow [6].

However, while arithmetic and sorting took significantly longer as microtasks, this was not the case for transcription. We hypothesize that users may have been implicitly breaking the transcription macrotask similarly to how the microtasks were structured (i.e. listening in parts): participants started, paused or stopped the audio a median of 5.3 times in the macrotask, but only 10.2 times in the microtask condition, where the minimum number of clicks is ten (to start and stop each of five segments).

Quality

The microtask structure produced higher quality work for all three task types, with participants making fewer errors when doing a task as a series of microtasks than as a macrotask (p<.001). The gray bars in Figure 3 represent the number of errors made for each task type in the uninterrupted condition. One explanation for this is that the additional work required to support the microtasks helped externalize some of the mental processing necessary to complete the tasks, which improved performance. In the case of transcription, splitting audio at shorter segments of about six seconds at prosodic pauses may have been be a good balance between keeping subtasks relatively short, while still maintaining adequate context.

In summary, with macrotasks, people can use any strategy they want, but these strategies vary in effectiveness, and tend to be faster but less accurate. With microtasks, the strategy is set and enforced by the system. If this strategy is similar to how a person would break the task down (e.g., transcription), task time is likely to be similar.

Preference

In addition to producing higher quality results, the microtask format also made each task type easier to complete. When asked to rank the task structure in terms of difficulty, an average of 77% of participants preferred the microtask format to the macrotask format ($p<.01$). Likewise, on the NASA TLX scale, the microtask format was consistently rated as easier than the macrotask format, with the microtask score being 6.2% lower for the arithmetic tasks, 9.2% lower for the sorting task, and 5.7% lower for the transcription task ($p<.01$).

Interruptions

Finally, we see a trend that completing a task via microtasks may be more robust to interruption than completing it as a macrotask. The amount of time it took to complete a task when it was broken down into microtasks was very similar regardless of whether the participant experienced interruptions or not (Figure 2). In contrast, in many cases it took longer to complete a task in the macrotask format when the task was interrupted than it was not. The weak significance of the "Format × Interruptions" interaction effect (Table 1) suggests that overall, interruptions may slow down task completion when a task is performed as a macrotask, but not as a series of microtasks ($p<.10$). Still, a separate analysis found that interruptions significantly slowed down the arithmetic macrotask ($t(41) = 3.67$, $p<.001$).

One possible explanation is that because task boundaries are clearly delineated for microtasks and the individual tasks themselves are short, participants regularly found themselves at a task boundary when interrupted using the microtask structure. While interruption costs can also be reduced by scheduling interruptions at subtask breakpoints [4] or using goal reminders [1], the inherent structure of microtasks results in more explicit breakpoints, making them more interruption-friendly than larger tasks. Across all conditions, the interruptions themselves took similar amounts of time to complete (μ=7.4s), and do not appear to impact the number of errors made. In both cases, we observe no significant differences.

CONCLUSION

We explored the impact of breaking macrotasks down into microtasks. For three common task types, we find it tended to take longer to perform a task using microtasks than macrotasks. However, the structured microtasks enabled participants to produce significantly higher quality work than they did using macrotasks, and participants found the microtasks easier to complete. Additionally, microtasks may be more robust to interruption, as there was some evidence that interruptions impacted the time it took participants to complete the macrotasks but not the microtasks. If differences exist even at this task size boundary, benefits may increase as the macrotask increases in size.

This paper presents a first step at studying the effect of task decomposition. Future work includes better understanding when this is beneficial. For example, while sorting seven lines of text is easier when done as a series of microtasks, this may not be the case for sorting only three lines where the content of each line can be held in short term memory. Additionally, many complex tasks do not have obvious structure that can be used to support microtasking. Cognitive modeling techniques (e.g., GOMS) may provide finer insight into how a particular task decomposition affects performance. Our findings suggests a future where microtasks could enable people to complete tasks in interruption-driven environments in a structured way that requires less cognitive effort, and in spare moments of time.

REFERENCES

1. Cutrell, E., Czerwinski, M., and Horvitz, E. Notification, disruption, and memory: Effects of messaging interruptions on memory and performance. In *INTERACT* (2001).
2. González, V. M., and Mark, G. Constant, constant, multi-tasking craziness: managing multiple working spheres. In *CHI* (2004).
3. Hart, S. G., and Staveland, L. E. Development of NASA-TLX (Task Load Index): Results of empirical and theoretical research. *Adv. Psychol.* (1988).
4. Iqbal, S. T., and Bailey, B. P. Effects of intelligent notification management on users and their tasks. In *CHI* (2008).
5. Lasecki, W., Miller, C., Sadilek, A., Abumoussa, A., Borrello, D., Kushalnagar, R., and Bigham, J. Real-time captioning by groups of non-experts. In *UIST* (2012).
6. Lasecki, W. S., Marcus, A., Rzeszotarski, J. M., and Bigham, J. P. Using microtask continuity to improve crowdsourcing. Tech. rep., 2014.
7. Little, G., Chilton, L. B., Goldman, M., and Miller, R. C. Turkit: human computation algorithms on mechanical turk. In *UIST* (2010).
8. Martin, D., Hanrahan, B. V., O'Neill, J., and Gupta, N. Being a turker. In *CSCW* (2014).
9. Sakai, K., Rowe, J. B., and Passingham, R. E. Parahippocampal reactivation signal at retrieval after interruption of rehearsal. *J. Neurosci.* (2002).
10. Teevan, J., Liebling, D., and Lasecki, W. Selfsourcing personal tasks. In *CHI* (2014).
11. Vaish, R., Wyngarden, K., Chen, J., Cheung, B., and Bernstein, M. Twitch crowdsourcing: Crowd contributions in short bursts of time. In *CHI* (2014).
12. Wickens, C. D. Multiple resources and performance prediction. *Theor. Issues. Ergon.* (2002).
13. Zacks, J. M., Tversky, B., and Iyer, G. Perceiving, remembering, and communicating structure in events. *J. Exp. Psychol. Gen.* (2001).

DIYbio *Things*: Open Source Biology Tools as Platforms for Hybrid Knowledge Production and Scientific Participation

Stacey Kuznetsov[1], Carrie Doonan[2], Nathan Wilson[2], Swarna Mohan[2], Scott E. Hudson[1], Eric Paulos[3]

Human-Computer Interaction Institute[1]
Carnegie Mellon University
Pittsburgh, PA, USA
{stace, hudson}@cmu.edu

Department of Biological Sciences
Carnegie Mellon University[2]
Pittsburgh, PA, USA
{cbd, njwilson, swm}@andrew.cmu.edu

Electrical Engineering and Computer Sciences[3]
University of California
Berkeley, CA, USA
paulos@berkeley.edu

ABSTRACT
DIYbio (Do It Yourself Biology) is a growing movement of scientists, hobbyists, artists, and tinkerers who practice biology outside of professional settings. In this paper, we present our work with several open source DIYbio tools, including OpenPCR and Pearl Blue Transilluminator, which can be used to test DNA samples for specific sequences. We frame these platforms as *things* that gather heterogeneous materials and concerns, and enable new forms of knowledge transfer. Working with these hybrid systems in professional and DIY settings, we conducted a workshop where non-biologists tested food products for genetic modifications. Our findings suggest new design directions at the intersection of biology, technology, and DIY: i) DIYbio platforms as rich tools for hybrid knowledge production; and ii) open source biology as a site for public engagement with science.

Author Keywords
DIYbio, publics, design things

ACM Classification Keywords
H.5.m. Information interfaces and presentation (e.g., HCI): Miscellaneous.

INTRODUCTION
The past decade has seen a shift from biology being treated as a natural science and towards domains within biology—*e.g.*, computational biology and synthetic biology—being framed as engineering fields. For instance, complex biological systems are being modeled *in silico* with modern computational platforms, while synthetic biology treats biological elements as engineered building blocks, enabling the design of new biological organisms. Alongside these advancements in professional research, new initiatives—from health advocacy groups to low-cost genetic testing services and biology hobbyist communities—involve members of the general public in various practices that interpret, critique, and construct scientific knowledge.

One way of orienting this space for HCI is in terms of *publics*—groups of people who come together around issues and work towards resolving shared concerns [5]. Within this larger framing, we focus on DIYbio (Do It Yourself Biology) as a movement that is concerned with enabling open access to biology [7]. Emerging publics of hobbyists, artists, and scientists explore this issue by experimenting, tinkering, and playing with biology outside of professional laboratories. These efforts innovate low-cost tools and materials for at-home experimentation, share expert and amateur knowledge, conduct public outreach events, or address biology problems such as genetic health testing, bio-fuels, or food production with DIY tools.

DIYbio things
DIYbio coalesces around diverse materials, methods, and people. Not unlike Latour's hybrid assemblies [8], which materialize heterogeneous ideas and relationships between human and non-human actors, DIYbio projects gather organic and digital components, expert and amateur knowledge, and public and professional concerns. This aligns DIYbio tools with *design things*: modifiable, active, and evolving artifacts, rather than the finished outcomes of professional science [1]. Framed in this way, *things* can produce new knowledge beyond their function, "opening to its users new possibilities of action and interaction" [1]. Within CHI literature, DiSalvo et al. discuss designing *things* to engage HCI with issues and support publics [6]. In this paper, we explore how DIYbio *things* materialize concerns regarding open access to biology and give rise to discourse around the future of biotechnology.

We present our work with several DIYbio platforms (Fig. 1): OpenPCR [9], an open source thermal cycler for replicating

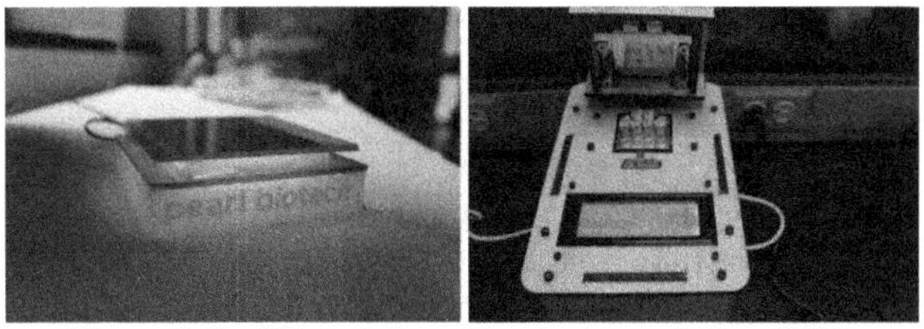

Figure 1. PealBiotech transilluminator and OpenPCR.

CHI 2015, April 18 - 23 2015, Seoul, Republic of Korea
Copyright 2015 ACM 978-1-4503-3145-6/15/04…$15.00
http://dx.doi.org/10.1145/2702123.2702539

specific strands of DNA (*e.g.*, genes); the Pearl Blue transilluminator [10], a tool for visualizing the results via gel electrophoresis; and the Dremelfuge, a 3D-printed attachment for a dremel, which serves as a centrifuge. We first studied these tools in a university biology laboratory and compared them against professional equipment. We then conducted a workshop whereby non-biologist participants used these tools, along with several other off-the-shelf kits and parts, to test food products for genetic modifications. With a framing of DIYbio platforms as *things*, our findings reveal that tools such as OpenPCR give rise to heterogeneous ideas, expertise, and concerns. We conclude by discussing how HCI research can re-envision open source biology tools as platforms for i) constructing hybrid knowledge, and ii) supporting public engagement with biology and other scientific domains.

RELATED WORK

DIY initiatives have been of great interest to the CHI community [3]. We see open source biology tools as parallel to the more widely-studied DIY platforms— Arduino, Raspberry Pi, PICAXE, or the dot.NET gadgeteer, which support hardware prototyping outside of professional settings. DIYbio tools such as OpenPCR enable non-experts to screen organic materials for genetic traits such as GMO's, diseases, or genealogy and can be seen as parallel to other citizen science sensors (e.g., air quality monitors). This DIYbio "sensing" is not unlike low cost monitoring of factors such as air quality [e.g., 14]. Similar to how current HCI systems allow crowdsourcing of ecological and environmental data collection [e.g., 13], low-cost biology tools can serve as platforms for collecting and analyzing biological data on a larger scale. Prior work has explored the intersection between DIY, computation, and biology through an earlier study of DIYbio initiatives [7], or the development of computational biology tools [12]. We contribute by examining how DIYbio tools can support community engagement with science from the bottom up.

EXTRACTING AND VISUALIZING DNA

PCR (Polymerase Chain Reaction) is a process that enables testing a DNA sample for a specific sequence or gene. The results of PCR can be visualized with gel electrophoresis, which applies a high voltage across a gel. This process separates DNA segments based on their size, which can in turn be visualized by staining and illuminating the gel.

OpenPCR and Pearl Biotech

While PCR is a well-known, 30-year-old established procedure, recent DIY innovations have made work with DNA more accessible outside of professional settings. OpenPCR is an open source, low-cost (600$) thermal cycle kit, which requires simple assembly before use. Arduino (a low-cost microcontroller) serves as its backbone, regulating a peltier heating/cooling element based on temperature data from a thermocouple sensor. OpenPCR can be programmed using a simple GUI interface on a Mac or PC. Likewise inspired by the open hardware movement, the Pearl Blue Transilluminator provides a safer and more affordable ($300) way to visualize electrophoresis results. The device relies on blue light transillumination and works with non-toxic SYBR safe DNA stains such as GelGreen. After electrophoresis, gel can be placed over the device, with DNA segments appearing as illuminated "bands". While lab-quality equipment for testing DNA (*e.g.,* centrifuges, PCR machines) can cost thousands of dollars, these open source tools are more accessible to the general public, especially if shared by DIY collectives.

TESTING FOOD FOR GENETIC MODIFICATIONS

Motivation

Our research aims to understand how open source biology tools might catalyze broader scientific participation as we envision near term consumer-level technologies for DNA testing. We chose GM food as an example use case for these platforms for several reasons. First, many off-the-shelf kits, primers, and protocols already exist for GMO analysis, making food testing more accessible than other types of tests. Second, the use of GMOs is a widely debated topic in the United States: the potential for GMOs to produce higher food yields and alleviate world hunger problems is often pitted against the drawbacks of heavier reliance on pesticides, un-anticipated mutations, or the risk of invasive species effecting local ecosystems.

Background and initial testing

Our work uses an off-the-shelf ($200) primer and reagent kit from Carolina Biological [4], which supports testing up to 24 samples for the CaMV 35S promoter, a sequence present in transgenic plants. In addition, this kit includes a control primer for tubulin, a gene present in all plant material. A positive PCR reaction for tubulin thus confirms that DNA was extracted correctly from the food product.

Prior to organizing the workshop, our interdisciplinary team of interaction designers and biologists tested the DIYbio tools and the GMO kit in a professional laboratory over the course of four months. We experimented with several DNA extraction protocols, PCR settings, and gel staining procedures and compared results from the DIYbio tools against output from professional biology equipment. Our final PCR reaction consists of 40 cycles: 94C 20 seconds; 54C 40 seconds; 72C 60 seconds. With these settings, we were able to accurately isolate the tubulin and 35S sequence from control genetically-modified corn leaves. A base pair ladder, which consists of known-size DNA sequences, was used to determine a best-fit equation for computing the size of PCR product based on the distance it travels through the gel. Our isolated tubulin and 35S PCR results were within 7 and 6 base pairs of the expected primer lengths, respectively, which is within the acceptable margin of error in biology research [2].

WORKSHOP WITH LOCAL DIY COMMUNITY

Working with a local DIY community, we organized a workshop whereby participants were invited to bring food products for genetic testing. The workshop was held at a local hackerspace, with 4 participants (1 female) completing the entire workshop from start to finish, and 4 others stopping by and participating in some of the steps throughout the day. In addition to the GMO testing kit and the DIYbio tools, we also provided an electrophoresis apparatus and micr pipettes from a laboratory.

Goals and methods

Our workshop goals were twofold. First, for the participants, the aim was to learn about available DIYbio tools and to determine whether their food items were genetically modified. Second, the researchers' goal was to understand the challenges and opportunities for public participation in biology. The workshop began with a brief overview of the steps involved in DNA extraction, PCR, and electrophoresis. Participants then extracted DNA from their food products, following our printed instructions and demonstrations. Participants were shown how to use the OpenPCR machine and load their samples. During the PCR reaction, which lasts about two hours, participants practiced loading samples into an electrophoresis gel, using food coloring for demonstration. Upon completion of the PCR, participants ran electrophoresis on their DNA samples. The gel was stained and visualized using the PearlBiotech transilluminator. An image of the gel and calculations of the PCR product size were emailed to participants.

Participants brought in a range of food samples for testing: an organic persimmon, organic pasta, chocolate, and cheese crackers. The electrophoresis results indicated that all participants successfully isolated DNA from their samples (based on the tubulin positive control reaction). The pasta, chocolate, and cheese cracker samples also turned out positive for the 35S promoter (GMO). The workshop was audio-recorded and photographed. Workshop audio was transcribed and coded to themes using an open coding scheme. This data, along with post-workshop feedback was used to synthesize three areas within our findings (below).

DIY making

Throughout the workshop, participants emphasized wanting to make all the tools involved in the protocols completely DIY. First and foremost, participants brainstormed ways to replicate the professional lab equipment we brought (gel box and pipettes) using off the shelf and cheaper components. For instance, participants discussed ways to create DIY pipettes by milling out fixed-volume indentations on a metal tray (5ul, 10ul, etc.) and then using an eyedropper to extract and apply these volumes. Likewise, participants discussed ways to build the electrophoresis apparatus from scratch using a laser cut casting tray or tupperware. Interestingly, participants also talked about reverse-engineering the DIYbio tools themselves. Having learned the steps of PCR, for instance, participants discussed how they could create an even cheaper and more transparent PCR machine using Arduino, thermocouple, computer fan, and heating elements.

Knowledge sharing

In addition to ideating new DIY tools, the workshop also led to many instances of knowledge and expertise sharing. Our workshop relied heavily on the expertise of and feedback from professional biologists. In addition to the text-based instructions that we provided for the protocols, and every step had to be demonstrated by the workshop organizers. Participants relied on demos from biologists to learn basic lab techniques such as pipetting, and to understand how to set up the PCR reactions and load their samples into the electrophoresis gel. In addition, participants also discussed and shared their own understanding of biology concepts, and researched information online during the workshop. For instance, it was not uncommon to hear participants discuss questions such as the difference between DNA and RNA, the base pairs and their role in the human genome, inherited traits, or the difference between mitochondrial and cell DNA.

Engaging with broader issues and concepts

Finally, our workshop resulted in discussions surrounding the broader scientific and socio-political issues related to genetic testing. Participants discussed a host of GMO-related topics, including the US legal system which enables patenting of certain genes, or Monsanto's monopoly on some types of corn and the effects of cross-pollination with organic farms. Several conversations also addressed the use of OpenPCR more broadly, such as, for instance, running genetic tests on human DNA, or speculating on DIYbio tools given the FDA's most recent regulation of 23andme.com, a public genetic testing service for diseases and ancestry. These and other examples show how the workshop and DIYbio tools were situated within broader contexts by participants.

DISCUSSION AND IMPLICATIONS

We began this paper by discussing DIYbio communities as *publics*: motivated by enabling open participation in biology, practitioners are making, experimenting, and Some of these efforts have effectively innovated low-cost tools that replicate the functionality of hard-to-access lab equipment. Returning to our initial framing of DIYbio platforms as *things*, our work offers several points of reflection for HCI. First, the tools themselves are assemblies of hybrid elements: electronics (e.g., the Arduino) interface with organic and chemical materials (e.g., DNA, primers), and the steps for testing DNA require organic, plastic, digital, and analog components. Hands-on work with these heterogeneous materials led participants to share and co-construct knowledge, as well as to reflect on the broader issues at the intersection between biology, technology, and DIY (e.g., government regulation of genetic testing). Finally, the DIY nature of the work inspired participants to ideate ways to modify the tools to support broader access and transparency. These findings reveal how DIYbio platforms are aligned with a view of *things* as artifacts that materialize relationships between human and non-human actors, and continue to evolve rather than being treated as finished products. For HCI, this suggests opportunities to re-envision DIYbio platforms as i) rich tools for expertise sharing; and ii) instruments for public engagement with science.

Rich tools for hybrid knowledge production

Our workshop participants relied on demos from professional biologists in addition to text-based descriptions, and inspired participants to research and share biology information independently. For HCI, this presents opportunities to apply tablets, phones, and PCs as education and outreach tools for disseminating biology knowledge. Going beyond text-based tutorials, these can capture the unique hands-on nature of wetlab biology work and appropriately fit into a lab or hackspace setting. For instance, within the context of extracting DNA, certain techniques such as pipetting, vortexing, or centrifuging could be presented on multi-touch tables, phones, or tablets. These tools can also be deployed in laboratories and hackspaces to collect data from biology experiments and share this information between professionals and amateurs.

More broadly, scaffolding tools can serve to connect hobbyists with professionals and enable new forms of mentorship and learning. For example, social media or crowdsourcing systems might be used to troubleshoot problems in biology protocols, optimize procedures, or make certain steps easier or safer. The design of systems that can be situated in and fluidly drawn upon in a (DIY) lab space presents new challenges and opportunities. How might technology be embedded in a laboratory setting and easily accessible and interacted with during biology work? How can new interaction techniques and data visualization methods be leveraged to foster productive collaborations between biologists and designers, as well as artists, hobbyists, tinkerers, and hackers?

DIYbio as a site for public engagement with science

With open access being a key concern for DIYbio, HCI systems can invite members of general public—beyond people already interested in GMOs and tinkering—to participate in biology projects. On one hand, new interactions and data visualizations can shift scientific machines (microscopes, PCR machines, etc.) from collecting data and towards also sharing information with larger audiences. At the very least, foregrounding interactions with tools in DIY and professional settings can demystify lab practices and involve a range of stakeholders in scientific discourse. Moreover, virtual and physical assemblies can support in-silico modeling and crowdsourced DNA analysis. Finally, as primer design still remains a challenge (for both professionals and amateurs), and new sharing and collaboration tools can be deployed to make this process easier for non-experts.

The challenges for HCI range from the practical considerations for fluidly attributing metadata (e.g., GPS, time or care instructions) to the information collected by distributed groups; to the mechanisms for sharing this information with stakeholders such as novice practitioners, policy makers, or the wider public; and the higher-level implications of mediating dialogues across these groups. This presents opportunities to rethink hardware platforms (e.g., microscopes) as instruments of public debate, and in turn re-envision modes of science making across DIY and professional labs.

CONCLUSION

In this paper, we presented our work with several DIYbio tools and protocols. We frame these platforms as *things* that coalesce hybrid materials, knowledge, and concerns. Aligned with this framing, our workshop shows how involvement with these tools supports ideation, expertise sharing, and engagement with broader biotechnology issues. Our findings suggest DIYbio tools as platforms for hybrid knowledge production and public engagement with science, in and outside of biology domains.

ACKNOWLEDGEMENTS

This work was supported by NSF IIS-1211047.

REFERENCES

1. Binder, T., De Michelis, G., Ehn, P., Jacucci, G., Linde, P., Wagner, I. Design Things, MIT Press, Cambridge, MA, 2012.
2. Brandner, D. L. 2002. PCR-Based detection of genetically modified foods. Pages 69-84, in Tested studies for laboratory teaching, Volume 23 (M. A. O'Donnell, Ed.), ABLE.
3. Buechley, L., Rosner, D. K., Paulos, E., Williams, A. DIY for CHI: methods, communities, and values of reuse and customization, CHI '09, 4823-4826.
4. Carolina Biological Supply. http://www.carolina.com
5. Dewey, J. The Public and Its Problems. NY: Holt, 1927.
6. DiSalvo, C., Lukens, J., Lodato, T., Jenkins, T., Kim, T. 2014. Making public things: how HCI design can express matters of concern. CHI '14, 2397-2406.
7. Kuznetsov, S., Taylor, A. S., Regan, T., Villar, N., Paulos, E. 2012. At the seams: DIYbio and opportunities for HCI. DIS'12, 258-267.
8. Latour, B. and Weibel, P. (eds.) Making Things Public: Atmospheres of Democracy, MIT Press, 2005.
9. OpenPCR. http://openpcr.org
10. Pearl Biotech Blue Transilluminator. http://pearlbiotech.org
11. Shaer, O., Mazalek, A., Ullmer, B., Konkel, M. 2013. From big data to insights: opportunities and challenges for TEI in genomics. TEI '13, 109-116.
12. Taylor, A. S., Piterman, N., Ishtiaq, S., Fisher, J., Cook, B., Cockerton, C., Bourton, S., Benque. D. 2013. At the interface of biology and computation. SIGCHI, 493-502.
13. Wiggins, A. 2011. eBirding: technology adoption and the transformation of leisure into science. In Proceedings of iConference '11. ACM, NY, 798-799.
14. Willett, W., Aoki, P., Kumar, N., Subramanian, S., Woodruff, A. 2010. Common sense community: scaffolding mobile sensing and analysis for novice users. Pervasive'10, 301-318

Designing for Citizen Data Analysis: A Cross-Sectional Case Study of a Multi-Domain Citizen Science Platform

Ramine Tinati
University of Southampton
r.tinati@soton.ac.uk

Max Van Kleek
University of Southampton
emax@soton.ac.uk

Elena Simperl
University of Southampton
e.simperl@soton.ac.uk

Markus Luczak-Roesch
University of Southampton
M.Luczak-Rosch@soton.ac.uk

Robert Simpson
University of Oxford
rob.simpson@ox.ac.uk

Nigel Shadbolt
University of Southampton
nrs@soton.ac.uk

ABSTRACT
Designing an effective and sustainable citizen science (CS) project requires consideration of a great number of factors. This makes the overall process unpredictable, even when a sound, user-centred design approach is followed by an experienced team of UX designers. Moreover, when such systems are deployed, the complexity of the resulting interactions challenges any attempt to generalisation from retrospective analysis. In this paper, we present a case study of the largest single platform of citizen driven data analysis projects to date, the Zooniverse. By eliciting, through structured reflection, experiences of core members of its design team, our grounded analysis yielded four sets of themes, focusing on *Task Specificity*, *Community Development*, *Task Design* and *Public Relations and Engagement*. For each, we propose a set of design claims (DCs), drawing comparisons to the literature on crowdsourcing and online communities to contextualise our findings.

Author Keywords
Citizen science, crowdsourcing, online communities

ACM Classification Keywords
H.5.m. Information Interfaces and Presentation (e.g. HCI): Miscellaneous

INTRODUCTION
Online citizen science (CS) has proven to be not only a practical and effective means of solving previously infeasible, large-scale scientific problems, but also a valuable education tool [46], and, for the scientifically curious, an entertaining, and sometimes addictive, past-time [42]. While we can find exemplars of such systems in many shapes and forms, those that have seen the greatest success have excelled at (at least) two things: first, they managed to accomplish the particular set of scientific objectives sought, and, second, they were able to attract and sustain the interest and support of a critical mass of volunteers over time.

CHI 2015, April 18–23, 2015, Seoul, Republic of Korea.

http://dx.doi.org/10.1145/2702123.2702420

Jointly achieving these two goals is a difficult task. The design of a CS project requires consideration of a great number of factors. This makes the overall process unpredictable, even when a sound, user-centred design approach is followed by an experienced team of UX designers. As a result, it poses significant barriers towards establishing CS as a valid and widely accepted scientific methodology, as smaller research groups appreciative of the CS concept cannot be expected to have the expertise and resources that are essential for a purposeful design and user engagement strategy.

This situation is due to the novelty of the field as well as the challenges associated with recruiting a volunteer participant population. Most citizen science projects rely on contributions primarily driven by intrinsic motivations [42, 49]. Their design has to reflect the values of the community of amateur scientists supporting them, and, in the same time, to enable effective problem solving through the crowd. Even if we consider the large body of literature that offers advice and experience reports in building online communities and similar systems [29, 25], many of the issues, including the feasibility of the tasks to be accomplished, the skills they require, or the process used to launch and advertise the project, are unique to the context of citizen science [7, 10]. The aim of this paper is to come up with a set of design guidelines by which this high-dimensional design space can be better understood.

To do so, we studied the largest single platform of CS projects to date, the Zooniverse. Through a process of structured reflection, we elicited insights and experienced deemed most important from core members of its design team. Our grounded analysis of these experiences yielded four sets of themes, comprising *Task-Community Integration*, *Community*, *Task Design* and *Public Relations and Engagement*, supported by two-to-four specific design claims each. Based on these findings, we synthesised a set of design recommendations, drawing comparisons to literature on crowdsourcing and online communities to gain a better understanding and inform the development of future systems in this space.

BACKGROUND AND RELATED WORK
We consider two perspectives on CS initiatives: a crowdsourcing perspective that views CS as large-scale volunteer-driven human computation systems, and an online communities perspective, that considers the social and other communication activity that supports CS work around the tasks.

Citizen Science

Unlike in traditional scientific collaboration, citizen science is characterised by a majority (or significant constituency) of participants engaging with a scientific investigation on 'an avocational basis' [17]. Online citizen science systems, in which participants engage in scientific activities through the Web, have typically enlisted the help of participants with three kinds of activities: data collection/curation (e.g., [55]); data analysis (e.g. [52, 15]); and problem-solving (e.g., [21, 8]). The Zooniverse platform [12] fits the second category; small professional science teams, who provide the raw digital artefacts for each project, such as images, video and audio recordings, light curves, and other data representations, are supported by vast numbers of members of the general public who voluntarily identify, classify, and label the data according to instructions and loose direction provided by the science teams.

Previous work has studied a variety of different aspects of CS systems. Analysis of the factors that most influence accuracy and completion of tasks, as well as methods for improving such performance such as through refined task selection have been studied [7, 20], as well as task scheduling heuristics [21]. Wiggens et al. [53] analysed CS projects as online communities and modelled CS community organisation through the relationship between volunteering, digital technologies, and workplaces. Other studies have sought to understand the core motivations of citizen scientists (e.g. [41, 43]), while others have focused on documenting the increasingly common citizen-initiated serendipitous scientific discoveries [45]. Such studies often reference the vast psychology and social psychology literature relating to human motivation to provide a theoretical grounding for continued engagement with CS systems [11].

Online Communities

Online communities studies include the analysis of how members cooperate, compete, and form and re-form groups (e.g., [1]), to how information is shared within and across groups [26], to how characteristics of communities change over time [28]. Others have looked at, to name a few, question-answering communities such as Yahoo! Answers [13], knowledge sharing on expert sites such as Stack Overflow [50], Wikipedia [22], MOOCs [35], MUDs [3] and MMOs [47]. There are also several studies which have identified how the characteristics of an online community during the early stages of its formation can indicate its future growth and stability [18, 2].

The core of this paper derives inspiration from Kraut, Resnick et al.'s *Building Successful Online Communities* [25], which addresses the idea of *designing from evidence*, providing a synthesis of relevant theory pertaining to the understanding of communities, alongside methods for translating such theory into design practice. We have structured our main results as *Design Claims* about citizen science platforms to facilitate comparison with their more general counterparts in their volume.

THE ZOONIVERSE PLATFORM

The Zooniverse is a web-based platform that hosts many citizen science projects. The first Zooniverse project, *Galaxy Zoo*, was launched July 2007 and invited volunteers to participate in the morphological classification of images of galaxies [31, 12]. The early success of Galaxy Zoo led the Zooniverse team to branch out to new domains and task types. Table 1 lists all Zooniverse projects order by their launch date, and indicates their status, subjects processed, and domain. As of August 2014, Zooniverse has gained over one million active volunteers. *Retired* projects have achieved their classification goals and are now closed. *Active* projects are those still open for new contributions.

Project	Launch	Domain	Users	Subjects	Task
Galaxy Zoo*	07-07	S	165,000	890,000	C
Galaxy Zoo* 2	02-09	S	223,965	304,122	C
GZ Mergers*	11-09	S	20,588	58,956	C
Solar Stormwatch	02-10	S	65,971	N/A	C/M
GZ Supernova*	03-10	S	37,150	76,376	C
GZ Hubble*	04-10	S	2,735	200,000	C
Moon Zoo	05-10	S	121,251	435,314	M
Old Weather	10-10	C	32,076	1,090,745	T
Milky Way	12-10	S	66,495	109,459	M
Planet Hunters	12-10	S	167,354	3,063,759	M
Ancient Lives	07-11	H	24,983	153,885	T
Ice Hunters*	08-11	S	15,276	6,300,518	C/M
NEEMO*	10-11	S	485	N/A	C
Whale FM	11-11	N	2,150	15,531	C
SETI Live*	02-12	S	63,609	27,004	C
Galaxy Zoo 4	09-12	S	85,758	365,193	C
Seafloor Explorer	09-12	N	21,112	123,077	M
Cyclone Center	09-12	C	7,210	84,231	C
Bat Detective	10-12	N	2,500	491,221	C
Cell Slider	10-12	B	19,368	275,702	C
Andromeda Project*	12-12	S	10,547	20,106	M
Snapshot Serengeti	12-12	N	31,559	1,545,399	C
Planet Four	01-13	S	43,975	59,442	M
Notes from Nature	04-13	N	6,090	188,551	M/T
Space Warps*	05-13	S	27,514	479,469	M
Worm Watch Lab	06-13	B	6,425	74,016	C
Plankton Portal	09-13	N	5,227	338,060	C/M
Radio Galaxy Zoo	12-13	S	5,044	174,821	C/M
Operation War Diary	01-14	H	10,528	94,656	M/T
Disk Detective	01-14	S	5,252	278,121	C
Condor Watch	04-14	N	3,059	264,066	M
Sunspotter	06-14	S	3,067	210,793	C
Asteroid Zoo	06-14	S	5,332	90,000	M
Floating Forests	08-14	N	1,924	778,506	M
Chicago Wildlife Watch	09-14	N	81	4,052	C
Penguin Watch**	09-14	N	–	178,061	C/M
Higgs Hunters**	10-14	P	–	80,445	C/M

Table 1. Summary of Zooniverse projects past and present, including each project's status as of September 2014. Domains: S – space; C – climate; H – humanities; N – nature; B – biology; P – physics. Tasks: C – classifying; M – marking; T – transcribing. Projects marked with a * have been retired; ** indicates a project that had not launched at time of writing; in more recent projects where participation is possible without logging in this is a lower bound to the total participation rate.

METHODOLOGY AND ANALYTICAL FRAMEWORK

Since our goal of identifying the critical decisions, supporting rationale, key internal, external and other factors that most influenced the development of the Zooniverse platform over its first 5 years potentially involved many project-related sources, as well as insights from those who were involved in its creation, we adopted a structured reflection [16] approach to our investigation, with two foundational members of the Zooniverse team. These individuals were selected because they were responsible for nearly all decisions at the beginning of the project, and remained highly integral throughout. These reflection sessions took place over two days; audio was recorded during the sessions, and later transcribed and annotated. During these sessions, we encouraged the individuals to draw upon their own notes, meetings, design decisions, and internal communication records in order to translate their actions into a systematic order, providing the analysis with the required information to bridge the theory-practice gap [4]. During each session, we asked clarification questions in order to connect recollections and thoughts with documents where possible.

The transcripts then underwent a thematic coding processes to elicit the core topics discussed. Based upon a grounded theory approach [34], the coding process was conducted by three members of our research team. Each member initially coded the transcripts individually and their list of codes were then compared, discussed, and adjusted until consensus was reached. In addition to the interview data, we were granted access to several core project data repositories prior to the aforementioned sessions, including discussion boards for four Zooniverse projects, *Talk* pages for 14 projects, as well as 26 Zooniverse-related blogs. These data represented a snapshot of the entire Zooniverse system from September 2013, encompassing 250,044 Zooniverse users, 50,995,591 completed tasks, and 650,243 Talk pages. Such artefacts were used primarily to derive a high-level summary of the project's evolution, and to identify evidence that might support or contradict the design claims derived from the coding process.

Analytical Framework

We derived our framework from Kraut, Resnik et al. [25] study of online communities. Our design claims (DCs) were mapped, through a thematic coding process, to a set of emergent topics which we organised into different categories based on their content and context (e.g., community structure, external communications, task design). Some of our findings overlap with Kraut's existing guidelines, while, the rest, which we designate as "New" below in results, are new observations specific to CS communities.

RESULTS: KEY THEMES AND DESIGN CLAIMS

We present our analysis based on the structured reflection and the thematically coded interviews. In collaboration with the Zooniverse team, we have organised design claims around four themes corresponding to *Task Specificity*, *Community Development*, *Task Design* and *Public Relations and Engagement*. The choice of these themes pertained to the corresponding discussions and examples provided by the interviewees regarding (user) activity in a system, problems identified during system deployment, the solutions they adopted, or a behaviour that was unique to a system. Table 2 summarises the themes and Design Claims assigned to each.

Theme 1: Task Specificity

DC1: a) Citizen science participants want and need the ability to discuss aspects of projects and tasks. b) Standard message boards work well for small online citizen science communities, but do not scale well as communities grow; c) Lack of integration between discussion and task interfaces impedes communication and wastes community effort. During the launch of the first Zooniverse project in July 2007, there was no discussion space to accompany Galaxy Zoo. A groundswell of volunteers requested a forum, and so the researchers set up a standard, open-source, PHP Simple Machines Forum (SMF) in the early days of the project. PHP SMFs became the standard discussion tool for the first Zooniverse projects (Galaxy Zoo 2, Solar Stormwatch, Moon Zoo, and Old Weather) and provided a space for peer question-answering support, serendipitous collaboration, and social community building and sharing. The forums were low-cost to deploy, and low buy-in for new users, given the popularity of the forum interface in 2007.

As the forums expanded, it became clear that aspects of the PHP SMF design impeded their effective use for Zooniverse discussion. The linear, message-board format became difficult to navigate as the size of these forums grew. Moderators struggled to keep boards thematically consistent, with threads often ending up in different boards, duplicated, or with blended themes. Such problems, including fragmentation and duplicity mirror those well-known in many other large, online threaded discussion boards (e.g., [37]), and posed a serious challenge as some Galaxy Zoo boards expanded to over 5000 threads, collectively comprising over 650,000 posts. After several of the serendipitous discoveries were made, other problems such as the lack of integration between the forums and tasks became apparent. By early 2010, less than 10% of users were active in both classification and discussion.

In response, in August 2010 the Zooniverse team developed a bespoke forum, *Talk*, which contained object-specific discussion boards, in addition to more typical forum structure. Talk's purpose was to promote Zooniverse discussion. As described by a member of the Zooniverse team, the initial stage of combining the forums with the task aimed to make it straightforward for a individual to enter a discussion relating to a particular subject or topic. The second goal, was to make discussions a part of the task workflow, by making discussions around the relevant subject salient during a tasks, making it possible to initiate new discussions in-situ within the task interface [38]. Talk was integrated into the workflow process of new Zooniverse projects (starting with the Milky Way Project in December 2010); in September 2012, 40% of users were active in both classification and discussion. The same figure held true in June 2014.

In August 2014, the original Galaxy Zoo forum was retired, and turned into a read-only archive. This was done at the request of the Galaxy Zoo forum participants who wanted to migrate to Talk, where more discussion was happening. Among those requesting the forums be retired were several of the original members who requested the original forum in 2007, and who helped to moderate and keep it alive.

DC2 (New): Task workflows which encourage discussion facilitate citizen-led discovery. Whilst the primary goal of a citizen science project is to complete the task within the pre-defined workflow, the Zooniverse experienced a number exciting *citizen-led discoveries* as a consequence of users going beyond the requirements of the task and asking questions about unusual objects within an observation. Originally, the workflow of a Zooniverse project contained a series of tasks selected by the science team, which were devised to investigate a preselected set of problems. This workflow, the conventional path of most human computation systems, successfully yielded a majority of the findings for Zooniverse. However, the addition of discussion facilities opened a second pathway, which became apparent under a month after the Galaxy Zoo Forum first launched. By providing users with the tools to communicate, a user-driven process led to the discovery of a peculiarity object known as "Hanny's Voorwerp" [32]. This would ultimately mark the project's first citizen-initiated discovery.

The research following the discovery of the *Voorwerp* unfolded as it did because, being a rare astrophysical body quite unlike others, the science team quickly noticed it. In this case, citizen contributions were limited due to lack of access to other data sources, or telescopes for further follow-up or expertise. Moreover, being such an unusual form, most amateur scientists had never seen anything like it, and to validate the finding, the science team cross-referenced databases and tools that volunteers didn't have access to, running their own analyses before eventually applying for and scheduling time on telescopes with colleagues to gather more data.

In contrast, other serendipitous discoveries have been made due to the self-organised effort of volunteers. The Galaxy Zoo *Green Peas* [5, 6] discovery emerged because, whilst not common, pea galaxies were seen regularly enough that they were recognised by other citizens, which sparked a "pea hunt" amongst the self-titled "pea corps". According to a science team member, the discovery was initially overlooked as the science team were busy processing data being generated through the "main path", but also partially because it was believed the greenish appearance of the peas was merely artefactual of the imaging apparatus, as "green glitches" were quite common in the images.

Group-search based discoveries have been successful as well. On Old Weather, for example, a mass-tagging campaign took place to tally the number of men who were in sick bay on board the various ships. When huge spikes were seen in sick bay stays, this resulted in an independent rediscovery of the 1918 Spanish Flu. Similarly, a new type of emerging star-forming region was identified by volunteers on the Milky Way Project when citizens self-organised to seek "yellow balls" seen in the data. The discovery of a circumbinary planet on Planet Hunters [45] stands out from the rest in that the citizens derived their own astronomical models, generated from light curves autonomously without science team intervention. This example highlighted to the Zooniverse and its science teams that citizen volunteers could be true collaborators, and that citizen science systems served another important purpose, which was to bring users with varied capacities together around common problems of interest, across traditional organisational, national, and cultural boundaries.

In several of the examples (Voorwerp, yellow balls etc.), the initiating user simply asked for help in identifying an unknown object they saw. With the Peas discovery, meanwhile, the intention at the beginning was primarily social, commenting that she found things that "looked like peas". In the circumbinary planet findings, by comparison, the citizens already had a hypothesis about what they had found, and had conducted a partial analysis prior to first posting. Each of the citizen-led discoveries exhibit several underlying differences among the situations, yet they were shaped by a common constraint; immediate access to scientific expertise when progress stalls or problems arise, a problem that the Zooniverse overcame with the social mechanisms described in the next section.

Theme 2: Community Development

DC3: (a) Granting roles and privileges with experience can motivate contributors to effectively assume community leadership and maintenance roles. (b) Volunteer moderators can effectively filter issues requiring the science team's attention. Given that the science team responsible for a Zooniverse project are limited in resources, establishing a community which functions semi-autonomously and even supports the science team in running the project can be highly beneficial. Across all Zooniverse projects analysed, the volume of posts and threads on the discussion forums (usually over 300 posts per day) meant that it was not feasible for the scientists to monitor all discussions in order support all possible serendipitous leads. To overcome this, certain members of the community were promoted to a *Moderator* status, whose role was to filter and signal potential findings to the science team. However, in all four of the citizen-led discovery examples, at different stages of the process, the moderators lacked the necessary knowledge to answer the questions of their peers. However, when this situation occurred, the moderators were able to notify or consult the science team for their help.

DC4 (New): Timely support from science team members is essential to enable citizen-led discovery. Based on their experiences with a number of citizen-led discoveries, the Zooniverse team came to the conclusion that the amount of effort that needs to be invested in supporting the community is relative to the rate at which progress occurs. Although moderators are helpful, the science team is still required to intervene when progress stalls or when unexpected issues arise in the line of scientific enquiry. They are also indispensable as discoveries eventually run their course and the only thing left to do is publish a result - something the public are not comfortable with at present.

The degree to which the science teams are involved in the discovery process varied amongst the examples provided. For the Voorwerp discovery, the science team took over the investigation shortly after the citizen pointed it out. In the other examples, however, there was more autonomous action by citizens; in the Peas case, for example, citizens self-organised a collection of samples before the science team took significant interest in their findings [6]. Alternatively, in the case of the convict worm, the science team intervened early and then immediately solicited to identify similar subjects. This was done because the science team did not know whether this was a one-off worm or common enough to constitute a distinct species. Finally, with the circumbinary planet discovery, the users conducted an entire hypothesis validation process, consisting of modelling and light curve analysis, using their own sets of tools.

Theme 3: Task Design

***DC5 (New): Designing tasks to encourage* best guesses *avoids the* don't know *effort trap*.** One common request that the team intentionally did not honour was to add a *I don't know* or "Skip to next" button in task interfaces. The omission of such a button was a deliberate design decision based on early testing, which demonstrated that (as explained in a blog post [24]) the presence of such a button discouraged participants from attempting a *best guess* to the more challenging exercises. When present, it was too easy for participants just to press the button to see more subjects, essentially providing a motivation loophole that allowed the reward of access to new subjects without doing any work. Such a loophole reduced a major source of motivation, which was gaining access to previously unseen subjects. Not having a button, meanwhile, encouraged users to consider difficult cases and to submit a best guess. Such "best guesses" were ultimately useful to the science team, because they could be checked with other participants' best guesses, which would not have been captured without them. (In lieu of a "Don't know" button, the team added a "Discuss this" prompt, which allowed people to post about and discuss more difficult cases, further improving the likelihood of their disambiguation.)

DC6 (New): Multiple factors influence the perceptions of a project, including memorability/interestingness of subjects, task difficulty, speed, and amount of feedback provided. The analysis of the user growth per project found that not all projects gained immediate uptake, and some were vastly more successful at securing long-term participation than others. As the team sought to identify the factors that influenced participants' perceptions the most through all the Zooniverse projects launched, several themes emerged. These were, first, the *interesting-ness of subject, speed and difficulty of task*, and related to these two, the *frequency and form of implicit reward*. Other factors, such as type of task, domain of origin, worthiness of cause (e.g., cancer research or deep space research), and source of data, did not generate conclusive findings. (One additional factor that emerged was media type - image-orientated tasks were much more likely to sustain participation than audio tasks.)

The first factor, *interestingness*, pertains to how likely the subjects being classified would be likely to be perceived to the general populace as interesting, or have aesthetic or emotional value, such as "beautiful and mysterious" photos of deep space, or the "cute" candid photos of animals of *Snapshot Serengeti*. This interestingness metric was also affected by *how often* interesting subjects came up amidst tasks with less interesting ones; specifically, some projects which sought to identify rare interesting objects which were only likely to come up once in a hundred or thousand subjects were perceived as less interesting than projects that had at least somewhat interesting subjects on every task.

Such insights led the Zooniverse team to re-design some of the tasks to avoid long stretches of monotonous subjects, that might influence participants to get bored and leave. To do so, for such rare-object search tasks, the team interspersed subjects in which objects were found by other users into the task queues of those who had not encountered such an interesting subject in a while. In *Worm Watch Lab*, for example, an algorithm was devised that would take subjects that were classified by at least one user to contain egg-laying events, and scheduled these into the queues of users who had not witnessed egg-laying events in their most recent classifications.

However, even monotonous sequences of subjects sustained participation if they could be performed quickly. The team's interpretation of this result was twofold, first, that with quick tasks it was easy to gain an accrued sense of accomplishment, and such a feeling could be sustained with less effort. This factor was used to explain the high levels of participation in projects such as *Ice Hunters* and *Moon Zoo*, which had long sequences of extremely similar-looking subjects, that, although monotonous, could be completed quickly. The second interpretation was that since such tasks were conceptually simple, they offered a lower barrier of engagement, which encouraged more casual participation [27], both from new and existing players.

***DC7 (New): Avoiding upfront tutorials in lieu of in-task UI guidance and interposed instructional tasks improves participant experience*.** In a majority of the Zooniverse projects, effective task completion required some degree of specialised knowledge about a particular scientific domain. For example, Space Warps required the identification of rare celestial phenomena called *gravitational lenses*, while Snapshot Serengeti involved spotting and classifying animals particular to the Serengeti. New users to citizen science platforms were by and large unlikely to have the expertise necessary to complete such tasks a priori [39]. A simple approach to solving this problem, and one that was initially taken in Zooniverse, was to provide an instructional video for new participants. However, adding such a video meant postponing actual task, and consuming valuable minutes of participants' attention that might potentially be better put to use if such tutorials could be avoided.

In particular, project analytics revealed that a significant proportion of users left within 90 seconds of first visiting the site, and a video tutorial would likely consume a significant portion if not the entirety of such a duration. Two strategies were devised in response to this need; the first was to re-design task interfaces to reduce the need for tutorials, by increasing *in situ* guidance. An example of this was the Snapshot Serengeti interface, which guided participants through a graphical decision-tree process to narrow down the species by identifying specific characteristics, such as the presence and kind of antlers/horns, size, colour and shape. However, a selection process of this nature would slow down experienced users who might immediately identify an animal they had seen before, the team introduced a second interaction path, a visual matrix designed to allow direct selection for expert participants.

In addition to guided task interfaces, a second approach was to make tutorials short, interactive, and "feel" like real tasks. The benefit of doing this would be that participants would feel like they were contributing immediately, making them likely to stay longer. A particular variation that was adopted was one the interspersing of real tasks with gold standard tutorial tasks, an approach proposed in the crowdsourcing community [40]. The Zooniverse team found that this strategy was particularly appropriate for bringing new participants into tasks involving rare object searches, that is, in which participants would likely have to sift through a large number of subjects prior to encountering the sought phenomena, such as the aforementioned gravitational lenses in Space Warps. In such tasks, interspersing gold standard true positives at a much higher hit rate than random helped not only teach individuals but also to keep them motivated to look for more.

DC8 (New): Periodic feedback can motivate continued participation. The Zooniverse team found that interspersing diagnostic "gold standard" tasks periodically among the real tasks, to provide participants feedback about their performance, caused an increase in sustained participation. This complements earlier studies showing that participants' performance may increase, e.g., that participants will be more accurate and faster at completing tasks with such feedback [23]. Introducing "gold standard" tutorial tasks on several projects, including Galaxy Zoo, Planet Hunters, the Andromeda Project, and Space Warps also enabled first-time users to jump immediately into real tasks, even with no prior experience. The overwhelmingly large proportion of such users was reflected in the fact that an estimated 6,620,423 (or 15%) of the total task classifications came from such transient users who never ultimately signed up.

DC9 (New): Adding context to a task adds value and improves community engagement. Providing contextual information about tasks and subjects were often seen to benefit participant engagement at multiple levels, often in unexpected ways. In the Old Weather project, the primary goal was to transcribe sea captains' meteorological readings of 19th and 20th century, to build long-term models of ocean climate. However, many of the ship logbook pages also included other information about minor events on ships, such as crew and cargo movements, ship damage, and so on, as well as the occasional draft personal letter from a sailor on the ship. Initially, the team intended to remove this irrelevant information; however, due to the difficulty in doing so (being a task suitable for human-computation work in itself), it was decided to simply leave it in. This additional info intrigued many participants, who saw them as clues to a partially-obscured history. Discussions quickly grew on the forums about the significance of particular letters and activities on the ship, and participation in the project increased substantially. Participants exchanged thoughts on who the recipients of the letters may have been, the meanings of particular terminology, and gathered the histories of ships and crew members, drawing upon diverse information sources in their investigation.

While this kind of participation may have not directly benefited the project's objectives, it drove significant attention to the subjects, and managed to patch together several significant events in history from the perspective of ship logs, which may ultimately be of use to historians. The design of the Old Weather interface fostered this growth in several ways; first, an early decision to organise ship logs by ship, route, and date allowed users to reference logs by the same date, crew and route. By comparison, most other projects displayed subjects randomly based on classification need. Thus, preserving the context and provenance of information was seen to be effective towards engaging interest from a wide and varied participant community.

Theme 4: Public Relations and Engagement

Strategies for publicising and gathering attention to citizen science projects across media channels, including traditional broadcast media, is often overlooked in smaller citizen science projects. However, the Zooniverse team found that, perhaps unsurprisingly, such a PR strategy was rather essential to driving substantial uptake. Cross-media PR played multiple roles, including bootstrapping fresh projects with a wider demographic than "digital natives" who are active on social media, but also to get users back who had been previously active and forgotten about the platform. The following design claims summarise PR and attention, and discusses the role of the first 24-hours after launch (project launch profiles) in determining and assessing success.

DC10 (New): Launch performance indicative of success; pre-launch PR important for recruiting new members and old. Performance during the launch of each Zooniverse project served a valuable indicator of its likely future success, as well as an opportunity to reflect on and assess the project's pre-launch PR activities. The team build up launch profiles by measuring, per project, the number of active and new participants per minute, identifying, where possible, how each new participant had heard about the project, average time spent on the site, discussion volume, and volume of social media. These metrics were monitored continuously over the first 24 hour period, and for the following month. Using such analysis, the team were able to effectively compare project launches, build models to predict short-term outcomes, and create strategies they called *launch campaigns*.

Successful launch campaigns included Snapshot Serengeti and Space Warps, which each experienced over 80,000 users during their respective first 24-hour "launch days". The Space Warps project experienced a initial surge of participants from other projects, in May 2013, with 10,000 people collectively contributing approximately 500,000 classifications in the its first 24-hour period. Participation in Space Warps continued beyond the immediate launch period, with more than 10,000 people unique visitors daily even three weeks later, a majority of whom were seasoned "Zooites". In January 2014, Space Warps was featured as part of BBC One's prime-time "Stargazing Live" event and at its peak received 1,000,000 classifications in just an hour. The experience rendered the Zooniverse platform in-operational for about 3 minutes, as tens of thousands of existing Zooniverse users simultaneous attempted to reset their Zooniverse account password. Analysis revealed that a majority of the surge of participants consisted of existing Zooniverse users, who had learned of the new project via the launch announcement newsletters. Such observations led to an effort to synthesise effective "launch campaigns" that would both publicise new projects and time them in a way to gather the greatest number of initial users.

Coverage from traditional media outlets and online media aided the launch and growth of these projects. This included international media networks such as the BBC (on *The Sky At Night* and *Click*), widely-read scientific magazines including regular coverage in the "Citizen Science"' column of *Scientific American*, and featured articles in *National Geographic*. Such coverage regularly resulted in traffic spikes and influxes of new large numbers of new users, some of whom will continue to participate for weeks or months. In Snapshot Serengeti, the science team submitted 12 images to the BBC's *Camera-trap Photo of the Year* competition, based upon recommendations by users. This not only raised the profile of the project, but also had a positive effect on the active number of users, and the discussion activity within the forums.

DC11 (New): Citizen science communities are the most effective at leading their own social media campaigns. Early on, the team noticed that many participants liked to copy images out of tasks and to share them on social media, such as images of galaxies they thought were beautiful. Such posts sometimes generated small boosts in participation, as people discovered the project through their friends/followers' posts. A secondary effect of such posts was that, based on forum discussions, already active users were also motivated to continue to perform tasks with the hopes of encountering similar beautiful subjects.

Dedicated participant communities sometimes even saved projects from termination by sustaining them financially. When Snapshot Serengeti, a project that had attracted top participation levels, ran out out of funding, the science team turned to crowd-funding it. This marked the first participant-funded citizen science campaign for Zooniverse. To gain more widespread support, the team added a "meme this" function to allow participants to create Internet memes out of Snapshot subjects. The resulting campaign ended up very successful, and has sustained the project to date.

DISCUSSION

Several of the DCs derived in our analysis directly support Kraut et al.'s claims for building successful online communities [25]. For example, *giving individuals space to discuss and socialise* was seen in (DC1), while *granting specific roles and privileges to particular individuals* further encouraged these participants to fulfil their given roles (DC3). Support for the suggestion to *make easy-to-use tools for finding and tracking work* was seen in (DC2); the integration of Talk made it significantly easier to track subjects that needed disambiguation by allowing disparate subjects to be easily cross-referenced and collated by hashtag. It was seen that this functionality alone allowed the discussion volumes to grow without need for moderator involvement. Moreover, several of the insights pertaining to tutorial design, such as introducing gold standard tasks, coincide with the suggestions towards enhancing intrinsic motivation, including *providing clear feedback and goals* (DC8). The idea of *quickly grabbing participants' attention and keeping it throughout* was supported by DC7; upfront tutorials, by postponing the actual task, failed to get participants engaged and caused them to leave often before performing any tasks at all. Pertaining to anticipating and handling *perverse incentives* and participants *gaming the system*, this was seen as less of a concern in general in Zooniverse due to there being little incentive to do so; participation in Zooniverse is inherently non-competitive, and was found to be motivated by altruism, curiosity and other intrinsic drives. Despite this, the mere ability to see new, previously unseen subjects still served a kind of reward for performing tasks that would be devalued with the introduction of *Don't know* or *Skip* functionality.

Among the other DCs from Kraut et al., some did not see much support in our findings. For example, propose that it is important to *emphasise the importance of contributions*; the Zooniverse team, on the contrary, found that such emphasis seemed have little effect on participation. For example, the Cell Slider, despite being clearly oriented around an important altruistic cause, to benefit global cancer research, experienced among the lowest participation levels of the projects.

Several of the DCs also support findings from human computation and microtask crowdsourcing. Understanding the motivations of participants are central to achieving successful participation, not only in citizen science platforms [43], but in peer-production and microtask systems such as MTurk, as highlighted by Schroer et al.'s study of participation in Wikipedian [44] and Kraufmann et al.'s [19] study of Human Intelligence Tasks (HITs) on MTurk. Such studies reveal how task specificity as well as task significance play an important role in participation, aligning with (DC6), the interestingness and complexity of a task and DC9, adding context to the task.

Effective crowdsourcing requires both high accuracy and sustained work volume. The state of the art for crowdsourcing typically recommends providing clear instruction along with some amount of background context about each task (which complements our DC6), information about the ways in which the results will be used (DC8), and, most of all, timely and relevant feedback (DC8) [9].

Relating our findings to *games with a purpose* [51], which are human-computation platforms structured in game-like environments, the level of participant engagement has been found to vary considerably on the perceived interestingness of subjects being classified or examined [48], much in accord with our DC6. In addition, engagement was shown to depend on aspects of its representation, including the way questions/tasks were presented [30]. Rapid feedback (DC8) and minimally invasive tutorials (DC7) were also shown to boost engagement [54].

Our findings regarding the vital importance of social features and community support to project success complement other citizen studies of CS, including that by Mugar etc al. [36] which documented the use of social features of CS platforms for varied kinds of engagement, including new types of practice. Furthermore, as DeVries et al. [14] describes in their user participation activity model, the ability for a user to participate in discussion and analysis in parallel to task workflow (DC2) faciliates user generated queries and analysis.

Limitations

Despite the diversity represented by the various Zooniverse projects, similarities among them, such as their all being of the data analysis variety, means that our observations may not generalise to other kinds of CS. For example, in DC5, we described that the team found that *not* providing a *don't know* mechanism encouraged educated guessing, resulting in substantial effort savings. However, or data collection projects, it may be important for such uncertainty to be explicitly expressed and handled differently as found by Lukyanenko et al. [33]. Moreover, since Zooniverse's primary aim was *scientific outcomes and discovery*, this has very likely influenced the team's decision and perspective; other systems may have

Theme	Design Claim	System Benefit
Task Specificity	*1. Focus on supporting community development and sociality early, using standard forum software if necessary; switch to bespoke tools as the community grows.*	Bootstrapping community
	2. Task workflows which encourage discussion facilitates citizen-led discovery	Serendipitous scientific discoveries
Community Development	*3. Granting roles and privileges with experience can motivate contributors to effectively assume community leadership and maintenance roles*	Engaging with users, supporting professional team
	4. Timely support from science team members is essential to enable citizen-led discovery	Supporting users, finding new scientific discoveries
Task Design	*5. Designing tasks to encourage best guesses avoids the "don't know" effort trap*	Obtaining new users
	6. Factors that influence project engagement include memorability/interestingness of subjects, task difficulty, speed, and amount of feedback provided.	Retaining users
	7. In-task UI guidance and interposed instructional tasks improves participant experience, and increases the number of completed tasks	Supporting users, Improving task completion
	8. Providing users with periodic feedback can motivate continued participation	User retention
	9. Adding context to a task adds value and improves community engagement.	Improving user engagement, Finding new scientific discoveries
Public Relations and Engagement	*10. Launch performance indicative of success. Pre-launch PR important for recruiting new and previous participants*	Obtaining new users
	11. CS communities are effective at leading their own social media campaigns	Obtaining new users

Table 2. ***Summary of Design Claims*** **- Design claims grouped by thematic category.**

different, even multiple, priorities. Educating users, for instance, was not among the team's design goals, which was reflected in decisions such as reducing tutorials to minimum in-situ guidance to complete tasks. While effective at increasing users' task time, this had the effect that users did not readily gain skill in task performance over time, as evidenced by a study showing that experienced users rarely outperformed new ones.

In addition, the use of structured reflection as a methodology requires consideration of several potential limitations; for example, the process may be influenced by selection biases that may effect the identification and reported importance of findings [16]. For example, recency, saliency and memory effects may have made more recent observations seem more important than older observations from earlier projects, for example. In order to counter such effects, we encouraged the design team to re-visit their log notebooks from the beginning during the exercises.

Finally, the DCs presented in this paper should be treated as *claims* that warrant further study, rather than as empirically-validated *laws*. In this sense, they complement Kraut's et al.'s DCs as a theoretical basis; while their work synthesises a survey of a wide selection of studies, however, ours derives from a single team's first-hand experiences with a smaller-variety of projects. In order to further investigate our results, we are planning to work with the team on several controlled studies to validate and measuring effects of particular task-community design choices to follow on from this work.

CONCLUDING REMARKS AND FUTURE WORK

The Zooniverse project provides a particularly important case study for citizen science not only due to its breadth, longevity, and success, but because it stands alone as an example where a single, small core team has been able to design, launch and conduct a large number of citizen science projects, using past experience to guide the next development. Such an allowed the team to gain extensive cumulative experience, and explore many design alternatives and strategies throughout.

Among the most valuable lessons learned for the team was the fundamental shift from viewing CS participants "crowd workers" to true peers in the scientific process. Throughout Zooniverse's projects, community members often took up responsibilities previously among those of science teams, such as creating tutorial material for newcomers, cross referencing scientific data sources, killing false leads, and, even devising models to test hypotheses. Perhaps most unexpectedly, citizens led their own investigations that sometimes independently re-discovered something previously known (e.g. the Spanish Flu), but other times resulted in new, publishable science. In more than a few instances, participants took their investigations "off the board" and into their own tools to test hypothesis, bringing results and evidence back to the project for discussion.

To support the goal of having citizens become peers in the scientific process, the Zooniverse team have started two initiatives; first, to develop new Web-based links to essential scientific tools previously only available to science teams. The second, an experiment called *Galaxy Zoo Quench* aims to involve citizens in the scientific journal preparation process themselves. The outcomes of these projects may empower participants to finally become true partners in the scientific process.

ACKNOWLEDGEMENTS

Support for this study was provided by the *SOCIAM: The Theory and Practice of Social Machines* (EP/J017728/1) grant from the UK Engineering and Physical Sciences Research Council (EPSRC). We would also like to thank the Zooniverse team for their time and effort.

REFERENCES

1. Arguello, J., Butler, B., and Joyce, E. Talk to me: foundations for successful individual-group interactions in online communities. *Proceedings of the ...* (2006), 1–10.
2. Backstrom, L., Huttenlocher, D., Kleinberg, J., and Lan, X. Group formation in large social networks: Membership, growth, and evolution. In *Proceedings of the 12th ACM SIGKDD*, KDD '06, ACM (New York, NY, USA, 2006), 44–54.
3. Bruckman, A., and Resnick, M. The mediamoo project constructionism and professional community.

Convergence: The International Journal of Research into New Media Technologies 1, 1 (1995), 94–109.

4. C, B. *Helping to get you started reflecting on your experiences*, 3rd edition ed. Oxford Blackwell, 2004.
5. Cardamone, C., Schawinski, K., Sarzi, M., Bamford, S. P., Bennert, N., Urry, C., Lintott, C., Keel, W. C., Parejko, J., Nichol, R. C., et al. Galaxy zoo green peas: discovery of a class of compact extremely star-forming galaxies. *Monthly Notices of the Royal Astronomical Society 399*, 3 (2009), 1191–1205.
6. Cardamone, C. N. The story of the peas: Writing a scientific paper. `http://blog.galaxyzoo.org/2009/07/02/the-story-of-the-peas-writing-a-scientific-paper`, 2009.
7. Cooper, C. Zen in the art of citizen science: Apps for collective discovery and the 1 percent rule of the web. `http://blogs.scientificamerican.com/guest-blog/2013/09/11/zen-in-the-art-of-citizen-science-apps-for-collective-discovery-and-the-1-rule-of-the-web/`, 2013.
8. Cordero, P., Lucks, J. B., and Das, R. An rna mapping database for curating rna structure mapping experiments. *Bioinformatics 28*, 22 (2012), 3006–3008.
9. Dawson, R., and Bynghall, S. *Getting Results from Crowds*. Advanced Human Technologies, 2012.
10. Druschke, C. G., and Seltzer, C. E. Failures of engagement: Lessons learned from a citizen science pilot study. *Applied Environmental Education & Communication 11*, 3-4 (2012), 178–188.
11. Ebner, W., Leimeister, J. M., and Krcmar, H. Community engineering for innovations: the ideas competition as a method to nurture a virtual community for innovations. *R&D Management 39*, 4 (2009), 342–356.
12. Fortson, L., Masters, K., Nichol, R., Borne, K., Edmondson, E., Lintott, C., Raddick, J., Schawinski, K., and Wallin, J. Galaxy zoo: Morphological classification and citizen science. *arXiv preprint arXiv:1104.5513* (2011).
13. Harper, F. M., Moy, D., and Konstan, J. A. Facts or friends?: Distinguishing informational and conversational questions in social q&a sites. In *Proceedings of the SIGCHI Conference on Human Factors in Computing Systems*, CHI '09, ACM (New York, NY, USA, 2009), 759–768.
14. Hassman, K. D., Mugar, G., Østerlund, C., and Jackson, C. Learning at the seafloor, looking at the sky: The relationship between individual tasks and collaborative engagement in two citizen science projects. In *Computer Supported Collaborative Learning* (2013).
15. Heinzelman, J., and Waters, C. Crowdsourcing crisis information in disaster-affected haiti. `http://www.humanitarianforum.org/data/files/crowdsourcinghaiti.pdf`, 2010.
16. Hilliard, C. Using structured reflection on a critical incident to develop a professional portfolio. *Nursing standard 21*, 2 (2006), 35–40.
17. http://OpenScientist.org. Finalizing a definition of 'citizen science' and 'citizen scientists'. `http://www.openscientist.org/2011/09/finalizing-definition-of-citizen.html`.
18. Kairam, S. R., Wang, D. J., and Leskovec, J. The life and death of online groups: Predicting group growth and longevity. In *Proceedings of the Fifth ACM International Conference on Web Search and Data Mining*, WSDM '12, ACM (New York, NY, USA, 2012), 673–682.
19. Kaufmann, N., Schulze, T., and Veit, D. More than fun and money. worker motivation in crowdsourcing-a study on mechanical turk. In *AMCIS* (2011).
20. Kawrykow, A., Roumanis, G., Kam, A., Kwak, D., Leung, C., Wu, C., Zarour, E., Sarmenta, L., Blanchette, M., Waldispühl, J., et al. Phylo: a citizen science approach for improving multiple sequence alignment. *PloS one 7*, 3 (2012), e31362.
21. Khatib, F., Cooper, S., Tyka, M. D., Xu, K., Makedon, I., Popović, Z., Baker, D., and Players, F. Algorithm discovery by protein folding game players. *Proceedings of the National Academy of Sciences 108*, 47 (2011), 18949–18953.
22. Kittur, A., and Kraut, R. E. Harnessing the wisdom of crowds in wikipedia: Quality through coordination. In *Proceedings of the 2008 ACM Conference on Computer Supported Cooperative Work*, CSCW '08, ACM (New York, NY, USA, 2008), 37–46.
23. Kluger, A. N., and DeNisi, A. The effects of feedback interventions on performance: a historical review, a meta-analysis, and a preliminary feedback intervention theory. *Psychological bulletin 119*, 2 (1996), 254.
24. Kosmala, M. We need an 'i dont know' button! `http://blog.snapshotserengeti.org/2012/12/14/we-need-an-i-dont-know-button/`, 2012.
25. Kraut, R. E., Resnick, P., Kiesler, S., Burke, M., Chen, Y., Kittur, N., Konstan, J., Ren, Y., and Riedl, J. *Building successful online communities: Evidence-based social design*. Mit Press, 2012.
26. Krieger, M., and Stark, E. Coordinating tasks on the commons: designing for personal goals, expertise and serendipity. *Proceedings of the 27th International Conference on Human Factors in Computing Systems (CHI)* (2009), 1485–1494.
27. Kuittinen, J., Kultima, A., Niemelä, J., and Paavilainen, J. Casual games discussion. In *Proceedings of the 2007 Conference on Future Play*, Future Play '07, ACM (New York, NY, USA, 2007), 105–112.
28. Kumar, R., Novak, J., and Tomkins, A. Structure and evolution of online social networks. *Proceedings of the 12th ACM SIGKDD international conference on Knowledge discovery and data mining - KDD '06* (2006), 611.
29. Lampe, C., Wash, R., Velasquez, A., and Ozkaya, E. Motivations to participate in online communities. In *Proceedings of the SIGCHI Conference on Human Factors in Computing Systems*, ACM (2010), 1927–1936.
30. Law, E., and von Ahn, L. Input-agreement: A new mechanism for collecting data using human computation games. In *Proceedings of the SIGCHI Conference on Human Factors in Computing Systems*, CHI '09, ACM (2009), 1197–1206.

31. Lintott, C. J., et al. Galaxy zoo: morphologies derived from visual inspection of galaxies from the sloan digital sky survey. *Monthly Notices of the Royal Astronomical Society 389*, 3 (2008), 1179–1189.

32. Lintott, C. J., et al. Galaxy zoo:hanny's voorwerp, a quasar light echo?. *Monthly Notices of the Royal Astronomical Society 399*, 1 (2009), 129–140.

33. Lukyanenko, R., Parsons, J., and Wiersma, Y. F. The iq of the crowd: Understanding and improving information quality in structured user-generated content. *Information Systems Research 25*, 4 (2014), 669–689.

34. Mazzolini, M., and Maddison, S. Sage, guide or ghost? the effect of instructor intervention on student participation in online discussion forums. *Computers & Education 40*, 3 (2003), 237–253.

35. Milligan, C., Littlejohn, A., and Margaryan, A. Patterns of engagement in connectivist moocs. *MERLOT Journal of Online Learning and Teaching 9*, 2 (2013).

36. Mugar, G., Osterlund, C., Hassman, K. D., Crowston, K., and Jackson, C. B. Planet hunters and seafloor explorers: Legitimate peripheral participation through practice proxies in online citizen science. In *Proceedings of the 17th ACM Conference on Computer Supported Cooperative Work*, CSCW '14, ACM (New York, NY, USA, 2014), 109–119.

37. Murphy, E., and Coleman, E. Graduate students' experiences of challenges in online asynchronous discussions. *Canadian Journal of Learning and Technology 30*, 2 (2004).

38. Norman, D. A. *The design of everyday things*. Basic books, 2002.

39. Ockerman, J., and Pritchett, A. A review and reappraisal of task guidance: Aiding workers in procedure following. *International Journal of Cognitive Ergonomics 4*, 3 (2000), 191–212.

40. Oleson, D., Sorokin, A., Laughlin, G. P., Hester, V., Le, J., and Biewald, L. Programmatic gold: Targeted and scalable quality assurance in crowdsourcing. In *Human Computation*, vol. WS-11-11 of *AAAI Workshops*, AAAI (2011).

41. Raddick, J., Lintott, C., Bamford, S., Land, K., Locksmith, D., Murray, P., Nichol, B., Schawinski, K., Slosar, A., Szalay, A., et al. Galaxy zoo: Motivations of citizen scientists. In *Bulletin of the American Astronomical Society*, vol. 40 (2008), 240.

42. Raddick, M. J., Bracey, G., Gay, P. L., Lintott, C. J., Murray, P., Schawinski, K., Szalay, A. S., and Vandenberg, J. Galaxy zoo: Exploring the motivations of citizen science volunteers. *Astronomy Education Review 9* (2010), 010103.

43. Rotman, D., Preece, J., Hammock, J., Procita, K., Hansen, D., Parr, C., Lewis, D., and Jacobs, D. Dynamic changes in motivation in collaborative citizen-science projects. In *Proceedings of the ACM 2012 conference on Computer Supported Cooperative Work*, ACM (2012), 217–226.

44. Schroer, J., and Hertel, G. Voluntary engagement in an open web-based encyclopedia: Wikipedians and why they do it. *Media Psychology 12*, 1 (2009), 96–120.

45. Schwamb, M. E., Orosz, J. A., Carter, J. A., Welsh, W. F., Fischer, D. A., Torres, G., Howard, A. W., Crepp, J. R., Keel, W. C., Lintott, C. J., et al. Planet hunters: A transiting circumbinary planet in a quadruple star system. *The Astrophysical Journal 768*, 2 (2013), 127.

46. Silvertown, J. A new dawn for citizen science. *Trends in ecology & evolution 24*, 9 (2009), 467–471.

47. Szell, M., Lambiotte, R., and Thurner, S. Multirelational organization of large-scale social networks in an online world. *Proceedings of the National Academy of Sciences 107*, 31 (2010), 13636–13641.

48. Thaler, S., Simperl, E., Siorpaes, K., and Wlger, S. *SpotTheLink: A Game-based Approach to the Alignment of Ontologies*. IGI Global, 2012.

49. Tinati, R., Luczak-Roesch, M., Simperl, E., and Shadbolt, N. Motivations of citizen scientists: A quantitative investigation of forum participation. In *Proceedings of the 2014 ACM Conference on Web Science*, WebSci '14, ACM (New York, NY, USA, 2014), 295–296.

50. Vasilescu, B., Filkov, V., and Serebrenik, A. Stackoverflow and github: associations between software development and crowdsourced knowledge. In *Social Computing (SocialCom), 2013 International Conference on*, IEEE (2013), 188–195.

51. von Ahn, L., and Dabbish, L. Designing games with a purpose. *Communications of the ACM 51*, 8 (2008), 58–67.

52. Westphal, A. J., Butterworth, A. L., Snead, C. J., Craig, N., Anderson, D., Jones, S. M., Brownlee, D. E., Farnsworth, R., and Zolensky, M. E. Stardust@ home: a massively distributed public search for interstellar dust in the stardust interstellar dust collector. In *36th Annual Lunar and Planetary Science Conference*, vol. 36 (2005), 1908.

53. Wiggins, A., and Crowston, K. From conservation to crowdsourcing: A typology of citizen science. In *System Sciences (HICSS), 2011 44th Hawaii International Conference on*, IEEE (2011), 1–10.

54. Zichermann, G., and Cunningham, C. *Gamification by Design: Implementing Game Mechanics in Web and Mobile Apps*, 1st ed. O'Reilly Media, Inc., 2011.

55. Zook, M., Graham, M., Shelton, T., and Gorman, S. Volunteered geographic information and crowdsourcing disaster relief: a case study of the haitian earthquake. *World Medical & Health Policy 2*, 2 (2010), 7–33.

Is This How We (All) Do It?: Butler Lies and Ambiguity Through a Broader Lens

Megan French[1], Madeline E. Smith[2], Jeremy Birnholtz[2], Jeff T. Hancock[1]
Communication Department
Cornell University, Ithaca, NY 14853
Department of Communication Studies
Northwestern University, Evanston, IL 60208
mrf239@cornell.edu, jeremyb@northwestern.edu, jth34@cornell.edu, madsesmith@u.northwestern.edu

ABSTRACT
The ubiquity of mobile devices has resulted in more opportunities to interact with more people than ever before. Given a finite capacity for interaction with others, people commonly manage their availability by limiting others' access to them. Prior work has demonstrated the importance of doing so in a relationally sensitive way and identified the butler lie, in which deception is used to manage availability, as a common linguistic strategy. Two key limitations of existing exploratory work, however, are limited samples of primarily students and a focus on media properties in understanding ambiguity that enables butler lies to be plausible. This paper aims to address these issues via a broad field study of deception and butler lies using a novel message-sampling method employed via a custom mobile app. Results show clear evidence of butler lies occurring in a broader population, with some gender differences; and urge adoption of a multi-level framework for understanding ambiguity that also includes private information and infrastructure-level attributes of interaction media.

Author Keywords
Texting; butler lies; availability; deception; CMC

ACM Classification Keywords
H.5.3. Information interfaces and presentation (e.g., HCI): Group and Organization Interfaces

INTRODUCTION AND BACKGROUND
One of the most basic features of mobile phones – allowing interaction with nearly anybody at nearly any time – is both a benefit and drawback. On one hand, social coordination is easier and people can stay in touch in novel ways [7]. On the other hand, constant connection can overwhelm users with interaction opportunities and interruptions. Mobile phone users must maintain a delicate balance between the desire to avoid interaction and the possible consequences of offending their contacts [2]. To maintain this balance, people use relationally sensitive strategies, such as what have been called "butler lies," for managing availability [3].

CHI 2015, April 18 - 23 2015, Seoul, Republic of Korea.

ACM 978-1-4503-3145-6/15/04…$15.00.
http://dx.doi.org/10.1145/2702123.2702368

Several studies of butler lies have investigated their use and perception [reviewed in 2] but our understanding of this everyday behavior remains constrained in important ways. First, prior work has been exploratory in nature, relying primarily on student participants whose media use and social coordination may be different from other adults' [2].

Second, drawing on Aoki & Woodruff [1], we know that butler lies and other lies online are plausible because they reference ambiguous information that is not verifiable by the recipient (e.g., [3]). Prior work on butler lies has focused mainly on ambiguities related to media themselves, extending work by [5]. For example, the fact that mobile phone users are physically separated makes a lie about one's current location difficult to verify, whereas this lie is essentially impossible when partners are co-present. Literature on deception, however, suggests several other kinds of information that is unverifiable, particularly lies based on private information (e.g., one's feelings) [4]. A clearer picture of how people use private information in butler lies will help us understand how people draw on ambiguity to manage availability.

These open issues are of interest to the CHI community in that butler lies, and availability management strategies more generally, can influence the design of tools to provide awareness and availability information such as interruptions, read notifications, and typing-in-progress indicators. By improving our understanding of how people manage availability, we can design interaction tools that better support people's needs and behavior; and extend our theoretical understanding of how people strategically use media and language to advance relational goals.

Does Everybody Really Do it?
A consequence of prior research on butler lies being exploratory is that all participants in these studies were students at US universities. Given documented differences in deception, texting and other online communication behavior [4, 9], it is important to explore more broadly how these messages are used by different generational and demographic groups. We therefore asked:

***RQ1**: What is the frequency and nature of butler lying behavior in a broader population?*

Ambiguous Ambiguities

Secondly, Birnholtz et al. [3] argued that butler lies are constructed by drawing on the ambiguities inherent in media, such as SMS mobile texting. These ambiguities do not refer to the content of the lie, but rather what makes the lie uncertain enough to be plausible. They presented a taxonomy of ambiguities used in butler lies that largely stem from properties of the communication medium, including: timing (e.g., when something happened), location (e.g., where a person is texting from), and activity (e.g., what the sender is doing). While these ambiguities clearly appear in butler lies, there is arguably an important omission in this taxonomy. Prior work on deception shows that lies are often about private states or information known only to the liar, such as beliefs (e.g., "I really want to see you"), preferences (e.g., "that party will be great"), and intentions (e.g., "yep I'm planning on going") [4].

This omission matters because the ambiguity of private information is distinct from ambiguity related to media. Deception about private information is plausible even face-to-face, as with "white lies." Such lies, when told in mediated interactions, may remain plausible even after the conversation is over because the information is more difficult to verify. Better understanding and capturing this distinction can shed light on how people manage availability strategically. Given the common use of private information in deception, we would expect to see evidence of this in a larger sample. We asked:

RQ2: *What types of private information are the subject of butler lies and what are the sources of ambiguity?*

THE PRESENT STUDY

To these questions, we introduce a novel message-sampling method using a custom-developed texting application that collected participants' text messages over seven days, and asked at send time if each outgoing message was deceptive.

Participants. We recruited people to participate in a study on text messaging via e-mail listservs, Craigslist ads in 10 cities, and a web-based recruitment system. There were 248 participants, of whom 47 were removed for insufficient activity (< 10 messages) or attempting to participate twice. The remaining 201 included 92 males and 103 females (six did not report gender), and were aged 19 to 63 (M=31, SD=8.9). Participants had, on average, 7.5 years of texting experience. Sixty-six percent indicated they were non-students, 6% part-time students, and 28% full-time students. The racial/ethnic background of participants was: White (51%), African American (19%), Asian (14%), Hispanic (9%), and Other (7%). Participants were located throughout the United States: 40% in the midwest, 22% in the west, 20% in the northeast, and 18% in the south.

Message Sampling. We developed Butler Messaging, a custom Android app that was substituted for participants' ordinary SMS app during the study. The app interfaced with our secure database, to which each sent or received message was automatically saved. To protect privacy, common proper names were removed and phone numbers were one-way hashed. To allow for send-time identification of deception, a pop-up dialog appeared when send was clicked that asked if the message was deceptive. Deceptiveness information was stored in the database, but not stored on the participant's phone or shared with contacts.

Procedure. After consenting, participants were instructed to install Butler Messaging, import their existing messages, and make it their default messaging app for seven days. Afterwards, participants were completed an online post-study questionnaire and received instructions to uninstall the app. The questionnaire presented them with specific deceptive messages they had sent, and asked them: 1) if they recognized each recipient, 2) their relationship to each contact (e.g. friend, family, etc.), and 3) closeness to each contact. For each deceptive message, participants were asked to explain why it was deceptive.

Data Analysis. Two coders independently coded all deceptive messages for butler content, jocularity (e.g., jokes or sarcasm) and messages accidentally marked as deceptive, using a prior coding scheme [3]. Next, butler lies were coded for the type of ambiguity that enabled plausibility [3]. Ambiguity types from prior work included activity (what the sender was doing), location (where the sender was) and time (when something occurred). Following RQ2, we identified two additional sources of ambiguity: private information and infrastructure, described further below. Of 401 butler lies, 40 could not be coded for ambiguity because participants did not provide enough detail. Inter-coder reliability for ambiguity was acceptable (77% agreement, Cohen's $kappa$=0.65).

RESULTS

In all, participants sent 12,587 and received 29,050 messages, exchanged with 1,661 distinct contacts.

Did Everybody Do It?

Our first research question was about the frequency of butler lies in a sample that extended beyond a predominantly student demographic. We first looked at the prevalence of general deception in our data. Of the 12,587 sent messages, 769 messages were deceptive, with a mean general deception rate of 8% (SD=13%). Of these deceptive messages, on average, 56% (SD=37%) were identified as butler lies. It should be noted that the rate of butler lies in this study is distinctly higher than past studies, which have averaged around 39% [3, 8].

Deception Across Demographics

We wondered if, in a broader sample with more messages, there were differences across demographic categories for deception or butler lie rates [see Table 1]. Looking first at gender differences using a t-test, we see that that men told significantly more lies in their text messages overall than women [$t(128)$=2.78p<0.01]. For butler lies data, however, the reverse was true. Women told significantly more butler lies on average than men [χ^2= 5.3, p<0.05; Kruskal-Wallis test was used due to bimodal distribution of butler lies]. Using ANOVA, we examined differences across previously under-represented racial or ethnic groups. The difference in rates for butler lies across ethnic groups approached significance [F(4,131)=2.1, p=0.08].

	Deception Rate		Butler Lie Rate	
Gender	*M (SD)*	*N*	*M (SD)*	*N*
Male	0.11 (0.18)**	92	0.48 (0.35)*	63
Female	0.06 (0.08)**	103	0.58 (0.36)*	71
Age				
Under 25	0.09 (0.11)	57	0.55 (0.35)	46
25-30	0.09 (0.16)	58	0.50 (0.35)	37
31-40	0.10 (0.16)	52	0.50 (0.37)	37
Above 40	0.05 (0.10)	29	0.60 (0.44)	17
Ethnicity				
African American	0.08 (0.15)	38	0.61 (0.39)	26
Asian	0.12 (0.17)	29	0.50 (0.37)	20
Hispanic	0.10 (0.18)	18	0.26 (0.32)	12
White	0.08 (0.12)	103	0.55 (0.36)	71
Other	0.06 (0.04)	8	0.55 (0.30)	7
Student				
Full Time Student	0.08 (0.10)	55	0.54 (0.38)	44
Non-Student	0.09 (0.15)	144	0.57 (0.36)	93

Note: For butler lies only participants who told at least one lie were included, ** p<0.01, * p<0.05

Table 1. Demographic breakdown of average rate of deceptive messages and butler lies.

We believe this was driven in part by the lower rate found for Hispanic participants. However given the small sample of Hispanics, we hesitate to draw any conclusions about this marginally significant relationship.

Despite a large number of non-students, comparing across age groups, using ANOVA, and status as full-time student, using a t-test, findings revealed no significant differences for deception or butler lies.

Understanding Ambiguity

Our second research question addressed the nature of private information and the kinds of ambiguity that people drew on to make their butler lies plausible. To compare the frequency of different types of ambiguity, we ran a mixed model with the five ambiguity categories as a fixed factor and participants as a random factor, revealing significant differences [F(4,535)=41.2, p<0.001]. Private information was used most (45%), followed by activity (26%), time (15%), location (5%), and infrastructure (4%) [see Figure 1]. Pairwise comparisons, using a Least Significant Difference correction (p<.05), showed that private information, activity, location, and time all significantly differed from each other. There was no significant difference between location and infrastructure.

Private Information

What is most striking in these results is that the most frequent category was private information. We saw that

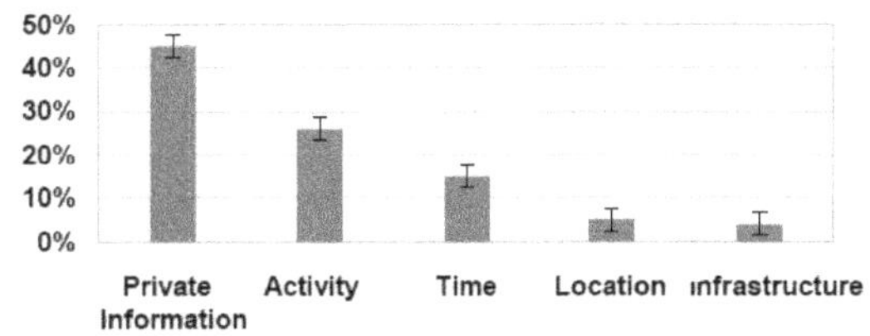

Figure 1. Estimated mean proportion of each participant's butler lies drawing on ambiguity types.

participants regularly drew on private information that was not verifiable, either because it was private to the individual (e.g., intent, feelings) or because it is not visible or normatively acceptable to verify (e.g., money troubles).

Participants drew on ambiguity from private information when being deceptive about their true feelings or intentions, such as a participant who said she was "still interested!" in a social event even when she indicated in the post-study questionnaire that she had known she was not. The same was true for knowledge of future plans. One participant – regarding his availability for later activities– said "not sure where ill be. Maybe," but told us he had knew then he would not be available.

Another use of private information was to ask questions where the answer was already known, but the question served to support conversational goals. One participant, for example, said "you working today…?", but indicated to us they already knew the recipient was not working. This is interesting, in that it does not contain false information. The participant likely rated it as deceptive because the question falsely implies that the recipient's work status is unknown.

Infrastructure

Another novel form of ambiguity we saw here was related to infrastructure. Where prior work did not draw a distinction between attributes of a medium and attributes of the underlying infrastructure, we believe the distinction captures an important phenomenon. Mobile phones have batteries that can fail, for example. Those batteries are an attribute of the phone itself, not an attribute of texting. The ambiguity stems not from the medium, but the functioning of the device or its infrastructure.

While butler lies drawing on this type of ambiguity were not frequent (see Figure 1), considering this allows us to better capture how people take of advantage of device characteristics to manage availability within different contexts. We saw people blame both the infrastructure, as with a participant who falsely said "Hey, sorry -- I was having all kinds of issues with texts going through yesterday…"; as well as the device, as with another that said "the phone keeps freezing" even when it had not.

DISCUSSION

This work has several implications for our understanding of and ability to support availability management. First, we presented Butler Messenger, a message sampling method that allowed for in-the-moment data collection across geographic regions.

Second, in using our message-sampling method we show a clear difference in the rate of butler lies as compared with prior studies. This raises the question of whether this is due to our experiential sampling rather than retrospective survey method (e.g., [3]); or due to an actual change in texting behavior. Given the relatively short time since prior work, smaller sample and other prior methodological limitations, we argue that the present study presents a more accurate depiction of deception and butler lies in texting.

In addition to overall higher rates of butler lies, we found that gender differences in rates of deception and butler lies. Men lied at almost twice the rate that women lied. However, a higher proportion of women's deceptive messages were butler lies. There were no age, ethnicity, or student status differences for either of our dependent measures. This was surprising both in that one might expect group differences and in that it stands in contrast to work suggesting that students lie at a higher rate [4]. Our result provides some evidence that deception as a strategy for availability management is common across demographics.

Third, we build on prior work by illustrating two distinct ways in which people use ambiguity in crafting plausible butler lies. To our surprise, we found that our participants drew on ambiguity related to private information more frequently than any other type of ambiguity. This suggests that, even when interactions are mediated in ways that provide additional ambiguity, people still frequently use private information strategically, perhaps because of the difficulty that such lies could be detected even face-to-face.

We also saw participants draw on ambiguity related to infrastructure. This distinction is useful because many common communication media (e.g., Skype, WhatsApp, SMS, etc.) run on different types of devices and depend on infrastructures with varying technical properties. Where past research has focused on media features [3, 5], our work considers the reliability and attributes of the devices and infrastructures that underlie these features.

A more complete taxonomy of ambiguity types can inform designers about the potential impacts of making certain information visible to interaction partners. We urge researchers and designers to consider the multiple levels at which ambiguity occurred here in availability management and deception, including private information, details obscured by media properties, and attributes of infrastructure. With a multi-level approach to ambiguity, we can better understand the relationship between media (e.g. GlancePhone [6]) and availability management. One issue this highlights is the way that available/busy status indicators conflate private information with media features that serve to provide or obscure this information.

Limitations and Future Work

While butler lies and deception in texting were examined on a larger scale than prior studies [2, 3, 8], there are limitations to consider. Despite a broader sample, the participants in this study are still not representative of the US population. Our methodological and theoretical contributions provide a foundation for future work.

We also acknowledge the possibility that asking people about deception during the study may have altered their texting behavior. We do not believe this was the case, however, as we saw a noticeable difference only for butler lies, and not for deception overall. In addition, the overall average rate of lying was not significantly different between the first and second half of the study (M=0.08, SD=0.01; M=0.09, SD=0.01, p>0.10). An alternative approach for future work to address this issue would be to have the app query participants about a range of topics at send time (e.g., "Did this message contain humor?"), asking about deception only for a random subset.

ACKNOWLEDGEMENTS

We acknowledge NSF funding (IIS-0915081 and DGE-0824162) and valuable research assistance from Scott Cambo, Jon Culver, Jared Kass, Weili Shi, and Jessie Taft.

REFERENCES

1. Aoki, P. & Woodruff, A. Making spaces for stories: Ambiguity in the design of personal communication. *Proc. ACM CHI* (2005), 181-190.
2. Birnholtz, J., Reynolds, L., Smith, M. & Hancock, J. (2013). "Everyone has to do it:" A join action approach to managing social inattention. *Computers in Human Behavior, 29,* 2230-2238.
3. Birnholtz, J., Guillory, J., Hancock, J., & Bazarova, N. "on my way": Deceptive texting and interpersonal awareness narratives. *Proc. ACM CSCW (2010)*, 1-4.
4. DePaulo, B., Kashy, D., Kirkendol, S., Wyer, & Epstein, J. (1996). Lying in everyday life. *Journal of Personality and Social Psychology, 70,* 979-995.
5. Hancock, J., Thom-Santelli, J., & Ritchie, T. Deception and design: The impact of communication technology on lying behavior. *Proc. ACM CHI (2004)*, 129-134.
6. Harper, R. & Taylor, S. Glancephone – an exploration of human expression. *Proc. ACM MobileHCI (2009),* 24-32.
7. Ling, R. (2004). *The Mobile Connection: The Cell Phone's Impact on Society*. San Francisco: Morgan Kaufmann.
8. Reynolds, L. Smith, M, Birnholtz, J., & Hancock, J. Butler lies from both sides: Actions and perception of unavailability management in texting. *Proc. ACM CSCW (2013)*, 769-778.
9. Zickuhr, K., & Smith, A. (2012). Digital differences. *Pew Internet & American Life Project, 13.*

CrowdMonitor: Mobile Crowd Sensing for Assessing Physical and Digital Activities of Citizens during Emergencies

Thomas Ludwig, Christian Reuter, Tim Siebigteroth, Volkmar Pipek
University of Siegen, Institute for Information Systems
Kohlbettstr. 15, 57072 Siegen, Germany
{thomas.ludwig; christian.reuter; tim.siebigteroth; volkmar.pipek}@uni-siegen.de

ABSTRACT
Emergencies such as the 2013 Central European flood or the 2013 typhoon Haiyan in Philippines have shown how citizens can organize themselves and coordinate private relief activities. These activities can be found in (physical) groups of affected people, but also within (digital) social media communities. There is an evident need, however, for a clearer picture of what exactly is going on to be available for use by the official emergency services: to enlist them, to keep them safe, to support their efforts and to avoid needless duplications or conflicts. Aligning emergency services and volunteer activities is, then, crucial. In this paper we present a mobile crowd sensing based concept, which was designed as well as implemented as the application CrowdMonitor and facilitates the detection of physical and digital activities and the assignment of specific tasks to citizens. Finally we outline the findings of its evaluation.

Author Keywords
Emergency Management; Crowdsourcing; Mobile Crowd Sensing; Social Media; Design Case Study

ACM Classification Keywords
H.5.3 Group and Organization Interfaces.

INTRODUCTION
Various events during recent emergencies show that in addition to formal crisis management through emergency services, citizen-based crisis management, characterized by situated altruism [8], is a common behavior. Individuals and groups get together to form emergent and temporary organizations [30] for improvised relief and rescue activities [37]. Although citizen-initiated activities have always existed during emergencies [34], the sheer pervasiveness of social media and mobile devices has changed the kinds of mobilization possible during and after emergencies. Via social media, volunteers can now quickly establish self-help groups and relief communities for dealing with response and recovery activities [25, 26]. It is already possible, to a degree, for volunteers to integrate such activities with those of the emergency services. Citizens can either help physically, e.g. by filling sandbags [25], or online, e.g. by providing crisis-related information [11]. Although emergency services have recognized the relevance and importance of citizen-initiated physical and digital activities, problems still arise. How to identify, integrate and manage on-site as well as online activities into official work practices in time-critical and uncertain situations remains an open question. Not least, this is important to prevent the disruption of both official interventions and existing volunteer work.

CHI 2015, April 18 – 23, 2015, Seoul, Republic of Korea.

ACM 978-1-4503-3145-6/15/04...$15.00.
http://dx.doi.org/10.1145/2702123.2702265

This design case study [39] aims to address this issue and examines how physical as well as digital activities of citizens can be made manageable for emergency services. In what follows, we analyze related approaches to crowdsourcing, mobile crowd sensing and use of social media in emergencies. In a qualitative empirical study of emergency services, we then explore the impact of citizen-generated content from social media as well as on- and off-site volunteer involvement. Based on our pre-studies we derive an approach, which allows monitoring and aligning of both civil on-site as well as digital activities. We use the empirical findings to implement the web-based application "CrowdMonitor", which is based on a mobile crowd sensing concept and is intended to support collaboration between emergency services, volunteers and others.

SOCIAL MEDIA, CROWDSOURCING AND MOBILE CROWD SENSING IN EMERGENCIES
In the recent years, open innovation concepts – emerging from Web 2.0 – have been geared to citizen involvement as well as community engagement. Those concepts mainly comprise support for a greater participation and integration of citizens into the tasks and activities of professional organizations [3]. *Crowdsourcing* is a "type of participative online activity in which an individual, an institution, a non-profit organization, or company proposes to a group of individuals via a flexible open call, the voluntary undertaking of a task" [9]. There are several approaches of crowdsourcing, which we will discuss below.

One subset of crowdsourcing, which emerged with the ubiquity of smart mobile devices is *participatory sensing* [4] in which individuals are asked to gather, analyze and share data and information using the integrated sensor capabilities of their mobile devices. Application areas for participatory sensing include, for example, GPS or speed data from cyclists to infer route and traffic noisiness [24], audio data from microphones to discover biodiversity [19] or to measure the air quality [14]. The presence of such multimodal sensors is enabling a broad range of possibilities through the automatic collection of sensor data. The concept of *mobile crowd sensing* [40] combines the participatory sensing concept with a "collective" sensing view by supplementing sensor data collected via mobile devices on the ground with citizen-generated content from social media, such as opinions or experiences [12].

Social media are – of course also during emergencies – already widely used [22]. Facebook, Twitter and other services are used in different ways [13] and cover both real and virtual activities [25] such as the provision of on-site information or the reporting of news in order to achieve situational awareness [36]. Citizens can communicate and share information directly from an incident's location often before other data is available [18]. Furthermore digital volunteers can organize themselves [31] to generate collective pictures of events [32]. How emergency services use this available data and how they establish relationships with volunteers, however, can result in a variety of outcomes [7]. Although organizational and structural obstacles exist [15], there are already approaches that focus on useful relations between officials and citizens during emergencies [28], which we will outline in the following.

CROWDSOURCING SYSTEMS WITHIN EMERGENCIES

Various crowdsourcing systems (which often base on social media) for the use in emergencies exist that try to support the actions of emergency services and volunteers, especially in time-critical situations. *Twitinfo* [17] is a platform for exploring Twitter in real-time. It "extracts the posts that match keywords in the query and provides a graphical timeline interface that labels peaks of high-volume posts as sub events and highlights important terms and tweets". Although providing important information, it supports no interaction or sensing. In *Twitcident* [1] tweets relevant to an automatically broadcasted crisis event are collected in real time. By analyzing and filtering tweets, a crisis profile is created to support awareness. Like Twitinfo, it does not support any sensing functionality. *Ushahidi* is a platform that supports emergency services in requesting citizens to gather and structure information [21]. It mainly contains reports about, for instance, local or medical needs. In addition, it encompasses different sources, like social media, E-Mail or SMS. In Ushahidi, reports are visualized on a map to improve the situation overview [5]. Ushahidi was used, for example, for the allocation of food during the tsunami in Japan 2011 [11]. In Ushahidi, information from individuals is embedded, but aggregated social media data is not. With *Mobile4D* [10], emergency services request reports about the local situation from members of the public via a dedicated mobile application. Emergency services can use this application to directly communicate with people and verify submitted information. In addition Mobile4D supports broadcast warnings based on submitted reports or directly via integrated communication channels. Mobile4D was used in Laos in 2013, where reports about floods and the avian flu were collected. Providing an appropriate participatory sensing functionality using social media is not part of the approach. Existing reverse-911 systems use telephone numbers and addresses of residents within a geographical area to be able to send out warnings to specific groups, but lack a dynamic response capability and do not monitor social media.

CROSS [6] does use social media to initiate the participation of members of the public by a call to use a mobile application. Users can then collect local information and transmit it, enriched with data about their location. The location allows emergency services to purposefully coordinate participants. But potentials of digital volunteers were not addressed. *DIADEM* [38] represents another means to gather and validate information. Here, a pre-selected group of volunteers is requested by emergency services to use a mobile application for identifying strange smells during chemical disasters. Information obtained can be shared between experts and visualized on a map so that emergency services can locate the source of the smell [38]. Microtasking applications like *MicroMappers* [23] where emergency services ask digital volunteers to perform small tasks by submitting requests to a crowdsourcing-platform. Such applications were used during the 2013 typhoon in the Philippines to check relevant tweets and categorize photos.

These approaches are mainly used for data gathering or evaluation purposes. The potential, we argue, for using the social media to integrate crowdsourced information and to integrate local "on the ground" activities is still substantially unexplored. Nevertheless, "the incorporation of social media into pre-existing emergency management systems is inevitable" [2]. Our research question was therefore how the digital and physical activities of volunteers and other citizens might be integrated within the practices of emergency management through IT.

EMPIRICAL STUDY: INTEGRATION OF ACTIVITIES OF VOLUNTEERS AND OTHERS DURING EMERGENCIES

Our objective is to examine the potential of social media generated information for situation assessment and at the same time the potential for involving volunteers into the current work of emergency services. We therefore conducted and analyzed 42 interviews (Table 1) with different organizations involved in emergencies (police, fire department, authorities and emergency call center) in Germany (Bonn, Dortmund, Kerpen, St. Augustin, Siegen) as well as in the European Union (Amsterdam, Antwerp, London, Ljubljana, Oslo, Twente, Warszawa) with a view to establishing, inter alia, the potential for volunteer-initiated activities as well as other content from social media in emergency management. We focused on collecting responses from a wide range of authorities.

Name	Title and Focus	Year	Quantity	Place
I1-24	Work Practices and IT Support	2010/11	22	GER
IM1-5	Mobile Collaboration practices	2012	5	GER
C1-11	Social Media in Emergencies	2014	11	EU
IS1-4	Citizen involvement in Crisis	2014	4	GER
Sum:			42	

Table 1: Interviews (2010-2014)

We aimed for a cross selection of hierarchical units ranging from a (lower level) Head of Section to a (high level) Head of Control Center. The aim was to get a comprehensive overview of the entire organization. Each interview lasted between 1 and 2 hours and followed a guideline. I1-24 focused on the participants' role and work activities under normal conditions; participants' tasks during emergencies in our scenario framework; applied information and communication systems and perceived problems with these tools. To study mobile collaboration practices more closely with regard to the creation, exchange and use of information by response teams and control centers, five additional interviews were conducted (each 1 hour; IM1-5) [27]. C1-11 and IS1-4 focused on different types of official users and their motivation for using social media and involving volunteers during emergencies.

All interviews (I1-24; IM1-5; IS1-4) were audio recorded and transcribed or documented (C1-11) for subsequent data analysis. The analysis was based on the inductive approach of *grounded theory* [33], at least to the extent that we used open coding associated with grounded theory to derive categories from empirical data by the careful reading aggregation of categories. Transcripts were therefore open coded and the statements of the agents were divided into text modules and later into categories. The knowledge previously acquired in the literature study was used to heighten *theoretical sensitivity* [33]. *Theoretical sampling* led us to select certain interviews for further analysis as our categories emerged.

Integration of Citizens into work Practices

Currently, volunteers and other citizens are de facto not integrated into the everyday work practices of emergency services due to their lack of qualification (IS03). During large-scale emergencies or long-term disasters, however, collaboration with volunteers is seen as important:

"During our everyday work actually not, because one cannot work for fire services without any qualification. During major emergencies such as floods one can certainly fill sandbags, for instance. Then we really seek for the collaboration with citizens" (IS03).

In order to participate appropriately in such emergency situations, however, it is *"extremely important that we instruct the citizens"* (IS04), because otherwise they lack sufficient knowledge (IS01):

"For instance, we also have to control the sandbags. What's the use of having 150 people and 50 bags or maybe nothing to do at all? I must get an overview on the entire area of operations and the situation itself" (IS01).

The handling of resources with regard to volunteers requires coordination efforts by the officials. From the point of view of professional emergency services, too little is known about the actions of volunteers and others and the existing organizational capabilities of volunteers, and therefore *"[we can] allow them to act under our supervision, to try to convince them through conversations and to help them adapt our operational strategy"* (IS01).

This is necessary, not least, because of possible danger. For an integration of citizens on the ground it is necessary to detect possible danger areas (IS01), since volunteers must not put themselves in danger.

"If it is about clearing something away or protecting something or something like this, we can include citizens who are already there wherefore we avoid that they only stand there and look around" (I11).

For simple tasks the on-site integration of citizens makes sense, but even here this kind of danger exists: *"because they probably do not have the adequate equipment they would need. Or maybe because they do not have the necessary information"* (IS04).

Furthermore, an official integration of civil activities currently must not happen before emergency service units arrive *"because we would expose them to a risk which we could not assess if we are not there [on-site]"* (IS04). Citizens entering danger areas could interfere with the actions of relief forces (IS04) and *"there also are legal issues"* (IS02) such as insurance coverage.

Integration of volunteers is initially established in two different ways. The first is the physical contact on-site: *"We had that during the Oder floods when a few volunteers came and said: 'Here I am, I would like to help!'"* (IS01). The second way is to monitor citizens organizing themselves through social media. From the emergency services' perspective it is important to know *"where people are organizing themselves so that they can be coordinated somehow"* (IS02). Social media are already monitored spontaneously (IS02) and some attempts are made to explicitly coordinate citizens e.g. via Facebook pages: *"I become a member [of a group] and then I identify myself as emergency service and say: 'Okay, I need help there'"* (IS04).

In urgent situations *"people frequently want to receive really up-to-date and detailed information: 'What are we supposed to do now? What does that mean for us?'"* (IS02). Adequately data about the current situation as well as anticipated dangers is vital. Within large-scale emergencies such involvement of volunteers in simple tasks is straightforward: *"You don't need any special qualification for filling sandbags. We give a short instruction and then the citizens know how it can be done"* (IS03).

Apart from this, special local knowledge and abilities (e.g. foresters, chimney sweepers) or language skills might be needed in this situation (IS01):

"There are many special things for which you need basic knowledge or foreknowledge. But there are also things for which you can make use of the knowledge and skills of citizens because it is their daily bread" (I11).

Enhanced Situation Assessment by Volunteers On-site

Besides physical relief activities, local citizens can provide important information. In major incidents the emergency services normally receive a large amount of emergency calls from citizens (IS03, IS04), which are used as initial situation overviews. The emergency services always ask five specific questions to get the needed information:

"There are five questions: What has happened? Where did it happen? How many injured people are there? And at the end we wait, so that dispatchers at the control center, who are receiving the call, can ask further questions, that they actually know how the situation on-site looks like" (IS03).

Based on information from those calls *"an assessment of the situation and appropriate measures such as sending an ambulance are taken"* (IS03). Call takers will continue to ask questions until official emergency forces arrive on-site.

"But when the fire and rescue services are on-site, then our people are there. Why shouldn't I talk to them if they are there? So the question will only arise if we aren't there. That means to fill this time gap until we are there" (IS04).

Consequently, acquiring information from the public makes sense until the official emergency services arrive. In major incidents local people can also provide information on poorly accessible areas:

"Imagine we have an emergency over a large area – again I take Fukushima as an example. The fire service cannot be everywhere at the same time and there might be several separated areas. Then, of course, it is great if citizens tell us that unfortunately 20 dead bodies have already been found or we are having 500 injured here" (I10).

However, there are often differences between the actual situations on-site and descriptions offered (I04) because members of the public do not always find it easy to assess the situation (IS03, IS04) or might be most useful (IS03). For that reason it is sometimes necessary that information is explicitly requested (IS01, I02), which becomes clear in an example about the reporting of car fires:

"Somebody is driving on the highway and sees someone with a smoking engine on the breakdown lane. [...] That means we have to go out because we can't rule out that the car really is on fire and the guy just doesn't know that white smoke might just be steam" (IS03).

Thus, any input from the public has to be validated by further inquiries (IS04), sometimes even after relief forces arrive on-site.

Integration of Off-Site Citizen Activities

In addition to the integration of on-site activities, the current practices of emergency services comprise requests to digital volunteers on social media. This can be seen in the provision of information: *"Authorities invoke the users on its Facebook page: 'Please give us some information on this and that topic'"* (IS02).

This information may contain impressions, feelings or pictures from incident locations (IS02). Citizens, for instance, can be asked about the evolving pattern of smoke to be seen (C02). However, such data requires validation:

"This is our computer, on which we receive this Facebook comment that 630 sandbags are missing. Then we contact the control center and say: 'Please check with Bad Laasphe [German city], what is going on there and there?'" (IS04).

Verification is always important. *"[We use] ... other [...] reliable or official sources"* (IS02) to verify information. These might be other official sources (IS02) or the social media (IS03). Monitoring of social media, something that can be done by volunteers, allows emergency services to gain further knowledge about the situation on-site (S01). In doing so, they can either make use of existing data or actively make requests:

"One can just say: 'Please tweet information about how you feel or what problems you have on-site and label it with this or this hashtag', so that we can filter it more easily" (IS02). Needs and concerns are actively requested: *"What is the public thinking? What do they want? What do they probably need what we don't know about?"* (IS02).

The reason for integrating volunteers into a monitoring role is that currently the emergency services do not have any special staff for doing this (IS02, C07). Monitoring is carried out on an ad hoc basis by individual members (IS01, IS02, C10) of the incident command or the section staff of the control center (IS04), and is not part of the official structural plan (IS03):

"I was in Dresden [German city – flooded in 2013] for 14 days and we had selected a colleague who didn't do anything else but pay attention to Facebook or the media. He participated in press work, but he kept an eye on the monitor and was always browsing on Facebook: 'What is happening there? Where are they meeting?'" (IS01).

Consequently there is less time available for primary tasks of the control center (I02). As a result, monitoring and especially work with social media arguably needs to be done by specialized and focused volunteers:

"I tell you, the guys, who currently do this stuff and take it seriously, say that it should be done by people who only do social media" (IS02).

This task could also be taken over by citizens because no special knowledge is needed but only a common sense:

"If something like this happens, we need smart people on the platforms who read along, moderate and publish press releases. [...] They don't have to be firefighters. They just need a firefighter as a contact person" (IS04).

Since tweets are publicly accessible, Twitter is more suitable for monitoring than Facebook where relevant information is mostly exchanged between friends and *"is actually not distributed publicly"* (IS02). Nevertheless, the emergency services use Facebook more often than Twitter due to its popularity within Europe (IS02):

"The vast majority of colleagues, who do this, definitely use Facebook and Twitter. I mean Facebook is simply the most popular" (IS02).

It has been shown that critical information, such as warnings or reports about an incident are often distributed to friends by liking a Facebook page and so on:

"But on Facebook everyone has this message on their timeline who has subscribed to us and who liked our news time. That's why we had such a wide audience. Although we only have 1,400 fans we could reach 14,000 people, because our users have shared it on their profile" (IS03).

During more routine work, social media are already used for publishing summaries of daily operations (IS03) and requests to the public, for instance, for the purpose of information provision or blood donation requests (IS01). When large-scale incidents happen, many of our respondents point to the potential of social media as they can be used by the emergency services for the search for missing persons (IS01), the support of evacuation measures (IS03), or for warning the public (IS03, IS04, C02, C09, C10). The latter is fostered, for example, by the distribution of critical information, citizen to citizens (IS03).

In large-scale emergencies, this information means that emergency services *"can better understand the activities of independent volunteers. I mean we can monitor them better because we have better information on what they are planning"* (IS02). Information containing *"location data is very important because in this way [...] we can draw a more precise picture of the situation"* (IS02, C02, C11).

When communicating via social media, several aspects have to be considered, e.g. data privacy (IS04). Names or streets with house numbers, for instance, are not to be mentioned explicitly (IS03). Furthermore it should be noted that expertise in the use of social media is not evenly distributed. Officers sometimes lack daily experience (IS02). Moreover, when communicating with the public, technical terminology needs to be avoided:

"For example, when I'm posting something, I must be careful that I write it in a way that a citizen can understand it and it's not in a technical language" (IS03).

Discussion

Regardless of privacy and other concerns, volunteers and others could offer several benefits for integration into official crisis management from the emergency service's perspective. They can take over both real physical activities on-site, such as filling sandbags (IS03) or taking clearance measures (I11) as well as digital activities off-site, such as sharing (IS02, IS03) or validating (IS02) information that improves overall situation assessment (IS02, IS04) – especially during large-scale emergencies where certain areas might be difficult to access (I19) or relief forces have not yet arrived at the scene (IS03, IS04). Individual assessments can diverge from actual situations considerably and so constant interaction between officials and others has to be supported (IS03, IS04).

Several problems can arise when volunteers are engaged in activities on the ground. They can operate in dangerous areas and get hurt or interfere with the actions of emergency services (IS04) and vice versa. It is all the more important, therefore, that volunteers are sufficiently informed about the overall situation (IS02), advised in accordance with organizational demands, and integrated into the operational strategy (IS01). The careful coordination of their activities is therefore absolutely necessary (IS01, IS02, IS04). Currently, however, civil community work is a kind of black box for many of emergency services (IS02). Initiatives to foster collaborations between emergency services and citizens happen through local on-site collection points and direct contact (IS01) or (relatively) rarely via social media in a rather ad hoc fashion as coordinators of Facebook pages or within groups. (IS02). There is an evident need for a more systematic approach (IS04). Not least, as pointed out, information has to be validated in some fashion (IS02, IS04) and besides, information overflow (IS01) is always likely due to the independent actions of volunteers [29].

CROWDMONITOR: A CONCEPT FOR ASSESSING PHYSICAL AND DIGITAL ACTIVITIES OF CITIZENS

Our empirical study demonstrated the need for an integrated approach for handling citizen-generated content from social media and advising on the ground civil activities in order to collaborate with them in an appropriate manner. The existing current approaches do not facilitate a combined assessment and management of social media and volunteer-initiated activities. On the basis of our findings, therefore, we designed – with regard to the current state of the art – the mobile crowd sensing application CrowdMonitor.

For improving situation awareness (IS02, IS04), CrowdMonitor seeks to passively collect and display social media information (from ordinary people without their knowledge) alongside volunteered information in response to public requests via a mobile application (i.e. from knowledgeable volunteers). Formal responders of official emergency services, the main operators and users of the tool, can create requests for particular information or targeted alerts, which can then be pushed to users of the mobile app within a particular location. Such requests are necessary to prevent volunteers engaging within dangerous areas or interfere with actions of formal emergency services (IS04) or to validate citizen-generated information from social media (IS03, IS09). The aim of CrowdMonitor is to synchronize and harmonize actions performed by emergency services and those of the public by (1) monitoring social media and (2) integrating volunteers into activities coordinated and led by emergency service officials. The following will describe the detailed functionalities of CrowdMonitor.

The central part of CrowdMonitor is an Open Street Map, which displays information on different layers (**A**). As literature has shown, a layer-based map is an important part for situation assessment activities during emergencies. Those layers (**B**) contain, on the one hand the well-known map types (roads, satellite, topographic view) and standardized map services (like web feature services, e.g. hydrant layers), but also time-critical data (citizen-generated content from social media, volunteered report responses to prior requests or movement data) to which we will refer later. Time-related information can be selected by date and time (**C**) and displayed as clusters (with regard to the zoom level) based on their type, amount and location. Depending on the selected layers, the legend (**D**) aligns itself. The information is visualized by markers and details will be shown in the detail view (**E**). On the left side, the user has the option to load map extracts and related data for a specific type of emergency, e.g. displaying flood-areas, water levels or water protection authorities for a flood situation (**F**). It is possible to save the current map, which can then be recalled at any time.

The search functionality offers a query for 'locations of interest' or for specific 'citizen-generated content' (**G**). The search for social media content uses an implemented social media API that returns all message results for different social media services by a keyword. Due to performance issues, the values are returned always based on the current visible map area as well as defined time. The results are displayed and sorted on the right side as a list (**H**) and at the same time visualized directly on the map. To help validate the results they are sorted by a simple algorithm that ranks the messages by e.g. number of retweets and their up-to-datedness. In the detail view, the entire content of a message as well as the author are displayed. A button in the detail view (**I**) allows immediate access to the corresponding platform on which any particular message can be accessed and the user can immediately use established communication channels.

The aforementioned visualization and searching functionalities are not, we acknowledge, particularly novel and are to some degree already addressed in previous literature, e.g. [16, 17]. The actual innovative functionality, that we argue goes beyond the current state of the art, is the combination of the social media content and the emergent civil activities on-site as well as the inclusion of options for instructions and advice. For example, movement data of volunteers can be collected via the mobile part of CrowdMonitor, a module with an emergency app, providing additional information during emergencies. Within this app it is possible to select whether – during an emergency and in an anonymized way – the movements of participating volunteers can be tracked. Volunteers use the app always voluntarily, are constantly aware of being tracked and have options to quit tracking anytime.

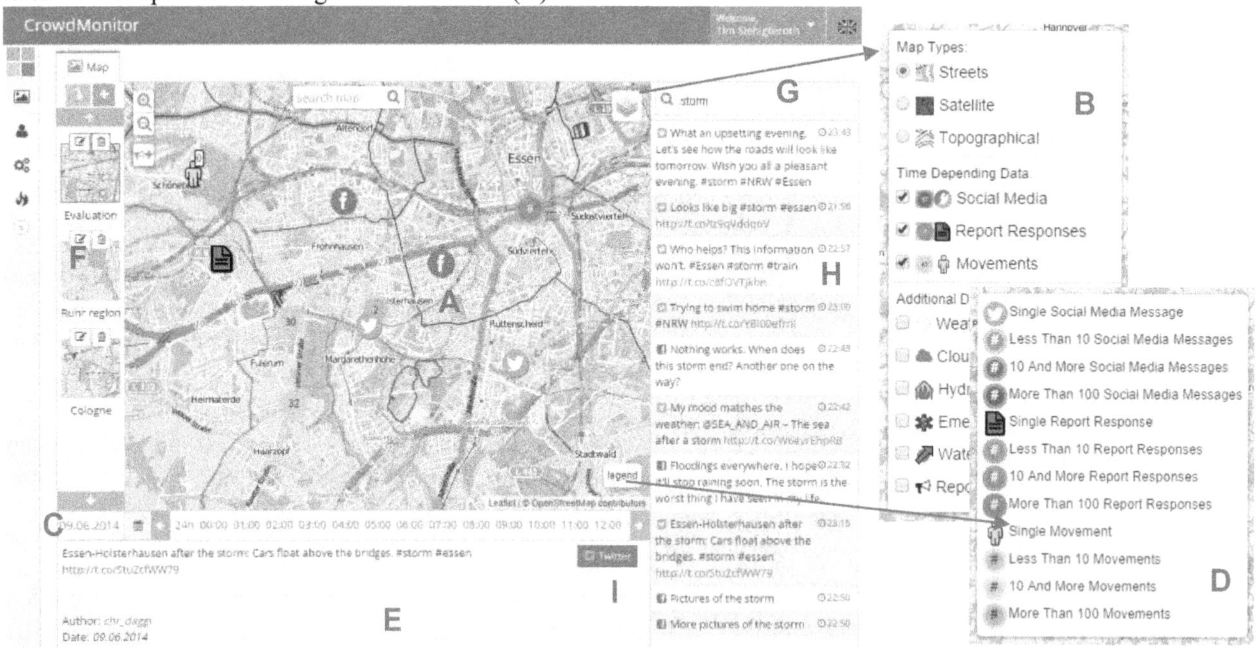

Figure 1: CrowdMonitor: Assessing of Digital Activities during Emergencies

The individual movements of volunteers are presented as persons (**J**) related to a certain location and time. The small box represents the anonymous identification number. In addition, the path of a volunteer's movement and direction (**K**) is presented within the selected period of time between two time stamps. The speed with which the volunteer on the ground has moved between different locations is displayed (**L**). This data is also listed in the detail view of a marker with an accurate date and time to discover potential local patterns of movements. Officials further have the option to contact volunteers directly via chat functionality (**M**).

Public calls to the crowd can be initiated either by requesting all mobile app users or by defining a rectangle on the map (**N**). This rectangle presents the intended area where users should be notified about defined public calls or instructions. After defining an area, a dialog pops up to further specify the call (**O**). Emergency services must define a title, a description and the specific questions (include multiple choice, single choice or open questions). If a volunteer enters the pre-specified location, the request or instruction will start automatically and the volunteer can respond to it. All responses are displayed on the map by time and its location (**P**). The detail area contains the report's title, description and corresponding questions along with the responses of participating volunteers.

EVALUATION OF CROWDMONITOR

In order to evaluate CrowdMonitor, we conducted several evaluations, mainly with emergency services as they are the primarily users of such an application. The conceptual basis has been evaluated in two iterations (first with 12 and second with 16 emergency service officials) focusing on aspects of information gathering and sharing as well as situation assessment [16, 27]. To evaluate the mobile crowd sensing, we made an additional evaluation with a total of eight people. We aimed at testing both usability, for which we used a group of four students (E1-4), and practice relevance, for which we enlisted four emergency services units (E5-8). In the second instance, we were primarily concerned with identifying in what ways CrowdMonitor would be used, and what difficulties in use might be encountered. The philosophy behind the evaluation was derived from the notion of 'situated evaluation' [35] in which qualitative methods are used to draw conclusions about the real-world use of a technology using domain experts. The aim was not to measure the relationship between evaluation goals and outcomes but to derive views from experts about how useful the tool might be in use. Although our system had been fully implemented, IT security regulations of the emergency services prevented us from conducting an in-use and real-world evaluation.

The evaluation was therefore predicated on a scenario-based walkthrough coupled with subsequent semi-structured interviews. The scenario was designed to introduce the participants to the context of a disaster and to simulate the special characteristics of a crisis situation. The scenario was based on a big storm in western Germany, which caused heavy floods and damages. During the storm, it was intended that participants should manage four tasks: (1) getting an overview about the current situation, (2) creating and saving an appropriate map, (3) creating a public request and (4) making an informed decision based on the reports that are received. During this exploration of CrowdMonitor the participants were asked to 'think aloud' [20] and were audio-recorded. Further, the semi-structured interviews focused on a deeper understanding of usability issues (students) as well as application fields, potentials and obstacles in using the system (emergency services).

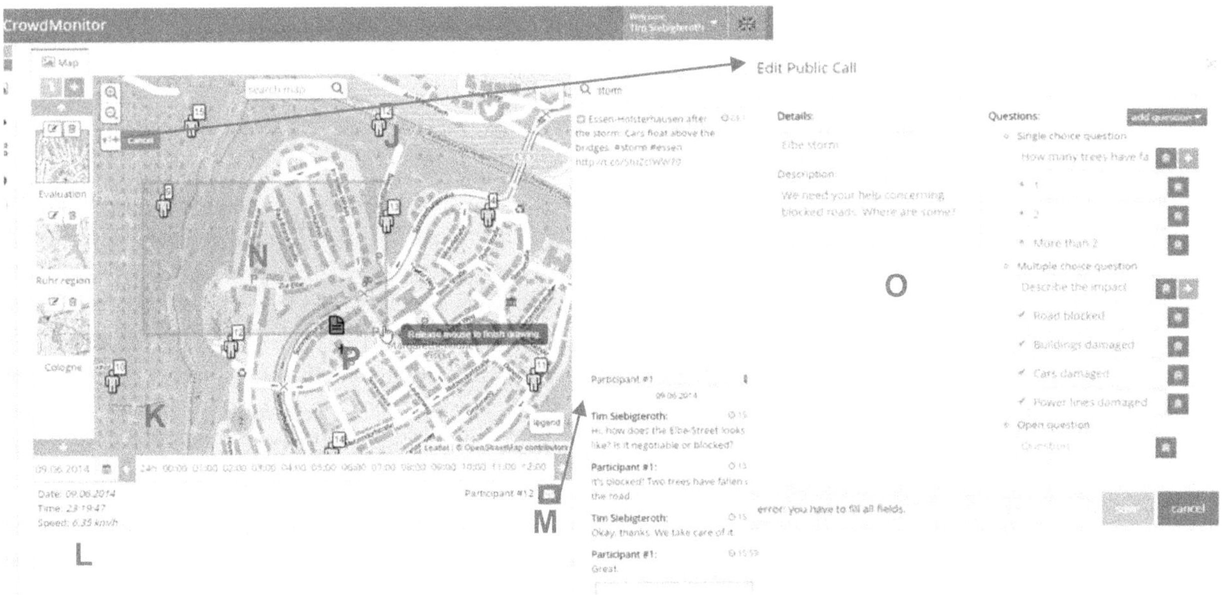

Figure 2: Crowd Monitor: Assessing of Physical On-site Activities

Overall the participants praised the system's usability. They argued that it is intuitive (E5), simple to use (E8), and easy to understand (E2). As a result, the given scenario was generally solved without need for supervision, which is a precondition for its deployment during crisis management. The options for public calls (E8) and the color chosen for the visualization of movement paths and directions were criticized for not standing out from the background (E2).

Results I: Advanced Situation Assessment

The potential for emergency services during large-scale emergencies, such as storms or large fires (E5) was apparent. Supporting emergency services, e.g. for localizing smells, was mentioned as a concrete use case:

"I think of Cologne [German city], where we had this odor nuisance last year. We could make requests here, where does the smell come from, where do we need to perform actions?" (E5).

Displaying citizen-generated content from social media in combination with volunteered movement data and reports provides a good overview about the current situation of actions on-site: *"It surely makes a lot of sense for the initial rough assessment to find out where my priorities are"* (E8).

During use, the participants particularly emphasized the value *"that the messages, when I zoom out, are more summarized. Then I don't have 20 markers next to each other"* (E5). In this way, it is possible, on the one hand, to assess a situation and, on the other hand, to differentiate between affected areas and to react correspondingly:

"[...] that I know which districts are more affected than others. From where are we receiving more extreme damage reports, then I would see that I quickly send an authority's car to check whether it's really like this or not" (E8).

Results II: Facilitate Coordination with Volunteers

The potential of a synchronized view on citizen-generated data, volunteered on-site information and subsequent possibilities to for coordinating with volunteers were identified, because if social media data or emergency calls do not fulfil the emergency services' needs, they have with CrowdMonitor an additional information source:

"If it is described inaccurately within social media, I could ask persons, who are near that place, for more details [...] otherwise I have to send somebody to check it" (E5).

Citizens providing information need always feedback from the officials: "*In any case they need a feedback, regardless of whether a message was helpful or not. Otherwise – I think – he would lose the motivation after two times"* (E6).

With regard to the feedback to citizens, the functionality for defining an area for targeted instructions as well as the anonymous chat become important, because if citizens have a feeling that no one cares about them, they feel isolated:

"You can be addressed directly with this chat. This is very positive, because you directly have the feeling that someone takes care of you, if one someone writes" (E7).

Public calls are important not only for provision of information by volunteers, but also for monitoring their activities and collaborating with them during emergencies. With the overview of social media data and options for public calls, a 'bridge' (E6) is built that allows interacting with online as well as offline self-help communities:

"*To get a bridge to social media and prevent a bit of this [uncoordinated] self-help and help organize. We can initiate public calls to manage it a bit.*" (E6)

With approaches for coordinating with citizens, locations and points of interest can be announced and directed:

"You could, if you have food stores somewhere at five sand packing stations and then you would start a public call, you can directly specify the address. He [volunteer] knows right where he must go" (E6).

Results III: Individual and Targeted Warnings

With an application that provides information about locations, citizens and volunteers can be specifically and – above all – individually be warned in case of dangers:

"If I know here is a river that will overflow within the next two hours, and then I can start this public call, frame the area and then notify the people: 'The river will overflow!' And then the people can react and ask themselves: 'Will I leave the house or will I seal it off somehow and get sandbags?' That is definitely very practical" (E7)

Such individual targeted warnings will potentially mean that warnings are more likely to be noticed. In serious situations, a display of movement data enables the monitoring of individuals to determine whether there are persons in danger areas or not:

"The movement data of people certainly are very nice. If someone fell into the water or something like that, then that would certainly be very useful" (E7).

Moreover the possibility of providing an overview of the current situation with the aid of social media was emphasized: *"I can see directly on Facebook and Twitter what people are posting and what their concerns are"* (E7).

However, it was remarked that right now the deployment of the system in real world situations is still not sure "*because currently too many things take place in parallel via phone and radio. This would require some alignment in a realistic and sufficient way"* (E2).

Results IV: Pictures enhance Citizens' Activities

Emergency services wanted volunteers to be able to transfer multimedia content as additional responses to public calls:

"I think a picture would be helpful for situation assessment. Especially for power lines or cars when you don't know

whether you need a tow-truck, whether you need an energy operator for disconnecting the power or whether the power has already been turned off" (E6).

The need for pictures also becomes apparent in the context of messages from social media: *"Probably there are pictures in the posts. It would certainly be perfect if I could look at the pictures from here [system]"* (E1).

In addition, the need for a classification of the responses of public requests was mentioned, because it would allow a more effective reaction to the reports:

"That I know: 'There is only a small branch on the car; he has sent me a photo; it's not that bad. But behind, a tree has fallen on a house and it must be removed first'. I can say which is important and which can be done later" (E7).

DISCUSSION AND CONCLUSION

In recent years, the work practices of emergency services have been confronted with (at least) two separate issues: The first and newly emergent issue is the appropriate handling of citizen-generated content from social media. The second is the need for the appropriate management of on-site activities by volunteers (newly coordinated through social media). Our paper focuses on both types of citizen involvement (social media / on-site) during emergencies and contributes with an approach how a combination of digital and physical activities as well as the content generated in social media could support the work of emergency services and vice versa volunteers.

Based on our empirical work, which outlines current intersections between volunteer activities and the actions of emergency services, we have developed the web application CrowdMonitor that develops the concept of mobile crowd sensing [40] to create coordination mechanisms for interacting and collaborating with the public during emergencies. It provides functionality for gathering 'on the ground' movements, requesting data publicly and access to social media information and therefore covers real and virtual activities. The evaluation of our approach showed its potential and suggested possible improvement, such as a better first overview of incidents or warnings geared to individual needs of citizens. We outline four lessons learnt when designing approaches that deal with combining physical and digital citizens' activities during emergencies:

(1) For situation assessment, emergency services can use the crowd by official public calls that request gathering, or validating of citizen-generated social media content. Additionally, volunteered individual reports, especially pictures, are of particular value.

(2) Combined visualization of social media and volunteer activities, especially movements on-site, enables the monitoring of and coordination with citizens on an individual as well as collective level.

(3) Monitoring of individuals as well as the crowd is appropriate for a first overview and less so during the entire progress of an emergency, because officials arriving on-site will act as contact persons to emergency management and the importance of volunteer generated content decreases. Later coordination with volunteers becomes more important than the overview, so as to align their activities with the emergency services.

(4) When considering volunteer integration into the current work practices of emergency services, large-scale and long-term situations provide more potential (and traffic) than daily or small incidents.

Misinterpretation remains a problem, even with CrowdMonitor. Citizens using social media or the mobile app (with tracked positions) are more likely technophile. This will not be true for all people affected and we cannot assume that an accurate picture will always be possible. A retirement home, for instance, creates less information, but is more affected by most kinds of emergencies.

Based on our results, a next version of CrowdMonitor must provide options for enhanced responses with multimedia information to public calls and mechanisms for movement predictions based on the provided location information. One limitation of our approach is that social media, in the context we examined, are currently not part of the official work structures (which is about to change), and is only informally used for getting an unofficial situation overview.

ACKNOWLEDGEMENTS

The research project EmerGent' was funded by a grant of the European Union (FP7 No. 608352).

REFERENCES

1. Abel, F., Hauff, C., and Stronkman, R. Semantics + Filtering + Search = Twitcident Exploring Information in Social Web Streams Categories and Subject Descriptors. *Proc Hypertext* (2012), 5–8.
2. Alexander, D.E. Social Media in Disaster Risk Reduction and Crisis Management. *Science and Engineering Ethics*, 20, 3 (2013), 717-733.
3. Brabham, C.D. *Crowdsourcing*. The MIT Press, Cambridge MA, London, 2013.
4. Burke, J., Estrin, D., Hansen, M., et al. Participatory Sensing. *Proc. Sensys* (2006), 1–5.
5. Chohan, A.F., Hester, V., and Munro, R. Crowd-sourcing for Multipurpose and Multicategory Climate related Disaster Reporting. Manchester (2010), 1–9.
6. Chu, E.T., Chen, Y., Lin, J., and Liu, J.W.S. Crowdsourcing Support System for Disaster Surveil-lance and Response. *Proc. WPMC*, IEEE (2012), 21–25.
7. Denef, S., Bayerl, P.S., Kaptein, N. Social Media and the Police-Tweeting Practices of British Police Forces during the August 2011 Riots. *Proc. CHI*, ACM (2013).
8. Dynes, R.R. Situational Altruism: Toward an Explanation of Pathologies in Disaster Assistance. 1994, 18–23.

9. Estelles-Arolas, E. and Gonzalez-Ladron-de-Guevara, F. Towards an integrated crowdsourcing definition. *Journal of Information Science* 38, 2 (2012), 189–200.
10. Frommberger, L. and Schmid, F. Mobile4D: Crowdsourced Disaster Alerting and Reporting. *Proc. ICTD* (2013), 29–32.
11. Gao, H. and Barbier, G. Harnessing the Crowdsourcing Power of Social Media for Disaster Relief. *Intelligent Systems*, IEEE 26, 3 (2011), 10–14.
12. Guo, B., Yu, Z., Zhou, X., and Zhang, D. From Participatory Sensing to Mobile Crowd Sensing. *Proc. Workshop: Social and Community Intelligence* (2014).
13. Hughes, A.L., Denis, L.A.S., Palen, L., and Anderson, K.M. Online Public Communications by Police & Fire Services during the 2012 Hurricane Sandy. *Proc. CHI* (2014), 1505-1514.
14. Kuznetsov, S., Davis, G.N., Cheung, J.C., and Paulos, E. Ceci N'est Pas Une Pipe Bombe: Augthoring Urban Landscapes with Air Quality Sensors. *Proc. CHI* (2014), 2375–2384.
15. Latonero, M. and Shklovski, I. Emergency Management, Twitter, and Social Media Evangelism. *IJISCRAM* 3, 4 (2011), 1–16.
16. Ley, B., Ludwig, T., Pipek, V., Randall, D., Reuter, C., and Wiedenhoefer, T. Information and Expertise Sharing in Inter-Organizational Crisis Management. *JCSCW*, Springer, 23, 4-6 (2014), 347–387.
17. Marcus, A., Bernstein, M., Badar, O., Karger, D.R., Madden, S., and Miller, R.C. Twitinfo: aggregating and visualizing microblogs for event exploration. *Proc. CHI*, ACM (2011).
18. Mills, A., Chen, R., Lee, J., and Rao, H. Web 2.0 emergency applications: how useful can twitter be for emergency response. *JIPS*, 5, 3 (2009) 3-26.
19. Moran, S. et al. Listening to the Forest and its Curators. *Proc. CHI* (2014), 2387–2396.
20. Nielsen, J. *Usability Engineering*. MKP, 1993.
21. Okolloh, O. Ushahidi, or 'testimony': Web 2.0 tools for crowdsourcing crisis information. *Participatory Learning and Action* 59 (2008), 65–70.
22. Palen, L. and Liu, S.B. Citizen communications in crisis: anticipating a future of ICT-supported public participation. *Proc. CHI*, ACM (2007).
23. Poblet, M., García-Cuesta, E., and Casanovas, P. IT Enabled Crowds: Leveraging the Geomobile Revolution for Disaster Management. *Proc. WG5 CI* (2014), 16–23
24. Reddy, S., Shilton, K., and Denisov, G. Biketastic: sensing and mapping for better biking. *Proc. CHI* (2010), 1817–1820.
25. Reuter, C., Heger, O., and Pipek, V. Combining Real and Virtual Volunteers through Social Media. *Proc. ISCRAM* (2013), 1–10.
26. Reuter, C., Ludwig, T., Kaufhold, M.-A., and Pipek, V. XHELP: Design of a Cross-Platform Social-Media Application to Support Volunteer Moderators in Disasters. *Proc. CHI* (2015).
27. Reuter, C., Ludwig, T., and Pipek, V. Ad Hoc Participation in Situation Assessment: Supporting Mobile Collaboration in Emergencies. *TOCHI* 21, 5 (2014).
28. Reuter, C., Marx, A., and Pipek, V. Crisis Management 2.0: Towards a Systematization of Social Software Use in Crisis Situations. *IJISCRAM* 4, 1 (2012), 1–16.
29. Schulz, A., Paulheim, H., and Probst, F. Crisis Information Management in the Web 3.0 Age. *Proc. ISCRAM* (2012), 2–6.
30. Stallings, R.A. and Quarantelli, E.L. Emergent Citizen Groups and Emergency Management. *Public Administration Review* 45 (1985), 93–100.
31. Starbird, K. and Palen, L. Voluntweeters: Self-Organizing by Digital Volunteers in Times of Crisis. *Proc. CHI*. ACM, Vancouver, Canada, 2011.
32. Starbird, K. Delivering patients to sacré coeur: collective intelligence in digital volunteer communities. *Proc. CHI*, ACM (2013), 801–810.
33. Strauss, A.L. *Qualitative Analysis for Social Scientists*. Cambridge Press, 1987.
34. Tierney, K.J., Bevc, C., and Kuligowski, E. Metaphors Matter: Disaster Myths, Media Frames, and Their Consequences in Hurricane Katrina. *AAPSS Journal* 604, 1 (2006), 57–81.
35. Twidale, M., Randall, D., and Bentley, R. *Situated evaluation for cooperative systems Situated evaluation for cooperative systems*. Lancester, UK, 1994.
36. Vieweg, S., Hughes, A.L., Starbird, K., and Palen, L. Microblogging During Two Natural Hazards Events: What Twitter May Contribute to Situational Awareness. *Proc. CHI* (2010), 1079–1088.
37. Wachtendorf, T. and Kendra, J.M. *Improvising Disaster in the City of Jazz: Organizational Response to Hurricane Katrina*. 2006..
38. Winterboer, A., Martens, M.A., Pavlin, G., Groen, F.C.A., and Evers, V. DIADEM: A System for Collaborative Environmental Monitoring. *Proc. CSCW*, ACM (2011), 589–590.
39. Wulf, V., Rohde, M., Pipek, V., Stevens, G. Engaging with Practices: Design Case Studies as a Research Framework in CSCW. *Proc. CSCW*, ACM (2011).
40. Zaslavsky, A., Jayaraman, P.P., and Krishnaswamy, S. ShareLikesCrowd: Mobile Analytics for Participatory Sensing and Crowdsourcing Applications. *Proc. ICDEW*, IEEE (2013), 128–135.

XHELP: Design of a Cross-Platform Social-Media Application to Support Volunteer Moderators in Disasters

Christian Reuter, Thomas Ludwig, Marc-André Kaufhold, Volkmar Pipek
University of Siegen, Institute for Information Systems
Kohlbettstr. 15, 57072 Siegen, Germany
{christian.reuter; thomas.ludwig; marc.kaufhold; volkmar.pipek}@uni-siegen.de

ABSTRACT
Recent disasters have shown an increase in the significance of social media for both affected citizens and volunteers alike in the coordination of information and organization of relief activities, often independently of and in addition to the official emergency response. Existing research mainly focuses on the way in which individual platforms are used by volunteers in response to disasters. This paper examines the use of social media during the European Floods of 2013 and proposes a novel cross-social-media application for volunteers. Besides comprehensive analysis of volunteer communities, interviews were conducted with "digital volunteers" such as Facebook moderators of disaster-related groups. Based on the challenges identified, we designed and implemented the cross-social-media application "XHELP", which allows information to be both, acquired and distributed cross-media and cross-channel. The evaluation with 20 users leads to further design requirements for applications aiming to support volunteer moderators during disasters.

Author Keywords
Social Media; Emergency Management; Digital Volunteers, Cross-Platform, European Floods, Design Case Study

ACM Classification Keywords
H.5.3 Group and Organization Interfaces.

INTRODUCTION
Social media can be described as a "group of Internet-based applications that build on the ideological and technological foundations of Web 2.0, and that allow the creation and exchange of user-generated content" [17]. Salient examples include Facebook with about 1.35 billion active users monthly, and the microblogging platform Twitter numbering approximately 284 million active users monthly. The functionalities they offer are demonstrably suitable to support communication and coordination between the people affected by and volunteers helping during emergencies. They enable real and virtual help activities to be addressed [30, 49] although some limitations have also been recognized [11]. Their emergent relationship with official responders has also been well-attested [47]. Social media have been extensively used during various disasters, such as the 2010 Haiti earthquake [44, 49] or 2012 hurricane Sandy [16]. The 2013 European floods are one of the latest examples [10]. During the flood, not only did a great number of professionals engage in building up flood barriers but volunteers and the people affected by the floods participated too. In situations where the scale and extent of difficulties are emergent and therefore not completely known; or where resources may be scarce or inappropriately allocated; and where information unfolds rapidly, the role of unofficial actors can be critical.

This design case study [48] aims to examine how real and virtual relief activities might be supported by specific tools. These activities are initiated and coordinated through the use of social media. Based on a review of related work, which helped us frame some of the relevant questions, we conducted an empirical study concerned with the role of volunteers and use of social media during the 2013 European floods. This was accomplished by analyzing content from social media as well as conducting interviews with "digital volunteers". Challenges were identified based on this study and an attempt was made to address these challenges by means of XHELP, our cross-social-media application for volunteers in emergencies, especially for moderators of emerging groups. We finally evaluated XHELP with 20 users.

CHI 2015, April 18–23, 2015, Seoul, Republic of Korea.

ACM 978-1-4503-3145-6/15/04...$15.00.
http://dx.doi.org/10.1145/2702123.2702171

RELATED WORK: VOLUNTEERS AND SOCIAL MEDIA

Digital and Real Volunteers in Emergencies
Substantial, organized volunteering during disasters is not a novel phenomenon: Nearly 40 years ago, these "emergent groups" were characterized as "private citizens who work together in pursuit of collective goals relevant to actual or potential disasters but whose organization has not yet become institutionalized" [36]. According to Quarantelli [28], the essential conditions for their emergence are (a) a legitimizing social environment, (b) a perceived threat, (c) a supporting social climate, (d) a network of social relationships, and (e) the availability of specific (immaterial) resources. The broad acceptance of social media has, however, widened the possibility for crisis communication from authorities to citizens as well as the coordination of voluntary activities [31]. Reuter et al. [30] distinguish between activities in the "real" and the "virtual" world. A distinction

becomes apparent between real "emergent groups" [36], which usually act in the form of neighborly help and on-site work, and virtual "digital volunteers" [37], who originate from the Internet and work online. Accordingly, one of the main challenges is to combine these communities.

Volunteers and Social Media

The emergence of digital volunteers and "voluntweeters" [37] (digital volunteers in the Twitter sphere) and their use of social media has been studied in the context of various disasters: Users organize and disseminate crisis-related information [13], seek information about peoples' status [27], express solidarity [38] or coordinate both material and immaterial resources [25]. Starbird & Palen [37] suggested that personal relationships with people affected and the pure desire to help were the initial reasons for using Twitter. The prospect of *identifying, amplifying and redirecting information* was examined in multiple studies, which highlight the role of retweeting, outline the phenomena of information *broadcasting* or information processing through filtering [38]. Another important aspect is the *verification* of information as there are obvious issues with regard to the perceived credibility of social media content in comparison with other media. Information with no clear source, for instance, can be implicated in the spread of rumor [23]. Even so, activities of *structuring and synthesizing* become apparent [45]. These studies analyzed how Twitter can contribute to the production of an overall, coherent picture which enables an appropriate response to the developing situation [29], and indicates that tweets including situational updates or geolocations are more likely to be retweeted than others. Volunteer role classifications include "helper", "reporter", "retweeter", "repeater" and "reader" [30] as well as "information broker", gathering and reporting information [46]. Kaufhold & Reuter [18] suggest "moderators", who establishes supportive platforms for real and virtual activities, mediates offers of and requests for assistance, mobilizes resources and integrates information of various sources.

Volunteers – Potentials and Obstacles

Digital volunteerism, then, might have both positive and negative consequences. Many studies highlight the "chaotic" or disorganized work of volunteers [4, 44], whose activities are indisputably valuable, but which also often lead to confusion. Activities in danger-zones have the potential to increase not only the complexity of tasks but also uncertainty and the pressure on emergency services, especially if the volunteers themselves are endangered [25]. Valecha et al. [44] suggest that "whenever there is greater uncertainty reduction needed, there will be a larger amount of collaboration on the platform", while uncertainty can be generated by redundant information and mistakes due to the chaotic "disorganized" work of volunteers. Accordingly, Chen et al. [4] describe the actions taken by the emergency services to correct the mistakes caused by the "emerging risks of the chaotic use of social media". Another suggested remedy lies with so-called "community scouts" [31]. In one case, a group of "trusted volunteers" was respectively formed to monitor social media and transfer "semi-official" reports to officials [7]. Different social media entail different forms of communication [16]. Nevertheless, most studies focus on the use of Twitter, perhaps due to the ease of data access or the frequency of use [31]. However in many European countries such as Germany – where our study pertaining to the European floods was conducted – 56% of all Internet users actively use Facebook, whereas the active usage of Twitter is significantly lower at just 6% [2]. Yet, Birkbak [1] claims to be one of the first comparative case studies of public Facebook groups in emergencies, showing that more research is needed. The use of more "closed" social media creates new design requirements, e.g. to make them more listenable. Thus, "data showed that replies by emergency managers to questions from the public were often buried within response threads to individual messages" [16]. They suggest that, "to make online media streams more "listenable" for on-the-ground emergency managers, new [...] tools are needed that allow emergency managers to better track, respond to, and document public information".

Research efforts have been largely geared to identify as design requirements. Reuter et al. [30] propose, (a) the integration of ICT for volunteers into existing networks, (b) the fostering of voluntary groups coming into existence, (c) connection between virtual and real activities, and (d) interfaces with official crisis management. Furthermore, based on interviews with emergency services and digital volunteers, Cobb et al. [5] suggest (a) the coordination and integration of voluntary activities, (b) the connection between different tools and tasks as well as (c) the option to share their own activities in order to generate learning effects for spontaneous and often less experienced volunteers. They argue to query multiple social networks with filter options.

Existing Approaches and Tools

A number of public, scientific or commercial applications have been developed for coping with social media [26]. They are being directly or indirectly developed for crisis management, but have limitations, as will be explained in the following. They have (a) syntactical requirements, (b) do not support cross-media communication, or (c) are not integrated in networks users are familiar with (Table 1).

Tool and Reference	a	b	c	Tool and Reference	a	b	c
Brandwatch [3]			x	Tweak the Tweet [39]	x	x	
Geofeedia [12]			x	TweetDeck [42]		x	x
Hands2Help [14]	x	x	x	Twitcident [40]		x	x
HierarchicalTopics [9]			x	TwitInfo [20]		x	x
Hootsuite [15]			x	UberMetrics [43]			x
SensePlace2 [34]		x	x	Ushahidi [24]		x	x
Sproutsocial [35]			x	Visual Backchannel [8]		x	x

Table 1: Several existing Approaches and Tools

TweetDeck [42] is a publicly available tool for real-time tracking, organizing, and engagement. It enables Tweet publication, management, and search (based on quantitative criteria). Multiple approaches aim to provide visualization which supplements the common activity- or list-based view of social media. For instance, *Visual Backchannel* [8] offers a multi-faceted visual overview enriching queried tweets with a temporal topic stream, a spiral of involved people, and an image cloud. *TwitInfo* [20] additionally presents a message frequency graph and evaluates the overall positive and negative sentiment of the analyzed set of tweets in a pie chart. *HierarchicalTopics* [9] is an approach to visually exploring large text collections; however, the system is not customized for citizens. Other platforms concentrate on the map-based visualization of data: *Ushahidi* [24] is a platform for the collection and visualization of information and interactive mapping. Supporting multiple data streams, e.g. text messages via smartphone app, email, Twitter, and web forms, it allows the dissemination of reports which can be displayed via list or geo-reference in a map view. Similar to *SensePlace2* [34], Ushahidi enables the chronological filtering of messages. The downside of Ushahidi is, however, that it requires the deployment of a separate platform, while SensePlace2 is not publicly available. Although a closed system, *Hands2Help* [14] is a mobile app concept which intends to coordinate volunteers in terms of supply and demand of help, enabling ad hoc registration and allowing efficient allocation and monitoring. An exceptional solution is the *Tweak the Tweet* [39] micro syntax for Twitter, allowing the automatic classification of information by means of specific hashtags and tweet structure. It is the only approach which is integrated in an existing network, but has syntactical requirements and is limited to Twitter.

Furthermore, there are plenty of commercial platforms providing cross-media functionalities: Hootsuite, Sproutsocial, *Brandwatch* [3], Twitcident and *UberMetrics* [43]. Each supports the monitoring, filtering and analysis of various social media utilizing a dashboard feature. However, these dashboard reports and visualizations focus on categories such as business performance, competitor benchmarking, and brand analytics. Using dashboards for volunteer activities therefore requires the identification of relevant information categories. Additionally, *Geofeedia* [12] focuses on the monitoring of specific and configurable geographic locations. In addition to the presented functionalities, *Hootsuite* [15] and *Sproutsocial* [35] both provide message publication and scheduling for public engagement as well as a team collaboration module which, for instance, allows the setup of permissions and roles, additional to the assignment and management of tasks. Moreover, *Twitcident* [40], which addresses emergency services, contributes the functionalities of event and incident detection. In conclusion, these approaches provide the aspect of dashboards, geographic monitoring, bidirectional message publication and task management. This could all be useful in supporting volunteer activities, but as commercial B2B products they are not available to a broad audience and do not address all requirements for volunteer moderators.

To summarize, almost all approaches (Table 1) have limitations when used by volunteer moderators in disasters: They either demand syntactical requirements from the user [39]; do not provide cross-platform structures, e.g. focus solely on Twitter [8, 20, 24, 34, 40, 42], or require the use of a new platform and therefore fail to integrate ICT for volunteers into existing networks (almost all).

State of Play

Despite the outlined design requirements mentioned above, there is little existing research which focuses on the development of technical artifacts to support the rich coordination activities of digital volunteers - especially how to support the "community scouts" [31] or "trusted volunteers" [7] who appear in the form of very active "moderators" [18] during crises. Thus our design case study seeks to enhance the state of the art by providing a cross-social-media case study based on the 2013 European floods in order to derive challenges, which in turn inform the design, development and evaluation of a technical artefact to support the current practices of volunteers in disasters and "to make online media streams more 'listenable'" [16].

THE STUDY CASE: EUROPEAN FLOODS 2013

The European floods in June 2013 were an event in which self-help activities played a major role. 35 federal states of seven European countries had to declare a state of disaster in multiple districts; including 55 districts in Germany, notably the Federal States of Bavaria, Saxony and Saxony-Anhalt. This disaster caused the deaths of eight people in Germany and cost the states an estimated 6.7 billion Euro. The German armed forces (19,000 soldiers) and fire services (75,000 firefighters) participated in the relief efforts. The German Red Cross and further relief organizations were involved in medical care. Besides the large number of professional forces and voluntary organizations, many volunteers and affected people participated in building up flood barriers, filling and piling up sandbags, donating work material and goods for victims, distributing food and providing emergency shelters. The use of social media in this case has been acknowledged and even utilized by the traditional media. Volunteer activities were planned and coordinated, emotional support was given and eyewitness reports were shared. Using this case, Fuchs et al. [10] confirm the potential of Twitter as a distributed "social sensor".

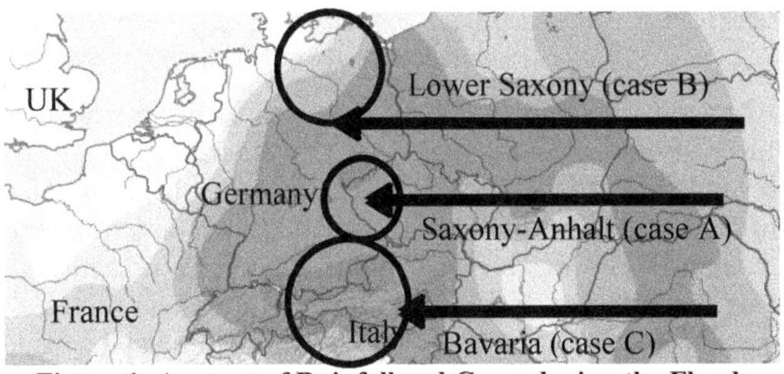

Figure 1: Amount of Rainfall and Cases during the Floods

EMPIRICAL STUDY: USE OF SOCIAL MEDIA DURING THE EUROPEAN FLOODS IN GERMANY 2013

Our empirical study, which has partly been reported [18], aims to examine the usage of social media for the coordination of volunteer relief activities. In the period from June 6th to June 27th 2013, nearly 80,000 tweets containing the term or hashtag "hochwasser" (English: flood) were archived with the tool "Tweet Archivist Desktop". We used the term "hochwasser" because it was listed among the top trends in Twitter and was mentioned in several media. Facebook group and page activities were downloaded as complete HTML docs. Additionally, news articles in the context of the floods were archived as PDFs and more than 50 screenshots were saved in order to document the use of Google Maps in the affected areas.

Our Twitter analysis focused on how and in what ways relief activities are shaped in and by Twitter. In doing so, we also looked at other related technologies. The Facebook analysis explored messages in three groups from three federal states in order to analyze processes regarding interaction, structuring, and task sharing (Figure 1, Table 2). In the third step of our empirical study we conducted phone interviews with moderators of the analyzed groups to gain insights into their work practices, ways of mobilizing resources [25] and self-organization processes [37] as well as identifying the potential for supporting them (Table 2). The interviews were designed to specifically address our interests. At the beginning, the interviewees were asked whether they belonged to an organization of civil protection or had competencies regarding professional crisis response. The subsequent part focused on the tasks and activities of the respondents; here, we were particularly interested in the relationship between online or virtual activity and mobilization 'on the ground'. The third part concentrated on task-sharing processes, during which the potential cooperation with emergency services was discussed. Finally the interviews posed questions at an ICT level by evaluating FB functions and discussing technical support potential.

Case/State	**A:** Saxony-Anhalt	**B:** Lower Saxony	**C:** Bavaria
Facebook Pages	Hochwassernews Magdeburg *(Flood News Magdeburg)*	Hochwasser Niedersachsen (*Flood Lower Saxony*)	Infoseite-Hochwasser Bayern 2013 (*Infopage Flood Bavaria*)
Facebook Groups	Hochwasser Magdeburg – HilfsGESUCHE (*Flood Magdeburg – Requests for help*)	Hochwasser Niedersachsen - BIETE/ SUCHE (*Flood Lower Saxony Offer/ Search*)	Mamas Helfen (*Moms help*)
Interviews	A (moderator)	B (moderator)	C (moderator)

Table 2: Empirical Study in Facebook

Although Twitter was extensively used in flood situations for distributing information and situational updates, our results show that it tended to mainly take the form of a broadcast medium for shaping cross-platform structures and extending coverage. The coordination of relief activities was rarely observed in the Twitter sphere alone, but took place within a complex ecology of both online and offline facilities. This could, to some extent, be a corollary of low Twitter penetration in Germany, but it is consistent with Hughes et al. [16] showing differences of use across media platforms. Accordingly Twitter is used for real-time notification, and FB for community engagement [6]. In our case, local and subject-specific groups emerged on FB, which cooperated extensively with other groups/pages. These observations lead to our design challenges:

First, *clarity and representation of relevant content*: The issue of "collective activity", so that all participants, officials and volunteers can access accurate and up-to-date information, can be supported by the identification or the assessment of information through search and filter functions. The interviews indicate that information tends to be sorted thematically with the aid of files. Additional functions for organizing information with search and filter options especially with geographical references are desirable. The purpose of such functions would be to render relevant help requests more available and listenable [16] to the users, to maintain a clear overview within the interaction platform and to support the interaction between moderators, helpers and people in need. These people are currently organized in different groups and use a variety of pages - and sometimes several pages - to articulate their demands.

Second, *moderation and autonomous work*: Interviews show that the moderator's role (an extension of the Reuter et al. [30] role model) is to mediate demands, requests and offers for help; to mobilize volunteers as well as material and immaterial resources and to integrate information from media, official authorities and other organizations. This is evidently a serious role and entails considerable overhead. It is noticeable that private rooms are sometimes used for coordination, especially when privacy is of importance or sensitive data needs to be available on a limited basis. It is obvious that moderating a group is a very time-consuming process. ICT could reduce the amount of moderation activities by fostering the self-regulation of the participants.

Third, *feedback and updates in interaction relationships*: Incoming messages from people not appearing on one's friends list are not flagged and are filtered into the residual FB folder "other". This process impedes the giving of timely feedback. Regarding Google Maps, the requirements for up-to-datedness of geo-referenced objects could, in addition, be supported by notifications or time-based filtering.

Fourth, *integration of technologies and interaction types*: It is apparent that, in a complex ecology, different tools are used for different purposes. Twitter is particularly used for distributing situational updates. Interviewees saw the benefit of an embedded FB application as long as it is quickly accessible and fills feature gaps. Using maps such as Google Maps could also tighten the connection between real and virtual volunteer activities. When integrating these services, additional accounts should be avoided because not every user has accounts on networks such as Twitter or Google+. It should be remembered that not everyone is equally "savvy"; imposing an unnecessary learning overhead during a crisis situation is not to be recommended.

Figure 2: Search settings and results

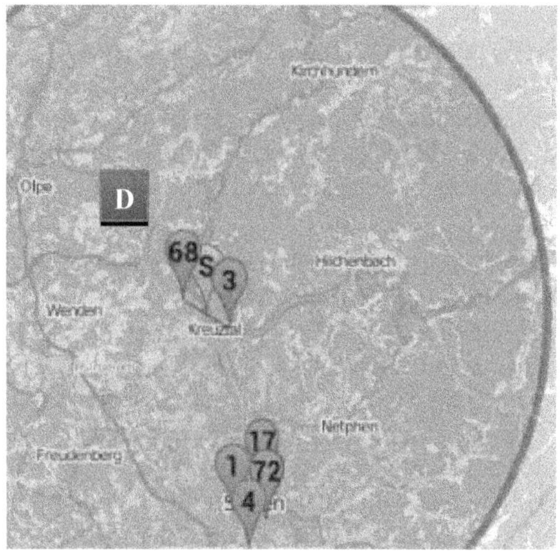

Figure 3: Geo-localization

XHELP: DEVELOPMENT OF A CROSS-SOCIAL-MEDIA APPLICATION FOR VOLUNTEERS

We developed the platform XHELP in order to support these requirements and with the overall aim of supporting the role of group moderator through functionality for assessing and distributing information. We are aware that such functionalities might also be of interest to other target groups. However, based on our research, volunteer moderators are our main target group so far. A cross-platform search and posting function should simplify the current practices and reduce organizational efforts. Since most of the relief activities we saw were organized via FB groups and pages, XHELP has been implemented as an embedded FB application. The advantages of such an approach are that an additional registration process is not necessary and potential entry barriers will be reduced. To evaluate the potential synergy effects of integrating several social networks, the functions of the web application will not just relate to FB, but will also integrate Twitter. Besides using XHELP inside FB, the user can also assess XHELP as an ordinary web version.

Cross-Social-Media Search and Filter Function

To support the relief activities of volunteers and group moderators in particular, a function for searching and filtering information is needed, as we have seen. Groups and pages are often regionally based and therefore require filtering by location, while time-based filtering enables a further selection of the information supply. As moderators in particular search their groups for information in order to coordinate offers of and demands for help, it is essential to include data from groups and pages of the specific user in the search. The search function obtains the data from a social media API developed for this purpose. The API provides relevant messages from Facebook and Twitter in the OpenSocial format (http://opensocial.org/) and offers parameters for the time- and location-based filtering of posts. Using tokens, we can also access data from the user's restricted FB groups, if s/he has agreed and installed the XHELP FB app. In order to further support the aspects required for filtering and assessing information by users, the social media API is combined with an *quality assessment service* [32]. This tool enables the weighting of 12 different assessment criteria (time, space, reputation, metadata, sentiment analysis, fear factor, happiness factor among others) for search requests in addition to the filter options mentioned above. This means that the order of the search results can be controlled (Figure 2).

In the *general* section, users can type in search strings, choose the media to be searched and specify both a search period and a location, including a search radius (**A**). It is also possible to relevant FB groups or pages. The subsequent collapsible field-sets offer optional assessment criteria to impact the order of search results. Alternatively, the search results can be sorted by time, local proximity, and platform (**B**). If a user defines more than one criterion, the degrees of fulfillment will be shown in percentage and color during a mouse-over (**C**). Next to the list of the search results is a map (Figure 3) visualizing the set location as a green marker, the search radius as a blue circle, and the search results with geo-coordinates as red markers (**D**).

Publication and Management of Relevant Messages

The empirical study revealed that groups are closely linked to regional areas, but information requirements cannot always be met within the confines of the area in question. The posting function (Figure 4) of the application aims to support information retrieval by moderators and volunteers by providing the opportunity of publishing messages on multiple channels simultaneously. Here Twitter is provided as a publication channel in our evaluation without the need of a Twitter account. In a real-world setting, this would not be feasible or would at least be legally difficult. Clicking the label "Create new posting" (Figure 5) on the left navigation bar shows the view of a message publication. The user types the message into a text box before selecting the channels for publication (**E**).

Closely tied to the posting function is a dashboard view that summarizes created posts along with relevant metadata. Since postings are published cross-platform, the user has to be supported in the management of these postings and related comments by providing an overview. The dashboard is intended to give the user an overview of his/her activities and to enable direct interaction with the responding authors without visiting each channel individually.

The dashboard contains the overview "My Postings" (Figure 5). Alongside the postings published within XHELP, it contains the user's postings or commented postings that were created beyond the application on the source platform to give an entire overview of the user's activities. Once a post is commented on, it will be attached chronologically with a reference to its source platform (**F**). For the sake of clarity, the dashboard displays a maximum of five comments per posting; and with an arrow symbol in the top right hand corner of a posting, the user can collapse or expand the comments on a posting. The user can respond to each comment and delete their own. The top right hand corner of a posting contains symbols for deleting and finalizing the correspondent posting (**G**). With the "finalize posting" function, the user has a dialog-based opportunity to write a concluding posting informing all related groups, pages and media. The empirical study showed that users published their requests in multiple groups but neglected to inform each group individually whether requests had been settled. In order not to waste resources on matters already dealt with and to prevent *dead postings*, XHELP supports the user in finalizing and/or deleting successful requests or postings and informing the participants of interaction. The posting will not be displayed in "My Postings" anymore, but is still accessible in the left navigation bar.

In summary, XHELP blends together multiple aspects of existing (commercial) approaches within the scope of volunteer activities: It provides dashboard features [3, 42, 43], bidirectional and cross-media communication [35], and with "finalize posting" a basic task management function [15]. Moreover, the information search is enriched by map-based visualization [12, 24]. Additionally XHELP has no syntactical requirements and is embedded into an established context of use.

EVALUATION WITH VOLUNTEERS AND CITIZENS

To assess the concept and the potential value of the web-application XHELP, an evaluation of the search for, filtering and assessment of information functions and of cross-channel functionality (Facebook, Twitter) was conducted. The philosophy behind the evaluation process was derived from the notion of "situated evaluation" [41] in which qualitative methods are used in order to draw conclusions about real-world use of a technology using domain experts. The aim here is not to measure the relationship between evaluation goals and outcomes but to derive subjective views from experts about how useful and relevant the technology might be in use. XHELP was therefore evaluated with 20 users (E01-E20) whereof six participated on a first version of the prototype and were not involved in the follow-up. Of the remaining 14, four participants had been initiators and moderators of Facebook pages during European floods (three of them had already been interviewed during the empirical case study). Their experience as active volunteers generated some valuable feedback.

The evaluation was based on a scenario-based walkthrough coupled with subsequent semi-structured interviews. The scenario was designed to introduce the participants to the character of a disaster and the role of the volunteer (only if he/she was not already an experienced volunteer). It was based on hurricane Xaver which caused heavy damage on the coast of Germany in December 2013. The participants were given a general description of their role with regard to dealing with the information demands of affected citizens with the help of XHELP. The participants were then given the opportunity to explore the application, on the basis that they would be given a concrete task to tackle afterwards. The first step of the task required them to search for and filter specific information pertaining to water levels. For this purpose, the search function was extended with an evaluation mode. Search results were premised on preselected data records to ensure the comparability of the participants' results. The second step instructed them to ask for additional information about the condition of the dikes using the publication function, whereupon our team created some responses from both

Figure 4: Create new posting

Figure 5: Dashboard with "My Postings"

platforms to enable the use of the response and finalize functions. Following the think-aloud protocol [16], participants were asked to express their thoughts while completing the task.

The semi-structured interviews which followed were intended to encourage reflection on the evaluation process, on ease of use and on the overall value of the application. The questions were specifically oriented towards overall impressions, the advantages and disadvantages of XHELP, coverage of information demands, possible overload and problems of cross-platform information acquisition. The interviews were analyzed and categorized systematically. We employed "open" coding i.e. gathering data into approximate categories to reflect the issues raised by respondents based on repeated readings of the data and its organization into "similar" statements. We clustered positive and negative aspects of the (a) search and (b) dashboard functionality, as well as the (c) usability and (d) potentials of functional enhancement. Taking into account the quantity and originality of aspects as well as the participants' domain expertise, we created a rating for each cluster. The most noteworthy contributions will be presented subsequently and thereafter shaped into design requirements.

Results I: Cross-Platform Search and Assessment

Ten interviewees regarded the search refinement and sorting of results as being valuable, especially when dealing with large amounts of data. In contrast, some negative views were expressed. Eight interviewees deemed the selection of criteria to be too extensive, resulting in complex searches which might hamper quick results. Additionally, E20 suggested that some means of assessing the emotional content of messages was needed, since it bore some consequences for perceived accuracy:

"If someone is upset about something that isn't correct at all and then spreads wrong information and next other people follow it, it has to be counteracted rapidly" (E20).

Two participants argued that an automatic information assessment might result in over-reliance on the application and could potentially result in the loss of relevant search results. E20 doubted that an information search with search terms was useful for identifying offers of, and demands for donated items:

"But then, if I search for donations, they don't show up, but rather I have to enter 'dusk mask'. But I cannot always search through all search terms. If it is somehow possible to reasonably filter offers of donation computer-linguistically, that would be certainly handy" (E20).

More positively, nine interviewees deemed search functions based on chronological and regional proximity to be important. The visualization of a search radius, the ability to identify their own location and see search results on a map were all seen as enriching information value. Broadly, this is because these functions enabled better judgment about information relevance in relation to rationality, priority and reliability (E17). A search for general, repeated and crisis-specific verbs or syntaxes, that *"are easily and always tracked in the background for a certain disaster"* (E20), would therefore be a useful addition.

Results II: Cross-Platform Dissemination of Posts

Altogether, we saw benefits in terms of the reduction of the overhead. Publishing posts in multiple groups, pages and platforms simultaneously was seen to be much easier. Through the centralized presentation, an overview could also be obtained:

"I really like it. It saves a lot of work, because before, you had to visit every single page and that wasted too much time: You do not have enough people that can help" (E19).

Seven interviewees thought that the application speeded up their information searches over different information sources and the broader bandwidth of platforms. During the selection of dissemination channels, six participants selected Twitter to increase the audience of readers. Three people indicated explicitly that they value the opportunity to publish postings in Twitter without owning an account:

"You essentially built a bridge [...]. This is awesome, because many distribute their information through Twitter and have the opportunity to use Twitter without even owning an account or looking for followers or whatever" (E18).

Further, four participants expressed a positive attitude towards finalizing a posting, or at least the opportunity to publish summary messages, on all channels simultaneously. This circumstance and the resulting reduction of effort are emphasized by E18:

"What I really liked was the function to finish a posting, or to extend or change the demands; you did not need to search in twenty groups 'Where is the post?' to edit or comment it, but rather it was done immediately" (E18).

Results III: Reliability of Gathered Information

During the evaluation, eight participants expressed concerns about the reliability of information, which they gathered with the search or dissemination functionality, and identified different ways in which they went about validating information. Two navigated the public profile of the message author to gain an impression of this person:

"Then I would try to evaluate the information based on the history of the person, which means if a person published quite a few postings in the past that were meaningful and correct, then I would be more likely to believe in the correctness of information" (E12).

Three interviewees wanted to check the reliability by confirmation from other users and two sought direct contact with the author. The consultation of other sources is linked to some other concerns as stated by E16:

"Someone might ascribe too much weight to information on these networks which has not been validated officially. Be-

cause I remember that there were several false reports [...]. That could raise panic or something" (E16).

E16 suggests (similarly to E8) that false reports are a serious problem. Beyond that, she considers local information to be more reliable than remote information.

Results IV: Potential of Functional Enhancement

A number of comments were made about improving XHELP's functionality. Five participants requested the possibility of self-selecting groups, pages and networks, ensuring that only relevant crisis information is managed within the application:

"An incredible amount of people [...] have hundreds of groups. To select the relevant groups again and again from post to post [...] is too time-consuming. Maybe you can select [...] groups to be associated with the app" (E18).

Further, three interviewees see potential in the integration of additional social networks, e.g. Google+. Another person mentions the integration of news webpages within the search functionality (E15). To increase XHELP's breadth of usage, E18 wishes "*that if the application is released, it will be released on smartphones [...], because many people are on the road and do the whole [response work] not at PC or laptop, but on a smartphone*" (E18).

Furthermore, E18 suggests improved contact support among the users of the application to connect people with similar objectives. Thus new relations between volunteers or communities can emerge:

"Maybe it would be interesting to see other users of the app [or] who are searching for the same thing and using the app and who have the same interests as me" (E11).

If task completion is to be achieved cooperatively, E20 asked for a joint view within the application:

"It would be very important for the organizers of the same group [...] to have the same overview, because otherwise you do things twice or three times [...], so you simply need the same information" (E20).

Overall five participants asked for the ability to evaluate obtained information. Three of them explicitly mentioned the ability to sort comments or select a "best answer":

"It would be nice [...] if you had the option to actually mark the question answered or to highlight the respondent who answered the question. So that anybody searching for the answer does not have to go through all the comments initially" (E12).

Concerning the search function, two interviewees requested the ability to manually evaluate search results along with the automatic assessment and to be able to put selected results into a favorite view (E08). Similarly E20 proposes a function to exclude unreliable sources and to purposefully search for messages of certain, reliable or official authors. Authorities themselves are seen to be reliable information sources. Thus E15 wishes "*that the corresponding official establishments such as police, fire service etc. write appropriate messages, in the knowledge that people can access them in any case through this application*" (E15). E19 complains that otherwise official information is disclosed *"much too late and not comprehensively"* (E19) to self-organized helpers.

DISCUSSION OF DESIGN REQUIREMENTS

The evaluation reveals four design requirements as being essential to enhance the value of an application that provides a cross-social-media support for volunteers during emergencies:

First, *overview and avoiding barriers of usage*: The basic principle of a Facebook application that enables interaction patterns, the display and content of social media already in use is demonstrably beneficial, according to our respondents. The evaluation, however, showed that there is need for an information management tool which allows some kind of overview and transcends existing barriers. Extended configurations imply further possibilities for improving the information overview, especially in terms of providing a common overview that moderators and teams can rely on.

Second, *user-defined information management*: A custom information management is required because of the varying preconditions, assessments and working procedures of the participants. Options were requested for selecting relevant application channels to include or exclude information from groups or sites that they saw as relevant or irrelevant to their demands. Furthermore, the scenario showed that users wanted a component to manage favorites, e.g. storing valuable search results or relevant answers obtained using the cross-platform posting function.

Third, *support for self-assessment* and *information verification*: The participants wanted support for information assessment according to specific qualitative criteria to enable them to search purposefully through the vast flood of data in social media. At the same time, they expressed a desire to self-evaluate posts or comments and to highlight relevant comments. Such a function could be used to improve the filtering and classification of upcoming search queries [5]. As the data is investigated, the process can be assisted by giving easy access to a message creator's public profile, supporting the establishment of contacts and enriched information about the poster. Since official crisis response information is considered to be more trustworthy, the integration of that data into the process of information assessment or into the application is preferable.

Fourth, *amplify potential for cross-platform networking*: Interviewees see advantages in cross-platform information processing because faster responses are possible and the general view of the integrated platforms reduces management effort. The functionality of finalizing postings is perceived as assistance to formulating cross-platform status updates and to finishing help activities.

CONCLUSION

Our paper examines the work of volunteer communities in disasters focusing on the empirical analysis of social media activities as well as interviews with moderators of volunteer groups in Facebook and the evaluation of the novel web-application XHELP. This is intended to support volunteers during crisis events.

The case study of the European floods in 2013 [18] emphasizes the relevance of social media in Germany for the first time. Twitter has been used broadly as a platform for status updates, while Facebook pages gave a situational overview and Facebook groups coordinated a multitude of virtual and real help activities. This confirms the findings of Hughes et al. [16]. Among affected citizens and volunteers, some particularly motivated people adapted the role of "moderators" to mediate offers of and demands for help with the use of the technical functions of the social networks. This extends the role model of Reuter et al. [30]. Our examination shows the main challenges, which are (1) clarity and representation of relevant content; (2) moderation and autonomous work; (3) feedback and updates in interaction relationships and (4) integration of technologies and interaction types for the design of social media for volunteers in crisis.

Evaluating our web-application XHELP, we showed that a cross-platform search, especially with time and location filtering options, contributes to the channeling of the information flow. Furthermore, cross-platform posting provides an overview and reduces overhead with its centralized management. The embedding of Twitter is seen as an opportunity to increase the range of search and distribution activities. The interviewees mentioned the reduction of search criteria and possibility of self-assessment and filtering of information to gain an overview of the relevant activities as potential sources for improvement. The main results of the evaluation can be summarized as (1) avoiding barriers of usage with supportive tools; (2) user-defined application configuration and information management; (3) support for self-assessment and information verification and (4) amplifying the potentials of cross-platform networking.

Compared to related work, our approach provides several contributions: Addressing the "chaotic" use of social media [4, 44], we implemented functionalities to render social media "more listenable" as suggested by Hughes et al. [16] (which is also interesting for crowd monitoring [19]), e.g. by showing related discussions in various social media and by using a cross-social-media function to finalize postings. In order to support current working practices, Cobb et al. [5] suggests querying multiple social networks with filters. We have implemented such a function. Our app enables its users to disseminate messages (including backchannel [8]) to various social networks. We propose that our approach enhances the state of the art in presenting empirical data, a concept and its implementation, which e.g. amplify the potential of cross-platform networking. Other tools, such as Ushahidi, automate the collection of incident reports and facilitate the mapping of report locations [21] but are developed as external platforms which have to be deployed manually. Our app is integrated into Facebook and supports established interaction types [30] while still having a cross-platform focus without the burden of syntactical requirements [37]. The integration of additional social media platforms promises to further enhance the cross-platform concept in future. XHELP will then be able to support volunteer's emergent collaboration [33] not only across time and space, but also across platform, group and page.

ACKNOWLEDGEMENTS

The research project EmerGent' was funded by a grant of the European Union (FP7 No. 608352).

REFERENCES

1. Birkbak, A. Crystallizations in the Blizzard : Contrasting Informal Emergency Collaboration In Facebook Groups. *Proc. NordiCHI* (2012), 428–437.
2. BITKOM. Soziale Netzwerke 2013 - Eine repräsentative Untersuchung zur Nutzung sozialer Netzwerke im Internet. Berlin, 2013.
3. http://www.brandwatch.com/brandwatch-analytics
4. Chen, C., Carolina, N., and Ractham, P. Lessons Learned from the Use of Social Media in Combating a Crisis: A Case Study of 2011 Thailand Flooding Disaster. *Proc. ICIS* (2012), 1–17.
5. Cobb, C., McCarthy, T., Perkins, A., and Bharadwaj, A. Designing for the Deluge: Understanding & Supporting the Distributed, Collaborative Work of Crisis Volunteers. *Proc. CSCW* (2014), 888-899.
6. St. Denis, L., Anderson, K.M., and Palen, L. Mastering Social Media : An Analysis of Jefferson County's Communications during the 2013 Colorado Floods. *Proc. ISCRAM* (2014), 737–746.
7. St. Denis, L., Hughes, A., and Palen, L. Trial by Fire: The Deployment of Trusted Digital Volunteers in the 2011 Shadow Lake Fire. *Proc. ISCRAM* (2012), 1-10.
8. Dörk, M., Gruen, D., Williamson, C., and Carpendale, S. A Visual backchannel for large-scale events. *IEEE TVCG 16, 6* (2010), 1129–1138.
9. Dou, W., Yu, L., Wang, X., Ma, Z., and Ribarsky, W. HierarchicalTopics: Visually exploring large text collections using topic hierarchies. *IEEE TVCG 19, 12* (2013), 2002-2011.
10. Fuchs, G., Andrienko, N., Andrienko, G., Bothe, S., and Stange, H. Tracing the German Centennial Flood in the Stream of Tweets: First Lessons Learned. *SIGSPATIAL GeoCrowd* (2013), 2–10.
11. Gao, H., Barbier, G., and Goolsby, R. Harnessing the Crowdsourcing Power of Social Media for Disaster Relief. *IEEE Intelligent Systems* 26, 3 (2011), 10–14.
12. http://geofeedia.com/how-it-works
13. Heverin, T. and Zach, L. Microblogging for Crisis Communication: Examination of Twitter Use in Response to a 2009 Violent Crisis in the Seattle-Tacoma, Washington Area. *Proc. ISCRAM* (2010), 1-5.

14. Hofmann, M., Betke, H., and Sackmann, S. Hands2Help – Ein App-basiertes Konzept zur Koordination Freiwilliger Helfer. *i-com 13*, 1 (2014), 29–36.
15. https://hootsuite.com/products/platform
16. Hughes, A., Denis, L.A.S., Palen, L., and Anderson, K.M. Online Public Communications by Police & Fire Services during the 2012 Hurricane Sandy. *Proc. CHI* (2014), 1505-1514.
17. Kaplan, A.M. and Haenlein, M. Users of the world, unite! The challenges and opportunities of Social Media. *Business Horizons* 53, 1 (2010), 59–68.
18. Kaufhold, M.-A. and Reuter, C. Vernetzte Selbsthilfe in Sozialen Medien am Beispiel des Hochwassers 2013 / Linked Self-Help in Social Media using the example of the Floods 2013 in Germany. *i-com 13*, 1 (2014), 20–28.
19. Ludwig, T., Reuter, C., Siebigteroth, T., and Pipek, V. CrowdMonitor: Mobile Crowd Sensing for Assessing Physical and Digital Activities of Citizens during Emergencies. *Proc. CHI* (2015).
20. Marcus, A., Bernstein, M., and Badar, O. Twitinfo: aggregating and visualizing microblogs for event exploration. *Proc. CHI* (2011), 227-236.
21. McClendon, S. and Robinson, A.C. Leveraging Geospatially-Oriented Social Media Communications in Disaster Response. *Proc. ISCRAM* (2012), 1-10.
22. Nielsen, J. Usability Engineering. Morgan Kaufmann, San Francisco, 1993.
23. Oh, O., Agrawal, M., and Rao, H.R. Community Intelligence and Social Media Services: A Rumor Theoretic Analysis of Tweets during Social Crises. *MISQ* 37, 2 (2013), 407–426.
24. Okolloh, O. Ushahidi, or 'testimony': Web 2.0 tools for crowdsourcing crisis information. *Participatory Learning and Action* 59, 1 (2009), 65–70.
25. Perng, S.-Y., Büscher, M., Wood, L., et al. Peripheral response: Microblogging during the 22/7/2011 Norway attacks. *Proc. ISCRAM* (2012), 1–11.
26. Pohl, D. Social Media Analysis for Crisis Management: A Brief Survey. Special Technical Community on Social Networking. IEEE STCSN E-Letter 2, 1 (2013).
27. Qu, Y., Huang, C., Zhang, P., and Zhang, J. Microblogging after a Major Disaster in China: A Case Study of the 2010 Yushu Earthquake. *Proc. CSCW* (2011), 25–34.
28. Quarantelli, E.L. Emergent Citizen Groups in Disaster Preparedness and Recovery Activities. 1984.
29. Reilly, W.S.N., Guarino, S.L., and Kellihan, B. Model-Based Measurement of Situation Awareness. *Proc. WSC* (2007), 1353-1360.
30. Reuter, C., Heger, O., and Pipek, V. Combining Real and Virtual Volunteers through Social Media. *Proc. ISCRAM* (2013), 780-790.
31. Reuter, C., Marx, A., and Pipek, V. Crisis Management 2.0: Towards a Systematization of Social Software Use in Crisis Situations. *IJISCRAM* 4, 1 (2012), 1–16.
32. Reuter, C., Ritzkatis, M., and Ludwig, T. Entwicklung eines SOA-basierten und anpassbaren Bewertungsdienstes für Inhalte aus sozialen Medien. *Informatik* 2014 (LNI) (2014), 977–988.
33. Reuter, C. *Emergent Collaboration Infrastructures: Technology Design for Inter-Organizational Crisis Management (Ph.D. Thesis).* Springer Gabler, Siegen, Germany, 2014.
34. Robinson, A., Savelyev, A., Pezanowski, S., and MacEachren, A.M. Understanding the Utility of Geospatial Information in Social Media. *Proc. ISCRAM* (2013).
35. http://sproutsocial.com/features
36. Stallings, R.A. and Quarantelli, E.L. Emergent Citizen Groups and Emergency Management. *Public Administration Review 45*, Special Issue (1985), 93–100.
37. Starbird, K. and Palen, L. Voluntweeters: Self-Organizing by Digital Volunteers in Times of Crisis. In *Proc. CHI*. Vancouver, Canada (2011), 1071-1080.
38. Starbird, K. and Palen, L. (How) Will the Revolution be Retweeted ? Information Diffusion and the 2011 Egyptian Uprising. *Proc. CSCW* (2012), 7–16.
39. Starbird, K. and Stamberger, J. Tweak the Tweet : Leveraging Microblogging Proliferation with a Prescriptive Syntax to Support Citizen Reporting. *Proc. ISCRAM* (2010), 1-5.
40. Terpstra, T., Vries, A. de, Stronkman, R., and Paradies, G.L. Towards a realtime Twitter analysis during crises for operational crisis management. *Proc. ISCRAM* (2012).
41. Twidale, M., Randall, D., and Bentley, R. *Situated evaluation for cooperative systems Situated evaluation for cooperative systems.* Lancester, UK, 1994.
42. https://about.twitter.com/products/tweetdeck
43. http://www.ubermetrics-technologies.com/en/product
44. Valecha, R., Oh, O., and Rao, R. An Exploration of Collaboration over Time in Collective Crisis Response during the Haiti 2010 Earthquake. *Proc. ICIS* (2013), 1-10.
45. Vieweg, S., Hughes, A., Starbird, K., and Palen, L. Microblogging During Two Natural Hazards Events : What Twitter May Contribute to Situational Awareness. *Proc. CHI* (2010), 1079–1088.
46. Vieweg, S., Palen, L., Liu, S.B., Hughes, A., and Sutton, J. Collective Intelligence in Distaster: Examination of the Phenomenon in the Aftermath of the 2007 Virginia Tech Shooting. *Proc. ISCRAM* (2008), 44–54.
47. White, C., Plotnick, L., Kushma, J., Hiltz, S.R., and Turoff, M. An online social network for emergency management. *IJEM* 6, 3/4 (2009), 369–382.
48. Wulf, V., Rohde, M., Pipek, V., and Stevens, G. Engaging with Practices: Design Case Studies as a Research Framework in CSCW. *Proc. CSCW* (2011), 505–512.
49. Yates, D. and Paquette, S. Emergency knowledge management and social media technologies: A case study of the 2010 Haitian earthquake. *IJIM* 31, 1 (2011), 6–13.

Building a Birds Eye View: Collaborative Work in Disaster Response

Joel E. Fischer, Stuart Reeves, Tom Rodden, Steven Reece[+], Sarvapali D. Ramchurn[*], David Jones

The Mixed Reality Lab
School of Comp. Sci.
University of Nottingham
{jef,str,tar}@cs.nott.ac.uk

[+]Patterns Analysis & Machine Learning
University of Oxford
reece@robots.ac.uk

[*]Electronics and Computer Science
University of Southampton
sdr1@soton.ac.uk

Rescue Global
London, UK
co@rescue global.org

ABSTRACT

Command and control environments ranging from transport control rooms to disaster response have long been of interest to HCI and CSCW as rich sites of interactive technology use embedded in work practice. Drawing on our engagement with disaster response teams, including ethnography of their training work, we unpack the ways in which situational uncertainty is managed while a shared operational 'picture' is constituted through various practices around tabletop work. Our analysis reveals how this picture is collaboratively assembled as a socially shared object and displayed by drawing on digital and physical resources. Accordingly, we provide a range of principles implicated by our study that guide the design of systems augmenting and enriching disaster response work practices. In turn, we propose the *Augmented Bird Table* to illustrate how our principles can be implemented to support tabletop work.

Author Keywords

Tabletop; disaster response; ethnography; collaboration; situation awareness; uncertainty; crisis informatics

ACM Classification Keywords

H.5.m. Information interfaces and presentation (e.g., HCI): Miscellaneous.

INTRODUCTION

Command and control environments and operational settings have long been of interest to HCI—and particularly CSCW—as rich sites of interactive technology use embedded in work practice [13,15,25,40]. Shared wall displays and tabletop surfaces are a common feature of many of these settings and these are used to support situational awareness, decision-making, and collaboration amongst teams [30,37]. This has not gone unnoticed by HCI and the ITS (Interactive Tabletops and Surfaces) communities as an opportunity for deploying the considerable body of research into the natural interaction practices [32,44], interaction techniques [22,36] and technical innovations [1,17,20]. Consequently, designing for disaster response settings has gained increasing currency in HCI [5,7,27,38]. Accordingly, there are a number of recent examples of interactive surfaces being developed that draw their motivation from the need for situational awareness in emergency response situations [2,23,24,26,28].

CHI 2015, April 18 - 23 2015, Seoul, Republic of Korea
Copyright 2015 ACM 978-1-4503-3145-6/15/04...$15.00
http://dx.doi.org/10.1145/2702123.2702313

We complement these interests by focusing on the everyday practices involved in command and control in disaster response. We are particularly interested in unpacking the ways in which the responders cope with contingencies inherent to these settings. Surprisingly, we find this a domain that has received little attention, despite its acknowledgement by disaster response professionals [16]. In order to examine the practical nature of these settings we embedded with Rescue Global, a disaster response organisation in a 2-week long Search and Rescue (SAR) training exercise. We wish to balance the emergence of new capabilities with an understanding of how *existing* practices are actually constituted as a matter of disaster responders' work and the impact this might have for future technologies.

The first contribution of this paper is a study of the practical reasoning and action of disaster responders' work practices that surface ***management of uncertainty***. To do so we focus our study on responders' work around a 'bird table'—an analogue tabletop. We highlight how *four different uncertainties* impinge upon team members' interactions: 1) uncertainty around infrastructures and logistics (e.g., with implications for mobility and form factor); 2) uncertainty of the actual availability of resources to construct an operational picture; 3) uncertainty as to whether the equipment remains operational over time; and 4) uncertain validity of the information drawn upon to construct the operational picture.

Drawing on our first contribution, our second is a set of principles for design of technologies in uncertain environments. These principles can be summarised as a recommendation broadly to *augment and enrich* existing sites of the operational picture (e.g., the tabletop). Given the emphasis on collaborative interaction around shared surfaces and the growing interest in disaster response as an application domain for interactive tabletops we illustrate this by reference to digital, interactive tabletop design for disaster response.

In the following sections we firstly cover in greater detail the literature at the intersection of disaster response settings and interactive tabletops. We then present our study, providing an overview of the setting followed by a series of data fragments that highlight aspects of uncertainty in disaster responders' work.

RELATED WORK

We briefly review research on collaboration in command-and-control settings. We then focus on research to support hybrid physical-digital work, and review tabletop systems, particularly to support disaster response.

Studies of Command and Control Settings

Command-and-control settings have been a mainstay of CSCW research focusing of how operators manage and control safety-critical systems. This paper aligns with the long-standing tradition to study these complex settings to identify implications for technology support. Heath and Luff's study of London Underground shows for example how co-orientation among operators is critical in this "multimedia environment" [13].

Tolcher [37] showed in his PhD thesis how military planning around bird table maps is accomplished through collaboratively developing and analysing courses of actions. Tolcher's work is particularly relevant to our study, in that there is significant overlap between the planning process employed by Rescue Global and the UK military Standard Operating Procedures (SOP).

Collaborating across the physical-digital divide

Related to the prevalence of paper resources (especially maps) in our study, MacKay's work on the use of flight strips in air traffic control has highlighted the kind of physical interaction afforded by paper [25], also relating more broadly to research on the role of paper in knowledge work collaboration [33].

The challenge to overcome what might be termed the *physical-digital divide* in tabletop work has driven much technical innovation and research (cf. [14]). Often this work has attempted to combine the advantages of paper and electronic documents [42], including hybrid interaction techniques [22], interaction frameworks for pen-and-paper user interfaces [36], and integrated prototypes for collaborative annotating, linking and tagging digital and printed documents [35].

Tabletop systems for situational awareness

More recently, research has emerged that focuses on situational awareness in incident management as an important application domain for tabletop systems. Most of these systems are implemented on large multi-touch tables with a GIS base system, and allow for example the browsing and annotating of maps [28], spatial information overlays [24], automatic placement of annotations to avoid occlusion [19], and integration of digital pens for precise interactions [9]. While most of these systems are aimed at supporting map-based situation assessment and planning of operations, some are specifically designed to support simulation of disaster scenarios for training purposes [4,23]. However, the work has in common that it assumes a relatively *permanent* control room or portable incident vehicle in which bulky hardware is installed and remains set up. Yet, in the setting we studied, a *temporary* control room was set up for not much longer than the duration of the operation. This fundamental difference already anticipates substantially different design implications for this setting.

Given the current role of shared surfaces in incident response the capabilities offered by interactive surfaces are obviously appealing. However, the challenge remains as to the extent to which these might actually mesh with work practice. Although we have seen some engagement with practitioners include the development of guidelines [2], interview with experts [9], and a user-centred design process with the German Technical Relief agency (THW) [26], there has been little emphasis in understanding the nature of the setting into which these technologies will be deployed.

At present we have little insight into how responders socially organise their work. Understanding the social organisation of work has been central to grounding the design of interactive tabletops. Scott et al. for example found that people structure the (analogue) table space into 'personal', 'group' and 'storage territories' [32]. Similarly, research showing that task time pressure has an observable impact on group dynamics [44] is relevant in disaster response. Insights that emerge from our study relate to ways in which one of the fundamental challenges of any disaster is dealt with: the inherent uncertainty of the situation [18].

STUDYING DISASTER RESPONDERS' WORK

Disaster response may be understood as a stage in the broader disaster management cycle, which includes prevention, preparedness, response and recovery/relief [41]. The response includes activities such as Search and Rescue, medical support, reconnaissance to assess the situation, and providing assistance to restore infrastructure.

Rescue Global (RG) is a disaster response organisation. They are a UK charity and a US not-for-profit headquartered in London, UK. Their remit is to provide "*immediate crisis and disaster reconnaissance ability, delivering accurate and timely information and risk data, as well as performing emergency search and rescue operations where needed to save life.*" [30]. RG has adopted a framework of procedures that implements ISO 9001 Quality Management (QM) principles, which commits RG for example to conduct risk assessments and to record decisions for accountability purposes. This has implications on the ways in which missions are planned and carried out (the focus of our field work).

RG's organisational structure represents a typical hierarchy found in emergency services (cf. [39]), termed Gold, Silver and Bronze. Gold denotes the strategic lead, which is associated with RG's senior officers (often referred to as the 'head shed') and the headquarters in London, Silver is the tactical lead, which is 'spun up' for mission planning, both to assess feasibility of deployments and when actually deployed onsite. Bronze refers to the operational level, in which 'Pathfinders' (field responders) carry out operations 'on the ground' supported by Silver command [29]. RG's core staff consists of around 20 highly specialised experts and admin support, many of whom have had prior careers in the military, and emergency and first response services.

As part of our collaboration with RG we were invited to accompany RG to a large training exercise—"Angel Thunder"—in order to observe aspects of their work practice (albeit in a training context) in the field so as to inform technology design. Angel Thunder (AT) is a yearly inter-agency two-week Search and Rescue (SAR) event involving military, and personnel recovery agencies mainly from the US, but also from many nations around the world. Continual training, including in skills outside individual member's area of expertise is part of RG's strategy. The goal is that staff can flexibly take on multiple roles. While RG staff engaged in many different activities during the AT period, we focus in this paper on one particular three-day exercise, "Operation Praesidio", as it presented the most comprehensive training operation.

Our specific interest within this is in unpacking a key feature of disaster response work: the 'Commonly Recognised Information Picture', or 'CRIP' [18]. This is a domain-specific term referring to situational awareness held in common by the members of involved disaster response organisations. *Just how* the CRIP was constructed as a social object—preserving uncertainty and constituted of formal planning, various digital and non-digital resources, and tabletop representations—is subject of our analysis.

Our approach

We conducted an ethnographic study so as to inform the design of technology to support RG's work [8]. To this end we collected field notes, photos, video recordings, and audio, and copies of documents. We present our findings, particularly drawing on video data to focus on the interactional accomplishment of activities [12], and from back briefing this analysis to RG about 2 months after the operation (a 'member checking' meeting). Our analytic orientation is informed by ethnomethodology; which here means we investigate the practical action and reasoning of RG staff. During our ethnography, RG were practicing a new planning procedure—"7 Questions"—which had the advantage for us as ethnographers that it enhanced the observability of RG staffs' reasoning around the production of the CRIP.

The RG team attending the broader AT exercise comprised 13 members. Five members were senior 'head shed' (Gold/Silver), Six members were junior (Silver/Bronze), and two admin staff.

Silver (tactical command-and-control) was set up close to a small municipal airport with skydiving facilities associated with AT, in a large room (approx. 538 sq ft / 50 m^2) with good amenities and infrastructure, including power, Ethernet, air conditioning, a fridge, tables, chairs, whiteboards, flipcharts etc. RG brought and set up their own office and communications equipment. Areas of the room were designated to certain activities and roles.

The training exercise context: 'Operation Praesidio'

One of RG's main internal learning and training objectives for participating in AT and specifically deployed in Operation Praesidio was the "7 Questions" (7Q) planning procedure. To this end, one of RG's senior officers—Eric—who was familiar with the planning procedure acted as a 'trainer' during the exercise. The 7 Questions, as a process-oriented planning procedure, has been linked to good response practices in uncertain events [21]. We present the 7Q here so as to contextualise subsequent aspects of the ethnographic work we describe later. Each of the 7Q is associated to tasks, resources used, outputs and milestones achieved (see Table 1).

Tactical mission planning procedures such as the 7Q are aimed at supporting members in aligning information about the situation (environment, structures, hazards, people, third parties) to the organisation's own capabilities and resources to deliver a certain kind of operation in a way that makes optimal use of resources, whilst managing uncertainty (e.g., being risk averse) at the same time. We found that in practice tasks in the 7Q planning procedure may be done concurrently in anticipation of certain outcomes. As the outputs of previous stages are used for further planning, they remain open for scrutiny and refinement.

Operation Praesidio itself proceeded in the following way. On the morning of Day 1, Eric briefed the designated Incident Commander (IC) to conduct a reconnaissance operation ('recce') on the third day, and that the team is to progress to complete Q5 at the end of Day 1. The Incident Commander then delivers the following scenario as a 'Request Order' that spins up tactical planning (Silver):

The international community plans to evacuate the town of Coolidge (~3,000 inhabitants) to save them from an imminent threat posed by hostile forces via air transport from the nearby disused Municipal Airport. RG has been requested to provide early reconnaissance to enable planning and execution of the evacuation. Specific tasks for the recce include:

- **roads** in and out of the town,
- **holding and camping areas** (for people and vehicles),
- **water** sources to enable life support of camps,
- **alternate landing sites** (for helicopters and planes).

Question	Task(s)	Resources	Output(s)	Milestone
1. What is the situation?	Terrain analysis, risk mngmt	Digital + paper tools, maps, info	Situation Overlay (SO)	Team issued notice to move
2. What action has been requested?	Requirements analysis	Request order	Confirmation order	Client back briefed
3. What effects are required?	Define activities	SO + Request	CO's intent and endstate	Endstate defined
4. Where can the effect be best achieved?	Integration of SO and CO's intent	SO + intent	Decision Support Overlay (DSO)	Areas of interest defined
5. What resources are required?	Resource allocation, risk mngmt	SO + intent + DSO	Decision Support Matrix (DSM)	Warning Order
6. What coordination is required?	Sequencing, 3rd party liaison	DSM	Synchronisation matrix	Task complete
7. What control measures are required?	Comms procedure, risk mngmt	DSM	Comms plan, Risk analysis	Go/no go brief

Table 1. The "7 Questions" (7Q) planning procedure.

After delivering the scenario, the IC (Dom, Pathfinder team leader with a background in alpine mountaineering) handed out individual taskings to begin the planning process. Bill, (Pathfinder with military experience) is tasked with geography, terrain analysis, roads in/out, and water. Clive, the RG information manager is to look at the airport, potential campsites, holding areas, food and water storage, and power. Andy (pilot) is to provide a detailed weather report, and identify potential alternate landing zones.

BUILDING THE CRIP

A key goal for the RG team at the Operation Praesidio exercise was the construction of the Commonly Recognised Information Picture. The primary artefact around which the CRIP's construction is shared and (literally) made visible amongst the team is the **bird table**, a large tabletop surface located in the centre of the main planning area of the Silver command-and-control operations room. The physical centrality of the bird table makes it a natural coordination point for the on-going work observable in face-to-face discussions, annotating acetates placed on paper maps, and digital work on laptops placed on the bird table, and on surrounding desks.

In order to understand how the CRIP is co-constructed, displayed, and refined on and around the bird table, we turn to three aspects of its construction and use: first, the mixed resources drawn together to constitute the CRIP itself; second, the introduction of uncertainty into the transferral of resources to the bird table; and third, its resolution in decision making processes around the bird table. As part of this we must also introduce the bird table itself.

Working up the CRIP: Digital and physical resources

The members of Silver went about constructing and making the CRIP visible on the bird table in what we might term as a 'mixed media' environment.

The bird table: Paper maps and acetate overlays

The central feature of the bird table is a set of maps and overlays that are used to highlight information relevant to the mission. The bird table's map is overlaid with two separate layers: a 'Situation Overlay' and a 'Decision Support Overlay'. These are both practically realised through annotating an acetate sheet that is then placed over the map, thus offering a set of removable annotations (see Figure 1). The Situation Overlay is constructed by highlighting geographical features that are relevant to the initial Request Order, e.g., roads for the evacuation and water features such as a reservoir, wells, rivers, and canals.

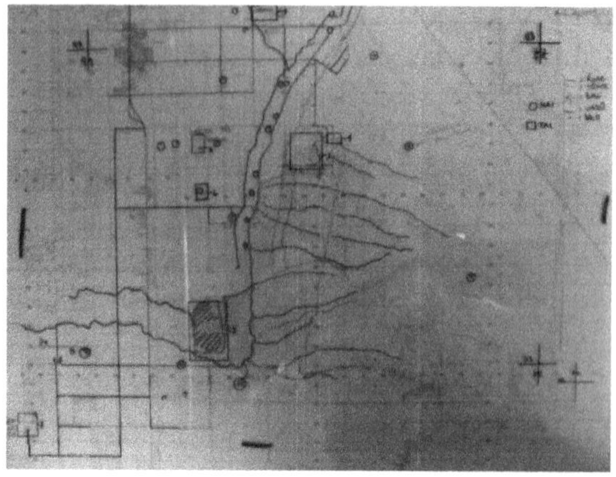

Figure 1. Bird table map with the Situation Overlay (highlights relevant roads, water, wells, base, etc.), and the Decision Support Overlay (highlights areas of interest).

Consider the following fragment, in which the Commanding Officer (CO), Fred—who had been busy during the Request Order briefing—delivers his 'intent' (Q3, see table 1) to the IC (who is in the process of constructing the Situation Overlay), after showing a visitor around Silver, and thereby briefs his team on the mission goals.

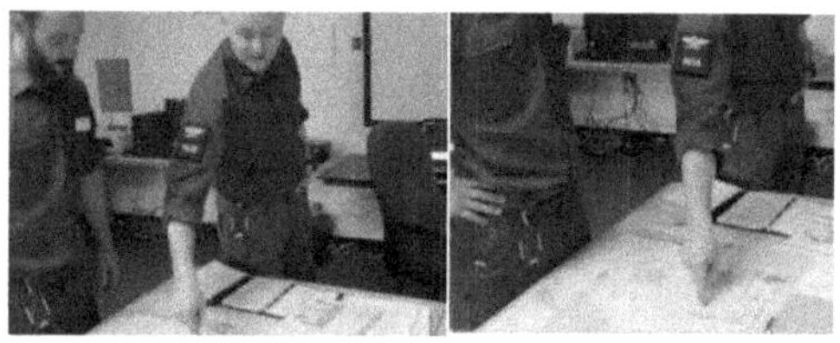

Figure 2. Fragment 1 a) CO delivering his intent (mission goals); b) pointing at airport on Situation Overlay map.

```
Fred: Reassure that population ((points at town on map,
  fig. 2a)), prepare them to move within three weeks.
  Check at least 2 routes from there to this location
  ((traces routes to airport)), Secure this location
  ((points at airport, fig. 2b)) with an airborne inser-
  tion of pathfinders because assume the roads aren't
  clear. Pathfinders when they parachuted in to secure
  this area ((points at airport)) to allow the infillers
  of Silver. When Silver is here them to then brief the
  Pathfinders to do reconnaissance of this area ((points
  at town)) and the hill area which is 450 metres that
  direction ((points off map)) to do water samples.
```

Fragment 1 shows how the CO was able to orientate to the on-going construction of the Situation Overlay on the bird table and deliver his intent 'off the cuff', despite him being busy and absent up to this point.

The Decision Support Overlay is then constructed to 'integrate' the relevant mission goals (i.e., the CO's intent) with the Situation Overlay. In effect, the Decision Support Overlay further highlights specific areas of interest that are relevant to the mission goals. The areas of interest represent potential candidate site for 'recces', operations in which Pathfinder team(s) investigate on site, in this case to find (access to) water sources and test its potability. In a sense, it represents a further filter on the more general geographic information presented on the Situation Overlay. Figure 1 shows the map with both the Situation Overlay and the Decision Support Overlay fully annotated after Q4.

The bird table map and overlays are a key shared resource for RG team members to read and align to the progress in the 7Q planning procedure; it forms an accessible, common frame of reference, including for members more peripheral to its ongoing construction (cf. the CO delivering the intent). The use of the acetate sheets enables the team to simply and flexibly add and remove annotations to the map, and incrementally render the various resources (particularly the Request Order, the CO's intent) to a shared resource.

The bird table: Use of digital tools

A core part of what gets rendered to the bird table is resourced via digital means. Digital tools were routinely used by RG staff to further enrich the CRIP. For example, the pilot used Google Earth to study satellite imagery of the surrounding area in his task to find alternate landing zones (ALZs). This involved assessing the condition of the ground, measuring the length and width of potential strips (which has implications on which kinds of aircraft can safely land), finding distances and routes to base (Silver), and retrieving geo-coordinates. Having been asked what he was doing, he offered the following account.

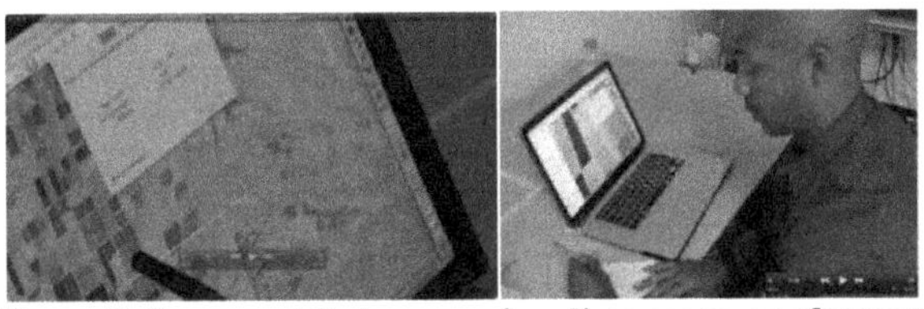

Figure 3. Fragment 2 a) measuring distance to an alternate landing zone; b) copying info to notebook.

Andy: In all these operations, what we do is we try and find as many landable airstrips, helipads, flat areas that we can. (...) And normally there are alternatives. Google Earth is a great little tool for that. And like we look here ((zooms in)), and we see within ((selects 'ruler' tool)) a relatively short distance (1.0) find out how short ((selects scale)) in miles. Right so just three-and-a-half miles away we have something ((taps on location on screen, fig. 3a)). We don't know how usable it is, but we can work it out by zooming in ((zooms in)). And then you can see, it's reasonably long but it's incredibly narrow. Won't be good enough for big transport, but we could get something smaller in like the King Air. So I'm just- basically measuring (.) airfields and plotting them on the map at this stage so we can use it for planning later on. ((measures length)) See that's 800 metres. That's kind of usable for us ((takes a note in notebook, fig. 3b)).

The pilot proceeded to save the location, compile the information into a (Word) document, and email it to admin and the Incident Commander. The landing zones were then transcribed onto the Situation Overlay acetate, indexing the availability of further information on the matter.

The use of digital tools is not limited to planning: they were also used extensively to communicate with Pathfinders and track their locations. Consider the following fragment from Day 3, in which Clive uses IncaX Geocaster on a laptop to track the Pathfinders, and transcribes their locations to the Decision Support Overlay on the bird table. As the Pathfinders are en route to do a 'confirmatory recce' of the water reservoir (which we return to shortly), Eric walks up and stands next to Clive, looking at his screen.

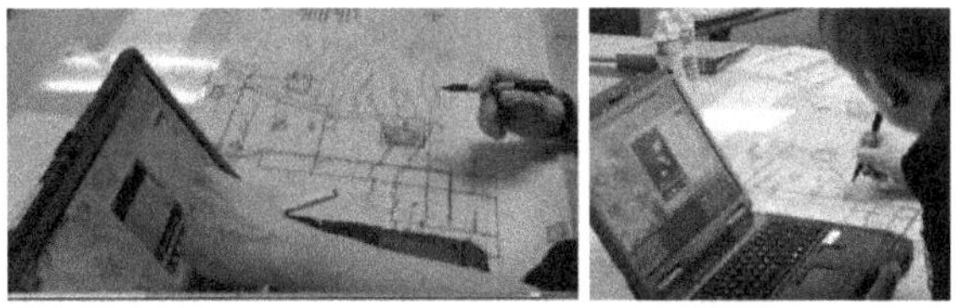

Figure 4. Fragment 3 a) pointing out travel direction on tracking software UI; b) transcribing tracking to map.

Eric: Have they turned south yet?

Clive: Yep. See ((points pen downwards, fig 4a)) that's the direction they're looking in (...). So they'll be joining the 87 in erm (1.0) a very short time. (...) Do you see what I mean ((pointing at screen)), they'll be joining this ((traces route on acetate)). (...) So they're now driving south on 87 (2.0) At approximately 55 miles per hour.

Eric: Northing?

Clive: Northing would be ((leans in to screen)) 45th northing. Just crossed the 45th northing. ((looks at watch, transcribes tracking point as "[time]:IncaX" to map, fig 4b)).

Some time later Clive comments on this process, "Even if you loose comms you should be able to estimate where they are. And with an increasing degree of uncertainty as they may have taken different routes and stuff".

The fragment shows how Clive uses the tracking software to offer to Eric the Pathfinders' current location, translating this location first by pointing, and then transcribing it to the acetate. The annotation "IncaX" points to the provenance of the track point, indexing its information source. Slightly later on Clive comments on the 'boundary' of the training exercise, noting that information on the Pathfinders' current location could become increasingly uncertain in particular circumstances, yet various methods could be employed to mitigate this. This point anticipates an informational uncertainty in the resourcing process when building the CRIP, which we will return to shortly.

In summary, then, we have shown how the CRIP is constructed and maintained or updated by drawing on a mix of physical and digital resources. This can be thought of as a 'sources and sinks' arrangement. The annotations on the acetates serve as indices of the 'sources' (e.g., IncaX in Fragment 3), and 'sinks' of information (e.g., the pilot's tacit domain knowledge and his further documentation in Fragment 2). We also have seen how the bird table's physical accessibility enables peripheral members to readily engage and contribute to building the CRIP (Fragment 1).

Uncertainty in CRIP resources

Working in a mixed digital-physical information environment, members routinely transfer information resources across the 'seams' from one medium to the next. A complicating factor is that secondary—i.e., unconfirmed and therefore uncertain—information may be inconsistent. The work of transfer not only preserves this uncertainty when translating across seams, but also offers a moment of reflection on the veracity of the information being added / shared.

Consider the following fragment, drawn from the afternoon of Day 2. Three team members are in the process of discussing the risk assessment for Q7 (see Figure 5). Bill brings up the issue of the water reservoir. This has been highlighted on the Situation Overlay during the Terrain Analysis (Q1) as a potential water source (see fig. 1), but when Andy (the pilot) used Google Earth on the previous day to identify landing zones on satellite imagery, he discovered that "the reservoir is a forest now".

```
Bill [left]: Erm. We need to (.) redo this. ((points at
  water reservoir, fig. 5a)) (...)
Dom: Why?
Bill: Because it's suggested we are not doing this (1.0)
  ((retracing reservoir outline with finger)) any more
  (...) we don't need to highlight it. In fact we need to
  cross it out ((makes crossing-out gesture)) and make it
  green ((laughs)).
Andy: We left it in deliberately to show the water supply
  ((taps on reservoir)) ( ) as a point of note.
```

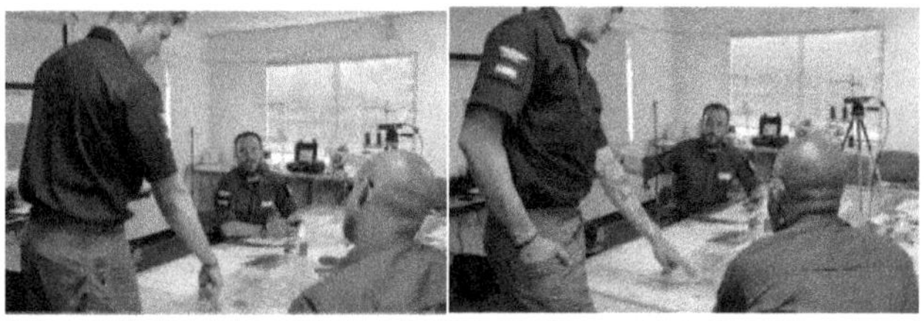

Figure 5. Fragment 4 a) pointing at the contested water reservoir; b) Dom suggesting to keep it as a point of note.

```
Dom: Yeah.
Bill: ( ) Google Earth. More updated imagery?
Dom: Exactly. And hopefully that will just lead to the
  whole can we have Falcon View please.
Andy: Well in this case we found it and then found out
  that it wasn't the case.
Bill: We do in fact have Google Earth? Real world and
  scenario yes?
Dom: ((nods))
Andy: Ya-ya.
Bill: So we've already (...) done (...) our map recon our
  most basic recon that we always do before we go any-
  where and found that that's ((points at reservoir)) not
  there. So. ((makes crossing out gesture))
Dom: ((tuts, nods))
Andy: Yah. We made a point of note already ( ) so you can
  get rid of it as well. Well. ((shrugs))
Bill: We are in fact briefing this right? Or no.
Dom: We are. And I was gonna put that into the briefing-
  that (...) when doing lat longs (...) and looking fur-
  ther afield than just the airfield we found this on
  Google Earth. Therefore point of note (.) we need to
  get some really up to date current maps ((talk omit-
  ted))
Bill: So you wanna keep this on there ((points at reser-
  voir, fig. 5b))?
Dom: Yeah. ((talk omitted))
```

Bill initiates this dialogue by suggesting to change the highlight of the reservoir on the Situation Overlay from signifying a body of water to land ("we need to redo this (...) we don't need to highlight it (...) we need to cross it out and make it green"). Andy points out (and Dom agrees) that this was left on deliberately as a 'point of note', which also refers to a specific kind of item in the risk/QM management procedure. Google Earth is then brought up, the information source that is seen to refute the existence of the water reservoir. The way Dom responds anticipates a potential outcome of relaying this point of note to the 'head shed', that this might emphasise the need for a specific mapping application ("hopefully that will just lead to the whole can we have Falcon View please"). Andy then points out that ("we found it and then found out that it wasn't the case") as if to offer an account of how the refutation was arrived at, perhaps in anticipation of the briefing. Bill then raises the question of the training exercise 'boundaries', and whether Google Earth is 'permitted' (which his teammates confirm). However, Bill reiterates the point that their initial map recon revealed that the reservoir is "not there", and concludes by repeating the 'crossing-out' gesture. Dom and Andy's responses do not indicate their full agreement. Bill's question whether this will be briefed prompts Dom to anticipate what he might offer when briefing the 'head shed' on the following day ("when doing lat longs (...)we found this on Google Earth. Therefore point of note we need to get some really up to date current maps."). Subsequently Dom and Bill agree to keep the reservoir as is (not shown in this transcript).

The interaction in Fragment 4 illustrates how members resolve the challenge of dealing with conflicting information. While conferring an epistemic authority to Google Earth, nevertheless, the team achieves a form of 'resolution' precisely by *postponing resolution* purposefully. They agree to 'brief it' as a 'point of note' to the higher ups, rather than by acting on it directly, here and now, which in this instance means erasing the reservoir from the Situation Overlay. By doing this postponement, the original conflict is preserved, and indicates in turn their preference for actively *preserving* conflict and therefore the essential uncertainty of the informational resources they draw upon.

The second point we note is that the team is continually and reflexively working with reference to the boundaries of the training scenario (e.g., whether Google Earth is 'allowed'). This is important because it helps decide which conflicts or uncertainties are to be preserved and which are irrelevant.

Resolution: Deciding 'what to do'

The previous fragment showed how secondary (i.e., 'unverified') information results in uncertainty in the CRIP. The resolution of this can be achieved either by verification from a trusted source, or conducting missions to investigate the situation on the ground. In the case of the reservoir, the following fragment from Day 3 shows how Dom (the IC), the CO and Eric achieve such a resolution.

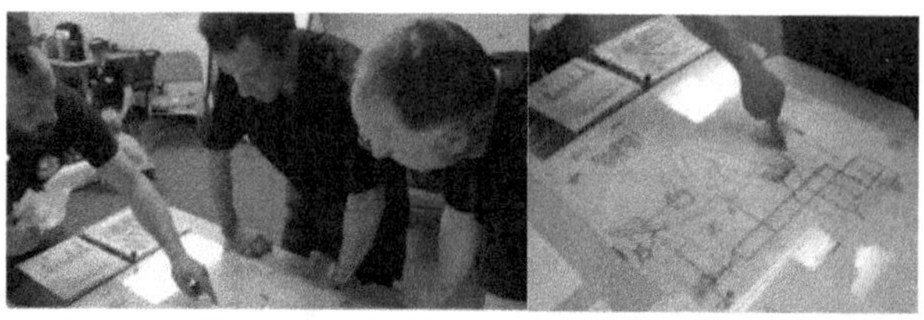

Figure 6. Fragment 5 a) Dom briefing senior officers; b) pointing at secondary water source close by reservoir.

```
Dom: We left this on as part of (.) a reference for when
  we do the debrief. We got excited about this ((points
  at reservoir – fig. 6a)) feeding all of this stuff
  here. This looked cool. On later inspection with Google
  Earth as were trying to get lat longs we found that
  this is just a field ( ).
Eric: Let's do a confirmatory recce.
Fred: Ya. That's good idea. That's a nice location. (...)
  That's a target.
Dom: But we know from Google Earth (.) that it's not.
Fred: Yea but we might assume that we don't have that
  connectivity.
Eric: Also Google Earth changes as well.
Dom: Yea.
Fred: And if you didn't have that connectivity anyway
  you'd have to go physically eyes on (...) Okay so have
  that as a confirmatory recce is it usable ( ).
Eric: ((nods)) or there might be pockets of water in the
  area ( ).
Dom: Yea. We know that there's- (1.0) ((points at well
  below reservoir, fig. 6b)) Well we don't know (.) but
  there might be.
Eric: Well that's it. Seek out a- seek out a water sup-
  ply. If you go there ((points at reservoir)) and
  there's nothing there then there's your secondary
  ((points at well)).
```

Here Dom offers his conclusion that the reservoir "is just a field", embedded within his account of the work process through which he arrived at this conclusion. Thus, map annotations are indexical to the tacit part of the CRIP developed through collaboration earlier. Immediately after the end of Dom's turn (i.e., his briefing to the senior officers), Eric states "do a confirmatory recce", with which the CO agrees. As Dom interjects "But we know from Google Earth that it's not", Fred points to the boundaries of the training scenario as a way of introducing uncertainty over available infrastructure ("we might assume that we don't have that connectivity"). Eric builds on Fred's utterance by introducing a different kind of uncertainty around the information presented by Google Earth, i.e., that it "changes". Fred then returns to his earlier point on infrastructural uncertainty to establish grounds for Eric's idea of a "confirmatory recce". By way of reinforcing what the projected work of the recce might do, Eric hypothesises "pockets of water in the area". This culminates in Dom *repairing* his utterance: from "we know that" to "we don't know but there might be". Dom builds the emerging sense of informational uncertainty into his talk.

Two important points are being made here. First, Fred challenges Dom in stating that the connectivity required for a tool like Google Earth might not be available. The uncertainty of which tools are available in the scenario (cf. Fragment 4) should not be misread as resulting from a lacking definition of the rules of the training scenario. The point made by Fred stresses that this uncertainty is realistic in that the availability of certain resources cannot be assumed in real operations. Second, Eric, by questioning how up-to-date Google Earth is, he also makes explicit its status as a non-primary source of information. This is made evident by suggesting the confirmatory recce as a primary source.

This fragment exhibits a persistent matter for disaster responders: *uncertain, unverified secondary information must often be used to plan an operation to obtain primary information*. During our back brief, the CO responded to the issues raised by this fragment in the following way:

```
Fred: The mapping issue is kind of one of the main rea-
  sons we exist ((talk omitted)) it doesn't really matter
  what Google Earth says, it doesn't really matter what
  Falcon View says, it doesn't really matter what the lo-
  cal person says we get the intelligence from. It's
  actually all bollocks until we've gone out and looked
  at it and confirmed it. This goes to the provenance as-
  pect. ((talk omitted)) no matter how good Falcon View
  or Google is, it's wrong when the disaster's here, be-
  cause it's now secondary data, it's no longer primary.
```

The CO here is describing the *organisation of uncertainty* in disaster settings, i.e., how they go about designating categorisations of primary and secondary. Categorisations are made in ways that are sensitive to the practicalities of the (real or prospective disaster) situation, meaning that use of resources like Google Earth, Falcon View or paper mapping comes to require a novel visual sensibility.

PRINCIPLES FOR SYSTEMS IN UNCERTAIN SETTINGS

We have examined key practices employed by RG members during the training exercise, particularly focusing on the co-construction of the CRIP ('Commonly Recognised Information Picture'). The bird table is the site at which the CRIP is co-constructed and updated by assembling and making use of a complementing set of physical and digital resources. Yet the CRIP is *not* just a collection of documents, it is a socially shared object. The CRIP also includes collective team members' experience, skills, practices, and understandings. The bird table is used to make elements of the CRIP visible to all. As such the CRIP acts as a 'boundary object' in the classic sense [34], offering a common point of reference for responders and their collaborators, yet *retaining* conflicting and unresolved perspectives (i.e., not just 'interpretative flexibility').

The bird table itself is developed through methods of 'filtering' and 'indexing', where in-depth work procedures are reduced and transcribed to bird-table-compatible annotations (such as a suitable landing strip, cf. Fragment 2; and tracking, cf. Fragment 3). While there is a sense in which the bird table only partially surfaces *particular aspects of* the CRIP, the annotations are taken as indexical—i.e., they are tied to, or 'documents of' [10]—the team's work practices (exhibitions of knowledge, competencies etc.), and are readily brought to articulation in discussion (e.g., the reservoir debate in Fragments 4 and 5).

In summary, a central feature of this work is the *management of uncertainty* inherent in the CRIP. Much of this is practically achieved by the construction of the bird table, which—as we have shown—is used to support the teams in retaining and preserving *uncertainties* across seams. This maintenance of uncertainty leads to a principle of generally avoiding premature resolution, and instead postponing non-resolution until it becomes critical to do so.

Principles for systems design

We propose four principles for systems design in uncertain settings that foreground different forms of uncertainty, based on the setting we encountered. We explain each form of uncertainty and its corresponding principle (see Table 2). We then map these to the HCI literature to illustrate their relevance beyond disaster response.

Uncertainty of environment (1). In planning deployment, there is a need to consider how the infrastructure in the destination environment might constrain equipment operation. This has implications on the logistics of what equipment to take; for example, in extreme circumstances Rescue Global may parachute with all their kit to set up Silver (cf. the CO's intent, Fragment 1). Therefore the first principle is to design technology support that is, ideally, *deployable anywhere*. In relation to RG's practice, this rules out bulky, heavy, large kit such as multi-touch surfaces in favour of portable, light-weight solutions, including energy efficient computers, and offline functionality.

Uncertainty of resources (2). The uncertainty of what local resources (e.g., satellite imagery, local maps, and population) are available poses a further challenge. In RG's case, the design needs to provide *flexible support for situation analysis*. In practice, paper maps could be augmented with projected information. A technical challenge would be how to calibrate a potential underlying digital GIS system to capture the same topographical space of the paper map, so that *geographically accurate* projections could me made. Aside from projecting maps onto special paper for digital pen interaction [23], a proof-of-concept augmenting actual paper maps appears to be lacking from the literature to date.

Uncertainty of equipment (3). Technology support for uncertain operational environments needs to adhere to the principle of *redundancy and graceful degradation*. This reflects RG's practice to have (at least) a secondary for each of their primary tools. Again, this supports projected augmentation in favour of replacement with devices—if the digital projection fails to work for whatever reason, the 'analogue' workflow (e.g., annotation of acetates) is still intact. This principle has further implications for possible solutions, from supporting a rich mixed-media environment (for redundancy), through to a modular software architecture that is robust to failure of individual components.

Uncertainty of information (4). Perhaps most significantly, any technology to support uncertain information needs to *support articulation work* [31] *and accountability* [10]. Our analysis showed that these features of the work are central to managing the uncertainties inherent in disaster situations. In practice, projected augmentation could for example visualise the Points of Note that index the sources and sinks of the information. Thus, providing provenance (where is it from?), and capture surrounding articulation work (who put this on here, and why?). This is similar to the design requirement by Bader et al. to *make interaction and communication attributable and recordable* [2].

Principle	Uncertainty	Practitioner's Questions	Example solution
1. Deployable anywhere	Environment (e.g., logistics and local infra-structure)	What do we take with us? How do we operate it?	Portable, light-weight, low power, offline functionality
2. Flexible support for situation analysis	Availability of resources	What local resources are available?	Projections on any paper maps
3. Redundancy and graceful degradation (primary/ secondary)	Equipment	What tools work, what if they fail?	Loose digital-physical coupling
4. Support articulation work and accountability	Information	What is the situation?	Visualise points of note indexing info sources and sinks

Table 2. Principles for system support in uncertain situations.

Relevance beyond Disaster Response

Dealing with uncertainty in systems design is a challenge faced by HCI researchers more broadly. For example, on reflecting on the challenges of deploying a location-based experience, Benford et al. propose five principles for managing uncertainty ('remove it, hide it, reveal it, manage it, and exploit it') [3]. The authors encounter uncertainties in the local infrastructure (GPS and Wi-Fi) and the equipment (hardware failures through physical strain); these uncertainties map to those in our setting (environment and equipment). Lending further support to the relevance of our principles beyond the disaster response domain, Gaver et al. also discuss the challenges of 'ambiguous information' by example of GPS-tracked players in a location-based game (cf. our principle dealing with uncertain information) [11]. In turn, our work also speaks to the broader debate in mobile and ubiquitous computing on 'exploiting' uncertainty (rather than hiding it) that was developed in reflection to—for instance—the 'seams' in the infrastructure [6], and ambiguity as a resource in design [11]. In contrast, we suggest that the sensitive nature of the collaborative work we observed renders the setting less appropriate for attempts to 'exploit' uncertainty as a resource. Our four principles are more closely aligned with strategies to 'manage' and 'reveal' uncertainties (rather than to 'exploit' them) [3], and elaborate them in the disaster response context.

Considering an Augmented Bird Table

By way of example, our principles suggest we should *augment, rather than replace* the bird table, and its constituting work practices. Our principles are also complementary to more general findings on how tabletop interaction is naturally organised [32], and more specific design guidelines for tabletop systems for emergency management [2], and crisis response [9].

Augmenting instead of replacing established and functioning paper-based workflows has been demonstrated in particular by the work around air traffic controllers' use of flight strips. From MacKay's early study that suggested to "turn the physical flight strip into an interface to the computer" [25], to Hurter et al.'s state-of-the-art realisation of StripTIC, that provides augmentation through projections onto physical strips, input through digital pens, and tracking of strips through computer vision [16].

Inspired by this work and to support the work practices described in our study we developed design requirements that we presented in the back brief to RG. The feedback provided by RG validated our requirements analysis and the efficacy of our design suggestions. RG members identified the desired prototype to be built: the *Augmented Bird Table* is a projection-vision system (e.g., similar to the PlayAnywhere system [43]), that adheres to our principles in that it

- requires only a camera, a projector, and a lightweight computer (such as a laptop) (Principle 1),
- uses computer vision to process annotations on physical acetates placed on any paper map (Principle 2),
- degrades gracefully to the standard work practice of annotating acetates if it fails (Principle 3),
- visualises points of notes that link to information sources and authoring team members (Principle 4).

The *Augmented Bird Table* uses an underlying GIS system to transform the input into geo-coded references, such as geo-locations, lines, and areas. This offers instant digital recording of geo-information for auditing purposes, for example to comply with QM processes, and to re-use this information in other forms, for example to communicate to third parties, and to connect to mapping applications for further processing (e.g., to compute routes, distances, travel times etc.). Also, it allows for projections of real-time locations (tracking). Connecting the GIS to a directory of RG's assets and tasks further allows to support resource allocation and synchronisation of reconnaissance tasks. Further, the 'provenance' of the sources and sinks of situational information is retained to aid articulation work, particularly around uncertainty. The feedback provided by RG helped to articulate priorities and refinement of key features for the upcoming implementation phase of our collaboration (e.g., tracking, provenance, integration with existing systems).

CONCLUSIONS

We have presented ethnographic findings from embedding for two weeks with Rescue Global, a disaster response organisation. Our observations of a training operation reveal how the CRIP ('Commonly Recognised Information Picture') is co-constructed as a shared social object by drawing on a variety of digital and physical resources, and rendering the results to the bird table. The bird table becomes the focal point for members to read progress, align their own contributions, and co-orient to teammates' contributions, as well as a 'boundary object' resource to negotiate how to proceed. Our fieldwork revealed uncertainty as a particular challenge that cuts across different aspects of the situation encountered in responding to a disaster. We identified four forms of uncertainties: uncertainty in the environment (e.g., the local infrastructure), resources (whether and what is available), equipment (whether it is operational), and information (whether it is accurate).

In response, we suggested four principles for designing systems for uncertain settings such as disaster response that take into account the four forms of uncertainty we identified. We exemplified how these might be implemented by way of the *Augmented Bird Table* that we are developing in future work with Rescue Global.

ACKNOWLEDGMENTS

We are grateful for the collaboration with Rescue Global. Thanks to Andy Crabtree and Peter Tolmie for providing valuable advice. This work is supported by EPSRC grants EP/I011587/1, and EP/K025848/1.

REFERENCES

1. Avrahami, D., Wobbrock, J.O., and Izadi, S. Portico: tangible Interaction on and around a Tablet. *Proc. UIST '11*, ACM Press (2011), 347–356.
2. Bader, T., T. Digital map table with Fovea-Tablett®: Smart furniture for emergency operation centers. *Proc. ISCRAM 2008* , 679–688.
3. Benford, S., Crabtree, A., Flintham, M., Drozd, A., Anastasi, R., Paxton, M., Tandavanitj, N., Adams, M., and Row-Farr, J. Can you see me now? *ACM Trans. on Comp.-Hum. Interact. 13*, 1 (2006), 100–133.
4. Bortolaso, C., Oskamp, M., Graham, T.C.N., and Brown, D. OrMiS: A Tabletop Interface for Simulation-Based Training. *Proc. ITS '13*, ACM Press (2013), 145–154.
5. Carver, L. and Turoff, M. Human-computer interaction: the human and computer as a team in emergency management information systems. *Comm. of the ACM 50*, 3 (2007), 33–38.
6. Chalmers, M. and Maccoll, I. Seamful and seamless design in ubiquitous computing. *Workshop at the crossroads: The interaction of HCI and systems issues in UbiComp*, (2003).
7. Convertino, G., Mentis, H.M., Slavkovic, A., Rosson, M.B., and Carroll, J.M. Supporting common ground and awareness in emergency management planning: a design research project. *ACM Trans. on Comp.-Hum. Interact. 18*, 4 (2011), 1–34.
8. Crabtree, A., Rouncefield, M., and Tolmie, P. *Doing Design Ethnography*. Springer, London, UK, 2012.
9. Doeweling, S., Tahiri, T., Sowinski, P., Schmidt, B., and Khalilbeigi, M. Support for collaborative situation analysis and planning in crisis management teams using interactive tabletops. *Proc. ITS '13*, ACM Press (2013), 273–282.
10. Garfinkel, H. *Studies in Ethnomethodology*. Polity, 1967.
11. Gaver, W.W., Beaver, J., and Benford, S. Ambiguity as a resource for design. *Proc. CHI '03*, ACM Press (2003), 233-240.
12. Heath, C., Hindmarsh, J., and Luff, P. *Video in qualitative research*. Sage Publications, 2010.

13. Heath, C. and Luff, P. Collaboration and Control: Crisis Management and Multimedia Technology in London Underground Line Control Rooms. *Computer Supported Cooperative Work 1*, (1992), 69–94.
14. Hilliges, O. Bringing the Physical to the Digital. 2009. PhD Thesis. Ludwig-Maximilians University Munich.
15. Hughes, J., King, V., Rodden, T., and Andersen, H. Moving out from the control room: ethnography in system design. *Proc. CSCW '94*, ACM Press (1994), 429–439.
16. Hurter, C., Lesbordes, R., Letondal, C., Vinot, J.-L., and Conversy, S. Strip'TIC: exploring augmented paper strips for air traffic controllers. *Proc. AVI '12*, ACM Press (2012), 225–232.
17. Izadi, S., Hodges, S., Butler, A., West, D., Rrustemi, A., Molloy, M., and Buxton, W. ThinSight: A Thin Form-Factor Interactive Surface Technology. *Comm. of the ACM 52*, 12 (2009), 90–98.
18. Jones, D. Multi-agency command support. *Crisis Response 9*, 3 (2014), 20–23.
19. Kaneider, D., Seifried, T., and Haller, M. Automatic annotation placement for interactive maps. *Proc. ITS '13*, ACM Press (2013), 61–70.
20. Karnik, A., Martinez Plasencia, D., Mayol-Cuevas, W., and Subramanian, S. PiVOT: Personalized view-overlays for tabletops. *Proc. UIST '12*, ACM Press (2012), 271–280.
21. Kartez, J.D. and Lindell, M.K. Planning for Uncertainty: The Case of local Disaster Planning. *Journal of the American Planning Association 53*, 4 (1987), 487–498.
22. Khalilbeigi, M., Steimle, J., and Mühlhäuser, M. Interaction Support for Hybrid Groups of Paper and Digital Documents on Tabletops. *Proc. ITS 2009*.
23. Kobayashi, K., Narita, A., Hirano, M., Tanaka, K., Katada, T., and Kuwasawa, N. DIGTable: A Tabletop Simulation System for Disaster Education. *Proc. Pervasive Computing* 2008.
24. Kunz, A., Yantaç, A.E., Alavi, A., Woźniak, P., Landgren, J., Sárosi, Z., and Fjeld, M. Tangible tabletops for emergency response: an exploratory study. *Proc. MIDI '13*, Article No. 10, ACM Press (2013).
25. MacKay, W.E. Is paper safer? The role of paper flight strips in air traffic control. *ACM Trans. on Comp.-Hum. Interact. 6*, 4 (1999), 311–340.
26. Nebe, K., Klompmaker, F., Jung, H., and Fischer, H. Exploiting new interaction techniques for disaster control management using multitouch-, tangible- and pen-based-interaction. *Proc. HCII* 2011, Springer (2011), 100–109.
27. Palen, L., Vieweg, S., Liu, S.B., and Hughes, A.L. Crisis in a Networked World: Features of Computer-Mediated Communication in the April 16, 2007, Virginia Tech Event. *Social Science Computer Review 27*, 4 (2009), 467–480.
28. Qin, Y., Liu, J., Wu, C., and Shi, Y. uEmergency: a collaborative system for emergency management on very large tabletop. *Proc. ITS '12*, ACM Press (2012), 399-402.
29. Rescue Global. *An introduction to Rescue Global.* 2013.
30. Schafer, W.A., Ganoe, C.H., and Carroll, J.M. Supporting Community Emergency Management Planning through a Geocollaboration Software Architecture. *CSCW 16*, 4-5 (2007), 501–537.
31. Schmidt, K. and Bannon, L. Taking CSCW seriously. *CSCW 1*, 1-2 (1992), 7–40.
32. Scott, S.D., Sheelagh, M., Carpendale, T., and Inkpen, K.M. Territoriality in collaborative tabletop workspaces. *Proc. CSCW '04*, ACM Press (2004), 294-303.
33. Sellen, A.J. and Harper, R.H.R. The Myth of the Paperless Office. (2003).
34. Star, S. and Bowker, G. *Sorting things out: Classification and its consequences.* MIT Press, Cambridge, MA, 1999.
35. Steimle, J., Brdiczka, O., and Muhlhauser, M. CoScribe: Integrating Paper and Digital Documents for Collaborative Knowledge Work. *IEEE Trans. on Learning Technologies 2*, 3 (2009), 174–188.
36. Steimle, J. Designing pen-and-paper user interfaces for interaction with documents. *Proc. TEI '09*, ACM Press (2009), 197-204.
37. Tolcher, R.J. Ethnomethodological Studies of Conventional Software Engineering Methods in Military C2 Work Settings. 2005. PhD Thesis. University of Oxford.
38. Toups, Z.O., Kerne, A., and Hamilton, W.A. The team coordination game: Zero-Fidelity Simulation Abstracted from Fire Emergency Response Practice. *ACM Trans. on Comp.-Hum. Interact. 18*, 4 (2011), 1–37.
39. U.S. Department of Homeland Security. *National Incident Management System.* 2008.
40. Vinot, J.-L., Letondal, C., Lesbordes, R., Chatty, S., Conversy, S., and Hurter, C. Tangible augmented reality for air traffic control. *interactions 21*, 4 (2014), 54–57.
41. Waugh, W. and Hy, R. *Handbook of emergency management: programs and policies dealing with major hazards and disasters.* Greenwood Pub. Group, 1990.
42. Wellner, P. Interacting with paper on the DigitalDesk. *Comm. of the ACM 36*, 7 (1993), 87–96.
43. Wilson, A.D. PlayAnywhere: a compact interactive tabletop projection-vision system. *Proc. UIST '05*, ACM Press (2005), 83-92.
44. Zhang, X. and Takatsuka, M. Put That There NOW: Group Dynamics of Tabletop Interaction under Time Pressure. *Proc. TABLETOP'07*, IEEE (2007), 37–43.

Success & Scale in a Data-Producing Organization: The Socio-Technical Evolution of OpenStreetMap in Response to Humanitarian Events

Leysia Palen, Robert Soden, T. Jennings Anderson & Mario Barrenechea
Department of Computer Science
University of Colorado Boulder
{Leysia.Palen, Robert.Soden, Jennings.Anderson, Mario. Barrenechea}@colorado.edu

ABSTRACT
OpenStreetMap (OSM) is a volunteer-driven, globally distributed organization whose members work to create a common digital map of the world. OSM embraces ideals of open data, and to that end innovates both socially and technically to develop practices and processes for coordinated operation. This paper provides a brief history of OSM and then, through quantitative and qualitative examination of the OSM database and other sites of articulation work, examines organizational growth through the lens of two catastrophes that spurred enormous humanitarian relief responses—the 2010 Haiti Earthquake and the 2013 Typhoon Yolanda. The temporally- and geographically- constrained events scope analysis for what is a rapidly maturing, whole-planet operation. The first disaster identified how OSM could support other organizations responding to the event. However, to achieve this, OSM has had to refine mechanisms of collaboration around map creation, which were tested again in Typhoon Yolanda. The transformation of work between these two events yields insights into the organizational development of large, data-producing online organizations.

Author Keywords
Crisis Informatics; Crowdwork; Geospatial Data; Mapping; Open Data; Organizational Behavior; Social Computing

ACM Classification Keywords
H.5.3. Groups & Organization Interfaces—collaborative computing, computer-supported cooperative work; K.4.2. Social Issues

General Terms
Human Factors

A DATA-PRODUCING ORGANIZATION UNDER CHANGE
OpenStreetMap (OSM) sees itself as a global community that creates a common open digital map of the world. OSM is therefore understood to be both a *volunteer-driven organization* as well as *the map* it produces for anyone to use: its members work collaboratively to create a high-resolution, global cartographic representation of the planet. Computer scientists in the UK who were frustrated by the licensing restrictions placed on government data by the national mapping agency created OSM in 2004 [5]. In the years since OSM has expanded to a global organization with over 1.5 million registered users and local groups active in over 80 countries, stretching far beyond the initial group of London-based collaborators who could meet in person to discuss problems or plan mapping strategies. In tandem with this growth in membership, OSM map data have also grown to serve a wide range of uses, including adoption by government [9]; private sector organizations including Microsoft Bing, Foursquare, and Telenav; and, of most relevance to this paper, humanitarian organizations working on disaster relief and international development [27,29]. OSM has sought to manage this expansion of scale and scope through a series of efforts to attract new members, articulate the work of ever-larger numbers of volunteers, and deliver map data in more accessible and reliable ways to a growing user base.

OSM is often called "the Wikipedia of Maps" because it is a volunteer-driven platform where users collaborate to create freely accessible information. The OSM community is segmented into subgroups that self-organize around geographical areas or themes such as mapping wheelchair accessibility or cycling routes. People are motivated to contribute for a variety of reasons but many cite the value of open spatial data as an important factor for their participation [4]. As a geowiki [24], OSM appears to operate similarly on its surface to Wikipedia, though a great deal less is known about OSM's normative and social structures—including its reward systems, the details of its array of collaborative practices to generate and edit data, and the manner in which it sees and conducts itself as an organization. As a subject of research, it has not yet gained the attention that Wikipedia has in the social computing literature, perhaps because geography in HCI is relatively new (see Hecht's calls for *geo-HCI* [11]).

However, the study-ability of OSM is also likely an issue. That the primary site of collaboration is the map database itself rather than human-readable text significantly complicates analysis. Unlike Wikipedia's articles, the individual objects that comprise the OSM map do not have

CHI 2015, April 18 - 23, 2015, Seoul, Republic of Korea

ACM 978-1-4503-3145-6/15/04…$15.00
http://dx.doi.org/10.1145/2702123.2702294

Talk pages that would allow researchers to view the objects' change histories, nor the rationales of the editors who modified them. These factors complicate both the study of cooperative behavior in OSM as well as the community's own ability to organize, as we will discuss.

Furthermore, the form that the data take makes analysis complex: OSM datasets are unwieldy, and each geographic entity—even down to the level of a building for example—is a series of *nodes* and *ways* with their own attributes and revision histories. Analyzing user activity and map changes is therefore a computationally demanding task with few agreed-upon analytics for the meaningful study of map data creation and in-map interaction.

A Brief Overview of Everyday Remote Mapping in OSM

Mappers can work from anywhere in the world using OSM tools and high-resolution satellite imagery to digitize roads, building footprints, and other identifiable features to add to the database. This work is interdependent in that, although contributors work in a distributed manner, there is only one database in which to represent a finite number of objects in the world. The simplest form of coordination occurs when each feature is traced once; then, when different mappers trace additional portions of the same or a related feature—a long road for instance, or surrounding buildings in a complex—their contributions are connected and internally consistent. Ideally, features are tagged in a fashion consistent with best practices as defined by the community through discussion on the wiki page and mailing lists. Simple coordination like this between mappers does take place, but back-and-forth editing and overwriting are not unusual. However, the degree and nature of interaction are unknown because it is hard to extract meaningful behavioral patterns from the database. Observationally, we see that activity "in the map"—the map database—as well as discussions "off the map"—email, chats, conferences—are sites of articulation work that affect OSM's evolution.

Organizational Growth vis-à-vis Open Data Ideals

At the time of this writing, OSM is ten years old and maturing rapidly. In its early days, OSM's focus was on simply gaining ground on the practicalities of collaborative spatial data production among a distributed volunteer base. Its members were the primary consumers of the map, so the relationship between creation and use was closely knit. Today OSM sits in a broader arena of actors where the implications of the ideals of open data come differently into view, requiring greater internally- and externally-coordinated work. Humanitarian activities have been a driver of OSM's evolution, in part because open data and participatory ideals align with humanitarian work, but also because disasters are catalysts for organizational innovation generally speaking [20]. Humanitarian events thus become useful lenses for isolating strategies that the wider OSM community has adopted to cope with growth in membership as well as geographic and thematic scope.

Disasters as Windows into Organizational Evolution

The 2010 Haiti Earthquake was a significant event for OSM [29]. In this research, we take the collaborative work [25] happening on and through the map during this timeframe along with another major disaster—the 2013 Typhoon Yolanda—as windows into OSM's organizational growth and evolution. To illustrate rationale and foreshadow the discussion to come, we draw attention to the map data creation during the one-month periods following each event in Figure 1. The orderings are remarkably different. Notice how in Port-au-Prince, the data by mappers—who are represented by color—are distributed across the area. In the Tacloban region of the Philippines, mapper activity is far more clustered, with little overlap. How this reordering came about was, on first glance, a straightforward technical solution, but we will show how it is rather *a socio-technical outgrowth of OSM's tacit and explicit organizational objectives.*

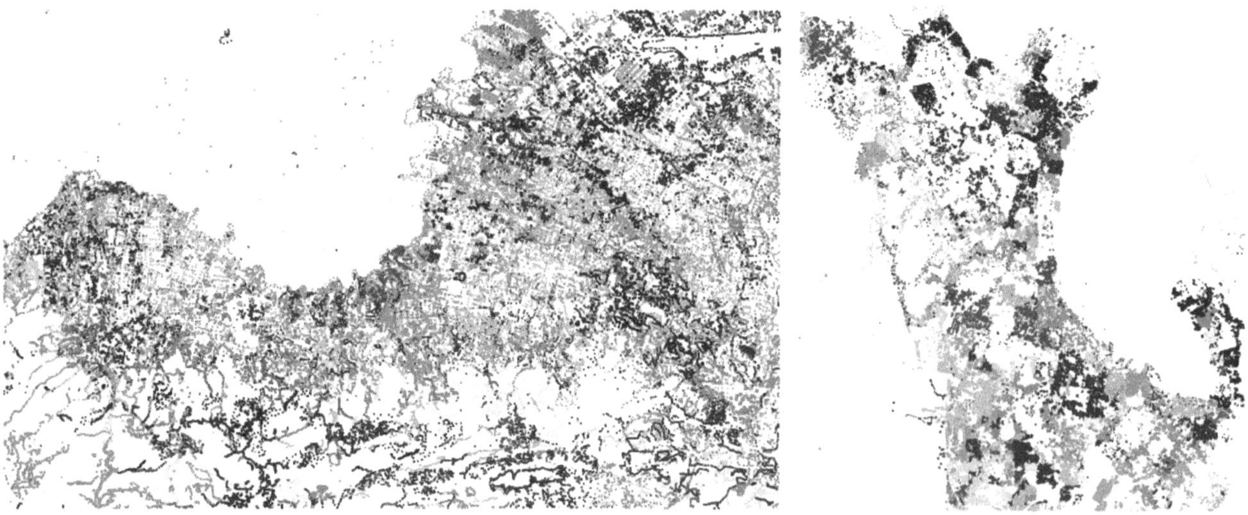

Figure 1. Marked differences in map data creation by users (colorized) across two disaster events reflect evolution in OSM organizing. Visualization compares 116k node additions in Port-au-Prince, Haiti (left) & Tacloban, Philippines (right).

Research Objective

This paper describes the socio-technical evolution of the OSM community, and addresses how this large, distributed data-producing organization manages its growth. We examine mapping activity during two disaster events, and consider how and why it shifted over the four-year period.

SITUATING OSM IN RELATION TO WIKI & DISASTER VOLUNTEER SCHOLARSHIP

To consider OSM's growth, we must consider the current research on OSM and how it compares to a similar organization—Wikipedia. Because we recognize that disasters are drivers in organizational change, we also too must consider the particular nature of digital volunteerism in the humanitarian sphere and its effects on OSM.

Though there is a growing body of research on OSM, the literature tends to be quantitative in nature and focus on its map data quality or aggregate measures of contributions across time and space. For example, Haklay [8] studied OSM data in comparison to official sources and found OSM coverage to be uneven but its quality generally high. Though this is important, the literature describing the *social and organizational life* of OSM is relatively thin, especially when compared to the CHI and CSCW communities' deep knowledge of Wikipedia.

Mooney and Corcoran attempted to describe OSM's organizational life, arguing it is "fragmented…comprising of individuals performing...tasks in isolation with little collaboration or interaction with each other" [21]. We take issue with this observation, which bases its understanding of collaboration solely on cases of "edit interaction," or when one user modifies an object in the map that was previously created or edited by another. This limited framing misses an opportunity to unravel the true nature of collaboration, especially from a computer-supported cooperative work perspective. Some scholarship [13,19] but indeed even casual interaction with the OSM map and community reveals that both "in the map" and "off the map" interactions with others are sites of articulation work [25] that, albeit sometimes slowly, critically drive OSM's organizational future. Humanitarian events accelerate some matters, as we will discuss.

The research on Wikipedia has useful points of comparison for understanding social interaction and organizational growth in OSM. Specifically we see that Wikipedia and OSM show different ways in which very large, volunteer-based data-producing organizations can grow. As the Wikipedia community grew, governance policies were central to its strategy for managing contributions [7]. Some observe that these processes for maintaining quality may now have deleterious impacts on Wikipedia's ability to retain new contributors [27]: In particular, the growth of algorithmic monitoring and the increasing rigidity of policies have been shown to reduce the number of new contributors who continue editing [10]. Further, Wikipedia faces a significant challenge with respect to encouraging diversity among contributors. A 2011 study showed that only around 7% of editors were women and that, unlike gender gaps in other online communities at the time, this ratio was not improving [17]. OSM offers an interesting counterpoint to Wikipedia, as it has made decisions to deliberately keep what it sees as bureaucracy at bay in part to encourage diverse participation.

Finally, disaster events have affected OSM in particular ways because of the high value of the geospatial data it produces. Crisis informatics research has examined the emergence and convergence of "digital volunteers" who mobilize via social computing platforms to report on events, search and distribute situational information, and articulate unspoken needs on behalf of victims [30,31]. The work of digital volunteerism is diverse, but can be thought of as information tasks that can be done remotely, including generating data by combining existing sources anew. Disasters often attract new digital volunteers; many disperse after an event is over, but some continue to help from event to event [31]. It is with respect to "high tempo" events like disasters that Wikipedia activity might reflect the greater diversity we see in disaster volunteerism: Keegan et al. describe the shared editorial work to be executed by members with "profound differences in perspectives and norms" [16]. OSM has drawn both experienced and new mappers to humanitarian causes, shaping the orientation of experienced mappers to OSM in new ways, and creating the need to make mapping simple for new mappers who know little about OSM otherwise.

We will discuss how OSM has responded to membership growth and diversity, and to the management of distributed responsibility across a loosely connected organization comprised of individuals with varying goals. Such a contribution offers further ways beyond the rich but dominant Wikipedia literature to think about how large data-producing organizations could work in the future.

THE STUDY

We now describe the disaster events that serve as the temporal and spatial constraints for examining OSM's evolution. We describe data collection and provide an overview of the OSM data structure.

Two Disaster Events: Overview of Conditions

Haiti Earthquake

Just before 5pm local time on January 12, 2010, a 7.0 magnitude earthquake struck Haiti. The heavy block and concrete style construction—intended to withstand hurricanes—collapsed and caused massive loss of life and injury. Over 40,000 people died and over 1 million were displaced. As many as 40% of Haiti's civil servants were injured or killed, and the majority of government buildings were damaged or destroyed [14], rendering access to government documents (including maps) difficult. The UN and other international organizations launched one of the largest relief efforts in history.

Typhoon Yolanda

On November 8, 2013, one of the strongest storms ever recorded hit the Visayas region of central Philippines: Typhoon Yolanda (also known as Haiyan). The storm itself affected more than 8 million people and killed over 7,000 [33]. The subsequent flooding, landslides and storm surge affected an estimated 14 million people, over 14% of the country's population [32]. Over 50 international groups have contributed to the response and recovery efforts [32].

Data Collection

Our methods rest on significant participant observation in OSM between 2009 and 2014. An author of this paper was a founding member of the Humanitarian OpenStreetMap Team (HOT) and a regular attendee of OSM conferences and meetups throughout this time period. This was supplemented by content analysis of blogposts, listserv conversations, and wiki pages. To understand OSM activity during crisis situations, we also examined records in the OSM database during the one-month long periods following the onset of each disaster. The dataset includes all edits from January 12-February 12, 2010 for Haiti, and November 8-December 8, 2013 for the Philippines. Data were imported into an instance of the Mongo database, where we used Ruby, R, and custom queries to analyze.

OSM Data Structure

We analyzed all unique versions of *nodes*, the building blocks of all OSM data. A node represents a single geographic point. Roads, paths, buildings, and areas are represented as a string of several nodes; in OSM, this entity is called a *way*. Our database contains entries for every version of all nodes and ways in the study areas for Haiti and the Philippines, whose structure is shown below (Figure 2). This allows us to reconstruct the modification history of objects. The *changeset id* for each node or way is unique to a set of edits committed to the database by a user. Large automated data imports that represented macro features like country boundaries were not included because they did not represent contributions by individual mappers and therefore skewed results.


```
{"id": 1333723135,
"lat": 18.5342186, "lon": -72.3673319,
"timestamp": 2013-06-24T02:49:56Z, "changeset":
16677898,
"version": 2,
"user": "jaakkoh_massedits",
"tags": {"source": "cosmha_iom",
          "amenity": "drinking_water",
          "pump_type": "manual",
          "operational_status": "open",
          "water_quality_issue": "yes"} }
```


Figure 2. A distilled JSON representation of an OSM node

ANALYTICAL DISCUSSION

Next, in this main section, we inductively weave together the quantitative and qualitative content to describe the socio-technical evolution of OSM across the four years bounded by the two disaster events.

A Catalyzing Event: OSM & the Haiti Earthquake

The Haiti Mappers

In the month following the earthquake, 491 OSM users contributed 12,858 distinct changesets. This included edits to 1,217,448 nodes, 956,725 of which were new additions. The mappers created the most detailed map of the quake-affected area in existence [29]. User contributions varied dramatically, with a mean of 2,471 nodes edited, but a median of just 223, exhibiting a long-tail distribution.

OSM Experience Level	Num. of Mappers	Total Nodes Edited	Total Changesets Made
New	119	126,392	891
Experienced	372	1,091,056	11,967

Table 1. Experience & Contribution during the Haiti window

Of the total Haiti mappers, 24% were new to OSM, seemingly drawn by a desire to help that we see in other digital disaster response efforts [30]. New mappers—those who joined OSM following the disaster—contributed 10.4% of all node edits, meaning that experienced mappers—those who already had accounts at the time of the earthquake—conducted the vast majority of mapping.

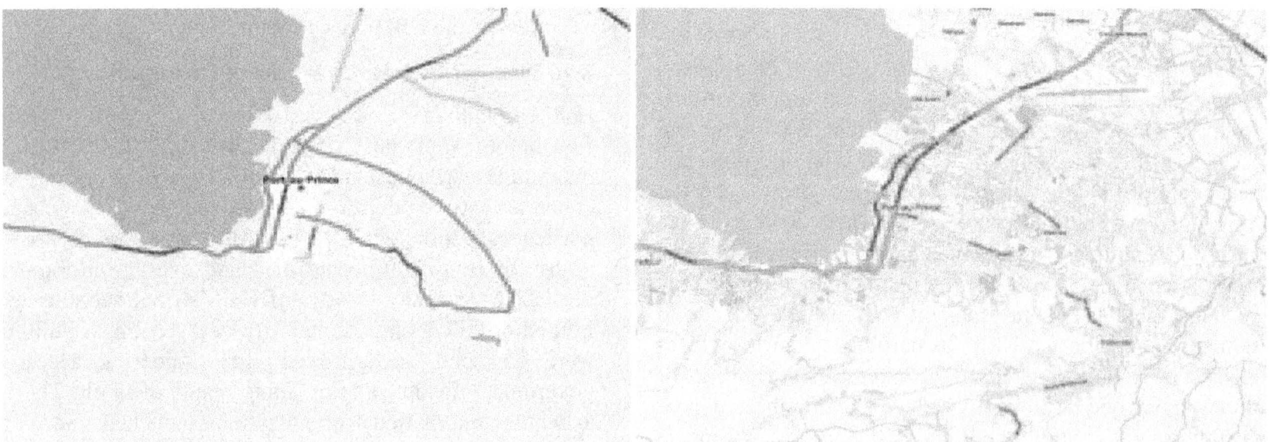

Figure 3. Rendering of Port-au-Prince before & after earthquake, a 9-fold increase in *node* content. 1/9/2010, 1/20/2010 [15]

High Tempo Mapping: Collisions in Simultaneous Work

Though their accomplishments were remarkable, the high tempo activity by numerous mappers in a constrained geography was perceived by some mappers as problematic. Moments of conflict, collision, and duplicated efforts happened at a very low-level, in pieces and parts of a building or road, which can be hard to detect by the mappers. Normally, interaction through map conflict can be valuable for establishing and regulating OSM's norms and practices for map creation. They can be opportunities to teach newcomers how to map well. However, in the matter of disaster events, where maps are readily needed for on-the-ground humanitarian work, such conflicts can get in the way of working efficiently.

Figure 4 shows a simple case of duplication that eventually reached resolution. Here, two changesets less than 1 minute apart contained 4 duplicate road sections created by two mappers (one red, one blue). The duplicate sections in this case were resolved when the second mapper returned to delete the first mapper's traces 4 hours later.

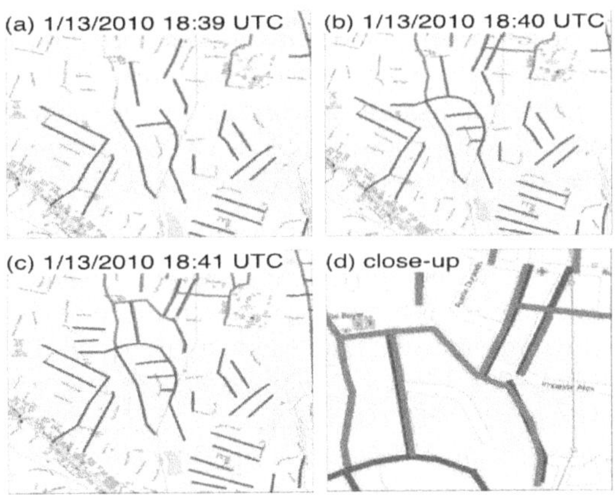

Figure 4. Four overlapping roads by two mappers

A second case (Figure 5) shows how a road was produced by three mappers, but the entirety of the tracing remained unresolved. Here, a remote mapper working the southwest area of Port-au-Prince mapped and tagged the highlighted feature as "highway: unclassified" (Fig 5b). Three minutes later, a different mapper created another way for the same feature, but tagged it "highway: road" (Fig 5c). Working at nearly the same time, the mappers probably were unaware of the collision. Five hours later, a third mapper deleted the road by the second mapper, and created yet a third road that used only some of the nodes from the first road. This final road was also tagged as "highway: unclassified," meaning that the resolution of the duplication remained incomplete.

These selections illustrate how high tempo mapping work in constrained geographies can result in map collisions. Though collisions often get resolved, the experiences reported by mappers who worked on the Haiti event in combination with evidence of duplication throughout the database indicate that valuable time was spent on producing the map erratically. These collisions were not a matter of

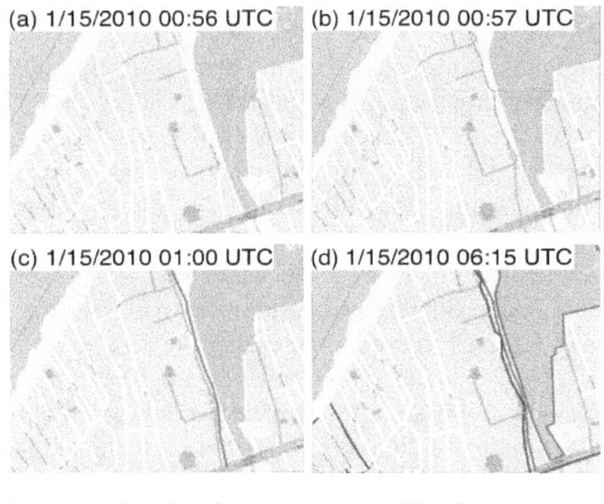

Figure 5. Overlapping roads created by three mappers

inexperience: practiced mappers were at work here. What is important to appreciate about what is otherwise normal and even organizationally beneficial in-map collision is that disaster-area maps are needed for immediate use and decision-making. OSM's success as a data provider meant that it had to directly address its organizational growth in relation to these external demands.

Collaboration "Off the Map"

The Haiti earthquake mappers loosely organized their work through public listservs, IRC discussion, and a wiki page—what we call collaboration "off the map." There they strove to motivate the community to contribute with prioritization of features that international responders especially needed, including spontaneous settlements of those displaced by the earthquake ("tent cities"). They also needed to manage the high volumes of donated satellite imagery that was the basis for their mapping. Though those tasks were critical to the overall effort, they still could not address the pervasive problem of "in-the-map" collisions. Indeed, one of the organizers wrote to the general OSM mailing list asking:

> What tools are available to see in real time which areas have been mapped recently? ... Any ideas on another tool that would allow people to "check out" an area for a period of time? ... This would be helpful for general coordination among us mapping in Haiti.

This request was unfulfilled, though not for long, and the challenges that OSM faced as it found itself in new territory were coming into view.

Organizational Changes to OSM in the Wake of Haiti

Lessons from Haiti gave rise to socio-technical changes within the organization. In addition, other changes were afoot that, in total, paint a picture of evolution toward more clearly articulated implications of OSM's ideals.

The Formalization of the Humanitarian OSM Team (HOT)

OSM was the de facto basemap for humanitarian groups working in response to the earthquake. It was used by first responders during search and rescue, to plan and manage camps for displaced Haitians, and in response to the Cholera outbreak that began in October 2010 [29]. As discussed extensively in our prior work [29], a group that called themselves the Humanitarian OpenStreetMap Team

(HOT) traveled to Haiti six times with long stays during the 18 months following the disaster to help not only responding organizations adopt OSM, but also to generate Haitian interest in developing a local OSM chapter. They hoped that a local community could maintain and update the map for the indefinite future. During this time HOT worked closely with partners in humanitarian organizations to understand their data needs. They adapted OSM's practices accordingly, including building a new data model of map features as well as releasing the data more rapidly [29]. This objective represented an important turn, as it shows how OSM's purpose was expanding from a primary focus on map creation to now include a focus on situated, localized data use by organizations that, in this case, a newly instituted Haitian OSM community could support.

HOT formally registered as a non-profit organization that following August, just 7 months after the earthquake [29]. It now employs an executive director, consultants, and a Board of Directors elected by the OSM membership. It has worked in a number of countries in Africa and Asia where, as in Haiti, they sought to encourage the growth of local OSM communities and bring contributors to the effort. By the time of Hurricane Yolanda, HOT had become the locus of activity within the OSM community for disaster response and international development concerns.

Innovating to Manage High Tempo Mapping Conflicts

The map congestion experienced in the aftermath of the Haiti earthquake led the newly formed HOT to create *The OSM Tasking Manager* to help mappers more efficiently coordinate simultaneous work. This innovation coincided with the growing popularity of microtasking as a solution to conduct distributed work (e.g., [1]). The design resembles microtasking environments that have people working in parallel with little knowledge of what others are doing. Administrators create "jobs" for a large geographic area, with written instructions about the features to be prioritized and tagging schemas if they differ from global OSM practice. The Tasking Manager then divides each job into a grid of "tasks" which mappers can select (Figure 6). Yellow means the task is taken; red denotes that it is complete but awaits "validation" by another; green denotes that it has been inspected in the OSM database for completeness and compliance. The first version of the Tasking Manager launched in September 2011 and was used to help in a number of smaller emergencies, but was not used during a crisis on the scale of the Haiti earthquake until Yolanda struck.

Other Notable Changes within OSM at Large

The period between the disasters was also an important time of change for the wider OSM community. The growth of both map creators and the users who relied on OSM data were driving a number of parallel efforts to meet desires for attracting and retaining new participants, and making data more reliable and accessible.

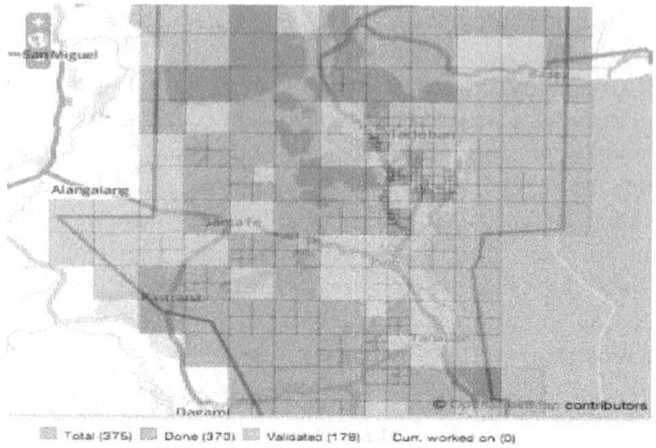

Figure 6. The user interface of the Tasking Manager [12]

Legal Status of OpenStreetMap Data. Underway for several years but finalized in September 2012, OSM moved away from the Creative Commons and towards ODBL—the Open Database License. This significant change was controversial within the community, but was motivated by concern that Creative Commons Licenses were created for works of art rather than databases and therefore did not properly protect the data and those who created it [23]. This move indicates additional orientation to downstream activities of data consumption once the efforts of the organization were gaining significant ground.

Broadening Appeal. In May 2013, an updated OSM editing interface was released to make it easier for new participants to map. Improvement of the openstreetmap.org website carried out at the same time had a similar goal. A private company called Mapbox, with funding from the Knight Foundation, carried out both of these projects. The announcement of the project on the Mapbox blog reveals the growing support and stronger orientation toward not only data creation, but also consumption:

> Our goal is to use this investment to make it easier to add data to OpenStreetMap, make OpenStreetMap.org more social to support the community as it continues its rapid growth, and make it easier for people to get data out of OpenStreetMap to make their own maps.

A website called LearnOSM was built by HOT to consolidate the great deal of documentation and training materials to help new mappers. Launched in June 2012, LearnOSM materials are translated into 9 languages to reach people from disparate linguistic backgrounds. In another attempt to broaden appeal, a new email list was launched in June 2013 after discussion at OSM conferences earlier that year to promote inclusion of a more diverse mapping population, particularly women. Some estimates put the number of female contributors to OSM as low as 3-5% [26], below even Wikipedia's numbers. These efforts again suggest an orientation toward better mapping contributions by a diverse population, a major driver for sustaining a viable community that would not suffer from some of the problems Wikipedia has faced.

Other Support for Collaboration. In its own parallel effort distinct from the Tasking Manager, the development of *Notes*, a drop-pin annotation feature, is described as an issue-tracking feature to point out improper tagging or to suggest additional information that could be added to the map. In addition, guests are able to create Notes such that "everyone can add their local knowledge to the map" [6] without having to learn how to edit in OSM. Here we see OSM attempting to facilitate what Lave and Wenger refer to as "legitimate peripheral participation" [18], a growth pattern in communities of practice in which new members are given meaningful but simple tasks to perform. New participants learn about the community while creating the possibility for richer, more central, future engagement. The Notes feature also enables meta-conversation that sits on top of the map and is not encoded in the database. The creation of Notes suggests that OSM is exploring new approaches to collaboration that are based on the map but take place a step removed from the database itself. We will return to the use of Notes in our discussion of Yolanda.

Resistance to Expansion of Governance Structures. Unlike Wikipedia, which has sought to manage community growth through the creation and clearer articulation of policies [2], the OSM governance structure remained largely the same during this period and still today. The mission and responsibilities of the OSM Foundation, a small elected body and its working groups, has remained narrowly scoped: to maintain server infrastructure, host the annual State of the Map conference, and act as a legal and fiscal entity for the effort. Debates on the OSM listserv and at the State of the Map indicate a strong desire to avoid what are seen as bureaucratic solutions to project governance in favor of social and technical approaches.

These socio-technical activities illustrate how OSM was seeking non-bureaucratic ways to promote and cope with growth—changes that were then in place and had repercussions in the response to Typhoon Yolanda.

Another Trial 4 Years On: OSM & Typhoon Yolanda

Almost four years after the Haiti earthquake, Typhoon Yolanda struck the Philippines. Over this period, OSM membership quadrupled to over 1.2 million users. The response to the event was significant, with the work of the volunteer mappers led by the now well-established HOT.

The Yolanda Mappers

In the month following the typhoon, 1,574 mappers made 3,648,537 node edits, including adding 3,294,981 new nodes to the map, averaging 2,292 edits per mapper, with a median of 426. This again signals a long-tail distribution. Figure 7 shows the results of their mapping contributions.

OSM Experience Level	Number of Mappers	Total Nodes Edited	Total Changesets Made
New	663	491,404	14,562
Experienced	911	3,157,143	22,266

Table 2. Experience & Contribution during Yolanda window

We see a roughly 3-fold increase in both the number of mappers as well as node edit contributions between Haiti and Yolanda. This tracks with overall OSM membership growth, but was likely also influenced by HOT's recruiting and organizing efforts. As with Haiti, experienced users made the majority of contributions with new mappers contributing just 13.5% of the total node edits.

Use of the New Tasking Manager

HOT coordinated the OSM community's response during Yolanda using email and an IRC chatroom to motivate volunteers, discuss imagery issues or finer technical details of mapping, and direct contributors to the Tasking Manager. Because the OSM database does not record whether a mapper's edits are directly related to the Tasking Manager, we compared the history of the Tasking Manager database with the OSM changeset history to determine how much this new tool was used. During the study window, 1,354 or 86% of the mappers checked out tasks and made changesets that geographically coincided with one or more

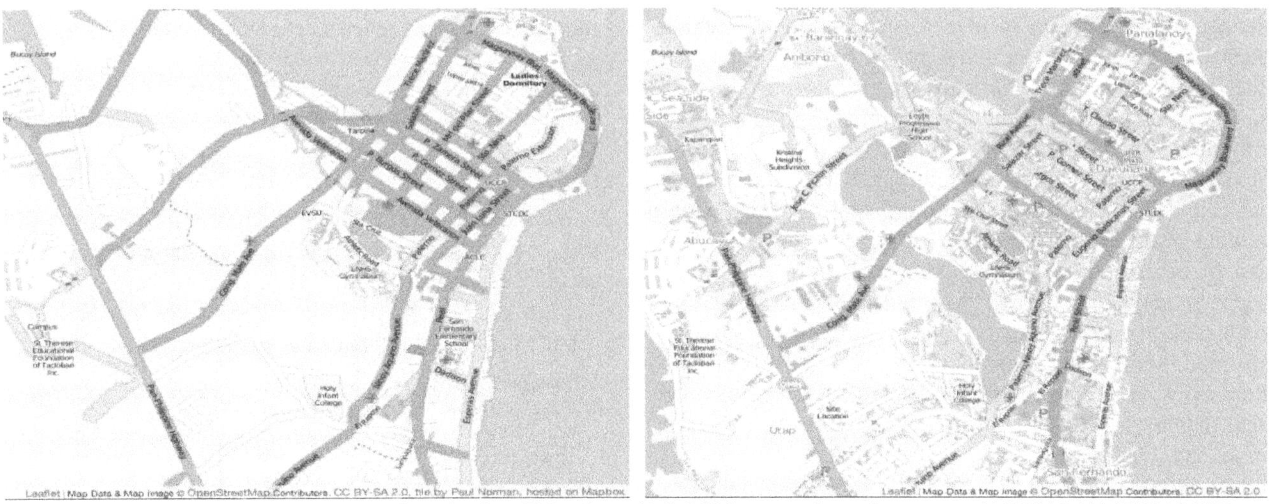

Figure 7. Rendering of Tacloban before & after Yolanda, a 11.5-fold increase in *node* content. 11/7/2013,11/ 17/2013 [22]

of the Yolanda Tasking Manager jobs. Mappers who did not appear in the Tasking Manager database contributed only 6% of the Philippines OSM changesets. These results indicate that the Tasking Manager was widely used by those who participated in remote mapping.

A changeset can illustrate not just what mappers edited but *how* they edit the map. We employed several metrics to study editing patterns, including nodes per changeset, area of the changeset bounding box, and the quotient of the two: what we call the "density of the changeset." Within both datasets, some changesets reflect large automated imports of data. For the purposes of the node count, area, and density analyses, the changesets we observed were greater than $1m^2$ and limited to those containing less than 10,000 nodes to avoid inclusion of automated imports.

The median area for changesets in the Philippines was $0.5km^2$, significantly lower than for Haiti where the area was $3km^2$. In addition, changesets in the Philippines were, on average 9 times denser than changesets in Haiti. These numbers indicate that the Philippines mappers tended to be more geographically focused, a likely impact of Tasking Manager use. Furthermore, when looking at simply the number of changesets that geographically overlap, we see that in the Philippines, an average changeset intersects with 67% fewer changesets than in Haiti.

Returning to the first visualization offered in this paper (Figure 1), we see the vivid before-and-after effect of the Tasking Manager intervention that illuminates these figures reported here. (The bounds of each figure were chosen so that they would have a common number of nodes—116K—for consistent comparison.) For Haiti, there is a great deal of dispersed mapping. In the Philippines, however, a different ordering emerges, with patterns of concentrated mapping by people working (virtually) side-by-side.

Lessons Learned from the Tasking Manager in Yolanda

HOT reflected on the Yolanda experience in early 2014 (not long before the time of this writing), and has developed a set of priorities to improve the Tasking Manager. Among them include a new addition by which mappers working on the same task can talk with each other—asynchronously through comments—to discuss uncertainties. Identification of this priority is consistent with something we anticipate: Our observation is that the microtasking environment so reduced mapping collisions that opportunities for deliberation and organizational learning from those erstwhile "entanglements" could be lost. In other words, when seeking to address collisions, mappers may be required to revisit mapping activity conducted by themselves or others; reflect on available information about the geographic area and make decisions about how best to represent it in the map; or work with other members of OSM to resolve disagreements. The task comments could be a way to reintroduce benefits of collaboration without cost to the efficiency that was otherwise gained for time-critical mapping.

Also on the list of priorities was an item that we think signals a very important concern about higher order issues of coordination. Since all the jobs are put into one instance of the Tasking Manager no matter where on the globe the work is, there could be yet a new form of traffic within the confines of the microtasking tool. Here, the team is considering how to specify division for bigger geographic or population segments ("for Haiti," or "by the ugrad course at University X") to mitigate this potential problem.

These solutions reinforce three things with respect to analysis of OSM's evolution: 1) that OSM is thinking about how to scale as its mapping population grows; 2) that the database, though powerful for what it offers as an open spatial data repository, will become only increasingly problematic with respect to how it supports and reveals social interaction as OSM grows; and 3) that OSM is struggling again with technical solutions for collaboration.

Use of the New Notes Feature

Recall that the Notes feature was invented in April 2013 as yet another solution for supporting collaborative activity, with a specific goal of encouraging legitimate peripheral participation. There was some use of Notes in Yolanda, though not extensive (30 registered accounts, compared to the 1554 total mappers for that event). Though the number of Notes created was small, the activity happening here by both new users and experienced users is a sign of issues that OSM will have to wrestle with in the future.

Of the 241 Yolanda Notes, we see different, critical examples of legitimate peripheral participation. Here we see an interaction in which a guest user who is perhaps Filipino notes a missing feature on the map; two OSMers move the problem to solution in two steps, and resolve it:

> **Anonymous** (2013-11-15 21:30:39) [action:opened]: mao ni ang buray bridge
>
> **GoMap** (2013-11-16 05:45:14) [action:commented]: translation: "this is Buray bridge"
>
> **brianlopes** (2013-11-19 05:55:57) [action:closed]: bridge name added

In other exchanges, guests demonstrated that they see OSM *as a map to appropriate and personalize*, not a map to directly create. They are acting more as "involved viewers" rather than as data producers who view the map more functionally. One tagged his residence "Home Sweet Home," while another marketed his cockfight arena.

In other cases, we see guests cautiously interacting with the map, which was sometimes taken as cues for experienced users to train them. Here, after one types in "asdasdasdasd" to apparently test out the feature, an experienced OSM explains his envisioned use of Notes:

> **GoMap**(2013-12-05 03:01:24) [action:closed]: Use this feature to report an error in the data or to give some additional information, for instance the name of a street or an address etc. When available, an OSM contributor will attempt to resolve it.

Though in the Yolanda response it was clear that some mappers strove to make Notes a mechanism for coordination, norms around its use have yet to stabilize. We predict that Notes will continue to have a degree of volatility because guests might see Notes as an opportunity for personalization, or for noting information that is transient, rather than permanent (such as a school marked as a temporary disaster shelter). This differs from the prevailing view of the map as encoding physical structures that are permanent and visually verifiable. We see both the conceptualized and actual use of Notes as expressions of a desire to support legitimate peripheral participation [18].

CONCLUSION

This account of the socio-technical evolution of a large, volunteer-based data-producing organization yields new insight about how such entities emerge, and provides another site of observation beyond OSM's closest cousin of Wikipedia. Like Wikipedia around 2007, OSM has experienced rapid growth and has had to find ways to cope with and maximize this opportunity. In the early days of OSM, many of the important *users* of the data were members of the community and thus also directly involved in the *creation* of the data. As new groups began to rely on OSM data, such as the humanitarian organizations operating in Haiti and the Philippines, OSM has had to make itself more accessible to outsiders. It has attempted to address these twin challenges of community growth and accessibility to an array of new users (both mappers and data consumers) by focusing on the usability of its tools, addressing legal questions around usage and distribution of the data, and working to attract and retain participants.

We find evidence that OSM is increasingly orienting to the obligations that come about when open data—freely available data—is an organizational value. We argue that to see such a value through, an organization must come to see itself as part of a constellation of data use relationships that place demands on such issues as data integrity, availability and accessibility. Unlike commercial efforts that are perhaps necessarily oriented toward its customers, volunteer-based open data efforts may be able to suspend orientation to that goal while they are bootstrapping data production and building their community, but to remain sustainable and indeed to have the meaning that open data values connote, a hard turn toward the demands of data consumption is inevitable. As a participant at the State of Map Conference 2010 said of OSM to great applause:

> Aren't we just hitting puberty? We were born 4 years ago; we are growing up...Look at what we've accomplished. We are growing appendages and we don't really know what they do. And we are trying to figure them out and occasionally they don't work like they should...[but] we've put people in Haiti, we're putting people in Kibera...[so] we're growing up... [But] it's not just [about] the language *we* are speaking, it is about the language *that everyone else is speaking*. So yeah, we do need to have that culture where we just don't "do it," but we also need to present that to the [for example] "assistant under secretary of management" for the UN, because we do have to speak that language as well.

To these ends, OSM took measures to facilitate improved collaboration. Different parts of the organization have created different tools to manage work in an effort to "realign" [3] with its expanding user base as the organization envisions how to proceed in relation to larger goals of data reuse that are coming into view. In effect it is creating and maintaining the kind of cyberinfrastructure that Bietz, Ferro and Lee describe [3]. However, we speculate that some of OSM's current solutions might be closing out opportunities that spring from *beneficial entanglements*. Some entanglement in distributed work can benefit organizational evolution, because it is through those rich interactions on the map that trust and familiarity are first staged, and which later support substantive deliberations about mapping practices, policies and "speaking other languages" of all stakeholders.

However, the work of OSM is hard to assess quantitatively or qualitatively because so much of it is written in at the lowest levels *into* the database. Even core members struggle with understanding the nature of the work and how it comes about because it is simply so hard to perceive it. The power of the database as the repository for open spatial data has both propelled OSM forward, but also creates special challenges. OSM as an organization cannot easily separate itself from how it encodes its data.

To move forward then, OSM's solutions are sitting "on top" of the map. Though this abstracted approach to supporting articulation work thereby is more visible, and easier both for participants to conduct and researchers to observe, the view of the work at the level of map genesis is still obscured. This paper, en route to explaining organizational evolution, offers some measures for mappers and observers to understand map-based interaction as it is inscribed in the database, and we hope to further facilitate analyses of OSM's rich organizational life. We see such contributions as belonging to the important call to better understand matters of geospatial data [11]—its creation, its reuse, and the social infrastructure that surrounds it—as a growing issue in human-computer interaction.

In contrast with Wikipedia's policy-driven strategy for managing rapid community growth, OSM has developed a range of socio-technical interventions aimed at easing learning by new contributors, streamlining adoption of its data by new users, and assisting the articulation work of a growing community of mappers. It is too early to tell if this approach will address problems of policy rigidity and unfriendliness to newcomers that Wikipedia has faced. We also do not yet know what new problems these interventions could cause, such as the reduction of situations in which potentially beneficial entanglements might occur. This study of organizational development does illustrate a potential alternative to the policy-driven strategy adopted by Wikipedia. Time and future research will be necessary to understand its full implications.

ACKNOWLEDGMENTS
This research is funded by US National Science Foundation grants 0910586, 1331490, and 1441263. We thank our Project EPIC colleagues at the University of Colorado Boulder for support and critique. We thank reviewers and particularly Irina Shklovski for her insightful assistance.

REFERENCES

1. Bernstein, M., Little, G., Miller, R., Hartmann, B., Ackerman, M., Karger, D., Crowell, D., Panovich, K. Soylent: a word processor with a crowd inside. *Proc. of UIST* (2010), 313-322.
2. Beschastnikh, I., Kriplean, T., McDonald, D. W. Wikipedian Self-Governance in Action: Motivating the Policy Lens. *Proc of ICWSM.* (2008).
3. Bietz, M., Ferro, T., Lee, C. Sustaining the development of cyberinfrastructure: an organization adapting to change. *Proc of CSCW* (2012), 901-910.
4. Budhathoki, N., Haythornthwaite, C. Motivation for open collaboration crowd and community models and the case of OpenStreetMap. American Behavioral Scientist 54, 5 (2013), 548-575.
5. Chilton, S. Crowdsourcing is radically changing the geodata landscape: case study of OpenStreetMap. *Proc. of UK Cartographic Conf,* (2009).
6. Fairhurst, R. OpenStreetMap opens up to more contributors with easy 'add a note' feature. *OSM Foundation Blog.* (4/29/13).
7. Forte, A, Bruckman, A. Scaling consensus: Increasing decentralization in Wikipedia governance. *Proc of HICSS*, 2008.
8. Haklay, M. How good is volunteered geographical information? A comparative study of OpenStreetMap & Ordnance Survey datasets. *Environment & Planning B: Planning & Design* 34, 4 (2010), 682-703.
9. Haklay, M., Antoniou, V., Basiouka, S., R Soden, R., Mooney, P. Crowdsourced Geographic Information Use in Government. *World Bank.* (2014).
10. Halfaker, A., Geiger, R. S., Morgan, J. T., Riedl, J. The rise and decline of an open collaboration system: How Wikipedia's reaction to popularity is causing its decline. *American Behavioral Scientist.* (2012).
11. Hecht, B., Schöning, J., Erickson, T., Preidhorsky, R. Geographic Human Interaction. *Ext. Proc, of CHI* (2011).
12. HOT Tasking Manager. Typhoon Haiyan. *http://tasks.hotosm.org/job/350.*
13. Hristova, D., Quattrone, G., Mashhadi, A. J., Capra, L. The Life of the Party: Impact of Social Mapping in OpenStreetMap. *Proc of ICWSM* (2013).
14. Human Rights Watch (HRW). *World Report 2011.* Seven Stories Press (2011).
15. ITO World Blog. January 20, 2010. http://itoworld.blogspot.com/2010/01/mapping-crisis-openstreetmap-response.html.
16. Keegan, B, Gergle, D, Contractor, N. Hot off the wiki: dynamics, practices, and structures in Wikipedia's coverage of the Tōhoku catastrophes. *Proc of WikiSym,* (2011).
17. Lam, STK., Uduwage, A., Dong, Z., Sen, S., Musicant, D. R., Terveen, L., Riedl, J. WP: clubhouse?: An exploration of Wikipedia's gender imbalance. *Symposium on Wikis & Open Collaboration.* (2011).
18. Lave, J., Wenger, E. Situated Learning: Legitimate Peripheral Participation. Cambridge Univ, (1991), 138.
19. Lin, Y. A qualitative enquiry into OpenStreetMap making. *New Review of Hypermedia and Multimedia* 17, 1 (2011), 53-71.
20. Mileti, D.S. 1999. *Disasters by Design: A Reassessment of Natural Hazards in the US.* Joseph Henry D.C.
21. Mooney, P, & Corcoran, P. How social is OSM. In *Proc of AGILE Conf on GIS.* 2012. (24-27).
22. OpenStreetMap Development. *http://pierzen.dev.openstreetmap.org/hot/leaflet/OSM-Compare-before-after-philippines.html.*
23. OSM Foundation. *We are Changing the License.* (2012).
24. Priedhorsky, R., Jordan, B., Terveen, L. How a personalized geowiki can help bicyclists share information more effectively. *WikiSym,* (2007), 93-98.
25. Schmidt, K, & L Bannon. "Taking CSCW seriously." *Journal of CSCW,* 1.1-2 (1992): 7-40.
26. Schmidt, M., Klettner, S. Gender and Experience-Related Motivators for Contributing to OSM. *ACTIVITY* (2013).
27. Simonite, T. The Decline of Wikipedia. *MIT Technology Review.* October 22, 2013.
28. Soden, R., Budhathoki, N., Palen, L. Resilience-Building and the Crisis Informatics Agenda: Lessons Learned from Open Cities Kathmandu. *ISCRAM,* (2014).
29. Soden R., Palen, L. From crowdsourcing to community mapping: the post-earthquake work of OpenStreetMap Haiti. In *Proc. of COOP,* (2014).
30. Starbird, K. Palen, L. "Voluntweeters": self-organizing by digital volunteers in times of crisis. *Proc. of CHI,* (2011), 1071-1080.
31. Starbird,K, Palen,L. Working & Sustaining the Virtual "Disaster Desk." *Proc. of CSCW* (2013), 491-502.
32. United Nations Office for Coordination of Humanitarian Affairs (UNOCHA) 2013. https://docs.unocha.org/sites/dms/CAP/SRP_2013-2014_Philippines_Typhoon_Haiyan.pdf
33. USAID Yolanda Factsheet - http://www.usaid.gov/haiyan/fy14/fs20
34. White, J., Palen, L., Anderson, K. M. Digital mobilization in disaster response: the work & self-organization of on-line pet advocates in response to hurricane sandy. *Proc. of CSCW,* (2014), 866-876.

Physio@Home: Exploring Visual Guidance and Feedback Techniques for Physiotherapy Exercises

Richard Tang[1] Xing-Dong Yang[1] Scott Bateman[2] Joaquim Jorge[3] Anthony Tang[1]
[1]University of Calgary
Alberta, Canada, T2N 1N4
{richard.tang, xdyang, tonyt}
@ucalgary.ca
[2]University of Prince Edward Island
Charlottetown, Canada, C1A 4P3
sbateman@upei.ca
[3]IST/INESC-ID/U Lisboa
Lisbon, Portugal
jaj@inesc-id.pt

ABSTRACT
Physiotherapy patients exercising at home alone are at risk of re-injury since they do not have corrective guidance from a therapist. To explore solutions to this problem, we designed Physio@Home, a prototype that guides people through pre-recorded physiotherapy exercises using real-time visual guides and multi-camera views. Our design addresses several aspects of corrective guidance, including: plane and range of movement, joint positions and angles, and extent of movement. We evaluated our design, comparing how closely people could follow exercise movements under various feedback conditions. Participants were most accurate when using our visual guide and multi-views. We provide suggestions for exercise guidance systems drawn from qualitative findings on visual feedback complexity.

Author Keywords
Physiotherapy; movement guidance; visualization; augmented reality;

ACM Classification Keywords
H.5.m. Information interfaces and presentation (e.g., HCI): Miscellaneous.

INTRODUCTION
As people age, they are more susceptible to joint and muscle injury. While improvements in healthcare mean that people can survive these injuries, many live longer while recovering from such injuries [20]. Physiotherapy is a post-injury rehabilitation activity that improves and restores physical function after injury or surgery [7, 20]. For example, after a dislocated shoulder is put back in place, a patient is taught several shoulder exercises to help restore strength and range-of-movement. In these sessions, the physiotherapist teaches and demonstrates exercises. A patient will then perform the exercise, and while they practice, the physiotherapist provides immediate feedback and correction to ensure the patient performs the exercise correctly.

CHI 2015, April 18 - 23 2015, Seoul, Republic of Korea
Copyright 2015 ACM 978-1-4503-3145-6/15/04$15.00
http://dx.doi.org/10.1145/2702123.2702401

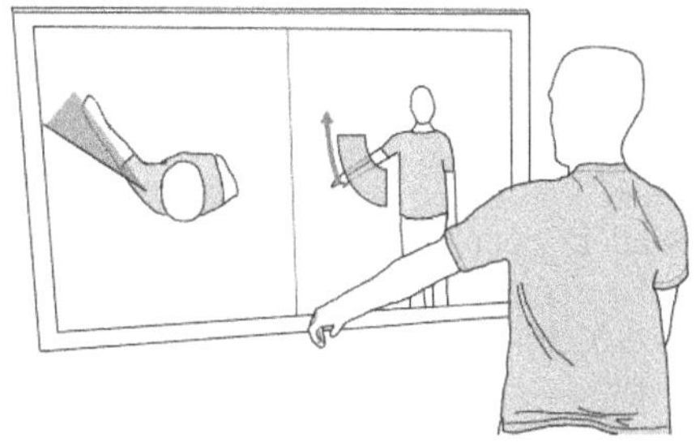

Figure 1: Our prototype shows front + top camera views of the exerciser with visualizations overlaid on their body.

This feedback ensures the patient will be able to recover physical functioning and avoid re-aggravating their injury [4]. In addition, the feedback can provide the patient with motivation to continue their exercises.

The problem is that patients also need to perform these exercises at home, without the guidance of a physiotherapist. Without guidance, patients risk performing their exercises incorrectly—at best without gaining restorative benefits, and at worst re-injuring themselves. Early technology explorations to help patients have used on-body sensors to provide movement and guidance feedback (e.g. [1, 9, 16, 29]). Yet, many of these initial explorations employ technologies that are expensive and unwieldy for home use.

The commoditization of computer vision technologies makes encumbrance-free, low cost body tracking a promising and viable alternative. Several researchers have explored the use of the Microsoft Kinect in this way—tracking motion, and then providing visual feedback to help teach and guide new movements (e.g. [3,21,25]). However, most of this prior work has focused on gross motor movements (e.g., dance), and in contexts forgiving to movement errors. In contrast, physiotherapy demands careful and controlled movements due to a patient's reduced mobility and the potential for re-injury. Given this focus, what are the kinds of feedback and guidance that physiotherapists are concerned with? How can we design effective visual feedback that allows people to take meaningful corrective actions during exercises?

Based on discussions with a physiotherapist, we derive five features of movement guidance and feedback. We realize these ideas in the design of Physio@Home, a prototype system for guiding and aiding proper performance of basic physical therapy exercises. As people perform exercises (mimicking pre-recorded movements), the system provides several views with a real-time, on-screen 'Wedge' visualization which provides corrective guidance (Figure 1).

To evaluate our design approach, we conducted a study with 16 participants. Our results show that using the Wedge and multi-view camera allows people to perform exercises with the least amount of error compared to using video alone. While our strong results demonstrate the potential of our approach, we have identified several outstanding issues that need to be addressed in systems providing visual guidance for precise movements. These include the visual complexity of guides and avoiding information overload.

This work makes three contributions: first, we developed Physio@Home, a novel system that demonstrates the viability of visual feedback for guidance of physical therapy exercises in the home; second, we contribute a study of our system, which highlights the utility of visual feedback and multi-view for movement guidance, and finally, we identify a set of challenges for the design of similar systems.

RELATED WORK

Rehabilitation Systems Requiring Worn Sensors

There has been a recent push to develop rehabilitation solutions for treating patients at home. Examples include [4, 29], which use wearable kinematic sensors to track and visualize knee angles during exercises. These systems visualize the knee angle on a computer monitor to indicate whether the patient is correctly performing their exercises. Ayoade & Baillie [4] evaluated their system with patients undergoing knee rehabilitation over a six-week period and found that patients working with their system were recovering better than patients without. Pt Viz [2] also uses wearable sensors, but visualizes the correct knee angle directly on the wearable using lighted fabric.

BASE [9] was another kinematic sensor-based system that focused on supporting exercises at home. The system was designed for older adults, a population commonly requiring physiotherapy care, and focused on strength and balancing exercises. BASE displayed real-time feedback based on the alignment and angle of their legs.

Some rehabilitation systems were also designed as exergames to encourage and motivate patients. Alankus et al. [1] designed interactive games for stroke patients using webcams and Nintendo Wii remotes to track arm motions. Uzor and Baillie [24] implemented simple exergames for elderly patients using knee bending, sit-to-stand, and marching exercises and found that their exergames encouraged adherence to rehabilitation programs and would have the potential to improve mobility.

These systems demonstrate the benefits of computer-based rehabilitation systems over traditional methods. They also emphasize the importance of measuring the angles of joints, and using interactive visual cues that directly show progress in an exercise. However, these systems are limited to simple, coarse-grained movements such as bending a knee [4, 29] or aligning a patient's entire body [9]. Our work focuses on precision for more complex shoulder exercises.

Vision-based Systems for Rehabilitation

The Microsoft Kinect is a viable sensing platform capable of full-body and limb tracking. The Kinect also benefits from being readily available, easy to setup, and low-cost. For example, Huang [12] developed Kinerehab to track arm-based exercise movements. Similarly, Lee et al. [13] used the Kinect to track Tai Chi motions for physical rehabilitation. Rector et al's Eye-free Yoga [19] made use of the Kinect and audio feedback to develop an exergame for visually-impaired persons to match yoga postures. Similarly, MotionMA [25] uses the Kinect to focus on movement interpretation and feedback for performing repetitions. Work by Camporesi et al [6] studied how Kinect systems may be customized to improve treatment. Overall, rehabilitation systems have taken advantage of the Kinect's depth-sensing and skeletal tracking capabilities to develop easy to use and deploy systems for patients with a variety of conditions.

However, the Kinect is still subject to inaccurate tracking and skeleton placement. As noted in [12], the Kinect had difficulties tracking patients with walkers or wheelchairs. Work by Tao and Levin [23] found the optimal position of the Kinect to be between 1.45 and 1.75 meters in front of the user and 0.15 meters left or right. These area requirements may restrict their deployment in patient homes and introduces sources of error that must also be considered when used for rehabilitation. Despite these disadvantages, performance studies of the Kinect suggest that it has sufficient overall tolerance that it can be used for encouraging and maintaining exercise compliance [17].

Our project focuses on precise exercises that involve movements with a higher number of degrees-of-freedom. To eliminate tracking problems inherent with current iterations of the Microsoft Kinect, particularly with fine-grained rotation exercises, we use Vicon cameras. This allows us to design our system with a best-case motion tracker. We may soon have smaller, commodity-level sensors that near the Vicon's precision, without its extensive infrastructure.

Movement Instruction

The broader HCI community has also explored movement guidance. Early work explored techniques to teach gestures (e.g., for touchscreens), while more recent work has explored approaches for providing hints/guidance for full body movement. Various projects have explored different mechanisms for providing feedback, though in general, this work focuses on visual feedback. For example, OctoPocus [5] and ShadowGuides [10] are concerned with teaching gestures on touch screens. These systems present dynamic, real-time guides when the screen is touched to help teaching people gestures and movements.

Others have explored different ways of presenting this feedback—often in egocentric ways. For instance, rather than relying on the interaction surface as the output space for the feedback, LightGuide [21] projects guidance on people's body (i.e., their hands). Here, the researchers studied how guides such as arrows and lines projected directly on the body can help guide arm motions. While effective, this projection approach may not be appropriate when body parts cannot be seen (e.g., the back of one's shoulder). Just Follow Me [28] taught movement using a head-mounted display and virtual reality. Just Follow Me uses ghostly arm outlines to convey movement instructions to the wearer. Similarly, White et al. [27] evaluated visual hints for instructing physical gestures with cards, while Henderson and Feiner [11] displayed arrows and visual guides directly on objects to complete assembly tasks.

These projects introduce the concepts of *feedback* and *feedforward*. Feedback is information conveyed during or after the execution of movement indicating what gestures the user is close to performing (e.g., OctoPocus) and the visualization of current posture (e.g., ShadowGuides). Feedforward provides information about how to complete future movements: OctoPocus realizes this through possible tracing paths, while ShadowGuides and Just Follow Me realize these as future hand poses and ghostly arm images, respectively. We drew on the richness of these past uses of feedback and feedforward information to advise the design of our visualizations for guiding precise arm movements.

Most close to our work, YouMove [3] is a full-body movement instruction system with personalized recording, annotation, and gradual learning using an augmented mirror. The feedback is presented in a "mirror" that allows people to see themselves. Their system taught movement in gradual steps by scoring movement similarity and removing guides as the performer becomes proficient. We build on this approach of an "augmented mirror" in three ways: first, we focus on finer-grained physio exercises (rather than gross movements like yoga and ballet); second, we focus on guiding movement through dynamic guides (as with [5, 10]) as opposed to teaching through repetition; and finally, our work explores the use of multi-view cameras for feedback.

DESIGN

Physiotherapists often provide patients with pamphlets [26] containing drawings of exercises, but it can difficult to understand these movements based only on a few snapshots. A better option is to refer patients to online videos that demonstrate complete exercises; however, this lacks the feedback necessary for precise movement guidance. Our goal was to design visual guidance that could be used at home to guide careful movements such as those required in physiotherapy. We envision such a system would be displayed on a television screen so that it functions like a mirror in their physiotherapist's office (e.g. [3]). Ideally, the system would not require on-body sensors or complex setup, instead relying on low-cost cameras (e.g., Kinect).

We took an iterative approach to realize our final design. We worked with a practicing physiotherapist to learn the basic exercises they teach patients, how to perform them correctly, and how they teach and correct their patients.

Example: shoulder abduction & adduction. For the purpose of this section, we describe one simple physiotherapy exercise: a shoulder abduction followed by adduction. This is a strengthening exercise that involves raising the arm (abducting) along the frontal plane (Figure 2) up to shoulder level while keeping elbow locked, and then lowering (adducting) the arm back down to the patient's side. This exercise may be performed with the arm being raised along the frontal plane, or 45 to 60 degrees from the patient's front. They are also often performed with thumb facing upwards in order to work the muscles in the shoulder. Other exercises are described in our Evaluation.

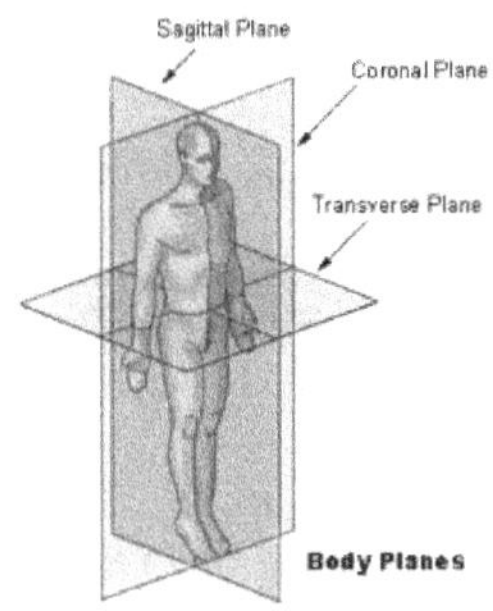

Figure 2: Anatomical body planes. Coronal plane is referred to in paper as 'Frontal plane'

Characteristics of Guidance

Based on how physiotherapists train and correct exercise movements, we classified four guidance characteristics they communicate to patients: *plane (and range) of movement*, *maintaining position/angle*, *extent of movement*, and *movement speed*.

Characteristic	Realized in Physio@Home
Plane of movement *Path and direction that the user needs to move*	Wedge, Movement arc, Directional arrow
Range of movement *Start and finish of a movement*	Wedge
Maintaining position/angle *Joints to keep still/keep at a particular angle*	Nearest Arm
Extent of movement *Limits on error in movement*	Movement arc, Nearest arm, Top-down angle
Rate of movement	N/A

Table 1: Summary of guidance characteristics

We summarize these in Table 1 and explain them in the context of the shoulder exercise described previously.

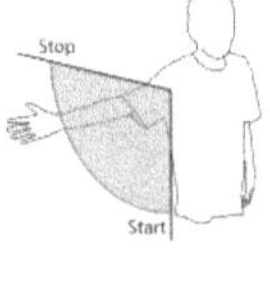

Plane or Range of Movement. The *plane of movement* refers to the plane the body part will move along during the exercise. The *range* refers to the "start point" and "end point" of this movement. For instance, during non-angled shoulder abduction, the patient's arm moves up along the frontal plane (Figure 2), starting from resting position to where it is exactly aligned with the shoulder.

Maintaining position or angle. For many exercises, certain joints need to be kept in either a fixed position, or at a fixed angle. In the case of a shoulder abduction/adduction, the arm must be kept straightened, and the shoulder kept level with the ground. Other exercises are stricter—for example, with an external rotation exercise, the elbow needs to stay next to the body, and be bent at 90°.

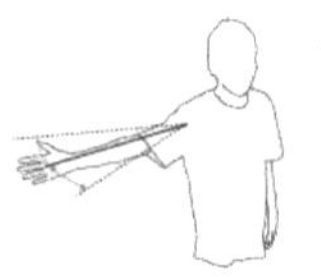

Extent of movement. The *extent of movement* limits how a body part's motion can and should deviate from the plane of movement. For example, during an angled shoulder abduction, the arm must maintain its angle relative to the body's sagittal plane.

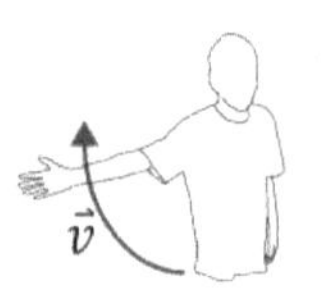

Rate of movement. This refers to how fast a body part must move. For some exercises, performing them slowly ensures the right muscles are being used. This characteristic applies to a variation of the shoulder adduction where the arm must travel slower as it returns to the patient's side. In many cases, the patient is free to proceed at their own pace.

Wedge Visualization

We designed a guide called the 'Wedge' to be displayed on-screen to convey an exercise's movement characteristics in real-time (Figure 3). We chose to use a dynamic visual guide instead of video so that the guide can be adjusted for a user's size and position and provide contextualized movement guidance while the patient is moving. The Wedge consists of several distinct parts: the Movement Arc, Directional Arrow, Nearest Arm, and Topdown Angle.

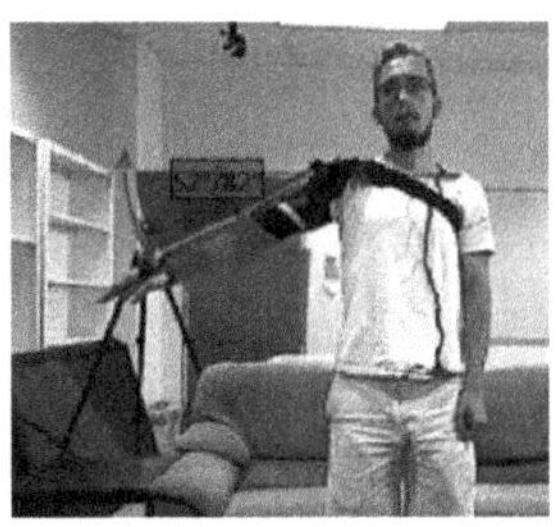

Figure 3: Wedge visualization. The dynamic visual guide is overlaid on top of a user's arm

Movement Arc. The central arc shape of the Wedge conveys the plane of movement for each part of an exercise. It is based on the motion of the arm with either the shoulder or elbow as the center of its radius and where the moving arm forms the shape of the arc.

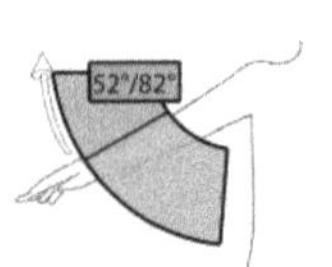

The Movement Arc is divided into two parts: one section for the completed portion in green, and the other for the incomplete remainder of movement. As the user follows the plane, the green completed section grows to indicate progress, while the grey incomplete section shrinks to show how much of the movement still remains. This conveys both feedback and feedforward, and offers motivation for the user. In addition to the shape and fill of the Arc, we also provide a numeric angle indicator of their current and required arm angles to complete exercise.

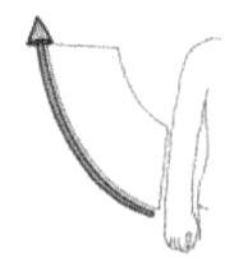

Directional Arrow. We draw an arrow on the outside of the Movement Arc to show the direction the user must move in. Similar to the Movement Arc's feedforward, the Directional Arrow shows where to move to and how much of the movement is left as the stem shrinks with user progress.

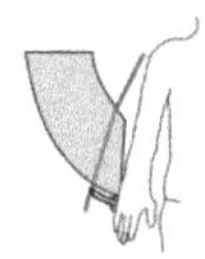

Nearest Arm. We draw a red stick figure of the nearest correct arm from the exercise to the user's when they are in the wrong position. This guide provides feedback on the user's movements by letting them know if they are in the incorrect place and where they should be. When they are properly aligned, this guide disappears.

Topdown Angle. Similar to the Nearest Arm, we show a red arc in the top-down view when the user's arm is moving along a vertical plane and is not on the same angle. This arc grows and becomes more visible if the user is further away so their arm may maintain the required angle from their forward direction. This provides corrective feedback on the extent of the movement.

By design, the Wedge and its separate parts encapsulate all our movement characteristics except for rate of movement. We envision the latter being conveyed by animating sections of the arc and arrow to imply required movement speed. The Wedge uses simple visual elements to avoid screen clutter, and so that its components do not interfere with each other.

Multiple Camera Views

Most vision-based systems, particularly those using the Kinect, consist only of a single perspective view facing the user (e.g. [3,12,13,19,25]). While these systems are sufficient for exercise movements where the movement is perpendicular to the camera, depth perception is a challenge. Difficulty with understanding depth, combined with mirroring by the camera, a limited field-of-view, and angle of tilt, means users can have difficulty identifying if they need to move closer or further away from the camera.

To address this problem, we explored the use of multiple camera views. Multiple camera views are sometimes used in dance instruction [8] to show footwork from an alternate angle. PTMotions [18] developed an iOS app for viewing common physiotherapy exercises from front and side views for better viewing angles of posture. We extend this concept in Physio@Home (Figure 4) using the Wedge visualization by also adding real-time feedback. By using multiple views, an exercise movement may be clearer and easier to understand. For instance, a front-facing view may be better for movements on the frontal plane, while a top-down view may better for interpreting forward and backward depth.

Chapters: Reducing Visual Clutter

In early iterations of Physio@Home, we noted that the Wedge, even with its simple visual elements, exhibited a high level of visual clutter. To simplify what was being displayed, we decided to split exercises into a sequence of 'chapters', where each 'chapter' represents a single one-dimensional movement step. This reduces the amount of visual clutter on the screen. For example, the shoulder abduction/adduction exercise becomes two chapters: for the abduction chapter, it shows a Wedge with a directional arrow pointing up; for the adduction chapter, it shows the Wedge with a directional arrow pointing downward.

IMPLEMENTATION

Tracking. We implemented our prototype system using Vicon motion tracking cameras, the Proximity Toolkit [14], WPF, and the Helix3D toolkit. To track joints, users wear markers mounted on shoulder, elbow, and wrist support braces. The tracking system provides x, y, z coordinates for each joint in millimeters within the testing space. These coordinates are then used in the 3D viewport to place 3D elements in corresponding positions to the real world.

To set the 3D viewport camera, we applied Vicon markers to the corresponding RGB camera. We used the Proximity Toolkit to retrieve position and orientation and set the 3D camera properties to these values. We then manually adjust the pitch, yaw, and roll of the 3D camera to align its image with the RGB camera. We overlay the 3D viewport atop the video feed and aligned the Helix 3D and RGB cameras to appear as though they originate from the same location.

Vicon vs. Kinect. Our initial prototypes used the Microsoft Kinect depth cameras [22] (see [27] for more), but we opted to use the Vicon tracking system for this iteration due to the Kinect's inadequate tracking. We found that the Kinect had problems accurately placing joints when these were obscured by the user's body. For instance, when the user holds their hand perpendicular to the Kinect—either fully stretched out or with their elbow tucked against their side—the Kinect cannot see their elbow and misplaces it as it tries to track their skeleton. This problem complicated the placement of visual guides and error calculations. Smoothing data with filters and using multiple Kinects were inadequate; they both considerably slowed down the software.

To assess the accuracy, we conducted a small experiment where we completed five repetitions of the Elbow exercise (see below), recording the reported length of both forearm and bicep at 0.1s intervals. The Kinect produced lengths of high variability (bicep standard deviation = 10.8mm, forearm standard deviation = 28.9mm), whereas the Vicon produced a far more stable result (bicep SD = 1.9mm, forearm SD = 0.7mm). Therefore, we chose the Vicon tracking system. We were interested in evaluating the extent to which the visualization would improve the accuracy in movement guidance. In addition, the Vicon tracker uses multiple cameras and could thereby track obscured joints more easily. We envision that over time, tracking will achieve Vicon-like accuracy with commodity-level costs.

Figure 4: Top (right) and front (left) camera views, as displayed on TV screen in front of user.

Wedge Visualization. The Wedge visualization is rendered using the Helix3D toolkit. It consists of four visual elements: two pie slice elements that form the entire Movement Arc, one for percentage of chapter completed, and one for the chapter remainder; a pipe for the stem of the Directional Arrow; and, a cone for the Direction Arrow's head.

The first and last frames of the exercise chapter are used to create the start and end points for the Wedge's movement arc. To show percentage of the completed chapter, the user's live arm position is matched by vector to the most similar arm posture from the chapter.

Multi-view. We implemented our multi-view setup using two commercial RGB cameras mounted in front of and above the user. The top perspective was selected as the second view due to the exercises requiring more movements related to the transverse plane. In principle, it is possible to show more camera views; however, we limited this to first understand how a second view would be used.

Recording and Playback. Our system records movements captured by both the RGB and Vicon cameras at a rate of 60fps. For each frame, the raw images and x, y, z positions of the shoulder, elbow, and hand markers are captured.

Scaling. We transform recorded exercises to account for variations in a recorded participant's arm length and location to compute error. We first compute the length of the participant's bicep and forearm using the absolute Euclidean distances between the x, y, z positions of their shoulder, elbow, and wrist. We then iterate through each pre-recorded frame to compute normalized 3D vectors of the bicep and forearm, and then using the participant's shoulder as an origin, we multiply the bicep vector by the participant's bicep length and add it to their shoulder position to get a new elbow position from the exercise, now scaled to the participant's bicep length. We do the same with the forearm vector to get a scaled wrist position, and repeat over all frames of the recorded exercise until the exercise has been transformed and scaled to the participant.

Error metric. We implemented a tool to compare a user and exercise recording and compute average errors between them to show how closely the user was able to follow the exercise. Our tool uses the previously described scaling algorithm to scale and transform the exercise to the user's size and position. It then iterates through each recorded user frame; for each user frame, it searches through the scaled exercise frames to find a frame with the least error between elbow and wrist—the shoulder is excluded because our scaling algorithm uses the shoulder as the origin. This error is computed by absolute Euclidean distance in millimeters. This allows us to focus on how closely they could follow the exercise. Errors are accumulated and averaged by the number of user frames.

Authoring. We developed an authoring tool (similar to [3]) to encode playback instructions for each recorded exercise. This tool allowed us to seek frame-by-frame through a recorded file to mark groups of frames as 'chapters' in order to distinguish separate, single-dimension movements as independent parts of each exercise. Further, our tool allowed us to indicate which joints are to be kept stationary during an exercise, which is similar to physiotherapists highlighting arms and legs on diagrams of exercises.

EVALUATION

Our design process produced a rich, but relatively complex, visualization: the Wedge. The Wedge communicates several aspects of movement, and can be augmented by a secondary overhead camera view. We were interested in three specific questions: Does the Wedge help people to perform the exercises with increased accuracy? If so, are both the Wedge and multiple views necessary, or is one sufficient? Does the Wedge and multiple views perform differently for different types of exercises?

We recruited 16 graduate students from a local university through email lists. Each study lasted an hour and participants were paid $20. We used a within-subjects design to evaluate both accuracy and subjective preference with four different combinations of the Wedge and the number of views (Interface condition): *single view with video playback* (VideoSingle), *single view with Wedge visualization* (WedgeSingle), *multiple views with video playback* (VideoMulti), and *multiple views with Wedge* (WedgeMulti). The conditions were presented in a Latin Square ordering to avoid bias.

Participants would complete the exercises while following an on-screen guide (either a video recording of the exercise being demonstrated or the Wedge visualization system). In the video conditions (i.e., the ones that did not use the Wedge visualization), participants would see a main video of themselves (like a mirror), with an inset video of the prerecorded exercise, allowing them to mimic the exercise. In the Wedge visualization conditions, the visualization (based on the pre-recorded video) is overlaid atop the live video.

Procedure

Participants were introduced to the system with a short demonstration and, after being fitted with markers, completed a trial run of each condition. Participants were allowed to spend as much time as they needed to test and understand the visualization. During this phase, each participant was taught how to interpret the Wedge. Participants were also instructed not to move, turn or sway during the experiment to ensure accurate data collection.

Each participant provided 48 recorded exercise trials: 4 interfaces × 4 exercises × 3 trials. In some cases we recorded additional trials when tracking errors occurred with the Vicon system. The study concluded with a questionnaire and semi-open interview on their subjective preferences and experiences using the different conditions.

Exercises

Participants completed four real physiotherapy exercises. These four exercises help rebuild shoulder mobility after injury (e.g., a dislocated shoulder). Our study was designed to examine our systems under distinct and progressively more complex exercises to understand any potential limitations.

We focused on exercises relating to the shoulder, because participants can easily make the movements while standing. The shoulder is also a ball-socket joint (unlike, say, the knee) meaning that a wide range of movements and variation from a prescribed motion is possible (i.e., there is more possibility of error and, therefore, need for guidance). In addition to being an extremely common subject of rehab, the shoulder allowed us to control individual differences in physical abilities between participants: a person only needs to be able to stand and move their arm comfortably. For these reasons we felt the representative set of exercises in shoulder rehab would allow us to go in-depth with a single but potentially useful application of our system design, rather than focusing on a general motion feedback system.

Straight. Abduction of arm along the frontal plane up to shoulder level, followed by adduction of arm back to the participant's side. This is a simple frontal plane exercise.

Angled. Abduction of the arm at 45° from the frontal plane, followed by adduction back to the side. This is an angled variation of the *Straight* exercise, where interpreting the angle may be difficult.

Elbow. External rotation of forearm away from the center of the participant's body until 90° from the sagittal plane, followed by an internal rotation back to center. This exercise requires the participant to keep their elbow tucked against their side and is a difficult exercise to understand without depth cues (i.e., with just a frontal view).

Combo. Abduction of the arm along the frontal plane up to shoulder level, internal rotation of the arm until pointing forward, followed by an external rotation of the arm back to the frontal plane, and adduction of the arm back to the participant's side. This is a more complex exercise than the previous three, involving many components.

Performance measurements

We collected three performance measures: two distance error metrics (one for the hand and one for the elbow), and a measurement of the maximum angle of rotation achieved. We ignore speed as a measure because we are mainly interested in how closely participants can follow an exercise. The two error metrics captures how closely a participant can follow a pre-recorded exercise delivered either by video or the Wedge system: one for the error from the hand and one from the elbow. For the Elbow exercise, we also recorded a separate metric—the maximum angle reached by participants during the external rotation. Because the Elbow exercise relies on a patient rotating outwards to their farthest extent, we were interested in evaluating how clearly our participants could interpret the required angle with the different interface conditions.

Data Analysis

Performance data were analyzed using 4×4 RM-ANOVA, with interface (VideoSingle, VideoMulti, WedgeSingle, WedgeMulti) and exercise (elbow, combo, angled, straight) as factors. Violations to sphericity used Greenhous-Geisser corrections to the degrees of freedom. Post-hoc tests used Bonneferoni corrections for multiple comparisons; only significant pairwise differences are reported. Post-hoc analysis was only performed to compare levels of the interface condition, as we were only interested in the performance of the different interfaces overall and within the different exercise conditions, and less interested in differences between different exercises. Subjective responses were analyzed using Friedman's test, and post hoc comparisons were done using the Wilcoxon signed-rank test. Before analysis, outlier trials were removed that were > 3 sd. away from the mean for any given exercise, this resulted in the removal of 24 of 1920 records (1.25%).

Results

We first present the performance results—including hand error, elbow error, and maximum rotation—we then present the analysis of subjective response data. We present our observations and the responses we received from participants during our semi-structured interviews in the discussion to help explain our results.

Performance Results

Hand Error: Across all exercises, the WedgeMulti had the lowest mean hand error improving error by ~1.7cms over the baseline VideoSingle (see Figure 5, left). While this difference is not large, it is reduced by the poor performance by all conditions for the elbow exercise, as larger difference can be seen in other exercises (e.g., WedgeMulti reduced error by 50% over VideoSingle in the angled exercise); see Figure 6. There was a significant main effect of both interface ($F_{3,45}$=20.15, p<.001) and exercise ($F_{1.77,26.54}$=7.012, p=.005) on hand error. Pairwise comparisons of interface showed that WedgeMulti had significantly lower hand error than WedgeSingle (p<.05), VideoMulti (p<.001), and VideoSingle (p<*.001*). Hand error was lower for WedgeSingle than VideoSingle (p<.05).

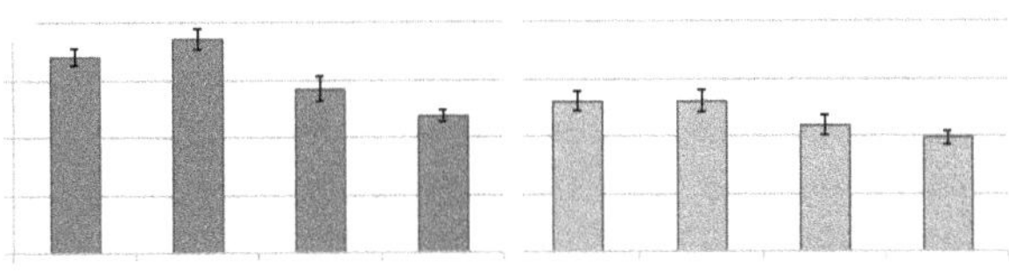

Figure 5: Performance by Condition (Left) Mean Hand Error ±SEM (Right) Mean Elbow Error ±SEM. Lower is better.

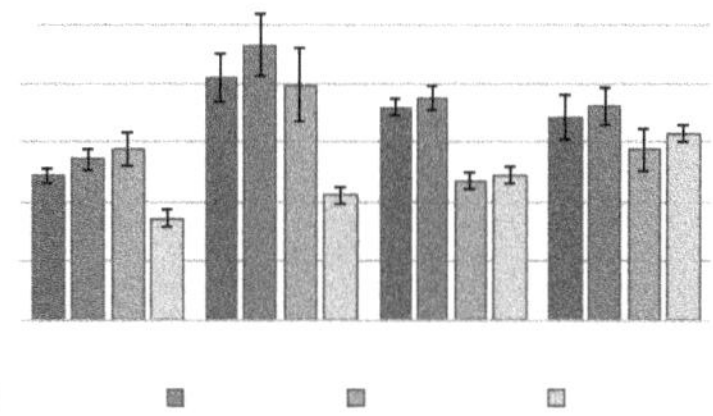

Figure 6: Mean hand error in mm (±SEM) for each interface grouped by exercise. Lower is better.

There was a significant interaction effect between interface and exercise ($F_{4.05,60.69}$=6.026, p<.001) for hand error. Within all exercises pairwise comparisons showed that WedgeMulti had consistently lower hand error than VideoMulti (p<.001), VideoSingle (p<.001), and WedgeSingle (p<*.05*, not combo*)*, with the exception of the elbow exercise, where no differences were observed. For combo, WedgeSingle had significantly lower hand error than both VideoMulti (p<.001) and VideoSingle (p<.001).

Elbow Error: Overall exercises, WedgeMulti had the lowest mean hand error improving error by ~1 cm over the baseline VideoSingle (see Figure 5, right). However, again this number was reduced by performance in the elbow exercise (see Figure 7). There was a significant main effect of interface ($F_{3,45}$=9.895, p<.001) on elbow error. However, there was no effect observed for exercise ($F_{1.5,23.01}$=2.073, p>.05) on elbow error. Pairwise comparisons again showed that WedgeMulti had significantly lower elbow error than VideoMulti (p<.005) and VideoSingle (p<.001), but no other pairwise differences were observed. See Figure 7.

There was an interaction effect objected between interface and exercise for elbow error ($F_{9,135}$=2.091, p<.05). Pairwise comparisons within the groups show that WedgeMulti had significantly lower elbow error than VideoMulti (p<.05, for combo and straight), VideoSingle (p<.05, for angled, combo and straight), WedgeSingle (p<.05, straight). The only other pairwise differences observed was for WedgeSingle, which had significantly lower elbow error than VideoMulti (p<.005) and VideoSingle (p<.05), but just during the combo exercise.

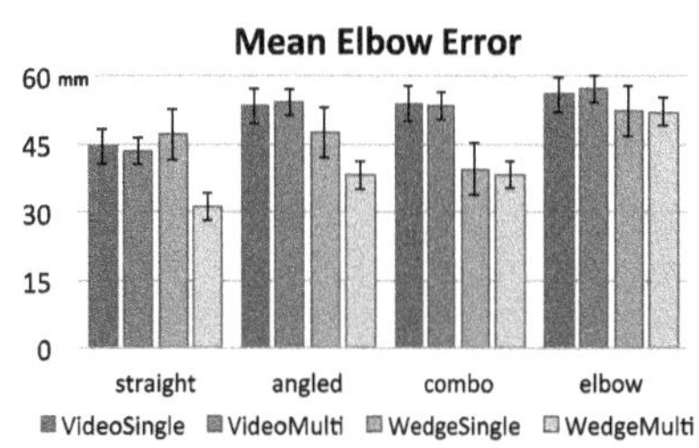

Figure 7: Mean elbow error in mm (±SEM) for each interface grouped by exercise. Lower is better.

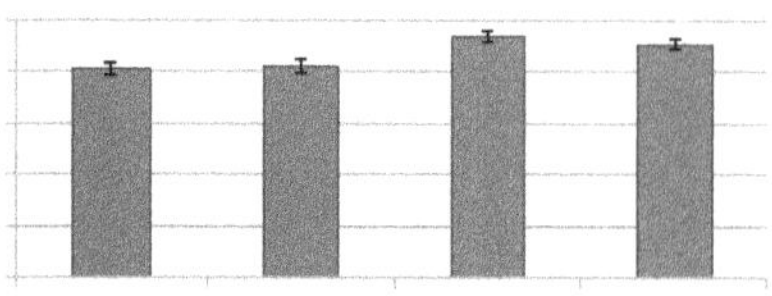

Figure 8: Mean max rotation angle ±SEM. Higher is better.

Rotation Angle: Figure 8 presents the mean maximum rotation angles obtained by participants. Analysis showed a significant effect of interface on max rotation angle during the elbow exercise ($F_{3,45}$=13.285, p<.001). Pairwise comparison showed that participants made significantly higher rotations with WedgeMulti than VideoSingle (p<.05), and that WedgeSingle had higher rotation than both VideoSingle (p<.005) and VideoMulti (p<.005).

Subjective Response Results

At the end of the experiment participants were asked to rank each condition on two criteria. First, participants ranked the interfaces on how accurate they felt the interface allowed them to be. Second, they also ranked the interfaces based on their subjective preference. The mean ranks can be seen in Figure 9, where 4 is ranked highest, and 1 is ranked lowest. We also asked participants their favorite visualization (video / Wedge) and view (single / multiple).

Subjective Accuracy: Analysis found a significant effect of interface on accuracy rankings ($\chi^2(3)$=22.754, p<.001). Pairwise comparisons showed participants felt they were more accurate with WedgeMulti than VideoMulti (z=-2.61, p<.01) and VideoSingle (z=-3.20, p<.001). Participants also felt they were more accurate with WedgeSingle than VideoSingle (z=-2.83, p<.005) and with VideoMulti than VideoSingle (z=-2.97, p<.005).

Subjective Preference: Participants were split on their most preferred methods. The rankings in Figure 9 show no clearly preferred method. There was no effect of interface observed on preference ranking ($\chi^2(3)$=5.0, p>.05).

Preferences for Visualization and Views: 14 participants responded to which group of interfaces they preferred, 9 chose the Wedge visualization interfaces (WedgeSingle and WedgeMulti) and 5 chose the simpler video-only interfaces (VideoSingle and VideoMulti). Eleven indicated they preferred using multiple views, while 5 selected a single view.

Limitations

Our recruited participants were local graduate students rather than on-going physiotherapy patients or seniors. We selected this participant pool due to the early state of our prototype and difficulties recruiting and working with these populations. This is notable limitation, as these participants were healthy and may not have the same appreciation for the stricter requirements for physiotherapy patients. However, 5 out of 16 participants had prior physiotherapy experience, and we discuss their experiences below.

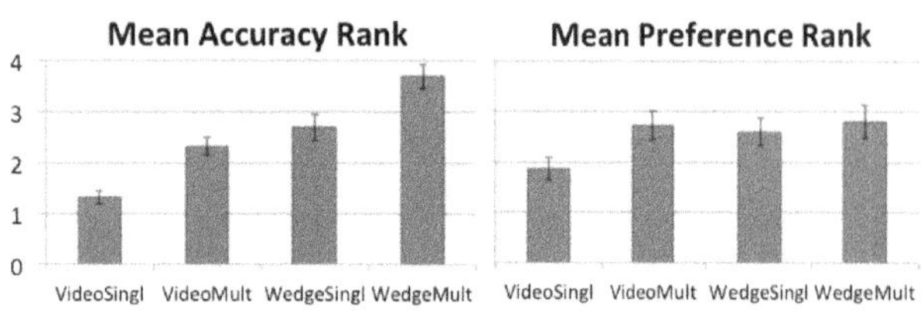

Figure 9: Subjective Rankings (Left) Mean Accuracy ±SEM (Right) Mean Preference ±SEM; 4 is best.

Our system was also limited due to the placement of our markers. While our current Vicon setup were able to reliably track our wearable marker patterns, they still required participants to keep the markers visible at all times to ensure tracking would not be lost.

DISCUSSION

Our results show that both the Wedge visualization and multiple views may be needed in combination to improve guidance. Our study highlight four main findings: the Wedge visualization with multiple views performed consistently as the most accurate technique; no technique performed better than any other for the elbow exercise based on our error metrics; both Wedge conditions improved the ability to perform the rotation movements found in the elbow exercise; and despite performing the best and participants feeling that they were most accurate with the Wedge, participants were split on which visualization they prefer.

We discuss these findings below with observations from the study and participant comments from the semi-structured interview to help explain the results.

Why was the Wedge with multi-view the most accurate?

The Wedge interface with multiple views (front-on and top-down) was the most accurate in terms of both hand and elbow errors (for 3 of 4 exercises). Participants effectively interpreted the information from the Wedge, and multiple views added benefit. The required angle for participants' abduction/adduction movements of the exercises were clearly conveyed by the top-down view available with the multi-view version, while the Wedge's Topdown Angle and Nearest Arm guides provided the necessary information to better allow participants to keep their arm aligned.

Visual guidance from the Wedge resulted in participants stopping as soon as any corrective guides appeared, realigning themselves, and then resuming the movement. These actions ensured they would stay on the correct path at all times. Without corrective guides (in video condition), participants had no direct indication of how far off their movements were, and would continue through the exercise.

Why didn't the Wedge perform better in the Elbow exercise?

The Wedge did not perform better than the other interface conditions for the Elbow exercise due to our current implementation. While the Wedge shows the required vertical angle for the other exercises via its Topdown Angle guide, it does not provide an analogue for the front view. This meant participants did not have sufficient feedback for maintaining their horizontal angle. As a result, the Wedge did not perform any better than video.

We also suspect that our mechanism for tracking the elbow (trackers affixed to participants' forearms closest the elbow) caused problems. During rotation, the markers would sometimes shift position, resulting in a potentially misleading change in the visualization of arm position. Because of this problem and the fact that this exercise is mainly focused on rotation of the forearm, we believe evaluating participant performance for the Elbow exercise is best done by the maximum angle of rotation.

Why did the Wedge help for rotation movements?
While Wedge errors for the Elbow exercise were not much lower than the Video, participants were able to rotate roughly 10 degrees farther during the exercise using either Wedge conditions. Using only the Video conditions, the participant can see that they must rotate outwards during the exercise, but not how far they must go. This often resulted in participants stopping early. Both Wedge conditions showed the fully required extent of the rotation; the Movement Arc in the top-down view showed how much rotation is still required, and the Directional Arrow in both views showed when movement in a direction was needed.

Why did people not prefer the Wedge?
While the Wedge conditions were rated the most accurate, preferential rankings were split due to their difficulty and complexity. Even though some participants were able to follow movements more accurately by performing short 'micro-corrections' whenever a guide appeared, these corrections required noticeable attention on their part. The guides appear whenever there is the slightest misalignment and do not disappear until it is corrected, leading to comments that the Wedge was "too strict." Still, some participants felt this could be a potential benefit for a physiotherapy patient, as it would force them to follow exercise movements carefully and pay close attention to the feedback.

A related complaint about the Wedge was that its Nearest Arm guide felt misleading. While this guide helped participants see when their movement was incorrect, it did not tell them how to correct themselves. This resulted in several participants trying to align themselves with the Nearest Arm, but finding it difficult to get their arms in the correct position. The five participants preferring Video felt that it was more straightforward. Participants reported being more comfortable following video because it allowed a more fluid movement—more fun than the stricter Wedge.

How did physiotherapy patients feel about the Wedge?
Five participants had prior physiotherapy experience. Their feedback was consistent: all rankings indicated that Wedge with multiple views as the most accurate; furthermore, three preferred WedgeMulti, one preferred video, and one liked every technique. Two of these participants also indicated that all techniques could have a role in an effective physiotherapy: video provides an easy-to-understand demonstration of the movement that would introduce a patient to a new exercise and help them adjust to a learning curve, while the Wedge would be helpful later in follow-up sessions to understand the finer-grained movement characteristics. This feedback is important as exercises are sometimes painful to perform correctly—the feedback provides reassurance that things are moving forward (P14). Finally, these participants were notably more forgiving of momentary tracking and visualization errors by the Wedge, because it helped overall with accuracy.

Challenges for Design
Our findings build on prior work by demonstrating that on-screen visualizations *can* work for high-precision movements, e.g. in physiotherapy. Our process has helped us to uncover several design implications and challenges for systems that guide or correct movement and exercises through visual feedback overlaid on live video (e.g. [3]).

Reducing Visual Complexity. Even with the simple movements that we were exploring in our work, participants were sometimes overwhelmed with the complexity and amount of information presented. Given the guidance characteristics outlined in Table 1, this should probably not be too surprising—it is possible to perform exercises incorrectly in many different ways. Enabling all aspects of the Wedge visualization at once means that there may be simply too many things to attend to at once.

Balancing visual complexity with sufficient guidance is the central challenge to our approach. In our work, we explored one way to do this, by separating different parts of an exercise into segments, and presenting only the parts of the visualization that were relevant given where the participant was in the exercise. Yet a scaffolding approach might be appropriate too: for instance, providing only the wedge part of the visual guide until a person has mastered the basic motion—once this is accomplished, then showing visualizations that illustrate the extents, and so forth. This would only show visualizations piecemeal so as to not overwhelm the user. Another approach might be to show only corrective feedback visualizations (e.g. Nearest Arm) once a person had already mastered the exercise.

Semantics of Visual Illustration. Although we articulate the aspects of movement guidance that need some sort of visualization feedback (Table 1), we did not thoroughly explore the space of visual illustration. While our visual guides are somewhat rudimentary, they were designed strictly to address each aspect of the movement guidance framework that we outlined. Nevertheless, a lot of work has explored how illustrative techniques from comics can be used to suggest, convey, and communicate movement (e.g. [15]). Exploring this rich vocabulary may lead to more concise and intuitive visualizations.

Depth Perception and Capture. We also saw that participants had a hard time interpreting depth easily from video (and to a lesser extent, our visualization). This is perhaps a consequence of the 2D camera capture and the 2D representation/rendering on the screen of the video. In practice, we use head motion to gain a better understanding of depth when, for example, looking in a mirror. It may be possible that combining head tracking with depth video capture will allow people to better understand what is going on in regard to the playback video and/or the visualization.

Camera Placement. A single video feedback window is insufficient to accurately perceive movement—both one's own movement, and that of the on-screen guide. The exception to this is when the movement happens strictly on the plane perpendicular to the camera. In the general case, multiple cameras—particularly when one is perpendicular to movement—are useful to improve the accuracy of movement. From a hardware standpoint, this is not far-fetched: most modern phones come equipped with powerful cameras that could be used. One trade-off is that multiple cameras add to the visual clutter and complexity of the scene.

CONCLUSIONS

Physiotherapy patients exercising at home do not have the benefit of guidance and feedback, and there is a strong possibility of re-injury with incorrect exercise movements. Physio@Home explores the use of a dynamic on-screen movement guide called the Wedge and multiple camera views to guide movements, with attention to supporting depth perception and precision. We found that participants performed exercises with the least error using the Wedge and multi-camera views. From this, we identified several characteristics required for accurate movement guidance, and challenges for exercise guidance systems. Physiotherapy services will continue to be in high demand as the population ages. With increasingly capable and inexpensive motion tracking cameras on their way, the concepts from Physio@Home will be able to help meet the needs of physiotherapy patients in the future.

ACKNOWLEDGEMENTS

We thank Homebody Health and our participants, and NSERC and GRAND for generously funding this work.

REFERENCES

1. Alankus, G., et al. (2010) Towards Customizable Games for Stroke Rehabilitation. *CHI*, 2113-2122.
2. Ananthanarayan, S., et al. (2013) Pt Viz: towards a wearable device for visualizing knee rehabilitation exercises. *CHI*, 1247-50.
3. Anderson, F., et al. (2013) YouMove: enhancing movement training with an augmented reality mirror. *UIST*, 311-320.
4. Ayoade, M. & Baillie, L. (2014) A novel knee rehabilitation system for the home. *CHI*, 2521-2530.
5. Bau, O., Mackay, W.(2008)OctoPocus: a dynamic guide for learning gesture-based command sets. *UIST*, 37-46.
6. Campresi, C., et al. (2014). Motion Parameterization and Adaptation Strategies for Virtual Therapists. *IVA*. 99-108.
7. Canadian Physiotherapy Association. http://www.physiotherapy.ca/About-Physiotherapy
8. Diddlyi. Online Irish Dance Workshops. http://www.diddlyi.com
9. Doyle, J., et al. (2010). BASE - An interactive technology solution to deliver balance and strength exercises to older adults. *PervasiveHealth*, 1-5.
10. Freeman, D., et al. (2009) ShadowGuides: visualizations for in-situ learning of multi-touch and whole-hand gestures. *ITS*, 165-172.
11. Henderson, S.J., & Feiner, S.K. (2011). Augmented reality in the psychomotor phase of a procedural task. *ISMAR*, 191-200.
12. Huang, J-D. (2011) Kinerehab: a kinect-based system for physical rehabilitation: a pilot study for young adults with motor disabilities. *ASSETS*, 319-320.
13. Lee, J-D., Hseih, C-H., & Lin, T-Y. (2014) A Kinect-based Tai Chi exercises evaluation system for physical rehabilitation. *ICCE*, 177-178.
14. Marquardt, N., et al. (2011) The Proximity Toolkit: Prototyping Proxemic Interactions. *UIST*, 315-326.
15. McCloud, S. (1993) Understanding Comics.
16. Nicolau, H., et al. (2013). Computer-assisted rehabilitation: towards effective evaluation. IJCPS, 11-26.
17. Nixon, M.E., et al. (2013) Quantitative evaluation of the Microsoft KinectTM for use in an upper extremity virtual rehabilitation environment. *ICVR*, 222-228.
18. PTMotions. Program Viwer. http://ptmotions.com/ptm_pv.html
19. Rector, K., et al. (2013) Eyes-free yoga: an exergame using depth cameras for blind & low vision exercise. *ASSETS*. 8 pages.
20. Services Canada. (2013) Physiotherapists. http://www.servicecanada.gc.ca/eng/qc/job_futures/statistics/3142.shtml
21. Sodhi, R., et al. (2012) LightGuide: projected visualizations for hand movement guidance. *CHI*, 179-188.
22. Tang, R., et al. (2014) Physio@Home: Design explorations to support movement guidance. *CHI EA*, 1654-1656
23. Tao, G., et al. (2013) Evaluation of Kinect skeletal tracking in a virtual reality rehabilitation system for upper limb hemiparesis. *ICVR*, 164-165.
24. Uzor, S. & Baillie, L. (2014). Investigating the long-term use of exergames in the home with elderly fallers. *CHI*, 2813-2822.
25. Velloso, E., et al. (2013) MotionMA: motion modelling and analysis by demonstration. *CHI*, 1309-1318.
26. Vines, A. (2013) Rehabilitation after shoulder dislocation: information for patients. Prepared for UK National Health Services, Oxford Radcliffe Hospitals
27. White, S., et al. (2007) Visual Hints for Tangible Gestures in Augmented Reality. *ISMAR*, 1-4.
28. Yang U. & Kim, G-J. Implementation and evaluation of "just follow me": an immersive, VR-based, motion-training system. Presence, vol. 11, issue 3, 304-323
29. Yeh, S-C., et al. (2012) A lower limb fracture postoperative-guided interactive rehabilitation training system and its effectiveness analysis. Healthcom, 149-54

Lessons Learnt from Deploying an End-User Development Platform for Physical Rehabilitation

Daniel Tetteroo[1], Paul Vreugdenhil[1], Ivor Grisel[1], Marc Michielsen[2], Els Kuppens[3], Diana Vanmulken[4], Panos Markopoulos[1]

[1]Eindhoven University of Technology
Eindhoven, The Netherlands
{d.tetteroo, p.e.vreugdenhil, i.g.j.grisel, p.markopoulos}@tue.nl

[2]Revalidatiecampus St. Ursula
Herk-de-Stad, Belgium
marc.michielsen@jessazh.be

[3]MS-Reva Overpelt
Overpelt, Belgium
els.kuppens@msreva.be

[4]Adelante Centre of Expertise in Rehabilitation
Hoensbroek, The Netherlands
d.vanmulken@adelante-zorggroep.nl

ABSTRACT
Clinical researchers in rehabilitation technology have often called for exercise customization to address patient specific needs. Where such customization transcends simple parameter setting, the need for End-User Development (EUD) arises. EUD in this field can potentially tap on the expertise of highly skilled workers, but presents serious challenges regarding acceptance by end users and the feasibility of embedding EUD in their professional practice. This paper describes the deployment and adoption process of TagTrainer, a physical rehabilitation technology that supports EUD. TagTrainer was deployed in four rehabilitation clinics and was used by 24 rehabilitation therapists. We analyze how they engaged in EUD activities and we discuss decisions that we took in the design and deployment of TagTrainer. Based on these case studies, we present guidelines for the deployment of EUD systems.

Author Keywords
End-user development; physical rehabilitation; field study; socio-technical environment; meta-design

ACM Classification Keywords
H.5.m. Information interfaces and presentation (e.g., HCI): Miscellaneous; J.3 Life and medical sciences: Health

INTRODUCTION
End-user development (EUD) is a socio-technical paradigm focused on enabling end-users of interactive systems to engage in the modification, extension, and even creation of interactive artifacts [20]. The aspiration for this field is that EUD shall bridge the divide between design-time and use-time by extending the evolution of interactive systems beyond the initial software development, allowing continuous adaptation of these systems to evolving and context specific end-user needs [21]. Although the evolution of end-users' needs is a phenomenon occurring in almost any domain, certain domains have been identified as especially suitable for the application of EUD practices [10]. One of these domains is healthcare, were the greatly varying needs of individual patients present a design problem of a scale unmanageable with a traditional technology design process. The specific domain that we address in this paper is that of physical rehabilitation after stroke, multiple sclerosis (MS), and spinal-cord injury (SCI).

CHI 2015, April 18 - 23 2015, Seoul, Republic of Korea

ACM 978-1-4503-3145-6/15/04...$15.00
http://dx.doi.org/10.1145/2702123.2702504

Persons who have been diagnosed with stroke, MS or SCI often suffer from cognitive and/or motoric function loss. In order to regain some of the lost functionality, they usually engage in a physical rehabilitation program as soon as possible. Previous research points at the importance of patient customized exercises and sufficient exercise variability in physical rehabilitation [7,32]. Patients might have their own, personal goals for rehabilitation (e.g., relearning to eat with knife and fork, relearning to play the guitar, etc.) and will vary in the extent to which their cognitive and motoric functions are affected.

Customization can be supported at multiple levels. To start with, therapists typically do not rely on a singular device or exercise approach for a patient, but combine one or more of these to address the patient's condition and training needs. Increasingly over the last decade, a task-oriented training approach is adopted in which patients train on specific daily skills of their choice, that can provide them benefits in terms of their ability to function independently and to integrate socially [31]. For technologies that are integrated in such a training program, the level of challenge should ideally be adapted to the patients' needs [1], or even adjusted automatically as patients progress through a game [18]. Such parameter adaptations pertaining to range of movements, or the speed and accuracy required, do not fully address the pragmatic concerns of patients relating to the very content and nature of exercises. Being able to change the content, purpose, and difficulty of exercises to match patient interests requires a higher level of customizability that can better be thought of as EUD.

Designing EUD solutions for professional use represents several challenges. An important one for the given domain is to enable novice programming [30]: in the domain of rehabilitation, the vast majority of professionals do not have any affinity with programming. To overcome this challenge, the usability of systems has to be ensured, so that programming presents a low threshold and allows them to easily map concepts from the domain of their professional expertise to that of the programmable environment. Beyond making programming easier, there are further challenges regarding the feasibility of adopting EUD as part of their professional practice, pertaining to motivation, peer and organizational support, culture, and the effect on the productivity of health professionals. While earlier research has identified the importance of such a broader perspective (e.g., [11]), there is as yet little empirical research to document the issues at play, to show the feasibility of EUD as a professional practice in a clinical setting, and to guide future design efforts.

Therefore, we present a multi-site deployment study of TagTrainer: an EUD system to support upper extremities training for patients suffering from stroke, SCI or MS. TagTrainer (see [29]) supports arm-hand rehabilitation through the manipulation of physical objects. It allows therapists to author exercise content, and tailor exercises to the needs of their individual patients. The overarching aim of the four deployment studies presented in this paper was to identify the factors that influence therapists' decisions to engage in EUD practices.

In the next sections we first summarize related work on introducing EUD in different professional contexts. We then present TagTrainer, and detail its deployment in four clinical settings. Finally, we discuss the overall lessons learnt and provide pointers for future EUD deployments.

RELATED WORK

Many researchers have studied how end-users can be enabled to engage in EUD (e.g., [4,19]), and have studied EUD practices as they occur (e.g., [15], [27]). Blackwell introduced the Attention Investment model [3], that describes from a cognitive psychology perspective the suitability of EUD practices. He claims that the decision to engage in EUD depends on the result of a cost-benefit analysis involving costs for doing a task manually, EUD investment costs, EUD payoff and risks associated to the EUD process. While this model is unspecific regarding how to quantify attention investment and so far little empirical evidence has been presented to support it, it presents a useful starting point for the design and evaluation of EUD systems.

Further, others such as Mehandjiev (e.g., [22]) have developed substantial knowledge on the organizational aspects of EUD. Meta-design [11] looks at EUD from a socio-technical perspective, putting the end-user developer on a spectrum with on one end the end-user, and on the other end the meta-designer of an extensible socio-technical system. Rather than treating the end-user developer as a particular species of its own, in meta-design theory users may assume and switch between multiple roles on this spectrum, depending on the context. In this theory, end-user development may become a shared effort amongst users that occupy different positions on the developer-spectrum.

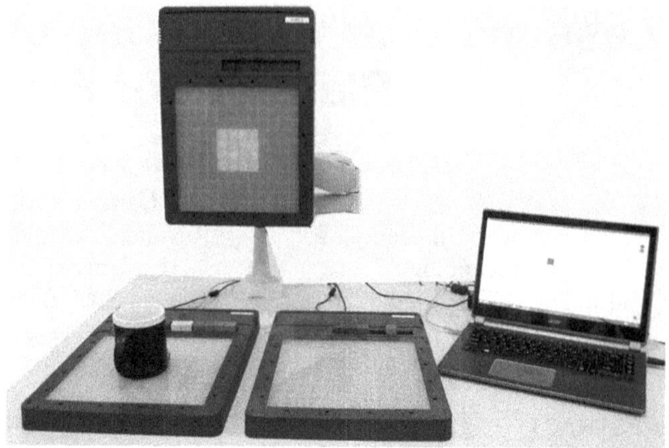

Figure 1: A TagTrainer system with three TagTile boards connected to a laptop running the TTPI software.

Although the before mentioned research provides us with valuable insights on factors that influence the EUD process, they mostly study EUD in a lab setting, or in situations in which EUD is already practiced, and therefore do not help understand what is required for EUD technology to be adopted in the first place. There are just a few studies that report on the deployment of EUD environments and study their adoption. For example, [6] studied the adoption of a system that allows caretakers to create prompting scripts to enhance the independence of cognitively disabled persons. Amongst others, they confirm the importance of a holistic view on EUD – thus considering technology as well as context. Another study reports on the deployment of a platform that allows business users to create custom widgets [27]. The authors conclude that, for the case of small and medium enterprises, a properly led deployment can lead to a self-sustainable EUD environment were users take on different roles, from 'widget consumers' and 'widget creators', to 'service creators' that are similar to what Fischer et al. call 'meta-designers' [11].

TAGTRAINER

TagTrainer is a tangible, extensible, interactive training platform for arm-hand rehabilitation therapy [29], consisting of: 1) **TagTile boards**: interactive boards (24cm x 24cm) that can give visual and audio feedback, and are able to detect RFID-tagged objects (see Figure 1). The boards provide feedback through full-color LEDs, as well as the possibility to playback audio. 2) The **TagTrainer Patient Interface** (TTPI), which manages personalized *exercise programs* (i.e. series of exercises) and provides feedback to patients about their progress. 3) The **TagTrainer Exercise Creator** (TEC): a visual programming tool that supports authoring and modification of exercises to be executed on the board (see Figure 2). 4)

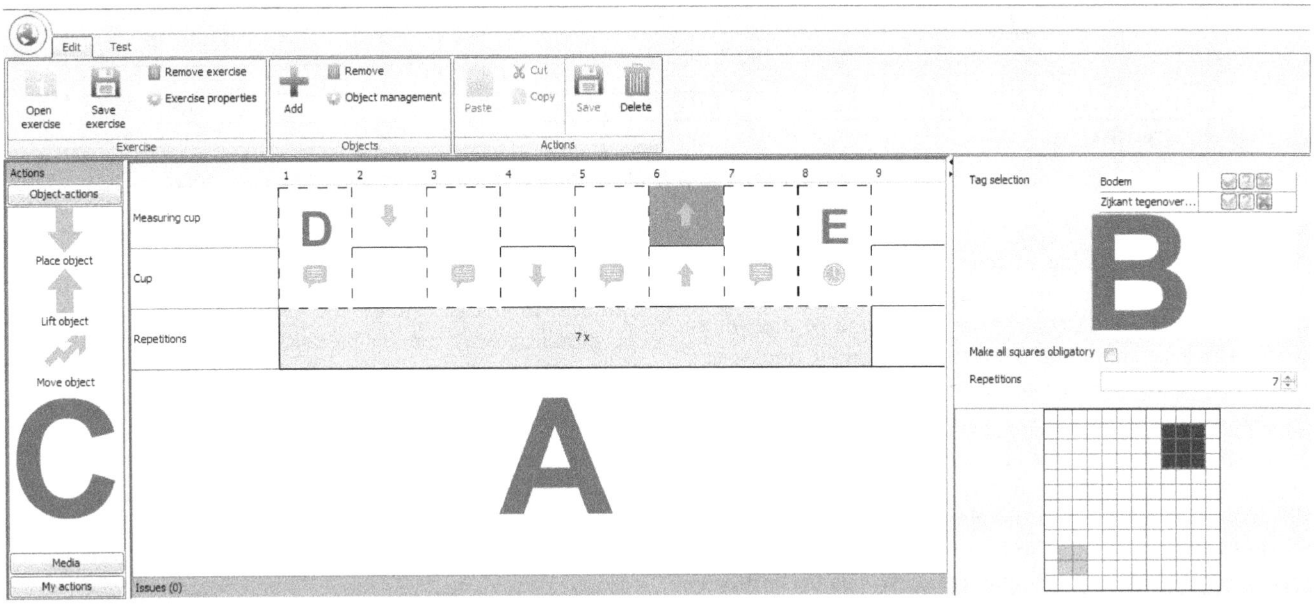

Figure 2: The TagTrainer Exercise Creator (TEC) software. The center area (A) shows the workspace with the exercise, featuring a timeline with actions associated with the objects ('measuring cup' and 'cup') involved in the exercise. Properties of the selected action (in this case 'lift object') such as position on the board are displayed to the right (B). Finally, additional actions can be dragged from the library (C) into the workspace to extend an exercise. Note that beyond actions involving manipulations on the board, other actions such as giving instructions (D) and pausing (E) can be used.

An extensible and customizable collection of **objects** with RFID-tags attached to them.

TagTrainer was developed in response to a request for patient-tailorable rehabilitation technology by rehabilitation clinics. Although TagTrainer is by default provided with a base set of about 150 exercises, the TEC allows therapists to create custom exercises that match the skill level and rehabilitation goals of individual patients.

Exercises for arm-hand training involve physical objects; the therapist creates a simple model of an exercise using TEC, as a sequence of object movements on target areas on the board and repetitions thereof. The board recognizes movements such as placing, moving, removing or rotating objects on the board. In principle, any number of objects can be used within an exercise and an unlimited amount of actions can be added to each of the objects. In addition to the object-related actions, instructions, pauses and sound can be added to an exercise (see Figure 2–D, E).

TagTrainer is designed to present a low-threshold for new users while still accommodating for the creation of relevant and engaging training content. Following a usability evaluation of an early version of the system [17], complex control structures are not supported and only sequential, stepwise execution of actions is possible using a timeline based scripting - similar to what can be found in animation software. For example, actions scheduled to occur in step 2 of an exercise can only happen after the first step has been completed. Repetitions of (parts of) an exercise can be programmed to increase training intensity. Users are further aided by an automated validation tool that notifies them about errors or inconsistencies in their creations. Errors by patients in the execution of an exercise (e.g. using an incorrect object) are handled automatically through default routines (such as repeating the instructions for the current step) and need not be addressed by the creator of an exercise.

	Location	Length	Participants	Pathology	Notes
Case 1	Hoensbroek, Netherlands	3 w		SCI, stroke	Research team had participated in the design and development of TagTrainer [29].
Case 2	Herk-de-Stad, Belgium	8 w	Aged 25-32	Stroke	Aim: to assess EUD practices in a different health system and organizational context. We focused on the rehabilitation of stroke patients.
Case 3	Overpelt, Belgium	5 w	Aged 24-54	MS, stroke	Aim: to study a different patient population and organizational context.
Case 4	Hoensbroek, Netherlands	8 w	Aged 26-44	SCI, stroke	Follow up to case 1. Aim: to assess the spontaneous and unguided use of the system, post initial deployment.

Table 1: Characteristics of the four case studies (/ = physiotherapist, / = occupational therapist).

Case 1	S+T	S+T	S+T+CE					
Case 2	S+T			S+T				S+T+CE
Case 3	S+T		S+T		S+T			
Case 4	S+T			S+T				S+T+CE
Week (relative)	**1**	**2**	**3**	**4**	**5**	**6**	**7**	**8**

Figure 3: Administration of self-efficacy (S), UTAUT (T) and credibility/expectancy (CE) questionnaires.

METHODS

A field study consisting of four cases was carried out to evaluate whether and how therapists can act as end-user developers of training content, in the context of their daily work. The case studies lasted for three to eight weeks, and took place in The Netherlands and Belgium, see Table 1.

An important motivation for the fourth study was that the simultaneous introduction of a new technological artefact and EUD practices in the first three cases made it hard to distinguish to what extent the observed practices related to the introduction of EUD, versus the use of a new training technology. Therefore, a follow-up study was performed at the clinic of the first case study, to see whether prolonged use of TagTrainer would cause a change in EUD practices.

Participating professionals

Therapists working in the clinics could participate on a voluntary basis after agreement with their management. In total 24 health professionals participated, see Table 1. Participating therapists had no previous experience with TagTrainer, except for two participants in Case 4, who had also participated in Case 1. The participants' computer experience was limited to using general office software, email, internet and online social networks.

Materials

In the first three cases, which studied initial deployment, two systems per clinic were deployed consisting of one TagTile board connected to a laptop and an initial set of about 150 exercises that were ready to be used. For case 1 this was in two different treatment rooms, while in the 2nd and 3rd case the boards were available in a space in between treatment rooms. The exercise set was iteratively improved between deployments. Importantly, beyond the initial set of exercises, the therapists in the latter three cases were also provided with the (unaltered) exercises created by therapists in earlier studies. For the 4th case, upon request of the therapists, three boards were combined into a single system, providing the therapists with greater flexibility in the design of therapy exercises. This system was placed on a table with wheels such that it could be moved between the two treatment rooms in which the participating therapists worked.

Procedures

The procedures for the four studies varied slightly, gradually reducing the involvement of the non-clinical researchers.

In the first three case studies, therapists received at the start of the study a two-hour long introduction to the TagTrainer system that included simple hands-on practice. One week after the start of these studies, therapists received additional training for the creation and modification of therapy exercises. Therapists were free to decide whether and when they would use TagTrainer during their therapy sessions.

In the first case study the designer and developer of TagTrainer was on site, holding a scheduled weekly information session, observing the use of TagTrainer and conducting fixes and iterative design of the system as this was necessitated in practice. In the 2nd and 3rd case study a researcher was present one to three times weekly for trouble shooting, observations, and situated interviews. In the fourth case, a researcher was only present for initial training, data collection, and remote technological assistance.

Measures

In their stepwise guidance to facilitate successful implementation of technology in therapy, [17] argue that after the initial phases, during which awareness and insight about the new technology are spread amongst therapists, a phase of acceptance follows. During this phase, therapists' attitude, motivation, and willingness to change are crucial factors in the success of the implementation process. Since we were interested in factors that influence therapists' decisions to engage in EUD practices, the focus of the research efforts has been on measuring factors that predict technology acceptance and on collecting in-depth information about the practices, events, and opinions that underlie the therapists' decisions.

Logging – We logged the use of TagTrainer (storing time of use, exercises used and the therapist using TagTrainer) and the creation and modification of exercises, including the time of creation/modification, the content created and the author.

Self-efficacy – The degree to which therapists felt able to create exercises with the program was measured using a questionnaire based on [2], which measures self-efficacy on thirteen scales, ranging from 0 to 100. We took measurements at three different moments, see Figure 3.

Technology acceptance – Technology acceptance refers to the intent of individuals to use a particular technology, and to a number of determinant factors. These were measured using UTAUT questionnaire [33] was administered three times during the studies, see Figure 3.

Credibility/expectancy – A credibility/expectancy questionnaire [9] was administered at the end of each study that measures the degree to which therapists believe that TagTrainer is credible as a therapy aid and that they expect it will help patients recover.

Observations – A researcher was present for at least one day a week at every clinic to observe TagTrainer use by participating therapists. Field notes and photographic records were kept as a reference.

Semi-structured interviews were conducted with individual therapists, as well as in groups. These interviews discussed therapists' general experience of using TagTrainer, as well as their experiences with modifying and creating exercises. Depending on their availability and level of involvement in the study, up to four interviews per therapist were conducted.

RESULTS

Quantitative results

Table 2 shows the most important statistics on TagTrainer usage and exercise creation / modification. Table 3 shows the results from the questionnaires. The UTAUT scores for effort expectancy, facilitating conditions and behavioral intent were slightly above average for all cases. Social influence and performance expectancy were slightly negative in all cases. Overall, little change can be observed over the course of each case. Only during the second case, behavioral intent dropped significantly as was shown by a Wilkoxon signed-rank test ($Z=-2.041$, $p<0.05$). Interviews revealed that therapists in this case were unaware that the TagTrainer systems would remain at their clinic post-study, hence they gave low scores for behavioral intent.

Credibility scores were between neutral and positive, while expectancy scores ranged from neutral to slightly negative. Overall, self-efficacy increased significantly in all cases apart from the last, where it decreased somewhat from moderately high to neutral. However, when excluding one participant not actively involved for the last part of the study, the results show a slight increase in self-efficacy ($M=69.2$, $SD=9.3$). The low score at the start of case 3 is caused by the therapists' interpretation of the questionnaire; since they had not yet worked with TagTrainer, they gave a score of 0 for all self-efficacy questions at the start of the study.

Motivation towards EUD

The first case resulted in a lot more exercise creation than the latter three studies. One possible explanation could be a possible 'demand effect' (see [23]) because therapists were instructed on how to modify and create therapy exercises with TagTrainer, regardless of their actual need to do so. To probe whether EUD practices could develop spontaneously, participants in the fourth case were instructed on how to create exercises only upon their specific request.

Case study #	1	2	3	4	Total
Participants	4	5	9	6	24
Exercises carried out	n/a*	203	171	92	466*
Training sessions	34	50	34	28	146
Patients treated	13	19	5	8	45
New exercises	20	3	11	1	35
Modified exercises	3	1	0	1	5

Table 2: Usage and EUD statistics. *Software used in case 1 did not allow for logging use of individual exercises.

Although therapists created and modified exercises, they mentioned that this took a considerable share of the already limited time they had for patient treatment (cases 1 and 2). Despite the benefits they expected for training patients, they would not be willing to divert time from patients to programming in the future. As they do not spend much time behind a computer, for therapists the threshold for engaging in EUD was higher compared to office workers with whom EUD is typically studied.

Furthermore, therapists remarked that many of the exercise modifications they required could be achieved in less time by using different objects, or by modifying the physical context in which the systems were located (cases 2 and 4).

In case 3, where therapy sessions often involved one therapist attending to multiple patients simultaneously, therapists indicated that TagTrainer allowed patients to work independently, which gave therapists the opportunity to look after other patients. They also indicated to be content with the option to create patient-tailored exercises. One therapist remarked: *"The return-on-investment is clear to me. By creating patient-tailored exercises, I can have patients work independently. For example, I might spend five minutes on the creation of an exercise. If a patient uses the exercise twice for five minutes, I save five minutes."*

In case 3, therapists were spontaneously and actively exploring the limits of what they could use TagTrainer for. For example, one therapist created an exercise in which TagTrainer was placed on the floor and used to train a patient's legs rather than his hands. In another case, a therapist created an exercise in which two patients would train together; the exercise was designed so that it would only progress if both patients would perform a given movement. Although not planned by design, the technology supported these uses. However, therapists in the fourth case doubted the usefulness of TagTrainer for lower-limb training.

Mostly therapists were content with the existing set of generic exercises and saw no need for additional ones (except for personalized exercises). In case 4 however,

Case study #		1	2	3	4
Effort exp.	start	5.20 (1.39)	4.70 (0.76)	4.60 (1.18)	5.00 (0.57)
	end	5.30 (1.08)	4.60 (1.14)	5.00 (0.71)	4.00 (1.04)
Facilit. cond.	start	4.60 (1.27)	5.10 (1.08)	4.50 (1.22)	5.00 (1.14)
	end	4.80 (1.47)	4.80 (1.20)	4.90 (0.48)	5.00 (1.49)
Behav. intent	start	4.80 (1.29)	6.00 (1.00)	4.50 (0.93)	6.00 (1.09)
	end	5.50 (1.23)	2.00 (1.00)	3.80 (2.22)	5.00 (1.91)
Social infl.	start	3.90 (0.78)	2.50 (1.27)	4.40 (1.20)	3.00 (1.15)
	end	4.00 (1.34)	2.20 (1.30)	3.90 (0.25)	3.00 (1.58)
Perform. exp.	start	3.60 (1.03)	2.60 (1.47)	3.30 (0.92)	4.00 (1.04)
	end	3.80 (0.98)	1.70 (0.76)	3.30 (0.87)	3.00 (1.19)
Credibility		14.8 (5.70)	19.5 (3.11)	n/a	18.0 (3.60)
Expectancy		10.1 (3.00)	13.9 (5.22)	n/a	11.0 (5.60)
Self-efficacy	start	52.3 (37.60)	23.2 (14.20)	0.0 (0.00)	61.7 (11.00)
	end	75.4 (19.10)	64.1 (13.50)	61.7 (3.94)	54.6 (32.10)
t-test SE start/end		t=-2.356 p=0.05	t=-3.434 p<0.05	t=-68.783 p<0.001	t=0.439 p=0.704

Table 3: Means (standard-deviations) for UTAUT, credibility, expectancy and self-efficacy.

some therapists expressed a wish for more generic exercises, especially ones that would use all three TagTile boards.

In case 4, the two therapists with previous TagTrainer experience were regarded as experts in exercise creation, both by themselves and by their colleagues. These therapists were willing to support colleagues and even create exercises for them, provided that they would receive managerial support, and time would be reserved for these activities. One of the 'expert therapists' had even trained an intern in exercise creation with TagTrainer, without this intern having received any training by the researchers. The decision to train an intern was fueled both by the therapist's drive to spread knowledge about TagTrainer, as well as the intern's curiosity. Therapists also sketched another scenario for exercise creation: the appointment of a dedicated 'technology manager'. This person, not necessarily a therapist, but someone within the clinic and knowledgeable about rehabilitation therapy would be assigned the task of creating and modifying exercises.

Usability

The successful use of the TEC by therapists who had never received formal training by the researchers confirms the usability of the tool. However, some of the exercises that therapists created had poor usability. E.g., in one exercise the visual confirmation provided upon the correct placement of an object was covered by the object itself. Further therapists lacked programming skills and had no expertise in interaction design; as a consequence they were unable to provide the level of usability that is required by their patients. Moreover, the resulting training content has to bear two levels of correctness: software quality (i.e. being 'bug-free' and being usable as argued by [14,25]) and clinical effectiveness (i.e. helping rather than hampering a patient's recovery process).

Sharing EUD creations

Therapists expressed varying opinions about sharing custom-created exercises. They reported that in principle they had no objections to sharing their creations with colleagues within or outside their own clinic, as long as other therapists would share as well. One participant (case 4) especially liked the idea of other therapists being able to review the exercises that she created, such that she would learn to create better exercises. However, they doubted the further usefulness of sharing, since they expected that working out the details of a colleague's exercise would cost them more time than creating an appropriate exercise from scratch. Additionally, participants expected that a lack of knowledge about the local patient population would make it harder for external colleagues to interpret the meaning and value of a given exercise. Rather than sharing exercises, therapists proposed an inter-clinic collaboration aimed at identifying 'gaps' in the exercise database that could be filled by the therapists themselves.

Reuse

One would expect therapists to prefer the use of existing exercises over creating new exercises. Paradoxically, therapists were less enthusiastic about reusing peer-created exercises. For example, one therapist in case 3 remarked: *"Finding out the details about a peer-created exercise would take me more time than creating a suitable exercise myself."* Therapists expected reuse to be difficult, since exact knowledge about an exercise (e.g., tag placement on an object) is required to get the desired effects of an exercise. Additionally, they envisioned problems in standardizing the categorization of exercises. Nevertheless, they used extensively the exercises pre-installed in TagTrainer at the start of the study, which had been created by other therapists.

DISCUSSION

We have examined the challenges surrounding the introduction of EUD to support therapists in creating and customizing exercises on TagTrainer, a tangible interactive platform for rehabilitation training. Contrary to situations where EUD practices emerge bottom up, amongst communities and individuals with a high exposure to informatics, the context of rehabilitation training is characterized by relatively low familiarity and affinity to programming and informatics, and by a higher level of formality and management involvement in inserting new technologies in daily work. Still it is a professional context in which a lot of major benefits can be reaped from EUD, because of the need to tailor training programs to individual patients and local clinical practices of highly specialized and trained professionals.

By means of four case studies we studied the deployment and adoption of TagTrainer. The aim of these studies was to identify the factors that influence therapists' decisions to engage in EUD practices. In all cases the results of the UTAUT questionnaire show a positive acceptance of TagTrainer: therapists used TagTrainer extensively as a tool for daily therapy, illustrating the potential of tangible rehabilitation technology. Furthermore, we have demonstrated the feasibility of EUD in a clinical environment, as in all four studies new exercises were created independently by participating therapists. These exercises complemented the collection of exercises available to them at the start of the study period, and matched the needs of the specific patients they were working with.

Interestingly, our studies revealed several challenges that need to be overcome before therapists engage successfully in EUD. Therapists reported to be confident about their EUD skills; nevertheless, the amount of development taking place in the three latter studies was less than had been anticipated based on the initial deployment study. Over a combined duration of 21 weeks, the 20 participants from the three latter studies created just 15 new exercises, compared to 20 new exercises in three-week long first case study. Furthermore, the results on self-efficacy and the reported and observed EUD behavior are remarkably consistent amongst all three latter studies, despite considerable differences of culture, healthcare system, socio-technical context and deployment strategy.

In the following paragraphs we discuss more closely the EUD related decisions that our participants have been making, and the options that we provided them through the deployment of TagTrainer. Finally, we discuss, based on our experiences and previous work, the need for deployment guidelines for designers of future EUD environments.

To develop or not to develop – that is *a* question

Our studies have provided many examples of end-users that faced decisions related to EUD. These decisions often had the nature of a trade-off: the user would face a number of options with different costs and benefits, from which the best option needed to be selected. Often, these choices were not binary, but multinomial. For example, a therapist might face the need for a patient-tailored exercise. At this point, the therapist might have the following four options: modifying an exercise in his collection to fit the patient's needs, creating an entirely new exercise, finding a matching exercise created by a colleague, or taking an existing exercise and accept that it is non-optimal for the patient.

The Attention Investment model by Blackwell [3] considers the decision of end-users to engage in programming on a cognitive level. Blackwell argues that people constantly have to evaluate the tradeoff between investing time in automation and performing a task manually, since our cognitive resources are limited. However, Blackwell's model takes the perspective of a single user facing a very clear and well-contained choice. Many EUD systems, such as TagTrainer, are part of more complex socio-technical environments where decision options become fuzzy. Although a similar tradeoff plays out in our cases, we think the factors involved transcend the cognitive effort as discussed by [3]. Further, a positive evaluation of the tradeoff may not be enough: our participants indicated that they see a positive return-on-investment for EUD activities with TagTrainer regarding the effort they spend on it. In the terms of [3], the cognitive resources spent on creation activities are perceived to be less than the resources that they would spend to train patients without TagTrainer. Still, therapists often did not engage in EUD activities because of external reasons: for example because the clinic's management did not free them from part of their regular activities to perform EUD activities.

On the other hand, therapists saw the opportunity to provide patients with better treatment by offering patient-tailored exercises with TagTrainer. Therefore, an alternative tradeoff appears to emerge between the treatment quality versus compliance with the culture of the clinic and performance indicators adopted by the management (in this case fully allocating the therapists' time to patient treatment). This tradeoff is not about efficient use of one's cognitive resources, but cost-benefit equity at an organizational level. The presence of other factors beyond end-users' cognitive resources that influence their decision to engage in EUD implies that units of attention, the 'currency' used in the Attention Investment model, might not be the only one for determining an end-user's decision to engage in EUD in context. Examples of non-cognitive factors that influenced therapists' decisions to (not) engage in EUD are plentiful: managerial issues, caring about a patient's wellbeing, plain curiosity, etc.

Such a broader perspective on EUD practices has been discussed by Fischer et al., in their manifesto for end-user development [11]. Based on results from several surveys, they propose a model which, further to the trade-off between user costs and user motivations, acknowledges management issues, context issues, technology etc. Fischer et al. [11] argue that critical success factors for the adoption of EUD depend very much on the domain considered. In cultures with high end-user motivation and low managerial influence (such as in engineering and scientific domains, or creative communities), EUD practices might simply develop by end users taking development into their own hands. In other cultures that are usually the domain of *non-information workers* [30], a larger distance has to be bridged for EUD to take place. The unifying property that characterizes this latter group is that interacting with computer technology is not the main focus of its members' work, with the majority of their work happening off-screen, embedded in social interactions, communicating, observing etc. (e.g., primary school teachers, rehabilitation therapists).

Our study seems to confirm Fischer et al.'s argument in [11] that for domains dominated by non-information workers in general, contextual and managerial issues play a large role in an end-user's decision to engage in EUD. Further the model of [11] is in line with general models of technology acceptance [33] and the more general model of theory of reasoned action (TRA, [13]); contrary to the literature on technology acceptance, there has been little attempt to validate this model quantitatively. On the one hand this calls for future empirical research to fill this gap. On the other, we note that technology acceptance models provide little guidance to designers as to how to design EUD technology to ensure acceptance. Therefore, in the following paragraphs we elaborate on some of the tasks that our participants faced, as well as on the particular design choices that enabled our users to perform these tasks.

End-user tasks in EUD environments

Using existing exercises

Some therapists remarked that because a substantial set of exercises was already available, there was less of a need to create new exercises. Although not all participants shared this opinion, it highlights an important design decision that was made for the deployment of TagTrainer. An initial set of about 150 exercises was included upon deployment of the TagTrainer systems in our studies. These exercises were developed in close collaboration with therapists, to cater for a set of basic arm-hand therapy demands. The idea was that, as described in [12], these exercises would act as the 'seed' from which TagTrainer could grow, through the development of additional exercises by therapists. In hindsight, it might have been that our 'seed' had satisfied the current demands of some therapists – thus the system that we deployed was not sufficiently 'underdesigned' [11] for EUD practices to occur amongst all therapists.

Reusing others' exercises

While therapists found exercise reuse beneficial in principle, they feared that assessing whether the content of peer-created exercises was suitable for any particular patient would take longer than it would take them to create an exercise from scratch. The difficulty in re-using code and sharing code between programmers is well known [16], and has motivated engineering practices such as component based software development [28], API usability [8], and at a more operational level commenting and documenting of source code. However, it is questionable whether such engineering practices should be expected by health professionals. Moreover, there are major differences to how therapists will explain an exercise, versus what could constitute a suitable documentation of the relevant software. Indeed one of the most prominent problems that therapists encountered in the exercise creation process was the translation between different 'languages' applying to their problem: i.e. handling the translation between intrinsic meaning (what does the exercise do?), programming language (how was it built?) and natural language (how can I explain it to a colleague?), see also [24,26].

Though therapists voiced negative opinions concerning exercise reuse, these opinions form an apparent discrepancy with the behavior displayed by participants. The therapists' attitude would lead one to expect that therapists would engage vigorously in EUD and use their own exercises, rather than those made by others. However, for most of the training carried out during the study, participants relied on the exercises already available in the TagTrainer system.

There could be several explanations for this, the most obvious one that attitudes do not always succeed in predicting behavior, which is emergent and contextualized. Another one would be that software creation was just not thought to be feasible in the time available for training a patient (one session typically lasts 30 minutes). Perhaps a therapist would need more time to organize a training session in such a way that creating a new exercise would not take away any training time from the patient (e.g., while the patient is carrying out another task). Consistently with the TRA, a person's belief in their ability to engage in a specific behavior is a major predictor of them actually engaging in it. But this belief depends on a very specific behavior and context (following the behavior compatibility principle discussed in [13]), rather than the more general conception of self-efficacy of EUD that was measured in this study.

An alternative explanation is that our own expectations of what constitutes re-use are different than those held by therapists. Surely, the 'ready exercises' that were made available in TagTrainer at the start of the studies described here, had been tested and refined to remove technical or usability errors. However, these exercises also had been developed by rehabilitation therapists. Could then the therapists' reservations towards reusing end-user software be a matter of perception regarding the software creation process and trust towards its outcomes, rather than having its roots in any negative experiences?

The intent to use TagTrainer is largely affected by its perceived credibility and this seems to be, at least in part, influenced by the perceptions therapists have about how it was created. For example, evidence of clinical effectiveness in terms of clinical trials was often mentioned as a prerequisite for using TagTrainer, which is consistent with the standard approach for implementing technology in healthcare [17]. Even though pre-installed exercise content was to our eyes the product of EUD as much as what was created during the study period, therapists perceived this very differently. Future research could shed light into these considerations by measuring credibility and expectancy specifically for end-user developed software itself, versus one that others have created. It could also consider how end-users evaluate any curation process by software professionals. More generally, technology acceptance models for EUD need to account for perceptions of the software creation process held by end-users.

Modifying exercises

An interesting phenomenon that occurred in all of our studies was the modification of therapy exercises by substitution of the physical objects involved. The 'tags' included in TagTrainer can quickly be attached to any object of choice, and thus allows therapists to use different objects with the same exercise software. Therapists remarked that these 'modifications' allowed them to create patient-tailored exercises without the need for delving into the software, thereby allowing them to save time. Although traditionally the physical modification of TagTrainer would not be considered EUD, we argue to broaden the scope of this term for interactive physical systems [30]. We believe that the possibility of physical modifications has facilitated the EUD engagement by smoothing the transition between exercise consumerism and exercise creation.

Creating new exercises

Not all customization needs can be addressed by just using different physical objects. For example, in the fourth case, two existing TagTrainer systems with each one TagTile were merged into a new system with three TagTiles. However, all pre-installed exercises had been created for a single-TagTile system and did not make use of the two additional TagTiles. Therapists felt that more multi-TagTile exercises were required – especially for training the relatively skilled patients. Still, only two new exercises were created for the three-board TagTrainer system during the fourth case study. Therapists remarked that, although they had a need for new exercises, they were unable to create them because they would not divert from patient treatment to engage in exercise creation. They suggested, beyond providing them with time dedicated to the development of new exercises, to employ a dedicated TagTrainer responsible with whom they together could develop new exercises.

Cabitza et al. have recently proposed such an extension to the meta-design paradigm, in which a *maieuta-designer* (derived from *maieutics*, a Socratic form of inquiry and discussion between individuals) acts as a complementary role to the meta-designer [11], but *"more oriented to the social aspects of EUD practice than to the technical ones"* [5]. Such a maieuta-designer would be tasked with facilitating the shift from consumerism to EUD on a social and managerial level, just as a meta-designer does on a technical level. This relates to the role of *contact person* that Spahn and Wulf [27] have introduced in their work on the deployment of an EUD environment in mid-sized German companies. The contact person acts as an evangelist, promoting and supporting the use of an EUD environment, and assisting end-users in the creation of new software artifacts.

Curation

In all studies, therapists remarked that it was hard to find the right exercise for a particular patient. Although exercises are described and categorized by means of a title, a category and keywords, therapists had difficulties finding applicable exercises. One reason was the lack of a uniform classification scheme to categorize and describe exercises; as a result, suitable exercises might have been available, but would not be found because therapists described their needs in terms different from those used in exercise descriptions. Furthermore, the value of certain exercises was contested by some therapists. For example, therapists who were part of the third study had developed exercises that used TagTrainer for training a patient's legs. However, when therapists from the fourth study were confronted with these exercises, they dismissed them as being 'not useful', and 'not in line with their intended use for TagTrainer'.

These notions indicate that there is a need for curation in EUD environments like TagTrainer. This curation, that relates to the 'reseeding' phase in Fischer et al.'s SER model [12], could be implemented in many different ways, such as through a community review, by a dedicated curator, or by an external validation body.

Success or failure?

Although the adoption of TagTrainer as a rehabilitation technology can be considered successful by all means (e.g., usage statistics, questionnaire ratings), it is hard to qualify its success as a tool for EUD. After all, what constitutes a *successful* EUD deployment? If it is simply a high number of EUD creations, then what would be the minimal value for this number to declare success? Indeed, the sheer number of EUD creations in our studies (40) was somewhat limited compared to the number of participants (24) and the lengths of the case studies. We argue however, that such numbers have little value in determining the success of an EUD deployment. Rather, we think that the success of an EUD system depends on its impact on the goals its users want to accomplish. In our case, EUD *did* help therapists to provide personalized training content to their patients - a goal that could not have been achieved without EUD. Whether more patients could have been helped, and whether the efficiency of the EUD process could have been improved are equally important questions, though currently hard to answer.

The difficulty in defining the success of TagTrainer as an EUD environment illustrates the discrepancy between our expectations as researchers and designers (success meaning widespread uptake of EUD activities) and those of the our end-users (success meaning improved treatment quality and efficiency). Acknowledging the existence of this discrepancy for the larger EUD community (and in particular in environments with non-information workers) should be a first step towards a set of guidelines for future EUD deployments. Currently, such guidelines are lacking, and the result of EUD deployments is based largely on the experience and intuition of the researchers, rather than scientific evidence. We call upon the research community to collect experiences from EUD deployment studies and to use these experiences to formulate a set of general guidelines for the deployment of EUD environments.

CONCLUSION

This paper has demonstrated the feasibility of EUD in the context of rehabilitation training through four case studies extending from three to eight weeks, in three different rehabilitation clinics located in two different countries. Through these field studies, we have gathered significant experience in what it means to deploy EUD environments in the context of a domain that is dominated by *non-information workers*, such as rehabilitation therapists.

Our studies have revealed the relatively large influence of external (e.g. managerial and contextual) factors on an end-user's decision to engage in EUD practices. We have also shown that what constitutes end-user development is different from the first person perspective of the therapist compared to what we anticipated, showing how important their perceptions and evaluations of the software creation process are for adoption. For improving the EUD systems created, more attention needs to be paid towards guiding end-users to address usability, as well as towards supporting the browsing, locating, and comprehension of existing solutions.

ACKNOWLEDGEMENTS

We acknowledge the support of the Innovation-Oriented Research Programme 'Integral Product Creation and Realization (IOP IPCR)' of the Netherlands Ministry of Economic Affairs.

REFERENCES

1. Alankus, G., Lazar, A., May, M., and Kelleher, C. Towards Customizable Games for Stroke Rehabilitation. *Proc. CHI '10*, ACM (2010), 2113–2122.
2. Bandura, A. Guide for constructing self-efficacy scales. *Self-efficacy beliefs of adolescents 5*, (2006), 307–337.
3. Blackwell, A.F. First Steps in Programming: A Rationale for Attention Investment Models. *Proc. HCC '02*, IEEE Computer Society (2002), 2–10.
4. Burnett, M.M. and Myers, B.A. Future of End-user Software Engineering: Beyond the Silos. *Proc. ICSE 2014*, ACM (2014), 201–211.
5. Cabitza, F., Fogli, D., and Piccinno, A. Fostering participation and co-evolution in sentient multimedia systems. *J. Vis. Lang. Comput. 25*, 6 (2014), 684–694.
6. Carmien, S.P. and Fischer, G. Design, adoption, and assessment of a socio-technical environment supporting independence for persons with cognitive disabilities. *Proc. CHI '08*, ACM (2008), 597–606.
7. Cott, C.A. Client-centred rehabilitation: client perspectives. *Disabil Rehabil 26*, 24 (2004), 1411–1422.
8. Daughtry, J.M., Farooq, U., Stylos, J., and Myers, B.A. API usability: CHI'2009 special interest group meeting. *CHI '09 Extended Abstracts*, ACM (2009), 2771–2774.
9. Devilly, G.J. and Borkovec, T.D. Psychometric properties of the credibility/expectancy questionnaire. *J Behav Ther Exp Psy 31*, 2 (2000), 73–86.
10. Fischer, G. Understanding, fostering, and supporting cultures of participation. *ACM interactions 18*, 3 (2011), 42–53.
11. Fischer, G., Giaccardi, E., Ye, Y., Sutcliffe, A.G., and Mehandjiev, N. Meta-design: a manifesto for end-user development. *Commun. ACM 47*, 9 (2004), 33–37.
12. Fischer, G., McCall, R., Ostwald, J., Reeves, B., and Shipman, F. Seeding, evolutionary growth and reseeding: supporting the incremental development of design environments. *Proc. CHI '94*, ACM (1994), 292–298.
13. Fishbein, M. and Ajzen, I. *Predicting and Changing Behavior: The Reasoned Action Approach.* Taylor & Francis, 2011.
14. Fisher,II, M., Rothermel, G., Brown, D., Cao, M., Cook, C., and Burnett, M. Integrating automated test generation into the WYSIWYT spreadsheet testing methodology. *ACM Trans. Softw. Eng. Methodol. 15*, 2 (2006), 150–194.
15. Gantt, M. and Nardi, B.A. Gardeners and gurus: patterns of cooperation among CAD users. *Proc. CHI '92*, ACM (1992), 107–117.
16. Haefliger, S., Krogh, G. von, and Spaeth, S. Code Reuse in Open Source Software. *Manage Sci 54*, 1 (2008), 180–193.
17. Hochstenbach-Waelen, A. and Seelen, H.A. Embracing change: practical and theoretical considerations for successful implementation of technology assisting upper limb training in stroke. *J Neuroeng Rehabil 9*, (2012), 52.
18. Jacobs, A., Timmermans, A., Michielsen, M., Vander Plaetse, M., and Markopoulos, P. CONTRAST: Gamification of Arm-hand Training for Stroke Survivors. *CHI '13 Extended Abstracts*, ACM (2013), 415–420.
19. Ko, A.J., Abraham, R., Beckwith, L., et al. The state of the art in end-user software engineering. *ACM Comput. Surv. 43*, 3 (2011), 21:1–21:44.
20. Lieberman, H., Paternò, F., Klann, M., and Wulf, V. End-User Development: An Emerging Paradigm. In H. Lieberman, F. Paternò and V. Wulf, eds., *End User Development*. Springer Netherlands, 2006, 1–8.
21. Maceli, M. and Atwood, M.E. From Human Crafters to Human Factors to Human Actors and Back Again: Bridging the Design Time – Use Time Divide. *Proc. IS-EUD 2011*, Springer Berlin Heidelberg (2011), 76–91.
22. Mehandjiev, N., Sutcliffe, A., and Lee, D. Organizational View of End-User Development. In *End User Development*. Springer, 2006, 371–399.
23. Orne, M.T. Demand characteristics and the concept of quasi-controls. In *Artifacts in Behavioral Research: Robert Rosenthal and Ralph L. Rosnow's Classic Books*. Oxford University Press, 2009, 110–137.
24. Pane, J.F., Ratanamahatana, C., and Myers, B.A. Studying the language and structure in non-programmers' solutions to programming problems. *Int J Hum-Comput St 54*, 2 (2001), 237–264.
25. Rothermel, G., Burnett, M., Li, L., Dupuis, C., and Sheretov, A. A methodology for testing spreadsheets. *ACM Trans. Softw. Eng. Methodol. 10*, 1 (2001), 110–147.
26. De Souza, C.S., Garcia, A.C.B., Slaviero, C., Pinto, H., and Repenning, A. Semiotic traces of computational thinking acquisition. *Proc. IS-EUD 2011*, Springer-Verlag (2011), 155–170.
27. Spahn, M. and Wulf, V. End-User Development of Enterprise Widgets. In V. Pipek, M.B. Rosson, B. de Ruyter and V. Wulf, eds., *End-User Development*. Springer Berlin Heidelberg, 2009, 106–125.
28. Szyperski, C. *Component software: beyond object-oriented programming.* ACM Press/Addison-Wesley Publishing Co., New York, NY, USA, 1998.
29. Tetteroo, D., Markopoulos, P., Timmermans, A., and Seelen, H. Rehabilitation Therapists as Software Creators? Introducing End User Development in a Healthcare Setting. *Int J of Sociotechnology and Knowledge Development 6*, 1 (2014), 36–50.
30. Tetteroo, D., Soute, I., and Markopoulos, P. Five Key Challenges in End-User Development for Tangible and Embodied Interaction. *Proc. ICMI '13*, (2013).
31. Timmermans, A.A., Seelen, H.A., Willmann, R.D., et al. Arm and hand skills: training preferences after stroke. *Disabil Rehabil 31*, (2009), 1344–52.
32. Timmermans, A., Seelen, H., Willmann, R., and Kingma, H. Technology-assisted training of arm-hand skills in stroke: concepts on reacquisition of motor control and therapist guidelines for rehabilitation technology design. *J Neuroeng Rehabil 6*, 1 (2009), 1.
33. Venkatesh, V., Morris, M.G., Gordon B. Davis, and Davis, F.D. User Acceptance of Information Technology: Toward a Unified View. *MIS Quarterly 27*, 3 (2003), 425–478.

Exergames for Physiotherapy and Rehabilitation: A Medium-term Situated Study of Motivational Aspects and Impact on Functional Reach

Jan David Smeddinck, Marc Herrlich, Rainer Malaka
Research Group Digital Media, University of Bremen, TZI, Bibliothekstr. 1, Bremen, Germany
{smeddinck,mh,malaka}@tzi.de

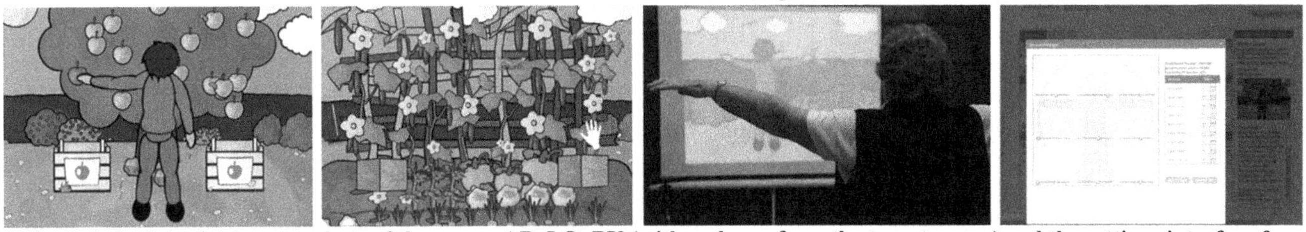

Figure 1: Left to right: screenshots of the games AP, LO, BU (with a player from the target group) and the settings interface for controlling adaptations and adaptivity (settings were defined via individual milestones; the window shows the sub-view for range of motion settings via body zones; all other settings were expressed as percentages and modified via standard WIMP components).

ABSTRACT

Exergames are increasingly considered as an exercise instruction modality in health applications. Studies are typically conducted in non-situated contexts and capture short-term effects. We present first results from a medium-scale study conducted over the course of 5 weeks and integrated into a normal rehabilitation program. The study features three groups, comparing manually adjustable exergames with the identical games in adaptive versions and manual physiotherapy interventions without games. The results indicate that the exergames and traditional therapy are comparable regarding measures of competence and enjoyment, while exergames led to significantly higher scores for autonomy, presence, and in a functional reach test. With traditional therapy, scores for tension-pressure and effort-importance were significantly higher. The initial results of the broader study presented in this paper deliver insights regarding motivational aspects of exergames and traditional therapy and point out which motivational aspects could be strengthened in future implementations.

Author Keywords

Exergames; games for health; player experience; balance.

ACM Classification Keywords

K.8.0 [Personal Computing]: General – Games.

INTRODUCTION

Full-body motion-based games for health (MGH) have emerged as an alternative means for exercise instruction in application scenarios such as physiotherapy (PT) or rehabilitation. Target groups range from the general population, over older adults [2] to specific groups such as people with Parkinson's disease [13] or children with cerebral palsy [5]. All these groups have in common that the heterogeneous abilities and requirements of their members must be met [13]. This requires mechanisms for adaptation that surpass the flexibility of consumer market (e.g. dance/fitness) games. Automatic adaptivity ensues as an additional requirement to lower the burden that frequent manual adjustments place on therapists, doctors or other caregiving staff. Solutions for both challenges, and insights on the general acceptance and effectiveness of MGH, require medium- to long-term studies and evaluations which are still rare.

We present initial results from a study on the therapy experience, and impact on physical function, comparing a suite of manually adjustable MGH (condition: *normal*) with semi-automatically adaptive versions (*adaptive*) and manual PT interventions without games (*control*), all for upper-body back and neck afflictions. The study was performed in the situated context of a large PT practice with professional therapists (TPs) and real patients. The intervention period lasted for five weeks. The outcomes discussed here are *motivational components*, which were differentiated via measures for the components of self-determination (SDT) [8,10] and *functional therapeutic effects*, which were differentiated via *Timed Up and Go* (TUG) [9] and *Functional Reach* tests (FRT) [7]. We expected the MGH to result in comparable levels of motivation despite less direct personal interaction. The autonomy component of the SDT needs satisfaction model was expected to be increased while others were expected to be decreased with casual game style implementations. Dimensions where the MGH are lacking can hint at future improvements and the dimensions where games are doing well can hint towards design guidelines. We also expected that functional results in the areas targeted by the games can be as good as, or even better than,

CHI 2015, April 18 - 23 2015, Seoul, Republic of Korea.

ACM 978-1-4503-3145-6/15/04...$15.00. http://dx.doi.org/10.1145/2702123.2702598

conventional PT for comparable therapy targets. The initial results of the broader study presented in this paper deliver insights in two areas: How to design for motivation in terms of motivational dimensions and which motivational aspects should be strengthened in future implementations.

STATE OF THE ART

MGH have been used with various target groups in research projects and early clinical applications [1,2,5,13]. The approach of using games for serious purposes in kinesiatric health applications is mostly cited for the potential to provide motivation to execute repetitive exercises [15]. Games (or playful apps) can also offer guidance via immediate custom performance feedback, and objective means of analysis via the collection and processing of performance data [12]. MGH can augment traditional treatments, but they can also allow for improved home/remote exercising. Studies have confirmed that they can be superior to traditional means of exercise instructions, e.g. instruction sheets [14]. While adaptable and adaptive MGH have been designed and evaluated in short-term studies [3,4,13], medium- or long-term situated studies are rare. Yet, these are much needed to confirm the lasting impact and effects. First longer-term studies for MGH indicate positive results (e.g. [5,14]), but real-world situated use is still underreported, esp. in the setting of busy practices, and a detailed motivational dissection has not yet been done. We were motivated to perform such a (rather difficult to organize and control) study since it offers much better comparability with true "in-the-wild" use that cannot be obtained from laboratory studies alone. Therapists and patients have more realistic motives and it is known from related work (and we experienced this in prior studies of our own) that some biases of lab studies are amplified with special target groups such as older adults (e.g. good participant effect). In addition, emotion research with isolated individuals is highly problematic due to the social functions of emotional regulation [6].

SETUP AND PROCEDURE

A suite of three casual MGH was used (Figure 1). Set in a garden scenario, which had been tested to be accepted by a wide range of older adult players, the games were: (a) An apple picking game (AP) which allows players to move at their own speed while picking ripe (red) apples from a tree and placing them in baskets near the ground. (b) A locust catching game (LO) where players were asked to collect locusts from a garden, requiring them to move their hands slowly and in a controlled manner towards the locusts, so as not to scare them away. (c) A butterfly balancing game (BU) that required players to match and hold poses performed by a virtual instructor in order to attract butterflies to sit on the player avatar. The games are part of a larger suite of games developed at the University of Bremen with the support of the "Spiel Dich Fit!" (SDF) project consortium [cf. to ACKNOWLEDGMENTS] over a period of two years. They were created in a player-centered iterative design approach and prior evaluations had shown that they facilitate positive therapy experiences. The selection of games set a focus on upper body flexibility and range of motion relating to the selection criteria for the study into which only patients with recurrent upper-body back and neck afflictions (a common PT target group) were admitted.

The study was performed at a large PT practice in Delmenhorst, Germany led by an experienced and renowned physiotherapist. It included 12 TPs and 29 patients (9 male, 20 female, median age 66 [1st Qu. 59, 3rd Qu. 73]). Patients were split into three groups (*normal* (9), *adaptive* (9) and *control* (11)) by random assignment. A therapist from the same pool was present in each session (S1-5). Patients in all groups were in treatment for chronic spine afflictions and treated following a (pro-active) progressive adaptations therapy approach aiming to reduce pain and to improve flexibility and balance (which continued as usual in the control group and TPs employed the games to continue working towards their goals with the patients in the other groups). Therapists were free to interact with patients as they saw fit in all groups, although they showed less direct interaction with patients in the game groups. They provided frequent verbal feedback and guidance in all sessions. With the games, the patients also received general feedback on their gameplay performance after each round of play but no further feedback on their exercise performance. For the normal group TPs were regularly reminded that they could use a calibration tool to manipulate personalized settings for *range of motion* (by active game screen zones; cf. Figure 1), required *speed*, *motion accuracy*, *endurance* (level duration) and *complexity* (amount of active objects) for each level. These settings were subject to a pre-study with 10 TPs and were evaluated as being easily understandable, useful for making meaningful adjustments, and allowing for efficient configurations. For the adaptive group, TPs were asked to make initial settings in S1 and to define a target milestone for S5. An automatic rubber-banding adjustment system then aimed at step-wise increasing game settings (in software) while guaranteeing a fair amount of success. In weeks 1 and 3, TPs were reminded that they were always invited to re-adjust the milestones / settings.

Weekly sessions of 20-25 minutes with 10-15 minutes play time per participant (playing each game if in a game group) were held over five consecutive weeks and substituted regular therapy appointments. The games were played in a separate section of a training room at the practice. The measures ranged from affect to exhaustion, self-efficacy, game performance, observational protocols and therapist reports on each patient and have been employed successfully in related work. In this initial report, we focus on two categories of measures collected after S1 and S5 of each participant respectively: (a) *Motivational measures* from instruments rooted in self-determination theory, namely the *competence*, *intuitive control*, *autonomy* and *presence* dimensions of the Player Experience of Needs Satisfaction (PENS) questionnaire [10] and the *tension-pressure*, *interest-enjoyment* and *effort-importance* dimensions of the intrinsic motivation inventory (IMI) [8]. Items of both questionnaires were adjusted to refer to "movement applications" in order to match the settings of all groups. (b) *Functional measures* for evaluating therapeutic effect, namely TUG and FRT. Both categories reflect important aspects of the targeted therapy. SDT motivational measures have been shown to impact exercising adherence [8] and the FRT is a validated indicator for balance and fall prevention [7].

RESULTS

A mixed-model analysis of variances (ANOVA) was conducted to check for statistically significant differences. Independent variables were 'group' (between subjects), and 'session' (within subjects) as the reported measures were collected after S1 (pre) and S5 (post). Data imputation (max. 1 case per participant on a sub-item in max. 2 participants per measure) was performed using group means. Variances were winsorized [2] (leveling outliers in the top/bottom .1 quantiles to the trim edge values).

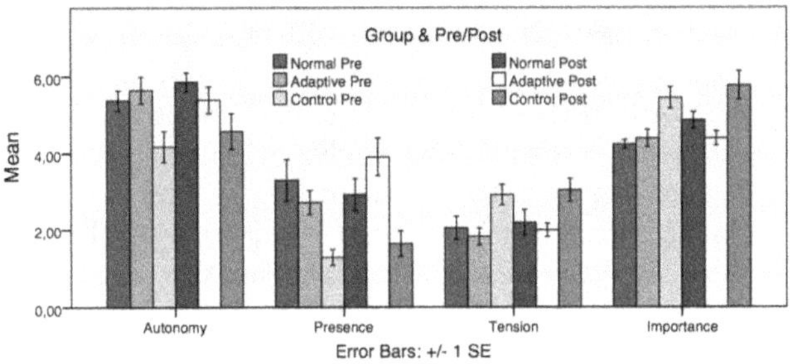

Figure 2: Means and standard errors for autonomy, presence, tension-pressure, and effort-importance collected in the first session (pre) and in the last session after five weeks (post).

ANOVA revealed no statistically significant differences regarding pre and post measures for PENS and IMI. For the independent variable 'group' the conducted ANOVA revealed statistically significant differences (Figure 2) for *presence* ($F(2,23)=7.725$; $p=0.003$; partial $\eta^2=0.402$; Levene fail.), *tension* ($F(2,23)=5.584$; $p=0.011$; pt. $\eta^2=0.327$; Lev. pass.), and *effort imp.* ($F(2,23)=7.037$; $p=0.004$; pt. $\eta^2=0.380$; Lev. fail.). The *autonomy* measure very narrowly failed the alpha level for sig. ($p=0.089$) while competence and enjoyment were not significant. Looking at S1 and S5 individually for autonomy revealed statistically sig. diffs. for S1 ($F(2,28)=5.204$; $p=0.013$; Lev. fail.) and a trend ($F(2,25)=3.521$; $p=0.058$; Lev. pass.) for S5. Post-hoc tests confirmed sig. diffs. for presence (Dunnett-T3 test used because of failed Lev.; groups normal and control: $p=0.022$; groups adaptive and control: $p=0.001$; groups normal and adaptive: n.s.), for *tension* (Bonferroni corrected; groups *normal* and *control*: $p=0.049$; groups *adaptive* and *control*: $p=0.013$; groups *normal* and *adaptive*: n.s.), and for *effort importance* (Dunnett-T3 test used because of failed Lev.; groups *normal* and *control*: n.s.; groups *adaptive* and *control*: $p=0.040$; *normal* and *adaptive*: n.s.).

An ANOVA for FRT differences (cf. Figure 3) between S1 and S5 revealed statistically sig. diffs. for the indep. var. 'group' ($F(2,26)=3.539$; $p=0.045$; pt. $\eta^2=0.228$; Lev. fail.). Post-hoc tests confirmed sig. diffs. for groups *adaptive* and *control* (Dunnett-T3 test used because of failed Lev.; $p=0.001$), all remaining group combinations were not sig.. Table 1 presents the descriptive statistics for measures not shown in Figure 2 or 3 that were comparable across groups.

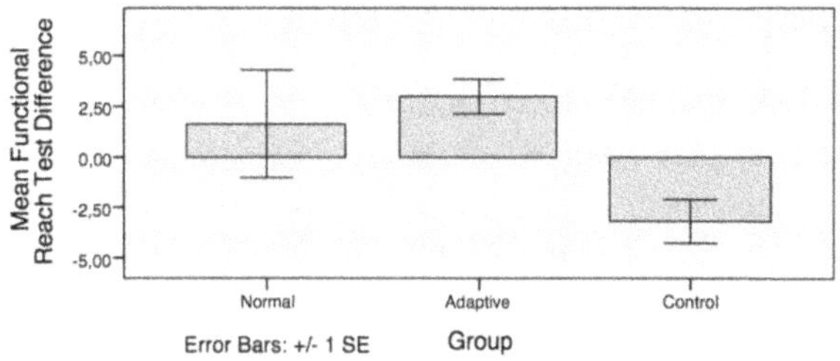

Figure 3: Means and standard errors for the pre-post-differences of the functional reach test for all groups.

	Week	*Normal*	*Adaptive*	*Control*
Competence	1	Mean = 5.6 SD = 0.8	Mean = 5.7 SD = 0.8	Mean = 5.6 SD = 0.6
	5	Mean = 5.4 SD = 0.7	Mean = 5.6 SD = 0.8	Mean = 5.7 SD = 0.5
Intuitive control	1	Mean = 6.0 SD = 0.5	Mean = 5.9 SD = 0.7	Mean = 5.2 SD = 0.9
	5	Mean = 6.6 SD = 0.5	Mean = 5.9 SD = 0.6	Mean = 5.4 SD = 1.0
Interest-enjoyment	1	Mean = 6.0 SD = 0.7	Mean = 5.9 SD = 1.0	Mean = 5.6 SD = 0.9
	5	Mean = 6.3 SD = 0.6	Mean = 5.6 SD = 0.9	Mean = 5.3 SD = 1.1
Timed Up and Go Test	W5 - W1	Mean = 0.2 SD = 2.0	Mean =-0.8 SD = 2.1	Mean = 0.2 SD = 3.2

Table 1: Means and std. dev. for competence, intuitive control, interest-enjoyment and the TUG test for weeks 1 and 5.

DISCUSSION

The results indicate that the measures of motivational components are not unanimously in favor of either games or regular PT sessions, pointing to the need to consider motivational aspects of MGH in detail. An explanation for the observed higher mean responses on the tension-pressure dimension in the control condition might be the impact of the strong role of a human instructor. If external pressure induced by the presence of an authority is internalized by the patients (e.g. patients believing that following the lead of their TPs is essential to their own well-being), this does not contradict the increased effort-importance (intrinsic motivation is usually not undermined by internalized extrinsic motivation [11]). Coupling the motivational measures that were significantly in favor of the games conditions could offer an explanation for the observations on these scales. The increased presence in the games conditions is perhaps not surprising and it was also measured with less question items than usual (only two matched the general "movement applications" wording). However, it goes along well with the result of increased autonomy: If a player is getting immersed in a game, it allows them to behave on their own accord. Drawn together, the results suggest that the current generation of games for health (at least the casual style games, which resemble typical applications in this domain) might be a good match for augmenting traditional therapy. Future generations of MGH that are, from the start, designed for patient-therapist and patient-patient interaction through the game might improve results in the other motivational measures and thus facilitate even more captivating exercise instruction. However, partial improvements, or equal performance in MGH already allow for them to be used to augment traditional therapeutic exercise instructions with a new palette of diverse experiences.

Some limitations apply to our study. Our sample shows a gender imbalance. While the split represents the gender distribution in patients of the targeted age group well, further studies are needed to research effects of gender (and age) in more detail. Due to the situated nature of the study and our aim to observe realistic usage, we did not enforce a controlled set of exercises across all groups. The differences we observed can thus only be attributed to the treatment complex of therapy games plus the exercises they implemented as a whole. A more detailed separation requires further (likely lab) studies with a much more controlled approach. Our results also indicate that we cannot clearly separate the *normal* and *adaptive* groups on any measure. While this points to future work, for now the automatic adaptivity does not appear to significantly decrease the PT experience or functional development. At the same time, TPs repeatedly indicated that they appreciated the adaptive version, since it reduces burden on their schedules. The situated context of a busy practice produces a noisy and difficult environment for scientific study. The notable variance in the data we gathered underlines these challenges and the need for improved research methods for situated studies, if more subtle differences are to be detected. Yet, game design for health applications is bound to remain a problem where clear lines are difficult to establish.

CONCLUSION

We presented first results from a medium-term study of full-body motion-based games for physiotherapy and rehabilitation. With a custom-built suite of MGH and a flexible configuration tool, the situated usage in a PT practice was studied over the course of five weeks. Results on the measure of functional reach appear to be increased in the game conditions, hinting at improvements, but further studies are needed in order to generalize this finding. The results of experiential measures rooted in needs-satisfaction models of SDT are mixed and appear to hint at the role of human involvement, indicating directions for future study.

ACKNOWLEDGMENTS

We thank the members of SDF (abraxas Medien Hamm & Wächter GbR and vacances GmbH), Rehamed Delmenhorst (Wolters / Eybe / Schröder-Wolters GbR), Simon Hermsdorf, Sophie Janzen and all participants. The SDF project received funding from the Wirtschaftsförderung Bremen and the EU fund for regional development (EFRE).

REFERENCES

1. Alankus, G., Lazar, A., May, M., and Kelleher, C. Towards customizable games for stroke rehabilitation. *Proc. of the 28th international conference on Human factors in computing systems*, (2010), 2113–2122.
2. Gerling, K.M., Livingston, I.J., Nacke, L.E., and Mandryk, R.L. Full-Body Motion-Based Game Interaction for Older Adults. *CHI'12: Proc. of the 30th int. conf. on Human factors in computing systems*, (2012).
3. Göbel, S., Hardy, S., Wendel, V., Mehm, F., and Steinmetz, R. Serious games for health: personalized exergames. *Proc. of the int. conf. on Multimedia*, ACM (2010), 1663–1666.
4. Hardy, S., Göbel, S., Gutjahr, M., Wiemeyer, J., and Steinmetz, R. Adaptation Model for Indoor Exergames. *Int. Journal of Computer Science in Sport 11*, 1 (2012).
5. Hernandez, H.A., Ye, Z., Graham, T.C., Fehlings, D., and Switzer, L. Designing action-based exergames for children with cerebral palsy. *Proc. of the Conf. on Human Factors in Computing Systems*, (2013), 1261–1270.
6. Kappas, A. Smile when you read this, whether you like it or not: Conceptual challenges to affect detection. *IEEE Trans. on Affective Computing 1*, 1 (2010), 38–41.
7. Katz-Leurer, M., Fisher, I., Neeb, M., Schwartz, I., and Carmeli, E. Reliability and validity of the modified functional reach test at the sub-acute stage post-stroke. *Disability and Rehabilitation 31*, 3 (2009), 243–248.
8. McAuley, E., Duncan, T., and Tammen, V.V. Psychometric properties of the Intrinsic Motivation Inventory in a competitive sport setting: a confirmatory factor analysis. *Research quarterly for exercise and sport 60*, 1 (1989), 48–58.
9. Podsiadlo, D. and Richardson, S. The timed "Up & Go": a test of basic functional mobility for frail elderly persons. *Journal of the American Geriatrics Society 39*, 2 (1991), 142–148.
10. Rigby, S. and Ryan, R. *The Player Experience of Need Satisfaction(PENS): an applied model and methodology for understanding key components of the player experience.* 2007.
11. Ryan, R.M. and Deci, E.L. Intrinsic and Extrinsic Motivations: Classic Definitions and New Directions. *Contemporary Educational Psychology 25*, 1 (2000), 54–67.
12. Smeddinck, J.D., Gerling, K.M., and Malaka, R. Anpassbare Computerspiele für Senioren. *Informatik-Spektrum 37*, 6 (2014), 575–579.
13. Smeddinck, J., Siegel, S., and Herrlich, M. Adaptive Difficulty in Exergames for Parkinson's Disease Patients. *Proc. of the 2013 Graphics Interface Conf.*, Canadian Information Processing Society (2013), 141–148.
14. Uzor, S. and Baillie, L. Investigating the long-term use of exergames in the home with elderly fallers. ACM Press (2014), 2813–2822.
15. Yim, J. and Graham, T.C.N. Using games to increase exercise motivation. *Proceedings of the 2007 conference on Future Play*, ACM (2007), 166–173.

Resilience Ex Machina: Learning a Complex Medical Device for Haemodialysis Self-Treatment

Paul Noble
UCL Interaction Centre
University College London
Paul.Noble@cs.ucl.ac.uk

ABSTRACT
Resilience, the ability to bounce back or manage sufficiently despite ongoing adversity, has received considerable interest from several domains over the last two decades. A concept that is easily and widely applicable, it has evolved a variety of nuanced interpretations. Recent work in the systems theory and resilience engineering domains has moved towards some sharper definitions. This paper discusses and develops these definitions, and by contrasting with robustness, applies them as an approach for HCI evaluation. Observational data from a hospital training environment is used to examine how patients learn to operate home haemodialysis devices, and how patients' safety is managed and maintained. This paper concludes that to improve recovery of adverse situations within the home, there is a necessity for design to support the acquirement of resilient reaction as a skill, in hand with temporal management. These ideas are developed in conjunction with the consideration of how technology can support, or nudge, the expression of resilient behaviours.

Author Keywords
Resilience; Human Error; Medical Devices; Haemodialysis

ACM Classification Keywords
H.5.3 Group and Organization Interfaces - Computer-supported cooperative work, Evaluation/methodology, Synchronous interaction, Theory and models

INTRODUCTION
Over the past two decades the concept of resilience has received attention in various domains such as psychology, ecology, systems theory, and safety engineering. In particular, the recent arrival of resilience engineering [4] has stimulated a new research impetus, with many published papers investigating resilience characteristics of a variety of complex systems. As a concept resilience is one that has suffered loose definition, with re-contextualisation across domains leading to various nuanced interpretations. Resilience and resilience engineering appear exciting as theoretical instruments of systems analysis, but what does it mean to apply these instruments to HCI (human computer interaction) at levels of fine granularity? The title of this paper is a play on the Latin phrase 'Deus Ex Machina' or 'God from the Machine'. This phrase refers to a scaffolding device used behind the scenes in ancient Greek theatre, which lowered an actor playing a God onto the stage who saved the day. Often used by playwrights of the age to resolve a badly written plotline where the hero faced certain death, the phrase was employed disparagingly by critics. Considering HCI and the design of sociotechnical systems, what should a resiliently engineered design aspire to; does such a design expect that there be some ingenious intervention saving the user and system from certain failure? If not, who engineers resilience within a socio-technical system, is it the system designer, user, or other actors? How can resilience expressed from the 'machine'?

CHI 2015, April 18 - 23 2015, Seoul, Republic of Korea Copyright 2015 ACM 978-1-4503-3145-6/15/04...$15.00
http://dx.doi.org/10.1145/2702123.2702348

This paper evaluates observational data obtained from a case study of a home haemodialysis (HHD) medical training environment. Resilient activities are identified and explored as to how they can yield insights into system safety and performance. A specific focus examines the strategies and behaviours of the actors inside the system in making the system safe, and also in how they cope with the transfer of responsibility of HHD device operation. Resilience engineering encompasses a variety of potentially applicable concepts, which are initially contextually reviewed. Topical discussion in resilience engineering theory argues for the definition of resilience as largely the ability to manage functional trade-offs in order to combat adverse events [6][5]. The concept of robustness is introduced and contrasted with this in order to sharpen the conceptual distinction. Design considerations are drawn and the locus of resilience reflected upon.

Resilience and Robustness
De Haan et al. [3] demonstrate that resilience is a concept that is highly correlated with short timescale system recovery after shocks or disturbances. A resilience *engineering* (RE) perspective aims to determine the factors behind successful system operation and thus improve recovery performance. Resilience can be considered something that a system *does,* not what a system *has* [4]. In contrast, conventional safety perspectives focus on the root cause of system failure, the fixing of which progressively improves system robustness.

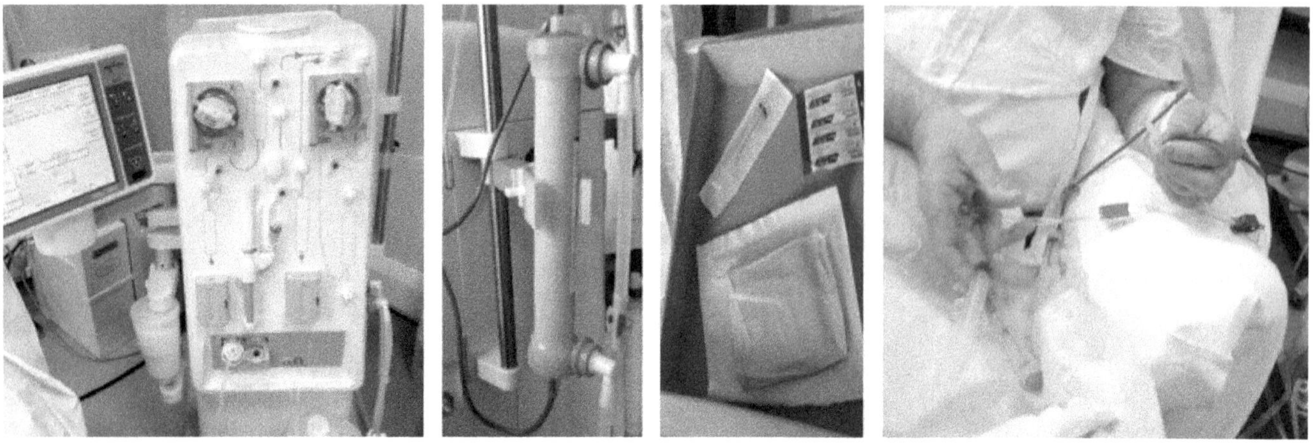

Figure 1: a) Home haemodialysis machine. b) Device artefacts. c) Patient artefacts. d) Handling lines & syringes

RE consists of a broad range of concepts, of which resilience is one, that examine how to avoid and anticipate complications, minimising the need for recovery. Hollnagel et al. [4] offers four principles (anticipation, monitoring, learning, response) considered instrumental in this endeavour. Regrettably, as a consequence of the wide-ranging and nuanced use of the resilience concept, it was observed that almost every action can be considered 'resilient' [2]. To clarify, Wears [6] makes the distinction between 1st and 2nd order resilience, where 1st order resilience that 'many would not consider resilience at all' is described as simple corrective measures concerned with stability. 2nd order resilience is considered by Wears to include responding to unforeseen situations, and also monitoring and anticipating for related threats or advantageous opportunities. Morel et al. [5] also explores resilience as decision making, describing resilient behaviours as a trade-off between risk and reward founded upon the level of experience of actors within the system.

Developing this distinction in this paper this 1st order resilience is considered to be equivalent to the established concept of robustness or 'adaptive robustness' [3]. This concept is associated with continuity of system operation, but is not linked with any *additional* anticipatory or trade-off activities managed by actors outwith system design. In this sense monitoring and anticipation are applicable to both robust and resilient interpretations. A process of monitoring tackles expected (robust) and unexpected (resilient) system events in the present. Anticipation through requisite imagination [1] supports robust design and underpins the capacity for resilient recovery.

Home Haemodialysis Training

Recent advances in technology have led to a renewed effort to encourage capable renal patients to switch from hospital treatment to self-care at home. Hospital treatment for end stage renal disease (ESRD) typically involves patients attending 3 dialysis sessions per week, each of 5-6 hours duration. HHD benefits patients in that life and care quality improves, while also incurring reduced cost to healthcare providers. Patients who are offered HHD training must be able to demonstrate a range of competencies on completion. Operation of the medical device (Figure 1a), along with the various procedures and artefacts surrounding use (Figure 1b/c), is challenging, with the most capable and dexterous (Figure 1d) patients selected for the program. Due to a projected future increase in number and age of dialysis patients, it is important to discover ways for reducing the learning burden regarding the safe use of such devices. Furthermore, limited research has examined how the design of these machines can support a learning process that assists with transfer of the experience of safe use and recovery.

The activity of dialysing can be thought of as being analogous to an aeroplane flight. There are many safety procedures, preparations, and actions at the beginning and end. Equally, in the middle there are long periods (4-5 hours) of quiet treatment time where the blood is cleansed. This time is punctuated intermittently by monitoring activities, or the occasional device alarm. The systematic structure of haemodialysis treatment consists of independent patient and device procedural setup tasks, with the human-machine interface being the 'fistula'; a surgically constructed access chamber located within the patients' arm, where inserted needles allow blood exchange to take place.

Considering the home dialysis context, the home device environment is unique and offers potential for unusual occurrence. Dialysis patients are highly resistant to equipment change, as they have worked hard to obtain consistent and safe device practices through iterative cycles of appropriation and customisation. The focus of this paper is on examining the process of safety enskilment in such an environment. In this endeavour it is considered that:

Robustness concerns itself with the continuity of a system function, including adaptations in order to maintain that function.

Resilience describes the management of trade-offs in which a variation in system function takes place for the purpose of recovery from an event.

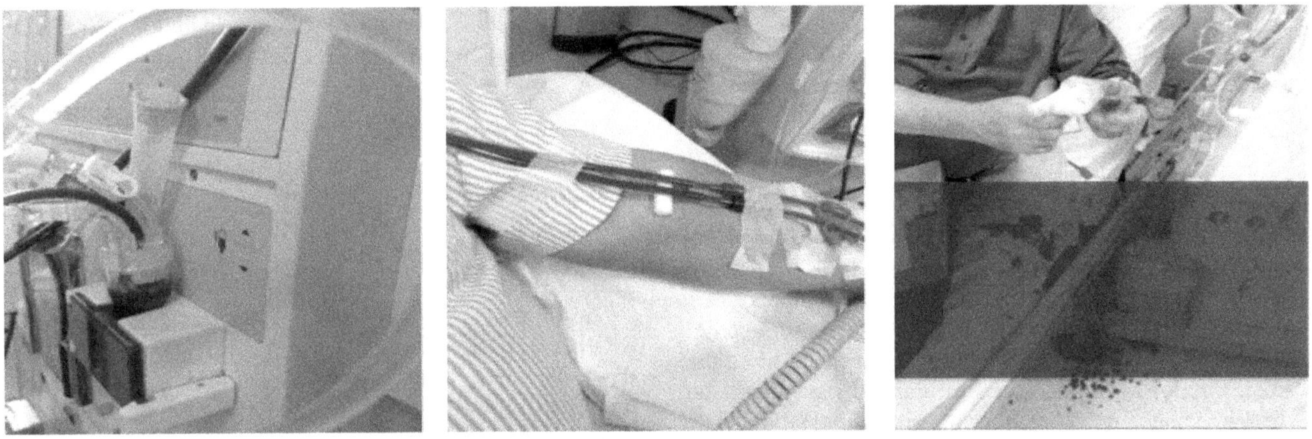

Figure 2: a) Customisation. b) Improvised solution. c) 'Learning the hard way' [partially masked]

METHOD

The context for this observational study was a specialist training suite situated within a dialysis unit in a London hospital. The suite contained two home dialysis units placed side by side, with the training nurse seated opposite.

Observational data was collected by the author who attended every session of a four-week training course conducted for two patients. Patients attended the course 3 times a week for approximately 5 hours per session. Patients' start times were staggered by 1 hour in order to assist the training nurse in supporting device setup and completion tasks with each patient individually. Consequently, 2 discrete task sets were observed per session by the author, along with any alarms and difficulties encountered during dialysis. Notes on dialogue, artefact photographs, and training materials were also gathered. The patients were selected as an opportunity sample based upon those attending the hospital course over the duration of the study. Both male patients were of similar age (65) and had been undergoing dialysis for approximately 18 months. Patient 1 worked together as a team with his wife who provided assistance. Patient 2 has no family support and so learnt independently.

A thematic analysis of the data was conducted, and the sensitising concept of resilience-robustness applied. Prominent themes were initially drawn out from the data, before cyclically returning and identifying themes of robustness, resilience, monitoring, and anticipation. In addition to the observational data, the author also drew upon an auto-ethnographic component derived from his active participation with the patients in operating the machine, learning procedure, and identifying events. Field notes were reviewed daily, reflecting on taught procedure and the operation of artefacts and actions not understood. This data was instrumental in understanding particular incidents through reflection, and in probing depth of patient knowledge as opposed to procedurally robust learning from training materials. Semi-structured exit interviews were conducted with the training nurse, patients and spouse.

RESULTS

Analyses reveal a variety of robust and resilient activities. Supplementary HHD themes identified correspond well with prior studies [7]. A clear distinction can be drawn between the activities in that the patients specifically focused on procedural robustness, whereas the trainer would additionally attempt to impart resilient practices. However, the extra 'work' of resilience activities were interpreted as optional in comparison with 'essential' procedures. Robustness strategies observed were:

Customisation for Robustness: Patient 2 often overlooked the final step after initiating treatment, which is to inject anti-coagulant into the tubing. He created a storage position out of the tubing for the anticoagulant container tube in order to keep it in his line of sight (Figure 2a).

Adaptive Robustness: Patient 1 suffered a kink in the tubing carrying his blood to the dialyser. A consequence of this was that the device alarmed and stopped dialysing multiple times. In an attempt to prevent the line from kinking again, a fix was improvised where gauze was placed under the tubing for reinforcement (Figure 2b).

Shared Responsibility: While both patients preferred to work from memory, Patient 1's wife made copious notes as she was 'scared that the children would blame me if anything happened'. She quizzed patient 1 about procedures in order to strengthen memory and distribute responsibility.

Resilient practice is dependent upon acquired experience [5]. The trainer would encourage patients to attempt challenging steps within a safe environment:

Learning and Experience: In isolation Patient 2 decided to go ahead and connect himself to the machine as encouraged by the trainer (who was absent but nearby). He neglected to close one clamp on the tubing, which led to blood flowing freely out of his arm. A small amount of blood was lost but for him this was quite a shocking sight. However, it was also a valuable learning experience. He called it 'learning the hard way'. This experience reassured the patient that adverse events are recoverable (Figure 2c).

Monitoring and anticipation processes were again split between 'essential' robustness and 'optional' resilience activities. Both patients were content to passively let the limited alarm functionality of the device inform them of any adverse events, instead of actively monitoring for potential troubles ahead. Patients separated resilience from robustness very early. 'I just want to get the basics' was a common response from Patient 1. Considering that if the device has been made 'safe' by increased procedural robustness, then this places strain upon the patients. This was particularly observed in Patient 1's wife. At some point the level of strain requires redesign. Resilience enters the system through two main avenues; Patient knowledge and experience, and active monitoring and anticipation. The former is particularly emphasised within the training environment. The trainer purposely sits with her back to patients in order to allow them to make mistakes. Frequent exposure to failure allows one to develop confidence and strategies for coping with failure. Frequent exposure to small failures is therefore a good way for patients to develop resilient practice. In addition, patients also gained knowledge regarding rare circumstance. In the example with the kink in the tubing they responded robustly; after review with the trainer they would perhaps next act resiliently. The robust response to discard the tubing and restart is extremely time consuming. Alternately they could resiliently manage the situation by assessing and reconciling dialysis time remaining, the severity of the kink (with its potential for red blood cell damage through haemolysis), and the speed of the pump. Haemodialysis is also a particularly embodied practice. Resilient trade-off often requires awareness of the body's physical limits in combination with decisions made on the machine. Patient 2 always dialysed for some 'extra' time. On occasion this made his hands cramp and so he required assistance to remove the inserted dialysis lines upon completion. This experience develops awareness of physical limits supporting potential future decisions.

RESILIENCE EX MACHINA

So how can we design to foster resilient practice from the machine? We can support the transfer of experiential practice, active monitoring, and diminish robustness strain:

System Education Points. There is potential for the designer to be aware of device error reporting as system education points, where device interruption occurs and discussion is likely to take place. An example of this was the observed use of the alarm points for imparting system knowledge by the trainer. The trainer would observe and let the patients make mistakes that were then captured by the device. Tracing back through cascading alarms developed deeper knowledge of machine operation.

Resilient Monitoring: There are opportunities for the development of device functionality to support (or nudge) the integration of resilience effort into those of essential procedures. Attention drawing interface designs can bolster scanning behaviours during device operation. The study device defaulted to displaying 'Dialysis Time Remaining'.

Temporal Awareness: When responding resiliently, management of trade-offs occur with respect to time. Systems that support superior time tracking in order to assist timely decision-making are advantageous. When the device in the study undergoes power failure, there is a 30-minute battery reserve. Device power source and battery reserve time remaining are not displayed on the device.

CONCLUSION

HCI has long been concerned with the recovery from device error, but resilient error recovery in haemodialysis is itself a skill forged through experience. This ability is particularly important within unpredictable home environments. Design can assist with the transfer and development of resilient practice, while also reducing cognitive demand. Resilience can be expressed 'from the machine' through assisting trade-off recovery from adverse events in hand with augmentation of temporal awareness.

ACKNOWLEDGMENTS

Thanks to Ann Blandford, NHS staff and patients. Study conducted under NHS ethics (11/LO/0329) and supported by EPSRC CHI+MED grant (EP/G059063/1).

REFERENCES

1. Adamski, A. and Westrum, R. 2003. Requisite Imagination: The Fine Art of Anticipating What Might go Wrong. *Handbook of cognitive task design*. LEA
2. Comfort, L.K., Boin, A., and Demchak, C.C. 2011. *Designing Resilience: Preparing for Extreme Events.* University of Pittsburgh Press, Pittsburgh, PA
3. De Haan, J., Kwakkel, J.H., Walker, W.E., Spirco, J., and Thissen, W.A.H. 2011. Framing flexibility: Theorising and data mining to develop a useful definition of flexibility and related concepts. *Futures 43*
4. Hollnagel, E., Woods, D., and Leveson, N. 2006 *Resilience Engineering: Concepts and Precepts.* Ashgate
5. Mörel, G., Amalberti, R., and Chauvin, C. 2008. Articulating the differences between safety and resilience: the decision-making process of professional sea-fishing skippers. *Human Factors 50*, 1, 1–16.
6. Wears, R.L. and Morrison, J.B. 2013. Levels of Resilience: Moving from Resilience to Resilience Engineering. *Proceedings of the 5th Resilience Engineering Symposium*, Soesterberg, The Netherlands
7. Wong, J., Eakin, J., Migram, P., Cafazzo, J. a, Halifax, N.V.D., and Chan, C.T. 2009. Patients' experiences with learning a complex medical device for the self-administration of nocturnal home hemodialysis. *Nephrology Nursing Journal 36*, 1, 27–32.

Understanding Design Tradeoffs for Health Technologies: A Mixed-Methods Approach

Katie O'Leary[1], Jordan Eschler[1], Logan Kendall[2], Lisa M. Vizer[2], James D. Ralston[3], and Wanda Pratt[1]

[1]The Information School; [2]Biomedical and Health Informatics
University of Washington| DUB Group
Seattle, WA 98195 USA
{kathlo; jeschler; kendall5; lmvizer; wpratt}@uw.edu

[3]Group Health Research Institute
Seattle, WA 98101 USA
ralston.j@ghc.org

ABSTRACT

We introduce a mixed-methods approach for determining how people weigh tradeoffs in values related to health and technologies for health self-management. Our approach combines interviews with Q-methodology, a method from psychology uniquely suited to quantifying opinions. We derive the framework for structured data collection and analysis for the Q-methodology from theories of self-management of chronic illness and technology adoption. To illustrate the power of this new approach, we used it in a field study of nine older adults with type 2 diabetes, and nine mothers of children with asthma. Our mixed-methods approach provides three key advantages for health design science in HCI: (1) it provides a structured health sciences theoretical framework to guide data collection and analysis; (2) it enhances the coding of unstructured data with statistical patterns of polarizing and consensus views; and (3) it empowers participants to actively weigh competing values that are most personally significant to them.

Author Keywords

Design methodology; Q-methodology; Health attitudes; Technology adoption; Mixed-methods; Health Informatics.

ACM Classification Keywords

H.5.2 [Information interfaces and presentation]: User interfaces—*evaluation/methodology, theory and methods, user-centered design.*

INTRODUCTION

Personal health technologies are designed to support people to attain personally significant health goals, such as staying fit, aging in place, and managing chronic diseases. However, it is challenging for designers to support personal health goals with new technologies because, unlike objectively measured productivity goals, health goals are highly subjective, contextual, and situated within competing values. For designers of personal health technologies, it is critical to understand people's subjective perspectives that are likely to influence health goals and subsequent behaviors, such as attitudes toward personal accountability, health information use, and technology adoption in the context of health self-management.

CHI 2015, April 18 - 23 2015, Seoul, Republic of Korea.

http://dx.doi.org/10.1145/2702123.2702576

Current HCI and social scientific methods for gathering subjective perspectives to inform the design of personal health technologies include interviews, focus groups, attitude measurement scales, and participatory design techniques. However, these methods are not always optimal for gathering highly structured data for understanding design *tradeoffs* based on how individuals weigh and compare the relative value of health information and technology to attain health goals.

We introduce a mixed-methods approach that combines ethnographic interviews with Q-methodology [21], a quantitative technique for finding clusters of subjective perspectives distinguished by polarizing opinions. We followed each in-depth interview with the Q-methodology procedure wherein participants chose how to normally distribute a set of statements about health and technology. This structured data collection method empowered participants by allowing them to weigh the statements most closely aligned with their personal beliefs, and to guide the discussion in explaining their health beliefs and attitudes with the interviewer. The relative ranking of subjective statements about health within a forced distribution forms the foundation of our mixed-methods approach. The quantitative analysis techniques of Q-methodology provided statistical patterns of statement rankings that we applied to thematic analysis of the ethnographic interviews. Thus our approach enhances qualitative data analysis with powerful statistical techniques for the purposes of creating a rich, holistic picture of polarizing and consensus health and technology attitudes.

We leveraged Q-methodology specifically for personal health technology design in HCI in the following three ways: (1) to discover how patients understand, value, and relate concepts from health sciences theories; (2) to provide structure for qualitative data analysis that enhances subjective coding of unstructured data with statistically significant patterns of polarizing and consensus attitudes; and (3) to provide opportunity for participants to take control and actively define and prioritize the health and technology values that are most significant to them.

We demonstrate the use of our mixed-methods approach in an ethnographic study of attitudes toward self-management of chronic diseases. In this study, we conducted 18 in-home interviews using Q-methodology: 9 with older adults with diabetes, and 9 with mothers of children with asthma. Using Q-methodology to structure the data collection and analysis of interviews, we observed and quantified how people prioritize competing values related to accountability, information, and technology for personal health care. We also identified and probed apparent contradictions in beliefs that can influence health behaviors and technology adoption. We demonstrate how these insights are unique to our mixed-methods approach, and how they are applicable to technology design for personal health care.

BACKGROUND TO Q-METHODOLOGY

Q-methodology uses a set of statements about a topic to elicit people's points of view [21,22]. The purpose of Q is to understand what attitudes people feel most strongly about. Participants rank the statements in a forced distribution from Most Disagree to Most Agree, with statements of relative insignificance in the middle. This ranking procedure is captured in a table, called a "forced distribution" because participants are forced to place the statements in a normally distributed pattern around a zero-point, with a standard deviation (Figure 1). The advantage of the forced distribution is that each person's point of view can be compared using the powerful statistical technique of factor analysis to reveal patterns of subjective opinion.

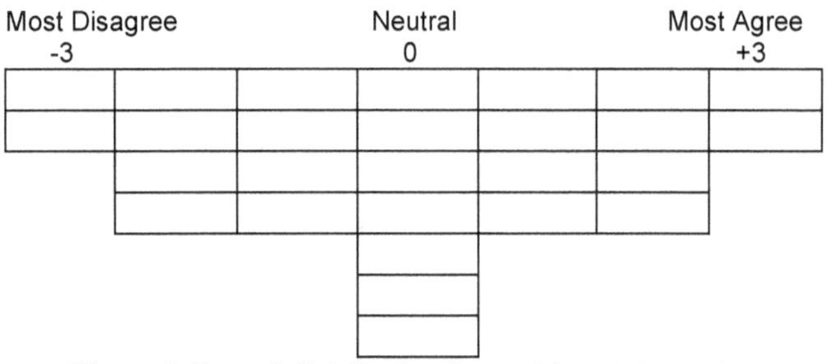

Figure 1. Forced distribution for ranking statements.

Factor analysis is a statistical technique for reducing large amounts of data by clustering similar data and extracting a small number of unique clusters that explain most of the variance, or differences, in the data. Thus, factor analysis can be used to objectively discover patterns in large data sets and to focus attention on the most statistically significant comparisons and contrasts in the data. Q-methodology is unique in its application of factor analysis to the discovery of patterns in subjectivity.

In Q-methodology studies, a factor is a cluster of participants who have ranked statements in a similar pattern, and therefore share a common point of view on a topic. Each cluster has a set of "distinguishing statements" that characterizes the unique point of view it represents. The distinguishing statements for each cluster are statistically significant, meaning that participants ranked those statements much higher or lower than participants in other clusters, at a minimum threshold of $p<0.05$. Thus Q-methodology affords the use of quantitative analysis techniques to reveal differences in subjective perspectives. Q-methodology is not an inferential statistical technique. Rather, it is similar to qualitative techniques because it works with a small-sample size ($n<50$), and has limited generalizability. The clusters that emerge from factor analysis reveal statistically significant variations in patterns among statements, not patterns among populations of people. Q-methodology provides many of the same advantages of qualitative methods, such as discovering themes in rich subjective data. However, it accomplishes this theme detection by leveraging the objective pattern identification afforded by quantitative analysis.

Q-methodology Adapted for Health Technology Design

Our mixed-methods approach to using Q-methodology with ethnographic interviews introduces two enhancements of traditional Q technique: (1) a health-sciences theoretical framework for structuring Q data collection, and (2) an application of Q factor analysis to coding interview data.

First, to enhance Q data collection for health technology design, we created a health-sciences theoretical framework to guide selection and creation of the statement set. We analyzed concepts from self-care literature to find high-level categories (e.g. accountability) that grouped similar concepts. We focused on concepts informed by grounded theory analyses of patients living with chronic illness [14], and on validated constructs from the Patient Assessment of Chronic Illness Care [7], and the Patient Activation Measure [9]. We created a range of statements for each high-level category to capture the theoretical polarity of self-care attitudes, e.g., high to low accountability. Our previous research with these participants [5,10] helped us to create relevant, naturalistic statements using participants' words. The theoretical framework helped us to ensure that we sampled a representative and comprehensive set of statements—the two cornerstones of validity in Q [22]. Moreover, the intersecting categories in the framework helped us to gain a greater understanding of trade-offs in how patients prioritize self-care and technology in everyday life (see Table 2). We describe the framework in more detail below.

Second, to enhance the analysis of interview data with significant differences in health perspectives, we applied the distinguishing statements discovered in the Q statistical analysis to the coding of interview data. Statements such as "I want to be educated about my health," that distinguished the unique attitude of a cluster of participants, were linked with corresponding utterances in those participants' interview transcripts that confirmed or contradicted this point of view. This novel data analysis technique allowed us to observe nuances in participants' perspectives and to understand their most polarizing opinions in the context of other competing values and beliefs. We illustrate this technique and its advantages below.

RELATED WORK

Q-methodology Studies in HCI

An adaptation of Q-methodology for HCI, called HCI-Q [17], was tailored for the specific purpose of empowering stakeholders to critically reflect on designers' assumptions about desirable and undesirable features of a design. The topic of the statements for HCI-Q studies is the designer's *a priori* hypotheses about the implications and uses of a design idea that are likely to be significant to stakeholders. HCI-Q is well-suited to design ideation with stakeholders, and supports designers in being transparent about their biases. Furthermore, it reveals the features of a design that are most controversial among stakeholders and provides practical insights for what to design and for whom. However, HCI-Q relies on concrete design ideation to create statements for ranking, and focuses on gathering attitudes toward design features, rather than attitudes toward behaviors and beliefs that may influence technology adoption and use. Our approach to using Q-methodology is different from HCI-Q in that we used a structured theoretical framework, informed by theories of chronic illness and the Technology Adoption Model [3], to create a set of statements specifically tailored to revealing insights for designing health technologies. We also differentiated our situated ethnographic approach from the online HCI-Q approach by using a set of paper cards that participants sorted and ranked on their kitchen tables during in-home interviews.

Q-methodology Studies in Health Sciences

Q-methodology has been used in health sciences research to investigate patient perspectives of a variety of health topics, including chronic pain [18], cancer-related fatigue [13], medication adherence [2], weight [6], and symptoms of acute myocardial infarction [19]. These studies feature the traditional data collection procedure of Q-methodology, including the common practice of conducting short interviews or surveys *after* participants rank-order subjective statements in a forced distribution. In the traditional approach, interviewers use the ranked data to probe further into statements that the participant ranked highly. For example, after the ranking procedure, Bullington et al [2] instructed participants: "In a sentence or two, describe why you selected the two items that are scored 'most like my feelings.'" This structured qualitative data is used to interpret why participants felt strongly about particular statements. We pursue an alternative mixed-methods approach that significantly deepens the role of qualitative data collection for the purposes of understanding strong attitudes toward health self-management. We used the standard Q data collection procedure, but we conducted semi-structured interviews *before* participants rank-ordered the statements. Our approach enables researchers to understand participant's significant opinions in the context of their broader health goals and experiences.

Moreover, our mixed-methods approach uses the quantitative data from Q-methodology to help interpret the *qualitative* data. This new approach to qualitative data analysis offers the advantages of a structured coding scheme derived from statistical patterns of polarizing and consensus opinions. These patterns, which were captured by the Q-methodology, then provide valuable insight about how participants make tradeoffs among their health and technology values. Not only is this approach to qualitative coding efficient, it also builds a rich and nuanced picture of participant experiences based on the values that they asserted to be most significant.

Design Studies of Health Self-Management

Researchers in HCI have explored a range of patient perspectives to inform technology designs that empower patients to take control of their chronic illness. Their studies have yielded valuable insights for technology designers to support people with a chronic illness. For example, in a study of people with cancer, Klasnja et. al. [12] found that patients need health information management support for easy capture of a range of informal information, for integration among that data, and for linking the data to upcoming events. In another example, Maitland et al [15] used ethnographic interviews and inductive analysis to discover tensions and competing values that influenced the heath-related behaviors of cardiac rehabilitation patients. For people with diabetes, Mamykina et. al. [16] used interviews, observations, and a cognitive probe to discover that people need help in understanding the connection between their everyday activities and blood sugar values. However, the methods used in those studies do not help us understand the relative value or priorities that patients place among the discovered technology needs, attitudes, and beliefs and the patient's health goals or attitudes.

In studies of health self-management, like those listed above, researchers commonly apply qualitative methods, such as interviews and focus groups, to explore stakeholders' perspectives of technologies and health. Unstructured data is collected and then analyzed using an inductive approach, allowing themes to emerge through a reflexive coding process. In our study, we demonstrate that one of the advantages of applying Q-methodology during ethnographic interviews is that researchers can directly

	Technology Statements	Self-Management Statements
Accountability The degree to which an individual feels accountable for his or her health care. <u>Covers concepts</u>: Lorig et al [13]: Medical and behavioral management Hibbard et al [9]: Believes active patient role important	1. I'll forget to do a health task unless someone checks in with me. 2. I'm more likely to follow through on paper mail reminders than other types of reminders. 3. I'm more likely to take action when I get a phone call. 4. My cell phone is essential for managing my health.	5. I only follow doctor's orders if I believe they will help. 6. I'm the one who is responsible for taking care of my health. 7. I should be asked to repeat health instructions to make sure I understand them. 8. I need follow-up from my doctor to stay on track with my health. 9. I rely on my doctor to take responsibility for my care.
Resource Use The degree to which an individual uses resources (tools and information) to manage his or her health. <u>Covers concepts</u>: Lorig et al [13]: Resource utilization Hibbard et al [9]: Confidence and knowledge to take action	10. I put things where I can see them if I need to remember a health task. 11. I mostly keep track of health tasks in my head. 12. Paper calendars are useful for keeping track of my health. 13. Online calendars are the best way for me to keep track of my health. 14. I like using electronic communication with my doctor.	15. I'm an expert in my health care. 16. I want to be educated about my health. 17. I want to know the science behind health advice. 18. I want to know why I need a health test or procedure.
Performance Expectancy The degree to which an individual believes that using a tool or information will help him or her to improve health. <u>Covers concepts:</u> Lorig et al [13]: Problem solving, self-efficacy, emotional management Glasgow et al [7]: Patient activation Davis [4]: Perceived usefulness of tools for attaining goals.	19. I would feel more in control of my health if I had better reminders. 20. I'll get better at managing my health with a better calendar system. 21. My health will improve if I get better at mobile technology. 22. I will feel more positive about my health if I have more online social support. 23. Electronic reminders will reduce the stress of managing my health.	24. The more information I have about my health, the better. 25. My health will improve if my friends and/or family support my health goals. 26. My health will improve if I set health goals with my doctor. 27. I'll make better health decisions if follow-up notices are easier to understand.

Figure 2. Theoretical framework with statements for eliciting participant's opinions during the Q-methodology task.

observe participants negotiate and weigh the tradeoffs of competing values. Additionally, researchers can use a *deductive* analytic approach to categorize themes and surface competing and conflicting viewpoints. By affording a structured way to capture participants' views of health, our mixed-methods approach can enrich qualitative data collection and analysis procedures with statistical patterns of significant differences in patient perspectives.

Understanding patients' priorities is important for designers and developers who will need to make resource-allocation and design decisions about which opinions are most important to support. We contribute an approach that supports designers in making those choices by capturing the ways in which participants relate health and technology attitudes in the context of chronic disease self-management.

THEORETICAL FRAMEWORK

The health-sciences theoretical framework, with statements arranged in a grid of intersecting categories (see Figure 2), was designed to highlight attitudes and tensions that can influence technology adoption and provide insights for design. To observe how attitudes toward accountability and resource use interact with the acceptance and use of technology for health self-management, we used the concept of performance expectancy from the Technology Adoption Model (TAM) [3] to reveal attitudes toward future technology adoption to support heath goals.

The concepts of accountability, resource use, and performance expectancy are inherently entwined in the management of chronic conditions. Based on our synthesis of self-management theories [1,4,7,8,9,14], we define accountability as the degree to which an individual feels accountable for his or her health care; resource use as the degree to which an individual uses resources (tools and information) to manage his or her health; and performance expectancy as the degree to which an individual believes that using a tool or information will help him or her to improve health outcomes. We used these three concepts to frame the statements for the Q-methodology data collection procedure and to frame our interpretation of results. Figure 2 shows how we categorized the statements for the Q-methodology procedure into six intersecting categories of the framework. Below, we describe the use of the framework and mixed-methods approach in the context of an ethnographic study of attitudes toward self-management of chronic diseases.

METHOD

Participants

We recruited nine older adults with Type 2 diabetes, and nine mothers of children with asthma. Older adults (5 male) had a median age of 82 years old (μ=79.89), and mothers had a median age of 38 years old (μ=38.67). Participants were from diverse races and educational backgrounds (see Table 2). This maximum variation sampling strategy had two purposes: (1) to identify challenges and opportunities for designing technologies that are meaningful to a broad spectrum of users, and (2) to highlight edge cases that may usefully bound the design space of technologies for self-management of chronic illnesses.

Apparatus and Procedure

We travelled around Washington State to people's homes in urban and rural settings, and sat at their kitchen tables to conduct the interview and Q-methodology procedure. Each session lasted 45-75 minutes in length, and was structured as follows: (1) a semi-structured interview to understand participants' personal health goals and preferences for information; (2) an artifact discussion about a health task list to probe whether nationally recommended health care activities for diabetes and asthma management matched with their most significant health concerns and priorities; and (3) facilitation of the Q-methodology procedure.

We began with a series of semi-structured questions prior to the Q procedure to help the participants reflect on their health goals. This gave participants time to think about their health activities and reduced the likelihood that the structured statements in Q would solely frame the conversation. This strategy also gave the interviewer an opportunity to follow-up on the Q ranking procedure with questions that incorporated both participant comments at the beginning of their interview and during their sorting of statements.

For the Q procedure, we gave participants 27 statements printed in large font (size 16) on laminated cards. We chose to be conservative with the number of statements in our theoretical framework to avoid fatiguing participants, half of whom were over 70 years old, and 2 had low literacy and low vision. This approach is validated by Watts & Stenner [22] who demonstrate a robust analysis derived from a 25-item Q-set. In accordance with standard Q protocol, we instructed participants to read and sort the statements about health and technology into three piles: agree, disagree, and neutral.

Then, we instructed participants to place statements from their disagree pile into the nine spaces available in the table for disagreeable statements, along a spectrum from Most Disagree (-3) to Disagree (-1). They then repeated this procedure for their agree pile (+3 to +1), and iterated the process until they were satisfied with the result. Participants moved statements in and out of the neutral pile (0) as necessary to normally distribute the statements in the table. After the participants had ranked all statements, we took a picture to capture their data (Figure 3). Mothers found that their self-care attitudes differed from those when caring for their child's health, so we directed them to do 2 sorts—one for themselves (the one used in this paper) and for their child. Many participants commented on the method, and we have included those comments in our discussion.

Analysis

Data analysis began with factor analysis of the Q-methodology data. Pictures of each participant's arrangement of statements were transcribed and entered into PQMethod software, a common statistical package for analyzing Q data [20]. Factors, which are clusters of similar perspectives, were identified using Principal Components Analysis, and rotated using the varimax method [11]. Then, we used the distinguishing statements (Table 1) for each cluster to code the interview transcripts. Each distinguishing statement was associated with three sub-codes: "Q" for quotes from the Q procedure directly related to the statement; "Complement" for quotes from the interview that complimented the sentiment of the statement; and "Conflict" for quotes that conflicted with the sentiment of the statement. We grouped and coded transcripts by cluster, for example, distinguishing statements for the first cluster (called "Attitude 1") were used to code transcripts for participants grouped in that cluster.

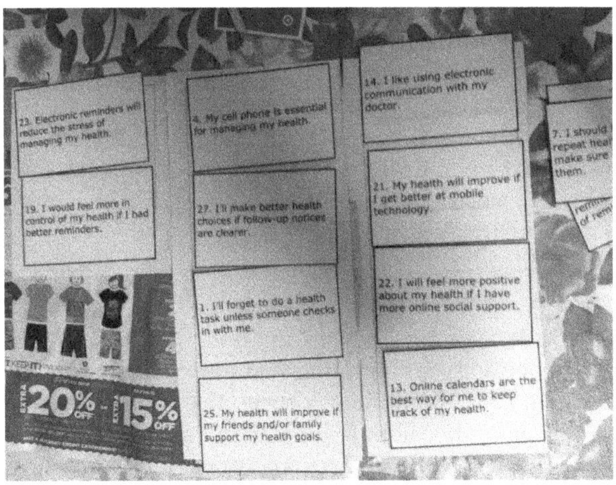

Figure 3. D4's distribution of disagreeable statements.

Attitude Cluster	Statement	Ranking (-3 - +3)
Attitude 1	I want to be educated about my health.	+3
	I want to know the science behind health advice.	+2
	I'll forget to do a health task unless someone checks in with me.	-2
	I'm more likely to follow through on paper mail reminders than other types of reminders.	-3
Attitude 2	My health will improve if I set health goals with my doctor.	+3
	I need follow-up from my doctor to stay on track with my health.	+3
	I mostly keep track of health tasks in my head.	-3
Attitude 3	I mostly keep track of health tasks in my head.	+3
	Electronic reminders will reduce the stress of managing my health.	-3
Attitude 4	I want to know why I need a health test or procedure.	+3
	My cell phone is essential for managing my health.	+2
	I rely on my doctor to take responsibility for my care.	-3

Table 1. Distinguishing statements used for coding.

FINDINGS

We used the factor analysis of the Q methodology to identify four clusters that represent four different attitudes toward health and technology for self-management of chronic illness. The four attitude clusters accounted for 68% of the variance in the data. Attitudes 1 and 4 were shared by members from both age cohorts suggesting that, for our sample of participants, health attitudes were not necessarily age or disease specific. Attitudes 2 and 3 were each represented by two members of the older cohort whose perspectives differed significantly from each other. Health perspectives represented by these four unique attitudes do not appear to differ based on characteristics such as education level, gender, or race, as each cluster has a diverse demographic profile (See Table). Two participants were confounded (D8 and D5) meaning that they had too much in common with every cluster, rather than correlating highly with one cluster. These participants were therefore excluded from further analysis because their perspectives were ambiguous.

Attitude 1: "It's my decision, my body"

The participants in this cluster had a strong preference for education (+3), scientific evidence (+2), information (+2), and taking responsibility (+3). They agreed that online calendars (+1) and electronic communication with providers (+2) are important for managing their health. Despite having a dislike of paper calendars (-1) and paper mail reminders (-3), they disagreed that cell phones (-2) or better use of mobile technology (-3) are related to health outcomes, and do not necessarily expect that electronic reminders will reduce the stress of managing health (0).

Attitude	ID	Age	Gender	Race	Education
1	A3*	36	F	Black	HS
1	A9	36	F	White	4YR
1	A1	38	F	White	4 YR
1	A7	46	F	Hispanic	HS
1	D3	85	F	Black	+4YR
1	D9	88	F	White	Some HS
2	D1	69	F	Hispanic	+4YR
2	D2	82	F	Black	+4YR
3	D6	71	M	White	HS
3	D4	88	M	White	Some HS
4	A5[t]	31	F	Black	Some College
4	A2	38	F	Black	+4YR
4	A6	40	F	White	4YR
4	A4	41	F	White	+4YR
4	A8	42	F	Black	+4YR
4	D7	73	M	White	HS
X	D5	89	M	Asian	+4YR
X	D8	74	M	White	Some College

Table 2. Participants grouped by attitude. X=confounded; *=low vision; [t]=low literacy.

Participants explicitly voiced relationships between significant concepts, especially between health information, education, and responsibility. For example, D9 said of the importance of being educated about her health: *"if I went in and the doctor's over here, deciding everything and not telling me anything, it's not doing me a bit of good. I've got to know what's going on and why my body is acting that way. I guess that's the same as number 6, 'I'm responsible for taking care of it.'"* A3 agreed, "Yeah, because I feel like as individuals we are responsible for ourselves, so being educated and knowing options—." A7 articulated the relationship between responsibility and resource use in a similar way to A3, *"If there's a decision to be made, I feel ultimately it's my decision, my body, right? I like to know the science behind what the options are."*

This cluster is characterized by a strong sense of responsibility and resource use for health self-care. However, participants that defined this factor felt uncertain about whether they are experts in their health care (0). The qualitative data helped us to dig deeper into this apparent contradiction. A9 explained that she gets the doctor's opinion after she gathers health information from multiple sources: "*The Internet, the nurse hotline, my mother-in-law. Those will probably be my first three... You can put them together and see what feels right, kind of thing...then you get into the doctor, and he puts all of it together even better".*

A1's comment about her preference for speaking with a nurse, also sheds light on the difference between the role of patient, doctor, and technology in health self-management: *"I'm not big on Dr. Google, I'm much more likely to call the consulting nurse if it's something more urgent. I correctly self-diagnosed my lupus in the early days of the Internet. But that scared me so much with everybody's stories..."* These perspectives helped us to understand that performance expectancy for self-management was not highly related to technology for this cluster.

The interview data also helped to corroborate the surprising finding that, despite being a cluster of participants that is very diverse by traditional demographics, they indeed shared the same preference for health information. For example, a 46-year-old Hispanic female with a high school education (A7) and an 85-year old African American female with more than 4 years of college (D3) shared the practice of comparing different sources of information. A7 said, *"I guess for me, finding different resources that say the same thing helps back what was said, you know, the [doctor's] answer."* In a similar vein, D3 said *"I use just about every source I can. I'll go to friends who have been in the profession that I'm interested in just finding out about, I'll go to friends. I'll go to the Internet. I'll go to my physicians, my providers. I'll go to family. I'll seek it wherever I can."* It is hardly surprising to find that people who value health information are comparing information sources; however, it is surprising evidence that people with less than a high school education share similar attitudes toward health information as people with doctorate degrees. This finding displays the strength of Q for undermining stereotypes and for facilitating universal design approaches that emphasize diversity. It also suggests that there is value in combining participants from different generations who may adopt similar strategies to using health information and technologies to manage their care.

Attitude 2: "I'm assuming my doctor will tell me"

Participants with Attitude 2 felt most strongly that they need follow-up from their doctor to stay on track with their health (+3), and that their health will improve if they set goals with their doctor (+3). Their preference for doctor engagement in their care was reinforced by their strong disagreement with the statement "I'm an expert in my health care" (-3). In contrast to Attitude 1, the two participants who shared Attitude 2 expressed low self-efficacy, for example, during the interview, D1 said: *"I'm not an MD, I don't have any clue. I just try to learn, but I really don't know."*

This attitude appears to have a low sense of responsibility and resource use for their care. However, surprisingly, they did not perceive themselves as reliant on their doctors, as evidenced by their disagreement with the statement "I rely on my doctor to take responsibility for my care" (-1). This finding appeared contradictory, but the interview data helped us to understand nuances in health accountability from the patient perspective. For example, D1 explained how goal-setting helped her to clarify her responsibility: *"I think that's important to know what the expectations are...I know she [the doctor] sets goals, like your A1c needs to be under 8, she says, so when it gets close to 8 I have to start watching it. I watch it anyway, but just be more diligent."* This contradiction between the Q statement and the participant's interview statement demonstrates the value of our mixed-methods approach for discovering how patients prioritize and operationalize core health self-management concepts like accountability.

Similarly, in the interview, D2 explained how having goals set by her doctor is at the core of self-management: *"Whatever the major problem was the doctors can see in the past year, and say... 'why don't we work on X, Y or Z because there's been very little change in that'... That's what to me self-care management should be."* Rather than viewing self-management as a personal responsibility, participants with Attitude 2 perceived it as a partnership with the doctor who is *"watching over us,"* as D1 put it. In the interview, she reinforced this attitude by saying that, when she needs health information, *"I'm assuming my doctor will tell me when I don't have enough."*

People with Attitude 2 made primary use of visual and paper systems like wall calendars and sticky notes to manage their care; however, they had moderate performance expectancy regarding future use of electronic reminders (+1) and calendars (+1). The interviews revealed that both participants in this cluster used email with their providers to stay on track with their health. D2 described how she asks for follow-up from her doctor by email: *"if I have an ailment I don't call for an appointment, I send an email and tell him what it is, how long I've had it, how I feel with it and what steps I have taken for it, and then I'll say 'recommendation?'"* This example illustrates the strong connection between technology use and self-management attitudes for Attitude 2.

Attitude 3: "It's just automatic"

Attitude 3 was characterized by self-reliance and a strong preference to be independent with their care. The participants who shared this attitude preferred to be in control of defining their goals and priorities for health. This was the only cluster that agreed with the statement "I only follow doctor's orders if I believe they will help" (+1), which gives evidence of their strong sense of independence in their care. Their self-reliance did not stem from a belief that they are experts in their health (-2), rather, it was rooted in a desire to manage their chronic disease without compromising a sense of identity. D4 explained in the interview, *"It's just I get up in the morning and do the daily routine. There's no - basically my life has been the same for the last 88 years, I don't really dwell on any - just get up and do my routine and what I normally do, a little slower than I used to and that's about it."*

In contrast to Attitude 2, participants who shared Attitude 3 did not desire follow-up from providers to stay on track (-1), and had personalized strategies and habits for keeping track of their chronic diseases. For example, D4 showed us the paper form that he created to track his blood pressure and glucose *"I'll show you I've got a blood pressure machine and a glucose machine in my office...so that's what I do with getting up in the morning and making a record of and take that in [to the doctor] at the end of the month and start over the following month, do that over again."*

In the interview, D6 shared how he responds to doctor's orders: *"When I need to do something that I can fathom, they seem to get it through to me and it's my choice to ignore it or do something about it, and for the most part I try to get in and take care of it."* He emphasized his sense of self-reliance again in the interview, when asked whether he would speak with his doctor about weight management, *"I guess I would. I don't like it, but I need to, I know that."*

Participants who shared Attitude 3 kept track of health tasks in their heads (+3), and used visual cues (+1) and paper calendars (+3) to remember health tasks. D4 explained in the interview, *"I don't have a computer so they send me out the mail, they'll give me a date when to go for the appointment and mail the results of the blood test."* Their strong sense of responsibility for their health (+2) was characterized by low resource use. They strongly disagreed with relying on cell phones (-3) and electronic reminders (-3) for managing their health. The dislike of technology is not surprising considering the ages of the participants who defined this cluster (71 and 88 years old). However, the 62- and 88-year old participants who defined Attitude 2 had a significantly different point of view, characterized by reliance on health providers. The Q technique is valuable for observing such significant differences in perspectives for the purposes of understanding the very different roles that technology might play in the health self-management of elder patients.

Attitude 4: "When should I be worried?"

This cluster had a strong sense of responsibility for their care (+3) and had a strong preference for technology such as cell phones (+2) and electronic communication with their doctors (+2). They want to be educated about their health (+2) but, unlike the participants with Attitude 1, they do not have a preference for knowing the science behind health advice (0). Like the people with Attitude1, the people with Attitude 4 had as strong sense of responsibility (+3), but they were not as confident about their self-management.

For example, in contrast to participants with Attitude 1, their need for information and sense of responsibility stemmed from a desire to feel at ease with the care process. A2 explained, *"I want to know...When should I be worried? When is it okay to say that's a fine result? Those things really matter to me."* In the interview she provided a story that reinforced the significance of the need to feel reassured, *"We were getting [daughter's] test in for celiac disease. That just sounds really scary we get a piece of paper that has numbers - that doesn't tell me whether she has it or doesn't have it."* A4 also shared a story to explain why she needs to be informed: *"I don't know that these health care providers have my best interest in mind,"* she continued, *"I had a really bad experience with my dad who was diagnosed really late with cancer and it went for a long time undetected and he was rushed to the emergency room and I know that a lot of that could have been prevented if someone had been at the office with him."* Our mixed-methods approach helped us to identify these narratives underlying the patients' most deeply held beliefs and values.

Other narratives were more positive. For example, in the interview, D7 explained how his doctor helped him to understand the need for his knee surgery: *"when he talked to me about doing that, he went in his office and pulled open a drawer that had a bunch of plastic replacement parts in it and showed me how they were worn differently and whatnot, and how important it was. Yeah, he did a heck of a job."* Individuals who shared this attitude valued information for forming realistic expectations and for building empathetic relationships with providers.

Finally, Attitude 4 was the only cluster characterized by a strong reliance on cell phones for the purposes of scheduling and remembering health tasks. A2 said "*I like ease. It's really easy to communicate electronically because I'm busy, so it helps.*" A6 said, "*My cell phone is essential for managing my life,*" and A4 agreed, "*I do everything on my phone.*" However, in the interviews, participants shared two barriers to using their cell phones for health – one was that keys were too small for typing, and the other was that the health system's mobile application had limited functionality, and was not usable for scheduling. The use of the theoretical framework to structure the Q-methodology data collection procedure helped us to observe that participants sharing Attitude 4 had a strong interaction of high performance expectancy for self-management and technology use. Unlike their highly motivated peers in Attitude 1, participants of Attitude 4 emphasized a strong relationship between mobile technology and personally significant health goals.

DISCUSSION

Our study demonstrates that our mixed-methods approach has several advantages for investigating attitudes toward health and technology in the context of chronic disease management. First, the factor analysis allowed us to find meaningful comparisons and contrasts within an extremely diverse cohort of participants, with ages ranging from 31 to 89, with two different chronic diseases, and with a variety of racial and educational backgrounds. Attitude 1 was a good example of the ways in which factor analysis identified meaningful connections among diverse participants. Their preference for scientific evidence and education was especially surprising given that three of the participants in the Attitude 1 cluster had a high school education or less. Without the objective assessments that the Q-methodology affords, researchers' bias could easily cause us to overlook such strong values and preferences that do not match our preconceived notions.

Second, the factor analysis in Q provided an efficient way to identify a small number of statistically significant and unique attitudes toward health self-management among these patient stakeholders. For example, each cluster was characterized by different values and motivations for both engaging in self-management and using technology to manage chronic illness. The analysis helped to tease apart not only the more obvious differences in motivations—such as the motivation to have shared responsibility with providers in Attitude 2 versus the strong sense of self-reliance in Attitude 3—but also more nuanced perspectives on the role of information in chronic disease management. For example, the participants with Attitude 1 were highly intrinsically motivated by an intellectual desire to be informed about medications, diagnoses, and treatments. They also used a variety of resources to satisfy their desire to learn about options for their health. In contrast, the participants with Attitude 4 were motivated by an emotional desire to feel comfortable with the care plan. They sought transparency about realistic expectations and empathy for the anxiety experienced when receiving test results.

Finally, our use of a theoretical framework—combining theories for self-management of chronic illnesses and technology adoption—helped us to understand how traditional concepts of self-management in chronic illness are intertwined with use and perceptions of technologies. For example, the self-reliance evident in Attitude 3 can be interpreted as self-reliance *of necessity* because those participants also tended to be relatively isolated from electronic communication and information. In contrast, the significance of communication technology for self-management in participants with Attitude 4 can be understood in light of their desire to be reassured; the communication technology serves to enhance an empathetic relationship with providers. For Attitude 2, the expectation of improved health performance with new technologies makes sense when understood in relation to their need for follow-up and structured guidance from their providers. Finally, the high resource use yet low salience of technology found in participants with Attitude 1 can be reconciled in light of their emphasis on the in-clinic educational dimension of the doctor-provider relationship.

By having participants weigh the tradeoffs of competing values regarding their health and their use of technology for self-care, our approach provides implications for health technology design. The most extreme-ranked statements (i.e. ranked -3 or +3) and related qualitative data provide strong rationales for the type and range of designs during prototyping. For example, Attitudes 2 and 4 helped us to understand that, rather than encourage independence from health providers, technologies could be most beneficially designed to *enhance* the relationship between providers and patients by supporting follow-up communication that is actionable and empathetic. Attitudes 1 and 2 suggest that technologies for health self-management, such as for tracking health indicators, need to support both patient and provider-directed goal-setting, depending on the patient's motivation for taking responsibility for their health. Attitude 3 suggests that technology are desirable only when memory or routines become unreliable aids, such as when people are on vacation or during significant changes in medications—scenarios in which patients are situationally impaired.

Strengths and Weaknesses of the Approach

Q-methodology provides advantages over pure qualitative research, but it comes with limitations as well. One limitation is that some participants had a difficult time sorting the statements because they either agreed or disagreed with *most* of the statements in the initial sorting phase. For example, D2 had an overwhelming number of statements in her disagree pile to choose from. She asked, "So you want *two* here [in Most Disagree]? I could put *all* of these in those." Another limitation is that the theoretical framework is designed for investigating subjective perspectives of chronic disease self-management, and might not be applicable to technology design studies focused on supporting wellness.

Our approach of combining Q-methodology with interviews provided several advantages over other approaches to health technology design. First, the playfulness of Q-methodology resonated with participants and changed the dynamic of the interviews by engaging them in an activity. For example, D8 jokingly suggested, "*Should I get the poker chips out?*" Second, the Q-methodology helped participants take control over the direction of the conversation. For example, D6 expressed his authority: "*The first one is easy, 'My cell phone is essential' - I don't believe in that at all. And then 'I'm an expert in my health' is probably the next one I would mostly disagree with.*"

In addition, our inclusion of observations and interviews regarding participants' reflections allowed us to understand their interpretations of each statement, such as when D9 commented on relying on her doctor to take responsibility for her care: "*I guess I'm having trouble, not understanding them [the statements], but the way I **feel about** them. I expect my doctors to take responsibility when I ask him a question - but he's not a super being, all he can do is do what I tell him.*" As another example, at the end of the procedure, A2 commented on the first-person wording of the statements, "*I had to keep [the statements] in perspective, too. It kept saying 'my' - so it's me, not my child's, so my opinions are different.*" We had each mother conduct two sorts – from the perspective of her role in her child's health and her own health – so that we can conduct a future analysis of the differences in perspectives based on different roles in care.

In addition, we used our mixed-methods approach with a diverse set of people. We demonstrate that it is accessible to adult and elderly individuals, including people with low vision, low education level, and low literacy. This flexibility for use with a diverse population is an asset for health-related research that engages a broad spectrum of patients, clinicians, and caregivers. Our work demonstrates that using Q-methodology can help designers to quickly and efficiently identify commonalities and differences that are not based on traditional participant segmentation by age, ability, gender, or disease.

CONCLUSION

In this paper, we introduced a new approach that combines the quantitative advantages of the Q-methodology with the nuanced interpretations afforded by interviews. We see several ways to build upon this work in the future. For example, the identification of the factors using the Q-methodology could be used to develop personas that are grounded in the perspectives of study participants. Personas created with our technique could provide designers with highly opinionated representative users to inform personal health technology design.

We contribute a mixed-methods approach that is uniquely suited to understanding how people weigh competing health values, and how they articulate connections between self-efficacy and performance expectancy for health self-management. These insights lead to understanding design tradeoffs for health technologies based on the values and motivations that govern different strategies for self-care. With our mixed-methods approach, researchers can start from core self-care theories that help structure data collection and analysis, to discover meaningful connections among stakeholders, regardless of age or disease. Our technique can support designers to understand the polarizing and consensus views that influence stakeholders' adoption and use of personal health technologies for chronic disease management.

ACKNOWLEDGMENTS

This work was supported in part by the AHRQ grant (R01 HS 021590). We also thank the iMed research group and the REMIND team at the Group Health Research Institute.

REFERENCES

1. Bandura, A. Self-efficacy: toward a unifying theory of behavioral change. *Psychol Rev. American Psychological Association 84*, 2 (1977), 191–215.
2. Bullington, P., Pawola, L., Walker, R., Valenta, A., Briars, L., and John, E. Identification of medication non-adherence factors in adolescent transplant patients: the patient's viewpoint. *Pediatric Transplantation 11*, 8 (2007), 914–21.
3. Davis, F.D. Perceived Usefulness, Perceived Ease of Use, and User Acceptance of Information Technology. *MIS Quarterly 13*, 3 (1989).
4. Deci, E. and Ryan, R. The support of autonomy and the control of behavior. In E. Higgins and A. Kruglanski, eds., *Motivational Science: Social and Personality Perspectives*. Psychology Press, Philadelphia, PA, 2000, 128–146.
5. Eschler, J., Kendall, L., O'Leary, K., et al. Shared calendars for home health management. *CSCW'15*, (2015).
6. Van Exel, N.J. a, de Graaf, G., and Brouwer, W.B.F. "Everyone dies, so you might as well have fun!" Attitudes of Dutch youths about their health lifestyle. *Social science & medicine 63*, 10 (2006), 2628–39.
7. Glasgow, R.E., Wagner, E.H., Schaefer, J., Mahoney, L.D., Reid, R.J., and Greene, S.M. Development and validation of the Patient Assessment of Chronic Illness Care (PACIC). *Medical care 43*, 5 (2005), 436–44.
8. H, L., Nerenz DR, Steele, D., Taylor, S., and Singer, J. Illness representation and coping with health threats. In Baum A, ed., *Handbook of Psychology and Health.* Lawrence Erlbaum Associates, Killsdale, NJ, 1984, 219–252.
9. Hibbard, J.H., Mahoney, E.R., Stockard, J., and Tusler, M. Development and testing of a short form of the patient activation measure. *Health services research 40*, 6 Pt 1 (2005), 1918–30.
10. Kendall, L., Eschler, J., Lozano, P. et al. Engineering for reliability in at-home chronic disease management. *AMIA'14,* (2014).
11. Kim, J. and Mueller, C.W. *Factor analysis: Statistical methods and practical issues.* Sage, Newbury Park, CA, 1978.
12. Klasnja, P., Hartzler, A.C., Unruh, K.T., and Pratt., W. Blowing in the wind: unanchored patient information work during cancer care. *CHI'10*, (2010), 193–202.
13. Lai, J.-S., Kupst, M.J., Cella, D., Brown, S.R., Peterman, A., and Goldman, S. Using Q-methodology to understand perceived fatigue reported by adolescents with cancer. *Psycho-oncology 16*, 5 (2007), 437–47.
14. Lorig, K.R. and Holman, H. Self-management education: history, definition, outcomes, and mechanisms. *Annals of behavioral medicine : a publication of the Society of Behavioral Medicine 26*, 1 (2003), 1–7.
15. Maitland, J. and Chalmers, M. Self-monitoring, self-awareness, and self-determination in cardiac rehabilitation. *CHI'10*, (2010), 1213–1222.
16. Mamykina, L., Mynatt, E.D., and Kaufman, D.R. Investigating health management practices of individuals with diabetes. *CHI'06*, (2006),927–936.
17. O'Leary, K., Wobbrock, J.O., and Riskin, E.A. Q-methodology As a Research and Design Tool for HCI. *CHI'13,* (2013), 1941–1950.
18. Risdon, A., Eccleston, C., Crombez, G., and McCracken, L. How can we learn to live with pain? A Q-methodological analysis of the diverse understandings of acceptance of chronic pain. *Social science & medicine 56*, 2 (2003), 375–86.
19. Ryan, C.J. and Zerwic, J.J. Knowledge of symptom clusters among adults at risk for acute myocardial infarction. *Nursing research 53*, 6 (2004), 363–9.
20. Schmolk, P. PQMethod Software. 2014. http://schmolck.org/qmethod.
21. Stephenson, W. *The study of behavior: Q-Technique and its methodology.* Univ. of Chicago Press, Chicago, IL., 1953.
22. Watts, S. and Stenner, P. *Doing Q methodological research: Theory, method and interpretation.* Sage, Los Angeles, 2012.

G-raff: An Elevating Tangible Block for Spatial Tabletop Interaction

Chang-Min Kim
CIDR Lab, Dept. of Industrial Design,
KAIST, Yuseong-gu, Deajeon,
305-701, Republic of Korea
peterkim12@kaist.ac.kr

Tek-Jin Nam
CIDR Lab, Dept. of Industrial Design,
KAIST, Yuseong-gu, Deajeon,
305-701, Republic of Korea
tjnam@kaist.ac.kr

Figure 1. G-raff: A Tangible Block Supporting Spatial Interaction in a Tabletop Computing Environment

ABSTRACT
We present an elevating tangible block, G-raff that supports spatial interaction in a tabletop computing environment. The elevating head part of G-raff moves according to the given height and angle data. We adopted two rollable metal tape structures to create large movements with a small volume block. On the head part, a smartphone can be mounted either horizontally or vertically. G-raff becomes a device that can connect a mobile device with a tabletop computer, thus a new spatial representation and control interaction is made. This paper introduces the design details, key features and applications of G-raff. We report on the results of a preliminary user study and discuss future work to improve the elevating device. This work contributes to maximizing the availability of augmented reality space above the tabletop display.

Author Keywords
Tangible interface; spatial interaction; interface devices;

ACM Classification Keywords
H.5.2. User Interfaces: Input devices and strategies

INTRODUCTION
Multi-touch sensing and new display technologies have accelerated the development of the tabletop computing environment. The tabletop computing environment offers collaborative and augmented reality interaction space that can seamlessly integrate digital and real worlds. One of the notable application domains of tabletop computing is for domains using 3D information space, such as architecture, product design and fields using volumetric data. For these domains, tabletop computing often requires additional interface devices as conventional 2D touch is limited in supporting spatial interactions.

Previous research, such as Lumino[1], CapStones and ZebraWidgets[2], Tangible bots[8] and Touch bugs[7] use tangible above the tabletop surfaces to augment 2D interactions. However, they are still limited in supporting full 3D tabletop interactions. Some researchers introduced interaction techniques and devices allowing the use of 3D volumetric information space on tabletops; HATs[6], Tangible 3D tabletops[3], Use your head[9] and Tangible views for information visualization[10]. They proposed an additional handheld display on Tabletops for spatial interaction. However, a handheld device occupies a user's hands and causes fatigue in long term use. Also, it is hard to sense exact 3D position due to the floating condition. Recent work such as Hoverpad[5] and Inform[4] addressed some of the problems by height adjustable interaction devices with self-actuation. However, these systems require cumbersome and expensive equipment which makes them impractical for wide adoption.

We present an elevating tangible interaction device, G-raff, to maximize the potential of 3D information space above the tabletop display. G-raff features a head part to which a mobile display can be attached to make up-and-down movements. It allows a tabletop computer and a smartphone to be complementary to each other and support tangible 3D interaction on the tabletop display. In the following, we introduce G-raff's design details, key interaction features

CHI 2015, April 18 - 23 2015, Seoul, Republic of Korea
Copyright 2015 ACM 978-1-4503-3145-6/15/04...$15.00
http://dx.doi.org/10.1145/2702123.2702444

and applications. We also report on a preliminary user study and discuss implications and further issues for improvement.

G-RAFF

G-raff is a small tangible interface device that supports 3D spatial interaction on tabletop display. Above the Graff's body, an elevating head part can be controlled both actively and passively. Small display devices such as smartphones or tablet computers can be simply attached to the head part horizontally or vertically, and can be linked to and used together with a tabletop computer. With elevation and links between devices, new tabletop user experiences (spatial data navigation, manipulating physical height data) can be made.

Hardware

G-raff is separated into a body and head part. The body part is comprised of control switches, two rollable metal ribbon structures (Figure 2), and a metal pointer in the base that indicates the location and orientation of G-raff. The head part is a representative part; it makes movements according to the data that corresponds to the G-raff's location.

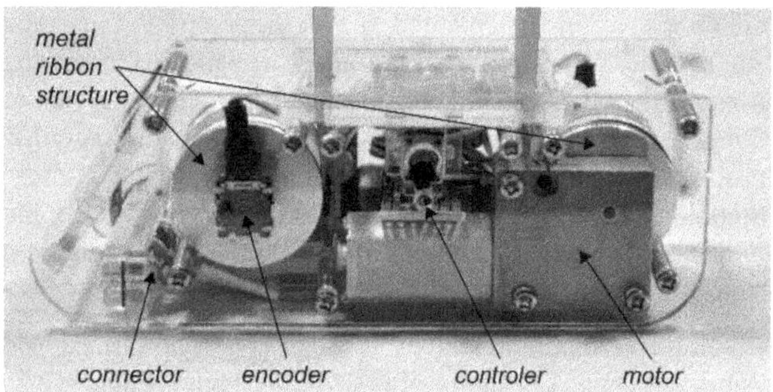

Figure 2. Hardware structure of G-raff

A metal ribbon rolled in a cylinder lengthens or shortens by rotating a motor and creating height/angle movements (Figure 1a). With the help of this structure, G-raff can actively translate digital data into physical movements. Users can directly manipulate the height and angle of G-raff's head part and update the associated data.

G-raff's dimensions are: width 70mm, length 140mm and height 58mm. G-raff can stably elevate its head part to 350mm and can reach up to a maximum of 800mm. G-raff actuates in speeds of 80mm/s and carries a maximum weight of 250g. Elevation is made by two WGM33-2032 motors controlled by a L293D motor driver. To share height and angle data, Arduino and serial communication was used between G-raff and the computer. Location and orientation is recognized by three small thumb-like metal pointers at the bottom, connected to a common ground. With these pointers, G-raff can be used with both capacitive touch displays and IR reflection touch displays.

G-raff is a connecting device for multiple devices (e.g. a tabletop computer with a smartphone). Smartphone displays can be horizontally or vertically linked to G-raff by using two types of head parts. G-raff uses location and height of head display and shows a corresponding portion of 3D spatial data.

User Interface and Software

We added some GUI elements to enhance the usability of linking multiple devices. To accurately map the tabletop location of G-raff's elevated head part, we used pointing cross hairs (Figure 3a). Also, a vector arrow was drawn to express the incline of a surface or spot. The length of arrow depends on the degree of the head angle (Figure 3b).

Figure 3. Pointing cross hairs (a), vector arrow (b)

Software is developed using Processing (computer) and Processing for Android (smartphone). OSC library was used to exchange data between devices. Through real-time device communication, location and height data is shared. Each device uses the shared data and updates the contents in the display. System configuration is shown in (Figure 4).

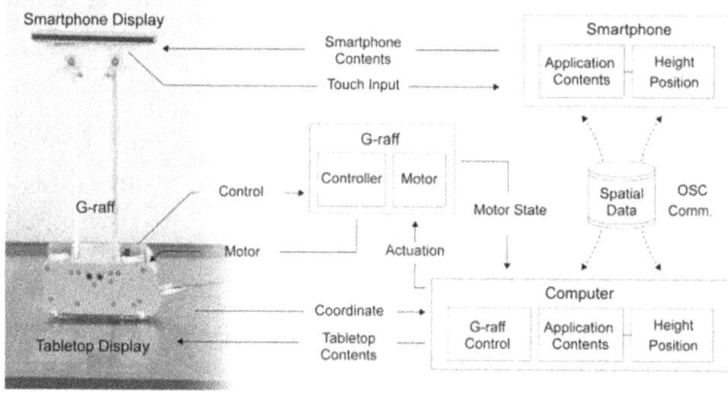

Figure 4. System configuration of G-raff

Key Features and Applications

3D Data Exploration with Actuated Display on Tabletop

G-raff makes interactive 3D data exploration possible. The small actuated display features content according to G-raff's position and orientation on the tabletop surface. The elevating display shows a portion of data in the tabletop screen; and it can show augmented information on the elevating display. Users can search through buildings and floors by controlling height and position (Figure 5.). The head part can be controlled via the smartphone screen with touch inputs or via the controller on the body part. Also, for 3D models, height position and angle can be substituted for the camera's view coordinates and the model can be freely observed from an arbitrary plane (Figure 1.d).

Figure 5. Spatial data mapped over tabletop display

Tangible Representation of Digital Contents in 3D Space

The third dimension (z-axis) data can be physically represented by both the screen displayed data itself and the height of G-raff's head part. For 3D bar chart navigation, the z-value can be expressed as the height of G-raff. Building height can be physically shown in a town planning application.

The head part can be tilted so it is possible to show the tangent plane in a certain position. While exploring 3D mesh data, curvature of a certain point can be represented by the angle of the head part and vector arrow in the head display (Figure 3.b). Also, it is possible to express other types of information such as air flow in a 3D position through head movement (Figure 6).

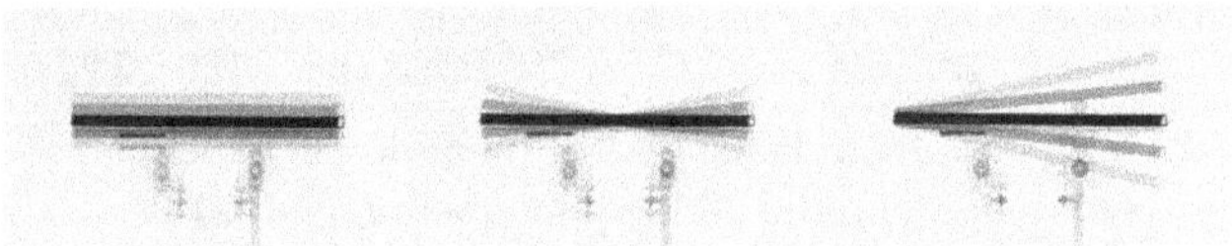

Figure 6. Creating surface motion with G-raff

Direct 3D Manipulation and Connected Interaction with Tabletop

G-raff allows users to directly create or control the data in the 3D space. 3D bar charts can be edited by controlling z-values. Touch and slide down interface can be used for controlling the height. When the z-value is changed on either the tabletop or the smartphone, the physical height is also changed. Users can directly leave annotation or draw a new sketch in an arbitrary 3D plane. Localized zoom can available when independent view control is necessary.

G-raff provides a new type of interaction when two displays are connectively used. In the case of the copy and paste functions, G-raff physically indicates the copy and paste by small up down movements. When graphical data of the tabletop display is copied, the buffered data can be shown on the mobile display. When necessary, the data can be directly edited in the middle of the copy and paste process (Figure 7).

Figure 7. Contents editing during copy and paste

PRELIMINARY USER STUDY

A preliminary user study was conducted to explore G-raff's user experience issues for developed applications and to collect feedback on how to improve the device. Six college students participated in the study. They all had experience with touch based tabletop or tablet computers. Google Nexus 5 was used as the smartphone and Wacom CINTIQ 24HD as the tabletop display. In the first practice session, participants were introduced to the basic interactions of G-raff. In the main session, the participants used the site navigation, 3D graph and 3D model navigation applications. They were asked to find certain content in 3D information space and to leave annotation on a certain building floor. Another task was to directly manipulate graph data. After the main session, they were interviewed on the usability, satisfaction and limitations of G-raff compared to conventional 2D touch interactions.

Understanding the system and interface of G-raff took a very short time. Participants easily recognized that the height of the smartphone display represents the data above the tabletop display. Also, learning how to use G-raff did not take much time. P1 said "I could use the device due to the similarity between G-raff and a conventional mouse."

Participants claimed that the physical movement of G-raff yielded a fun and novel effect. Given tasks were much more engaging with G-raff than with 2D touch interaction. Features such as exploring above the tabletop display and creating a data in a new plane were highly evaluated. Participants liked height (z-axis) data being expressed in the real world, not by not by perspective drawings over a display. P2 claimed, "Representing and authoring content over spaces is the unique experience obtained from the device."

Several limitations of the device were also found. Most notable was the size and the not fast enough elevating speed. P3 said, "G-raff requires a large moving lines and actions. Also before reaching the height, there are delays." There were opinions about making the tabletop display bigger or G-raff smaller. P6 said, "Size of G-raff is quite bigger than a conventional mouse." Some of the participants pointed out G-raff's limited 3D interaction. P4 said, "It's more like 3D plane navigation rather than 3D navigation." P5 said "Unlike expectation, what I learn is more dependent on the GUIs on the screen, less from the height. I think scenario with angle is more compelling."

DISCUSSION AND FUTURE WORK

Based on G-raff's design and the user study, we identified several issues that need to be resolved before G-raff can support rich tabletop spatial interaction.

Connected use of multiple devices

Participants in the user study easily understood and preferred the connected use of the two displays. However, the height difference and bezel of the smartphone hinders visual connectivity. To indicate and guide the connected usage, we used GUI elements such as a cross hair cursor and an up-vector. It may be necessary to investigate other UI and hardware aids for the integrated use between tabletop and smartphone. Our prototype used a 24 inch tabletop and a 5.5 inch smartphone display. It may be necessary to test screen combinations and find optimal combination for various applications and contexts. In those contexts, it is necessary to investigate the physical and functional requirements, and design guidelines for better tabletop spatial interaction.

Stability of the Elevating Head
One major challenge in the design and the user study was to provide stable, accurate and fast vertical movement of the head part. The metal ribbon structure is compact and enables a large degree of height change. The drawback is the stability. Depending on the weight of the display, the structural stability can change. The current prototype often experiences swinging and inaccuracy in a high position. Power supply and the position detection with the encoder influence the movement too. Compared with other elevating structures (e.g. antenna, motorized potentiometer structure), optimal movement speed and structure should be refined. Making the device wireless also needs to be considered.

Seamless interaction model change
G-raff allows smartphones to be mounted on its head part to be used for both representation and control. Often it is necessary to change the interface modes. Intuitive ways of natural mode change should be considered. Currently the height of the head can be controlled by buttons and the touch interface on the smartphone. The dial and the touch input are used for angle change. One of the key features of tangible interface is seamless coupling of representation and control. To maximize the TTI benefit, further exploration is necessary in physical and software interfaces for the mode change.

Other Tabletop 3D Applications by G-raff
G-raff provides benefits of spatial interaction on tabletop displays. However, even in that situation, multi-touch is often more effective. It is necessary to further explore specific applications and contexts in which G-raff can be most beneficial. One useful context for tabletop computing is multi-user collaboration. Multiple G-raffs can effectively support such collaborative tasks as navigation or a co-located multi-user game. G-raff can be easily extended to a rich multi-user situation without adding extra equipment. Other tabletop applications with 3D information can get benefit from G-raff interaction. In such contexts as building plan, space simulation and edutainment application in a museum, G-raff can provide an intuitive and engaging user experience. Practical application developments for real context and structured evaluation of G-raff's impacts on people's experience will be covered in future work.

CONCLUSION
In this paper, we presented a tangible block providing a new user experience in a tabletop computing environment, G-raff, a compact tangible interaction device with a height-controlling feature. G-raff can be a new type of active interface device for the tabletop computing environment that efficiently integrates three-dimensional information. We expect G-raff to be applied in various contexts, including educational software, navigation systems and data visualization in tabletop computing environments.

ACKNOWLEDGMENTS
This paper is based on a research which has been conducted as part of the KAIST-funded K-Valley RED&B Project for 2014, and by ICT R&D program of MSIP/IITP [2014. 10041313, UX-oriented Mobile SW Platform]

REFERENCES

1. Baudisch, P., Becker, T., & Rudeck, F. Lumino: tangible blocks for tabletop computers based on glass fiber bundles. In *Proc. CHI 10'* ACM Press (pp. 1165-1174).
2. Chan, L., Müller, S., Roudaut, A., & Baudisch, P. CapStones and ZebraWidgets: sensing stacks of building blocks, dials and sliders on capacitive touch screens. In *Proc. CHI 12'* ACM Press (pp. 2189-2192).
3. Dalsgaard, P., & Halskov, K. Tangible 3D tabletops: combining tangible tabletop interaction and 3D projection. In *Proc. CHI 12'* ACM Press (pp. 109-118).
4. Follmer, S., Leithinger, D., Olwal, A., Hogge, A., & Ishii, H. inFORM: dynamic physical affordances and constraints through shape and object actuation. In *Proc. UIST 13'* ACM Press (pp. 417-426).
5. Julian, S., Sebastian, B., Christian, W., Florian, S., Fabian, S., Steffen, H., ... Enrico, R. Hover Pad: interacting with autonomous and self-actuated displays in space. In *Proc. UIST 14'* ACM Press (pp.139-147).
6. Mi, H., & Sugimoto, M. HATs: interact using height-adjustable tangibles in tabletop interfaces. In *Proc. ITS 11'* ACM Press (pp. 71-74).
7. Nowacka, D., Ladha, K., Hammerla, N. Y., Jackson, D., Ladha, C., Rukzio, E., & Olivier, P. Touchbugs: Actuated tangibles on multi-touch tables. In *Proc. CHI 10'* ACM Press (pp. 759-762).
8. Pedersen, E. W., & Hornbæk, K. Tangible bots: interaction with active tangibles in tabletop interfaces. In *Proc. CHI 11'* ACM Press (pp. 2975-2984).
9. Spindler, M., Buschel, W., and Dachselt, R. Use your head: tangible windows for 3D information spaces in a tabletop environment. In *Proc. ITS 12'* ACM Press (pp. 245-254).
10. Spindler, M., Tominski, C., Schumann, H., & Dachselt, R. Tangible views for information visualization. In *Proc. ITS 10'* ACM Press (pp. 157-166).

Modeling Distant Pointing for Compensating Systematic Displacements

Sven Mayer, Katrin Wolf, Stefan Schneegass, Niels Henze
VIS, University of Stuttgart
Stuttgart, Germany
{firstname.lastname}@vis.uni-stuttgart.de

ABSTRACT

Distant pointing at objects and persons is a highly expressive gesture that is widely used in human communication. Pointing is also used to control a range of interactive systems. For determining where a user is pointing at, different ray casting methods have been proposed. In this paper we assess how accurately humans point over distance and how to improve it. Participants pointed at projected targets on a wall display from 2m and 3m while standing and sitting. Testing three common ray casting methods, we found that even with the most accurate one the average error is 61.3cm. We found that all tested ray casting methods are affected by systematic displacements. Therefore, we trained a polynomial to compensate this displacement. We show that using a user-, pose-, and distant-independent quartic polynomial can reduce the average error by 37.3%.

Author Keywords

distant pointing; mid-air gesture;

ACM Classification Keywords

H.5.2. Information Interfaces and Presentation (e.g. HCI): User Interfaces

INTRODUCTION

Human communication is often supported by gestures. Probably the most common gestures is the pointing gesture selecting an object, place, or person. One of the earliest examples of absolute distant pointing is used in Bolt's seminal 'Media Room' [2]. Users could interact with the system through a combination of distant pointing and speech input. A large body of human-computer interaction research further advanced Bolt's work for various tasks and investigated its usability. With the rise of ubiquitous computing, pointing at real world objects is also a topic worth to be investigated, for example, to switch the light on and off through pointing at the light source [7]. Since the introduction of the Wii Remote and the Kinect, absolute distant pointing at virtual objects is also widely used in consumer products.

CHI'15, April 18 - 23, 2015, Seoul, Republic of Korea

ACM 978-1-4503-3145-6/15/04...$15.00
http://dx.doi.org/10.1145/2702123.2702332

Figure 1. The study setup with the motion capture marker shown as white circles.

Work in psychology shows that pointing is such a fundamental activity that it is already developed in early childhood [6]. Already at this age, children begin to express themselves through pointing gestures. Haviland, however, also emphasizes that '*pointing may seem a primeval referential device, it is far from simple: It is complex*' [6, p. 156]. Foley and Held further show that humans do not point at targets with perfect accuracy [5]. Even if a person tries to point straight at a distant target, a ray cast that virtually extends a person's arm or finger does not necessarily hit the center of the target.

Humans' limited accuracy when pointing does not necessarily pose a problem for human communication. Through context and inference humans are excellent in resolving potential ambiguities when the intended target is not clear. Current computing systems, however, lack this understanding of the situation. Targets in graphical user interfaces, for example, are typically dense and require highly accurate input techniques. Therefore, it is crucial to precisely determine where a user intends to point at. While previous work developed interaction techniques to allow distant pointing (e.g., [13]), increasing the accuracy of absolute distant pointing itself has not gained much attention in human-computer interaction research.

In this paper we analyze and improve the accuracy of selecting targets through absolute distant pointing. First, we present a target selection study to determine precise body postures while pointing using a motion capture system. Analyzing the recorded data, we describe the pointing accuracy when using different ray cast approaches. We show that simple ray casting is limited to an average error of 59.7cm when standing 3m in front of the target. Using the collected data we developed a model that compensates systematic displacements to reduce the inaccuracy. We show that the developed model improves users accuracy by 37.3% which corresponds to an average absolute error of 23.7cm. We discuss the implication on current consumer products and close the paper with an outlook on future work.

RELATED WORK

A substantial body of research investigated selection of distant targets. One strand of research focused on the use of relative input devices to steer a cursor (e.g., [3]). In contrast, we are interested in absolute distant pointing as it is not only already used in commercial devices but also in human communication. Another strand of research investigated users' performance with absolute pointing devices that provide visual feedback about the location the user points at. Myers et al., for example, compared users' performance when using laser pointers or similar devices [11]. Vogel and Balakrishnan [13] investigated absolute pointing without a device by steering a cursor that provides feedback. In contrast, we also focus on situations where no visual feedback can be provided.

Distant pointing has been widely addressed in other domains. Kendon [9], for example, provides a general overview about the body posture when a person points. Absolute distant pointing with and without visual feedback has intensively been addressed in psychology and psychophysics. In particular, psychology aims to understand cognitive and physical processes while humans are pointing at distant targets. Foley and Held [5], for example, found that direction of the sighting eye doses appear to have a large in uence on the pointing direction. Psychology focuses on qualitative models that increase our understanding of how humans point but provide no quantitative models compensating systematic errors.

In HCI, previous work on absolute distant pointing without visual feedback mainly focus on casting a ray out of a body posture. Using the direction of the ray the intersection with potential targets can be determined. Argelaguet et al. [1] classify ray cast techniques by the origin of the ray. They distinguish between *hand rooted techniques* and *eye rooted techniques*. Corradini and Cohen describe the most common hand rooted technique as *'passing through the base and the tip of the index nger'* [4]. We will refer to this ray casting approach as index finger ray cast (IFRC). There are commonly two different *eye rooted techniques* used. First, the direction of the eyes [12] which is also known as 'gaze ray cast'. The second technique uses the eyes as root and the tip of the index finger as direction of the ray cast. In this case it is common to use the point between the eyes as eye root point, Kranstedt et al. [10] described this as 'Cyclops eye'. We refer to this technique as eye finger ray cast (EFRC). Nickel et al. [12] further investigated *elbow rooted techniques* by using the ray between the elbow and the hand (forearm ray cast (FRC)). Furthermore, previous work also compared different ray casting approaches and assessed their accuracy showing that the technique needs to be selected depending on the task [8].

Overall, a significant body of work investigated the selection of distant targets. In particular, previous work proposed different ray casting approaches and investigated their accuracy. In contrast, we do not only aim to assess users' accuracy but also improve it by compensating systematic displacement.

METHOD

We conducted a study to accurately determine the body posture while pointing at distant targets using a motion capture system. The aim is to use this data to determine the accuracy of different ray casting approaches, determine systematic displacements, and to develop a model to compensate the displacement. In the study participants pointed at targets projected on a large screen in front of them from different distances and with different body postures.

Design & Task

As we aimed to get a spectrum of body postures while pointing we varied the distance between the participant and the projection screen (2m and 3m). In addition, participants pointed at the targets while sitting and while standing. Participants took part in all four conditions resulting in a 2x2 repeated measures design. The Targets were arranged in a 7x5 (column x row) grid resulting in 35 target positions. We show a red cross at one of these positions minimizing the size of the target to the center of the cross. Participants pointed three times at each target resulting in a total of 420 target selections per participant. We counterbalanced the order of the four conditions using Latin square and randomized the order of target positions. The targets were projected on a 4.5m x 3m large screen (see Figure 1). The spacing of the target grid was 0.7m x 0.6m. Thus, the distance between the leftmost and the rightmost target was 4.2m. To reduce carryover effects from one selection to the next, participants had to come back to a starting posture before pointing at the next target.

Apparatus & Measurements

As apparatus, we used a Windows 7 PC connected to a projector and the marker based motion capture system OptiTrack by NaturalPoint. The tracking system delivers the absolute position of the markers attached to the participant at 30 FPS. We calibrated the system as suggested by the manufacturer resulting in millimeter accuracy. Therefore we used 17 cameras which were positioned in the way that each spot was covered by at least 4 cameras. We equipped each participant with 16 markers (cf., Figure 1) to get a precise description of the participants' posture (marker count and positions: 4 hand, 2 wrist, 2 elbow, 4 head, 2 shoulder, and 2 hip). We implemented a tool in C# to project the targets and to record the tracking data, which recorded all markers at 30 FPS. In addition to recording participants' body posture while pointing, we asked them to fill a NASA Task Load Index (NASA-TLX) after each condition to check for fatigue effects.

Procedure & Participants

We recruited participants with various professions including mechanical engineers and judicial assistants. In total, 12 participants took part in the study (6 female, 6 male). The age of the participant was between 16 and 27 (M = 24.4, SD = 2.7). The body height was between 167 and 194cm (M = 177.6, SD = 9.9). All of them were right handed and none of them had any locomotor coordination problems.

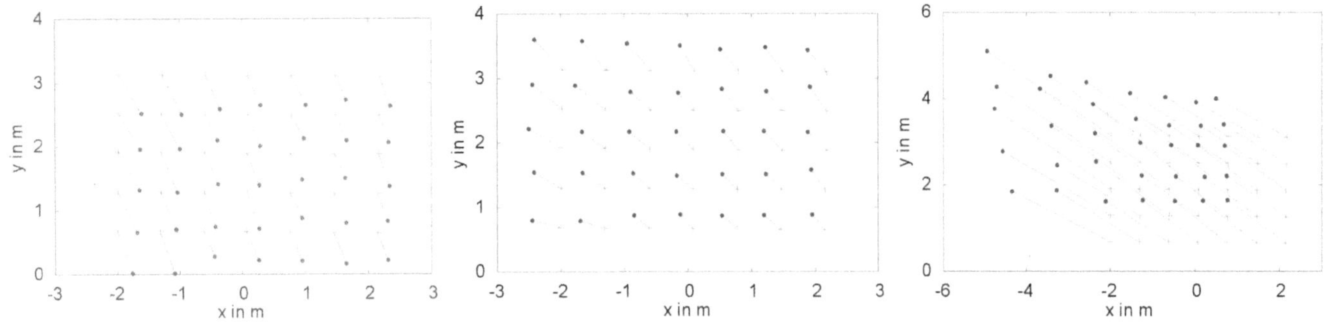

Figure 2. The average intersection point (gray dot) and the targets (red cross) for the ray casting methods EFRC (left), IFRC (center), and FRC (right).

After welcoming a participant we explained the procedure of the study and asked to fill an informed consent as well as a demographic questionnaire. Afterwards, we asked them to stand or sit at a specific position and point at the targets using their dominant hand. To compensate for natural hand tremor they had to hold the pointing position for at least one second. To ensure this time span, the participant had to click with the non-dominant hand on a button of a remote control when they started holding. The target disappeared after one second. We instruct the participant to point as they would naturally do in other situations. We intentionally did not restricted participants pose to record a range of pointing postures. While the experiments we observe it procedure from behind of the participant.

ANALYSIS & MODELING

We first analyzed the NASA-TLX to determine if we have to consider fatigue effects. The average NASA-TLX score was M = 31.0 (SD = 13.2) after the first, M = 29.0 (SD = 15.3) after the second, M = 29.9 (SD = 16.6) after the third, and M = 27.2 (SD = 15.3) after the fourth pass. As a repeated measures one-way ANOVA did not reveal a significant effect ($F_{3,33}$ = 1.740, p = .178), we assume that the effect of participants' fatigue is negligible.

Throughout analysis and modeling, we used the three ray casting methods EFRC, IFRC, and FRC that have been used in previous work. In total we collected 5040 pointing gestures. As a first step we filtered the data to remove outliers using the distance between position where the ray cast intersects with the projection screen and the position of the target. We removed outliers for each ray casting method, condition, and target individually that are more than two standard deviations away from the average. Thereby, we removed 38 trials for EFRC, 12 trials for IFRC, and 39 trials for FRC

Accuracy of Ray Casting

We determined the distance of the point where the ray cast intersects with the projection screen for the three ray casting EFRC, IFRC, and FRC. Table 1 shows the average distances for the three methods and the four conditions. The average distance is 58.1cm for EFRC, 61.4cm for IFRC, and 278.9cm for FRC. For EFRC and IFRC the distance is smaller for 2m than for 3m and also smaller for standing than for sitting. For FRC the average distance between ray cast intersection is more than four times higher than for the other methods and lower for standing than for sitting.

To determine reasons for the large deviations, we further analyzed the displacement for the individual targets. Figure 2 exemplarily shows the average intersection for the standing 3m away condition. For all three methods, the displacement is similar for all targets. The average intersection point is 23.4cm to the right and 49.7cm below the target for EFRC, 34.7cm left and 31.2cm above the target for IFRC, and 200.4cm left and 140.1cm above the target for IFRC.

Model for Improving Pointing Accuracy

As we found that the accuracy of the three ray casting methods is limited, we investigated approaches to compensate systematic displacements. In a first step we transformed each pointing gesture in the two angles α_{lr} (horizontal deviation) and α_{bt} (vertical deviation) to get a distance-invariant measure of the individual trials. Thereby, we can derive the according two correction angles Δ_{lr} and Δ_{bt} that describe the deviation between pointing ray and a ray to the target.

After transformation to angles, we fit a function that removes systematic displacement and thereby improves the accuracy. This requires one function for the horizontal deviation and one function for the vertical deviation. We generated 4 models by fitting the data to 4 different functions using *ordinary least squares*. The first function f_1 is a one-dimensional polynomial complete function of second degree. For the model we fit α_{lr} to Δ_{lr} and α_{bt} to Δ_{bt}. The functions f_2 to f_4 are complete two-dimensional polynomial functions. f_2 is of degree 1, f_3 of degree 2, and f_4 of degree 4. For these three functions we fit both α values to the Δ values.

		EFRC	IFRC	FRC
sitting	2m	53.8 (45.0)	57.9 (31.4)	353.4 (445.0)
	3m	69.8 (63.8)	72.6 (38.7)	334.4 (265.2)
standing	2m	48.6 (45.8)	55.4 (20.7)	222.9 (182.5)
	3m	60.1 (59.7)	59.7 (27.4)	204.9 (71.8)

Table 1. Mean distances between ray cast and target. SD in brackets, all distances are in cm.

		EFRC	IFRC	FRC
sitting	2m	37.9 (25.8)	35.6 (12.5)	53.6 (21.6)
	3m	41.4 (27.5)	47.2 (15.7)	59.2 (30.9)
standing	2m	36.7 (12.5)	35.0 (10.0)	44.7 (21.2)
	3m	40.4 (12.8)	36.0 (9.2)	45.1 (20.2)

Table 2. Mean distances between ray cast and target when using the model with f_4. SD in brackets, all distances in cm.

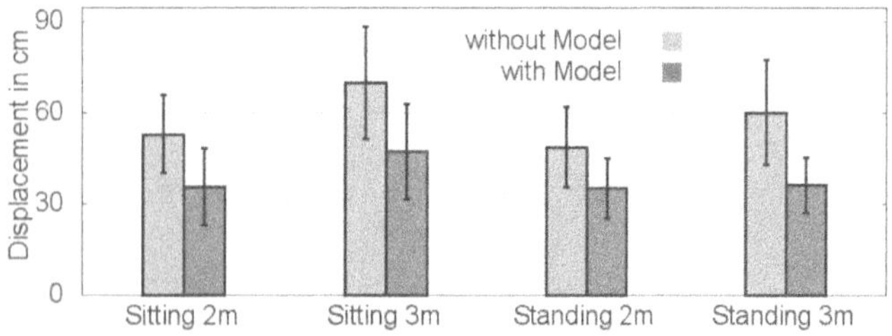

Figure 3. The improvements of the model when using index finger ray cast (IFRC) and fitting function f_4 (error bars show the standard error).

Evaluating the Model's Performance

We tested the four functions using leave-one-out cross-validation. For each participant, we fitted a model using the data of the 11 remaining participants. Afterwards, we determined the remaining error for the participant's trials. Thereby, we determined the performance of the four function if used as a user-independent model to compensate systematic displacement. For all three ray casting methods, the performance of the four functions follows the same trend. For IFRC, for example, The two linear functions already reduce the mean error to 40.8cm for f_1 and 40.6cm for f_2. The two-dimensional polynomial f_3 reduces the mean error to 40.4cm. The two-dimensional polynomial f_4 results in the smallest mean error (38.5cm): $f_4(x,y) = ax^4 + by^4 + cx^3y + dxy^3 + ex^3 + fy^3 + gx^2y^2 + hx^2y + ixy^2 + jx^2 + ky^2 + lxy + mx + ny + o$. The coefficients for the correction functions ($f_{4,lt}$ & $f_{4,bt}$) are show in Table 3 when using α_{lr} as x and α_{bt} as y.

The average distance for the four conditions are shown in Table 2. Compared to the displacement of the standard ray casting methods (see Table 1) the accuracy is improved for all methods. IFRC results in the smallest error with and without compensating systematic displacement. On average over all conditions the model reduces the error by 37.3% when using IFRC. Figure 3 contrasts displacement for IFRC. One of the origins of the remaining error is the free choice of pointing posture. Forcing specific postures can reduce this error.

CONCLUSION

In this paper, we aimed to improve the accuracy of absolute distant pointing. In a study we asked participants to point with their dominant hand at project targets from 2m and 3m while sitting and while standing. Testing three commonly used ray casting methods, we found that even the most accurate ray casting method (index finger ray cast) had an average error of 61.3cm. We found that all tested ray casting methods are affected by systematic deviations. Therefore, we trained a polynomial to compensate systematic displacement. We show that using a user-, pose-, and distant-independent quartic polynomial can reduce the average error by 37.3%.

We aimed to find a user- and pose-independent model and did not force participants to point in a specific way. Considering each of these aspects could further improve the pointing accuracy. If a system, for example, recognizes if the user is sitting or standing, it could select a corresponding model and thereby further improve accuracy. Furthermore, most systems that use absolute pointing for input provide the user with visual feedback. The effect of such a model on pointing with visual feedback needs to be investigates in the future.

coef.	lr	bt	coef.	lr	bt
a	0.0296	−0.0439	i	−2.6181	−1.1506
b	0.0190	0.1070	j	−144.4819	−72.1956
c	−0.0258	−0.0070	k	239.7431	310.0211
d	−0.0634	0.0212	l	77.4749	151.2857
e	−7.7225	−2.2891	m	2863.6584	−1495.0381
f	−3.0723	−19.5427	n	4786.0898	−8136.1496
g	−0.1239	0.0598	o	528615.8408	−522112.5319
h	−2.4860	−0.6280			

Table 3. The coefficients for the correction function f_4 (in 10^{-5}). The coefficients are rounded with in the 95% confidence bounds.

ACKNOWLEDGMENTS

This work is partly supported by DFG within SimTech Cluster of Excellence (EXC 310/2).

REFERENCES

1. Argelaguet, F., Andujar, C., and Trueba, R. Overcoming eye-hand visibility mismatch in 3d pointing selection. In *Proc. VRST* (2008).
2. Bolt, R. A. Put-that-there: Voice and gesture at the graphics interface. In *Proc. SIGGRAPH* (1980).
3. Boring, S., Jurmu, M., and Butz, A. Scroll, tilt or move it: using mobile phones to continuously control pointers on large public displays. In *Proc. OzCHI* (2009).
4. Corradini, A., and Cohen, P. R. Multimodal speech-gesture interface for handfree painting on a virtual paper using partial recurrent neural networks as gesture recognizer. In *Proc. IJCNN* (2002).
5. Foley, J., and Held, R. Visually directed pointing as a function of target distance, direction, and available cues. *Perception & Psychophysics 12*, 3 (1972).
6. Haviland, J. B. *Pointing: Where Language, Culture, and Cognition Meet*. Sotaro Kita, 2003, ch. Pointing Is the Royal Road to Language for Babies.
7. Holzapfel, H., Nickel, K., and Stiefelhagen, R. Implementation and evaluation of a constraint-based multimodal fusion system for speech and 3d pointing gestures. In *Proc. ICMI* (2004).
8. Jota, R., Nacenta, M. A., Jorge, J. A., Carpendale, S., and Greenberg, S. A comparison of ray pointing techniques for very large displays. In *Proc. GI* (2010).
9. Kendon, A. *Gesture: visible action as utterance*. Cambridge University Press, 2008.
10. Kranstedt, A., Lücking, A., Pfeiffer, T., Rieser, H., and Staudacher, M. Measuring and reconstructing pointing in visual contexts. In *Proc. SemDial* (2006).
11. Myers, B. A., Bhatnagar, R., Nichols, J., Peck, C. H., Kong, D., Miller, R., and Long, A. C. Interacting at a distance: measuring the performance of laser pointers and other devices. In *Proc. CHI* (2002).
12. Nickel, K., and Stiefelhagen, R. Pointing gesture recognition based on 3d-tracking of face, hands and head orientation. In *Proc. ICMI* (2003).
13. Vogel, D., and Balakrishnan, R. Distant freehand pointing and clicking on very large, high resolution displays. In *Proc. UIST* (2005).

Is Moving Improving? Some Effects of Locomotion in Wall-Display Interaction

Mikkel R. Jakobsen & Kasper Hornbæk
Department of Computer Science, University of Copenhagen
Njalsgade 128, DK-2300 Copenhagen, Denmark
{mikkelrj, kash}@di.ku.dk

ABSTRACT
Physical movement plays an important role in interaction with wall-displays. Earlier work on its effect on performance has been inconclusive, however, because movement has not been experimentally controlled. In a first experiment, we controlled participants' ability to physically move in front of a 3-meter wide 24-megapixel wall-display. Participants performed a classification task involving navigation using a zoom-and-pan interface. Results suggest that the ability to move does not increase performance, and that a majority of participants used virtual navigation (i.e., zooming and panning) and little or no physical navigation (i.e., moving their bodies). To isolate the effects of physical and virtual navigation, a second experiment compared conditions where participants could navigate using either only physical movement or only virtual navigation. The second experiment showed that physical movement does benefit performance. The results from the experiments suggest that moving may not be improving performance, depending on the use of virtual navigation.

Author Keywords
Large display; wall-display; physical navigation; virtual navigation; user study

ACM Classification Keywords
H.5.2 [Information Interfaces and Presentation]: User Interfaces

INTRODUCTION
Physical movement plays an important role in interaction with high-resolution wall-displays. A key benefit of wall-displays is that they allow more information to be shown at the same time, thereby reducing the need for virtual navigation (e.g., zooming and panning). Users can physically navigate the display through *locomotion*. Previous research has concluded that locomotion increases performance in search and navigation tasks [2,5], and in classification tasks [17].

The effects of locomotion in wall-display interaction and the reasons why locomotion may benefit interaction (e.g., through use of spatial memory [23] or other "embodied resources" [3]) are not well understood. In particular, we see two key concerns for current research. One concern is that most conclusions about physical navigation around wall-displays come from studies that do not experimentally control locomotion. In these studies, locomotion has resulted from an increase in display size, but increasing the display size may bring other benefits. For example, Liu et al. [17] found that a wall-display enabled users to reach targets at a distance without moving. Ball et al. [5], likely the most widely cited study on the idea that physical navigation increases performance, studied only correlations among performance and physical navigation, precluding any causal conclusions about the effects of locomotion. The extent to which locomotion contributes to performance thus remains unclear.

A second concern is that some empirical studies have used information spaces that fit on the display (e.g., [17]), where navigation can be done exclusively by locomotion, whereas others have used information spaces that do not fit on the display (e.g., [2]), requiring users to combine virtual and physical navigation. Work on navigating large information spaces suggests that these conditions lead to different behavior [13] and might also require users to use different strategies for navigation. Thus, comparing results is hard and muddles the picture of the benefits of moving.

Figure 1: Participants in the experiments used a gyroscopic mouse for interacting with the wall-display, wearing a cap with markers used to track movement.

CHI 2015, April 18 - 23 2015, Seoul, Republic of Korea
Copyright 2015 ACM 978-1-4503-3145-6/15/04...$15.00
http://dx.doi.org/10.1145/2702123.2702312

This paper investigates the effects of locomotion in wall-display interaction through two experiments. One experiment controls users' ability to move in front of a wall-display in order to examine the relative use of physical navigation and virtual navigation in a pan-and-zoom interface (see Figure 1). The experiment also varies the scale of information space used, thus manipulating the need for virtual navigation. A second experiment compares the relative performance of using either physical or virtual navigation. The results from these experiments show that users do not choose to use locomotion instead of virtual navigation in wall-display interaction, as previous research suggests, and that the performance effects of locomotion are small.

RELATED WORK

Physical movement of the body at a coarse scale (locomotion) is important in many user interfaces, including movement-based gaming [20] and virtual environments [24]. The present paper focuses on locomotion in interaction with large displays, extensively discussed in earlier work (e.g., [5,17]).

For large displays, locomotion may be beneficial because it can replace virtual navigation (e.g., with a mouse) with physical movement [2,5], because users may benefit from moving when working together on a shared task [14], and because users may step back to gain an overview and closer in order to view details or for direct interaction with touch displays. Next we discuss the technologies for supporting locomotion, the empirical studies of its effect, and some concerns about earlier work.

Input Technologies that Allow Users to Move

Some input options for large displays do not allow users to move in front of large displays, for instance, if they are using mouse or keyboard while seated at a desk. Although this use situation has been improved by using chair rotation [8] or having mouse and keyboard on a rolling stand [26], physical movement is nevertheless limited to head turning.

At least three approaches avoid tethering the user to a particular location and thus support locomotion. First, input devices such as a gyroscopic mouse [5], handheld devices [6,21,22], and tangibles [15] have been used as input.

Second, mid-air gestures with free hand movements have been explored. Nancel et al. [22] compared alternative mid-air pan-and-zoom techniques; they found two-handed linear gestures, using 1D or 2D movements on an input device instead of free-hand movements, to perform the best. Other mid-air techniques likewise allow users to move freely [18].

Third, research has explored using whole-body movements to navigate, where the locomotion is tracked and used as input [12,16,25]. For instance, Lehmann et al. implemented zooming based on zones of distance to the display and a lens based on gaze [16]. Research has used proxemics to exploit users' movement relative to other users or to devices in order to support interaction [9].

Empirical Studies of Locomotion

Independently of the above approaches, it remains an empirical question if locomotion benefits interaction. Ball and North [4] proposed that "physical navigation promotes higher order thinking, such as investigating data points that hold the most promise for solving a task, virtual navigation promotes more simplistic algorithmic strategies that are less efficient" (p. 16). The key benefits of locomotion seem to concern navigation performance, spatial memory, benefits contingent on display size, and input mode.

Locomotion may benefit *navigation*, in particular because users may rely less on virtual navigation. Ball and North studied peripheral vision and physical navigation [4]. They found that physical navigation had a positive effect on performance while peripheral vision did not. Ball and North [2] compared visualization and navigation tasks between displays consisting of 1, 3, and 9 tiled monitors. They concluded that larger displays that allow physical navigation perform better than smaller displays that use pan and zoom navigation. Ball et al. [5] compared performance in search and navigation tasks across different widths of a wall-display. Participants used a wireless gyromouse for zooming (with scroll wheel) and panning (by dragging the mouse). Results showed an increase in performance and physical navigation as display width increased. Increased virtual zooming was more strongly correlated with increased task time than was physical movement. Moreover, in tasks where virtual navigation was not required participants chose physical navigation over virtual navigation.

Spatial memory may also benefit from locomotion as opposed to virtual navigation. In virtual navigation with a tablet in front of a wall-display, Rädle et al. [23] found egocentric movement to improve navigation performance and spatial memory recall after a 15-minute distraction task.

The positive effects of locomotion also relate to *display size*. Liu et al. [17] compared physical navigation in front of a wall-display with virtual navigation using pan-and-zoom on a desktop display for a classification task. Participants could only navigate through movement in the wall-display condition (which fits all data) and through zoom-and-pan in the desktop condition. The input methods differed between the conditions: Participants used a mouse for manipulating data and for panning and zooming on the desktop display, but used a trackpad for controlling the cursor on the wall-display. Liu et al. found that a wall-display increased performance for more difficult classification tasks and for smaller labels that users could not read without navigation. Liu et al. pointed out that the wall-display enabled users to reach targets at a distance without moving while on the desktop they must pan and/or zoom. Andrews and North [1] found physical navigation on a large desktop-display to impact spatial organization for a sensemaking task, using a 17" display zoom-and-pan workspace as baseline for comparison. Shupp et al. [26] compared different display sizes with different curvatures. A curved wall-display performed faster than a flat. They observed that participants tended to do more rotational movements and less walking in the curved condition and more walking in the flat wall-display condition. Overall, these results show that the specific configuration of the large display may have different effects on performance.

The *input mode* used also shape locomotion. As mentioned, for wall-displays, such modes include free-hand gestures [27], input devices [6,21,22], tangible user interfaces [15], and whole-body movements for interacting with wall-displays [12,16,25]. Most work on using touch input for interacting with wall-displays has investigated indirect input through hand-held devices used in mid-air. Apart from studies of collaboration [14] and public displays [11], direct touch on wall-displays has been largely overlooked. This is curious, because touch-based interaction is familiar to most users and allows freedom of movement, except that the display has to be within reach of the user. The relation between physical movement and different input modes, including touch, remains unclear.

Two Concerns with Earlier Work

While the above empirical studies show benefits of locomotion, we raise two concerns about these findings: one about the experimental control of locomotion and one about the information spaces used in the studies.

Earlier studies of locomotion have treated it as a dependent variable, typically derived from tracking of users' movement (e.g., [4,5,17]). In these studies, physical movement is associated with an increase in display size, but increasing the display size may bring other benefits. Had locomotion been manipulated as an independent variable, then causal conclusions about its effect would have been possible. At the moment, though, mainly evidence about positive correlations between locomotion and performance [5] or spatial memory [23] exists.

The second concern is about the information spaces used in the studies mentioned above. The key take away from previous research is that reduced virtual navigation improves performance. However, even wall-sized displays may not always fit a large information space and users may want to view information at multiple scales. Most experiments have used information spaces that fit the largest display condition, which means that tasks have not required virtual navigation [2,17,28]. In studies of navigation techniques, a choice is whether to use tasks where data fit on the largest display condition or tasks where data do not fit [13], thus requiring virtual navigation also with a wall-display. Also, even if data fit on the wall-display, one can still support virtual navigation so that tasks can be completed without physical navigation.

Summary

Earlier work has shown various benefits of locomotion for interacting with large displays. It has not, however, experimentally controlled locomotion, nor has it explored the influence of information spaces of varying sizes that may or may not require virtual navigation. The experiments presented next aim to address those concerns.

EXPERIMENT 1: CONTROLLING PHYSICAL MOVEMENT

The first experiment investigated how physical movement affects performance by varying participants' ability to move. The ability to move was controlled by dimming the display if the participant's head moved outside of an allowed region.

Participants

Sixteen volunteers (5 female), 19–40 years old (M = 25.3, SD = 5.5), participated in the experiment. Their average height was 175cm (SD = 8cm). Participants were screened to have normal or corrected to normal vision. Participants were recruited by word of mouth and were provided the equivalent of €25 in compensation.

Apparatus

Participants used a 2.8m×1.2m display with 24 megapixels (see Figure 1). The bottom of the active display area is 89cm above the floor. The display consists of 4×3 tiles projected from the back by 1920×1080 projectors, manually aligned so as to minimize seams between tiles. The display is run by a single computer running Microsoft Windows 7. The room in which the display is set is 3.5m wide and the distance from the display to the back wall is 2.95m. Office ceiling light fixtures illuminate the room.

We used a NaturalPoint OptiTrack motion capture system (www.naturalpoint.com/optitrack/) for tracking the location and orientation of the participant's head via reflective markers attached to a baseball cap. Tracking had an average error around .5mm for each marker.

Participants used a Gyration Air Mouse Elite wireless gyromouse. The mouse pointer was enlarged and mouse acceleration in Windows 7 settings was set to maximum. We decided on a gyromouse for several reasons: it is designed for single-handed use; typical operations like pointing, zooming, and panning work similar to a normal mouse; and it has been used in previous work [5], thus allowing comparison. We decided against using a trackpad [17], which would require use of both hands. Free-hand mid-air techniques and touch are interesting alternatives that however would be less familiar to participants and would make the results harder to relate to earlier work.

Main Experimental Conditions: Allowing Movement

In the *Move* condition, participants could move freely. In the *NoMove* condition, the display was dimmed to black if the participant's head moved outside of an allowed region. The region was located 1.5m from the center of the display.

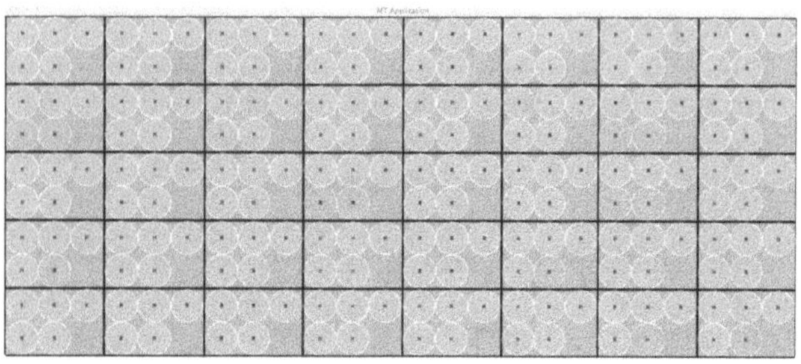

Figure 2: Display layout at the beginning of a task. Participants must move pink discs to their correct containers.

This distance was chosen to be far enough to ensure uniform luminosity in the back-projected image while retaining a wide field of view angle. The region covered a circular area with 40cm diameter, which was empirically defined to allow participants to comfortably turn their head and shift between standing poses. The display was gradually dimmed over 5cm so as to avoid abrupt changes. Also, when the display was dimmed a visual indicator appeared to guide the participant back to the allowed region. Although this control likely is artificial for participants, we found it preferable to alternatives such as fixing participants' head (which would be intrusive), physically constraining movement by fencing in the participant (which would allow leaning and therefore not as strict control), or having participants sit (which would impact comparison, e.g., with respect to fatigue). The display was dimmed at least once in 10% of the tasks (1.14 seconds per task on average for those tasks).

Task and Information Space

Participants performed the classification task described by Liu et al. [17]. We chose this task because it involves a combination of search, navigation, and manipulation of data. For each task the display shows a scene consisting of 40 containers arranged in an 8×5 matrix. Each container fits six labeled items represented as discs. Items are labeled according to class. The task requires participants to move items between containers so that each container holds items of the same class. Correctly and incorrectly classified items are green and pink, respectively; colors were chosen to be safe to color blindness. Figure 2 shows an example task.

Tasks begin with a layout of containers holding five items each. Twelve incorrectly classified items are evenly distributed across classes, but randomly distributed among containers: Four containers hold two incorrect items and four other containers hold one incorrect item. We generated a random layout for each task that satisfied a similar constraint as in Liu et al. [17].

Task difficulty: Number of classes

Items are labeled according to class. The number of classes was varied in order to vary the level of difficulty: *Easy* (two classes labeled "C" and "D") and *Hard* (four classes labeled "H", "K", "N", and "R"). The difficulty affects how much of the information space needs to be searched for the correct container. The average distance between an incorrectly classified item and the closest suitable container is between 1.2 and 1.4 for Easy tasks and between 2.4 and 2.6 for Hard tasks (distance calculated as the Euclidian distance between containers, where the distance between two adjacent containers is 1). Thus, more difficult tasks are expected to require more navigation.

Scale of the information space (Label size)

The scale of the information space also influences the need for navigation. We varied the scale of the information space by using different font sizes and thus control the level of navigation needed to read labels, similar to the approach of Liu et al. [17]. Legibility may be limited not only by distance to the display, but also by other factors such as viewing angle and not least display resolution: For very small font sizes, reducing the distance does not make text readable and virtual navigation is required. We therefore determined font sizes empirically so as to control the need for virtual navigation in both movement conditions. We used font sizes varying from 4pt to 32pt (letter size varying from 1mm to 9mm in height). Larger-scale information spaces contain higher levels of detail, with labels in a smaller font size. The levels are as follows:

- *Large-scale (4pt)* is not readable, regardless of the viewing distance, unless zoomed to at least 1.5× magnification. Virtual navigation is therefore always required, in both Move and NoMove conditions—participants cannot complete the task by physical navigation alone.
- *Medium-scale (8pt)* is readable from around 1m distance or closer to the display. The task can therefore be completed through physical navigation alone in the Move condition, but requires virtual navigation in the NoMove condition.
- *Small-scale (32pt)* can be read without navigation in both Move and NoMove conditions when the participant is standing in the starting position (the allowed region in the NoMove condition). This level therefore acts as a control condition. Letters at this scale have the same size at 1× magnification as letters of Large-scale at 8× magnification.

Interface

Participants pan and zoom the display content (the groups of items) using the mouse. To pan the user clicks and drags the mouse opposite the panning direction. The user scrolls the mouse wheel forward to zoom in and backward to zoom out. Each notch on the mouse wheel changes magnification by 25% and it is possible to zoom from highest to lowest level in one scrolling motion of the mouse wheel. The mouse cursor is used as the center of zooming. Zooming is constrained between the lowest level of 8× magnification and the highest level at which all containers fit the display. Each task starts with all contents shown (1× magnification).

Participants manipulated discs as described by Liu et al. [17], except that they click on a disc to highlight it; a second click moves the disc to another container (or leaves it in its original position if the clicked container is full).

Design

A within-subjects design was used in which the ability to move (Move, NoMove), scale (Small, Medium, Large), and task difficulty (Easy, Hard) were varied. Participants completed 12 tasks for each movement condition, the order of which was systematically varied across participants. Participants performed two tasks for each combination of label size × task difficulty, the order of which was systematically varied using a Latin square in order to reduce learning effects. In all, this resulted in 16 (participants) × 2 (movement conditions) × 3 (label sizes) × 2 (levels of difficulty) × 2 (repetitions) = 384 task trials.

Procedure

Participants were first given an introduction to the experiment. The interface and the task were explained to them. Participants first used the display while moving freely: they performed three training tasks in the Move condition, first using a Medium-scale information space in which they were encouraged to move in front of the display, moving closer to read the labels, etc. This was followed by three tasks in the NoMove condition. After the introduction, participants completed two blocks of 12 tasks, one block for each of the movement conditions. Participants were told before each of the two blocks whether they could move. To begin a task, participants had to stand in the starting position 1.5m from the center of the display and click a button on the screen, whereby the groups of items were presented. After completing all tasks in a movement condition, participants were administered a questionnaire with four questions from NASA TLX [10] asking about mental demand, physical demand, effort, and frustration. After completing all tasks, participants were asked about performing tasks in each of the conditions. We probed for reasons if they had not moved much. We explicitly asked whether it was clear if they could move or not; none of the participants were confused about the conditions. The experiment lasted around 75 minutes for each participant.

Hypotheses

Tasks can be solved using virtual navigation in both Move and NoMove conditions. However, previous research raises several expectations about how participants would use, prefer, and benefit from locomotion compared to virtual navigation:

H_1: The wall-display affords physical navigation: participants will move, if allowed to, when solving the tasks. This hypothesis is based on previous research that has found wall-displays to afford physical navigation [5,17].

H_2: Participants choose locomotion over virtual navigation in the Move condition. Ball et al. [5] found that when virtual navigation is not required and users have a choice to either virtually navigate or physically navigate, they prefer to physically navigate. Also, Liu et al. [17] found that participants moved even for tasks that could be completed without any navigation.

H_3: Participants perform better in the Move condition where they can physically navigate. An increase in physical navigation (and a decrease in virtual navigation) has been correlated with an increase in performance [5].

Results

We performed a 2 (movement) × 3 (scale) × 2 (difficulty level) repeated measures analysis of variance on the task completion times and virtual navigation actions ($N = 384$).

Performance

Surprisingly, we found no main effect for movement, $F(1, 15) = 1.69$, ns. H_3, which states that physical movement results in better performance in the Move condition (M = 101s, SD = 63s) compared to the NoMove condition (M = 105s, SD = 63s), is not supported. The benefit of movement might depend on level of difficulty and the scale of information space (label size), as can be seen in Figure 3, which shows mean task completion times for the different conditions. We found main effects for both label size, $F(2, 30) = 83.9$, $p < .001$, and for difficulty, $F(1, 15) = 87.3$, $p < .001$. However, no interaction was found between neither movement and scale, nor movement and difficulty.

Locomotion

We analyzed participants' locomotion to find a possible explanation for the lack of difference in performance between the two movement conditions. We computed the length of participants' movement paths (from tracking their head) filtered using the Douglas-Peucker algorithm [7] with

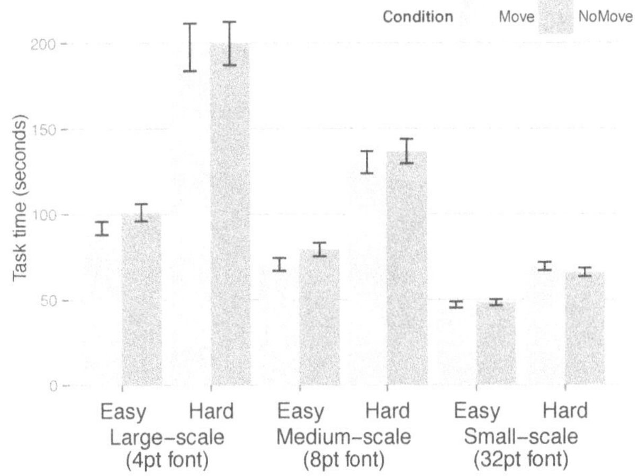

Figure 3: Mean task completion times for Move and NoMove condition across different levels of difficulty (Easy, Hard) and scale of information space (Large-scale, Medium-scale, Small-scale). Error bars show standard error of the mean.

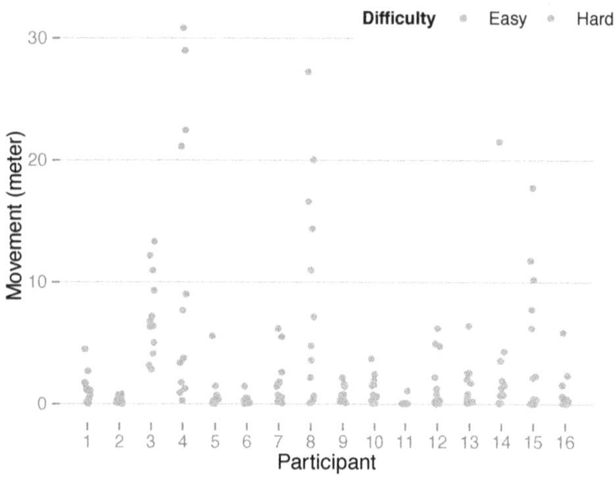

Figure 4: Locomotion in meters per task (all tasks, each represented as a point) for each participant.

a 10cm tolerance. The tolerance level was set so as to give an overall low measure of locomotion (M = 0.3m) in the NoMove condition—ideally this measure should be zero since participants were restricted from locomotion.

In the Move condition, participants moved 2.9m on average (SD = 5.4m) per task, so the display did afford physical navigation, giving support for H_1. However, there was great variation in locomotion across participants, see Figure 4. Five participants moved much (3.0m – 10.9m), whereas the others moved little or not at all (.1m – 1.8m). It seems participants either chose to use locomotion (and did so extensively for many of the tasks, e.g., participants 3, 4, 8, 15), or to not move at all (e.g., participants 2, 6, 11). Figure 4 shows examples of locomotion in a two Large-scale tasks for one of the participants that moved the most.

Participants moved more for Hard tasks (M = 4.4m, SD = 6.0m) than Easy tasks (M = 1.4m, SD = 2.2m) and moved more for Large-scale (M = 4.4m, SD = 6.5m) and Medium-scale spaces (M = 3.4m, SD = 6.0m) than Small-scale spaces (M = 0.9m, SD = 1.8m) that require no navigation.

	Zoom		Pan	
	Move	NoMove	Move	NoMove
Average	14	15	22	28
Difficulty				
Easy	9	10	12	18
Hard	19	20	32	38
Scale				
Large	28	30	41	50
Medium	14	14	20	28
Small	0	1	4	5

Table 1: Average number of virtual navigation actions performed in each task for the Move and NoMove conditions.

Virtual navigation

The two movement conditions required participants to use the mouse for navigating to varying extent, as can be seem from Table 1, which summarizes zoom and pan actions performed across the different conditions (consecutive scrolling events using the mouse wheel in the same direction, with less than 1s in between events, count as one zoom action). We found a main effect of scale on the number of zoom actions, $F(2, 30) = 48.6$, $p < .001$, and pan actions, $F(2, 30) = 9.44$, $p < .001$. The number of navigation actions performed increase as the information space increase in scale (smaller label sizes). We also found a main effect of difficulty on number of zoom actions, $F(1, 15) = 36.3$, $p < .001$, and pan actions $F(1, 15) = 10.0$, $p < .001$. Harder tasks required more navigation actions. Small-scale tasks required no actions, yet participants panned the view 4-5 times on average in both conditions—these are likely accidental panning actions where participants actually wanted to pick or drop an item.

We expected that the ability to move would offset the need for virtual navigation (H_2), but this was only partly the case: No main effect was found for movement condition on the number of zoom actions performed, $F(1, 15) = 3.72$, p = .07, or on pan actions, $F(1, 15) = 3.76$, $p = .07$. Participants tended to do more panning actions, and panning across a larger distance, in the NoMove condition (M = 27.6, 42012 pixels panned in motor space) than in the Move condition (M = 21.9, 50089 pixels).

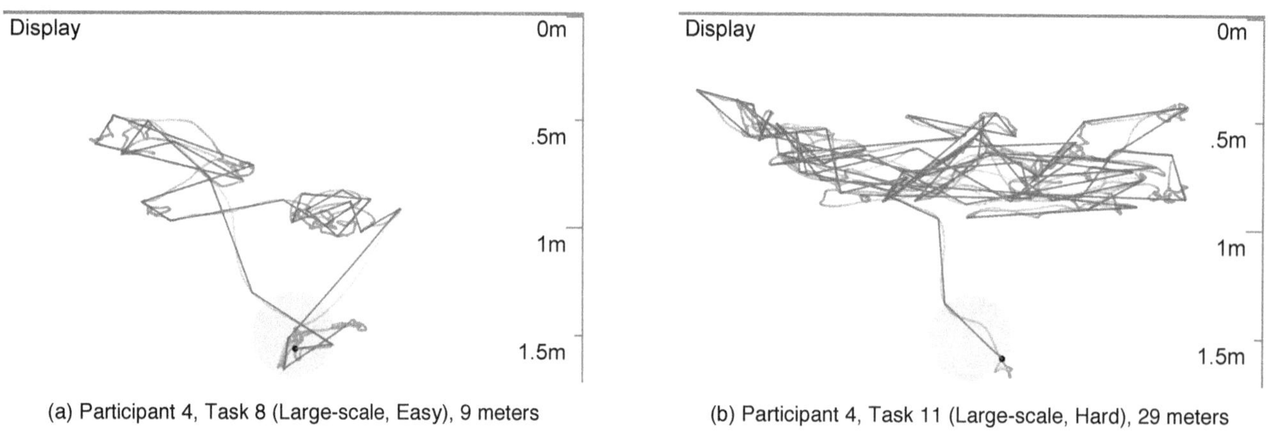

(a) Participant 4, Task 8 (Large-scale, Easy), 9 meters

(b) Participant 4, Task 11 (Large-scale, Hard), 29 meters

Figure 5: Movement path of two tasks. Blue paths show data filtered using the Douglas-Peucker algorithm with a 10cm tolerance, which measure 9m and 29m, respectively; gray paths show the logged data points. The orange circle indicates the starting position.

	Move			NoMove		
	Large	Med	Small	Large	Med	Small
1×	11%	25%	98%	10%	17%	100%
2×	17%	50%	2%	16%	55%	0%
3×	39%	23%	0%	33%	22%	0%
4×	25%	1%	0%	24%	6%	0%
5×	6%	0%	0%	12%	0%	0%

Table 2: Time spent at different magnification levels for the Move and NoMove conditions and for different scales of information space (label size). Time spent at the 6 – 8× magnification levels accounted for less than 2% for Move and 4% for NoMove.

Participants spent time at different magnification levels, determined mainly by the scale of the information space (see Table 2). For Small-scale, no zooming was required, whereas more time was spent at higher magnification levels for Medium-scale and still higher levels for Large-scale. However, this did not vary between Move and NoMove conditions. When allowed to move, participants could have move closer in order to reduce the amount of magnification required through zooming, but they did not—not even for the Medium-scale information space for which virtual navigation could be completely replaced by locomotion. The affordance of physical navigation did therefore not appear to offset the need for virtual navigation.

Subjective satisfaction

The average of the TLX questions suggests differences between the movement conditions, $F(1, 15) = 5.15, p < .05$. Individual analysis of variance suggests significance only for the question about physical demand: the Move condition was rated as less physically demanding ($M = 2.81$, $SD = 1.47$) than the NoMove condition ($M = 3.75$, $SD = 1.34$). In comments after the experiment, seven participants said that it was quite tiring to have to hold the same posture (e.g., "tiring to stand still") and not move just a little bit. However, eight participants emphasized that even when they were allowed to move, they did not (e.g., it was "easier to stay in the same place").

Summary

Participants did not solve tasks faster when they could navigate using locomotion (H_3). Our data could not confirm the positive relation between increased physical movement and task performance found in earlier work [5,17].

The display afforded physical navigation (H_1), but did it promote physical navigation (H_2)? Not really. It seems participants to a large extent preferred virtual navigation over locomotion. Only five participants used locomotion extensively to navigate. We do, however, note that the participants generally used and express satisfaction with moving, such as leaning closer to better be able to read text. Also, participants used a large amount of virtual navigation, even those that also used locomotion. This runs counter to earlier findings of significant decreases in virtual navigation when users can physically navigate.

EXPERIMENT 2: PHYSICAL VS. VIRTUAL NAVIGATION

One key difference between Experiment 1 and earlier work is that we included information spaces that did not fit the display and required virtual navigation also in the Move condition (e.g., Liu et al. [17] fitted data on the wall-display, whereas Ball et al. [5] required semantic zooming in all conditions). Because participants thus used physical and virtual navigation in combination, we do not know how participants would perform if navigating only by locomotion or navigating only by zooming and panning using a mouse. Perhaps participants in the first study performed in a way that resulted in less than optimal performance, for instance by using virtual navigation when locomotion would have been faster. To investigate this, we conducted a second experiment in which we manipulate whether participants could use *either* physical navigation *or* virtual navigation, but not both, for solving the tasks.

Participants

Ten volunteers (4 female), 18–32 years old, participated in the experiment. Their average height was 174cm (SD = 7cm). Participants were screened to have normal or corrected-to-normal vision. Participants were recruited by word of mouth and compensated the equivalent of 25€.

Design

The experimental design was similar to that used in Experiment 1. The conditions used, *Physical* and *Virtual*, were similar to the Move and NoMove conditions, respectively, except that participants in the Physical condition could not zoom and pan using the mouse, but only navigate through locomotion; in the *Virtual* condition, participants could zoom and pan with the mouse, but were kept from physically moving by dimming the display if they moved outside of an allowed region. Another difference is that tasks that used a small-scale information space (4pt font) were excluded, because they can only be completed with the use of virtual navigation.

A within-subjects design was used in which the type of navigation (Physical, Virtual), scale (Medium, Large), and task difficulty (Easy, Hard) were varied. For each navigation type, participants completed eight tasks—two for each combination of label size × task difficulty. In all, this resulted in 10 (participants) × 2 (navigation types) × 2 (scales) × 2 (levels of difficulty) × 2 (repetitions) = 160 task trials.

The hypothesis was that participants would perform better in the Physical condition than in the Virtual condition.

Interface

The interface used was the same as in Experiment 1, except that the mouse-functionality for zooming and panning the view was disabled in the Physical condition; participants could still select and move items, necessary for completing the task.

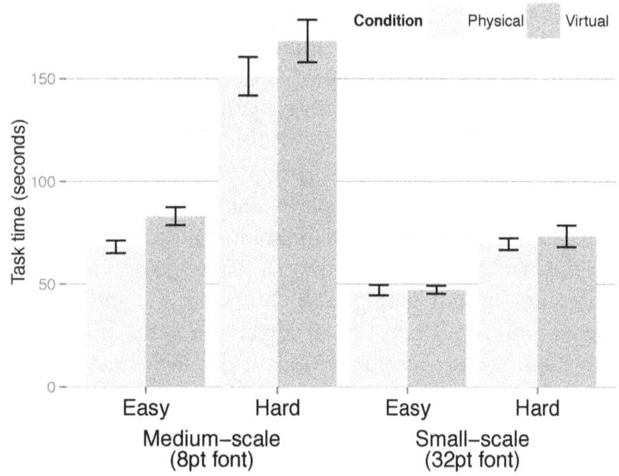

Figure 6: Mean task completion times for the Physical and Virtual navigation conditions across levels of difficulty (Easy, Hard) and scale of information space (Medium-scale, Small-scale). Error bars show standard error of the mean.

Procedure

The procedure was as in the first experiment. The experiment lasted around 45 minutes per participant.

Results

We performed a 2 (navigation type) × 2 (scale) × 2 (difficulty level) repeated measures analysis of variance on the task completion times ($N = 160$).

Performance

We found a main effect of navigation type, $F(1, 9) = 7.29$, $p < .05$, $\eta^2 = .04$. The hypothesis was supported: Participants completed tasks faster using Physical navigation ($M = 84$s, $SD = 46$s) than using Virtual navigation ($M = 93$s, $SD = 53$s), although the effect size is low. Mean completion times for different levels of difficulty and scale of information space can be seen from Figure 6. We found main effects of scale, $F(1, 9) = 145.2$, $p < .001$, $\eta^2 = .64$, and difficulty, $F(1, 9) = 100.2$, $p < .001$, $\eta^2 = .60$. There was a marginal interaction between the navigation type and scale of information space, $F(1, 9) = 4.85$, $p = .055$, $\eta^2 = .02$. As expected, participants performed tasks equally fast using physical and virtual for small-scale information spaces where there was no need for navigation. In contrast, for medium-scale spaces participants were slower using virtual navigation ($M = 126$s, $SD = 56$s) than using physical navigation ($M = 110$s, $SD = 52$s).

	Exp. 2, Physical			Exp. 1, Move		
Small-scale	Easy	Hard	*M*	Easy	Hard	M
M	0.7m	1.7m	1.1m	0.5m	1.3m	1.0m
SD	(0.6)	(1.7)	(1.3)	(0.8)	(2.3)	(1.5)
Medium-scale						
M	6.7m	23.8m	15.2m	1.5m	5.2m	3.3m
SD	(3.1)	(8.8)	(10.8)	(1.9)	(7.9)	(6.1)

Table 3: Locomotion in the Physical condition and the Move condition (experiment 1) for comparison.

Locomotion vs. Virtual Navigation

Participants in the Physical condition moved 8.23m ($SD = 10.41$m) on average per task. This is noticeably more than in the Move condition of the first experiment ($M = 2.9$m, $SD = 5.4$m), likely because participants used both physical and virtual navigation in the Move condition. The amount of movement across task conditions is shown in Table 3, compared to the Move condition in Experiment 1. Participants moved more for Medium-scale than Small-scale, and they moved more for Hard than Easy tasks.

Participants could only use virtual navigation in the Virtual condition. Table 4 summarizes the number of zoom and pan actions performed across the different task conditions. Participants did as much virtual navigation as in Experiment 1 (cf. Table 1). For Medium-scale, participants zoomed 14 times on average, similar to the NoMove condition in Experiment 1, and they panned 23 times on average, compared to 20 times in the NoMove condition.

Subjective Satisfaction

We found no difference for the reported workload values, $F(1, 9) = .53$, ns. Participants were also split in their preference for the navigation types: six preferred physical navigation, three preferred virtual, one preferred a combination. One factor that shapes these preferences is the ability to keep an overview; three participants said this was a benefit of physical (e.g., "easier to keep the big picture") and a drawback of virtual navigation (e.g., "the overview is lost"). Another factor was movement, which four participants said required excessive effort.

Summary

We have found a clear difference in performance between physical navigation and virtual navigation using a mouse to zoom and pan by experimentally controlling participants' ability to use *only* physical *or* virtual navigation. The results provide evidence supporting earlier work [5,17] that has shown that physical navigation can have a positive, if small, impact on performance.

DISCUSSION & CONCLUSION

The purpose of this paper has been to investigate the use of locomotion for interaction with large displays and its effect on task performance. The key findings of the two experiments can be summarized as follows:

(a) Locomotion does not seem to improve performance when users can choose to virtually navigate (or when the scale of the information space requires them to).

	Zoom			Pan		
	Easy	Hard	*M*	Easy	Hard	*M*
Medium	9	19	14	11	35	23
Small	1	0	1	3	5	4
M	5	10	7	7	20	13

Table 4: Mean number of virtual navigation actions for each task in the Virtual condition.

(b) Physical navigation is not preferred over virtual navigation, neither in behavior nor in stated preferences.

(c) Locomotion seems to improve performance when users could not use virtual navigation, that is, when the information space fit the display.

Differences to Earlier Work

Our findings contrast those of earlier work, in particular the studies by Ball et al. [5] and by Liu et al. [17]. Ball et al. [5] concluded that "larger displays lead to more physical navigation, which reduces the need for virtual navigation, which offers improved user performance" (p.199). We cannot comment on the first step of this inference, as we did not manipulate display size. However, the last two steps are not consistent with our findings. Although participants in Experiment 1 used physical navigation, there was no significant difference in the amount of zooming and panning they did compared to that in the condition that prevented them from navigating physically. Perhaps for that reason, physical navigation did not lead to improved performance.

Liu et al. [17] compared physical and virtual navigation indirectly because their main focus was on comparing wall-size displays (which allowed only physical navigation) with desktop (which had only virtual navigation). They reported an interaction with task difficulty so that desktop is more efficient for easy tasks whereas the wall is more efficient for hard tasks. In some parts of their paper, Liu et al. attribute this difference to navigation (e.g., "Experiment 1 showed a strong performance advantage of physical navigation on a wall-size display when compared with pan-and-zoom navigation on a desktop interface for difficult classification tasks", p. 4155). Our Experiment 2 suggests an advantage of physical navigation for the same task, which is not contingent on a large difference in display size.

What might be behind the differences between our experiments and earlier work? Several factors vary between our paper and the work of Ball et al. and Liu et al., including:

- *Experimental Design.* A key difference to Ball et al. [5] and Liu et al. [17] is that we experimentally manipulated locomotion and isolated it from display size. The artificial control of telling people not to move might influence their behavior throughout the experiment (e.g., they may be unsure if they are allowed to move in the Move condition). However, we got not such indications when probing participants and find it unlikely to have had much effect.
- *Display Characteristics.* With regard to size, the display in the present study is comparable in width to that used by Ball et al. [5], but only around half the width of the display used by Liu et al. [17]. Participants did not move for large label sizes, as participants in the study by Liu et al. did. Because their display is almost twice as wide as the one used in this study, it requires a larger field of view. Perhaps our display width better accommodates a sweet spot in field of view, whereas wider displays require movement?
- *Room Characteristics.* Ball et al. commented that a key factor in encouraging physical navigation was that there was "large physical space for range of motion" (p. 199). The room the experiments were set in was smaller than that of Liu et al. and possibly also to that of Ball et al. (though it is not clear from their paper). However, in the sample plots of movement provided by Liu et al. ([17], p. 4153), participants seem to not back up more than 2.5m, less than the space available in front of the display in the present study.
- *Task.* Our experimental task differs from that of Ball et al. [5]. They emphasized that physical navigation was useful to users for scanning large amounts of information at multiple levels of scale. The task proposed by Liu et al., which we also used, asks participants to use information at one level of detail only. If the task were extended to include classification at several scales (e.g., hierarchies of containers), that might promote multi-scale navigation, with different physical navigation behavior to follow.
- *Size of information space.* Only in our Experiment 2 did we find a performance benefit of physical navigation. However, the benefit of physical navigation is tied to the information space being of a scale so that it fits the display, a precondition of most of earlier research that shows benefits of physical navigation. In fact, when given the means to virtually navigate participants did not use physical navigation to significant advantage (Experiment 1).

Open Questions

We have investigated a classification task, which requires participants to inspect and move objects. Thus, locomotion may have several other benefits that we have not discussed. For instance, Rädle et al. [23] looked at memory in large display navigation and found a benefit of egocentric movement.

Earlier work has manipulated display size (e.g., desktop vs. wall [17], columns of display [5]). Obvious future work is to include display size as a parameter. This would allow a better understanding of the difference to in particular the work of Liu et al. [17], where both display size and navigation type were manipulated.

Some forms of input affect movement patterns more than the use of a gyro-mouse, used in the present study. Touch on wall-displays are rarely studied (though see [14]), and affect physical movement by requiring users to move to the display to touch. Touch may, however, be combined with other techniques, such as mid-air gestures [19], which might completely change the interplay of physical and virtual navigation. We see a need to study this.

ACKNOWLEDGEMENTS

This work has been supported in part by the Danish Council for Strategic Research under grant 10-092316. We thank Dan-Adrian Avram for his assistance with the experiments and the reviewers for helping us improve this paper.

REFERENCES

1. Andrews, C. and North, C. The Impact of Physical Navigation on Spatial Organization for Sensemaking. *IEEE TVCG 19*, 12 (2013), 2207–2216.
2. Ball, R. and North, C. Effects of tiled high-resolution display on basic visualization and navigation tasks. *CHI extended abstracts*, ACM (2005), 1196–1199.
3. Ball, R. and North, C. Visual Analytics: Realizing embodied interaction for visual analytics through large displays. *Comput. Graph. 31*, 3 (2007), 380–400.
4. Ball, R. and North, C. The effects of peripheral vision and physical navigation on large scale visualization. *Proc. GI*, Canadian Information Processing Society (2008), 9–16.
5. Ball, R., North, C., and Bowman, D.A. Move to improve: promoting physical navigation to increase user performance with large displays. *Proc. CHI*, ACM (2007), 191–200.
6. Baudisch, P., Sinclair, M., and Wilson, A. Soap: A Pointing Device That Works in Mid-air. *Proc. UIST*, ACM (2006), 43–46.
7. Douglas, D. and Peucker, T. Algorithms for the reduction of the number of points required to represent a digitized line or its caricature. *Cartographica 10*, 2 (1973), 112–122.
8. Endert, A., Fiaux, P., Chung, H., Stewart, M., Andrews, C., and North, C. ChairMouse: leveraging natural chair rotation for cursor navigation on large, high-resolution displays. *CHI extended astracts*, ACM (2011), 571–580.
9. Greenberg, S., Marquardt, N., Ballendat, T., Diaz-Marino, R., and Wang, M. Proxemic interactions: the new ubicomp? *interactions 18*, 1 (2011), 42–50.
10. Hart, S.G. and Staveland, L.E. Development of NASA-TLX: Results of empirical and theoretical research. *Human Mental Workload*, Elsevier (1988), 139–183.
11. Jacucci, G., Morrison, A., Richard, G.T., et al. Worlds of information: designing for engagement at a public multi-touch display. *Proc. CHI*, (2010), 2267–2276.
12. Jakobsen, M.R., Haile, Y.S., Knudsen, S., and Hornbæk, K. Information Visualization and Proxemics: Design Opportunities and Empirical Findings. *IEEE TVCG 19, 12* (2013), 2386-2395.
13. Jakobsen, M.R. and Hornbæk, K. Interactive Visualizations on Large and Small Displays: The Interrelation of Display Size, Information Space, and Scale. *IEEE TVCG 19*, 12 (2013), 2336–2345.
14. Jakobsen, M.R. and Hornbæk, K. Up Close and Personal: Collaborative Work on a High-resolution Multitouch Wall Display. *ACM Trans. Comput.-Hum. Interact. 21*, 2 (2014), 11:1–11:34.
15. Jansen, Y., Dragicevic, P., and Fekete, J.-D. Tangible remote controllers for wall-size displays. *Proc. CHI*, ACM (2012), 2865–2874.
16. Lehmann, A., Schumann, H., Staadt, O., and Tominski, C. Physical navigation to support graph exploration on a large high-resolution display. *Proc. AVI*, Springer-Verlag (2011), 496–507.
17. Liu, C., Chapuis, O., Beaudouin-Lafon, M., Lecolinet, E., and Mackay, W.E. Effects of Display Size and Navigation Type on a Classification Task. *Proc. CHI*, ACM (2014), 4147–4156.
18. Markussen, A., Jakobsen, M.R., and Hornbæk, K. Vulture: A Mid-air Word-gesture Keyboard. *Proc. CHI*, ACM (2014), 1073–1082.
19. Marquardt, N., Jota, R., Greenberg, S., and Jorge, J.A. The continuous interaction space: interaction techniques unifying touch and gesture on and above a digital surface. *Proc. INTERACT*. Springer, 2011, 461–476.
20. Mueller, F. and Isbister, K. Movement-based Game Guidelines. *Proc. CHI*, ACM (2014), 2191–2200.
21. Nancel, M., Chapuis, O., Pietriga, E., Yang, X.-D., Irani, P.P., and Beaudouin-Lafon, M. High-precision Pointing on Large Wall Displays Using Small Handheld Devices. *Proc. CHI*, ACM (2013), 831–840.
22. Nancel, M., Wagner, J., Pietriga, E., Chapuis, O., and Mackay, W. Mid-air pan-and-zoom on wall-sized displays. *Proc. CHI*, ACM (2011), 177–186.
23. Rädle, R., Jetter, H.-C., Butscher, S., and Reiterer, H. The Effect of Egocentric Body Movements on Users' Navigation Performance and Spatial Memory in Zoomable User Interfaces. *Proc. ITS*, ACM (2013), 23–32.
24. Ruddle, R.A., Volkova, E., and Bülthoff, H.H. Walking improves your cognitive map in environments that are large-scale and large in extent. *ACM Trans. Comput.-Hum. Interact. 18*, 2 (2011), 10:1–10:20.
25. Shoemaker, G., Tsukitani, T., Kitamura, Y., and Booth, K.S. Body-centric interaction techniques for very large wall displays. *Proc. NordiCHI*, ACM (2010), 463–472.
26. Shupp, L., Andrews, C., Dickey-Kurdziolek, M., Yost, B., and North, C. Shaping the Display of the Future: The Effects of Display Size and Curvature on User Performance and Insights. *Human-Computer Interaction 24*, 1 (2009), 230–272.
27. Vogel, D. and Balakrishnan, R. Distant Freehand Pointing and Clicking on Very Large, High Resolution Displays. *Proc. UIST*, ACM (2005), 33–42.
28. Yost, B., Haciahmetoglu, Y., and North, C. Beyond visual acuity: the perceptual scalability of information visualizations for large displays. *Proc. CHI*, ACM (2007), 101–110.

Selective Undo Support for Painting Applications

Brad A. Myers[1], **Ashley Lai**[1], **Tam Minh Le**[1], **YoungSeok Yoon**[1], **Andrew Faulring**[1], **Joel Brandt**[2]

[1]School of Computer Science
Carnegie Mellon University
5000 Forbes Avenue, Pittsburgh, PA 15213
{bam, youngseok, faulring}@cs.cmu.edu, {ashleyhlai, minny.le}@gmail.com

[2]Creative Technologies Lab
Adobe Research
San Francisco, CA
joel.brandt@adobe.com

ABSTRACT

Today's widely deployed painting applications use a linear undo model that allows users to backtrack previous operations in reverse chronological order. This undo model is not useful if the user has performed desired operations *after* undesired ones. Selective undo, in contrast, allows users to select specific operations in the past and only undo those, while keeping the remaining operations intact. Although selective undo has been widely explored in the context of text editing and object-oriented drawing, we explore selective undo for painting (bitmap) editing, which has received less attention and introduces many interesting user interface design challenges. Our system, called Aquamarine, explores the script model for selective undo, where selectively undone operations are skipped in the history, rather than the more explored inverse model, which puts an inverse of the selected operations at the end of the history. We discuss the design implications and show through two informal user studies that selective undo is usable and desirable.

Author Keywords

Selective Undo; Bitmap Editor; Creativity Support.

ACM Classification Keywords

H.5.2 User Interfaces (Graphical user interfaces (GUI)); I.3.4 Graphics Utilities (Paint systems); I.3.6 Methodology and Techniques (Interaction techniques).

INTRODUCTION

The *undo* operation has long been understood to be a required command in applications, especially to support creative exploration. Studies have shown that when users have the ability to undo, they are more comfortable exploring and trying new commands [16]. Ideally, any previous operation should be able to be undone. However, most applications use the same *restricted linear undo model* [3], primarily due to the user interface challenges of presenting a more powerful undo model in a way that it is easy for the user to understand. In the linear undo model, multiple operations are saved on the undo stack and can be undone, and after undoing some operations, users can change their mind and start redoing those operations again. However, if a *new* operation is performed after undoing some operations, the undone operations are discarded and are no longer available for redoing. This makes it impossible for the user to undo the undo. Another limitation of the linear undo model is that all operations must be undone in order. This makes it impossible to keep any operations that happen *after* an operation to be undone. That is, if there are a mixture of wanted and unwanted operations, users cannot use undo to achieve their desired result [24].

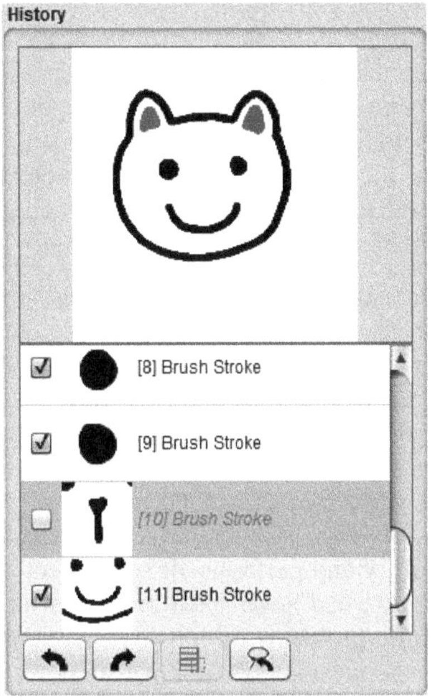

Figure 1. Aquamarine's History Panel showing operation #10 (brush stroke for the nose) selectively undone.

The limitations of linear undo have motivated research on *selective undo*, where the user can specifically select which of the previous operations to undo and which to keep [1-3, 5, 19, 25]. However, this prior work has primarily focused on object-oriented drawing programs, like PowerPoint or Adobe Illustrator [3, 19], where selective undo is more easily achieved by selecting and changing objects' properties. New work has started to address selective undo in text [17, 25], but there is little work on selective undo in painting applications like Photoshop which lack the structures used by object editing programs, and where operations tend to affect overlapping spans of pixels. This makes it much

CHI 2015, April 18 - 23 2015, Seoul, Republic of Korea
Copyright 2015 ACM 978-1-4503-3145-6/15/04...$15.00
http://dx.doi.org/10.1145/2702123.2702543.

more difficult for users to identify which operations to undo (since there may be many small edits) and to predict the outcome of selectively undoing something in the past. Furthermore, it is challenging to provide understandable user interfaces for any selective undo model. Note that throughout this paper, we are deliberately distinguishing the term *drawing* from *painting*. Drawing programs have identifiable objects in the picture that can be selected and manipulated later, whereas painting programs convert objects into pixels immediately, and subsequent selections and operations are at the pixel level. Many painting operations cannot be naturally converted into objects with a distinct shape. For example, the paint bucket tool and filters do not create or even necessarily modify objects; instead they manipulate pixels. Aquamarine focuses on painting only. Note that modern image manipulation programs like Photoshop actually have a mixture of drawing and painting features.

Another interesting issue is the distinction between the *inverse* and *script* models of selective undo. In the *inverse model*, supported by most previous selective undo systems [3, 19, 25], a selective undo causes the inverse of the selected operations to be added to the end of the history. For example when the user selectively undoes a delete, a create operation is performed and added to the end of the history. In contrast, the *script model* removes the selected operation from the history and performs all subsequent operations as if that operation had never been performed [15]. This can cause semantic problems in drawing programs (for example, what is the meaning of a change-size operation applied to an object if the previous creation of that object is selectively undone, and thereby removed from the history?), but may be more appropriate when painting (since there are no objects to which operations are applied). We are not aware of any previous research on supporting selective undo in a paint program using the script model.

We created *Aquamarine* (see Figure 1) to study these issues. Aquamarine, which stands for Allowing Quick Undoing of Any Marks And Repairs to Improve Novel Editing, is a new prototype painting program that supports selective undo using the scripting model. We first performed semi-structured interviews with student and professional graphic artists to see what they would want and expect in such a tool. We then implemented the Aquamarine prototype based on those findings, and ran usability evaluations to assess its features and design decisions.

The contributions of this paper include:

- Results of semi-structured interviews, which show that users have a significant need for selective undo capabilities in painting programs, and compensate with workarounds such as using many layers, saving the whole file to disk, or just starting over.
- A discussion of the design space for selective undo and tradeoffs among the design decisions.
- A design and implementation for a selective undo mechanism using the script model in a prototype paint program called Aquamarine, which explores the design space for how the script model should operate.
- A usability evaluation that demonstrates the aspects of the selective undo mechanism which are most usable and useful, and areas where more research is required. All users expressed a desire to have a form of selective undo in their everyday programs.

RELATED WORK

There has been significant work on undo and edit history over the years, in a variety of application domains.

Selective Undo

One of the earliest efforts in this area investigated the script model [2], which tries to guarantee that the final result be as if the prior command had never been performed in the context of text editing for a code editor, and identifies issues specific to that domain. The Emacs text editor has long had an "undo-in-region" command, where the user undoes the most recent operation that affected a specific selected region of text. Other text editors such as DistEdit [21] have provided this feature. Regional undo is useful and also relatively easy to implement compared to the generic selective undo, because it always undoes the most recent operation performed in the selected region, which reduces the possibilities for conflicts. In regional undo, however, there can be an ambiguity if the user selects a region that partially overlaps with an operation's effective region. Li and Li refer to this problem as "region overlapping" and introduce the idea of *partial undo* as a solution, which undoes only the overlapped part of the operation when an operation partly falls in the given undo region [17]. Regional undo was applied in spreadsheets [12] by allowing users to select a region in the spreadsheet and perform undo only on those cells. Our new system, Azurite [24, 25], provides general selective undo (not just region undo) in a code editor. Azurite uses the inverse model, by adding the inverse text editing operation to the end of the history, and provides a variety of user interfaces to resolve conflicts.

Probably the most work on selective undo has been in the context of graphical (object-oriented), interactive editors. Berlage introduced the selective undo model that adds the reverse operation of the selected command to the current context [3]. The Amulet [20] and Topaz [19] systems had a similar selective undo feature, but these allowed repeating a selected command even on a new object. All of these use the inverse model, with the undos added to the end of the history. Dwell-and-spring [1] provides an interface that is limited to undoing only press-drag-release interactions, and it does not deal with any conflicting operations. All of these approaches also assume that there is an object on which the operations can be performed: primitive graphical objects such as shapes in graphical editors, and individual cells in spreadsheets. In contrast, there is no clear notion of objects in painting programs, since edit operations typically affect areas of pixels.

Another important difference between object-oriented and painting systems is that detecting and handling conflicts and dependencies among the operations is important for all object-oriented selective undo systems. Whereas early systems using simple dependency models [3, 19], later work focused on formal, sound and complete modeling of dependencies, and even automatically cascading the selective undo when necessary for consistency [6]. User studies showed that people could predict and understand what these selective undo systems will do [7]. Whereas in one sense, painting systems do not have such dependencies since all actions operate on pixels, we do study the issue of conflicts when the boundaries of actions overlap, as discussed below.

There are other undo models that support selective undo by providing additional commands beyond undo and redo. The US&R model [22] allows users to *skip* redoing an operation, using a complicated tree-based data structure. Users can selectively undo an isolated operation by undoing multiple steps until the target operation gets undone, skipping the redo command once, and then redoing the rest of the operations. The triadic model [23] uses a simpler structure composed of a linear history list, and a circular redo list which can be *rotated* by users. Undoing an operation puts the operation at the beginning of the redo list, and rotating the redo list takes one operation at the beginning of the list and puts it at the end. Since the rotate command can be used to skip a redo command, users can selectively undo a certain operation in a similar way. However, both models require deep understanding of the underlying history structure to correctly perform selective undo. In addition, selective undo cannot be done in one step, which can be cumbersome for users.

Adobe Photoshop provides a history window with a mode for "non-linear undo", but this is different from selective undo—when the user undoes operations and then does new ones, Photoshop's non-linear undo retains the undone operations on the undo stack rather than remove them. However, future undos still start at the last operation and continue backwards through all previous operations in order.

Another use of selective undo is in collaborative editing, where multiple people can edit a document concurrently, which has been studied by various systems [4, 10]. When user1's and user2's edits are intermixed, it is not clear whether user1's undo command should affect user2's operations. Surprisingly, the Google Docs text editor does not seem to do anything sensible when multiple people edit in the same region and then one performs undo.

A revision control system for images based on a directed acyclic graph (DAG) enables users to make forks and joins, and then move around in the history and see various versions of images [8], but it does not support selective undo or the script model.

Graphical Edit Histories

Aquamarine displays the past interactions in a graphical History pane (see Figure 1). There has been significant research on such displays. Chimera provided graphical histories as thumbnail snapshots which could be edited and reused, and past actions could be modified [15], but conflicts among operations were not specifically identified. The Designer's Outpost shows snapshots of the history of states of a web editing session with multiple users and keeps track of forks among versions [13]. Systems have also used graphical histories to foster learning [9, 11] and creating macros for later reuse [15, 18].

INITIAL SEMI-STRUCTURED INTERVIEWS

In order to get a better idea about how people might use a selective undo mechanism in painting applications, we first performed semi-structured interviews of nine people. Our last author from Adobe reports that there are three primary uses of Photoshop: (1) to design and prototype user interfaces, (2) as a painting tool to create art, and (3) to edit and retouch photographs. We were careful to recruit participants from all three groups (see Table 1).

ID	Experience	Student or Prof.	Des?	Art?	Photo?	Ctrl-Z	Step-Back	Hist. Panel	Hist. Brush
1	Intermediate	student	Yes	Yes			Yes	Yes	Yes
2	Intermediate	student	Yes	Yes		Yes			
3	Intermediate	student			Yes			Yes	
4	Expert	student	Yes			Yes	Yes		
5	Expert	prof.		Yes		Yes	Yes	Yes	
6	Novice	student		Yes			Yes		
7	Expert	prof.	Yes				Yes		
8	Expert	prof.	Yes				Yes		
9	Expert	prof.	Yes				Yes		

Table 1. Participants in our semi-structured interviews.

All of our participants were frequent users of Photoshop, with four self-rating as expert users, four as intermediate and one as novice. Four were professionals and five were students. Photoshop provides four undo mechanisms: an old-fashioned toggle undo (Ctrl-Z), which undoes and then redoes the last operation, a normal linear undo, which it calls "Step Backwards" and "Step Forwards" (Shift/Alt-Ctrl-Z), a history panel which enables undoing back multiple steps (with a fixed maximum limit that defaults to 20), and a "history brush" where users select a point in the history panel and then paints, which restores the pixels back to that point in time, as a form of regional undo. As previously mentioned, Photoshop provides an optional non-linear history mode. No participant (in this or the final study) had ever used or had even heard of this feature, which is turned off by default. Three of the participants reported using the toggle undo, five reported using step-backwards and step-forwards, three used the history panel, and one reported using the history brush.

In the first part of our interviews, we asked participants to work on one of their own tasks using Photoshop, in a form of contextual inquiry, and they were encouraged to think aloud. We told them we were particularly interested in situations where they would "explore different ideas and test out different alternatives."

The more experienced users exclusively used the shortcut keystrokes to invoke commands. Only two participants had the history panel displayed, but both of them used it to undo multiple operations. We did not see any use of the history brush. Some participants erased areas rather than using undo, whereas others made significant use of the step-backwards commands. They recognized the limitations: "I don't want to use the undo button if there's a part that I drew after that I like." Another said: "It's more of a short-term memory [issue] for me. I don't usually undo more than five steps back."

Participants used the layers mechanism to group items together when they anticipated a need to selectively change an area or a shape, and experienced users grouped and named layers to keep the large number of layers organized. When beginning a creative exploration, participants often duplicated layers or saved a version of the whole picture, to facilitate backtracking. Users often hid layers instead of deleting them; one said: "I don't like deleting things; it feels too permanent—even if it was a mistake."

In the second part of our interviews, we gave the participants a series of tasks designed to elicit selective backtracking behaviors and strategies. We told them to imagine they were creating images for a company that is run by a very indecisive boss. We would repeatedly instruct them to create something, then change it, then do other things, and finally to change it back. This cannot be supported with any of Photoshop's existing undo mechanisms. As in the first part, when participants anticipated that something would need to be undone, they put it on a separate layer. If we asked them to undo something that was not on a separate layer, they expressed regret that it was not separated and usually started over from scratch. Users considered using advanced editing tools such as Photoshop's Color Replacement Tool, but often decided it would not work sufficiently well, and just painted over items, or deleted and redrew them from scratch. These results reveal the reliance on layers to simulate selective undo, and the need to start over and lose desired work when undesired operations precede the desired ones.

In the third part of our interviews, we explained the concept of selective undo and asked if they thought it would be useful in their own work. Six participants said it would be useful frequently or almost every day, and the other three said maybe not since they achieved the same functionality with layers or by frequently saving their work to disk.

In the fourth part of our interviews, we asked a series of questions about what they thought would happen as a result of performing a selective undo. In particular, we were exploring whether they expected the *script model* or the *inverse model* of behavior. For example in Figure 2, if the stars were created by duplicating the original star, what should happen if the creation of the original star was selectively undone? All participants thought the other stars should *not* disappear, so they were endorsing the *inverse* model in this case, since under the script model, there would be nothing to duplicate. On the other hand, if we added a recolor step for the star between steps 1 and 2, and then selectively undid the recoloring, all but one of the participants expected the stars in step 2 to also change color, requiring the script model to hold. When this inconsistency was pointed out, most participants agreed that their preference would change based on the situation.

Finally, we explored a number of features that might be used in a selective undo mechanism. Most participants agreed that the ability to identify which operations had contributed to a selected region of the picture would be useful, as a way to find which operations to selectively undo. About half thought the reverse operation was needed – to select an operation in the history panel and highlight what area of the picture it affected. Few participants saw any need to search for commands in the history by name (to enable searches like "find the last time I used the brush tool"). Also deemed unnecessary would be a need to view different versions of a picture side-by-side, or automatic version control tools, as are commonly used for source code and which are provided by third party tools like LayerVault (layervault.com) and Pixelapse (www.pixelapse.com).

Discussion

In an object-oriented drawing program, users can generally get the effect of undoing operations by manually performing the opposite operation. Thus, the "undo" of resizing can be achieved by just resizing it back, which can generally be performed at any time. Photoshop and other painting programs try to provide this capability for as many operations as possible by having many operations act like they are object-oriented instead of pixel based (that is, like a drawing program instead of a painting program). For example, text in Photoshop is kept as objects on its own layer until the user explicitly flattens it into a bitmap. However, this means that many bitmap operations, like blurring or erasing, would not be available until the image is flattened, and changing the text would not be possible after blurring.

Similarly, in our study, we saw participants using layers to try to make painting operations have the ability to be selectively edited. However, layers do have significant limitations. We saw frequent errors where participants would accidentally draw into the wrong layer, merge layers and regret it later, or realize too late that a new layer should have been created. Also, the large number of layers became difficult to manage.

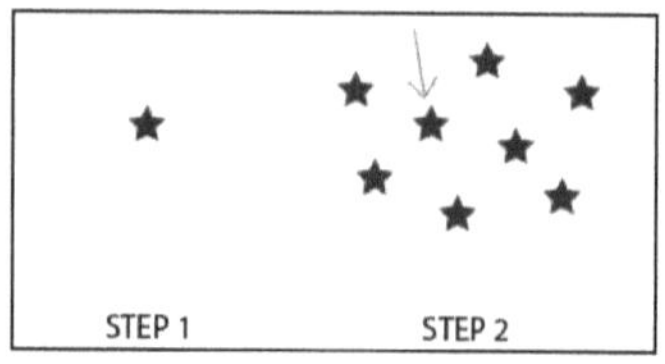

Figure 2: Multiple steps to create a drawing.

In addition, users were wary of the Photoshop history tool, since it only keeps a limited number of steps backwards, the history is not preserved when a document is closed, and it can be difficult to identify which step to go back to. One participant noted: "If you rely on history, you're asking to get burned by it." Therefore, there is an opportunity to provide a new way for users to backtrack.

Participants agreed that there would be significant value in having a selective undo tool that would provide the ability to change what was done in the past, without the requirements of pre-planning to use layers and without giving up the advantages of bitmap editing.

DESIGN TRADEOFFS

In designing and implementing the selective undo feature, we had to make a large number of design decisions, across a number of different dimensions. In many cases, we needed to decide what a selective undo for painting applications should mean since this has never previously been explored. This section presents the design dimensions, the various options and tradeoffs, and justifications for decisions implemented in Aquamarine.

Which Operations to Explore?

We classified all Photoshop operations into eight categories with respect to their interaction with Undo (as has also been explored previously by others [8]). The categories are:

1. Creation/painting, which cause pixels to be drawn
2. Local-adjustment tools, which change existing pixels
3. Global commands, which affect all pixels in the image
4. View control commands, which do not change pixels
5. Selection tools, which control subsequent operations
6. Mode changes, like picking a color or current layer
7. Conversion tools, like Flatten and Convert to Smart Object
8. Miscellaneous, like 3D tools

The first three are most relevant to selective undo, so we implemented at least two operations from each of these categories. We expect that operations in Photoshop or other full-featured paint programs would have identical issues with respect to selective undo, so we believe the HCI issues we have identified will generalize to all other commands.

Script Model versus Inverse Model?

The most important decision was which kind of selective undo model to support. As discussed above, the primary choices are to use some form of script model or some form of inverse model.

The inverse model seemed inappropriate for a painting program, since so many operations cannot be undone by adding a new command to the end of the history. For example, take color change. In a painting program, a color change using the Paint Bucket Tool (more formally called flood fill), changes the color of the area defined by the contiguous pixels that match, within a tolerance, the color of the clicked pixel. This operation often *cannot* be undone with a new flood-fill at the end of the history (that is, "now"). For example, in Figure 3, the flood fill of step 2 cannot be undone with another flood fill after all of the actions in step 3, because flood-filling now will only change parts of the former blue t-shirt, and the long sleeves added to the shirt might also be flood-filled. Similarly, other bitmap editing operations, like blurring the image, cropping, etc. may be impossible to reverse in the current state. Other operations, even creating new shapes, cannot necessarily be undone in the current state, because of other paintings drawn on top of them may compute the new pixels using the existing pixels.

However, a script model *can* be used to selectively undo the flood fill operation—we can undo all the operations back to before step 2 was done (so the image looks like step 1), skip doing step 2, and then do the remainder of the operations.

Note that using layers to separate operations as in Photoshop and other programs, so the user can simulate selective undo by turning off or deleting layers, will not help with selective undoing of painting-based operations like flood fill or blur, since these operations must work on the same layer as the pixels to be modified.

Since Aquamarine specifically focuses on these painting operations, we decided to use the script model. Another motivation is that the script model has rarely been investigated in previous research or commercial systems, and it brings up many more interesting and challenging design decisions, which we discuss next.

Note that providing selective undo with either model can work with the regular linear undo command. Thus, if the user does not use selective undo, it can be ignored entirely, and the normal way of using undo/redo can be utilized.

Another issue is that some commands have side effects *external* to the editor. For example, File Save should not be re-executed each time the system reruns the script to perform a selective undo. Fortunately, it turns out that these operations are actually not put into the undo stack anyway (see also the discussion of copy and paste below). For a few *internal* operations with side effects, like Create Layer, we must disable all the other operations on that layer if the create is selectively undone.

Handling Region Conflicts among Operations

As discussed in the related work section, an important concern in object-oriented editing is dealing with dependencies and conflicts [3, 6, 19]. Bitmap operations do not have this kind of conflict, since they work on pixels, which will still

(1) (2) (3)

Figure 3. In a painting program, (1) paint a shirt, (2) flood fill it with a new color, (3) then do a variety of other actions.

be there. However, it is possible to have *region conflicts* [25], which are where a later operation's scope overlaps the selected operation in such a way that it is not clear what the selective undo should do. For example, in Figure 3, if the user tried to selectively undo the painting operation (step 1), what should the flood fill (step 2) do, since the t-shirt is no longer on the screen?

There are a variety of possible outcomes for step 2 in a script model when step 1 is removed:

1. Cancel the selective undo due to the conflict. That is, do nothing.
2. Perform the selective undo, and also undo the conflicting operations, which includes at least step 2.
3. Perform the conflicting operations as dictated by the script model with the selected operation removed. In this case, it would probably flood-fill the whole canvas since there would be nothing (only background) at the pixel where the flood fill operation happened.

There is actually a 4th possibility, which we discuss in Future Work: allow the user to *modify* the conflicting operation or *add* entirely new operations into the history. For example in Figure 3, the user might select a new pixel at which to apply the flood fill, or paint a brand new shape where the shirt used to be as a new step 1.

We investigated providing a popup dialog to help the user resolve these conflicts and pick one of the three options, as in Azurite [25], but it proved quite difficult to identify exactly which operations should be marked as conflicting with the undone operation, resulting in very expensive pixel operations and too many false positives. Therefore, we decided to use a much simpler approach of just comparing bounding boxes of all subsequent operations, and highlighting the operations in the history which *might* conflict, to help the user find them if they want option 2 (see Figure 4).

To reduce the number of operations that are highlighted, we developed a set of heuristics for the kinds of region conflicts that should be brought to the user's attention based on the operation categories discussed above. The heuristics are as follows: first, we do not highlight creation/painting operations. For example, if a new shape is painted on top of an old shape, and the painting of the old shape is selectively undone, even though overlapping pixels are affected, we do not alert the user, and simply remove the old shape and repaint the new shape. Similarly, global operations affect all pixels, but we do not alert users to these region conflicts either. The main issue is when the later operation is a *local-adjustment tool*, which modifies only some of the pixels of the picture. Flood-fill and smudge are examples of this, and there are many others. When such operations affect the same area that the selective undo will affect, we alert the user of all conflicting operations using orange highlights.

As future work, we plan to support allowing the user to select *multiple* operations to be selectively undone together [25]. For example, the user might select both Steps 1 and 2

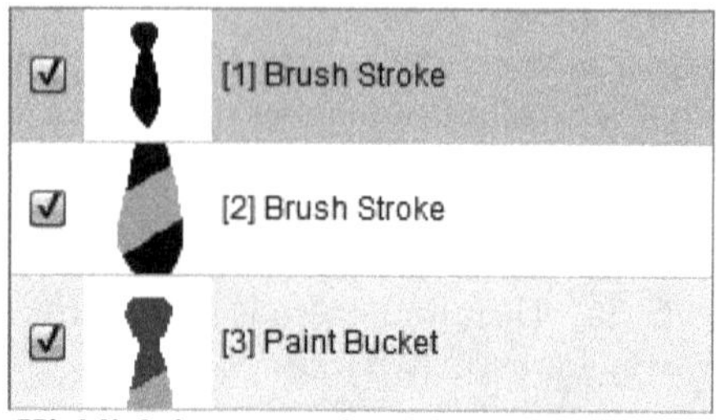

Figure 4. Highlighting operation 3 in orange since it conflicts with the selected operation 1 (shown in blue).

together in Figure 3. When all the region conflicts are internal to the selected operations, there is no ambiguity of what to do, so the user does not have to be alerted. In our usability evaluation, this was a much-requested feature.

Copy and Paste

Another interesting design issue revolves around copy and paste. In most existing applications, the copy operation is *not* put on the undo stack, and whatever is copied is retained independent of what the user subsequently undoes. For example, in Microsoft Word, a user can type some text and copy it, and then invoke undo one or more times so that the text is all removed. However, the clipboard will still retain the text, which can be pasted later. Of course a cut operation goes on the undo stack, but only the deleting part of the cut is undone—again the clipboard is not affected by undoing the cut operation. Users have developed strategies for clever ways to use this feature, so we decided to retain it in Aquamarine.

Therefore, Aquamarine makes what we call a *deep copy* of whatever is selected when the user performs a copy operation, and the copy operation is not put into the undo stack. That means that the script model will not re-execute the copy operation, so the clipboard will continue to have a copy of the pixels as they were originally copied, no matter what happens subsequently to that part of the image. Similarly, the paste operation retains a deep copy of what was in the clipboard when the operation is first invoked, so it continues to paste the *same* picture if it is reinvoked later due to the script model.

Another reason we felt that we needed to adopt this model for copy is that the clipboard is globally shared by all programs, and the user might change the clipboard by doing a copy in *another* program, and in that case, we would not want to change the clipboard as a result of a selective undo.

Selective Undo/Redo Operations in the History Panel

In Topaz [19] and Azurite [24] and many other systems that implement the inverse model, the selective undo and redo operations themselves are added to the end of the undo history, and shown in the history panel (see Figure 5). This seems to make sense in those programs since the inverse operation is actually performed at that point in the history, and so a representation like Figure 5 should reinforce this mental model for users. Another advantage of this approach is that the selective undo operation itself can be selected and undone, which would then add another selective undo to the end of the history, restoring the effect of the original operation. Alternatively, the user could select the original operation (#5 in Figure 5) and selectively *redo* that operation, which has the same effect as selectively undoing the undo. A final advantage of this design is that it is clearer what a regular linear undo command will do – it works up from the bottom, undoing each of the operations in turn (selective and regular operations alike).

Given these advantages, we first tried adapting this style of history panel for the script model of Aquamarine, as shown in Figure 5. In this design, the user can select an operation (e.g., #5), and invoke selective undo on it, which adds the selective undo operation to the end of the history (shown as operation #7). Unlike in the inverse model, the selective undo is not really on the history, but instead the referenced operation is skipped (in Figure 5, only operations 1 through 4 and 6 are executed). We try to visualize this by graying out the referenced operation. If the user wants to reverse this operation, the selective undo (#7) can be selectively undone or the original operation (#5) can be selectively redone, and these operations would be also added to the history. However, we felt it was getting complicated to understand what was done and not done, and we also felt that this design might give the wrong mental model to users, since the selective operations are not really in the history.

Therefore, we designed a different history panel, shown in Figure 1, where the original operations can simply be unchecked to selectively undo them, or rechecked to be selectively redone. This matches the design for the layers panel in Photoshop, where layers can be made visible or not with a toggle button next to each layer's name. This should do a better job of matching the appropriate mental model for users: that the current picture results from the operations being executed from the top down, skipping operations that are not checked. Another advantage is that we do not need explicit selective undo or selective redo commands, but instead the user just toggles the appropriate checkbox.

It is less clear what the regular linear undo should do in this model. We decided linear undo should undo the most recent operation shown in the history panel that is still in effect. Therefore, the selective undo is not directly undoable by Ctrl-Z. This again mimics the default behavior of turning on and off layers, which are not put on the history stack (although Photoshop has a setting to enable this). Similarly, the regular linear *redo* moves down the history stack re-enabling operations, no matter how they were undone. Thus, it redoes operations that were disabled either by selective undo or regular undo. Of course, the user can always go to any individual operation and toggle its checkbox, no matter how it was disabled.

Since the "right" design for this feature is not clear, we decided to include questions about this in our usability evaluation, discussed below, which came out strongly in favor of the checkbox version shown in Figure 1.

Figure 5. An alternative form of history panel where selective undo/redo operations are included in the history.

Thumbnail Images

One small design issue is: what to display for each operation in the history panel. A common complaint about Photoshop's history panel from our initial semi-structured interviews was that it only shows an icon for the tool used, so it is impossible to tell which operation is for which part of the drawing, for example when there are many brush strokes. Therefore, we wanted to show a thumbnail representation of what the operation did, along with some context, as has been done previously [15].

A new complication for Aquamarine that has not been previously reported arises from the scripting model of selective undo—what should be shown in the thumbnail when a selective undo causes a previous operation to be turned off? Should the thumbnails of the subsequent operations be changed? We decided to update all the thumbnails, since that is the more correct (and interesting) design. Ironically, in the usability evaluation, users almost universally said they did *not* want *any* context to be shown in the thumbnails, completely eliminating this problem. Instead, they preferred seeing only the specific output of the current operation. The preview window (the upper panel of Figure 5), however, should continue to show what the complete picture would look like up to the selected operation.

Identifying Desired Operations

Azurite [24] provides elaborate ways to *search* for the operations that the user might want to undo. However, in our initial semi-structured interviews, the key way that users wanted to search for operations in a painting program was by selecting an affected region on the screen. Therefore, we provide commands in Aquamarine for identifying the set of operations that affect the selected region on the screen. We

Figure 6. Pixelitor modified with our history panel.

also provide the reverse operation which shows the region on the screen that any operation affects. Note that both of these are based on the specific pixels on the screen, which may no longer hold that operation's result. For example, if the user paints a shape, but later selects and moves it, the region for the original painting operation will remain where the shape started. In a painting program, it seems impossible to identify where the pixels that result from an arbitrary operation might have gone, and it seems more useful to help users find where things used to be, in case they want to get back to that state. Note that if the user selects the region on the painting where the shape was originally painted, both the painting and the move operations will be identified, so users can selectively undo/redo any operations that are desired.

IMPLEMENTED SYSTEM

Our original hope was to implement Aquamarine as a plugin to Photoshop since it supplies a variety of APIs. Unfortunately, none of Photoshop's APIs provided sufficient access to the undo stack and the result of each operation to support the desired features. Therefore, we needed to find an open-source paint program we could modify. We required sufficient functionality so that the design issues discussed above would emerge (which eliminated simple painting programs like the Java Paint program used in other studies [14]), and we needed access to the full source to be able to implement the selective undo.

We selected Pixelitor 2.0.0 in Java by László Balázs-Csíki (http://sourceforge.net/projects/pixelitor/) (see Figure 6). The original version of Pixelitor used the built-in Java Swing undo model, which uses command objects [20]. We were able to replace this with our own undo implementation which supports our novel selective undo mechanism.

One complication is that Pixelitor, like other painting programs including Photoshop, implements undo by simply having most operations save a bitmap of the picture before the operation executed. This is sufficient for the regular linear undo model, since it can always be sure that when it places the bitmap into the correct position, that the context will be correct and the full image will be restored. However, this is insufficient for any selective undo model, especially for the script model, since we need to be able to re-execute all commands later. Therefore, we had to modify each command to remember all of its parameters so it can be re-executed when needed. For example, the Shape and Brush stroke tools must save the path and all the properties of the pen (color, transparency, etc.). Similarly, the Paint Bucket tool needs to remember the color, start pixel, etc. Further, we had to refactor the application so all operations could get their parameters from the global widgets (like the current color) or from the saved command objects. We still save the bitmaps so they can be used for regular undo.

Another implementation tradeoff was whether each operation should save the entire bitmap of the whole picture, or only the portion affected by this operation. If each operation saved the entire picture, then our script model could implement the selective undo of an operation by simply reinstating the full picture before that operation, skipping the operation, and then re-performing all enabled subsequent operations. However, saving the entire bitmap wastes a lot of memory, since most operations only affect a tiny part of the picture. Pixelitor only stores bitmaps for the regions affected by each operation (which it uses for undo), which we retain. Therefore, implementing the script model selective undo does not require any significant amount of extra space. The tradeoff is that for selective undo, we must internally roll back to the selected operation, by doing a linear undo all the way back, in order to restore the picture to the original state. This is a classic space-time tradeoff, and in practice, we found it to be sufficiently fast. If it turns out not to be fast enough in the future, there are many obvious optimizations that could be implemented.

Some Photoshop operations can be quite slow and expensive, so there is a question about the efficiency of reapplying all the operations each time a selective undo is invoked, which is required for the script model. In our unoptimized prototype implementation, selective undo slows down noticeably on a big image if there are over 100 operations. Although we focus on the user interface aspects here, we have considered some performance optimizations that could be applied in a real implementation. Obviously, the length of the history can be limited, as is already the case in Photoshop, but that is not desirable from a UI standpoint. Instead, slow operations could be approximated on downsized images, to show quick previews which estimate what the results will be, with the real result calculated in the background once the user stops undoing and redoing.

USABILITY EVALUATION

Since our initial semi-structured interviews and other prior work had clearly identified problems that our mechanism addresses, we felt the key issue to evaluate was whether users could understand and successfully apply our new script-model selective undo, and whether users can think of strategies that would make effective use of it. Therefore, we felt the appropriate evaluation would be to do think-aloud usability evaluations of various versions of the features which embody the design decisions discussed above.

We recruited eight participants (see Table 2), one of whom was also part of our initial semi-structured interviews (participant 5 in Table 1 is participant 2 in Table 2). We specifically picked users across a wide range of experience. None of the new participants were students. Four were professional graphic artists and the other four were professionals who only used Photoshop or equivalent occasionally. All participants were familiar with conventional undo models, as supported by Photoshop and most applications, but three participants were not familiar with Photoshop's special undo features.

ID	Experience	Prof.	Des?	Art?	Photo?	Ctrl-Z	Step-Back	Hist. Panel	Hist. Brush
1	novice	other			Yes	Yes	Yes		
2	expert	prof.		Yes		Yes	Yes	Yes	
3	expert	prof.	Yes			Yes	Yes	Yes	
4	expert	prof.	Yes	Yes		Yes	Yes	Yes	
5	intermediate	prof.	Yes			Yes	Yes	Yes	
6	novice	other	Yes			Yes	Yes		
7	intermediate	other	Yes	Yes		Yes	Yes		
8	expert	other			Yes	Yes	Yes	Yes	

Table 2. Participants in our usability evaluation.

We asked the participants to "try drawing a few things" with Aquamarine, and then undo operations using a variety of commands. Most participants just drew random lines and shapes, but p5 drew animals like Figures 1 and 6. We then asked them what they would expect to happen with various undo commands (regular Ctrl-Z and our new selective undo) and then to try them out to see what happens. We had about half of the participants use the checkbox version of the history first (Figure 1), and the other half tried the in-history version first (Figure 5). Then they tried the other version. The order had no effect, and *all* 8 participants strongly preferred the checkbox version. Everyone understood the operation of the checkboxes and how they would affect the picture, although some expressed a preference to using an "eyeball" icon as used to toggle layer visibility (see Figure 6). In the in-history version, they found the presence of the "selective undo" and "selective redo" operations in the history to be confusing, and also felt that this would clutter up the history without being useful.

All users found the script model to be understandable and preferable in general, but all users were surprised by the operation of the paint bucket, when the area underneath where it was applied was selectively undone (a situation in which there is a region conflict). In this case, the paint would typically fill the whole background, which was not something anyone wanted. Some participants wanted the paint bucket to just remember the shape it had filled and reuse that, even if the area was no longer there, but most people wanted the system to be smarter about undoing the paint bucket operation with the previous operation. In discussions, however, they agreed this would be tricky in practice, and that the orange highlighting of the conflicting operations (Figure 4) would be a reasonable way for users to manually find and fix conflicts.

Interestingly, all but one participant was surprised by the operation of copy-and-paste, even though everyone was familiar with the way copy-and-paste works in other programs (where the copy ignores undo). However, participants agreed that our design was consistent and would sometimes be useful.

The main requested feature was a way to *group* actions. For example, selecting multiple operations together and undoing them all at once, or collecting operations into named groups, like layers can be in Photoshop.

In summary, the evaluation showed that with the check-box version, the script-model selective undo was understandable and usable, and that people understood how the issues from the semi-structured interviews would be addressed by our tool. All participants expressed a strong desire to have this kind of selective undo in Photoshop, and even in their other editing programs. They said that selective undo could substitute for some of the ways they now use layers.

FUTURE WORK

Currently, Aquamarine is an early prototype, sufficient to explore the design issues discussed here, but not yet ready for deployment. The current work includes making the rest of the features of Pixelitor work with selective undo, and then releasing Aquamarine as open source for general use and a full field test.

Photoshop has an option to add the operations that enable and disable layers onto the undo history, and Topaz [19] even could put changes of selections and the "find" operation into the undo history. Some of our participants expressed the desire to have state changes that do not affect the current painting, such as changing the current color or the radius of the brush, included into the history so they could be undone. We propose to explore these in the future.

We also want to investigate how to allow operations in the past to be *modified.* For example, some participants in both studies expressed a desire to be able to change the color of an operation done in the past, and see that propagated through the rest of the edits. The next step is to enable *new* operations to be inserted into the past, or existing operations to be reordered, for example to put something behind other painting in the stacking order. Although other research systems have tried some of these [15], a key usability challenge remains of how the user would be able to understand, undo and selectively undo changes to the history.

Another requested feature from our participants was some way to collapse long histories. For example, text editors coalesce multiple keystrokes into a single undoable action, and we would like to explore the ability to collapse and expand multiple small brush strokes. This might be supported both automatically and manually, so the user could achieve the desired level of granularity when navigating.

Finally, we would like to explore saving and restoring histories. The history might be stored in the image document, to enable cross session undoing. This could also enable someone later to explore how an effect was achieved. Similarly, a saved script could be converted into a tutorial [9]. Sections of a history could also be selected and converted into parameterizable reusable macros, as in Topaz [19].

CONCLUSIONS

Providing selective undo in a painting program brings up a surprising number of design challenges. Aquamarine shows that UI research can address those challenges and usable interfaces can be provided that can have benefits for users. We hope this research will inspire others to investigate providing selective undo in a variety of domains.

ACKNOWLEDGEMENTS

We thank Min Jeong Kim for her help with the figures used in this paper. Funding for this research comes in part from NSF grant IIS-1314356, from the Korea Foundation for Advanced Studies (KFAS), and from Adobe Research. Any opinions, findings and conclusions or recommendations expressed in this material are those of the authors and do not necessarily reflect those of the NSF, KFAS, or Adobe.

REFERENCES

1. Appert, C., Chapuis, O., and Pietriga, E., "Dwell-and-Spring: Undo for Direct Manipulation," in *SIGCHI'2012*. Austin, TX. pp. 1957-1966.
2. Archer Jr., J.E., Conway, R., and Schneider, F.B., "User Recovery and Reversal in Interactive Systems." *ACM Trans. Program. Lang. Syst.*, 1984. **6**(1): pp. 1-19.
3. Berlage, T., "A Selective Undo Mechanism for Graphical User Interfaces Based on Command Objects." *ACM Trans. on Comp. Human Inter.*, 1994. **1**(3): pp. 269-294.
4. Berlage, T. and Genau, A. "A Framework for Shared Applications with a Replicated Architecture," in *ACM UIST'1993*. Atlanta, GA: pp. 249-257.
5. Cass, A. and Fernandes, C., "Using Task Models for Cascading Selective Undo," in *Inter. Conf. on Task Models and Diagrams for UI Design*, K. Coninx, et.al, Eds. 2007. Springer Berlin / Heidelberg: pp. 186-201.
6. Cass, A.G. and Fern, C.S.T., "Modeling Dependencies for Cascading Selective Undo," in *IFIP INTERACT 2005 Workshop on Integrating Soft. Eng. and Usability Eng.*
7. Cass, A.G., Fernandes, C.S.T., and Polidore, A., "An Empirical Evaluation of Undo Mechanisms," in *NordicCHI'*2006. Oslo, Norway. pp. 19-27.
8. Chen, H.-T., Wei, L.-Y., and Chang, C.-F., "Nonlinear Revision Control for Images." *ACM Trans. Graph.*, 2011. **30**(4): pp. 1-10 (Article 105).
9. Chi, P.-Y., *et al.*, "Mixt: Automatic Generation of Step-by-Step Mixed Media Tutorials," in *UIST'2012*. ACM: Cambridge, MA. pp. 93-102.
10. Choudhary, R. and Dewan, P., "A General Multi-User Undo/Redo Model," in *ECSCW'1995*. Springer Stockholm, Sweden. pp. 231-246.
11. Grossman, T., Matejka, J., and Fitzmaurice, G., "Chronicle: Capture, Exploration, and Playback of Document Workflow Histories," *UIST'2010*. pp.143-152.
12. Kawasaki, Y. and Igarashi, T., "Regional Undo for Spreadsheets (Demo)," in *Adjunct Proceedings UIST'2004*. 2 pages.
13. Klemmer, S.R., *et al.* "Where Do Web Sites Come From?: Capturing and Interacting with Design History," in *CHI'2002*. Minneapolis, Minnesota: pp. 1-8.
14. Ko, A.J., *et al.*, "An Exploratory Study of How Developers Seek, Relate, and Collect Relevant Information During Software Maintenance Tasks." *IEEE Trans. on Soft. Eng.*, 2006. **33**(12): pp. 971-987.
15. Kurlander, D. and Feiner, S. "Editable Graphical Histories," in *1988 IEEE Workshop on Visual Languages*. Pittsburgh, PA: pp. 127-134.
16. Kuttal, S.K., Sarma, A., and Rothermel, G., "History Repeats Itself More Easily When You Log It: Versioning for Mashup," in *IEEE VL/HCC'2011*. pp. 69-72.
17. Li, R. and Li, D., "A Regional Undo Mechanism for Text Editing," in *Inter. Workshop on Collaborative Editing Systems*, 2003.
18. Lieberman, H. "Dominos and Storyboards: Beyond Icons on Strings," in *1992 IEEE Workshop on Visual Languages*. Seattle, WA: pp. 65-71.
19. Myers, B.A. "Scripting Graphical Applications by Demonstration," in *SIGCHI'1998*. pp. 534-541.
20. Myers, B.A. and Kosbie, D., "Reusable Hierarchical Command Objects," in *CHI'1996*. pp. 260-267.
21. Prakash, A. and Knister, M.J., "A Framework for Undoing Actions in Collaborative Systems." *ACM Trans. on Comp.-Human Inter.*, 1994. **1**(4): pp. 295-330.
22. Vitter, J.S., "Us&R: A New Framework for Redoing (Extended Abstract)." *SIGSOFT Software Engineering Notes*, 1984. **9**(3): pp. 168-176.
23. Yang, Y., "Undo Support Models." *Inter. J. of Man-Machine Studies*, 1988. **28**(5): pp. 457-481.
24. Yoon, Y., Koo, S., and Myers, B.A., "Visualization of Fine-Grained Code Change History," in *IEEE VL/HCC'2013*. pp. 119-126.
25. Yoon, Y. and Myers, B.A., "Supporting Selective Undo in a Code Editor," in *ICSE 2015*, Florence, Italy, to appear.

Designing for Exploratory Search on Touch Devices

Khalil Klouche[1,3], Tuukka Ruotsalo[2], Diogo Cabral[1]
Salvatore Andolina[1], Andrea Bellucci[4], Giulio Jacucci[1,2]
[1]Helsinki Institute for Information Technology HIIT, Department of Computer Science,
University of Helsinki, PO Box 68, 00014 University of Helsinki, Finland
[2]Helsinki Institute for Information Technology HIIT, Aalto University,
PO Box 15600, 00076 Aalto, Finland
[3]Aalto University, School of Arts, Design and Architecture, Media Lab Helsinki,
Hämeentie 135 c, 00560 Helsinki, Finland
[4]Universidad Carlos III de Madrid, Av. Universidad 30, 28911 Leganés (Madrid), Spain
[1]first.last@helsinki.fi, [2]first.last@aalto.fi, [4]abellucc@inf.uc3m.es

ABSTRACT

Exploratory search confront users with challenges in expressing search intents as the current search interfaces require investigating result listings to identify search directions, iterative typing, and reformulating queries. We present the design of Exploration Wall, a touch-based search user interface that allows incremental exploration and sense-making of large information spaces by combining entity search, flexible use of result entities as query parameters, and spatial configuration of search streams that are visualized for interaction. Entities can be flexibly reused to modify and create new search streams, and manipulated to inspect their relationships with other entities. Data comprising of task-based experiments comparing Exploration Wall with conventional search user interface indicate that Exploration Wall achieves significantly improved recall for exploratory search tasks while preserving precision. Subjective feedback supports our design choices and indicates improved user satisfaction and engagement. Our findings can help to design user interfaces that can effectively support exploratory search on touch devices.

Author Keywords

User Interfaces; Exploratory Search; Touch Devices

ACM Classification Keywords

H.5.2. Information Interfaces and Presentation: User Interfaces; H.3.3. Information Storage and Retrieval: Information Search and Retrieval

CHI 2015, April 18 - 23, 2015, Seoul, Republic of Korea

http://dx.doi.org/10.1145/2702123.2702489

INTRODUCTION

Surface computing technologies hold great potential for enhancing information retrieval activities. Devices with touch interaction capabilities make possible to design engaging direct manipulation interactions, facilitate awareness of information available for the user beyond conventional search engine result pages, and afford visualization and spatial organization of content. However, conventional search user interfaces rely exclusively on typed-query interaction and result presentation as ranked list of documents [24], and thus they present challenges when transferred to touch devices.

These design conventions are pernicious for many search scenarios, in particular, *exploratory search* scenarios, that describe a class of search activities that go beyond basic lookup, typically involving the user in a field with which she is not familiar [38]. Exploratory search patterns are very diverse, but share together common complex user-centered challenges: The need to overcome difficulties in formulating queries in unknown information spaces, ways to learn about the information space and identify possible search directions beyond the entry point specified by an initial query [28].

Causes of inadequacy of classical search interfaces for touch-enabled devices are the poor substitutes for keyboard and mouse inputs. Virtual keyboards are reported to be less performing then their physical counterpart [34], and do not provide usual text editing shortcuts (e.g., copy, cut, paste, cancel). As for mouse-based interactions, touch-based substitutes constrain natural touch interactions and prove difficult for quick and accurate text selection [10]. Also, the lack of window management on touch devices does only allow the visualization of a single query at a time, which hinders comparison and revisiting previously retrieved information.

As a consequence, the fluidity and search performance expected while searching with surfaces is hampered [38]. Therefore, it becomes crucial to design new solutions that overcome the limitations of conventional search user interfaces and bring in forefront the potential of multi-touch interaction.

We present the design of Exploration Wall, a novel search user interface for facilitating exploratory search tasks on touch devices. Exploration Wall is based on the following design principles targeting above-mentioned challenges:

1. Flexible reuse and combination of items to facilitate query formulation.
2. Result sets of not only documents but most relevant entities to foster iterative query reformulation.
3. Use of spatial configuration of multiple search streams to identify search directions and learn about the information space.

Our design was found to facilitate exploratory search behavior when compared to the conventional baseline search user interface, as indicated by measured system effectiveness. Moreover, users were found to be more engaged with the task and subjectively more satisfied by their exploratory search. Our findings suggest that our principles can be effective when designing search user interfaces for touch devices, and can overcome many limitations of the direct adaptation of conventional search user interfaces to surfaces.

BACKGROUND

Exploratory Search

Most available tools for information retrieval focus on lookup retrieval, such as looking up the address of a restaurant or reminding a historical fact, while many users search to solve more complex tasks that require exploration of the information space. White [38] describes exploratory search as activities that move beyond basic lookup retrieval. Such activities rely on learning and investigation [22]. Exploratory search activities have no predetermined goals and are described as open-ended [38]. Therefore, the absence of clear user intents leads to difficulties in formulating queries.

Exploratory search processes are considered dynamic. As the information space is unknown or unfamiliar to the user, the query formulation evolves iteratively as the user becomes more familiar with the context [7]. In addition, exploratory search tasks include cognitive and behavioral attributes [40]. Cognitive attributes can be defined as those that have the reasoning associated with conducting an exploratory search and involve learning and investigation as goals; general and ill-structured problems; uncertainty; dynamic, multi-faceted and complex search tasks and are accompanied with sensemaking, decision making or other cognition.

As stated, in the context of exploratory search users need particular support in formulating queries, learning about the information space and identifying possible search directions. Next we review how visual interfaces have been developed to address these issues.

Visual Interfaces in Search

Recently, a variety of search systems have been developed in order to enable faster relevance judgment and effective feedback [12, 17, 19, 23, 32]. Several visualization approaches have been explored including multiple linked lists, scatter plots, graphs and their combinations [31, 19]. These types of visual search systems are distinguished from familiar query composition ones (e.g., Project Blacklight [30]) because of their emphasis on rapid filtering to reduce result sets, progressive refinement of search parameters, continuous reformulation of goals, and visual scanning to identify results [1].

Currently, visual approaches attempt to better support exploration in different ways: supporting sense making by incrementally and interactively exploring the network of data [8], showing how visualization support user involvement in the recommendation providing rationale behind suggested items [35], visualizing relations of different queries and result sets [2]. Recent work shows how to support users to view and manipulate their search intent models as viewed by the system [2, 3, 29, 11] . This work attempts to combine personalization of search with visualization approaches offering support to formulate queries and learning about the information space helping users in directing their search [29] . While these systems demonstrate the importance of investigating visual user interfaces in exploratory search, they have not been considered for multi-touch devices.

Recent visual interfaces in search have shown the effectiveness of interacting visually with query elements and results combined with computational techniques that support exploration. Multi-touch devices could provide an opportunity for visual interactive search for their capability to encourage manipulation of visual elements and for the limits posed by the absence of mouse and keyboard. In the next section we inspect previous work on search interfaces on touch-enabled devices.

Search with Touch Devices

The workshop on exploratory search and Human-Computer Interaction at the 2007 CHI conference [37] demonstrates the interest in the research community on extending search interfaces to new kind of interactive environments. One of the discussed topics, in fact, was about the need to better understand how to design exploratory search systems for beyond-the-desktop interaction. There is a raising need for search system designs on interactive displays that take advantage of the idiosyncrasies of multi-touch interactions [39] instead of simply being directly ported from desktop-based interfaces.

One of the critical issues is to reduce the need for text entry, which is not suitable for touch-based interaction [42]. In the case of a small form-factor, FaThumb [18] explores web browsing on mobile phones by providing an interface that exploits facet navigation and limits text entry only to further narrow search results. Findings from the user evaluation demonstrated that text entry is more efficient for direct search while for open-ended search facet navigation offers better performances. Multi-touch gesture-based interaction has also been exploited as a mean to improve targeted search of specific content. For instance, Gesture Search [20] is a tool that allows users to define personalized touch gestures to quickly access data items on their mobile phone. The Questions not Answers (QnA) [16] prototype is an interesting instance of a system that exploits social interactions and context-awareness capabilities of mobile devices in order to offer reuse of previous queries based on geographical locations. The system maps other users' queries to their physical location and provides an interface to display them on an interactive map. Results from the user study demonstrated that displaying previous query result in less need to formulate new query or to a better formulation, which is influenced by the displayed queries.

Concerning large surfaces, like in public display settings, surface computing has been examined particularly for open-ended information exploration [14, 9]. Especially interesting cases are the EMDialog [13], which provides a visual exploration environment for an artist's work in a museum via temporal and contextual dimensions, and the Bohemian Bookshelf [33], which is designed to systematically support serendipitous discoveries while searching in a book collection through different interlinked visualisations. Insights from these research works led to several design principles for search interfaces in public spaces, such as combining different search strategies, rewarding short-term and long-term exploration and making information exploration appealing through engaging multi-touch interaction and information visualizations. Research literature emphasized on the use of large interactive surfaces for collaborative search tasks. Morris et al. [24] have conducted extensive empirical research on collaborative information seeking using horizontal surfaces, providing discussions on opportunities, challenges and design principles for the development of co-located search systems on tabletops along different dimensions such as collaboration styles, search input, group size and application domains. Efficient text entry by enabling the reuse of existing text instead of typing all searches on a virtual keyboard is also a leading design goal in the case of large surfaces [25].

From the state of the art, it is manifest that current solutions are modelling search systems for small or large surface and there is a lack of investigation on touch interfaces for medium-sized display screens, such as tablets. They present different affordances if compared to smaller or larger form-factor, and therefore need a different design approach. For instance, they do not support collaborative tasks as large surfaces do —given the limited screen size— but the display dimension is still bigger than mobile phones —while supporting users mobility— thus allowing richer visualisations, arrangements of interface elements and touch-based manipulations (e.g., two-handed gestures).

DESIGN CHALLENGES

From the state of the art, we identified three main challenges:

1. Formulating queries in unknown information spaces
Activities considered as related to exploratory search are very diverse and hard to define in a consolidated way. But unlike basic lookup search, they usually take place in areas that are unfamiliar to the user and are characterized by the frequent need to reformulate the query.

2. Learning about the information space and identifying possible search directions
The spatial metaphor of exploration applied to information retrieval well describes the need for steering the exploratory evolution in the information space. Narrowing possibilities to make steering decisions implies continuous gain of topical information.

3. Going through long lists of results with low information gain
In current search systems, users are forced to invest significant cognitive efforts in acquiring cues to formulate queries from the intermediate results, instead of focusing on collecting and learning from relevant information. Long lists of results conflict with the idea of a dynamic steering by slowing down the iterative process of query reformulation.

4. Typing and manipulating queries
Exploratory search activities performed on a traditional typed-query search interface require a lot of text entry and text manipulation. On touch devices, text manipulation is made difficult by the absence of a physical keyboard, hotkeys or shortcuts, and the lack of an accurate selection tool.

GENERAL DESIGN PRINCIPLES

From the above mentioned challenges, we came up with targeted design principles to guide the implementation of our prototype:

A. Flexible reuse and combination of information items to facilitate query formulation
To reduce the need for text entry (challenge 4), we chose to itemize information into entities of different types that can be flexibly manipulated and "dragged around" to support and facilitate all fundamental tasks like selection, duplication, grouping, deletion. Entities would be used to formulate queries, either individually or combined, to get a set of new entities as search results. An existing query could then be easily refined or reformulated by addition or removal of such entities and the results would update accordingly.

The possibility to input text is still necessary in some situations, for example when the system fails to make the proper suggestions or when specifying a first query. We decided our design should thus support it as an alternative and as a way to instantiate a search session.

B. Result sets of not only documents but most relevant entities to foster iterative query reformulation
To foster iterative query reformulation (challenge 3), we introduce the notion of *search streams* which describes an interactive structure supporting a query and related results: the query itself is formed of one or more entities and is composed by the user, while the results are shown as a vertical arrangement of entities related to the query and positioned above it. In the query area, items can be moved freely. Under a certain horizontal distance threshold, those entities are considered as a single query. The unity of a query is visualized through a network of thin lines linking the entities together. At first the query visually leads to a button that triggers the retrieval. The search engine then returns a set of entities related to the query. Those represents not only retrieved documents but also new entities, such as keywords or persons. They are vertically ordered by type and relevance. The flexibility of the search stream comes from its two level structure. It acts partly as a consolidated unit which can be moved around and considered as an almost traditional list of results, but each document or

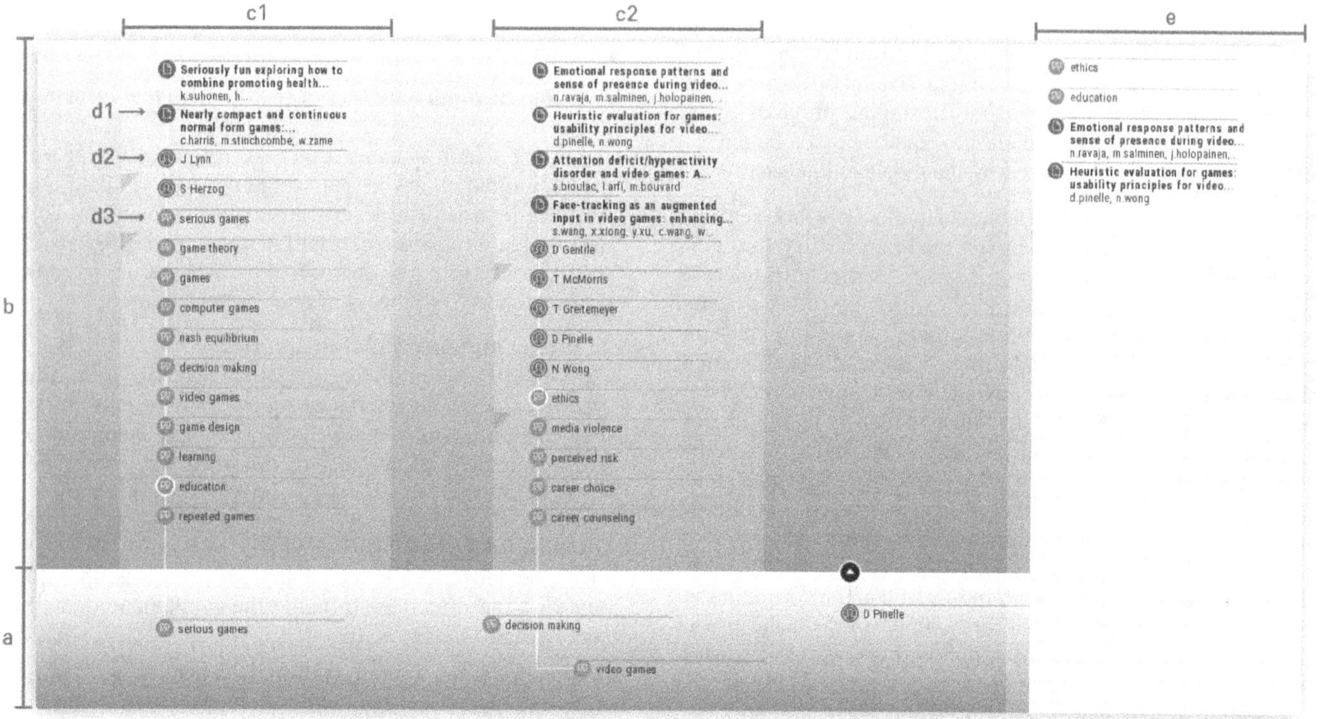

Figure 1. The Exploration Wall interface is composed of the (a) query area, (b) the results area, (c1, c2) search streams, three types of entities: (d1) documents (brown icon), (d2) authors (red icon), and (d3) keywords (blue icon), and (e) the reading-list drawer. The user can move any information item to compose queries by spatially grouping them on the query area. The whole workspace is scrollable and unlimited. Multi-touch gestures allows user to easily add or remove space between streams, or combine streams.

entity can become a new query, or part of an existing query, in the same stream or a parallel one.

C. Use of spatial configuration of multiple streams to identify search directions and learn about the information space

To facilitate steering decisions (challenge 2) and help the user formulate queries (challenge 1), our design supports search on simultaneous parallel streams. Persistency of search and context improves exploration by fostering trials without fear of losing current work, and supporting information comparison and entity association leading to quick instantiation of new queries or quick query re-formulation. It also allows the user to keep track of former queries and results while supporting unconstrained branching and revisits in the actual search process.

EXPLORATION WALL

Here we describe the interactions and implementation of the system based on the above mentioned design principles.

The User Interface

The interface of Exploration Wall is entirely dedicated to its main workspace (Figure 1), which is divided in two areas: the query area at the bottom (Figure 1-a) and the result area on top (Figure 1-b). The workspace supports information in the form of parallel search streams (Figure 1-c1 and c2) organized by taking advantage of the multi-touch ability: it can be scrolled on the horizontal axis with a simple swipe gesture on the background, horizontal space can be added or removed at will from a specific location using a conventional pinch gesture, the same pinch gesture can also be used to dilate or contract space (e.g., to quickly improve legibility of an area cramped with information).

In current instantiation, entities are of three types (Figure 1): Documents (Figure 1-d1), Authors (Figure 1-d2) and Keywords (Figure 1-d3). Each entity is represented by a pictogram, a label and a relevance gauge. One can move an entity by dragging its pictogram. Additional interactions include: tap on the title of a document to reveal additional information like source and content, tap on the icon to store the entity. Stored entities appear highlighted and can be found in the storage drawer described below.

The storage drawer (Figure 1-e) offers an unobtrusive solution that acts as a reading list as well as an always accessible storage area for information transit. One opens and closes it by performing a swipe gesture from the right edge of the display.

The Search Engine

The search engine was designed to support multi-touch interaction design of Exploration Wall and is based on two design rationale. First, the *entity ranking* where entities that are returned for the user to manipulate and use to formulate queries should be as central to the topic as possible. For example, if the user searches for "information retrieval", she is not expecting back only entities that occur in the top ranked

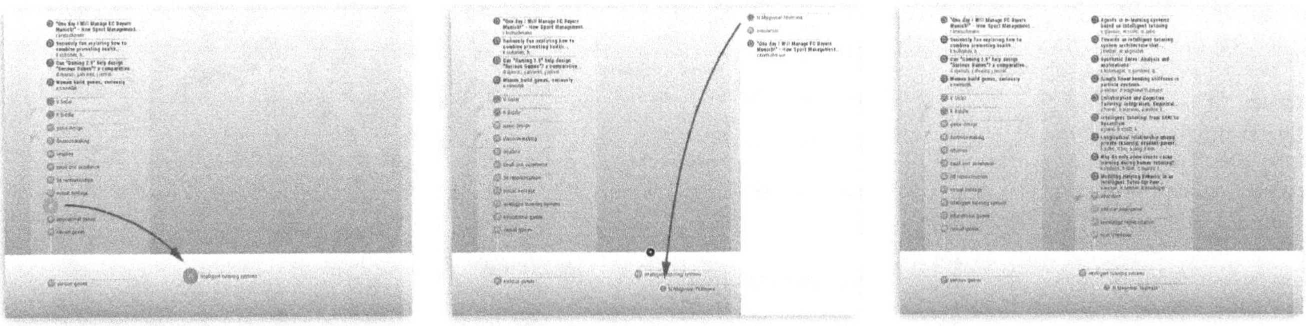

a b c

Figure 2. An exemplary search scenario illustrating the functionality of the Exploration Wall system. (a) After initiating a query the user receives a set of results, the user notices a keyword-entity that tackles her interest and drags it to the query area. (b) The user investigates the selected keyword in relation to an author entity that has been formerly saved in to the reading list by dragging the author entity to the query area as well, close enough so they become visually associated. (c) The user taps on the trigger to retrieve a new set of documents and entities (authors and keywords), that can be further manipulated and used to combine with an existing search stream or to create a new search stream.

documents, but that are central for the field of information retrieval. Second, the *document ranking* where the documents that are returned for the user as results after making some query, say "information retrieval" and "relevance feedback" should be not the most central entities, but the most relevant documents matching the query.

Entity Ranking

We represent the data as an undirected graph, where each document, keyword, and author are represented as vertices and the edges represent their occurrence in the document data.

The centrality ranking is based on the user's relevance feedback on vertices determined by dragging them into the query area. Each cluster in a query area represents a separate query that consists of a set of vertices. We use the personalized PageRank method [15] to compute the ranking of the vertices. The set of nodes that the user has chosen to be part of an individual query form the personalization vector that is set to be the prior for the PageRank computation [15]. We compute the steady distribution by using the power iteration method with 50 iterations. The top k=10 nodes from each entity category (keyword, author) are selected for presentation for the user.

Document Ranking

The document ranking is based on language modelling approach of information retrieval [41], where a unigram language model is built for each document and the maximum likelihood of the document generating the query is used to compute the ranking. We use Jelinek-Mercer smoothing to avoid zero probabilities in the estimation.

Intuitively, separating the entity ranking and document ranking approaches makes it possible to compute a limited set of entities that are likely to be the most important in the graph given the user interactions and allows users to target their feedback on a subset of the most central nodes given the interaction history of the user in any subsequent iteration. At the same time, the document ranking enables accurate and well-established methodology for ensuring relevance of the documents.

EVALUATION

The main purpose of the evaluation was to observe the effects and implications of the design of Exploration Wall on search performance and search behavior. Therefore, Exploration Wall was compared to a conventional search interface which was used as a baseline. The experiment concerned the following factors: effectiveness, expert rating, search behavior, usability and user engagement. The evaluation was composed of two tasks, a short one (5 minutes) and a long one (20 minutes).

Dataset

We used a document set including over 50 million scientific documents from the following data sources: the Web of Science prepared by Thomson Reuters, Inc., the Digital Library of the Association of Computing Machinery (ACM), the Digital Library of Institute of Electrical and Electronics Engineers (IEEE), and the Digital Library of Springer. The information about each document consists of: title, abstract, author names, and publication venue. Both the baseline and Exploration Wall used the same document set.

We decided to limit the data to scientific literature for two reasons. First, the data should allow retrieval tasks that result in exploration, and scientific search tasks are suitable for scenarios where users' goals are uncertain and require exploratory search behavior. Second, experts were available for providing high quality relevance assessments for task outcomes.

Baseline

The baseline, shown on Figure 3, was implemented following the interface principles of traditional search tools: typed query and resulting list of returned documents presented by title, with authors and keywords. The system uses the same dataset used by Exploration Wall to permit comparability. Also, the ranking is based on the same document retrieval model as in Exploration Wall, but to mimic traditional search engines it ranks only documents, while authors and keywords are only shown as additional information associated to each document. Last, our system did not allow dynamic updates of the search result when typing the query. All these factors aimed to create a baseline allowing us to focus the evaluation solely on the user interface design of Exploration Wall.

Tasks

The evaluation was composed of two tasks, a short one and a long one. We chose 6 possible different topics for the two tasks: *crowdsourcing*, *smartphones energy efficiency*, *diagrams*, *semantic web*, *lie detection* and *digital audio effects*. In order to ensure that participants were not experts in the topics and could perform a real exploratory search, they pre-rated their familiarity with the topics on a 1 (less familiar) to 5 (most familiar) scale. The four less familiar topics were used in the tasks. Both tasks were performed with different topics, so the participants did not the know the results from the previous task.

Short Task

For this task, we asked the users: "Search and list 5 relevant authors, documents and keywords that you consider relevant in topic Y." The time limit for this task was 5 minutes.

Long Task

For this task, we asked the users: "Imagine that you are writing a scientific essay on the topic X. Search and collect as many relevant scientific documents as possible that you find useful for this essay. During the task, please, list what you think are the top five key technologies, persons, documents and research areas and write five bullet lines, which would work as the core content of the essay." The time limit for this task was 20 minutes.

Participants and Procedure

We recruited 10 researchers from the computer science departments of two universities with a range of research experience. The 20% of them were females, which matched the gender ratio of both departments, and the mean age was M=30.5, SD=5.52. For the experiment participants used an iPad Air Wi-Fi tablet, as shown on Figure 4.

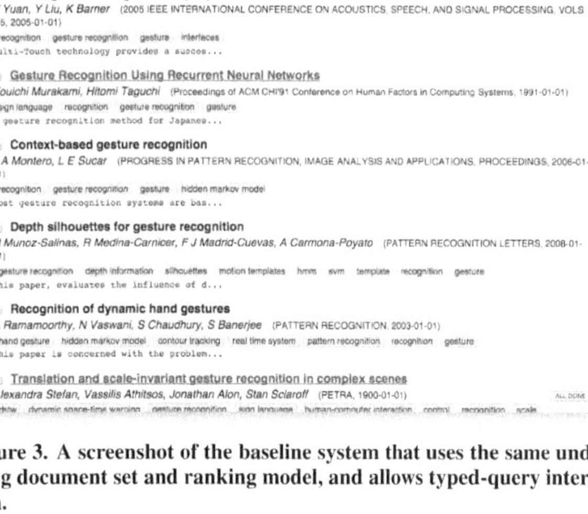

Figure 3. A screenshot of the baseline system that uses the same underlying document set and ranking model, and allows typed-query interaction.

Figure 4. Exploration Wall was evaluated using using the iPad Air Wi-Fi tablet.

In this study, we followed a within-subjects experiment design, counter-balanced by changing the order of the two tested interfaces, as well as the order of the two tasks. Before starting the main tasks, users received detailed instructions on how to use the interface and performed a 5 minutes training task on each interface. For text entry, we relied on the native virtual keyboard of the tablet. At the end of the sessions participants were asked to answer the UES and SUS questionnaires for each interface via on-line forms (Google Forms). We used the API and service of logentries.com to log all actions and data.

MEASURES

The experiment considered the following factors: effectiveness, expert rating, search behavior, usability and user engagement which were measured as follows.

Effectiveness

The effectiveness refers to the quality of the information retrieved and displayed by a system. Since our baseline system returns lists of documents while Exploration Wall returns lists of mixed-type entities, we chose to solely measure the quality of the displayed documents. We created ground truth by pooling the retrieved documents from the system logs. Domain experts were then asked to assess the relevance of the retrieved documents on a binary scale (relevant or irrelevant). Effectiveness was measured by precision, recall and F-measure at two levels [21]. First, we measured the average retrieval effectiveness at a query level as an average quality of the documents returned in response to a user interaction. Second, we measured the retrieval effectiveness at task level as an cumulative quality of documents retrieved within the whole search session.

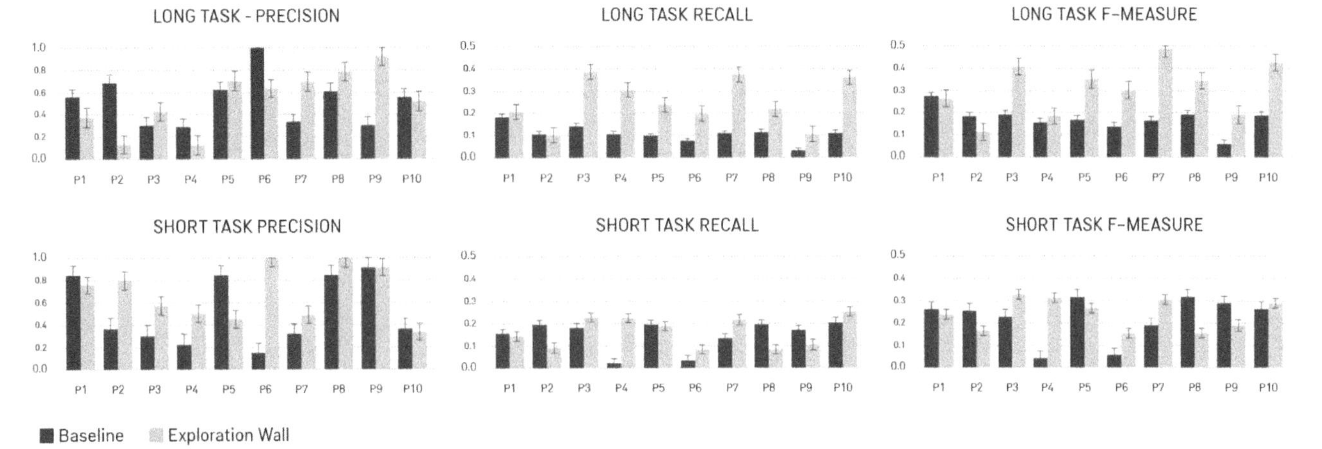

Figure 5. Effectiveness results for the short and long tasks split by participants. Results are reported as the mean of every query-response of each participant during the task.

Expert Rating

Experts were asked to rate the task outcome. For the short task, the outcome was a list of documents, and two types of entities: authors and keywords. The relevance of each item was evaluated on a 5-point scale (1 less relevant - 5 most relevant). The outcome of the long task was an essay, a set of documents, and a set of entities: keywords representing technologies and research areas, and persons. The sets of documents and entities were evaluated in the same way as in the short task, while the essay was evaluated on a different 5-point scale (5=Excellent, 4=Good, 3=Satisfactory, 2=Deficient, 1=Failing).

Search Trail Analysis

In order to understand and compare users' search behavior, we logged user actions and extracted corresponding search trails using a method resembling White's [36]. In a similar manner, we then looked for descriptive statistics of the search trails by selecting six parameters relevant to both interfaces.

- Number of queries: the total number of queries that were submitted during each task on both interface.
- Number of text entries per query
- Number of revisits: The number of revisits to a query or stream consulted earlier in the current trail.
- Number of branches: The number of times a subject revisited a query or stream on the current trail and then proceeded with formulation of a new query.
- Number of queries/min: the number of queries per minute that were submitted during each task on both interface.
- Number of parallel queries: Number of parallel streams produced with Exploration Wall or number of tabs opened with the baseline.

Usability and Engagement

As usability assessment questionnaires we used the standard System Usability Scale (SUS) [6] and the User Engagement Scale (UES) for exploratory search [26]. SUS consists of a ten item questionnaire and is a widely used and validated for measuring perceptions of usability. Since the degree of user engagement is a strong indicator of exploratory search performance [38], we chose to use UES for exploratory search. The User Engagement Scale (UES) questionnaire include 27 questions considering six different dimensions: Aesthetics (AE), Focused Attention (FA), Felt Involvement (FI), Perceived Usability (PUs), Novelty (NO) and Endurability (EN) aspects of the experience.

RESULTS

In this section, we present results from the user experiments divided according to the different factors: effectiveness, expert rating, search trail analysis, and usability and engagement.

Effectiveness

The effectiveness results are given in Table 1. The results show that Exploration Wall shows substantial improvement in the long task. The improvement was found to hold for task-level measurement, but also for averaged interaction-level measurement for which the recall and the F-measure were found to be significantly higher compared to the baseline. On average at the query level, the F-measure for the Exploration Wall was improved (M=0.136, SD=0.122). This im-

	Long Task			Short Task		
	BL	EW	p	BL	EW	p
P (Task)	0.40	0.42	0.85	0.52	0.58	0.67
R (Task)	0.13	**0.38**	**<0.01**	0.18	0.21	0.59
F (Task)	0.17	**0.34**	**<0.01**	0.25	0.26	0.90
P (Query)	0.53	0.53	0.96	0.52	0.69	0.16
R (Query)	0.11	**0.25**	**<0.01**	0.15	0.16	0.69
F (Query)	0.17	**0.31**	**<0.01**	0.22	0.24	0.41

Table 1. Effectiveness results for the short and long tasks. Results are reported cumulatively for the whole duration of the task and as a mean of every query-response during the task. P=Precision, R=Recall, F=F_1 measure, EW=Exploration Wall, BL=Baseline.

	Long Task						
Search Trail Features	BL			EW			BL vs EW
	M	SD	Median	M	SD	Median	Wilcoxon Test
No. of queries	4.30	3.09	4.50	12.10	6.97	**13.50**	**Z = -2.76, p <0.01**
No. of text entries/query	1.00	0.00	1.00	0.36	0.35	**0.27**	**Z = 2.67, p <0.01**
No. of branches	0.10	0.31	0.00	5.70	4.55	**6.00**	**Z = -2.68, p <0.01**
No. of revisits	0.70	1.64	0.00	7.00	6.09	**6.00**	**Z = -2.67, p <0.01**
No. of queries/min	0.26	0.17	0.26	0.63	0.36	**0.70**	**Z = -2.70, p <0.01**
No. parallel queries	1.70	1.06	1.00	8.50	5.89	**7.00**	**Z = -2.76, p <0.01**
	Short Task						
Search Trail Feature	BL			EW			BL vs EW
	M	SD	Median	M	SD	Median	Wilcoxon Test
No. of queries	2.50	1.58	2.00	3.50	2.12	4.00	Z = -1.46, p >0.05
No. of text entries/query	1.00	0.00	1.00	0.55	0.35	**0.47**	**Z = 2.55, p <0.05**
No. of branches	0.00	0.00	0.00	0.8	1.03	**0.5**	**Z = -2.21, p <0.05**
No. of revisits	0.20	0.42	0.00	1.1	1.10	1.0	Z = -1.81, p >0.05
No. of queries/min	0.59	0.33	0.45	0.86	0.36	0.93	Z = -2.24, p >0.05
No. of parallel queries	1.30	0.67	1.00	2.70	2.00	**2.00**	**Z = -2.40, p <0.05**

Table 2. Results of the search trail analysis for the short and long tasks. Means, Standard Deviation, Median (used in the Wilcoxon Matched-Pairs test) as well as Significant differences of search trail feature considering both interfaces. The values in bold show the significant differences. BL=baseline, EW=Exploration Wall.

provement was statistically significant, $t(9)$=3.519, $p < 0.01$. This is a direct consequence of the improvement in the recall (M=0.142, SD=0.094, $t(9)$=4.790, $p < 0.001$). The difference in precision was not significant (M=0.005, SD=0.366) which indicates that while Exploration Wall improves recall it retains precision. In terms of effectiveness, no statistically significant differences between the systems were found in the short task.

Figure 5 shows the query-level effectiveness for the long tasks and the short task split by participants. Exploration Wall constantly outperforms the baseline system in terms of recall and F-measure in the long task. The effect is steady across participants. No significant differences between the systems were found in the short task.

Expert Rating

Unlike the effectiveness, the expert rating showed no significant differences between the Exploration Wall and the Baseline. Regarding the relevance of selected items, the mean values for the long task were M=3.54, SD=0.67 for Exploration Wall and M=3.45, SD=0.82 for Baseline, while for short task they were M=3.60, SD=1.23 for Exploration Wall and M=3.83, SD=0.99 for Baseline. Regarding the the relevance of the essays produced in the end of the long task the mean values were M=3.90, SD=0.75 for Exploration Wall and M=4.05, SD=0.69 for Baseline.

Search Trail Analysis

Table 2 shows the results of the search trail analysis. The Shapiro-Wilk test indicated that the search trail data did not follow a normal distribution, and the Wilcoxon Matched-Pairs test was used for significance testing. The users in the Exploration Wall condition were found to use all of the measured interaction features significantly more than the users in the baseline condition in the long task. Differences were also found in the short task. The users in the Exploration Wall condition typed less, branched more, and used more parallel queries.

Usability and Engagement

The results for the mean of answers of the SUS questionnaire, i.e., for usability, were M=78.85, SD=12.43 for Exploration Wall and M=62.25, SD=15.65 for the baseline. A paired t-test showed a significant difference ($t(9)$=2.36, $p < 0.05$) between the two systems, revealing higher usability for Exploration Wall. The results of the UES questionnaires are also favorable for Exploration Wall. Wilcoxon Matched-Pairs test shows that in 70% of the questions there is a significant difference between the interfaces, all in favour of Exploration Wall.

DISCUSSION AND CONCLUSIONS

Challenges in supporting exploratory search include providing resources for formulating queries in unknown areas [11], learning about possible directions in the information space [29], and going through long list of results with low information gain [38, 5]. In particular on keyboard-less touch devices the challenges are aggravated by typing efforts. We introduced Exploration Wall a novel user interface that addresses these challenges with a principled design. The founding principle is to transform results into entities that can be flexibly manipulated and used for creating queries and search streams. The wall is a canvas where parallel and previous search streams are juxtaposed and provide a spatial exploration of the information space and possible exploration directions. The manipulation includes inspecting relationship between entities and facilitating the creation of new search streams.

The study shows how Exploration Wall is an effective tool for exploratory search on touch surfaces. Participants using Exploration Wall were able to exploit parallel search streams to iteratively refine their queries and deeply explore the search tree. The difference in recall proves that more relevant documents were retrieved when using Exploration Wall.

Exploration Wall also led to a more active search behavior, with more queries per minute and more branches. In addition, if we consider the fact that participants used more parallel queries with Exploration Wall (parallel streams) than with the baseline (parallel tabs), we can conclude that the participants took advantage of parallel streams with consequent avoidance of text input.

Results from the UES questionnaire also show a better user engagement, a factor that is likely to have contributed to the more active search behavior. In addition, the SUS scale shows that Exploration Wall presents a better usability than conventional search interfaces on tablets.

The study confirms how our design approach facilitates query formulation, by directing exploration in unknown areas, and providing alternatives to text inputs. While little or no differences were appreciated in short tasks, Exploration Wall proved to be an effective tool for long tasks by showing improved recall while preserving precision, as well as improved user engagement and satisfaction.

In addition to the positive results, this work is adaptable to many applications and setups that would enable new possibilities to be found through deeper study of user behavior (e.g. search strategies and nature of composed queries). It has important implications for future development of exploratory search systems in particular considering multimodal interaction and user interface for entity oriented search [27]. The principles are applicable to other datasets such as for example news search [4] as well as other devices and sizes (e.g. large multi-touch screen for collaborative work, mobile devices for mobility and privacy, combinations of devices, desktop).

Considering this, as well as the growing popularity of touch devices, our work offers a powerful and flexible template to be considered when designing user interfaces supporting exploratory search.

ACKNOWLEDGMENTS

This research was partially funded by TEKES (through the Re:KnoW project), the European Commission through the FP7 Project MindSee 611570, the Academy of Finland (Multivire, 255725 and 278090), TIPEx Project (TIN2010-19859-C03-01) and "Postdoc Mobility Scholarship Programme" of Universidad Carlos III de Madrid. Certain data included herein are derived from the Web of Science prepared by THOMSON REUTERS, Inc., Philadelphia, Pennsylvania, USA: Copyright THOMSON REUTERS, 2011. All rights reserved. Data is also included from the Digital Libraries of the ACM, IEEE, and Springer We would like to thank Kumaripaba Athukorala for her valuable suggestions.

REFERENCES

1. Ahlberg, C., and Shneiderman, B. Visual information seeking: Tight coupling of dynamic query filters with starfield displays. In *Proc. CHI*, ACM (New York, NY, USA, 1994), 313–317.
2. Ahn, J., and Brusilovsky, P. Adaptive visualization for exploratory information retrieval. *Information Processing & Management 49*, 5 (2013), 1139–1164.
3. Ahn, J.-w., and Brusilovsky, P. Adaptive visualization of search results: Bringing user models to visual analytics. *Information Visualization 8*, 3 (2009), 167–179.
4. Andolina, S., Klouche, K., Peltonen, J., Hoque, M., Ruotsalo, T., Cabral, D., Klami, A., Głowacka, D., Floréen, P., and Jacucci, G. Intentstreams: smart parallel search streams for branching exploratory search. In *Proc. IUI*, ACM (2015).
5. Athukorala, K., Oulasvirta, A., Głowacka, D., Vreeken, J., and Jacucci, G. Narrow or broad?: Estimating subjective specificity in exploratory search. In *Proc. CIKM*, ACM (New York, NY, USA, 2014), 819–828.
6. Brooke, J. Sus-a quick and dirty usability scale. *Usability evaluation in industry 189* (1996), 194.
7. Capra, R., Marchionini, G., Oh, J. S., Stutzman, F., and Zhang, Y. Effects of structure and interaction style on distinct search tasks. In *Proc. JCDL*, ACM (2007), 442–451.
8. Chau, D. H., Kittur, A., Hong, J. I., and Faloutsos, C. Apolo: Making sense of large network data by combining rich user interaction and machine learning. In *Proc. CHI*, ACM, ACM (New York, NY, USA, 2011), 167–176.
9. Coutrix, C., Kuikkaniemi, K., Kurvinen, E., Jacucci, G., Avdouevski, I., and Mäkelä, R. Fizzyvis: designing for playful information browsing on a multitouch public display. In *Proc. DPPI*, ACM (2011), 27.
10. Esenther, A., and Ryall, K. Fluid dtmouse: Better mouse support for touch-based interactions. In *Proc. AVI*, ACM (New York, NY, USA, 2006), 112–115.
11. Głowacka, D., Ruotsalo, T., Konyushkova, K., Athukorala, K., Jacucci, G., and Kaski, S. Directing exploratory search: Reinforcement learning from user interactions with keywords. In *Proc. IUI*, ACM (New York, NY, USA, 2013), 117–128.
12. Havre, S., Hetzler, E., Perrine, K., Jurrus, E., and Miller, N. Interactive visualization of multiple query results. In *Proc. InfoVis*, IEEE Computer Society (Washington, DC, USA, 2001), 105.
13. Hinrichs, U., Schmidt, H., and Carpendale, S. Emdialog: Bringing information visualization into the museum. *Visualization and Computer Graphics, IEEE Transactions on 14*, 6 (2008), 1181–1188.
14. Jacucci, G., Morrison, A., Richard, G. T., Kleimola, J., Peltonen, P., Parisi, L., and Laitinen, T. Worlds of information: designing for engagement at a public multi-touch display. In *Proc. CHI*, ACM (2010), 2267–2276.
15. Jeh, G., and Widom, J. Scaling personalized web search. In *Proc. WWW*, ACM (New York, NY, USA, 2003), 271–279.

16. Jones, M., Buchanan, G., Harper, R., and Xech, P.-L. Questions not answers: A novel mobile search technique. In *Proc. CHI*, ACM (New York, NY, USA, 2007), 155–158.

17. Käki, M. Findex: Search result categories help users when document ranking fails. In *Proc. CHI*, ACM (New York, NY, USA, 2005), 131–140.

18. Karlson, A. K., Robertson, G. G., Robbins, D. C., Czerwinski, M. P., and Smith, G. R. Fathumb: A facet-based interface for mobile search. In *Proc. CHI*, ACM (New York, NY, USA, 2006), 711–720.

19. Kules, W., Wilson, M. L., Schraefel, M. C., and Shneiderman, B. From keyword search to exploration: How result visualization aids discovery on the web. Tech. rep., University of Southampton, 2008.

20. Li, Y. Gesture search: a tool for fast mobile data access. In *Proc. UIST*, ACM (2010), 87–96.

21. Manning, C. D., Raghavan, P., and Schütze, H. *Introduction to information retrieval*, vol. 1. Cambridge university press Cambridge, 2008.

22. Marchionini, G. Exploratory search: from finding to understanding. *Commun. ACM 49*, 4 (Apr. 2006), 41–46.

23. Matejka, J., Grossman, T., and Fitzmaurice, G. Citeology: Visualizing paper genealogy. In *CHI '12 Extended Abstracts on Human Factors in Computing Systems*, ACM (New York, NY, USA, 2012), 181–190.

24. Morris, M. R., Fisher, D., and Wigdor, D. Search on surfaces: Exploring the potential of interactive tabletops for collaborative search tasks. *Information processing & management 46*, 6 (2010), 703–717.

25. Morris, M. R., Lombardo, J., and Wigdor, D. Wesearch: supporting collaborative search and sensemaking on a tabletop display. In *Proc. CSCW*, ACM (2010), 401–410.

26. O'Brien, H. L., and Toms, E. G. Examining the generalizability of the user engagement scale (ues) in exploratory search. *Information Processing & Management 49*, 5 (2013), 1092 – 1107.

27. Ruotsalo, T., and Hyvönen, E. Exploiting semantic annotations for domain-specific entity search. In *Proc. ECIR*, Springer (2015).

28. Ruotsalo, T., Jacucci, G., Myllymäki, P., and Kaski, S. Interactive intent modeling: Information discovery beyond search. *Communications of the ACM 58*, 1 (Jan. 2015), 86–92.

29. Ruotsalo, T., Peltonen, J., Eugster, M., Głowacka, D., Konyushkova, K., Athukorala, K., Kosunen, I., Reijonen, A., Myllymäki, P., Jacucci, G., et al. Directing exploratory search with interactive intent modeling. In *Proc. CIKM*, ACM (2013), 1759–1764.

30. Sadler, E. B. Project blacklight: a next generation library catalog at a first generation university. *Library Hi Tech 27*, 1 (2009), 57–67.

31. Stasko, J., Görg, C., and Liu, Z. Jigsaw: supporting investigative analysis through interactive visualization. *Information visualization 7*, 2 (2008), 118–132.

32. Terveen, L., Hill, W., and Amento, B. Constructing, organizing, and visualizing collections of topically related web resources. *ACM Transactions on Computer-Human Interaction 6*, 1 (1999), 67–94.

33. Thudt, A., Hinrichs, U., and Carpendale, S. The bohemian bookshelf: supporting serendipitous book discoveries through information visualization. In *Proc. CHI*, ACM (2012), 1461–1470.

34. Varcholik, P. D., LaViola, J. J., and Hughes, C. E. Establishing a baseline for text entry for a multi-touch virtual keyboard. *Int. J. of Human-Computer Studies 70*, 10 (2012), 657 – 672.

35. Verbert, K., Parra, D., Brusilovsky, P., and Duval, E. Visualizing recommendations to support exploration, transparency and controllability. In *Proc. IUI*, ACM, ACM (New York, NY, USA, 2013), 351–362.

36. White, R. W., and Drucker, S. M. Investigating behavioral variability in web search. In *Proc. WWW*, ACM (2007), 21–30.

37. White, R. W., Drucker, S. M., Marchionini, G., Hearst, M., and schraefel, m. c. Exploratory search and hci: Designing and evaluating interfaces to support exploratory search interaction. In *CHI '07 Extended Abstracts on Human Factors in Computing Systems*, ACM (New York, NY, USA, 2007), 2877–2880.

38. White, R. W., and Roth, R. A. Exploratory search: Beyond the query-response paradigm. *Synth. Lec. on Inf. Conc., Retr., and Serv. 1*, 1 (2009), 1–98.

39. Wigdor, D., and Wixon, D. *Brave NUI world: designing natural user interfaces for touch and gesture*. Elsevier, 2011.

40. Wildemuth, B. M., and Freund, L. Assigning search tasks designed to elicit exploratory search behaviors. In *Proc. HCIR*, ACM (New York, NY, USA, 2012), 4:1–4:10.

41. Zhai, C., and Lafferty, J. A study of smoothing methods for language models applied to information retrieval. *ACM Trans. Inf. Syst. 22*, 2 (2004), 179–214.

42. Zhai, S., Kristensson, P.-O., and Smith, B. A. In search of effective text input interfaces for off the desktop computing. *Interacting with computers 17*, 3 (2005), 229–250.

Clutching Is Not (Necessarily) the Enemy

Mathieu Nancel
Cheriton School of Computer Science
University of Waterloo, CANADA
mnancel.liu@uwaterloo.ca

Daniel Vogel
Cheriton School of Computer Science
University of Waterloo, CANADA
dvogel@uwaterloo.ca

Edward Lank
Cheriton School of Computer Science
University of Waterloo, CANADA
lank@uwaterloo.ca

ABSTRACT

Clutching is usually assumed to be triggered by a lack of physical space and detrimental to pointing performance. We conduct a controlled experiment using a laptop trackpad where the effect of clutching on pointing performance is dissociated from the effects of control-to-display transfer functions. Participants performed a series of target acquisition tasks using typical cursor acceleration functions with and without clutching. All pointing tasks were feasible without clutching, but clutch-less movements were harder to perform, caused more errors, required more preparation time, and were not faster than clutch-enabled movements.

Author Keywords

clutching; pointing; performance; trackpad; touchpad

ACM Classi cation Keywords

H.5.2. Information interfaces (e.g., HCI): User Interfaces.

INTRODUCTION

Relative pointing is the mapping of physical motion to cursor displacement using a Control-to-Display (CD) transfer function. It is common with mice and trackpads and proven efficient for mid-air interaction [1, 6, 7]. One characteristic is that a discrepancy builds between the relative location of the cursor on the display and the position of the input device (e.g. finger on trackpad). To stay within an optimal range of input sensing or comfort, this discrepancy must be reset at regular intervals with a clutch'. This is a break in control-to-display mapping when the input device can be moved independently of the cursor (e.g. lifting the finger to reposition it on a trackpad). Based on observed correlations between increased pointing time with increased clutching [1, 3], the belief is that clutching impairs performance since input time is "lost" when clutching. For this reason, researcher and designers typically view clutching as the enemy', seeking to avoid it entirely or minimize its frequency or effect.

Avoiding clutching completely usually requires using absolute mappings [5–7] or rate-based mappings [3]. Since clutching is expected when there is not enough physical input space to perform a pointing movement [2, 3], a commonly proposed solution is to increase the CD gain [2, 6] since low gains cause more clutches. However, the interaction between CD gain, clutching, and pointing performance is not that trivial. For example, Chapuis *et al.* observed performance decreased with low gains even without clutching [4]. Since clutching cannot be avoided with relative pointing, work has considered it when designing transfer functions and performance modeling [5] and methods have been proposed to improve the clutching mechanism itself [8] or make up for lost pointing time by gliding the cursor during a clutch [1].

Yet despite encouraging results for these reduced-clutching pointing techniques [1, 3, 6], what causes clutching and whether clutching is responsible for lost performance remains hypothetical: (i) Casiez *et al.*'s model of clutching [3] was originally evaluated in limited input and task conditions, and in [1] Beaudouin-Lafon *et al.* were unable to show that this model fits their data better than Fitts' law despite a significant number of clutches; (ii) the clutch-avoidance effectiveness of recent approaches [2, 6] remains to be quantified, and (iii) it remains unclear whether the performance gain in clutch-minimizing techniques is entirely due to reduced clutching, or simply due to faster cursor movements.

We investigate the cause and effect of clutching independently of the transfer function. We ran a controlled experiment using a laptop trackpad where all target acquisition tasks could be performed without clutching. In the first condition, clutching was permitted to observe if participants clutched by choice and how clutching was affected by the transfer function. In the second condition, clutching was not permitted to produce hypothetically ideal clutch-less motions to directly compare performance with and without clutching.

Our results indicate no clear time improvement between movements with "unnecessary" clutching and ideal clutch-less movements on a trackpad. Yet, clutch-less movements are harder to produce, cause twice as many errors, and require more planning time. Therefore clutch-less movements are not necessarily an optimal pointing strategy. This calls for a reconsideration of clutching and for deeper investigation of its causes and effects in relation to input devices, transfer functions, physical space, and input speed.

MOTIVATION

Causes of clutching

Clutching is usually attributed to insufficient physical space to make the cursor travel a given distance with a transfer function [3], whether the function is linear [2] or acceleration-based [6]. This is easy to verify with linear functions, as cursor motion with constant CD gain is only affected by the physical amplitude of the input movement (provided that input events and cursor updates have the same frequency). This

CHI 2015, April 18–23, 2015, Seoul, Republic of Korea.

ACM 978-1-4503-3145-6/15/04...$15.00
http://dx.doi.org/10.1145/2702123.2702134

effect is less trivial to model with acceleration because the amplitude and speed of the input movement are co-dependent when considered in the resolution of cursor motion: user performance might vary depending on ability to perform fast input motions or to control wide ranges of speed, but approximations can be made using the highest accessible gains [2, 6]. In these cases, clutching is unavoidable and prior research suggests minimum bounds for gain values to avoid it [2], based on the sensing or operating range of the input device. Another plausible purpose for clutching is to minimize the control-display discrepancy by readjusting the location of the user's limb relative to the input sensor or to the user's body. This cause is similar but depends on the *remaining* physical space available in the sensing range in the direction of the pointing motion, rather than its total size.

We suspect clutching is caused by more than mechanical limitations. This is based on informal observations: the acceleration settings of operating systems generally allow the cursor to go through the whole display with a short wrist or finger ick, often of less than half the operating range of the mouse or trackpad; yet users using such normal settings appear to clutch more often that would be accounted for by simply needing to minimize the control-display discrepancy. Similar observations were reported for mid-air pointing [1, 6], where participants clutched even though the transfer functions theoretically allowed them to perform all tasks without clutching. We evaluate whether this informal observation holds with the more common laptop trackpad, and if so, whether clutching really re ects suboptimal pointing behavior.

Effects of faster transfer functions

Clutching is assumed to lower pointing performance and it is often advocated to avoid it when designing relative pointing techniques [2, 3, 6]. A common guideline is to use higher CD gain values, because these generally result in better performance. However it is unclear why. Less clutching and faster cursor motions are both trivial consequences of higher gains, but the exact causation from these intermediate effects to increased performance remain to be quantified. We need to control for clutching when evaluating the effects of faster transfer functions, but even more strictly than Chapuis *et al.* [4].

Effects of clutching on performance

The specific assumption that clutching lowers pointing performance remains to be formally asserted and quantified. Since time is spent clutching while the cursor remains static, it must be that performance is reduced (barring inertial pointing, like [1] or trackballs). However, there are other aspects to consider. For example, the effective operating range decreases, potentially lowering the number of joints and muscles in use. Also, people may unconsciously optimize the amount of effort or attention required to perform difficult tasks like selecting small targets over large distances. This requires both high and low input speeds, and clutching could be used to divide the pointing movement into sub-movements of more controllable speeds [5]. Therefore, to assess the effectiveness of the hypothetically optimal clutch-less behaviour, we need to evaluate conditions where participants are specifically instructed not to clutch.

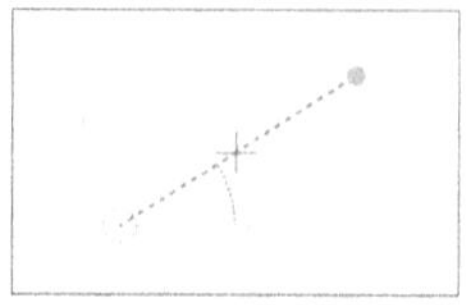

Figure 1. Pointing task: all tasks were centred around the screen centre; participants had to click the pre-target then the target. Targets scale increased for readability and in experiment, the background was black.

STUDY

Our experiment investigates four research questions:

Q1 Is clutching only triggered by transfer functions that are too slow or the physical range being too small?

Q2 What are the effects of transfer functions on clutching?

Q3 At equal difficulty and transfer function, is there a systematic advantage to performing clutch-less movements?

Q4 What are the effects of clutching on performance?

Participants

We recruited 12 participants (1 female), aged 23 to 39 (mean 26.8, SD 4.4), all right-handed and using computers more than 30 hours a week (mean 51.4, SD 15.9).

Apparatus

Participants used a MacBook Pro Retina with 115×85 mm trackpad and OSX 10.8 acceleration settings. In order to accurately differentiate tapping events from clutch events, we disabled tap-to-click and instructed participants to click using the embedded physical button on the trackpad. Thus, a clutch was detected any time participants lifted their finger. Software was developed in Java 7 using the Java Native Interface[1] to access low-level trackpad events.

Task and Stimuli

The task was consecutively clicking inside a *pre-target* (circle, ⌀10 mm) then a target (disc) of variable width and distance (Fig. 1). Both were displayed at the beginning of the task trial; the pre-target disappeared when it was clicked. We ignored the time taken to reach the pre-target in our analyses. We chose a randomized target presentation over a repetitive, reciprocal one for two reasons. First, people do not necessarily plan pointing trajectories far ahead, but trajectories can be artificially learned with repetitive tasks. Second, this ensures that pointing motion is not constrained by the physical location of the hand at the end of the previous task.

Design

We used three ACCELERATION levels: 5th, 7th and 9th notches on the slider of the Mac OS 10.8 trackpad speed settings. Participants first performed 50 trials with each ACCELERATION level as accurately and quickly as possible without any specific instruction about clutching (CLUTCH condition). The cursor was a white cross. After we brie y explained clutching, participants were instructed to perform the same trials without clutching between the pre-target and target (NOCLUTCH condition). In pilot studies, participants tended to overlook

[1] http://docs.oracle.com/javase/7/docs/technotes/guides/jni/

the NoClutch instruction after a while, so the cross cursor was surrounded with a white circle as soon as they clicked the pre-target, as a visual reminder. If a clutch was detected in the NoClutch condition, the whole cursor turned red and thicker until they resumed pointing. We discard NoClutch trials with clutches from analysis (i.e. when this extra feedback is shown). Clutches occurring before the pre-target was clicked are not considered.

The ordering of the CanClutch factor was not counterbalanced. Pilot tests showed that pointing on a trackpad is such a common task that no amount of training could prevent normal pointing habits (i.e. Clutch) to in uence the NoClutch condition. Conversely, pilot tests confirmed that practising with NoClutch does affect further "normal" pointing behaviour. While interesting, the real-life implications of that effect do not answer our research questions. The first 15 trials of all CanClutch × Acceleration conditions were excluded as training, resulting in 2 CanClutch{Clutch, NoClutch}× 3 Acceleration {Acc5, Acc7, Acc9}× 35 trials = 210 data points per participant. The experiment lasted 40 min, participants did not report substantial fatigue.

Distributions of Independent Variables

To minimize loss of information or effect, we generate uniform distributions for Width, Amplitude, Fitts's ID, and direction to obtain an all-inclusive, equally-likely sample of the observed effect (rather than extrapolate from a regression line based on a small number of aggregates). Widths are chosen to be realistically hard to acquire, from the size of a desktop icon (12 mm) to a very small size visible with normal eyesight (1.5 mm). Amplitudes are chosen to re ect realistic pointing tasks on a 13" laptop (43 to 239 mm on a 285 × 175 mm screen) while limiting edge pointing, known to affect pointing behaviour and performance.

Since $ID = f(A, W)$, the uniformity of all three variables cannot be strictly maintained. We focus on Fitts's ID and relax the uniformity constraint on Amplitude and Width as follows. In all trials, Fitts's ID is chosen randomly between 2.2 and 7.32 bits (best- and worst-case scenarios). In odd trials, Width is chosen randomly between 1.5 and 12 mm and Amplitude is computed as $A = W(2^{ID} - 1)$. In even trials, Amplitude is chosen randomly between 43 and 239 mm and Width is computed as $W = \frac{A}{2^{ID}-1}$. In all trials, direction angle is chosen randomly: pre- and actual targets are centred on screen Amplitude mm apart on a random angle between -180 and 180 degrees (Fig. 1); if the resulting targets are partially or completely out of the screen, a new angle is chosen. Pilot tests revealed the trackpad button is much harder to use when near the top of the trackpad, especially problematic with NoClutch. To compensate, we added an additional condition to angle selection: the target had to be more than 15 mm from the top of the display.

This produced uniform distributions for Fitts's ID (M 4.74 bits, SD 1.45 bits). The distribution of angles was affected by the screen aspect-ratio, favouring horizontal angles for high Amplitude (M 7.4 deg, SD 106.7 deg). As expected distributions were skewed for Amplitude (M 130.6 mm, SD 63.5 mm, skewness .17) and Width (M 5.6 mm, SD 3.4 mm, skewness .41), which remain close to uniform distributions.

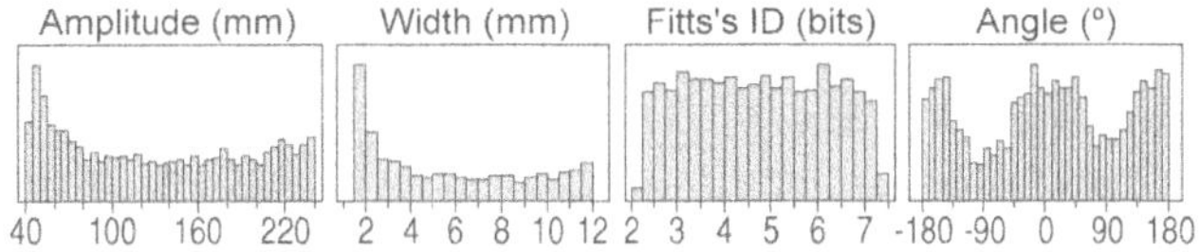

Figure 2. Distributions for A, W, ID and angle.

Results

We found no order effect of Acceleration on task time. All analyses are multi-way ANOVA: participant is a random variable using the REML procedure of the SAS JMP package. Post-hoc Tukey tests are used unless stated otherwise.

Amount of clutching

We found significant effects of CanClutch ($F_{1,11} = 36.5$, $p < 0.0001$), Acceleration ($F_{2,22} = 15.4$, $p < 0.0001$) and CanClutch×Acceleration ($F_{2,22} = 14.6$, $p < 0.0001$) on the number of clutches. Post-hoc tests show that Acceleration did not significantly affect the number of clutches in the NoClutch condition (mean .2 clutches per trial), that NoClutch caused significantly less clutches than Clutch (mean 1.24 clutches per trial) overall and that, in the Clutch condition, Acc5 caused significantly more clutches (mean 1.6 clutches per trial) than Acc7 (1.18) and Acc9 (.94). A nominal logistic test showed that Fitts's ID had a significant (decreasing) effect on whether participants clutched or not in the Clutch condition ($\chi^2 = 57.8, p < .0001$). Overall, 14.7% of the NoClutch trials had one or more clutches: 14.9, 17.6 and 11.5% for Acc5, Acc7 and Acc9.

Error rate

We consider the Error rate as the ratio of trials where one or more clicks missed the final target. We found a significant effect of CanClutch on Error ($F_{1,11} = 7.1, p = .0222$) and no effect of Acceleration. A Student t-test revealed that participants made almost twice as many errors in the NoClutch phase (4.2%) than in the Clutch phase (2.6%). All trials with Errors are ignored in the following analyses.

Time performance

We measured Movement Time (MT) as the time between clicking the pre-target and clicking the target, Preparation Time (PT) the time between entering the pre-target and clicking it, and Start Time (ST) the time between clicking the pre-target and leaving it. No aggregation was performed before running regressions with Fitts's ID, on account of our continuous Fitts's ID range. For other within-subject ANOVA, we used medians to compensate for skewed distributions.

We excluded 183 NoClutch trials where a clutch occurred (14.7%) in order to obtain a corpus of ideal clutch-less pointing motions regardless of the cursor transfer function. Clutch-less motions also occurred in the Clutch condition, more often (but not exclusively) in the easier tasks, as reported above.

We found no significant effect of CanClutch and Acceleration on MT, and an equivalence test with 200 ms threshold finds MT equivalent for Clutch and NoClutch ($p = .0406$).

Fitts's law regressions are very similar: MT$= 461.6+394.8 \times ID(r^2 = .41)$ for NoClutch and MT$= 348.6 + 433.8 \times ID(r^2 = .39)$ for Clutch, see Fig. 3.

Neither CanClutch and Acceleration had any significant effect on ST, but PT was significantly affected by CanClutch ($F_{1,11} = 7.8, p = .0176$) and CanClutch×Acceleration ($F_{2,22} = 5.5, p = .0113$). Participants took significantly more time to click the pre-target in the NoClutch condition (834.7 ms) than in the Clutch condition (654.1 ms). More precisely, the condition Acc5×NoClutch (936 ms) was significantly slower than every other combination (mean 676.2 ms) except Acc7×NoClutch (825.6 ms). Fitts's ID also has a significant effect on PT for Clutch ($F_{1,11.85} = 6.42, p = .0265$, PT$= 590.8 + 25.9 \times ID$) and NoClutch ($F_{1,9.48} = 33.22, p = .0002$, PT$= 610.2 + 68.3 \times ID$), see Fig. 3.

We hypothesize that participants spent more time above the pre-target in the NoClutch condition to prepare for difficult tasks, either to relocate their finger on the trackpad or to plan a fast movement. This indicates that pointing actions started before the pre-target was clicked. We thus introduce another time measure, Task Time (TT=MT+PT). We found no significant effect of CanClutch or Acceleration on TT, and an equivalence test with 200 ms threshold finds TT equivalent for Clutch and NoClutch ($p = .0073$). Again, Fitts's law regressions are very similar: TT$= 1071.8 + 463.1 \times ID, r^2 = .38$ for NoClutch and TT$= 939.4 + 459.6 \times ID, r^2 = .31$ see Fig. 3. On average, TT was higher for NoClutch (Fig. 4).

Finally, CanClutch had a significant effect on cursor-moving time ($F_{1,11} = 8.2, p = .0152$), which was significantly higher in the NoClutch condition (3606.8 vs. 3391.5 ms) (Fig. 4).

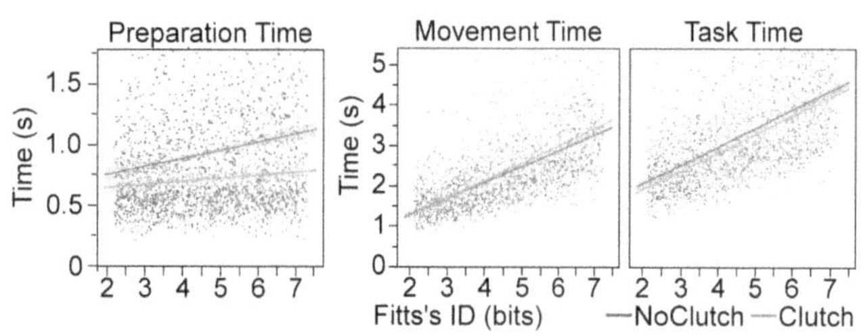

Figure 3. Fitts's law regressions for Preparation Time (PT), Movement Time (MT) and Task Time (TT). Outlines represent the confidence of fit.

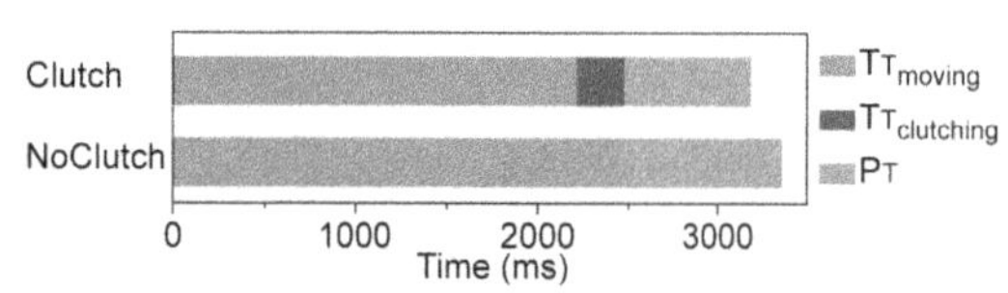

Figure 4. Mean Task Time when moving the cursor (TT_{moving}) and when clutching ($TT_{clutching}$), and Preparation Time (PT).

Summary

Almost all participants felt that the Clutch condition was faster (P9 felt otherwise), more precise (P2 felt otherwise), easier to use, less tiring (P2 felt otherwise), and preferred it over NoClutch. All aspects rated on 7-point Likert scales. One participant (P4) felt no difference at all since they always try to avoid clutching.

All tasks were feasible with a single finger motion, yet we found that participants clutched often when not instructed otherwise (M 1.24 clutch/trial, **Q1**). Unsurprisingly, lower pointer accelerations increased clutching (**Q2**), but faster accelerations did not cancel it (.94 clutch/trial with Acc9). Despite previous assumptions, we did not find explicitly clutch-less pointing motions to be significantly beneficial to pointing time. On the contrary, they caused twice as many pointing errors (**Q3**). Clutch-less movements were also harder to produce (14.7% failed) and necessitated more preparation time. Despite not "loosing" any time from clutches, the time spent actually moving the cursor (TT_{moving} in Fig. 4) was about 200 ms longer in average with clutch-less pointing (**Q4**).

DISCUSSION AND FUTURE WORK

These results challenge the current belief that clutching is detrimental to pointing performance. Clutching is a favoured and effective trackpad pointing strategy, not just a method to compensate for limited physical space. The hypothetically optimal clutch-less movements turn out harder to perform, causing more errors and no time improvement. Possible causes, including optimization of motor resources (fewer joints and muscles put in use) or psycho-motor resources (splitting a difficult movement into more controllable chunks) will be investigated in future works. This work is a first step towards formulating a more comprehensive model of clutching and pointing. Given these encouraging first results, we are pursing expanded analysis of different input devices, transfer functions, and tasks where clutching is unavoidable.

REFERENCES

1. Beaudouin-Lafon, M., Huot, S., Olafsdottir, H., and Dragicevic, P. Glidecursor: Pointing with an inertial cursor. In *Proc. AVI'14*, ACM (2014), 49–56.
2. Casiez, G., Vogel, D., Balakrishnan, R., and Cockburn, A. The impact of control-display gain on user performance in pointing tasks. *HCI 23*, 3 (2008), 215–250.
3. Casiez, G., Vogel, D., Pan, Q., and Chaillou, C. Rubberedge: Reducing clutching by combining position and rate control with elastic feedback. In *Proc. UIST'07*, ACM (2007), 129–138.
4. Chapuis, O., and Dragicevic, P. Effects of motor scale, visual scale, and quantization on small target acquisition difficulty. *ACM ToCHI 18*, 3 (Aug. 2011), 13:1–13:32.
5. Nancel, M. *Designing and combining mid-air interaction techniques in large display environments*. Ph.D dissertation, Université Paris Sud - XI, Dec. 2012.
6. Nancel, M., Chapuis, O., Pietriga, E., Yang, X.-D., Irani, P. P., and Beaudouin-Lafon, M. High-precision pointing on large wall displays using small handheld devices. In *Proc. CHI'13*, ACM (2013), 831–840.
7. Vogel, D., and Balakrishnan, R. Distant freehand pointing and clicking on very large, high resolution displays. In *Proc. UIST'05*, ACM (2005), 33–42.
8. Woźniak, P., Fjeld, M., and Zhao, S. Limiting trial and error: Introducing a systematic approach to designing clutching. In *Proc. Chinese CHI*, ACM (2014), 35–39.

Visual Grouping in Menu Interfaces

Duncan P. Brumby and Susan Zhuang
UCL Interaction Centre
University College London
London WC1E 6BT UK
Brumby@cs.ucl.ac.uk

ABSTRACT
Menu interfaces often arrange options into semantic groups. This semantic structure is then usually conveyed to the user by supplementary visual grouping cues. We investigate whether these visual grouping cues actually help users locate items in menus faster, and whether there is potential for these powerful grouping cues to impede search when used inappropriately. Thirty-six participants performed known-item searches of word menus. These menus differed along three dimensions: (1) whether visual grouping cues were used, (2) whether items were semantically organized, and (3) the number of items belonging to each semantic group. Results show that the usefulness of visual grouping entirely depends on the underlying semantic structure of the menu. When menus were semantically organized, having visual grouping cues delineate the boundaries between large semantic groups resulted in the fastest search times. But when semantically unrelated items were visually grouped together, participants took far longer to locate targets. Menu designers should therefore take great care to avoid visually grouping semantically unrelated items as this has the potential to hinder menu interactions.

Author Keywords
Visual search; menus; eye-tracking; interaction science.

ACM Classification Keywords
H.5.2 User Interfaces: evaluation/methodology, screen design, theory and methods.

INTRODUCTION
Menu interfaces appeared in the earliest personal computers and are still in widespread use today. They are used in all desktop applications, on most websites, on smartphones and tablets, and even on home heating control panels and medical devices. Regardless of the application domain, menu interfaces should allow the user to locate and select the desired item as quickly and easily as possible.

CHI 2015, April 18 - 23, 2015, Seoul, Republic of Korea Copyright 2015 ACM 978-1-4503-3145-6/15/04...$15.00
http://dx.doi.org/10.1145/2702123.2702177

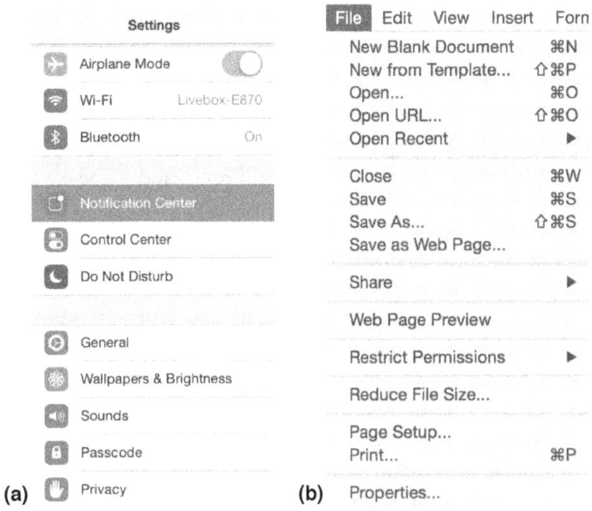

Figure 1.(a) Settings menu from Apple iPad iOS7 and (b) File menu from Microsoft Word Mac 2011. Both menus group semantically related content together and use visual grouping cues (either spatial proximity or common region) to communicate the intended structure.

An extensive literature has sought to understand the factors that influence search time during menu interactions [2,3,4,6,7]. One important finding is that organizing the content of menus into semantically related groups helps users locate items faster [4]. This semantic grouping effect has been replicated numerous times [2,6], and examples of semantically arranged menus abound. For instance, Figure 1 shows two common menu interfaces (the Settings menu from Apple iPad and the File menu from Microsoft Word). Both group functionally related items together (e.g., *Airplane Mode*, *WiFi*, and *Bluetooth* are all concerned with managing radios of the iPad, whereas the next group of items is concerned with managing notifications).

The menus shown in Figure 1 also use visual grouping cues to make the intended semantic organization of the menu pop out. The Settings menu of the iPad uses spatial proximity (i.e., spacing) to group items, while the desktop application menu bar of Microsoft Word uses common region (i.e., dividing lines). Despite the apparent widespread use of visual grouping cues in menu interfaces, we wonder whether these cues actually help users locate items faster. An early study by Parkinson, Sisson, and Snowberry [7] found that visual grouping can facilitate menu search performance. Participants searched menus that organized content into semantically related groups. Visual grouping cues were then used to reinforce this coherent structure, helping participants locate items faster.

In practice though it is often quite challenging for designers to get the semantic structure of a menu interface right [5]. Examples of menus that group semantically unrelated items together are surprisingly common. For instance, the final group of items in the Apple iPad Settings menu (i.e., *General*, *Wallpaper*, *Sounds*, *Passcode*, *Privacy*) might best be described as the 'everything else' group. Previous research has used unordered (randomized) menu layouts to capture the situation in which menu items have weak semantic congruence [2,4,6], finding that users are slower at locating targets in unordered menus. Is there a danger that inappropriate visual grouping cues might compound the problems of poor semantic grouping and slow search time yet further?

A menu search experiment was designed to unpick the influence of visual grouping effects from the influence of semantic ordering effects. Participants performed known-item searches in menus that differed in terms of: (1) whether visual grouping cues were present, (2) whether items were semantically organized, and (3) the number of items belonging to each semantic group. This last factor was included to reflect the variability that is usually seen in how items are grouped in menus (e.g., Fig. 1 shows group sizes of between one and five items).

Following Parkinson et al. [7], we would expect visual grouping cues to help participants locate targets faster when menu items are arranged into cohesive semantic groups. But when semantically unrelated items are visually grouped together we might expect search times to increase because these cues will give the impression that there is a meaningful structure to the menu (even though there is none).

In designing the experiment we sought to replicate and extend Halverson and Hornof [6]. But unlike in this previous study, we choose to use line boxes to group items (as shown in Fig. 2). Using boxes is this way is known to be a particularly effective visual grouping cue for communicating informational structure [1]. A further benefit of using boxes is that the presence/absence of visual grouping can be varied without impacting other aspects of the display. In contrast, using spatial proximity to group items would increase the physical distance between groups of items, and this is known to affect search behavior [3].

METHOD

Participants

Thirty-six participants (nine male) aged between 19 and 23 years were recruited through the UCL Psychology Subject Pool. All were native English speakers, with normal or corrected-to-normal vision, and experienced computer users.

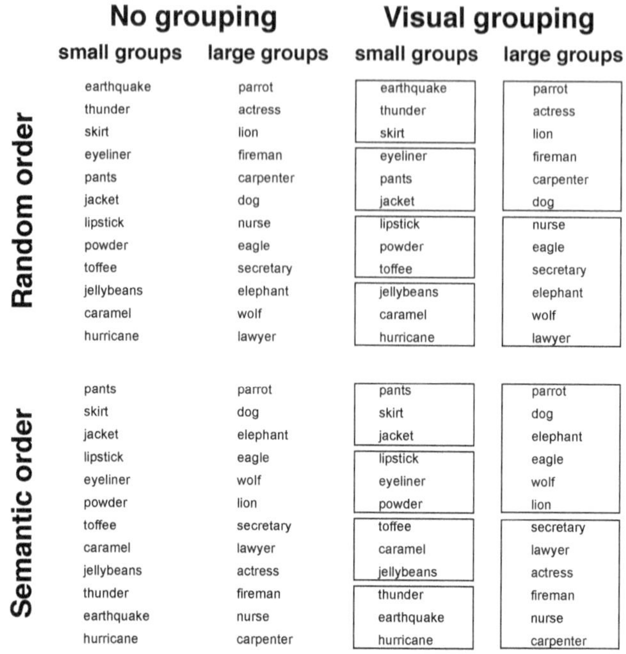

Figure 2. Illustration of each experimental condition (semantic order × semantic group size × visual grouping). Actual menus contained 3 columns of 12 menu items each, all conforming to one of the conditions depicted above.

Materials

All menus contained 36 single-word items. We generated these menus from the same database of words as used in previous studies [2,3,6]. This database is useful because it contains 560 unique words (with character length $M = 6.2$, $SD = 2.0$, range: 2 – 12), organized into natural categories. There are 14 top-level categories (e.g., animal, building, entertainment), with each of these separated into four mid-level categories (e.g., bird, farm animal, tropical fish, and wild animal are all members of the animal category). Finally, for each mid-level category there are 10 instances (e.g., bluebird, canary, starling, eagle, hawk are all members of the bird sub-category). Human ratings have previously been gathered for these materials and confirm that items from the same semantic groups are judged as being more closely related than items from a different semantic group (see [2] for details).

Each menu contained 36 items that were arranged as three columns of 12 items each. The horizontal separation between items in each column was 30 pixels (0.70° of visual angle), with the first item being 80 pixels from the top of the screen. The vertical separation between each column was 250 pixels (6° of visual angle). All text was presented in an Arial font, size 10. Items had to be arranged across multiple columns (giving a 2D menu); had we presented all 36 items as a single 1D list the font would have been far smaller and items much closer together.

Stimuli were presented on a 17-inch monitor (1024 x 768 resolution). Eye movements were recorded using a Tobii 1750 eye tracker. The sampling rate of the eye tracker was 50 Hz, with gaze point accuracy of less than 0.5° of visual angle. The experimental software ran on Microsoft Windows XP. An optical mouse was used, set at the 'medium' speed via the system control panel.

Design

A 2×2×2 (*semantic order* × *semantic group size* × *visual grouping*) mixed design was used. Semantic order and group size were both manipulated as within-subjects factors. In the semantic order condition, items belonging to the same group were listed together, whereas in the random condition, items were jumbled and presented in no order. Menus differed in terms of the number of items that came from the same top-level category (i.e., semantic group). Menus contained either six groups of six related items (large groups), or were made up of 12 groups of three related items (small groups). Visual grouping was manipulated as a between-subjects factor. This meant that half of the participants searched menus that always had boxes grouping sets of items, while the other half of participants searched menus that did not have boxes.

Procedure

Participants were informed that they would be required to search menus to locate a given target. At the start of each trial, participants were told what word they were looking for, as well as a top-level category description of that word (e.g., "Find a type of animal, wolf"). After reading this, participants started a trial by clicking a button on the screen. This made the target description disappear, and the menu appeared beneath it. Participants were told that there was only a single target item in each menu and that they had to locate it as quickly as possible. Participants selected an item by clicking on it with the mouse. If an incorrect selection was made, participants were instructed to make another selection from the same menu after being shown the target information again. The trial ended when the participant had successfully selected the target. Before proceeding to the next trial, participants were given feedback on the time taken to locate the target. The purpose of this feedback was to reinforce the instruction to locate the target quickly.

Each participant completed 100 search trials, divided into two blocks of 50 trials each (grouped by semantic order condition). The sequence in which each semantic order condition was experienced was counter-balanced between participants: half of the participants did all of the semantic order searches before the random order searchers, and vice versa. The presentation order of different semantic group size conditions was randomized within a given semantic order condition. The eye tracker was calibrated before the start of each block to ensure accurate gaze tracking. Participants were seated approximately 60-70 cm from the monitor throughout the experiment, and were given the opportunity for a short break in between blocks. The entire experiment took approximately 30 minutes to complete.

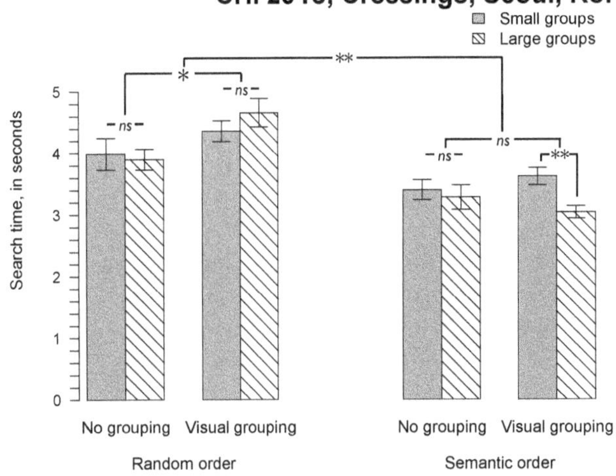

Figure 3. Mean search time across conditions. Error bars depict standard errors. *$p < .05$ **$p < .001$

RESULTS

A mixed ANOVA was used, with a significance level of .05 for judging the significance of effects. We excluded trials from the analysis in which the participant did not correctly select the target on the first attempt. Accuracy was generally very high: mean accuracy for each condition was between 98–100%, and data from only 44 trials were excluded (from a total of 3,600).

The primary measure of interest was search time (i.e., how long it took participants to correctly locate and select the target item). Figure 3 shows mean search time data for each condition. It can be seen in the figure that participants were significantly faster at locating targets in menus that were semantically organized (M = 3.34, SD = 0.56) than menus that were randomly organized (M = 4.23, SD = 0.80), $F(1, 34) = 79.52$, $p < .001$, $\eta_p^2 = .70$. While there was not a significant main effect of either semantic group size or of visual grouping, F's < 2, there was a significant three-way interaction, $F(1, 34) = 3.94$, $p = .05$, $\eta_p^2 = .10$.

The significant three-way interaction suggests that the effects of semantic group size and visual grouping are dependent on whether or not the menu is semantically organized. We therefore separate the analysis of semantically organized menus from the randomly organized ones, and for each, consider the effect of semantic group size and visual grouping. For semantically organized menus, there was a significant two-way interaction between group size and visual grouping, $F(1, 34) = 4.23$, $p = .05$, $\eta_p^2 = .11$. Follow-up tests of this interaction show that when there was visual grouping in the menu, participants were significantly faster at searching menus with larger semantic groups ($M = 3.04$, $SD = 0.41$) than menus with smaller semantic groups ($M = 3.62$, $SD = 0.60$), $F(1, 34) = 13.78$, $p < .001$, $\eta_p^2 = .28$. However, there was no effect of group size when there was no visual grouping, $F < 1$. For randomly organized menus, there was a different pattern of effects. Participants were now significantly *slower* at searching menus that had visual grouping cues ($M = 4.51$, $SD = 0.73$) than those that did not show grouping cues ($M = 3.95$, $SD = 0.78$), $F(1, 34) = 5.00$, $p = .03$, $\eta_p^2 = .13$.

Finally, eye movement data are considered to understand the effects of semantic and visual grouping. In general, fixation count data revealed the same pattern of statistical effects as the search time data. This is because there is a simple linear relationship between fixation counts and search time, $R^2 = .45$, $t(34) = 5.41$, $p < .001$. A more interesting finding from the eye movement data is that the mean distance (in pixels) between contiguous fixations was greater when participants searched semantically organized menus ($M = 6.66$, $SD = 1.58$) than when they searched randomly organized menus ($M = 5.94$, $SD = 1.41$), $F(1,34) = 18.83$, $p < .001$, $\eta_p^2 = .36$. This suggests that participants were adapting their search strategy to the semantic structure of the menu. This makes sense: encountering a semantically unrelated item during search informs the searcher that the target is unlikely to be in that part of the menu, and that attention should be directed elsewhere, allowing the target to be located faster. There was however no effect of either grouping or semantic group size on mean distance between fixations, F's < 1.

DISCUSSION

Consistent with previous research [2,4,6], we found that organizing the content of menus into semantically related groups helped participants locate items faster. Consistent with [7], adding visual grouping cues to semantically organized menus helped further speedup search times, but only when menus contained fewer, larger groups. Being able to easily see the boundaries between semantically distinct groups presumably helped participants to systematically assess each group in turn. This meant that groups containing an irrelevant item could be dismissed, so helping participants quickly hone in on the target group.

The results of this study also highlight the potential for visual grouping cues to hinder menu interactions when used inappropriately. In particular, we found that when semantically unrelated items were grouped together, participants took far longer to locate targets. This is an important finding because in practice it is often difficult to get the semantic structure of a menu interface right [5]. Adding visual grouping cues to an already poorly organized menu can make matters worse and should be avoided.

Limitations

Menus are used in a variety of settings, by a variety of users, to achieve a variety of goals. We end by considering how some of the decisions made in designing this experiment might warrant further investigation.

First, the study reported here used line-drawn boxes to group items. There are of course other visual cues that can be used. In Figure 1a, for instance, spatial proximity is used. Color can also be used (as in [6]). It is presently not clear how the choice of visual grouping cue might influence the pattern of results reported here, although we suspect it will make little difference.

Second, participants were given a precise description of the item that had to be located in the menu (known-item search). But often the user only has a vague idea of how the target will be specified (semantic search). This distinction is interesting because users adopt different eye gaze strategies depending on the kind of activity they are engaged in [3]. We might expect visual grouping cues, which highlight the fine-grained semantic structure of the menu, to offer even greater benefit to users engaged in a semantic search (because they cannot adopt simple letter-matching strategies that would be otherwise insensitive to visual grouping effects).

Finally, we had participants interact with each menu only once. While this is representative of many infrequent or first time menu interactions, there are many occasions in which users frequently interact with the same menu. Previous research has shown that some menu layout effects are diminished when users repeatedly interact with the same menu [2]. Usually this is explained by assuming that users learn over time the spatial location of targets in the menu [2]. Would we find a similar reduction in effect size here? All of these avenues require further empirical work.

ACKNOWLEDGEMENTS

This work was supported by the UK Engineering and Physical Sciences Research Council grant EP/G059063. We thank Gilles Bailly, Antti Oulasvirta, and Andrew Howes for encouraging us to publish this work, as well as our reviewers for their constructive feedback.

REFERENCES

1. Bae, J. & Watson, B. Reinforcing visual grouping cues to communicate complex informational structure. *IEEE Transactions on Visualization and Computer Graphics, 20,* (2014), 1973-1982.
2. Bailly, G., Oulasvirta, A., Brumby, D.P., & Howes, A. Model of visual search and selection time in linear menus. *Proc. CHI '14*, ACM (2014), 3865-3874.
3. Brumby, D.P., Cox, A.L., Chung, J., & Fernandes, B. How does knowing what you are looking for change visual search behavior? *Proc. CHI '14*, ACM (2014), 3895-3898.
4. Card, S.K. User perceptual mechanisms in the search of computer command menus. *Proc CHI '82*, ACM (1982), 190-196.
5. Chi, E.H., Rosien, A., Supattanasiri, G., et al. The bloodhound project: Automating discovery of web usability issues using the infoscent simulator. *Proc CHI '03*, ACM (2003), 505-512.
6. Halverson, T. & Hornof, A.J. The effects of semantic grouping on visual search. *Proc CHI EA '08*, ACM (2008), 3471-3476.
7. Parkinson, S.R., Sisson, N., & Snowberry, K. Organization of broad computer menu displays. *International Journal of Man-Machine Studies, 23,* (1985), 689-697.

Color Portraits: From Color Picking to Interacting with Color

Ghita Jalal, Nolwenn Maudet, Wendy E. Mackay
Inria, Université Paris-Sud, CNRS
F-91405 Orsay, France
{Jalal, Maudet, Mackay}@lri.fr

ABSTRACT

Although ubiquitous, color pickers have remained largely unchanged for 25 years. Based on contextual interviews with artists and designers, we created the *Color Portraits* design space to characterize five key color manipulation activities: *sampling and tweaking* individual colors, *manipulating color relationships*, *combining colors* with other elements, *revisiting previous color choices,* and *revealing a design process through color*. We found similar color manipulation requirements with scientists and engineers. We designed novel color interaction tools inspired by the design space, and used them as probes to identify specific design requirements, including: interactive palettes for sampling colors and exploring relationships; color composites for blending and decomposing colors with other elements; interactive histories to enable reuse of previous color choices; and providing color as a way to reveal underlying processes. We argue that color tools should allow users to *interact* with colors, not just pick or sample them.

Author Keywords

Color picker; Color tools; Creativity; Generative Design

ACM Classification Keywords

H.5.2 [User Interfaces]: Theory and Models

INTRODUCTION

Desktop computing suppports the creation of diverse types of digital media, including drawings, spreadsheets, photographs, video and multimedia documents. Applications for creating digital media usually include a *color picker*, with three common features: a visual representation of a specified color model, the organization of displayable colors into a three-dimensional color space, and controls to change parameter values within that space [6]. Users can select individual colors from the color space, either with the mouse or by specifying a three-digit code, such as an RGB value. Some color pickers also allow users to select a color from a pixel in an image or from existing color swatches.

CHI 2015, April 18 - 23 2015, Seoul, Republic of Korea
Copyright 2015 ACM 978-1-4503-3145-6/15/04...$15.00
http://dx.doi.org/10.1145/2702123.2702173

Despite being ubiquitous, color pickers have changed little over the past 25 years. Fig. 1 shows almost identical layouts and controls for three common color pickers; the only new features are their underlying color spaces, which have been updated according to research in color perception [7] and representation [20].

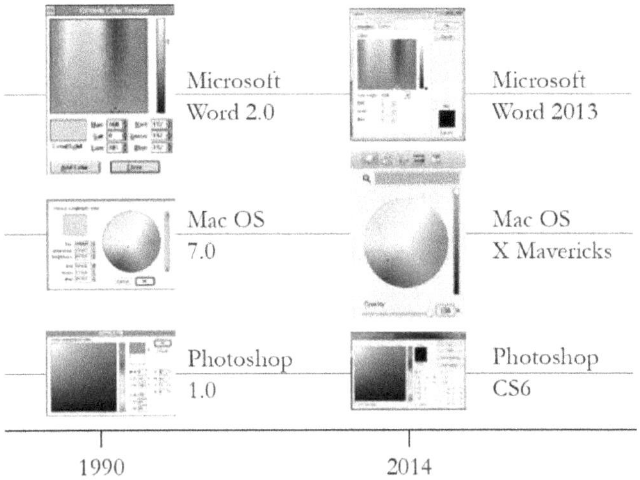

Figure 1: Today's color pickers have changed little since 1990.

Of course, one reason that color picker design is static could be that color picking is a "solved" problem—users can successfully manipulate color in digital documents. However, Bailey et al. [2] show that untrained users still have trouble selecting particular colors, and Albers [1] argues that professional artists do not want to simply follow prescribed color systems and theories.

We are interested in how users, especially artists and designers, manipulate color as part of their creative process. We begin with a review of related research on color perception, techniques for visualizing color spaces, and the design of specialized color manipulation tools. We describe our findings from interviews with artists and designers who focus on color, and frame the results as a design space, called *Color Portraits*. We verify our design space through a second set of interviews with non-expert color users, and an analysis of current color tools. Finally, we present a set of novel color-manipulation tools that test the generative power of the design space. We presented these to users as probes and conclude with implications for the design of more advanced color manipulation tools.

RELATED WORK

Color is a deceptively complex domain, studied from a variety of different perspectives. Psychologists seek to understand how humans sense and perceive color whereas human factors experts codify this knowledge into simple, easy-to-apply design rules. Computer scientists and mathematicians build upon our understanding of color perception to create multi-dimensional color spaces that can be represented on the screen. Artists and designers work with the resulting color representations to explore color relationships and generate aesthetically appropriate colors for each individual artifact.

Sensation and Perception of Color

Color perception is more complex than directly sensing wavelengths of light. Instead, the brain interprets signals from individual photoreceptors as distinguishable, subjectively different colors [16]. Psychologists study optical illusions, where color perception differs from the physical signal. For example, the McCollough effect [18] involves staring at a colored test image, looking at a different background, and seeing new, non-existent colors. The simultaneous contrast illusion [8] presents a solid color bar on a gradient background, from dark to light, making the bar appear as a gradient from light to dark. Human factors experts create guidelines based on these physiological and psychological studies of color [17]. However, artists and designers often break these rules, playing with optical illusions to achieve specific effects.

Representing and Visualizing Color

Color can be displayed according to mathematically or perceptually based coding schemes. RGB is a device-dependent color model comprised of additive primary colors, red, green and blue, which combine to create various colors, including white. HSV describes color as hue, saturation and value (brightness), defined arbitrarily in different tools or standards [15]. Both models emphasize color generation, not color perception. For example, RGB produces a wide variety of greens, but very few reds.

An alternative strategy is to define color spaces in terms of color perception [21]. For example, perceptually uniform color spaces, such as CIELUV and CIELAB, create equal perceptual distances among the colors [27]. Other coding schemes reduce cognitive effort by mapping the represented data set to the capabilities of the human vision system [5, 26]. Color is also affected by how it appears on a computer screen [25]. For example, data visualization researchers use computer-aided color-coding to represent and interact with their data [11] or to map data along color dimensions to create a pictorial representation [3]. The print industry defines standard color references, such as the PMS Pantone Matching System, according to specific ink formuli or a CMYK mix [22], with corresponding reference guides for various print devices and substrates.

Many color tools are based on computational algorithms that hide the complexity of color manipulation. If users do not understand the underlying models, they have trouble using them to achieve specific effects. ACE (*A Color Expert*) [20] addresses this by automatically selecting colors based on a model of the functional relationships among components of a design drawing. Wang et al.'s [26] interactive colorization process lets users choose hues from a color wheel. Then, an expert system calculates optimal brightness and saturation. These expert systems support clearly defined tasks but are less helpful for creative tasks in which users define their own rules and constraints.

Interactive Color Tools

Several web-based tools allow users to experiment with different color combinations. Adobe *Kuler*[1] lets users combine colors around a particular theme: they can manipulate multiple color swatches sampled from images or generate palettes based on color rules, e.g., color triads or complementary colors. Other tools pre-select sets of colors to address specific requirements. *Color Brewer* [10] helps users choose effective color schemes for coloring maps, based on specific properties of the data being represented and human color perception. *IWantHue*[2] helps users generate palettes with optimally distinct colors. Both have the advantage of simplicity, but with a very limited scope.

Several recent tools explore innovative ways of manipulating color. For example, *Histomages* [4] allows users to edit images by modifying a histogram of the colored pixels within the image. Users can select and change subsets of colors, such as turning the sky from shades of blue to shades of orange. Pouli and Reinhard [24] demonstrate how to transfer color by progressively matching a histogram to a target image's color, and Meier et al.'s *Interactive Color Palette Tools* [19] offer additional techniques for interacting with color. Although these tools offer promising new techniques for manipulating color, they remain isolated from mainstream authoring applications.

Designing with Color

Color is often fundamental to an artist's or designer's work. According to Itten [14], artists must control *impression* (perception of color), *expression* (emotional reaction to color), and *construction* (conveying meaning), combining all three to create each desired effect. Albers argues that color is *"the most relative medium in art"* [1] and uses practical exercises to teach novice artists about the nature of color and to explore how it can convey mood and meaning. Artists and designers thus develop nuanced understandings of color perception through intensive practice and experience.

Our goal is to improve how authors of digital media manipulate color to achieve desired effects. This requires a more detailed understanding of current color practices, beyond the use of the ubiquitous, but unchanging color tool: the color picker.

---

1 www.kuler.adobe.com
2 www.tools.medialab.sciences-po.fr/iwanthue/

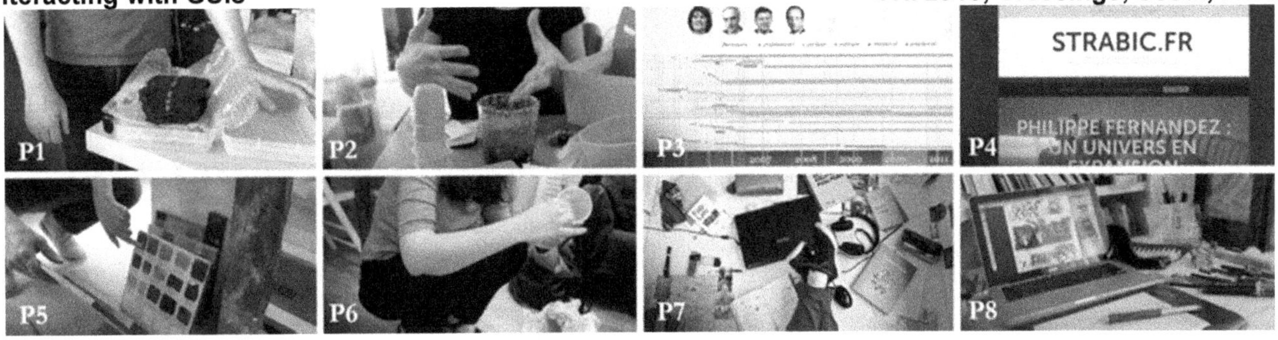

Figure 2: Eight artists and designers demonstrated how they manipulate color to achieve effects in both physical and digital media.

HOW DO ARTISTS INTERACT WITH COLOR?

Participants: We observed and interviewed eight artists and designers (4 men, 4 women; age 23-45) who consider color an essential part of their work practice (see Fig. 2). Their professions included painter, illustrator, ceramist, spatial designer, graphic designer, product designer, service designer and interaction designer.

We are interested in the tools and techniques artists use to incorporate color into their work, especially how they produce specific color effects. Although digital color tools are our primary concern, we also want to understand physical color practices that have evolved over centuries and may inspire new ways to manipulate color online.

Procedure: We interviewed participants in their studio or office for about one hour. We asked participants to tell stories about their use of color in recent projects and to show us the resulting artifacts. We probed for situations in which their interaction with color was particularly effective, but also when it was extremely difficult or impossible.

Data Collection: We recorded audio for each interview and took written notes. We also recorded video of participants' interactions with the objects they had created, and photographed each artifact and any related color creation or manipulation tools.

Analysis: We created a storyboard to illustrate each story, with a photograph of the artifact, as well as drawings to describe each step in the color creation and manipulation process (see Fig. 4). We later showed these storyboards to the participants to verify the details. We used a grounded theory [9] approach to define ten different color manipulation categories and mapped each story to one or more categories. We chose the five most representative categories to create the *ColorPortaits* design space.

RESULTS: COLOR PORTRAITS DESIGN SPACE

We collected 35 separate stories from eight participants. We identified several surprising practices: one artist explicitly chose an 'incorrect' color to indicate to the client that the final color had not yet been chosen, and several participants moved back and forth between physical artifacts and digital colors. However, our analysis here focuses on the most common color manipulation practices, chosen because they appeared for half or more of the participants, usually with multiple examples per participant.

Samples: Picking and Tweaking

One of the most common tasks is simply to choose a particular color. Colors are derived from different sources, either from the color space provided by a color picker or from an existing sample. Although users can apply these colors directly, they more often tweak them before applying them to an artifact. Fig. 3 defines two activities related to color selection, including:

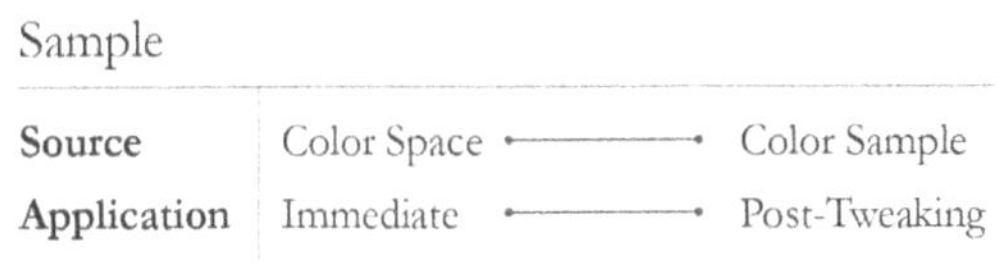

Figure 3: Users pick colors from diverse sources, and often tweak them later.

Surprisingly, only two participants mentioned cases in which they selected a color from the color picker and used it without further modification. P6 (Product Designer) used Adobe Photoshop's color picker to recreate a particular blue she had already used for a website, and P4 (Graphic designer) tried to create 'unusual colors' by using Adobe Illustrator's color picker.

The remaining participants used commercial color pickers, but only as a small part of a much more elaborate color manipulation process. Most (7/8 participants) chose from a variety of samples, including online websites, color palettes and photographs, as well as physical objects, such as ceramics or textiles. Occasionally, participants used the sample color directly, such as when P4 (Graphic designer) chose a blue from a catalog to ensure that the printed version of his poster would appear exactly as he wanted.

More often (7/8 participants), participants started with a sample and then tweaked it before applying it to the artifact. For example, P2 (Exhibit designer) sampled colors from paintings she had found online, and then used the color picker's design space to modify the samples before adding them to her mood board. P7 (Service designer) created a palette using *Kuler*, extracted colors from the screen with *InDesign*, changed one of them, and then used the resulting palette in his final design. P1 (Painter) selected a set of three tubes of oil colors and mixed them to obtain the final colors for his painting (see Fig. 4).

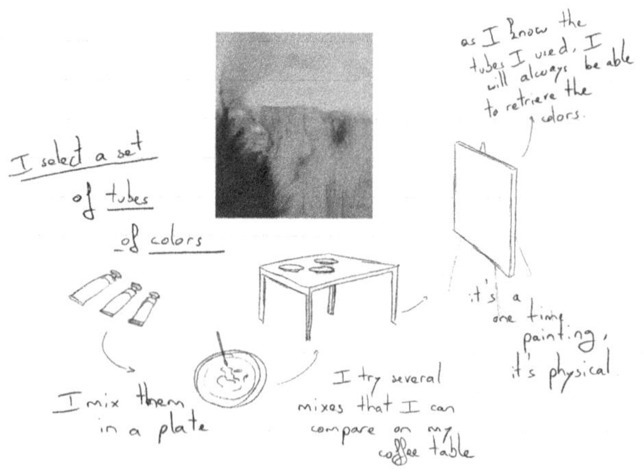

Figure 4: Each storyboard includes a photograph of the artifact and drawings of each step in the color process

Most participants preferred to select a color from a sample, but some found the color picker useful for modifying colors. For example, P8 (Illustrator) used the eyedropper tool in the Macintosh OS color picker to select a colored pixel from an image in a magazine. She decided to purify it by *"removing the black"*, which she accomplished by placing the color in CMYK color space and sliding the black (K) parameter to zero.

Palette: Manipulating color relationships

Participants rarely worked with individual colors. Instead, they created coherent sets of colors and manipulated them in groups, called palettes. Fig. 5 defines five activities related to color palettes, including: comparing swatches of different sizes, layering or repositioning colors, manipulating groups of colors as a unit, and interacting with color independently, such as within a color picker, or in the context of the remaining colors.

Most participants (7/8) created related sets of colors rather than separate individual colors. Color pickers provide a list of past color choices, but with no context. Participants wanted to create coherent sets of colors, according to the characteristics that they specify. For example, P2 (Exhibit designer) took photographs of related colored objects. For her, *"each picture is a different palette."[P2]*. Although the pictures contained the same objects, their positions differed, which resulted in different color compositions.

Palette

Size	Fixed	⟶	Resizable
Layout	Juxtaposed	⟶	Layered
Position	Static	⟶	Dynamic
Manipulation	Individual	⟶	Group
Context	Independent	⟶	Dependent

Figure 5: Users adjust size, layout and position of one or more colors, ideally in context.

Participants were very concerned with how different colors appear when used together. For example, P8 (Illustrator) had a restricted palette of one blue and one red for a set of book illustrations. She bought a variety of blue and red pencils and tested how they looked together, before making a final choice.

Participants also wanted to apply a single color change to affect an entire palette. For example, P8 (Illustrator) created one palette and then modified the hue of each color by the same amount, which generated a new palette. Simultaneously adjusting one property for the entire set of colors allowed her to maintain a related, harmonious color palette.

Participants often wanted to manipulate spatial dimensions and contextual characteristics of each palette to control color relationships. Unfortunately, color pickers do not allow users to resize or reshape color swatches, nor do they let users explore color variations in context.

Composites: Assembling disparate elements

Colors are affected both by their surrounding colors and by other adjacent elements. Fig. 6 defines two activities related to color composites, including: composing and decomposing multiple components, and manipulating these components individually or together.

Half of the participants (4/8) wanted to couple color with other elements, such as texture, and manipulate the resulting combination. P2 (Exhibit designer) described the screen as *"a flat surface that does not always transpose the richness of the physical world"*. To reproduce the yellow texture of a tablecloth on the screen, she scanned it and used the resulting image to provide the effect she wanted. For her, the color did not exist without the underlying texture. P8 (Illustrator) used Photoshop to manipulate a color and a texture that she paired together in several illustrations, which she had to manipulate separately each time. P1 (Painter) created a special preparation that added a particular type of light reflection to each color. He considers this combination of color-plus-reflection as his personal signature.

Composites

Creation	Color & Component	⟶	Composition
		⟶	Decomposition
Manipulation	Color	⟶	Composite

Figure 6: Users combine and decompose colors with disparate components.

Unfortunately, color tools are designed to manipulate properties based on pure colors. They do not support creation of complex color-texture composites, nor can users manipulate individual elements as separate subcomponents that can be assembled and disassembled as needed.

History: Interacting with past actions

Participants often performed similar tasks again and again, or revisited old artifacts when creating new ones. They needed to remember both how they initially created colors and also how the colors were applied in the final artifact. Participants were also interested in intermediate steps, which would let them explore alternative paths without starting over. Fig. 7 defines two activities related to history, including: preserving source materials and final artifacts, and capturing intermediate steps in the selection process.

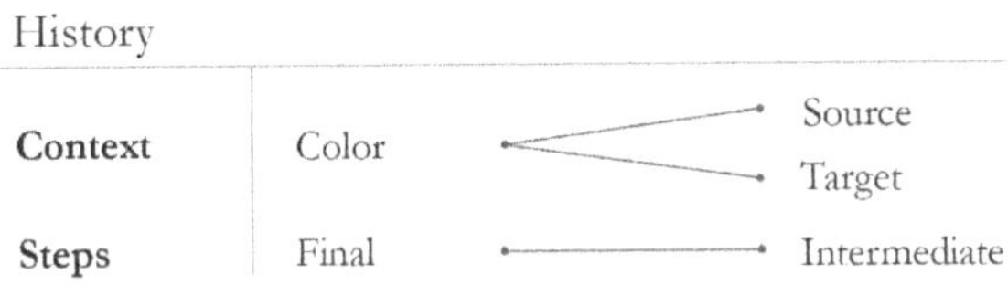

Figure 7: Users record color sources and targets, as well as intermediate steps.

Half the participants (4/8) sought ways to save meaningful intermediate steps in the process of creating a final color. For example, P5 (Ceramist) kept samples of every color she created over the past decade, as well as notebooks containing personal names, codes and the numbers of trials needed to obtain each color.

A few participants (2/8) also kept track of source colors. For example, P7 (Service designer) saved images he downloaded from the internet: *"I use these images to extract colors for my palettes and I keep them for later reuse."[P7]*. Other participants saved their final palettes with the resulting artifact. For example, P4 (Graphic designer) placed different-sized rectangles with each final color into the unused space beyond the margins, and saved them as part of the final document.

Some participants (2/8) wanted to return to a previous use context, with both the initial color source and the final artifact. For example, P5 (Ceramist) used several previously created red tiles to develop a nuanced set of three slightly different red tiles for another client.

Unfortunately, color pickers support only the most limited form of history. Although many provide slots for recording previous color choices, these colors are devoid of context about their sources, the sequence of steps necessary to recreate them, and the final result.

Process: Revealing activity over time

Sometimes participants who create physical objects observed color changes that revealed useful information about interim states. Unlike previous dimensions, color here is not the focus, but rather a means to an end. We are interested in how this physical use of color can affect electronic media. Fig. 8 defines two activities related to the color change process, including: manipulating color that results from other activities and revealing on-going processes.

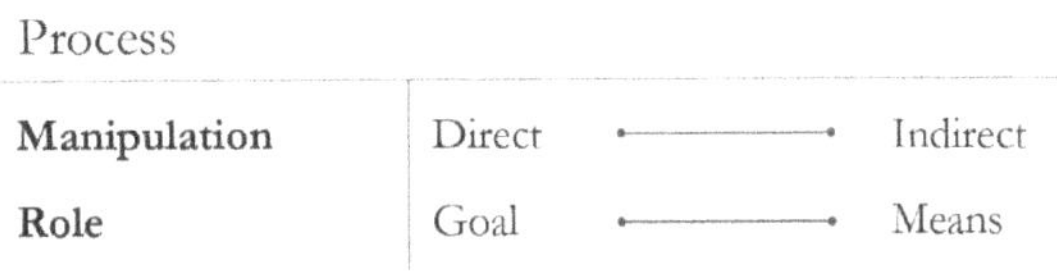

Figure 8: Users react to naturally occurring changes in color to indicate progress.

Half the participants used color to indicate how they created an artifact or the amount of time spent on its creation. P6 (Product Designer) observed colors to determine important details about her design process: *"Just by looking at the pot, you can see how many layers I used"*. In another project, she heated metal chairs, which caused the metal to change colors. She stopped the process when she liked the color and applied a coating to stabilize the color. Here, she manipulated color indirectly though changes in temperature. This suggests an interesting opportunity for electronic color manipulation tools, in which color change reveals the underlying changes in an online activity.

Color Portraits Design Space: We observed multiple examples of each design category, which form the five key dimensions of the Color Portraits design space:

Sample	start from an initial color; tweak properties to obtain a final color.
Palette	manipulate relationships among groups of colors.
Composite	combine colors with other elements such as texture; decompose to disparate elements.
History	capture and reuse source and target color contexts; preserve meaningful interim steps.
Process	reveal progress through color changes.

EVALUATING COLOR PORTRAITS

Color Portraits reflects core color manipulation needs for a specific user group: artists and designers. We are also interested in whether other users who create digital content use similar techniques, and how well current color tools meet the needs we have identified. We would also like to explore how this design space can offer new insights into the design of more powerful color manipulation tools.

Testing with non-color specialists

To test the broader applicability of the *Color Portraits* design space, we interviewed eight scientists and engineers (6 men, 2 women, aged 23-45), from the following disciplines: biology, biochemistry, computer science, data visualization, game developing, virtual reality engineering, automatics and information theory. Each interview lasted approximately one hour, in the participant's office. As before, we asked participants to show us recent artifacts they had created and to describe the steps they followed to incorporate color. At the end of the interview, we asked for additional stories related to each design space category. We recorded audio for all interviews and recorded video of participants' interactions with the resulting artifacts.

Results and Discussion

We collected a total of 34 stories, three to five per participant. Fig. 9 shows that scientists and engineers have similar color manipulation requirements as artists and designers. We saw similar proportions of activities for both groups and were surprised at how important these participants consider color manipulation. For example, P10 (Biochemist) organized a full afternoon with his colleagues to choose colors to represent different molecules. P15 (Information theorist) found choosing a color for a figure very time-consuming: *"I might spend half an hour to find the right amount of blue in my color"*.

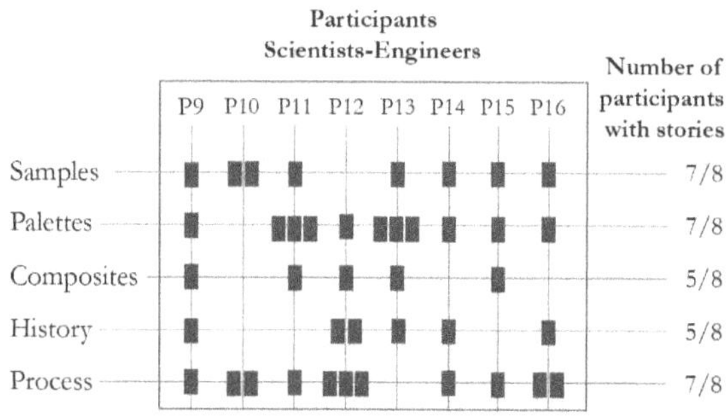

Figure 9 Mapping stories from scientists and engineers, to the Color Portraits design space. One story can map to more than one category.

Samples

Scientists and engineers, like artists and designers, actively sample and then tweak colors (7/8). For example, P10 (Virtual reality engineer) looked for images on the Internet to find inspiration. He sampled several colors as initial references and then adjusted them to create his own set. P13 (Data visualization researcher) wanted to visualize data about cycling teams, so he began by sampling an image of the team t-shirt. He then modified the colors to make them easier to distinguish from each other.

Palettes

Although none of these participants referred to a palette explicitly, almost all (7/8) interacted with sets of colors. For example, P9 (Programmer) created a palette for a user interface design by selecting a few primary colors. He then programmed a script to add a small amount of black to all of his colors to increase legibility. P12 (Geologist) scanned an image from a microscope image of a rock, using polarizing paper to change all colors simultaneously: *"This lets me preserve the relationships among the colors"*.

Composites

Many participants (5/8) were interested in achieving a particular effect that they then explored by interacting with color and a second element. P10 (Virtual reality engineer) combined a grass texture with green to create the grass for his 3D space: *"I played with the combinations to get this effect with my 3D rendering software."*

History

Over half the participants (5/8) kept track of interim steps in the context of previous color manipulations. For example, P14 (Game developer) created folders of colors where she recorded her color choices and later reflected on them, in the context in which they had been created: *"I look at the colors, dates of creation and names I gave the colors to see how my perception of these names changed over time."*

Process

Interestingly, almost all scientists and engineers (7/8) used color to indicate the progress of an on-going activity. P9 (Programmer) used highly distinctive colors for his Java classes in order to quickly check the complexity of a piece of code: *"If the class has many colors, it means that it has a large number of dependencies and it will be hard to test"*. Similarly, P16 (Information theorist) used a colored pen to mark variables in her equations, which helped her communicate and follow the evolution of her calculations.

In summary, seven participants described color-manipulation stories related to at least four of the five dimensions. This suggests that the color manipulation activities we identified for artists and designers, for whom color is a major focus of their work, also obtain for scientists and engineers, for whom color is more of a means to an end.

ANALYSIS OF CURRENT COLOR TOOLS

All 16 participants in the previous studies managed to manipulate color in creative ways, as expressed in the *Color Portraits* design space. We analyzed six existing color tools to see how many support the five key activities: Two for the general public (color pickers for *Macintosh OS X* and *Microsoft Word)*; two for scientists and engineers (*Color Brewer* [10] and *IWantHue*); and two for artists and designers (*Adobe's Kuler* and *Photoshop* color tools).

Fig. 10 maps the characteristics of each tool according to the *Color Portraits* design dimensions, based on type of interaction: *System*: Does the tool offer specific, ready-to-use features that support the activity? *User*: Can users personalize their activity? *User-System Interaction*: Can users capture and reuse previous interactions with the tool?

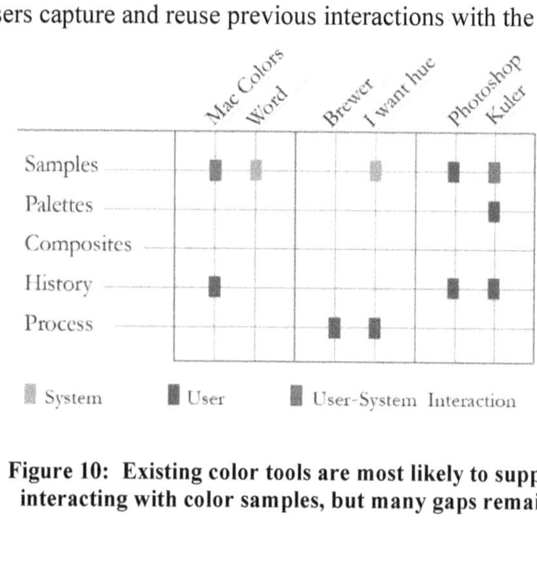

Figure 10: Existing color tools are most likely to support interacting with color samples, but many gaps remain.

Color pickers for the general public

Microsoft Word and *Macintosh OS X* both provide sets of color pickers designed to support color selection from either a limited set of pre-defined colors or else from an extremely wide range of colors within mathematically defined color models. Both tools provide swatches of pre-determined colors, with shades of gray and sets of primary and secondary colors. Users can use the mouse or adjust sliders to select individual colors and create subtle variations, but even with domain knowledge, they have difficulty selecting a precise color, and in many cases, the desired color does not even exist.

The *Macintosh OS X* color picker includes an eyedropper for selecting the color of any pixel on the screen. Users can also save colors as a list of swatches that are accessible from different applications. This offers limited, but somewhat cumbersome, support for history. Thus *Microsoft Word* offers only system-level support for sampling colors, whereas the *Macintosh OS X* color picker also features interaction-level support for sampling and user-level support for history. Neither tool supports interacting with palettes, composites or process. Thus, the most common color tools for the general public support only a small proportion of the color manipulation requirements identified by in the *Color Portraits* design space.

Color Tools for Scientists and Engineers

Color Brewer provides suitable color palettes for online maps and *IWantHue* offers optimally diverse color palettes for data scientists. Unlike other color tools, both explicitly support use of color to represent process: *Color Brewer* helps scientists and engineers to color maps and *IWantHue* supports exploratory data visualization.

On the other hand, neither tool allows users to interact with palettes, make composites or preserve a history of their previous interactions. They offer only a cursory use of samples, which are restricted to a limited set of system-generated colors. Both make a trade-off between simplicity and power, supporting a restricted set of color manipulation activities, but offering little flexibility if the specific tasks require more advanced color experimentation.

Color Tools for Artists and Designers

The *Adobe Photoshop* color tool is embedded within a professional application designed to help artists and designers edit photographs. *Adobe Kuler* is an online tool with a large library of themed palettes contributed by users as well as an interactive tool that incorporates color theory to generate new color palettes. Both support sampling at the system and user level: users can not only select from pre-defined sets of colors, but also create their own.

The *Photoshop* color tool lets users import their own palettes and *Kuler* lets users upload images and extract color samples. *Kuler* also offers advanced interaction capabilities for manipulating samples and can also generate new palettes. However, *Kuler* does not meet the most advanced level of interaction with palettes: Users can change one color to affect the rest of the palette, but cannot control the spatial arrangement. Although they can take advantage of pre-defined color rules to create certain types of palettes, such as complementary colors, they cannot define their own rules to determine their own personally defined color relationships.

Although *Photoshop's* color tool and *Kuler* both allow users to save colors as they progress through a task, which they can reuse later, neither preserves context. We thus categorize these tools as providing user-level support for history. Neither tool supports creating or disassembling composites of multiple colors and textures, nor do they support the use of color to reveal activity. Not surprisingly, these two professional tools cover a larger portion of the *Color Portraits* design space when compared to tools intended for the general public or for scientists and engineers. However, they still lack support for many color manipulation activities that were identified by the participants.

Although they do not comprise an exhaustive set, these six color tools are widely available and represent the most common strategies for helping users manipulate color. However, when we examine their specific capabilities, we see that many gaps remain in the *Color Portraits* design space (Fig. 10), suggesting opportunities for the design of innovative color tools.

TOOLS FOR INTERACTING WITH COLOR

In order to test the generative power of the *Color Portraits* design space, we created a set of four probes [13], each designed to explore an activity that is not well supported by current tools. The probes were inspired directly from the color manipulation stories, and represent different requirements specified by the *Color Portraits* design space. Note that our goal was not to fully support all possible color manipulation activities, but rather to illustrate how color tools might inspire new directions for designing color manipulation tools. The probes support the following activities: designing and interacting with palettes, assembling and disassembling composites, creating interactive histories, and applying color to reveal the process as users progress through a particular activity.

Palette Explorer – Interacting with Palettes

Almost all participants (14/16) actively created sets of colors and manipulated the relationships among them, but usually in an ad hoc way, combining features from multiple tools or creating their own techniques. *Palette Explorer* lets users create groups multi-colored swatches of different sizes and shapes. In Fig. 11a, the user creates a large green foreground swatch, with a pale blue background and red and blue intermediate elements. The user can move, resize and adjust layers to explore the effects of different spatial relationships. In Fig. 11b, the user changes the background to red and the remaining elements are smaller and repositioned in layers next to each other.

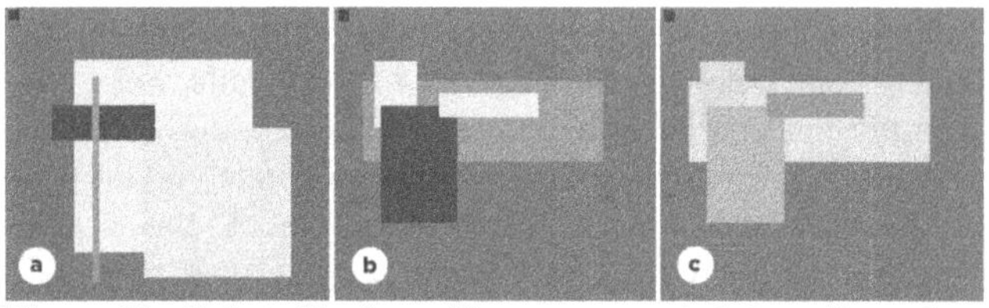

Figure 11: ***Palette Explorer*****: Users can create interactive color palettes with dynamic swatches, enabling them to explore spatial relationships and manipulate sets of swatches.**

Users can modify a color in the context of the remaining colors by moving the cursor along three axes: X for hue, Y for saturation and mouse wheel for brightness. Users can also select sets of swatches or the whole palette and modify them at the same time, retaining the harmony and other characteristics of the original palette. In Fig. 11c, the user has shifted the main foreground blue to orange, and the remaining colors have changed accordingly.

Color Compositor – Interacting with composites

Although some color pickers allow users to include a limited set of patterns or textures [23], they do not allow users to incorporate their own material. *Color Compositor* lets users combine colors and textures to create their own novel composites.

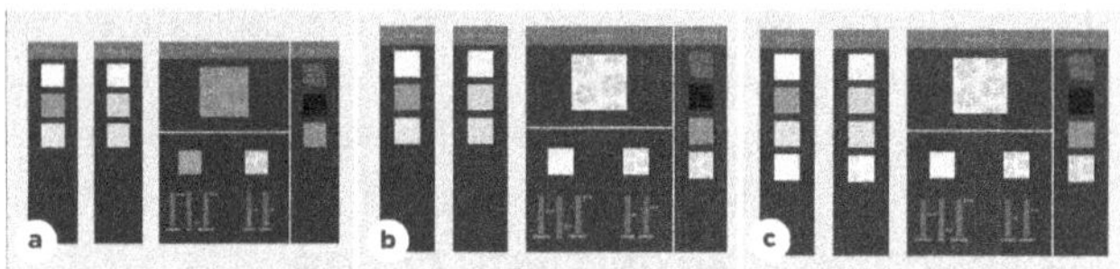

Figure 12: ***Color Compositor*****: Users combine colors and textures to create and manipulate composites.**

In Fig. 12a, the user combines orange with an image containing slices of a citrus fruit. The user can also modify the colors and textures independently. In Fig. 12b, the user turns the orange into a lemon. Users can also decompose the resulting textured image into its component parts. In Fig. 12c, the user extracts color and texture for later reuse.

Color Partner – Interacting with History

Participants often reuse previous material from earlier projects and develop their own ad hoc techniques for capturing a history of their actions. *ColorPartner* lets users capture these interim steps in their color exploration process. Users identify a starting point by specifying two colors, after which *ColorPartner* generates novel, related colors. In Fig. 13a, the user creates a white and a black dot. In Fig. 13b, the system generates a set of related dark colors.

Users can guide which colors are generated through proximity to previously generated colors: moving the cursor closer to a dot produces more similar colors whereas moving the cursor away results in more diverse colors. In Fig. 13b, the user generates paler colors in the red range by moving from the red dot on the right, towards the white dot.

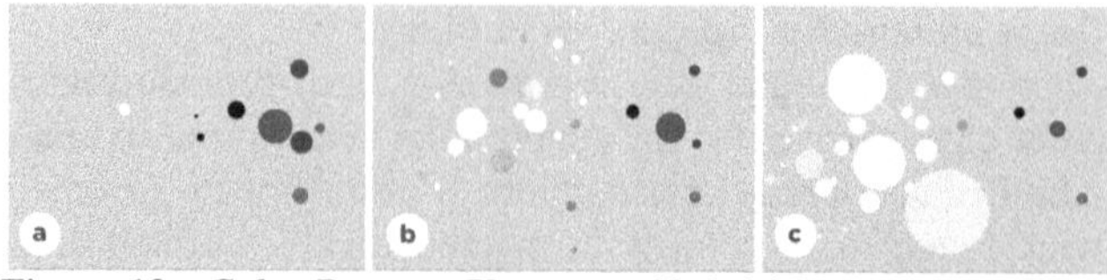

Figure 13: ***Color Partner*****: Users specify initial colors and move the cursor to control generation of new colors. They can save interesting intermediate colors by clicking on the dot.**

Over time, colors become smaller and disappear. However, the user can save colors by clicking on them; multiple clicks enlarge the size of the dot. In Fig. 13c, the user indicates a strong preference for three yellow and pale orange colors. *ColorPartner* allows users to return to intermediate color choices and use them to create new colors. *ColorPartner* offers an interesting partnership between users and the system, since they both collaborate on the creation and reuse of collections of colors.

Color Revealer – Interacting with Process

Unlike the other activities in the *Color Portraits* design space, process does not treat color as an end in itself, but rather as a means to an end. Color changes reveal intermediate steps or the overall state of an activity as it occurs over time. Like *EditWear* [12], which uses color to support annotation, *ColorRevealer* captures traces of the user's writing process, modifying hue and intensity. Characters each appear in a subtle, colored layer in the background.

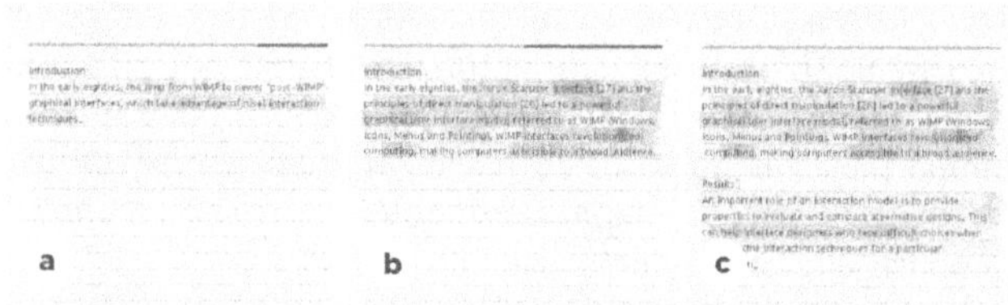

Figure 14: ***Color Revealer*****: Users' hesitations and corrections are revealed through changes in hue and intensity.**

In Fig. 14a, the user writes with very little hesitation, so the layers behind the text appear as a pale green. Additional layers appear as the user deletes or rewrites words. In Fig. 14b, the user has repeatedly deleted and corrected a number of words in his introduction, which introduces blue and purple text. *Color Revealer* allows users to control the mapping of colors to their writing activities and provides an adjustable timeline that lets them scroll back through earlier stages in the writing process. In Fig. 14c, the user needs additional time and has adjusted the time scale accordingly.

These four color tools embody different aspects of the *Color Portraits* design space. We treat them as probes to help us evaluate how color manipulation activities are represented in the design space and, to understand color manipulation more generally.

INTERACTING WITH PROBES

We selected participants from the two earlier studies to try the probes. We wanted to get an idea of how they interpreted each tool in general, and also in the context of their current work.

Participants: We re-interviewed eight participants, half from each of the two previous studies (5 men, 3 women, aged 23-40). Professions included: product designer, illustrator, painter, service designer, researcher in data visualization, information theorist, virtual reality engineer and programmer.

Procedure: Each session lasted approximately one hour in the participant's studio or office. We presented each tool, in turn, and gave the participant five minutes to experiment and perform short tasks with each tool, as follows: *Palette Explorer*: Create a book's cover page. *Color Compositor*: Design a textured color for the background of the book cover. *Color Partner:* Create your favorite red and favorite blue. *Color Revealer*: Write a summary of a recent project. After each task, we asked participants to think of recent color projects in which they manipulated color and show us how the tool might, or might not, be useful for those tasks. We counter-balanced the order of tools across participants.

Data collection: We collected audio recordings of each session and screen captures of their interactions with each color tool. We also took notes based on participants' answers to a common set of interview questions.

RESULTS

Participants suggested different ways of using the color probes both conceptually, by explaining what the tool does, and practically, to solve problems for their current projects. Interestingly, all participants wanted to interact with the color tools immediately, to manipulate swatches, dots or textures to obtain a desired effect.

Palette Explorer – Interacting with Palettes

Most participants (7/8) viewed *Palette Explorer* as a space for sketching color relationships relevant to those in their daily work. P5 (Product designer) described *Palette Explorer* as *"a tool for projection and sketching that allows rapid visualization of scale relationships among colors."* She wanted to create a color chart to establish a digital identity for a client and was particularly interested in using it to see how the colors look together in different contexts. For example, she wanted to establish a set of colors and then experiment how they would look with different versions of her client's logo.

Color Compositor – Interacting with composites

Half the participants in each of the earlier studies reported developing ad hoc strategies to combine colors and textures, but felt that *Color Compositor* greatly simplified the task. P3 (Service designer) was happy to avoid using *Photoshop* layers when creating and experimenting with a textured color. P5 (Product designer) wanted to use *Color Compositor's* texture library to group similar components for future use.

Although *Color Compositor* focused on texture, participants had a number of suggestions for combining color with other elements, especially images. They also offered innovative ideas for how to extend it. For example, three participants suggested reproducing these patterns on very large surfaces, to establish color and texture relationships when creating wallpaper.

Color Partner – Interacting with History

Participants viewed *Color Partner* as a space for exploring color. P1 (Painter) appreciated how suggesting colors helped him make color-related decisions. However, he *"would not share the result of generation. The colors I get are more personal"*. *Color Partner* also allowed participants to create interesting clusters of colors and to preserve those they would later use to create a new color exploration chain. P16 (Information theorist) felt that the tool would help her get "*little by little to the color I want*".

Color Revealer – Interacting with Process

Color Revealer encouraged participants to reflect on how they type and write. P16 (Information theorist) compared *Color Revealer* to an eraser: *"When I erase an area several times, I end up seeing the trace on paper"*. She also noticed that she always deleted the whole word when she makes a typo, which she had not realized before. P5 (Product Designer) explained that *Color Revealer "projects your thinking as you write. It helps you feel the intensity of your writing and gives it meaning through making this process visible."*

All but one participant described how they would use *Color Revealer* in their current projects. P1 (painter) wanted to use it when collaborating on a course he is teaching. Since his colleague is a fast typist, he wanted her to use the tool to take notes during class. He would like to then read the notes and use the change of color to help him understand when she hesitated, just as in a face-to-face conversation.

IMPLICATIONS FOR DESIGN

Our observations of how users interacted with the color probes suggest the following directions for designing interactive color tools:

Experimentation: explore color relationships; compare alternatives; and support user-defined constraints.

Ownership: personalize colors; capture interim creative steps; embed meaning; retain context; and support reuse of color creation chains.

Partnership: select within meaningful subsets of colors suggested by the system; and guide the system in new directions.

Integration: combine diverse elements; manipulate composites; and decompose into component parts.

SUMMARY AND FUTURE WORK

We created the *Color Portraits* design space to help identify color manipulation requirements that are poorly addressed by today's color manipulation tools. We conducted contextual interviews with 16 participants, who provided detailed examples of how they used color to create 69 different artistic or technical artifacts.

We also created a set of four color probes: *Palette Explorer* manipulates color relationships within a shared context; *Color Compositor* composes and decomposes diverse colors and textures; *Color Partner* generates and captures chains of color, guided by the user; and *Color Revealer* reveals underlying processes by subtly changing hue and color intensity.

The *Color Portraits* design space demonstrates the scope of as-yet unmet color manipulation needs, and the color tools demonstrate the generative power of this design space. In the future, we hope to build upon this work to design innovative new color manipulation tools for creative professionals, moving beyond simply picking colors to truly interacting with color.

ACKNOWLEDGMENTS

This research was supported by ERC grant n° 321135 *CREATIV: Creating Co-Adaptive Human-Computer Partnerships*. Our thanks to the participants for sharing their creative uses of color, and to Inria's Insitu research lab for fruitful discussions throughout the project.

REFERENCES

1. Albers, J. *Interaction of Color: 50th Anniversary Edition*. Yale University Press, New Haven, CT, 2013.
2. Bailey, P., Manktelow, K., & Olomolaiye, P. Examination of the color selection process within digital design for the built environment. In *Proc. IEEE, Theory and Practice of Computer Graphics* (2003), 193–200.
3. Bergman, L.D., Rogowitz, B.E., & Treinish, L.A. A rule-based tool for assisting colormap selection. In *Proc. Visualization* (1995), 118.
4. Chevalier, F., Dragicevic, P., & Hurter, C. Histomages: fully synchronized views for image editing. In *Proc. ACM UIST* (2012), 281–286.
5. Della Ventura, A. & Schettini, R. (1992) Computer-aided color coding for data display. In *Proc. IAPR (1992)*, 3: 29–32.
6. Douglas, S.A. & Kirkpatrick, A.E. Model and representation: the effect of visual feedback on human performance in a color picker interface. *ACM Transactions on Graphics* (1999), 18(2): 96–127.
7. Faul, F. & Ekroll, V. Psychophysical model of chromatic perceptual transparency based on substractive color mixture. *JOSA A* 19,6 (2002), 1084–1095.
8. Frisby, J.P. & Clatworthy, J.L. Illusory contours: curious cases of simultaneous brightness contrast? *Perception 4*, 3 (1975), 349 – 357.
9. Glaser, B. & Strauss, A. The Discovery of Grounded Theory: Strategies for Qualitative Research. Aldine Transaction, Chicago, 1999.
10. Harrower, M. & Brewer, C.A. ColorBrewer.org: An Online Tool for Selecting Colour Schemes for Maps. *The Cartographic Journal 40*, 1 (2003), 27–37.
11. Healey, C.G. Choosing effective colours for data visualization. In *Proc. Visualization* (1996), 263–270.
12. Hill, W.C., Hollan, J.D., Wroblewski, D., & McCandless, T. Edit Wear and Read Wear. In *Proc. ACM SIGCHI* (1992), 3–9.
13. Hutchinson, H., Mackay, W., Westerlund, B., Bederson, B., Druin, A., Plaisant, A., Beaudouin-Lafon, M., Conversy, M., Evans, H., Hansen, H., Roussel, N., & Eiderbäck, B. Technology probes: inspiring design for and with families. In *Proc. ACM CHI* (2003), 17–24.
14. Itten, J. Art de la couleur, *édition abrégée*. Bordas Editions, Paris, 1996.
15. Jirousek, C. Color, Value and Hue. *Art, Design and Visual Thinking,* 1995.
16. King, T.D. Human color perception, cognition, and culture: why red is always red. *Electronic Imaging, Inter. Soc. Optics & Photo.* (2005), 234–242.
17. Kubat, R., Mirman, D., & Roy, D. Semantic context effects on color categorization. In *Proc. CogSci* (2009).
18. McCollough, C. Color Adaptation of Edge-Detectors in the Human Visual System. *Science* (New York, N.Y.) 149, 3688 (1965), 1115–1116.
19. Meier, B.J., Spalter, A.M., & Karelitz, D.B. Interactive color palette tools In *Proc. IEEE Graphics and Applications*, 24, 3 (2004), 64–72.
20. Meier, B.J. ACE: a color expert system for user interface design. In *Proc. ACM SIGGRAPH symposium on User Interface Software* (1988), 117–128.
21. Meyer, G.W. & Greenberg, D.P. Perceptual color spaces for computer graphics. In *Proc. ACM SIGGRAPH Computer Graphics* (1980), 254–261.
22. O'Neill, J., Martin, D., Colombino, T., Roulland, F. & Willamowski, J. Colour management is a sociotechnical problem. In *Proc. ACM CSCW* (2008), 599–608.
23. Pang, W. M. An intuitive texture picker. In *Proc. ACM IUI* (2010), 365–368.
24. Pouli, T. & Reinhard, E. Progressive histogram reshaping for creative color transfer and tone reproduction. In *Proc. ACM Symposium on Non-Photorealistic Animation and Rendering* (2010), 81–90.
25. Robertson, P.K. Visualizing color gamuts: A user interface for the effective use of perceptual color spaces in data displays. *IEEE CG&A*, 8, 5 (1988), 50–64.
26. Wang, L., Giesen, J., McDonnell, K.T., Zolliker, P., & Mueller, K. Color design for illustrative visualization. *IEEE Vis. Comp. Graph*, 14 6 (2008), 1739–1754.
27. Wijffelaars, M., Vliegen, R., Van Wijk, J.J., & Van Der Linden, E.-J. Generating color palettes using intuitive parameters. *Comp Graph. For.* (2008), 743–750.

The Emergence of Interactive Behaviour: A Model of Rational Menu Search

Xiuli Chen[1], **Gilles Bailly**[2], **Duncan P. Brumby**[3], **Antti Oulasvirta**[4], **and Andrew Howes**[1]

[1]University of Birmingham, Birmingham, UK. xiuli.chenuk@gmail.com
[2]CNRS LTCI, Telecom-Paristech, Paris, France.
[3]UCL Interaction Centre, University College London, UK.
[4]Aalto University, Helsinki, Finland.

ABSTRACT

One reason that human interaction with technology is difficult to understand is because the way in which people perform interactive tasks is highly adaptive. One such interactive task is menu search. In the current article we test the hypothesis that menu search is rationally adapted to (1) the ecological structure of interaction, (2) cognitive and perceptual limits, and (3) the goal to maximise the trade-off between speed and accuracy. Unlike in previous models, no assumptions are made about the strategies available to or adopted by users, rather the menu search problem is specified as a reinforcement learning problem and behaviour *emerges* by finding the *optimal policy*. The model is tested against existing empirical findings concerning the effect of menu organisation and menu length. The model predicts the effect of these variables on task completion time and eye movements. The discussion considers the pros and cons of the modelling approach relative to other well-known modelling approaches.

Author Keywords

menu search; cognitive modelling; visual search; eye movements; Markov Decision Process; reinforcement learning; interaction science

ACM Classification Keywords

H.5.2 Theory and methods: H.1.2 User/Machine Systems: Human Information Processing

INTRODUCTION

Over the past few years, a trend has been for models of human performance to encompass the *adaptive* nature of interaction [15, 22, 31, 32, 34, 41]. In these models a sequence of user actions is predicted from an analysis of what it is rational for a user to do given an interface design and given known constraints on human cognition. These analyses take into account the costs and benefits of each action to the user so as to compose actions into efficient behavioural sequences. Examples include models of multitasking in which the time spent on each of two or more tasks is determined by their relative benefits and time costs [24, 42]. They also include models of the search for information on the web in which the benefits include information gain [34] and even models of how to use a visual programming language [14]. The analysis of rationality has also informed empirical studies of tasks such as driving while using a phone or iPod [9], studies of Powerpoint use [11], and of interactive planning [30]. In each case human behaviour is shown to be an *emergent* consequence of adaptation to the task environment and psychological constraints.

CHI'15, April 18 - 23 2015, Seoul, Republic of Korea.
Copyright © 2015 ACM 978-1-4503-3145-6/15/04 $15.00.
http://dx.doi.org/10.1145/2702123.2702483

The goal of the current paper is to explain menu search as an emergent consequence of adaptation to these same constraints. Understanding menu search is important for HCI because menus are the primary interaction method in most computer technologies and because there are outstanding design issues; issues concerning both organisational and layout factors.There are also many empirical studies of the use of menus and they continue to present design challenges [6, 10, 17, 20, 28]. Understanding menu search is also important, because many menu commands are used infrequently and users often have to search for commands that are new or that have forgotten locations. Sometimes the search will be localised to a particular menu and sometimes not. A predictive model of menu search could assist in research aimed at improving this ubiquitous and powerful interface technology [3].

Evidence suggests that there is substantial scope for strategic adaptation in menu search [6, 10, 17, 20, 28]. Despite deceptive simplicity, menus invite a flexible range of behaviour. Even, for example, the seemingly mundane task of searching through a vertically arranged textual menu can be achieved by starting at the top and considering each item or, alternatively, by guessing where the desired item will be in an alphabetically ordered or semantically grouped list. Sometimes users appear to skip over some items but not others [6]. They also search differently when looking for a known-word than when looking for a semantically related item [7]. There are many further possibilities and refinements and many subtle variations that determine, for example, where to look next, when to make a guess, and when to search in a different menu entirely. For many users, these are choices that are made quickly and implicitly.

In the current article we show that the range of observed behaviours emerges through psychologically constrained interaction with menus. Specifically, we report a cognitive model of rational menu search that offers the first account in which predictions of search time and eye movements emerge from assumptions about the user's task environment and limitations.

Another goal of the paper is to advance the role of cognitive models as a method for explaining interactive behaviour. Modelling is important to HCI because it has the potential to offer more systematic, rigorous and general explanations of interaction than, for example, verbal descriptions. It is *rigorous*, because modeling uses computational methods to simulate cognitive processes and thereby reduce the potential for ambiguity and miscalculation. It is *systematic*, because otherwise disparate theoretical commitments can be brought together into a single explanatory framework. Lastly, it is more *general*, because the systematicity of theory allows a large body of facts, e.g., about performance time, sometimes on very different tasks, to be given a single explanation.

Despite their potential strengths, cognitive models have been under-exploited in HCI. While there has been a substantial effort to model menu search and related visual search tasks [8, 10, 15, 18, 25, 28], these existing models have tended require the modeler to explicitly define the set of available strategies. For example, the ACT-R model reported in [10] implemented a set of production rules to decide which item to assess next. One of these rules would direct gaze to the next item in the menu while the other would move gaze to a randomly selected (and previously unassessed) item. Because these production rules competed stochastically, the resulting behaviour was a mix of systematic top-to-bottom scanning with occasional jumps. The EPIC model reported in [18] captured item skipping in a different way. Production rules were used to implement a visual search strategy in which fixations were constrained to fall on new items that were outside the current field of view (even though they might not be directly fixated). Despite these differences in the production rule specifications, the behaviour of both of these models is restricted to the strategy alternatives that were explicitly defined (hand-coded) by the modeler.

In contrast to the previous models of menu search, the model reported in the current article has two advantages: (1) it does not require the modeller to hand-code production rules and, as a consequence, (2) there are no arbitrary restrictions on the range of possible behaviours. Instead control knowledge, and therefore predicted effects for a particular menu design, is an emergent consequence of rational adaptation to the structure of interaction, cognitive and perceptual limits, and the goal to maximise the trade-off between speed and accuracy. In other words, the model shows how user strategy might emerge from constraints. Therefore, while the proposed model builds on a number of insights concerning cognitive mechanisms that were first proposed with ACT-R and EPIC models [8, 10, 15, 18, 25, 28], it does not require any hand-coded production rules to make predictions.

In what follows we first review the background to the work. In particular, we focus on contributions to understanding Human-Computer Interaction as a rational adaptation to constraints. Subsequently, we report a model of menu search which shows how visual search behaviour is an emergent consequence of adaptation. Critically, the model does not make any a priori assumptions about either eye movement strategy or when to select an item (which are usually thought of as a *stopping rule* problem). The model is tested with two studies one of which was chosen to demonstrate that the model can generate predictions for common computer application menus and the second of which was chosen so as to provide a comparison to existing data sets. The first study generates predictions for users of an Apple Mac who have experienced a number of applications and a number of the menus deployed by those applications. The second study tests the model's predictions against data from participants in a laboratory experiment reported by [2]. Detailed comparisons to human performance metrics (including performance time and eye movements) are provided.

Our primary contributions are:

1. A novel computational model, based on machine learning, of menu search showing how behaviour is an emergent consequence of environment, cognition, and utility.
2. A quantitative account of how existing empirical findings concerning menu search can be explained as rational adaptation to constraints.
3. The further development of a general computational modelling framework for explaining the emergence of rational interactive behaviour.

BACKGROUND

The idea that human interaction with technology can be understood as a rational adaptation has strong roots in the HCI and Human Factors literatures [5, 15, 26, 32, 31, 34, 33, 40, 41]. One way to summarise the framework adopted in this literature is with Figure 1 [31]. In the figure there are four components to an explanation of behaviour: Environment, Utility, Mechanism and Strategy. *Utility* concerns assumptions about what a person wants to do. *Ecology* concerns the statistical structure of the environment. *Mechanism* concerns human information processing capacities. These three components determine a space of strategies, which is the fourth component, and with a principle of rationality they then jointly determine the *strategy* (also called a *policy*) and therefore a sequence of *actions*. In the framework the strategies are an emergent consequence of rational adaptation to the other components.

The successful application of this framework requires a theory of each of the components in Figure 1. One key set of constraints are those imposed by the human visual system. In the vision research literature there has been much recent interest in explaining visual search as an adaptation to visual processing mechanisms and reward [19, 29, 37, 39]. Key

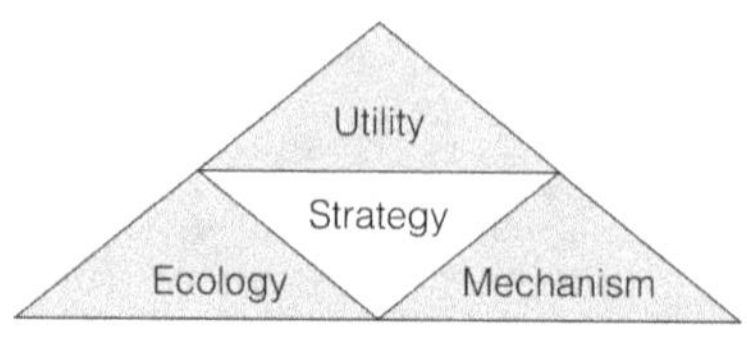

Figure 1: The Adaptive Interaction Framework [31]

constraints imposed by the mechanisms concern saccade and fixation latencies [35] and also the reduction of acuity with eccentricity from the fovea [25]. It has been shown that given these constraints, strategies can be derived through the use of reinforcement learning algorithms [12, 19, 37], though it is possible that strategies may be acquired by other learning mechanisms, for example, by cultural transmission, through instructions, or by evolution.

The approach that we take is also influenced by ideas in optimal control and Machine Learning [5, 36, 38]. A key contribution of this literature has been to provide a formal basis for learning an optimal control policy given only a definition of the reward function, the state space, and the action space. Control knowledge is simply knowledge that determines what-to-do-when. In the case of menu search it concerns where to move the eyes and when to select an item. In this framework, the expected value of an action given a state is the sum of the immediate reward plus the rewards that would accrue from subsequent actions if that action were selected. This simple assumption has provided a means of deriving human visual search strategies in well-known laboratory tasks [12]. It also provides a means by which to derive rational menu search behaviour given assumptions about utility, ecology and psychological mechanisms but only if the user's menu search problem can be defined as a reinforcement learning problem. In the following section we report a model that does just that.

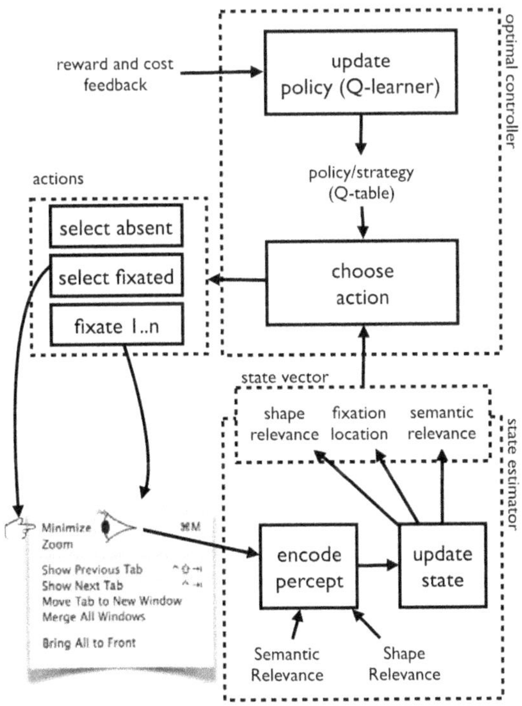

Figure 2: An overview of the adaptive menu search model.

THEORY AND MODEL

Imagine that the goal for a user who is experienced with menus, but who has never used Apple's OS X Safari browser before, is to select 'Show Next Tab' from the Safari Window menu. This task and menu are illustrated to the bottom-left of Figure 2. A user might solve this goal by first fixating the top menu item, encoding the word 'Minimize'; rejecting it as irrelevant to the target, moving the eyes to the next group of items, that begins 'Show Previous Tab', noticing that this item is not the target but is closely related and also noticing, in peripheral vision, that the next item has a similar word shape and length to the target; then moving the eyes to 'Show Next Tab', confirming that it is the target and selecting it. The aim of the modelling is that behaviours such as this should emerge from theoretical assumptions. Importantly, the aim is not to model how people learn specific menus and the location of specific items, rather the aim is to model the menu search task in general. The requirement is that the model should learn, from experience, the best way to search for new targets in new, previously unseen, menus.

To achieve this goal we use a *state estimation and optimal control* approach. In Figure 2 an external representation of the displayed menu is fixated and the state estimator encodes a percept containing information about the relevance of word shapes ('Minimise' and 'Zoom', for example have different lengths) and semantics (word meanings). This information is used to update a state vector, which has an element for the shape relevance of every item in the menu, an element for the semantic relevance of every item in the menu, and an element for the current fixation location. The vector items are null until estimates are acquired through visual perception. Updates are made after every fixation, e.g. after fixating 'Minimize' in the above example. After having encoded new information through visual perception, the optimal controller chooses an action on the basis of the available state estimate and the *strategy* (i.e., the policy that determines a state-action value function). The chosen action might be to fixate on another item or to make a selection, or to exit the menu if the target is probably absent. State-action values are updated incrementally (learned) as reward and cost feedback is received from the interaction. The menu search problem is thereby defined as a reinforcement learning problem [38].

The paragraph above offers only a very brief overview of the theory and it leaves out many of the details. In the following subsections more detail is provided about how the state estimation and optimal controller work. Subsequently a model walkthrough is provided.

State estimator

The state estimator (the bottom right of Figure 2) encodes semantic, alphabetic and shape information, constrained by visual and cognitive mechanisms.

Semantic relevance

In common with many previous models of menu search [8, 15, 28, 34, 33], our model assumes that people have an ability to determine the semantic relevance of items by matching them to the goal specification. To implement this assumption, we used average pairwise relevance ratings gathered from human participants (which are taken from [2]). These relevance ratings are described in detail below. For now, consider the following example: if the model sampled the goal Zoom and foveated the word Minimize then it could look-up the relevance score 0.75 which was the mean relevance ranking given by participants. The level of this relevance score will only acquire meaning (whether it is considered a good or bad match) during learning. We also assume that people are able to maintain a short term representation of the semantic relevance of items that have been perceived. These are encoded in the state representation. No capacity limitations are assumed in this version of the theory.

Note that while the pairwise relevance ratings provide the model with a substantial database of information they do not specify the actions that should be taken on the basis of this information. How the best actions are found is described below in *The Optimal Controller* section.

Alphabetics and Shape relevance

The shape of each menu item was represented by its length in characters. No effort was made to model the shape of individual characters. The shape relevance had two levels, [0 for non-target length; 1 for target length]. The alphabetic relevance of two items was determined using the distance apart in the alphabet of their first letters. This was then standardised to a four-level scale between 0 and 1, i.e., [0, 0.3, 0.6, 1].

Saccade duration

The saccade duration D (in milliseconds) was determined with the following equation [4]:

$$D = 37 + 2.7A \tag{1}$$

where A is the amplitude (in terms of visual angle in degrees) of the saccade between two successive fixations.

Fixation duration

It is known that the average fixation duration for reading is 200-250ms [35]. However, menu search involves some matching process and so some additional latency per menu item gaze is expected. In fact, in a typical menu search task the mean duration of item gazes was reported as about 400ms [7] and this is the fixation duration assumed in our model.

Peripheral vision

Visual acuity is known to reduce with eccentricity from the fovea. In our model, the acuity function was represented as the probability that each visual feature of the item was recognised. Our model made use of semantic features and shape features but could easily be enhanced with other features such as colour. Semantic acuity (the semantic relevance of the item to the target) was specified as being available within $1°$ of the current fixation [23]. The model predictions were compared with the empirical data from Bailly et al. [2]. In their experiment, the height of the items in the menu was about $0.7°$. Hence, our model assumed that the semantic of item was obtained only when it was fixated. Shape acuity was specified as a quadratic psychophysical function from [25]. This function was used to determine the availability of the shape of the item based on the eccentricity and the size of the item (Equation 2).

$$\begin{cases} P(available) & = P(s + X > threshold) \\ threshold & = ae^2 + be + c \\ X \sim \mathcal{N}(s, v \times s) \end{cases} \tag{2}$$

where, s is the item size; e is eccentricity; X is random noise with standard deviation $v \times s$ (v is a constant).

The parameters in Equation 2 were chosen so as to fit the materials used in Bailly et al. [2]. In their experiment, the height of an item was 0.75 cm; the distance of the users eyes from the screen was 65 cm. Participants should therefore have been able to simultaneously gather information about the shape of 3 items given a fovea of $2°$. Parameters for Equation 2 were set as follows, $v = 0.7$, $b = 0.1$, $c = 0.1$, $a = 0.3$ and $s = 0.75$. These parameter settings resulted in the following availability probabilities: 0.95 for the item fixated, 0.89 for items immediately above or below the fixated item, and 0 for items further away. On each fixation, the availability of the shape information was determined by these probabilities.

The optimal controller: Strategy/Policy Learning

The function of the optimal controller (top right in Figure 2) is to choose which action to do next (e.g. to fixate or select an item). It does so by looking up a value for each action available and picking one. These values are called *q-values*, or state-action values, and are stored in a q-table. A row in the q-table might, for example, specify that in a state with many low-relevance items ending the search by exiting the menu has a high value. One important question concerns how these q-values are learnt and why they implement the optimal menu search policy. However, to answer this question we must first briefly describe how learnt q-values are used to control search. Doing so requires us to introduce the concept of a Markov Decision Process (MDP); see Figure 3.

Recall the task illustrated in Figure 2 of selecting 'Show Next Tab'. The model starts in state $s1$ (Figure 3), which is the *initial state*. As no visual information has been encoded the state vector [semantic relevance, fixation, word shape relevance] is null (See the top row of Table 1).

The next step is to choose an action. From each state the available actions include: an action for fixating on each menu item, an action for selecting the fixated item, and an action for stopping the search because the item is believed to be absent. In the figure, the state-action values (q-values) are represented on the arcs from states (red circles) to actions (green circles). (How these q-values are learnt is explained below but for now assume the values presented in the figure.) If the menu searcher is greedy then it will select the most valuable actions as represented by larger q-values. It follows that, using the MDP in the figure, the model will first fixate on the first menu item; that is it will choose the 'fixate 1' action (with value q=8) in the uppermost row of green actions in Figure 3 and as a consequence it would fixate the 'Minimize' item in Figure 2.

Having fixated 'Minimize' the model encodes the semantic and shape relevance for the fixated item. The goal is 'Show

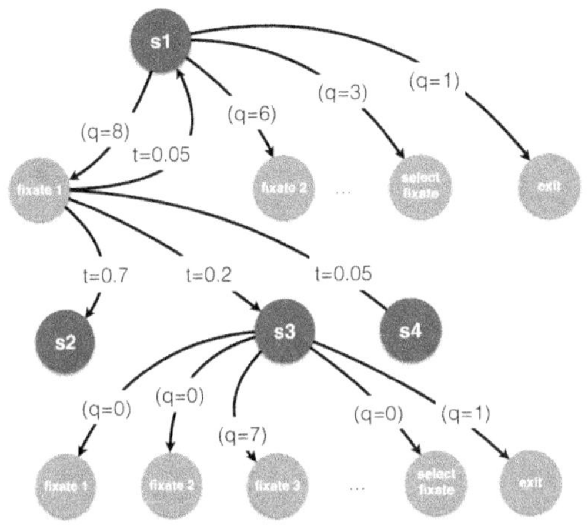

Figure 3: A part of a solution to a Markov Decision Process (MDP) for searching the Safari Window menu. Red circles labelled 's' represent states. Green circles represent actions. 'q' values represent learned state-action values. 't' values represent state-action to state transition probabilities. Action 'fixate 1' is the consequence of choosing the highest value action. The model subsequently transitions to state 's3' with probability 0.2.

Action	*Semantic relevance*	*fixation*	*Shape relevance*
start	N, N, N, N	N	N, N, N, N
fixate 1	$0, N, N, N$	1	$0, 0, N, N$
fixate 3	$0, N, 0.3, N$	3	$0, 0, 1.0, 1.0$
fixate 4	$0, N, 0.3, 1.0$	4	$0, 0, 1.0, 1.0$
select 4			

Table 1: Example changes in the state representation for a 4 item menu ($N = null$). The semantic relevance had 5 levels [Null, 0, 0.3, 0.6, 1].

Next Tab' and so the relevance of 'Minimize' relative to this goal is likely to be low. The model also encodes shape relevance about neighbouring items in accordance with Equation 2. However, the exact values encoded are subject to noise because visual information processing is uncertain. As a consequence, the model might end up in either state $s2$, $s3$, or $s4$, or perhaps back in state $s1$ if no new information was encoded after the previous action. The transition probabilities to these states, t, are shown in the figure. These transition probabilities are a consequence of the interaction between the model of the visual system and the external environment. After any action the model is more likely to transition to a state that is (a) more likely in the environment and (b) more likely to be encoded by the perceptual model.

Subsequently, assuming that the model has transitioned to state $s3$ representing low semantic and low shape relevance, then the highest value action from this state is to fixate on item 3 (q=7). In other words, because of the low relevance of item 1, the model has skipped item 2 and focused on an item in the next semantic group.

Assumption	*Description*
Utility	Utility = $10000 \times correct - 10000 \times error - time$, where *correct* and *error* are Boolean variables; the unit of *time* is *ms*.
Ecology	The ecology concerns the statistical structure of menus. Menus, in the world, have a distribution of length (number of items) and a distribution of group size. Menu items have a distribution of semantic relevance and shape/length (number of chars). See Figure 4.
Mechanism	People can estimate the semantic relevance of the foveated menu item. They can also estimate the shape/length of items in the periphery, although acuity decreases with eccentricity. See Equations 1 and 2.
Strategy	A strategy (or policy) for menu search is optimised to Utility, Ecology and Mechanism assuming a state space that consists of the relevance vectors and the fixation.

Table 2: Summary of assumptions for the adaptive model of menu search.

Table 1 gives an example of how the state vector is updated as information is gathered through eye movements and visual perception.

State and action space

For a set of menus that have a maximum of n items, a state is represented as a vector V with $2 \times n + 1$ elements. This consists of n elements for the shape, n for the semantic relevance, and 1 for the fixation location. The semantic/alphabetic relevance had 5 levels [Null, 0, 0.3, 0.6, 1]. The shape relevance had 2 levels [0 for non-target length; 1 for target length]. The fixation was an integer representing one of the menu item locations [1..n]. From each state there were $n + 2$ actions, including n actions for fixating on n menu item locations, an action for selecting the fixated item, and an action to exit the menu without selection (target absent).

Learning

The q-values, as illustrated in Figure 3, represent control knowledge and are learnt with a reinforcement learning algorithm. The reinforcement learning algorithm used was a standard implementation of Q-learning. We do not present the details of the algorithm here but they can be found in any standard Machine Learning text (e.g. [38]).

Q-learning requires reward and cost feedback so as to learn the state-action values. A state-action value can be thought of as a prediction of the future reward minus costs that will accrue if the action is taken. The rewards and costs must be combined into a single utility score. We assumed a simple utility function in which there is a reward for success, a penalty for an error, and a penalty for time. The time cost is measured in milliseconds and is determined by the visual information processing and motor assumptions and by the number of fixations made. The reward for a correct menu item selection was $+10000$; the penalty for an incorrect selection was −10000. These numbers are large so as to emphasise accuracy over time. Indeed in the studies reported below the model achieved 99% accuracy.

Before learning, an empty Q-table was assumed in which all state-action values were zero. The model therefore started with no control knowledge and action selection was entirely random. The model was then trained until performance plateaued (requiring 20 million trials). On each trial, the model was trained on a menu constructed by sampling randomly from the ecological distributions of shape and semantic/alphabetic relevance defined below. The model explored the action space using an ϵ-greedy exploration. This means that it exploited the greedy/best action with a probability $1-\epsilon$, and it explored all the actions randomly with probability ϵ. q-values were adjusted according to the reward and cost feedback. The optimal policy acquired through this training was then used to generate the predictions described below. To do so the optimal policy was run on a further 10,000 trials of newly sampled menus, and its performance was recorded.

While we used Q-learning, any MDP solver that is guaranteed to converge on the optimal policy is sufficient to derive the rational adaptation [38]. The Q-learning process is not a theoretical commitment. Its purpose is merely to find the optimal policy. It is not to model the process of learning and is therefore used to achieve methodological optimality and determine the computationally rational strategy [16, 27].

In summary, Q-learning was used to learn (or estimate) the value of each state-action pair by simulated experience of interaction with a distribution of menu tasks, where the interaction is mediated by the theory of visual perception and knowledge. The optimal policy is then the greedy policy given the q-values. The assumptions are summarised, briefly, in Table 2 and explained fully below. (The model was implemented in Matlab and can be downloaded on request from the first author.)

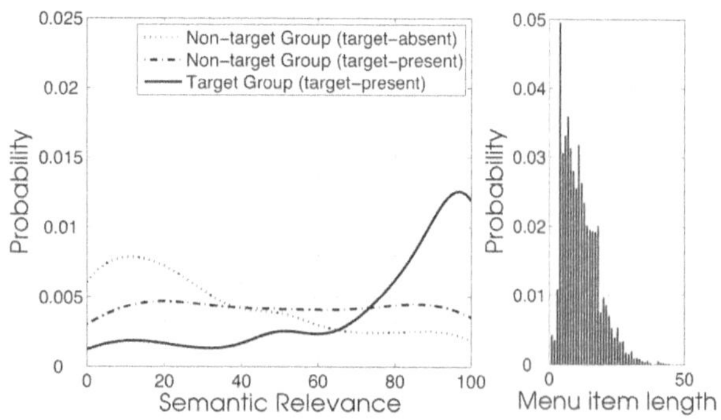

Figure 4: Menu ecology of a real-world menu task (Apple OS X menus). Left panel: The distribution of semantic relevance. Right panel: The distribution of menu length.

STUDY 1: PREDICTING REAL-WORLD MENU SEARCH

The purpose of this first study was to examine the model's predictions on commonly used computer application menus. The task was to search for specific target items in a vertically arranged menu. How items were organised in the menu was

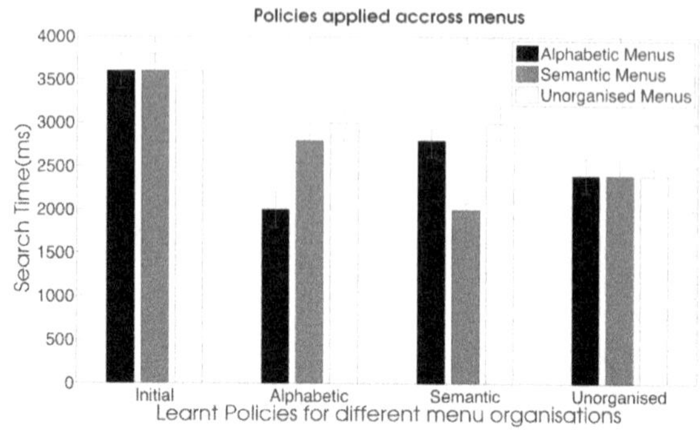

Figure 5: The search duration taken by the optimal strategy for each type of menu (95% confidence intervals (C.I.s))

varied. Items could be unorganised, alphabetically organised, or semantically organised. To determine the statistical properties of a menu search environment we used the results of a previous study [1] in which the menus of 60 applications from Apple OS X were sampled. Together these applications used a total 1049 menus, and 7802 menu items. We used these to determine the ecological distribution of menu length, item length, semantic group size and first letter frequencies (for alphabetic search). The probability of each length (number of characters) is shown in Figure 4 right panel. The mean item length was 11.5, the median was 10 and the standard deviation was 6.82. The most frequent menu item length was 4 characters. As should be expected the distribution is skewed, with a long tail of low probability longer menu items.

We then ran a study in which we asked 31 participants to rate how likely two menu items were to appear close together on a menu. Each participant rated 64 pairs that were sampled from the Apple OS X Safari browser menu items. The probability of each semantic relevance rating is shown in Figure 4 left panel. These ratings were used both to construct example menus and to implement the model's semantic relevance function.

Results

All results are for the optimal strategy (after learning), unless stated otherwise. The optimal policy achieved 99% selection accuracy. The utility of all models plateaued, suggesting that the learned strategy was a good approximation to the optimal strategy.

Search duration

Figure 5 is a plot of the duration required for the optimal policy to make a selection given four types of experience crossed with three types of test menu. The purpose of this analysis is to show how radically different patterns of behaviour emerge from the model based on how previously experienced menus were organised. Prior to training (the left most *Initial* set of three bars in the figure), the model offers the slowest performance; it is unable to take advantage of the structure in the alphabetic and semantic menus because it has no control knowledge. After training on a distribution of *Unorganised* menus (far right set in the figure), performance time is better

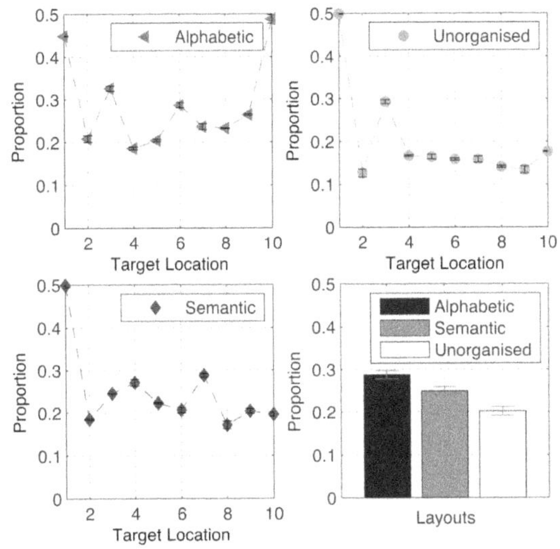

Figure 6: The proportion of gazes on the target location for each type of menu (95% C.I.s).

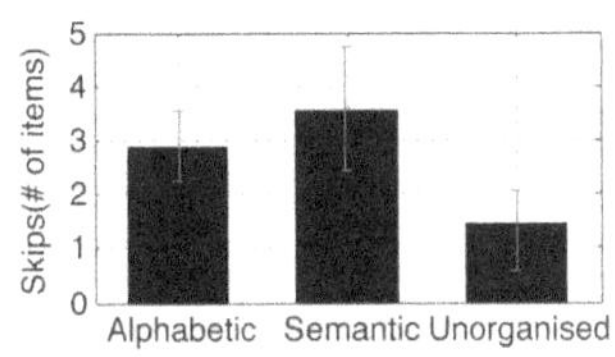

Figure 7: The model's prediction of skipping (mean gap between fixations).

than prior to training. However, there is no difference in performance time between the different menu organisations. After training on a distribution of semantically organised menus (middle right set in the figure), the model is able to take advantage of semantic structure, but this training is costly to performance on alphabetic and unorganised menus. After training on a distribution of alphabetically organised menus (middle left set in the figure), the model is able to take advantage of alphabetic ordering, but this training is again costly to the other menu types. The optimal policy must switch the policy depending on the menu type.

Gaze distribution

Figure 6 shows the effect of the menu organisation/layout on the distribution of gazes landing on target items. This is one measure of the effectiveness of each menu organisation for finding the target. A higher proportion of gazes on the target suggests a better organisation for search. The plots show the advantage of the alphabetic and semantic menus over the unorganised menus. The reason that there is higher proportion of gaze on the target item in the alphabetic and semantic menus is that in the emergent policy more low relevance items could be skipped (See Figure 7).

Effect of semantic grouping

Figure 8 shows the effect of different semantic groupings on performance time. It contrasts the performance time predic-

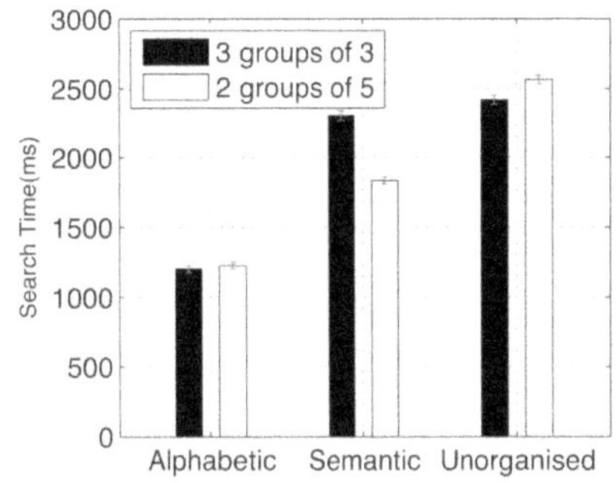

Figure 8: The effect of semantic group size (95% C.I.s).

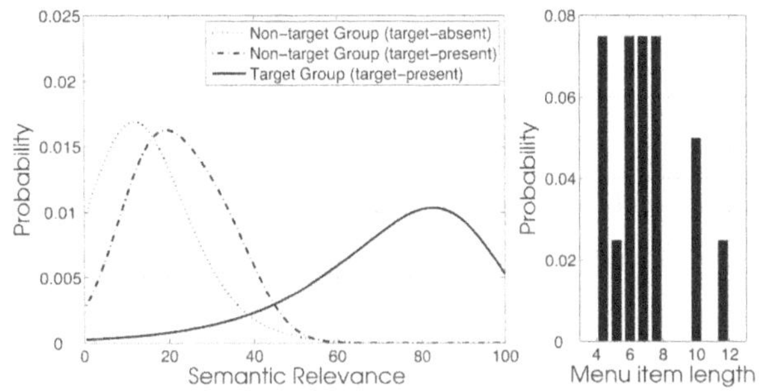

Figure 9: Menu ecology for the experimental menu search task. Left panel: The distribution of semantic relevance. Right panel: The length distribution.

tions for menus that are organised into 3 groups of 3 or into 2 groups of 5. The contrast between these kinds of design choices has been studied extensively before (See e.g. [28]). What has been observed is an interaction between the effect of longer menus and the effect of the number of items in each semantic group (See [28] Figure 8). As can be seen in Figure 8 while the effect of longer menus ($3 \times 3 = 9$ versus $2 \times 5 = 10$) is longer performance times in the unorganised and alphabetic menus, the effect of organisation (3 groups of 3 versus 2 of 5) gives shorter performance times in the semantic condition. This prediction corresponds closely to a number of studies (See [28] Figure 8).

Discussion

The results show that deriving strategies using a reinforcement learning algorithm, given plausible assumptions about the menu search problem (Table 2), can lead to reasonable predictions about human behaviour in ecologically valid task environments. In the following section we test these predictions against data from a study of human participants using a small set of representative menus.

STUDY 2: TESTING THE MODEL AGAINST HUMAN DATA

While the previous model demonstrated the viability of the approach it did not provide an opportunity to test the predictions against human data. In this section we test the model against two previously reported data sets [2, 7]. The data set reported by Bailly et al. [2] has the advantage that it includes eye movement and task performance time data. However, it

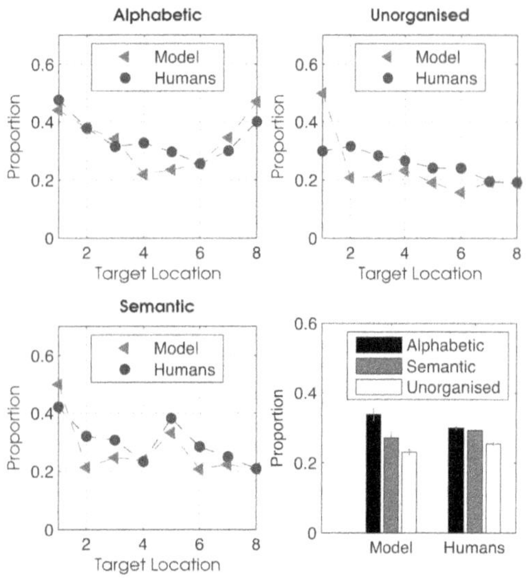

Figure 10: The proportion of gazes on the target location for each of the three types of menu (95% C.I.s).

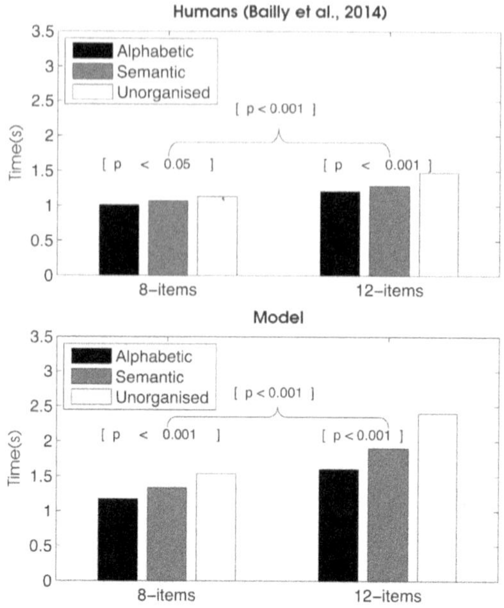

Figure 11: Search time for 8 and 12 item menus each organised in three different ways. Top panel for humans [2], bottom panel for the model. The predict effects are long but the directions are confirmed.

has the disadvantage that the distributions of menu length, menu item length and semantics do not correspond to the ecological distributions. Therefore, while this model shares all of the cognitive, visual, and utility assumptions with the above model, it does not share the same assumptions about the environment. Instead, for the experimental environment the distributions of semantic relevance and menu length was determined using relevance ratings reported in [2]. In addition, the experiment menus were 8-items (2 groups of 4) and 12-items (3 groups of 4). The distribution is plotted in Figure 9. The data set reported by Brumby et al. [7] reveals the effect on search of whether or not the exact target word is known.

As with the previous model, this model was trained on distributions of menus and menu items sampled from the ecological distributions. It was trained on 20 million samples. The optimal policy was then used to generate the predictions described in the following results section.

Results

We report a range of effects predicted by the optimal policy and compare them to the human data. As before, the optimal policy achieved 99% accuracy which corresponded with the reported participant accuracy level [2]. We report effects of menu layout on performance time and also effects on gaze distribution. The gaze distributions provide evidence that both model and people strategically adjust behaviour to the particular menu organisation.

Target location effect on gaze distribution

Figure 10 shows the effect of target position on the distribution of item gazes for each menu organisation. The model is compared to human data reported in [2]. The adjusted R^2 for each of the three organisations (alphabetic, unorganised, semantic) are $0.84, 0.65, 0.80$. In the top left panel, the model's gaze distribution is a consequence of both alphabetic anticipation and shape relevance in peripheral vision. Interestingly, both the model and the participants selectively gazed at targets at either end of the menu more frequently than targets in the middle. This may reflect the ease with which words beginning with early and late alphabetic words can be located. In the top right panel, there is no organisational structure to the menu and the model's gaze distribution is a consequence of shape relevance only in peripheral vision. The model offers a poor prediction of the proportion of gazes on the target when it is in position 1, otherwise, as expected, the distribution is relatively flat in both the model and the participants. In the bottom left panel, the model's gaze distribution is a function of semantic relevance and shape relevance. Here there are spikes in the distribution at position 1 and 5. In the model, this is because the emergent policy uses the relevance of the first item of each semantic group as evidence of the content of that group. In other words, the grouping structure of the menu is evidence in the emergent gaze distributions. The aggregated data is shown in the bottom right panel; the model predicts the significant effect of organisation on gaze distribution, although it predicts a larger effect for alphabetic menus than was observed.

Effect of length (8 v 12) on duration

It is known that people take longer to search menus with more items. Figure 11 shows that the model predicts the effect observed by [2].

Effect of known- versus unknown-target on duration

Using the same materials as [2], Brumby et al. [7] have shown that people are slower at searching menus when given only a semantic description of the target (rather than being told the exact target word). To capture this effect, we implemented a variant of the model that was given a semantically related word rather than the target word. The model could therefore not make use of the shape of items located in peripheral vision during search. All other assumptions remained the same. This meant that the model had to directly fixate items in order to assess them. We found that this variant of the model performed slower (M = 2183 ms, SD = 777 ms) than the standard model (M = 1458 ms, SD = 760 ms). It predicted known- versus unknown-target effect observed in [7].

DISCUSSION

We have reported a model in which search behaviours were an emergent consequence of a combination of three sources of constraint: the ecological structure of interaction, the cognitive and perceptual limits, and the goal to maximise the trade-off between speed and accuracy. The model was tested with two studies of its predictions. The first study involved applying the model to a real world distribution of menu items and in the second study the model was compared to human data from a previously reported experiment. The model was thereby tested against existing empirical findings concerning the effect of menu organisation, menu length, and whether or not the target is a known word. The predictions of the model were largely supported by the experimental evidence.

Unlike in previous models, no assumptions were made about the gaze strategies available to or adopted by users, rather the menu search problem was specified as a Markov Decision Process (MDP) and behaviour emerged from solving the reinforcement learning problem. The states of the MDP were defined by a theory of foveal and peripheral vision that encoded information about semantic and word shape relevance. Unlike production system based approaches (ACT-R and EPIC) there are no rules programmed by the modeller, rather the strategy is emergent from the constraints.

While the reported models demonstrate that it is possible to predict user behaviour with both a real world and a laboratory menu system the method also has potential to predict performance with interesting design variations. It could be used, for example, to verify performance predictions with automatically designed interfaces [3]. It could also be extended to predict visual search of icons [25] or any other means of laying out options spatially on a display. It could also be used to predict rational strategies in aimed movement required for using a mouse or a touch surface [31, 39].

Also, while we have reported a model of menu search, the theory that underpins the model and much of the way in which the problem was solved using machine learning, is potentially general to many modelling problems in HCI. Indeed elements of this argument have been made by a number of authors [12, 31, 33, 41]. A key property of the approach is that behavioural predictions are derived by maximising utility given a quantitative theory of the constraints on behaviour, rather than by maximising fit to the data. Although this *optimality* assumption is sometimes controversial, the claim is simply that users will do the best they can with the resources that are available to them. Further discussions of this issue can be found in [21, 27, 31].

Finally, there are many issues that need to be resolved. For example, the conversion of the Partially Observable Markov Decision Process (POMDP) into an MDP by assuming a psychologically plausible state estimation is known to fail to achieve an exact solution to the POMDP. Further work is required to understand the properties of a model in which, unlike ours, an optimal action is found for each possible belief over the states of the world (a belief state). Further work is also required to understand how this approach can be extended to capture the range of phenomena associated with skilled menu use [13]. Scalability is also a concern and the analyses presented in the paper required substantial computation. As noted above, the semantic relevance had 5 levels and shape had 2 levels. Therefore, the state space for an 8-item menu is $5^8 \times 2^8 \times 8$ states. But, this is an upper-bound and because the menus have structure, the state space experienced during training is much smaller.

ACKNOWLEDGMENTS

This research was supported by Air Force Office of Scientific Research (AFOSR#12RH05COR) and the EU-funded SPEEDD project (FP7-ICT 619435).

REFERENCES

1. Bailly, G., Malacria, S., et al. Menuinspector: Outil pour l'analyse des menus et cas d'étude. In *25ème conférence francophone sur l'Interaction Homme-Machine, IHM'13* (2013).
2. Bailly, G., Oulasvirta, A., Brumby, D. P., and Howes, A. Model of visual search and selection time in linear menus. In *ACM CHI'14* (2014), 3865–3874.
3. Bailly, G., Oulasvirta, A., Kötzing, T., and Hoppe, S. Menuoptimizer: Interactive optimization of menu systems. In *ACM CHI'13* (2013), 331–342.
4. Baloh, R. W., Sills, A. W., Kumley, W. E., and Honrubia, V. Quantitative measurement of saccade amplitude, duration, and velocity. *Neurology 25*, 11 (1975), 1065–1065.
5. Baron, S., and Kleinman, D. L. The human as an optimal controller and information processor. *Man-Machine Systems, IEEE Transactions on 10*, 1 (1969), 9–17.
6. Brumby, D., and Howes, A. Strategies for guiding interactive search: An empirical investigation into the consequences of label relevance for assessment and selection. *Human-Computer Interaction 23*, 1 (2008), 1–46.
7. Brumby, D. P., Cox, A. L., Chung, J., and Fernandes, B. How does knowing what you are looking for change visual search behavior? In *ACM CHI'14* (2014), 3895–3898.
8. Brumby, D. P., and Howes, A. Good enough but i'll just check: Web-page search as attentional refocusing. In *ICCM* (2004), 46–51.
9. Brumby, D. P., Salvucci, D. D., and Howes, A. Focus on driving: How cognitive constraints shape the adaptation of strategy when dialing while driving. In *ACM CHI'09* (2009), 1629–1638.

10. Byrne, M. D. ACT-R/PM and menu selection: Applying a cognitive architecture to HCI. *International Journal of Human-Computer Studies 55*, 1 (2001), 41–84.

11. Charman, S. C., and Howes, A. The adaptive user: an investigation into the cognitive and task constraints on the generation of new methods. *Journal of experimental psychology. Applied 9*, 4 (2003), 236–48.

12. Chen, X, Howes, A., Lewis, R.L., Myers, C.W., Houpt, J. Discovering computationally rational eye movements in the distractor ratio task. In *RLDM* (Princeton, 2013).

13. Cockburn, A., Gutwin, C., and Greenberg, S. A predictive model of menu performance. In *ACM CHI'07* (2007), 627–636.

14. Fu, W.-T., and Gray, W. D. Resolving the paradox of the active user : stable suboptimal performance in interactive tasks. *Cognitive Science 28* (2004), 901–935.

15. Fu, W.-T., and Pirolli, P. SNIF-ACT: A cognitive model of user navigation on the World Wide Web. *Human–Computer Interaction 22*, 4 (2007), 355–412.

16. Gray, W. D., Sims, C. R., Fu, W.-T., and Schoelles, M. J. The soft constraints hypothesis: a rational analysis approach to resource allocation for interactive behavior. *Psychological review 113*, 3 (2006), 461–82.

17. Halverson, T., and Hornof, A. J. A minimal model for predicting visual search in human-computer interaction. In *ACM CHI'07*, ACM (2007), 431–434.

18. Halverson, T., and Hornof, A. J. A computational model of active vision for visual search in human–computer interaction. *Human–Computer Interaction 26*, 4 (2011), 285–314.

19. Hayhoe, M., and Ballard, D. Modeling task control of eye movements. *Current Biology 24*, 13 (2014), 622–628.

20. Hornof, A. J., and Halverson, T. Cognitive strategies and eye movements for searching hierarchical computer displays. In *ACM CHI'03*, ACM (2003), 249–256.

21. Howes, A., Lewis, R. L., and Vera, A. Rational adaptation under task and processing constraints: implications for testing theories of cognition and action. *Psychological Review 116*, 4 (2009), 717–751.

22. Howes, A., Vera, A., Lewis, R. L., and McCurdy, M. Cognitive constraint modeling: A formal approach to supporting reasoning about behavior. *Proc. Cognitive Science Society* (2004), 595–600.

23. Inhoff, A. W., and Rayner, K. Parafoveal word perception: A case against semantic preprocessing. *Perception & Psychophysics 27*, 5 (1980), 457–464.

24. Janssen, C. P., Brumby, D. P., Dowell, J., Chater, N., and Howes, A. Identifying optimum performance trade-offs using a cognitively bounded rational analysis model of discretionary task interleaving. *Topics in Cognitive Science 3*, 1 (2011), 123–139.

25. Kieras, D. E., and Hornof, A. J. Towards accurate and practical predictive models of active-vision-based visual search. In *ACM CHI'14* (2014), 3875–3884.

26. Lelis, S., and Howes, A. Informing decisions: how people use online rating information to make choices. In *ACM CHI'11* (2011), 2285–2294.

27. Lewis, R., Howes, A., and Singh, S. Computational rationality: linking mechanism and behavior through bounded utility maximization. *Topics in Cognitive Science 6*, 2 (2014), 279–311.

28. Miller, C. S., and Remington, R. W. Modeling information navigation: Implications for information architecture. *Human-Computer Interaction 19*, 3 (2004), 225–271.

29. Nunez-Varela, J., and Wyatt, J. L. Models of gaze control for manipulation tasks. *ACM Transactions on Applied Perception (TAP) 10*, 4 (2013), 20.

30. O'Hara, K. P., and Payne, S. J. The effects of operator implementation cost on planfulness of problem solving and learning. *Cognitive psychology 35*, 1 (1998), 34–70.

31. Payne, S. J., and Howes, A. Adaptive Interaction: A Utility Maximization Approach to Understanding Human Interaction with Technology. *Synthesis Lectures on Human-Centered Informatics 6*, 1 (2013), 1–111.

32. Payne, S. J., Howes, A., and Reader, W. R. Adaptively distributing cognition: a decision-making perspective on human-computer interaction. *Behaviour & Information Technology 20*, 5 (2001), 339–346.

33. Pirolli, P. *Information foraging theory: Adaptive interaction with information*, vol. 2. OUP, USA, 2007.

34. Pirolli, P., and Card, S. Information foraging. *Psych Review 106* (1999), 643–675.

35. Rayner, K. Eye movements in reading and information processing: 20 years of research. *Psych. Bulletin 124*, 3 (1998), 372.

36. Russell, S., and Subramanian, D. Provably bounded-optimal agents. *Journal of Artificial Intelligence Research 2* (1995), 575–609.

37. Sprague, N., and Ballard, D. Eye movements for reward maximization. *Advances in neural information processing systems 16* (2004), 1419–1433.

38. Sutton, R. S., and Barto, A. G. *Reinforcement Learning: An Introduction*. MIT Press, 1998.

39. Trommershäuser, J., Maloney, L. T., and Landy, M. S. The Expected Utility of Movement. *Brain* (2009), 95–111.

40. Tseng, Y.-C., and Howes, A. The adaptation of visual search strategy to expected information gain. In *ACM CHI '08* (2008), 1075–1084.

41. Vera, A., Howes, A., McCurdy, M., and Lewis, R. L. A constraint satisfaction approach to predicting skilled interactive cognition. In *ACM CHI'04* (2004), 121–128.

42. Zhang, Y., and Hornof, A. J. Understanding multitasking through parallelized strategy exploration and individualized cognitive modeling. In *ACM CHI'14* (2014), 3885–3894.

Selective Undo Support for Painting Applications

Brad A. Myers[1], Ashley Lai[1], Tam Minh Le[1], YoungSeok Yoon[1], Andrew Faulring[1], Joel Brandt[2]
[1]School of Computer Science
Carnegie Mellon University
5000 Forbes Avenue, Pittsburgh, PA 15213
{bam, youngseok, faulring}@cs.cmu.edu, {ashleyhlai, minny.le}@gmail.com
[2]Creative Technologies Lab
Adobe Research
San Francisco, CA
joel.brandt@adobe.com

ABSTRACT
Today's widely deployed painting applications use a linear undo model that allows users to backtrack previous operations in reverse chronological order. This undo model is not useful if the user has performed desired operations *after* undesired ones. Selective undo, in contrast, allows users to select specific operations in the past and only undo those, while keeping the remaining operations intact. Although selective undo has been widely explored in the context of text editing and object-oriented drawing, we explore selective undo for painting (bitmap) editing, which has received less attention and introduces many interesting user interface design challenges. Our system, called Aquamarine, explores the script model for selective undo, where selectively undone operations are skipped in the history, rather than the more explored inverse model, which puts an inverse of the selected operations at the end of the history. We discuss the design implications and show through two informal user studies that selective undo is usable and desirable.

Author Keywords
Selective Undo; Bitmap Editor; Creativity Support.

ACM Classification Keywords
H.5.2 User Interfaces (Graphical user interfaces (GUI)); I.3.4 Graphics Utilities (Paint systems); I.3.6 Methodology and Techniques (Interaction techniques).

INTRODUCTION
The *undo* operation has long been understood to be a required command in applications, especially to support creative exploration. Studies have shown that when users have the ability to undo, they are more comfortable exploring and trying new commands [16]. Ideally, any previous operation should be able to be undone. However, most applications use the same *restricted linear undo model* [3], primarily due to the user interface challenges of presenting a more powerful undo model in a way that it is easy for the user to understand. In the linear undo model, multiple operations are saved on the undo stack and can be undone, and after undoing some operations, users can change their mind and start redoing those operations again. However, if a *new* operation is performed after undoing some operations, the undone operations are discarded and are no longer available for redoing. This makes it impossible for the user to undo the undo. Another limitation of the linear undo model is that all operations must be undone in order. This makes it impossible to keep any operations that happen *after* an operation to be undone. That is, if there are a mixture of wanted and unwanted operations, users cannot use undo to achieve their desired result [24].

CHI 2015, April 18 - 23 2015, Seoul, Republic of Korea
Copyright 2015 ACM 978-1-4503-3145-6/15/04...$15.00
http://dx.doi.org/10.1145/2702123.2702543.

Figure 1. Aquamarine's History Panel showing operation #10 (brush stroke for the nose) selectively undone.

The limitations of linear undo have motivated research on *selective undo*, where the user can specifically select which of the previous operations to undo and which to keep [1-3, 5, 19, 25]. However, this prior work has primarily focused on object-oriented drawing programs, like PowerPoint or Adobe Illustrator [3, 19], where selective undo is more easily achieved by selecting and changing objects' properties. New work has started to address selective undo in text [17, 25], but there is little work on selective undo in painting applications like Photoshop which lack the structures used by object editing programs, and where operations tend to affect overlapping spans of pixels. This makes it much more difficult for users to identify which operations to undo (since there may be many small edits) and to predict the outcome of selectively undoing something in the past. Furthermore, it is challenging to provide understandable user interfaces for any selective undo model. Note that throughout this paper, we are deliberately distinguishing the term *drawing* from *painting*. Drawing programs have identifiable objects in the picture that can be selected and manipulated later, whereas painting programs convert objects into pixels immediately, and subsequent selections and operations are at the pixel level. Many painting operations cannot be naturally converted into objects with a distinct shape. For example, the paint bucket tool and filters do not create or even necessarily modify objects; instead they manipulate pixels. Aquamarine focuses on painting only. Note that modern image manipulation programs like Photoshop actually have a mixture of drawing and painting features.

Another interesting issue is the distinction between the *inverse* and *script* models of selective undo. In the *inverse model*, supported by most previous selective undo systems [3, 19, 25], a selective undo causes the inverse of the selected operations to be added to the end of the history. For example when the user selectively undoes a delete, a create operation is performed and added to the end of the history. In contrast, the *script model* removes the selected operation from the history and performs all subsequent operations as if that operation had never been performed [15]. This can cause semantic problems in drawing programs (for example, what is the meaning of a change-size operation applied to an object if the previous creation of that object is selectively undone, and thereby removed from the history?), but may be more appropriate when painting (since there are no objects to which operations are applied). We are not aware of any previous research on supporting selective undo in a paint program using the script model.

We created *Aquamarine* (see Figure 1) to study these issues. Aquamarine, which stands for Allowing Quick Undoing of Any Marks And Repairs to Improve Novel Editing, is a new prototype painting program that supports selective undo using the scripting model. We first performed semi-structured interviews with student and professional graphic artists to see what they would want and expect in such a tool. We then implemented the Aquamarine prototype based on those findings, and ran usability evaluations to assess its features and design decisions.

The contributions of this paper include:

- Results of semi-structured interviews, which show that users have a significant need for selective undo capabilities in painting programs, and compensate with workarounds such as using many layers, saving the whole file to disk, or just starting over.
- A discussion of the design space for selective undo and tradeoffs among the design decisions.
- A design and implementation for a selective undo mechanism using the script model in a prototype paint program called Aquamarine, which explores the design space for how the script model should operate.
- A usability evaluation that demonstrates the aspects of the selective undo mechanism which are most usable and useful, and areas where more research is required. All users expressed a desire to have a form of selective undo in their everyday programs.

RELATED WORK

There has been significant work on undo and edit history over the years, in a variety of application domains.

Selective Undo

One of the earliest efforts in this area investigated the script model [2], which tries to guarantee that the final result be as if the prior command had never been performed in the context of text editing for a code editor, and identifies issues specific to that domain. The Emacs text editor has long had an "undo-in-region" command, where the user undoes the most recent operation that affected a specific selected region of text. Other text editors such as DistEdit [21] have provided this feature. Regional undo is useful and also relatively easy to implement compared to the generic selective undo, because it always undoes the most recent operation performed in the selected region, which reduces the possibilities for conflicts. In regional undo, however, there can be an ambiguity if the user selects a region that partially overlaps with an operation's effective region. Li and Li refer to this problem as "region overlapping" and introduce the idea of *partial undo* as a solution, which undoes only the overlapped part of the operation when an operation partly falls in the given undo region [17]. Regional undo was applied in spreadsheets [12] by allowing users to select a region in the spreadsheet and perform undo only on those cells. Our new system, Azurite [24, 25], provides general selective undo (not just region undo) in a code editor. Azurite uses the inverse model, by adding the inverse text editing operation to the end of the history, and provides a variety of user interfaces to resolve conflicts.

Probably the most work on selective undo has been in the context of graphical (object-oriented), interactive editors. Berlage introduced the selective undo model that adds the reverse operation of the selected command to the current context [3]. The Amulet [20] and Topaz [19] systems had a similar selective undo feature, but these allowed repeating a selected command even on a new object. All of these use the inverse model, with the undos added to the end of the history. Dwell-and-spring [1] provides an interface that is limited to undoing only press-drag-release interactions, and it does not deal with any conflicting operations. All of these approaches also assume that there is an object on which the operations can be performed: primitive graphical objects such as shapes in graphical editors, and individual cells in spreadsheets. In contrast, there is no clear notion of objects in painting programs, since edit operations typically affect areas of pixels.

Another important difference between object-oriented and painting systems is that detecting and handling conflicts and dependencies among the operations is important for all object-oriented selective undo systems. Whereas early systems using simple dependency models [3, 19], later work focused on formal, sound and complete modeling of dependencies, and even automatically cascading the selective undo when necessary for consistency [6]. User studies showed that people could predict and understand what these selective undo systems will do [7]. Whereas in one sense, painting systems do not have such dependencies since all actions operate on pixels, we do study the issue of conflicts when the boundaries of actions overlap, as discussed below.

There are other undo models that support selective undo by providing additional commands beyond undo and redo. The US&R model [22] allows users to *skip* redoing an operation, using a complicated tree-based data structure. Users can selectively undo an isolated operation by undoing multiple steps until the target operation gets undone, skipping the redo command once, and then redoing the rest of the operations. The triadic model [23] uses a simpler structure composed of a linear history list, and a circular redo list which can be *rotated* by users. Undoing an operation puts the operation at the beginning of the redo list, and rotating the redo list takes one operation at the beginning of the list and puts it at the end. Since the rotate command can be used to skip a redo command, users can selectively undo a certain operation in a similar way. However, both models require deep understanding of the underlying history structure to correctly perform selective undo. In addition, selective undo cannot be done in one step, which can be cumbersome for users.

Adobe Photoshop provides a history window with a mode for "non-linear undo", but this is different from selective undo—when the user undoes operations and then does new ones, Photoshop's non-linear undo retains the undone operations on the undo stack rather than remove them. However, future undos still start at the last operation and continue backwards through all previous operations in order.

Another use of selective undo is in collaborative editing, where multiple people can edit a document concurrently, which has been studied by various systems [4, 10]. When user1's and user2's edits are intermixed, it is not clear whether user1's undo command should affect user2's operations. Surprisingly, the Google Docs text editor does not seem to do anything sensible when multiple people edit in the same region and then one performs undo.

A revision control system for images based on a directed acyclic graph (DAG) enables users to make forks and joins, and then move around in the history and see various versions of images [8], but it does not support selective undo or the script model.

Graphical Edit Histories

Aquamarine displays the past interactions in a graphical History pane (see Figure 1). There has been significant research on such displays. Chimera provided graphical histories as thumbnail snapshots which could be edited and reused, and past actions could be modified [15], but conflicts among operations were not specifically identified. The Designer's Outpost shows snapshots of the history of states of a web editing session with multiple users and keeps track of forks among versions [13]. Systems have also used graphical histories to foster learning [9, 11] and creating macros for later reuse [15, 18].

INITIAL SEMI-STRUCTURED INTERVIEWS

In order to get a better idea about how people might use a selective undo mechanism in painting applications, we first performed semi-structured interviews of nine people. Our last author from Adobe reports that there are three primary uses of Photoshop: (1) to design and prototype user interfaces, (2) as a painting tool to create art, and (3) to edit and retouch photographs. We were careful to recruit participants from all three groups (see Table 1).

ID	Experience	Student or Prof.	Des?	Art?	Photo?	Ctrl-Z	Step-Back	Hist. Panel	Hist. Brush
1	Intermediate	student	Yes	Yes			Yes	Yes	Yes
2	Intermediate	student	Yes	Yes		Yes			
3	Intermediate	student			Yes			Yes	
4	Expert	student	Yes			Yes	Yes		
5	Expert	prof.		Yes		Yes	Yes	Yes	
6	Novice	student		Yes			Yes		
7	Expert	prof.	Yes				Yes		
8	Expert	prof.	Yes				Yes		
9	Expert	prof.	Yes				Yes		

Table 1. Participants in our semi-structured interviews.

All of our participants were frequent users of Photoshop, with four self-rating as expert users, four as intermediate and one as novice. Four were professionals and five were students. Photoshop provides four undo mechanisms: an old-fashioned toggle undo (Ctrl-Z), which undoes and then redoes the last operation, a normal linear undo, which it calls "Step Backwards" and "Step Forwards" (Shift/Alt-Ctrl-Z), a history panel which enables undoing back multiple steps (with a fixed maximum limit that defaults to 20), and a "history brush" where users select a point in the history panel and then paints, which restores the pixels back to that point in time, as a form of regional undo. As previously mentioned, Photoshop provides an optional non-linear history mode. No participant (in this or the final study) had ever used or had even heard of this feature, which is turned off by default. Three of the participants reported using the toggle undo, five reported using step-backwards and step-forwards, three used the history panel, and one reported using the history brush.

In the first part of our interviews, we asked participants to work on one of their own tasks using Photoshop, in a form of contextual inquiry, and they were encouraged to think aloud. We told them we were particularly interested in situations where they would "explore different ideas and test out different alternatives."

The more experienced users exclusively used the shortcut keystrokes to invoke commands. Only two participants had the history panel displayed, but both of them used it to undo multiple operations. We did not see any use of the history brush. Some participants erased areas rather than using undo, whereas others made significant use of the step-backwards commands. They recognized the limitations: "I don't want to use the undo button if there's a part that I drew after that I like." Another said: "It's more of a short-term memory [issue] for me. I don't usually undo more than five steps back."

Participants used the layers mechanism to group items together when they anticipated a need to selectively change an area or a shape, and experienced users grouped and named layers to keep the large number of layers organized. When beginning a creative exploration, participants often duplicated layers or saved a version of the whole picture, to facilitate backtracking. Users often hid layers instead of deleting them; one said: "I don't like deleting things; it feels too permanent—even if it was a mistake."

In the second part of our interviews, we gave the participants a series of tasks designed to elicit selective backtracking behaviors and strategies. We told them to imagine they were creating images for a company that is run by a very indecisive boss. We would repeatedly instruct them to create something, then change it, then do other things, and finally to change it back. This cannot be supported with any of Photoshop's existing undo mechanisms. As in the first part, when participants anticipated that something would need to be undone, they put it on a separate layer. If we asked them to undo something that was not on a separate layer, they expressed regret that it was not separated and usually started over from scratch. Users considered using advanced editing tools such as Photoshop's Color Replacement Tool, but often decided it would not work sufficiently well, and just painted over items, or deleted and redrew them from scratch. These results reveal the reliance on layers to simulate selective undo, and the need to start over and lose desired work when undesired operations precede the desired ones.

In the third part of our interviews, we explained the concept of selective undo and asked if they thought it would be useful in their own work. Six participants said it would be useful frequently or almost every day, and the other three said maybe not since they achieved the same functionality with layers or by frequently saving their work to disk.

In the fourth part of our interviews, we asked a series of questions about what they thought would happen as a result of performing a selective undo. In particular, we were exploring whether they expected the *script model* or the *inverse model* of behavior. For example in Figure 2, if the stars were created by duplicating the original star, what should happen if the creation of the original star was selectively undone? All participants thought the other stars should *not* disappear, so they were endorsing the *inverse* model in this case, since under the script model, there would be nothing to duplicate. On the other hand, if we added a recolor step for the star between steps 1 and 2, and then selectively undid the recoloring, all but one of the participants expected the stars in step 2 to also change color, requiring the script model to hold. When this inconsistency was pointed out, most participants agreed that their preference would change based on the situation.

Finally, we explored a number of features that might be used in a selective undo mechanism. Most participants agreed that the ability to identify which operations had contributed to a selected region of the picture would be useful, as a way to find which operations to selectively undo. About half thought the reverse operation was needed – to select an operation in the history panel and highlight what area of the picture it affected. Few participants saw any need to search for commands in the history by name (to enable searches like "find the last time I used the brush tool"). Also deemed unnecessary would be a need to view different versions of a picture side-by-side, or automatic version control tools, as are commonly used for source code and which are provided by third party tools like LayerVault (layervault.com) and Pixelapse (www.pixelapse.com).

Discussion

In an object-oriented drawing program, users can generally get the effect of undoing operations by manually performing the opposite operation. Thus, the "undo" of resizing can be achieved by just resizing it back, which can generally be performed at any time. Photoshop and other painting programs try to provide this capability for as many operations as possible by having many operations act like they are object-oriented instead of pixel based (that is, like a drawing program instead of a painting program). For example, text in Photoshop is kept as objects on its own layer until the user explicitly flattens it into a bitmap. However, this means that many bitmap operations, like blurring or erasing, would not be available until the image is flattened, and changing the text would not be possible after blurring.

Similarly, in our study, we saw participants using layers to try to make painting operations have the ability to be selectively edited. However, layers do have significant limitations. We saw frequent errors where participants would accidentally draw into the wrong layer, merge layers and regret it later, or realize too late that a new layer should have been created. Also, the large number of layers became difficult to manage.

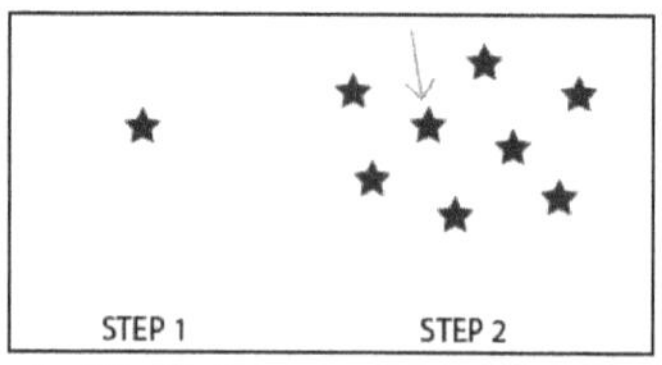

Figure 2: Multiple steps to create a drawing.

In addition, users were wary of the Photoshop history tool, since it only keeps a limited number of steps backwards, the history is not preserved when a document is closed, and it can be difficult to identify which step to go back to. One participant noted: "If you rely on history, you're asking to get burned by it." Therefore, there is an opportunity to provide a new way for users to backtrack.

Participants agreed that there would be significant value in having a selective undo tool that would provide the ability to change what was done in the past, without the requirements of pre-planning to use layers and without giving up the advantages of bitmap editing.

DESIGN TRADEOFFS

In designing and implementing the selective undo feature, we had to make a large number of design decisions, across a number of different dimensions. In many cases, we needed to decide what a selective undo for painting applications should mean since this has never previously been explored. This section presents the design dimensions, the various options and tradeoffs, and justifications for decisions implemented in Aquamarine.

Which Operations to Explore?

We classified all Photoshop operations into eight categories with respect to their interaction with Undo (as has also been explored previously by others [8]). The categories are:

1. Creation/painting, which cause pixels to be drawn
2. Local-adjustment tools, which change existing pixels
3. Global commands, which affect all pixels in the image
4. View control commands, which do not change pixels
5. Selection tools, which control subsequent operations
6. Mode changes, like picking a color or current layer
7. Conversion tools, like Flatten and Convert to Smart Object
8. Miscellaneous, like 3D tools

The first three are most relevant to selective undo, so we implemented at least two operations from each of these categories. We expect that operations in Photoshop or other full-featured paint programs would have identical issues with respect to selective undo, so we believe the HCI issues we have identified will generalize to all other commands.

Script Model versus Inverse Model?

The most important decision was which kind of selective undo model to support. As discussed above, the primary choices are to use some form of script model or some form of inverse model.

The inverse model seemed inappropriate for a painting program, since so many operations cannot be undone by adding a new command to the end of the history. For example, take color change. In a painting program, a color change using the Paint Bucket Tool (more formally called flood fill), changes the color of the area defined by the contiguous pixels that match, within a tolerance, the color of the clicked pixel. This operation often *cannot* be undone with a new flood-fill at the end of the history (that is, "now"). For example, in Figure 3, the flood fill of step 2 cannot be undone with another flood fill after all of the actions in step 3, because flood-filling now will only change parts of the former blue t-shirt, and the long sleeves added to the shirt might also be flood-filled. Similarly, other bitmap editing operations, like blurring the image, cropping, etc. may be impossible to reverse in the current state. Other operations, even creating new shapes, cannot necessarily be undone in the current state, because of other paintings drawn on top of them may compute the new pixels using the existing pixels.

However, a script model *can* be used to selectively undo the flood fill operation—we can undo all the operations back to before step 2 was done (so the image looks like step 1), skip doing step 2, and then do the remainder of the operations.

Note that using layers to separate operations as in Photoshop and other programs, so the user can simulate selective undo by turning off or deleting layers, will not help with selective undoing of painting-based operations like flood fill or blur, since these operations must work on the same layer as the pixels to be modified.

Since Aquamarine specifically focuses on these painting operations, we decided to use the script model. Another motivation is that the script model has rarely been investigated in previous research or commercial systems, and it brings up many more interesting and challenging design decisions, which we discuss next.

Note that providing selective undo with either model can work with the regular linear undo command. Thus, if the user does not use selective undo, it can be ignored entirely, and the normal way of using undo/redo can be utilized.

Another issue is that some commands have side effects *external* to the editor. For example, File Save should not be re-executed each time the system reruns the script to perform a selective undo. Fortunately, it turns out that these operations are actually not put into the undo stack anyway (see also the discussion of copy and paste below). For a few *internal* operations with side effects, like Create Layer, we must disable all the other operations on that layer if the create is selectively undone.

Handling Region Conflicts among Operations

As discussed in the related work section, an important concern in object-oriented editing is dealing with dependencies and conflicts [3, 6, 19]. Bitmap operations do not have this kind of conflict, since they work on pixels, which will still

Figure 3. In a painting program, (1) paint a shirt, (2) flood fill it with a new color, (3) then do a variety of other actions.

be there. However, it is possible to have *region conflicts* [25], which are where a later operation's scope overlaps the selected operation in such a way that it is not clear what the selective undo should do. For example, in Figure 3, if the user tried to selectively undo the painting operation (step 1), what should the flood fill (step 2) do, since the t-shirt is no longer on the screen?

There are a variety of possible outcomes for step 2 in a script model when step 1 is removed:

1. Cancel the selective undo due to the conflict. That is, do nothing.
2. Perform the selective undo, and also undo the conflicting operations, which includes at least step 2.
3. Perform the conflicting operations as dictated by the script model with the selected operation removed. In this case, it would probably flood-fill the whole canvas since there would be nothing (only background) at the pixel where the flood fill operation happened.

There is actually a 4th possibility, which we discuss in Future Work: allow the user to *modify* the conflicting operation or *add* entirely new operations into the history. For example in Figure 3, the user might select a new pixel at which to apply the flood fill, or paint a brand new shape where the shirt used to be as a new step 1.

We investigated providing a popup dialog to help the user resolve these conflicts and pick one of the three options, as in Azurite [25], but it proved quite difficult to identify exactly which operations should be marked as conflicting with the undone operation, resulting in very expensive pixel operations and too many false positives. Therefore, we decided to use a much simpler approach of just comparing bounding boxes of all subsequent operations, and highlighting the operations in the history which *might* conflict, to help the user find them if they want option 2 (see Figure 4).

To reduce the number of operations that are highlighted, we developed a set of heuristics for the kinds of region conflicts that should be brought to the user's attention based on the operation categories discussed above. The heuristics are as follows: first, we do not highlight creation/painting operations. For example, if a new shape is painted on top of an old shape, and the painting of the old shape is selectively undone, even though overlapping pixels are affected, we do not alert the user, and simply remove the old shape and repaint the new shape. Similarly, global operations affect all pixels, but we do not alert users to these region conflicts either. The main issue is when the later operation is a *local-adjustment tool*, which modifies only some of the pixels of the picture. Flood-fill and smudge are examples of this, and there are many others. When such operations affect the same area that the selective undo will affect, we alert the user of all conflicting operations using orange highlights.

As future work, we plan to support allowing the user to select *multiple* operations to be selectively undone together [25]. For example, the user might select both Steps 1 and 2 together in Figure 3. When all the region conflicts are internal to the selected operations, there is no ambiguity of what to do, so the user does not have to be alerted. In our usability evaluation, this was a much-requested feature.

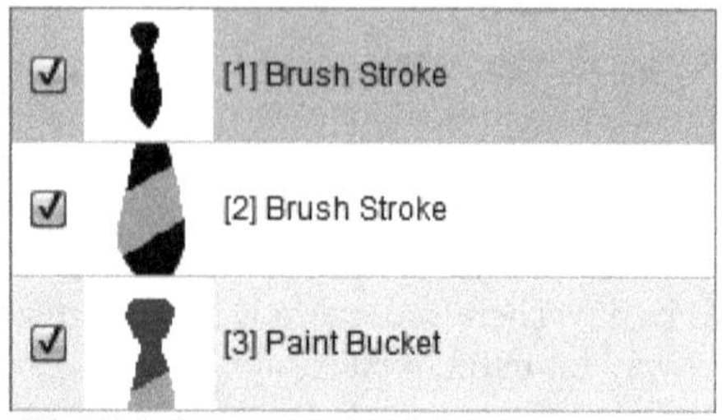

Figure 4. Highlighting operation 3 in orange since it conflicts with the selected operation 1 (shown in blue).

Copy and Paste

Another interesting design issue revolves around copy and paste. In most existing applications, the copy operation is *not* put on the undo stack, and whatever is copied is retained independent of what the user subsequently undoes. For example, in Microsoft Word, a user can type some text and copy it, and then invoke undo one or more times so that the text is all removed. However, the clipboard will still retain the text, which can be pasted later. Of course a cut operation goes on the undo stack, but only the deleting part of the cut is undone—again the clipboard is not affected by undoing the cut operation. Users have developed strategies for clever ways to use this feature, so we decided to retain it in Aquamarine.

Therefore, Aquamarine makes what we call a *deep copy* of whatever is selected when the user performs a copy operation, and the copy operation is not put into the undo stack. That means that the script model will not re-execute the copy operation, so the clipboard will continue to have a copy of the pixels as they were originally copied, no matter what happens subsequently to that part of the image. Similarly, the paste operation retains a deep copy of what was in the clipboard when the operation is first invoked, so it continues to paste the *same* picture if it is reinvoked later due to the script model.

Another reason we felt that we needed to adopt this model for copy is that the clipboard is globally shared by all programs, and the user might change the clipboard by doing a copy in *another* program, and in that case, we would not want to change the clipboard as a result of a selective undo.

Selective Undo/Redo Operations in the History Panel

In Topaz [19] and Azurite [24] and many other systems that implement the inverse model, the selective undo and redo operations themselves are added to the end of the undo history, and shown in the history panel (see Figure 5). This seems to make sense in those programs since the inverse operation is actually performed at that point in the history, and so a representation like Figure 5 should reinforce this mental model for users. Another advantage of this approach is that the selective undo operation itself can be selected and undone, which would then add another selective undo to the end of the history, restoring the effect of the original operation. Alternatively, the user could select the original operation (#5 in Figure 5) and selectively *redo* that operation, which has the same effect as selectively undoing the undo. A final advantage of this design is that it is clearer what a regular linear undo command will do – it works up from the bottom, undoing each of the operations in turn (selective and regular operations alike).

Given these advantages, we first tried adapting this style of history panel for the script model of Aquamarine, as shown in Figure 5. In this design, the user can select an operation (e.g., #5), and invoke selective undo on it, which adds the selective undo operation to the end of the history (shown as operation #7). Unlike in the inverse model, the selective undo is not really on the history, but instead the referenced operation is skipped (in Figure 5, only operations 1 through 4 and 6 are executed). We try to visualize this by graying out the referenced operation. If the user wants to reverse this operation, the selective undo (#7) can be selectively undone or the original operation (#5) can be selectively redone, and these operations would be also added to the history. However, we felt it was getting complicated to understand what was done and not done, and we also felt that this design might give the wrong mental model to users, since the selective operations are not really in the history.

Therefore, we designed a different history panel, shown in Figure 1, where the original operations can simply be unchecked to selectively undo them, or rechecked to be selectively redone. This matches the design for the layers panel in Photoshop, where layers can be made visible or not with a toggle button next to each layer's name. This should do a better job of matching the appropriate mental model for users: that the current picture results from the operations being executed from the top down, skipping operations that are not checked. Another advantage is that we do not need explicit selective undo or selective redo commands, but instead the user just toggles the appropriate checkbox.

It is less clear what the regular linear undo should do in this model. We decided linear undo should undo the most recent operation shown in the history panel that is still in effect. Therefore, the selective undo is not directly undoable by Ctrl-Z. This again mimics the default behavior of turning on and off layers, which are not put on the history stack (although Photoshop has a setting to enable this). Similarly, the regular linear *redo* moves down the history stack re-enabling operations, no matter how they were undone. Thus, it redoes operations that were disabled either by selective undo or regular undo. Of course, the user can always go to any individual operation and toggle its checkbox, no matter how it was disabled.

Since the "right" design for this feature is not clear, we decided to include questions about this in our usability evaluation, discussed below, which came out strongly in favor of the checkbox version shown in Figure 1.

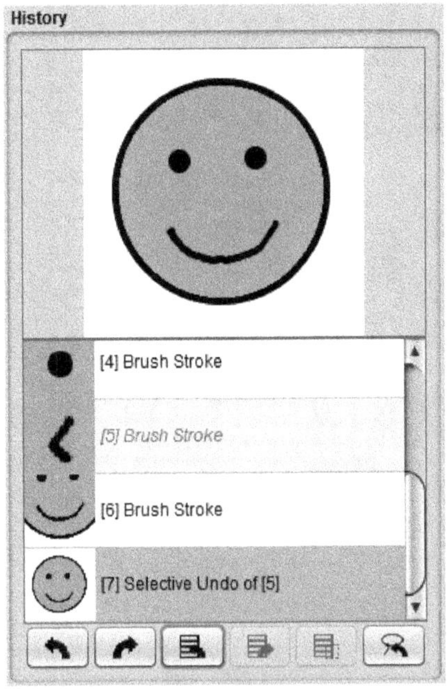

Figure 5. An alternative form of history panel where selective undo/redo operations are included in the history.

Thumbnail Images

One small design issue is: what to display for each operation in the history panel. A common complaint about Photoshop's history panel from our initial semi-structured interviews was that it only shows an icon for the tool used, so it is impossible to tell which operation is for which part of the drawing, for example when there are many brush strokes. Therefore, we wanted to show a thumbnail representation of what the operation did, along with some context, as has been done previously [15].

A new complication for Aquamarine that has not been previously reported arises from the scripting model of selective undo—what should be shown in the thumbnail when a selective undo causes a previous operation to be turned off? Should the thumbnails of the subsequent operations be changed? We decided to update all the thumbnails, since that is the more correct (and interesting) design. Ironically, in the usability evaluation, users almost universally said they did *not* want *any* context to be shown in the thumbnails, completely eliminating this problem. Instead, they preferred seeing only the specific output of the current operation. The preview window (the upper panel of Figure 5), however, should continue to show what the complete picture would look like up to the selected operation.

Identifying Desired Operations

Azurite [24] provides elaborate ways to *search* for the operations that the user might want to undo. However, in our initial semi-structured interviews, the key way that users wanted to search for operations in a painting program was by selecting an affected region on the screen. Therefore, we provide commands in Aquamarine for identifying the set of operations that affect the selected region on the screen. We

Figure 6. Pixelitor modified with our history panel.

also provide the reverse operation which shows the region on the screen that any operation affects. Note that both of these are based on the specific pixels on the screen, which may no longer hold that operation's result. For example, if the user paints a shape, but later selects and moves it, the region for the original painting operation will remain where the shape started. In a painting program, it seems impossible to identify where the pixels that result from an arbitrary operation might have gone, and it seems more useful to help users find where things used to be, in case they want to get back to that state. Note that if the user selects the region on the painting where the shape was originally painted, both the painting and the move operations will be identified, so users can selectively undo/redo any operations that are desired.

IMPLEMENTED SYSTEM

Our original hope was to implement Aquamarine as a plugin to Photoshop since it supplies a variety of APIs. Unfortunately, none of Photoshop's APIs provided sufficient access to the undo stack and the result of each operation to support the desired features. Therefore, we needed to find an open-source paint program we could modify. We required sufficient functionality so that the design issues discussed above would emerge (which eliminated simple painting programs like the Java Paint program used in other studies [14]), and we needed access to the full source to be able to implement the selective undo.

We selected Pixelitor 2.0.0 in Java by László Balázs-Csíki (http://sourceforge.net/projects/pixelitor/) (see Figure 6). The original version of Pixelitor used the built-in Java Swing undo model, which uses command objects [20]. We were able to replace this with our own undo implementation which supports our novel selective undo mechanism.

One complication is that Pixelitor, like other painting programs including Photoshop, implements undo by simply having most operations save a bitmap of the picture before the operation executed. This is sufficient for the regular linear undo model, since it can always be sure that when it places the bitmap into the correct position, that the context will be correct and the full image will be restored. However, this is insufficient for any selective undo model, especially for the script model, since we need to be able to re-execute all commands later. Therefore, we had to modify each command to remember all of its parameters so it can be re-executed when needed. For example, the Shape and Brush stroke tools must save the path and all the properties of the pen (color, transparency, etc.). Similarly, the Paint Bucket tool needs to remember the color, start pixel, etc. Further, we had to refactor the application so all operations could get their parameters from the global widgets (like the current color) or from the saved command objects. We still save the bitmaps so they can be used for regular undo.

Another implementation tradeoff was whether each operation should save the entire bitmap of the whole picture, or only the portion affected by this operation. If each operation saved the entire picture, then our script model could implement the selective undo of an operation by simply reinstating the full picture before that operation, skipping the operation, and then re-performing all enabled subsequent operations. However, saving the entire bitmap wastes a lot of memory, since most operations only affect a tiny part of the picture. Pixelitor only stores bitmaps for the regions affected by each operation (which it uses for undo), which we retain. Therefore, implementing the script model selective undo does not require any significant amount of extra space. The tradeoff is that for selective undo, we must internally roll back to the selected operation, by doing a linear undo all the way back, in order to restore the picture to the original state. This is a classic space-time tradeoff, and in practice, we found it to be sufficiently fast. If it turns out not to be fast enough in the future, there are many obvious optimizations that could be implemented.

Some Photoshop operations can be quite slow and expensive, so there is a question about the efficiency of re-applying all the operations each time a selective undo is invoked, which is required for the script model. In our unoptimized prototype implementation, selective undo slows down noticeably on a big image if there are over 100 operations. Although we focus on the user interface aspects here, we have considered some performance optimizations that could be applied in a real implementation. Obviously, the length of the history can be limited, as is already the case in Photoshop, but that is not desirable from a UI standpoint. Instead, slow operations could be approximated on downsized images, to show quick previews which estimate what the results will be, with the real result calculated in the background once the user stops undoing and redoing.

USABILITY EVALUATION

Since our initial semi-structured interviews and other prior work had clearly identified problems that our mechanism addresses, we felt the key issue to evaluate was whether users could understand and successfully apply our new script-model selective undo, and whether users can think of strategies that would make effective use of it. Therefore, we felt the appropriate evaluation would be to do think-aloud usability evaluations of various versions of the features which embody the design decisions discussed above.

We recruited eight participants (see Table 2), one of whom was also part of our initial semi-structured interviews (participant 5 in Table 1 is participant 2 in Table 2). We specifically picked users across a wide range of experience. None of the new participants were students. Four were professional graphic artists and the other four were professionals who only used Photoshop or equivalent occasionally. All participants were familiar with conventional undo models, as supported by Photoshop and most applications, but three participants were not familiar with Photoshop's special undo features.

ID	Experience	Prof.	Des?	Art?	Photo?	Ctrl-Z	Step-Back	Hist. Panel	Hist. Brush
1	novice	other			Yes	Yes	Yes		
2	expert	prof.		Yes		Yes	Yes	Yes	
3	expert	prof.	Yes			Yes	Yes	Yes	
4	expert	prof.	Yes	Yes		Yes	Yes	Yes	
5	intermediate	prof.	Yes			Yes	Yes	Yes	
6	novice	other	Yes			Yes	Yes		
7	intermediate	other	Yes	Yes		Yes	Yes		
8	expert	other			Yes	Yes	Yes	Yes	

Table 2. Participants in our usability evaluation.

We asked the participants to "try drawing a few things" with Aquamarine, and then undo operations using a variety of commands. Most participants just drew random lines and shapes, but p5 drew animals like Figures 1 and 6. We then asked them what they would expect to happen with various undo commands (regular Ctrl-Z and our new selective undo) and then to try them out to see what happens. We had about half of the participants use the checkbox version of the history first (Figure 1), and the other half tried the in-history version first (Figure 5). Then they tried the other version. The order had no effect, and *all* 8 participants strongly preferred the checkbox version. Everyone understood the operation of the checkboxes and how they would affect the picture, although some expressed a preference to using an "eyeball" icon as used to toggle layer visibility (see Figure 6). In the in-history version, they found the presence of the "selective undo" and "selective redo" operations in the history to be confusing, and also felt that this would clutter up the history without being useful.

All users found the script model to be understandable and preferable in general, but all users were surprised by the operation of the paint bucket, when the area underneath where it was applied was selectively undone (a situation in which there is a region conflict). In this case, the paint would typically fill the whole background, which was not something anyone wanted. Some participants wanted the paint bucket to just remember the shape it had filled and reuse that, even if the area was no longer there, but most people wanted the system to be smarter about undoing the paint bucket operation with the previous operation. In discussions, however, they agreed this would be tricky in practice, and that the orange highlighting of the conflicting operations (Figure 4) would be a reasonable way for users to manually find and fix conflicts.

Interestingly, all but one participant was surprised by the operation of copy-and-paste, even though everyone was familiar with the way copy-and-paste works in other programs (where the copy ignores undo). However, participants agreed that our design was consistent and would sometimes be useful.

The main requested feature was a way to *group* actions. For example, selecting multiple operations together and undoing them all at once, or collecting operations into named groups, like layers can be in Photoshop.

In summary, the evaluation showed that with the check-box version, the script-model selective undo was understandable and usable, and that people understood how the issues from the semi-structured interviews would be addressed by our tool. All participants expressed a strong desire to have this kind of selective undo in Photoshop, and even in their other editing programs. They said that selective undo could substitute for some of the ways they now use layers.

FUTURE WORK

Currently, Aquamarine is an early prototype, sufficient to explore the design issues discussed here, but not yet ready for deployment. The current work includes making the rest of the features of Pixelitor work with selective undo, and then releasing Aquamarine as open source for general use and a full field test.

Photoshop has an option to add the operations that enable and disable layers onto the undo history, and Topaz [19] even could put changes of selections and the "find" operation into the undo history. Some of our participants expressed the desire to have state changes that do not affect the current painting, such as changing the current color or the radius of the brush, included into the history so they could be undone. We propose to explore these in the future.

We also want to investigate how to allow operations in the past to be *modified*. For example, some participants in both studies expressed a desire to be able to change the color of an operation done in the past, and see that propagated through the rest of the edits. The next step is to enable *new* operations to be inserted into the past, or existing operations to be reordered, for example to put something behind other painting in the stacking order. Although other research systems have tried some of these [15], a key usability challenge remains of how the user would be able to understand, undo and selectively undo changes to the history.

Another requested feature from our participants was some way to collapse long histories. For example, text editors coalesce multiple keystrokes into a single undoable action, and we would like to explore the ability to collapse and expand multiple small brush strokes. This might be supported both automatically and manually, so the user could achieve the desired level of granularity when navigating.

Finally, we would like to explore saving and restoring histories. The history might be stored in the image document, to enable cross session undoing. This could also enable someone later to explore how an effect was achieved. Similarly, a saved script could be converted into a tutorial [9]. Sections of a history could also be selected and converted into parameterizable reusable macros, as in Topaz [19].

CONCLUSIONS

Providing selective undo in a painting program brings up a surprising number of design challenges. Aquamarine shows that UI research can address those challenges and usable interfaces can be provided that can have benefits for users. We hope this research will inspire others to investigate providing selective undo in a variety of domains.

ACKNOWLEDGEMENTS

We thank Min Jeong Kim for her help with the figures used in this paper. Funding for this research comes in part from NSF grant IIS-1314356, from the Korea Foundation for Advanced Studies (KFAS), and from Adobe Research. Any opinions, findings and conclusions or recommendations expressed in this material are those of the authors and do not necessarily reflect those of the NSF, KFAS, or Adobe.

REFERENCES

1. Appert, C., Chapuis, O., and Pietriga, E., "Dwell-and-Spring: Undo for Direct Manipulation," in *SIGCHI'2012*. Austin, TX. pp. 1957-1966.
2. Archer Jr., J.E., Conway, R., and Schneider, F.B., "User Recovery and Reversal in Interactive Systems." *ACM Trans. Program. Lang. Syst.*, 1984. **6**(1): pp. 1-19.
3. Berlage, T., "A Selective Undo Mechanism for Graphical User Interfaces Based on Command Objects." *ACM Trans. on Comp. Human Inter.*, 1994. **1**(3): pp. 269-294.
4. Berlage, T. and Genau, A. "A Framework for Shared Applications with a Replicated Architecture," in *ACM UIST'1993*. Atlanta, GA: pp. 249-257.
5. Cass, A. and Fernandes, C., "Using Task Models for Cascading Selective Undo," in *Inter. Conf. on Task Models and Diagrams for UI Design*, K. Coninx, et.al, Eds. 2007. Springer Berlin / Heidelberg: pp. 186-201.
6. Cass, A.G. and Fern, C.S.T., "Modeling Dependencies for Cascading Selective Undo," in *IFIP INTERACT 2005 Workshop on Integrating Soft. Eng. and Usability Eng.*
7. Cass, A.G., Fernandes, C.S.T., and Polidore, A., "An Empirical Evaluation of Undo Mechanisms," in *NordicCHI'*2006. Oslo, Norway. pp. 19-27.
8. Chen, H.-T., Wei, L.-Y., and Chang, C.-F., "Nonlinear Revision Control for Images." *ACM Trans. Graph.*, 2011. **30**(4): pp. 1-10 (Article 105).
9. Chi, P.-Y., *et al.*, "Mixt: Automatic Generation of Step-by-Step Mixed Media Tutorials," in *UIST'2012*. ACM: Cambridge, MA. pp. 93-102.
10. Choudhary, R. and Dewan, P., "A General Multi-User Undo/Redo Model," in *ECSCW'1995*. Springer Stockholm, Sweden. pp. 231-246.
11. Grossman, T., Matejka, J., and Fitzmaurice, G., "Chronicle: Capture, Exploration, and Playback of Document Workflow Histories," *UIST'2010*. pp.143-152.
12. Kawasaki, Y. and Igarashi, T., "Regional Undo for Spreadsheets (Demo)," in *Adjunct Proceedings UIST'2004*. 2 pages.
13. Klemmer, S.R., *et al.* "Where Do Web Sites Come From?: Capturing and Interacting with Design History," in *CHI'2002*. Minneapolis, Minnesota: pp. 1-8.
14. Ko, A.J., *et al.*, "An Exploratory Study of How Developers Seek, Relate, and Collect Relevant Information During Software Maintenance Tasks." *IEEE Trans. on Soft. Eng.*, 2006. **33**(12): pp. 971-987.
15. Kurlander, D. and Feiner, S. "Editable Graphical Histories," in *1988 IEEE Workshop on Visual Languages*. Pittsburgh, PA: pp. 127-134.
16. Kuttal, S.K., Sarma, A., and Rothermel, G., "History Repeats Itself More Easily When You Log It: Versioning for Mashup," in *IEEE VL/HCC'2011*. pp. 69-72.
17. Li, R. and Li, D., "A Regional Undo Mechanism for Text Editing," in *Inter. Workshop on Collaborative Editing Systems*, 2003.
18. Lieberman, H. "Dominos and Storyboards: Beyond Icons on Strings," in *1992 IEEE Workshop on Visual Languages*. Seattle, WA: pp. 65-71.
19. Myers, B.A. "Scripting Graphical Applications by Demonstration," in *SIGCHI'1998*. pp. 534-541.
20. Myers, B.A. and Kosbie, D., "Reusable Hierarchical Command Objects," in *CHI'1996*. pp. 260-267.
21. Prakash, A. and Knister, M.J., "A Framework for Undoing Actions in Collaborative Systems." *ACM Trans. on Comp.-Human Inter.*, 1994. **1**(4): pp. 295-330.
22. Vitter, J.S., "Us&R: A New Framework for Redoing (Extended Abstract)." *SIGSOFT Software Engineering Notes*, 1984. **9**(3): pp. 168-176.
23. Yang, Y., "Undo Support Models." *Inter. J. of Man-Machine Studies*, 1988. **28**(5): pp. 457-481.
24. Yoon, Y., Koo, S., and Myers, B.A., "Visualization of Fine-Grained Code Change History," in *IEEE VL/HCC'2013*. pp. 119-126.
25. Yoon, Y. and Myers, B.A., "Supporting Selective Undo in a Code Editor," in *ICSE 2015*, Florence, Italy, to appear.

Author Index

www.ingramcontent.com/pod-product-compliance
Lightning Source LLC
LaVergne TN
LVHW080101011026
849160LV00013B/1009
* 9 7 8 1 4 5 0 3 3 7 7 7 9 *